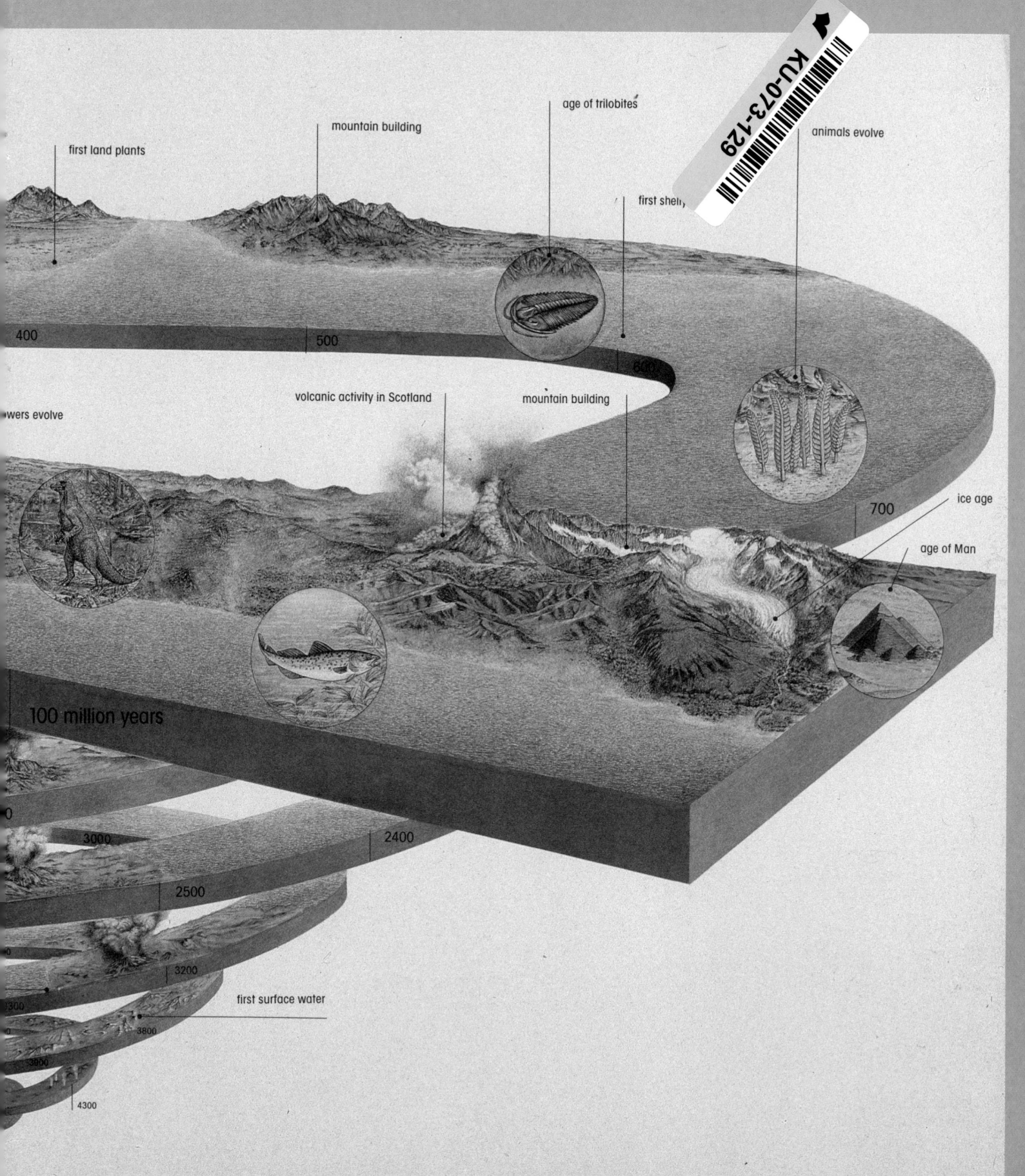

first land plants

mountain building

age of trilobites

animals evolve

first shel...

400

500

600

volcanic activity in Scotland

mountain building

...wers evolve

ice age

700

age of Man

100 million years

3000

2400

2500

3200

first surface water

3800

3900

4300

Humans are newcomers to the planet Earth, appearing towards the end of its development and hundreds of millions of years after the first life forms. Some of most crucial and
dramatic phases of the Earth's evolution are shown on this spiral diagram of geological
time, reproduced by courtesy of the Geological Museum, London.

Chronicle

of the World

Longman

Chronicle

How to use this book

The book is arranged chronologically from 3.5 million years BC to 1945. The world before that and post-1945 is covered by several essays; key events since 1945 are summarised beside the essays. At the beginning a double-page spread may cover hundreds of thousands of years; by the end of the 18th century coverage averages two years a spread, with the occasional one being devoted to a single particularly eventful year. On each spread there are one or two left-hand columns containing short "chronology" entries. These serve both to list dates in their own right, such as deaths, production of works of art, inventions, etc., and to trace the events that come between the stories, so if you are following the the American civil war, for instance, it is worth reading not only the main stories but also the "chronologies", which detail some of the lesser developments.

Each story is written to a particular date (which may well be approximate – indicated by c. (circa) – in the earliest periods) as if it were being told by a modern journalist reporting the event at the time, so no information is contained in the story that comes after that date. To follow further developments consult the index although this inevitably concentrates on events reported as stories rather than chronology summaries. There are over 50 essays included within the text which give an overview of subjects which are either particularly complicated, such as the 100 Years' War, or not easily covered purely by reference to specific events, such as trade or philosophy.

Where possible we have used pictures that are contemporary. But before the invention of photography there were no pictures made precisely at the time of an event, so until the 19th century we have used visual material produced in the relevant era, such as the Assyrian's bas-reliefs of their victories or engravings of colonial battles. Where this has not been possible we have used later representations of an event, such as Victorian paintings of early British scenes. In these cases we have indicated that the picture is from a later period. Buildings present a particular problem; we have occasionally used a finished building to illustrate a story about work starting on it. There are also problems with buildings or cities that are now ruins and of which there are no contemporary pictures such as the walls of Great Zimbabwe.

With names of both people and places we have generally used the one current at the time and, if it is different from that used today, we have indicated today's equivalent in brackets after it. But there are a few places where – because of the rise and fall of empires and constantly shifting borders – equivalence between ancient and modern usage is vague and confusing; Mesopotamia covers an area approximate to Iraq and Syria today, while Anatolia, Asia Minor and Turkey have all been used to indicate a roughly similar area at different times. We have not always identified Asia Minor with Turkey nor have we identified Persia with Iran. We have tried to strike a balance between historical accuracy and clarity for the modern reader. Charlemagne, for example, was not actually called by that name until after his death, but he is so well known as Charlemagne that we felt to call him Charles would be perverse. Similarily, stories set in prehistory are located by a modern placename.

In transliterating names from non-alphabetical scripts such as Egyptian, Chinese, or Mesopotamian there is considerable room for variant spellings. For Chinese we have followed the new Pinyin style in which Peking becomes Beijing and where we have felt there might be confusion have put the old style in brackets. Sometimes in the interest of accuracy we have used variants on familiar names, hence Nebuchadrezzar.

At the back of the book there is a gazetteer which lists all the nations of the world under the names by which they are known today and which gives the broad geographical and political details of each with a summary of their history.

Acknowledgements

Assembling a book of this size inevitably makes special demands on many people's time and patience, as well as their expertise. I would like to thank everyone involved for their whole-hearted response. In particular, in addition to those mentioned opposite, we would like to acknowledge the following people and sources of information.

We obviously made use of a large number of specialist reference books – which frequently differed over dates – but we owe a particular debt to the following volumes: *An Encyclopaedia of World History,* William L. Langer, (Harrap/Gallery Press); *An Eyewitness History of Australia,* Harry Gordon (Penguin); *Chambers Biographical Dictionary; Dictionary of British History,* (Pan Books); *Dictionary of Wars,* George C. Kohn (Anchor Books); *Dictionary of World History,* (Nelson); *Great Battles of the World,* John Macdonald (Guild Publishing); *Grove Concise Dictionary of Music,* Edited by Stanley Sadie (Macmillan); *The Longman Handbook of Modern European History* 1763-1985, Chris Cook and John Stevenson; *Reportage,* edited by John Carey (Faber); *The Pelican History of the World,* J.M. Roberts; and the *Oxford Classical Dictionary.*

In "The Nations of the World" section of the book the general text was checked by our consultants with additional facts, such as population figures and religions, cross-checked with books such as the Statesman's Yearbook and Britannica Yearbook.

The maps which appear in *Chronicle of the World* were drawn by specialist map-makers in Paris and checked against a variety of sources. These included previous Chronicle books, the *Collins Atlas of World History,* the *Penguin Atlas of World History* and two volumes from Times Books: *Past Worlds: The Times Atlas of Archaeology* and *The Times Concise Atlas of World History.* More specific sources are given where appropriate.

Chronicle of the World is an entirely new volume, but it has its ancestors in the Chronicle family around the world. *Chronik der Menscheit* in Germany and *Chronique de l'Humanité* in France first ventured down the path we now tread. We drew upon the French text in many of our reports, although it hardly ever, if at all, appears simply as a translation. Nonetheless we are indebted to our French colleagues for their earlier work and, especially, for their assistance in the production of this book; Henri Marganne deserves a particularly honourable mention in dispatches. We are also grateful to colleagues in our sister company in New York who made available to us proof pages of their forthcoming book, *Chronicle of America.*

The photographic agencies which supplied pictures are credited at the end of the book, but we are particularly grateful to a number of individuals who toiled nobly to answer our sometimes arcane and invariably urgent requests for photographs. They are Caroline Geary, Jane Ward (Bridgeman Art Library); Fiona Purvis (E T Archive); all at Mary Evans Picture Library; Michael Holford (Michael Holford Photographs); Anna Calvert (Hulton Picture Company); Peter Newark (Peter Newark's Pictures); Mike Dixon (Photoresources); Liz Moore, Dawn Wyman (Popperfoto); Barbara Heller, Lawrence Jarosy (Werner Forman Archive).

Other individuals and organisations whose help we would like to acknowledge are the staff of the Readers' Digest in London (whose offices we shared when this book was commenced); Marion Dain, Vanessa Kelly, Caroline Mardon, John McCormack and Frank Tricot.

JB, July 1989

First published in 1989 jointly by Longman Group UK Ltd and Chronicle Communications Ltd.
ISBN: 0-582-05884-8

(Also published solely by Chronicle Communications Ltd., London, in Australia, Canada and New Zealand
ISBN 1-872031-00-5; and in the United States.)

Typesetting: Berger-Levrault, Nancy, France.
Colour process work: Christian Bocquez.
Printing & Binding: Brepols, Turnhout, Belgium.

Chronicle Communications Ltd.,
154, Clerkenwell Road,
London EC1R 5AD.

Longman Group UK Ltd.,
Longman House,
Burnt Mill,
Harlow,
Essex CM20 2JE.

Chronicle of the World

has been conceived and co-ordinated by Jacques Legrand

Editor: Jerome Burne

Picture Editor: Ruth Darby

Chronology Editors: Hazel Bedford, Henrietta Heald

Assistant Editors: Peter Bently (Essays), Denis Pitts (Text)

Writers: Frank Barber, Adam Curtis, Christopher Dobson, Peter Evans, Tony Geraghty, David Gould, Richard Grant, Jonathon Green, Robert Jones, Peter Lewis, Charlotte Veysey May, John Miller, Rupert Morris, Warren Pitts, Richard Trench

Consultants: Dr Raymond Allchin, Reader in Indian Studies, Faculty of Oriental Studies, Cambridge (India to 1200 AD); Dr Oriana Baddeley, Senior Lecturer in South American Art History, London (Latin America); Prof Tim Barrett, Professor of East Asian History, School of Oriental and African Studies, London (China 300BC-1800AD); Dr Paul Cartledge, Lecturer in Ancient History, Clare College, Cambridge (Europe 2000BC-300BC); Dr Christopher Cullen, Lecturer in History of Asian Technology, School of Oriental and African Studies London (China to 300BC); Dr Gillian Darcy, Lecturer in History, Middlesex Polytechnic (Women); Peter Evans, Presenter "Science Now" BBC Radio 4 (Science); Victor Harris, Dept. of Japanese Antiquities, British Museum, London (Japan 700BC-1000AD); Dr Rosemary Horrox, Lecturer in History, Cambridge (Europe 1000 to 1500); Mark Jenner, Lecturer, St. John's College, Oxford (Europe 1500-1600); Dr Hugh Kennedy, Lecturer in Medieval History, St. Andrew's (Islamic World); Dr Peter Kornicki, Lecturer in Japanese, Faculty of Oriental Studies, Cambridge (Japan 1000-1945); Dr Jaromir Malek, Ashmolean Museum, Oxford (Ancient Egypt); Dr Tim Murray, Lecturer, Department of Archaeology, La Trobe University, Australia (Australasia); Dr Neil Parsons, Hon. Research Fellow, Institute of Commonwealth Studies, London (Africa south of Sahara); Dr John Patterson, Assistant Lecturer in Ancient History, Magdelene College, Cambridge (Europe to 1000BC to 300BC); Dr Tim Potts, Research Lecturer, Christ Church, Oxford (Mesopotamia); Dr Francis Robinson, Reader in History, Royal Holloway and Bedford New College, London (India 1200-1945); Dr Derek Roe, Honorary Director, of Donald Baden-Powell Quarternary Research Centre, Oxford (World to 10,000BC); Amanda Sackur, Teaching Assistant, School of Oriental and African Studies, London (West Africa 200BC-1850); Dr Andrew Sherratt, Department of Antiquities, Ashmolean Museum, Oxford (Europe 10000 to 2000BC); Dr John Spurr, Fellow St. Edmund Hall, Oxford (Europe 1600-1800); Dr R. G. Tiedeman, Lecturer, School of Oriental and African Studies, London (China 1800-1945); Philip Waller, Tutor in Modern History, Merton College, Oxford (Europe 1800-1945); Dr Bryan Ward-Perkins, Tutor in History, Trinity College, Oxford (Europe 300-1000).

Researchers: Michael Berlin, John Castleford, P. Gaucci, Penelope Glare, Louise Holloway, Andrew Hope, Niall McKeown, Dr Simon Loseby, Brendan Marshall, Dr Dermot Quinn, J. V. Stokes, Matthew Strickland, Edward Vincent, John Watts

Essayists: Dr Peter Andrews, Dept. of Palaeontology, British Museum (Natural History), London; Dr Jeremy Black, Lecturer in Akkadian, Oxford; Patrick Brogan, A Washington Correspondent for The Observer; Dr Bernard Dixon, European Editor, Bio-Technology; Godfrey Hodgson, writer and broadcaster; Dr John Maddicott, Exeter College, Oxford; Dr Rosalind Miles, Head of Centre for Women's Studies, Coventry Polytechnic; Brian Moynahan, Foreign Correspondent, The Sunday Times; Sue Rigby, Department of Earth Sciences, Cambridge; Anthony Smith, President, Magadelen College, Oxford; David Styan, School of Oriental and African Studies, London; Dr Christopher Tyerman, Hertford College, Oxford; Justin Willis, School of Oriental and African Studies, London; plus many of the consultants and researchers listed.

Editorial production: Bronwen Lewis (Production Manager), Joan Thomas (Editorial Manager), Christian Danger, Maud Escalona, Laura Hicks, Martine McManus, Francesca Odell, Nathalie Palomba

Art: Henri Marganne (Manager), Christian Baude

Computer systems: Catherine Balouet (Manager), Dominique Klutz (Software Engineer), Martine Colliot (Assistant)

Index: Ian Crane

Translators: Jennifer Barnes, Oxford; First Edition, Cambridge; Material Word, Birmingham; Kathryn Ross, Oxford; Ros Schwartz, London; Tino's, London.

Editor-in-Chief: Derrik Mercer

Igor, a figure from Russian national myth, fighting the Tartars.

Wax portrait on a mummy case of a young man from 2nd cent AD.

Angel with a gun: South America, in the 17th century.

Chinese technology from the 13th or 14th centuries for rice irrigation.

Index to the Essays

and National Histories

Jaundiced English view from 1828 of the future of steam-powered travel.

How the British saw travelling in Africa in 1821 – by W. Hutton.

A recruiting poster issued by the American army in World War One.

Cixi, Dowager Empress of China at the time of the Boxer rebellion.

5

Introduction

This book is the product of a curious paradox. On the one hand news and current affairs are a billion pound business while for many people history is composed of confused schoolday memories of long-lost battles and numbered kings. Yet history is just yesterday's current affairs and without it today's news, especially in places like Israel or Northern Ireland, is incomprehensible. Similarly, while everyone in the West sides with Poland's attempt to assert its independence in the face of Soviet might, its efforts are even more impressive with the historical knowledge that Russia has been attempting to crush Polish independence for at least three hundred years. In fact, Russia's forays into Poland were often combined with successful attacks on the old Islamic Turkish empire along her southern border which is of course why Russia has so many Moslems in the southern states who are also asserting their identity in the wake of perestroika.

The major aim of *Chronicle of the World* is to bring such great current events of the past to life for the ordinary reader and to infuse them with the same sense of drama and excitement that now surrounds a Gorbachev peace initiative or events in Tiananmen square. In some cases an extraordinary sense of *deja vu* makes the connection with today very powerfully. "American-backed adventurer seizes power in Nicaragua" could be taken from today's front page; actually it refers to an event in 1856. When was this story "Russia puts down uprising in Hungary"? In fact, it was 1849. All the stories in *Chronicle* are reported as though they had just happened, free of any hindsight or historical analysis.

Compiling this book has been a fascinating and humbling experience; not only did it make us aware of our enormous ignorance, but it gave us a sense of the vast span of history. We are closer to the ancient Greeks than they were to Sargon, the legendary first-ever emperor to emerge in Mesopotamia, while Sargon in turn is closer to us than he was to the first farming villages. In one sense what we are telling is a horror story, a tale of endless battles, massacres and unimaginable cruelties, as powerful men sacrificed their relatives, their subjects and anyone else in their bid to stay on top; from the Chinese to the Zulus the royal family was a dangerous place to be. It was in order to provide something of an antidote to world history as an account of the doings of aggressive men that we hired a consultant whose speciality was the history of women.

Counter-balancing the slaughter was the art that each culture produced and one of the delights of producing this book has been to see the context from which not only the great art of Europe emerged but that of other cultures, such as the extraordinary Benin bronzes, the temples of India, the delicate painting of Japan and so on. As well as art there is science and the development of the scientific method – one of Europe's unique intellectual contributions. Watching the rationalist answer to the religious world view emerging through the 17th century, the nature of the divide separating the two sides in the Salman Rushdie affair became very clear.

Writing histories of the world has an honourable tradition going back at least to 100BC when the Chinese – for whom, of course, China *was* the world – wrote a two million-word history. A pre-enlightenment Sir Walter Raleigh wrote one while in prison in 1608 which was mainly concerned with asserting the truth of the Biblical account. In 1920 the English writer H G Wells published *The Outline of History*, in an attempt to gain a longer perspective on the disillusionment in the West that followed the Great War. Wells was not too concerned with the Bible, but there are a couple of striking differences between his view of world history and our own.

To begin with, 70 years ago it was generally agreed that the first ancestors who could be called humans appeared about 500,000 years ago whereas recent research has pushed the date right back to 3.5 million years BC. Ironically, the period during which conventional academic wisdom changes the fastest is pre-historic. Even while we were compiling the book at least three stories from pre-10,000BC had to be changed to incorporate the very latest findings. The second point is the extent to which his book is essentially a history of Europe with references to the rest of the world when they impinge on the European saga. So, to take just two major events, there is no mention of any of the South American wars of Independence nor is there even a line about the Taiping rebellion in the last century in China, during which about 20 million people died and which was a forerunner of the Chinese Communist revolution.

When we began the book we started with the intention to make it as much of a world history as possible and to keep the European bias to a minimum. We soon found that it wasn't that easy. Not only are information and illustrations relating to Europe – and Britain in particular – far more readily available than anywhere else (hardly surprising) but in some areas we found that proper records only began with the arrival of Europeans and that when there were local accounts they were often not available in English. Just the fact that we had necessarily adopted a European calendar rather than an Islamic or Japanese one confirmed our bias.

Within these constraints we have endeavoured to give the non-European world as much coverage as possible. In selecting stories we have sometimes deliberately excluded interesting British events on the grounds that they would be covered in the future *Chronicle of Britain*. However, our story selection has also been governed by journalistic principles, so with the European bias in mind, we have sometimes given more space to stories that have good pictures or a vivid eyewitness account than might otherwise have been warranted by a strictly historical perspective. This book also complements *Chronicle of the 20th Century,* providing a wide-angle view of this century as well as the different perspective that comes from seeing it as just one century out of the several thousand that have gone before.

It is the mix of the familiar great European stories with less well-known ones from elsewhere in the world that provides much of the fascination of the book. For example, from the beginning of the 1400s the Chinese sent a number of large-scale expeditions to explore the eastern coast of Africa. These took hundreds of ships and thousands of men; they were, in terms of resources, the equivalent of moon-shots. In 1433 the faction at court which had opposed them on the grounds they were a waste of money took power and further expeditions were forbidden. The following year the Portuguese made a breakthrough in their exploration of the western coast of Africa and the torch of discovery passed from the old world to what was then the new.

Closer to home, while Queen Elizabeth I, one of the few fixed points in most people's historical galaxy, was holding Britain together in the face of religious conflicts, Akbar, a Moghul emperor of India who was just as successful as Elizabeth but far less familiar in the English-speaking world, temporarily solved the even more complex religious disputes that wracked his country by proclaiming himself both a god and infallible.

We now live in a world where the focus of attention is becoming increasingly global whether it is concern for the greenhouse effect, the ozone layer and the lack of respect nuclear radiation has for national boundaries or the impossibility of avoiding Dynasty anywhere. The inescapable message of the last twenty years is that we are all in it or rather on it together and if that is the case then perhaps it time for history, that most insular and nationalistic of disciplines, to take a more global view.

Jerome Burne

Earth before the human race appeared

The planet on which humans evolved has a long and complicated history in which they play no part. The original formation of the Earth remains obscure: no rocks remain from that time. It probably occurred about 4,500 million years ago, as the Sun condensed from a cosmic dust cloud. As the Sun's gravitational energy increased, the "spare" dust began to spin around it, and collide with itself to form larger and larger blobs. Some of these eventually became large enough to have high gravitational attraction themselves, and so to grow even faster. Eventually, the few large blobs which remained exhausted the supply of dust, and could grow no further; these were the planets of the Solar System.

Just after it was formed the earth must have been largely molten, with elements of all weights scattered through it. Gradually, the heaviest elements were pulled by gravity into the centre to form the core, the lightest elements (the gases) drifted up to create a primitive atmosphere, while the rest made up an inner mantle and an outer, solid crust.

A world of huge volcanoes

The oldest rocks in the world are found in Greenland. They are 3,700 million years old and reflect a world very different from our own. Nothing on the planet was alive and the atmosphere was mostly methane and hydrogen sulphide, with very little oxygen. Huge volcanoes were in continuous eruption, and only a smear of solid crust separated the surface from molten rock in the mantle.

But these eruptions were changing the primitive conditions all the time. They were pumping out water to form oceans, and low density rocks to form the continental crust. Water and carbon compounds came into contact on the surface of the Earth. In the oceans and in sulphurous springs they combined to form new and complicated organic molecules. Eventually a molecule must have formed which had the ability to make accurate copies of itself. Life had evolved almost imperceptibly.

Rocks from 600 million years ago record a more recognisable Earth. Although the atmosphere was still poor in oxygen, water was abundant and though the continents were barren, there was thriving life in the seas. This life left little trace in fossils because it was all soft-bodied. No hard parts like teeth or bone or shell had evolved. But at the beginning of the Cambrian period, about 570 million years ago, that changed abruptly.

The first shells were tiny and composed largely from phosphate; but they quickly got larger as the major component changed to calcium, and suddenly most major groups of animals had them. The reason is not known. Perhaps a set of "super predators" evolved, against whom protection was needed. Alternatively, perhaps the composition of sea water changed, so that there were greater supplies of calcium available for the first time in sufficient quantities.

Whatever the reason, the effect was profound. For animals, a skeleton means being able to become larger and more complex. It provides not only protection, but also surfaces for attaching muscles which make locomotion more efficient. A great burst of evolution followed, in which many familiar forms, like bivalves (clams and mussels) and arthropods (the marine ancestors of spiders and scorpions) appeared.

The cockle and world history

For geologists the result was just as important – similar to the appearance of written records for the historian. A cockle is much more likely to become fossilised than a worm because of its durable shell; with the appearance of the hard parts, the quality and quantity of the fossil record improved dramatically. The change is so profound that all rocks older than this are called Pre-Cambrian while those that come after are Phanerozoic, which means "the age of revealed life".

A world map of the Cambrian period would not be recognisable as the world of today. Africa, South America, Antarctica, India and Australia were joined together into "Gondwana", a large continent which straddled the equator. The other continents also lay along the equator. Gradually, the plate on which Gondwana sat drifted southwards until it lay across the South pole. One by one, the plates carrying the remaining continents collided into Gondwana, until 300 million years ago all of them were linked together into a giant continent which has been called Pangaea. This massive land mass stretched from the south pole to high northern latitudes, and along the equator for 8,000 miles (13,000km).

Life was abundant in the seas around Pangaea, and on the continent itself. In the oceans, fish and animals without backbones had evolved into many of the species which live today. They were preyed upon by sharks and now extinct swimming reptiles. Tree ferns and gymnosperms (like pines and cedars) covered the land, but there were no flowers or grass. The surface was dominated by huge dinosaurs.

Even when fossils are available, it is difficult to tell how long ago an event occurred. It is relatively easy to see that the dinosaurs are younger than the earliest shelled creatures, but by how much? The key lies with the igneous rocks – those which form from molten rock, either from volcanoes on the surface or deep underground. As they cool, minerals form; some of these contain small quantities of radioactive isotopes which immediately begin to decay and in doing so produce a distinctive "daughter" element.

The clocks buried in the rocks

The longer the time since an igneous rock formed, the more "daughter" atoms will have been created. So providing the rate of "parent" decay is known, their relative proportions will give the age of the rock. For the distant past, slow-decaying uranium, thorium and rubidium are used. For slightly more recent events, potassium is more useful. For anything in the last 100,000 years, a similar technique can be used with carbon, found in living things.

The super-continent of Pangaea lasted for almost 100 million years before it began to break up in the Jurassic period about 180 million years ago. Gradually, Eurasia and North America drifted to the north, away from the rest, and a seaway formed between them, along the line of the present Mediterranean. The Atlantic began to form as well, first in the Caribbean, then from there to both north and south. Finally, the remaining southern continents began to separate and India moved north to collide with Asia 50 million years ago producing the Himalayas.

These continental movements laid the foundations of the world we see today. By this time mammals and birds had taken over from the dinosaurs, and flowering plants and birds were abundant. Fifty million years ago the world must have looked rather similar to today with the exception of the climate which was generally warmer; tropical birds, snakes and turtles lived in the London area even though it was at about the same latitude as today. But for reasons that are still not fully understood, the climate began to cool until around 12 million years ago; ice spread out from both poles towards the equator, covering much of the northern hemisphere. The ice advanced and retreated in a series of cycles each lasting several hundred thousand years. It was in one of the advances around 3.7 million years ago that humans first appeared in Africa. The surrounding ice made it wet and temperate allowing forest and grassland to flourish in what is now the Sahara.

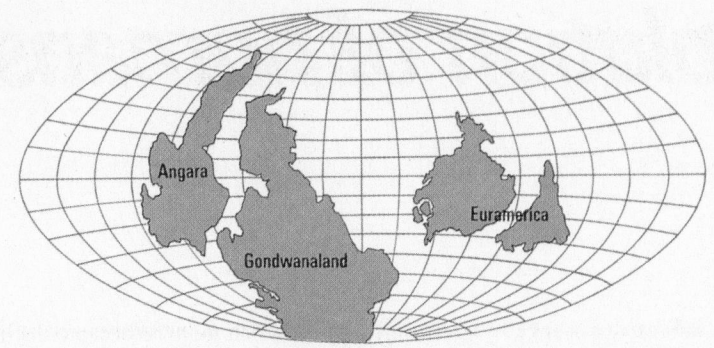

How the continents are thought to have looked 500 million years ago: evidence about the origins of China and South America is very tentative, however.

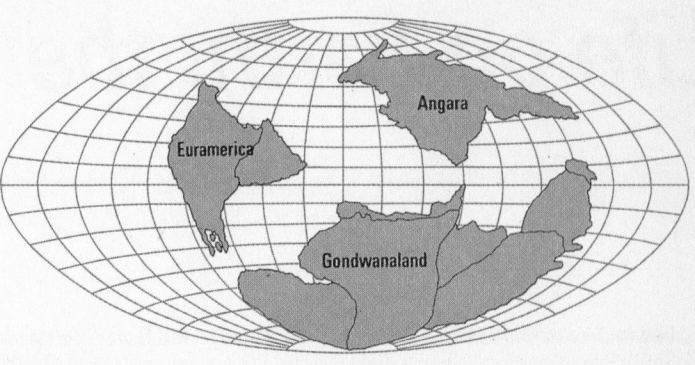

The continents take shape: 325 million years ago and the continents can be plotted with greater accuracy by carboniferous dating in terms of latitude.

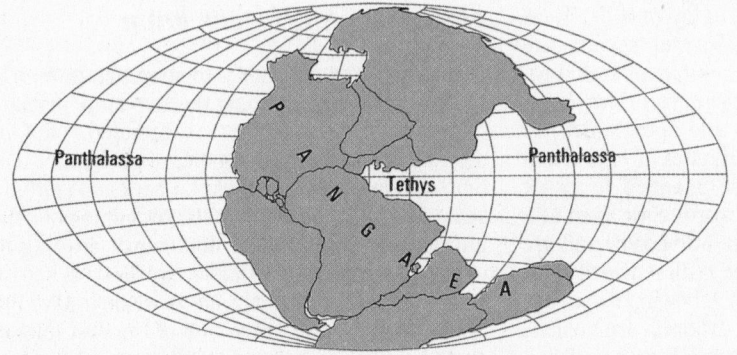

The continents collide: about 275 million years ago the three land masses which had existed in the Palaeozoic period have fused into one continent.

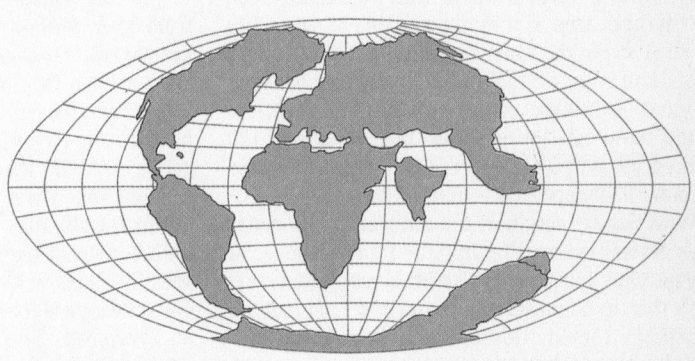

The Earth as we know it takes shape: this detail shows the English Channel some 50 million years ago after the continent of Pangaea had broken up.

The surface of the Earth begins to crust over: an artist's impression of a process which took over aeons of time before land masses were formed.

Life on Earth: the evolution of humans

Life began on earth more than 3,500 million years ago. For a long time it was restricted to simple life forms such as bacteria and algae, and it was not until 570 million years ago that the first shelled creatures appeared, 100 million years later, before the first vertebrates (animals with backbones such as fish) appeared. For many millions of years, life on land and in the water was dominated by amphibians and reptiles, the age of dinosaurs between 300 and 70 million years ago being the most extreme manifestation of this; but by about 120 million years ago a group of small warm-blooded animals had appeared – mammals.

With the extinction of the dinosaurs, the mammals diversified rapidly, initially into a number of groups that subsequently themselves became extinct, then by 55 million years ago into such modern groups as rodents, insectivores, horses and primates – to which humans belong.

In fact, the fossil history of the primates can be traced as far back as 70 million years ago. These early primates were rather like the modern tree shrew. They were a widespread and successful group, living in tropical forests and eating insects and plant foods, but they began to change in ways that led to their subsequent success. Of particular importance was their development of grasping hands, with tactile pads on the ends of the fingers (producing finger prints) and nails protecting the backs of the finger tips.

Along with these improvements to the hand was a change to taking more of the body weight on the legs rather than the arms, which in time led to a more upright posture in most primates. Another fundamental change was the development of the primates' unique stereoscopic vision. Both the shift towards vision rather than smell as the dominant sense, and the greater sensitivity of the hands led to an increase in brain size. There were also other changes such as a decline in the importance of hearing and reduction in the numbers of teeth in the jaws, probably due to an increasingly vegetarian diet.

Primates go largely vegetarian

Many of these primate adaptations cannot be identified in the fossil record, and we do not have an exact record of how and when they developed. It can be said, however, that since they are present in all living primates, they must have arisen by the time of the common ancestor for living primates between 55 and 45 million years ago. At this time there began a shift towards eating more vegetation

and fewer insects, and with this shift came a change in anatomy towards more robust jaws and larger body size, which culminated in the emergence of the higher primates, most of which are primarily vegetarian.

The Old World higher primates are first known from 35-30 million years ago in Egypt with a form known as *Propliopithecus*. Several species are known from tropical forest habitats of that time. Still primarily fruit eaters, they are evidently related to the living monkeys and apes, which together make up the higher primates of Africa and Eurasia, but they cannot be assigned to either group specifically. In other words they lived at a time before monkeys and apes diverged, and are broadly ancestral to both. The earliest evidence for any fossil ape is found in East Africa in an ape called *Proconsul*. This was an arboreal fruit eater, like the earlier forms, but it was bigger and had much more robust jaws than Propliopithecus. The earliest known species lived 22 million years ago, but very soon afterwards the diversity of species was already so great, that it is supposed that they had been distinct as a group some millions of years before then, since diversity is a product of time.

Primate teeth become stronger

Around 14 million years ago an important change in primates' teeth took place. The enamel covering them began to thicken, probably because of changes in the diet as they moved out of the forests. At the same time some began to move out of Africa and into Europe and Asia. Those that stayed behind, such as *Kenyapithecus* became the forerunners of humans, while those that left, such as *Sivapithecus* (and the closely related *Ramapithecus*, now regarded as a smaller species of *Sivapithecus*), went on to become the ancestors of today's orang-utan.

We know very little of exactly how the very earliest hominids split off from those apes that remained in Africa, as there is no good fossil evidence from 14 million years ago. All we can do is to draw conclusions from the more complete fossils that are available before and after the missing period. These suggest that long before they separated, the ancestral apes were already becoming partly terrestrial and living on non-forested areas, so clearly the old idea of "man coming down from the trees" is no longer tenable. The ancestors of living apes and humans were already down and thriving long before humans came on the scene. So rather than being on the ground, it seems likely that the most

significant way by which humans became distinguished from the apes was in developing still further the ancient primate characteristic of mobile and sensitive hands.

Humans get a bigger brain

It is the human ability to manipulate that is so distinctive, and in doing this two more primate trends have been further exaggerated. One of these is the increased dominance of the hind or rear limb seen in early primates as far back as 45 million years ago; this has been taken by humans to the ultimate extreme of total dominance, leading to upright posture and walking on two legs. All known early hominids walked upright as we do today, and this is likely to have been one of the first human characteristics to have evolved.

The other major change related to the freeing of the hands is the increase and modification of the brain. This change apparently came after walking upright, for the earliest fossil hominids had brains little changed from those of living apes. At this early stage in their evolution, humans could probably vocalise no more than apes, and their social structure would have been ape-like as well. They retained the same sort of teeth with thickened enamel and the environment they lived in – open woodland – and the food they ate – nuts, berries and vegetation – was probably little different.

Which apes did humans diverge from? The evidence of genetics, the structure of our DNA, shows very clearly that humans are much more similar to the African apes, the chimpanzees and gorillas, than to the Asian apes, orang-utans and gibbons. There is still controversy, though, over which African ape humans are close to for, while the genetic evidence shows greater similarity between humans and chimpanzees, the evidence of anatomical characteristics that we can actually see and measure shows greater similarity between chimpanzees and gorillas than chimps and man.

What can be said, however, is that humans evolved in Africa from a common ancestor shared with one or both of the African apes, probably between six and seven million years ago. There is one fossil from northern Kenya from that period that supports this: it appears to be a gorilla ancestor, and on negative evidence it can be said that if gorillas were already distinct by this time, the line leading to modern humans must have been also. One day, perhaps, some direct evidence may be found.

Chimpanzees with their young: one link in the evolutionary chain.

A young chimpanzee using a hand-tool: a significant skill in animals.

Chimpanzee: Pan troglodyte.

Chimpanzee: Dwarf Siamang.

Gorilla: young female lowland.

Orang utan: pongo pigmaeus.

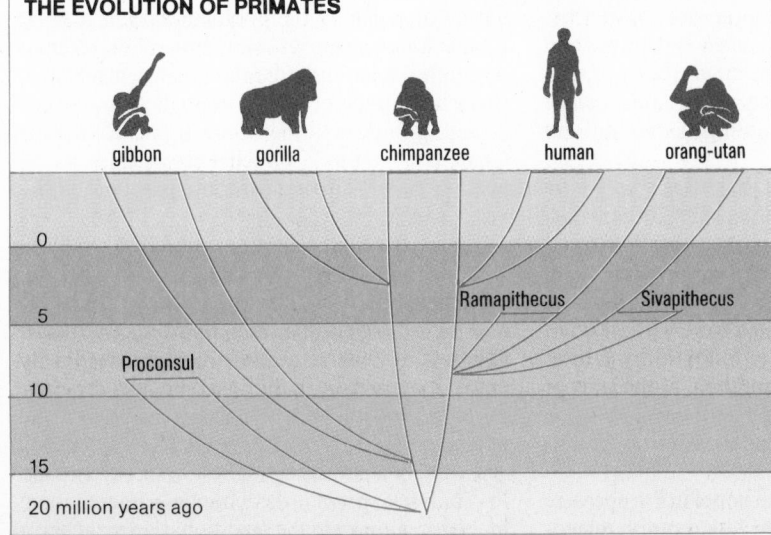

THE EVOLUTION OF PRIMATES

gibbon   gorilla   chimpanzee   human   orang-utan

0

5   Ramapithecus   Sivapithecus

Proconsul

10

15

20 million years ago

This chart shows the genetic similarity between different primates. Source of this and diagram right: "Past Worlds: The Times Atlas of Archaeology".

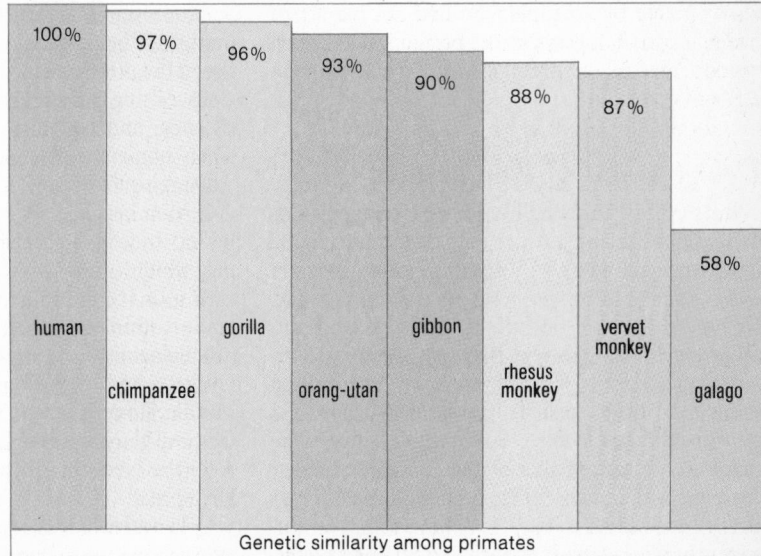

100%   97%   96%   93%   90%   88%   87%   58%

human   chimpanzee   gorilla   orang-utan   gibbon   rhesus monkey   vervet monkey   galago

Genetic similarity among primates

This diagram shows a hominid family tree with the relationship, based on genetic and anatomical factors, between apes, humans and their ancestors.

From Genesis to the Stone Age

The idea that there was anything other than a biblical beginning to human history originated in the 19th century. Until then, there was a general belief that God had created the world in seven days, just as set down in the Old Testament Book of Genesis. The story of a universal deluge, Noah's Flood, was also believed, even by many, such as William Buckland, who called themselves geologists. As for dating the past, archbishop James Ussher had worked out in the 17th century, from the generations listed in the Old Testament, that the Creation took place in 4004 BC: this date can be seen printed in the margins of the old Authorized version of the Bible. Several different lines of evidence led to the abandonment of such views.

From time to time, isolated discoveries had been made in various parts of Europe that appeared to show humanly manufactured implements in association with the fossil bones of extinct and clearly very ancient animals, but such reports were regarded as heretical and either ignored or explained away. For example, when a Mr Conyers found a fine Old Stone Age flint hand axe with fossil elephant bones near Grays Inn Lane in London in the late 17th century, it was regarded as being an Ancient British weapon of Roman age, on the grounds that the elephant must have belonged to the invading armies of the Emperor Claudius.

When, in 1797, John Frere, at Hoxne in Suffolk, England, found many flint hand axes, together with extinct animal bones, buried some 12 feet (3.6 metres) down in ancient lake sediments, and claimed that they were "weapons of war fabricated and used by a people who had not the use of metals ... (in) ... a very remote period indeed; even beyond that of the present world", no one took any notice of him.

Deluge is out of the question

But during the first half of the 19th century, finds of implements and extinct animal bones became more frequent, notably in Britain, France, Belgium and Germany. In Britain, Kent's Cavern at Torquay, Devon, produced important finds as did another Devonshire cave at Brixham, where a committee of scientists was appointed to supervise an excavation which verified the claims. From 1838 at Abbeville in France, comparable finds were made in ancient gravels of the River Somme by Jacques Boucher de Perthes. Though most of his French colleagues refused to believe him, two Englishmen, Sir Joseph Prestwich and Sir John Evans, visited the site of his discoveries in 1859 and published a report authenticating them.

Meanwhile, a few geologists, notably Sir Charles Lyell, had begun to demonstrate that the various slow geological processes which could be seen at work today had also operated in the past, which meant that the age of the earth must be very great indeed, and Biblical events like the miraculous creation of the world and a universal deluge were open to question. At the same time, though quite independently, biologists and zoologists like Charles Darwin and Alfred Wallace, supported by T H Huxley, were putting forward their theories of evolution, which could be seen to involve slow processess of development affecting all living things, including humans.

Great antiquity of human race

Darwin's *The Origin of The Species* was published in 1859, and by the 1870s, his work and the finds of the palaeontologist had combined to break down the old Genesis view, and create a climate in which there was a growing acceptance of the great antiquity of the. human race. In various parts of Europe, sequences of archaeological sites were becoming known, as opposed to the single unrelated occurrence. Such discoveries – for example, those made by J J A Worsaae in Denmark – showed that the prehistoric past could be divided into the stages of Stone Age, Bronze Age and Iron Age.

These labels soon passed into general use, although they originally only referred to the materials out of which some of the more striking weapons and tools found at ancient sites were made. A more important basic division of prehistory is that between the more recent stage, when agriculture and stock raising provided the economic basis of subsistence, and the much longer preceding period when humans relied on hunting, gathering and scavenging for food.

It soon became clear that there was a very long period indeed before metal-working began during which some stone was the chief material used to make durable tools. Broad divisions were made within the Stone Age: the Old Stone Age (the Palaeolithic period) lasted from earliest times until the end of the Ice age, followed by a brief Middle Stone Age (the Mesolithic), at the start of the post-glacial period lasting until the New Stone Age (the Neolithic), when mixed farming gradually spread.

Discoveries of fossil human bones in Europe were made sporadically during the 19th century, including some of the best known Neanderthal specimens. That from Gibraltar was first in 1848, fol-lowed by the Neander Valley remains in 1856. Upper Palaeolithic burials, featuring essentially modern human types, were found at Pavilland Cave (Wales) in 1823, Cro-Magnon (France) in 1868, and Menton (France) in 1872. The first find of a European pre-Neanderthal hominid was the famous Heidelberg jaw in 1907.

The cradle of the human race

Finds of *Homo erectus* (then called *Pithecanthropus*) in Java were made by a Dutchman, Eugene Dubois, in 1891-2, but it was not until the 1920s that areas outside Europe became a major focus of attention, with Raymond Dart's discovery of *Australopithecus* at Taungs in South Africa, and the first find of hominid remains, now recognised as *Homo erectus*, from Zoukoudian in China. Africa has since yielded large quantities of the earliest human types, notably in Kenya, Tanzania, Ethiopia and South Africa. Sub-Saharan Africa is now generally regarded as the "cradle of the human race".

The work of members of the Leakey family in East Africa over some 60 years has been particularly important, notably by Louis and Mary Leakey at Olduvai Gorge and by their son Richard in the Lake Turkana basin. Important finds have also been made in Ethiopia by Don Johanson, Tim White and others.

In the second half of the 20th century, many important scientific techniques have become available to Palaeolithic research, ranging from the dating of rocks by the potassium-argon method, to the microscopic examination of use-damage on stone tools, and computer-based methods of processing data of every kind. Palaeolithic archaeology can now be seen as one element of Quatenary research, which encompasses all aspects of natural history over the past two million years or so.

The work of the American anthropologist Lewis R Binford has been influential since the 1960s in directing archaeologists away from culture history and the simple classification of artefacts, towards attempts to understand how human societies operated dynamically in the past, and how they have developed by adapting themselves under pressure of changes in their environments. Current research accordingly has a strong interest in theory and also in studying present-day hunter-gatherer communities, alongside the traditional approaches of discovery and excavation of sites and detailed analysis of artefacts.

Archbishop James Ussher: putting a date to the biblical Creation.

Primeval chaos: one artist's view of the world of the Old Testament.

Gentlemanly study: early archaeologists compare notes in Britain.

Stone Age flint hand-axe: identified as Romano-British in 17th century.

Charles Darwin as a young man breaking down the Genesis view.

Darwin: not everybody believed or approved of his theory of evolution.

Outrage over Darwin is seen in this "Punch" cartoon of a "scientist".

Darwin in old age: scientific acclaim followed the early popular abuse.

Louis Leakey: African finds.

Richard Leakey: following father.

Raymond Dart: with Taungs skull.

Searching for fossils in the 1980s.

Early humans stand tall on rear legs

East Africa, c.3.5 million BC
Hominids are walking upright on two feet, according to the evidence of footprints left in volcanic "tuff" – a sort of consolidated ash – at Laetoli, Tanzania.

Together with the tracks of a large number of animals and birds taking part in an annual migration, the tracks of three hominids, all of them heading north, have been preserved in rain-hardened ash. Although it is not quite clear to which species of hominid the footprints belong, they were left, apparently, by two adults and a juvenile, with the smaller of the two adults deliberately treading in the steps of the biggest of the three.

The largest footprints are between seven and nine-and-a-half inches long and their depth in the ash indicates that the hominids are between four and five feet in height. Also in the volcanic ash, left over a period, are over 18,000 individual tracks of a wide range of animal species, ranging from insects such as the ant to the elephant.

The footprints show that while crossing the expanse of ash one of the three hominids stopped to look to the left, possibly to check for predators, which are common in this area. The hominid trail itself is crossed by that of a horse with a foal trotting beside it.

The ability of hominids to assume this upright posture is important for several reasons. Firstly, it gives them extra height and affords them the ability to spot possible dangers from potential carnivorous enemies; and it will assist them in their quest for food.

Walking on two legs is likely to add to their endurance, and the ability to stride out, or even run for many hours, is another advantage in their fight for survival.

Hominids are terrestrial animals whose ancestors left their life in the trees as the forests became increasingly arid. Now, for the first time, they are able to compete with other species, although mostly they tend to be scavengers living in small groups. Their ability to stand upright is significant because the stance has freed their hands for future evolution. Although they have gained the ability to grip with their thumbs, they do not yet appear to be using the stones available to them for the manufacture of hand-held tools or weapons.

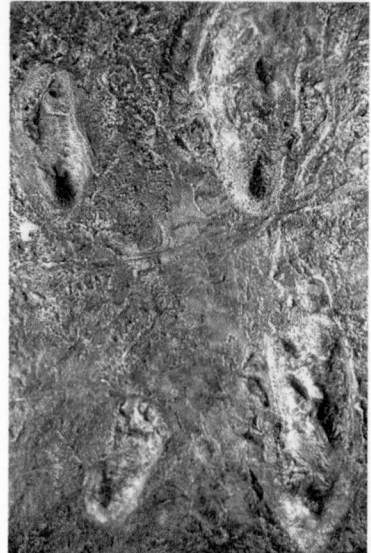
Footprints in the ash at Laetoli.

It seems likely that they can already use existing objects, like stones or pieces of wood, to assist them in their quest for food; but there is no clear evidence upon which to judge their full abilities. Here at Laetoli we know they walked across the land, but not where they came from, or where they were going, or what they were carrying on their travels.

Basic stone tools of volcanic rock appear and their use spreads

Ethiopia, 2.9-2.5 million BC
A novel technological aid is being employed by hominids living in the Awash river valley in the Afar region of northern Ethiopia. The device, probably used for hunting and cutting up flesh, consists of pieces of stone crudely chipped into the desired shapes from quartzite or basaltic lava. This is believed to be the first time that stone tools have been used.

Accounts of this ingenious invention may have been passed on by word of mouth to other parts of Ethiopia and perhaps beyond. Hominids living further south in fertile lakeside settlements in the Omo river valley which drains into Lake Turkana *(mainly Kenya)* are believed to have begun to develop their own version of the stone tool, sometimes using lava drawn from the many volcanoes in the region which were active between 2.4 and 2.0 million BC. The Omo valley

Early stone tools – made by crudely chipping flakes off a pebble core.

tools are small and some are made of quartz, which can be broken into sharp pieces by striking it with another stone. These make highly effective cutting tools without needing to be shaped further. Tools can also be made by working pebbles on one or both faces to provide cutting edges and perhaps a point or two.

It is not known exactly what the early humans are using these tools for, but there is no doubt that they are used to break up rock.

"Handy man's" brain grows bigger

Southern Africa, c.2 million BC

It has taken more than a million years for hominids to develop larger brains and to improve their manual dexterity, but now, on the African continent, *Homo habilis*, the earliest member of the genus *Homo*, is making basic stone tools by the simple device of chipping pebbles to produce a sharp cutting edge.

Homo habilis – the name means "handy man" – is now capable of a precision grip. Toolmaking is a regular activity and considerable evidence of "handy man's" primitive skills is being left across a wide swathe of Africa from Olduvai in Tanzania and Lake Turkana in Kenya, together with other settlements in Ethiopia and Kenya, to as far south as Sterkfontein in South Africa.

Homo habilis differs considerably from the *Australopithecines* in several ways. The average brain capacity is 700cc as opposed to 450-500cc, the brow ridges are far less pronounced and there is no shelf of bone at the rear of the skull

Twentieth-century painting of homo habilis hunting in the Olduvai gorge.

to anchor the strong jaw muscles – a feature shared by both apes and *Australopithecines*.

There is a difference in diet too. "Handy man" is omnivorous (eating both meat and plants) unlike *Australopithecus* and the apes whose large teeth are better suited to a diet of rather more gritty vegetable matter.

Humans move into the Olduvai area

East Africa, 1.9-1.0 million BC

New species of human creatures are appearing on the luxurious lake margins of Olduvai, on the edge of the Serengeti Plain in Tanzania. The first stone building has also been erected there. It is a ring of basaltic rocks, nine feet in diameter, and is probably a windbreak, with tree branches on top.

The hominids include *Australopithecus boisei*, who is a vegetarian despite massive teeth and jaws, and *Homo habilis*, whose tools are crudely flaked pebbles with sharp edges and who seems mainly to get food by scavenging.

More recently (about 1.5 million years ago) *Homo erectus*, a hominid who stands upright and walks on two feet, has appeared. The new arrival's tools include handaxes and cleavers; he may also have begun to hunt elephants and other large game, and to butcher the remains of animal "kills" or attack prey trapped in marshland.

Homo erectus has an even bigger brain

![Homo erectus skeleton]

Homo erectus, in life, walks tall.

Kenya, c.1.65 million BC

A new sort of hominid is emerging in Kenya. A specific example (at the site of Nariokotome III, to the west of Lake Turkana) is a 12-year-old who differs markedly from his forefathers in both height and brain capacity. He was almost six feet in height and thus one of the tallest specimens of hominids known in the early prehistoric period. The species *Australopithecus* usually grows to little more than four feet in height. Finds of skulls attributable to this new variety of higher primate indicate a brain capacity of at least 900cc.

This is *Homo erectus*, or "upright man", named because of changes in the body structure; there is no stoop to the shoulders and the arms are much shorter, relative to the legs, than those of earlier hominids.

The width of the sacrum (the bone which forms the keystone of the pelvic arch) in *Homo erectus* differs little in the male and female of the species. The birth canal of the female is quite small, but as the skull of the grown species is relatively large it seems that significant brain growth must take place after birth. This indicates a prolonged period of infant dependency on its parents.

Walking hominid "Lucy" dies at the age of 25 years

Ethiopia, c.3.1 million BC

"Lucy" was a hominid who died recently at the age of about 25. Her stature was small – she was hardly four feet in height – and her brain capacity was limited to no more than 400cc. Her teeth and jaws were huge and primitive.

What makes "Lucy" special is that she is known to have walked upright and her skeleton provides the earliest actual skeletal evidence of bipedality – the hominids' capacity to walk upright on two legs – although footprints from 500,000 years earlier demonstrated this ability among hominids.

"Lucy" belongs to the *Australopithecus afarensis* species, a population known to live in this region, Hadar. A complete family of at least nine adults and juveniles was killed at about this time in some sudden disaster, perhaps a flash flood or similar calamity.

These particular *Australopithecines* live in an environment of wooded and waterside settings. This hominid species is strongly sexually dimorphic, males and females showing distinct physical differences.

The possibility that some early member of the *Homo* lineage has also been living in this area – where the oldest stone tools are to be found – still remains.

How four-foot tall "Lucy" might have looked reaching for fruit.

Europe, c.800,000BC. The hunting settlements at Isernia in southern central Italy and Vallonnet cave in southern France are occupied by some of the first humans in Europe. Large game such as elephant and bison is hunted or scavenged on the open steppe.

North Africa, c.700,000BC. *Homo erectus* now inhabits Ternifine in Algeria and other sites on the coastal plain north of the Atlas mountains.

Europe, c.600,000BC. Handaxe industries are spreading over western and southern Europe. A great advance in stone-tool manufacture, these all-purpose cutting tools are being increasingly well made in a variety of sizes and shapes.

Pakistan, c.500,000BC. Stone handaxes, as well as other stone tools, are being made in northern Pakistan.

Britain, c.450,000BC. Human groups arrive in Britain and settle at Kent's Cavern in Devon, High Lodge in Suffolk and Boxgrove in Sussex.

China, c.350,000BC. The caves of Zhoukoudian (Dragon Bone Hill), north of the Yellow River in north-east China, have been occupied by *Homo erectus* for 100,000 years. These humans seem to have mastered the use of fire.

Germany, c.300,000BC. The people living in the lakeside settlement of Bilzingsleben are using tools made of wood and bone, as well as a great number of stone implements.

Spain, c.300,000BC. Elephant-hunters are active in the area of Torralba and Ambrona, some 60 miles north-east of Madrid. Elephants and other big game are stampeded to deep mudflats, where they are killed and butchered.

France, c.300,000BC. On short annual visits to Terra Amata, near Nice on the south coast, hunting people have taken to building temporary shelters which contain hearths.

Europe, c.250,000BC. *Homo sapiens* is now fully developed in parts of western Europe: for example, in Britain – at Swanscombe in Kent and Pontnewydd cave in Wales – at Tautavel in France, and at Steinheim in Germany.

Europe, c.150,000BC. Caves, as well as open sites, are being used as dwellings. In Lazaret cave, near Nice in France, a dwelling structure inside the cave itself has been built.

New types of stone tools are invented

Hand-axes used at Swanscombe, England, made with new techniques.

Europe, c.250,000-100,000BC
Homo sapiens, the latest in a line of evolving hominids, who is settling in Europe, Asia and Africa, is developing new toolmaking techniques using hammers of stone and antler to make flat, shaped axes of chipped stone.

At many sites in Western Europe, tools are being made by striking a flake from a flint nodule after preparing it for the required shape or size. It is clear that this technique represents an important innovation, showing that the tool makers start with a precise idea of how they want the finished product to turn out. They seem to have a set sequence of flaking operations that reduces the risk of mistakes.

Another technique uses disc-shaped nodules, or cores, which allow many more flakes to be struck than is possible by other methods. These improvements in productivity and precision working are bound to have beneficial effects on food supplies, so an increase in the population can be expected to begin soon.

Another sign of increasing sophistication is displayed by river-side dwellers in Britain who have developed a wooden spear with a fire-hardened tip for hunting. Wooden tools and weapons have also been seen in Germany, Spain and Africa. The use to which the early Britons put their spears is vividly illustrated by the bones of elephant, deer, horse and rhinoceros scattered around their homes.

For increasing numbers of Europeans, home is where the caves are found

Europe, c.150,000BC
Everywhere in Europe caves have become the favourite dwellings for humans during the present Ice Age, when winter snows and frosts are occurring as far south as southern France. Some of the best known cave communities have been seen at Crvena Stijena, Yugoslavia, La Cotte de St Brelade, Jersey, and Le Lazaret, France.

The cave dwellers have discovered that, quite apart from the protection caves provide during wet weather, temperatures remain remarkably constant. While outdoor temperatures can vary by up to 30 degrees during the year, inside the cave the variation is no more than four degrees. And, of course, with a good fire kept going, a considerable degree of comfort can be enjoyed. In some caves small huts have been erected to provide protection from the inevitable chill.

Life is not without hazards, though, for the cave dweller. Many animals, including bears and hyenas, have a fancy for cave life, especially for winter hibernation. Also, in some caves, flooding and rock-falls present a hazard. But since cave dwellings for human groups have a long history – limestone caves at Sterkfontein, South Africa, were occupied 1.5 million years ago – there must be plenty of folklore to help today's dwellers. And a roaring fire can be counted on to keep even the fiercest animal at bay.

Homo sapiens is proving a sucess

Budapest, c.450,000BC
Homo sapiens is proving a very successful species and is living all over the world. What makes this hominid different from its immediate ancestor, *Homo erectus*, who first came out of Africa a million years ago, is the size of the brain. Here, in Hungary, Vertesszolos Man has a cranial capacity of 1,400cc, markedly different from *Homo erectus*' 840-1066cc.

These people live near a shallow, pit-like depression beside a hot spring which they occupy during the cold weather. They use stone tools to butcher carcasses and can light open fires. Although their

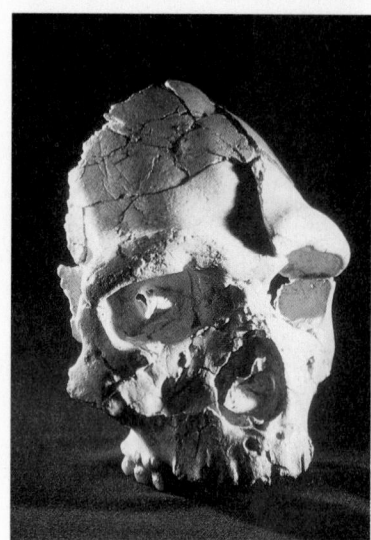

Homo sapiens skull from Tautavel, France: brains are getting bigger.

occiput – the bones at the base of the skull – is thick, with a prominent bony shelf for the attachment of powerful muscles, it indicates a distinct evolutionary trend. Their teeth are smaller, possibly indicating a diet of cooked food.

Groups of *Homo sapiens* are now living in Java (Ngandong), China (Mapa), Greece (Petralona), France (Tautavel and Biache), Germany (Steinheim) and Britain (Swanscombe). At Bodo, in Ethiopia, one *Homo sapiens* has been scalped by some one using a a stone knife.

Where and when this species first emerged during the distant past remains a mystery, since the latest examples of *Homo erectus* may date from as late as 250,000 years ago.

Out of Africa: Humans begin to explore the world

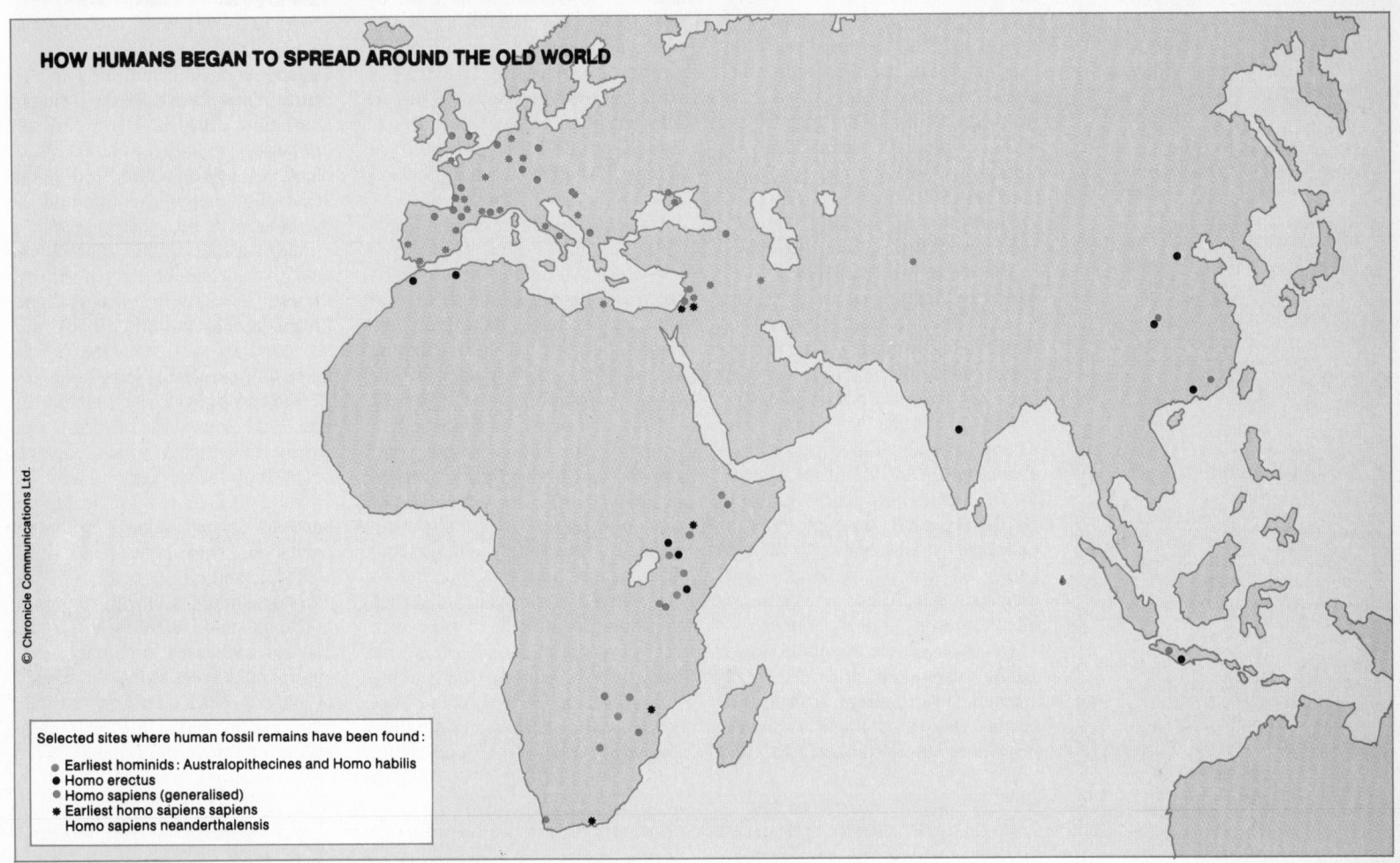

HOW HUMANS BEGAN TO SPREAD AROUND THE OLD WORLD

© Chronicle Communications Ltd.

Selected sites where human fossil remains have been found:

- Earliest hominids: Australopithecines and Homo habilis
- Homo erectus
- Homo sapiens (generalised)
- ✳ Earliest homo sapiens sapiens
  Homo sapiens neanderthalensis

Asia: first human beings arrive in China

Shaanxi, China, c.900,000BC
The increasingly inventive and adaptive humans have discovered fire and are using it to keep warm and perhaps to cook in the bitter Chinese winters. How they learned the secret remains something of a puzzle – although it is most likely that they took advantage of natural brush and forest fires started by lightning. Their diet is believed to include vegetables such as hackberries.

Bands of *Homo erectus* have left their warm homelands in East Africa and embarked on tremendous migration. They have passed through North Africa and India to Java, and now they have reached China; however, they have left the landscape virtually untouched by their passing.

They presumably took with them the capacity to make handaxes, although now they are equipping themselves with choppers and chopping tools, perhaps because the local stone is not suitable for flaking handaxes. With the aid of these, they are currently producing much sharper multi-purpose implements, which are more akin to cleavers and which they may use to sharpen bamboo for spears for hunting.

In Java, these people have established settlements in several places, including Sangiran, Modjokerto and Trinil in the Solo River Valley.

Here, in China, they are cave dwellers they are to be found at Xihoudu, Yumou and Tsingtun, and are occupying sites in Yuanmou in western China and Lantian on the Yellow River.

They tend to live in small groups of between 20 and 40 in number. They are hunters, short and stocky (averaging five feet six inches), and well-built in stature.

Europe: hunters cross the Mediterranean

Europe, c.680,000BC
Hominids, in the form of *Homo erectus,* have arrived in Europe, almost certainly via the Straits of Gibraltar. By about 1,000,000BC *Homo erectus* had left East Africa, and may already have reached China and Java, but only now is the colonisation of this continent beginning.

Some of these early settlers have established themselves at Vallonet Cave (*near the coast of southern France*) where they use crudely made stone tools, such as choppers and flake implements, which allow them to butcher a variety of animals such as wild cattle, bear, horse, rhinoceros, hippopotamus, deer and monkey.

These hominids have clearly been drawn to this site by the coastal location and the wide variety of animals which flourish in this area during the warm weather.

Another group was already living in central Italy (Isernia) for 50,000 years earlier than this, and there may already be people both at Mauer in Germany and at several places in central and eastern Europe. All of them use simple stone tools.

There are a number of ways in which these people could have arrived in Europe. One is via south-west Asia. The second possibility is a journey from north-west Africa via the narrow Straits of Gibraltar; or, thirdly, a route from Libya to Sicily when sea levels were lower and a land bridge existed.

The fact that there are settlements of *Homo erectus* at Ternifine and in other parts of north and north-west Africa, together with the lack of evidence for humans living on the Mediterranean islands, suggests the westernmost route.

Europe, c.128,000BC. Sea levels rise dramatically as temperatures warm at the end of the recent ice age.

South Africa, c.125,000BC. Hunters and gatherers living in caves at the mouth of the Klasies river on the southern African coast systematically collect shellfish to supplement a diet which includes both terrestrial and marine animals.

Asia/Europe, c.120,000BC. Some of the first Neanderthal humans, of the sub-species *Homo sapiens neanderthalensis*, are present in western Asia. Members of the same large-brained species living in Europe are stockier and more rugged than their Asian counterparts.

Britain, c.120,000BC. Since the intense warming trend began about 8,000 years ago, Britain has been colonised by a number of warm-adapted animals.

Africa, c.100,000BC. A new sub-species of human, called *Homo sapiens sapiens*, has put in an appearance in eastern and southern Africa. Compared with Homo sapiens, the new species, *Homo sapiens sapiens* has a smaller face, higher forehead, lighter skull and straighter limbs.

Near East, c.90,000BC. Members of the sub-species *Homo sapiens sapiens* have reached the Near East and are living at, for example, Qafzeh cave and Skuhl cave in Israel. They share the region with the Neanderthal population.

Europe, c.80,000BC. Neanderthals have now been living in Europe for perhaps 40,000 years. They are particularly associated with Le Moustier and many other caves and rock-shelters in the Dordogne region of France. Neanderthal settlements are also known to exist in Belgium, Spain, Britain and central and eastern Europe.

Yugoslavia, c.70,000BC. The violent deaths of a group of Neanderthals living at Krapina – and the treatment of the bodies after death – have led some to suspect that the local people practise cannibalism.

Europe/Asia, c.50-30,000BC. The climate in Europe and central Asia is growing steadily colder again. Adaptation to the cold has led to the development of the most sophisticated Neanderthals yet seen. But *Homo sapiens sapiens* has now moved into Europe.

The world changes as it grows warmer

Europe, 128,000-118,000BC

The highest temperatures for several hundred thousand years are causing drastic changes to the landscape. As the ice retreats the meltwater is raising the level of the oceans by up to 26 feet and causing extensive flooding. The low-lying land between Britain and France is gradually being eroded and may soon turn Britain into an island.

The higher sea levels are accompanied by radical changes in the climate, with dry, settled weather patterns being replaced by wetter, more turbulent conditions as the moist sea winds carry rain inland.

This rain and the warmth are having a dramatic effect on the animal and plant life of the region. Where mosses and lichens growing on the icy rocks once provided a precarious subsistence for scattered herds of grazing animals, lush grasslands and forests now support many different types of animals.

The sheer variety of animal life is astonishing. Deer and elk have appeared in profusion, growing fat on the rich vegetation, providing in their turn succulent meals for the lions and wolves which have colonised these new hunting grounds. Bears feast on the salmon which run up the rivers to spawn, and exotically feathered birds fill the air with song. Even elephants, rhinoceroses and hippopotami are finding Europe congenial, moving north year by year as the ice retreats and warm savannah lands replace the harsh ice age wastes.

If these conditions persist, it is likely that human communities will soon move north to exploit the bountiful supply of meat, clothing and other benefits provided by the animal population and the harvest of fruits and berries in the woods.

Surely the hardy men and women who survived the rigours of the ice age will take advantage of this storehouse of exploitable resources. One thing holding them back may be that they became so well adapted to the ice age that they are finding it difficult to cope with the new conditions. However, with their growing skills in the making of weapons and their ability to hunt as a team they must soon take their place at the head of the food chain.

Hippos wallow in tropical Thames

Britain, 128,000-118,000BC

Hippopotami are flourishing in the warm, marshy areas of the Thames and other British rivers. These lumbering aquatic animals find plenty of vegetation to feed upon and wallow happily in the mud of the Thames as it crosses low land.

They co-exist with other new animal colonists, brought north by the retreat of the ice age glaciers. Lions, deer, hyenas and aurochs are all found in this area. One of the more unusual of the new colonists is the straight-tusked elephant, which is quite different from the woolly mammoths which roamed here during the ice age.

The area favoured by the hippopotamus is well suited to human habitation, with good water and plentiful food, while the forests on the surrounding hills provide both sanctuary and building materials. The only drawback to human habitation would seem to be the clouds of stinging black flies and mosquitoes which make life extremely uncomfortable in the summer.

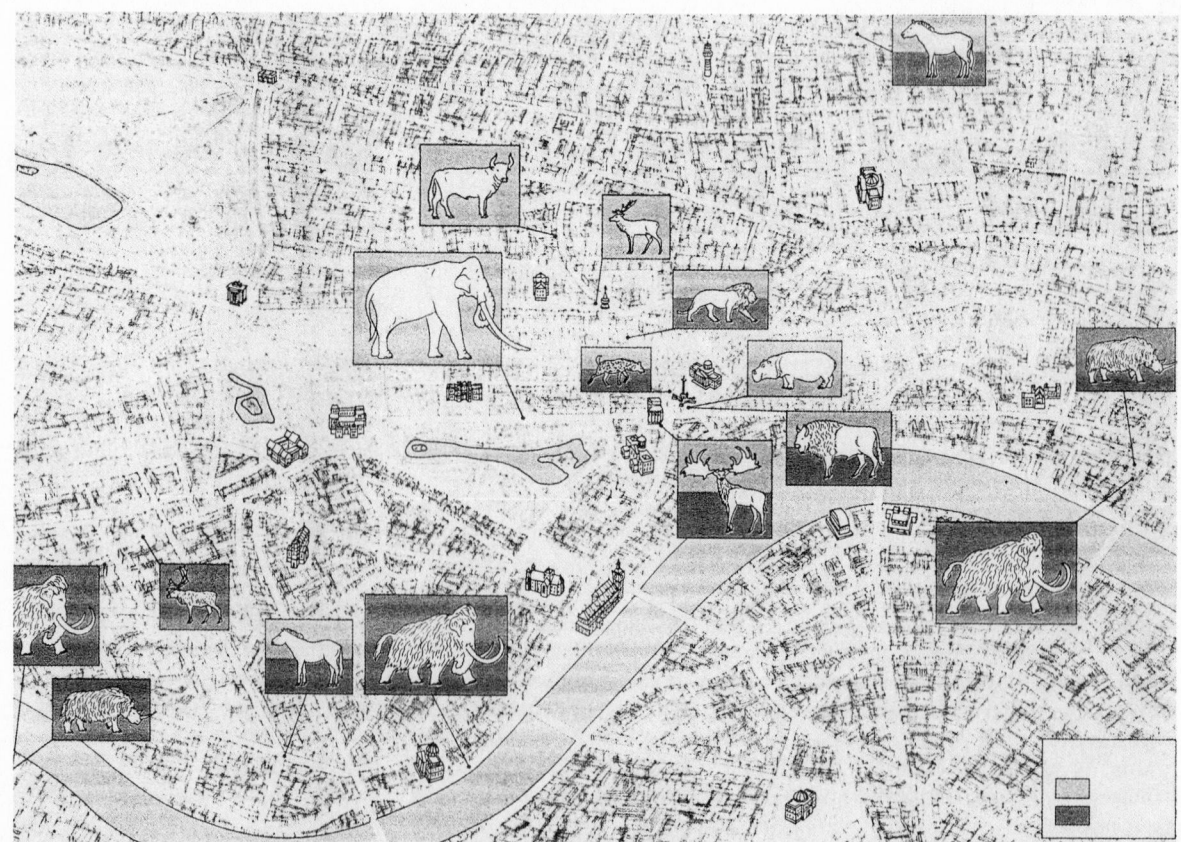

Warmer climates brought animals later associated with more southerly latitudes to Britain; this detail is from an illustration in "Past Worlds – The Times Atlas of Archaelogy".

Neanderthals are in the ascendant

Europe, 120,000-80,000BC
A robust *Homo sapiens* sub-species has taken over as the dominant group in Europe, North Africa and south-west Asia. Known as Neanderthal after the valley near Dusseldorf in Germany where they are known to have lived, they are taller than other species – about five feet eight inches – with aarge brain, powerful jaws and large teeth, a forward-projecting face and a heavy brow ridge running right across above a broad, flat nose. In the warmer climes of south-west Asia, however, they are less stocky and have less rugged features.

Other than this, little is known at present as to their habits and skills, though it is a fair guess that they move about in groups as a necessary safeguard against attacks by wild beasts. Their stone weapons and other implements will be used not only for cutting meat to get tastier food, but also for scraping skins to make themselves articles of clothing – surely necessary in chilly Europe.

An early 20th century view of how Neanderthal man may have looked.

The Neanderthal folk living in Western Europe are generally very much more robust than their brethren in North Africa and Asia. Some observers believe these tough Europeans have acquired their physical characteristics as an adaptation to the continent's colder conditions, since stockily-built people find it easier to keep warm. With the climate apparently set for yet another big change, possibly to another Ice Age, the Neanderthals in Europe will have to consider whether to join their brethren in warmer climes or stick it out in surroundings which, though familiar, become increasingly hostile.

Homo sapiens sets out for Australia and New Guinea

Australasia, c.50,000-30,000BC
In a remarkable feat of ocean-going navigation, the first humans have arrived in Australia, crossing from south-east Asia.

Much of the journey was made on land, however, because the icesheets around the poles have caused the sea level to drop by 390 feet. Despite this the journey involved crossing at least 30 miles of open sea.

The crossing has brought them to an unbroken landmass called Sahul (*Australia, New Guinea and Tasmania*). Here the explorers are encountering animals hitherto unknown to man, including mar-

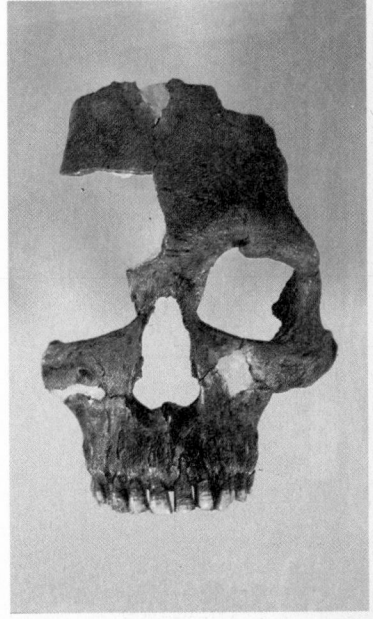
Skull of Australian Homo sapiens.

supials which have evolved in total isolation from neighbouring species in Asia. These include giant species of the kangaroo.

The human groups, who on occasion cremate their dead, have reached Lake Mungo (*southern New South Wales*). The migrants can travel either directly across the continent or by following the coastline.

They are also moving towards the southern reaches of Sahul, and more still are expected to reach Kosipe in eastern New Guinea, as well as south-west Australia and Tasmania, in due course.

Fine flint tools become the hallmark of the Neanderthal era

Cutting and scraping instruments put Neanderthals ahead in the tool race.

Europe, 80,000-32,000BC
More is becoming known about the new sub-species of *Homo sapiens* known as the Neanderthals. Its craftsmen have been observed at work in and around Le Moustier cave, in the Dordogne, France, and Neanderthal settlements have been found in Britain, Belgium, Spain, Germany and Eastern Europe. Lively accounts of their cultural and technological innovations describe new levels of skill in stone tools.

Earlier toolmakers had struck flakes randomly with hard hammerstones from suitable chunks of rock and had used some to make tools. Now good flint is used when avail-able and the Levallois and disc-core methods are employed to obtain flakes of specific shape and size.

The Neanderthals seem to have lost interest in handaxes and are manufacturing a variety of stone tools from these flakes. These include saw-like cutting instruments, scrapers and pointed projectile heads. It is apparent that a good deal of ingenuity must have gone into the development of these tools, which put the Neanderthals well ahead in the race for technological superiority.

It seems certain that the new tools have been developed to enable new jobs to be undertaken or old jobs carried out more efficiently. The cutting and shaping of wood is an obvious need, in order to make weapons and fashion rough shelters against the elements. Where wood is hard to get, the Neanderthals sometimes use large bones and tusks of mammoth to build themselves huts, covered by hides. These enterprises are greatly improving the standard of living of the average Neanderthal family.

Australia, c.50-30,000BC. The first humans arrive from south-east Asia by sea and spread out over the continent.

Russia, c.45,000BC. Large circular dwellings are under construction on the open Russian steppelands near Moldova. The builders use mammoth skulls, tusks and other large bones to support a cover of animal skins. The houses have hearths inside.

South Africa, c.45,000BC. Humans have extracted red ochre from mineral deposits in Swaziland.

Near East, c.42,000BC. Although blade tools have occasionally been used in sub-Saharan Africa and parts of the Near East, only now is a systematic change from flake tools to blade tools under way, principally in Israel and Lebanon. Blades make possible a new range of tool types.

India/Pakistan, c.40-25,000BC. Groups of hunter-gatherers in central India are living in painted rock shelters. Similar groups in northern Punjab, Pakistan, are working at open sites with the protection of windbreaks.

Europe, c.30,000BC. After occupying Europe, the Near East and North Africa since c.120,000BC, the Neanderthals have disappeared without trace. *Homo sapiens sapiens* is the sole remaining hominid.

Mexico, c.30,000BC. A human settlement has been established at El Cedral, San Luis Potosi.

Australasia, c.30,000BC. The southernmost settlements in the world are developing at Bluff Cave and Shannon in southern Tasmania.

Czechoslovakia, c.26,000BC. Substantial huts are being built at Dolni Vestonice and Pavlov, in Moravia. Sculptors from Dolni Vestonice are making female figurines from bone and ivory, and from good-quality clay tempered with powdered animal bone and fired.

Australasia, c.25,000BC. The emergence of land bridges, resulting from a dramatic fall in sea levels, has brought about a rapid expansion of settlement in Australia, Tasmania and New Guinea. All the major environmental zones are now under human occupation.

Australia, c.22,000BC. Ground-edge axes are being used at Malangerr, Northern Territory.

Humans begin to honour their dead with ceremonial burials

Europe, Asia, c.50,000BC
Elaborate burial rituals have been adopted by Neanderthal communities in Europe and Asia, indicative of a growing respect for the dead and suggesting that ideas about some form of life after death are now being generally accepted.

At Shanidar Cave, in the Zagros mountains of Iraq, a man has been buried amidst brightly coloured and sweet-scented garlands of flowers. Some Neanderthal people at Shanidar suffered severe afflictions during their lives and must have been cared for by relatives or friends.

At Le Moustier in France a young man is accompanied by tools made of flint, and animal bones are scattered around him as a form of tribute. In a rock shelter at La Ferrassie, also in France, a man, a woman, two children and a new-born infant are interred in a small cemetery, one grave being covered with a stone slab. In Central Asia, at Teshik Tash, Uzbekistan, a child is interred with a ring of goat horns

Remains of a Neanderthal man who was ceremonially buried in France.

set in the earth about his head. Whether or not these are burials of especially important members of the community is not clear, but one distinction has been noted. Men are usually buried with meat, tools or other items; women do not appear to get the same treatment. Not all

Neanderthal communities show such respect for the dead. At Krapina, in Yugoslavia, smashed bones have been tossed aside along with animal bones with no attempt to bury them; some show cut marks. Cannibalism has been suspected, but this is far from certain.

Temperatures fall and ice encroaches

Britain, 70,000-30,000BC
It is growing colder and the glaciers are marching south again, changing the climate and the environment. The temperate woodland which sustained such a rich variety of animals and plants is giving way to cold tundra where only the hardiest creatures and vegetation can survive.

The hippopotami and elephants which once browsed over southern Britain have been replaced by mammoths, woolly rhinoceroses, bison, reindeer and horses, all well able to cope with the cold.

It remains to be seen what effect the encroaching ice will have on the Neanderthal groups of humans who are living in caves in the west country and the midlands. Armed with characteristic stone tools, they lived by hunting and gathering. These groups are, however, coming under pressure, not only from the changing climate, but also from more advanced human types. The likelihood is that no humans will be able to remain in Britain if the ice continues to advance.

Strange case of vanishing Neanderthals

Europe, Asia, c.30,000BC
As the latest Ice Age enters its closing stages, a considerable mystery surrounds the sudden disappearance of the Neanderthal folk, who flourished for around 100,000 years and had apparently adapted so well to the cold. Their place is rapidly being taken by an entirely new subspecies, the straight-standing, agile and ingenious *Homo sapiens sapiens*. Human beings look set to inherit the planet.

Several theories have been offered to explain the disappearance of the Neanderthals. They do not seem to have interbred and merged with *Homo sapiens sapiens*, as nobody has ever seen a mixed type and the skeletons of each species seem quite distinct.

One theory is that the Neanderthals have been killed off by the newer humans, but no evidence of massacres has come to light. Is disease a possibility?

Two theories rest on special qualities of the Neanderthals. They were tough folk, who had lived through the Ice Age; perhaps they could not adapt to a temporary

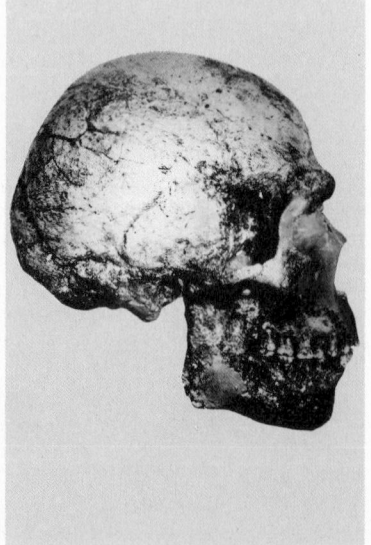

New breed: Homo sapiens sapiens.

warming of Europe's warmer climate. Neanderthals also had a very large brain, which might have continued to increase in size, to such an extent that it became too big for the female birth canal. This last theory is very unlikely. At all events, *Homo sapiens sapiens* is now spreading round the world.

Deep in caves artists paint by flickering lamplight

Europe, c.20,000BC

It was probably before the present Ice Age that people first began to make artificial representations of the world which sustained them. But the first true artistic traditions have emerged only during the last 20,000 years, and key areas of life are now portrayed with a realism and skill previously unheard-of.

Part of this artistic breakthrough lies in the fact that these Ice Age artists are beginning to analyse their environment, as well as carefully observing its physical details; in other words, their work can be symbolical as well as simply figurative, just recording what they see.

Working by lamp-light, deep within the dark recesses of cave systems, they paint mysterious symbols as well as naturalist pictures of the rich panorama of mammoths, reindeer, bison and other beasts they encounter in their daily lives. Indeed, it may be that they believe in painting animals as a sort of charm to increase the likelihood of a successful hunt, possibly because the cold weather is making life more difficult for cave dwellers.

Cave decoration began in earnest about 10,000 years ago. At Les Combarelles, in southern France, the outlines of animals are engraved with flint burins on the rock walls. At Lascaux, in the Dordogne valley in south-west France, cave artists use scaffolding to reach otherwise inaccessible areas of cave walls. The paintings are done – and are only visible afterwards – with the aid of stone lamps, with wicks of lichen and animal fat for fuel, which illuminate only a very small area of wall at a time. This may explain why paintings often overlap and vary greatly in size.

The pigments available to the cave artist include yellow, red, and black made from minerals such as powdered haematite, calcium phosphate and manganese dioxide, some of it brought in from nearly 30 miles away. Large game animals such as woolly mammoths, horses, bison, deer and wild oxen are the usual subjects for the cave artist, although lions and even fish also feature. Although the artists have shown themselves capable of painting, engraving and even sculpting both animal and human figures, images of people are notably rare. Where they do occur, they are nearly always female.

Cave paintings and engravings are generally restricted to southern France and northern Spain. In other parts of Europe and in Russia three-dimensional forms of art are widespread: the inhabitants of Dolni Vestonice in Czechoslovakia are among those who make human statuettes from baked clay. Especially common are bone or ivory "Venus" figurines, so-called because they may be fertility symbols. Often faceless, they are stylised representations of the female form with greatly exaggerated buttocks and breasts.

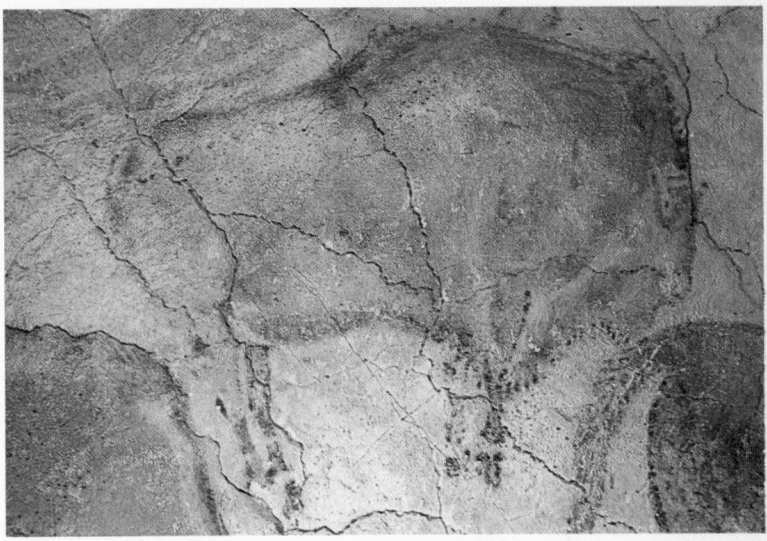

Large game, such as bison, is the most popular subject for cave artists.

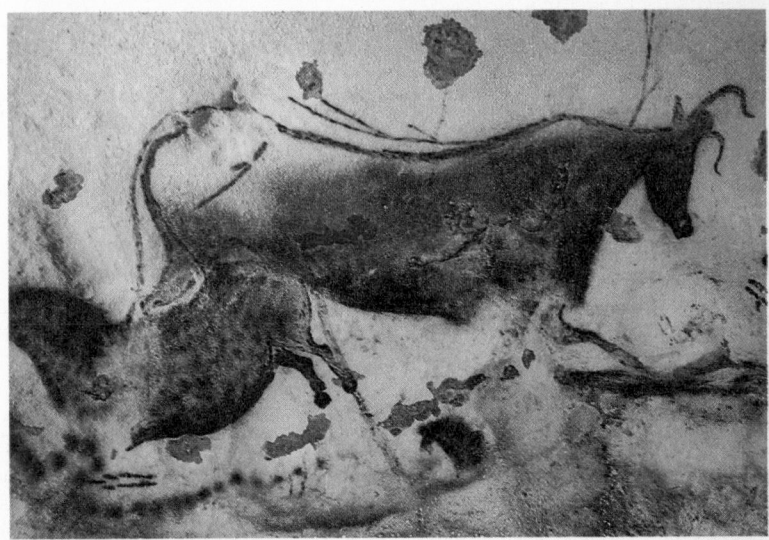

Red, used here to depict cow and horse, is one of the commonest pigments.

Goats and horses at Lascaux: scaffolding lets artists reach high spots.

This bison licking its side was carved from a reindeer antler in the Dordogne.

Fossilised clocks on the sea bed

The story of our early ancestors involves a substantial period of time. The first tools were made at least two and a half million years ago, and human or proto-human creatures were walking upright at least a million years before that. Such statements are easily made, but the vast stretches of time that they take for granted are not easy to comprehend, and it is helpful if these can be divided into a succession of more manageable units. One thing that makes this easier is the fact that there have been numerous major changes of climate, on a global scale, during the last few million years, and these have left abundant evidence in the geological record.

These climatic changes include what are usually known as the Ice Ages: long periods, many tens of thousands of years, of conditions much colder that those of the present day, which caused the polar ice and the local ice caps of the higher mountains to expand greatly, while new ice masses formed on mountain ranges that are today ice-free and spread out over the landscape.

In the case of the British Isles, such local centres of glaciation included the higher mountains of Scotland, Wales, Ireland and even Cumbria; the ice margins on one occasion even reached as far south as the Thames Valley and what are now the outer edges of London, at Finchley and Upminster. During these glacial phases, or glaciations, the other climatic zones of the earth contracted and shifted substantially towards the Equator.

Another ice age is coming

There were several separate glaciations during the last two million years. They were not periods of unbroken intense cold, but show cold peaks separated by less severe conditions and even brief mild oscillations. The various glaciations are separated from each other by substantial periods that were as warm as, or even warmer than, the conditions we experience today: these warm phases are called interglacials; we are living in one at the present.

The causes of the past glaciations are still debated but in general they seem related to variations in the amounts of solar radiation reaching the earth and also possibly to irregularities in the earth's orbit or other changes in its behaviour as a planet. Whatever the factors involved it seems likely enough that they will continue to operate and therefore that glaciation on a massive scale will eventually affect the world again, though probably not within the next 2,000 to 3,000 years.

For a long while it was believed that there had been only four separate glaciations during the Pleistocene period (the geological epoch that occupies most of the last two million years), but it is now known that there were ten periods at the very least.

Easily the best record of all these past changes in world temperatures is preserved in sediments on the beds of certain deep areas of the oceans, which is unfortunate from the archaeologist's point of view, since the ocean beds are hard to relate to archaeological sites on land.

The record is held in the bodies of certain tiny creatures called plankton that live in the surface waters of the oceans. When the temperature changes, it causes variations in the proportion of two oxygen isotopes present in the carbonate of their body structure. After death they sink to the bottom, accumulating in vast numbers to form the "fine ooze" chalk-like sediments on the deep sea floor where, as teh sediments build up, they preserve a continuous record of actual temperature changes over the whole Pleistocene period, and indeed longer, always provided that the sediments remain undisturbed. Samples ("deep sea cores") can be taken through the sea bed sediments for laboratory study and the resulting "palaeo-temperature curve" has shown us how complicated the climatic sequence of the Pleistocene period is.

On land there is no such continuous record; the glaciations involved erosive processes on a massive scale and, as the ice sheets expanded or melted, each one tended to destroy the evidence of its predecessors. Only the last of the series, which ended some 10,000 years ago, can be studied in detail.

Fortunately, other kinds of evidence exist. When such vast and long-lasting changes in climate take place animals and plants are profoundly affected, and leave behind remains of "cold" or "warm" fauna and flora which make it easier to work out what the climate was like at those times. In certain types of deposit animal bones and teeth survive in excellent condition, though very acid surroundings may destroy them completely. Wood and other plant remains are more fragile, although they survive well in waterlogged deposits. Pollen grains however have a high survival capacity and are often easy to identify. But the plants and animals are not only reacting to the climate, they were also evolving. As a result, it may be possible to tell from the contents of a given deposit not merely that it was formed under cold or warm conditions, but to which part of the Pleistocene period it belongs.

Thus for example, in Europe *Elephas meri-*

dionalis, a tropical elephant associated with warm conditions, is present only in the very early part of the Pleistocene period, and its successor is *Palaeoloxodon antiquus*; or again, the particular kind of mammoth that abounded at the height of the last glaciation, is very clearly identifiable. When human bones or tools are found in close association with remains of plants or animals, this can help to date them. Just as important, it may also reveal what kind of environment the humans had chosen; a lake margin in a well-wooded landscape, a river bank in open grassland, or whatever it may be.

Clues in the rocks

These methods, however, do not provide us with direct "chronometric" dates - that is to say, actual statements of age in years. These can sometimes be achieved using one or another form of "natural clock" - usually a radioactive decay process that began when some particular rock was formed and has been continuing at a known and constant rate ever since. This applies especially to rocks of volcanic origin, which, together with some sedimentary rocks, may also preserve a record of past changes of direction in the earth's magnetic field ("palaeomagnetic reversals"), of which the ages are now all known. These help greatly in establishing correlations between Pleistocene sequences, both locally and around the world. It is particularly fortunate, for all these reasons, that the origin and early development of the first human groups took place in East Africa at a time when many volcanoes were active, producing dateable lavas and ash-falls, often the most helpful proximity to undisturbed sites.

The close of the Old Stone Age lies within the range of radiocarbon dating, which relies on the measurable and constant decay of an unstable isotope of carbon, not in rocks this time, but absorbed from the atmosphere to a constant level by all living things up to the time of death. Since the decay rate of the carbon isotope in question is relatively rapid, dates older than about 40,000 years are hard to obtain by currently available techniques.

These few examples will show the variety of ways in which we can hope to solve problems concerning dating, environmental interpretation and correlation between areas; they will also reveal the extent to which archaeologists are dependent on their colleagues working in quite different disciplines.

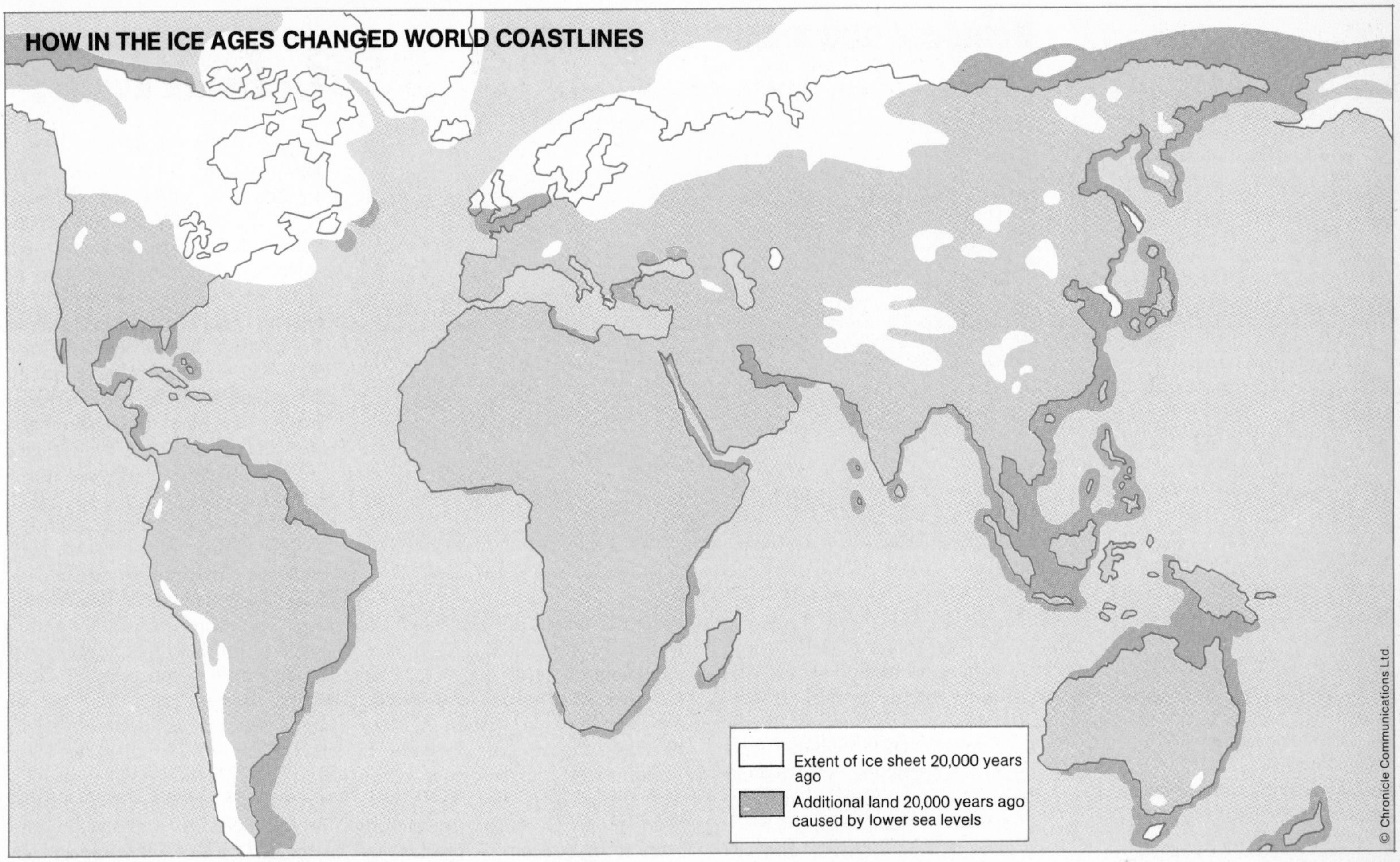

HOW IN THE ICE AGES CHANGED WORLD COASTLINES

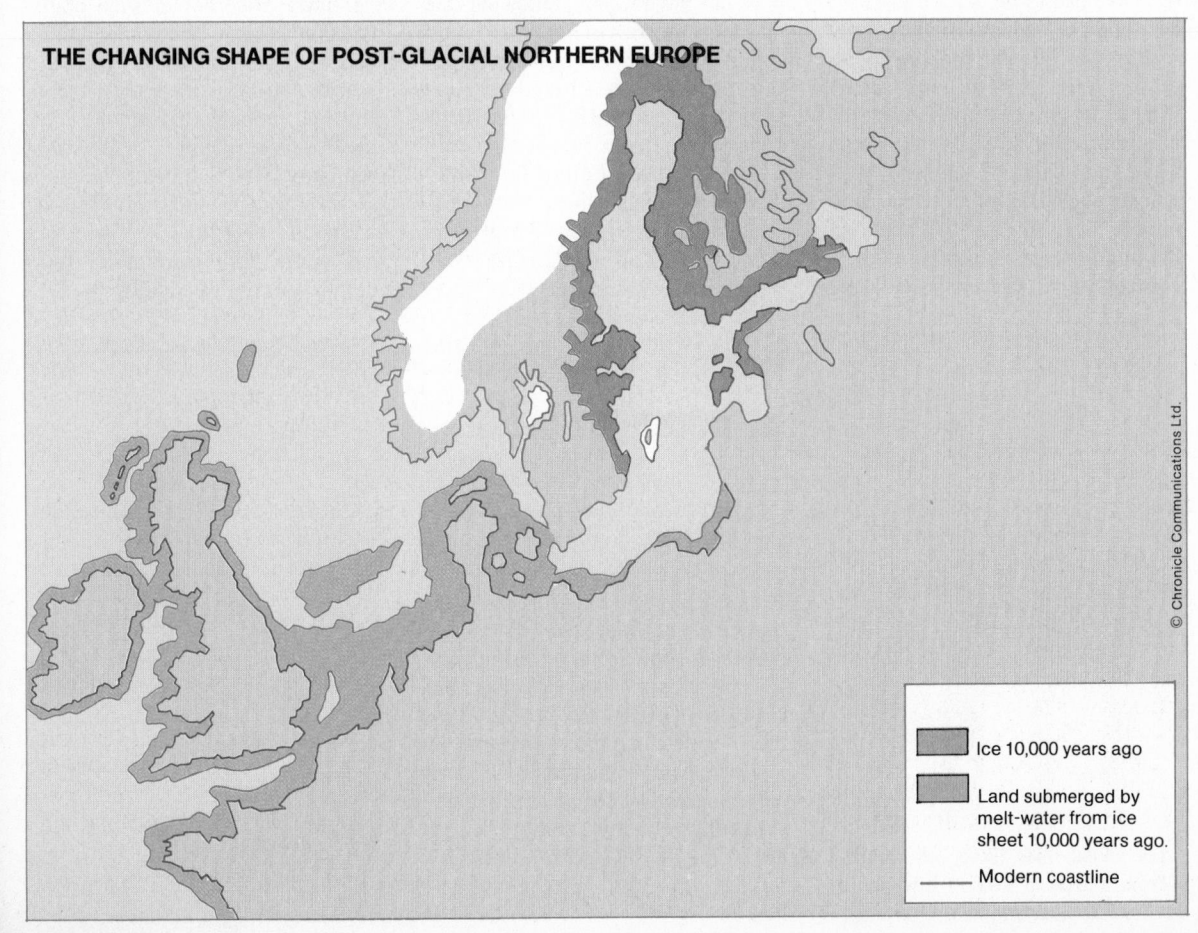

	Extent of ice sheet 20,000 years ago
	Additional land 20,000 years ago caused by lower sea levels

© Chronicle Communications Ltd.

THE CHANGING SHAPE OF POST-GLACIAL NORTHERN EUROPE

© Chronicle Communications Ltd.

	Ice 10,000 years ago
	Land submerged by melt-water from ice sheet 10,000 years ago.
	Modern coastline

Climatic change has literally shaped the world. As ice sheets spread from the poles, some land masses were linked by ice. Elsewhere the freezing of so much water meant that sea levels fell, allowing new coastlines to emerge as what were once sea-beds were exposed. In places, straits ceased to exist and islands became connected to each other, or to neighbouring continents, in the form of "land bridges". One such land bridge was between the British Isles and Europe; others linked North America to Asia, Australia to Tasmania. These land links enabled peoples, animals and plants to spread around the globe.

The most recent of several Ice Ages ended in approximately 10,000BC. Then, as ice retreated, sea levels rose, forcing coastlines back, drowning river valleys and swamping land bridges. In places the land remaining exposed had been affected by the ice, as glaciers gouged deep valleys. With the change in climate came a change in potential animal and plant life – and that, too, had incalculable consequences for the way in which Man learnt to live on planet Earth.

Europe/Asia, c.20,000BC. The cold trend which began about 20,000 years ago is now seeing its lowest temperatures so far. Mammoth-hunters living on the open tundra of eastern Europe and Russia are building houses by fitting mammoth bones together. World sea levels have been drastically reduced, and much of northern Europe has been depopulated.

France, c.18,000BC. Hunting of horses is popular at Solutre in western France; a natural cliff is believed to have been used as a fall trap. High and low relief friezes of horses, bison and other figures are being sculpted at the Roc de Sers cave in the Charente valley. Flutes and the first eyed needles are being made from bone at Pair-non-Pair.

North Africa, c.15,000BC. The tradition of Oranian industries, characterised by the use of blade tools, geometrically shaped microliths and bone points, is spreading across much of the North African coast. The Oranians move between coastal and inland areas to exploit seasonally available resources.

North America, c.11,000BC. Up to 4,000 years ago, while sea levels were low, Asian big-game hunters colonised North America via the Beringia land-bridge. A rapid expansion of settlement is now under way.

Europe, c.10,000BC. The return of a temperate climate is modifying the ecology of Europe. Forests of birch, hazel and oak begin to replace the steppe. The reindeer retreat to the north and the mammoths have disappeared totally. As the forests spread, these animals are replaced by red deer, wild pig and cattle.

Near East, c.8500BC. The past 1,500 years have seen large encampments of hunter-gatherer groups in the Negev desert adopt a more setled lifestyle based on collecting natural resources, such as wild grasses and grains which grow locally. This reflects a period of higher rainfall as the climate grows warmer.

Europe, c.8000BC. Hunters are finding that the bow and arrow is more appropriate than the spear for stalking animals in the forest. The new weapon has been known for at least 1,000 years: a hoard of 100 wooden arrow shafts was left at Stellmoor, near Hamburg in Germany, c.8500BC.

Reindeer and mammoths: a way of life

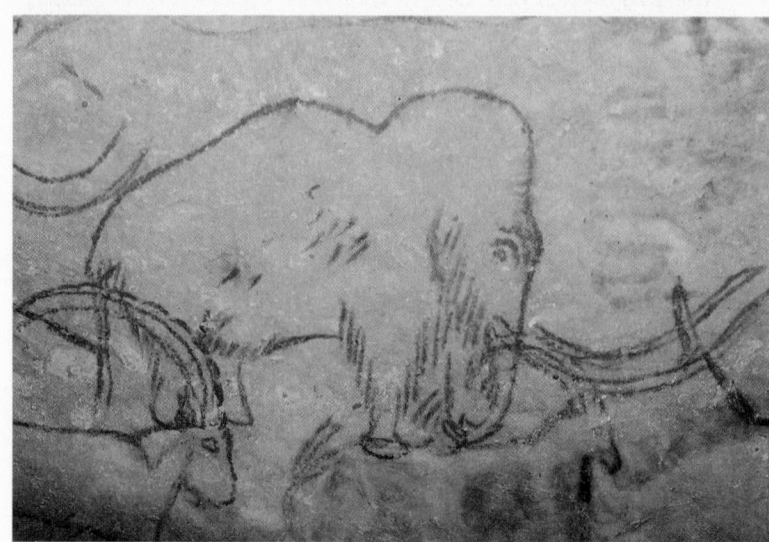

Woolly mammoth: the favourite quarry for hunters in central Europe.

Europe, 20,000-12,000BC
In the later stages of the Ice Age, the vast plains of Europe and Asia are being overrun by herds of reindeer, horses, bison and woolly mammoths, and humans have seized the opportunity of exploiting these animals to acquire rich supplies of food, hides, bone, and ivory.

New hunting strategies and tactics have had to be devised to tackle the mighty mammoth and bison and to overcome the running speeds of the horse and the reindeer. If somebody chances upon a particularly effective way of dealing with a certain kind of animal, it is quickly copied by others in the community. In this way, success in hunting encourages communities to concentrate on certain species and disregard others. Occasionally, for hunters in the Ukraine, bison were the favourite prey, but both here and in central Europe it is usually the mammoth. In western Europe, reindeer and horses are preferred.

Groups of hunters from caves and rock-shelters like La Madeleine in the Dordogne, south-west France, have been taking part in seasonal migrations, following the reindeer north in summer and south in winter. Several camps for the hunters (the Magdalenians) have been established in the Paris region of northern France.

The Magdalenians are also fishermen. From their living sites near river banks they can harvest the salmon that now run up the rivers of the south-west to spawn.

Harpoons, like these, are made from antlers in western Europe.

Pottery developed as nomads settle

Japan, c.12,000BC
Crude pottery vessels impressed with cord are appearing in Japan among settled fishing and food-gathering people. Although the properties of fired clay have been known in some areas for more than 10,000 years, it has only become used for pottery as people have taken to leading more settled lives in permanent communities. Pottery has apparently been invented independently in many other regions of the world as well, most notably by farmers who also make mud-brick houses.

Horses are quarry for French hunters

France, 20,000-10,000BC
The people of eastern France, who are known as Solutreans after one of their main sites at Solutre, near Macon, have taken to hunting the horse, which is now to be seen in large numbers over much of Europe. Solutreans have acquired an intimate knowledge of their prey, and have set up camps along the migration trails of the herds. The remains of over 100,000 horses are scattered near a cliff at Solutre, perhaps driven over it by Solutrean hunters.

The Solutreans are also acquiring a fine artistic tradition and their craftsmen are turning out beautifully fashioned flint implements, especially the projectile points made to tip their hunting weapons. At first such points were of fairly simple designs; now they are of laurel leaf and willow leaf shapes, and a few are over 13 inches long. The best laurel leaves, it is generally agreed, are masterpieces, trimmed on each side by very fine pressure strokes. One can only suppose that the finest examples of such craftsmanship have a ceremonial, rather than a merely utilitarian, function.

Over 500 miles away, in Czechoslovakia, people living at Predmosti, whose culture is somewhat like that of the Solutreans, are also hunters, though their prey is the mammoth. After the kill the tusks and bones have many uses, from making tools to building huts.

How Solutre might have looked.

Hunters reach Americas' southern tip

America, c.10,000BC

After a journey of 10,000 miles from Alaska, America's earliest inhabitants have arrived at Monte Verde in Chile. It seems to have taken them less than 15,000 years.

The origins of the migration go back to when hunters from Siberia crossed Beringia, a strip of land 600 miles wide created by the advancing ice sheets which had lowered sea levels. The hunters travelled across this land bridge to arrive in Alaska. Over the years the hunters trekked south via the coast and along a narrow ice-free corridor, bounded by the great Cordilleran glacier of the Rocky Mountains and the Laurentide ice-sheet covering most of Canada, proceeding west to California, south to New Mexico and east to Pennsylvania.

They were mobile hunters, using distinctive arrow-heads, double-faced with longitudinal grooves. Their prey included mammoths, bears, horses and beavers the size of donkeys – and they hunted them to extinction. Only the bison survived, providing the hunters with meat, marrow, hair and horns.

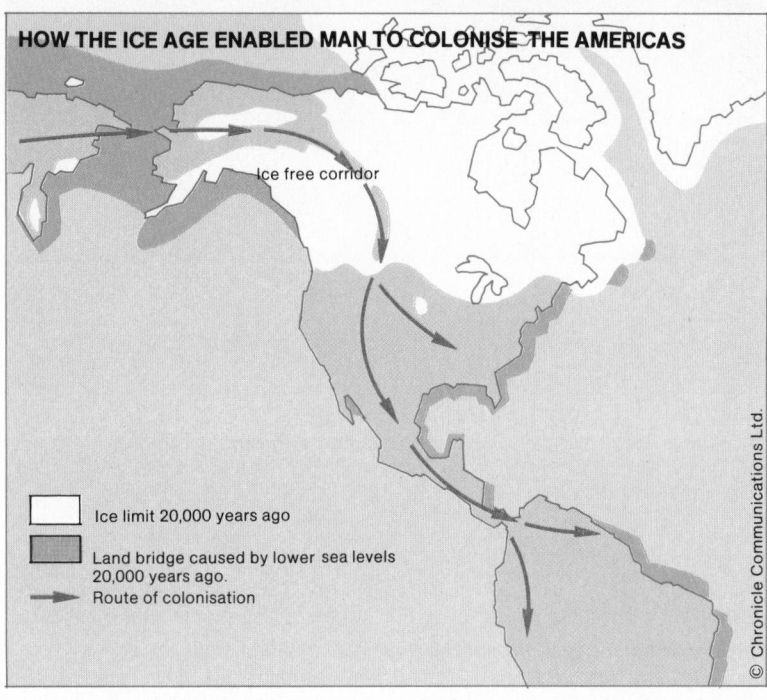

HOW THE ICE AGE ENABLED MAN TO COLONISE THE AMERICAS

Ice free corridor

Ice limit 20,000 years ago

Land bridge caused by lower sea levels 20,000 years ago.

Route of colonisation

© Chronicle Communications Ltd.

A thousand years ago Palaeo-Americans had already passed the Panama Isthmus, and all of the Americas have now been reached. Recent arrivals in Patagonia have been hunting wild animals with bolases and slings, and using the split ivory tusks of the local mastodon, one of the last of the dwindling mammoth family, as chisels for woodcarving, joinery and making weapons.

The Big Chill warms up, but life gets even tougher

Northern Europe, 10,000-6000BC

Great changes are taking place in the lives of human beings as the ice retreats once again. The herds of reindeer which were able to survive in the bleak and and inhospitable environment of Europe are following the ice northwards, depriving the humans of their meat for food, hides for clothing and bones, antlers and sinews for tools.

However, as the steppe tundra turns to grassland, then to forests of birch and pine, and eventually to mixed deciduous woodland, the inhabitants are turning to hunting the new types of animals which inhabit the forests. such as elk, deer and aurochs (a wild ox).

They have been forced to adapt their methods of hunting to suit the environment and these animals, which are less gregarious than the reindeer.

These hunters are supplementing their diet with fish and birds and are relying far more on gathering the abundant fruits of the forest.

New techniques can now process grain

Nile Valley, 15,000-10,000BC

Food production has acquired a novel dimension for the river people of Egypt. On the lower Nile, the Halfan folk are harvesting wild cereal grasses and then using grinding stones to produce a powder-like substance. On the upper Nile, in Nubia, local communities are using flint-bladed reaping knives, and their upper and lower grinding stones are made from limestone.

As the climatic belts shifted after the end of the Ice Age, the weather along the Nile became more moist, and this probably led to wild cereals growing in abundance. This in turn gave rise to big increases in population.

But whether the abundance will continue is in doubt. Drier weather seems to be on the way, which will mean less plentiful cereals. Local communities may shrink and people return to hunting and fishing for their livelihood.

Cereal grasses cultivated for first time

Near East, c.8000BC

For the first time, in a major break with the two-million-year tradition of man as a hunter and gatherer, the people of Palestine have started to clear ground, sow seeds and cultivate small plots of land.

This slow transition from hunter to farmer began about 7,000 years ago, when Kebaran hunters incorporated wild cereal grasses into their standard diet, using flint blades set in wooden hilts as sickles to harvest the grain.

Soon cave-dwelling people in sites such as Hayonim or the caves of Wadi el Mughara, near Mount Carmel, were making depressions in their rock floors for the grinding of grain.

Within 3,000 years wild cereals had become a vital part of the Levantine diet. By 2,000 years ago sedentary Natufians had established larger and more permanent settlements on the grain-rich slopes of the Judaean hills, building circular and semi-circular dwellings of

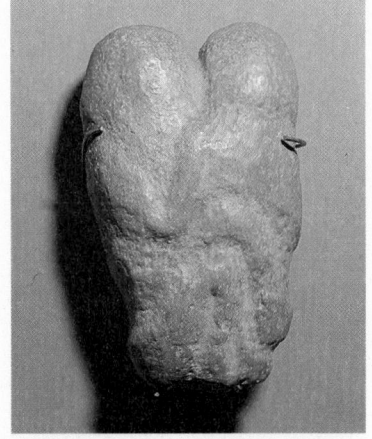

A Natufian kiss captured in stone.

stone, mud and timber, such as they built at Jericho. In addition to flint-bladed sickles they used pounders, pestles and mortars, increasingly supplementing their diet of meat and fish with cultivated cereals.

It was a crucial step in the journey from hunter to farmer, gatherer to producer, which has taken 7,000 years.

Hunting nomads move northwards

Northern Europe, c.8000BC

As the Ice Age recedes and temperatures become more equable, the ice sheets are retracting northwards and the empty landscape in the more northern reaches of Europe – including Britain – is quickly being occupied by humans. A few hunters have stayed with the cold-adapted reindeer and moved to the sub-Arctic areas of Scandinavia and the northern Russia.

As the landscape gradually changes from tundra to woodland in the warmer climate, human technology is adapting and the bow and arrow is established as an effective weapon. The new arrivals are fishing with traps, hooks and gorges. Wood is being used extensively, and axes and adzes to work it are being made from flint and other flakeable rock. Dug-out canoes are being made from tree trunks, allowing the rivers to be used to gain access to the forests.

Jericho, c.8000BC. Centred on the perennial spring of Ain-es-Sultan, in the Jordan valley, the oasis of Jericho has been inhabited for about 1000 years. A permanent village of circular mud-brick houses has now developed here, replacing the semi-nomadic camps.

South America, c.8000BC. Human communities are now established as far south as Tierra del Fuego. In Peru beans and root crops, including potatoes, are under cultivation.

Europe, c.8000BC. Hunting groups are moving into Lappland from the east, south and west.

Jericho, c.7500BC. The inhabitants of Jericho, numbering perhaps 2000, fortify their village with a high stone wall several feet thick, topped by a massive tower almost 30 feet in diameter and 25 feet in height. The scale of the collective effort and the care for common security reflect a society with a previously unparalleled degree of social organisation.

Sahara, c.7000BC. Pottery is being produced for the first time by people in the central Saharan massifs of Air, Hoggar and Tadart Acacus in northern Niger and southern Algeria. Its most distinctive feature is a wavy-line decoration.

New Guinea, c.7000BC. Peasants are cultivating root crops and have begun to domesticate pigs.

Pakistan, c.7000BC. At Mehrgarh, on the western fringes of the Indus valley, a farming village has been established. The inhabitants grow barley and raise sheep and goats; they hunt antelope and other animals. They use stone tools, baskets and mud bricks.

Asia, c.7000BC. Wheat, barley and pulses are under cultivation from Anatolia to Pakistan.

Near East, c.7000BC. As settlements become better established, pottery is used increasingly for storage and for cooking cereals. In regions where stone is scarce, clay, present in abundance, proves an excellent material for fashioning vessels and making them watertight. With refinement, the containers become sturdy and diverse; covered vessels improve both hygiene and insulation.

Bows and arrows boost hunter's kill ratio

Hunters with bows and arrows in a later cave painting from Spain.

Europe, c.8000BC

A new and deadly weapon is being adopted by the people of Europe. Travellers who have seen this invention describe it as a piece of wood, probably a small tree branch, with considerable elasticity, to which a strand of thread-like material is attached at either end and used to bend the wood. A stick is then placed against the bow and drawn back with the thread. When it is released the stick is driven forward with great velocity and is capable of penetrating the hide of an animal. In the wrong hands the bow and arrow, as it is called, could pose a serious threat to human life.

Just when the bow and arrow was invented is not known. It may have developed from the discovery that a tree branch could be tied back and released with great force when the quarry approached. This might have been combined with experience gained from a much older weapon, the spear thrower, a device that enables the hunter to gain extra power in directing the spear at his target.

During the Ice Age in Europe, the spear was widely used in hunting, especially in the open landscapes of the treeless tundra. But as the ice sheets withdrew and forests spread, the large herds of reindeer and similar animals were replaced by more solitary forest species, such as red deer, which had to be hunted by an more adaptable weapon. The bow and arrow, which probably originated in Asia, has now been taken up by European hunters who have greatly improved the design by the use of miniaturised flints.

Composite weapons, made by using resin to stick sharp pieces of flint in wooden or antler shafts, have been in use for many thousands of years. Gradually these bits of flint have become smaller, so that a piece only an inch long can be produced. Given a triangular shape, it is fastened to a stick to produce a light, symmetrical projectile with a good trajectory. This must be the first invention of a device in which energy can be accumulated slowly and released suddenly at the target.

Miniature flints: handy projectiles.

Hammered copper makes its debut

Iran and Turkey, c.7000BC

Astute hill dwellers are prospecting for copper deposits in the mountain chains that form the backbone of the Middle East and south-east Europe.

The prospectors are on the lookout for nuggets of pure copper that can be shaped by hammering. Specialist craftsmen use this method to produce novelties like beads, and awls – handtools for driving holes in leather and wood. So far manufacture of these items has been confined to sites closest to the veins of copper ores that proliferate in this region.

The prized nuggets of "native" copper that can be easily hammered are most commonly found in the upper, weathered veins of ores such as malachite and azurite. Until now the only attraction for collectors of these copper ores has been the decorative stones they provide.

African fishermen improve their diet

East Africa, c.7500BC

A greatly improved diet is being enjoyed by the people living around Lake Turkana in northern Kenya. Not only are there more fish than ever before, but the people are using clay pots for the first time and so are able to have soups and stews.

Because the area has recently been getting wetter the rivers and lakes have swollen, and this in turn has led to a great increase in the number and variety of fish.

The local people have not been slow to take advantage of this and have established fishing communities in the Upper Nile basin and the rift valleys of Kenya. They have developed a new weapon – the harpoon – which has a serrated point carved out of bone, with a notch or grove at the blunt end to enable it to be tied to the shaft of a spear or arrow. From boats, or standing in the shallows, they now use harpoons to spear their prey.

The development of such weapons enables the fisherfolk to enjoy a high protein diet of Nile perch and tilapia, as well as delicacies like waterfowl and turtle.

Skull and fertility cults

Anatolian fertility symbol: pregnant woman with huge breasts and thighs.

Near East, c.7500BC

Now that people of the Near East have given up the nomadic existence and settled down to farming, they tend to spend their whole lives in the same place. The ancestor cult has assumed a great importance for them, and the skulls of relatives are preserved and treated with veneration.

At Jericho, in the Jordan Valley, a particularly strange skull cult has emerged. The skull is filled with clay and the outside painted with a flesh-coloured substance to represent a face, almost certainly that of the dead person. Shells are placed in the eye sockets, and the skull is then set on a small pedestal of red clay on the floor of the family dwelling. The exact purpose of this custom is not clear, though it is possible that the skull of a relative treated in this way may be thought to give protection.

Further east, in the valley of the Euphrates, it is the bull that has become a cult object. The people from the village of Mureybat are gazelle hunters and do not use the bull for food. Instead, they bury the skulls and bones of bulls in the clay walls of their houses. In central Anatolia, at Catal Huyuk, images of bulls are everywhere. Giant bulls are painted on the walls of buildings that appear to serve as sanctuaries. Bulls are modelled in clay and given the horns of real bulls. In some parts of the Near East a female fertility figure appears alongside that of a Bull God, evidently a symbol of power.

The worship of a female deity or spirit seems to have spread throughout much of the Near East. Many Mother Goddesses are to be seen, as well as numerous statuettes of women with huge breasts, thighs and bellies, but with the face touched in only vaguely. At Catal Huyuk statuettes portray women in childbirth. More recently, statuettes of women with slim bodies have appeared. These new women are often holding infants, but, bizarrely, they have been given wigs and the faces of reptiles. They are seen as fertility symbols.

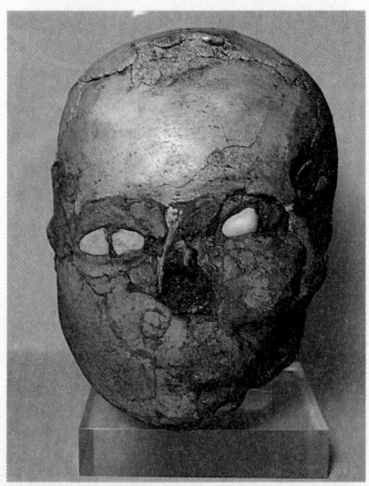

Shell eyes adorn a painted skull.

Farming villages develop in Near East

Near East, c.8000BC

People are beginning to live in substantial, permanent settlements as they move from a life centred on the constant need to hunt and gather food to a more secure existence based on agriculture. Dependence on farming, which consists mainly of growing crops and keeping animals, has two key effects. Firstly, it means that farming people are tied to the land on a permanent basis. Secondly, farming gives rise to larger communities living together, with perhaps hundreds of people in a single settlement. The hunting-gathering lifestyle depends on chasing and killing animals over a wide area, which means that hundreds, even thousands, of acres of land are required to sustain just one human family. But a farming family can grow enough to support itself on as little as 25 acres; as well as allowing for a more settled existence, this makes possible a great boost in the population.

Not surprisingly, the first villages are springing up in the areas most favourable for growing crops, lowland areas with rich soil within the Near East from the Mediterranean to the Persian Gulf. The lush forests of Syria are home to wild elephants; more important for people, though, are the region's wild barley and a plant similar to wheat which grow in southern Anatolia. Another type of wild wheat, emmer, grows in Palestine.

The villages usually consist of little mud-brick houses, which are

Interior of stone tower at Jericho.

round or oval in shape like the tents of more nomadic hunting communities. The large village of Jericho in Palestine, which has probably existed for centuries, has grown to around nine acres of mud-brick houses built on stone foundations.

As well as sustaining themselves, the inhabitants can produce more food than they need, unlike the hunting societies which preceded them and which still persist in some favourable areas. As well as encouraging population growth, this means that, again unlike hunting peoples, it is not essential for everyone to be constantly employed in the production of food, and some people can devote all their time to pursuing other activities and acquiring other skills and abilities. The social make-up of these first farming villages has great potential for diversification.

Settlements are established in Pakistan

Pakistan, c.7000BC

A valuable discovery has been made by the inhabitants of Mehrgarh, a village on the banks of the river Bolan by the western fringes of the Indus valley. These people have found that they can cultivate two wild grasses, barley and wheat, the seeds of which form a part of their diet. Cultivation means they can grow as much of the two plants as they wish, rather than simply gathering what happens to grow wild; this should allow them to boost their food supply and lessen their dependence on the tiring business of constantly hunting antelope and other game.

Their hunting activities have been reduced anyway since they successfully domesticated sheep and goats not long ago, and they are trying the same experiment on the local humped cattle as well.

The villagers of Mehrgarh live in mud-brick dwellings. They store their grain and entomb their dead in separate buildings, also made of sun-baked mud bricks. The main tools used by these resourceful people are axes and scythes made of stone, which are stuck to bone or wooden handles with locally-dug bitumen. The nearby river provides plentiful supplies of rushes for weaving mats and baskets.

Europe, c.7000BC. Pine and hazel trees are flourishing as the climate warms; oak, elm and lime have also appeared.

Japan, c.6500BC. A society has grown up in the Japanese archipelago based on hunting, fishing and gathering. Objects of stone and bone are made, as well as pottery decorated with geometric motifs.

Near East, c.6500BC. Rectangular mud-brick houses replace round huts, as settled villages based on farming and the cultivation of annuals spread through the region. The people make pottery and small clay figurines, as well as large clay figures which sometimes incorporate human skulls.

Greece, c.6500BC. Farmers gradually clear the forests and begin to cultivate corn, barley and millet; in some places they plant lentils and peas. Wild fruits are still collected but horticulture is making good progress: pears, almonds, figs and olives have become part of the daily diet. Shepherds take herds of goats, cattle and pigs to pasture.

Mediterranean, c.6500BC. In rudimentary dug-outs humans take to the sea. Sailing along the shores and from island to island, they colonise new lands. The use of ceramics spreads from the Near East to various regions of Europe.

Europe, c.6500BC. The North Sea plain is inundated by ice meltwater and Britain is cut off from the continent, both physically and culturally. Settlements emerge on the Atlantic coast of France, at places such as Hoedic and Teviec, and at Kongemose and Ertebolle in Denmark. Marine resources are becoming increasingly important.

Europe, c.6300BC. While continuing to hunt, western Europeans are starting to produce their own food and to share out tasks within the community. But there is no clean break with past nomadic life: areas are cleared for cultivation by burning; when the soil is exhausted, the farmers move on in search of other, fertile lands.

Crete, c.6300BC. Seafarers, thought to be from Anatolia, sail along the north coast of Crete and settle at Knossos. They live in dried-mud huts, working the land and growing cereals. They make ceramic vessels and large pots in which to store provisions.

Catal Huyuk sets new rural standards

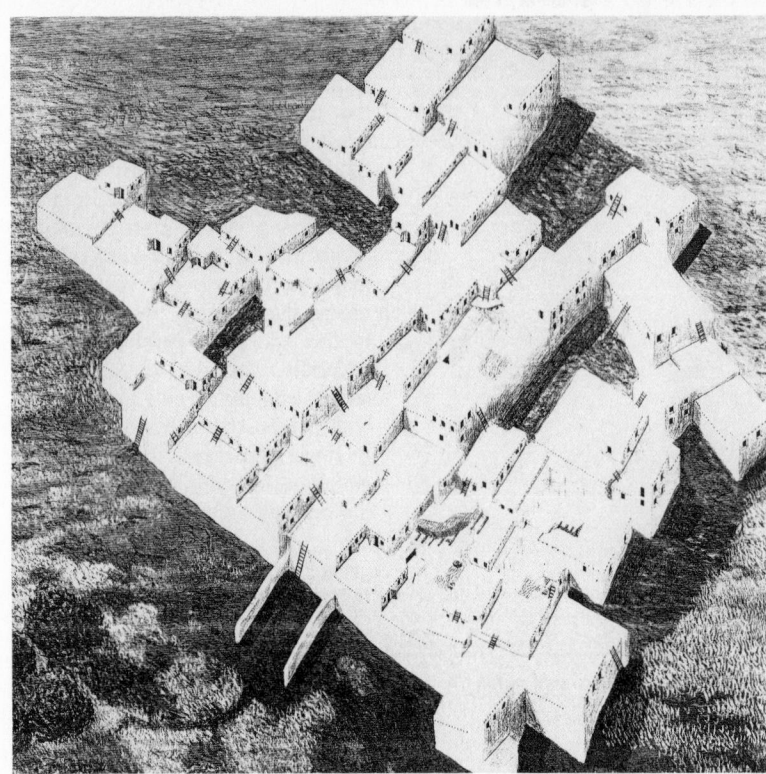

Catal Huyuk seen by "Past Worlds – The Times Atlas of Archaeology".

Anatolia, c.6000BC

The town of Catal Huyuk in central Anatolia is a spectacular example of a large farming community, with a population possibly running into the hundreds. It covers 32 acres, with densely-packed houses located in an area which is very productive for farming, where a river crosses an otherwise arid plain. Unlike the round or oval houses of earlier towns like Jericho, Catal Huyuk's dwellings are rectangular, with rooms often grouped around a courtyard. Most of the houses are entered not through a doorway in the wall but down ladders through an opening in the roof. The inhabitants live partly through hunting, but mainly by farming and breeding cattle, which live in large numbers in nearby swampland. The town is one of the first centres of cattle domestication, which may explain its great wealth, because it can afford to import obsidian, a black volcanic glass used for making cutting-tools and objects such as mirrors. Other sought-after stones, such as apatite and stalagmite, are used to make beads which decorate the bodies of the dead, who are buried under the floors of the houses.

Catal Huyuk possesses an extraordinary series of shrines, which include bull skulls set in clay together with wall paintings of stag-fights and vultures pecking at human corpses. These shrines are all in houses; the town seems to have no religious or administrative centre, which points to a relatively egalitarian society of farmers bound by a common cult or religion.

Thaw brings bounty to northern hunters

Britain, c.7000BC

The ice has melted and forests have sprung up in the warmer weather to provide a new, rich source of prey for the hunter-gatherers of northern Europe. Star Carr in Yorkshire is one place regularly visited by hunters in search of deer, boar, elk and aurochs, a type of ox. Britain is connected by land to the rest of the continent, and the Star Carr hunters exploit similar new techniques and tools to those of other groups in Europe; among the weapons used to hunt the greater number of animals to be found in the forests are bone or wooden-hafted flint arrows and knives.

Sea levels rise as glaciers melt away

Worldwide, c.6000BC

The great Antarctic and Arctic ice-caps, vastly swollen by the last Ice Age, are releasing their waters as the world warms up, and once again the shape of the continents and oceans is being drastically altered as water floods over land which has been dry for thousands of years.

Coastal plains, among some of the world's most productive areas, supporting large herds of game, have been inundated. The most spectacular land loss has taken place in south-east Asia where a whole continent has been submerged, leaving only the tops of its mountains and volcanoes to form an archipelago stretching down towards Australia.

In many areas, islands which had been joined to the mainland are once again cut off and their animals and plants are developing highly individual characteristics.

The rising seas have also cut off human populations and they too are developing individual characteristics, often dependent on the climate and terrain of the land. The sea has almost succeeded in dividing Britain from the rest of Europe, but at present a land bridge still exists. However, it is only a matter of time before this land bridge is eventually covered by the sea and Britain, like many other marooned areas, goes its own separate way.

One of the baked clay bricks used for the walls of Jericho's oval or round houses. The houses are built on stone foundations.

Breeding revolution changes lives

Farmers learn to tame the "wild" sheep of Asia

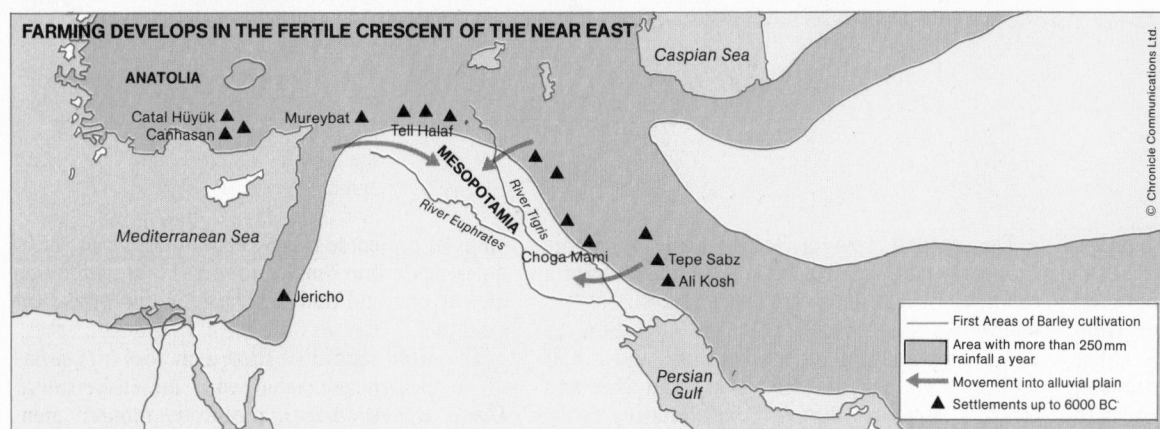

FARMING DEVELOPS IN THE FERTILE CRESCENT OF THE NEAR EAST

ANATOLIA

Caspian Sea

Catal Hüyük
Canhasan
Mureybat
Tell Halaf

MESOPOTAMIA

River Tigris
River Euphrates

Mediterranean Sea

Choga Mami
Tepe Sabz
Ali Kosh

Jericho

Persian Gulf

© Chronicle Communications Ltd.

First Areas of Barley cultivation
Area with more than 250mm rainfall a year
Movement into alluvial plain
▲ Settlements up to 6000 BC

Greece, c.6000BC

Near East farmers, who pioneered the cultivation of wild cereals and sedentary living, are now breeding a complete range of domesticated animals, sheep, goats and cattle. Now they are travelling north with their flocks through the Levant and Anatolia in search of good farmland and pasturage to settle in the Balkans.

Their ancestors were nomadic hunters and gatherers, following the herds and collecting cereals on a seasonal basis. Then they began settling in fertile areas and collecting wild cereals. After a while they learned to cultivate their own cereals, clearing and planting land and harvesting the crops. There was more than enough land, so farmers cultivated patches until the

soil became exhausted and then moved on to the next patch to repeat the production cycle.

Cultivation meant that people became tied to the land, and to secure their supply of meat they began to rear in captivity animals they had once hunted in the open. These domesticated herds are maintained in flocks guarded by shepherds, leaving the flocks to graze on the mountain slopes in the summer and bringing them down to the valleys in the winter.

When humans began hunting in the Near East it teemed with gazelle, which naturally became the staple meat diet. But gazelles proved unsuitable in captivity, and were replaced by the wild goats which roamed through most of the lands around the Mediterranean. Goats

in turn were supplemented by sheep from Khuzistan (*Iran*). The final phase came with the introduction of cattle from the Tigris and Euphrates valleys and central Anatolia. Thus the new stockbreeders are rearing three basic meats: goat, mutton and beef.

Now livestock provides not only a variety of meat dishes, but also leather for clothing and makeshift tents, horns for agricultural equipment and everyday utensils, and milk. However, the consumption of animal milk by humans is only very slowly catching on.

In addition, these domesticated flocks are now used as both a universally accepted medium of exchange and a rough, but ready, way of calculating a man's wealth and power.

Southern Europe, c.7000BC

Domesticated sheep, first reared in Iran, have spread through western Asia and southern Europe to reach the shores of the western Mediterranean.

Wild sheep, restricted to western Asia, have been hunted for their mutton since the closing phases of the last Ice Age. As agriculture developed, people became increasingly confined to plots around their villages and unable to follow the herds. The wild sheep were therefore brought down from the mountains to be reared as livestock, becoming the preferred animal for religious sacrifices.

From Khuzistan (*in south-west Iran*) domesticated sheep spread with trade and barter into the Levant, Anatolia and Greece, where sheep were raised not only by farmers, but also by hunters and fishermen.

The sheep, with their distinctive spiral horns and hairy coats, are valued exclusively for their meat. With the practice of domestication spreading through the Balkans and around the Mediterranean to Italy, Sardinia, southern France and Spain, mutton has become a staple part of the diet of people in Europe and the Near East.

Farming begins in south-east Asia

South-east Asia and Australasia, c.6000BC

In the last thousand years or so, agriculture has begun in the region stretching from Indochina to New Guinea where, in some cases, humans have been since before the last Ice Age. The warmer weather that followed the thaw led to a great growth in the density and types of plant life; particularly along the coasts. People moved towards deliberate cultivation of food crops, although, farming does not supplant food obtained from hunting and gathering. In the highlands of New Guinea, drainage trenches have been dug for crops, presumably taro, for perhaps 1000 years.

Dug-out canoes catch on as transport for trade and animals

Mediterranean, c.6300BC

During the summer months, when the sea is not too rough, fishermen living in the Franchthi cave in the Peloponnese paddle out to sea in canoes made from hollowed-out tree trunks. Usually they go fishing, especially for tunny fish, but sometimes they make a special voyage to the island of Melos where there are outcrops of a black volcanic glass called obsidian, particularly useful for making sharp-edged tools.

The dug-outs, which are widely used by coastal people from the Mediterranean to Denmark, are sturdy boats, quite stable enough to carry the domestic livestock of farming groups who have begun to colonise the uninhabited islands of Cyprus, Crete and Sardinia.

An early 20th century French view of how the first dug-out canoes in the Mediterranean might have been made. They were used for fishing.

Making knives as sharp as steel

One favourite definition of the earliest humans relies on the phrase "Man the Toolmaker". This implies that the ability to make tools, as opposed merely to using them, distinguishes humans from other members of the animal kingdom. Other animals do sometimes use tools: for example, chimpanzees will use a stick or a grass stem to "fish" for termites in termite mounds, and may even break a stick to adjust its shape or length for the task.

But human tool-making from the start involved higher levels of perception, besides greater persistence and accuracy in the manufacturing process. It is one thing to see that an existing stick will be more useful if the end is broken off, but quite another to realise that within a rounded cobble or pebble there are sharp cutting edges waiting to be released.

Workable rock is readily available in most parts of the world. The best and easiest kinds to use are hard, glassy and almost grainless, such as chert and flint, but quartzites, fine-grained volcanic lavas and many others are also effective. Rocks with natural flaws, bedding-planes that split unevenly or variable internal structures, are to be avoided. Flakes can easily be detached, with a suitable hammer-stone, from the edge of any piece of appropriate rock that affords an angle of less than 90 degrees on to which to strike.

For some kinds of flaking, softer hammers of bone, antler or wood can be used. Freshly struck flakes are extremely sharp and will cut wood, meat, hide and many other substances as effectively as a modern steel knife. Their edges can also readily be shaped by further flaking ("retouching").

Recognising the genuine article

When flakes are struck from a piece of stone in the course of tool manufacture, the flakes themselves and the scars left by their removal show characteristic technical features which enable them to be distinguished from rock broken by such natural processes as the action of frost or fire. These features provide the key to our recognising genuine stone implements and understanding exactly how they were made.

The earliest traces of stone tool manufacture yet known come from East Africa: the oldest implements found so far, at least two and a half million years old, are from Kada Gona in northern Ethiopia. Stone tools are much more frequent in the archaeological record from about two million years ago, after the appearance of *Homo habilis*.

The earliest sets of tools included simple choppers, made by detaching a few flakes from a cobble to leave a sharp edge. Such flakes were also themselves used, with hardly any alteration, as knives and scrapers. After about one and a half million years ago, the first true hand-axes and cleavers appeared: these are large cutting tools, more systematically flaked on both faces, showing approximate symmetry and having reasonably straight cutting edges round the circumference or across the top.

They were probably originally made by the *Homo erectus* populations. Hand-axes, accompanied by neatly made flake tools, were widely used, over an immense period of time, in Africa, India, Europe and southwest Asia, by later *Homo erectus* and the earliest *Homo sapiens* people, in places until less than 100,000 years ago. Some of the later examples are made with great skill and elegance, and the latest of all were made by a few of the Neanderthal groups in Europe.

New techniques developed

From about 250,000 years ago new techniques for striking flakes of predetermined size and shape began to be introduced - the so-called Levalloisian technique, for example, in which selected pieces of stone were carefully shaped and prepared until an accurate blow could remove a large oval or pointed flake from the upper surface, requiring little further adjustment to become a finished implement.

This and comparable techniques of flake production enabled the Neanderthal population, in particular, to fashion elaborate sets of flake tools, precisely made and showing great consistency of shape, size and edge angle; many of them have been found in the caves of southern France, though their distribution also includes Europe, North Africa and western Asia.

Between 45,000 and 35,000 years ago an important new technique of stone toolmaking spread rapidly over the Old World. It involved the striking of long, narrow blades, rather than broad flakes, from carefully prepared blocks of stone which are called "blade cores". Many blades could be obtained from a single core, and they were struck with the aid of a punch rather than directly with a hammerstone.

Their nature permitted the design of many new kinds of tools: penknife-like backed blades, delicate engraving tools and awls, elegant scrapers with long handles and several different kinds of projectile points. Blades were also sometimes made into "multiple tools" - an engraving tool at one end and a scraper at the other, for example.

The rapid spread of these new tool-kits seems to be clearly associated with the dispersal of *Homo sapiens sapiens*, physically modern man, over most of the Old World and eventually parts of the New World, during the Upper Palaeolithic period. Many of the blade tools seem to have been designed to work bone and antler, and sometimes to decorate them, since it was at this time that objects made of these materials became abundant.

Durable and vital evidence

Blade tools continued in use until the end of the Old Stone Age, and indeed beyond; different types and styles were characteristic of different peoples and regions during the closing 30,000 years or so of the last Ice Age. Some clever techniques were invented, such as "pressure flaking", in which fine, flat retouch flakes were removed by pressing, rather than striking, on the edge of a blade, to obtain a very accurate and beautiful finish in making projectile points.

It was also discovered that some rocks, particularly flint, would flake much more easily if they were gently heated on a hearth for several hours. That process certainly made pressure flaking easier to achieve. At the very end of the Old Stone Age various tiny tools, made from small bladelets, came into use: these are called *microliths* ("literally, little stones"), and were often of geometric shapes like crescents, triangles or rectangles. They were hafted in groups to make composite projectile points.

Stone tools are extremely durable as archaeological evidence and provide an important source of information. While it is true that their typology and technology may reflect their age or characterise some particular region or people, it is important to remember that they were made for use and their nature is strongly influenced by the particular tasks in view at the time.

The fracture characteristics of locally available rock may also affect their form. Archaeologists are increasingly concerned with studying such aspects of stone tools: for example, microscopic traces on their working edges can sometimes show how they were used and on what kind of substance. Such evidence is vital to our understanding of the remote past.

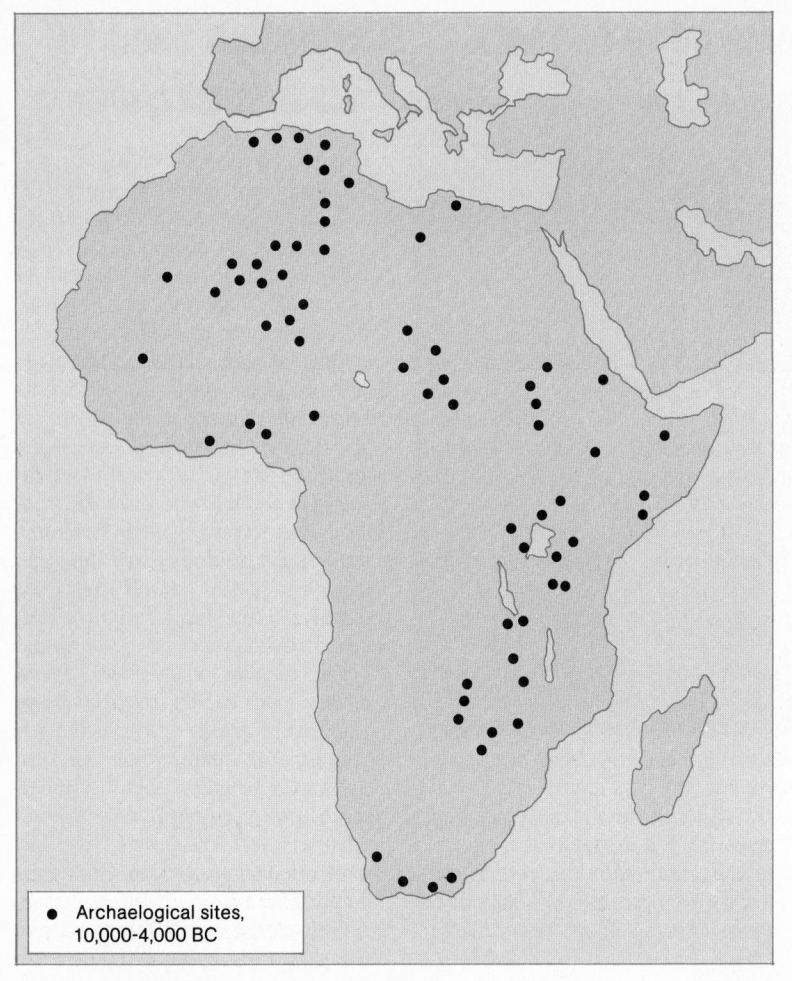

● Archaelogical sites,
    10,000-4,000 BC

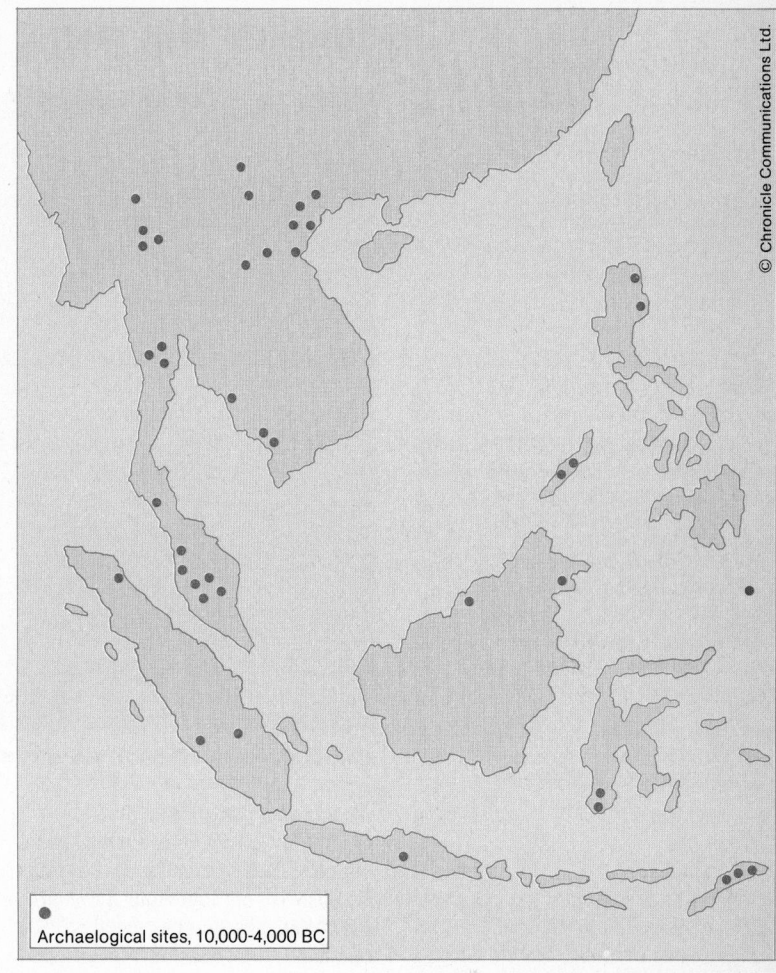

● Archaelogical sites, 10,000-4,000 BC

© Chronicle Communications Ltd.

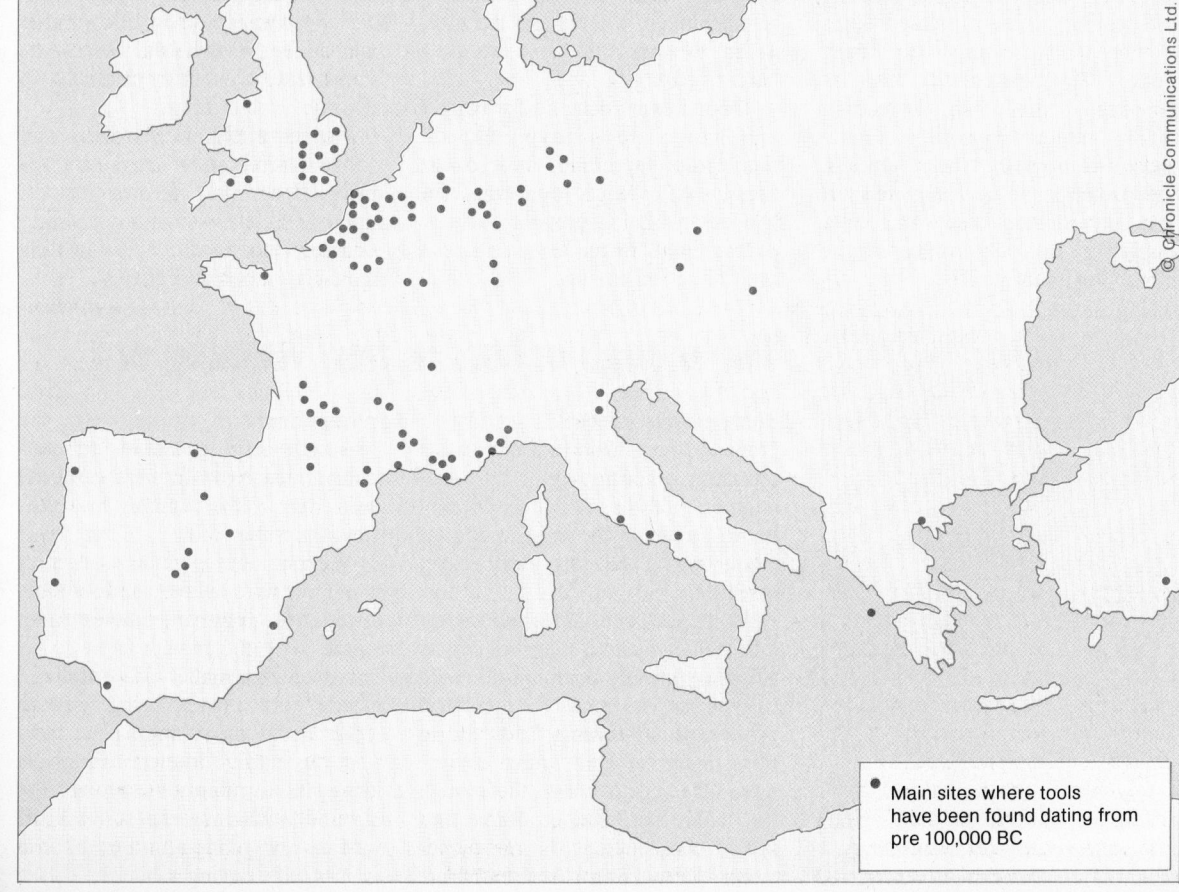

● Main sites where tools
   have been found dating from
   pre 100,000 BC

© Chronicle Communications Ltd.

Early Man lived by hunting and gathering, but evidence of his settlements is hard to find. The best clues to his presence are finds of primitive tools, such as stone axes and tools to cut down trees for fires. Although the first communities were nomadic in the sense that they moved around their territories, rivers and lakes were popular sites for more permanent settlements.

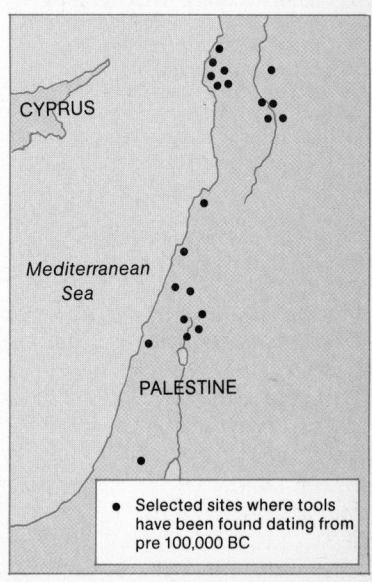

CYPRUS

Mediterranean
Sea

PALESTINE

● Selected sites where tools
   have been found dating from
   pre 100,000 BC

North America, c.6000BC. A climatic change brings a spread of forests in eastern North America, but increased aridity to central and western parts. Hunters make use of smaller game and vegetable foods as larger grazing animals such as the mammoth become extinct.

Mexico, c.6000BC. There have been cave-dwellers in the arid region of Tamaulipas since c.7000BC. Primarily hunters and gatherers, they have now begun to grow peppers, marrows and pumpkins.

Cyprus, c.5800BC. Coming by sea from Asia, farmers have set up villages on the island of Cyprus. They live in small round huts with stone foundations and walls of clay or dried mud. They make stone tools and stone vessels.

Pakistan, c.5500BC. The inhabitants of Mehrgarh, on the edge of the Indus valley, have learnt how to make pottery from burnt clay, and small clay female figurines. They carry on long-distance trade in precious stones and sea shells.

Mesopotamia, c.5400BC. Settlers have appeared for the first time on the banks of the Euphrates, at Kish, Eridu, Ur and al-Ubaid. They produce buff-coloured pottery with abstract, red-brown painted decoration.

Mexico, c.5000BC. Maize is becoming an important crop in the Tehuacan valley.

China, c.5000BC. Rice is put under cultivation in the Homudu region of China.

Europe, c.5000BC. Along the Mediterranean coast from Spain to Tuscany settled communities are emerging. People still live in caves, but outdoor shelters, in the form of round huts, are appearing. Sheep, oxen and pigs are raised, and wheat and barley grown. Potters make bowls, bottles, cooking pots, ladles and amphorae, decorating the clay with the imprint of shells.

Near East, c.5000BC. Copper is being used for the casting of objects such as mace-heads.

Egypt, c.5000BC. The village communities recently set up in Egypt are working the land, cultivating wheat and barley.

Americas, c.5000BC. As rudimentary cultivation of corn develops, formerly nomadic people are establishing fixed settlements.

Coppersmiths give a new edge to tools

Copper sceptre and "crown" found in a valley cave near the Dead Sea.

Near East, 5000-3000BC
Communities are producing more copper-based tools and weapons because of an ingenious new process that allows the metal to be extracted by heating rocks that contain copper ores.

The process involves placing ore-bearing rocks in closed kilns similar to those used for firing pottery. Temperatures as high as 800 degrees centigrade are reached before molten copper is finally separated from the rocks. Once it has cooled it can be hammered flat and cut with stones, as with copper nuggets – the only source of the metal previously worked.

Coppersmiths are also using the discovery that copper can be melted to create new tools, by casting molten copper into moulds shaped like tools such as adzes and hammer-axes.

Other materials, such as arsenic, are being added to copper while it is still molten; these make the tools easier to cast and give them a harder finish.

The increased demand for copper ores has led to quarrying expeditions into mountain and desert areas, with large quantities of copper ores being brought back by pack animals to the smelting ovens at farming settlements.

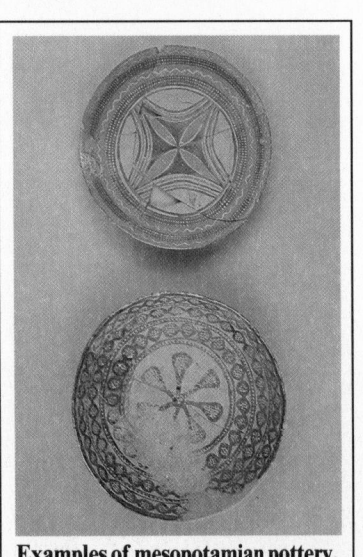

Examples of mesopotamian pottery.

Irrigation used to boost farm yield

Mesopotamia, 6000-4000BC
Farming communities can look forward to higher crop yields and opportunities to bring more land into cultivation with the introduction of increasingly ingenious and sophisticated largescale irrigation schemes.

One of the largest man-made schemes in Mesopotamia now harnesses the annual floodwaters of one of the two major waterways, the Euphrates, allowing cereal crops in fields some distance from the banks to be irrigated. While the technology behind these artificial irrigation canals is not new, the scale of the work involved is unprecedented.

The digging of miles of dykes, ditches and canals required huge amounts of labour and considerable organisation. Before the lowland Euphrates scheme could be undertaken, prototype artificial irrigation schemes were constructed at sites where small streams could be easily diverted.

One of the first projects was at Choga Mami, near Mandali, in Iraq. Started in 6000BC, it has trenches dug at right angles across a slope where a stream flows. The natural lie of the land forces the water sideways into channels to irrigate fields of crops.

Further afield, in the Nile and Indus basins, water engineers are using dykes and ditches for the opposite effect – damming watercourses to prevent floodwaters damaging crops and homes.

The plough ushers in new farming era

Mesopotamia, c.6000BC
Nobody knows who first thought of attaching a hoe to a pair of yoked animals, but the plough is turning out to be one of the most important labour-saving farming devices yet invented.

Along with the increasing use of artificial irrigation schemes, it is allowing farming communities both to increase enormously agricultural production on existing fields and to bring marginal land under cultivation. One region where the plough has had widespread economic and social consequences is the wind-swept Near-Eastern steppes. Here ploughing has opened up the seasonally arid grasslands to crop cultivation. Now farmers turn the soil over in the autumn in readiness for winter rain.

Without the plough, soil preparation was tedious and labour-intensive, requiring hoeing by hand. How the plough came to be invented is a matter of conjecture. Cattle were already being used to drag loads, and it may have been that a badly loaded hoe was dragged accidentally along the ground, scratching the soil off the surface and giving a farmer the idea of properly rigging a hoe.

Peasant-farmers import ceramic skills into river valleys of Eastern Europe

Model of a head in painted baked clay produced by potters in the Balkans.

Eastern Europe, c.5000BC
A great migration is taking place in central Europe. Bands of peasants from the Balkans are trekking north across a broad front to set up farming communities along the rivers which link the plains of Hungary, Czechoslovakia, Poland and Germany. They are drawn here by the fine, mineral-rich soil known as loess which was blown here by the wind from the edges of the recently retreating ice sheet.

Driven by the need to find new land, the farmers build villages in forest clearings along the banks of major rivers, like the Danube, and their tributaries. These settlements are characterised by large timber buildings which, apart from housing the inhabitants, also serve as barns, cowsheds and cornlofts. Stone wedges are used for splitting and working the timber. Sickles, scrapers and blades of various kinds are made from flint.

Farmers employ the technique of ring-barking to kill trees, thereby creating enough light in the forest to grow crops. Small fields are cultivated and used as grazing for sheep, goats and oxen. These people live a peaceful existence, and feel no obligation to build defences around their settlements; the only purpose of the palisades which sometimes surround the settlements is to corral their livestock.

The settlers devote much of their energy to making tools for their work on the land, but their skills are best demonstrated by their techniques for making pottery, many of which are derived from their ancestors in the Balkans. Early examples of their tableware have been decorated with ribbon-like patterns and dots incised into the clay.

Recently they have been elaborately decorated, by using a pointed stick, in horizontal or vertical bands, garlands, and herringbone patterns. Sometimes they are highlighted in white.

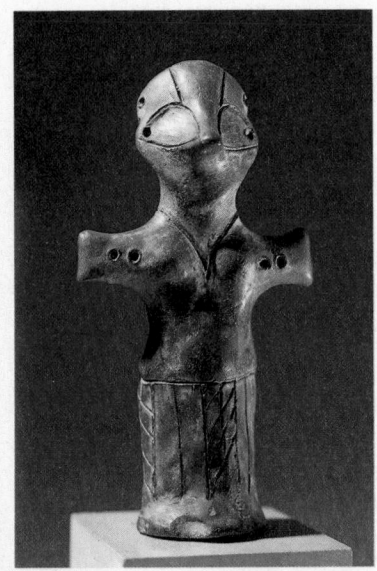

An anthropomorphic idol made of painted clay, from Yugoslavia.

Pottery is now decorated and practical

Near East, c.6000BC
One of the signs of a wealthy community these days, in many parts of the world, is the presence of beautiful vases covered with brightly coloured geometric or animal designs. Hollowed stone bowls are obsolete, as are wicker baskets smeared with clay for carrying water.

Pottery first appeared in Japan and China around 4,000 years ago, but subsequently a number of other settlements discovered how to make it quite independently. What they had in common with the Japanese and Chinese potters, however, was a settled way of life because, since earthenware pots are both fragile and heavy, they are of little use to a nomadic people constantly on the move.

Once people settled down and started lighting fires in mud-brick houses, they discovered that the clay near the flames became hard. From that it was only a short step to making crude pots by coiling strips of moist clay on top of one another. They then smoothed and decorated the sides before briefly heating them over an open flame. Alternatively, they built a mould of the desired shape and spread the clay around it.

Pottery was first made in the Near East, about 1,000 years ago in Syria and Palestine, and its use spread rapidly to Mesopotamia and Anatolia. At first it was used mainly for religious and aesthetic purposes, but recently improved techniques have made the pots more durable and now highly decorated pots are being used domestically.

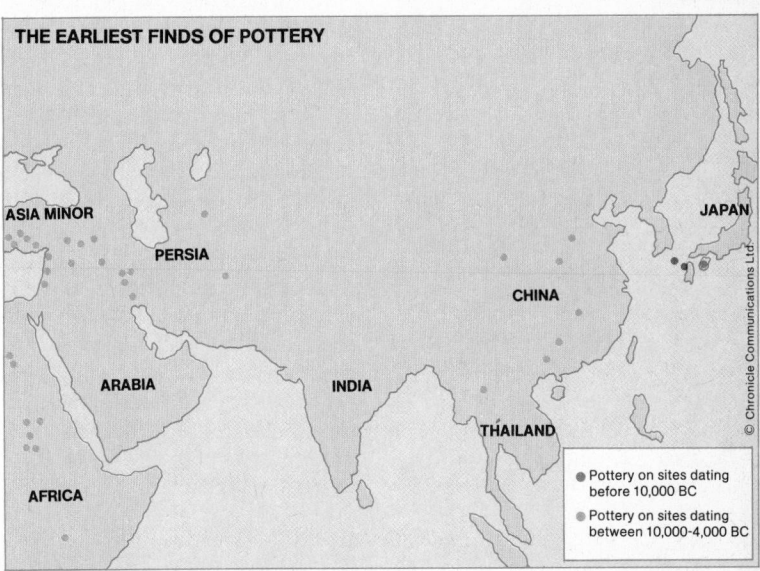

THE EARLIEST FINDS OF POTTERY

Sailing boats flourish on the River Nile

Egypt, c.4500BC
The Egyptians are using more sophisticated boats on the River Nile. The Nile is Egypt's chief internal artery of communication as well as the provider of life-giving water to sustain the people. It is probably the importance of river traffic that has led to the development of more efficient vessels. The primitive reed boats which have long plied the river are giving way to ones in which the muscle power of oarsmen is backed up by shortmasted square sails. The prows and sterns of these vessels are raised and the hulls streamlined for greater speed.

This Egyptian pot is decorated with a painting showing the type of sailing boat now in use on the River Nile.

Metal-working spreads towards Europe

Europe, c.4000BC

Metal is beginning to rival stone as a material for making tools as more craftsmen acquire skills in working bronze, copper and gold. Copper is now being smelted on a sufficiently large scale to produce copies of everyday stone stools. Chief among these are shafthole axes. The copper versions are cast in simple open moulds. Once the copper has cooled they are turned out of the mould and hammered into shape.

The increased demand for copper has led to new methods of prospecting for the carbonate-rich copper ores, such as malachite, which are relatively easy to smelt.

Instead of looking for ore veins on the surface and hacking away at the rocks, prospectors now drive shafts a yard or so wide into the rock along the prominent veins of ore. The veins, which prospectors recognise by their colour and texture, are then excavated using stone mauls – heavy two-handed hammers.

Some of the largest mines, as these excavations are called, are in the Balkans, which is rich in copper-bearing ores.

Ironically, the shafthole hammer-axes which are eventually cast from copper are too soft for use in the copper mines. Nonetheless the copper versions are much-prized as status symbols, sometimes serving as symbols of authority for heads of families and clans. In keeping with

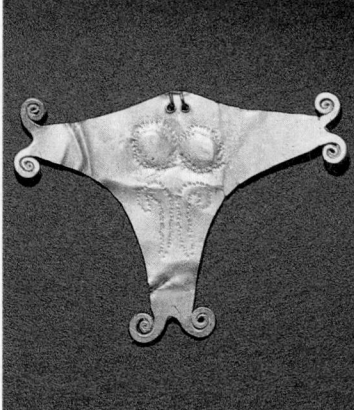

Gold plaque of a stylised female.

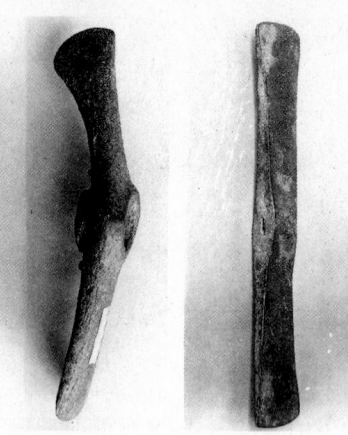

Axes are now made from iron.

tradition these chiefs are often buried with their copper axes and other items of personal equipment.

Gold nuggets, found by panning in streams, are being beaten into shape to make ornaments.

Headache? Try a hole in the head

France, c.4000BC

A brain "operation" has been carried out in Montpellier-le-Vieux on a patient. The illness from which the patient was suffering was madness. The treatment: drilling or trepanning into the skull with sharpened flints in a neat circle to let the demons out.

Priests pronounced the operation a success. The patient, who had been anaesthetised by a carefully mixed dose of plants and herbs, is reported to be much quieter than before. He cannot remember a thing.

This kind of treatment, now said to be practised around much of the Mediterranean, is regarded as further evidence of man's growing medical expertise. Other treatments in use – less spectacular than trepanning skulls, but possibly more effective – have been devised to try to prolong or improve the quality of life.

Thorns have been used to pierce abscesses and draw blood, sharpened flints have been deployed on teeth, and serrated slate has been used to make amputations quicker and easier. None of these advances would have been possible if it had not been for an increasing knowledge of the medicinal properties of plants, which not only anaesthetise but also heal wounds, cure fevers and provide antidotes to poisons.

Hunter-gatherers put down roots and begin to farm in China

China, c.4000BC

The people of China have become more settled in the 6,000 years or so since the last Ice Age. When the ice melted, Chinese hunter-gatherers were quick to exploit the boost to plant and animal life brought by warmer weather. There were rich pickings for some from the sea around southern China; others began to develop agriculture with the plants and animals found in their areas, and as farming became more established communities settled down. The villagers of Banpo in northern China keep pigs and dogs, as well as growing various types of millet in the dry climate. In the wetter south other crops have become popular, especially rice.

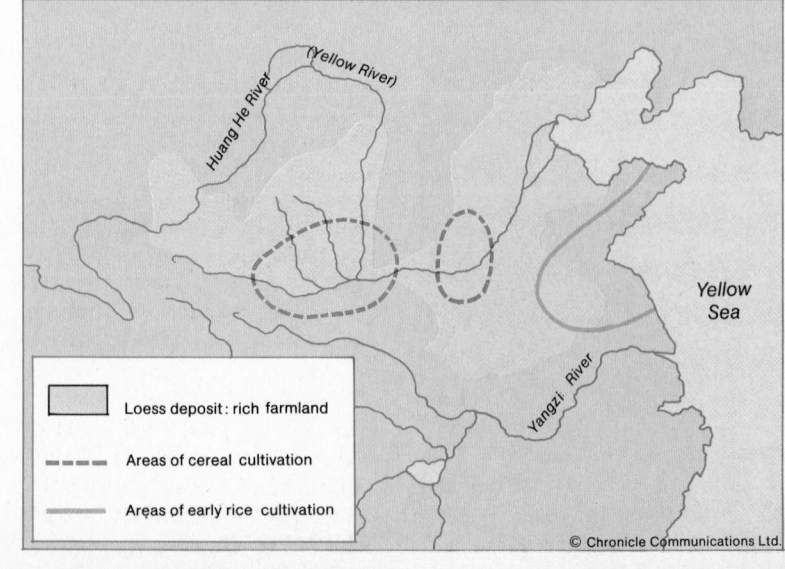

Loess deposit: rich farmland

Areas of cereal cultivation

Areas of early rice cultivation

© Chronicle Communications Ltd.

Stones mark holy sites

The entrance to a grave at Locmariaquer, near Carnac, in Brittany.

Europe, c.4000BC

Massive stone monuments marking graves and religious sites are being erected by the peoples native to the coastal regions of Europe. This development is part of the changes taking place in these regions following the arrival of the farmers who have spread across Europe from the east.

The original inhabitants, largely fishermen and hunters, have learnt how to grow cereals and rear livestock from the newcomers and have prospered. It is thought that their use of stone for monuments is a jealous reaction to the timber houses built by the people from the east.

Whatever the reason, these monuments are skilfully made and will no doubt last for thousands of years. In some of them the dead are buried in small chambers which can be re-opened to take further bodies.

The burial chambers are made out of huge stones and are called megaliths. They are encased in mounds of earth and stones, usually circular, which are built up in tiers to form a tall landmark. Often situated on prominent hills, they can be seen for many miles.

Other stones, up to 35 feet high (menhirs), are dragged to places of worship and set up singly. Some are engraved with geometric designs while others are shaped in human form.

The influence of the eastern immigrants can be seen most clearly in the north, where the stones are incorporated in long burial mounds resembling the long-houses of the immigrants.

What is so remarkable about this development is that the houses of the native people remain insubstantial. It seems that they would rather provide secure places of rest for their dead than shelter for themselves while they live.

Massive standing stone (menhir) near Dol-de-Bretagne in Brittany.

Wild horses come under human control

Eastern Europe, c.4000BC

Man has found a new way to travel without having to walk. Tame horses which allow humans to ride them are in use from the Black Sea to the Mediterranean, as Russian horse experts trade their mounts with Balkan farmers.

A horse is usually ridden by a single rider, sitting astride the horse's back. The rider holds on and stays upright by holding two leather straps, which are attached to a piece of antler secured across the horse's mouth. This allows the rider to control the movement of the horse's head and with it the direction in which the horse will travel. If the horse runs too fast a jerk on the reins will bring its head up and make it slow down.

Credit for first taming horses is given to people on the banks of the rivers Dnieper and Don and in the steppes north of the Black Sea. They have long been skilled in animal breeding, and taming wild horses seems to be an extension of this.

The ability to travel by horse has given these communities greater access to the grasslands of the steppes, where they use their horses for looking after their herds of cattle, sheep, goats and pigs.

Neolithic villages flourish in the Balkans

Balkans, c.4000BC

The first farmers settling in south-eastern Europe are building free-standing houses with pitched roofs. Some are laid out in a square, with four entrances to surrounding palisades, aligned to the cardinal points of the compass. These village layouts do not appear to be dictated by practical considerations, nor are they merely accidental. They might well be inspired by ideas about an afterlife or the spirit world, and linked to male and female principles, since burials follow a strict pattern of orientation, men and women being placed in graves facing in different directions.

Female statuettes of clay have become familiar household ornaments. They are thought to have been treated as "mother goddesses" and, although there is unlikely to be any notion of a supreme being, either male or female, it is clear that women play an important part in the mythology of these communities and are closely related to ideas about house, health and home. Other evidence of magic and ritual is seen in symbols inscribed on clay tablets.

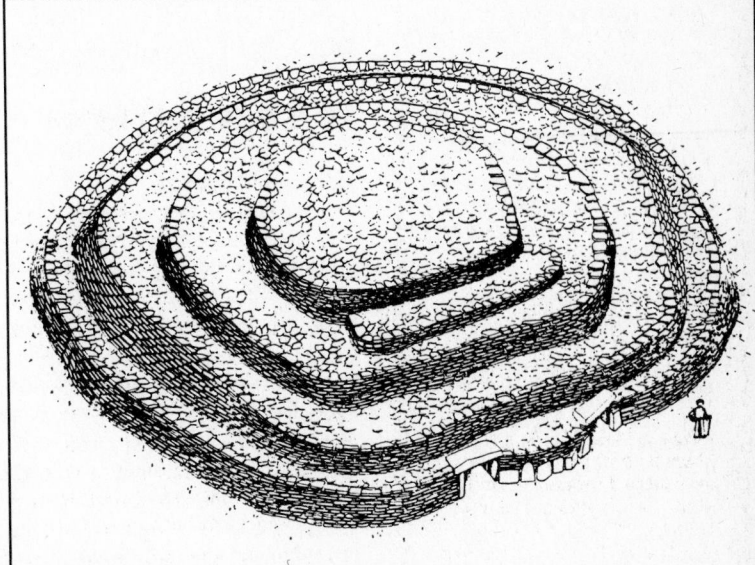

A typical passage grave set in a round mound, at Dissignac, western France. The grave has a chamber approached by a passage from the front, and the mound is built of successive tiers of rubble. It will serve as a communal tomb for several generations of a small family.

West Africa, c.4000BC. Coastal people are making pottery at Tema, on the ocean shore of Ghana.

Egypt, c.4000BC. Two large cultural groups are forming and settling along the Nile valley. One of these is concentrated around the Nile delta and near the Faiyum oasis, while the other group occupies the upper Nile valley.

Australia, c.4000BC. Small finely worked stone tools are becoming more popular in Australia after first appearing in Arnhem Land, Northern Territory, 1,000 years ago.

Mesopotamia, c.3500BC. Towns and cities, new forms of civilisation, are developing. Each town is a religious centre, and its two main monuments are a temple and a royal palace. They are also centres of trade where peasants and citizens can exchange goods.

China, c.3500BC. The Longshan people in the east and north-east, noted for their use of fine black ceramics, are setting up the first towns in China. The Yangshao culture of Henan in the north was established about 500 years ago; its pottery is distinctive for its geometric painted patterns. The peasants in these regions grow millet and raise dogs, pigs, sheep and oxen.

India, c.3500BC. Mountain-dwellers from Baluchistan and southern Afghanistan are moving into the Indus valley, where wild animals abound in the forests. The soil here is fertile and well irrigated, and the newcomers are busy clearing land suitable for cultivation. Some of the villages are growing into small towns.

Europe, c.3400BC. Along the Atlantic coast of western Europe, complex architectural structures are being built in which to bury the dead. Most consist of a rectangular or round funeral chamber reached by means of a corridor. The body is surrounded by polished hatchets, objects made of precious stones, necklaces and pieces of pottery.

Egypt, c.3300BC. Metallurgy of copper, bronze and iron, perhaps originally imported from western Asia, has become well established in Egypt, but without any substantial innovations in form or technique. The Egyptians continue to use farm tools made of finely polished stone or of flint, which has the cutting quality of metal.

Saharan art styles alter with climate

Recent Saharan rock paintings.

Sahara, c.3700BC
Cave paintings in the Sahara are changing. For 5,000 years people have been decorating rocks with pictures of the wild animals they see around them, such as giraffes and elephants. Now, however, the climate here is getting drier and some of these species are disappearing from both the landscape and the paintings.

Their place is being taken by desert animals which are now appearing on the rock walls along-side religious images and scenes from everyday life. Among the newcomers are domesticated cattle, symbolising the fact that the people have begun to live in farming communities.

Heady brew found in fruity ferment

Near East, c.3500BC
People have discovered bizarre properties in the dates, grapes, figs and other tree-crops they have learnt to cultivate in recent times. If these fruits are left lying around in pots or jars, it seems their juice will often ferment; the fermented juice can form the basis of a brew which, it has been found, has a curiously narcotic effect when drunk. Such potions are now being deliberately made, and have become very popular, although the drinks from the vine and dates are dear to produce. But fermenting techniques can also be used on more plentiful malted cereals to make a cheaper brew, even if its thick sediment means it has to be drunk through a straw.

Animal traction opens up Europe to trade

Europe, c.3500BC
Farmers are starting to rear livestock for their potential pulling power as well as the meat and milk they can yield.

Two innovations – the plough and the cart – have made farmers appreciate the value of animals as a source of traction. Oxen are proving especially useful for pulling heavy carts. These vehicles, with their large solid disc-shaped wheels, can carry greater loads than either humans or horses, enabling communities to trade and barter agricultural and metal goods on a much larger scale than hitherto.

The ox-drawn plough is making it possible for small groups to cultivate larger areas of land than was once thought possible. This has provided the incentive for opening up the forests, and people have begun chopping down trees to clear areas for farmland. The plough also allows farmers to grow crops on land where the soil, until recently, has been considered too light or too poor for cultivation. As forests are cleared, the land can be used for grazing as well as cultivation and herding becomes more important.

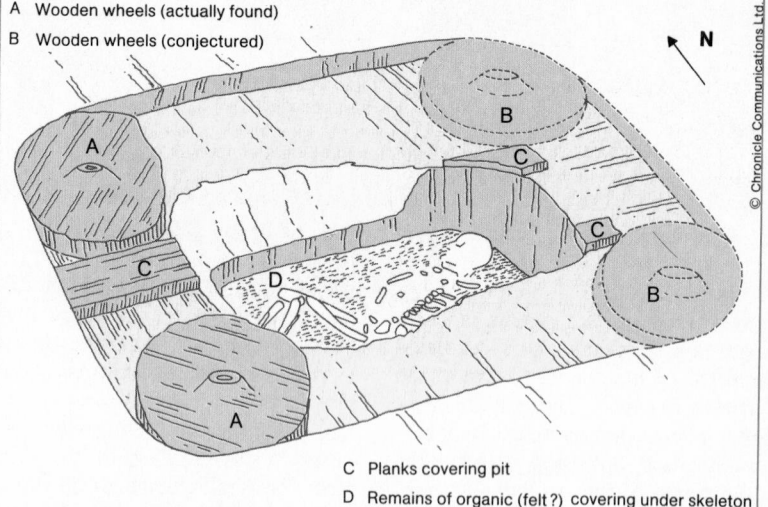

A Wooden wheels (actually found)
B Wooden wheels (conjectured)
C Planks covering pit
D Remains of organic (felt?) covering under skeleton

© Chronicle Communications Ltd.

Wheels transported their masters even unto an afterlife: remains of some of the earliest wheels have been found in a burial grave as shown in the diagram above. The skeleton rested on something organic, possibly a form of felt.

The Sahara: how the climate changed

Africa, c.3000BC
Bad news for humans and animals living in northern Africa: the Sahara is drying up after a spell of moist, hospitable weather. During the last Ice Age, which ended about 6,500 years ago, the lack of rainfall in the Sahara causesd by the freezing of so much water further north meant that the area was hardly suitable even for the adaptable human race. It was only as the ice began to retreat that the climate became significantly more moist, leading to the creation of many lakes. Lake Chad, for instance, reappeared about 8,000 years ago (after drying up completely when the Ice Age was at its peak about 12,000 years ago), and 1,000 years ago covered over 600,000 square miles.

Humans have been in the Sahara for about 6,000 years. The climate improved for the first 4,000 years or so after they came, leading to the spread of grassy areas around the edge of the Sahara and of woodland similar to that of the Mediterranean in mountainous parts. Lions, elephants, rhinoceroses and hippopotami are among the animals who took advantage of the better environment. However, in the last 1,000 years the Sahara has become remarkably drier, and the levels of the Saharan lakes appear to be dropping sharply.

Written language invented in Sumer

Mesopotamia, c.3200BC

For many generations the Sumerian people dwelling in the city of Uruk would make a mental note whenever they paid tribute to the priests to intercede for them with the gods who kept the soil fertile. But even the best of memories can sometimes fail or mislead, especially if a bad harvest should give rise to doubts about whether the priests are doing their job.

From now on the problem should be a thing of the past, for the people of Uruk have devised a system of signs for putting important transactions on record. The priests use a sharp reed pen to make "pictographs" – marks on clay tablets. These marks, which represent numbers, objects and even ideas, are used to keep the grain accounts and other business matters, including land sales.

The invention has been an instant success, so that now no business deal is accepted as genuine unless it has been written down. The Sumerians are believed to be the first people to have devised a system of writing. One theory is that they stumbled on the idea after a period when they kept records by using clay tokens, which they impressed into wet clay.

At all events, the discovery is being widely copied by others, and the Sumerian script is becoming increasingly sophisticated. About

Slate plaque engraved with an offering scene and pictographic writing.

the same time as the Sumerians hit upon their new system for keeping records, a very similar one appeared in the city of Susa, in neighbouring Elam.

Reports from Susa speak of pictographs on clay tablets much like those adopted in Sumer. Since Sumer is no more than a few days' travel from Susa, and the two places have many cultural affinities, it seems likely that travellers spread the word among the people of Susa.

Writing is essentially a series of drawings, crude outlines of familiar objects, such as plants, human heads and animals, which are used as "ideograms", pictures expressing ideas. Childbirth is suggested by an egg next to a bird, and darkness by fine parallel lines beneath the arc of a circle – perhaps an image of sunset. However, these images are becoming increasingly schematic, and a script made up with wedge-shaped ("cuneiform") marks is developing. Cuneiform signs are even capable of representing distinct sounds, rather than standing for single words and ideas.

Cities emerge in Euphrates valley of Mesopotamia

Mesopotamia, c.4000BC

Larger, more highly organised population centres are growing up in the southern part of Mesopotamia, where the twin valleys of the rivers Euphrates and Tigris run down to the sea. It is an area which has supported farming villages for many centuries, because soil deposits washed down to the coastal plain from further inland and frequent floods have created a soil of great richness where it is easier to farm than in other parts. Sea fishing has added to a food surplus.

The and co-operation and organisation needed to control the flooding of the two rivers, by banking and using the water for irrigation,

Alabaster "eye-idol" from Syria.

may have played its part in bringing people together in bigger communities, as has the need to stick together for strength against rival groups of people seeking to tame the marshlands by the river.

The village life common throughout the Middle East has altered in Mesopotamia to a life based in mud-walled towns, raised on platforms to keep out floodwaters and possible enemies. The sites for these towns may be the shrines of local gods; a prominent place of worship is certainly a distinct feature of Mesopotamian urban settlements. In fact, it could be that places like Eridu in the Euphrates valley are religious centres more than genuine cities.

The Sahara: where there are signs of human settlement

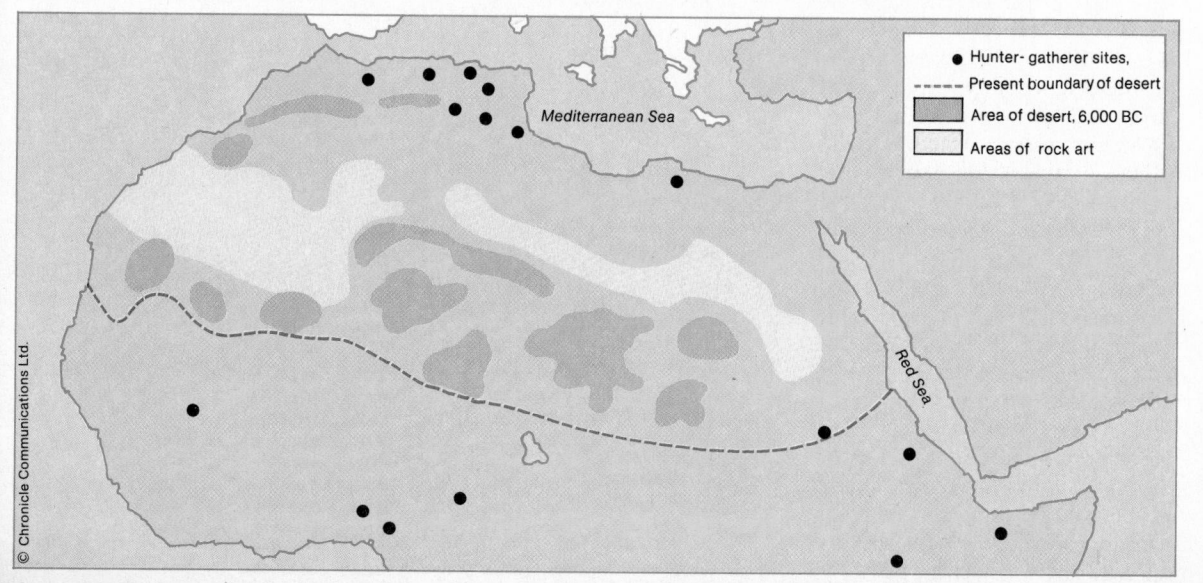

- Hunter- gatherer sites,
- - - - Present boundary of desert
- Area of desert, 6,000 BC
- Areas of rock art

Mediterranean Sea

Red Sea

Mesopotamia, c.3200BC. At Uruk in southern Mesopotamia graphic signs are appearing on stone or slate tablets. They are pictograms representing objects in the concrete world.

South America, 3114BC, August 13. Mythical founding of the Maya dynastic calendar.

Mexico, c.3000BC. The cave-dwellers of Tehuacan, long familiar with wild maize, have identified a variety with larger ears, which they have put under cultivation. Maize is becoming the staple diet of this fast-growing population.

Sahara, c.3000BC. The progressive desiccation of the Sahara region is leading to an extension of the desert and the migration of cattle-breeding populations to more fertile areas such as Egypt.

India, c.3000BC. During the past 500 years farming villages have appeared all over the Indus valley. Exploiting the fertile soil and annual river floods, the population is steadily growing, so that there are now many larger settlements, often surrounded by brick walls. With increasing trade and contact between the villages, a common style of life has been established.

Europe, c.3000BC. Although they have been breeding cattle and sheep for some time, Europeans are only now coming to recognise the value of the horse for its strength and meat. Wild horses are still hunted, but a widespread domestication of the animal is under way.

Australia, c.3000BC. Australians are using new types of stone tools with handles.

Korea, c.3000BC. Agriculture has begun in Korea with the cultivation of millet. Although pottery was made here as early as 6000BC, hunting and gathering continued until now to be the basis of subsistence.

Ecuador, c.3000BC: The inhabitants of Valdivia on the Pacific coast are producing pottery.

Egypt, c.3000BC. The use of bricks in architecture has developed and is assuming impressive proportions. Egyptian art is affirming itself magnificently in works such as the "Palette of Narmer", in which Narmer (Menes) wears white and red crowns, linked with north and south – showing that he controls both Lower and Upper Egypt.

Egypt pioneers use of hieroglyphs

Egypt, c.3000BC

Using drawn symbols, scribes in Egypt are beginning to write and record everyday life on a form of paper made from reeds. A system of hieroglyphs, a form of writing inextricably linked to art, could develop in the form of engravings on temple walls and in a parallel form (known as hieratic) on papyri. This form of "paper" is made by soaking and pressing the papyrus reeds from the Nile before drying them.

The classical language (*Middle Egyptian*) uses some 700 hieroglyphic signs, but the number will have to increase considerably if the technique is to prove useful. The hieroglyphs show, for example, human figures, parts of the human body, animals, birds, trees and plants, as well as various tools, vessels and items of furniture.

These symbolic images are used in horizontal or vertical lines which can be read either from right to left or from left to right, with a human or animal head indicating the direction by pointing to the beginning of the line. Words and sentences are not separated.

The scribes use hieroglyphs as an art form as well as a means of communication. They endeavour to group the signs into an imaginary

Egyptian hieroglyphic inscriptions carved in stone, from Karnak.

square; the sign for the king or a god may precede other words. A sign can have several meanings: it can express an idea or a sound, and can be used to explain other signs.

The "grammar" of hieroglyphs is complex. A sign used to convey the name of an object or action (an ideogram) cannot be easily used, for instance, to convey abstract notions such as thoughts, feelings, professional or family relations and

proper names. A sign representing a sound (a phonogram) expresses only consonants, not vowels. Some signs determine the sense of the sounds which precede them and are not pronounced.

The verbal sentence is constructed to a very strict order: verb, subject, direct object and complements. Only priests and scholars use heiroglyphs in a population which is 99 percent illiterate.

Megalithic monuments leave their marks on north-west Europe

Europe, 3000-2000BC

The megalith builders are reaching fresh heights of artistic and engineering skill and their new creations are places of awe and mystery. They are building monuments on a much larger scale than ever before with avenues of massive standing stones.

One of these structures on the southern coast of Brittany is made up of three separate sections, each with a dozen lines of stones which march in powerful array across four miles of the landscape.

The practice of building megaliths of the passage grave type is also spreading, reaching as far as Ireland and the Orkneys. Their brooding presence is a reminder of how far man has come since the end of the ice age. From simply struggling for survival he now honours his dead and worships his gods.

Mystery swirls like the mists of dawn around the stone alignments at Carnac, in Brittany, erected some time between 3000 and 2000BC.

Booming trade routes herald new epoch of prosperity for islands of Greece

Pottery of the Cyclades.

Carved steatite model, probably of a granary, the Cyclades.

Aegean Sea, c.2800BC

The Cycladic Islands, astride the major trade routes between Greece, Anatolia and Crete, have become the economic centre of the eastern Mediterranean, and are beginning to develop their own indigenous Aegean civilisation.

The cluster of islands, lying in a circle around Delos, has long been rich in materials. Volcanic glass from Melos, marble from Paros and Naxos, and silver, copper and lead from Seriphos and Siphnos are exported to the surrounding areas.

The growth of cities in Mesopotamia, Egypt, the Levant and Anatolia a millennium ago produced a corresponding growth in trade. Sea transport is more efficient than land transport, and the Cycladic Islands have prospered as their canoe-like vessels hopped from island to island.

The group of islands became rich, famous for its boat-building, and changed from a producer of raw materials into a major trading culture.

The islanders, inside their fortified hill settlements, have become ever more skilful makers of silver ornaments, lead model boats and marble figurines. Meanwhile, their boats wait in the bay for further trading expeditions.

Uruk is the home of the goddess of love

Mesopotamia, c.3100BC

Monumental temples have been built at Uruk in Sumer, symbolising the importance of a settlement which has grown out of the villages of Eanna and Kulaba to become the centre of Mesopotamian culture. It is the legendary home of Inanna, goddess of love and procreation, known to the Semites as Ishtar. Her power, according to tradition, derives from her seduction of the god Enki when he was drunk at a banquet he gave in her honour.

The most spectacular buildings are in the part of Uruk still known as Eanna: a vast enclosure surrounded by two temples, a hall with rows of columns, and a third and larger temple, 80 metres by 30 metres, towering above the others. These temples, with their large

The hero Gilgamesh with animals.

halls and smaller rooms, are dedicated to the patron deities of Uruk – An and Inanna. Some buildings are decorated with mosaics made of stone or clay cones with coloured heads, sunk into the clay walls.

King Menes unites Egyptian kingdoms

Memphis, c.2950BC

Menes (Horus Narmer), the first king of Egypt, has succeeded in uniting the whole of this country under one rule. The new state combines Upper and Lower Egypt, the Nile valley and delta. This union is indicated by the white and red crowns of Upper and Lower Egypt worn by the king.

King Menes has founded the Thinite dynasty – perhaps named after the district of This el Birba, in Upper Egypt, from where the kings of this dynasty come. His capital is established at Memphis (the Inebhedj or "White Wall") at the apex of the Nile delta.

This king uses several names. The name Narmer is inscribed on ceremonial palettes and mace heads at Hierakonpolis (in Southern Egypt) in honour of his jubilee, a festival intended to rejuvenate and re-invigorate him for the next part of his reign.

These palettes and mace heads are exquisitely carved with scenes in raised relief and represent the most accomplished examples of this dynasty's art. The name Horus

King Narmer with Horus as a god.

equates Menes with the god Horus, the falcon-god with whom all Egyptian kings have identified and to whom the temple at Hierakonpolis is dedicated.

Under Menes' rule, Egypt enjoys a simple administrative system. After death high officials are interred in brick tombs at Saqqara.

Battle-axes accompany European dead

Northern Europe, c.3000BC

Right across the North European plain, from Holland to Moscow, a new form of burial has appeared. Adult men are being placed in individual graves under small, round mounds, and are accompanied by articles from daily life, including drinking cups decorated with a pattern of twisted cord and stone battle-axes with a carefully drilled shafthole.

At first it was thought that these new burial practices, appearing after long years when stone tombs were common, had been brought about by a massive invasion of a new race from Central Asia. Now it seems that the changes have been taking place in existing communities, and that the weapons and drinking equipment preserved in graves serve to emphasise the importance for the community of the competitive spirit and individual leadership.

The new practices have grown up in the wake of changed lifestyles as farming has grown in importance

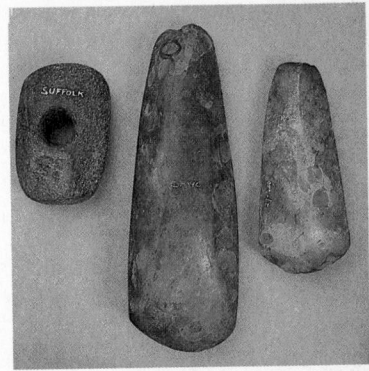

Axes, mace-head from England.

with the introduction of the plough and the keeping of livestock. The new farms are often seen in places never before settled by cultivators, and the burial sites are smaller and less permanent than in the past, which indicates a greater readiness by people to move on and clear a fresh site for cultivation. When harvests begin to decline, another move takes place. But if the dead are left behind, at least they have been given weapons to defend themselves and cups to drink from.

Civilisation in a grain of wheat

Humans evolved into their present form during the Ice Ages - a cycle of cold and warm periods through which we are still living. The last ten thousand years represent one of the warm intervals, of which there have been many earlier examples. During this period human culture has evolved uniquely quickly and human numbers have multiplied at an unprecedented rate.

The reason for this extraordinary development lies principally in the way that human beings have learned to bring plants and animals under their control and use them for their own ends - in other words, agriculture.

Agriculture was not invented in a single place to then spread around the globe; many areas contributed to the stock of domesticated plants and animals, and agriculture can be said to have been invented independently in half a dozen areas. In each one, particularly productive species were taken out of their natural habitats and raised in conditions which were to some extent artificial.

Farming usually began with the cultivation of plants - often the large-seeded grasses of the cereal family, though also root crops in the tropics. Pulses, such as lentils, beans and peas, provided a protein-rich complement to these suppliers of carbohydrates. By moving these productive species to habitats where they would not normally grow, their yield could be increased and made more dependable.

An amazing parallel

Other aspects of the subsistence economy then had to be adjusted to fit this new dependence on cultivation; animals had to be kept near at hand, and thus species which could be herded and tamed were selected for their compatibility with cultivation. In this way a complementary package of different plant and animal species was put together into a viable farming economy. This demanded both organisation and the exchange of seeds, tubers and young animals between different communities. This process happened within a similar timescale in the Near East, the Far East, sub-Saharan Africa and the Americas. In Palestine the process was under way by 7000BC, in the Americas by 6000BC, and in Africa by 4000BC. In comparison with the speed of earlier developments in human culture during the Ice Ages, this was amazing parallelism.

The emergence of *Homo sapiens* - the modern form of the human species - seems to coincide with the appearance of more complex forms of culture and social organisation, reflected most powerfully in the astonishing art of the last glacial period which has been preserved on the walls of caves in Spain and southern France. Other, less obvious, traces of the new potential of human populations are the types of stone and shell which were obtained by exchange with people living some distance away. These demonstrate an ability to organise some form of trade in valued items, well beyond the boundaries of the immediate social group.

These abilities are the clue to why human populations were able to respond in similar ways to the problems of gaining a living in the post-glacial world. It was the organisation of trade between communities which was crucial for any more complex system of exploiting the environment, and moving plants and animals from one habitat to another. Once the experiment had proved successful, the formula could be repeated and the innovation diffused outwards through trade.

The spread of humanity

The incentive to carry out such experiments came about as a result of the growing size of human populations as the climate warmed up. During the last phase of this Ice Age the human species had spread to new continents - Australasia and the Americas - and occupied a much greater proportion of the earth's surface than ever before. Long inhabited regions such as the Near East were also populated at a higher density than earlier, and a much broader range of natural resources was being exploited. It was no longer sufficient to live only by hunting a few favoured species; now many smaller items of food had to be collected, including seeds, nuts and shellfish. Climatic fluctuations also caused great variations in the abundance of important food species. A period of higher rainfall from 14,000 to 10,000 years ago created large stands of wild cereals, which encouraged the formation of large groups of people who could collect them where they grew; but as the local climate became drier, these groups were faced with the choice of either trying to maintain their supplies, or moving out.

The stark juxtaposition of different types of environment provided one local solution. By transferring wild cereals to nearby lowland locations, where there were rich soils and abundant water, they could be grown artificially with minimum disruption to the way of life of these groups. But by making this change, early farmers unconsciously began a process of increasing commitment to particular plots of land, forgoing the mobility which came from ranging widely over the landscape to hunt or collect whatever foods were available on a seasonal basis.

Enter the wheel and the plough

This process had important consequences, social as much as economic. People came together in larger communities then ever before, and on a more permanent basis. Indeed, the areas of prime agricultural land which could be cultivated by simple techniques were so valuable that the sites which were occupied in this move often remained centres of settlement for many years to come. This new form of society had to be regulated by social institutions, which were often based on an extension of relationships within the family; religion, too, was important in maintaining the bonds of common belief and action within an enlarged community, since individual people or families had little opportunity for gaining power and there were few divisions of rank or status to provide the basis of a social hierarchy.

There were also innovations in technology. Along with permanent settlement came architecture and the building of houses, with their fireplaces and ovens from bricks made out of the local mud. Experience of the effects of fire on dried clay resulted in the invention of pottery - a suitable set of containers for a settled lifestyle, and useful in cooking the cereals which now formed an important component of diet.

Soon these craft skills would be transferred to other materials, with the development of carpentry, and the exploration of mineral pigments and their alteration by fire which provided the basis for discoveries in metallurgy. The provision of water supplies led to the development of irrigation techniques; the existence of domestic animals allowed animal power to be applied to dragging loads, and so gave rise to the technologies of the plough and the wheel.

From a small initial change, therefore, an ever-widening set of consequences was put in motion. Agriculture populations multiplied and displaced the remaining hunting groups; they became socially and technologically more diverse, and set up networks of trade and exchange which disseminated a wide range of innovations. As these interactions grew in scale, so changes occurred at an ever-faster rate.

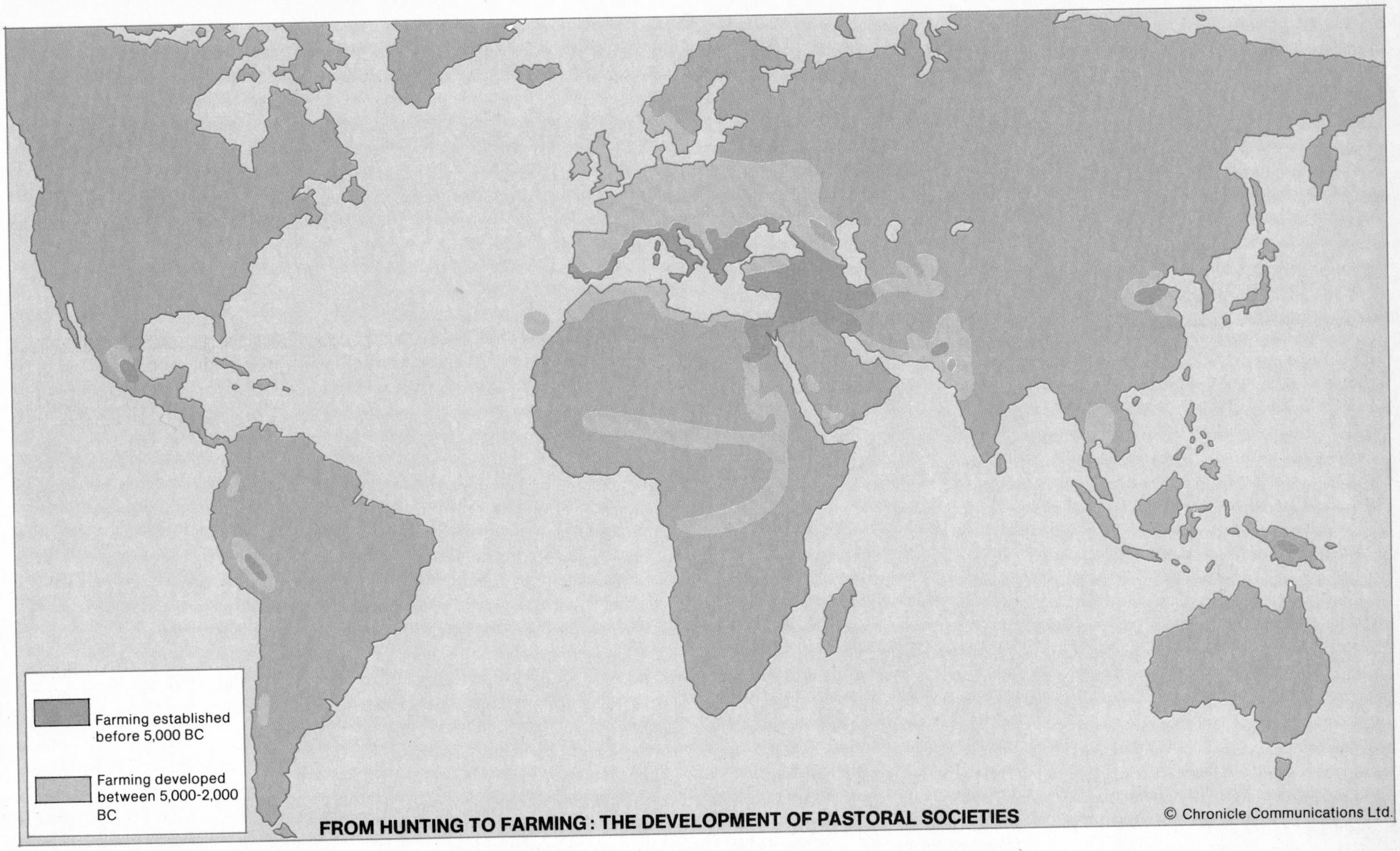

Farming established before 5,000 BC

Farming developed between 5,000-2,000 BC

FROM HUNTING TO FARMING : THE DEVELOPMENT OF PASTORAL SOCIETIES

© Chronicle Communications Ltd.

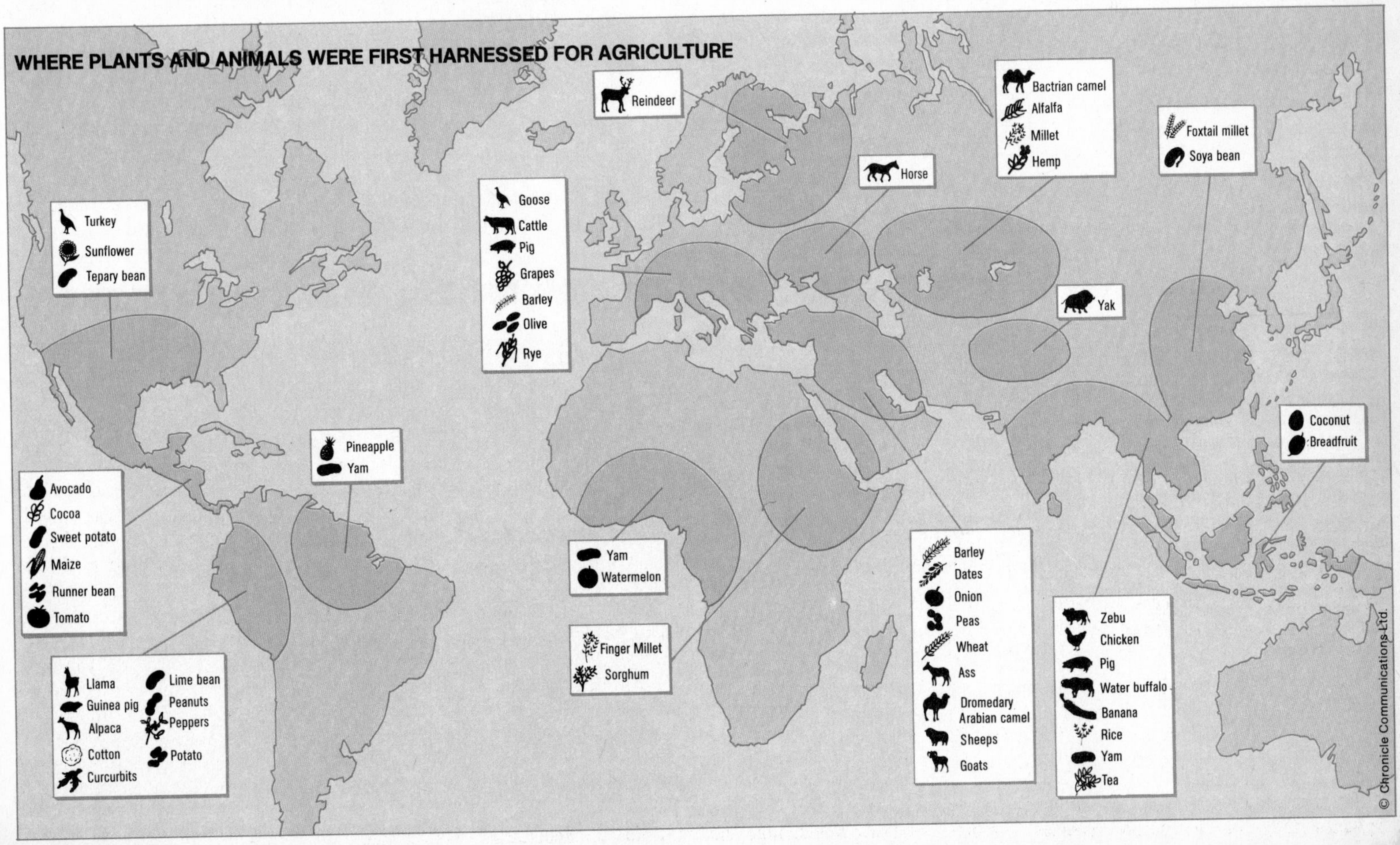

WHERE PLANTS AND ANIMALS WERE FIRST HARNESSED FOR AGRICULTURE

Reindeer

Bactrian camel
Alfalfa
Millet
Hemp

Horse

Foxtail millet
Soya bean

Goose
Cattle
Pig
Grapes
Barley
Olive
Rye

Yak

Turkey
Sunflower
Tepary bean

Pineapple
Yam

Coconut
Breadfruit

Avocado
Cocoa
Sweet potato
Maize
Runner bean
Tomato

Yam
Watermelon

Barley
Dates
Onion
Peas
Wheat
Ass
Dromedary
Arabian camel
Sheeps
Goats

Zebu
Chicken
Pig
Water buffalo
Banana
Rice
Yam
Tea

Finger Millet
Sorghum

Llama
Guinea pig
Alpaca
Cotton
Curcurbits
Lime bean
Peanuts
Peppers
Potato

© Chronicle Communications Ltd.

Egypt, c.2800BC. During the reign of the Thinite king Den many new forms of art and architecture are starting to develop, among them relief-carving, metal craftsmanship, sculpture in the round and furniture-making. Tombs known as *mastabas* are being specially made for members of the royal family and other important people.

Mesopotamia, c.2800BC. A great flood is rumoured to have occurred in Mesopotamia, causing extensive destruction and wiping out most of the population. It is believed to have been sent by the gods in order to destroy the sinful human race.

South America, c.2800BC. Village societies based on horticulture are becoming established in the Amazon region.

China, c.2700BC. The inhabitants of China have mastered the art of silk weaving. They are also making bronze artefacts for the first time. Production of hempen ropes began here about a century ago.

Egypt, c.2650BC. Start of the Egyptian Old Kingdom – the great period of the pyramid builders.

Mesopotamia, c.2600BC. After the time of the deluge, when the waters had subsided, kingship again "descended from the heaven", this time at Kish. This is recorded in the Sumerian King List, which preserves the names of the sovereigns who rule over the land as kingship is "carrried" from one place to the next. Enmebaragesi became king of Kish c.2700BC. He is the author of the first royal inscription in Mesopotamian history.

Malta, c.2600BC. At Hal-Saflieni an underground temple, or hypogeum, is being cut into the rock. It covers more than 1,500 square feet and is designed on three levels. The elaborate stone temple above ground at nearby Tarxien is one of several similar buildings under construction.

India, c.2600BC. Farmers in the thriving agricultural communities of the Indus valley are now making use of the plough.

Egypt, c.2600BC. Builders are at work on the Pyramid of Maidum, the first true pyramid.

Huge pyramid to house a dead king

Memphis, c.2620BC

The great step pyramid of Saqqara is almost complete. Its architect is the high priest, Imhotep. The dimensions of this tomb for the late King Djoser of the third dynasty are enormous. The site of the pyramid and its funerary temple covers more than 180,000 square yards of desert. A special closed room (*serdab*) contains a magnificent seated statue of the king. A second tomb has been built to the south, and there are chapels dedicated to different gods to the east of the pyramid.

The design of the Saqqara pyramid is based on those of tombs built in previous dynasties. These consisted of burial mounds of sand consolidated by brickwork and were finally replaced by rectangular mounds with walls sloping towards the centre. The *mastaba* (a free-standing tomb with sloping sides) symbolises the mound emerging from the liquid chaos created by the god Atum during the very first days of the earth.

Imhotep has used similar principles in his design, but the Saqqara pyramid has been constructed of stone to ensure that this spectacular royal tomb will be eternal. In the later stages of the design, the architect has emphasised the symbolism of the *mastaba* by adding several layers which evoke a "stairway to heaven" used by the soul of the

Djoser's pyramid, monument to the genius of its architect, Imhotep.

pharaoh to rise up to his father, Re. The pyramid has perhaps also been designed to represent the beams of light shooting out from the sun.

King Djoser did not live to see the completion of his spectacular tomb. Imhotep plans to cover the pyramid in limestone, and several blocks have already been prepared, carefully adapted to size. His design is much concerned with security against future robbers and vandals. At the bottom of a huge 90-foot shaft, an intricate network of galleries leads to the burial chamber in which the mummified body of the King will lie. The glazed tiles, the

reliefs on the walls, the false doors and the niches will testify for ever to the care taken in the construction of this monument.

The pyramid and its funerary temple are at the centre of a complex of buildings surrounded by a 30-foot high enclosure wall which is crenellated like a fortress. Imhotep has included 14 false doors in order to achieve a symmetrical appearance to the building. The second tomb built to the south is also within the wall, and contains an underground shaft and burial compartment decorated to the same high standard.

Avebury: a temple is built amid the hills of southern England

Britain, c.2600BC

A magnificent henge or ceremonial structure is being built at Avebury. The first phase of the building of this monument was the erection of two stone circles, but since then an outer stone circle has been built, with a massive earth bank and ditch enclosing the ceremonial area and approached by two avenues of stones.

The whole work covers 28 acres and is a marvel of artistry and engineering. The pairs of stones which make up the grand avenue alternate between tall thin stones and broad, lozenge-shaped ones, representing men and women. Further tombs and stone circles are under construction in the area.

The stone circle at Avebury, with its massive bank and ditch.

Religion and myths thrive in Sumer

Gilgamesh: an epic tale of Babylon

A cuneiform tablet of part of the epic of Gilgamesh, telling Babylon's account of a great flood sent by the gods to destroy the earth.

Babylon, c.2750BC
Gilgamesh, a king of the Sumerian city of Uruk in southern Mesopotamia, has become the subject of a great epic told in Babylon. The real man fought against the kingdom of Kish and was deified after his death for his heroic exploits. In the epic Gilgamesh sets out to defy the gods in his quest for immortality.

With his friend Enkidu he kills Huwawa, guardian of the cedar forest, and when the goddess Inanna sends the "Bull of Heaven" to kill the two heroes it, too, is slain. But Enkidu dies, and a distraught Gilgamesh seeks out Utnapishtim, an old man who, according to Sumerian legend, survived a great flood by building an ark for his families and animals, and was therefore granted eternal life by the gods.

Utnapishtim gives Gilgamesh a magic plant which restores youth, but a serpent steals the plant and Gilgamesh again becomes distraught. He goes once more to Utnapishtim for the secret of immortality, which he is promised if he stays awake for six days and seven nights. Gilgamesh is only human, and falls asleep. But when he awakes he is reconciled to his mortality:
"O Gilgamesh ... you were given the kingship, such was your destiny; eternal life was not your destiny."

Mesopotamia, c.2700BC
Sumerians are guided in their daily lives by a host of gods, who are worshipped in a hierarchy according to the importance of the field of human life each looks after. In earlier times each of the Sumerian cities originally had its own particular deity, but political changes in the relations between the cities may have led to the present hierarchy of several gods. Sumerian gods have human forms and express people's relationships with each other and with Nature. Chief among them are Anu, Enlil and Enki. Anu, the god of the sky, is also the father of the gods. Enlil is the god of air, who makes everything possible. It is he who creates the order of things which is administered by Enki, god of wisdom, cunning and underground waters essential to Sumer's well-being. Another important one is Inanna, goddess of love and war.

Sumerians worship their gods in complex ceremonies. In return for these rituals and a life of propriety,

Statue dedicated to the goddess Inanna (Ishtar) of a priest wearing a sheepskin garment, c.2500BC.

they believe the gods will give them longevity and prosperity. The rebirth of creation is celebrated in an annual festival of spring, which reassures Sumerians that their existence, vulnerable at all time to natural disasters such as flooding, will continue for another year.

Slaves follow royal masters to the grave

Mesopotamia, c.2600BC
King Mes-kalam-dug and his brother King A-kalam-dug are dead, but they have not gone alone to whatever existence they believe awaits them. They are accompanied in death by a large number of their faithful relatives and servants who dutifully followed their late sovereigns in solemn procession into their magnificent hecatombs in the city of Ur. In the corridors and access shafts, close to the funeral chariots and harnesses, they took poison and perished alongside their dead masters. In one tomb no fewer than 74 of the king's retinue have been buried in accordance with this custom.

To meet death in this way must be considered a great honour for a king's family and retainers, because the subterranean funeral chambers built by Mes-kalam-dug and A-kalam-dug are sumptuously furnished, as befits kings' status and wealth. The fittings include elaborate jewellery of gold, silver, lapis lazuli and carnelian, vases of precious metal and gold ceremonial weaponry. For the kings' pleasure

A lyre inlaid with lapis lazuli, gold and shell from the tombs at Ur.

there are musical instruments and gaming boards encrusted with lapis lazuli and mother-of-pearl. It could be that some of this finery is meant as an offering to the gods. In the great epic of Gilgamesh, the dead hero presents the gods with gifts on behalf of himself and all those buried with him: his wives, concubines, children and servants.

"Pit graves" are hallmark of people from the steppes

Eastern Europe, c.2800BC
A substantial migration of herdsmen seems to be under way into parts of Eastern Europe previously unoccupied or recently abandoned. The migrants have apparently domesticated the horse, and are using wheeled vehicles for transport.

The evidence for this migration is provided by the unusual burial methods practised by these people, notably in the Ukraine, a region thought unfit for settlement because the land is too dry for simple farming techniques. Now there are hundreds of burial grounds where the dead are enclosed in timber chambers and laid out in a distinctive position with the legs drawn up.

Similar burials are now making an appearance in more westerly parts of eastern Europe, in areas abandoned by farming populations, probably because of soil deterioration. It is the newcomers' burial method that makes them stand out from earlier settlers with more conventional methods of burying their dead.

Little is known about these new arrivals from the steppes, except that they seem to speak a language quite new to the peoples whom they are coming into contact with as they move into Europe.

Fine jewellery of gold and lapis lazuli, positioned as worn in the royal tomb of Queen Pu-Abi in Ur, Mesopotamia, c.2600BC.

Egypt, c.2580BC. While the pharaohs have started to build pyramids, noblemen continue to be buried in *mastabas* — underground chambers with chapels above ground. The chamber holds the sarcophagus and articles indispensable in the afterlife. The chapel houses a statue of the deceased. Incense, food and drink are regularly taken there.

India, c.2550BC. The substantial towns at Mohenjo-Daro and Harappa are surrounded by defensive walls of baked brick.

Mesopotamia, c.2500BC. A westerner from the steppelands by the name of Ur-nanshe seizes control of Lagash, one of the largest and most important city-states of Sumer. Until now Lagash has been governed by local princes who succeeded one another without any major dynastic disruptions. They devoted their energies to improving the land.

Mesopotamia, c.2500BC. The world's first libraries are being set up at Shuruppak (Fara) and Eresh (Abu-Salabikh). They include texts concerned with the trials of daily life reflected in proverbs: "My wife is in the temple, my mother is by the riverside, while I am here dying of hunger"; "A spendthrift housewife adds illness to worries"; "You can have a master, you can have a king, but a man to be feared is the tax collector".

Peru, c.2500BC. The inhabitants of Waywakas are fashioning objects from gold.

Near East, c.2500BC. Bronze is becoming a popular material for the manufacture of arms and tools.

Mexico, c.2500BC. Pottery and weaving are developing in central Mexico.

South America, c.2500BC. The selection and hybridisation of maize have given a great boost to crop yields. As a result the population is growing and large permanent villages have been set up. Long-distance trade routes are being forged.

Mesopotamia, c.2450BC. Eannatum, a member of the dynasty founded by Ur-nanshe at Lagash in Sumer, has recorded an account of his victorious wars on the "Stele of Vultures". He tells how he tried to dominate the whole of Sumer and led his armies as far as Mari to the north-west and Elam (Iran) to the east.

Farmers till the fertile banks of the Indus

India, c.2500BC

A remarkable farming civilisation is flourishing in the fertile plains of the valley of the river Indus in north-western India. Spread over half a million square miles, it is sustained by its agriculture and centres on the two important cities of Harappa and Mohenjo-Daro, which have a circumference of around two and a half miles and contain as many as 30,000 people each. The similar street plans of both cities bear witness to the highly-developed administration and organisation of the inhabitants; both are arranged on a grid pattern with wide streets, and have dwellings built of kiln-fired bricks, much more solid and durable than the sun-baked mud bricks of Mesopotamia. Citadels built on artificial mounds over ten feet high dominate both cities. The kiln-fired bricks are also used in complex dyke systems to ward off the dangers of flooding from the Indus. The drainage of the cities shows that people are keen on personal hygiene; many houses are equipped with a specific room for bathing.

It is hard to say whether this civilisation can be called an empire rather than a group of towns, but this belief is supported by the similarity of building methods and the use of standardised weights and measures over a vast area. A great port four hundred miles south of Mohenjo-Daro, connected to the sea by a canal, shows that the Indus people trade abroad, and the embel-

Votive figure from Mohenjo-Daro.

A seal bearing the image of a bull.

lished seals used for marking merchandise indicate a unified, literate culture which may use a Dravidian language. It is probably the first civilisation to make cotton cloth, and its craftsmen produce beautiful decorated earthenware vessels and elegant bronze statuettes.

Egyptian hieroglyphs inside the coffin of steward Seni; the texts are supposed to keep the dead man from harm. Such texts for kings should ensure they retain their royal status; at first added to the walls of temples in burial complexes, the texts were later inscribed inside royal pyramids.

Mesopotamia torn by 100-year war

Mesopotamia c.2350BC

For 100 years war has been the normal state of affairs in Mesopotamia. The first dynasty of Ur brought peace under Mesanne-padda for a while; he overthrew the last king of Uruk, as well as Mesalim, the king of Kish, an important city of Akkad, north of Sumer. But since then a persistent, seemingly interminable, war has prevailed.

The main conflict has involved the neighbouring states of Lagash and Umma which were vying for control of the irrigated border territory of Guedin. Mesalim of Kish tried to resolve the dispute by measuring the ground with a rope, and putting up boundary posts to

Portrait-relief of King Eannatum of Lagash with pictographic script.

mark the border. But around 2450BC, Enakalli, the king of Umma, seized the land and ripped up the posts. Eannatum, king of Lagash, supported by infantry armed with long spears and protected by heavy shields, defeated him so that Lagash held sway for a while.

Umma fought back under their king Urlumma, but its victory was reversed by Enmetena, grandson of Eannatum, in about 2400BC.

Influence over the area continued to swing between Lagash, Umma, and Mari, in the north-west. At one stage Ila, who came from Lagash, took possession of Umma and became its king. He turned against his former country, only to be defeated. The see-saw continued until Lugalzagesi came to power in Umma. He now claims control of all Mesopotamia.

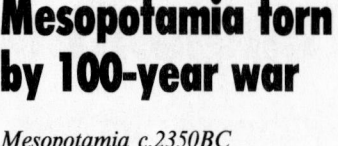

Tombs fit for pharaohs

The great sphinx and one of the pyramids of the pharaohs at Giza.

Egypt, c.2580BC
Eternity is assured for the kings of Egypt who, embalmed and mummified using simple techniques, are being laid to rest in colossal stone-built tombs in the desert near the river which has made this country fertile. These pyramids, the tallest of which, built by Khufu (Cheops), is over 480 feet in height, are built of limestone quarried in the vicinity of the building site. Stone of better quality is transported from quarries on the opposite bank of the Nile. The remainder of the blocks of stone – each weighing over two tons – are transported by logs.

The workers employed in this great task are not slaves. This is sacred work. The men who toil to raise these vast stones to such heights – using a combination of girders and ropes – are free to work the soil during the rest of the year. They labour for their king, whose influence assures peace, civil order and harmony of the country within the universe.

The Egyptians believe in life after death, and the pharaoh will then accompany the sun god during the day. Thus it is essential that his body is preserved and that he has everything within his tomb that is necessary for life, like the food and drink left within his reach.

At death the royal body is mummified by being treated with drugs and filled with aromatic substances and bandaged. The people of this country also believe that the pharaoh is reborn at the time of his death, allowing him once again to occupy his royal throne. The social order he has maintained in life must continue; and thus the king's wife and his most important officials are also buried close to him.

Wit and wisdom of an Egyptian vizier

Egypt, c.2350BC
Ptahhotpe, the vizier, has written down some words of advice – ostensibly for his son, but also with an eye on future generations. His maxims, recorded in hieratic script on papyrus, make a moving document.

In a prologue Ptahhotpe bewails the limitations of old age. "You doze during the day, the eyes are dim, the ears are deaf ... the mouth is silent and cannot speak, the mind is empty and no longer remembers the past ..." he writes.

He goes on to caution against intellectual arrogance and recommends a good time: "Do not be proud on account of your knowledge; consult the ignorant and the wise ... Entertain your friends with that you possess because you only have these possessions as one whom God favours ... bow before your superior ... wretched is he who challenges a superior ..."

The Nile brings life to Egyptian society

Egypt, c.2580BC
For over 400 years since the time that King Menes introduced water engineering to Egypt, the Nile, bringing alluvial silt and fish to the delta, has brought life and prosperity to the people of Egypt. This is a peasant economy, and the *fellahin* (mostly small farmers and fishermen) make maximum use of the annual floods for their food.

The land is well irrigated by a system of canals and reservoirs which capture the water and silt. Wheat, barley, emmer (a wheat species) and flax are the main harvests. Orchards and vegetable gardens flourish by the riverside, with broad beans, lentils, chickpeas, lettuces and cucumbers growing in great quantities. Vineyards are a common sight – wine has been produced here for nearly 500 years.

Most peasants live in mud-brick houses, keeping their own goats, sheep and even pigs. Oxen, working in pairs, are the main power source for the wooden ploughs. Fish products, dried or preserved, and eaten

A man with a basket of fledglings.

with bread and beer, are an important part of the country's diet.

The Egyptian economy depends greatly on the pharaoh, national stability and good adminstration by officials. The people depend on them to supervise the maintenance of canals and reservoirs. In times of crisis agriculture suffers and famine threatens.

Mystery surrounds the "Beaker Folk"

Europe, c.2500BC
The settled way of life of the megalith builders is under attack from the new mobility which is bringing to northern Europe goods and customs which have never been seen before in these remote parts. Traders are bringing copper from the south to replace stone for the blades of their daggers and axes.

Most symbolic of the new way of life, however, is the spread across most of western Europe of beaker drinking cups made in the shape of an upturned bell. No one seems to know where these cups come from, but it is possible that they were originally made in the Low Countries, which have a tradition of beaker making going back to the older tradition of cord-decorated pottery.

The beakers are decorated with characteristic zoned designs, have thin walls and are well-fired. The latest types have either short or long necks added to the original bell style.

Despite the mystery surrounding the origin of these beakers there is no doubt that they are prized by

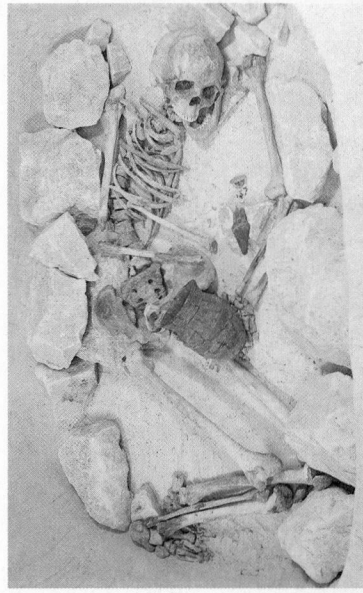

A burial with beaker in England.

their owners. When a warrior dies his beakers are buried alongside him with his weapons.

This affection for the beaker may well have something to do with another new practice, that of making an alcoholic drink from fermented barley.

Ebla scribes keep records on clay tablets

The inscribed tablet from Ebla details activities of Sumerian professions.

Syria, c.2350BC

Although the oldest cities in the world are in Sumer, in southern Mesopotamia, flourishing influential towns have sprung up in other parts of the great Fertile Crescent between the Mediterranean and the mouths of the Tigris and Euphrates.

One of these is Ebla, a town of over 120 acres in north-western Syria, dominated by a citadel with a royal palace, massive oval ramparts and four fortified gates.

What makes Ebla remarkable is the great state archive of clay tablets kept on wooden shelves in the royal palace. They are written in the cuneiform script devised for

official records by Sumerian scribes in recent centuries. Now, however, there are many small states around Mesopotamia, especially along the trade routes carrying valuable raw materials. Many of the documents are therefore concerned with trade and diplomacy.

The library itself is an official archive of Ebla's history and considerable influence on – and perhaps also aggression towards – other powers in the region.

In one letter to the king of Ebla a neighbour, the king of Mari, appears to warn his counterpart against any act of aggression by reminding him of the exploits of his royal predecessors.

Kings no longer double as priests

Mesopotamia, c.2350BC

Kings of Mesopotamia are ceasing to be substitute gods and are beginning to cast off their priestly functions. This separation of palace and temple was accelerated by the reforms of King Uru'inimgina of Lagash and has outlived his fall.

Under Enmetana, a previous king, Lagash had had a separate high priest called Dudu. After Enmetena's death the priests of Ningirsu seized the throne of Lagash, and for the next two decades they enlarged their own influence and property at the expense of the gods and the people. Officials interfered in every facet of life: heavy taxes were levied on burials and weddings, and corruption was rife.

When Uru'inimgina came to the throne he launched an ambitious reform programme, removing superfluous officials, cutting taxes, and restoring land and property to the gods. An inscription of the time reads: "He freed the citizens of Lagash from usury, monopoly, hunger, theft and assault; he established their freedom."

Uru'inimgina's reign lasted only eight years before he was driven out of Lagash by the invading army of Lugalzagesi of Umma. Lugalzagesi has gone on to conquer Uruk and the main Sumerian states, but now faces a battle with Sargon.

Troy destroyed by fire: valuable jewellery is left in the ruins

Anatolia, c.2300BC

The fortified citadel of Troy has been destroyed by fire. The flames obviously swept through the buildings very rapidly, for the inhabitants had no time to save their valuables and left behind an impressive collection of jewellery.

There are bronze daggers and axes, as well as silver ingots, and drinking vessels beaten out of gold and silver – compelling evidence of the riches and power which have accrued to this fortress in north-western Anatolia.

Troy has been enjoying a period of great prosperity, due to exploiting successfully its dominance of the important trading passage from the Aegean to the Sea of Marmara

and the Bosporus. The citadel, built about 700 years ago, was surrounded by walls 12 feet thick; it had a roofed ceremonial gateway opening onto a gravel courtyard around which the main buildings were arranged. The main structure was built of plastered mud-brick in a timber framework, with a slate roof or cornice. There was a separate complex probably providing residential accommodation for court officials or members of the royal family.

The craftsmen responsible for the beautiful metalwork were skilled in the complex techniques of filigree and granulation and were clearly familiar with contemporary styles in Mesopotamia.

A pot from the city of Troy in the form of a human being; one of the many artefacts abandoned by the inhabitants as they fled from the fire which destroyed their homes.

Sargon, the first emperor, has died

Goldsmiths scale new heights of artistry in Agade

Bronze head of King Sargon.

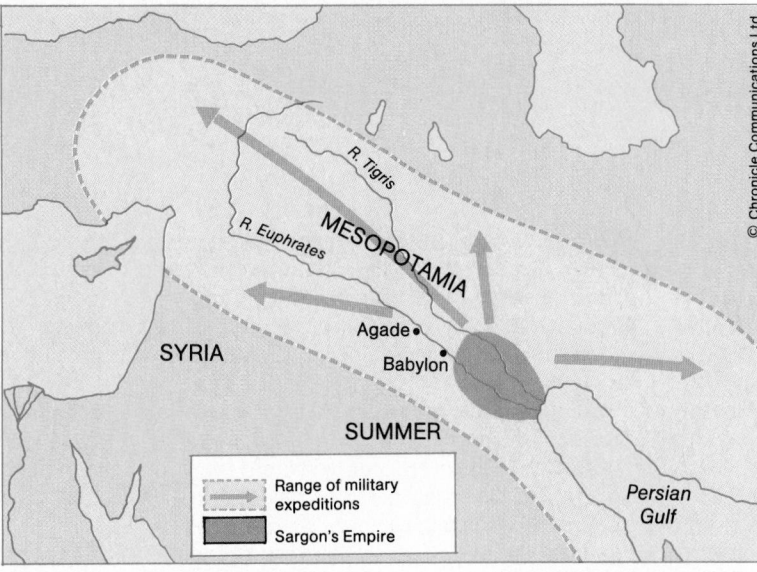

Mesopotamia, 2279BC

Sargon, who rose from being a humble cup-bearer to found the greatest empire Mesopotamia has known, is dead. For 50 years he ruled his empire from the city of Agade, or Akkad, which he had also founded. Even before his death Sargon, whose name means "righteous" or "true king", had become a figure of such legendary power that his origins are shrouded in myth.

He is said to have been an illegitimate child who was abandoned in a rush basket, rescued by a well-drawer, and brought up by the goddess Ishtar (Inanna). He was the cupbearer of Ur-Zababa, the king of Kish, whom he overthrew before marching on Uruk with an army of followers and defeating King Lugalzagesi, then overlord of Sumer.

Conquering in rapid succession Ur, Lagash and Umma, Sargon went on to found a new city at Agade, on the Euphrates, where he built a palace and temples to Ishtar and Zababa, the warrior-god of Kish. Agade became the first true capital of Mesopotamia and for the first time has given the Semites ascendancy over the Sumerians.

Sargon was more than a great warrior. He respected the religious institutions of Sumer, making his daughter the priestess of Nanna, moon-god of Ur. He was also aware of the importance of good (and loyal) administration. After he consolidated his authority over

Sumer, and enlarged his army, he advanced across the Tigris towards Iran, and along the Euphrates towards Syria, appointing Akkadians (inhabitants of Agade) as governors of conquered territories.

Sargon's campaigns were directed against regions rich in metals, stone and timber, some of which could be floated down the Euphrates to Agade. Royal wealth was the foundation of an imperial economy, with the governors growing increasingly rich, yet knowing they owed it all to their king.

From the Mediterranean to the highlands of Persia, from the foothills of the Caucasus to the Persian

Gulf, Sargon became unchallengeable. He was even able to leave his palace at Agade to retreat to the provinces, where he encouraged art to flourish. Sargon was, in short, the first absolute monarch and reigned for 55 years, defeating revolts even in his old age.

The empire he has bequeathed to his son and successor, Rimush, is wealthy, but it is not without internal difficulties. Constant funnelling of wealth from the conquered lands to the heart of the Akkadian empire has stirred discontent. His successor will be well advised to maintain a high level of military prowess and vigilance.

Mesopotamia, c.2200BC

Gold, silver and bronze are being worked into a remarkable variety of shapes, often with highly complicated methods, as craftsmanship prospers in Agade. Just as Lugalbanda, the legendary king of Uruk, travelled abroad several centuries earlier in search of fine objects and the men who could make them, so the king of Agade has been recruiting craftsmen from the surrounding regions.

By the time the royal tombs of Ur were built – around 300 years ago – metalworking techniques of considerable sophistication had been invented. Over the next few centuries, in the palace and temple workshops, craftsmen have been perfecting them.

Metal can now be hammered into relief, known as repousse, and gold and silver made into thread (filigree). Granulation (small globules), cloisonne (inlaid cavities), engraving and welding are also skills now being developed.

The silversmiths of Agade work long hours in response to fluctuating, sometimes heavy, demand. One text records that 29 kilograms of fine gold were delivered to the town of Nippur, in Sumer, to be worked into several thousand small crescents and suns.

Sargon's successor adds new lands to Mesopotamian empire

Near East, c.2200BC

With the establishment of the Akkadian dynasty, wars have been waged over a much larger area. The kings of Agade are warmongers with a double purpose. Firstly, they need constantly to destabilise enemy forces, thereby ensuring the security of their commercial centres; secondly, they want to bring back to Agade as many riches as possible. Thus their whole economy is based on war.

Since Sargon founded the empire a century ago, Akkadian armies have campaigned all the way to the Mediterranean coast in the northwest, eastwards well into Persia, and across the Gulf to Magan *(Oman)*. Not even Sargon's great

conquests can match the reputation of his grandson Naram-Sin, around whom an epic literature grews up, extolling his deeds of arms.

His long reign of at least 36 years seems to have been almost entirely filled with military operations. In the west, he conquered Arman and Ebla, in Syria, where he plundered the palace before forcing his vanquished enemies to work for him. In the north, he campaigned against Hurrian Namar and built a royal residence in the Khabur basin, controlling all the roads of Jazirah. In the south, he conquered Magan. But his most important victory was over the powerful Lullubi in the east, commemorated in rock sculpture.

Naram-Sin and a defeated people.

Water cradles first civilisations

Although the first farming settlements in the Middle East, like Jericho and Catal Huyuk, often attained a remarkable size, they could not be described as cities. They had no special central functions, reflected in administrative buildings or palaces, temples or market places; they were simply large farming settlements, often the only ones in their immediate region, where population was concentrated around areas of particularly fertile soil.

By contrast, the large settlements which appeared in Mesopotamia from 4000BC onwards in the vast alluvial plain of the Euphrates and Tigris were true cities, set in the middle of a network of rural settlements which were subordinate to them.

Here there were to be found major public buildings such as temples and the seats of rulers, stores of agricultural produce and imported materials, as well as workshops and facilities for manufacturing activity. These more complex forms of economic activity required the use of written records, whose development can be traced from simple pictorial symbols to abstract signs.

The form of social organisation which could cope with the complexities of administration, the production and exchange of goods, the defence of territory and the mounting of expeditions to look for raw materials was clearly beyond that of tribal institutions based on ties of family and kinship. The appearance of cities and the economic systems behind them presupposes the existence of the state. Indeed, when the written records are sufficiently developed to be translated and read, we find records of rulers who controlled the territory around the cities, developed its potential by promoting irrigation schemes, and engaged in warfare with their neighbours. The dawn of history thus began soon after the emergence of cities and the state.

Economy, politics and culture

Another word is often used to describe these early urban societies: the first civilisations. The city-dwelling elites, whether priestly or secular, developed a culture and lifestyle in which art and the production of specialist craft-made goods played a similar role to these aspects of our own society. Prehistoric art is often enigmatic; it rarely consists of whole scenes, and often the representations are so schematised that the message is hard for us to grasp. The art of even the earliest civilisations is immediately more meaningful to us: it consists of scenes, and often includes narrative

sequences. Even where the conventions are unfamiliar, and the identities of the figures portrayed are unknown, we recognise a method of portraying events which is not completely alien to our own culture. This familiarity is aided by the presence of inscriptions. Thus we recognise religious scenes, or royal propaganda, portrayals of historic events or depictions of everyday life.

These three elements - an economy based on cities, a political system based on the state, and an elite culture involving literacy and representational art - mark the appearance of new sorts of complex societies which were made possible by agriculture. These appeared a few thousand years after the appearance of farming itself, in several parts of the world; and those in the Old and New Worlds - eastern and western hemispheres - arose completely independently of each other. While the cities of Mesopotamia were the first in the world, they were soon followed by similar phenomena in Egypt and the Indus valley (Pakistan and north-west India), somewhat later in China (around 2000BC), and in the Americas (Mexico and Peru) after 1000BC.

Water: the essential factor

These centres of development were closely associated with the areas where farming itself had begun; but the first cities usually appeared in particular sorts of locations, especially where highly productive techniques of irrigation agriculture could be applied. These were often fertile lowland plains, usually in dry regions watered by rivers or lakes, and often requiring the importation of resources from a wide hinterland. It was in these circumstances that the decisive shift to more complex forms of society occurred.

Various explanations have been put forward as to why this should have come about. One is the growth of population in geographically circumscribed territories: each of these early civilisations arose in an area sharply demarcated, often by deserts, and with a restricted extent of fertile soil. Another theory stresses the effects of irrigation in creating social inequality, since some villages and landowners had better access to high-quality land than others, and were in a position to control water.

A further aspect was the need to organise trade, to ensure supplies of essential raw materials, often from mountainous areas or better watered zones beyond the centre's immediate territory. All these factors probably operated together, and such explanations are not mutually exclusive. Some

theories stress the beneficial and managerial qualities of elites, organising the exchange of commodities for the general good and promoting greater efficiency in the use of resources. Others stress the element of exploitation and monopoly power inherent in the growing inequalities between different social groups. Whether these developments constitute "progress" is thus a complex moral and philosophical question.

Textile industries began

In the case of Mesopotamia, these developments were accelerated by technical advances which made possible a new scale of production and the transfer of products between regions. Already by 5000BC it seems that the plough and simple irrigation systems were in use. The combination of these two techniques made possible the growth of population in the alluvial plain of Mesopotamia. In addition, a new generation of domestic plants and animals came into use after 4000BC, which offered scope for the manufacture of distinctive products from the raw materials they supplied. Tree crops, such as date, fig, vine, olive and pomegranate, came into cultivation and were used to produce new commodities such as oil and wine. New breeds of sheep came into existence, with woolly fleeces rather than the hairy coats which the earliest varieties had shared with their wild ancestors. These made possible the first large-scale textile industries. Transport animals such as the donkey, horse and camel were domesticated, facilitating contacts across deserts and steppe areas; and wheeled vehicles were developed for transporting heavy loads. Water-borne transport was even more effective than overland carriage, however, and this was made more efficient by the use of the sail. Thus new sources of energy were tapped, both animal and wind power. These technologies interacted and produced further innovations; for instance, the wheel could be applied to the mass production of pottery.

Because of the rapid pace of technological change, as well as for political reasons, these early states were relatively unstable. The extension of trade routes often produced competition from secondary centres which developed at choke-points on the supply network, which either themselves grew into small states, or had to be incorporated in larger political units of alliances or empires. Political unity alternated with fragmentation; but cultural and artistic development (like technical advances) was more continuous, and began to foster tradition.

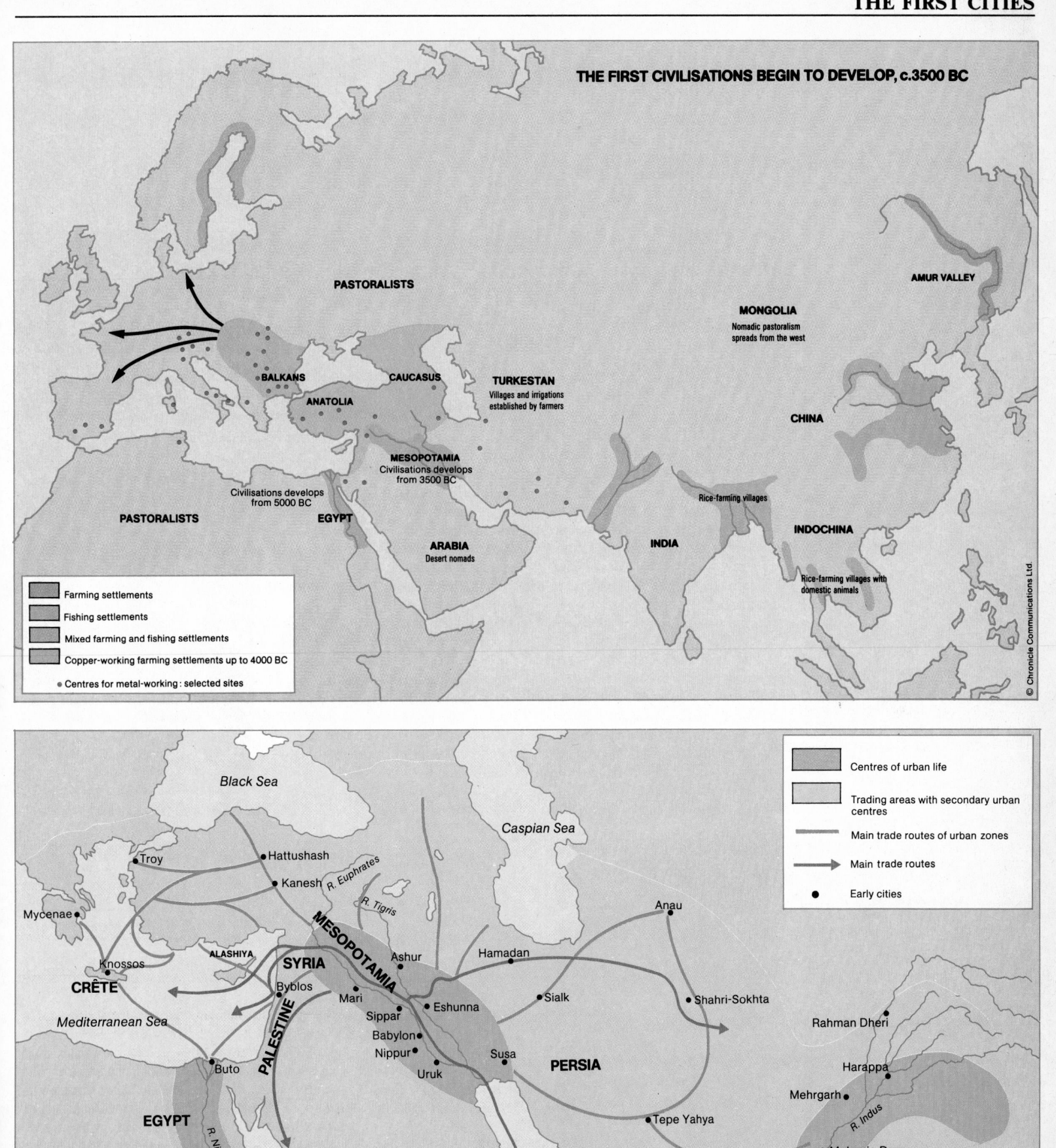

THE FIRST CIVILISATIONS BEGIN TO DEVELOP, c.3500 BC

PASTORALISTS

AMUR VALLEY

MONGOLIA
Nomadic pastoralism
spreads from the west

BALKANS

CAUCASUS

TURKESTAN
Villages and irrigations
established by farmers

ANATOLIA

CHINA

MESOPOTAMIA
Civilisations develops
from 3500 BC

Civilisations develops
from 5000 BC

EGYPT

Rice-farming villages

ARABIA
Desert nomads

INDIA

INDOCHINA

PASTORALISTS

Rice-farming villages with
domestic animals

	Farming settlements
	Fishing settlements
	Mixed farming and fishing settlements
	Copper-working farming settlements up to 4000 BC
●	Centres for metal-working : selected sites

© Chronicle Communications Ltd.

Black Sea

Caspian Sea

	Centres of urban life
	Trading areas with secondary urban centres
	Main trade routes of urban zones
→	Main trade routes
●	Early cities

Troy

Hattushash

Kanesh

R. Euphrates

R. Tigris

Mycenae

Anau

ALASHIYA

SYRIA

Ashur

Hamadan

MESOPOTAMIA

Knossos

CRÊTE

Byblos

Mari

Eshunna

Sialk

Shahri-Sokhta

Mediterranean Sea

Sippar

Rahman Dheri

Babylon

Susa

Nippur

PERSIA

Harappa

Buto

Uruk

PALESTINE

Mehrgarh

R. Indus

EGYPT

R. Nile

Tepe Yahya

Mohenjo Daro

Dilmun

Persian
Gulf

Amri

Red Sea

ARABIA

Arabian Sea

Allahdino

INDIA

THE GARIGST CIVILISATIONS AND THEIR INTERCONNECTIONS

© Chronicle Communications Ltd.

China, c.2200BC. The Longshan people in the north and north-east of China are building walled settlements and developing sophisticated crafts such as metalworking and wheel-thrown pottery.

Egypt, c.2155BC. Pepi II is dead after a reign of 94 years. He came to the throne at the age of six and was king during a glorious period, when Egypt experienced intense commercial activity, particularly with Byblos, and Punt in East Africa. The close of Pepi's reign was very troubled and his death marks the end of the last illustrious reign of the Egyptian Old Kingdom.

Mesopotamia, c.2150BC. The Akkadian empire, founded about 200 years ago by Sargon, has been overthrown by an invasion of the Guti, high-landers from the Zagros mountains, who have pillaged and sacked the land.

Mesopotamia, c.2120BC. Utu-hegal, king of Uruk, drives out the last armed Guti band still wandering over the Sumerian territory of Umma. In Mesopotamian eyes, Guti are coming to symbolise evil and disorder.

Egypt, c.2040BC. The Thebans have gained control of the kingdom of Egypt, which has just emerged from 100 years of violence and economic recession, exacerbated by famine. After the death of Pepi II the country disintegrated into a multitude of battling principalities. The dynasties inaugurated c.2135BC by Khety had to face the growing power of the local princes from Thebes in the south, who have now proved victorious in the struggle.

Egypt, c.2010BC. The death of Mentuhotpe, the Theban ruler, after a 50-year reign, marks the conclusion of a momentous time in Egyptian history. Mentuhotpe crushed the rival kingdom of Herakleopolis, reunited Egypt and re-established centralised rule. Thebes, Mentuhopte's native city, functions as capital.

Mesopotamia, 2004BC. The supremacy of Ur is at an end. The Elamites *(from Iran)* – with the support of a group of Guti called the Amorites – have overthrown the armies of Ur and taken the king prisoner. The dynasty founded by Ur-Nammu saw a century of relative peace and prosperity in Mesopotamia and a renaissance in Sumerian art and literature.

New temples adorn Egyptian capital

Thebes, c.2000BC

Thebes is now the capital of Egypt and massive building work is under way to create the temple of Karnak to celebrate the god Amun's elevation to the country's principal god, a change from his minor status when Thebes was no more than a provincial town.

Legend has it that Amun takes part in a public procession in his barque each year; in fact he is brought in statue form on the occasion of the procession of the feast of Opet, the greatest of Thebes' festivals.

The pharaohs are enlarging Karnak into a major complex of temples and building themselves funerary temples on the west bank – large rock-cut tombs with magnificent facades at el Taraf. It was Mentuhotpe I who developed Thebes as the capital, although one of his successors, Amenemhet, abandoned the city and set up his capital at el Lisht close to the Faiyum Oasis. (The reasons for this move were mainly administrative, due to its strategic location between the Nile delta and Nile valley.)

Thebes' advantages as the capital during political crises are its basically Egyptian character and its proximity to trade routes, mineral and other resources, and to Nubia, with its supply of mercenaries.

Nonetheless, a major reorganisa-

A papyrus showing a wealthy citizen and his wife adoring Osiris.

tion of the kingdom has been taking place in Egypt, with the kings aiming to consolidate a single political unit around themselves. Centralisation has eventually become less excessive, however, and the Egyptian middleclasses are becoming more involved with affairs of state.

Significantly, the god Osiris – at one time the "exclusive property of the kings" – is now associated with every dead person in the kingdom. The problems of royal succession – which have contributed to anarchy in the past because of the pharaohs' longevity and proclivity to fatherhood – have been resolved by a system of co-regency between a king and his son.

A priest with an image of Amun.

A stone statuette, apparently of a harp player, made out of Parian marble from Keros near Amorgos, both islands in the Cyclades group off Greece.

Stone-bowl culture comes to east Africa

East Africa, c.2000BC

The use of stone for tools and other objects still survives among several peoples in East Africa, especially among the cattle-farmers along the Great Rift Valley and surrounding areas. The Njoro River cave people, for instance, who may originally come from the Sudan, hollow their bowls out of local stone and use stone to make tools for cutting, scraping and boring. Obsidian, a black volcanic glass, is an especially popular material, not only because it is readily available but because it provides very sharp edges. Other tools are made from wood, and the Njoro people also make decorated wooden and earthenware vessels, although they are much less common than the stone bowls. Other artefacts include basketwork and cords, and gourds are also used.

The skills of the Njoro River people do not stop there. Although they still hunt, their communities are founded on agriculture, which may have spread from regions to the north. They have learnt how to keep cattle, as well as sheep and goats. They also grow cereals, for which they have grindstones and pestles. Curiously, though, they appear not to eat fish, a taboo also observed by peoples further north in the Sudan.

Apart from the more practical side of life the "stone-bowl" people spend time on less essential activities; they love to decorate themselves with many different forms of beads made from local materials.

Peaceful interlude marked by Gudea's earthly temples

Sumer, c.2144-2124BC

While the Guti were wreaking havoc throughout Mesopotamia, the city of Lagash under King Gudea, was an oasis of peace and civilisation. During his 20 years of power, Gudea engaged in only one military campaign – in Iran – and devoted the rest of his time to building temples.

Gudea built about 15 temples in Lagash, but his pride and joy was the E-ninnu, the dwelling of Ningirsu, patron god of the city. The temple is the earthly home of the god, and its building was accompanied by elaborate ritual inspired

King Gudea with spurting vase.

by a dream of Gudea's. After consulting the goddess Nanshe, interpreter of dreams, Gudea sought to purify the city by encircling it with fires, before building a temple of unparalleled extravagance.

Craftsmen and materials were gathered from far afield and everything was done in accordance with plans drawn up by Gudea. He, as Ningirsu's earthly messenger, was architect and master of the project: he made the mould which was used to shape the first brick, and he laid the foundations.

The result is a temple of awesome size, on seven levels, decorated with images of demons and animals, including a lion with seven heads, bison and dragons.

Bureaucracy instils order in Sumer

A cuneiform tablet with a receipt for tools, including 327 copper sickles.

A list of amounts of grain paid out to temple officials and servants.

Mesopotamia, c.2100BC

A new order is emerging in Mesopotamia after the fall of Agade. The death of Naram-Sin precipitated a series of rebellions and palace revolutions, climaxing in victory for the Guti highlanders, invading from the Zagros mountains, over the Akkadian forces. Ur-Nammu, founder of the city of Ur in Sumer, eventually restored native authority, but it was his son, Shulgi, who was able to reorganise the administration of the state into the most efficient and comprehensive bureaucracy yet seen.

During a long and mainly peaceful reign, Shulgi started by completing the temples and monuments begun by Ur-Nammu and building some of his own. He reinstated the Sumerian gods in their proper shrines, reformed the calendar, and introduced new measures for grain. He mixed the inevitable military campaigns with diplomacy, marrying his daughters to the governors of Barahshe and Anshan, and building temples in Susa to the native Elamite *(Iran)* gods.

The Sumerian empire is not as large as the the empire of Agade, but it is much more coherent in terms of the way in whuch it is governed. Under an omnipotent monarch, a network of city states is administered by governors chosen equally from Sumerians and Akkadians or, in outlying areas, from the native population. Communications are improved by garrisons on main routes, and alliances and commercial relations are often cemented by marriage.

Power is highly centralised. The king owns all the estates, and has factories, workshops and trading

centres both in Mesopotamia and abroad. The power structure, from the top downwards, then comprises the king's grand vizier, who is the empire's chief bureaucrat or administrator; the prefects, senior civil servants who can afford houses, fields, asses and slaves; and the local governors of the different parts of the empire, who pay themselves from the taxes they levy, and can become quite rich in spite of having to send a certain number of cattle to the capital, Ur.

The temples, too, are run according to their own bureaucratic structure: an administrator or prefect, an archivist, a registrar, a tax inspector, an army captain, a works manager, a sub-registrar, a head gardener, an agricultural supervisor, a post manager, throne bearers and foremen. Alongside the growing bureaucracy a middle class of merchants is emerging. The pyramid is sustained at the bottom by freemen, serfs and slaves.

King promulgates first legal code

Mesopotamia, c.2100BC

The world's first known legal code has been introduced in Sumer. Corrupt men who have stolen property are dismissed, the poor are protected, and a new system of punishments is laid down. Although Ur-Nammu has been credited with these reforms, it appears more likely that it was his son, Shulgi, who drew up the new legal code. Now certain categories of crime are punished by fines levied according to the nature of the crime.

Whoever initiated the legal reforms, Ur-Nammu was certainly noted for reviving agriculture, digging canals, fortifying towns and rebuilding. His most startling innovation was the ziggurat, a three-storey temple at Ur which is the world's first multi-storey building.

Officials presented to Ur-Nammu.

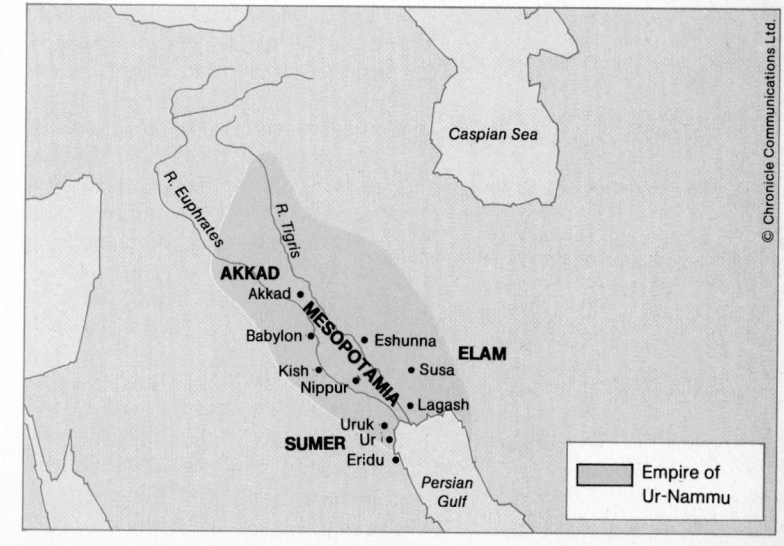

Caspian Sea

R. Euphrates
R. Tigris

AKKAD
Akkad

MESOPOTAMIA

Babylon • • Eshunna

ELAM

Kish • • Susa

Nippur •

• Lagash

Uruk •

SUMER Ur •

Eridu •

Persian Gulf

Empire of Ur-Nammu

First palaces begin to be built in Crete

Goblet from Phaestos palace.

A vase, also from Phaestos.

Crete, c.2000BC

New standards of luxury are appearing in Crete as the island takes over the leadership of Aegean trade. Palaces are being built in several parts of the island near to the small towns which are its manufacturing centres. The largest is probably that at Knossos, on a fertile plain in the centre of the island. The palace is built around a courtyard, with storerooms and luxurious apartments; but it is also a religious centre.

Craftsmanship has reached very high levels: tiny seals in semi-precious stones are carved with great accuracy and show plants, animals, birds, boats, shells and geometric patterns. The walls of the palaces are covered in frescoes, and the finely made pottery in bright colours on a dark background echoes the patterns on the walls.

It also reflects skills in other crafts – the manufacture of stone vases and shapes that were first used in metalwork, particularly silver. Ships with sails carry these commodities along the coast of Anatolia to Syria where they are exchanged with Egyptian traders.

Assyrians set up merchant colonies

Assyria, c.1900BC

The commercial tentacles of the Assyrian empire have spread into Cappadocia, the wild heart of eastern Anatolia. Merchants from the capital at Ashur have recently set up a trading settlement near Kanesh (Kultepe), exporting textiles and tin and importing copper.

The trade is tightly controlled from Ashur by a few powerful families, who take the profits in the form of gold and silver. The pioneering merchants have formed small colonies which in turn control a network of agencies throughout the country. The close Assyrian control of operations is made easier by the fact that the area is divided into relatively weak principalities.

Each colony has its own shops and banks which do business with the local authorities as well as collecting taxes. Business houses, run along family lines, earn substantial profits. Although financed on a modest scale, there is nothing modest about their interest rates which may be as high as 100 per cent.

The colonies are responsible to the main settlement at Kanesh, which answers to Ashur, which supplies any necessary finance, but leaves the day-to-day trading operations to the merchants.

Wooden models carve out a new Egyptian art form

Egypt, c.1900BC

Egyptian craftsmen are creating a new style: wooden models, which are placed in tombs next to the dead. Originally such models were carved in limestone, but these new ones show complex scenes involving day-to-day activities in miniature settings: houses and gardens, granaries and boats, all of them showing ordinary people and tradesmen going about their business.

There is the butcher slaughtering an ox; or the carpenter sawing through a plank of wood; or a musician with his wind instrument. All human life is here: women grinding corn; the baker kneading dough which he will pass to the brewer who is seen to sieve the fermented dough to make beer, a favoured drink in the Egypt of today.

A realistic wooden funerary model of two men at the plough.

Amun becomes king of Egypt's gods

Egypt, c.2000BC

The god Amun now reigns supreme. He was originally a minor god, worshipped in Thebes, but as the town grew in status to become the capital of Egypt Amun's prestige grew with it. Now he is king of the gods – at the top of the Theban trinity with his wife, the goddess Mut, and his son Khons.

Amun is regarded as the physical father of every pharoah; and thus he receives many gifts from his grateful sons in their temples which accounts for the enormous privileges granted to his priests. The temples dedicated to him are huge, their wealth ever-increasing, and the priests have become a political power to be reckoned with. The name Amun is an important element of royal names.

Amun is most frequently portrayed wearing a cap decked with two tall feathers (symbols of the gods of the air), with his body sometimes shown as ithyphallic in token of fertility. The ram and the white goose are the two animals associated with him.

His power was great indeed, as this prayer from a supplicant shows.

A priestess and the monkey god Hapi adore the Eye of Amun-Re.

"O Amun," it reads, "lend thine ear to one who stands alone in the court, who is poor while his adversary is rich. The people of the court oppress him; silver and gold for the scribes of the accounts; clothes for the attendants! But it is found that Amun has changed into Vizier in order that a poor man shall not be crushed."

Another prayer confirms the popular faith in Amun's justness. "Amun-Re judges the earth with his finger, and speaks to the heart. He assigns the wicked to punishment, but the righteous to the West," it reads.

A singer of Amun-Re from Thebes.

Sinuhe becomes an heroic figure in early literature

Egypt, c.1960BC

A story written at this time has become a "best seller". The tale of Sinuhe is being copied out by scribes and shows every sign of being popular for many years to come.

According to the story, Sinuhe was a courtier of King Amenemhet I. When the king dies Sinuhe, fearing national turbulence surrounding the accession, flees from Egypt and crosses the delta and Suez isthmus. He finds himself in the desert which, at first, strikes him as being hostile, dangerous and full of fantastic animals.

He almost dies of thirst, but he is made welcome and cared for by Bedouin tribesmen. After fathering a family, Sinuhe becomes the Bedouin leader. It is a fascinating account in which every stage of his journey and new life is recorded, with his thoughts and feelings on every occasion copiously described.

Despite his success in the desert, Sinuhe does not forget his native Egypt. When he receives an edict from the new king, Sesostris I, granting him an amnesty, he happily returns. He has been promised an important position and a tomb similar to those reserved for children of the royal family.

Sinuhe's adventures typify a form of literature popular in Egypt. Prophecies are eagerly read – describing dramatic events from the past as if they predict the future.

A "plank idol", from the island of Cyprus, made from red polished terracotta which has been incised with the design.

Social differences increase among the peoples of Yellow River

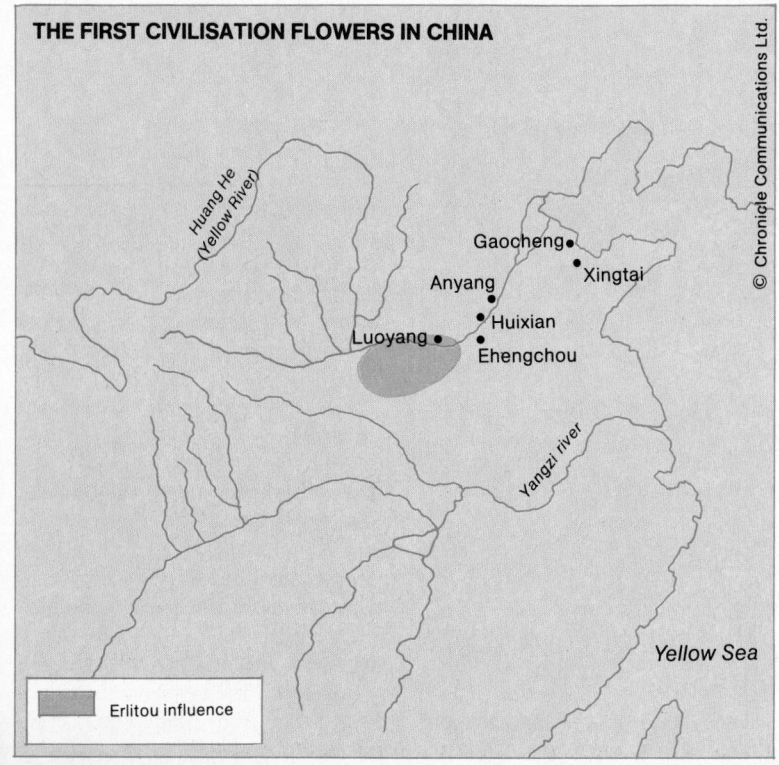

THE FIRST CIVILISATION FLOWERS IN CHINA

© Chronicle Communications Ltd.

Huang He (Yellow River)

Gaocheng
Xingtai
Anyang
Huixian
Luoyang
Ehengchou

Yangzi river

Yellow Sea

Erlitou influence

China, c.2000BC

A flourishing culture with a complicated social hierarchy has emerged on the central plain of the Yellow River in the area inhabited by the Longshan people. They have a well developed agriculture, with millet as their main crop, and they have succeeded in domesticating the dog, pig and cattle.

Their best pottery is finely crafted blackware, thin-walled and delicately shaped, much more sophisticated in design than the clumsy pottery of earlier farming settlements.

Social divisions are apparent, with the rich occupying much more lavish homes than the poor. This division extends to the grave. The poor are placed in simple pits, while the rich are set to rest with their wealth about them. Polished stone implements, beads, shell ornaments and jade discs accompany them to the hereafter. Women are not highly regarded. Rich or poor, they are buried with little ceremony.

Mesopotamia, c.1900BC. Farming is intensified to meet the needs of the fast-growing population. Where rainfall is poor, complex irrigation systems are installed. In the state of Larsa an office responsible for developing canals has been created.

Mesopotamia, c.1900BC. Farming is intensified to meet the needs of the fast-growing population. Where rainfall is poor, complex irrigation systems are installed. In the state of Larsa an office responsible for developing canals has been created.

Egypt, c.1840BC. During his reign of nearly 40 years Sesostris III, descended from Amenemhet I, has annexed Lower Nubia to Egypt and built fortifications on the Nile to secure his country's southern border. He undertook a military expedition into Palestine. At home he suppressed moves towards provincial independence.

Peru, c.1800BC. A large temple complex dedicated to a feline deity cult has been built at Chavin de Huantar on the eastern slopes of the Cordillera Blanca, northern Peru. Animal and human sacrifice is practised here. Chavin people trade with coastal settlers.

Egypt, c.1800BC. Egyptian prosperity has reached new heights during the reign of Amenemhet III, just ended. Amenemhet promoted international trade, bringing an influx of foreign peoples into the country. He masterminded massive irrigation and land reclamation projects, in particular at the Faiyum oasis, where he also built his pyramid and funerary temple.

Egypt, c.1800BC. Egyptians are using mathematics, based on decimals and addition, to keep temple accounts, for architecture and for land surveying.

Mesopotamia, c.1800BC. The ruling dynasties of Isin and Larsa, who had continued the policies of the kings of Ur, have been overthrown and Mesopotamia is being divided into a large number of city-states. The Amorite nomads who swamped the kingdom of Ur from 2004BC are now the ruling class in most of the great cities of Sumer and Akkad.

Assyria, c.1800BC. Shamshi-Adad, an Amorite prince, has seized power in Assyria. He is planning to conquer the city-state of Mari and regain possession of his kingdom of Terqa on the Euphrates, from which he was ousted by an ambitious neighbour.

Sahara, c.1730BC. People in the Air massif of Niger have begun to use copper, melting the ore in open pots.

Stonehenge built from giant rocks

Britain, c.1700BC
Much work is being carried out at this ancient religious site. Gangs of men are dragging huge bluestones from many miles away and setting them up in a great circle. A pathway lined with standing stones is being built so that it faces the rising sun at dawn on the longest day. A horseshoe of local stones capped with lintels is also being erected, creating an impressive enclosure. This work will certainly make Stonehenge one of Britain's most celebrated places of ritual worship.

Bluestone circle at Stonehenge.

Pacific opens to traders

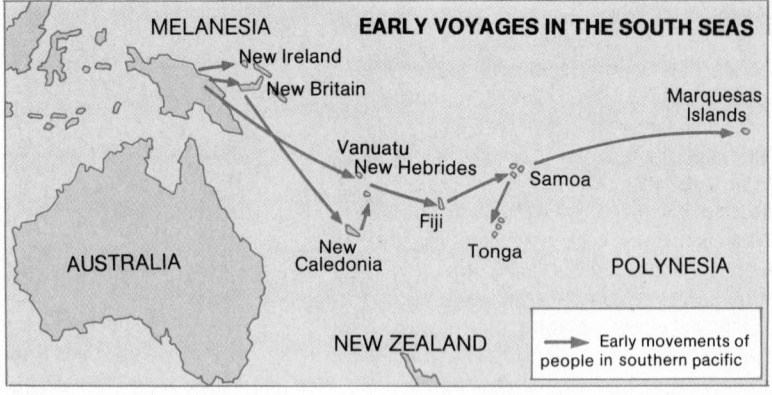

EARLY VOYAGES IN THE SOUTH SEAS

MELANESIA
New Ireland
New Britain
Vanuatu
New Hebrides
Fiji
Samoa
Tonga
New Caledonia
AUSTRALIA
Marquesas Islands
POLYNESIA
NEW ZEALAND

→ Early movements of people in southern pacific

Melanesia, c.1700BC
Traders from the Bismarck Archipelago have started migrating into the uninhabited islands of the south-west Pacific. Moving swiftly, the tribes, members of the Lapita people, have already established themselves across a wide swathe of islands.

The Lapita tend to build their settlements in coastal areas or on small offshore islands. Here they rear pigs and cultivate root crops such as yams and taro, as well as nut and fruit bearing trees, many of which they have brought from their homeland. They collect shellfish, hunt green sea turtles and fish with intricately designed shell hooks. These foods are supplemented by domestic chickens, pigs and dogs, which they have also brought with them.

Apart from bringing human life to these empty islands, the Lapita also carry a number of distinctive stones, notably obsidian, a volcanic glass of great value in making stone tools, and own their unique style of pottery ware.

Books for the hereafter accompany the dead to their tombs

From a Book of the Dead: the dead woman prays to the hippopotamus goddess, Tauret, while Hathor, goddess of love, in cow shape, looks on.

Egypt, c.1700BC
Egypt's dead are offered more than food, drink and ceremonial boats for their passage to any afterlife. They are provided with a spiritual guide in the form of a collection of religious texts.

At first these were inscribed on coffins ("Coffin Texts"), but later they are written on *papyrus* and placed in the sarcophagi or coffins with them – the Book of the Dead.

The texts range over a wide variety of subjects. Some themes recur frequently, in particular precepts to protect the spirit of the deceased and safeguard him in the hereafter.

Many texts are beautifully illustrated, with the names of the dead owners inserted at appropriate places. The magic spells included are required reading for the dead. Learned by heart, they are supposed to ensure the dead a safe escape from the darkness of the tomb and a return to their homes and gardens where they enjoy "the sweet breezes of the north wind".

King lays down the law

Babylon, c.1760BC

The laws of Hammurabi, king of Babylon, are engraved on stone slabs. Hammurabi promoted Marduk, god of Babylon, to the head of the pantheon, thereby legalising his dynasty. Then, like other Mesopotamian kings, he "ordained justice" by remitting various debts and fixing prices of commodities in the markets.

His laws are essentially a collection of ad hoc edicts, often based on existing laws and customs in order to ensure continuity. They relate to three classes of citizen – free men, serfs or villeins, and slaves. Fees and punishments vary according to class.

Compensation in kind, or money, which was the basis of the Sumerian system, is partially replaced by the Law of Retaliation. Thus a surgeon or architect whose work results in injury or death to his client is liable to have his hand cut off or, in extreme cases, to be executed.

Adulterous wives can be saved from sentence of death by their husbands, but their lovers can be spared only by the king. A prisoner's wife can sleep with another

Laws engraved on a stone slab.

man "if there is nothing to eat in her house". Men wishing to divorce their wives have to compensate them financially. Widows have use of their husbands' property as long as they live.

People in certain positions are granted "ilkum" – corn, land, sheep and cattle – from the king in return for their loyalty.

Literary buds begin to bloom in Sumer

A cuneiform tablet from Sumer.

Mesopotamia, 1900-1800BC

The Sumerian language is dying, and to immortalise its intellectual achievements the Houses of Tablets have been instituted.

These literary workshops are organised like family units, with scribes working under a "father",

and an internal hierarchy distinguishing between the most talented and experienced pupils, known as "elder brothers", and the beginners, known as "younger brothers". Pupils begin their instruction by learning to write, handle words and understand grammar. A select few will go on to create literature.

Wherever a temple is built there is work for copyists. Gradually a network of tablet houses is being created: they propagate myths and stories explaining man's beliefs, his relationship with nature, and the origins of the universe. Hymns extolling gods or kings are set down; lamentations describing in detail the pestilences and afflictions of the day; prayers; fables in which animals, plants and men engage in debating contests; proverbs and maxims; and stories like the *Epic of Gilgamesh*, a legendary tale of a great hero from the past in the city of Uruk.

Soothsayers see shape of things to come

Babylon, c.1800BC

The work of soothsayers, or diviners, is an important part of Babylonian scholarship and philosophy. No king will embark on a major undertaking – a war, or the building of a temple – without consulting these men. Previous disasters have been attributed to failure to consult the oracles.

The diviners believe that man, nature and the cosmos have a reciprocal relationship. The whole universe is conceived as a huge, complex network of sympathetic forces which draw disparate things together. So man is related to animals, which are related to elements, which are related to each other.

At the same time there are antipathetic forces working through the same relationships. Diviners believe they can make deductions about the human condition from omens in nature.

The examination of a sheep's entrails provides an example: "If

Clay model of sheep's liver inscribed with omens and magical formulae.

the entrails are burst at the point of entry, a king's son will succeed to the throne, If they are burst at the navel, a madman will rule the land. If the small intestine is burst, a peasant's son will take the throne."

Mesopotamian diviners claim to understand man's relationship with nature so well that they can deduce from a human situation precisely what omen the oracle will offer.

Grasshoppers tickle Mari's royal palates

Mari statuette: the "great singer".

Mari, Mesopotamia, c.1780BC

The kings of Mari rule from a 300-room palace, the finest in the world, with courtyards covering about seven acres.

There are official audience rooms, the king's private apartments, guest suites and garrison quarters, a school, royal chapels, kitchens, servants' quarters and workshops. The great courtyard, 4,500 square feet, is planted with palm trees; another is decorated with frescoes showing the king pay-

ing homage to the gods. The buildings are made of mud bricks with plastered faces, and the outer palace wall is 40 feet thick. Rooms have no windows, relying on light from tall doorways and holes in the ceilings. Bitumen-lined clay pipes and gutters provide drainage.

Food is one of the luxuries of court life. Beef, mutton and gazelle are eaten frequently, fish only rarely; skewered grasshoppers are a favourite delicacy, as are ostrich eggs. Vegetables, breads and sweetmeats accompany the main dish. There is a great variety of beers made from fermented barley; wine is imported chiefly from Syrian vineyards, kept in cellars and stored according to its year and place of origin.

The king eats with his court dignitaries, while the queen eats at another table. He dresses simply, wearing a Babylonian bonnet and a single garment wound round his body, with a belt at the waist. He hardly moves except in one small part of his palace. He does not meet his people, and because he does not visit his temples or capital city, the gods have to come to see *him*.

Near East, c.1700BC. A tribal chieftain and religious leader called Abraham is reputed to have led his tribe out of the city of Ur in Sumer and settled at Hebron in Canaan.

Greece, c.1650BC. Greek mainland culture is breaking free of Cretan influence and developing new forms. One example is the domed beehive tomb known as the *tholos*. This type of monument began at Pylos. Here and at Mycenae craftsmen also make vases, with figurative decorations.

Anatolia, c.1620BC. The Indo-European intruders known as the Hittites have become a force to be reckoned with. They laid the foundations for a kingdom under Labarnas I, who died c.1650BC after notable conquests in central Anatolia. His son won further victories south towards Syria and founded a capital at Hattusas (Boghazkoy).

China, c.1600BC. A large building, believed to be a palace, has been built on a platform of earth at Erlitou, near Yenshi in Henan (Honan), a site which has already been occupied for several centuries. The palace inhabitants use bronze to make carefully crafted ritual vessels as well as a variety of tools and weapons. They also produce fine jade work.

Near East, c.1595BC. Mursilis, the Hittite king, has taken the town of Babylon, bringing to an end the dynasty of Hammurabi. Earlier, Mursilis brought down the kingdom of Aleppo in northern Syria. He has now returned to Hattusas, his capital in Anatolia, leaving the Kassites, a people originating from the Zagros area, to assume control of Babylon.

India, c.1500BC. The cities of the Indus valley have been abandoned. Whether the cause was some natural catastrophe, an internal breakdown of order or attacks by marauders from the hills to the west is unknown. While city life has come to an end, however, the population of the countryside seems to have survived.

North America, c.1500BC. People living in the regions of Minnesota and Wisconsin have started to learn the techniques of metallurgy.

Sicily, c.1500BC. Local Sicilian chiefs have begun to receive visits from traders coming from the Aegean. They barter local products for pottery and metalwork.

Palaces are jewels of Minoan Crete

Crete, c.1700BC

After a massive earthquake which brought ruin and desolation to Crete, the island's palaces are being rebuilt on an even more magnificent scale than before. King Minos, at Knossos, has engaged the architect Daedalus to construct a vast complex of buildings set around a central court running north and south.

Besides the Throne Room and the royal apartments there are shrines, administrative offices, an arsenal, granaries, warehouses and workshops. Near the central court is the Snake Goddess, a statuette of a narrow-waisted woman with a long, flounced skirt and a tight fitting blouse, cut away to expose the breasts. In her hands she holds out wriggling snakes.

As well as the palaces there are also country houses, which are the centres of estates that produce olive oil and wine, in addition to rearing the large flocks of sheep whose wool is the basis of the local textile industry. Writing, in a local script based on Egyptian models, has been introduced to keep track of these ever more complex arrangements.

The present palaces, at Knossos and elsewhere on the island, are being built on the sites of the original ones, so much of the evidence of the past is being buried it is known, though, that the old palaces, like the new ones, consisted of buildings arranged round a large rectangular courtyard.

At Malia on the north coast there

Statue of a bronze bull with acrobatic figure, from a Cretan palace.

was a group of administrative buildings separate from the palace complex. Cemeteries were located in a rocky area by the sea. In eastern Crete, at Gournia, a village of narrow winding streets and rough steps has been built on a hillside overlooking the sea. Some of the houses are furnished with materials brought over the mountains from Knossos, some 30 miles distant across the island.

The labyrinthine passages of Knossos are said to have given rise to the legend that King Minos had them built to hide the monster he had fathered, the Minotaur, with a man's body and the head of a bull.

Throne room interior at the Royal Minoan Palace, Knossos.

Egyptian tomb obelisk given as reward to royal scribe, 1585BC.

Hittite potters set new artistic styles

Anatolia, c.1600BC.

Hittite culture is developing in an original way, notably expressed in pottery. Techniques are derived from the Hittites' predecessors, the Hatti, who travelled through regions that produced copper and silver, and developed metalwork, under Anatolian, Indo-European and Mesopotamian influences.

Vases with spouts, whether used for practical or ritual purposes, often depict the daily life of the Anatolian people, in their typical clothes and pointed head-dresses.

Fortresses rule Carpathian passes

Carpathians, c.1700BC

A series of stone-built fortresses and strong-points has been constructed along the passes in the Carpathian mountains in Czechoslovakia to safeguard the vital trade routes northwards to Germany and Denmark, where substantial markets have opened up for bronze tools and weapons made from Transylvanian copper and tin deposits in Rumania. Sometimes these fortified settlements are attacked and burned, leaving objects of amber and gold behind in the ashes.

Volcano buries island

A fresco buried by the volcano.

Aegean Sea, c.1500BC

A huge volcano has destroyed the island of Santorini, leaving its inhabitants buried under a huge layer of lava and debris. Much of the island has disappeared, submerged under the sea.

First indications of the disaster came when the ground began to shake violently as though from an earthquake. People began to flee from the principal town of Akrotiri, taking a few precious possessions. Then came the explosion, which hurled out huge boulders smashing down on the houses. Day became night as a huge blanket of ash covered the island. Thousands of tons of molten lava poured down towards the helpless town, and the sea began to pour in as the sides of the volcano collapsed.

A way of life has disappeared with Santorini. Food supplies – vegetables, dried fish, cereals, oil, wine and olives – were stored in earthenware jars in the ground floor rooms, with the people living up-stairs. Each house had a room which appeared to serve as a shrine. It was decorated with frescoes of landscapes showing animals, boats, growing lilies or papyrus, crocuses being picked, a small catlike animal stalking ducks and a fisherman with his arms full of fish.

Akrotiri and its people have been entombed, sealed in a time capsule which later generations may discover and learn about a society that once flourished on a small and prosperous Aegean island.

Egyptians drive out their unwelcome Hyksos overlords after lengthy siege

The invasion of the Hyksos kings, as seen by a much later German artist.

Egypt, c.1550BC

After a lengthy siege the Hyksos defenders of the fortress capital of Avaris in the north-eastern delta have capitulated, bringing to an end some 140 years of foreign domination of Egypt.

The victorious Egyptian army is now poised to cross the Sinai and invade Palestine and Syria in pursuit of the Hyksos and their allies in western Asia. Tribes from Asia had taken advantage of weak Egyptian leadership to infiltrate the Nile delta and finally to conquer the whole of Egypt, using war chariots and other forms of weaponry unknown to Egypt.

Reports speak of the "infliction of every kind of barbarity upon the inhabitants, slaying some, and reducing the wives and children of others to a state of slavery". Others speak of the destruction of the great temples built by previous Egyptian rulers, although many of these claims are unproven and may be no more than Egyptian propaganda.

It was 90 years ago that King Salitis established a Hyksos dynasty which ruled Egypt with garrisons built along the entire length of the Nile. The Hyksos, mostly an illiterate race, adopted Egyptian customs, took Egyptian names and learned to use the hieroglyphic script. The "Shepherd Kings" as they were known – although "Hyksos" derives from the Egyptian for "ruler of foreign lands" – were Salitis, Bnon, Apakhnan, Apophis, Iannas and Kertos. Princes ruled provincial Egypt.

Organised resistance began in Thebes. The Egyptians had learned the value of the horsedrawn warchariot, of bows and arrows and slings, from their Hyksos masters. Now they turned these same weapons on the invaders, driving them north. Most of the delta was liberated by the Egyptian king, Amosis, before he laid siege to the Hyksos stronghold at Avaris.

Life begins after death for pharaohs in Valley of the Kings

Egypt, c.1550-1070BC

A pharaoh is dead; and now, here in the Valley of the Kings, he begins his voyage to the hereafter, taking with him his earthly possessions and servants to care for him. But first comes the involved ritual in which he is embalmed, mummified and prepared for the journey to the underworld through which the sun god, Re, passes each night in his barque before rising again at dawn.

The funerary process alone takes 70 days, the first 40 of these devoted to the embalming of the pharaoh, the last 30 taken up with the complicated bandaging of the body, each bandage requiring separate prayers and ceremonies.

A pharaoh's funerary bandages are woven especially for him from the finest linen. The embalming involves the removal of the pharaoh's entrails, the lungs, liver, stomach and intestines, each placed in individual canopic jars, their lids depicting the four sons of Horus who will protect the royal entrails. These will be placed near the sarcophagus together with *shawabtis*, mummy-shaped statuettes who will do agricultural work for the deceased in the hereafter.

As the mummification continues, the preparation of the tomb involves an equally intricate level of planning. The pharaoh will take with him his personal equipment: his weapons, games, jewels, usical instruments, clothes – even his toilet case. These will be placed close to the body as essential requirements for the afterlife.

At the conclusion of the 70 days he will be brought to the entrance of his tomb, which consists of a series of corridors and halls cut into the rock. Here, to the chanting of incantations, with the air heavily scented with purifying incense, the ceremony of "opening the mouth" – in which the mummy is believed

Valley of the Kings: a last journey.

to regain the use of its senses – is conducted. Fully prepared for the journey, the pharaoh is then carried to his burial chamber through passages illustrated with scenes in which the gods protect him.

Britain, c.1500BC. As demand for jewellery grows, goldsmiths are hard at work making diadems, necklaces, pins and bracelets, as well as fine plate. The most highly regarded craftsmen export their wares to mainland Europe.

Mediterranean, c.1500BC. The people of Sardinia, Corsica and the Balearic Islands are building fortresses, usually on hilltops, with blocks of roughly hewn stone. In Corsica there are also a large number of *menhirs* cut to form the shapes of noses, mouths and eyes – giving them a rudimentary human appearance.

Syria, c.1500BC. Idrimi, the son of a king of Aleppo, driven from his kingdom by the Mitanni, settles at Alalakh, where he founds the kingdom of Mukish and wages sporadic campaigns against the Hittites.

India, c.1500BC. The arrival of the Indo-Aryans in Punjab is simultaneous with the end of the Indus civilisation. Hitherto mainly animal breeders and pastoral nomads, the Aryan invaders introduce a new culture and show their military superiority by using war chariots. When they settle in India, the Aryans start to compose the *Rig-Veda*, a distillation of their religious beliefs.

Europe, c.1500BC. Modern farmers in western Europe have stopped using sickles or scythes fashioned from flint; instead they use bronze sickles, which are much tougher and cut better.

China, c.1450BC. The Shang dynasty establishes its capital at Zhengzhou (Cheng-chou) in Henan (Honan). The city is surrounded by a stamped earth wall and centres on a palace. The Shang gained ascendancy over other tribes in the Yellow river valley over 200 years ago.

Near East, c.1450BC. The region of Syria and Palestine, because of its geographical position, is constantly being preyed upon by its neighbours. At present divided between the Hittites, the Mitanni and the Egyptians, it is going through an extremely troubled period.

Crete, c.1450BC. The palatial complexes are destroyed, apart from Knossos which is taken over by Mycenaeans from the mainland. The Mycenaeans adopt bureaucratic techniques such as writing from the older Cretan culture, and the Greek language is now being written down for the first time.

Beard masks female role as pharaoh

Egypt, 1458BC

The name of Hatshepsut, daughter of Thutmose I, is being systematically hammered from monuments all over Egypt on the orders of her successor and half-nephew, Thutmose III, clearly resentful at being kept in a subordinate position during his aunt's reign.

In every respect the beautiful Hatshepsut was a pharaoh in her own right. Statues and paintings show her as a bearded Osiris in the traditional manner. She is not buried with royal women in the Valley of the Queens, but lies in her spectacular tomb among male pharaohs in the Valley of the Kings.

But how did a woman achieve such power and influence in a country in which the male line is so dominant ? The answer is found in the complicated marital situation which governed at the time. Hatshepsut married her half-brother, Thutmose II, who died prematurely leaving a son, Thutmose III, the child of another wife. Thutmose III was a child, incapable of ruling; and thus the forceful, charismatic Hatshepsut stepped in and officially took power until her death.

Hatshepsut's reign was marked by the expansion of trade and the erection of one of the finest temples in Egypt – its great doors fashioned from black bronze, its inlaid figures in electrum – built for her by

Relief from the temple of Queen Hatshepsut showing the Queen of Punt and gift-bearers on an expedition from East Africa to Egypt. Expeditions also went to Punt to bring back myrrh trees to plant on the temple terraces.

Senenmut, her daughter's tutor. A trading expedition to the land of Punt (*perhaps in the region of Somalia or further inland*) which brought back gold, ivory, incense, apes, birds and trees to the pharaoh is recorded in some detail among the inscriptions. They show the very fat queen of Punt, together with the Egyptian envoy, displaying beads and other articles used in the trade.

Hatshepsut's reign was also marked by her encouragement of architecture and other art forms throughout Egypt. At Karnak, for instance, she was responsible for the erection of two monumental obelisks.

Hatshepsut: queen with a beard.

Funeral temples enshrine the glory and deification of pharaohs

Queen Hatshepsut's mortuary temple cut into the cliffs at Deir el-Bahri.

Egypt, c.1460BC

The vast mortuary temple built for Queen Hatshepsut is complete, dominating the cliffs overlooking Karnak, its height and splendour indicating the prestige in which the queen was held. The building is partly cut into the rock and fits perfectly with its surroundings.

The architect, Senemut, has excelled himself. A great central ramp links the terraces. The pillared porticoes are decorated with painted reliefs, and the overall effect is one of careful thought for both the site and the importance of its occupant.

With this temple, the glory of the pharaohs and their deification in the hereafter leaves the obscure darkness of the pyramids to be displayed to the light of day.

Mitanni kingdom emerges in Near East

Mesopotamia, c.1500BC

A new and embattled kingdom, called Mitanni, has been established in the Near East. It is centred on the capital of Washukani, but its influence extends as far away as Jerusalem, to Alalakh on the coast of the Mediterranean, and to Arrapkha, on the lower Zab, a tributary of the Tigris.

For most of the century the new kingdom has been plagued by wars, mostly arising from conflicts about the succession to power amongst the ruling families. Each clique has sought the help of either the Hittites or the Egyptians in the internal struggles, and the Egyptians and the Hittites have not been slow to use this as an excuse for extending their own power in the region.

The Mitanni, most of whose population speaks the local Hurrian language, are ruled by an immigrant people whose language is Indo-European and is related to Vedic which is spoken as far away as India.

Typical names are Artatama, which means "he who resides in divine law", and Tushratta, "he who possesses the splendid chariot". The members of the new landed aristocracy who fight in war chariots are known as "maryannu",

Mitannians hunting and drinking.

which is related to the Vedic "young man". Mitannis also worship the great Indo-Iranian gods, such as Mitra, Varuna and Indra, as well as the Hurrian goddess, Hepat, but few of them have a chance to do so in peace. Only a few cities have managed to avoid incessant wars.

The most notable of these is Nuzi, south of the lower Zab, a river in Mesopotamia. The peace has been kept there thanks to the protection of the King of Assyria who recognises Nuzi as his suzerainty; the Assyrians seem to be increasing their influence.

Northerners buried in everyday clothes

Bounty from a Danish grave.

Denmark, c.1450BC

When people die in Denmark and northern Germany they are buried under round burial mounds, or tumuli, in coffins made from hol-

lowed, out tree trunks. Corpses are interred wearing the woollen clothes which are commonly worn in everyday life; for the men this means brown cloaks and kilts, while the women wear skirts – short ones for the young and long ones for older women – secured by a woven belt with an elaborate tassle. The women's hair is sometimes secured with a snood, a sort of hairnet or headscarf.

For burial, a flayed cow-hide usually covers the body. The dead are accompanied in their graves by a variety of artefacts, such as gold ornaments and combs, and circular birch-bark containers for food and drink – things possibly believed necessary for an afterlife. Men are often buried equipped with their bronze swords and wooden scabbards, although perhaps only for show, since in one case the sword has been swapped for a dagger.

Egyptian rule stretches to Euphrates

Egypt, c.1460BC

After 17 campaigns, Thutmose III has extended the Egyptian empire to the banks of the Euphrates and proved himself an outstanding military leader. The campaigning began when Egypt was threatened by an alliance of the princes of Megiddo and Kadesh. Thutmose took preemptive action and attacked Megiddo, leading his army in single file along a narrow defile – "horse behind horse, man behind man, his Majesty showing the way by his own footsteps" – and captured the city after a short siege.

Following a strategy of creating "buffer states" around Egypt – primarily to defend his country against any repetition of the invasion which produced the Hyksos dynasty – Thutmose has created a novel system, under which Syria and Palestine have been forced to keep the peace and smaller king-states have been kept under order. The pharaoh has established an inspection system for collecting tributes from defeated nations.

After so many years of subordination to his aunt, Queen Hatshepsut, Thutmose's emergence as the the fighting head of such a great empire has come as something of a surprise to observers. The pharaoh is not merely a great general: he is a statesman who treats his defeated enemies with considerable humanity. Even those leaders who fought against him were not executed.

Thutmose III – outstanding leader.

They were deposed, and their sons and brothers brought to Egypt and held hostage. Under Thutmose the smaller states are said to be enjoying a kind of prosperity previously unknown.

Thutmose has had several close escapes from death. In Syria, for instance, he encountered a herd of wild elephants – only to be rescued by his bodyguard, Amenemhab. In a battle with a coalition of Mitanni, the prince of Kadesh and the prince of Tunip, a mare in season was released to create havoc among the Egyptian chariots. It was the loyal Amenemhab who saved the day by catching and killing the animal.

Father is master of the Nuzi household

Mesopotamia, c.1450BC.

In Nuzi, a Mesopotamian city of the Mitanni empire, the man is head of the family, owner of goods and chattels, master of his wife, sole fount of family authority and controller of all in his house.

Paternal will is imposed by perpetuating the worship of ancestors, and by direct communication with the gods. It is the father's responsibility to ensure that his house meets with the gods' approval. The father forgives or punishes. Should he fall into debt, he can sell members of his family as slaves.

The husband's privileges are not so brutally asserted as they are in Assyria, where he is free to beat or disfigure his wife, sometimes by cut-

ting off her nose or ears. But the woman is subject to the will of men throughout her life: first her father, then her father-in-law, her husband and, finally, her sons. In Nuzi, a father foreseeing his imminent death can decide to endow his wife with paternal power.

There are important limits, however. A widow can neither sell nor give away any part of the goods or chattels for which she is responsible. If she were to exceed her rights, her sons could chase her naked from the house.

Children are brought up very strictly. If they are disobedient the father can flog them, or shackle them, or shut them away in a dark cave.

Babylon, c.1450BC. Gulkishar, king of Babylon, is busy compiling recipes for glass-making. All the recipes begin with a short introduction on how to construct a furnace. Then comes the list of ingredients required for making glass, sometimes with instructions about the quality of ingredients to select or how to use them.

Egypt, c.1430BC. Amenhotep II, son of the great soldier Thutmose III, is thrusting on with his father's work. He has kept a tight grip on southern Palestine, harshly repressing any rebellion, and fought a successful campaign on the Euphrates. A fine marksman with bow and arrow, he extols the values of "sport".

Egypt, c.1410BC. The recent marriage of Thutmose IV – who now rules over the flourishing empire founded by his grandfather, Thutmose III – and the daughter of the Mitanni king promises to promote good international relations. Thutmose IV has erected a monumental stele, or pillar, between the feet of the Giza sphinx, after a dream in which the sphinx confided its regret at being covered by sand.

Anatolia, c.1400BC The Hittites have learned how to smelt and forge iron for practical purposes. The first use of the metal in the Near East dates back to c.2500BC, when a king of Agade made an iron statue of a god. The key discovery of the Hittites is a technique to increase the carbon content of iron, making it much harder.

Greece, c.1400BC. The Mycenaean civilisation on the Greek mainland is opening up to the outside world and establishing trading contacts over large parts of the Mediterranean, especially in the Aegean, Cyprus and the Near East. The Mycenaeans exchange fabric, perfumed oils, cereals and wine for basic materials which they lack, such as copper, tin, gold, ivory, amber and jewels.

Greece, c.1400BC. The administrative officials based at the Mycenaean palaces are using a form of writing based on ideograms representing men, animals, objects, products and numerical signs. Painted inscriptions in the same style have been made on oil jars exported from the Chania area of Crete to a large part of the Aegean.

Egyptians battle Hittites for supremacy

The Hittites mark their military prowess in warrior carvings ...

... such as these from Tell Halaf, which also act to protect palaces.

Egypt, c1400BC

Two great world powers confront each other in the Near East today, with Palestine and Syria the eagerly sought prizes. After a series of campaigns by Egypt's Thutmose III, it is Egypt and the Hittite kingdoms that dominate the world.

The death of Thutmose, the military genius, sparked off fresh uprisings and internecine warfare between the Syrian princes. Though these were quelled by an operation led by Thutmose's son, Amenhotep II, tension remains throughout the Middle East as the Hittites seek to expand.

The interests of both countries are focused on the Mitanni kingdom which dominates much of Syria and Mesopotamia. Thutmose never succeeded in conquering the Mitannis and now his successor,

Amenhotep II, anxious to befriend the nation, has arranged to take a Mitanni princess into his harem. Meanwhile, King Shuppiluliumash has founded a new Hittite kingdom after 20 years of civil war and has covetous eyes on Mitanni. His excuse comes with an alliance he makes with a pretender to the Mitanni throne.

Shuppiluliumash's first attack was a failure. The Mitanni succeeded beating off his army, but a second battle – with the Hittite armies crossing the Euphrates and attacking the city of Washshukani – was a spectacular success, however. The city capitulated, and Shuppiluliumash gained control of most of the Mitanni empire.

An uneasy state of truce exists between the Hittite and Egyptian armies.

Rock carvings reach new heights in Alps

Maritime Alps, c.l400BC

Shepherds and peasants struggle 8,775 feet to the top of Monte Bego to carve their faces into the sides of the mountain. They use sharp metal and stone implements to scrape and dig deep into the schist and sandstone rock.

The stream of pilgrims to the mountain has left this open-air sanctuary decorated not only by vast numbers of faces, but with pictures of people at work, battle and prayer. Other engravings show cows harnessed to the plough and tools of bronze and copper.

A tribal chief engraved in the Alps.

Phoenicians give alphabetical order to their language

Syria, c.1400BC

Scribes working in the Levantine port of Ugarit (Ras Shamra) in Syria have invented a new system of signs which for the first time have made it possible to write down the local language, one of a number of semitic tongues.

Ugarit is one of the most prosperous of Syria's ports, manufacturing and exporting weapons and a variety of luxury metal objects, notably its renowned bronze vessels. Given the city's role as a major port, with access to major caravan

The Phoenicians record an offering to a god using alphabetic writing.

routes, the traders of Ugarit have welcomed this new, flexible writing system, which should make commercial transactions much easier.

The new system is not the first means of setting down the spoken word, but it is an alphabet, a system that arranges the signs used in a specific language in an order that is always the same. This represents a great advance over its predecessors, the Mesopotamian syllabic cuneiform and hieroglyphic systems developed by the peoples of Egypt.

Under the new Syrian system the number of signs has been drastically reduced; it uses only about 30 signs to write down the sounds of the spoken language.

Further south, in Phoenicia and Palestine, a linear script is being developed that does not make use of cuneiforms. This involves the scratching of curved or straight lines rather than using wedges. As this is not restricted to writing in clay, it may be more successful and spread more widely.

Pharaoh dedicates temple at Thebes

The Colossi of Memnon: the giant statues of Amenhotep III at Thebes.

Egypt, c.1390BC
Under Amenhotep III Egypt is enjoying an artistic and architectural renaissance. The new pharaoh has inherited the most wealthy and powerful country in the Near East. Egypt has excellent diplomatic and economic links with all of her neighbours who acknowledge the pharaoh's total authority.

With his wife Teye – surprisingly, a non-royal choice – Amenhotep is making a marked impression on Egyptian art. The colonnades of his palace at el-Malqata in Thebes and his mortuary temple, as well as the tombs of his officials, all testify to the pharaoh's taste for the grand and the excesssive. They demonstrate, too, the affectation of his artists, particularly the architect of the

same name, Amenhotep, who may be deified for his work.

The crowning glory of Amenhotep is his great temple at Luxor. The original design of this temple was less complex than that of the temple of Karnak. But now it is rebuilt in sandstone to a monumental scale. The rooms at the rear are decorated with exquisite reliefs, and a courtyard is surrounded by a magnificent colonnade. The whole edifice is connected to the temple at Karnak by a two-mile pathway bounded by sphinxes, with resting places for boats. This spectacular pathway was built during the reign of Queen Hatshepsut.

It is small wonder, therefore, that Amenhotep, who has more statues of himself than any other pharaoh, is known as "The Magnificent."

Horse-power changes life for peasants

Central Asia, c.1400BC
The tough little Steppe horse has changed an entire way of life in grassland and semi-desert from the Black Sea to India and Syria. Many small peasant farmers have given up tilling the soil for the wide open spaces. Thanks to the horse they are now nomads, taking their flocks and herds hundreds of miles.

They use the horse for riding and pulling chariots, and the reverence

in which they hold it is shown by the fact that horses are often buried with their rich owners.

The dominant tribes, who trade with the cities and towns on the fringe of the steppe, are related to the Aryans in India. They worship the ancient Indian gods of Mitra, Varuna and Indra. They have learned many skills and are able to cast their own bronze tools and weapons.

Technical strides change Egyptian art

Egypt, c.1390BC
Pictorial art is reaching new heights in the reign of Amenhotep III. Compositions are larger than ever before; the gestures of the subjects more supple; and the range of colours more subtle.

But how are Egyptian painters managing to produce such exquisite work? The answer is found in the natural elements available to them from the land itself: reed stems with pulped ends; brushes of palm fibre; naturally occurring pigments, and various binding agents like gum arabic and gelatine. Finely ground mineral substances are mixed with water, with gelatine, gum or white of egg added.

The crumbly limestone of the walls of Thebes will not allow bas-relief work. Instead, the cracks are filled with mud which is then covered with plaster which becomes the base for the pigments. Under this pharaoh, the white background is preferred to the grey-blue of the early days of Egyptian art.

Naturalistic art is at its height, as shown in the fowling scene of Nebamun hunting birds with a throwstick. There is a cat snaring birds, butterflies taking flight; everything is recorded in the minutest detail.

Another main motif reflects the Egyptian obsession with death; mourners follow a funeral pro-

Theban mayor smelling a lotus.

Harvest scene with oxen and boat.

cession, and pictures in the tomb of the vizier Ramose show the unrestrained grief, with tears flowing down the cheeks of the wailing women. The artistry is powerful and symbolic of this pharaoh.

Hunting birds in the marshes: naturalistic art, crammed with detail.

1390 (1390-1350)

China, c.1390BC. Writing has made an appearance in China: the Shang people are making inscriptions on oracle bones and bronze ritual vessels.

Crete, c.1375BC. The palace of Knossos – the only Minoan palace to survive the 1450BC devastation – is destroyed. The introduction of the *tholos* (stone-built beehive tomb), the wide use of metal in warriors' tombs and the economic, military and political organisation on the island bear witness to the recent domination of Crete by the Mycenaeans.

Syria, c.1360BC. The kingdom of Mitanni is breaking apart. The Mitanni have never recovered from the plundering of their capital by the Hittite king, Shuppiluliumash, c.1370BC. Ever since, the country has been riven by civil war. Palace intrigues have culminated in the death of its king, Tushratta. Now large numbers of people are making for Babylon, while others find refuge in Hittite lands – leaving the country at the mercy of the Assyrians.

Egypt, 1353BC. Amenhotep III is buried at Thebes, in the largest tomb ever prepared for a king. During his reign Egypt continued to expand its influence and prosperity.

Anatolia, c.1350BC. The bold soldier and diplomat Shuppiluliumash, who became king c.1380BC, has founded a new Hittite kingdom.

Syria, c.1350BC. The scribes in the Syrian port of Ugarit (Ras Shamra) are developing multilingual skills. Besides their own tongue, written in a cuneiform alphabet, they are using the foreign languages of the Babylonians and the Hittites.

Assyria, c.1350BC. During the reign of Assur-Uballit, who founded a new kingdom c.1365BC, Assyria has freed itself from the domination of Mitanni, of which it had been a vassal state for 200 years. The king is the driving force behind the resurgence and expansion of Assyria, which is gradually asserting itself as a great power. He has built a wall around his capital, Assur, and entered into diplomatic relations with Egypt.

Anatolia, c.1350BC. The Hittites have repelled an onslaught by the Ahhiawa people, whose kingdom lies to the west of the Hittite heartland and presents a continuing threat.

Pharaoh changes Egypt's religion

Colossal statue of Akhenaten, the champion of a new solar cult.

Akhenaten, Nefertiti and daughters beneath the rays of the sun god Aten.

Egypt, 1353BC
Egyptians, who for centuries have worshipped the great god Amun Re, have changed their religion under their new ruler, Amenhotep IV. He, in turn, has changed his name (which means "Amun is Satisfied") to Akhenaten ("He who is acceptable to the Aten") and moved his capital from Thebes to a newlyfounded desert town, el-Amarna, which he intends to rename after himself. The Aten, the actual disc of the sun, providing heat and prosperity, is the new deity; Amun is regarded as a deity too intimately connected with the old religion to be capable of change. Solar worship had gained greater influnce already under Amenhotep III, and may prove to be more universal in its appeal.

The name of Amun is being erased from monuments, and suddenly he is a non-god. The new temples dedicated to the Aten are open and filled with light. Nefertiti, Akhenaten's queen, comes to them to offer gifts of flowers and fruits to the god. The worship of the sun-disc is a religion of life, freedom and love of nature; elements of it appear to have been developed by the priests of Heliopolis who worshipped the sun god Re-Harakhi.

Akhenaten's refusal to leave the new capital is causing serious political problems, however. The wealth of the occupied territories in the Levant and other lands in the eastern Mediterranean used to enrich Thebes and the priests of the Amun cult. Now the tributes and taxes stop at the new capital. Akhenaten's pacifism – and isolation – is another problem. For although he maintains poetic correspondence with the vassal princes of Asia, the great Egyptian empire is breaking up, threatened by the Hittites.

In his desert capital Akhenaten is unaware of the potential danger. He has vowed to remain there, never to travel; and thus he remains largely ignorant of what is happening in his own country and abroad. In Thebes and elsewhere taxpayers are at the mercy of government servants while the pharaoh writes poetry in praise of the new god, the Aten.

Nefertiti, mother of six princesses.

The Hittites go on to the offensive

Lions at the Hittite capital's gates.

Anatolia, c.1380BC
A bold new ruler, Shuppiluliumash, is starting a drive south to extend the territory of the Hittite Empire. He is aiming for the rich cities and manufacturing centres of north Syria. The Hittites have been steadily expanding their power from Anatolia to kingdoms on the fringes.

Now Shuppiluliumash is seeking to establish vassal states in Syria, driving a wedge between the powerful but strife-torn Mitanni kingdom and the Mediterranean Sea. He can expect some fierce opposition from the Egyptians who are also keen to expand their influence in the Levant. He will also have to deal with Assyria which has encroached on Mitanni from the east.

Cruelty marks Shang rule in China

China, c.1384BC

A powerful but cruel society is flourishing in Henan Honan province, some 75 miles north of the Yellow River. A remarkable people have established a society known as the Shang dynasty centred on their king, a semi-divine ruler who is regarded as the channel of communication with the ancestors of the royal clan.

In order to keep on good terms with these powerful gods the Shang offer them human sacrifices, usually prisoners taken from the neighbouring peoples with whom they wage constant war.

The sacrifices are carried out in a solemn ritual by the priest-warriors of the ruling caste. Beautiful bronze vessels decorated with animal designs are used to hold offerings of food and wine.

The Shang converse with their gods by writing questions on bones and tortoise shells, applying a hot iron and then analysing the resultant cracks. The answer given by the cracks is written on the bone or shell which is then carefully filed.

The questions, and therefore the gods, seem to control every aspect of Shang life. The "oracle bones" are consulted before the army sets out on a campaign, at the start of an elephant hunt, and to ask the gods for rain.

Craftsmanship is highly regarded, with bronze and jade being worked into utensils and jewellery. Mulberry trees are cultivated and silk is used for clothing, while many of the surrounding peoples still wear only coarse hemp clothes.

Shang society, however, is also

Bronze ritual vessel of tiger protecting a man, covered with animal motifs.

marked by cruel customs. The servants and concubines of the rulers are often buried alongside their dead masters, to serve them in the afterlife, along with their weapons and cooking utensils.

There is also no such thing as equality in this society. The lower classes live in pit-dwellings with few possessions. They spend their days labouring in the fields while the ruling aristocrats live in luxury and devote themselves to warfare and ritual.

Princesses become diplomatic tools

Egypt, c.1350BC

As Egypt strives to maintain excellent relations with its neighbour states, a trade in princesses is growing throughout the Near East. Princesses of the royal lines are exchanged between Egypt and other countries in return for gold which enables the Kassite princes of Babylon to finance their prestigious building programmes.

The princesses, often infants, are much sought after on the basis of exchange. The alliance between the courts of Babylon and Thebes has been reinforced by successive marriages occurring with such regularity that they can only be regarded as a cynical, though pragmatic, form of diplomacy.

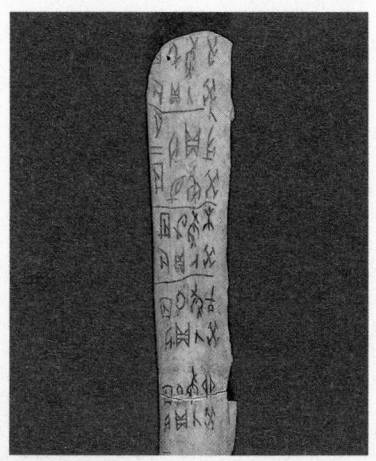

An oracle bone with inscriptions.

A royal marriage of convenience.

Colossal sculptures celebrate Hittite culture in Anatolia

Anatolia Turkey, c.1380BC

Giant figures carved in the rock face dominate the Hittite sanctuary at Yazilikaya (*near Boghazkoy*), the most important holy place in the Hittite empire. The first temple was built here about eighty years ago and there are many spectacular examples of Hittite sculpture.

The main sanctuary is partly a cave cut into the rock face. The figures are amazingly lifelike, their arms and legs shaped to give a constant illusion of movement.

In the capital itself there are around thirty temples, with central courtyards surrounded by colonnades of columns. Nearby is the royal palace, with pillars of wood in its immense parade hall. The city wall is built of stone blocks on an

Stag goblet showing a ritual scene.

earth embankment some 20 feet high. The gates are decorated with giant sculptures, of which the most impressive are found in the representation of the God of War at the royal gate.

Hittite art is well represented in the objects of daily life. The seal stones used for stamping documents are delicately carved round or square blocks. Some of these have the royal insignia. The local rich metal reserves have been drawn on to make small figurines of the gods shaped to form ceremonial drinking vessels. One of the best of these is a goblet decorated with the sculpture of a stag and an elaborate ritual scene in low relief.

Iron enters Greek soul and scabbard

The idea that iron could have moral as well as purely functional properties - as expressed in Sartre's novel *Iron in the Soul*, for instance - received its first developed articulation within the western tradition among the ancient Greeks. Hesiod, the Boeotian shepherd-poet who flourished about 700BC, borrowed and manipulated the oriental myth that mankind had successively degenerated since its primordial Golden Age through generations of Silver and Bronze Men.

To this inherited schema Hesiod added an Age of Heroes (itself a borrowing, but in this case from the Greek epic tradition that culminated in Homer's *Iliad* and *Odyssey*) and an Age of Iron, the age in which he and his listeners had the misfortune to live.

Archaeologists and historians do not normally lack soul, or Hesiod's tender concern for moral issues. But for them the coming of iron tends to represent the very opposite of a degeneration. It is a mark, rather, of advance both technological and cultural, an essential stage in the story of civilised mankind's increasing control over raw nature.

Iron - the "democratic" metal

This is not so much, or only, because iron tools and equipment were always, everywhere, necessarily superior in quality and efficiency to their bronze counterparts. Instead, it is because iron ores are far more liberally distributed beneath the earth's crust than the ores of copper and tin which are the principal constituents of bronze, so that the ability to extract and exploit the cheaper and more plentiful iron ores potentially expanded vastly a society's productive capacity. Speaking metaphorically, iron has rightly from this point of view been hailed as a "democratic" metal, the metal of the common man.

In Greek myth a people called Chalybes were famed as the first workers of iron on a regular basis. They lived, according to legend, along the southern shores of the Black Sea in what is now north-central Turkey. Behind the myth and legend there may dimly be seen a confused reminiscence of an historical fact: that it was the Indo-European Hittites of central Anatolia who, in the later second millenium BC, first mastered iron technology for utilitarian, everyday purposes, not for use in warfare.

But in about 1200BC the Hittite empire came crashing down, and the shock reverberations of its fall were felt all round the eastern Mediterranean

basin. The Hittite secrets of iron working did not survive the disaster and had to be re-learned by trial and error. The second discovery, according to the best interpretation of the latest archaeological evidence, was apparently due to Greeks residing on the island of Cyprus (some of them refugees from the destruction and desolation of mainland Greece in the years around 1200BC) during the twelfth century BC.

Greece: first Iron Age dawns

Both copper and iron ores were to be found in plenty and in close proximity on Cyprus. But copper without tin was relatively useless, and tin supplies had temporarily been completely cut off in the century or so of broken communications that afflicted the eastern Mediterranean and Near East after 1200BC.

Necessity, therefore, mothered the invention of practicable ironworking, which was in turn passed on to, and adopted and improved by, the Cypriot Greeks' cousins in Old Greece. By 900BC in the most progressive Greek areas (Attica, Euboea, the Argolid) we may speak properly of the dawning of an Iron Age - several centuries ahead of a similar development in Europe to the north and west of Greece, and even in once-mighty Egypt, Anatolia and the Levant.

The manufacture of bronze implements and equipment did not simply cease overnight in Greece - far from it. In the first place, existing stocks of bronze could be recycled to some extent. But, secondly, the techniques of successful iron-working are considerably more tricky than those required for the manufacture of serviceable bronze.

The case-hardened "sandwich"

To start with, the smelting of iron ores is more complicated than that of copper, and to convert the ore to metal by means of carbon monoxide gas demands careful control of atmospheric conditions in the furnace. Then the molten metal must be heated to not less than 1100-1500 degrees Celsius and carburised by using charcoal for fuel and reducing the draught to the fire so as to increase the carbon contents and therefore the hardness of the metal.

Next, several small carburised laminations must be piled on top of each other and forged by hammering into a "club sandwich" of iron and mild steel. Finally, this mixture must be quenched by

dousing in water, again in order to increase the hardness, and tempered (ie reheated) before being hammered again until the desired combination of strength, hardness, shape and sharpness has been achieved.

In these circumstances, therefore, it is not altogether surprising that the Greeks (unlike the Chinese) never learned to cast iron. So they retained bronze for vital items of military and cultural significance like the hoplite infantryman's breastplate and the ritual cauldrons used for cooking sacrificial meat in religious sanctuaries.

When one says, therefore, that the Iron Age had dawned in Greece by 900BC, what is meant is that for the basic classes of edged cutting tools - swords, knives, spearheads, ploughshares and so forth - iron massively and irreversibly preponderated over bronze by and from that date.

Even so, the Greeks did not entirely abandon the attitude of awe towards the mysteries of iron-working expressed in the Chalybes myth. The Spartans, a martial and bellicose community that depended on iron for its utilitarian functions in warfare, yet persisted in regarding iron as a precious metal too. For the square-section spits on which they roasted sacrificial meat in honour of the gods also servied in Sparta as a primitive system of money - a system which was retained for some three centuries after the Lydian invention of coinage had been widely adopted in Greece.

The value of Sparta's iron-spit money was low in relation to its bulk - so low that it took wagonloads and housefuls of the stuff to make a poor man rich! But the idea behind the low valuation of an individual spit was precisely to emphasise the high value of the spit-money as such, since it could not lightly be either accumulated or discarded. Nor, of course, could it be easily exchanged outside the community, which begins to explain Sparta's much prized insularity.

Elsewhere in Greece, though, the impact of iron was exactly the opposite. No doubt it was the doleful effects of iron on the battlefield, rather than its peaceful applications in agriculture and religion, that cast gloom and despondency over the sensitive spirit of Hesiod. But from the less involved standpoint of the historian, the Greeks' pioneering achievement in iron technology unarguably enabled their remarkable demographic and political expansion at home and their yet more extraordinary expansion all round the Mediterranean and Black Seas, until - as Plato would graphically put it - Greeks could be found sitting "like frogs or ants round a pond".

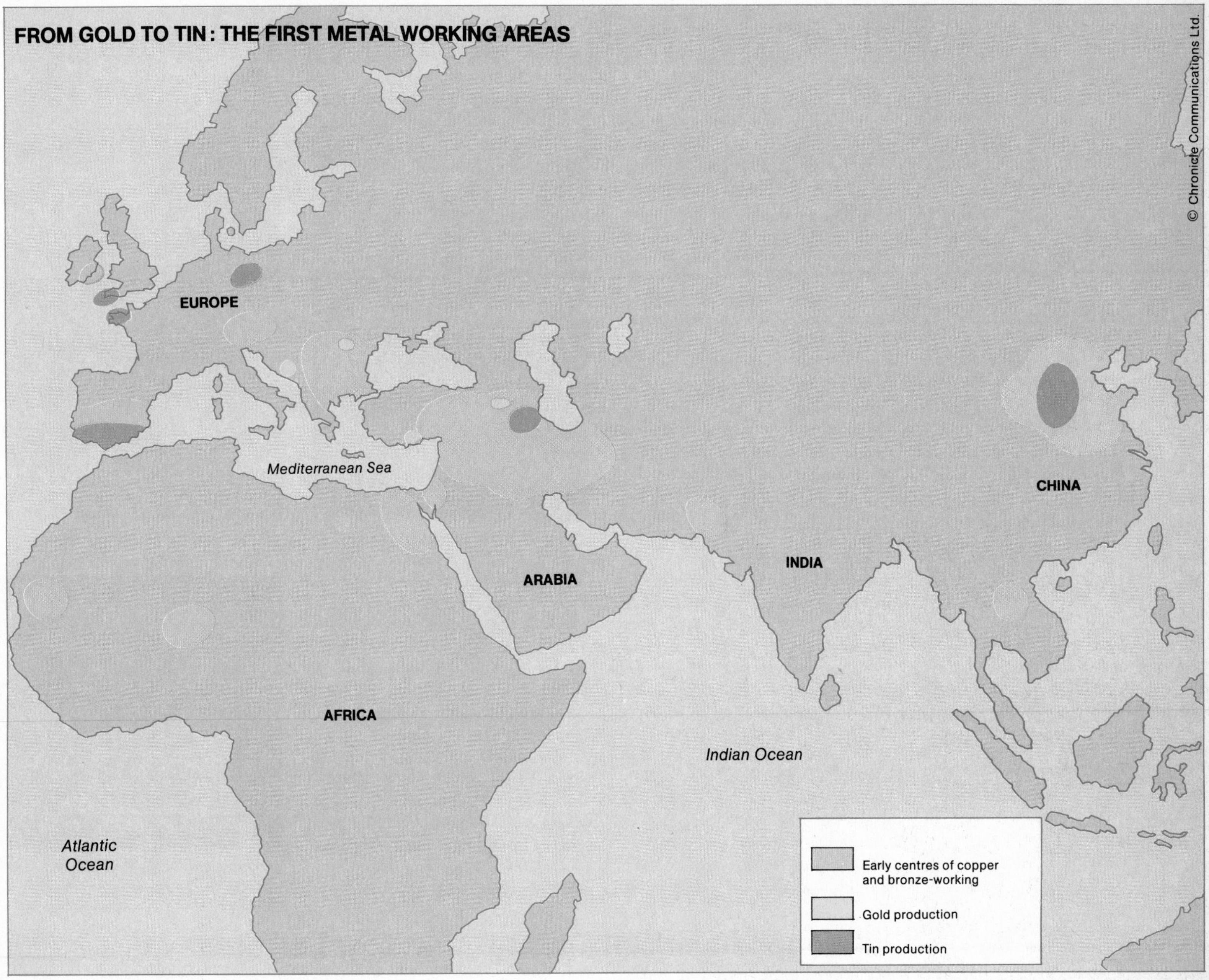

FROM GOLD TO TIN : THE FIRST METAL WORKING AREAS

© Chronicle Communications Ltd.

EUROPE

CHINA

INDIA

Mediterranean Sea

ARABIA

AFRICA

Indian Ocean

Atlantic
Ocean

Early centres of copper
and bronze-working

Gold production

Tin production

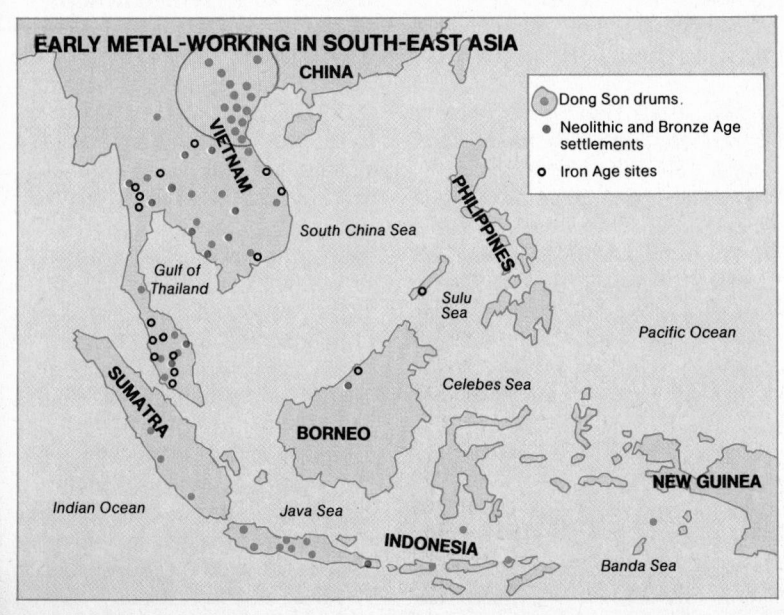

EARLY METAL-WORKING IN SOUTH-EAST ASIA

CHINA

VIETNAM

South China Sea

PHILIPPINES

Gulf of
Thailand

Sulu
Sea

Pacific Ocean

SUMATRA

Celebes Sea

BORNEO

NEW GUINEA

Indian Ocean

Java Sea

INDONESIA

Banda Sea

Dong Son drums.

Neolithic and Bronze Age
settlements

Iron Age sites

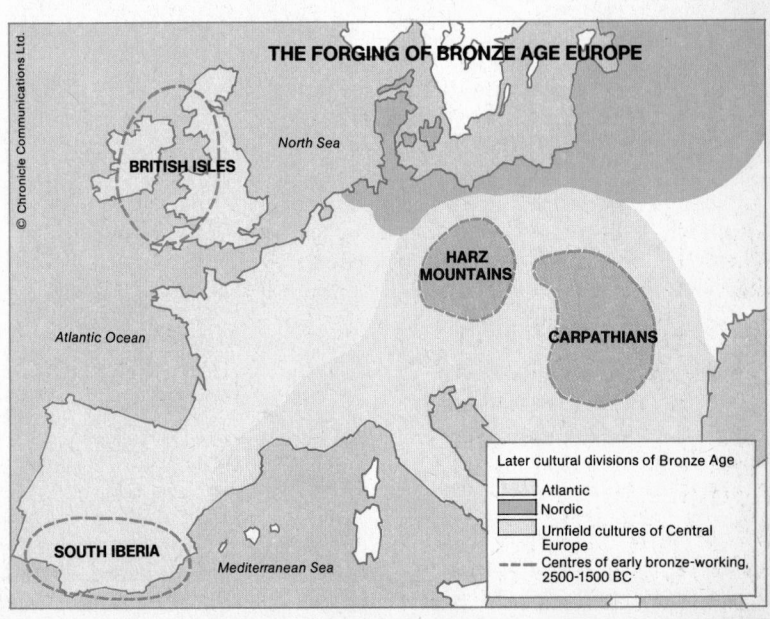

THE FORGING OF BRONZE AGE EUROPE

© Chronicle Communications Ltd.

North Sea

BRITISH ISLES

HARZ
MOUNTAINS

CARPATHIANS

Atlantic Ocean

SOUTH IBERIA

Mediterranean Sea

Later cultural divisions of Bronze Age

Atlantic

Nordic

Urnfield cultures of Central
Europe

Centres of early bronze-working,
2500-1500 BC

Mesopotamia, c.1345BC. Assur-Uballit, king of Assyria, provoked by the murder of his grandson, marches on Babylon and sparks off a brief war – the first open conflict between the two kingdoms. The dead child was the son of Assur-Uballit's daughter, whom he gave in marriage to the king of Babylon, Burnaburiash.

Egypt, c.1335BC. The reign of the controversial pharaoh Amenhotep IV, who succeeded his father, Amenhotep III, ends when the Egyptian sphere of influence is crumbling.

Syria, c.1335BC. On the death of Shuppiluliumash, king of the Hittites, the whole of Syria up to the region of Damascus is under Hittite control.

Mesopotamia, c.1330BC. The Kassite king Kurigalzu II leaves Babylon and founds a new capital 100 miles to the north-west. He calls it Dur-Kurigalzu (Aqarquf) and builds there a vast palace, far larger than the palace at Mari, which had been regarded as one of the wonders of the world. A 170-foot-high ziggurat, erected just beside the palace, dominates the surrounding plain.

South America, c.1300BC. At Santarem, in the lower Amazon region, potters are producing complex vessels decorated with human figures, caymans, frogs, monkeys, jaguars and birds.

Egypt, c.1290BC. The young and ambitious Ramesses II succeeds his father, Seti, to the throne of Egypt. These two kings are members of the dynasty founded c.1307BC by Ramesses I. Seti's most pressing concern during his reign was to maintain Egyptian control of Palestine.

Egypt, c.1256BC. Ramesses II marries a Hittite princess, the daughter of Hattusilis III of Hatti. This consolidates the good relations between Egypt and the Hittites, recently sealed in a peace treaty settling the differences which reached their climax in 1285BC at the battle of Kadesh.

Europe, c.1250BC. Warrior elites are emerging in Europe as society becomes increasingly militaristic. New types of weapons and armour, such as bronze swords, helmets and greaves, are becoming popular. Europeans have adopted the practice of cremating their dead and placing the remains in funerary urns.

Boy pharaoh is buried in splendour

Egypt, c.1338BC

Tutankhamun has died at the age of 18 and the following words have been inscribed on the mask of solid gold under which his body is enshrined: "... *your right eye is the boat of night (of the sun god), your left eye is the boat of day, your eyebrows are those of the Ennead of Gods, your forehead is that of Anubis, the nape of your neck is that of Horus, your locks of hair are those of PtahSokar. You are in front of the Osiris (Tutankhamun); he sees thanks to you, you guide him to the good paths, you smite for him the confederates of Seth so that he may overthrow your enemies before the Ennead of the Gods in the great mansion of the Prince which is in Heliopoli ...*"

They will serve to protect the mask and its owner by identifying its various parts with the corresponding parts of the bodies of the gods themselves. Such is the total belief in Egypt today that the king, even a minor ruler like this boy-king, will be transported to the hereafter and become a god.

The personal and ritual objects in Tutankhamun's tomb are richly decorated, many of them covered in gold leaf. The items deposited in the burial chamber are decorated with scenes showing the pharaoh with his queen, Ankhesenamun,

The gold mask of Tutankhamun.

Detail from the boy-king's throne.

daughter of Akhenaten, who is seated at his feet drinking a beverage he is pouring for her. In another decoration, the young king is seen depicted in the process of killing a lion he is holding by the tail – a favourite theme of the kings of Egypt at this time.

The coffins of Tutankhamun are protected by four gilded shrines. The first is decorated with "djed pillars", symbols of the god Osiris and of stability, and with the so-called knots of Isis. The others portray deities of the hereafter.

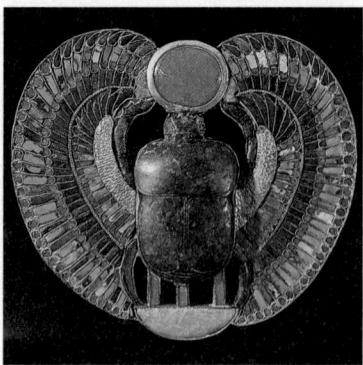
Magnificently embellished chest ornament in the shape of a scarab.

Hittite spy trick nearly destroys the Egyptian army

Later impression of the battle.

Kadesh, Syria, c.1285BC

A cunning piece of disinformation brought near disaster to Ramesses II's armies today as they prepared to assault this Hittite stronghold on the Orontes river. As the advance guard of the Egyptian army approached the city, two Hittite spies told Ramesses that the entire Hittite army had fled, leaving the city at his mercy.

It was not until Ramesses was preparing to march into Kadesh that the Hittites struck. Their leader, Muwatallis, sprang his trap, ordering a powerful force of war chariots from its hiding place to cut Ramesses's armies into two. The crack Egyptian Re division was wiped out crossing a ford.

As his armies regrouped – the Amun division was completely in disarray after the surprise attack – Ramesses, now left in command of a small force, was encircled by the entire Hittite regiment of more than 2,500 chariots.

In the fierce hand-to-hand fighting that followed Ramesses, leading his men from his war chariot, made two desperate charges and eventually managed to drive the Hittites back across the river. Even so, the Egyptian king's army remained in grave danger.

As they prepared what must have been the final attack, the Hittites paused to sack the Egyptian tented camp. Only then did Ramesses hear the sound of bugles and drums of an Egyptian division marching from the coast. Despite further fighting, Kadesh remained in Hittite hands.

Mycenae is richest fortress in Greece

Drought drives the Saharan nomads to new pastures

Mycenae, Greece, c.1300BC

Established in their strategically-sited citadel at the head of the Plain of Argos, the lords of Mycenae have achieved fame and prosperity without equal on mainland Greece. Not only do they hold sway over the fertile plain, with its cornfields and horse ranches, but they also dominate the trade routes from the south-eastern ports through the mountain passes northwards to the Isthmus of Corinth.

They have fostered a vigorous enterprise culture, forging links deep into Europe for trade in gold, bronze and amber, some of which they re-export, along with their pottery, to the islands of the Aegean and the eastern Mediterranean.

The opulence of the Mycenaean lords' burial customs has become legendary. In the so-called shaft graves, now enclosed in stone circles, men and women are buried with gold and silver vases, gold rings and necklaces, crowns and tiaras, and bronze daggers with gold inlays. One Mycenaean dignitary has been buried with his face covered by a heavy mask fashioned from solid gold.

More recently the Mycenaeans have been building massive beehive shaped vaulted tombs, 49 feet in diameter, outside the citadel itself. Again, the dead are buried with a rich assortment of weapons, tools, jewellery and vases containing food and drink. Some observers believe that the people buried in the bee-hive tombs are later moved to the shaft graves when new burials take place.

The Mycenaean ruling classes

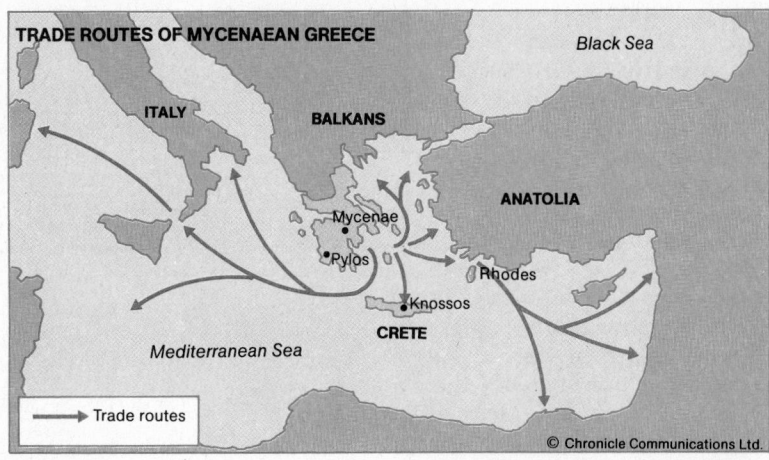

TRADE ROUTES OF MYCENAEAN GREECE

Black Sea

ITALY

BALKANS

ANATOLIA

Mycenae

•Pylos

Rhodes

•Knossos

CRETE

Mediterranean Sea

→ Trade routes

© Chronicle Communications Ltd.

generally enjoy a full life of sport and games, spiced by wars with the hill-folk to the north. Boar-hunting expeditions and armed combat, with lance and body shield of bull's hide, are portrayed on palace frescoes, tombstones and vases, which show the womenfolk as large-eyed, with flowing hair, flounced skirts and low-cut bodices. The women are shown dancing and feasting with the men.

However, there are signs that life is becoming less secure. The citadel is surrounded by massive walls, recently rebuilt, which incorporate some of the latest novelties in military architecture from the Hittites. The nearby port of Tiryns also has a heavily fortified citadel built in the same style. And there are rumours of unrest.

Mycenaean gateway graced by lions

Sahara, c.1300BC

Fierce heat, constant drought and the ever-advancing sands of the Sahara are driving herders from their pastures north into the Magreb, south into west and central Africa and east into Egypt where the new migrants are threatening political upheaval and potential anarchy.

A millenium ago the Sahara was occupied by mixed farmers. The inhabitants used caves as shelters and their cave paintings tell the story of the Sahara's decline. The earliest paintings show elephants, rhinoceros and the now extinct *Bubalus antiquus*, some of them dating back to 3700BC. Later the *Bubalus antiquus* disappeared, replaced by domestic cattle. The most recent paintings show men on horse-drawn chariots.

This gradual Saharan migration has profoundly influenced the out-lying regions. In west and central Africa it brought new agricultural techniques, and in Egypt the need to feed the growing population brought an agricultural revolution. But in the north the migration's influence been anything but bene-ficial and peaceful. There the immigrants, fair-skinned Berbers mounted on chariots, have dev-eloped into a powerful military force and now threaten Egypt.

Egyptian surveys give map-making a fresh geometrical angle

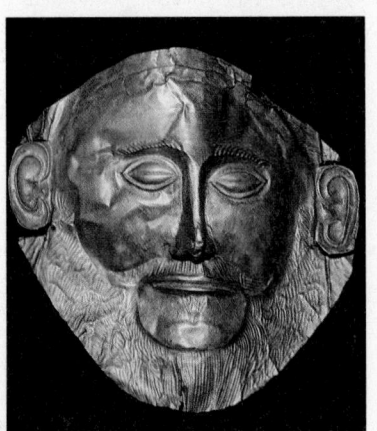

Death mask made of solid gold.

Egypt, c.1150

Map-making has become an art form in Egypt and the country's surveyors are producing the first topographical maps, geometrically exact, with selective use of colours, captions naming important features, and roads indicated.

One map represents a plan of the gold mines situated between the River Nile and the Red Sea, to-gether with access routes. It shows roads, the mineworkers' houses, the sanctuary of Amun, the *stele* of Sethos I, and another road leading to the sea.

The mountains where the gold is mined are coloured red, with other colours used to indicate other features of the landscape.

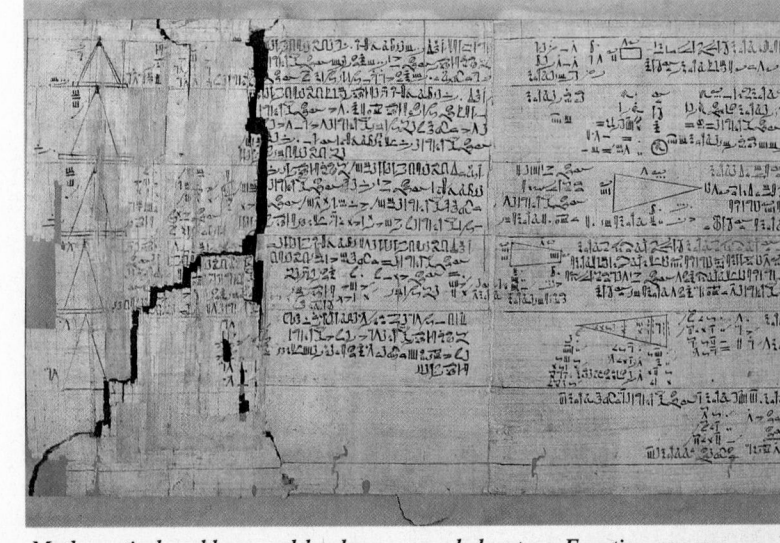

Mathematical problems and land areas puzzled out on Egyptian papyrus.

Assyria, c.1250BC. The Assyrians have continued their energetic campaign of conquest under the great warrior King Shalmaneser. After subduing the northern mountainous region of Urartu (in Armenia), Assyria has turned on its former allies, the Hurrians, and their Hittite mercenaries, and annexed their lands.

Babylon, c.1235BC. Tukulti-Ninurta, who became king of Assyria in 1244BC, marches on Babylon, seizes its king, Kashtiliash IV, whom he deports to Kalah (Nimrud), and takes control of the kingdom. He is the first Assyrian to be named king of Babylon.

Babylon, c.1225BC. The Babylonians revolt against the Assyrian puppets who have ruled their kingdom since the invasion of the Assyrian king, Tukulti-Ninurta. Kassite supremacy is restored.

Sahara, c.1200BC. Paintings of chariots have begun to appear in the Hoggar Massif of the western Sahara, as the use of light, two-wheeled vehicles spreads south from the Mediterranean.

Near East, c.1200BC. The Israelite tribes, who were driven out of Egypt c.1230BC by Rameses II, are reputed to have arrived in Canaan. They are fighting to take control of the country under the leadership of Joshua, who is believed to have performed various miracles, such as causing the walls of Jericho to fall at the sound of trumpets.

Greece, c.1200BC. The four palaces of Mycenae, Tiryns, Pylos and Thebes have been destroyed and the Mycenaean civilisation has collapsed. Some regions, such as that around Pylos, have been almost abandoned. Elsewhere, in Argolis and Attica, people have regrouped in the shelter of the citadels. An economic crisis and social problems are thought to be at the root of the upheaval.

Anatolia, c.1200BC. The Phrygians, from Thrace in the Balkans, have invaded the Anatolian plateau, overthrown the Hittite kingdom and sacked its capital, Hattusas (Boghazkoy).

Asia, c.1200BC. Travellers from the central steppe lands, where a sophisticated bronze industry is evolving, are known to have made contact with the Shang people in China.

Hebrew tribes tell of Red Sea miracle

Sinai, c.1200BC

Twelve tribes of nomadic Hebrews, calling themselves the Children of Israel, are wandering in the deserts of Canaan and tell this story of their escape from many years of captivity and persecution in Egypt. They worship one god – Jehovah – and credit him with a number of miraculous acts without which their escape and subsequent survival would have been impossible.

They arrived in Egypt, they claim, under their patriarch Jacob around 500 years ago, were subjected to increasingly unbearable hard labour, and longed to escape. Their leader, Moses, appealed in vain to the pharaoh, Ramesses II, to permit an exodus from Egypt. Only after the country suffered ten plagues, destroying crops, cattle and finally first-born children, did Ramesses relent.

When the Egyptians then pursued the Hebrews to the Red Sea the waters, they claim, miraculously parted, permitting them to cross safely, only to swamp the

The parting of the Red Sea, as seen by a film-maker of the 20th century.

Egyptians. The Hebrews have been in the desert near Mount Sinai for some years – protected, they say, by their highly unusual god Jehovah, who is quite different from other gods in that he looks after not just a tribe or a family but all of them. As well as making a number of religious laws, Moses has given them what he says is a divinely inspired table of laws called the Ten Commandments which forbids them, among other things, to kill, rob or commit adultery.

Great builder Ramesses II constructs massive new temple

Egypt, c.1250BC

To cope with the ever-present danger of invasion threatening Egypt, Ramesses II has moved the country's capital to Pi-Ramesse, in the north-eastern delta, as Egypt enters its biggest-ever period of building and re-building.

The great temple of Abu Simbel in Nubia typifies the scale of Ramesses' approach to architecture. The entire edifice, with its colossal statues both inside and outside the temple, is carved into the rocks overlooking the Nile, facing the sunrise with the falcon-headed Re-Harakhti stepping forward to face the morning sun. The shrine is superbly designed to ensure that the the first rays of light fall on the four gods inside – Amun-Re of Thebes, Ptah of Memphis, Re-Harakhti of Heliopolis and Ramesses, himself who will join the others in eternity as a god in his own right.

The entire temple is dominated by four massive statues of this pharaoh on his throne – carved from a different stratum of rock to allow them to stand out in every

Monumental statues of Osiris at the mortuary temple of Ramesses II.

condition of light. A small temple has been dedicated to Queen Nofretari on the same site. Ramesses has built his mortuary temple – the Ramesseum – west of Thebes. Here, once again, monumental figures of the king dominate the entire scene – one of them (of him seated) bigger than any other statue carved in Egypt. The temple's surrounding wall also encloses a great many houses and workshops.

Egypt defeats alliance of nomads and sea raiders

Nile Delta, c.1220BC

After a prolonged period of conflict with Saharan Libyans, Egypt has defeated an alliance of Libyans and Mediterranean pirates at Pi-yer, killing 6,000 and capturing 9,000. For Egypt's pharaoh, Merenptah, it is a magnificent victory, but the campaign has so exhausted Egypt that the price of victory may be the loss its empire.

The pressures on Egypt go back a thousand years, when the fertile plains of the Sahara dried up. The result was a movement of people eastwards, the pressure increasing over the centuries. Brilliant horsemen and charioteers, they regularly ravaged the country before being turned back by Merenptah's depleted forces.

In their most recent attempt the Libyans allied themselves with sea raiders from Corsica, Sardinia and Sicily – veterans of the sackings of the Levantine cities, who were to provide the navy that would carry the Libyans around Egypt's flank – and with Asian migrants from Persia threatening Egypt from the east. Merenptah's land victory against the Asiatics in southern Palestine, and his sea victory against the Libyans and their maritime allies at Pi-yer, have secured Egypt's frontiers for the time being.

Collapse ends Hittites' years of glory

Anatolia, c.1200BC

The mighty Hittite Empire is no more. The kings who from their remote power-base on the Anatolian plateau in central Turkey humbled the proud pharoahs, and dealt on equal terms with the Babylonians, have been scattered by newcomers arriving across the sea from the wilds of Europe.

The end came in a confusion of local rebellions and economic chaos triggered by the growing political instability in eastern Mediterranean states, on which the Hittites depended for much of their trade. These widespread disorders gave opportunities for movements of population, as former mercenaries became settlers or pirates.

The Hittite king, Dudkhalias, striving to repel a local invasion, appealed in vain for military help from the Ugarit people in neighbouring Syria; that signalled the end. Invaders from the sea swarmed across the land, followed by Thracians and Armenians, and the Hittite capital of Hattusas (Bogazkoy, the village in the gorge) was sacked, reportedly by Phrygians, a people who came from the Balkans.

The Hittites were an unprepossessing race, as they portrayed themselves on steles and bas-reliefs, with heavy features, great curved noses, sloping foreheads and huge beards, clothed in close-fitting, sleeveless, jerkins, but in their time as a great

Relief of Hittite king hunting lions.

Hittite pendant of a goddess.

power they were notably efficient administrators. In the state archives at Hattusas the tens of thousands of clay tablets inscribed in cuneiform record treaties with foreign powers, diplomatic correspondence, royal proclamations and judgements on disputes between cities, as well as lexicons for the translation of Babylonian and Sumerian into the Hittite language.

The Hittite legal code is much less harsh than that devised by Hammurabi in Babylonia or the eye-for-an-eye Israelite laws. The Hittites seldom imposed the death penalty, and the laws relating to sexual crimes have been described as indulgent.

In the beginning the Hittites were favoured by geography; in the end they were brought down it. In Hattusas they had a natural stronghold protected by deep ravines and precipitous escarpments, while to the east and south their empire was guarded by mountains.

In the west, however, the Anatolian plateau falls away to sheltered estuaries on the Aegean coast. When the people from the sea arrived, the Hittites, lacking naval power, were unable to defend the Levantine forts crucial for bringing up supplies and protecting trade. As Hittite power waned, the rulers hired mercenaries from neighbouring barbarian tribes who, becoming embroiled in internal feuds, compounded the chaos that was afflicting the whole region from Egypt to the Aegean.

Phoenicians rise as empires decline

The Levant, 1200BC

The crisis in the Egyptian and Hittite empires has proved a blessing to the Phoenicians, a nation of traders living on the eastern Mediterranean coast. In spite of the chaos caused by war and raids by pirates from Corsica, Sardinia and Sicily, the Phoenicians have successfully established their independence and have become powerful.

The Phoenicians are sailors and middle-men. Their ports, each one an independent city-state, are equi-distant from Egypt and Mesopotamia and perfectly placed to cast out trade lines across the Mediterranean.

Many of the city states, such as Ugarit, Aradus and Sidon, were too jealous of their independence to unite against a common foe and fell victims to the invasions of Mediterranean pirates and Asian settlers. Tyre survived and, strengthened by refugees from Sidon, it is becoming the most powerful state in the Levantine region.

Phoenicians are trading as far as Spain from newly-founded bases along the African and Sicilian coastlines, from Tyre and Cyprus to the Iberian peninsula, where they trade copper from Spain and tin from Britain and Brittany for textiles and spices from the Orient.

A warship, used by Phoenicians to defend their large trading network.

Egyptian officials accused of complicity in robberies from royal tombs in Thebes

Egypt, c.1110BC

Allegations of complicity by high officials in the robbing of royal tombs were made in an Egyptian court today when eight men were acquitted of theft.

The accused were brought to face a special commission ordered when Paser, the mayor of Thebes, learning that the royal tombs had been desecrated and robbed, sent a report to his superior, Khaemwese. The hearing exposed considerable rivalry between Paser and the mayor and chief of police of the cemeteries on the west bank, Paweraa.

After investigation it became clear that only one royal tomb – that of Sebekemsaf II had actually been robbed. Nonetheless, several graves of ordinary people had been desecrated.

Paweraa made a list of suspects, and they were rounded up and brought to the court. One mason, Amenpanufer, confessed that he had been stripping the necropolis for several years. Others, however, appear to have made false confessions after repeated torture with the bastinado (a method of beating the soles of the feet). One man was no longer able to find the grave he was alleged to have robbed.

Although Amenpanufer managed to bribe his way to freedom, the case was regarded as a victory for

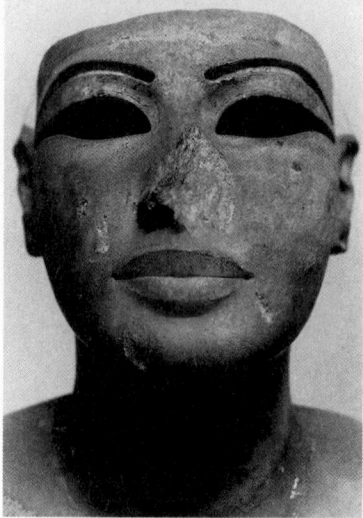

Alabaster head of Sethos I – one suspected victim of tomb-robbers.

the necropolis police. A furious Paser accused the police chief of complicity. Paweraa complained to Khaemwese, who closed the trial by acquitting all the prisoners.

The verdicts have brought justice into disrepute in this part of Egypt where the royal tombs, with their treasures, are vulnerable to robbers so much so that the violation of burial chambers and mortuary buildings is increasing daily. The government may be forced to move many mummies, in order that the day may sleep peacefully in secret hiding places.

"Endless tide" of nomads scares Assyrian rulers

Near East, c.1100BC

Groups of nomads from the west are infiltrating the lands of Assyria in increasing numbers. They have established themselves in control of some major cities of Syria including Damascus, pushing out the neo-Hittite population.

They bring with them a new language, Aramaic, related to the Hebrew spoken by the tribes of Israel which is written with a linear alphabetic script adopted from the Phoenician. With far fewer signs than the cuneiform style, this is easier to write and may well enjoy a wide currency.

Bands of these invading Aramaeans were defeated by the Assyrian kings of the 13th century BC, but they continue to push into the steppe lands of western Assyria (the Jasirah Plain) and south towards the major cities.

They bring no culture of their own, simply adopting the lifestyle and arts of the lands they occupy. King Tiglath-Pileser I has fought 28 battles against the Aramaeans, but the tide of nomads continues to stream undiminished into his country. With an Aramaean already occupying the throne of Babylon, it seems unlikely that the Assyrians will be able to resolve this serious threat to their sovereignty.

Babylonians losing faith in the power of their gods

Babylon, c.1200BC

Confidence is beginning to wane in the notion that worshipping the gods guarantees divine protection from an unkind fate involving death and destruction.

Pessimistic trends in recent popular works portray the gods as sometimes deceitful.

One of the gloomiest poems of the new pessimists is *The Just Sufferer*, in which a distinguished and god-fearing noble finds himself abandoned by his god. Depressed and unhappy, he loses the confidence of the king and his court, becomes destitute and falls ill. The poem has a fairly happy ending, but the message is that, when it comes to deciding our fate, we are power-

less in front of the gods.

The idea that the gods dictate fate dominates another popular text based on a debate between two scholars, one an unhappy, luckless melancholic, the other a respecter of morals and religion. It decides that, while the gods are responsible for justice, they are also to blame for evil.

A similar conclusion is reached in an epic poem dedicated to the plague god Era, who deceives the hero Marduk into abandoning Babylon to his mercy. Plague strikes the city, but eventually Era relents. By then the point has been made: the gods cannot always be trusted, even by the most devout of believers.

Symbols of gods invoked to protect the dead – are they trustworthy?

Sea peoples are crushed in bloody clash

Triumphant Ramesses III, here hunting bulls in a detail from his tomb.

Egypt, c.1187BC

In a bitterly fought, bloody encounter at the very mouth of the Nile, Egyptian combined forces led by Ramesses III have smashed an invasion attempt by the sea peoples. At the head of his army, Ramesses is now driving far into Palestine and Syria on a punitive expedition against these foreign invaders.

The sea peoples are an alliance of tribes living along the Eastern Mediterranean coast. For years they have been terrorising neighbouring countries in a orgy of pillage and looting. In the eighth year of Ramesses reign they joined together for a mass attack on Egypt. It was a two-pronged attack, with the main body of the invaders marching along the coast, accompanied by ships offshore.

They had clearly assumed that the Egyptians were unprepared, and that landing on the Nile delta would be an easy affair. They had not reckoned with Ramesses' excellent intelligence. The Egyptians were ready and allowed the sea peoples' boats to be lured into the Nile before the fleet struck.

The invaders were completely outnumbered, and those who managed to struggle ashore were quickly mopped up by war chariots and foot soldiers. The defenders showed no mercy. The sea peoples' bodies were stripped, their hands and other parts cut off. This was not the first attempt at an invasion by these Levantine tribespeople, but it was the most dangerous. The invaders were accompanied by their families, and so almost certainly intended to settle in what they expected to be the newly-conquered lands. The coalition included the peoples of Tjekker, Sherden, Sheklesh, Weshesh, Denen and others.

But now, under Ramesses' firm control, Egypt and the whole of the troubled Near East can look forward to a period of stability.

Olmec culture emerges in the Americas

Olmec hallmarks include jade sculptures such as this ceremonial adze.

Gulf of Mexico, 1200BC

Great basalt heads, 12 feet in height, have been placed next to pyramid temples near the religious centres at La Venta, San Lorenzo and Tres Zapatas in the Central American region of Mexico.

The devotion inspired by the religious cults of central America is spectacularly demonstrated by these huge sculptures carved in the Gulf of Mexico, some of which weigh several tons.

The interiors of the buildings are decorated with finely carved pillars, altars and coffins. Jade, terracotta and bone sculptures show religious beliefs and fat eunuchs with innocent expressions as well as jaguars and serpents.

The Olmecs have designed an accurate calendar from their study of the stars and are beginning to count, calculate and write.

Many of the ideas and beliefs of these highly developed people have spread to neighbouring eastern and central Mexico and further afield to central America, as far as Guatemala and El Salvador.

Holy ziggurat tells of the resurgence of Elamite civilisation

Elam, c.1180BC

The capture of Babylon by Shutruk-Nakhunte makes the Elamites masters of Mesopotamia.

Elamite civilisation, first came to prominence just over 800 years ago when they destroyed the Third Dynasty of Ur but in recent decades its influence has grown dramatically.

Untash-napirisha, who became king in about 1240BC, founded the holy city of Dur-Untash, where stands the ziggurat of the temple of the god Inshushinak.

This is perhaps the greatest Elamite monument to be seen anywhere in the Middle East. The city, surrounded by a high defensive wall, has at its centre the main sanctuary, sheltered by a further wall.

In the middle of the sanctuary stands the ziggurat. Its first floor comprises a number of vaulted rooms, reached by stairways embedded in the main construction – an architectural innovation.

Shutruk-Nakhunte has devoted his whole reign to the successful pursuit of the Babylonian war. He is a great soldier, and no town in Babylonia has been able to resist the forces of Elam. Shutruk-Nakhunte has completed his conquest of Mesopotamia and taken the principal records of Mesopotamian history, from Naram-Sin of Agade to Hammurabi of Babylon, back to his capital at Susa.

Elamite religious figure: bronze ornament in the form of a seated goddess, with a fish tail.

Solomon and David create Israelite power

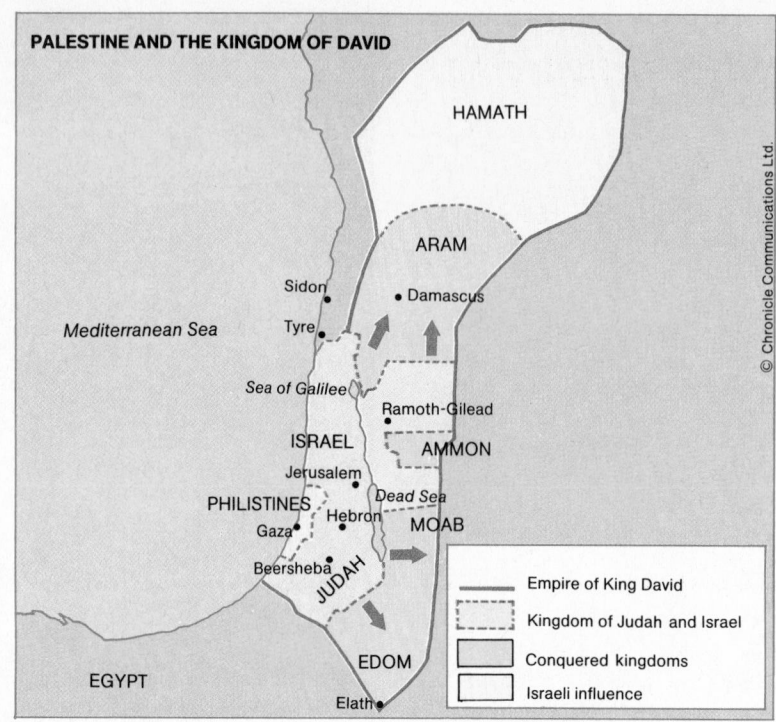

PALESTINE AND THE KINGDOM OF DAVID

Legend:
- Empire of King David
- Kingdom of Judah and Israel
- Conquered kingdoms
- Israeli influence

© Chronicle Communications Ltd

Israel, c.925BC

The kingdom of Israel was once no more than a home for 12 tribes of nomadic Hebrews, who escaped from bondage in Egypt only to wander for 40 years in the desert. Over the last 50 years, however, it has established itself as one of the great nations of the eastern Mediterranean. The former nomads have settled down and established a stable state, which is administered by an increasingly complex bureaucracy and defended by a substantial standing army.

This transformation has been largely achieved through the efforts of two kings: David, who died 40 years ago after a 40-year reign, and his son Solomon, who has just died.

King David's major achievement was the unification of twelve disparate tribes, especially those in the northern part of the kingdom, who resented the increasing power of his capital Jerusalem.

His son Solomon, who was forced to overcome his own half-brother in the struggle for the throne, built on David's success to preside over what is seen as a golden age for Israel and to establish himself as a monarch whose influence extends far beyond his own nation.

Under Solomon the state has enjoyed unprecedented stability, with a strictly hierarchical bureau-cracy, arranged in nine departments and based on an Egyptian model, creating a fully unified kingdom. This unity is backed by a professional army which boasts an elite chariot corps of 4,000 horses and 1,400 vehicles.

Against this background Israel has undergone an economic boom. Using slave labour, drawn from prisoners of war, the country has developed copper mines at the Wadi Araba, and Israelite craftsmen have become well-known. Trading is extensive, and close-knit relations have been developed with neighbouring Phoenician states.

The most notable example of such trade links was the visit of the legendary Queen of Sheba, who travelled 1,500 miles to meet Solomon and to experience for herself his fabled wisdom and wealth.

Solomon's greatest memorial may turn out to be his extensive programme of building. Apart from his own palace, the Temple of Jerusalem, built on Mount Moriah to house the Ark of the Covenant, is known throughout the world. Over seven years in the making, the Temple combines a vestibule, a cella (or internal area) and the Holy of Holies. Here too Solomon benefited from his trading partners: King Hiram of Tyre provided craftsmen, raw materials and the boats to transport them.

Cyprus is melting pot for the arts

Bronze incense-burner stand shows Phoenician carrying copper ingot.

Cyprus, c.1075BC

The island of Cyprus in the eastern Mediterranean has always been a great crossroads for people and cultures, situated as it is between Europe, Africa and the Levant.

The recent collapse of the Hittite and Mycenaean empires has increased this tendency, especially since the collapse of Greek domination at sea has opened up Cyprus to opportunities and influences from as far afield as Sardinia and Egypt.

This is reflected in the island's art, in which Mycenaean Greek styles are mingled with oriental and Egyptian influences. Greek names are written in the local script and Greek influence is evident in the spread of chambered tombs with long entrance passages.

Carved bulls on ivory box: another product of the cultural crossroads.

Assyrians set new imperial bounds in Near East

Feast welcomes ascendancy of new king

Ashurnasirpal II rules vast empire.

Nimrud, Assyria, c.879BC
Ten days of feasting begin today in the opulent new capital Nimrud to celebrate officially the realisation of Assyria's 200-year-old dream of once again controlling an empire that reaches to the Mediterranean.

More than 60,000 guests have descended on the capital for its inaugural feast and to pay homage to King Ashurnasirpal II, one of the most effective Assyrian rulers in recent times.

Since he ascended the throne four years ago he has consolidated past gains and extended Assyrian authority over an empire that now stretches from the Mediterranean city-states of Phoenicia in the west to the Zagros Mountains of Armenia and Lake Urmia in the east.

The new capital, which replaces Assur as the seat of Assyrian power, reflects the strength of the Assyrian revival and the huge resources the empire now controls. It is here that conquered peoples now bring their annual tributes of gold, silver, and other precious metals, along with raw materials, goods, herds, flocks and produce.

The most breathtaking symbol of this new wealth is Ashurnasirpal's new palace which dominates the city's five-mile perimeter. The palace gates are guarded by colossal alabaster lions and bulls. Inside, the porticos are decorated with cedars, cypress, boxwood, mulberry and pistachiowood. In the throne room and reception rooms the walls are decorated with lifesize bas-reliefs depicting religious scenes, battles and royal hunts.

The fortified acropolis contains several temples, including one to Ninurta, god of war, who has smiled on Assyria in recent times. The last time Assyrians had access to the Mediterranean was two centuries ago under Tiglath-Pileser I. Infighting among his successors weakened the kingdom and led to loss of control of surrounding lands.

The modern revival began in 911BC, under Adad-Nirari II, whose six campaigns established strategic strongholds in northern Syria. His grandson Ashurnasirpal consolidated these before fortifying the eastern border to leave himself free to re-open the route to the sea.

Theft of holy statue alarms Babylonians

Sippar, Babylon, c.879BC
The removal of the statue of the god Marduk by plundering Assyrians continues to worsen the economic crisis in this war-torn region.

Without his statue to worship Babylonians say that Marduk has gone and they no longer have his divine protection.

For the local economy this sense of desolation has proved dire. Without a god to serve and feed farmers have lacked sufficient motive to bring in harvests. The crisis has been further compounded by the arrival of marauding Aramaean and Sutaean nomads plundering granaries and burning buildings on the outskirts of towns.

Babylonians fear that by not being able to worship Marduk they have called the balance of the cosmos into question. Speculation is rife as to how an angry and hungry Marduk will react for being deserted by his faithful followers and shipped to a place where he has no power.

In better times worshippers at the temple of Shamash brought Marduk two meals of choice cuts of meat and arrangements of fruits each day, while musicians performed for him.

ASSYRIAN EMPIRE AT THE HEIGHT OF ITS POWER

Map showing:
- Caspian Sea
- ANATOLIA
- Nineveh
- R. Euphrates
- MESOPOTAMIA
- Ashur
- R. Tigris
- Sidon
- Damascus
- Mediterranean Sea
- Babylon
- Susa
- Jerusalem
- Persian Gulf
- R. Nile
- Red Sea
- © Chronicle Communications Ltd.

Legend:
- Area of Assyrian Empire, 650 BC
- Area of Assyrian homeland

Reign of terror grips entire empire

Assyria, c.879BC
One of the more spine-chilling inscriptions to stop a visitor as he enters Ashurnasirpal II's new palace reads: "I flayed all the chief men who revolted, and I covered the pillar with their skins, some I walled up within the pillar, some I impaled upon the pillar on stakes, and others I bound to stakes round about the pillar; many within the border of my own land I flayed, and I spread their skins upon the walls; and I cut off the limbs of the officers who had rebelled ..."

The effect of the message is deliberate. The Assyrian empire now operates a conscious policy of terror. Its army, which has the enviable reputation of being the most effective in the Near East, also has the unenviable reputation of being the most repressive in the region.

If this army has a heart it is an equine one. Horsedrawn two-wheeled chariots and, to a lesser extent, cavalry have proved unbeatable at breaking through enemy lines in highspeed phalanxes. This has made horse supply a major priority. Trusted nobles scour the empire, shipping back horses, with the royal stables being replenished at the rate of 100 horses a day. It is

An Assyrian soldier kills a captive.

not only horses that are transported. Whole communities are uprooted as part of Assyria's security strategy of bringing conquered peoples completely under its control. Non-Assyrians are considered barbarians and subjected to ruthless treatment; official reports detail massacres and mutilation.

To the Assyrians, who see themselves as being engaged in a cosmic fight against evil on behalf of the supreme god, Ashur, their wars are divinely inspired, the stuff of ceremonies. Soldiers now bring back soil from pillaged towns and spread it outside the capital's gates so people can daily tread it underfoot.

Egypt, c.874BC. Osorkon II succeeds Takelot I on the throne of Egypt and places his son Nimlot at the head of the priests of Amun. He extends the temples built at Tanis and Leontopolis (Tell el-Muqdam) and builds a jubilee hall at Bubastis (Tell Basta).

Assyria/Syria, c.838BC. Shalmaneser III, son of Ashurnasirpal II, makes a third vain attempt to conquer Syria.

Armenia, c.830BC. Sardur founds a neo-Hurrian kingdom at Urartu in Armenia, on the northern fringes of the Assyrian empire. He chooses as his capital Tushpa, on the banks of Lake Van.

Assyria, c.827BC. A revolt of the rural nobility, fuelled by a son of Shalmaneser III, breaks out against the great barons of the kingdom.

North Africa, c.814BC. The Phoenicians found Carthage.

Mesopotamia, c.811BC. The death of Shamshi-Adad V, who succeeded his father Shalmaneser III, as Assyrian king, sees Babylon crushed and power restored to Assyria. Shamshi-Adad had to subdue an internal uprising led by his own brother. Taking advantage of the civil war, Babylon imposed a humiliating treaty on Assyria. Before he died Shamshi-Adad wreaked his vengeance by pulverising the Babylonian forces.

Assyria/Syria, c.806BC. Adad-Nirari III, who has just assumed full power as king of Assyria, invades Syria and enters Damascus, where he succeeds in imposing taxes and tributes. When his father died in 811BC, Adad-Nirari was too young to rule, so for five years Assyria was governed by his mother, Sammuramat (also known as Semiramis).

Iran, c.800BC. The Medes and the Persians, Indo-European peoples who began to enter Iran from the north 300 years ago, are now firmly settled on the Iranian plateau.

India, c.800BC. The Indo-Aryans who first appeared in India and Pakistan several hundred years ago have spread through northern India. They are integrating with the local agricultural population and establishing permanent farming settlements. Many have reached the Ganges valley where, after clearing the dense forests, they are laying the basis of an urban civilisation.

Baal banished: Jehovah returns to power

Bronze statuette of the god Baal.

Israel, c.842BC

Jehovah has been restored to his status as Israel's only god, following years of intense religious strife. This followed the marriage over 30 years ago of the late King Omri's son Ahab to Jezebel, a Phoenician who worshipped Melkart, god of Tyre.

On Jezebel's instructions a temple to the Phoenician god Baal was erected in Samaria, where Omri set up a new capital to replace Jerusalem, and its priests gained increasing influence at court. The worship of Jehovah, once the state religion, declined to the status of a persecuted minority cult.

Opposition to Jezebel and her husband King Ahab was spearheaded by two fundamentalist prophets: Elijah, who claimed descent from Moses, and his successor Elisha. Both challenged not only Baal, but also every aspect of the undeniable sophistication that Jezebel has brought to Israel's court. Their efforts appear to have won: Baal has been banished and Jehovah returned to power.

Poem celebrates the virtues of Marduk

Babylon, c.850BC

As the New Year approaches, priests at Babylon's great Esagila temple are preparing for the most important date in their calendar – the fourth day of the festival – when they will recite *When on High*, the epic poem to the great god Marduk.

The poem, on seven tablets, describes how Marduk defeated the forces of chaos among the gods before creating the cosmos and fashioning the human race.

It tells of a time when the sweet waters, the salt waters and the clouds were all one. From this chaos emerged the first gods, including Ea the all-wise, who with his wife Damkina created Marduk.

When war is declared by Tiammat, a god thwarted by Ea, all the

A great god: Marduk?

others decline to fight. Marduk accepts the challenge, provided he is made supreme god. After defeating Kingu, Tiammat's son, he uses his blood to make the first man for "the service of the gods".

Pharaohs buried in temples of Tanis

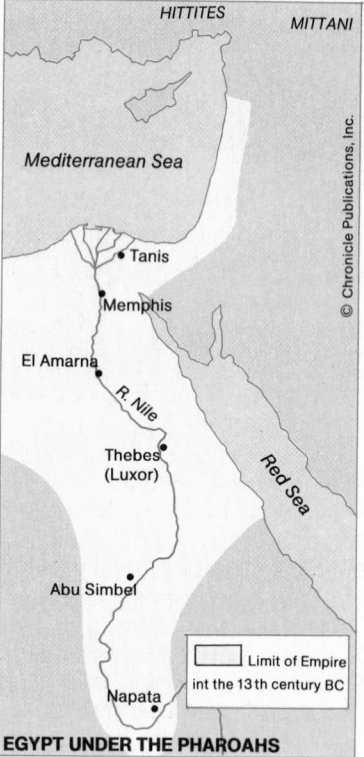

EGYPT UNDER THE PHAROAHS

Egypt, c.840BC

A new line of kings in the north of Egypt has established Tanis (*San el-Hagar*) in the north-east of the Nile delta as the capital of the kingdom.

Here a great temple of Amun dominates the skyline, together with temples dedicated to Mut and Khons in which Anta, a Canaanite goddess, is also worshipped.

Four pharaohs are buried here – Amenophis, Shoshenq III, Osrokon II and Psusennes I – all surrounded by the treasures which accompany them on their last voyages.

Sacred beliefs of India are combined in "Upanishad" writings

India, c.800BC

The *Rig-Veda*, the most sacred, though unwritten, text of the peoples of northern India, has given rise to a great deal of religious discussion since its hymns were first collected at least two hundred years ago. The latest development in the spiritual debate is a varied group of devotional hymns, sayings and reflections called the *Upanishads*, which are the work of holy men and philosopher-kings. The word literally means a session in which religious teachers pass on their wisdom to their pupils, and the 250 or so *Upanishads* are composed as dialogues, with questions and answers as if in a class. They are aimed, essentially, at finding deeper religious truth in the traditional framework of belief centred on the concept of life and existence known as *brahma*. They are more spiritual than earlier texts, for example laying less stress on gods and goddesses. *Upanishads* pose questions such as "what is the origin of the universe?" and "what is the nature of the soul?".

Glimpses of light seen in Greek Dark Age

Dorian decorations are stilted compared with the lifelike Mycenaean art.

Greece, c.800BC

The Greek lands are beginning to regain a little of the organisation that they displayed during the Mycenaean civilisation. For 400 years the inhabitants of Greece have been illiterate, living largely in villages and knowing nothing of Greece's illustrious past. The palaces have disappeared and the towns have been depopulated as Greece slid into a Dark Age.

Much of southern Greece is now dominated by the Dorians, invaders from the north. Just how this relatively primitive people came to dominate the Peloponnese is not known, but it seems likely that the Mycenaeans were overwhelmed by internal crises and domestic revolts, creating a power vacuum for the Dorians to fill.

Like other Dark Age Greeks, the Dorians have come to rely on iron to make their tools and weapons. They live in small communities with land divided into plots owned by the community. But some individuals have begun to grab larger chunks of land so that a more hierarchical society is developing.

Phoenician traders have visited Greece, bringing jewellery, pottery and other objects, but Greek art is only slowly re-emerging from its hibernation. As yet there is nothing comparable with the Mycenaean era in terms of architecture, wall-paintings or decorative metalwork, although there is some painted pottery, bearing rather stilted decorations of funeral processions and fighting by land and at sea.

However, the Dark Age Greeks have perpetuated the Mycenaean religion and emulate their predecessors through a cult of heroes, their tombs marked by great burial mounds like that covering the grave of a chief and his wife at Lefkandi in Ebbua. This has a temple-like structure with a wooden colonnade. Even in the Dark Age, there are glimpses of light.

East meets West at trading crossroads

Near East, c.825BC

A major channel for the exchange of all sorts of commodities has been established at Al Mina at the mouth of the river Orontes in Syria. Here Greeks from the island of Euboea, near Attica, meet other Greeks and Phoenicians from Cyprus and the Levan, to trade slaves, metals, cloth, perfumes and other valuable goods. Contact with other peoples for the exchange of goods also entails an exchange of ideas, and it was perhaps at Al Mina that the use of a Phoenician-style alphabet first occurred to the Greeks. At Al Mina the Aegean world also meets oriental literature, philosophy and social customs – such as reclining while eating and drinking.

Urn-field culture spreads through Europe

Central Europe, c.800BC

Life has been changing in Europe north of the Alps. The 400-year recession in the Mediterranean has scarcely affected the economy here. Indeed, bronze production has soared as new deep mines for copper have been opened up in Austria and returning mercenaries have introduced new techniques of making sheet-bronze armour and helmets. Bronze swords are plentiful and warriors are learning the techniques of fighting from horseback.

Ownership of land is important, as better crops can be grown with new varieties of wheat grown over the winter. Fields are dominated by hillforts – fortresses of earth and timber where the warriors feast and drink from gold and bronze vessels.

This way of life is spreading out from central Europe to the west and north. Some tribes, such as Celtic-languge speakers in France, expand against less powerful neighbours in Spain and the British Isles. A common burial ritual has become characteristic. Instead of burying the dead under mounds, the body is burnt and the cremated remains are put in a pottery urn. The large cemeteries of pits, each with its burial urn and objects left with the dead, are known as urn-fields.

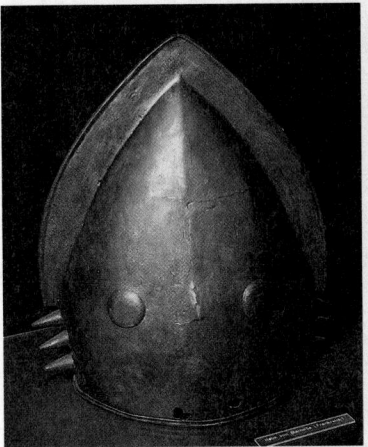

War gear of a French warrior.

Bronze Celt with horned helmet.

Detail from the golden vase of Hasanlu, a masterpiece created by the Mannean people who inhabit a small kingdom in Iran. The vase includes scenes of divinities as well as fighting warriors.

Fertile Crescent nurtures warring empires

There can be no doubt that the area called the Fertile Crescent, tracing an arc from southern Mesopotamia along the foothills of the Zagros Mountains upwards and round across into western Syria, was the scene of the earliest high civilisations in the history of mankind. This was the area where the "Neolithic revolution" - the change to farming - gradually took place, perhaps from as early as 6500BC. The advent of civilisation is usually reckoned to be marked by the development of cities, the invention of writing, the construction of monumental architecture and, in low-rainfall areas, the organisation of large-scale irrigation.

It is probable that the development of cities and the construction of monumental buildings led to the need to organise administration and recording, and hence to the invention of writing. Although writing is first attested at Uruk in southern Mesopotamia, (present day Iraq), almost certainly in the Sumerian language, just before 3000BC, and shortly afterwards in Elam (south-western Iran), there are recording practices, involving the marking of clay tablets, that go back perhaps as early as 5000BC.

The first written language

The first great literate civilisation of the Near East was that of the Sumerians, speakers of the earliest written language, a language none of whose relatives was ever recorded in writing. The Sumerian city-states were conquered by Sargon of Agade about 2300BC. The people of Agade spoke the Semitic language of Akkadian, which was to dominate Mesopotamia thereafter with the single exception of the Third Dynasty of Ur, a neo-Sumerian revival (2113-2006BC) whose kings left an indelible imprint on the history of Mesopotamia as notable builders of temples and ziggurats.

During the second and first millenia BC, northern Mesopotamia was the centre of successive Assyrian empires, and southern Mesopotamia of Babylonian empires. Babylonia always remained the cultural centre of Mesopotamia and of the civilisation transmitted in the cuneiform writing, even during the period of rule by the Kassites, an intrusive people of unknown origin (c.1600-c.1250BC), and ultimately in 612BC the Assyrian Empire fell to a combined alliance of the Babylonians and the Medes. This gave the opportunity for the development of the last great Babylonian Empire (626-539BC).

Babylonian civilisation was complex and long-lived, absorbing many influences from surrounding peoples. The extensive literature preserved in cunei-form writing on clay tablets is sometimes in the Babylonian language, sometimes in Sumerian with an inter-linear translation into Babylonian.

Divination, from the entrails of slaughtered animals, or else from observation of the movements of the heavenly bodies, was extensively used to interpret the future, both by ordinary individuals and by the king and his generals and ministers. Through this astrological divination, Babylonian astronomy became relatively advanced.

Magic and religion

Babylonian religion was excessively polytheistic - the names of over 3,000 deities are known - partly through the gradual amalgamation of numerous local cults. The many temples had a large clergy of priests who performed daily sacrifices and liturgies, many of which are preserved on tablets. Magic was an accepted aspect of religion, both because it was believed that many diseases were caused by demons and because it was thought that human beings could be bewitched by sorcerers. The powers of demons and sorcerers could be broken by magic. Medicine was thus a mixture of magic and genuine herbal medical practices, involving potations and poultices with some surgery.

From the earliest times the necessity of accurately dividing up precious arable land, in this highly bureaucratic civilisation, had led to the development of surveying, and, as a result, Mesopotamian mathematics was rather advanced; it has now been shown that the Babylonians must have been familiar with theorems previously attributed to Euclid or Pythagoras.

Throughout Mesopotamian history, its societies took slavery for granted. Slaves might be captured in war, or might have sold themselves when their debts became too great. Babylonian and Assyrian women seem to have been more secluded than their Sumerian predecessors, although not without exceptions. Babylonian religious women could inherit property and conduct business transactions. Monogamy was normal, although a man might sometimes take a concubine in order to produce children.

The discovery, in AD 1975, of extensive archives at Tell Mardikh has revealed the existence during the third millenium BC of an empire in Syria centered on Ebla. It gave way in time to other Syrian empires, sometimes sub-Assyrian, sometimes Hurrian or, later, neo-Hittite in origin, but always owing a great cultural debt to Mesopotamia. In return the Syrian empires could act as channels of a vigorous trade in metals and other western goods. The Hurrians, a people of otherwise unknown connections, were spread over Syria and northern Mesopotamia by about 2000BC. A number of Hurrian states came into existence in Syria, the most significant of which was the kingdom of Mitanni, which controlled a substantial area of northern Syria, Mesopotamia and south eastern Anatolia from c.1500 to about 1250BC. During this time the kings of Mitanni corresponded on equal terms with the kings of Egypt, exchanged gifts and traded princesses in marriage.

Nomads and traders

In central Anatolia the Hittites, an Indo-European people, formed their empire which spread to control most of Anatolia until its demise about 1200BC. The neo-Hittite empire found itself thereafter controlling an area slightly to the south east on the border between Anatolia and Syria. The Aramaeans were nomads, who began to move eastwards into Mesopotamia in about 1100BC, until they formed the majority of the population, and Aramaic became the most widely spoken language in the Near East.

The division of Israel into two kingdoms (Israel and Judah), in about 930BC, coincided approximately with the rise of Phoenician prosperity (under Hiram of Tyre, 980-936BC), but, although the Phoenicians traded and colonised abroad (for example later at Carthage), these and other coastal kingdoms lived in the constant shadow of Egypt or Assyria or Babylonia.

On the northern fringes of the Assyrian Empire from 800BC was the growing kingdom of Urartu, a neo-Hurrian civilisation of eastern Anatolia, finally overthrown about 585BC. The Urartians were evidently in touch with Assyria's and Babylonia's great army, the powerful kingdom of Elam, with its capital at Susa in south-western Iran. The civilisation of Elam was devastated by Assyria in 639BC.

The Iranian Medes, originally allies of the Babylonians, were overthrown by the Persians under Cyrus in 550BC, and the Persians ultimately gained control of the Babylonian Empire when Cyrus captured Babylon from Belshazzar, son and viceroy of its last king, Nabonidus, in 539BC. From then on almost the whole of the Near East came under the control of the Persians - Iran, Mesopotamia, Syria, Palestine, Asia Minor - and the Persians controlled the whole of the Fertile Crescent until the conquests of Alexander the Great 200 years later.

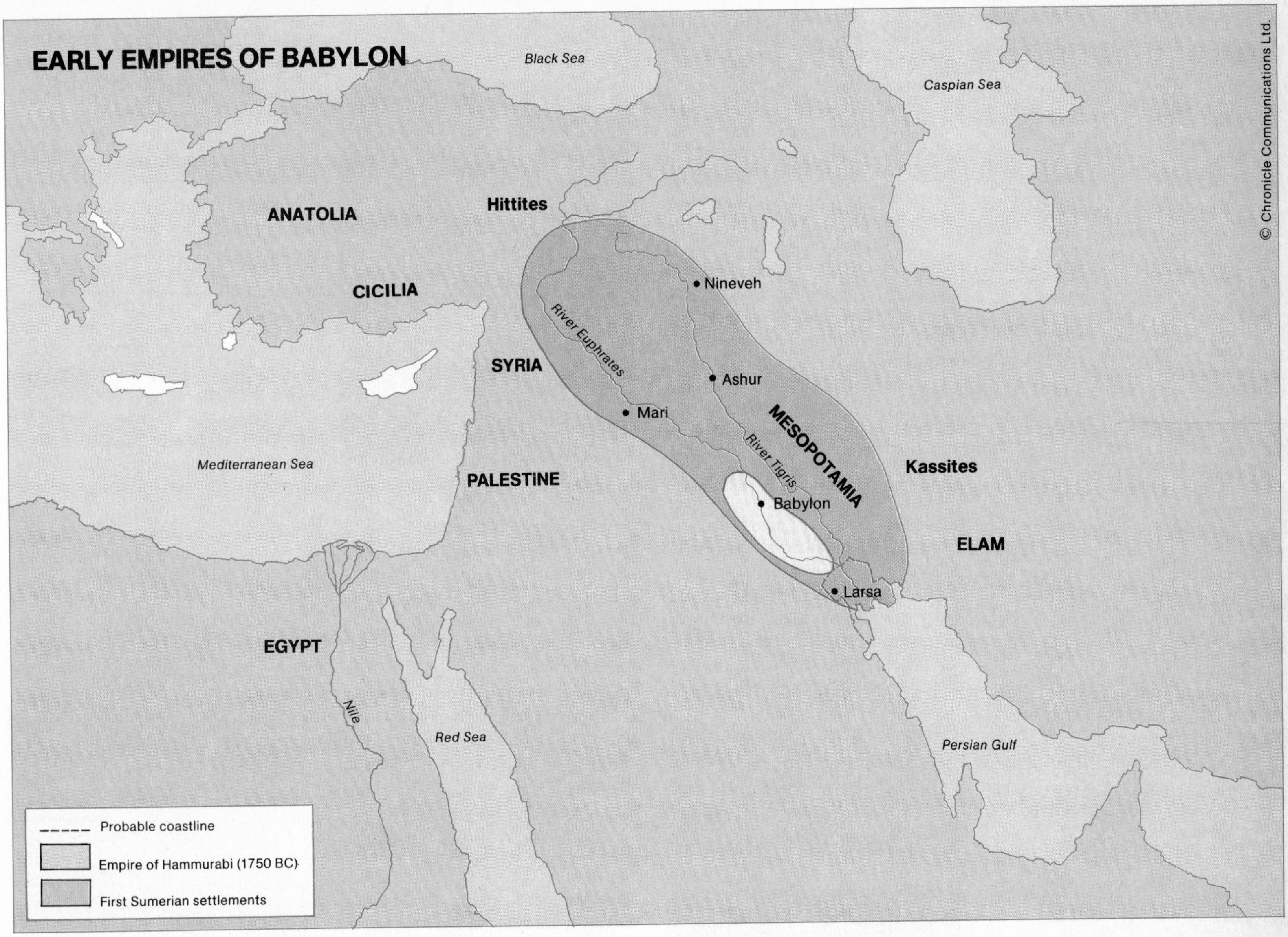

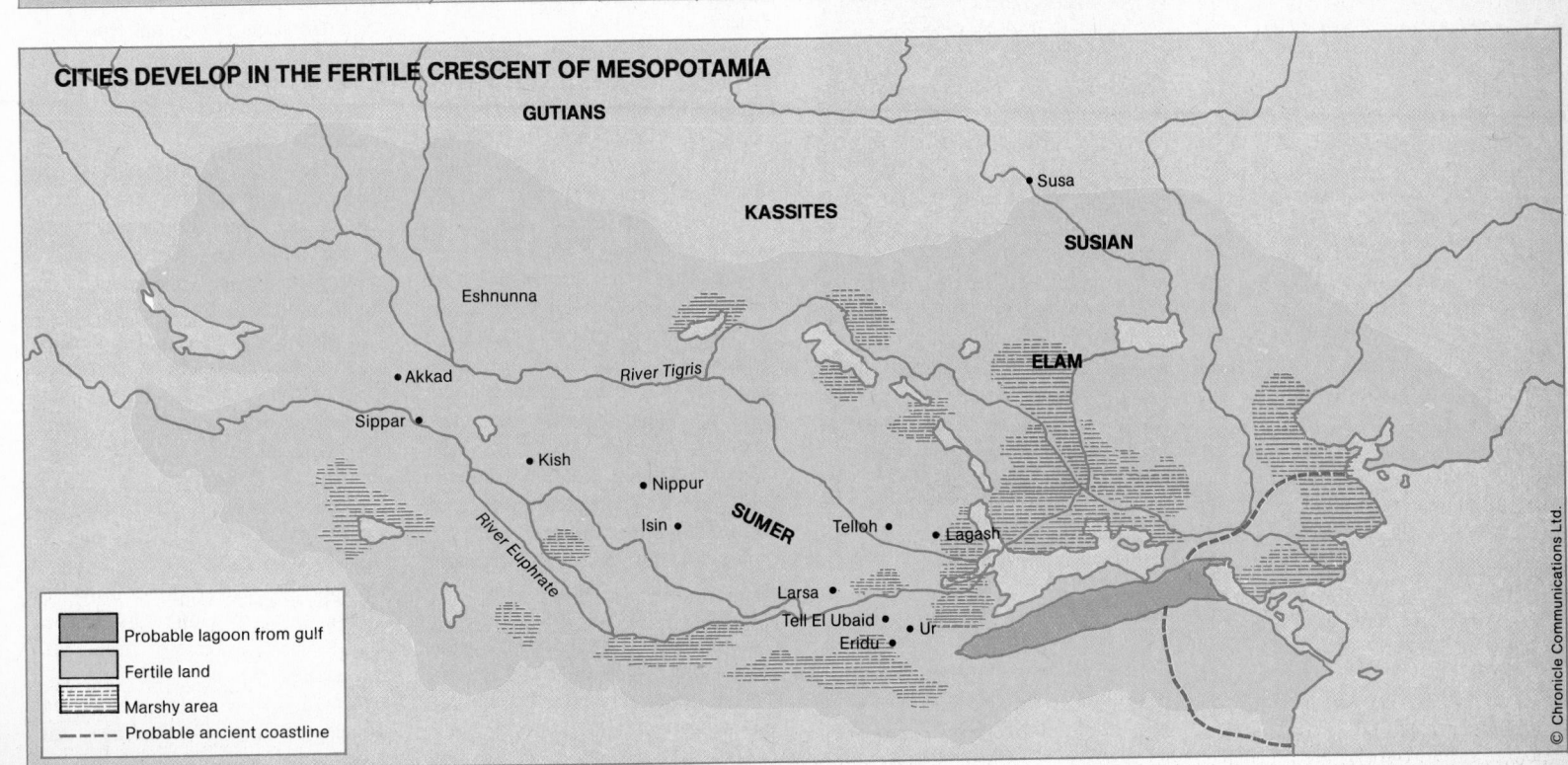

EARLY EMPIRES OF BABYLON

Black Sea

Caspian Sea

© Chronicle Communications Ltd.

ANATOLIA

Hittites

CICILIA

• Nineveh

River Euphrates

SYRIA

• Ashur

MESOPOTAMIA

River Tigris

• Mari

Kassites

Mediterranean Sea

PALESTINE

Babylon

ELAM

• Larsa

EGYPT

Nile

Red Sea

Persian Gulf

- - - - Probable coastline

Empire of Hammurabi (1750 BC)

First Sumerian settlements

CITIES DEVELOP IN THE FERTILE CRESCENT OF MESOPOTAMIA

GUTIANS

• Susa

KASSITES

SUSIAN

Eshnunna

ELAM

• Akkad

River Tigris

Sippar •

• Kish

• Nippur

Isin •

SUMER

Telloh •

• Lagash

River Euphrate

Larsa •

Tell El Ubaid •

• Ur

Eridu •

Probable lagoon from gulf

Fertile land

Marshy area

- - - - Probable ancient coastline

© Chronicle Communications Ltd.

Sardinia, c.800BC. For 200 years a civilisation distinctive for its original architecture and sculpture has been evolving in Sardinia. The Sardinians build dry-stone towers in the shape of truncated cones and surrounded by stone walls. Sculptors create bronze statues of men, animals and divinities, including a "great goddess" portrayed as a woman cradling a child in her arms.

Italy, c.790BC. Small villages of primitive thatched huts are appearing on the Palatine and neighbouring hills overlooking the Roman countryside. As well as fishing, hunting and gathering, the inhabitants grow wheat and barley and raise goats and pigs.

Greece, 776BC. Athletes compete in the first Olympia Games.

China, c.770BC. After the fall of the Western Zhou capital at Hao, a new Zhou capital is set up at Luoyang. The state of Qin (Ch'in) is established in the area of the former capital in the Wei valley.

Iran, c.770BC. The Manneans, who live in a small kingdom to the south of Lake Urmia, rear horses and are experts in the art of metalworking. Their country has seen several wars between the Assyrians and the Urartians, and they are subject to diverse cultural influences: Assyrian, Greek, Scythian and others. At Hasanlu they have built an fortified citadel sheltering temples and a palace.

Mediterranean, c.770BC. The Greeks are creating colonies all over the Mediterranean world and in parts of western Asia.

Italy, c.770BC. Central Italy is dominated by a civilisation centred on Villanova, near Bologna. The Villanovans live in villages of huts, on hills. Their way of life is based on agriculture, but they are also keen traders and metalworkers. They value martial art and maintain a detachment of combat cavalry. The Villanovans cremate their dead and consign their ashes to urns.

Italy, 753BC. Legendary founding of Rome.

Italy, c.750BC. The Etruscan civilisation is taking root as immigrants who arrived by sea from the Near East establish settlements in Tuscany. The newcomers are integrating with the Villanovan people and spreading their knowledge of goldworking and other skills.

Western Zhou dynasty reigns in China

China, 775BC

Hao, the capital of the Zhou dynasty, has become established as the cultural as well as the political centre of China since the Zhous overthrew the ruling Shang dynasty 250 years earlier.

The Shangs ended in fire and blood when the dissolute Emperor Chou Hsin, reputed to be so strong that he could slay wild beasts with one blow of his fist, was deserted by his warriors. He went out literally in a blaze of glory. Putting on his most splendid robes and jewels, he set fire to his palace and perished in the flames.

Since then the Zhou have ruled wisely, delegating authority over much of China to junior members of the royal family and to nobles who have been given fiefs to rule.

The Zhou emperors have not, as yet, abandoned the practice of human sacrifice, but it is much less common than it was in the days of the Shangs whose regime was hallmarked by cruelty.

One of the reasons for this is that they have abandoned the old Shang religion of ancestor worship and

Zhou bronze of man holding lamp.

have developed a theology in which they worship Tian or "Heaven", a semi-personal divinity.

The Zhou also take a pride in recording their history, inscribing their achievements on ornate bronze vases and for the first time providing accurate dates.

There is much to be recorded for the ambitious nobles of the Zhou empire are continually expanding its boundaries.

Etruscan city states rise to power in Italy

An ornately elegant Etruscan vase.

Italy, c.750BC

The Etruscans, a mysterious people who have apparently migrated to Italy from the east, have set up a series of flourishing city-states in the rolling country and volcanic uplands of Etruria (Tuscany). The

states are united in a religious league, but each controls its own destiny.

This political system lends itself admirably to economic and military growth. The Etruscans are skilled ironworkers and their traders carry on commerce with the Greeks and Phoenicians while their heavily armoured soldiers use chariots to expand south into Campania.

Culturally, the Etruscans have borrowed from the Villanovans, the people they displaced, and the Greeks. The Hellenic influence is especially noticeable in their tomb paintings which show not only portraits of the dead men and their wives at banquets, but also scenes of daily life with vivid pictures of boating, fishing and hunting.

These tomb paintings highlight the Etruscans' character for they live well, enjoying luxury for its own sake, their jewellery and goldwork being much prized. They are fond of music, games and gambling, and women play an important role in Etruscan life.

Greeks learn their alphas and betas

Greece, c.775BC

As trade continues to increase between the world's nations, the need for a simple written language has continued to grow. The Phoenicians already have an alphabetical system and now the Greeks have created a unique system of their own.

In Mycenaean times the Greeks depended on the 88 character syllatic system, which had become increasingly unwieldy and ill-adapted to modern needs. Like a number of similar systems it has simply too many signs for clarity and ease of use. Systems that depend on pictures (like Egypt's hieroglyphs) or on representing syllables (like Mesopotamian cunei-

New Greek script includes vowels.

form) are too cumbersome. Today Greece is benefiting from the Phoenician invention.

Greeks first discovered the new system as part of their trading with Phoenicia. Later, Phoenicians who settled in Greece offered their discovery to native Greeks who went on to modify it for their own uses, although the origins of the new alphabet have not been forgotten. One of the names for the alphabet is *Phoenician objects*, and the words for "writing" and for "scribe" both incorporate *Phoenician*.

The most obvious difference between the Greek system and its model is in the way the alphabet looks: the different sounds of Greek produce differently shaped letters. Greek scribes have also augmented the basic 22-letter system with five vowels. Semitic languages, of which Phoenician is one, have chosen to ignore the vowels.

Greek audiences are enthralled by tales of daring

Greece, c.750BC

The Greeks now have a chance to read two magnificent poetic epics which have been written down for the first time: the *Iliad*, about the Trojan war, and the *Odyssey*, which relates the adventures of Odysseus, a Greek prince who fought at Troy.

Greeks have long been thrilled and moved by legendary exploits and adventures. The stories they like to hear best – of invincible warriors, steadfast heroines, awesome gods and terrible monsters – are told by professional bards. These reciters and singers of poetry are also known as rhapsodes, a word which means "stitchers of songs", and part of their fame rests on an immense skill in "stitching" great epic tales together from a rich repertory of characters, themes and linguistic formulas. A bard's memory has to be almost as phenomenal as the deeds of which he tells.

The Greeks consider the *Iliad* and *Odyssey* to be the best of these "stitched together" compositions. They draw on elements from every age since the time of Mycenae, five centuries ago; these elements are nostalgically fused as an idealistic, but supposedly real, age of heroes. Every Greek says that the two epics are the work of the greatest of the bards, a blind poet called Homer. But that is all they seem to know of him, and although the style of these great works implies that one man wrote them, it is hard to be sure.

Achilles spears the Amazon queen Penthesilea during the Trojan war.

Odysseus and his companions blind the cyclops Polyphemus with a stake.

The heroic legends of the Iliad

Greece, c.750BC

The *Iliad*, a great poem about the siege of the city of Troy, is one of the two Homeric epics which have gripped the imaginations of the Greeks and set new standards of literary expression. Like its counterpart the *Odyssey*, the *Iliad* consists of previously unwritten legends of the past, and its story moves quickly in a language which, although capable of great clarity and simplicity, is rich in drama, excitement, humour and sorrow.

It is essentially a war poem, in which the heroes of Greece vanquish the heroes of Troy across the sea. The war is sparked by the abduction of the beautiful Helen, wife of Menelaus, by Paris, one of the 50 sons of King Priam of Troy. A great hero, the partly divine Greek warrior Achilles, goes to Troy with 50 ships as an ally of the Greek king Agamemnon, Menelaus's elder brother. Achilles is distinguished by his youth, height, flashing eyes and flame-red hair, as well as by his uncontrollable fury when provoked.

When Agamemnon takes the slave girl of Achilles, the hero refuses to fight for him, but eventually, after the Trojans have scored a run of successes, Achilles agrees to let his friend Patroclus borrow his armour and lead his men in an action to protect the Greeks. Patroclus is killed by Hector, Priam's son and the greatest Trojan warrior; Achilles, frenzied with grief, makes it up with Agamemnon. The next day he smashes the Trojans and kills Hector, giving his corpse to Priam after Patroclus has been buried.

Odyssey of Ulysses wins popular acclaim

Greece, c.750BC

Just as popular as the heroic derring-do of the *Iliad* are the adventures recounted in the *Odyssey*, the epic tale of the travels and exploits of Odysseus, or Ulysses. He is the son of King Laertes of Ithaca, and appears in the *Iliad* as a brave and wise Greek warrior in the service of Agamemnon and Achilles.

On the fall of Troy, where the *Odyssey* begins, he sets off to return home to his wife Penelope and son Telemachus. He fights the Cicones soon after leaving Troy, but is beaten off and carried by a storm to the land of the Lotus Eaters from where he wanders to the land of race of one-eyed cyclops.

The cyclops Polyphemus takes Odysseus and his men and begins to eat them. But the heroes blind Polyphemus and escape, eventually reaching the isle of the divine sorceress Circe. She turns Odysseus' men into swine until he forces her to change them back, after which he lives with her for a year. He sets out again, careful not to succumb to the Sirens, whose singing attracts sailors to land, where they die. Later, his hungry crew eat cattle belonging to Helios, the Sun.

In revenge Helios shipwrecks Odysseus, killing his companions, and he drifts to the island of the nymph Calypso. She keeps him there for seven years, after which he sails away and is again wrecked; but he swims ashore and is tended by the King of Phaeacia, who sends him home clad as a beggar. In a violent denouement Odysseus and his son kill his wife's suitors and, ten years after leaving Troy, he is reunited with his family.

Israel, c.750BC. Amos, a peasant prophet from Judah, warns of a coming Day of Judgement. On that day, according to Amos, the justice of the Lord will be seen to be done, and the children of Israel will suffer for their unrighteous ways.

Europe, c.750BC. Ironworking, which began in southern Europe over 200 years ago, reaches Britain. The abundant sources of iron in the continent have led to its gradually replacing bronze as the favourite material for weapons.

Armenia, c.745BC. Urartu, in Armenia, has reached new heights under Sardur III, a descendant of Sardur I, who founded the kingdom about 100 years ago. Sardur III has now formed a vast coalition with Syria against their common enemy, Assyria.

Syria, c.743BC. Tiglath-Pileser III, king of Assyria, defeats Arpad after a three-year siege. Arpad was the centre of an anti-Assyrian coalition headed by Sardur of Urartu.

Mesopotamia, c.740BC. The Medes and the Persians, the Indo-European peoples who have been settling Iran for the past few hundred years, have now reached the frontiers of Assyria.

Syria, 732BC. With the fall of Damascus to the Assyrians, Syria is finally subjected. Samaria, Tyre and Byblos recognised Assyrian authority when Tiglath-Pileser broke up a second Syrian coalition.

Babylon, 729BC. After stamping out a Babylonian revolution, Tiglath-Pileser III, king of Assyria, names himself king of Babylon.

Assyria, 727BC. At his death Tiglath-Pileser III leaves behind him a vast and prosperous empire.

Rome, c.716BC. Romulus, the legendary founder and first king of Rome, is reputed to have been carried up to heaven in a chariot of fire. Romulus and his twin brother Remus were said to have been suckled by a she-wolf.

Assyria, c.710BC. Sargon II, the brilliant soldier who ascended the Assyrian throne c.721BC, moves his capital from Nimrud to Khorsabad, 15 miles north-east of Nineveh. Khorsabad, built on a previously virgin site, includes a vast palace and a ziggurat.

Scythian warriors storm into Middle East

Scythian amphora showing a warrior horseman unhobbling his mount.

Middle East, c.715BC
A new force has appeared to disrupt the existing order in the Middle East and the Caucasus. Groups of nomadic warriors, the Scythians, are pouring into western Asia to threaten the frontiers of Assyria as well as heading for the Black Sea to harry the peoples of Europe. The Scythians appear to come from the steppes of central Asia, around the River Volga, but since they are nomads, living in tents and shifting from pasture to pasture with their herds of animals, it is hard be sure of this. Nor does anyone know what, in recent years, has prompted them to move southwards; perhaps they have been displaced by other wandering peoples.

The Scythians themselves have forced others to move on, such as the Cimmerians of southern Russia – to the dismay of people like King Midas of Phrygia in Anatolia, whose kingdom the Cimmerians are currently ransacking.

The Scythians have acquired a reputation as fearsome mounted warriors. Especially admired – not to mention dreaded – is their ability to fight on horseback with powerful bows, which are made of both wood and bone rather than single pieces of wood, to give them greater strength and accuracy. But the Scythians are also considerable craftsmen, with vigorous and individual styles of pattern and design, often based on animal motifs.

Thracians find new homeland in the west

Eastern Europe, c.715BC
Thracian families are fleeing to eastern Europe after crossing the Caucasus mountains. These nomadic tribesmen are one of the peoples being forced from their lands by advancing Scythian horsemen, as they move from their native steppe region beyond the Black Sea with herds of fine and highly bred horses.

The land where the Thracians are settling is rich in gold, silver and copper deposits. This has encouraged Thracian craftsmanship of a high standard.

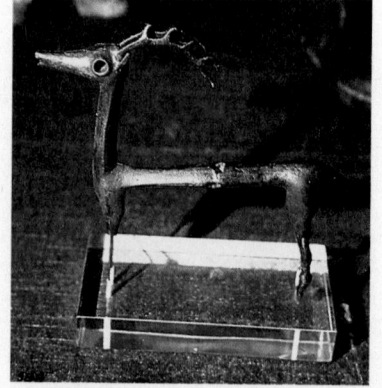

A bronze stag exemplifies the fine craftsmanship of the Thracians.

A Kushite armada has captured the capital of Egypt

Memphis, Egypt, c.730BC
Piankhy, or Piye, the king of Kush, has defeated the Egyptian army at Memphis, and his troops have gained control of the Nile. "I will take it like a flood of water," Piankhy announced before the battle, and, gathering an armada of small boats, he assaulted Memphis from the river Nile.

For over a thousand years the two nations of the Nile, Egypt and Kush, have maintained a see-saw relationship. When Egyptian power was weak, Kush asserted its independence; when it was strong, Kush accepted its dependency. Throughout those centuries Egypt never effectively colonised Kush. Egypt's interest was in what it

Graphite vessel cover from Kush.

could take – gold, ivory and timber – and Kush never lost its sense of national and cultural identity.

The decline in Egyptian power following the Libyan invasions gave Kashta, brother of Piankhy, the opportunity to re-assert Kushite independence. The Kushites grew rich from their gold mines and established a court at Napata, across the Nile from their sacred mountain, Gebel Barkal. Kashta expanded Kush, occupying Thebes and Upper Egypt.

Piankhy has completed the campaign. "He to whom I say "thou art a king" shall be a king." Now the capital Napata is taking on all the pretensions of Egyptian fashions and to some, the new conquerors are trying to be more Egyptian than the Egyptians themselves.

Mystery man seizes Assyrian throne

Nimrud, Assyria, c.721BC

Stability is beginning to return to Assyria following the overthrow of Shalmaneser V, one of the most incompetent monarchs of recent times. His successor, who styles himself Sargon II, is a mystery man whose background is unknown. But his title may be a clue to the type of kingdom Assyria can now expect.

The name Sargon – the legitimate king – is a deliberate echo of the glory days of Sargon of Agade, founder of the Akkad dynasty. The new Sargon has moved fast to end the domestic disorder that helped him ride to power and oust Shalmaneser V.

His first move has been to overturn the unpopular decision to curtail the privileges of Assyria's holy cities, which led to last year's civil unrest. Sargon II has assured the citizens of the temples and city states that he will not restrict their traditional immunity from taxation and conscription. With domestic issues settled, observers now expect Sargon II to turn his attention to the two major threats that confront his empire.

To the west the Egyptians, still smarting from the loss of Phoenicia to the Assyrians, are lending covert support to the princes of Palestine

Gateway figures from the imposing palace of Sargon II at Khorsabad.

in the hope of starting a rebellion that could embarrass Sargon II and leave his forces stretched.

On his eastern front Sargon II faces similar interference from the Elamites in the affairs of Babylon. An independent Babylon would help restore their trade routes which were cut when Assyria conquered the city.

Kingdom of Uratu falls to the might of Assyrian power

Urartu, c.714BC

Victorious Assyrian forces have won complete control of the kingdom of Urartu in Armenia, ending over 150 years of conflict. The fall of Urartu on the shores of Lake Van marks the collapse of Assyria's main enemy and a personal triumph for Assyria's king, Sargon II, who has succeeded where his predecessors failed.

Shrewd use of military intelligence is believed to have played a key role in the successful timing of the Assyrian assault, with Sargon II at his new palace at Nineveh monitoring reports from his scouts along the Urartian border. Recent reports that Cimmerian nomads had inflicted a heavy defeat on Urartian forces, and one report from Crown Prince Sennacherib listing the names of Urartean commanders killed in battle, convinced Sargon II that the time was ripe to move against his weakened enemy.

The conquest of Urartu gives

Weird bronze beast from Urartu.

Assyria control of a flourishing economy. Urartu's farming infrastructure is well-organised, with secure granaries and artificial lakes and reservoirs that have removed the threat of drought. Its metal workers are world-famous. Strategically placed on the major trade routes, its annexation will further enrich Assyria and help to secure its northern border.

Mass deportation of Israelis after two-year siege

Samaria, c.721BC

The once-proud northern kingdom of Israel is being effectively wiped off the map by an Assyrian army of occupation, following the surrender of the city of Samaria after a siege lasting two years.

Assyrian forces acting on the orders of their new king, Sargon II, have begun mass deportations of captured Israelites, removing every trace of its tribes from Samaria. Latest official figures put the number of Israelites deported to Assyria at 27,290. Most of them will be used as slaves in forced labour camps.

To complete the sweeping cultural changes to the area, Assyria has re-designated Samaria a province and begun repopulating it with foreign deportees from Syrian, Babylon and Arabia. Where once

there were two Israelite kingdoms there is now only one – Judah, to the south, which opted for Assyrian protection 15 years ago.

The surrender of Samaria is Sargon II's first victory since becoming king. The collapse of the siege was the last act in the Israelite

uprising that began six years ago when King Hoshea ben Elah, a vassal king installed by TiglathPileser III, refused to perform an act of allegiance to his son Shalmaneser V on his accession. Hoshea was captured three years ago, but the city of Samaria held out.

Phrygia becomes latest Assyrian victim

Gordium, Phrygia, c.709BC

King Midas is dead. The Phrygian monarch, whose fabulous wealth inspired legends that he could turn things to gold, has committed suicide here in the capital after Cimmerian hordes from the north ransacked his kingdom.

Midas's suicide represents the end of Phrygian independence. The country has now been forced to sign

a peace treaty with its southern neighbour, Sargon II of Assyria, that guarantees protection in return for Phrygia paying him tribute.

In many respects Midas *was* Phrygia. He enhanced the reputation of this kingdom high on the Anatolian plateau by his wealth, his marriage to a Greek princess and by being the first non-Greek to make offerings at Delphi.

Near East, c.705BC. The Cimmerians, a warlike people from southern Russia, have crossed the Caucasus and entered western Asia. In Anatolia they are harassing Phrygia and the rich new kingdom of Lydia. In Iran they are busy making alliances with the Manneans and the Medes.

Assyria, c.700BC. Nineveh, rebuilt out of the ruins of the old city, has been restored as the capital of Assyria. The capital created by Sargon II at Khorsabad was deserted soon after the old king's death and is now falling into ruins.

Assyria, c.700BC. Sennacherib has swiftly put an end to the sporadic revolts that broke out after he ascended the Assyrian throne in 704BC, following the death of his father, Sargon II. Sennacherib is well informed about the situation prevailing in the provinces because, while crown prince, he was for a long time in charge of the reconnaissance service of the Assyrian army.

Asia, c.700BC. The fierce warrior horsemen known as the Scythians, whose way of life has so far been mostly nomadic, are forming large permanent communities in the western steppelands. As well as rearing cattle, sheep and horses, they do some farming and hunting. Their settlements are rich and hierarchical.

Greece, c.700BC. The poetry of Hesiod, a former shepherd born near Mount Helicon in Boeotia, central Greece, is gaining in influence. The first western writer to embody didacticism in his work, Hesiod has an essentially serious outlook on life and exalts honest labour. His epic poem *Works and Days* creates a vivid impression of everyday life in a contemporary Greek village.

Anatolia, c.700BC. A substantial number of Greek colonies are being set up in Anatolia, in Thrace and on the shores of the Black Sea and the Propontis (Sea of Marmara).

Sicily, c.690BC. A branch of the Greek people known as the Dorians, who have already established communities at Sparta and Argos in the Peloponnese area of Greece, found the city of Gela. Their intervention in the island of Sicily was made under the guidance of Antiphemos of Rhodes and Entimos of Crete.

Splendid new Assyrian capital at Nineveh

Archers and slingers in action – from Sennacherib's palace at Nineveh.

Nineveh, Assyria, c.700BC

A new Assyrian capital has risen here out of the ruins of the old city, reviving the tradition of Nineveh as the home of Assyrian kings. Under the direction of the new king Sennacherib, who is maintaining the royal tradition of surpassing his predecessors, a "palace without a rival" has been built according to the positions of the stars in the skies and the gods in the heavens.

The most magnificent Assyrian capital yet built, it is surrounded by a two-mile-long wall. At the heart of the city the Tebiltu has been diverted and a rock platform built into the old riverbed to give the palace citadel a natural riverside terrace. The foundations measure 360 by 204 yards, more than twice the size of the old royal residence.

Two enormous copper pillars, each resting on four bronze lions, form the uprights to the palace gates, which are topped with two great cedars. Four mountain sheep, cast in silver and copper and pointing in the directions of the four winds, adorn the entrances.

At the side of the palace is a great park boasting "all kinds of herbs and fruit-trees". Major irrigation works for it include a 300-yard-long aqueduct, canals, dams, basins and the straightening of two rivers.

Babylon's rebellion crushed by Assyrians

Elam, Persian Gulf, c.694BC

A massive Assyrian combined sea and land operation aimed at securing access to the Persian Gulf has also succeeded in consolidating Assyrian control over Babylonia by crushing allies of the rebel leader.

The Assyrian forces, led by King Sennacherib, pillaged Elamite cities along the Gulf, but failed to find Merodach-Baladan, the renegade Chaldean chieftain. He has been sheltered by the Elamites for the past six years since Assyrian troops crushed his 700BC attempt to regain control of Babylonia. Then Merodach-Baladan was forced to flee with the statues of his gods and the bones of his ancestors, his family falling into Assyrian hands.

This latest Assyrian expedition against the one-time king of the Sea-Land marshes of southern Iraq involved building open-sea boats at Nineveh and then sailing them down the Tigris as far as Opis. They were then hauled overland to the Arahtu canal before continuing down the Euphrates to the Gulf.

Merodach-Baladan has long been a thorn in Assyria's side, first seizing Babylon in 721BC. He was overthrown by Sargon II ten years later, but returned again in 704BC.

Bronze gives way to iron in Europe

Europe, c.700BC

Peasant farmers are suffering under the shadow of the new iron sword as a rising class of unscrupulous warriers seizes economic and political power.

Iron manufacture, once a Hittite military secret, has now been mastered by Celts all over western Europe. Blades of knives and long slashing swords can be ground sharper – and therefore deadlier – than ever.

After the collapse of the Hittite Empire in the east it took 350 years for the strong and cheap iron-making method to be used more widely. Italy was ahead of the game when it began using iron 150 years ago, and it has been followed by Spain, Britain, Brittany, Germany and Poland.

While the new iron technology was confined to Anatolia, the brilliant kingdoms of Mycenae had time to flower and die. In their heyday they were great importers of precious minerals from eastern Europe. They bought amber from the Baltic, tin from Czechoslovakia and gold from Hungary.

Years later, once these fabulous kingdoms had disappeared, there was a gradual recession in the Mediterranean. This resulted in an expansion of Europe and coincided with the arrival of iron from the east.

Ceramic face surrounded by dragons – a cult object from the civilisation centred on Chavin de Huantar in the Cordillera Blanca, northern Peru. Chavin influence now stretches over a wide area of the country.

Greeks yearn for mythical "golden age"

Hesiod, harbinger of men's doom.

Greece, c.700BC

The poet Hesiod has already sought to explain what all the gods stand for in his work *Theogony*, and he has now set about explaining the state of human existence in his book *Works and Days*. He ascribes man's present woeful, weary lot to two causes. The first is the jar of evils opened on the world by the woman Pandora. Secondly, Hesiod says men have generally deteriorated since the "first age" of mankind.

The people of this wonderful Age of Gold were made by the gods, and lived "with carefree heart, remote from toil and misery". They never grew old, but died "as if overcome by sleep". Back-breaking work on the land was unknown since the soil gave them all the food they needed of its own accord. When these people passed from the earth Zeus made their spirits divine.

The Age of Gold was followed by the inferior Silver Age. The men of silver lived through a childhood of 100 years, and then died shortly afterwards because their witlessness led them to folly and immoderation and they would not honour the gods. Zeus put them away beneath the earth as the "mortal blessed", and then made a third, bronze, race of men. These were "terrible and fierce" warriors, who slew each other until none was left.

Zeus improved on the men of bronze with a fourth race, the "godly race of heroes", who were the predecessors of modern men. But these "righteous and noble" men were destroyed by "ugly war and fearful fighting" before the seven gates of Thebes or at Troy "on account of lovely-haired Helen". Those who did not perish were granted a blessed life in the islands at the ends of the earth.

Now men suffer in the Age of Iron, and despite some good things "will never cease from toil and misery". But Hesiod warns that men will soon succumb to envy, dishonour, hatred and lawlessness. When this happens Zeus will destroy them as surely as he has destroyed their predecessors.

Greek nobility lies in working the land

Bearded Greek ploughmen painted on an amphora made in c.600BC.

Greece, c.700BC

"Work and let work follow work": this is the key to a decent life of reasonable prosperity, according to Hesiod, a shepherd poet from the agricultural area of central Greece. The advice comes in his poem *Works and Days*, in which he gives a detailed account of the yearly calendar of hard work which should serve as an example to moderately well-off peasant smallholders.

He aims his lesson at his brother Perses in particular. Perses has tried to persuade the ruling *basileis*, or nobles, to give him more than his fair share of the farmland left by their father when he died. Hesiod seeks to prevent him and to convert him from idleness to diligence, spicing his more practical advice with proverbs, allegories and legends, such as the stories of Pandora and the Five Ages of Man.

Of foremost importance are "the clearing of debts and avoidance of famine", which requires application, because "a postponer does not fill his granary". If you do not do this, Hesiod says, you may have to go begging to your neighbours, who will eventually turn you away.

But the prosperous peasant owns a few slaves, or hires labourers, and produces all the food he and his family need, such as wheat, barley, vegetables, fruit and grapes. He keeps sheep for wool, goats for milk and cheese, oxen or mules for pulling and carrying.

Each part of the year has its allotted task: ploughing, sowing, harvesting, threshing and storing grain and straw. The women of the household prepare food, spin flax and wool and weave cloth to make garments. The yearly grind is relieved, however, by numerous festival days when the peasant families can enjoy the fruits of their toil.

Brave new world of Sparta is based on inflexible discipline

Greece, c.700BC

Order has come to the lives of the people of Sparta, a city in the far south of Greece. They have adopted a new constitution aimed at what they call *eunomia*, "good order", and attributed to a great lawgiver called Lykourgos. It has two main principles: equality and strict discipline, organised along military lines. The machinery of the constitution is an odd mixture of monarchy, oligarchy and democracy. There are two kings, who seem to have more military than governmental power. Alongside them are five annually-elected magistrates, and a council of elders whose members are elected for life but must be at least 60 years old. The final say in legislation is had by an assembly of 9,000 citizens or "Equals". However, most of Sparta's inhabitants are not citizens and are excluded from government; they are the freemen and serfs who grow the food for everyone else. Women, as in other Greek states, are excluded from all political power, although their lives are less constrained than in many other places.

The city is run along austere, disciplinarian lines. Commerce and the possession of gold and silver are forbidden and people's clothes do not vary much. Male citizens are brought up as soldiers from the age of seven, live in dormitories and eat together in communal messes, even when they marry.

Women in Sparta are excluded from politics, but the regime demands that they take athletics seriously.

Italy, c.690BC. The Etruscan states are introduced to alphabetical writing by Greek settlers from Euboea. As a result, the Etruscans adopt the Chalcidian (from Euboean Chalcis) version of the Greek alphabet to transcribe their own language onto stone, bronze, wood, papyrus and even gold.

Mesopotamia, c.689BC. Following Assyria's near-defeat in a great battle with the Babylonians and the Elamites (Iranians) on the Tigris, Sennacherib, king of Assyria, takes his revenge by destroying the city of Babylon.

China, c.687BC. A spectacular fall of meteors – part of what are known as the Lyrid showers – has occurred.

Anatolia, c.687BC. Gyges, bodyguard of the Lydian king, Candaules, kills his master and takes his place. Rumour has it that this was the outcome of a plot devised by Candaules' wife at the time of the plot, whom Gyges has now married. The queen wanted revenge on Candaules for allowing Gyges to see her naked.

Judah, c.687BC. Manasseh, aged 12, becomes king of Judah in succession to his father, Hezekiah.

Mesopotamia, c.680BC. Esarhaddon, youngest son of Sennacherib, with the help of his mother, Naqia (Zakutu), is victorious in a dynastic feud and becomes king of Assyria. The feud broke out after the murder of Sennacherib by his own sons in 681BC – in revenge for the late king's destruction of Babylon. Esarhaddon is now putting all his energies into restoring the city.

Greece, c.680BC. Archilochus, who was born on the island of Paros c.705BC, has become well established as a lyric poet. Writing in the Ionian dialect, he composes short elegies and couplets in a sometimes mordant tone. He inveighs against the object of his unrequited love: "Already the beauty of your skin is fading and sad old age is ploughing its furrows in it."

Africa, c.680BC. The smelting and use of iron and the making of pottery are spreading rapidly among farmers around Lake Victoria in East Africa and the Termit massif in south-east Niger. Copper smelting is also becoming popular. Until now copper ore has been melted in open pots.

New temples rise on older sacred sites

The spectacular terrace of lions on the Greek island of Delos.

Greece, c.690BC
In recent years the Greeks have been active in building temples to their gods. The sacred sites chosen for these sanctuaries have generally been used as places of worship by previous inhabitants.

They are usually in the open air, in positions with outstanding natural features related to the particular deity with whom the place is connected. The rustling of the leaves on the sacred oak trees at the oracle of Dodona is ascribed to the greatest of the gods, Zeus, to whom the site is dedicated. Delphi, the greatest of the oracles, is now dedicated to Apollo, although in former times it was the shrine of an earthspirit, as was Olympia, the most important shrine of Zeus.

Most Greek temples are based on the idea of a rectangular room with an entrance at one end, and a porch created by extending the two side walls, between which there are often columns.

The temple is built as the house of the god rather than as a place in which people congregate to worship. Acts of worship normally take place at a separate altar which stands opposite the front of the building; only members of the priesthood and lay officials are allowed into the temple itself. At more famous shrines some cities have built "treasuries" next to temples; these are miniature temples to display the cities' piety and wealth.

Feuding warlords in China recognise ruler

China, c.679BC
Duke Huan of Qin Ch'in, a state on the eastern seaboard, has been recognised as "Ba", or ruler, at a meeting of feudal warlords anxious to bring order to the country which has been in turmoil since around 771BC when the Zhou king was killed and his capital sacked by disaffected vassals and hostile neighbouring peoples.

A prince of the line was rescued by a loyal feudal lord and a new capital was established in the east. However, while the warlords continued to pay ceremonial deference to the Zhou, the dynasty never regained its effective central power.

The result has been that the warlords have fought among themselves and with the non-Chinese people who still occupy some parts of the country. Cities have been destroyed, the countryside ravaged.

Now the powerful Duke Huan, who succeeded to the rule of Qin six years ago, will rule while still owing allegiance to the Zhou dynasty. He has pursued a vigorous policy of building up the military and economic power of his state, encouraging agriculture, developing the sea-salt industry and introducing the first cash economy. Qin is now the most advanced and powerful of the Chinese states.

Greek citizens have voice in city life

Greece, c.690BC
The market places of city-states throughout Greece are ringing with the cries of protesting peasants who are demanding more civil rights. They are primarily angry about being continually unsettled by continual feuding between landowners over boundaries. Indeed, it is the turmoil in the countryside which has given them the opportunity to challenge the city-state governments.

Formerly, only male property owners who worshipped the local patron god or goddess were allowed to attend political meetings and elect officials.

Free public meetings then began in city squares, where slaves, peasants, artisans, traders and even aristocrats all had a chance to speak. The ruling assemblies were made up of aristocrats who had taken over the power of the king.

At the same time, one government officer had to be called king in order to continue ancient religious rites with the gods. Others were made the generals, civil heads, directors of the law and supervisors of state cults.

The city-states, centres of territorial government were built around groups of villages, ideally on a hill for defence reasons.

Hieroglyphs from the Saite dynasty (c.664-c.525BC), when Egypt saw a cultural and economic renaissance.

Carthage thrives as trade expands

Carthage, c.677BC

Within little more than a hundred years of its foundation, Carthage has overtaken Tyre as the leading city of Phoenician civilisation.

In the centuries since Phoenician power first asserted itself, the city-states of the Levantine coast have grown rich, trading in tin, lead, copper, gold, textiles and timber. Of all the states Tyre dominated, and continued to dominate while Assyrian pressure crushed her lesser neighbours. Then the Assyrians turned on Tyre.

Faced with possible annihilation a Phoenician colony led by Elissa, or Dido, a royal princess, left Tyre on an epic voyage to the small Phoenician staging post on the North African coast, situated in the bottleneck between the eastern and western Mediterranean. There the colonists established a settlement on a sandstone peninsula jutting out into the sea. The site formed a natural harbour and was easy to defend. They called it Carthage,

Phoenician art: woman in ivory ...

which means "new capital". Carthage quickly became a self-sufficient community, cutting its ties with Tyre and establishing satellites along the North African and Sicilian coasts, from where it controlled the eastern and western Mediterranean.

It has now become the major trading port of the Mediterranean,

... and man with sacrificial animals.

with gold, slaves, ivory and ostrich feathers coming from across the desert to the south and tin, copper, lead and textiles coming in from across the sea to the north. Its ships, known in every port in the Mediterranean, have sailed beyond the Pillars of Hercules into the Atlantic Ocean, and its merchants cross deserts and mountains.

Swords and ploughshares change Africa

Rock painting from the Sahara depicting a two-wheeled horse chariot.

Egypt, c.678BC

Within a couple of decades of Egypt's defeat by an Assyrian army fighting with iron swords and spears, iron smelting is spreading through Africa, heralding the end of the Stone Age. It has transformed the Egyptian agricultural economy and has brought great wealth to Kush, whose new capital at Meroe is surrounded by iron-ore deposits. Kush has already established the beginnings of an iron industry.

The arrival of iron has revolutionized African agriculture and society. Iron bladed weapons have given new and terrible powers to men, but wrought-iron agricultural implements, plough-shares in particular, have given them the opportunity to clear more scrubland, produce more food, and create wrought iron artifacts.

Curious burial rites practised in Peru

Peru, c.690BC

Dead men's bodies are mutilated and preserved by the Paracas tribe in curious burial rituals on the Southern Pacific coast. Indians on the Paracas Peninsula dig subterranean vaults through desert rock to fill with precious "mummy bundles" of their dead.

The hot dry desert climate helps in the mummification process which involves the removal of the internal organs, after which the body is tied up in a foetal position. Circular holes are gouged out of the top of the skull of the corpse with bone tools.

Bundles of these bodies have been brought from north and south of the peninsula to be buried in the tomb at Paracas Cavernas.

At Paracas Necropolis vaults are filled with a rich assortment of burial offerings: gold ornaments, weapons, pottery and textiles. Long mantles are packed with beautifully embroidered cotton and brightly patterned textiles woven in elaborate designs.

Phalanxes present disciplined front line of the Greeks

Greece, c.675BC

Greece with its city-states has become a nation of citizens' armies. Military service has become compulsory and every Greek is required to take part in the defence of his city. Many cities are now organised so as to produce as large an army as possible. Usually, all men who own a moderate amount of land must equip themselves as heavily-armed footsoldiers called *hoplites*.

The hoplites wear bronze helmets, breastplates and greaves (leg-armour) and are armed with long lances, for stabbing rather than throwing, and short swords. They carry stout, circular shields of wood on their left arms.

The key to the hoplites' success in battle is their formation into compact, highly-disciplined formations called phalanxes. A typical phalanx is deeper than it is wide; the soldiers stick very close together, each protecting himself and the man on his left with shield. The fighting itself is a matter of shoving and pushing with the shield, accompanied by stabbing with the spear or sword.

If the front rank falls it is trampled underfoot as the next rank replaces it, and so on until one side gives way. Death in battle can be particularly nasty. Because of the hoplite's shield, most wounds are either in the neck or genitals.

Suit of armour worn by a hoplite.

Egypt, c.671BC. Esarhaddon, king of Assyria, has invaded Egypt and driven out the pharaoh, Taharqa. This is in retaliation for Taharqa's attempt to restore Egyptian influence in Asia by stirring up revolt among the Assyrian vassal states.

Sahara, c.670BC. North-south trade by two-wheeled horse chariots is thriving in the central Sahara. This activity has been stimulated by the rise of the Phoenician colony of Carthage on the North African coast, as has the production in the Sahara of copper and iron.

Egypt, c.667BC. Thebes has fallen to the Assyrians, who have inflicted great damage on the holy sanctuaries. Not long ago Ashurbanipal, king of Assyria, invaded Egypt with Syrian support to put down a revolt led by the pharaoh, Taharqa – back in Egypt after his ejection in 670BC. After a great battle Taharqa and his followers were forced to take refuge in Thebes. Now the pharaoh is on the run again.

Japan, c.660BC. The legendary prince Jimmu Tenno, who is descended from the solar goddess Amateratsu, ascends the throne of Japan after vanquishing the Yamato kingdom. He is reputed to have been born in Kyushu, which he left c.667BC to conquer eastern Japan.

Anatolia, c.660BC. The king of Assyria, Ashurbanipal, has refused to answer an appeal for help from Gyges, king of Lydia. Lydia is under severe pressure from the Cimmerians, who have already invaded the young kingdom several times. The Assyrian armies, however, are fully occupied in putting down the revolt in Egypt.

Egypt, c.656BC. Psammetichus has driven the Assyrians out of Egypt and restored his country's independence. After an oracle advised him to ally himself with men of bronze who came from the sea, he enlisted the help of Ionian and Carian mercenaries. He has now pursued the Assyrians as far as Ashdod in Palestine.

Anatolia, 652BC. The Cimmerians capture the city of Sardis, capital of Lydia, and kill the king, Gyges. The most notable events of Gyges's reign were his invasions of Miletus, Smyrna and Colophon. More recently he sent troops to help Egypt in its attempt to free itself from Assyrian control.

Athletes compete at Olympic Games

Greece, 648BC

The Olympic Games have seen two outstanding performances in Zeus's sacred grove this year. The formidable Krauxidas of Krannon triumphed in the new sport of pankration, a combination of boxing and all-in wrestling, while Lygdamis from Syracuse won the horse-race.

The Syracusans, who claim that Lygdamis is the equal of Hercules in size and strength, are delighted with his performance and propose to erect a statue in his honour.

The games are a most remarkable institution. Held every four years to the glory of Zeus, they bring together athletes from all the Greek cities. Old animosities are put aside when heralds proclaim the sacred truce for the games and for a time the Greeks, so often bitterly divided, are reconciled by the accomplishments of the athletes.

The athletes must be Greek and must be free men. Visitors from all over the known world flock to see them compete, although married women are barred from the arena.

The games are strictly controlled by the people of Elis who run the festival. The athletes are required to train for ten months, spend the 30 days before the sports in Elis, and swear by the gods that they have not broken their training.

The competitions last for between five and seven days, of which the first is given over to ceremonial with blasts on the trumpet, sacri-

Long-distance runners: foot races form the basis of the Olympic Games.

fices and banquets. Originally the events consisted only of foot races, but over the years since 776BC when the games were instituted, more sports have been added.

The foot races, with the young men running naked, still form the basis of the games, but there are also boxing and wrestling, the pentathlon, the race in armour and the various horse and chariot races.

The "Olympionicae", the winners, are rewarded on the last day of the games with simple olive wreaths but when they go home they are feted as heroes, the equals of warriors, and are awarded valuable gifts and privileges.

The boxers wear himantes, gloves made of ox-hide bindings laced around their hands. They are not confined to rounds or rings.

Oriental influences begin to give Greek jewellery a new look

Necklace strung with a row of gold plaques showing the goddess Artemis.

Greece, c.650BC

Contact with the Near East and further afield has been a feature of Greek life for probably at least 150 years, especially with the development of commerce and colonial expansion by various city-states. Oriental influence has clearly rubbed off on the jewellery and other artefacts now being made in Corinth, Rhodes and other places with well-established connections with the Levant. Eastern decorative motifs are common, including friezes of animals such as lions, tigers and ibexes, and mythical beasts such as sphinxes and griffins. For the first time since the age of Mycenae floral patterns also appear in Greek art.

Mediterranean lands colonised by Greeks

Greece, c.650BC

Greek expeditions are setting sail to all parts of the known world to set up colonies, some cities founding as many as four or five colonies in one generation. The settlers, young men of fighting age, set out in bands of up to 200 under the command of an "oikistes", or founder, to a place chosen by the elders of their city.

Corinth, for example, established Syracuse in Sicily; other colonies have been founded in southern Italy, North Africa and on the shores of the Black Sea. These colonies are essentially agrarian, the land being allotted equally among the settlers.

Sometimes they are welcomed by the original inhabitants, who give them grants of land, but in other cases they have to fight their way ashore and if they are successful they use the conquered natives as slave labourers in the fields.

Once established, the new colony becomes completely independent of its metropolis or mother city. The settlers retain close links with their old homes, taking with them their traditional institutions and even carrying their gods with them in the form of wooden statuettes.

This amazing movement, which is spreading Greek civilisation to all parts of the Mediterranean world, began with social pressures, quar-

Greek in style, but made locally in Metapontium, a Greek colony.

rels over the distribution of land and the fear of starvation.

There is, however, another form of Greek colonisation – trade, which is marching hand in hand with the agricultural settlements. These commercial settlements, or "emporia", usually owe their existence not to a mother city, but to groups of businessmen who see an opportunity for profitable trade.

One such "emporion" has been set up at Naukratis in Egypt. It is strictly a commercial enterprise and, although the pharaoh allows the Greeks to worship their own gods, he does not allow mixed marriages and maintains strict control over their activities.

Delphic oracle guides Aegean explorers

Greece, c.650BC

The most revered oracle in Greece foretells the future in the temple of Apollo at Delphi. There, every month, ordinary people and delegates from the cities come to ask the advice of the god as he speaks by way of the Pythia, a peasant woman chosen for her purity.

The applicant, always a man, must follow a precise ritual. First he must make an offering, in money or in kind. City spokesmen pay more than private individuals, but they are ushered to the head of the queue. Then he makes a sacrifice, usually a goat, which is examined by the priests, and if the portents are good he is allowed to enter the temple.

There the Pythia, carefully purified, sits on a bronze tripod awaiting his question. Some say she is in a state of trance brought on by chewing bay leaves; others insist that her tripod is placed over a fissure in the rock which gives off trance-inducing fumes. She listens to the question and then makes a series of strange utterances which are interpreted and transcribed in verse by her attendant priests.

However, even after the priests have made their interpretation the Pythia's utterances can be read in many different ways, and often the wrong conclusion is drawn, with

A suppliant pouring a liberation to the oracle in the temple at Delphi.

disastrous results. The questions that are asked cover many subjects. Cities will ask if they should go to war or make peace. Individuals want to know if they should make voyages or should marry.

One of the oracle's most important tasks is to advise cities where to set up colonies. There is a practical aspect to these consultations as well as the religious function, for the priests keep copies of all the Pythia's utterances, and much general information is filed in the temple's library, thus enabling them to make a rational judgement.

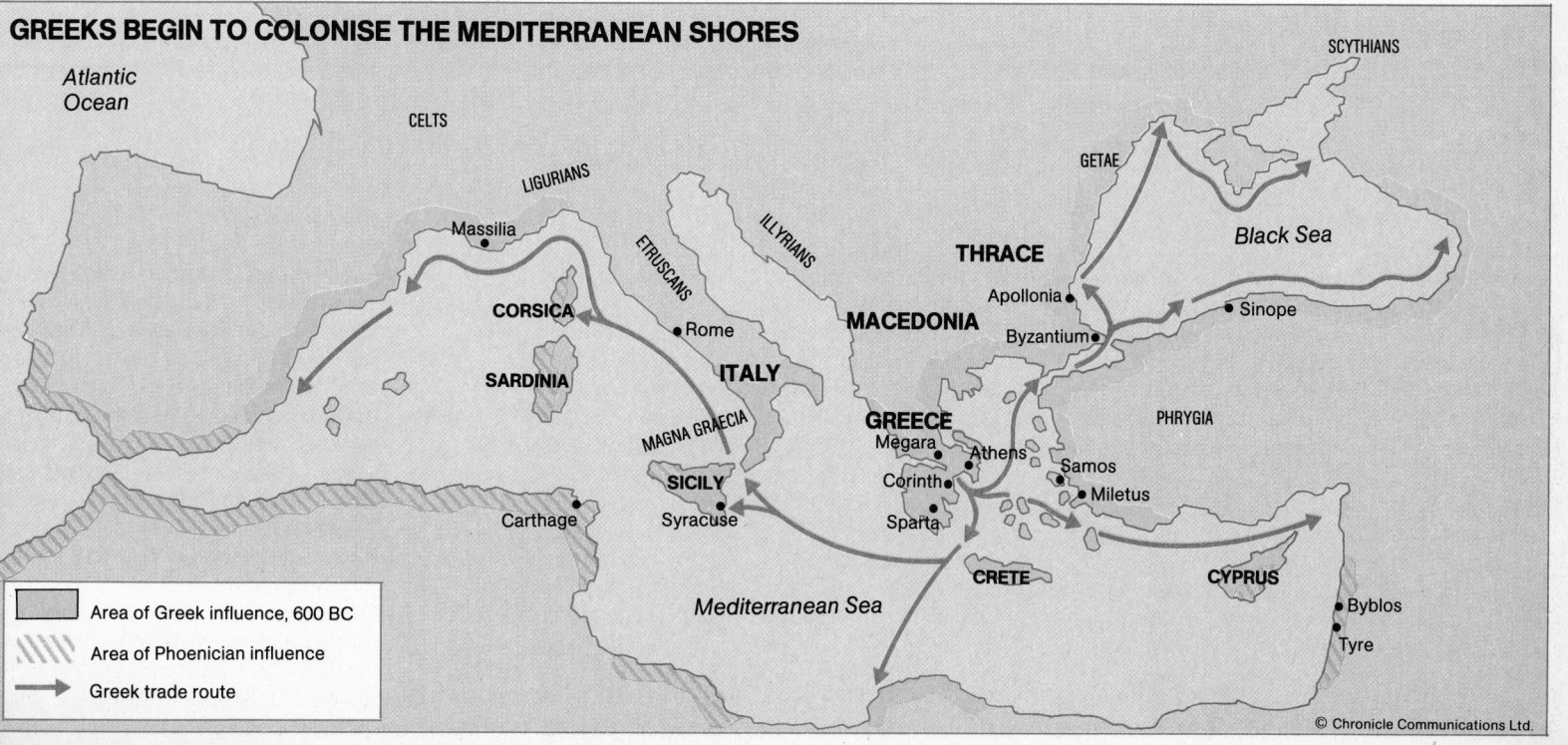

GREEKS BEGIN TO COLONISE THE MEDITERRANEAN SHORES

Atlantic Ocean

CELTS

SCYTHIANS

LIGURIANS

Massilia

ETRUSCANS

ILLYRIANS

GETAE

Black Sea

THRACE

CORSICA

Rome

MACEDONIA

Apollonia

Sinope

Byzantium

SARDINIA

ITALY

MAGNA GRAECIA

GREECE

PHRYGIA

Megara

Athens

Samos

SICILY

Corinth

Miletus

Carthage

Syracuse

Sparta

CRETE

CYPRUS

Byblos

Mediterranean Sea

Tyre

Area of Greek influence, 600 BC

Area of Phoenician influence

Greek trade route

© Chronicle Communications Ltd.

Unravelling Egypt's past

The ancient Egyptians did not know the concept of written history and, indeed, their world outlook and attitudes were not compatible with such an approach to the past, present or future. The start of the reign of each new king was regarded as a re-enactment of the mythical beginnings of the world, with chaos being replaced by the traditional order (maet), and resulting in a return to static normality of which the new king now became the champion and protector.

This view was officially affirmed in elaborate rituals enacted at the coronation and jubilee festivals, but it did not encourage observation, recording and interpretation of events over a longer period of time or attempts at seeing them as elements of a larger pattern. Events recorded in writing on stelae, or shown in scenes on the walls of temples (such as victories over external enemies), had another purpose: they proclaimed the king's success in maintaining the desired state of affairs. The presence of these texts and representations in temples was to ensure that the gods continued to be favourably disposed towards the ruler and his reign. These may be valuable historical materials, but their aim was not to record history. Some of the most significant developments were disregarded completely.

Constructing a chronology

The chronological framework of the history of ancient Egypt is now known in considerable detail and can be used as a yardstick for establishing fixed points of chronological systems of other areas of the ancient Near East. It also provides a sufficiently long and precise calibrating scale for modern scientific dating techniques. Much of Egyptian history and chronology has been constructed in a painstaking way by combining information of varying kinds. In the early stages of the study of ancient Egypt the dynastic framework of Egyptian chronology derived nearly exclusively from Manetho, a priest living in Ptolemaic Egypt of the 3rd century BC. Inspired by non-Egyptian tradition, Manetho compiled the first history of Egypt, written in Greek, but based on ancient Egyptian sources, most of which we now can verify and thus check his historical accuracy.

Our knowledge of Egyptian relative chronology, i.e. the order of kings, is greatly helped by records which list successive rulers or give details of their reigns. The most informative, but unfortunately very incomplete, are the "annals" engraved on the so-called Palermo Stone (the name derives from its present location) and associated fragments. Here

selected events of each regional year are described (the emphasis is on religious occasions) and accompanied by a note recording the height of the Nile measured at an unspecified point. Egyptian thinking was not historical, but practicalities of a complex society required such lists for administrative and religious purposes. The surviving fragments of these "annals" refer to the earliest periods of Egyptian history, the first 600 years of the 3rd millenium BC, but the monument itself probably is a much later copy. The other examples of regularly kept records, the war journals of the military expeditions of Thutmosis III and Rameses II into Syria, are of a different nature, but were also created for practical purposes.

King-lists show sense of past

An abstract of a document similar to the "Palermo Stone" annals is preserved on a Ramesside papyrus in Turin known as the "Turin Canon". It starts with the mythical rules of gods and demigods, but then it covers the period from the beginning of the 1st Dynasty (c. 2950BC) to the end of the 17th Dynasty (c.1550BC) and systematically lists the names of kings and the lengths of their reigns. By arranging the rulers in groups, albeit mainly geographical, and providing them with chronological summaries, the list betrays awareness of continuity and thus displays its compiler's rudimentary historical sense. Even less detailed are the king-lists known from the temple of Thutmosis III at Karnak, the temples of Sethos I and Rameses II at Abydos, and a tomb of an official of the reign of Rameses II at Saqqara. These are extensive selections of royal names made for a specific purpose and this, to some extent, affects the degree to which they can be relied on. Nevertheless, all these records show that the Egyptians were conscious of their past and at least some of them were reliably informed of its main features. A popular reflection of this feeling can be detected in literary works inspired by folk stories.

Important information on royal succession can be gleaned from biographical texts inscribed in the tombs of ancient Egyptian officials whose careers spanned the reigns of two or more kings. Their accounts supply details of historical events unknown from other sources. Such inscriptions and other similarly explicit texts are, however, rare. For some periods we are helped by the existence of joint rules during which some monuments bearing royal names have also been used to clarify problems. Some questions still remain unanswered, but on the whole the order of the more important Egyptian

kings is now established. The main exceptions are the three prolonged "intermediate periods" of political instability during which large numbers of rulers reigned for short periods and left few monuments.

Clues from calendars and cows

The task of establishing Egyptian absolute chronology, ie the dating of events in years BC, is facilitated by the use of a "civil calendar" (as opposed to one based on purely astronomical observations) throughout almost all Egyptian historic periods. A year consisted of 365 days, and the difference of about 1/4 day between this and the true astronomical year caused the two to get more and more out of step every year. The Egyptians did not date events in the form of a continuous numerical series of years. At first they described each year by its chief characteristics, and later they used the biennial property assessment (mainly a cattle-count) for the same purpose. From about 2200BC they dated by numbering the regnal years of individual kings. This, however, means that without knowing the precise length of each reign the chronological sequence becomes quite uncertain. Fortunately, the imperfection of the Egyptian artificial calendar is the modern historian's boon. The correspondence between the Egyptian "civil calendar" and our dating system was noted in the Roman period. The date of an astronomical observation recorded by regnal years of a king and the days and months of the "civil calendar" can be compared with a date calculated in years BC and thus provide a fixed point around which the absolute chronology can be built. Such an event is the pre-dawn rising of the Sothis star (Sirius) which heralded an annual inundation. Two notes to this effect provide the backbone of Egyptian absolute chronology: one from the 7th year of Sesostris III, the other from the 9th year of Amenhotep I. Other, though less helpful, observations are those of the phases of the moon.

Among modern scientific methods radiocarbon dating makes the greatest contribution to the chronology of the predynastic period and the early stages of Egyptian history, but has had little impact on the more recent periods. Synchronisms with other countries are most significant for Egyptian history during the 1st millennium BC.

The precision of Egyptian absolute chronology declines the further back one looks. The error may be as much as 200 years for the reigns of the early kings; from the mid-7th century BC the chronology may be regarded as certain.

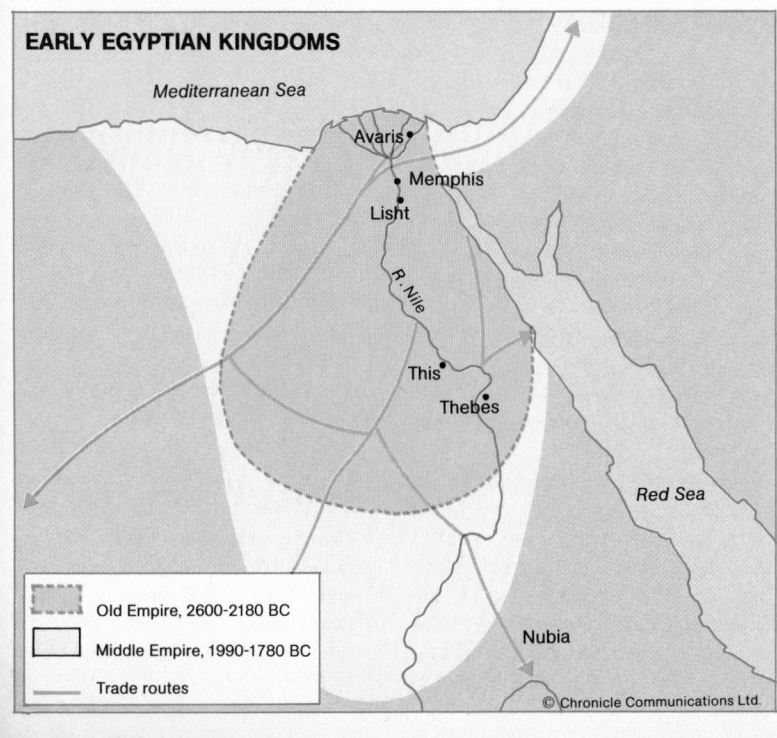

EARLY EGYPTIAN KINGDOMS

Mediterranean Sea

Avaris

Memphis

Lisht

R. Nile

This

Thebes

Red Sea

Nubia

▨▨ Old Empire, 2600-2180 BC

☐ Middle Empire, 1990-1780 BC

── Trade routes

© Chronicle Communications Ltd.

One of the most important lists of Egyptian Kings can be seen in the picture above which shows King Seti I in his memorial temple at Abydos. He is wearing the Blue Crown, on the front of which is the cobra, or Royal Uraeus, for protection. He is wearing a short kilt (shendyp) which is a sign of kingship, over a faintly drawn, longer skirt and is holding an arm-shaped censer in his left hand. In front of him walks his son Prince Ramesses (the future Ramesses II who was to be the great builder) with a papyrus scroll open in front of him, from which he is reciting. A lock of hair falls over the prince's right shoulder – a characteristic of royal princes – and he is wearing a long pleated kilt.

The contents of the papyrus are displayed in the hieroglyphics above their heads which record offerings, of bread, cake or fruit, which Seti has made to his ancestors – the past

kings of upper and lower Egypt. The fact that the prince is reciting is important as that in itself magically delivers the offerings to the kings.

The names of the kings themselves are written in the top two rows of hieroglyphics in front of the royal pair; each king has two of his several names enclosed by the oval frames, or cartouche, probably as a word play on the phrase "to encircle" refering to the Egyptian king's sovereignty over the world. The symbols above the frames mean "this is for" while the third row contains the alternative names of Seti himself – the person who has been doing the offering.

The names of the kings are chronologically placed starting with the legendary Menes at the left end of the top row and lists 76 kings in all. It was not intended as a historical record but was copied and partly edited from a reliable document.

Pharaohs rekindle echoes of golden age

A glazed clay model of a sow with piglets, sacred to the sky-goddess Nut.

Egypt, c.640BC

Egypt's pharaohs are seeking to emulate the country's past glories as the country becomes unified once more under a central administration. This is based in Memphis, although the kings live (and will be buried) at Sais (*Sa-el-Hagar*) in the western Delta.

The nature of this renaissance can be seen in religious worship in particular. The texts in pyramids built in the golden age of Egypt are being copied and inscribed on the walls of tombs and sarcophagi. Private statuary, too, is heavily influenced by the past, with poses and costumes more reminiscent of earlier kingdoms. No longer is mainly soft, perishable limestone used, however. The favoured stones are hard and polished – basalt, serpentine or breccia marble. The basalt relief often derives its inspiration from the scenes in early tombs. Administrative titles which were common in earlier periods of Egyptian history are used once again. Egypt thrives under these new rulers, with the country's resources more fully exploited, trade developing – especially with the Aegean world – and agriculture flourishing.

Eastern tastes reshape Corinthian art

A jug depicting lions, from Rhodes.

Greece, c.640BC

Ties between Greece and the Near East have grown remarkably in the last century, and some of this close contact with the Orient has rubbed off on the current style of Greek art. The geometric patterns of earlier pottery, for instance, are giving way in Corinth and other cities to motifs and patterns borrowed from the ceramic art of the east, bringing a new vitality to decorated vases.

Animals are especially common in the new style, in particular ibexes, panthers, lions (the Corinthians have adopted the Assyrian design of a square-headed lion with lolling tongue and heart-shaped ears) and fantastic beasts such as griffins and sphinxes.

The geometric style had incorporated animals at times, but never floral designs, which are making their appearance in Greek decoration for the first time since the Mycenaean age. Assyrian-style lotuses are most common, but one can also find palms, buds and pine cones.

Book of Songs put together in China

China c.630BC

A remarkable selection of ancient poems has been collected into one volume, the *Shi jing* or *Book of Songs*. Some of the most archaic verses are said to be from the sacrificial hymns used in the ancestral temples of the Shang dynasty over five hundred years ago. Those in more modern style range from court love poetry to peasant folk-songs.

The book is essential reading for the educated Chinese, particularly for those involved in political life. Quotations from the verses have become common currency in the complicated political world of the feudal states into which China is divided. To someone without the required education in poetry a tense diplomatic confrontation involving the fate of whole states might seem no more than a desultory swapping of literary quotations.

Dynastic hymns describe elaborate ceremonies in the temples of the royal clan. Folk songs record peasant festivals "In the tenth month they clear the stackgrounds. With twin pitchers they hold the village feast, killing for it a young lamb."

There are complaints from soldiers at the front, and amorous songs for the spring match-making games: "Plop go the plums; but there are still seven. Let the boys who want to court me come before it is too late."

Bronze ornaments and animal bones – the remains of joints of meat – have been hoarded in the hollowed-out trunk of an alder tree as part of a sacrificial well in Moen, Denmark.

Triumphant Assyrians are more secure than ever

King Ashurbanipal feasts with his queen in this relief from Nineveh.

Nineveh, Assyria, 640BC

The streets of Nineveh were treated to a symbolic and ruthless display of imperial power today as three captured Elamite princes and a former king of Arabia were shackled like cart-horses to King Ashurbanipal's chariot and made to pull him around the capital.

The parade, celebrating the sacking of Susa, the Elamite capital, follows news that an Assyrian force controlling the northern front in Anatolia has routed the Cimmerian chieftain Lygdamis' army, which had burnt down Ephesus.

These victories for King Ashurbanipal, coupled with the solution of the long-term Babylonian problem, mean that Assyria's 1,200-mile northern and eastern frontiers are more secure than ever. Ashurbanipal, now in his 28th year on the throne, claims to be Assyria's most powerful emperor yet.

Nineveh is certainly the richest city in the world and is overflowing with treasure, including booty taken from Memphis, Thebes and Susa during the Egyptian and Elamite wars, tributes from the vassal princes of Judah, Phoenicia and Lydia, and gifts from the princes of Media and Persia who have recently pledged their allegiance. However, some believe that the empire is overstretched and the army exhausted, and that Assyria's use of force rather than assent is only just keeping the lid on a cauldron of dissent that could become rebellion.

Internal splits undermine Elamite revolt

Nineveh, Assyria, c.645BC

The head of Tempt-humbanin-shushinak was hung in the royal garden of King Ashurbanipal as a warning to the princes of Elam not to take on the Assyrian empire.

The death of Tempt-humbanin-shushinak at the battle of Tulliz on the Kerkha river brings to an end one of the few periods in Elamite history when this uneasy coalition of small principalities has been ruled by one man. Assyria plans to split Elam into two subject territories to be ruled by the sons of Urtaki, Humbanigash and Tammaritu, who fled to Nineveh seven years ago when the throne was seized by Tempt-humbanin-shushinak. It was the Elamites' attempts to have them extradited and Ashurbanipal's refusal which led to Elam declaring war on Assyria. Assyria's strategy has long been based on the

Another city falls to Ashurbanipal.

notion of a divided Elam, too absorbed in its own dynastic squabbles to coordinate attacks against Assyria.

It engineered many of Elam's palace plots, with rival factions tearing each other to pieces as they fought for the throne.

Fratricidal war rages for Assyrian throne

Babylon, 648BC

The rebel Assyrian prince Shamash-shuma-ukin committed suicide in the viceroy's palace today after ordering his men to set fire to it as Assyrian forces, led by his brother King Ashurbanipal, made their final assault on the capital.

Shamash-shuma-ukin's death ends four years of warfare between the two brothers and leaves the multi-national cast of conspirators who had hoped to overthrow

Ashurbanipal without a leader.

The grandiose scope of the plot Shamash-shuma-ukin devised was in keeping with a man born second-in-line to the Assyrian throne. It relied on a huge coalition of anti-Assyrian interests – Phoenicians, Philistines, Judaeans, Arabs, Chaldeans, Elamites, Lydians and Egyptians along with the Babylonians – to mount a concerted and simultaneous attack against Assyria. Had it succeeded, the empire would certainly have been vanquished.

Only the plot's discovery four years ago prevented it being implemented. Few suspected that Shamash-shuma-ukin, who had appeared content to serve as his brother's viceroy in Babylon for 17 years, was prepared to rebel.

One theory is that he had become infected by Babylonian nationalism, believing that Babylon should be the seat of world power rather than Nineveh. Court insiders point out that Shamash-shuma-ukin's father was well aware of his son's Babylonian leanings when he ignored his claims, preferring the third-in-line Ashurbanipal to succeed him as king of Assyria.

Royal bones scattered in desert as 3,000 years of feuding end

Susa, Elam, 639BC

Assyrian forces under King Ashurbanipal are carrying out a scorched-earth policy against the Elamites following the capture of Susa, Elam's capital and home of its gods.

The Assyrians appear determined to wipe their sworn enemy off the face of the earth and finally end the 3,000-year feud between the two peoples.

It is in marked contrast to the situation eleven years ago when the Assyrians restored their own client king, Tammaritu, as ruler of Elam.

Now, in Susa, the enamelled brick temple has been destroyed and the statues of all of Elam's gods have been removed to Assyria, where they are powerless. The graves of generations of Elamite kings have been destroyed and their bones strewn across the desert.

Those Elamites who survived the massacres are being deported to Assyria, while the Assyrian army carries out a defoliation programme in Elam, scattering salt so that it will be desert for years to come.

Elamite troops grovel in defeat.

Anatolia, c.630BC. The Greeks are busy setting up colonies and trading posts along the shores of the Black Sea, the Bosporus and the Propontis (Sea of Marmara), at places such as Byzantium, Sinope, Olbia and Amisus.

Syria, c.630BC. The Scythians enter Syria and cross the country, reaching the Egyptian border with minimal resistance from the Assyrian armies.

Syria, c.630BC. An important library has been established at Sultan Tepe, near Harran. In addition to medical and divinatory texts, it includes editions of the great epic and mythological works such as the *Epic of Gilgamesh*, the *Tale of the Righteous Sufferer* and the *Myth of the Descent of Nergal into Hell*.

Egypt, c.630BC. The king of Egypt, Psammetichus, wards off a threatened Scythian invasion by means of bribes. After his successful attempt, with the help of the Lydians, to expel the Assyrians from Egypt in 655BC, Psammetichus founded a capital at Sais, in the Nile delta region, and reunited his country. He has also encouraged an influx of Greeks into Egypt.

Assyria, 629BC. King Ashurbanipal dies in obscure circumstances in his palace at Nineveh.

Judah, c.628BC. The prophet Jeremiah receives the word of Yahweh (God) and begins his ministry.

Babylon, 626BC. A Babylonian governor called Nabopolassar, the leader of an insurrection against Assyrian domination, enters Babylon, where he is crowned king. With this event, which follows a year of guerrilla war, the old dream of the Semitic people known as the Chaldeans to ascend the throne of Babylon is at last realised.

Greece, c.620BC. Alcaeus, who was born on Lesbos, is gaining a reputation as a lyric poet. His work includes religious hymns, in which he sings of Athena, Apollo, Hermes and Aphrodite. As with other poets of his generation, however, his own feelings and experiences are also a fertile source of inspiration. He recalls, for example, an encounter with the Athenians in which he had to throw away his shield in order to make a quick escape. Alcaeus also sings of the pleasures of love and honey-scented wine.

Scholar king bequeathes priceless library

Nineveh, Assyria, 629BC

King Ashurbanipal, who ruled Assyria for 39 years, is being mourned as both a warrior and a scholar. A priceless library containing over 25,000 works of literature has been discovered among his possessions. Many of the works are rare, the result of painstaking searches ordered by Ashurbanipal throughout Mesopotamia.

Ashurbanipal's love affair with literature began in childhood. Born the third son of the emperor Esarhaddon, he was originally destined for the priesthood and his education involved learning to read and write. The premature death of his eldest brother, and his surviving brother's appointment as viceroy of Babylon, changed Ashurbanipal's destiny. As a warrior king he was innovative, directing strategy from

The late king on a lion hunt.

his palace and leaving his generals in the field to take care of tactics. Scholars believe his library is a national treasure that will allow future generations to learn of the legends and gods of his time.

Scythian troops reach Egyptian borders

A golden panther from a shield or breastplate, in typical Scythian style.

Syria, c.630BC

Smooth talking and a huge bribe in gold by Psammetichus, the king of Egypt, have saved his country from domination by the Scythians, the nomadic people from central Asia, who have swept through Syria crushing all opposition. They move swiftly, riding on horseback and using their bows and arrows from the saddle.

The Scythians have also made successful raids into Assyria and Palestine, and their advance guard had reached the Egyptian border. With his country in imminent danger of invasion, the Egyptian king

went out to meet them in Palestine and bought them off.

The Assyrians have not been so lucky. King Ashurbanipal made an alliance with the Scythian chief, Madyes, but this has not prevented successful raids into Assyrian territory. Despite their riches and sophisticated system of government, the Assyrians have not been able to hold back the Scythians.

The Scythians are no respecters of property. They live in tents themselves and move wholesale into settled territory, plundering villages and terrorising the local inhabitants.

Judaean king bans all pagan priests

Jerusalem, 621BC

In a move that overturns nearly 60 years of pagan worship in Judah, King Josiah has launched a programme of wholesale religious reforms aimed at returning the country to the worship of a single god: Yahweh.

These reforms follow the discovery in the Temple of a "Book of the Covenant". This book, allegedly the words of Yahweh himself, attacks the Judaeans for their worship of idols and threatens national disaster if true religion is not restored. The king's first steps have been to read the Book to the assembled population and to make a public vow promising to obey Yahweh and pledging Judah to follow all the god's commandments.

He has purified the Temple, destroying everything in it that was related to pagan gods. All the pagan holy places which have grown up around the country have been suppressed: temples have been desecrated, idols destroyed and priests stripped of their religious authority.

It is now illegal to practise divination – prophesying the future on the basis of various signs – and the old festival of Passover, celebrating the exodus of the Israelites from captivity in Egypt, has been restored to its full importance.

A Greek model of a woman in the throes of childbirth; another figure holds the mother firmly from behind as the child is born.

Greeks love (and hate) their tyrant rulers

Greece, c.630BC

A new type of ruler has appeared in the Greek city-states. He is the tyrant, usually an aristocrat, who seizes power in a period of crisis. The first of these tyrants emerged in 655BC at Corinth on mainland Greece, where Cypselus took over the government. Then Theagenes became the ruler of Megara in 640BC, and ten years later supported an unsuccessful coup by his son-in-law Cylon at Athens.

The curious thing about tyrants is that they all seem to follow the same pattern. Anarchy is their breeding ground; they are nurtured on discontent. The tyrant seizes power with the support of a faction of the quarrelling aristocracy or the poor and dispossessed, or sometimes with the sword-power of a band of foreign mercenaries.

His immediate task is to solve the particular crisis which brought him to power and, once he has got rid of his immediate opposition, he usually has the people's support while he does so. He is, in fact, often a popular figure.

As he strives to re-establish order and stability he is likely to institute radical measures, in-

Pittakos, philosopher and tyrant.

volving the redistribution of land. He will set economic and social measures in motion with large-scale building projects, and will often look abroad to increase his city's international prestige.

He will also promote the arts and popular religious cults. Some tyrants even pass on their rule to their sons, but their rule rarely extends beyond one generation because Greeks are freedom-loving people and tyrants grow burdensome to them once their task has been completed. So they are overthrown and the political round resumes.

Corinthian tyrant needs no bodyguard

Greece, c.630BC

The rule of the tyrant Cypselus at Corinth is already becoming enshrined in myth. His mother, Labda, was a member of the ruling family, the Bacchiads, who kept power within the family by intermarrying. But Labda was lame and was spurned by her kinsmen, so she married Aetion, a non-Bacchiad.

Her family, says the myth, took no notice of this until she became pregnant and the Delphic oracle told Aetion that "Labda will bear a rock which will roll down upon those who rule alone and will set Corinth to rights".

The Bacchiads were enraged by this prophecy, and when Cypselus was born they sent men to the village of Petra where Aetion lived to kill the baby.

Their plan was to ask Labda if one of them could hold the child out of affection for its father, and then whoever was given the baby would dash him to the floor.

Chance saved him for, as Labda handed him over, the baby enchanted his would-be killer with his smile and he was returned safely. Then, when a second attempt was made, Labda hid her

A decorated vase made in Corinth.

son in a chest and he was saved. It is said that Labda named him Cypselus after the word meaning chest.

The Bacchiads were right to fear him. When he grew to manhood the Delphic oracle hailed him as king of Corinth and, armed with this prophecy and the support of the army, he overthrew his kinsmen, who had become increasingly unpopular, and made himself master of Corinth.

His rule so far has been mild towards the ordinary people. He is popular and it is written of him that he walks without a bodyguard, which indicates that he still enjoys the support of the soldiers.

However, he has been ruthless towards the Bacchiads, killing many of his relations, exiling others, and stripping them of their property. He is making sure that they will never again return to power. He is now at the height of his power and prosperity; it is of such stuff that myths are made in a nation that thrives on them.

The "black blood of the Greeks" flows as social divisions grow

An Athenian smith at his furnace.

A girl prepares for her wedding.

Greece, c.627BC

Homer has described it as the "black blood of the Greeks"; and now it is flowing in abundance. There is turmoil everywhere in Greece, but especially in the countryside. No one is secure in this country, from the plains of Boeotia to the hills of Attica.

The poor have to look for protection to the ever-quarrelling aris-

tocrats, and these powerful nobles exact a heavy price for their uncertain help. These "eaters of gifts" demand ever greater shares of the poor man's harvest and he slides deeper and deeper into debt.

He mortgages himself; and when he cannot pay he is forfeit to the great estates and the freeman becomes a serf. Like the helots of Sparta and the hectemores of

Athens, the serfs are Greeks who have lost their status. The helots are sometimes treated as quarry by young Spartan warriors who ambush them at night and kill them to prove their manhood.

In the Athenian countryside there is a growing reluctance by former soldiers turned farmers to pay the customary one-sixth tirbute demanded by landowners. These independent-minded men regard the tribute as degrading.

The discontent in the country is spilling into the cities and leading to political instability with the *stasis*, or rupture, of the civic community. This situation is made worse by the rivalry between the various aristocratic factions.

The people are beginning to demand political equality and a fairer distribution of the land. The old certainties are being questioned, with the *demos*, the people, challenging the powers of the old ruling factions.

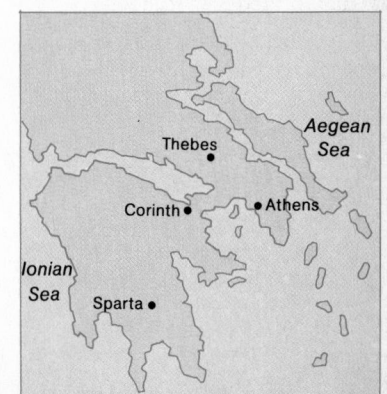

Greeks reach gods via animal sacrifices

Greeks stand before an altar with animals to be sacrificed solemnly.

Greece, c.600BC
Animal sacrifice is an important part of daily life, both as a tribute to the gods and as a source of food. No important political decision or military initiative is taken without first conducting a sacrifice.

The ritual slaughter of domestic animals – goats, sheep or oxen – is also the principal way of preparing meat for eating. Every butcher conducts sacrifices.

The precise form of the sacrifice will depend on the animal, the god or gods addressed, and the occasion. A common feature, however, is that the animal victim should be festively prepared, groomed, perhaps even have its horns gilded, and be led with apparent willingness to the altar.

The place of slaughter is marked out by carrying round a sacred basket and sprinkling water over both victim and participants. Barley grain is thrown at the animal to secure its acquiescence. A priest cuts a few hairs from its head. Then the head is pulled back to point towards the sky, and the throat is cut. The silence is broken by women screaming.

The animal is immediately skinned and butchered. The heart, lungs, liver and kidneys are removed, skewered and roasted, before being tasted by every participant. The tail, gall-bladder and thighbones are burnt on the god's altar. The prime lean cuts are roasted, distributed and eaten. Finally, the remains are boiled and made into sausages or puddings for the less favoured.

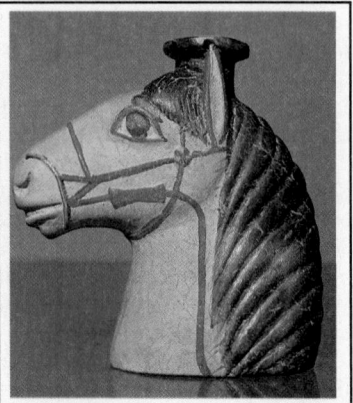

This elegantly-crafted model of a horse's head is a scent bottle, made on the Greek island of Rhodes, a leading trade centre.

Scribes write Greek laws in stone

Greece, c.620BC
A new figure is beginning to appear in Athens and other developing city-states of Greece. He can be seen regularly engraving the new laws on stone pillars or columns in public places. Some of these scribes, as they are called, are craftsmen hired for the job who travel from place to place. Others are resident officials.

They are all skilled in alphabetic writing and are responsible for publishing official decrees, lists of magistrates, religious instructions and commemorative notices affecting the daily lives of citizens. The texts, picked out in red and blue lettering to attract attention, appear in the busiest parts of the cities, in front of public buildings and in the *agoras*, or city forum.

So the art of writing, no longer a privilege of royal archivists and similar experts, is now being used to tell the people of laws that are the same for all.

A section of a Doric law code.

Athenians welcome Draco's written laws

Athens, 621BC
The man of the year in Athens is the *archon*, or magistrate, Dracon, who has devised the first written code of laws for the people. After the attempted coup by the ambitious young aristocrat Cylon, and the subsequent upheavals, there was a need for firm rules, widely understood and generally accepted.

Dracon, a deeply religious man, has set out a new legal concept that makes a clear distinction between manslaughter and premeditated murder. For murder there is a scale of penalties that even takes into account the weapons used. Other crimes, from assault and battery, robbery and theft, on to personal insults and sacrilege, are all identified and allocated appropriate penalties, which include fines that vary according to the importance of the victim, as well as imprisonment, enslavement and execution.

Some people have criticised these Draconian laws as too severe, but they have given Athenians a set of rules applicable to all. They should bring to an end the settling of differences by blood feuds and acts of personal revenge.

Assyrian empire has been destroyed

Nineveh, Assyria, 609BC

The once-mighty Assyrian empire which dominated the Eastern world for 200 years is no more. The last remnants of its army, many of them Egyptian conscripts, lie dead outside the gates of Nineveh after King Ashur-uballit's desperate last-ditch attempt to regain his capital failed. The king, the last of the house of Sargon, is believed to have died on the battlefield.

Without Nineveh, Ashur-uballit had little chance of restoring his throne. He is thought to have been encouraged by a number of minor victories after he rallied his forces at Harran, west of the capital, following the fall of Nineveh to Median forces in 612BC after two years of bitter house-to-house fighting.

For the Medians and their Babylonian allies this latest battle represented a mopping-up operation. The high point for the Medes had been the storming of Nineveh's temple of Ashur, where Median soldiers smashed into tiny pieces the tablet containing the oath of

The fall of Nineveh, as imagined by the painter John Martin (1789-1854).

allegiance which the Median people have been forced to swear to the Assyrians for the past 70 years.

The decline in Assyrian fortunes goes back to the death of the last great emperor, Ashurbanipal, 20 years ago. His two sons who succeeded him both proved ineffective while in neighbouring Babylon the arrival of a strong ruler, Nabopolassar, altered the balance of power in the region. His move against the city of Nineveh in 616BC failed, but his alliance with the Medians, led by Cyaxares, ultimately sealed the fate of Assyria.

Key Egyptian town falls to advancing Babylonian troops

Carchemish, Syria, 605BC

Babylonian troops led by Crown Prince Nebuchadrezzar have crossed the Euphrates and captured the strategically important town of Carchemish from the Egyptians, putting the two-year-old Syrian war on a new footing. During the battle for Carchemish the Egyptian garrison, reinforced by Greek mercenaries, put up a strong fight, but was overrun. Defenders who escaped were massacred in the desert.

The victory at Carchemish by Nebuchadrezzar, who has recently begun to share the reins of power with his ageing warrior father

Finely-clad Babylonian archers.

Nabopolassar, is a breakthrough for the Babylonians who have tried several times to create a bridgehead across the Euphrates into Syria-Palestine to re-open their traditional trade routes to the Mediterranean.

Despite taking control of the old Assyrian empire four years ago, the Babylonians have shown little interest in occupying or redeveloping vast tracts of Assyria. Their allies in the overthrow of Assyria, the Medes, have been contained by a pact giving them the land east of the Zagros mountains. Most of Babylon's efforts instead have been concentrated on ousting the Egyptians from Syria-Palestine, which the Egyptians occupied in 609BC in a belated attempt to help their Assyrian allies.

Nebuchadrezzar II makes Babylon a flourishing artistic centre

An impression of the Hanging Gardens by a French engraver in 1886.

Babylon, c.605BC

Babylon is being turned into the greatest city in the world by its new king, Nebuchadrezzar II. Since ascending the throne to succeed his late father Nabopolassar, who re-established Babylonian independence 20 years ago, the young king has thrown himself into turning the city into the most imaginative masterpiece in the world.

Much of the work surpasses the glory of the old city, destroyed 80 years ago. The centrepiece of the city is the Hanging Gardens, only accessible via the royal apartments and regarded as one of the wonders of the world. Filled with luxuriant vegetation, including many exotic plants, these artificially irrigated terraced roof gardens offer a stark contrast to the desolation of the surrounding countryside.

The new Babylon contains more than 50 temples dedicated to the gods. The most striking is the Tower of Babel dedicated to the god Marduk. It has seven storeys and is built in the form of a step-pyramid that tapers towards the top and contains the Marriage House of the God, with a separate temple to Marduk at the base.

In the temple of Ishtar, the goddess of fertility and voluptuousness, local tradition demands that a Babylonian woman offers herself once in her lifetime to a stranger within the temple, the man having to pay for this fleeting union.

A gate dedicated to Ishtar, who is also a goddess of war, is one of the sights that greets the visitor to Babylon. All the gates have been enlarged and embellished, standing further out as Nebuchadrezzar II has increased the city's perimeter and raised the external fortifications to bring the rural population under his protection. The shimmering blue enamelled brick decoration of Ishtar's gate depicts symbolic animals of myth and legend, such as griffins and bulls, and cannot fail to impress the visitor to this new city of wonders.

600

India, c.600BC. As the population of the Ganges plains expands rapidly, the dominant Aryan tribes create numerous small kingdoms. Each state centres on a capital city, surrounded by ramparts and moats. Royal power is limited by the influence of Brahmans and by palace officers and courtiers. There is a tendency towards specialised employment, with workers becoming, for example, artisans, artists or merchants.

India, c.600BC. The Indians have started to use the elephant in warfare.

Europe, c.600BC. Celtic people living north and west of the Alps are establishing direct trading contacts with the Greek colonies of the western Mediterranean.

Persia, c.600BC. The teachings of the prophet Zoroaster are gaining in influence. Zoroaster argues that the struggle between the benevolent creator and the evil principle is the core of history. He prophesies that good will eventually triumph and evil be destroyed.

Greece, c.600BC. On becoming tyrant of Sicyon, near Corinth, Cleisthenes moves against the growing Dorian power in the area. The three traditional Dorian tribes are renamed Piggites, Swinites and Assites.

Greece, c.600BC. The poet Alcman, who is thought to hail from Lydia in Anatolia, has settled in Sparta and is writing poems in the Doric dialect. He excels in "partheneia", hymns sung by choirs of maidens. In Greece, poetry, dance and music constitute both an entertainment for the young and an important aspect of religious and political life.

Greece, c.600BC. The poet and lyre-player Arion has had a miraculous escape from death. A disciple of Alcman, Arion travelled from city to city performing his choral lyrics. He even made a tour of Italy, where his talents made him rich. On his return journey to Greece the sailors tried to murder him and steal his money. He was granted a request to sing one last time. Then he threw himself overboard – but a dolphin, transfixed by his music, carried him to the shore on its back.

Germany, c.600BC. Peasant farmers are establishing the first settlements in the central lowlands of northern Europe, where ironworking has recently started to develop.

Sappho, poetess who loved women, dies

Greece, c.600BC

Sappho, the poetess and founder of a unique school for women on the island of Lesbos, is dead. Although she was a wife and mother, she will be remembered best for her poems referring to love between women.

Born into one of the best families in Lesbos, Sappho is said to have been the wife of a rich man from Andros, by whom she had a daughter. She founded a boarding-school for well-born young women of the island, and taught them poetry, music and social graces under the watchful eyes of the Muses, the Graces and Aphrodite.

Pupils were being groomed for marriage, which Sappho exalted in her poems. But Sappho also encouraged the girls to show affection for one another.

This may have involved sexual contact and, if so, it would have been no more unusual than male homosexuality which was more or less institutionalised in Greece at this time. Sappho's poems were not

Sappho, the great Lesbian poetess.

explicitly physical, but full of passion and sensuality. They described the torments of love, with tremulous outpourings of emotion, and were often dedicated to her pupils.

A Spartan education for a fighting nation

A young Spartan woman athlete.

Sparta, c.600BC

After years of near-oriental luxury, Sparta is experiencing a puritanic revival, with the ruling class giving itself over entirely to military training. New-born babies judged to be weaklings are left to die, and at seven a boy is taken from his family to live among children of his own age. At 12, training proper begins.

Dirty, barefoot and ill-clad, the boy sleeps on a mat of reeds, and learns to read and write, but only in order to express himself "laconic-

ally" in a few pointed words. At 20, after many painful ordeals, he is given the title of *eiren*, and put in charge of younger boys. They are encouraged to steal food, but if they are caught they are flogged.

During their training the youths have other young men as lovers. Elders keep watch on gymnastic contests and the naked battles between rival teams. In religious ceremonies the boys flog each other until blood is drawn, or even until one of them dies. The system is designed to turn out soldiers who are tough, obedient and resourceful.

The girls of Sparta are trained in running, wrestling, javelin-throwing, and casting the discus, so they will develop strong, healthy bodies that will deliver strong and healthy babies.

Only the warrior class has legal and civil rights. Below are so-called "Dwellers Round About", who carry on trade, and helots, who are serfs tied to the land. Some believe it was fear of an uprising by these subject classes that caused the rulers to introduce the strict Spartan regime that has turned the city-state into an armed camp.

Greeks set up a colony at Massalia

Marseilles, c.600BC

A new colony has been established by the Greeks of Phocaea (Anatolia) at Massalia (Marseilles). The site, on a small coastal plain alongside deep water and protected by rocky hills, is within easy reach of the Rhone, the river which has opened up southern Gaul to trade.

The founding of the colony is already legend. The daughter of the local king, Princess Gyrtis, fell in love with one of the Phocaean leaders, Protis, and married him. Massalia, the story goes, was the princess' dowry. It seems more likely that the marriage was part of an astute deal by the Phocaeans involving negotiations for property and trading rights.

Since then this new Phocaean outpost of Hellenic progress has

A Greek coin from Massalia.

had no shortage of enemies, attacked from the sea by the Carthaginians and from the land by the local tribes led by Gyrtis's own brother. Jealousy of the Phocaeans, who trade from men-of-war rather than merchantmen, is increased by their success in opening up the silver supplies of Tartessos on the Atlantic coast of Iberia.

Despite these problems, the colony has thrived. The vine and olive have taken root in the Rhone valley and, with the establishment of new colonies along the southern shore of Gaul and the northeastern coast of Iberia, the Phocaeans are rapidly becoming the major economic power in the western Mediterranean.

Rome flourishes under Etruscan influence

Rome, c.600BC
Under the influence of its northern Etruscan neighbours, Rome is developing from a collection of mud-hut villages into a major city. The Forum is nearing completion and the city now has a unique drainage system which began as a single ditch before its expansion into a more sophisticated form which drains the whole city. Pavements have been built for its populace; and the city-state has its own army.

Rome has always attracted the enigmatic Etruscans, whose descent is uncertain, although their forebears are certainly eastern Mediterranean in origin and Greek influence is paramount in their culture. Geographically, this collection of villages, built on seven hills, is attractive to them because the Tiber river is easily forded, allowing them access to the rich lands of Latium (an area south of Rome).

Rome is surrounded by land which can produce as many as three crops per year, and there are valuable salt-deposits close by. Three neighbouring towns, Tarquinii, Caere and Veii, are playing

Etruscan model of female warrior.

a major part in Rome's development. The Etruscans have passed on their alphabet – derived from the Greeks – to the Romans, as well as an adminstrative framework, the work of Servius Tullius, a representative in Rome of the Tarquin dynasty which rules Etruria. Even the name Rome – despite the legend of Romulus ("man of Rome"), the city's supposed founder – is Etruscan in origin.

Boar-hunting trains Greeks for manhood

Greece, c.600BC
Hunting, especially of the dangerous wild boar, is considered a vital part of the training of young Greeks. The chase, on foot or horseback, tests their courage and endurance and teaches them how to judge the lie of the land and how to use their weapons against live quarry.

In a country where every man is expected to take to the field in defence of his city at a moment's notice, this training is essential to his survival.

So important is hunting that it has been decreed that the huntsmen may even ride through standing crops, and that there should be no catching of animals by stealth at night near the city so that the sportsmen's game is preserved.

It is considered that hunting also has a beneficial effect on a young man's character, making him confident and, at the same time, just. Hunting is, therefore, an initiation rite, through which the virtues of the young are recognised.

Even the slaughtered quarry has

Hunters returning from the chase.

a place in this philosophy of hunting, for it is a sign of social prestige and is among the most acceptable of lovers' gifts.

However, it is pointed out by some cynics that while Athenians hunt in the open with javelins, Spartans, renowned for their cunning as well as bravery in war, are taught the skills of poaching when young.

Celtic chieftains control central Europe

Europe, c.600BC
The Hallstatt civilisation dominates central and western Europe. These Celtic chieftains have been influenced by eastern culture and, like the chieftains of the Russian steppes and the Scythian and Cimmerian nomads, they are becoming increasingly reliant on the horse.

The horses that run freely across the steppes are rare in central Europe, and only the privileged few keep them, immortalising them in the carving of their furniture. These Celtic aristocrats like to be buried in their wagons, with harnesses and bits beside them.

The warlike leaders of these people feast freely and drink wine imported from Greece and Italy, although they sleep on animal skins in crude houses. The hilts of their swords might be decorated with fine geometric patterns, however, and the bronze urns used in their houses are decorated in the Veneto-Illyrian style. Their pottery, with decorative circles, lozenges, chevrons and hatching, is even finer than their jewellery.

Greeks relax in an orgy of food and drink

A woman flute player entertains men at a drinking party, or "symposion".

Greece, c.600BC
The *symposion* is a Greek institution which is of considerable social importance. Men gather on these occasions to eat, drink, sing, discuss the affairs of the day, and be entertained by beautiful young boys and girls.

There is a strict order for these occasions. The host will invite his friends to an "andron", or men's room, where they lie, propped on their left arms, on couches piled high with cushions. Slaves serve them with delicacies, and light snacks are laid out on low tables.

Then the real business of the evening begins. A toast is made to Dionysus, the god of wine, and a "king" is elected for the evening to mix the wine and water in a large *krater*, or mixing bowl. When he has done his work, young boy and girl slaves pour the wine into fine pottery or metal goblets.

The drinking follows well-established rituals common to many all-male gatherings, and many *symposions* have their own song books. No free women are allowed to attend, but some men take their "hired women" with them.

As the wine circulates the gaiety increases. There are games, like flicking wine at a target, music, dancers and jesters. But the *symposions* can also have a serious aspect. They are often intellectual gatherings at which poets and authors read out their latest work. Sometimes the great philosophers will attend *symposions* to dispute their theories, and then the conversation reaches a very high level.

Other sources for Bible stories

The cuneiform script was used in Babylonia and Assyria, as well as parts of Syria, Anatolia and Iran, for nearly three thousand years, to write the Sumerian, Akkadian and other languages.

With the deciphering of these languages during the 19th century, and the progress of excavations from then until the present, scholars now have a fund of many hundreds of thousands of original documents dating from the periods of history referred to in the Bible. Many of these have not even been read yet, but among those that have been studied it is not surprising that contemporary confirmation is found of many events recounted in the Bible. Relevant cuneiform texts can be divided roughly into two groups: historical annals, and works of literature reflected in the Bible.

The statue of Idri-mi, the ruler of Alalakh, a city in Syria, in about 1550BC, is inscribed with Idri-mi's autobiography. He was born in Aleppo, when difficulties arose there he escaped first to Emar, then to the "land of Kin'anu" (Canaan), finally taking refuge with people he called "Hapiru warriors".

After seven years he was able to return and gain possession of the city of Alalakh, which was his by birthright. It appears that the term Kin'anu included for him approximately the area of modern Lebanon and Israel. The "Hapiru people" are mentioned in cuneiform texts (and appear as "pr" in Egyptian texts) as workmen, soldiers or bandits, and the term is probably generic rather than ethnic.

Confirmation of the Exodus?

It is very probable that the term Hapiru is the ancestor of Biblical "'ibrim" (Hebrews). A stele of the Egyptian pharaoh Merneptah (c.1208BC) celebrates his triumphs over a list of various Asiatic peoples. All their names are written with the hieroglyph for "land" except that of Israel, written with the sign for "people", which might suggest that the Israelites were a wandering, nomadic group. The order of names in the list suggests that by this date they were already in Palestine, possibly confirming an exodus from Egypt by about 1250BC. Merneptah succeeded Rameses II (1279-1212BC).

An illuminating picture of the Biblical world in the fourteenth century BC, probably to be reckoned as before the Exodus, is gained from the so-called Amarna Letters. This collection of over 350 letters on clay tablets was found in 1887 at el-Amarna in Egypt, the site of the new capital which the pharaoh Akhenaten built to celebrate his religious reforms. The letters, mostly in a Babylonian lingua franca,

are addressed to Akhenaten (Amenhotep IV) and his father Amenhotep III from the Babylonian, Mitanni and Hittite kings and from rulers in Palestine, Phoenicia and Syria subject to the Egyptians.

Many cities known from the Bible are mentioned, as are the land of Kin'anu (Canaan) and the group of marauding nomads called Hapiru. Jericho's ancient name is not known, but the site has been excavated and found to be a walled city of extreme antiquity, although evidence to confirm or deny the Bible account of its capture has not been trace.

A caged bird in Jerusalem

The Assyrian kings gradually managed to extend their empire over the whole Near East, including Palestine. Their inscribed monuments give (often one-sided) accounts of their military campaigns. The Black Obelisk of Shalmaneser III (858-824BC) records campaigns against Ben-Hadad of Damascus and his successor Hazael (2 Kings 9:14, 10:32, 12:17, 13:22), and its bas-relief sculpture shows tribute brought by the Israelite king Jehu "son of Omri", ie Jehu of the house of Omri. (In fact Jehu was an usurper.) Sargon II (721-705BC) claims in his annals to have deported 27,280 Israelites to Assyria and to have conquered Samaria (2 Kings 17), although the Samaria may have been taken by his predecessor Shalmaneser V (726-722BC).

The annals of Sargon's son Sennacherib (704-681BC) give a detailed account of his siege of Hezekiah in Jerusalem "like a caged bird" (cf 2 Kings 18:17-19:36 and Isaiah 36:1-37:37) and his claimed deportation of 200,150 people. His siege and capture of Lachish (2 Chronicles 32:9) are illustrated by an elaborate series of bas-relief sculptures now in the British Museum.

The Assyrian empire fell to the combined attack of Babylonians and Medes in 612BC. The Babylonians under Nebuchadrezzar II (605-562BC) soon extended their empire nearly as far afield as the Assyrians. Nebuchadrezzar's siege and capture of "the city of Juda", Jerusalem, in 598BC is recorded in the Babylonian Chronicle. The last king of the Babylonian empire was Nabonidus (556-539BC), who was actually absent from Babylon when Cyrus the Persian captured the city; instead the city was under the temporary control of his son, Belshazzar.

In the Bible Belshazzar is described as "king" of Babylon (Daniel 5:1 etc), and he was king in all but name, since it is clear that his father was often absent in Arabia, apparently for religious reasons. Thus Daniel is described as "third ruler in the king-

dom" (Daniel 5:29). Belshazzar is mentioned in a surviving prayer of Nabonidus to the moon-god Sin.

Babylonian literary works shed a different sort of light on the contents of the Bible. The Babylonian *Epic of Creation*, entitled from its first words "Enuma elis" "When on high the heavens and, below, the earth had as yet no name .... ", may date from 1300BC (it survives in tablet form from the seventh century BC). It tells quite another story of the beginning of the world, in which the creation of Man follows the destruction by the god Marduk of a brood of monsters spawned by the primeval ocean goddess Tiamat.

A forerunner to Noah?

Of especial interest for the Bible are two Babylonian literary works which deal with the theme of the Flood which destroyed all but one family of mankind. One of these is the *Epic of Atra-hasis*, the earliest version of which was probably composed in the 19th or 18th century BC. According to this, the god Enlil puts the lesser gods to work digging and labouring and eventually they go on strike and refuse to work any longer. The god Enki suggests that Man should be created to solve the problem; however, mankind, once created, multiplies until the noise it makes proves unacceptable to the gods. A plague, a famine, a drought and finally a flood are sent to destroy mankind, but each time Enki leaks the gods' plans to the man Atra-hasis. When the flood comes, Atra-hasis builds a boat and takes on board his family, possessions and animals. They survive while the rest of mankind is destroyed. In time the gods regret the destruction of mankind, since no one is left to provide sacrifices for them, and eventually Enlil accepts the existence of man in the shape of Atra-hasis and his descendants.

The Flood story was also incorporated into the *Epic of Gilgamesh* at least as early as the 18th or 17th century BC. In this epic the hero Gilgamesh, afraid of death, travels to the end of the world to visit the survivor of the Flood (this time called by the name Utnapishtim), who alone of mankind has been granted eternal life. Utnapishtim tells Gilgamesh the story of the flood to make it clear that the grant of immortality to him was a unique event and can never be repeated for another human being. Gilgamesh returns home depressed by mortality. The Biblical account of Noah is clearly adapted to a different purpose, but is often so similar to the Mesopotamian myth that it is hard to believe that the Biblical authors were not familiar with it.

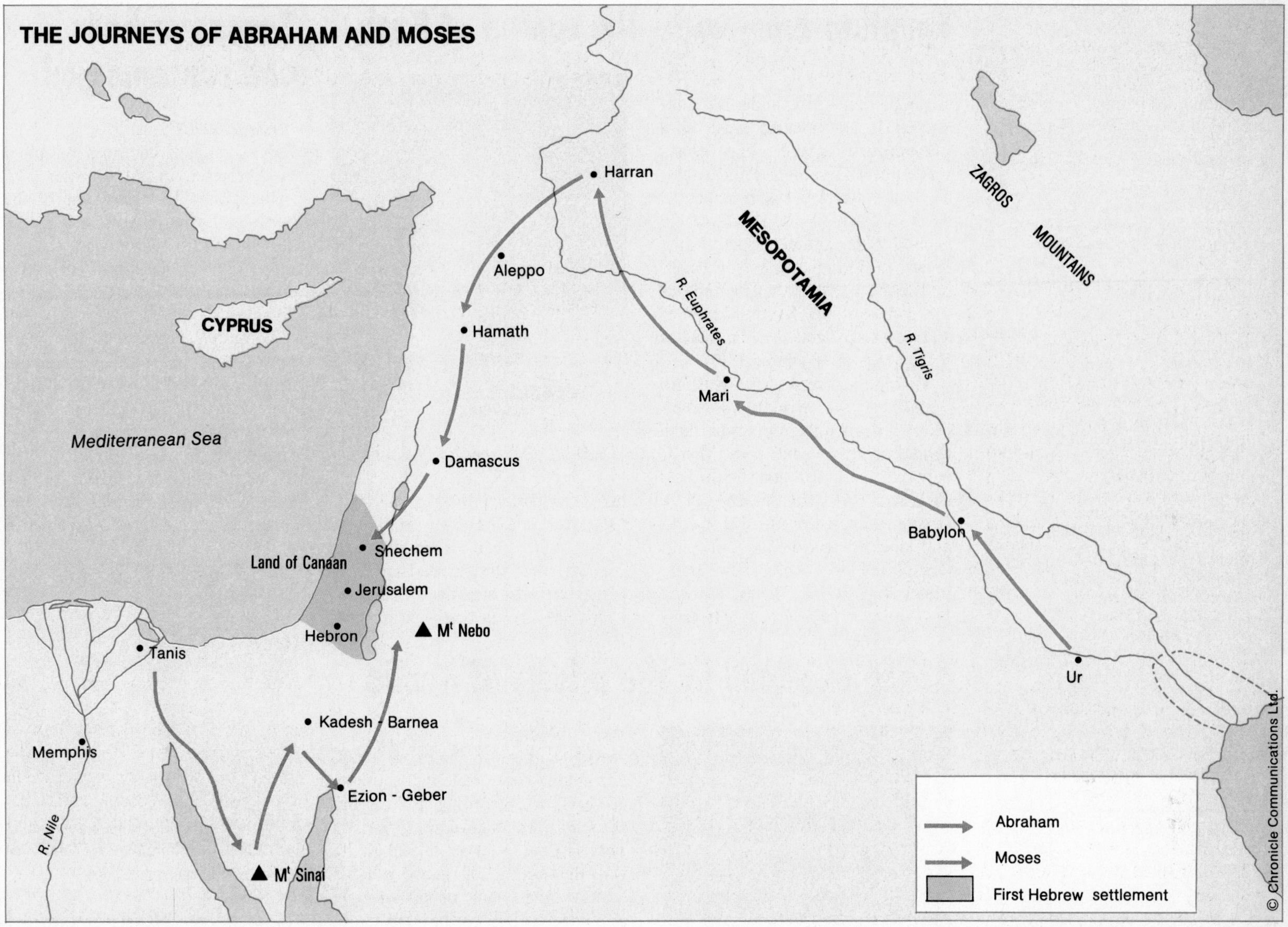

THE JOURNEYS OF ABRAHAM AND MOSES

Harran

Aleppo

MESOPOTAMIA

ZAGROS MOUNTAINS

Hamath

CYPRUS

R. Euphrates

R. Tigris

Mediterranean Sea

Damascus

Mari

Shechem

Land of Canaan

Jerusalem

Babylon

▲ Mᵗ Nebo

Hebron

Tanis

Ur

Kadesh - Barnea

Memphis

Ezion - Geber

R. Nile

▲ Mᵗ Sinai

© Chronicle Communications Ltd.

→ Abraham

→ Moses

First Hebrew settlement

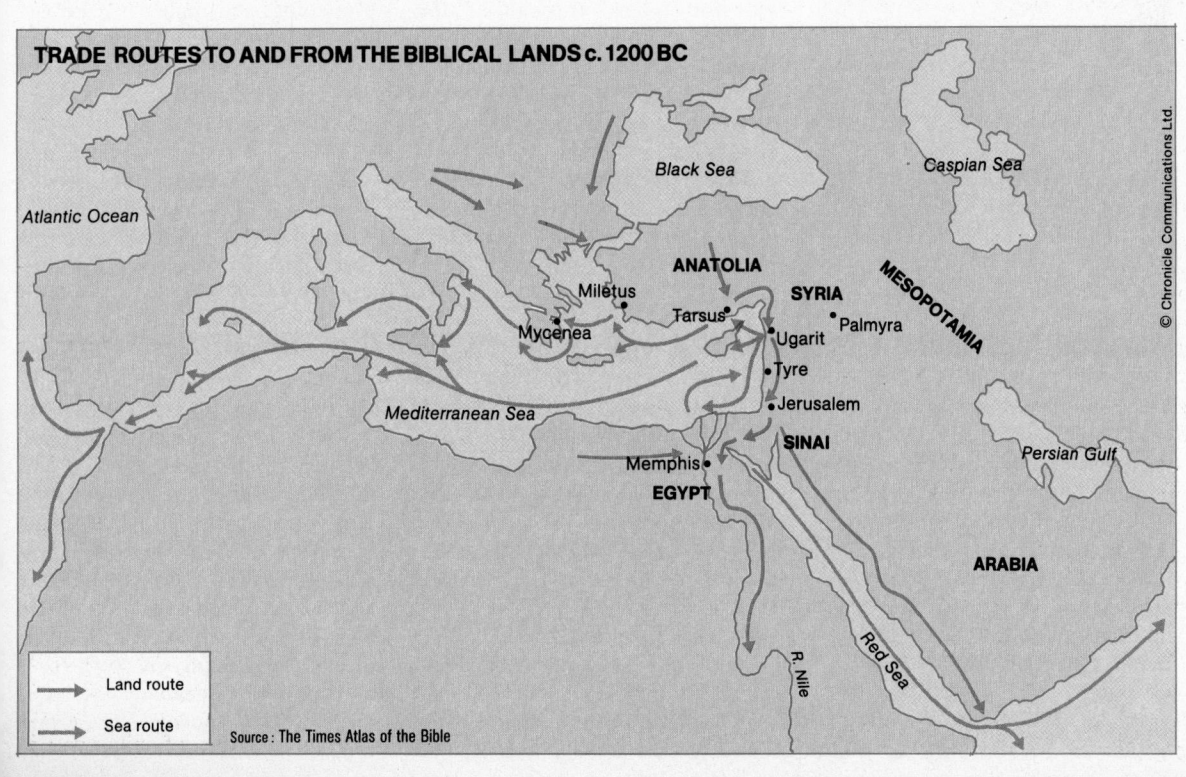

TRADE ROUTES TO AND FROM THE BIBLICAL LANDS c. 1200 BC

Black Sea

Caspian Sea

Atlantic Ocean

ANATOLIA

Miletus

SYRIA

MESOPOTAMIA

Tarsus

Ugarit

Palmyra

Mycenea

Tyre

Mediterranean Sea

Jerusalem

SINAI

Memphis

Persian Gulf

EGYPT

ARABIA

R. Nile

Red Sea

© Chronicle Communications Ltd.

→ Land route

→ Sea route

Source : The Times Atlas of the Bible

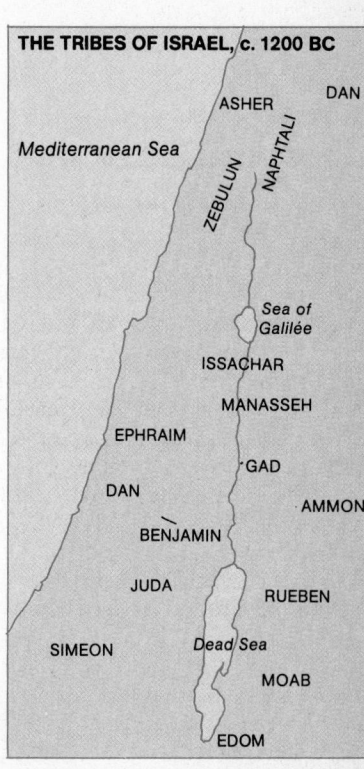

THE TRIBES OF ISRAEL, c. 1200 BC

DAN

ASHER

Mediterranean Sea

ZEBULUN

NAPHTALI

Sea of Galilée

ISSACHAR

MANASSEH

EPHRAIM

GAD

DAN

AMMON

BENJAMIN

JUDA

RUEBEN

SIMEON

Dead Sea

MOAB

EDOM

Africa, 594BC. Phoenician ships are reported to have circumnavigated Africa. As they rounded the southernmost point of the continent, the sailors noted how the sun rose on a different side of the ship.

Anatolia, c.590BC. After several failed attempts to conquer the Lydians, Cyaxares, king of the Medes, agrees to fix a frontier with the kingdom of Lydia; it follows the course of the river Halys.

Near East, 587BC. Nebuchadrezzar II, king of Babylon, destroys Jerusalem after a Jewish revolt and carries off the tribes of Judah into captivity. Under the leadership of Nebuchadrezzar, Babylon has secured an empire running from Suez, the Red Sea and Syria across the border of Mesopotamia and the old kingdom of Elam.

Anatolia, c.585BC. In the Greek cities on the eastern shores of the Aegean, in particular at Miletus, an intense intellectual life is developing. Mathematicians, physicians and philosophers are imposing a new rationality upon matters once conceived in mythical terms.

Phoenicia, 573BC. The king of Babylon, Nebuchadrezzar II, captures the city of Tyre after a 13-year siege. Situated on an island and containing two seaports, Tyre has grown into a major trading and political power in Phoenicia. Until now its privileged location has kept it well protected from invasion.

Egypt, c.570BC. The massacre of an Egyptian army by the Greeks of Cyrene provokes a general revolt in Egypt, whose people hold their king, Apries, personally responsible. Apries is forced to depend for his protection upon Greek mercenaries. After he came to the throne in 589BC, Apries sent a military expedition to Palestine. When Jerusalem was destroyed by Nebuchadrezzar, he welcomed Jewish refugees into Egypt.

Samos, c.570BC. The architects Rhoikos and Theodorus are commissioned to rebuild the sanctuary of the goddess Hera, destroyed in a fire. The new temple will have a deep porch leading to a main chamber divided by a double colonnade into three naves. The two architects have discovered how to hollow-cast bronze in moulds – an important advance in the sculpting of statues.

Egyptian army sacks the capital of Kush

Egypt, 593BC

An Egyptian army under Psammetichus II has invaded Kush in a pre-emptive strike. The army, made up of Egyptians, Phoenicians, Jews and Greeks, has reached the town of Pnubs in the region of the Second Nile cataract. Such is the hatred of Psammetichus for Kushite treachery that he has hacked out the names of the Kushite kings of 100 years ago from the temples, as if they had never existed.

This latest defeat of the Kushites underlines the wisdom of their recent decision to move their capital further south to Meroe, between the Fifth and Sixth Nile cataracts. Already Meroe is a sizable town with a royal palace and, located astride the Nile and well-placed to exploit the trade routes of both the Nile and the Red Sea, the new capital is fast becom-

Sheath of King Aspelta of Kush.

ing the commercial centre of Kush. Moreover, the Egyptian army was armed with iron weapons, and beneath the silt-enriched soil of Meroe are vast deposits of iron ore, which are already being excavated.

Aesop executed by the priests of Apollo

Corinth: a scene from Aesop.

Delphi, 585BC

Aesop, author of fables, is dead, executed by the Delphians, priests of Apollo. According to varying accounts, he was a Phrygian, a Thracian, or a slave; although he was the author of many notable fables, others are being wrongly attributed to him as they are retold by story-tellers throughout the Greek-speaking world. Aesop's fame is founded on his anthropomorphic tales, in which animals behave in ways which offer morals about human behaviour. He is believed to have offended the Delphians, who accused him of sacrilege and cast him to his death from a rock.

Zoroaster hails one supreme god

Persia, c.600BC

Persian religion has been reformed by Zoroaster, or Zarathustra, who is thought to hail from one of the north-eastern provinces. He makes the god Ahura-Mazda into a single supreme deity, the creator of everything, who obliterates all other divinities.

Zoroaster, priest and theologian, well versed in religious tradition, bases his doctrine on free will, as opposed to the prevailing religion which worships many gods and is dominated by ritual, animal sacrifice and drugs. Polytheism is thus replaced by monotheism. Zoroaster conceives of Ahura-Mazda as a

Zoroastrian coin of c.224AD.

transcendent being, creator of everything and father of Entities personifying abstract ideas such as justice. Zoroaster thus advocates resistance to the law when it denies essential justice to people.

And he conceives of good and evil as twin spirits, again with Ahura-Mazda as their father, who divide up the entire universe between them.

Pharaoh's fleet completes a three-year voyage around Africa

Nile Delta, 595BC

An Egyptian-backed Phoenician fleet has returned to Egypt after circumnavigating with dramatic reports of Africa – from the Red Sea, back to the Nile delta.

The arduous voyage had lasted three years, taking the fleet from the Red Sea down the length of the Indian Ocean and back northwards to the Pillars of Hercules (the Straits of Gibraltar) and along the length of the Mediterranean to

Egypt. Sailors in the fleet believe that they have succeeded in sailing around the neighbouring country of Libya. They tell of the sun rising on the left-hand side of their ships, only to rise on the right hand as they rounded the coast. To feed themselves, they landed each autumn and planted crops.

This epic voyage was commissioned by Necho II, who has long been anxious to extend Egypt's authority and trading links to the

southern seas. It was Necho who ordered the building of a canal between the Nile and the Red Sea, following a dried-up bed of an old arm of the Nile. This undertaking – starting at Bubastis and returning eastwards – was abandoned after 120,000 men had died and the pharaoh had been told by an oracle that he was "doing the work for a barbarian" – meaning, perhaps, that he was leaving his country exposed to enemy invasion.

Athenians lay groundwork for democracy

Solon: poet and law-maker.

Athens, 592BC

Solon, the poet-statesman who was elected *archon*, or chief magistrate, of Athens two years ago, has introduced a completely new set of laws. These laws guarantee the freedom of every citizen of Athens, and in a poem commemorating this radical move he says: "I wrote down laws alike for base and noble, fitting straight judgement to each."

His dislike of the greed and pride of the Athenian rich recurs throughout his poetry; some of the lower classes had expected him to be even more radical and are disappointed with his new laws.

It seems that the reality of office has forced him to compromise. Nevertheless, his social reforms are now known as the *Seisachtheia* – "the shaking off of burdens". Possibly the most welcome is the abolition of the system whereby a man and his family could fall into slavery through the non-payment of debts or mortgages.

Solon has also reorganised the distribution of political power, taking it from the old aristocracy and dividing it between four new property-owning classes according to the yields from their lands.

Actual power now resides in the first three of these classes, who fill the public posts either by election or by casting lots, "the choice of the gods". But even the lowest class, the *thetes*, are admitted to the judicial tribunals and Assembly.

They take part in the appointment of magistrates and members of the Council. Foreigners are also granted civil rights. These laws can be read by everybody. They are written on wooden tablets set in rotating four-sided frames.

It is said that Solon has brought democracy to Athens. There remain, however, two classes who are still denied any part in the political process and have no control over their lives. These are the slaves and the women of Athens.

Vanquished Jews deported to Babylon

Nebuchadrezzar takes Jerusalem – from Calmet's Bible Dictionary, 1732.

Jerusalem, Judah 587BC

Jerusalem, the holiest city in Judah, has fallen to the invading armies of King Nebuchadrezzar of Babylon. The city has been utterly destroyed and its entire population deported.

Nebuchadrezzar, under whose rule Babylon has grown ever more mighty, with its Hanging Gardens and many other glories, has always wished to include Jerusalem in his empire. In 597BC he raided the city, replacing the young King Jehoiachin with his uncle Zedekiah, who was to rule as a Babylonian puppet. In the event Zedekiah, backed by his court, preferred rebellion to Babylonian rule, although the prophet Jeremiah constantly preached that submission to Babylon was the only way Judah could atone for years of what he condemned as moral laxity.

Nebuchadnezzar had no doubts: his armies invaded two years ago, taking the cities of Azekah and Lachish before starting an 18-month siege of Jerusalem. Now that too has fallen and nothing remains but smouldering ruins.

Indian society divides into caste system

India, c.575BC

Society is being organised here according to a caste system, a complex mixture of religious, social and ethnic factors. Marriage is forbidden outside one's own caste; certain professions are restricted to a single caste; and it is supposed to be impossible to change from one caste to another.

A caste is a social unit or category, determined at birth. By tradition there are four principal castes, headed by the Brahmans, who are thought to wield divine power. They have the duties of studying and teaching the *Rig-Veda*, an ancient collection of priestly hymns composed in Punjab, and offering sacrifices. A sacrificial offering is food given to gods who cannot sustain themselves in any other way, and is therefore considered essential to the smooth running of the cosmos.

Next after the Brahmans are the Kshatriya, their chief task being to bear arms; they also have the right to offer sacrifices and to study the *Rig-Veda*. Third are the Vaisyas who can also make sacrifices and study the *Rig-Veda*; their job is to generate the wealth and means of support for the superior castes through commerce and agriculture.

Members of these three castes are known as the "twice-born", or *Dvija*, because they are eligible for a ritual "second birth" at their initiation ceremony.

At the bottom of the system are the Sudra, or "once-born",

High caste Brahman (1837).

Low caste bangy man (1837).

the most numerous. Their sole function is to serve the three superior castes without tainting them. Reference in the *Rig-Veda* to a fourfold division of Aryan society is the earliest known mention of the caste system. Since then the rise of the cities has brought different groups to specialise in certain professions, creating new castes and sub-castes.

Greek glory symbolised by temples

Greek world, c.560BC

The civilisation of the Greeks in the Mediterranean is flourishing, and there are no more potent and beautiful displays of Greek genius and prestige than the many temples now being built.

In Mycenaean times, around 700 years ago, people, including kings, worshipped at shrines in their own homes, or at sacred sites like caves or mountain tops in the open air. But 200 years ago, when Greek culture re-emerged from obscurity after the fall of the Mycenaean empire, a new architectural form, the temple, emerged with it. This was probably one of the first symbols of the collective government of the *polis*, or city-state, which replaced the monarchy of earlier times. Instead of palaces and tombs of kings, monuments were now to be built to the gods who protected the *polis*. Indeed, some of the first temples were built on the foundations of old Mycenaean palaces.

Except in Crete, however, temples have not brought religion indoors. They are simply the houses of the gods, where their images are kept, and only priests are normally allowed in. Religious ceremonies are performed at separate altars outside the temples, a survival of earlier open-air worship.

The earliest ones were made of mudbrick, often painted, on stone foundations, with wooden pillars supporting steeply-pitched thatched roofs. Decorated clay was often

A Doric temple from Sicily, still unfinished (note the bosses left on stones).

used for the *metopes*, designs on a frieze between the pillars and the roof. The basic ground plan, which persists in the temples now going up, was of a rectangular main room, or *naos*, with a projecting porchway on pillars. Later, an added colonnade, or peristyle, around the *naos* allowed a lower-pitched roof and offered better protection for the mud walls. Later still, the use of heavy clay tiles for the roof led to the replacement of the wooden pillars by stone columns;

with a few exceptions, Greek temples are now made entirely of stone.

Two distinct styles or "orders" of temple architecture have developed in the last century. On mainland Greece and in the western colonies the *Doric* order is popular; its columns, stubby and fluted with plain, cushion-like "capitals" (column-tops), are reminiscent of Mycenae or Egypt. In Anatolia and the Greek islands the *Ionic* order prevails; its columns are slimmer, with bases and curled capitals. It is more oriental in style and more ornamented (for example, with floral designs) than the Doric order.

A completed temple, at Agrigento in Sicily, typically Doric in design.

Athena, from the Athens acropolis.

Philosophers and scientists challenge Greek gods

Anatolia, c.560BC

A group of Greek intellectuals in the Ionian cities of Asia Minor (*Anatolia*) is radically changing the way men think about the world around them and the universe beyond. With their searching questions, Thales, Anaximander and Heraclitus are challenging traditional myths and legends, familiar to readers of the poet Hesiod, who catalogued some 300 gods, with Zeus as their king.

Besides Atlas, who holds up the sky, and Astraeus, who takes care of the stars, Hesiod has gods for the physical world: Earth, Sea, Mountains and so on.

The Ionian intellectuals will have none of that. They reject the notion of the gods meddling with the natural world. Thunder is not a loud noise made by an angry Zeus; it is to be explained in natural terms. Likewise, Iris may be goddess of the rainbow, but a rainbow is simply a multicoloured cloud of moisture. The Ionians have a word for their new way of looking at things. *Kosmos* means "the universe", but it also means something more; it comes from the Greek word meaning "to order" or "to arrange" things. So the universe, including our own world, is seen as arranged in an orderly fashion; it can be studied and explained by reasoning. The philosophers do not simply make assertions; they support their opinions with reasoned argument.

Pythagoras: mathematical legend inspires a political movement.

World map drawn by Anaximander

Miletus, c.550BC

In the seaport town of Miletus all the talk is of the controversial map of the world engraved on a tablet of stone by Anaximander, the philosopher. He sees the world as rounded, like a pillar, with the inhabited part on one side. But the unusual feature of his world is that it is represented as being viewed from on high, as though by a bird or a god.

Nobody seems to have thought of doing this before. The idea probably came to Anaximander because, as a pupil of Thales, who devised a system of geometry, he was familiar with geometric shapes, such as the circle. He suggests that the earthly cylinder lies at the centre of a celestial sphere in a position of perfect equilibrium.

Another of Anaximander's theories is that humans were developed from animals, because animals can look after themselves very soon, while humans need to be nursed for a long period of time.

Pythagoras founds a scientific sect

Southern Italy, c.560BC

The mathematician Pythagoras is becoming a legendary figure in the Greek settlements of Southern Italy, chiefly because of the missionary zeal of his followers, who have become a political force in several cities. Not only do they expound the Pythagorean theorem (that the square on the hypotenuse of a rightangled triangle is equal to the sum of the squares on the other two sides), but they also tell of his discovery that musical harmonies can be expressed mathematically.

The Pythagoreans are vegetarians and are opposed to the killing of any living creature. They also carry out physical exercises similar to the yoga practices said to be carried out in the Far East. But numbers are at the centre of their beliefs: numbers, they claim, can explain the working of the universe.

Anaximander: map-maker and inventor of a sundial to measure time.

Thales fashions the science of geometry

Miletus, Anatolia, 560BC

Whether or not the philosopher Thales did predict the eclipse of the sun 25 years ago on May 28, as is said, his fame has spread far and wide in the Greek colonies of Asia Minor (*Anatolia*). His disciples gather round as he draws various shapes on tablets: straight lines, points, triangles and circles. He then discusses problems of measurement and relationship involving these diagrams.

Unlike the Egyptians, who used the skill for building and land surveying, Thales does not see a practical use for geometry. It is theoretical knowledge that will help in the understanding of the universe. He does not believe the generally accepted mythological explanation for the creation of the world. He says it was born of a single material substance, probably water.

Xenophanes probes secrets of Nature

Anatolia, c.560BC

The poet Xenophanes, who travels about Greece reciting his verses, has upset the traditionalists by ridiculing their religious beliefs. He notes that men give their gods bodies, voices and clothes like their own. Thracians think of their gods as having red hair and blue eyes, while Ethiopians have gods with snub noses and black faces. Homer and Hesiod even have the gods behaving badly, like humans, committing adultery, stealing and deceiving one another.

Xenophanes derides these notions by suggesting that, if cows, lions and horses had hands and could paint, they would paint the gods as cows, lions and horses. He believes there is one god, more powerful than all other gods and men, who is different from mortals in mind and body.

Greece, c.550BC. An alliance of Peloponnesian states is formed under the control of Sparta, which aims to counter the influence of Argos and help the Greek cities to get rid of their tyrants so pro-Spartan rulers may come to power. The alliance also has military implications for combined attack on external foes and defence against aggressors.

Ethiopia, c.550BC. Arabs from the Yemen cross the Red Sea and settle in northern Ethiopia. Intermarriage with the local Habashat tribe leads to the creation of a new people, the Geez, who found the kingdom of Axum (Aksum).

Cyprus, c.540BC. Amasis II of Egypt captures the island of Cyprus and forces it to pay tribute. A huge limestone statue of the Egyptian god Bes is constructed at Amathus on the eastern coast of the island.

Persia, 539BC. Cyrus, king of Persia, conquers Babylon after defeating King Nabonidus near Sippar. Cyrus secured control of the whole of Persia after vanquishing his grandfather, Astyages, at the battle of Hamadan (Ecbatana) in 548BC. He is now master of all Asia from the Hindu Kush to the Mediterranean.

India, 538BC. Thanks to the skill and ambition of its new king, Bimbisara, the state of Magadha wins a war with the Vrjji people over control of the Ganges valley. A firm friend of the religious leader Buddha, Bimbisara establishes a hierarchical system of administration whose object is to maintain order in the provinces and organise the collection of taxes.

Persia, 538BC. Cyrus issues an edict putting an end to the Jews' captivity in Babylon and granting them permission to return to their own country.

Rome, 534BC. Servius Tullius, the Etruscan king of Rome, is assassinated by patricians made jealous by his reforms. The sixth king regulated the calendar, the priesthood and the sanctuaries. He created four districts in Rome and divided the people into five property classes. He also formed the first civic army in the Roman state.

Egypt, 526BC. Six months after the coronation of Psammetichus III, the Persians, led by Cambyses II, son of Cyrus, invade and conquer Egypt. Cambyses is declared king of Egypt.

Joyful Dionysus stirs female frenzy

Athens, 534BC

This year's festival of Dionysus has seen a startling innovation. Along with the usual dance, mime and choral song, there was a single person, Thespis, speaking his own lines as a counterpoint to the chorus. It is perhaps a sign that the Dionysus cult is becoming civilised. The god of drunkenness, dance and joy is being harnessed to another kind of illusion – drama – in which reality is imitated.

However, in some parts of the country, the festival of Dionysus is still an old-fashioned orgy of terrifying violence. Groups of women go to the forests or mountains outside the town. They become totally ecstatic on a diet of wine, dance to frantic rhythms, and sing out "Hail Bacchus!".

They throw away all their normal restraints. Sometimes they capture rabbits, hinds and fawns, and in their delirium tear them to pieces with their bare hands. They eat them raw and bloody in a ritual which perhaps harks back to an ancient cannibalism.

In ancient myth Dionysus has particular power over women, causing them to reverse their usual protective behaviour towards their children. In myth it is not animals, but their own children, whom they tear to pieces in their frenzy.

Dionysus is unusual amongst Greek gods and is widely thought to be of foreign origin. He is the only one born of a mortal woman. He was the son of Semele, daughter of Cadmus, the King of Thebes. She coupled with Zeus, but was punished for wanting to see her divine lover by being killed by a

First century AD relief of baby Dionysus held by a maenad and a satyr.

thunderbolt. Zeus rescued the child from her womb and it was born again from his thigh.

Dionysus is one of many Greek gods of fertility, but his particular importance is his celebration of creativity without restraint. In his entourage there are satyrs, quasi-human beings something like two-legged centaurs. They are the spirits of the rural wild life

Drinking vessels with pictures of them are very popular here. They are shown as male, always obviously sexually excited. Sometimes they have goats' legs and horses' tails depicted in scenes of dancing and revelry.

Dionysus with symbols of rebirth.

Tyrant tricks gullible Athenians in "I was robbed" farce

Athens, c.550BC

Solon's legacy of open government for Athens has been swept aside by his kinsman, Peisistratos, who has seized power and become "tyrant" of the city. It must be admitted that so far his rule has not been too cruel and has been marked more by farce than by tragedy.

The Athenians have only themselves to blame for allowing him to seize power. At a time of quarrelling between the people who live on

the plain and those who live along the shore, he formed a third faction drawing strength from the poor farmers and the men of the hills who felt they had not benefited from Solon's reforms.

Then, inflicting some cuts and bruises on himself and his mules, he drove his cart into the meeting place, the *agora*, and claimed that he had barely escaped with his life from a band of assassins.

The good citizens were horrified,

and when he demanded a bodyguard they allowed him to form a band of tough men armed with wooden clubs. Backed by these roughs he then seized the Acropolis and power over Athens.

He seems determined, however, to rule fairly, and so far has maintained a tranquil atmosphere. He is beautifying the city and encouraging sculptors and poets, so that the citizens are beginning to talk of his rule as a "Golden Age".

Jews allowed back to Jerusalem after exile in Babylon

Jerusalem, c.538BC

Fifty years after their forefathers were deported from a devastated Jerusalem to exile in Babylon, the Jews have returned to their holy city. Persia's King Cyrus, conqueror of Babylon last year, has repatriated the Jews, as he has done others formerly held captive.

More than ever determined to adhere to the worship of their one god, Yahweh, the Jews attribute their return to their Lord, and they tell this story of their deliverance.

During a banquet given by King Nabonidus' son Belshazzar a mysterious hand wrote on a wall the words *mene mene tekel upharsin*. The prophet Daniel explained that God had "weighed the king in the balance and found him wanting" so his kingdom had been handed over to Cyrus.

Ex-spearbearer seizes throne

Persia, 522BC

Darius, a former spearbearer to King Cambyses, has seized power in the second revolution in this country in only three months.

In July Bardiya, a brother of Cambyses, proclaimed himself king. In September Darius put it about that Bardiya was an impostor, a religious leader called Gaumata. According to Darius, Cambyses had killed Bardiya seven years ago. Along with six other nobles, Darius stabbed Gaumata (or Bardiya) to death.

All this time Cambyses has been in Egypt. He has been king of Upper and Lower Egypt ever since he defeated the Egyptian king, Amasis, at the battle of Pelusium in 525BC. As soon as he heard about Bardiya's coup he hurried back to Iran, but is thought to have died on the way.

Cambyses was not popular in Egypt, where his troops often plundered villages. Local rumours there say he killed the divine bull, Apis, and was sent mad in divine retribution. He is also said to have killed his pregnant sister.

Cyrus dies, but Persian empire lives

Persia, c.530BC

Cyrus the Great, founder of the Persian Empire, is dead. The king, whose conquests stretch from Greece to India, and whose reputation for mercy and justice is summed up in his decision to end the Jewish exile in Babylon, has been killed fighting the Scythian tribes of the Aral Sea. He has been succeeded by his son, Cambyses II.

Like other great leaders – Moses and Sargon of Agade – legend has it that Cyrus was found abandoned as a child on a river, though some writers dismiss this as fantasy. Whether adopted or not, he was brought up as the son of King Cambyses, a member of Persia's Achaemenid dynasty (founded c.700BC) and the first of their kings to rule all the Persian tribes. In 550BC, when Cyrus succeeded his father, the Persians were still subject to the rule of the Medes, who had dominated the area around Iran for the previous century since Cyaxares II (653-585BC) had defeated the Assyrians in 612BC. But when in 550BC King Astyages, whose daughter he had married, proved unable to control the

Later British view of the Persian conqueror Cyrus entering a defeated city.

Median empire, Cyrus led a Persian revolt, crushing the Medes and capturing their king. Cyrus allied himself with Babylon and in 547BC began a campaign against Lydia, ruled by King Croesus, whose wealth was of proverbial size. It failed to save his kingdom, which fell in fourteen days, although Cyrus spared his life and employed him as an adviser. As Cyrus' power increased, with conquests reaching as far as Gandara in north-western India, he abandoned his alliance with King Nabonidus of Babylon and attacked him in July 539BC. On October 29 the war was over, Cyrus triumphant and Nabonidus dethroned. Among other reforms Cyrus sent home the Jews, ending a 50-year exile. Still eager for conquest, Cyrus began a new campaign last year. Tragically, it has proved his last.

Egyptian influence gives a new sensuality to Greek statues

Greece, c.530BC

The Greeks are developing greater realism and subtlety in their statues, under the influence of what they have seen and learnt from other civilisations, especially the Egyptian one. With more skills and techniques the sculptors of Greece have created an individually Greek style of statue, which is breaking away from the remarkable, but rather staid and stylised, sculptures of about 70 years ago. The use of the iron chisel and increasing confidence in carving marble are allowing a more realistic treatment of anatomical details, which are better related to the mass and structure of the body. The traditional fixed smile of Greek statues is relaxing into an expression more apt for funeral monuments.

The changes in style are most obvious in the *kouros* figures of young male nudes, because they are still made in the set symmetrical pose of 70 years ago, with the arms

A statue of a youth, or kouros ...

... and a female kore, from Athens.

held at the sides and hands clenched, one foot generally in front of the other. But the female figure, or *kore* – traditionally a quite clumsily stylised representation, sexu-

ally distinguished from the *kouros* almost only by its female clothes – is acquiring more sexuality as male sculptors become able to express greater sensuality.

Greece, c.520BC. Born in Teos, Ionia, Anacreon has become a court poet in Athens. His favourite theme is love, "which masters the gods and tames men". He extols the charm of young girls who are wilder than unbroken mares. If a rival is more favoured than himself, he accuses him of dallying with bakerwomen and "frequenting prostitutes".

Samos, c.516BC. The island of Samos, last bastion of Hellenic independence, falls victim to Persian domination. All Ionia is now divided into satrapies and heavily taxed to fill the royal coffers of Susa.

Iran, 515BC. King Darius lays the foundation stones, of gold and silver, of a new capital at Persepolis. Darius came to the throne in 522BC, after a bout of palace intrigues following the death of Cambyses II, to whom he is distantly related.

Greece, c.513BC. Restoration of the temple of Apollo at Delphi, destroyed by fire in 541BC, is completed. Much of the work was funded by international subscription.

Asia/Europe, c.513BC. At the head of a large army, Darius, king of Persia, crosses the Bosporus and heads for the Danube, aiming to wage war on the Scythians, who inhabit central Asia and northern Europe. However, the elusive Scythians get the better of him and the Persians are only saved from disaster by the treacherous Greek tyrants who rule the cities of Ionia in the Persian interest.

Italy, c.510BC. Sybaris, one of the wealthiest Greek cities in southern Italy, is razed to the ground and its inhabitants are massacred. Sybaris had become infamous for its decadent lifestyle. Under the guise of a religious crusade, the cities of old Greece and of the local region joined forces to beat down the upstart.

India, c.510BC. With the annexation of the Indus valley by Darius of Persia, the Achaemenid empire embraces all the lands from the Indus to Thrace in Europe, and Egypt and the Libyan coast in Africa.

Rome, 510BC. Tarquinius Superbus, seventh king of Rome, and all his family are banished from the kingdom. Tarquinius was the third member of an Etruscan dynasty to rule in Rome. His tyrannical behaviour provoked an uprising led by his nephew, Brutus.

Roman revolt causes king to flee city

Rome, 510BC

Rioting and demonstrations rocked Rome today after the rape of an officer's wife by a fellow officer. Tarquinius Superbus, the seventh king of Rome, has fled from the city and a republic is about to be declared. The story behind this dramatic turn of events began at Delphi where a young courtier, Lucius Junius Brutus, the king's nephew, was told by the oracle that one day he would rule Rome. Fearing for his life, Brutus chose to bide his time, playing the role of court dullard and allowing the king to seize his possessions.

During a drinking session, a number of officers taking part in a siege argued as to which of them had the most virtuous wife. They rode to Rome, where they found most of their wives socialising, and then to Collatia, where Lucretia, the wife of Tarquinius Collatinus, was discovered with her hand-maidens working on wool. Lucretia was the unanimous winner. It was on the following night that one of the officers, Sextus Tarquinius, rode with a slave to Collatia, where he was greeted by Lucretia who gave him dinner and a bedchamber.

When the house was still, Tarquinius woke the sleeping Lucretia and told her: "Be still! My sword is in my hand. Utter a sound and you die!" He threatened to kill her and his slave so that she would be thought to have been killed in adultery with a "base person".

Lucretia was forced to succumb; when her husband returned with Brutus they found her distraught and wracked with guilt. Demanding pledges of vengeance from them, she said: "For my part, though I acquit myself of the sin, I do not absolve myself from punishment." She took a knife and plunged it into her heart.

Brutus drew the knife from

Romulus, Remus and the she-wolf: legends invoked against the king.

Lucretia's breast and vowed to pursue Sextus and his family. They would never achieve power, and Rome would return to the fine ideals of its founders, Romulus and Remus. The sight of the body displayed in the market place was the signal for the people to revolt.

Gold and bronze pay tribute to Celtic royalty in lavish burials

Europe, c.520BC

Celtic chieftains of tribes have been building up riches in hilltop palaces throughout Europe. Their wealth is being buried with them – in the form of gold and bronze objects and other precious possessions.

The Greek *krater* of Vix has been buried with an unknown prince or princess. It is a superb example of the fine art of this age. The *krater* – about five feet high, its neck decorated in relief with warriors, and chariots on the lid – has as its handle a statuette of a young woman, with a gold diadem on her head.

Bronze cauldrons from regions of Greece, Etruscan bronze vases and clay Athenian cups are among the treasures buried in the graves of Celtic rulers from Bohemia to Burgundy.

They are part of a military aristocracy which controls the trading routes between Europe and the Mediterranean, and builds fortifications at strategic points, usually on hilltops.

In exchange for raw materials like tin and amber, Greek and Etruscan traders export to the north luxury items, works of art, and wine – adding to the considerable wealth (and lifestyles) of the Celtic princes.

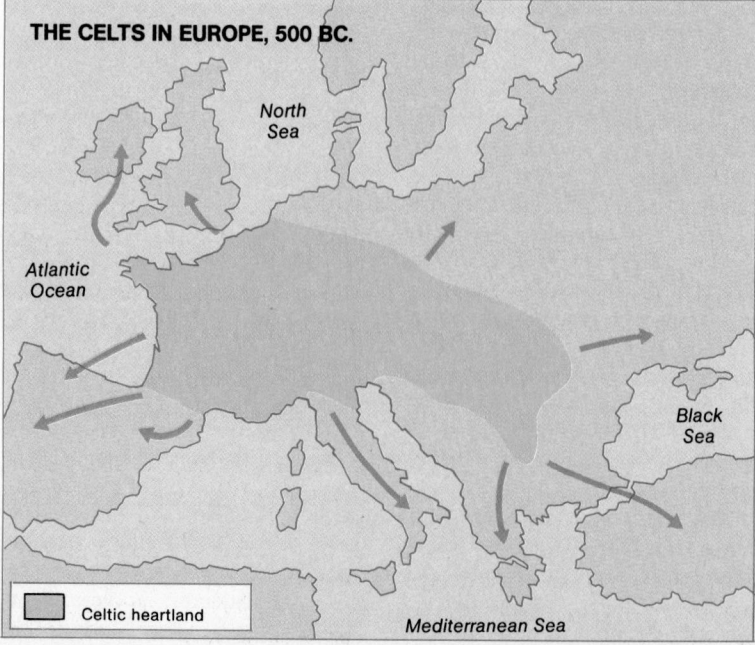
THE CELTS IN EUROPE, 500 BC.

North Sea

Atlantic Ocean

Black Sea

Celtic heartland

Mediterranean Sea

A gorgon stares out from this bowl.

Power given to the people in Athens

Athens, 507BC

Cleisthenes, the aristocrat who last year enlisted the help of the *demos*, the people, to wrest power from his rival, Isagoras, has embarked on a programme of far-reaching reforms which will give more power to the people and at the same time consolidate his rule over them.

He has broken up the city-state into administrative units called the *deme*, which may consist of a village or a section of Athens. These units are then combined into 30 groups called *trittyes*, which themselves form ten new *phylai*, or tribes, replacing the old division of four tribes.

Each tribe now chooses 50 men by lot to send to the Council, and this means that all the citizens of Athens, from the richest to the poorest, are represented on the Council. All are now equal in the eyes of the law.

However, while it is thought by some that this proves that Cleisthenes has been genuinely converted to the cause of the *demos*, there are others who believe it is merely a device to curb the power of his rivals among the landed gentry.

Cleisthenes is also thought to be about to introduce the system of ostracism, under which, once a year, a man considered to be dangerous to Athens could be sent into exile for ten years. This will be done by citizens scratching the name of the man they want exiled on a potsherd. The man who receives the most votes will be exiled.

Athens is crowned by Democracy.

Theseus hailed as father of democracy

Some of the heroic deeds of Theseus. In the centre he slays the minotaur.

Athens, c.507BC

The fame of the mighty Theseus, slayer of the minotaur and hero of many myths, is growing every day in Athens. His deeds are represented on Attic pottery, festivals are held in his memory and sacrifices are devoted to him.

Skilfully promoted, this cult has to do not so much with his heroism as with his rule as king of Athens. For it was Theseus who unified the city-state, and he has established Athens as the sole centre of political life.

This fits in well with the radical reforms instituted by Cleisthenes, and Theseus has, at it were, been annexed as the hero-father of the new democracy.

Campaign of terror after plot fails

Athens, 514BC

Hipparchus, the artistic son of the "good tyrant" Peisistratos, has been murdered, stabbed to death during a religious procession, and his elder brother, Hippias, who succeeded their father 14 years ago, has unleashed a campaign of terror against their enemies.

The reason for the murder was originally sexual rather than political. Hipparchus fell in love with a handsome young Athenian called Harmodius, but his advances were rejected as Harmodius was already locked in a passionate affair with a man named Aristogeiton.

Hipparchus determined to have his revenge after being twice rejected. He offered Harmodius' virginal sister a place of honour in the procession, and then rejected her because "she was far too wicked". This enraged Harmodius, who plotted with Aristogeiton and a group of friends to kill the brothers and overthrow the dynasty.

They murdered Hipparchus, but their plot failed. Harmodius was killed on the spot and Aristogeiton was caught and tortured to death. Since then there have been many killings as Hippias seeks to destroy his enemies. His actions, however, are serving only to strengthen the opposition to his rule.

Love between men symbolises courage for Greek soldiers

Athens, c.515BC

Love between men is as common as heterosexual love in many areas of the Greek life, and is positively encouraged among students and soldiers.

The most common form of homosexuality is pederasty, in which a man (*erastes*) forms an attachment to a youth (*eromenos*) between the ages of 12 and 18. In Athens this is seen as an integral part of a young man's education. The relationship is ideally Platonic, such as that between Socrates and his followers. More often, however, it also involves mutual masturbation.

Young men are legally protected against rape and certain forms of abuse, and they are not expected to submit to an older man's advances. But if they do, there is no opprobrium attached.

In the Dorian cities, notably in Sparta, pederasty is favoured, and bonds of love between soldiers are guarantees of solidarity and bravery in combat.

Attic vases frequently depict naked young men, with the exclamation *"kalos"* (meaning "beautiful"), and partners are shown either exchanging gifts or, just as likely, making gestures indicating sexual contact.

A young athlete and a boy slave.

Greece, c.505BC. Sparta and its Peloponnesian allies invade Eleusis and ravage the north and west of Attica. Active on all fronts, the Athenians put the aggressors to flight and take many prisoners, whom they exchange for hefty ransoms. The Peloponnesians, chastened by the experience, abandon their attack for the time being, while Athens inflicts further defeats in Boeotia and Euboea.

Greece, c.500BC. A new magistracy/public office is instituted in Athens. Elected by the popular assembly, it is made up of ten *strategoi* (generals) who are under the direction of the *polemarchos* or supreme commander.

Sahara, c.500BC. As the Sahara turns to desert, the transport of goods by horse chariot becomes increasingly impractical. Trade looks likely to survive, however, as a result of the increasing use of camels.

Mexico, c.500BC. Temple complexes are being built at Monte Alban in the valley of Oaxaca, in southern Mexico. The mountaintop has been flattened and levelled and the temples have been designed around a large plaza. The settlers have evolved distinctive styles of pottery, sculpture and architecture; they are also formalising astronomical observations and a calendar system.

Italy, c.500BC. Etruscan art, especially statuary, develops more lifelike and rhythmical forms under Greek influence. An example of this is the terracotta Apollo at the temple in Veii, which has a feeling of charm as well as of physical strength; its face is lit up by almond eyes and a mysterious smile. The use of terracotta, rather than stone or bronze, is an Etruscan peculiarity.

Rome, c.500BC. The Chalcidian version of the Greek alphabet, adopted by the Etruscans under the influence of Greek settlers almost 200 years ago, is now being used in Rome.

Anatolia, 498BC. In an atmosphere of mounting revolt against the Persians, the Greeks launch a surprise attack on the Lydian town of Sardis. The Greek cities on the Bosporus and Hellespont also rebel, threatening the Persian trading routes. Elsewhere, there is unrest both in Caria and on the island of Cyprus.

Mystery surrounds claim of record voyage

Africa, c.500BC

Hanno of Carthage claims to have completed the greatest voyage of exploration yet undertaken. Heading what he describes as a large fleet, he says he ventured beyond the Mediterranean to the Atlantic coast of Africa. His tales of encounters with humans and a sub-human race are being treated with some scepticism. Nonetheless this is the story he tells.

Hanno says he set sail with 60 ships with the intention of exploring beyond the Pillars of Hercules (*the Straits of Gibraltar*) and founding new cities that would extend Carthage's trading empire.

Two days after leaving the Mediterranean, Hanno landed and founded his first city, called Thymaterion, above a broad plain. He established settlements at five points along a coast that varied from overgrown headland to reedy lagoon. When Hanno's fleet arrived at the mouth of a large river, called the Lixos, he enlisted the help of Lixian nomads as guides and interpreters.

But after sailing up a great river to a lake, surrounded by crocodiles and hippopotami, the explorers were confronted by savages clad in animal hides who threw stones and would not let them land.

As they headed back along the coast, they failed, even through Lixian interpreters, to communicate with any natives. They fled from one island after being terrified by a nocturnal clamour: pipes, drums, shouting and fires. At their last stop they pursued some gorillas; the males escaped, but two females were killed and their skins brought back to Carthage.

Etruscans face life after death in style

A woman and her husband on a fine Etruscan sarcophagus from Caere.

Italy, c.500BC

Etruscan tombs testify to the strong belief that the spirit survives after death. The dead are interred in barrow-like tombs with everything necessary for a comfortable life in the afterworld. Where the Etruscans differ from the Egyptians and Greeks, however, is in that they represent the material needs of the dead in pictorial form; extremely realistic paintings are designed to re-create the forces of life such as birds and vegetation, together with a funerary portrait.

Cremation is a normal practice throughout Etruria, some believing that this is the point at which the soul is liberated from the shackles of life towards a celestial sphere. Nonetheless, the ashes of the dead are often put into "house-shaped" urns, or into vases representing the face of the dead person, suggesting a return to the original Mediterranean concepts of death.

Iron forges new African societies

Nigeria, c.600-500BC

In the forests of West Africa the arrival of iron among farmers using stone tools has revolutionised society and a new culture is flowering in Taruga and the Nok valley. Iron came to Taruga with the blacksmiths, credited by the local population with stealing fire from the gods and possessing magical powers. The smiths, making full use of their new prestige, have become the religious leaders in the region and forged a very strict hierarchical society.

It was iron that made this sophisticated society possible, providing the technology to clear the forest and produce the agricultural surplus that allows people to think further than where their next meal is to come from, and to fulfil their spiritual and artistic ambitions.

The beautiful terracotta figures which can be found all over the region epitomise these spiritual and artistic ambitions. The human face is elaborately stylised, but the animals – elephants, monkeys and snakes – are naturalistic, possibly derived from wood-carving styles.

Yet there is a price to pay for these artistic achievements: conformity. The dress-styles of both sexes may be ornate, but they are totally uniform; and behaviour is more subdued than might have been expected now that the smiths have established a firm hierarchy.

A terracotta statue of the god Apollo from Veii. Only nine miles north of Rome, the large Etruscan town of Veii is renowned for the quality of its statuary.

Greeks rebel against Persian rulers

Greece, 500BC

The Greeks are locked in a bitter conflict with the mighty King Darius of Persia that seems set to last for many years. Wealthy cities on the coast of Asia Minor (Anatolia) have been laid waste, and city-states in Greece are being drawn into what some see as a struggle between burgeoning Greek democracy and eastern despotism.

As the tide of Persian expansion swept over the Greeks of Asia Minor there was grumbling at the disruption of old trading links with Egypt, but the Persians kept things under control through pliant local tyrants.

All this changed when the tyrant of Miletus, Histiaeus, was held hostage by Darius in the Persian capital of Susa. A cousin, Aristagoras, took over in Miletus, and set out to gain favour with the Persians by proposing that they join with him in an expedition to capture Naxos and other Aegean islands.

The Persians agreed, but bad blood developed between the Persian admiral and Aristagoras; as a result the Persians betrayed him, the expedition was a disaster, and Aristagoras found himself in a very shaky position.

Just then a slave arrived from Susa. "Shave my head, master," the slave said. Aristagoras did so and found a message from Histiaeus tattooed on the scalp, urging his cousin to lead a revolt against the Persians. To win the support of the people for this, Aristagoras overthrew all the tyrants in cities around Miletus and proclaimed *isonomia*, equality under the laws.

He then sought help from King Cleomenes of Sparta, showing him a bronze map and pointing out the expedition route, which seemed short. But the wily king asked how long the journey would be in marching days. Three months, said Aristagoras.

The king turned him down. He had better luck with the Athenians, who agreed to provide 20 warships.

A Greek warrior, from Thebes.

So Aristagoras, having been first a tyrant in the pay of the Persians, and then an ambitious adventurer, became the champion of equality and leader of the Greek revolt against Persia.

Greek myths fall flat when written down for first time

Miletus, Greece, c.500BC

For the first time the Greek myths have been put in writing, and fun has been poked at their contradictions by Hecataeus of Miletus.

In his *Genealogiae* he classifies the traditional stories chronologically – from Deucalion, the first man after the flood, to the children of Hercules.

What is more, he has written them in a way which is more true to life, ironing out inconsistencies and purging them of their fantastic elements on the grounds of commonsense, to make them seem more sane and credible.

Written, or "laid down flat", the old myths can be compared, and so writing is seen as a means of interpretation and criticism. Hecataeus applies this critical approach in his *Journey round the world*, in which he catalogues the names of people and places, mainly around the eastern Mediterranean regions, and observes the local flora and fauna as well as the differences in religious traditions.

People are now able to study humanity in its historical, as well as its physical, environment and Hecataeus expedites this process by bringing critical faculties to bear on genealogical claims made by the aristocratic families, asserting truth and individual opinion at a time when privileges are being challenged.

Zeus, Apollo and Aphrodite look down on Man from Olympus

Zeus watches as the goddess Hera lifts her veil, from the Parthenon.

Greece, c.500BC

The Greeks worship a multitude of gods who they believe are human in form and live in various parts of the universe. They display human traits and habits, despite being immortal – the radical difference which makes them divine. Homer and other writers provide images of some of the principal gods. They hold court on Mount Olympus in Thessaly, the highest peak in Greece, where Zeus is father of both gods and humans. His wife and sister, Hera, is the guardian of women and marriage. Zeus' sons and daughters are: Apollo, god of the sun, music, medicine and divination; his twin sister, Artemis, a hunting goddess, identified with the moon; beautiful Aphrodite, goddess of sexual love; Hermes, the god of travellers; and Ares, the warrior. But most astonishing is Athena, a virgin with no mother who sprang from the head of Zeus: she symbolises intelligence and is the patron of artisans.

Gods undertake tasks according to their particular attributes: thus Hermes carries messages and conveys the souls of the dead to Hades (the underworld). All like to visit their own sanctuaries and receive sacrifices from faithful humans.

Assuming human or animal disguises they intervene in worldly affairs, punishing, or assisting by use of miracles. Zeus likes to seduce women, who then give birth to demi-gods such as Hercules, son of Alcmene. Gods feed on ambrosia and drink nectar, which bestows eternal youth. When they quarrel Zeus, who creates storms and hurls thunderbolts, settles all disputes immediately.

The **monstrous head of the gorgon, or Medusa, a popular motif in Greek art. Legend has it that the snake-haired gorgon, whose stare could turn men to stone, was slain by Perseus.**

Aegina, c.495BC. A temple to Aphaea, protectress of hunters and fishermen, is built on the island of Aegina in the Saronic gulf, between Attica and the Peloponnese. Britomartis, the Cretan nymph and daughter of Zeus, hid here when fleeing from Minos. The original sanctuary commemorating this myth was destroyed long ago. The new temple has a double interior colonnade and splendid marble statues of the heroes of Athenian myth.

Anatolia, 494BC. The Persians inflict a severe defeat on Greek rebels in Miletus. The city is razed to the ground and its population deported to Mesopotamia.

Athens, 493BC. The tragic poet Phrynichus stages his play *The Sack of Miletus*. Its topicality marks a departure from the traditional subject matter of tragedy: myth. The Athenians, who feel partly responsible for the disaster at Miletus, are both moved and guilt-stricken by the play. To salve their consciences, a fine is imposed on the poet.

Greece, 492BC. The Greeks fear an attack on Athens by the Persian general Mardonius, who is travelling west at the head of a large army and fleet. In fact his mission is to subdue Thrace and Macedonia in the aftermath of the Ionian revolt. He achieves this aim but retreats after the Persian fleet is dashed to pieces on the rocky promontory of Mount Athos in a storm.

Greece, 489BC. Miltiades, the hero of Marathon, dies from a wound sustained in an abortive attack on the island of Paros. He led an expedition to destabilise Persian influence in the Cyclades and capture the gold reserves of Paros and Thasos. Before his death Miltiades was fined heavily by the Athenians for his failure.

India, c.486BC. Ajatasatra, ambitious son of Bimbisara, deposes his father, and has him thrown into prison, before making himself king.

Egypt, c.486BC. Profiting from Persian weakness after the defeat at Marathon, the Egyptians rebel against Persian domination of their country. The foreign presence has been marked by the completion of a canal, begun by Necho, from the Nile to the Red Sea.

Persia, 486BC. Xerxes becomes king on the death of his father, Darius, the architect of the modern Persian empire.

Plebs rebel against Roman aristocrats

Rome, 494BC

The entire future of republican Rome hung on a knife-edge today as plebeians, who make up more than 90 per cent of the city's population, withdrew to the Aventine, a working-class stronghold outside the city. The plebs were protesting against the "weighting" of voting rights, which gave the well-to-do patricians far greater power than themselves in the Assembly.

Despite the republican nature of Roman society since the fall of the Etruscan kings, the patricians have worked hard to ensure their monopoly of power by keeping the plebs from positions of importance, particularly membership of the Senate, and by creating a second group of "clients" – a "middle-class" that enjoys the patronage of wealthy Romans. The patricians, suffering heavy financial losses from foreign wars, have made increasing demands on the plebs: and the latter, in turn, have been more and more vocal in their insistence on a bigger say in government.

They argue that high interest rates on loans have forced more and more of them into near-slavery – debtors are frequently forced to pledge their bodies if they cannot meet their debts – and that collective protest is the only answer. On the Aventine Hill, the plebs have sworn a corporate oath of mutual support. They are armed, following a recent campaign.

After a moving speech by the consul, Agrippa, it is reported that the plebs have accepted the idea of "Tribunes of the Plebs" – designed to protect them from patrician excesses.

Poet Pindar lauds winners of the Games

A horse race on an amphora, or vase, given as a prize at the games.

Greece, c.490BC

Greece's athletic Games, host to the achievements of so many great competitors, have gained a new talent: the genius of the Theban poet Pindar, the glory of whose verses pays fitting tribute to the efforts of those whom they immortalise.

Throughout his career, Pindar has been a follower of the four major athletic festivals, penning triumphal odes or *pinicians* in honour of the victors at the Olympic, Pythian, Isthmian and Nemean Games. Indeed, if an athlete is rich enough, he can commission the poet himself, and a choir will sing the resulting ode for the public's enjoyment.

All Pindar's odes follow the same pattern: after calling up visions of splendour, they tell of the victor's home and family and the city in which he lives; then they deal with the contest itself, usually in terms of a famous mythical exploit, well known to all. As well as descriptions Pindar refers to religious and moral themes, and stresses that victory comes only to those whose way of life deserves it.

The god Pan prowls Greek countryside

Pan is famed for his amorousness, but if angry he can cause "panic".

Greece, c.490BC

Many are the tales told by shepherds on the remote hillsides and wastelands of Arcadia of the goat-god Pan, famed for his potent, bestial sexuality, who spreads panic among those who encounter him. Around this time he appears before the runner Philippides as he races to summon the Spartans to resist the invaders from Persia.

On this occasion Pan shows the benign side of his nature, but it is usually considered wise to make oneself scarce when this uncouth god of savage beasts, and of shepherds, sheep and goats, puts in an appearance. In the presence of Pan there is nothing a general can do but order his men to lay down their arms.

A small, horned creature, with the legs of a goat and the torso of a man, he lives in caves far away from the cities, in a twilight world inhabited by nymphs and satyrs. Sacrificial banquets take place in honour of his sexual potency, the rituals of worship apparently being particularly attractive to women. Any isolated nymph or goatherd is liable to fall prey to his carnal appetite.

Pan lives at the frontier between the human, the divine and the bestial, embodying the uncivilised but fascinating power of procreation.

Greeks repel Persians at Marathon

Marathon, 13 September 490BC
There was wild rejoicing in Athens today at the news of a great Athenian victory over the huge Persian army. The hero of the day was Miltiades, who persuaded nine other generals to fight now and not to wait for help from the Spartans, who had said they would not come until their religious festivities were over despite the extraordinary run by Philippides who covered 150 miles in two days to beg assistance.

The army of the Persian King Darius had sacked the town of Eretria on the island of Euboea and landed on the eastern coast of Attica. Today the Persian army was massed on the marshy plain of Marathon and the Athenian force of some 10,000 was in the hills above.

Miltiades had heard that the Persians had withdrawn some of their cavalry to the ships to prepare for an attack on Athens from the sea.

He chose this time to attack, relying on surprise, speed and a three-pronged assault across a wide

The Athenian general Miltiades.

Weapons from the battlefield.

front. His forces ran towards the Persian archers, getting underneath their arrows.

At first the Persians broke through in the centre and pursued the Athenians inland. The two armies on the flanks, however, defeated the Persian flanks and made a concerted attack on the main force from the rear. They then captured seven Persian ships. Some 6,400 Persians were killed, against the Athenian army's losses which numbered fewer than 200.

Athenians erect a treasury at Delphi to honour Apollo

Delphi, 490BC
The Athenians, triumphant after their victory over the Persians at Marathon, have shown their gratitude to the god Apollo by building a treasury in his honour at Delphi. Inside the miniature temple, they leave offerings of silver, plundered from the abandoned Persian camp.

The sculptures which decorate the building, made from Parian marble, are as fine as any in Greece at this time. They depict scenes from the exploits of the Greek heroes, Theseus and Heracles.

A "treasury" building at Delphi.

Two hundred ships built to spearhead Athenian battle fleet

Athens, 483BC
Athens is planning to have the largest fleet in Greece, seven times bigger than that of its rival, Aegina. There is to be a crash building programme of 200 *triremes* to be completed in only three years. The *triremes* are long fast ships, each requiring some 200 oarsmen. They are built for fighting, and the square sail is often left on the beach when they go into battle.

The programme is the brainchild of Themistocles, the *archon* of Athens, who has persuaded his fellow citizens to fund it with the recent big find of silver at the Laurion mines. He is also raising money by the *trierarchy*, a tax levied on those who own very large amounts of property. Effectively it is a tax on the hundred or so wealthiest citizens.

To house the new fleet the port of Athens, Piraeus, is being extensively modernised. The Bay of Mounychia will be dredged and enormous repair yards built there.

Themistocles launched his plan ostensibly to help in the war against

An oarless merchant ship, and a warship with a bronze prow for ramming.

Aegina. But his real purpose is to build up Athenian defences against the much stronger potential enemy – Persia. His new navy will require 40,000 rowers, more than Athens herself could provide even if all able-bodied men were drafted. If Athens were ever to be defeated by the Persians, or any other power, the *triremes* could be used for mass emigration of the Athenians to the west of Greece.

A new memory aid invented by poet

Greece, 489BC
A useful new memory aid has been invented by Simonides of Ceos, the poet, following a disastrous recital. He had been giving the recital at the home of a nobleman named Scopas, in Thessaly, and there had been an argument over his fee. As Simonides departed the roof collapsed, killing the entire audience which was still inside.

The victims were crushed beyond recognition, but the poet was able to identify their bodies because he could remember where each guest was sitting. This made him realise that memory could be improved by forming mental images of the required facts and arranging them in an imaginary set of pigeon holes.

Chivalry dies as Chinese states go to war

The traditional scheme of Chinese history divides the five and a half centuries between the fall of the Western Zhou (Chou) capital at Hoa (near modern Xi'an) in 771BC and the establishment of the Qin (Ch'in) dynasty in 221BC into two main periods. The first of these is the Chungiu (Ch'un-ch'iu) "Spring and Autumn" period, named after the official "Spring and Autumn Annals" of Confucius' home state of Lu, which cover the years 722-481BC. The second period is that of the Zhanguo (Chan-kuo) "Warring States". This is usually taken as beginning in 453BC when the ancient state of Jin (Chin) split into three as the result of a coup d'etat.

As its name suggests, the Warring States period was a time of increasingly violent and ruthless political and military conflict between the rulers of the seven major feudal states into which China was divided. In the process smaller units were absorbed or annihilated until finally Qin succeeded in crushing its rivals and creating a united empire. The royal house of Zhou continued to be treated with at least a ceremonial deference throughout this period, until it in turn was destroyed by Qin in 256BC. Since the Zhou kings had moved east to a new capital at Luoyang (Lo-yang) after the disaster of 771BC, the Spring and Autumn and Warring States periods are often referred to jointly as the Eastern Zhou.

The Warring States period was a time of rapid change on many fronts. While changes in the field of power politics are the most conspicuous in the selective historical record that has come down to us, equally important change in other areas were taking place. Nevertheless, it is to politics that we inevitably turn first in an attempt to characterise the age. During the Spring and Autumn period the rulers of the feudal states of China had gained de facto independence from the Zhou kings, who had lost effective power in the aftermath of the collapse of the Western Zhou.

The Zhou royal line continued, but its rulers were puppets in the hands of their more powerful vassals. In the Warring States period the process of destruction of the Zhou world order went much further, as the ancient ruling men whose power rested on military and political skills rather than on right of birth.

Ruthless, yet competent, officials

Despite the fact that all political power was theoretically held through feudal investiture conferred by the Zhou kings, they were in practice quite unable to block such changes. For example,

when the Han, Wei and Zhao (Chao) families in the state of Jin seized power from the legitimate ruler in 453BC, the Zhou kings were forced to recognise the creation of three new feudal states as Jin was carved up amongst the victors in the power struggle.

Similarly, the offices of state which had previously been held on an hereditary basis for generation after generation were increasingly filled by men selected on the basis of perceived competence and ruthlessness in carrying out the policies of the new rulers. There was a free market for new ideas as well as new skills: it was in this atmosphere of innovative ferment that Chinese philosophy enjoyed an unprecedented period of creativity.

Under the old system, each state had been in part further subdivided into the feudal holdings of the hereditary state officers. Under the new arrangements, states came to be divided into administrative districts, *xian (hsien)*, which were themselves grouped into commanderies, *jun (chun)*. These new units were controlled by salaried officials directly responsible to the ruler of the state rather than to a powerful family.

A vigorous reformer

Reforms such as these were carried out most vigorously in the state of Qin under Duke Xiao (Hsiao) (ruling 361-338BC), when the statesman Shang Yang was at the height of his influence. This drive towards increased centralisation of power was associated with the so-called "Legalist" school of thought, and was to shape the organisation of the empire Qin and of all its successor dynasties.

The nature of Chinese warfare changed in step with changing patterns of political power. In the Spring and Autumn, period warfare had been an aristocratic affair in which relatively small numbers of warriors fought from chariots with bronze weapons. Such infantry as there had been little more than support troops. Campaigns were short and seasonal, and fighting was to some extent governed by a code of chivalry. The new rulers wanted nothing less than total victory over their opponents, and they had often destroyed the aristocracy of their own states who would previously have led their supporters into battle.

The Warring States period armies were led by professional soldiers, and their ranks were filled by peasant infantry who increasingly held land as a reward for their effectiveness as soldiers. These infantrymen had new and more effective weapons, the crossbow and the long sword replacing the old

halberd *ge (ke)*. To replace the chariot corps some northern states organised cavalry along the lines of the barbarians with whom they were in close contact.

To support this growing and active military establishment demanded a rapid expansion of the economic base of each feudal state. Efforts were made to expand agriculture, both by bringing new land into cultivation and by improving productivity. During this period China was suffering from a shortage of skilled labour, and each state was anxious to attract and retain migrants who might open new land, and so increase the state revenues, as well as add to the population available for military service.

Tax "holidays" for persons settling newly cleared land was one amongst several measures used for this purpose. Canals were dug to drain marshes and to irrigate dry areas. Soil fertility was cared for by greater attention to manuring and crop rotation, as well as to techniques of ploughing and sowing.

A superior kind of iron

Closely connected with the increased effectiveness of agriculture and warfare as core state activities was the great improvement in the quality and quantity of tools and weapons available during this period. Whereas these had previously been made of bronze at best, and wood or stone at worst, the implements of the Warring States period were for the first time made of iron. The iron age in China started relatively late: one text giving the first likely mention of iron refers to events in 513BC, and the first firm archaeological evidence does not appear until the fourth century BC. However, when iron did appear in China it is highly noteworthy that it was cast iron, poured into moulds, from a high temperature blast furnace, as a liquid which would set into any desired shape. No European saw cast iron until the 14th century: until then the only iron available came from low-temperature furnaces which produced spongy blooms full of slag, requiring prolonged working before it was of use. China, in contrast to Europe, was a land in which iron was readily available in quantity. This basic technological fact was clearly linked with the high efficiency of Chinese agriculture and the disappearance of an aristocratic ethos of war in China. Together with the persistence of a centralised bureaucratic state, these were features of China that had their origins firmly in the time of the Warring States.

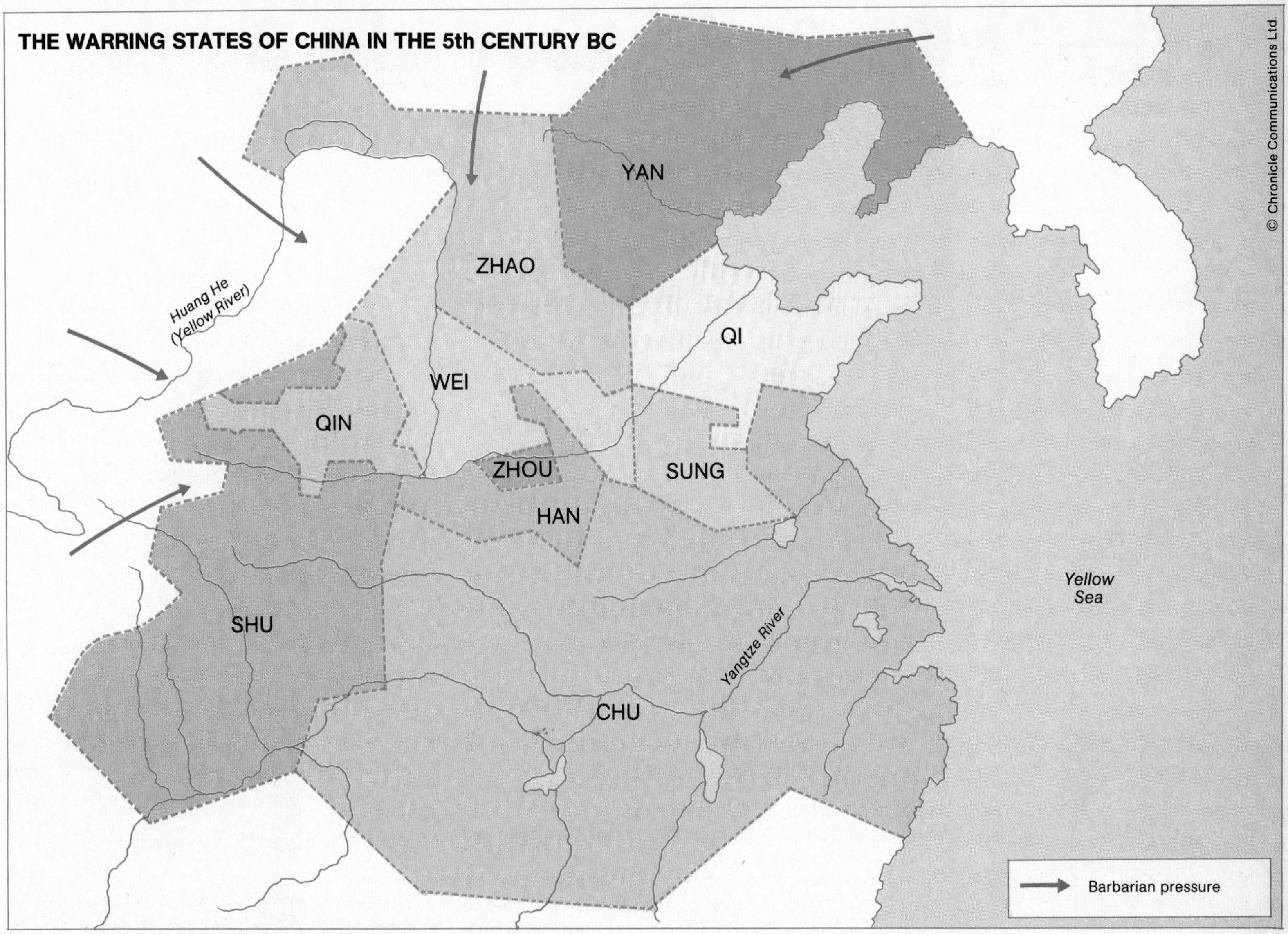

THE WARRING STATES OF CHINA IN THE 5th CENTURY BC

YAN

ZHAO

QI

WEI

QIN

ZHOU

SUNG

HAN

SHU

CHU

Huang He (Yellow River)

Yangtze River

Yellow Sea

→ Barbarian pressure

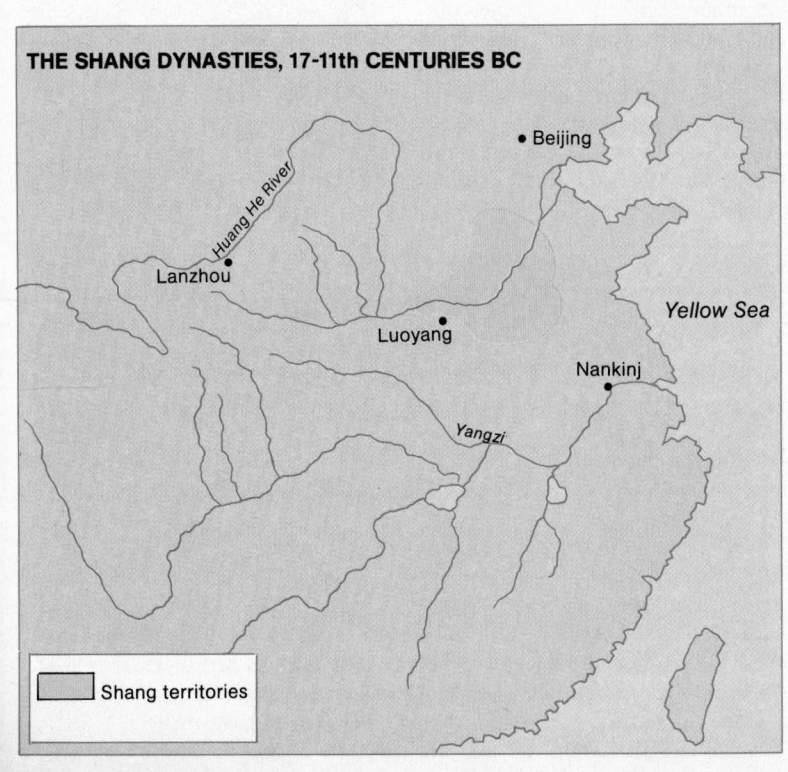

THE SHANG DYNASTIES, 17-11th CENTURIES BC

• Beijing

Huang He River

Lanzhou

Luoyang

Nankinj

Yangzi

Yellow Sea

☐ Shang territories

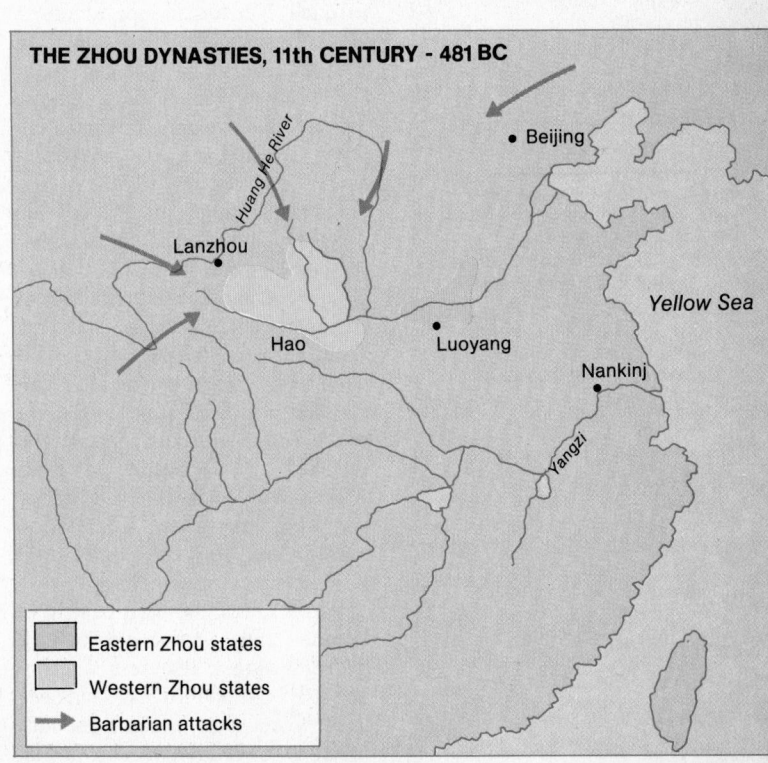

THE ZHOU DYNASTIES, 11th CENTURY - 481 BC

• Beijing

Huang He River

Lanzhou

Hao

Luoyang

Nankinj

Yangzi

Yellow Sea

☐ Eastern Zhou states

☐ Western Zhou states

→ Barbarian attacks

Babylon, 482BC. In an attempt to put down a Babylonian rebellion against Persian domination, Xerxes, king of Persia, destroys the temples of Babylon, including the temple to Marduk.

Anatolia, c.480BC. The Greeks are baffled by the theories of Heraclitus, a philosopher from Ephesus nicknamed "the Riddler". He argues that the universe is governed by the conflict of opposites and that everything is achieved by discord. He believes that the elements are caught up in an endless cycle of transformation which starts from fire, the primordial element.

Greece, c.480BC. The philosopher Parmenides has written an epic poem, *On Nature*, expounding his belief that nothing changes. It begins with a revelation: Parmenides' chariot is carried towards daylight by the daughters of the sun and arrives at the palace of Dike, goddess of justice, who proclaims that his destiny is to know everything. Parmenides learns that all one is entitled to do is affirm existence.

Greece, c.480BC. Zeno, a philosopher from Elea, a Greek colony in Italy, is tortured for his part in a conspiracy against a Greek tyrant. A disciple of Parmenides, Zeno opposes the Pythagoreans and tries to demonstrate that unity is self-contained. Fond of paradox, he argues that, even by running, Achilles will never catch up with a tortoise if it sets off before him because, in theory, the distance between them is infinitely divisible.

Sicily, c.480BC. Gelon, tyrant of Syracuse, in alliance with Theron, tyrant of Acragas, inflicts a crushing defeat on the Carthaginians under Hamilcar at the battle of Himera. Gelon is the successor to Hippocrates, the tyrant of Gela, who, profiting from a serious social crisis earlier in the century, seized power at Syracuse also. The Punic threat has been growing ever since.

Greece, c.480BC. A cult is developing centred on the worship of Demeter, goddess of the earth's fertility, and her daughter Persephone, who was carried off by Hades, god of the underworld. The new spirituality finds its most complete expression in the rituals known as the Eleusinian Mysteries.

New Persian king crushes Babylon

A relief of Darius at Persepolis.

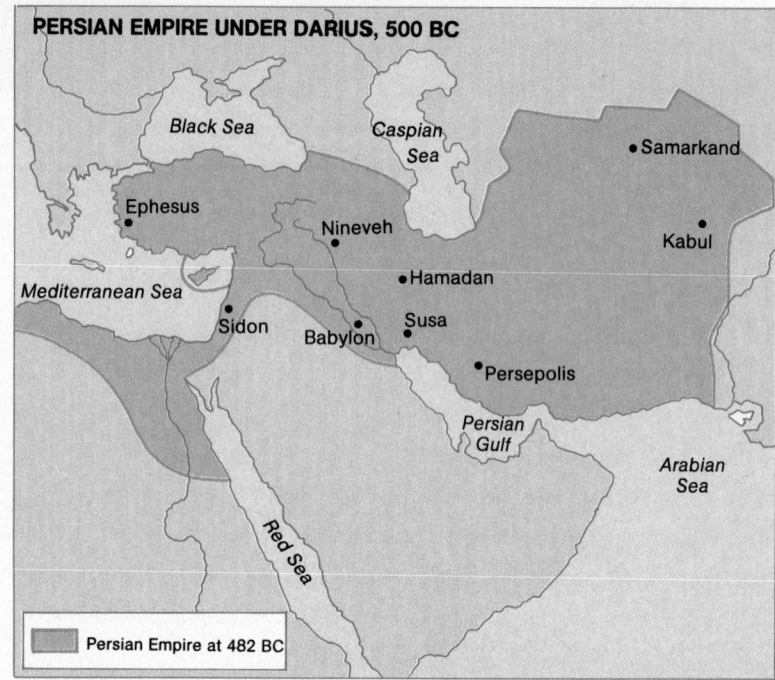

PERSIAN EMPIRE UNDER DARIUS, 500 BC

Black Sea · Caspian Sea · Samarkand · Ephesus · Nineveh · Kabul · Mediterranean Sea · Hamadan · Sidon · Babylon · Susa · Persepolis · Persian Gulf · Arabian Sea · Red Sea

Persian Empire at 482 BC

Near East, 482BC

Xerxes, inheritor of the Persian empire, has brutally put down a revolt in Babylon – launched to recover the freedom lost to Persia in 539BC. Many rebels have been tortured and slain, the city walls have been destroyed and temples razed to the ground. Xerxes has carried off the vast gold statue of the god Marduk and the temple to Marduk, the largest and most prestigious in the oriental world, lies in ruins.

The uprising has revived old enmities. Xerxes' father, Darius, who died in 486BC, used military force to quell Babylonian opposition to his accession 40 years ago, and Babylon has since remained quiet. On his death, Darius left an empire whose limits extended beyond even those created by Cyrus and Cambyses.

Darius, another member of the Achaemenid royal house, succeeded to the throne in 521BC, following the collapse of the brief reign of Cambyses II into civil war, and set about consolidating his power.

As the dominant people in an empire that stretched from Greece to India, all Persians were given special privileges. The aristocracy were advisers and officials, who made up the cavalry in time of war. Commoners were exempt from taxes and served as the army's heavy infantry.

Where Cyrus had been content to conquer lands, Darius systematically exploited their resources. The empire itself was divided, as it had been under Cyrus, into 20 satrapies, each under its own *satrap*, or governor,

who was often a member of the royal family. Each satrapy had to provide money (collected as taxes), horses, produce, ships and soldiers. Individual *satraps* ruled virtually as local kings, administering law and order, commanding troops and conducting local diplomacy.

An extensive system of new roads crossed the empire, establishing unprecedented standards of communication, and a stable coinage underpinned the flourishing economy.

The Babylonian rebellion and the manner of its suppression threaten to destabilise the empire and undermine Darius' great achievements.

A beautifully-made Persian vase.

An Eskimo bone comb, incised with the figure of an archer standing over a man and a variety of animals. The bow and arrow were probably first used in America by the Eskimos, who brought them from Asia.

Outwitted Persians routed at sea

Salamis, 29 September 480BC

The ships of the combined Greek fleet have today won a great victory over the Persian navy. The waters of the Strait of Salamis are littered with the wreckage of Persian ships and the bodies of King Xerxes' sailors. The Persians lost 200 ships, compared to 40 Greek vessels.

The Greeks won the battle as much by cunning as by bravery and seamanship. They tricked the Persians into believing that they had the Greek fleet bottled up in the straits, but when the battle started it was the Persians who were trapped. Much credit must go to the sailors of Corinth who headed north into the Bay of Eleusis, deceiving Xerxes' commanders into thinking they were running away, and then turning and striking at the Persians with great ferocity.

There are some Greeks who also think the Corinthians were running away and were stopped only by the appearance of a mysterious ship sent by the gods to order them back into battle. This story reflects the disunity of the Greeks before the battle, when it was obvious that

Late 19th century British impression of the Greek victory at Salamis.

many of the commanders feared for the safety of their own cities while they were absent.

They were as divided over tactics as they were over strategy, and the debate went on late into the night. In the end the Athenian commander, Themistocles, prevailed, and the Greeks sailed out from their anchorages off Salamis to give

battle in the main channel. There were 380 Greek ships opposed to some 800 Persian men of war. But the Persians split their forces and, in the confused melee which ensued, the Athenian *triremes* with their great prows rammed the Persian ships, sending 200 to the bottom and making the remnants flee to the Bay of Phalerum.

Persians held up by heroic Greeks at Thermopylae

Thermopylae, 480BC

The battle of Thermopylae is over and Leonidas and his 300 Spartans are dead. They died as only Spartans can die: sword in hand, glorying in battle, defying death, seeking only honour.

King Leonidas, commander of the Greek forces holding the pass, had withstood the attack of the Persian hordes for two days. The contours of the narrow pass and the fighting skill of his men enabled him to repel the enemy with great loss.

On the second day, however, a Greek traitor, Ephialtes, revealed the existence of a mountain path which would enable the Persians to

A bronze helmet from Salonika.

take the Greeks in the rear. That night a hand-picked force made its way along the path and brushed aside the Phocians who had been posted to guard the path.

When scouts came running with news of Ephialtes' treachery, Leonidas knew that he was doomed. His force was only 4,000 strong, an advance guard designed to hold the Persians until the main force, which was busy with religious celebrations, arrived.

He sent away the men from other cities, keeping with him only the Thebans, whom he mistrusted, and the valiant Thespians, who refused to go. The end was inevitable. The Thebans went over to the Persians, but the Thespians and the Spartans fought till they died, overwhelmed by numbers and treachery.

Indian prince spurns riches to become preacher called Buddha

Central India, 482BC

A mendicant monk, once a prince, is travelling the roads of India preaching a new path to enlightenment. The prince, Siddhartha Gautama, was born in Kapilavastu, at the foot of the mountains of Nepal. His father was a wise and illustrious ruler; his mother, Maya Devi, died a week after his birth, according to legend "that she might not have her heart broken by seeing her son leave home and take to the life of a beggar".

Quiet and reflective, he was brought up for a life of pomp and politics for which he was temperamentally unsuited. His father, fearing his son would renounce the throne for a contemplative life, attempted to isolate him from all human suffering. He failed. One day, driving in his chariot through the eastern gate of Kapilavastu, he was confronted by the sufferings of an old man. Another day, driving through the southern gate, he was confronted by the sufferings of a dis-

eased man. A third time, driving through the western gate, he was confronted by a dead man. Finally, at the northern gate, he passed a monk with a begging-bowl. The four sights concentrated his mind; he renounced his princely inheritance and became a monk.

Religion in India was the monopoly of the Brahman caste, who taught that birth and rebirth were eternal cycles from which there was no escape. Siddhartha rejected their teachings and withdrew to the village of Urevela, on the banks of the Nairanjana, where he stayed for six years. There, under a fig tree, he achieved enlightenment, becoming "the" Buddha, the "Enlightened One", and entering the state of Nirvana, or Nothingness.

To "the" Buddha there were four essential holy truths: everything is suffering; the cause of suffering is desire; the suppression of desire brings about the suppression of suffering; and to suppress suffering you must follow the noble eightfold

A near-lifesize head of the Buddha.

path of right opinion, intention, speech, action, livelihood, mindfulness, effort and concentration. The Buddha preaches that enlightenment and salvation are not exclusive to the Brahmans, as the latter preached, but open to all.

Greece, 479BC. After their defeat at the battle of Salamis, the Persians try unsuccessfully to negotiate a treaty of alliance with the Athenians against the rest of the Greek world.

India, c.478BC. Siddhartha Gautama Buddha, the founder of Buddhism and one of the great spiritual masters of Asia, dies in Oudh. Aged 30 he abandoned all earthly ambitions for the life of an ascetic. Finding in the contemplative life the perfect way, he spent over 40 years teaching and gained many disciples.

Sri Lanka, 478BC. Prince Vijaya sails from India with a party of companions and lands in Sri Lanka, where he founds a new kingdom.

Greece, c.477BC. The wealthy Aegean island of Thasos, off the coast of Thrace, forms an alliance with the Delian league of Greek maritime states and provides the alliance with a strong contingent of ships.

Greece, c.477BC. The Athenian sculptor Critios is commissioned to replace, with a composition of his own choice, the bronze group raised by Antenor to the glory of the tyrannicides – which has been carried off to Persia by Xerxes.

Mediterranean, 474BC. Hieron, who became tyrant of Syracuse on the death of Gelon in 478BC, wins a great naval victory over the Etruscans, destroying Etruscan sea power. Despite his violent nature, Hieron is a lover of poetry and patronises Pindar, Aeschylus, Simonides and Bacchylides. Pindar and Bacchylides have written odes in praise of Hieron's success in the horse races at Olympia.

Athens, 472BC. In his play *The Persians* Aeschylus presents the Athenian public with a Persian view of the battle of Salamis. The vanquished appear on stage, and the main body of the drama consists of one long, gloomy complaint. The play offers a moral lesson in moderation, caution and respect for the gods – all those qualities which ought to have dissuaded the Persians from such a disastrous undertaking.

Greece, c.470BC. Pausanias, who led the Greeks to victory against the Persians in the battle of Plataea, is accused of fomenting a helot revolt in his native Sparta. He takes sanctuary in a temple, where he is left to starve to death.

Confucius looks back to a golden age

China, 479BC

A great intellectual ferment is currently under way in China, which is in the grip of nationwide discontent and political instability. In this climate it is probably not surprising that people have taken to speculating on the best way to govern their lives and live together in harmony. One philosopher in particular, who died recently at the age of about 70, has aroused great attention with his teachings and recommendations for order accompanied by fair and stable government.

This man, called K'ung-fu-tzu or Confucius, was born into the lesser nobility of the principality of Lu in the region of Shandong. He worked for a time as a civil servant in charge of supervising granaries. It is said that he turned to private teaching after failing to find a single Chinese ruler who would follow his advice on how to institute sound government; he then went on to refine his doctrines even further until his death.

Confucius believed that long ago people lived in a serene age when everyone knew his place in society and carried out the duties that went with it. His doctrines seek a return to that time, the principles of which he claims have been forgotten or obscured over the centuries. At the heart of Confucian teaching is order – the position of everything in its rightful and natural place in the universe.

To ensure order some people, especially those in government, must stick to their moral obligations towards each other and towards society as a whole. In prac-

Lao-tse, Buddha and Confucius depicted on a 19th century sword guard.

tical terms this ideal favours those institutions which are most inclined to lead to the persistence of order, such as the family group and social hierarchy. It requires honesty, integrity and respect for elders and betters, as well as an unpatronising fairness towards people in lower social positions.

As far as those in government are concerned, Confucius is said to have asked for four qualities in both rulers and administrators: care and respect for records, decency of conduct, loyalty, and faithfulness towards superiors and colleagues. Confucius takes a very dim view of naked ambition, because a good administrator who carries out his duties scrupulously can expect to be rewarded without pursuing success.

The great philosopher Confucius.

Athens organises an alliance to rebuff the Persian threat

Greece, 478BC

Athens has taken the lead in forming an alliance of Greek cities against the Persian King Xerxes who, despite his defeats at Plataea and the great sea battle of Salamis, remains a threat to Greece.

Aristeides the Just has convinced Athens' Ionian allies of the need for such a *symmachy*. Delos, the small island home of a religious community, has been chosen as the administrative headquarters of the alliance. It has been agreed that the

congress of this "Delian League" will meet once a year on the island. The alliance was sealed by sinking pieces of iron in the sea to symbolise the fate of those who break oaths.

The first problem to be faced by Aristeides is that it is essential for the league to have a fleet capable of protecting its cities against the Persians, but some of its members are too small to be able to provide the necessary ships and men.

Aristeides has therefore pro-

posed that each member should pay an annual *phoros*, or tribute, to finance a fleet of *triremes*, with the contribution of each city fixed according to its means.

The Spartans, believing that the war against Xerxes is over, are playing no part in the League's affairs. They may well regret their typically independent attitude, however, for it seems likely that the Athenians' leadership of the league will result in all of Greece being gathered under Athenian hegemony.

Athenians triumph again over Persians

Detail of an Athenian frieze showing Greeks and Persians in battle.

Plataea, 479BC

The Greeks have won another crucial victory against the invading Persians. After Salamis, Xerxes withdrew his main force to Asia Minor (Anatolia) to protect his lifeline, the bridges across the Hellespont, but left behind a force of 50,000 troops under Mardonius to continue the war.

Mardonius ravaged the countryside, setting fire to Athens, and then retreated to Boeotia to force the Greeks to fight in country more suitable to his tactics in which he could employ his numerical superiority – the Greeks could field only 39,000 men. It is the Greeks who have triumphed, however. Under the command of Pausanias, the regent of Sparta, they met the Persian army outside Plataea at the foot of Mount Cithaeron and, despite some initial setbacks against the Persian cavalry, have inflicted a terrible defeat on Xerxes's army.

The phalanxes of heavily armed Greek infantry, among whom the Spartans, as usual, distinguished themselves, slaughtered the Persians, who were demoralised by the death of Mardonius. Only 3,000 of the Persians remained alive at the end of the day.

The Greeks also won another victory, catching the Persians off guard at Samos where they burnt the Persian fleet and massacred the garrison, thus securing control of the Aegean.

Creator of Athenian navy is "ostracised"

Athens, 474BC

In a surprise decision, the Athenians have voted to banish Themistocles, the man who devoted his time as *archon* to building up the Athenian navy and other defences to protect it from the Persians. He fell victim to ostracism, which has been used increasingly as a political weapon in recent years.

The ostracism law first came into use 13 years ago, introduced in case there was ever a need to remove a despot. In practice, however, it is used by jealous politicians to settle scores with rivals. Hipparchos, son of Charmos, was the first to be ostracised. He fled to Persia.

Sometimes the pendulum swings later in favour of the victim, who can then be restored to his rights. Aristeides the Just, who was banished in the decade after the battle of Marathon, was later recalled. The victim keeps the major part of his wealth in Athens, and can make his home in a place of his own choosing. Ironically, Themistocles chose to go to Persia, the home of his former enemy.

Ostracism is set in motion by the President of the Council, once victims' names begin to be mooted in the Assembly. Six months later a gathering of all citizens in the *agora*, the meeting place, takes the final decision. At least 6,000 citizens must voice an opinion. Everyone who wishes to inscribes, or has inscribed, the name of the person he wants banished on a fragment of pottery called an *ostrakon*. The person who gets the most votes is banished.

Religious festivals shape the calendar

Demeter and Persephone, part of the mystic cults of Eleusis near Athens.

Greece c.480BC

Although the struggle against the Persians endangers the country's very existence, religious festivals and sacrifices not only continue regardless, but also shape the annual calendar of events. The Athenian year begins in Hecatombaion (July) when Kronos, father of Zeus, is honoured. Masters and slaves feast at the same table, often in the fields where they work. At the end of the month is a national festival, the Panathenaea, a procession to the Temple of Athena on the Acropolis.

Religious attention switches to Eleusis in Boedromion (September), but the rites are for initiates only. People meanwhile celebrate Apollo's "sure resource" in battle.

Pyanepsion (October) opens with another festival for Apollo, when the god is presented with a vegetarian meal of beans, legumes, wheat flour, figs and pots of honey. In the Oschophoria of Dionysus, a procession of adolescents bearing heavy bunches of grapes is greeted with wild cries. And, in honour of Demeter, married women exclude men as they observe abstinence and fertility rites.

Terracotta phalluses are planted in Poseideion (December) in another festival reserved for women, particularly those of dubious virtue. And both Gamelion (January) and Anthesterion (February) bring hectic wine festivals.

Spring arrives in Elaphebolion (March), when Athena is thanked and foreigners flock to see performances of Greek theatre. Cakes are offered to Artemis in Mounychion (April); two "scapegoats" laden with evils are expelled in Thargelion (May), before Apollo is feasted and the statue of Athena bathed in the sea and fed dried figs. The year ends in Skirophorion (June) with sacrifices to commemorate the first killing of a plough-ox and the first sacrifice.

A charioteer, from a sculpture of a victorious chariot team offered to the shrine of Delphi by the tyrant Polyzelos of Gela.

Greece, 468BC. The great Athenian politician Aristeides dies in poverty. Known as Aristeides "the Just", he was a general at the battle of Marathon before being elected *archon* (chief magistrate) in Athens, but his rivalry with Themistocles and the democrats led to his exile. Recalled to command the Athenian forces at the battle of Plataea in 479BC, he helped to make Athens the ruling state of the Delian League.

Greece, 467BC. Cimon, son of Miltiades, the conqueror at Marathon, destroys or captures most of the Persian ships at the mouth of the River Eurymedon, off the coast of Pamphylia, securing Athenian dominance in the Aegean. Having taken advantage of Themistocles' political decline, Cimon is currently the most powerful man in Athens.

Athens, 467BC. Aeschylus wins the dramatic competition of the Great Dionysia with his trilogy on the Theban legend. The last of the three plays, *Seven Against Thebes*, deals with the final confrontation between the two accursed sons of Oedipus. Eteocles, king of Thebes, and his brother Polynices kill each other in battle and the terrible curse on the house of Laius dies with them.

Persia, 465BC. Xerxes, king of Persia, is assassinated. Xerxes never fully recovered his power after the Persian defeats by the Greeks, and palace intrigues and revolts followed one another thick and fast. His son, Artaxerxes, succeeds.

Greece, 465BC. The states of the Delian League make their payments to the shrine of Apollo on Delos. These payments can be in money or in kind, for example by supplying ships to the common fleet. Although the original aim of the League was to protect Greek cities against Persian invasion, it is rapidly becoming an instrument to bolster the power of Athens.

Greece, c.465BC. A new realism is asserting itself in Greek painting. Scenes from everyday life are popular and there is a concern to paint individual faces. Experiments in polychrome on a white ground have paved the way for the special funerary oil-vases called *lekythoi*. A painting of the slaughter of the children of Niobe superimposes different planes of action and makes use of a variety of perspectives.

Temple of Zeus depicts Herculean labours

Hercules, or Herakles, overcomes one of his labours, the Erymanthian boar.

Olympia, 460BC
Work on the temple of Zeus continues. A collection of sculptures has just been added, containing 12 *metopes* depicting the "Labours of Hercules". Born of Zeus' union with a mortal, Hercules becomes a victim of Hera's jealousy as Hera is the god's lawful wife.

However, his early misfortunes are as nothing compared with the labours which Eurystheus imposes upon him.

The first *metope* shows Hercules strangling the Nemean lion with his bare hands; the well-known image of him holding a club is fixed by this episode. He slays the nine poisonous heads of the hydra of Lerna, and captures the wild boar of Mount Erymanthus and the golden-horned stag of Arcadia before shooting the man-eating birds of Stymphalia.

Then he succeeds in cleansing the cattle stables of King Augeus by diverting two rivers through them; captures the mad bull that terrorises Crete, and the man-eating mares of King Diomedes; slays the Queen of the Amazons and takes her girdle; seizes the cattle of Geryon beyond the pillars named after him (*Gibraltar*); retrieves the golden apples guarded by the Hesperides; and, finally, manages to recover from the underworld the dog Cerberus which guards its gates.

He dies when his wife Deianeira gives him a love potion which turns out to be poison. Zeus removes him from his funeral pyre and he is immortalised as a god.

Power passes to people in Athens

Athens, 462BC
A major political upheaval has taken place in Athens. In recent years the conservative aristocratic faction has regained much of its lost power, but, taking advantage of the absence of Cimon, the faction's leader, on a military expedition to Messenia, an attack has been mounted on its position by Ephialtes, a radical reformer.

Ephialtes, respected for his integrity by his fellow-citizens, has forced a fundamental law through the Assembly which is designed to establish a new fairness among Athenian political institutions. His main target is the Areopagus.

This ancient, aristocratic council and court, whose political powers have been codified since the days of the great Solon, has been taking advantage of the turmoil created by the unrest following the Persian wars to extend its powers.

Ephialtes' new law will deprive the Areopagus, composed of former magistrates, of its principal judicial powers. From now on everything concerning the administration of Athens, even the supervision of public affairs, will be handled either by the Council of Five Hundred or the popular court, the Heliaia.

What this means is that the power of the people will be increased while that of the aristocracy, as expressed through the Areopagus, will be curtailed. But Ephialtes has made many enemies.

Slave revolt unsettles the city of Sparta

Greece, 464BC
Sparta, the most powerful city of the Peloponnese, is plunged into crisis as slaves take advantage of an earthquake to rise up in rebellion.

The violence of the tremor has devastated the city and killed thousands of its inhabitants. The helots of Laconia and their fellow-slaves in Messenia rise up, too, converging on the city from the surrounding countryside to attack the survivors.

But King Archidamus quickly rallies his warriors, forcing the helots to withdraw and wage open war. The slaves are joined in the rebellion by members of the Perioecic community, who have also been debarred from positions of power in the Spartan state. They take up positions on the slopes of Mount Ithome in Messenia.

The Spartans, failing to take the place by direct assault, are forced to ask their Athenian allies to help them lay siege.

This bronze figure of an archer comes from Sardinia, where an original culture has flourished for more than 500 years.

World envoys join Persia's celebrations

Persians, with characteristic fluted hats, on a grand stairway at Persepolis.

Capital buildings symbolise empire glory

A glazed-brick griffin from Susa, the administrative capital of Persia.

Persia, 465BC

Persepolis, the City of the Persians, is finally complete. The New Year celebrations, which coincide with the spring equinox, are more spectacular than ever and last for 11 days.

There are parades of unparallelled magnificence, with delegations from all the known world arriving to pay tribute to the mighty Persian empire.

Persepolis was started in 516BC by Darius I at Stakhr-i-Parsa, to take the place of Cyrus's old capital of Pasargadae. The building of the city continued through three reigns. While Susa remains the administrative capital, it is Persepolis, the ceremonial capital, which epitomises the grandeur of the greatest empire the world has seen, stretching from the Caspian Sea to the Nile, from India to the Aegean.

Ceremonial life in the palace revolves round the two great audience halls. The *apadana* is where the king receives his dignitaries and the annual tributes of his subject peoples, and where he gives an annual banquet for the people of Persia and Medea.

It is reached by flights of steps with friezes depicting tribute-bearers: Medes, Susians, Arabs, Armenians, Babylonians, Egyptians, Scythians, Indians, Libyans, Ethiopians and Ionians.

The other great hall is known as the Hall of 100 Columns and is used for receiving the peoples of the Empire.

Persia, 465BC

The greatness of Persia is displayed in the monumental architecture of its twin capitals, Susa and Persepolis. The enormous variety of artistic influences reflects the extent of the Persian empire.

Cyrus had employed teams of Lydian and Greek masons on his palace at Pasargadae, and Darius continued the Greek tradition with great columnar halls flanked by colonnaded porticoes.

At Persepolis, however, his palace is distinguished by Egyptian cavetto mouldings, and the carved frontages of his cruciform tomb in a huge cliff nearby also look Egyptian.

Susa, the political capital and administrative centre of the empire, had been destroyed in 640BC by the Assyrian Ashurbanipal, but was rebuilt by Darius. A low hill was levelled with gravel to a height of about 65 feet above the stream bed to form a terrace of ten acres. Darius's palace was built on the north side, its rectangular rooms arranged round several courtyards.

The *apadana*, or audience hall, at Susa is surrounded by a triple row of columns of black and white stones. Each column is 65 feet high, with a pair of bulls at the top supporting the roof beams. Stone was in short supply, and the mud walls of the palace are decorated with enamelled bricks depicting bulls, griffins and the "Immortals",

A Persian archer from Susa.

Darius's personal bodyguard. Labour and materials were provided by 26 or 27 different peoples.

Despite Susa's importance, not only as a capital city but also as the commercial centre of the empire, the greatest architectural magnificence was reserved for Persepolis. Here the terrace is three times the size of Susa's, reached by twin returning staircases of 111 steps and surmounted by the immense Gate of Xerxes, with colossal cherubim and Assyrian-type monsters.

Island rebels give in after two-year siege

Thasos, 463BC

The two-year siege of Thasos is over, with the rebel islanders forced to accept Athenian terms. The city walls have been demolished, financial penalties levied, and the island surrenders its navy and its rights on the mainland.

Tension between Athens and Thasos dates back to the aftermath of Salamis in 477BC, when the Thasians joined the Delian League of Greek maritime states and provided the confederacy with a powerful fleet. Hostilities broke out in 465BC over Thasian claims to markets and mines on the mainland. The Athenians sent a fleet to Thasos, won a naval battle and laid siege to the city.

The Thasians appealed to Sparta for help, and the Spartans promised to invade Attica in order to persuade the Athenians to lift their siege. The Spartans' efforts were thwarted, first by an earthquake and then by a revolt of helots and others in Ithome. Without Spartan help, the people of Thasos had to sue for peace.

Egypt, c.460BC. Athens sends a fleet to support an Egyptian revolt against the occupying Persian forces. In response, the Persians now have an army of 300,000 men in Egypt.

India, 459BC. Ajatasatra, who became king of India after deposing his father, is dead. Ajatasatra secured the final defeat of the Vrjji people. He fortified his capital, Rajagrha, and built a fort at Pataligrama.

Egypt, 459BC. After helping the Egyptian rebels to defeat the Persians at Papremis, the Greeks are put to flight and take refuge on an island in the delta, sustaining heavy losses.

Greece, c.458BC. As part of its campaign to attack the states of the Peloponnesian League individually, Athens wins a naval victory over Aegina, an island in the Saronic gulf, and goes on to defeat the Corinthians at Megara.

Greece, c.458BC. After intervening in Phocis and Doris, the Spartans confront and vanquish the Athenians at Tanagra, in Boeotia.

Athens, 458BC. Aeschylus again wins first prize in the tragedy competition, with the *Oresteia* trilogy. In the first play, *Agamemnon*, the Achaean king is murdered by his wife, Clytemnestra, and her lover. In *The Libation Bearers* Agamemnon's son, Orestes, avenges his father by matricide. *The Eumenides* is a drama of reconstruction.

Sicily, 456BC. Aeschylus dies at Gela in odd circumstances. According to the Greeks, an eagle spotted a rock against which to smash the shell of a tortoise it was carrying and hurled the animal at it. Its target was not a rock, however, but Aeschylus' bald head shining in the sunlight. The poet did not survive the blow.

Greece, 454BC. The Delian League's treasury is moved from Delos to the Acropolis of Athens. The official reason is the threat to its security. More likely, Athens intends to use the funds to further its imperialist policy.

Egypt, 454BC. The Persians regain control of Egypt, practically annihilating the Greek troops sent to support the Egyptian rebels.

China, 453BC. As a result of a seizure of power, the kingdom of Jin (Chin) splits into three warring principalities: Han, Wei and Zhao.

Temple glorifies Zeus

Poseidon is among the onlookers as Athena is born from the head of Zeus.

Olympia, 470BC
The architect Libon has designed a new temple of Zeus. An artificial mound raises the building 10 feet above ground level, and its monumental size is further emphasised by its massive proportions, by the contrast of white walls against violent blue and red triglyphs and dripstones, and by the majesty of sculpted pediments and metopes. The temple is designed to house a gold and ivory statue of Zeus by the great sculptor Phidias.

The size and grandeur of the building emphasise the fact that

Victorian recreation of the extraordinary Olympian statue of Zeus.

Zeus stands above all other gods. Even gods who are not his children address him as father and stand in his presence. He unites many divine attributes. If on a physical level he is the god of the sky, of rain and of thunder, he is more usually a benign god who watches over the universe and is concerned with maintaining peace between people.

He is thus the god of justice, assisted by Themis, goddess of law, and by his own daughter, Dike, who is goddess of justice. He hates crime and murder, and always punishes those guilty of opposing established order by sending the avenging Erinyes, or Ate, who drive individuals to distraction, causing them to destroy themselves.

Zeus presides over relationships, watching over families with his wife Hera, goddess of marriage, and over friendship in his capacity as Zeus Xenios, who makes it an obligation to offer hospitality to strangers. He grants authority to kings; cities are placed under his protection. In Athens he is worshipped in the form of Zeus Polieus, god of the city, as god of the *agora*, or meeting place, and as god of the *boule*, where he presides over debates. He is general protector of all Greeks, and is Soter, or Saviour, who averts danger. The temple reflects the fact that his name is on the lips of all Greeks.

Poseidon rules the waves from golden maritime palace

Greece, 477-467BC
When Zeus came to the throne of Olympus he entrusted the rule of the sea to his brother, Poseidon, who exercises an unpredictable authority over his maritime kingdom and its inhabitants. According to Homer he lives in the depths, near Aegae in northern Greece, in an indestructible golden palace, and drives a golden chariot across the seas without its getting wet.

He is a formidable god, married to Amphitrite, and usually manifests himself in the unleashing of the waves. For the Greeks he is the

A bronze of Poseidon, the mighty maritime god of the Greeks.

incarnation of the anguish the sea always causes, unpredictable and subject to sudden changes of mood. He uses a trident to strike the waves and raise the storm.

Poseidon's power extends onto land, where blows from his trident provoke earthquakes. He is also the god of horses, and terrifies or calms them at will. Horsemen and sailors alike are powerless against his sudden anger and can only offer up prayers. The great white temple of Poseidon on Cape Sunium can be seen by all ships heading for Athens, and the first catch of the tunnyfishing season is offered to him. Woe betide any mortal who, like Odysseus, makes an enemy of Poseidon.

Olympia: a Greek shrine for religion and sport

Chariot-racing is a highly popular event at the Olympic Games.

Olympia, Greece, 452BC

Every four years, from all over the Hellenic world, Greeks flock to Olympia, to the Games where the flower of Greek manhood competes. Olympia, in the Alpheus Valley in the north-west of the Peloponnese, is a holy place, a shrine to the god Zeus, attracting thousands of pilgrims each year; but it is in the Games that Olympia comes into its own. A month before the Games open, heralds and religious ambassadors announce the date of the great gathering. A holy truce is proclaimed, warring states put aside their weapons, and competitors, spectators and pilgrims are given safe conduct to the Games.

The athletes themselves must all be of Greek blood, free men, legitimate and of impeccable character. Already they have spent ten months in rigorous training in their own city-states. After the proclamation they gather in the gymnasium of the neighbouring state of Elis for the final month of training. During that month they are forbidden any stimulants and are fed a diet of barley bread, wheat porridge, dried figs, nuts and cheese.

Responsibility for overseeing the Games lies with the aristocracy of Elis, who preside over all religious ceremonies at Olympia, of which they are the earthly guardians. United in an "Olympic senate" they elect nine *hellanodikai*, or judges, three for the chariot and horse racing, three for the Pentathlon and three for the other events.

Dressed in their purple robes, with laurel wreaths on their brows, they set the rules, give the starting signals, judge the competitions, and award the prizes of wild olive wreaths to the victors. The opening ceremonies begin at Elis two days before the start of the Games. There – to the order: "Forward to Olympia! Enter the stadium and prove yourselves victorious men! But anyone who is not prepared may go where he will!" – the competitors selected by the *hellanodikai* set out on their two-day march to Olympia.

The march, over 35 miles, takes the athletes through Pieria, the sacred spring on the frontier between Elis and Pisa, where they wash themselves and sacrifice a pig, and Letrini, where they rest for the night before continuing to Olympia the following morning.

Arriving at Olympia the athletes are greeted by the roar of 20,000 spectators packed into the stadium. A *keryx*, or servant of the *hellanodikai*, raises his arm for silence and reads out the names of the competitors, the cities they come from and the events they will take part in. Then the *keryx* takes each competitor into the centre of the arena and asks the thousands assembled if there are any who object to the athlete taking part. Finally the athletes, led by the *hellanodikai*, go to the altar of Zeus where they swear to keep the Olympic ideal.

Throughout the Games the virtues of modesty and good nature are regarded by the athletes as essential complements to victory. Victory belongs primarily to the gods and secondarily to the city-states. The ego of the individual

The passageway into the stadium.

A bronze helmet from Olympia.

athlete is considered the least important. The Games over, the final task belongs to the *hellanodikai*, to enter the results in the victory lists and set up the statues of the victors.

Temple of Zeus, with the stadium in the background (20th century model).

The temple of Hera at Olympia is a reminder that Olympia is a holy place.

Athens, 451BC. Pericles, leader of the democrats, is shoring up his position in Athens and restoring order in the Aegean after signing a five-year truce with Sparta. He is faced with an aristocratic opposition led by Cimon who, back in Athens after ten years of ostracism, acted as principal negotiator in the Spartan truce talks.

Athens, 450BC. Sophocles' tragedy *Ajax* deals with an episode in the Trojan war. After the death of Achilles, the Greeks decide to give the hero's armour to the man with the greatest cunning, Ulysses (or Odysseus), rather than to Ajax, the most courageous. Ajax flies into a fit of rage, slaughters all the army's livestock and then commits suicide.

Athens, c.450BC. The work of the sculptor Pheidias expresses the grandeur of Athens. He projects a new grace and serenity onto the faces of the gods and mythological figures, creating a moral and spiritual ideal. Among his masterpieces are the statues of Zeus and Athena at the temples of Olympia and Athens, and the Parthenon sculptures.

Sicily, c.450BC. Empedocles, a poet born at Agrigentum, is regarded as a great philosopher and magician. In his didactic poem *On Nature*, he maintains that the four elements of which the world is composed – air, fire, earth and water – are governed by the opposing forces of love and discord.

Greece, 449BC. Persia and Athens conclude the Peace of Callias, marking the official end to the Persian wars and acknowledging Athenian supremacy in the Aegean.

Greece, 446BC. Athens and Sparta sign a 30-year peace treaty which obliges Athens to withdraw its troops from territories belonging to the Peloponnesian League.

Athens, c.445BC. The Athenians build a temple on a hilltop in honour of their divine patron of crafts. It is known as the Hephaisteion.

Rome, 443BC. The office of censor is created. The elected official is responsible for taking a census of the nation, for maintaining a list of senators and for purifying the Roman people. He can exclude from the senate any citizen thought likely to blemish the common good and transfer such a person to a different tribe or social class.

All life is sacred, says ex-warrior

Tenth century Indian goddess.

India, c.450BC

Two new philosophies have grown with the rise of new cities in India in the past century. One of these is Buddhism, and the other is based on the teachings of Vardhamana, known to his followers as *Mahavira*, "the great man".

Mahavira's life has parallels with that of the Buddha. He was born at Bihar into the warrior caste about 50 years ago. At the age of 30 he abandoned his life of ease and retired for a year of meditation, before devoting himself to asceticism and experiencing "enlightenment". His followers are called *Jainas*. A key tenet of what is called Jainism is the "theory of approach", according to which the appearance of a thing depends not on its essence but on the individual's approach to it.

Image of Mahavira, c.500-700AD.

It follows that what the individual perceives is not necessarily reality.

Mahavira teaches, therefore, that the sacred *Rig-Veda* texts cannot be divine revelation; nor can the priests, the Brahmans, be the only mediators between gods and men. The ways to enlightenment are right faith, right knowledge and right conduct, accompanied by *ahimsa*, non-injury to all living creatures.

In the growing towns the wealthy merchants are especially attracted to Jainism, not least because it frees them from the crushing obligations of supporting the Brahman priests and their costly services.

Legal changes give rights to plebeians

Rome, c.449BC

Twelve tables setting out the laws are being displayed in the forum, ending years of injustice to the plebeian classes in Rome. Until now the law has remained the preserve of the patricians, unwritten, transmitted in speech only and passed down through generations of pontiffs and magistrates.

Ignorance of the law, claim plebeian leaders, has led to the poor being enslaved for debt and being deprived of any say in government. Nonetheless, plebeians can still be sold for slavery if a debt is not paid within 60 days.

Rome finally beats warlike neighbour

Rome, c.450BC

After almost a century of wars, Rome has finally defeated the Sabines. This fierce alliance of pastoral people living in the Apennines has long coveted Latium's access to the sea, its fertile land and winter pastures. They also seek the salt available to the Romans at Ostia. Now they finally seem prepared to accept Romanisation, and the Romans themselves have adopted a Sabine god, Sancus.

The victory must represent a considerable relief for the Romans. During the countless campaigns the Sabines have often succeeded in getting to the city walls, and on one occasion actually occupied the Capitoline citadel itself before Rome could call in allies from Tusculum – which has also been constantly threatened by these "foreigners" – to assist in their ejection.

Rome has come to terms with its Latin neighbours and has reluctantly accepted equal political status with 30 Italian states; but, even so, Rome is gradually imposing its supremacy in Latium, particularly in the area of religion, much of which has been "borrowed" from other states. This Roman policy – aimed at attracting to itself the power and divinities of defeated states – has brought from Tusculum the worship of Castor and Pollux, the Greek Dioscuri.

A detail from a beautifully decorated Chinese silk, embroidered with pheasants and phoenixes, buried in the tomb of a Scythian chief and preserved by the freezing climate of northern Asia.

Miletus is showcase for urban planning

Greece, c.450BC

A native of the city of Miletus on the Ionian coast, the architect Hippodamus, is developing a new way of laying out the towns and cities of Greece. Using a rectangular grid, Hippodamus brings together a number of large units, each of which is dedicated to some function of the city's life, to create the entire plan, accentuating both orderliness and harmony.

What has become known as the Hippodamian system was first seen in the architect's home town, which had been razed to the ground by a Persian attack in 494BC. In 479BC, with a blank sheet, Hippodamus was able to start from first princi-

Lion and column from Miletus.

ples. Working from a pattern of right-angled, intersecting streets, Hippodamus has created a chessboard effect, onto which are placed all the most important buildings. At the centre of town, where the various types of buildings, such as houses and religious institutions, meet, stands the *agora*, or meeting place, the natural focus of urban life. With its new plan Miletus has begun flourishing again.

The Hippodamian system is being adapted throughout Greece and its colonies and is proving itself an ideal, uncomplicated method of town planning, incorporating as it does all the basic urban needs and solving with the minimum of fuss the problem of how best to divide up the amenities of a new city site. Among Hippodamus' other commissions is the replanning of Piraeus, the port of Athens.

Pericles strengthens democracy in Athens

Athens, 443BC

Pericles, the great orator and statesman, has confirmed his position as the most powerful man in Athens by engineering the ostracism, or exile, of his rival Thucydides. He will now be able to continue the democratic political reforms begun by his friend, the murdered Ephialtes.

His talents extend far beyond domestic reform. It is his intention to make the Athenians fully aware of their power and to use the principle of democracy to bring unity and glory to the city-state.

He has already demonstrated his ability to think beyond the confines of Athens. In 449BC he organised a congress of all Greek states to plan the rebuilding of the temples destroyed by the Persians, the establishment of the freedom of the seas, and peace among the states.

Although nothing came of this, Pericles gained much honour and four years ago was appointed commissioner for the building of the

Pericles, orator and statesman.

Parthenon. He is an incorruptible man, but, despite his democratic principles, remains a rich and haughty aristocrat. Consequently he has many enemies, who slander him.

New walls built to protect port of Piraeus

A 19th century view of how Piraeus and its long walls may have looked.

Athens, 449BC

The Middle Wall, the third of the long walls which protect roads between Athens and its port of Piraeus, is now complete. It is parallel to the original Northern Wall started by Themistocles 30 years ago. That was in 479BC, the year that the Athenians finally threw out the Persians and returned to their city, which had been

devastated in the invasion of 480BC. The Spartans were arguing then that the old fortification walls should not be rebuilt since they could provide a defence for the Persians if the latter captured the city again. Themistocles, however, led the whole population in working on the new walls, even demolishing public and private buildings to help to provide materials.

Athens holds power over neighbours

Athens, c.450BC

Athens has now consolidated its power after successful battles with the Persian invaders, and dominates several city-states in the Aegean in a loosely-structured empire. Its power is based on the biggest navy in the area, including the 200 *triremes* built between 483BC and 480BC. This fleet enabled Athens to recover from invasion and win great naval battles against the Persians at Salamis and Mycale.

The Delian League was originally a defensive alliance of Greek cities, which paid a tribute to Athens mainly to support the navy. The Athenians have developed it over the years to exert economic

Athena and Hera, from a decree.

and political power over the other city-states, some of which, like Athens, are democracies and others oligarchies. In most of the other cities there are resident Athenians who wield influence in the local assemblies.

Athens is the judicial capital of the region and its focal point. The Athenian currency is used in all trade in the empire. Thanks to its rich silver mines and the business and craft skills of its citizens, Athens can buy wheat for everyone.

Power still resides with old families, from which both Pericles and Cimon, the two main leaders of the last 30 years, came. But they depended for their power on oratorical skills, which won them support in the Assembly, rather than upon any hereditary right to govern.

Funerals seen as the key to an afterlife

Athens, c.430BC

The Athenians believe that everyone, apart from certain criminals, is entitled to a decent burial. Like most Greeks, they think that without burial the deceased cannot gain access to the afterlife in the house of Hades, the lord of the underworld. A corpse is regarded as having nothing further to do with the gods of the living, and therefore must be hidden in the earth to avoid pollution or offence to them.

Funerals tend to follow the same pattern. The body is first bathed, then dressed in clothes such as would have been worn in life. It is then laid on a couch, and a honeycake or other offering is placed in the mouth for Charon, the boatman who ferries the dead across the subterranean river Styx to Hades.

Lamentations follow, together with libations – ritual pourings of various liquids, such as wine, milk, honey and water. The funeral then sets off in procession to the cemetery, which is outside the city walls to avoid pollution. There the body is either buried in a coffin, or cremated and the bones buried in a jar or urn. The grave is marked by a stone *sema* (sign), with an inscription and often a statue, for example of a youth, girl, lion or sphinx. The relatives re-enact the first ritual at increasing intervals for a month afterwards, and then every year on

Urn depicting a funeral procession.

the anniversary of the death. In Athens, those who have reached the highest level of value and selflessness by being killed in battle are buried with a public display of mourning and reverence which culminates in a funeral oration.

A particularly fine example of such a speech was given this year by the Athenian leader Pericles, shortly after the outbreak of war with the Peloponnesians. Pericles praises the dead as worthy of their city, the great free democracy of Athens, but warns that "freedom depends upon being courageous".

Hippocrates founds science of medicine

Greece, c.430BC

The teachings of Hippocrates and other physicians who have adopted his methods have transformed the approach to sickness in the city-states of Greece. Hippocrates insists that disease has natural causes and is not to be explained by divine intervention. His book *On the Sacred Disease* caused a sensation by rejecting the common belief that epilepsy was caused by the gods. Calling the disease sacred, he says, is a cover for ignorance.

Hippocrates, born on the small island of Cos, off the south-west coast of Anatolia, has travelled widely in mainland Greece, teaching medical students to study their patients carefully, record their symptoms dispassionately and treat them sympathetically. A code of ethics, which is increasingly being referred to as the Hippocratic Oath, is now regularly adopted by doctors. It says: "I will use my power to help the sick, according to my ability and judgement, and not for their injury or any evil purpose ... Whatever I see or hear in my attendance on the sick, which ought not to be divulged publicly, I will keep secret and tell nobody ..." Busts of the great physician show him bearded, with a grave and thoughtful expression.

Migrations cause social tensions to intensify in western Europe

Europe, c.440BC

Rebellions against many Celtic rulers have ushered in a new cultural phase in northern Europe, typified in the architecture and artefacts of La Tene, beside Lake Neuchatel, in Switzerland.

From the beginning of the century, the older centres of Celtic power in Burgundy and southern Germany began to lose their importance. Social inequalities and tensions which the greedy princes did nothing to mitigate coincided with large growths and movements in population. There were sporadic uprisings. Fortresses like the Heuneburg in Bavaria were overrun, looted and razed to the ground. Sculptures were violated, and many dynasties overthrown.

It was the beginning of a new and

more aggressive phase of Celtic culture, based on developing warrior societies whose members launched raids to capture slaves, and who ventured into Italy and parts of Asia Minor, (*Anatolia*) clashing with Romans and Greeks. Some then ended up as mercenaries in Greek armies.

There were significant regional differences among the Celts, but one unifying factor was religion. They believed in rebirth after death, and worshipped various gods. The priesthood of the Druids had great power, being the educators of the young and having the power to order human sacrifices.

Symbols of this emergent civilisation can be found at La Tene: long double-edged iron swords, and artistic decorations derived

Decorated helmet from La Tene.

from Etruscan, south Russian and native sources; fantastic stylised animals are common, as well as heavy necklaces of solid gold or bronze.

Athens and Sparta torn apart by war

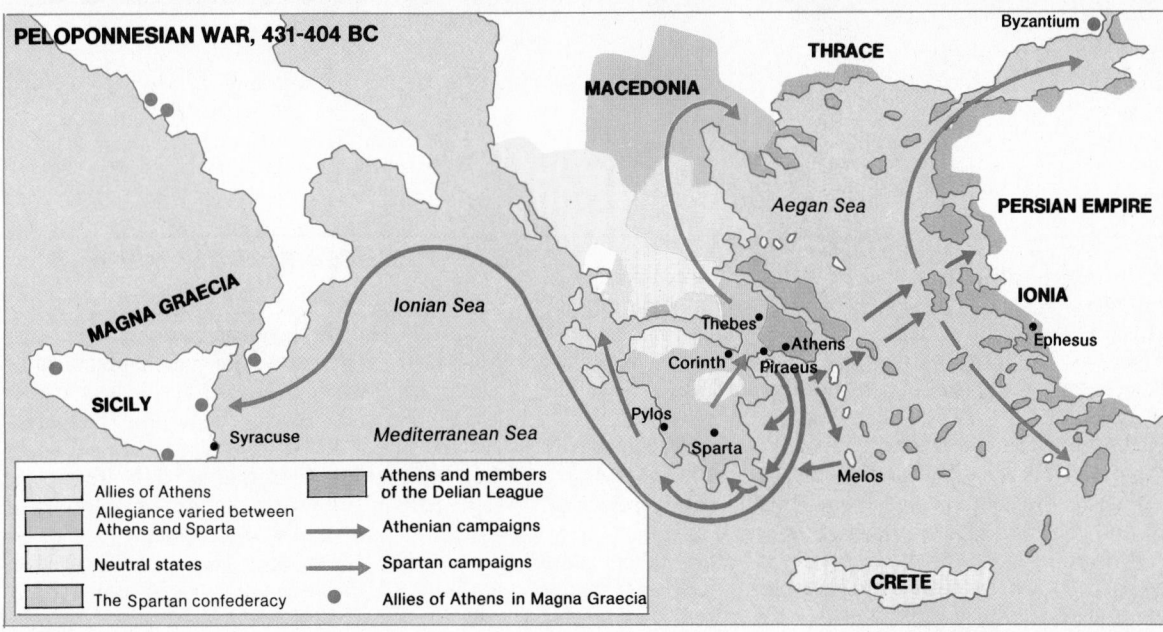

PELOPONNESIAN WAR, 431-404 BC

Byzantium

THRACE

MACEDONIA

Aegan Sea

PERSIAN EMPIRE

MAGNA GRAECIA

Ionian Sea

IONIA

Ephesus

Thebes

Corinth   Athens
           Piraeus

SICILY

Syracuse   Mediterranean Sea

Pylos

Sparta

Melos

CRETE

Allies of Athens
Allegiance varied between Athens and Sparta
Neutral states
The Spartan confederacy

Athens and members of the Delian League
Athenian campaigns
Spartan campaigns
Allies of Athens in Magna Graecia

Thucydides records the war to become first war reporter

Greece, 430BC

A Greek soldier, Thucydides, is revolutionising the annals of warfare by bringing back on-the-spot reports from the battlefields of the war between Athens and Sparta, which, as he puts it himself, is "the greatest disturbance in the history of the Greeks". A devoted follower of the Athenian commander Pericles, Thucydides was born around 460BC and has been writing for a decade. Now he is proving himself not just one more enthusiastic young soldier, but a brilliant reporter of current events.

Thucydides has no doubts about the importance of his work. He says: "It is better evidence than that of the poets, who exaggerate the importance of their themes, or of the prose chroniclers, who are less interested in telling the truth than in catching the attention of their public." Their authorities cannot be checked, he claims, while his own work, based on personal experience, is far more accurate.

As well as eye-witness reports, Thucydides includes many of the speeches delivered in assemblies or on the battlefield, and although, as he admits, his imperfect memory may mean that the exact text has been lost, "what, in my opinion, was called for in each situation" has been properly included.

Greece, 429BC

The brutal war between Athens and Sparta and their allies is devastating Greece. The city-state of Plotidaea has been forced to surrender to the besieging Athenians after being reduced to such a state of hunger that its people have been eating the bodies of their dead.

The Athenian generals have allowed the inhabitants to leave the town without massacring them, but have imposed such harsh terms – the men are allowed to take only one garment – that many will die in this harsh winter. Even so the victorious generals are being criticised in Athens for not insisting on the unconditional surrender of the city. The truth of the matter is that the Athenian soldiers were suffering almost as much as the Plotidaeans, such is the condition into which this Peloponnesian War has plunged the Greeks. Much of the blame for the war must be attributed to the Athenians, whose empire-building brought them into conflict with other city-states such as Sparta, Corinth and Thebes.

Now Athens itself is suffering cruelly. When the war started Pericles gathered the people of Attica behind the defensive walls he had built, allowing the superior Spartan army to ravage the countryside while the Athenian fleet harried the enemy coastline. But Athens now has an enemy inside the walls. Plague has broken out, killing thousands; among them is the man who led them into war – Pericles.

A warlike figure of Athena.

Plague strikes besieged Athenians: one in four feared dead

Athens, 430BC

Driven into their city by the Peloponnesian invasion of Attica, the people of Athens are succumbing to a devastating plague.

The invasion under the Spartan king, Archidamus, appears to have coincided with the arrival of the disease from Ethiopia, via Egypt and Libya and lands held by the King of Persia.

The disease appeared first in the port of Piraeus. When it reached Athens, the influx of people from the surrounding countryside pro-

vided just the conditions in which it can flourish: overcrowding, with people crammed together in badly ventilated huts during the heat of summer.

The historian Thucydides, who caught the disease but survived, described its symptoms: "People in perfect health suddenly began to have burning feelings in the head; their eyes became red and inflamed, there was bleeding from the throat and tongue, their breath became unnatural and fetid. As the disease progressed from chest to stomach,

it would cause vomiting and spasms. The skin would break out into pustules and ulcers."

Driven by thirst and heat people plunged into cisterns, where they spread the disease. While the enemy is ravaging Attica, more than a quarter of the population is dying in Athens.

Doctors have been badly hit. Prayer to the gods seems ineffectual and, as despair grows along with the piles of bodies in the streets, there is looting, robbery and sexual abandon.

A Greek physician, holding a bleeding-cup, tends a standing patient in the 5th century BC.

How Greek trade gave rise to Homer

Homer and Hesiod, our earliest surviving Greek literary sources (datable at about 700BC), present an unfavourable, indeed hostile picture of traders. Sea-battered and out of condition, Odysseus finds his way at last to the relative safety of Phaeacia, a never-never island set somewhere in the golden west, only to be abused by a Phaeacian aristocrat for resembling a sordidly mercenary merchant skipper rather than a gentleman-amateur sportsman. Hesiod was prepared to concede that a moderately prosperous peasant-farmer might load a surplus of grain into his own modest boat and dispose of it somewhere down the coast during the dead part of the agricultural year, but to be a full-time trader rather than a respectable farmer was for him completely socially unacceptable.

This aristocratically-inspired prejudice against trade and traders has to be set in its historical context, a world ruled and dominated by landed aristocrats. Thus it was perfectly all right for a Greek aristocrat to visit his peers in other communities and come home laden with richly woven garments or finely wrought metalwork, given and received in the expectation that a comparable counter-gift might some day be required.

But to spend most of the recognised sailing season from April to October plying the Aegean or eastern Mediterranean with a cargo of, say, perfume flasks, hides, salt fish and wine amphoras, making only a humble living and unable to take part in the military and political activities that defined the citizen elite of a Greek *polis*, was considered an occupation suitable only for the lowest echelons of Greek society, the dependants perhaps of a great landlord.

Trade: a vital agent of change

Yet, though the personnel involved full-time in commerce during the era of Homer and Hesiod were socially inferior and politically negligible, the commerce they engaged in was itself of the utmost historical significance. Without it there would have been no opening to east and west, beginning in the half century between about 825BC and 775BC, no movement of colonisation to southern Italy, Sicily and the Black Sea, no comparative knowledge of other cultures and social practices, and thus no alphabet and, maybe, no Homer or Hesiod. Traders, therefore, may have been despised by their social superiors, but trade was vital to political, economic and cultural change in post-Dark Age Greece.

By 600BC, however, the situation of traders had

markedly, though not entirely, altered for the better. The aristocratic monopoly of political power was almost everywhere a thing of the past, and Greek societies were in general more open-textured. Aristocrats still travelled to visit their peers and exchange valuable gifts and mutual support, but some aristocrats were also travelling for different purposes and with different results. Solon of Athens, for example, visited Egypt for sightseeing and self-improvement; travel broadened, rather than narrowed, his mind at least.

Charaxos, brother of Sappho of Lesbos fame, used a cargo of wine from his ancestral Lesbian vineyards to finance a trip to Egypt which yielded a Thracian slave Rhodopis, whom he discovered selling her charms for the profit of her Greek master at the Greek port of Naukratis and whose freedom he had been moved to buy.

The very existence of a new settlement at Naukratis on the Nile delta is a crucial index of the change that had overtaken Greek seaborne commerce by the later seventh century. For this was not an autonomous Greek city but an emporium, a port of trade. It was founded in about 630BC by Greek traders from Asia Minor (Anatolia), the adjacent Greek islands and Aegina, under the auspices of the Egyptian pharaoh Psammetichus (Psamtik).

Oil and wine for slaves

In return for Greek oil, wine and luxury goods, the Greek traders of Naukratis received Egyptian grain, metals and slaves - an exchange from which the Egyptian treasury derived extra value in taxes. Soon Naukratis had a counterpart at Gravisca in Italy, where Greeks and Etruscans exchanged commodities. This professionalisation of commerce, in the shape of permanent market-centres linking dissimilar economies, corresponded to an upgrading in status of Greek full-time traders.

They are henceforth typically free citizens, literate (batch-marks and individual merchant-marks now regularly appear on the base of clay drinking cups or transport amphoras), and independent entrepreneurs owning purpose-built sail-driven round-hulled merchantmen. For the first time we learn the names of individual citizen-traders. Most famous were Colaeus of Samos, who opened up the silver-route to south-western Spain, and Sostratus of Aegina, who specialised in the run between Etruria and the Aegean by means of the haulway built across the Corinth isthmus in about 600BC.

The first trading wars begin

Not all Greek seaborne commerce, however, was conducted in the new-style merchantmen after 600BC, because not all Greek trade, by any means was carried on in peaceful conditions. The success of traders from the Greek settlement at Phocaea in Asia Minor, in particular, aroused the ire of their Carthaginian and Etruscan rivals for the routes to southern France and eastern Spain.

These Phocaeans had led the way to Provence, precipitating the foundation of Massalia (Marseilles) in about 600BC and perhaps introducing the grapevine to those parts. But the jealousy of their non-Greek competitors forced them to trade in converted fifty-oared longships, with the inevitable reduction of profit margins. In 540BC military conclusions were tried at sea off Alalia (Aleria) in Corsica. The Phocaean defeat spelt the end of Greek westward commercial expansion.

Within the Aegean and eastern Mediterranean, however, trade and commerce began to intensify, perhaps aided by the introduction into the Greek world of the idea of coined money invented by the Greeks' Lydian neighbours and (in some cases) overlords. Two items of the utmost significance, which helped to shape the whole character of Greek history in the succeeding classical epoch, should be singled out at this point: wheat and slaves.

It was from 600-500BC, especially toward 500BC, that the grain route from the points of production in the rich black-earth lands of the Crimea and Ukraine through the Bosporus and Hellespont (Dardanelles) into the Aegean was first opened up on a substantial scale and a regular basis. This grain supply provided better bread and compensated for the shortfalls in Athens' unpredictable domestic production of cereals (chiefly barley), eventually enabling Athens to become, in the fifth century BC, the most densely populated state in the ancient world, with perhaps a quarter of a million souls.

About one third of these were slaves, and it was also in the sixth century BC that there had first developed a regular traffic in "barbarian", that is non-Greek, slaves from Thrace (roughly modern Bulgaria) and Asia Minor. The growth of freedom for Greek citizens, which culminated in the world's first citizen democracy at Athens shortly before 500BC, thus went hand-in-hand with the growth of unfreedom for non-Greeks. In this political and ideological sense, as well as in terms of their economic contribution, slaves formed the essential basis of Classical Greek civilisation. Without developed commerce that would have been impossible.

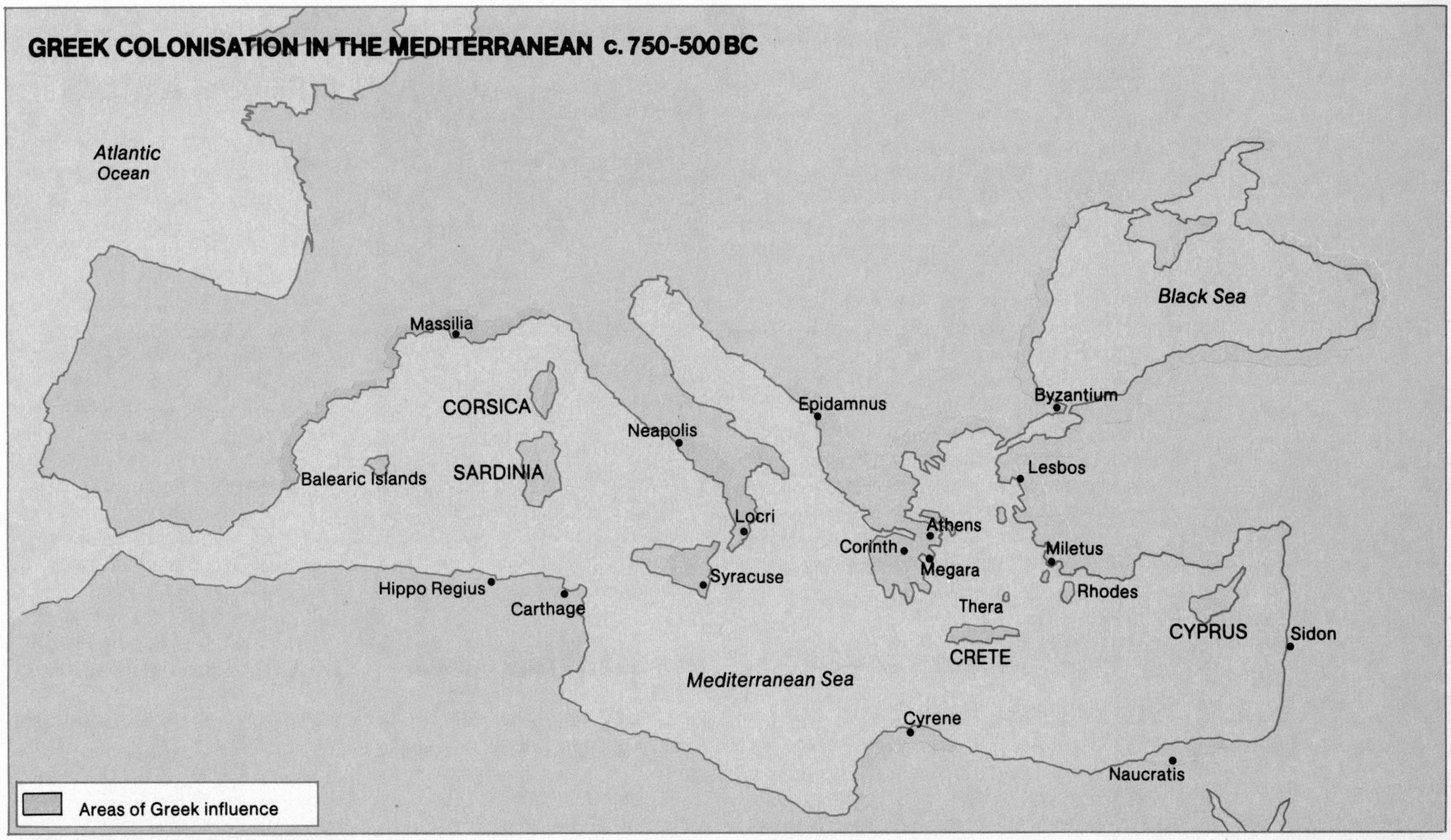
GREEK COLONISATION IN THE MEDITERRANEAN c. 750-500 BC
Atlantic Ocean
Black Sea
Massilia
CORSICA
SARDINIA
Balearic Islands
Neapolis
Epidamnus
Byzantium
Lesbos
Locri
Athens
Corinth
Megara
Miletus
Rhodes
Syracuse
Hippo Regius
Carthage
Thera
CRETE
CYPRUS
Sidon
Mediterranean Sea
Cyrene
Naucratis
Areas of Greek influence

ΠΡΟ ΤΟΥ 480 Π.Χ.
BEFORE 480 B.C.

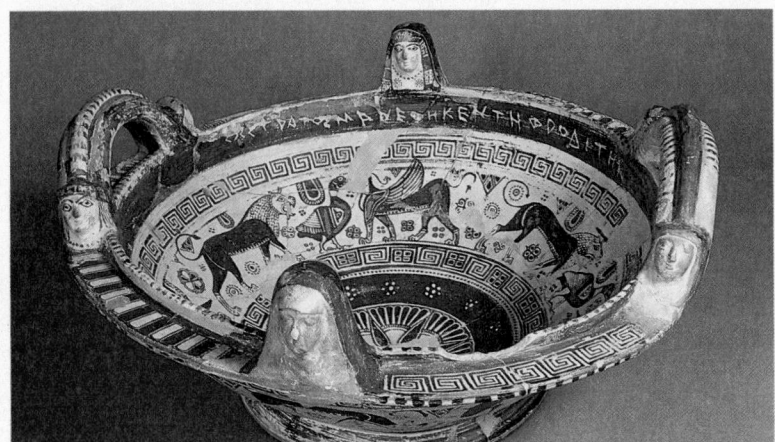

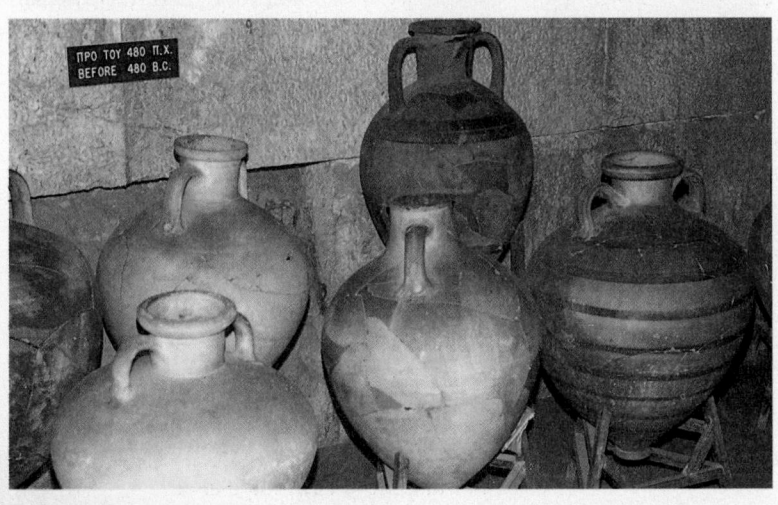

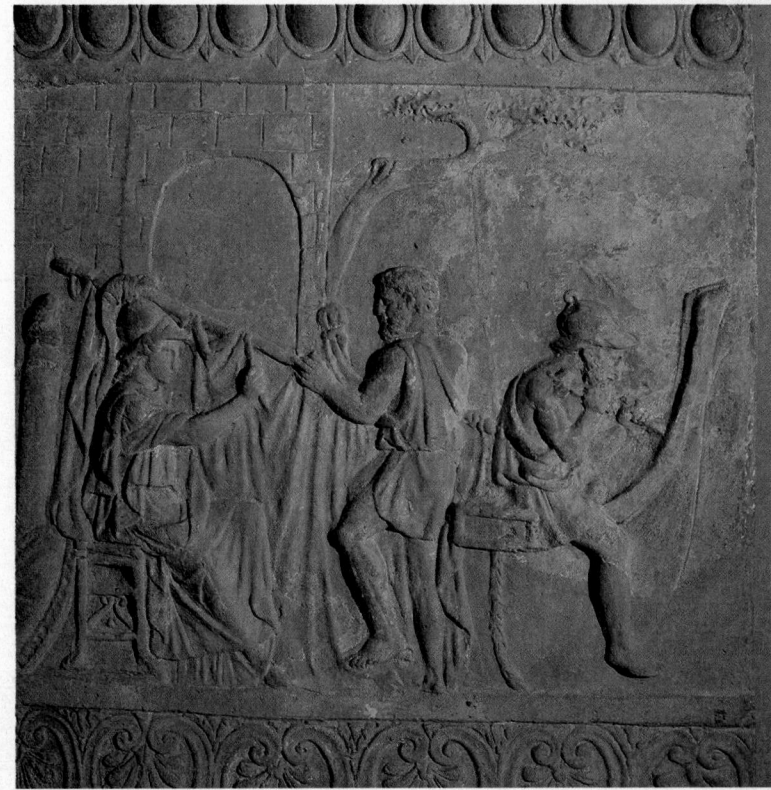

(Upper left): An Aphrodite bowl made in the greek island state of Chios and found in Naukratis in Egypt, where there was a sanctuary dedicated to Aphrodite, at which the prostitute Rhodope would have plied her trade. (Bottom left): Amphorae, or clay jars used to transport wine or oil and found all over the Mediterranean. (Above): The building of the legendary ship Argo by the goddess Athena, the helmsman Tiphys and shipwright Argos.

Greece, 425BC. Athens has inflicted several defeats on the Peloponnesian league. Aware of an Athenian plot to spark a *helot* revolt in Laconia and Messenia, the Spartans hastily evacuated Attica, but too late to stop the occupation of Messenian Pylos. Subsequent Peloponnesian attacks were driven back by the Athenians under Demosthenes. Survivors have been taken to Athens as hostages against reinvasion.

Greece, 424BC. Athens' plan to weaken the Peloponnesian alliance by backing revolutionary democrats in the Boeotian city-states misfires, and Athens is forced to send two armies to the region. The column led by Hippocrates is halted at Delium by a phalanx of the pro-Spartan Boeotians. Over 1,000 Athenians die in the ensuing battle.

Athens, 424BC. Euripides stages the tragic masterpieces *Hecuba*, *Suppliant Women* and *Heracles*. He treats the great mythological subjects in a new way, stressing passion, troubles of the soul and psychological developments, but includes sharp political comment.

Athens, 422BC. Aristophanes violently denounces the alleged abuses of the legal system in his satire *The Wasps*. He claims that the financial indemnities paid to Athenians who sit on the tribunals have corrupted their sense of justice. They are just like wasps: their stylus is their sting, and they are reduced to stinging their fellow citizens to earn a living.

Greece, 421BC. Athens and Sparta sign the peace of Nicias, marking at least a truce in the Peloponnesian war. The two camps agree to return to their original positions and to exchange prisoners of war.

Greece, c.420BC. Threatened with a charge of impiety, the Sophist Protagoras flees Athens. A believer in the doctrine that "Man is the measure of all things", Protagoras has written about the art of dialectic and eristic, a rhetorical technique enabling one to get the better of an opponent in an argument.

Athens, 420BC. The peace of Nicias enables the completion of the temple of Athena Nike, the jewel of the Acropolis, which was begun almost 30 years ago. Adorned by a carved frieze around its top, this miniature building embodies all the grace and harmony of the Ionic style.

Egypt rebels against Persian domination

Egypt, c.424BC
Egypt is in revolt against its Persian oppressors today after 100 years of occupation. The people have risen up against the tax-collectors and, with Athenian assistance, they are fighting for their freedom along the entire length of the Nile.

This is not the first Egyptian revolt against Persian rule; nor does it seem likely that it will be the last. Whenever there is a crisis over succession amongst their Achaemenid overlords, as there is in this "Year of the Four Emperors", the Egyptians raise the banner of rebellion to escape the burden of crushing taxation and to regain some political and religious autonomy.

A decorated Egyptian scent flask made out of green opaque glass.

Nehemiah lays down new religious code

Jerusalem, c.425BC
Ninety-one years after the Jews returned from their Babylonian captivity, the walls of Jerusalem, their most holy city, have been rebuilt. The newly-confident people are enjoying fresh enthusiasm for their faith. Responsibility for both the building and the religious revival is due to Nehemiah, a senior Jewish official at the Persian court and now governor of Judah.

The reconstruction of the Temple was completed in 515BC, but not until Nehemiah's arrival did the Jews really return to their traditional worship. Just as Nehemiah involved the whole community in the 52-day rebuilding of the city walls, an unprecedented effort of construction, so he has capitalised on Jewish national feeling to reinstitute religious observances, notably keeping the Sabbath and outlawing mixed marriages.

Above all, the governor has re-written many of the sacred texts, combining old and new writings to create an authoritative basis for a newly-flourishing Judaism.

A jade disc, or *pi*, sawn with rare skill from a block of jade using a cord sprinkled with sand. This disc dates from between 481-221BC.

Children of Athens enrol for lessons

Athens, c.420BC
Growing numbers of Athenian parents are sending their sons to school. Primary education is available for boys only, and it is up to the family to foot the bill.

Boys go to school accompanied by their slave-tutors, carrying tablets and styluses. They meet at the house of the *grammatistes*, the master who is paid a modest fee by the parents. They begin by learning the alphabet, then move on to reading, writing and arithmetic.

Teaching is basic, with the children progressing as rapidly as possible from simple learning by rote to much more difficult logical and rational problems. After learning the alphabet they move on to syllables, before tackling whole

Two boys on a vase (c.450BC).

words. Arithmetic consists of counting and the learning of fractions. However, little attempt is made to make adult language more intelligible, and the chief instrument of motivation is the rod.

Handwriting may be practised on fragments of broken earthenware pots, or on wax tablets. Pupils move on to write on papyrus leaves with quills made of reeds. The boys recite passages from Homer, Hesiod or Solon, from which the master draws moral and religious lessons.

Although richer families may have private tutors, most Athenian children receive this rudimentary education, and very few will have the opportunity to study beyond their early teens.

Alcibiades whips up anti-Sparta anger

Athens, 415BC

Alcibiades, the brilliant, impetuous scion of one of Athens' richest families, has succeeded by the power of his oratory in persuading the Athenians to send a powerful naval expedition to Sicily.

Always opposed to the peace with Sparta made by his great rival Nicias, he has been demanding a resumption of hostilities for the greater glory of Athens. Now he has triumphed and the *triremes* will sail to do battle with Syracuse.

Alcibiades finally persuaded the assembly that the expedition should go ahead in a debate during which Nicias, one of Athens' ablest generals, pointed out the dangers of the expedition and called into question Alcibiades' extravagant lifestyle.

It was exactly the sort of challenge that Alcibiades relishes. He boasted of the honour that he had recently brought to Athens, when his chariots came first, second and fourth in the Olympics.

"Though it is quite natural," he said, "for my fellow citizens to envy me for the magnificence with which I have done things in Athens ... yet to the outside world this is evidence of our strength."

He went on to argue passionately that it was the Athenians' duty to "raise this city to even greater heights". His fiery words were greeted with acclaim, forcing Nicias to bow to his arguments and even to propose that the power of the expedition be increased. There is little doubt that hostilities will now resume throughout war-ravaged Greece.

Alcibiades holds the people of Athens in awe with his rhetorical powers.

Greek god loses his virility overnight

Athens, 415BC

A great scandal has broken out in Athens. A number of statues of the god Hermes, a common sight in Athens, have been mutilated. Their faces have been hacked and their prominent, erect symbols of manhood have been broken off.

Political significance is being given to this sacrilege as, even though it might be merely the result of drunken hooliganism by young men, it is being taken as a bad omen for the naval expedition about to set out for Sicily.

At the same time rumours are sweeping the city about mock celebrations of the holy Eleusinian Mysteries being held in private homes. These mysteries symbolise the annual rebirth of life, and are believed to ensure a happy life after death for the initiated. Any mockery of them is punishable by death.

It is believed that a small group of high-living Athenians has been profaning the ceremonies with prostitutes and drunken behaviour. Chief among them, according to a slave questioned by torture, is Alcibiades, one of the leaders of the Sicilian expedition. His enemies – and they are many – are whipping up the case against him.

Athens shaken by failure of Sicilian foray

The Athenian warrior Demokleides, who perished in the war against Sicily.

Athens, 413BC

The Athenian expedition to Sicily has suffered a catastrophe. The Syracusans with their Spartan allies have destroyed Nicias' forces in a great land and sea battle. With Nicias himself captured and executed, thousands of Athenian prisoners are being held in appalling conditions in stone quarries, where they are dying of their wounds and disease.

Much of the blame for this defeat must go to those politicians who schemed to have Alcibiades tried for sacrilege. Although he offered to stay in Athens to face these charges, they made him take command so that they could plot against him in his absence.

They then recalled him from Sicily, but on the way he learnt that he had already been sentenced to death and so defected to the Spartans. Nicias, left in sole command of the expedition, has led it to disaster. The fleet is destroyed and it is unlikely that any of the soldiers will return. All Athens mourns, but already new ships are being built.

Polyclitus takes sculpture into bronze age

Greece, c.415BC

Polyclitus of Argos has revolutionised Greek sculpture by his use of bronze and his radical approach to this art form. And unlike Phidia of Athens, who specialised in images of the gods, Polyclitus uses men, athletes in particular, as his subjects.

Symmetria, he states in his treatise, the *Canon*, is the philosophical principle behind all artistic composition, and he uses symmetry to create works of art where not only are the proportions and balance exact, but there is a sense of both harmony and movement.

Though far more natural than anything preceding it, the figures of heroes and athletes remain idealised, almost godlike, which possibly explains his largest statue, a gold and ivory colossus of the goddess Hera for her temple in Argos.

Although his subjects are idealised, Polyclitus has brought a new verve to the art of sculpture, as shown by this bronze, "The Spear Carrier".

Athens, c.413BC. "Torotoro-torotorotix! Kikkibau, kikkibau!" Athens cannot believe its ears. In his latest play, Aristophanes presents two Athenians who decide to go and live in the land of the birds. They involve the birds in the building of an aerial city, Cloudcuckoobury, halfway between men and the gods. The play deals with the serious political and moral problems of Athens as it remains caught up in an exhausting war.

Greece, 413BC. While the Athenians are busy fighting in Sicily, the Spartans invade Attica, acting on the unseemly advice of the defector Alcibiades. They establish themselves at Decelea and set about devastating the region.

Athens, 411BC. A disastrous economic situation and the intrigues of Alcibiades provoke a revolt in Athens. The magistracies are suspended and replaced by a council of co-opted members called the Four Hundred. The revolt's leaders argued that political life was reserved for the propertied rich and the *hoplites*, and denied to the poor, who row on board the *triremes*. The fatal decision was taken when most of the Athenian rowers were abroad on campaign.

Sicily, 410BC. Among the oligarchs exiled from Syracuse by the democrats since the defeat of the Athenian expedition three years ago is the general Hermocrates, who played a large part in bringing about the Syracusan victory.

Athens, 410BC. Democracy is restored in Athens after the fall of the Four Hundred and its successor, a moderately oligarchic regime known as the Five Thousand. The Spartans refused to help the co-opted council by concluding peace. Athens, meanwhile, suffered a crushing naval defeat in Etetria in September 411BC. The alienation of Theramenes, one of the coup's leaders, precipitated the demise of the Four Hundred.

Asia Minor, 410BC. Alcibiades, appointed general by the Athenian fleet at Samos, annihilates the Peloponnesian fleet at Cyzicus in Asia Minor (Anatolia).

Sicily, 409BC. Called in by the citizens of Segesta in northwest Sicily, the Carthaginians under Hannibal sack the city of Selinus, a long-standing enemy of Segesta.

Dancing by torchlight launches days of celebrations, as Athens pays homage to the gods through religion and entertainment

Athens, c.410BC

The greatest of the state festivals being held at this time in Athens is the Panathenaea, a celebration of the splendour and solidarity of the city-state under the protection of the great goddess Athena whose birthday it marks.

Established, according to legend, by Theseus, and reorganised in 566BC, it is an expression of religion, patriotism and pride involving the whole community.

The festival takes place every year at the end of July and lasts for two days. But every fourth year it is celebrated with extra splendour over four days: this is the Great Panathenaea. So massive and magnificent are the proceedings that there is a general belief that the gods themselves gather to watch.

The festival begins with a night of dancing, singing and torchlit races. At dawn, a huge procession sets off from the Cerameicus across Athens towards the Acropolis. At its head are the bearers of ritual offerings, the foreigners with trays of cakes and honeycombs, and officials carrying the paraphernalia of the priests. Others bring sacred branches of olive or oak, and the whole population of Athens follows behind.

The central purpose of the procession is to present a new robe to to the goddess. Woven, with much ritual, by girls chosen from the Athenian aristocracy, the robe will be draped over Athena's statue at the Acropolis. These young virgins are escorted by horsemen as they lead the procession up to the Acropolis.

Afterwards, the festival reaches another climax with the sacrifice of large numbers of cows at the great

Riders prepare to form a procession: a detail from the Parthenon frieze.

altar near the Parthenon. Many of the beasts have been contributed by Athenian communities overseas; others have been bought with the proceeds of rents on public land.

Some of the meat is set aside for religious and secular officials; the rest is distributed among the people of the city.

Meanwhile, a series of contests and competitions is held in honour of various gods. Some involve feats of athletics, others take the form of recitals of heroic poetry. The winners are awarded with jars of oil pressed from Athena's sacred olive trees.

Frieze shows Athena's robe.

Sophists are the paid talkers in Greece

Athens, c.410BC

If you want to know which came first, the chicken or the egg, ask a Sophist. He won't have the answer, of course, but he'll argue, conjecture and pontificate for hours in the market place if you wish – for a fee. Sophists are travelling intellectuals who go from town to town here in Greece, making their living by showing off their knowledge.

They offer exclusive seminars to the rich; or they will happily set up a public debate with each other on any subject under the Athenian sun – mathematics, astronomy, genealogy, politics ... and that insoluble chicken.

Their philosophical arrogance is gargantuan. Plato dismisses them as pretentious; and because they

sell wisdom for money, Socrates likens them to prostitutes. Yet Sophists like Protagoras, Prodicus and Hippias can attract big audiences wherever they appear. They teach the art of rhetoric – argument that appears convincing regardless of the subject matter – a valuable aid in a country in which few decisions are made without much discussion.

Aristophanes, in his comedy *Clouds*, referred to them as "pseuds with bare feet and pale faces ... who maintain that heaven is shaped like a bread oven, placed all around us as if we were coal".

Pseuds or otherwise, Sophists take enormous pleasure in creating puzzles and debating them for hours on end – generally to no real purpose except, perhaps, the fee.

The great procession under way.

Glory of Athens reaches zenith at the Acropolis

The Parthenon, crowning glory of the Acropolis and its biggest building.

Athens, 408BC

The Erechtheum, the last building in the magnificent complex of temples on the Acropolis which towers over the city of Athens, is now virtually complete. The three temples, and the superb entrance structure with its huge Doric columns, have been completed in just over 40 years, making this one of the architectural feats of the age.

The whole structure is a monument to the recovery of Athens from the devastation of the Persian invasion of 480BC. Building began just over 40 years ago on the initiative of Pericles, the aristocratic leader. He diverted some of the funds raised for defence by other Greek cities in the Delian League to this prestige project.

He saw it as a massive public works project, providing employment not only for architects, sculptors and painters, but also for craftsmen and labourers. His critics alleged that it was a vanity and a misuse of the allies' money. He replied: "They do not give us a single horse, nor a soldier, nor a ship. All they supply is money, and this belongs not to the people who give it, but to those who receive it, so long as they provide the services they are paid for." This, he maintained, Athens had done through building up the finest navy in the region.

His arguments did not silence his critics. They said he favoured his friends, like Pheidias, the sculptor who directed the erection of many of the buildings. They said Pheidias arranged love affairs for Pericles with the Athenian women, when they came on the pretext of looking at the works of art.

The Acropolis, which has steep cliffs on three sides, was a fortress for many years. In the Bronze Age it was topped by a Mycenaean palace. Pericles determined to make it a shrine to the city's patron goddess, Athena, and a showplace for the art of its citizens.

The biggest structure is the Parthenon, flanked on all sides by towering columns of white pentelic marble. The gold and ivory statue of Athena, standing helmeted and armed, was sculpted by Pheidias himself. The architrave is dominated by a frieze showing the struggle between the Athenians and the Barbarians and symbolising the triumph of reason over brute force. Other scenes show the capture of Troy, and the birth of Athena among the Olympians.

The columns are arranged with a grace and symmetry which mark the finest achievement of the classical period. The statues are a celebration of the human body, male and female, showing a keen attention to anatomy and movement.

A 19th century "reconstruction" showing the sculptor Pheidias' gold and ivory statue of the city's patron goddess, Athena, dominating the Parthenon interior.

In the Erechtheum, the last building to be completed on the Acropolis, the graceful female forms of the caryatids are beautiful alternatives to columns.

Athens, 407BC. Alcibiades, now an Athenian general, returns to the city which he betrayed a few years ago. His welcome amounts to a pardon and reflects the euphoria in Athens after recent victories over the Peloponnesians in Asia Minor (Anatolia) and the restoration of democracy.

Athens, 406BC. The tragedian Euripides, successor to Aeschylus and Sophocles, is dead. Focusing more on men's passions that on the great myths, Euripides challenged conventional assumptions and introduced a new tone into Attic tragedy. Among his great works are *Electra* and *The Trojan Women*.

Sicily, 405BC. Since the Carthaginians resumed their offensive against Sicily in 409BC, cities have been falling one after another. A Syracusan officer called Dionysius takes advantage of the situation by getting himself elected absolute ruler of his native city.

Greece, 403BC. The success of the Athenian democrats, led by Thrasybulus, over the Spartans at the battle of Munychia presages a political change. An amnesty is declared – except for the surviving members of the pro-Spartan gang known as the Thirty Tyrants, and some other oligarchic extremists, who take refuge at Eleusis, while Thrasybulus tries to reconcile the citizens of Athens. The restoration of democratic institutions marks the end of a very bloody era.

Persia, 401BC. Two brothers, Artaxerxes II and Cyrus the Younger, governor of Asia Minor since 407BC, dispute the Achaemenid inheritance. Artaxerxes became king on the death of his father, Darius II, in 404BC. Cyrus plans a coup, for which he raises a force of Asiatic and Greek mercenaries. The decisive battle is fought at Cunaxa, near Babylon. Cyrus wins but is himself killed.

Athens, 401BC. Sophocles' last tragedy, *Oedipus at Colonus*, a drama of guilt and destiny, is staged posthumously for the first time. Sophocles, who died five years ago, also wrote about the man who killed his father, married his mother and fled from Thebes in his masterpiece *Oedipus Rex*, first shown c.430BC.

India, c.400BC. The scholar Panini analyses and organises the grammar of the Sanskrit language, formulating 4,000 grammatical rules.

Socrates takes poison after verdict

Athens, 399BC

One of the best-known figures in Athens, the 70-year-old moral philosopher Socrates, is dead, condemned by his fellow citizens after a trial in which many believe he had been framed. He was accused of corrupting the youth of the city and failing to worship the proper gods. He denied the charges, but devoted most of his long speech to the court to defending his life-style, saying that he preferred to live in poverty and go barefoot rather than to seek honours and riches.

In fact, Socrates seems to have made a nuisance of himself to a number of self-important politicians, who took the opportunity to get their revenge. He served in the Peloponnesian War and briefly as a city councillor. But it was a remark by the Delphic Oracle that changed his life.

When the Oracle said no man was wiser than Socrates, he could not believe it. He called on some of the policitians who had a reputation for wisdom and questioned them. The effect of his questioning was to bring out the fact that though they thought they were wise they were in fact ignorant, and

A relief from the 4th century BC of Socrates drinking the fatal cup of hemlock.

Socrates, who acknowledged his ignorance, had the advantage. The politicians, thus humiliated, nursed their grievances.

In time the Socratic method of getting at the truth by repeated questioning gained him a high reputation among young Athenians, who flocked to his side to study his methods. They would then go off and make people contradict themselves as they struggled to answer

question after question. Socrates might have been let off with a fine or exile, but he cheekily suggested his sentence should be a pension for life as a reward for helping Athenians to find virtue and wisdom.

The court promptly voted for the death sentence and later, in prison, he was handed the statutory cup of hemlock. He refused to take the opportunity to escape and raised the cup to his lips.

The Orphic sect puts its faith in self-denial and the afterlife

Athens, c.400BC

It is rare these days to walk for long down any Athens street without meeting strange figures, dressed all in white, who may well engage one in conversation. They are members of the Orphic sect, which daily increases its numbers here and in other Greek cities. They are vegetarians and sexual puritans, and hold a belief in reincarnation like some Indian religions. According to gossip, they also indulge in Bacchic rites.

The cult derives from the poet Orpheus, who charmed animals and cast spells over nature, and then descended into the underworld where he met a terrible death. He was torn to pieces by infuriated women.

According to Orpheus, the origin of man was equally bloody. The child Dionysus was beaten by the Titans, cut into pieces, skewered on spits and grilled. Zeus struck down

Orpheus, wounded, runs from a Thracian woman who will finish him off.

those who did it with lightning, and the human race was born from their ashes.

To the Orphic cult animal sacrifice is akin to cannibalism, and members refuse even to eat meat.

They protect their dead with tablets inscribed with ritual formulae placed on tombs. They believe the individual human soul will eventually find peace after many reincarnations.

Athens sentences her victorious generals to death

Athens, 406BC

The Athenians have put to death six of the men who commanded their victorious fleet against the Spartans at the battle of Arginusae in the narrow channel between Lesbos and Asia Minor (*Anatolia*). They were charged with failing to rescue the crews of ships disabled in the fight, and sentenced to death at the Assembly in Athens.

The generals pleaded that they had despatched ships to pick up the sailors while they pursued the Spartans, but that a great storm had sprung up making the rescue impossible. However, although Socrates spoke on their behalf, the crowd, whipped up by the generals' enem-

Athena mourns her fallen citizens.

ies, refused to listen to their defence which was shamefully curtailed.

The trial reeked of corruption, with false witnesses and the crowd baying for blood. It was an affair symptomatic of these degrading times in Athens. How could there be justice when Theramenes, who had been ordered to pick up the survivors, was one of the chief accusers?

Already the Athenians are beginning to regret their action. But their regret will not bring Pericles, Diomedon, Lysias, Aristocrates, Thrasyllus and Erasinides back.

Athenian fleet crushed

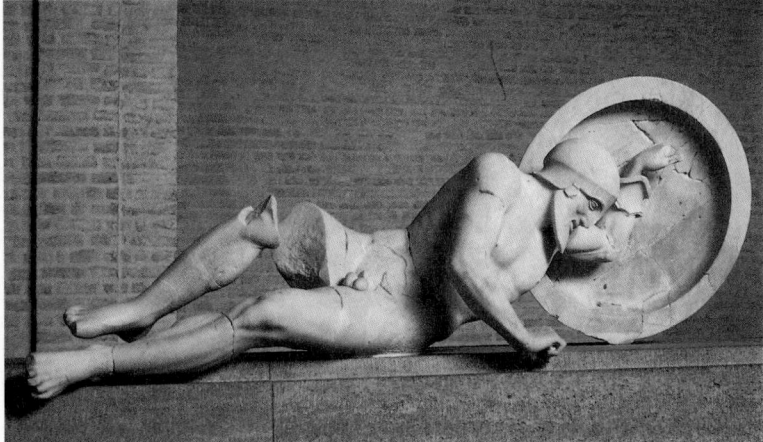

The dying moments of a warrior: a sculpture from a temple at Aegina.

Athens, 405BC

The Athenians have suffered a crushing defeat at the hands of the Spartans. They have lost all but ten of their *triremes*, suffered many casualties, and are now facing defeat in this cruel, long war.

The battle was fought on land and sea at Aegospotami, in the Hellespont, where the Spartan commander, Lysander, at the head of a fleet built with Persian money, first destroyed the Athenian vanguard under Philocles and then caught the rest of the fleet by surprise before it was ready for sea.

He landed soldiers at the Athen-

ian fortress of Eteonikos, seized part of the palisade, and then fixed grappling irons to the Greek ships and dragged them away. While he was doing this his soldiers routed the Greeks, who resisted as well as they could, but were disorganised by the surprise attack and soon broke and fled.

Conon, the Athenian commander, escaped in his *trireme*, but fearing the consequences if he returned to Athens he has fled to Cyprus. The unfortunate Philocles has been executed by Lysander. With its fleet destroyed, and morale at a low ebb, Athens faces a bleak future.

Spartan gang is spreading terror

Athens, 404BC

The glory of Athens has been humbled. Forced to capitulate under the threat of starvation, the Athenians must live under Sparta's dictates. The long walls have been torn down. Exiled opponents of democracy are returning in great numbers, and the city is being ruled by a gang of reactionary extremists imposed on it by the victorious Lysander. This gang, the Thirty Tyrants, rules by fear. Critias, leader of the tyrants, was once exiled by the *demos*, and now he is taking his revenge. He has acquired a taste for killing large numbers of people and is indulging it with great cruelty. Among his victims is Theramenes, the moderate leader who was once his friend.

The Tyrants are systematically eliminating the democrats. Only a privileged 3,000 are allowed to bear arms, and anyone not among those 3,000 may be summarily executed. Others are ordered to despatch themselves with a fatal draught of hemlock, often without a trial. The Tyrants are also murdering immigrants who have served Athens well, and seizing their possessions for personal gain. It is a shameful chapter in the Athens story.

Short-back-and-sides forms part of adult initiation ceremonies

A young man, his hair cut short in preparation for his military training, is given a riding lesson in this scene depicted on a 5th century BC vase.

Athens, c.400-350BC

The Spartans were probably the inspiration for the Athenian system of military, or *ephebic*, training. It has now become the practice for young men of 18 to have their hair cut short and to embark on a two-year training course.

Each Attic *deme*, or township, draws up a list of young men when they reach 18, the age of civic majority. Provided they are eligible for Athenian citizenship they become *ephebes*, drafted for two years. Their service begins with an expedition to the Attic borders, followed by instruction in barracks at the Piraeus, before they spend a year in the wild – hunting, and doing various military duties. They wear black cloaks and special hats.

The *ephebe* takes oaths of loyalty, and at the end of his training is ready to become a *hoplite*.

399 (399-390)

China, c.399BC. China is undergoing a period of political and moral crisis and profound anarchy. Since the state of Qin (Ch'in) was split into three by a coup d'etat in 453BC, the great feudal lords have been tearing each other apart.

Persia, 398BC. Less than a century after Marathon and Salamis, the Persian fleet has an Athenian admiral. After the disaster of Aegospotami in 405BC, Conon judged it unwise to return to Athens. He went into exile with some of his followers and became a mercenary to the Persian king.

Greece, 395BC. The Spartan general Lysander is killed and his army routed near the city of Haliartos. This follows a growth in anti-Spartan feeling which culminated in the invasion of Phocis by the Boeotian league with Athenian support. Lysander's death is a severe blow to Sparta, which has affirmed its hegemony through his military victories in the Aegean and the generalship of King Agesilaus in Asia Minor (Anatolia), where he defeated the Persian cavalry on the Pactolus river.

Greece, 394BC. In the aftermath of their recent successes, the opponents of Sparta launch an attack which sparks off the Corinthian war. The coalition's troops are crushed, however, first near Corinth, then at Coronea by the Spartan king, Agesilaus.

Athens, 393BC. Isocrates, a former law-court speechwriter and an opponent of the Sophists, founds Athens' first institute of higher learning, a school of rhetoric.

Persia, 393BC. Led by its exiled Athenian admiral, Conon, the Persian fleet defeats a Spartan fleet off Cnidos, Asia Minor, ending Sparta's attempt to extend her hegemony from the Aegean to the Asiatic mainland. As a mark of gratitude, and in order to support an anti-Spartan coalition in Greece, Persia provides money for the leading states – Athens, Argos, Thebes and Corinth.

Athens, 392BC. Aristophanes has written another comedy about women, called *Women in Parliament*. In this, as in *Lysistrata*, first staged in 411BC, he makes fun of the political role played by women – inconceivable in reality in a city where only men take part in public debates and political decision-making.

Sexual wars change Greek theatre

Greek playwrights: Aeschylus, Euripides, Sophocles and Aristophanes.

Greece, 398BC
With the production of *Lysistrata*, in the middle of the Peloponnesian Wars, Greek theatre has reached new dramatic heights – or, some would say, depths. The play, by the playwright Aristophanes, describes an imaginary peace movement in which the women of Greece force peace on their warring men by denying them sex. The result is inevitable.

Lysistrata, which concludes with peace breaking out everywhere, has been so successful that Cleophou, the leader of the Athenian pro-war party, has denounced it as morally offensive and called for Aristophanes' deportation as an alien.

Drama in Greece is only a century old. Earlier, Greek plays had only one actor. Aeschylus added a second, and Sophocles a third. Actors wore masks, each actor playing several parts. Props and scenery were so minimal as to be symbolic; subtle facial expressions and nuances were impossible, everything depended upon the lines. Drama was still serious and tragic, the protagonists pawns of the gods.

Euripides, who only died eight years ago and whose life spanned most of the fifth century BC, added a new tone to tragedy, focusing on the passions of men rather than celebrating the greatness of myths. *Iphigeneia in Aulis*, in which Agamemnon must choose between the defeat of his army or the death of his daughter, epitomised the new tone.

It is only in the last few decades that theatre has established its reputation for comedy and satire, and this is largely due to Aristophanes.

Before Aristophanes, satire – particularly in the hands of his older rival, Cratinus – was totally crude. Aristophanes, in such plays as *Frogs*, *Birds* and *Peace*, raises bawdiness to a higher level, giving it a political edge that the Athenian public love and their rulers detest.

Masks worn on the Greek stage.

A later actor from a comedy, raised to new heights by Aristophanes.

Sacrifice of a wife in a play by Euripides, painted 350-325BC.

Bronze of a comic actor in a mask dating from the 5th century BC.

134

Rome defeats the Etruscans in Veii war

A bronze of two Etruscan soldiers carrying a fallen comrade from the field.

Italy, c.396BC

The ten-year siege of the Etruscan hilltop city of Veii came to an abrupt end today when Roman soldiers tunnelled their way into the very centre of the Temple of Juno and began the systematic sacking of Rome's archrival. The fall of Veii brings to an end a war between the two cities lasting more than 80 years in which fortunes have see-sawed continually.

Roman fortunes changed when Furius Camillus, the newly-appointed dictator, assumed command and created Rome's first professional army in order to maintain the siege. Until then military service in Rome had been confined to short summer campaigns.

The tunnel was Camillus' inspiration. He organised his men in six-hour shifts, digging continually until his sappers were close enough to hear the king of Veii preparing to offer a sacrifice to victory in the temple above them. In the fierce fighting that followed, women and slaves were burned alive after they had hurled stones down from roof-tops. Despite the success the dictator is in disgrace, exiled in Rome for holding on to too much of the huge booty taken at Veii.

Etruscan decline sets in after fall of Veii

Etruria, c.392BC

The great Etruscan civilisation is in a slow and sad decline as Rome increases in power and extends its influence beyond the city-state into the rest of Italy.

Little is known about the origins of the Etruscans, although it is generally believed that they are descended from Asiatic immigrants who came to Italy at the end of the Hittite empire. Whatever their history, they were a talented and hard-working people. Seven hundred years ago they had developed their own iron-working culture and were busily exploiting ore deposits on the island of Elba.

It was this knowledge of metallurgy that gave the Etruscans the weapons that allowed them to rule much of the central peninsula of Italy through the kings of small city-states.

They were skilled traders who established strong links – both in trade and culture – with Greek Sicily and Phoenicia. Their language is based on the Greek alphabet, their culture distinctly Hellenic in its origins.

It was 109 years ago that Rome expelled its king and joined other city-states in a rebellion against its Etruscan masters. Now, after the fall of Veii, Etruria is undergoing a major series of changes as it is integrated into the Latin world.

An incised Etruscan bronze box.

Rome's democratic ideals have diminished the role of the *lucumon*, the political and religious leader.

Women, who enjoyed a considerable level of liberty in Etruria, now find themselves subjugated.

Funeral practices are also changing, with burial replacing cremation. Sarcophagi are replacing funeral urns. Etruscan art – noted for its realistic and spontaneous qualities – is under threat.

Etruria may be doomed – but, already, Rome is adopting many aspects of the much older Etruscan civilisation. It has "borrowed" the "century" system of organising its armies, as well as gladiatorial games and military *triumphs*.

Athenian historian glorifies retreat of leaderless Greeks through Persia

Athens, 392BC

Xenophon, the great Athenian warrior-historian, has produced a remarkable account of the expedition of the "Ten Thousand" – the Greeks who fought for Cyrus the Younger in Persia and then, when Cyrus was killed, battled their way home through hostile terrain.

Xenophon obviously studied well when, as a rich young man, he sat at the feet of Socrates. He went off some ten years ago as a gentleman volunteer with the army of impoverished Greek peasants recruited by Cyrus to depose his older brother, King Artaxerxes II.

The "Ten Thousand" were deceived by Cyrus, who told them that they were merely going to deal with some troublesome tribesmen. Only gradually did they realise the extent and danger of their enterprise and become mutinous. They had gone too far to turn back, and agreed to fight on for double pay.

The story of their ascent, *Anabasis*, into the heart of Persia gives the book its title, and, in it, Xenophon tells of their adventures in vivid detail. Commanded by Clearchus, they marched, virtually unopposed, to Cunaxa on the outskirts of

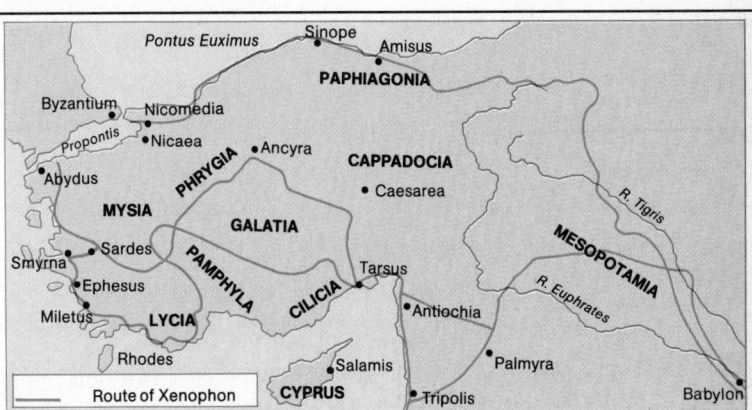

Babylon where Artaxerxes at last gave battle. The Greeks, on the right wing of Cyrus' army, shouted their warcries, "clashed their shields and spears" together, and drove their opponents from the field.

They virtually won Persia's crown for Cyrus. But "Cyrus was killed himself, and eight of the noblest of his company lay dead upon his body".

The Greeks were allowed to leave after Clearchus and his captains had been killed. Xenophon was then elected general and, in an epic march, led the survivors home.

Athenian woman is queen bee in her hive

Greek ladies playing at "knucklebones" in a rare moment of leisure.

Athens, c.400-300BC

A woman's place is in the home. Outside, she has no independent status, is not allowed to enter into any transaction worth more than one *medimnos* of barley, and cannot own any property other than her own clothes, jewellery and slaves.

A girl of good family lives among the servants and learns domestic chores from them. In the *gynaeceum*, where men are not admitted, she learns to spin, weave and cook. She also learns to manage the workshops and slaves.

When she is 15 her father will seek a husband for her. She will not be consulted. As a wife, she is in charge of her children's education, and the running of the home. She supervises everything, from baking the bread to making the clothes. She is said to be "queen bee in her hive".

A well-born Athenian woman is well-versed in religion. She worships Hestia, goddess of the hearth, and is constantly confined within the *gynaeceum*. Religious festivals, funerals, or visits to other *gynaecea* are her only opportunities for feminine socialising in a fundamentally masculine society.

The peasant women of Attica, by contrast, will help their husbands in the fields – in addition to the housework expected of them.

Virgin huntress protects the young

Greece, c.378BC

Young girls of marriageable age are flocking in increasing numbers to the Brauron sanctuary, near Philaidai, on the east coast of Attica. There, under the aegis of Artemis, the virgin huntress goddess, they take to the woods, pretending to be she-bears and dancing naked to rhythmic music.

It is all supposed to help to prepare the pubescent girls for marriage. It helps them to experience their animal natures, including their ripening sexuality, and shows them the need for "taming" by men in marriage if they are going to take their places in society.

Artemis is the goddess of transitions and mistress of the wild animals. She is said to live in the marshes between dry land and lakes, or the fringe between the forest and the town. She rules over wild animals and hunting, but also protects the young animals whom hunters are not allowed to kill.

Artemis is associated with taming sexuality, but some myths have heroines who reject her and devote themselves entirely to hunting, killing the young men who seek their hands. In Sparta, Artemis ceremonies train both young men and young women in near-impossible endurance and combat tests, to help them to master their instincts. The wild life must precede maturity.

Birth ritual purifies house and integrates newborn into the clan

Greece, c.500-200BC

The birth ritual, which is of ancient origins, is an important aspect of family life. Its dual purpose is to purify the house after the messiness of the birth and to integrate the new-born child into the family.

When a child is born, the father, absolute head of the family, decides whether or not he wants to keep it. He may test its fitness by various tests – for example, rubbing it with icy water, pure wine, or urine. Sometimes he will abandon it.

The usual reason for abandoning a child is in order not to divide up an already small estate. A daughter is more likely to be rejected in this way. An abandoned child will be taken to a wild spot and left, probably in a pot known as a *pithos*, in the hope that a passing shepherd may take pity on it. Childless couples may be quietly alerted to an impending abandonment.

After a birth, a sign will be put on the door: an olive branch for a boy, wool for a girl, and a smear of pitch to ward off evil spirits.

On the seventh day the whole family joins in the ceremony of *amphidromia*. The women having swept the house and sprinkled water in ritual cleansing, the father carries the infant round the hearth at a run, while the family sing in thanksgiving.

On the tenth day, or thereabouts, the child is fully integrated into the family and given a name. A boy will

Twentieth-century AD baby in 6th-century BC Athenian potty-chair.

usually be given the same name as his paternal grandfather in order to ensure the continuity of the family name in a society with high mortality rates.

Noisy geese save Rome

Gauls battle with Etruscans as they advance southwards towards Rome.

Rome, c.390BC
The clacking of the sacred geese of the Roman capitol saved this fortress from a surprise attack by besieging Gauls tonight. With Rome abandoned to the invaders from the north, the city's able-bodied men are the sole defenders. They owe their lives to Manlius Capitolinus who heard the geese and raised the alarm.

Rome has been virtually evacuated after its heavily outnumbered army of 10,000 men – the biggest ever in Rome's history – was defeated at the Battle of Allia and scattered throughout the province. The Gauls, who fight naked, drove their war chariots into the city to find only its senators sitting quietly on their thrones awaiting their deaths with dignity.

As the siege of the Capitol enters

Later image of Capitoline geese.

its tenth month, Furius Camillus, the former dictator, has been recalled from exile. His newly reformed army has forced the Gauls to withdraw to the north.

New law says plebs can be consuls

Rome, 370BC
The plebeians, for centuries the underdogs, have won a major victory in their fight for a bigger say in the government of Rome. Despite powerful opposition from the wealthy patrician class, a new law has been passed which allows a pleb to be elected one of the two consuls (senior magistrates), thus ending years of class struggle in the city.

The heroes of the struggle are Gaius Licinius and Lucius Sextus, the plebs' tribunes, who have sought to erode the power and influence of the patricians by the shrewd use of the law of veto which allows an assembly of plebs to vote down measures such as the election of military tribunes.

The patricians' desperate answer was to appoint a dictator, Camillus, who confronted the two tribunes at an assembly of plebs. According to one witness, Camillus "breathed wrath and menaces" as he took his seat. Licinius and Sextus stood their ground, however. Despite the dictator's threat to expel the plebs from the meeting and force the young plebs into the army, the assembly refused to give way and continued to vote for the new laws.

As well as meeting the demand for a plebeian consul, the new acts allow for changes in the harsh debt laws which have enslaved many plebs, and also for land reform. When the dictator resigned, Lucius Sextus became the first plebeian consul.

Plato heads a new academy in Athens

Athens, 385BC
After his years of foreign travel, the wealthy aristocrat Plato has returned to his native Athens to open his own school just outside the city in a garden dedicated to the mythical hero Academus. Plato expresses his philosophical views in lectures that take the form of conversations, or dialogues, in which he does not appear to take part. His favourite interrogator in the dialogues, in fact, is his idol and former teacher, Socrates.

Plato's wide-ranging dialogues discuss such questions as the theory of knowledge, the acquisition of wisdom, the difference between

Pompeii mosaic of Plato teaching.

right and wrong, and whether democracy or autocracy is better. He argues that ideas have an independent existence and are the archetypes of all concrete things. He ponders on the relationship between the human soul, the state and the universe.

After he left Athens at the time of Socrates' death, he spent some time at the court of Dionysius, the tyrant of Syracuse in Sicily. That experience led him to argue that a just state will only come into existence when philosophers – who comprehend the harmony of the universe – become the rulers and abolish private property and the family, and introduce eugenic mating and an educational system to train each citizen for his place in society. It is at his Academy that he has brought together like-minded scholars to talk about this ideal Republic.

Well-treated slaves underpin booming economy of Greece

Greece, 4th century BC
The Greek economy is booming, but while freeborn Greeks control the country's commercial success, nothing would be possible without the large community of slaves who actually perform the vital labour.

Slaves are almost always non-Greeks; without liberty, rights or property, they are traded like any other commodity. There are as many as 100,000 in Athens alone and they make up a third of the total population. Despite their numbers they never revolt. Some may escape, but these are always caught and returned. Slaves are

vital to the community's smooth operation and, while they are exploited to the full, their conditions are not wholly unpleasant.

The elite of public slaves, the property of the state and essential to the bureaucracy and the police, are highly emancipated. They may start a family, and earn money and buy their freedom with it. Similarly privileged are those with special skills in crafts or financial services.

Less privileged are domestic servants or farm labourers. As private property they are never really emancipated. Lowest of all are the 30,000 working in the mines.

Athenian mistress and her slave.

Two Greek geniuses invent history

"History", wrote the famous American archaeologist Samuel Noah Kramer, "begins at Sumer." By this he meant, above all, that the Sumerian civilisation of the fourth millennium BC was the first to produce and bequeath one of the essential raw materials for the writing of any history of the human past - namely, written documentation. However, a sharp distinction must be drawn in principle between the mere fact of written documentation and historiography (the writing of history) proper. The reason is that self-aggrandisement, political propaganda and religious devotion were among the primary motives and objectives in the creation, publication and preservation of written documents. And not only at Sumer, but in all the successive oriental civilisations (including those of, say, the Jews and the Persians) where this sort of public and official literacy was regarded as both normal and indispensable. Yet today those motives would be considered not merely dispensable, but utterly incompatible with the proper standards of the profession, by all serious practitioners of the historian's craft. When and why did this crucial change in attitudes to historiography come about?

The "when" question is fairly simple to answer. The first work of history, in something like its modern sense of a critical, disinterested account and explanation of what actually happened, is the *Histories* (literally Researches) produced by Herodotus, in about 430BC. Herodotus is rightly feted, in Cicero's phrase, as the "Father of History" and his work - an account of the wars between Greece and Persia from 490 to 479BC - perceived as the very denial of "official" history in the oriental, propagandist mode. But the "why" of Herodotus' invention is much more difficult; there was no Herodotus before Herodotus, who belongs to that elite handful of fifth-century BC Greek innovating geniuses in drama, philosophy and scientific medicine.

Herodotus: fruitful comparison

Clearly, the timing and location of Herodotus' birth were vitally relevant. For he was born in the culturally mixed Graeco-Carian city of Halicarnassus (modern Bodrum in south-west Turkey), which then lay within the Achaemenid Persian empire, shortly before King Xerxes sought and massively failed to add all mainland Greece to his vast domains. It was this combination of familiarity with and yet distance from an alien edifice of imperial rule, spiced by the experience of enforced exile and extensive travel, which crucially developed Herodotus' instinct for fruitful comparison between and contrast of, incompatible systems of political and social organisation.

Yet, despite his critical objectivity, and his unquenchable thirst to understand and explain why the Greeks and the "barbarians" (non-Greeks) had come into catastrophic collision during the second half of the sixth and first quarter of the fifth centuries Herodotus remained rooted BC mentally speaking, in a more ancient Greek past. To his way of thinking, it was as important to emulate Homer in preserving from oblivion the "wondrous deeds of mankind", and to echo the dramatists in their exploration of man's relations with the superhuman and the divine, as it was to write a "scientific" history of the Graeco-Persian Wars. The fact that Herodotus composed primarily for oral recitation before large audiences, rather than for private and individual reading, helped to ensure that his *Histories* remained imbued with a strongly archaic coloration of divine agency and intervention in human affairs.

Thucydides: dispeller of myths

Almost totally different in conception and atmosphere, as in style and execution, was the life work of Herodotus' greatest ancient successor, Thucydides of Athens. The differences are explained by their backgrounds. Thucydides was not just an Athenian, a citizen of the most powerful and most cosmopolitan Greek state of the Aegean world, but a brilliantly clever Athenian of the post-modernist intellectual Enlightenment, a child of the rationalist intellectual revolution encapsulated in Protagoras' limitlessly bold claim that "Man is the measure of all things".

The gods, and indeed the supernatural generally, are not entirely absent from the pages of Thucydides, but they are there marginalised severely as explanatory factors. In the view of Thucydides', man makes himself (not herself, since Thucydides' laser-like concentration on war, politics and diplomacy served practically to exclude from consideration the other half of the human race), and so, from an historiographical point of view, human, secular explanations of the past he chose to write about are all that count.

Moreover, in determining what had actually happened, Thucydides applied far more rigorously critical standards of enquiry into and evaluation of (largely oral) testimony that Herodotus had thought fitting. Aware of humanity's, or at any rate most Greeks', propensity for turning fact into myth and legend, Thucydides decided that only what happened in one's own lifetime, and within the experience and memory of intelligent and articulate witnesses, could legitimately be known, discovered and written up with sufficient accuracy to qualify as history proper.

An historian's war

That was the technical ground on which he elected to compose a history of the great war between Athens and Sparta and their respective allies which broke out in 431BC (when Thucydides was probably in his mid-twenties) and lasted with intermissions until 404BC. It is in Thucydides' honour that we still call it the "Peloponnesian War" - the war against the Peloponnesians - composed by Thucydides the Athenian, for had Thucydides been a Spartan it would of course have been the "Athenian War". Few wars, in fact, have been so much the creation of their historian.

On the other hand, it would be quite wrong to exaggerate the similarities of approach and outlook between Thucydides and the canonical modern historian as if, for all the world, he were a colleague in the faculty of history at any university. True, he was decisively influenced by Protagorean secular rationalism and by the empirical precision of the Hippocratic School (hence, for example, his meticulous and flesh-crawling description of the symptoms the Great Plague of Athens, which he himself caught, but survived). But, like Herodotus, he also shared the preoccupation with human pride and excess, and the problems of free will and determinism which exercised his tragedian contemporaries such as Euripides.

Moreover, especially in the speeches and dialogues which he wrought into works of dramatic art, Thucydides used his history as a vehicle for reflection in a vein that would be today considered appropriate for a moral philosopher or political theorist but not, strictly, for an historian.

Therein, however, lies his peculiar greatness, never to be matched in antiquity even by that most acute observer of human foibles and most successful of Roman narrative historians, Tacitus. As long as the ancient Greek classics are judged worthy of study, whether in the original language or in a modern vernacular translation, Thucydides' history bids fair to fulfil its author's hubristic claim to be "a possession for all time".

Bust of Herodotus, celebrated as the 'Father of History': he was the first to write history that was not official propaganda, but his works were linked to a more ancient Greek past in that they were written for oral recitation.

Bust of Thucydides of Athens, a rationalist historian who decided that only what happened within one's own memory, or the memory of intelligent and articulate witnesses, could legitimately be thought of as history.

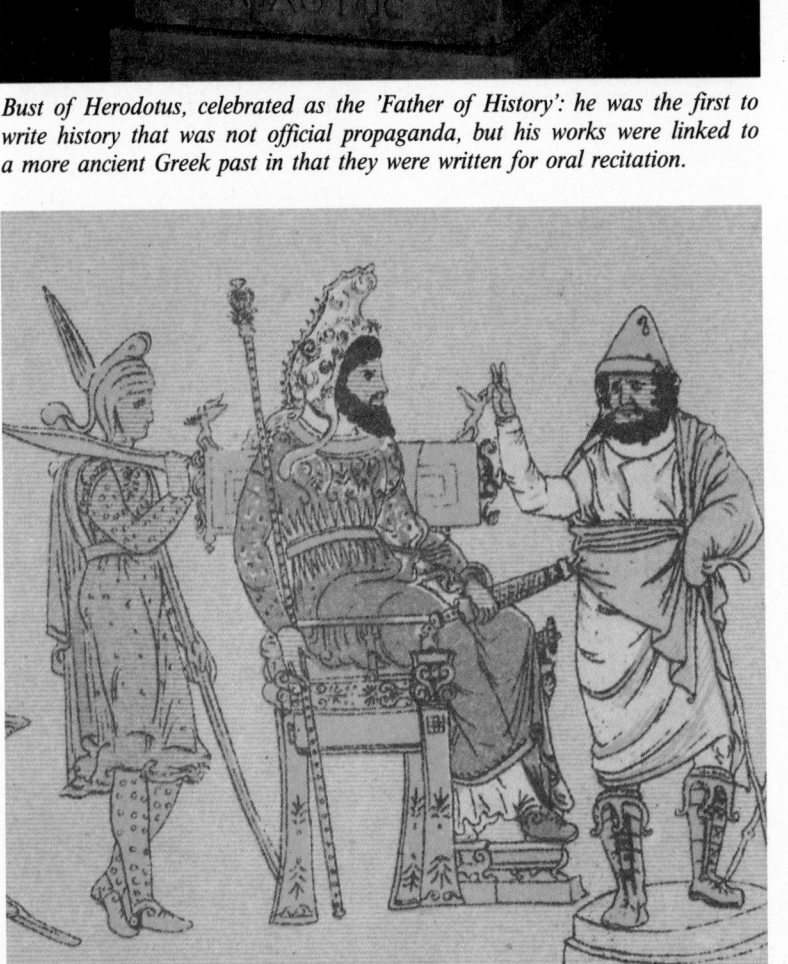

Great King Xerxes of Persia and his council during the wars with Greece: he succeeded when his father Darius died while still preparing for a third expedition against Greece. After two years of fighting Xerxes was defeated.

A relief of the young Xerxes standing behind the throne of his father, Darius the Great of Persia. Darius reorganised the Persian Empire making Susa the capital, and pushed his conquests as far as Caucasus and the Indus.

Greece, 369BC. After a recent defeat by Thebes at Leuctra, the Spartans are hemmed into their part of the Peloponnese by two new city foundations: Megaopolis, an amalgam of 40 villages in south-west Arcadia, and Messene, capital of the reborn nation of Sparta's former *helot* serfs.

Sicily, 367BC. The reign of Dionysius, tyrant of Syracuse, is at an end. After his election in 405BC, Dionysius attacked the propertied rich and freed their slaves. He concluded a peace treaty with Carthage, opening the way for Syracuse to become one of the dominant cities of southern Italy.

Greece, 362BC. The Theban general Epaminondas loses his life in the defeat of breakaway Arcadian, Athenian and Spartan contingents at Mantinea. The battle of Mantinea enshrines the eclipse of Spartan power and the independence of the Peloponnesian regions, and aggravates the conflict between Thebes and Athens.

Athens, 360BC. The great orator Lysias has died. After his brother was killed by the Thirty Tyrants Lysias fled into exile, but returned to Athens with the democrats. He prosecuted Eratosthenes, the tyrant chiefly to blame for his brother's murder, and went on to write many speeches for private litigants, which often included telling points on morals and politics.

Macedonia, 359BC. Philip becomes regent of the small kingdom of Macedonia on the death of his brother, King Perdiccas, whose son is a mere child. Philip, aged 22, already displays unusual diplomatic and military acumen.

Egypt, 359BC. Nectanebo II has scarcely ascended the throne when he is forced to put down a significant revolt. He then sets about pursuing the building policy of his predecessor, Nectanebo I.

Persia, 358BC. Artaxerxes III succeeds Artaxerxes II and ends the *satraps'* revolt which has poisoned the life of the empire for the past decade. Fearing possible rivals, he has his whole family massacred.

Greece, 357BC. Supported by Byzantium and Mausolos of Caria, Chios, Rhodes and Cos leave the Athenian alliance. Meanwhile, Philip of Macedon captures Amphipolis and allies himself with the Chalcidians and the Thessalians.

Theban empire expands

Greece, 360BC

With Athens ruined by war and Sparta become decadent, Thebes has taken these ancient rivals' place as the dominant power in Greece. The Thebans used their new "phalanx" tactic to defeat the Spartans at the battle of Leuctra 11 years ago. The Spartans, their military prowess eroded, relied on mercenaries and were no match for the fresh and confident Thebans.

As the Thebans expanded their empire and made allies under their two great generals, Pelopidas and Epaminondas, the Spartans and Athenians, after years of bloody strife, joined forces to fight the upstart Thebans. But even together they were defeated at the battle of Mantinea two years ago.

One of the Thebans' most powerful weapons on the battlefield is The Sacred Band, a force of 300 shock troops founded in 378BC after the Thebans had expelled the Spartans then occupying their city.

The men of this band are homosexuals, "lovers and their beloved", and they are renowned for their fierce loyalty to each other. Trained

Epaminondas dies (later portrayal).

to fight as a single unit by Pelopidas, they have yet to be defeated.

However, despite the Thebans' mastery of the Greek battlefield, there is concern for the future of their empire. Both Pelopidas and Epaminondas have been killed in battle, and Thebes shares in the confusion which rules Greece.

Athens dominated by complex goddess

Athens, 300-200BC

This city is still dominated by the Parthenon on the Acropolis which was completed 70 years ago. In translation it is the "maiden's apartment" built in honour of the city's patron goddess, Athena, and still today Athena towers over religious and secular life here. Athena is a complex goddess, whose example still nourishes the virtues which have made Athens pre-eminent.

She is a warrior, often depicted in helmet and breast-plate holding spear and shield. But she is also the supreme judge, who ensures that justice is done. Athena is also believed to have an inventive practical intelligence. She inspires craftsmen, potters and weavers, and guides pilots safely through currents.

According to myth, it was Athena who, through the use of her wiles, convinced Odysseus that he had finally ended his journey and arrived back in his homeland. Athena's mother, Metis, was renowned for her cunning. Zeus was

Athena, warrior and arts patron.

frightened of her, and he swallowed her when she was pregnant. She retaliated by giving him a headache, and he was then struck on the head by an axe. Athena sprang forth fully formed from the wound in his head.

Winged messenger looks after thieves

Greece, c.370BC

The Greeks worship many gods, all of whom inhabit Mount Olympus under the rule of their lord, Zeus. Among the foremost of these is Hermes, the divine trickster, not merely a god, but a friend of mankind as well.

Hermes, the son of Zeus and the nymph Maia (herself the daughter of a Titan), is the messenger of the gods. He is always on the move, and watches over travellers and the roads they follow. He takes his name from a Greek word meaning "pile of stones", and the roads of Greece are dotted with such cairns, often in the shape of an erect phallus, marking the midpoint between the country's villages and the

Hermes, in a less excited pose.

centre of Athens. Worship of Hermes centres on these symbols, and he is known for his sexual success.

With the helmet of Hades to make him invisible, the winged sandals with which he flies, and his staff, a real magic wand, Hermes is the very spirit of communication. He is the patron of ambassadors and messengers. He also watches over trading of all kinds, treaties, oaths and any sort of bargain.

But he has a darker side. The Greeks tell of his theft, while still a baby, of the sacred cattle of his fellow-god Apollo (for whom he created the lyre from a tortoise-shell), and while shepherds take him as their special god so, too, do robbers. Hermes is Olympus' very own thief and there are many stories of the gods using him to carry out special tasks that require his swift cunning and resourcefulness.

Shang Yang rules in Qin

China, 356BC

Shang Yang, chancellor of the western state of Qin (Ch'in), has introduced a remarkable series of reforms to this area, which is usually regarded as being on the fringes of Chinese culture and administration. But there is nothing accidental in this development. Shang Yang has carefully planned his programme to make his state a great economic and military power.

He has cunningly strengthened the power of the central government by dividing the state into 31 counties, each governed by a magistrate directly responsible to himself,

and he brooks no inefficiency or the slightest whiff of disloyalty.

He is also taming the old landowning families, by making the sale and purchase of land easier and insisting that agricultural taxes are collected in cash rather than in kind or by working them off in the fields.

He has also instituted a strict penal code which is applied to everyone regardless of their social status. These new laws are rigorously enforced by "mutual responsibility groups". Good work is rewarded. Success in farming and in warfare brings not only a grant of land, but also a non-hereditary title.

Crossbow transforms Chinese warfare

Brick from 100-200AD showing a Chinese archer with crossbow, on horseback.

China, 360BC

Warfare in China is now dominated by the crossbow – an arrow-firing device so deadly that a soldier can rely on a bolt fired from it to kill or maim an enemy on the other side of a battlefield. With entire armies equipped with this remarkably accurate weapon, the crossbow has become both the means and the end of war in China. The key to its effectiveness is the pressure-sensitive trigger that releases the string of the short bow mounted crosswise on a wooden stock.

Mass-production of these triggers and other components has turned Chinese cities into centres for the manufacture of and trade in weapons. This has led to military

commanders concentrating campaigns on capturing cities in order to destroy their opponents' ability to wage war. This, in turn, has led to developments in siege warfare techniques.

Defenders have been bombarded with missiles, including incendiary devices catapulted from giant slings with 30-foot-long throwing arms. Attackers have been met by ingenious counter-measures, including giant crossbows fired from battlements and tunnels dug beneath city walls pumped full of poisonous smoke. A by-product of these changes is the renaissance of the humble infantryman. Equipped with armour, a sword and a crossbow, he has come into his own.

Greek sculptors turn to secular subjects

The head of Mausolus, from his tomb, the Mausoleum, at Halicarnassus.

Greece, c.510-350BC

Statues in city squares throughout Greece mark a new development in artistic life. Sculpture is no longer confined to representations of the gods, but may depict all the varieties of the human form.

From earliest times, sculpture was an essentially religious art. Statues were the property of the gods whom they represented, or to whom they were dedicated. They were made in wood, marble or bronze, and decorated in many colours for the gods' greater delight. They were almost invariably confined to sanctuaries or cemeteries.

In Greek temples, statues were placed inside the *naos*, or inner chamber, where the god lived; other votive statues, donated either in thanksgiving by private individuals, or by cities to commemorate great victories or peace treaties, were distributed round the rest of the sanctuary. In the cemeteries,

statues idealised the dead in the beauty of their youth.

The first secular sculptures began to appear at the start of the fifth century BC in public squares. In 510BC the *agora* in Athens was the chosen site of a statue of Harmodius and Aristogeiton, commemorated as tyrannicides. The tyrant in question was actually killed by Spartans, but Athens needed heroes, so when Harmodius and Aristogeiton killed the tyrant's brother they were chosen for immortality. Xerxes of Persia stole the statue, but it was replaced in 477BC and now stands in the *agora* again, alongside statues like that of Conon, an Athenian admiral who fought for Persia with Athens against Sparta.

By 350BC Praxiteles, the Athenian sculptor, was able to make a statue of Aphrodite, clearly modelled on his mistress, Phryne, a well-known figure in the city.

Macedonia conquers Thrace, a flourishing kingdom of contrasts renowned for warlike shepherds and sophisticated jewellery

Thracian gold and silver statuette.

Panels showing the high level of Thracian craftsmanship in precious metal.

Balkans, c.340BC

After 20 years at war, Macedonians under Philip II are beginning to take stock of the huge and wealthy Thracian empire they now control.

With lands that stretch from the Danube to the Bosporus, Philip II now rules one of the most culturally, economically and politically advanced regions in the world.

Thracian treasure with its fine filigree work in silver and gold is internationally famous, with Thracian craftsmen setting new standards in fashioning jewellery, helmets and breastplates in gold and silver. Much noted are those decorated with unusual combinations of human and animal subjects, reflecting Thrace's eastern influences.

This ability to generate items of wealth was a weapon in the unsuccessful campaign by Thrace's last overall ruler, Kotys, to win allies and influence friends.

Kotys tried to unite Thrace's tribes of wild shepherds into an empire, reminiscent of the Persians' that would extend from the Black Sea to the Mediterranean.

The Eleusinian Mysteries enshrine the secrets of Greek religion

Greece, c.340BC

The Greeks love a mystery – and there is no greater mystery cult than that of the Mystae, who are celebrating in Athens and Eleusis. An elaborate religious festival, the "Greater Eleusinian Mysteries", continues over a period of nine days every September in honour of Demeter, goddess of fertility and resurrection, and her daughter Persephone.

Only the initiated are allowed to attend, but the cult is open to all Greek-speakers, even slaves, regardless of age and gender. They receive preliminary instruction during smaller festivals at Agrae at the end of the winter. After their initiation they are sworn to silence.

The principal festival begins in Athens and on a beach at Phaleron, where the Mystae sacrifice a pig and bathe in the sea to purify themselves. Then, on the fifth day, they march in procession to the sanctuary of Demeter and Persephone at Eleusis. It is there, in the Hall of Initiation, that the Eleusinian Mysteries reach their climax.

Details of the rites are shrouded in great secrecy, but the priests probably mime the legend of Persephone and unveil sacred symbols of fertility.

According to the legend, the original temple was built by the Eleusinians to placate Demeter after they had rejected her gift of eternal life for the King's son, Demophon.

Demeter had been given refuge in Eleusis after her daughter, Persephone, was abducted by Hades and made queen of the underworld. In return for their hospitality she had given her favourite, Triptolemus, an ear of corn, the symbol of renewed life. But then Zeus inter-

The Eleusinian initiation ritual.

vened with Hades, and persuaded him to allow Persephone to visit her mother every summer in Eleusis. Her return each year is held to symbolise the annual rebirth of the corn crop.

Persian invasion ends Egyptian revival

Egypt, 342BC

After 60 years of rebellion Egypt has been invaded again and is once more under the oppressive rule of its Persian masters. The cultural revival under Nectanebo I and his successor is at an end as the Persians plunder and pillage.

Nectanebo I, a brilliant commander in the field, had succeeded in fighting off the first Persian attempt at re-conquering Egypt 30 years ago by holding back the invaders until the annual flooding of the Nile delta – giving his navy the considerable advantage of local knowledge in the marshes. After his death, however, the Persians persisted and succeeded in deposing Nectanebo II, who has fled south.

Without the burden of paying tithes to foreign rulers, Egypt prospered under Nectanebo who ensured that much of the country's revenue went into new building. So much fine red granite was taken from the first Nile cataract for the erection of huge temples that the king ordained that no more be cut.

Nonetheless, Nectanebo built a great temple to Isis, the Iseum of Behbeit al-hagar in the delta, entirely of granite, one of two buildings in Egypt – the other being the great Sphinx of Saqqara – to be completed in this lovely stone. Another of his great achievements was the "House of the Divine Birth", the temple annex at Denderah in Upper Egypt where the mysteries of Osiris' birth were celebrated.

Egypt is paying a high price for its years of revolution. The temples of Nectanebo and all the splendour of Egypt are being systematically destroyed, and a proud people is being forced by its masters to worship a donkey.

Selk, a deity who guards coffins.

The Egyptian crocodile god Sebek.

New Greek music outrages elders

Greek musicians in procession: carved in 100AD.

Athens, 340BC

A new and outlandish form of music, rejecting traditional forms and values, is being taken up by Athenian youth. Two leading philosophers, Plato and Aristotle, have expressed their outrage.

Plato believes that the three years which the young devote to music are inadequate to protect them from the boorish emotionalism of the new wave of musicians, such as Timotheus of Miletus, whose music so shocks the older generation. Aristotle has said that music has such an emotional effect on people that it should be censored.

This public debate would never have taken place a generation ago. Since Orpheus charmed the beasts, the birds, even the trees and the streams, in the days of the Argonauts, music has been the predominant art in Greece. Orpheus' lyre was given to him by Apollo; his music even enchanted the underworld. The *Iliad* and the *Odyssey* were chanted to the music of the lyre. Music was the most important part of an Athenian's education. In addition to the lyre, Athenians played the *aulos* (oboe) while country people played the *syrinx* (panpipes). To many the century before the wars with Sparta were a halcyon age of Greek music.

It is only in recent times, in the period of Athens' self-doubt following her defeat by philistine Sparta in the Peloponnesian War, that the role of music in Athenian society has been questioned; and, significantly, it has been out of this period of self-doubt that the new-wave music of Timotheus of Miletus has emerged.

Despised Macedonia crushes the Greeks in the "Sacred War"

The Temple of Apollo: the legendary home of the Delphic Oracle.

Greece, 346BC

The Sacred War, waged for the last ten years for possession of Greece's supreme oracle at Delphi, has ended with Philip of Macedon, despised as a barbarian by the Athenians, winning ascendancy over Greece. This unforeseen result of yet another internecine quarrel bodes ill for the city states.

It started when the Thebans, who controlled the *Amphictiony*, the multi-state council which administers the shrine, forced through a threat of war against the Phocians unless they paid a fine for cultivating sacred ground.

The Phocians, who had once had control of Delphi, chose to go to war to re-establish their position, but there then followed a period of cruel, confused warfare during which the Phocians were generally successful. But then the war drew in the ambitious Philip, who saw his opportunity to seize Greek territory.

His advance and involvement in Greek affairs drew bitter attacks from Demosthenes, who issued the first of his "Philippics" in 351BC. Athens belatedly sent an army to help Athens' allies besieged by Philip at Olynthus.

It was too little and too late. Philip captured the city and razed it to the ground. Phocis has now been forced to sue for peace and Philip the Barbarian holds power in Greece.

Euterpe, flautist-Muse of poetry.

Greece, 339BC. Hostilities are renewed between Athens and Macedonia, marking the start of the fourth Sacred War. Philip II occupies Elateia, two days' march from Attica. Demosthenes saves the day for the panic-stricken Athenians by engineering an alliance between Athens and Thebes.

Persia, 338BC. Artaxerxes III is poisoned to death by his favourite eunuch. During his reign he did much to rebuild the empire, which was disintegrating on his accession.

Greece, 338BC. Philip II of Macedon defeats the combined forces of Athens and Thebes at the battle of Chaeronea. With the surrender of Thebes the Boeotian league is dissolved. Philip imposes peace terms on Athens which include allying with Macedonia and dissolving the Athenian league. Struck by the generosity of their conqueror, the Athenians offer citizenship to Philip and his son, Alexander.

Athens, 338BC. The orator Isocrates, who began his career by writing law-court speeches, dies at 98. After opening his school of rhetoric in 393BC, he felt impelled to prove his worth by writing "display" speeches for big occasions. Among the most famous are the *Panegyricus* and the *Panathenaicus*, which hymn the glories of Hellenism and the city of Athens. Isocrates made a major contribution to developing Panhellenism, according to which a united Greece should conquer Persia.

Italy, 338BC. Rome, which has become the main power in Italy, succeeds in dissolving the Latin league and uniting Latium.

Macedonia, 337BC. Philip's decision to marry Cleopatra, a woman from the Macedonian nobility, causes a stir at court. The marriage, which will be polygamous, stems from Philip's concern about his line of succession. Alexander is his heir-designate but, as his second son, Arrhidaeus, suffers from epilepsy, he thinks it wise to have a third son.

Rome, 336BC. Plebeians are allowed to become *praetors* (magistrates closely connected with military affairs). This is the latest step in a gradual recognition of plebeians' rights. The office of dictatorship was opened to them in 356BC, and the censorship in 351BC. One plebeian, Quintus Publilius Philo, holds all three offices.

Philip of Macedon conquers the Greeks

King Philip, the unifier of Greece.

Athens, 337BC

After a decisive defeat by Philip II of Macedon, Athenian leaders have accepted peace on terms which effectively end the traditional independence of Greek city states. In a war which began more than 20 years ago, the Macedonian "barbarian" has proved himself a master of political strategy as well as a military genius. He has used the wiles of diplomacy, marriage, banking, corruption and sabotage. His military coups include the defeat of Illyria to the north, together with Athens' maritime ally, Chalcidice, to secure his southern Aegean flank and the remorseless occupation of mainland cities.

Athens, a tardy opponent, held his advance after a long battle in 352BC to control the strategic Thermopylae Pass. Philip used a temporary peace with Athens to join Thebes in its "Sacred War" against Phocis. Thebes, a hollow victor, was spent. The real winner was Philip.

Other governments anointed him as a peacemaker, but in 341BC he attacked Athens' allies in Thrace-Gallipoli. Renewed warfare culminated in an evenly-matched combat at Chaeronea last year. The turning point was a feigned retreat by Philip behind piles of corpses, enticing the Athenians into hot pursuit and an ambush. This was sprung by seasoned Macedonian cavalry, led by Philip's son Alexander.

In the immediate aftermath of the war, Thebes has been occupied by Macedonians. Nominal self-government continues elsewhere, but without autonomy overseas. Most states must join Philip's new League of Corinth as he prepares to repay Persia for its earlier attacks. Greece is unified, but at a great cost.

"Puny village" becomes a hub of empire

Macedonia, 346BC

Athenian propaganda asserting that the Macedonian capital, Pella, is "a puny little village" (as Demosthenes, the anti-Macedonian lobbyist, has suggested) is contradicted by eye-witness accounts of recent travellers who visited it.

Far from its being an inaccessible shanty town, they say, it is approached by a well-engineered road some 30 feet wide. It is on a vast fertile plain flanked by the sea, with a thriving port. This prime site was developed some 50 years ago by King Archelaus. Elegant buildings, with walls six feet thick, are decorated with rare pebble mosaics, Ionic and Doric colonnades, and three-foot roof tiles stamped "Pella".

The palace contains murals by the great artist Zeuxis. Standards of public hygiene, water supply and

Part of Pella, Macedonia's capital.

drainage match the aesthetic quality of the city. The plays of Euripides are performed and the heir to the throne, young Alexander, has Aristotle as a visiting tutor. Pella is unquestionably the hub of a growing empire.

Demosthenes leads fight for freedom

Roman portrait of Demosthenes.

Athens, 337BC

Athenian civilisation and the defence of freedom are embodied in one man – the lawyer, statesman and orator Demosthenes.

Even after the defeat of the combined Athenian and Theban army by Philip of Macedon at Chaeronea in 338BC, Demosthenes holds a unique position of trust and respect among his people. He was chosen to deliver a funeral oration for the dead of that battle, and was granted a crown of gold for his efforts to organise and defend the people of Athens.

Demosthenes learned his legal skills as a young man in a prolonged battle to recover his patrimony from dishonest guardians. He won his case, but there was no money left, and so he began to earn his living by writing speeches.

At 30 he rose to the rostrum of the assembly, and learned to improve his diction. Although his arguments often failed – anti-war in 354BC, and pro-war in 351BC – he gradually won a reputation for speeches of powerful logic, withering sarcasm, and use of dialogue that kept his audience enthralled.

From 351BC onwards, his was the one insistent voice warning Athenians not to trust Philip of Macedon, to support cities threatened by him, and to build up their army for the inevitable war with Macedonia. It appears that Athens heeded his advice too late.

Philip slain: Alexander is in power

Statues get human faces in Greece

Macedonia, 336BC

King Philip II of Macedon has died at the hands of an assassin in his hour of triumph. After attending a state ceremony at which his own statue was displayed as a new Olympian god, he was stabbed by Pausanias, a royal bodyguard with a grudge. Philip is succeeded by his son Alexander, aged just 20.

In spite of his youth Alexander is already a veteran of warfare and of government. Four years ago, while Philip was on an expedition to Byzantium, Alexander acted as regent of Macedonia and fought his own local war against the Thracian Maedi. His role in the battle of Chaeronea spread his reputation throughout Greece.

Alexander has had a rich and complex education. Along with the studies normally pursued by a young aristocrat he has been exposed to hard lessons in practical politics within the family circle. In his early years at Pella, the Macedonian capital, he came under the influence of his mother, Olympias.

Her kinsman Leonidas introduced him to the Homeric legends as a guide to practical living, from the art of war to navigation. At the age of 13 he was taken by his father to become a pupil of Aristotle. A liberal education with others in residence at Mieza included medicine, geometry, rhetoric and literature.

Throughout his formative years his mother's influence remained. When Philip married a younger woman named Cleopatra polygamously last year, it provoked a near fatal division between the two men. At the wedding feast, the bride's uncle unwisely predicted a "legitimate heir to the throne". An enraged Alexander, war veteran as well as true heir, started fighting. Philip intervened but collapsed, drunk. Alexander left, saying: "Here's the man who was making

Alexander, the 20-year-old king.

ready to cross from Europe to Asia, and who cannot cross from one table to another without losing his balance." Only recently was Alexander persuaded by his father to come out of self-imposed exile in Illyria, after escorting his mother to sanctuary.

Greece, 390-335BC

Athens, where glorious statues are already a commonplace of the city's renown, has a new artistic prodigy: the sculptor Praxiteles, himself the son of the famous sculptor Cephisodotos. Praxiteles' work shows that he has both learned from his father and added his own personal style, which reflects a contemporary, sophisticated personality.

He works in marble, creating statues which are ornamented, primarily in red or black, by the painter Nicias. Unlike many of his peers, Praxiteles is unimpressed by traditional militaristic or athletic themes. Instead his works, such as "Hermes with the Infant Dionysus" and "Aphrodite of Cnidos", project a very human, even tender, quality, and in many statues Praxiteles has even given the sculpted marble a degree of humour.

Gods these figures may be, but under his hands they become almost mortal. No one has ever sculpted goddesses with such sensual beauty, and no one, certainly, has ever revealed them without their clothes. For the first time Athens has a sculptor whose aim is less to honour the gods than, unashamedly, to delight the viewer.

Aristotle's writings lead logically to new school of philosophy

A statue of Aristotle, philosopher, scientist, physician and teacher of Alexander, son of Philip of Macedon.

Athens, 335BC

Students at the new college opened by Aristotle in the Athens Lyceum park are being taught a new method of reasoning, called logic. It is part of Aristotle's innovative approach to the whole question of human knowledge. In every branch of learning on the Lyceum curriculum Aristotle rests his teaching on close observation of facts.

This is especially noticeable in his book *Historia animalium*, a detailed record of the behaviour and habits of animals, which has led to Aristotle being called the world's first biologist. "Even in the study of animals unattractive to the senses," he writes, "the nature that fashioned them offers immeasurable pleasure to those who can learn the causes ..."

His family background doubtless encouraged his pragmatic approach to problems. His father was physician to King Philip of Macedon. When he was 17, Aristotle came to Athens to study under Plato and remained until Plato's death 20 years later. Many expected Aristotle to succeed Plato as head of the Academy. When that did not happen, Aristotle left and became tutor to Alexander, heir to the Macedonian throne.

Aristotle is changing the way in which scholars think. He divides knowledge into two categories: theoretical and practical. Theoretical knowledge seeks knowledge for its own sake; it includes philosophy, the theory of mathematics and theoretical chemistry. Practical knowledge deals with such matters as building, politics and economics.

Aristotle also makes a distinction between theoretical and practical knowledge. The mental calculation $2 \times 2 = 4$ leads to a universal conclusion – a result that is always true. But practical knowledge deals with everyday things that can vary a great deal; they are to some extent unaccountable.

In his lectures on logic, Aristotle introduces his students to the syllogism: All men are mortal *(major premiss)*; Socrates is a man *(minor premiss)*; therefore Socrates is mortal *(conclusion)*. The syllogism shows the students what they must do in order to prove something. Had the major premiss been "Some men are mortal", it would not have been possible to show that Socrates was a man.

For the study of politics Aristotle has directed his students to collect no fewer than 150 different constitutions of Greek city-states in order to discover the best system of government.

The humanity of Praxiteles' work is seen in "Aphrodite of Cnidos".

Macedonia, 335BC. After succeeding his father as king of Macedonia, Alexander sets out on his first military campaign, aiming to punish the Triballi for their rebellion of 339BC and re-establish order in the Balkans. His victory reinforces Macedonian power in the region of the lower Danube.

Asia Minor, 333BC. Already in control of a large part of Asia Minor (Anatolia), Alexander defeats Darius III of Persia at Issus. This follows his great victory over the Persians last year at the river Granicus. Darius is put to flight and Alexander captures his camp and family, sleeping in the Persian king's tent on the night of his victory.

Phoenicia, 332BC. Alexander has taken the city of Tyre after an eight-month siege. It is reported that 8,000 citizens have been killed and 30,000 sold into slavery. After Alexander's recent rout of the Persians the cities of Phoenicia – except for Tyre – wisely surrendered to him.

Persia, 331BC. After his unopposed expedition to Egypt, Alexander moves into Persia and defeats the Persian army at Gaugamela. Babylonia and Susa surrender to him.

Persia, 330BC. Alexander marches on Persepolis and allows his army to pillage the royal city. He wants to take Darius alive, but the Persian king is assassinated by rebels. His death marks the collapse of the Achaemenid dynasty.

Central Asia, 327BC. Alexander secures the conquest of Bactria and Sogdiana, begun two years ago when he crossed the Hindu Kush after conquering the eastern states of the Persian empire.

Persia, 327BC. The official historian of Alexander's expedition, Callisthenes, is executed for his alleged complicity in a conspiracy.

China, 325BC. The prince of Qin (Ch'in) takes the title *wang* (king), thereby making a claim to be the legitimate ruler of the whole of China.

Persia, 324BC. Alexander organises an unprecedented move to forge links between the Greeks and the barbarians: 90 of his Graeco-Macedonian companions marry, or are forced to marry, daughters of the Medean and Persian nobility. Ten thousand soldiers also embark on marriages with Persians.

Alexander subdues restless Greeks

Greece, 335BC

In an eventful few months the young monarch Alexander has moved swiftly to put his personal stamp on the Greek empire unified by his late father, Philip. He has purged politically unreliable individuals and launched swift punitive expeditions against any regions even hinting at disloyalty.

Two Macedonian nobles have been executed for failing to make public homage promptly enough. Others at risk are relatives of King Philip's last wife, Cleopatra. Her uncle Attalus, serving with the Greek advance guard in Asia, is suspected of plotting with the Athenian lawyer Demosthenes. An army unit has been sent to bring Attalus home.

Alexander's attacks on regional enemies have been bold. He led a pre-emptive attack against the Triballi and the Illyrians which took him across the Danube. In his absence, however, there was disaffection in Sparta and Athens.

It was in Thebes that the most serious trouble occurred, ignited by rumour that Alexander had been killed in action. Thebes promptly split from the Greek federation. After a forced march of 310 miles (500 km) in 13 days, Alexander

Alexander: a conqueror's image.

stormed the city and systematically destroyed everything except temples and the home of Pindar the poet. The city's 8,000 people were sold as slaves and their homeland split into lots which were also sold. Other states tempted to dissent hastily sought the king's pardon.

To complete preparations for his campaign against Persia, Alexander consulted the Oracle of Delphi, but chose a day regarded by temple authorities as inauspicious for any "reading". The king promptly summoned the presiding priestess, who refused to perform the ceremony. Alexander manhandled her towards the temple. The frightened woman shouted words to the effect that Alexander

Later portrayal of the warrior king.

was "invincible". A delighted Alexander released her and said he had no further need of prophecies.

Beneath his confidence, though, it is clear that Alexander is not ready to place people from the old city-states of Athens, Sparta or Thebes in positions of trust. Regiments from these areas are now second-rate members of his expeditionary force, or potential hostages.

Egyptian city commemorates triumphs of Macedonian conqueror

Egyptian statue of Alexander.

Egypt, 331BC

Foreigners from all parts of the eastern Mediterranean are flocking to a splendid city which the conquering Macedonian king, Alexander, is building on the Egyptian coast in the west of the Nile delta. A great harbour, being created by constructing a mole linking the mainland with the island of Pharos, will be used as a naval base for Alexander's war against the Persian empire.

The architect Dinocrates, who gained notoriety when he suggested that Mount Athos be carved into a gigantic seated statue, is marking out the new city, to be called Alexandria, in a grid pattern of straight streets intersecting each other at right angles.

Alexander's decision to found the city was announced after he had visited the oracle of Ammon, at the Siwa oasis in neighbouring Libya. The Greeks identify Ammon with their own Zeus, and it is said that Alexander wanted to trace his birth back to Ammon. He was not disappointed. Having been guided to

the oasis by two black crows, he was greeted by a priest who hailed him as a "son of the god".

The new city, set at the crossroads between the Hellenistic world of Greece and Asia Minor (Anatolia) the rich valley of the Nile, and the markets of the east, seems certain to become a great trading centre. Already a substantial Jewish quarter is growing up in the north-east of the city, while Egyptian fishermen are settled in the south-west. The Greeks are in the central sectors around the royal palaces and surrounding gardens.

The city is far from complete, but its founder has already departed to resume his campaign to destroy the Persian empire. He has appointed a viceroy, the youthful Cleomenes, and instructed him to spare no expense in pressing on with the immense task of construction.

Military genius wins war against Persians

The might of Persia crumbles before the onslaught of Alexander's troops.

Asia Minor and Persia, 330BC

Early on a summer's morning, Alexander and his army, crossing the mountainous region of western Iran, came upon the remnants of the once-mighty forces of Darius III. Most of them fled, and when Alexander caught up with the Persian wagons he found Darius in one of them, dead from stab wounds inflicted on the orders of his cousin Bessus. The campaign that had begun three years before, when Alexander crossed into Asia Minor with 30,000 men, was over. At last he was master of the Persian empire.

The Persians had the bigger army, but Alexander had the better one. The first battle took place at the Granicus river, near the Sea of Marmora. Alexander, with 13 troops of horse, plunged into the swiftly-running waters and with a feint attack on the Persian left caused the enemy to weaken its centre, where the main Greek blow came. It was the first battle of the war in which the phalanx was used. This close formation of long spears behind a wall of overlapping shields devastated the Persian lines.

From Granicus, Alexander went south, liberating the Greek cities of Asia Minor and planning for the following year's campaign, which would begin at Gordium. There he was told of Gordius, the mythical king of Phrygia, whose wagon was fastened to the yoke by a knot that defied all efforts to untie it. An oracle said that whoever untied the knot would rule Asia. Alexander simply cut the Gordian knot with his sword.

Alexander expands his empire into India

Susa, Persia, 325BC

Alexander has arrived back in this capital, his army victorious in their Indian campaign – but almost halved in numbers by the toll taken on them by heat, hunger and thirst on the long march from the Punjab.

Alexander had fought his way across Afghanistan and penetrated the Khyber Pass to descend on to the Punjab plain where he vanquished Porus, the last rajah to have been brought under Persian influence. Porus met him on a river bank with 40,000 men and 200 elephants, but Alexander secretly crossed the river by night and swept down on Porus' exposed flank. Some 20,000 Indian infantry and 3,000 cavalry were killed, for the loss of about 80 of Alexander's men.

It has been an heroic saga, with Alexander winning battle after battle, year after year. He struck through the Hindu Kush into Turkestan, crossed the Oxus river to reach Samarkand and captured the Scythian chief Oxartes, whose daughter Roxana he married.

In his desire to unite his newly-conquered empire he encouraged his men to form marriage alliances with Asian women. He himself has adopted some Persian customs. As king of the rugged Macedonian tribes he had striven to gain acceptance by the cultivated Greeks.

Later portrayal of Alexander.

Now he seems to be betraying that ideal, and discontent is growing in his army. He has begun to scent conspiracies and has even had Parmenio, his faithful chief of staff, put to death. Alexander's ambition was to penetrate as far as the Ganges, where he expected to find the eastern limit of the inhabited world. But his troops refused to go further. For three days he sulked in his tent before giving way.

He divided his forces. He sent the main body back through Afghanistan, and dispatched a fleet down the Indus river with orders to sail along the coast to reach the Persian Gulf. A third force he led across the desert of Baluchistan. It was to be a terrible three months' march.

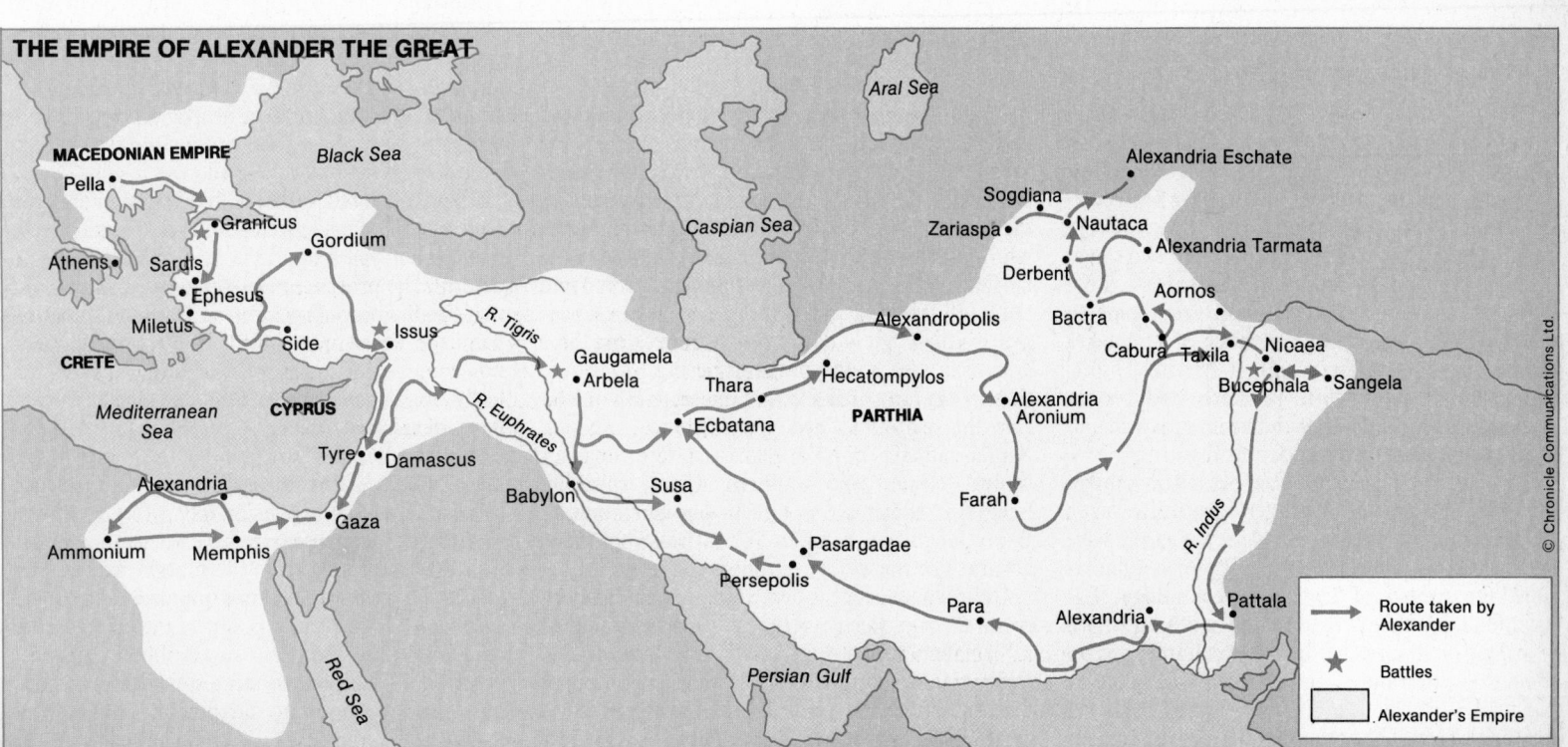

THE EMPIRE OF ALEXANDER THE GREAT

Route taken by Alexander

Battles

Alexander's Empire

© Chronicle Communications Ltd

Mystery surrounds Africa's language

It is strikingly apparent from the linguistic map of Africa that nearly a quarter of the 1,650 languages spoken there belong to a sub-group of one family. Moreover, this sub-group dominates roughly half the continent. These languages, called Bantu, from the common stem for the word for person (*ntu*), are all very closely related, as close to each other as the Germanic languages in Europe. The way in which this came about has intrigued many generations of scholars and is still not entirely clear.

However, thanks to the work of comparative linguists, it has been established that the ancestral language from which they are derived, called Proto-Bantu, can be reconstructed using vocabulary which forms a common base. By comparing Proto-Bantu with other languages it became clear that those closest to it were to be found in the area which now forms south-eastern Nigeria and western Cameroon. From this it appears that the ancestral language from which all the Bantu languages developed was originally spoken in this small area of West Africa. Confirmation comes from analysis of the vocabulary of Proto-Bantu: words for canoes, fishing equipment and certain types of plants are common, indicating that it was spoken in the forest or on the forest margins. Moreover, the close links between Bantu languages suggest recent and rapid expansion from the original homeland.

Two stages of expansion

In fact, Bantu languages can be divided into two groups. The western, or forest, languages have less in common with each other, and so have been evolving for longer than the eastern ones which are very close to each other indeed; this points to two stages in the expansion of Bantu languages. How did a language spoken in such a small area come to develop into such a large number of languages dominating the southern half of Africa? Unfortunately there are no written records, and it is not easy to reconcile the scanty archaeological evidence with what can be deduced from linguistics.

For this reason, attention has focused on another historical process which left very distinct traces in the archaeological record and which appears to have been occurring in much the same region at a similar time: the spread of Iron Age technology. Excavations throughout eastern and southern Africa reveal the rapid spread of Iron Age culture, bringing food production and the use of pottery into a region believed to have been inhabited previously by hunter-gatherers. The origins of this culture appear-

ed to be the lake region of East Africa at the end of the first millennium BC, and by about AD300-400 the technology and its associated material culture had reached modern South Africa.

The rapidity of the spread of Iron Age culture, and its association with a single pottery tradition and with the introduction of fully domesticated animals and crops, lends much weight to the assumption that it was brought by a new group of people moving into the area. Since the expansion of Bantu languages is also seen as a rapid but coherent population movement, it seems logical to link the two.

According to the hypothesis, the first stages of the expansion of Bantu-speaking peoples, along the northern margins of the forest and following rivers through the forest, was a movement of Late Stone Age vegeculturalists who kept goats but probably not sheep or cattle. Somewhere along the northern forest margins these people came into contact with others, through whom they adopted cereals and, possibly, sheep and cattle. Even more significantly, they learnt the use of iron, knowledge of which had spread from Meroe.

The expansion so far may have been a relatively slow process. However, the combination of agriculture and Iron Age technology would have stimulated population growth, giving an impetus to expansion.

Bringers of iron?

Bantu-speaking peoples moved both south and east, selecting only the best sites and so occupying a wide area relatively quickly. Since agricultural settlements were fixed and comparatively compact, these villages tended to attract hunter-gatherers who gradually adopted both the culture and the language of the newcomers, becoming absorbed into the Bantu-speaking population. This was a slower process than that of occupying territory, and there is evidence of hunter-gatherers using Stone Age technology long after the first introduction of iron into the region. Indeed, the existence today of hunter-gatherer populations in a few areas of central, eastern and southern Africa, speaking languages which are not related to surrounding Bantu languages, is taken as confirmation of the accuracy of the model outlined above.

Unfortunately for the peace of mind of historians, research over the past few years has produced information which does not fit into this picture. Excavations in Rwanda and Tanzania have produced evidence of Iron Age culture which is significantly earlier than previously thought possible. If these

dates (some as early as the second millennium BC) are confirmed, then knowledge of iron-working could not have been diffused from Meroe. Work on the western edges of the forest has also produced dates for food-producing and iron-using peoples which do not fit the rough chronology established in the 1970s. Taken together, these discoveries raise doubts about the link between Bantu expansion and that of the Early Iron Age complex.

New linguistic evidence

Linguists and historians are also becoming more cautious in their conclusions. It is now recognised that although linguistic changes in Europe can be dated, the same is not true in Africa. All that can be said is that by about AD700 people on the coast of East Africa were speaking a Bantu language.

Caution is also necessary when looking at the so-called remnant populations of hunter-gatherers. Peoples such as the San in the Kalahari and the "Pygmies" of the Ituri forest have been seen as surviving pockets of a once widespread non-Negro population, living a lifestyle unchanged for thousands of years. However, biologists are increasingly unhappy with the whole concept of race, particularly when it is based on physical criteria. Historians also challenge the idea that modern hunter-gatherers are "survivals" from an earlier period. In fact, specialisation in hunting and gathering may even be a recent development, stimulated by the presence nearby of specialists in a variety of types of food production with whom products could be exchanged.

Thus the overall picture of the expansion of Bantu languages is much less clear than it appeared to be five or ten years ago. Yet it is still possible to describe the process in general terms. It is obvious that the Bantu tongues evolved from one ancestral language which was spoken in the area which is now south-eastern Nigeria and Cameroon. Absolute dating is not possible, but these languages must have developed relatively recently and rapidly, certainly compared to the other members of the same branch of the Niger-Congo family. In fact, it is probable that expansion took place in at least two stages. There appears to have been a slow spread into the forest area from the margin with a later and much more rapid expansion into eastern and southern Africa from a point on the eastern edge of the forest. The first stage almost certainly involved food producers using stone tools; whether the second was linked to the spread of iron remains to be seen.

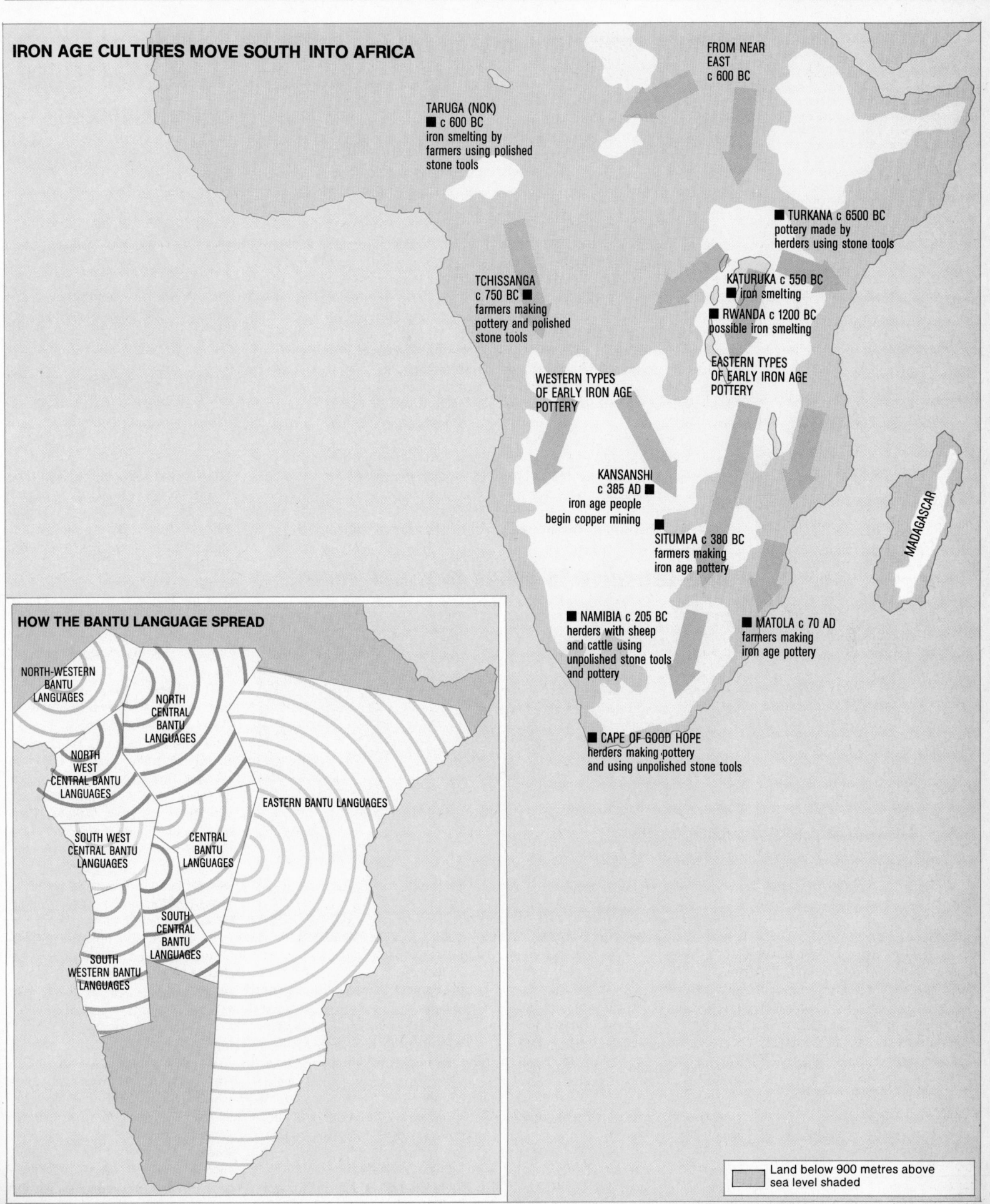

IRON AGE CULTURES MOVE SOUTH INTO AFRICA

FROM NEAR
EAST
c 600 BC

TARUGA (NOK)
■ c 600 BC
iron smelting by
farmers using polished
stone tools

■ TURKANA c 6500 BC
pottery made by
herders using stone tools

TCHISSANGA
c 750 BC ■
farmers making
pottery and polished
stone tools

KATURUKA c 550 BC
■ iron smelting

■ RWANDA c 1200 BC
possible iron smelting

WESTERN TYPES
OF EARLY IRON AGE
POTTERY

EASTERN TYPES
OF EARLY IRON AGE
POTTERY

KANSANSHI
c 385 AD ■
iron age people
begin copper mining

SITUMPA c 380 BC
farmers making
iron age pottery

MADAGASCAR

■ NAMIBIA c 205 BC
herders with sheep
and cattle using
unpolished stone tools
and pottery

■ MATOLA c 70 AD
farmers making
iron age pottery

■ CAPE OF GOOD HOPE
herders making pottery
and using unpolished stone tools

HOW THE BANTU LANGUAGE SPREAD

NORTH-WESTERN
BANTU
LANGUAGES

NORTH
CENTRAL
BANTU
LANGUAGES

NORTH
WEST
CENTRAL BANTU
LANGUAGES

EASTERN BANTU LANGUAGES

SOUTH WEST
CENTRAL BANTU
LANGUAGES

CENTRAL
BANTU
LANGUAGES

SOUTH
CENTRAL
BANTU
LANGUAGES

SOUTH
WESTERN BANTU
LANGUAGES

Land below 900 metres above
sea level shaded

149

Babylon, 323BC. There is division about who should succeed Alexander. The choice is between his epileptic half-brother, Arrhidaeus, and the child expected by his Persian wife, Roxana. It is decided to await the birth. Perdiccas is regent in Asia; Antipater remains regent in Europe. Ptolemy becomes ruler of Egypt, Lysimachus of Thrace, Antigonus the One-Eyed of Asia Minor (Anatolia).

Athens, 322BC. Zeno of Cyprus founds the Stoic school, named after Athens' painted portico, Stoa Poikile, under which he usually teaches. Stoicism centres on the doctrine that virtue, which is based on knowledge, is the only good.

Greece, 322BC. Athens, which led a Greek revolt on learning of the death of Alexander, has lost the Lamian war. Demosthenes commits suicide, the diehard adversary of Macedon surviving Alexander the Great by a single year.

Italy, 321BC. The Romans suffer a humiliating defeat by the Samnites from the southern Apennines. They are trapped by the enemy in a pass near Caudium, the Caudine Forks, in Campania. They are forced to pass beneath a yoke of spears erected by the enemy.

Athens, 321BC. Theophrastus succeeds Aristotle, who died last year, as head of the Lyceum. He emphasises the scientific orientation of research and much work is done on plants and minerals. Theophrastus has written a series of caricatures of stock types entitled *Characters*.

Athens, 320BC. Menander, a former pupil of Theophrastus, is attracted by the Epicurean philosophy. At the age of 22 he withdraws from public life to his villa in Piraeus, with a courtesan called Glycera, and begins to write plays.

Central Asia, 320BC. The Greeks build a town on the shores of the Oxus (Amu Darya) believed to be called Alexandria in Sogdia. On the pattern of a Greek town, it includes an acropolis, public monuments, lower town and outer wall.

India, 317BC. Chandragupta, who founded the Mauryan dynasty in 321BC with a capital at Pataliputra (Patna) in the east of the country, drives the Greek garrisons out of India.

Athens democracy dies on field of battle

Greece, 321BC

Athens, defeated on land and sea by Antipater, the regent of Macedon, has been forced to sue for peace under terms which entail the end of democracy. This sorry tale started with the news of the death of Alexander. The Athenians, who had gradually been rebuilding their military and financial power, now considered the time was ripe to free themselves from Macedonian rule.

Although there were some in Athens, mainly belonging to the propertied classes, who would have preferred peace and a quiet life, the Athenians organised a league of allies which went to war under the leadership of the Athenian mercenary, Leosthenes.

He won some quick victories over Antipater, who was short of troops and forced to retreat to Lamia. Demosthenes, who was in exile, returned to Athens and, with the orator Hyperides, became the mainstay of the struggle against the Macedonians. However, the war soon began to go badly for the Athenians as Antipater received reinforcements. Leosthenes was killed, and last year the Greek fleet was beaten off the island of Amorgos. It may be said that, if the battle of Salamis in 480BC laid the foundation of Greek glory, then the battle of Amorgos has destroyed that glory for ever.

Antipater then marched into Greece and forced the reluctant allies to give battle at Crannon in Thessaly. It was a scrappy affair with neither side gaining a clearcut victory, but the Greek commanders decided to sue for peace.

Antipater, cunningly, would only make peace with individual cities, and so divided his enemies. Now the Athenians have been forced to accept his terms. Hyperides has been executed and Demosthenes has committed suicide.

Everyday skills win praise from nation of philosophers

Athena born from Zeus's head.

Greece, c.400-300BC

This nation of philosophers and geometricians is learning to respect the more down-to-earth, practical kinds of skill. There is a new admiration for the cunning of the hunter or fisherman who knows how to keep his concentration as he lies in wait for his prey, ready to pounce. The same goes for the craftsman who understands raw materials and knows how to weave and to decorate.

The Greeks have developed a high regard for resourcefulness of every kind. The quality is *metis*, a term meaning cunning intelligence. In legend, Metis was the first wife of Zeus. She was swallowed by her husband after becoming pregnant with their daughter, Athena. Zeus had realised that Metis could give birth to a son stronger than himself. By swallowing her, he made sure that no trick in the world could be plotted without its first passing through his mind.

In the *Iliad*, Homer describes how the old sage Nestor advises his son Antilochus in the skills of *metis*, helping him win a chariot race against faster opponents.

Antilochus triumphs by swerving in front of a rival on a narrow stretch of the course, forcing him to rein in his horses. Afterwards he is scolded for his unfair manoeuvre, and finds himself obliged to make amends. But the lesson is that, when the odds are unfavourable, success can be won through cunning. *Metis* is the ultimate weapon in any contest.

Hills are alive to sound of Greek theatre

Greeks take great pride in their theatres, such as this one at Epidauros.

Greece, c.320BC

Theatre design has reached a new degree of perfection at Epidauros, Greece, where the architect Polykleitos has constructed an amphitheatre of local limestone which provides seating for over 13,000 people, giving each member of the audience an equal view.

The banks of seating rise at an angle of 26 degrees, fitting snugly into the slope of the hillside, and converging on the circular space known as the *orchestra* where the Chorus dances its dramatic odes. This has a floor of beaten earth with a small altar in the centre. Behind it is the raised stage building, incorporating three doors from which the actors enter. There is a ramp at either side of the stage providing entrances under double Ionic gates.

The great glory of the theatre is its perfect acoustics, created by the bowl-shape of the auditorium, which is divided into two levels.

Alexander dies aged 32

A later Roman statuette believed to be of "Alexander the Great".

Babylon, 323BC

In the spring Alexander came down to Babylon, where embassies from all parts of the known world were waiting to pay homage to the conqueror of the east. He was already planning his next great enterprise, the exploration of the seas around his empire.

In the year since he had returned from India he had devoted himself to overhauling the imperial administration, dismissing officials judged to be incompetent and dealing with complaints of corruption. He sought to bind the conquered Persians to his cause by offering satrapies to Persian grandees and recruiting 30,000 Persian youths for his armies. He took another oriental wife, Satira, daughter of Darius, before leaving Susa for Babylon.

In Babylon he ordered the construction of an immense fleet, and under his supervision a great basin was excavated in the Euphrates capable of taking 1,000 ships. He wanted to open a maritime route from Babylon to Egypt, round Arabia. Later, in the far north of his empire, he would seek a passage from the Caspian Sea to the Northern Ocean.

By the summer everything was ready and a date fixed for his departure. He spent two nights carousing with friends. Afterwards he awoke with a fever, which at first he dismissed as trivial. But soon he became delirious. The palace swarmed with generals, soothsayers, and priests making sacrifices and uttering incantations. Once, during a lucid moment, he was asked who should inherit his empire. He replied: "The best man."

One by one the men of his Macedonian army passed through the sick chamber, bidding him farewell. It is said that he recognised each man by name. He died as the sun was setting on the plain of Babylon. He was 32 years old.

A bust of the dying conqueror.

Ten years of war that wrought an empire

Near East, 323BC

Alexander was 20 when he ascended the throne of Macedonia after the assassination of his father Philip. He gained the support of the army, put to death two potential rivals, suppressed rebellions by hill tribes in the north and crushed a revolt by Thebes. The Greek city-states then recognised him as captain-general for their war against the Persian empire.

Macedonia, once a wild frontier kingdom outside Greek proper, had been transformed by Philip into a powerful military state. Now it was Alexander's ambition to be accepted as a true Greek. Having been tutored by the greatest philosopher of the age, Aristotle, he brought Greek culture and learning into the distant lands of Asia conquered by his army.

His army was unique. Besides the infantrymen, archers and javelin throwers, and the 18-foot spears of the phalanx, there were engineers, architects, surveyors, scientists and historians. When in the spring of 334BC he crossed the Hellespont into Asia Minor (Anatolia), it was the start of ten years of war that would spread Hellenism far and wide.

He swept through Syria and Palestine to subdue Egypt. He conquered Asia Minor (Anatolia), defeated the Persians, penetrated Afghanistan, and reached Samarkand before descending into India. Everywhere he founded cities to guard his communications. Veterans from his army were left to garrison these Greek outposts that were, more often than not, named after the conqueror, the most famous of these being Alexandria.

Alexander was a military genius and a man with a vision. He left such an impression on the conquered Persians that they adopted his name, calling members of the royal family Iskander.

A battle scene from a carved sarcophagus, possibly depicting Alexander.

Apelles hailed as supreme Greek artist

Greece, 325BC

The painter Apelles is at the peak of his career, working in the court of Alexander the Great at Pella. The king will allow no other artist to paint his portrait. One depicts him on horseback, another holding a thunderbolt, and there are many others. The two often met in the artist's studio to talk about art and painting.

When Apelles fell in love with Alexander's favourite mistress after being commissioned to paint her in the nude, the King allowed him to take her over.

Born into a family of painters, Apelles was taught in Ephesus by Ephoros, and later by Pamphilus at Sicyon. His work combines all the grace of the Ionian tradition with an emphasis on movement and an attempt to achieve true likenesses.

Apart from his portraits, Apelles also produces large-scale religious works and allegories.

Macedonia, 316BC. Olympias, Alexander's mother, is stoned to death on Cassander's orders. This act of revenge stems from the succession crisis created by the death, in 319BC, of Antipater, made regent of Macedonia and Greece on Alexander's departure for Asia.

Palestine, c.315BC. The *Song of Songs*, a collection of love poems, appears. Compiled anonymously from different sources, these profane poems are presented under the prestigious name of Solomon.

Carthage, 310BC. Agathocles, ruler of Syracuse, attempts to ward off the threat posed to Sicily by the Carthaginians. He lands his troops in Carthage and worries the Carthaginians sufficiently to obtain a peace treaty and war indemnities.

Kush, 308BC. The last royal burial – of King Natasen – takes place at Napata. Future kings will be buried at Meroe.

Athens, 307BC. After the failure of its struggle for independence, Athens falls under Macedonian control: Demetrius Poliorcetes, son of Antigonus the One-Eyed, takes command of the city.

Cyprus, 306BC. Ptolemy, a former Macedonian general who became ruler of Egypt on the death of Alexander, is defeated in a sea battle off Salamis by the Greeks under Demetrius.

Athens, 305BC. Epicurus, the philosopher who believes that pleasure is the chief good, founds a school in Athens.

Rhodes, 305BC. After a failed siege of Rhodes, Demetrius is forced to recognise the island's independence. Rhodes was defended by Ptolemy of Egypt, who was given the title Soter (Saviour) by the Rhodians.

India, 302BC. Chandragupta, founder of the Mauryan dynasty, signs a peace treaty with Seleucus, the former Macedonian general who now rules Babylon.

Asia Minor, 301BC. Antigonus the One-Eyed dies at Ipsus, in Phrygia, in a battle with the other successors of Alexander, who agree on a new division of the world. Cassander keeps Macedonia; Lysimachus has Thrace and Asia Minor (Anatolia) as far as the Taurus mountains; Seleucus gets only northern Syria, the southern part being held by Ptolemy. Demetrius keeps areas of Asia Minor, Greece, the Cyclades and Phoenicia.

Syracuse and Carthage square up for war

A street on the acropolis of Selinunte, one of the Greek cities in Sicily.

Cape Bon, North Africa, 310BC
An army of 14,000 mercenaries led by Agathocles, the self-proclaimed king of Sicily, has invaded North Africa in a daring strategic move designed to wrongfoot the Carthaginian forces now besieging his Sicilian capital, Syracuse.

The Greek-born Agathocles, the first European to invade North Africa, is now marching his troops on Tunis, which it is thought he intends to use as his base for his retaliatory campaign against Carthage.

By taking the battle to the enemy, Agathocles has changed the familiar pattern of the century-old conflict between the Carthaginians and the Greek rulers of Sicily, with both camps for once having enemies at their gates as they fight over a divided Sicily.

This latest outbreak began last year when the wealthy Greek oligarchies controlling Sicily's city states of Akragas, Gela and Messina refused to pay dues to Agathocles, whose climb to power in Syracuse seven years ago had been accompanied by a popular uprising in which 4,000 nobles were slaughtered. The oligarchs of Akragas, fearing a similar fate, then successfully sought protection from Carthage, which sent its fleet.

Generals carve up Alexander's empire

Macedonia, 306BC
Almost 20 years after Alexander's death his generals, the *Diadochi*, or Successors, are still intriguing and fighting to gain the lion's share in the partition of the empire. In western Asia the most powerful of the *Diadochi*, Antigonus, has assumed for himself the title of king, a move which has encouraged others.

In Egypt, Ptolemy now calls himself king, as do Seleucus in Babylon and Lysimachus in Asia Minor (Anatolia). In Greece and Macedon, Alexander's viceroy Antipater has died and been succeeded by his son Cassander. He has murdered Alexander's mother Olympias, who had earlier murdered Alexander's epileptic half-brother Philip Arrhidaeus and his wife Eurydice. Alexander's widow, Roxana, and his son, briefly known as Alexander IV, have also been murdered.

Alexander's empire has disintegrated in a welter of bloodshed. For the poast eight years, an intermittant war has been going on between Antigonus and his rivals and lasy year his son Demitrius, joined in by invading Greece in a bid to expel Cassandra. In Babylon, however, Seleucus has had no hand in the string of assassinations among the Diadochi. He is devoting himself to the spread of Hellenism in the East.

Censor Appius gives his name to a road that leads to Rome

Rome, 312BC
Rome's censor Appius Claudius, who mixes a patrician background with a reputation as the people's friend, has inaugurated the latest of his city's public works. This, among the most important of all, is a road linking Rome to Capua. Running for 132 miles through difficult coastal terrain, and paved throughout with stone, it will bear his name: the Appian Way. Better protected from attack than the inland Via Latina, it will serve as a secure route south, less vulnerable to the Samnite tribesmen of central Italy with whom Rome is currently at war.

Appius is not just a builder, although a nine-mile aqueduct near Rome also carries his name. Despite his background he has campaigned to increase the part played by plebeians in public life. No previous reformer has ever tried to help these urban poor, although some critics say that his efforts were simply a way of keeping the masses from rebellion and note that, for all his liberal views, he refuses to permit plebeians to join the traditionally patrician priesthood. His defenders suggest he simply fears an alliance of plebs and aristocrats.

Appius is also a literary man, author of many pithy moral sayings, but above all it is as censor that he is making his mark. The censor, an office established in 443BC, is responsible for regulating much of Roman life. As well as taking the census he lays down the

The Appian way to more freedom?

regimen morum, the moral standards governing all citizens.

Appius is a revolutionary censor, and has alienated many patricians by allowing the sons of freed slaves into the senate.

Looking for signs in dreams and stars

Mesopotamia, c.300BC

In a world of increasing complexity human beings are both fascinated and confused by what they see as a wide range of different signs occurring around them. These signs obviously have some meaning, but it is left to specialists to decipher it. In Mesopotamia there has emerged a group of such specialists: the seers or soothsayers.

The vocation of such seers is the study of every variety of sign. They interpret the content of dreams, which are seen as a direct link to the divine world. Seers often use special "dream books" in which are listed

List of lucky and unlucky dates.

the omens attached to the most common dreams. *Hepatology*, studying the meaning found in the livers of sacrificed animals, is equally popular, and fresh offal or clay models are both used.

The skies and the heavenly bodies that move there are especially important, and the Mesopotamians have evolved the science of what the Greeks call *astrology*, literally the "account of the stars", to interpret these activities. They are particularly interested in the appearance and disappearance of the stars and planets, and whether this happens before or after sunset.

Studying the heavens has developed a number of *ephemerides* (from the Greek "diary" or "calendar"), or astrological tables. These plot the way in which these bodies seem to move in fixed orbits, and help the astrologers to base their opinions on the position of each star at any given moment of its course. Each planet has its own importance; Jupiter, for instance, regulates the life of the king.

Indian king abdicates to become monk

India, 297BC

King Chandragupta, the first man to unite the Indian sub-continent, has abdicated in favour of his son Bindusara. His reign has been notable for military success, and for stability achieved through peace treaties. It has also seen the rise of the great religions of Buddhism and Jainism.

From the fourth century BC, northern India was divided into 16 large states, under one monarch. Government was decentralised, however, with much day-to-day decision-making in the hands of local deputies. Buddhism and Jainism were taking root. The Ganges valley fell under the sway of the Magadha kingdom, until Chandragupta Maurya destroyed the Nanda dynasty and won control of much of central and northern India.

In 305BC Chandragupta fought Seleucus Nicator, a former general of Alexander who had remained in north-western India. A peace treaty established friendly relations between the Mauryan dynasty and the Seleucid kingdom.

Kautilya, Chandragupta's prime

A Maurya terracotta mother-deity.

minister, wrote a treatise, the *Arthasastra*, describing the Mauryan ideal of government. Shortly before his abdication, Chandragupta converted to Jainism. He now says that he is firmly resolved to pursue an ascetic existence for the rest of his life.

Greek artists acquire taste for realism

Wall painting of a chariot race from Southern Italy, in the new style.

Greece, 300-100BC

Just as Greece's traditional art form – sculpture – has seen a revolution in style and content, so too has painting. The old heroic themes – the gods, great battles and sporting victories – are now rivalled by ideas on a more human scale. Painters seek realism, showing how people are, rather than an ideal of

how they ought to be. Portraiture is also becoming very popular.

The way in which artists paint has also altered. Classical painting was usually found on pots; now artists prefer to paint on marble or on walls. Overall style has changed too: pictures have backgrounds, not simply figures – man is no longer the sole focus.

Greek envoy tells of Indian glory

India, 302BC

The magnificence of Pataliputra, capital of the Mauryan empire, is described by Megasthenes, the ambassador of King Seleucus Nicator.

Megasthenes' mission was the result of the peace treaty in 305BC between Seleucus Nicator, one of Alexander's generals to be bequeathed kingdoms in distant provinces, and Chandragupta, founder of the Mauryan empire and ruler of much of India. The two kings exchanged gifts and ambassadors.

According to Megasthenes, this great city extends for ten miles along the Ganges, surrounded by a massive palisade with 64 gates and 570 large towers, and a broad moat. The magnificent royal palace is built of timber and stone, with richly gilded ornamentation.

Megasthenes is impressed with the organisation of the army, which includes a large number of elephants. His observations are corroborated by contemporary Indian writings.

Rather more extraordinary are Megasthenes' observations on life at the court of Seleucus Nicator. He tells how the king likes being rubbed with sticks of wood by attendants while hearing cases. His recreations are equally eccentric. He enjoys hunting from his chariot, surrounded by two or three armed women, in an enclosure with the quarry surrounded by spearcarriers – or, in the wild, from the back of an elephant.

Detail of a felt wall-hanging from the Altai Mountains in northern central Asia.

Italy, 295BC. In the third Samnite war – which began three years ago, prompted by the expansionist policies of Rome – the Romans defeat a large army of Gauls and Samnites at the battle of Sentinum. They then force the Etruscans to accept peace.

Macedonia, 294BC. Demetrius Poliorcetes seizes the throne of Macedonia – a feat he has been trying to accomplish since the death of Cassander in 297BC.

Peru, c.290BC. The Chavin culture, whose roots date back 1,500 years, is falling into decline.

Greece, c.290BC. Euhemerus has sown the seeds of a new theology. He argues that the stars alone are immortal gods. the Olympian gods of the traditional religion are, in reality, human kings deified for their civilising role. His theory has political implications, justifying the cult of sovereigns which is beginning to spread in the Hellenistic monarchies.

Alexandria, c.290BC. The mathematician Euclid sets out the principles of geometry in his *Elements*.

Alexandria, 290BC. Ptolemy founds the Museum of Alexandria and dedicates it to the Muses. The museum welcomes scholars who wish to devote themselves to study in exceptional surroundings.

Rome, 287BC. The law of Hortensius, according to which the decisions of the plebeians have legal standing, is vigorously promulgated.

China, 287BC. To protect themselves against barbarian invasion, the northern states of China begin to build sections of a "Great Wall".

Egypt, 285BC. Ptolemy, who became ruler of Egypt – one of the richest Greek kingdoms – on the death of Alexander, abdicates in favour of his son. During his reign, Ptolemy devoted himself to annexing neighbouring territories and fostering Greek immigration. His capital, Alexandria, is the centre of commerce and Greek culture.

Alexandria, 285BC. Sostratus of Cnidus builds a lighthouse, linked by a dyke to dry land, on the island of Pharos. The three-storey building is over 300 feet high. At the top an arrangement of convex mirrors reflects the light from a wood fire. The lighthouse will be a landmark for all ships crossing this part of the Mediterranean.

Philosophy blossoms in Greek cities

Greece, c.290BC

Alexander's empire is no more but the cities he founded are flourishing in Asia Minor (Anatolia), Syria, Persia, Mesopotamia, Persia and Egypt, where power has passed to princes steeped in Greek culture. Men of enterprise are migrating from the cities of mainland Greece to seize the opportunities offered by the wider Hellenistic world.

Made restless by the promise of wealth and power, and no longer upheld by the old certainties, people have begun to lose their moral bearings and are seeking reassurance and happiness in new beliefs.

The most fashionable of these is Stoicism, founded by a business-man who left his native Cyprus and settled in Athens as a young man. Observing the decay of religious faith and social ties, Zeno took to explaining his ideas in the painted *stoa*, or colonnade, of the market place. Zeno offers to deliver men from fears and desires that make them unhappy by telling them to accept the world as it is and seek happiness within themselves. So long as happiness depends on others, or on anything over which men have no control, they will be a prey to anxiety and disappointment.

Epicurus, a native Athenian, also offers release from fear and worry. He tells his listeners, who include women as well as men, that although people seek pleasure they must avoid excesses which lead to pain. One should lead a simple life and avoid public ambition, the pursuit of success, and such entangle-

The Stoic Chrysippus, said to have died from laughing at his own joke.

ments as marriage. Other views are being aired in the Lyceum, where Aristotle once lectured, and in Plato's old Academy. But the Academy has been taken over by a group calling themselves Sceptics, who say that whatever argument

may be produced in support of a belief, just as strong arguments can be found to refute it. The wise man, they say, has no opinion about anything other than that which he has seen and felt.

More recently, groups of wandering preachers have appeared in the streets of Athens. Calling themselves Cynics, they profess indifference to all worldly things – riches, honour, freedom, health – in their pursuit of virtue. They live without family or religion, and make great show of their poverty. One Cynic was asked by an acquaintance what he could do for him. "Step out of my sunlight," replied Diogenes. He caused some less than sympathetic comments when he threw away his last possession, a cup, and took to living in a tub. Despite their differences, these new philosophies do have one thing in common: a mistrust of today's autocratic regimes.

Bronze portrait of a philosopher.

Epicurus: the simple life is best.

Rome's legions smash Samnites to control Italy

Rome, 295BC

As two great opposing armies lined up against each other – the Roman legions facing a powerful alliance of Gauls and Samnites – a wolf chased a hind across the battlefield. The wolf escaped through the Roman lines and was seen as a lucky omen by the legionaries. The criti-cal battle of Sentinum was about to begin – and despite the omens, Roman victory was in doubt until the very end.

The two Roman commanders applied markedly different tactics in this savage battle against the coalition. Decius Mus, the younger of the two, attacked at once with his cavalry, only to see them beaten back in confusion by Gallic war chariots. Decius died with his infantry. Fabius, on the other hand, fought defensively, advancing prudently until his army was able to drive a wedge between the enemy and attack the Gauls from the rear.

Victory finally went to Rome at the cost of nearly 8,000 dead, although 25,000 coalition soldiers were slain on the field of Sentinum. With much of Samnium laid waste by a previous campaign by Decius, and Etruria cut off from its allies, Rome is now in a position to control most of its neighbouring states.

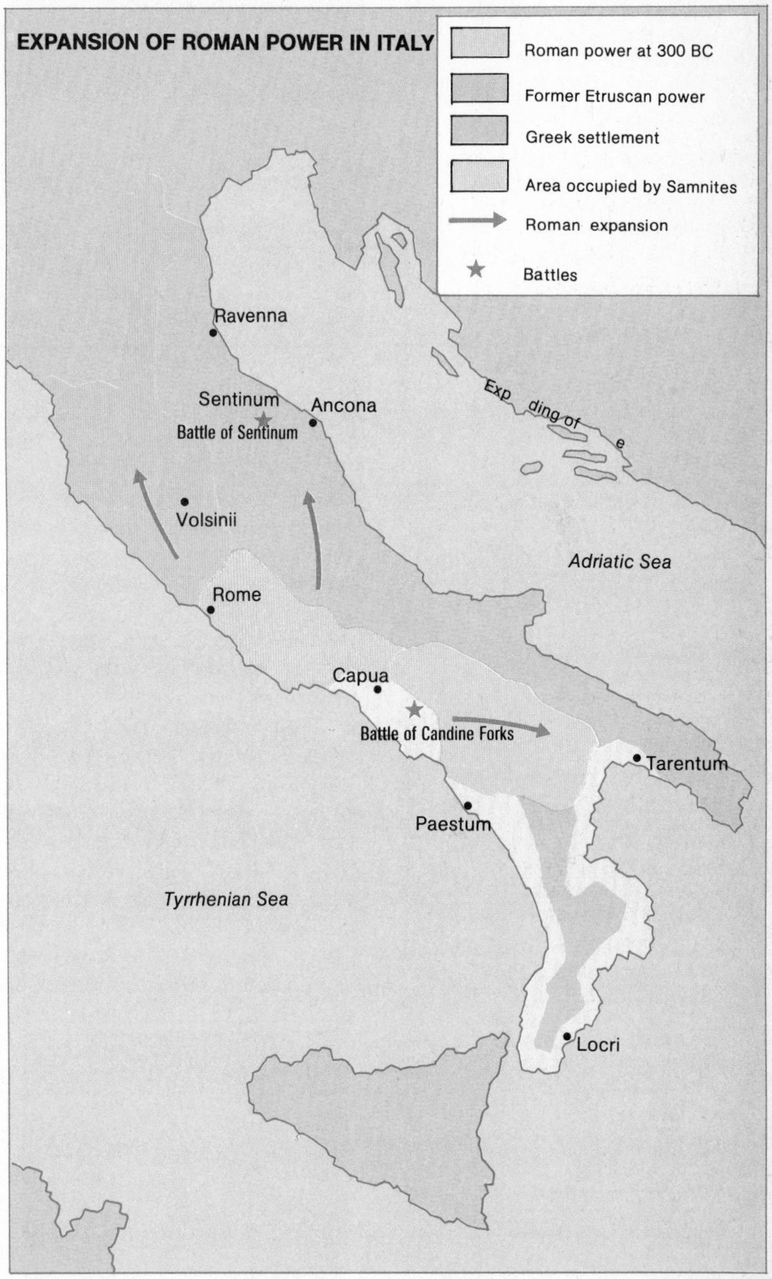

A consul of the Roman republic.

The trap which rankles in Roman breasts

Rome, 295BC

Rome's crushing victory over the Samnites – the mountain people who have brought war to the city and Latium for nearly 20 years – finally avenges the humiliation of the Caudine Yoke which has long rankled in every Roman breast.

This black hour in the city's history happened 18 years ago at the height of the war when an entire legion was led by its officers through a short cut in the Appennines – only to find the path at the Caudine Forks blocked by boulders and felled trees and an entire Samnite army at their rear.

The Roman army was helpless, its leaders impotent to make decisions and displaying their frustration to the soldiers under their command. The troops themselves, angry with the surrender-or-die situation in which they found themselves, frequently came close to mutiny.

The Samnites themselves were hard-pressed to know what to do with an army that lay at their mercy. Their leader, Gavius Pontius, proposed first mercy, then the slaughter of every Roman, and fin-ally the taking of 600 aristocratic Roman hostages followed by the yoke under which the Roman troops, humbled and vanquished by their officers' misjudgement, would be forced to walk through enemy lines. Officers were stripped of their finery and forced to walk half-naked through the throngs of the jeering Samnites. The legionaries were given similar treatment, except that those who showed pride or contempt were hacked down. Rome's humiliation was complete.

EXPANSION OF ROMAN POWER IN ITALY

Legend:
- Roman power at 300 BC
- Former Etruscan power
- Greek settlement
- Area occupied by Samnites
- → Roman expansion
- ★ Battles

Map labels: Ravenna · Sentinum · Battle of Sentinum · Ancona · Volsinii · Rome · Adriatic Sea · Capua · Battle of Candine Forks · Tarentum · Paestum · Tyrrhenian Sea · Locri · Exp...ding of...e

Menander, father of new form of Greek comedy, dies at 50

Athens, 292BC

One of Greece's most prolific playwrights, the poet Menander of Athens, has died at the age of 50. He was the author of 108 plays, and the ease with which he scripted a piece once he had thought up the plot was proverbial. Among his best-known works are *The Shield* and *The Misanthrope*.

Menander's dramas, with their blend of humour and sympathy for the twists and turns of the human condition, have come to be known as the "New Comedy". His plays are comedies of manners, poking gentle fun at contemporary society and each depending on an apparently endless series of surprises and barely plausible coincidences.

Menander's plots are certainly complex, but what is most important is the way he handles his characters. Many dramatists seem to write for books of fine sayings; Menander's characters are flesh and blood people who talk and act like real human beings.

Menander, the leading playwright of the "New Comedy" of manners.

Egypt, 283BC. In honour of his dead father, Ptolemy II institutes the Ptolemaia, on the model of the Olympic Games, starting a cult among Egypt's Greek subjects.

Italy, 283BC. In retaliation for the annihilation of a Roman army beneath the walls of Arretium (Arezzo) two years ago, the Romans massacre or disperse the Gallic people known as the Senones.

Egypt, 283BC. A translation of the Hebrew scriptures into Greek is begun. It is known as the Septuagint after the number of translators: seventy.

Greece, 281BC. The Achaean league has established a federal assembly, a council and a general, all elected annually, enabling it to control the whole of the Peloponnese.

Macedonia, 281BC. Seleucus Nicator dies after falling into a trap set by Ptolemy II of Egypt. Seleucus – the last surviving general of those appointed by Alexander – became king of Syria after defeating Lysimachus at Corupedium in Asia Minor (Anatolia) earlier this year.

Italy, 280BC. Pyrrhus, king of Epirus, has sent troops to aid Tarentum and the other Greek cities of southern Italy against Rome. At the battle of Heraclea, Pyrrhus' elephants terrorise the Roman soldiers.

Greece, 279BC. The mountain people known as the Phocians and the Aetolians halt the spread of the Celtic hordes through Macedonia and northern Greece by engaging them in fierce battles. Finally rebuffed, the Celts head for the east, via Thrace and the Hellespont region.

Italy, 272BC. Tarentum, the leading Greek city in southern Italy, falls to the Romans, fresh from their defeat of the Samnites. The fall of Tarentum follows the withdrawal of support by Pyrrhus, king of Epirus. The Romans pillage the city and have a taste of Hellenistic Greek luxury.

Epirus, 272BC. King Pyrrhus of Epirus is dead. A brilliant strategist and administrator, he made a great power of his mountainous kingdom, one by one annexing the provinces under Macedonian control.

Asia Minor, 270BC. Seleucus II successfully subdues the upstart Gallic forces who settled in Asia Minor after their attack on Delphi.

Elephants put Gallic invaders to flight

A masterly statue of a dying Gaulish warrior. The Gauls fight in the nude.

Asia Minor, c.275BC
An uneasy peace reigns in Greece and Asia Minor (Anatolia), with the old Alexandrian empire fragmenting and menaced by the ever-encroaching Gauls.

Following the assassination of Seleucus in 281BC, Antiochus, his successor, became embroiled in wars with Ptolemy II and a revolt in Syria. The Seleucid empire also faced hostility from Greek cities on the coast.

More dangerous, however, was the threat from by Nicomedes of Bithynia, in northern Asia Minor, who had formed an alliance with marauding tribes of Celts to come and deal with a pretender to his throne, Zipoetes. The tribes, the Trocmi, Tolistoagii, and Tectosages, began a warlike progress through Asia Minor, plundering and exacting tributes by threats of terror.

They were repulsed by the infantry and elephants of Antiochus, but at considerable cost, and have been confined to a region of Phrygia now renamed Galatia.

Songs of Ch'u win Chinese plaudits

China, 274BC
A remarkable anthology of poems has been compiled in the principality of Ch'u in the basin of the Yangtze River. Called the *Ch'u tz'u*, or the Songs of Ch'u, they are among the most prized examples of Chinese literature.

The anthology is particularly notable for the works of Ch'u Yuan, the most famous poet of his time. He had a brilliant career, becoming a chief minister of Ch'u, and was renowned for the lyric beauty of his poetry.

His sheer brilliance aroused much jealousy among less-gifted men and a whispering campaign was mounted against him by his fellow poets. Alas; the slanders were believed and, in disgrace, he committed suicide.

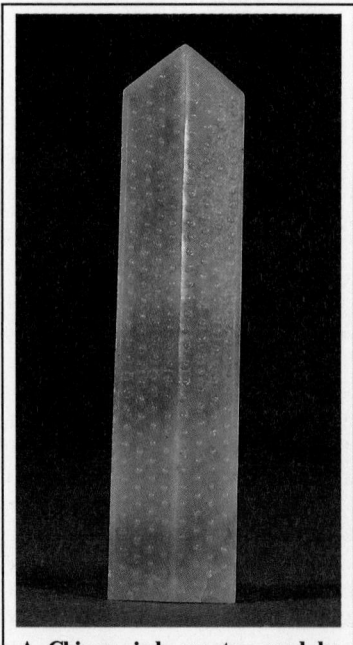

A Chinese jade sceptre, used by the emperor when sacrificing to the east: a symbol of "Spring and the awakening of life".

Elephants used as weapons of war

Asia Minor, 350-150BC
Elephants, first encountered when Alexander invaded India, have become increasingly popular as weapons of war.

Oriental rulers used them for many years, but the first time that the Greeks saw them was at the Battle of the Hydaspes, in the army of the King of Punjab Poros, in 326BC. India remained the chief supplier of elephants to the Hellenistic armies, particularly for the Seleucids and the Ptolemies.

Equipped with a tower for the soldiers, elephants allow archers to dominate a battlefield. But probably their most important function is to intimidate opponents by their sheer size and the awesome power of their charge.

A war-elephant from Galatia.

The most celebrated instance of elephants winning a battle was in 275BC, when Antiochus let them loose against a superior army of Celts, turning their chariots and cavalry against their own troops. When the battle was won, Antiochus insisted on a carved elephant as the sole memorial.

Elephant trainers, brought from the Indian sub-continent, are highly regarded by their Greek masters and given honoured status in every regiment, with substantially better pay than foot-soldiers. Attempts to enslave them have always failed because of the close relationship between the trainer and his beast which begins when the elephant is very young, growing up to understand one language only – that of his master.

Romans repel Pyrrhus

A later engraving of King Pyrrhus.

Benevutum, c.275BC

Rome's legions have finally held off the superbly trained Greek army of Pyrrhus of Epirus. After successful – though costly – campaigns in Sicily, Pyrrhus returned to help fellow Greeks in their fight against a Rome-Carthage alliance on the Italian mainland. The outcome was a draw.

Roman soldiers first faced the tactics of Alexander the Great – including war-elephants – when they battled with Pyrrhus's phalanx at the battle of Heraclea, facing elephant charges which scattered their cavalry. The short Roman swords could not cope with the long spears of the Greeks. Seven thousand Romans died in that battle. Despite the heavy Roman losses, Pyrrhus' army suffered casualties of more than 4,000 – men whom he could ill-afford to lose, as he began his crusade against Rome with an army of 25,000.

Pyrrhus, a relative of Alexander the Great, was invited to lead his army into Italy by the leaders of Tarentum, the Greek city in the south of the country which had won a major sea battle against the Romans and expected massive retaliation. At the same time, Rome was beginning to extend its interests southwards with the clear aim of uniting the whole of Italy. The clash became inevitable.

Pyrrhus followed up his victory with a dash to Rome, hoping – in vain – to gain support on the way from other states. Even so, his forces were victorious in several engagements with the Romans, particularly at Asculum where rough ground made going difficult for his phalanx until Pyrrhus could move the fight to level ground.

Rome looks south to war with Carthage

A 20th century model of a punic galley sailing into Carthage.

Messana, Sicily, 264BC

Two Roman legions have arrived in this Sicilian seaport, encountering scant resistance from the Carthaginian garrison. Reports from Carthage, however, indicate that the Punic commander will be crucified for cowardice.

Despite treaties of friendship and trade, the two great Mediterranean powers of Rome and Carthage are squaring up for what is likely to be a major confrontation.

The trouble began when the Mamertines – Campanian mercenaries – occupied Messana (Messina). They were then besieged by the Syracusans and appealed to Carthage for help. The Carthaginians came to their aid, but some dissident Mamertines expelled them and invited the Romans. With some people in Rome fearing that Carthaginian control at Messana poses a threat to Roman interests in southern Italy, the Romans quickly came to Messana.

The scene is thus set for a direct clash in an area which King Pyrrhus has called "a cockpit".

Ethiopian port is world trade centre

Ethiopia, 264BC

The port of Adulis on Ethiopia's Red Sea coast, a collection of huts until a decade ago, has become a centre of world trade. Anchored in the harbour are dhows and galleys bringing frankincense and cinnamon from Arabia, silks and spices from India, and manufactured goods from Europe. Rarely a day goes by without a caravan arriving from Kush, carrying wrought iron and gold, or from Ethiopia, carrying timber and ivory.

The opening up of the Red Sea began a quarter of a century ago when Ptolemy I of Egypt, interested in securing elephants for his army, established a series of elephant-hunting base-camps along the African coast. Equally significantly, he built a permanent fleet on Egypt's south coast to protect traders from pirates, and recut the canal linking the Gulf of Suez with the Nile, thus allowing ships to sail direct from the Red Sea to Alexandria and the Mediterranean.

His son, Philadelphos, the present Ptolemy, has continued his father's policies, and under his admiral, Eumenes, his father's elephant-hunting bases have been turned into trading and staging posts.

Adulis is the most southerly of these posts. Beyond the Bab el Mandeb, the Red Sea bottleneck where Africa and Arabia almost touch, the Arabian dhows maintain their monopoly of trade with India, Persia and the rest of Arabia. It was thus that Adulis, an obscure and godforsaken outpost, became the entrepot of East and West.

Children are sacrificed in Carthage

Carthage, c.264BC

The city of Carthage has grown great and powerful from the spoils of its empire and the skill of its traders. The empire now covers much of North Africa and extends across the Mediterranean to include much of Spain together with Sardinia, the Balearics, Malta and Sicily.

The huge Carthaginian fleet enforces a "closed sea" policy which allows its traders a virtual monopoly. The city has sealed the Straits of Gibraltar, giving its cargo *triremes* freedom to trade without competition along the western coast of Africa and as far north as Britain.

Carthage came into being as an offshoot of the Phoenician city of Tyre, another important trading centre; and descendants of the original Phoenicians are among the

A Carthaginian ceramic amulet.

aristocrats who seized power here over 100 years ago. Carthage worships Baal Ammon, a formidable god who demands human sacrifices, especially of children.

Rome, 264BC. The Romans have discovered a new kind of spectacle: gladiatorial combat. A violent and cruel sport, often seen at funerals, it is becoming enormously popular.

Asia Minor, 262BC. Following a victory over the Seleucid army, Eumenes, nephew of Philetaeros – who saved Pergamum from the Gauls in 276BC – declares Pergamum independent and founds a fourth Hellenistic kingdom in Asia Minor (Anatolia).

Athens, 262BC. Antigonus Gonatas, the Macedonian ruler whose authority now extends over a good part of the Greek world, takes possession of Athens after a long siege. Five years ago Antigonus quelled an uprising aimed at expelling the Macedonian garrison from Greece. The rebels – an Hellenic coalition which included Sparta, the Arcadians and the Achaeans – were led by Athens.

Sicily, 260BC. Rome wins its first great naval victory, over the Carthaginians at Mylae. "Ravens" – grappling hooks designed to hold together Roman and enemy ships – allowed the Romans to fight hand-to-hand on board ship.

Alexandria, c.260BC. The poetry of Callimachus, which illuminates the legends and cults of the principal divinities, is gaining influence.

Syria, 254BC. A six-year war between the Seleucids and the Ptolemies for possession of Syria is concluded by a marriage alliance between Antiochus II and Berenice, a daughter of Ptolemy II.

Syria, 247BC. On the death of Antiochus II, his Ptolemaic wife, Berenice, is threatened by Queen Laodice, the wife Antiochus repudiated in favour of Berenice. Ptolemy III rushes to his sister's aid. Seleucid power is now holding up only in the city of Antioch.

China, 247BC. Prince Zheng (Ch'i Huang-ti) ascends to the throne of Qin (Ch'in).

Greece, 243BC. Aratus of Sicyon, a partisan of the Achaean league, takes Acrocorinth, the two ports of Corinth and the Macedonian fleet, thereby liberating the Peloponnese from Macedonian domination. This is a response to the capture by Antigonus Gonatas, in 245BC, of Acrocorinth, the mountainous acropolis towering over the city of Corinth.

Ptolemy dies, having led Egypt's revival

Alexandria, 246BC

Ptolemy II has died, leaving the vast museum and library in this city of Alexander as his monument. This remarkable pharaoh did much to enhance Egypt's prestige and influence abroad during his reign.

His achievements in Egypt were considerable. He re-opened the disused canal from the Nile to the Red Sea and encouraged trade with the Orient. He rebuilt many of the temples destroyed by previous invaders. He made Alexandria one of the great cultural centres of the world, encouraging writers, artists and scholars of all nations to visit the city and work here.

Despite these achievements, Ptolemy was a bureaucrat who imposed heavy taxes on his people.

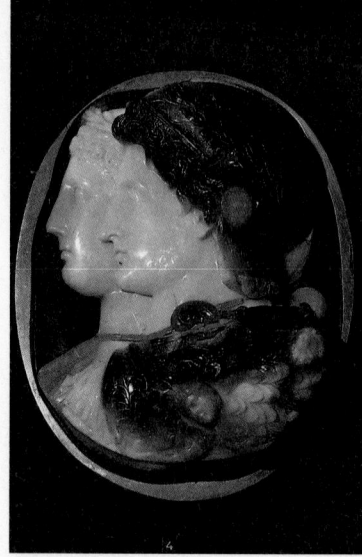

Ptolemy II and his wife.

Greek civil servants run Egypt

Two figures of women from Alexandria in typical Hellenistic dress.

Egypt, c.246BC

Egypt under King Ptolemy II Philadelphus is a Hellenistic state, with a bureaucracy to match. The life of Zenon, a middle-rank civil servant, provides the ideal case study. Zenon, a Carian from Asia Minor, came to Egypt in 261BC to work for Apollonius, the finance minister. His talent and efficiency as an archivist and manager were quickly recognised and he was put in charge of the administration of a model farm created on the heights of Philadelphia.

Here, like everywhere else in Egypt, the native workers (*fellahin*) are ruthlessly exploited. Local officials called *oikonomoi* extract taxes and rents from them for flocks, harvests and transport.

Zenon oversees the cultivation of gardens, wheatfields and orchards; the grafting of plants; irrigation; the budget; and the workers. But he is not above cheating the taxman himself, and giving and receiving favours from friends. In such ways the Greek elite stays rich, and continues to run the country.

Poet sings praises of everyday life

Alexandria, c.260BC

Alexandria, among the greatest centres of modern intellectual life, has now produced a poet whose own greatness lies in his celebration of less academic, but equally important, themes. The *Idylls* of Theocritus have gained immense popularity with their tales of everyday life in both town and country.

Born in Syracuse, Sicily, Theocritus now works at the court of Ptolemy Philadelphus, where he has become particularly renowned as the inventor of what are called "pastorals", poems that essentially take sophisticated urban attitudes and place them against a simple rural background.

Thyrsis, The Herdsmen and *The Harvest* are perfect rural idylls. As the peasants talk of their lives, readers can revel both in the poet's rural imagery and the earthy conversations of his shepherds and goatherds.

Urban life is there, too. *The Festival of Adonis* is a dialogue between two young wives who have come from Syracuse to the festival at Alexandria, and Theocritus enjoys the wonder of two country bumpkins in the big city. Other favourites are *The Sorceress*, in which a discarded mistress urges her spinning wheel "Turn magic wheel, and force my lover home"; and *Cyclops in love*, in which the poet pokes fun at the oafish gallantry of the mythical monster.

Theocritus, poet of pastoral idylls.

Rome crushes its old rival, Carthage

Urns of sacrificed babies' ashes.

Rome, 241BC
With a spectacular defeat of the enemy's fleet at the Acgadian Islands, Rome has finally triumphed over Carthage and has emerged from 23 years of war as a major sea power. An exhausted and humiliated Carthage has surrendered Sicily and agreed to pay reparations to its great rival.

The Punic War – named after the Greek *poeni*, meaning Cartha-ginians – began with the Roman occupation of Messana in Sicily. The Roman senate had hesitated to take this move; but the Assembly, concerned about Carthage's activities so close to the Italian mainland, voted for action. Rome continued its campaign in Sicily with considerable success, but Carthage's ability to supply its land forces showed up a key Roman weakness: the lack of a navy.

With the war in its third year, Rome set about building a fleet of 100 heavy *quinqueremes* – in which each oar was pulled by five men – and 20 *triremes*. Crews were trained in wooden "mock-ups" on the shore – and Rome's new naval strategists even devised a boarding gangway in the bows.

The Roman fleet's first major engagement took place off Sicily, where it heavily defeated the Carthaginian fleet commanded by Hannibal. Five years later, after another naval victory, Roman troops landed in Carthage. The legions were less fortunate; they were beaten by a force of elephants and cavalry and evacuated by their navy. Rome's fortunes reached a low ebb after this, with hundreds of her ships perishing in storms.

In one last desperate attempt, Rome borrowed heavily from her people to build a new fleet of 200 ships which succeeded in destroying much of the remaining enemy naval force.

Column marking Rome's victory.

Priests and pontiffs extend secular powers over Rome

Rome, 300-250BC
Religion in Rome is a public affair, and the priests enjoy political as much as spiritual power. The colleges of pontiffs and augurs, first established under Numa Pompilius, the second king of Rome, are the chief administrators of the state.

At their head is the pontifex maximus, so called after his historic duty of organising the repair of wooden bridges. Elected for life by the college of pontiffs, he fixes calendar and feast days, nominates Vestal Virgins and priests, and supervises ceremonies.

The number of pontiffs has, over the years, been increased to nine, including the rex sacrorum who leads religious ceremonies. The

A calf is prepared for sacrifice.

pontiffs administer the sacral law and have a powerful influence over the private and criminal law. Under them are the flamines and Vestal Virgins.

The 15 flamines are priests who serve particular gods and conduct sacrifices. The three most senior are assigned to Jupiter, Mars and Quirinus. There are six Vestal Virgins, who live in the temple of the goddess Vesta, for whom they must remain virgins for 30 years.

Arguably most important of all are the augurs, who interpret the auspices and must be consulted before any public act.

Indian king Asoka becomes the world's first Buddhist monarch

The capital of a pillar erected to proclaim King Asoka's conversion.

PIndia, c.262BC
Asoka of India, third king of the Mauryan dynasty, has become a Buddhist. Shocked by the horrors of the Kalinga war, in which 100,000 were slain, he has merged spiritual and temporal power, establishing a state based on "universal order".

Asoka succeeded to the throne ten years ago. His empire, encompassing all of India, was so vast that it was divided into four provinces, each administered by a prince of the royal blood. Its population, in turn, was divided into seven castes, of which two, the Brahmans and the Kshatriyas, monopolised spiritual and temporal power respectively. Rule was paternal, carried out by a centralised bureaucracy.

All over India rocks and stone pillars engraved with Prakrit inscriptions announce Asoka's conversion to Buddhism, pledging that he will rule his empire through the principles of "kindness, liberality, truthfulness and purity of deed and thought".

From his capital at Pataliputra, where he is building palaces of stone, the philosopher-king is practising what he preaches: he is now founding monasteries, financing irrigation schemes, establishing a health service, creating a welfare state, and practising the principle of universal toleration – "the very essence of religion" – to all religions in his kingdom.

Gautama Buddha with disciples.

Round up of suspects in republic's death

In the middle of the second century BC, the Roman state was organised under a republican system which in essentials was not much different from the one adopted when the Etruscan kings were expelled from the city in 509BC. Writers of the time tried to categorise it according to the traditional divisions of Greek political analysis - was it a democracy, an aristocracy, or a monarchy?

Polybius identified elements of each type: in his analysis, power was shared by the Senate (a body of landed aristocrats with political authority), the consuls (two executive magistrates elected annually) and the assembly of the people (which made laws and declared war or peace). But little more than a century later, Rome had its first emperor - Augustus - with effective control of armies, provinces and finance. How did such a dramatic change - especially surprising in the case of a people so devoted to tradition as the Romans - come about? Explaining the collapse of the republican system has been a major concern for historians since antiquity. One influential view was that of the historian Sallust, who considered the political crisis which struck Rome in the first century BC to be a result of the avarice and love of luxury which became widespread in Rome once foreign rivals had been eliminated. Sallust himself was no stranger to the life of luxury - after being expelled from the Senate in 50BC, he retired to his grand estates on the outskirts of the city of Rome. Whether or not the fall of the Roman republic was due to luxury, it certainly seems likely that there were links between the growth of Rome's empire in the second and first centuries BC and the dramatic changes in Roman politics and society in the same period.

From hill town to world power

By about 264BC, Rome was in control of virtually the whole of the Italian peninsula south of the Po valley, and the First Punic War saw Roman forces operating overseas for the first time - in Sicily, against the armies of Carthage and Syracuse. Victory in the war allowed Rome to take control not only of Sicily, but of Corsica and Sardinia too - so the Romans now had an overseas empire. When Rome defeated Hannibal in the Second Punic War, the way was open to expand still further, and more foreign wars followed. Roman society was exceptionally militaristic - political credibility was intimately linked to success in war - and a collective paranoia about potential rivals had survived Rome's rise from minor Italian hill town to world power. The ambition of individual generals led to spectacular Roman successes, especially in Greece and Asia Minor (modern Turkey) - Roman armies returned laden with loot and with vast numbers of slaves.

This new-found wealth had an enormous impact on Rome itself and on Italy in general. In many areas slaves were used to replace the peasants, who had in the past cultivated small tracts of land - so wine and oil could be produced on a large scale and sold in the expanding market provided by the city of Rome. Areas close to the city were worst affected - Tiberius Gracchus, the tribune of the people in 133BC, had been shocked when travelling through Etruria to see how many barbarian slaves were tilling the land. Traditionally, ownership of land had been a prerequisite for military service - so, as the peasants lost their estates and drifted into Rome, it became much more difficult to recruit soldiers.

Political consequences

The Roman authorities responded by gradually reducing the level of the property qualification, and a series of military crises at the end of the second century BC led the general Marius to abolish it altogether. This reform resolved the immediate difficulties. But since many soldiers now had no land to which they could return at the end of their service, they had to rely on their generals to obtain land for them as a discharge bounty. Friction resulted - the Senate was generally unwilling to confiscate large areas of land to give to veterans, and so the association between generals and their soldiers became closer than ever.

There were other political consequences. As the number of provinces to be administered grew, the number of junior magistrates increased - but the number of consuls elected each year remained static at two. The consulship was traditionally considered the peak of the aristocrat's political career, and competition for it increased as junior magistrates vied with their contemporaries for this high honour. With the increase in wealth available to successful provincial commanders, the level of bribery and corruption in public life increased, and candidates strove to outdo each other in providing lavish entertainments to impress potential voters.

When Julius Caesar was *aedile* (superintendent of public buildings and other matters) in 65BC, his term was marked by gladiatorial shows involving 320 pairs of fighters - and the theatrical shows and processions he arranged outclassed all previous attempts to impress in this way. Cultivating the people of Rome had become increasingly important as the aristocracy became more disunited - the electoral system was organised in such a way as to favour the wealthy, provided that they all voted for the same candidate. When the votes of the rich were split, however, the outcome was much less of a certainty. Besides, the initiatives of Tiberius Gracchus (who had caused a political storm in 133BC by proposing a measure, the redistribution of land, before the assembly of the people rather than before the Senate) had emphasised the authority of the Roman *plebs*, the common people.

Murder on the Appian Way

But another feature of this new political importance of the assembly of the people was that political violence and intimidation became an increasingly serious problem. Traditional elements in the Senate had roused a mob to kill Tiberius Gracchus in 133BC, and from the 70s BC onwards rival gangs clashed in the streets of Rome. In 52BC Clodius, one of the chief leaders in this gang warfare, was murdered in a riot on the Appian Way, and his supporters cremated his body in the Senate house, which was burnt down in the process. Pompey, the consul, had to draft in troops to restore order - unheard of - in a city which traditionally banned armed soldiers from crossing city limits.

The situation in the countryside was not much better - continued civil strife, and in particular the "Social Wars" which set Romans against their Italian allies (*socii*), meant that the hills of Italy were infested by bandits and desperate peasants and slaves. Even the grant of Roman citizenship to the allies, which ended the Social war, had the effect of aggravating the political tensions at Rome, since many of the wealthiest Italian citizens joined in political competition at Rome too.

So increased political competition, reduced loyalty of armies to the state, and the rising climate of violence in the city of Rome and the Italian countryside, all contributed in different ways to the collapse of the republic. But the ambitions of the individuals played a major part, too. Plutarch records a story that once, when Julius Caesar was crossing the Alps on his way to the province of Spain, his party passed through a tiny, squalid mountain village. Caesar's friends joked that perhaps here, too, there were struggles for political office. But Caesar, quite seriously, observed: "I would rather be first here than second in Rome." Caesar's heir was the Emperor Augustus.

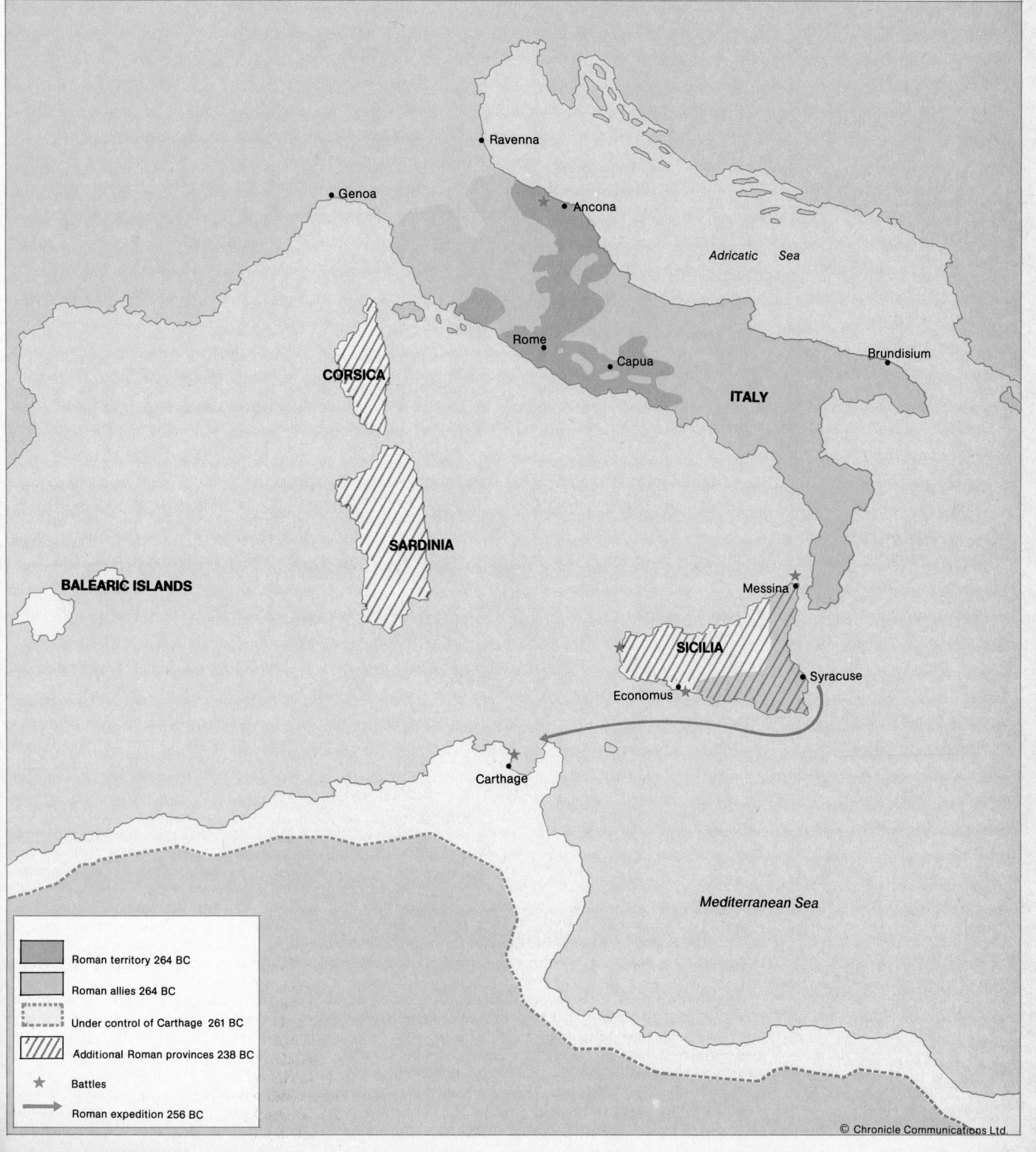

Ravenna

Genoa

Ancona

Adriatic Sea

CORSICA

Rome

Capua

Brundisium

ITALY

SARDINIA

BALEARIC ISLANDS

Messina

SICILIA

Syracuse

Economus

Carthage

Mediterranean Sea

Roman territory 264 BC

Roman allies 264 BC

Under control of Carthage 261 BC

Additional Roman provinces 238 BC

★ Battles

Roman expedition 256 BC

© Chronicle Communications Ltd.

Rome, 240BC. At the time of the Roman games, by official command, the poet Livius Andronicus stages the first tragedy and the first comedy in Latin literature: *Trojan Horse* and *Achilles*. This import of specifically Greek art forms into Rome is a huge success.

Mediterranean, 238BC. While Carthage is embroiled in a revolt by mercenaries led by Matho and Spendius, Rome establishes a presence in Sardinia and Corsica.

Asia Minor, 238BC. Coveting the kingdom of Pergamum, Antiochus Hierax, king of the part of Asia Minor (Anatolia) held by the Seleucids, forms alliances with the bands of Galatian brigands who flourish in the region.

Carthage, 237BC. After putting an end to the mercenaries' revolt with the aid of Hanno the Great, Hamilcar, the Carthaginian general defeated by Rome in Sicily, embarks for Spain.

Greece, 235BC. A war between Demetrius II of Macedonia and a coalition of the Aetolian and Achaean leagues ends without a decisive battle. It broke out soon after Demetrius ascended the throne in 239BC.

Athens, 232BC. Chrysippus of Soli, in Cyprus, succeeds Cleanthes as head of the Stoic school.

Greece, 229BC. On his ascension to the Macedonian throne, Antigonus III Doson is confronted by revolts in Greek cities: Thessalians, Athenians and Achaeans want to be free of Macedonian tutelage.

Greece, 228BC. Antigonus III Doson inflicts a defeat on the rebellious Aetolians and Thessalians, but the Achaean league is steadily gaining strength. Meanwhile, Athens has expelled the Macedonian garrison from Piraeus.

Greece, 225BC. Sparta, which wants to control the Achaean league, intervenes in the conflict between Macedonia and the Greek cities, forcing Aratus of Sicyon, an Achaean partisan, to seek Macedonian aid.

Greece, 224BC. Antigonus III Doson and Aratus of Sicyon agree on a plan to reorganise Greece so that the Achaean league and the Macedonians can co-exist.

Greece, 222BC. Antigonus and the Achaean league defeat Sparta.

The Celts no longer pose a threat to northern Italy

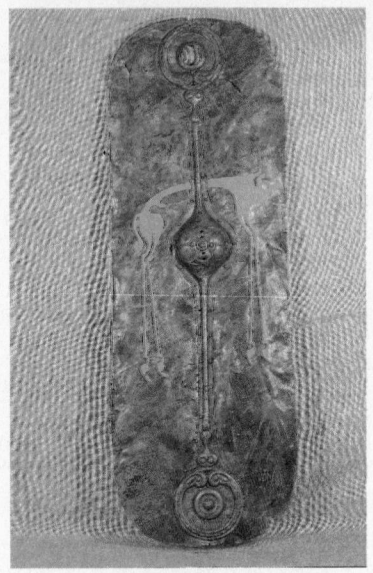

Celtic enamel-inlaid bronze shield.

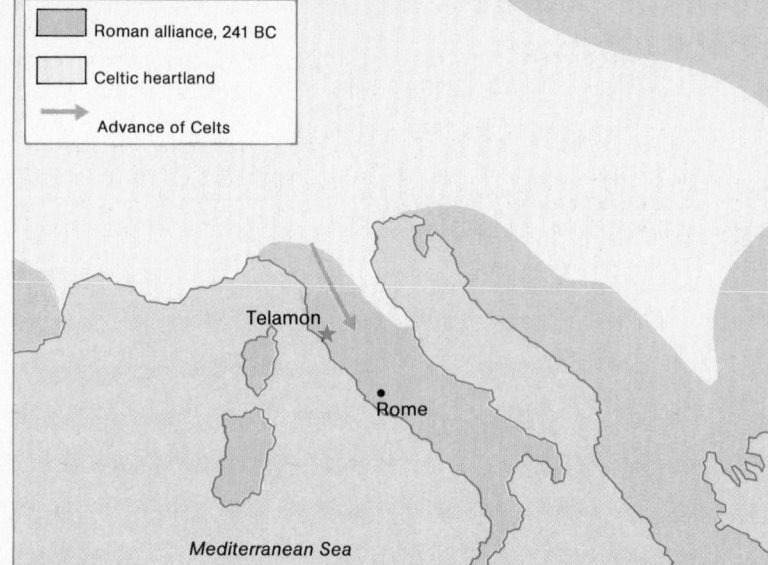

Northern Italy, 225BC

The Celtic threat to northern Italy is over. A powerful army of Gallic tribes has been defeated by Roman legions at Lake Telemon. Over 40,000 Gauls lie dead on the battlefield. This bloody battle is the latest episode in a conflict which has been simmering since around 400BC when the Gauls started to arrive in northern Italy. In 295BC they allied with the Samnites and won a skirmish with the Romans before two consular armies defeated them the following year at Sentinum.

In 284BC the Romans took revenge for Gallic raids by crushing the Senones, then the Boii. After a further defeat, at Delphi in 279BC, the Gauls settled in Cisalpine Gaul around the Po plain. They were policed by Roman garrisons, and the area named Ager Gallicus was colonised by Roman citizens in 232BC. There was panic in Rome this year when Gallic tribes joined forces and invaded Etruria with 70,000 men – until they were trapped between two armies at Lake Telemon.

Colossus of Rhodes destroyed by quake

A later impression of how the Colossus may have looked with his torch.

Rhodes, 224BC

The Colossus of Rhodes, rightly numbered among the Seven Wonders of the World, has been destroyed in a massive earthquake.

The Colossus, a 100-foot-high statue of a young man representing the sun-god Helios, was erected in 304BC. It commemorated the successful resistance by the people of Rhodes to a year-long siege by Demetrius, who wished to bring the islanders, whose prosperous and independent merchant republic was allied to Ptolemy of Egypt, into the Greek empire.

A new culture appears in Peru

Peru, 221BC

A new culture is blossoming on the narrow coastal plain between the Andes and the Pacific Ocean. Irrigation canals are spreading outwards from the Nazca river, and maize crops are flourishing.

This desert has been the nursery of every major civilisation in Peru since immigrants came from Mexico 1,500 years ago. They brought with them farming techniques and a religion that worships the jaguar.

Nazca society is well-organised, its survival depending on effective irrigation. Power is centred on the capital, Cahuachi, whose 20-metre-high stepped pyramid dominates the city.

The country's textiles are bright and multi-coloured, and usually embroidered with jaguars. Its pottery is gaily painted, simple pots moulded and decorated as trophy heads. The more sophisticated ware is given the image of the mythical being, the Nazca god.

Zheng builds great wall in the north

Scholarly book emerges from a barbarous land

China, 239BC

A remarkable book has just been published in the state of Qin (Ch'in). It is called *The Spring and Autumn Annals of Mr Lu,* and is the work of a team of scholars who were brought together to summarise all their knowledge of statecraft and philosophy.

What is especially remarkable about this work is that is should be produced in Qin, which is generally considered a barbarous state. The man behind the enterprise is Lu Buwei (Lu Pu-Wei), a merchant who became Chancellor of Qin in 250BC and, ashamed at Qin's reputation for coarseness, determined to raise its cultural standards. His own adventures make interesting reading for, while he was still a merchant, he befriended the young prince of Qin who had been driven into exile. Lu sealed the friendship by presenting the prince with his own favourite concubine and, when the prince ascended the throne, Lu rose with him.

The new king married the concubine, who presented him with a son who looked like Lu. When the king died the queen showed renewed interest in Lu. He, fearing the consequences, introduced her to a man of almost legendary virility whose sexual powers were seemingly unquenchable. And it seems that everyone was satisfied.

Prolific poet dies

Alexandria, c.240BC

Callimachus, the versatile and original scholar-poet who wrote over 800 volumes of verse, is dead. Born in Cyrene, North Africa, c.305BC, Callimachus moved to Alexandria early in life and, after a spell as a schoolmaster, became head of the famous Alexandrian library.

An advocate of small-scale perfection, as exemplified in his epigrams, Callimachus engaged in heated rows with champions of the epic form. Marked by ingenuity, wit, realism and expression of personal emotion, his poetry is rich in mythical allusions and all sorts of curiosities.

China, 221BC

Work has begun on a great wall, 2,600 miles long, to keep out the fierce hordes of nomads who threaten China from the north. Three hundred thousand men have been conscripted for this mammoth project on the orders of Zheng, ruler of Qin (Ch'in), who has proclaimed himself "First August Lord" – emperor of China. Defence in the north is one of his first priorities. The wall, made of packed earth, will stretch from Liaodong in the east to Lintao in the west, in a single line of frontier defence.

Fortunately the builders are not having to start entirely from scratch, as they will be able to incorporate smaller-scake fortifications constructed over past centuries. But the idea of a unified defence system covering the whole of northern China is quite new. When the wall is garrisoned its soldiers will have an important intelligence gathering role. Regular patrols will be sent out to watch nomad movements, and near important passes areas of raked sand will be maintained to reveal the tracks of enemy scouts creeping in under cover of darkness. Watchtowers will pass on messages by a complex system of flag, smoke signals or torches.

The warrior state of Qin has finally succeeded in conquering all its rivals after decades of ruthless war in which hundreds of thousands have been slaughtered.

After his final victory Zheng held a great assembly of his ministers to decide how his conquests were to be governed. Their decisions are far-reaching and will undoubtedly have a profound effect on the future history of this vast land.

Zheng rejected the proposal put forward by a group of conservative advisers which would have entailed the division of the empire into fiefs governed by his family and supporters in the old feudal style. He thus displayed his wisdom, for it was this very system which led to the war between the old fiefdoms.

Instead, he has set up a system of commanderies and prefectures run by salaried civil servants responsible to the central government. By this method he has gathered the reins of power into his own hands. He is, indeed, the emperor, and to

The Great Wall of China snakes its massive way across the landscape.

make sure there will be no rebellion against his strict rule he has ordered that all weapons must be handed in and melted down.

He is also taking no chances with the powerful families of the defeated states, gathering them together in the capital of Qin where they are lodged comfortably but under close supervision.

Civil laws are being enacted to turn China into a genuinely unified state. A single standard script is being used for all official documents, and local variants are being suppressed.

Weights and measures are also being standardised, and even the axle-width of carts is being regulated so that they fit the established road-ruts. To make all these measures work the strict system of Qin law is being made to apply to every part of China.

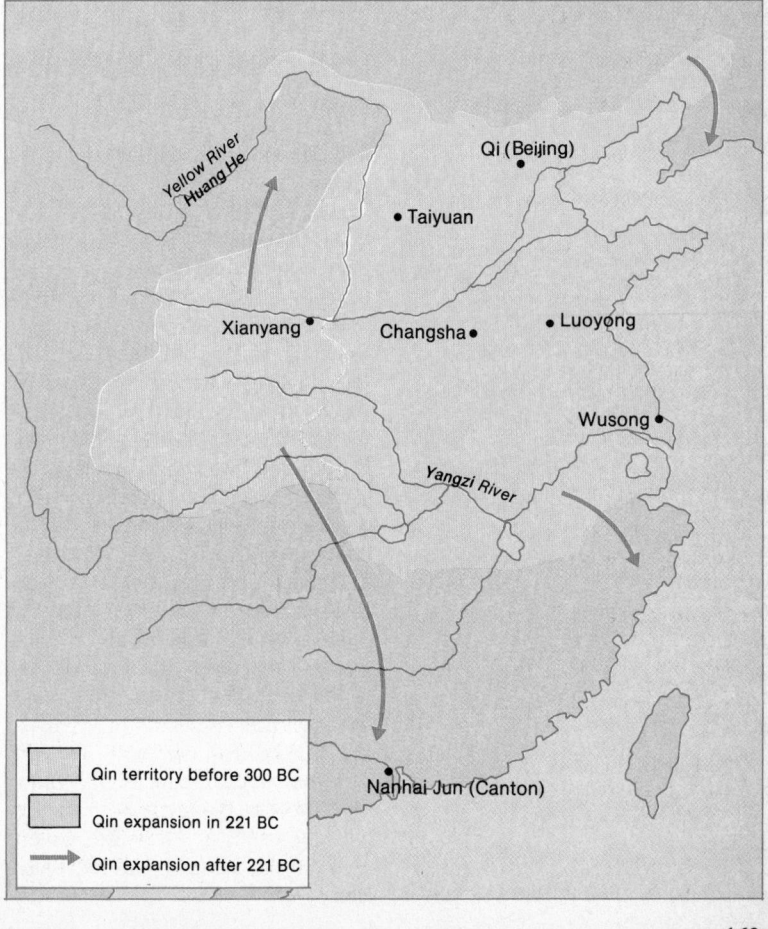

Qin territory before 300 BC

Qin expansion in 221 BC

Qin expansion after 221 BC

Spain, 219BC. In an effective declaration of war on Rome, the Carthaginian general Hannibal besieges the pro-Roman town of Saguntum. Since Spain became a province of their empire in 236BC, the Carthaginians have been exploiting the economic resources of the peninsula and swelling the ranks of their army with local recruits.

Palestine, 217BC. Egyptian *hoplites*, led by the young Ptolemy IV Philopater, crush the Seleucid army under Antiochus III at Raphia. Two years ago, in pursuit of his dream of restoring the grandeur of the Seleucid empire, Antiochus initiated the fourth Syrian war and took possession of the coveted province of Coele Syria at the expense of Ptolemaic Egypt.

Italy, 217BC. Hannibal takes the Roman general Flaminius and his legions by surprise near Lake Trasimene in Umbria. The ensuing battle, in which 15,000 Romans are killed and 15,000 taken prisoner, marks the loss to Rome of the whole of Etruria. In Rome itself, in anticipation of imminent assault, the bridges over the river Tiber are cut and the city walls repaired.

China, c.215BC. Shi Huang Di, the architect of Chinese political and administrative unity, joins together the separate parts of the Great Wall.

China, 213BC. On the orders of Shi Huang Di all books, other than those on useful subjects, such as medicine, agriculture and divination, are burnt.

Sicily, 212BC. The Roman general Marcellus captures the city of Syracuse after a siege. Archimedes, a mathematician who used his expertise to construct formidable war machines to resist the Roman onslaught, dies in the battle. Syracuse, ally of Carthage, had hoped to negotiate with the Romans, but this was vetoed by pro-Carthaginian factions.

Italy, 212BC. War breaks out between Rome and Macedonia. Philip V of Macedon – an ally of Hannibal since 215BC – intends to gain control of Illyria and the Greek cities along the Adriatic coast, an area of Roman influence. In response, Rome has formed an alliance with the Aetolians and promised to cede to them any land which it may conquer in the region.

Egypt's old enemy is on the decline

Syria, c.212BC

It is now over a hundred years since the death of Alexander the Great, and for much of this time Syria has swung to and fro between competing rulers. For most of the period the most consistent leaders have been the descendants of a Macedonian general called Seleucus. Currently, however, they are in decline and have been ousted by the Egyptians both in Syria and along much of the coast of Asia Minor (Anatolia)

Seleucus himself had taken full control of northern Syria 90 years ago, but his successor, Antiochus I, not only failed to conquer southern Syria, but also found it difficult to maintain control in the north. Since then the military power of the Seleucids has waxed and waned until today, when they are clearly no match for the Egyptian Ptolemies.

They have, however, left a legacy in the area with the building up of the cities, mostly under the rule of the first three Seleucid kings. These cities include Antioch, the capital, famous for its park at Daphne, Seleuceia-in-Pieria with its harbour, and Apamea, a big military centre

Antiochus III, the king of Syria.

on the middle Orontes, where the Seleucids keep their war animals.

These cities are mostly well managed, with local magistrates responsible for the condition of the streets, the water supply and public sanitation. They have powers to fine people for breaking the laws Their populations show a mixture of Greek, Macedonian and oriental influences, and they depend mostly on agriculture.

Alexandrian library has 200,000 books

Alexandria, 220BC

The world-famous library at Alexandria is celebrating its sixtieth anniversary this year. The library is part of the Museum of Alexandria, founded by Ptolemy II Philadelphus 50 years ago, although it has been suggested that the concept of a library was mooted even earlier, by Ptolemy I, 65 years before.

Today's library is the greatest in the world, making Alexandria an unrivalled intellectual centre. It allegedly holds 200,000 (some even say 490,000) volumes, although given that each "volume" is, in fact, a papyrus scroll, several of which may be needed for a single work, and that there are many duplicates, the true number may be nearer 120,000 individual books.

Working under a chief librarian, the library staff carry out an enormous task. New acquisitions arrive continually. All are catalogued as to their origins, former owner and edition, as well as by author and subject-matter. Often they must be recopied by hand and deviant editions corrected.

Alexandria becomes the scientific capital of Hellenistic world

Alexandria, 212BC

The city founded by Alexander the Great over a century ago has become the scientific capital of the Hellenistic world, largely owing to the support and encouragement of Egypt's rulers, the Ptolemy dynasty, founded by one of Alexander's generals. Having inherited the trading links of Phoenician Tyre in Lebanon after the siege by Alexander, the city has acquired great wealth and fine public buildings.

The Ptolemies have made the museum into the leading Greek university, with schools of medicine, mathematics, astronomy and geography. Scholars from all over the Greek world, attracted to the university, are paid by the king.

The man in charge of the famous library, Eratosthenes of Cyrene, has caused a sensation by measuring the circumference of the earth. He recorded the angle of a shadow cast by a stick at Alexandria on the day of the summer solstice, when there was no shadow at Aswan,

The "Antikythera Mechanism", possibly an instrument of navigation.

about 500 miles (800km) to the south. Then he divided the figure – 7.5 degrees – into 360.

The king has also encouraged the study of biology by providing the university with convicted criminals who were cut open while they were still alive. By this means much knowledge about the brain and

other organs, including the reproductive system, was acquired.

In another discipline, the lecturer on geometry was once asked by the king whether there was no easier way than ploughing through figures and angles. Euclid answered: "Sire, to Geometry there is no royal road."

Hannibal shocks Rome

Rome, 218BC

In a brilliant and daring manoeuvre, Hannibal, the Carthaginian general, has led an army of 25,000 men with war-elephants and horses across the snow-covered Alps and invaded Italy from the north. His army has linked up with Gallic allies in the Po valley and is poised to strike at Rome. Despite Rome's superior army – mobilised and numbering a potential 600,000 men, including allies – Hannibal's move makes the second Punic War a much more evenly matched encounter.

Rome had relied on its superior sea-power to fight off any invasion from Carthage. At the outset of the campaign – the cause was Roman interference with Carthaginian activities in Spain – Rome prepared squadrons to invade both Carthage and Spain. One of the objectives of the latter attack was the arrest of Hannibal. They had not reckoned with the speed at which the fiery young Hannibal could move. Although there was a Roman army stationed in the south of Gaul, he

Hannibal: elephantine successes.

made his way with a veteran army of African horsemen and infantry from Spain across the Rhone to the Alps.

Hannibal's losses were considerable. Thousands were killed by hostile Gauls, more still on the ice-covered passes. So serious is his threat, however, that Rome has abandoned its projected invasion of Carthage and has diverted its army northwards – only for it to be cut to pieces in a Carthaginian ambush at the Tretia river.

Defeat at Cannae puts Romans in peril

Rome, 216BC

Two years after his brilliant Alpine crossing into Italy, Hannibal's armies have inflicted a crushing defeat on the Roman legions. Forty-five thousand Romans lie dead on the fields of the battle of Cannae. A further 20,000 legionaries have been captured, and the future of Rome itself is in grave doubt as its former allies turn on it.

The Roman army, under its new commander, Fabius, had carefully avoided direct confrontation with the invaders, preferring to harass the enemy until they could be attacked in their winter quarters. Hannibal succeeded in fooling the Romans at night-time when he tied torches to the horns of a herd of cattle to simulate an army on the move – meanwhile escaping in another direction.

It was August 2 when the two armies finally came to grips, Hannibal's Gauls fighting naked from the waist up with long spears, his mercenary Spaniards dressed in scarlet and white. Rome's forces numbered 60,000; the Carthaginians and their allies, 45,000.

Victorian view of elephants in action.

Blinded by the dust of battle, the Romans were out-manoeuvred and out-generalled, with Hannibal's infantry deliberately retreating in the centre to allow the cavalry on the flanks to encircle the Romans.

So grave is the news that human sacrifices are being offered in Rome for the first time in living memory.

Comic theatre finds a new stage in Italy

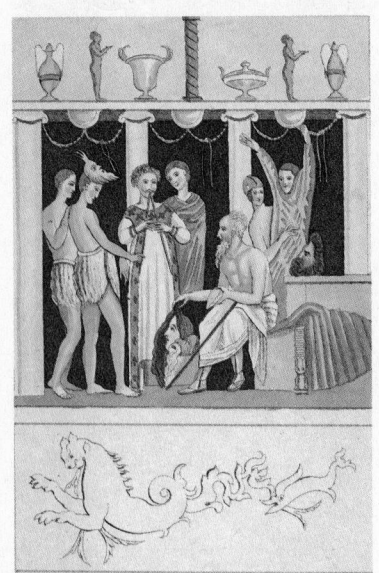

A mural at Pompeii showing actors.

Rome, c.212BC

"New Comedy" – a form of entertainment in which live actors perform as gods and mortals in absurd situations – is now established in Rome as a favourite pastime. The most prolific writer of such stories,

Titus Maccius Plautus, is notorious for his audacious treatment of once-sacred Greek myths. The pioneer of the genre was Menander (c.342-292BC), who inspired the writer Terence as well as Plautus. In most of their work the crafty slave, errant son, cuckolded husband and motherly whore are stock figures. The magic lies in an author's treatment of such familiar material.

In Plautus' *Amphitryon* a Theban general of that name has gone campaigning with his servant Sosias, leaving their womenfolk, including the general's wife Alcmene, unattended. The gods Jupiter and Mercury (father and son) adopt the likeness of the absentees. Alcmene shares her bed with her "husband", but the real Amphitryon and Sosias return next day. For Sosias, arriving ahead of his master, the first shock is to be greeted at the door by his double. The plot, laced with song and reed music, thickens nicely and the action is non-stop: unlike the Greeks, Plautus does not like intervals.

Sculptors put humour before religion

A child grapples with a goose.

Greece, c.220BC

Greek sculpture, one of the glories of the contemporary world, has been taking a new direction in recent years. Modern sculptors are turning away from the classical tradition, with its emphasis on the great themes of religion, war and sporting contests, and concen-

trating on more spiritual concepts. Human beings, their trials and tribulations, are the preferred subject matter of today's statues.

Sculptors today are far freer than their predecessors to portray scenes and themes they like. On the other hand they are in some ways more restricted, since they must bow to the demands of the rich patrons who commission their work.

Statues have become less idealised and far more relevant to everyday feelings. While gods and goddesses still have their place, sculptors like Praxiteles have given them a more human feel. They are no longer examples of how mankind ought to live, but relate to how people actually are. New themes, such as those of old age, childhood, sadness and suffering can all be seen. Humour, which classical works would not permit, is found more and more.

Sculptors also deal in portraits – carved heads – and in group statues, telling a story and revealing the emotions of those involved.

Terracotta army guards tomb of Qin

A vast army of terracotta soldiers and their animals stand in formation between walls of unexcavated figures, awaiting a command from their dead master, Chinese Emperor Qin Shi Huang Di.

China, 210BC
The first emperor of China, known as Qin Shi Huang Di, the First August Lord of Qin, has died, aged 49, in the eleventh year of his reign over the unified empire. He is to be given a funeral fitting for his accomplishments in a vast tomb beneath a man-made mountain near his capital, Xianyang (Hsien-yang).

The constellations of the heavens are pictured on the interior of the dome which forms the roof of his tomb, while the mountains and rivers of China are modelled below. Rich grave-goods surround the body of the emperor, ready for him to use in the afterlife.

He is to be guarded by an army of soldiers, made out of terracotta and buried in the ground around the tomb, ready to spring to their master's aid.

A warrior from the imperial tomb.

Another soldier in the tomb-army.

Pottery culture spreads south in Africa

Namibia, c.205BC
Cattle, sheep and a new way of life are spreading towards the southernmost tip of the continent. Herding people are also making pottery for the first time in southern Africa. Cattle and sheep were brought from East Africa and were adopted with enthusiasm by the hunting and fishing peoples around the marshes of the northern Kalahari. The great lake covering the Okavango and Makgadikgadi areas has begun to dry up, revealing lush pastures for grazing animals. People have begun to herd domestic livestock, as well as fishing and hunting zebra, hippo, gnu and antelope.

The human and livestock populations of these pastures have swelled in size and are moving southwards in search of new pastures. Some indigenous people in the south have joined them, adopting the language and lifestyle of the northerners.

A life-size terracotta horse, saddled and ready for action.

Romans win Punic Wars

Carthage, 201BC

The once-proud city of Carthage bowed to its Roman victors today and accepted terms of surrender. Despite the reverses suffered during Hannibal's early campaign in northern Italy, Rome has triumphed in the second Punic War, and the great Carthaginian empire appears set to fade into the dust of the North African deserts.

Carthage has already lost Spain to the victorious Roman general, Scipio Africanus. Now it is forced to surrender almost of all of its fleet and the elephants which made its army such a formidable fighting force. It must pay massive reparations to Rome; and it can no longer declare war without the prior authority of Rome. The terms of the surrender allow Carthage to retain control of its cities in Africa, together with slaves, herds, flocks and other property; no Roman garrison will be based in the city.

When these terms were put to the Carthaginians, one senator was about to speak against them when he was pulled from the rostrum by Hannibal, the general who had come so close to winning the war.

The responsibility for defeat, he said, was his. The Roman terms were generous. "It seems to me amazing that anyone who is a citizen of Carthage should not thank his stars that now we are at their mercy we should receive such leniency," he added.

Hannibal surrenders at battle of Zama

Carthage, 202BC

A brilliant young Roman general has changed the entire course of the war which has raged between Rome and Carthage over the past 17 years. His name is Scipio – he has adopted the surname Africanus – and he was only 25 years old when he led a legion behind the lines in Spain and gained the upper hand over what the enemy had called "New Carthage".

An attempt by Hasdrubal, Hannibal's brother, to lead a relief column across the Pyrenees failed, leaving Carthage open to Roman invasion. It was Scipio who took the Roman army back to Africa. The Romans had learned a great deal from Hannibal – particularly in the use of cavalry – and when the two generals met at Zama, the two armies were equally matched.

For once, Hannibal's elephants

Punic grave stone from Carthage.

– he used 80 in the front line – were of no avail to him. They panicked, scattering their own infantry. Scipio used Hannibal's own cavalry tactics on the flanks, and it was the Carthaginian army that collapsed.

Roman culture begins to find its voice

A sarcophagus with a sculpted frieze of the nine female Muses of the arts.

Rome, c.202BC

Scipio's epic victory and the collapse of the Carthaginian empire have produced an epic writer – Gnaeus Naevius, a former actor, whose *The Punic War* is the first real attempt at a classic poem in the Greek tradition.

Naevius served in the first Punic War, but since then his outspoken views have made him singularly unpopular with the influential Metelli family of noblemen and he was imprisoned, and later exiled, for libel.

His major work is *Bellum Poenicum*, a curious mixture of fact – about the war – and mythology in which he writes of Troy and Carthage as fictional cities.

A literary tradition is beginning to emerge in Rome. Although heavily influenced by Greek classicism – with the emphasis on tragedy and the epic – literature and the theatre are reflecting Rome's history. Many writers are inhibited by the paucity of today's Latin – and, significantly, Fabius Pictor, the senator who wrote *The History of Rome*, used Greek to write in. The cultures of the two countries have always been intertwined since Etruria welcomed its first Greek traders; and Hellenic communities still flourish in southern Italy.

It is 40 years since Livius Andronicus – a Greek born in one such community – produced the first Roman tragedy. Although this was written in Greek, he followed it up with a translation into Latin of Homer's *Odyssey*. Although a highly inventive work – the Muses become fountain goddesses, for example – the Latin style lacks much of Homer's grace.

Roman empire gains a foothold in Asia

Attalos I, king of Pergamum.

Rome, 201BC

Having built up a massive fleet of warships during the second Punic War, and secured a grip on Sicily, Sardinia and Spain, it seemed inevitable that Rome would begin to look further into the Mediterranean for alliances – or conquests.

The opportunity came when an alliance of Rhodes and Pergamum (*Bergama*) appealed to Rome for help against a potential invasion by Macedonia and the Seleucids – who had allied themselves to attack Egypt.

In Rome, the assembly of the people, exhausted by the war against Carthage, voted heavily against any military action, but the people were overruled by a warlike Senate. Roman legions were dispatched to fight on Greek soil. It now remains to be seen whether the flexible tactics devised by Scipio in the last war, and used so sucessfully in Carthage and Spain, will pay off against the hitherto invincible Macedonian phalanx.

A gold head from a shrine to the river Oxus in Bactria (Afghanistan), part of a hoard dating from the age of the Persian empire to Hellenistic times.

Syria, 200BC. Antiochus III conquers Coele Syria by winning a victory over the Egyptians at Panion.

Kush, c.200BC. The rule of King Arkamani (Ergamenes) at Meroe is at an end. Over his 25-year rule he fostered friendly relations with the Ptolemaic pharaohs at Alexandria down the Nile.

Mexico, c.200BC. The merging of a number of villages in the Teotihuacan valley, with a total population of about 50,000, has given rise to a large-scale building programme. The people follow the cult of the rain-god Tlaloc.

Mexico, c.200BC. Urban centres are emerging in the Maya area. At the city of El Mirador, the Tigre and the Danta pyramids (respectively 178 and 136 feet high) are under construction.

Greece, 197BC. Defeated by the Romans at the battle of Cynoscephalae, Philip V is forced to accept all the conditions insisted upon by the consul Flamininus in exchange for peace. Macedonia is stripped of its possessions in European Greece and Asia Minor (Anatolia). This puts an end to three years of fighting between Rome and Macedonia in Illyria.

Greece, 194BC. The last Roman soldiers leave Greece and return to Rome, taking with them many Greek works of art.

Greece, 191BC. Antiochus III, the territorially ambitious Seleucid king, is forced to abandon Greece after a defeat by the Romans in the pass of Thermopylae. Antiochus sent 10,000 men to Greece last year after forging an anti-Roman coalition with the Aetolians, Spartans and Macedonians. The Aetolians in particular felt frustrated at the political reorganisation of Greece by Rome, which has declared all Greek cities free.

Asia Minor, 190BC. After a defeat by the Romans at Magnesia, Antiochus III gives up his claim to Thrace and evacuates Asia Minor as far as the Taurus mountains. The credit for this development goes to Publius Cornelius Scipio and Publius Scipio Africanus, who were sent by Rome to Greece and then to Asia Minor in order finally to settle the Seleucid problem. The Romans were supported in this task by the kingdom of Pergamum.

From Peru to Ohio, new cultures stir

Central America, 200BC

Four thousand years after American man first cultivated the soil, sophisticated societies have grown up from the Rockies to the Andes.

One and a half thousand years ago immigrants from Mexico came to the dry coastal strip of Peru, and built temples at Chuquitanta and Las Aldas and pyramids at Rioseco. Six hundred years later Chavin culture established itself in the Andes, building a magnificent temple at Chavin de Huantar. Chavin culture decayed and civilisation shifted to the desert, where the Paracas culture created exquisite fabric designs and colours before evolving into Nazca culture.

While Chavin culture dominated the Andes, Olmec culture was developing on the east coast of Mexico, its colossal sculpted heads looking out over the Gulf of Mexico. Olmecs were replaced by Zapotecs, who built a city at Monte Alban on the west coast, and in turn gave way to Mixtecs, who carpeted their buildings with exquisite mosaics.

North of Mexico, in Ohio, the Adena culture has built towns and villages, and inters its dead in burial mounds. The Adenas are now declining and being replaced by the Hopewell culture, trading people who smoke tobacco and use copper.

Most recent of the American civilisations are the Mayas, whose enormous pyramid complexes in Guatemala are already more magnificent than anything so far.

A mask made of gold with inlaid eyes and owl decoration, from Peru.

A pearl-eyed raven or crow cut from a sheet of copper made in Hopewell.

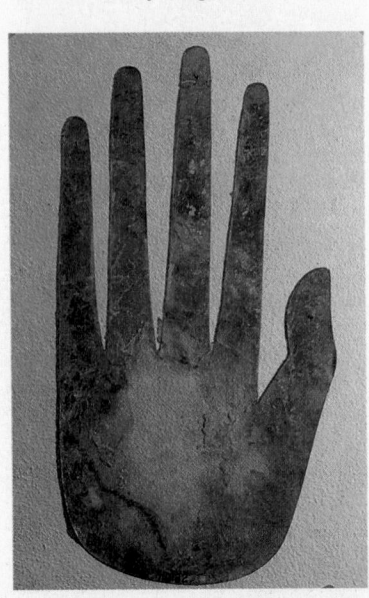

Symbolic mica hand, from Ohio.

A Mayan pottery vessel in the shape of a sitting man, from Guatemala.

Peruvian ceramic of a standing person clutching a bowl.

Orgiastic cults cause uproar in Rome

Rome, 186BC

Bacchanalian orgies that have corrupted thousands in the city have been outlawed by decree. A purge of the priests and instigators of these cults is under way, and the Senate has ordered a complete ban on Bacchanalian festivities unless properly authorised.

Although Dionysus (also known as Bacchus) has long been honoured in Rome, it is only recently that drunkenness, crime and immorality of all kinds have become associated with the celebration of the Bacchanalia. It is variously said that these depraved practices are of Asian origin, or come from southern Italy, via Etruria and Campania, or were introduced by a low-born Greek.

Whatever the origin, religious festivals have been turned into occasions of wine and feasting, with promiscuity between men and women, youths and their elders, accompanied by loud music. Further debaucheries have become associated with these occasions, including fraudulent plots, forgeries, and murders of kin.

So great was the sense of outrage at these revelations that the Senate decided to take urgent action to safeguard public morals, and to prevent the orgies from being

One woman is whipped – for immorality? – while another dances nearby.

exploited by enemies of the state. Two consuls ordered a search for the priests involved; those caught were to be kept under arrest pending a full inquiry.

Watches were posted throughout the city, and rewards offered for information. It was said that more

than 7,000 people were involved, and so many fled from Rome that the consuls had to search country villages and conduct trials there. Those guilty of fraud, forgery, debauchery or murder are to be put to death. Anyone initiated into the cults will be imprisoned.

General Liu Bang founds the Imperial Han dynasty in China

This bronze model of an elk from Han China was made as part of the harness of a Chinese horseman.

China, 200BC

There is a new, strong, emperor of China. He is Liu Bang, who has named his dynasty the Han after the river which gave its name to the first state over which he ruled during his rise to power.

That rise was completely unexpected, for when the first emperor, the great First August Lord of Qin died in 210BC, power passed to his son. But he was weak and fell under the influence of the court eunuch, Zhao Gao (Chao Kao), who had designs on the throne.

The tight hold maintained by the first emperor fell away. Different factions struggled for power. First his son and then the eunuch were assassinated. The shockwaves then spread to the far corners of the empire and the conquered states began to rebel against the oppressive rule of Qin.

From all this turmoil there emerged two main contenders for supreme power. One was an aristocratic general, Xiang Yu (Hsiang Yu), and the other was Liu Bang, a man of humble peasant origins who, nevertheless, was a forceful leader.

Liu's cautious approach and careful choice of subordinates brought him victory over Xiang Yu, and he was proclaimed emperor two years ago. At the time there were those who thought that his humble origins would lead to a relaxation of the harsh laws of Qin, and, indeed, Liu promised that he would repeal those laws.

However, in the two years that he has occupied the throne he has made it quite plain that he will rule China's reunified empire just as harshly as the first emperor, the great First August Lord of Qin.

Roman army helps to free Greeks from rule by Macedonia

Greece, 196BC

There are celebrations at the Isthmian Games as a decree is issued declaring freedom and autonomy for the Greeks after the defeat of the Macedonians by Rome.

The Roman proconsul, Titus Quinctius Flamininus, is hailed as the country's liberator. He had taken command of the Roman army after his election the previous year, and had led it to a crushing victory over the Macedonians at Cynoscephalae.

This effectively brought an end to the Second Macedonian War, forcing Philip V of Macedon to make peace and promise to stay out of Greece.

The Romans came to the aid of the Greeks after a joint appeal in 201BC by the city-state of Rhodes and King Attalus of Pergamum. They had themselves declared war on Philip in an effort to halt his conquest of the minor independent states of the Aegean, but with little success.

The Roman army was, at first, poorly disciplined and poorly led. Not all Greeks supported their campaign, and the Macedonians had held their own until the arrival of Flamininus. Now, with Rome victorious, the Greeks are hoping to re-establish their independence.

A stone inscription from Rosetta in Egypt, by the priests of Memphis in honour of Ptolemy V, in two Egyptian scripts (hieroglyphic and cursive), and Greek.

Rome, 189BC. Eumenes II, king of Pergamum, is received by the Senate. They reach an agreement whereby control of Asia Minor will be shared between Pergamum and Rhodes.

Asia Minor, 188BC. After his defeats at Thermopylae and Magnesia, Antiochus III concludes a peace treaty with the Romans at Apamea in Phrygia. The treaty effectively puts an end to Seleucid influence in the Mediterranean. The Thracian peninsula and most of Seleucid Asia Minor are now controlled by Pergamum.

Rome, 187BC. The Roman general Publius Cornelius Scipio and his brother Lucius, who commanded the victorious Roman armies at the battle of Magnesia, are accused of accepting bribes from Antiochus III, the vanquished Seleucid king.

Italy, 187BC. The Via Aemilia is constructed from Placentia to Ariminum (Rimini).

Rome, 184BC. Marcius Porcius Cato (the Elder), the censor, endeavours to restore moral virtue in Rome by taxing luxury. He also builds the first basilica in the Forum – the Basilica Porcia. The basilica, which becomes a popular meeting place, reflects the growing Greek influence on the architecture of Rome.

Italy, c.180BC. Over the past 20 years the Romans have been occupied in subjugating the Italian Celts and annexing the region between the Apennines and the Alps known as Cisalpine Gaul. Among the colonies they have founded are Bononia (Bologna) in 189BC and Parma and Mutina in 183BC.

Egypt, c.180BC. Under Ptolemy VI Philometor, who became king last year, Egypt is continuing its decline. The country is beset with internal disputes and fiscal and military crises.

China, 180BC. Following the death of Empress Dowager Lu, who has dominated court politics since the death of Liu Bang, founder of the Han dynasty, Emperor Wendi succeeds to the throne.

Macedonia, 179BC. Despite plots against him, Perseus succeeds his father, Philip V, as king of Macedonia. Perseus earlier persuaded Philip to execute his pro-Roman brother, Demetrius. Perseus is now sending agents all over the Mediterranean in order to raise a coalition prepared to mount an assault on Rome.

Rome, 173BC. The authorities expel two Epicurean philosophers from Rome, alleging that their moral code, which is based on the theory that pleasure is the highest good, corrupts the young.

Italy, 172BC. In the first confrontation between Rome and the Macedonian king, Perseus, the Romans land at Epirus. Perseus has restored to power the pro-Macedonian factions in Greek cities. He is in a strong position but too hesitant. Some of his allies move over to the Roman camp.

Rome, 169BC. The poet Quintus Ennius, who was born at Rudiae in Calabria in 239BC, is dead. Ennius served with the Roman army in Sardinia and was brought from there to Rome in 204BC by Cato the Elder. Ennius will be best remembered for his historical epic poem *Annales*, in which he introduced the hexameter into Latin literature.

Macedonia, 168BC. Macedonia surrenders to the Romans after its defeat at the battle of Pydna, which saw 20,000 Macedonians dead. Perseus attempts to flee but, abandoned on all sides, ends up surrendering to Aemilius Paullus, the consul who led the Roman legions into battle. Perseus takes part in the general's triumphal march in Rome – as a prisoner. The empire of Alexander the Great has finally disintegrated.

Judaea, 167BC. Antiochus IV, the Seleucid king of Syria, dedicates the Temple of Jerusalem to the Olympian Zeus.

Delos, 167BC. The Romans declare Delos a free port.

Rome, 167BC. Direct taxation of Roman citizens is abolished.

Greece, 167BC. The Romans restore order to Greece. The pro-Macedonians are hunted down remorselessly. Exiles, summary executions, forced residence in Italy: every course is pursued to eliminate the slightest opposition.

North Africa, 167BC. Masinissa, king of Numidia, takes possession of the emporia of Syrtis on the coasts of Tripolitania and Cyrenaica, at Roman expense.

Italy, 166BC. Perseus, former king of Macedonia, dies in captivity at Alba Fucens in central Italy.

Judaea, 165BC. Judas Maccabaeus enters Jerusalem, purifies the temple and re-establishes Judaism. This is the outcome of his rebellion against the Hellenisation of the country and the prohibition of Judaism promulgated by Antiochus IV.

Syria, 162BC. Demetrius, son of Seleucus IV – who succeeded Antiochus III to the Seleucid throne but was later murdered – escapes from captivity in Rome and regains control of his kingdom. To do so, he has to oust his cousin, Antiochus V, who took power last year.

Booming city grows quickly in Mexico

A mask made of clay from Teotihuacan in Mexico, which shows the sort of facial adornment worn by the nobility: a nose pendant and ear spools.

Mexico, 170BC

The largest and most populous city in the Americas is growing quickly in Teotihuacan, a city of 5-10,000 inhabitants. Nor is it the only city in Mexico to be prospering. In Cholula and Remojadas, too, new civilisations flourish.

Nowhere is this more apparent than in Teotihuacan, a city covering three and a half square miles whose wealth is based on making knives and tools from the hard volcanic rock, obsidian.

The city is cut in two by one grand avenue leading to the imposing pyramids of the sun and moon. The avenue is lined with lesser pyramids and palaces where the ruling caste of priests lives. The palaces are built around courtyards, with walls of stone bright

A decorated pot from Teotihuacan.

with murals. The vast wallpaintings depict jaguars as priests and other mythical beings, and priests reciting sacred texts.

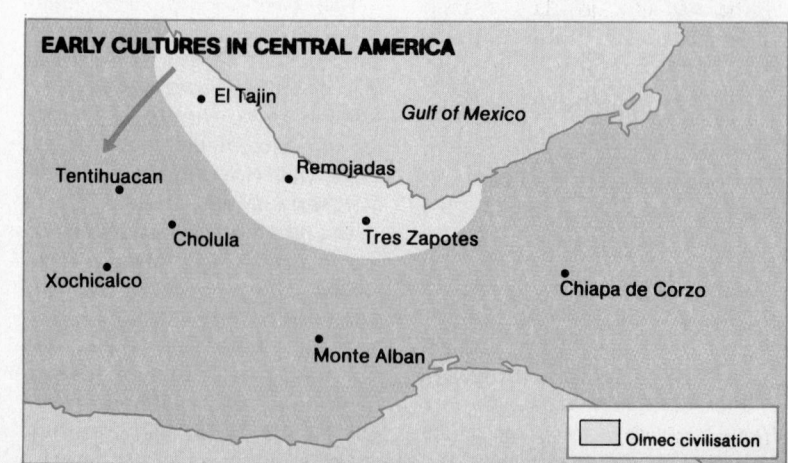

EARLY CULTURES IN CENTRAL AMERICA

- El Tajin
- Gulf of Mexico
- Tentihuacan
- Remojadas
- Cholula
- Tres Zapotes
- Xochicalco
- Chiapa de Corzo
- Monte Alban

Olmec civilisation

Indian emperor killed

A fresco from the porch of a cave at Ajanta, India, 200BC-900AD.

India, 185BC
Brihadratha, last of the Mauryan emperors, has been assassinated by his commander-in-chief, Pushyamitra, at a military review. The assassin has founded a new imperial line, the Shunga dynasty.

Mauryan power has been in decline for half a century since the death of Asoka, the first Indian monarch to be converted to Buddhism. The seeds of that decline can be found in Asoka's own enlightened policies. His concentration of power created an administration too brittle and distant to adapt to changing circumstances. His welfare state, based on the teachings of the Buddha, impoverished the treasury, while war with the Greek kingdom of Bactria has lost the Punjab. Brihadratha's death thus seemed inevitable – the logical conclusion of the decline.

Jewish guerrillas beat Syrian overlords

Judaea, 165BC
The Jews in Judaea have rebelled against their Syrian rulers and have successfully rebuffed attempts to turn their holy city, Jerusalem, into a Greek colony. Led by Judas Maccabaeus, a priest of the house of Hashmon, Jewish partisans have defeated a large Syrian army under generals Gorgias and Nicenor and rejected all efforts to dedicate their Temple to the Olympian Zeus and suppress the worship of Jehovah.

Maccabaeus, whose name in Hebrew means "the Hammerer", is one of the five sons of the priest Mattathias, who has been a major opponent of the Syrian occupiers since 169BC when King Antiochus sacked the Temple and began his attempt, spear-headed by the high priest Jason, to impose Hellenism on the Jews. Antiochus showed himself utterly intolerant of Jewish tradition. After plundering the Temple of its treasures and, in 167BC, installing a garrison in Jerusalem, he systematically desecrated the holy places.

Prostitutes have set up shop within the Temple precincts, a pig has been sacrificed on the altar, and Jews throughout the country have suffered wholesale persecution.

The Syrian king Antiochus, notorious for his persecution of the Jews.

Urged on by his father to resist the king, Maccabaeus and a few companions began living as guerrillas in a mountain hideout, and gradually built up an army of some 6,000 partisans. Now, after a two-year campaign, against which Antiochus has found himself increasingly powerless, the partisans have won. The Syrians remain in power, but Maccabaeus has entered Jerusalem in triumph and has promised to restore the Temple soon.

Delos becomes the hub of Aegean trade

Delos, 166BC
Boom times have come to Delos, the smallest and most central of the Cyclades islands, now that Rome has declared it a free port. This tiny city-state of the Aegean is now the pivot of east-west Mediterranean trade and has a cosmopolitan population.

The island's major claim to fame is founded on the myth that it is the place where Leto gave birth to the divine twins Apollo and Artemis. Having become the site of a great panhellenic shrine, and a place of pilgrimage, it was for long under the direct control of Athens. But this ended when Athens lost her sea power.

For the last 150 years Delos has been administered by local officials, who have promoted it as a centre of the corn trade. This in turn has attracted a foreign colony, including financial firms. Slaves have also become one of the chief commodities of exchange. Rome's decision to hand back Delos to Athens and declare it a free port has substantially boosted the island's economic links with both Asia Minor and the far western Mediterranean. It has been accompanied by a new influx of seamen and merchants.

The island's good fortune is at the expense of Rhodes, Rome's long-time ally in the Hellenistic world, which has also been a formidable trading state. However, four years ago the Rhodians upset the Roman senate and tried to negotiate a peace between Rome and Perseus of Macedonia. With the war ending in a Roman victory the Rhodians were stripped of their territories in Asia Minor.

An even worse punishment was to have Delos declared a free port. This decision is likely to mean Rhodes losing its position as a major trading nation in the region.

Temples of Pergamum now rival Athens

Pergamum, 160BC
Pergamum (*Asia Minor*), under the Hellenistic King Eumenes II, is reaching levels of artistic magnificence that, in some cases, not even Athens can match. Among the theatres, palaces, temples and libraries of the acropolis is its greatest glory, the great altar of Zeus.

This enormous, almost square building is decorated with more than 425 feet of bas-relief frieze, the work of many artists, under the direction of Menecrates of Rhodes.

In honour of Zeus and Athena, patron deities of Pergamum, it commemorates victory over the Gauls by depicting the Olympian gods triumphing over giants representing the forces of barbarism.

Reconstruction of the great altar of Zeus, in the city of Pergamum.

Asia Minor, 160BC. The decline of Ptolemaic power in Egypt has encouraged the rise of a new cultural centre to compete with Alexandria: Pergamum, capital of the Attalid dynasty. The library in Pergamum, however, has difficulty in obtaining books, for they have almost all been bought by its Egyptian rival. The fact that royal representatives have been paying for books in gold has given birth to a thriving industry of forgeries.

Greece, 159BC. The Roman dramatist Terence dies on a journey to Greece. He wrote his first comedy, *Andria*, only seven years ago, since when he has produced about a play a year. While his work is highly derivative – based directly on the original Greek of Menander – Terence is distinguished for the purity and elegance of his use of the Latin language.

Athens, 155BC. Attalus II, who succeeded his brother Eumenes II as king of Pergamum in 160BC, has a portico built on the *agora* (marketplace), the ancestral arena of Athenian democracy.

Rome, 155BC. Athens sends representatives of its three great schools of philosophy – the Academy, the Stoa Poikile and the Lyceum – on a mission to Rome. Epicureans, who are not in favour with the Roman authorities, are excluded.

Balkans, 155BC. In retaliation for Dalmatian attacks on their allies, the Romans invade Dalmatia on the eastern coast of the Adriatic and destroys the capital, Delminium.

China, 154BC. The king of Wu – whose son and heir has been killed in a quarrel over a game of chess with the imperial heir-apparent – stages a revolt in concert with six other kings against the imperial house. The failure of the revolt marks a new stage in the centralisation of imperial power.

Rome, 153BC. As a result of a rebellion in Spain, the consuls enter office on 1 January, instead of 15 March, establishing 1 January as the beginning of the civil year.

North Africa, 151BC. Masinissa, king of neighbouring Numidia, invades the city of Carthage and achieves a military victory. The Numidian invasion has its roots in the king's desire to annex Carthage – which, despite the harsh peace conditions imposed by Rome after the Second Punic War, is on the road to recovery.

Syria, 150BC. Demetrius, king of Syria, dies in a battle against Alexander Balas, a pretender to the Seleucid throne.

Africa, c.150BC. Immigrant Bantu-speaking farmers from the north have brought the first iron tools to the Zimbabwean plateau. They have settled with Khoisan-speaking herders who are still using stone tools. The distinctive Bambata bowl, with its thin clay body and intricate decoration, is a product of the intermingling of these two cultures.

North Africa, 149BC. Rome takes the decision to intervene in the dispute between Numidia and Carthage, triggering off the Third Punic War.

Rome, 149BC. The tribune Lucius Calpurnius Piso has set up a permanent commission to hear complaints from provincials concerning money exacted by their governors. This commission differs from previous boards of investigation in being always available without the need for special legislation.

Rome, 149BC. Marcus Porcius Cato, who performed his duties so rigorously that he acquired the permanent surname of "Censor", is dead. After visiting Carthage in 153, he made the statement: *"Delenda est Carthago* (Carthage must be destroyed)."

Macedonia, 148BC. Macedonia becomes a Roman province after a royal usurper has been put to flight. Following their defeat of the Macedonians in 168BC, the Romans divided Macedonia into four closely supervised federations. Andriscus, who called himself Philip and said he was the son of Perseus, staked his claim to the throne and sought to form an anti-Roman alliance. When a military victory put Andriscus briefly in control of Macedonia, the Romans were forced to respond vigorously.

North Africa, 146BC. Under the leadership of Scipio Aemilianus, the Romans capture and destroy Carthage after a hard-fought battle with Hasdrubal, bringing the Third Punic War to a conclusion. They then establish the province they call Africa (northern Tunisia).

Mesopotamia, 146BC. Mithridates the Philhellene has laid the basis for a Parthian empire. After defeating the Seleucids to gain control of Media and Babylonia, he went on to add Elam, Persia and parts of Bactria (northern Afghanistan) to his kingdom. The Parthian capital is the city of Ctesiphon-Seleucia on the banks of the Tigris.

Central Asia, c.146BC. A group of Scythian warriors called the Tochari have invaded the Seleucid *satrap* of Bactria. They invaded Sogdiana, the kingdom to the north, several years ago.

Carthage left in ashes

Carthage, 146BC

Carthage is no more. Every building in this city has been flattened, and the ashes of the great citadel are being ploughed into the ground. The 50,000 inhabitants – men, women and children – are being sold into slavery. Carthage, once the brightest jewel in North Africa, has suffered the full brunt of Roman fury, and Rome is now the undisputed ruler of the Mediterranean.

The Roman Senate ordered the sacking and razing of Carthage following a bloody and bitter battle in which a defiant Hasdrubal, the Carthaginian leader, refused to surrender his garrison to Scipio's legions. For six days and six nights the Romans fought from house to house, until the citadel itself capitulated.

Even then fighting continued, with 900 Roman deserters occupying the temple of Aesculapius – knowing the death penalty was certain if they surrendered. They fought on for several days until they set fire to the temple, burning themselves to death. When Hasdrubal brought an olive branch to the Roman leader, Scipio ordered him to sit at his feet. With contempt for her husband's surrender, Hasdrubal's wife threw herself and her children into the flames of the temple.

Rome declared war on its old adversary when Carthage, making a fast recovery from the Second Punic War, was provoked into attacking one of Rome's allies, Masinissa. Cato, the Roman senator, had reported his concern about possible Carthaginian aggression after a visit to Africa.

Despite Scipio's outstanding generalship, the campaign began badly for the Romans. The army was dispirited, lacking experience, and suffered several defeats before Scipio instituted strict discipline and retraining. The move paid off. Scipio's legions captured a strategic fort and began the lengthy blockade of Carthage. A vast mole was built across the harbour to stop supplies arriving by sea. The Carthaginians responded by building a fleet of 50 ships, only to see them smashed by the Roman fleet in a bitter battle. Carthage was doomed.

Gilded bronze armour worn to protect the back, of the style used by the Carthaginians against Rome.

Punic art: a tablet depicting a funeral banquet, c.250BC. Carthage now has good cause to mourn.

A Carthaginian religious carving of a figure performing a cult, c.250BC.

Rome falls captive to style of conquered Greece

Greek plays find new audiences in Italy

Rome, 159BC

For most Romans the patrician Scipio family is best known for its military prowess. But the present Scipio, grandson by adoption of the great Scipio Africanus, is also an admirer of Greek culture and became the patron of the writer Terence, who won great popularity by presenting Greek plays to Latin-speaking audiences in Italy.

Terence, who has just died, was born in North Africa and given a Greek education. Brought to Rome as a slave, he was freed when his talents were discovered. His story is by no means unusual. As Roman power has spread abroad, Greek culture and customs have fed back into almost all aspects of Roman life.

Greek influence goes back many years and is reflected in the many Greek words that have passed into Latin: *pirata*, pirate; *emblema*, ship's ensign; *prora*, prow. Greek deities have also been adopted by the Romans, who send an embassy to consult the Oracle of Apollo at Delphi in times of danger. Now Greek artisans as well as writers are settling in Rome, and Greek architecture is being widely copied. As the poet Horace later said: "Graecia capta ferum captorem cepit" – captive Greece took captive her conquerer.

Bacchus, alias the Greek Dionysus.

Greek art is much admired in Rome: this scene on a vase shows Cheiron and the god Apollo.

Cato, guardian of morality, is dead

Rome, 149BC

Cato the Censor, who campaigned against Greek influence in Roman life, imposed heavy taxes on luxuries and demanded the destruction of the old enemy Carthage, has died aged 85. Of provincial peasant stock, he came to Rome as a young man, fought in the Second Punic War, and held a number of public offices before becoming censor and fiercely defending traditional values in Senate speeches delivered in broad rustic tones.

He wrote several books, in one of which, on agriculture, he advises his son: "Sell off promptly old or sick cattle, old farm stock, old or sick slaves, and any other superfluity."

Later portrait of Cato, who said "Carthage must be destroyed".

Senate acts against "indecent" theatre

A later view of the unfinished theatre being demolished on the orders of the Senate, convinced that it would corrupt public moralty.

Rome, 154BC

Roman senators have delivered a sharp rebuff to the city's censors, Cassius Longinus and Valerius Messala. The two planned to build a permanent theatre of stone, with proper seats, to allow the public to enjoy the seasonal round of games and shows in comfort.

But the consul, Scipio Nasica, got up in the Senate and called for a ban on the building. The senators agreed and ordered that the stone for the building be sold off. They also decreed that no seats should be provided, even in the temporary theatres of wood which are set up for each performance.

The city fathers seem to believe that comfort at the theatre would encourage idleness and thus be harmful to public morals. The two censors must be reflecting ruefully on the frustration of their enterprise, since one of their duties is to supervise public morals.

Stoicism spreads among intellectual elite

Rome, 149BC

Greek academics visiting Rome to lecture on Stoic philosophy are provoking controversy with their views, but they are drawing big audiences. The central feature of Stoicism – that man lives to do his duty, not to pursue pleasure – has a strong appeal for many Romans, particularly when it is joined with the notion of serving one's country.

Inevitably, perhaps, personalities have become involved. When a party of Greek philosophers, including prominent Stoics, visited Rome a few years ago, they were guests of the Scipio family. That angered Cato the Censor, a long-time critic of the Scipios, whom he denounces not only for fostering Greek influence but also for clemency in war. Stoicism, which was developed by Zeno of Citium during lectures in Athens around 300BC, has been adapted to serve the needs of statesmen and soldiers by Panaetius, a Greek philosopher now living in Rome.

Through him, Stoicism has spread widely among the Roman upper classes. Panaetius and his disciples discuss such questions as how a good man would act in circumstances where he faces a conflict of duties. They also believe that the philosopher should try to help people who fall below the lofty ideals espoused by pure Stoics. In other words, sinners should be offered hope of salvation.

The golden age of Chinese thought

The centuries from about 500BC to 200BC were marked by great developments in the history of human thought. At about the beginning of this period Buddhism started to spread in India; Socrates lived in Athens from 469 to 399, and was followed by Plato and Aristotle in the next century. In China, too, there was a great intellectual ferment, which was eventually brought to a forcible end in 213BC, when the first emperor of the Qin dynasty banned philosophical discussion and burnt the books of those thinkers whom he considered dangerous to the state.

The age of the philosophers in China begins with Confucius, the latinised name of Kong Fu Zi (K'ung Fu Tzu), who lived from about 551BC to 479BC. He was the first Chinese thinker to gather disciples around him as a private initiative rather than as a government official training subordinates. The disciples recorded his teachings and passed them on, thus creating the first identifiable philosophical school.

The Confucian "gentleman"

Confucius' teaching was essentially an attempt to save something of value from the decay of the old aristocratic order at the end of the Spring and Autumn period, when warfare between the Chinese feudal states was becoming more and more ruthless. He urged that everybody, of no matter what social origin, could practise the morality of the *jun zi (chun tzu)*, or gentleman. Like the English word, this began with the simple meaning of "aristocrat" and ended by meaning a person who behaves in a decent and moral manner.

Large-scale philosophical debate does not begin until there is more than one school of thought in the field, and in the time of Confucius his opponents were individuals as isolated as he was himself. By around 300BC, however, the situation was entirely different. Chinese society was in an ever more rapid state of change – or decay, as some saw it – and many different groups of thinkers struggled to gain the patronage of rival feudal lords in search of new ways of governing their realms effectively. This was the age when, as the Chinese saying has it "a hundred flowers blossomed and a hundred schools of thought contended". To follow some of the main threads in the debate, we may turn to a contemporary witness and follower of Confucius, Mencius.

Mencius is the latinised name of Meng Ke (Meng K'o), who lived from about 372BC to 289BC. Whereas the disciples of Confucius gave us only short notes of the master's sayings, Mencius recorded his ideas in a fairly long book which is still extant. He developed and expanded Confucius' social and political ideas, and expounded them in vigorous debate both in private and at the courts of various feudal rulers. When asked why he devoted so much energy to his task, he said that he was concerned because China was full of "the words of Yang and Mo", and he felt that they were endangering the true doctrine of the ancient sages.

A new moral basis

We know more about Mo than we do about Yang. His full name was Mo Di (Mo Ti), although following the same pattern as other philosophers he was frequently known as Mo Zi (Mo Tzu) – Master Mo. He lived from about 479BC to 381BC, so that he was born about the time of Confucius' death. Whereas Confucius had tried to rescue something from the wreckage of the old feudal order, Mo Zi believed that a new basis for morality had to be found. His idea was that actions were to be judged by whether or not they produced useful results for people in general. Thus the old customs of elaborate funerals, long mourning and expensive religious rituals and musical performances were all to be discarded. The greatest waste of resources for no good purpose was, of course, warfare, and the followers of Mo Zi (known as Mohists) were staunch anti-militarists. They even went so far as to organise themselves into groups of specialists in defensive warfare, who would hire out their services to anybody who suffered aggression. They also undertook rigorous training in techniques of logical debate in order to beat opponents from other schools of thought. Lest all this should sound too modern, we must remember that a central plank in Mo Zi's platform was that people should be encouraged to believe in the existence of ghosts and spirits, since this might frighten them into moral behaviour.

Both Confucians and Mohists believed that one had to be prepared to face death if necessary in the cause of right, and in the ruthless world of Warring States China this was often more than a theoretical possibility. Mencius' other opponent, the somewhat shadowy Yang mentioned above, took a very different view. Yang Zhu (Yang Chu) may have lived around 375BC, and his position was that, for any individual, the highest possible goal was his personal survival in a difficult world. His opponents accused him of saying that he would not pull out a single hair from his leg even if it would benefit the whole Chinese empire if he did so. Yang's real position seems to have been rather less obsessively selfish than this. He was probably saying that even if he was offered the imperial throne at the cost of pulling out a hair he would not do it, the point being that great political power is a risky and possibly fatal possession, and that people with a care for their own safety should be very cautious in taking it on.

The way to higher truth

At some time around 300BC two books were written which were to have great influence on the subsequent history of Chinese thought. Both of them can be seen to some extent as tracing back their origins to the "survivalist" thinking of Yang Zhu, although in later times they were considered as belonging to a separate school known as Daoism (Taoism). The word *dao*, which means way or path is used by many Chinese philosophical schools to refer to their particular doctrine. For Daoists, the Way was the essentially unknowable reality beneath the surface of things. It could not be understood by logical debate, or pinned down by a precise description, so Daoist writers resorted to paradox or poetic language in an attempt to convey something of its significance. Zhuang Zi (Chuang Tzu) lived from about 369BC to 286BC, and may well have written major parts of the book which bears his name today. He stressed the relativity of all judgements of what was desirable or undesirable, and urged that right decisions could not be made by any attempt to observe rigid rules of morality or proper behaviour. Zhuang Zi and his disciples frequently told stories in which the revered figure of Confucius was made fun of, or even made the spokesman for Daoist doctrines. The other basic work of the Daoists comes from about the same time as Zhuang Zi. It has two titles; the first is *Lao Zi (Lao Tzu)*, which could mean either Master Lao or The Old Master. The other is *Dao De Jing (Tao Te Ching)* – The Way and its power. By about 100BC a legend was current to the effect that the book had been written by an actual person called Lao Zi, who was supposed to be an older contemporary of Confucius. There is no reliable evidence for this, and it is far more likely that the book was compiled by an anonymous group over a fairly lengthy period. The book is short, and often obscure and aphoristic, but the poetic power of its attempts to convey what is meant by the Dao have inspired many translations, and it is probably the most widely read and influential philosophical work outside China today.

Figures from Chinese philosophy. Left: a bronze figure of Lao Zi, the mythical founder of Daoism (Taoism), riding on a water buffalo, from the Ming dynasty in the 17th century. Upper left: a statue of Confucius, Kong Fu Zi, who lived from about 551 to 479BC; he was the first Chinese thinker to establish a philosophical school by educating a group of disciples who went on to spread his teachings themselves. Upper right: a silk painting of Confucius with his disciples; he was trying to save something of worth from the decay of the old aristocratic order, and believed that everyone should practice the morality of the gentleman. Above: a painting with Wen Ch'ang the Chinese god of literature on the left, and, again, Lao Zi on his water buffalo; he was popularly believed to be the author of one of the first Daoist texts, though these are probably the work of a group of writers.

Syria, 145BC. Alexander Balas, the pretender to the Seleucid throne, is killed by Demetrius II, who himself ascends the throne.

Judaea, 142BC. The Jews liberate Jerusalem and make it their capital.

Spain, 140BC. The Roman general Fabius has been defeated by a strong rebel force led by Viriathus. Originally a Lusitanian shepherd, Viriathus has been waging a successful campaign against the Romans for seven years. He has now secured a favourable peace with Rome and been recognised as an ally.

China, 136BC. Confucianism becomes the state religion. Emperor Wudi changes the system of officially appointed academicians, of whom there were traditionally 72, establishing chairs for only the five main classical traditions.

Asia Minor, 133BC. Attalus III Philometor, last sovereign of the Attalid dynasty in Pergamum, has a nasty surprise in store for his subjects after his death. In his will he bequeaths Pergamum to Rome. It is rumoured that his motive may have been to create an insurance against social revolution while he survived.

Spain, 133BC. The Romans capture Numantia, in central northern Spain, after a long siege. This marks a decisive turning point in the guerrilla war which they have been fighting in the mountains since the creation of two Roman provinces in Spain in 197BC. It also puts an end, for the time being, to revolts such as that led by Viriathus, provoked by hardening repression.

Rome, 133BC. After his election as tribune, Tiberius Sempronius Gracchus attempts to introduce reforms to alleviate the plight of the thousands of Roman citizens living in hopeless poverty.

Asia Minor, 131BC. The Romans send an army to quell the unrest in Pergamum caused by the will of Attalus III. Aristonicus, natural son of the former king, Eumenes II, has seized the kingdom at the head of an army of slaves.

India, c.130BC. The reign of Menander, the great Indo-Greek king, is at an end. He came to power c.155BC and led an expedition into the Ganges valley, reaching Pataliputra (Patna). Menander will be remembered for his conversion to Buddhism by a scholar-priest by the name of Nagasena.

Asia Minor, 130BC. The Roman consul Publius Licinius Crassus, a supporter of Tiberius Gracchus, is captured and executed by allies of the pretender Aristonicus.

Asia Minor, 129BC. The Romans regain control of the situation in Pergamum. The pretender Aristonicus is taken prisoner and beheaded in Rome. The Roman province of Asia – comprising Mysia, Aeolis, Lydia, Ionia, Caria, the islands along the coast and the Troad (a mountainous region in the north-east) – is created.

China, 128BC. The Chinese have constructed a magnificent canal, over 100 miles long, linking the Han capital of Changan with the Yellow river.

Parthia, 127BC. Phraates II, king of Parthia, is killed in a battle with the Tochari, who proceed to devastate his kingdom. Phraates' greatest achievement was his defeat of the Seleucid king Antiochus VII in Media, which excluded the Seleucids from the lands east of the Euphrates.

China, 126BC. Zhang Qian returns from intrepid feats of exploration in central Asia. His initiative leads to the establishment of the "Silk Roads" to central Asia, and China's knowledge of the world now extends to the Mediterranean.

India, c.125BC. A Scythian tribe known as the Sakas invades the Punjab from Baluchistan and Sind.

Italy, 125BC. Fregellae, a Latin colony in central Italy which remained loyal to Rome against Pyrrhus and Hannibal, has now revolted against it. The Roman general Gaius Opimius has succeeded in suppressing the rebellion, but so brutally that Fregellae now lies in ruins.

Gaul, 123BC. The Romans put an end to a series of attacks by the Celto-Ligurian tribe known as the Salluvii on the people of Massilia (Marseilles). This expedition brings Rome's military campaigns in Gaul to a successful conclusion.

Mediterranean, 123BC. The Balearic islands are conquered by the Romans.

Rome, 121BC. The tribune Caius Sempronius Gracchus, brother of Tiberius, is killed by a slave after a riot in the Forum in which 3,000 of his supporters died. They were protesting about the Senate's decision to repeal laws enacted by Gracchus, in the tradition of his brother, to lighten the burden of the poor.

Rome, 120BC. Lucius Calpurnius Piso, who has recently been appointed censor, has completed seven books of *Annales*, which cover the history of Rome from its origins to recent times. Piso rationalises Roman legends and sets the ancient virtues against contemporary vices.

Corinth is destroyed as Rome quashes Greek revolt and plunders its riches

Greek warriors, c.150BC. Their bravery has been outmatched by Rome.

Corinth, 146BC

Rome's patience with her Greek subordinates came to a savage end today with the sacking and destruction of Corinth. The city's male inhabitants have been slaughtered; its women, children and slaves sold; and its masterpieces removed and taken to Rome.

This drastic action followed years of war between states, in addition to political unrest, in Greece, which had been allowed to manage its own internal affairs until a pretender tried to seize the Macedonian throne. Rome crushed this uprising, reducing Greece to provincial status. Even so, the Achaean League continued to agitate against the detention of 1,000 deported prisoners and fanned the flames of revolt in Greece. Believing that Rome was fully occupied in Africa and Spain, the Achaeans opposed Roman orders to free Sparta, Corinth and Argos.

It was when anti-Roman demonstrations began in Corinth that Rome acted. A Roman army led by Metellus was held back by Corinthian forces, but four legions led by Mummius routed the defenders at the Isthmus and began the systematic destruction of the city.

Slaves crucified after uprising in Sicily

Sicily, 132BC

Twenty thousand slaves will be hanged from crosses in this province under a savage reign of terror by Consul General Rupilius. No one defies Rome. After three years of guerrilla warfare, the slaves' rebellion has been been put down. The rebel leader Eunus ("King Antiochus") from Syria has died in captivity. He led the first revolt, which turned into an orgy of rape, murder and looting. Over 70,000 slaves are said to have taken part.

Rome's huge population of slaves includes educated Greek prisoners of war and foreigners seized by pirates for sale to Rome. Some are well treated and become Roman citizens, but many are tortured for sadistic pleasure or die through overwork by cruel slave-owners.

The lessons of this rebellion are clear. With so many hostile slaves harvested from the battlefields of the Second Punic War, Rome's labour intensive estates are growing bigger, more cost effective and profitable – but at a potential price.

A common saying in Rome goes: "Every slave we own is an enemy we harbour."

Land reformers killed

Rome, 133BC

A young tribune, the leader of a people's movement for land reform, was assassinated with 300 of his followers today after a successful attempt by the Senate to block a critical election. Their bodies were thrown into the Tiber.

Although an aristocrat by birth, Tiberius Gracchus was a plebeian tribune, a powerful speaker on behalf of hundreds of small farmers, many of whom have been forced to sell out because of an agricultural recession. Much of this fallow land has been seized by the wealthy classes, who have also taken possession of the *agar publicus* – common land or people's property.

Gracchus and the *populares*, the "People's party", had demanded that this land should be redistributed among the poor in lots of 18.5 acres and that ownership of common land be restricted to 308 acres.

Although the need for land reform has long been admitted, and Gracchus's "Land Bill" was heavily backed by the assembly of the people, the Senate blocked attempts to change the situation. Much of the land had been mortgaged, senators argued, and more had been pledged as dowries for daughters of the rich.

Despite their opposition, a land commission was established. Gracchus was fighting for more finance for its work when he was murdered after a march on the Capitol.

Five thousand dead is price of "Triumph"

Part of a Roman triumphal arch showing the figure of winged victory.

Rome, c.129BC

For the Roman victor the spoils – and the *Triumph*. No country in the world honours its successful generals like Rome. The *Triumph* is the pinnacle of every officer's ambition. To achieve it, his army must have killed at least 5,000 men in battle.

On the morning of the celebration, the general will parade his troops and present them with their share of the spoils. Then he will march at the head of his army with magistrates, senators, musicians, slaves and eminent captives along a time-honoured route through the Forum to the Temple of Jupiter where sacrifices take place. Like the statue of Jupiter, his face will be painted red, he will be dressed in lavish gold and purple robes, and paintings of his achievements will be carried aloft together with booty he has brought back to Rome.

The victor is "god for the day" – although he is accompanied by a slave who whispers to him continually: "Remember thou art mortal." A bell and a whip are also tied to the chariot as reminders that Rome can still punish him.

At the height of the celebration, the loser – a defeated enemy general – is put to death in a prison cell below the Capitol.

Southern Gaul falls to the power of Rome

A Celtic warrior fighting a Roman. The Gauls are Rome's latest victims.

Provence, 123BC

Rome has occupied southern Gaul and its legions are garrisoned throughout the province. Gaul was taken by an army led by the consul Domitius Ahenobarbus who, like Hannibal, used elephants to cross the river Rhone. Strong resistance by Gallic tribesmen was put down by another army led by Quintus Fabius Maximus who returned to Rome to receive a *Triumph* – Rome's greatest honour.

Rome's latest conquest followed a now traditional pattern. A plea for help was received from Massilia (Marseilles), a Greek ally which was threatened by Gallic invaders. The plea was opportune. Rome was anxious for good communications with its legions in Spain. Its merchants were keen on control of a region to which it has been selling wines and ceramics; and the Senate, under constant pressure for land reform, sees the fertile lands of southern Gaul as a ideal place to settle farmers and thus satisfy the *populares*' demands which led to riots ten years ago.

Portraits give realistic face to Greek art

The Greek World, 200-100BC

A realism which had its origins 200 years ago now holds sway in Greek sculpture. It was in response to the diversity of the Hellenistic world, in which Greeks lived alongside many different races, that artists chose to represent the many facets of humanity rather than the idealised forms of the Greek classical period.

There are still imaginary effigies of long dead heroes, like Homer, but more recent figures, like Plato, are accurately represented. Family portraits are realistic, as are those of shepherdesses, fishermen, sleeping children and even drunken people.

Bronze head of Aphrodite c.100BC: even a goddess has a human face in the new realistic sculpture.

China, 119BC. The Chinese, led by the "Martial Emperor" Wudi, have been waging successful but costly wars in central Asia, expanding their territories considerably. The Han empire now replenishes its coffers by turning the salt and iron industries into state monopolies and levying taxes on boats and carts.

China, 119BC. The Xiongnu, long-standing enemies of the Chinese who formed the first Turkish empire in Mongolia a century ago, have been driven north of the Gobi desert by Huo Qubing, a 20-year-old hero.

North Africa, 118BC. On the death of the king of Numidia, his adoptive father, Jugurtha acts against his two brothers, who are joint heirs with him to the Numidian throne. He has one murdered and attacks the other, Adherbal, forcing him to flee to Rome.

Gaul, 118BC. A new Roman province, Gallia Narbonensis (Provence), is created between the Maritime Alps and the Pyrenees. The Romans begin building roads here to link Italy with Spain. Massilia (Marseilles) is made responsible for maintaining a coast road that runs from the Alps to the Rhone.

Balkans, 117BC. The province of Dalmatia on the east coast of the Adriatic is once again under attack from Rome.

Egypt, 116BC. Against her will, Cleopatra III rules Egypt jointly with her son, Ptolemy VIII Soter II. Ptolemy's younger brother, Alexander, governor of Cyprus, is a contender for the throne.

Asia, 115BC. The Parthians, whose ancestors were no more than tribesmen from the east of the Caspian Sea, have established themselves as rulers of Bactria (northern Afghanistan), Persia and Mesopotamia.

Gaul, 113BC. The Cimbri, the Teutons and the Ambrones, Celtic and Germanic tribes which have migrated to the eastern Alps, are growing restless and posing an increasing threat to Rome.

North Africa, 112BC. Jugurtha, who has been given control of western Numidia by Rome, again attacks Adherbal, his brother and rival for the Numidian throne. Despite Roman opposition, Jugurtha besieges Adherbal in Cirta, captures the city and kills his brother.

China, 110BC. China has conquered the kingdoms of Yue (Fukien) and Nanyue (Canton and North Vietnam). All the best lands in their known world now belong to the Chinese.

China, 108BC. The Chinese are pursuing a ruthless policy of expansion. They have now taken Zhaoxian, a border kingdom in the Korean peninsula.

Egypt, 108BC. Alexander, governor of Cyprus, expels his brother, Ptolemy VIII, from the Egyptian throne and takes his place as Ptolemy IX Alexander.

Gaul, 105BC. The Cimbri, Teutons and Ambrones win a great victory over the Romans at Arausio (Orange) and enter Spain, from where they are swiftly expelled by the Celtiberians.

Sicily, 103BC. An army of 14,000 Romans lands in Sicily to quell a revolt of slaves.

Gaul, 102BC. The Roman general Marius inflicts a decisive defeat on the Teutons and Cimbri at Aquae Sextiae (Aix-en-Provence).

Italy, 102BC. Gaius Lucilius, inventor of a new literary form – satire – dies in Naples. An outstanding feature of Lucilius' work, which comprises 30 books written in hexameters and gives an illuminating critical insight into his times, is his extensive use of autobiography.

Asia Minor, 101BC. Mithridates, king of Pontus (on the Black Sea coast), is pursuing an expansionist policy in the region. To protect both the province of Asia and seaborne trade in the Aegean, the Romans create a new province, Cilicia, in southern Asia Minor.

Sicily, 101BC. The Roman consul Manius Aquillius crushes the second slave revolt on the island, personally killing the rebel leader.

Italy, 101BC. The Germanic tribe known as the Cimbri, who have travelled round the Alps and entered Italy from the north-east, is destroyed by the Romans.

China, 101BC. The Chinese have conquered yet more lands. The capture by Li Guang-li and his large army of the states of the Tarim basin and Ferghana makes China the master of most of central Asia.

Rome, 100BC. Saturnius and Glaucia, this year's plebeian tribune and praetor, are determined to continue the policy of the Gracchi. Their proposal to introduce new social laws – above all, a reduction in the price of corn for the poorest people – provokes resistance by the nobles, and civil strife breaks out.

South Africa, c.100BC. Khoisan herding culture has now spread, together with the speaking of northern Kalahari Khoisan languages, as far as the south coast of the continent.

African revolt sparks crisis in Senate

A later view of Bocchus, the king of Numidia, with whom Jugurtha took refuge after his defeat, handing the rebel over to the Romans.

Numidia, North Africa, 105BC
The repercussions of a raid on the market centre in a small town here are still being felt in distant Rome. It began as a limited local problem when Jugurtha, the late king's adopted son, organised a coup, seized Cirta and massacred the merchants. Some of these were Roman *equites* (knights) who – like many other Romans – had taken advantage of Rome's victory over Carthage to move in.

To the fury of other nobles in North Africa, the Senate in Rome quavered when punitive action was demanded against Jugurtha. Four senators were impeached for graft and the people's assembly nominated the consul, Gaius Marius, to take over command in Numidia. The ambitious Marius was in conflict with other generals at the time, but won command. War was declared on Jugurtha, and Marius' army systematically destroyed the rebel fortresses until Jugurtha was beaten.

The episode has given Marius star status but, more seriously, has dented senatorial credibility and set the precedent of public disagreement in Rome's ruling elite about running a foreign war.

Polybius, historian between two worlds

Rome, 120BC
Polybius, the Greek historian and diplomat whose life's achievement was the monumental *Histories* recording the rise of Rome, has died aged 82, after a fall from his horse.

He achieved the rare distinction of spanning two cultures, feted both by Roman society and by his fellow Achaeans for the adroit way he reconstructed their political system after Achaea's crushing defeat by Rome in 146BC. A member of a wealthy Achaean family, he first set foot in Rome 22 years ago. A chance meeting with the young Scipio, a future general, blossomed into a lifelong friendship that led to Polybius travelling throughout the empire as Scipio's mentor.

Polybius, the historian, soldier and diplomat, celebrated by Greeks and Romans (18th century portrait).

General announces Roman army will recruit the poor

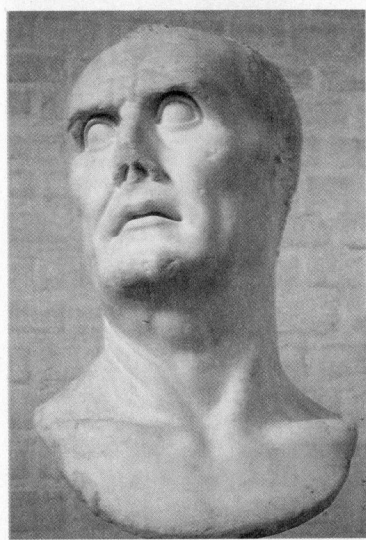

The reforming general Gaius Marius.

Rome, 107BC

The defence review announced by General Gaius Marius creates a new model army offering military training to working-class Romans for the first time. Traditionally, only the five wealthiest classes in the census were accepted for war service and then only while hostilities continued. The idea of allowing the poor to join up has been debated for over a century. Marius' great African campaign across sea, desert and mountain forced him to sign up men without observing the niceties.

Difficulties in recruiting soldiers have finally forced this major reform, and it is thought that any crises such as invasions could make it permanent. But critics believe that class loyalty, the army's bonding agent, is being corroded. Men who like soldiering as a way of life rather than as a duty to country might be more professional fighters but – without pension or private income – loyal to whom? Pessimists suggest that they will be loyal at a price to generals, who will thereby enjoy political power. Rome has no standing army, but there are already more likely lads to volunteer than places available.

For those who do join up, Marius proposes membership of bigger formations of 6,000 men. They will also be licensed to carry silver standards.

China's greatest traveller has died

China, 100BC

Zhang Qian, the "Great Traveller" of China, has died, little more than a year after his triumphant return from the last of his expeditions to the unknown lands outside China. His travels have changed this vast country's relations with the rest of the world for ever.

A strong, resourceful man, he faced great dangers to open up trade and diplomacy with India and Parthia and as far west as Syria. He made contact with the Hellenistic world and brought the grapevine and alfalfa to China.

His adventures started in 138BC when he volunteered to pass through the land of China's enemies, the nomadic Xiongnu (Huns), to make an alliance with the Yuezhi.

He was captured almost immediately and taken to the Great Khan who treated him kindly and gave him a wife, but kept him prisoner for ten years. Zhang Qian then escaped with his wife and one ser-

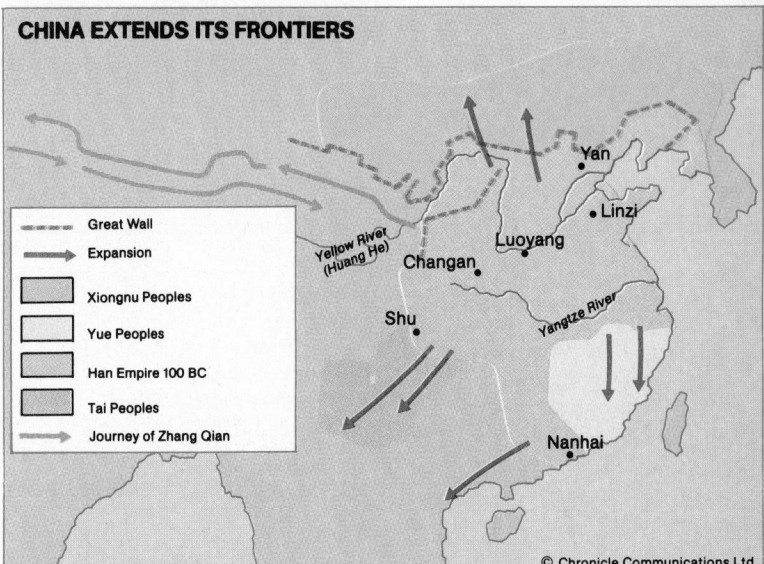

vant, but instead of fleeing to safety he continued his journey, spending a year in Bactria (Afghanistan), where he found that smugglers had established a route from China. On his journey home he again fell into the hands of the Xiongnu, but escaped after a year in captivity.

The emperor made him Marquis of Bowang and, after the Xiongnu had been defeated, he led another expedition with 300 men and gifts of gold and silk to dazzle the west with China's riches.

The making of a citizen: how Rome educates sons for civic duty

Children in a religious procession.

Rome, c.100BC

The family is the foundation on which Roman society rests. It is in the family's bosom that children grow up and are educated.

A son is an absolute necessity for the perpetuation of the family line, so a father can always adopt a son

A relief of children playing, from a Roman sarcophagus.

if he has none of his own. A few days after the birth of a child it is given a first name, along with a small bag of lucky charms. A boy remains for the first seven years with his mother, who may also suckle the children of the family slaves, so that they feel brotherly love for the boy.

For his proper education, the boy comes under the care of his father, the *paterfamilias*, who should inculcate in him a sense of piety, civic duty and love of his native land. In

due course he might accompany his father into the senate, and take part in feasts, singing and serving at table.

At the age of 16 the young man sets aside his *toga praetexta*, the uniform of childhood, and dons the *toga virilis*, symbol of the citizen. Shortly afterwards, he will leave his family to do military service.

Girls remain under the care of their mothers until they are married, spinning wool and doing housework.

Rome, 100BC. The Senate outlaws the popular leaders Saturninus and Glaucia. Before they can be arrested, however, the tribune and praetor are murdered.

North Africa, 98BC. Ptolemy Apion, illegitimate son of Ptolemy VII Euergetes of Egypt, bequeaths Cyrenaica, over which he has ruled since his father's death, to Rome.

China, 97BC. Despite having been castrated by the emperor for sponsoring the cause of a disgraced general, Sima Qian completes an historical record known as the *Shiji*. His work, which is half a million words long, establishes a new form of historical writing.

Rome, 91BC. Livius Drusus, tribune of the people, has been assassinated. Although a rich aristocrat by birth, Drusus renewed some of the most liberal measures of the Gracchi and advocated the claims of the Italians to Roman citizenship. The day before his death, the Senate withdrew its support from the reformer and revoked all of his laws.

Rome, 90BC. The consul Lucius Julius Caesar passes the *Lex Iulia*, offering basic citizenship to the Italian allies.

Rome, 89BC. The tribune Marcus Plautius implements the *Lex Plautia Papiria*. The new law supplements the *Lex Iulia* of last year and gives satisfaction to many of the Italians seeking Roman citizenship. It grants the freedom of the city of Rome to everyone whose name is entered in the praetor's register.

Rome, 88BC. As the Social War approaches its end, Lucius Cornelius Sulla is elected consul. He is given the responsibility of promoting internal recovery and, above all, of standing up to the threat from Mithridates. Sulla reacts to attempts by the general Marius to block his command against Mithridates by marching on Rome with an army and taking the city by force. Marius is forced to flee.

Asia Minor, 88BC. Mithridates, the ambitious king of Pontus (on the Black Sea), routs Nicomedes of Bithynia, in north-west Asia Minor. He then invades the Roman province of Asia and massacres 80,000 Romans and Italians.

Delos, 88BC. Mithridates' fleet lays siege to Delos and his troops kill 20,000 of the island's inhabitants.

Egypt, 88BC. Ptolemy IX, who ousted his brother, Ptolemy VIII, from the Egyptian throne 20 years ago, is killed by the people of Alexandria, and the former king is restored to power.

Greece, 87BC. Prepared to take on Mithridates, who is now in control of much of Greece, Sulla disembarks at Epirus with a large army. He swiftly gains control of the European part of Greece, with the exception of Athens and the port of Piraeus, to which he lays siege.

China, 87BC. The "Martial Emperor" Wudi is dead. His long and successful reign began in 140BC and has been marked by numerous foreign conquests and by the establishment of Confucian scholarship as a control over civil administration.

Rome, 87BC. Lucius Cornelius Cinna, who distinguished himself in the field during the Social War, is elected consul after swearing to Sulla not to disturb the constitution. Soon after taking office, however, he impeaches Sulla and agitates for the recall of Marius.

Rome, 87BC. Octavius, Cinna's colleague as consul and a supporter of Sulla, attacks Cinna and his followers, whom he either kills or drives out of Rome. He then has Cinna deposed and replaced.

Athens, 86BC. The Athenians, made hungry by a long siege and blockade of their city, and following a breach of the city wall of Piraeus, surrender unconditionally to Sulla. After allowing the Roman troops to loot and pillage Athens, Sulla magnanimously gives the city back its freedom.

Rome, 86BC. Marius and Cinna march against Rome and declare themselves consuls after a brutal massacre of aristocrats. A fortnight later Marius dies of natural causes.

Sahara, c.86BC. With their Berber allies, the Garamantes, the Romans make an expedition from Carthage into the Sahara. Apparently confusing the Air massif with "Agisymba" (Abyssinia), they try to reach Ethiopia by a roundabout route, avoiding the Nile, throught the central Saharan massifs.

Asia Minor, 85BC. Mithridates makes peace with the Romans, on Sulla's terms, at Dardanus, giving up all the territories he has conquered. This follows two defeats of Mithridates' general Archelaus, at Chaereonea and Orchomenos in Boeotia.

Rome, 84BC. The tyrannical consul Cinna, former ally of Marius, is killed in a mutiny.

Rome, 82BC. At the battle of the Colline Gate, Sulla repulses from Rome a large force of Samnites. This is the culmination of a brilliant campaign to subdue his opponents, whom he severely punishes before having himself appointed dictator.

Great general involved in double murder

Marius is carried aloft by his jubilant troops after inflicting a crushing defeat on the Cimbri. By Saverio Altamura (1826-97).

Rome, 100BC

With the complicity of the Roman general Gaius Marius, the praetor Glaucia and the tribune Saturninus have been brutally murdered.

In the past two years, Marius, at the head of Rome's first long-term professional army, has won sensational victories over a Germanic alliance of Cimbri and Teutons, who swept over Gaul annihilating two Roman armies. In a battle at Aquae Sextiae (Aix-en-Provence), the Roman legions slaughtered 200,000 Teutons and took 90,000 prisoners. In a further battle, the combined armies of Marius and Catulus killed 140,000 Cimbri.

The defeats are a remarkable vindication of Marius's policy of enlisting an army from the poor and training it in Africa. The hitherto invincible barbarians from the north had Italy at their mercy until faced with this toughened army – fresh from a campaign in Numidia.

Back in Rome as consul, Marius was faced with a bitter dispute over land reform. Glaucia and Saturninus had stirred up public opinion to the extent that the very fabric of the country was in danger. Although a former tribune himself, Marius played a major part in the killing of the two men, even though it has cost him popularity.

The "Venus de Milo": a statue of Aphrodite, by Alexandros of Antioch, from Melos, a Greek island.

A Gallic prisoner (c.50BC).

Roman citizenship is worth the fight

Italian allies in revolt demand vote

Italy, 91BC

The Roman Senate is meeting in emergency session to tackle what has been described as the most serious military peril since Hannibal's invasion. Armed rebellion has broken out in central and southern Italy and is spreading fast. There are threats of a complete break with Rome. A rebel Senate is planned, and a capital to be called Italica.

The Italians' grievances go back many years, but have been exacerbated by the Roman officials' abuse of their powers. When an enraged mob lynched a Roman official who was visiting Asculum, all hope of a peaceful settlement was lost.

In the past two centuries, as Rome extended its power over the rest of Italy, its policy was *divide et impera*. Each conquered tribe or city became bound to Rome by a separate treaty, so that a network of isolated allies, or *socii*, was created. These allies have long resented the fact that they are denied Roman citizenship. In the Senate, moderates, led by Livius Drusus, proposed to extend the franchise to all

Coin struck by one of the "socii".

Italians. He was denounced as a traitor and assassinated.

To a man the *socii* have risen in revolt – hence "Social Wars", the name given to the uprising. They have fielded some 100,000 men, many of them battle-hardened veterans who have fought alongside Roman legions. They will certainly give the Romans a run for their money. In the face of danger, the Senate has closed ranks, but the gossip in the Forum has it that sooner rather than later the Italians will have to be given the vote.

Some citizens more equal than others

Rome, 88BC

In the aftermath of the Social War, the Roman Senate has had to consider the question of citizenship. Laws have been passed bestowing Roman citizenship on all who wish to receive it. But some citizens are more equal than others. At the top are probably 200,000 Roman men who have the full protection of the law, and the right to vote and hold office. At the bottom are the slaves with no rights whatsoever. In between are non-Romans, often conquered people, who have been given citizenship, but without the right to vote, though they are liable for military service. Roman women have the full protection of the law, but cannot vote or stand for election. Even within the ranks of full citizens there is a hierarchy set by the amount of wealth each group possesses. This derives from Rome's old military organisation: wealthier groups used to provide themselves with more expensive equipment.

Scythian invaders surge south from Asia into India

Gold buckle, c.100BC-100AD.

India, 88BC

Pushed west by the relentless pressure of nomadic tribes from central Asia, Scythian invaders have overrun the Greek kingdom of Bactria and defeated the Parthian army, killing Mithridates II, king of Parthia.

The great movement of peoples began seventy years ago when Hun hordes, blocked from invading China by the Han emperors, turned westwards, driving Yuezhi nomads before them into the lands of the Scythians. Unable to beat the great westward migrations, the Scythians joined them, re-establishing themselves in Bactrian territory on the west bank of the Oxus. They remained here for forty years, until pushed south by further Yuezhi pressure into Parthia.

Two Parthian kings, Phraates II and Artabanus I, died defying the invaders. Now a third is dead, and there is nothing left to stop the Scythians from overrunning all the Indus Valley.

Senate establishes itself as the powerhouse of the republic

Some members of the Senate, guardians of free speech in Rome.

Rome, c.85BC

The Roman Senate is the powerhouse of the Mediterranean. Decisions taken in the Senate House affect every man, woman and child in this vast republic. The Senate controls foreign policy, supervises military operations, fixes the status of conquered territories, and secures the management of the treasury. On the domestic front, it is the Senate which must guarantee order and can therefore decree public safety measures.

Who are these men who rule Rome? The Senate is made up of magistrates and former magistrates and is dominated by the Roman noble families. It consisted originally of 100 members, although this was later increased to 300.

Senators wear the toga and special shoes. They have reserved seats at religious ceremonies and public entertainments. Acting as magistrates they have the power of life and death over their fellow citizens.

Despite the apparently oligarchal nature of the Senate, a careful system of checks and balance has evolved over the years. The senators must answer to the tribunes of the plebs, who have represented the interests of the people for the past 200 years; and they are always aware that 80 elite officials – consuls and military tribunes – are elected annually and, above all, that Rome's victorious army is a powerful force to be reckoned with.

Free speech is unlimited in the Senate of Rome and the law insists its doors must be left open.

Scythian plaque, c.200BC-100AD.

Asia Minor, 81BC. Rome signs a peace treaty with Mithridates ending the second Mithridatic war, which broke out two years ago.

Rome, 81BC. Julius Caesar, the son of a Roman praetor, has angered the dictator Sulla by marrying Cornelia, daughter of Sulla's enemy Cinna. Caesar decides to lie low in Asia.

Egypt, 80BC. No sooner has he succeeded to the Egyptian throne than Ptolemy X Alexander II is killed by the people of Alexandria. His place is taken by Ptolemy XI, illegitimate son of Ptolemy VIII.

Italy, 78BC. After his resignation of the dictatorship last year, Sulla retired to his estate at Puteoli. The dissipated life he led there has now been the death of him.

Rome, 78BC. Marcus Aemilius Lepidus is elected consul for 78BC, in succession to Sulla. He proposes recalling exiles, re-establishing the wheat distribution laws, and restoring to the Italians land which has been confiscated. The Senate approves only the first measure.

Rome, 77BC. Angered by the Senate's refusal to implement his proposed reforms, Lepidus marches on Rome at the head of an Etruscan army, demanding to be elected consul for a second year. His enterprise is halted by the distinguished general Pompey, who has executed several successful campaigns for Sulla and last year supported Lepidus in his election as consul.

Spain, 77BC. Pompey enters Spain and attacks the army of the rebel general, Quintus Sertorius, a former rival of Sulla.

North Africa/Asia Minor, 74BC. Cyrenaica, which was bequeathed to Rome in 98BC, and Bithynia, whose king, Nicomedes III, has recently died, are organised as Roman provinces. Mithridates, king of Pontus, regards these acts as blatant provocation.

Asia Minor, 74BC. Mithridates has invaded the Roman province of Bithynia. The general Lucullus is faced with the task of ejecting him.

China, 74BC. The great general Li Ling dies tragically, a captive among his adversaries. Li Ling's deep penetration into central Asia at great odds ended in his surrender to a nomad confederacy, the Xiongnu, after a heroic feat of arms near Dunhuang in 99BC. The historian Sima Qian paid the price of castration for having extolled Li Ling's exploits.

Asia Minor, 73BC. After being driven back by the Romans, who are occupying his kingdom of Pontus, Mithridates flees to the court of Tigranes in Armenia.

Italy, 73BC. A gladiator from Thrace by the name of Spartacus has seized Mount Vesuvius and set off a revolt, supported by many fugitive slaves. The rebels defeat two Roman armies and devastate southern Italy.

Italy, 72BC. The rebel Spartacus has conquered three more Roman armies to reach Cisalpine Gaul. He is now marching south again.

Spain, 72BC. Quintus Sertorius, who was given control of the province of Spain in 83BC, is murdered by Perperna, a jealous rival, at a banquet. After rebelling against Rome, Sertorius ruled Spain as an independent state with a senate and magistrates. Despite the intervention of Pompey in 77BC, Sertorius used his genius as a strategist to resist the Roman armies.

Rome, 71BC. Pompey returns from Spain and cooperates with Crassus in finishing off the revolt of slaves led by Spartacus. Pompey, after crucifying many surviving fugitives, claims credit for the victory, thereby making an enemy of Crassus.

Rome, 70BC. In the face of a prosecution launched by the orator Marcus Tullius Cicero, Gaius Verres, governor of Sicily, flees to Massilia to avoid trial. Reputed to have plundered and bribed his way to the top, and to have made unscrupulous use of his wealthy connections, Verres trampled on the rights of Roman and provincial alike during his time in Sicily. Despite the defendant's flight, Cicero proceeds with his prosecution and brilliantly succeeds in proving Verres' guilt.

Rome, 70BC. Julius Caesar, who returned to Rome from Asia on Sulla's death, has become active in campaigning for the overthrow of Sulla's constitution.

Parthia, 70BC. The kingdom of Parthia has suffered a collapse and been greatly reduced in territory by Tigranes, king of Armenia.

East Africa, c.70BC. The pottery associated with the early users of iron in the continent is now being made as far south as Maputo, south of the mouth of the Limpopo river in Mozambique. This coastal type of pottery derives from Malawi, eastern Tanzania and Kenya.

Rome, 69BC. The flamboyant orator Quintus Hortensius, who has dominated Rome's law courts for the past decade, is elected to the consulship. Hortensius unsuccessfully defended his friend Verres against Cicero.

Crete, 67BC. Crete, which was captured by the Romans last year, becomes a Roman province.

Spartacus leads revolt of 100,000 slaves

Rebel slaves attack Roman soldiers in the film "Spartacus".

Rome, 71BC

Along the Appian Way today there hangs a grim warning to any slave minded to rebel: 6,000 men, the equivalent of an entire legion, are dying slowly on the cross after making a break for freedom and war against Rome. This rebellion was different from other such wars in being started and led by one of the servile elite, a Thracian member of the gladiator school at Capua. His name was Spartacus.

A former auxiliary (non-legion) soldier, he absconded two years ago with ten others and hid in Vesuvius, an extinct volcano. He soon collected an irregular army which scored local victories over official forces. He dominated Campania and Luc-ania and frightened Rome. In fact Spartacus wanted to vanish across the Alps, but was overruled by Germans and Gauls in his force who preferred plunder in Italy to farming at home.

With 70,000 men he defeated Roman armies and bought time to escape to a better life. He could not elude the brigands in his own ranks and was still in southern Italy when two Roman armies (one landing by sea from Thrace) trapped him. Spartacus' army, facing two fronts, fragmented. His main force lost three successive battles to the six legions led by Crassus, a soldier-politician. Spartacus died like a gladiator; his "legion" now hangs like carrion along the Appian Way.

Chinese state debates role of monopolies

China, 81BC

A profound debate has taken place, on the emperor's orders, into the intellectual, political and social issues of the day. Hidden in the pages of an edict carrying the boring title *Discussions on Salt and Iron*, the record of this debate between the most brilliant minds of the empire reveals a deep split on almost every aspect of life between the supporters of the government and the powerful reform movement.

The emperor ordered the debate to look into matters such as the state's monopoly of the salt and iron industries, but made it plain that he wanted an examination of the suffering of the people.

The debate developed along the lines of state pragmatism opposed to reformist idealism. The government officials argued that their duty lay in satisfying the people's practical needs. The critics replied that the present government, with its stern rule and profit-seeking, was unfit to uphold the principles of humanitarian rule. The critics are judged to have won the debate but, officially, they compromised.

Sulla presides over a reign of terror

The dictator Sulla, now the most feared man in the city of Rome.

Rome, 82BC

The consul Lucius Cornelius Sulla, disowned by his government, has returned from his wars in the east to wreak vengeance on his enemies in Rome and to impose discipline, as he sees it, on Roman society. In a desperate battle under the walls of the city, at the Colline Gate, he finally scattered his foes; now master of the Roman world, he has unleashed a reign of terror. Enemies, real and imagined, are killed and their lands and goods given to Sulla's war veterans and political supporters.

Now he has set about reforming the constitution. A diehard conservative, he is giving the whole power of the state to the Senate and effectively rendering impotent the Assembly of Tribes. There are to be no more repeated consulships, like those of his rival Gaius Marius.

The feud between the two men began when Sulla, expecting to command the campaign against the Asian potentate, Mithridates IV, found Marius had been appointed. The rivalry was intensified by the fact that Marius, of humble birth, had risen to become Rome's first commander of a professional army, unlike Sulla who gained command in the traditional fashion, as one of the upper classes. In the end Sulla got the command by bringing his army into Rome, thereby violating the city's sacred precincts.

Townhouses give new style to daily life

Rome, c.70BC

As the Roman republic lurches from one crisis to the next, the division between rich and poor ever widening, a new and ostentatious style in architecture is spreading through Italy. Already the sprawling ultra-modern villas of the new rich line the coast from Rome to Naples.

Until recent times Roman domestic architecture was characterised by its austerity and modesty, reflecting the lifestyles of the Romans themselves.

The first Roman dwellings were primitive huts of wood, slay and straw. With the defeat of the Etruscans, the Romans began to adopt Etruscan architecture as their own.

The style was uniform: a simple rectangular building with a short vestibule leading directly to the main room of the house, the *atrium*. In the middle of the *atrium's* ceiling was an opening for letting out smoke and cooking smells, and letting in light and rain water, which collected in a small *impluvium*, or water tank.

The *atrium* was the focus of the household, combining the roles of kitchen, dining room and living room. Furniture was minimal: a stove, simple pedestal tables, a couple of couches and the *lararium*, or altar, where the household gods were worshipped.

Opening onto this *atrium* were the family bedrooms. The splendid new villas and townhouses which have been built for the very rich have grown out of these simple Etruscan-style dwellings. To begin with, the number of rooms off the *atrium* was increased, first to provide store rooms and then – significantly – to give more servants' quarters. Next, extensions were built behind the house, for baths, wine presses and separate kitchens, as well as additional store rooms and servants' quarters. The extensions enclosed a peristyle of columns around an urban style garden.

Now some big houses boast of two or three peristyles, a *tablinum*, or grand chamber, for public business, separate *triclinia*, or dining rooms, summer houses, and even libraries; and it is not unusual for a luxurious villa to have as many as 60 rooms.

A colourful fresco from Pompeii of the type painted in rich men's houses.

Roman villas have outgrown their simple Etruscan predecessors and have become luxurious living-complexes, such as this villa in Herculaneum.

Young Pompey is Rome's rising star

Pompey, the youngest-ever consul, as a later artist saw him.

Rome, 70BC

Pompey has been elected consul, one of the two chief magistrates of Rome. His rise to power has been so swift that, at 36, he is not yet of legal age for the post, neither has he held one of the senatorial positions normally required of a man wishing to become consul.

He owes his success not only to his family connections – his father was consul ten years ago – but also to his prowess on the battlefield where he first appeared at the head of three legions raised and equipped from his father's dependants.

He fought for the dictator Sulla so successfully in Sicily and Africa that Sulla granted him the right to enter Rome in triumph in 81BC and gave him the title of Magnus – the Great.

Four years later he helped to drive Sulla's enemy, Lepidus, from Italy and destroyed the army of Sertorius, another of the dictator's rivals, in Spain. He then returned to Rome to mop up the slaves' revolt led by Spartacus, the gladiator. Six thousand of the slaves were crucified along the road to Rome.

Pompey remains an unknown quantity as a politician. His fellow consul is Crassus, who is reputed to have profited financially from seizing the property of men proscribed by Sulla. There is likely to be much jealousy between these two ambitious men.

Mediterranean, 67BC. The Roman general Pompey clears the sea of pirates. Recently there has been a rapid increase of piracy in the Mediterranean – a prime aim being kidnapping for the slave market at Delos. Centred on Crete and Cilicia, the activity has been interfering with Rome's grain supply. Attempts to put a stop to it proved fruitless, but the tide turned earlier in the year with the capture of Crete.

Rome, 67BC. After spending a year as *quaestor* in Spain, Julius Caesar returns to Rome and marries Pompeia, a relative of Pompey and Sulla.

Asia Minor, 66BC. Pompey vanquishes Mithridates, king of Pontus, and drives him out of Bithynia. He then goes on to capture Tigranes, king of Armenia, who has been attempting to annex Cappadocia and Syria. Tigranes is deprived of all territories except Armenia.

Rome, 66BC. Lucius Sergius Catilina (Catiline), appointed governor of Africa last year, is disqualified for the consulship by charges of maladministration and extortion.

Judaea, 63BC. After nearly a century of freedom, the Jews have once again been conquered by a foreign power. To pacify the country, Pompey has captured Jerusalem and annexed Judaea to the Roman empire, leaving in charge the Maccabaean high priest Hyrcanus.

Rome, 63BC. Fearful of extremists, the Romans elect the famous statesman and orator Cicero to the consulship. The former "knight", who has held all the main magistracies, puts into effect a moderate policy and unites the Romans against Catiline.

Rome, 63BC. The tribune Marcus Porcius Cato (the Younger) denounces Julius Caesar as an accomplice of Catiline.

Asia Minor, 63BC. Mithridates, king of Pontus, who has fled to the Crimea to escape Pompey, commits suicide by stabbing himself. A constant diet of poison – to protect himself against assassination attempts – meant he was immune to drugs.

Italy, January 62BC. The notorious rebel Catiline is slain in battle with a republican army at Pistoria (Pistoia) and his troops are routed.

Asia, 62BC. Pompey has now established four Roman provinces: Bithynia-Pontus (excluding eastern Pontus), Asia, Cilicia and Syria. Eastern Pontus, Cappadocia, Galatia, Lycia and Judaea remain client states.

Rome, 61BC. After his brilliant victories in the east over Mithridates, Tigranes of Armenia and Antiochus of Syria, and his capture of Jerusalem, Pompey returns in triumph to Rome. The senators, however, are in no hurry to organise a celebration to mark his achievements. At the instigation of the tribune Cato, moreover, measures are taken to undermine Pompey's patrician supporters.

Rome, 60BC. Julius Caesar forms a triumvirate with Pompey and Marcus Licinius Crassus. Caesar is elected consul for next year, with the support of Crassus.

Egypt, 59BC. The king of Egypt, Ptolemy XI Auletes ("the flute-player"), is awarded the prestigious and politically useful title of "friend and ally" of the Roman people. In return, Ptolemy pays Caesar and Pompey the fabulous sum of 6,000 talents.

Rome, 59BC. Caesar neutralises the second consul, Calpurnius Bibulus. His concern to please the *populares* has led him to propose to the Senate a law by which land would be given to veterans of Pompey's wars. Caesar has given his daughter Julia in marriage to Pompey, and has himself married Calpurnia, daughter of Lucius Calpurnius Piso.

Cyprus, 58BC. Marcus Porcius Cato annexes Cyprus to Rome. The island is attached to the province of Cilicia.

Egypt, 58BC. On account of his friendly relations with Rome, Ptolemy XI is expelled from his country by the Alexandrians.

Gaul, 58BC. Having won control of the provinces of Cisalpine Gaul, Transalpine Gaul and Illyricum, Caesar opens a military campaign in Gaul, conquering the Celtic tribe known as the Helvetii at Bibracte (Mont Beuvray) and the German leader Ariovistus near Vesontio (Besancon).

Rome, 57BC. The tribune Titus Annius Milo secures the recall of Cicero, who withdrew to Epirus last year as a consequence of his dispute with Clodius.

Parthia, 57BC. Phraates III, king of Parthia since 70BC, is dead. During his reign he restored order to Parthia, but was too weak to resist the Roman advance led by Lucullus and Pompey.

Italy, April 56BC. The triumvirs meet at Lucca, in Etruria, to renew the clauses of their agreements. They decide that Crassus and Pompey will jointly hold the consulship for the year 55BC. Caesar's command in Gaul is prolonged for five years.

Cicero unmasks plotters

An imaginative later impression of Cicero, famed – and feared – for his oratory, denouncing the conspirator Catiline.

Rome, 5 December 63BC

Cicero is relentlessly pursuing the conspirators who plotted to seize power in Rome. Despite a moving plea for moderation by Julius Caesar, five of them were condemned to death by the Senate today and have already been executed. This drama started on October 21 when Cicero, in his role as consul, revealed to the Senate the details of a conspiracy led by Catiline, the former governor of Africa, a man who so desperately wanted to be consul that he was prepared to overthrow the state.

Cicero, famed for his oratorical skills, launched a direct attack on Catiline in the Senate two weeks later with details of the plot which he had learnt from Catiline's mistress. This speech, *The First Oration Against Catiline*, won instant fame, and Catiline fled to Etruria where he had raised a force of bribed soldiers. The following day Cicero made his second speech against Catiline, this time addressing the people of Rome. He told them what had happened, and in vitriolic fashion listed the groups involved in the plot. Of those closest to Catiline he said: "They devote their whole lives and all their waking hours to the vast labour of banqueting. In this herd is found the gambler, the adulterer, and all the filth of Rome."

Nevertheless, Cicero still did not have enough evidence to arrest the plotters and they continued their activities in Rome. They made a great mistake, however, in attempting to involve a deputation from the Gallic tribe of the Allobroges. The latter reported everything to Cicero and he set up an ambush in which the plotters were caught red-handed. Now they have paid for their conspiracy with their lives.

Cicero banished after feud with Clodius

Rome, 58BC

Cicero has been forced into exile by the tribune Clodius who, without naming Cicero, proposed a bill to outlaw anyone who had killed a Roman citizen without trial. This was obviously aimed at the execution of the five Catilinian conspirators in 63BC, which was based on a Senate ruling rather than a trial. This is not simply a legal matter, but one of personal enmity, for in 62BC Cicero prosecuted Clodius for sacrilege after Clodius entered the house of Julius Caesar disguised as a woman during the women's Bona Dea ceremony.

Cicero destroyed his alibi, but Clodius won an acquittal through bribery and has hated Cicero ever since. Now he has had his revenge. He has burnt down Cicero's house and the former consul, deserted by many of his friends and unable to move the ruling triumvirate of Caesar, Pompey and Crassus, is not allowed to come within 400 miles of Rome.

Scathing attack on inadequate oratory

Later image of Cicero, statesman and Rome's finest public speaker.

Rome, 58BC
Is the art of public speaking a natural talent or a discipline to be studied? That's the question being posed to Rome's orators by one of the capital's most gifted lawyers and public speakers as he employs all his oratorical skills in a campaign to improve the standards of debate in Roman society.

In his recently published three-volume dialogue *De Oratore*, Cicero, a leading figure at the Roman bar, delivers a scathing attack on the poverty and paucity of speech-makers among Rome's leaders as he sets out a codified view of oratory capable of being taught as an academic discipline to would-be orators.

Fundamental to his principles of oratory is the belief that the successful public speaker requires a broadbased education with a thorough grounding in philosophy, law and history. "Eloquence," he holds "is dependent upon the trained skills of highly educated men."

Adopting the rhetoricians' classification of oratory into five elements – the use of invention, disposition, memory, elocution and actions or gestures – Cicero calls for more imagination, flexibility and scientific planning by orators in developing lines of argument. The three aims of oratory he defines as to prove, to please and to stir – a feat he has achieved.

Lust for power cements triumvirate

Rome, 60BC
Julius Caesar has returned from his successful year a governor of Spain and brought off a brilliant coup. He has allied himself with Pompey, a distinguished and successful military commander, and Crassus, the richest man in Rome, in a triumvirate, thus forming the most powerful political military and social force in Rome. It bodes ill for the Senate's oligarchy.

Caesar's ambitions have been apparent for a number of years. While Pompey was campaigning in the east, Caesar made himself popular with the people with a series of measures aimed at corrupt members of the Senate. He won Pompey's friendship by supporting him when the Senate delayed awarding the victorious general the *Triumph* he deserved on his return to Rome and refused to give his soldiers the grants of land he had promised.

While Caesar's friendship with Pompey seems wholly admirable, he has bound himself to Crassus in a fashion better understood by that greedy and ambitious nobleman. Deeply in debt, Caesar has borrowed the considerable sum of 830 talents from him.

The short-term ambitions of the three men are well understood. Caesar wants first to be consul, to consolidate his political base, and then to be commander of a major province such as Gaul in order to enhance his military standing.

Pompey wants the Senate to ratify the settlement he made in the East after his defeat of Mithridates and to make good his promises to his veterans. Crassus' ambitions are more venal. He wants the Senate to permit the renegotiation of a bad deal concerning the collection of tithes struck by a company of tax-collectors with which he is involved.

In the long run, all three men want power. Caesar wants it more than the others and is more single-

Julius Caesar, most ambitious of Rome's new governing triumvirate.

minded. Much depends on his ability to keep the triumvirate together. Crassus and Pompey have been jealous of each other since their joint consulship ten years ago. They will not make easy partners.

Amorous ambitions provoke a scandal at the house of Caesar

Rome, 61BC
The great scandal of the Bona Dea religious celebrations at the house of Julius Caesar last year is still titillating Roman society and seems likely to have serious political repercussions. The cult of Bona Dea, the Earth Mother, is strictly confined to women and her name is never spoken in a man's presence.

The ceremonies to the goddess are supervised by the wife of the magistrate, with the vestal virgins playing a prominent role. In a room decorated with vine-leaves and flowers, a sow is sacrificed.

Given this background, it is not surprising that there was uproar when the notorious Clodius tried to enter the house, dressed as a woman, while the goddess's mysteries were being enacted. It appears that he intended no sacrilege, but had amorous designs on Pompeia, Caesar's second wife.

Whatever his intentions, Clodius was charged with sacrilege and prosecuted by that great lawyer and orator, Cicero, who destroyed his alibi. Clodius escaped, however, because he bribed the jurors.

In a letter to his friend Atticus

Clodius, in the guise of a woman, is unmasked (engraving, c.1800).

after Clodius was acquitted, Cicero wrote: "You've never seen a shadier set of characters sitting down together, even in a third-rate nightclub. There were senators with a mark against their name, bankrupt knights, treasury officials hunting for treasure."

The latest development is that Caesar has divorced Pompeia. It would seem that this is not because he felt aggrieved at being cuckolded – his sexual prowess is the source of pride to his soldiers – but because, as he told Pompeia, "Caesar's wife must be above suspicion".

Clodius was at one time a close friend of Cicero. After the trial, however, the rakish dissolute has vowed vengeance on the lawyer.

Love is explicit in new wave poetry

Rome, 54BC.
The poems of Catullus represent a new wave in Roman literature. Drawing his inspiration from the Hellenistic poet Callimachus of Cyrene, who lived 200 years ago, Catullus is making poetry out of subjects that conservative Romans would not have considered sufficiently serious.

Gaius Valerius Catullus was born in Verona in 87BC, and became a cultured man of leisure, fond of literary banter. He developed a great admiration for Callimachus who first composed short lyrics, epigrams, literary hymns and miniature epics as alternatives to the grand epic poetry exemplified by Homer.

Because there was scarcely any tradition of small-scale Roman poetry, Catullus was obliged to borrow heavily from Callimachus, as in poems like *The Lock of Berenice*. He consciously imitated the Greek syntax and diction, but because of his Italian passion and originality, his poems are distinctly Roman.

Although Catullus is a learned man, he enjoys poking fun at his literary rivals. He can make memorable poems out of trivial, everyday subjects.

Roman camps become towns on the move

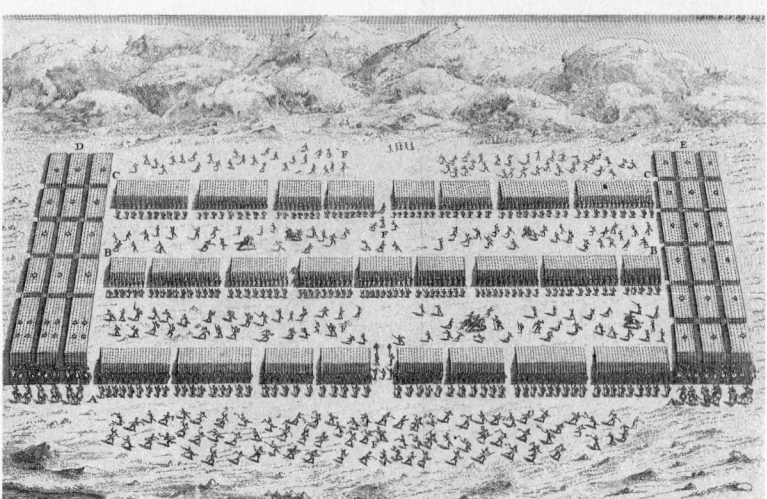

Part of the success of the Roman legions derives from their discipline in battle, as shown here in a later engraving, or when establishing a camp.

North Africa, c.55BC
Some of the worst defeats suffered by Roman columns, particularly in desert warfare, occur when the column, much of it on foot and carrying 100 pounds of gear per man, is ambushed by enemy cavalry. The most vulnerable moment for the regiment is when it makes camp.

The Roman army has a drill for this which has become a sort of ritual. Although sentries are kept posted, most soldiers must fall to their allotted building jobs while keeping weapons handy. The lay-out never varies. The reference point is the commander's quarters, the *praetorium*. From here the two lines of dwellings run to four gates.

The camp is surrounded by a deep ditch dug by the auxiliaries. The spoil makes a steep defensive wall topped by a fence. Building tools, such as picks, turf-cutters, metal spikes (to buttress walls) and baskets for moving earth, are normal marching kit as well as weapons, rations and water vessels. For every eight men a mule will carry a leather tent and millstones for sharpening – and punishment.

Cheering crowds greet husband and wife in mid-river reunion

Edfu, Egypt, c.150-c.10BC
This town deep in Lower Egypt attracts big crowds each year for the annual festival of the "Good Reunion" between the god Horus and his wife Hathor of Dendara. It happens in the second month of the Egyptian year, when the sacred statue of Horus is taken from his magnificent temple here and rowed up the Nile to meet Hathor's sacred statue in mid-stream. It is a time of great joy for the thousands who line the banks of the Nile. Once the couple have been reunited, the entire population gathers to watch the priests carry the statues into the temple.

Of all the temples built in Egypt since the earliest pharaohs', none is more magnificent than this. It contains some of the finest art and architecture of the Ptolemaic period and is dedicated to the two loving gods

The Ptolemaic Temple of Horus at Edfu: reliefs of the king and prisoners.

and their son, Horus the younger – "the uniter of two lands".

It is the two gods who figure in one of the most striking reliefs in the temple. They watch as the king grabs an enemy by the hair and prepares to strike him. Offerings are made to the gods on a giant altar in a spacious enclosure with a gallery supported by 32 columns.

Mortal man need not fear vengeance of gods, says poet

Rome, c.55BC

A major new philosophy has been expounded by Lucretius, based on Epicurean ethics and the laws of physics. He contends that man is mortal, and need not fear the vengeance of the gods.

Titus Lucretius Carus, like Catullus, enjoyed the support and friendship of Gaius Memmius, but little is known of his life apart from his great didactic poem *De natura rerum*. In this work he explains the atomic view of the universe: that

Lucretius, Epicurean philosopher, by a later artist.

an infinite number of atoms move constantly in space, creating things by combining together, and ending by splitting apart. Man, being made up of atoms, is mortal.

Lucretius accepted Democritus' material philosophy based on the laws of physics, but rejected his determinism. He postulates free-will, and advocates Epicurus' belief in the pursuit of pleasure.

But Epicurus' philosophy was not hedonistic. His conclusion was that, to achieve the maximum pleasure and cause the least possible distress, it was advisable to lead a simple life, free of ties and un-encumbered by wealth. Lucretius enlivens Epicurus with imagery and wit, and is hailed by Cicero for his artistry and genius.

Parthians humiliate legions of Rome

Carrhae, Mesopotamia, 53BC

An expeditionary force led by one of Rome's three most powerful commanders, the ex-consul Crassus, has been wiped out by heavy Parthian cavalry in the Mesopotamian desert.

In a military disaster unprecedented in Roman history, the 40,000-strong column of seven legions died over several days. The Parthian horses, fitted with equine armour and bearing mail-clad warriors equipped with lances long enough to skewer two men, systematically tore the column to pieces. Those taking flight were brought down by mounted archers.

At one stage the enemy beheaded Publius, Crassus' son, and taunted the Roman commander by parading past him with his son's head on a spear. Crassus died in combat soon afterwards, his decapitated head in turn being used as a theatrical prop during after-dinner entertainments at an Armenian banquet attended by Pomaxathres, the Parthian who killed him. Mean-

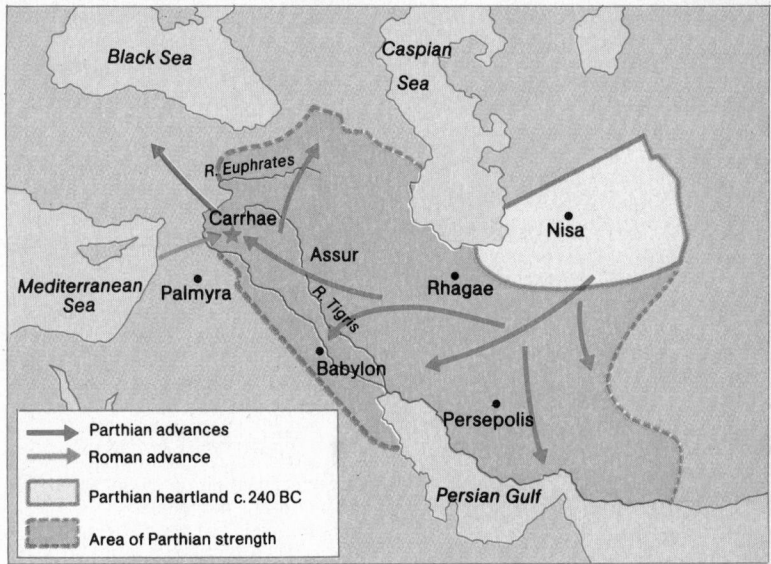

while a Roman prisoner who resembled Crassus was forced to imitate him at a victory parade.

It was a dreadful price for Crassus to pay in his search for a victory famous enough to compare with those of his fellow consuls Pompey and Caesar. Pompey, the second member of the ruling triumvirate, opted to stay in Rome while delegating his duties as consul for Iberia to deputies.

Already, following Crassus' defeat, there are rumours of civil disorder in the capital. Caesar, meanwhile, stays in Gaul.

How Rome's provincial governors can line their own pockets

Rome, c.55BC

The provinces of the Roman Empire, for many years under no more than military control, are now effectively exploited by governors with three years' tenure. These men can make a lot of money out of the local populace – as Verres showed from 73BC to 71BC, until Cicero successfully prosecuted him for defrauding the people of Sicily.

Traditionally, a province was not a piece of territory, but simply a command allotted to a consul or praetor, usually for a year. But from the beginning of the first century, the duties of governor changed from military surveillance to administering law and overseeing tax collection.

When a province was annexed by Rome, its administration would be defined by charter, varied to accommodate local laws and customs where possible.

Two groups were particularly favoured: the *civitates foederatae* and the *civitates liberae*, both of whom could use their own laws and were normally exempt from taxat-

A provincial Roman temple at Nemausus (Nimes) in Gaul.

ion and the requirement to quarter Roman troops. Taxes on the remainder varied from fixed taxes to tithes on agricultural land, and border tolls. They were normally levied by the hated *publicani*, individuals who bid at auction for the right to collect taxes. Thousands of *publicani* were massacred in 88BC by Asiatic rebels under Mithridates.

The governor has a large staff: a *quaestor* to deal with financial

Bronze head from the North African province of Cyrenaica, c.200BC.

administration; three *legati*, usually senators chosen by him; an inner council of friends and relatives known as *comites* or *contubernales*; prefects, clerks, secretaries and minor officials. He has enormous powers of patronage.

Caesar's *Lex Julia* of 59BC, a law requiring governors to balance and publish accounts, will make abuses rarer, but Roman politicians still hope to finance their careers through lucrative governorships.

Gaul, 53BC. Caesar puts down a rebellion among the Belgic tribes after fierce fighting. Three years ago he defeated the Belgic league and the Nervii in Alsace and Belgium. He undertook to conquer the lands to the west, along the Channel and the Atlantic coast, achieving military victories over the Veneti and other peoples of Britanny and Normandy. He then proceeded to drive two invading Germanic tribes across the Rhine.

Rome, 53BC. The holding of elections in Rome is prevented by riots and fighting between the gladiators of Publius Clodius and those of Titus Annius Milo, a former supporter of Pompey who successfully engineered Cicero's recall to Rome in 57BC.

China, 52BC. Last year the *shanyu* (ruler) Huhanye of the Xiongnu confederacy of nomads sent his son to the Han court. He now pays personal homage to the Han emperor, who treats him more as a rival head of state than as a vassal and rewards him generously for his participation in the Han tributary system. The nomad threat to China is thereby diminished.

Athens, 52BC. The Roman orator, poet and literary patron Gaius Memmius – supporter of, among others, Catullus and Lucretius – goes into exile in Athens. A former governor of Bithynia, Memmius stood for consul two years ago, but his chances were ruined by an electoral scandal which he himself brought to light. He was condemned for involvement and is now suffering the punishment.

Gaul, 52BC. A serious revolt breaks out in Gaul under the leadership of Vercingetorix, who is declared supreme commander of the Gauls at Bibracte (Mount Beuvray). Vercingetorix is the son of Celtillus, a former king of the Gallic tribe known as the Arverni.

Italy, 52BC. Publius Clodius, the political opportunist whose name has been tinged by scandal, is murdered by Titus Annius Milo, who was a candidate for the abortive elections to the consulship last year.

Rome, 52BC. Pompey is illegally appointed sole consul – in effect, dictator – by the Senate. Two years ago a theatre built in his honour in the Campus Martius was dedicated.

Rome, 52BC. Milo is found guilty of the murder of Clodius and exiled to Massilia (Marseilles). His friend Cicero did not dare to defend him at his trial because, on the orders of Pompey – who spearheaded the prosecution of his former ally – the court had been strongly reinforced for the occasion.

Rome, 52BC. Pompey rescues Metellus Scipio, whose daughter Cornelia he has married, from a bribery charge and makes him his colleague in the consulship. Scipio stood against Milo in the elections last year which had to be abandoned.

Egypt, 51BC. On his death, Ptolemy XI Auletes leaves his throne jointly to his children, Cleopatra VII and Ptolemy XII.

Rome, 51BC. In his *De Republica*, just completed, Cicero reflects on contemporary political problems. He advocates a constitution which combines monarchy, oligarchy and democracy, and he asserts the importance of human rights and the brotherhood of man.

Rome, 51BC. On completing his conquest of Gaul, Caesar decides to leave behind him a monumental account of the task he has accomplished. The dry and elegant style of *De Bello Gallico* is reminiscent of *communiques* from staff headquarters. The battles are described in full, with an eye for dramatisation and theatrical detail. Despite his claim of objectivity, Caesar has another motive for writing his memoirs: to make the victor of the Gallic wars into a national hero.

Rome, 50BC. On the orders of Caesar, a new Forum is under construction in Rome. Its site, at the foot of the Capitol, was occupied by houses belonging to the nobility. It took Caesar three years to persuade the nobles to let him demolish their houses – a very expensive operation. The centre of the new Forum will be occupied by a temple dedicated to Venus Genetrix, the legendary "patron" of the Julian family. The Forum is also intended as the site of a new senate house.

Italy, 50BC. The consul Gaius Claudius Marcellus sends Pompey to command the two legions stationed at Capua and to raise more troops for the Roman army.

Red Sea, c.50BC. Alexandrians from Egypt are quarrying porphyry stone for export to Rome for buildings. Over 200 years ago, in 264BC, the Egyptian port of Ptolemias Epitheras was founded on the Ethiopian coast of the Red Sea (Eritrea). From there the Egyptians have been conducting a flourishing trade in ivory and skins. The pharoahs Ptolemy III and Ptolemy IV sent further trading expeditions to the Red Sea and the Ethiopians of Axum.

East Africa, c.50BC. Some Alexandrian sailors have sailed down the east coast of Africa to reach Rhapta (*probably the Rufiji river mouth in Tanzania*) on the Indian Ocean.

Political gang leader killed in streets

Milo's men drag Clodius from the inn (C18th engraving).

Rome, 52BC

The gang warfare in Rome between the supporters of Clodius and those of Milo has resulted in the death of Clodius in a brawl at Bovillae on the Appian Way between his gang and one led by Milo. Some say that Milo himself cut down Clodius.

Few tears will be shed for the notorious Clodius, whose bullyboy tactics have kept Rome in uproar for months. His tactics have prevented the proper conduct of political life and Milo, who, as tribune, was responsible for the recall of Cicero from the exile forced on him by Clodius, raised his own band to fight Clodius' thugs on the streets.

Milo, who has been charged with the murder of Clodius, will no doubt be defended by Cicero, but the lawyer is already being threatened by Clodius' men. They have marked their leader's cremation by rioting and burning down the Senate House. There seems to be little hope for a peaceful solution of Rome's political problems.

Legions increase as army is reorganised

Rome, c.50BC

They call themselves "Marius' Mules". Today's infantrymen carry chains, spears, swords, shields and their body armour as well as trenching tools and survival gear as they march across the plains and deserts behind the shimmering eagle.

As the republic grows, so does the army's importance – in spite of the recent disaster at Carrhae. After the Second Punic War, 150 years ago, there were 23 legions. Gaius Marius made nonsense of this figure when he created a legion of 6,000 men (double the size of the first legion formed) and opened the doors to a formation of classless professionals prepared to serve for 20 years. The spread of Roman citizenship through much of Italy has increased the manpower pool and the potential armed forces even further.

A legionary in armour, c.200AD.

Rebels surrender to Caesar: Gaul is conquered

Alesia, Gaul, September 52BC
Julius Caesar has destroyed the rebellion in Gaul led by the young nobleman Vercingetorix. It was a near run thing, settled by one day's fierce fighting at Alesia where the Romans laid siege to Vercingetorix.

This rebellion in the name of liberty from Roman rule had been growing for some time. Following his successes in 56BC and 55BC, Caesar was able to sail across to Britain for the second time in 54BC and bring several British tribes to heel.

However, when he returned to Gaul he scented trouble and dispersed his troops to quell local uprisings. But they were attacked everywhere and Ambiorix, chief of the Eburones, massacred a legion and a half of Roman soldiers.

Caesar called for reinforcements and stamped out the uprising with great severity. But the Gauls now came together under the command of Vercingetorix.

Early this year they murdered Roman merchants who had set up business in Orleans. The rebellion spread rapidly south and west as Vercingetorix attempted to cut off Caesar, who was wintering at Ravenna, and drive the legions out by pursuing a scorched earth policy.

He failed because Caesar eluded him and the Gauls refused to burn their crops. He did, however, score one significant victory over Caesar at Gergovia (Clermont-Ferrand) which led some of Rome's allies among the Gauls to defect.

Caesar now demonstrated his generalship. He drove the Gauls into the hill-town of Alesia and laid siege to them with a double row of fortifications, with strong points

Vercingetorix, the last hope of Gallic freedom (C19th statue).

protected by pits studded with sharp stakes. The inner ring faced Alesia, the other pointed outward to hold off the warriors who were gathering to raise the siege. They attacked in great strength – Caesar's own estimate is that they numbered a quarter of a million – but they were beaten off and dispersed.

Vercingetorix now tried to break out. His men advanced with great courage under cover of darkness, but fell into the pits and sustained many casualties from spears thrown from Caesar's ramparts.

When it grew light the Gauls tried again, this time filling in the pits with brushwood, but they took too long; the Romans got amongst them with their swords and they retreated into the town.

Vercingetorix then chose 60,000 of his best fighters to creep out at night and hide themselves, ready to

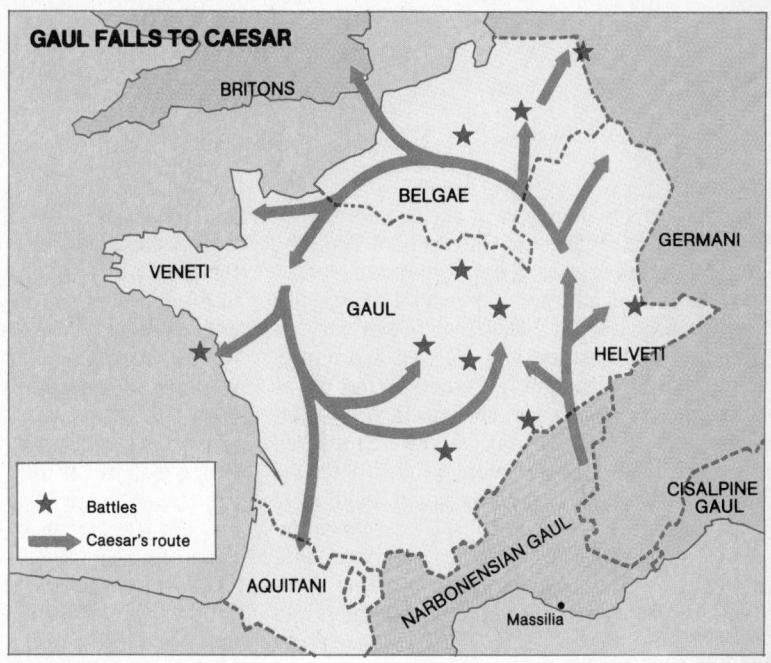

GAUL FALLS TO CAESAR

BRITONS
BELGAE
GERMANI
VENETI
GAUL
HELVETI
CISALPINE GAUL
AQUITANI
NARBONENSIAN GAUL
Massilia

★ Battles
→ Caesar's route

attack the most vulnerable point in the Roman lines. They rose from their hiding places and attacked at midday. Then Vercingetorix led his main force out to give battle. The fighting raged all along the line. At times it seemed that the Romans would be broken, but Caesar, dis-

tinctive in his scarlet cloak, conducted the battle brilliantly and the Gauls were driven off with great loss.

The next day Vercingetorix surrendered, anxious to save his men. He is now Caesar's prisoner and Gaul belongs to Rome.

Sanchi takes shape as Buddhist shrine

India, c.300-50BC
A hundred and fifty years after Emperor Asoka founded it, the shrine of Sanchi, in the state of Madhya Pradesh, has become one of the great religious centres of Indian Buddhism. Now surrounded by lesser shrines, the original *stupa*, or monument, to Sanchi still dominates. It was first built of brick and topped by a stone umbrella-canopy. Since then it has been extended and embellished. Now it is a solid construction of bricks and rubble, faced in concrete, 54 feet high, shaped like a dome and still shaded by a stone umbrella. Buried within it are the relics of the Buddha, kept in a casket. A stone railing ten feet high encircles the shrine. It is broken by four exquisite gateways of stone, their pillars and crossbars carved with lions, elephants, demi-gods, caryatids and var-

A gate at the shrine of Sanchi.

ious forms of erotica, admired without reservation by the thousands of pilgrims who flock to Sanchi from all over India.

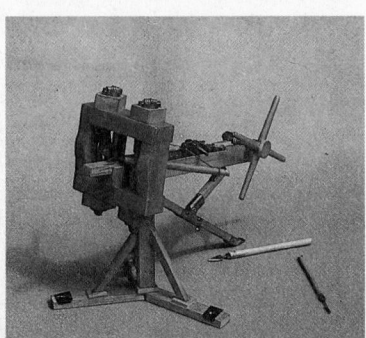
Model of a Roman battle catapult, with its sharp, lethal projectiles.

Captive Gauls and their weapons, on a coin commemorating Caesar.

The dawn of woman

The story of the human race begins with the female: DNA research at the University of Berkeley, California, has now established that one woman was the common ancestor of our entire species. She lived in Africa about 200,000 years ago and, although short, squat, heavily muscled and doubtless not visibly distinguished from the rest of the early humans around her, she was in fact faster, fiercer, and cleverer than any before her. She killed more swiftly and foraged more efficiently for the food that she needed; she kept her children alive when others died; she established a safe settlement where she took sexual partners at will, strengthening the gene mix of her offspring. And, when the time was ripe, she led her daughters and her daughters' daughters out of Africa to overrun the whole globe.

The story of this "gene fount mother", nicknamed "Eve" by the scientists who discovered her, was repeated worldwide as early humans struggled out of darkness towards full humanity. For under primitive conditions, where the sole imperative of the tribe is survival, the leadership of women is, to this day, very marked. Women's skills – food gathering, handwork, plant knowledge – are the principal tribal resource. Above all, they alone can renew the tribe. The success of the early "Eves" in mothering the increasingly complex human baby is attested by the fact that we are here today.

As the struggle for survival gave way to the struggle for understanding, the female of the species was again to the fore. Nothing seemed more mysterious than woman, with her power of generating life from within her own body, and her secret of shedding blood in a regular, predetermined flow, without injury, pain, infection or death. Before the male role in human reproduction was understood, woman took on the aura of something superhuman, sacred and divine.

The Great Goddess

For at least 20,000 years, then, from the early carvings and statuettes to the overthrow of the last shrines with the fall of the Roman empire, God was a woman. The power and centrality of the first divinity, the Great Goddess, is one of the best-kept secrets of history. Modern textbooks record a number of goddesses, all with different names – Isis, Juno, Demeter – and suppress what 5,000 years ago every girl knew, that there was only one God, and her name was Woman. Contemporary accounts consistently refer to "The One Being", "The Universal Mother" and "The Mistress of All Elements, Queen of All Things, Living and Dead".

The primary incarnation of the first woman-god was as the Great Mother – the so-called "Venus figurines", discovered in their tens of thousands in Europe alone, display the outsize breasts, pregnant belly, and tree-trunk thighs of the female form at its most fecund. But the Goddess was never wife – in the myths of every land, she chose and discarded young and potent lovers. Her high priestesses selected annually the handsomest young man of the tribe to share the sacred couch for one year. After this he was put to death, and his body was ploughed into the fields to regenerate the crops in the ritual which anthropologists call "The King Must Die".

As this shows, the Great Mother was not always the Good Mother. In about 2300BC she was honoured by Enheduanna, the high priestess of Sumer and the world's first known poet, for "filling the rivers with blood". In Ireland, the Great Goddess in her threefold incarnation (the earliest holy trinity) haunted battlefields, rounding up those about to die. The Great Mother's blood thirst could be appeased by sacrifice: in about 1500BC at Hal Tarxien, in Malta, the ministers of a seven-foot statue of the goddess, her belly obesely pregnant over pear-shaped legs of massive stone, caught the blood of slaughtered victims in a deep vessel symbolic of the divine vagina. Bloodiest of all was the Indian Dark Mother, Kali Ma, with skulls around neck and waist, her huge tongue lolling for the last drop to be wrung from her millions of victims.

Yet, life-giver or bearer of death, this was one and the same divine being, attested in the myths and archaeological remains of every known country. Later commentators dismissed goddess-worship as "minor deities" and "cults". But Sir Arthur Evans, the discoverer of the Minoan civilisation of Crete, where goddess-worship is attested in every statue and carving, revealed that the goddess of Crete represented "the same Great Mother, whose worship under various names and titles extended throughout Asia Minor and the regions beyond". Subsequent scholarship has revealed not just a pattern but a network of worldwide goddess-worship, with priests from Celtic Britain travelling to ceremonies of the Great Mother goddess as far afield as Anatolia, for instance.

The Rights of Woman

Where the Great Goddess held the power of life and death, the status of all women was commensurately higher. In Egypt and many other countries, inheritance passed through the female line, with queens such as Cleopatra VII (*the* Cleopatra) ascending the throne in their own right, not as consorts to kings. Non-royal women owned and controlled money and property, their rights enshrined in the earliest known laws. The code of Hammurabi of Babylon of about 1700BC, for instance, laid down that any woman's property or money remained hers even on marriage, and passed at her death to her children – rights that women in the west were still fighting for in the 19th century.

Strangest of all, perhaps, were the physical freedoms which the women of the earliest civilisations enjoyed, again in contrast to later social controls. In seventh-century BC China, the young women would adjourn in bands to nearby woodlands to size up the males, and to spend the night with any who took their fancy. Only if they found themselves pregnant would they even consider marriage. In Greece, women hunted, rode as jockeys in championship races, and practised the ancient Cretan sport of bull-leaping. And throughout the world, tales of breastless man-haters notwithstanding, women fought as soldiers from Britain to Peru – Celtic women, for instance, proving so formidable that the Roman historian Tacitus doubted whether even the famed Roman legions would be a match for them.

End of the Golden Age

This long period, from pre-history up to the emergence of the first civilisations and beyond, has been described by Simone de Beauvoir as "the golden age of woman". Later historians, dealing with accounts of matriarchies and amazons, and evidence of cultures so much at variance with our own, decided that the "Age of Queens" was too good to be true. And so it proved. At some unidentified point in history, the power of woman was overthrown.

Undoubtedly a major factor in the loss of woman's divine status was the gradual dawning of realisation of the truth of biological fatherhood, described by the French historian Jean Marks as the "greatest revolution in human thought". So came about what Engels called "the world historic defeat of the female sex". Thrusting first into the field came the petty phallic deities, the Apollos and the Visnus, to be followed by the power-hungry Father Gods of Judaism, Christianity and Islam. Thus came the rise of value systems which enshrined maleness as power and defined woman as its opposite, setting every man over every woman, husband over wife, brother over sister, son over mother.

Images of the ancient powers of women. Left: a stone carving now known as the "Venus of Laussei", from the hunter-gatherer settlement in Aurignac in southern France about 25,000 years ago; pendulous breasts and heavy buttocks symbolise her all-powerful fecundity. Upper left: finely carved head of a woman thought to be Cleopatra, the queen of the Nile, who came to the throne in her own right, rather than as consort to a king. Upper right: the Indian "Dark Mother" Kali Ma, the bloodiest and most terrifying of the goddesses, wielding a sword and wearing a necklace and belt of skulls, seated here with the double corpse Shiva. Right: a female fertility figure from Alaska about two thousand years ago, known as the "Okvik Madonna", from St Lawrence Island: she clasps her baby against her chest.

Rome, 50BC. Alarmed by Caesar's desire to remain in Gaul in command of his army and the province, his opponents in the Senate strive to get him recalled to face charges of wrongdoings during his consulship. Caesar's interests are defended in the Senate by the tribune Marcus Antonius.

Rome, 7 January 49BC. The Senate says that Caesar will be declared a public enemy unless he disbands his army. This prompts the tribunes who support him to flee to Ravenna, where Caesar is waiting.

Italy, 10 January 49BC. Caesar crosses the Rubicon.

Italy, 49BC. Lucius Domitius, formerly a bitter opponent of the triumvirate, who has been granted command of Gaul by the Senate, confronts Caesar's troops at Corfinium but is defeated.

Italy, 49BC. In fear of Caesar's large forces in Gaul, Pompey leaves Italy for Greece, followed by most of the Senate.

Rome, 49BC. With the support of the *praetor* Marcus Aemilius Lepidus and sympathetic senators remaining in Rome, Caesar is appointed dictator. This follows his investiture with magistracies which make him a lawful representative of republican powers.

Spain, 2 August 49BC. Caesar, who marched to Spain earlier in the year leaving Marcus Antonius in charge of Italy, defeats Pompey's generals Afranius and Petreius at Ilerda (Lerida) north of the Ebro river.

Gaul, 49BC. Massilia (Marseilles) surrenders to Caesar on his way back to Gaul after his victorious campaign in Spain.

Greece, 9 August 48BC. Having landed in northern Epirus in June, Caesar defeats Pompey's troops and those of his father-in-law, Metellus Scipio, at Pharsalus. Pompey flees to Egypt.

Egypt, 28 September 48BC. On landing in Egypt, Pompey is murdered on the orders of Ptolemy XII.

Spain, 47BC. Lepidus becomes governor of a province of Spain.

Egypt, 47BC. Caesar, who has pursued Pompey to Egypt, insists that Cleopatra VII be returned to the throne of Egypt to rule jointly with her brother, Ptolemy XII, by whom she had been expelled.

Egypt, 47BC. Caesar, who has been besieged in Alexandria over the winter by an Egyptian force, is relieved by an army from Asia. The young Ptolemy XII is killed during the fighting.

Egypt, 47BC. After the death of Ptolemy XII, Caesar arranges that a younger brother, Ptolemy XIII, should rule jointly with Cleopatra.

Egypt, 47BC. Cleopatra charms Caesar into spending three months with her as her lover in Egypt.

Syria, 2 August 47BC. At Zela, Caesar defeats Pharnaces, son of Mithridates the Great, who has earlier invaded Pontus. Caesar's comment on the victory is: "*Veni, vidi, vici* (I came, I saw, I conquered)."

Rome, 46BC. Caesar returns to Rome to quell a mutiny. Among the reforms he undertakes is the abandonment of the old calendar of the pontiffs in favour of a calendar in which there are 365 days in a year with a extra day every four years.

North Africa, 46BC. Determined to track down the surviving supporters of Pompey, who are led by Labienus and Cato, Caesar disembarks in North Africa. The fugitives have found refuge in Numidia with King Juba.

North Africa, 6 April 46BC. Metellus Scipio and other Pompeian leaders, including Afranius, are killed in a battle with Caesar's troops at Thapsus. Pompey's son, Sextus Pompey, flees to Spain to join his brother, Gnaeus.

North Africa, 46BC. The kingdom of Numidia is added to the Roman province of Africa after the suicide of its king, Juba. The rest of the country comes under the control of eastern Mauretania.

North Africa, 46BC. On hearing of Caesar's decisive victory at Thapsus, Marcus Porcius Cato (the Younger), a former supporter of Pompey, commits suicide at Utica by stabbing himself in the chest.

Rome, 46BC. Caesar is again appointed consul, together with Lepidus. He uses his right, with the people's consent, to extend his title of dictator for ten years. Celebrations are held in Rome to mark his four great triumphs – in Gaul, Egypt, Asia Minor and Africa.

Spain, 15 March 45BC. Caesar wins his last victory over Pompey's armies, defeating the great general's sons, Sextus and Gnaeus, at Munda.

Rome, 45BC. Caesar, who has recently been made consul for ten years, adopts his great-nephew, Octavius. Apart from other royal tributes, Caesar's head appears on Roman coins.

Rome, 44BC. Marcus Antonius becomes Caesar's colleague in the consulship.

Nomads finally pay tribute to emperor

China, 50BC

The Xiongnu, the warrior nomads of the north, have at last been forced to pay tribute to the Han emperor of China. Weakened by war between two brothers claiming to be the *shanyu*, or ruler, of the Xiongnu, the nomads can no longer frighten the Chinese with their swift cavalry raids.

This change has been marked by the appearance at the emperor's court of Huhanye, one of the rival *shanyus*, to celebrate the New Year.

The Chinese are fully aware of the importance of this event, and have gone out off their way to treat Huhanye more as the head of a rival state than as a vassal.

He has even been given the great honour of not having to prostrate himself before the emperor and was seated higher than all the other

A silver plaque of the Xiongnu, showing a yak among trees, c.50BC.

nobles at court. He has also been given more tangible marks of the emperor's appreciation: gold, silk, suits of clothes, 15 horses and wagon loads of grain will accompany him on his journey back to the wild steppes.

Steps to power on Rome's political ladder

A portrait, probably of an official and his aristocratic wife (c.50AD).

Rome, c.50BC

The ambitious Roman politician recognises that, if he wants to get on, he should have some well-placed relatives. He also needs money because, quite apart from the fact that the great offices of state are unpaid, election campaigns can be expensive. Also, and most vitally, a politician has to be the right age. In Rome it is simply out of the question for him to make a pitch for high office by parading his youth.

The strict hierarchies of Roman society ensure that the rising politician almost always finds himself competing with men of his own age.

Even before embarking on a political career proper, he must do his military service, maybe ten years. After that, at 30, he can stand for one of the 20 posts of *quaestor*, or financial administrator. Next, at 36, he will seek election to the quartet of *aediles*, who are responsible for organising games and supervising public works. Now our politician is approaching the summit. When he is 39 he could find himself elected as one of Rome's eight *praetors*, who are senior magistrates, just below the two *consuls* who are elected annually and exercise the highest authority in the republic. Consuls must be 42 years old.

This tidy ascent of the political ladder is not always observed in practice. The careers of men without connections and wealth may often be held back. It is exceptional for someone like the orator Cicero, who does not belong to a senatorial family, to become consul at 43, as he did. Others have found means to bend the rules. Pompey was 34 when he crushed the Spartacus slave revolt, and he was unwilling to start a political career at the bottom of the ladder. By a scarcely-disguised threat of force he secured election to the consulship at 36, without having served in any of the junior magistrates' posts.

Civil war erupts as Caesar challenges Pompey

Caesar crosses the Rubicon at the head of the 13th Legion

Italy, 12 January 49BC
Julius Caesar has taken a fateful step. He has crossed the Rubicon, the little river dividing Gaul from Italy, at the head of his battle-hardened 13th Legion. Civil war between the former allies, Caesar and Pompey, is now inevitable.

Some people say that it became inevitable with the death in battle of Crassus, the third member of the triumvirate, four years ago. Others say that the death of Julia, Caesar's daughter and Pompey's much loved wife, broke the marriage bond and, with it, the alliance.

What is certain is that neither Caesar nor Pompey wanted to go to war. Caesar has been conciliatory and Pompey, commander of the Senate's forces, has vacillated, but both have been pushed into war by the feuding factions in Rome. The deadline was set by Caesar's impending return to Rome after his victory in Gaul.

Fearing his return, his opponents wanted him to come home as a private citizen, without his loyal legions, but that would have put him at the mercy of his enemies. He retaliated by proposing himself for election as consul, a move which provoked a series of motions against him in the Senate. Eventually his enemies forced through a motion making him a public enemy if he did not lay down his command.

Two of his friends, the tribunes Quintus Cassius and Marcus Antonius, vetoed the motion, to which the Senate replied by declaring martial law. Cassius and Antony fled, taking the news to Caesar. Now he is marching on Rome ready to confirm the worst fears of his enemies.

Julius Caesar: man of destiny.

New calendars begin year in January

Roman calendar: pegs mark the day (top), date (right) and month (left).

Rome, 46BC
This year, says Julius Caesar, is "the last year of confusion", for it marks the introduction of his new calendar. It replaces the old calendar of Numa, based on a 12-month lunar year of 355 days with provision for an extra month of 22 or 23 days every two years to make it agree with the solar year.

However, the religious authorities who controlled the calendar had allowed this system to fall into chaos, so in his role as *pontifex maximus* – the official head of religion – Caesar decided to make the year conform to the course of the sun. Helped by his secretary, Marcus Fulvius, and the Egyptian mathematician Sosigenes, he has made his year 365 days long, with an extra day every four years. This "Julian" calendar comes into effect on January 1 next year.

Cicero refashions Roman philosophy

Rome, c.44BC
Greece's traditional monopoly of the study of philosophy, the pursuit of wisdom itself, is being steadily eroded by a succession of papers by Cicero ranging from the nature of the state to questions of man's immortality.

This intellectual *tour de force* by one of Rome's most eminent public figures constitutes the first serious attempt to add a Roman dimension to the philosophical debates concerning the nature of life and the individual.

Ever since his first book on current philosophical issues, in 54BC, Cicero's main concern has been to extract practical applications from the ideas he explores. In *De Republica* he views the successful government of the Rome of a century ago as being the ideal balance between a monarchy (the consuls), an oligarchy (the Senate) and the people. To him, justice is the basis of society, with citizens putting the needs of the state above their own. Cicero, who studied philosophy in Greece, has recently explored the nature of good and bad.

Pompey is killed as his army is routed

Pelusium, Egypt, 48BC
Pompey has been treacherously murdered on the orders of the Egyptian king, Ptolemy, as he sought asylum after defeat by Caesar. The great general was stabbed as he was being carried to shore in a small boat from his *trireme*.

Ptolemy, an inexperienced young man, was persuaded to kill Pompey by his advisers, who argued that if they allowed the Roman to land they would have him for a master and Caesar for an enemy. On the other hand, if they killed him they would please Caesar and have nothing to fear from Pompey, for "a dead man does not bite".

So Pompey has been murdered and his head cut off and sent to Caesar, who is reported to be disgusted at the fate of the man who was once his ally and son-in-law. This is not Caesar's way of making war. He had defeated Pompey through the fortitude and fighting skill of his veterans and his own brilliant tactics at the battle of Pharsalus in Thessaly.

It was a battle which Pompey should have won, because his army outnumbered Caesar's and he had the advantage of seapower. He could have starved Caesar into submission, but chose glory on the battlefield and was defeated. Now Caesar is master of Rome.

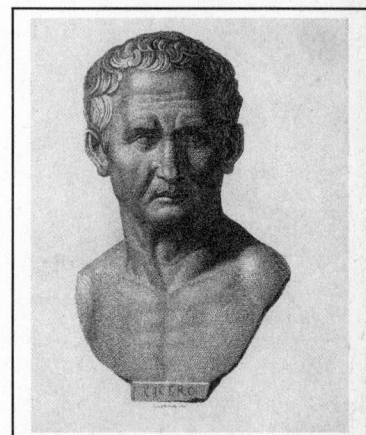
44BC. Later portrait of Cicero who, recalled from exile, has added to his standing as a thinker with his "De Republica".

Rome, 15 March 44BC. Caesar is murdered by conspirators.

Rome, 44BC. A succession crisis breaks out after Caesar's death. Marcus Antonius stakes his claim against that of Octavian, Caesar's great-nephew and adopted son, who has arrived in Rome to receive his inheritance.

Rome, 44BC. Cicero has no qualms about revealing his preferred choice to succeed Caesar. In his polemical works known as the *Philippics* he strongly denounces Marcus Antonius and his followers.

Rome, 44BC. The Senate gives superior commands to the murderers of Caesar so that they can raise armies against Marcus Antonius. After the murder Decimus Brutus fled to Cisalpine Gaul, Marcus Brutus to Macedonia and Cassius to Syria – provinces which were already assigned to them and where they are now established as governors.

Rome, 44BC. Marcus Antonius secures from the Roman people the transfer of Cisalpine Gaul and Macedonia to himself and of Syria to Publius Cornelius Dolabella.

Egypt, 44BC. Ptolemy XIII, who shares the throne of Egypt with his sister Cleopatra, is murdered by her.

Italy, 21 April 43BC. Octavian emerges the victor in a battle with Marcus Antonius near Mutina (Modena) in which the new consuls, Hirtius and Pansa, are killed. To end Antonius' ambitions, Octavian has put together a powerful coalition, which includes many former followers of Pompey.

Rome, July 43BC. After marching on Rome and compelling the senate to hold special elections, Octavian is elected consul with Pedius. A law is passed declaring vengeance on Caesar's killers.

Italy, November 43BC. Octavian meets Marcus Antonius and Marcus Lepidus, governor of Transalpine Gaul, at Bononia (Bologna), and forges with his former foes an alliance of interest known as the second triumvirate.

Rome, 7 December 43BC. Cicero is assassinated on the orders of Marcus Antonius.

Gaul, 43BC. On the site of one of Caesar's army bases, at the confluence of the Rhone and Saone, the Roman colony of Lugdunum (Lyons) is founded.

Army veterans are colonising Gaul

Gaul, 43BC

Thousands of the tough, highly-trained and disciplined veterans of the Roman army are being being put to use in the colonisation of the empire. In Gaul, as well as back home in Italy, vast numbers of Roman soldiers are being settled in towns which are bearing the title of colonia, or colonies. At the same time some "new towns" are being created from scratch.

One such colony taking shape is Lugdunum (Lyons) where the rivers Rhone and Saone meet in central Gaul. It is being hailed as a model colony and settled by Lucius Munatius Plancus, one of Caesar's officers in the Gallic Wars, who was also at his side during the civil war with Pompey. After these events, Rome has been in chaos. Hordes of soldiers are clamouring for their rewards, which include being given land on their discharge. Caesar's friends have also expected generous treatment.

Plancus has also taken over land at Beneventum, in southern Italy, where several nearby towns have been appropriated and given to large numbers of veterans. This resettlement programme helps the state to extend its power and goes some way towards satisfying the land-hunger of a growing population. It is turning out to be very popular with the depressed urban and rural poor.

Wax portrait of an adolescent boy on a mummy, from Hawara, El Faiyum in Egypt, in the Roman period, c.100.

Outlawed Cicero beheaded by assassins

Gaeta, Italy, 7 December 43BC

Cicero, one of the greatest sons of Rome, has been barbarically put to death today on the orders of his enemy, Marcus Antonius. Cicero had fled to his country estate in this small town after being proscribed on Antonius' orders, but Antonius' men found him, dragged him from his litter and killed him.

They cut off his head, and the hands with which he wrote his warnings about Antonius' ambitions, and they are to be hung on the Rostra in the Forum where he made his passionate, lucid speeches. Many men are being killed after being made outlaws in the reign of terror in Rome which has followed Caesar's murder. None of them served Rome as well and honourably as Cicero.

Rich prosper as social divisions widen

The daughter of a rich family has a lesson on the "cithara", a type of harp.

Rome, c.44BC

As Rome reflects on itself following the assassination of Julius Caesar, it sees an increasingly divided society where the rich get richer and the poor poorer.

The earliest ideals of the Roman republic had been egalitarian. Plebeians and equites were equal under the law. There was a written constitution. Tribunes of the people possessed real powers. One of Rome's greatest tribunes, Gracchus, had been assassinated for advocating land reform. One of her greatest consuls, Marius, was said to have been the son of a labourer.

Since Marius' death forty years ago there has been a gradual erosion of civil liberties, an increase in the prestige and political influence of the Roman army, and an acceptance of corruption among public servants that would have shocked the founders of the republic. At the same time vast fortunes have been accumulated by a small group of men who use their wealth, mostly from land, to control the Senate. At

Fresco of a poor traveller or tinker.

first it seemed that Julius Caesar, Marius' nephew, would inherit Marius' egalitarian ideals. Instead he allied himself with Crassus, the richest Roman of them all, placating the plebeians with bread and circuses as they sank from proletariat to undisciplined mob. Egalitarian Rome is dead.

Caesar stabbed to death in Senate

Marcus Antonius hunts murderers

Julius Caesar: victim.

Marcus Junius Brutus: assassin.

Gaius Octavian: successor.

Marcus Antonius: avenger.

Rome, 15 March 44BC

Julius Caesar has been assassinated. He was stabbed to death by a group of conspirators, some of them his closest friends, as he took his seat in the Senate House today, the Ides of March. The soothsayer Spurinna had warned him of danger that would come to him not later than this day, but he ignored the warning, calling Spurinna a false prophet, and went to meet his death.

It was Tillius Cimber, pretending to plead the cause of his brother whom Caesar had exiled, who made the first move as the assassins gathered round the dictator. As Caesar waved him away Cimber seized hold of his toga as if to insist. Caesar protested at this indignity and, as he did so, Casca struck the first blow. The wound was not serious and Caesar struck back with his stylus, driving it into Casca's arm. He tried to get to his feet, but another dagger thrust drove him down. Then they all thrust at him, for they had decided that no one man should be responsible for his death.

When he saw the daggers he pulled the top part of his toga off his face and and let the lower part fall so that he would die with his legs decently covered. He said nothing while 23 daggers thrust home until, as Marcus Brutus prepared to strike for the second time, he reproached Brutus in Greek, saying "You too, my son?".

So Caesar died at the foot of Pompey's statue. He lay there for some time, with no-one daring to approach his body, until three common slaves carried him to his

Caesar's rule ends as he is struck down in the Senate (C20th engraving).

home in a litter. The assassins had planned to throw his body into the Tiber, confiscate his property and revoke all his decrees. But fear of the revenge of Marcus Antonius and Lepidus, Master of the Horse, made them run away.

There were some 60 men in the plot, led by Marcus Brutus, whom Caesar had raised to high rank, and Cassius, to whom Caesar had promised the governorship of Syria. They think of themselves not as murderers but as tyrannicides, duty bound to rid Rome of a dictator who they feared was about to make himself king of Rome.

They had some reason for their fear for, although he had refused to wear the crown offered to him in public by Marcus Antonius, Caesar had accepted other emblems of royalty – a purple robe, statues, and his head embossed on coins. He had

also given his power a religious basis by organising his own cult and, if he was feared as a would-be king, he was feared even more as a potential god.

Rome, 43BC

Marcus Antonius is hunting down the men who murdered Caesar. At first he seemed conciliatory towards them. He persuaded them to leave the Capitol where they had taken sanctuary, dined with Cassius and spoke in favour of an amnesty.

He also favoured the distribution of provinces between Brutus and Cassius and their supporters; when the Senate agreed, voting also that Caesar's decrees should stand, he was hailed for preventing civil war.

However, when he saw the mood of the people at Caesar's funeral where he delivered the eulogy, he mingled indignation at the murder with his praise for the dead man, holding up Caesar's bloody toga and inciting the people to fury. They seized torches from the pyre and set fire to the houses of the assassins. Brutus and Cassius have fled and now the hunt is on.

Young Octavian named as Caesar's heir

Rome, 44BC

Julius Caesar's will, which was guarded by the chief Vestal Virgin, has been read in Marcus Antonius' house by the dictator's father-in-law, Lucius Piso, and it has caused a sensation by naming Gaius Octavian, Caesar's great-nephew, as his chief heir.

Octavian lost his father when he was a boy and Caesar took great interest in his upbringing. But even Octavian was surprised when, under the terms of the will, the dead Caesar adopted him as his son. So

Caesar's mantle falls on the slight shoulders of an 18-year-old, inexperienced in the ways of the world. Some people think that he is too young to play an important role in Rome, and that Antonius will inevitably succeed Caesar.

Octavian must not, however, be disregarded. He was learning the art of war with the army in Illyricum when Caesar was killed. He promptly left for Rome and it is significant that when he landed at Brundisium (Brindisi), the soldiers hailed him as leader.

Rome, 42BC. Caesar is officially recognised as a god and, at the instigation of the triumvirate, it is decided to erect a temple in his honour in the forum.

Sicily, 42BC. Sextus Pompeius, son of Pompey, occupies the island of Sicily with a force of fugitive Pompeians who survived Caesar's victory in 45BC.

Greece, 42BC. Octavian and Marcus Antonius defeat Cassius and Marcus Brutus, two of Caesar's murderers, at the battle of Philippi. Decimus Brutus, the other most prominent conspirator, was killed in Italy last year.

Italy, 41BC. Lucius Antonius, brother of Marcus, takes advantage of a revolt of peasants dispossessed of their land to further the struggle against Octavian. With the help of Marcus Antonius' wife, Fulvia, he provokes the war of the Veterans.

Asia Minor, 41BC. In the course of reorganising the eastern part of the empire, Marcus Antonius meets Cleopatra VII, the Egyptian queen, at Tarsus in Cilicia.

Italy, 40BC. Octavian triumphs over Lucius Antonius at the battle of Perusia (Perugia), thanks to the skill of his two lieutenants, Agrippa and Rufus. He shows great cruelty towards the veterans and peasants who opposed him.

Syria, 40BC. Parthian troops, led by the king's son Pacorus and Quintus Labienus, a former ally of the conspirator Cassius, invade Syria. Decidius Saxa, appointed governor of Syria by Marcus Antonius, is defeated and killed in the ensuing battle.

Italy, October 40BC. A peace treaty is concluded at Brundisium (Brindisi) by which Octavian and Marcus Antonius share the Roman world between them. The west will be controlled by Octavian and the east by Marcus Antonius. Lepidus takes control of the African possessions.

Italy, 40BC. Following the recent death of his wife Fulvia, Marcus Antonius marries Octavian's sister Octavia.

Rome, 40BC. The historian Sallust publishes a history of the Jugurthine war which covers both the Roman campaigns in Numidia at the end of the last century and events in Rome at the time. Sallust served in Caesar's campaign in North Africa in 46BC and became the first governor of the enlarged province of Africa.

Asia Minor, 39BC. Sent by Marcus Antonius to drive the invading Parthians out of Syria and Asia, Publius Ventidius inflicts two crushing defeats on the enemy in Cilicia.

Italy, 39BC. Sextus Pompeius is now in control of Sicily, Sardinia, Corsica and the Peloponnese. By the pact of Misenum the triumvirs formally recognise these possessions. In exchange, Pompey must cease his interruption of Rome's grain supplies in the Mediterranean and halt attacks on the Italian mainland.

Rome, 38BC. Octavian, now almost in full command of the western part of the Roman empire – except for the possessions of Sextus Pompeius – takes the title "son of the divine Julius [Caesar]".

Syria, 38BC. Ventidius expels the Parthians from Syria.

Italy, 37BC. Under a pact reached at Tarentum, Octavian provides Marcus Antonius with troops for the war he is conducting against the Parthians.

Rome, 37BC. The triumvirate is renewed for five more years.

Judaea, 37BC. The Romans drive the Parthians, who invaded Judaea in 40BC, out of Jerusalem. Herod, who escaped to Rome after the invasion, becomes king.

Sicily, 36BC. Octavian accuses Sextus Pompeius of breaking the agreement of 39BC and negotiates with Marcus Antonius for the provision of 120 ships. With the help of Agrippa, who is promoted to admiral, and Lepidus, he defeats Sextus' fleet at Naulochus. This opens the way for the safe transport of supplies to Rome.

Armenia, 36BC. Marcus Antonius retreats to Armenia after suffering a severe defeat by the Parthians.

Asia Minor, 36BC. Sextus Pompeius flees to Miletus, where he dies.

Sicily, 36BC. Despite Lepidus' attempt to seize control of Sicily after the flight of Sextus Pompeius, Octavian annexes the island and takes Lepidus captive.

Italy, 36BC. Octavian sets about consolidating Roman power in the Alps and in Illyricum.

Egypt, 36BC. After suffering a defeat by the Parthians, Marcus Antonius goes to live in Egypt with Cleopatra, whom he weds despite still being married to Octavia. Cleopatra seeks to establish a Hellenistic monarchy with Antonius, who is building up alliances in the East.

Rome, 35BC. Sallust, author of histories of the Catiline conspiracy and the Jugurthine war, is dead. He was acquitted of oppression and during his governorship of Africa, but he made enough money at that period to lay out imposing gardens on the Quirinal and to build a fine mansion.

Rome's high-rise slums are death traps

Rome, c.40BC

The Roman town, planned and laid out in orderly fashion around major thoroughfares and served by impressive networks of sewers and aqueducts, ought to be a healthy and edifying place to live in.

But a major fire which hit part of Rome this year has highlighted serious urban problems in older, unplanned towns. In many cities the grand public works stand side by side with sprawling, narrow streets in which the less well-off citizens live, often in conditions of misery and squalor. In Rome, which contains perhaps a tenth of the entire population of Italy, pressure on space has led to the building of overcrowded and dangerously high blocks of flats, known as *insulae*, or "islands".

In these *insulae*, which are sometimes of concrete or brick, but most often flimsily built of wood and wattle, tenants rub shoulders without proper heating, lighting or cooking facilities. Worst of all, these tenements have no toilets and no connection to the great Roman sewerage network. Water has to be brought in by bearers; piped water from the aqueducts is a luxury for most people, because householders have to pay a fee to get their houses connected to the water supply.

Even without the ever-present danger of disease, *insulae* are potential death traps because of their tendency to collapse without warning.

Better-quality housing at Herculaneum, a town south of Naples.

And should a fire break out, as it did this year, it spreads rapidly to other buildings along the winding, congested, ordure-filled alleys.

The tenants pay high rents to live in their hovels, and wealthy landlords have little interest in the upkeep of cheaply-built high-rise shacks, the loss of which they can easily afford. Even such a famous landlord as Cicero is remarkably unconcerned that his buildings, at Puteoli in southern Italy, may simply collapse. He said recently: "Two of my shops are falling down, and the rest are cracking ... Other people call it a calamity, but I don't count it even a nuisance."

Vitruvius, great architect of Rome

Rome, c.35BC

A treatise has been published, dedicated to the Roman Emperor Augustus which seems likely to influence the development of architecture for centuries to come. Its author is an engineer and architect, Marcus Vitruvius Pollio, and the work, *De architectura*, a ten-volume monument to his immense learning and experience.

Vitruvius has never been much of a practising architect – with only one building of any real note – the Basilica at Fanum (Fano) – to his personal credit. Since the time of Julius Caesar, he has been amassing a vast body of theoretical and practical information on all aspects of architecture and related subjects including geography, climate, people and medicine. He is also an expert on perspective, mathematics, optics and astronomy.

His field of knowledge is extraordinary. He is steeped in mechanics, hydraulics and ballistics, as well as acoustics which he has turned to practical effect by devising systems for the improvement of sound quality of both closed halls and open theatres.

His remarkable work deals with general principles and theory, the history of building practice and materials. Other books books deal with temple construction and public buildings such as prisons, theatres and bath-houses. One is dedicated entirely to interior design.

Brutus dies at Philippi

Philippi, 42BC

Octavian and Antonius have crushed the republican army of Cassius and Brutus at Philippi in Macedonia in a confused battle which lasted for several days.

Cassius was routed on the first day and his camp sacked and, thinking that Brutus was also defeated, he ordered his shield-bearer to cut his throat. Brutus, however, had inflicted severe casualties on Octavian's legions. He mourned over the body of Cassius, declaring him to be "the last of all the Romans".

Then it was his turn to die. Trapped in the mountains with a small force, he accepted defeat and died on the sword of his friend, Strato. His epitaph came from his victorious foe, Antonius: "This was the noblest Roman of them all."

So Caesar's murder has been avenged by his adopted son and his chief lieutenant who, with Lepidus, Caesar's Master of Horse, now form the second triumvirate.

The first act of the triumvirs was to sweep Rome clean of their enemies. They did not make Caesar's mistake of forgiving their opponents, but killed them and confiscated their property. Cicero was perhaps their most famous victim.

Now they have swept Cassius and Brutus from the scene and the cause of republicanism is lost. But cracks are already appearing in the alliance and all Rome is betting on who will be its next ruler.

Herod makes Judaea a Roman enclave

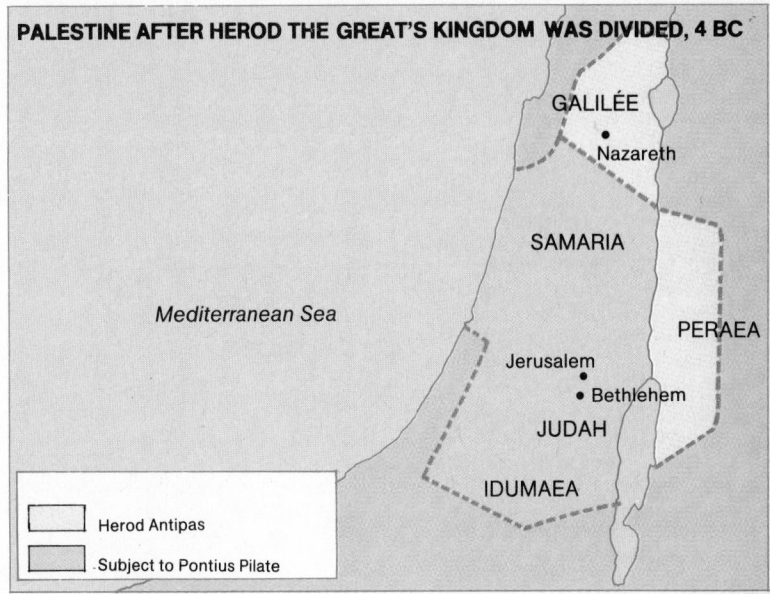

PALESTINE AFTER HEROD THE GREAT'S KINGDOM WAS DIVIDED, 4 BC

- GALILÉE
- Nazareth
- SAMARIA
- Mediterranean Sea
- PERAEA
- Jerusalem
- Bethlehem
- JUDAH
- IDUMAEA

☐ Herod Antipas
☐ Subject to Pontius Pilate

Judaea, 35BC

The land which is the home of the world's Jews, is becoming an increasingly Romanised country, as dependent on Rome as any other part of the republic. One man alone can take responsibility for this development: Herod the Great, King of Judaea since 37BC and unashamed client of the Senate.

Herod, heir to the royal line of the Idumaean Antipater, has been a Roman citizen since 47BC, but, although nominated by Marcus Antonius as king in 40BC, was unable to take power until Roman troops drove a Parthian invasion force out of Jerusalem.

King Herod is a brutal ruler but a subtle diplomat, keeping his subjects quiet and his Roman allies satisfied. Military power rests on a group of forts, notably the Antonia in Jerusalem, manned by a gentile mercenary army. He governs with an efficient bureaucracy and a highly effective secret police.

He is also an enthusiastic builder, who has restored the Temple and created several new cities.

Virgil eulogises the life of the countryside

A pastoral landscape, inspired by one of Virgil's rustic poems (C15th).

Rome, 37BC

A new style of poetry, which paints a romantic picture of the lives of ordinary Italian shepherds and peasants, has just been published by Virgil (Publius Vergilius Maro). The anthology of ten poems, called the *Eclogues* or *Bucolics*, tells of shepherds who suffer the pangs of love and political oppression and find happiness in inner peace. Virgil's shepherds are in fact poets who address their mistresses in song, and the countryside is an idyllic *Arcadia*.

The *Bucolics* were inspired by the *Idylls* of Theocritus, a Sicilian poet who lived in Alexandria around 270BC. Virgil goes much further, however, in giving the peasants tender and sentimental feelings and creating an imaginative pastoral world.

At the same time he is much more of a realist, introducing actual people into his poems. He makes a passionate plea for those who have been dispossessed of their land in the region of the Po valley near Mantua, where he was born in 70BC. He makes a hero of a godlike youth who helped them, who is obviously meant to be Octavian Caesar, the great-nephew of Julius Caesar, who came to power soon after the latter's murder in 44BC.

Virgil's own father was a farmer who was wealthy enough to send him to complete his education in Milan and Rome. In Rome he came under the influence of the Epicurean philosophy, which stresses the dangers of the passions and the need for the development of the inner life. He went to live in an Epicurean colony on the Bay of Naples. The *Bucolics* took him about five years to write.

Royal tomb is built on mountain summit

Asia Minor, 35BC

Antiochus, who has been King of Commagene (*eastern Turkey*) for 27 years, has just had a magnificent tomb built for himself.

It is on the two-mile-high hill of Nimrud, built on top of a conical mass of stones 170 feet high. The tomb is flanked by colossal statues of gods, eagles and lions. The king's Persian and Greek ancestors are shown in bas-reliefs. Antiochus himself is shown shaking hands with a god.

Antiochus has prospered as one of the "client kings" on the fringes of the Roman empire. These kings, nominally independent, but actually bowing to Rome, provide buffer areas between Rome and the barbarians. They save Rome the expense of maintaining permanent garrisons in the area.

The head of a god from the tomb of King Antiochus of Commagene.

Rome, 33BC. Charges by Octavian that Marcus Antonius is under the control of the Egyptian queen, Cleopatra, spark off a campaign of abuse between the two leaders.

Rome, 32BC. Marcus Antonius divorces his wife, Octavia, the sister of Octavian.

Italy, 32BC. After discovering that Antonius' will contains provisions in favour of Cleopatra, Octavian arranges for the whole of Italy, Gaul, Spain and the African possessions to make an oath of allegiance to him. This oath recognises Octavian as leader and entails the obligation to support him in case of war.

Greece, 31BC. Octavian declares war on Marcus Antonius and Cleopatra, who are now in Greece, and moves into Greece with his general Agrippa; they choose Actium as a base. Antonius and Cleopatra are defeated in the ensuing sea battle and flee to Egypt.

Egypt, 31BC. Marcus Antonius, after his defeat at the battle of Actium, and in the belief that Cleopatra has taken her own life, commits suicide.

Egypt, 30BC. Having failed to seduce the young Octavian, Cleopatra commits suicide. Her death brings to an end the last of the Hellenistic monarchies.

Rome, 30BC. The suicides of Marcus Antonius and Cleopatra leave Octavian as sole master of the Roman world.

Egypt, 30BC. Egypt becomes a Roman province. Henceforth it will be directly under the authority of Octavian and its administration will be entrusted to a prefect.

Rome, 30BC. Octavian's friend Maecenas uncovers a plot by Lepidus, the son of the former triumvir, to assassinate Octavian. Maecenas and Agrippa, the general responsible for the victory at Actium, have been put in charge of affairs in Rome and Italy during Octavian's absence.

Rome, 29BC. A temple in the heart of the forum is dedicated to Julius Caesar.

Rome, 29BC. The publication of Virgil's *Georgics*, which deal in verse with agricultural matters and animal husbandry, confirms his position as the foremost poet of the age. A protege of the knight Maecenas, Virgil, whose own farm was confiscated by the triumvirs, has already gained recognition for his *Eclogues*.

Rome, 29BC. By closing the temple of Janus for the first time since 235BC, Octavian signals the achievement of peace throughout the empire.

Rome, 13 January 27BC. Octavian transfers the state to the free disposal of the Senate and the people. He receives Spain, Gaul, and Syria as his province for ten years.

Rome, 16 January 27BC. The senate bestows on Octavian the title of *Augustus*, in recognition of his superior position in the state. He will henceforth be known by the new name.

Greece, 27BC. Augustus wins back Achaea for Rome and makes it into a new Roman province.

Spain, 26BC. Augustus embarks on a military campaign which takes him into the region of the Cantabrian mountains. He puts all his efforts into subjecting the Cantabrian people and the Asturians, who are continuing to rebel against his authority.

Rome, 26BC. The poet Cornelius Gallus, under threat of a treason charge, takes his own life. A one-time friend of Augustus, Gallus recently incurred the emperor's wrath, perhaps because of his high opinion of himself, which he was not ashamed to make public. Gallus, who also made a name for himself on the battlefield, is best known for the love poems to his mistress, the actress Cytheris. He was a firm friend of Virgil.

Egypt, 25BC. The Roman general Petronius secures the frontiers between Egypt and Ethiopia. His campaign consolidates the position achieved by Cornelius Gallus in the region in 29BC.

Asia Minor, 25BC. Despite his desire to instigate a regime of vassal states, Augustus reduces Galatia to a Roman province, taking advantage of the weakness of the local powers.

Italy, 25BC. The Roman general Terentius Varro Murena defeats the Gallic tribe known as the Salassi in the Val d'Aosta.

Rome, 25BC. The historian Livy embarks on a monumental history of Rome since its foundation.

Rome, 25BC. The poet Horace, who was born in southern Italy, is carving out a brilliant career for himself in Rome. Like Virgil a protege of Maecenas, he has rapidly gained entry to Augustus' entourage. Already famed for his *Epodes* and *Satires*, Horace has recently undertaken the composition of a book of *Odes* addressed to Maecenas. He claims that his models are the early Greek lyric poets Sappho and Alcaeus.

Kush, 23BC. The Romans, led by the general Petronius, invade the Meroe kingdom of Kush and sack its capital, Napata.

Petra prospers on Arabian trade routes

Petra, c.25BC

From their extraordinary rock-hewn desert city of Petra, the Nabataeans are continuing to spread their commercial empire far and wide and maintain their independence against allcomers. This vigorous race of desert Arabs is growing rich from the caravan trade which is developing with southern Arabia and involving Arabian incense and myrrh, Persian pearls, Indian spices and cotton, and Chinese silk.

Petra lies hidden in great folds of mountains, and with their wealth the Nabataeans have hollowed caves out of the sides of the ravines and created a whole city in the rock with villas, temples, markets and tombs. The city is a marvel.

Petra means simply "rock", an apt name for a city hewn from stone.

In Rome, married life can begin at 12

Painting of a Roman wedding ceremony, now with ever-younger brides.

Rome, c.25BC

They marry young in modern Rome. One girl in ten now gets married by the time she reaches the legal age of 12, according to a survey of 145 marriages. In it, a further eight per cent admitted living with their future husbands while under age. However, the most popular ages for girls to marry are 13 and 14, according to the survey. Boys, who can marry from 14, prefer to wait until even later.

For Rome's child brides the transition from childhood to wedlock is often as fast as that from night to day. On the eve of her wedding the pre-teen bride is expected to give back her toys to Lares, the household god. The next day she is taken to her bridegroom's home for a ceremony requiring her to adopt her future husband's gods and ancestors. The newlyweds follow their vows with an animal sacrifice and a mock abduction for the benefit of cheering relatives before the bride is carried over the threshold into the bridal suite. There the groom hands her bread, fire and water, while she hands him a spindle, as a symbol of her virtue and domesticity.

Many young marriages are arranged, with the city keen to maintain a healthy population rate. Divorce, however, is becoming more common, with couples able to dissolve a marriage simply by consent.

Cleopatra bids for glory

Rome, 32BC

All Rome is intrigued and concerned at the romance between Cleopatra, the alluring Queen of Egypt – who has already given birth to a son by Julius Caesar – and Marcus Antonius, Rome's consul in the east. The scandal threatens to embroil the whole Roman republic in a civil war.

After Caesar's assassination, Antonius, a popular figure who had been the dictator's first lieutenant, had agreed to share the Roman world with Caesar's adopted son, Octavius. Neither had reckoned with the seductive power and the fierce ambition of the queen on the Nile.

Cleopatra dreamed of an Egypt restored to its original splendour under the Ptolemies; and through Antonius she saw a way in which Alexandria could become the centre of the entire Graeco-Roman world. The equally ambitious Antonius saw the wealth of Egypt as a potential springboard to ultimate power.

Antonius' dallying with the Egyptian queen was a clear factor in the failure of his campaigns against the Parthians in northern Persia, in which he lost a third of his legions. And neither had reckoned with Antonius' wife, Octavia – Octavian's sister – whose fury knew no bounds when Cleopatra contracted a form of marriage with Antonius and bore him twins.

Civil war is inevitable. Octavian is preparing to sail east, where Antonius and Cleopatra are making ready for the final showdown.

The beguiling – and very clever – queen of Egypt, in command of the Egyptian fleet. When she saw Antonius losing, she fled (C19th engraving).

Cleopatra, last queen of Egypt?

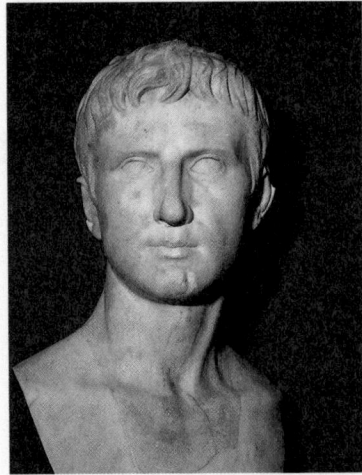

Octavian, the Roman leader.

Octavian is victorious

Actium, 2 September 31BC

Octavian and his general, Agrippa, have won an absolute victory over the fleet commanded by Antonius and Cleopatra at a great sea battle off Actium.

Antonius' ships were at a disadvantage from the beginning of the battle, for Agrippa's ships had been raiding the Egyptian lines of communication, so they were short of supplies. They were also short of rowers for the *triremes*, as plague had run through their decks.

In a skilful campaign Agrippa bottled up Antonius' fleet on the west coast of the Balkans until it was in such a poor state that he was forced to break out.

As soon as Cleopatra saw which way the fight was going, she turned her ship towards Egypt and fled. Antonius, seeing his lover sail away, followed her, deserting his men who fought on until they were persuaded to capitulate with the promise of honourable treatment.

Antonius' cause is ruined. There is little doubt that the cold, implacable Octavian will pursue him to Egypt and to his certain death. Octavian, a poor commander, must give thanks to Agrippa for his naval victory, but he has also waged a brilliant political and propaganda campaign against his former allies in the triumvirate.

First he neutralised Lepidus and then he convinced the Romans that Antonius was betraying them to serve Cleopatra's interests. Now is he what Caesar aspired to be: master not only of Rome but of all its possessions.

Governors keep provinces in order

Rome, 27BC

Augustus, ruler of Rome, has come up with a scheme which will maintain his power and at the same time bow to demands for more power from the Senate in the old republican tradition. He is vesting the rule of ten or so of the biggest provinces in governors selected in the old way by drawing lots in the Senate.

Responsible for law and order, the governors, will hold office for one year and are watched over by *procuratores*, knights appointed by Augustus. The *procuratores* look after the emperor's personal possessions in the province, dealing with much of the administration, as the governors are often away.

Regions shared out include Sicily, Narbonne, and parts of Africa and Macedonia. Augustus retains control of the other provinces for several years through legates he shrewdly appoints himself.

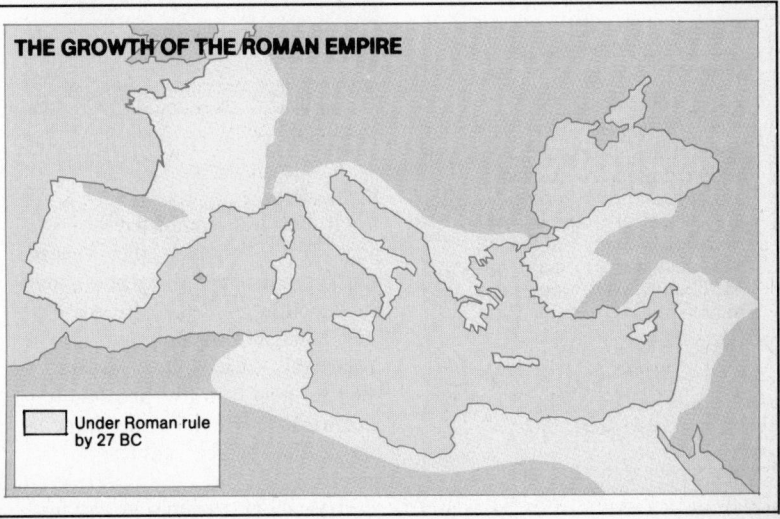

THE GROWTH OF THE ROMAN EMPIRE

Under Roman rule by 27 BC

Republican fiction masks imperial power

Rome, 23BC

Is Rome still a republic? Or have the Roman people been deluded into believing that they still have a say in the destiny of this city? The Romans have always been hostile to monarchy or any leader with absolute power. They exiled their last king, and Julius Caesar was killed in the name of liberty.

Octavian, the victor of the sea battle of Actium and vanquisher of his arch-rival Marcus Antonius, has held the consulship of Rome for eight years – even though the consul has to be elected annually. After holding every public office, he has now been given for life the title and powers of the tribunes and the title of *imperium maius proconsulare*, which carries absolute power.

Throughout this period Octavian has remained wholly modest, proclaiming his respect for the Senate and people. Even when the empire invited him to receive an extraordinary *imperium* (emperorship) – to be renewed every ten years – he made a dramatic show of laying down his power before the Senate.

Augustus: a man of the people?

Four years ago he was awarded the title of *Augustus* – based on *auctoritas* (authority) – a title which he can now use as his name.

Nonetheless, he prefers to assuage republican feelings by the use of *princeps* ("first citizen"), even though Augustan Rome is clearly no longer a republic.

Virgil's new poem tells of Rome's origins

Virgil and Muses (c.200AD).

Rome, 19BC

Virgil has just completed an epic poem in 12 books, the *Aeneid*, which builds on the legends about the founding of Rome. He has created a magnificent myth which will inspire all citizens here. It shows how the poet can give patriotic service to his country equally important to that of the soldier and the statesman.

The poem, which took him nearly a decade to write, marks a big change from the rural bliss of the *Bucolics*. He hesitated more than once before writing it; indeed the god Apollo at one point warned him to stick to pastoral poetry.

Virgil was inspired by the great epic poems of the Greek poet, Homer. His hero, the Trojan, Aeneas, was a relative of Hector, an important character in Homer's *Iliad*. Aeneas leaves Troy for long wanderings over the sea, just as Odysseus did in the *Odyssey*, though for different reasons.

In Virgil's poem Aeneas is near Italy when a storm begun by the goddess, Juno, casts him onto the shore of Africa. Venus then puts a spell on him which makes him fall in love with Dido, the queen of Carthage. He tells her the story of the fall of Troy and his wanderings. But Jupiter tells him to get on with his mission of founding a new kingdom. The grief-stricken Dido kills herself when he leaves. After many battles Aeneas arrives in Latium and founds Rome with the help of the Arcadians and Etruscans.

Horace says simple pleasures are best

Rome, 13BC

Speaking the language of the common people, the poet Horace is the most influential writer of the day. Without appearing to moralise, he advocates the virtues of the simple life. His poems amuse and instruct simultaneously.

Born in Apulia in 65BC, Horatius Flaccus was of modest family, but went to university in Athens, and served in the army under Brutus. His poetic gifts were noticed by Maecenas, who made him part of the writers' circle round Augustus, and gave him a Sabine farm, to which he often refers in his poems.

In the *Satires*, written between 35BC and 30BC, Horace contrasts the pleasures of country life with

Horace (engraving, c.1800).

the hectic, frustrating cares of the city. He relates conversations from life, and mixes dialogue with irreverent observations on people and the way they behave.

Horace's *Odes* and *Epodes* show his concern with form. In satirical vein, he borrows from the Greek Archilochus, who wrote poems of scathing abuse. He adheres rigidly to the constraints of meter. But his lightness of touch never leaves him.

In his latest work, *Epistles*, the poet rejects the Platonic theory of inspiration, and declares that poetry should be the work of reason, written with care and modesty. It should be useful and pleasing. To this end, he offers some down-to-earth hints on avoiding folly, vice and guilt.

Coca-leaf ritual is celebrated by artists in Peru

A Mochica stirrup-spout vessel of a fox with a cap and ear-plugs.

Peru, c.10BC

The finest artisans and craftsmen in the Americas are to be found among the Mochica people on the north-east coast of Peru, most of whom habitually chew the coca-leaf, which grows in abundance.

Their regular coca rituals are recorded on painted ceramics showing figures wearing ritual clothing and the local Mochica god – a cat-like being, its belt with snake-like forms dangling from it. Not all the ceramics are coca-related, however. Some show domestic scenes, house-forms, figures holding vessels, a man with a cat, a figure pecked by vultures and a curious "moon animal".

The Mochica potters have mastered some remarkable techniques – perhaps acquired from previous cultures like the Huantar and Recuay – including modelling in high-relief with low-relief created by stamping. Some scenes are painted on flat surfaces; some are moulded; some hand-modelled. All show a wide variation in form.

Related subjects are sometimes depicted in a strip of overlapping illustrations. One picture may show the coca-ritual, the next the bag in which the coca-leaves are collected; and the next may show a battle scene and the taking of captives for sacrificial beheading.

German campaign grinds to a halt

Germany, 9BC

Rome's drive to extend its empire and protect it by easily defensible natural barriers has come to a halt in Germany. Drusus, the audacious commander who has been leading the Roman campaigns in Germany has died in summer camp.

He was the emperor's stepson and Augustus also considered him to be one of his finest generals. He entrusted him with the invasion of Germany three years ago, but it has proved a formidable task and its problems appear to have been underestimated. After three successive campaigning seasons designed to secure a front line on the river Elbe, Drusus leaves the country unconquered.

In the first campaign Drusus' chief base was Vetera (Xanten), and then Mogontiacum (Mainz). He succeeded in routing the Sugambri and then sailed from the lower Rhine along a specially constructed canal to the North Sea where he won over the Frisii. His fleets explored the North Sea, from the Zuyder Zee to the mouth of the Elbe, with the aim of landing troops with fresh supplies and attacking the enemy from the rear.

Last year he invaded the land of the Chatti, and in his last and greatest campaign he had beaten several tribes and reached the Elbe before falling victim to a German counter-attack.

He has died as a result of an illness which began when he was thrown from his horse. News of this brought his brother and fellow commander Tiberius hastening from Ticinum, and he reached Drusus just before he died.

Traders and craftsmen flourish in Rome

Rome, c.10BC

The expansion of Rome's empire overseas is having a marked effect on prosperity at home, with more of the population enjoying Rome's new-found wealth.

Observers of Rome's carefully stratified society note that beneath the landed ruling classes, a whole new class of urban plebs – many of them freedmen – are cashing in on the economic boom created by Rome's flourishing empire.

Nowhere typifies this better than modern Ostia, whose port facilities service Rome's overseas trade. Around the port roadside businesses have sprung up, providing services and products to satisfy almost every need. Most of the goods have been produced locally by the occupants. Prospective purchasers can watch bakers, fullers, goldsmiths, launderers, blacksmiths and tanners at work in their shops.

In certain well-established trades skilled craftsmen have formed themselves into associations, governed by strict rules of conduct, and designed to give mutual protection in times of hardship. One of the most flourishing is Ostia's wine guild. Membership is confined to importers and merchants, entitling them to attend wine auctions. It also accords status, with members displaying signs on their premises.

A relief of Roman builders using a heavy hoist and a treadmill on the Aterii monument.

A Roman butcher at his slab chopping meat: joints are hung hyhienically above his head.

Jewish religion is divided by sects

A C20th impression of the Jewish sect known as "Scrollmakers".

Judaea, c.10BC

The Jews pride themselves on the worship of a single god, but Judaism, their religion, is becoming increasingly divided by rival sects, each of which claims to preach the one true faith. Their only link is the common belief, based on a number of prophecies, that a Messiah ("anointed one" in Hebrew) will appear to free the Jewish nation and establish Jehovah as the true Lord of the world.

Among the most prominent of these sects are the Pharisees ("separate" in Hebrew), whose origins lie in the popular uprising of Judas Maccabaeus in 165BC. They believe that everyone should receive a proper religious education, suitably adapted for the needs of everyday life; religious devotion should be a personal, inner emotion. Some believe in resurrection after death and what they term the Last Judgement, when everyone, alive or dead, will face the Almighty.

Opposed to them are the Essenes, who reject a worldly, social life in favour of religious communes where the Law can be studied in depth without interference from externals. They predict the imminent end of the world and believe in two Messiahs, one descended from King David, the other from Aaron. Between them lie the Sadducees, a priestly caste, and the Zealots, who combine Pharisaic beliefs with militaristic nationalism.

Germany, 9BC. Tiberius succeeds Drusus, stepson of Augustus, who died after reaching the Elbe, as commander of the Roman army stationed in Germany. Drusus had been engaged in establishing Roman supremacy in Germany. Tiberius is now making great inroads into the territory beyond the Rhine.

Rome, 9BC. An altar of peace, for which the senate voted four years ago, is dedicated in Rome.

Rome, 8BC. Horace and Maecenas die within a few months of each other. The two men, bound by a strong friendship, each made a distinctive mark on the artistic history of the empire. Maecenas became a patron of a circle of fine poets, including Virgil, Propertius and Horace himself, whom he brought to the notice of his friend Augustus. Horace, famed for his *Satires*, *Epodes*, *Odes*, *Epistles* and the *Ars Poetica*, owed to Maecenas his good fortune in becoming the poet of the national renaissance.

Armenia, 6BC. Tiberius, engaged for the past two years in continuing the conquest of Germany, has now been sent to Armenia.

Asia Minor, c.5BC. Strabo, a Greek born in Amaseia, northern Asia Minor, has written a vast *Geography*. A general survey of Hellenistic geography and cartography, his work examines the controversies between Eratosthenes, the first systematic geographer, who was writing 200 years ago, and his successors. Regional descriptions cover physical geography, ethnographic features and myth. Its wide range makes the *Geography* an effective census of the world.

Judaea, 4BC. The brutal reign of Herod the Great, king of Judaea, is at an end. On his death, his kingdom is divided between his three sons.

Judaea, 4BC. A Jewish couple, Joseph the carpenter and his wife Mary have a baby in a stable in Bethlehem and name him Jesus. New tax legislation had required all Jews to return to their home town and the resulting overcrowding meant that there was no room for them at the inn.

Rome, 2BC. In recognition of his Roman virtues, Augustus is endowed with the title *pater patriae*, "father of his country".

Gauls abandon their beards and take up togas, as Roman ways transform the administration and architecture of their land

Gallic sculpture – in Roman style.

Aqueducts are among the Roman engineering marvels brought to Gaul.

Gaul, c.1BC
You have to travel a long way through Gallia Narbonensis (Provence) these days before you meet any citizens sporting beards or even moustaches. In the capital here, the citizens long ago began to shave and abandoned the traditional breeches for the toga. Although Rome annexed the region some 120 years ago, many of the inhabitants continued to fight with legendary fierceness, and to maintain their own dress and customs. Today, however, Roman ways have been accepted throughout the area, and the population is such a model of submissiveness that only a few Roman garrisons remain.

It marks a success for the conciliatory policy adopted by the Roman authorities which offered citizenship rights to local leaders who, in turn, began to imitate the ways of their Roman occupiers.

Latin, long the administrative language, is now taught widely in higher education, and the ordinary people have begun to pick it up from soldiers and traders. Wealthy citizens are building Roman villas with their delightful warm baths. They have also begun to worship Roman gods. There are temples with huge statues, through which local artists are seeking to reproduce the splendours of Graeco-Roman work. Local craftsmen are making Roman-style glassware.

King Herod the Great, ally of Rome, unmourned in Jerusalem

Judaea, 4BC
Herod the Great, during whose 33 years of rule Judaea came fully under the influence of Rome, has died in Jerusalem aged 69. Herod, who was appointed king by the Roman Senate in 40BC, is unlikely to be mourned by all his subjects, many of whom regret the alliance with Rome. He was also very unpopular with the extreme Jewish factions, the Saducees, Pharisees, Zealots and Essenes.

His greatest monument remains in the architecture of his capital city. Herod's palace, where he lived and ruled, is well known, but his supreme achievement is the reconstruction of the Temple. Though not yet quite complete, it is being glorified and enlarged to cater for the hundreds of thousands of pilgrims who visit every year. It is planned to be the largest structure in the known world.

A model of the Antonia Fortress in Jerusalem at the time of the Great King Herod, who was also responsible for the rebuilding of the city's temple.

Antilles, c.1. Arawak peoples, originating from the Orinoco basin, migrate to the Antilles, gradually driving out the earlier Ciboney settlers of the islands.

Mexico, c.1. Hieroglyphic writing and the use of the "Long Count" calendar is developing in the Maya area of south-east Mexico. Hieroglyphs are carved or painted on monuments and also used on screenfold "books". The Long Count calendar, a highly complex and accurate method of recording time in calendrical cycles, forms the basis of Maya religious life and records Maya dynastic and political history.

South America, c.1. On the Pacific coast of Colombia and Ecuador the inhabitants have learnt how to smelt platinum at very high temperatures.

Rome, 2. On the death of Lucius Caesar, one of Augustus' two grandsons, Tiberius – the son of the emperor's wife – becomes a contender for the succession. Another possible successor is Gaius Caesar, the second grandson of the *princeps* (as Augustus is known).

Rome, 4. The death of Gaius Caesar, Augustus' second grandson, combined with his own receipt of tribunician power, puts Tiberius in a strong position to succeed as emperor. Augustus formally adopts Tiberius, his stepson, giving him the name of Tiberius Julius Caesar. Augustus also adopts Agrippa Postumus, son of Agrippa, who was born after his father's death in 12BC, and insists that Tiberius adopts his own nephew, Germanicus.

Rome, 5. The *Lex Valeria Cornelia* is promulgated. Under this law, ten centuries (voting groups of the Roman people), formed by senators and the wealthiest knights, choose the candidates whom they consider worthy of the consulship or prefecture. It is an attempt by Augustus to modify the functioning of the *comitia*, an assembly of the people whose main purpose is to ratify or veto decrees of the senate. The role of the *comitia* is already restricted by the *princeps'* right to decide who shall stand for election.

Rome, 6. To streamline urban administration, Augustus creates a reserve nocturnal police force and a prefecture responsible for fire-fighting, called the *vigiles*.

Massacre in the forest

Romans attacking under their shields, from the column of Marcus Aurelius.

Germany, 9

An entire Roman army of three legions campaigning in the fledgling province of Germany has been ambushed in a forest and wiped out by a German tribe. News of the defeat has come as a shock to Rome and is a damaging blow to Roman prestige and its hold on Germany.

The force, which was led by General Quinctilius Varus, was trying to pacify a region neglected because of revolts elsewhere. Varus had struck camp in the Teutoberg Forest when he was attacked by the Cherusci, a tribe led by a young German prince, Arminius. Hemmed in by forests and marshes, the Romans were exterminated almost to a man. Varus, who had deluded himself into thinking the tribesmen were grateful for Roman rule, killed himself with his sword.

His head was cut off and sent to Rome by the victors. Augustus was so overcome by the defeat that he refused to cut his beard or hair for several months and walked about muttering: "Varus, give me back my legions." The Romans will now try to mantain the Rhine as their frontier with Germany.

Livy completes 16-year history of Rome

A later image of the chronicler.

Rome, 9

A new chronicle of Rome and the glorious deeds of the Romans has just been completed and is already proving a great success.

The author of the 142-book *History of Rome*, from the city's foundation to the present age of Augustus, is a 50-year-old native of Padua, in north-east Italy, called Titus Livius, or Livy. Unlike some annal-writers he is not a public figure dabbling in history for political ends, but a serious, dedicated historian. About 16 years ago, Livy decided that Rome deserved a new history. It was to be worthy of the prosperity and imperial greatness of the new Augustan era, which he hopes will see a restoration of old Roman moral virtues.

Despite his deep seriousness and overall moral tone, Livy's *History* is rich in humanity and variety. He uses a wide range of Latin styles, depending on the circumstances: orators use elaborate rhetoric, but a military man talks in the colloquialisms of a soldier. Livy has come under fire for alleged provincialism; to most Romans, though, this is the liveliest and most realistic history they have read.

African kingdom enjoys renaissance

Sudan, 9

Over 30 years after Kush was devastated by Roman invaders, King Natakamani is rebuilding the country, and re-establishing its economic prosperity.

The war between Kush and Rome began with an ill-advised Kushite border raid on Syene, near Aswan, while the main Roman army in Egypt was engaged in battle against the Arabians. Having defeated the Arabians, the Roman legions, under Publius Petronicus, the governor of Egypt, recaptured Syene and marched south into the

Roman-influenced Kushite temple.

Kushite heartland, sacking the capital, Napata.

According to the geographer Strabo, who was with the legions, the inhabitants of Kush were nomads, river people and troglodytes (no doubt a reference to Meroe iron miners). They were neither numerous nor warlike and, though they collected an army of 30,000, they were ill-equipped and easily defeated by Petronicus' 10,000 infantry and 800 cavalry.

For ten years the country lay at waste until Natakamani ascended the throne and, adopting the technology of his enemy, began a programme of reconstruction that is making Kush stronger and wealthier than before the invasion.

Nakatamani is using the revenues of the country's gold and iron mines to renovate cities, secure trade routes and re-establish law and order. He has already built more than any other Kushite ruler, founding temples and palaces at Amara, Meroe and Naqa, and the shrine of Jebel Barkal near Napata.

Rome, 9. Augustus decides to abandon the attempted conquest of Germany after the recent devastating defeat of the Roman army on the Rhine by Arminius, a chieftain of the Cherusci tribe.

China, 9. The regent and acting emperor Wang Mang, legitimising his action on the pretence of fabricated omens, usurps the throne from the young prince and imperial heir-apparent, Liu Ying. Declaring the Han defunct, he ascends the throne himself and calls his dynasty the Xin, or New. Wang Mang's usurpation is made possible by his family's relationship of marriage to the imperial line.

Balkans, 9. The Roman general Tiberius crushes a revolt in the central European region of Pannonia after three years of fighting.

Balkans, 10. Pannonia becomes a Roman province, linking Illyricum, on the Adriatic coast, with Moesia, on the shores of the Black Sea. The administration of Pannonia is independent of that of the province of Dalmatia.

Parthia, 12. The victor in a struggle with Vonones, leader of the Pahlavas (a tribe related to the warrior horsemen known as the Scythians), Artabanus III becomes king of Parthia. Artabanus is a descendant, on his mother's side, of Arsaces, who founded the royal dynasty of Parthia c.250BC.

Rome, 13. Augustus appoints Tiberius his successor by giving him a proconsular *imperium maius*, thus creating a joint regency. Augustus has taken advantage of the ten-yearly renewal of his power to bring Tiberius into the fold.

Italy, 14. Immediately after the death of Augustus, his adopted son, Agrippa Postumus, is put to death. Some years ago Agrippa Postumus was disinherited by Augustus because of his depraved behaviour and sent into perpetual exile on Planasia.

Rome, 14. On the proposal of the consuls, Tiberius is proclaimed emperor.

Rome, 14. The Senate decrees that Augustus should be deified.

Kush, c.15. King Natakamani of Meroe, who shared power with Candace (Queen Mother) Amanitere, is dead. He restored the kingdom of Kush after the Roman invasion of Napata in 23BC and has traded as far east as India, via Axum.

Rome, 15. Tiberius brings back into force the law of *maiestas*, which punishes acts which undermine the sovereign power and dignity of the Roman people.

Rome, 15. The younger Drusus, son of Tiberius, becomes consul after successfully putting down a revolt of the Pannonian legions.

Rome, 16. A slave of Agrippa Postumus, by the name of Clemens, is captured and killed after impersonating Agrippa in an attempt to overthrow Tiberius.

Germany, 16. While on the Rhine with his parents, Germanicus (adopted son of Tiberius) and Agrippina, four-year-old Gaius is nicknamed "Caligula" ("Little Boots") by the soldiers because of the military boots he wears.

Italy, 17. The historian Livy, who chronicled the history of Rome since its foundation, dies at his birthplace, Patavium (Padua).

Rome, 26 May 17. Germanicus, the son of Drusus who was adopted by Tiberius, celebrates a great victory over the Germans under Arminius – the latest in a two-year campaign to avenge the Romans for the crushing defeat they suffered at the hands of the Germans in the Teutoberg forest eight years ago. Tiberius, jealous of Germanicus' popularity, has now recalled him to Rome.

Asia Minor, 17. On the deaths of the kings Archelaus of Cappadocia and Antiochus of Commagene, their kingdoms are annexed to the Roman empire. Cappadocia is established as a province and Commagene becomes part of Syria.

Asia Minor, 17. The prolific poet Ovid dies in exile at Tomis on the Black Sea. Before embarking on his controversial love poems, Ovid was a distinguished lawyer and scored his first literary success with the tragedy *Medea*. His epic poem *Metamorphoses*, written in hexameters, is a collection of stories from classical and Near Eastern legend. Since his banishment by Augustus, Ovid has written, among other things, a five-volume work of elegies called the *Tristia*.

Greece, 18. While at Nicopolis in Epirus, Germanicus becomes consul for the second time.

Armenia, 18. Germanicus instals Artaxias (Zeno) on the throne of Armenia. Despite his designs on Armenia, the Parthian king, Artabanus III, acquiesces and renews his friendship with Rome.

China, 18. Wang Mang's imperial forces fail to quell an uprising in Shandong of the rebel bands of peasants known as the Red Eyebrows.

Rome, 19. Germanicus incurs the wrath of Tiberius by travelling, out of romantic curiosity, to Egypt, which Augustus had barred to senators.

Cult of the emperor unites Roman world

Later idea of a celebration glorifying Augustus in Rome.

Gythium, Greece, 17

Emperor Tiberius has issued new guidelines to provincial officials on how far to take the cult of emperor-worship, which is fast becoming Rome's single most successful cultural export to its empire.

The guidance is contained in a letter to the people of Gythium. Last year their leaders sacrificed a bull to Tiberius as the finale to six days of worship in the Temple of Caesar celebrating the Emperor and his imperial ancestors.

Emperor Tiberius applauds the Gytheates for treating his late father Caesar Augustus as a god, but says: "For myself I am contented with more modest and human honours." He is prepared to accept sacrifices and oaths in the name of his Genius, his guiding spirit, but finds the adulation that comes with being treated as a deity not to his taste. The elaborate ceremony laid on by Gythium's councillors and magistrates reflects current Greek enthusiasm for the benefits of Roman rule.

Throughout the empire similar ceremonies are held annually, with the emperor and his ancestors frequently worshipped alongside local gods. By not disrupting local patterns of worship proconsular officials have been able to retain the loyalty of provincial peoples, at the same time using emperor-worship to ensure loyalty to Rome.

Reports from across the empire suggest that the cult of emperor-worship is strongest in recently conquered provinces, which have yet to be Romanised, and weakest in Rome itself where the emperor, sensitive to upper-class attitudes, has been careful only to allow worship of his Genius, rather than himself.

How Rome flourished under the rule of Augustus

Augustus, diplomatic emperor, is dead

Rome, 14

As he lay on his deathbed this August, the Emperor Augustus summoned a group of friends and asked them wryly: "Have I played my part in the farce of life creditably enough?" Augustus could look back at a life in which the Roman empire became stable and prosperous and continued to grow.

Augustus was concerned with reducing internal friction within the Roman world. He forcibly pacified Spain and Gaul, and annexed several other countries, including Egypt. But in his latter years his external policy tended to be diplomatic rather than warlike. In the north-east he gave up grandiose plans for the invasion and occupation of Parthia (Iran), and settled for the return of trophies and prisoners captured in earlier campaigns

A pacified barbarian offers a child in tribute to the emperor Augustus.

and the evacuation of Armenia. The Euphrates is now Rome's eastern border. Augustus was a strong believer in the traditional Roman policy of encouraging local self-rule vassal states, a system which is working well in Judaea and Galicia.

Erotic poems that led to a poet's exile

Rome, 17

Among those to suffer the wrath of Augustus – allegedly for his writing of erotic verses – was Rome's leading poet, Publius Ovidius Naso, known as Ovid. Instead of being allowed to enjoy popular acclaim in Rome, nine years ago Ovid was banished to the Black Sea colony of Tomis, where he has now died.

Ovid's greatest work, the *Ars Amatoria* (The Art of Love), is said to be the poem which angered Augustus. It is a guide to seduction in three books: the first two for

men, the third for women and written at the request of women. Much more than a poetic sex-manual, however, *Ars Amatoria* is filled with Ovid's vibrant wit and can be seen as a satire on Roman life.

Ovid's friends, puzzled at the savagery of the exile, believed that Augustus was furious because of the poet's alleged interference in political matters. From exile, Ovid wrote (to Caesar) in *Tristia*: "Though two crimes, a poem and a blunder, have brought me ruin ... I must keep silent."

Temples celebrate the glory of Rome

Reconstructed "Altar of the Peace of Augustus", imperial focal point.

Rome, c.10

After a century of turmoil, the Roman world is enjoying an unprecedented period of peace. A major building programme is under way, with the emperor pledging that he will leave Rome – a city built of bricks – "swathed in marble".

There can be no finer example of Augustus' taste than the *Ara Pacis* – an altar of peace built in 9BC to celebrate the emperor's return from "pacifying" Gaul and Spain. This half-religious, half-civil monument, erected by the Senate and people, represents the very soul of Rome at this time. On one wall, allegorical figures of Rome and the rest of Italy flank a door; by another are mythological scenes of

Romulus and Remus. Another wall shows a procession of senators, lictors, magistrates and priests, with a few "typical Roman people" in attendance. Most significant of all is the huge frieze depicting the emperor's family and relatives, sculpted life-size in "formal" poses.

A third Forum, to cope with the increase in population and number of legal disputes, has been completed. A new temple of Jupiter is under construction on the Capitol, together with a new Sanctuary and a temple of Mars in Caesar's memory.

Emperor controls the purse-strings in administrative shake-up

Rome, 14

With the streets of Rome thronged with people of all races and freed slaves, with the city burgeoning over its seven hills, the need for adequate administration was apparent even before Augustus began his reign. The emperor has created just such a bureaucracy, although every aspect of local government stems from his own office.

Rome is governed by prefects – chosen from knights of the equestrian order, who gave staunch sup-

port to Augustus during the civil war – each of whom has separate responsibilities. The emperor's chief-of-staff is a close political adviser and controls the imperial bodyguard. The adminstration of Rome is conducted by the prefect of the city, aided by two knights. Under him come the prefects of the *vigiles* (police and firemen) and corn supply. Roads, aqueducts and public buildings are dealt with by *curatores*, men with technical training. The vital province of

Egypt has its own prefect. Taxes are gathered and counted by freedmen assisted by slaves, and this same class handles the writing and classification of official texts.

Augustus has revised the roll of citizens on a ward-by-ward basis, and reorganised a welfare system involving the distribution of corn or money. And, determined to revive Rome's former glory, he has decreed that togas must be worn in the Forum. Cloaks are definitely out of favour in Caesar's Rome.

The ruined Temple of Mars, in the Roman Forum.

Italy, 19. Maroboduus, who migrated south from Germany with his tribe, the Marcomanni, c.9BC and built up a kingdom in land of Bohemia, seeks refuge on Roman territory after being expelled from his kingdom. Internal troubles in Bohemia were stirred up by the Romans, who now intern Maroboduus at Ravenna.

Syria, 10 October 19. The Roman general Germanicus dies near Antioch. He was convinced that the mysterious illness that ended in his death was a result of poisoning by the Syrian governor, Gnaeus Calpurnius Piso, whom he had ordered to leave the province.

Rome, 20. Gnaeus Calpurnius Piso, the former governor of Syria, is prosecuted by the Senate for fomenting a military revolt in Syria, but commits suicide during the trial. Piso is suspected of implication in the death of Germanicus.

Gaul, 21. A revolt among the Gallic tribes known as the Treveri and the Aedui is swiftly suppressed by Gaius Silius, the commander of upper Germany.

China, 22. The usurper Wang Mang is beaten and killed during a revolt by partisans of the legitimate Han regime. The revolt was provoked by merchants and capitalists employed as administrators, whose underhand practices Wang Mang was trying to curb. His death sparks off a quarrel between the Han princes over who should rule.

Rome, 23. Sejanus, the sole commander of the Praetorian Guard, concentrates the Guard – until now dispersed throughout Italy – in a permanent camp in Rome. Following the recent death of Tiberius' son Drusus (in which Sejanus may have been implicated), Sejanus occupies a position of enormous influence in the senate.

North Africa, 24. Tacfarinas, king of the Numidians, who seven years ago stirred up a revolt – which has been rumbling on ever since – in the province of Africa, is trapped and killed by Publius Cornelius Dolabella, the Roman proconsul in Africa. The province of Africa is brought to heel.

India, 25. In Gandhara, the Buddha is represented for the first time in human form.

China, 25. With the ascendancy of Liu Xiu over other rival protagonists in the struggle for power during the civil war at the end of the Xin dynasty, a new dynasty, known as the Later or Eastern Han, is established. The Han imperial line is restored, with the capital at Loyang.

Rome, 25. The historian Cremutius Cordus, prosecuted for treason on the instigation of Sejanus, takes his own life. He refused to glorify Augustus and wrote in praise of, among others, Brutus and Cassius, the murderers of Caesar. Many of his works are burnt.

Judaea, 26. Pontius Pilate, who has recently become the fifth Roman procurator of Judaea and Samaria, has offended the Jews by bringing images of the emperor into Jerusalem. He has shown his lack of sympathy with the Jewish religion in other ways.

Italy, 27. On the prompting of Sejanus, the prefect of the Praetorian Guard who has become his chief adviser, Tiberius decides to leave Rome for the island of Capri.

Judaea, c.27. Herod Antipas, who became tetrarch of Galilee on the death of his father, Herod the Great, in 4BC, divorces his wife and marries his niece, Herodias, the daughter of his brother Philip's wife.

Judaea, c.27. John the Baptist denounces Herod Antipas for marrying Herodias incestuously. John, a cousin of Mary, mother of Jesus, has gained a reputation for his baptisms and his preaching about repentance and forgiveness of sins.

Italy, 29. Agrippina, widow of Germanicus, who suspects Tiberius of responsibility for her husband's death, is arrested on the instruction of Tiberius and banished to Pandateria. Agrippina has lived in Rome since Germanicus died ten years ago, providing a rallying point for senators opposed to the growing power of Sejanus. Sejanus now sets about securing the arrest of her sons, Nero and Drusus.

Italy, 29. On the death of his mother, Livia, the former wife of Augustus, Tiberius refuses to carry out the terms of her will or allow her to be deified. Livia, who was also known as Julia Augusta, had been accused of attempting to dominate the empire after Augustus' death. Her first husband, and the father of the present emperor, was Tiberius Claudius Nero, who supported Marcus Antonius' brother against Augustus in the Perusian war of 41-40BC. Not long after this Livia divorced him to marry Augustus.

Rome, 30. Velleius Paterculus, former cavalry officer and legate in Germany and Pannonia, completes his *Historiae Romanae*. While claiming to be a universal history, his work concentrates largely on the exploits of Rome. He recounts the actions of Tiberius and the imperial family with uncritical admiration.

Peasants oust reformer

A beautifully-crafted Han dynasty bronze statuette of a flying horse.

Han terracotta model of a house.

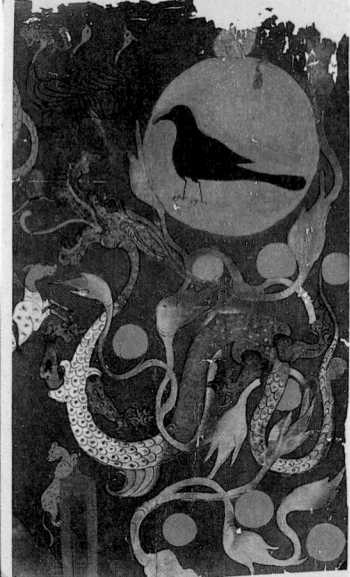

Han art: ink and colour on silk.

China, 25

The Han dynasty is once more on the throne of China from which it was ousted 16 years ago by the agrarian reformer, Wang Mang. The irony of this development is that the once popular Wang Mang was brought down by the forces of nature when the mighty Yellow River changed its course and inflicted catastrophe on the countryside.

Famine spread; peasants left the land and formed themselves into armed bands. They painted their foreheads red and became known as the "Red Eyebrows". As red was the colour of the Hans they became identified with the deposed regime. They became an army and defeated the government's troops.

Anarchy spread through the country until the Red Eyebrows and the disaffected gentry looked to the remote descendants of the Hans for leadership. Wang Mang was defeated and, amidst much intrigue by members of the Han family, Liu Xuan ascended the throne, only to be overthrown by his warrior cousin Liu Xiu, the new emperor.

Jewish preacher works "miracles"

Galilee, 29

A young Jewish preacher travelling through Judaea is winning widespread support and gaining a reputation as the most influential prophet of modern times. Some of his followers, who call themselves disciples, are even claiming that he is the long-awaited Messiah or, as the Greeks translate it, the Christ.

Jesus of Nazareth, a poorly educated carpenter, has already won the support of the ascetic preacher John the Baptist. Both men have urged the need for repentance and declared their belief that God's rule on earth is about to begin.

According to his followers Jesus teaches with a unique authority. He delivers his message with a sense of great urgency and lays claim to an unusually intimate relationship with God, whom he describes as 'father'. His relationship with Jewish religious leaders is inevitably uneasy.

Two things make Jesus more than just one more itinerant preacher. One is the intense popular appeal of his teaching, much of which is delivered as parables. Judaea's poor find lines like "the first shall be last and the last shall be first" irresistible, although the authorities, who have no desire to allow him to become a focus for

Jesus brings in a big catch, by Conrad Witz (C15th).

discontent, are becoming increasingly hostile. The other is his performance of alleged "miracles". Jesus has supposedly raised the dead, turned water into wine, cured fatal illnesses and exhibited other supernatural powers.

One remarkable example of the "miracles" performed by this man

involved turning a handful of loaves and a few fish into enough fare to feed a vast crowd of hungry people who had come to hear him speak.

For those who have witnessed such marvels and listened to the stories known as parables, Jesus is not just a powerful preacher, but the Messiah himself.

Fearful Rome ruled by Tiberius from self-imposed exile in Capri

Tiberius' decision to rule from Capri has been prompted partly by his obsessive fear of plots.

Capri, 27

Tiberius, who left Rome last year to live in Campania, has decided to settle in the island of Capri, off the coast of Naples. Rome is uneasy, and the most powerful man in the city is the corrupt Sejanus, Prefect of the Praetorian Guard.

Tiberius succeeded Augustus as princeps in 14. Born in 42BC into the patrician family of the Claudii, he was Augustus' stepson and the obvious heir, yet he seemed reluctant to assume power. A fine soldier, with an exemplary record in the east, Germany and the Balkans, he seems a troubled soul, dour and introspective. His face is ravaged with sores.

Senators, whose decisions Tiberius promised to respect, and to whom he entrusted the election of magistrates, were initially well-

disposed towards him. But they found it increasingly difficult to understand him. The trial of Marcellus, accused of treason, is a case in point: Tiberius lost his temper and declared that he would vote on oath. "Caesar, will you vote first or last?" asked a senator. "If first, I shall have your lead to follow; if last I am afraid of inadvertently voting against you." Tiberius voted meekly for acquittal.

Meanwhile, Tiberius was making the prince's council a permanent feature of government, and reorganising the praetorian guard in Rome, thereby increasing his monarchical power. The senators became increasingly uncertain, and plotted against one another.

Into the power vacuum stepped Sejanus, who seduced Drusus' wife before having Drusus poisoned.

Tiberius linked to poisoning of Germanicus

Epidaphne, Syria, 10 October 19

Germanicus, conqueror of the German armies and best-loved of Roman princes, is dead. On his deathbed he accused Piso, the governor of Syria, of poisoning him. He is also reported to have warned his family against the Emperor Tiberius, who is now widely suspected of having ordered his death.

The son of Drusus the Elder, and brother of Tiberius, Germanicus married Agrippina, Augustus' grand-daughter, and was adopted by Tiberius. When he became a consul seven years ago, he was widely seen as the likeliest nobleman to inherit the Roman empire.

After Augustus' death it was Germanicus who quelled the mutiny of the Rhine legions and led a series of campaigns against the German peoples, avenging the defeat of Varus with two victories over Arminius of the Cherusci. When he might have completed the conquest of Germany, he was recalled by Tiberius and sent to the east, where he displeased Tiberius by venturing into Egypt and falling out with Piso.

Failed rebel nobles kill themselves

Augustodunum, Gaul, 21

Twin rebellions led by Romanised Gallic noblemen have been crushed, and both leaders have committed suicide. Capitalising on local grumbling about high taxation and the Roman ban on Druidism, Julius Florus and Julius Sacrovir persuaded a number of the Treveri and Aedui to revolt.

Florus was the first to fail when the Treveri fell into disarray after murdering a few Roman traders. The rebellion of the Aedui was more serious, and Sacrovir held a number of Gallic students hostage in Augustodunum to force their parents to join the revolt. He assembled a motley army of 40,000 men, including some *crupellarii* (troops with heavy body armour), but they were no match for the legions of Caius Silius.

International trade from Italy to the Indus

India's trade links with Mesopotamia go back to well before 2000BC, and during the life of the Indus valley civilisation there was regular trade, probably both by sea along the coasts and overland. We know more of what was exported to Mesopotamia than of what was imported into India. Certainly beads of carnelian were exported, as well as pearls and lapis lazuli, and probably also timber and cotton textiles, although evidence for these is lacking.

It seems likely that trade with the eastern Mediterranean continued in a somewhat irregular manner through the centuries, and received a further stimulus in the sixth century BC when Darius, the Achaemenid king of Persia, sent Scylax on an expedition to explore the Indus region. Trade between India and the west could either go overland by long and arduous routes, exposed to the taxes and depredations of local rulers and brigands, or follow the coastal route by sea, from the ports of Egypt and the Red Sea or the Persian Gulf. This trade was exposed to the hazards of piracy. One would have expected a marked increase in trade following Alexander the Great's campaigns in the east, but there is little evidence to support it, at least as far as the sea route is concerned.

As far as can be said, trade did not assume large proportions until the first century BC, and that it did so then was the result of two developments: the exploitation of the seasonal monsoon winds, and the growing wealth of Rome which led to a demand for all sorts of exotic luxury goods.

Winds of change

The discovery of the monsoon winds is attributed to an otherwise unknown Greek sea captain named Hippalus, who in around 50BC realised that with accurate navigation it was possible to sail from the Egyptian Red Sea ports to a selected point on the Arabian coast, whence, using the south-westerly monsoon winds blowing during the summer months, a ship might sail directly across open sea to the Indian port of Bharukaccha (Broach). This led in the next few years to other starting points being fixed from which one could sail directly to other Indian ports farther south. There were two great advantages in these new routes. Firstly, they were much quicker than the long coastal route and greatly shortened the time the voyage took, and secondly they largely cut out the danger of piracy, since the pirates preyed only upon the coastal traffic, and could scarcely lie in wait for ships on the open sea. Once this new route had been dis-

covered the volume of traffic rose dramatically. The ships were unloaded and remained in the Indian ports until the onset of winter when, laden for the return journey, they made use of the north-eastern monsoon winds for the return voyage.

The second factor in the growth of western trade with India was a natural concomitant of the growing power and wealth of the Roman empire, particularly during and after the rule of Augustus (27BC-AD14). Following his initial stimulation, Roman trade with the east rapidly expanded and began to create a trading imbalance, with Rome on the debit side. For, as Romans became used to luxury imports of textiles and spices, particularly pepper, they came to accept that such things were essential. This imbalance made itself felt throughout the life of the empire.

We owe much of this knowledge to a remarkable book, the *Periplus of the Erythraean Sea*, written in the late first century AD by an unknown writer who must have been a Greek or Alexandrian sea captain. This precious record also tells us about ports visited and the various goods imported or exported through them.

Regional differences

Indian imports and exports, according to the *Periplus*, varied from port to port and from region to region, depending on the local demands and on the hinterland which the port served. At Barbarike, on the Indus delta, imports included glass vessels, silver plate, wine, frankincense, storax and coins; exports included gems such as turquoise and lapis lazuli, spices, Chinese skins and yarns, and some cloth. The imports were probably in part destined for the Hellenic kingdoms of what is now north-western Pakistan and Afghanistan.

The next great port was Bharukaccha (Broach), on the mouth of the river Narbada. This port served several inland regions, including the Hellenic kingdoms, the whole Ganges valley and the Dekhan to the south. Imports at Bharukaccha included copper, tin and lead (the two latter were always in short supply in India and were at this time used as alloys in coinage, among other things), costly wine and silver plate, musicians and girls for the royal harem, and, as at Barbarike, gold and silver coinage. Archaeologists have discovered in the Begram treasure (from north of Kabul, in Afghanistan,) splendid glass vessels from Alexandria, typical Roman bronzes and vessels, and a collection of plaster models of classical Hellenistic

designs and themes, all of which may have come through Bharukaccha. Exports from Barukaccha included ivory, precious stones, several kinds of textiles, silk yarn and pepper. The discovery of an Indian carved ivory in the buried remains of Pompeii testifies to the export of ivory around this time.

Farther south the picture changes again. In this area, along with copper, lead and tin, some wine was imported. But the main feature was the importation of large quantities of coinage, attested by the discovery of many Roman coins in southern India, particularly from the first century AD. Exports from the southern ports include sapphires, diamonds and many other kinds of precious stones, as well as pearls, ivory, tortoise shell, spices and, above all, pepper. The tropical climate of the south and of neighbouring Sri Lanka makes the region still a great producer of black pepper today.

Greek factories in India?

Archaeology again supports the accuracy of the *Periplus* at the ancient port site of Arikamedu near Pondicherry, where the discovery of Roman *amphorae* (storage jars) vividly illustrates how wine was imported. Also found at Arikamedu, and at other sites in southern India, are large amounts of Roman Arretine ware, evidently imported as a fine ceramic product.

The *Periplus* refers to these trading ports as *emporia*. Contemporary Tamil literature of southern India indicates that there were actually small colonies of foreign traders (the texts call them Greeks) at such places, who seem to have operated "factories" rather like much later European traders in India. If this is correct, Arikamedu was almost certainly such a factory, and it is tempting to speculate that western merchants set up a ceramics industry on Indian soil, to supply the locally acceptable fine ceramic known as "rouletted ware".

There were probably two distinct types of trade between India and Rome: one was local trade of goods often destined to be taken overland from the Indian ports to remote areas, the other was transit trade. It seems clear that, as time went by, south-eastern Asia and China became important in the latter respect; goods were probably brought to the southern Indian ports and trans-shipped there, for onward dispatch to Rome or to the east depending on their origins. India seems in most respects to have been the net gainer in the trade, in that it received large quantities of gold and silver coinage in exchange for mainly raw materials, or locally made goods.

Left: Figures (c.350) of the Indian god Pangika, and the goddess Hariti, who was a protectress of children. The influence of Roman fashions is clear in the style of their clothes and the arrangement of their hair (compare above right). Above left: Roman wall painting of a girl bottling perfume. Above right: head of a Roman lady of the Flavian period with a sumptuous hair-do.

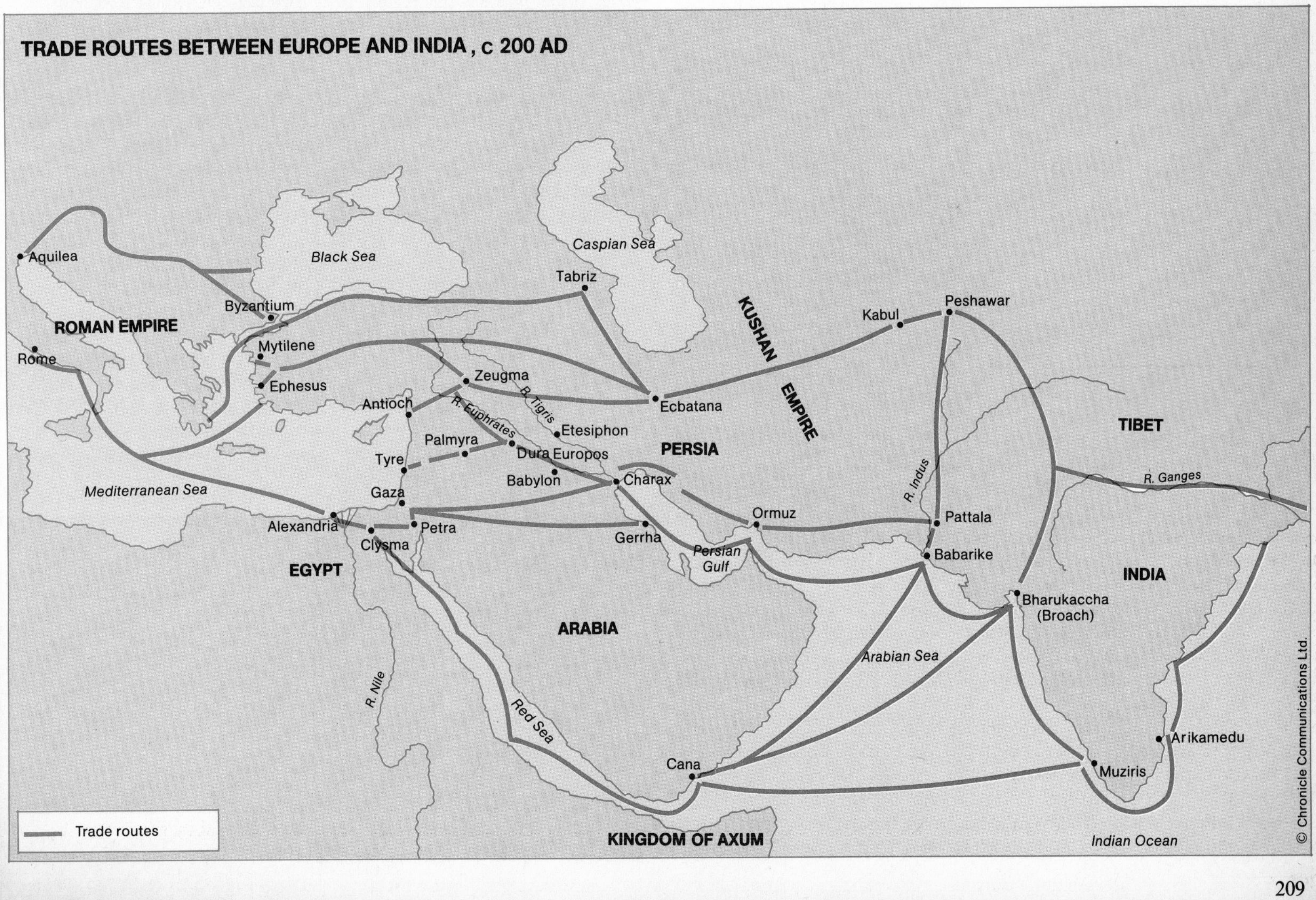

TRADE ROUTES BETWEEN EUROPE AND INDIA , c 200 AD

- Aquilea
- *Black Sea*
- *Caspian Sea*
- Byzantium
- **ROMAN EMPIRE**
- Tabriz
- **KUSHAN EMPIRE**
- Kabul
- Peshawar
- Mytilene
- Rome
- Ephesus
- Zeugma
- *R. Euphrates*
- *R. Tigris*
- Antioch
- Ecbatana
- **TIBET**
- Etesiphon
- **PERSIA**
- Palmyra
- Tyre
- Dura Europos
- *R. Indus*
- *R. Ganges*
- Gaza
- Babylon
- Charax
- *Mediterranean Sea*
- Alexandria
- Petra
- Ormuz
- Pattala
- **EGYPT**
- Clysma
- Gerrha
- *Persian Gulf*
- Babarike
- **INDIA**
- **ARABIA**
- Bharukaccha (Broach)
- *R. Nile*
- *Arabian Sea*
- *Red Sea*
- Arikamedu
- Cana
- Muziris
- **KINGDOM OF AXUM**
- *Indian Ocean*

— Trade routes

Judaea, 30. The procurator Pontius Pilate makes a vain attempt to transfer to Herod Antipas, tetrarch of Galilee – who is in Jerusalem for the Passover – the responsibility for trying the Galilaean, Jesus.

Judaea, 30 April 30. After being condemned to death by the Jewish court known as the Sanhedrin, Jesus of Nazareth is crucified at Golgotha.

Italy, 31. Nero, eldest surviving son of Germanicus and Agrippina, is put to death at Pontia, where he was deported after his arrest on the orders of Sejanus. Following the suspicious death, in 23, of Tiberius' 17-year-old son Drusus, Nero was next in line to become emperor. Tiberius, convinced by the accusations emanating from Sejanus, denounced him in 29.

Rome, 33. Drusus, second surviving son of Germanicus and Agrippina, and the likely successor to Tiberius after the death of his brother Nero, dies, a prisoner in the emperor's palace. Drusus was arrested in 30, a year after Agrippina and Nero.

Rome, 33. Interest rates rocket as a result of a currency shortage. Property prices fall as owners sell their land to pay off debts. Tiberius provides the bankers with 100 million sesterces to finance interest-free loans.

Italy, 18 October 33. Heartbroken by the deaths of her sons Nero and Drusus, and banished to the island of Pandateria by Tiberius, Agrippina, widow of Germanicus, dies of self-inflicted starvation.

Capri, 33. After the suicide of his mother Agrippina, Caligula (Gaius Caesar) goes to Capri to join Tiberius.

Armenia, 34. On the death of Artaxias (Zeno), a client of the Romans, Artabanus III, the king of Parthia, puts his son Arsaces on the Armenian throne. This action presents a direct challenge to Rome.

Parthia, 35. Overthrown by his cousin Tiridates III, who enjoys the support of Rome, Artabanus III, king of Parthia, escapes to the north-east, where he is given refuge by the nomadic people of Hyrcania.

India, c.35. After forcibly establishing unity among the five Indo-European tribes in Bactria known as the Yuezhi, Kujula Kadphises seizes control of the Kabul valley and adjacent regions from the Pahlavas (Parthians closely related to the Scythians). By setting himself up as ruler of Bactria and Sogdiana, Kadphises has laid the basis for a Kushan dynasty.

Syria, c.35. On the road to Damascus, the Jew Saul of Tarsus is converted to Christianity by a vision of Jesus Christ crucified. Formerly a strenuous Pharisee, Saul has assisted in the persecution of the Christians.

Armenia, 35. The Romans expel the Parthian prince, Arsaces, after toppling him from the Armenian throne. He is replaced by the Caucasian ruler Mithridates of Iberia (Georgia).

Rome, 35. Tiberius makes his great-nephew Caligula and his grandson Tiberius Gemellus heirs to his private estate.

Parthia, 36. Artabanus III regains his throne and comes to an agreement with Rome: he is recognised as king of the Parthians but accepts the Roman protectorate of Armenia.

Judaea, 37. Herod Antipas is defeated in a battle at Peraea with his former father-in-law, Aretas. With this victory Aretas exacts his revenge for Herod's divorce of his daughter to marry Herodias.

Italy, 16 March 37. On a trip to the Italian mainland from his home on Capreae (Capri), the emperor Tiberius – who has been of unsound mind for the past few years – dies at Misenum (on the bay of Naples).

Rome, 18 March 37. The Senate annuls Tiberius' will, disinheriting Gemellus, and proclaims Caligula emperor. Caligula then adopts his cousin Tiberius Gemellus.

Rome, November 37. His mind weakened by a serious illness – suspected to have been caused by his depraved style of life – the emperor Caligula has Tiberius Gemellus executed.

Rome, 38. In the year since he became emperor, Caligula has squandered the vast fortune left by Tiberius. He has also banished or murdered many of his relatives, except Drusilla and Claudius.

Rome, 23 September 38. Drusilla, Caligula's sister who died in June, with whom the emperor is said to have had an incestuous relationship, is deified.

Germany, 39. Caligula puts down a conspiracy led by Gaetulicus, governor of higher Germany. He then embarks on an abortive campaign against a German tribe called the Chatti.

Judaea, 39. At the instigation of his wife, Herodias, the tetrarch Herod Antipas asks Caligula for the title of king. However, he is deposed on a charge of treason trumped up by his nephew, Agrippa, who proceeds to inherit his tetrarchy.

Cities of Provence acquire Roman style

Romanisation is an essential part of the consolidation of Roman rule in Gaul. This gateway is at Autun.

A peristyle (in other words, bordered by columns) garden. The house of the Vetti, Pompeii.

Narbonne, c.30

The recently-completed triumphal arch, dedicated to the Emperor Tiberius, is only the latest example of the superb Roman-style building in all the major towns in Gallia Narbonensis (Provence). The new arch stands at the north of the city of Arausio (Orange), in the Rhone valley in the north of this region. It has Corinthian columns on all four sides, and several original features – notably it comprises three archways with two attics on top.

This arch commemorates the crushing of the revolt by Florus and Sacrovir six years ago. Originally colonised by Roman veterans 52 years ago, Arausio has many other fine Roman buildings, including a forum and a large temple. A huge theatre, capable of seating 20,000 spectators, is nearing completion.

Some of the most impressive building can be seen in Nimes, also founded as a veterans' colony in 16BC and now boasting a population of nearly 50,000. Nimes is enclosed by thick stone walls, six feet wide and with 19 towers along

them. The biggest of these is the Tour Magne, a 130-foot high octagonal tower built at the highest point in the town.

Nimes also has one of the region's best amphitheatres. This is the twin of the amphitheatre at Arles, unsurprisingly because they were both designed by the same architect, T Crispius Reburrus.

The best baths are at Glanum (St Remy) which was settled by the Greeks in the third century. Although it was sacked, reportedly by the Cimbri, in the late second century, some Greek houses with pebble mosaic floors still survive. Most of the buildings, however, were put up by the Romans in the last century. The impressive mausoleum has reliefs of Greek myths at the bottom and is capped by a statue of Julius Caesar.

Vasio (Vaison-la-Romaine) has some magnificent private houses. For example, the House of the Silver Bust has a fine entrance portico with shops behind, a superb bathing suite, and a peristyle garden with a small pool.

The magnificent Roman theatre at Arausio (Orange) in southern Gaul, capable of holding as many as 20,000 spectators.

Jesus, "Son of God", is crucified

Jerusalem, 30 April, 30

Jesus of Nazareth, called by his followers "the Son of God" or Christ (Greek for the Messiah), has been executed by the Roman authorities following a hearing before Jewish leaders. He was crucified at Golgotha at 9 o'clock this morning, together with two thieves. His mother was among a small crowd who witnessed the execution and heard his last words: "Father, into thy hands I commend my spirit."

Christ supposedly performed many miracles in his lifetime, and witnesses of his death claim that the three-hour eclipse of the sun which accompanied the crucifixion was a sign of God's anger. Certainly many of those who came to mock the "King of the Jews" left Golgotha highly moved. His body was claimed by Joseph of Arimathaea, a Jewish council member but an opponent of the death penalty.

Jesus, proclaimed as their saviour by an increasing number of Jews, was arrested on April 6 and tried by a Jewish council on blasphemy charges. Eyewitnesses claim that Jesus had prophesied the events surrounding his death. At the Passover supper the night before his crucifixion he foretold his betrayal by one of his disciples. His followers claim his life and death reveal him to be the Messiah promised by the Jewish scriptures.

All his prophecies have turned out to be true. Judas, a disciple, betrayed Jesus. Jewish leaders then alleged Jesus had called himself "Son of God" though the preacher apparently preferred the title "Son of Man". The high priest Caiaphas declared him guilty of blasphemy and subversion, claiming that he wished to overthrow Rome and establish himself as "king of the Jews". Since the Jews may not pass the death sentence, Jesus was handed over to Pontius Pilate, the Roman governor. Although Pilate told the authorities that he found Jesus innocent of all charges, suggesting that he be flogged and then freed, the Jewish leaders demanded the death penalty, making it clear that otherwise the Jerusalem mob would certainly riot. Pilate gave in, freeing instead Barabbas, a rebel and murderer, but a hero of the mob.

As seen by Mattias Grunewald (1455-1528), Jesus of Nazareth suffers appalling pain as he dies on the cross, watched by his mother and a follower.

Roman soldiers keep order as a crowd of priests, relatives and supporters of Jesus mingle around the crosses, from the film "King of Kings".

Praetorian Guard prefect executed

Rome, 18 October 31

The commander of the Praetorian Guard, Lucius Aelius Sejanus, has been executed after being arrested and accused of plotting to seize imperial powers. The death of Sejanus has come when he was at the height of his powers, and after being behind a reign of terror both in Rome and in its distant provinces.

Sejanus' fall from grace as prefect of the emperor's personal bodyguard was as sudden as his rise. As a good organiser and successful in gaining Tiberius' confidence, he was very much a prime minister. His influence steadily increased with Tiberius' retirement to Capri, and he brought about the disgrace and death of many eminent men and women – innocent and guilty – who stood in his way.

Only just appointed joint consul with Tiberius for five years, Sejanus was accused of plotting in a letter from the emperor's sister-in-law. He and his two children were strangled.

John the Baptist's head given as prize

Judaea, c.30

Salome, stepdaughter of Herod Antipas, tetrarch of Galilee, has won a gruesome and gory prize: the head of John the Baptist, presented on a platter. At the bidding of her mother, Herodias, Salome sought this trophy from her stepfather as a reward for pleasing him with her dancing.

During his ministry, John, who was a cousin of Mary, the mother of Jesus Christ, had become well known for performing baptisms, including that of Jesus himself. He preached repentance and the forgiveness of sins.

John came into conflict with Herod Antipas, son of Herod the Great, about three years ago, when Antipas divorced his Nabataean wife to marry Herodias. Herodias was the daughter of Antipas' brother Philip's wife, and John denounced the marriage as incestuous. Enraged by his attitude, Herodias has now succeeded in exacting her revenge.

Rome, 40. King Ptolemy of Mauretania, a Moorish kingdom in north-west Africa, is assassinated by Caligula during a visit to Rome.

Mauretania, 40. Under the leadership of Aedemon, the Mauri rise up against Roman annexation of their country after the murder of King Ptolemy.

Rome, 40. Messalina, 14-year-old granddaughter of Octavia on her mother's and father's sides, marries her second cousin Claudius, who is 48.

Rome, 24 January 41. Shortly after declaring himself a god, Caligula is assassinated by two Praetorian tribunes.

Rome, 25 January 41. After fruitless discussion about the re-establishment of a republic, the Senate recognises Caligula's uncle, Claudius, as emperor. The appointment is proclaimed by the Praetorians. Claudius was saved from Caligula's cruelty by his supposed mental deficiency. After his nephew's murder, he was found hiding in the palace by soldiers.

Judaea, 41. Agrippa, nephew of Herod Antipas and grandson of Herod the Great, is made king of all Judaea by the Emperor Claudius.

Britain, c.42. Cunobelinus, king of the Catuvellauni from Verulamium (St Albans), is dead. After moving against the the Essex tribe called the Trinovantes, Cunobelinus established a capital at Camulodunum (Colchester) and went on to conquer Kent.

North Africa, 42. Having eliminated Aedemon, leader of a revolt by the Mauri, and pacified Mauretania, the Roman general Paulinus advances as far as the Sahara.

Britain, 43. On the orders of Claudius, the Romans, led by Aulus Plautius, invade Britain.

England, 43. Maiden Castle in Dorset has been invaded by the Romans, and most of its defences have been destroyed. The construction of the castle was begun before 400BC and took 400 years to complete. As many as 5,000 people were living in wooden huts behind its ramparts before the Roman invasion.

Judaea, 44. On the death of Agrippa, who, with the help of Caligula and Claudius, re-established the kingdom of Herod the Great, Judaea is annexed to the Roman empire.

Arawaks canoe to the West Indies

Central America, c.40
The Arawak people have made their way in dug-out canoes down the length of the Orinoco river and have settled in the island that they call Iguana (San Salvador). They are spreading out to many of the West Indian islands, including Jamaica and Cuba. The canoes are an essential part of their life – used for migration, trade, fishing, hunting and the transport of food.

They are skilled farmers, too, growing maize, sweet potatoes and bean crops, peanuts, peppers and pineapples. Other favoured crops – though non-edible – are varieties of plant from which body-painting dyes are produced. The Arawaks have developed the skill of irrigation and use wooden farming implements – a digging stick for planting and a broadsword (which doubles as a weapon) for cutting.

Arawak religious ritual includes a variant of the Central American ballgame, played with rubber balls and involving human sacrifice.

Race riots quelled by emperor's plea

Alexandria, Egypt, 41
Following appeals from the Emperor Claudius, calm has returned to Alexandria after a period of inter-racial violence between the city's Greek and Jewish inhabitants.

Jewish unrest dates back to the time of Augustus. Thirty-five years ago he annexed Judaea, Samaria and Idumaea in Palestine as a new province, governed by Roman procurators. Although the Romans allowed the Jews to worship freely, discontent reached a crisis when Pontius Pilate was procurator under Tiberius from 26 to 36. Tiberius suppressed Judaism at Rome; Caligula, assassinated this year, almost sparked a rebellion last year by proposing to put a statue of himself in the Temple of Jerusalem.

Claudius has inherited the Jewish problem. Particularly troublesome are the followers of a man they call Christ – "the anointed" – who was executed by Pilate in Judaea and whom they claim is the long-awaited Jewish Messiah.

Caligula assassinated after bloody reign

How Caligula saw himself: Pompeii's statue of a dignified emperor.

Rome, 24 January 41
The Emperor Caligula is dead, struck down today in his own imperial palace at the age of 28. His death brings to an end a reign of tyranny, cruelty and depravity.

Gaius Julius Caesar Germanicus, nicknamed *Caligula*, or "Little Boots", by the soldiers with whom he was brought up, donned the imperial purple in 37. He was tall, with a massive hairy body but bald head, thin legs and neck and sunken eyes. He was always a sickly child, and a serious illness shortly after he became emperor is thought to have unhinged his mind; certainly he was much more autocratic than his predecessors, and regarded himself as a god. Indeed, he deified his sister – almost certainly his incestuous lover – when she died.

Caligula's cruelty was notorious. He had one senator torn to pieces, happy only when the limbs and entrails were piled before him. Others he simply had sawn in half, often for trivial reasons. He thought it too dear to feed cattle to the wild beasts for his shows, so they ate criminals instead. He threw a knight to the lions; the man protested his innocence, so Caligula withdrew him, had his tongue cut out, and threw him back.

Caligula suppressed a plot to kill him early last year while he was with his troops on the Rhine. This time the conspirators have hit their mark, to the relief of all.

Chinese crush Vietnamese rebellion

Vietnam, 43
A four-year Vietnamese revolt against China has been crushed by the veteran Chinese general Ma-yuan at Lang Bac. The revolt's leaders, the sisters Trung Trac and Trung Nhu, have been drowned, the traditional suicide for Vietnamese royalty.

The revolt came after a century of indirect Chinese rule, which characterised itself as efficient, reformist, and totally insensitive to the feelings and fortunes of the Vietnamese aristocracy. After decades of watching their power being whittled away by overzealous Chinese reformers, they rose under Trung Trac's husband, Thi Sach, the richest landowner in Vietnam. His brutal murder multiplied the ranks of the rebels, their leadership passing to the sisters.

The Trungs drove the Chinese out of Vietnam and proclaimed themselves queens. However, they were unable to gain the support of the peasantry who looked to the Chinese as their protectors against the landowners. Isolated from the masses, they proved easy prey to Ma-yuan's well-armed troops.

Power transforms Claudius, the unlikely emperor

Rome, 43

The Emperor Claudius, a despised and unknown figure two years ago, has transformed his reputation. Today he returned to Rome in triumph after having spent 16 days with his invading legions in Britain. He was with them for the capture of the capital of the Trinobantes, Camulodunum (Colchester).

Claudius became emperor almost by accident after his nephew Caligula's assassination two years ago. He ran away when he saw the assassins, and soldiers found him cowering behind a curtain in the palace. The senators wanted to restore the republic, but were squabbling among themselves. The Roman crowd preferred a monarchy; the soldiers saw him as a convenient figurehead.

As a child Claudius was kept out of public view by his great-uncle, Augustus. He had a tic, a speech impediment, and a mouth which was always open and dribbling. People thought him an idiot. For a long time he was almost imprisoned with tutors, which enabled him to

Claudius, the handicapped ruler who has shown he is nobody's fool.

become a scholar and an expert on Carthage and the Etruscans.

Now 53, Claudius is proving a shrewd ruler. On his accession he paid his troops 150 gold pieces to win their allegiance. He has set up central government and finance offices run by two loyal freedmen, Pallas and Narcissus. He is encouraging nobles from overseas provinces to enter the Senate.

Claudius builds a port for Rome at Ostia

Rome, 42

Work has just started on a new harbour for the port of Ostia, 16 miles south of here. Architects have opposed it, claiming that the site is unsuitable and that the Tiber river between Ostia and Rome is too narrow and winding for easy navigation. But Claudius, the new emperor, has stuck to his guns.

When he took over after the assassination of Caligula early last year, Claudius was much concerned at finding there was only eight days' supply of corn in the Roman granaries. He feels that the popularity of the emperor is dependent on providing food for the 200,000 free Romans. Much of this (some 12 million bushels) is supplied from Egypt, and a rising amount from other parts of Africa.

The present harbour at Ostia cannot accept the big ocean-going grain ships. The grain has to be unloaded at sea and brought in by lighter. Claudius is planning a new harbour two miles north of the existing docks. Two curving moles are being built out to sea. In the middle an island is to be made by sinking the huge merchantman which brought the Egyptian obelisk for Caligula's circus. It has been loaded with 120,000 bushels of len-

A view of the Via Decumanus at Ostia with a theatre on the left.

tils for ballast, and a four-storey lighthouse – like the one in Alexandria – will be built on it.

Claudius is also planning jetties, new docks and new storehouses. Ostia is not just important for grain. It is a shipping port for wines, spices, perfumes, cloth and precious objects from around the empire and from China and India. It is increasingly one of the major ports on the Mediterranean.

The new emperor is also acutely aware of the need to secure efficient food distribution. He has set up an office to control it, and has appointed a trusted equestrian officer as its head.

Rome's elite threatened by freedmen

A bronze model of a black Roman slave, busily cleaning a boot.

Rome, c.40

A new class of Roman citizen is treading on the toes of the aristocrats and arousing considerable hostility. They are freedmen, whose status is between that of the slaves and those free from birth.

Freedmen are highly educated former slaves and the Emperor

Claudius has given several of them, like Narcissus, Pallas and Callistus, important offices in his administration. They are undeniably talented, but the greed and arrogance of some of them is causing many to call for more power to go to the old elite of the equestrian officers.

A romance currently in vogue, the *Satyricon*, by Petronius, reflects some of the negative feelings the freedmen are arousing. The main character, Trimalchio, inherits wealth from his former master and enlarges it by commerce. He is portrayed as vulgar and ridiculous, inspiring hatred in a senator who is losing his power and fortune.

Meanwhile Claudius is more concerned to improve the lot of the slaves themselves, which means most of the peasants, craftsmen and domestic servants. Despite the Stoic influence, which has caused many Roman leaders to foster a more humanitarian spirit, many slaves are still treated badly, a situation which Claudius may well try to rectify.

Mosaic in the "Square of the Corporations" in Ostia, showing a lighthouse and shipping. A passage beneath the lighthouse breaks the sea's force.

Egypt, 45. The philosopher and commentator Philo dies in his native Alexandria. Philo headed a Jewish embassy to Caligula in 39 to ask for exemption from the duty of worshipping the emperor – an expedition which he described in his *De Legatione*. He attempted to reconcile Jewish and Greek thought.

Balkans, 46. Weakened by disputes among its princes, the kingdom of Thrace becomes a province of Rome.

Rome, 47. Alongside his secular games known as the Hilaria, the Emperor Claudius introduces worship of the Phrygian god Attis. He also restores the office of the censor.

Rome, 48. The sexual profligacy of Claudius' wife Messalina reaches a climax when, in Claudius' absence, she goes through the formalities of a marriage ceremony with one of her lovers, the consul-designate Gaius Silius.

Rome, 48. On the instigation of his freedman, Narcissus, Claudius has Messalina and her lover Gaius Silius put to death.

Rome, 48. Noblemen from Gaul are given access to the Senate on the orders of Claudius.

India, 48. On the death of Kujula Kadphises, the Kushan empire stretches from beyond the Hindu Kush to north-west India. He is succeeded by his son, Vima Kadphises.

China, 48. The Emperor, Guang Wudi, of the Later or Eastern Han dynasty, re-establishes Chinese domination over the peoples of inner Mongolia.

Rome, 48. Claudius marries his niece Agrippina II, the daughter of Germanicus.

Indian Ocean, c.50. The sea route between Egypt and India is becoming increasingly important for trade, in competition with the main land routes through Persia and central Asia.

Rome, 50. Claudius adopts his stepson Nero, the son of his wife Agrippina.

Rome, c.50. Phaedrus, a freedman from Macedonia, who has recently died, gained a high reputation for writing verse fables. He published five books consisting of short animal stories based largely on the works of Aesop.

Balkans, 50. A group of tribes – the Roxolani, Iazyges and Alani – collectively known as the Sarmatians, who until now have been settled in southern areas of Russia, reach the region of the Danube.

Parthia, 52. Vologeses, a Mede, comes to the throne of Parthia and restores order to his country after a period of dynastic disturbance.

Britain, 51. The British king Caractacus, son of Cunobelinus, who has been fighting the Roman invaders since 43, is taken prisoner at Ludlow. He had sought refuge with Cartimandua, queen of the Yorkshire Brigantes, who handed him over to the enemy. Most of Caractacus' family are already in captivity.

Italy, 52. Under the direction of Claudius, Lake Fucino in central Italy is drained. Despite a number of setbacks, the land is finally successfully reclaimed for cultivation.

Greece, 52. Paul of Tarsus lands at Corinth, which he intends to make his centre for the evangelisation of Greece.

Armenia, 53. In a challenge to Rome, Vologeses, king of Parthia, puts his brother Tiridates on the Armenian throne, laying the ground for an Arsacid dynasty in the country.

Rome, 53. Nero marries his stepsister Octavia, the daughter of Claudius and Messalina.

Rome, 13 October 54. After his murder by Agrippina, Claudius is succeeded by his adopted son, Nero, rather than by Britannicus, his son by Messalina.

Rome, 55. Britannicus, son of Claudius, is poisoned to death by Nero.

China, 57. An ambassador from the king of Nu, one of the countries of Wa (Japan), arrives at Loyang, capital of Han China. In return for homage paid, the king of Nu is given a seal confirming his kingship in the name of the Han emperor.

China, 57. The Emperor Guang Wudi dies, leaving his throne to Mingdi.

Greece, 58. Still based at Corinth and contemplating a visit to Rome, Paul writes an epistle to the Romans.

Armenia, 58. Corbulo, leader of the Roman armies in Syria, completes a successful invasion of Armenia and makes the country into a Roman protectorate.

Rome, 59. Nero murders his mother, Agrippina II, who herself poisoned her husband, Claudius, in 53.

Armenia, 60. The Roman general Corbulo drives Tiridates, brother of the Parthian king Vologeses, out of Armenia, replacing him by Tigranes V, whose grandfather ruled the country in the Augustan era.

Mark writes the story of Jesus' life

Palestine, c.60

Mark, one of the disciples of the Jewish preacher Jesus of Nazareth, has written down the history of his master's life and is using the story to help spread a new religion based on Jesus' teachings.

Jesus, who was known to his followers as Christ or the Messiah, was crucified in 30 after being condemned by the Jewish council on charges of blasphemy and sedition. His supporters have refused to abandon their faith and, despite his execution, Christ's cult is spreading rather than fading away.

Mark, along with ten others of Christ's original disciples, is now known as an apostle, from the Greek for "messenger". Their task, which they claim was entrusted to them by Jesus, is to spread Christ's teachings throughout the world.

Much of the material Mark has used for his story derives from his own translations of the apostle Peter's Aramaic sermons. Accompanying him on a mission shortly before he died, Mark translated Peter's accounts of Christ's teachings into colloquial Greek, and has

Mark begins his account of the life of Christ (1678 engraving).

now pieced them together to record the life and work of the Messiah.

He begins with the baptism of Jesus by John the Baptist in the wilderness, and goes on to set out the stories that have gathered round Jesus' life. The final section details the alleged resurrection after death, upon which miraculous rebirth Christ's followers base their belief in Jesus as the true Messiah.

Romans capture British resistance leader

Britain, 51

Caractacus, the leader of the British resistance to Roman occupation, has finally been taken prisoner, after eight years of fighting. He has been turned over to the enemy at Ludlow by Cartismandua, queen of the Brigantes.

The invasion of Britain began in 43 when Roman war galleys hove-to off the harbour at Rutupiae (Richborough near Sandwich, Kent) discharging thousands of legionaries. The Romans met little resistance until they crossed the River Medway where they were confronted by Caractacus and the British army.

For two days the Britons put up a determined fight, but they were heavily outnumbered and finally forced to retreat to the west. Here they regrouped to continue the resistance fighting which has now been effectively extinguished.

The Emperor Claudius visited his troops shortly after their landing and received the surrender of Camulodunum (Colchester), mak-

Celtic bronze from a Dorset castle.

ing the town his capital and declaring the island to be a province called Britannia.

Although Julius Caesar invaded Britain more than a century ago, the country was never completely occupied.

Claudius, poisoned by his wife Agrippina, is succeeded as emperor by stepson Nero

Rome, 13 October 54

The Emperor Claudius has died suddenly at the age of 64 after eating a dish of mushrooms. Rome is agog with rumours that he was poisoned by his wife, Agrippina. Despite the rumours Nero, Agrippina's son by a former marriage, is to be the new emperor, instead of Claudius' son Britannicus.

Claudius was pushed into marrying Agrippina in 48, though she was his own niece, by one of his freedmen, Pallas. She was a great-granddaughter of Augustus, and a dominating woman who had already got through two husbands. Ambitious and unscrupulous, she got rid of her enemies by poison or trumped-up charges. She had Nero made guardian of Britannicus, and arranged for him to marry Claudius' daughter Octavia.

Claudius was also unlucky in his first wife, Messalina. Claudius ignored her many infidelities until 48 when she went through a form of public marriage with her lover Silius, a politician. They were probably plotting to overthrow

Claudius and Agrippina, on a triumphal arch to a British victory in 51.

Claudius, so he had them both executed. Despite all these intrigues Claudius managed to be an efficient and forward looking ruler. He helped the slaves and freedmen at home and the provinces abroad. But his undermining of the power of the old governing class has given more power to the emperor.

Nero orders the murder of his mother

Rome, 59

Agrippina, widow of Germanicus and mother of the Emperor Nero, has been assassinated on her son's orders. She survived a complicated attempt to drown her in a sabotaged boat, but when she escaped with only a shoulder wound an assassin, a freedman called Anicetus, was despatched to her house.

Roman society is agog with rumours that Agrippina has left the manuscript of her autobiography, filled with revelations about life in the Caesars' palaces, including her many love affairs and her part in the poisoning of Claudius.

When Claudius died of poisoning in 54, Nero was only 17 and his position was fragile. The scheming Agrippina seems to have fomented jealousy between him and his potential rival Britannicus, son of Claudius. In 55 Britannicus was poisoned on Nero's orders.

The first five years of Nero's reign have met with senatorial approval. Astutely advised by his tutor, the philosopher Seneca, and Burrus, prefect of the Praetorians, the young emperor has shown an enlightened public face, declaring

Nero: an enlightened emperor or a vain and sinister tyrant?

allegiance to Augustus' principles, reprieving many from death sentences, abolishing oppressive taxes, and distributing money to the common people and extra grain to the Praetorian cohorts.

But Nero is excessively vain. He loves to declaim in public, and stage great spectacles, in which thousands of young men are paid to lead the applause. More sinister is his habit of roaming the streets at night in many disguises with a few cronies, beating, or even killing, innocent people.

Writer Seneca becomes princely adviser

Seneca: influential thinker.

Rome, 1 January 56

Seneca, the writer and philosopher, who is now nearly 60 years old, is fast becoming the most powerful man in Rome. His influence over the Emperor Nero, whom he has

tutored since 49, has increased, while that of Nero's mother, Agrippina, has diminished. Now Seneca and Burrus, the prefect of the Praetorians, are Nero's joint advisers.

Seneca was born at the end of the last century in southern Spain, but into a wealthy Italian equestrian family. He studied rhetoric and philosophy, and acquired a reputation as an orator and writer after he came to Rome as a young man. He was exiled to Corsica in 41 by the intrigues of Messalina, the first wife of the Emperor Claudius. He was brought back in 49, by Claudius' second wife, Agrippina, to help her to advance Nero to power.

Seneca wrote uplifting tracts on the brevity of life and human destinies. His latest work, on clemency, extols such Stoic virtues as reconciling power and reason. As a working politician, however, he cannot totally evade responsibility for Nero's nastier acts, such as the murder last year of Britannicus, the son of Claudius.

Japanese envoy pays homage at Chinese court

China, 57

An envoy from the king of Nu, one of the countries of Wa (Japan), has arrived at the court of the emperor Guang Wudi in Loyang, the capital of Han China.

The Chinese are fascinated by the foreign ambassador and many fabulous tales are being told about Wa and its people. It is said that they have a taste for strong drink and that they decorate their bodies with elaborately patterned tattoos and scarlet colouring. They show respect by kneeling with both hands on the ground before a person of higher rank.

In return for the homage he has paid, the king of Nu is given a seal confirming his kingship in the name of the Han emperor. More than 30 of the many autonomous tribes have to date made similar overtures to China.

This two-handled blue glass urn from Britain is an especially fine example of Roman cameo work.

Romans wipe out Boudicca's women freedom fighters

Britain, 61

Roman fury turned on Boudicca's army on a battlefield in the centre of Britain today. Eye-witnesses claim that more than 80,000 Britons – many of them women spectators who had joined their menfolk – were slaughtered by the javelin-wielding Roman army, against Roman losses of fewer than 400. The Iceni queen, seeking to avenge a flogging by the Romans and the rape of her two daughters, is reported to have taken poison rather than surrender to the Romans.

The fierce Celtic queen had taken advantage of Suetonius' absence – he was putting down a Druid revolt in Anglesey at the time – to wreak her revenge on the Roman garrisons at Camulodunum (Colchester), Verulamium and this town. Her army is said to have killed more than 70,000 Romans in these attacks and forced at least one Roman leader to flee to the relative safety of Gaul.

The defeated Iceni warriors have carried their queen to her burial place. Little is known about the late queen except that she was tall, and grim-faced in appearance with piercing eyes and a harsh voice. A Roman historian (who could not possibly have heard the actual words) claims that she told her army: "This land is familiar to us – but to [the Romans] it is unknown and hostile."

A later picture of Boudicca, the grim-faced queen of the Iceni.

Paul spreads the gospel in Roman world

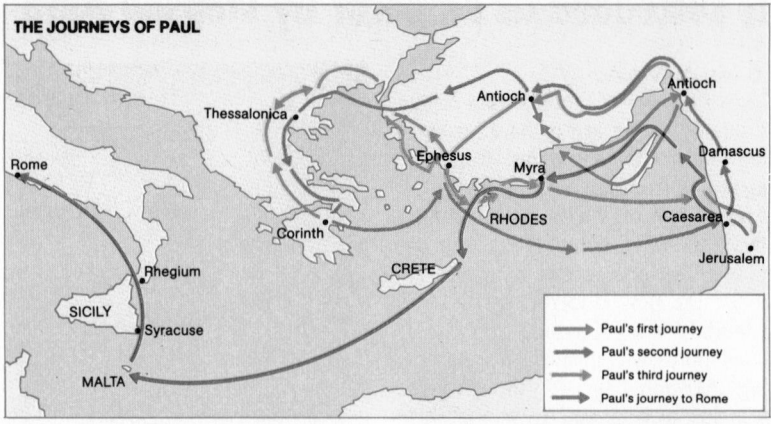

THE JOURNEYS OF PAUL

Paul's first journey
Paul's second journey
Paul's third journey
Paul's journey to Rome

Rome, Spring 60

Paul of Tarsus, a former Pharisee, is proving himself the most successful of all those attempting to win converts to the new faith based on the teachings of Jesus of Nazareth: Christianity. Some call him the true successor to Christ himself.

Paul, formerly Saul, was once a leading opponent of Christianity, but after a miraculous vision which he says occurred during a journey to Damascus, c.35, he changed both his name and his beliefs. For the last decade, taking advantage of the stability that Roman rule has imposed on the area, he has been travelling extensively around the eastern Mediterranean and Greece, preaching Christ's words with unrivalled enthusiasm.

Of all the apostles Paul has taken Christianity furthest from its Jewish origins, abandoning many traditions and concentrating on Christ's divinity. This has naturally alienated many Jews, and Paul was arrested on his last visit to Jerusalem. Only his Roman citizenship saved his life, and he was sent to Rome, where he now lives.

Paul (c.1300): zeal of the converted.

Roman senators lose some of their power

Rome, c.60

Nero, like his stepfather Claudius before him, has continued to centralise power in his own hands. Both emperors have steadily eroded the powers of the Senate, by a mixture of promoting the election of their favourites, giving some high offices of state to non-senators, and using their powers of patronage.

The Senate elects the magistrates, passes laws and acts as a court for major offences. Provincial governors are appointed by drawing lots in the Senate, and many high offices, such as quaestor, consul and prefect of the city, are reserved for senators. Although not an hereditary aristocracy, the membership of the Senate has been restricted until the last few years to a few hundred wealthy families. Sons have been encouraged to follow in their fathers' footsteps, wearing the *latus clavus* (purple sash) and attending Senate meetings.

Nero and Claudius have given important offices to many equestrians (the second in the Roman social pecking order), and even to freedmen in Rome and in the provinces. They have used the *adlectio*, which gives the emperor power to introduce men of loyalty and merit to the Senate, to put in powerful new men, especially those from abroad, able to sway the vote. Critics allege that the Senate of today simply passes any law that Nero wants.

Nero to rebuild fire-ravaged Rome

Rome, 64-68

The fire which destroyed most of Rome has given the Emperor Nero the opportunity to redesign the city, and to build himself the palace of his dreams. Though the Christians were blamed for the fire, many Romans still believe Nero himself was responsible.

Fire broke out in the Circus under a full moon on 18 July 64. Spreading rapidly through shops, and fanned by the wind, it went on to destroy ten of the 14 Augustan regions. On the sixth day, when the flames subsided on the Esquiline Hill and the fire seemed to be over, new fires broke out in open spaces and destroyed temples and arcades.

Nero, who was in Antium when the fire started, returned to direct fire-fighting, organise shelter for the homeless, and distribute food and cheap corn. But rumours circulated that he had ordered the fire,

and watched it from the Tower of Maecenas, singing his own aria to the Sack of Troy. To divert the citizens' anger, Nero made scapegoats of members of the new Christian sect, rounding them up and putting them to death in various cruel and spectacular ways.

In the wake of the fire Nero has been able to plan a more ordered city, with a rectangular street system and taller buildings. Closer to his heart, however, is his Domus Aureus, a palace of unparallelled grandeur, which he has ordered to be built between the Esquiline and Caelian hills.

It is a great architectural achievement, with an octagonal room in the east wing surmounted by a dome, and other rooms with domes, semi-domes, barrel-vaults and cross-vaults, showing a new flexibility in interior design which offers great scope for the future.

Citizens panic as they flee from the flames in the film "Quo Vadis".

There is inspired decoration by the court painter Fabullus. The palace is surrounded by colonnades, lakes and parks, and has a 120-foot high statue of Nero.

Buddhists begin to penetrate the Chinese empire

China, c.65

Over a hundred years after the first Buddhists came into China, Buddhist monasteries are multiplying through the country and a Chinese king has been converted to the new religion.

Buddhism came to China from the west along the string of oases called the Silk Road, running from the Buddhist Kushan empire in central Asia into China; from the east on the China Sea; and from the south via Burma. Its first practitioners were foreign merchants.

Soon indigenous monasteries were founded, a genuine Chinese Buddhism with a Taoist flavour emerged, and large sections of the population were converted.

The first Chinese king to become a Buddhist, Mingdi, has announced his conversion, following a dream in which he saw a golden deity flying by his palace. His brother, the maverick and unpredictable Liu Ying, Prince of Chu, who has not been not above conspiring to seize the throne of China himself in the past, was converted five years ago. Buddhist monks from Liu Ying's capital, Pengcheng, have founded a monastery at Mingdi's imperial capital, Loyang.

The new Chinese Buddhism is distinctly Chinese. Most of the Chinese translations of Buddhist texts use Taoist terminology. No longer seen as a foreign religion, its promise of freedom from pain and suffering has attracted millions of converts, making it the fastest growing religion in China.

New gourmet eating habits outrage Rome's moralists

Rome, 68

In spite of the suicide of the Emperor Nero, which has been greeted with some relief by much of the civilised world, the extravagances that characterised his reign continue, though in a marginally more modest form. Nowhere is this more apparent than in the Romans' eating habits.

Food for the Romans during the republic was frugal, eaten in the *atrium*, fields, or wherever they might be. Breakfast, the first break in their working day, consisted of bread dunked in wine and water. Lunch was almost as simple: boiled or raw vegetables, a cereal gruel, cheese and fruit. The evening meal was similiar, though a little more plentiful. Meat was reserved for feast days and celebrations.

In recent times the evening meal has taken on increasing importance among the affluent classes, though the plebeians continue to eat their frugal fare. Three couches are arranged in the *triclinium*, or dining room, in a horse-shoe fashion around a table. The guest of honour takes his place on the middle couch beside the host, and the feet of the guests are washed by servants. The dishes, like the wines, seem end-

A banqueting scene: prosperous Romans dine around three couches.

less: sucking pig, flamingos' tongues and mullets' livers, so disguised by herbs, wines and sauces that it is impossible to identify the source of the taste.

Conservatives condemn these new fashions as decadent, citing the *Satyricon*, but the excesses described by Petronius are by no

means typical. Petronius was one of Nero's sycophants, never content until he had passed the frontiers of gluttony. But the effects of Nero's excesses have permeated through to the upper classes, whose concern for the pleasures of the table and new gourmet delights would have shocked their ancestors.

Buddhist shrines (these are c.1000-1500) are familiar sights in China.

Rome, October 68. Servius Sulpicius Galba, known as the "legate of the Senate and the Roman people", has accepted the invitation of Vindex, the governor of Gallia Lugdunensis who rebelled against Nero, to succeed as emperor. He enters Rome with the support of Otho, governor of Lusitania in western Spain.

Germany, 3 January 69. The Roman legions on the Rhine refuse to declare their allegiance to Galba, instead proclaiming their legate, Aulus Vitellius, as emperor.

Rome, 15 January 69. Weakened by the revolt of the legions in Germany, Galba is overthrown and killed by the Praetorians, who offer the empire to Otho.

Judaea, 69. After his capture last year of Qumran, stronghold of the Essenes, and Jericho, Vespasian, the commander appointed to suppress the Jewish rebellion, lays siege to Jerusalem.

Italy, 16 April 69. Defeated by Vitellius' troops at Bedriacum, Otho commits suicide.

Egypt, 1 July 69. In Alexandria, Vespasian, the leader of the eastern army and son of a humble tax collector from the Italian municipality of Reate, is hailed as Roman emperor by the Egyptian legions under Tiberius Alexander.

Balkans, August 69. Gaius Mucianus, governor of Syria, which has come out in favour of Vespasian, leads his troops through Asia Minor and the Balkans to threaten Italy.

Italy, September 69. Antonius Primus, commander of a legion in Pannonia, declares his support for Vespasian and, having gained the backing of the other Danubian armies, leads an invasion of Italy.

Italy, October 69. The forces of Antonius Primus inflict a crushing defeat on Vitellius at Cremona.

Rome, 20 December 69. Vespasian's supporters enter Rome and discover Vitellius in hiding. He is dragged through the streets before being brutally murdered.

Rome, 21 December 69. Vespasian enters Rome and is adopted as emperor by the Senate.

East Africa, c.70. Pottery typical of the early users of iron in the continent is now being made as far south as Maputo, south of the Limpopo mouth, in Mozambique. This coastal type of pottery derives from Malawi, eastern Tanzania and Kenya.

Judaea, 7 September 70. Under siege by Vespasian's son, Titus, since his father's proclamation as emperor last year, Jerusalem finally falls to the Romans.

Germany, 70. Gaius Julius Civilis, a Batavian who led a great revolt of the Germanic peoples against the Romans, suffers a decisive defeat. The "war of liberation" began in 69 under pretext of providing support for Vespasian, and was joined by Gallic tribes such as the Treveri and Lingones.

Near East, 70. Vespasian strengthens Rome's eastern borders with Armenia and Parthia. He moves legions from Syria to forts on the upper Euphrates, puts Cappadocia under the control of the imperial governor of Galatia, and takes over several small principalities in Asia and Syria.

China, 73. General Ban Chao is sent to the western regions, where he establishes Chinese control over the oasis states. This marks a new peak in Later Han military success.

Rome, c.73. Helvidius Priscus, son-in-law of Thrasea, leader of the Stoic opposition to the empire, is banished by Vespasian.

Germany, 74. In order to reduce the salient between the Rhine and the Danube, the Romans occupy the Neckar valley.

Spain, 74. Vespasian introduces the status of "Latin rights", giving the inhabitants of towns civil rights identical to those of citizens, but not allowing them access to public office.

Rome, 75. Flavius Josephus, a Jewish historian and former fighter in the 66 uprising, now with the Romans, recounts the events in his *Bellum Judaicum* (History of the Jewish Wars). He has also written a history of his own people, from their origins until the present, the *Antiquitates Judaicae* (Early History of the Jews).

Rome, 75. Vespasian has completed his temple of peace in Rome. Begun in 71, the temple is part of an ambitious building programme.

China, 75. The Emperor Mingdi dies and is replaced by Changdi. General Ban Chao, who has been occupied in capturing the Tarim oases since 73, puts down a general uprising in the region.

Syria, 76. With the consent of Vespasian, Johanan ben Zakkai, former spokesman of the Pharisaic pacifist sect, sets up an academy at Jabneh and re-establishes the Sanhedrin. Johanan ben Zakkai took refuge at Jabneh before the Romans captured Jerusalem.

India, 78. The Kushan king, Vima Kadphises – a great conqueror who now rules the north of India as far as Benares and the Indus delta – sends a delegation to Rome to arrange a surprise attack on the Parthians.

General re-builds Rome

Rome, 70

Vespasian, a gruff-spoken general of (relatively) humble origins, is the new ruler of Rome.

This hero of campaigns in Judaea has arrived in the city to take the laurel wreaths of both emperor and triumphant victor.

Already he has set about the task of re-building the city of Rome and restoring its fortunes. Many of the city's great buildings suffered from Nero's pyromaniac excesses.

Vespasian has invited anyone who pleases to take over the vacant sites and build on them if previous owners fail to come forward. He himself collected the first basket of rubble and debris from the ruined Capitol and carried it away on his own shoulders.

Taxes have been drastically increased to recover the huge expense of the civil wars; Vespasian is searching industriously for new sources of revenue. And, in his role as censor, he has purged the Senate of enemies and introduced more non-Romans, provincials and Ital-

Vespasian: a portrait of the emperor by Rubens (1577-1640).

ians into the Senate House. Vespasian's progressive rule is marked by his interest in education – he has personally endowed several professorships – and by his humanity, which is demonstrated by a significant fall in the number of executions in Rome since his accession in November.

Jewish revolt ends in ruin of Jerusalem

The triumphal arch of Titus; the Jews do not regard him so highly.

Jerusalem, 8 September 70

After four years of bloody warfare, the Jewish revolt against Roman domination has been crushed. Jerusalem has been destroyed and, with it, the Temple, the holiest of all Jewish places.

The province of Judaea has always been seen as a problem by

Rome, but the authorities failed continually to take proper control. This new revolt broke out in 66, when the Jews, infuriated by the corruption of a succession of procurators, suffering after a number of famines, and stirred up by a variety of fanatical nationalist preachers, turned on their occupiers.

The first phase of the revolt ended two years ago, when troops under Vespasian and Titus defeated what were in effect no more than guerrilla forces, known as *sicarii*. Only Jerusalem remained, and it has been stubbornly defended during a two-year siege.

That siege ended today when Roman soldiers broke through the last defences and unleashed a terrible revenge on the defenders. Thousands have been massacred in an orgy of killing; the Temple has been looted, then burnt to the ground; the city itself is in ruins.

One solitary pocket of resistance remains. One thousand Jews are isolated in the southern fortress of Masada. They promise: "No surrender."

Pompeii buried under volcanic ash from Vesuvius

A street in the doomed town of Pompeii; Vesuvius looms on the horizon.

Colourful wall frescoes give a glimpse of prosperity before the eruption.

Pompeii, 24 August 79

Death came swiftly, mercifully so. For thousands, particularly in the heat of a Roman summer, Pompeii was the ideal holiday resort. Built on a hill overlooking the sea, it was a cool yet lively town, its streets ever busy with traders and craftsmen; its pottery was famed all over Italy, and its houses noted for their cloistered gardens and frescoes. The theatre was always filled in the season, and the town boasted the oldest stone amphitheatre in the Roman world – until today, when the sleeping mountain called Vesuvius vented its fury.

Some slept when the vast cloud of ash engulfed and choked them; some were gambling; some were sleepless in that unnatural heat and sat and talked until suddenly they died; many more were making love in their own beds, or in the many brothels of Pompeii, when the volcanic dust snuffed out their lives. Traders died instantly, some at the moment of the final haggle.

Everyone died in Pompeii; and such was the devastation and loss that the government in Rome has chosen to leave the town buried under the lava and ash. Few witnesses remain to tell the whole horrific story of the night that Vesuvius erupted. And yet the disaster claimed the life of one of Rome's greatest writers, Pliny, the author of *Natural History*, who was then the commander of a fleet nearby. Pliny died, but his nephew witnessed much of what happened.

As his uncle's ship drew towards Pompeii "... on Mount Vesuvius, broad sheets of fire and leaping flames blazed at several points, their bright glare emphasised by the darkness of night". Pliny the elder arrived where "... the buildings were shaking with violent shocks and seemed to be swaying to and fro as if they were being torn from their roots".

By this time Pliny was trapped. He went down to the sea to look for a possible escape route. The waves were too wild and dangerous. The night was "blacker and denser than any night that ever was" and Pliny, leaning on two slaves, was overcome and collapsed.

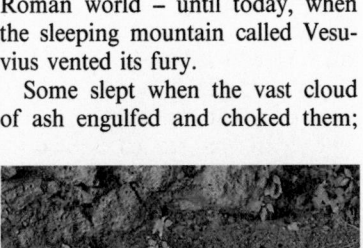

A victim of the calamity, buried in volcanic ash exactly where he died.

Wall-painting from the Villa of the Mysteries in Pompeii, showing the high quality of art lost with the town.

Egyptian scientist uses water power

Alexandria, c.80

This most innovative and cultured city has produced a remarkable inventor and scientist who had discovered forms of steam propulsion and systems of hydraulics. Hero – or Heron – has devised an ingenious apparatus called an "aeoliphile" – a steam source linked to a rotating sphere with two nozzles as outlets. A boiler generates steam that emanates from the outlets giving power to turn a wheel.

He is making other important contributions to the advancement of science. "Hero's formula" for finding the area of triangles is one accomplishment together with *Metrica*, a treatise which includes a method method for finding the approximate square root of any number and ways of computing the volume of cones, pyramids, cylinders, spheres and prisms.

Hero has made a considerable contribution to knowledge in the craft of surveying. In his *Dioptra*, he describes an instrument called a diopter which measures angles of elevation, essential to a surveyor's measurements. His knowledge of astronomy has enabled him to compute the distance from Alexandria to Rome through sightings of a lunar eclipse.

Perhaps the most valuable device he has produced is an sophisticated system of lifting weights by the use of water pressure, a system which will save countless man-hours.

Hero's famous "aeoliphile".

Romans push into Scotland after Agricola quashes Picts in fierce mountain battles

Horse-head bronze from a Pictish war chariot, c.50.

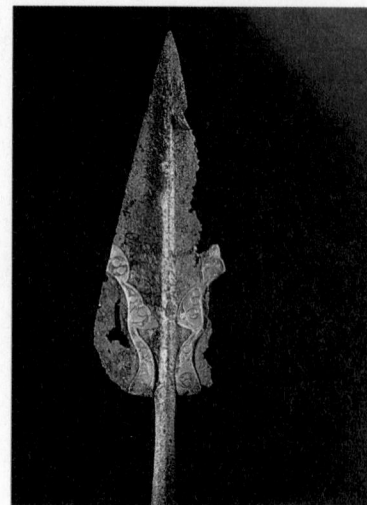

A Celtic spear used in Britain, of iron with bronze decoration.

Caledonia, 84

The victories of Agricola over the Picts, and the setting up of small forts along the Clyde-Forth line, mark the greatest extent so far of Roman advances in Britain.

The invasion of Britain in 43, with 50,000 men under Aulus Plautius, was ordered by the Emperor Claudius to protect Gaul and Roman merchants, exploit mineral resources, and bring greater glory to Rome.

Having established a foothold in the south-east, and extended westwards under Vespasian's generalship, the Romans attacked Wales in 48 under Ostorius Scapula, who also disarmed the Iceni in East Anglia.

Boudicca's rebellion in 61, when Suetonius Paulinus was stamping out Druidism in Anglesey and Roman forces were scattered, may have cost the lives of 70,000 Romans in the sack of London before Paulinus crushed the rebels in a bloody pitched battle.

By 74 Cerialis had subdued the Brigantes in the north; by 77 the Silures in Wales had yielded to Frontinus. Agricola's campaigns against the Picts have taken him to the Grampian mountains.

Poet Martial turns epigrams into art form

Rome, 85

A 46-year-old Spaniard is causing a stir with a recently-published collection of pithy epigrams depicting Roman society.

Marcus Valerius Martialis, or Martial, has lived in Rome for about 20 years. He first came to public attention six years ago with a book marking the opening of the Colosseum by the Emperor Titus, which was followed by books of suggestions for menus and gifts. With the first volume of his *Epigrams*, though, Martial breaks new ground with his brilliantly sharp and varied portrayals of the vices and virtues of all levels of Roman life, in which humanity and wit are combined with brevity.

Later portrait of Martial, whose epigrams amply demonstrate that brevity is the soul of wit.

New amphitheatre shows gory gladiatorial games

The Flavian Amphitheatre, or "Colosseum", spectacular setting for games.

Romans thrill to the excitement of chariot races in the film "Ben Hur".

Rome, 80

A capacity crowd of 55,000 roared its delight today as the Emperor Titus raised his hand to signal the opening of the biggest stadium in the world – the Roman Colosseum. Within minutes the huge arena was alive with colour, movement and spectacle as musicians, dancers, and soldiers of the Praetorian Guard, their armour gleaming in the Roman sun, together with elephants from Africa, camels from Egypt and horsemen from Spain, paraded before Caesar.

The biggest cheer of all came for the gladiators who raised their swords, spears, tridents and fighting nets in homage to the emperor, the assembled Senate and the crowd. Even as the crowd roared, it could hear another roar – of wild animals which had been kept starved in their cages.

The gladiators are the stars in this arena, in which they will fight in combat that has no rules except that the winner is the man who walks away alive. Many are ex-soldiers – professionals who travel to amphitheatres all over Italy to display their fighting skill. They have their own followers, and the victor can always be certain of free wine and the choice of pretty girls until his next encounter. Many more are slaves, fighting not merely for their survival but for the chance of freedom.

Here in this massive, purpose-built enclave the crowd will watch as the gladiators fight, sometimes one against one, often in gory multiple figures. Speciality acts are always in demand – brother facing brother, father facing son, can always be relied on to draw big crowds. And if the sight of men hacking at each other with swords or other weapons begins to pall, few spectacles appear to offer more pleasure to Roman audiences than the sight of Christians and criminals being ripped to pieces by wild animals. All Rome loves the games. The games *are* Rome. The emperor in his gilded box faces the senators in their special seats. When a kill or not to kill decision is required, only the emperor can decide; his up-turned thumb means mercy, down-turned is death.

Admission is by ticket only. Women – except for the Vestal Virgins (who are honorary men) – sit in the back rows. Togas are obligatory. The bodies are taken out through the Porta Libitinaria exit.

Charioteer in leather protective helmet and his sponsor's colours.

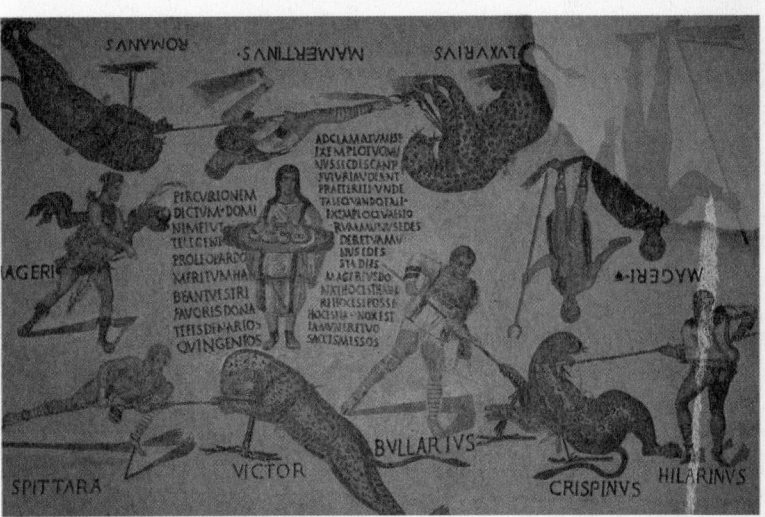

A mosaic from North Africa showing a gladiatorial troop killing leopards.

The gruesome "sport" of bear-baiting is a popular spectacle among the Roman public, as is depicted in this relief of the games from the imperial provinces.

Roman gladiator and his opponent in action in the amphitheatre.

Rome, 85. The Emperor Domitian appoints himself censor for life. This office gives him complete control of the composition of the Senate.

Balkans, 87. The Romans suffer a serious setback in the Dacian war, which broke out in 85. The Praetorian prefect, Cornelius Fuscus, who was entrusted with the Roman command, is defeated and killed.

Rome, 87. Domitian, jealous of Julius Agricola's successes as governor of Britain – where he has advanced far into Scotland – recalls him to Rome. After the Roman defeat of the Caledonians in 85, Agricola's fleet circumnavigated the coast, for the first time discovering Britain to be an island.

China, 87. Hedi succeeds as emperor on the death of Chongdi.

Germany, 88. Following the abortive revolt of Saturninus, the governor of upper Germany, Domitian declares that only one legion is to be quartered in each Roman camp. His motive is to prevent any commander from gaining influence over excessive numbers of troops.

Balkans, 89. The Romans have failed to wipe out the troublesome tribe known as the Dacians. Their kingdom has been saved from total destruction by the Marcomanni and the Quadi, who now occupy Bohemia, a western neighbour of Dacia. After defeating the emperor in battle, these peoples forced Domitian to sign a humiliating peace treaty with the Dacian king, Decebalus.

Rome, 90. Domitian has embarked on a campaign of persecution and execution of his opponents. Last year he expelled the philosophers from Rome.

Central Asia, 91. Continuing his conquest of the Tarim basin the Chinese general Ban Chao inflicts a defeat on the Indian Kushans under the leadership of Kaniska.

Rome, 92. The lawyer Quintilian, who was born in Spain c.30, has written the *Institutio Oratoria*, a programme of education for the future orator. Quintilian, who believes that the supreme orator represents all that is best in morals, education and stylistic judgement, holds the chair of Latin eloquence created by Vespasian in 72. Among his pupils have been Pliny the Younger and the two great-nephews and heirs of Domitian.

China, 92. The historian Ban Gu, who with his father and sister complied a history of the former Han dynasty, is executed for having supported the Dou faction at court.

Balkans, 92. The Iazyges, one of the two main branches of the Sarmatian tribe, who now occupy the plain between the Danube and the Theiss rivers, invade Dacia. Domitian takes the field against them in person and succeeds in driving them back.

Central Asia, 94. The Chinese general Ban Chao completes his conquest of the Tarim basin by capturing Karashahr.

Rome, 95. Domitian accuses the consul Flavius Clemens and his wife, Flavia Domitilla, of "atheism" (perhaps Christian or Jewish practices). Clemens – whose two sons Domitian had intended to be his heirs – is executed. Domitilla, meanwhile, is banished to an island.

Italy, 96. The poet Statius, a favourite at Domitian's court, dies in his native Naples. His best-known works are the occasional verses known as the *Silvae* and the epics *Thebais* and *Achilleis*.

Rome, 18 September 96. Domitian, who has been conducting a reign of terror for the past three years, is assassinated as the result of a plot by his wife Domitia and two Praetorian prefects. Among the many fine buildings constructed in Rome during his reign are the temple to Jupiter on the Capitol and a temple to Jupiter Custos on the Quirinal.

Rome, 19 September 96. Nerva, suspected of complicity in the death of Domitian, is declared emperor by the Senate. The Senate then annuls laws passed by Domitian and orders his statues to be destroyed.

Rome, 27 October 97. To placate the Praetorians and legions in Germany, Nerva adopts Trajan, the Spanish-born governor of lower Germany.

Rome, 97. Cornelius Tacitus, who has replaced Verginius Rufus as consul, delivers his predecessor's funeral oration. A former governor of upper Germany, Verginius Rufus crushed the uprising led by Vindex in 68. He twice refused to accept the title of emperor, but was chosen by Nerva as his colleague in the consulship earlier this year.

Rome, 98. Tacitus publishes an account of the life of his father-in-law, Julius Agricola, whose daughter he married in 77. Tacitus has also written a descriptive history of the various tribes north of the Rhine and the Danube, and recently started work on a monumental history of Rome.

Germany, 28 January 98. On the death of Nerva, Trajan is declared Roman emperor in Cologne, the seat of his government in lower Germany.

Empires of Rome and China nearly meet

Central Asia, 94
The Chinese general Ban Chao has extended Han power along the Silk Road through Turkestan to the west until only the Caspian Sea and the Armenian mountains separate the Han and the Roman empires.

Ban Chao has spent most of his life fighting the northern nomads, and 20 years ago he was sent to the border kingdoms to make alliances and gain recognition of Han supremacy. He is a man of great firmness and strength of character, and he won his way through the often hostile tribes as far west as Kashgar.

His success was not approved of by a faction at court which opposed expansion to the west, and he was recalled before he had time to consolidate his gains.

However, the accession of a new emperor, Han Zhangdi, enabled Ban Chao to mount another expedition. He subjugated the tribal

Han dinasty dancing figure.

kings and now, with an army of 70,000 men, stands on the shores of the Caspian Sea awaiting news from the envoy he has sent to make contact with the Romans.

Cruel emperor builds new palace

Rome, 85
Perhaps it was because the Emperor Domitian had a poverty-stricken youth – it is said that his family could not afford silver on their family table – that he has built such a magnificent palace on the Palatine. Whatever the reason, this despotic Caesar has now given Rome an official home for himself, from where he and his successors can effectively rule the city and its burgeoning empire.

The Palatine is an obvious choice. The highest of the seven hills of Rome, it has been a residential area for Rome's famous and infamous – like Cicero, Crassus, Sulla and Marcus Antonius – for centuries. Apart from its superb setting, the palace is remarkable in that it is built almost entirely of concrete, which has been developed rapidly during Domitian's reign as an efficient building material.

Visitors seeking an audience with Domitian can expect a nerveracking 120-foot walk down a marble-sheathed hall lined with statues before they reach the emperor on his throne. And if Caesar is so inclined, visitors will be taken into the courtyard with its elaborate fountain for a more informal talk. The

Later portrait of Domitian.

vast columns here have been lined with white moonstone, giving a mirror-like surface in which the emperor might see a possible assassin behind him.

Domitian has set a new standard for public building. His palace includes a great banqueting room, a garden designed as a stadium, baths and a forum. For all his energy in restoring Rome's glory, this Caesar's cruelty is notorious, especially his delight in torturing victims by burning their genitals.

Unchaste Vestal Virgin buried alive

Rome, 90
The Emperor Domitian has ordered the chief priestess of the Vestal Virgins to be buried alive following allegations of unchastity that have rocked the Roman establishment.

The Vestal Virgins are chosen by the emperor, in his capacity as *pontifex maximus*, Rome's high priest, to serve Vesta, the Roman hearth-goddess. Their term of service can last for 30 years, during which time they must remain virgins on pain of death, which means burial alive for a chief Vestal. The alleged affair between the chief Vestal Cornelia and a former magistrate is said to have left Domitian furious. Despite protesting innocence, Cornelia will be executed in the traditional way.

Statue of one of the Vestal Virgins.

Bid to curb Roman wine glut dropped

Rome, 92
The Emperor Domitian has dropped plans to slash wine production in the empire. His bid to curb viticulture in Italy and the provinces followed this year's glut of wine, which coincided with a dramatic shortage of corn. An edict ordered that no new vines should be planted in Italy, and that production in the empire should be halved. However, the edict has proved hard to enforce and has led to Domitian being lampooned by satirical Romans as a "vine-eating goat".

Christian writer predicts doom for Rome

A serpent, illustrating John's revelations, from Luther's Bible (c.1530).

Patmos, Aegean Sea, 97
A devastating attack on Rome and a rallying cry to the world's Christian community have emerged from the Aegean island of Patmos. The author is John the Apostle, known as "the beloved disciple", one of the four writers whose gospels tell the story of the Christians' alleged Messiah, Jesus Christ.

John, who was exiled to Patmos by the Roman Emperor Domitian as part of a general attack on Christianity, has written an *Apocalypse*, or book of prophecies. The book, which is intended to raise the morale of those Christians suffering persecution, is a collection of visions and symbols, all of which point to the destruction of Rome and the ultimate victory of Christ. Typically, the *Apocalypse* does not attack Rome directly, but in vivid, even terrifying, language speaks of the defeat by "the Lamb, the Lord of Lords and King of Kings" of "a woman mounted on a scarlet beast ... Babylon the great, mother of whores and of every obscenity on earth".

Further visions include the "four horsemen" who will announce the Day of Judgement, the appearance of two great beasts (representing Roman emperors), and a final battle in which Christ defeats Satan. There is no doubt that, symbolic or not, John's powerful book will be fully understood by Romans and Christians alike.

Soldier Trajan is named emperor

Roman Empire, 28 January 98
To avoid a ruinous power-struggle after his death, the Emperor Nerva last year named as his successor an army general from the provinces. Today the Roman Senate endorsed Trajan, the 43-year-old son of a Spanish mother and a Roman father, as the new Caesar.

Trajan is at present on the distant Rhine frontier building defences against the Germans. He has told the Senate he intends to finish the work before coming to Rome. He is said to feel more at home in camp with his legions than in the city. His marriage to Pompeia Plotina has so far remained childless; by reputation, the new emperor prefers wine and young boys.

Emperor Nerva: paving the way.

Settlers move into newly pacified areas near German border

Rome, 90
The Emperor Domitian has appointed Rome's first envoy to Germany, following recent conquests there. Most of northern Germany is still barbarian. What is new is that a huge triangle of territory encompassing the Black Forest, between the Rhine and the Danube, is now pacified, securing Rome's Alpine approaches. The conquest took 16 years. Alongside new roads and forts are farms where local people have now been resettled, working the land and paying tithes. The campaign needed nine legions, including four from Britain.

Roman troops attacking a village across the Roman frontier in Germany, a 19th century engraving of part of a Roman victory column.

Rome, 99. Having inspected and organised the frontiers of the Rhine and Danube, and subdued or executed mutinous Praetorians, Trajan – the former governor of lower Germany who succeeded Nerva as emperor early last year – leaves Germany and makes his entry into Rome.

Rome, 99. Julius Frontinus, a former governor of Britain who was made superintendent of Rome's water supply by the Emperor Nerva, has completed a detailed account of the city's water system, describing the aqueducts and their history. He has also written studies of land-surveying and of Greek and Roman military science.

India, 99. The Kushan king Kaniska, under whose rule the kingdom has reached great heights, sends a delegation to Rome to arrange a surprise attack on the Parthians.

Mexico, c.100. The Pyramids of the Sun and Moon are under construction at Teotihuacan.

Rome, 100. Among the many social reforms introduced by Trajan is a system of *alimenta*, which is designed to give allowances to children of the poor. Interest paid by landowners on mortgage loans made by the state is distributed among the children – primarily to increase the birth-rate in order to swell the ranks of the Roman legions.

Rome, September 100. On taking up the office of consul, the advocate Pliny the Younger, a pupil of Quintilian, delivers his *Panegyric of Trajan*, the portrait of an ideal prince, in which he contrasts the beneficial reforms of Trajan with the evil deeds of Domitian. Pliny has also written several books of literary letters, in which he comments on social, domestic and political events.

North Africa, 100. The Emperor Trajan bases the Roman legion known as the III Augusta, the only African legion, at Thamugadi (Timgad) in Numidia. The town built there according to a geometric plan is given the status of a colony. A Roman colony is also established at Lambaesis, 20 miles to the west.

Balkans, 101. Trajan, worried by the growing power of the Dacian king, Decebalus, invades Dacia at the head of the legions of neighbouring Moesia.

Italy, 102. Trajan gives orders for work to start on extending the port of Ostia.

Central Asia, 102. Having organised the Chinese territories of the Tarim basin, the general Ban Chao retreats.

Balkans, 102. After the capture of Sarmizegethusa, capital of Dacia, by Trajan's forces, King Decebalus is forced to sign a humiliating treaty by which he agrees to become an ally of the Roman people.

Spain, c.104. The poet Martial, who gained a reputation for his witty epigrams, dies at Bilbilis in his native Spain.

Spain, 105. The bridge of Alcantara, which has a straight floor, is constructed over the river Tagus.

Rome, 105. Plotina, wife of Trajan, who is admired for her simplicity and virtue, accepts the title of Augusta, which she refused five years ago.

Balkans, 105. Decebalus, king of the Dacians, attacks the nomadic people known as the Iazyges, who come from the lower Danube region, and besieges the Roman garrisons remaining in Dacia.

China, 105. A form of prototype paper is evolved and made known to the Han government by the eunuch Cai Lun.

Balkans, 106. Having relieved the Roman garrisons in Dacia, Trajan recaptures the Dacian capital and drives Decebalus to suicide. Dacia becomes a Roman province.

Arabia, 106. The kingdom of Nabataea, which has its capital at Petra, is invaded by Cornelius Palma, governor of Syria, and annexed by Rome. It becomes the Roman province of Arabia.

Mesopotamia, 107. Osroes succeeds to the throne of Parthia.

Rome, 107. Magnificent games are held in Rome to celebrate the Dacian conquest. Construction begins on new baths and a forum in which a column will be erected to mark the victory.

China, 107. An-ti (Ngan-ti), a young boy, becomes emperor, leaving the Dowager Empress Deng to rule. A Japanese prince sends a present of 160 slaves to the Chinese court.

Rome, c.107. The church father Ignatius, a disciple of St. John and former bishop of Antioch, dies a martyr in Rome.

India, c.110. At the instigation of the Kushan king, Kaniska, a grand Buddhist council is held in Kashmir. It proceeds under the direction of the Buddhist theologian Asvaghosha, a poet, dramatist, musician and friend of the king. The most important outcome of the council is the division of Buddhism into two branches of belief, those of the Greater and Lesser Vehicle, Mahayana and Hinayana.

Eunuch teaches Han how to make paper

Paper-maker working on the production of the new cheap writing material.

China, 105

Cai Lun, a eunuch serving in the imperial court, has invented *chih* (paper) by soaking and pounding flat the bark of trees, rag, hemp and old fishing nets.

This invention will bring great changes in the art of writing and painting, for until now heavy tablets of bamboo and expensive pieces of silk have been used. Now, large quantities of cheap, easily transportable writing material can be manufactured.

It also means the experts in calligraphy and painting will be able to use their brush strokes with even more pleasing results. The emperor has recognised the value of this new process and heaped praise on Cai Lun.

He is already renowned as a man of talent and learning and holds the important court position of *Shang Fang Si*, controller of the making of instruments and weapons. He is working now to refine the colour and texture of his invention, which has become generally known as "the paper of Marquis Cai".

Fugitive Dacian king takes his own life

Rome, 106

The severed head of Decebalus, the defeated king of Dacia (north of the Danube), was ceremonially hurled down the Gemonia Steps today as Rome celebrated the Emperor Trajan's conquest of the country.

Decebalus is reported to have slit his own throat with a curved dagger in his hideout in the Transylvanian mountains, where he had fled after Roman troops had overrun his royal palace.

The groundwork for Trajan's victory had been laid months before with the completion of a huge stone bridge across the Ister. It allowed Trajan to end the truce and march against the fortresses which Decebalus was rebuilding, which he had been forced to dismantle by the peace treaty of 102.

Scenes from the campaign against Dacia, on Trajan's victory column.

Trajan's rule wins support of people

Buddha in Greek robes is new form of art in India

Ruins of a temple built by the Emperor Trajan at Pergamum.

Trajan: enlightened emperor.

India, c.100
A new school of art, synthesising Greek and Buddhist ideals, has developed in the Gandhara province of north-west India. Until recently artists have closely followed Buddhist iconographical rules, representing the image of the Buddha symbolically. Now, in Gandhara, the Buddha is being portrayed with European features and replete with images of ancient Greece. These Greek Buddhas, both statues and paintings, are found all over Gandhara, particularly in Taxila and the great monastery of Takht-i-Bahi.

Rome, 101
In the three years since he became emperor, Trajan has gained wide popularity with his public work schemes and generous benefits for the poor. At the same time he has promised not to increase taxes. He is reforming the civil service to root out corruption and promote efficiency.

The emperor has increased the number of citizens eligible for the free distribution of corn. He has also produced a scheme for child benefits. Landowners are to be granted low-interest loans. The interest, probably five per cent, will be used to fund child benefits.

Some people question whether benefits should be paid to the well-to-do as well as to the poor. In fact, Trajan's scheme is intended to help children who will later serve in the armed forces. One commentator, Pliny the Younger, says: "Nearly 5,000 freeborn children have been entered on the lists through the generosity of their prince, to safeguard the state in war and adorn it in peace." The public works programme includes major schemes for roads and ports, and magnificent new baths and a forum in Rome.

Trajan has led successful military campaigns in Dacia (Rumania), Armenia and Mesopotamia, thus extending the empire's frontiers far beyond those of his predecessors.

A Gandhara Buddha (c.200).

Satires of Juvenal strike at excesses

Rome, 110
A devastating attack on moral standards is contained in a new book, *Satires*, the first volume of which has just been published here. It is written by Juvenal, who was born at Aquinum, in Campania, during the reign of Nero. He was trained as a teacher of rhetoric.

He paints a vivid picture of life amongst the lower classes, revealing avarice, vice and crime. There are witty gibes about the hypocrisy of the Stoics, and a savage polemic against sodomy. One amusing satire shows the Emperor Domitian summoning his cringing cabinet to discuss the cooking of a giant turbot. The most bitter satire reveals a city where an honest man cannot make a living and the poor are objects of scorn; a rich patron laughs as he orders insolent servants to bring cheap food to a poor client.

Egyptian publishes guide to Indian Ocean

Eritrea, 106
A Greek sea captain has published a *periplus*, or guide, to the Red Sea and India Ocean, which together he calls the Eritrean Sea.

The *periplus* provides information on the Eritrean port of Adulis; the Ethiopian capital, Axum; Somalia (where the people are "very unruly" and "each town is ruled by a separate chief"); Zanzibar ("the last market of the continent"); the Yemenite port Mocha ("crowded with ship owners and seafaring men"); south Arabia, and the Indian coast.

A man sailing a "corbita", a small coastal vessel, from Carthage (c.200).

Kingdom of Petra annexed by Rome

Petra, 106
After the death of Rabbel II, Petra, the capital of the kingdom of Nabataea, which has long been protected by Rome, is annexed by the Emperor Trajan to become the province of Arabia. Petra, an important trading post on the Bedouin caravan route, is renowned for its elaborate cave tombs; these are carved out of sandstone and have Greek sculpted decorations.

Asia Minor, 110. Pliny the Younger is appointed governor of Bithynia.

Rome, 113. The architect Apollodorus of Damascus completes Trajan's new Forum.

Rome, 114. The Senate votes to build a triumphal arch at Beneventum, at the end of the new Via Traiana, the construction of which has improved communications with Brundisium (Brindisi) and the east. Dedicated to "Trajan Optimus", it will depict imperial achievements in a series of allegories.

Armenia, 114. Osroes, king of the Parthians, dethrones the Armenian king, a vassal of the Romans, and replaces him with his nephew Parthamasiris. Trajan then declares war on the Parthians, and occupies Armenia aided by the people of Colchis in the Caucasus.

China, 115. Ban Zhao, China's leading polymath, historian, mathematician, astronomer and poet, dies at the age of 70, following an arduous journey to be with her son, a provincial magistrate. The sister of Ban Gu, who was executed in 92, Ban Zhao was a model for the women of her time; her writings include a influential book on morality called *Lessons for Women*.

Mesopotamia, 115. With the collaboration of Abgar, king of Osroene – a kingdom in the north-west of the region with a capital at Edessa (Urfa) – Trajan occupies most of Mesopotamia.

Judaea, 115. Lusius Quietus, appointed governor by Trajan, undertakes a brutal repression in Judaea to maintain peace. This follows Jewish uprisings in Cyrenaica, Egypt and Cyprus against the Romans and the Greeks, which threaten to spread to the whole of the Jewish world.

Near East, 116. Trajan captures Ctesiphon, the capital of Parthia, and reaches the Persian Gulf. Armenia, Mesopotamia and Adiabene in Assyria become Roman provinces. Parthamasparthes, a vassal of Rome, is installed as king of Parthia and takes the title "Parthicus".

Syria, August 117. Hadrian, named by the dying Trajan as his successor, is declared emperor at Antioch. To establish peace on the frontiers of the empire, he abandons Mesopotamia and Assyria.

Glories of Rome reflected in Forum

Rome, 118

With a population of over a million Rome is the biggest city in the world, and the successors of the Emperor Augustus have continued to honour his pledge to "swathe the city in marble". The latest architectural masterpiece in this city is the Forum and market complex commissioned by Trajan and dominated by a 130-foot column surmounted by a statue of the emperor wearing a breastplate.

The complex is entered through a triumphal arch, and its most striking feature is the enormous basilica, its five naves decorated with marble brought from all over the empire. There are two libraries – one Greek, one Latin. The construction of the Forum involved the clearance of hundreds of dwellings in this part of Rome and the removal of thousands of tons of soil. The semicircular market, a strictly utilitarian building, is designed to hide the scars on the hill.

So much of Rome is taken up with public basilicas, temples, circuses, public baths and theatres that building land is at a premium, which has meant the building of tall blocks of apartments for the poorer classes. Overcrowding is endemic and the contrast between rich and poor is startling.

The wealthier Romans may occupy the whole ground floor of one of these buildings as a single family unit; but the apartments over them become smaller and more and more cramped, the higher they get. For the most part, they are dark and gloomy, lit by candles or smoky lamps. Cooking is done on open stoves, with an ever-present risk of fire. Although eight aqueducts bring 200 million gallons of water into the city each day, water has to be brought to most poorer homes by buckets filled at street fountains. Sewage disposal, too, is a bucket affair, with cesspools at regular intervals on the streets.

The streets of Rome are narrow, noisy and lively, with traders, craftsmen, jugglers, snake-charmers, acrobats and street vendors jostling each other for favoured pitches. Barbers, too, ply their trade in the streets – treating the inevitable cuts with spiders' webs soaked in oil and vinegar.

Ruins of the Forum, Rome's great public space, looking south-east.

Colosseum and Forum dominate this model of the 2nd-century Rome.

Ruins of Trajan's market.

The Forum, as it may have looked.

Hadrian inherits the largest-ever Roman empire

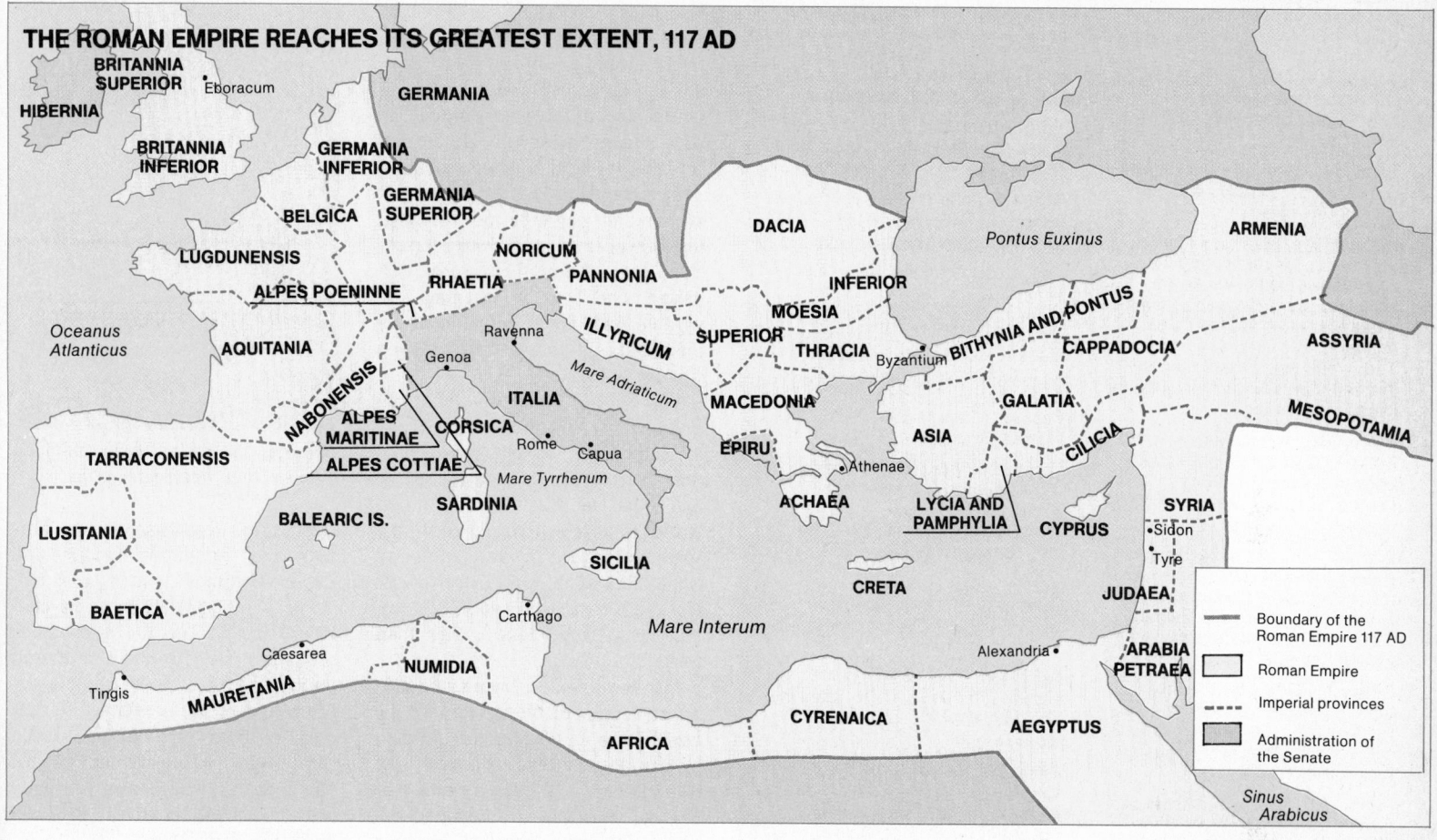

THE ROMAN EMPIRE REACHES ITS GREATEST EXTENT, 117 AD

Asia Minor, 8 August 117
The Emperor Trajan, returning from a military campaign against the Parthians, died today at Selinus in Asia Minor, and the succession has passed to his protege, the 46-year old Hadrian, at present in command of the legions in Syria. It was Trajan's widow, Plotina, who told the Senate of her husband's deathbed nomination of Hadrian.

The first and most urgent task is to stabilise the empire's frontiers. This calls for the abandonment of

Trajan's policy of expansion, which has bequeathed to Hadrian the biggest-ever Roman empire. Nothing is to be gained by scattering the barbarians on the frontiers and then seeking to occupy their territory. Better to have shorter frontiers that will keep the barbarian at bay; the empire's manpower resources have hardly increased at all in the century since Augustus.

In Parthia, beyond the Euphrates, the most recent conquest, the people are in revolt and the ter-

ritory is to be given up. The Jews of the Diaspora, from Mesopotamia down through Egypt to Cyrene in Libya, are also in rebellion. They can expect no mercy from Hadrian, who has been known to talk of a no-nonsense response to Jewish troublemakers.

The new emperor is also reported to be planning a visit to Britain, where he will consider constructing a new wall, from the Solway Firth to the Tyne, to keep the Picts of the Caledonian hills out of the colony.

There is no thought of giving up Britain; many soldiers in the army of occupation have taken native wives and settled in the country, and their sons have later become recruits for the legions.

It is said that, whereas Trajan was a born soldier who became a statesman, Hadrian sees himself as a statesman who must on occasion use military force. He is certainly more of an intellectual than his predecessor, and intends to become a patron of the arts.

Writer to rule disorderly province

Rome, 110
The Emperor Trajan has sent Pliny the Younger as legate to govern the disorderly province of Bithynia. Pliny has already made a formidable reputation for himself as a state prosecutor of provincial governors accused of extortion. He is also a prolific writer, and has published nine books of literary letters in the last decade. He was born in Como in 61 and came to Rome to

study advocacy under Quintilian. His letters give a detailed account of Rome's social, domestic and political life. It is mostly a favourable picture, showing Romans as being considerate of their wives and having a rich literary life. Pliny gives the Senate an heroic role in opposing Domitian. However, he censures the cruelty of the slave masters, the dodges of the legacy hunters and the meanness of the rich.

Historian completes account of empire

Rome, 115
Rome's most prolific historian, Cornelius Tacitus, has fulfilled his ambition of covering the history of imperial Rome from Augustus to Trajan. His *Annales* focusses on the Julio-Claudian dynasty. He avoids retailing the more extravagant rumours, but the facts he reports provide a catalogue of crimes, particularly by Nero and Tiberius.

His first historical work was a

graphic account of the conquest of Britain by his father-in-law, Agricola. This contained some fierce criticism of the Emperor Domitian. His *Historiae* covers the period from the death of Nero to the death of Domitian.

In *Annales* Tacitus reveals his heroes. He paints a glowing picture of the republic, of heroism amongst the lower classes and of the sturdy simplicity of Italy.

Rome, 9 July 118. Hadrian, who became emperor a year ago on Trajan's death, makes his entry into Rome. In his absence the Senate has ordered the execution of four provincial governors, including Trajan's generals Lusius Quietus and Cornelius Palma, convicted of conspiring against the new emperor.

Rome, 118. Hadrian takes an oath not to execute senators without trial by their peers.

Balkans, 118. Hadrian subdues an uprising in Moesia by the Sarmatian tribe known as the Roxolani. He then gives command of the provinces of Dacia and Pannonia to Quintus Marcus Turbo, who was recently sent by Trajan to settle Jewish disturbances in Egypt and Cyrenaica.

Rome, 122. Hadrian dismisses the historian Suetonius from his post as private secretary and the Praetorian prefect Septicius Clarus.

Britain, 122. On the orders of Hadrian, who is visiting Britain, construction begins on a frontier wall between the Roman province and the unconquered Caledonians. It will stretch from the Solway Firth to the river Tyne.

Armenia, 123. Under a peace treaty signed by Hadrian and the Parthian king, Osroes, Armenia again has an Arsacid ruler under the protection of Rome.

Athens, 124. During a journey to Greece, Hadrian is initiated into the ancient rites known as the Eleusinian Mysteries.

China, 124. A change in succession made earlier in the year by the Empress Yen is reversed after a violent uprising.

India, 125. Gautamiputra Satakarni, a king of the Andhra dynasty, destroys the Saka kingdom of Maharashtra near Bombay. The Andhra dynasty has dominated the eastern Dekhan region, between the Godavari and Krishna rivers, since c.100BC. Gautamiputra now occupies the whole of central India from coast to coast.

Central Asia, 125. The Chinese general Ban Yong, son of Ban Chao, repels an attempt by the Kushans of India to conquer the Tarim basin.

Greece, c.125. The philosopher and biographer Plutarch, a follower of Plato and author of the famous *Parallel Lives*, dies.

Rome, 127. Hadrian returns to Rome after seven years of touring the provinces. His travels have taken him to Britain, Holland, Gaul, Spain, Asia Minor, Greece and Sicily.

Athens, 128. Hadrian dedicates the Olympieum, the enormous temple of the Olympian Zeus. Work on construction of the temple started under the tyranny of Peisistratus over 700 years ago but was only recently completed. The emperor also accepts the title of *Olympius*.

North Africa, 128. Hadrian visits the Roman province of Africa to review the troops stationed there.

Near East, 129. Hadrian continues his travels, this time visiting Caria, Cilicia, Cappadocia and Syria.

Italy, c.130. On his property at Tibur (Tivoli) Hadrian has had a palatial villa erected to house reproductions of the monuments he has admired during his journeys. At Rome he has completely rebuilt the Pantheon, the temple in the Campus Martius built in 25BC by Marcus Vipsanius Agrippa.

Egypt, 130. While on a journey with the emperor up the Nile, Hadrian's lover Antinous is drowned. Rumour has it that he may have given his life for his master.

Egypt, 130. Hadrian founds the city of Antinoopolis in memory of his lover Antinous.

India, 130. Vasiska, king of the Kushans, the successor to Kaniska, dies, and Huviska comes to the throne.

Rome, 131. As requested by Hadrian, the young jurist Salvius Julianus has composed a revised version of the praetorian edict by which praetors announce new rules. Praetors have so far had the right to alter the edict, but on Julianus' recommendation it has now acquired a permanent form, depriving praetors of this right.

Judaea, 132. Incensed by the creation of a pagan Roman colony and the building of a shrine to Jupiter Capitolinus on the site of the temple at Jerusalem, the Jews rebel. Under the joint leadership of Simon Bar-Kochba ("Son of the Star") and the rabbi Eleazar, they take possession of Judaea.

Central Asia, 134. The Chinese domination of the Tarim basin is weakening.

Asia Minor, 134. Arrian, the governor of Cappadocia, beats off an attack by the Alans, nomadic pastoralists from south-eastern Russia.

Greece, c.135. The Stoic philosopher Epictetus dies at Nicopolis in Epirus, where he has lived since Domitian banished the philosophers from Rome in 89. A former slave, Epictetus advocated self-denial and indifference to suffering and taught that the universe is the work of God.

Plutarch, writer and moralist, is dead

Greece, c.125

The most famous citizen of Chaeronea, in Greece, is dead. Plutarch, writer, moralist, priest and politician, was known and respected in Greece and the Roman Empire. He was widely travelled. He served his philosophical apprenticeship in Athens, and lived for a time in Alexandria, where he met the great thinkers of the age. He was a teacher in Rome during the reign of Vespasian, and through teaching and writing had much influence over the minds of young men entering Roman politics.

For the last 30 of his nearly 80 years of life, Plutarch was a priest at Delphi. But he still spent much time here in his home town, as he had done all his life. His moral writings, such as *Ethica*, laid great stress on the idea of consolation and tranquillity of the soul. He wrote of vice and virtue, but with a warm and sympathetic tone rather than harsh moralising.

His most famous work, *Parallel Lives*, comprises biographies of the key figures in Greek and Roman history. It gave him an opportunity to celebrate the past glories of Greece, to which he remained devoted. He drew parallels between

Plutarch, the ethical writer and biographer, by a much later artist.

Greeks and Romans, such as Theseus and Romulus, Pericles and Fabius Maximus.

His work showed great psychological insight into the motivations of leaders. He also had a profound understanding of how cultures develop and of the continuity in political structures and art and social forms between Greece and Rome. His writings will almost certainly act as a major record of thess remarkable civilisations.

Trajan improved many roads and entirely rebuilt the road from Beneventum to Brundisium in southern Italy. This triumphal arch marks the start of the road and shows Trajan's work in Italy and the empire.

Rome basks in peace and prosperity

Radical edict spurs judicial reform

Rome, 132
The confusion which has reigned for so long in the Roman legal system has been brought to an end by the Emperor Hadrian. From now on there will be one law for the entire Italian peninsula – which Hadrian is proposing to divide into four provinces.

Until now, the city *praetor*, other city officials and the governors of provinces have set out annually the principles upon which they will administer justice. Only lawyers seem to have benefited.

Hadrian's arch at Athens, reminding Greeks that Rome is their master.

Hadrian the lawgiver, c.1400.

Travelling emperor inspects his empire

Rome, 132
Hadrian has returned to Rome, and it looks as though the emperor is planning to stay. If he does, it will be a rare change for a man who has travelled more than any other Roman ruler in history.

Hadrian has spent 12 of the 21 years he has reigned away from Rome, inspecting his empire and his army, marking his route with temples, basilicas and other Roman monuments. Twelve years ago he began his travels by visiting Gaul, Germany, Britain and Spain, following this up with travels to Asia Minor, the Aegean Islands, the Balkans and Greece, returning to Rome via Sicily.

Four years ago Hadrian set off once more – this time to Africa, the Orient, Syria and Egypt. The emperor had taken advantage of an unprecedented period of peace and prosperity in Rome to inspect the vast empire.

Chinese combine to beat nomads

Mongolia, c.123
The Xiongnu, the feared warrior nomads of Mongolia, have suffered a series of defeats at the hands of a dangerous neighbouring people, the Xianbei. Their downfall has been partly brought about by their warlike nature, for centuries of fighting have weakened them and left them open to attack.

They also divided their forces, enabling the Han armies to drive the northern tribes to the west and defeat them one by one. The southern Xiongnu then formed themselves into a confederation, but they were faced with a new alliance between the Han and the Xianbei, and even the fierce horsemen of Mongolia could not withstand such enemies.

Historian offends emperor's wife

Later artist's view of Suetonius.

Rome, 122
The emperor has abruptly dismissed his *magister epistolarum* (private secretary), the distinguished historian Suetonius. It seems that while Hadrian was absent from Rome, visiting Britain, Suetonius failed to observe court etiquette towards the emperor's wife, Julia. Suetonius, author of the *Lives of Famous Men*, says he will continue with his massive *Lives of the Caesars*, but he will have to do without access to official archives.

Wall built in Britain to separate warring Celtic tribes

Britain, 130
Nine years after the Emperor Hadrian's tour of inspection of the northernmost part of his empire, his army engineers have completed a defensive line stretching 73 miles across Britain from the Tyne to the Solway Firth.

This monumental wall – eight feet in width, with lookout points at half-mile intervals, and 16 forts built into it – was surveyed by the emperor and is designed to separate two tribal groups, the Brigantes of northern England and the Selgovae and Novantae of the central Lowlands. Roman legions based at Chester and York are backed up by auxiliary forces stationed on the wall itself.

Remains of Hadrian's Wall, marking the northern frontier of the Empire.

Speech tells of Rome's greatness

Rome, 21 April 143
Even the proudest Roman citizen walked taller today after a distinguished orator poured paean after paean of praise on the city, its emperor and people. The speech was more flattering in that it came from a Greek-born philosopher, Aelius Aristides, whose work, along with that of Dio of Prusa and Herodes Atticus, represents a renaissance in Greek letters.

Aristides, who named his speech "In praise of Rome", said that the government of Rome combined all the good qualities of kingship, aristocracy and democracy without their bad aspects. "For you alone are natural rulers," he went on. "Since you were free from the beginning and, as it were, were born directly to be rulers, you have well prepared all that pertains to this and have discovered a form of government which no one had before, and have imposed unvarying law and order on all men."

Aristides then turned to his native Greece and the benefits of being a Greek in a Roman colony: "Now all the Greek cities flourish under you, and the offerings in them, the arts, and all their adornments bring honour to you... You care for the Greeks as though they were your foster fathers."

He continued with the stirring declaration: "Those outside your empire should be pitied since they are deprived of such advantages."

Aelius Aristides, by a later artist.

Jewish expulsion creates the "diaspora"

The sack of Jerusalem in 70: a scene from the arch of Titus, Rome.

Roman Empire, 135
Simon Bar-Kochba, "Son of a Star", the latest Jewish rebel leader to pit his strength against Rome, has been defeated and killed, and his people have been expelled from their land by order of the Emperor Hadrian. Greek peasants have been moved into Palestine and the Jews dispersed across the empire. They call this scattered community of displaced persons the *diaspora*, from the Greek word for dispersal.

Bar-Kochba's revolt, which grew into a war, was the climax of years of guerrilla uprisings. These have continued for 18 years since Trajan suppressed a previous uprising, but it was Hadrian's attempt in 132 to replace Jerusalem by a pagan city – Aelia Capitolina – and his banning of circumcision that ignited Bar-Kochba's forces.

This exceptionally bloody war has lasted for three years, but now Julius Severus, a former governor of Britain, has crushed the rebels and given the Jews another martyr.

Waning of Greek influence on Persian art

Persia, c.140
Great changes have taken place in Persian art as the Greek styles inherited from the successors of Alexander the Great have mingled with more recent influences. When Alexander died, nearly 500 years ago, his vast empire was split up, chiefly among a few Macedonian generals. The bulk of the empire was ruled by Seleucus, and he and his descendants, the Seleucids, built or rebuilt great cities from Asia Minor to the Hindu Kush, where Greek culture flourished.

When the nomadic Parthians occupied much of the Seleucid kingdom 300 or so years ago a more Oriental "Graeco-Persian" style evolved. In recent decades this style has led to an original "Parthian" art, characterised by an almost sty-

Parthian gold on silver dish.

lised manner that contrasts with Greek expressiveness. In architecture the Parthians have developed the *iwan*, a vaulted hall with one of its four sides open, inspired by the nomadic tent.

New trade routes open up to the east

Wold map (Egypt on right), c.40.

Egypt, 137

Hopes that Egypt will soon begin to enjoy the same economic prosperity as its eastern neighbours have been boosted by the opening of a new road linking the Nile to the Red Sea. In recent times Egypt has been falling behind in world trade.

The new road, commissioned by the Emperor Hadrian, links the city of Antinoopolis with the Red Sea port of Berenice. It is expected to relieve traffic on the more northerly Coptos-Berenice trade route and to give Alexandria a more direct link with the Indian Ocean.

The new road threatens to end the Bedouin transport monopoly on Egypt's imports. Alexandrian merchants have long blamed Bedouin caravan freight charges for the high prices of such imported luxuries as spices, perfumes and slaves.

With direct access to a sea route to the Far East, Egyptian traders can now avoid the increasingly unsafe overland trade routes to China, especially northern Syria which imposes high taxes on Chinese silk passing through its territory.

Hadrian indulges his rage for building

The Castel St Angelo in Rome: originally the mausoleum that Hadrian had built for himself overlooking the river Tiber.

Ruins of Hadrian's villa: he could be monumental in private, too.

Gentle aristocrat took reins of power while Emperor Hadrian went slowly mad

Antoninus Pius: gentle emperor.

Temple of Antoninus in the Forum.

Rome, c.142

During the long illness that finally led to his death Hadrian adopted Antoninus as his successor and, as the emperor's madness increased, it was this gentle aristocrat who assumed control.

The contrast between the two is remarkable. Hadrian's reign began and ended with bloodshed; Antoninus is concerned with good administration and organising the coming 900th anniversary of Rome's foundation. Hadrian travelled extensively; Antoninus prefers the life of a country gentleman and is unlikely ever to leave Italy. Antoninus' relationship with the Senate is so good that it has conferred the title of *Pius* (devout) on him.

Wall joins Firth of Forth to River Clyde

Britain, 143

No more than five years after the accession of the Emperor Antoninus, civilisation has advanced 80 miles north of Hadrian's Wall with a new barrier from the Firth of Forth in the east to the River Clyde in the west, enclosing the lowlands of Caledonia.

This Antonine Wall, as it has become known, is 37 miles long, and was built of turf on a stone base in just one year. The legions which built it marked their sections on inscriptions measured to the last half pace.

In Rome itself a new coin is being designed, showing Britannia and Victory, and dated 143-4. It should help the Romans to expunge memories of their earlier defeats at the hands of the tribes in this northern outpost of the empire.

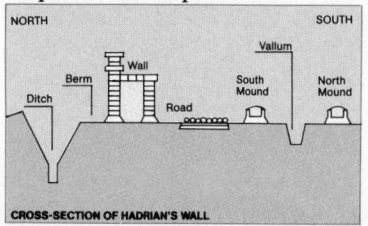

CROSS-SECTION OF HADRIAN'S WALL

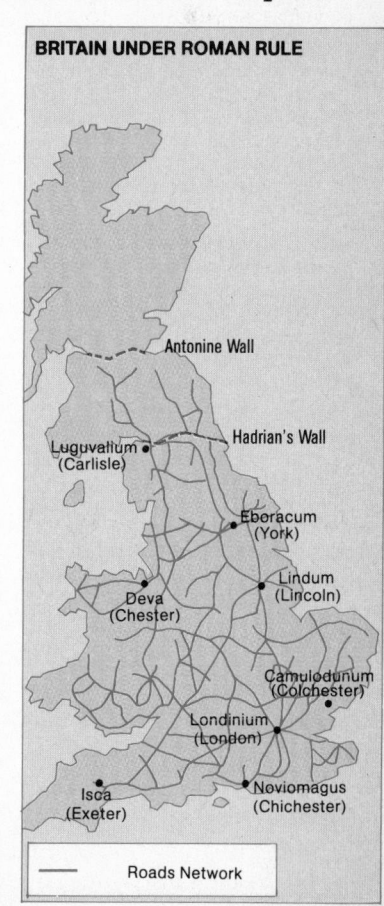

BRITAIN UNDER ROMAN RULE

Antonine Wall

Hadrian's Wall

Luguvalium (Carlisle)

Eboracum (York)

Lindum (Lincoln)

Deva (Chester)

Camulodunum (Colchester)

Londinium (London)

Isca (Exeter)

Noviomagus (Chichester)

— Roads Network

Britain, 143. Quintus Lollius Urbicus, the governor of Britain, has suppressed the revolt of the Brigantes which began last year. Lollius is also responsible for the construction of the turf wall which has been built across the country north of Hadrian's Wall.

Rome, 145. Marcus Aurelius marries his cousin Faustina the Younger, daughter of Antoninus.

Rome, 146. On the birth of his daughter, Marcus Aurelius receives the powers of a tribune and a proconsul, making him the most likely successor to Antoninus.

China, 147. The dowager empress, a member of the Liang family, puts the infant Huandi onto the throne of China. The Liangs have reached the summit of power under the leadership of the marshal Liang Chi, brother of the empress.

Rome, 147. Marcus Aurelius has developed an enthusiasm for Stoic philosophy. This displaces his earlier interest in rhetoric, which he studied under Marcus Cornelius Fronto, the foremost Roman orator of his day.

Rome, 21 April 147. Antoninus celebrates the 900th anniversary of Rome's foundation.

Mesopotamia, 148. By capturing the kingdom of Parthia, where Greek influence is in decline, the Arsacid king Vologaeses III puts an end to the succession struggle sparked off by the death last year of Vologaeses II.

China, 148. The Parthian monk An Shigao arrives in the capital Loyang and initiates the first project for a systematic translation of Buddhist texts into Chinese from originals either in Sanskrit, or more probably, central Asian Prakrits.

Asia Minor, 154. King Eupator of the Bosporus pays tribute to the Roman empire. Under threat from the Alans in the Caucasus, the kingdom of the Bosporus and the Greek cities on the Black Sea have turned to Rome for protection.

Palestine, 155. To appease unrest among the Jews, Antoninus re-authorises circumcision. Rome has acknowledged that, without being recognised as a legal religion, Judaism must be tolerated. The surviving leaders of the Jewish communities meet at Usha, a small village in Galilee, and decide to restore the court known as the Sanhedrin, along with the Patriarchy, which will be headed by Simeon ben Gamaliel.

Armenia, 155. Antoninus thwarts an attempt to conquer the country by Vologaeses III, the Arsacid king of Parthia. The struggle ends with an inconclusive peace.

Rome, 160. The lawyer Appian writes his *Roman History*, which includes the history of each nation conquered by Rome until the time of its conquest. Appian, Alexandrian by birth, is living in Rome and superintending the emperor's domestic affairs.

Germany, 160. The *limes* (fortified boundary) of the Rhine is extended beyond the valley of the Neckar.

Rome, 160. The writer Suetonius, a former secretary of Hadrian, is dead. He will be best remembered for his biographies of Roman emperors and literary men.

Rome, 161. The famous jurist Gaius composes a monumental record of law in the Roman empire entitled *Institutes*.

Italy, 7 March 161. On the death of Antoninus at Lorium, Marcus Aurelius becomes emperor.

Rome, 161. Marcus Aurelius invests his adoptive brother Lucius Verus with the powers of a tribune and makes him co-emperor. For the first time the imperial powers are fully shared.

Armenia, 162. Taking advantage of the death of Antoninus, Vologaeses III, king of the Parthians, instals his relative Pacorus on the throne of Armenia, and at Elegeia crushes the Roman army sent to dethrone him. He then launches a raid into Syria.

Athens, 162. In honour of his wife Regilla, who died in 160, the Greek orator Herodes Atticus builds an *odeon* (theatre), which, despite its enormous scale, is covered by a roof.

Syria, 162. Co-Emperor Verus disembarks in Syria at the head of an army sent to confront the Parthians.

Armenia, 163. Statius Priscus, the governor of Cappadocia, expels the Parthians from Armenia and instals Arsacidus Sohaemus, a Roman protege, on the throne. After destroying the Armenian capital, Artaxata, he founds a new one at Valarshapat.

Mesopotamia, 164. The governor of Syria, Avidius Cassius, one of Verus' generals, crosses the Euphrates, invading Parthian territory.

Asia Minor, 164. At Ephesus, Marcus Aurelius marries his daughter Lucilla to Lucius Verus, his colleague as emperor.

Rome, 165. The Christian apologist Justin is martyred. Born in Samaria, Justin was successively a Stoic and a Platonist. After his conversion to Christianity he became a travelling preacher. He wrote two Christian *apologias* addressed to the emperor.

Earthquake hits cities in Asia Minor

Asia Minor, 151

A major earthquake has recently destroyed a great temple in Cyzicus and caused serious damage to property in Bithynia, the Hellespont and other parts of Asia Minor. The disaster posed a great challenge to the administration of the Roman empire, but the hardship, though severe, would have been much worse but for the generosity of the Emperor Antoninus.

The rebuilding now under way provides a typical example of the Roman tradition of benefaction, from the emperor downwards. The maintenance of the role of emperor required that he be seen as a fount of generosity. This tradition was respected by emperors from Augustus to Hadrian, and continued by Antoninus. Records of imperial gifts were always kept.

Imperial largesse was reinforced by a system of *liturgies*, municipal offices whose holders were obliged from time to time to finance games and races, the distribution of money and wheat, or building. The great cities of Ephesus and Pergamum, with their market places, temples, city gates, baths and theatres, were built in this way.

Taxation was unpopular, and irregularly applied throughout the Roman empire. In times of peace it might provide enough, but economic depression, war or natural disasters would put a heavy burden on certain privileged individuals.

Eastern gods honoured in Roman empire

Lugdunum (Lyons), 160

Exotic Oriental religions, which have taken hold in Rome after being favoured by recent emperors, are spreading through western Europe. The worship of the Great Mother Cybele, from Asia Minor, involves the *taurobolium*, or baptism in bull's blood. A man jumps into a ditch, cuts the bull's throat and splashes the blood over himself. Another popular cult is that of the Egyptian Isis, goddess of fertility and protectress of commerce. These cults offer purification from sin and a universality lacking in the old Latin gods.

Shroud, with the bird-god Horus.

A 20th-century view from the Parthenon on the Acropolis at Athens of the theatre of Herodes Atticus, completed in 162.

Two emperors reign at the same time

Rome, 161
For the first time in Rome's 900-year history, two emperors share the throne. Immediately upon his accession, Marcus Aurelius surprised the Senate by petitioning it to accept his adopted brother, Verus, as co-emperor. Marcus is keeping to a promise made to his predecessor, Antoninus. Verus will hold the title of Augustus and every imperial title except that of *pontifex maximus* (high priest).

Both men come from wealthy, aristocratic backgrounds and are related to former rulers – but there the resemblance ends. It is hard to imagine two more differing characters.

Marcus is a brilliant philosopher – he impressed Hadrian at the age of eight with his serious approach to life – a quietly spoken, sickly young man with high moral values. He was the natural successor to the equally serious Antoninus.

Verus, on the other hand, is robust, cheerful and irresponsible; his interests seem confined to women, good wine and circuses.

Ptolemy's world: Britain is top left, the Indian Ocean at the bottom.

Ptolemy presents new view of the world

Alexandria, Egypt, 151
People will have to rethink their ideas about the known world, thanks to the work of Claudius Ptolemaeus, or Ptolemy, an astronomer and geographer living in Alexandria. Ptolemy has just published a work on map-making called *Geographia*, or "Geography". In it he improves on the accuracy of previous maps, using a grid system of latitude and longitude which should prove useful to navigators as well as cartographers. The world, according to Ptolemy, stretches from Iceland and the Canary Islands in the west to Ceylon in the east, with unknown lands south of North Africa and beyond India. Ptolemy is also renowned for his studies of astronomy, which further refine Greek ideas about the stars and planets moving in concentric orbits around the earth.

Africa produces superb sculpture

Nigeria, c.150
On the Bauchi and Jos Plateaux in Nigeria a 700-year-old Iron Age culture is reaching its highest level, its influence spreading throughout the region.

The Nok, descendants of the early black people who emigrated southwards during the desiccation of the Sahara, were the first to use iron in West Africa. The agricultural revolution brought about by their iron instruments has so enriched Nok culture that its people are producing the most exquisite terracotta sculpture yet seen in black Africa.

Nigerian terracotta Nok head.

Egypt crippled by heavy Roman taxes

Alexandria, 160
After 190 years of occupation, Rome's crippling tax demands are destroying the Egyptian economy. Initial judgements on the occupation were favourable. Administration was more efficient, canals were cleared and fields irrigated. Roman rule was indirect, Egyptian culture was respected, the priesthood protected, and the Greek and Jewish minorities used as administrators.

But Rome's demand for cheap corn is crippling the economy, agricultural taxes are depopulating the countryside, and Rome's policy of playing Jew against Greek is causing regular pogroms between the communities.

Emperor Marcus Aurelius revolutionises the Italian civil service

Rome, 163
Marcus Aurelius, the philosopher-emperor, has introduced sweeping changes in the admininstration of Rome and Italy. Like his predecessor, Antoninus, Marcus enjoys an excellent relationship with the Senate, and it is through it that he has instituted a system of *juridici* – a civil service that will act as an arm of government throughout Italy.

He has restored the consuls, the officers who control the bureaucracy, extended the judicial powers of the court of appeal, and increased the powers of the prefect of Rome. This conservative aristocrat has also taken the unusual step of introducing African and Oriental officers – even those from humble backgrounds – into the Senate and giving them responsible positions in government.

Marcus' peaceful reign is marred by war in the east, where the Parthians have destroyed two Roman armies. An expeditionary force has been despatched.

A bronze statue of the Emperor Marcus Aurelius in Rome, c.165.

China, 165. The Confucian philosopher Wangfu, who has recently died, will be remembered for his criticisms of the luxury of consumer goods and the exodus from the land.

Mesopotamia, 165. Avidius Cassius takes Nisibis and conquers the north of the country. The Romans establish a garrison at Doura-Europos on the Euphrates, a control point for the commercial route to the Persian Gulf.

Britain, 165. Following new incursions by the Brigantes, the Romans abandon the Antonine Wall, built in 143, and retreat to Hadrian's Wall.

China, 166. An embassy of Syrian merchants who claim to have been sent by Marcus Aurelius in 162 arrives in China.

Mesopotamia, 166. After Avidius Cassius' victories, including the partial destruction of Ctesiphon, the Emperor Verus enters the Parthian capital and makes peace with Vologaeses III.

Italy, 166. German tribes pour across the upper and lower Danube and invade northern Italy.

Asia Minor, 13 February 167. Polycarp, bishop of Smyrna, on the west coast of Asia Minor, since 110, is martyred by being burnt alive. A disciple of St John, Polycarp corresponded with the earlier martyr Ignatius of Antioch and was the dominant figure of eastern Christianity in recent times. He became involved in a controversy with Rome about the timing of Easter celebrations.

Rome, 167. Brought back from the east by Verus' army, the plague ravages Rome. Marcus Aurelius resorts to the most ancient rites to ward it off: *vota publica*, public vows to the gods, and *lectisternia*, by which gods are symbolically entertained as guests at a meal, couches being specially prepared for them.

Central Europe, 167. The German invaders in Pannonia are halted by Claudius Pompeianus, the governor of lower Pannonia.

China, 168. The Emperor Huandi dies at the age of 36. Having eliminated the Liang clan, he put an end to the dominance of dowager empresses and relied increasingly upon the power of the palace eunuchs.

China, 168. An attempt by Dou Wu, the empress dowager's father, to kill the leaders of the palace eunuchs fails, and the eunuchs reassert their power. As the Han dynasty declines, the struggles between the eunuchs and the mandarins who staff the bureaucracy are becoming more intense.

Italy, 168. At Aquileia, the Emperors Marcus Aurelius and Lucius Verus reach peace terms with the German invaders who entered northern Italy in 166, and the region is freed from foreign interference.

Rome, 169. Lucius Verus dies of apoplexy on his return to Rome.

Rome, 169. Marcus Aurelius marries his unwilling daughter Lucilla, the widow of Verus, to his friend Claudius Pompeianus, the governor of lower Pannonia.

Asia Minor, 170. The Christian Montanus begins to prophesy in Phrygia. Preaching asceticism and martyrdom, Montanus predicts the return of Christ. He fiercely criticises the hierarchies of the Roman state and of the Christian church, which is accused of being in league with them. "Montanism" is the first Christian heresy.

Rome, 170. Marcus Aurelius has an equestrian statue of himself erected on the Capitol.

Balkans, 172. Marcus Aurelius imposes peace on the Quadi and the Marcomanni. A strip almost five miles wide to the north of the Danube is forbidden to them.

Greece, 173. Pausanias, a Greek geographer and historian who was born in Lydia, finishes writing his *Itinerary* of Greece.

Egypt, 173. Invested with the control of the whole of the eastern empire since 166, Avidius Cassius, the governor of Syria, crushes the insurrections of the shepherd brigands known as the *boukoloi*.

Balkans, 175. Marcus Aurelius imposes a peace on the Sarmatian Iazyges in the Danubian region.

Syria, 175. At the false rumour of Marcus Aurelius' death, Avidius Cassius, the governor of Syria, has himself proclaimed emperor. However, three months after his accession, abandoned by his supporters, he is killed by a soldier.

Rome, 176. Marcus Aurelius puts his son Commodus on the throne, giving him the title of Augustus.

Rome, 177. The powers of a tribune are conferred upon Commodus, son of Marcus Aurelius.

Balkans, 177. The Quadi and the Marcomanni have again declared war on the Roman empire.

Gaul, 178. Irenaeus, a disciple of Polycarp, replaces the martyred Pothinus as bishop of Lugdunum (Lyons).

Greece, 180. The philosopher Celsus has written the first comprehensive and reasoned critique of Christianity, which he calls the *True Word*.

Parthian city burned in reprisal raid

Ctesiphon, Mesopotamia, 166

The burning of Ctesiphon and Seleucia marks the end of Marcus Aurelius' punitive expedition against the Parthians. Rome is once more protector of Armenia; part of Mesopotamia is annexed; and garrisons are established at Osroene.

Trouble began in 162 when the Parthian king, Vologaeses III, declared war, and his general Osroes invaded Armenia. The governor of Cappadocia was defeated and killed at Elegeia.

By the spring of 163 the imperial forces were ready, under the nominal leadership of Marcus Aurelius' brother Verus, but effectively organised by Marcus from Rome, and commanded by Avidius Cassius and other generals.

The Parthians were gradually forced out of Armenia and Mesopotamia. The Roman advance was

Co-Emperor Verus: victorious.

only halted in 165 by a plague emanating from Seleucia, which Cassius' troops carried back to Rome and passed through other legions to armies as far away as the Rhine.

Eunuchs battle with empress in China

China, 168

The empress dowager's fury at the behaviour of the eunuchs has led to a bloody revolution at court.

The Emperor Huandi died in January, leaving no named heir. The Empress Dou was declared dowager, which gave her a major say in the choice of successor. Lingdi, a 12-year-old boy of noble birth, was selected, and 1000 eunuchs were sent to Jieduting to bring him to the capital, Loyang.

The journey took two and a half weeks, and during this period the empress dowager tried to put her late husband's nine concubines to death. Only one was killed before two eunuchs intervened. Dou also ennobled her father, Dou Wu.

When the new emperor arrived at Loyang, a bitter power struggle ensued. Dou Wu resolved to kill the eunuchs; they were equally anxious to kill him and his family. After much bloodshed, Lingdi, supported by the eunuchs, emerged the victor. The empress is now in prison and Dou Wu has taken his own life.

Bronze model of a Han horse carriage with driver (c.150).

Christians die in arena

A 20th-century impression of Christians thrown by wild beasts.

Lyons (France), August 177

Feeling against the Christians has reached fever pitch here. Popular passions have been whipped up by rumours that Christians indulge in cannibalistic orgies and incest. There have been many instances of mobs stoning and raping Christians.

The Roman administration has finally bowed to this popular feeling. More than 20 Christians were arrested. Those who claimed Roman citizenship were tortured and beheaded in jail. The others were led into the amphitheatre and thrown to wild beasts in front of a howling crowd. One young woman, Blandina, was hung on a stake, but curiously the wild beasts would not touch her. Nothing has been heard of her since.

Local people say that some of the other prisoners have been strangled in their cells and others thrown to wild dogs.

Victory paves way for new province

Pannonia (Hungary), 179

Tarrutenius Paternus, prefect of the Praetorian Guard, has won a decisive victory over the Germanic Marcomanni at Vindobona on the Danube. It looks as if the Emperor Marcus Aurelius is within sight of fulfilling his ten-year-old plan to annex Bohemia and the Carpathians and create the provinces of Marcomannia and Sarmatia.

The Marcomanni, with their Germanic neighbours the Quadi and the Sarmatians, are being invaded from the east by European tribes of Goths, Burgundians and Vandals. They are fleeing west into Roman territory. In 169 the Marcomanni and the Quadi got as far as the plains of north Italy, causing panic in Rome.

Marcus Aurelius sold his valuable plate to help to equip an army

Marcus Aurelius: for secure peace.

to fight them, and he imposed a temporary peace five years ago. But he realised that a permanent solution depended on having strong Roman provinces on the frontier.

City of 100,000 dominates Mexico

Mexico, c.180

The great conurbation of Teotihuacan, the "City of the Gods" nestled in the folds of the Mexican plateau, is spreading over the entire valley of Teotihuacan. It is now recognised as the largest city in the Americas.

Set in the middle of the neck of Mexico, on the crossroads between North and South America, it has become the cultural and commercial capital of Central America. Yet little is known of the ancestors of the Teotihuacanians; their cultural, racial and linguistic origins are a mystery.

Wherever its founders came from, the city took shape over 200 years ago, following a massive population explosion, when the two-mile-long grand avenue that marks the city centre was built, lined with palaces, pyramids and temples. Since then the city has spread over 11 square miles, the grand avenue has been ennobled by even grander pyramids – all adorned with the sacred symbol of Teotihuacan, the plumed serpent – and the city's population is believed to have passed the 100,000 mark.

Now its colonies stretch as far as Kaminaljuyu in Guatemala (previously a Maya city-state), and its exports are to be found all over Central America. These exports are not merely agricultural and manufactured; Teotihuacan exports ideas, and the cult of the plumed serpent has spread all over Central America.

The Pyramid of the Sun at Teotihuacan, from the Pyramid of the Moon.

New version of the Confucian classics

China, 175

Cai Yong, a famous calligrapher, has been granted permission by the emperor to produce a standard version of the six classics of Confucianism. Cai Yong's aim is to remove the errors which have crept into the classics. He has gathered together a team of scholars and engravers, and work is to start immediately on the formidable task of collating the many versions of the classics.

"Ass" story means gold for the writer

Rome, c.175

Apuleius, an author born in the province of Africa about 50 years ago, is having great success with his picaresque novel *The Golden Ass*. It tells the tale of Lucius, who is accidentally turned into an ass. He goes through a series of adventures in which sex, magic, comedy and filth are mixed with great elegance. The story ends when Lucius vows to serve the goddess Isis and becomes human again.

Asia Minor, c.180. The Greek historian Arrian, who was born in Nicomedia in Bithynia, is dead. Arrian served as governor of Cappadocia under Hadrian and defeated the great invasion of the Alans from the Caucasus in 134. He was a pupil of the Stoic philosopher Epictetus, whose valuable *Discourses* he was responsible for preserving. His most important work is a history of the campaigns of Alexander the Great, called *Anabasis*.

Balkans, 17 March 180. At the death of his father, Marcus Aurelius, from the plague, Commodus is fighting the Marcomanni on the upper Danube. Commodus, who is now sole emperor, abandons plans for conquest, makes peace with the Marcomanni and hastens to Rome.

Black Sea, c.180. A Germanic people known as the Goths, who originated in southern Scandinavia, have migrated from the Baltic and are settling on the shores of the Black Sea. They are divided into Goths from the west (Visigoths) and Goths from the east (Ostrogoths), on either side of the Dniestr.

Rome, 180. Work begins on the erection in the Campus Martius of a column commemorating the wars conducted by Marcus Aurelius on the Danubian front.

Rome, 182. Lucilla, daughter of Marcus Aurelius, is exiled to the island of Capri after taking part in an unsuccessful conspiracy against her brother, the Emperor Commodus. Commodus' habit of governing by favourites has aroused Senate opposition.

Rome, 182. The Praetorian prefect Perennis – undoubtedly responsible for the fall of his colleague Tarrutenius Paternus, who served as prefect under Marcus Aurelius – becomes effective master of the Roman empire.

Rome, 185. The Praetorian prefect Perennis, victim of the hostility of the army in Britain and of the intrigues of the chamberlain Cleander, falls into disgrace. Cleander becomes the new favourite of Commodus.

Germany, 187. Clodius Albinus conquers the highly organised Germanic tribe known as the Chatti, which had been threatening the Agri Decumates region (*which includes the Black Forest*). The Rhine-Danube fortified boundary established by Domitian is abandoned for that of Antoninus.

India, 189. Demetrius, bishop of Alexandria, has sent the missionary Pantaenus to India, but his preaching is meeting with little success.

China, 189. Summoned by a faction at court, General Dong Zhuo puts an end to the rule of the eunuchs by massacring them and proceeds to take power.

Egypt, 190. The country is suffering worsening poverty as a result of the doubling of prices in the past decade. The proportion of silver in the denarius is lowered from 90 to 70 per cent.

China, 190. After the death of Lingti last year, Xiandi (Hienti) comes to the throne.

South Africa, c.190. The culture associated with the early users of iron in the continent has spread as far into the interior as the Limpopo valley – to Mabveni (*in southern Zimbabwe*) and Makodu (*in eastern Botswana*). The pottery produced here, which is distinct from the east coast tradition, derives from the region of the East African great lakes (*Zambia, western Tanzania and Uganda*).

Rome, 191. Considering himself the new founder of Rome, Commodus rebaptises the city in his own name, calling it *Colonia Lucia Aurelia Nova Commodiana*. He does likewise with the fleet, the wheat, the legions and all the months of the year.

China, 192. After allowing his soldiers to burn down the capital, Loyang, General Dong Zhuo is assassinated, and China descends into anarchy.

Rome, 31 December 192. His mind unhinged by power, Commodus, who sees himself as the incarnation of Hercules, has expressed a desire to sacrifice the new consuls on 1 January 193. Frightened by this mania for blood, his concubine Marcia and the Praetorian prefect Aemilius Laetus arrange for an athlete called Narcissus to strangle him in his bath. His death brings to an end the Antonine dynasty.

Rome, 1 January 193. Publius Helvius Pertinax is proclaimed emperor by the Praetorian Guard under its prefect Laetus.

Rome, 28 March 193. The Praetorian Guard, which now regrets the removal of Commodus, assassinates Pertinax after only three months in office. This is followed by the proclamation of Marcus Didius Julianus – a man unpopular with both the Roman masses and the provincial armies – as emperor.

Balkans, 9 April 193. The distinguished soldier Septimius Severus is proclaimed emperor by the army in Illyricum.

Syria, April 193. Pescennius Niger, who become governor of Syria two years ago, is proclaimed emperor by the army in the east.

Horses and carriages, a stone relief from a Han dynasty tomb (c.150).

Revolt of "Yellow Turbans" rocks China

China, 184

A peasant revolt led by Zhang Jue, an itinerant magician, is threatening the imperial government. Zhang Jue has an army of 300,000 fervent adherents known as the "Yellow Turbans" because of their distinctive head-dress.

He gained power over them by curing them of an epidemic which swept the central provinces, and now they believe that his spells have made them immortal.

These Yellow Turbans are fearless in battle and are making progress against the government forces. They are opposed not so much to the emperor as to the eunuchs and the officials who have imposed a tyrannical and rapacious administration on the countryside.

The revolt erupted when Zhang Jue sent a delegation of Yellow Turbans to the court and they were murdered by the eunuchs whose power has undermined the Han dynasty. Now the Yellow Turbans fight under the Daoist text "a new kingdom of harmony, justice and peace".

Equestrian Order attracts elite of Rome

Roman Empire, 192

The key role played by the *equites*, or knights, in the administration of the empire has been highlighted by their adoption of formal titles in the manner of their superiors, the senators, who are known as the Illustrious. Knights are now known as Outstanding, Most Perfect, or, highest of all, Most Eminent.

The Equestrian Order lost much of its financial importance when the old tax-farming privileges were curbed. But the emperors, in need of a reliable class of public servants to administer the vast territories of the empire, have used their control over admission to the Order to put the knights to work.

The Minister of Finance is a knight, as is the Minister of Food, who is responsible for Rome's corn supplies from distant provinces. The *cursus publicus*, the empire's communications network, formerly funded by local taxes, has been

A knight, from Pompeii.

made a charge on the state and placed under a knight. Shrewd emperors have drawn into the Equestrian Order many able Greeks, Jews and other non-Romans.

Emperor joins gladiators in the arena

Commodus as his hero, Hercules.

Commodiana, 189
Rome's addiction to the games is reaching new and absurd heights under the eccentric Emperor Commodus. The son of Marcus Aurelius believes that he is the god Hercules and has renamed Rome "Commodiana" after himself. He prefers killing captive men and animals, in his favourite role as gladiator, to running the empire.

Instead of politics there are games lasting 14 days in which men are chained together and obliged to kill one another. By way of change there are deadly chariot races led by the drunken ruler. Senators and nobles must attend, for no-one is safe. Indeed, most citizens must now pay "voluntary" sums to Commodus to avoid assassination.

Emperor throws chief adviser to mob

Rome, 189
Cleander, the former slave who rose to be the emperor's chancellor, has been decapitated by a lynch mob while Commodus looked the other way. Cleander was blamed for wheat shortages, while Commodus actually increased his popularity with the street gangs by his insatiable lust for blood and circus antics. It is said that one day recently he killed five hippopotami with his bare hands.

The advice of a Christian concubine and the dark rituals of Mithras are of more political moment to the emperor, while he acts out his Her-

cules fantasies, than the experienced counsel of General Ulpius Marcellus. Five years ago Marcellus suppressed a rebellion in Scotland after the Antonine Wall was overrun. It was the only military victory of this reign. Commodus then rewarded Marcellus with a capricious death sentence and a sudden reprieve.

Routine government is handled by the new chamberlain, Eclectus, and a Praetorian prefect named Laetus. With the examples of Cleander and Marcellus before them, it makes daily routine a matter of life or death.

Lucian, wandering satirist, is dead

Egypt, c.180
The death of Lucian the poet has deprived Greek literature of an amusing satirist who developed a new literary form, the humorous dialogue, which made him famous. He wrote dialogues of the dead, and of the gods and nymphs, and some between a young prostitute and her ambitious mother which are considered somewhat shocking.

Lucian made his living as a travelling reciter. He mocked belief in the gods of Olympus and in Hades as "vain Infernal trumpery". He wrote nearly 60 works.

A sculpted slab at the eastern end of the Antonine Wall, built by the Romans across the southern part of Caledonia, c.143.

Imperial estates give Africa a new face, but tenants resist power of the bailiffs

Ruins of the amphitheatre at olive oil-rich Thysdrus in Africa.

Africa, c.180
The long arm of the empire is changing the face of the province of Africa. The town of Thysdrus, near the Mediterranean coast, is a centre of the olive oil trade and has grown large enough to build an amphitheatre to hold 50,000 people, the largest in Africa.

The huge imperial estates are farmed under procurators, who parcel out the estates to bailiffs, who divide them among tenants. Under the law of Hadrian those who plant crops, such as olive orchards or vineyards, retain their harvests completely for the first five years, after which they must

give a third of it to the bailiff. The bailiffs cultivate part of the land and tenants must give up six days' labour per year to help them.

A group of peasants in the district of Carthage petitioned the Emperor Commodus because their landlord, supported by the procurator, "ordered some of us to be seized, tortured, fettered and beaten with rods and cudgels" because they had refused to work for longer periods or give up more of their crops. "We are poor peasants sustaining life by the work of our hands and no match for the bailiff," they wrote. The emperor decreed in their favour.

A healthy-looking peasant ploughing a field, on a Roman mosaic.

Rome, 1 June 193. The Emperor Marcus Didius Julianus is murdered in his palace.

Rome, June 193. After his uncontested entry into Rome, Septimius Severus dismisses the Praetorian Guard and replaces it with a new guard.

Britain, 193. Clodius Albinus, governor of Britain, is given the title Caesar.

Syria, 194. After several defeats by the army of Septimius Severus, Pescennius Niger, declared emperor by his troops last year, is overtaken and executed while fleeing towards the Euphrates. Syria is then divided into two provinces.

China, 195. The warrior nomads known as the Xiongnu are settled as confederates in the north of China, where they present a continuing threat.

Gaul, 196. In an attempt to secure the support of the German legions for a march on Rome, Clodius Albinus, the governor of Britain, who has been declared Augustus by his army, crosses to Gaul.

China, 196. The fugitive boy emperor is held captive by the warlord Cao Cao. The emperor is now a mere pawn in the hands of contending warlords.

Gaul, 19 February 197. With the conquest of his last rival, Clodius Albinus, in a battle at Lugdunum (Lyons), Septimius Severus reunites the Roman empire.

Britain, 197. After the defeat of Clodius Albinus, Britain, like Syria, is divided into two provinces.

Mesopotamia, 197. As retribution for their support of Pescennius Niger, Septimius Severus vanquishes the Parthians at Seleucia and Ctesiphon and wrests control of Mesopotamia from them.

Mesopotamia, 199. Mesopotamia becomes a Roman province.

Asia Minor, 200. A woman by the name of Aemilia Aureliana erects a carving at the temple of Tralles commemorating her act of sexual service (sacred intercourse) to the Great Goddess, like her mother and grandmother before her.

Madagascar, c.200. Over the past century, the first human settlements have been established on the island of Madagascar in the Indian Ocean. The immigrants are mostly Malayo-Polynesian sailors, from south Borneo in Indonesia. Trade across the Indian Ocean to East Africa and offshore islands has brought bananas, coconuts, yams and the playing of xylophones to Madagascar.

West Africa, c.200. The region known as Ghana in the Sahel savannah region (*where Mauritania and Mali overlap*) is gaining in wealth and power. Local Mandingo people have been influenced by incoming Berber traders from the north since c.600BC.

Rome, 202. An edict is issued against Christianity in the Roman empire. All Christian or Jewish proselytising is forbidden, opening the way for local persecutions in Africa, Gaul and Egypt.

Gaul, c.202. The Christian father Irenaeus is dead – perhaps martyred in the persecution. Since becoming bishop of Lugdunum (Lyons) in 178, Irenaeus devoted himself to the conversion of the Rhone valley. He will be remembered particularly for his controversy with the Gnostics, set out in his great treatise *Against Heretics*.

Rome, 203. An arch dedicated to Septimius Severus is erected in the Forum.

Rome, 203. The jurist Papinian becomes Praetorian prefect, in succession to Plautianus, who was executed in a plot. Papinian's recently published doctrinal analyses *Quaestiones* and *Responsa* link law and humanism.

Egypt, 203. Origen replaces Clement as head of the Christian school of Alexandria.

Britain, 210. Having suffered heavy losses since invading Scotland in 208, the Romans make peace with the Scots.

Britain, 4 February 211. Septimius Severus dies of natural causes at Eburacum (York) during his British campaign. He is succeeded by his sons Marcus Aurelius Antoninus – nicknamed Caracalla on account of his long-hooded Gaulish tunic – and Septimius Antoninus Geta.

Rome, February 212. Geta is murdered on the orders of his brother Caracalla, who proceeds to unleash bloody repression in Rome. Among the 20,000 victims is the famous jurist Papinian.

Rome, 212. Caracalla grants Roman citizenship to virtually all free inhabitants of the empire.

Palestine, 215. The church father Clement of Alexandria is dead. Born in Athens, Clement studied philosophy and later became head of the Christian school in Alexandria, where he taught for over ten years. He was forced to flee to Palestine in 203 to escape the persecution under Severus. His latest written work, *Miscellanies*, attempts to synthesise Christianity and ancient philosophy.

Popular emperor dies in Britain

York, 4 February 211

Roman legionaries in this northern garrison are mourning the death here of their emperor. Worn out by sickness and exhausted after two years of unsuccessful campaigning against the Caledonians, Septimius Severus – the first African to rule Rome – left a farewell message to his sons from his death-bed: "Live in peace. Enrich my soldiers and despise the rest of the world."

Any emperor who could raise his army's wages from 375 to 500 denarii a month was bound to be popular; none more so than Severus, who began the democratisation of the new guard, turning it into a seminary for officers. He permitted soldiers to marry during their service and they enjoyed special benefits on their discharge.

His rule was regarded as just and humane, although military campaigns throughout the empire involved substantial tax increases in Rome. For Severus, Rome could survive only with a large and powerful army and he was determined to keep it that way.

Septimius Severus' arch in Rome: he knew that a strong army was essential.

Great doctor Galen had humorous notion

Rome, 199

Claudius Galenus, or Galen, the leading physician of modern times, has died at the age of 70. Born at Pergamum, he studied in Alexandria before becoming physician to the gladiators in Pergamum. He went to Rome in his early 30s and won fame as doctor to the Emperor Marcus Aurelius. Galen revered Plato, Aristotle and Hippocrates, but was the first to regard all areas of medicine as part of the same science. He was a great physiologist, proving that the arteries as well as the veins carry blood. His pathology was based on the idea that temperament is a mixture of four humours of the body: blood, phlegm, choler and melancholy.

Later engraving of Galen.

Murderous ruler widens tax base

Roman Empire, 212

The year will be remembered for two things done by the 23-year-old Emperor Caracalla: he has had his brother and co-ruler Geta murdered, and he has granted citizenship to all freemen throughout the empire. He and Geta had just returned from York, where their father Severus had died. Geta was actually in the arms of their mother, Julia Domna, when Caracalla's assassins drove their daggers home. He then got the Senate to make him sole emperor. The citizenship decree has a scarcely less ignoble motive: the new citizens do not get the vote, they simply lose their exemption from taxes.

Caracalla: making his name.

Bandit "Lucky" to be thrown to lions

Italy, 206

The luck of Bulla Felix (Bulla the Lucky) has finally run out. He will be thrown to the lions in a public arena. After terrorising the towns and villages of northern Italy with a bandit force of some 600 men, many of them war veterans, he has been betrayed by a friend's wife, with whom he was having an affair.

While provincial governors and commanders of legions embrace treachery and murder in seeking to gain the imperial purple, the people live in fear. Bulla and his gangs roamed far and wide, plundering at will, "never seen when seen, never caught when caught", as the saying goes.

Soldiers join all-male secret cult

The slaying of a bull by the god Mithras, the centre of a new secretive cult.

Rome, c.200

An increasing number of influential Romans are turning to the worship of Mithras, the Persian god of light, who demands strenuous initiation rites of his devotees before they can join the all-male cult.

With initiates sworn to secrecy no exact figures exist on how widespread the cult has become. It is believed to be especially popular with the military and affluent businessmen. In Ostia, a major trade port, at least 15 underground chapels are dedicated to Mithras. The cult's appeal is based on its promise of help in both this life and in the after-life, plus the emphasis its services place on manly and moral virtues.

Initiates are pledged to secrecy before a seven-stage initiation process that includes periods of fasting and abstinence. Initiates have to survive being bound, stripped, blindfolded and thrown across a water pit before being branded on the hand or forehead.

Tertullian defends the Christian cause

Carthage, 197

A qualified lawyer, the son of a Roman centurion, has produced a daring and unprecedented defence of Christianity in a book published this year. Tertullian, whose hostility to the excesses of paganism made him a convert in 195, has used his *Apologeticus* to show Romans that the new faith is not a mixture of atheism and black magic, as its opponents suggest, but a respectable and moral religion.

Roman attacks are quite unjustified, he stipulates. Christians are admirable citizens, he claims, and their martyrs, for whom he has much respect, are most worthy of honour.

"Life is a dream" – Buddhist radical

India, c.200

A new way towards enlightenment is being proclaimed by the Buddhist philosopher and monk Nagarjuna. From his spiritual base at Dhanyakataka his *Mahayana*, or Middle Way, is spreading all over southern India.

Originally a Brahman, he was converted to Buddhism during the great renewal of the religion in India by Kaniska, the Kushan emperor, half a century ago, and was taught by some of Buddhism's most learned teachers.

He is now the spiritual adviser to the powerful Satavahana king, Gautamiputra Satakarni, and his ideas have become the official doctrine of that vast southern Indian kingdom.

Some of his ideas, contained in his book the *Prajnaparamita Sutra*, or Perfection of Wisdom, such as active compassion for all the creatures on the earth, and the conviction that laymen as well as monks can attain enlightenment, are natural developments from early Buddhism. Other ideas, such as the deification of the Buddha, the belief that the Buddha is himself the incarnation of a greater Buddha, and the theory of emptiness or void (all is delusion, life is a dream), are radical, and are rapidly changing the whole concept of Buddhism.

Ruins of the vast baths of Caracalla by his father in Rome. The building also houses a library and gymnasium.

Mesopotamia, 217. After the assassination of Caracalla, the Praetorian prefect Marcus Opellius Macrinus, who is implicated in the killing, becomes the first emperor from the Equestrian Order.

Syria, 218. Defeated in a battle near Antioch, Macrinus is captured and put to death by supporters of Elagabalus, who claims to be the son of Caracalla and has recently been hailed as emperor.

Palestine, 219. A Hebrew edition of the *Mishna*, a collection of sayings and teachings drawn from the Torah, is published. It was produced under the direction of Rabbi Yehuda ha-Qadosh.

China, 220. With the end of the Han dynasty the country is divided into three kingdoms – Wei, Shu and Wu.

Rome, 221. On the death of Elagabalus, Alexander Severus becomes emperor.

Rome, 222. Pope Callistus is killed during an anti-Christian popular uprising. This is at a time when the church is undergoing a great expansion and Christians are mostly tolerated by the authorities. They even have contacts with the powerful Empress Julia Mamaea, mother of the Emperor Alexander Severus.

Rome, 225. The first Christian paintings appear in Rome, adorning the catacombs.

Mesopotamia, 226. Ardashir overthrows Artabanus, the last of the Parthian kings, and founds a new Persian dynasty of the Sassanids.

China, 227. Cao Pi, founder of the Wei dynasty, is dead. He was the son of Cao Cao, the poet and general who conquered northern China.

China, 229. Following the assumption by Sun Quan of the imperial title of first emperor, there are three emperors reigning in China.

Near East, 232. The Romans expel the Sassanian king Ardashir from the provinces of Mesopotamia and Cappadocia, which he invaded in 230.

Germany, c.235. The Germanic Alamanni league mounts serious raids on the frontier of the upper Rhine and the Agri Decumates.

Germany, 235. Maximinus, a former Thracian peasant, is proclaimed emperor by the mutinous troops who overthrew Alexander Severus.

Murderous end to female dynasty

Rome, 235

The murder of Julia Mamaea by disillusioned Roman soldiers has brought to an end a remarkable dynasty of four women – two sisters and two daughters – all of whom wielded much power in the Roman empire. Julia Mamaea was the mother of Alexander Severus, who was made emperor at the age of 14. As regent, her policies brought about the defeat by the Persians in 232, for which the army never forgave her.

Her mother, Julia Maesa, the daughter of a Syrian consul, was influential in the proclamation of Elagabalus in 218 and served as his adviser. Her sister, Julia Soaemius, was killed in 222 – with Elagabalus – by Praetorian guards, for flirting with the emperor.

Her aunt, Julia Domna, mother of the Emperor Caracalla, died at Antioch in 217 after being informed of her son's brutal death at the hands of an assassin. She is rumoured to have starved to death with grief.

Politically ambitious, Julia Domna is best remembered as a highly intelligent and cultivated woman who patronised the leading scholars, artists, jurists and scientists of her day. These men included the Greek philosophers Diogenes Laertius, Flavius Philostratus and Athenaeus, as well as the great Greek physician Galen.

Julia Domna, starved to death.

Han emperor forced by army to abdicate

China, 220

The Emperor Han Xiendi has been forced to abdicate, and the Han dynasty which has ruled China for 400 years is at an end. The immediate cause of the emperor's downfall was the seizure of power by the battle-hardened army, which had put down a series of peasant revolts and then destroyed the power of the court eunuchs.

Behind these bloody events, however, the underlying reason for the failure of the Hans was the inability of successive emperors to cope with the financial and social problems of the empire.

Provincial governors waged war against each other while the emperors, cut off from the reality of the countryside, indulged in court intrigues. The country fell into anarchy. from which it was rescued by three generals. But now they, too, are contending for power.

The emperor became the puppet of the celebrated General Cao Cao and it is the general's son, Cao Pi, who has assumed the throne. But he has control only of Wei in the northern third of China.

Two other states, Shu-han in the south-west and Wu in the south-east, have been carved out of the Han empire by the rival generals, and divided China is now said to be entering a period of San Kuo, the three kingdoms.

Pottery model of a watchtower, c.150.

Jade head of a horse, c.200.

Bloodthirsty Caracalla stabbed to death

Mesopotamia, 217

The bloodthirsty Caracalla answered a call of nature today – only to meet his death at the hands of a vengeful legionary. The assassination happened near Arbela (Erbil) where Caracalla was heading his legions against the rebellious Parthians.

As he approached the temple of the moon, and left the column for a few vital moments, his escort withdrew discreetly. At that moment a centurion called Martialis broke ranks and charged at the emperor, stabbing him in the back. The assassin leapt on a horse, but was pursued and killed by spears.

The explanation for the emperor's murder is his execution of Martialis' brother a few days earlier. It is suspected that the centurion was put up to the assassination by Macrinus, a member of the court, who was under suspicion of treason.

Caracalla has governed Rome for 19 years with a ruthlessless which dismayed the Senate – he had many senators put to death – and delighted his army. He himself ordered his guard to cut the throat of his brother, Geta, in the arms of their mother, Julia – and demanded that the mother should not show grief, but rejoice and laugh in public, or she, too, would die.

Caracalla had long cherished ambitions to repeat the achievements of Alexander the Great and conquer the Parthian kingdom. His legions had already inflicted heavy casualties, and he seemed destined for success at the time of his death.

New Caesar is aged 12

Rome, 238

In a year of revolution and counter-revolution the ruthless Emperor Maximinus has been defeated by forces loyal to a 12-year-old pretender. Maximinus, the son of a Thracian shepherd, rose through the ranks of the Roman cavalry until, three years ago, he cut the throat of his commander and emperor, Alexander Severus, at Mainz. Severus was mother dominated to his death at the age of 27, and died with his mother.

Maximinus needed funds to keep the troops happy, so he imposed new taxes on the rich. Landowners in North Africa now forced an octogenarian proconsul, Gordian, to lead the opposition. Gordian and his son were soon killed by forces loyal to the Thracian ruler. The Senate responded by electing Gordian's grandson as Caesar in response to popular demand.

In the four-month civil war which followed in Italy, Maximinus was lynched by his Parthian

Severus Alexander: murdered.

legion during a siege. In the capital a pair of regent emperors, Maximus and Balbinus, were also lynched by Praetorian guardsmen. Remarkably, the great mass of the army did not disintegrate. It remained a solid, disciplined force which contributed to Rome's stability as well as challenging it.

Army kills debauched emperor

Rome, 27 June 221

The authorities in Rome are not expecting a great wave of public mourning in the wake of the assassination yesterday of the 19-year-old Emperor Elagabalus by a member of the Praetorian Guard. Investigators believe that the murderer was bribed by Elagabalus' aunt, Mamea, so that her son Alexander Severus, already Caesar, could succeed Elagabalus. Severus was proclaimed emperor yesterday.

In his four years as emperor, Elagabalus managed to alienate large sections of the establishment, including senators and prefects, by his abuse of power and debauched lifestyle. Many were relieved when last year Elagabalus' grandmother Julia Maesa – long regarded as controlling affairs of state – persuaded her grandson to hand over his secular duties as Caesar to his cousin Alexander Severus.

This left Elagabalus free to concentrate on the priesthood and promotion of the eastern sun-god El Gabal, from whom he had taken his own name, as the supreme god. His obsession with this god, and his

A 19th-century idea of Elagabalus.

habit of wearing rouge, plus his insistence that he be allowed to marry a Vestal Virgin – forcing her to break a vow of lifelong chastity – despite his own castration, were all factors in his unpopularity. Attempts to counter it with feasts and spectacles were offset by his ruthless habit of executing anyone he discovered disapproving of him.

Pope allows rich sinners to take Mass

Rome, 222

Fierce opposition is growing here to the authority of Pope Callistus. The ringleader is the theologian priest Hippolytus. He is accusing Callistus of indulging rich converts and being so lax as to allow adulterers and fornicators to take the Mass. Callistus is a controversial figure. He was a slave who was entrusted by his master with money to open a bank in the fish market. This got into difficulties and Callistus fled. He returned to Rome thanks to the intervention of Marcia, the mistress of the Emperor Commodus. He was put in charge of the first Christian cemetery, on the Appian Way, and became pope in 217.

Callistus, by a later artist.

Ancient dynasty is overthrown

Persia, 226

The Arsacids, the royal dynasty of Parthia which has ruled Persia for more than four centuries, have been overthrown. After years of defeats by the Romans, including the sack of Ctesiphon by Septimus Severus in 197, the Parthians have succumbed to the Sassanian forces of Aradashir.

Arsaces became the first king of Parthia c.250BC. His descendants and successors rapidly transformed Parthia into a world power second only to Rome. They expelled the Seleucids from Mesopotamia and their empire extended as far east as India.

Descended from nomadic tribes who came from east of the Caspian Sea, the Parthians established their capital at Ctesiphon on the Tigris.

The Persians, however, were never reconciled to the Parthian intruders and opposition has recently been gathering force under the Sassanian rebel leader Ardashir.

Now Ardashir has seized control

The features of a Parthian king, on in a gilt mask, c.100-500.

of the Parthian empire by defeating the Arsacids at Hormizdagan. The Sassanian armoured cavalry proved too strong for the mounted Parthian archers, and Artabanus, king of the Parthians, was killed.

Barbarians move across the Danube

Roman Empire, 238

Attempts by two recent emperors, Alexander Severus and Maximinus, to fight off barbarian incursions into Roman territory have not succeeded.

The first barbarian invasion came about five years ago, when the Germanic Alamanni tribe raid-

ed the frontier of the upper Rhine and area, the Agri Decumantes. Earlier this year the Goths and the Carpi, who have already taken possession of land north of the Black Sea, crossed the Danube and invaded the province of Moesia. The Romans have paid tributes to them to induce them to withdraw.

Roman engineering: imperial monument

The grandiose public monuments of the cities of the Roman empire, many of which survive today, have traditionally been considered among the greatest achievements of the Romans. But a point which is not so often considered is that perhaps the majority of buildings in the Roman empire, even some of the most impressive, were the result of local initiatives and local financial expenditure – and so the monuments of the Roman Empire in many cases tell us more about the subjects of Rome than they do about the Romans themselves.

One story illustrates the point neatly. In the mid second century AD, a Roman military engineer called Nonius Datus was sent to the town of Saldae, in North Africa, to resolve a problem. The municipal authorities had commissioned the building of an aqueduct, but the workmen had found themselves in difficulties. Two squads had started to excavate a tunnel through a hill, starting at opposite ends.

After several years' work, they found that the combined lengths of the two tunnels was more than the distance between the two entrances! The local council appealed to the Romans for help, and Nonius Datus was sent to the scene. His journey was interrupted by bandits who robbed and stripped him, but eventually he arrived at Saldae, and solved the problem by boring a hole sideways between the two tunnels, which had missed each other. A monument was set up to commemorate his achievement.

The story illustrates the technical capabilities of Roman engineers, but also shows the extent to which local initiatives lay behind public building projects.

The importance of engineering

From the earliest times the Romans used engineering techniques as a means of gaining, or exploiting, success in war. It may be that some of these techniques came from the Etruscans, their neighbours and arch-rivals: many drainage channels, cut through the soft volcanic rock, can still be seen in Etruria. Some of the best examples survive at Veii – the traditional story of Rome's capture of that city in 396BC, Livy reported, suggests that the Roman success was due to tunnelling below the walls of the otherwise impregnable citadel.

As Roman control over Italy increased, so engineering projects allowed Roman forces to control conquered territory. Together with military advances into Campania in the late fourth century, and the foundation of a series of colonial settlements in the area, came the building of the most famous of all Roman roads, the Appian Way, in 312BC. It ran originally from Rome to Capua, but was later extended to Brundisium (Brindisi).

The new road allowed effective and comparatively speedy communication between Rome and Campania, and seems to have had an entirely military purpose – there is no trace of an economic motive. During the following years the road network was extended further, and by the middle of the second century most of the Italian peninsula was criss-crossed by roads.

We find similar techniques of pacification being used under the empire, too. The siege of Masada, where enormous earthworks were created to besiege a small body of Jews, shows that the field-engineers of the Roman army were just as important to the imperial army as to the army of the early republic. Frontiers (essentially an imperial innovation, as the prevailing ideology of the republic was one of boundless conquest) were originally conceived as roads parallel to the frontier line which enabled rapid deployment of troops to take place in time of crisis.

Imperial or local inspiration

As Roman enthusiasm for conquest declined (except for a few campaigns designed to bring glory to otherwise unmilitary emperors like Claudius), so the frontiers were consolidated – the best-known example, Hadrian's Wall, in northern England, is also perhaps rather untypical, because of its vast size. But it shows splendidly the technical abilities of the Roman engineers who built it; and the fact that governors of comparatively peaceful provinces – Pliny in Bithynia (northern Turkey), for example – would call in a military architect when a project needed to be carried out, reinforces the point.

Sometimes buildings or other monuments in provincial towns were set up at the specific command of the emperor: perhaps to commemorate an imperial visit there, or in response to a disaster like an earthquake. Imperial benefactions were most often given to colonies of army veterans or other Roman citizens, as in the case of the Pont du Gard, which supplied Nemausus (Nimes) with water.

But despite the impressive buildings constructed by the Roman authorities in the provinces, it needs to be emphasised that most projects were civil in conception and locally funded. There are a number of reasons for this enthusiasm for public building in the towns of the empire.

Firstly, there was keen rivalry between provincial towns, and considerable snobbery about places which were inadequately provided with amenities like baths, aqueducts, fountains and so on. Despite the views of Frontinus, who argued that Roman architectural achievements (and aqueducts in particular) were by far superior to those of the Greeks, or to the frivolous pyramids of Egypt, it seems clear that the building of aqueducts and baths often said more about the style or image of a town than they did about its cleanliness – sometimes the water brought into the town at vast expense ran to waste in decorative fountains, while bath-houses functioned more as social centres than places to wash.

Individual enterprise

Urban pride, then, was an important motivating force behind the policies of ancient towns; but perhaps even more important was individual ambition. Just as a political career at Rome was helped by generous expenditure, so a local dignitary gained honour and advancement by generous funding of buildings in the Roman style. The disadvantage with this was that few benefactors could be found to pay for inglorious but essential amenities like sewers: Pliny reported that a town in his province, Amastris, was well provided with public buildings but a fetid drain ran down the middle of the main street.

The central question remains, though: how were the local aristocracies persuaded to spend their revenues on building Roman-style monuments? This may be comprehensible in countries like Greece, which already had a long tradition of urban life, but is more difficult to explain for places like Gaul, where populations were largely tribal before the Romans conquered them.

The short answer seems to be that it helped to consolidate their power over the local population, within the framework of Roman imperial rule. Once an area had been satisfactorily conquered, and it had begun to pay taxes, the Romans were on the whole happy to leave day-to-day control to the local elites – in areas which had once been organised tribally, the tribal leaders were simply transmuted into local councillors, and they acquiesced in this because it allowed them to keep their traditional local authority. Some provinces responded less readily than others – Tacitus, for example, observed that the governor, Agricola, had to make deliberate attempts to persuade the British chiefs to build temples and *fora*. But even the Britons were eventually convinced."This element of their slavery they called culture", he comments.

Aqueduct at Segovia, Spain, built under the Emperor Hadrian (96-117).

Ruined Roman baths at Aquae Sulis (Bath) in south-west Britain.

Remains of a Roman road not far from Eburacum (York) in Britain.

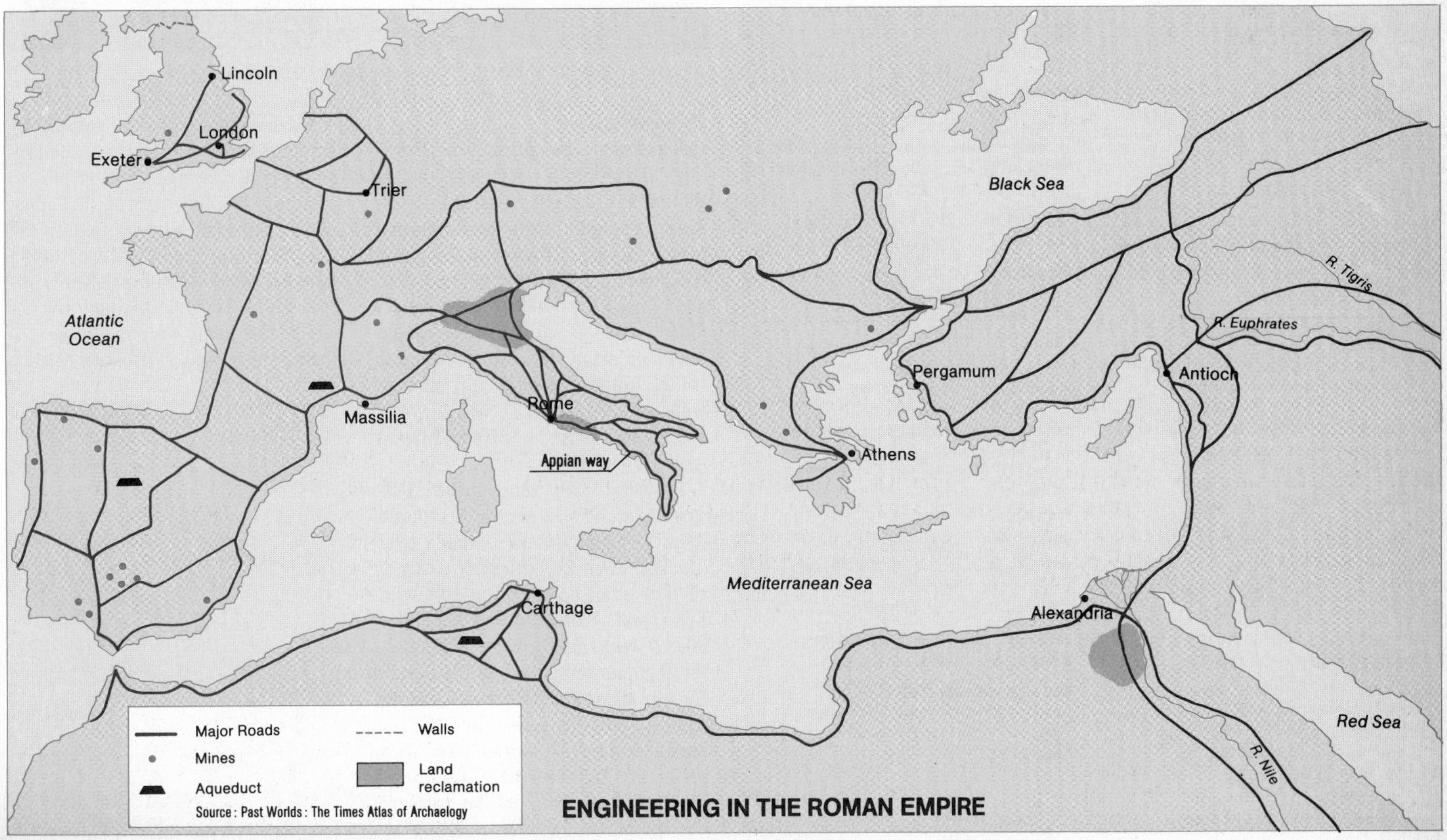

—— Major Roads	----- Walls
• Mines	
◣ Aqueduct	▨ Land reclamation

Source: Past Worlds : The Times Atlas of Archaelogy

ENGINEERING IN THE ROMAN EMPIRE

Lincoln · London · Exeter · Trier · Atlantic Ocean · Massilia · Rome · Appian way · Carthage · Black Sea · Pergamum · Athens · Antioch · R. Tigris · R. Euphrates · Mediterranean Sea · Alexandria · Red Sea · R. Nile

Balkans, 238. Despite the payment of tributes, the Romans have failed to persuade the barbarian Goths and Carpi to withdraw from the province of Moesia.

North Africa, 238. Gordian, the governor of the province of Africa, recently proclaimed emperor by rebels, dies after a defeat by the Numidians, bringing to an end his reign of 22 days.

Rome, 238. The Praetorian Guard mutinies at the Senate's choice of Balbinus and Pupienus as joint emperors, and appoints in their place Gordian III, grandson of the former governor of Africa, Gordian I. The Praetorians then kill Balbinus and Pupienus.

Italy, 238. Maximinus – made emperor in 235 – is killed by his troops while besieging Aquileia in northern Italy.

China, 239. Queen Himiko of Yamatai, in Japan, sends to China an envoy who is given a gold seal by the Chinese emperor confirming the queen as an ally of China.

Black Sea, 242. Gordian III evacuates the cities of the Cimmerian Bosporus (southern Russia). Cut off from the Roman world, the region falls under the domination of the Ostrogoths who are settling in the Ukraine.

India, 242. The Kushans come into confrontation with the Sassanian empire, which is conducting an aggressive campaign in Bactria.

Mesopotamia, March 244. Gordian is murdered by his own soldiers during a war against the Persians which began in 242. The Praetorian prefect, an Arab named Philip, is made emperor and makes peace with the Persians.

Japan, 247. Queen Himiko of Yamatai goes to war with the king of nearby Kunukoku, a state in the southernmost island of Japan. Her request to China for aid is sternly rejected.

Japan, 247. Civil war breaks out in Japan after the death of Queen Himiko when her brother usurps the throne, overthrowing the female right of inheritance. Peace is only restored when Himiko's daughter Iyo regains power as priestess-queen.

Rome, 27 April 247. Philip the Arab marks the millennium of Rome with a celebration of the *ludi saeculares*.

Italy, 249. Philip the Arab is killed in a clash with Decius, his commander in Dacia, at Verona. Decius becomes emperor.

China, 249. The brilliant philosopher Wang Bi dies in his early twenties after changing the course of Chinese thought.

China, 249. Descendants of the warlord founders of the Wei dynasty succumb to a palace coup initiated by their own chief general, Sima Yi. The Wei dynasty continues in name only.

Ethiopia, c.250. Axum is growing into a powerful kingdom under the rule of King Aphilas. Frankincense and myrrh are exported through the Red Sea to the Mediterranean, and Aphilas issues his own coinage. Magnificent obelisks and a royal palace are in the process of construction.

Balkans, 250. The Carpi invade Dacia; the Goths invade Moesia.

Balkans, 251. As a consequence of the disloyalty of Gallus, the governor of Moesia, Decius and his son are defeated and killed at the battle of Abrittus by the Goths under Kniva. Gallus becomes emperor.

Balkans, 253. During an attack on Aemilius Aemiliamus, his successor as governor of Moesia, Gallus is killed by his own troops.

Rome, September 253. Valerian is recognised as emperor by the Senate. He choses his son Gallienus as his colleague. This follows the death in a mutiny of Aemiliamus, emperor for just a few months.

Gaul, 253. The Franks and the Alamanni invade Gaul.

Palestine, 253. The theologian and philosopher Origen, who headed a Christian school in his native Alexandria for 28 years, dies as a result of torture suffered during the Decian persecution of 250.

Rome, 258. A second edict is issued, following one published last year, forbidding Christian worship. Pope Sixtus II is martyred.

North Africa, 258. Cyprian, the bishop of Carthage, is martyred.

Rome, 260. Gallienus issues an edict enshrining tolerance of the Christians. It is known as the "little peace of the Church".

Syria, 260. The Persians are repelled in Cappadocia by the Praetorian prefect Macrinus, who has his sons proclaimed emperors at Emesa (Homs). Odenaethus, the prince of Palmyra, attacks them while they are retreating and takes control of the Roman empire.

China, 265. The short-lived Wei dynasty is ousted by a Wei general, Sima Yan, who founds a new regime, the Jin or Western Jin.

Balkans, 267. The Goths pillage Thrace, Macedonia and Greece.

Italy, September 268. While besieging Aureolus, leader of the rebel cavalry, Gallienus is assassinated.

A Roman ally is stabbed after victory

A painted marble statue of a woman known as "The Beauty of Palmyra".

Palmyra, 267
Odenaethus, the prince of Palmyra, and long a vital ally of the Romans, has been stabbed to death, apparently on the emperor's orders, shortly after a victory over the Persians led to his being hailed as "Corrector of all the East". Odenaethus, of Arab blood, mixed with ancient Amorite and Aramaic stock, initially sought an alliance with the Persian king, Shapur, but when he was rebuffed turned towards Rome.

Protected by the feared Palmyran archers and by armoured cavalry, Palmyra prospered over the last three centuries as a result of its strategic location between Syria and Babylonia. Odenaethus, loaded with honours by Gallienus, the Roman emperor, led his Syrian forces alongside Roman legions against the Persians. In 262 he regained the Mesopotamian fortresses of Carrhae and Nisibis, and in 267 he marched to the gates of Ctesiphon, the Persian capital.

Odenaethus was so valued by Rome that he was awarded the title of *imperator*, which entitled him to wear the laurel wreath and diadem of the emperor. But his adding the title "King of Kings" to his Roman honours caused Rome some concern and led to his eventual murder which Gallienus ordered, fearing a forthcoming breach between them.

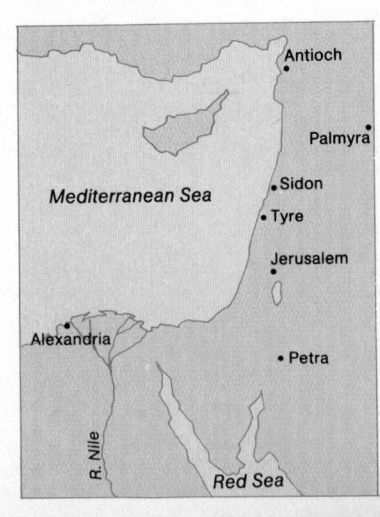

Rome shaken by invasions and internal divisions

Sacrifice or burn, Christians are told

Rome, 250
Failure to produce a simple document can mean torture and death to the Christians of Rome. The Emperor Decius has decreed that, on a given day, every Roman must make a sacrifice to the gods in return for a certificate. Some Christians have bowed to the emperor's will and laid a few grains of incense on the pagan altars; others, who refused, have been publicly whipped and burnt to death, sometimes by vigilante groups, sometimes by court order.

Later view of a crucifixion.

Roman soldiers kill their own general

Gaul, 269
General Postumus, who seized his share of power after the capture of Valerian nine years ago to rule the Roman empire with Gallienus, has been murdered by his own troops who resented "too much labour". Postumus was at the top for seven years. He ruled (and visited) Britain, Gaul and parts of Spain. He restored credibility to the "Gallic Empire", centred on Cologne and Mainz, after throwing German invaders out of Gaul. The Gauls killed him.

A general on a horse leads troops against shaggy-haired barbarians.

Empire comes under assault on all fronts

Rome, 260
The Roman empire is coming under more sustained attack than ever before. In the east, where the recently-founded Sassanid dynasty is determined to regain Asia Minor, Syria and Egypt, it has lost an emperor, flayed alive after being captured by the Persians (*see below*). Already Palmyra, the last Oriental province, has fallen – to Zenobia, the widow of Odenaethus, the Palmyran prince killed by Rome.

In Europe, the Franks have invaded Gaul, sweeping into Spain while the Goths and Vandals are attacking Italy and Greece. And in Africa it is Berber tribes who are attacking Roman land.

What makes the crisis so dangerous for Rome is that its armies are divided, often to the point of near civil war, as each elects its own "caesar". Military disasters have piled up unceasingly. Plague is also a constant companion of every legion, and much of the empire faces famine in the wake of pillaging armies of Rome and its increasingly potent enemies.

Roaring inflation hits small traders

Rome, c.260
With wars raging throughout the empire and inflation rampant at home, Rome is facing a major economic crisis which is compounded by the political and military troubles now besetting the empire which have resulted in armies electing their own "caesars".

The cost of maintaining fighting armies on so many fronts is not only crippling the Roman treasury, but also making it more difficult to achieve agreement on measures to combat inflation.

New coins are being produced in record numbers, but with their silver content reduced by more than 90 per cent. The depreciation of the denarius – combined with dangers on road and sea – has paralysed trade.

Plague has broken out again and food production has been hit by drought. Famines have become commonplace. Tradesmen, craftsmen and small farmers are all hard-hit by the depression.

With money becoming valueless, barter is commonplace throughout Rome. The bigger land-owners are thriving, however, and buying up cheap land to increase the sizes of their estates.

Emperor Valerian flayed alive after his capture by the Persians

Persia, 260
The capture of the Emperor Valerian by King Shapur of Persia has concluded a disastrous period for Roman arms. It is said that Valerian's skin was exhibited as a trophy with his stuffed body after he had been flayed alive.

Ardashir, the first Sassanian ruler of Persia, conducted several campaigns against Rome, taking Carrhae and Nisibis in 238. In 244 Shapur defeated a Roman army at Massice, after which the Emperor Gordian III died, perhaps murdered. His successor Philip paid Shapur a ransom of 500,000 gold dinars. Four years ago a Roman army of 60,000 was destroyed at Barbalissus.

Valerian submits to Persia's king: a Persian relief, c.260.

Balkans, 269. After crushing the Goths in two great battles, at Doberus and Naissus (Nissa), Claudius II – one of Gallienus' chief officers, who succeeded his master last year – wins the congratulatory nickname of "Gothicus". Soon after becoming emperor, Claudius defeated the invading Alamanni.

Egypt, 269. Zenobia, the widow of Odenaethus of Palmyra, a city centred on an oasis between Syria and Babylonia, conquers Egypt. She has already secured control of Syria and laid waste to the northern Arabia region of Bostra.

Balkans, 270. Claudius II dies from the plague at Sirmium (Mitrovica). The disease has been spread from the east by the Roman armies.

Balkans, 270. Lucius Domitius Aurelianus (Aurelian), who distinguished himself in the fight against the Goths after Claudius put him in charge of the cavalry, becomes emperor.

Asia Minor, 270. Zenobia gains control of most of Asia Minor, apart from Bithynia.

Balkans, 271. In their first important withdrawal since the beginning of the empire, the Romans evacuate Dacia.

Rome, 271. An attack by the Juthungi on northern Italy prompts Aurelian to order the building of a sturdy wall around the city of Rome.

Syria, 271. Zenobia declares herself empress and breaks with the Roman empire. She gives her son Vaballathus the title of Augustus.

Egypt, 271. Aurelian, who has decided to put a stop to Zenobia's activities, sends his troops into Egypt, but loses his general, Probus, in a battle for control of the country.

Syria, 272. Having reoccupied Anatolia and defeated Zenobia's troops in two battles, Aurelian captures Palmyra and takes the queen herself prisoner.

Syria, 273. Aurelian puts down a new revolt in Palmyra and deposes the new king. The city is reduced to a village.

Gaul, 274. After the desertion of his army by Tetricus, who was made emperor in Gaul in 270, Aurelian puts an end to the "Gallic empire", reunifying the Roman empire.

Rome, 274. The warrior-queen Zenobia dies quietly in Rome, where she had married a Roman senator. Earlier in the year she took part in Aurelian's *Triumph*.

Gaul, 275. The country is pillaged by the Franks and the Alamanni.

Asia Minor, 275. On his way to confront the Persians, Aurelian is murdered near Byzantium as the result of a military plot.

Asia Minor, 276. Tacitus, who was chosen by the Senate late last year to succeed Aurelian, is killed by his own troops after winning a victory over the Goths.

Persia, 26 February 277. Mani, the founder of Manichaeism, is put to death by the Sassanian Persians.

Gaul, 277. Marcus Aurelius Probus, who became sole emperor in 276 after outmanoeuvring his rival, Florian, liberates Gaul from the Franks and the Alamanni.

Balkans, 279. Probus expels the Burgundians and the Vandals from Rhaetia.

Palestine, 279. Johanan bar Nappacha, the Jewish doctor who masterminded and edited the Palestinian or Jerusalem *Talmud*, dies.

Egypt, c.280. The mathematician Pappus publishes his *Mathematical Collection*, a summary of the knowledge on the subject acquired to date.

Persia, 280. The Sassanian king Bahram II sends an envoy to make peace overtures to Probus.

Egypt, 281. Probus drives the people called the Blemmyes, who have made several recent conquests in Egypt, out of the country.

Mesopotamia, August 283. Carus, the Praetorian prefect under Probus, who declared himself emperor last year after his master's murder, dies during a successful campaign against the Persians, which has included the capture of Ctesiphon.

Asia Minor, 20 November 284. On the death at Nicomedia of Numerian, younger son and successor of Carus, Diocletian, the commander of the emperor's bodyguard, is proclaimed emperor by his soldiers.

Balkans, 285. Carinus, elder brother of Numerian, who was made Augustus of the west before the death of his father, Carus, is defeated by Diocletian at the battle of the Margus in Moesia.

Gaul, 1 April 286. Maximian is made emperor by Diocletian and placed on an equal footing with him, acquiring the title Augustus.

Britain, 287. Carausius, the admiral of the Channel fleet, seizes control of Britain and a part of northern Gaul.

Asia Minor, 1 March 293. Diocletian arranges for two Caesars, Galerius and Constantius Chlorus, to join the two Augusti in the rule of the Roman empire.

Chained Queen of Egypt paraded in Rome

Aurelian's walls protecting Rome.

A 19th-century idea of a "Triumph".

Rome, 274

Zenobia, the Queen of Egypt, was paraded in golden chains through the streets of Rome today in the most spectacular *Triumph* the city has seen. The Emperor Aurelian showed his captives to the crowd together with 20 elephants and 200 tamed wild animals. Zenobia, who had defied Rome until the moment of her capture, rode in a gold chariot, with slaves supporting the heavy chains. Tetricus, the rebel of Gaul, rode in another chariot. The emperor's jewel-encrusted chariot was drawn by four stags which he slaughtered in sacrifice on the altar of Jupiter.

New dynasty unites divided kingdom

China, 280

Sima Yan, the ruler of the northern kingdom of Wei, has reunited the Three Kingdoms of China into one empire and founded the Jin dynasty. Sima Yan usurped the throne of Wei 15 years ago and was proclaimed emperor with great ceremony.

Wei had already swallowed the western kingdom of Shu, and now Sima Yan has sent his army across the Blue River and crushed the forces of the southern kingdom of Wu to make himself emperor of all China. It will not be an easy throne on which to sit. China's strength is drained and the countryside devastated, and the nomads of the north are threatening the frontiers.

Pacification of Gauls celebrated

Rome, 281

The Emperor Probus has been hailed by a grateful Rome in a magnificent *Triumph* staged in the imperial capital to celebrate his victories over barbarian armies which threatened the empire. Most crucial of Probus' campaigns was the final pacification of Gaul in 277. This followed a decade of attacks by German tribes, chiefly Franks and Alamanni, which nearly led to civil war within the empire as a succession of Roman generals usurped imperial power in Gaul, Britain and part of Spain.

Probus spearing an enemy.

Four emperors rule Roman empire

Nicomedia, Asia Minor, 293
After a century of military anarchy, with frontiers crumbling under barbarian attacks, Diocletian has found an imaginative solution to the problem of keeping order in his far-flung empire. While he remained at Nicomedia, on the Propontis (Sea of Marmara), he chose Maximian as a second emperor in the west. Both emperors have the title of Augustus. Now two Caesars have been appointed as heirs apparent to the empire: Galerius and Constantius. Their loyalties have been cemented by marriages to the daughters of the Augusti.

Diocletian, born into a Balkan slave family and made emperor by his soldiers, will lead campaigns against the Persians. While Maximian tackles unrest in Africa, and Galerius fights on the Danube, Constantius is preparing an assault on Britain, where a mutinous admiral has seized power.

Just in case anyone should quibble over this system of government, known as the *tetrarchy*, Diocletian has announced that he is descended from the Olympian god Jupiter, while Maximian claims descent from Hercules, Jupiter's faithful strongman.

Diocletian (l.) and Maximian face each other on the side of a coin.

Founder of Persian sect has died in jail

Persia, 277
Mani, the founder of Manichaeism, has died in the jail of Bahram, king of Persia. Manichaeism, a religious sect related to Christianity but preaching redemption through knowledge rather than sacrifice, has been persecuted in Rome and Persia, but has acquired followers in Rome's eastern empire.

Mani was born in 216 in Babylonia, of Persian parents. His father belonged to a gnostic sect. Mani went east, towards India, to preach. In a world of light and darkness, he believed that demons had enclosed the light in matter; by an ascetic life devoted to the pursuit of truth, man could release the light. Mani believed that the world's many religions were not universal enough.

Division of empire brings huge increase in burden of taxation

The Augusti (r.) and their Caesars.

Rome, 293
Diocletian's decision to divide the empire may make sense as far as governing distant territories is concerned, but it has given rise to a massive increase in bureaucracy. Both Augusti require a large number of officers – keepers of their palaces, masters of the records, personnel officers (who play a major part in watching the emperor's personal and political security), magistrates and their officials, together with senators empowered to collect taxes.

Two Augusti and two Caesars and this doubling of the normal number of state servants has created a huge increase in taxation at a time when the value of money is rapidly diminishing. Tax is being

collected "in kind": members of municipal senates are expected to find quantities of wheat and other produce from farms already depleted of workers – who are being conscripted into the army in ever-increasing numbers.

Rather than face the burden of high taxes, many craftsmen have fled the country. Many more are going into monasteries, and some are accepting serfdom, preferring to await an invasion by barbarians whose harsh rule would probably not include heavy taxation.

This complacency, wholly untypical of Rome, is universal, spreading through the church, the intellectual and craftsmen classes. It does not bode well for a great empire.

Islamic view of Mani's death.

Romans abandon difficult province

Dacia, 271
The frontiers of the Roman empire seem more secure today after the announcement by the new emperor, Aurelian, that Rome is to withdraw from the province of Dacia beyond the river Danube. This is the first time that Rome has abandoned an entire province. However, the wild, mountainous terrain of Dacia has never been easy to govern since it was conquered in 106 by Trajan. As recently as 251, for instance, the Goths penetrated Dacia to invade Moesia, south of the Danube.

Huge collection of Jewish laws published

Palestine, 279
Jewish scholars based in Tiberias have issued a collection of laws, doctrines and legends, which they call the Jerusalem *Talmud*. The research for this *Talmud* (which comes from the Hebrew word *lamed*, or teaching) has occupied scholars since the return from Babylon more than 800 years ago.

The work has been masterminded by Johanan bar Nappacha ("the blacksmith's son"), who took over from Rabbi Yehuda ha-Qadosh who died in 219. With a team of assistants he has selected and edited a vast body of material.

Essentially this collection of oral and traditional material is an enormous footnote to the *Pentateuch*, the five books of Moses, notably Deuteronomy, which lay down Jewish law.

The material included in the *Talmud* is known as the *Mishna* (Hebrew for instruction). It is made up of the teachings of generations of rabbis, usually in the form of their interpretations of the *Pentateuch*. The *Mishna* is divided into two parts: the *Halachah*, which contains legal and doctrinal material, and the *Agada*, which centres on stories and legends.

Plotinus, the Greek thinker, is dead

Italy, 270
Plotinus has died of diphtheria in Campania. Born around 66 years ago in Egypt, he studied philosophy in Alexandria before settling in Rome and attracting a circle of intellectuals. He revived and extended the work of Plato. He believed that there are concentric circles of reality centred on the sublime source of existence and values, with an outer circle of bare matter. Man is a microcosm of this principle; he can attain the inner sublime state through ecstasy.

Persia, 293. Narses, the new Sassanian king, son of Shapur – who twice invaded Mesopotamia and Syria but was driven back – reverts to an anti-Roman policy.

Central America, c.295. The civilisations of Teotihuacan and Monte Alban, in Mexico and central America, are reaching new heights of prosperity. In the Maya area numerous city-states are developing, ruled by rival dynastic families.

Britain, 296. The Emperor Constantius Chlorus, Caesar of the west, recovers the province of Britain from the usurper Allectus, an officer in Carasius' army who had murdered the rebel leader and taken control himself.

Egypt, 297. A second revolt in Egypt, following one five years ago, is put down by the Emperor Diocletian.

Rome, 31 March 297. An edict is issued condemning as anti-Roman Manichaeism, a religion favoured by the Persians.

Armenia, 297. Capitalising on Roman involvement elsewhere, the Roman-backed Persian king, Narses, ousts King Tiridates from Armenia. The Caesar Galerius, sent by Diocletian to confront Narses, is beaten back by the Persians near Carrhae.

Armenia, 298. Utterly defeated by Galerius, who has reinforced his army, the Persian king, Narses, is forced to sign the treaty of Nisibis, which affirms Roman supremacy over the kingdom of Armenia and surrenders to the Romans some Persian lands beyond the Tigris.

Armenia, 300. Tiridates, king of Armenia, is converted to Christianity by Gregory the Illuminator, making his the first state to accept Christianity as the official religion.

Rome, 20 November 303. The Augusti and the Caesars, who are together for the first time, hold a festival in honour of the twentieth anniversary of Diocletian's accession.

Asia Minor, 304. Since his purge of the army and the court in 302, Diocletian has issued four edicts aimed at destroying Christianity in the Roman empire. Churches are dismantled, clergy arrested and Christians forced to sacrifice to the pagan gods on pain of death.

Pottery painting catches on among American tribes

North America, c.300

The craft of pottery-making is becoming increasingly sophisticated in the south-west region of North America, among a people whose way of life would seem to leave little time for the complexities of the potter's art.

The Mogollon Indians have been eking out a living in this mountainous terrain for some 500 years, surviving on what nature has to offer. Experiments with agriculture have not been wholly successful, partly because of the irregular rainfall, so they remain reliant on the food that they can gather from the wild, eating seeds, roots, nuts and occasional fruits. Meat is a rare luxury.

The art of pottery-making among the Mogollon people was probably initially learnt from neighbouring Mexican tribes, so they have not had to develop the skill from scratch themselves. They make jars and bowls by coiling the clay, and smoothing the vessels to their final shape with pebbles. This gives Mogollon ware a distinctively dimpled finish. Recently they have begun to add painted decoration to their pottery.

They also make clay pipes, and, occasionally, tiny clay dolls. The Mogollons live in small villages of pit houses which are partly underground, with their entrances facing east to catch the rays of the early morning sun.

Mosaic of a Roman girl athlete.

A scene from the "Kama Sutra", the guide to lovemaking, c.1780.

The "Kama Sutra" tells of erotic delights

India, c.300

An Indian sage, Vatsayana Mallagana, writing in the holy city of Benares, has produced a unique guidebook to the many and varied pleasures of sexual love: the *Kama Sutra*, or Aphorisms on Love.

The work runs to 1,250 *slokas*, or verses, divided into 36 chapters. Written in Sanskrit, it functions as a guide to every aspect of erotic etiquette. It has been composed very much from the male point of view, although the author suggests that brides-to-be should study it before their marriages.

The *Kama Sutra* is a veritable encyclopaedia of sexuality. Not only does it list literally hundreds of ways of sexual intercourse, but its pages include information on courtesans, go-betweens, the sexual preferences of different nationalities, courtship and kissing, marriage and seduction. The physical act of love is set out in unprecedented detail. There is even a selection of magic spells.

Underlying the book is the philosophy of the Hindu religion, which stresses that sexuality is a central part of human life, as fundamental as breathing. It is a basic part of nature, what Hindus call the Cosmic Dance of Shiva, the god of creation, and is as much a religious experience as it is a physical and sensual one.

Porphyry, critic of Christianity, dies

Rome, 304

Porphyry, meaning purple, was the nickname given to the philosopher born as Malchus in Tyre, the home of the Phoenician purple dye used to colour the robes of emperors. At his death he was the leader of the neo-Platonist school of philosophers and the closest disciple of their founder, Plotinus.

Porphyry taught the salvation of the soul through strict asceticism and piety, leading to a knowledge of God, but he wrote a celebrated treatise against the cult of the Christians, casting doubt on their sacred texts. A polymath, he also wrote lives of Plotinus and Pythagoras, treatises on vegetarianism, Homer, grammar and embryology, and commentaries on Plato, Aristotle and Ptolemy.

Roman empire at peace

Diocletian: imperial pacifier.

Rome, 28 November 303
Twenty years after coming to power, the Emperor Diocletian is visiting Rome for the first time. The occasion is being marked by feasts and games in his honour. At last, after many years of disorder and danger, the empire is at peace.

Diocletian has reformed the whole imperial administrative system, separating civil and military departments. For each department he has fashioned an unbroken chain of command, from the emperor down to the lowest official in the most distant province.

He has been less successful with his handling of the economy. In an attempt to tackle inflation he imposed wage and price controls. A wide range of goods, including bread, meat, vegetables, fruit, footwear, leather, carpets and clothes was covered by the edict of two years ago.

Maximum rates of pay were fixed for all, from labourer to lawyer. Punishment for violating the controls was death or exile. This ambitious bid to manage the economy collapsed under the combined pressures of shortages and a rampant black market.

Diocletian's attempt to reform the tax system has been effective but harsh. He abolished the old, complicated system and introduced a simplified one based on land acreage. In practice, this amounted to the legalisation of the practice of exacting contributions of produce and labour. The effect has been to tie country folk to their land, like serfs.

Trier, in Gaul, becomes imperial seat

The massive – though uncompleted – bulk of Trier's "Porta Nigra".

Gaul, 296
Constantius Chlorus, the Emperor Diocletian's Caesar (vice-emperor) for the western empire since 293, has announced that he is establishing his capital at Trier (Augusta Trevirorum) on the river Moselle.

Trier, which was founded in 44 by the Emperor Claudius, is already a city of considerable importance, with a vast circuit of walls built just under a century ago. These fortifications include the *Porta Nigra*, or Black Gate, and other monuments include an amphitheatre and baths. It is believed that Constantius plans several imposing new buildings, as befits what is now the second city of the western empire, after Rome itself. A new imperial palace and a vast new imperial bath-complex are thought to be in the pipeline. Before he turns to architecture, though, Constantius has to sort out problems with usurpers in Britain.

Trade boom throughout the Roman world

Rome, c.300
One quick way to gauge the annual turnover of trade in the empire is to visit the docks and examine the year-on-year growth of the Mons Testaceus. This huge mound has been built from broken pottery: bits of discarded *amphorae*, the nonreuseable vessels used to ship olive oil from Spain and Africa.

While Rome's oil trade provides one index of economic activity, several centres now produce and ship goods on a large scale. Britain is a major grain producer, shipping corn to troops on the Rhine frontier. In the Rhineland a major glass and pottery industry has emerged, while Africa also ships large quantities of grain to Rome.

Pay and prices curb to combat inflation

Rome, November 301
The Emperor Diocletian has instituted a prices and wages freeze in a desperate attempt to control the rampant inflation which has already resulted in a 50 per cent devaluation. His decree, which will be enforced throughout the empire, is quite unprecedented. It contains a very detailed list of prices for all major and many minor commodities. An egg is to cost one denarius; a lemon, 24; a chicken, 30; a pheasant, 250; a male slave, 30,000; and a racehorse, 100,000. As for wages, agricultural workers will get up to 25 denarii a day, and bakers 50 denarii a day; scribes 25 denarii per 100 lines; and teachers 50 denarii per pupil per month.

A Roman merchant vessel being loaded with grain at Ostia, c.200–300.

Money being counted in a Roman counting house, c.100–200.

Rome, 1 May 305. Diocletian becomes the first emperor to abdicate; he retires to a palace on the Adriatic. Maximian is forced to abdicate with him. The former Caesars Galerius and Constantius both receive the title of Augustus. The new Caesars are Severus, who is made prefect of Italy, and Galerius' nephew Maximin Daia, who gains control of Syria and Egypt.

Britain, 23 July 306. On the death of his father, the Augustus Constantius Chlorus, Constantine is proclaimed Caesar of the west by the army at York. Severus, the former Caesar, is recognised by Galerius as Augustus of the west.

Rome, 28 October 306. Maxentius, son of Maximian, is elevated to the throne by the Praetorian Guard and the people of Rome. He takes control of Italy, Spain and Africa.

Italy, 306. Severus surrenders to Maxentius at Ravenna after attempting to march on Rome. He is put to death.

Eastern empire, 307. Galerius is forced to abandon an invasion of Italy because of disloyalty in his army.

Rome, 308. Maxentius takes the title Augustus. His father, the former emperor Maximian, meanwhile, after failing to depose his son, has fled to Constantine.

Balkans, 308. Galerius confers with Diocletian and Maximian at Carnuntum on the Danube. Maxentius is declared a public enemy, and Licinius is proclaimed rightful Augustus of the west.

Persia, 310. After a crisis over the succession, the 17-year-old Shapur II, grandson of Narses, becomes king.

North Africa, 311. The election of Bishop Caecilianus of Carthage is contested by Donatus, a bishop from Numidia. This creates a serious split in the African church, known as the Donatist schism. The disagreement centres on responses to persecution. The extremist Donatist party holds that anyone who has sacrificed to the Roman gods should be refused readmission to the church.

Balkans, April 311. The Emperor Galerius issues the edict of Sardica, granting toleration to the Christians; he dies shortly afterwards. Maximin and Licinius hurry to divide up the eastern empire between them. Maximin resumes persecution of the Christians.

Italy, 28 October 312. After invading Italy, Constantine defeats Maxentius at the battle of the Milvian Bridge, making him master of the whole Roman west.

Milan, February 313. Licinius marries Constantine's sister, Constantia. The two emperors agree on a policy of religious toleration for Christians, known as the Edict of Milan.

Adrianople, 30 April 313. Licinius eliminates the Caesar Maximin Daia and unifies the whole of the eastern empire under his rule.

Balkans, 313. The ex-emperor Diocletian dies in Dalmatia.

Rome, 315. The arch of Constantine is built near the Colosseum. Constantine also completes the great basilica begun by Maxentius and places in it a huge statue of himself. These monuments commemorate his victory of 312.

China, 316. The Western Jin collapses following the capture of Changan by the Xiongnu.

China, 317. The survivors of the Western Jin re-establish themselves further south on the Yangzi river, and the prime minister, Sima Rui, succeeds to the throne of the Eastern Jin in Jiankang (Nanjing).

Egypt, 318. Arius, the priest of Alexandria, puts forward his doctrine which denies the consubstantiality of the Son with the Father and, therefore, Christ's fully divine nature.

India, 320. Chandragupta, king of Magadha, founds the Gupta dynasty.

Rome, 3 July 321. Sunday is made a day of rest throughout the empire.

Egypt, 323. Pachomius founds the monastery of Tabennesi in the desert.

Asia Minor, 324. After inflicting a series of military defeats on Licinius by land and sea, Constantine captures and soon executes his co-emperor. His hold on the east secured, Constantine is now sole ruler of the empire.

Asia Minor, May 325. Constantine summons and presides over a world council of bishops at Nicaea. An orthodox creed is established.

Palestine, 325. Eusebius, the bishop of Caesarea and a supporter of Arius, publishes his *Ecclesiastical History* and an historical *Chronicle*.

Rome, 25 July 326. Constantine continues the festivities celebrating his twentieth year in power and his triumphs over the barbarians and Licinius, but refuses to carry out the traditional pagan sacrifices in the temple of Jupiter.

Jerusalem, 326. Helena, mother of Constantine, discovers the Holy Cross and Jesus' tomb, the Holy Sepulchre.

Succession secure as Diocletian abdicates

Part of the magnificent palace built for Diocletian's retirement.

Rome, April 305

The Emperor Diocletian has announced that he is to abdicate after 21 years on the throne and retire to his palace near Salonae in his native Dalmatia. Diocletian's system of *tetrarchy* (four rulers) should ensure a peaceful transition of power. Under the *tetrarchy* there are two Augusti, or senior emperors, one for the east and one for the west, each with a junior, and heir, called Caesar. As well as smoothing the succession, having joint rulers in different parts of the empire allows local military rebellions to be put down more easily. Maximian, Diocletian's fellow Augustus, is also to abdicate, leaving the empire to the Caesars, Constantius in the west and Galerius in the east. So far, the *tetrarchy* seems to have worked.

Barbarians pillage Chinese capital

China, 311

Loyang, the imperial capital, has been pillaged by the Xiongnu, the barbarians from the north. Taking advantage of the political chaos under the Jins, the Xiongnu leader, Liu Cong, has burnt the imperial palace and taken the Jin emperor prisoner. The Great Wall was built to keep out these wild horsemen, and they were brought under control by the Han dynasty. But one of the warring Jin princes made the fatal mistake of employing Liu Cong as a mercenary, only for him to turn against his employer.

New coin minted to beat inflation

Trier, Gaul, 310

In an attempt to offset the depreciation of the denarius and restore stability to the imperial currency, the Emperor Constantine has ordered the minting of a new gold coin, the *solidus*, at his capital Trier. The introduction of the *solidus*, of which there are 72 to a pound of gold, means that from now on the imperial financial system will be once more based on the value of solid gold, which should increase the purchasing power of Roman currency. Civil servants and soldiers, who are paid in gold, are among those who will benefit.

A variety of imperial coinage.

Constantine alone rules over empire

Nicomedia, Asia Minor, 25 July 325
Sumptuous festivities are under way here, celebrating both 20 years in power for the Emperor Constantine and his victory last year at Chrysopolis over his former ally, Licinius. The final breach with Licinius, who controlled the eastern half of the empire, came when he broke his promise to Constantine to give toleration to Christians. Constantine defeated him and captured Byzantium. Today Christian priests, in council near Nicaea, will celebrate with him.

Constantine is the son of an emperor and his concubine, a Christian born in Bithynia of humble origins. His family was excluded from the succession by the Emperor Diocletian in 305. He fled to join his father fighting in Britain, and was proclaimed emperor there in 306 on the day of his father's death.

Triumphal arch in Rome to the man who restored imperial monarchy.

Edict of Milan grants toleration to Christians in Roman empire

Milan, 3 February 313
The Emperor Constantine, the master of the western empire, and Licinius, the most powerful man in the east, agreed a new policy here today of absolute toleration for Christians. They signed an edict guaranteeing it and restoring to them any confiscated property.

Persecution of the Christians in Rome began under Diocletian in 303 and reached its peak under his successors Galerius and Maximian. Constantine has been working hard for toleration for many years. He is himself the son of a Christian mother, Helena. He was born in 272 in Naissus (*in Yugoslavia*) and

educated at the imperial court of Diocletian. After he became emperor in 306 he became devoted to the cult of the Unconquered Sun.

His religious views changed radically in 312 when he was in Italy fighting Maxentius, the son of Maximian. Just before the battle he saw a cross of light superimposed on the sun. From then on he identified the sun with the Christian God. He ordered his men to go into battle with Christian symbols painted on their shields. They quickly won a famous victory at the Milvian Bridge, just outside Rome, on 28 October and Constantine became ruler of the west.

Constantine: policy of tolerance.

Clever compromise looks set to unify Christian Church

Nicaea, Asia Minor, 20 May 325
The Emperor Constantine, dressed in purple robes to stress the sacred nature of his power, today inaugurated the Ecumenical Council of Nicaea. He has summoned bishops from all over the empire to meet here to settle the violent controversies which have been raging in the church for the past seven years.

The split has arisen because of the doctrine of an Alexandrian priest, Arius, who questions the full divinity of Christ. Arius argues that if Christ is the Son of God he cannot be eternal since he had a beginning. Therefore he was not wholly God, but was inferior to God the Father. What began as an academic theological debate has spread to Christian congregations throughout the empire and there is a real danger of a lasting schism. Constantine is now using his skills as a peacemaker in the spiritual sphere; his advisers have devised a compromise solution which looks likely to carry the Council.

He is urging the adoption of a new creed which affirms that Christ "is of one substance with the Father". Superficially this looks like a victory for the orthodox church over the Arians. In fact the cleverly-worded creed is much more ambiguous, and many leading Arians have already said that they are prepared to adopt it. As the Council opens there is a hard core of 200 Arians opposing it, but Constantine should win and achieve a strong unified church barely 12 years after the persecutions.

Christian lives as a hermit in desert

Egypt, 312
After 20 years alone in the desert, and seven more years establishing Christianity's first community of hermits, Anthony is retreating further into the desert. Born in Memphis 60 years ago, he spends his time rope-plaiting and meditating, his solitude occasionally interrupted by fellow hermits seeking moral strength.

ABC gives mathematician the answers

Alexandria, c.310
A Greek mathematician living in Alexandria has published a treatise outlining a fascinating new method of calculation which he calls *Arithmetika*. It is better known by its Arabic name of *algebra*.

In his 13-volume work, the author, Diophantus, is indebted to a tradition that goes back ultimately to Babylonian mathematics, but his method and approach are entirely original.

In the *Arithmetika*, letters are employed to express unknown quantities, connected by signs expressing their relations to each other. By constructing and solving equations, Diophantus shows how values for the unknowns can be determined.

His work is considered the biggest step forward in mathematics since the work of Euclid, another Alexandrian, who published his *Elements* 600 years ago.

New Roman capital to be at Byzantium

Byzantium, Asia Minor, 324
Constantine has officially founded a new capital of the empire, which is to be built on the site of the old Greek colony of Byzantium on the Propontis (Sea of Marmara). The city, called "Constantinople" or "city of Constantine", is near the scene of the emperor's victory this year over his rival Licinius, and is of great strategic importance.

Constantinople, 11 May 330. Constantine has chosen to make the town of Byzantium, on the southern end of the Bosporus, the new capital of his empire. It is now dedicated and is called Constantinople after the emperor.

Constantinople, 331. The philosopher Sopatrus, a pupil of Porphyry, who has been accused of practising magic, is beheaded, and the books of the neo-Platonists are burnt.

Constantinople, 331. In an open expression of hostility towards paganism, Constantine orders the confiscation of the temple treasures throughout the empire. He vigorously promotes the Christian faith.

Ethiopia, 333. Ezana, who became king of Axum in 320, is converted to Christianity by a Coptic missionary called Frumentius. Frumentius is then consecrated *abuna* (bishop) of Ethiopia by Athanasius, the patriarch of Alexandria.

Jerusalem, 335. The church of the Holy Sepulchre is consecrated.

India, c.335. Chandragupta, king of Magadha, who founded the Gupta dynasty in 320, is dead. He is succeeded by Samudragupta, who sets about creating an empire in the Ganges plain.

Constantinople, 336. Having been condemned by the council of Tyre for his uncompromising attitude to Arians and Melitans, Athanasius, patriarch of Alexandria since 328, appeals to Constantine. But the Arian bishop Eusebius persuades the emperor to exile Athanasius to Trier in Gaul.

Constantinople, 336. Despite the death of the Alexandrian priest Arius, the Arian heresy he propounded lives on.

Asia Minor, 22 May 337. After a deathbed baptism, Constantine dies in his villa near Ancyra in Nicomedia. He is buried in the church of the Holy Apostles in Constantinople.

Constantinople, 9 September 337. Constantine's three sons, already Caesars, each take the title of Augustus. Constantine II and Constans share out the west. Constantius II takes control of the east.

Italy, March 340. After defeating and killing his brother Constantine II at Aquileia in northern Italy, Constans unites the whole of the west under his rule.

Rome, 340. Pope Julius holds a synod attended by Athanasius and other exiled eastern bishops. In a letter to the eastern churches he supports their position and asserts the primacy of his see.

Mesopotamia, 341. Thousands of Christians die from persecution in Seleucia.

Balkans, 343. The emperors try to heal the split between the eastern and western churches by calling a joint council at Sardia in Thrace, but after much hurling of insults the only result is deadlock.

Egypt, 21 October 346. Under heavy imperial pressure, the eastern and western churches reach a nervous compromise at Alexandria. Athanasius is restored to his see.

Mesopotamia, 348. The bloody battle of Singara between Shapur II, king of the Persians, and Constantius II ends indecisively.

Kush, 350. Meroe, capital of Kush (Sudan), is destroyed by the Ethiopian forces of Axum under the leadership of King Ezana. Earlier, Axum allied itself with the Romans against Meroe, which succeeded in resisting Roman power.

China, 350. Wei Furen, the "mother of calligraphy", is dead. Honoured in the *Book of 100 Beauties*, she established the art of fine writing and inspired China's leading practitioners.

Gaul, 350. Constans is murdered in a coup d'etat by the military commander Magnentius, who defeats his rivals and usurps the western empire.

Gaul, August 353. Constantius II follows up his victory over Magnentius at Mursa in 351 by pursuing the usurper into Gaul. Defeated for the second time, Magnentius commits suicide. Constantius II becomes sole emperor.

Gaul, 355. The Alamanni, a Germanic barbarian tribe, cross the Rhine and wreak havoc in eastern Gaul.

Constantinople, 19 February 356. Constantius II issues a decree giving orders for all the pagan temples in the Roman empire to be closed.

Egypt, 356. Athanasius, the former patriarch of Alexandria, takes refuge in a remote desert in upper Egypt after being expelled again from Alexandria by the pro-Arian Emperor Constantius II.

Rome, 28 April 357. Constantius II visits Rome for the first time, to celebrate his victory over Magnentius and to address the Senate and the Roman people.

Gaul, 25 August 357. Julian, who was made Caesar on 6 November 355 by his cousin Constantius II, defeats the Alamanni at Strasbourg and drives them back behind the Rhine.

First Christian basilicas appear in Rome

Early Christian sarcophagus from Rome, showing the Good Shepherd.

Rome, 337
Although it is only 25 years since Christians were regularly persecuted in Rome, at least five Christian basilicas have now been built with the help of the Emperor Constantine. They are mostly outside the town walls, on the sites of Christian cemeteries. The only internal church, Saint John Lateran, is on imperial land next to the Lateran Palace and is the bishop's cathedral. Most of the basilicas have five aisles, like Saint Peter's on the Vatican Hill, which is built over the tomb of the Apostle. Other notable churches include Saint Agnes on the Via Nomentana, Saint Sebastian on the Appian Way and Saint Paul without-the-Walls.

Heretical bishop had emperor's ear

Nicomedia, 337
Shortly before his death at Pentecost the Emperor Constantine was baptised by Eusebius, the brilliant leader of the Arian heresy. It underlines how strong the Arians are, as orthodox church leaders had thought that they had won the day when they secured the adoption of the Nicene Creed in 325.

Eusebius has used his position at Nicomedia to gain Constantine's confidence and oust orthodox opponents. He discredited bishops from Antioch, Alexandria and Ancyra in his pursuit of power.

Italian mosaic showing a victorious gladiator kneeling beside the body of the opponent he has just defeated and killed in the arena.

New capital consecrated

Byzantine gold cup with a figure representing the city of Constantinople.

Constantinople, 11 May 330
The Roman empire, for so long centred on the town after which it is named, has a new capital: Constantinople, named after the Emperor Constantine and built over the ancient city of Byzantium.

The new capital is ideally situated. It stands on the Bosporus, the crossroads of Europe and Asia, of the Black Sea and the Mediter-

ranean, and of many land and sea routes. In imperial terms it is midway between the Danubian and Oriental frontiers.

The geographical move is also a religious one: this new city, its magnificent churches resplendent with masterpieces imported from every land, will be a truly Christian capital. Only its government duplicates that of Rome.

Maya live peacefully in city states

Central America, c.350
The Maya civilisation is flowering all over Honduras, Guatemala and southern Mexico, producing the most advanced urban civilisation in the Americas.

There is no one single dominant power among the Maya. The people live in city-states, at peace with one another and freely exchanging commerce and ideas. Political control is in the hands of the high priests, but they do not have political ambitions and their armies never go to war with each other, reserving their resources for colonial campaigns against subject tribes.

This new era of Maya civilisation is epitomised by the architecture in Maya cities. In Copan, Tikal, Chichen Itza and Quirigua are temples, pyramids and obelisks more elaborate, yet much more serene than anything before them. Outside the cities, in the surrounding farms, corn, cotton, tobacco, cocoa and fruit are cultivated, and bees are kept. In addition the Maya have created their own alphabet of

Maya jade bead of the Sun God.

syllables, symbols and pictures, and formulated a calendar of 365 days, based on the fifty-two week cycle common to all contemporary Mesoamerican civilisations.

Christian Ethiopia is trade centre

Ethiopia, 350
Since the defeat of Kush by Ezana, the first Christian king of Ethiopia, his capital Axum has become the commercial crossroads of north east Africa and capital of the most powerful independent African

state. Axum itself is an architectural wonder of towers, palaces and obelisks. Dominating it is the vast newly-built Cathedral of St Mary, the seat of Frumentius, the bishop of Ethiopia, who brought Christianity to the country 23 years ago.

Goths get new translation of the Bible

Eastern Europe, c.350
The Holy Scriptures are being expressed in a barbarian language for the first time. Ulfilas, the first Gothic bishop, has undertaken an astonishing labour as well as an act of faith in this Biblical translation into his people's vernacular.

He has had to create a new, holy

version of the Goths' language, since some Christian ideas can only be conveyed by adapting Latin words for use as part of Gothic vocabulary. And he has even had to expand that basic building block the alphabet, because the Gothic script was inadequate. It is not the complete Bible, but it is enough.

Some of the many obelisks which give Axum a distinctive skyline.

Pilgrims flock to church on Christ's tomb

Jerusalem, 17 September 335
Christians from every corner of the empire are expected to flock to Jerusalem to see Christianity's greatest shrine, the Holy Sepulchre, which was consecrated with great festivities today. Christ's tomb on Golgotha was discovered seven years ago, on the site of an old temple to Aphrodite. The Emperor Constantine declared the site a holy place and ordered the construction of a vast complex. Opened today, it consists of a rotunda which houses the Holy Sepulchre itself, and an attached basilica with five aisles and a large atrium.

The later church at the Sepulchre.

Syria, 359. Shapur II, the Sassanian king of Persia, invades Syria and captures the Roman town of Amida after a long struggle.

Italy/Mesopotamia, 359. Two separate councils of the western and eastern churches are held, at Rimini and Seleucia. Each is persuaded to accept a pro-Arian creed put forward by the advisers of the Emperor Constantius II.

Constantinople, 360. A council ratifies pro-Arian alterations to the Nicene creed.

Mesopotamia, 360. The Persians, under the leadership of Shapur II, capture Singara and Bezabde in battles with the Romans.

Gaul, February 360. In Paris, Julian – who, as Caesar in charge of Gaul and Britain, has subdued the Franks and the Alamanni and restored the Rhine frontier – is declared Augustus by his army. This follows a request by the Emperor Constantius II to send some of his men to the east, at which Julian's troops mutinied.

Asia Minor, November 361. Constantius II dies of fever on his way to fight Julian, who is marching east to attack him. Julian becomes sole emperor.

Syria, 17 June 362. The Emperor Julian passes an edict banning Christians from teaching grammar and rhetoric. He has already revealed himself to be a pagan and has proclaimed toleration for all religions.

Persia, 26 June 363. Julian has invaded Persia. Having defeated the Persians outside the walls of their capital, Ctesiphon, he is fatally wounded while retreating up the Tigris. His death brings an end to the pagan revival.

Persia, 363. Jovian, who served in the Persian campaign under Julian and was hastily chosen as emperor on his death, concludes a dishonourable peace treaty with Shapur II. He surrenders to the Persians all the territory which Diocletian had won in the east, as well as the imperial cities of Nisibis and Singara.

Asia Minor, 26 February 364. On the death of Jovian, a conference at Nicaea chooses Valentinian, an army officer who was born in the central European region of Pannonia in 321, to succeed him.

Constantinople, 28 March 364. Valentinian appoints his brother Valens to govern the east. For the first time, the division of rule over the empire is accompanied by a true division of resources and armies between the west and the east.

Gaul, 367. Hilary, who became bishop of Poitiers c.350 and won fame for his treatise on the Trinity, dies. A staunch opponent of the Arian heresy, he wrote three outspoken addresses to the Emperor Constantius II on the subject.

Gaul, 368. Valentinian, based at Trier, defeats the Alamanni in the course of a long series of campaigns against them on the Rhine frontier.

Roman Empire, 368. A *defensor civitatis* (defender of the city) is appointed in each city to protect humble people against the powerful and to provide them with an inexpensive and accessible court of justice.

Armenia, 369. Shapur II, the Sassanian king of the Persians, occupies the pro-Roman kingdom of Armenia.

Central Europe, 369. Valens forces the Visigoths of King Athanaric to accept an unfavourable treaty on the Danubian frontier.

Korea, 369. A Japanese expeditionary force lands in south Korea and establishes a colony, Mimama, bordered by the coast.

Gaul, 372. Martin, a disciple of Hilary of Poitiers, is made bishop of Tours. Born c.316 in Pannonia, Martin served in the Roman army before joining the clergy. He has established one of the first hermit communities in the west.

Egypt, 2 May 373. Athanasius, the patriarch who fiercely defended Nicene orthodoxy against the Arian heresy, dies at Alexandria. He played an important role in the spread of monasticism.

India, 375. Samudragupta, who came to the throne in 335 and created a vast empire in the Ganges plain, is dead.

Guatemala, 375. In the first recorded royal accession in a Maya city, "Curl Snout" becomes king of Tikal in the Peten jungle.

Ukraine, 375. The nomadic people known as the Huns, moving steadily eastwards from the steppes of central Asia, defeat and conquer the Ostrogoths. In consequence, the Ostrogothic king Ermanaric commits suicide.

Central Europe, 17 November 375. Enraged by the insolence of barbarian envoys, Valentinian dies of apoplexy in Pannonia. His elder son Gratian, aged 16, is proclaimed emperor of the west.

Balkans, 376. The Visigoths, who have been inhabiting part of Dacia for the past 150 years, are driven by the Huns to seek Roman permission to cross the lower Danube. Permission is granted.

The Huns invade Europe

Upper Danube Basin, 375

Roman forces on this boundary of the empire are watching an increasing horde of barbarians on the north bank of the Danube. They are their old enemies the Goths, but this time these warriors are themselves under attack and have become refugees seeking asylum on Roman territory from the attacks of new invaders – the Huns.

From desolate Siberian deserts around Lake Baikal, the Huns have driven westwards. They are perceived by their victims as subhuman – beardless, stocky figures hardened by cold, impervious to hunger and pain, who fight, hunt, kill, eat and sleep in the saddle. If these legends are to be believed, the Huns are unsurpassed marksmen with bow or lasso while on horseback. Certainly, they have swept aside peoples who themselves had won warlike reputations. Nomadic Alans living between the rivers Don and Volga were the first to confront the invasion, and prudently changed sides. The migration has become a tidal wave of Germanic tribes, from Ostrogoth to Visigoth – heralds of a storm to come. These heralds might not yet be at the gates of Rome, but they are just across the river and threaten to intensify the pressures on the empire.

Julian, the pagan emperor, has died

Cameo, probably of the anti-Christian Emperor Julian and his wife.

Antioch, Syria, 26 June 363

After less than two years as Roman emperor, Julian has died of wounds on his campaign against the Persians. He set out from here earlier this year and reached Ctesiphon, on the Tigris, before being forced to retreat. He was only 31.

Julian had also campaigned to restore pagan worship in the empire and reverse its conversion to Christianity. For this he was called "the Apostate", but his campaign is likely to die with him. Julian, a bookish intellectual, studied philosophy and occultism in the east and rejected his Christian upbringing.

He was a nephew of the Emperor Constantine, and on the latter's death saw the rest of his family massacred by soldiers on the orders of the new emperor, his cousin Constantius. Julian was only five.

He declared himself a pagan in 361, when his cousin's death left him sole emperor. He restored the old temples to the Olympian gods, revived the ritual sacrifices of oxen, which he performed himself, and decreed that school teachers should renounce their Christianity. He wrote many theological works and a diatribe against Christian belief, which he saw as atheism.

Dispute over Jesus splits Christians

Mesopotamia and Italy, 359
Christian communities are in turmoil as bishops engage in furious controversy over the true nature of Jesus. A priest in Alexandria, Arius, started the row by preaching that God had created Jesus from nothing. He was denounced, on the grounds that he had made Jesus not the equal of God the Father, but a rival demi-god.

Arius' teaching was condemned in 325 by the Ecumenical Council of Nicaea, which laid down that Jesus was "of the essence of the Father, not made, being of one substance ...".

Arianism, however, is still on top, because, in Constantinople, emperors have backed the heresy. Two church councils, one for the east at Selencia and one for the west at Rimini, have just declared that the Son is only "similar" to the Father, thereby overturning the decision of Nicaea. The opponent of Arianism, Jerome, complains: "The whole world groans and marvels to find itself Arian."

Civil servant army runs Roman Empire

Rome, c.373
The government of the Roman empire has reached new heights of centralisation and top-heaviness. With an army of 500,000 men to maintain, taxes are heavy and an army of officials runs the system.

The sophisticated civil service surrounding the emperor is headed by a *Consistory*, or Imperial Council, comprising the heads of departments of state. The head of the civil service is the Master of the Offices; the *Comes* (Count) of the Sacred Largesse controls the treasury and the mint; the Count of the Imperial Portfolio controls the vast public and imperial estates; the *Quaestor* of the Sacred Palace draws up the edicts of the emperor in literary form; the *Primicerius Notariorum* is in charge of the writing office, or chancery. The empire is administered by the three Praetorian Prefects, whose areas are divided into dioceses and provinces, each with its governor.

A row of stone buddhas from the imperial Gupta period.

Samudragupta leaves India a rich legacy

India, 375
Samudragupta, the Gupta monarch who extended his rule from a tiny kingdom to an empire dominating all northern and central India, is dead. The "Poet King", who was as much a patron of the arts as a warrior leader, died peacefully. Tributes extolling his virtues are already being engraved on a stone pillar originally set up by Asoka some six centuries earlier.

In his military campaigns he subdued the Vakatakas in central India, the Nagas in northern India, the Maghas of Kausambi, the Kosalas of the Ganges, and the remnants of the Kushan empire. Other territories came to Samudragupta through marriages and political alliances. Using his family to govern his provinces, and maintaining compliant rulers in his tributary nations, he ruled one of the largest empires India has seen.

On his return from an expedition in the Dekhan, he performed the ancient Vedic ritual of *asvamedha*, or horse sacrifice, abandoned since the second century, thus by implication proclaiming himself universal monarch.

Although a fervent worshipper of Vishnu, his policy of religious toleration as well as his role as a patron of the arts will also be remembered; the image of him, as depicted on his gold coins playing the lute, has become common currency among his people.

Rome and Persia sign peace treaty

Mesopotamia, Summer 363
Rome and Persia have signed a 30-year peace treaty. The terms are largely dictated by Shapur II, who has repulsed an attack on Mesopotamia by the legions of the Emperor Jovian. The *satrapies* annexed by Rome in 298 are returned to Persia, as are the fortresses of Nisibis and Singara, and half of Armenia. Rome is to pay a tribute to Persia to help fortify Caucasius against the Alans.

Shapur's treaty, the greatest triumph of his 30 years' rule, marks the high point of the Sassanian empire. The Persian nobles are loyal subjects at last; cavalry power ensures Shapur's dominance and Persian security.

Later impression of Jovian.

Anti-heretic bishop Athanasius is dead

Alexandria, 2 May 373
Bishop Athanasius, the patriarch of Alexandria, has died at the age of around 77. He was the most formidable and uncompromising opponent of the Arian heresy, championing against it the true divinity of Christ and his full equality with the Father. For this he suffered exile from Alexandria on five occasions on the orders of emperors unsympathetic to his extreme stand.

He also played a key role in the spread of monasticism, partly by his biography of St Anthony; through him that monasticism was introduced to the western empire.

SASANIAN EMPIRE · VAUDHEYAS · ARJUNAYANAS · MALAVAS · SAKAS · VAKATAKAS · KADAMBAS · R. Indus · NAGAS · NEPALA · R. Ganges · MAGADHA · R. Brahmaputra · KAMARUPA · DAVAKA · PARIVRAJAKAS UCCHAKAL PAS · PUNDRA VARDHANA · SAMATATA · SALANKAYNA · Bay of Bengal · Arabian Sea · PALLAVAS · Indian Ocean

Empire of Samudragupta,375
Tributary peoples of Samudragupta
Temporary tributary of Samudragupta

Asia Minor, August 378. Valens, emperor of the east, is defeated and fatally wounded in a battle against the Visigoths at Adrianople.

Balkans, January 379. To help him control the crisis within the empire, Gratian appoints the Spaniard Theodosius as the new Augustus of the east. Theodosius takes charge of the war against the Goths.

Gaul, 379. The poet Ausonius, a former tutor of the Emperor Gratian and governor of Gaul, is made consul. Ausonius taught for 30 years in his native Bordeaux and composed epigrams, idylls and letters in verse and prose.

China, 379. The celebrated calligrapher Wang Xizhi dies. He was one of the inventors of *cao shu*, a cursive type of handwriting, elegantly elongated, which breaks with the former rigid Han style.

Constantinople, 381. The new pro-Nicene Emperor Theodosius summons an ecumenical council to Constantinople, at which Arianism is finally condemned once and for all. Gratian follows suit in the west.

Italy, 382. Gratian formally moves the imperial court from Rome to Milan – probably to be nearer the frontier armies and ready to deal with any crises. Emperors now rarely visit Rome.

Balkans, 15 August 383. Theodosius signs a peace treaty with the Visigoths giving them land and political autonomy within the empire in return for military service.

China, 383. The non-Chinese warrior Fu Jian – whose empire, the Former Jin, has grown rapidly in northern China – is decisively defeated in his attempt to move southward in the battle of the Fei river in central Anhui. The threat of extinction of the Chinese Jin dynasty is removed.

Gaul, 15 August 383. After Maximus, proclaimed emperor by the troops in Britain, invades Gaul, Gratian is murdered by his troops at Lyons. Maximus is proclaimed emperor by the army.

Rome, 384. Pope Damasus II dies. He stressed Rome's primacy as the apostolic see and acquired increased juridical control over the church.

South Africa, 385. Copper mining and smelting has begun at Kansanshi in the Katanga (Shaba) copperbelt (*on the Zaire-Zambia border*).

Rome, 385. Ammianus Marcellinus begins to write a history, modelled on that of Tacitus, covering the years from 96 to 378.

Syria, 386. Libanius, a friend of the Emperor Julian and the mouthpiece of the pagans, makes an impassioned speech at Antioch "In defence of the temples". But his struggle against anti-pagan legislation is proving totally unsuccessful.

Italy, 387. Maximus invades Italy and drives out Valentinian II, Gratian's younger brother, who appeals to Theodosius.

China, 387. The Northern Wei dynasty is founded, with its capital at Pingcheng (Datong). Until now China has been a battleground for various short-lived dynasties of non-Chinese origin. The Toba people of Mongolian origin who found this dynasty prove to have a far greater capacity for bringing stability to northern China.

Italy, 388. After two defeats by Theodosius, Maximus surrenders and is executed at Aquileia.

Armenia, c.390. Theodosius and Shapur III sign a treaty agreeing on a partition of Armenia between the Roman and Persian empires.

Milan, 25 December 390. Ambrose, bishop of Milan, forces the Emperor Theodosius to perform public penance for his massacre of thousands of the rebellious citizens of Thessalonica.

Japan, 391. Invaders from Yamato overrun Silla and Paekche and start an expedition into Kokuri.

Italy, 392. Valentinian II, Augustus of Italy and Illyricum, is murdered on 15 May by his Frankish military commander Arbogast, who proclaims Eugenius, a Roman professor of rhetoric, emperor. Eugenius makes vain attempts to restore paganism.

Italy, 8 November 392. Theodosius passes legislation prohibiting all pagan worship in the empire.

Greece, 393. As part of Theodosius' drive against paganism, the Olympic Games are suspended for the first time in their 1,000-year history.

Italy, 6 September 394. Theodosius defeats and kills the usurper Eugenius and his general Arbogast at the battle of the River Frigidus. Theodosius is now sole emperor.

Milan, 17 January 395. Theodosius dies and is succeeded by his two sons. The empire is once again divided. Arcadius, aged 18, controls the east; Honorius, aged 10, takes the west. The border dividing the empire crosses the Balkans and the Libyan desert.

Milan, 4 April 397. Ambrose, bishop of Milan, aristocrat and theologian, dies. He has been a dominant force in ecclesiastical and secular affairs for 20 years.

Emperor Valens defeated and dies in fire

Valens offers the hand of asylum to the Visigoths in this 19th-century view.

Rome, August 378

The Emperor Valens, who gave sanctuary to the Visigoths after their flight from the Huns, has been killed by barbarians. Three years ago Valens responded to their pleas for asylum, and many thousands crossed the Danube to reach Thrace.

Local Roman commanders took advantage of the situation to impose slavery on some refugees. The rest ran wild. At a banquet hosted by Roman officers some Visigoth leaders learned that their bodyguards had been butchered. Hostilities followed and, in the battle of Adrianople, the Visigoth King Fritigern, aided by Alans and Ostrogoth cavalry, defeated the Romans led by Valens. The wounded emperor was carried to an house which the enemy then burnt down. The defeat has caused panic in Constantinople where Gothic troops serving in the Roman army have been massacred as a precaution, lest they join the enemy.

The emperor Theodosius at the Constantinople hippodrome, c.399.

Buddhist shrine at Loyang in China, where Buddhism is becoming popular.

Monk introduces Buddhism into China

China, 399
Buddhism is spreading through China, working its way along the trade routes from central Asia and India. Regarded as something of an intellectual curiosity by the Han court, it is now a recognised religion, and Indian translators are working on the huge task of providing Chinese versions of the original teachings in Sanskrit.

Paradoxically, Buddhism owes much to the fall of the Hans and the "age of confusion" which followed, for when the Xiongnu occupied Loyang the Confucian scholars fled, leaving the field open to Buddhist monks who provided the barbarian conquerors with a literate civil service.

The small states of the north which have easy contact with India are particularly receptive to Buddhism. Kumarajiva, a monk of Indian descent born in central Asia, is teaching at Changan in Shensi province, preaching versions of the religion previously unknown in China. Chinese monks are also finding their own path to the secrets of Buddhism, travelling along the Silk Road to study the true doctrine at the sources of their religion.

One such monk, Faxian, has just set out from Changan on this long pilgrimage. Although he is over 60 years old he plans to spend several years walking the Silk Road, visiting temples, studying with holy men, and recording the traditions and customs of the countries through which he passes.

Theodosius becomes sole ruler of empire

Italy, 391
Theodosius, born in Spain, the son of an army general, has needed all his military skills to defeat his rivals for the imperial purple and hold the splitting empire together. After killing usurpers and puppets, as he calls them, he has reunited the empires of east and west. But he has been compelled to make some risky concessions.

After a three-year war with the Goths in Thrace, who threatened Constantinople, he signed a treaty accepting them into the empire, which has never before accepted undefeated barbarian tribes within its frontiers, and recruiting them into the army.

Theodosius, depicted on a dish.

A bishop forces emperor to do penance

Roman Empire, 25 December 390
The Emperor Theodosius was today forced to do penance for a massacre which he ordered. It was the culmination of events which began when a charioteer, accused of indecency after the emperor had banned homosexuality, was arrested by an over-zealous army officer.

The citizens of Thessalonica rioted, and Theodosius ordered a massacre to teach the people a lesson. That upset Bishop Ambrose of Milan, and today the bishop made his emperor pay public penance.

Theodosius is a devout Christian, and one of his first actions after he had established himself in power was to call an Ecumenical Council in Constantinople in 381 to unite the Church and denounce the Arian heresy, which denies that Jesus shared God the Father's divinity. Theodosius set about rooting out Arianism, which still exists among many barbarian peoples.

A 14th-century statue of Ambrose.

Emperor bans all forms of pagan ritual

A pagan couple, c.390.

Roman Empire, 391
Declaring that Christianity and paganism cannot live side by side, Theodosius has seized pagan temples, broken up the statues of their gods and prohibited on pain of death the practising of pagan rites, even in private at home. The traditional faiths have survived among senators with their nostalgia for the days when they enjoyed power and prestige. Now the Altar of Victory, on which incense was burned at the start of each session of the Senate, has been taken away.

Woman teaches philosophy in Alexandria

Alexandria, c.395
Students of mathematics and philosophy at the university here have an unusual and extremely popular teacher. She is a woman, Hypatia, daughter of the mathematician Theon. Scholars from all over the Greek world attend her lectures, and she is known simply as "The Nurse" or "The Philosopher".

Hypatia established her reputation as a mathematician while in Athens studying under Plutarch the Younger and his daughter Asclepegeneia. On returning to Alexandria she was invited to lecture at the university, and now teaches geometry, astronomy and the new science of algebra. She has also invented two astronomical instruments, an astrolabe and a planisphere.

Her philosophy is neo-Platonic, embracing a scientific rationalism which runs counter to Christian beliefs. Cyril, the Patriarch of Alexandria, would like nothing better than to rid the city of her.

The barbarian conquest of Rome

After the death of Augustus in AD14 the Rhine and the Danube essentially marked the limits of the Roman empire in Europe. This frontier was not seriously breached until the 250s, a time of civil war and economic and social crisis within the empire.

The wealth and luxury of the empire were the main attractions for the barbarians. Many of them had experience of Roman wealth at first-hand, fighting as mercenaries for Roman armies against other barbarians or rival claimants to the imperial throne. Trade with Roman merchants also illustrated what luxuries lay just across the frontier. Germanic rulers depended on the support of their warrior followers, which could only be obtained and kept if suitable rewards were provided. Leadership was therefore dependent on the continuous acquisition of plunder.

Early in the third century barbarian groups like the Franks and the Alamanni appeared on the frontier for the first time. These were not new arrivals, but new combinations of several long-established smaller tribal units. The wealth and weakness of the empire in the third century made it the obvious target for these more powerful confederations.

The frontier temporarily collapsed and barbarians penetrated the empire at various points; the Goths ravaged Greece and Asia Minor (258-69), the Franks cut a swathe through Gaul and reached Spain (268-78), the Alamanni went over the Alps into Italy and even menaced Rome itself (260-78), and the seaborne Saxons began their raids along the coasts of Britain and Gaul.

False sense of security

A series of effective emperors arrested the crisis and restored the frontier. Diocletian (268-304) completely re-shaped the internal structure of the empire in order to increase its military effectiveness. But the events of the third century prefigured what was to come: the notion of imperial invincibility had been destroyed.

For almost a century after Diocletian's reorganisation the empire's frontiers remained more or less intact. The Alamanni repeatedly crossed the Rhine, but each time they were successfully repulsed. On the Danube a treaty was established with the Goths. But around 370 the situation changed dramatically with the arrival of the Huns on the eastern fringes of Europe. This tribe, squat, ugly and strange to European eyes, came from the steppes of central Asia; they terrified Romans and barbarians alike. Defeated by them in the Ukraine in 375, the Goths and Alans panicked and rushed westwards. A chain reaction was set in motion; in their eagerness to get away from the Huns, the barbarians now became all the more anxious to cross the frontiers of the Roman empire.

Their primary objective now was not booty but land on which to settle. The Visigoths offered to serve in the imperial army in return for land within the empire; they were formally permitted to cross the Danube in 376. They were exploited by the imperial administration and two years later they revolted, killed the Emperor Valens and slaughtered his army outside Adrianople. The Visigoths spent the next forty years wandering across the empire, from the Balkans into Italy, where they sacked Rome (410), and then on into Gaul (412) and Spain (415), looking for somewhere to settle.

Meanwhile, the Huns had continued their rapid progress westwards as far as Pannonia on the upper Danube. The pressure now increased on the peoples behind the Rhine frontier. On the last day of December 406 the Rhine froze; the Vandals, Sueves and Alans took advantage of the fact to sweep across it in vast numbers and hurtle through Gaul. The frontier was lost.

The West caves in

The ensuing conflict took place within the former borders of the empire, but it was not a straightforward struggle for supremacy between Romans on one side and united barbarians on the other. The Roman forces were often involved in civil wars against other Romans, and the imperial army had in any case long been dependent on mercenary barbarian troops and commanders for its defence. This policy was now extended, and for a time the empire was able to survive by exploiting the long-standing feuds which divided the various tribes. But the price of barbarian support was not just tribute; the Barbarians wanted formal grants of land within the empire. Visigoths, for example, were used against the Alans and Vandals in Spain, and were ceded Aquitaine in return (418). The Huns were allowed to consolidate in Pannonia and were paid by the Romans to keep the Burgundians and Franks out of the empire.

When the Huns themselves advanced into Gaul under Attila, a great alliance of Romans and barbarians united to win a decisive victory at the battle of the Catalaunian Fields (451). But defence of the peripheral regions of the Western empire had become impossible. Roman troops were pulled out of Britain early in the fifth century, never to return. The Saxon raiders soon began to stay and overrun the island. The Vandals crossed the Straits of Gibraltar (429) and rapidly conquered the coastal province of Africa. From this base they controlled the western Mediterranean and menaced Italy with their fleet. The Visigoths and the Sueves were left to dispute control of Spain.

The barbarians consolidate

Behind these deep thrusts into the heart of the empire, a second group of invaders was slowly consolidating its positions on former imperial territory west of the Rhine: the Burgundians, the Alamanni and the Franks. Only between about 480 and 507 did this last group become dominant and rapidly advance from its heartland in modern Belgium. Under Clovis they defeated the remaining GalloRoman forces in northern Gaul (486), pushed the Alamanni into what is now Switzerland (506) and drove the Visigoths back into Spain (507). Clovis' successors finished off the Burgundians (534). Meanwhile in Italy the barbarian commander of the imperial forces, Odoacer, had finally dispensed with the fiction of imperial rule. The last puppet emperor of the West was deposed (476), and Odoacer ruled in the name of the Eastern emperor, but in reality as absolute ruler of Italy.

The Eastern emperor's response to Odoacer's seizure of power was to turn to the time-honoured imperial policy of playing the barbarians off against each other. The second branch of the Goths, the Ostrogoths, had been allowed by the Roman government of the East to settle in the Balkans, but under their king Theodoric they had begun to threaten Constantinople itself.

The Emperor Zeno solved the problem by employing Theodoric to go to Italy and deal with the upstart Odoacer. By 493 Italy had fallen to the Ostrogoths; Theodoric became the doyen of all the barbarian kings.

With the triumph of the Franks in Gaul the territorial situation was further resolved: almost the whole of Gaul was theirs, the Vandals controlled Africa, the Visigoths most of Spain and Septimania (Languedoc), the Sueves north-western Spain, and up in Britain the Anglo-Saxons were steadily driving the Romano-British population westward. Protected from barbarian invasion by the Caucasus Mountains, the Bosporus and the Persian empire, the richer Eastern empire was able to survive. The Western empire was in barbarian hands.

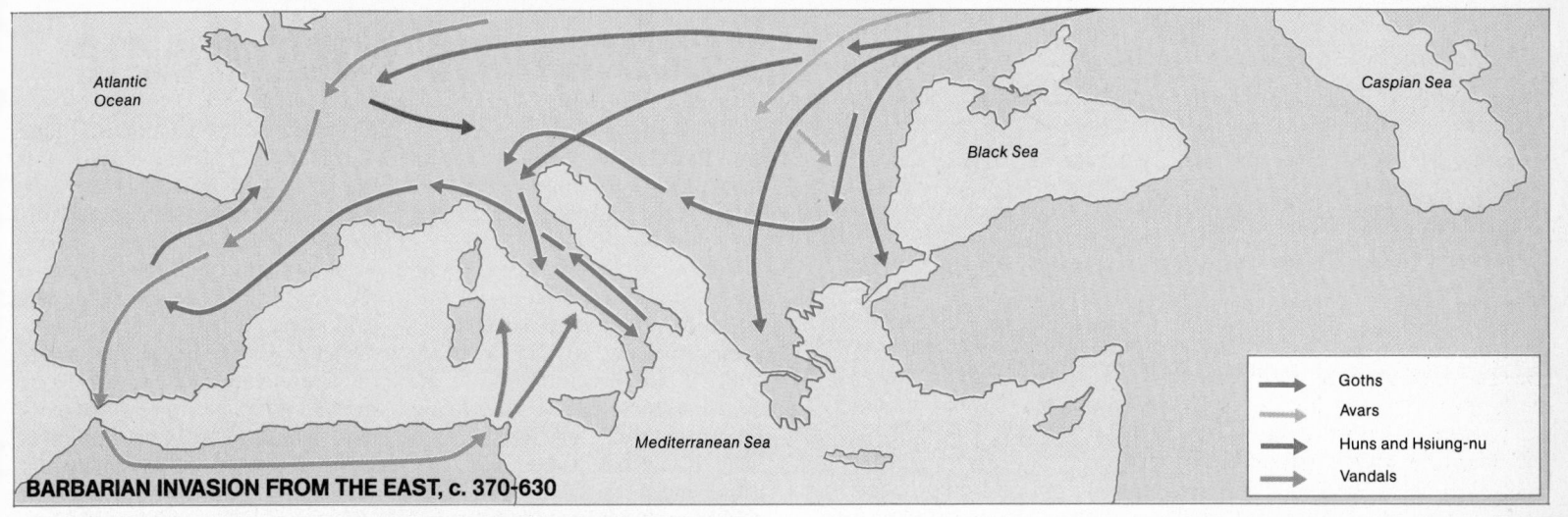

BARBARIAN INVASION FROM THE EAST, c. 370-630

→	Goths
→	Avars
→	Huns and Hsiung-nu
→	Vandals

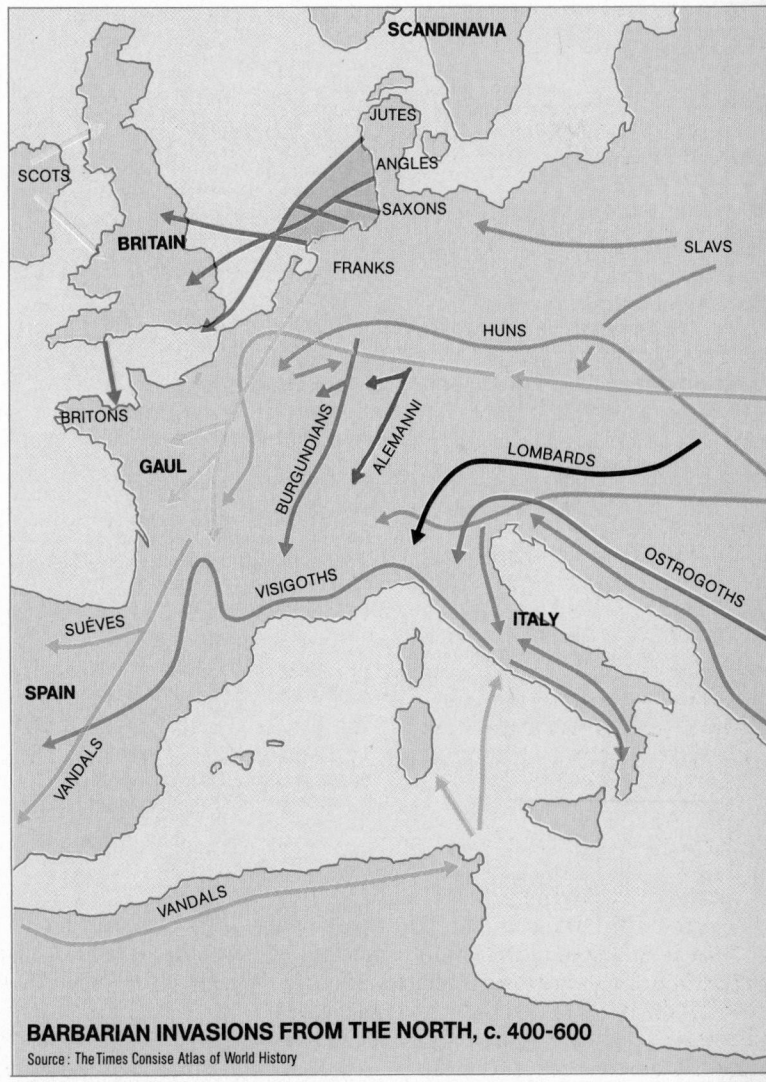

BARBARIAN INVASIONS FROM THE NORTH, c. 400-600

Source : The Times Consise Atlas of World History

A Roman soldier frog-marches a captured barbarian into captivity, from the Arch of Constantine, erected in Rome in 312 to commemorate the emperor's many victories. The pressure from the nations jostling on the "limes" – frontier – of the empire has been a constant headache to Rome since the early days of imperial conquest.

The barbarians fought for land and riches: neighbouring tribes coveted the wealth that they knew existed within the empire, and their leaders were driven by a real need to plunder sufficient booty to keep their soldiers loyal. This led to some trouble in the east, where Persian pride refused to accept Roman domination; in Britain, where persistent assaults on Roman positions *made it necessary to build physical frontiers to repel Caledonian tribes; and on the Danube, leading to the eventual evacuation of an entire province, Dacia, in 271.*

The situation on the Danube was again exacerbated a century later when the Huns arrived in eastern Europe from central Asia. The marauding newcomers drove terrified barbarians ahead of them and westwards into the empire. Many Germanic tribes, including the Goths and Vandals, crossed the imperial frontiers in an attempt to flee the Huns; it was on the western frontier that the flow of migrants finally turned into a tidal wave which the empire was powerless to stop.

Persia, 399. Yezdgerd succeeds to the throne of Persia. Tolerant of Christianity, he builds up good relations with the Romans.

Rome, 399. Fabiola, the first known woman surgeon, dies in Rome, where she is also famous for founding hospitals for the poor.

Central America, c.400. Building activity is reaching new heights at the Mexican city of Teotihuacan – with a population of 250,000, the sixth largest city in the world. People from the area are setting up colonial or trading posts 600 miles away at Kaminaljuyu. Teotihuacan is also exerting a strong cultural influence on Maya city-states such as Tikal and the Zapotec capital Monte Alban.

Italy, 401. The Visigoths under Alaric invade northern Italy from the Balkans.

Italy, 402. To escape the Visigothic threat, the court of the western empire is moved again, from Milan to Ravenna, a naturally well-defended site.

Verona, 402. The Visigoths are defeated in battle by the Roman army of the west, led by the Vandal Stilicho, supreme military commander and effective ruler of the western empire. He forces them out of Italy.

Constantinople, 404. The patriarch John Chrysostom is banished from Constantinople.

Italy, 23 August 406. On a march to Rome, pillaging barbarians from various tribes under the leadership of King Radagaisus are crushed by Stilicho with the aid of mercenary barbarian troops at Fiesole, near Florence.

Gaul, 31 December 406. Hordes of Vandals, Alans and Sueves take advantage of the exceptional cold to cross the frozen Rhine. The frontier is lost. Gaul is open for pillaging.

Gaul, 407. The usurper Constantine III leaves Britain, where he has been declared emperor by the army, and sets about saving Gaul from the barbarian invaders.

Constantinople, 1 May 408. On the death of Arcadius, the eastern emperor, his eight-year-old son Theodosius II, succeeds to the throne under the protection of the Praetorian prefect Anthemius, who has been in real control in the east since 405.

Ravenna, 23 August 408. With the Emperor Honorius, the aristocracy and the Roman troops against him, Stilicho is arrested and executed. The Roman forces foolishly massacre the families of the barbarian mercenaries who go off and join Alaric's army.

Gaul, 408. Constantine III moves the capital of Gaul from Trier to Arles and extends his authority into Spain.

Spain, 409. The Vandals, Alans and Sueves move from Gaul into Spain.

Rome, 24 August 410. The Visigoths under Alaric sack Rome.

Gaul, 411. The usurper Constantine III is besieged at Arles and finally captured by forces loyal to the Emperor Honorius.

Rhineland, 413. The Burgundians make a treaty with the empire by which they are allowed to settle on former imperial land beside the Rhine.

Constantinople, 413. The Praetorian prefect Anthemius has built the great walls of Constantinople, known as the Theodosian walls.

China, 413. The great Kuchean translator Kumarajiva dies. His excellent translations of Buddhist texts finally allow the Chinese to gain a real understanding of Buddhism as a philosophy.

Gaul, 1 January 414. At Narbonne, Athaulf, Alaric's successor as king of the Visigoths, marries Galla Placidia, the sister of the Emperor Honorius, who was taken hostage during the sack of Rome in 410. Athaulf led the Visigoths into Gaul in 412 and has seized the south-west of the country.

Constantinople, 414. At the age of only 15, Pulcheria, the sister of Theodosius II, becomes ruler of the eastern empire as regent for her weak-minded brother.

Alexandria, 415. The Greek mathematician and philosopher Hypatia, the leading intellectual of Alexandria, is tortured to death by a mob of Christian zealots incited by the patriarch Cyril. The fatal attack was provoked by Hypatia's scientific rationalism and authority as a woman, both of which ran counter to the dogma of emerging Christianity.

India, 420. A masterpiece of Indian literature, *The Ring of Sakuntula* by Kalidasa, is published. This drama illustrates the pious and chivalrous ideal of the Brahmans, and is at once acclaimed as peerless.

China, 420. Eastern Qin (Ch'in) is overthrown by its general, Liu Yu, who becomes the first Liu Song emperor. Liu Yu, born into great poverty, owes his rise to power to an exceptional military career. Fourteen years ago he temporarily recaptured the former capital of Loyang in northern China from its non-Chinese occupiers.

Barbarians sack Rome

Rome, 24 August 410

For three days German hordes have roamed the streets of Rome, burning and pillaging the greatest city in the known world.

Under their leader, King Alaric, the Visigoths have been an internal threat to the empire since being given sanctuary in 375, roaming from Thrace (where they had internal autonomy) to Illyricum. Epirus was theirs, but they invaded Italy. Rome has had to hire barbarian mercenaries, including Vandals, to meet the Visigoth threat.

The Emperor Honorius was with his army at Ravenna when he rejected Alaric's demands for gold and honours. Alaric instantly turned his followers loose on undefended Rome. Optimists (and there are still some) observe that the sacking of Rome has "no military significance" because the core of the Roman army and government are intact and unassailable at Ravenna. Few people elsewhere will assent to that.

Many people blame the growth of Christianity and the neglect of the old gods for Rome's weakness, but realists know that Romans have abdicated responsibility for defending themselves. Before the reforms of Gaius Marius the aristocracy fought its own corner – but that was 500 years ago. For six years entire tribes of Goths have been enrolled as protectors, but now they are taking over.

Chinese artist excels at religious themes

"The Lessons of the Instructress to the Ladies of Court", by Gu Kaizhi.

China, c.410

Figure painting, as well as landscape art, is a strong tradition in China. At the court of Nanking the painter Gu Kaizhi is admired for the certainty of his brushstrokes and his "fine wire line".

One of his best works is a scroll depicting "The Lessons of the Instructress to the Ladies of Court" in which she is giving instructions on how to appear beautiful. A poem accompanying the picture laments that, while many ladies know how to adorn their persons, few know how to beautify their souls.

Romans withdraw troops from Britain

Britain, 407

A letter home by a Roman centurion from a fort on Hadrian's Wall says it all: "The climate is cold, the men are cold and bored and long for the good wine and warm women of the southlands."

Led by Constantine, the common soldier whom they elected "emperor", the Roman army is leaving Britain – but not for Rome. Constantine is seeking to extend his authority and deal with the barbarians who have invaded Gaul.

The inhabitants of Britain have been left to organise their own defences against the Saxons and Picts.

Hebrew Bible is put into Latin

Antonello Da Messina's "Jerome".

Bethlehem, 414
The only translation of the scriptures to be authorised by the Church, the Latin version of the Hebrew Bible, has finally appeared. The life's work of the ascetic philologist Jerome, one of the "four Doctors" of the Church, it is the most important work of Christian Latin literature. It has taken him forty years to complete. Jerome was born in Strido, Dalmatia, in about 342. He studied grammar and theology, and after two years as a hermit in the Syrian desert was called to Rome by the Pope. In 377 he began his great work.

Barbarian state set up within the Empire

Bordeaux (France), 418
The troublesome Visigoths have been bought off at last with land of their own. The province is called Aquitaine II and extends from Toulouse to the Atlantic. Under an agreement between the barbarian King Wallia and the Emperor Honorius, the Visigoths are to defend the Atlantic coast from raids by Saxon pirates and have been given a fund for this purpose.

An earlier deal involved Honorius and Wallia's predecessor, Athaulf. Honorius broke his word that time, so the Visigoths occupied Narbonne, Toulouse and Bordeaux. A marriage between Athaulf and the Emperor's sister, Galla Placida, briefly restored good relations. Soon, however, a new quarrel began and Honorius drove the Visigoths into Spain, where famine awaited them. Three years ago the Visigoths murdered Athaulf and made a new start with Wallia: he is the first barbarian to set up an independent barbarian state within the borders of the Roman empire.

An even greater triumph was to establish peaceful co-existence with Aquitaine's existing ruling class, an old aristocracy combining Roman and Gallic stock. The province has two distinct religious communities. The Visigoths, although Christian, are of a different sect from the established community. Like most Goths they follow Arius, a recent philosopher, who argued that Jesus the Son did not share fully God the Father's divinity.

Rome's western regent is beheaded

Ravenna, 23 August 408
Stilicho, the Vandal who became a Roman general, was beheaded here today, and Rome lost its most effective defender against the attacking Barbarians. Stilicho, a favourite of Theodosius, was appointed tutor to the emperor's son Honorius, aged ten, and regent of the Western empire in his name, in 394. He defeated the invading Visigoths, but later his army rose against him.

Armenia rallies to support its church

Armenia, c.400
In spite of years as a battleground between Romans and Persians, and the recent partition of the country between them, Armenia retains its culture and Christianity. In the Persian zone, the larger of the two, Christianity and nationalism have become inseparable, the Armenians preserving their national consciousness through their alphabet, patriarchs and church.

Sun Temple built of 150 million bricks

Mochican ceramic of a warrior.

Peru, 419
Moche culture has spread south from the Chicama and Moche valleys in the narrow arid coastal strip of Peru. After a hundred years of conquests it now extends from the Andes to the Pacific.

In the Moche valley, cut by roads and irrigation canals, are temples dedicated to the Sun and Moon. The temple to the Sun is 150 feet high and built with fifty million bricks. Inside, its frescoes painted in seven different colours repeat the realistic motifs used in Mochican ceramics, depicting people and animals at everyday tasks.

A manuscript written on codex, which is replacing papyrus scrolls in the Mediterranean world. The codex is made up of square or rectangular sheets of papyrus or parchment, which are laid flat and then bound at one edge. The leaves are kept flat by being bound again between thick covers, which are often elaborately decorated. This particular exemple comes from St. Catherine's monastery, Sinai, c.400.

Exile for bishop who attacks empress

Constantinople, 404
John Chrysostom, patriarch of Constantinople and one of Christianity's most compelling preachers, has been expelled from the city. The former monk, named *Chrysostom*, or golden-mouthed, from his eloquence, has gone too far in his criticisms of the Empress Eudoxia. Now, enraged by his attacks on her sumptuous lifestyle, she has persuaded her husband Arcadius to send him into exile.

Chrysostom was born in Antioch 54 years ago, and after a pagan upbringing had himself baptised as a Christian in 370. He spent ten years studying in the desert before beginning his career as a preacher in Antioch. He was made bishop of Constantinople six years ago.

John: a 19th-century illustration.

Japan, c.421. On his death, the Emperor Nintoku is entombed in the largest mound yet known to man.

Rome, September 421. Constantius III dies just a few months after being made co-emperor of the West by Honorius. Appointed supreme commander of the Western army in 411, Constantius had married Galla Placidia, sister of Honorius, in 417.

Persia, 422. After two years of war caused by Persian persecution of the Christians, Theodosius II, the Roman Emperor of the East, and King Varahran of the Persians conclude a peace treaty which is intended to prevent fighting between them for 100 years.

Constantinople, 422. The Emperor Theodosius agrees to pay an annual tribute to the Huns in order to buy peace.

Constantinople, 27 February 425. Encouraged by his wife Eudoxia, Theodosius effectively founds a university in the capital by employing a greatly increased number of professors and giving them a monopoly over higher education in Constantinople.

Italy, 23 October 425. A pretender named John, who had seized control of the West on the death of Honorius in 423, is defeated, and Valentinian III, infant son of Constantius III and Galla Placidia, is installed as Augustus of the West with the backing of Theodosius II. His mother is appointed regent.

Constantinople, 428. Nestorius, the patriarch of Constantinople, preaches a new doctrine of Christ which emphasises the distinction between his divine and human natures. Nestorianism is immediately condemned by Pope Celestine and Cyril, the patriarch of Alexandria, as heresy.

North Africa, May 429. The Vandals, led by King Gaiseric, cross the Straits of Gibraltar from Spain into Africa. They are said to number 80,000.

Italy, 429. Aetius, who has defeated the Visigoths and the Franks and re-established the frontier of the Rhine with the help of Hun mercenaries, is appointed commander of the armies of the Western empire.

North Africa, 28 August 430. Augustine, the bishop of Hippo, dies while his town is under siege by the Vandals.

Persia, 430. The Hephtalite Huns, who are established in central Asia, attack Persia.

Rome, 431. Pope Celestine sends his deacon Palladius to Ireland as its first bishop.

Asia Minor, June 431. The Third Ecumenical Council, meeting at Ephesus, condemns the Nestorian doctrine as heresy.

Balkans, 434. The armies of Theodosius II are defeated by the Huns in Thrace. Attila and his brother Bleda set the peace terms: the Romans' annual tribute to the Huns is doubled and a series of other concessions are made.

Constantinople, 29 October 437. Valentinian III, the ruler of the Western empire, marries Licinia Eudoxia, the daughter of Theodosius II, the ruler of the Eastern empire.

North Africa, 19 October 439. The Vandals, led by King Gaiseric, take Carthage.

China, 439. With the fall of the Northern Liang to the Northern Wei rulers, the Toba, the northern and southern courts stand in direct conflict. The Northern Wei complete their unification of north China under a single regime.

India, 440. A great centre of Buddhist studies is founded on the plain of the Ganges at Nalanda. It consists of some ten monasteries and a group of shrines, all enclosed within a surrounding wall.

North Africa, 442. The Vandal king, Gaiseric, signs a peace treaty with Valentinian III, with the approval of Theodosius II. He is granted full rights as an independent ruler over most of the Roman province of Africa (Tunisia and western Libya). In return, he hands back Sicily, recently invaded by the Vandals, Numidia and the two provinces of Mauretania (Morocco and Algeria).

Gaul, 443. After suffering a defeat by the Huns – who are fighting for the empire as mercenaries – at Worms in 436, the Burgundians began to move from the upper Rhine. They are now given imperial land in the Geneva area by Aetius and become allies of Rome under a special treaty, serving in the Roman army.

Balkans, 447. The Huns, under Attila, cross the Danube frontier, invade Thrace and force the Romans to pay them a heavier tribute and withdraw from a wide strip of land beside the Danube. The annual tribute paid to the Huns by the eastern empire had already been trebled from 443 onwards.

Asia Minor, 449. At a council held at Ephesus, under the leadership of Dioscurus, patriarch of Alexandria, the Monophysites push through the acceptance of their doctrine. This takes place in the absence of Pope Leo, a fierce opponent of Monophysitism.

Saxon mercenaries rebel and seize Kent

Kent, Britain, c.450

Saxon mercenaries led by Hengest ("The Stallion") and Horsa ("The Horse") have seized Kent, destroying the local infrastructure of Roman government. When the Romans left, over 40 years ago, the Romano-British people had to fend for themselves. Led by Vortigern, they hired about 140 Saxon warriors to combat Pictish raiders from the north. Soon more Saxons, with their neighbours the Jutes and Angles, were crossing to Britain in search of easy money. But when their demands for more supplies were refused, the mercenaries rebelled and, as one observer writes, "towns were laid low, as swords glinted and flames crackled".

Hengest and Horsa (r.) negotiate with Vortigern (19th-century print).

Patriarch of Constantinople is banished

Asia Minor, June 431

At a general ecumenical council summoned by Nestorius, patriarch of Constantinople, at Ephesus, the patriarch himself has been deposed – accused of heresy.

Nestorius was made patriarch in 425 by the Emperor Theodosius II. An ascetic and intolerant man, he raised a storm in the church three years ago by preaching a new doc-trine according to which there are two distinct natures in Christ. One is completely human, the other completely divine. The Virgin is therefore only the mother of Christ, not of God.

Antagonists – including Pope Celestine and Cyril, patriarch of Alexandria – were quick to condemn him, and Nestorius has now been banished to Egypt.

Christians told to ignore worldly matters

Hippo, North Africa, 426

Bishop Augustine of Hippo has completed his great work *De Civitate Dei* (The City of God) which has taken him 13 years. It is a series of meditations inspired by the question "Why did God allow Rome to fall to the Barbarians?". Ever since Alaric sacked the city, in 410, refugees have swarmed to Africa, and a Vandal invasion of Africa is expected. Non-Christians blame the fall of Rome on the fact that Romans had deserted the worship of their old gods, such as Jupiter, who consequently withdrew their centuries'-old support. Augustine, himself a pagan until the age of 32, demolishes this belief by arguing that the old gods did not save Troy or prevent Roman defeats in the past. He says Rome fell by God's will because no earthly city is founded on goodness or justice. Only the City of God, to which all Christians aspire to be-

Augustine with the Virgin and Child.

long, is eternal and will survive the ruin of the old order. He asks: "In this short life what does it matter under whose dominion a man lives, so long as he does not commit impious acts?"

Vandals capture the city of Carthage

Carthage, 19 October 439
The Roman city of Carthage has fallen to the Vandals, putting the whole of North Africa under the control of this wandering Germanic people. A Vandal state has come into being under the ruthless rule of Gaiseric, who has brought 80,000 people – including 15,000 warriors – with him from Spain. He crossed the Straits of Gibraltar in 429 and marched along the North African coast, sacking and looting city after city.

It took Gaiseric 11 years to reach Carthage, pausing for an entire year to besiege and capture Hippo (430). Five years ler, in 435, a desperate Rome came to terms with the Vandal king and formally granted him the areas already conquered. But Gaiseric was not satisfied for long: now, with the loss of Carthage, Rome has given up sovereignty over much of its former territory in Africa, including the lush wheat fields upon which the empire depended for its bread.

The population continues to live under Roman law, however, and

A Roman mosaic from Carthage of a Vandal horseman leaving his villa.

the existing administration is largely maintained by Romans, to the profit of Vandals. Meanwhile, Gaiseric's men have confiscated Roman estates and live in unaccustomed luxury and idleness. Unfortunately for the locals, the Vandals are fervent followers of the Arian

heresy and have begun to persecute the Catholics in the community, many of them facing death or exile if they refuse to recant their faith.

Nor is the Vandal threat confined to Africa. Gaiseric is building a fleet of fast ships to try to control the western Mediterranean.

Buddhism is set to revive in China

China, 448
The Daoist court official Gou Qianzhi, who succeeded in establishing his doctrine as the dominant faith in China, has died. It was Gou who converted the Emperor Wu to Daoism eight years ago and established such a hold over him that four years later the emperor conducted a service marking the supremacy of Daoism.

The emperor had already taken measures against the spread of Buddhism, and in 446 the apparent involvement of a Changan monastery in a rebellion led him to order the destruction of the monasteries and the execution of every monk in the empire.

Even Gou was appalled by this decree and, supported by other officials, managed to delay the executions until many of the monks had been able to escape.

There have been signs recently that the emperor's devotion to Daoism has been waning. It seems probable that Gou's death will bring a revival of Buddhism.

Empress who maimed kidnappers, dies

Ravenna, 27 November 450
The Empress Galla Placidia died today at Ravenna, aged 60, after an eventful life, during which she married one of her Visigoth kidnappers and, after her release, reluctantly married the suitor chosen by her half-brother Honorius, the Roman emperor of the West.

The daughter of Theodosius I, she was 20 when Alaric the Goth subjected Rome to a three days' sack and took her hostage. Four years later, in 414, she married Alaric's brother-in-law and successor as king of the Goths, Athaulf. In 415 Athaulf was murdered and Placidia was sent back by the Visigoths to Ravenna, where she unwillingly married Constantius, an army general with aspirations to the throne. He died soon after the birth of their son, Valentinian.

Placidia now had to reject the amorous advances of her half-brother. She sought refuge in Constantinople, where her nephew Theodosius II was emperor of the East. Soon, however, Honorius

died and she returned to Ravenna to act as regent for the new Western emperor, her infant son Valentinian. Her regency was undermined by court intrigue, rebellion and invasion. Finding her power waning, she devoted her last years to acts of piety and concern for the welfare of the Church.

A tomb in Ravenna: Placidia's?

Literary emperor writes legal code

Constantinople, 25 December 438
Theodosius II, it is said, reigns, but does not rule; that task is performed first by his sister Pulcheria and then by his wife Eudoxia and the ministers. The emperor, meanwhile, is devoted to literary and theological pursuits. Still, his reign has seen notable achievements: the foundation of a university, the building of Constantinople's great walls, and the publication of the Theodosian Code of imperial laws, the first for over a century.

The Code sets out the laws in chronological order, and if laws appear contradictory then the most recent are to be applied. It is hoped that laws passed in the East will also apply in the West, and vice versa. The Code also shows how the once-efficient Roman administrative system has been weakened and local government fallen into decay. Emperors have been impotent to restrain the avarice and abuse of power of provincial governors.

Easterners triumph at Church council

A Christian tapestry from Egypt.

Ephesus, 8 August 449
Supporters of Monophysitism, the Christian philosophy teaching that the incarnate Christ is of a single, divine nature, have won an important theological battle at the Council of Ephesus. The Council has backed the Monophysite patriarch of Alexandria, who is supported by Egypt's monastic movement, and has also insulted the representatives of Pope Leo, the bishop of Rome.

Constantinople, 28 July 450. Theodosius II falls off his horse and dies, after ruling as emperor of the East for 42 years. He leaves no direct heir. Theodosius was prone throughout his reign to follow the advice of others, notably his sister and his wife, but also a series of imperial officials.

Constantinople, August 450. Marcian, a retired army officer, becomes emperor of the East thanks to the all-important backing of Aspar, the barbarian commander of the Eastern armies, and of the Empress Pulcheria, Theodosius II's sister, who duly marries him.

Ireland, c.450. Patrick founds the episcopal see of Armagh.

Gaul, 20 June 451. Having mounted an invasion of Gaul, Attila and the Huns are defeated in the battle of the Catalaunian Fields by a combined force of Romans, Visigoths and several other barbarian peoples, all under the command of Aetius.

Asia Minor, October 451. At Chalcedon, the Fourth Ecumenical Council, summoned by Pope Leo, condemns Monophysitism and completely reverses the decrees of the Council of Ephesus of 449.

Italy, 452. The Huns invade Italy and sack a series of northern Italian cities, including Padua and Verona, before Pope Leo persuades Attila to desist from his planned attack on Rome and withdraw.

Pannonia, 453. On the death of Attila, leader of the Huns since 434, the vast Hun empire is divided up between his sons.

Italy, 21 September 454. Aetius, the supreme army commander, is murdered at Ravenna by Valentinian III, the emperor of the West.

Pannonia, 454. The Germanic vassals of the Huns, inspired by Ardaric, the king of the Gepids, rebel against Attila's sons and defeat them in Pannonia. The Hun empire begins to fall apart.

Ethiopia, 454. Following the split in the Roman church, which became more pronounced three years ago after the Council of Chalcedon, the kingdom of Axum decides to give its support to the Coptic patriarch of Alexandria, who follows the Monophysite doctrine.

Rome, March 455. Valentinian III is assassinated by two barbarian retainers of Aetius. His death brings to an end the Theodosian dynasty. A very wealthy senator, Petronius Maximus, bribes the troops and is proclaimed emperor by them.

Rome, June 455. The Vandals, led by King Gaiseric, sack Rome. On the death of Valentinian III, they had immediately seized those parts of Africa still in Roman hands, together with the islands of Sardinia and Corsica. In the panic before their arrival in Rome, the new Emperor Maximus tried to flee and was killed by the mob, after a reign of 11 weeks.

Gaul, 9 July 455. Following a two-month period without an emperor, the Gallic senators proclaim Avitus, military commander in Gaul, as emperor of the West. Avitus has the support of Theodoric II, the king of the Visigoths.

Italy, 456. Avitus is defeated in battle at Placentia, in northern Italy, and forced to abdicate by the rebel general Ricimer, an Arian barbarian from the Suevian tribe. Ricimer aims to rule through a puppet emperor, Majorian.

Spain, 456. The powerful Suevian king Rechiarus is defeated and killed by the Visigoths, who begin to seize the upper hand in Spain.

Constantinople, 7 February 457. A Thracian officer by the name of Leo is proclaimed as emperor of the East by the army general, Aspar, on the death of the Emperor Marcian.

Italy, 2 August 461. Majorian is deposed and killed by his military commander, Ricimer, the man responsible for elevating him to the throne. In the event, Majorian had proved too independent for Ricimer's liking.

Italy, 15 August 465. Libius Severus, the puppet emperor elevated by Ricimer to succeed Majorian, dies after a reign of four years.

India, 467. On the death of Skanda Gupta, who succeeded his father Kumaragupta in 455, the Gupta empire is beginning to break up under pressure from the Hephtalite Huns, who have conquered a large part of western India. During the early part of his reign Skanda Gupta successfully repelled their attacks.

Rome, August 467. In return for military aid, Ricimer accepts Leo's nominee, the general Anthemius, as Western emperor. Anthemius marches west and is proclaimed Augustus.

Constantinople, 467. The Emperor Leo marries his daughter Ariadne to Tarasicodissa, who takes the name Zeno. He is an Isaurian from the mountains of southern Asia Minor.

Sicily, 468. The Vandals defeat the Western forces decisively and conquer the island of Sicily.

Victory for Catholic church at Chalcedon

Asia Minor, October 451
Catholic Christians have reversed the decisions of the Council of Ephesus at the Fourth Ecumenical Council held here on the orders of the Emperor Marcian. This time the bishops of Rome and Constantinople united to defend the Nicene Creed and in their view of the exact nature of the incarnate Christ.

Opposition came from Eutyches, whose Monophysite doctrine had been pushed through the Council of Ephesus two years ago in the absence of the bishop of Rome, Pope Leo. Monophysites assert that the person of the incarnate Christ has but a single, divine, nature, while orthodox Catholic teaching insists that after incarnation Christ had a double but indivisible nature, both divine and human. Monophysitism is the latest heresy arising from two difficult but crucial Christian mysteries: the Incarnation and the Trinity. Earlier heresies denounced by the Church were Arianism, concerned with the status of Christ within the Trinity, and Nestorianism (after Nestorius, patriarch of Constantinople 428-31), seeking

A later artist's impression of the bishop of Rome, Pope Leo I.

to separate the divine and human within the incarnate Christ.

But the orthodox Catholic victory at Chalcedon may be a hollow one. The heresies have followers on the fringes of the empire: Arianism amongst the barbarians, Nestorianism in Persia, and Monophysitism in Egypt, Palestine and Syria.

Patrick dies after converting Ireland

Ireland, c.461
Bishop Patrick, one of the most remarkable men ever to come to this country, is dead. Everyone who met him was impressed by his holiness, which came from a firm belief that he received direct and specific guidance from God in dreams and visions. It was one such vision that urged him to return to Ireland and convert the Irish, a task he has gone some way towards completing.

He was born near Carlisle, in Britain, and was the son of a landowner called Calpurnius. His grandfather, Potitus, was a priest. At the age of 14 Patrick was captured by Irish raiders and sold as a slave to Ireland. After about six years he escaped and made a three-day voyage to Gaul in a small boat.

He trained as a priest in Gaul and Britain and, prompted by his vision, he returned here about thirty years ago as a "bishop in Ireland". Since then he has successfully converted most of the kings in Ulster, Leinster and Munster, and they have allowed Christian priests

to take the word to their peoples.

Much of his thinking is recorded in two books written in Latin, *Confessio* and *Epistola*, the latter in the form of an open letter of vehement criticism to a British king, Coroticus.

A later portrait of Patrick, who brought Christ to the Irish.

Romans and barbarians halt Attila

Aetius stabbed to death by emperor

Italy, 21 September 454
The Emperor Valentinian III today stabbed to death his commander-in-chief, Aetius, during a meeting of the imperial council at Ravenna. A heated argument erupted after the emperor accused Aetius of plotting to take power. Some claim that he was a victim of court intrigues, and servants vow they will avenge his death by killing Valentinian.

For 30 years Aetius defended the empire against the Burgundians, Visigoths and Vandals, becoming ruler in all but name. He was Italian, born in the Danubian province of Moesia, and married into the Gothic nobility. He spent many years as a hostage of the Huns, during which time he formed a close friendship with Attila. This stood him in good stead during his struggles with the barbarian invaders.

A later artist's view of the Roman army, under Pope Leo I, halting Attila – with saintly reinforcements.

Champagne, Gaul, 20 June 451
After a furious battle here at the Catalaunian Plains, Attila the Hun, the most feared man in Europe, is retreating under cover of darkness. His vast army has met its match in an extraordinary alliance of Romans and barbarians, with imperial troops fighting alongside Visigoths, Franks, Burgundians and others to save the Western empire from Attila's hordes. The Visigoth king, Theodoric, died in the battle, but Gaul is saved. The Roman General Aetius has allowed Attila to retreat to Pannonia (*Hungary*).

It is two years sce Attila abruptly changed his policy of maintaining friendly relations with the Western empire while bleeding the Eastern empire dry. He had demanded to marry Honoria, the sister of the Emperor Valentinian III, with a dowry of half the empire. Although Honoria was apparently willing – perhaps because Valentinian had had her lover murdered – Attila was refused and invaded Gaul. The Hun troops, fearsome in animal skins and with faces slashed to avoid growing beards, were returning eastwards, their baggage trains laden with booty, when the alliance struck.

Uncertainty in Hun empire as Attila dies

Pannonia, 453
The Hun troops cut their hair and slashed their faces to "mourn with blood rather than tears" their leader Attila who has died after a wedding feast. Few others will mourn the stocky warrior-diplomat who used cunning and violence to sack the Balkans regularly and extort vast sums in tribute from the Eastern empire. Hun warriors, experts at shooting with bows from swift Steppe horses, were unified by Attila, who ruled a powerful yet precarious empire. But with his death many of his Germanic subjects, kept under Hun control for the past 50 years, are said to be plotting revolt. The Huns themselves are already arguing over his successor.

Rome is sacked for the second time in less than 50 years

Rome, 16 June 455
The Vandal army, laden with booty and taking thousands of captives, among them the Empress Eudoxia and her daughters, is leaving Rome. For two weeks its troops have plundered the great city, although they agreed not to burn it after a plea by Pope Leo.

This is the second sack of the city in 50 years, the first being in 410 at the hands of the Visigoths. The Vandal king, Gaiseric, took the city with an army landed by the powerful Vandal fleet after the murder of Valentinian III four months ago. Gaiseric was the emperor's ally and regarded all treaty obligations as cancelled by his murder.

The inability of the empire to defend the most prestigious city in the world against such a swift and brutal attack is symptomatic of its present decayed state. Spain has fallen, Gaul has been abandoned, and North Africa is in the hands of the Vandals.

Now Gaiseric's fleet is roaming freely throughout the western Mediterranean, with rich island prizes at its mercy.

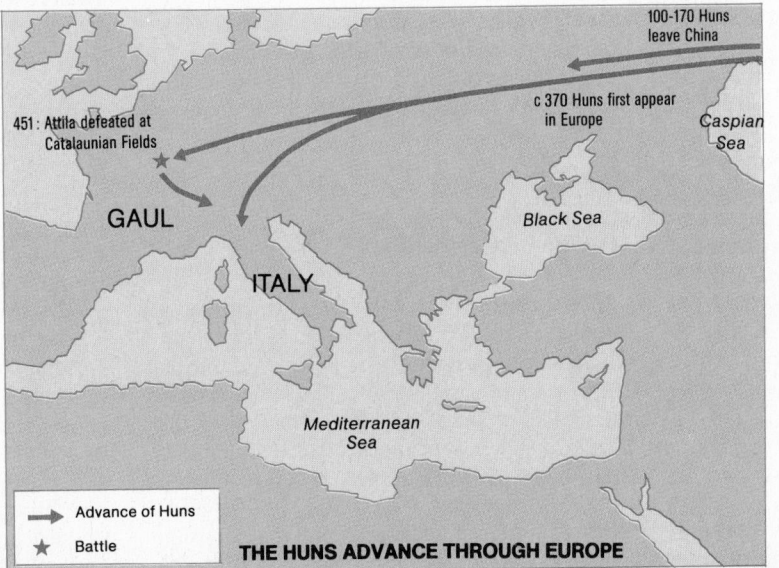

THE HUNS ADVANCE THROUGH EUROPE

The sunset of the Roman World

The period between 400 and 700 saw an extraordinary change in Europe and the Mediterranean: the Roman empire, which had ruled over millions of people, was reduced to a beleaguered capital, Constantinople, and a few outlying territories, all threatened by attack from Arabs and Slavs.

The power of Rome had been challenged in the years around 250, when barbarians breached the frontier; they were beaten back, and for a century the empire seemed secure. But in 378 the Visigoths, pushed across the Danube and into the empire by nomadic Huns, defeated and killed the Emperor Valens outside Adrianople.

Political and military decline

From then on the military position of the West and the Balkans slowly disintegrated, and by 500 there had emerged in the Western empire a number of barbarian kingdoms, most notably those of the Vandals in North Africa, the Visigoths in Spain and southern Gaul, the Ostrogoths in Italy, the Franks in northern and central Gaul, and the Anglo-Saxons in Britain. These kingdoms for the most part closely imitated Roman administration, employing Romans to maintain a bureaucracy and the profitable tax-system. Gradually this Roman style of government disintegrated, to be replaced by more primitive systems in which direct and personal obligations of service replaced taxation and the maintenance of a bureaucratic state.

The reconquest by the Eastern Emperor Justinian of the western provinces of Africa (534-5), Italy (535-53) and southern Spain (551) had little long-term effect on political geography in the west – much of Italy soon fell to barbarian newcomers, the Lombards, while the south of Spain was recaptured by the Visigoths.

The eastern provinces remained Byzantine for much longer. Only in the years around 600 did the Balkans and much of Greece succumb to Slav invaders. Central and eastern North Africa and the Near East (Syria, Palestine and Egypt) fell between 634 and 689 to the Arabs, recently united under a new faith, Islam. The Byzantines were hard pressed to prevent the Arabs taking over Asia Minor (Anatolia), and in 673-7 the Arabs repeatedly besieged Constantinople itself. Having taken Carthage in 689, the Arabs took over the rest of North Africa and began to expand into Visigothic Spain.

Roman economic collapse

In 400 the Roman economy was still very complex and flourishing. Although some western provinces, such as Italy, were perhaps less prosperous than they had been, other areas, such as the east, North Africa and the Rhineland, flourished in the century from 300. Some of these areas were clearly dependent for their wealth, at least in part, on the production and export of specialised goods – the east produced wine and oil; Africa was a source of oil and domestic pottery; and the Rhineland made fine glassware and pottery. Great cities flourished: Alexandria, Antioch and Constantinople in the east, Carthage, Rome and Trier in the west.

By 700 the picture was bleak. In some areas, such as Britain and the Balkans, economic sophistication had disappeared entirely – the old industries, trade, coinage and towns were no more, although in Britain there were signs of a long-term revival. In other areas, particularly around the Mediterranean, the economic disaster was less complete, and Arabs and Lombards proved ready to adapt to urban ways. But almost everywhere towns had shrunk in size – even Constantinople – and long-distance trade, except in a few exotic luxuries, had virtually collapsed. Even local trade had declined. The Roman copper coinage, for instance, which once sustained and aided exchange, had disappeared in the West, where barbarian kings minted only in gold, and was very rare in the Byzantine world.

Constant warfare (with its pressure on money and manpower), conquest and insecurity were undoubtedly prime causes of this dramatic change – Europe and the Mediterranean were no longer protected by the stability of the *Pax Romana*, the Peace of Rome. In addition, the population shrank, partly devastated by plague, and land fell out of use all over the old empire. This led to environmental problems: rain and rivers carried down soil from abandoned upland fields and dumped it in valleys and deltas. And the rich fens of Britain, partly drained and cultivated by the Romans, reverted to swamp.

The end of Roman culture?

In 400 most of Europe and the Mediterranean was part of a single cultural world, dominated by the classical thought and art of Greece and Rome. There was, of course, much regional diversity within this world, for instance in architecture. Similarly, in literary culture an ancient divide between Greek and Latin speakers still to some extent persisted; even a great scholar like Augustine admitted to considerable problems in understanding Greek. But in 400 the empire was still essentially united by a centuries-old classical cultural tradition and, more recently, by the new religion of Christianity.

Again, by 700 the story was mostly one of fragmentation and decline. In the Western provinces knowledge of Greek had virtually disappeared, and with it almost all understanding of the philosophical tradition of Aristotle and Plato; at a more basic level, few people could even read or write in any language, and spoken Latin was fast diverging into a string of distinct dialects; Gallo-Romans and Italians, for instance, probably already found it hard to understand each other in the vernacular. Although jewellery and weaponry were produced to superb standards in barbarian kingdoms, there was very little activity in other spheres of the arts – painting and mosaic outside Italy were extremely rare, and even in the most sophisticated of towns, such as Rome itself, the only new buildings were tiny, ill-constructed chapels which would have been laughed at by classical Roman architects.

In the Byzantine East, the Greek language of the empire preserved some of the traditions of ancient Greek culture. However, very little new work was being written – and what there was, often very derivative and skimpy – and very few new churches were being built, again all tiny in comparison with the buildings of the late empire.

In the provinces newly under Arab rule, the Arab impact was initially not very marked. Arabia was scarcely sophisticated, and the Arab invaders were at first happy to adopt and even develop the Byzantine artistic tradition of their conquered peoples. However, the first signs of a distinctive Islamic and Arab culture were emerging by 700, with Arabic as its literary language and with an art dominated by non-figurative decoration, since Islam expressly forbade all representations of the human form.

But between 400 and 700 not every development in the cultural world of the former Roman empire was part of a downhill slide. The Christian church survived in all provinces, and was reintroduced to those, such as Britain, where it had been temporarily submerged. It preserved a great deal of the classical tradition, such as the habit of writing in Latin or Greek: the books of classical antiquity were copied and read, particularly in monasteries. The church also kept open channels between different peoples; it spread its religion, and with it literacy and part of the old classical culture, beyond the former imperial frontiers. A new Europe began to emerge, based no longer on political unity but on a new sense of shared religion and culture.

Sixty-five emperors who ruled the Roman empire

Rome, once a republic, rose to its greatest power under these emperors who ruled until the empire was divided in 395.

27BC	Augustus
14AD	Tiberius
37	Caligula
41	Claudius
57	Nero
68	Galba
	Otho
	Vitellius
	Vespasian
79	Titus
81	Domitian
96	Nerva
98	Trajan
117	Hardrian
138	Antoninus Pius
161	Marcus Aurelius
180	Commodus
193	Pertinax
	Didus Julianus
	Niger
	Septimius Severus
211	Caracalla
	Geta
217	Macrinus

Augustus Caesar, the first emperor of Rome, 27BC-14AD.

218	Elagalabus
222	Alexander Severus
235	Maximin I
238	Gordian I and II
	Balbinus
	Pupienus
	Gordian III
244	Philip

Constantine I (309-337), who made Constantinople capital.

249	Decius
251	Gallus
253	Aemilian
	Valerian
	Gallienus
260	Gallienus alone
270	Aurelian
275	Tacitus

276	Florian
	Probus
282	Carus
284	Carinus
	Numerian
	Diocletian
	Maximian associated with
286	Diocletian
305	Constantius
	Galerius
306	Severus
309	Constantine the Great
	Licinius
	Maximin
	Galerius
	Maxentius
	Maximian
323	Constantine alone
337	Constantine II
	Constantinus II
	Constans
353	Constantius alone
361	Julian
363	Jovian
364	Valens
	Valentinian I
367	Gratian
375	Valentinian II
379	Theodosius the Great

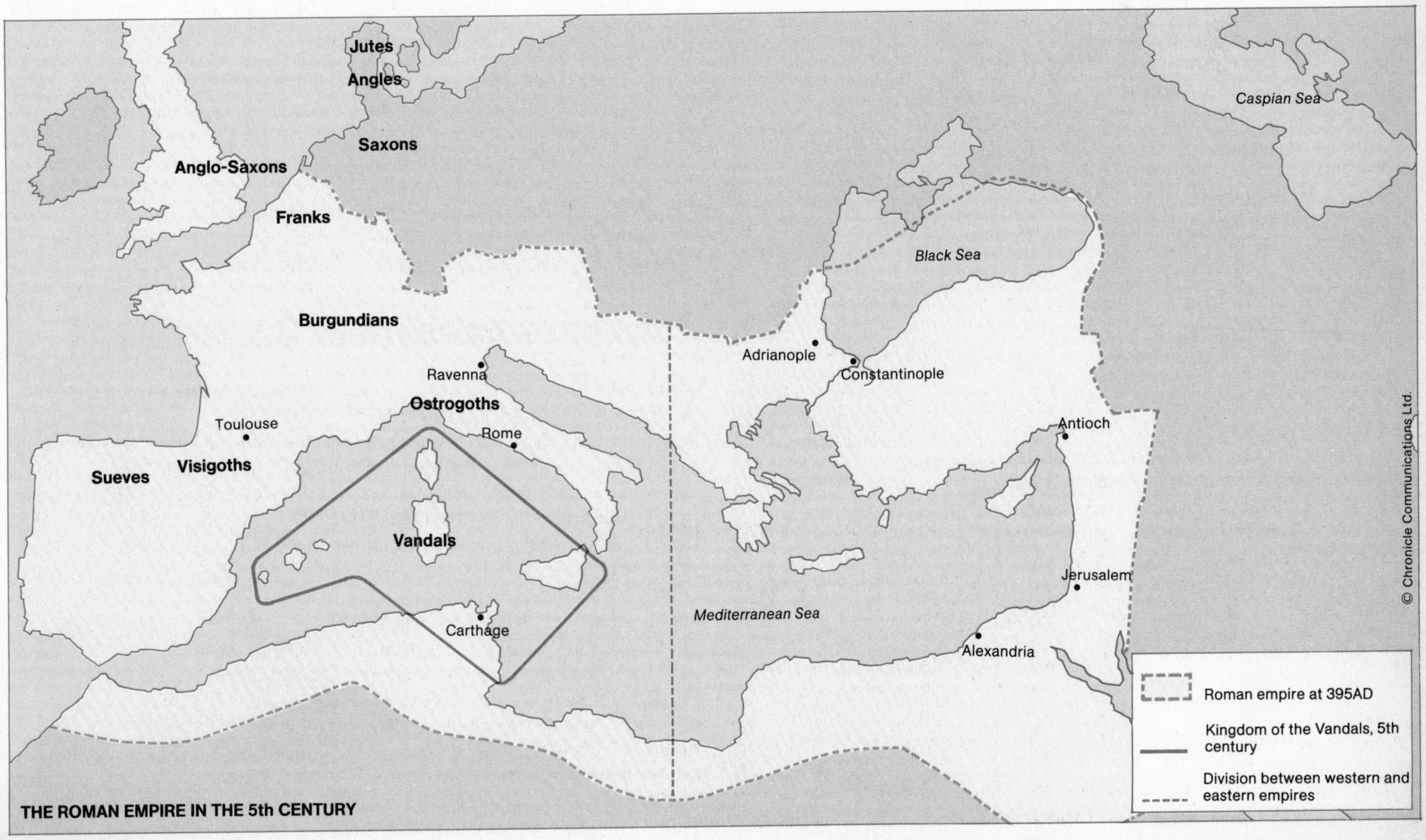

Jutes
Angles
Caspian Sea
Saxons
Anglo-Saxons
Franks
Black Sea
Burgundians
Adrianople
Constantinople
Ravenna
Ostrogoths
Toulouse
Rome
Antioch
Sueves   Visigoths
Vandals
Jerusalem
Carthage
Mediterranean Sea
Alexandria

© Chronicle Communications Ltd.

Roman empire at 395AD

Kingdom of the Vandals, 5th century

Division between western and eastern empires

THE ROMAN EMPIRE IN THE 5th CENTURY

Constantinople, 471. On the orders of the Emperor Leo, the army commander Aspar is assassinated.

Rome, 11 July 472. The barbarian general Ricimer kills the Emperor Anthemius in civil war. He replaces him with Olybrius.

Rome, 19 August 472. The kingmaker Ricimer, who has been responsible for raising a series of emperors to the Western throne, dies. Another barbarian, the Burgundian Gundobad, takes over supreme command of the Western army.

Rome, 2 November 472. Olybrius dies. No emperor is immediately appointed to succeed him.

Rome, 24 June 473. Julius Nepos, backed by Leo, emperor of the East, marches on Rome and ousts Gundobad's nominee Glycerius, becoming emperor of the West himself.

Constantinople, 473. Leo appoints another Leo – the son of his son-in-law Zeno – co-emperor.

Constantinople, 474. Leo II, who became sole emperor of the East following the death of Leo I earlier in the year, dies after reigning for only a few months and is succeeded by his father, Zeno.

Gaul/Spain, 475. Euric, king of the Visigoths since 466, is granted legal tenure of his conquests by Julius Nepos, emperor of the West. The Visigoths now control south-western Gaul and most of Spain, except for the Suevian kingdom in the north-west.

Rome, 475. The Roman army commander Orestes drives Julius Nepos out of Italy and puts his own son, Romulus Augustus, on the throne.

Gaul, 476. The Visigothic king, Euric, conquers the remainder of southern Gaul, up to the Italian frontier.

Italy, 476. The imperial army at Ravenna mutinies and proclaims Odoacer, a barbarian officer from Germany, king. Orestes is killed; his son, Romulus Augustus, is deposed and exiled to Campania by Odoacer. Odoacer chooses to do without a puppet emperor and formally recognises Zeno as sole emperor, while holding real power himself.

North Africa, 477. The Vandal king, Gaiseric, dies in the province of Africa. His son Huneric, who is an Arian Christian, succeeds him and embarks upon a policy of violent persecution of the Catholics.

China, 477. The Liu Song dynasty collapses when General Xiao Daocheng has the emperor killed and sets himself up as regent.

China, 477. Buddhism becomes the state religion.

China, 479. Xiao Daocheng has the boy emperor and all the members of the imperial family murdered and creates the Southern Qi dynasty. Fighting between the Toba and the south begins again.

Britain, c.480. Saxons under the leadership of Aelle land on the south coast and drive the Britons westward. The kingdom of the South Saxons (Sussex) is established.

Dalmatia, 480. Odoacer occupies the Dalmatia region on the death of the exiled former emperor Julius Nepos, who had controlled it.

Gaul, 480. Gundobad, the former Western commander, succeeds his brother Chilperic as king of the Burgundians. The Burgundian kingdom now extends over much of eastern Gaul, with two capitals, at Lyons and Geneva.

India, c.480. Nestorianism – the Christian doctrine which emphasises the distinction between Christ's divine and human natures, and thereby denies that the Virgin is the mother of God – has reached India.

Gaul, 481. Childeric, king of the Franks, dies at his capital, Tournai, and is succeeded by his son Clovis.

Constantinople, 482. In order to settle the violent conflict between the Chalcedonian Monophysites and Catholic believers, the Emperor Zeno promulgates a compromise edict of union known as the *Henotikon*.

Constantinople/Rome, 484. A schism splits the Churches of Constantinople and Rome. The pope refuses to accept Zeno's *Henotikon*, which he regards as heretical.

Gaul, 486. The Frankish king, Clovis, defeats Syagrius, leader of the Gallo-Romans, at Soissons and conquers much of northern Gaul, except for Armorica (Brittany).

Persia, 486. The second Council of Seleucia brings together the Christians of Persia who adhere to Nestorian heresy.

Constantinople, 488. The Catholic usurper Leontius and the Isaurian patrician Illus, who opposed the emperor, are executed. The Monophysite party wins the day. Zeno is restored.

Constantinople, 488. Having survived a series of attacks by rebels and barbarians, Zeno finally ends the troubles besetting his reign by paying the Ostrogothic king Theodoric to go and expel Odoacer from Italy.

Huge grotto celebrates Buddhist revival

Inside a Chinese Buddhist pagoda.

China, 489

The rulers of Wei, now firmly restored to Buddhism after their brief flirtation with Taoism, have started a monumental project to honour their religion. Thousands are employed in fashioning a huge cave temple in a sandstone cliff at Yungang in northern Shanxi.

Imposing figures are being carved out of the rock. Curiously, they depict Indian gods carved in a style which owes much to Greek statuary. The artists are somewhat naive and often incorporate Greek mythological themes without understanding them.

There is a much more Chinese feel to the smaller figures, which are being carved by native craftsmen who are not inhibited by the Indian origins of Buddhism. Whatever the artistic merits of this project, there seems no doubt that it is a vast enterprise which may last for many centuries.

Desert monastery holds 100's of monks

Near East, 473

A great *lavra*, or monastery, has been founded in the Judaean desert by the wandering hermit Sabas of Cappadocia. The monastery will house hundreds of monks, each in his own accommodation.

The idea of retreating from public life to spiritual centres provided by such monasteries has become increasingly popular among Christians for 25 years. Religious communities have emerged all over the eastern Mediterranean, many also becoming economic centres.

Not all monks choose the communal life. Some, the *gyrovagues*, wander from monastery to monastery. Others, known as *stylites* from the Greek for pillar, sit for years on pillars; Simeon, who died in 459, lived on top of his column for 37 years. Some, the *anchorites*, live as solitary hermits.

Pope ousts patriarch of Constantinople

Rome, 484

A rift has occurred between the Eastern and Western Churches after Pope Felix III's decision to excommunicate Acacius, the patriarch of Constantinople, and Zeno, the Eastern emperor. The split began in 482, when Acacius issued an edict, the *Henotikon*, without consulting the Pope. The edict aimed to soften the Church's decision, made at the Council of Chalcedon in 451, to brand Monophysitism as a heresy. Acacius' formula on the nature of Christ was acceptable to the Monophysite churches of Egypt and Syria, which Zeno wished to please for political reasons.

Felix III: break with the East?

Pope orders ruler in East to be killed

Constantinople, 471

Aspar, the barbarian commander and, for a long period, *de facto* ruler of the Eastern empire, has been assassinated with his son Ardabur on the orders of the Emperor Leo. The murder ends the effective control of the empire by German generals.

This barbarian influence began in 421-2 when the German soldiers Areobindus and Ardabur (father of Aspar) led Roman forces against the Persians. Aspar served as his father's lieutenant in the ensuing campaign to get rid of the usurper John and put Valentinian III on the throne of the Western empire. In 431 Aspar was given command of an expedition to Africa, and in 434 he became a consul. His position as commander-in-chief was reinforced by the support of the powerful army of the federate Goths.

When the Theodosian line died out in 450, Aspar was the most powerful figure in the empire. As a barbarian Arian Christian he did not seek the throne for himself, but secured it for Marcian, the head of his guard. When Marcian died in 457, Aspar nominated as emperor the obscure tribune Leo.

But in 466 Leo married his daughter to Tarasicodissa, a member of the powerful Isaurian tribe, who took the Greek name Zeno and became Leo's favourite. Isaurian troops were soon based in the capital; although Aspar took steps to consolidate his position, his days were numbered.

Western emperor deposed by barbarian

The end of an epoch: Romulus – named after Rome's founder – abdicates.

Ravenna, September 476

The Western empire has seen ten emperors come and go in the past 21 years; now it has as ruler a man who refuses to call himself emperor. Odoacer, a barbarian born in the middle Danube, joined the imperial army after Severinus, the bishop of Noricum, told him "Thou who art now clothed in vile raiment will give precious gifts to many", and rose to become commander of the barbarian mercenaries in imperial pay. Last year Orestes, a leading citizen, overthrew the Emperor Nepos and gave the purple to his own teenage son Romulus. Odoacer mutinied, promising his mercenaries land; Orestes has been beheaded, and today Odoacer arrived in Ravenna, the Western capital, and sent Romulus packing. He denies the need for separate Eastern and Western emperors, and will rule as the lieutenant of the Emperor Zeno in Constantinople. He only asks that he should be recognised as a Roman citizen, though born a barbarian. Many believe that this signals the end of the empire in the West, although imperial rule is nominally maintained.

King of the Franks defeats Romans

Gaul, 486

The kingdom of the Roman Syagrius in northern Gaul has been crushed at Noviodunum (Soissons) by Clovis, the king of the Franks, who now rules from the Somme to the Loire. His victory spells the end of Roman rule in Gaul.

Clovis, aged 21, is the grandson of Merovech, the founder of the Merovingian dynasty of Franks, a Germanic people who had reached the northern edge of Gaul by 350. His son, Childeric (Clovis' father, who died in 481), led a Frankish section of the Roman army, establishing the Frankish foothold to which Clovis has been adding.

Clovis, youthful new ruler of Gaul.

Bishop Apollinaris dies at Clermont

Gaul, 486

Sidonius Apollinaris, poet, bishop and statesman, has died aged 54 at Clermont, in the Auvergne. He was a son of the prefect of Gaul and son-in-law of an emperor, and prefect of Rome before his election in 472 as bishop of Clermont, a natural step at a time when the Church is a more effective guardian of Roman values than the state. It was that state which, to his disgust, conceded the Auvergne to the Visigoths in 475. He wrote: "Our slavery is the price of others' security."

Frescoes in the vast Buddhist cave temples of Ajanta, central India.

Archangel Michael as Byzantine protector (ivory panel, c.500).

Constantinople, 491. After the death of Zeno, his widow, the Empress Ariadne, chooses the elderly Anastasius as emperor. Anastasius, a convinced Monophysite – whom Ariadne marries after his coronation – sets about bringing some order to the ramshackle finances of the empire.

Asia Minor, 491. The Isaurians, a warrior people from the mountains of southern Asia Minor, revolt against Anastasius, the new emperor of the East, who has put an end to Isaurian power in Constantinople. The rebels are crushed at the battle of Cotiaeum.

Italy, 25 March 493. After defeating him in battle and then besieging him in Ravenna for two and a half years, the Ostrogothic king, Theodoric, persuades Odoacer to surrender by offering him a share of the government. He then promptly murders him at a banquet. The Ostrogoths now control Italy.

Rome, 3 May 495. The Italian bishops support Pope Gelasius in his refusal to yield to the Emperor Anastasius, who wants to establish the Monophysite doctrine. The pope asserts that his spiritual authority is superior to the emperor's temporal authority.

Gaul, 496. Clovis allies with the Franks of the Rhineland to defeat the Alamanni in battle at Tolbiac near the Rhine. The Alamanni are driven back beyond the Rhine.

Italy, 497. Anastasius sends the imperial insignia of the West to King Theodoric, thus recognising him as his representative in Italy.

Asia Minor, 498. The mountain strongholds of the Isaurians are finally pacified. The Isaurian threat to the Eastern empire is removed.

Gaul, c.500. Clovis, the Frankish king, is converted to Catholicism, becoming the only orthodox Catholic Christian sovereign. The kings of the Visigoths, Vandals, Burgundians and Ostrogoths are Arians, while the emperor follows the Monophysite doctrine.

West Africa, c.500. A dynasty of Hagha kings is beginning to rule Ghana, in the Sahel savannah region. They trade in gold and salt by camel trains to North Africa.

North America, c.500. The Anasazi culture is developing in Utah, Arizona and New Mexico. For protective reasons the Anasazi construct their villages on cliffs.

South America, c.500. The Huari civilisation, based in the Ayachucho valley of the central Andean region, is expanding its power by conquest as far as the northern coastal region of Peru and the Nazca area to the south.

South America, c.500. The Tiahuanaco civilisation, centred on the south coast of Lake Titicaca, shares religious and cultural beliefs with the Huari society and is also building up a large empire. There are signs that the power of Tiahuanaco, at 12,000 feet the highest city in the world, derives from its control of trade in hallucinogens for ceremonial purposes. Its influence spreads south from Bolivia into Argentina and Chile.

Britain, c.500. The Britons defeat the Saxons at Mount Badon and check the Saxon advance westwards, following the recent founding of the kingdom of the West Saxons (Wessex).

Persia, c.500. Led by Mazdak, a Zoroastrian high priest, the social and religious Mazdakite movement, which advocates the sharing of property, is gaining in popularity.

Gaul, 29 March 502. At Lyons, Gundobad, the king of the Burgundians, issues a new legal code bringing the Romans and Burgundians under the same law.

China, 502. Xiao Yan marches on Nanjing, forcing the Qi rulers, his own kinsmen, to cede their power. He founds the Liang dynasty.

Mesopotamia, 502. The Persians, having declared war on the Eastern empire for its failure to keep to the terms of the treaty of 442, sack the frontier town of Amida in northern Mesopotamia.

Balkans, 502. The Bulgars, a Mongolian people who have absorbed the remaining Huns, ravage Thrace, unopposed by the Eastern armies which they had already defeated in 493 and 499.

Mesopotamia, 506. After a Roman counter-offensive, peace is re-established between the Roman and Persian empires.

Gaul, 506. Alaric II, the king of the Visigoths, publishes a code of laws, the "Breviary of Alaric", inspired by the Theodosian code.

Gaul, 507. Allied with Gundobad, the Burgundian king, Clovis crushes the Visigoths and kills their king, Alaric II, at the battle of Vouillé. The Franks take Aquitaine; the Visigoths are pushed back into Spain.

Gaul, 508. At Tours, Clovis receives imperial recognition from Anastasius of his rule over Gaul.

Gaul, 508. Theodoric the Ostrogoth drives the Franks out of Provence and takes it over. His armies also rapidly recover Septimania (Languedoc) for the Visigoths, and Theodoric acts as regent for the infant Visigothic king, Amalaric, his grandson.

Working class of Teotihuacan, largest city in Americas, are talking of revolution

Image of the plumed serpent Quetzalcoatl from a Teotihuacan temple.

Central America, c.500
Teotihuacan in Mexico, the biggest city in the Americas, now controls the largest empire Meso-America has seen. Its gods – Tlaloc, the Rain God; Chalchiuhtlicue, the Water Goddess; Mictlantecuhtli, Lord of the Underworld, and Quetzalcoatl, the Plumed Serpent – have become the accepted gods of all Central America. Teotihuacan is not merely a political capital but also a religious one, with thousands of pilgrims flocking there every year. Society in this sprawling conurbation of nearly 250,000 people is rigidly hierarchical. The high priests live in mansions and palaces along the prestigious Avenue of the Dead. The proletariat is squashed into inner city rabbit warrens. The middle classes occupy the suburbs.

Many of the pilgrims have stayed in Teotihuacan, swelling the underclass in the inner city; there are now murmurs of discontent and threats of revolution, things never before known in Teotihuacan.

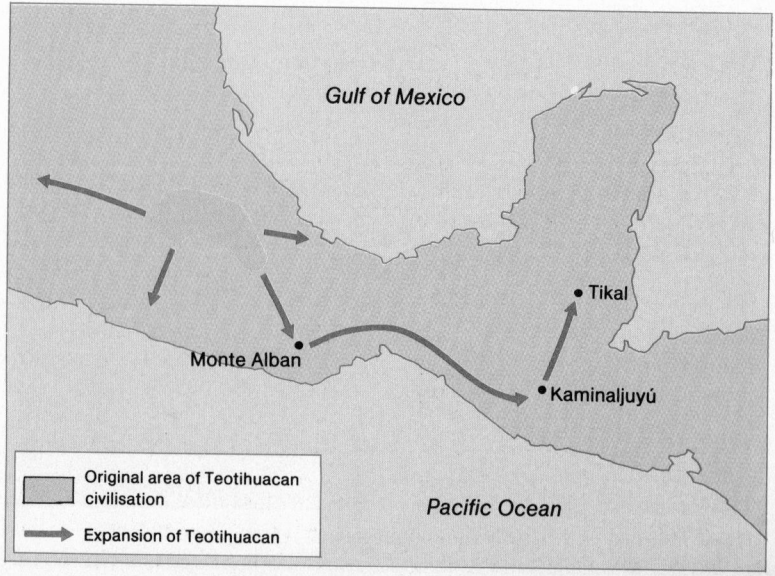

Gulf of Mexico

Tikal

Monte Alban

Kaminaljuyú

Pacific Ocean

Original area of Teotihuacan civilisation

Expansion of Teotihuacan

India and Persia attacked by Huns

Combat: Sassanid dynasty sculpture from Nagh-e-Rosta in Persia.

Hephtalites conquer the Sassanid empire

Persia, c.500
Hephtalite Huns, led by Toramana, have invaded India and made substantial inroads into Persia. The Persian Sassanid empire is in their thrall. The Hephtalites are fair-skinned nomads, not directly related to the Huns of Attila, who originated in central Asia and crossed the Oxus 160 years ago. The Persian king, Shapur II, was obliged to make them a federate state in Bactria 30 years later.

Towards the end of the last century they moved into Afghanistan, occupying Begram, near Kabul, and destroying the Kushan kingdom. The Hephtalites now control a vast area extending from Bactria through Persia, Afghanistan and India to the Indus. They extort taxes from the Sassanids, having placed their client Kavadh, the son-in-law of their chief, on the Persian throne. Their intrusions into India, where they have settled in the Malwa plain, spell the collapse of the Gupta empire.

At the same time, Persian and Indian art continue to flourish. Statues at Bamyan, in northern Afghanistan, show both Sassanid and Buddhist influences. The Hephtalites worship the sun in the form of Mithras or the Buddha; wives are shared among brothers.

"Glorious" Goth is master of the west

Italy, 510
The Ostrogoths, now the most powerful nation in western Europe following their annexation of southeastern Gaul. The move, aimed at containing the Franks, puts the Ostrogothic king, Theodoric, in control of a kingdom that stretches from Gaul to Illyricum *(Yugoslavia)*. To this may be added Spain, which Theodoric governs as regent for his grandson Amalaric, a child.

The son of King Theodomir, Theodoric united his fellow tribesmen. He threatened Constantinople for many years, but was bought off by the Emperor Zeno in 476 and made a general and consul in 484. In 489 Zeno sent him to Italy in his name to deal with the upstart Odoacer, whom he defeated in 493. Theodoric, who respects Roman customs, has since been hailed in Italy as "most glorious king".

Goths and Romans strictly divided in Italian life. Goths run the army, Romans the civil service. Goths own a third of Italy, but old Roman families enjoy traditional powers. Goths are Arian Christians – considered as heretics – while Romans are orthodox Catholics.

The Gupta empire heads for collapse

India, c.500
The Gupta empire, the cradle of Buddhist art and culture for more than a century, is disintegrating as the Huns advance ever deeper into India. Since the end of Buddha Gupta's reign, in 496, various small kingdoms have tried in vain to lay claim to his dynasty.

Under the tolerant rule of the Gupta emperors Sanskrit literature enjoyed a renewal, notably when the great poet Kalidasa was one of the "nine jewels" around King Chandragupta II. Hindu art gradually grew more specifically Buddhist, and the first small temples were built.

Under the Guptas, Buddhist art reached the peak of its development, with a distinct iconography. The Buddha was represented in a series of gestures, called *mudras*, relating to different episodes in his life. He was shown sitting, meditating, teaching, or standing, his arm halfbent in a compassionate gesture. He had a majestic silhouette, with broad shoulders, and long streamlined legs. His face was finely drawn, with an enigmatic smile, his eyes half-closed in deep meditation.

Mathura and Sarnath were the two great schools of Buddhist art, with the latter finding the finer balance between beauty of form and spiritual suggestion.

A Hindu deity in Gupta style.

King Clovis founds Frankish kingdom

Gaul, 507
Clovis, the king of the Franks, has defeated Alaric II, the king of the Visigoths, who died in a fierce battle at Vouille, ten miles from Poitiers. which leaves Clovis master of all but the south-east of Gaul.

Clovis was regarded with terror by civilised society after he defeated Syagrius's Roman army at Soissons in 486, advancing the Frankish frontier to the Loire. In 502 he pushed further east by defeating the Alamanni, another Germanic tribe.

A Frankish claw-beaker from Gaul.

Clovis, who had married Clotilda, a Catholic Burgundian, said during the battle that he would be baptised if God helped him to beat the Alamanni. He kept his word, and the Franks marched southwards under their Christian king to defeat the Burgundians at Tolbiac last year. Clovis then turned on the Visigoths. Like most Germanic invaders, the Visigoths are Arian Christians, denying the Trinity, which gave the orthodox Catholic Clovis theological justification for his conquests. "It grieves me to see that the Arians still possess the fairest portion of Gaul. Let us march against them, vanquish the heretics, and share out their fertile lands," he announced from his capital, Paris, before marching to Poitiers.

Clovis's conversion has hardly made him into a model of Christian meekness. Of Christ's crucifixion he once exclaimed: "Had I been there at the head of my army of valiant Franks, I would have avenged his death!"

510 (510-537)

Paris, 27 November 511. Clovis, king of the Franks, dies and his kingdom is divided up between his four sons: Theuderic in Reims, Chlodomer in Orleans, Childebert in Paris and Lothar in Soissons.

Korea, 512. The Japanese imperial chieftain Otomo no Kanamura agrees to the accession of the four provinces of Mimana in southern Korea to Paekche, a larger state in south-west Korea.

Burgundy, 516. Gundobad, king of the Burgundians, dies. His son Sigismund, who had shared power with his father, succeeds him and establishes Catholicism in place of Arianism among his people.

Constantinople, 9 July 518. Anastasius, who came to the throne of the Eastern empire in 491, dies. Anastasius re-established the empire's finances, reforming the coinage and taxation systems.

Constantinople, 519. The new emperor, Justin, opposed to the Monophysitism of his predecessors, re-establishes orthodoxy and relations with Rome. The 35-year schism between the western and eastern churches comes to an end.

North Africa, May 523. Hilderic succeeds Thrasamund as king of the Vandals.

Burgundy, June 524. After killing King Sigismund, the Frankish kings Chlodomer and Theuderic invade Burgundy, but Chlodomer dies in battle at Vezerone, and the Burgundian king, Godomer, holds on to his kingdom.

Italy, 524. King Theodoric imprisons his minister Boethius, a Roman aristocrat and philosopher of the old school, on a charge of plotting with the eastern emperor.

Arabia, 525. The Ethiopians win back the Yemen from the Jewish prince, Dhu Nuvas, and re-establish Christianity there.

Italy, 30 August 526. King Theodoric dies of dysentery. His daughter Amalasuntha becomes regent for her young son Athalaric.

Rome, 526. Dionysius Exiguus, a monk of Scythian origin, produces Easter Tables and propounds the AD system of dating from the birth of Christ.

Constantinople, 4 April 527. Justin, seriously ill, crowns his nephew Justinian as his co-emperor. He dies later the same year.

Japan, 529. A serious revolt in Kyushu prevents a Japanese army from crossing to Korea to support the group of southern states known as Mimana, which are now under threat of domination by Silla, a powerful kingdom in the south-east of the country.

Athens, 529. The city's school of philosophy is closed on the orders of Justinian. This is the last formal act in the breaking away from pagan culture.

Persia, 530. Under the leadership of Belisarius, the Byzantines defeat the Persians, with whom they have been at war for the last five years, at Dara.

Rhineland, 531. Thuringia is conquered by the Franks Theuderic and Lothar.

Ethiopia, 531. The Byzantine Emperor Justinian tries to recruit Axum to help him in his fight against Persia.

China, 531. Xiao Tong, the elder son of the Liang emperor and author of the *Wenxuan*, an anthology of the past 500 years, dies aged 30.

Constantinople, January 532. A popular revolt against Justinian's rule causes panic in the capital, until 30,000 rebels are massacred in the circus by imperial troops.

Persia, 532. After a seven-year war, the new Persian king Khosrow signs a "treaty of eternal peace" with Justinian.

Burgundy, 534. The kingdom of the Burgundians, founded in 442, is annexed by the Franks.

North Africa, 534. The Byzantine forces, led by Belisarius, conquer the Vandal kingdom and capture the last Vandal king, Gelimer. Much of North Africa is now controlled by the Byzantines.

China, 535. The Northern Wei dynasty splits into Eastern and Western halves, which are dominated by the Gao and Yuwen families respectively.

Italy, 30 April 535. Theodahad, the new king of the Ostrogoths, has his wife, Queen Amalasuntha, the daughter of Theodoric, strangled. His action gives Justinian a pretext for his planned invasion of Italy.

Sicily, 535. Belisarius begins the conquest of the Ostrogothic kingdom by occupying the island of Sicily.

Rome, 9 December 536. Having captured Naples earlier in the year, Belisarius takes Rome. The Ostrogoths depose their inactive king, Theodahad, and elect a general, Vitigis, to replace him.

Ethiopia, 536. By its persecution of the Coptic church in Egypt, Rome has alienated the kingdom of Axum, which now severs its connections with Rome.

Italy, 537. Benedict, the abbot of Monte Cassino, draws up his monastic rule (the Benedictine Rule).

Philosophy consoles writer in prison

Pavia, Italy, 524
Anicius Boethius, the Roman senator who rose to be Master of the Offices for Theodoric, the Ostrogothic ruler of Italy, finished his most important work in prison just before his execution.

Boethius was largely responsible for making the rule of the Gothic king relatively easy for his fellow countrymen to bear, but last year his forthrightness cost him his freedom. He was stripped of power and accused of treasonable contacts with the Eastern empire. His downfall came when he spoke up in defence of Albinus, who was himself accused of high treason. Boethius stated that, if Albinus was guilty, so was he, and indeed, so was the entire Senate.

De Consolatione Philosophiae (The Consolation of Philosophy) is written in the form of a conversation with Philosophy on the trans-

The philosopher Boethius, as seen by a late 16th century artist.

ience of earthly fortune, and it concludes that nothing except virtue has permanence; Boethius accepts his fate stoically. His translations of Aristotle, Euclid and Ptolemy are already renowned.

Barbarians record their laws in Latin

Western Roman Empire, c.520
The barbarians have begun to record their laws in Latin. Previously, these illiterate people relied on specialists to commit the law to memory.

The Visigoths were the first to document their laws, in King Euric's Code, some 40 years ago. The Burgundians were the next, about 20 years ago, and now the Salic Franks (the more powerful of two main Frankish groups) are doing the same. The Visigoths also recorded the laws of the Romans in the *Breviary of Alaric* for their own use in 506.

Barbarian trial is by oath-swearing and, if that fails, ordeal by fire and water. To prevent vendettas, compensation is paid to the families of crime victims.

Wrangle over date of Easter settled

Rome, 525
The monk Dionysius Exiguus has published a table aimed at settling the controversy about the date of Easter which has been raging for at least a century. In 325 the Council of Nicaea decided that Easter should be the Sunday following the first full moon after the spring equinox on the Julian calendar authorised by Julius Caesar. Dionysius numbers his calendar from Christ's birth, which he estimates was 48 years after the death of Caesar. This would replace traditional methods of numbering by the years of emperors' reigns or by the terms of the consuls.

Monastery built on burning bush site

Sinai, c.530
Justinian, the Byzantine emperor, has founded a monastery in the Sinai desert on the spot where the burning bush is said to have appeared to Moses. St Catherine's monastery has been built nearly 5,000 feet above sea level at the foot of Mount Sinai. It is fortified, and decorated with mosaics of the Transfiguration. Icons are also being painted, and St Catherine's could become an anchorage point of Christianity. Justinian, who has just become emperor, is bent on reasserting imperial authority and regaining former Roman possessions in North Africa.

Tax rebels are massacred in stadium

New rules for life in monk's "family"

Constantinople, 532

The dead lay in their thousands in the hippodrome here after a massacre of the huge crowd attending the chariot races. Armies commanded by the generals Belisarius and Mundus broke up a riot which followed three days of burning, and attacked the mob, even as the Emperor Justinian was preparing to flee from the city.

The cause of the riot was the ever-growing conflict between "Greens" and "Blues" – the two sides who have for so long demonstrated their political differences in the hippodrome. Emperors are traditionally above such conficts – but Justinian, by his harsh system of taxation, has been shown to be a "Blue". Through a particularly cruel tax-collector, John of Cappadocia, Justinian has incensed Constantinople by demanding heavy taxes to support his wars in Persia. This was a root cause of the hippodrome massacre and the emergence of Belisarius.

Justinian assumed the mantle of emperor five years ago, on the death of his uncle, Justin, and has long yearned for the return of the grandeur of a Rome that was.

A brilliant, if autocratic, admin-

Justinian's basilica of St Apollinaris in Classe, at Ravenna, in Italy.

istrator and a learned theologian, he is a hard worker, yet intensely emotional and unstable. Rome to him is the cradle of culture, Christianity and civilisation; he aims to restore it to its former glory.

As Belisarius prepares to fight the Vandals in Africa, Justinian continues to seek a reason for invading Italy and re-taking Rome. And even now, as he watches his invading fleet sail down the Bosporus, Justinian is planning the re-

form of Roman law, the restoration of the empire's boundaries, a better administration and the unification of its Christian faith.

Encouraged in all his aims by his wife Theodora, Justinian is a vain man, an irritable despot who trusts no-one except his wife in a palace renowned as a hot-bed of intrigue. Theodora has lived in Syria and Egypt: perhaps it was she who inspired Justinian's dream of a Rome he has never seen.

Italy, 537

Monasticism has taken a step towards playing a full and active part in the life of the Church with the appearance this year of a new rule to govern monastic life. The Rule has been set out by Benedict, the head of the monastery of Monte Cassino in central Italy. He was born into an aristocratic family at Nursia, in about 480, and educated at Rome. The licentiousness of society led him to become a hermit in a mountain wilderness for several years. A community grew up around him, and he set up 12 monasteries of 12 monks each. But local jealousies forced him to flee, and with a small band of monks he founded Monte Cassino, a monastery intended for laymen, in 529.

Benedict's Rule is similar to other codes, but less rigid and austere, and is a powerful expression of monastic joys and ideals, insisting chiefly on inner discipline. The monastery is a "family" governed by an abbot elected for life by the monks. After a probationary year a new monk takes his vows, but there is no particular vow of poverty; all the monastery's goods are held in common. Central to a monk's life is the Divine Office, the many services he attends throughout the day and night, which inspires the work, study and private prayer which take up the rest of his day.

Belisarius defeats Vandals in North Africa

Justinian adds final touch to legal code

North Africa, March 534

A Byzantine army under the command of Belisarius has smashed the Vandal armies of King Gelimer and looks set to free North Africa from Vandal domination. The relatively small invading force – numbering about 18,000 troops, 1,000 barbarian allies and Belisarius' own bodyguard, carried in 500 ships – landed in Byzacenum last August. Within a month, the imperial force had crushed a large Vandal army at Ad Decinum and the gates of Carthage were opened to the empire.

Belisarius is a brilliant strategist, but he was helped in his attack on the Vandals by the absence of their king who was putting down a revolt in Sardinia. Gelimer returned to Africa this month, blockading Carthage in the process, but his armies were defeated within an hour of meeting the imperial army at Tricamarum. Gelimer has fled and the

empire is poised to recover all its lost possessions in the imperial province of Africa (*Tunisia*). An overjoyed Justinian has awarded himself the title of *Vandalicus* (conqueror of the Vandals), and Belisarius will receive a *Triumph* on his return.

A victory medallion of Belisarius.

Constantinople, 534

The confused state of Roman law has been ended by the final revision of Justinian's mighty *Codex*. When his reign began the empire had a baffling mixture of old and new Roman laws, some dating back to the days of the republic and the early emperors, much of its records scarce or lost. Added to this were the ordinances of the emperors of the last 200 years, which often conflicted with previous laws.

Justinian appointed a commission of eminent advocates under Tribonian to reconcile all these edicts. They also simplified the commentaries of the classical jurists, some of which are in force as civil law. The results are a unified Code of Statutes, a digest of legal commentaries, and a summary, all valid for the entire Roman world.

Benedict: laying down the law.

Rome, 537. Having secured his rear by conceding Provence, in Ostrogothic hands since 508, to the Franks, Vitigis moves on Rome and lays siege to it. The Franks now control all of Gaul except Visigothic Septimania (Languedoc) and Armorica (Brittany).

Rome, 538. Vitigis abandons his siege of Rome.

Japan, 538. Gilded bronze Buddhist images and *sutras* start to arrive in Japan from Korea.

Italy, March 539. Milan, one of the most important cities in Italy after Rome, is recaptured by the Ostrogoths and destroyed. The men are massacred and the women sold as slaves.

Italy, May 540. Vitigis, king of the Ostrogoths, is tricked into surrendering to Belisarius, who takes possession of Ravenna. The reconquest of Italy south of the Po seems complete. Belisarius returns to Constantinople, taking Vitigis with him.

Constantinople, 540. A great Bulgar horde ravages Thrace and Macedonia and reaches the walls of Constantinople before returning home laden with booty.

Ethiopia, c.540. Ethiopian scholars have begun to translate the Bible into their Geez language.

Kush, 540. Kush, to the south of Egypt, is divided into three Nubian kingdoms – Nobatia, Alodia and Mukurra (Dongola).

Syria, 540. Khosrow, king of the Persians, resumes the war against Justinian by invading Syria. Antioch, the most important city in the area, is sacked.

Italy, 541. The senator Cassiodorus, once the chief minister of Theodoric, king of the Ostrogoths, founds a monastery and famous library in his retreat at Vivarium in southern Italy.

Spain, 541. The Franks attack the Visigothic kingdom in northern Spain, but are driven back at Saragossa.

Constantinople, May 542. An epidemic of bubonic plague, which started in Egypt in 541, reaches Constantinople, killing hundreds of thousands of people. It spreads throughout the empire and is carried to Italy.

Italy, 543. With the departure of Belisarius, the imperial forces are in disarray. Totila, the new king of the Ostrogoths, advances to Italy, where he takes Naples after a siege. Belisarius is forced to return to Italy.

Kush, 543. The Nubian kingdom of Nobatia is converted to Christianity by Coptic missionaries from Egypt.

Rome, 17 December 546. The Ostrogothic king, Totila, captures Rome after a year's siege. The city has been deserted by all but 500 of its civilian inhabitants.

Rome, 547. Belisarius, the Byzantine general, reoccupies and repairs the defences of the deserted city of Rome.

North Africa, 547. The Berber tribes of the interior, which have long been rebelling against the Byzantines, are crushed. After a series of civil wars and revolts, Africa is now at peace.

Constantinople, 548. Justinian summons Pope Vigilus from Rome and induces him to sign his edict condemning "The Three Chapters": certain theological works accepted at the Council of Chalcedon in 451, but regarded as Nestorian heresy by the Monophysites. In this way Justinian hopes to reconcile the Monophysites to the Catholic faith as expressed at Chalcedon. This action causes protests in the West.

Constantinople, 28 June 548. Theodora, wife of the Emperor Justinian, dies. She had been a highly influential figure at court, but was unable to get Justinian to favour her Monophysite faith.

China, 548. General Hou Jing, a Toba northerner who has entered the service of the Chinese Liang in the south, heads a rebellion against his masters and leads his troops on Nanjing.

China, 549. Hou Jing lays waste to Nanjing.

China, 549. During the reign of Wudi, who has died after 47 years as emperor, Mahayana (the "Greater Vehicle") has become the predominant form of Buddhism.

Italy, 550. After Belisarius, frustrated by lack of imperial money and reinforcements, is recalled from Italy, Totila proceeds to recapture Rome and to complete the reconquest.

Britain, c.550. The Anglo-Saxons again begin to push westwards, driving back or subjecting to their rule the Romano-British population.

Kush, 550. The Nubian kingdom of Alodia is converted to Christianity by Coptic missionaries.

Egypt, 552. The patriarch, Apollinarius, re-establishes Catholicism in Alexandria by bloody repression, with the help of imperial troops. Coptic resistance, however, remains strong.

Italy, 552. Justinian finally responds to the crisis in Italy by sending out a huge force led by Narses. He defeats and kills Totila in battle at Busta Gallorum.

Emperor opens the church of St Sophia

Constantinople, 27 December 537
The finest church in Christendom, St Sophia's, was dedicated today with great ceremony by the Emperor Justinian, just five years after building started.

The original church of *Hagia* (Saint) Sophia was built by the city's founder, Emperor Constantine in 330, but was severely burnt, with much of Constantinople, during the rebellion of the circus factions in 532, when the Emperor was nearly overthrown.

Justinian charged the architects Anthemius of Tralles and Isidore of Miletus with St Sophia's rebuilding; despite some architectural difficulties, they have produced a truly magnificent, richly decorated monument.

St Sophia, with Islamic additions.

Japanese look to Buddha for wisdom

Japan, 538
Buddhism has been officially recognised here with the Emperor Kimmei's acceptance of a gold and copper image of the Buddha from King Syong Myong of Paekche, a Korean state. There is a practical reason for the gift: Syong Myong needs military help. But the message with it, that Buddhism can lead "to a grasp of the highest wisdom", has sparked much debate at court.

Courtesan who maimed emperor, dies

Constantinople, 28 June 548
Theodora, the pious and powerful empress and courtesan, who outraged Constantinople opinion when she married the Emperor Justinian, has died of cancer in her early forties. She was a woman of great character and beauty, small and rather pale, with a piercing gaze.

She had considerable influence over her husband and certainly saved his crown during the so-called Nika riots, when the city was taken over by the mob, churches and public buildings were put to the torch and the palace was besieged. When courtiers urged flight, Theodora cried: "Reflect whether, once you have escaped, you would not prefer death to safety." Her brave words persuaded the emperor to stay and fight.

Theodora, the daughter of the bear-keeper at the circus, took to the stage while still a child. When Justinian wanted to marry her, the law forbidding patrician marriage to an actress had to be repealed. Although 20 years younger than the emperor she was no mere consort, but became actively involved in the imperial government. She supported the Monophysites, and endowed Christian institutions and monasteries in Constantinople.

Theodora: woman of influence.

Invaders push out Celts

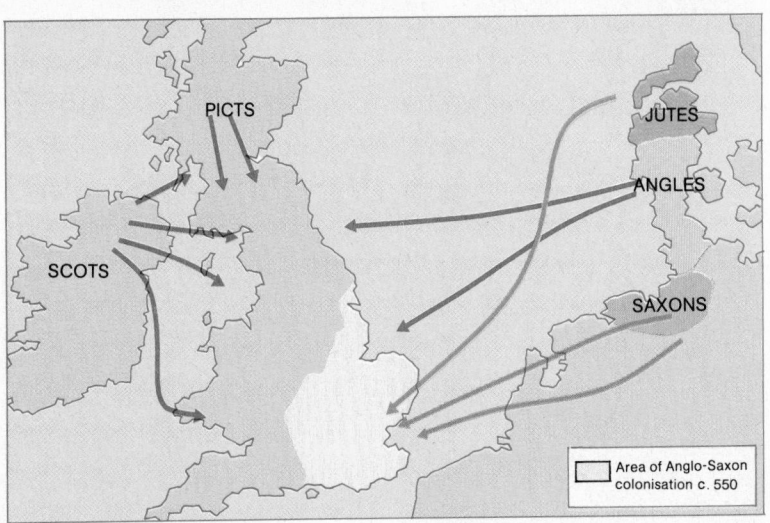

Area of Anglo-Saxon colonisation c. 550

Britain, c.550

Piecemeal colonisation of Britain by North German tribes has changed the face of the country. Since the middle of the last century, Angles, Saxons and Jutes have crossed the North Sea and sailed up big rivers, such as the Thames and Humber, in search of new lands.

The invaders live mainly in the countryside and farm the heavy soil of the river valleys, with the result that they have largely ignored the old Romano-British towns and villas, many of which have fallen into ruins. Those Romano-Britons and Celts not wishing to live alongside the Germanic invaders he mi-

grated to western Britain, or to Armorica (Brittany). As if to show that they are here to stay, the Germans refer to British natives as *Welsh*, or foreigners.

Natives and newcomers co-existed reasonably well until King Maelgwyn of Gwynedd died three years ago. That prompted renewed German advances and a *Welsh* defeat at Catterick, which has threatened to cut off the British tribes north of Hadrian's Wall from their fellow Celts in the west. The Germans boast that the last local to win a battle was a Romanised Celt called Artorius or Arthur, about 50 years ago.

Epidemic of plague spreads from Egypt

Constantinople, 542

At least half the population of the imperial capital is believed to have been wiped out in an epidemic of plague that has left thousands of rotting corpses in the streets and brought normal life to a standstill. The plague has now spread to Antioch and the rest of Syria.

This is the latest, and most catastrophic, of a series of disasters which has struck the empire in the last 30 years; it appears to have begun in Egypt, and arrived in Constantinople early this year. Hallucinations may precede an attack. On the first day of the plague the victims have a fever and feel languid; then, or on the next day, they

begin to suffer from buboes, or swellings, in the groin, the armpit, the thighs, or by the ears – these have proved fetid when lanced after death. The fever grows more violent and the patient sometimes falls into a deep coma, or becomes violently delirious, and may suffer from black pustules or carbuncles. Death is often, but not always, rapid.

In four months people have died more quickly than they can be buried, sometimes at the rate of 16,000 a day. Those living in close quarters, such as the poor and soldiers, have been especially hard hit. The current death toll, as the plague abates, may be around 230,000 of the city's 400,000 inhabitants.

African farmers make terracotta heads

Africa, 540

Agricultural communities are growing up in the western foothills of the Drakensberg Mountains in southern Africa. These farmers, recent immigrants from the north, own sheep, cattle, goats and dogs, and use iron and copper implements. They make pots and ceramics decorated with intricate motifs.

The women have elaborate hairstyles, and adorn themselves with many-coloured bead necklaces, held together by thin copper bands, and facial incisions.

Society is organised along tribal lines, and every year the youth of the community mark the arrival of adulthood with sacred initiation rites. Terracotta heads are placed on the high totem poles rising above the villages, and stay there throughout the ceremony before being returned to the pits where they are kept for safety. The terracotta heads are as exquisite and elaborate as the hairstyles of the women, the same motifs appearing on them as adorn both the pottery and the cheeks of the women.

Mosaics adorn regal Ravenna

Italy, 548

Following his reconquest of much of Italy, the Emperor Justinian has set about adding to the monuments of Ravenna, the seat of his viceroy in the West. Chief among these is the church of St Vitalis, begun under Ostrogothic rule by a rich banker. The interior is decorated with beautiful mosaics made from thousands of coloured glass cubes, reflecting the light and bathing the church in their rich colours, mainly green and gold. Justinian and the Empress Theodora stare down from the chancel. New mosaics are also planned for the basilica of St Apollinaris.

The mosaics of the Baptistry in Ravenna are among the splendours of the city. The dome shown here (l., and detail, r.) illustrates the baptism of Christ and the Twelve Apostles.

552 (552-580)

China, 552. While General Chen Baxian drives out the mutinous Toba general, Hou Jing, from Nanjing in the south, Gao Yang deposes the last emperor of the Northern Qi, thereby gaining control of most of northern China.

Italy, 553. The Byzantine general Narses defeats Teias, Tortila's successor as king of the Ostrogoths, at Mons Lactarius. The reconquest of Italy is almost complete.

Constantinople, 553. The historian Procopius completes his *Wars*, an account of Justinias conquests.

Italy, 13 August 554. The Emperor Justinian launches a programme to reorganise the administration of Italy after the chaos of the 20-year war with the Ostrogoths.

Spain, 554. Justinian's troops, invited to Spain two years ago by Athanagild, the pretender to the Visigothic throne, continue to occupy the southern part of the country after Athanagild becomes king and has no further use for them. They establish their capital at Cordoba.

Constantinople, December 557. An earthquake rocks the city, damaging the great church of St Sophia.

China, 557. Yu Wenjue deposes the last emperor of the Western Wei and sets up the Northern Zhou dynasty. In the south, Chen Baxian ousts the contending heirs to the throne and creates his own dynasty, the Chen.

Constantinople, 7 May 558. The dome of the church of St Sophia collapses. Its immediate rebuilding is ordered by Justinian.

Constantinople, 558. Another epidemic of plague breaks out in the city.

Central Asia, c.560. The enormous Turkish race breaks its ties with the Juan-Juan or Avars, who created the first Mongol empire shortly after 400, and founds two states. One is based in Mongolia (eastern Turks) and the other in Zungaria (western Turks). These events cause the migration of the Avar people towards the Caucasus.

Central Asia, 560. Khosrow, the king of the Persians, allied with the western Turks, destroys the empire of the Hephtalites, which was set up on the borders of Persia and India about 100 years ago.

Gaul, 561. Lothar, who has been the sole king of the Franks since 558, dies at Compiegne. The Frankish kingdom is divided between his four sons.

Balkans, 561. The Avars appear for the first time on the Danube frontier of the Eastern empire.

Constantinople, 561. Justinian establishes a new treaty with Khosrow by which the Persian frontier with the Byzantine empire is restored. The Byzantines, however, now undertake to pay an annual tribute.

Constantinople, 562. Justinian attends the second consecration of St Sophia's Church after the restoration of its dome.

Constantinople, 565. Justinian dies after a reign of 38 years. He leaves to his successor, Justin II, his nephew, an empire at its territorial peak, but facing serious barbarian threats to its overstretched resources on most frontiers.

Gaul, 567. On the death of their brother Charibert, the sons of Lothar re-divide the Frankish kingdom. Sigibert takes Austrasia (eastern Gaul), Chilperic takes Neustria (western Gaul) and Guntram takes Burgundy (south-eastern Gaul).

Pannonia, 567. The Lombards and Avars combine to crush the Gepids. The Avars take over their territory on the middle Danube.

Italy, 568. Under their king, Alboin, the Lombards abandon Pannonia (Hungary) to the Avars and invade northern Italy.

Sudan (Kush), 569. Following the conversions of Nobatia, in 543 and Alodia, in 550, the Nubian kingdom of Makuria (Dongola) is converted to Christianity.

Japan, 570. The Korean kingdom of Koguryo sends its first embassy to Japan.

West Africa, c.570. Sef ibn Dhi Yazan founds the first Bornu kingdom of Kanem.

Arabia, 570. Mohammed is born in Mecca.

Arabia, 572. The Axumites are expelled from Yemen back across the Red Sea by the Persians.

Italy, 572. After a three-year siege Pavia falls to the Lombards, who have overrun northern Italy; but their king, Alboin, is murdered by his Gepid wife.

Constantinople, 573. Despite the Lombard invasion of Italy, the Visigoths recapture Cordoba in Spain, and revolts in Africa, Justin II provokes war with the Persians, who ravage Syria and capture the strategic city of Dara.

China, 577. The dynamic emperor Wu of the Northern Zhou conquers the Northern Qi and reunifies China.

Constantinople, 578. Tiberius II succeeds Justin II as ruler of the Byzantine empire. He has effectively ruled since 574, when Justin II became insane.

Emperor dedicates St Sophia's new dome

St Sophia's main dome rises majestically above a smaller eastern dome.

Constantinople, 24 December 562
The ageing Emperor Justinian today dedicated the new dome of the church of St Sophia, four and a half years after the roof of his great basilica collapsed. St Sophia's has now been rebuilt twice. Between 532 and 537 the original church was completely replaced after being destroyed in a riot; the architects of the new building were Anthemius of Tralles and Isidore of Miletus. An earthquake in 557 severely weakened the perhaps over-ambitious structure, which led to the collapse of the dome and much of the roof the following year.

Isidore's son was commissioned by Justinian to repair the damage. Among other things, Isidore the Younger supported the new dome on four massive pillars, skilfully concealed and in turn supported by buttresses. His dome is narrower and steeper than its predecessor and perhaps less striking; on the other hand, it is still an imposing feature, and much safer structurally than its predecessor.

The effects of light and space inside the church are described by the historian Procopius as of "an ineffable beauty". It seems, he says, as if "radiance is generated within, so great an abundance of light bathes this shrine all round".

A mosaic in St Sophia of Justinian (l.) and Constantine before the Virgin.

Khosrow, King of Persia is dead

Persia, 579

Khosrow, the king of the Persians, has died during a third war with the Romans. His 48-year reign has seen a return to the grandest days of the Persian empire, which now stretches from the river Oxus to the shores of the Red Sea.

In 531, when Khosrow came to the throne, the Sassanid empire was embroiled in seemingly endless conflict with Rome, was paying tribute to the Hephtalite Huns, and was suffering internal disturbance from the Mazdakite revolutionary movement. His first step was to make peace with Rome – the "Eternal Peace" concluded with Justinian in 532.

Turning to domestic matters, he restored to their owners all goods confiscated by the Mazdakites, who believed in sharing everything; abducted women were allowed to choose whether or not to return to their husbands. Khosrow reduced taxes, especially for the old. He kept the aristocracy under control by installing four military governors, answerable only to him. He was tolerant towards the Christians and had a good relationship with the patriarchs of the Nestorian Church, one of whom was his old doctor. He ordered the construction of many fine new buildings,

The Takhti Khesra, residence of the Persian kings at the city of Ctesiphon.

including the Takhti Khesra at Ctesiphon. In alliance with the Turks, Khosrow withdrew tribute from the Hephtalites, whom he went on to destroy in campaigns between 565 and 568, when he annexed Bactria.

Persia's greatest glory under Khosrow came with the renewal of war with the old enemy, the Eastern empire, under the Emperor Justinian. In 540 he attacked Syria, sacked Antioch, and deported its citizens to Ctesiphon. He made peace again in 562.

King Khosrow among dignitaries.

Foreign ideas split the Japanese court

Japan, 552

Unrest is brewing at the court of the Emperor Kimmei over a small matter, but one which has unleashed open hostility to foreign ideas.

The argument centres on a gilded bronze statue of the Buddha and some Buddhist texts which Syong Myong, the king of Paekche in Korea, has given to Kimmei in the hope of securing an alliance against a rival king. The emperor is thought to be impressed by Buddhism, to the dismay of opponents of the recent influx of mainland ideas. Indeed, Syong Myong's statue has split Kimmei's court, with those who favour Buddhism and new ideas opposed to those bound to traditional Shinto beliefs and hostile to alien influences.

Christian sect converts Nubian kingdoms

Nubia, c.569

The last of the three Nubian kingdoms, Mukurra, has been converted to Christianity by missionaries from Egypt who uphold the Monophysitic belief in the one nature, both human and divine, of Christ.

In conflict with orthodox, Melkite Christians, the Monophysites first gained a hold in Nubia because of scheming by the Emperor Justinian's wife, Theodora, in 543. In defiance of her husband she arranged for Julian, a Monophysite to reach the kingdom of Nobatia before his opponents, and the conversion was soon accomplished. The kingdom of Alodia followed suit in 550.

New book celebrates Justinian's wars

Constantinople, 553

A new account of the conquests of the Emperor Justinian has just been completed by Procopius, an historian who was born at Caesarea, in Palestine. *The Wars* is written in Greek, and is in eight volumes divided into three parts. Each part covers one of Justinian's campaigns: against the Persians in the east, the Vandals in North Africa, and the Goths in Italy.

Much of Procopius' account has the liveliness of an eyewitness, because he is a longtime companion of Justinian's general, Belisarius, who led the reconquest of North Africa. His stylistic predecessors are the writers Herodotus, Thucydides and Polybius.

Justinian realises dream to recapture Italy for the empire

Italy, 554

The Emperor Justinian has realised his dream of reconquering Italy – a land which he has never even seen, ravaged and close to economic ruin after 20 years of bloody conflict – for the empire.

After Belisarius had vanquished the Vandals in Africa, Justinian found a pretext for invading Italy in the murder of the pro-Roman Ostrogothic queen, Amalasuntha, by her husband Theodahad. Belisarius sailed from Africa to take Sicily and Naples before he marched, unopposed, into Rome. Thus began a war that see-sawed the length of Italy. Justinian's forces pushed right through Italy, while the Goths, under their new leader, Witigis, counter-attacked and unsuccessfully besieged Rome.

Justinian boastfully assumed the title *Gothicus* (conqueror of the Goths), but his enemy was by no means defeated. Regrouping in the north under King Totila, the Goths struck again, capturing Naples (543) and Rome (546), which became deserted. Belisarius only just held on to Ravenna. By 551 almost all Italy was back in Totila's hands. Justinian finally provided the money for an army of at least 20,000 under General Narses, an Armenian eunuch, to recover Italy again. Totila fell in a two-day battle; his successor was killed on the slopes of Vesuvius. Justinian had won, but the price of his imperial dream was a wrecked country on the verge of collapse.

The Basilica of St John at Ephesus, built by the Emperor Justinian.

Spain, 580. Bishop Martin, who converted the Arian Sueves to Catholicism in the 560s, dies at Braga in north-western Spain.

Balkans, c.580. The Slavs, a people who have been threatening the Danube frontier for the past 30 years, begin to settle in the Balkans; they recognise Avar supremacy.

Italy, c.580. Cassiodorus, founder of a monastery and renowned library on his estate at Vivarium, dies. He leaves a series of literary, grammatical and historical works of his own, and many classical works survive in his library to be copied by future monks.

China, 581. The last emperor of the Northern Zhou is overthrown by one of his own partly Chinese generals, Yang Jian.

Balkans, 582. The Emperor Tiberius II surrenders Sirmium to the Avars and pays them a huge tribute to safeguard the rest of the Balkans. In August he dies and is succeeded by Maurice, the general on the eastern frontier.

Spain, 585. Leovigild, the Arian king of the Visigoths, conquers the kingdom of the Sueves, in the north-west of Spain.

Spain, 586. Leovigild dies and the persecution of the Catholics ends with the accession of his Catholic son Recared.

Central Asia, 589. At the head of a vast empire, the western Turks, based in Zungaria, take control of the Silk Road.

Spain, May 589. The Visigothic king Recared imposes the Catholic faith on his Gothic subjects at the Council of Toledo. Arianism, which has long hindered the fusion of the conquered peoples of the empire and the barbarians, is now virtually extinct, except among the Lombards.

China, 589. After launching a successful combined naval and land attack against the Chen capital on the Yangzi river, Yang Jian takes the south and reunites China under the Sui dynasty.

Persia, 589. Khosrow II is deposed from the throne of Persia in a military revolt and flees to Constantinople to seek support.

Italy, 590. The Lombards survive a combined attack by the Franks and the Byzantines by retreating behind their city walls. They pay the Franks tribute to withdraw.

Rome, 590. Gregory, who founded six monasteries in Sicily as well as St Andrew's in Rome, of which he is now abbot, is elected pope against his will.

Burgundy, c.590. Columban founds a monastery at Luxeuil.

Persia, 591. The Byzantine Emperor Maurice restores Khosrow II to the throne of Persia. In return he receives significant territorial concessions; peace is once again established between the two empires.

Balkans, 592. Maurice begins warfare against the Avars and the Slavs, who have been periodically ravaging the Balkans and threatening Constantinople for the last decade.

Japan, 592. The emperor of Japan has been put to death by Soga Umako. This is the latest stage in the continuing friction between the clans of the Soga, who support Buddhism, and the Mononobe, who maintain the supremacy of the indigenous *kami* deities.

Britain, 597. Augustine, sent by Pope Gregory, arrives in Kent on a mission to convert the pagan Anglo-Saxons to Christianity.

Italy, 598. After steady Lombard advances under King Agilulf since 591, the Byzantines finally conclude a treaty conceding northern Italy.

Britain, c.600. Augustine converts King Aethelbert of Kent to Catholic Christianity.

North America, c.600. Hohokam culture, which shows signs of Mexican influence, emerges in the south-west Arizona desert. Social organisation is at a chieftainship level. At Snaketown and Pueblo Grande ball courts are erected, while at Mesa Grade low pyramid-type buildings are under construction.

North America, c.600. Hopewell has ceased to be the dominant culture of the Midwest and has almost disappeared as a cultural style.

South America, c.600. On Marajo island, in the mouth of the Amazon, social organisation has developed to a chieftainship level. Very large and elaborate pottery styles are produced.

Peru, c.600. The Moche empire has collapsed as a result of Huari expansion. Another possible cause of the collapse is a major environmental change which has caused the canals that irrigated the city of Moche to silt up.

Asia Minor, 27 November 602. In the midst of a lengthy war against the Avars in which they have the upper hand, the Byzantine troops in the Balkans mutiny and choose the centurion Phocas as their leader. They march on Constantinople, where they get popular support. The Emperor Maurice flees but is captured and executed. Phocas becomes emperor.

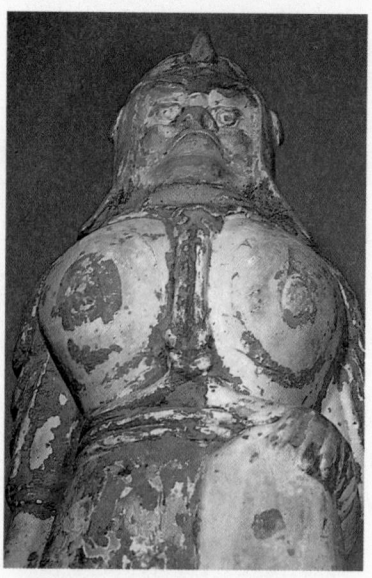
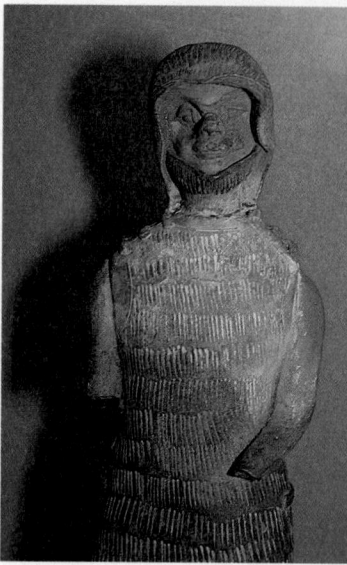

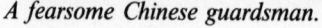
A fearsome Chinese guardsman.   *Chinese infantryman in armour.*

Chinese empire reunified by Sui dynasty

China, 589
Yang Jian, a ruthless warlord of mixed Chinese and Tartar blood, has reunified China after 400 years of division and civil war. Naming himself Emperor Wendi, he has founded a new imperial dynasty, the Sui.

He first claimed the throne eight years ago when he overthrew the ruler of the Northern Chou kingdom and massacred the Yu-wen royal family. However, it has taken him until now to subdue the rest of China, although the final resistance of the discredited Ch'en dynasty in the south was ineffectual.

Wendi has now embarked on a campaign of reorganising the administration and restoring the economy. Much needs to be done, but the emperor, who is described as miserly as well as despotic, has already established an efficient tax-gathering system.

The government warehouses are filling up with rice and silk, and China is enjoying a strength and prosperity it has not seen since the start of the long Period of Division.

This new strength is being displayed in the confident manner in which Wendi is dealing with China's troublesome neighbours. One grave danger still faces him. It is the danger common to all China's emperors: a son overly-impatient for the throne.

Japanese emperor killed by his uncle

Japan, 592
Soga no Umako, a powerful figure at the Yamato Court, has had his nephew, the Emperor Sushun, assassinated. A devout Buddhist, but ruthless politician, Umako's ambition is to establish the Soga family's supremacy at court.

Sushun was put on the throne by Umako five years ago when the Sogas overcame the anti-Buddhist Mononobe family. But he overstepped his role as puppet emperor and has been replaced by the Empress Suiko, Umako's niece, from whom more cooperation is expected. Umako is her chief minister.

Gregory writes a Frankish history

Tours, 593
Bishop Gregory of Tours who has died has written a remarkable book about the Frankish kingdom. "History of the Franks," which he has been working on over the last 20 years, records events, and the reigns, of the Frankish sovereigns and their ancestors in vivid detail. The book is one of the few sources of the period.

Bishop Gregory was by birth a Gallo-Roman aristocrat. During his time as bishop he defended the rights of the Church against infringements by the kings and their representatives. He died aged 58.

Spanish Visigoths impose Catholic creed

Augustine converts pagan king of Kent

A decorated Visigothic cross.

Toledo, May 589
Spain, its faith for so long split between the Arianism of its Visigothic occupiers and the orthodox Catholicism of its subject population, is at last to have a single creed. From now on, as laid down by this month's council at Toledo, Spain is a Catholic country.

The conflict between Arians and Catholics – the former refusing to accept the full equality of the Son with the Father – has persisted since the Council of Nicaea in 325. The Visigoths, who have occupied Spain since 458, have always been Arians, but until the reign of Leovigild (568-586) their faith had not been a contentious issue.

In 578, having successfully fought off the Franks and the Byzantines, Leovigild decided that religious unity would promote national solidarity. He began persecuting Catholics, but few changed their beliefs. His elder son Hermenegild actually converted after marrying a Frankish Catholic princess, and attempted to overthrow his father in 583. The revolt ended in 585 and Hermenegild died in prison, still a stalwart Catholic.

Leovigild himself died in 586 and was succeeded by Recared, his younger son. Recared, too, saw the need for religious, and thereby national, unity, but in 587 he chose the Catholicism of the majority. He summoned Spain's leaders to Toledo to declare their adherence.

Some Visigoth priests remain diehard Arians, but most were prepared to accept the declaration.

A cross commemorating Augustine.

Canterbury, England, c.600
Christianity is becoming firmly established here, thanks to the efforts of Augustine who was sent three years ago by Pope Gregory to evangelise the Anglo-Saxon kingdoms. He landed at the Isle of Thanet in the kingdom of Kent, ruled by King Aethelbert, who was initially very suspicious because of his pagan belief that priests practised magic. However, thanks to his wife, Bertha, a Frankish Christian, he was converted.

The king has provided a house

The baptism of Aethelbert in 597.

for Augustine at Canterbury, and churches have been built in the area. So successful has Augustine been that Christianity is also becoming established in the neighbouring kingdom of Essex. However, Pope Gregory's master plan of setting up a network of bishoprics throughout the country, with archbishops at York and London, seems totally impractical in current circumstances. Most old Roman towns are in ruins, and most of the many small Anglo-Saxon kingdoms are still firmly pagan.

Columba dies at his monastery on Iona

Iona, 597
Columba has died in the monastery which he established on this beautiful remote island off the western coast of Scotland. It is said that he delivered a final message to the community of monks and rushed to the church where he was found dying on the altar steps, his eyes radiant with joy.

Although only a priest, Columba, who was over 60, was recognised as the religious authority over monastic communities throughout western Scotland and the north of Ireland. He successfully evangelised south-western Scotland, and the new king of the Scots of Dal Riada so respected him that he came to Iona for his blessing.

Columba was born in Ireland of a noble family. When young he killed a man while defending his kin. Consumed with guilt, he banished himself to Iona and there founded a new evangelistic community.

Lombards extend control of Italy

Italy, 598
The Byzantine viceroy in Italy, Callinicus, has signed a truce with the Lombard king, Agilulf, that establishes effective Lombard control over northern Italy. The empire retains control over most of central and southern Italy.

The Germanic tribe of Lombards, or *Langobardi* (Longbeards), left Pannonia (Hungary) under Avar pressure in 568. Alboin, the Lombard king, took Milan in 569 and proclaimed himself "Lord of Italy". The march southward continued until the empire, paralysed by wars against the Slavs and Persians, was forced to negotiate.

One view of Columba's departure from Ireland en route for Scotland.

Part of a Chinese Buddhist obelisk showing the figure Maitreya (Chi period, 550-571).

The triumph of The Cross

Before joining battle with his rival Maxentius at the Milvian Bridge just outside Rome (312), the Emperor Constantine had a vision in which he was told that his soldiers should paint the Christian *chi-rho* symbol (a monogram of Christ) on their shields. The order went out: although heavily outnumbered, Constantine won the day and became master of the western empire. This was the single most momentous event in the triumph of Christianity.

Prior to Constantine's conversion the Christian faith was still only one of the many cults observed within the empire. There were many more Christians in the east than in the west, but overall the Christians remained an insignificant minority, concentrated among the urban lower classes. What marked the Christians out as far as the authorities were concerned was their refusal to worship the traditional Roman gods. But persecution was usually rare and localised until the Great Persecution instituted by Diocletian (303) and prosecuted with rigour in the east by Galerius and Maximin (305-12); many were martyred. Only with the victories of Constantine in the west and Licinius in the east was a policy of religious toleration for all agreed under the terms of the edict of Milan (313).

Christianity consolidates

When Licinius reverted to persecution, Constantine launched a crusade behind his Christian banner and defeated him at Chrysopolis (324). Constantine now bestowed enormous benefactions on the church; he built numerous churches; he founded Constantinople, a new Christian capital to supersede pagan Rome. Positive steps against paganism followed. Temple lands and treasures were confiscated (331); pagan sacrifices were banned (337). It was no longer risky to be a Christian, but a considerable advantage to one's career prospects. Whether from self-interest or deep convictions, the number of converts rapidly increased, especially among the middle and upper classes and in the army.

Constantine's sons continued and extended his policies (337-62); Constantius II ordered all temples to be closed (356). A network of bishops, based directly on the imperial administrative system, was gradually established at cities throughout the empire. This tightly-organised ecclesiastical hierarchy strengthened Christianity in the towns; under the pagan Emperor Julian (361-3), Christianity was probably already too well-established for his revivalist policies to succeed. Under

Gratian, and especially Theodosius, decisive action was taken against paganism, culminating in Theodosius' orders banning all forms of pagan cult, private and public, including the Olympic Games (393). A senatorial revolt was crushed (394).

It is doubtful whether this anti-pagan legislation was ever strictly observed, and paganism died a slow death – some pagan customs survived into modern times as superstitions. But after Theodosius the empire was nominally a Christian empire, although, particularly in the west, the real process of conversion, the adoption and understanding of Christianity by the mass of the people, was only just beginning. It was to be continued and eventually completed under barbarian rule.

The faith beyond the empire

The early church made little attempt to evangelise the barbarians beyond the frontiers. God was thought to have chosen the empire to receive the Christian faith; those who remained outside its frontiers remained, by God's will, outside the faith. When the church did consecrate bishops to serve beyond the frontiers of the empire, like the Arian Ulfila to the Goths (341) or Palladius to Ireland (431), the intention was not that they should convert the barbarians but that they should minister to existing Christian communities, made up largely of prisoners. In Ireland it was one of those prisoners, Patrick, who succeeded Palladius; he was the first Catholic to see it as his moral duty to go out and convert the heathen, and he began the distinctive missionary tradition of the Irish church, adopted later by the Anglo-Saxons. Within the empire, the tendency seems to have been to ignore the paganism of the barbarians until they crossed the frontier, when there were sound spiritual – and political – reasons for converting them.

Armed with Ulfila's translation of the Bible into Gothic, his pupils soon succeeded in converting the Visigoths after they had come within the empire (around 385). But these missionaries were not Catholics but Arian heretics, and so it was that, after it had been condemned by the empire (381), Arian Christianity continued to spread among the invading barbarians, perhaps largely through Visigothic influence. The Visigoths certainly sent missionaries to the Ostrogoths and Gepids; the Vandals were convinced Arians by 417, the Burgundians by around 430, the Sueves by 465. Except in Africa, where the Vandals intermittently inflicted violent persecution upon their Catholic subjects, Arian barbarians and the Catholic population

generally co-existed peacefully. By 600 Arianism was almost extinct, either through the military conquests of the Catholic Byzantines and Franks or population integration. It lived on among the Lombards, before eventually dying out (around 675).

Catholic conversions

We know far more of the conversion of the Franks and the Anglo-Saxons, who were converted directly from paganism to Catholicism. Gregory of Tours reported how, when the Frankish King Clovis' army was facing defeat at the hands of the Alamanni and prayers to his ancestral gods had proved worthless, Clovis wept and called on Christ for aid, promising adherence to Christianity in return for victory. The Alamanni immediately began to flee; Clovis was duly baptised and the conversion process began at once among his people (in around 500). Once again there is no indication in Gregory's story of any attempt at evangelisation of the Franks by the Catholic Church until Clovis' own conversion.

The papacy and the Church of Rome were not directly involved in missionary activity until the time of Gregory the Great. He sent Augustine to Britain to convert the Anglo-Saxons (597), something which the surviving British had again made no attempt to do. Augustine and his companions succeeded in converting Aethelbert of Kent, assisted by Athelbert's Catholic wife, the Frankish princess Bertha (in around 600). Like Constantine, Aethelbert showed favour to converts, helped in the building of churches and used his political hegemony to extend the faith into neighbouring kingdoms. But AngloSaxon England was much less of an entity than the Roman empire, and conversion was very gradual. But through the combined and contrasting efforts of the Canterbury-based Roman Church and the monastic Irish missionaries who came across to Lindisfarne from Iona, all the Anglo-Saxon kingdoms were finally won over (by around 680). With the rise of Islam in the east and the vigorous missions from Britain to pagan tribes beyond the Rhine, the identification of the Christian faith with the borders of the empire was finally worn down. Christianity had survived the fall of the Roman empire and even emerged refreshed from the barbarian invasions. But the real process of conversion, the training of priests to preach to the common folk, the extension of the faith into the countryside, the teaching of Christian doctrine, and the elimination or adaptation of pagan festivities, shrines and, most difficult, customs – went on for centuries.

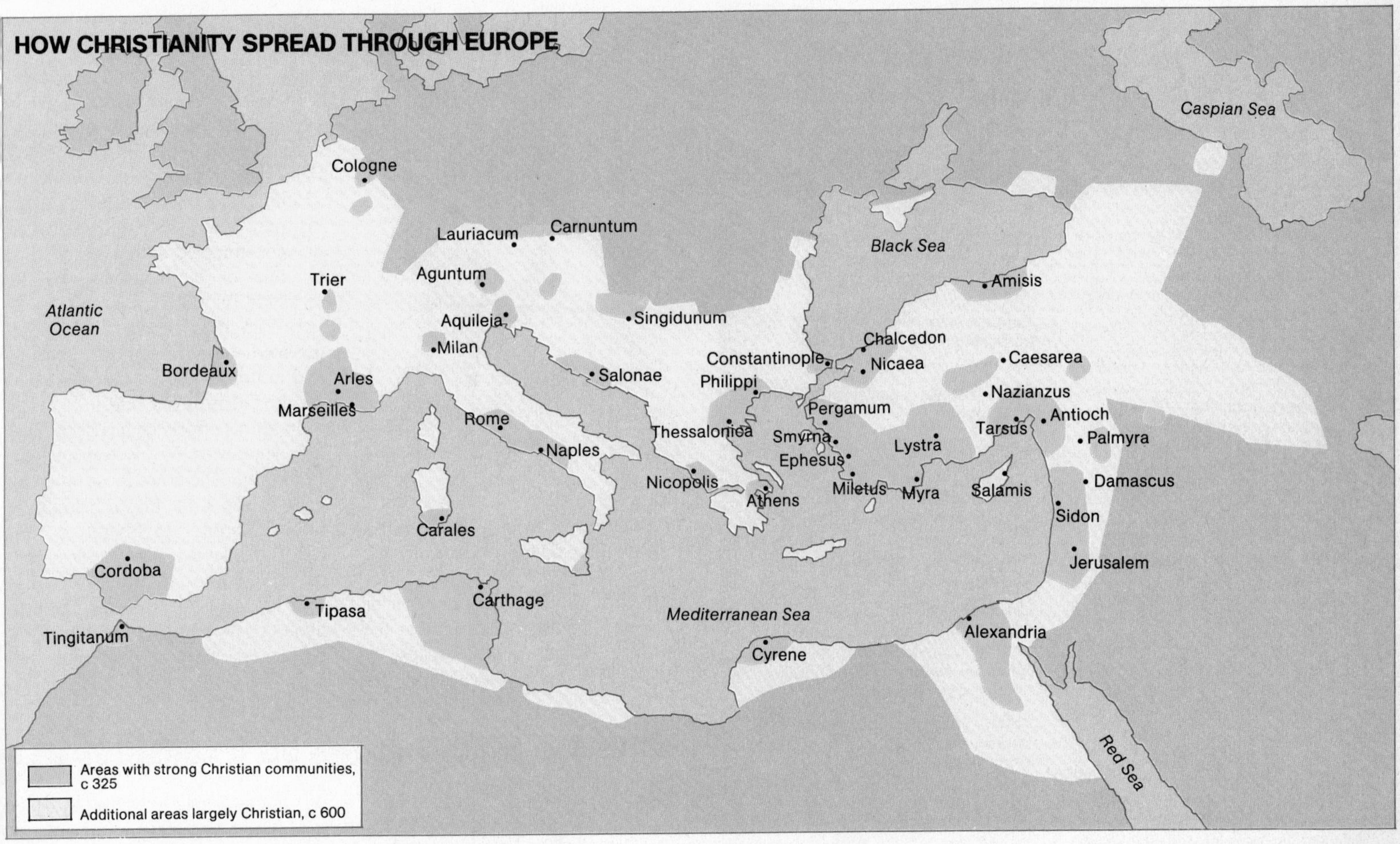

HOW CHRISTIANITY SPREAD THROUGH EUROPE

Caspian Sea

Cologne

Lauriacum   Carnuntum

Trier   Aguntum   *Black Sea*

Atlantic Ocean   Aquileia   Singidunum   Amisis

Bordeaux   •Milan   Chalcedon

Arles   •Salonae   Constantinople Nicaea   Caesarea

Marseilles   Rome   Philippi   Nazianzus

Thessalonica   Pergamum   Antioch

•Naples   Smyrna   Tarsus   Palmyra

Nicopolis   Ephesus   Lystra

Athens   Miletus   Myra   Salamis   •Damascus

Carales   Sidon

Cordoba   Jerusalem

Tipasa   Carthage   *Mediterranean Sea*

Tingitanum   Cyrene   Alexandria

Red Sea

| | Areas with strong Christian communities, c 325 |
| | Additional areas largely Christian, c 600 |

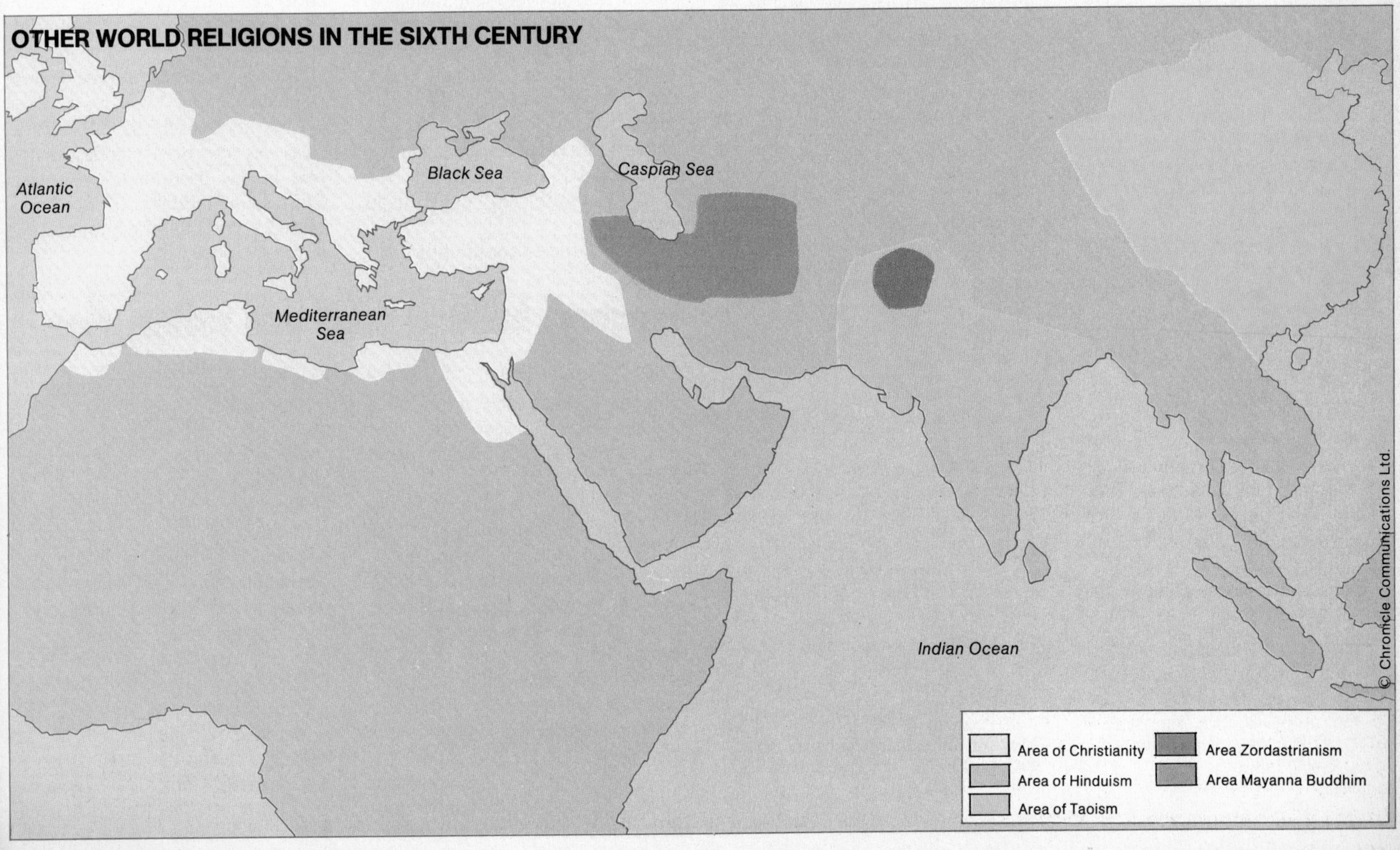

OTHER WORLD RELIGIONS IN THE SIXTH CENTURY

Atlantic Ocean   *Black Sea*   *Caspian Sea*

Mediterranean Sea

Indian Ocean

© Chronicle Communications Ltd.

	Area of Christianity		Area Zordastrianism
	Area of Hinduism		Area Mayanna Buddhim
	Area of Taoism		

Britain, 603. Aidan, the king of the Scots, attempts to stop the expansion of the Northumbrians under Aethelfrith, but is defeated at Degsastan and forced to flee.

Persia, 605. The Persians under Khosrow II resume the war against the Byzantines.

China, 605. The second emperor of the Sui, Yangdi, expands and reorganises the Confucian civil service examinations, introducing the prestigious Jingshi degree.

China, 607. A Japanese emissary, Ono no Imoko, is sent to China by Shotoku Taishi – crown prince under Suiko, the first officially recognised empress of Japan – in order to further good relations between the two countries.

Japan, 607. The Horyuji monastery is established at the instigation of Shotoku Taishi, who has done much to encourage the spread of Buddhism in Japan and the adoption of Chinese forms of culture and politics.

Asia Minor, 608. Having seized Armenia and Syria, the Persian army crosses the Taurus mountains into Asia Minor. Under the brutal, unpopular Phocas, the Byzantine empire is in total disarray.

Arabia, 610. Mohammed, a preacher of the Quraysh tribe of the Bedouin, begins to preach in Mecca, a prosperous oasis town and centre of pilgrimage. He calls for an end to the demons and idols of Arab religion and conversion to the ways of the one god, Allah.

China, 610. The Emperor Yangdi completes the earlier version of the Chinese grand canal system.

Constantinople, 5 October 610. Heraclius, son of the governor of Africa, attacks Constantinople with his fleet. The people rise in his favour: Phocas is seized and executed. Beset by barbarian attacks and religious and political divisions, the empire is on the point of collapse.

Spain, 612. Sisebut, a poet and great patron of learning, becomes king of the Visigoths. He begins campaigns against the Byzantines and the Basques.

Paris, 15 October 614. Lothar II, now sole king of the Franks after the execution of Queen Brunhild, issues the Edict of Paris in an attempt to stamp out corruption in his kingdom. He establishes mayors of the palace to act as his chief ministers in the three parts of his united kingdom, Neustria, Austrasia and Burgundy.

Palestine, 5 May 614. The Persians complete the conquest of Syria by capturing Jerusalem. They seize the True Cross, the most holy Christian relic.

Ethiopia, 615. Moslem refugees from Arabia are given refuge in the independent state of Axum.

China, 616. A rebellion breaks out throughout China against the Emperor Yangdi, who is building a great canal connecting the Blue river with the Yellow river.

Constantinople, June 617. The Avars and the Slavs arrive beneath the walls of the imperial capital and ravage the suburbs. The Balkans have been overrun by the barbarians; only a few towns remain in Byzantine hands.

China, 618. Li Yuan founds the Tang dynasty.

Egypt, 619. The Persians complete their conquest of Egypt.

Constantinople, 619. The Emperor Heraclius buys off the *kagan* (ruler) of the Avars, so that he can concentrate on defending the empire against the Persians.

Constantinople April, 622. Having raised money by melting down church treasures to mint coins, Heraclius launches a counter-attack on the Persians.

Arabia, 16 July 622. Mohammed is forced to leave Mecca and take refuge at Yathrib (Medina). His flight is known as the *Hegira*.

Asia Minor, c.625. To reduce its dependence on barbarian mercenaries, the Byzantine empire is reorganised. In Asia Minor it is divided up into military territorial districts, known as *themes*.

Constantinople, August 626. The Persians ally with the Avars and launch a combined assault on Constantinople, but the Avar fleet is destroyed and the kagan raises the siege. Constantinople is saved.

China, 626. Li Yuan's second son, Li Shimin, engineers a coup d'etat, known as the Xuanwu Gate incident, in which he kills his brothers. Shortly afterwards he forces his father to abdicate.

Britain, 627. King Edwin of Northumbria is converted to Christianity and baptised by Paulinus, who becomes bishop of York.

Persia, 9 December 627. Heraclius, allied with the Khazars, a people of Mongolian origin, penetrates deep into Persian territory and annihilates the fleeing Persian army at Nineveh. This victory opens up for Heraclius the route to the Persian capital, Ctesiphon.

Persia, 3 April 628. Following the murder of Khosrow II, his son and successor, Kavadh, sues for peace with the Byzantines. He hands back Armenia, Byzantine Mesopotamia, Syria, Palestine and Egypt, as well as the True Cross.

New dynasty ends period of anarchy

Li Yuan, the first of the Tangs.

China, 618

Li Yuan, the governor of the province of Shanxi, has overthrown the shortlived Sui dynasty and proclaimed himself the first emperor of the Tang dynasty. His claim to the throne is being accepted because of his family's aristocratic blood ties with two previous dynasties, and because the people are anxious to end the anarchy brought upon them by Yangdi, the profligate second Sui emperor, who paid for his many sins earlier this year when he was strangled with a silken cord by one of his courtiers. In the scramble for power that accompanied Yangdi's demise, Li Yuan defeated other ambitious generals and put down the peasants who had revolted against Sui rule.

In all his efforts he has been most ably supported by his teenage son, Li Shimin. There are those who say that the son is the power behind the father's throne. Li Shimin is certainly displaying his Tartar ancestry in the way in which he deals with his father's enemies as the new dynasty sets about consolidating its power. His elder brothers may well regret his ruthlessness.

Japanese regent draws up a constitution

Japan, 604

The governing classes of Japan have a new constitution, thanks to the prince regent, Umayado. Prince Umayado, aged 34, has ruled Japan for his aunt, the Empress Suiko, since the year after the assassination of the last emperor. He is a scholarly Buddhist of great administrative skill who admires the Chinese model of centralised government.

His 17-article constitution directs the members of the ruling class to believe in Buddhism and to unite under the authority of the emperor. The constitution also stresses the virtues of harmony and obedience, elements which derive from Confucianism.

Umayado's keenness on Chinese ideas has also been manifested this year by his decision to adopt the Chinese calendar. It confirms 660BC as the date of the foundation of the Japanese state.

Gregory, brilliant pope and writer, dies

Rome, 12 March 604

Gregory, a remarkable pope and a brilliant theologian and writer, died today after 14 years on the papal throne. He was 64.

The son of a senator, Gregory sold off his vast property when he was 33 and gave all the money to the poor. He founded several monasteries, including one in Rome which he himself entered. Gregory held a senior position as papal envoy to the emperor in Constantinople before returning to Rome to become an abbot and, five years later, pope.

At this time Italy was in an alarming state, devastated by famine, pestilence and the Lombard invasion. Gregory organised charitable relief for the afflicted and military resistance against the invaders.

He will also be remembered for his missionary work. One of his greatest successes was to begin the conversion of the Anglo-Saxons, a task which he gave to Bishop Augustine of Hippo and about 40 missionaries from his own monastery.

As well as being renowned for his energy as an administrator, Pope Gregory was also one of the most esteemed writers of his day. His works include commentaries on the book of Job and the life of St Benedict. Perhaps most notable is his work *Pastoral Care*, a book on the duties of a bishop.

Mohammed flees Mecca

A miniature depicting Mohammed visited by holy men and an angel.

Mecca, Arabia, 622

Mohammed, a preacher who has been advocating an end to Arab polytheism and the worship of one God, has fled from the town of Mecca and headed north.

Born in around 570, Mohammed belongs to a branch of the Quraysh, one of the many Bedouin tribes in the vast Arabian peninsula. In 610 he began preaching in Mecca, a remote but important trading and cultural centre where the Quraysh have recently become prosperous as entrepreneurs, sending caravans to Syria, Iraq, Egypt and Yemen; indeed, Mohammed is married to a wealthy Qurayshi widow with money in the caravan business. But Mecca is also important as a place of pilgrimage, for it is here that Arabs come to venerate the temple of the Kaaba, a black meteoric stone central to their religion, of which the Quraysh are guardians.

Mohammed has denounced the idols associated with the Kaaba and urged people to turn to *Allah*, "the One and Only God", and help the poor. This has not endeared him to some rich and powerful Meccans, and his enemies have increased over the years. His decision to flee with his followers is a prudent one.

Civil administrators transform economy

China, 605

The death of the Emperor Wendi has brought to an end a remarkable reorganisation of China's civil service. A strong central bureaucracy has been established, and its officials have carried out sweeping reforms which have transformed the economy of the nation, now unified under the Sui dynasty.

While keeping the reins of power in his own hands, the emperor built up an efficient army of administrators able to carry out his orders in every part of his empire. It remains to be seen if his heir, Yangdi, will carry on his good work.

Irishman builds monastery in Italy

Italy, 612

The Irishman Columban has established a monastery at Bobbio in the Apennines here, thanks to the permission of the Lombard king, Agilulf. His monastic rule is very austere, with harsh penances, beatings and fasts and extremely long services. But his fiery brand of asceticism is still very popular.

He left Ireland in about 590 to do pioneering work in converting the rural areas of the Vosges in Gaul. He founded three monasteries, but his Celtic practices and the antagonism of the Frankish queen led to his expulsion to Italy.

Burial treasures stowed inside a ship at Sutton Hoo give a glimpse of Saxon life

England, c.625

The body of a king has been interred here in an extraordinary manner – inside the hull of a long ship on top of a cliff at Sutton Hoo in East Anglia. The ship is 90 feet long and up to 14 feet wide. It was hauled out of the River Deben to the top of a 100-foot bluff overlooking the estuary and the sea. A wooden hut with gables was built to house the great coffin and a hoard of treasure. Then the whole was covered with a burial mound, visible from far away.

The king commemorated in such splendour is Redwald, one of the kings of East Anglia, who had a residence at Rendlesham nearby and was perhaps the most powerful of the Anglo-Saxon kings at the time of his death.

The objects buried in the grave show how rich the East Angles are in foreign articles as well as in ornaments of fine English workmanship. The beautifully engraved gold ornaments are English, but there are bowls from Constantinople and Alexandria and coins from Gaul, and the king's helmet and shield were probably made by Swedes.

This way of burying the great is not unusual. The Anglo-Saxon epic poem, *Beowulf*, refers to the burial of the hero with much treasure on a similar headland "high and broad and visible to those journeying the ocean".

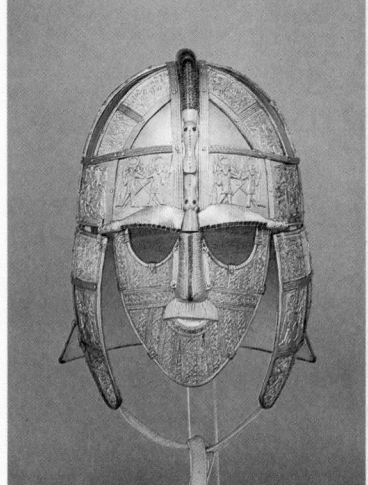

The tinned-bronze covered iron helmet from Sutton Hoo.

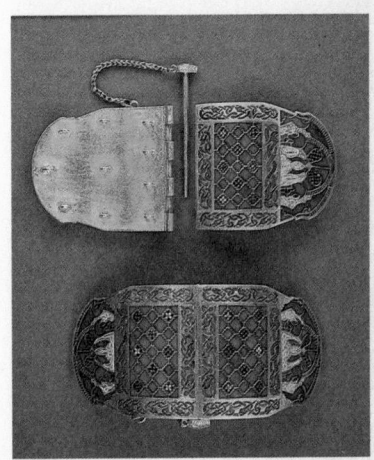

Gold shoulder clasps inlaid with garnet, glass and gold filigree.

This solid gold belt-buckle buried at Sutton Hoo weighs nearly a pound. It is covered with an intricate interlaced design of various stylised animals.

Arabia, 628. Mohammed and his supporters are granted permission to make a pilgrimage from Yathrib (Medina) to Mecca. This follows the lifting of a siege of Yathrib by the Meccans.

Gaul, 629. Dagobert, son of Lothar II, succeeds to the Frankish throne.

Spain, 629. The Visigoths complete the recovery of southern Spain from the Byzantines.

Constantinople, 629. The Byzantine emperor, Heracli, abandons the Latin imperial form of address – Imperator Caesar Augustus – and takes the Greek title of Basileus.

Jerusalem, 21 March 630. Heraclius restores the True Cross, which he has recaptured from the Persians.

Arabia, 630. Having defeated the Meccans, Mohammed takes control of Mecca.

Arabia, 632. Mohammed's closest followers select the ageing Abu Bakr to succeed the Prophet as leader of Islam. He takes the title of *caliph*.

Britain, 633. King Edwin of Northumbria is killed in battle by the Britons in alliance with the Mercians. Oswald becomes king after a brief pagan revival and restores Christianity with the help of Irish monks from Iona led by Aidan, who founds a monastery on Lindisfarne.

Red Sea, 634. Arab Moslems take Massawa on the Red Sea from the Ethiopian Axumites.

Balkans, 635. Aiming to keep the Avars out of the Balkans, Heraclius forms an alliance with Kuvrat, the Bulgar king.

Syria, 15 August 636. The Byzantine army is crushed by the Arab Moslems at the battle of Yarmuk. The Arabs, who took Damascus last year, now control all of Syria.

Persia, 637. The Arabs destroy the Persian army at the battle of Qadisiyya.

China, 638. The Emperor Taizong commissions the great scholar Yan Shigu to establish definitive versions of the classics, and orders Kong Yingda and other scholars to write detailed commentaries on them. Known collectively as the "Correct meaning of the five classics", these provide the foundation for classical Confucian education.

Jerusalem, 638. Jerusalem falls to the Arabs under Caliph Umar.

Ceremonial mounds popular among new Mississippi settlers

North America, c.640
The city of Cahokia, founded in southern Illinoi about 50 years ago, is fast becoming one of the most heavily populated of the communities now springing up in the central Mississippi valleys. Settlers have been attracted to the region by the climate, which is ideal for the newly available strains of maize, and the rich soil, which is suited to hoe agriculture.

Cahokia is a religious, political and economic centre with prosperous quarry and salt industries. Social organisation is at a chieftainship level and the city is establishing outlying colonies and trading posts.

Its most distinctive feature is a large number of flat-topped mounds of varying sizes, some of them associated with plazas, which provide the focus of civic and ceremonial life. These mounds serve as platforms for major buildings, residences of the community leaders and shrine houses, known as "temples", dedicated to the veneration of ancestors of the elite. The bones of rulers and their close relatives are placed in the temple shrines after death.

Leaders of Mississippian villages derive much of their authority from the belief that they embody sacred forces.

Michtlanticultli, lord of the dead, made by the Totonac people of Mexico, 400-1000.

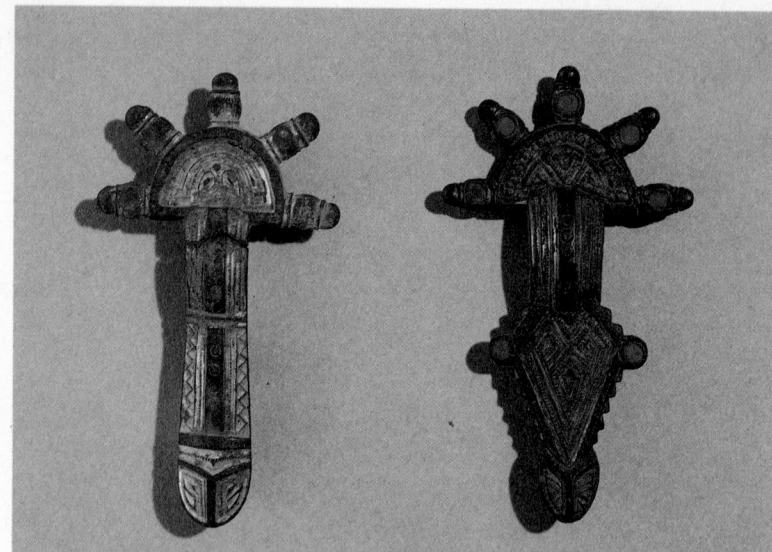

A pair of Frankish silver brooches decorated with garnet and niello work.

Frankish kingdom thrives under Dagobert

Gaul, 639
Dagobert, the son of Lothar II and king of the Franks since 629, has died after suffering an attack of dysentery. During his reign the Franks in Gaul have become a more unified people and, if he has alienated some of the aristocracy and senior clergy by diminishing their powers and possessions, to the masses he has been a wise and just king, touring his dominions and stamping out the injustices of the rich. One visit is said to have caused "profound alarm" to local dignitaries, but brought "great joy" to the poor.

Dagobert abandoned the usual Frankish practice of dividing the kingdom between all those in the direct royal line. He insisted that he should be made the sole king and took absolute power, and, although he extended his father's policy by creating sub-kingdoms to satisfy nationalist tendencies in Aquitaine and Austrasia, real power remained firmly in his hands. With this power the king was able to control rebellions and resume campaigns against the Celts of western Gaul, the Basques and the Visigoths. He allied with the Eastern emperor, Heraclius, in striving to hold the Slavs, a traditional enemy, at bay.

Isidore, greatest scholar of his age, dies

Spain, 636
Isidore of Seville, probably the most learned scholar of the age, has died aged 66. Drawing on his encyclopaedic knowledge he wrote many books, including a dictionary of synonyms, a treatise on astronomy and physical geography, histories and many theological works. He was a renowned teacher and proposed a liberal curriculum attempting to embrace all learning.

Isidore's greatest work is undoubtedly the 20-volume *Etymologies*, or Origins, in which he shows that the nature of all things can be derived from tracing their names back to the original roots and forms. Embracing all contemporary knowledge, it is an incomparable book by an unrivalled intellect.

Isidore: an encyclopaedic mind.

Arabs extend the frontiers of Islam

Mohammed, unifier of Arabia, is dead

Medina, Arabia, 8 June 632
Mohammed, the founder of Islam, died today at the age of about 62. Born of poor parents, he was soon orphaned. He came to settle in the oasis town of Mecca, a centre of the Arabs' polytheistic religion. In 610 he began to preach, calling for Arabs to turn to Allah, the one true God who had revealed Himself to the Christians and the Jews (who had both misinterpreted His word) and was now revealing Himself through Mohammed. He became increasingly unpopular and in 622 fled to Medina, 200 miles north of Mecca, with loyal companions.

Mohammed continued to receive revelations from Allah, and they began to be recorded. He saw himself as an instrument of God and submitted to His will, and the new faith became known as *Islam* (submission). Its adherents were called *Moslems* (they who submit).

Medina and most Arab tribes have come to accept his authority. He finally made peace with the Meccans a couple of years ago, when they agreed to recognise him as Prophet of God. In return, Mohammed accepted that the Kaaba, the former temple of polytheism in Mecca, should remain a place of pilgrimage for the new faith.

Caliph Umar enters Jerusalem, heralding the end of Byzantine Palestine.

Syria and Jerusalem fall to Arab invaders

Near East, 638
The Byzantine empire is reeling under the breathtaking advance of the Moslem Arabs, who, only six years after the death of Mohammed, have almost chased the imperial armies from the Near East.

When the first caliph, Abu Bakr, sent out troops from Medina to impose his authority on rebellious Arab tribes, he followed up his success by raiding parties against the Byzantines in Syria and the Persians in Mesopotamia. These revealed the weakness of the Byzantine defences, and Abu Bakr's suc-cessor Umar despatched better forces under the great General Khalid ibn al-Walid. In 635 the Arabs besieged and conquered Damascus; the fall of Syria was completed in 636 when the Moslems defeated the main Byzantine army on the river Yarmuk, east of the sea of Galilee. The emperor, Heraclius, was powerless to prevent further advances and the capture of Jerusalem was almost inevitable. Byzantine Palestine is now limited to an area around Caesarea, on the Mediterranean, which also seems certain to fall to Islam's conquering zeal.

Abu Bakr, successor to Mohammed, dies

Medina, 22 August 634
Abu Bakr, the man chosen to succeed Mohammed as head of the Moslem community, died today after ruling for only two years.

A mild and courteous old man, Abu Bakr achieved much during his short tenure and has almost certainly ensured the survival of Islam. At the Prophet's death it was not clear whether there should be a successor to Mohammed at all, and the community looked as if it might collapse. But a group of the late leader's closest companions chose Abu Bakr as head of Islam, giving him the title *Caliph*, or Successor. The claims of Ali, Mohammed's cousin and son-in-law, were brushed aside. Many Arab tribes immediately rejected the new faith and the authority of the Moslem leaders in Medina. Abu Bakr launched successful military expeditions, led by the brilliant General Khalid ibn-al Walid, to bring them back into line. The caliph decided to keep up the momentum of conquest by sending raiding parties to attack the Byzantine empire in Syria and the Persians in Mesopotamia.

Abu Bakr is succeeded by Umar, another of the Prophet's followers, a rather stern and puritanical figure. He seems likely to step up the first caliph's Syrian and Mesopotamian campaigns.

Mohammed's ascent to heaven.

Buddhist monk in India collects Sanskritscriptures

China, 640
Hsuang-tsang, a Buddhist monk from China, is in the twelfth year of his travels outisde his native country. He set off for the "lands beyond the snowy peaks" of the Himalayas in 628 in order to study his religion in the region where it began.

Before he left, Hsuang-tsang sent petitions to the Emperor Taizong several times requesting imperial approval for this journeys, but this was repeatedly refused. Finally, the monk left for India without informing the Emperor, so great was his conviction that Buddhism in China would benefit from his travels.

One of the most important aims of this mission is to collect Buddhist scriptures that are written in Sanskrit so that he can translate them into Chinese when he returns to this homeland.

Heraclius reclaims the "True Cross"

Jerusalem, 21 March 630
The Emperor Heraclius has recaptured the "True Cross" – said to be the one on which Christ died – from the Persians, and returned it to Jerusalem.

This is the triumphant climax to a military campaign which has restored imperial power in the Near East. Rumours of Arab unity and power are the only clouds on the horizon.

When Heraclius overthrew the Emperor Phocas in 610, the Persian army was advancing southwards; they took Syria, with Jerusalem and the True Cross, in 614. They then moved armies into Palestine and Egypt, and advanced into Asia Minor.

In 622 Heraclius began his counter-moves. After an attack on Constantinople by the Avars – allies of the Persians – had been repulsed in 626, Heraclius marched on the Persian capital of Ctesiphon in 628. A treaty restored conquered territories, and the Cross, to the empire.

640 (640-655)

Central Europe, c.640. Led by Samo, a merchant of Frankish origin, the Slavs have established a kingdom in Bohemia independent of the Avars and the Franks.

Constantinople, 641. Heraclius dies after a 30-year reign. Despite his spectacular successes against the Persians, he leaves an empire beset by religious controversies and now threatened by the Arabs. After a brief period of confusion – during which his two sons die within months of each other – he is succeeded by his youthful grandson Constans II.

China, 641. The influence of the Tang dynasty, which is conquering the Silk Road, extends westwards. Nestorian Christianity reaches China.

Egypt, 641. Egypt, invaded two years ago, surrenders to the Arabs, who proceed south to Nubia.

Persia, 642. The Arabs defeat the Persians at Niharvand and put their king, Yazdgard III, to flight. This victory puts an end to the Sassanid dynasty.

Britain, 5 August 642. Oswald, the Christian king of Northumbria is killed by Penda, the pagan king of Mercia, at Maserfelth.

Egypt, 642. The Arabs capture Alexandria, the last Byzantine outpost in Egypt.

Italy, 643. Rothari, king of the Lombards, publishes an edict codifying the laws of the Lombards in Latin. Meanwhile, he is busy expanding his kingdom at the expense of the Byzantines.

North Africa, 643. The Arabs reach Cyrenaica and Tripolitania.

Arabia, 4 November 644. Umar is assassinated at Medina and is succeeded as caliph by Uthman.

North Africa, 646. With the support of the African Church and the Berbers, Gregory, the *exarch* (governor) of Carthage, rebels against the Emperor Constans II, who has espoused the Monothelete doctrine, a watered-down version of the Monophysite heresy which is regarded as heretical by the orthodox Catholic African Church, in an attempt to reconcile the Monophysites with within the Byzantine empire.

Japan, 646. The "Taika Kaishin" brings all private land under public ownership. Power is centred on the emperor in imitation of the Chinese system.

North Africa, 647. The Arabs launch a raid into the Byzantine province of Africa, killing the usurper Gregory and effectively ending the African rebellion against Constans, the Byzantine emperor.

Syria, 647. Mu'awiyah, the Arab governor of Syria, lays waste to Cappadocia in Asia Minor and takes the spoils home to Damascus.

India, 647. The Indian ruler Harsha, who became king of Kanauj in 606, dies after creating an empire in the north comparable to that of the Guptas.

Constantinople, 648. In an attempt to restore church unity Constans II promulgates a doctrinal edict called the *Type*, but this simplistic attempt to prohibit discussion of the problem satisfies neither the orthodox nor the Monopheletes.

Rome, October 649. Pope Martin calls a council at the Lateran Palace which condemns the Monothelcte doctrine and the recent compromise edict the *Type*, imposed by Constans II.

Cyprus, 649. The Arabs, who have assembled a formidable fleet under the leadership of Mu'awiyah, the governor of Syria, storm the island of Cyprus.

China, 649. After the death of the Emperor Taizong, Gaozong succeeds to the throne.

North Africa, 651. Nubia is again invaded by Arab Moslems.

Italy, 652. Aripert, who has succeeded the Arian Rothari, the king of the Lombards, is baptised a Catholic at Pavia. Catholicism has almost vanquished Arianism among the Lombards.

Spain, 653. At Toledo, Recessuinth, the king of the Visigoths, draws up a code, the *Liber ludiciorium*, based on Roman law, aimed at achieving complete equality between all subjects, both Hispano-Romans and Goths. It is the first territorial law code which applies to all regardless of racial and cultural differences.

Rome, 653. Pope Martin is arrested by the *exarch*, the governor of the imperial territory in Italy, and sent to Constantinople, where he is convicted of high treason. His death sentence is commuted to banishment.

Rhodes, 654. The Arabs invade Rhodes and set about systematically pillaging the island.

Central Asia, 655. Yazdgard III, the last Sassanid king, who fled from Persia after its defeat by the Arabs in 642, is assassinated. The Arabs take Kabul and Kandahar.

Crimea, 655. Pope Martin dies in exile of cold and starvation.

Asia Minor, 655. In a major sea battle off the south coast of Asia Minor the Byzantines, led by Constans II, are defeated by the Arabs whose fleet now commands the eastern Mediterranean.

Persian Empire falls to soldiers of Islam

Persia, 642

The empire of the Sassanid dynasty of Persia is broken. Arab armies under their great commander, Khalid ibn al-Walid, known as "the sword of Allah", began raiding Mesopotamia, part of the Persian empire, in 633, and finally defeated the Persian armies, despite their numbers and their elephants, at Qadisiyya, in 637.

After the Persian armies had been put to flight, the Bedouin invaders took the ancient capital of Ctesiphon with its sumptuous royal palace. They pillaged its treasures, and cut up the famous jewelled carpets that adorned it so that each of the Bedouin victors could be given a share.

Following the victory there has been a mass migration of Arab tribes into the fertile lands between the Tigris and Euphrates. But the Arab armies, rather than mingle with the local people, have set up military encampments on the edge of the desert at Kufa and Basra. From here they can control and tax the country and mount Bedouin raids into Persia. The Sassanid king, Yazdgard III, counter-attacked this year, and his armies were again defeated at Nihavand.

Persian silk showing the mythical "senmurv", a Sassanid royal device.

Alexandria capitulates to Arab invaders

Alexandria, 642

The fall of Alexandria – the great metropolis of Byzantine Egypt and centre of Greek culture – marks a climax to the Moslem conquests achieved since Mohammed's death in 632.

In Syria and Palestine all resistance to the invaders ceased with the surrender of the coastal city of Caesarea in 640 after a long siege.

Already, despite the opposition of the caliph Umar, a plan was afoot to attack the rich province of Egypt. The fortress of Babylon – key to central Egypt – was besieged and taken last year, and now the supreme prize of Alexandria has fallen into Moslem hands.

The Byzantine army put up considerable opposition to the attack, but the local people were much more equivocal. Most of them are members of the Coptic church – long persecuted by the Byzantine authorities as heretical – and many hope for religious freedom and lower tax rates under the new conquerors. While not actively assisting the Moslems, they offered the Byzantines little support.

It remains to be seen whether these conquests will be lasting or whether Byzantine command of the sea will enable them to make a counter-attack and recover the lost territories, some of the richest in their empire.

China enjoys golden age

China, 649
The great Emperor Taizong has died after a glorious, if ruthless, reign of 22 years. It was his father who won the scramble for power as the Sui dynasty collapsed and established the Tang dynasty, but it was always Taizong, then known as Li Shimin, who wielded the power.

Impatient at not being made heir to the throne, he killed his elder brothers and their families and deposed his father in 627. He then set about consolidating his grasp on China, making the borders safe, defeating the Turks and penetrating into central Asia. Trade followed his conquests; soon caravans bringing goods from the west streamed into China. Foreign traders came too, establishing their own colonies along the commercial network that sprang up under China's new and highly efficient bureaucracy.

Well aware that the Sui dynasty was brought down by peasant unrest, Taizong instituted a land reform programme which shares abandoned land among the poor farmers. His reign has also proved to be a golden age for culture. Poetry, painting and philosophy have flourished.

The last years of his life were taken up with his war against Korea, which brought that country under Chinese control. It was his last great success. His son Gaozong now succeeds to a united, prosperous and self-confident empire.

A Chinese pagoda of the Tang dynasty at Sian Tang Dyn.

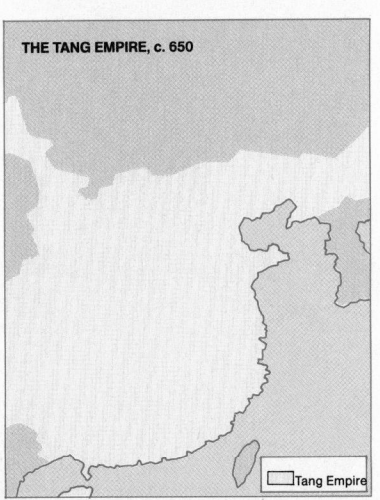
THE TANG EMPIRE, c. 650

Tang Empire

Ceramic models of Chinese cavalrymen in the service of the Tang dynasty.

Koran text written down for first time

Medina, 651
The Koran, the set of sacred revelations believed to have been given directly to Mohammed by Allah, has been collected and written down for the first time.

The revelations were somewhat haphazardly recorded, or memorised by Mohammed's secretaries as he uttered them. But Uthman, who succeeded Umar as caliph in 644, feared that the conquests of Islam might not last if the new faith, like Christianity and Judaism, did not have a single, unifying sacred text. Last year he appointed a committee under one of Mohammed's old secretaries to assemble the scattered texts. From now on, all non-standard versions of the Koran have been banned from Uthman's lands.

Pope dies of cold and hunger in Crimea

Crimea, 655
Pope Martin has died in exile after clashing with the Emperor Constans II. Martin, who succeeded Theodore, angered the emperor by speaking out at the Lateran Council in Rome against the heresy of Monothelitism, popular in the east, which insists that Jesus Christ had only a single will. Constans, a champion of Monothelitism, had him arrested. He was taken to Constantinople, charged with high treason and deported to the Crimea where he died of cold and hunger.

Murder fells family at Yamato Court

Japan, 645
The tyranny of the Soga family over the imperial throne has finally broken. Soga no Iruka has been murdered in the palace's crowded audience hall in a coup d'etat staged during a reception for Korean envoys. Iruka and his father, Soga no Emishi, had enraged the court by manipulating state affairs for themselves. Iruka was killed by Prince Naka no Oe and Emishi committed suicide the next day, having been deserted by his supporters following his son's murder.

Architect of vast Indian empire dies

India, 647
Harsha of Kanauj has died after a 41-year reign which has seen the unification of India under one ruler.

When Harsha came to power in 606, he inherited a small principality north of Delhi. He gradually built a vast empire in northern India, stretching from the Indus valley in the west to Orissa in the east. With his demise India is once again in danger of fragmenting into tiny states.

Harsha was a man of letters; he wrote three dramas in Sanskrit. Although he was a disciple of Siva, one of the dramas shows a lively interest in Buddhism. Harsha's life and deeds have been recorded by Bhana in the *Harshacarita*.

Pope Martin: clash with Constans.

Tibet emerges as independent state

Lhasa, 650
A new power combining strong centralised government with potent religious ritual in organised communities is replacing the old order from western Tibet to upper Burma. Srong-btsan Sgampo, the king of Tibet, having married a Chinese princess and a Nepalese princess, now has an army conquering lands far beyond Nepal. After the sword comes the word, in the sacred Sanskrit tongue, chanted in monasteries by monks called *lamas*. The *lamas* blend Buddhism with the sorcery of Bon.

655 (655-680)

Britain, 655. At the battle of the river Winawed, Oswy, the king of Northumbria, defeats and kills Penda, the pagan king of Mercia.

Asia Minor, 655. The Arabs defeat a Byzantine fleet, commanded by the Emperor Constans II himself, off the coast of Lycia.

Arabia, 17 June 656. Caliph Uthman is assassinated and succeeded by Ali ibn Abi Talib, Mohammed's cousin and son-in-law.

Arabia, 9 December 656. Rebels who dispute the succession of Ali are defeated by the caliph's forces at the battle of the Camel, near Basra.

Mexico, 657. Pacal becomes king of the Maya religious centre of Palenque. In southern Mexico a Maya city and astronomical observatory are established.

India, 657. Brahmagupta, a great mathematician, establishes the rules of calculation by introducing the concept of zero.

Central Europe, 658. Samo, who reigned over the Slav kingdom of Bohemia which he had created, is dead.

Syria, 659. The Byzantines reach a truce with the Arab commander in Syria.

Mesopotamia, 24 January 661. Ali is assassinated in Kufa by an ex-supporter who has become a Kharajite.

Syria, 661. Mu'awiyah succeeds Ali as caliph and founds the Umayyad dynasty. He moves the seat of government to Damascus.

Italy, 663. Unpopular in his capital, and with Syria and Egypt under Arab control, Constans II sails west to Italy and makes a vain attempt to reconquer mainland Italy, which is now largely Lombard territory, for the empire.

Britain, 664. The plague which began in Egypt in the 540s and devastated Constantinople in 542 ravages the British Isles, having crossed Europe.

Britain, 664. King Oswy of Northumbria presides over the Council of Whitby, at which important decisions affecting the Anglo-Saxon church are taken.

China, 664. The Chinese monk and pilgrim Xuanzang, who founded the Wei-shih school of Buddhism, dies at the age of 68. Xuanzang travelled to India in 629 to bring back sacred Sanskrit texts.

Korea, 668. The king of Silla recaptures Koguryo and Paekche, adjacent kingdoms in Korea, with the help of China, whose sovereignty he recognises.

Sicily, 668. The Emperor Constans II is assassinated during a mutiny at Syracuse. He is succeeded by his son Constantine IV, who is in Sicily to put down the revolt that led to his father's death.

Central Asia, 670. Qutlugh re-establishes the *khanate* of Orkhon, an eastern Turkish empire which had been destroyed by the Chinese Emperor Taizong.

Central Asia, 670. The Tibetans take control of the Tarim basin and drive the Chinese from their four garrisons.

North Africa, 670. The Arabs complete their conquest of the region they call Ifriqiyah on the coast of North Africa (*which stretches from eastern Algeria to Egypt*).

Spain, 672. On the death of Reccesuinth at Toledo, Wamba is elected king of the Visigoths.

Britain, 673. Benedict Biscop founds a monastery at Monkwearmouth in Northumbria.

China, 673. Yan Liben, a painter of the Tang dynasty, is dead. He presided over the public works committee entrusted with the task of constructing the imperial palaces of the capital. He leaves his famous hand scroll of the Thirteen Emperors.

Constantinople, 678. The Arabs have attacked Constantinople by sea annually since 674. The Byzantines use "Greek fire" – a new weapon invented by the Syrian Callinicus – to defend themselves. This is an incendiary mixture, fired from guns, that is fuelled, rather than extinguished, by sea water. It is a violent storm, however, rather than this lethal weapon, that destroys the Arab fleet and puts an end to their harassment. The Arabs and the Byzantines sign a peace treaty.

North Africa, 678. Arab armies commanded by Uqba ibn Nafi sweep across North Africa to the Atlantic, Uqba spurring his horse into the waves.

Syria, 678. Yazid succeeds as caliph on the death of his father, Mu'awiyah, in Damascus.

Constantinople, 680. Constantine IV, until now forced to share power with his younger brothers Heraclius and Tiberius, becomes sole emperor.

Constantinople, 680. With the main Monophysite parts of his empire, Egypt and Syria, lost to the Arabs, the Emperor Constantine IV abandons his support for the now redundant Monothelete compromise. He holds the Sixth Ecumenical Council, condemning Monothelitism and restoring orthodox Catholicism.

Northumbrian Church chooses Roman over Celtic teachings at Whitby Council

Whitby, 664

After a dramatic debate at the council convened here, the powerful Northumbrian king, Oswy, has decided in favour of the Roman teachings put forward by the ambitious priest Wilfrid.

Some of the Irish priests have walked out, but most seem ready to accept the decision, which will end differences between the Irish and Roman missionaries over the date of Easter and other customs.

Christianity had taken a hold in Northumbria with the baptism of King Edwin at York, in 627, by a Roman mission backed by his Kentish wife. But Edwin was killed in battle in 633 by Penda, the pagan king of Mercia. Prince Oswald re-turned from exile on Iona to become king and brought over Irish missionaries, led by Aidan, who set up the great monastery on Lindisfarne. Penda killed Oswald too, but his brother Oswy avenged him in battle in 655. Like his brother, he vigorously fostered Christianity.

Christianity's fortunes have been mixed in the south of England. Augustine was sent by Rome in 597, soon converting King Aethelbert and establishing a see at Canterbury. After the king's death in 616 his successors reverted to paganism, but the Romans went on converting people, and have now again won royal approval. And, with Penda's death, Mercia has also converted to Christianity.

Whitby Abbey, which was founded in 657 by Abbess Hild.

Grimoald beheaded after coup attempt

Gaul, 656

An attempt by Grimoald, the rich and powerful mayor, or prime minister, of the Frankish kingdom of Austrasia in eastern Gaul, to seize power at Vienne has failed. Grimoald has been executed by Lothar III, the king of the neighbouring Frankish kingdom of Neustria in north-western Gaul, who has handed over the throne to his own brother Childeric.

The coup shows the discord and decay of the Merovingian kingdom since the death of Clovis 150 years ago. The kingdom was divided into three main parts: Neustria, Austrasia and Burgundy. With a few exceptions, like Dagobert, the kings lacked the power to cow their nobles, who bolstered their positions by allying with mayors, often the real rulers in the states.

Grimoald, the son of Pepin of Landen, the hereditary mayor of Austrasia, was the most powerful. When the ineffectual Sigibert III died, aged only 26, Grimoald took over the kingdom and sent the crown prince, Dagobert, to a monastery in Ireland. He installed his own son as king, but his reign was short: Lothar trapped both men within a few months of the coup. Childeric II now rules Austrasia; the Merovingians remain in power.

Islamic world rocked by bitter power struggles

Besieged caliph is killed by rioters

Medina, 17 June 656

The 82-year-old Caliph Uthman was hacked to death today by Moslem rebels from Mesopotamia who broke into his Medina home as he sat studying the Koran. The death of the Islamic scholar has thrown the Moslem world into confusion. The rebels' attack followed their blockade of his home throughout the hot Hijazi summer, which forced the caliph to suffer from protracted hunger and thirst. He is expected to be succeeded by the Prophet's son-in-law Ali.

Ali is outwitted at the battle of Siffin

Mesopotamia, 26 July 657

The long stalemate between the two Moslem factions led by Caliph Ali and Mu'awiyah ended in a battlefield truce today as Mu'awiyah's Syrian troops attached copies of the Koran to the ends of their spears in a reluctant and symbolic attack on Ali's forces.

The Syrians and Ali's Mesopotamian supporters have been at enmity over Mu'awiyah's insistence that Ali must hand over the assassins of Caliph Uthman. Both sides have agreed to arbitration.

A Moslem preacher in a mosque.

Arabs swear allegiance to Ali after the murder of Caliph Uthman.

Ali assassinated outside Kufa mosque

Kufa, 24 January 661

Exiled Kharajite rebels have assassinated Ali, the leader of the Moslem world and son-in-law of the Prophet Mohammed, the founder of Islam. He died after being stabbed with a poisoned sword as he left the mosque at Kufa in Mesopotamia. The Kharajites – so-called because they have splintered from the Moslem community – decided on assassination as revenge for Ali's attack on them at Nahrawan. This

attack had been Ali's attempt to punish them for the way they had turned against him after the symbolic battle of Siffin, where, to their anger Ali had chosen arbitration in preference to fighting on. The Kharajites believed that Ali's refusal to continue the war and accept its outcome was an outrage against divine justice. A Kharajite plan to kill Mu'awiyah, the other signatory to the Siffin agreement, as well is reported to have failed.

Governor of Damascus is elected caliph

Damascus, 678

Oaths of allegiance have been pledged to Yazid, the new governor of Damascus, after he was elected unopposed to succeed his late father Mu'awiyah as caliph.

Yazid's confirmation in office is seen as continuing evidence of the Umayyad family's dynastic ambitions. These first became apparent in Mu'awiyah's 18-year rule with a succession of political manoeuvres

designed to secure oaths of allegiance from potential rivals for the succession. Chief among these was al-Husayn, the son of the late Caliph Ali, who was bought off for an unspecified, but substantial, sum of money. These political moves, coupled with a remarkable flair for administration, plus a calm and intelligent manner served to make Mu'awiyah one of Islam's most respected statesmen.

Moslems conquer North Africa

North Africa, 670

The Byzantine empire is once more smarting from the onward, seemingly unstoppable, march of the armies of Islam. This time it is the turn of North Africa to fall to the caliphs.

The march into Africa began in 640, after the Byzantines had been expelled from Syria and Palestine, when an Arab army under Amr ibn al-'As invaded Egypt. The great Greek-founded city of Alexandria finally fell in 642, and in the same year the Arabs conquered the former Roman province of Cyrenaica, west of Egypt. The city of Tripoli fell soon after, and in 647 an Arab expeditionary force entered Tunisia and defeated the Byzantine army under Gregory, the governor of imperial Africa. Gregory was killed, and the empire offered the Arabs a ransom not to continue with their invasion; having little knowledge of the land ahead, they accepted.

However, in 665 the Arab armies carried out a reconnaissance raid against the towns of northern Tunisia; the Arabs now knew the land and could organise a proper conquest. The empire of Islam now stretches from Kairouan in the Tunisian desert to Kabul in Afghanistan; its expansion shows no sign of abating.

The Great Mosque of Kairouan.

Mesopotamia, 10 October 680. Al-Husayn, the son of Ali, is killed in combat at Karbala. His death gives birth to Shi'ism: a dissident group called the Shi'ites claims that the right of interpreting the Koran is confined to Mohammed's descendants. They maintain that Ali was immune from sin and error and had been divinely chosen as *Imam* to transmit his office to his descendants. Al-Husayn is therefore regarded as a martyr.

Spain, 680. Count Ervig, taking advantage of an uprising by the Basques and of the discontent caused by reforms of the church and the army, overthrows Wamba, the king of the Visigoths, and as king makes concessions to the rebellious aristocracy.

Balkans, 681. After defeating the Byzantine army, the Bulgars found a new state on the delta of the Danube.

Britain, 682. The controversial prelate Wilfrid, exiled from his Northumbrian bishopric, converts the South Saxons of Sussex to Christianity.

Near East, 682. Abdullah ibn Zubayr, who is supported by the people of Mecca and Medina, is acclaimed as caliph in Arabia, Mesopotamia and Egypt, and by the members of the Qais tribe in Syria.

Britain, 683. Benedict Biscop founds the monastery of Jarrow in Northumbria.

Central Asia, 683. Qutlugh, the Turkish *khan*, sacks the Chinese region of Chan Yu.

China, 683. On the death of the Emperor Kaozong at Loyang, his concubine Wu Zhao takes possession of the throne and founds the Zhou dynasty.

Syria, 684. The Qais tribe, who support ibn Zubayr's claim to the caliphate, are heavily defeated by the Umayyads at Marj Rahit.

Britain, 685. The Picts defeat the Northumbrians in battle near Forfar and kill their king, Ecgfrith. The Northumbrians are forced to retreat from conquered Pictish territory.

Syria, 685. Abd al-Malik succeeds his father, Marwan, a distant cousin of Mu'awiyah, as caliph of the Umayyads. The supporters of the Umayyads, the Sunnites, believe – in contrast to the Shi'ites – that doctrinal authority changes hands with the caliphate.

Syria/Constantinople, 685. Abd al-Malik and Constantine IV agree to share the taxes from Armenia, Iberia (Georgia) and Cyprus.

Japan, 685. Buddhism becomes the state religion.

Constantinople, 685. At the age of 16, Justinian II succeeds his father, Constantine IV, on the throne of the Byzantine empire.

Britain, 687. After its conquest by Caedwalla, king of Wessex, the Isle of Wight is the last area of Anglo-Saxon England to be converted to Christianity.

Britain, 20 March 687. The saintly Cuthbert, who lived as a hermit on the Farne islands and became bishop of Lindisfarne in Northumbria, dies.

Gaul, 687. After a series of conflicts between the Austrasian and Neustrian mayors of the palace – the real rulers of the Franks behind the facade of the increasingly ineffectual kings – Pepin II, mayor of Austrasia, wins a decisive victory over his Neustrian rival at the battle of Tertry. The Franks are now united under one king and, more importantly, under one mayor.

Italy, 689. King Cunipert of the Lombards defeats a rebellious duke and succeeds in establishing religious unity. Arianism is finally stamped out.

Gaul, 690. Willibrord, a Northumbrian monk, travels to the continent and, with Frankish encouragement, begins to preach the Gospel to the heathen Frisians (*of Friesland*).

Sumatra, 690. The Malayan kingdom of Srivijaya conquers the Indianised kingdom of Malayu, setting up its capital at Palembang and adopting Buddhism.

Balkans, 690. The Byzantine emperor, Justinian II, defeats the Slavs, who are based in Macedonia and Thrace.

Mesopotamia, 690. Mus'ab, the governor of Mesopotamia and brother of the rebel ibn Zubayr, is defeated on the Tigris by the caliph Abd al-Malik.

Arabia, 690. Abd al-Malik's general al-Hajjaj captures Medina.

West Africa, c.690. The state of Gao is founded on the upper Niger.

Central Asia, 691. Bek Tchor becomes khan on the death of his brother Qutlugh, the great khan.

Palestine, 691. The Dome of the Rock is completed in Jerusalem.

Central Asia, 692. China recaptures Tarim.

Constantinople, 692. An episcopal council meeting confirms eastern customs against western ways and asserts that the patriarch of Constantinople is equal to the pope. The papacy rejects the canons passed.

Former concubine seizes Chinese throne

China, 690

The beautiful Wu Zhao, who has been in the past the concubine of both the Emperor Taizong and his weak son Kaozong, has declared herself ruler of China as "Holy and Divine Emperor". She is a woman who combines great cruelty with equally great intelligence.

In her relentless determination to achieve power, she has destroyed most of the Tang princes and gone so far as to overthrow two of her own sons. She has also transformed one of her rivals in love into a "human swine" by chopping off her arms and legs.

But, whatever else she may be, Wu Zhao is certainly a most efficient administrator and a capable ruler.

The former concubine Wu Zhao.

Pictish army defeats the Northumbrians

Forfar, Britain, 21 May 685

Thirty years of Northumbrian domination of Picts ended yesterday when the aggressive Northumbrian king, Ecgfrith, was killed in battle by King Bridei, son of Bili. Bridei tricked Ecgfrith into chasing him into a remote valley in Angus before he sprang a reinforced ambush. Ecgfrith's body is to lie in a monastery, unmolested, because both sides are Christian converts thanks to the Irish missionary, Columba.

The Picts are an enigmatic people. Originally they came from northern Europe to Ireland; then they migrated to the wilderness of northern Britain. They were unconquered by the Romans and carried out raids across Hadrian's Wall.

After the Romans left the Picts made a string of short-lived treaties with the powerful Anglo-Saxons of Northumbria, with the old Celtic kingdom of Strathclyde, and even with the Scots, a Celtic people from Ireland who migrated to north Britain about 200 years ago. They were unified in 550. Aidan the Scot led a combined force of Scots and Picts against King Aethelfrith of Northumbria, and was beaten 82 years ago. King Oswy repeated the lesson in 657, giving Northumbria control of an area up to the river Forth.

Three warriors on a Pictish stone from Birsay, a settlement in Orkney.

Bulgars defeat Byzantine emperor

Balkans, July 681

The Bulgars, descendants of Asiatic nomads of the Steppes, like the Huns of an earlier period, have defeated the Byzantine empire, and it looks as if they will settle on the delta of the river Danube in eastern Europe. Led by Asparukh, the Bulgars had carried out raids into Byzantine territory for booty; as a result the Emperor Constantine IV launched a huge offensive against them. Defeated, Constantine has returned to Constantinople.

English priest is hailed as saint

Britain, 687

Cuthbert, the bishop of Lindisfarne, has died at his hermitage on Farne Island and immediately been hailed as a saint. Originally a noble soldier, Cuthbert entered Melrose Abbey in 651. Later, at Ripon, he worked tirelessly, preaching and healing plague-victims, before returning to Melrose as prior in 661. He moved on to the monastery of Lindisfarne, but after 676 chose to live at his remote island hermitage, where King Ecgfrith of Northumbria visited him and persuaded him to become a bishop. Cuthbert took up his new duties with zeal, but fell ill after two years and returned to Farne shortly before his death.

Great Turkish khan dies in his eighties

Central Asia, 691

The Great Khan, Elterich Kaghan, nicknamed Qutlugh, meaning "the fortunate", has died in his eighties, leaving a Turkish empire restored in the east. He is succeeded by his brother, Bek Tchor.

When he was a young Turkish prince, Qutlugh had been forced underground with various supporters to wage the fight against Chinese cultural domination. In 670 he re-established the khanate of Orkhon, empire of the eastern Turks. This stimulated a renewal of traditional religion, and a return to the Turkish language.

The Dome of the Rock, adorning one of the holiest shrines of Islam.

Dome of the Rock erected in Jerusalem

Jerusalem, 691

A magnificent new religious monument has been built in Jerusalem. Commemorating epochal events of two religions – Islam and Judaism – the Dome of the Rock, or *Qubbat as-Sakrah*, is the first such shrine to be constructed on the orders of a Moslem ruler.

The new building is the creation of Caliph Abd al-Malik, the third caliph of the Islamic Umayyad dynasty which has ruled the eastern Mediterranean since 660. The Dome commemorates two events which allegedly took place here. One is "the binding of Isaac" by the Jewish patriarch Abraham, whose willingness to sacrifice his son was rewarded by Yahweh's mercy; the other is the ascent to heaven of the prophet Mohammed.

The shrine is an octagonal building, notable for its harmonious proportions, covered by a dome. The walls and dome are similarly covered with glass mosaics, inlaid with gold.

Prophet's grandson dies as Moslems battle for power

Mesopotamia, 10 October 680

Divisions within Islam deepened today with the death of the Prophet's grandson, al-Husayn, in battle against the forces of his rival, Yazid, whose claims as caliph he refused to acknowledge. The battle was fought at Karbala, near Kufa, and alHusayn, whose forces were only some 70 strong, is being talked of as a martyr.

The previous caliph, Mu'awiyah, set up an Umayyad dynasty by insisting that his son, Yazid, should succeed him. Al-Husayn raised a rebel force against Yazid and advanced on Kufa, where his father Ali, the Prophet's son-in-law, had briefly been caliph.

Supporters of Ali, called Shi'ite Moslems, resent the rise of the Ummayad dynasty and believe themselves to be truer to Islamic law than Sunnite Moslems.

Before al-Husayn could reach Kufa, he was confronted by the governor ibn Ziyad, with a large force. Al-Husayn and all his companions were killed fighting heroically against hopeless odds.

Constantinople bishops vote to allow priests to get married

Constantinople, 692

Bishops meeting here have voted for many changes in the Church which are bound to anger Rome. Priests and deacons are going to be allowed to marry, and they will no longer be obliged to keep the Saturday fast in Lent. However, the representation of Christ as a lamb, very common in western churches, will be banned.

These changes will prove a headache for the Emperor Constantine IV, who has been working hard to conciliate Rome. His father, Constans II, had Pope Martin arrested in 655, and Constantine has tried to reduce Roman fears of Constantinople. In 680 he called an ecumenical council which made changes favourable to Rome.

Pope Sergius will undoubtedly resist the new measures. Rumour has it that he is already enlisting the help of the military in case attempts are made to arrest him.

The order of Christian society, with priests, nobles and citizens.

Rome, 692. The missionary monk Willibrord travels to Rome to meet Pope Sergius.

Asia Minor, 693. The Byzantines break their treaty with the Arabs, but are crushed in battle at Sebastea. Armenia falls to the Arabs.

Arabia, 693. The Umayyads, led by al-Hajjaj, put down the ibn Zubayr rebellion. Mecca is besieged and captured, and ibn Zubayr is killed. Abd al-Malik becomes master of the Umayyad empire.

Spain, 694. The Visigothic Council of Toledo decrees the enslavement of all Spanish Jews and orders their property to be confiscated. This is the culmination of a century of anti-Jewish legislation in the Visigothic kingdom.

China, 694. Manichaeism is introduced into China.

Mesopotamia, 694. Al-Hajjaj is made governor of Mesopotamia.

Constantinople, 695. The Byzantine emperor, Justinian II, is overthrown by the general Leontius. His nose is cut off and his tongue cut out. He takes refuge in the Crimea with the Bulgars.

Rome, 695. The pope consecrates the Northumbrian monk Willibrord as bishop of Utrecht, to serve his new converts to the Christian faith in Frisia.

Arabia, 696. The first Moslem dinar is minted. Abd al-Malik imposes Arabic as the official language in the Umayyad empire. The Koran is re-edited with vocalic symbols.

Venice, 697. The first *doge* is elected.

North Africa, 698. The Arabs occupy Carthage and bring an end to Byzantine rule in North Africa.

North Africa, 698. The Arabs put down a revolt by the Berbers in the Aures mountains, in the region which they call Ifriqiyah, on the North African coastline.

Constantinople, 698. Following another military revolt, the admiral Tiberius III becomes emperor. Leontius has his nose cut off.

Ireland, c.700. Adamnan, abbot of Iona, persuades much of the Irish church to come over to the Roman method of calculating the date of Easter, but fails to convince his own community and its daughter monasteries in Ireland.

North America, c.700. The use of bows and arrows, which are gradually replacing spears as the favourite weapons for hunting, has transformed activities in Indian society. The invention of the hoe has improved the efficiency of agriculture.

Mexico, c.700. The city of Teotihuacan is largely destroyed by fire and deserted by most of its inhabitants. The cause may have been social insurrection. Another theory is that the valley of Mexico could no longer sustain the huge population of Teotihuacan. Environmental deterioration caused by deforestation – to produce the vast amounts of lime plaster needed to cover the city walls – may also have been a factor.

Mexico, c.700. Possibly as a consequence of the collapse of Teotihuacan, Monte Alban is abandoned.

Mexico, c.700. The Temple of the Inscriptions and Temple of the Cross are under construction at Palenque, an important Maya religious centre.

Mexico, c.700. Shield Jaguar becomes king of Yaxchilan in the Peten jungle of southern Mexico.

Britain, c.700. The Lindisfarne Gospels, the finest of all Anglo-Saxon illuminated manuscripts, are produced.

West Africa, c.700. The kingdom of Ghana is growing in strength because of its control of trade routes, in particular the gold trade route.

Japan, 701. The Taiho code covering civil and criminal matters is issued. The Ommyoryo (Ministry of Divination by Yin and Yang) is set up.

Constantinople, 705. Tervel, the Bulgar khan, attacks Constantinople in support of the exiled Justinian II. The ousted emperor regains the Byzantine throne and Tervel receives the title of Caesar.

China, 705. The Empress Wu is deposed in a coup d'etat organised by her own ministers, who have grown sick of her frivolous excesses. The Tang dynasty is restored in the person of the son she had previously deposed, Zhongzong.

Syria, 8 October 705. The Umayyad caliph Abd al-Malik dies in Damascus. He is succeeded by his son Walid.

Syria, 705. Work starts on the construction of the Great Mosque in Damascus.

Gaul, 710. Hubert becomes bishop of Liege and continues his work of converting the heathen peoples on the eastern fringes of the Frankish kingdom.

Spain, 710. The rebel Roderic, the duke of Baetica, is elected king of the Visigoths, although his kingdom remains divided by internal unrest. His rival Agila rules part of the north.

Flourishing Venice elects its own leader

Venice, c.700

The city-state of Venice, founded as a refuge for families fleeing the Hun invasions of the fifth and sixth centuries, has developed into one of the world's great trading centres. In a move that reflects this increasing importance and the growing independence of the population from its ostensible rulers in Constantinople, the citizens have elected their own ruler, the *Doge*, a word derived from the Latin *dux*, "leader, duke".

A unique city, set among the coastal lagoons of the river Po, Venice is built on many tiny islands and its buildings, each shored up by great wooden piles, are connected by a network of canals.

As well as capitalising on the local environment, rich in fish and water-fowl, the Venetians benefit from the ideal position their city occupies: linked by sea to Byzantium and the east, by land and the river Po to wealthy northern Italy. They trade in salt, produced locally, and in exotic goods, notably spices and silks, imported from the east.

Reforming Caliph Abd al-Malik dies

A silver coin of the Umayyads.

Damascus, 8 October 705

The death of Abd al-Malik ends a 20-year reign that saw the breathtaking expansion of the Umayyad empire and its Arabisation. Abd al-Malik substituted Arabic for Greek as the language of administration, and abolished Byzantine coinage. His successor, Caliph Walid, has begun to build a Great Mosque, which will be constructed at enormous cost on the site of a Christian church, in Damascus.

Irish monks finish the Book of Kells

Ireland, 700

Irish monks in the Abbey of Kells have just completed the *Book of Kells*, a most beautiful example of the art of illumination in which the decorated initial letters sometimes take up a whole page. It took ten years to produce and is a testimony to the learning and skills of Irish monks, who have made Ireland without doubt the greatest centre of monastic life in Europe.

Irish life is tribal, with no towns, which makes it unsuitable for conventional bishoprics. Great monasteries have been established by such people as Finnian of Clonard, and they in turn have spawned satellite monasteries. The abbots of these extended monastic communities have become much more powerful than the bishops and have much influence with the tribal kings.

Through royal support the monasteries have become wealthy; this allows them to foster learning, finance book production and send monks out to spread Christianity.

Berber heroine dies from battle wounds

Aures, Ifriqiyah (North Africa), 698

Al-Kahina, the symbol of the Berber revolt in North Africa, has died in battle. Her forces were crushed 30 miles north of Tomba. Little is known of the origins of al-Kahina ("The Diviner"), except that she was at the forefront of Berber resistance after the fall of Carthage to the Arabs and the collapse of Byzantine power in North Africa.

Her first victory was won with the help of the Byzantine landowners of Hasan ibn Nu'mana. But she subsequently accused them of betraying the Aures people, and led her supporters against them.

Deprived of powerful allies, al-Kahina resorted in desperation to a scorched earth policy, destroying the town of Baghaya where most of her support came from.

Rich and diverse cultures flourish in the Americas

New communities grow in North America

A coiled basket with bird decoration: Anasazi culture, Colorado.

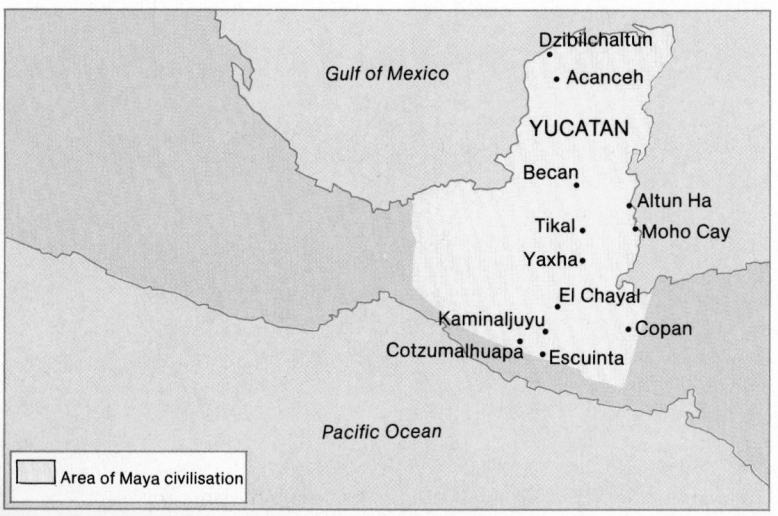
A typical Maya stone pyramid: this one is in the city of Cichen Itza.

Maya civilisation reaches new heights

Central America, c.700

Since their culture first began to flourish, in about 100, the Maya people have succeeded in creating a splendid civilisation which has reached heights of glory in the last century or so. Maya states now stretch over a vast area whose main administrative and religious towns are Copan, Tikal, Quirigua, Palenque and Uxmal. The various states are governed by kings, who bear the title of "great sun", backed by a political and religious elite.

The Maya have to clear dense,

inhospitable rain forest to farm; once cleared, the land becomes barren after only one or two harvests. It is in the forests, too, that they build great religious complexes whose stone pyramids, ziggurats and towers rival those of ancient Egypt, although they have no knowledge of the arch. As impressive as their buildings is the calendar which the Maya have worked out through skilled astronomical observation and mathematics. They record time by erecting a dated monument every 20 years.

A bowl of the Mogollon culture.

Three distinct cultures have emerged among farmers in the southwest regions of North America: the Hohokam, the Mogollon and the Anasazi. The Hohokam have lived here the longest, and they have imported many skills from Mexico, from where it is thought they may have originated. While the Hohokam live in the desert, the Mogollon are people of the mountains. Recent crop failures have forced them to find their food in the wild as their ancestors did. The Anasazi live to the North of the Mogollon, but they too are in contact with Mexico.

Map:
Gulf of Mexico
Dzibilchaltun
• Acanceh
YUCATAN
Becan
•Altun Ha
Tikal •
•Moho Cay
Yaxha•
El Chayal•
Kaminaljuyu•
•Copan
Cotzumalhuapa•
•Escuinta
Pacific Ocean

☐ Area of Maya civilisation

A representation on a pot of a ritual dance: Hohokam culture, Arizona.

Asia Minor, 711. Bloody acts of suppression by Justinian II provoke a serious revolt in the Crimea, which is supported by the Turkish Khazars. After marching on Constantinople, the rebels defeat and kill the emperor in a battle in northern Asia Minor.

Spain, 711. A small Arab expeditionary force under Tarik crosses the Straits of Gibraltar and crushes Roderic's Visigoths in battle on the river Euadelete. Much of Spain rapidly capitulates to the Arabs.

India, 711. Led by Mohammed ibn al-Kassim, the Arabs invade India.

Japan, 712. The *Kojiki*, an astonishing account of the history of Japan from its birth, is completed.

Italy, 712. Liutprand becomes king of the Lombards. He aims to reunite Italy by conquering the Byzantine territories and the semi-independent dukedoms of Spoleto and Benevento.

China, 712. The Emperor Xuanzong succeeds to the throne, bringing to an end a period of instability during which the nominal emperors, Zhongzong and Ruizong, were forced to share power with the corrupt Empress Wei and the formidable Taiping princess, both of whom aspired to follow the Empress Wu's example.

Gaul, 714. On the death of Pepin II, one of his illegitimate sons, Charles Martel ("The Hammer"), overcomes the other claimants and succeeds his father as mayor of the Austrasian palace, the effective power behind the Frankish throne.

India, 715. Mohammed ibn al-Kassim, the leader of the Islamic army which has conquered Sind and part of the Punjab for the Arabs, dies.

Gaul, 716. Charles Martel, mayor of Austrasia, defeats his Neustrian rivals at the battle of Ambleve.

Britain, 716. The wandering bishop Egbert, Northumbrian by birth, wins the monks of Iona and the monasteries under its jurisdiction over to the Roman Easter.

Britain, 716. Aethelbald becomes king of Mercia and begins to make it the most powerful of the Anglo-Saxon kingdoms.

Constantinople, 717. An Arab army of 80,000 men and a fleet of 1,800 ships besiege the capital of the Byzantine empire.

Constantinople, September 718. The latest Byzantine emperor, Leo III the Isaurian, triumphantly raises the Arab siege of Constantinople, thanks to Byzantine superiority at sea. Further Arab expansion is blocked.

Spain, 718. Pelagius, a Visigothic noble, leads a rebellion against the Arabs and defeats them at Covadonga. He founds the tiny independent Christian kingdom of the Asturias in northern Spain.

Rome, 719. The West Saxon monk Winfrid is sent by the pope to preach the Christian faith to the heathens in Germany. The pope gives him the name of Boniface.

Japan, 720. A history of Japan called the *Nippon Shoki* is published. Much of the content of both this history and the *Kojiki* is apparently based on collections of legends and hearsay. The authors describe the establishment in 660BC of the Japanese nation under the first of the imperial line, Jimmu Tenno.

Constantinople, 720. Leo III orders the execution of the ex-Emperor Anastasius II.

Gaul, 721. Having overrun Visigothic Septimania (Languedoc), the Arabs attack the Franks, but Duke Eudo defeats al-Sanh ibn Malik outside Toulouse and prevents an Arab invasion of Gaul.

Central Europe, 721. Legendary founding of Prague by Princess Libousa.

Rome, 30 November 722. Boniface is ordained as bishop of Germany by the pope and sent back to continue his work of conversion.

Britain, 725. The Northumbrian monk Bede publishes a treatise entitled *De ratione temporum* (On the reckoning of time). He follows Dionysius Exiguus in reckoning dates from the birth of Christ. Through his works this AD system is rapidly disseminated throughout western Europe.

Constantinople, 726. Leo III the Isaurian bans the worship of religious images. His measures meet violent popular opposition throughout the empire.

Italy, 727. Pope Gregory II condemns iconoclasm. Byzantine Italy breaks with the empire.

Italy, 728. King Liutprand of the Lombards occupies all the *exarchate* (imperial territories in Italy) except the capital, Ravenna. He retires, but keeps the western parts of the area.

Germany, 730. Charles Martel, the effective ruler of much of the Frankish dominions, defeats the last independent dukedom of the Alamanni. He launches raids on the Saxons beyond the Rhine.

Britain, 731. At Jarrow, Bede completes his *Ecclesiastical History*.

Rome, 731. Pope, Gregory III condemns iconoclasm and excommunicates its supporters.

Nara becomes the first capital of Japan

Japan, 710
The court and the government have moved to Nara, a pleasant rural site which was chosen under the Taika administrative reforms of 646 to be the first permanent capital of Japan.

Until then, the choice of capital had been influenced by the ancient Shinto belief that a dwelling place is polluted by death and so, each time a ruler died, his successor moved to another place.

It has taken all this time for Nara to be prepared for the move into what is virtually a purpose-built capital, based on Chang'an, the great capital of Tang China.

Great care was taken in choosing the site, and the Chinese art of "geomancy" was used to make sure the surrounding hills and streams were auspiciously formed.

The choice of Nara also reflects the growing influence of Buddhism, for it is the home of several major Buddhist temples, including the beautiful shrine of Horyuji.

With its five-tiered pagoda and

The five-tiered pagoda of Horyuji.

octagonal Pavilion of Dreams, the Horyuji, founded in 607, is the seat of Buddhist power in Japan. Now Nara is to be the seat of temporal power.

Christian hermits seek safety in caves

Cappadocia, Asia Minor, 716
As Arab raids on the vulnerable eastern fringe of the Byzantine empire continue, Christian hermits have taken to a novel form of self-protection. In face of the ever-present danger of attack many of them have become cave dwellers, or *troglodytes*, taking advantage of the soft volcanic rock, or tuff, with which the region abounds. Over thousands of years the tuff has been eroded into needles, cones and pyramids which, when hollowed out – not difficult, given the softness of the rock – provide quite passable dwellings. People have exploited the local rock in this way for a long time; the first to do so were the ancient Hittites.

Christian hermit dwellings carved out of volcanic rock in Cappadocia.

Moslems continue to advance in Europe and Asia

Spain capitulates to Arab invaders

Saragossa, Spain, 714
With the fall of Saragossa to the Arab armies of Musa ibn Nusayr, almost the whole of Spain has been conquered in a mere three years. Musa ibn Nusayr was governor of Ifriqiyah (*Tunisia*) when he sent a small expedition across the Straits. The expedition leader, Tariq ibn Ziyad, took up position on Mount Calpe, which was then named by the army "Mount of Tariq" or "Jebel Tariq" (Gibraltar).

From there Tariq took Algeciras and headed inland towards Cordoba. He did battle with the Visigoths under their king, Roderic, in July 711, and continued on a victorious march, capturing the towns of Ecija, Toledo, Alcala de Manares and Cordoba.

In 712 Musa followed him with new troops, and last year took the towns of Seville and Merida, followed by Saragossa. Only the mountainous regions of northern Spain remain so far unconquered, and it seems that the Arabs have no desire to penetrate them.

The Arabs' method of pacifying the country is enlightened. They offer to grant religious freedom for both Jews and Christians in return for a town's capitulation. In the countryside, most of the peasants are prepared to adopt the faith of Islam. The kingdom of the Visigoths is at an end.

Clash of armies – and cultures – at Poitiers; the Franks won the day.

Charles Martel halts the Arabs at Poitiers

Gaul, 25 October 732
The Frankish general, Charles Martel ("The Hammer"), has gained a brilliant victory at Poitiers over the seemingly unstoppable Arab forces, whose battlecry (from the Koran) is "Paradise lies in the shadow of the sword".

In the century since the death of the Prophet Mohammed, the Arabs have carried their faith to the limits of the known world, with the exception of the Byzantine empire and northern Europe. A few years ago they crossed the Pyrenees from Spain and seized Narbonne. This year, led by Abd al-Rahman, a member of a fanatical Moslem sect, they sacked Bordeaux and Poitiers and advanced on Tours, with its monastery of St Martin – one of Christendom's richest.

Eudo, the duke of Aquitaine, reeling under the Arab onslaught, sent a desperate appeal to Charles, who came riding south with his Frankish warriors. Tours was saved, and for six days the two armies skirmished warily. On the seventh, Abd-el-Rahman attacked Poitiers. In the day-long battle, the Arab leader himself was among the dead. The next morning the Arabs had decamped. They are said to be off to North Africa to put down a Berber uprising. It looks as though Charles Martel has put paid to Arab ambitions in Europe.

Bad image bans Byzantine icons

Constantinople, 730
Four years after the Emperor Leo III officially banned the worship of religious images, a mass-meeting of the churchmen of the empire has upheld Leo's revolutionary and and controversial decree. From now on all visible symbols of Christ, other than the Eucharist, are forbidden. Icons are to be smashed, and statues taken down. Anyone who refuses to comply will be guilty of paganism and idolatry.

Leo's move is primarily a religious one, and he is certainly not alone in feeling that what were once only symbols of the divine have become divinities in themselves. Furthermore, in the face of the seemingly inexorable spread of the Arabs and Islam, people have begun to wonder about the power of the icons in which they once put their trust. Leo wants to strengthen Christianity's resistance to the appeal of Islam, which forbids any portrayal of the human form. Leo also wishes to check the growing power of the monasteries whose monks threaten the division between Church and state.

A painting of the richly-arrayed Roustem, or the God of Silk, on a wooden panel from Dandan-Oiliq in Turkestan. It is typical of the region's art.

Moslems lay siege to Constantinople

Constantinople, 717
Moslem armies have moved into Syria and Asia Minor (Anatolia) and are besieging their ultimate objective, Constantinople. But the city is confident of checking Islam at its gates. It is the largest and most powerful of European cities, although it has undoubtedly decayed considerably in size and splendour since the great days of Justinian. Twelve miles of city walls should foil Arabs intent on seizing the "city of the world's desire".

Islamic empire now greater than Rome's

Damascus, 711
While the Moslem armies in Spain are fighting the Visigothic King Roderic, another expedition has set out eastwards towards the mouth of the river Indus in the country of Sind. The army has been mustered by the governor of Mesopotamia from the restless Arabs of Kufa and Basra and is led by Mohammed ibn al-Kassim.

From the mouth of the Indus the troops are spreading over the plains to the capital, Multan. Meanwhile, further north, other Moslem armies are pushing east from the Persian plateau into the steppes of Turkestan and the valleys of the Oxus and Jaxartes. Commanded by Qutayba, they have penetrated to the cities of Tashkent, Bokhara and Samarkand, on the Silk Road from China, which have been occupied, as well as the fertile oasis of Khwarazm, on the Aral Sea. Here the Moslems have encountered the Turks.

So the empire of Islam now stretches from the Atlantic coast to the Indus and as far north as the Aral Sea; its boundaries are set wider even than those of the Roman empire.

Britain, 732. Egbert, a member of the Northumbrian royal family, becomes bishop of York. He makes York a renowned centre of learning and founds a library there.

Constantinople, 733. In response to a revolt in Italy against iconoclasm supported by Pope Gregory III, Leo III withdraws all the Balkans, Sicily and Calabria from the jurisdiction of the pope and puts them under the control of the church at Constantinople. The break between the papacy and the empire is almost complete.

Gaul, 737. After the death of Theuderic IV, the throne of the Frankish kingdom is left vacant for a time by Charles Martel, the mayor of the palace and the effective ruler.

Egypt, 737. Christians invade Egypt from the south to protect the patriarch of Alexandria.

Spain, 739. Alfonso (the Catholic), the son-in-law of King Pelagius, becomes king of the Christian kingdom of the Asturias. He makes frequent raids on Arab territory.

Asia Minor, 739. The Arab invaders of Asia Minor are defeated by the Byzantine forces at the battle of Akroinon.

Rome, 739. The pope vainly appeals to Charles Martel for help against the expansionist policies of Liutprand, king of the Lombards.

Gaul, 739. The Anglo-Saxon monk Willibrord, who evangelised Frisia, dies at the age of 81 in the Echternach monastery which he founded in 698.

East Africa, 740. Moslems form Arabia and Persia are trading on the coast.

Japan, 741. The Japanese government decrees that Buddhist temples shall be established throughout the nation.

Gaul, 22 October 741. Charles Martel dies at Quiezy. His mayoral power is divided between his two sons, Pepin III and Carloman.

Constantinople, 741. Constantine V succeeds his father, Leo III the Isaurian, on the throne. A supporter of iconoclasm, he begins to persecute the image-worshippers.

Mesopotamia, 741. Zayd, grandson of the Shi'ite martyr al-Husayn, is killed in a Shi'ite revolt at Kufa.

Gaul, 742. Chrodegang, the former chancellor of Charles Martel, is appointed bishop of Metz and embarks on a reorganisation of the corrupt Frankish church.

Italy, 742. King Liutprand of the Lombards marches south and subjects the independent duchies of Spoleto and Benevento to his rule.

China, 742. Xuanzong's reign sees various measures taken against Buddhism in favour of Daoism. Moreover, the emperor now adopts a new reign title, *Tianbao* ("Heavenly Treasures"), with Daoist connotations, to symbolise the changed nature of his divine mandate to rule.

North Africa, 742. The Arabs put down a revolt of Kharajites and Berbers.

Constantinople, 742. Constantine V storms the capital, which has been seized by his rebel brother-in-law Artavasdus and the opponents of iconoclasm. Having regained control, he intensifies his attacks on image-worship.

Constantinople, c.745. An outbreak of bubonic plague sweeps Constantinople and spreads through Europe.

Egypt, 745. Nubians invade Egypt and temporarily occupy Cairo.

Cyprus, 746. The Greeks, having destroyed a large Arab fleet, regain control of Cyprus.

Gaul, 747. Carloman, who was sharing power with his brother Pepin, abdicates and retires to a monastery in Rome. Pepin III (the Short) becomes sole effective head of the Frankish kingdom.

Persia, 747. Abu Moslem leads a revolt of the Abbasids against the Umayyads at Khurasan.

Syria, 748. Wasil ibn Ata, founder of the liberal religion known as Mu'tazilism, dies. Mu'tazilites believe in free will and hold that God's actions are dictated by justice and reason.

Japan, 749. The reign of Shomu Tenno, who came to the throne in 724, is at an end. It was dominated by a widespread imitation of Chinese culture.

Syria, 749. Marwan, the last Umayyad caliph, is defeated by the Abbasid at the battle of the Zab.

South Africa, c.750. The culture associated with early users of iron in Africa reaches the Transkei area of the eastern Cape. This culture developed around Durban in Natal from about 380. Further south it is becoming increasingly mixed up with and indistinguishable from Khoisan herding culture. Bantu languages of the area borrow the click sounds of the Khoisan languages.

Palestine, c.750. John of Damascus, the author of a general survey of religion entitled *The Fount of Wisdom*, dies at the monastery of St Sabas in the valley of Cedron near Jerusalem. At the time of the iconoclastic crisis, he was one of the principal opponents of Leo III the Isaurian.

One of the many obelisks for which the Ethiopian city of Axum is famous.

Eygptian Moslems surrender to Nubians

North Africa, c.745

Caliph Marwan II of Egypt has capitulated in the face of an invading army of Christians from Nubia and Ethiopia, and released Michael, the patriarch of Alexandria, from captivity.

The caliph had imprisoned Michael in retaliation for local Coptic resistance to Moslem rule, and refused the request of a Nubian embassy that he be released. Undeterred, Kiriakos, the king of Nubia, sent an army to Egypt which picked up more recruits on the way in Christian Ethiopia. The army entered Egypt and had reached Fustat (Cairo) when the caliph finally released the patriarch.

The Christians and Moslems of the Nile delta have been in conflict for over a century now, since Egypt was taken by the Arabs in 641. Nubia narrowly escaped occupation by the Arabs in 651 after an attempted invasion, and was forced to agree to pay an annual tribute of 400 slaves. The patriarch is of particular importance to them because he appoints their bishops.

Abu Moslem leads revolt in Khurasan

Persia, 747

Abu Moslem ("Father of Moslem") has seized Merv, the capital of Khurasan, in north-east Persia, from the Umayyad caliph, 68 years after the Umayyads first conquered the area. The Arab invaders promised equality to any embracing the Koran, but their assurances were left in complete tatters by jealous conflicts among the Arab settlers and their army. A few months ago Abu'l-Abbas, a descendant of the Prophet's uncle al-Abbas, seized the chance to send Abu Moslem to exploit the unrest and begin an insurrection against the Umayyads.

Islam is rocked by murder of Caliph

Bakhra, Syria, April 744

The Umayyad Caliphate has been shaken by the murder of Caliph al-Walid II. Walid succeeded his father, the shrewd and puritanical Hisham, last year, and soon became notorious for his extravagance. He moved from one desert palace to another, spending a fortune on building, poets and – against Islamic laws – wine. One story claims he dived into a pool of wine and drank himself unconscious. He loved hunting, girls and even boys. His shocked family had him murdered, and various factions now seek to take advantage of his death.

Historian Bede dies in Jarrow Abbey

Jarrow, England, 25 May, 735

He was teaching until the very end. Yesterday was Ascension Day and, as he taught, Bede told his pupils: "Learn quickly – for I do not know how long I shall live or if my maker will soon take me away." The 63-year-old monk rose at dawn this morning and dictated for three hours. A monk suggested that it might be too tiring for him to dictate the final chapter of his book. Bede answered: "Take up your pen and ink and write quickly."

Six hours later, Bede said: "I have a few treasures in my wallet – some pepper, some napkins and some incense – so run quickly and bring the priests of our monastery so that I can distribute such small gifts as God has given me." He dictated one final sentence, knelt on the floor, prayed and breathed his last.

This devout scholar will be sadly missed in the Anglo-Saxon community. At the age of seven, Bede was entrusted by his family to the monastic life and he and the abbot were the only monks to survive an outbreak of the plague at Jarrow. Bede became a deacon at the early age of 19 and a priest at 30.

Bede only left his monastery on brief visits to Lindisfarne and York, but never left Northumbria, devoting his life to the study of scripture, commentaries on the Bible and an

The great monk and scholar Bede, as portrayed by a later artist.

important treatise on chronology which dates history from the time of the birth of Christ. It was an earlier, shorter version of this which brought a charge of heresy against Bede, a charge which he dismissed as "made by rustics wallowing in their cups".

He wrote a history of the Abbots of Jarrow and the life of St Cuthbert; but he will most likely be remembered for his Ecclesiatical History of the English Nation, a remarkable account of the early history of the Anglo-Saxon kingdoms and their conversion to Christianity which Bede compiled

A doorway of Jarrow monastery, founded by Benedict Biscop.

with the help of correspondents throughout the country.

This revered teacher was greatly helped in his work by the library at Jarrow founded in 683 by Benedict Biscop, who brought back books and relics from Rome to create an endowment unparalleled in Britain.

Bede is perhaps the greatest product of a time of cultural flowering in the fields of scholarship, sculpture and manuscript illumination, which have developed in Northumbria under the combined influence of the Roman Church and of Celtic monasticism from Ireland.

Death of Martel, the mightiest ruler in western Europe

Gaul, 22 October 741

The ruler of the Franks, Charles Martel ("The Hammer"), whose empire is now the dominant power in western Europe, died today in his country palace at Quierzy, aged 53. Despite his great power he never took the title of king, but called himself simply mayor of the palace, or duke. The old Merovingian dynasty continues to exist, but its kings wield no power.

Charles, the illegitimate son of the Frankish ruler Pepin II, fought his rivals for three years before gaining possession of the Frankish territories between the Rhine and the Loire. He went on to subjugate Burgundy and Provence and force German tribes to pay tribute.

He fostered good relations with the papacy, having repelled the Arab threat, but refused to aid Pope Gregory III against King Liutprand of the Lombards, with whom he chose to stay on good terms.

He protected the Anglo-Saxon missionary Boniface as he spread the Gospel in southern Germany. He set up an annual assembly of nobles, known as the *Campus Martius*, and angered the priests by giving his vassals confiscated Church land to keep them loyal.

Monasticism plays a growing role in western European society

A Bible made by monks at Jarrow.

Western Europe, c.750

Monasteries have now spread throughout western Europe and are taking an increasing role in social and intellectual life. Monasticism has spread mainly because of the spiritual impulse of men to give their lives to God in meditation. Ever since early Christian times there has existed in the Church a tradition of withdrawal from the world, in order to worship God more effectively. At a more prosaic level it also provides material security from the uncertainties of the times, and has been found to be a useful way of securing family land under the guise of "religious" foundations.

Most monastic founders make their own rules, and discipline can be very varied in its severity. How-

ever, all monastic orders live as communities, under abbots, dedicated to the service of God and the spiritual development of the monks. In the west the Rule issued in 537 by the monastic founder Benedict, the abbot of Monte Cassino in Italy, has found particular favour for its directness and clarity, and it is gradually being adopted by other monastic houses.

The other big influence has been the Irish monks, who have long established monasteries on different, but parallel, lines. Some of them, like Columban, have emigrated and set up monasteries in Europe, notably in the Vosges region and at Bobbio in Italy. In Celtic monasteries more severe and ascetic rules, like that of Columban, are generally followed.

A later image of Charles Martel.

750 (750-760)

East Africa, c.750. Over the past 20 years, Arabs and Persians have been taking control of coastal trade along the coast they call Zanj (*from Somalia through Kenya and Zanzibar to southern Tanzania and Mozambique*).

West Africa, 750. Arabs from North Africa have begun crossing the Sahara in large numbers to trade in gold.

Mesopotamia, 750. The Abbasids overthrow the Umayyad sect and gain spiritual and political control of most of the Moslem world.

Japan, 751. The Toshodaiji temple is built in Nara.

Gaul, 751. After obtaining papal approval, Pepin III, the mayor of the palace, dispenses with the fiction of rule by the long-ineffective Merovingian king, and takes the title king for himself, founding a new royal dynasty: the Carolingians.

Italy, 751. Ravenna, the last Byzantine possession in northern Italy, falls to the Lombards under King Aistulf.

Central Asia, 751. After having occupied Tashkent, Samarkand and Bokhara, the Chinese are crushed by the Arabs on the river Talas. Islamic influence spreads through central Asia.

Japan, 752. The Empress Koken attends a ceremony before the great bronze Buddha in the Toshodaiji temple in Nara. She attests that she, as empress, is the servant of the Three Jewels of Buddhism.

Arabia, 752. Two Chinese prisoners reveal the technique of making paper to the Arabs. The first paper mill in the Arab world is established.

Japan, 754. The Chinese monk Chien-chen, who is almost blind, reaches Japan after making five unsuccessful attempts.

Gaul, January 754. Assailed by the Lombards, and with little prospect of help from the Byzantines, Pope Stephen II appeals to the Franks for help. He and Pepin conclude a treaty to their mutual advantage, and the Lombard king Aistulf swiftly submits.

Germany, 754. Having embarked on yet another mission, this time to the unevangelised tribes of north-eastern Frisia, Boniface is killed by the heathens.

Mesopotamia, June 754. Al-Mansur, the brother of Abu'l-Abbas, the first Abbasid caliph, succeeds to the caliphate.

Tibet, 755. The reign of Khri-Ide gtsug-brtsan, which saw the building of the royal fortress of Lhasa, is at an end.

China, 755. Rivalry between the Mongol general An Lushan and the minister Yang Guozhong leads to a conflict between An Lushan and the court. After invading Hebei, An Lushan quickly moves south and captures Loyang, where he enthrones himself as emperor of a new Xia dynasty.

Balkans, 755. Constantine V embarks on a determined campaign against the Bulgars.

Mesopotamia, 755. The Abbasid leader Abu Moslem, who has recently put down a revolt in Syria, is assassinated in Baghdad on the orders of Caliph al-Mansur.

Persia, 755. Following the death of their leader, Abu Moslem's supporters in Khurasan revolt against the Umayyads.

Spain, 756. The Umayyad prince Abd al-Rahman creates the emirate of Cordoba.

Italy, 756. After the Lombard king Aistulf, resumes his attacks on the pope and marches on Rome, Pepin III intervenes and forces Aistulf to surrender. The pope is given control over an enlarged papal state under Frankish protection. The link between the empire and the papacy has gone.

China, 756. On the death of the imperial concubine Yang Guifei, the Emperor Xuanzong abdicates. An Lushan seizes the capital and proclaims himself emperor.

China, 756. Wu Daogi, one of the great masters of painting of the Tang period, dies.

Britain, 757. After a very successful 40-year reign King Aethelbald of Mercia is murdered at Seckington by his bodyguard. He is succeeded by his kinsman Offa.

China, 757. With the assassination of its leader, the An Lushan rebellion comes to an end, leaving millions dead. Millions more refugees are now fleeing to the south.

Gaul, 759. The Franks recapture Narbonne, which has been in Arab hands since 720, and take control of Septimania (Languedoc).

Japan, 759. The Chinese monk Chien-chen is granted a centre of studies and an ordination platform in the Toshodaiji temple.

India, 760. On the orders of the Emperor Krishna of the Rashtrakuta dynasty, the temple of Kailasa at Ellora is carved entirely out of the living rock, as if it were a statue.

Mesopotamia, 760. The Indian system of numerals is adopted in the Abbasid empire.

Pepin the Short enters alliance with Pope

Pepin: short stature, great mind.

Gaul, 754
Pope Stephen II and King Pepin III of Gaul, the son of Charles Martel, have concluded a treaty that is expected to have far-reaching effects on the balance of power in northern Europe and is almost certain to lead to war with neighbouring states.

Under the treaty Pepin the Short, as he is known, has vowed to give 23 towns in central and northern Italy to the pope. One snag is that the towns are held by King Aistulf of the Lombards, who has been threatening the pope, and Pepin will have to invade Lombardy to keep his word. If and when these towns are handed to Rome, they will be added to the pope's existing lands to form a sizable papal state, with security provided by Pepin.

In return, a new dynasty of Frankish kings has been given the legitimacy it craves. Although effective rulers for years, Pepin's line remained in name only mayors of the palace (chief ministers). Then, in 751, the Pope authorised the ousting of the last Merovingian king in favour of Pepin. Now Pepin and his heirs will be styled "Patricians of the Romans".

For Pepin, the treaty will also mean breaking the alliance that his father Charles Martel signed with with the Lombards 15 years ago.

Emperor abdicates over lover's death

China, 756
The Emperor Xuanzong, the grandson of the cruel Empress Wu, has abdicated after 44 years on the throne, his heart broken by the death of his beautiful concubine, Yang Guifei. She had been his son's wife, but the emperor fell in love with her, made them divorce and took her into his harem.

She became the patron, some say the lover, of An Lushan, a Mongol general who eventually rebelled against the emperor. Xuanzong and Yang Guifei fled, but their bodyguard mutinied and, blaming her for their plight, demanded her death. The terrified emperor gave in and she was strangled by the chief eunuch.

The temples of the Kailasa at Ellora in central India: carved out of the living rock, it is one of several similar temple complexes in the region.

New rulers dine over their victims

Kufa, Mesopotamia, 750

A new caliph now rules over the Islamic world, following the defeat and annihilation in the past year of the Umayyads, the former rulers.

For many Moslems the Umayyads had come to be seen as unworthy rulers. Their ancestors had been among the bitterest enemies of the Prophet Mohammed, and some of them had been godless and debauched. Many felt that true Islam could only be restored when the family of the Prophet held the reins of power.

The Alids, descendants of Fatima, the Prophet's daughter, and Ali, her husband, had tried and failed to topple the Umayyads. But another branch of the family, the Abbasids, also had their eyes on power. Abu'l-Abbas, descended from the Prophet's uncle al-Abbas, had lived in obscurity in southern Jordan until, in the late 740s, he took advantage of unrest in Khurasan, in the east of the Umayyad empire. He sent his brilliant but rather sinister envoy, Abu Moslem, to inspire the people of Khurasan to march west and overthrow the Umayyad caliphs. Cleverly, the Abbasids urged them to do this in the name of the "Family of the Prophet", thereby winning support

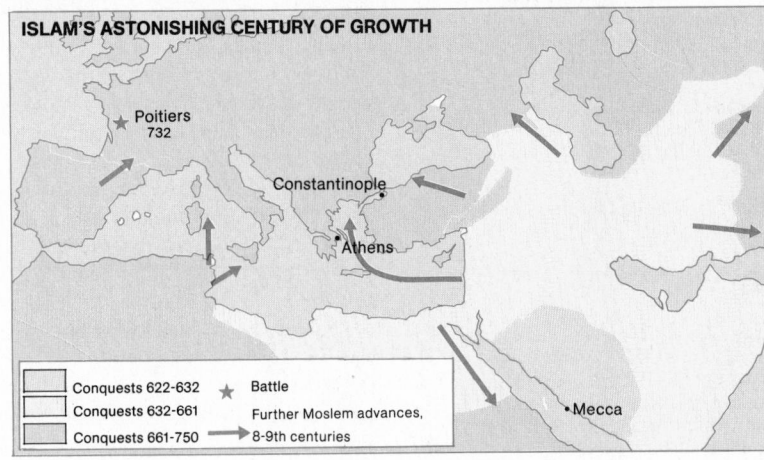

ISLAM'S ASTONISHING CENTURY OF GROWTH

Poitiers 732

Constantinople

Athens

Mecca

Conquests 622-632
Conquests 632-661
Conquests 661-750

★ Battle

Further Moslem advances, 8-9th centuries

from the Alids. The Abbasid armies overran Mesopotamia and defeated the caliphate, killing the last Umayyad caliph. But, to the indignation of the Alids, Abu'l-Abbas announced it was to be his branch of the Family of the Prophet that would be the rulers of the Islamic world from now on. At Kufa, last year, Abu'l-Abbas was proclaimed caliph, with the auspicious title *al-Saffah*, "Shedder of Blood".

Since then the new caliph has been consolidating his power and mopping up the remnants of the old dynasty, thoroughly earning his title. His armies have swept west, obliterating members of the Umay-

yad family wherever they have found them; they have even dug up the bodies of the Umayyad caliphs and publicly flogged their remains, before scattering the bones to the elements. Recently, in an apparent act of reconciliation, Abu'l-Abbas invited the surviving male members of the Umayyad dynasty to a dinner party. But even before the first course the guests were massacred; the new rulers then carried on with the feast over the corpses.

The Abbasid revolution has been a popular one. Nonetheless, many former supporters of the Alids feel they have been duped, and remain a potential source of trouble.

Umayyad prince is emir of Cordoba

Spain, 15 May 756

Abd al-Rahman, a Syrian prince, has been proclaimed emir of Cordoba. The only member of the ousted Umayyads to survive a massacre by the Abbasids in 750, he came to Spain last year with other Arab clans. When he first fled from his homeland he took refuge in Egypt, and then at Kairouan, before arriving in Spain on 14 August. He profited from division among the Arabs to make his way via Seville to Cordoba, the capital of Spain. He is also a poet, and has written poems lamenting the loss of Syria.

Porcelain bottle from Arab Spain.

Arab writer thrown into burning oven

Basra, 757

The greatest contemporary writer of Arabic prose has been killed at the age of 39. Ibn al-Mukaffa was tortured to death on the orders of Caliph al-Mansur. Under the supervision of the governor of Basra, a long-time enemy, his limbs were cut off before he was thrown, still alive, into a burning oven.

Ironically, ibn al-Mukaffa's writing caused his death. Commissioned by the caliph to write a pardon, or *aman*, for a rebellious noble, al-Makaffa surrounded the caliph's promise with so many solemn oaths that al-Mansur was outraged. He ordered the writer to be executed. Among al-Mukaffa's works are legal and philosophical treatises and the *Kalila wa Dimna*, a collection of Indian fables.

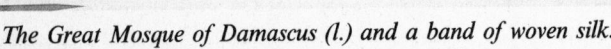

The Great Mosque of Damascus (l.) and a band of woven silk.

An Arabian band of woven silk.

Japan, c.760. Following the death of the Emperor Shomu a wooden structure has been built near the Toshodaiji temple to house his possessions. It is called the Shosoin treasure house. The store includes objects which travelled the Silk Road from the Near East. There are silk kimonos, lacquered vessels, musical instruments, swords, furniture and items used in dramatic performances.

North Africa, 761. Ibn Rustum founds the dynasty of the Rustumides at Tahert in Algeria.

Mesopotamia, 762. Baghdad is chosen as the capital of the Abbasid empire.

Mesopotamia/Arabia, 762. The Shi'ites revolt against the Abbasids in Mesopotamia. A similar revolt is in progress at the town of Medina in Arabia.

China, 763. After sacking the eastern Chinese capital of Loyang, the central Asian people known as the Uighurs are converted to Manichaeism.

Balkans, 764. After conducting a series of military campaigns against the Bulgars over the past decade, the Byzantine Emperor Constantine V forces them to sign a peace treaty.

India, 765. The Pala dynasty is founded in Bengal and Magadha (*Bihar*).

Asia Minor, 765. Constantine V steps up his persecution of the image-worshippers. Icons and mosaics are smashed. The monastic order as a whole is violently attacked; many are martyred in the process.

Britain, 765. Aethelbert succeeds Egbert as bishop of York. He greatly enhances the library there and puts his pupil Alcuin in charge of the cathedral school.

Gaul, 768. With the defeat and death of Weifar, duke of Aquitaine, Pepin III and the Carolingians finally establish control of the area after a series of invasions over the past 20 years.

Gaul, 24 September 768. Pepin the Short dies. His dominions are divided, according to custom, between his sons, Charles (Charlemagne) and Carloman.

Rome, 769. At a church meeting at the Lateran Palace the laity lose the right to participate in the election of the pope.

China, 770. The great Chinese poet Du Fu dies alone, possibly of malnutrition. His poetry embraces a great breadth of sympathies and his own life mirrors the sudden change from prosperity to uncertainty brought about by the An Lushan rebellion.

India, 770. The reign of Nandivarman II, who became king of the Pallava dynasty in 720, is at an end.

Mesopotamia, 770. The first public pharmacy is opened in Baghdad.

Gaul, 4 December 771. With the death of his brother Carloman, Charlemagne becomes sole ruler of the Frankish empire.

Rome, 772. Pope Hadrian appeals to Charlemagne for help against the Lombard king, Desiderius, who has taken over part of the Papal States.

Italy, 774. Charlemagne conquers the Lombard kingdom and makes it part of the Frankish kingdom. He then declares himself king of the Lombards. He now controls much of Italy.

Rome, 774. Charlemagne becomes the first Frankish king to visit Rome. He confirms the "donation" of the Ravenna region to the pope, which was made by Pepin the Short, his predecessor.

Iraq, 772. Al-Mahdi succeeds his father, al-Mansur, as caliph of the Abbasids.

Constantinople, 775. On the death of Constantine V, his eldest son, Leo IV, succeeds as Byzantine emperor. Although an iconoclast like his father, he pursues a more conciliatory religious policy.

Malaysia, 775. The kingdom of the Srijaya (*in Sumatra*) conquers the whole of the Malaysian peninsula.

Britain, 777. Alcuin publishes a treatise on musicography entitled *De Musica*, in which he expounds the theories of his time.

Constantinople, 777. Telerig, the khan of the Bulgars, is baptised and becomes an ally of the Eastern empire.

Spain, 778. Charlemagne's forces invade Spain, where an Umayyad dynasty was established in 756, but meet heavy resistance at Saragossa.

Spain, 778. As the Franks retreat from Spain, Roland, one of Charlemagne's most trusted generals, is killed in an ambush by the Basques at Roncesvalles.

Asia Minor, 778. The Byzantine forces defeat the Arabs at the battle of Germanikeia.

Gaul, 779. Charlemagne issues the *Capitulary of Herstal*, which includes an edict attempting to enforce the payment of tithes by each man to the church.

Central Asia, 780. Alp Qutlug, the *kagan* (emperor) of the Uighurs, opens up his country to Sino-Persian influence by adopting Manichaeism as the official state religion.

Land of gold lies south of the Sahara

Western Sudan, 770
Arab traders returning from the caravan routes across the Sahara tell of a magnificent kingdom known as "Ghana" – land of gold. The people gain their wealth by acting as middlemen; they take salt, cloth and other commodities from the Mediterranean traders in the north and exchange these for the gold produced by Ghana's neighbours in the south.

The origins of the kingdom are lost in legend. Kings known as Hagha rose to power among the Soninke, the local farmers of the Western Sudan. These kings controlled trade with Berber and Jewish traders who came from North Africa to buy gold and salt.

A royal city, called Al Ghaba by the Arabs, north-west of the great bend of the River Niger, is surrounded by wells of drinking water and vegetable gardens. An efficient army supports the rule of the Hagha.

The gold trade has increased because of demand from the flourishing economy of Moslem Spain and North Arica. Muslim influence in Ghana is growing with the conversion of some leading Soninke and the building of mosques.

The penny is new Anglo-Saxon coinage

England, 778
As Mercia, under the tough rule of King Offa, enjoys an unprecedented trading boom with Europe, a new silver coin is being minted. It is called a penny and is replacing an earlier, smaller, silver type of coin, the *sceatta*.

The new coin, minted in London, Kent and the kingdom of the East Angles, clearly imitates the deniers of the Franks in size and weight, and sometimes shows the influence of Roman imperial designs. Offa's name is always featured on this coinage, which is testimony to the growing wealth of the Anglo-Saxons and their trading contacts with the rest of Europe, and to the desire of kings like Offa to tap the wealth to their advantage.

Four silver "sceattas".

Baghdad chosen as Abbasid capital

Baghdad, 762
Al-Mansur, the second caliph of the Abbasids, has chosen Baghdad as his new capital. It is on the banks of the Tigris, close enough to the Euphrates for canals to link the two rivers; a pass leads through the Zagros mountains to the Persian plateau and beyond. A formal, ceremonial round city is being built for al-Mansur's court and army, with four vast gates, and a mosque and palace at the centre. Baghdad is an Arab city, but the Abbasids are heavily influenced by Persian culture and political ideas.

Islam's strongman has died at Mecca

Mecca, Arabia, 775
Al-Mansur, the Caliph who has ensured the survival of the Abbasid dynasty, has died on a pilgrimage. He succeeded his brother al-Saffah in 754, at a time when the new Abbasid dynasty was under pressure from outside and from those who wanted to make the Caliph a puppet. Al-Mansur, tall, gaunt and swarthy, showed no mercy to his rivals, who included the great general Abu Muslim. But he was supportive to servants and loyal commanders. His son al-Mahdi should find the succession easy.

Charlemagne expands his empire

Western Europe, 778

Charles, the king of the Franks, is facing a new threat from the peoples across the river Rhine. Having brought the pope under his control, subjected the Lombards to his rule and united northern Italy to his realm, thereby making Frankish Gaul (or *Francia*, as it is now often called) a major force in western Europe, he is turning his armies on the troublesome Saxons who have always threatened the growth of the Frankish kingdom.

Since the death of his brother, Carloman, seven years ago, Charles, or *Charlemagne* (Charles the Great) has been the sole ruler of the Franks. Using supreme diplomacy and styling himself "King of the Franks and Lombards and Patrician of the Romans" he succeeded in bringing the Lombard kingdom to heel. He thus broke the vital connection of interests between the pope and the Byzantine empire. Charles was now the protector of the pope, but not yet an emperor. Internecine fighting between provincial rulers ensured that Italy was constantly divided between north and south.

Despite the frequent punitive raids of the Franks and the valiant efforts of a succession of Anglo-Saxon missionaries, many of the Saxons worshipped the same gods that they had worshipped for hundreds of years, believed in oracles and held sacrificial feasts; in short,

Charles of the Franks: reviving the idea of empire in western Europe.

they believed in everything that was anathema to the Christian Charles. Worse still, they tended to plunder his wealthy kingdom, particularly when he was away.

In his most recent campaign (772-5) he marched to the river Weser and destroyed the column of Irminsul – a tree worshipped by pagans as the tree that supported

the world. No sooner had he advanced into Italy, however, than the Saxons again began to venture into Frankish territory.

Two years ago Charles established fortresses on the river Lippe from which missionaries could operate. Despite this, a tribal chief, Widukind, has emerged as a new leader of the Saxon resistance.

Roland, ally of Charlemagne, killed in surprise Basque attack

Spain, 15 August 778

Roland, one of the most loyal followers of the Frankish king Charles, or *Charlemagne*, has died in a surprise attack in the Pyrenees. With his army, Roland was returning to France after scoring several successes against the Arabs in Spain. The quickest way back is through dangerous territory occupied by the Basques, a proud people with their own distinct language and traditions, unconquered even by the Romans. It appears that, as Roland was crossing the pass of Roncesvalles, his rearguard was ambushed by Basques. Many Franks are believed to have been killed, including Roland himself.

Roland, Charlemagne's general, in battle, as portrayed by a later artist.

Great Chinese poet drowns in river

China, 762

Li Bai, the greatest of China's poets, has died, reportedly of drowning while drunkenly trying to capture the reflection of the moon in the waters of the Yangtze. His death in this fashion surprises no-one, for his love of wine and eccentric behaviour are part of the myth which surrounds this extraordinary man. His spontaneous poetry is full of fantasy and reflects the dashing image of his carefully cultivated personality. He surrounded himself with convivial companions and lived life to the full.

It was not until he was already famous as a poet that he visited the capital, where he was introduced to the Emperor Xuanzong as a "banished immortal" and was made court poet. He fell foul of Yang Guefei, the emperor's concubine, and was banished. Later he was imprisoned for his involvement in the Prince of Yong's attempt to seize power. He ended his days in exile, dying as he lived – outrageously.

"Gregorian" chant devised for Church

Monks: changing their tune.

Rome, 778

Christian worship is being sung to a new set of chants, named *Gregorian* after Pope Gregory the Great. When he died 174 years ago an earlier liturgy, *Cantus romanus*, was evolving. To standardise ritual, two bishops, aided by monks of St Gallen abbey in Switzerland, created a chant peculiarly suited to the Latin tongue, used by the Church. The name *Gregorian* lends the new chant authority.

China, 781. Christianity spreads to the Chinese court. Christian monasteries are built.

China, 781. Attempts by the Emperor Dezong to bring territory held by warlords under central control meet with rebellions and a tacit acceptance by the emperor of local autonomy.

Saxony, 782. After three years of fighting, Charlemagne makes Saxony a Frankish province and imposes the Christian faith on the natives. But their leader Widukind soon leads a revolt and massacres a Frankish army. Charlemagne slaughters rebel prisoners and invades again.

Saxony, 785. Widukind is baptised and reconciled to Charlemagne. The Saxons have submitted once more.

Britain, 786. Papal legates visit Britain for the first time since Augustine. They hold councils in Northumbria and Mercia and attempt to correct abuses.

Saxony, 786. The term *deutsch* (German) appears for the first time, in Saxony, used to distinguish the vernacular from the Latin used by priests.

Byzantine Empire, 787. After heated debate, the second Council of Nicaea, called by the Empress Irene, condemns iconoclasm and restores the veneration of images.

Gaul, 789. Charlemagne issues the *Admonitio generalis*, a decree setting out his plans for the revival of culture and education in his dominions.

Britain, 789. Coming from Scandinavia, three ships of Vikings launch a raid on the south coast. The king's retainers ride from Dorchester to meet them, believing them to be traders, and are killed.

Britain, 8 June 793. Vikings raid the Northumbrian coast, sacking the monastery on Lindisfarne and slaughtering many of the defenceless monks.

Japan, 794. The Emperor Kammu moves the capital to Kyoto, away from the power of the Buddhist sects of Nara.

Spain, 795. Charlemagne creates a frontier province, "the Spanish march", south of the Pyrenees, between the Frankish and Arab empires.

Ireland, 795. After attacking the Shetlands, the Vikings sail down the west coast of Scotland, sack the monastery on Iona, and plunder Ireland for the first time.

The dyke builder King Offa, has died

Offa: keeping the Welsh at bay.

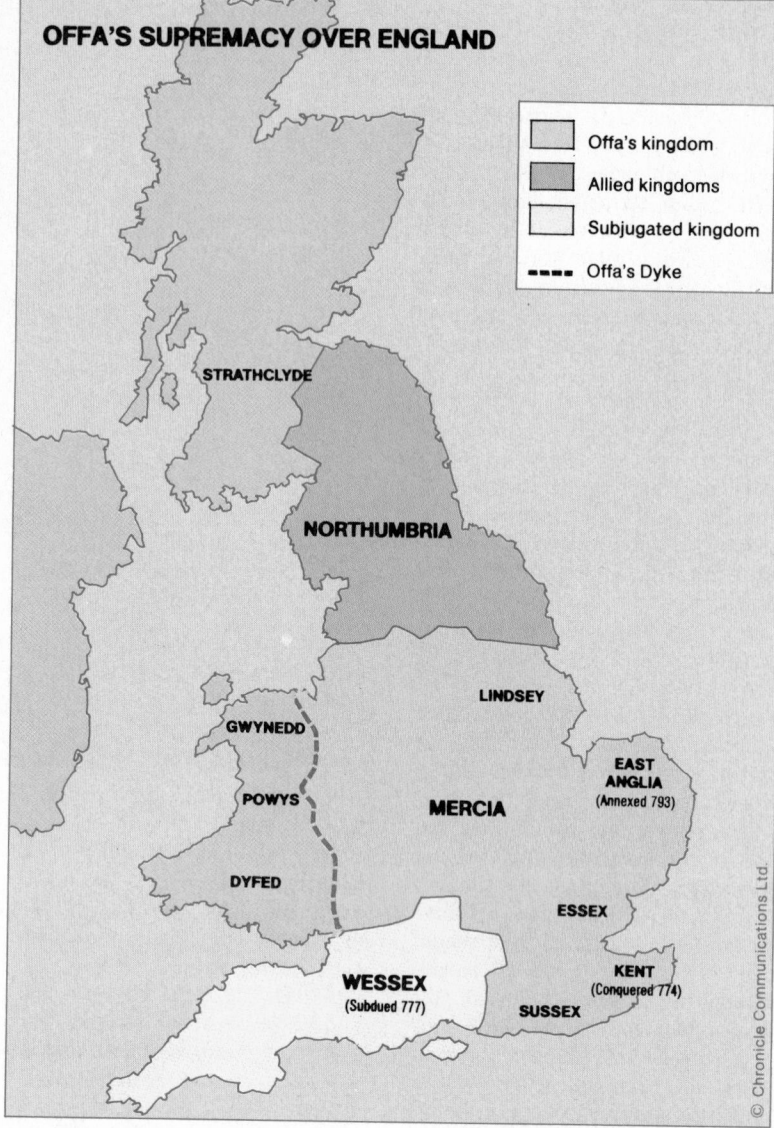

OFFA'S SUPREMACY OVER ENGLAND

Offa's kingdom
Allied kingdoms
Subjugated kingdom
---- Offa's Dyke

STRATHCLYDE

NORTHUMBRIA

GWYNEDD
LINDSEY
POWYS
MERCIA
EAST ANGLIA (Annexed 793)
DYFED
ESSEX
WESSEX (Subdued 777)
KENT (Conquered 774)
SUSSEX

© Chronicle Communications Ltd.

Mercia, England, 26 July 796
Offa, the first Anglo-Saxon king to call himself *rex Anglorum* (king of the English), has just died, after completing a massive 150-mile-long dyke to mark the border between his kingdom and various Welsh territories. Already known as Offa's Dyke, it extends from the Severn to the Dee Estuary, and for long distances runs above the 1000-foot contour line.

During his 40-year reign, Offa brought Kent, Sussex, Essex and East Anglia directly under his control, and latterly gained influence in Wessex. But the kingdom he leaves extends no further northwards than the Humber, beyond which Northumbria remains independent. Offa thus built on the foundations of Mercian control over the rival kingdoms of southern England laid by his predecessor Aethelbald.

He dealt on equal terms with the powerful Charlemagne, the king of the Franks. Just recently Charlemagne and Offa concluded the first commercial treaty in English history. They agreed that traders visiting Gaul from England or England from Gaul should have official protection during their travels.

Poisoned toothpick kills dynasty founder

Morocco, June 791
Imam Idris, the founder of a new Arab dynasty in Morocco, has been murdered, apparently by a poisoned toothpick sent by Caliph Harun al-Rashid of Baghdad. Originally from Medina, in Arabia, Idris was a descendant of the Prophet Mohammed. In 786 he took part in a failed revolt against the caliph – the monarch of Islam, descended

from Mohammed's uncle – and fled in disguise to Egypt and thence to Morocco. The Awraba tribe of Berbers hailed him as their religious and political leader, or *imam*. Idris established himself at the old Roman town of Volubilis and built a new capital, Fez, from which to win over other Berber tribes. Idris has left no son, but one of his concubines is heavily pregnant.

Title page of the Gospel According to St Matthew, from the magnificently illuminated Book of Kells, made by Irish monks.

Charlemagne encourages education

A partly gilded silver goblet.

Aachen, c.789
Charlemagne, king of the Franks, has issued the *Admonitio Generalis* (General Reminder), a declaration of his plans for the encouragement of learning throughout his dominions, part of a wider programme to revive scholarship and the arts.

Many of the most learned men in Europe have come to his court in Aachen, where a school has been established for the education of his sons, young nobles, and even poor boys if they have talent. The writing of books is encouraged and a new, standardised, script is being adopted by monastic scribes.

Yet Charlemagne himself is illiterate. He has made several attempts to learn to write, but is now resigned to the fact that he began too late in life. Even so, he has learned to speak Latin and some Greek and is familiar with mathematics and astrology.

Charlemagne's first concern is to create an educated clergy with a proper understanding of the Bible and the Christian faith. In his message to priests calling on them to study literature, he says he receives badly-written and uncouth letters from monasteries. "Let men be chosen who have the will and the ability to learn and also the desire to instruct others," he says.

Charlemagne is also a great patron of the visual arts. In the field of architecture he has built a palace church at Aachen in the style of Justinian's St Vitalis at Ravenna; a

An ivory symbol of St John the Evangelist made by a north Italian craftsman.

The so-called "Lothair crystal", depicting the biblical story of Susanna.

man of action as well as culture, he enjoys hunting in the forests near his court. He dislikes elaborate banquets, preferring a four-course meal with venison, served on a spit by his huntsmen, while listening to readings from St Augustine's *City of God*. His private life is robust and active. Though he is said to be a devoted husband, he has had several mistresses and illegitimate children.

Caliph succeeds by fair means or foul

Baghdad, 4 September 786
Rumours of foul play surround the announcement this morning of the death in the night of the Abbasid Caliph al-Hadi. His younger brother Harun al-Rashid succeeds.

Harun's accession ends a decade of uncertainty and rivalry. When Caliph al-Mansur died in 775, factions which he had kept under control began to re-emerge under his son, Caliph al-Mahdi. The military backed al-Mahdi's elder son, the dull but competent al-Hadi, as heir. But the caliph's favourite wife, Khayzuran, and palace bureaucrats favoured the retiring Harun. When al-Mahdi died last year, al-Hadi duly became Caliph. Although he had been ill, his sudden death has sparked a host of rumour. Did Khayzuran have him suffocated? Why has his son been arrested? Whatever the truth, Harun is in charge, and faces the task of winning over the military.

The new caliph: Harun al-Rashid.

Long vigils for Sufis

Islamic world, c.780
A new form of ascetic mysticism has sprung up in the Islamic world, practised by people who are known as Sufis from the habits made of coarse wool (*suf*) which they wear. Sufism is an Islamic form of contemplative life which takes many of its outward forms from Christian monasticism. This influence is seen in the practice of solitary meditation, long vigils and celibacy, as well as in the woollen habits. Sufis seek a life inspired only by God and unhindered by materialism.

Scholarly English monk dies in France

Alcuin: the learned monk from York.

Tours, Gaul, 804

The learned English scholar Alcuin has died in the abbey of St Martin of Tours, given to him by Charlemagne in 796. Born in Northumbria and educated in York, Alcuin took charge of York cathedral school and became its leading scholar. His life was transformed when he met Charlemagne at Parma in 782. The Frankish king was impressed by Alcuin's piety and scholarship, and persuaded him to join the group of leading scholars at the Frankish court. Alcuin took charge of the palace school which the king had founded for the education of his sons and boys of the nobility, and acted as his main adviser, notably on religious issues.

Through Alcuin, political and cultural links were also developed between Gaul and England. He never forgot the school at York, and wrote a long poem in praise of its saints and bishops.

From Tours, Alcuin wrote to the king: "I, your servant, miss to some extent the rarer books of scholastic learning which I had in my own country." He was granted permission to send some of his pupils to York to choose the books needed. Highly developed Northumbrian culture thus came to influence continental scholarship.

Pact gives Islamic state independence

One of the reservoirs built at Kairouan for the new rulers of Ifriqiyah.

North Africa, 800

The caliph, the ruler of the Islamic world, has reached an agreement with the province of Ifriqiyah (*Tunisia*) which gives it virtual autonomy under its governor, Ibrahim ibn-al Aghrab.

Ibrahim was appointed governor of Ifriqiyah (an Arabic corruption of "Africa", an old Roman province) this year and has been energetic in restoring order and calm after a period of turbulence. But the threat of unrest from Berber tribes and others still remains in the capital, Kairouan, and elsewhere, and Ibrahim has built up a guard of black slaves to tackle it.

His military power puts Ibrahim in a strong bargaining position with the caliph. In exchange for 40,000 dinars, Caliph Harun al-Rashid has granted Ibrahim almost complete autonomy and the right to bequeath the province to his son. Spain, Morocco and, effectively, Ifriqiyah are now independent; the caliph's authority stops at Egypt.

Culture threatened high in the Andes

Tiahuanaco spouted pottery jaguar.

Peru, c.811

On the shores of Lake Titicaca, 11,700 feet above sea level, the Tiahuanaco civilisation has reached its peak and spread down to the Pacific coast.

Centred in the city of Tiahuanaco, the first planned city in South America, the Andes civilisation has been maturing over 1,000 years, watched over by the sun god Viracocha. How long Tiahuanaco can retain its power is uncertain. Wars with its Huari neighbours are weakening it, and the more it expands, the weaker is the centre.

A Norse carved stone from the island of Gotland, with the god Odin's eight-legged horse.

Pope crowns Charlemagne in Rome

The new emperor of the West.

Rome, 25 December 800

On this Christmas Day, when Mass was finishing in St Peter's, Rome, Pope Leo III suddenly produced a crown and, placing it on the head of Charlemagne, the king of the Franks, who was kneeling before the high altar, proclaimed him emperor of the Romans. The Roman notables there assembled cried in unison: "To Charles, the most pious Augustus, crowned by God, the great and peace-loving emperor, life and victory."

This dramatic scene came as the climax to an extraordinary series of events which began when hostile aristocrats had Leo seized, beaten so severely that he almost lost his sight and speech, and then deposed. Saved by Frankish envoys, the terrified Pope sought refuge with Charlemagne, who restored him to the Holy See after Leo had sworn he was innocent of the charges of perjury and adultery made by his enemies.

Charlemagne claims to be displeased with Leo's gesture in proclaiming him Roman emperor. It is thought that he does not wish the title to be seen as a gift of the papacy. He sees the Church as having been entrusted to him by God to defend and to direct. His official scribes style him "Leader and Guide of all Christians".

To the Christmas Day congregation in St Peter's, Charlemagne is

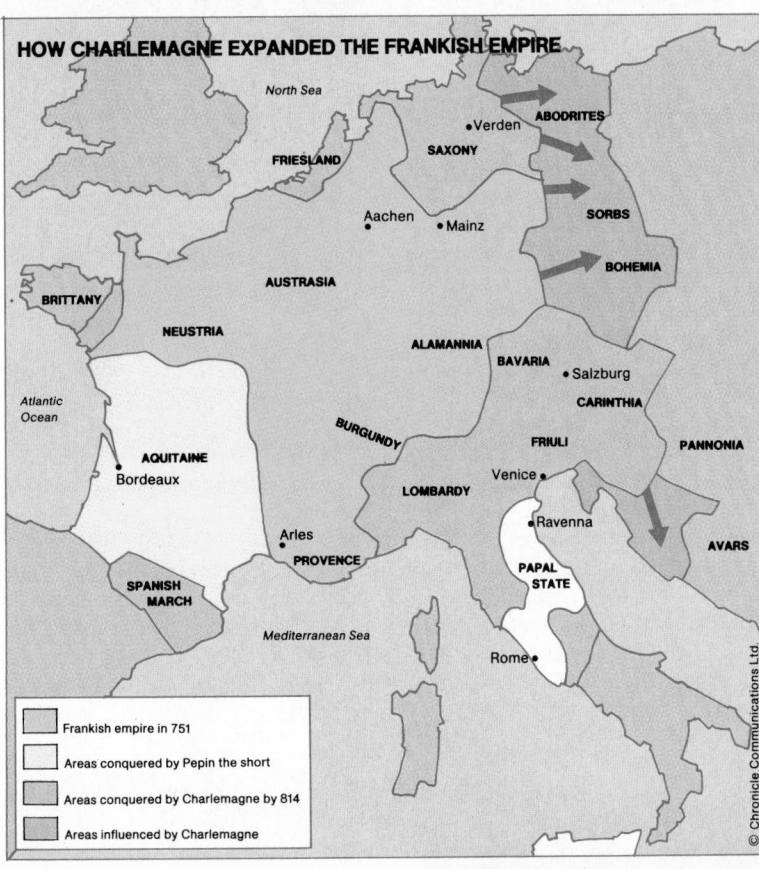

HOW CHARLEMAGNE EXPANDED THE FRANKISH EMPIRE

North Sea
Verden
ABODRITES
FRIESLAND
SAXONY
Aachen · Mainz
SORBS
AUSTRASIA
BOHEMIA
BRITTANY
NEUSTRIA
ALAMANNIA
BAVARIA
· Salzburg
Atlantic Ocean
CARINTHIA
BURGUNDY
FRIULI
PANNONIA
AQUITAINE
Bordeaux
LOMBARDY
Venice ·
· Ravenna
AVARS
Arles
PROVENCE
PAPAL STATE
SPANISH MARCH
Mediterranean Sea
Rome ·

Frankish empire in 751
Areas conquered by Pepin the short
Areas conquered by Charlemagne by 814
Areas influenced by Charlemagne

© Chronicle Communications Ltd.

the peace-loving emperor; to the rest of Europe he is the warlord who has spent the last 30 years subjugating Saxons, Italians, Bavarians and Slavs, so that his empire now equals that of the Byzantines. Much of it has been done in the name of God. The pagan Saxons, who have repeatedly rebelled, are Christianised by the thousand or mercilessly punished if they resist. Charlemagne has always regarded his rule as divinely sanctioned; now it is also styled "imperial" and "Roman", although at a practical level little has changed.

Charlemagne reaps for Christ.

Charlemagne's son overcomes the Avars

Pannonia (Hungary), 805

The armies of Charlemagne under the command of his son Pepin have completed the subjugation of the Mongolian Avars of Pannonia and taken vast quantities of gold and silver, which the Avars acquired in their years of pillaging neighbouring countries.

The Avars appeared in the sixth century, being pushed west by the Turks, eventually settling in the

Pannonian plain between the Danube and the Carpathians. They were splendid horsemen, always ready to move on with their ruler, the *khagan*, whose capital, known as the Ring, moved with him.

Pepin's victory has been celebrated in a long poem, which portrays the khagan as saying to Pepin: "Hail prince, be our lord! I hand over to you every straw and leaf of my kingdom."

Mother blinds her son, the emperor

Constantinople, July 797

Irene, the mother of the Emperor Constantine VI, ordered her son to be blinded and deposed before proclaiming herself the supreme ruler of Byzantium. The cruel Irene has achieved her ambition at last.

When Irene's husband, Leo IV, died 17 years ago, Constantine, then ten years old, inherited the throne with Irene acting as regent. In 790 the young emperor sought to gain control by ousting his mother's adviser, Stauracius. The attempt failed. Constantine was flogged, and Irene declared herself empress until the army threatened rebellion.

For the rest of his reign, Constantine weakly allowed himself to be influenced by his mother. She persuaded him to blind the general who had backed him and to infuriate the army by harsh repression. She took advantage of her son's love for his attendant, Theodote, and inveigled him into a bigamous marriage which enraged both the public and the church.

Irene is a devout *iconodule*, an image worshipper, who had concealed her beliefs during the years of repression by iconoclasts when Leo III condemned the veneration of icons as idolatrous.

Ruthless Irene: an image worshipper.

North Africa, 817. Ziyadat Allah becomes the third Aghlabid king of Ifriqiyah (*Tunisia*). The Aghlabids, have broken free of the Abbasid empire to form an autonomous Moslem dynasty.

Gaul, 817. The Emperor Louis issues the *Ordinatio Imperii*, his plan to divide up the empire between his sons while retaining its notional unity under a single emperor, the eldest, Lothar.

Italy, 817. Having been left out of Louis' proposed division of the empire, Bernard, the king of Italy, Charlemagne's grandson, rebels, but is captured and brought to Gaul. He dies three days after being blinded on Louis' orders.

Constantinople, 25 December 820. The unpopular Leo V, emperor since 813, is assassinated in St Sophia's by supporters of the Commander of the Guards, who becomes the Emperor Michael II.

China, 821. A Sino-Tibetan treaty recognising the independence of Tibet is ratified at Chang'an.

Gaul, 822. Racked by guilt, and influenced by the monastic reformer Benedict of Amiens, Louis does public penance for the death of Bernard.

Britain, 825. King Egbert of Wessex wins a decisive victory over King Beornred of Mercia at Ellendun (near Swindon).

Gaul, 826. Harald Klak, a pretender to the Danish throne who is backed by the Franks, is baptised at Louis' palace at Ingelheim. He takes back with him Anskar, a Frankish monk, who begins the slow and hazardous process of bringing Christian faith to the Danes.

North Africa, 827. The Aghlabid king, Ziyadat Allah, launches an expedition under Asad ibn al-Furat to capture Sicily from the Byzantines.

Morocco, September 828. On the death of King Idris II, his kingdom – which was founded as a refuge from Abbasid persecutions in the east – is divided between his sons. Idris' most notable achievement was his founding of Fez as the capital of his dynasty in 808.

Gaul, 829. Louis angers his three other sons by amending the inheritance settlement of 817 to make provision for Charles, his infant son by a second marriage to Judith of Bavaria.

Prince to be sole heir to Frankish empire

Frankish Empire, 817

In the three years since he inherited the crown from his father, Charlemagne, Louis has struggled to preserve the unity of the empire and yet uphold the Frankish custom of partible inheritance: the division of property between all direct male heirs in equal proportion. He has now told his sons of his plan: the eldest, Lothar, will rule Gaul with his father and be sole heir to the empire; his brothers, Louis and Pepin, will now take control of Bavaria and Aquitaine, but will be subject to Lothar on Louis' death.

Charlemagne had willed that, on his death, the empire be equally divided between his three sons, but, by chance, only Louis survived him, so the empire remained intact.

In his planned division Louis had not reckoned with Bernard, a grandson of Charlemagne, already the ruler of Italy. Bernard was provoked into revolt by the thought of

Louis: determined to keep his father's empire in one piece.

being subject to Lothar. His coup failed, and he was blinded in such a bungled fashion that he has died. The deeply religious Louis is reported to be distraught, but his plans seem likely to succeed.

Radical philosopher of Hinduism dies

India, 820

Shankara, the Hindu philosopher born in Cochin, whose exposition of the theory of Vedanta has revolutionised Hindu thought, is dead.

Though Shankara was only 32 years old, his commentaries on the *Upanishads* have given Hinduism a new coherence. Shankara travelled India preaching his message, and founded monasteries at Sringeri, Puri, Dwaraka and Badrinath. Synthesising Hinduism and Buddhism, he identified two levels of truth. At the lower level, the world was created by Brahma; at a higher level, all, including the gods themselves, was *Maya*, an illusion. The only reality was *Brahman*, the impersonal world soul. Shankara himself never achieved the higher level, and on his deathbed regretted going on pilgrimages and so forgetting that God is everywhere.

Magnificent Buddhist temple of Borobudur takes shape in Java

A statue of the Buddha preaching.

Java, c.811

A magnificent temple is being built in central Java by the island's Buddhist Sailendra rulers. They have named the temple *Borobudur*, meaning "Many Buddhas". The shrine, unlike anything previously built, and the embodiment more of earthly powers than of heavenly nothingness (*Nirvana*), epitomises the confidence and proselytising zeal of the Sailenda rulers, who have just declared Buddhism the official religion on the predominantly Hindu island. On a rounded

A view of the terraces of Borobudur with its many finely-carved sculptures.

hilltop, terraced and clad in stone, Borobudur rises out of the flat rice fields of the Kedu plain, girdled by distant volcanic cones.

The lower six terraces are cut square, with stairways on the cardinal points, and are adorned with an uninterrupted sequence of bas-reliefs portraying the life of the Buddha. Placed end to end, the re-

liefs stretch for three miles. The upper terraces are round, with 72 *stupas*, shaped like cupolas and carved in stone lattice work, each covering a seated Buddha. At the pinnacle is a larger *stupa*. Thus the temple, its skyline resembling the City of God, symbolises the pilgrim's progress from worldly life to ultimate enlightenment.

Pious Louis neglects court scholars

Aachen, c.828

Under Charlemagne's son Louis, the great intellectual flowering of Charlemagne's reign is changing in character. In part this is due to a decline of direct patronage by the imperial court, since Louis is less interested in assembling around himself a prestigious group of scholars, but it is also due to the development of several centres of local intellectual tradition. Consequently, several scholars have left the court at Aachen for monasteries at Tours, Rheims and Lyons.

The scholars at Louis' court are there to perform specific tasks. For example, one is tutor to Louis' youngest son, Charles, and another is chief religious adviser. Louis himself is said to spend most of his time reading works of religion, praying and listening to lawsuits.

But the legacy of Charlemagne is not lost. In the monasteries and bishoprics across the length and breadth of the empire, schools offer an education for would-be clerics, the gifted children of the poor as well as the aristocracy. First, the

Frankish pupils and their master: is learning under threat in Gaul?

child is given a good grounding in reading, writing and arithmetic. After this, Latin and rhetoric are introduced, then geometry, astronomy and music.

Ordinary folk who do not have the good fortune to attend a charitable school receive a less varied intellectual diet; for them, sermons delivered by the local priest in church remain the sole form of education.

Master of prose style dies in China

China, 824

The writer-politician Han Yu, who was renowned for his prose style, has died at the age of of 56. He was lucky to have lived this long, for, as an ardent supporter of Confucianism, he wrote a long polemic, *Memorial on the Bone-Relic of the Buddha*, in which he attacked the Emperor Xian-zong's worship of a Buddhist relic.

The emperor was furious, and only the intervention of powerful patrons at court saved Han Yu from being put to death. He was exiled to south China for five years, but when he was allowed to return in 820 he was given a number of official posts and was mayor of the capital, Chang'an, when he died.

He had a harsh early life, failing his civil service examinations and being forced to take a post on the staff of a provincial military governor. Nevertheless, he gathered round him a group of intellectuals and honed the clarity of his prose and poetic style until his genius was recognised throughout China.

Battle over Koran divides Moslems

Baghdad, 827

Caliph al-Ma'mun has proclaimed a new dogma about the Koran. This states that the Koran is not eternal with God, but was created by God at a certain time and revealed to the Prophet Mohammed.

The implications of this belief, called Mu'tazilitism, are great: if God created the Koran at one time, then it could be interpreted differently at another or supplemented by further revelation. And who would be worthier to receive this revelation than the caliph?

Mu'tazilitism seems to be a bid to boost the caliph's authority and win over the family of Ali, the Prophet's son-in-law, who already claim that they can supplement the Koran with their own comments. Opponents, led by the uncompromising lawyer Ahmad ibn Hanbal, accuse al-Ma'mun of altering God's word. Undaunted, the caliph has launched an inquisition, to ensure all officials agree with his doctrine.

Holy Koran produces superb calligraphy

Islamic world, c.820

Some of the world's most striking calligraphy is to be found in copies of the Koran, the sacred book of the Moslem faith. Moslems are prohibited from showing human or animal forms in their art, but this has not stopped them producing

beautiful images in their writing. The Koran is revered by Moslems as the actual word of God, which was passed on to their Prophet Mohammed. The full text was first set down 140 years ago by Caliph Uthman, the third in succession to the Prophet.

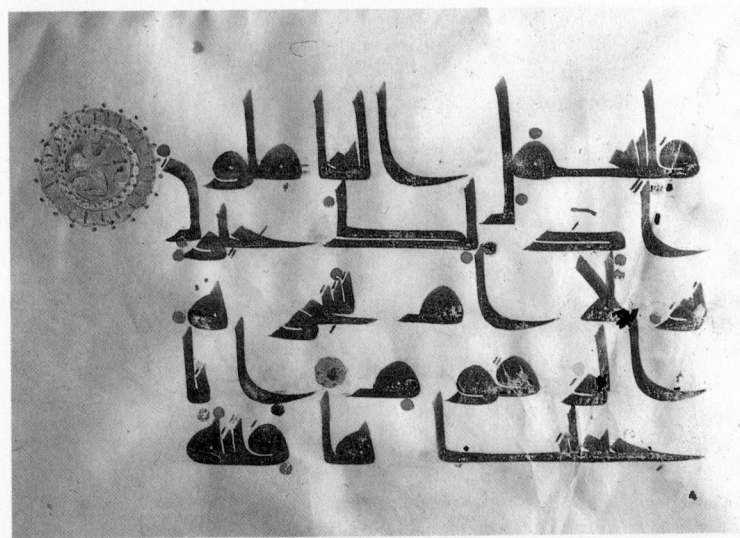

A page from the Koran, demonstrating the quality of Islamic calligraphy.

The military seize power in Persia

Persia, 822

Khurasan, the rich north-eastern province of Persia, has become effectively independent of Caliph al-Ma'mun in Baghdad.

The Persians, ironically, backed al-Ma'mun as caliph against his brother. In 819 al-Ma'mun left Persia for the old Abbasid capital of Baghdad, and many Persians felt he had abandoned them. Among these was Tahir, the brilliant general who did most to win al-Ma'mun the caliphate. Powerless at Baghdad, Tahir became governor of his native Khurasan. Recently, he renounced the caliph's authority by omitting his name from Friday prayers.

The caliph's agents were prompt and Tahir was dead the next day. But political pressure forced al-Ma'mun to appoint Tahir's son, Talha, to succeed him. Although nominally still under the caliph, Persia (at least part of it) now has its first native ruler since the Arab conquest 150 years ago.

830 (830-840)

A Greek miniature depicting a Sicilian city under siege from the Arabs.

Byzantines lose Sicilian cities to Arabs

Sicily, 831
The Aghlabid rulers of Ifriqiyah (*Tunisia*) have dealt a major blow to Byzantine prestige by capturing Palermo in Sicily, one of the few remaining parts of the empire in the western Mediterranean.

The bid to conquer Sicily began in 827 when Ziyadat Allah, the third Aghlabid sovereign, sent an expedition to the island under Asad ibn al-Furat, the religious magistrate of Kairouan famed for his spiritual fervour and military energy. Asad's campaign led to the fall of Mazara, before Asad died near Syracuse in 828. However, the whole island seems likely to fall under Arab rule before long. When it does, it will provide the Aghlabids with a base from which to harry the rest of the Mediterranean.

Scholars flower at "House of Wisdom"

Baghdad, c.832
The intellectual and astute Caliph al-Ma'mun, who succeeded Harun al-Rashid in 813, has founded a scholarly "House of Wisdom" to support efforts to translate ancient Greek wisdom into Arabic.

The texts are being translated not from the original Greek but from versions in Syriac, a tongue related to Arabic used by early Christians, and are mainly of practical value. They include works by Galen on medicine, Ptolemy on geography and astronomy, Aristotle on philosophy and Dioscorides on plants. History, poetry and drama are almost entirely neglected.

The translators are chiefly Christians. Some first efforts have been so literal as to be incomprehensible, but standards are improving.

An Anglo-Saxon carved whalebone casket. The inscriptions, in English, are written in runes, a Germanic script derived from the Greek alphabet.

Egbert dies leaving a greater Wessex

Wessex, England, 839
King Egbert of Wessex has died, ending a 37-year reign in which he reshaped the political history of southern England. His eldest son Aethulwulf is to succeed him. The united kingdom that Egbert leaves behind is remarkably different from the small, weak kingdom of which he took control in 802. For some time political supremacy in southern England remained in the hands of his Mercian neighbours. Then in 825 Egbert decisively defeated King Beornwulf of Mercia in a battle near Swindon over disputed territory. At once he sent his son to seize Kent which, with Essex, Surrey and Sussex, passed from Mercian to West Saxon overlordship. The East Angles reasserted their independence from Mercia and killed Beornwulf. Egbert was briefly able to annex Mercia itself in 829, but was soon driven out. Nevertheless, he had won control over southern England, and over the British kingdom of Cornwall, for Wessex.

Egbert, the king of Wessex.

Builder writes life story of emperor

Michelstadt, 14 March 840
Einhard, the scholar-builder from the Rhineland, retired after 40 years in the royal service at Aachen and settled down to write the biography of his hero, the late Emperor Charlemagne. *Vita Caroli* is a brilliant portrait of a great man, modelled on the style of the Roman author Suetonius, and unusually down-to-earth and secular in its portrayal of the emperor. The writer has died today, aged 70.

Viking raiders come by night to terrorise the west

A Viking longboat: built to carry warriors and booty in heavy seas.

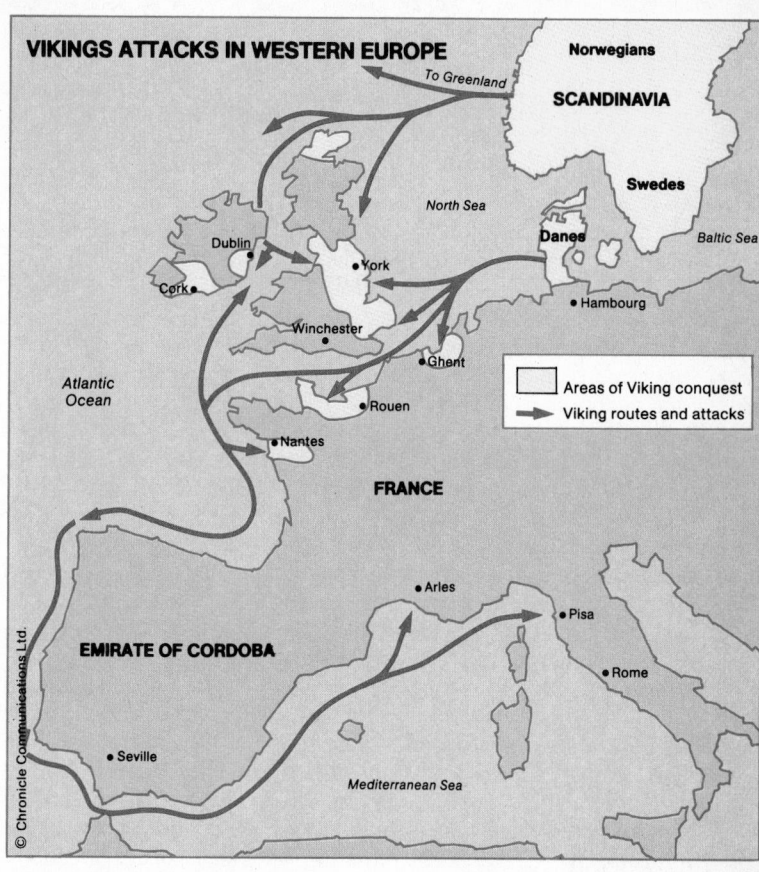
VIKINGS ATTACKS IN WESTERN EUROPE

Norwegians
SCANDINAVIA
To Greenland
Swedes
North Sea
Danes
Baltic Sea
Dublin
York
Hambourg
Cork
Winchester
Ghent
Atlantic Ocean
Rouen
Nantes
FRANCE
Arles
Pisa
EMIRATE OF CORDOBA
Rome
Seville
Mediterranean Sea

☐ Areas of Viking conquest
→ Viking routes and attacks

© Chronicle Communications Ltd.

England, 840

English defenders led by the *ealdorman* (duke) Wulfheard have repulsed the latest Viking raid in a battle at Southampton against the crews of 33 longships. Initial reports speak of a "great slaughter" at the scene.

Wulfheard's victory is a rare success in the increasing struggle to keep the terrible Vikings at bay. More typically, further west at Portland, after a protracted struggle with the raiders, the ealdorman Aethelhelm has been killed and his army put to flight, leaving the Vikings to ravage the area before returning to their ships.

The Vikings travel long distances in their longboats in search of plunder, and attack by night without warning and with unbridled ferocity. Their attacks have been a regular hazard in most of western Europe for 47 years. Nowhere is beyond their reach. In 818 an Irish mystic, Blathmac, went to Iona in search of martyrdom at Viking hands. He waited seven years before they landed and tore him to pieces for refusing to reveal where the monastery's treasure was hidden.

Churches have always been respected by warring Christian factions, but they are singled out as soft targets for easy loot by the Vikings. Captured leaders are sacrificed to their god Odin in the rite of blood-eagling, slicing down the victim's back and spreading out his entrails in the form of an eagle.

What the Vikings cannot use or understand they burn, and that includes priceless libraries such as Iona's. The list of once peaceful, but now ruined, places is long. It includes Lindisfarne (in 793); Jarrow; the Shetlands, Hebrides and Orkney (about 794); Skye (795); Rathlin (Antrim); Iona (at least four times from 795 onward); most of Scotland; much of Ireland, including Armagh; Sheppey; the English Channel coast; Dorestad, the west's greatest trading centre, near the mouth of the Rhine, and, in Gaul, monastic and commercial centres including Noirmoutier and Rouen.

The victims can only guess at the reasons for this sudden waterborne terror. Alcuin of York suggested in a letter to the King of Northumbria, Ethelred, that it was God's judgement on the English for widespread fornication.

There are also more secular explanations. Population growth in Scandinavia coincided with a quick solution to hunger: the development of the longboat. The Viking craft can sail with the wind or into it, or be rowed; it holds 30 warriors, has a hull flexible enough to bend in heavy seas without leaking, and draws only three feet of water below the waterline while carrying ten tons of booty.

Danish warriors coming ashore.

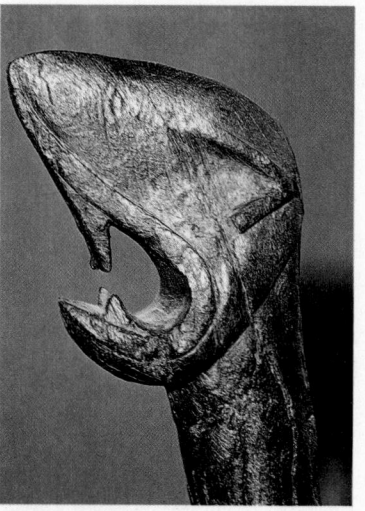
The wooden prow of a Norse vessel, in the shape of a fearsome beast.

The elaborately-decorated helmet of a Viking from the Vendel boat.

The onward march of Islam

From its birthplace in western Arabia in the early seventh century, Islam spread rapidly throughout the Near East and beyond. By the dawn of the 13th century it stretched from Persia and central Asia in the east to north and sub-Saharan Africa and the Iberian peninsula in the west.

Much of this expansion occurred within a century of the death of Islam's founding prophet, Mohammed. Mohammed was born around 570 into the Quraish clan of merchants who then governed the strategic city of Mecca. After a series of divine revelations at the age of about 40, Mohammed began preaching against the idolatry and the multiplication of pagan gods then worshipped by Arabian tribes. His criticism of Quraish custom soon led to his expulsion from Mecca and he sought refuge among the rival tribes in the town now known as *Medina*, (the town of the prophet), 250 miles to the north. Mohammed's flight – *hejira* in Arabic – marks the beginning of the Islamic calendar. Mohammed converted the tribes of Medina to his monotheistic beliefs, which acquired the name *Islam* – literally, giving oneself up (to God). As Christianity had done in Europe, Islam incorporated many long-established pagan practices then common in Arabia. These included the annual pilgrimage to the shrine of the Kabaa stone in Mecca, from which the ruling Quraish drew both prestige and wealth.

The essence of Islam

The *Koran*, Islam's holy text, is for *Moslems* (those who give themselves up to God) God's word as transmitted through the angel Gabriel to Mohammed. As opposed to the Christian vision of Jesus Christ, Mohammed was a mortal human being who was chosen by God to receive and record his revelations. The Koran, which includes narratives common to Christianity and Judaism – both then practised in Arabia – was completed after the death of Mohammed and the official version appeared around 650. The sayings – *hadiith* – of Mohammed himself constitute the second source of Islamic authority.

A belief in *Allah* (God) and in his revealed word, the Koran, is one of the key articles of Islamic faith. Others include the acceptance of God's division of good and evil, and a belief in the resurrection of the dead and the day of judgement. Five practises are essential to a Moslem: reciting the *Shahada*, the reaffirmation that there is only one God; praying at five preordained times of the day; giving alms to the poor; fasting from dawn to dusk in the

holy month of *Ramadan*; and making the *Haj*, the pilgrimage to Mecca, at least once in a lifetime.

Mohammed died in 632. The first four *caliphs* (successors) to follow him assured the spiritual consolidation of Islam and its propagation throughout the Near East. The speed and success of the Arab invasions was in large part due to the weakness of the Byzantine empire, and frequently the Arabs were seen by the people whom they conquered – even Christians and Jews – as liberators from Byzantine or Persian oppression.

Islamicisation occurred in most cases only a century or so after these early conquests. The motives of the invasions were thus not to propagate Islam, nor were they planned in advance. Rather it was the political cohesion provided by the new faith which contributed to the series of victories.

The pace of conquest faltered slightly as the first serious schisms emerged over rival claims to Mohammed's succession. Ali, the cousin and son-in-law of the prophet, had become the fourth caliph in 656. Ali's rule was challenged by Mu'awiya, his predecessor's governor in Damascus, and he was murdered not long after. Mu'awiya founded a new dynasty, the Umayyads, based in Damascus, but the *Shi'ite* sect upheld Ali's claim to the fourth caliphate. *Sunni*, or orthodox, Moslems accepted the Umayyad succession. (Over 80 per cent of Moslems are Sunnites. Shi'ites are split into numerous "schools", the largest of which recognises the succession of 12 spiritual leaders, or *imams*. It has been dominant in Iran since the 16th century.)

The end of Arab dominance

Caliph Umar II (717-20) realised the increasingly precarious position of an Arab elite dominating such a vast and heterogeneous empire. He advocated the conversion to Islam of all populations in western Asia to provide a broad Islamic, rather than a purely Arab, foundation to the empire. This move undermined the dynasty's financial base – taxation of non-Moslems – and encouraged dissent. The harsh rule of the Umayyads alienated many Sunnites, and Shi'ite movements fermented revolts which erupted in Kufa in 740. The dynasty disintegrated amid factional fighting.

The subsequent rise of the Abbasid dynasty of caliphs in 750 marked a geographical and ethnic shift in the foundations of Islamic power. Based in their magnificent new capital at Baghdad on the Tigris, the Abbasids recruited non-Arab troops and slaves, notably Turks. This ethnic mix initially per-

mitted the co-option of local leaders in many parts of the empire, but eventually, as provincial rulers rejected central control, Abbasid rule disintegrated into a multitude of rival Moslem states with diverse regional and ethnic bases, such as Turkish, Afghan and Mongol. The Abbasids clung to a shrinking empire until Baghdad fell in 1258 to the Mongols.

By the 12th century warriors, trading caravans and inspired Moslem scholars had carried Islam to the hinterlands of West Africa. The Almoravid *emirates*, formed between 1039 and 1049 by a confederation of North African tribes, were instrumental in the spread of Islam to sub-Saharan Africa. There it was adopted by the ruling elites of states such as Takrur, Ghana and Kanem.

In Asia, Islam had penetrated only as far as Sind by the early eighth century, and the major Moslem expansion began in the 11th century. In 1030 Lahore fell under the rule of an Islamic military regime invading from Afghanistan, where it had established a state in the wake of the fragmentation of the Abbasid empire. Consolidation of this initial invasion led to the establishment of the Delhi *sultanates* from 1206 onwards. Thus northern India, ruled by Afghan and Turkish sultans, adopted Islam as its state religion.

Cultural flowering

While Islam expanded politically, it also flourished culturally. Perhaps the most spectacular flowering of Islamic culture occurred in Spain in the tenth century, where advanced irrigation and other agricultural techniques provided the material basis for a new civilisation characterised by fine poetry, art and architecture. Many Moslem intellectuals and scientists from the Near East migrated to Islamic Spain, which became a bridge for the transfer of ancient Greek thought from the former Hellenic world to mediaeval Europe.

By the eighth century Moslem traders were established in Canton, and by the 13th century Islamic influence was to be felt in central Asia via Turkestan and the successive Mongol conquests. Arabian trade with China brought Islam to the islands of southeast Asia. By the beginning of the 13th century Islamic belief and practice, albeit in many different forms, extended across a considerable stretch of the globe. While it no longer held together a single, cohesive political empire, Islam had become a common religious and cultural trait for many diverse peoples, and the seeds of further expansion were firmly in place.

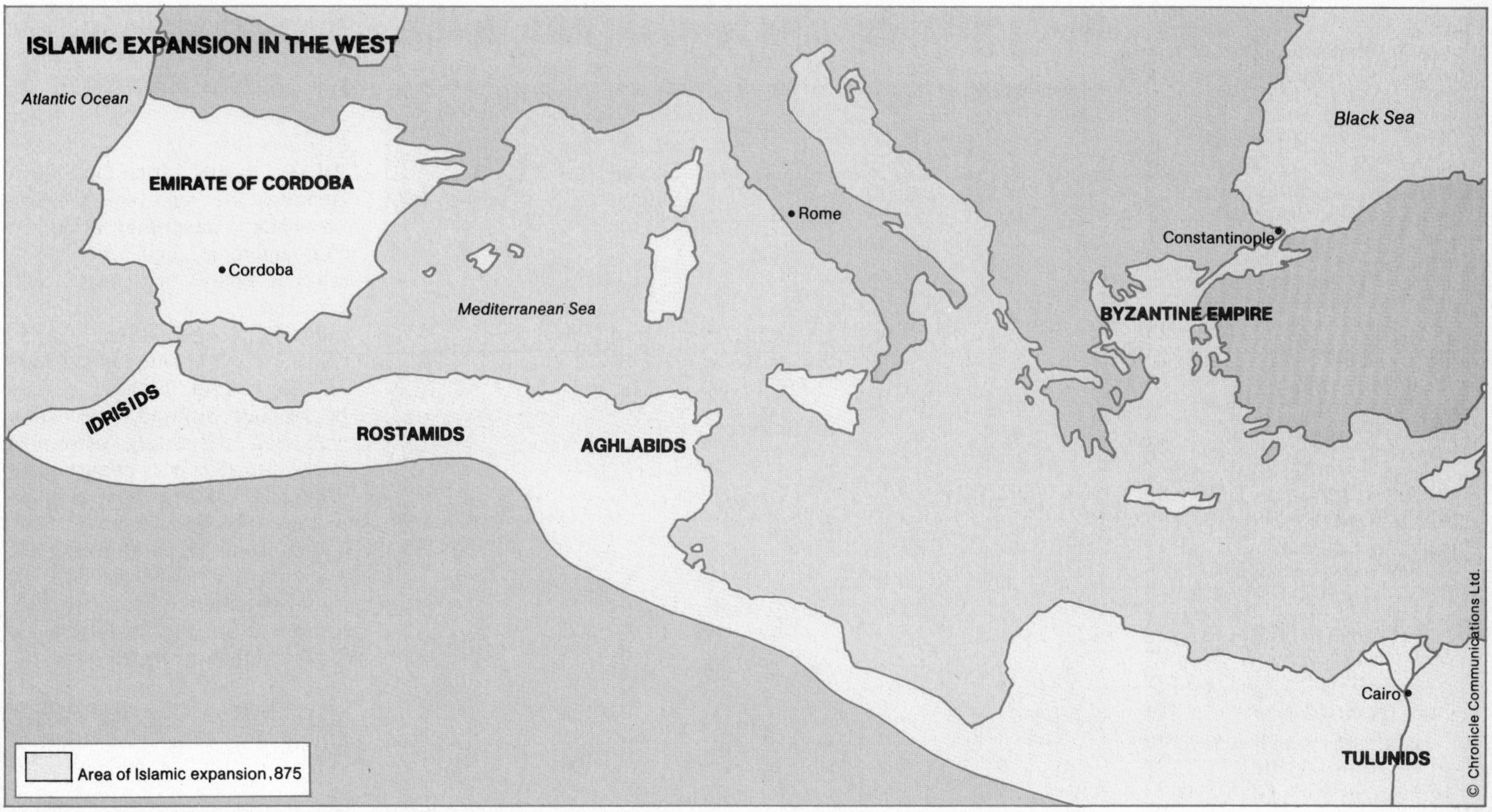

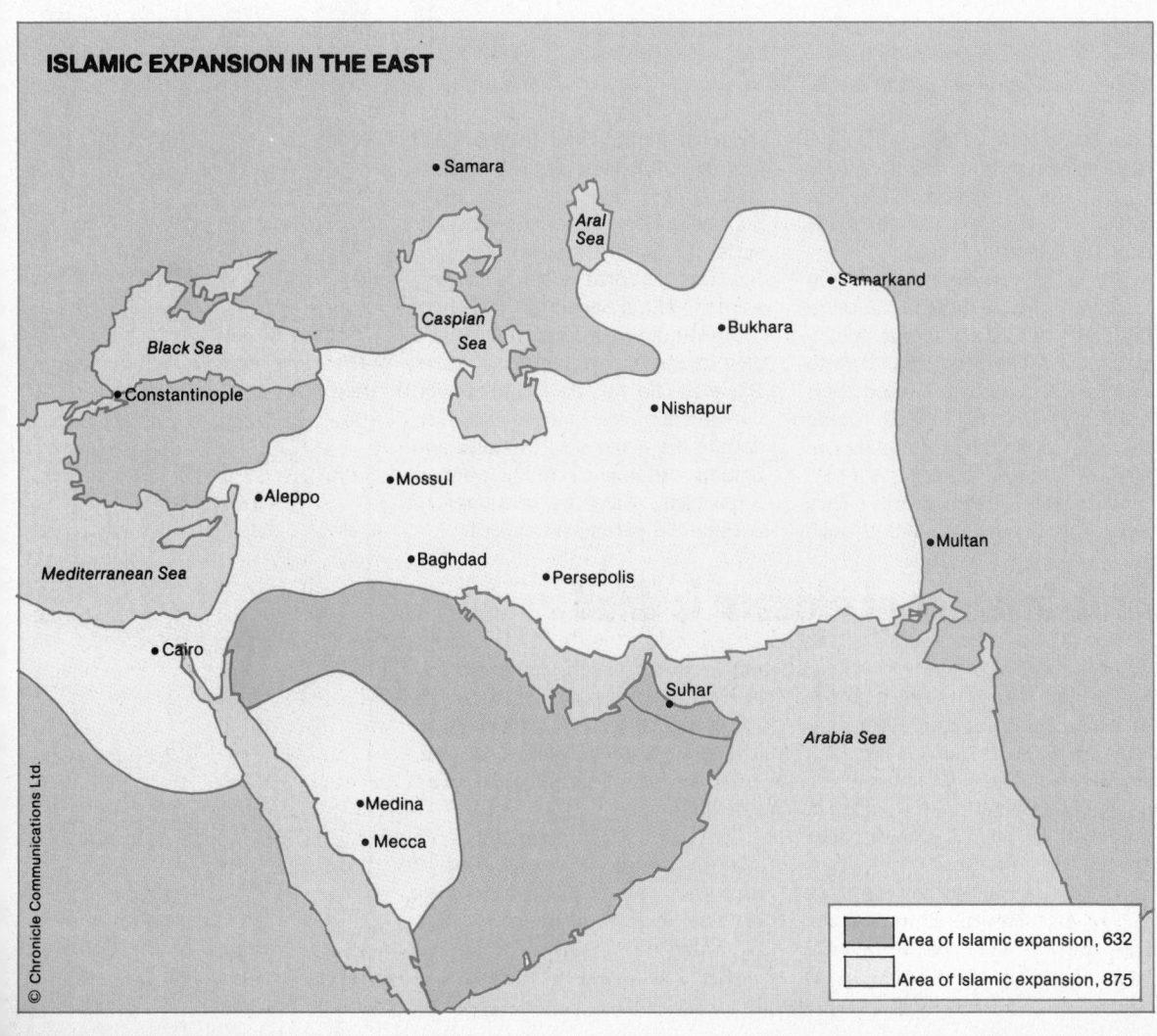

ISLAMIC EXPANSION IN THE WEST

Atlantic Ocean

Black Sea

EMIRATE OF CORDOBA

• Cordoba

• Rome

Constantinople •

Mediterranean Sea

BYZANTINE EMPIRE

IDRISIDS

ROSTAMIDS

AGHLABIDS

Cairo •

TULUNIDS

☐ Area of Islamic expansion, 875

© Chronicle Communications Ltd.

ISLAMIC EXPANSION IN THE EAST

• Samara

Aral Sea

• Samarkand

Caspian Sea

• Bukhara

Black Sea

• Constantinople

• Nishapur

Mediterranean Sea

• Aleppo

• Mossul

• Baghdad

• Persepolis

• Multan

• Cairo

• Suhar

Arabia Sea

• Medina

• Mecca

© Chronicle Communications Ltd.

☐ Area of Islamic expansion, 632
☐ Area of Islamic expansion, 875

Christianity took about 400 years to become established in the Roman empire. Islam, on the other hand, in the century following the death of the Prophet Mohammed, spread with quite astonishing speed from its Arabian heartland, and by 732, when the Frankish king Charles Martel ended the Moslem advance northwards from Spain, the new religion was firmly entrenched from Iberia to India.

632: Death of Mohammed.
636: Defeat of Byzantines at Yarmuk and Arab settlement in Syria.
637: Sack of Ctesiphon in Mesopotamia, capital of the Sassanid empire.
640: Arabs enter Egypt and found Fustat (Old Cairo).
642: Capture of Alexandria, the greatest city in North Africa.
644-56: Conquest of Persia and of Cyrenaica (eastern Libya).
660: Beginning of the Umayyad caliphate, with its capital at Baghdad.
670: Conquest of Ifriqiyah (Tunisia) and founding of Kairouan.
685-705: Consolidation of Arab rule under Caliph Abd al-Malik.
711-14: Conquest of all but northern Spain; the river Indus is reached.
732: Arab defeat at Poitiers in France by Charles Martel.

Gaul, 25 June 841. Charles the Bald and Louis the German, sons of Louis the Pious, defeat their elder brother, Lothar, the emperor of the West, at Fontenay.

Constantinople, 20 January 842. The Emperor Theophilus dies; iconoclasm dies with him. His wife Theodora, ruling as empress regent on behalf of their infant son Michael III, soon restores image-worship.

Britain/Gaul, 842. The Vikings ravage London and Rochester and the Frankish Channel port of Quentovic.

Gaul, 842. Having sacked the monastery of Noirmoutier, the Vikings winter on occupied territory for the first time.

Gaul, August 843. Lothar, Charles and Louis conclude the treaty of Verdun. Lothar is recognised as emperor, but has no power over the kingdoms of his brothers.

Spain, 844. The Vikings raid Spain for the first time.

Gaul, 845. Hamburg is sacked by the Vikings. Anskar's church is destroyed and he is forced to flee. But his missionary work to Denmark and Sweden continues from a new base at Bremen.

Rome, 847. On becoming pope, Leo IV sets about repairing and extending the city walls which were badly damaged by Arab pirates last year.

Mesopotamia (Iraq), 847. Caliph al-Mutawakkil tries to restore Abbasid authority by winning the support of the orthodox Sunnis. He persecutes the Mu'tazilites and the Shi'ites.

Peru, c.850. The Sican culture, centred on Batan Grande, is developing in northern Peru.

India, c.850. The Chola people, in Tamilnadu, are gaining power under King Vijayalaya.

China, 850. The Arab navigators Wahab and Abu Said travel to southern China and take home tea, brandy, rice and porcelain.

Gaul, 28 September 855. The Emperor Lothar dies. His kingdom is divided between his three sons, the eldest, Louis II, taking Italy and the title of emperor.

Baghdad, 856. The uncompromising theologian Ahmad ibn Mohammad ibn Hanbal dies. One of the four rites of Islam is based on his works.

New capital founded to avoid race clashes

The unusual spiral minaret of one of the many new mosques at Samarra.

Mesopotamia (Iraq), 842
A great new mosque has been built at the Caliph al-Mu'tasim's new capital in Samarra. It is made entirely of unfired bricks.

The caliph left his old capital at Baghdad for a new site 60 miles up the Tigris in 836, mainly for political reasons. The son of a Turkish slave woman, he had succeeded his brother al Ma'mun in 833, having risen to power by recruiting an army of Turks from the eastern borders of the Moslem world. They were loyal warriors and superb mounted archers and they enabled him to sidestep his nephew and become caliph. But the Turks spoke no Arabic and were only recent converts to Islam; many people in Baghdad resented them and there were violent clashes.

Al-Mu'tasim decided to found a new capital to take the Turks out of Baghdad. So far, only soldiers and bureaucrats have moved up-river, despite the many new mosques and palaces. Although running water is a problem, Samarra looks set to become the permanent capital.

Arab inventor of algebra is dead

Baghdad, 847
One of the greatest scientific minds of Islam, Mohammed ibn-Musa al-Khwarizmi, has died. Little is known about his life: although he wrote in Arabic and worked in Baghdad, he may well have been Persian by birth.

Al-Khwarizmi wrote the first known astronomical tables and the first known work on arithmetic, which includes the calculation of square roots. He introduced Hindu numerals to the Moslem world and earlier Hindu mathematicians inspired his chief work, called *Hisab al-Jabr w-al-Muqabalah* (The calculation of integration and equation).

This area of mathematics – *al-Jabr* for short – is unknown in the west, and al-Kharizmi's work on the subject demonstrates how far ahead of Christendom are the current intellectual achievements of Islam.

Icon-painters back in Constantinople

Constantinople, 843
Painters, banished from the Eastern empire by the iconoclastic Emperor Theophilus, are drifting back into Constantinople, and once again religious images are appearing in churches.

The Empress Theodora, ruling as regent for her infant son, Michael III, has reversed the harsh policies of her late husband, Theophilus, who had relentlessly persecuted image worshippers, closing convents and inflicting cruel penalties on those who defied him.

The iconoclast controversy has raged for over a century since the Emperor Leo III banned image-worship in the belief that it brought God's wrath upon the empire.

The apse mosaics in St Sophia's, celebrating the return of images.

Celtic art: page of St. Matthew, from the Macgregor Gospels.

Sons divide up empire

EUROPE AFTER THE TREATY OF VERDUN, 1843

Verdun, August 843
After violent struggles, Louis the Pious' three surviving sons have met at Verdun and agreed to partition the empire. Bavaria and other eastern lands go to Louis the German; the west, including much of old Gaul, goes to Charles the Bald; the eldest son, Lothar, retains the title of emperor and takes the territory between the other two, from Italy to the Channel coast, keeping the Frankish capital, Aachen, and Rome.

So the divisions which have split the Frankish empire for thirteen years are over. The brothers' ambitions, and the problems caused by Louis' attempt to provide for his young son Charles, frequently led to civil war in Louis' last ten years of power. When he died, three years ago, his sons Louis and Charles combined against Lothar, and they and their armies swore oaths at Strasbourg, in local languages rather than Latin so that the troops

Charles the Bald enthroned as monarch of the French kingdom.

could understand. Louis addressed Charles' men in *lingua romana* (early French) and Charles spoke in *lingua teudisca* (early German). They forced Lothar to renounce sovereignty over their kingdoms.

Slavs join forces to form Great Moravia

Moravia (Czechoslovakia), 846
Mojmir, the prince of Moravia, is dead, having united for the first time the Slav tribes of Bohemia, Moravia, Slovakia and Pannonia. This important military and political federation is known as Great Moravia.

From the beginning of the century, attempts have been made to convert the pagan Slavs to Christianity, first by missionaries sent by Rome, and then by the Frankish monarchs.

Mojmir became a Christian convert, but turned against the Franks, defeating his neighbour and rival, Prince Pribina, who enjoyed Frankish backing. Rastislav, Mojmir's successor, is backed by Louis the German, who hopes to restore Frankish influence over the area.

Buddhas melted into coins as ruler cracks down on "idolatrous religion"

Buddhist stone carvings from Sichuan province, now under imperial attack.

China, 845
The Emperor Wuzong has ordered the suppression of Buddhism and all other "foreign religions". This crippling blow to Buddhism has been foreshadowed for some time, with the emperor showing an obvious preference for Taoism.

The Buddhist cause was not helped by the monk Xuanxuan, who claimed he could defeat the feared Uighurs with a magic sword. His failure gave the emperor another reason for persecuting Buddhists. It is the Buddhists' wealth, however, which has been the main cause of their downfall. Their rich temples and extensive lands have proved irresistible to Wuzong.

His decree banning "this idolatrous religion" calls for the temples' bronze images to be handed over to the Salt and Iron Commissioner for melting into coins. Those made of gold, silver and jade go to the Bureau of Public Revenue.

Leading scholar on heresy charges

Frankish Empire, 856
John Scottus Eriugena, one of the most original thinkers of the times, is facing charges of heresy based on his book *De divina praedestinatione*. In it Eriugena, an Irishman who came to Charles the Bald's court in 843, refutes the extreme views of the monk Gottschalk, who rejected the notion of divine redemption.

Eriugena has offended some by asserting man's complete freedom to choose between good and evil. But it is likely that he will continue to be favoured at the court, for his knowledge of Greek is unparalleled, and his reputation as a scholar will save him from severe penalties.

John Scottus Eriugena: he insists we can choose between good and evil.

Iceland, c.860. Intrepid Viking sailors land on Iceland (as they call it) for the first time.

Constantinople, June 860. Two hundred ships of the Rus (Russians) besiege Constantinople.

Eastern Gaul, 862. The Maygars (Hungarians), a nomadic people based in the Ukraine, launch their first raid on the west, attacking the kingdom of Louis the German.

Constantinople, September 867. Having risen spectacularly to power the emperor's favourite, Basil, murders his benefactor and takes the throne.

Mesopotamia, 868. Al-Jahiz, author of the *Book of the Misers* and other works on history, sex and literature, dies.

Constantinople, 869. The Eighth Ecumenical Council, called by the Emperor Basil and Pope Adrian II, papers over the divisions between the Eastern and Western Churches which have come to a head over Plotius, the irregularly appointed patriarch of Constantinople. Plotius has been deposed, but the divisions remain.

Gaul, 870. With Lothar II dead, Charles the Bald and Louis the German divide up his kingdom between them. Lothar's only surviving son, the Emperor Louis II, controls Frankish Italy.

Britain, 871. Despite winning a great victory with his brother King Aethelred, the new king of Wessex, Alfred, is forced to pay tribute to the Danes.

Britain, 874. The Danish army moves into Mercia, meeting little resistance. Burgred, the king, abdicates and goes on a pilgrimage to Rome. The Danes appoint a puppet king, and effectively control Mercia.

Central Asia, 874. The Moslem Samanids establish their rule in Transoxiana, east of the Oxus.

Rome, 25 December 875. With the death of the Emperor Louis II, Charles the Bald hurries to Italy and is crowned emperor by Pope John VIII.

Gaul, August 876. After the death of Louis the German, his three sons divide up his kingdom.

Gaul, 6 October 877. Charles the Bald dies and Louis (the Stammerer), his only surviving son, succeeds him.

Bodhisattva on an elephant, from Japan: ink, gold colour and silver on silk.

Fujiwara family controls Japanese royals

Japan, 866
The great clan of landowners, the Fujiwaras, has become the most powerful family in Japan with the appointment of Yoshifusa as the *Sessho* (regent) of the nine-year-old emperor, Seiwa.

This appointment has set many precedents, for Seiwa is the first child emperor, and the first male ruler to be placed under the wing of a regent. It is also significant that Yoshifusa is the first regent not of the blood royal.

The rise of the Fujiwaras has been accomplished by careful politics rather than violence. Wealth, land and the marriage of their daughters into the royal line have brought them close to the throne.

Monk invents Slav "Cyrillic" alphabet

Moravia, 869
The Slav peoples of Moravia have been converted to Christianity and given the foundations of their own literature, thanks to the work of two Byzantine monks. The scriptures can now be read in the "Cyrillic" alphabet, named after Cyril, the younger of the two, who has died in Rome, aged 42.

Cyril, whose name was Constantine until he became a monk last year, was born in Thessalonica, of Bulgarian extraction. He and his brother Methodius, who was a provincial governor, both spoke Slav.

They were chosen as missionaries by the Emperor Michael III, at the request of Prince Rastislav, who wanted to counteract Frankish influence in Moravia.

The brothers worked together to compose a Slavonic alphabet, which has become known as the "Glagolitic". This used Greek lettering, combined with the phonetic sounds of the Slavonic dialect of southern Macedonia, and is now being simplified into the "Cyrillic" alphabet.

Bulgarian "czar" is Christian convert

Bulgaria, 866
Boris, the *czar* of Bulgaria, has been converted to Christianity. It remains unclear, however, whether he is loyal to the Christian authority of Rome or that of Constantinople. When Boris succeeded his father Malomir in 852, Bulgaria's foreign policy seemed to be pro-Frankish. In the early 860s Boris reaffirmed his allegiance to Louis the Pious. But Bulgaria has posed a threat to the Byzantine empire for many years, and in 864 the Emperor Michael sent an army to the frontier. This immediately persuaded Boris to be baptised by a Byzantine bishop and renounce his Frankish alliance. A pagan revolt by the old Bulgar clans was brutally crushed last year, and the ringleaders executed. But Boris is now corresponding with the pope and seems to be flirting with the Western church again, to emphasise his independence from Constantinople.

Crisis hits Tang dynasty

A figurine of a Chinese warrior.

A woman, in similar glazed style.

China, 875

The Emperor Xizong has come to the throne of the Tang dynasty at a troubled time. The provinces are wracked with drought and famine, local administration has broken down, and the tax-gatherers are becoming ever more avaricious.

The scholar Lu Xi has been bold enough to present a memorial to the emperor painting in relentless detail the picture of the crisis which has been building for the last ten years.

Lu Xi's account of the people's privations so impressed the emperor that he issued an imperial relief edict to provide help for the peasants. Now he has issued an "Act of Grace" which discusses the country's many problems and the way in which they should be tackled.

It is a wise document, but, like the relief edict, it seems doomed to failure because the countryside is slipping out of the grasp of the cen-

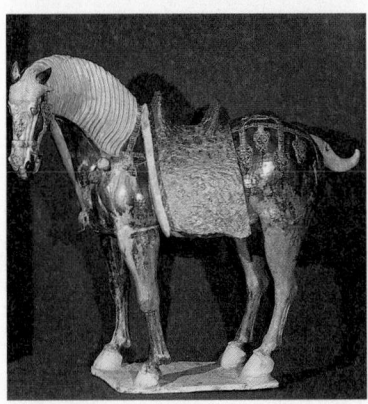

A saddled horse, another fine example of Tang ceramic ware.

tral administration. Bandit groups composed of landless, starving peasants have banded together until they now form small armies which ravage the countryside and attack walled cities, challenging the imperial forces. Chaos now reigns where once the Tangs were all-powerful.

Nothing changes things in Arab maths

Near East, c.873

Arab mathematicians have introduced a magic new number – zero. Their name for it is *sifr*, meaning nothing, or empty. It can also mean "it is not", or "it cannot be". The Arabs used Greek numerals before devising their own, around 770.

The Arabs write the figure zero with a dot or point, but Hindu mathematicians express zero with a circle.

The introduction of the zero marks a fundamental advance for mathematicians, enabling a decimal system to be used. This, however, has not yet reached Europe, where men of learning and the Church refuse to change from complex Roman numerals.

Son of Turkish slave takes power in Egypt

Fustat, Egypt, 877

Egypt is now fully independent again for the first time since the reign of Cleopatra. Ahmad ibn Tulun, the governor of Egypt, has decisively defeated an attempt by the Abbasid caliph, the ruler of the Arab world, to remove him from office. He has pressed home his military advantage and gone on to take over Syria as well. Ibn Tulun is the son of a Turkish slave who became a soldier in the caliph's army at Samarra, rose quickly through the ranks, and was sent to be governor of Egypt in 868.

Since taking over from his father, ibn Tulun has won the loyalty of the people here by administrative reforms, stopping the drain of Egypt's wealth to the caliph and building up a strong army. He has established the capital at Fustat (Cairo) and is building a mosque here which promises to be the rival of those in Baghdad and Samarra.

How ibn Tulun's new mosque – planned to rival any in Islam – will look.

Great Arab thinker dies in disgrace

Baghdad, c.869

Ya'qub ibn Ishaq, widely known in the Arab world as *Sabah al-Kindi*, or the philosopher of the Arabs, has died here in official disgrace. His thinking was considered too radical by the conservative Caliph al-Mutawakkil, but amongst intellectuals he is still regarded as a master of compromise who has done more than anyone to incorporate classical thought into Islam.

Al-Kindi declared his respect for the Prophet Mohammed, but emphasised that "true knowledge" can come from secular thinkers as well as prophets. He pioneered the translation of Greek works into Arabic. His own *On the first philosophy* was inspired by Aristotle's *Metaphysics*. Despite official displeasure his works are still read by Arab thinkers everywhere.

Polychrome vessel in animal form of the Nicoya people from Costa Rica, c.800-1100, showing the high standards of craftsmanship that have developed in Central America.

Britain, May 878. King Alfred of Wessex emerges from hiding and decisively defeats the Danes at the battle of Edington. The Danes agree to evacuate Wessex.

Ethiopia, c.880. Falasha Jews have settled in Ethiopia.

Rome, 12 February 881. Charles III (the Fat), the son of Louis the German, becomes the first eastern Frankish ruler to be crowned emperor. But his "empire" is in reality divided into a series of small completely independent principalities.

Ukraine, 882. Under Oleg, Kiev replaces Novgorod as the main centre of the Rus (Russians).

France/Germany, 887. With the deposition of the influential Charles the Fat late in 887, the Carolingian empire has finally fallen apart. Arnulf becomes king of Germany, and a non-Carolingian, Odo, the count of Paris, becomes king of France. The rest of the empire, in southern France, Burgundy and Italy, is subdivided into a series of warring kingdoms.

West Africa, 890. The Songhay kingdom (*Mali and Niger*) conquers Gao, on the right bank of the Niger.

Germany, 891. King Arnulf defeats the Vikings in battle on the river Dyle and expels them from his kingdom.

Baghdad, 892. The Abbasid caliphs move their capital from Samarra back to Baghdad.

Balkans, 894. Having succeeded his brother last year, Symeon, the czar of Bulgaria, invades Thrace. The Byzantines appeal to the Magyars for help.

Bulgaria, 895. Attacked by the Magyars in the rear, Symeon makes peace with the Byzantines.

Balkans, 897. Symeon allies with the nomadic Pechenegs who force the Magyars across the Danube where they establish their homeland (Hungary). With the Magyars out of the way, Symeon is able to defeat the Byzantines and exact tribute from them.

France, 1 January 898. With the death of Odo, the Carolingian Charles (the Simple) is recognised as king.

North Italy, 899. The Magyars invade North Italy, crushing the army of the Carolingian king of Italy, Berengar.

Alfred repels the Danes

A royal gift: gold, enamel and crystal with the legend "Alfred had me made".

England, 896
The Danes are finally giving up their assault on southern England, thanks to King Alfred of Wessex. In 865 they had dramatically changed their policy when, instead of plundering the coasts, they ravaged the country far inland and settled. They rapidly overwhelmed Northumbria and East Anglia and forced the Mercians to pay tribute.

The West Saxons, under King Aethelred and his brother Alfred, resisted, and won a famous victory at Ashdown in 871, but the war as a whole was going badly for them. When Aethelred died, the new king, Alfred, won a temporary respite by buying off the Danes. But, after subjugating Mercia, they launched a surprise winter attack early in 878, forcing Alfred to flee into the Somerset fens. At this critical moment Alfred emerged from his hiding place, rallied his people and won a crushing victory at Edington. A treaty was made by which Mercia was restored to Alfred, who could consider himself the only king of the Anglo-Saxons.

One image of Alfred the Great.

The Danes retained the *Danelaw*: Northumbria, East Anglia and the East Midlands. But the war was by no means over. The Danes continued to strike, mostly by sea. Alfred met this threat, with limited success, by ordering the construction of 60-oar longboats similar to those used by the Danes. A learned scholar and devout Christian, Alfred owes much of his success to a policy of creating defensive *burghs*, fortified towns like Winchester and Buckingham.

Indian king killed, kingdom annexed

Southern India, 885
Aparajita, the king of the Pallavas, has been killed in battle, leading his army on his war elephant, his once-great empire dying with him.

Since 640, in the reign of Narasimhavarman, when Pallavan art, literature and political power was at its zenith, constant conflict with the neighbouring empire of the Pandyas weakened both empires while destroying neither. They were further weakened by a new power in the region, the Cholas, under their ambitious king, Aditya, who astutely played the two powers off against each other. A Chola alliance with the Pallavas destroyed the Pandyas; now the Cholas have turned on the Pallavas, killing their king and destroying his army.

Though the Pallavan dynasty is no more, its glory outlives it. The great sculptures and reliefs in the Mahabalipuram caves, the countless *rathas* – shrines built like pyramids – and magnificent temples still remain, enduring memories of a lost empire.

A Pallavan temple.

Shepherds seeking new pastures have invaded Germany

Germany, c.899
The Carolingian rulers of Germany have a new worry to add to their troubles. A nomadic people from the east has invaded the eastern part of their domains and won control of nearly all of Frankish Pannonia (*western Austria and eastern Hungary*). The unwelcome newcomers call themselves Magyars and, although their precise origins are unclear, they seem to have begun as shepherds in the northern Caucasus.

As had happened to other peoples in the region, the Magyars were displaced – in this case by the Turkic Pecheneg tribes – and moved west in search of pastures new. This migration began about ten years ago under the man believed to be their leader, Arpad. About five years ago they reached the Danube and invaded Pannonia. It is unlikely that the weak Carolingian rulers of the east German kingdom will halt further Magyar advances.

Vikings head eastward

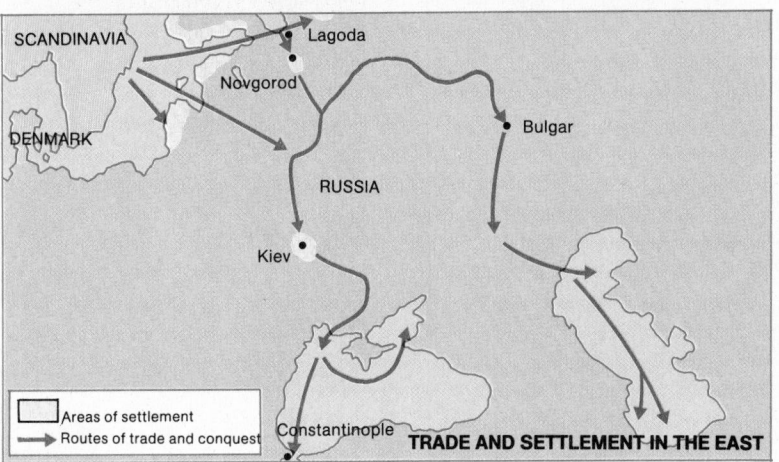

TRADE AND SETTLEMENT IN THE EAST

Areas of settlement
Routes of trade and conquest

Kiev, c.899
Descendants of Swedish Vikings known as Varangians (or Rus) have opened up a north-south trade route linking the Baltic to the Black Sea and beyond. The route follows the rivers Dnieper and Volga across the interior, but often the boats must be hauled overland.

Between 852 and 862, against localised opposition, the Varangians, led by Rurik and his brothers, first pioneered a route to their capital Novgorod via the Baltic and Lake Ladoga.

Twenty years later, Rurik's successor Oleg took Kiev from the Khazars and made it his new capital. This created the first Russian state and a regular route from the Gulf of Finland via the River Dnieper to the Black Sea. The ultimate target is Constantinople, the capital of the Byzantine empire and repository of fabulous riches.

One Rus attack on Constantinople 40 years ago, by a fleet of 200 ships across the Bosporus, almost succeeded. Sporadic attacks continue. As traders, the Varangians

Rurik: the Varangian leader.

have even reached Baghdad. Some Rus now adopt Christianity, but an Arab scholar notes that others still relish the ritual of collective rape and strangulation of a chieftain's concubine immediately after his death so that she can be buried with her master. Moslems view this barbaric northern practice with disbelief.

Slaves are vital to the Songhay economy

Western Sudan, c.880
Slaves play a vital role in the empire of Songhay in the western Sudan. So valued are they that royal slaves are even appointed as commissioners overseeing local rulers in the provinces – many of whom are the king's hostages.

Slaves are of prime importance to the empire's economic, military and political spheres. With no shortage of good fertile land, the

need is for manpower to provide the produce essential for the local chiefs to maintain their courts, so slaves are at a premium in Songhay. Slave settlements are often given by the ruler as gifts to his favourites.

Slaves, too, are at the very heart of the army – as bowmen – with freed slaves making up the cavalry. With horses fetching huge prices in Songhay, it is not uncommon for slaves to be exchanged for them.

Eastern and Western churches in dispute

Basil (c.) is faced with the hostility of Rome and, as shown here, Islam.

Constantinople, 878
The religious and political schism between Rome and Constantinople has opened up again with the death of Ignatius and the reinstatement of Photius as patriarch.

Since Basil became emperor in 867, having murdered Michael III, he has repeatedly been embroiled in religious arguments. His chief problem was Photius, who was excommunicated by the pope in 863 and persuaded a council in Constantinople to reject Rome.

On his accession Basil repudiated Photius and reinstated Ignatius, but disputes with Rome have continued. The real problem remains Byzantine refusal to accept the primacy of Rome.

Armenia cuts ties with its Arab masters

Close ties with the Byzantine empire: an earlier emperor Michael I Rhagabe crowns an Armenian co-emperor Leo V.

Armenia, 885
The Armenians, mountain people on the fringes of the Moslem and Byzantine worlds, have set up an independent state under Prince Ashot Bagratuni who has been governor of the region for nearly 25 years under the authority granted to him by the caliph of Samarra. He was

crowned king in the cathedral at Bagaran, the Armenian capital, and was immediately recognised by the Byzantine Emperor Basil, himself an Armenian.

This marks the end of direct domination by the Arabs, although the Armenians will continue to pay tribute to them.

900 (900-911)

Norway, c.900. Harald Fairhair wins a decisive victory at Hafrsfjord and becomes the first king of Norway, uniting the various princedoms.

South Africa, c.900. The Toutswe state (*Botswana*) has become established on the western edge of the Kalahari.

Peru, c.900. Arriving on a balsa raft, Taycanamo founds the Chimu city of Chan-Chan.

North Africa, 901. Abu 'Abd Allah rouses the Berbers against the Aghlabid *emir* in Ifriqiyah (*Tunisia*).

Sicily, 1 August 902. The Aghlabid rulers of Ifriqiyah capture Taormina, thus completing their conquest of the island from the Byzantines.

Byzantine Empire, 31 July 904. The Arabs capture Thessalonica, the greatest city of the empire after Constantinople, and ravage it before withdrawing.

Japan, 905. The *Kokin Wakashu* anthology of pure Japanese poetry is completed.

Constantinople, 907. Oleg, the prince of Kiev, besieges Constantinople, but is bought off by the payment of tribute and the offer of a trade treaty.

China, 907. The Tang dynasty, in power in China for almost 300 years, is at an end.

India, 907. The Rastrakutas now occupy most of the Dekhan, having repulsed the Chalukyas to the east, who have re-grouped around Vengi.

East Africa, 908. The Arabs settle in Somalia.

France, 910. The monastery of Cluny is founded by William, the duke of Aquitaine.

Britain, August 910. Edward, Alfred's successor as king of Wessex since 899, defeats the Danes at Tettenhall. With the aid of his sister Aethelflaed, the regent of Mercia, he begins to drive the Danes back, reoccupying London and Oxford.

Germany, November 911. Louis (the Child), the last Carolingian to rule Germany, dies. The nobles meet at Forchheim and agree to elect Conrad, the duke of Franconia, as their king, but part of the kingdom, Lotharingia (Lorraine), is seized by Charles the Simple, the king of France.

Copy of a fresco originally from a Zapotec temple in southern Mexico.

Maya man's head from Palenque.

Abandoned city signals collapse of a Mexican civilisation

Mexico, c.900

The great city of Monte Alban has been abandoned, sacked by the neighbouring state of Mixtec.

The capital of the Zapotecs for over 500 years, Monte Alban dominated the Pacific coast of Mexico from its heartland in the Oaxaca Valley. In its heyday it had been a prosperous and cosmopolitan city. From Teotihuacan came its pottery styles, and from the Maya a calendar and glyphic script.

Monte Alban itself was originally a shrine to the gods, in particular Cocijo, the rain god. Over the centuries it grew into a major city, its dwellings packed on the narrow terraced slopes of the Oaxaca Valley. In the centre was a magnificent courtyard, surrounded by platforms, pyramids and triumphal staircases. The buildings are austere, with few embellishments, though the tombs are decorated with frescoes of men and gods. Now Monte Alban lies in ruins.

King boosts Hindu revival in Java by building 150 monuments

The central tower of the Hindu temple of Prambanan, dedicated to Siva.

The statue of an elephant-god.

Java, c.900

A new dynasty, the Mataramas, has supplanted the Buddhist Sailendras. Java, now called Mataram, has reverted to Saivite Hinduism, after over a century of Buddhist domination. The earlier Hindu rulers, the Sanjayas, had been driven into the mountains, preferring exile to submission. Now, with the Sailendras overthrown, they have returned, and their new king, Balitung, who practises both Hindu devotion and religious toleration, has built over 150 Saiva temples.

The greatest of these is the Chandi Lara Longgrang at Prambanam, the capital, comparable in magnificence and ostentation to the Buddhist shrine of Borobudur, built 100 years earlier. There are eight temples surrounded by side chapels. The largest, dedicated to Siva, stands in the centre: a square pyramid, ennobled by friezes illustrating the *Ramayana*, even finer than those at Borobudur.

Vikings settle in France

A beautiful silver arm-ring made by Viking craftsmen in Denmark.

France, 911

The veteran leader of a Viking warrior band and the king of the western Franks have concluded a treaty at St-Clair-sur-Epte which could end nearly 50 years of violent Viking assaults upon the Franks. Charles the Simple has conceded some western territory to Rollo, who in return has sworn homage to Charles, accepted baptism and agreed to defend his kingdom against other Vikings. *Normandy*, the duchy of the Northmen, or *Normans*, is thus created.

A similar process of Viking settlement on conquered or unoccupied territory has been taking place over the last 50 years in the British Isles and beyond. Formerly the Vikings had arrived in the summer, plundered along the coasts and up the rivers, and sailed home with their booty, but gradually they chose to winter on unoccupied territory. Their raids, now carried out from nearby bases, continued with unceasing frequency and ferocity, with numerous towns, including Cologne, Paris, Nantes and London suffering bloody assaults. To the north, Iceland was occupied, the Scottish highlands and islands were colonised, and Vikings sailed around Ireland, creating new coastal towns such as Dublin. In England they overran more than half the country before being checked by Alfred, the king of Wessex. But

Rollo, the first duke of Normandy.

under the treaty of 886 the former Anglo-Saxon kingdoms of Northumbria and East Anglia, and the east Midlands, were yielded to Danish rule and called the *Danelaw*. Alfred died 13 years ago; his son, King Edward, has been driving the Vikings back once more. There are signs that they may have their positive side: where they have founded permanent settlements they are turning their energy and sailing skills to commercial activity, bringing prosperity to towns such as Dublin and York.

Indian prince inherits rich legacy of land

India, 906

The great Chola king, Aditya, has died. The land he inherited 35 years ago was an impoverished statelet squashed between two powers, the Pandyas and Pallavas. The land his son Parantaka inherits is an empire embracing all south-east India.

His reign was an epic one. After defeating first the Pandyas and then the Pallavas, and marrying a Pallavan princess, he expanded his empire into one of the most powerful in India. Already the foundations for a temple to serve as his sepulchre have been laid at Tondaimanad, near Kalahasti, where he died.

A Chola bronze figure of Siva Nataraja, the lord of the dance.

Samanids found an imperial dynasty

Central Asia, 900

The Samanid family have firmly established themselves as rulers of an empire centred on Transoxiana, roughly the region between the Caspian Sea and the Hindu Kush.

Originally Persian landowners from Samarkand, the Samanids have been increasing their power for the last century. Now Isma'il ibn Ahmed, the head of the family, has defeated the last of his local rivals and established his capital at Bokhara. The Abbasid caliph in Baghdad has formally recognised him as ruler of Transoxiana.

The Samanid empire is fast becoming a rich trading centre for goods from China and the far north, from where pagan merchants calling themselves Rus are bringing furs and iron along the river Volga in exchange for gold and silks from the Moslem east.

Samanid mausoleum at Bokhara.

Isma'il is a man of culture as well as an astute politician: he is a patron of the new Persian poetry and is building a stately and beautiful family mausoleum in Bokhara.

Ethiopia signs trade pact with the Yemen

Ethiopia, 901

Surrounded on the north, east and west by Moslem powers, Ethiopia has survived the Moslem onslaught into Africa. A new trade treaty with the Yemen amounts to recognition by Islam of Ethiopia's right to exist. The price has been high: Ethiopia is now completely cut off from Christian Europe. The Ethiopians survived the Moslem wave by shifting south. They abandoned the capital, Axum, Eritrea and the Red Sea coast, retreating into the Highlands, whence the Moslem armies are unable to dislodge them. In spite of these wars there is still extensive trade between Ethiopia and Islamic countries, hence the treaty with the Yemen. Al-Yaqubi, the Arab historian, writes of vast cities with colonies of Moslems, their numbers growing every year. Nor are they the first Moslems in the country: it was Ethiopia which gave refuge to the Prophet's followers after they had been driven from Arabia in the infancy of Islam.

The new Europe, 800-1000

The two centuries after 800 saw great changes in Europe. By the year 1000 the Carolingian empire had disintegrated into smaller kingdoms, duchies and counties and, on the fringes of Europe, new Christian states had emerged among once pagan and disunited barbarians. The economy was reviving, with population and agriculture increasing, and trade and towns acquiring new importance.

Carolingian Europe breaks up

Even at its height in 800, the year in which Charlemagne was crowned emperor in Rome, the Carolingian empire was a fragile creation, dependent on the military might and prestige of its ruler. Through successful conquest, Charlemagne was able to cow dissenters and reward and keep together his followers. However, the divisions of the empire after his death and the civil wars between his grandchildren very severely weakened the power of the kings, since they now needed to bid for their nobles' support in internecine strife. A new wave of invaders – Vikings in the north, Magyars (Hungarians) in the east, Arabs in the Mediterranean – complicated the military and political struggle, and further weakened the centralising powers of kingship.

By 900 the empire had split into three main kingdoms – France, Germany and Italy. Italy corresponded roughly with the old Lombard kingdom (conquered by Charlemagne in 774), and France and Germany with a linguistic division between Romance (French) speakers and German speakers.

In Germany the century after 900 saw the slow emergence of a dynasty, the Ottonians, who forged a new unity out of the German duchies, which in around 900 had seemed set to become independent states. Once mere dukes of Saxony, the Ottonians' power and prestige, like that of Charlemagne, rested substantially on military prowess. The dynasty's founder, Otto I, confirmed his position firstly by crushing the Magyars in 955, ending their raids on Europe, and then by conquering Italy and accepting the Holy Roman imperial crown from the pope in 962. By 1000 the Ottonians were firmly established as emperors, controlling both the eastern and Italian parts of Charlemagne's former empire. At the same time they had begun, slowly and painfully, to extend German influence and settlement east of the river Elbe, and their wealth was enhanced both by tribute from the Slavs and by the discovery of rich silver deposits in the Saxon Harz mountains.

Within the western part of the former Carolingian empire (roughly the area now called France), no mighty dynasty had emerged, by 1000, to reforge a centralised and powerful kingship; instead civil wars continued and did not abate with the establishment of a new dynasty, the Capetians, in 987. The weakness of central royal power meant that France was a single kingdom in name only – the orders of the king in Paris were accepted only within a small region around the city, and beyond this, France had effectively disintegrated into autonomous little states ruled by dukes and counts. Of these the greatest were Aquitaine, Flanders and Normandy.

Italy in 1000 was for the most part in the hands of the German emperors, although the far south and Sicily were ruled by Arabs or Byzantine Greeks. The north and centre had been conquered by Otto I in 961-2, and in 1000 they were ruled over by his grandson, Otto III, whose zeal for his title of "Roman emperor" led him to transfer his main residence from Germany to Rome itself. But the foundations of German power in Italy were not firm; too much royal land had been lost in the civil wars during the 50 years before Otto I's invasion, and a powerful merchant class was emerging capable of challenging the established order. The merchants of Cremona, for instance, extorted important political and economic concessions from their bishop before 1000; this did not bode well for the future, since bishops were the backbone of Ottonian rule.

The new states

In the two centuries from 800 to 1000, beyond the borders of the old Europe, wholly new states emerged and adopted Christianity and Christian culture, thus bringing them firmly into the fold of a new and wider Christian Europe. In the north, Christian kingdoms developed in Norway and Denmark. In Denmark the dynasty of Harold Bluetooth, who united Denmark and accepted Christianity in about 960, became a formidable power which in 1000 was engaged in an ultimately successful war of conquest in England. England was itself a new state; although long Christian, it was only unified politically by Alfred the Great and his successors in the decades after 900. Of all the states of Europe at the time, it had claims to being economically and culturally the most sophisticated.

On the eastern border of Germany, the Magyars, after their defeat at Lechfeld by Otto I in 955, ceased their raids into the west and established a duchy of Hungary under Duke Geza (972-97). His successor, Stephen, accepted a crown from the pope and made Hungary a kingdom.

To the north of Hungary, Slav Bohemia was firmly established as a Christian state by 1000, though it was often threatened by its powerful German neighbour. Slav Poland was also a Christian nation, ruled over by the powerful Boleslav Chobry.

Further east and south the new states took their Christianity from Constantinople rather than Rome. In north-west Asia Viking traders and conquerors – the Rus – forged a new political and economic power, Russia, by uniting and expanding the small Slav towns on the trade route of the river Don. They were gradually assimilated with their Slav subjects, and accepted Christianity through their links with the Byzantines. A huge area of Asia thus came into the sphere of Christian European culture.

In the Balkans, the powerful state of Bulgaria accepted Christianity as early as 864. Its *czars* or kings posed a formidable threat to Constantinople for centuries until they finally bowed to the Byzantines under the Emperor Basil II in 1014.

A growing economy

From as early as 700 there were signs of new growth in the European economies. By 800 new coastal towns had developed, such as Hamwic (Southampton) in England and Venice on the Adriatic, dependent on a newly flourishing trade. Civil wars and invasions, particularly by the Vikings, disrupted economic growth but did not destroy it. Indeed, once settled, the Vikings made a positive contribution to the European economy, opening up new trade routes to Constantinople and the caliphate, and through the Baltic, across Asia, the North Sea and even the north Atlantic.

Long-distance trade flourished, and Italian cities like Venice grew rich on the import of exotic goods, such as silks and spices, from the Islamic and Byzantine worlds into northern Europe. At the same time, a vast network of local trade prospered, based on a rising population, a sophisticated new coinage and the growth of markets and specialised production for local needs. In England, for example, a dense network of market-settlements was established, often with their own mints.

One sign of change was renewed urban growth, revitalised by rising trade and population. In some areas outside the old Roman empire towns appeared for the very first time, for example Kiev and Novgorod in Russia and Gniezo and Poznań in Poland. These new towns, solidly European in appearance, symbolised the integration of a vast new area into the economy and culture of a new Europe.

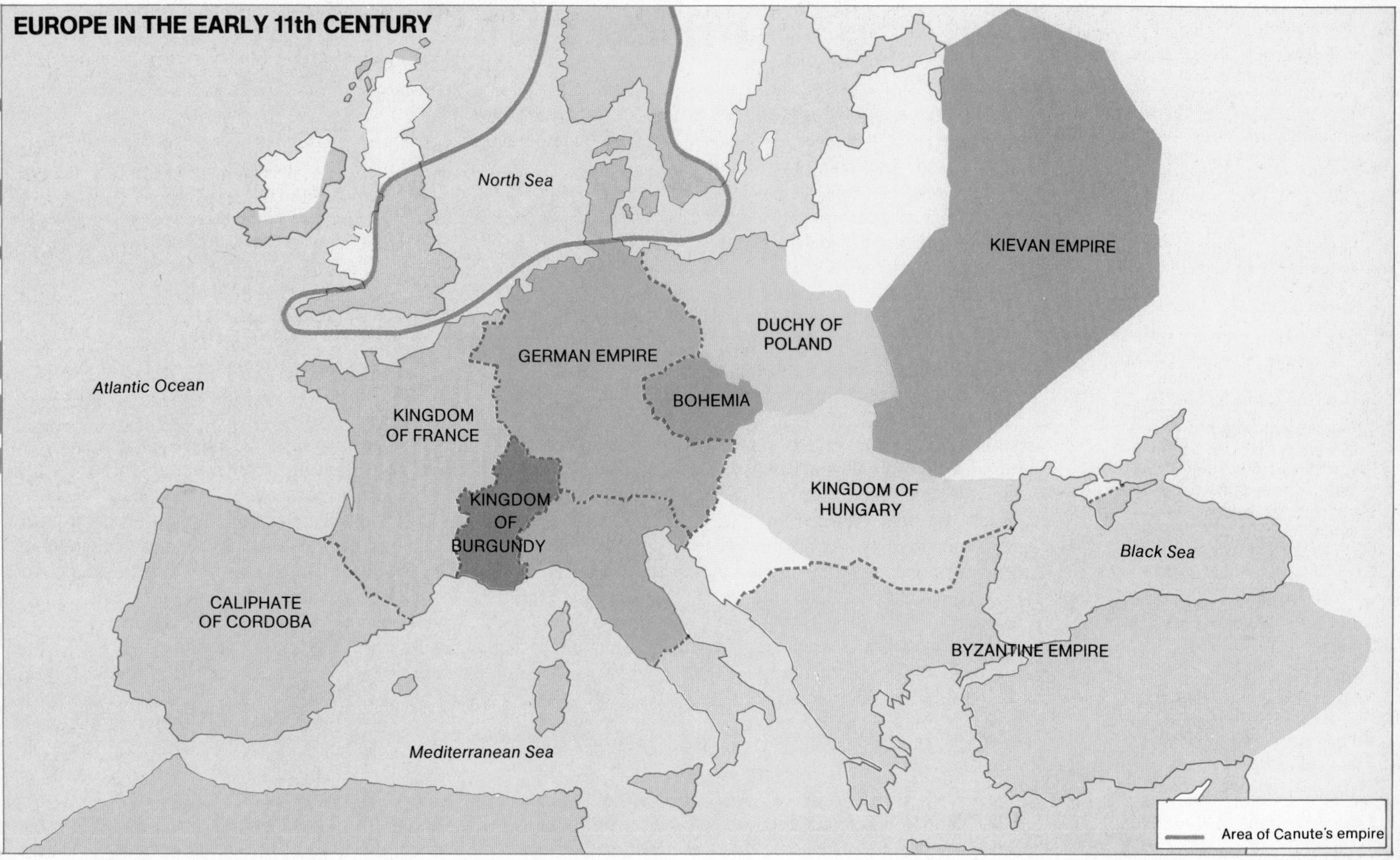

EUROPE IN THE EARLY 11th CENTURY

North Sea

KIEVAN EMPIRE

DUCHY OF POLAND

GERMAN EMPIRE

BOHEMIA

Atlantic Ocean

KINGDOM OF FRANCE

KINGDOM OF BURGUNDY

KINGDOM OF HUNGARY

Black Sea

CALIPHATE OF CORDOBA

BYZANTINE EMPIRE

Mediterranean Sea

— Area of Canute's empire

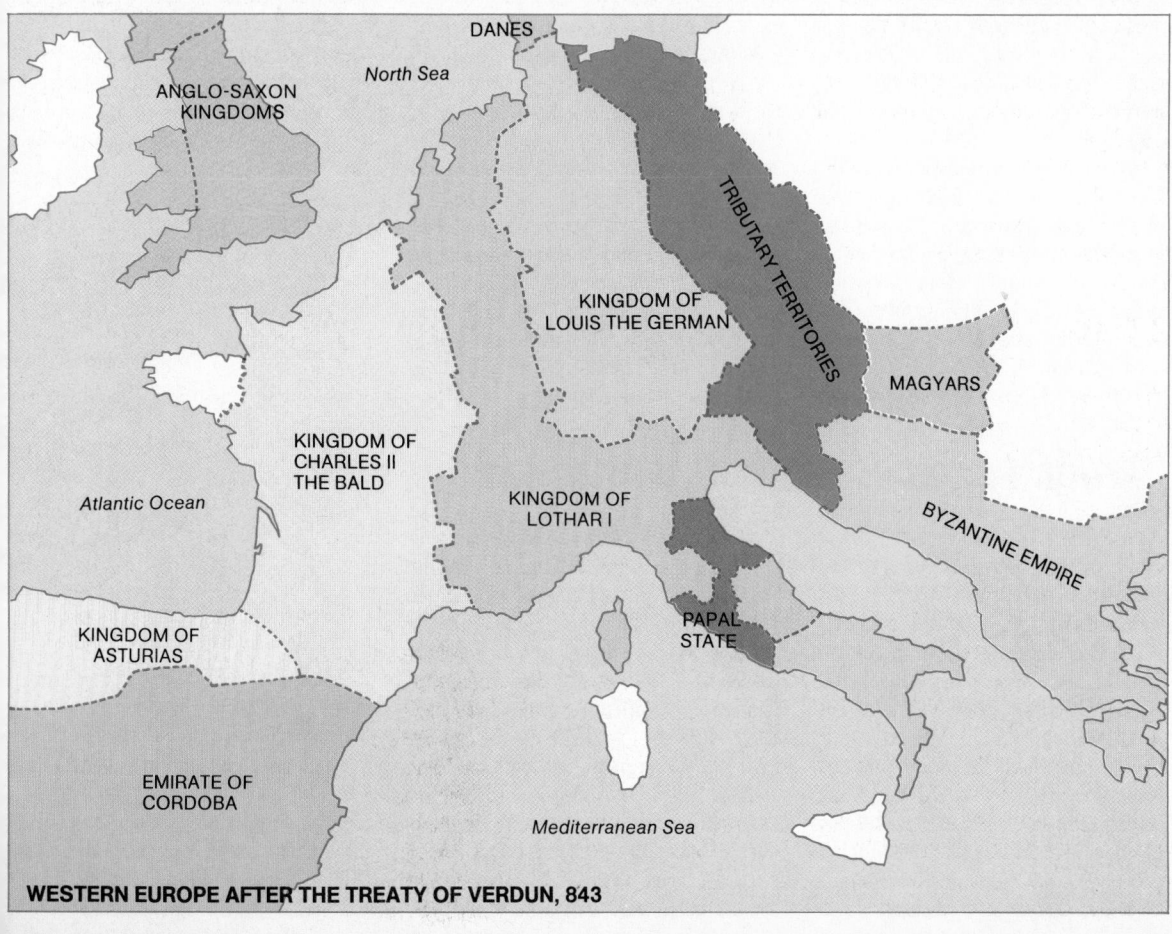

WESTERN EUROPE AFTER THE TREATY OF VERDUN, 843

DANES

North Sea

ANGLO-SAXON KINGDOMS

TRIBUTARY TERRITORIES

KINGDOM OF LOUIS THE GERMAN

MAGYARS

KINGDOM OF CHARLES II THE BALD

Atlantic Ocean

KINGDOM OF LOTHAR I

BYZANTINE EMPIRE

KINGDOM OF ASTURIAS

PAPAL STATE

EMIRATE OF CORDOBA

Mediterranean Sea

Frankish tradition demanded that Charlemagne split his empire among his sons, but all of them died save Louis (the Pious), who in 814 inherited an undivided empire. However, partitions into sub-kingdoms among Louis' sons Lothair, Louis (the German), Pepin and Charles (the Bald) followed before Louis the Pious died in 840. Lothair succeeded as emperor, but Charles and Louis (Pepin had died in 838) formed an alliance against him and, in 843, he was forced to agree to the Treaty of Verdun.

This deal created, broadly, an idea of Germany, France and Italy. Louis became ruler of the East Frankish kingdom (Germany) while Charles was confirmed as ruler of the West Frankish kingdom (France). Lothair remained emperor (an empty title) and ruler of Italy and of a broad strip of territory between his brothers' lands (Provence, Burgundy and an area called, after him, "Lotharingia" [Lorraine]). Lothar's lands were the subject of dispute for centuries and, until the 19th century, only Charles' kingdom – France – proved viable as a single nation.

Constantinople, 913. Provoked by the Byzantines' failure to pay their annual tribute, Symeon, the czar of Bulgaria, invades, but is stopped by the walls of Constantinople. He obtains major concessions from the regent, the patriarch Nicholas Mysticus.

Spain, 914. Ordono II becomes king of Asturias and makes Leon the capital in place of Oviedo.

North Africa, 916. 'Ubayd Allah, the first Fatimid caliph, makes Mahdia the capital of Ifriqiyah (*Tunisia*).

Bulgaria, 20 August 917. Having gone back on the agreement of 913 and seen Thrace overrun by Symeon as a result, the Byzantines launch a counter-offensive, but are routed by Symeon at Anchialus. Symeon controls the Balkans.

France, 15 June 923. Charles the Simple kills the rebel leader Robert, who usurped his throne last year, but loses the battle at Soissons. The rebels elect Ralph of Burgundy as king; Charles is imprisoned, but conflict soon resumes.

France, 924. The Magyars cross the Alps and devastate Provence.

Britain, 17 July 924. Having recovered East Anglia and the whole of Mercia from the Danes, Edward (the Elder) dies at Farndon. His son Aethelstan is chosen to succeed him as Anglo-Saxon king.

Constantinople, 924. Symeon attacks the Byzantine empire and is halted again by the walls of Constantinople.

Germany, 925. Henry, the king of Germany, annexes Lotharingia (Lorraine) from the divided French kingdom.

East Africa, 925. The island of Zanzibar is colonised by Arabs from the Gulf.

Balkans, 926. After crushing the Serbs, who had unwisely turned towards the Byzantines, Symeon attacks the Croats, loyal allies of the Byzantines. He is roundly defeated.

Mongolia, 926. Manchuria and northern Korea are annexed to the Mongol Khitan empire.

Bulgaria, October 927. Symeon died in May and was succeeded by his son Peter, who now makes a peace treaty with the Byzantines.

Morocco, 931. The caliph of Cordoba wins Morocco from the Fatimids.

Heart attack kills czar after defeat

Bulgaria, 27 May 927
Symeon, the emperor, or *czar*, of the Bulgarians, master of the Balkans and inspiration of Bulgarian power, has died of a heart attack. It is a grim conclusion to last year's unexpected defeat of his invading army by the Croats.

But this was Symeon's first failure. His power rivalled and at times surpassed that of the Byzantines, and he forged an empire stretching from the Ionian to the Black Sea.

Educated to be a monk in Constantinople, Symeon gained a solid grounding in both religious and secular affairs. Abandoning the Church, he was crowned in 893, and began to play Constantinople at its own game, mixing military might, diplomatic intrigue and an expanding commercial empire to establish Bulgaria's importance. He also defeated the Byzantines in a

Bulgarian cavalry in battle.

series of battles. Symeon's court at his capital, Great Preslav, imitated Byzantine pomp, and the cultured czar encouraged both Greek and home-grown Slavonic literature.

Persian mystic decapitated for heresy

Baghdad, 27 March 922
Al-Hallaj, the Persian mystic, was executed today in a gruesome public ceremony. Sentenced to death after a long trial, he was flogged, mutilated, then tied to a gibbet and beheaded. His body was burnt and his ashes scattered in the Tigris.

Abu al-Mughith-al-Husayn ibn Mansur, known as al-Hallaj, was a wool carder, born in 858 in a small village in southern Persia. He became a travelling preacher, crossing Persia and Turkestan and even venturing into India; he also made the holy pilgrimage to Mecca.

Adapting the Sufi doctrine, al-Hallaj went further and advocated the pursuit of ecstasy through a personal fusion with God. "I am the Truth," he said. "I am the One that I love, and the one that I love is me. We are two spirits and one body."

He was condemned as a heretic, and the civil authorities saw him as a potential rabble-rouser, particularly since he supported caliphal reform.

Al-Hallaj was arrested once, but escaped and hid at Susa. When he was arrested a second time, in 913, there was no escape. He had been in prison ever since. He has left a *Diwan*, and fragments of a treatise called *Kitab al-Tawasin*.

"World's greatest doctor" dies in bed

Persia, c.925
One of the most controversial figures in Islamic science, Abu Bakr Mohammed ibn Zakariya ar-Razi, has died peacefully in Khurasan. He was widely regarded as the greatest doctor in the world and was in demand at the caliph's court in Baghdad and in other capitals. His treatise on smallpox and measles is a standard work; his medical encyclopaedia brought together for the first time the best of Greek and Arabic medicine.

Ar-Razi also had a reputation as a heretic. His initial studies were in philosophy and he remained a great admirer of Plato, angering both Islamic conservatives and those radicals who favoured Aristotle. In his chemistry and medicine he based his work on experiment and exposed the difference between magical spells and genuine remedies. This won him grudging admiration from some Aristotelians. Others were prepared to forgive him anything because he was such a good doctor.

Revolt breaks out in North Africa

Ifriqiyah (Tunisia), January 911
The last of the Aghlabid rulers of Ifriqiyah has been driven out of the Kairouan by a popular revolt. The man now installed in the princely residence of Rakkada is 'Ubayd Allah, known as the *Mahdi* – "Prince of the Faithful".

The Aghlabids, long since effectively independent of the caliphate, were still known as "governors". The Mahdi, however, is styling himself "caliph" in a direct challenge to the authority of the Abbasid caliphs of Baghdad. He is a Fatimid, claiming descent from the Prophet Mohammed's daughter Fatima, and thus, he believes, more entitled to the caliphate.

The Mahdi's origins are obscure; he lived in Syria until 902, and when he travelled west he was taken prisoner at Sijilmassah. He owes his prominence entirely to his chief propagandist, Abu 'Abd Allah, who forged links with the Ketama Berbers from 894. The Ketama, old adversaries of the Aghlabids, looked forward to being an elite army under a new regime.

'Ubayd Allah settled in Ikjan, won over the people, and proceeded to advance into Aghlabid territory. He entered Rakkaba in 909, having crushed the army of the dynasty's last sovereign.

The new church of the Holy Cross on Aght'amar Island in Lake Van, seat of the Armenian Church, built by the powerful local monarch Gagik Ardzrouni.

Pilgrims massacred in mosques at Mecca

Arabia, 930

A breakaway group of revolutionary Moslems, known as the Carmathians after its founder Hamdan Karmat, has shocked the Islamic world with its week-long sack of the holy city of Mecca and the theft of the Ka'aba, the Black Stone which is the focus of pilgrimage. Many pilgrims were killed.

The Carmathians, possibly allied to the Fatimids of Ifriqiyah (*Tunisia*), totally reject the caliphate. In 899 they established their own state of Bahrain in eastern Arabia. Here they live in a type of oligarchical republic, where the ruler is seen only as the first among equals. There are no taxes, but this "society of equals" relies heavily on slaves.

The Carmathians have become increasingly aggressive, attacking Mecca-bound pilgrims and, in 923, sacking the port of Basra. Their motives for the theft of the Ka'aba is uncertain. On the one hand, it could be because they consider Moslem reverence for a stone to be idolatrous; on the other, they may

A manuscript showing the Ka'aba.

simply be hoping to divert Mecca's lucrative pilgrimage traffic to Bahrain.

Whatever the truth, this attack underlines the growing impotence of the Abbasid caliphs, unable even to protect their holiest shrine.

Spain is Moslem, says Cordoba's caliph

Cordoba, 929

Abd al-Rahman III, the Umayyad *emir* of Cordoba since 911, has proclaimed himself caliph, establishing Spain as a major Moslem power and an independent rival to the expansionist Fatimids of Ifriqiyah.

Spain has had a succession of emirs since the Arab invasion of 711, but the last century has seen a prolonged political crisis. The new caliph has ended that, crushing his rivals and re-establishing the authority of Cordoba, his capital. Spain, with its flourishing commerce, fertile agriculture and thriving intellectual life, is a force to be reckoned with.

The dome of Cordoba's great mosque towers above the city.

King Wenceslas is overthrown by pagan

Bohemia, 929

Wenceslas, the king of Bohemia, has been murdered by his pagan brother Boleslav.

Wenceslas was the grandson of Borivoy, the first known prince of Prague, and was brought up as a devout Christian by his grandmother Ludmilla. Wratislaw, Wenceslas' father, was killed fighting the Magyars. Wenceslas restored order and built a number of churches.

He also pursued an alliance with the Christian King Henry of Germany, and this may have been his undoing in the eyes of Boleslav and the jealous nobles.

Papal decadence dents authority of Rome

Rome, December 932

Unrest in Rome against the papacy and the noble family which controls it came to a head this month when a mob stormed the castle in which Hugh of Provence, the king of Italy, and his bride were installed. Hugh has escaped with his life. His bride, the scheming Marozia, has been jailed with Pope John XI.

Apart from Roman fears about foreign rule, Hugh was the bride's brother-in-law. The marriage contravened Church teaching, and once again the reputation of Rome's rulers, together with that of the papacy, is at a low ebb. Life in papal circles has hardly been saintly since the notorious "cadaver council" of Pope Formosus 35 years ago. Nine months after the aged pope's death, his body was exhumed, propped up on a throne in full papal vestments and solemnly arraigned on charges of perjury. A deacon stood by the body and spoke for it. Formosus' corpse was found guilty. The three fingers he used for blessing were chopped off and his body was thrown into the Tiber.

Since then the Vatican has been rocked by death and scandal. Formosus' successor and prosecutor, Stephen VII, was deposed and strangled; Benedict IV is believed to have been murdered; Leo V was

Pope John X: suffocated.

thrown into jail after only 30 days as pontiff, and later executed with Christopher, the anti-pope, by Sergius III. Sergius was so intimate with the wealthy, corrupt Theophylact family that it is believed that he fathered a son by their 15-year-old daughter, Marozia – a name that has figured more and more in the sordid papal scene.

John X, the ex-lover of Theodora, Marozia's daughter, was suffocated at Marozia's behest; and it has been revealed that the present pope, John XI, is Marozia's illegitimate son by Sergius III.

Byzantines win peace at a price

Constantinople, 2 December 911

Oleg, the leader of the Rus people and prince of Kiev, has used his naval power to gain a favourable commercial treaty from Byzantium in return for peace.

This treaty marks a change in Byzantine foreign policy. For the last 200 years Constantinople has allied with the Khazars, an Asiatic people speaking a Turkic language, Christian-influenced but largely Judaic. The Khazar empire, a vast area between the rivers Don and Volga, stood against the Arabs and then the Magyars and Vikings. But in the 850s the Rus took Kiev from the Khazars, whose empire is now in decline and faces various threats on all its borders. The Byzantines have little choice but to come to terms with the powerful Rus.

A crown, made of silver and originally decorated with semi-precious gemstones, probably made for the Silla dynasty, the current rulers of Korea.

Mystery sect gives up meat and sex

The tombstone of a Bogomil, a member of the strange sect which has aroused the Church's wrath.

Bulgaria, c.940
A strange religious sect, known as the Bogomils after its founder, a priest called Bogomil, is gathering followers all over Bulgaria. They are denounced as heretics by the Orthodox Church and are persecuted, but nothing will make them give up their fervently held beliefs.

They are "dualists", believing in a good God and in an almost equally powerful Satan, who created the world, the body and all material things. Their more fervent members, the "Perfect", abstain from almost all the things of this world, including sex, meat and wine. They believe that they are the only true Christians, and that when they die they will become ethereal bodies. Accepting only the New Testament, the Psalms and the prophetic books, they believe most of the Old Testament to be Satan's work. It is not surprising, therefore, that they are persecuted by the Church.

But the Bogomils are more than just a bizarre group of heretics. They are fiercely nationalistic, and their movement reflects Bulgarian resentment at Byzantine culture, imperial power and Slav serfdom.

It is said that "they teach their people not to obey their lords, they revile the wealthy, hate the czar, ridicule the elders, condemn the boyars, regard as vile in the sight of God those who serve the czar, and forbid every servant to work for his master." The Bogomils are, in fact, peasants united in a political movement by their religious beliefs.

Anglo-Saxons smash invasion force

England, 937
Anglo-Saxon forces under King Athelstan have annihilated a combined invasion force of Irish-based Vikings, Scots and Britons in the kingdom of Strathclyde. Both sides suffered severe losses, but eventually the invaders were forced to flee from the field.

Since coming to the throne in 925, Athelstan has rapidly brought to fruition his father Edward's counter-attacks against the Danes. Uniting Wessex and Mercia behind him, Athelstan rapidly recovered Northumbria and, with it, the key Viking centre at York. He then subjugated the Welsh princes and the Britons of Cornwall before leading a punitive expedition into Scottish territory. Having now crushed his main enemies, Olaf of Dublin (once of York) and Constantine of the Scots, Athelstan can justly call himself "King of the English and ruler of all Britain".

Athelstan is an administrator and diplomat as well as a warrior. His military renown led kings of Frankia, Germany and Norway alike to seek alliance with him. He

Art under Athelstan: a psalter.

held national councils to encourage the unification of the various peoples under his rule. He issued many detailed law-codes, and divided up his kingdom into large regions administered by *ealdormen* with wide authority for the local maintenance of order. Some claim he is greater even than his grandfather, the mighty Alfred.

Fisherman's son takes power in Baghdad

Baghdad, December 945
The capital of the once-mighty Abbasid caliphs is now in the hands of a Shi'ite fisherman's son from northern Persia. The power of the caliphs has long been on the wane, and recent attacks have shown their impotence even in their home territory of Mesopotamia (Iraq). In the last ten years real power in the region has been in the hands of local warlords, who have ravaged the countryside.

The new conqueror, Ahmad ibn Buwayh, has already exploited the

region's chaos to take most of western Persia. His father is a Caspian sea fisherman who claims descent from ancient Persian kings. However, the new Buwayhid, or Buyid, dynasty – Shi'ite Persian Moslems in a predominantly Sunni Arab Moslem land – may face resentment as Ahmad tries to restore peace. Perhaps for this reason, Ahmad – who has been granted the title *Mu'izz al-Dawla* ("He who makes the state mighty") – has clearly decided to keep the caliph as a figurehead.

"Greek fire" destroys the Russian fleet

Constantinople, 941
The Rus, or Russian, fleet has been all but annihilated after another abortive attack on Constantinople. In a plundering campaign which reached the city gates, Igor, prince of Kiev, crossed the Black Sea towards the Bosporus and went on to butcher and burn his way through Bithynia. The Byzantine fleet was

in the Aegean at the time.

When the Byzantine forces had reassembled and driven the Russians away from the city and back out to sea, the Greek navy under Theophanes destroyed their ships with the aid of "Greek fire", an incendiary liquid which burns even on water and can be directed through long metal tubes.

Monks who go it alone

A monk carries out the methodical, painstaking task of manuscript copying.

France, 942

Odo, the abbot of Cluny, who has died at the age of 63, made Cluny one of the most influential monasteries in Europe during his fifteen years of office. Several French monasteries are now under the direct control of the abbey of Cluny, and even such renowned Italian monasteries as Monte Cassino have been deeply influenced by the practices at Cluny.

It is only 32 years since Cluny

was founded. Berno, a Benedictine monk, had started a monastery in the Jura which had become too small for the many monks whom he attracted to it. In 910 he persuaded William the Pious, the duke of Aquitaine and count of Macon, to give him a hunting lodge at Cluny.

On 11 September 910 he won a unique charter for his new abbey there. It was put under the direct authority of the pope, but he could only intervene in cases of "great disorder" amongst the Cluny monks. Otherwise Cluny was to be free of interference from both princes and pontiffs.

Berno established a monastic life devoted to prayer and religious services. The vow of silence encouraged meditation. External work and manual labour were more or less forbidden. Book production was restricted to religious works.

Berno's spiritual leadership caused him to be made abbot of several other monasteries. Odo went further. In 928 he got Pope John X to confirm the unusual charter, and in 931 he persuaded Pope Leo VII to allow him to bring the other monasteries under the direct control of Cluny. In the last decade he has expanded the network of satellite monasteries. The new abbot to be elected at Cluny inherits the world's biggest monastic order.

Cluny Abbey, a centre of learning.

Late night tales save life of a Queen

Moslem world, c.950

Unhappy with every new wife, a king kills each one on the first morning of their marriage. Only the clever Sheherezade keeps her head: every night she tells the king a new, enthralling tale. Thus runs the story behind the *Hazar Afsanah*, or the Thousand and One Nights, a new collection of Arab folk tales which is delighting the whole Moslem world.

Sheherezade's tales, with titles like *Ali Baba*, *Sinbad the Sailor* and *Aladdin*, draw on many cultures, including those of India, Persia, Mesopotamia, Syria and Egypt. The tales have no single author, although it has been suggested that Abu Abd Allah, author of the *Book of the Viziers*, is the main compiler.

A later view of Aladdin's genie.

Slim chance for anti-sacrifice king

A stone pillar in the Toltec capital.

Mexico, 950

Mixcoatl, the ruler of the Toltec empire, has been assassinated in his capital, Tula. Shocked by his death, his people have deified him as the god of hunting. The Toltec civilisation over which he ruled is worthy of the Teotihuacan civilisation which his ancestors overthrew 300 years ago, when Toltec nomads swarmed down from the northwest destroying all that was left of Teotihuacan, already weakened by discord and revolution. Founding a new city at Tula, they adopted Teotihuacan gods as their own, giving Quetzalcoatl, the Plumed Serpent, the chief place.

Far more militarist than the Teotihuacans, preferring statues of warriors to temples of gods, the Toltecs are unlikely to take kindly to their new ruler, Topiltzin, a philosopher prince, known for his disgust at human sacrifices.

Otto crushes German lords in battle

Germany, 939

The Saxon Otto, crowned German king at Aachen three years ago, has scored a resounding victory over Eberhard of Franconia and other rebellious dukes at the battle of Andernach. From the start Otto made clear his determination to rule all Germany, not just Saxony.

This approach upset Bavarians,

Franconians and even some Saxons; Otto's own brother Henry joined the unsuccessful rebellion. Years of anarchy, foreign invasion, and not least the rivalries of royal pretenders, have featured in the gradual break-up of the vast Frankish empire. Now in Germany a single ruler and a single dynasty seem to be asserting themselves.

India, c.950. The central Indian kingdom of Chandela reaches new heights of influence and prosperity.

England, 954. With the murder of Eric Bloodaxe, York is taken from the Vikings. King Eadred rules all of England.

Germany, 10 August 955. Otto unites his nobles against the Magyars and defeats them in battle at Lechfeld. They retreat to Hungary and abandon the raids which have caused havoc for 56 years.

East Africa, 957. The Kilwa sultanate is founded (on the southern Tanzanian coast) by Ali ben al-Husain ben Ali.

Constantinople, 959. The Emperor Constantine VII dies. His son Romanus II succeeds.

Poland, 960. Prince Mieszko defeats the Slav tribes between the rivers Oder and Vistula, and founds the Piast dynasty.

China, 960. Faced with an invasion from the north, the palace guards of the Later Zhou mutiny and place their commander, Zhao Kuangyin, on the throne. He founds the Northern Song dynasty, with its capital at Kaifeng.

Crete, 961. The Byzantines recover Crete from the Arabs, checking their naval power.

Rome, 2 February 962. After an appeal by Pope John XII for aid against Berengar, the king of Italy, Otto invades Italy again and this time is crowned emperor in St Peter's.

Central Asia, 962. Alptegin achieves independence from the Samanids and makes Ghazna his capital.

Rome, 963. Pope John XII is deposed on charges of murder, incest and perjury.

Constantinople, 963. With the death of Romanus II, the ageing General Nicephorus marches on the capital, seizes the throne and marries his ally the Empress Theophano, thus legitimising his rule.

Rome, 964. Otto starves Rome into surrender and reinstates his nominee, Leo VIII, as pope. He is soon succeeded by Otto's choice, John XIII.

Cyprus, 965. The Byzantine fleet takes Cyprus from the Arabs while the army recovers Cilicia.

Vietnam, 968. Dinh Bo Linh adopts the title of emperor of Dai Viet (northern Vietnam), which is now independent. He founds the Dinh dynasty.

Danish king becomes a Christian

Denmark, c.960

Harald Bluetooth, who succeeded his father, Gorm the Old, in 935 as king of Denmark, and has survived 25 long years of warfare, has forsaken the old gods of the north and become a Christian.

Some say he was converted as the result of an argument with a missionary, Bishop Poppo, during which Harald challenged Poppo to prove his faith by ordeal. The missionary agreed, and the next day he thrust his hand into a white-hot iron glove, when he withdrew his hand, the story goes, it was unharmed, and Harald, in a state of astonishment, conceded that Christ was the one true God and that He alone should be worshipped in Denmark.

Another version of the story, however, is that Harald, recently defeated in an expedition against the German emperor, Otto, has

A "runestone" of Harald Bluetooth.

Harald's baptism by Bishop Poppo.

been forced to become a Christian as part of the price of defeat. There is much grumbling among those who fear the revenge of the old gods, but Harald is eager to be on good terms with Otto while he expands his influence in the north. He remains the undisputed master of Denmark, and has spread his influence by supporting his widowed sister Gunnhild and her five sons in their fight for the Norwegian throne. He is also thought to have territorial designs on Sweden.

German king is new Western emperor

Rome, 2 February 962

Amidst widespread speculation as to his motives in taking the imperial title, the powerful German king, Otto, was crowned Roman emperor by Pope John XII in Rome today.

Some believe Otto is motivated by aggrandisement pure and simple; others see him as having made a shrewd assessment of the political situation in Europe. When he became king he was bent on gathering Saxons, Franconians, Bavarians and others into one German kingdom. He also had an eye on the conquest and subjugation of Slav lands in the east. And finally he sought to legitimise his claim to the lands of Lotharingia, the middle kingdom of the Frankish empire, comprising Italy, Burgundy and eastern Gaul, by being crowned in Rome by the pope, like previous Frankish rulers of that kingdom.

Otto took control of Italy in 951 when Adelaide of Burgundy was kidnapped by the Margrave of Ivrea, Berengar, who was out to become king of Italy. Adelaide appealed to Otto, who rescued her, married her and annexed part of the country. On his second visit, the pope appealed for help against trouble-makers in Rome. After his coronation Otto made it clear who

Otto's new imperial headgear.

was master; he announced that in future no papal election would be valid until an oath of allegiance to the emperor had been taken. His rule is proving very unpopular.

Death claims great Arab philosopher

Damascus, 950

The great Moslem philosopher al-Farabi has died at the age of around 80. A Turk by birth, he was educated at Baghdad and flourished at the court of Saif-al-Dawlah al-Hamdani at Aleppo. In his philosophy he integrates Islamic and Greek thought, mixing Platonism and Aristotelianism with Islamic Sufism. Apart from commentaries on Greek thinkers, al-Farabi wrote psychological, metaphysical and political works. Plato's *Republic* and Aristotle's *Politics* inspired him to imagine an ideal city organised like the human body; the heart is the sovereign, perfect morally and intellectually. Al-Farabi was also a physician, mathematician, occult scientist and musician.

Christianity becomes Polish state religion

Poland, 966

Miezsko, who has made Poland into a unified and powerful state, has now adopted Christianity and turned to Rome. Poland has become a diocese directly attached to the Holy See.

Miezsko's decision was prompted by fears of Otto's expanding German kingdom. But there was also the attraction of the superior level of civilisation associated with Christianity, such as its books and ceremonies and the links with a Roman past. His wife has taken the lead and has already been baptised.

Magyars routed by Otto

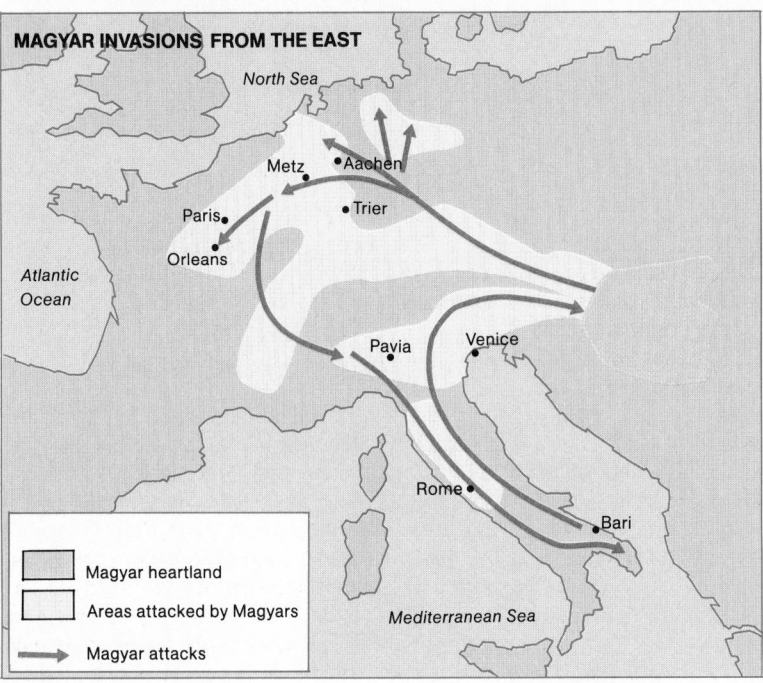

Germany, 955

The Magyar army, ravagers of Europe for over half a century, has been destroyed on a Bavarian battlefield by King Otto of Germany.

When the migrant Magyars conquered and settled in the Frankish region of Pannonia, east of the Alps, about 60 years ago, they used their new homeland as a base for raids that reached as far west as Orleans in France.

Germany bore the brunt of Magyar ferocity, despite a brief truce between the raiders and King Otto's father Henry "the Fowler". Otto came to the throne in 936, and managed to beat off renewed Magyar attacks. They switched their attention to France and northern Italy, where last year they carried out devastating raids. They returned briefly to their homeland, and prepared to assault Germany again. In August this year 50,000 Magyar troops besieged Augsburg-

A later image of Otto as Caesar.

in Bavaria, but its bishop held them off until Otto arrived – with only 10,000 troops. But, at nearby Lechfeld, Otto's mail-clad cavalry inflicted heavy losses on the lightly-protected Magyar army, which fled in disarray. Its survivors have limped back to their homeland. The Magyar menace is over.

Arabian poet killed by Baghdad bandits

Baghdad, 965

Al-Mutanabbi, one of the Arab world's greatest poets, has been murdered by bandits near Baghdad. He was returning from a visit to Shiraz, where he met the Buyid Emir Abdud al-Dawla. Born Abu al-Tayyin Ahmad ibn Husayn al-Gu'fi at al-Kufah 45 years ago, the poet was involved as a young man in a Carmathian rebellion in Syria. After being imprisoned for two years he abandoned his revolt on his release in 933, and for the rest of his life produced the verses for which he is celebrated.

Christian art adopts a Moslem style

A page from the Beatus Apocalypse, a Mozarabic illuminated manuscript.

Spain, c.951

Christian communities living in Spain under Moslem rule have adopted Arab culture, but kept their Christianity. In enclaves in such cities as Toledo and Cordoba they have their own churches, bishops and monks. They are known as *Mozarabic*, a word which comes from the name that the Arabs call them, *Musta'ribs*, meaning would-be Arabs.

One of the monks, Beatus of Liebana, wrote a commentary on the Book of Revelation in 786. This text has now been illustrated as the *Beatus Apocalypse* in manuscripts beautifully illuminated in Gerona and Valladolid, with glowingly painted pictures of saints and of the beasts of the Revelation.

Churches have been built in Mozarabic style, combining Moslem horseshoe arches and ribbed domes with Roman columns. Mozarabic chant is used for the Latin liturgy.

Page with Mozarabic decorations.

The Christians are moving out of Andalusia to Northern Spain, bringing with them remarkable techniques of Islamic decoration applied to Christian subject-matter.

East Africa and the Indian Ocean

From October to March each year, the Indian Ocean winds blow from the north-east, carrying sailing ships from India, the Gulf and the Red Sea to Africa's eastern coast. From April to June the southern monsoon winds push ships back to the north and east again. These steady, reliable winds carry boats past the long and generally inhospitable coast of Somalia, to the more fertile coast and better landing-places of Kenya and Tanzania. The clockwise summer equatorial current, far out in the Indian Ocean, helps vessels returning to India, and makes possible journeys as far as China.

In the second century, and perhaps earlier, these winds were used by traders from the Mediterranean world to visit East African ports – Opone in the north, and the island of Menouthias and port of Rhapta further south. They came in search of the ivory of East African elephants, which was, and still is, valued for the ease with which it can be worked and the size of the tusks.

We know of this trade, and of Menouthias and Rhapta, from two sailing manuals of the time, but no traces of these sites have ever been found. Menouthias may have been Zanzibar, and Rhapta has been said to lie on the north Kenyan coast, or further south in the Rufiji delta of Tanzania. However, the kingdom of Aksum was mentioned in the same accounts that tell of Rhapta, and its dramatic ruins still stand in Ethiopia. It was the rise of Aksum in around 500 that plunged the Indian Ocean coast of East Africa back into a period of obscurity, for the world described by the sixth-century Greek writer Cosmas Indicopleustes ended at Aksum.

Re-emergence under Islam

By the ninth century the rise of Islam had re-shaped the economy of the Red Sea and the Mediterranean, and the coast of East Africa reappears in the writings of Moslem geographers and traders. They tell of the development of a number of towns along the coast, to which came traders from Persia, Arabia and India in search of leopard-skins, tortoise-shell, timber and, most of all, ivory. These travellers' stories are often second or third-hand, yet give a clear overall impression of a growing number of towns involved in Indian Ocean trade.

The area south of modern Somalia was known as *Zanj* to these writers. To the south again, beyond *Zanj*, lay *Sofala*, the "low-lying land," and beyond this lay the mysterious and unreached land of *Waqwaq*. Details of the *Zanj* people are confused – some were fishers, some herders, some filed their teeth, and there was at least one *Zanj* king.

The travellers and traders were Moslems, but the *Zanj* were not. On the island of Qanbalu (possibly Pemba) there was, in the tenth century, a Moslem royal family and a pagan population, but it is unclear whether any of the Moslems were *Zanj*. However, over the following centuries, many of the towns of the coast became Islamic. A 13th century account mentions towns identifiable as Mombasa and Malindi, which were apparently pagan, yet the 14th century traveller Ibn Battuta, who visited the coast, found Moslem rulers and people in towns from Mogadishu in the north to Kilwa in the south.

The splendours of Kilwa

Kilwa, in modern Tanzania, impressed Ibn Battuta as one of the most beautiful towns in the world. Since the tenth century, there had been buildings of coral and cement in some of the towns of the Lamu archipelago, and by the 15th century there were dozens of Moslem settlements all along the East African coast. Houses and mosques built from coral blocks, and grandiose tombs with ornate inscriptions, stood alongside houses of mud and wood. The towns were all independent, some ruled by hereditary sultans, some by councils of older men. Coins of silver and bronze, inscribed in Arabic, were issued by the sultans of some of these towns. In the 13th and 14th centuries the sultans of Kilwa rose to prominence, building a palace which was perhaps the most splendid building on the coast at this time. Their rise was due to a trade more valuable even than that in ivory – the gold trade.

Mined in the area of modern Zimbabwe, this gold came to the coast around Sofala, considerably to the south of Kilwa. Yet Kilwa was the effective limit that could be reached by sailing vessels coming from the Gulf and wishing to return in a single season, and the rulers of Kilwa came to dominate this trade, a role which they may have taken over from the sultans of Mogadishu. The sultan of Kilwa taxed the trade, and grew rich. Later, the Portuguese heard that 3,000 pounds of gold came from Sofala each year, and in the 16th century they sought to monopolise this trade by conquering Kilwa.

However, although the intercontinental trade in gold and ivory made the coastal towns famous and their rulers wealthy, they owed their origins and continued existence to a vigorous local trade in less glamorous goods, traded up and down the coast. These included pottery, food and possibly cattle. The 16th century Portuguese raiders who seized ships in search of bullion and ivory found mostly grain. The reports of the gold trade had clearly been exaggerated, for the Portuguese never handled more than about 40 pounds of gold a year.

Origins of the coastal towns

Traditions which link the foundation of the coastal towns with the coming of settlers from the Gulf are common, and the coastal towns were, certainly, curiously isolated. Islam, firmly established in the towns, never spread inland. The coral buildings and Arabic inscriptions, the coins, imported ceramics and glassware found in the archaeological record of the coastal towns are absent even ten miles inland in Kenya and Tanzania. Only in the south, where the gold trade flourished, have imported goods been found any significant distance inland.

There are some ecological explanations for this: through most of modern Kenya, and into Tanzania, the relatively fertile coastal strip gives on to the *nyika*, a badly watered and inhospitable bushland that makes travel difficult between coast and hinterland. Items from the hinterland came to the towns via a chain of small local exchanges, not through long-distance trade or caravans to the interior.

There is also ample archaeological and linguistic evidence that, although there was settlement by immigrants from the Gulf, the coastal towns were in fact African in origin and in the bulk of their population. The cultural and religious influence of traders and settlers from overseas was considerable, but the language of these coastal towns was and is Swahili, part of the Bantu group of languages widespread in sub-Saharan Africa. Swahili seems to have developed as a separate language in the area of the northern Kenya coast. From there it spread to the south as far as modern Mozambique, as the language of a coastal maritime culture. Archaeologists have found evidence of the spread of this culture in the striking similarity in the locally-made pottery of ninth to 11th century settlements all along the coast from Shanga in the Lamu archipelago to Chibuene in Mozambique in the south.

Archaeological evidence has shown that Shanga grew from an African herding and fishing community in the eighth century into a large town by the 14th century whose Moslem population boasted three coral-built mosques. But there is a remarkable continuity of design between these remains and Swahili buildings of more recent times: this architecture is a distinctive product of the coast and not a style imported by an immigrant population.

A dhow, the vessel used by Arab and East African sailors for centuries, off Lamu, a key mediaeval trading centre (south of the equator in "Baru" on the map opposite).

Ruins of the great mosque of Kilwa (modern Tanzania), a monument to Arab influence. Most of the mosque was built in the 15th century, but parts go back to the 12th.

A tomb at the 16th-century trading post of Kunduchi (Tanzania). The embedded plates are of late Ming type from China, striking evidence of the extent of East African trade.

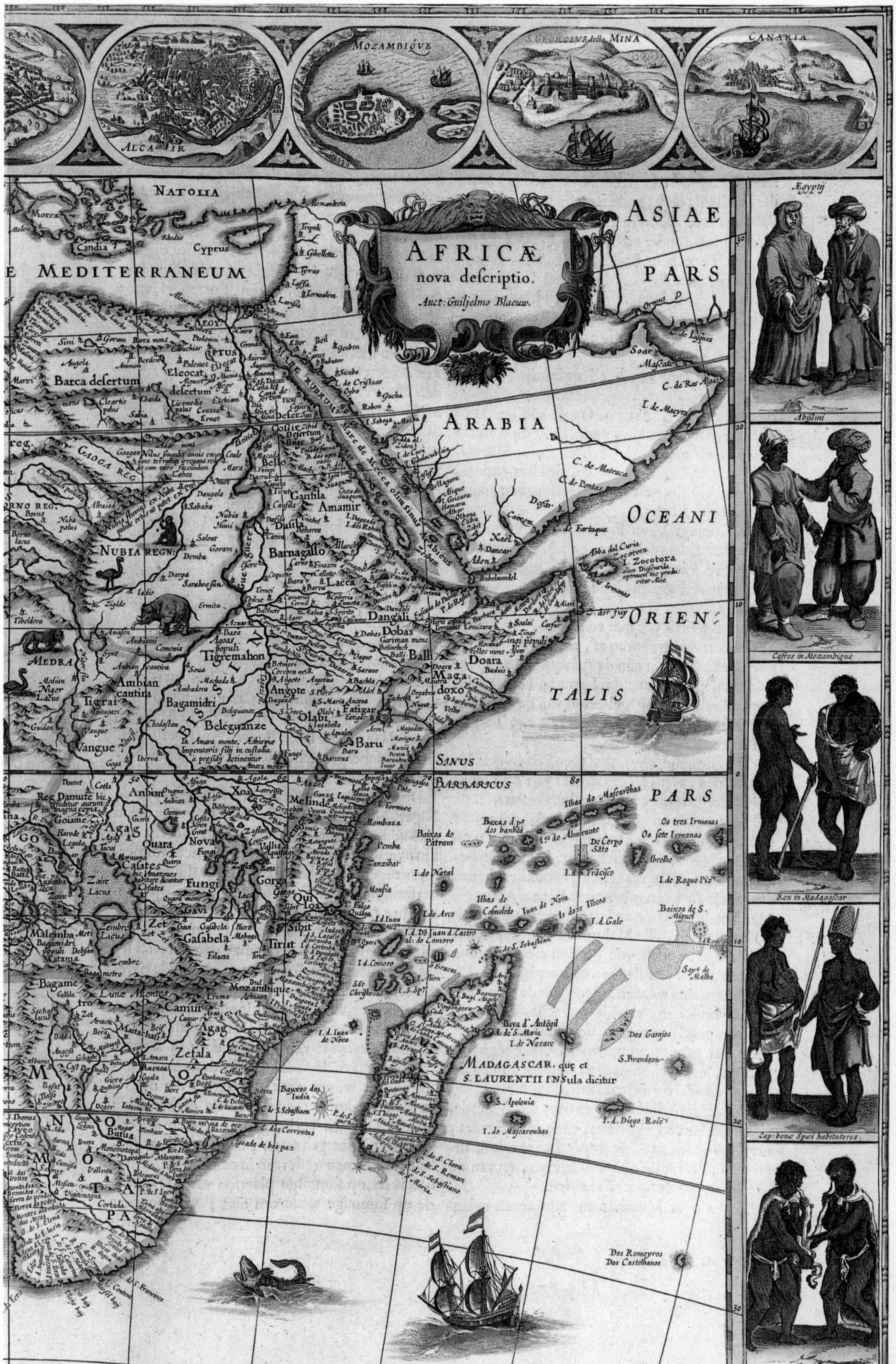

Part of a map of Africa published in 1650 by the Dutch mapmaker Willem Blaeuw. European interests in the continent built on existing trade relations in the region. Important older centres are Sofala ("Coffala", opposite southern Madagascar), Kilwa ("Quiloa") and Lamu ("Lamo", below the equator).

968 (968-990)

Ifriqiyah caliphs conquer Egypt and found a new city at Cairo

A plate with a picture of a Fatimid horseman, from near Kairouan, in Ifriqiyah.

The porch of the new university.

Egypt, 969

The Fatimids, Shi'ite Moslems from Ifriqiyah (*Tunisia*), have now conquered much of Egypt and set about making their capital of Cairo one of the most important cities in the Arab world. The able, well-led Fatimids are from a line of caliphs claiming descent from Fatima, the daughter of Mohammed, and they are building a palace and a mosque-university, *Al Azhar*, (the Splendid), which is seen as becoming the centre of Moslem learning in the world.

But one of the main reasons for building a solid stone-walled city is fear of trouble from the local Sunni, or orthodox, Moslem population which has owed its allegiance to the caliphs of Baghdad. These links have now been cut, but the Fatimids are prepared for riots.

Before work on the city was started an astrologer was consulted. Stakes were driven into the ground with ropes strung between them to which bells were attached. Work would start only when the bells rang. A crow landed on a rope, bells rang and work began on building Cairo. The astrologer's forecast of time and date was wrong.

Emperor is murdered by wife's lover

Two Byzantine warships. Nicephorus was famed as a naval commander.

Byzantium, 969

The Emperor Nicephorus has been brutally murdered in his palace by his wife's lover, his own right-hand man, the Armenian general John Zimiskes. His death brings to an end a brilliant reign which has seen the revival of the Byzantine empire through a series of victories against the Arabs. He smashed the Arab pirates and reconquered Crete, boasting "To me alone belongs the command of the sea". He recovered Cyprus for the empire and then attacked northern Syria. Earlier this year he brought the great city of Antioch back to the Christian fold. He was a man of many enemies, but he was killed as a result of a peculiarly squalid personal plot.

Arab pirates seize abbot in the Alps

The Alps, 972

Maiolus, the abbot of Cluny, has been captured with a large caravan in the Great St Bernard Pass in the Alps by Saracen (Arab) pirates. Local monks have already raised the ransom to secure his release, but that will not be an end to the affair. The monks of Cluny, whose influence extends through France and Italy, are putting pressure on the emperor Otto the Great to use his army to repel the pirates once and for all. For more than a century now the Saracens have dominated the western Mediterranean, as they have captured much of Spain and Italy. Ports on the south coast of Frankia have been dominated by them. Not content with piracy at sea, from their base at Fraxinetum, they have also extended their activities inland, terrorising travellers as far north as the Alpine passes.

Religious revival under King Edgar

Chester, England, 973

After his coronation at Bath on Whit Sunday, 11 May, the Anglo-Saxon King Edgar sailed with his fleet to Chester, where eight British kings came and swore fealty to him. To demonstrate their submission they rowed him on the river Dee from his palace to the church of St John, while he held the rudder.

Edgar actually became king 14 years ago on the death of his brother, Eadwig; some believe the coronation was delayed by divisions caused by Eadwig's behaviour on *his* coronation in 957. He left the solemn feast to be with a married woman and her daughter (whom he later married). The monk Dunstan reproached him, a furious row took place, and Dunstan was banished.

After this episode Eadwig lost the allegiance of Mercians and Northumbrians, who followed Edgar. But Eadwig soon died and at once the kingdom was reunited. With the kingdom at peace after the death of the last great Viking, Eric Bloodaxe of York, Edgar was able to throw all his energies into foster-

Eight Celtic kings row King Edgar.

ing a revival of monasticism led by Dunstan, whom he has recalled and made archbishop of Canterbury.

With the aid of other bishops, like Oswald of Worcester and Aethelwold of Winchester, Dunstan has set about sacking lax secular priests and installing monks who adhere strictly to the rule of St Benedict. The results are beginning to show in a revival of culture, learning and art, and in the development of new monasteries.

French choose new king and new dynasty

Rheims, 3 July 987

Hugh Capet, the most powerful of the French lords, was crowned king of France here today, bringing a new dynasty to power. Louis V is dead; with him the last vestige of Carolingian power has faded – though Duke Charles of Lower Lotharingia (Lorraine) is threatening to dispute the coronation, claiming right of descent.

From Paris, Hugh sought the support of wealthy landowning bishops in his quest for kingship. Despite his recent triumph, it is unlikely that he will be able to create any real unity in France, which is divided into numerous effectively independent principalities.

A later image of Hugh Capet.

Deposed prince turns captivity into verse

China, 978

Li Yu, the last emperor of the southern Tang, has died in captivity three years after his deposition by the Songs. He will be remembered not as a failed emperor, but as the master of the *ci* (lyric) style of poetry. Originally the poetry of the teahouse, it was often trivial, but Li Yu in his captivity turned it into a medium of self-expression in which he examined the downfall of his dynasty in poems filled with sorrow and nostalgia.

Russian prince converts

Kiev, Russia, 989

Vladimir, the prince of Kiev, the first Christian ruler of Russia, has married the sister of the Byzantine emperor, Basil II, in Kherson, which he has returned to the emperor. He has thus obtained his reward for helping the emperor to defeat a military rebellion. But, for the marriage to take place, he has had to agree to accept Christianity and impose it on his people.

When Vladimir arrived back in Kiev with his princess he ordered that the idols should be overturned, cut to pieces or burnt. The great idol Perun was tied to a horse's tail and dragged to the river. Twelve men were appointed to beat the wooden idol with sticks to chastise the demon which had deceived its worshippers. It was then cast into the river Dnieper.

The next day Vladimir proclaimed that all the citizens of Kiev

Icon of the Virgin. Georgia, c.950.

should assemble on the river bank, whence he then led them into the water. In an act of mass baptism some went in up to their necks, with children in their arms.

Chinese make advance in art of printing

China, 985

The master printers of Chengdu in Szechwan have at last finished their great work, the printing from wood blocks of the entire Buddhist scriptures, the *Tripitaka*. It has taken them 12 years to complete, and the result is a beautiful example of the advances made in printing in China.

The completed work has been transported by ox-cart to Kai-feng and formally presented to the Emperor Taizong. A special Court for Printing the Scriptures is being built to house the 130,000 blocks needed to print the 60-foot-long scrolls.

While this is the most splendid of the great printing projects, many others are at present under way. Dictionaries, encyclopaedias and literary anthologies are all being printed from the finely crafted wood blocks typical of the Song dynasty.

Making an impression: the frontispiece of the world's first printed book.

West Africa, 990. The kingdom of Ghana (*Mali and Mauritania*), under Soninke rulers, conquers Awdaghost, the trading gateway to Saharan salt and gold trade routes.

England, 991. Olaf the Norseman overcomes an heroic defence at Maldon and advances deep into England, now ruled by Aethelred (the Unready). He is likely to be bought off.

Indonesia, 992. The Sumatran Sailendras attack the rival kingdom of Mataram in Java and kill the Mataram king.

Poland, 992. Boleslav succeeds Mieszko as ruler of Poland.

Korea, 993. The Khitans annex Korea to their Mongol empire.

England, 994. The Norseman Olaf and the Dane Sweyn fail to take London, but ravage throughout southern England and are paid a massive tribute. The attacks continue.

India, 994. The city of Delhi is founded by the Tomaras.

Ethiopia, 996. Copts flee from Moslem Egypt to Ethiopia.

Greece, 997. Samuel, the Bulgarian czar, raids Byzantine possessions in Greece, but is defeated and severely wounded. The struggle for supremacy in the Balkans between Samuel and Basil II goes on.

Afghanistan, 998. Mahmud ascends the throne of the Turkish Ghaznavid people and starts new conquests.

Syria, 999. Basil II drives back an Arab counter-offensive against Aleppo and Antioch.

Eastern Europe, 999. Boleslav, ruler of Poland, exploits Bohemian anarchy to attack Silesia, Moravia and Krakow.

Central Asia, 1000. The Seljuk Turks occupy Transoxiana, east of the Oxus river.

North America, c.1000. The Southern Cult develops in the southern Mississippi area. Characterised by Mexican influence, it is concentrated at sites such as Grand Village and Emerald. Artefacts in carved shell, pottery and metalwork display a marked fascination with death.

North America, c.1000. Iroquois peoples in north-eastern North America form village communities and cultivate maize and beans.

Ethiopia, 1000. Ethiopia is almost overrun by pagan tribesmen from the south.

Vikings sail west across the Atlantic

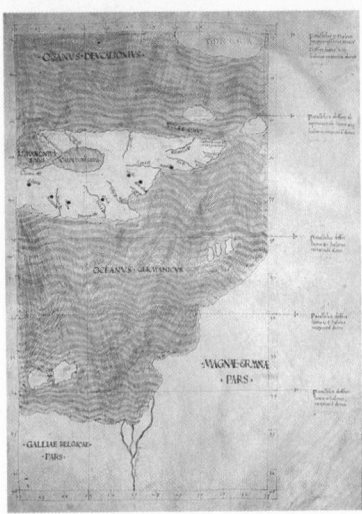

Map of "Thule", possibly Iceland.

The inscriptions on this rock in "Vinland" were made by Viking visitors.

Norway, c.1000

Tales are spreading that land-hungry Vikings have found a "lush land" after sailing far west across the Atlantic. Until now no-one has explored so far, or returned to tell the tale. The latest expedition has told of a native people with whom it traded goods and milk – from cows it took with it – for furs and skins. The Viking leader, Thorvald, was killed by an arrow in a fight with the natives.

It is almost 20 years ago since Erik the Red used his period of banishment for murder to seek out new land to the north-west. He discovered a good farming country since colonised by 3,000 Vikings and known as "Greenland".

Soon afterwards, in 986, Bjarni Herjolfsson, sailing from Iceland in search of Greenland, was blown too far south and saw a country "well forested with low hills". Some years later Erik's son, Leif, bought Bjarni's ship in Greenland, sailed west and discovered what he called Vinland – "land of wine" – where he stayed through the winter. His brother, Thorvald, repeated the journey in the following year, intending to set up a colony.

Thorvald's crew also spent the winter in Vinland before returning with news of his death. Further expeditions seem sure to follow.

Philosopher prince founds new dynasty in Mexico

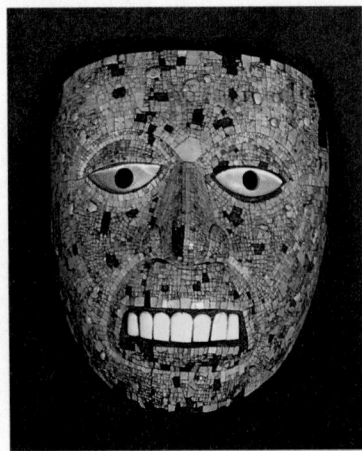

A Maya mosaic mask with shell teeth.

The astronomical observatory in the wealthy Maya city of Chichen Itza.

Mexico, 999

Topiltzin, the philosopher prince who was driven into exile in 987 by the Toltecs for his opposition to human sacrifices, and crossed the Gulf of Mexico to the Yucatan peninsula, has founded a new kingdom at Chichen Itza. The native Maya people call him *Kukalkan*, which means Plumed Serpent.

Synthesising imported Toltec culture and the local Maya culture (which had been in decline for over a century), a new civilisation is growing up. Already the capital Chichen Itza, with its vast pyramid crowned by a temple, rivals Tula in grandiose opulence

Young emperor in Rome

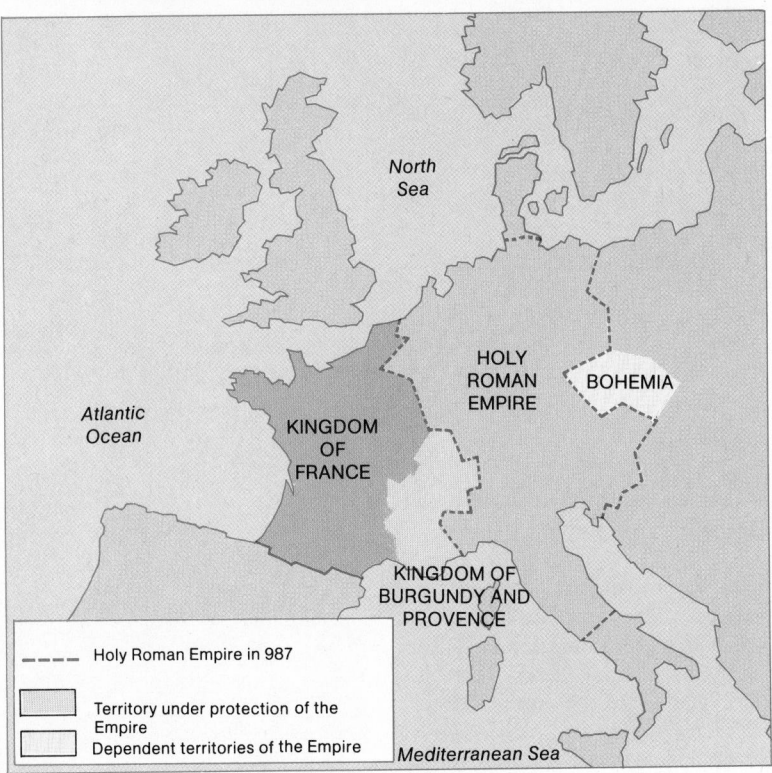

North Sea

Atlantic Ocean

KINGDOM OF FRANCE

HOLY ROMAN EMPIRE

BOHEMIA

KINGDOM OF BURGUNDY AND PROVENCE

Mediterranean Sea

- - - - Holy Roman Empire in 987

Territory under protection of the Empire

Dependent territories of the Empire

Rome, 21 May 996

A 16-year-old boy, who dreams of making Rome once again the capital of a universal empire, was today crowned Roman Emperor. Otto III is a child of East and West: his mother Theophano is the daughter of a Byzantine emperor, and his father was Otto II, the son of the first, great, Otto, the German king who sought to restore the empire of Charlemagne.

Otto III, schooled by bishops, has been described as "the wonder of the world". He was only three when his father died, and his succession was disputed by the duke of Bavaria, deservedly known as Henry the Troublemaker, who kidnapped the infant. He reckoned without two formidable women: Otto's mother Theophano and his grandmother Adelaide, the widow of Otto the Great. They forced Henry to return the child, and ruled as regents with the support of clerics.

Otto has been unlucky with his popes. John XV died before he could crown him. Otto then installed as Gregory V his cousin Bruno, who was driven from Rome by a clique of disgruntled patricians. Gregory was reinstated, but died a year later. Otto then installed his former tutor, Gerbert, the archbishop of Ravenna, as Sylvester II, a name chosen to evoke the grandeur of ancient Rome; the first Sylvester baptised Constantine the Great. Otto's visions, nevertheless, seem unrealistic. His empire lacks the sinews of the old: the educated ruling class, the bureaucracy, the communications. Like his father and grandfather before him, Otto faces a struggle to impose unity on strong provincial barons hostile to notions of a world empire which would diminish their local power.

The new emperor, Otto III.

Gold "grows like carrots" in rich Ghana

Western Africa, 990

The Berber town of Awdaghost has been captured by the king of Ghana. He is now the most powerful ruler in non-Islamic Africa, and his kingdom spans the area roughly between the upper reaches of the rivers Niger and Senegal, protected to the north by the Sahara.

Ghana dates back to the late pre-Christian era and owes its prosperity to its gold mines. Nomadic Berbers and Arab traders brought Ghana's gold to the Mediterranean, and Ghana was the first African state mentioned by Arab writers. Its wealth became so fabled that al-Hamadhani, who died in about 903, claimed that "gold grows in the sand like carrots". The capital, also called Ghana, consists of two towns: one for Moslem traders, and the other the seat of the fetish-worshipping king. He has a palace which consists of a castle and round huts surrounded by a wall.

Devout Stephen is new Magyar ruler

Hungary, 997

The Christianised Magyar Duke Geza – whose conversion might have been political expediency – has been succeeded by his truly devout son Vaik, also known as Istvan, or Stephen.

Baptised at the age of ten, in a ceremony which he shared with his father, Stephen is now aged 22. Two years ago he married Gisela, the sister of the duke of Bavaria.

The first task of Hungary's new ruler, great-great grandson of the legendary Magyar leader Arpad, is to consolidate his rule over the many powerful – and pagan – semi-independent Magyar chiefs.

Classic tale of Genji

An illustration of "The tale of Genji".

Japan, c.1000

Murasaki Shikibu, a noblewoman who is a tutor at the imperial court, has written a novel called *The Tale of Genji* which tells the story of the love affairs of a Prince Genji and of his son Kaoru. Genji is an emperor's son who is not in the line of succession to the throne, and is therefore able to follow a political career while still enjoying royal privileges. The author has used her own position at court to provide a fascinating picture of court society. It is already considered a classic of Japanese literature.

Pacific colonised

Pacific Ocean, c.1000

Polynesians have arrived in New Zealand, the last stage of what has been the greatest migration and navigational feat in history. Their ancestors began to disperse from the eastern islands of south-east Asia in about 1500BC, in the wake of a population explosion caused by the growth of rice cultivation. Probably sailing in open canoes, they had reached Hawaii and Easter Island by AD400. Polynesians are now the most widely-spread race on earth.

A Polynesian statue on Easter Island.

Hungary, 25 December 1000. Duke Stephen, in power since 997, is crowned Hungary's first king with regalia sent by Pope Sylvester II.

Balkans, 1001. Basil II, the Byzantine emperor, reembarks upon the conquest of Bulgaria.

Italy, 23 January 1002. The Emperor Otto III dies at Paterno.

Spain, 1002. Mohammed ibn Abu Amir, popularly known as al-Mansur, the chief minister of Caliph Hisham II and effective ruler of the Umayyad caliphate of Cordoba, dies at Medinaceli. He is succeeded by his son Abd al-Malik.

Rome, 12 May 1003. Sylvester II (Gerbert of Aurillac), the first French pope, is dead. Elected in 999, with the backing of Otto III, he encouraged the Holy Roman emperor's ambition to recreate the empire in the West and authorised the title of king for Duke Stephen of Hungary.

Italy, 1004. After the coronation of Henry II as emperor on 14 May, at Pavia, a quarrel develops between the Germans who are accompanying him and the Pavese. This grows into a full-scale battle in which much of the city is burnt and hundreds of citizens are slaughtered.

China, 1006. Granaries for emergency famine relief are set up throughout the country.

Persia, 1008. Al-Hamadhani (Ahmad ibn al-Husayn), the writer who acquired the nickname "the Wonder of the Age", dies at Harat. He invented the literary form known as the *maqamah* – a short anecdote written in rhyming prose, inspired by the Koran.

India, 1008. The armies of the Turkic Ghaznavid people sweep through India from their base in Afghanistan under their ruler Mahmud, defeating the armies of a Hindu confederacy on the plain of Peshawar.

Jerusalem, 1009. The Fatimid Caliph al-Hakim destroys the church of the Holy Sepulchre, apparently in a fit of madness, prompting calls for a Christian crusade to recover the Holy Land.

Ireland, 1014. The Vikings are defeated at the battle of Clontarf by the Irish army of King Brian Boru, who is killed in the battle.

Arts flower in brief reign of Otto III

Rome, 23 Jan 1002
Otto III, the Saxon emperor who has died of malaria while preparing to retake his capital, Rome, was only 22. He dreamed of recreating the empires of Constantine and Charlemagne. He settled in Rome, restored its palaces, and struck seals proclaiming *Renovatio Imperii Romani*.

Despite his youth, the half-Saxon, half-Byzantine Otto was a strong and able leader who inherited from his grandfather, Otto the Great, the capacity to form wide political conceptions, in particular the re-creation of the Roman empire incorporating Germany and the Slav countries under his kingship.

The political restoration of the empire led to a revival of arts and letters. Classical texts have been translated into High German and the deeds of the Ottonian dynasty chronicled as the *Res Gestae Saxonicae*. Huge basilicas have been built and decorated by artists from the great monasteries. But the people of

Ottonian illustrative art: St Luke.

Rome revolted at Otto's interference with papal matters. Otto was besieged in his palace and forced to leave for Paterno, where he died. He is to be buried beside Charlemagne, his hero, whose body he had had disinterred so that he could pray before it. Otto was a romantic emperor.

Doors in Hildesheim Cathedral.

East and West mate in slow chess moves

Chess. Arabs say "Shah mata!" (the king is dead!) on winning.

Madrid, c.1010
East and west may be divided by religious differences, but at least one cultural activity has crossed the great divide between Christianity and Islam more than once. It is a board game which some call *Ya, Shah* (Oh king!: a challenge) and others *chess*. The game might have its origins in ancient Greece, but it has returned to the west in several

slow moves from India, where it was known as *shatrandj*, by way of Persia. Two centuries ago Caliph Harun alRashid presented a chessboard to Charlemagne. More recently an Arab scholar, al-Biruni, rediscovered the game in India, much elaborated, with 64 squares. Pieces include an elephant and camels as well as a magic bird called *rukh*.

China gets worst of border peace with northern neighbour

China, 1004
The Song emperor, Zhenzong, has concluded a peace treaty, which is regarded as humiliating by many court officials, with the northern Liao empire of the Khitan nomads.

The emperor had led his army to force the Khitan to abandon land which they had seized in the province of Hopeh. But, well aware of the Khitans' martial prowess, he decided he would rather negotiate than fight. The Khitan Dowager Empress Xiao, an able regent for her young son, was of like mind and, after several skirmishes for honour's sake, envoys were exchanged, and a treaty of "sworn letters" has been agreed which returns Hopeh to the Song and establishes the basis of a lasting peace. But it also stipulates that the Song must pay the Khitans 100,000 ounces of silver and 200,000 bolts of silk every year – a "tribute" which offends many Song officials.

Danes invade England

London, December 1013
Danish forces under King Sweyn are claiming control of the whole of England following the surrender of London. The deposed king of England, Aethelred, is reported to have fled to France to join Queen Emma and their children, who have taken refuge with her brother, the duke of Normandy.

Most of the population, who surrendered rather than resisted, fear that, unlike previous invaders, the Danes will not be prepared to be bought off with bribes. Instead it is thought that King Sweyn plans to consolidate his hold on England as an act of revenge against Aethelred.

The enmity between the two goes back to 1002 when Aethelred, his rule weakened by frequent Viking attacks, ordered the secret St Brice's Day massacre of Danes living in England. Among those murdered was Sweyn's sister, Gunnhild.

A Danish-style tombstone.

Sweyn retaliated by burning homesteads throughout the south for four years before accepting a substantial bribe to withdraw.

The uneasy truce was broken last year when Aethelred persuaded one of Sweyn's top commanders, Thorkell the Tall, to defect. This led to the invasion, with Sweyn landing men on Humberside before marching south.

Irish beat back Viking invaders

Dublin, 1014
Brian Boru, the high king of Ireland and leader of the Dal Cais dynasty, was killed in a vicious all-day battle at Clontarf on Good Friday between two Irish factions, one of them with Viking support. Boru's victorious Munster army has seriously weakened the Norsemen's grip on Ireland. This was the second such victory for Boru. Fifteen years ago, his army defeated the Norsemen occupying Dublin together with Mael Morda, the king of Leinster.

Morda recently formed an alliance with Sitric, the Norse ruler of Dublin. Sitric summoned Sigurd of Orkney, Brodir of Man, and even Thorstein Hallsson of Iceland.

Boru died when Morda broke through his bodyguard and stabbed him. Morda was later tortured to death by the King's furious army.

Kingdom prospers in South India

A statue of Siva seated, from Chola.

Southern India, 1010
Under King Rajaraja of Chola, who extended the Chola domains to all southern India, the Chola empire has become the most powerful and prosperous in India. A Brihadisvara temple 200 feet high has been completed in the capital Thanjavur, a symbol of Chola grandeur.

On Rajaraja's accession in 985, Chola power was in retreat after the initial expansion by Aditya a century earlier. He first turned south, defeating a revived Pandya power and invading Sri Lanka; then east, against the Gangas; finally north, reducing the powerful Vengi state to a mere protectorate. His land conquests complete, he has built a fleet that dominates the Indian Ocean, making Chola rich from Chinese and Near Eastern trade.

On death of caliph Cordoba is jewel in Arab Spain's crown

Cordoba, 1002
Mohammed ibn Abu Amir, known as *al-Mansur* (the Victorious), the dictator of Moslem Spain for the last quarter-century, is dead. Under his rule Spain has reached unprecedented importance, but experts fear that in the power vacuum that now threatens Cordoba, since al-Mansur has left no specific successor, this importance may simply collapse into political in-fighting.

Al-Mansur gained power in 978 when, as chamberlain to the ten-year-old Caliph Hisham II, and backed by the caliph's Basque mother Aurora, he became the effective ruler of the country.

Although al-Mansur ruled as a dictator, he did not abuse his power, but instead worked to increase the influence of his country. Talented and efficient, he expanded Cordoba's power: in the north he took Leon and Compostela away from their Christian rulers, while in the south he expanded the power of Andalucia into western Maghreb.

Al-Mansur's success has not merely been as a conqueror. Cordoba has become a booming city of some 500,000 inhabitants, the largest in western Europe. Its craftsmen are renowed for their work,

Detail from the front of a Hispano-Arab ivory casket made at Cordoba.

producing exquisite goods and specialising in textiles, leather and ivory. Streets are clean and safe, and there are many mosques and public baths.

Spain's reputation for learning has also benefited. Hakam II, the father of the young caliph, who died in 978, left an important intellectual legacy. An enthusiastic bib-

liophile, he collected some 400,000 volumes, a library that covers every aspect of Islamic scholarship, from theology to science. The library is a centre for many scholars, although local Moslem fundamentalists fear that, so wideranging is the collection, many of its works may be heretical. They would purge the library if they could.

A Cholan three-headed brahma.

Russia, 1015. Vladimir, the prince of Kiev, dies. He was converted to Christianity in 988 when he married Anne, the sister of the Eastern Emperor Basil II, thus opening Russia to Byzantine influences.

India, 1015. The Ghaznavid army invades Kashmir, but is forced to retreat.

Britain, 30 November 1016. Edmund Ironside, who succeeded Aethelred as king of England earlier in the year, dies, leaving Canute as unchallenged ruler of England.

Bulgaria, 1018. The Eastern Emperor Basil II completes the conquest of Bulgaria.

India, 1018. Mahmud, leader of the Ghaznavids, sacks Kanauj and breaks the power of the Hindu states.

Sri Lanka, 1018. Rajendra Chola conquers Sri Lanka.

Europe, 1019. England and Scandinavia are unified under the rule of Canute.

France, 1019. Saracens attack the Mediterranean port of Narbonne.

Afghanistan, 1019. Mahmud founds the great mosque at Ghazni, capital of the Ghaznavid domains. His armies now occupy most of northern India.

India, 1021. The Cholas invade Bengal.

Central Asia, 1023. Mahmud and the Ghaznavids turn north and occupy Transoxiana.

North Africa, 1023. Soon after returning from a pilgrimage to Mecca, the Tarsina king of Zanata, a mountain nation on the borders of Morocco and Algeria, dies in battle.

Italy, 1024. Emperor Henry II dies on 13 July; a revolt then breaks out in Lombardy.

India, 1024. The Ghaznavids sack the great Hindu religious centre of Somnath, carrying away vast treasure after slaughtering over 50,000.

Constantinople, 15 December 1025. Basil II is succeeded as emperor by Constantine VIII, his brother and co-ruler.

Persia, 1025. Ferdowski, the author of the *Shahnameh* (Book of Kings), dies at Khurasan. His book charts the history of Persia from its mythical origins up to the Arab conquest.

Syria, 1027. Salih ibn Mirdas, the governor of Aleppo, besieges the city of Marras.

The Emperor Henry, whose majesty is well caught by this later portrait.

Henry crowned as Holy Roman emperor

Rome, 14 February 1014

Yet another German king has travelled to Rome to have himself crowned Holy Roman emperor. With his wife Cunigunde, the daughter of the count of Luxembourg, Henry II was today met on the steps of St Peter's by Pope Benedict VIII, who asked him if he would be a faithful defender of the Church. Henry and his wife were then admitted into the church and anointed. The pope placed in Henry's hand a golden orb surmounted by a cross, symbolic of his rule over the world's empire.

Behind this solemn ceremonial lies the reality of a ruler who faces an endless struggle to contain rebellions and feuds by powerful nobles. Henry, the son of that duke of Bavaria known as the Troublemaker, is pious, well-meaning and in poor health. He was destined for the Church when Otto III died without children. The Bavarians and the Franks called on Henry, who by concessions and favours won the dubious allegiance of Saxons, Thuringians, Swabians and Lotharingians.

Henry came to the throne faced by wars on every frontier. Italy had been lost, Boleslav of Poland was seizing lands in the east, and the count of Flanders was moving on Lotharingia. Henry has responded by seeking the support of the Church. Lavish in his grants of land and titles to bishops and abbots, he seeks to make them servants of the crown.

Turks find a new aggressive leader

Afghanistan, 1024

Mahmud of Ghazni, who defeated his elder brother to seize the throne of Afghanistan, is expanding his empire into Persia and India, raiding from his mountain fastness down into the rich agricultural plain of the Punjab. His conquests are religious as well as territorial, for he is a zealous Moslem and on his forays into India he destroys Hindu temples, carrying off their treasures and forcing their monks to convert to Islam.

His latest campaign in India has taken him to the shores of the Indian Ocean, and to the famous temple of Siva at Somnath in Gujarat where he horrified the Hindus by destroying the temple and carrying away its celebrated golden gates.

Mahmud is also, however, a patron of literature and art. This son of a Turkish slave become king has built a magnificent mosque, the Celestial Bride, at Ghazni, and splendid palaces at Bust and Ghazni, and at his court live the greatest scholars of the age.

Caliph disappears, feared murdered

Cairo, 14 February 1021

Searchers for the missing Fatimid Caliph al-Hakim of Egypt have lost hope of finding their irascible leader alive. Clothes last worn by al-Hakim have been found slashed by a dagger on the Mukattam hills outside the city and it seems almost certain he was murdered, apparently while on a nocturnal walk.

The caliph's sister, Sitt al-Mulk, may have decided to kill her brother to put to an end what many saw as his capricious and cruel rule. He made decrees at whim to ban chess or keep markets open all night, but gained real notoriety for carrying out sudden and brutal executions, and outraged Christians by ordering the demolition of their holiest shrine, the church of the Holy Sepulchre in Jerusalem.

Not everyone has given up hope for Al-Hakim. The Syrian Druze sect believe he is a divine monarch who has simply gone into hiding and is sure to return.

Prisoners blinded as Bulgars are crushed

Bulgaria, 6 October 1014
A sightless army returned from battle today – 15,000 men blinded on the orders of a Byzantine emperor. As the pathetic regiments made their way home, their ruler, Czar Samuel, was so shocked that he died, apparently of apoplexy.

Even the worst excesses of the most evil Caesar could not match the calculated cruelty which took place on the banks of the river Strymon after Basil's forces had surrounded and defeated the Bulgarians. One man in every 100 was left with one eye to guide his pathetic comrades on their long march home to Samuel.

To celebrate his victory and its horrific aftermath, Basil, who is described as a "humane and benevolent" man, has been given the title of *Bulgaroctonus* – slayer of the Bulgars.

For the past 13 years Basil has sought to vanquish Samuel's Bulgarian empire. Once he had secured his eastern borders, the tough and resourceful emperor drew up plans for the attack and led his well-

Bulgarians cower before Basil.

trained armies personally in a series of summer campaigns. His skill was in his ability to divide enemy forces and surround them with fast-moving infantry and cavalry.

At the beginning of the war Basil used a soft approach to the Bulgarian chiefs, offering them honours and titles. Believing that they had betrayed him, he began a campaign of unprecedented terror in which massacre became the norm.

King Canute unites England, Denmark

England, 1019
Canute is now king of England and Denmark. Three years ago the Danish prince, the son of Swein, was offered the English throne after defeating Edmund Ironside. Now the death of Harald of Denmark has enabled him to unite the two countries. It is the high point of a reign which has been distinguished by skilful statecraft and utter ruthlessness.

Since 995, England under Aethelred had been unstable, liable to frequent Viking incursions. Aethelred ordered every Dane in the country to be killed. At the time of Aethelred's death, in 1016, there were fluctuating alliances between Saxons and Danes, many of whom had intermarried. While Canute's army ravaged the south, Edmund controlled most of the north of England; the treacherous Eadric supported first one, then the other.

Canute defeated Edmund at Ashingdon in Essex, and the two agreed to divide the country. Edmund was murdered soon afterwards, and Canute eliminated

Dual monarch: King Canute.

potential rivals, including Eadric. In 1017 he married Aethelred's widow, Emma of Normandy. Since then he has espoused Christianity, established equal rights for Danes and Englishmen, and, confident of his position, sent most of his army back to Denmark.

Indian temple highlights erotic joys – and varieties – of love

The main tower of the temple.

One of the friezes which viewers at ground level are less likely to see.

Central India, c.1020
The stupendous Kandariya Mahadeva Hindu temple at the Chandela capital of Khajuraho is complete. Surpassing the smaller temples built by the Chandela dynasty over the last 100 years, it is the Chandelas' great masterpiece. Built in fine cream-coloured sandstone, its

phallic spire rises for 116 feet, though it appears even higher because of the deep basement and the vertical lines on the spire. It is surrounded by lesser spires.

Inside the temple is a *pradaksina*, or walkway, provided with shaded balconies. Outside are the friezes and sculptures. At the lower levels

scenes from hunting, warfare and courtly life are depicted. The higher friezes are reserved for representations of gods and goddesses, along with scenes of lovemaking, depicting couples and trios indulging in all the erotic variety which the vivid imagination of the gods has ordained.

Poland becomes independent state

Poland, 1025
Boleslav the Brave is dead, only a few months after being crowned king of Poland. Having received the pope's blessing a year earlier, he had established Poland as a sovereign state independent of the Holy Roman empire. He is succeeded by his son, Mieszko II. When Boleslav became Poland's ruler 33 years ago, he continued the alliance with the empire.

In 1000 the Emperor Otto III came to Gniezno to visit the grave of St Wojciech. But Otto's successor, Henry II, backed by German nobles, and ever anxious to recreate the Frankish kingdom, went to war with Poland.

In successive campaigns against the empire lasting for 14 years (1004-18), Boleslav held his own, occupying parts of Moravia and Bohemia, Lusatia and Milsko. These gains were consolidated in the Peace of Bautzen in 1018. The death of Henry II last year finally allowed full recognition of Poland.

Canute's empire grows

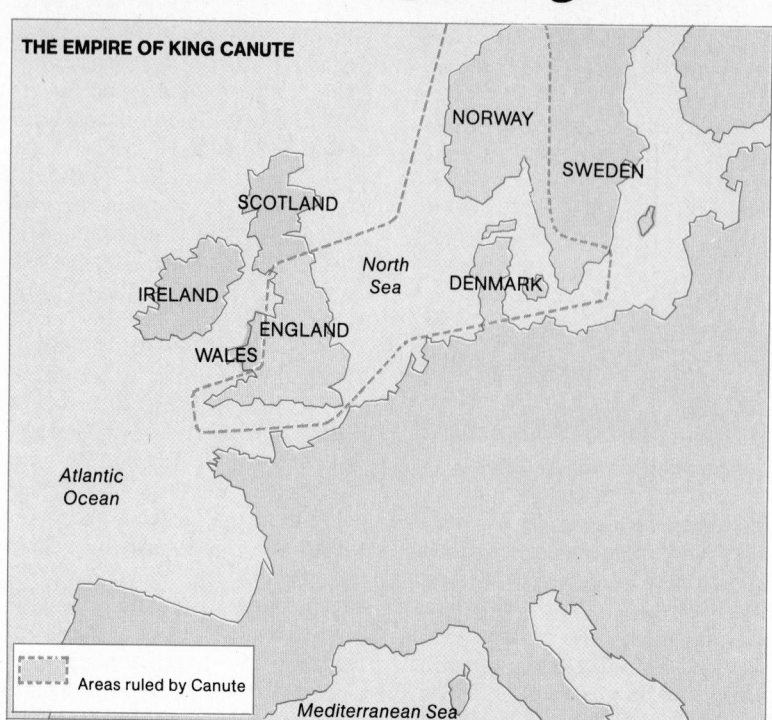

THE EMPIRE OF KING CANUTE

NORWAY

SWEDEN

SCOTLAND

IRELAND

North Sea

DENMARK

ENGLAND

WALES

Atlantic Ocean

Areas ruled by Canute

Mediterranean Sea

Great master of medicine has died

A later portrait of Avicenna: the Persians revered his vast learning.

Persia, 18 June 1037
Ibn Sina or, as Europeans call him, Avicenna, "the great master", has died at Hamadan and is mourned throughout the Islamic world.

His knowledge in every field of learning was encyclopaedic. He was particularly revered as the greatest modern medical mind through his treatises on the pulse, fevers, symptoms and diagnosis, wounds, fractures, bites, poisons and diarrhoea, among the many conditions listed in his *Canon of Medicine*.

Ibn Sina was also famed as a philosopher, influenced by the Greeks. He believed that human knowledge could be unlimited. He also believed that the saint and the sage could both attain perfect clarity equal to that of the Prophet.

He was born in Alshana, near Bokhara, and spoke Persian. He taught himself medicine. By 16 he had mastered all known science. He wrote his works at night very rapidly, while by day he served several princes as minister. He was often envied and forced to flee and hide, giving medical consultations to earn his living. He spent most of his last years at Isfahan.

Norway, 1030
Olaf, the former king of Norway, has died at the battle of Stiklestad, his ramshackle forces hopelessly outnumbered by a Norwegian army loyal to Canute. Canute is now master of England, Denmark, Norway and possibly Sweden.

Olaf, who took to the sea aged 12, and fought in Denmark, Sweden, Gotland, Finland, England and France, where he was baptised, returned to Norway to claim the throne 15 years ago.

Within a year Olaf was king of Norway. Although a ruthless warrior, he was an enlightened king, and a firm believer in the law. He not only introduced Christianity to Norway; he created a state church. He fought the Swedes, then married their king's daughter.

But joining the Swedish King Onund in an attack on Denmark was a mistake. Rapidly gaining control of the seas, Canute sub-

A later view of Olaf's death.

orned many of the Norwegian nobles, and landed unopposed in 1028 to claim the throne. When Hakon, made governor of Norway by Canute, died this year, Olaf made his final, ill-fated attempt to reclaim the throne.

Arab philosopher who wrote handbook on India is dead

Ghazni, Afganistan, 1048
Abu Raiham Mohammed al-Biruni, the author of treatises on astronomy, geography, history, chemistry, philosophy and mathematics, is dead. In the roll-call of Islamic thinkers, he is amongst the very first. Al-Biruni was born in 973 in Khwarizm, and became fluent in Arabic and Greek. His brilliance was recognised by Mahmud, the sultan of the Ghaznavids, who devoted his life's energies to expanding his Afghan empire to the Indus. As Mahmud's armies advanced, so al-Biruni followed, learning Sanskrit and studying Indian philosophy for his great work, *Tarikh-ul-Hind*, the acclaimed handbook on India that has become his memorial.

Holy fist-fight greets German ruler

Conrad: the hawkish Emperor.

Rome, Easter 1027
Amid imperial pomp and religious fist-fighting, Conrad, the king of Germany, was crowned emperor here in the presence of two crowned heads, Rudolf of Burgundy and Canute of England. Queen Gisela has been made empress of Rome. Two archbishops (of Milan and Ravenna), who had vied for the honour of leading the king to the altar, exchanged harsh words and even punches outside St Peter's cathedral.

Conrad began his march on Italy a year ago – ostensibly to claim his rightful crown of Lombardy. He came up against stiff opposition from the inhabitants of Pavia, who closed the city gates to his army' and later from Ravenna, where his men hacked down people running to safety. Conrad ordered survivors to parade before him in hair shirts, barefoot, with unsheathed swords hung around their necks, and beg for forgiveness. Much the same ordeal befell the people of Rome today after a riot which followed a dispute between a German and a Roman over the price of a hide.

Pagan is heart of new Burmese empire

A Buddhist temple at Pagan, showing Khmer and Hindu influences.

Burma, 1050
The strictly disciplinarian regime of the new king, Anawrahta, is bringing stability and power to Burma. From its capital, Pagan, the king is extending his empire from as far as the Mons kingdom of Thaton to the Indian Ocean.

Anawrahta has made good economic use of the crossing at Pagan of trade routes to Yunnan, Assam and the Shan States. He is advancing farming techniques, and is in process of strengthening his army by appointing four tough generals. His revolutionary use of elephants adds even greater power to his army.

Conversion to Theravada Buddhism inspired Anawrahta to begin building the Shwezigon pagoda. Worship of many gods was tolerated inside the pagoda. The king said: "Men will not come for the sake of the new faith. Let them come for their old gods and gradually they will be won over."

"World will end" fears grip Christians

Christ: a new earthquake in store?

Burgundy, France, 1033
Panic is spreading through the kingdom this summer. Many people here believe that this year, the thousandth anniversary of the death of Christ, will mark the end of the world. Their belief was nurtured by the famine arising from the torrential thunderstorms which flattened crops in much of France in the spring. Huge crowds are now making public displays of repentance, swearing to keep the peace of God. Thousands more have gone on pilgrimages to the Holy Land.

Similar fears were prevalent 33 years ago on the anniversary of

Tongues of flame – or hellfire?

Christ's birth. That year passed without mishap, but the destruction of the Holy Sepulchre in Jerusalem in 1009, by Caliph Hakim, produced a new nervousness.

Radulph Glaber, a Burgundian who now lives in the abbey of Cluny, expressed the feelings of his countrymen when he wrote about the earlier panic which hit the kingdom in the spring: "Men thought that the very laws of nature and the order of the seasons were reversed, that those rules which governed the world were replaced by chaos. They knew then that the end of the world had arrived."

African hilltop town rises on gold trade

Southern Africa, c.1050.
The Indian Ocean trade network is bringing riches to the people of the Limpopo river basin in south-east Africa. The most prosperous area is known as Mapungubwe, and trades both with merchants from the coast, and, indirectly, with lands on the other side of the Indian Ocean.

The area has been well-populated for several hundreds of years by farmers of cattle and caprines (goat-like sheep). But they are increasingly reaping the benefits of trade, exporting both rough and finely wrought ivory ware in exchange for large quantities of glass beads, ceramics from the Persian Gulf and other exotic commodities. The people thrive and the towns grow.

A Jewish school: Jewish teaching is now centred on North Africa, Spain and the Rhine. Only one school remains in Babylon, the former centre.

Norman pact with pope

Italy, August 1059
The Normans have achieved a vital agreement with their old enemy, the pope. One of their number, Robert Guiscard, has brought off a brilliant diplomatic coup by agreeing the terms of the Treaty of Melfi with Pope Nicholas II. Robert defeated the papal army six years ago at Civitate, but he has chosen the statesmanlike route of a peaceful alliance with the papacy.

In the treaty Robert promises to be faithful to the Catholic Church and to the pope. In return the pope recognises him as duke of Apulia and Calabria, which he has already conquered, and duke of Sicily, which is today occupied by the Saracens.

Pope Nicholas has been under pressure, thanks to continuing quarrels with Byzantium in the east and the military threat from the Arabs in much of the Mediterranean. He is only too thankful to have one less enemy. For Robert it means he can now push on to drive the Saracens from Sicily without the fear that the papal armies will attack his rear.

Roger Guiscard lands in Sicily.

The Normans are descendants of Viking mercenaries – like Robert's father, Tancred of Hauteville – who began to leave Scandinavia some 50 years ago to plunder in France and Italy. A few, like Robert, and William, the duke of Normandy, have now settled down and set up stable governments.

English king exiles his close adviser

Bosham, England, 1051
Under a royal safe-conduct, Godwin, the earl of Wessex, the second most powerful man in England, boarded his ship here – exiled by the king whose accession he had arranged. King Edward had for years been heavily influenced by the ruthless and wealthy earl. The king married Godwin's daughter, Eadgyth, though the marriage has remained childless, and watched helplessly as the earl and his family extended their estates and power in the west.

This power began to wane when Godwin's elder son, Swein, outraged religious feeling by seducing the abbess of Leominster and murdering his cousin.

Then, last year, Godwin went too far. The monks of Christ Church elected a Godwin kinsman as archbishop of Canterbury. The king refused to accept him and appointed a Norman, Robert. This, in turn, infuriated Godwin, who was bitterly opposed to the promotion of Normans in the church. Godwin

Edward: a later impression.

and his sons mounted an army and prepared to fight near Hereford. The king rallied other earls to his side. Surprised by this royal firmness, outnumbered, and condemned by the church, Godwin chose to flee.

Chivalry is the code for jousting knights

Europe, c.1065
Improvements in cavalry techniques have led to a major increase in the social status and prestige of mounted warriors. Behind the shift lies the introduction to Europe of the stirrup, from the Orient, in the early 700s; this gave horsemen far greater control, and greatly enhanced the importance of cavalry.

However, it is only recently that full advantage has been taken of the stirrup. It is now possible to deal an enemy a fierce blow with a heavier spear or lance couched under one armpit without falling out of the saddle. But buying all the relevant equipment for this technique, especially protective armour, is a costly business; only wealthy men can really afford to equip themselves or others as knights and hold the tournaments and jousts – essentially training sessions – which have become great social and courtly occasions. Horsemanship – or, as the Normans call it, *chivalrie* – is now a prestigious occupation, and new codes of behaviour are reinforcing the common bonds of the increasingly aristocratic knights.

A Japanese painted wooden statue of the Bodhisattva Jizo – who administers to those in need – dressed as a mendicant.

East-West Church split is threatened

Constantinople, 16 July 1054
Cardinal Humbert, the papal legate, today marched into the cathedral of Saint Sophia here and placed on the altar a bull of excommunication against Michael Cerularius, the patriarch of Constantinople. Local observers see this move as the final gesture of a desperate man who realises that his mission has failed.

Humbert was sent by the pope to try to bring the Eastern Church to heel. Since he became pope, in 1048, Leo XI has aspired to take firm overall control of the Christian Church throughout the world. His ambition takes little account of the prestige and independent behaviour of the Byzantine Church. It also shows little awareness of the deep distrust in the East of the papal alliance with the German emperor.

Patriarch Michael enjoys the support of his people, and the most likely outcome of today's move is the final split between the Eastern and Western arms of the Church. Their differences have been unresolved for some 400 years. Rome believes in the twofold nature of Christ which the East rejects. Rome insists on celibate priests, while the East has continued to allow its clergy to marry. The union of the Churches has depended on both sides turning a blind eye to the reality of the respective practices of East and West.

West: Venetian mosaics of Noah.

East: Christ at Constantinople.

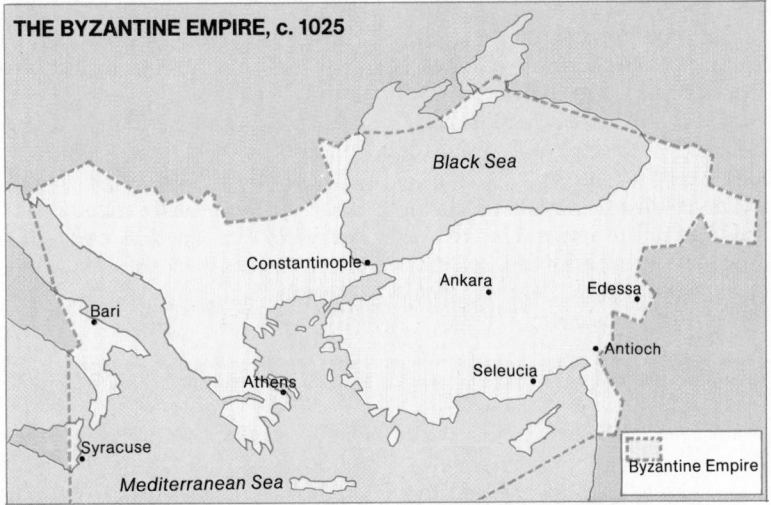
THE BYZANTINE EMPIRE, c. 1025
Black Sea
Constantinople • Ankara • Edessa • Antioch
Bari • Seleucia • Athens • Syracuse
Mediterranean Sea
Byzantine Empire

While Christendom is torn between popes, patriarchs and emperors, Islam flourishes. This bowl of sandy earthenware is from Nishapur, in Persia.

Blind hermit poet wrote dark verse

El-Marra, Syria, 1056
After half a century of living in ascetic seclusion, the poet Abu L'Ala al-Ma'arri has died aged 77. Blinded by smallpox at the age of four, the poet refused to compromise his nihilism for money.

Human life and nature were to al-Ma'arri the vanities of the world. He wrote cynically: "Better for Adam and all who issued forth from his loins that he and they never had been created!" The intensely dark, 13,000-verse *Luzumiyyat*, written to glorify God, was al-Ma'arri's antidote to the conventional poets' preoccupation with love, battle and frivolity.

Anarchy spreads through Tunisia

Tunisia, 1057
The decision of the defeated Tunisian ruler al-Mu'izz to retreat into an enclave at al-Mahdiya has left the country in disarray, with large areas controlled by the Banu Hilal. These southern Arabian tribesmen have steadily reduced Tunisia to a state of anarchy since they arrived seven years ago aided by the Cairo caliph, al-Mustanisir.

For al-Mu'izz it represents defeat for his policy of trying to integrate the Banu Hilal. When the tribesmen arrived he gave three daughters to their leaders, but this failed to stop them wiping out his army.

Victories of Spanish King putting the Arabs on the run

Iberia, 1055
Great progress has been made by Ferdinand in his campaign to regain Moslem territories in Spain for the Christians. After a six-month siege the king, who is 40, has just captured Coimbra, which means that he has enough territory under his control in Portugal and the south to exchange his title of "king" for that of "emperor".

Ferdinand's campaign of reconquest got under way when he imposed his authority over the old Leonise empire, ruling Galicia, Leon, Castile and the Rioja. He has not set out to conquer the territories merely by force of arms, preferring to get his way by extracting tribute from them in return for protection. Coimbra, however, resisted his overtures, and it took battering-rams to bring it to its knees. The conduct of the siege could have important consequences for the future. It suggests that if the citizens of a Moslem city surrendered immediately they would be allowed to stay and carry on as normal. If they surrendered during the siege they could depart with their lives and what they could take away with them. But if they went on fighting their city would be stormed and they themselves killed or enslaved.

Ferdinand is also demonstrating that he is not trying to force the Moslems to change their religion. Instead, he is showing himself to be a reconquerer wishing to spread the political power of a Christian community rather than belief in the religion.

A later portrait of King Ferdinand, who is bringing Spain's Moslems under his control.

England, 14 October 1066. William of Normandy defeats King Harold at Hastings and becomes king of England.

China, 1067. The poet Wang An-shih campaigns to stem widespread corruption in the administration and the army.

Asia Minor (Anatolia), 1067. The Seljuk Turks take Caesarea in Cappadocia.

England, 1070. The Danish fleet sent against England in 1069 is bribed to depart. This leads to the collapse of the opposition to King William in the fens led by Hereward the Wake.

France, 1071. The death last year of Baldwin VI, the count of Flanders, opens a succession dispute. Baldwin's widow, Richilda, ruling on behalf of his son, is opposed by Robert the Frisian, the son of Baldwin V. Robert defeats Richilda at Cassel and is recognised as count by King Philip.

Italy, 16 April 1071. The Norman Robert Guiscard takes Bari after a three-year siege. Byzantine rule in southern Italy is thus brought to an end after five centuries.

Asia Minor, 1071. The Seljuks defeat the Byzantines under Romanus IV Diogenes at Manzikert. Taken prisoner, Romanus is replaced as emperor by his stepson Michael VII. He is freed and returns home aiming to regain power from Michael, but dies in the ensuing struggle.

Sicily, 10 January 1072. Robert Guiscard and his brother Roger take Palermo.

Spain, 1072. Alfonso VI becomes king of Leon and Castile after the assassination of his brother Sancho. On the death of their father, Ferdinand, in 1065, Alfonso received Leon but lost it to Sancho (who received Castile) shortly afterwards.

Italy, 1073. Robert Guiscard takes Amalfi from Gisulf II of Salerno, securing Norman control of the maritime trade routes, but alienating the pope.

Rome, March 1075. Pope Gregory VII declares that the bishop of Rome is absolute sovereign over the Church.

West Africa, 1077. The nomadic Almoravids seize the kingdom of Ghana.

Italy, 1077. The Emperor Henry IV, excommunicated by Gregory VII, submits to the pope at Canossa.

Byzantines fight Turks, who use stirrups and can shoot with great accuracy.

Turks take Byzantine emperor captive

Eastern Turkey, 26 August 1071
Asia Minor is at the mercy of the Turks after the defeat today of the army of the Byzantine Emperor Romanus IV at Manzikert, north of Lake Van. The emperor himself has been captured.

This conclusive battle was the result of years of tension between the Armenian and Greek-speaking people of Asia Minor and Turkish nomads infiltrating from the east with their flocks.

The enormous distances involved made it almost impossible for the Byzantine government to take effective punitive action against these nomadic bands, and gradually the indigenous population was being forced westward.

Earlier this year, the new emperor resolved to drive the Turks out, and raised a large army for the purpose. The Turks appealed for help to the Seljuk Sultan Alp Arslan, who came in person, with his army.

Meanwhile, the Byzantine army appears to have been crucially weakened by internal squabbles and treachery. The Dukas family and their followers, political opponents of Romanus IV, deserted him just before the battle.

Pope bids to curb the power of princes

Rome, April 1075
Pope Gregory VII is making a strong bid to establish the primacy of the papacy and its authority over kings and princes as well as archbishops. *Dictatus Papae* (Sayings of the Pope) contains 27 short and pithy sentences which leave no doubt at all where the ultimate authority lies.

The assertions include: "That he [the pope] alone may use the imperial insignia."; "That he may depose emperors, that he himself may be judged by no one."; "That the pope may absolve subjects of unjust men from their fealty."

Although he has only been pope for two years, Gregory has been a powerful voice in papal reforms for more than 30 years. He was born in Tuscany, as Hildebrand, and became a monk, spending time at Cluny. In 1046 he went into exile with Pope Gregory VI, and every pope since then has followed his advice. Gregory sees the papacy

A later view of the formidable pope.

primarily as a governmental institution which must be backed by laws. He has renewed the drive against non-celibate priests and against the sale of church offices. His reforms are likely to renew the smouldering conflict between the papacy and the German emperor.

New emperor halts Fujiwara clan rule

Japan, 1068
The hold of the Fujiwara clan over government and imperial throne has been broken with the crowning of Emperor Sanjo II, who is not the son of a Fujiwara mother. The clan have maintained indirect control in Japan for over a century.

As recently as 1062 the Fujiwara appeared to have strengthened their power with a major victory by the Minamoto, a military clan known as the "claws and teeth of the Fujiwara". In a battle which marked the end of nine years of fighting, the Minamoto defeated the rebellious Abe family by destroying their last fortress on the banks of the Kuriyagawa river in the northern province of Mutsu. They were acting on imperial orders.

The Abe resistance was fierce, and the defence was overcome only when the Minamoto general, Yoshiiye, the son of the clan's leader, Yoriyoshi, diverted the water supply and set fire to the stockade.

The Minamoto emerged battlehardened and politically powerful. But this has not lasted as long as they might have hoped.

Barefoot king bows to papal command

Italy, 28 January 1077
King Henry IV of Germany has finally bowed to the authority of the pope. For the last three days he has stood barefoot in the snow, a penitent in sackcloth, at the gate of the castle of Canossa in the Alps. Pope Gregory VII finally chose to pardon him and withdraw the excommunication order imposed on him last year. That was when the struggle between the two men broke out in earnest; Henry then persuaded German bishops to renounce their obedience to the pope at a council in Worms.

Gregory responded by releasing his German subjects from their allegiance to their King. His action served as an excuse for a rebellion by many of the German nobility who were already unhappy about the increase in the king's power since the defeat of the Saxons. They forced Henry to submit to the pope.

New emperor faces foes on all sides

A model of a Byzantine vessel.

Constantinople, 1081

The Eastern Empire has a new emperor: Alexius Comnenus. He comes to the throne beset on all sides by dangers and difficulties.

The Seljuks Turks are established in the Taurus; the Serbs are causing trouble on the Danube and Bulgaria is threatened by the Patzinak nomads. But most serious is the ambition of the Norman Robert Guiscard to invade the empire itself. The Emperor will have to use all his talents as a soldier and diplomat if he is to preserve the empire.

Nomads smash Ghana's empire, and reach Spain

Ghana, 1077

Thousands of Saharan nomads have swept through Ghana, destroying the richest empire in West Africa. The Almoravid conquests began 20 years ago when Abdullah ibn Yasim, preaching holy war and spiritual renewal, united the tribes of the western Sahara and advanced into Morocco with 30,000 zealots.

While one Almoravid army crossed the Straits of Gibraltar into Spain, a second crossed the Sahara into Ghana, occupying its gold-mines, making the Almoravids richer than the degenerate sultans they vowed to overthrow, and creating an empire stretching from the Niger to the Ebro in Spain.

William conquers English at Hastings

Hastings, 14 October 1066

Duke William II of Normandy, commanding a mixed force of around 7,000 French, Breton and mercenary soldiers, crushed the army of his rival for the English throne and erstwhile lieutenant, King Harold, on windswept Sussex downland yesterday. The Normans claim that William is the rightful heir to the English throne and that Harold had conceded this.

The battle was a struggle between two opposed styles, mobile French Norman archers against stoical, close-packed ranks of English infantry armed with lances and axes. Yet for much of the day it seemed that the English had the upper hand. They approached through a wood near the top of Sandlake Hill, eight miles inland, dismounted and formed up in tight formation on the high ground. William's troops attacked with archers in front followed by armour-clad infantry. They rolled uphill in human waves which broke time and again. William, on horseback, stayed close and so kept control. He was a conspicuous target and had three horses killed under him. As the French front ranks at last panicked and fled, their own knights cut them down. William dismounted, removed his helmet in order to be recognised and, spear in hand, ordered them back into battle.

Many of the English, observing – so they thought – the beginning of a rout, and freed at last from their role as bowmen's targets, ran forward in hot pursuit, only to be hit on both flanks by French cavalry. It was probably the decisive moment of this battle. The French, turning near-disaster to advantage, now used the ploy to encourage the English to break ranks. In the confusion the English leaders were exposed as ready targets. Harold's two brothers were killed in a hail of arrows and spears. Harold himself, despite having lost one eye, fought on magnificently. His body, when recovered, was virtually unidentifiable.

Towards evening, the French continued to squeeze the core of Harold's army until only a few dozen remained standing. These survivors, who knew that all was lost, retreated in good order to

The Bayeux Tapestry (in fact embroidered) tells of the fall of the Anglo-Saxon kingdom. Here, William's ship sails for Pevensey, where the French landed.

The English held off the French on high ground at Sandlake Hill for much of the battle, but in the end the Norman attack proved too relentless.

Harold, his two brothers already slain, is struck in the eye by an arrow; the wound was probably fatal, but he fought on with great bravery before dying.

make a last stand on ground which gave them the best chance to sell their lives dearly. This was a steep valley cut by ditches and unsuitable for cavalry. William, his lance broken, led a party of men from Boulogne into the enemy redoubt.

The battle provokes many questions about recent events in Eng-land. Why did Edward the Confessor, on his deathbed, disinherit his cousin, the duke, and nominate Harold? Why did Harold, after marching to York to defeat the Norwegian King Hardrada at Stamford Bridge only three weeks ago, rush tired troops to Hastings and not wait for reinforcements?

1082 (1082-1087)

Trouble-shooting ruler goes to war

Japan, 1083

Yoshiiye, the warrior leader of the Minamoto clan, who won his spurs in the earlier Nine Years War against the rebellious Abe clan 20 years ago, has set out at the head of another expedition to put down trouble in the north.

This time his opponents are the Kiyowara family who were his allies in the war against the Abes. The emperor rewarded the Kiyowaras for their loyalty, but over the years they have fallen from grace by misruling the province of Matsu.

However, the emperor decided to move against them not so much because of their misrule, but because continuous dynastic squabbles within the clan led to open warfare between its different branches.

So Yoshiiye has been made governor of Matsu with orders to bring peace to the northern provinces. He has taken up his post backed by the prestige and military power of his warrior clan, but so far he has no commission from the court to go to war against the Kiyowaras.

His first efforts, therefore, have been to bring about a truce between the quarrelling factions, and he has had some success in calming the leaders of the factions. But the hotheads among the Kiyowaras are always drawing their swords, and it seems inevitable that Yoshiiye will have to intervene militarily.

Exile completes epic history of China

Silk scroll depicting spring festival celebrations in Tsu-ma Kuang's time.

China, 1083

The revered statesman-scholar Sima Guand has at last finished his epic history of China. It is called the *Comprehensive Mirror for Aid in Government*, and it has taken him 17 years to fulfil his commission from the Emperor Ying Zong to make a "record of events, of rulers and ministers in successive ages".

Sima Guand was helped by several dedicated assistants whom he urged to consult every type of source for, he argued, official records and histories "are not necessarily to be relied upon and anecdotes are not necessarily without foundation. Make your choice by your own scrutiny".

Ironically, he was able to complete his great work because of a political defeat. A conservative, he was sent into exile when the reformer Wang Anshi came to power, but was allowed to take his library with him. The result of his enforced political idleness and his questing methods is a superb chronicle.

Domesday Book gives William a record of conquered England

England, 1086

Every horse, cow, pig and hen in England is being counted in a massive audit of the nation's wealth being carried out by King William's officials.

The survey, on an unprecedented scale, is expected to take two years to complete and will constitute a comprehensive census of all landholdings and livestock in the kingdom.

The results of the Great Survey, as it is being called in court circles, are being compiled into two volumes, popularly titled the Domesday Book. With information arranged geographically, by shire, hundred and village, the Domesday Book will provide the king with a

quick and reliable reference system for levying military taxation. To avoid fraud the king's officials plan to make at least two inspection trips to each shire, using a standard questionnaire to establish the exact state of England's wealth.

Despite his successful conquest of England at the Battle of Hastings 20 years ago, King William believes that he has not yet consolidated his hold on the country or harmonised its feudal system with that of his native Normandy.

The Great Survey will allow him to do both. The terms of the survey overhaul land tenure, with all land in England now deemed to be held directly by the king or by his subjects on his behalf.

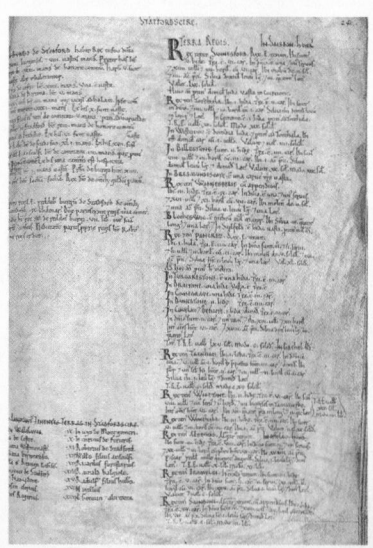

Domesday Book: Staffordshire.

New art favours fabulous monsters

Europe, c.1060-1100

A new style of architecture – Romanesque – now dominates Europe. As the name indicates, it is derived from the round Roman arch, which it repeats in series to divide church naves and abbey cloisters into bays. Half-columns are built against flat wall surfaces, with capitals which are no longer in classical Roman styles.

Very large abbey churches have been built in this style at Rheims and at the great Benedictine abbey at Cluny, which is the largest in Christendom, although the cathedral built at Speyer by the German King Henry IV is the highest, with its nave reaching 107 feet.

Normandy has raised the masterpiece of St Etienne at Caen. The church of Our Lady, crowning the rock of Mont St Michel, is a place of pilgrimage. So is the cathedral of Santiago de Compostela in Spain.

Three great Romanesque cathedrals are being built in England – Winchester, Norwich and Durham. At Durham clusters of columns up the nave alternate with massive piers decorated with carved zig-zag chevrons.

Carved capitals are appearing on church columns and around the arches of Norman churches in England. They take the form of demons, dragons and fabulous monsters, such as centaurs, symbolising drunken lechery, or the basilisk, a mixture of cock and serpent. The crypt at Canterbury is carved with goats and she-devils.

A sanctuary knocker, fashioned as a monstrous head, on the north door of Durham cathedral, a masterpiece of Romanesque architecture.

"The Mouth of Hell", a detail from the grotesque carving of the Last Judgement in the recently built Romanesque abbey at Conques in France.

Monreale, in Sicily, where Norman rule has put its mark on architecture.

Romanesque painting: St Matthew.

Rome raped after pope's cry for help

Rome, 1084

A pall of smoke covers Rome and thousands of bodies lie putrefying in the streets after three days in which much of the world's greatest city has been devastated by the Norman army of Robert Guiscard. Pope Gregory is the most hated man in Rome, for it was he who invited the Normans into Rome to protect him against the armies of the Emperor Henry IV – only to see his city destroyed and burnt by the so-called protectors.

Guiscard, the son of a minor Norman landowner, was the scourge of Calabria and had driven the Byzantines out of much of southern Italy before emerging as the most powerful Norman in the country. When Henry had himself crowned emperor he deposed the pope and installed an anti-pope, Clement. Gregory called on Robert for help. Realising that he was outnumbered, Henry left Rome, followed by a terrified Clement. Despite a massive uprising by the Roman citizens, there was no stopping the fury of the Normans.

Christian king wins Moslem Toledo

Spain, 1085

King Alfonso VI of Leon and Castile, the most powerful of Spain's Christian monarchs, has wrested Toledo from its Moslem rulers.

Alfonso inherited Leon in 1065, and fought his brother Sancho for Castile until Sancho's murder in 1072. Alfonso then turned southwards to Toledo, one of the many *taifas* (Moslem petty-states) which followed the break up of the caliphate of Cordoba about 50 years ago. Christian rulers in the north demanded tribute from the taifas, and five years ago, complaining that its tribute was paid in debased coin, Alfonso set out to conquer Toledo.

Alfonso has promised tolerant rule to Toledo's Moslem and Mozarabic (Arabicised Christian) populations. But he has also demanded increased tribute from the taifas, and many are considering an appeal for aid to the Almoravids, the new Berber rulers of North Africa.

France/England, 1087. On his death, William the Conqueror is succeeded in Normandy by Robert Curthose and in England by William Rufus.

Malta, 1091. Roger of Sicily, brother of Robert Guiscard, takes control of the island.

France, 1091. William Rufus invades Normandy and gains a foothold in the duchy.

Near East, 1092. The Islamic sect known as the Assassins murder the Seljuk vizier, Nizam al-Mulk.

Rome, 1094. The anti-pope Clement III is deposed. Urban II is installed in Rome.

Venice, 1094. The basilica of St Mark is consecrated.

France, 27 November 1095. Pope Urban II calls for a crusade to free the Holy Places.

Italy, 1096. The world's first university is founded at Salerno.

West Africa, 1097. Umme, the first king of Kanem-Bornu (in Nigeria and Niger), who was converted to Islam, dies.

Portugal, 1097. Alfonso VI of Leon gives his son-in-law Henry of Chalon the land between the Minho and Tagus rivers to hold as an hereditary county, known as Portugal.

Near East, 30 June 1097. The Crusaders defeat the Turks at Dorylaeum, opening the way to Asia Minor (Anatolia).

France, 1098. The Cistercian order is founded at Citeaux.

Near East, 1098. The Fatimids recover Jerusalem from the Turks. The Byzantines retake Smyrna, Ephesus and Sardis. The Crusaders take Antioch.

Jerusalem, 15 July 1099. The city falls to the Crusaders.

Near East, 12 August 1099. At Ascalon, the Crusaders defeat al-Afdal, the Fatimid vizier of Egypt, who was bringing an army to relieve Jerusalem.

Italy, 1100. Genoa, Venice and Pisa, whose fleets have helped the Crusaders to capture ports south of Beirut, are rewarded with trading privileges.

Jerusalem, 18 July 1100. On the death of his brother Godfrey of Bouillon, Baldwin becomes king of Jerusalem.

England, 2 August 1100. William Rufus is killed in a hunting accident in the New Forest. He is succeeded by his brother Henry.

"El Cid" triumphs in siege of Valencia

Valencia, Spain, 17 June 1094

The great Arab city of Valencia is in Christian hands today, defeated by starvation after a 20-month siege. The new ruler of the city is a man whom, ironically enough, the Arabs themselves dubbed *el Cid Campeador* (Lord Champion).

El Cid was born Don Rodrigo Diaz de Bivar about 54 years ago, the offspring of a noble Castilian family. He entered the service of King Alfonso VI of Castile and Leon. In 1081 Alfonso banished him for unauthorised raiding and, while nominally still in Alfonso's service, Don Rodrigo in effect became an independent travelling knight, serving both Moslem and Christian masters. He earned the title el Cid (from the Arabic *sayyid*, or *sid*, lord) in the service of the Moslem rulers of Saragossa.

El Cid saw the chance to conquer the Moslem city of Valencia in 1092 when its ruler, al-Kadir, was under threat from the Berber Murabits (Almoravids) from North Africa, who had already conquered much of Moslem Spain. In October 1092 al-Kadir was killed by rebel Valencians with Almoravid backing; but before the Almoravids could seize the city it was besieged by el Cid. Magnanimous in victory, el Cid has promised freedom of worship for his Moslem subjects.

Pope seeks "crusade"

Urban II presides over the Council of Clermont to launch the First Crusade.

Clermont, 27 November 1095

Pope Urban II got a tumultuous reception to his call for a crusade to the Holy Land in a major speech here today. For days it has been known that he was to make an important announcement. The papal throne was set on a platform in an open field, outside the eastern gate of the city, which was packed to capacity.

Pope Urban spoke with great fervour, using all his oratorical skills. He talked movingly of how it was no longer safe for pilgrims to visit the Holy Places in Jerusalem owing to the atrocities and disorganisation of Turkish rule there. He talked of the need to help the Byzantine emperor in the struggle of Christendom against the infidel Moslems.

The response has exceeded the pope's best hopes. So moved was the crowd that cries of "*Deus le vol!*" (God wills it!) punctuated his speech. As soon as he had finished the bishop of Le Puy jumped up and knelt before the throne begging permission to join the crusade. Emissaries from Raymond, the count of Toulouse and St Gilles, offered his services.

Most of the people at Clermont were the poor, and the pope is now seeking more noble support. Each crusader will be expected to wear a red cross sewn onto his coat and to vow to go to Jerusalem.

William, the Norman duke who became king of England, dies

Normandy, 9 September 1087

The king who transformed the face of England in 20 years of repression and reform died today at Rouen. William the Conqueror, aged 60, had gone to Normandy to lead a punitive raid against the French; he was badly hurt when his horse stumbled on the burning cinders of a town which he had sacked. William spent the first years of his reign putting down rebellions by English landowners. Sometimes he was satisfied to seize the land and give it to his Norman retainers; but in Yorkshire the scale of his devastation was so great that the desolation can be seen to this day. To keep the people in subjection, 80 castles have been built throughout the length and breadth

of the land. The Conqueror and his queen, Matilda, and two half-brothers came to own a quarter of all the land in England. Another third has been granted to 15 comrades-in-arms from the Battle of Hastings. The rest is in the hands of Norman barons and churchmen.

William retained such English institutions as the sheriffs and shire courts. He improved agriculture and made a wide-ranging record of social and economic life in the *Domesday Book*. The social divisions produced by the conquest are reflected in language: a few craftsmen, such as bakers, smiths, salters and skinners, have kept their Old English names, but butchers, carpenters, grocers and tailors take theirs from French.

A later picture of King William.

Christians take Antioch

Knights of the Order of the Holy Ghost embarking for the Crusade.

Antioch, June 1098

After a bitter five-month siege, the fortress city of Antioch in southern Turkey has fallen to the Crusaders. Today, there is not a Moslem left alive in the city and the air is thick with the stench of corpses rotting in the sun. Antioch is Christian again.

The city was gained by treachery. The Crusaders, led by Frankish and Norman knights, marched across Europe last year to join up with a

Crusader: Godfrey de Bouillon.

motley band of Germans, Flamands and other followers of the itinerant monk Peter the Hermit. Crossing the Anatolian plateau in high summer they reached Antioch in October, but winter was coming.

Cold and starvation dashed the enthusiasm aroused by Pope Urban's call for Europe to unite to deliver the Holy Land from the bondage of the Moslem Turks. Desertions increased as reports multiplied that Turkish reinforcements were near. The Crusade looked about to collapse.

But Prince Bohemond, the fairhaired Norman from Taranto, had secretly made a deal with a captain inside the city. After dark Firouz, an Armenian converted to Islam, opened windows in a tower, and the knights climbed in after scaling the walls by ladder.

The Crusaders are supposed to be helping the Byzantine Emperor Alexius Comnenus to regain territory seized by the Turks. But relations are deteriorating: the ambitious Bohemond intends to keep the city he captured and make himself prince of Antioch.

China divided by proposals for reforms

China, 1100

The new emperor, the artistic Huizong, has mounted the throne of a country bitterly divided over the reforms introduced over 30 years ago by the innovator statesman Wang Anshi.

Among his innovations, which shocked the conservatives of the court, were measures to grant low interest loans to peasants, land registration to uncover tax evasion by the rich, the establishment of

official pawnshops and grain markets, and fair taxation for property.

The controversy about these reforms has bedevilled China's administration ever since their introduction. Wang Anshi and his chief opponent, the historian Sima Guand, are long dead, but their successors continue the argument. The danger is that it is diverting attention from the growing threat posed by the northern nomads.

Crusaders in Holy City

A later French view of the siege of Jerusalem by the Crusaders.

Jerusalem, 15 July 1099

Late this afternoon the Holy City was restored to Christendom, and the massacres have already begun. When the Moslems and Jews have all been killed, the Crusaders will go to the church of the Holy Sepulchre to give thanks to God and to decide who shall rule Jerusalem. There is some feeling among the Crusaders that Tancred, the nephew of Bohemond the Norman, should not be allowed to keep all the treasure he has looted from the Dome of the Rock mosque.

In the year since they captured the fortress city of Antioch, the Crusaders have passed through Syria and the Lebanon, sometimes making deals with local Arab rulers who were pleased at the prospect of Turkish power being curbed. But in Jerusalem great changes took place during the Crusaders' long march. The Fatimids of Egypt, who lost the city to the Turks, now saw their chance to retake it.

When, on 7 June, the Crusaders arrived outside Jerusalem, they found the Fatimids in possession behind heavily fortified walls. It

The world, centred on Jerusalem.

was another six weeks before the Crusaders had built siege towers and scaled the walls under a storm of fire. In those weeks the knights in their heavy armour suffered greatly from the heat. Now, in the hour of victory, the Crusaders number no more than 12,000 foot soldiers and 1,200 knights, a small force to garrison vast tracts of territory in Asia Minor (Anatolia), Syria and the Holy Land.

Saragossa falls to conquering Christians

Spain, 18 December 1118
Saragossa has fallen to the Christian King of Aragon, Alfonso (the Battler), in a major blow to Ali ibn-Yusuf, the ruler of Moslem Spain.

The loss of Saragossa is the first serious reversal in the fortunes of the Almoravids, the North African Berber dynasty which was invited to aid the Moslem states of Spain after the fall of Toledo in 1085. Ali's father, Yusuf ibn-Tashufin, defeated Alfonso VI near Badajoz in 1086; he decided to reunite Islamic Spain, taking Valencia – whose conqueror, El Cid, had died in 1099 – in 1102 and the north-western city of Saragossa in 1110.

But Yusuf was not strong enough to occupy parts resettled by Christians, such as Toledo, before his death in 1106. Alongside this, the Berbers began to prefer Spanish luxuries to battle; disaffection spread among the troops, and it seemed that the Almoravid regime was already beginning to lose its grip.

The regime's unruly soldiers and growing financial difficulties led to widespread disloyalty among the people. This was a key factor in the fall of Saragossa, which will be a boost to the morale of Spain's embattled Christian rulers.

Jin dynasty is founded in China

China, 1115
Akuta, the chieftain of the Jin nomads, has enthroned himself as first emperor of the Jin state, ruling over land seized from the Liao empire. He had previously been employed by the Liao emperor to keep order on his northern frontier, and showed his independence three years ago by refusing to dance for the emperor at a banquet. Akuta launched his warriors against his former master last year, and now the Liao empire is in ruins and the Jin have started a dynasty.

Fast-growing monastic sect builds abbeys in lonely places

France, 1116
A young Burgundian nobleman, Bernard, has just established a new abbey at Clairvaux which is the third daughter monastery of Citeaux, the home of the Cistercian order. As recently as a few years ago the Cistercians seemed to be dwindling in numbers, but the inspired teaching of Bernard and the organising talent of the English abbot, Stephen Harding, have transformed them into the fastest-growing of all of the monastic orders.

The first Cistercian monastery was founded at Citeaux in a desolate swamp some 14 miles from the town of Dijon on Palm Sunday in 1098. That date was also the feast day of St Benedict, which was appropriate since the 21 monks, led by Robert from the Benedictine abbey of Molesme, saw themselves as renewing the Rule of St Benedict.

The monks subject themselves to severe discipline: they eat no meat or fat, and wear no comfortable clothing such as breeches or coats. They observe strict silence while they work; sloth is the great enemy, so all the monks have to do physical labour in addition to their devotions. They choose remote deserted sites and lonely valleys for their abbeys. They will not use slave labour, and they do much of their own farming and are adept at building and civil engineering. They have instituted a system of lay monks. The abbot of the mother house visits once a year. There is a

The ruins of the library of Citeaux Abbey from the fifteenth century.

general chapter once a year at Citeaux which is the supreme authority. The thrust of the movement has been a focus on the inner life, to be fostered by the severe discipline and inspired by awe of nature. Bernard is proving one of the most eloquent exponents of it.

He wrote recently: "Believe one who has proved it, you will find among the woods something you never found in books. Stones and trees will teach you a lesson you never heard from masters in the school. Think you that honey cannot be drawn from the rock, and oil from the hardest stone? Do not the mountains drop sweetness, and the hills flow with milk and honey?"

A Cistercian monk in his cowl; breeches and coats are forbidden.

Emperor funds war on all fronts with church treasure

Constantinople, 1118.

The Emperor Alexius Comnenus has died after 37 long years of fighting enemies of Byzantium.

He came to power surrounded by hostile peoples, but he has used every available means to preserve the Empire. He made peace with the Seljuks, established in uncomfortable proximity in the Taurus mountains. He held off the ambitious Robert Guiscard, the Norman Duke of Apulia, by funding rebel-

A detailed miniature from a Byzantine manuscript of three men fishing.

A typical "sweet-embrace" icon.

Treasures worth fighting for: a mosaic of an earlier emperor.

lion in his enemy's dukedom and by allying with Venice. In 1091 he finally subdued the Patzinak nomads who had threatened Bulgaria. He also had to deal with the Cumans, a tribe in the Ukraine who attacked the Empire in 1114.

He took advantage of civil war among the Seljuks in 1091 to retake some of the lost lands in Asia Minor. Two years before his death he made peace with them, having recovered the Asiatic coastline from Cilicia to Trebizond. Thousands of prisoners returned home. Alexius made himself less popular in his financial dealings. He confiscated Church treasure to fund his military operations and imposed extortionate taxes. But it was this or ruin for the Empire.

Mosaic art reaches new heights in today's Byzantium

Constantinople, c.1115

Byzantine art has been enjoying a second golden age under Alexius, the first emperor of the Comnene dynasty. The art of mosaic, along with that of goldsmiths and icon painters, has attained new brilliance, and Byzantine craftsmen are in demand in many lands.

St Mark's basilica in Venice, for instance, is being enriched by Byzantine mosaics, as is the cathedral of Torcello on an island in the Vene-

tian lagoon. Goldsmiths are working on a great treasure for St Mark's, the *Pala d'Oro*, a huge panel of enamelled figures set in a framework of gold and silver adorned with precious stones.

New mosaics are required for Ravenna, and in Sicily at the cathedral of Monreale. The abbot of Monte Cassino has sent to Constantinople for craftsmen to decorate the great monastery, and Salerno cathedral has been supplied

with its great bronze doors. The Russians, converted under Vladimir, are building basilicas in Byzantine style at Kiev and Novgorod, both dedicated to St Sophia. Icons, such as the Virgin of Vladimir, are being sent to Russia.

In Daphni, near Athens, a church founded by the emperor has been decorated throughout with the hierarchy of Byzantine sacred portraits, beginning at the dome with Christ Pantocrator.

A Byzantine relic of John the Baptist.

Mosaics in the monastery of St Luke ("Hagios Loukas") at Phocis in Greece.

1118 (1118-1130)

Pope and emperor end 50-year dispute over power of Church

Worms, 23 September 1122

A compromise solution to the struggle between the papacy and the German king has emerged at the *diet* (council) here.

The battle has raged since Pope Gregory VII excommunicated Germany's king, Henry IV, in 1076, seeking to impose papal power over kings. Both Henry V, the present king, and his father have on occasion set up an anti-pope and forced the real pope to take refuge in a monastery. Now Pope Callixtus II has persuaded Henry to renounce his right to invest bishops with the ring and crozier and allow their free election. In return the pope will allow the king to be present at the election of bishops and to intervene in disputes, which have occurred regularly over the years.

In practice this solution leaves kings with some influence. However, it goes some way towards establishing the papacy as the supreme Christian authority. It makes a distinction between *temporalia* (temporal power) and *spiritualia* (spiritual power).

A later portrait of Pope Callixtus II.

Pilgrimages establish network of roads and taverns in Europe

Statue of a pilgrim in the cathedral of St James in Compostela.

Spain, 1126

More than four decades of building reached their climax this year when the new cathedral of St James the Great was completed at Compostela in Spain. It stands on the site of a primitive church, destroyed by the Moslems in 907.

The site of the saint's remains has been among the most important of Christian shrines ever since Gottschalk, the bishop of Puy, came here in 950. Now this magnificent cathedral is bound to increase the flow of pilgrims along the roads of Europe, all eager to claim the cockle-shell badge that indicates their successful visit to St James' shrine. Indeed, many of these roads and the thriving towns that lie along them have developed specifically for the use of pilgrims. Many routes now lead to Compostela, running from Paris, Burgundy, the Auvergne and the south of France. Travellers can follow special guides which list inns, abbeys and churches where they may rest or pray.

It is not only pilgrims who follow the new roads that link Castile to the rest of Europe. Trade has benefited greatly, as has communication, both of information and ideas. And every traveller appreciates the relative safety of these well-maintained routes, on which the bandits who prey on many lesser roads fear to trespass.

Mathematician Umar Khayyam, author of the "Rubaiyat", dies

Eastern Persia, 1126

Future scholars trying to assess the life of the late Umar Khayyam may have to choose between his two lives – as mathematician and poet.

Born at Nishapur, in eastern Persia, Umar Khayyam was for many years best known as a mathematician and astrologer. Among his scientific works is a major treatise on algebra, and he headed a committee of scientists appointed by the *shah* to reform the calendar. However, he also had a second prolific career as a poet and turned out a vast number of *rubaiyats*, quatrains celebrating with a touch of melancholy the pleasures of life. In one he tells an apocryphal story of how wine was first discovered by a king who planted seeds left by a grateful phoenix which he had saved.

A scene from one of the "rubaiyats", in which the poet praises the wilderness.

Fighting monks win pope's approval

Crusading Knights Templars in Jerusalem, with Saracen cavalry outside.

Jerusalem, 1128
Two French knights have gained the pope's approval for their order of chivalry, which will now be officially known as "Knights of the Temple of Solomon of Jerusalem".

Ten years ago Hugh of Payens and Geoffrey of St Omer renounced all worldly ambition and, living as monks, determined to protect and aid Christian pilgrims who travelled to the Holy City. They took their vows of poverty, chastity and obedience before the patriarch in Jerusalem, who gave them a residence near the temple of Solomon.

Another task was added – to fight infidels at all times, even though Christians were not threatened. This latter duty was soon to become the Knights Templars' major occupation.

The progress of these crusading Templars was slow. Only last year the two knights had no more than nine supporters, and it was not until Hugh secured an audience with Pope Honorius II that the church council approved the new order. Now, though, the Templars are rapidly gaining popularity throughout the Christian world.

Pioneer of new love poetry dies

Southern France, 1127
The duchy of Aquitaine is mourning the death of its sovereign, Duke William IX. Whatever his knightly achievements, William was best known as the pioneer of a new style of love poetry which has begun to be written in recent years at the courts of southern France, and which is catching on among poets and reciters called *jongleurs*, or minstrels, who wander from court to court to sing or pass on the latest news.

The new poetry is written by *troubadours*, a southern French word meaning inventor (of poetry). It probably began as a means of entertaining the wealthy – and idle – courtiers. The poets sing short, pithy songs of elevated, courtly love and its accompanying moods, which, while aristocratic and feudal in imagery, express universal emot-

Minstrels: society's artistic nomads.

ions. They are often addressed to local women, which may explain why they are written in the *langue d'oc*, the language of southern France, and not in Latin.

New king crowned in Sicily by anti-pope

Palermo, Sicily, 25 December 1130
Amid splendour and pageantry, the Norman Roger II has been crowned king of Sicily and anointed by the special envoy of the anti-pope, Anacletus. The ceremony is of special significance to both Roger, who gains respectability, and Anacletus, who now has an influential supporter in his struggle for the true papacy with Innocent II.

The new king is the son of Roger I, the count of Sicily, who won the island from the Moslems, and Adelaide, who went on to marry Baldwin of Flanders, the king of Jerusalem, in 1113. Roger II fought the Moslems in North Africa in 1123, and claimed his inheritance on the death of his cousin, Duke William of Apulia, in July 1127. He defeated Pope Honorius II at Benevento and became duke of Apulia in August 1128.

Roger II's kingdom stretches

Christ crowns Roger II in Palermo.

from the Abruzzi to Malta and from Tripoli to Kabylia. His court is based on the French feudal system, but his Byzantine administration includes Greeks, Arabs and many other races.

Horse soldiers double-cross the Song

China, 1126
The Jin have captured Kaifeng, the capital of the Song dynasty, seized the two Song emperors, Huizong and his son Qinzong, and looted the imperial treasury. The Song offered little resistance to the Jin horsemen, having bought them off with a huge ransom only a few months previously.

The Jin had gratefully accepted five million ounces of gold, 50 million ounces of silver and a million bolts of silk. They had then retired from the gates of the capital, pillaging the countryside as they went. Then they came back, and this time they have taken everything.

A Jin jar decorated with phoenixes.

Drunken sailors put a king on the rocks

England, 25 November 1120
The succession to the throne of England has been thrown into confusion by the death of Henry's only son, drowned in the Channel when drunken seamen drove his boat, the *White Ship*, onto rocks. The prince got away safely, but his boat foundered when he insisted on returning to the wreck to rescue his sister.

Henry now has no legitimate sons to succeed him, and there is speculation that one result of the

disaster will be a hasty marriage in the hope of another heir. Meanwhile, one obvious candidate for the throne is his nephew William Clito, whose father lost Normandy to Henry 20 years ago.

Clito is unlikely to find favour with his uncle, however, and the prince's death may provide an opening to another royal nephew, Stephen of Blois, who has already emerged as a great favourite of the king's.

Almoravid rule ends in Spain and Africa

An imaginative later view of Moslems before King Roger II of Sicily.

North Africa, April 1147
The Almoravid empire is dead, following the fall of its capital, Marrakesh, to the Almohads.

Originally a Moslem sect, the Almoravids were nomadic Berber tribesmen. About 100 years ago they began to carve an empire covering much of western North Africa, and by 1090, Moslem Spain. But Almoravid strength in Spain was weakened by material luxury, self-interest and financial problems. Christian rulers launched new raids, and revolts in 1144 and 1145 effectively ended Almoravid rule in Moslem Spain.

The Almohads, also in origin a Berber Moslem sect, founded towards 1120 by Ibn-Tumart, steadily eroded Almoravid power in Africa under Ibn-Tumart's successor Abd al-Mu'min. Further expansion seem1inevitable, especially into Spain, where al-Mu'min is already recognised as caliph by some Moslem rulers. To the east, Almohad growth will come up against the Mediterranean's mightiest Christian king, Roger II of Sicily.

Lisbon's Moslems fall to Portuguese

Lisbon, 28 October 1147
The 17-week siege of Lisbon has ended with a peaceful mass evacuation of its Moslem inhabitants after they surrendered to an allied Christian force under Portugal's Afonso Henriques.

With the Moslems having abandoned both shores of the Tagus and been forced to give up bases at Sintra and Palmela, Afonso now controls most of the country's northern and western seaboard from his capital at Coimbra. The Moslems' northern border has been forced back to Evora. Christian forces forecast a Moslem surrender early on after allied troops overran the main Moslem food cache stored in caves, but the defenders held out until English troops finally managed to get a mobile tower up against the walls close enough for a drawbridge to be dropped over the parapet.

Now Afonso's task is to settle his debts with the large combined force of English, Flemish and German Crusaders – 13,000 men in 164 ships – whom he persuaded to help him. Under the alliance terms, which gave the Crusaders the spoils of the city, they can also opt for land in Portugal. The new settlers are being given incentives to stay, including the right to go on enjoying the customs and liberties of their native lands. Several Crusaders have already accepted the offer, with a group of Englishmen settling at Vila Verde.

Church court condemns Abelard, theologian and philosopher

Sens, France, 3 June 1140
Abelard, one of the most famous French philosophers and teachers, was today condemned for heresy by the church court here. He is to appeal to the pope, but there is little hope among his friends that the decision will be overturned.

The critical move was yesterday, when Bernard of Clairvaux persuaded bishops to support the heresy charge. Abelard had hoped to make a laughing stock of Bernard in theological debate. Today he was accused, like a criminal, of heresy, and refused to say anything.

The theological differences are not the root cause of the conflict. It is Abelard's personal style. He is widely loved by his students for his brilliance and willingness to attack orthodox leaders. His personal life has also been highly controversial.

Twenty years ago Abelard, then 40, fell in love with Heloise, a student aged 20, and fathered her child. Her uncle, a canon of Notre Dame cathedral, had Abelard castrated in revenge. Abelard went into the monastery at St Denis and Heloise became a nun. She is now the abbess of the convent of the Paraclete. Their love has survived as a spiritual passion and Abelard writes regular letters to Heloise, "once his wife, now his sister in Christ".

Peter Abelard and his former lover Heloise, now an abbess.

Heart of Mediterranean trade now controlled by the Italians

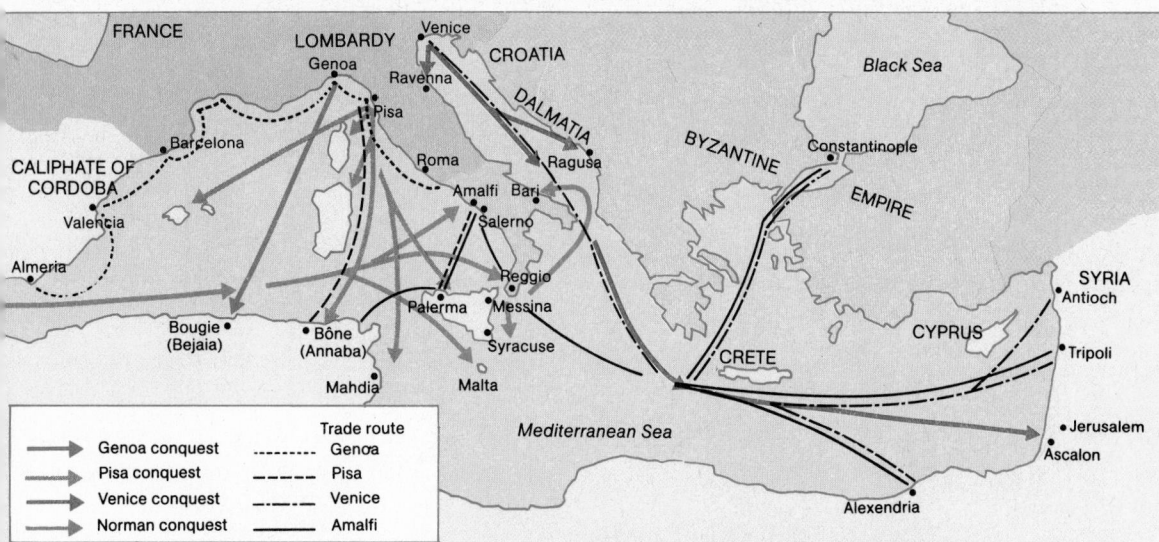

Fine bronzes cast by Igbo in Nigeria

A ritual bronze from the Niger.

River Niger, Africa, c.1139
A remarkable culture is flourishing among the Igbo people of the lower Niger in West Africa. The Igbo have probably been settled in this area for at least 350 years, but appear to have no formal system of government. However, this has not prevented them from developing a high standard of craftsmanship in the working of bronze artefacts, which are the first to be made in this part of the continent.

If the Igbo lack political unity, they are spiritually united by a religious leader called the *Eze Nri*. The Eze Nri may have something to do with a recent tomb which shows the quality of Igbo bronzework. The body, if not the Eze Nri's, is that of some important person who has been buried with slaves.

Among the regalia and ornaments buried with him are a bronze leopard skull, used as the top of a staff, and a finely decorated fly-whisk handle with a figure on horseback. Other items are a copper crown, vessels, armlets and anklets.

Not far from this tomb, a store of ritual objects further displays the astonishing technique of the Igbo metalworkers.

The Mediterranean, c.1140
As Christianity has been driving ever deeper into Moslem lands, control of the sea, and consequently of the world's most important trade routes, has passed into the hands of the Italian coastal cities of Venice, Pisa and Genoa.

The Moslem fleets, which plundered Pisa in 1001 and 1011, and attacked the northern shores of the Mediterranean in 1015, were defeated the following year by the Genoan and Pisan fleets off Sardinia. It was the turning of the tide.

In the western Mediterranean, while the Normans made war o land, the Italians conquered the sea. Pisa and Genoa vied for the cereals, salt, metal, coral and slaves of Corsica and Sardinia, and the grain of Sicily. By the time of the first crusades, when the maritime cities of Genoa, Pisa, Salerno and Amalfi attacked the Tunisian coast, extracting taxes from the emir of Kairouan, Christian fleets dominated the Mediterranean, and all the islands were in Christian hands. The Moslems lacked wood for their ships; their exports of wool and leather were in the hands of Italian merchants.

In the east, the Venetians, privileged traders in Constantinople by courtesy of the Byzantine empire, gradually gained footholds in the markets of Alexandria, Antioch and Tripoli. When the Crusaders invaded the Holy Land, the merchants of Venice, Pisa and Genoa sent relief fleets and were rewarded with quarters, warehouses, markets

Loading up a merchant vessel at a port city, from a French manuscript.

and churches in conquered towns. In 1123 Venice destroyed the Egyptian fleet off Ascalon, capturing a large merchant convoy and driving the last Moslem ships from the Mediterranean.

The scope of trade has been steadily increasing, with imports of spices, cotton, silk and fabric from the east balanced by exports of wool, flax and hemp cloth as well as older-established provisions like corn, salt, oil and wine. With increasing riches, the towns have cast off feudal ties, and are minting money, fixing tolls and controlling the surrounding country.

Lincoln ravaged as royals duel for power

England, 1 November 1141
England has fallen into anarchy as Matilda, the daughter of the late King Henry, and her cousin Stephen fight for the throne. At Lincoln, in February, Stephen's cavalry fled in panic when Matilda's forces charged. He was taken prisoner, while Matilda's men, led by the earl of Chester, slaughtered many of the citizens of Lincoln.

Matilda, though disliked for her temper, became *Domina Anglorum* (Lady of the English) and prepared

for her coronation. It never came; little more than seven months later her half-brother, the earl of Gloucester, was captured. He was released today in exchange for Stephen, who is now back on the throne. But he is no more popular than Matilda. At one time he was quarrelling with four powerful bishops, including his brother, the Bishop of Winchester. The country seems set for years of turmoil as barons rob and burn not only villages but even abbeys.

1148 (1148-1155)

North Africa, 1148. Roger II of Sicily takes Susa and Sfax in Ifrikiyah (Tunisia).

Near East, June 1149. Nur ad-Din kills Raymond of Poitiers, the prince of Antioch, near Apamea. Last year Raymond urged the leaders of the Second Crusade to join him in an attack on Nur ad-Din, whom he saw as the major threat, but they had preferred instead to attack Damascus.

England, 1149. A university is founded at Oxford.

Germany, 4 March 1152. Frederick (*Barbarossa* – Red Beard), the nephew of Conrad III, who died in February, is chosen as emperor and unites the two factions which emerged after the death of Henry V.

France, 1152. Louis VII secures the dissolution of his marriage with Eleanor of Aquitaine on the grounds of their consanguinity. Eleanor marries Henry of Anjou.

Jerusalem, 31 March 1152. Baldwin III, king of Jerusalem, besieges the citadel and exiles his mother, Melisande, with whom he had been reigning since 1144, to Nablus.

Afghanistan, 1152. Alauddin of Ghur sacks Ghazni and drives out the last Ghaznavid ruler. The empire won by Mahmud, who came to the throne in 998, and his father has therefore vanished after little more than a century.

Near East, 19 August 1153. Ascalon, the last Fatimid possession in Palestine, is taken by Baldwin III.

France, 20 August 1153. Bernard dies at the monastery of Clairvaux, of which he had been abbot since 1115.

England, 1153. The death of King Stephen's son Eustace leads Stephen to recognise Matilda's son, Henry Plantagenet, as heir to the English throne. Henry and his allies do homage to Stephen at Winchester.

Sicily, 26 February 1154. Roger II dies at Palermo. He is succeeded by his youngest son, William (the Bad).

Near East, 23 April 1154. Nur ad-Din seizes Damascus.

England, 25 October 1154. King Stephen dies at Dover.

Rome, 14 December 1154. Nicholas Brakespear, an Englishman, is elected pope. He takes the name Hadrian IV.

The third and highest terrace of Angkor Wat, the spiritual heart of the magnificent Khmer shrine complex.

Stunning temple of Angkor Wat is completed by Khmer king

Cambodia, 1150

The largest and most magnificent Hindu temple in Asia has been completed at Angkor Wat, the Khmer capital. Commissioned by King Suryavarman II as his funeral temple, its size alone makes it a suitable monument for the king who extended the frontiers of the Khmer empire beyond those of any other monarch. The moat encircling the temple and its edifices is 12 miles in circumference.

The grand entrance, over a paved bridge guarded by parapets depicting the part-dragon, part-human Hindu divinities, the Nagas, leads to a magnificent gatehouse, itself one of the grandest Khmer buildings ever erected. It is flanked by galleries, and its triple openings are surmounted by towers.

Beyond the gateway a paved causeway, protected by representations of the Nagas and flanked by two libraries, leads to a raised courtyard surrounded by a gallery. On ground level and gallery level are exquisite reliefs representing the great epics of Hindu mythology: the delights of paradise, the pains of purgatory, the battles of Devas, Asuras and Visnu, the legend of Garunda and Banasura, and Devas and Asuras churning the ocean.

Within the court is a second court, also raised and galleried, the gallery as richly and elaborately sculptured as the outer gallery.

Inside this court is the third, innermost, and highest of the courtyards. Here, standing on a pyramid, is the great temple itself, dedicated to Visnu and marked by five bellshaped towers, one at each corner and one in the centre, over 200 feet high: a testimony to man's search for beauty and for God.

A frieze of dancing female figures.

A many-armed god surrounded by various fabulous animals and demons.

Knights are humiliated

A later view of French and German troops at the ill-fated siege of Damascus.

Damascus, September 1148
The Second Crusade has ended in humiliating failure, and an angry King Conrad of Germany today left the Holy Land, bound for Europe. The other crusading king, Louis VII of France, remains in Jerusalem, putting off the day when he must face the nobles and clerics who had opposed the adventure.

The royal Crusaders attended a great assembly of the Frankish kingdom of Jerusalem in June when it was foolishly decided to attack Damascus. The Frankish barons of northern Syria refused to take part; after all, the emir of Damascus, Unur, was an ally of Palestine against the dangerous ruler of Aleppo, Nur ad-Din.

When they arrived outside Damascus, the Crusaders learned that Unur had appealed to Nur ad-Din, who had despatched a relief force. At the same time Unur was secretly in touch with officials of the court of Jerusalem, and vast sums of money were being paid by him. After only four days the Crusaders abandoned the siege and retreated, harried by Unur's bowmen. The road to Galilee was littered with corpses. The legend of valiant knights from the west lies shattered.

Empire-building Roger of Sicily is dead

Palermo, February 1154
King Roger of Sicily is dead. The nephew of the great Norman conqueror Robert Guiscard, he made Italy and the Mediterranean his target, and became one of the great rulers of his generation. He is succeeded by his son, William.

Roger inherited control of Sicily from his father, who drove out the Moslems. Recognised by Anacletus II as king of Sicily in 1130, he used it as a base to conquer southern Italy. More recently he invaded Tunisia, capturing several cities, with the apparent intention of establishing an African empire.

In keeping with Norman tradition, Roger established a feudal power structure. But there was a strong Egyptian or Byzantine influ-

Cathedral at Cefalu built by Roger.

ence in his highly organised civil service and extravagant court, with rich costumes, a mosaic-encrusted private chapel and, rumour has it, a harem.

Crusading abbot ends life at monastery

Dijon, 20 August 1153
Bernard of Clairvaux died today, aged of 63 in Clairvaux, a few miles from here. He has been a towering church figure for nearly 40 years and is most recently remembered for his preaching of the Second Crusade seven years ago.

Bernard came from a noble family and when his mother, of whom he was very fond, died when he was only 17 he decided to become a monk. Four years later he joined the Cistercians and was chosen by them to set up a new abbey when he was still only 25. Clairvaux now has 68 monks and is one of the most celebrated centres of learning.

Bernard's teaching put great emphasis on a severe life style, with the purpose of achieving spiritual marriage with God. In the schism of 1130, when two popes were appointed, he was the principal supporter of Innocent II, who favoured the monastic party. In 1140 he arranged the condemnation of Peter Abe-

Bernard the Cistercian monk.

lard for heresy at the court in Sens. Abelard had upset the church by his controversial style, but Bernard genuinely believed that his ideas were dangerous.

Kano walled to keep tribes at bay

Part of the fortification wall around the Hausa city-state of Kano.

Kano, Nigeria, 1150
Tsaraki dan Gijimasu, the ruler of Kano, has completed the city's walls. After five generations of interminable warfare between the Hausa citizens and the surrounding chiefs, the continued existence of the city state is guaranteed.

Kano has been inhabited since the eighth century when iron workings were established. It was not until the 11th century – when Hausa immigrants arrived from the east under their legendary leader, Bayajida, whose seven sons founded the seven city states of Hausa – that the city developed its sophisticated urban civilisation.

Gijimasu (1095-1134), the city's third ruler, began the walls; Tsaraki, his grandson, has completed them, providing the population of aristocrats, merchants, weavers, scholars, smiths and slaves with protection from the barbarians outside the gates.

One thousand Romans die in riot after emperor crowned

Rome, 18 June 1155
A comedy of errors preceded a bloody massacre here today as Hadrian, the English-born pope, crowned the German-born Frederick Barbarossa as emperor.

The comedy involved the ancient custom in which the king holds the stirrups on the pope's horse for as far as he can throw a stone – as a mark of respect for the head of the church. Barbarossa refused what he regarded as an act of vassalage; and Hadrian, in turn, refused to give the king the traditional papal kiss of peace.

Much discussion ensued among the attendant priests and princes and the emperor gave in, duly leading the pope for a short distance and holding his stirrup. Protocol now satisfied, it was the turn of the Roman people to upset the red-bearded king. Their delegation said that they would accept him as emperor – but for 15,000 pounds of silver. Barbarossa refused. "You men of Rome make large demands on our emptied treasury," he said.

When he had arrived at Rome Barbarossa had found the gates of the city closed to him, so he had had to trick his way into the Vatican. A troop of soldiers entered the city by a secret gate and occupied St Peter's. The imperial coronation took place on a Saturday instead of a Sunday – with the soldiers in the congregation whispering their joy rather than shouting it and letting the Romans know what was going on.

But the news got out, and crowds streamed across the Tiber, killing two German guards on St Peter's bridge. Only then did Barbarossa order his army to hack a way out of Rome. At least 1,000 Romans died.

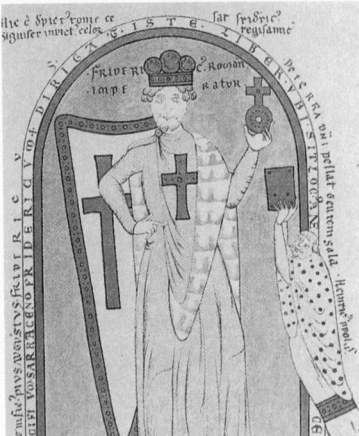
Frederick: the fiery Barbarossa.

Priest who preached poverty is burned

Rome, 1155
An idealistic priest who preached the joys of purity and poverty and created an "alternative Rome" has been sentenced to death and burned for heresy. The ashes of Arnold of Brescia were thrown into the Tiber.

The Arnoldist movement – which stresses apostolic poverty for the clergy and holds sacraments administered by any priest owning worldly goods as invalid – has threatened to split the church since Arnold came to Rome and allied himself with an anti-papal party. His activities have long brought him into conflict with the church. He was banished from Italy and expelled from France before being excommunicated.

Japanese emperor flees his palace disguised as lady-in-waiting

Japan, 1159
The bloody violence which has been raging between the warrior clans of Taira and Minamoto has ended in the defeat of the Minamoto in what has become known as the Heiji Rising, so called from the era-name *Heiji*, which means Times of Peace. At one stage the Minamoto held both the Emperor Nijo and the ex-Emperor Go-Shirakawa prisoner, but the Taira regrouped and the emperor escaped from his palace disguised as a lady-in-waiting. The Taira now attacked the Minamoto stronghold and drove them from the palace.

The Minamoto leader, Yoshitomo, and his three sons fled from the palace under cover of a snowstorm.

Capital punishment

Japan, 1156
Capital punishment has been reintroduced after 350 years for offences committed by courtiers in the wake of the Hogen disturbances which arose from rivalries within the imperial family and the powerful Fujiwara, Taira and Minamoto families.

The defeated Tameyoshi, the leader of the Minamoto, has already been killed. His son, Yoshimoto, was ordered to kill him, but refused. One of his own officers then killed him, saying that it would be a disgrace for him to die at the hand of a Taira. The officer then took his own life.

The burning of the Sanjo Palace in Kyoto during the Heiji insurrection.

Sect takes North Africa

Morocco, 1163

At the end of the reign of Abd al-Mu'min, the Almohads – Berbers from the Atlas mountains – are masters of North Africa. Having supplanted the declining Almoravid dynasty, they have driven the Normans out of Tunisia.

Abd al-Mu'min was the protege of ibn Tumart, a pure Berber from the Anti-Atlas who was head of the al-Muwahhidun Islamic reformist movement. They met in 1117, and Abd al-Mu'min was made a member of the executive body.

Ibn Tumart's death in 1130 was kept secret for three years before Abd al-Mu'min was recognised as his successor. Once anointed, Abd al-Mu'min won the support of the important Zanata Berbers, and in 1145 he won a great victory at Tlemcen over the forces of the Almoravid sovereign, Tashfin ben Ali, who died shortly after the battle.

With the vital Fez route now at his mercy, Abd al-Mu'min took Morocco in 1146 after a nine-month siege. By way of Meknes and Sale he came to the capital, Marrakesh, which fell in 1147. Abd al-Mu'min's next move was against

Marrakesh mosque, taken in 1147.

the "infidel" Normans who had captured coastal ports for Roger II of Sicily.

He then recaptured much of the north of Africa, including the important cities of Algiers and Tunis, and went on to conquer Christian strongholds throughout what he and his followers regarded as rightfully their territory in North Africa.

Rich merchant extols virtues of poverty

Lyons, 1175

There is now a flourishing movement here of Waldensians, also called "poor men of Lyons", which is alarming local church leaders. The group lives the life of the early Christians, having given up all possessions in order to help the poor. Members consider that all believers should have the same rights as priests, and feel that the pope and other churchmen have lost touch with the real needs of the poor.

The movement began three years ago when a local money lender, Pierre Valdes, was converted. He was overcome with emotion on hearing a local storyteller talking about the death of St Alexis. He decided to take Christ's words – "Go sell what thou hast and give to the poor ..." – literally. He provided for his family and then used the rest of his wealth for bread and soup for the poor. The money ran out in August 1173. His example,

A later image of Pierre Valdes.

however, attracted a constant flow of other rich converts, so he has been able to continue his work. The poor are pleased, but the Church fears for its authority.

Emperor crushes rebellion of Italian cities

Crema, 3 February 1160

Prisoners, including children, were tied to huge siege machines and hurled at the walls of this northern Italian city during a siege which ended today after six long months of fierce resistance. A furious Emperor Frederick Barbarossa personally ordered the atrocity.

Horror was piled on horror as the German emperor sought to end Crema's status as one of the many powerful independent Italian city states.

Shocked by the sight of the heads of decapitated prisoners being thrown around by Barbarossa's troops, the Cremans retaliated by tearing their prisoners literally limb from limb on the city walls. Barbarossa ordered the mass hanging of prisoners, only to see German soldiers swinging from gallows. It was then that the emperor ordered the child hostages to be brought to the front line.

When Crema finally opened its gates, the inhabitants watched as their city was razed to the ground. Now it is the turn of another defiant city, Milan, Crema's ally, to face Barbarossa's wrath.

Thomas Becket murdered at Canterbury

Becket receives a fatal head wound from the sword of one of his killers.

Canterbury, 29 December 1170

Thomas Becket, the archbishop of Canterbury, was struck down by swords in the north transept of his own cathedral today as he stood by the altar of the Virgin Mary. His killers were four knights of the royal household, who rode here this afternoon and began a violent argument with the 52-year-old prelate.

The archbishop struggled for several minutes with his assailants, while a crowd of his men and townspeople who had come to attend evensong looked on. But when he realised that death was near, he bowed his head and joined his hands in prayer. "I commend myself to God, the Blessed Mary, St Denis and the patron saints of this Church," he said.

The murder comes as the brutal climax to a prolonged quarrel between Thomas and King Henry II. Becket, the London-born son of a Norman merchant, had risen rapidly in the royal service, and when Henry had him installed at Canterbury he believed he was getting a docile cleric. But Becket became a firm upholder of ecclesiastical privileges.

On one occasion Becket, waving his crozier at the king, told him he had no right to judge him. Last June Henry had his son and heir crowned in Westminster abbey by the archbishop of York, assisted by six bishops. Becket denounced the action and excommunicated the bishops.

In his fury the king uttered a fatal cry: "Who will free me from this turbulent priest?" The four knights gave him the answer.

Toltec empire crumbles

Pyramid in the Mexican city of Tula, surmounted by huge Toltec statues.

Central America, 1175

Famine, fire, anarchy and revolution are steadily destroying not only the Toltec city of Tula, but the whole Toltec civilisation.

Since 1120 the frontiers of the empire have been pushed steadily inwards under the relentless pressure of people moving southwards into Toltec territory, responding themselves to pressure from others behind. Many of these immigrants bear no loyalty to the state, some of them actively supporting the Toltec's rival state, Cholula, which casts covetous eyes at the Toltec's rich cotton lands, and is under the same pressure from the north. Added to this is a new spectre, famine. The result is thousands of refugees pouring into Tula, with insufficient food to feed them. The population is dividing along ethnic lines.

The brief reign of the enlightened Ce Acatl Topiltzin offered hopes of a national revival, that would provide the will and the way to solve the Toltec Empire's problems. Now it seems the renaissance was merely a temporary phenomenon, serving only to delay the inevitable end.

Maya city is sacked, burned, abandoned

Sacred site at Chichen Itza.

Central America, 1179

As Central America becomes engulfed in anarchy, the Maya city of Chichen Itza has been sacked and burnt by Hunac Ceel, the ruthless and ambitious Mayapan king.

Hunac Ceel's rise epitomises the disorders of the time. First he gained control of his own Mayapan people with cunning and courage, then he formed an alliance with the Izamal state to attack Chichen Itza. Now he has turned on the Izamal.

Chichen Itza, famed as the centre of Maya civilization and re-established by Toltec exiles from Tula 200 years ago, is now deserted. Its great monumental buildings, the Temple of the Jaguars, the Temple of the Warriors, the vast ballcourt, the pyramid-shaped Castillo and the Caracol, the sacred well, are deserted. Those who have survived the sacking have fled south into the wilderness around Lake Peten Itza, where the last survivors of Maya civilization maintain a precarious independence around their new capital, Tayasal.

Church condemns "perfect" heresy

Toulouse, 1179

Cathar leaders here are dismayed at the news from Rome that the Third Lateran Council has banned "dualism" as heresy. The Cathar movement is very strong in the region and particularly in the towns of Toulouse and Albi. It was at Saint-Felix de Caraman, a few miles away, that Cathar beliefs were first formulated by Niketas, a visiting bishop from Constantinople.

Cathars believe there are two principles in the universe, good and evil, spirit and matter. Jesus is pure spirit and man is imperfect. The Old Testament is seen as the work of the devil and many Church rituals are felt to be useless pomp.

It is Cathar practices which have raised most controversy. They make a distinction between the "perfect" and believers. The "perfect" devote themselves to manual labour and live a life of abstinence and fasting. Believers, because they are thought to be saved by the virtue of the "perfect" are given every liberty in their personal lives.

Enemies of the Cathars say that their believers live lives of perpetual debauchery.

Elaborately worked solid gold seated figure, possibly of a deity, from Quimbaya in Colombia.

Saladin dreams of a "free" Jerusalem

A presumed portrait of Saladin.

Damascus, 1175

A new leader of Islam, Salah ad-Din (or Saladin) has welded the complementary strengths of Egypt and Syria under one command. Such a regional pan-Arab power, combining Egypt's wealth and learning with Syria's army, has serious implications for Christian interests in the Holy Land.

Saladin is a Mesopotamian Kurd and soldier who campaigned with his uncle in Egypt eight years ago. Shirkuh was a general under the Syrian ruler Nur ad-Din. Both leaders died naturally. Saladin, a strong man with a hard line about ridding Palestine of infidels, took command in Egypt after Shirkuh and soon proclaimed himself the actual ruler of Egypt rather than military governor. When Nur died four years ago, Saladin emerged as supreme commander of both countries at the age of 43. Since then he has defeated internal opposition to his role without losing political momentum internationally.

Some observers, noting the benefits to western culture of Arab conquest, including a more flexible number system than the Latin one, as well as opportunities for polygamy among converts, argue that it would not be all loss if Saladin were to realise his dream of "liberating" Jerusalem. This is not a view shared by more devout Christian believers, however.

Beaten emperor bows to power of pope

Venice, March 1177

As thousands watched in St Mark's Square, an emperor kissed the feet of the pope whom he had loathed and fought against for the past 19 years. Frederick Barbarossa has finally succumbed to papal authority and accepted Alexander III as the one and only pontiff.

Frederick had long sought to establish his anti-pope, Victor IV, or the latter's successor, Paschal III, on the papal throne in preference to Alexander. He sought support from King Henry II of England and King Louis VII of France, and succeeded in driving Alexander into exile in Sicily, although he failed in his attempt to win a decisive victory in Italy.

Ten years ago 10,000 knights and mercenaries set out in two columns, beating the Romans at Tusculum and capturing the Vatican after a fierce battle. Paschal was enthroned and victory seemed assured until the German army was decimated by malaria. Two thousand of Frederick's knights are believed to have

The victorious Pope Alexander III.

died; and, with much of Italy uniting against him, Barbarossa fled, disguised as a servant. The indefatigable emperor tried yet another military venture, but has now accepted the right of cardinals to elect the new pope by a two-thirds majority – and not to support pretenders to the Holy See.

Five-year-old emperor drowned in battle

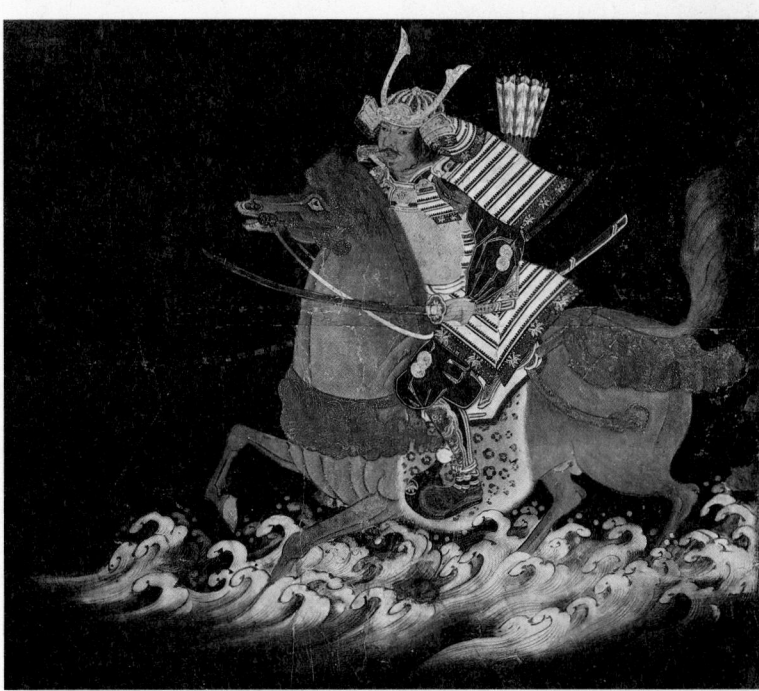

A later Japanese screen painting of a cavalryman in the current wars.

Japan, 1185

Antoku, the child-emperor, has perished in a great sea battle between the rival clans of Taira and Minamoto. With him died most of the Taira nobles and Taira power and ambitions. The Tairas, who had charge of the emperor and the regalia, the symbols of imperial legitimacy, had been beaten in a land campaign by the Minamotos acting on the authority of Go-Shirakawa, the "cloistered" emperor.

The Tairas, accomplished seamen, had taken to their ships with the regalia and Antoku, sure that they could defeat the Minamotos in a seafight, especially as they had 400 ships against their enemies' 300. When the fleets met at Dannoura, in the straits between Honshu and Kyushu, it seemed at first as if the Tairas were right to be confident. But when the tide changed and began to rip through the narrow straits, the Minamoto ships gained the advantage. The Taira fleet fell into disorder, its ships were sunk and the child-emperor drowned.

Detail of a Spanish woven silk with gold yarn from the tomb of Bishop Bernard Calvo of Vich, depicting a man apparently strangling two lions.

India, 1185. Mohammed of Ghur deposes the Ghaznavids by taking Punjab and Lahore.

Constantinople, 1185. The Emperor Andronicus is killed in a rebellion.

Japan, 1185. Minamoto Yoritomo annihilates the Tairas, establishes himself at Kamakura and sets up a "military government".

Balkans, 1186. The Bulgarians, led by Peter and John Arsen, rebel against the new Byzantine emperor, Isaac II.

Near East, 1187. After his victory at Hittin, Saladin picks off the Frankish garrisons. Soon only Tyre, Tripoli and Antioch still remain unconquered.

France, 21 January 1189. Philip Augustus, Henry II of England and Frederick Barbarossa assemble the troops for the Third Crusade.

France, 1189. Henry II is succeeded as king of England by his son Richard (Lionheart).

Sicily, 1189. William II, king of Sicily since 1166, dies. He fought against the Byzantines until his defeat at Mosinopolis in 1185 and aided the Latins against the Saracens.

Japan, 1189. Having helped his brother Yoritomo in his fight against the Tairas, Minamoto no Yoshitsune becomes the target of Yoritomo's attacks. Defeated, he commits suicide with his family and partisans.

Balkans, 1190. The Emperor Isaac II is vanquished by the Bulgarians at Stara Zagora.

Germany, 1190. The Teutonic Knights are established for the defence of the Holy Land.

Japan, 1191. Shortly after returning from a period of study in China, Eisai founds the Rinzai Zen sect.

Near East, 1191. Richard Lionheart seizes Cyprus. He and Philip Augustus then take Acre. Philip Augustus falls ill and abandons the crusade to return to France. His army remains, led by Hugh of Burgundy.

Rome, 1191. Henry VI, the son of Frederick Barbarossa, is crowned emperor in Rome by Pope Celestine III.

Near East, 1191. Richard Lionheart defeats Saladin at Arsuf.

Near East, 1192. Richard Lionheart seizes Jaffa but is defeated at Jerusalem.

Richard Lionheart is king of England after Henry's death

The effigy of Henry II on his tomb.

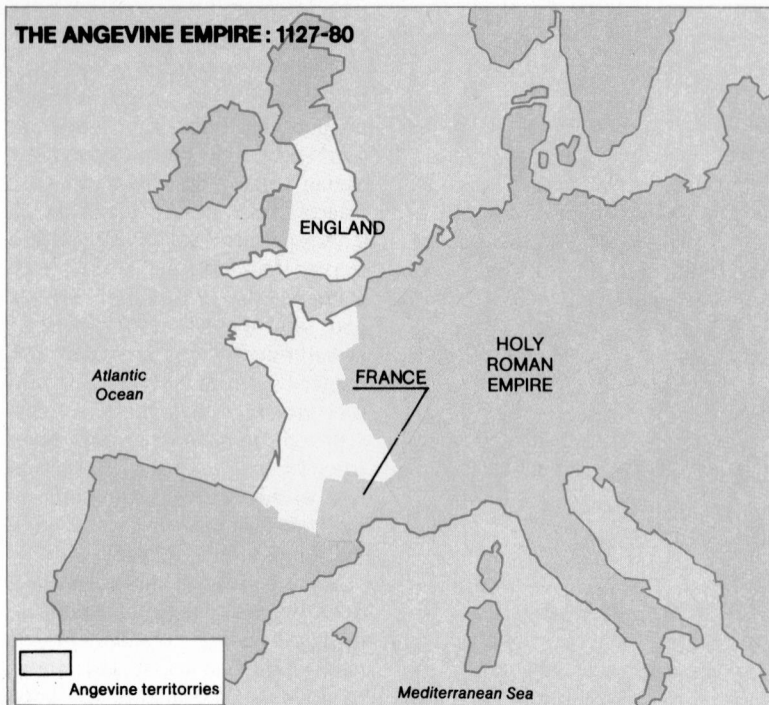

THE ANGEVINE EMPIRE: 1127-80

ENGLAND

Atlantic Ocean

FRANCE

HOLY ROMAN EMPIRE

☐ Angevine territorries

Mediterranean Sea

London, 3 September 1189

Richard Lionheart, crowned king of England today, knows little of the country he has inherited. He has spent most of his life in France, as duke of Aquitaine ruling the land of his mother, Eleanor, and fighting his father, Henry II, and his brothers. The old king's dying words to his pugnacious, disloyal son were: "God grant that I may not die till I have had a fitting revenge on you." Richard, aged 32, grew up in an atmosphere of intrigue. Henry had acquired vast territories in France by his marriage, and his sons were never satisfied with their shares. When Richard's elder brother Henry died and he became heir, his father wanted him to leave Aquitaine and come to England.

Richard scornfully refused and another family war, the last in fact, ensued. Richard's first act as king was to release his mother, who had been confined at Winchester for supporting him against her husband. He has been busy raising money for an expedition to Palestine. He can hardly wait to be off crusading once more. The nickname "Lionheart" was given to him in France, as *coeur de lion*, for his military prowess.

Anti-semitic riots spread in England as 500 Jews die at York

York, 17 March 1190

Six months of increasing anti-semitic agitation reached a climax today when more than 500 Jews – men, women and children – were massacred after they had taken refuge in York Castle. The massacre came at the end of a three-day siege of the castle by groups of young men about to depart on a crusade, backed by a number of people deeply indebted to Jewish moneylenders. Some Jews preferred to kill their families, and then themselves, rather than surrender to the mob. Those who did give in, promising to accept baptism if their lives were spared, were killed as soon as they left their sanctuary.

The Jews have never been fully accepted in England, but the uneasy tolerance they usually enjoy was shattered last September. King Richard forbade Jews to attend his coronation feast, but some of their leaders still attempted to enter his palace and offer him gifts. The London mob attacked these and other Jews, burning their houses and killing many of the inhabitants.

Since then the riots have spread through the kingdom, and Jews have been attacked from Durham in the north to Winchester in the south. The riots in Stamford and Newark were especially violent.

Many forces are exploiting the anti-semitic mood. Religious fanatics have convinced the simple-minded that the Jews are responsible for all their problems, and the image of the Jew as a wealthy usurer inevitably makes many people, especially those who use their services, very envious.

Those about to set off on crusades like to whip up their enthusiasm by attacking the Jews,

Jews choose suicide before murder.

whom they see as enemies of the faith, while those who cannot afford the journey find the vulnerable Jews a far more accessible target than the far-off Saracens.

Saladin becomes master of the Orient after battle of Hittin

Jerusalem, 2 October 1187
The Christian-Latin kingdom of Palestine is no more. A grand gesture intended to free a beleaguered queen caused an entire Christian army to be risked on an impossible march across the waterless, rocky heights of Hittin. It was a doomed expedition, surrounded and chopped to pieces by Saladin in July. As his enemies fell victim to heat exhaustion Saladin set fire to dry scrub and grass surrounding them. For men in chain armour this was torture.

After the inevitable surrender, Christian leaders such as Raymond of Tripoli, who had respected past treaties with Saladin, were treated correctly. Fanatics were executed, one of them (Reginald of Chatillon) by Saladin personally.

In the three months since then, Saladin's army of 30,000 has been able to pick off Christian citadels, from St Jean d'Acre to Beirut, and finally Jerusalem, with calm deliberation. Tripoli, Antioch and the port of Tyre remain in the hands of the Franks, but Saladin is convinced that it is extremely unlikely that the militant Christians will find support now for a costly third crusade.

Salah ad-Din (Saladin): victorious.

Crusade ends in failure for Richard

Acre, 9 October 1192
After 16 months' fighting, Richard Lionheart left Palestine today, with Jerusalem still in Moslem hands. The English king fought valiantly and won battles against Saladin, the sultan of Egypt, but the Christian armies failed to hold on to their gains and Richard quarrelled with his fellow Crusaders.

Richard has made the best of a bad job and patched up a truce with Saladin under which the Christians keep a few coast towns and are

Crusader king: Richard Lionheart.

promised free access to the church of the Holy Sepulchre in Jerusalem. Unarmed parties from the crusading forces are visiting Jerusalem, but Richard refuses to go.

Death of Kilwa sultan who won control of gold trade

The great mosque of Kilwa.

Kilwa Island, East Africa, 1188
Mourners are gathering from all over Islamic East Africa to pay their last respects to the late Sultan Ali bin Hasan, the architect of modern Kilwa.

The sultan, the first to have his head appear on all Kilwa coinage, was responsible for creating a powerful city-state by uniting Mafia Island, a prosperous trading centre 100 miles south of Zanzibar, with Kilwa Island – well-known for its iron smelting industry and cowrie shell trade – 60 miles further south. A key factor in Kilwa's growing prosperity under Sultan Ali bin Hasan has been its slow but steady annexation of the gold trade from Mogadishu.

Ali bin Hasan and his predecessors started this gradual takeover by encouraging a programme of intermarriage with the Moslems of Mogadishu until the Kilwans had learned enough of Mogadishu's secrets – such as the source of the gold, which was Sofala – to gain control of the gold trade. Much of the prosperity brought by this trade is reflected in Kilwa's elegant and stonebuilt capital, Kilwa Kisiwani.

Frederick Barbarossa drowns during Third Crusade

Asia Minor, 10 June 1190
The drowned body of Emperor Frederick – Barbarossa – was found on a river bank today. He died as he would have wished – on a crusade to save the Latin Kingdom of Jerusalem. His men believe he was thrown from his horse and sunk by his weighty armour.

Frederick's army, near exhaustion after crossing the Taurus mountains, was approaching the port of Seleucia when the emperor died. From the moment they left the Dardanelles straits they had been harried by Turkish tribesmen and suffered badly from hunger and intense heat. Now the commanders, demoralised by the death of their king, have decided to

A Low German manuscript account of the drowning of the emperor.

turn back. Barbarossa had organised this third crusade on the orders of Pope Gregory VIII. Jerusalem had fallen to Saladin after the defeat of a previous crusade. Two other kings, Richard "Lionheart" of England and Philip II Augustus of France, are leading their armies to the Holy Land.

The Japanese priest Hoshi, reputedly the incarnation of the deity emerging from his face.

361

Holy war: the crusades

The crusades were wars conducted against the enemies of the western Christian church from the late 11th to the 16th centuries. What distinguished the crusades from other "just wars" against heretics and infidels was the association of war with the idea of pilgrimage to Jerusalem and the Holy Places, which held an especially powerful attraction for Christian pilgrims.

Pope Urban II called the first crusade at the council of Clermont in November 1095. The response was overwhelming, and the idea captured the imagination of the increasingly distinct knightly classes of western Europe. Urban sought to raise an army to assist the Byzantine empire against the Seljuk Turks, the new Moslem power in Syria and Asia Minor, and he made Jerusalem, in Moslem hands since the seventh century, the ultimate goal of the expedition. He offered recruits the same spiritual advantages and ecclesiastical protection enjoyed by pilgrims to the Holy Land. Thus the campaign launched by Urban was an armed pilgrimage and those who volunteered to fight signalled their commitment by sewing a cross on to their clothes. They became *crucesignati*, "signed with the cross": crusaders.

The first and second crusades

The first crusaders fought to avenge the insult done to Christ by the occupation of his Holy Land and to earn themselves salvation. In subsequent centuries, however, crusaders' motives were more mixed, the crusade becoming a combination of holy pilgrimage, war, adventure, tourism and, for some, territorial and material gain. Urban II proposed the Holy War as an alternative to the customary military activities of the western warrior classes; soon that alternative became integrated as the highest expression of the martial values of those classes.

The first crusade (1096-99) was spectacularly successful, and took Jerusalem after a siege on 15 July 1099. Surrounded by visions and miracles, its path studded with deeds of heroism and signs of God's favour, the expedition quickly entered the realms of legend and romance. The first crusade also established Christian states: the kingdom of Jerusalem, the principality of Antioch and the counties of Tripoli and Edessa. These states grew in the early 12th century, but the Moslem powers of Syria began to reunite and in 1144 Edessa was captured by Zengi of Mosul, provoking a new large-scale expedition.

This second crusade (1145-99) was carefully prepared, yet the material results were negligible. The main German and French armies were decimated in Asia Minor; no attempt was made to recapture Edessa and the attempted seizure of Damascus (1148) ended in fiasco. The only gain from the Moslems was when a crusader fleet helped the king of Portugal capture Lisbon (1147). The disappointment and disillusion caused by the crusade's failure was profound, and although individuals and small contingents continued regularly to travel to the Holy Land, repeated requests for more substantial aid for the Christian settlements in the east – known as "Outremer" – went unanswered. The plight of the crusader states became even more precarious after Saladin united Moslem Syria and Egypt, and, increasingly, resources had to be poured into defence. Despite many ominous signs it came as a shock to the west when Saladin annihilated the army of Jerusalem at the Horns of Hattin (July 1187) and captured the Holy City itself (October 1187).

The third to fifth crusades

The third crusade (1189-92), dominated by the figure of King Richard I of England, failed to recapture Jerusalem, but brought Cyprus under western control and, by retaking Acre (1191), managed to reconstitute the kingdom of Jerusalem based on control of the major Syrian seaports. Despite their commercial wealth, these outposts of Christendom were beleaguered, especially by Egypt under the Mamelukes from 1250, and undermined by factional fighting among the nobility, the military orders and representatives of the cities of Venice, Genoa and Pisa, which had established trading bases in Outremer. Help from the west was inadequate.

The fourth crusade (1202-04), originally intended as an attack on Egypt, was diverted to Constantinople. The fifth crusade (1217-21) and the first crusade of Louis IX of France (1248-50) both succeeded in capturing, briefly, the Egyptian port of Damietta, but ended in ignominious defeat. Only the crusades of the Emperor Frederick II (1228-29), Count Theobold of Champagne (1239-40), Earl Richard of Cornwall (1240-41) and Lord Edward of England (1270-72) were aimed directly at the Holy Land and, in each case, they ended with negotiated treaties with local Moslem rulers and very little material results for Outremer. In 1229, Frederick II arranged for the return of Jerusalem, but as an open city which easily fell into Moslem hands again in 1244. Visiting crusaders, even Louis IX (1250-54) could do little more than strengthen existing fortifications. Gra-dually, the last great mainland outposts fell: Antioch in 1268; Tripoli in 1289 and, finally, Acre in 1291, after which the remaining Christian holdings in Syria were evacuated.

The crusades Peter out

Even the growing power of the Ottoman Turks in the eastern Mediterranean after the 1340s failed to extinguish hopes of a revival. King Peter I of Cyprus recruited western crusaders to assault Alexandria in Egypt in 1365. But the Hundred Years War, Black Death and Papal Schism prevented any concerted action by European powers. The last serious bid to recover the Holy Land ended when a Christian army was cut to pieces by Ottoman forces on the Danube in 1396. Thereafter, the ideal persisted, but ceased to be a political priority. However, the crusading order of St John, the Hospitallers, remained in the front line against Islam at Rhodes and, from 1522, Malta, until expelled by Napoleon in 1798.

The second reason why the crusades did not end in 1291 was that crusading as a form of penance, which could attract indulgences, was, as one historian has written, "part of the air men breathed". Although crusading armies were recruited, like any other, by lordship, loyalty and cash, the crusades can be considered a mass movement because the need to raise money, win penance or deliver up prayers could involve the whole of society. Also, the papacy used crusading privileges in a variety of contexts from the 12th to the 15th centuries, particularly against political opponents in Italy.

The destruction of the Byzantine empire by the fourth crusade has been seen as a catastrophe for western civilisation, a lasting consequence of which is the unhealed breach between the Catholic and eastern Orthodox churches. Under the guise of crusading, the Baltic was opened to German colonisation; rulers of northern France were able to subjugate the people and culture of Languedoc after the crusades against the Albigensian heretics (1209-29); and the Christian kings of the Iberian peninsula gained money, men and religious justification for their conquest of Moslem Spain. As an exercise in colonialism, the crusades were hardly successful, based as they were on the principles of the pilgrimage, from which most intended to return to their homes. One lasting legacy of the first crusade was anti-semitic pogroms; crusaders massacred Jews in the Rhineland in 1096 out of religious enthusiasm and material greed. Born of a rough, uncompromising faith, the crusades reflected an intolerance and violence that characterised mediaeval European society as a whole.

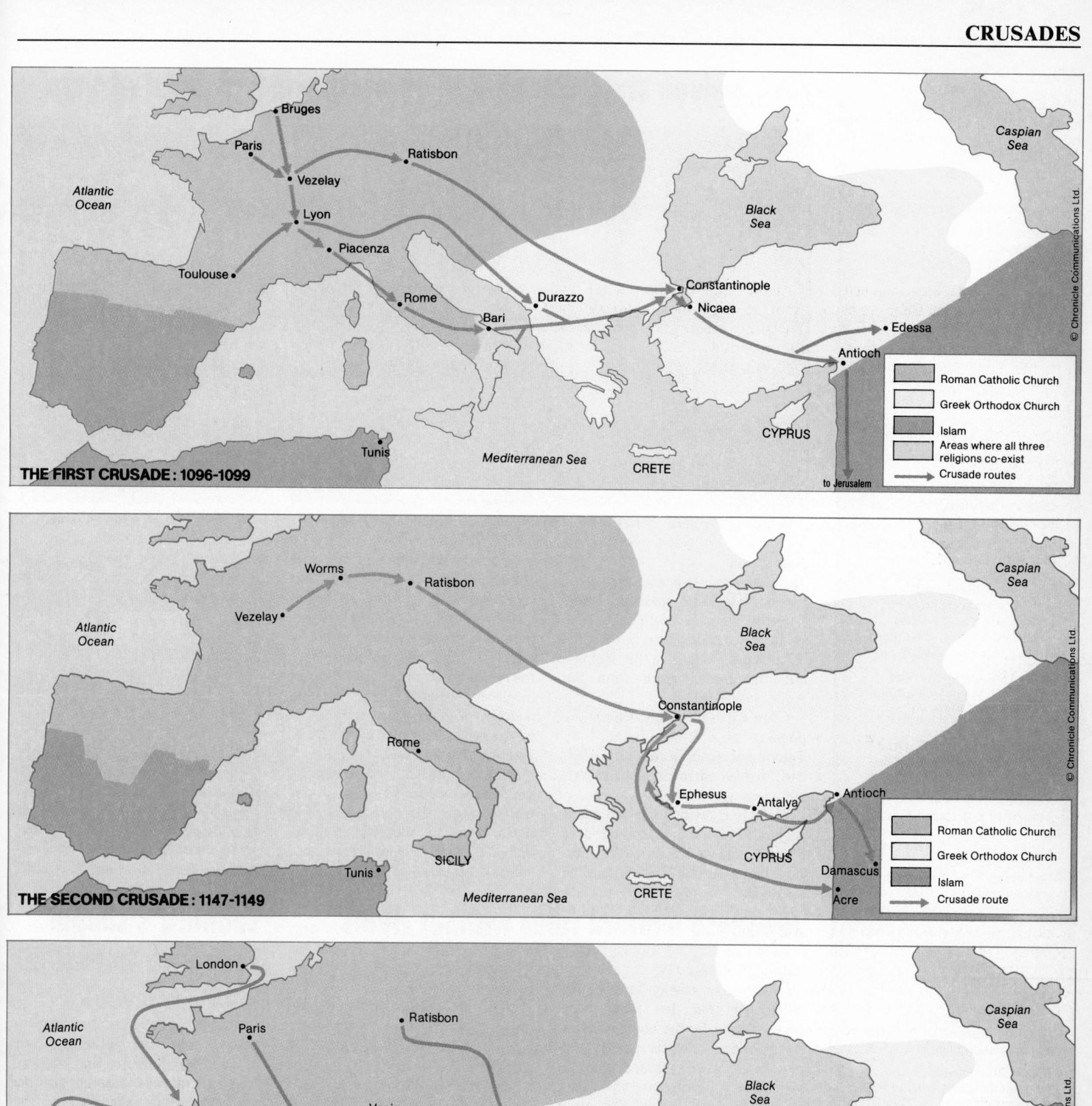

THE FIRST CRUSADE : 1096-1099

Atlantic Ocean

Bruges
Paris
Ratisbon
Vezelay
Lyon
Piacenza
Toulouse
Rome
Bari
Durazzo
Constantinople
Nicaea
Edessa
Antioch
Tunis
Mediterranean Sea
CRETE
CYPRUS
Black Sea
Caspian Sea
to Jerusalem

Roman Catholic Church
Greek Orthodox Church
Islam
Areas where all three religions co-exist
→ Crusade routes

THE SECOND CRUSADE : 1147-1149

Atlantic Ocean

Worms
Ratisbon
Vezelay
Rome
Constantinople
Ephesus
Antalya
Antioch
SICILY
Tunis
CYPRUS
Damascus
Acre
CRETE
Mediterranean Sea
Black Sea
Caspian Sea

Roman Catholic Church
Greek Orthodox Church
Islam
→ Crusade route

THE THIRD CRUSADE : 1189-1192

Atlantic Ocean

London
Paris
Ratisbon
Venice
Genoa
Marseille
Pisa
Nish
Adrianople
Constantinople
Rome
Lisbon
Konya
Reggio
CYPRUS
Tyre
Hattin
Acre
Tunis
CRETE
Candia
Mediterranean Sea
Black Sea
Caspian Sea

Roman Catholic Church
Greek Orthodox Church
Islam
→ Crusade routes

© Chronicle Communications Ltd.

363

First Andean state established on north-western coast of Peru

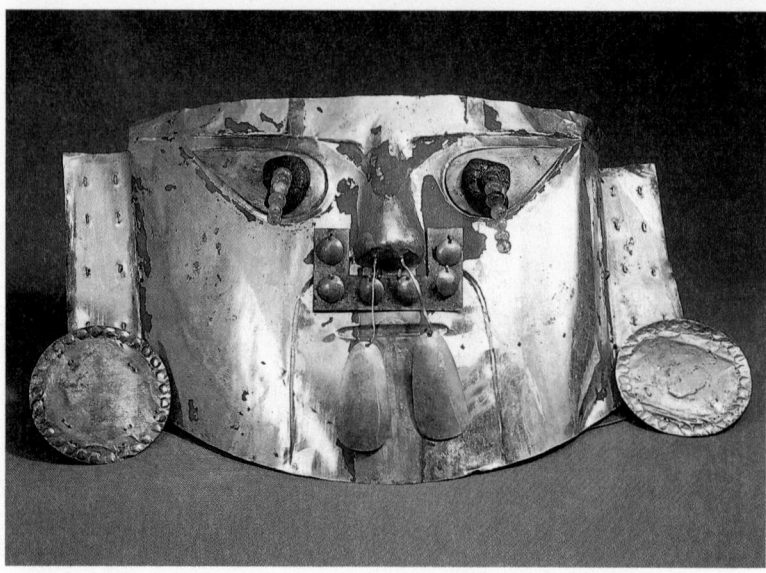

A gold funerary mask from Chimu, with emerald and traces of red colour.

A gold and turquoise ritual knife.

Peru, c.1200

The Peruvian state of Chimu, on the north-western coast of South America, has grown into an empire. Its capital, Chan Chan, in the Chicama valley near Trujillo, dominates the coastal plain from the Andes to the Pacific.

Chan Chan has been steadily expanding since it was founded by Tacayhamo who, according to legend, arrived there on a balsa raft 300 years ago.

The city is divided into ten quadrangles, each one extending over several acres and fortified by ramparts up to 50 feet high. Within the compounds the buildings are laid out according to a single plan, and in addition to the rows of houses there are miniature pyramids, storerooms, irrigated gardens, a public cemetery and stone-lined water reservoirs. For everything except the water reservoirs the building material is the same: rectangular adobe bricks reinforced with sand, gravel and straw.

Each compound is dominated by the fortified palace of the aristocrat who controls the compound. The palace walls are adorned with clay-moulded reliefs of birds, mammals, fish and flowers.

A Chimu breast cover with god-motif.

Japanese warlord rules without rivals

Japan, 21 August 1192

Yoritomo, the warrior head of the Minamoto clan, has today been made *shogun* by the emperor. This is a position of great power, and Yoritomo has established what is virtually a second capital at Kamakura in the lovely bay of Sagami.

With the Taira no longer able to challenge him, Yoritomo has no military or political rivals in Japan, and the ascendancy of the Minamoto is complete.

The shogun is too experienced a soldier to take chances, however, and so he has rewarded his followers with grants of estates at strategic points throughout the country. He is also planning an administrative network which could be the basis for a central government.

Yoritomo, the new "shogun".

Leonard's simple approach to maths

Italy, 1202

Leonardo Fibonacci, known as Leonard of Pisa, has published *Liber Abaci* (The Book of the Abacus), which promises to revolutionise the everyday use of mathematics.

Fibonacci's father, a Pisan merchant, worked in Bugia, in Barbary, where he met daily with Arab mathematicians. As a result of this Leonard learned about the Hindu system of numerals which, by including zero, makes calculations much simpler than by the Roman method.

Liber Abacci offers numbers, fractions, and methods of calculating prices, discounts and percentages.

Chivalrous Saladin dies

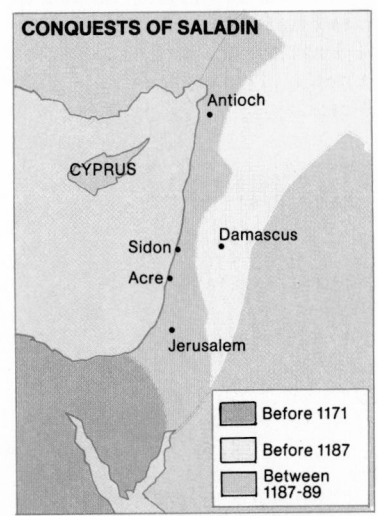

A manuscript depicting an imaginary combat between Richard and Saladin.

Damascus, 4 March 1193

Memorial services have been held in the great mosques of Damascus and Cairo following the death of Saladin. During the decade between his forties and fifties he had conquered a world. He had united the heart of Arabia and all but driven Christian fundamentalists out of Palestine.

Perhaps even more importantly, his chivalry won the respect of his opponents. Some were puzzled that a "pagan" (non-Christian) possessed chivalric virtues, wit and style, and suspected that he was a secret convert, knighted by one of his European captives.

Saladin needed no creed. He was that rare combination, a man of action who was mature enough to be generous to those he defeated. His only serious reverse was the unexpected success of the Christians' Third Crusade led by the English king, Richard Lionheart, among others.

This huge operation, launched through Tyre, has already retrieved the ports of Acre and Jaffa. Paradoxically, it seems to some observers that it was Saladin's very success at Hittin that provoked Europe's most powerful leaders into action. So Richard was joined by Frederick Barbarossa of Germany and Philip of France. Some of their allies, including King Guy of Jerusalem, were Saladin's prisoners who broke their word not to fight him again if freed.

CONQUESTS OF SALADIN

Antioch

CYPRUS

Sidon

Damascus

Acre

Jerusalem

Before 1171
Before 1187
Between 1187-89

King killed by an arrow

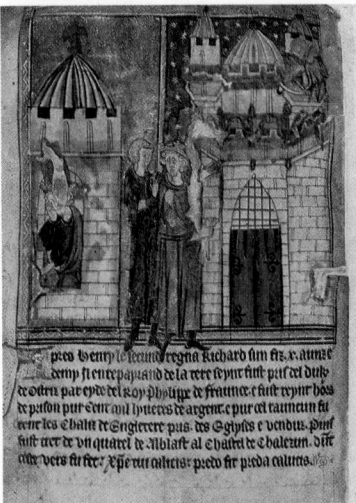

Two scenes from Richard's life.

Chalus, France, 6 April 1199

Richard Lionheart, who had not received Holy Communion for seven years, today called one of his chaplains and made his confession. With his soul thus at peace, he directed that his body be embalmed, his brain buried in the abbey of Charroux at Poitiers, his heart in the Norman capital of Rouen, and his corpse laid at the feet of his father in the abbey of Fontevrault. As darkness fell, the brave and often ruthless Richard breathed his last.

For ten years he was king of England, but he spent no more than six months in the country. At the time of his death he was besieging the castle of a disobedient baron

King Henry II, Richard's father.

when a bolt from a crossbow struck him in the left shoulder. When he tried to pull it out the wood broke, leaving the iron barb embedded. He survived for 11 days.

He almost bankrupted England when, returning from the Third Crusade, he was captured by the duke of Austria, who turned him over to the German Henry VI. A ransom of 150,000 gold marks was demanded. It was never paid in full, but even the first instalment strained the resources of England.

Richard was a favourite of the troubadours, and he himself composed lyrics. He gloried in war; he had little interest in women, but married Berengaria, the daughter of the king of Navarre.

Great Moslem thinker dies in Marrakesh

Marrakesh, 11 December 1198

Ibn Rushd, the greatest Moslem philosopher and scientist of his day, has died in Marrakesh, aged 78. Born at Cordoba in Moorish Spain in 1120, ibn Rushd as a young man rapidly became a favourite of the Almohed caliphs, Abu Ya'qub and his successor Ya'qub al-Munsur, who ruled Moorish Spain.

However, at the height of his powers ibn Rushd found himself briefly out of favour with Caliph Ya'qub al-Munsur and chose self-exile in Marrakesh instead. Observers believe that ibn Rushd was bracketed along with traditionalist philosophers by the caliph, who believed that the traditionalists were

opposed to his own philosophical viewpoint and were not being sufficiently dynamic in mobilising Islam against the mounting Christian offensive in Spain. Ibn Rushd chose Marrakesh because the more liberal and open atmosphere was more conducive to the line of thought which he was developing, but after a brief three years in exile he was recalled to Spain by Caliph Ya'qub al Munsur last year.

Among his contemporaries ibn Rushd was considered more than a mere commentator. His view, propounded in his lifetime, was that God made the universe, and it was for physical scientists to explain how it came about.

The magnficent gold and enamel Shrine of the Magi in Cologne Cathedral. It was begun by Nicolas Verdun, a master goldsmith and enameller in 1181 and was intended to contain the bones of the three kings, which had been brought to Cologne in 1164.

Innocent stamps his power on royals

Rome, 1202

Pope Innocent III has crushed the opposition of the German princes in a stinging letter to their leader, the duke of Zahringen. They were protesting at the astonishing increase in the temporal power of the pope during Innocent's four years of office. Innocent asserts that, since it is the pope's duty to crown the German emperor, it is only right that the pope should decide on his fitness for office. Otherwise a pope might have to crown an idiot, a heretic or a pagan.

Innocent has systematically extended the power of the papacy since he became pope in January 1198. He exploited the rapid decline in Germany's power in Italy, which had followed the death of the Emperor Henry VI in 1197. He persuaded Henry's widow, the Empress Constance, to recognise his authority over Sicily.

When Constance died Innocent became sovereign of Sicily and re-

A later image of ill-named Innocent.

gent of Germany while her son and heir, Frederick II, was a minor. He defeated protesting German nobles, and has since used his moral authority to get his suzerainty recognised by kings as far away as England, Portugal, Poland, Hungary and Denmark.

Finest Indian temple yet completed

The Chidanbaram Temple with one of its beehive-shaped gate towers.

Southern India, 1203

The spectacular temple of Nataraja has been completed at Chidambaram. It is the finest temple yet built by the Chola empire, surpassing even the magnificent and beautiful Rajaresvara temple, which was created by the famous Chola emperor, Rajaraja the Great, at

Thanjavur in about 1000. The Hindu temple, grand yet simple, is adorned with exquisite sculpture and is almost dwarfed by its four beehive-shaped *gopuras*, or gate towers. No gopuras so large, so intricately carved or so beautifully proportioned have been seen in India before.

Rabbi was doctor and spoke for Jews in sultan's court

Cairo, 13 December 1204

Maimonides, the controversial Jewish lawyer and philosopher, has died, aged 69. Known to Jews as Rabbi Moshe ben Maimon and to Arabs as Abu Imran al-Kutfuni, his rational teaching is seen by fundamentalists as being too unorthodox.

Born in Cordoba, but forced out by the Almohads, Maimonides lived at Fez for ten years, and his family were obliged to convert to Islam. In a *Letter to the Jews of Yemen*, he argued that forced conversion was no sin, if loyalty to Israel was secretly maintained.

In Cairo, he became a doctor in the sultan's court and spokesman for the Jewish community. He wrote the *Mishneh Torah*, summarising Jewish law and ritual, in Hishnaic Hebrew. His most famous work was the *Guide of the Perplexed*, written in 1190 in Arabic but aimed at Jewish intellectuals.

Maimonides justified the concept of the prophet-lawmaker, modelled on Moses, but played down traditional Jewish eschatology and stressed the eternal survival of the human soul.

The character Mahan meets a party of demons who turn his horse into a seven-headed dragon. (Persian miniature.)

Constantinople looted by Crusaders

Constantinople, June 1204

For three days, soldiers wrenched ornate crosses from the high altar, hacked anything of value from the walls, brought mules into the churches to carry the booty away and burnt works of art. A prostitute was enthroned in place of a religious patriarch. The surprise in all this was not the pillage as such, but the professed faith of the pillagers: all claim to be Christians who took religious vows three years ago to join a crusade and respect places of worship.

The vows were discarded on the road to Constantinople, the capital of Byzantium and hub of an empire in the eastern Mediterranean, which is also the seat of the Orthodox Christian Church. The pillage was carried out by Catholic Christians, mostly Frenchmen, with the backing of Venetian entrepreneurs. They did it in the name of religious unity. In fact, it was a short cut to repayment of a loan to fund a fourth crusade to the Holy Land which went very wrong.

Even before the expedition left six years ago, the whole expedition-

Delacroix's impression of the Crusaders entering the Byzantine capital.

ary force was excommunicated by Pope Innocent III, who had called for a crusade to Palestine. The Venetian doge, Enrico Dandolo, had contracted to supply ships for 30,000 men, but only 10,000 volun-

teered. Their leader Boniface, the marquess of Montferrat, agreed to seize Constantinople and share the city's wealth "to the honour of God, the pope and empire", and pay the Venetians.

Conquerors scramble to "share out" empire's remnants

"La Serenissima": the "most serene" republic of Venice, happy to reap a crop of territorial spoils from the plundered remains of the Eastern empire.

Constantinople, 1204

After the sack of its capital, the Byzantine empire itself is divided into three parts, like Roman Gaul, as war booty. Twelve Venetian leaders and a dozen non-Venetians representing their accomplices in the Fourth Crusade have formed a commission to allot some of the old empire to the new emperor and other shares to the Venetians and to non-Venetian Crusaders.

By this means, Venice has collected the Adriatic east coast, both shores of the Gulf of Corinth, islands such as Andros, and swathes of Albania.

Many territories "awarded" to the French Boniface and his henchmen – Macedonia, for example – have yet to be conquered. Greeks are no more ready to grovel to new masters than to old ones. Oblivious of that, Boniface and his comrade-in-arms, Baldwin, recently came close to war to establish who has Thessalonica. Whatever the new deal ensures, it is not stability.

Animals "talk back" to Francis

Rome, 1210

Pope Innocent III has approved a new order, the Friars Minor, based on a simple life derived from the gospel. They have given up all their possessions and go around ragged, barefoot and dirty like vagabond beggars, mixing with the poor and helping them. They are 12 in number, like the apostles, and came here with their leader, Francis of Assisi, to plead for papal recognition.

Francis was born in 1181, the son of a wealthy cloth merchant. He became uneasy about the contrast between his riches and the poverty and sickness he saw in the streets. One day he not only gave alms to lepers, but forced himself to kiss one on the lips. The act produced a sudden and profound conversion.

Later he had a second revelation when the crucifix of the church of St Damien spoke to him: "Francis, go and repair my house, which you see is in ruins." He first interpreted this literally and went through the streets begging for stones to rebuild the church. He sold some of his father's cloth to buy more stones.

His father was furious and demanded his money back. Francis gave it to him publicly in front of the bishop's palace. Dramatically, he also took off his clothes and gave them back as well, saying: "Naked I will go to the Lord." He now devotes himself to helping the poor and the sick – and also to animals. He talks to the birds, and they appear to listen to him and talk back.

A later view of St Francis receiving the stigmata by Cima da Conegliano.

Moslems crushed in Spanish crusade

Spain, 17 July 1212

Moslem power in Spain is near collapse following the victory today of a huge Christian army over the Almohad Caliph Mohammed an-Nasr, the ruler of an empire stretching from the south of the peninsula to Tripoli in North Africa.

The two armies met at the pass of Las Navas de Tolosa, near the river Guadalquivir between Toledo and Granada, and the odds were stacked from the start against the Almohads. In 1195 Mohammed's father, Abu-Yusuf Yakub, who established Almohad rule in Moslem Spain in the wake of the collapse of the Almoravid dynasty, inflicted a humiliating defeat on King Alfonso VIII of Castile at Alarcos. Exploiting the truce signed after the battle, Alfonso and other Christian rulers set about patching up their quarrels, determined once and for all to end Moslem domination of the peninsula.

Bishops and archbishops played key roles as mediators, calling for a crusade against the Moslems which gained the official backing of Pope Innocent III and drew supporters from beyond the Pyrenees. Thus it was that the Christian force which advanced from Toledo to meet the caliph included troops from all the Spanish kingdoms, boosted by contingents from France. Provided Christian rulers are not distracted by internal problems, the conquest of Islamic Spain now seems inevitable.

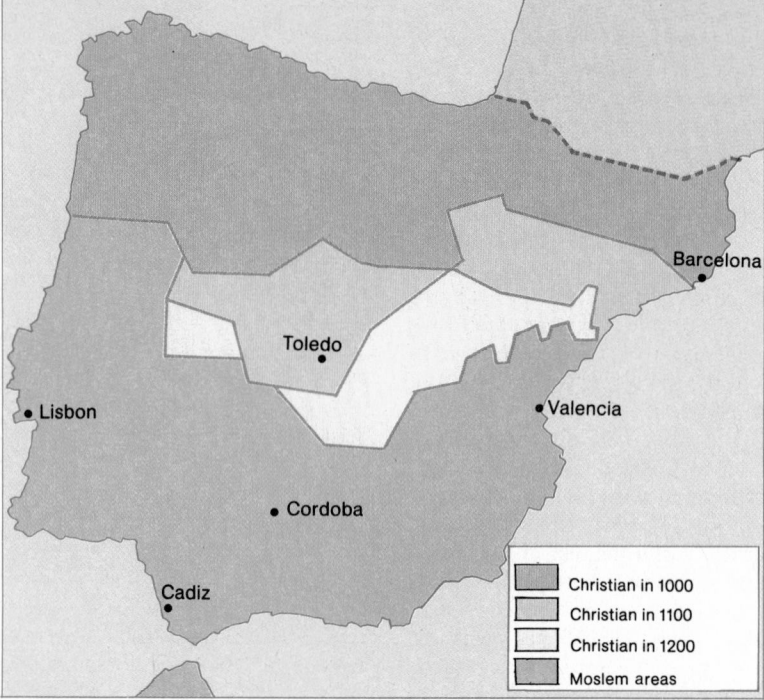

Christian in 1000
Christian in 1100
Christian in 1200
Moslem areas

Barcelona
Toledo
Lisbon
Valencia
Cordoba
Cadiz

Unknown from northern France is pope's supreme commander

Muret, France, 12 September 1213

The balance of power in southern France altered dramatically today after King Peter of Aragon died in a battlefield skirmish as he tried to lay siege to Simon de Montfort's fortress at Muret.

The shock defeat – Muret was defended by only 30 horsemen and a few foot soldiers – leaves Simon de Montfort in unchallenged control of southern France. King Peter of Aragon had been the southerners' last hope of ousting de Montfort, who they claim had perverted the crusade against the Albigensians – the heretical sect which has gathered much strength in southern France and Italy – for his own self-aggrandisement. Before the campaigns de Montfort was an obscure and minor noble from northern France. Today he is the pope's supreme commander.

In King Peter the southerners believed they had a champion with an impeccable anti-heretical pedigree capable of exposing de Montfort's so-called crusade. Many of the lands seized by de Montfort in his sweep for heretics in the dioceses of Carcassonne and Albi technically came within King Peter's fief.

For a short time it appeared that Pope Innocent III was prepared to back the Catalan king against de Montfort, accusing the latter of killing innocent people. But within a matter of months the pope, under pressure from his southern bishops, who owed their sees to de Montfort, switched sides.

A later artist's impression of an episode in the Albigensian Crusade.

English King John seals Magna Carta

Magna Carta: freedom for whom?

England, 15 June 1215

King John, known as John Lackland, has been forced to make a significant compromise in his struggle with the nobles who threaten his rule. After lengthy negotiations at Runnymede, in Surrey, near London, John today sealed *Magna Carta Libertatum* – the Great Charter of Liberties, which both guarantees to the barons their feudal privileges and promises to maintain the nation's laws.

John's bargaining position has been increasingly undermined by his loss of territories in France and by his highly unpopular attempts to tax those lords and knights who resist joining these costly and unsuccessful campaigns.

Magna Carta is essentially a peace treaty between John and his barons, with a committee of barons to ensure that it is carried out. Central to its 63 clauses are promises to administer an equitable legal system: everyone shall be entitled to the judgement of his peers; corruption will be ended; justice shall be available to all free men.

Mongols capture Peking

China, 1215

Ghengis Khan's Mongol horsemen have taken Peking. The imperial palace of the Jin emperor is in flames, the city has been razed, and its inhabitants have been butchered in a dreadful orgy of killing which accompanied the Mongol conquest.

The emperor's treasury of gold and precious stones, silver and silk, has been carried away to Ghengis where he relaxes near Lake Dolonor, beyond the Great Wall. He was so confident of victory that he did not even deign to appear before Peking, leaving the conduct of the battle to one of his captains, Muqali.

The fall of Peking was, indeed, inevitable. When Ghengis first mustered his army before the city a year ago, it was powerfully defended, and the Mongol leader cunningly sought easy ransom rather than a hard and expensive victory.

The Jin emperor gave him everything he asked for – treasure, horses, girls, a royal princess for his own bed – and he went away. But the Jin emperor knew that Ghengis

Ghengis and his Mongols in battle.

would be back and in June 1214 he fled from the city. His departure demoralised the citizens, the army mutinied, and when Muqali appeared Peking was ripe for plucking.

Mongol invaders look west for plunder

Ghengis praying to the sun.

China, 1218

Ghengis Khan, fretting at the slow business of laying siege to cities, has abandoned his pursuit of the Jin emperor and, leaving his forces in China under the command of Muqali the Jalair, has gone in search of further lands to plunder. He has led his unwashed horsemen, virtually invincible as light cavalry, back to the north, and has swung west towards Turkestan, Transoxiana and Afghanistan. It is a move which bodes ill for the flourishing Moslem states of central Asia, for wherever the Mongols pass they leave nothing but death and destruction.

They emerged from the edge of the Gobi desert, whose harshness may have penetrated their souls, as a feuding federation of tribes. It was Ghengis Khan who welded them together into the fearsome fighting force which is now rampaging across Europe and Asia.

Despite their conquest of many cities, and great stretches of China and the mountainous country to the west, the Mongols, unlike previous nomadic invaders, have not settled down and established their own civilisations.

For them cities are not places to be lived in but sources of plunder. Their organisation is purely military. They live and die in the saddle.

Young crusaders defy their king

France, 1212

A crusade of young people, led by Stephen of Cloyes, a 12-year-old shepherd boy, has set out by sea from Marseilles, determined to deliver the Holy Sepulchre from the infidels in Jerusalem.

This "Children's Crusade", as it has been named, is made up of few real children, but takes its title from the Latin word *infans*, literally meaning unable to speak and thus describing a variety of people – landless peasants, poor aristocrats and others – who have no real voice in society, but who have been attracted to the crusade.

King Philip II of France has banned the expedition, but Pope Innocent backs it, and many priests, peasants, women and assorted adventurers have joined in, following their leader, Stephen, who rides in a decorated cart with his bodyguard of young noblemen.

In Marseilles, where the crusaders won more support, they were helped by two merchants, Hugh Ferreus and William of Posqueres (known as William the Pig), who offered them transport.

Major drive against Jews and heresy

Rome, 1215

Major attacks on heresy, Jews and vice, plus moves to strengthen the church, have been announced by the pope in a communique following the Fourth Lateran Council in Rome.

The 1,200-strong council, called by Pope Innocent III, has issued declarations establishing and clarifying the church's teachings on several important issues. Its basic declarations are that:

*Each Mass is a miracle where consecrated bread and wine is miraculously changed into the flesh and blood of Christ whilst retaining the appearance of bread and wine.

*Every Christian must confess and take Communion at least once a year.

*Anyone propagating subversive ideas is automatically a heretic.

*Jews must be kept separate and be identifiable by special clothes.

1218 (1218-1228)

Japan, 1219. The Hojos assume the government at Kamakura after the death of Sanetomo, the third Minamoto shogun.

Egypt, 5 November 1219. The port of Damietta falls to the Crusaders after a siege.

Rome, 22 November 1220. Frederick II is crowned emperor by Pope Honorius III after promising to go to the aid of the Fifth Crusade within nine months.

South-East Asia, 1220. The first Thai kingdom of Sukhothai is established.

Italy, May 1220. Francis of Assisi resigns the leadership of the order which he created.

Italy, 1221. The Emperor Frederick II founds the university of Padua.

Near East, 1221. Sultan Kamil, Saladin's nephew and successor, offers to surrender Palestine to the Crusaders if the Egyptian port of Damietta is restored.

Egypt, 1221. Trapped in the marshes of the Nile delta, the Crusaders are forced to buy retreat by giving up Damietta.

France, 14 July 1223. Philip Augustus is succeeded as king by his son Louis VIII.

India, 1225. Iltutmish, the sultan of Delhi, repulses attacks by the Mongols.

Ethiopia, 1225. Lalibela, the emperor of Ethiopia, dies. He moved the capital from Axum to Lasta (Lalibela) and presided over the building of rock-hewn churches there.

France, 8 November 1226. Louis IX succeeds Louis VIII as king of France. His mother, Queen Blanche of Castile, acts as regent.

Japan, 1227. On his return from a journey to China, the Japanese monk Dogen introduces Zen Buddhism to Japan.

Rome, March 1227. On the death of Honorius III, Ugolini dei Conti, Innocent III's nephew, is elected pope. He takes the name Gregory IX.

North Africa, 1228. Having made himself independent of the Almohads, Abu Zakariyya Yahya founds the Hafsid dynasty and establishes a capital at Tunis.

Spain, 1228. James, who came to the throne of Aragon in 1213 at the age of five, resolves on a major offensive against the Moslems in Majorca.

Wandering Dominic "spoke only to God"

Bologna, 6 August 1221
Dominic, the founder of the monastic order that bears his name and one of the greatest of contemporary evangelists, has died in Bologna after falling ill during a mission in northern Italy. He was 51.

Born in Caleruega, in Castile, in 1170, he joined the church in 1196 and rose rapidly through its hierarchy, travelling widely on church business. This led to his development of an order of wandering preachers, known as the Friars Preacher, who were given papal recognition in 1217. For the next four years, until his death, Dominic devoted himself to expanding the order throughout Europe, spearheading its spread by his own constant journeying.

Dominic's personality was marked by his courage, his devotion to truth, his speedy analysis of every situation and the firmness with which he carried out his decisions. Devoted to the mendicant life, he accepted its privations, indulging in fasts, vigils, corporal penances and much other self-denial. Above all,

Dominic sees heretical books burnt.

Dominic was known for his ability to combine his personal religious feelings with an ability to spread the word of God to his fellow men. Absolutely committed to his work, he lived "in imitation of the apostles" and spoke "only of God or with God."

Japanese calligraphy reflects Zen spirit

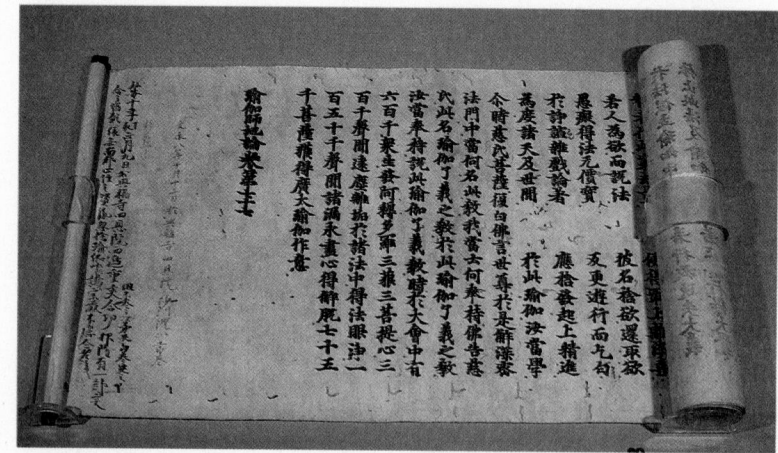
"Doctrine of Stages", by the Yogacara school of Japanese calligraphers.

Japan, c.1228
Calligraphy, the art of beautiful writing which has become such an important part of Japanese art and life, is undergoing a reformation under the influence of Zen culture which is spreading from China.

Zen Buddhism is being adopted by many of the powerful *samurai* warriors, who approve of its arduous mental discipline, and its qualities are being absorbed by artists, poets and calligraphers. Their work now displays the intensity of the Zen spirit, and its vigour is considered to be more important than the traditional skills of elegance and technique.

This new style is said to display both the writer's depth of conviction and his freedom of spirit. It adds a new dimension to the beauty and range of traditional Japanese calligraphy.

Ethiopian churches hewn from rock

Ethiopia, 1220
High in the mountains of Christian Ethiopia, hemmed in on three sides by Moslems, and bounded to the south by pagan tribesmen, a city of churches is being hewn out of raw rock: a symbol of the splendour and permanence of Ethiopia's church and of the dynamism and zeal of the country's rulers, the Zagwe dynasty. For three centuries Ethiopia had been in retreat, first from Moslems, and then, after the Moslems recognised its independence, from pagan Gallas; a few

A Labilela church hewn from rock.

pockets of Christianity survived in the north. By 1150 the Zagwes had reversed the process, regaining control of the Ethiopian Highlands.

Naturally, in a country where religion and national identity are one, political revival was matched by religious revival. Vast monasteries have been established at Tana Qirqos and Debre Libanos, and missionaries, aided by Egyptian Copts such as the saintly Gebre Menfas Qeddus (Servant of the Holy Ghost), are proselytising all over the newly liberated territories.

This city of churches, founded by the present emperor, Lalibela, and named after him, is the culmination of that revival. Here are 12 churches carved by monks out of solid rock. There is a Hill of Calvary, and a church called Golgotha. Running through the middle is a river named the Jordan. Many see this city as a new Jerusalem, and already the common people are calling it the work of angels.

Knight who jousts in dress and blond wig

Jousting knights and spectators.

A knight in full heraldic colours.

Bavaria, 1227
A Bavarian knight, dressed bizarrely in a long blond wig and a woman's dress, has been touring Europe and winning many new supporters for the martial sport of the tournament. Ulrich von Lichtenstein, who claims to be fighting for his own lady and all other women, calls his jousting tour the *Venusfahrt* (Venus tour) and offers a gold ring to anyone who can defeat him. Those who succumb to his lance must pay tribute to his lady. So far, if he can be believed, he has broken 307 spears, given away 271 rings, and dismounted four knights.

Von Lichtenstein's method of publicising his tour may seem extreme, and indeed his descriptions may not be wholly trustworthy, but this type of role-playing is certainly an important element in the growing enthusiasm for jousting among the aristocrats of Europe.

As well as providing excellent practice in the martial arts, and giving successful knights substantial prizes, tournaments offer chances for the upper classes to meet both socially and for political or diplomatic discussions. But tournaments have another task: promoting ceremony, the concept of chivalry and the kind of theatre epitomised by the Venusfahrt.

Von Lichtenstein is hardly the only or, indeed, the first performer of his type. The legend of King Arthur and his Round Table is especially popular, and a number of tournaments take place within an elaborate recreation of Camelot.

Islamic minaret rises from Hindu ruins

The new minaret in Delhi: the march of Islam continues.

Delhi, 1219
An imposing collection of new building is going up in Delhi, built out of material from 27 demolished Hindu temples. The most striking of them is a minaret which seems likely to become Asia's tallest building.

Started by Qutb-ud-Din in 1210 and continued under his heir the present Sultan Iltutmish, the project is a tribute to the confidence of the new Islamic regime in northern India, which gained control nearly 40 years ago when the Ghur tribe, originating from a remote part of Afghanistan, seized Punjab, Sind, Bihar and Bengal.

Great khan dies in bed

A European view of Ghengis Khan's fall from his horse. He never recovered.

China, 1227
Ghengis Khan is dead. The Mongol chieftain who carved out the largest empire the world has yet seen has died in his camp in the cool of the foothills of the Linbanshan mountains while his army besieges the Tangut king, Li Xian, in his capital of Ningxia.

The great khan, who had never fully recovered after a fall from his horse while hunting last year, knew death was upon him. He urged his officers to capture Ningxia quickly and, "warned by a dream", he summoned two of his three surviving sons, Ogodei and Toluy, who were campaigning nearby.

He dismissed his officers from his *yurt* where he lay in barbaric splendour and said to his sons: "My children, the end is near for me. Aided by the Eternal Heaven, I have conquered for you an empire so vast that from its centre to its bounds is a year's riding.

"If you would retain it, hold together, act in unison against your enemies, concert to further the fortunes of your followers. One of you must occupy the throne. Ogodei shall be my successor. Respect this choice after my death, and let Jaghatay [his third son], who is not here, make no trouble."

Then, even in great pain, on his deathbed, he outlined to them his plan of action for his last campaign against his old enemy, the Jin emperor. It was a typical Ghengis Khan strategy of sweeping cavalry moves combined with the cunning use of the Jin's fearful neighbours.

It was this inflexible spirit which had sustained him through many dangers to become chief of the Mongols and make them the conquerors of the world.

People shudder at his name, for death walked with him. Even now, his corpse brings death, for all those unfortunate enough to meet his cortege on the long road back to Karakorum are killed.

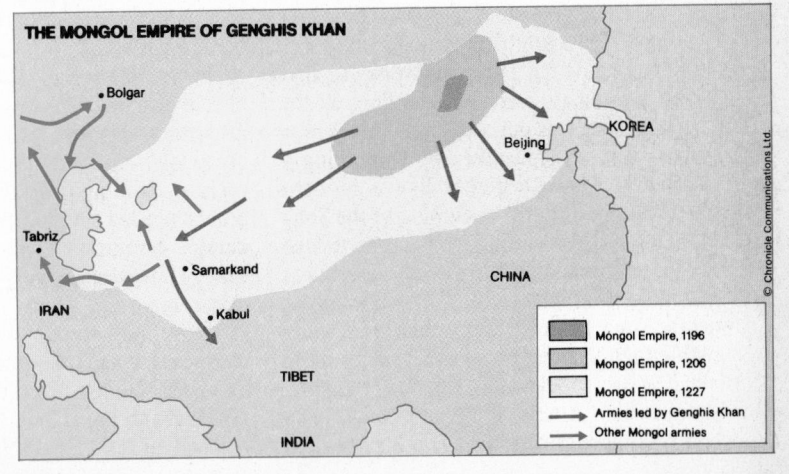

THE MONGOL EMPIRE OF GENGHIS KHAN

Bolgar

Tabriz

IRAN

Samarkand

Kabul

TIBET

INDIA

Beijing

KOREA

CHINA

Mongol Empire, 1196
Mongol Empire, 1206
Mongol Empire, 1227
Armies led by Genghis Khan
Other Mongol armies

© Chronicle Communications Ltd

China's scientific revolution

The Song and Yuan periods saw a great flowering of Chinese art and literature which has been called the "Chinese Renaissance". While many people know something about the arts of mediaeval China, few are aware that, like Europe during its own Renaissance, China also saw a rich growth of science and technology.

The importance of China's contribution to the scientific and technical development of the human race is given unwitting support by Francis Bacon, one of the founding figures of the scientific revolution in 17th century Europe. Writing in 1620, he urged people to see how different their world was from that known by the ancient Greeks, whose culture was still widely held to be superior to anything that had come later: "We should notice the force, effect and consequences of inventions, which are nowhere more conspicuous than in those three which were unknown to the ancients, namely printing, gunpowder and the compass. For these three have changed the appearance and state of the whole world..." Despite their importance, Bacon did not know where these inventions came from. Now we do. All three are Chinese, and all three reached their peak of development under the Song and Yuan.

Printing makes its mark

While paper was used in China during the first century BC, books continued to be copied by hand for centuries afterwards. It is the influence of Buddhism that seems to have led to the invention of a rapid means for reproducing both texts and pictures, since Buddhists believed that anybody who copied a sutra or an image of a divinity gained a great deal of merit for their work in propagating the faith. As early as the eighth century we begin to find specimens of short texts which have been produced in large numbers by the process of wood-block printing. A block of fine-grained wood had a whole page of text cut on it in reverse, so that the Chinese characters were left standing as the wood around them was cut away. The block was inked, and an impression taken by smoothing a sheet of paper over it – rather like a modern lino-cut. It was not until the beginning of the Song period that large-scale printing really began to take off. Soon the entire canon of Confucian classics was in print and the Buddhist canon followed shortly.

Under the Song, books became much more widely available than ever before, so that many more people had access to learning. This led to significant changes in Chinese society; whereas previously the Chinese government had largely been staffed by aristocratic appointees, from the Song onwards civil servants were recruited by a literary examination open to all. It was not a democratic system, but talent had a better chance of getting to the top.

Although the non-alphabetic Chinese writing system is not highly suitable for printing with movable type, the Chinese were well ahead there too: the first experiments with pottery type by Bi Sheng were described in the 11th century, and Wang Zhen printed lengthy works with movable wooden type in the early 14th century. The problem was, of course, that whereas later European printers (nobody printed books in Europe until the 15th century) needed only a few dozen kinds of type in his trays, a Chinese printer needed several thousand. This meant that carved wood-blocks printing a whole page at once were always more widely used in China.

The force of powder

Gunpowder seems to have been discovered by Chinese alchemists trying to "subdue" the activity of sulphur by mixing it with other ingredients. The addition of saltpetre (potassium nitrate) and substances containing carbon was found to result in a fire of such violence that alchemists were warned not to try it. This new "fire compound", *huoyao*, was soon used in weapons such as incendiary bombs hurled by catapults and flame-throwers, and the first gunpowder formula giving proportions of the ingredients is found in a Song dynasty military manual printed in 1044. Large numbers of gunpowder flame-throwers were used against the invading Mongols at the siege of Kaifeng in 1232. These were essentially giant – and highly lethal – Roman candles, giving a new twist to the old legend that the Chinese invented gunpowder but only used it for fireworks. Later, rockets came into use, often launched from great batteries of racks like the Russian "Katyushas" of the Second World War. At first the proportion of saltpetre used was low, so that the mixture went off with a "woosh" rather than a bang. This was obviously more suitable for incendiaries and rockets than an explosive mixture. Guns and bombs needed a high-nitrate mixture, and the first datable cannon is a small specimen dating from 1288. However, a newly discovered carving in a cave temple in Sichuan seems to show a cannon in action, and since this temple dates from 1128 it seems that such weapons are rather earlier than had been thought. This would mean that the Chinese had cannon at least two centuries before they reached Europe, in the 14th century.

A navigational aid

The Chinese were also undoubtedly the first with the compass. It is not mentioned in European writings until 1190, whereas it seems possible that Chinese diviners may have been using the directional properties of the lodestone as early as the first century. A clear description of the use of the magnetised needle is given by Shen Gua, writing in about 1086. He says that the needle can be balanced on any hard support, but that it is far better to hang it up by a single thread of silk. By the early 12th century Chinese writers are already telling us that the magnetic compass is in common use in ships. One interesting cultural difference: the Chinese always speak of the needle as pointing south, rather than north as in Europe. This is of course simply a matter of which way round one holds the needle when it is being magnetised, and has no scientific importance.

As in Europe, much scientific and technical discovery in pre-modern China was the result of the work of scholarly amateurs or individual craftsmen working at their trades. But although China had no Royal Society, scientific and technical activity was not completely unorganised. Illustrated agricultural handbooks were printed and distributed by government decree to popularise new crops and techniques of cultivation. In the field of astronomy the Chinese government maintained a department of specialists, and the state observatory kept careful records of observations which are still of use to astronomers today. The political importance of this branch of science stemmed from the fact that it was a central duty of the Chinese emperor to provide his people with an accurate calendar. The Chinese calendar was of the "luni-solar" type, which meant that although the year was based on the motion of the sun, as is our own, the month was supposed to keep in close touch with the variable and hard to predict motion of the moon. To make matters worse, it became customary for Chinese calendars to include tables of planetary motions as well, placing great demands on the skill of the official astronomers.

One of the greatest achievements of Chinese astronomy was the work of Guo Shoujing (Kuo Shou-ching) under the Yuan dynasty, who was asked to create a new system of mathematical astronomy for the empire founded by the invading Mongols. Instruments made by him in around 1270 still survive at the Purple Mountain observatory at Nanjing.

祈九京図揚枇宋
年重此懷杰穰稏
上農波之陳己
惕心農乃前擊
息喜功餘临糧
雲而細穀風

Yuan dynasty painting of rice harvesting. Chinese governments promoted the publication of agricultural treatises, which were often printed.

A compass, consisting of a movable magnetic stone and a figure pointing south according to Chinese custom, rather than north as in the West.

A model of the astronomical clock tower built by So Sung in 1088. China had a special government astronomy department and state observatory.

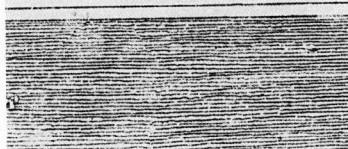

Chinese soldiers let off a gunpowder device, perhaps some sort of mortar. The first gunpowder formula appeared in a military manual of 1044.

A recent artist's impression of Bi Sheng, who invented movable type in the mid-11th century, although it took a long time to catch on.

King in bloodless coup

A French miniature painter's beautiful, idealised impression of Jerusalem.

Jerusalem, 12 March 1229
Frederick II of Germany – twice excommunicated by the pope for his delayed crusading – has arrived in Jerusalem at last.

It was in 1215 that the young king first vowed to fight in the Holy Land. He did not succeed in getting away as expected in 1221. In 1223 he said he would be ready to sail on 24 June 1225, but he was distracted by domestic problems including a Mongol invasion. A new date of 15 August 1227 was set. His troops sailed from Brindisi, without him, for he was unwell in Otranto. Without him, many others melted away.

Frederick finally reached the Christian port of Acre last September, but without much of an army.

However, he had a secret card to play. For more than two years he had been in clandestine diplomatic contact with the sultan of Egypt, al-Kamil. The sultan had been badly shaken by the Crusaders' advance into Egypt during the Fifth Crusade. He was happy to sign a treaty by which he surrendered Bethlehem and Nazareth and a corridor from Jerusalem to the coast as well as most of the city.

A bloodless coup of this sort is a novelty in the history of the Crusades, whose protagonists usually prefer to do things the hard way. It remains to be seen how the Vatican takes the news, for Frederick is still in disgrace, having dared to negotiate with an infidel.

Emperor's men kill pope's sailors

The papacy: imperial enemy.

Tuscany, 3 May 1241
With the red cross of the Crusades on their billowing white sails, a convoy of Genoese ships voyaged into disaster today. Trusting in the emblem of the Crusades to give them immunity, the convoy carried two cardinals and many bishops as well as large sums of money. It was destined for Rome where Pope Gregory IX had called a council seeking support against the Emperor Frederick II.

But the convoy never reached Rome. Off Tuscany it was attacked by a pro-imperial fleet from the rival city of Pisa and overwhelmed. Many Genoese sailors were slaughtered and the churchmen have been thrown into prison. Papacy and emperor have been enemies since soon after Frederick acceded at the age of 18. The emperor's hostages should guarantee the pope's failure to win the support he desperately needs.

The emperor: snub for the Vatican.

Mongols smash Teutonic Knights

Poland, 9 April 1241

Mongol horsemen from the Tartar region have broken an elite force of Teutonic Knights, contemptuously cutting off an ear from each corpse to be bagged and counted later like vermin's tails. Today, it is rumoured, nine bags were collected.

No-one seems sure where this force will strike when it has finished sacking the German city of Liegnitz. Mongol warriors ride four times faster than European heavy cavalry. This team has covered 400 miles from the Vistula River to Germany in a month. The invasion by this so-called "Golden Horde" started 18 years ago when Ghengis Khan crushed the Russians at the River Kalka after an expedition through Persia. With Ghengis' death in 1227, operations in the west were suspended. But after eight years, Tartar chieftains gathered at Karakorum agreed to ride under the command of Batu Khan, the grandson of Ghengis.

The new wave of Mongol attackers entered Russia through the Caucasus, rode north to sack Moscow, but was forced by floods to turn south, away from Novgorod, a trading centre. The Mongols then destroyed Kiev last year, before advancing through Poland to Liegnitz. The momentum of this invasion is such that there is a pervasive fear everywhere in Europe that it will not stop until it reaches the Atlantic. Ruling entire countries through the local aristocracies, now their vassals, the Mongols have created a vast empire which reaches from the Pacific to the Danube.

The skill of its mounted archers is crucial to the Mongol army's success.

First woman Moslem ruler and husband are killed by Turks

India, 13 October 1240

Sultana Raziyya, the first woman to rule a Moslem state, has been killed trying to regain control of Delhi. Turkish-backed Hindu troops murdered the sultana and her husband, Altuniyya, after a surprise attack near Kaithal today.

In 1236 Raziyya assumed this unique role when she succeeded her father Iltutmish to the sultanate of Delhi. The Turks did not share Iltutmish's high opinion of his emancipated daughter. They felt threatened by her popularity and were incensed by her administration.

Raziyya could crush Hindu and Moslem rebellions well enough, but she was no match for her noble Turkish enemies. Early this year they deposed and imprisoned her. The sultana later married her jailer, Altuniyya, and persuaded him and his army to accompany her on the fatal journey to Delhi.

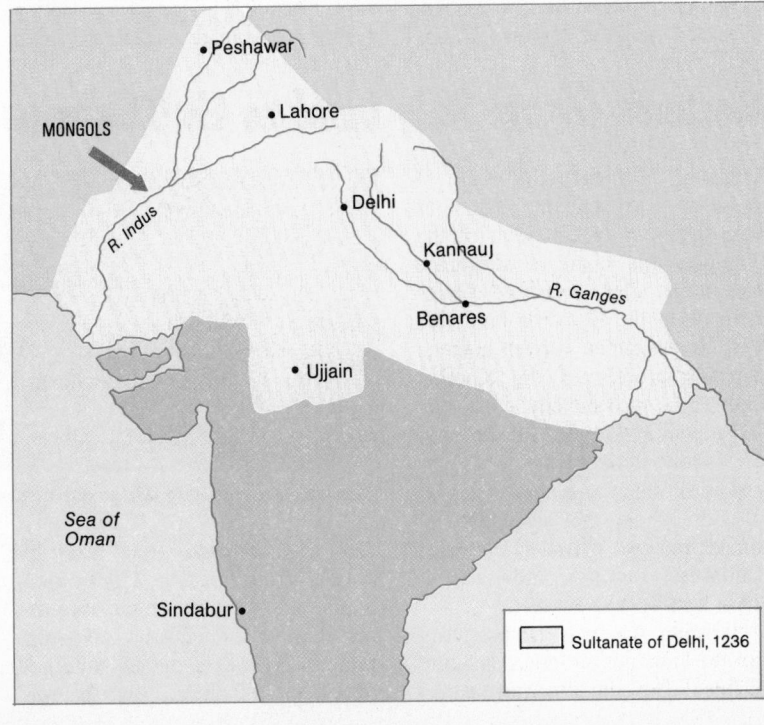

Peshawar
Lahore
MONGOLS
R. Indus
Delhi
Kannauj
R. Ganges
Benares
Ujjain
Sea of Oman
Sindabur
☐ Sultanate of Delhi, 1236

Khan's death saves Europe from horde

Vienna, Spring 1242

The Mongol advance across Europe has been halted, but not by force of arms. During the past winter, indeed, the Hungarian King Bela has been chased across the frozen Danube into Croatia while the main invading army occupied his country with chilling brutality. Winter over, the Mongols were expected to continue west, pushing a shield of prisoners before them if necessary. Instead, news that the great khan, Ogodei, had died in Mongolia started an unsavoury scramble to get home for the pickings.

Death of founder of the Sufi order

India, 1236

One of the world's most well-known ascetics, Khwaja Muinuddin Chishti, the founder of the fast-growing Chishti Sufi order, has died at Ajmir in Rajasthan, aged 97. It was at Ajmir that Chishti preached the mystic Sufi message, propounding a transcendental unity of being. Chishti also developed the nine ascetic rules of his order, requiring disciples to forsake money, never seek help and never possess more worldly goods than were required for a single day. Leading disciples of this mystical Islamic brotherhood want to spread Chishti's message throughout India.

Book of wisdom by master of Sufism

Damascus, 1232-1233

Ibn al-'Arabi has written *The Bezels of Wisdom*, a learned and metaphysical work defining the doctrine of Sufism.

Born in Murcia in 1165, ibn al-'Arabi has spent most of his life reading, meditating and writing. He believes in a God free of all attributes.

The Bezels of Wisdom sets out a Sufist view of the lives of 28 prophets, from Adam to Mahomet. For ibn Taymiyah, the Islamic fundamentalist, every word is a heresy.

Russian routs Teutonic Knights

The helmet of Alexander Nevsky.

Lake Peipus, Russia, 5 April 1242
In a dramatic ice-battle Russian troops led by Prince Alexander Nevsky have launched a successful counter-offensive against the Teutonic Knights, bringing to a halt their planned invasion of Russia.

Russian negotiators are forecasting that the routed Germans will be forced to give up all Russian lands that they have seized. The decisive clash between the Novgorod Russians and the Teutonic Knights came on the ice at Lake Peipus, in Livonia, where the German crusaders had concentrated several elite armies.

The turning point in the day-long battle came when Nevsky, whose Russian troops had borne the brunt of the German assault, unleashed his elite *droujina* troops

Alexander Nevsky, the prince of Novgorod and victor over the Tuetonic knights. His name comes from his defeat of the Swedes at Neva in 1240.

on the German flanks, crushing the enemy into submission. Nevsky, who less than two years ago was dismissed by Novgorod's republican people's council, is today being proclaimed a national hero after agreeing to come out of retirement to lead the counter-attack against the German invaders. In Novgorod, this victory is seen as the end of constant attacks by Catholic crusaders.

Moslems regain Holy Land as Christians are expelled by Turks

Jerusalem, 23 August 1244
Jerusalem, the religious totem of three faiths and focal point of the Crusades, has changed allegiance once more. The short-lived Christian rule of the Emperor Frederick II of Hohenstaufen is over, and the mercenary forces of the Khorezmian Turks hold the city.

Frederick's 15-year rule of the city followed the treaty he negotiated with Sultan al-Kamil of Egypt in 1229. Under this agreement he gained not just Jerusalem but also Bethlehem, Nazareth and parts of Sidon and Toron.

Christian rule was never strong and the kingdom of Jerusalem soon declined. The situation worsened in

The city of Jerusalem under siege, from a French illuminated manuscript.

1239 when Jerusalem was taken by the Ayyubid ruler of Transjordan. Skilful exploitation of the rivalries between the various Moslem princes meant that the city returned to Christian control, but this did not last. King Ayub of Egypt, a signatory to the treaty but still an enemy of Christianity, enlisted the Turks as allies and swept through Palestine. The fall of Jerusalem seals his triumph and that of Islam.

Seljuk army obliterated by Mongols after six-month campaign

A Seljuk Turkish mountain fortress.

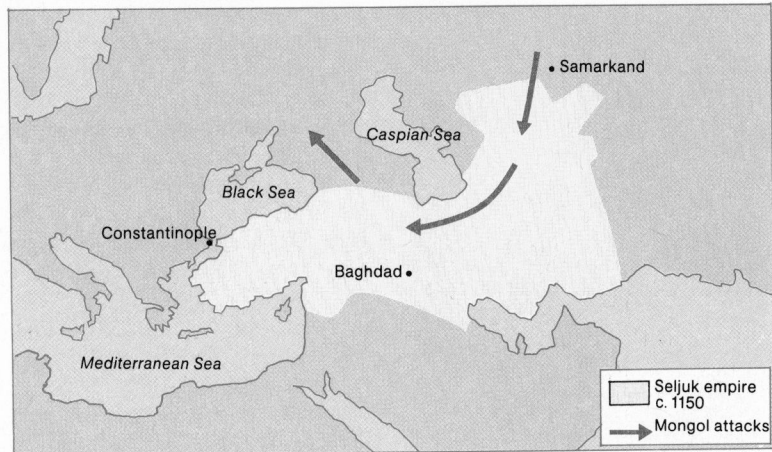

Seljuk empire c. 1150
Mongol attacks

Asia Minor, 26 June 1243

The Seljuk Turkish army has been wiped out by the Mongols. In a campaign which began last winter, the Mongols have advanced from Erzurum to Sivas, sacking this last city ruthlessly in punishment for the resistance that they met.

The Mongols took advantage of internal troubles in the Seljuk state to take Erzurum and managed, largely through treachery, to avoid a siege, which would have been un-wise at 3,000 feet in the winter. Well aware of the dangers of Mongol attacks, the Seljuks then tried desperately to rally all possible support around Sivas, where the sultan now went.

They were let down on several sides, including by the Armenians who were already busy trying to make peace with the Mongols, and had no intention of going to war with this terrifying people. It was a sizeable, but ill-assorted army that faced the Mongol leader Bayju and his invading horde.

Finally Bayju adopted the old strategy of a feigned retreat followed by a sudden advance. By this evening, the Seljuk army had been simply obliterated. The sultan and his mother have fled from the victorious Mongols.

Moslem rebels mix drugs and murder

Syria, c.1245

A rebel Moslem sect from Persia has established new headquarters at Jabal Ansariyah in Syria. Political leaders in the area now live in fear of receiving a "knife on the pillow" warning from the sect, an Isma'ili Moslem breakaway group which carries out ruthless murders for its cause against Islamic orthodoxy. Christians as well as Moslems are now threatened by this fanatical and dangerous sect.

Founded over 200 years ago, the sect was nicknamed the "Hashishin", or "Assassins", because its adherents were rumoured to take the drug hashish. The euphoria induced by the drug was said to give the men such ecstatic visions of eternal bliss that they could not wait to die.

Generals serving the Abbasid caliphs in Baghdad – who claim descent from the family of the Prophet Mohammed – and Seljuk Turkish mercenaries were despatched with ease by Assassin undercover agents planted in camps and cities in Persia. In 1092 the extremists killed their great enemy Nizam al-Mulk, minister to the

The Syrian fortress of the fiercely

Seljuk sultans.

In 1094 Hasan Sabah, the first grand master of the Assassins, captured the Persian fortress of Almut, below the Eldburz mountains at the southern end of the Caspian Sea. From this base Hasan commanded a growing network of guerrilla strongholds all over Persia and Mesopotamia.

Hasan, known as "The Old Man of the Mountain", built a library and encouraged learning amongst his men. The Old Man took Isma'ili free thinking to extremes, saying: "Nothing is true, everything is permitted."

Moslem Spain falls with city of Seville

Spain, 1248

Seville, the last great city in Spain under Moslem rule, has fallen to the army of King Ferdinand III of Castile and Leon. The Christian conquest of the Iberian peninsula is now all but complete.

The defeat of Las Navas de Tolosa in 1212 proved fatal to the Almohad rulers of Spain. In the 1220s ibn Hud overthrew the Almohad governors and set up a regime which, however, had to pay tribute to Ferdinand III, king of Castile from 1217 and of Leon from 1230. Ferdinand demanded Cordoba, the ancient capital of Moslem Spain; ibn Hud refused and Ferdinand captured the city in 1236.

Ibn Hud was ousted by his followers. He had no strong successor, and in 1238 King James of Aragon-Catalonia, Ferdinand's ally against the Moslems who had captured Majorca in 1229, seized Valencia. Also in 1238, the Portuguese took control of all of the Algarve.

Seville's fall leaves the small coastal kingdom of Granada as the only remnant of former Moslem Spain.

Franciscan friars report on Mongols

Kiev, June 1247

An elderly, fat Italian monk who speaks no Oriental languages has returned from an astonishing 3,000-mile mission across some of Asia's harshest terrain, on behalf of Pope Innocent IV, to the great khan, Guyuk.

John of Plato Carpini began his epic journey last year, setting out into the vast steppes with two fellow-monks. They had not travelled far when they met Guyuk's people, the Mongols, and were sent on their way to the city of Karakorum for Guyuk's inauguration as great khan.

The pope's envoys then rode for thousands of miles with very little respite, and little to eat and drink but millet mixed with salt and melted mountain snow – a remarkable achievement for a rather portly 66-year-old friar used to the comforts and luxuries of civilised Italy. John and his companions reached Guyuk on 22 July, just in time for his splendid inauguration at which they were the sole western witnesses.

Guyuk was keen to contact the great priest who rules the west, and sent John back with a letter to the pope in November.

A "stave-church" at Borgund, Norway, in the unique Nordic style of Christian architecture. These churches are typically made of rough timber with pyramidal, stacked roofs.

1248 (1248-1258)

Egypt, 1249. Louis IX of France, who left on crusade in June 1248, disembarks in Egypt and takes Damietta before advancing on Cairo.

Finland, 1249. After a century of warfare, Sweden, under Earl Birger, conquers Finland.

Egypt, February 1250. Louis IX is taken prisoner at the battle of al-Mansurah.

Egypt, 1250. The assassination of the last Ayyubid caliph of Egypt marks the takeover of power by the Mamelukes.

Italy, 1250. Following the death of the Emperor Frederick II, rebellions break out in northern Italy against the feudal lords.

Paris, 1252. The secular masters of the university of Paris begin a fight against the mendicant orders.

Italy, 1252. The first gold florin is struck in Florence. The minting of coins was an imperial right, which has been usurped by Florence in the confusion following the death of Frederick II.

Mongolia, 1253. The Franciscan William of Rubruck is sent by Louis IX of France to Mongke, the great khan of Mongolia, to conclude an anti-Moslem alliance.

Asia Minor (Anatolia), 1254. John III Vatatzes, ruler of Nicaea since 1222, dies at Nymphaeum near Smyrna. His alliance with Bulgaria in 1235 won much of Thrace. In 1246 he took Bulgarian territory and deposed Demetrius, the despot of Salonika. The Nicaean empire could claim to be the successor to the Byzantine empire.

West Africa, 1255. Sundiata Keita, the great king of Mali, dies.

Persia, 1256. Hulegu founds the Mongol dynasty of Persia.

Paris, 1258. Robert de Sorbon, Louis IX's chaplain, founds a college for students of theology within the university of Paris.

Baghdad, 10 February 1258. Hulegu seizes Baghdad, bringing an end to the Abbasid caliphate.

England, 1258. Led by Simon de Montfort, the rebellious English barons wrest various concessions, known as the Provisions of Oxford, from Henry III. They include the institution of a parliament meeting three times a year and the presence of a permanent council to advise the king.

Relief at the death of maverick emperor

A later portrait of Frederick II.

Italy, November 1250
The Emperor Frederick II – "The Wonder of the World" – died at Castel Fiorentino, near Lucera, today, leaving to his heirs the task of sorting out a chaotic Europe. In the Vatican there will be sighs of relief, for few emperors have caused as much havoc as this oft-excommunicated maverick of a monarch.

Although king of Germany, Frederick paid scant attention to that country, leaving it in the hands of the nobles, and concentrated on the reorganisation of Sicily and northern Italy. This, in turn, led the Vatican to suspect that it was his potential target in the middle. It was after the death of Pope Honorius III that Frederick met his match in Gregory IX, a ruthless and energetic pope who inherited Frederick's vow to mount a crusade. The emperor had been vacillating for years, and sailed – under the threat of excommunication – only to return when illness struck his fleet and himself. The pope carried out his threat; but, undeterred, Frederick set out once more. Gregory thereupon excommunicated him again – this time for crusading while excommunicated. Frederick negotiated a treaty with the sultan. A third excommunication followed – this time for dealing with an infidel.

Frederick was a scholarly king with a scientific curiosity. One experiment which he conducted involved rearing children in silence in an effort to discover what language was spoken by Adam and Eve.

King's ransom paid for Louis IX of France

Damietta, April 30, 1250
King Louis IX walked to freedom today after handing over the keys of the city of Damietta and a record ransom of one million dinars.

The king, looking tired and ill after his month in captivity, had been taken by his Egyptian captors to the city after ransom terms had been agreed for his release with Turan Shah, Sultan of Egypt, at his royal residence in Fariskur.

The payment of the ransom brings to an end one of the most humiliating episodes in Frankish history. It contrasts strongly with the start of the crusade a year ago when the Frankish army overran Damietta and King Louis was begged by the previous sultan Ayyub to barter Damietta in exchange for Jerusalem. King Louis refused to trade with an infidel.

This position of strength deteriorated in the long drawn-out siege between the two sides outside Damietta. The Franks, through poor intelligence, missed a golden opportunity to exploit disarray in the Egyptian ranks after Ayyub died

King Louis IX faces his captors.

and his successor Turan Shah was still out of the country.

With typhoid reducing the ranks of his army, Louis tried to cut his losses by taking up the old sultan's offer of Damietta for Jerusalem but was turned down and captured.

Death of king who owned gold trade

Timbuktu, 1255
Sundiata Keita, the founder of the empire of Mali, is dead. A Malinke chief who liberated his people from the yoke of Samunguru Kante, king of Sosso, he built an empire stretching from the Atlantic in the west to Gao in the east.

He should never have lived. The Sosso king, fearing the Malinke, killed the 11 heirs to the petty chiefdom, disdaining to kill the twelfth, Sundiata, a sickly, semi-crippled child. Sundiata thrived and escaped to exile. Called back by his people, he united the Malinke against the Sosso, leading them to victory in 1235 at Kirina. Victorious in every campaign, he expanded his kingdom, occupying the entire Ghana Empire by 1240 and all the major caravan entrepots of the southern Sahara by 1250.

His empire is not merely the biggest in Black Africa, but the richest: controlling the copper mines at Takedda, the salt mines at Taghaza and the gold mines at Bure. So rich is Mali, with its "mountains of gold", that the trans-Saharan caravan trade to Morocco is called in Europe "the golden trade of the Moors".

Part of a French illuminated manuscript of "The Romance of Lancelot", one of many versions of the popular legend of King Arthur and his knights.

378

Massacre follows fall of Baghdad

Church approves use of torture in hunt for heretics

Rome, 1255

In its constant fight against religious heresy the Roman Inquisition, founded more than 20 years ago, has authorised the use of a terrible new weapon: physical torture. Torture has been common in civil courts for some time, but the church has hitherto resisted its use. Now those accused of heresy who refuse to confess can be tortured until they satisfy the inquisitors.

"The question", as this interrogation is called, is just one part of the well-established inquisitorial

Heresy: a burning question?

process. Once the province of local bishops, the pursuit of heresy is now overseen by Rome itself.

Pairs of inquisitors, invariably Dominicans, tour a country, holding court in a succession of towns. On their arrival they deliver a public sermon on the evils of heresy, then offer a "period of grace" in which heretics can still confess.

Those who do confess gain an automatic pardon, but suspected heretics who still resist are pursued, often with the help of anonymous informers. This is a highly secretive process and the informers need never testify in public. After interrogation, sentence is announced during a second public sermon. Minor offenders receive no more than a penance and a fine; major heretics are imprisoned for life or burnt at the stake. The inquisitors may also impose collective punishments — fasts and pilgrimages.

A later Arab picture of Baghdad.

An engraving of a bird's eye view of the city of Baghdad.

Baghdad, February 1258

Baghdad has fallen to the Mongol hordes. Eye-witness accounts of the most appalling massacres have left the Islamic world trembling with shock.

Towards the end of last year Hulegu, the grandson of Ghengis Khan, occupied Persia and came to the outskirts of Baghdad. On 17 January his forces met the army of Caliph al-Musta'sim, the last of the Abbasids. The Mongols won a comprehensive victory, and went on to besiege the capital, Baghdad.

Eye-witnesses say that a thick cloud of dust engulfed the city, accompanied by a mighty rumbling. When the dust cleared, people who had climbed on to roofs and minarets saw the Mongol hordes in their city. When the invaders attacked, there was scarcely any resistance. Then the atrocities began. Those in the garrison who tried to escape were divided among the Mongols to be killed. When the caliph surrendered, on 10 February, Hulegu asked him to order his people out of the city, to lay down their arms. The majority obeyed and, once disarmed, were put to the sword. Three days later Hulegu's army moved into Baghdad, killing all who remained and starting fires. The sacking lasted for 17 days. On 20 February, al-Musta'sim was sewn into a bag and trampled to death by horses.

According to various accounts, the number killed varies between 80,000 and two million. The few who escaped have told their story throughout the Near East, and word has spread of Mongol savagery. Hulegu and his armies have acquired a reputation for invincibility. There is a crisis of morale through the Moslem world as the khan's hordes threaten to move further west.

Ex-monk leads ragged army on rampage

Picardy, France December 1251

This region is being frightened, not to say terrorised, by a ragged army numbering several thousands called *Pastoureaux* (Shepherds). Dressed as shepherds, they march into towns bearing pitchforks, hatchets, daggers and pikes. They beg for food, and if they do not get enough they take it by force.

It all began last Easter when a renegade Hungarian monk, Jacob, began preaching a new crusade. He played on local fears arising from the continued imprisonment of King Louis IX in the Holy Land. People were saying that Mohammed seemed stronger than Christ. Jacob claimed that God was angry at the pride of the nobles and churchmen and had called him to lead a crusade of the lowly. It was to be based on the shepherds, who first brought the glad tidings of the Nativity. He was soon joined by thieves and murderers as well.

The crusaders are supposed to be marching towards the Holy Land, and Jacob has told them that the sea will part for them so that they can walk all the way. Meanwhile they treat him as a messiah. He is said to heal the sick. He claims that their food will never grow less, like the loaves and fishes. He marries followers if they want it, and divorces them too. He even married 11 men to one woman.

Fisherman's son founds new sect

Japan, 1253

Nichiren, a Buddhist monk, has preached a remarkable sermon in which he denounced the traditional Buddhist sects of Jodo and Zen and established his own sect based on the Lotus sutra.

The followers of this fisherman's son are militant and intolerant of other beliefs, which he calls blasphemous. He insists that his disciples strengthen their faith by chanting "*Namu myoho rengekyo*", which means "I take my refuge in the Lotus sutra". His zealotry has already made him many enemies among powerful people.

Paris, 1259. By the treaty of Paris, Louis IX cedes the Agenais, Saintonge and parts of Quercy, Limousin and Perigord to Henry III of England. Henry gives up all claims to the Plantagenet fiefs of Normandy, Anjou, Touraine, Maine and Poitou.

Greece, 1259. Intending to conquer Salonika and regain Constantinople, Michael II of Epirus allies with the Frankish prince of Achaia, William of Villehardouin. They are routed by the Nicaean forces at Pelagonia.

West Africa, 1260. Mansa Ule, the king of Mali, who is based at Timbuktu, embarks on a pilgrimage to Mecca.

Italy, 4 September 1260. The Florentine Guelfs, who support papal power, are crushed by the Tuscan Ghibellines, who support the emperor, at the battle of Montaperto.

Italy, 1260. Charles of Anjou, the brother of the king of France, subjugates Piedmont.

Asia Minor (Anatolia), 1261. Michael VIII Palaeologus, proclaimed emperor of Nicaea in 1258, signs a treaty promising the Genoese all the trading privileges within the empire enjoyed by Venice.

Rome, August 1261. Urban IV, the son of a French shoemaker, is elected pope in succession to Alexander IV.

Constantinople, 15 August 1261. Michael VIII Palaeologus seizes Constantinople, putting an end to the Latin empire and restoring the Byzantine empire.

Italy, 1262. Supported by Pope Urban IV, the Guelfs return to power in Tuscany.

Greece, 1262. In return for his freedom, William of Villehardouin, in prison since his abortive attack on Nicaea in 1259, cedes part of Morea (the Peloponnese) around Mistra to Michael VIII Palaeologus.

Rome, 1263. Charles of Anjou – who is being groomed by Urban IV for the role of papal champion against German influence in Italy – is elected senator for life by the Romans.

Italy, 1263. The Venetians defeat the Genoese in a sea battle off Settepozzi.

France, 1264. Arbitrating in the dispute between the English barons and Henry III, Louis IX annuls the Provisions of Oxford, imposed on Henry in 1258.

Glorious cathedrals enhance splendour of European cities

Europe, c.1260

The great surge of Christian faith in this century has found expression in stone cutting, statuary and stained glass, put together to make cathedrals of a new lightness and grace.

It began 100 years ago with the abbey church of St Denis built by Abbot Suger outside Paris. Fifty years ago Bishop Regnault began to raise the two great spires of Chartres which can now be seen for 20 miles. He filled the 160 windows with stained glass, including the great rose window, bathing the interior with blue light. He had the portals decorated with holy statues.

Rheims, where French kings are crowned, has been rebuilt with 550 statues – "the smiling angels". Rose windows like those at Chartres and Rheims have now been added to Notre Dame de Paris.

Meanwhile, in England, King Henry III has begun rebuilding Westminster Abbey with soaring columns, ribbed vaulting, huge windows and flying buttresses. He is employing the French architect Henry of Rheims and plans a rose window copied from St Denis. The new style began in England at Canterbury under the French mason William of Sens, who fell from the scaffolding and was succeeded by William the Englishman. Lincoln, Wells and Salisbury are nearly complete.

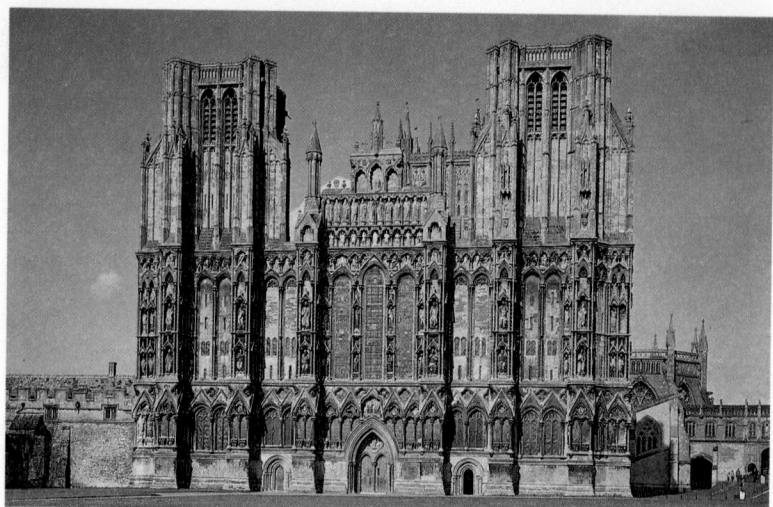

The west front of the spireless cathedral in Wells, Somerset: a magnificent English example of the new soaring, graceful style of church architecture.

The elegant clustered column in the chapter house of Salisbury Cathedral seems almost too delicate for the glorious vaulted ceiling it supports.

Amiens Cathedral: the west front.

Chartres Cathedral: the rose window.

Bourges Cathedral: the nave.

Kublai Khan heads Mongol empire

Ex-slave army routes Mongols and saves Egypt

China, 1260

Kublai Khan has succeeded his brother Mongke as ruler of the great empire founded by their grandfather, Ghengis, the fearsome first great khan of the Mongols.

Like all his family, Kublai is determined on conquest and has chosen his first victim, the remnant of the Song empire in southern China whose fall would bring the whole of China under Mongol rule.

The Mongols look at the great wealth of the Song and lick their lips in anticipation of the plunder, but Kublai is setting about the destruction of the Song with cunning rather than warfare.

He has sent an envoy, Hao Jing, to the Song court, ostensibly to discuss a peaceful settlement. He offered the Song a bargain: if they would acknowledge his reign as the "Son of Heaven" over all China, he would allow them a measure of self rule and the opportunity to benefit from the prosperity which would stem from a tolerant Mongol suzerainty.

Hao Jing embellished this offer by painting a picture of Kublai as a Chinese-style emperor, with Confucian advisers, governing in a civilised fashion.

However, Hao Jing also pointed out that any military resistance would be useless, for nothing could stand against the Mongol army which was now as skilled in siege warfare as it was in the field.

The Song, as aware of Mongol cunning as they are of Mongol ruthlessness, have refused to acknowledge Kublai's claim to be the Son of Heaven and have arrested Hao Jing, a move they will undoubtedly regret.

For the moment, however, the khan remains conciliatory, and is planning to send two more envoys to the Song. He is, in fact, quite unlike his grandfather, for he is an urban man rather than a horseman of the steppes.

He has shown an inclination for scholarship and the arts, and knows that commerce can bring as much profit as pillage. His entourage includes foreign scholars and experts of many races and religions. For all that, he is a Mongol and, like his forefathers, seems likely to wage war ruthlessly to achieve his ends.

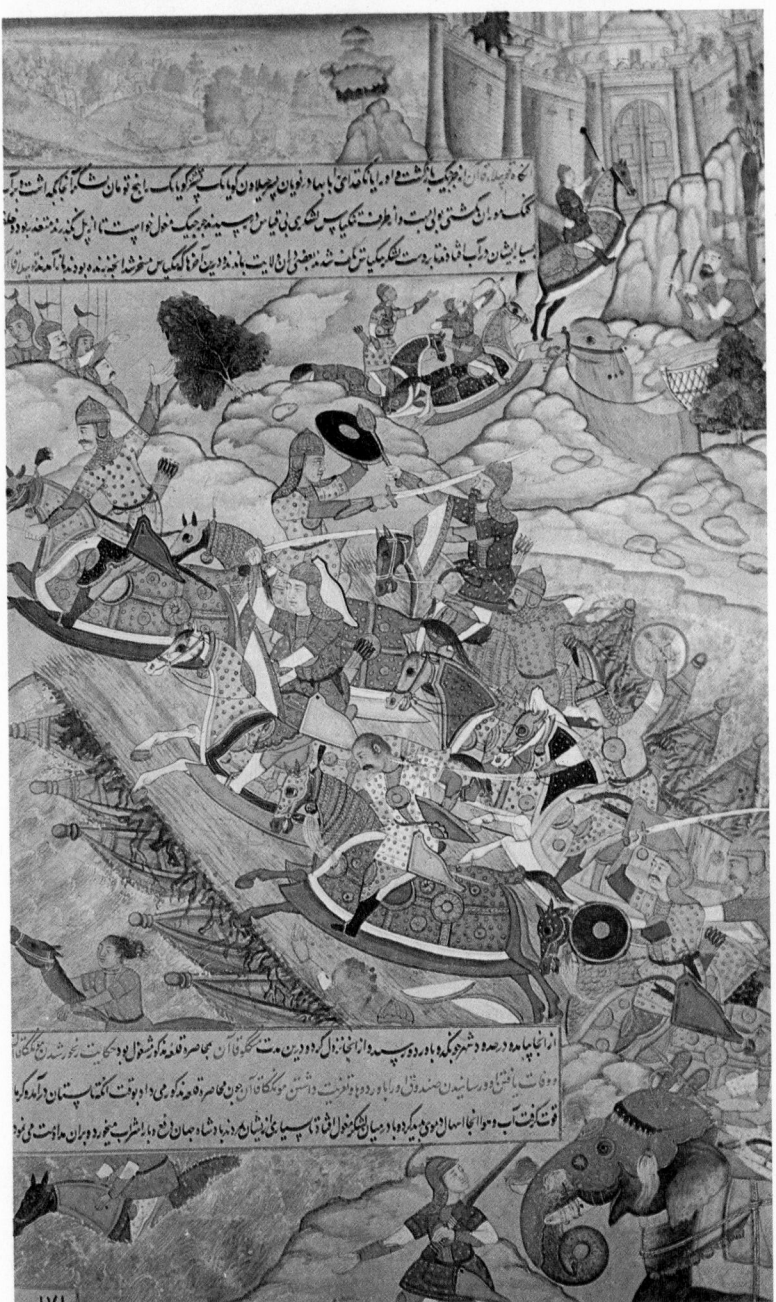

Kublai's armies attack a Chinese city in this later painting from India.

Nazareth, September 1260

A new Mongol offensive has been stopped in its tracks by an Arab army led by former Turkish slave mercenaries, the Mamelukes of Egypt. This was more than a military reverse: the mystique of Mongol invincibility has been utterly smashed.

The defeated Asiatic force was under the command of General Hulegu, the brother of the great khan, Mongke. Hulegu traversed the River Oxus on New Year's Day four years ago. It was an eventful trip across southern Asia. The Assassins challenged the Mongols and were wiped out. The Mongols invaded Baghdad next, sacked the city and defied local superstition by murdering the caliph. From Baghdad the invasion moved to the Syrian capital, Damascus, where Christian underdogs cheered foolishly and converted a mosque into a church. Aleppo also fell, and it seemed that Egypt was about to be raped as cruelly as Hungary.

The over-confident Mongols now made a fatal error. Hulegu, responding to word of Mongke's death, withdrew to Azerbaijan with many of his men and still sent the rest forward to crush the Mamelukes. The two forces met on a coast road in Palestine at Ain Jalut, which could mean "Goliath's Eye" or "Goliath's Spring." The Mongol Goliath was defeated by a hard man: Baybars, a product of several slave markets and an experienced assassin. The column commander, Ket Buqa, was last seen riding east, pursued by his bodyguard.

Constantinople falls: Venetian fleet saves some defenders

Constantinople, 15 August 1261

The Latin empire of Constantinople is no more. Michael VIII of Nicaea (Iznik, Turkey) was crowned emperor of Byzantium in the basilica of St Sophia today, his army having captured the city after a lengthy siege.

His agents are believed to have opened a gate from within to admit the Nicaean army. A Venetian fleet has taken off hundreds of women and children who cried for help as their shops and homes burnt behind them. Michael usurped the throne of Nicaea two years ago and made clear his purpose from the outset. The Emperor Baldwin II of Byzantium had assumed that the Nicaeans were the underdogs, and asked for the return of occupied lands. Michael ignored these requests and demanded half the customs dues and half the revenues from the mint. After signing a treaty of alliance with Genoa, Michael surrounded Constantinople. The city held out, although Baldwin was so short of funds that lead had to be stripped from roofs.

The emperor was among the survivors taken off by the Venetian fleet. He was wounded in the arm and leg, and left behind the imperial purple hat decorated with a priceless ruby.

Revolt of English barons ends in failure

Evesham, 4 August 1265
Simon de Montfort, the leader of the dissident barons who tried to curb the powers of King Henry III, died on the battlefield here today. He was beheaded and his body delivered to the monks of Evesham.

Though de Montfort's family was French, he inherited the earldom of Leicester through his mother, and the struggle against the king was in part motivated by a growing dislike of foreign influence, the heavy papal taxation of the church and the extravagance of the king's foreign dependants.

The king, meeting the discontented barons in a parliament at Oxford, made many promises, enshrined in the Provisions of Oxford, but reneged on them. De Montfort called his own parliament, which was notable for including knights and burgesses as well as barons.

De Montfort captured the king and his son, Edward, at the battle

King Henry III: keeping control.

of Lewes in 1264, but a year later the barons, perhaps mistrusting his efforts to gain broader popular support, were deserting him. Edward escaped, to lead the victorious army at Evesham.

Typhoon saves Japanese from Mongols

Japan, 1281
Kublai Khan's great invasion fleet has been wrecked by a typhoon on the Japanese coast. The grateful Japanese, who see the hand of God in their deliverance, have named the typhoon *Kamikaze*, the Divine Wind. The Mongol emperor's flotilla of Chinese and Korean ships carried 140,000 troops, and if this

army had got safely ashore there is little doubt that it would have conquered Japan despite the bravery of the *samurai* who, banners waving, prepared to meet the invaders.

Thousands of soldiers died when their ships foundered or were driven onto the rocks. The survivors who landed on Tsushima were cut down by the waiting samurai.

Some of the 1,001 gilded wooden statues of the Japanese deity Kannon in the temple of Sanjusangen-do in Kyoto, founded in 1164.

Man of God dies, admirer of pagans

Rome, 3 January 1274
Thomas Aquinas, the greatest European thinker of recent times, has died at the papal court at the age of 48. His work marks a major watershed in western thought because he succeeded in creating a synthesis of Christian theology and ancient philosophy, in particular that of Aristotle.

Aquinas was born of a noble family at Aquino, near Naples, in 1225 or 1226. He entered the Dominican order, and in 1245 arrived in Paris to study under Albertus Magnus, a fellow Dominican. Albertus had begun an attempt to bring Aristotle – recently available in new Latin translations from Arab sources – into scholasticism, the study of the meaning of Christian teaching. Aquinas studied the philosopher thoroughly when he was back in Italy at the papal court from 1259-

A later portrait of Thomas Aquinas.

68, before four more years in Paris. He returned to Italy in 1272.

From around 1260, Aquinas wrote his most monumental works: the *Summa contra Gentiles*, explaining Catholicism, and the unfinished *Summa Theologica*, summing up his whole work. By his profound argument that Aristotelian reason and Christian faith are complementary and confirm each other, Thomas Aquinas has forged a new bond between Christian Europe and one of the great philosophers of its pagan past.

Marco Polo at Kublai Khan's court

China, c.1280

Marco Polo, a young Venetian merchant, has become a favourite of Kublai Khan's at the Mongol emperor's stately capital of Cambuluc where once the Jin dynasty ruled.

Marco Polo arrived with his father and uncle five years ago. It is the older men's second visit. On the first, Kublai entrusted them with a message to the pope, and in 1271 they set out for the east again in the company of two missionaries, taking Marco with them.

The holy men soon abandoned their mission, but the adventurous Venetians eventually arrived at the khan's palace where he has gathered together an international group of advisers and military technicians like the experts in siege warfare whom he has hired from Baghdad.

The khan was much taken by young Marco's wonder at the glories of the capital he had built on the ruins of the city razed by his grandfather, Ghengis Khan, and he has employed Marco on a number

An imaginative, much later, view of Polo's presentation to Kublai Khan.

of diplomatic missions. The Venetian has travelled to India and Persia on Kublai's business and has become fluent in Persian and Mongolian although, curiously, he speaks no Chinese.

A sharp-eyed observer, he is impressed by the efficient Mongol administration with its roads and postal system, its census, markets and

paper money, all of which Kublai, a descendant of barbarians, has adopted from the Chinese.

However, of all the wonders of China, nothing has impressed Marco Polo more than Kublai Khan's marble pleasure palace in the city of Shangdu where, it is said, the khan can drink "the milk of paradise".

Reformed womaniser aims to convert the Moslem world

A later image of Raymond Lull.

Majorca, 1270

An extraordinary young man, Raymond Lull, is acquiring quite a reputation amongst the local intelligentsia. He is studying Arabic with a Moorish slave with the intention of going to convert the whole of the Moslem world to this version of Christianity. Meanwhile he is teaching, through stories and song, a new meaning of chivalry to any who come his way.

According to Raymond, it is the duty of the knight to be skilled not only in horse-riding and combat, but also in chivalry. Ethics and science go together in his view. One

man in a thousand is chosen to be a knight because he is "the most loyal, the most strong and of most noble courage". It is his duty to defend the people.

Raymond inherited wealth from his father, who helped King James of Aragon to take Majorca from the Moors. He himself was private tutor to the king's son. As a young man he sang in the manner of the troubadours and was renowned as a lover of women. One day in 1263 the looked up from the bed of one of his lovers and saw "the Lord God Jesus hanging upon the cross". Since then he has been devout.

Mameluke Sultan Baybars was a legend in his own lifetime

Damascus, 30 June 1277

Baybars, the sultan of Egypt and victor of Ain Jalut, has died. His name is revered throughout the Near East as the man who defeated the "invincible" Mongols and saved the civilised world from barbarism.

Like his fellow-Mamelukes who now hold power in Egypt, Baybars was a slave of Turkish birth. He

rose through army ranks to command the Egyptian forces against the advancing Mongols in 1260. At Ain Jalut, near the coast of Palestine, he won a vital victory, claiming the life of the great Mongol general, Ket Buqa, and scattering his army.

Buoyed by his success, Baybars organised the murder of this rival

Kutuz and became the army's choice as sultan. He campaigned against the Franks in the Holy Land, capturing Antioch in 1268 and the great fortress of Krak des Chevaliers in 1271. He died in Damascus after a short illness, leaving the Mameluke army the most powerful in the Near East and having prepared his son's succession.

Mystics who whirl way to ecstasy

Asia Minor (Anatolia), 1273

The great Persian poet Jalal al-Din al-Rumi, or Mawlana, founder of the so-called "whirling dervishes", has died at the age of about 66. Like most of the best Persian poets, Mawlana was a mystic, and a mystical Islamic fraternity, or *tariqah*, grew up around him at Konya (the ancient city of Iconium).

Members of the order were called Mawlawites after their leader, but the rotating dance that is a key part of their ritual soon earned them the nickname of "whirling dervishes" from outsiders. The hypnotic, whirling dance is in fact a liturgical service, with every gesture carefully and meticulously prescribed; through it, members of the fraternity seek to attain ecstasy and higher truth.

Music and dance are rare in Islamic ritual, but stranger practices than this are found among other of the permanent tariqahs which have grown up in the last hundred years or so, beginning as groups of disciples of some inspiring teacher. The first to appear was the charitable Qadirite sect of Baghdad, founded by Abd-al-Qadir al-Jilani, who died in 1166. This was followed by the Rifa'ites, founded by the Mesopotamian Ahmad al-Rifa'i, who died in 1183. Members of this sect, like those of other fraternities, can do bizarre things such as swallowing glowing coals, live serpents and glass, or passing needles and knives through their bodies.

From an Islamic manuscript: the Dance of the Dervishes.

Waiting for admission the garden: illustration from the "Roman de la Rose".

Bible of courtly love is brought up to date

Paris, 1281

The *Roman de la Rose*, the bible of "courtly love" for the past 44 years, has recently appeared in a new, revised edition. Its new author, Jean de Meun, has taken Guillaume de Lorris's earlier work and added 18,000 extra lines.

De Meun's lines are a continuation of Lorris' original work, with its allegorical characters and geometrical symbols. The book – "wherein the art of love is fully contained" – still presents lessons in love-making as well as a picture of today's social behaviour. But the new text incorporates major new attitudes. Lorris moved his characters within the closed boundaries of a square orchard, representing a monastic cloister and the life of contemplation lived within it. De Meun sets his story in a circular garden, representing the whole, infinite world.

He has also abandoned Lorris' belief in courtly love: it remains within the poem, but now it is deliberately debunked. Reason and Nature are de Meun's main characters; Lorris concentrated on courtly Joy. De Meun's encyclopaedic technique tries to take in every facet of modern thought.

Mongol conquest to outlast dead leader

Saray, Astrakhan, 1281

The death of the Golden Horde leader, Khan Mangu Temir, is not expected to impede Mongol conquest in central Europe, nor will Temir's successor be more free from the control exercised over all Tartar affairs by the great khan, Kublai Khan, in China.

A half century ago the eldest son of Genghis Khan, named Jochi, became ruler of the most westerly part of the Mongol empire, in the Urals. In 1236 Jochi's second son Batu pillaged eastern Europe on a scale that earned his army the name "the Golden Horde". Legends proliferated about the Mongols, but in fact most of Batu's soldiers were Turks.

The third pillar of this empire comprised compliant Russian princes, including Novgorod's hero Alexander Nevsky. Such vassals, summoned before their Mongol masters, never knew whether they were on their way to execution, or a party.

Carnage in Sicily on Easter Monday

Sicily, 28 April 1282

The whole of Sicily is in rebel hands after nearly a month of uprisings and massacres which have claimed the lives of several thousand French men, women and children. The bloodshed began on Easter Monday outside the church of the Holy Spirit in Palermo. A crowd was waiting to go inside when a group of French officials became insulting towards the local women. When a French sergeant began to molest one woman, her husband drew a knife and stabbed him to death. As the bells began to toll for the Vespers service, the other Sicilians fell upon the Frenchmen and butchered them.

This was the signal which the rebels had been waiting for. For the past 16 years, since Charles of Anjou won control of Sicily from the Hohenstaufen family, the native population has been encouraged to revolt by the Emperor Michael Palaeologus, in Constantinople, and by Pedro III of Aragon, whose wife was a Hohenstaufen. Messengers ran from the church square through Palermo and out into the towns and villages, and the Sicilians rose, killing their French masters and proclaiming themselves independent. Friars were dragged from Dominican and Franciscan monasteries, and were put to death if they could not pronounce the Sicilian word "ciciri". Messina was the last city to hold out, but now the revolt has begun there too, and already the Angevin fleet in the harbour has been destroyed.

A later Sicilian carving of the rebels plotting the Easter-time massacre.

Bacon's new book queries orthodoxy

Paris, 1292

The English philosopher and man of science Roger Bacon, for many years a controversial figure in academic circles in Paris, is reported to have completed a massive compendium of theological studies which promises to be every bit as challenging as his earlier works.

Bacon was condemned by his superiors in the Franciscan Order for "certain suspect novelties" in his writings, and he spent over ten years in prison. What these novelties were was not made clear, but Bacon has always been dismissive of his contemporaries – St Thomas is "a teacher yet unschooled", another scholar is "an absolute fool", and the Dominicans are the greatest corrupters of biblical texts. Such outspokenness has made him many enemies.

Bacon (who was born near Ilchester around 1214) had a powerful patron in Pope Clement IV. Soon after he moved from Oxford to Paris, the pope wrote to him asking to be sent reports on his scientific studies. Bacon, who argued that there could be no true understanding of religion without a solid grounding in natural science, wrote three major works for the pope and suggested a survey of the whole known world.

Bacon's science, like that of other men of learning, embraced astrology and alchemy. He argued, for example, that since deer, eagles and snakes could prolong their lives by using toads and stones, men should be able to discover an elixir of life. Unfortunately for Bacon, Pope Clement died and he was left without a powerful protector.

A later engraving of the scientist.

Acre falls to Egyptians

Calza's later view of cavalry skirmishes between Crusaders and Turks.

Acre, 5 May 1291

The last Christian bridgehead into Palestine, the great bastion of Acre, has fallen to a Moslem army after a siege of 53 days. Captive knights and foot soldiers alike are to become slaves, while their women and children are on their way to the Damascus slave market. So plentiful is the supply of Christian captives that girls are selling for a drachma apiece.

A year ago, drunken Italian Crusaders ran wild in Acre, dishonouring a truce which protected everyone including local Moslems. They murdered everyone who even resembled a non-Christian. The Sultan Qalawun of Egypt and his son Ashraf besieged the port with tens of thousands of troops and huge catapults to lob bombs over the walls. Up to 1,000 engineers were assigned to a single strongpoint to undermine it with gunpowder. Clouds of arrows fell continuously, as did their victims.

The defenders, including 1,000 knights and their soldiers, were steadily worn down until they could no longer man the walls. They retreated, setting fire to their own towers as 300 Moslem drummers signalled the final onslaught. On the seaward side of the fortress there was a desperate struggle for places aboard galleys escaping to the island of Cyprus.

England to expel affluent Jews

England, 1290

England's Jewish community, for many years an important part of the national economy, has been expelled from the country. Under law the Jews are the "property" of the sovereign, and now King Edward has chosen to banish them.

Under church law no Christian may operate as a usurer, lending money at interest. The Jews, who are not bound by such restrictions, have filled this necessary role with great skill. The community is small, perhaps 3,000 in all, but it plays a major role in financing the nation.

Now this situation has changed and several explanations for the expulsion have been offered. In the first place there is simple anti-Semitism, which has been increasing. But there are economic reasons too. Regular heavy taxation of the Jews has severely depleted their riches, and the king may well have decided that they were no longer wealthy enough to be worth tolerating. With the Jews gone, he has been able to sell off their confiscated property and, by calling in the debts that they were still owed, boost the royal coffers.

His action may also be justified by the Jews' refusal to comply with the Statute of Jewry of 1275. This abolished usury, offering Jews the chance to become merchants, artisans and even farmers. However, few have chosen to integrate in this way.

Rich European merchants are masters of craft and trade guilds

Europe, c.1290

If you live in a town, have not been born into the aristocracy or the merchant class, and want to get ahead in modern Europe, then make sure that you get into a guild – the new breed of professional society for members with a specific trade or craft.

Failure to join a guild in some towns can be the difference between prosperity and starvation. With the guilds frequently operating monopolies, the real power lies with the masters who run them. This is most pronounced in continental Europe where rich merchants dominate the master class. Acquiring master status requires submission of a masterpiece and payment of a large tax. The price may be high, but masters consider their status a passport to wealth. Guild masters fix prices, dictate standards of quality and decide on the eligibility of members.

In England guild membership, once granted to all free men with a trade, has become steadily harder to obtain. Weavers, especially, are being refused membership, and told to renounce their craft, by merchants worried that too many weavers will create a cheap and plentiful supply of labour likely to force prices down.

Aristocrats of trade: the seal of the Guild of Clothworkers in Bruges.

Glass discs offer new eyes for old

The first known picture of spectacles.

Rome, c.1299
It is now possible to correct far-sightedness by wearing specially-made glass discs set in a metal frame. Eye-glasses are thought to have been worn by the Chaldaeans several thousand years ago, and Nero, the Roman emperor was said to have improved his view of the gladiatorial contests by means of a curved, faceted jewel mounted in a ring.

Now a trend seems to be spreading from Italy, where corrective spectacles are being worn. They are making life much easier for both scholars and copyists, allowing them to work in poor light.

Byzantine shock defeat by new arrivals

Byzantine Empire, 1301
Byzantium is still trying to come to terms with the shock defeat of its imperial troops by a group of Ottoman Turkish tribesmen on its eastern border. First reports from the battlefield say that the Turkish attackers were about to raid a valley leading to the port of Nicomedia when they were stopped by imperial forces. The Turks then regrouped and made a swift cavalry charge which broke through Byzantine ranks. Looting is going on in the immediate area, but there has been no further advance on Nicomedia. Byzantium's sense of shock is compounded by its lack of knowledge about its new warlike neighbours under their leader Osman. Of Asian origin, they are descendants of the 400 horsemen who were allowed to settle in northwestern Asia Minor (Anatolia) 60 years ago as a reward for helping the local sultan defeat Mongolian invaders.

Pope held prisoner after French attack

Rome, 7 September 1303
Pope Boniface VIII is tonight a prisoner in his own palace in the hill town of Anagni near here. The palace was attacked at dawn by a band of mercenaries, 300 on horse and over a thousand on foot. They are led by Guillaume de Nogaret, the new minister of the French king, Philip the Fair, and some of the Pope's Italian enemies, notably Sciarra Colonna.

Despite the strong force, the palace's defences held out in the morning. A truce was declared while Boniface considered a demand that he renounce the papacy and hand over all the treasure. He refused.

This evening the attackers broke through, finding Boniface seated on his throne, clutching the papal cross. Colonna wanted to kill him in revenge for his condemnation of his brother, a cardinal. Nogaret insisted on taking him to France as a

A later bust of Pope Boniface VIII.

prisoner. The row began when the French king arrested the bishop of Palmiers and Boniface responded by threatening Philip with excommunication.

Drought brings death and destruction to North American towns

Arizona, c.1300
In the Mesa Verde and the Canyon de Chelly the towns and villages hewn out of rock are deserted. So, too, are the great semi-circular dwellings in the Chaco Canyon. The population, Anasazi Indians who have lived here for 1,500 years, have dispersed.

The same has happened in the southwest to the Hohokam Indians, who possessed one of the most sophisticated societies in North America. Their irrigation canals are dry, the mud walls surrounding their towns are crumbling, and their desiccated ball courts (an import from Mexico) are choked with weeds. In the south-east the story is similiar. The multi-room structures around Casas Grandes in Chihuahua, home for the Mogollon Indians since 1060, are dying in the sun. Drought is drying the land, spreading across the North American continent from east to west, and slowly destroying the Pueblo culture.

For 20 years Arizona and New Mexico have experienced climatic change. Rivers have disappeared, crops have failed, towns have declined, and now Navajo and Apache Indians have fallen on the weakened Pueblo peoples, driving them into the desert.

The remains of Pueblo Indian cliff dwellings at Mesa Verde.

Kublai Khan, Asian conqueror, dies

Enlightened rule by Mongol convert

THE MONGOL EMPIRE IN 1294

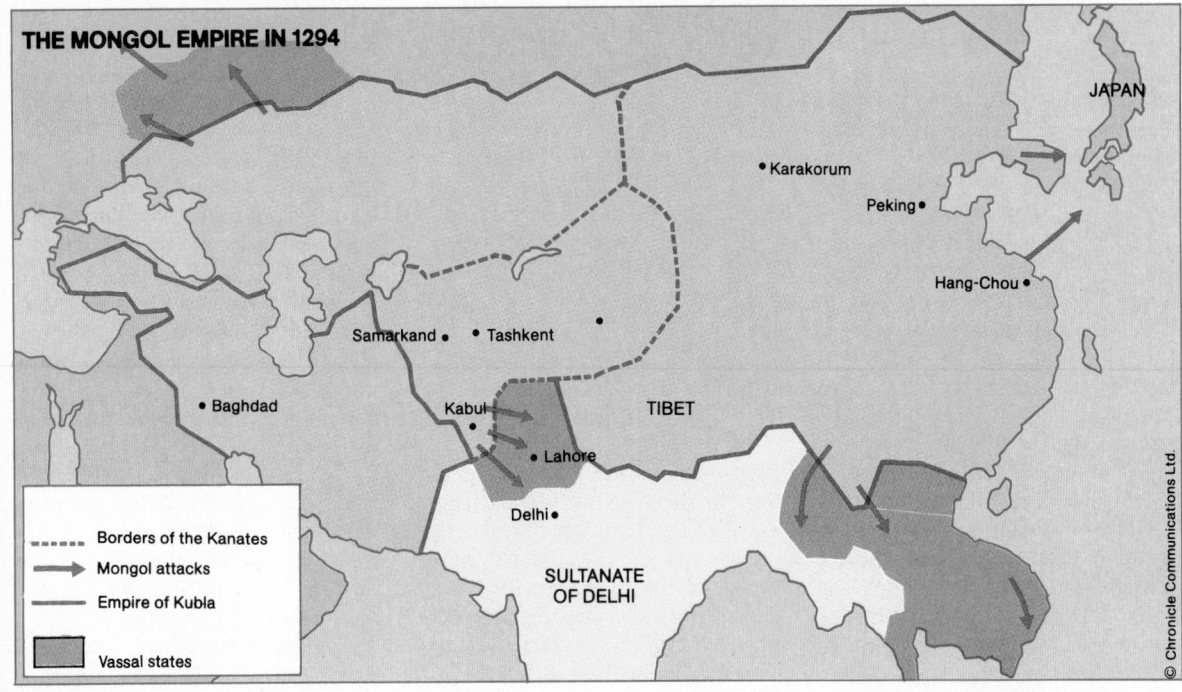

Legend:
- Borders of the Kanates
- → Mongol attacks
- — Empire of Kubla
- ▨ Vassal states

Map labels: JAPAN, Karakorum, Peking, Hang-Chou, Samarkand, Tashkent, Baghdad, Kabul, Lahore, TIBET, Delhi, SULTANATE OF DELHI

© Chronicle Communications Ltd.

Persia, 1304
The death of Ilkhan Ghazan brings to an end a nine-year reign which proved that the Mongols were capable of enlightened rule. Ghazan will be remembered chiefly for his reforms and his humanity towards his Persian subjects.

As a young prince in Khurasan, Ghazan was influenced by Nawruz, a powerful Mongol emir who persuaded him to convert to Islam. When he became *ilkhan* (subsidiary khan), in 1295, Ghazan and his emirs all became Moslems. Buddhists were ordered out, and Christians and Jews were made second-class citizens. Ilkhan Ghazan's conversion helped to bridge the gulf between the Mongol rulers and their Moslem Persian subjects.

Abroad, however, Ghazan continued the Mongols' feud with the Mamelukes of Egypt, even enlisting the help of the Christian powers of Europe. In 1300 he invaded Syria and drove the Mamelukes back, but was forced to retreat soon afterwards to quell an invasion from the Chaghatai khanate of central Asia.

At home, determined not to tax the peasants out of existence, he regulated the methods of taxation, and had all property registered for assessment. The postal courier system was improved, and the roads made safer. New coinage was introduced, and weights and measures standardised.

Beijing, 12 February 1294
Kublai Khan, the lord of all the world between the Danube and the East China Sea, is dead. He was 80 and, despite all his great achievements, he died a disappointed man.

The deaths of his favourite son, Zhenjin, and his beloved wife, Chabi, who made important decisions for him as he grew old, turned him into a recluse. He ate and drank to excess and became obese.

His sorrows were political as well as personal. His succession to his dead brother, Mongke, had been fiercely contested by another brother; then his cousins, Khaidu and Nayan, challenged his authority. Nayan was captured and smothered to death in a rolled-up carpet, but Khaidu waged war against the khan for many years. The failure of Kublai's attempts to invade Japan and Java also weighed heavily on him. Yet he conquered all China and established the Yuan dynasty, ruling from a glittering court in Beijing. He became more Chinese than Mongolian. He still hunted like his grandfather, Genghis, but his tent was lined with ermine and sable and so beautifully quilted that not a breath of wind, not a drop of rain, could disturb his comfort. Now, released at last from his luxurious melancholia, he is dead, leaving behind him a vast empire and a court whose brilliance and tolerance, portrayed by Marco Polo, have enthralled the western world.

What must be asked now, as his funeral procession winds its way to his secret grave in the Kentai mountains, is: how long can his empire hold together?

Black powder is changing warfare

London, c.1300
A black powder invented in China is likely to revolutionise the nature of warfare for ever. Gunpowder – a mixture of charcoal, sulphur, and saltpetre – is now being made in the west where it is rapidly changing the technology of military strategy. Contrary to popular belief, the inventor of gunpowder was not the celebrated Roger Bacon. Certainly he was aware of it, but so were many before him.

Indeed, as long ago as 1221 there are records of gunpowder arrows and packages being projected in battle, and before that, in the 12th century, descriptions of iron fragmentation bombs.

Gunpowder is now being manufactured on a considerable scale. This, in turn, is hastening the development of large metal-barrelled guns which are making existing weapons of war – such as the trebuchet, ballista and mangonet – completely obsolete. The force of the explosive means that attacks can be made at greater range. And the power of the impact of projectiles means that architects will have to revise their plans for fortifications, setting walls lower and curved to minimise damage. Military technology is changing rapidly with the introduction of gunpowder. Its possibilities in offence and defence seem boundless, and no doubt metallurgists are having to think hard about new ways of containing it within the weaponry now being devised as soldiers will require better protection.

An Italian "bombard": gunpowder has made warfare even deadlier.

Philip of France tortures Knights Templar

The death of Jacques de Molay.

Paris, 13 October 1307
Early this morning the members of the Order of the Knights Templar throughout France were arrested by officers of King Philip the Fair. The operation, which was carefully coordinated, came as a total shock. Only yesterday the grand master, Jacques de Molay, was a pallbearer at the funeral of the wife of the king's brother. Tonight he is being tortured in prison.

Few people believe the rumours being put out from the palace that the Templars are guilty of sodomy and other vile practices. Most observers think this is an excuse for Philip to justify crushing the order for financial and political reasons.

Only 16 months ago Philip took refuge for three days in the Paris temple when the mob was howling for his blood after the repeated devaluations. Not long after that he replenished the empty royal coffers by arresting all the Jews and seizing their money. Now it is rumoured that he is after the much bigger riches of the Templars.

The trigger for today's move came two days ago when de Molay had a friendly meeting with the pope at Poitiers to discuss a new crusade. Philip then decided to act immediately.

Chinese calligrapher and artist is dead

Chao Mengfu's "Sheep and Goat", showing his mastery of calligraphy.

China, 1322
The celebrated artist and calligrapher Zhao Mengfu has died at the age of 68. Descended from the founder of the Song dynasty, Zhao was prominent as a public figure as well as an artist, holding a government position under Kublai Khan. Zhao's work covers an extraordinary range of styles and subjects, as if in an effort to sum up all the traditional themes of Chinese paint-ing, although his originality means his paintings are rarely merely archaic. His use of colour and space is particularly effective in landscape painting, where he prefers clear brush strokes – not surprising, from the best calligrapher of his time – to washes, giving a realistic effect to scenery. His famous works include *Autumn Colours at the Qiao and Hua Mountains* (1296) and *Water Village* (1302).

Pope cracks down on "elixir" makers

Rome, 1317
The church has become very worried by the extensive practice of alchemy – an ancient body of knowledge that attempts, among other things, to discover the Philosopher's Stone, for transmuting base materials into gold, and an elixir of life, to confer immortality.

An edict has just been published by Pope John XXII banning alchemy because it clashes with orthodox religious teaching and observances. The pope contends that alchemy is not simply a quest for knowledge, but a dangerously superstitious and mystical exercise, with magical and immoral undertones. It will be interesting to see how far his ban affects the influential alchemists themselves.

Will they immediately renounce these practices? The chances are that they will not, whatever the church's official policy. Too many European rulers, eager to fill their coffers – even with fool's gold – will continue to employ them.

Bishop condemns begging sisterhood

West Germany, 1310
The bishop of Mainz has excommunicated Beguine beggars and threatened to evict them from his parishes. This is the second church crackdown on the activities of women who choose to live together in peace and prayer.

The communities are full of single women over thirty. Easily identifiable in black dresses and white veils, they are a familiar sight in the towns of Belgium, northern France and Germany.

Women are committed, after one year's initiation, to stay in the Beguinages for a further six. Some serve their communities by begging; most work in textiles.

The theological independence shown by the sisters in their translations of the Bible and at their street meetings worried the Catholic establishment. One bishop accused them of being idle, gossiping vagabonds who refused to obey men under the pretext that God is best served in freedom.

Swiss foot soldiers rout Habsburgs' army

Switzerland, 15 November 1315
A small army of Swiss footsoldiers at Lake Zug has routed an army which came to the valleys of Schwyz and Unterwalden to subdue the peasant farmers and to bring central Switzerland within the domain of the Habsburg empire. The Habsburgs have long enjoyed manorial rights in these valleys, but have never pressed their claim to political power.

The cantons of Switzerland were becoming increasingly independent; the inhabitants of Schwyz had begun to fortify the entrances to their valley. Conflict was inevitable, especially when a dispute over grazing rights involved the men of Schwyz in attacking an abbey and taking some of the monks hostage.

Leopold, the brother of Frederick of Austria, devised a plan, involving naval forces on Lake Lucerne, to block off Unterwalden and attack Schwyz. However, he did not reckon with the slaughter that followed – mostly of his own force and its noble leaders in the district of Morgarten.

Torrential rain causes famine in England

England, 1316
England is in the grip of famine. The farming economy has been plunged into depression by prolonged rainy spells which have ruined harvests. One in ten of the population is dying of malnutrition or disease. And still the rain is falling.

Bad harvests in recent years have caused hardship not only in England but also throughout northern Europe, where there is not enough to eat if corn crops fail. A wet autumn in 1314 was followed by the miserable summer of 1315. In England only the West Country escaped disaster. On the Bolton Priory estates in the north, wheat yields were a fifth of normal. This year another wet summer has caused unprecedented suffering. On top of bad harvests, there is now a shortage of salt, as salt pans have failed to evaporate, and livestock have been hit by disease. On the Clipstone estate, in Nottinghamshire, half the sheep have died.

Taxes are heavy, in order to finance royal campaigns against the Scots, and the rise in wheat prices – now 26 shillings and eight pence a quarter, compared with last year's already inflated 8/6d – has hit the poor hardest. Alms have been cut. In Berwick, the starving infantry garrison mutinied, and a wheat ship was attacked by a mob in Sandwich.

Calendar of labours (1460): famine means hardship all the year round.

Avignon new home for Pope Clement V

France, 9 March 1309
The Pope Clement V arrived in Avignon today to stay at the Dominican priory. Although there has been no indication that this is anything other than a temporary visit, there is a strong chance that the papal court may be set up here.

In his four years' reign, Clement has spent more time in France than in Italy. A lawyer by training, he was elected as a compromise candidate who might hold the peace between King Philip the Fair and the papacy. Philip is still trying to condemn the acts of the last pope, Boniface VIII. Clement is trying to stave off this move, and is also trying to restrain Philip's more recent excesses, such as the arrest and torture of the Knights Templar.

Avignon, en route from Paris to

The French-born Pope Clement V.

Rome, is an ideal centre for Clement's diplomatic efforts. It is also not too far away from his native Gascony, and there are many abbeys in the hills to provide refuges from the summer heat.

Divine poet Dante dies alone in exile

From "The Divine Comedy": Dante and the River of Blood in Hell.

Dante Alighieri, lover of Beatrice, as seen by Sandro Botticelli.

Ravenna, Italy, 14 September 1321
Dante Alighieri died peacefully today. He was in the 20th year of his exile from his native Florence, yet his is probably the most illustrious name of all Florence's citizens. He established the Italian language as spoken there as a vehicle for exquisite poetry.

His first collection of poems to his beloved Beatrice was published in his *Vita Nuova* (New Life) when he was 30, after Beatrice's early death in her mid-twenties. He tells us that he first set eyes on her when he was nine years old and nursed a pure passion for her ever afterwards, although both underwent arranged marriages to others.

He promised to say of her "What never yet was said of any woman" in *The Divine Comedy*, in which he voyages in the space of a week in 1300 through all the circles of Hell, or *Inferno*, meeting its famous inmates. Having passed through Purgatory he meets the shade of Beatrice, who conducts the reader through the nine heavens to a vision of the river of light.

English king killed by wife and her lover

England, 21 September 1327
The weak and foolish Edward II, the English king who was forced to abdicate earlier this year, was put to death today in Berkeley Castle, Gloucestershire, where he had been held prisoner. His young son, still a minor, with no real power, was crowned Edward III in January. Edward's fate was sealed a year ago when his wife Isabella and her lover, Roger Mortimer, landed in Essex with a band of foreign mercenaries and marched on London.

Isabella's cause found wide support among the barons and bishops and in the City. The king's favourites, upon whom he lavished lands and lordships, had caused great resentment, and Edward's weakness encouraged dissension, especially after a humiliating defeat by Robert the Bruce in Scotland. Isabella and Mortimer have represented their coup as having the support of parl-

A later engraving of Edward II.

iament and the people. Walter Reynolds, the archbishop of Canterbury, chose the text, "the voice of the people is the voice of God" for his sermon. An orgy of looting has broken out in London.

Giotto, who set painting free, is dead

Florence, 8 January 1337
Giotto, "the principal painter of our time" in the opinion of such poets as Petrarch and Dante, has died aged 70 with his major work, the campanile beside the cathedral here, only just begun. The painter-architect was appointed master of the cathedral works three years ago on his return from Naples where he was working for King Robert.

Giotto was discovered and apprenticed by Cimabue, and as a young man worked on the frescoes that depict the life of St Francis at Assisi. But his masterpiece, the frescoes that completely cover the interior of the Arena Chapel at Padua, changed the whole style of painting and freed it from icon-like formality into something far more naturalistic and dramatic. His crowded scenes, such as "The Adoration of the Kings", depict intensely lifelike figures and animals in bright colours against fragments of architecture and a background of intense blue.

A scene from the life of St Francis: one of Giotto's frescoes at Assisi.

Flemish rebels get English backing

Flanders, 1338
Shrewd economic power-play by the king of England has enabled a Flemish revolt to succeed against this country's French masters. An army of rich and poor led by Jacob van Artevelde, a wealthy burgher of Ghent, is besieging Tournai and has thrown out Louis of Nevers, the count of Flanders, a French ally. The revolt began when Edward III, seeking to force up wool prices, restricted wool exports to Flanders.

The Flemish weavers were badly hit, many of them facing starvation. With memories still fresh of a previous revolt ten years ago – when their peasant army was slaughtered by French cavalry and their leader horrible executed – the weavers prepared to fight back. They found a leader in van Artevelde. The revolt grew as other rich burghers took arms with them.

Edward's lifting of the wool blockade gave both employers and workers a cause to fight for, and van Artevelde, an eloquent and energetic leader, sees his opportunity to unite Flanders under one flag.

At war with France himself, over Philip VI's succession, an alliance with Flanders would be of advantage to Edward and to the Flemish freedom fighters.

Indian ruler shoots victim from cannon

Delhi, 1327
All the inhabitants of Delhi have been forced to leave their homes at a whim of their despotic ruler. The streets of the city are still and silent, and, looking over it, Mohammed bin Tughluq, furious at the citizens for threatening a revolt against him, said "My heart is satisfied, my feelings appeased".

The luckless citizens have been moved to Daulatabad, over 500 miles south, where the emperor is building a new capital. Two citizens unable to comply with the emperor's edict, one a blind man, the other a cripple, have been dispatched in ways much enjoyed by the ruler. One was fired from a cannon and the other had his limbs torn off.

Actors mock their Mongol overlords

Northern China, c.1330

When the Chinese were conquered by the Mongol invaders, and Kublai Khan founded the Yuan dynasty in 1279, they began to develop drama as a means of self-expression. Free of the constraints of Confucianism and censorship, dramatists are learning to explore the stage in a new atmosphere of imaginative invention. Drama grew out of poetry, but music also plays a large part.

Actors and actresses mime, sing, play instruments and dance as much as they speak lines. Music drama is played on several levels at once. There are about 100 Yuan dramatists and hundreds of plays are being performed, especially in the capital Dadu (Beijing). Most of them use legends and popular tales, often introducing satire on the ruling Mongols and their brutal methods. They also depict escapist fantasies of sexual love and the supernatural.

Passages sung by the leading actor or actress are linked by dialogue which narrates the story. On every entrance other characters introduce themselves to the audience, for the style is nonrealistic.

Moslems mourn mystic Indian poet

Delhi, 1325

Amir Khusrau, the "Parrot of India" has died at the age of 95. This great writer, composer and poet to six Delhi sultans was buried close to the grave of his spiritual master, the sainted Chishti Sufi, Nizamuddin Auliya.

Khusrau was the first artist to reflect the absorption of Islam into Indian life by mixing mystic themes and images from both cultures. His poetry and songs gained huge popularity. Khusrau's genius for writing in Persian shows in all his stories, *Laila and Majnun, Shirin and Khusrau*, and many more. Khusrau's devotion to the Sufis, a liberal Moslem sect, inspired his best work. The invention of the *sitar* and hypnotic *ragas* (poems of divine belief) were all intended to help Sufis reach mystical rapture.

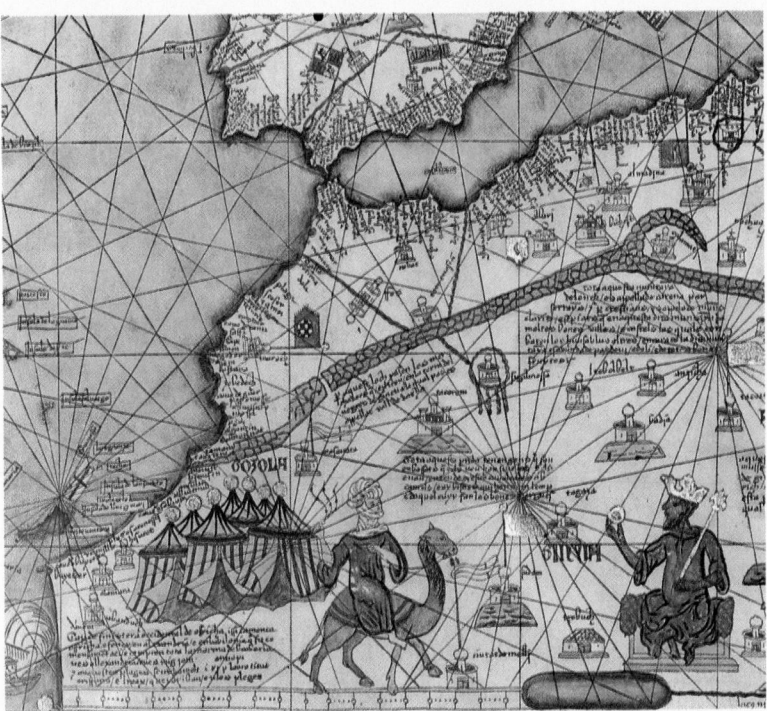

North-western Africa, from a Catalan atlas: Timbuktu is just left of the king.

King of Mali makes pilgrimage to Mecca

Timbuktu, Africa, 1325

Mansa Musa, the emperor of Mali and grandson of the great Suniata Keita, has returned to Timbuktu from his pilgrimage to Mecca. His entourage, preceded by 500 slaves, tailed by 100 camels carrying gold and escorted by 15,000 cavalry, was the most lavish recorded in the annals of the *haj*. Such was Mansa Musa's largesse that his visit caused inflation in Egypt. In Europe it is said that the price of gold is determined by "King Melli".

For most Moslem rulers the haj is more than a mere pilgrimage: it is an exercise in political prestige-building. Mansu Musa's haj is so lacking in political motivations that even the most cynical have been impressed by his sanctity. When he discovered that an audience with the Egyptian Mameluke Sultan al-Malik an Nisran meant kissing the ground in his honour, he refused, saying that he would only kiss the ground in honour of its creator.

Reaching Gao on his return, he has ordered the royal architect, as-Sahali, a Spaniard, to build a new mosque, while at Timbuktu, the main Saharan entrepot for Mali's gold exports, he is continuing the building of the university which is attracting scholars from all over the Moslem world.

Soldier monks beaten by five-foot sword

Japan, 1333

The soldier-monks of Enryakuji, have suffered a humiliating defeat at the hands of the rebels of Rokuhara. The monks, summoned to help the imperial force, marched in great strength from their mountain fastness, certain that the men of Rokuhara would flee.

However, the rebel commanders, knowing that the monks had no cavalry, planned to attack them with mounted archers who would gallop round them shooting arrows "as though at a dog shoot". The monks were so confident that they carried lodging signs to mark the houses which they planned to occupy. But when they reached a temple called the Hall of Eternal Reality the enemy cavalry swirled around them until the monks were utterly exhausted by fighting on foot and weighed down by their heavy armour.

They sought shelter in the temple, but were demoralised by a warrior called Saji Magoro who wielded a five-foot sword. They broke and ran, a defeated rabble.

Mystic heretical theologian is dead

France, March 1327

Meister Eckhart, the celebrated German Dominican mystic, has died in Avignon. It was only last month that he presented himself here to face his critics at the convocation called by Pope John XXII. The pope has condemned 28 of his views in the bull *In agro dominico*.

Eckhart saw the soul as the divine spark which enabled man to know God. To reach God meant turning inwards, doing nothing, owning nothing and knowing nothing. It meant being free of desire, even the desire for sanctity and God. It was the latter which set him apart from many monks who have chosen poverty and self-abnegation. Eckhart also said that the sacraments, though they played a part as preparation, must be cast off if man was to have direct access to God. This was seen as a direct threat to the authority of the church.

Short is beautiful, says thinker Occam

England, 1330

William of Occam, the scholar and philosopher, already established as one of England's most influential and controversial thinkers, has appealed to philosophers, scientists and other scholars to keep their theories as simple and short as possible.

Occam's law of economy (better known as "Occam's Razor") reads: "Entities are not to be multiplied beyond necessity." If, say, an astronomer were to have two explanations for the behaviour of a celestial body, one simple and direct, the other complex and convoluted, he should opt for simplicity, says Occam.

As it happens, this important philosophical rule is not new. The French theologian Durand de Saint-Pourcain has already preached the value of discarding unnecessary intellectual baggage. But it is Occam, who has relentlessly applied his razor to so much woolly thinking, who takes the credit for its widespread application.

Ivan raked in money for Mongol bosses

Moscow, 1340
They called him *Kalita* (Moneybags) – Ivan, the crafty prince of Moscow, born Ivan Danilovitch, who retired a year ago to a monastery to make his will. His death at the age of 36 ends a remarkable political career in which he manipulated both Russia's absentee Mongol masters and his countrymen's wealth.

The Rus tribes are still a series of separate kingdoms paying Tartar taxes. Just over 12 years ago Prince Alexander of Tver, sick of Mongol atrocities, led his people in a suicidal revolt which Ivan helped to crush. Within three years he was the Tartars' trusted tax collector throughout Rus territory, adding his own percentage. Most people benefited, even if the price of relative peace was Kalita's threats as

Moscow: cathedral of the Assumption.

well as penal taxation. In Rostov, however, plunder very similar to Mongol behaviour occurred.

With Kalita's death, Moscow wonders whether his precedent of local self-government will continue under his son, Simeon.

Sultan weds way into power block

Constantinople, 1341
A recent spate of marriage diplomacy – two cleverly arranged marriages in two years – has confirmed the gradual shift of power in the eastern Aegean from the Byzantine empire to Ottoman Turkey.

The main beneficiary of this bout of bloodless diplomacy has been Orkhan, the Ottoman sultan. He now has a secure threshold in Europe by marrying twice over into the Byzantine royal family. Last year he married Theodora, the daughter of Byzantium's new joint Emperor John Cantacuzene, whom he had lent 6,000 troops for his coup. The second marriage was this year when Orkhan's new sister-in-law, Helen, married the other joint emperor and coup victim, John Palaeologus.

Frescoes show "effects of good and bad government" in Italy

Siena, Italy, 1341
The artist Ambrogio Lorenzetti is being widely acclaimed for his magnificent new frescoes commissioned by the city government to decorate the council chamber of its headquarters, the Palazzo Pubblico. Called "Allegory of Good and Bad Government", the frescoes are immediately appealing for their robust naturalism which contrasts with the overworked Byzantine style of Lorenzetti's predecessors, or the strongly derivative style of some of his contemporaries.

The part of the mural showing the effects of good government depicts everyday life in a peaceful city – Siena – with merchants, builders, peasants and other citizens going about their everyday business under the eye of the allegorical figure of Security, one of the first female nudes in Christian art. The figure of Justice will remind the city fathers who use the chamber of the chief role of government, along with the Common Good and the Virtues. Various essential skills and professions are also depicted, such as weaving, agriculture, trade and metalworking. The fresco showing the effects of Bad Government similarly combines allegory and realistic detail, with tyranny, discord, treachery, rape, murder and plunder stalking a ruined landscape.

Lorenzetti's view of the harmonious effects of good government.

"Simple" palace hints at papal austerity

The chapel in the new papal palace.

France, December 1342
The new papal palace at Avignon is nearly complete. Although it is a most imposing building, with four wings built around a cloister, there are no extravagant sculptures. The atmosphere is rather of a monastic simplicity, even austerity. It is in marked contrast to the ornate pal-aces which many cardinals have built on the north bank of the Rhone, just outside the city.

The style may indicate that Pope Boniface XII, who has already installed himself in the pope's tower, is becoming sensitive to the critics of the papacy. It is now more than 30 years since the papal court first moved here, and the period has been distinguished by lawyer popes adept at running large bureaucracies, collecting huge taxes and otherwise vying with kings for temporal power.

Massive sums have been raised by taxes on bishops and priests and by the ubiquitous tithe. More controversially, there has been a big increase in the sale of church offices and dispensations, through which wealthy people are allowed to breach canon laws, such as those prohibiting the marriage of blood relatives.

Warring Hindu state building new capital

Southern India, 1343
A new capital is being built by Vijayanagara's monarch, Harihara. It will be called Vijayanagar. The collapse of the Delhi sultan's power in southern India around the year 1300 created a litter of petty statelets. Two dominated, the Moslem Deccan and the Hindu Vijayana-gara, separated by the Krishna river and regularly at war with each other. Under Harihara (a Hindu convert from Islam, which is unusual), Vijayanagara has become the preeminent power in the south; and in addition to building a new capital, he is clearing forests, irrigating drylands and reforming taxes.

English king bankrupts Italian banks

Bankers: counting their losses?

Florence, 1346
The great Italian banking houses are ruined. The bankruptcy of the Peruzzi in 1343 was followed by that of the Acciauoli and Bardi last year. Now the Florentine bankers alone have lost 1.7 million florins. The chief architect of their collapse is Edward III of England.

In Tuscany and Lombardy, bankers have been capitalising on European trade for nearly 100 years. The great Florentine firms are represented throughout Europe. But lending money to kings and princes has proved risky. To finance war against the Scots and French, Edward III has borrowed extensively from the Bardi and Peruzzi banks. He has now repudiated debts of 800,000 florins and imprisoned the banks' agents.

New Aztec capital fulfils old prophecy

A mosaic mask of an Aztec goddess.

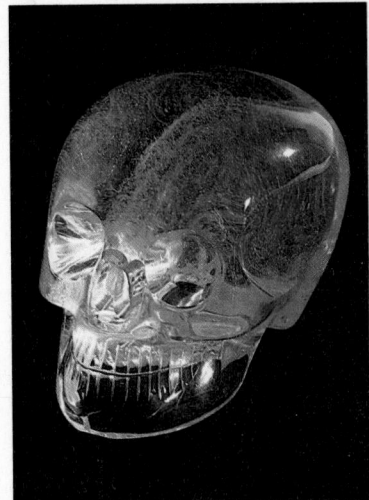

An Aztec skull carved from crystal.

Mexico, c.1345
On a marshy island in the Great Lake a new city is being built by the Aztecs. It is the fulfilment of a tribal prophecy that the Aztecs would found a capital on an island marked by an eagle on a prickly-pear cactus. They have called their city Tenochtitlan, which translates into English as "The Place of the Prickly-Pear Cactus".

The birth of Tenochtitlan marks the end of 200 years of Aztec wanderings through the Valley of Mexico, hiring themselves as mercenaries to the three leading powers in the region: the Tepanec at Atzcapotzalco on the northwestern shores of the Great Lake, the Toltec-derived state of Texcoco east of the lake, and the city-state of Culhuacan to the south. Now, under their priestking, Tenoch, they are a major power, maintaining semi-independence from the Tepanec.

The island city is magnificent, built on a grid and criss-crossed by

The serpent goddess Coatlicue.

canals and thoroughfares. Temples abound to the sun god Huitzilopochtli – who must be fed with human sacrifices. The streets are packed with Tenochtitlan's tens of thousands of citizens, the canals crowded with canoes.

A turquoise and shell chest ornament in the form of a two-headed beast.

Germany, 11 July 1346. Charles IV of Luxembourg is elected Holy Roman emperor at the instigation of Pope Clement VI, who has declared Lewis of Bavaria deposed. Most of Germany, however, continues to support Lewis.

France, 3 September 1346. Edward III of England, who invaded Normandy in July, begins the siege of Calais.

Constantinople, 1346. A violent earthquake strikes the Byzantine capital. The eastern arch of St Sophia's crumbles.

India, 1347. Bahman Shah establishes an independent sultanate, based on Bijapur, Bidar and Gulbarga in the Deccan.

Rome, 20 May 1347. The demagogue Cola di Rienzo, whose ambition is to revive Rome's classical role as capital of Italy, is given power by the people and takes the title of tribune.

Europe, September 1347. The Black Death arrives in Greece, Sicily, southern Italy and Livorno.

Germany, October 1347. The Emperor Lewis is killed in an accident, leaving the field clear for his rival, Charles IV.

Europe, January 1348. The Black Death spreads to Pisa, Venice, Avignon and Arles.

Europe, April 1348. The Black Death reaches Toulouse, Lyons and Spain.

Europe, June 1348. The Black Death arrives in England.

Prague, 1348. The Emperor Charles IV, who became king of Bohemia on the death of his father at Crecy, founds the university of Prague.

Europe, 1349. The Black Death comes to Germany and Brittany.

Germany, 1349. William of Occam, the Franciscan philosopher, dies at Munich. His will be best remembered for his law of economy (Occam's razor) in which he exhorted scholars to keep their theories short. He believed in the absolute power of God.

Germany, July/August 1349. Large-scale massacres of Jews occur in Frankfurt, Mainz and Cologne, associated with the activities of the Flagellants. Many survivors flee to Poland.

Avignon, October 1349. Pope Clement VI condemns the Flagellants and forbids their processions.

French beaten at Crecy

The Battle of Crecy: the English longbows (r.) proved decisive.

Crecy, 25 August 1346
Night has fallen on the battle field here, although the cries of the wounded continue to echo through the darkness until they are silenced by the swords and battle-axes of pillaging English footsoldiers. The out-numbered army of Edward III has won a great victory over French chivalry. Philip VI has fled, leaving over 1,500 dead, and the way is open for Edward to advance on Calais.

Two factors gave Edward his victory. The first was French pride and vanity, with Philip's knights ignoring orders and vying with each other to be first to confront the invaders. Confusion reigned in the darkness, and when the first ranks finally came across the English, they turned and ran into their own allies. The second factor was the English longbow. Philip had put great reliance on his 15,000 Genoese crossbowmen and ordered them to attack while he sorted out his divisions.

The Genoese were tired after an all-night march and at first refused to advance. When they finally made their move in a heavy rainstorm, their weapons were almost useless, their bow-strings soaked.

Only then did the English archers take one step forward and begin a rain of arrows on the hapless Genoese who fled into the swords of the French footsoldiers. In the melee that followed, the French presented a perfect target for the English bowmen. The French were already exhausted by the time that they began hand-to-hand combat against the well-prepared English knights and their infantrymen.

Abject burghers beg for mercy from English king

Calais, 3 August 1347
Six burghers of the besieged city of Calais surrendered to the English king, Edward III, today and were on the point of being put to death when Edward's wife, Philippa, sank to her knees, crying: "My dear lord, I ask you in all humility, in the name of the Son of the Blessed Mary and by the love you bear me, to have mercy on these men." The king's heart was softened and he granted her wish.

Calais had been under siege for a year and its citizens were dying of hunger when the governor, Sir Jean Vienne, offered to surrender if the king would spare their lives. Edward agreed on condition that six principal citizens, with heads and feet bare and halters round their necks, delivered the keys of the city and threw themselves on his mercy. Edward rejected all appeals for clemency from his own knights; then Philippa spoke up.

Six citizens of Calais are led to the English (19th-century engraving).

Mystery plague heads west after hitting Russian cities

Crimea, 1347
A new outbreak of plague has hit major cities in the Crimean area of southern Russia and is beginning to take hold in the Mediterranean. Reports state that the epidemic is spreading slowly westwards, engulfing city after city in its apparently unstoppable progress. It has al-

ready reached Sicily. The disease appears to be carried by merchant ships, which ply their trade between the Black Sea ports, to which Asian traders bring their goods, and those of the Mediterranean. Whether medicine can halt the epidemic is unknown. What is certain is that trading, upon which so many

depend, will continue. First reports of the plague, which has not been seen at this intensity for eight centuries, came in 1345, when it emerged in the cities of the Golden Horde in southern Russia. From there it moved to Armenia and Azerbaijan, Scythia, Byzantium and the Crimea.

Black Death claims third of European population

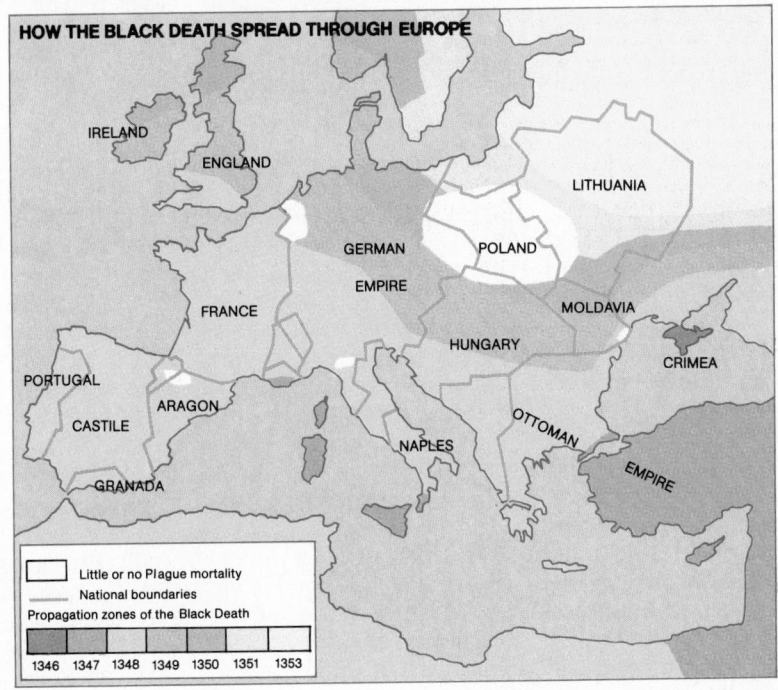

HOW THE BLACK DEATH SPREAD THROUGH EUROPE

IRELAND

ENGLAND

LITHUANIA

GERMAN
EMPIRE

POLAND

FRANCE

MOLDAVIA

HUNGARY

PORTUGAL

ARAGON

CRIMEA

CASTILE

NAPLES

OTTOMAN

GRANADA

EMPIRE

	Little or no Plague mortality
	National boundaries
	Propagation zones of the Black Death

| 1346 | 1347 | 1348 | 1349 | 1350 | 1351 | 1353 |

Flagellant Brethren: whipping up public remorse for the sins of the world.

Europe, 1348

Hundreds of thousands of people – men, women and children – are dying in every country in Europe, struck down by an epidemic of an apparently incurable plague which the healthy and afflicted alike call "the Black Death".

Not since the sixth century has such an epidemic attacked Europe. Spreading from Asia, and carried by rat-fleas via the ports of the Black Sea, the plague takes two forms. "Bubonic" plague is seen in the swellings, or buboes, that inflate the lymph nodes at the neck, armpit or groin, while the "pneumonic" plague affects the lungs, and victims choke on their own blood.

The plague has stunned Europe, and everywhere people are desperate for an explanation. Some blame invisible particles carried in the wind, others talk of poisoned wells. Many, inevitably, blame the Jews.

Immediate responses differ widely. Some choose to challenge the plague by bouts of riotous living, others seek protection by barring their doors and living as recluses. Neither method has halted the disease. Others have left home, seeking safety in the remote countryside, but often they too have fallen ill. Attempts to bar villages, towns, even whole cities, to sufferers have all failed. The plague moves on. The outbreak has shat-tered communities. Families have been set against each other – the well rejecting the sick. Essential services have collapsed; law and order, with so many administrators struck down, barely exist in some areas. A sense of panic pervades Europe and everyone, it appears, is struggling only for his own survival. Properties stand empty, deserted by desperate owners; the sick die alone, for even the most devoted doctors cannot save them; corpses are simply dumped in the street or buried in mass graves. Some depraved creatures, themselves already infected, break into houses and threaten to contaminate all within unless bribed to leave. Agriculture is at a standstill. Crops wither in the fields; cattle wander untended.

Doctors do what they can, but the plague seems irresistible. Even the most expert physicians can do little more than help strengthen people's resolve and build morale. Some recommend the burning of aromatic woods and herbs; others suggest special diets, courses of bleeding, new postures for sleeping and many other remedies. The very rich are trying medicines made of gold and pearls. The terrible truth is that nothing seems to work. Flight is the best option, and if one cannot fly, then all that remains is resignation and prayer.

Flagellants seek to appease angry God

Europe, 1349

Bands of hooded men, wearing white robes marked front and back with a red cross, are moving to and fro across Europe, attempting to atone for the ravages of the Black Death by whipping themselves in ritual public ceremonies.

The Flagellant Brethren, as they are known, believe that the plague is a punishment for human sin, and that by scourging themselves they can show mankind's repentance.

They travel in parties of anything from 50 to 500 men, and are highly organized. Led by a layman – the master – they move from town to town to perform their rituals. Singing hymns and sobbing, the men beat themselves with scourges studded with iron spikes. Blood gushes from their many wounds, and the spikes embed themselves in the torn flesh. The ritual is performed in public twice each day.

Such exhibitions are highly influential. The establishment may criticise their attacks on church corruption and their promotion of a wave of savage anti-Semitism, but the masses worship the flagellants as living martyrs. Their deeds are to be admired and their commands to be carried out.

English king founds new order of chivalry

A funerary badge, including King Edward's new Order of the Garter.

England, 1349

Competition is high among leading knights in the kingdom for invitations from King Edward to join his new Order of the Garter. Just 25 knights and the king are eligible for membership of the new elite order, which meets for the first time on St George's Day. The idea for the order reputedly came after the king, in a much-publicised moment of chivalry, rescued one of the countess of Salisbury's garters at a dance, rebuking onlookers with *Honi soit qui mal y pense* – Shame on whomever thinks this shameful.

Clash of kings: 100 Years War

The Hundred Years War owed its distant origins to disputes over the lands held by the English crown in France. Although Normandy, the homeland of the conquerors of 1066, had been lost to the French in 1204, English kings continued to hold Aquitaine (often known as Gascony) in south-western France. Taken over by the future Henry II when he married Eleanor of Aquitaine in 1152, this large slice of territory – perhaps a tenth of the area of modern France – was from 1259 held by the English king as a tenant of the French crown. This relationship between a French royal overlord and an English vassal, himself a king in his own country, was rich in possible conflict. To this cause for contention was soon added a more urgent dispute over the crown itself. Edward III, king of England from 1327, inherited a claim to the French throne from his mother Isabella, daughter of Philip IV of France; but on the death of Charles IV, the last of Philip's sons, in 1328, Edward's claim as Philip IV's grandson was ignored in favour of Philip's nephew, Philip VI. After a period of tension in the 1330s when each side supported the enemies of the other, a war was finally ignited by Philip VI's confiscation of Gascony in 1337.

The first two phases, 1337-60

The conflict which followed lasted until 1453, though campaigning was sporadic and truces frequent. At first the English had little success. In 1339 Edward took an army to Flanders, where he proclaimed himself king of France. But war was expensive, and Edward's initial attempts to rally support through a coalition of subsidised allies in the Low Countries and Germany proved impossible to sustain. Over-taxation brought a crisis at home, and although the English won a battle off Sluys, at the mouth of the Flemish river Zwyn, in 1340, the first phase of the war ended without much glory.

Not so the second phase. In 1342 Edward was able to intervene in Brittany, thanks to a disputed succession there, and in 1346 in Normandy. In August 1346 he shattered a French army at Crecy; in the same year the Scots, allies of the French, were beaten at Neville's Cross, near Durham, and their king, David Bruce, captured; Calais fell to the English in the following year; and in 1356 another French army was defeated at Poitiers by the Black Prince, Edward's eldest son. Poitiers, the greatest of the English victories, resulted in the capture of King John of France, Philip VI's successor, and the demoralisation of French political society. The treaty of Bretigny in 1360 was a recognition of Edward's successes. He was promised large new territories in western France and a huge ransom for King John. In return for these gains Edward was to give up his claim to the French throne.

English achievements were the product of good generalship, efficient fighting methods, and the skilful exploitation of large resources. Through grants of parliamentary taxation and the profits of a heavy export duty on wool, Edward was able to finance paid armies whose military capabilities exceeded those of the French. Campaigns were carefully planned and aimed at devastating the French countryside rather than at bringing the enemy to a battle whose outcome was unpredictable. The French were slow to adapt to English tactics of mobile raids and the use of archers; and they continued to rely on old-fashioned heavy cavalry, despite the vulnerability of mounted knights to English arrows. The size of France, the strength of provincial feeling, the difficulty of securing taxation, the existence of large semi-independent principalities within the country's boundaries – Flanders, Brittany, Gascony – all weakened the speed and cohesion of the French response. Edward confronted a country which lacked the long English tradition of tight, centralised government. That was his chief advantage.

Mixed fortunes, 1369-1420

The treaty of Bretigny preserved the peace for nine years. In 1369 the main conflict was resumed when some Gascon lords, aggrieved by the taxes levied by the Black Prince to pay for a Spanish expedition, appealed to Charles V of France for help. The fortunes of the war which followed turned against the English. The territories gained at Bretigny were lost and English Gascony was reduced to a narrow coastal strip. Raiding continued; but reforms within France – the growth of regular taxation and a new military emphasis on archery – reduced the disparities between the two powers, and there were no more English victories. By the mid 1380s a stalemate had set in. Richard II, king of England since 1377, favoured peace, and in 1396 a 28-year truce was agreed on. It lasted, precariously and with some breaches, until the accession of Henry V in 1413. Henry revived the claims of his great-grandfather Edward III to the French throne (never really abandoned, despite the settlement at Bretigny) and renewed demands for territory. When these were refused, he invaded France in 1415. After capturing Harfleur at the mouth of the Seine, he went on to defeat a French army at Agincourt, and by 1419 he had conquered Normandy: the most brilliant feat of sustained generalship in the whole war. By the treaty of Troyes of 1420 he was recognised as heir to the French throne after the death of the reigning king, Charles VI. His marriage to Catherine, Charles' daughter, did something to legitimise a position essentially based on conquest.

The tide turns against England

The treaty of Troyes was followed by the early deaths of both Henry V and Charles VI in 1422, leaving Henry's infant son, Henry VI, as titular king of France. For a few years the old king's brother, John, duke of Bedford, was able to maintain the English position in France against Charles VI's son, the dauphin. But from 1429 the war began to move decisively in favour of the French. In that year the charismatic figure Joan of Arc raised the English siege of Orleans and led the dauphin to his coronation at Rheims as Charles VII. In 1435 Bedford died and the Anglo-Burgundian alliance, vital to English strategy since 1419, broke down. In 1436 the English were driven from Paris and in 1445 Henry VI agreed to surrender Maine. In 1449 Normandy fell to the French; and in 1453 they reconquered Gascony. With Calais as their only remaining French possession, the English had lost the war.

The decline of the English cause reflected the changed nature of the war in the 15th century. Under Henry V and his successor it was a war for conquest, not a war of raids, as under Edward III. Forces had to be kept permanently in the field, castles manned, an administration maintained. Such a war was beyond the English crown's resources. After Bedford's death there was no outstanding military leader, and the home government was increasingly divided by faction: as the French government had been in Henry V's day, but was no longer. In France Charles VII secured regular taxes, reformed the army, developed a standing force of archers and a train of artillery. The English were literally outgunned.

For both England and France the war was a formative experience. In England it consolidated the role of parliament in the granting of taxes and contributed to the growth of a constitutional monarchy. In France it destroyed the provincial separatism which had formerly weakened the country and prepared the way for a more forceful monarchy, equipped with two of the main attributes of an absolutist state: taxation without consent, and a standing army. It thus did much to determine the future internal shape of both kingdoms.

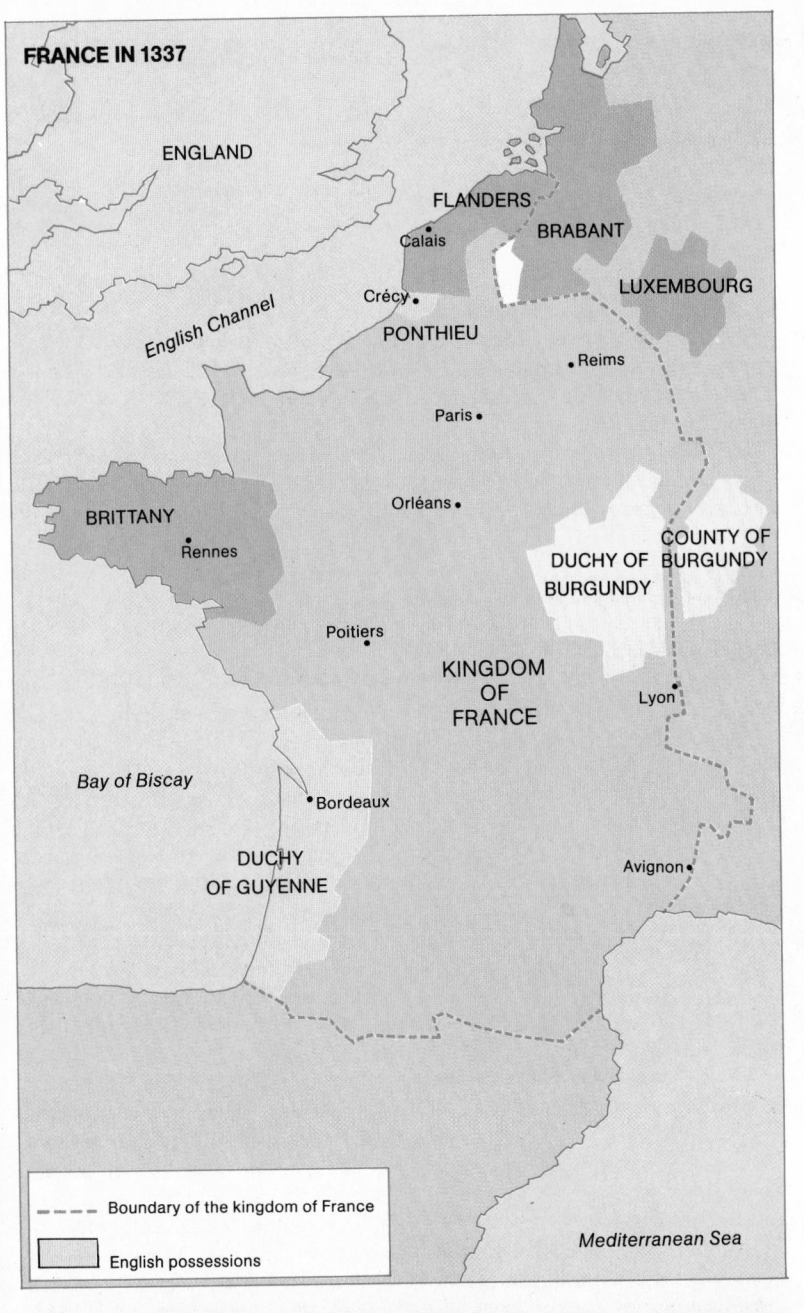

FRANCE IN 1337

ENGLAND

FLANDERS

Calais •

BRABANT

Crécy •

LUXEMBOURG

English Channel

PONTHIEU

Reims •

Paris •

Orléans •

BRITTANY

Rennes •

COUNTY OF
BURGUNDY

DUCHY OF
BURGUNDY

Poitiers •

KINGDOM
OF
FRANCE

Lyon •

Bay of Biscay

Bordeaux •

DUCHY
OF GUYENNE

Avignon •

Mediterranean Sea

- - - Boundary of the kingdom of France

English possessions

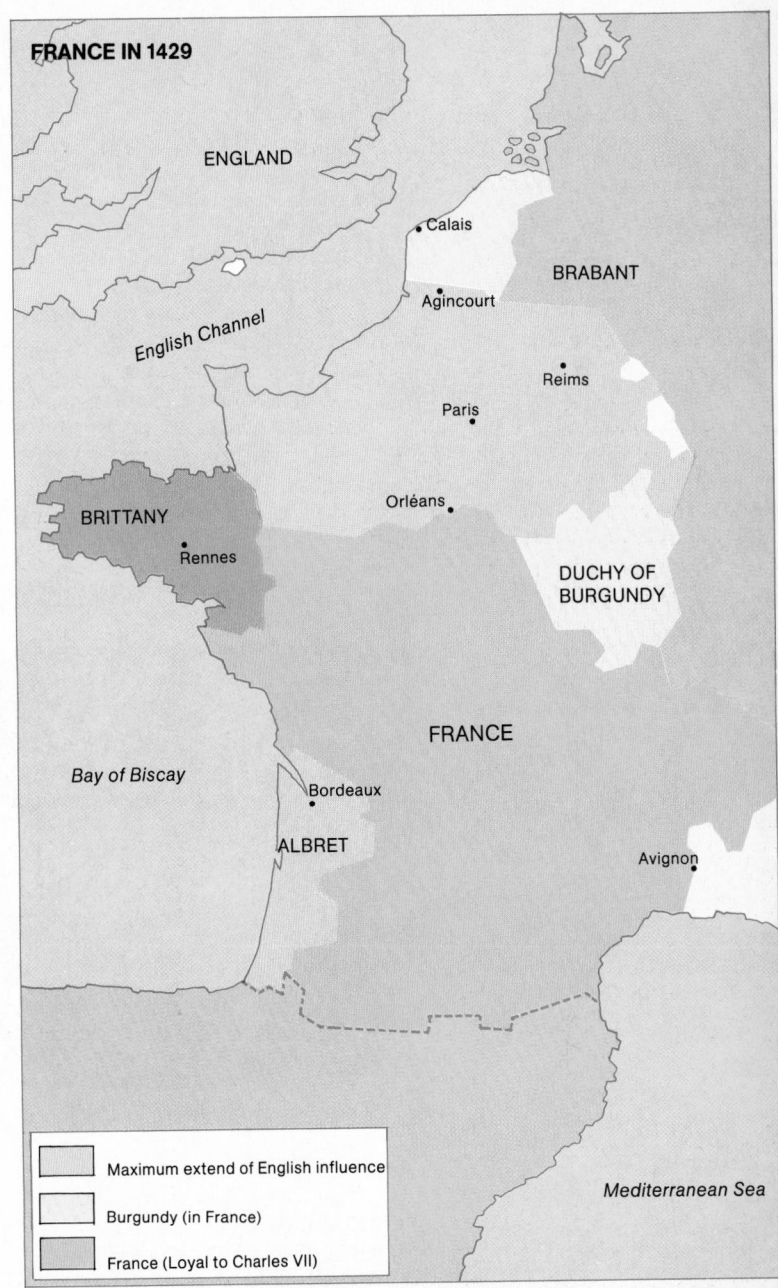

FRANCE IN 1429

ENGLAND

Calais •

BRABANT

Agincourt •

English Channel

Reims •

Paris •

Orléans •

BRITTANY

Rennes •

DUCHY OF
BURGUNDY

FRANCE

Bay of Biscay

Bordeaux •

ALBRET

Avignon •

Mediterranean Sea

Maximum extend of English influence

Burgundy (in France)

France (Loyal to Charles VII)

Left: a knight bids farewell, from the Luttrell Psalter. Above: Froissart's chronicle: the earl of Pembroke fights the Spanish at La Rochelle in 1372.

Red turbans rebel at taming Yellow River

China, 1351

A peasant revolt has broken out in the province of Huai where the government has sent 20,000 troops and coerced 150,000 men from the surrounding towns as labourers to re-route the mighty Yellow River.

The river has always been unpredictable and seven years ago it went on the rampage, bursting its dykes, flooding 6,000 square miles and inundating 17 walled cities. There was famine and plague. Many refugees turned to banditry.

Then the great river changed its course; the Grand Canal became useless and the waters threatened the vital salt works at Hejian. The emperor demanded that the river be tamed, and so began one of China's greatest projects.

But the assembling of the labour force has given the revolutionary "White Lotus" secret society the opportunity to cause trouble for the Yuan government. It has fomented a revolt among the peasants, who have taken the name of "Red Turbans", and trouble is spreading through northern China.

Moroccan traveller welcomed in Africa

Ibn Battuta, by a much later artist.

Timbuktu, 1352

Ibn Battuta, the great Arab geographer, has arrived in Mali. Born in Tangiers in 1304, he left for Mecca at the age of 21 and travelled through North Africa, Palestine, Persia, southern Russia, India, China, Indonesia, East Africa and Spain before returning to Tangiers.

Part private traveller and part unofficial ambassador for the Moroccan sultan, Abu Inan, ibn Battuta says he is now completing what he calls his last journey. At Sijilmasa, where his caravan set out across the Sahara, he met a man whose brother had given him hospitality in China; at Taghaza he saw the mines where the salt is hewn which, exchanged kilo for kilo for gold, makes Mali so rich; and in the southern sands his caravan almost perished of thirst.

In spite of the food, which he found disgusting, he appears to like the country. "The negroes have an abhorrence of injustice", the roads are safe, the merchants are honest, the women beautiful and "the men possess no sexual jealousy".

"Decameron" written while plague rages

A scene from a story in Boccaccio's "Decameron", by Botticelli (1440-1510).

Florence, 1353

Of the many ways of combatting the horrors of the plague, a book might seem the least likely. But the *Decameron*, written by the Florentine author Giovanni Boccaccio, is designed to do just that.

It consists of 100 amusing stories, supposedly told by seven young ladies and three young men taking refuge from the plague in the country, and, according to its author, is meant to console all unhappy lovers. The story-telling takes ten days, hence the name, which in Italian means ten days. But the *Decameron* is not all humour. Boccaccio, who lost his own mother to the plague, watched its ravages in Florence. The book's introduction is one of the finest eyewitness accounts to emerge from this terrible experience.

Boccaccio was born in Tuscany in 1313. His father worked for the bankers Bardi. Despite hopes that he might join either the church or the business world, Boccaccio preferred literature. He has spent many years in Naples, where he moved in court society and launched his literary career.

German emperor strengthens princely power with Golden Bull

Germany, 10 January 1356

The next king of Germany will be elected by an electoral college of seven, according to a new imperial edict – the Golden Bull – published today and designed to end the succession disputes that have plagued the Holy Roman Empire. Members of the electoral college are the archbishops of Trier, Cologne and Mayence and the rulers of Bohemia, the Rhine Palatinate, Saxe-Wittenburg and Brandenburg. Excluded from the Bull by Emperor Charles IV is the Pope who has frequently repeated his claim that he should be allowed to confirm whoever is elected. Under the Bull the seven electors cannot discuss their choice before casting their votes.

French king is captured

An effigy of the warlike Edward, the Black Prince, victor at Poitiers today.

France, 19 September 1356
The battle was almost won. The inhabitants of Poitiers had closed their gates to the French army and watched from safety as the English began a systematic massacre outside until the French surrendered.

Edward, the Black Prince of England, had fought "like a raging lion" all day and, hearing that victory was certain, he placed his banner on a bush to rally his army. A crimson tent was erected, drinks were brought, and he retired from the field of battle with his lords.

It was at that point that a mob of English footsoldiers appeared over a hillock with John the Good, the king of France, in their midst. In the true tradition of chivalry, the king was invited into Edward's tent where the two men drank wine and discussed the battle. At a banquet tonight, the king and most of his

Poitiers: a French manuscript.

captured counts and barons were honoured guests. The victorious Edward refused to be seated in the king's presence, even serving at table as a mark of humility. Tomorrow, after Mass, the prince, his captives, and a mass of booty will leave for London.

Mob kills Roman ruler in woman's dress

Rome, 1354
An innkeeper's son who dreamt of freeing Rome and uniting Italy has been stabbed to death by his former supporters. Cola di Rienzo had succeeded in convening an assembly of the people which elected him tribune and expelled the ruling nobles from the city. Rienzo then went on to challenge papal authority. He was imprisoned, but regained favour and once again ruled Rome. Prison had done much to damage his charisma, however. He emerged fat and flabby, with a huge paunch, his eyes wild and bloodshot from heavy drinking. It did not help his image with the sober Romans that he even washed in wine.

Rienzo's fate was certain when he introduced tax increases. A mob surrounded the Capitol, calling "death to the tyrant" and stoning Rienzo when he appeared on the balcony and tried to convince them that he, too, was a plebeian. Rienzo

Rienzo: republican dreams.

tried to escape, using tied table-cloths as a rope. That ruse failed. He put on his helmet and went to meet the crowd, sword in hand, but changed his mind at the last minute, cut off his beard and disguised himself as a woman before the crowd fell on him.

Prague to become "Rome of the North"

Prague, 1350
Prague has been named as the Holy Roman empire's imperial capital and looks like entering on an era of glory. The decision by the Emperor Charles IV is part of his plan to transform the city on the banks of the river Moldau, or Vltava, into the "Rome of the North".

Charles has already founded a university, the first in central Europe. It is composed of four faculties, philosophy, theology, law and medicine. He is also building new churches, including St Vitus', monasteries and fortifications, and spanning the Moldau with a stone

bridge which is carrying his name. As a result numerous and famous European artists, architects, sculptors and writers are flocking to Prague, and the cultural boom is being matched by a growth in trade and the increasing importance of artisans' guilds. For some 300 years Prague has been both a busy stone city, where Slavs, Russians, Moslems, Jews and Turks have traded, and a key religious centre.

Cathedral of St. Vitus in Prague.

Heirs of the great khan lose their Persian empire

Persia, c.1353
The Mongols' Persian empire, the *Ilkhanate*, has more or less disintegrated. A succession of short-lived pretenders has merely emphasised the power vacuum that has existed since Abu Said died in 1335 leaving no heir.

After Ghazan died in 1304, his brother Oljeitu ruled for 12 years. Oljeitu could claim two major achievements: he conquered the province of Gilan, on the Caspian

coast, the last significant expansion of the Mongol empire; and he left a magnificent memorial in his mausoleum at Sultaniyya, with its remarkable double-skinned dome.

Abu Said, the son of Oljeitu, was only 11 when he came to the throne, and effective rule was in the hands of the leading amir, Chopan. There was fierce rivalry between the Chopanids and the Jalayirids of Mesopotamia, which was to erupt again after Abu Said's death. In

1322 peace was made at last with the Egyptian Mamelukes, and in 1327 Abu Said overthrew and killed Chopan, and took full power himself. The rest of his reign was largely harmonious. There were no serious military rivals to the Mongols, but the Ilkhanate ultimately fell apart for purely dynastic reasons. Arpa Ke'un lasted for only a few months – the first of many distant descendants of Genghis Khan to claim the throne in vain.

London, 1358. France and England sign a treaty by which the ransom of John the Good is fixed at four million ecus and extensive French territories are ceded to England.

Balkans, 1358. Lewis of Hungary wins Dalmatia from Venice.

France, 1360. France and England reach accord in the treaty of Bretigny. John the Good is freed from captivity and returns to France.

France, 1363. When John learns that his son Louis of Anjou, whom he had agreed to deliver to the English as a hostage, has escaped, he keeps his word of honour and goes back to London as a prisoner.

Spain, 1363. Backed by Peter IV of Aragon, Henry of Trastamara, the illegitimate half-brother of King Pedro, lays claim to the throne of Castile.

London, 8 April 1364. John the Good dies in captivity at the Tower of London. He is succeeded as king of France by Charles V (the Wise).

Brittany, 12 April 1365. By the treaty of Guerande, the house of Blois cedes its rights in Brittany to John IV de Montfort.

Spain, 1367. Pedro the Cruel, aided by the Black Prince, defeats Henry of Trastamara at Najera.

China, 1368. Zhu Yanzhang captures Dadu (Beijing) from the Mongols and establishes the Ming dynasty, with a capital at Nanjing.

Spain, 28 March 1369. Henry of Trastamara defeats Pedro the Cruel and besieges him in his castle of Montiel. Pedro is captured trying to escape and knifed to death by Henry.

Denmark, 1370. The peace of Stralsund gives trading privileges to the Hanseatic league of German towns.

Balkans, 1371. The Ottoman Turks under Murat defeat the Bulgarian forces at the river Maritza. All Macedonia except Salonika falls to the Turks.

Scotland, 1371. The death of David Bruce brings a new dynasty to the throne: the Stewarts. David's heir is his nephew, Robert II Stewart, the hereditary steward of Scotland.

France, 1372. A Castilian fleet, acting in support of the French, defeats an English fleet off La Rochelle, reversing the effect of Sluys in 1340.

Ships from the Hanseatic league of trading towns in Copenhagen harbour.

German traders unite against competition

Lubeck, 1356
The German Hanseatic towns have formed an association to protect their trading network along the coasts of northern Europe from London in the west to Novgorod in the east. The Hanse is becoming an increasingly important commercial and military power.

German merchants have been extending their trading empire since the 12th century when they established a colony at Wisby on the island of Gotland. Trading with Novgorod and Finland, Wisby then became a link with western Europe, bringing Flanders cloths, salt and beer to the Slavs, and bringing back furs, hides, wax and amber.

Since the last century Hanseatic traders have become established at Lubeck, the focal point of Baltic commerce, Hamburg and Bremen, serving the North Sea and North Atlantic, and at Flanders, dealing with the river-borne commerce of northern Europe. London and Bergen in Norway are more recent additions to this fast-growing trade network.

The newly-formed federation allows competition, but it imposes severe penalties on any member violating a common decision.

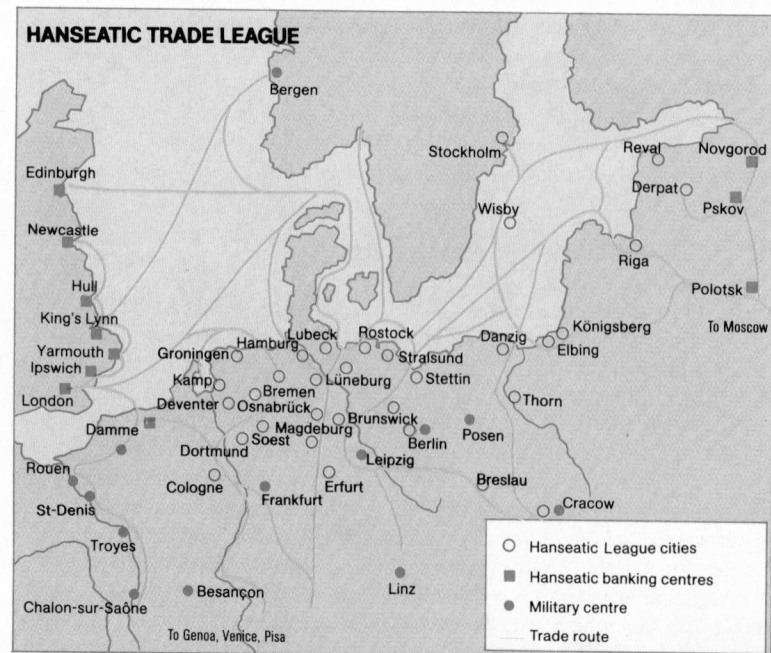

HANSEATIC TRADE LEAGUE

Bergen
Stockholm
Reval
Novgorod
Edinburgh
Derpat
Wisby
Pskov
Newcastle
Riga
Hull
Polotsk
King's Lynn
Königsberg
To Moscow
Yarmouth
Lubeck
Rostock
Danzig
Groningen
Hamburg
Elbing
Ipswich
Stralsund
Kamp
Lüneburg
Stettin
London
Bremen
Thorn
Deventer
Osnabrück
Damme
Brunswick
Magdeburg
Berlin
Posen
Dortmund
Soest
Leipzig
Rouen
Cologne
Erfurt
Breslau
St-Denis
Frankfurt
Cracow
Troyes
Besançon
Linz
Chalon-sur-Saône

To Genoa, Venice, Pisa

○ Hanseatic League cities
■ Hanseatic banking centres
● Military centre
— Trade route

Petrarch, poet who loved classics, dies

A later artist's view of Petrarch.

Arqua, near Padua, 1374
The classical scholar and lyric poet Francesco Petrarca, widely known as Petrarch, has died aged 70 in this small town. Born in Arezzo, the son of a Florentine lawyer, he passed his early life at the papal court at Avignon as a churchman living on benefices from rich patrons.

It was at Avignon in 1327 that he saw Laura, the wife of Hugo de Sade, and conceived a passion for her which he celebrated in Italian lyric poetry, madrigals and sonnets which became famous when collected as his *Canzoniere*. Like Dante's love for Beatrice, Petrarch's for Laura remained pure and distant; she became the mother of 11 children and died in the plague of 1348.

Petrarch wrote his learned works in Latin, including an epic poem in honour of Scipio Africanus and a series of prose biographies of famous Romans, *De Viris Illustribus*. He also wrote a treatise *On the Solitary Life*. He corresponded with his friend Boccaccio, the writer of the *Decameron*.

Petrarch's fame was such that he was an honoured guest at the courts of Europe where his hobby was to search libraries for forgotten Latin manuscripts. In Verona he discovered Cicero's letters, and in Liege some of his orations.

On Easter Day in 1341 he was crowned Poet Laureate on the Capitoline Hill in Rome, the first modern poet to be given the honour by the Senate.

Peasant revolt crushed

The "Jacquerie" rebels are crushed at Meaux: a later French portrayal.

France, June 1358
After three months of terror when rumours of rape, murder – even cannibalism – have spread rapidly through northern France with the speed of the plague, the country's nobles have united to put down a peasant revolt known as the *Jacquerie* with savage ferocity. Towns have been sacked, farmland laid waste and 20,000 rebels killed.

The beginnings of this rebellion are obscure. One report, widely circulated, suggests that peasants killed a knight, roasted him on a spit, gang-raped his wife and forced her to eat some of her husband's flesh.

With stories like this circulating from castle to castle, and with peasant mobs roaming freely through the land, fear became the norm.

Noblemen were helpless to act as the mobs broke into their homes, stealing food and wine and burning as the owners trembled behind locked doors. Towns were held hostage, forced to lay on feasts for the growing army of peasants.

Such a feast was taking place in the town of Meaux when two knights with a small army rode into the town and began to slaughter the Jacquerie. Other knights followed suit elsewhere. The revolt was over.

Much of North Africa is ruled from Fez

Morocco, 1358
The death of Abu Inan, the sultan of Morocco, leaves the Marinid dynasty still unsure of the extent of its power, although authority has been reasserted over the Ziyanids at Tlemcen where Arab tribes still block the path to Tunis.

It is exactly a century since the death of the first great Marinid chieftain, Abu Yahya, who led his Berber tribesmen in successful revolt, first against the Ziyanids and then against the Almohad caliphs at Marrakesh. The Marinids then extended their influence under Abu

Yahya's brother, Abu Yusuf. He took Marrakesh, defeated the Ziyanids and besieged Tlemcen before occupying the port of Ceuta and invading Spain, where he defeated the Castilians.

From their increasingly splendid headquarters at Fez, the Marinid sultans ruled by a combination of authority and patronage. Provincial governors imposed taxes in the sultan's name, and kept much of the proceeds. Lands and cities were frequently lost and recaptured, but the Marinids' right to the throne has remained unchallenged.

"Holy War" threatens Christian capital

Adrianople, 1361
One of the largest towns in Thrace, Adrianople, has fallen into Ottoman hands, giving the Turks their first major city in Europe and a capital from which to mount their European campaigns.

The fall of Adrianople, coupled with Ottoman control of the Gallipoli peninsula and both sides of the Sea of Marmara, now leaves Constantinople, the Byzantine capital, vulnerable to attack. In Rome the pope has declared that saving Constantinople from the Ottoman Moslems takes priority for crusaders over delivering the Holy Land from infidels. Constantinople is seen as vulnerable following the recent coup in which the Ottoman-backed John Cantacuzene was deposed. Adding to Rome's concern about the Moslem advance west is the frequent Ottoman declaration that it is an Islamic Holy War. One difficulty in ousting the Ottomans from

A Turkish Janissary soldier.

Thrace is lack of support from the Christian peasantry. They have been won over by the Ottomans' low taxes and fairer standards of law and order.

Polish hero dies in hunting accident

Poland, 5 November 1370
The Polish King Casimir III, whose reign has been marked by strong economic growth and the advancement of learning, died today in a hunting accident. He was 60. His kingdom was threatened on all sides when he ascended the throne at the age of 30. He repulsed a Mongol invasion, annexed Galicia and created well-defined national frontiers. He encouraged the immigration of Jews to serve as tax-collectors and bankers. He founded the university of Cracow, codified the laws of the land, established a firm, efficient administration and gave peasants the right to migrate from one place to another.

Casimir: firmness and efficiency.

Egyptians release king to life of exile

Armenia, 1375
Life in exile in Europe now awaits the deposed King of Armenia, Leon IV. His Egyptian captors plan to shortly release him from prison in Cairo, where he was taken after his capture at Gaban earlier this year.

The deposed king is expected to take refuge in the Christian courts of Europe where he will try to raise an army. However the Egyptians

and their new placeman on the Armenian throne, Achot, an Armenian noble who converted to Islam while in exile in Cairo, believe that the pleas will be politely rejected.

However ex-King Leon will be able to arouse considerable sympathy for the way the Egyptian forces destroyed and ransacked his country, including its once magnificent capital Sis.

Persians conquered by Timur the Lame

Persia, 1379

A Turkoman chieftain called Timur Lenk (Timur the Lame) has led an army from Bokhara, the second city of his homeland of Transoxiana, on a destructive raid on the Persian border town of Urgenj. The attack has sent rumours of conquest rippling across the country from Merv in the north to Shiraz in the south.

The auguries are not good. Timur has a taste for heads – other people's, detached from their bodies – as well as an appetite for territory. Students of the region's geopolitics perceive that the last of the Mongol dynasties are withering away. A power vacuum alongside an expansionist force such as Timur can have only one outcome: occupation. The still unresolved question is: occupation by whom? – for Timur is not the only predator.

In Egypt the Mamelukes are a vibrant economic and military power. To the north the Turkish Ottoman Sultan Bayezid has designs on the remnants of Christian Constantinople. Now Timur adds a

Mongol and Persian warriors.

third, terrifying, force to destabilise the Near East. The Christian powers of Europe are as uneasy as the Persians. From the days when two rival Christian churches – Rome and Constantinople – had power they have shrunk to a toe-hold in Asia Minor (Anatolia). Islam is one cause. Another is the greed of Venice and Genoa.

Moscow prince puts Mongols on the run

Moscow, 8 September 1380

On Curlew Field in Tula province today, exhausted Russian soldiers were treated to the novel sight of an entire "unbeatable" Mongol army galloping at speed – away from them.

The Russian leader, Grand Duke Dmitri, missed the great moment. He was lying under a tree, concussed. The outcome of Dmitri's war of independence against the Tartars was uncertain when the Mongol leader Mamay rode against Russia with 30,000 warriors, including Genoese mercenaries. (Some 34 years ago the Genoese also fought for France at Crecy, against England.)

To win, Mamay had to link with his Lithuanian allies coming the opposite way. Dmitri made a forced march to intercept Mamay, then staked everything on an opposed crossing of the Don river, straight into action. At the battle's climax, Dmitri's secret cavalry reserve swept onto the field to victory.

English surgeon seeks to revise odds against saints and shrines

London, 1376

John Arderne, the English surgeon, has published a lengthy treatise on his most successful operation, the lancing of an anal fistula. He has treated numerous knights, friars, merchants and priests, charging a considerable sum of £40, plus a suit of clothing and an annuity of £40 for as long as the patient survives.

In spite of his successes, he and other surgeons have failed to gain acceptance by physicians, who use elaborate medicines, bleeding and cauterisation to achieve the balance of humours which are believed to mean a healthy body.

Resort to physicians and surgeons is costly and their treatments often unpleasant. Most people rely instead on the healing powers of saints' relics or magic charms. Shrines claim a higher success rate than doctors. Even a specialist like Arderne can offer only a one in two chance of survival.

Arderne learned his surgical skills while serving with Edward the Black Prince during campaigns

A surgeon's clinic, from "Chirurgia" by the Frenchman Guy de Chauliac.

in France. After the Black Death he went to live in Newark, which had three hospitals and was a noted centre for surgeons.

He sets moral standards for his profession too, saying that surgeons

should never be foul-mouthed, never take advantage of female patients, should have a stock of comfortable sayings, but never allow themselves to forget that not every patient can be cured.

Two popes split church

English Lollards challenge papal power

Clement VII: the French usurper.

Urban VI: spiritual authority.

A 19th-century engraving of John Wyclif sending out some of his "Lollard" followers to spread his views on reform of church practices.

Rome, 20 September 1378

The Roman Catholic Church was split asunder today following the news that Robert of Geneva, a cousin of the French king, has been elected as Pope Clement VII.

His supporters claim that the election last June of Bartolomeo Prignano, an Italian, as Pope Urban VI was invalid, since the cardinals were acting under fear of the Rome mob. Pope Urban is determined to stay in office. His friends here say that Clement is an anti-pope illegally elected. They fear that this is a new attempt by the French king to usurp the pope's power. Until last year the papal court had been at Avignon for nearly 70 years, leaving the pope subject to French influence.

The dispute is more complex, however. French cardinals were in a majority at the conclave which elected Urban, but they were divided. Some supported Robert. The rest supported Urban, a man of lowly birth who they hoped would restore some spiritual authority to the papacy.

Since his election Urban has delivered a violent attack on the luxurious life of the cardinals and the sale of church favours. The French cardinals, many still living at Avignon, are understandably annoyed.

Lutterworth, England, 1379

John Wyclif, the renowned Oxford scholar, has moved from radical criticism of the church establishment to outright heresy in a series of lectures on the Eucharist. The orthodox view is that at consecration the bread and wine are miraculously changed, but Wyclif insists that they remain bread and wine. So far his views are not widely known beyond the academic community, but word is likely to spread and may well attract hostile attention to the university itself.

Wyclif, once master of Balliol College, is no stranger to controversy. Recently he has launched attacks on papal authority which have been sympathetically received in many quarters. The schism within the church has shocked people at all levels of society, while the English government has, for its own reasons, been willing to criticise the pope's temporal power.

Politically, Wyclif has powerful friends, including the king's uncle John of Gaunt. Their support helped him to weather papal condemnation of a series of errors. It remains to be seen, however, whether they will be as ready to back a declared heretic. Second thoughts may also be prompted by signs that Wyclif's teaching is acquiring elements of social dissent. An attack on papal power easily becomes a critique of state power. Wyclif's followers, known as Lollards, emphasise the importance of ordinary folk reading the Bible for themselves, raising the risk of a doctrinal free-for-all.

Workers take over the city of Florence

The Court of the Lions in the magnificent Alhambra palace in Granada, the seat of Arab rule of Spain. Mohammed V is constructing the Alhambra on the site of earlier Arab buildings on a hill overlooking the city, and work on the court began in 1377. It takes its name from its centrepiece, a fountain supported by 12 marble lions.

Florence, 1378

For over 100 years it has been the wealthy magnates who have ruled this city, but today Florence is in the hands of the Ciompi, the skilled artisans, cloth-workers in particular. If this revolution succeeds, only citizens who have actually worked for a living – either at trades or in business – will be able to hold office in the Florentine commune.

Conflict between the magnates ("The Hats") and the workers ("The Cloaks") had increased markedly in the wake of the Black Death, which considerably lessened the number of men in the cloth industry. In the rioting and burning that turned the tables on the aristocrats, the cry was "Death to the Hats and long live the Cloaks!"

As the inter-communal slanging match grew, the taunts continued. The Hats were given to shouting "Go back to your cloth-making", and "Go and grind the pepper" (to druggists), and one aristocrat lumped the workers together as a crowd of "robbers and traitors and murderers and assassins and gluttons and malefactors".

Such a shouting match had to end in violence. Traders, skilled artisans and the poor joined together to force their way into the palace and take over the city.

Venice bolsters trading power by victory in war with Genoa

The doge's palace in Venice.

Italy, 1381

The long-running bitter struggle between the republics of Venice and Genoa appears to have been resolved with the outcome of the War of Chioggia and the unconditional surrender of the Genoese force. Although the peace conference held in Turin has left the two exhausted protagonists politically where they were before the fighting, the Venetians have set about making a speedy economic recovery.

The two republics have been squabbling for a hundred years over who is to be the dominant trade power in the region. Venice's wealth has rested on the trade which flows through the city on its way from the east and Constantinople to markets in Europe and northern Italy. In order to protect these routes from piracy, Venetian power has been pushed south and east and ships have even broken into the Black Sea. The Genoese are also great traders and bankers, who import spices from the Far East, trade with Moslem states and have helped to re-establish the Byzantine empire. They were spoiling for a fight with the Venetians, and found one in the Chioggia lagoon in which their fleet was trapped by concrete-filled blockships and sunk by their enemies.

After ecstasy and revelation, leading mystic experiences death

Rome, 29 April 1380

The Christian mystic Catherine of Siena died today, eight days after being paralysed from the waist down by a stroke. She was only 33, but had been in poor health after years of tireless devotion to those in need and to the church, both in her native Siena and elsewhere in Italy. Most recently she had been active in seeking recognition of Pope Urban VI in the face of the breakaway papacy at Avignon. She was perhaps the greatest of the many Christian mystics who have glorified this age of mystical fervour, although mysticism itself is not new. Nor is it confined to Italy: famous mystics include the Germans Hildegard of Bingen (died 1180) and Henry of Suso (died 1365), and Bridget of Sweden (died 1373). England and the Netherlands have also produced eminent mystics, such as Julian of Norwich and John Ruysbroek.

Characteristics of mysticism are the twin experiences of ecstasy and revelation. Divine ecstasy involves a temporary loss of a sense of time and space by mystics in rapture. Divinely-inspired revelations do not necessarily give prophecies of the future; mystics also claim to have visions of contemporary or recent events at a great distance.

HILDEGARDIS a Virgin Prophetess, Abbess of St Ruperts Nunnerye. She died at Bingen A° D°: 1180 Aged 82 yeares.

The mystic Hildegard of Bingen.

Cleric turns study of the stars into science instead of prophecy

Astrological aid for sailors.

Paris, 11 July 1382

The death was announced today of the great French cleric, scholar and economist Nicolas Oresme. He was a thrilling preacher, a skilful debater and a subtle thinker, and made many contributions to the development of science, especially astronomy.

Born around 1320, he studied theology at the university of Paris. After various appointments in the church, he became chaplain to King Charles the Wise of France and later became bishop of Lisieux. Oresme was probably the first to think of the heavens as a gigantic clock mechanism. He carried out many mathematical calculations of planetary motions and, in doing so, concluded that the behaviour of the earth in relation to the universe was rather different from that depicted by astrologers. In his *Book on Divinations* he attacked the deterministic belief of astrologers that human actions are guided by the stars, as well as criticising the use of black magic.

One of his major achievements was his book *On the Heavens* in which he questioned Aristotle's view that the stars move around a stationary earth. And one of his most intriguing thoughts was that there may be universes other than our own. It is hardly surprising, therefore, that Oresme's many ideas and speculations have been widely discussed.

English peasants revolt

London, 15 June 1381

The head of the rebel leader Wat Tyler has been displayed on a pole in a London field today, and his followers are making their way home. The king is safe. The peasants' revolt is over.

It has been a bloody but short-lived affair which began – as far as London was concerned – two days ago when Tyler led his mob into the city after tricking his way across the bridge. On their march to London they had taken Maidstone, Rochester and Canterbury and opened the gates of the Marshalsea to free the prisoners. Hundreds of Londoners joined them in widespread looting.

Once in the city, Tyler's "army" marched through Fleet Street, burning shops and breaking into the Temple where legal documents were burnt – a protest against the poll tax which led to this rising. Then the horror began. A judge was beheaded with 18 other leading citizens. The mob vented their fury on the Flemish community, beheading 35 in the street. The archbishop was dragged from the Tower

Richard II sails to meet the rebels.

chapel and executed on Tower Hill. His head was set up on London Bridge, his mitre nailed to his skull.

As London burnt around him, Richard II, the king parleyed with the rebel leader, but, angered by Tyler's arrogant attitude, the mayor lunged with his sword. Tyler died soon afterwards, but the king has pardoned his followers.

High taxes provoke uprisings in France

Paris, 1 March 1382

A woman street merchant provoked a major riot today when a tax collector tried to seize her goods. She fought the man off with a cry of "down with taxes". Others took up the chant and, seizing mallets stored in the Hotel de Ville, the mob gave chase to tax-collectors throughout the city. The *Maillotins* thus became one more protest movement against the fierce taxation policies of Charles VI.

Elsewhere the *Tuchins*, peasants and craftsmen driven from the cities by taxation, are a loosely organised group making a living from robbery. Bound together by bloodcurdling oaths, the Tuchins operate in bands of no more than 20. They steal livestock, jewellery and cash, and capture churchmen and nobles for ransom.

Their favourite targets are the English and Gascon *routiers* – plunderers themselves, but vulnerable to attack by the Tuchins who claim patriotic motives. Tuchins

Parisians: up in arms against tax.

are not all peasants. One leader, Pierre de Bres, is connected with many leading families of the Auvergne and Languedoc, and is believed to have joined the anarchic movement after robbing his uncle, a bishop, and discovering his wife having an affair with his squire.

Portuguese freedom

The battle of Aljubarrota, as depicted in a later English chronicle.

Portugal, 15 August 1385

The firepower of 300 English archers has won the day in the battle of Aljubarrota and saved Portuguese independence. The army of John of Portugal has scored a decisive victory over that of John of Castile, who has fled to Seville. Now that Portugal is independent of its powerful neighbour, a new age of its history can unfold.

Portugal's affairs have long been bound up with those of Castile, and when King Ferdinand died two years ago Castile's John proclaimed himself king. This led to a popular revolt in favour of another John – the grand master of the Knights of Avis – whom the Castilians decided had to be overthrown. Lisbon was besieged, and only survived

because plague hit the Castilian army, killing over 2,000 men and its best commanders. The Portuguese were saved.

But the Castilian king was determined to risk everything on one more battle, and did so at Aljubarrota with a force of some 17,000 men. The Portuguese army was much smaller, but included a company of English archers sent by John of Gaunt who was pursuing his claims to Castile.

Although tired by a 12-mile march, the Castilians were ordered to attack. They came under terrible crossfire from English archers, and those not killed became entangled in a network of wolf-traps and trenches. The battle lasted for less than an hour.

Painter of austere landscapes has died

China, 1385

Ni Zan, currently one of the most revered Chinese artists, has died aged 84. He was born near Suzhou, and his early life was prosperous and comfortable. He knew many artists and scholars, and gained a reputation for being precious and faintly eccentric (he washed constantly) until 1356, when he left his home to live a simple life on a house-boat with his wife. He returned to his old home in old age after his wife's death.

Nearly all his works are small, delicately-toned, intimate and bare of people. There are usually just a few thin trees, a lake and low barren hills. The effect is of an understated, austere beauty.

"Autumn Landscape" (c.1360), typical of Ni Zan's spare beauty.

1385 (1385-1394)

Spanish mobs set Jewish ghettoes ablaze

Barcelona, 9 August 1391

The last four days here have seen the most violent anti-Semitic atrocities in what has been an appalling year for violence against the Jews. On 5 August Castilian sailors set fire to the ghetto, killing 100 Jews. They were joined during the night by a crowd on the rampage, and Jews fled to the royal castle.

The following day the ringleaders were arrested and imprisoned. However, on 7 August the mob freed them. They then besieged the royal castle and forced the Jews to march in procession to be baptised. The 300 who refused were killed on the spot.

This year's violence began when Ferrant Martinez became the temporary administrator of the diocese of Seville. Long known for anti-Semitic sermons, he called this year for the razing of the synagogues and urged the peasants to expel the Jews from their villages. By June,

One of the synagogues in Toledo.

Jews were being killed daily in Seville and mass hysteria was spreading. The Jewish community in Toledo was attacked and there were massacres in Valencia. Some people here think the rise of anti-Semitism dates from the need for the people to blame someone for the bubonic plague.

Private armies roam and plunder Europe

Paris, c.1391

Great swathes of Europe are being laid waste by armies of freebooting mercenaries who roam free, living off the land, terrorising the townspeople and peasantry, taking hostages for ransom and threatening to destroy the political fabric of much of the continent.

France, divided and made poorer by war and plague, suffers more than most – although German mercenaries operate in Italy, and private armies from Spain are causing havoc in Greece and elsewhere.

In France, the menace come from English *routiers* and French *echorcheurs* who, in the words of a contemporary writer, "resemble the passing of swarms of locusts ... they stripped the land bare and human government proved powerless to restrain them".

And therein lies the dilemma facing Charles VII. With an impoverished treasury, there is no way in which he can mount a royal expedition to clear France of these armies. Even so, most local people prefer to pay their ransom to the freebooters and stay quiet rather than complain and face punishment for the crime of paying it. If legal action is attempted against the

Knights: chevaliers or charlatans?

leaders, they generally claim that they are men of chivalry and acting on the king's behalf. Pardons are frequent, many bought for cash.

One routier captain who was not pardoned was Merigot Marches who was operating in the south of France – ostensibly in the names of the English king and the counts of Armagnac and Foix. He was tried in Paris and claimed (after torture) that he had sworn loyalty to England.

Poland grows after a royal marriage

Poland, 1386

A marrige has prepared the way for the union of the Polish and Lithuanian crowns and united the two countries against their common foe, the knights of the Teutonic Order, – the territory-hungry descendants of the Crusaders. At a ceremony in Cracow, Jagello, the 36-year-old grand duke of Lithuania, has married Jadwiga, the Polish queen, who is 12, and been crowned. The marriage ends the longstanding rivalry and means that the Lithuanians adopt Christianity.

Diplomatic manoeuvring over the union has been going on for several years, with Jagello out to save his own position as well as Lithuania's future. He has long wanted to enter the sphere of western civilisation.

Jadwiga, who had hoped to marry an Austrian prince, at first resisted the idea of union with the pagan Jagello. She was finally persuaded by Polish lords and priests to sacrifice herself for Poland's sake. Although she is still so young, her royal dignity, legally equal to that of her husband, is working out well in practice. At the same time Lithuanian nobles are proceeding to adopt the manners and traditions of the Polish aristocracy.

Sergius, the saintly Russian monk, dies

Russia, 1392

The Russian monk Sergius of Radonezh has died at the monastery of the Holy Trinity which he founded at Zagorsk, in central Russia. He was born at Rostov in 1314; civil war forced his parents to flee with him to Radonezh, north-east of Moscow. When he was 20 he and his brother Stephen became hermits in the neighbouring forest, where they eventually attracted followers. By 1354 Sergius led a proper monastic community, and his name spread across northern Russia; directly or indirectly he founded several other monasteries, and intervened to keep peace among quarrelling Russian princes. Renowned for his humility and simplicity, he taught his monks to be selfless.

Warlord who builds piles of heads

Samarkand, Central Asia, 1387

It is less than ten years since Timur the Lame (corrupted in Europe as Tamerlane) began empire-building, but already he has taken control of Persia, a task which took a mere two years, and secured the boundaries of his Transoxianan homeland against the Mongol horde, whose genes he shares.

However, these facts do not convey the bloodthirsty nature of the man. Like Genghis Khan, he offers his adversary a choice of prompt surrender or a bloodbath. Even a hint of token resistance provokes his fury. After capturing one city, Tamerlane ordered that 30,000 of its citizens – not all of them fighters – should be decapitated. He amuses himself by arranging severed heads in great mounds, like melons in a market place.

Physically he is a huge man, with a massive head and a formidable high forehead, his skin fair under his beard. He is devoutly religious. His ethic responds only to physical courage. Possibly this is because of

Tamerlane's war elephants, from a drawing by Raphael (1483-1520).

his chronic limp. Some think it was caused by a wound, but others believe that he was born like this. On bad days he cannot ride, but must be carried in a litter. He fights a campaign in advance, sitting immobile over his special chess board, then explodes into action.

It is odd that the man who delights in death takes his advice only from Islam's Sufis, who see God in living things.

Japanese rival courts are reconciled

Japan, 1392

The rival southern and northern courts of the divided imperial family are to be reunited after half a century of strife. Under the terms of the agreement the southern emperor, Go-Kameyama, was to perform a solemn act of abdication in which the imperial regalia held by the south were to be transferred to the north. He has already been be-

trayed, however, for the regalia have been returned to the north by a small escort of courtiers who carried them to the Tsuchi-mikado palace where the northern emperor, Go-Komatsu, was staying.

This bodes ill for the agreement which had stipulated that the succession was to alternate between the two lines of Japan's imperial family.

Serbians crushed by the Ottomans

Serbia, 15 June 1389

Serbia has been crushed by the Ottoman Turks after a battle at Kosovo, when the whole of the Serbian nobility was wiped out. The Turkish conquest is now sweeping rapidly over the Balkans.

Serbia has been the most brilliant, faithful and dangerous of Byzantium's Balkan heirs, but the Ottomans are becoming more bold in their attacks and a menace to both Greek and Slav. Having invaded Bulgaria last year, Sultan Murat turned against the Serbian leader Lazar.

At Kosovo ("field of the blackbirds"), fortune seemed at first to favour the Serbs. The sultan was killed, but led by the heir to the throne, Bayezid, the Ottomans achieved the upper hand. Lazar was taken prisoner and executed with his nobles. One feature of the battle was that the Janissary corps of forcibly recruited Christian boys fought very well for their Turkish rulers.

Koreans end years of Mongol control

Korea, 1392

The dictator Yi Song-gye has deposed King Kongyang and set himself on the throne of Korea, thus establishing a new dynasty untainted by subservience to the once-powerful Mongol empire.

Yi has been able to remove the last vestiges of Mongol rule by enacting a radical programme of land reform which has destroyed the economic power of the aristocratic families. These familes had flourished under the Mongols and Kublai Khan's Yuan dynasty, but now they have been swept away just like the descendants of Kublai. The money from their lands now goes into the treasury of the new dynasty.

A poet who revered God and the vine

Persia, 1389

The poet and Moslem mystic Shams al-Din Mohammed, known as Hafiz, has died at Shiraz, in southern Persia, aged about 70. He is regarded as the greatest master of the Persian *ghazal*, a lyrical short poem characterised by mysticism, richness and subtlety of imagery. Love and wine feature frequently in his work, as in the following lines:

Again the times are out of joint; and again
For wine and the loved one's languid glance I am fain to.

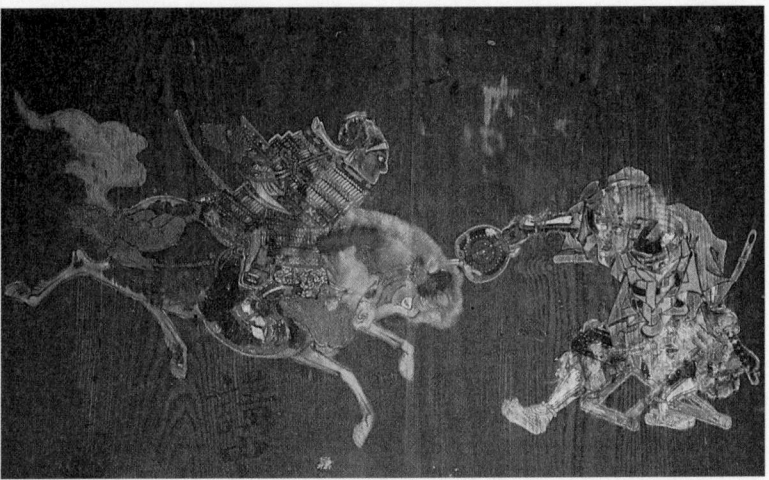

A painting from a Kyoto shrine, showing two warriors in close combat.

An illustration for a book by Hafiz.

Austria, 1394. The Habsburg dukes of Austria agree a 20-year truce with the Swiss confederation, which now comprises eight cantons: Uri, Schwyz, Unterwalden, Glarus, Zug, Berne, Zurich and Lucerne.

Florence, 1394. The English mercenary leader John Hawkwood, whose troops have become a force to be reckoned with in the politics of northern Italy, dies and is buried in an elaborate cathedral tomb.

Avignon, 1394. Benedict XIII succeeds Clement VII as pope.

France, 15 July 1394. Charles VI issues a decree of general expulsion of Jews from France.

Central Asia, 1395. Tamerlane destroys Astrakhan.

Italy, 1395. Gian Galeazzo Visconti buys the title of duke of Milan from King Wenceslas, which gives him the status of a legitimate prince.

Scandinavia, 20 June 1397. The Union of Kalmar unites Denmark, Sweden and Norway under one monarch.

Florence, c.1397. Giovanni de' Medici founds the Medici bank.

Paris, 1398. Earlier attempts to end the schism having failed, owing to the intransigence of the two popes, the university of Paris persuades the French king and clergy to withdraw their obedience from Benedict XIII, thus depriving him of much of his income.

India, 1398. Tamerlane invades India and sacks Delhi.

England, 29 September 1399. Richard II is deposed. His cousin Henry of Lancaster declares himself king under the name Henry IV.

Constantinople, 1399. John II of Boucicaut, the marshal of France, with western troops, holds Constantinople against the Ottomans. The Emperor Manuel II leaves for the west in an attempt to raise further help, leaving his nephew John VII as co-emperor.

Near East, 1400. Tamerlane takes Sivas from the Ottomans and ravages Syria.

Italy, 1400. Gian Galeazzo Visconti takes possession of Perugia, Assisi and Spoleto.

France, 1400. Jean Froissart finishes his *Chronicles*. Their picture of the chivalric world during the second half of the last century is proving immensely influential.

The poet who told Canterbury Tales dies

Chaucer at the court of Edward III, by Ford Madox Brown (1821-93).

London, 25 October 1400
Geoffrey Chaucer, a giant of English poetry, died today with his ambitious poetic cycle *The Canterbury Tales* still incomplete. As England's best-loved writer he is to be buried in Westminster Abbey.

Chaucer came from a well-to-do family of vintners with court connections (his father was deputy butler to the king). Geoffrey received a court education as a page and was put into the service of John of Gaunt.

He fought for England against France, was taken prisoner and later ransomed. He came back enthused by the French fashion for poems of courtly love. He also read in four languages and borrowed tales from Boccaccio.

Chaucer prospered at court, becoming a controller of customs and a magistrate, and was granted a daily jug of wine by Richard II. All this stopped when his patron, John of Gaunt, went to Spain in 1386.

The beginning of the Knight's Tale.

Chaucer was set at leisure. He had just completed *Troilus and Criseyde*, and now turned to his band of Canterbury pilgrims, whom he drew with a mixture of shrewdness and pithy humour.

Constantinople at mercy of Ottomans

Bulgaria, 25 September 1396
A disorganised and ill-led crusade against the Turkish Sultan Bayezid has ended in bloody disaster at Nicopolis. Constantinople is at the Ottomans' mercy.

Following the conquering path of Murad, his predecessor, Bayezid laid siege to Constantinople before capturing Nicopolis, the Bulgarian fortress on the Danube, in 1393, and imprisoning, then killing, the Bulgarian czar.

King Sigismund of Hungary eventually persuaded the French and reluctant vassal forces to join him in a crusade. But the French showed more appetite for pillage and plunder than for military strategy as the allies advanced down the Danube.

Having besieged the Turks in Nicopolis, the allies turned to face the sultan's arriving army. The French advance was brave, but blindly led, and was overwhelmed before the rest of the crusaders' army disintegrated. Bayezid took bloody revenge on his attackers, slaughtering the French captives by the hundred.

Marriages put duke on top in Italy

Italy, 1400
Northern Italy is dominated by Gian Galeazzo Visconti, a Lombard noble whose military prowess is outshone by his diplomatic skill and ruthless cunning. Only Florence stands between him and the title "King of Italy".

He inherited the lordships of Pavia and other northern Italian cities, and married Isabel of Valois, the daughter of the king of France. When she died, he married the daughter of his powerful uncle Bernabo, whom he imprisoned to acquire all the Visconti lands.

Having married his daughter to Louis of Orleans, the brother of the king of France, he has made more judicious alliances and, with a minimum of military effort, won control of almost every important city in northern Italy. He is recognised by the Emperor Wenceslas as duke of Milan and Lombardy.

English king abdicates

Richard II hands over his crown and sceptre to Henry, duke of Lancaster.

London, 29 September 1399

The turbulent reign of Richard II came to an ignominious end today in the Tower of London, where the king, under pressure from a delegation of nobles, signed a deed of abdication. Amongst the delegation was Henry, the earl of Hereford and son of John of Gaunt, who promptly claimed the crown for himself. A document of 32 articles accusing Richard of tyrannical rule has been prepared for presentation to parliament. Certainly his claim that the laws of England lay in his mouth, and the wanton luxury of his court, caused great resentment. But the immediate cause of his overthrow was his treatment of Henry of Hereford, whose estates he seized on the death of John of Gaunt.

Henry, who had been living in exile in Paris, set sail for England and landed at Ravenspur in Yorkshire. Richard's armies deserted him and he was brought to London a prisoner. Although his reign ended in disaster, he will be remembered for his courageous handling of the peasants' revolt, when he set himself at the head of the rebels and persuaded them to disband.

Kinkaku-ji: the Temple of the Golden Pavilion on the outskirts of Kyoto in Japan. It was built by the shogun Yoshimitsu after he had retired.

Ex-monk, first Ming emperor, dies at 70

China, 1398

Zhu Yuanzhang, the peasant who became emperor of China, has died at the age of 70. His rise to supreme power began when he was only 17, when all his family fell victim to the plague and famine. He became a monk in order to survive, but found his real role when he joined the peasant revolutionaries, the Red Turbans.

He rose to power by his military ability and bravery and, switching his forces' attacks from the landowners to overcoming the Mongol Yuan dynasty, he achieved such success that in 1368 he was able to take Beijing and drive the last Yuan emperor back across the Great Wall into the Gobi desert.

He named his own dynasty Ming (Brilliant) and ruled for 30 years. Scarred by the fate of his family, he spent most of his efforts in establishing a stable social and economic order based on agriculture.

He was always concerned with the common man and, even when he grew despotic towards the end of his life, his victims were the nobles rather than the peasants.

It has been suggested that he had been a member of the White Lotus

A statue on the way to Ming tombs.

secret society, and, although he denied this, he came to rely on his own web of secret agents and began to look upon any opposition as proof of a conspiracy against him.

He is to be buried in the Purple Mountains outside Nanking, his power base. He leaves this world feared, but respected as the man who reunified China.

Kalmar treaty unites Scandinavian states

Sweden, 20 June 1397

Three Scandinavian kingdoms have come together under a single sovereign with the signing of the Union of Kalmar. Denmark, Sweden and Norway now constitute the second largest accumulation of European territories under one leader, Queen Margaret of Denmark. The three states will have a common foreign policy, and matters of royal succession must be settled by consensus.

The agreement is a triumph for Margaret, an ambitious and skilful politician and gifted diplomat. She became regent of Denmark on the death of her father, and of Norway on the death of her husband. She gained possession of Sweden after deposing King Alfred. Her 15-year-old great-nephew, Duke Erik VII of Pomerania, has been crowned King of Scandinavia at Kalmar.

Margaret's intention from the beginning has been to provide the union with a suitable male head. But the union also grew to some

Swedish embroidery from Uppsala.

extent out of a general trend towards the creation of larger political entities such as the formation of Poland-Lithuania and the expansion of Moscow.

South-East Africa, c.1400. A thriving gold trade has been established down the Zambezi valley to the Sofala coast.

Germany, 1400. Wenceslas IV, an indolent drunkard, is deposed as king of the Romans (the title held by emperors not crowned as emperor), though he remains king of Bohemia. The choice of Rupert of the Palatinate to replace him causes a schism when Wenceslas and his supporters refuse to accept the election.

Baghdad, 1401. Tamerlane takes Baghdad for the second time.

England, 1401. A statute is passed authorising the handing over of obdurate heretics to the secular authorities to be burnt.

Asia Minor (Anatolia), 1402. The Ottoman sultan, Bayezid, is defeated by Tamerlane in battle near Angora. Tamerlane captures Smyrna and reaches the Bosphorus. Bayezid is taken prisoner and dies in captivity.

China, 1402. After a long period of civil war, Zhu Di, the uncle of the second Ming emperor, Jianwen, usurps the throne to reign as the Yongle emperor.

North Atlantic, 1402. Henry of Castile sends an expedition to conquer the Canary Islands.

Prague, 1402. The reformer Jan Hus begins to preach in the Bethlehem chapel, founded in 1391 by two laymen as a centre of religious revival.

Japan, 1404. Japan starts to trade with Ming China.

France, 27 April 1404. John (the Fearless) becomes duke of Burgundy.

Florence, 1406. A copy of Ptolemy's *Geography* is brought to Italy from Constantinople and is translated into Latin by James Angelus. Its availability gives an important boost to geographical knowledge in Europe.

Italy, 1407. No longer able to compete effectively with its rival, Venice, Genoa forms its own private banking company of St George.

Paris, 23 November 1407. Louis, the duke of Orleans, is murdered on the instigation of John the Fearless, the duke of Burgundy. With Charles VI prevented from governing by madness, a deadly struggle developed between Louis and John. Their supporters have formed factions known as the Armagnac and Burgundian parties.

Seven years later Delhi still in ruins

Delhi, 1405
The sultanate of Delhi is collapsing. Half a century ago it encompassed almost all India, save the southern tip. Today its capital, Delhi, is still in ruins, too weak to recover from the ravages of Tamerlane the Great seven years earlier.

Rebellions in Gujarat, Jaunpur, the Punjab and the Deccan had already whittled away its territory before Tamerlane's invasion. Corruption, regicide, overtaxation and the vast cost of protecting the Moslem state against its Hindu majority had weakened it from within.

Tamerlane crossed the Indus in December 1398. His pretext was the toleration by Delhi's Moslem rulers of Hindu idolatry. His object was plunder. On 17 December he scattered the sultan's army of 10,000 cavalry, 40,000 infantry and 120 war elephants; the elephants, according to Tamerlane, were "driven off like cows". Next day the city was sacked, Tamerlane leaving behind pillars of skulls.

Since then Mallu, the humiliated sultan, and his sucessor, Mahmud, have regained a fraction of the sultanate, but after the ravages of Tamerlane there seems nothing left with which to rebuild the sultanate.

Deccan art: a female drummer.

Defeated sultan is Tamerlane's footstool

Tamerlane the Great enthroned, from a Moghul manuscript (c.1600).

Angora (Ankara), Turkey, 1402
The great Ottoman leader, Sultan Bayezid, is Tamerlane's prisoner after a quarrel between the two mighty moslem neighbours which, for once, Tamerlane did not initiate. Bayezid rejected an offer of compromise over a border dispute three years ago by questioning Tamerlane's sexual virility. Now the Ottoman sultan is obliged to act as Tamerlane's footstool while his favourite wife, the beautiful Serbian Despina, is a naked waitress at the victor's table. When Tamerlane received Bayezid's insulting letter he was not deflected from his immediate objective: seizure of Syria, including Aleppo and Damascus, destruction of Baghdad, and creation of another of the pyramids of severed human heads which serve as signposts from the Great Wall of China to the borders of Asia Minor.

This year Tamerlane assembled an army of 20,000 men and a team of elephants to move the baggage. By a remarkable bluff he contrived to march into the heart of Anatolia and occupy a position behind his opponent and upstream, across the only water source in that desolate plain, which he diverted. Turkish morale was at rock bottom when

A Turkish prisoner, by a later artist.

the fighting started. Bayezid put Tartar cavalry – of the same blood as Tamerlane – at the front and they promptly changed sides, reducing the Ottoman force by a quarter. Bayezid was still swinging his battle axe like a killing machine when his army collapsed and the Ottoman leader was about to face the ultimate humiliation at the hands of his victor.

Timur the Lame is dead

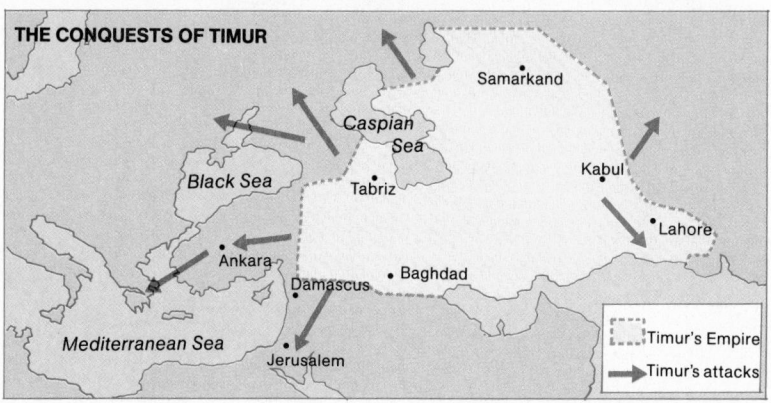

THE CONQUESTS OF TIMUR

Samarkand
Caspian Sea
Black Sea
Tabriz
Kabul
Ankara
Lahore
Damascus
Baghdad
Mediterranean Sea
Jerusalem

- - - Timur's Empire
→ Timur's attacks

Samarkand, Central Asia 1405
Word has reached the homeland of the great Timur the Lame that he has died during his most ambitious expedition yet.

Having defeated Anatolians, Turks, Persians, Arabs, Mamelukes and Mongols to create an empire stretching from Tartary to India, he wanted to take on the Chinese. In China, the ruling Ming awaited with interest this lost son of Mongolia who now appeared to threaten them from the west.

Timur, known in the west as Tamerlane, was born in Turkestan 69 years ago into the Barlas tribe, a clan originating from Mongolia which had adopted the Islamic religion and the Turkish language. He was a strange human cocktail: a white-haired illiterate who impressed the scholar ibn Khaldun with his wit; a greater tactician than Genghis Khan; a man who made a cult of atrocious cruelty, but who loved philosophy and brooded over chess; a lifelong nomad who was a patron of architecture. He was also

A European view of Tamerlane.

a collector: Samarkand is full of elegant loot from Delhi. But he saw little of his treasures; after 1370 he spent most of his next 35 years on the road.

Tamerlane died somewhere in Asia of a fever and "an indiscreet use of iced water". The ruler who dealt deaths of excruciating pain to thousands of innocent people had a peaceful end.

Teutonic Knights defeated by the Poles

Prussia, 15 July 1410
The Poles and Lithuanians have defeated their most powerful and dangerous enemy, the Teutonic Order, at Tannenberg, and ended its two centuries of rule in the region. The battle lasted for a day and resulted in the death of some 200 Teutonic Knights, including their grand master.

Both sides had been preparing for a decisive battle for some time, and had even submitted their cases to public opinion throughout Europe in memoranda sent to several

countries, including England. At the same time military preparations were also going on, with the order recruiting Western knights and the Poles enlisting some Czech mercenaries.

When it came to the battle the united Polish and Lithuanian army was larger than the German force, but not as experienced. However, Jagello decided to thrust at the order's capital at Marienburg, and the Polish gentry finally carried the day when the German grand master's charge failed.

Three popes reign in latest church crisis

The three popes. From left to right: Benedict, Gregory and Alexander.

Pisa, August 1409
The Council of Pisa has ended on a sad note, with delegates forced to admit that they have failed. Several hundred bishops, lower churchmen and royal envoys have been meeting here for the last four months seeking to heal the schism in the church. Neither of the two popes (Benedict XIII, based in Avignon,

and Gregory XII, the Roman pope) is strong enough to oust the other. The council thought it had found a solution by deposing both popes and electing a Cretan, Petros Philargos, as Pope Alexander V. However, Benedict and Gregory have refused to be ousted, so Alexander is setting up his court here, making three popes in all.

Arab with new historical theory dies

Cairo, 17 March 1406
Abd al-Rahman ibn Mohammed ibn Khaldun, historian, diplomat, judge and administrator, has died aged 74. Born in Tunis into a family of Spanish Arabs, ibn Khaldun held high office in Morocco, Spain and Egypt, invaluable experience for the work for which he is best known: a three-volume history of the Arabs, Persians and Berbers.

The first volume is the most famous, because it presents a new theory of historical development taking notice of physical influences, such as climate and geography, as well as moral and intellectual ones. Ibn Khaldun endeavoured to formulate the cycles of national progress and decay, and can be said to have discovered the true scope and nature of history and society.

A pharmacy: the Arabs have excelled in all branches of learning.

Italy, May 1410. Following the death of Alexander V at Bologna, John XXIII – said to have poisoned Alexander – is elected pope. His election marks an important stage in the rise of the Medici family, his backers.

Peru, c.1410. Under the leadership of Viracocha Inca, who became ruler of the Incas in 1400, the Inca empire is expanding and the rigidly hierarchical structure of Inca society is growing more formalised.

West Africa, 1410. Kanajejdi, the king of Kano, who introduced iron helmets and quilted horse armour to the Hausa cavalry, dies.

Hungary, July 1411. Sigismund of Hungary, the brother of Wenceslas, is elected Holy Roman emperor. Of the two candidates who were rivals for the title in 1400, Rupert died last year and Wenceslas is retired with a pension.

Portugal, 1411. Aragon and Portugal make peace after some 30 years of wars and truces. John of Portugal, now secure at home, begins a policy of overseas expansion.

England, 20 March 1413. On his death, Henry IV is succeeded by his son Henry V.

Paris, 1413. Demands for reform of finance and justice made by the Paris craftsmen under the patronage of the Burgundian faction result in an ordinance that all officials, both central and local, should be elected. This utopian measure is overturned when the Armagnac faction seizes control of Paris.

England, 1414. Henry V adopts the French claims of Edward III as his own and asserts his right to the inheritance of the Plantagenets.

England, 1414. A Lollard revolt, led by Sir John Oldcastle, discredits the movement by linking it with social radicalism.

Germany, 6 July 1415. Having appeared before the Council of Constance, Jan Hus is convicted of heresy and burnt.

Morocco, 1415. King John of Portugal conquers Ceuta in Morocco. Keen to acquire gold and slaves from Africa, he is also motivated by a dream of allying with Africans against the Moslems of the Maghreb.

East Africa, 1415. An embassy is dispatched from Malindi (Kenya) to China.

Czech reformer is burnt at the stake

Constance, Germany, 6 July 1415
Today Jan Hus, scholar, teacher and popular preacher, was condemned by the Fathers of the Council of Constance as a heretic. He was immediately stripped of his vestments and turned over to the king's men. By order of King Sigismund he was led out of the city to a pyre and offered a last chance to recant. He refused and was burnt to death. He died singing a hymn.

Hus was condemned for his theological ideas just like John Wyclif, the Englishman, some of whose ideas he adopted. But the underlying causes were political. Hus had spoken out strongly against corruption in the church, such as the selling of indulgences and the buying of offices. This made him a popular figure with the discontented poor and a threat to both church and secular leaders. In addition Hus, born of a peasant family in a Bohemian village, was closely identified with Czech nationalism, a clear threat to the German-dominated royal court.

Jan Hus is led to the stake.

Small is beautiful: a miniature entitled January in "Tres Riches Heures".

Miniatures adorn French duke's library

France, 1415
The Limburg brothers are busy preparing a new book, the *Tres Riches Heures* (Very Rich Hours), for the Duc de Berry. It is, as its name suggests, a richly illustrated "book of hours", religious texts and prayers to be read at various set times of the day. It is a masterpiece of miniature painting, and joins other fine books of hours in the duke's well-stocked library.

Peninsula of Malacca converted to Islam by Indonesian prince

Malacca, South Malaya, 1414
Paramesvara, the exiled Indonesian prince who founded a kingdom on the Malaccan peninsula, has been converted to the Moslem faith – but with Paramesvara seeking to counteract the influence of Malacca's ally China, and of her enemy Siam, it is a conversion of convenience. However, for Paramesvara, the prince of Palembang, it has been an epic journey. First he declared Palembang independent from the Hindu kingdom of Majapahit on Java. When Majapahit destroyed Palembang in 1390, he fled to Tumasik on the Malaccan peninsula, and was again pursued. Finally, in 1401, he reached Malacca where, with the help of the Chinese who needed a friendly port in so strategic a place, he established his new state. Malacca has grown prosperous thanks to Arab traders. Paramesvara's shrewd change of faith is likely to increase his country's prosperity considerably.

Krishna is beaten by the god Indra, who rides on the bird-deity Garuda.

Russian icons, including (bottom right) one of the Holy Trinity.

Bengali bard sings of the love of Krishna

India, c.1415

The Bengali poet and singer Baru Chandidas has written a beautiful set of songs about Krishna, one of the incarnations of the Hindu god Visnu, whose cult has become very popular in north-eastern India in recent years. Chandidas, a high-caste Brahman, is among the first

Bengali writers of Visnuite poetry, and his *Shrikrishnakirtan*, in which he retells the traditional story of the cowherd Krishna and his love for the shepherdess Radha, is unusual in its down-to-earth language. However, Chandidas stresses the importance of human emotion which is free from base desires.

Calm ecstasy evoked by icon of Trinity

Russia, c.1411

The icon painter Andrei Rublev has confirmed his reputation as the greatest Russian artist of his day with his latest work, *Trinity*, commissioned by the monastery of the Holy Trinity at Zagorsk, near Moscow. Rublev made his name through his work with Theophanes the Greek on the cathedral of the Assumption in Moscow, in 1405, and with Daniel Chorny in Vladimir-Volynsky in 1408. His work is more intimate and realistic in its contemplation of the divine than that of other icon painters, and he makes use of the technique known as *sfumato*, the soft blending of light and shade. The *Trinity*,

however, radiates light with an almost total absence of shadow, the rhythmic brushstrokes creating an impression of calm ecstasy in the three finely-drawn angels representing the Holy Trinity itself. It is a wonderfully simple expression of a theologically complex idea.

Lollard coup foiled

England, 13 January 1414

An attempted coup by the heretical Lollard sect has been foiled and 45 of the rebels were executed today. The uprising was led by Sir John Oldcastle, who was sentenced to death for his reformist beliefs last September.

Granted 40 days respite by the king, Henry V, Oldcastle lost no time in forming a last-ditch plan to take power. He escaped from the Tower and gave out word to Lollards across the country. But Henry, alerted to the plot, was waiting for the rebels when they met outside London. Some died in the fighting that followed, and many more were captured. Oldcastle, however, escaped.

African king who gave his army chain mail is dead

Kano, Nigeria, 1410

Kanajeji Sarki, the ruler of Kano, has died after a reign of 20 years. The West African monarch, who gave his soldiers the protection of helmets and chain-mail and introduced war horses protected by quilted body armour, raised the power of Kano to new heights. Two cen-

turies ago Kano was an insignificant city-state, whose writ ran little further than its city walls.

Steadily Kano expanded its territories. By Kanajeji's accession it dominated most of Hausaland (north-western Nigeria). By his death it had surpassed the power of the empire of Mali, dominating

West Africa. Not afraid of innovation, he imported chain-mail from Mameluke Egypt, and, recognising the tactical value of the horse, built a superb cavalry, its horses upholstered in quilts. None could withstand them, and Kanajeji's army is now one of most powerful on the whole of the African continent.

Spain, 1416. Alfonso V succeeds his father Ferdinand on the throne of Aragon. The election of Ferdinand, the son of John of Castile, in 1412 ended the succession dispute which broke out in 1410 on the death of Martin of Aragon without direct heirs.

France, 1418. John the Fearless of Burgundy, an ally of the English, seizes control of the government in the name of the queen, Isabel of Bavaria. The dauphin Charles escapes from Paris and sets up his base at Bourges, where he takes the title of regent.

Normandy, July 1419. With the exception of Mont St Michel, all of Normandy is now under the control of Henry V of England.

France, 10 September 1419. After a bad-tempered meeting with the dauphin, John the Fearless is murdered at Montereau by supporters of the dauphin. He is succeeded by his son Philip (the Good).

China, 1420. The Yongle emperor moves his main capital to the former Yuan capital Dadu, renaming it Beijing ("northern capital"), the better to defend the country against resurgent Mongol power. Nanjing becomes the secondary capital.

North Atlantic, 1420. Prince Henry of Portugal encourages the settlement of Porto Santo and Madeira.

Florence, 1420. Cosimo (the Elder) becomes manager of the Medici bank.

Paris, 1 December 1420. Henry V makes a triumphant entry into Paris.

Asia Minor (Anatolia), 1421. Murat II succeeds his father, Mahomet, as Ottoman sultan and resumes a policy of expansion.

Central Europe, 1 June 1421. At a meeting at Caslav, the representatives of Bohemia and Moravia renounce the Emperor Sigismund as their king and found a government.

Italy, 1421. As part of his campaign to restore the duchy of Milan, which fragmented into city-states after the death of Gian Galeazzo Visconti in 1402, Filippo Maria Visconti subjugates Genoa.

Flanders, 1421. Gypsies have been recorded as arriving in the city of Bruges. Established in eastern Europe by the end of last century, the gypsies started to move westwards early in the present century.

Church schism is healed at Constance

Martin V: habemus papam.

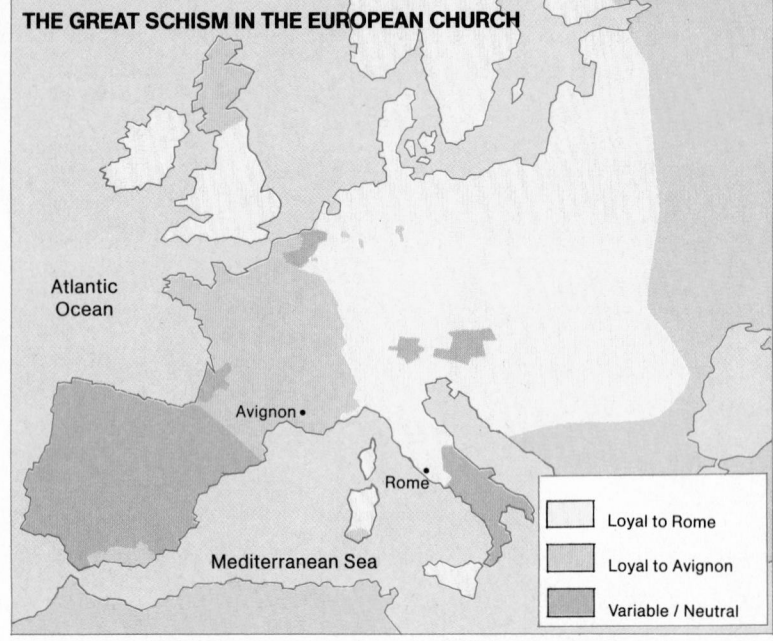

THE GREAT SCHISM IN THE EUROPEAN CHURCH

Atlantic Ocean

Avignon •

Rome •

Mediterranean Sea

☐ Loyal to Rome

▨ Loyal to Avignon

▨ Variable / Neutral

Constance, 11 November 1417
The "Great Schism" in the Christian Church, which began when two rival popes were elected in 1370, is over. Today the Italian Cardinal Oddone Colonna was elected Pope Martin V by the conclave with the support of the major national and clerical factions.

Unlike the ill-fated Council of Pisa, which elected a pope in 1409 and then found that the two existing popes refused to be ousted, the council here started pragmatically. It set out to remove the existing three popes first. The Pisan pope, John XXIII, was the first to fall. He was found guilty by the council in May 1415 of adultery, incest, sodomy, the poisoning of Pope Alexander V and the denial of the immortality of the soul. Gregory XII, the Roman pope, then decided that discretion

was the better part of valour, and resigned voluntarily in June. Benedict XIII, the Avignon pope, proved more obdurate, but he was finally deposed on 26 July 1417 as a heretic.

The new pope has no great reputation as a scholar or preacher. Here at Constance, in Germany, he has been seen running with the hare and hunting with the hounds. He is amiable and colourless, perhaps an ideal compromise figure. The key figure in securing unity has been the German King Sigismund, in alliance with England's Henry V, acting for political not theological reasons.

Chinese treasure fleet lands in Africa

China, 1422
Zheng He, the grand eunuch of the Three Treasures, has reached Malindi on the East African coast with his Star Raft, the great fleet sent to spread the Emperor Yunglo's prestige to the west.

This is Zheng He's sixth great expedition and it is no haphazard exploration. The huge treasure ships, with five or six decks, weigh about 1,500 tons each and are provisioned for ocean cruising. They carry a year's supply of grain, herds of pigs and jars of fermenting wine.

They are also equipped with the latest magnetic compasses and are

accompanied by auxiliary and store vessels, including horseships for the mounts of the expedition's 27,000 soldiers.

Malindi is a special place for the Chinese, for it is from there that the emperor has been sent giraffes, thought in China to be sacred unicorns. Zheng He ships are filled with porcelain, silks and satins, gold and silver, to trade for lions and rhinos, myrrh and ambergris.

The trade is symbolic as well as profitable, for by accepting the Chinese goods the local chieftains are deemed to have paid homage to the emperor.

Defenestration of Prague Catholics

Prague, 30 July 1419
The conflict between the Czech nation and the Church of Rome has come to a head with an uprising by followers of Jan Hus, the executed reformer. During a mass demonstration in Prague, thousands of Hussites marched on the New Town Hall. After demands for the release of several of their preachers were ignored, the crowd forced its way into the building and threw the Catholic councillors and others whom the Hussites hated out of the windows into the square.

A meeting of townspeople was held and appointed four captains to administer the city. The rising was in protest against the recent pro-Catholic policies of King Wenceslas IV, including the restoration of many churches in Prague and elsewhere to the Catholics.

The king's hard line was prompted by fears of a papal crusade against the country. Now, however, although shocked and frightened by the new Hussite militancy, he is taking no action against it. He has been convinced by his courtiers and members of the conservative Hussite group that, if he does not accept the new pro-Hussite council, the mutiny may even grow.

English win at Agincourt

The film of Shakespeare's "Henry V" evokes the English camp at Agincourt.

France, 25 October 1415

There could have been no greater contrast between these two armies as they awaited battle at Agincourt on the eve of this, St Crispin's Day. The English, numbering 12,000, were well-disciplined and prepared to die, knowing that they were grossly outnumbered by the French. As they lay silent as commanded, their king, Henry V, walked among their lines, talking quietly to archer, footsoldier and knight alike. He had not wanted this battle and had been prepared to strike bargains to avoid it. Half a mile away the French were jubilant, even parading a cart in which they intended to drag the English king through Paris. They had reason: they numbered 60,000. But they had learned little since Crecy, 69 years ago.

This morning Henry attended Mass and, like most of his army, confessed. He donned his armour and a bejewelled helmet and took his position in front of his army as the French began their advance – into a rain of English arrows. The French cavalry panicked, smashing their way through their own infantrymen, causing great breaches in the forward ranks which were quickly filled by English soldiers wielding swords and axes. The battle lasted until four o'clock today, when English victory was assured. A final push by the French forced the English to cut the throats of some 1,000 prisoners.

England and France sign perpetual peace

Philip of Burgundy: co-signatory.

Henry V: chief beneficiary.

France, 21 May 1420

After months of patient negotiation, Henry V, the victor of Agincourt, has brought England and France under one crown. And to cement the agreement, signed with Philip, the duke of Burgundy, the English king is to marry Catherine of Valois, the king of France's daughter. Henry believes that the agreement will bring "perpetual peace" between the two kingdoms. The customs and kingdoms of England and France are to be kept entirely separate, the union of the two crowns to be personal.

The agreement does not tackle the question of succession, however; and no woman can succeed to the French throne. This could prove to be a major stumbling block.

Pleasure-loving sultan broken by battle

Central India, 1420

Sultan Firuz Bahman, ruler of the Deccan (central India), has suffered a crushing defeat at Pangal, north of the River Krishna. The eighth sultan in the powerful Brahmani dynasty, Firuz is unaccustomed to defeat. He came to power in 1397 and immediately established his authority with a thorough-going re-organisation of administration in his lands.

The following year Harihara II, ruler of Vijayanagar (in southern India) tried to invade. Firuz slew the leader's son and, aided by heavy seasonal rains, drove a bedraggled Hindu army back to the south. His own expansionist ambitions were only temporarily halted by an alliance between Vijayanagar, Malwa and Gujarat. In 1406 he defeated his enemies and established his southern border on the river Tungabhadra.

Firuz is not only a war-monger. He has a passion for building and has filled his capital Gulbarga with many splendid edifices, the most remarkable of which is the main mosque, a copy of the one in Cordoba in Spain. He also has a taste for hard drinking, music and women, keeping a huge harem.

But his most recent defeat may change all this. He has returned from the battle a broken-down old man, with little enthusiasm left for his former pleasures.

"Hannya": a demon mask from the Japanese Noh theatre.

Mongol power in Persia and Russia slips

Saray, Astrakhan, c.1420

A century of abrasive border disputes in Azerbaijan and Transcaucasia between two expansionist Mongol powers has weakened both to a point where they no longer control events inside their own boundaries. The punch-drunk opponents are the *ilkhans* (subsidiary khans) of Persia and the Golden Horde in Russia and eastern Europe.

Some think that the death of Kublai Khan in 1294 damaged Mongol solidarity. At its peak, the Horde's writ ran from the Danube to the Baltic and from Kiev to the Urals. The Horde's most potent source of wealth, apart from loot and Russian taxation, was the trade link, via Italian middlemen, with Mameluke Egypt. It also controlled trade routes similar to that followed by Marco Polo from Europe across Asia into China.

As Horde domination collapses, the situation is reverting to the position before 1236: semi-independent Turkish nomads, loyal to clan chiefs, roam the steppes. What is new is the identity being forged by Russia.

Joan of Arc is victorious at Orleans

Orleans, France, 8 May 1429

In a full suit of armour, a young peasant girl knelt and prayed today as her victorious army celebrated the defeat of the besieging English. Many believe that France owes this critical victory to "voices" heard in her father's garden by the girl, Joan of Arc, since she was 13.

The retreating English army of 5,000, led by the earl of Salisbury, had sought to establish a foothold on the river Loire and open up Anjou to occupation. They had not reckoned with a revitalised, well-disciplined French army, spiritually transformed by Joan's voices.

The voices told Joan that it was the will of heaven that the English should be thrown out of France and that she, Joan, was in some way to be instrumental in their eviction. She must tell the Dauphin that he must be anointed with holy oil at Rheims – after which the English would not be able to stand against him. Four months ago Joan succeeded in reaching the Dauphin near Tours and convinced him of her devoutness and sincerity.

It was indeed a very different army that Joan rode with to Orleans. Whether they viewed the slight young 17-year-old as a mascot, a saint or an inspired leader cannot be said. But this was an elated, ecstatic, crusading army that foreswore swearing and harlots and attended Mass at which they vowed to follow Joan's "voices".

Joan, by a 19th-century artist.

Henry V, English soldier of genius, dies

King Henry V (1387-1422), from a painting in Chichester cathedral.

France, 31 August 1422

Henry V of England has died at the very moment when the crown of France was within his grasp and he was about to realise his ambition to rule over both kingdoms. He is best remembered for his stunning victory at Agincourt, but his reconquest of Normandy was achieved by less spectacular means – the besieging and capturing of castles and walled towns. Last year he married Catherine, the daughter of the imbecile Charles VI of France. He was to have acted as regent and to have succeeded to the throne on Charles' death. Henry's piecemeal conquest of France continued until May this year, when he fell ill. He struggled on for three months until he was too weak to ride his horse. He was 35 and had ruled England for nine years. His son is aged just nine months; this is causing widespread fears of a collapse of English power in France.

Aztecs forge triple alliance in Mexico

Central America, 1428

The Tepanec empire in the Valley of Mexico has been overthrown by a triple alliance of the Aztec island-city of Tenochtitlan, the exiled army of Nezahualcoyotl, the leader of Texcoco, and the disaffected Tepanec city of Tlacopan.

Tepanec tyranny ignited the revolt. The Emperor Maxtla was both cruel and short-sighted, with an unfailing gift for turning friends into enemies. He continued his father's policy of trying to subject Texcoco, his daily atrocities turning the population against him.

At about the same time Tlacopan, overburdened by taxation, revolted against the Tepanecs. Itzcoatl, the Aztec leader, whose militarist island-city has been asserting increasing independence from Tepanec suzerainty, seized the opportunity created by Tepanec weakness to bring the three enemies of the Tepanecs together.

For all three – particularly Tenochtitlan and Texcoco, who are former enemies – it is an alliance of convenience, combining the commercial prosperity of Tlacopan, the prestige of Texcoco and the military might of Tenochtitlan. Nor is there any doubt who has gained the most, and the Aztec state of Tenochtitlan now dominates the Valley of Mexico.

Joan is burnt at stake

Rouen, France, 30 May 1431
After a year of inquisition, torture and imprisonment, Joan of Arc was taken to the stake in the market square here today and burnt to death as a witch. Only two years ago this daughter of a peasant family was acclaimed as the heroine of Orleans. It was then that the French king took note of "voices" heard by Joan that could lead him to drive the English from France.

No one doubts that this was a political trial and execution, or that Charles VII's complacency was one of the main causes of Joan's ordeal. She had played a major role in the attempted recapture of Paris – in which she was wounded – and had fought in minor engagements before being taken prisoner by the Burgundians. They were allied to the English and sold her to the duke of Bedford for 10,000 gold crowns. An English escort took Joan to Rouen, and it was here that she faced the hostile questioning of Bishop Cauchon, a Burgundian, in a secret trial conducted according to the rites of the Inquisition.

Joan conducted her own defence and stressed her purity and her devotion to France, but to no avail. The bishops sentenced her to life

Joan the Martyr, from a miniature.

imprisonment, but even then they had not finished with her. She resumed the wearing of men's clothing – possibly this was all that she was given. This was taken as evidence of her relapse and she was condemned to the stake. There she asked for a cross to be held before her to see through the flames. Her last word was "Jesus".

Ruler takes his cut on paradise island

The ruins of Kilwa's 13th-century great mosque; Islam was brought by Arabs.

Kilwa, 1430
The merchant visiting Kilwa who stops to admire its fine buildings, its beautifully dressed and bejewelled inhabitants, its magnificent 100-room stonewall palace or the great mosque being rebuilt with a vaulted dome soon discovers his role in the wealth-creation process that has made the island states of Kilwa the most prosperous in the Indian Ocean.

For whatever he trades, whether he buys or sells, he has to pay his duty to the sultan of Kilwa's treasury. On gold the sultan takes five per cent, on ivory the rate is 14 per cent – one tusk in seven.

It is not only Kilwa that has benefited from 200 years of gold trading. Along the Mozambique coast 37 towns have sprung up. Most of their trade, which Kilwa dominates, is with fellow Moslems from west India. Some is with Europe where there is also huge demand in court circles for spices and slaves. Chinese trade is increasing; Ming emperors have sent two expeditions and another is expected soon.

Tough new armour is developed for Europe's armies

French soldiery in armour.

Europe, c.1430
Complete suits of armour made of metal plate are now being worn on the battlefield with considerable success. They have been developed

A knight in full military splendour.

to overcome the weakness of chain-mail armour, which provides only limited protection: an arrow or a crossbow bolt can penetrate the openings in chain mail. The new

harnais blanc, or white armour, as it is called, has been made possible by greater sophistication in metal manufacturing techniques.

Tougher iron and steel are being produced using a new carburising process and blast-furnaces. The white hot plates are then hardened by "quenching" in fluid. Improvements are also taking place in the workshops where the plate is fashioned, so that the armour offers greater resistance to missiles.

Of course, the use of full-plate body armour is not without some drawbacks. It is heavier and more tiring to wear. On the other hand, the incorporation of a lance rest at the side of the breastplate, now standard practice, has made heavy lances easier to handle. Cavalry can now lower their lances from the vertical to the horizontal and take accurate aim while charging at speed towards the enemy.

The Florentine artist Tommaso Masaccio died 1n 1428, aged 27. He revived Giotto's ideals of expressiveness in art, as in his "Virgin and Child", above.

North Atlantic, 1432. The Portuguese discover an archipelago which they name the Azores.

West Africa, 1433. The Tuaregs, desert camel-riders from the north of the continent, capture the city of Timbuktu.

Rome, 31 May 1433. Sigismund is crowned emperor by Pope Eugenius IV, who hopes for his support against the council at Basle.

Switzerland, 30 November 1433. The readiness of the Council of Basle to open negotiations with the Hussites splits the movement between the moderate Utraquists and the radical Taborites.

Bohemia, May 1434. The Taborites are defeated at Lipany by the army of the Emperor Sigismund, with the support of both Catholics and Utraquists.

South-East Asia, 1434. The capital of the Khmer kingdom is moved from Angkor to Phnom Penh.

Florence, 1434. Cosimo de Medici, who was exiled by his enemy Rinaldo d'Albizzi in 1433, returns and seizes power in the city. Although strictly Cosimo remains a private citizen within an independent republic, in effect his power is complete.

France, 19 September 1435. The duke of Bedford, the English lieutenant in France, dies. He had been the one man capable of controlling the factions within the minority government of his nephew Henry VI and his death fuels impatience for the king himself to take power.

France, 21 September 1435. By the treaty of Arras, Philip the Good breaks with the English and recognises Charles VII as the only king of France.

Scandinavia, 1435. Eric of Scandinavia makes peace with the Hanse and restores their privileged position. The Hanse had been drawn into a war between Eric and the count of Holstein over possession of Schleswig.

Bohemia, 5 July 1436. The agreement made with the Hussites in 1433 is confirmed and Sigismund is recognised as king of Bohemia.

West Africa, 1436. The Portuguese, having passed the Sahara coast, begin to explore the Rio de Ouro (the Gold River).

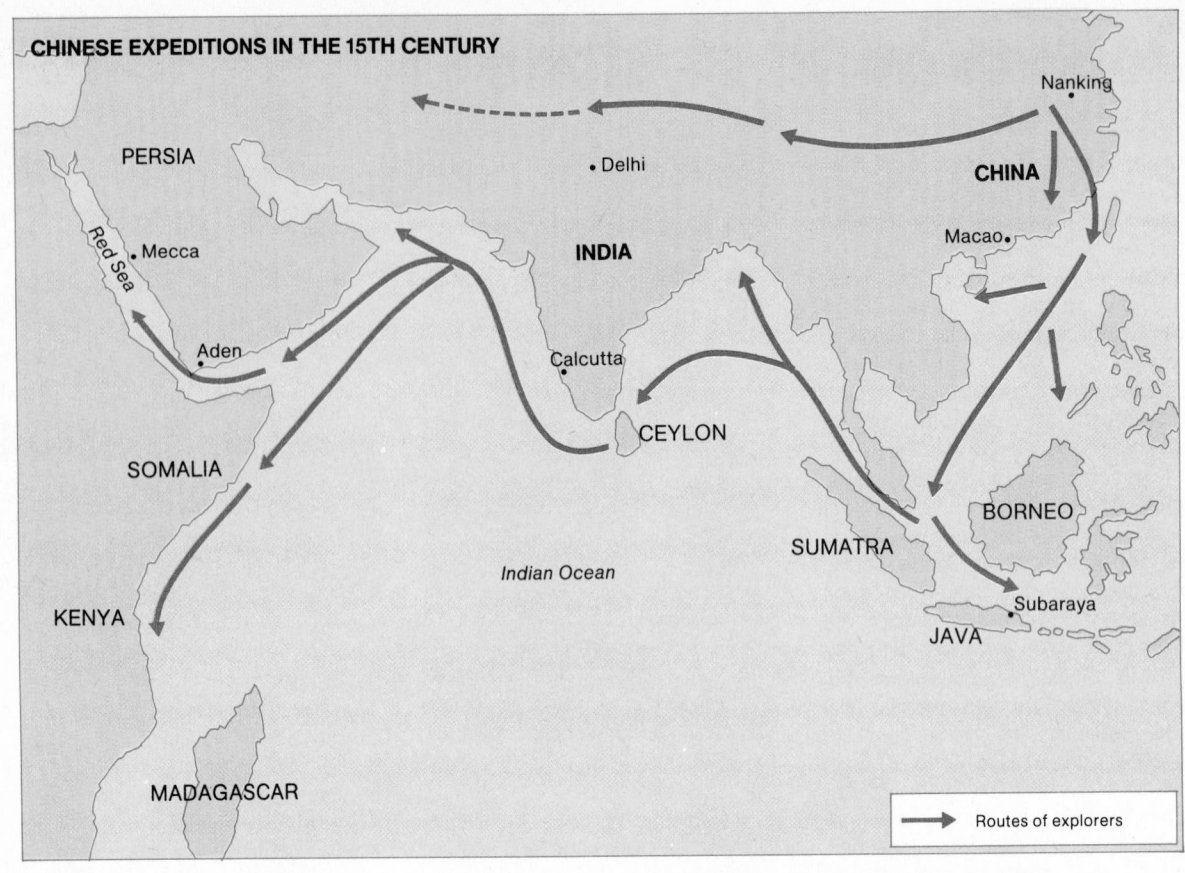

CHINESE EXPEDITIONS IN THE 15TH CENTURY

PERSIA · Delhi · Nanking · CHINA · Macao · INDIA · Red Sea · Mecca · Aden · Calcutta · CEYLON · SOMALIA · BORNEO · SUMATRA · Indian Ocean · Subaraya · JAVA · KENYA · MADAGASCAR

→ Routes of explorers

China bans voyages to the west, shuts out rest of world

China, 1433
Zheng He, the eunuch admiral, has returned safely with his fleet for the seventh time. But this will be the last of his voyages to the exotic lands of the west, for the emperor has forbidden him to sail again.

His voyages have always been opposed by the powerful Confucian bureaucrats at court who viewed them as adventures in trade rather than diplomacy and therefore, according to Confucian doctrine, both wasteful and frivolous. When Zheng He's patron, the Emperor Yangle, died, the civil servants persuaded his successor to stop the voyages, but when the latter too died, Zheng He was able to get permission to undertake one last expedition.

He set out with his huge treasure ships two years ago for Arabia and the east coast of Africa, exploring far to the south. He has returned with his ships filled with strange animals, scents and spices, and with much knowledge of the far lands. However, any hopes that he had of being allowed to continue his voyages have been dashed. He is to be honourably retired as military commander of Nanjing.

The civil servants have won such a complete victory that all records of his travels are being expunged and the plans of his ships are to be destroyed. China is shutting itself off from the world.

Empire that bans collections of luxury goods is set to expand

Cuzco, Peru, 1438
Pachacuti, the new ruler of the Incas, has pledged to extend the Incas' territory and build an empire. Already his capital, Cuzco, dominates the Andes. Its stone architecture, going back to 1200, is bleak, unadorned with decoration. The nearest there is to art is the pleating on the thatched roofs. Above the thatches rise the limestone ramparts of the fortress of Saccsailhuaman, a symbol of Inca might.

Pachacuti's Inca administration is well-organised and perfectly capable of expanding into an imperial bureaucracy with power deriving from the emperor, a descendent of Manco Capac, the legendary founder of the dynasty. He is the divine representative of the sun on earth. An hereditary aristocracy takes policy decisions, and local subject aristocracies ("Incas by privilege") carry them out.

Strict rules prohibiting the accumulation of luxury goods discourage both selfishness and crime. The population provides labour in lieu of taxes, with the sick and the old being cared for by the state.

An Inca pot in the form of a head.

Portuguese find new way to the east

Moslem conqueror of Cyprus is dead

Portugal, 1434

One of Henry the Navigator's captains has at last rounded the feared Cape Bojador, on the coast of West Africa, thus fulfilling one of Henry's most fervent ambitions.

The great sailor sent ship after ship out from his palace-observatory at Sagres to sail beyond the sandy bulge of the cape. Not one of them succeeded, and Henry listened patiently to his captains' tales of the dangers of that awful place. But the dangers were in their minds.

They were terrified of the legends of the Sea of Darkness which lay beyond the cape. It was a place where white men turned black and the currents would prevent any ship from returning.

Henry sent Eannes, one of his squires, out to this awesome place last year, but he, like the others, failed to conquer his fears and got no further than the Canaries.

Henry summoned him again this year and, chiding him gently about his fears, sent him out once more. This time the shamefaced Eannes rounded the cape. He found no indication of human habitation there, bringing back only some plants called St Mary's roses.

The importance of his voyage,

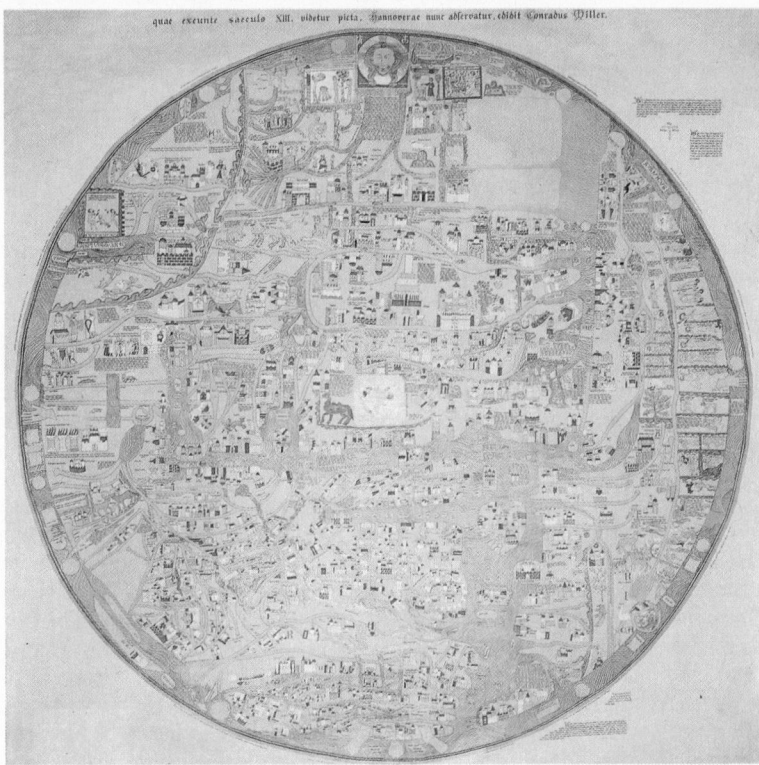

The world according to the 13th-century "Ebstore Map"; east is at the top.

however, is that he has disproved the belief that ships could not sail the seas beyond Cape Bojador. The way south is now open.

Henry has reacted promptly to Eannes' news. He has sent him to sea again along with another ship commanded by Afonso Baldaya, his cupbearer, with orders to explore beyond the cape.

Bruges prospers as leading commercial crossroads in Europe

Bruges, Flanders, c.1435

Bruges, the richest commercial staging-post in Europe, has become a world city, prosperous not only in commerce but in the arts, in a new international culture and lifestyle. This is exemplified in the sumptuous court of Philip the Good, the duke of Burgundy.

Developed in the 13th century because of its geographical position between England, France, Italy and the Rhine states, Bruges gave its merchants the chance to become landowners and members of the nobility.

English wool was delivered here so regularly that London ceased to be important to traders in the Hanseatic League. They brought timber, wheat, smoked fish, metals and furs from Germany, Russia and Sweden while spices and oriental products were brought by the Italians, either by sea or up the

Van Eyck's "Arnolfini Wedding".

Rhine. Bruges could export tapestries, cloth and material from Flanders, Brabant and Hainault.

In 1336 the Hanseatic League built a factory here, since when international commerce and bank-

ing have expanded enormously. The Flanders Council gave foreign merchants significant privileges: import tolls were reduced, accounting methods simplified, and bills of exchange introduced. The Teutonic Knights opened a bank, and papal tithes from all over Europe were banked here.

In 1369 Louis de Male married his daughter to Philip the Bold, the duke of Burgundy, the brother of Charles V of France. The dukes of Burgundy worked to establish Flanders' independence from France, but came into increasing conflict with the English, who were expelled in 1383. Intermittent warfare caused hardship among the native population, who had no share in the trade bonanza.

Today, Philip the Good is the patron of all woodcarvers, metalworkers and artists like Jan van Eyck.

Cairo, 1438

Barsbay al-Zahiri, one of the greatest Mameluke sultans, is dead. His 16-year reign has not merely kept a fragile empire intact, but has seen the conquest of Cyprus and considerable commercial success.

When he came to the throne, Frankish corsairs were making damaging attacks on Moslem shipping. Barsbay took reprisals against Frankish traders in Syria, Alexandria and Damietta. But it was the pirates operating out of Cyprus who were causing the damage.

In three expeditions between 1424 and 1426, Barsbay prepared the way for two conclusive battles, one on land, one at sea, which brought Cyprus under effective Mameluke control. King Janus was captured, obliged to pay public homage to the sultan, and reinstated as a vassal ruler.

In the Arabian lands beside the Red Sea, Barsbay ensured that Mameluke influence was not undermined. When Shah Rukh of the Yemen tried to send a *kiswa*, a ceremonial cloth, to Mecca, he told him that its sacred purpose was the sole prerogative of the sultans of Egypt. He acted with even greater firmness in a dispute over customs dues on ships trading with Jeddah and Mecca. Barsbay's forces occupied both cities and imposed the sultan's own duties. He enforced a royal monopoly to bypass the profiteering Karimi merchants.

An enamelled glass mosque lamp of the kind used in the 14th century by the Islamic conquerors of Cyprus.

Language and nationhood in Europe

Most European languages belong to the same group, known as Indo-European or (formerly) "Aryan", a family of languages stretching from Iceland to India, and, in modern times, to the Americas, Australasia and parts of Africa. They have a common ancestor in dialects spoken by a nomadic group somewhere in what is now the southern USSR, which subsequently split up during a large-scale migration westwards and southwards, probably from around 2000BC.

The European branch subdivided into five main groups: Balto-Slavonic, Celtic, Germanic, Hellenic and Italic, which in turn subdivided even further. The Baltic branch of the Balto-Slavonic group includes Lithuanian, the most complex and archaic of all modern Indo-European tongues in Europe. The main Slavonic languages are Bulgarian, Czech, Polish, Russian, Slovak and Serbo-Croat. Celtic, the most endangered of the great Indo-Germanic groups, is now almost exclusively spoken in the remoter parts of the British Isles and Brittany and includes Breton, Irish and Scottish Gaelic, and Welsh. Cornish and Manx died out in about 1800 and 1960 respectively.

The Germanic languages include Dutch/Flemish, English, German, and the Scandinavian tongues, Danish, Icelandic, Norwegian and Swedish. The most successful member of the ancient Italic group was Latin, which displaced Celtic tongues in Gaul and Spain as the Roman empire expanded.

From Latin the Romance languages developed in the former empire; the most important are French, Italian, Portuguese, Rumanian and Spanish. Greek is the most important offshoot of the Hellenic group. Albanian is also an Indo-European tongue, while Hungarian and Finnish are related members of an entirely different family, the Finno-Ugric languages. The origins of Basque are a mystery; it predates the Romans and one theory claims it may be related to Etruscan, another mysterious tongue supplanted by Latin under the Romans.

Linguistic dominance

In the early middle ages, regional linguistic differences were enhanced by political disunity and, in an age of poor communications, by isolation. For example, the disintegration of Roman government in the fifth century hastened the divergence of the Latin dialects of the empire. But the consolidation of some dialects into distinctive languages was often the result of the political or economic success and prestige of those who spoke them. A Romance language, Provencal (also called *langue d'oc* or *Occitan*), was for a long time the language of southern France, and was a major literary language from the 11th to the 13th centuries, used by acquisitive, cultured and successful rulers.

Catalan, Provencal's Spanish neighbour, was the language of the Aragonese merchants and diplomats who played a powerful role in Mediterranean politics from the 13th to the 15th centuries. The low German of northern Germany, closer to Dutch than to High German, the ancestor of modern German, developed into a thriving literary language in the middle ages because it was used by assertive and effectively independent merchants and regional rulers within the Holy Roman empire.

However, as political fortunes changed, formerly dominant languages and dialects declined in importance. This was the fate of Provencal, Catalan and Low German, as respectively French, Castilian and High German rulers came to the fore. The Celtic tongues were similarly encroached upon by English as new rulers came into power.

Cultural prestige

Cultural prestige also played its part in promoting dialects; for instance the dominance of Florentine Italian in Italy from the 14th century owed much to Dante and later humanists, just as standard English derives from the central-southern dialect of Chaucer and the courtiers, scholars and lawyers of late mediaeval England.

Writers such as Dante and Chaucer were key figures in the literary development of their own national languages. But in England, Italy and elsewhere, this development was delayed by the persistence of Latin as the universal language of Church, government and the intelligentsia. For most of the middle ages an illiterate, *illiteratus*, specifically meant one ignorant of Latin, and writing in Latin ensured a wide readership for academic works; Thomas More and Erasmus, for instance, communicated in Latin. However, with the growth in the proportion of educated laymen and women, who had little use for Latin but much use for literacy, the vernacular triumphed.

The Reformation, and the abandonment in many lands of Latin for common worship, and the spread of bibles translated into the vernacular, spurred the shift from Latin, although it remained the language of diplomacy until the 17th century and of the scientific world for a little longer.

National mythologies

Whether or not the peoples of Europe inherited any folk-memories of their origins, it is evident that the mediaeval national myths that have survived were designed to explain existing political structures rather than any historical reality. Most successful political groups either invented or were given suitable creation myths to explain their distinctiveness. They were three main models.

The first derived from the first century Roman historian Tacitus who traced the Germanic barbarians back to a progenitor called Mannus, later sometimes called Alanus. A second source was the Bible and, in particular, the story of Noah from whose sons Ham, Shem and Japheth a number of peoples traced their origins. The third, and most widespread, model was provided by the legends of Troy (particularly of the founding of Rome by descendants of Aeneas, who had fled from Troy after its fall), popularised by Virgil, the first century Roman poet whose works were widely read by the educated in the middle ages.

Within this basic structure of classical and biblical stereotypes, each myth displayed suitably individual characteristics, often including an appropriate founder of the *gens* or nation. Tacitus's derivation of the Germani from Mannus is matched by Scottish legends of descent from Scota, daughter of the pharaoh of Egypt, Frankish legends of the settlement in the Rhineland of a Trojan prince who found refuge in and gave his name to the island of Britain.

Many other peoples were given more exotic ancestry. In the tenth century some claimed that the Saxons of Germany descended from the soldiers of Alexander the Great, which explained their military prowess. In the 12th century, the Bavarians were traced back to the son of Hercules.

Such myths did not just appear by accident. Most commonly, the myth was deliberately created by intellectuals to explain current political dominance and to justify and praise their own political values and leadership. In the early 11th century, when the Normans were beginning to establish themselves as a potent force in Europe, their historian, Dudo of St Quentin, invented a descent from the Greeks and Trojans. For people who, after 1000, were coming under more codified legal systems and the stronger central authority of sovereigns, such myths helped consolidate a growing sense of national identity and prestige.

Detail of a carving from a stave-church portal, illustrating the story of the Norse hero Sigurd. The northern Germanic tongue of the Vikings was first manifested as a literary language in Scaldic verse and in the great Norse sagas of the 12th and 13th centuries.

"Leaving the Ark", an illustration from the French work known as the Bedford Book of Hours, c.1420. Noah's sons Ham, Shem and Japheth were once believed to be the ancestors of the world's races.

"Dante and his poem", by Domenico di Michelino. Dante's fame contributed to the popularity of the literary dialect of mediaeval Florence in Tuscany, which provided a model for the rest of Italy. There, as in many other parts of Europe, Latin was still the predominant written language.

A physician, from the Ellesmere Manuscript of Chaucer's "Canterbury Tales". Chaucer demonstrated brilliantly the literary potential of English, a Germanic language greatly enriched by French, Latin and Norse. All major languages are represented in the vocabulary of modern English.

Greek and Roman Churches reach formal agreement to unite

The 13th-century "Epitaphios of Thessaloniki", one of the great works of Byzantine religious textile art.

Florence, 1439
A demoralised delegation from the Eastern (Byzantine) Church, led by the Emperor John VIII, has now agreed to all the major demands of Pope Eugenius. The Greeks recognise the pope as the head of the whole Christian church. Union of the two churches, split on doctrinal issues for a thousand years, has been solemnly proclaimed. In fact, the Greeks have finally realised that they cannot deny the awful reality behind the words of a previous pope, Martin V, who wrote in 1422 that "the Turks will fear to attack you ... and Christians will come to your help with more eagerness if they know you are united with other Christians". Unity is the Greeks' last hope of saving themselves from the Turks. The Greeks have capitulated to the Roman view of the Trinity. Their one real concession is over the marriage of priests which is not mentioned in the agreement. There is no doubt here where the power lies, but whether Greek priests will conform is a more open question.

Matchmaker Warwick, "the father of chivalry", dies in France

France, 31 May 1439
Richard Beauchamp, the earl of Warwick, known as "the father of chivalry", and England's most powerful nobleman, has died at Rouen, where he was resident as lieutenant of France and Normandy. Born in 1381, Beauchamp became the fifth earl of Warwick in 1401. After fighting at the Battle of Shrewsbury, in 1403, he set out in 1408 for the Holy Land and spent six years touring the courts of Europe. On his return he was made captain of Calais by the new king, Henry V, and there organised a *pas d'armes* (a series of formal personal combats, a surrogate for actual war).

The king then sent him as ambassador to the general council at Constance where he met the pope and the emperor and was offered by the latter the heart of St George. Warwick declined and the emperor himself brought the heart to England in 1416. Warwick also helped to arrange Henry's marriage to Catherine, the daughter of the king of France. In 1429 Warwick became guardian of their son, Henry VI, then aged seven – a tribute to his chivalric pre-eminence.

He also accompanied Henry to France for his coronation, and was the English commander at Rouen during the trial of Joan of Arc when a widespread French uprising seemed imminent.

Despot scars his people's faces as slaves

Benin, Nigeria, 1439
Ewuare has taken over the kingdom of Benin, killing the previous incumbent, his own brother, and becoming *oba*. There was heavy fighting, many have been killed, and the capital, Urbini, has been taken by storm.

The coup brings Benin not only a new ruler but a new kind of government. The old constitution, with the power of the ruler limited by the *ozama*, or hereditary chiefs, has been abolished, and Ewuare has ordered all free-born citizens to be scared with facial markings as "slaves of the oba". There is no doubt that Ewuare is making a bid for absolute power.

Already Ewuare has shown himself to be the most energetic ruler the 300-year-old state has known. To offset the power of the ozama, he has established a new order of "town" chiefs directly responsible to him. He has announced that he will be rebuilding the capital, and has already given it a new name, Edo. Finally, he is expanding the army that brought him to power, talking of new conquests beyond Benin's borders.

The myth of the birth of Mahavira, founder of Indian Jainism, as seen in Jain scriptures.

Rise of Italian city-states heralds art renaissance

Florence, c. 1440-1450

The cities of northern Italy are in competition not only for wealth and power, but also in an artistic revival in which their richest families vie with one another as patrons of art and learning.

Foremost of them is Florence, whose patron is the banker Cosimo de Medici, the *Pater Patriae* (Father of the Republic). The Florentines at last consecrated their cathedral, Santa Maria dei Fiore, in 1436, on completing the self-supporting octagonal dome designed by Filippo Brunelleschi. The bronze doors of the Baptistry alongside are the life's work of his friend, Lorenzo Ghiberti. The first, with scenes from the New Testament on its bronze panels, was finished in 1424, but the second, Old Testament, door is only just nearing completion, with as many as 100 figures to a panel. Ghiberti is using Brunelleschi's discoveries to give them perspective.

Paolo Uccello is applying the laws of perspective to painting. He has decorated the church of Santa Maria Novella and is now working on a big battlepiece for the Palazzo Medici showing the cavalry charge at San Romano where Florence defeated Siena in 1432. Meanwhile the decorations of the convent of St Mark by its Dominican prior, Fra Angelico, include a remarkable *Annunciation*.

The sculptor Donatello decorated the cathedral facade and campanile with statues and is in great demand in many cities for his bronzes, such as the *David* he cast for the Medicis – the first life-size, naked statue since Roman times. For Padua he did a massive statue of Gattemelata, the soldier of fortune, and the *Miracles of St Anthony* to adorn the high altar.

Arezzo is employing Piero della Francesca on a sequence of frescoes in the church of St Francis. He, too, used perspective in his *Baptism of Christ* beneath a tree set in a receding landscape. Siena is amazed by the precocity of Andrea Mantegna, who began painting a chapel for his master, Squarcione, at the age of 12, as if fully mature. In Venice the Grand Canal has seen the erection of the richest *palazzo* yet, the Ca' d'Oro, painted in gold.

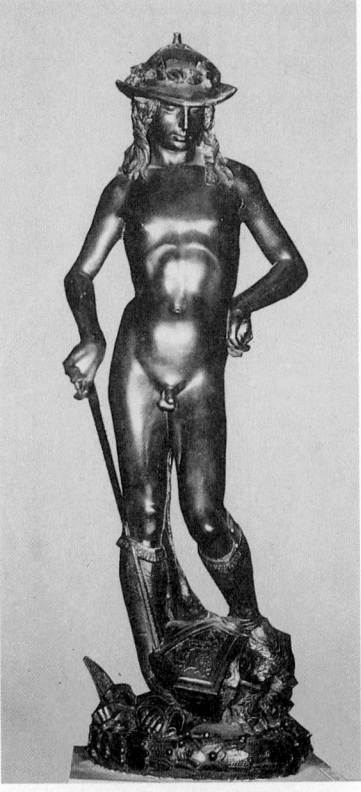
Donatello's bronze, life-size David.

Florence's magnificent cathedral.

The Ca' d'Oro in Venice.

Florence cathedral: ceiling mosaics in Brunelleschi's octagonal dome.

"The Birth" by Fra Angelico in the convent of St Mark in Florence.

1440 (1440-1450)

Portugal, 1441. For the first time, slaves and gold are directly imported from West Africa into Portugal.

Florence, 1441. The Ethiopian Church sends a representative to the Church council. An act of union is signed between the Church of Ethiopia and that of Rome.

Naples, 12 June 1442. Alfonso V of Aragon is crowned king of Naples after conquering the town.

Hungary, 1442. Janos Hunyadi – the general of Vladyslav, the king of Poland and elected ruler of Hungary – wins two victories over the Turks. First he routs Mezid Bey, who had invaded Transylvania; then he overcomes the army sent to avenge the bey's defeat.

Bulgaria, 1444. The Ottomans defeat the Hungarians at Varna on the shores of the Black Sea. This opens their way to Constantinople.

West Africa, 1444. Portuguese explorers reach the mouth of the Senegal and reach Cape Verde.

Poland, 1447. Casimir IV Jagiellonian becomes king of Poland, in succession to his brother Vladyslav III, the king of Poland and Hungary, who vanished in the defeat at Varna.

Milan, 1447. On the death of Filippo Maria Visconti, the last of the male line, a republic is proclaimed by the citizens, who hire Francesco Sforza as their general.

Germany, 1448. Leaving Strasbourg, where he has lived for the past few years, Johannes Gutenberg – who has recently invented moveable printing characters – returns to his native town of Mainz.

Serbia, 19 October 1448. The Hungarian general Janos Hunyadi, who has been the effective ruler of Hungary since the disappearance of Vladyslav at Varna, is defeated by the Ottoman Sultan Murat II at Kosovo.

Constantinople, 6 January 1449. Constantine XI succeeds his brother John VIII Palaeologus as emperor.

Lausanne, 25 April 1449. The rump of the Council of Basle (which was expelled from that city last year) recognises Nicholas V as pope and dissolves itself. Felix V, the pope elected by the council in 1439, abdicates.

"The Adoration of the Lamb", painted for the cathedral of St Bavo, Ghent, was the creation of two van Eycks – Jan and his elder brother, Hubert.

Jan van Eyck, the first oil painter, dies

Bruges, Flanders, 1441
Jan van Eyck, who has died here, took painting an enormous stride forward when he experimented with oil as the medium for his colours. Until then painters had mixed paint with water for frescoes or egg-yolk for tempera. Both Jan and his elder brother Hubert van Eyck painted with oil on wooden panels, which were prepared with plaster and glue. This gave a glowing effect not achieved before.

Their greatest joint work is the altarpiece for the cathedral of Ghent, *The Adoration of the Lamb*, consisting of a landscape and 16 portrait panels, covering over 1,000 square feet, the first oil painting on such a scale. Jan completed the work after Hubert's death in 1426, and settled at Bruges where he developed the new art of secular portrait painting. No-one had seen such realism before – all the wrinkles and warts are rendered so faithfully that the sitters, such as the *Man with Carnations*, seem about to speak.

Jan van Eyck also took delight in his ability to render domestic interiors in gleaming detail. His double portrait *The Arnolfini Marriage* shows the couple in their best robes holding hands. The lady's little terrier stands at her feet and there are oranges scattered by the windowsill. The scene is reflected in miniature in a convex mirror behind the couple, which also shows the painter, who signs himself "Jan van Eyck was here".

Science mourns stargazer khan

Samarkand, Central Asia, 1449
Ulugh Beg, the astronomer khan, is dead, executed on a trumped-up legal charge at the instigation of his own son, Abd al-Latif. Ulugh Beg ruled for only two years after the death of his father, Shah Rukh.

A scientist rather than a warrior, Ulugh Beg faced political chaos on his father's death and had to fight for his inheritance, succeeding in maintaining control of only a part of the empire left by his cruel grandfather, Tamerlane the conqueror.

His reign has now been brought to a swift and shameful end. Abd al-Latif revolted against him, defeated him and has killed him. Abd al-Aziz, the khan's favourite son, has also been put to death.

To murder one's father and brother is regarded as excessive even by Mongol standards, and it is suggested that Abd al-Latif is also not long for this world.

Ulugh Beg was happiest working in his observatory just outside the city of Samarkand where Tamerlane lies in his black onyx tomb. He built a telescope sunk into the hillside to study the stars, and with four other scholars produced a volume of astronomical tables.

These tables, the first since those of Ptolemy, are remarkably accurate. Ulugh Beg was also a patron of architecture and built the beautiful teaching colleges at Samarkand and Bokhara. His death is a great loss to science and the arts.

Tamerlane's tomb in Samarkand.

424

Mongols' victory threatens Peking

China, 1449

A powerful Chinese army, led by the young emperor, Yingzong, has been ambushed by the Mongol chieftain, Esen. Thousands of men have been killed and the emperor has been captured. It is reported that the Mongols found him seated on a carpet surrounded by the bodies of his slaughtered bodyguard. Now Peking itself is in danger.

This was a wholly unnecessary affair mounted by the overweening eunuch Wang Jin who, against the advice of court officials, persuaded the emperor to lead the army against the raiding Mongols.

The expedition was a shambles from the start. Wang Jin had no military experience and, brushing aside the protests of officers with long experience of frontier war, he exposed the army to attack in a position where it had neither food nor water.

The disaster is complete. Wang Chin is dead and so are most of the experienced generals. The emperor is held hostage and the road to the capital is open.

Ambassador visits splendid Indian city

Southern India, 1443

The seasoned traveller and Afghan ambassador, Abdur Razzaq, has had the enviable experience of visiting one of India's greatest cities, Vijayanagar, capital of the great Hindu empire in the south.

Razzaq was summoned to Vijayanagar by the king, while on a mission to Calicut. He was to see a city that was founded over a hundred years ago in 1336. It lies on the south bank of the Tungabhadra river and is famous across the continent for the grandeur of its buildings, its bazaars teaming with luxurious imported goods and the sheer number of its citizens, enjoying the prosperity.

Early this century, Bukka II, then ruler, embarked on an extensive programme of improvement and expansion. His most remarkable addition to Vijayanagar was a vast dam in the Tungabhadra. Water from the reservoir thus created was brought to the city by acqueduct, over a distance of 15 miles (24km). Razzaq could not but be impressed on this visit.

Albania breaks free from Turks

Kruje, Albania, 28 November 1443

A 38 year-old Albanian noble, taken hostage by the Turks and educated as a Moslem, has led his people in a revolt against their occupiers. George Kastrioti or Skanderbeg (a title he earned at the Turkish court), governor of Albania since 1438, has today proclaimed the restoration of the free principality of Albania.

The son of an Albanian prince, Gjon Kastrioti, Skanderbeg was held as a hostage by the Turks to ensure that his fellow-Albanians would not revolt. A successful career in the Turkish civil service was capped by his appointment as governor of Albania.

Now, it seems, the Turkish plan has backfired. Taking advantage of the Turks' preoccupation with their hostile Hungarian neighbours, Skanderbeg has declared Albania independent, announced himself a Christian, and challenged the occupier to suppress his people. The two-headed eagle of the Kastrioti is flying over the citadel of Kruje and Skanderbeg is a national hero.

Black magician and child killer burnt

Gilles de Laval, Seigneur de Rais.

France, 26 October 1440

One of France's most respected and beloved knights was executed today at Nantes. Condemned for the murders of at least 200 children, and for heresy, sodomy, apostasy, sacrilege and violation of clerical immunity, Gilles de Laval, seigneur de Rais, was garrotted and burnt with his two accomplices.

A man of supposedly unassailable piety, a former commander of Joan of Arc's troops, a marshal of France who boasted a 200-strong retinue, a friend to beggars and patron of the arts, de Rais appeared to embody the chivalric ideal.

But, apparently, behind the goodness lay an inner man as depraved as his external image was pure: a satanist who experimented in alchemy and black magic, and who claimed to model himself upon the Caligula, the most perverse and cruel of Rome's emperors.

De Rais is alleged to have killed at least 200 children. Some were abducted, and some were sold – often for a dress or a loaf of bread – by impoverished parents. Once entrapped, they were sodomised, then slowly tortured to death. De Rais' real pleasure was watching his victims' slow death agonies.

Throughout his trial de Rais professed devout Christianity. He confessed, and claimed to see his execution as God's fitting punishment.

State scholars join sons of the nobility at king's Eton College

Eton, 1440

A new school is to be founded at Eton, Buckinghamshire. Eton College is the brainchild of King Henry VI. As well as housing clerks to pray for the king, 25 poor scholars are to be taught grammar there. The school master is also required to teach other applicants on demand.

Education is a fashionable area of concern. Henry's initiative was prompted by William of Wykeham's foundation of Winchester school. Attention is also focussing on the importance of good teachers. Clergymen who set themselves up as schoolmasters may well perform quite adequately, but in the end they lack the real teaching qualifications.

This problem, especially in the important area of the teaching of Latin grammar, was noted last year in a report by William Bingham, who sent in to the King a petition detailing the extent of the problem. He noted that some 70 schools had been forced to close down because of the scarcity of masters, and stressed that without good teachers, the Church would be weakened, since no new clergymen would be taught.

He has called for the establishment of a special college, not for the young, but for the training of the teachers who will be sent out to educate them.

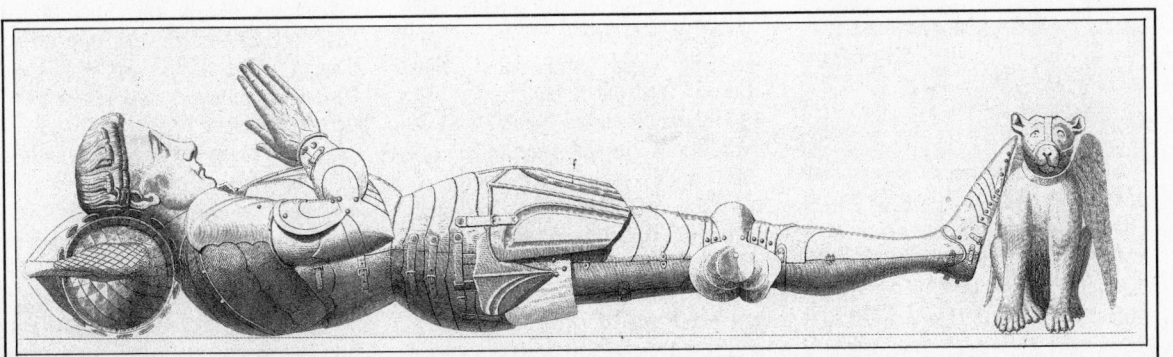

The tomb effigy of Richard Beauchamp, earl of Warwick, soldier and statesman, who died in 1439.

Milan, February 1450. Francesco Sforza, hired as military leader by the republic of Milan, stages a coup and takes the title "Duke of Milan".

South-East Africa, 1450. Mutota, conqueror of the northern Zimbabwe plateau, is succeeded by his son Matope who also takes his father's title of Munhumutupa.

Normandy, 15 April 1450. With a victory over the English at Formigny, the French complete their reconquest of Normandy.

Scandinavia, August 1450. Norway accepts an act of union by which Denmark and Norway will always have the same king. Sweden, meanwhile, is in a state of civil war.

England, 1450. Resentment at Henry VI's incompetent government erupts into open rebellion. Several of the king's advisers are murdered.

Asia Minor (Anatolia), 2 February 1451. Mohammed II succeeds Murad II as sultan of the Ottomans.

Austria, 6 January 1453. Frederick III, crowned Holy Roman emperor last year, confirms privileges granted to Austria in 1359 and raises it to the rank of archduchy.

Constantinople, 29 May 1453. The Ottoman Turks seize the city. The Byzantine empire is at an end.

France, 17 July 1453. France defeats England at Castillon, ending the 100 Years' War.

Burgundy, 17 February 1454. At a grand feast, Philip the Good of Burgundy takes the "vow of the pheasant", by which he swears to fight the Turks.

England, March 1454. The duke of York is appointed protector when Henry VI suffers a mental collapse.

Venice, 18 April 1454. The doge Francesco Foscari signs a treaty with the Ottoman Sultan Mohammed II on terms generous to Venice.

Spain, 21 July 1454. John II, the king of Castile, and Leon, who fought against the Aragonese and the Moors, is succeeded by his son Henry.

Rome, 18 February 1455. The painter Fra Angelico dies.

Rome, 24 March 1455. Pope Calixtus III succeeds Nicholas V, who sent the cardinal Nicholas of Cues on a successful mission to lead reform in Germany.

Zimbabwe is strangled by its own wealth

Part of the massive, abandoned structures of the city of Great Zimbabwe.

Zimbabwe, c.1450

Great Zimbabwe, the African kingdom set in the gold and copper-bearing country between the Zambezi and Limpopo rivers, is slowly dying. In the capital, also called Great Zimbabwe, the streets are deserted and the population dispersed.

For more than 200 years the Zimbabwe state has been growing, its growth reflected in the expansion of its capital city. The city began as a hill fortress built with rough stone walls. It then spread into the valley beneath. The rich lived in homes with elaborate winding walls of stone and clay; outside their gates the poor were huddled in flimsier dwellings made from wattle and daub.

The state expanded; so did the city. The more that Zimbabwe controlled, the richer it became; its subject peoples paying tribute in gold, copper and iron. The very wealth Zimbabwe accumulated is causing her downfall.

The city has attracted so many courtiers, politicians and craftsmen that the surrounding lands are unable to feed them. Thus the city is dying, and with it would die the state.

Bronze doors are complete after 50 years

The magnificent new doors of the Baptistry by Lorenzo Ghiberti.

Florence, 1452

Lorenzo Ghiberti has completed his greatest work, the second bronze door of the Baptistry of the cathedral of Santa Maria del Fiore, nearly 50 years after he began work on the first door as a young man. Now, at 74, he has surpassed all his previous achievements.

The second door is more ambitious than the first, which depicted the New Testament. This one has only ten much larger panels, each of which contains a whole world of amazing depth and detail, illustrating the Old Testament. The Flood panel shows Noah, with his family and animals leaving the ark, offering a sacrifice beneath the rainbow, planting vines and then sprawling in drunken abandon.

The compositions recede from foreground figures in half-relief to low relief for those in the distance. There are architectural views, mountains, trees and above all people, all in astonishing realism.

Peace-loving ruler preferred poetry

Adrianople, Turkey, 1451

Sultan Murad II has died of apoplexy after a 30-year reign. Under him, the military might of the Ottoman empire has been transformed into an enlightened and civilising force. He is succeeded by his more volatile son, Mohammed II.

Murad, lover of peace, was constantly obliged to make war. He swiftly defeated a pretender to the sultanate in Constantinople and briefly besieged the city, before returning to defeat, then hang, his rebellious younger brother Mustafa, in Anatolia. Mustafa's Karamanian allies were granted vassal status. A treaty was also made with

A 1687 portrait of Murat II.

the new emperor, John VIII. In 1430 the city of Salonika, over which Greeks and Turks had been battling for years, was sold by the emperor to the Venetians. Murad won it back, prevented a massacre, and granted the Venetians trading rights throughout his empire.

The Christians of northern Europe, led by Ladislas III of Poland, and inspired by the Hungarian warrior leader Hunyadi, made a daring expedition across the Danube in 1443, which ended with a truce at Szeged. The following year the Christians reneged, and marched to defeat at Varna.

At last Murad was able to retreat to Magnesia, where he built a palace and surrounded himself with poets, mystics, theologians and men of letters, while his son ruled. But two years later Grand Vizier Halil persuaded him to return. A successful campaign against the Greeks was followed in 1448 by defeat of the Hungarians at Kosovo.

Constantinople falls to the Ottomans

Constantinople, last remnant of the Roman empire, falls to the Turks.

Mohammed II, by an Italian artist.

Constantinople, 29 May 1453
Constantinople, the capital of the once-great Byzantine empire, has fallen to the Ottoman invaders. After brave but doomed resistance, the garrison has been overwhelmed, and the head of the Emperor Constantine is displayed on the column of the Augusteum.

It is the end of an era. With its soldiers' armaments outdated, its former allies deserting, Constantinople has been in decline for some time. Exploited by the Venetians and Genoese, betrayed by Slav and Byzantine princes, the city was friendless and hopelessly outnumbered by the armies of Sultan Mohammed II.

The siege of Constantinople was the realisation of a long-held ambition. The Ottoman army spent February and March manoeuvring its heavy artillery into position, while several towns on the Sea of Marmara and the Black Sea were overrun. On April 6, the siege began in earnest, the sultan's great cannon directed at the Gate of St Romanus, where the emperor and his Genoese soldiers had mustered.

Initial resistance was strong. A surprise attack was repulsed, and walls damaged by cannon fire were rebuilt. At sea the Turkish fleet suffered a reverse on April 20 when four relief ships battled through to the harbour. Then the sultan decided to transport 72 ships overland from the Bosporus to the Golden Horn, penetrating the harbour defences. A group of captured Venetians were executed in view of the city, so the Greeks did the same with their Ottoman prisoners. The sultan's cannon kept up the bombardment, and the besiegers dug in under the city walls.

Early this morning, the storming of the city began. There was fierce fighting until the Byzantine commander, Giovanni Giustiniani-Longo, left the field to tend his wounds. The emperor was killed in the thick of battle. Then the looting began. People huddled in the church were dragged off to slavery, killed, or assaulted on the altar.

But the sultan curbed some excesses. When the imprisoned Lucas Notaras, grand duke and admiral, was brought before him, Mehmet promised to put him at the head of the city's administration, with the state and court officials.

Defeat ends English rule in France

Charles II of France: the victor.

France, 17 July 1453
The French army of Charles VII defeated the English army at Castillon near Bordeaux today, bringing nearly 100 years of hostilities to a conclusion. Four years ago, Henry VI's armies occupied nearly a third of France; today, as French troops round up English survivors from the battle of Castillon, only Calais remains in English hands. It was the death of the English commander, John Talbot, the earl of Shrewsbury, that made a French victory certain.

Talbot, a general much respected by both sides, had led an expeditionary force which had been welcomed into Bordeaux by its inhabitants, a welcome that began to cool when it became known that three French armies were approaching.

Bordeaux and the walled city of Castillon were threatened with siege; and it was a reluctant Talbot – he had planned to take on all three armies in one battle – who went to Castillon's aid.

Talbot had reckoned with neither the firepower of the 600 cannon that the French brought with them nor the skill of his opponent, Jean Bureau, who succeeded in drawing his enemy between his artillery and the Dordogne river. It was a French cannon ball that killed Talbot's horse, pinning the aged general beneath it. The battle was lost.

Battling Italian city states make peace

Italy, 9 April 1454
As the Habsburg empire continues to grow in strength and France emerges as one of the major European powers, Italy remains fragmented by fierce rivalries between its numerous city states. For the past half century, wars have been frequent and destructive; but now, under a treaty negotiated by Pope Nicholas V and signed at Lodi, peace reigns.

Three bitter rivals – Venice, Milan and Florence – are the signatories, with Rome and Naples likely to join the peace. This newly formed "Italian League" has agreed to recognise and maintain the position of the major states as they exist at the moment. The members have also agreed to protect each other against outside aggression.

Significantly, the League has recognised that there are common interests between its members and that "Italy" is a geographical entity – albeit divided by trade rivalry, countless dialects, the lack of a generally-accepted written Italian language (most business is still conducted in Latin) and the fierce loyalty to city rather than a non-existent Italian state. Trade rivalry is likely to be the most formidable barrier to further agreement.

Blinded prince wins Russian civil war

Novgorod, Russia, 1453
A long-running civil war between Vasily II, the grand prince of Moscow, and his cousin, the "Pretender" Dmitry Shemyaka, has concluded in Shemyaka's death after being exiled and poisoned.

Vasily and Shemyaka had been locked in rivalry for some 20 years. After Vasily was captured by Khan Ulag-Mahmed, the Mongol leader, but freed on payment of a huge ransom, Dmitry began plotting in earnest. Vasily was arrested and blinded, but again freed. This was Dmitry's biggest mistake because his cousin raised an army and one year and one day after being blinded he returned to Moscow in triumph. He is now planning to expand Muscovite territory.

Hungarians defeat Ottomans at Belgrade

Belgrade, 14 July 1456

The bloody battle of Belgrade, the Hungarian fortress on the Danube, has ended in a clearcut victory for John Hunyadi over a huge Ottoman army and navy. Sultan Mohammed's first large-scale campaign after the conquest of Constantinople has come badly unstuck after a retreat which degenerated into a rout.

The sultan's campaign was prepared largely in secret and he managed to muster some 150,000 men as well as a fleet of 60 ships to blockade the city. Hunyadi, who heads the Hungarian regency council, gathered an army of only some 60,000 men, mostly volunteers and peasants, and a much smaller fleet.

The Turks also had some 300 siege guns, including 27 giant cannon, and catapults and other weapons which were all entrusted to Italians and Germans. Huge boulders were also hurled at the fortress but were ineffective because of a successful warning system, using bells.

After Hunyadi's navy broke the blockade, his troops relieved the fortress and blunted a series of Turkish attacks. Finally, the siege guns were overrun.

Delicate Ming pottery is export success

Ivory Buddha on turquoise throne.

Elaborately glazed and painted jar.

China, c.1460

The imperial porcelain works at Ching Te Chen are turning out marvels of delicacy and skill for both the domestic market and export to distant lands.

The court takes a keen interest in the blue and white ware developed under Ming rule and paintings are sent from the palace for the potters to copy. Flowers, birds and insects are transferred to cups and vases with incredible delicacy.

Porcelain is only one aspect of Ming craftsmanship. Chinese workers are also carving objects of extraordinary beauty and delicacy, showing a marvellous sensitivity to the texture of ivory, jade, turquoise or other material.

Zara, Ethiopia's reforming emperor, dies

Ethiopia, 1468

Zara Yaqub, the greatest of the Solomonic emperors of Ethiopia, has died. In his reign of 34 years he centralised the imperial bureaucracy, reformed the church and, using his skills in war and peace, brought all the Ethiopian Highlands under his rule. Though Yaqub advocated religious toleration to all Moslems in his empire who posed no threat, Ethiopia under Yaqub became a bulwark against a resurgent Islam, defeating Moslem armies in the Horn of Africa and guaranteeing the freedom of Egypt's Copts. Ethiopian power has thus won the admiration of Christendom. The Pope sent an ambassador, ending centuries of isolation for the mythical kingdom of "Prester John".

Famine hits Aztecs in Central Mexico

Mexico, c.1455

After four years of drought in the Valley of Mexico, the Aztecs are suffering terrible privation. Thousands of people are dying of starvation, their unburied bodies falling prey to vultures and packs of wild boar.

So great is the famine that these once powerful people have been driven to desperate measures to survive. Some have retreated into the forests to try to scrape a living. Others have sold themselves into slavery to the Totonacs from the Gulf Coast area.

The Aztecs have traditionally been hunters, relatively unskilled in agriculture. But the famine has persuaded them to enlist the help of the Texcocans from across the lake in building an aqueduct and irrigation system.

Once-exiled sultan was tolerant ruler

Kashmir, 1467

Zian ul Abidin, the eighth sultan of Kashmir, has died. An exile in his youth from the paranoia of his elder brother, Ali Shah, the previous sultan, he had the unusual distinction of being the prisoner of Tamerlane and surviving.

In his exile Zian ul Abidin's courage, compassion and culture won him the support of Jasrat, the chief of the turbulent Khokar tribe. When Ali Shah tried to seize Zian ul Abidin the Khokar defeated Ali Shah, giving the throne of Kashmir to their young and unusual refugee.

Kashmir was a Moslem state with a Hindu majority. Zian ul Abidin promptly reversed Ali Shah's policy of persecuting Hindus, Brahmans and Buddhists. He founded universities, built bridges, distributed alms, and even restored Hindu temples. He was fluent in Arabic, Persian, Tibetan and Hindu, and the arts and sciences have flourished in his reign. Under Zian ul Abidin, Persian has become the official language of the court.

His subjects loved him, and his delight was to turn war technology into a peaceful art and give them firework displays.

Germans print the Bible

An illustration of Noah's Ark, from a Bible printed at Nuremberg in 1483.

Mainz, Germany, 1468

A German craftsman, writer and inventor, Johann Gutenberg, from Mainz, has died in obscurity. It was Gutenberg who devised a mechanical method of printing – based on the presses already in use for wine and paper-making – and using a revolutionary system of producing metal type-faces. His first publication, in 1455, was a Bible with 42 lines on each page printed in a typeface called "Gothic".

The use of a press for printing was not new – but making type had always involved laborious hours of carving letters from wood; and earlier versions of the Bible had always been handwritten. The new system allowed the printer to make type by pouring molten metal into punchstamped moulds, giving a limitless supply of letters. Gutenberg also developed an oil-based printing ink. Apart from the Bible, Gutenberg's system is in use for publishing religious tracts.

Gutenberg ran into major financial difficulties during the process of invention. He was forced to borrow money heavily, particularly from a rich goldsmith and financier, Johann Fust. The backer became increasingly impatient with the inventor – who was also working on a copperbased system of reproducing etchings on a mass basis – and sued Gutenberg for the return of his 800 guilders. The courts found for Fust and it is he who is making a fortune from sales of the Bible and producing a book of psalms on the Gutenberg system.

Johann Gutenberg, whose invention means that accurate texts can now be produced in great numbers.

A page of the 42-line Bible printed by Gutenberg at Mainz in 1455; it still has the look of a manuscript.

Explorer-prince dies

This early 15th-century bowl from Valencia shows a Portuguese sailing ship.

Portugal, 13 November 1460

Prince Henry knew the end was near. He granted two islands in the Azores to his nephew and heir Fernando, and assigned the spiritualities of the Madeira islands to the Order of Christ. He provided for Masses to be said for his soul and then made his will. He died today, aged 66, and his remains were taken to the church of St Mary at Lagos. It is said that he remained a virgin throughout his life.

For 40 years Henry, who was the third son of John of Portugal and Philippa, the daughter of England's John of Gaunt, devoted his wealth and his energies to maritime exploration. He grew up at a time when the Moors had at last been driven from Portugal and much of Spain, and the crusading spirit was still vigorous. The navigational enterprises with which he came to be associated began with a crusade against North African Moors.

Though he saw himself as a Christian knight dedicated to the struggle against Islam, his vision carried him beyond old horizons. He brought cartographers from Sicily and elsewhere to train his seamen. He found shipwrights to build craft strong enough to remain at sea in rough weather. Year after year Henry sent expeditions southward along the West African coast. The island groups of Madeira and the Azores became the first overseas colonies claimed by Henry, who dreamed of reaching the legendary Christian kingdom ruled by a priest king, Prester John, which was believed to exist in the heart of Africa. He never found it, but by his death his navigators had explored the coast of Africa as far south as the rugged mountain chain they called Sierra Leone; the Christian message was being carried to the heathen.

Prince Henry (C16th manuscript).

Florence, 3 December 1468. Lorenzo (the Magnificent) and his brother Giuliano succeed their father, Piero de Medici, as rulers of Florence.

Scandinavia, 1468. Christian, the king of Scandinavia, cedes Orkney and Shetland to the Scots in pledge for the dowry of his daughter Margaret, who is to marry James III.

Balkans, 1468. The death of Skanderbeg, the "prince" of the Albanians, opens Albania to the Turks.

West Africa, 1468. Sonni Ali, the king of Songhai, drives the Tuaregs out of Timbuktu.

Italy, 9 December 1469. The painter Fra Filippo Lippi dies.

Spain, 1469. Isabella of Castile marries Ferdinand, heir to the throne of Aragon.

England, c.1470. Thomas Malory completes the *Morte d'Arthur*, a retelling of the Arthurian legends.

France, January 1471. Louis XI declares war on Charles the Bold, the duke of Burgundy, and occupies the towns of Picardy.

Anatolia, 1471. Mohammed II conquers the last surviving Turkish emirate, Karamania. All the lands from the Taurus mountains to the Adriatic are now under Ottoman rule.

Germany, 1473. In a bid to acquire the title "King of the Romans", Charles the Bold arranges to meet Frederick III at Trier; but the emperor gives Charles the slip, making him the laughing stock of Europe.

Mexico, 1473. Ayacatl, Aztec ruler since 1468, defeats the neighbouring city of Tlatelolco.

France, 11 June 1474. Louis XI ratifies the "Perpetual Peace", signed by the Habsburgs and the Swiss.

England, 1474. The treaty of Utrecht gives the Hanseatic league (Hanse) generous trading privileges in England.

France, 29 August 1475. Having bought off Edward IV of England, who has been fighting in support of Charles the Bold, Louis XI signs the treaty of Picquigny with him.

France, 1476. The Swiss, now allied with France, open a campaign against Burgundy, seizing the district of Vaud. In response, Charles the Bold seizes Lorraine.

France, January 1477. On the death of Charles the Bold, Louis XI invades Burgundy, Franche-Comte and Artois.

Wolves feed on Charles the Bold

Switzerland, 7 January 1477
Two days after the battle of Nancy, an Italian page has found the body of Charles the Bold, the duke of Burgundy, naked on a frozen pond, half eaten by wolves, his skull cloven by a Swiss battle-axe. The duke was unrecognisable and was identified only by the scars on his body.

Thus ended the career of the turbulent duke who wanted so badly to be a king, a successful general and a conqueror and who failed in all three ambitions. The downfall of this ruthless commander – who modelled himself on Julius Caesar and other great Roman conquerors – began at the battle of Grandson last year, when Swiss pikemen bore down the heavily-armoured Burgundian cavalry. Charles sought revenge for "shameful defeat" by besieging Morat – and was again routed by the Swiss. Half his army died, and Charles fled.

Encouraged by his defeats, Charles' rival, Rene II of Lorraine, reoccupied Nancy and called for Swiss and French help against Burgundy. The army arrived while Charles was besieging the city and, in his third defeat in under a year, the duke lost his life and army.

Mass murderer Prince Dracula dies

Transylvania, 1477
The people of central Europe are sleeping a little easier with the news that its most notorious mass murderer, Vlad the Impaler, has died aged 45 in exile.

Dubbed *Dracula* (from the Rumanian for the Devil), he died after a short campaign to regain his native Wallachia. Crowned Vlad IV there 21 years ago, he was deposed and imprisoned by his Hungarian neighbours. They freed him last year after serving 14 years for conspiring with the Turks to take Hungary, which he coveted and terrorised.

Vlad was at the height of his powers in 1461 when he formed a defensive alliance with the Hungarians and marched across the Danube devastating Turkish Bulgaria and killing 25,000 people by impaling them on stakes. His cruelty and bloodlust – such as forcing child-

Dracula before his impaled victims.

ren to eat their roasted mothers – was downfall. A Turkish emissary refused to take off his turban, so Vlad had it nailed to his head, thereby angering the Turks.

Death of Bohemian king may start war

Prague, 22 March 1471
Jan Hus may have been burnt at the stake for his heretical beliefs in 1415, but his doctrine – which, among other things, allows for the taking of both wine and bread by the laity at mass – lives on, and has been threatening to bring Bohemia into a major war, with the Ottoman empire prepared to join in.

The Hussites lost a great champion today, however, in the form of George Podebrad, a leading Czech politician who in 1444, at the age of 24, formed a Hussite league – "the Union of Podebrad" – which defied the Catholic party in Prague and the rest of the country. With its backing George made himself master of Prague, driving out the Catholics and restoring the cardinal.

In 1458, Bohemia's young King Ladislas died of plague. George, who had been regent for the last five years, was elected king in his stead. Papal condemnation of George as a heretic in 1466 strengthened his enemies within Bohemia, who also won the support of George's son-in-law Matthias of Hungary. George's party remains in power, but his death may lead to renewed conflict.

Incas extend power over South America

The grassy slopes of Machu Pichu.

Peru, 1470
The Inca army under Topa Inca, son of the great Pachacuti, has overrun the kingdom of Chimor. The Chimu state on the Pacific coast was the most developed in the region. Its defeat by the Incas, bringing to an end eight years of war, has made the Incas the dominant power in South America.

The Inca expansion began 32 years ago when Pachacuti took over the state and, from his capital at Cuzco high in the Andes, built an empire throughout the southern Highlands. Topa Inca has continued his father's policy, leading Inca armies north into the rest of the Andes and west onto the coastal plain. With the inclusion of Chimor in the empire, Inca rule stretches from the Andes to the Pacific.

Inca society could not be more suitable for empire building. It is austere and rigidly, even militaristically, organised. It appears to have little concern for art, except perhaps the art of war. Political and sexual deviance is punished with torture and death by varying methods of execution.

Loyalty to the emperor, the representative of the sun on earth, is absolute. The administrative class of the empire is divided between "Incas by blood", and "Incas by privilege", collaborators drawn from subject peoples. Everything Topa Inca needs to expand his empire is already there.

Usurper executes king in Wars of Roses

London, 21 May 1471
King Henry VI has died, presumably murdered, in the Tower of London and the usurper Edward IV once more occupies the throne.

Henry's death is the latest episode in the dynastic struggles between the houses of York and Lancaster, or "the Wars of the Roses" as they are called from the emblems of the two sides (the white rose for York, the red for Lancaster). Back in 1454 the Lancastrian Henry VI was stricken with a mental illness and Richard, the duke of York, laid claim to the throne. Richard was killed at the battle of Wakefield in 1460, but his son Edward beat Henry's forces in 1461 and became king as Edward IV.

With French aid, the earl of Warwick and Edward's brother, the duke of Clarence, deposed Edward and restored Henry VI last year. Edward returned with Burgundian backing earlier this year and was reconciled with his brother; he defeated Warwick at Barnet, near London, on 13 April. Warwick died in the battle.

On 3 May, the Lancastrians were trounced at Tewkesbury and Prince Edward, Henry VI's son, was killed. With the death of a dangerous potential rival claimant to the throne, Edward IV had no need to keep the captive Henry VI alive.

Henry VI's widow, Queen Margaret.

Usurper: Edward IV in council.

Lone Russian merchant arrives in India

Bidar, India, 1470
After an epic journey of 3,000 miles Afanasii Nikitin, a Russian trader, has arrived in Bidar. Leaving his home at Kalinin near Moscow in 1466, he joined an embassy sent by Ivan the Great to Tartary and followed the Volga, past Horde (the summer camp of the Mongol emperor), into the Caspian Sea. They were attacked and imprisoned by Tartar pirates.

Nikitin was released and continued alone. Hugging the shore of the Caspian, he took a boat to Persia, watching the flames from leaking oil deposits as he sailed past Baku. At Chapakur he disembarked and rode south across Persia, through Kashan and Yazd, to Hormuz. There he took a ship, first to Muscat and then India, landing at Chaul, 300 miles south of Bombay.

After two months at Junnar he has come to the Moslem state of Bidar. His arrival coincides with a Hindu invasion from Vijayanagar, and the Russian traveller has watched the Moslem army, hundreds of thousands of infantry and cavalry supported by armourplated elephants, march out to battle in barbaric splendour.

Venetian Caterina is queen of Cyprus

Cyprus, 1477
Despite the ever-present military threat from the Turks, Cyprus is prospering under Caterina Cornaro, its intellectual Venetian queen. Born in 1454 into a family with financial interests in Cyprus, she was taught by her brothers.

In 1468 she was engaged to King James II of Cyprus. The couple were married in 1472, but James II died just a few months after the wedding. Caterina was entangled in a web of intrigue as she endeavoured to exercise her authority; her young son, King James III, was taken from her by the council of regency, and her cousin and uncle were murdered. In 1474 she regained power for her son, but he died of malaria, leaving her to rule alone.

A later portrait of Caterina.

Plato translated into Latin for Medici

Florence, 1469
As fascination with the ancient world grows among educated Italians, a dedicated priest, Marsilio Ficino, has completed the monumental task of translating the complete works of Plato from Greek into Latin. He is following it up with a substantial philosophical work of his own, *Theologia Platonica de immortalitate animae* (Platonic theology concerning the immortality of the soul), a metaphysical work which argues for the freedom of the soul from the body.

Ficino is a leading member of the Florence-based Platonic Academy founded by Cosimo de Medici, who died three years ago. He saw only the first fruits of Ficino's Plato translation, but his grandson Lorenzo de Medici, the academy's new patron, has continued to fund Ficino's work.

The Platonic Academy, which has no buildings or teachers, con-

A later print of Marsilio Ficino.

sists of a small group of men with a common interest in Plato and respect for Ficino as their mentor. It has exercised a major influence over Italian philosophical thought and has made a significant contribution to intellectual humanism.

Music, maps and posters roll off the new printing presses

Europe, 1477
Gutenberg's movable type printing press has quickly caught on around Europe. Initially printers used the new technology to disseminate a great variety of devotional texts such as Bibles. But the range of printed subjects knows no bounds. In 1472 the first printed music appeared in Bologna, Italy; then followed the printed map; and now a printed poster has rolled off the press of the Englishman William Caxton and advertises the thermal cures at Salisbury.

Caxton is also credited with the first dated book printed in the English language, *Dictes and Sayings of the Philosophers*, which appeared on 18 November of this year. From his printing works and offices in Westminster he is also publishing foreign works. His ambition is to make all kinds of writings widely available, chivalric romances, history, philosophy, and even an encyclopaedia.

Flanders, 18 August 1477. Maximilian of Austria, the son of the Emperor Frederick III, marries Mary of Burgundy, the daughter and heir of Charles the Bold. The house of Habsburg is now heir to the duchy of Burgundy, one of the richest states in Europe.

Florence, 1478. Giuliano de Medici is killed as a result of the Pazzi conspiracy against him and his brother Lorenzo.

Spain, 1479. Ferdinand, the husband of Isabella of Castile, succeeds his father, John II, as king of Aragon. Ferdinand and Isabella last year introduced the Inquisition into Spain.

France, 7 August 1479. Maximilian of Austria halts Louis XI's incursions into Burgundian territories.

Milan, 1479. Ludovico Sforza seizes power from his nephew Gian Galeazzo, the youthful grandson of Francesco Sforza.

Russia, 1480. Ivan the Great stops paying tribute money to the Mongols.

Portugal, 1481. John II succeeds his father, Alfonso V, as king of Portugal. His accession gives a boost to voyages of exploration.

Constantinople, 3 May 1481. Mohammed II is succeeded as sultan by his son Bayezid II.

Flanders, 27 March 1482. Mary of Burgundy dies after a hunting accident. Her husband, Maximilian, becomes regent of the Low Countries in the name of their son, Philip.

France, 23 December 1482. Burgundy and Picardy are absorbed into France by the treaty of Arras. Artois becomes the dowry of the two-year-old Margaret of Burgundy, daughter of Mary and Maximilian, who has been promised in marriage to the dauphin. The rest goes to her brother Philip.

England, 9 April 1483. Edward IV dies at Windsor. During his second reign he re-established stability after the upheavals of the Wars of the Roses, but his achievements are threatened by the fact that his heir, Edward V, is aged only 12.

Rome, 9 August 1483. Pope Sixtus IV celebrates the first mass in the Sistine Chapel, which is named after him.

France, 30 August 1483. On the death of Louis XI, Charles VIII is placed under the guardianship of his elder sister, Anne de Beaujeu.

Moneylenders face small farmers' rage

Japan, 1481

Peasant communities throughout the rural areas are rising in violent protest against punitive taxation and the grasping moneylenders who are foreclosing on mortgages and seizing their land.

These moneylenders, who combine usury with brewing *sake*, lend money to the peasants to "tide them over". But natural disasters, wars and predatory landlords have combined to ruin the peasants and whole communities have fallen into the power of the moneylenders.

So the dispossessed farmers are arming themselves and forming bands powerful enough to challenge large armies and to intimidate the ruling classes. The first of their demands is the destruction of the pawnshops.

Rival banking firm plot church stabbing

Florence, 27 April 1478

The palaces of Florence are festooned with corpses of rebels hanged from their windows, following the murder in the cathedral yesterday of Giuliano de Medici and the attempt to assassinate his brother, Lorenzo, joint rulers of the city.

The assassins were members of the rival banking family of Pazzi and their confederates, including the archbishop of Pisa. Francesco Pazzi walked Giuliano de Medici to the cathedral arm-in-arm for High Mass attended by a cardinal from Rome (the pope is believed to have encouraged the conspiracy).

During the Mass the plotters plunged their daggers into Giuliano 19 times while two priests attempted to stab Lorenzo. He escaped, gashed in the neck, and ran to the sacristy for safety. In the stampede from the cathedral the assassins

Lorenzo de Medici by Vasari.

escaped, but the people of Florence turned against the Pazzi and hunted them and their friends down. In the violence which followed there have already been 70 deaths.

Death of "Conqueror" sultan leaves great but troubled empire

Ottoman Empire, 1481

The death of Mohammed the Conqueror leaves the Ottoman empire powerful but uncertain. His two sons, Bayezid and Jem Sultan, must fight for the throne, while their subjects grumble about the confiscations and currency debasement that financed Mohammed's wars.

The capture of Constantinople in 1453 earned Mohammed II his title of "Conqueror", and gave him the prestige to dispense with his old adversary, Grand Vizier Halil Pasha. He had previously quelled a revolt among the elite army corps of Janissaries, and bound them

closer to him. Mohammed saw himself as *khan*, lord of the nomadic steppes, *ghazi*, fighter for Islam, and *basileus*, emperor of Byzantium. This allowed for religious toleration, but not for the possibility of revolt. He therefore codified Ottoman secular law to apply throughout his lands.

Most of his energies were successfully devoted to warfare, so that by the end of his reign he had taken most of Serbia, Albania, Herzegovina, much of Bosnia and Greece (including Athens and the Peloponnese). Anatolia was subdued, and Venice paid tribute.

Conquering sultan, Mohammed II.

Man seen in terms of Zodiacal symbols, from the guild book of the barber-surgeons of England.

Spain gives up new African territories

Portugal, 4 September 1479

After almost four years of bitter warfare, Spain has agreed to a Portuguese monopoly of trade and navigation along the whole West African coast, and Portugal has acknowleged Spanish rights to the Canary Islands.

The immediate cause of the war had nothing to do with territorial claims overseas. It arose from a dispute over the succession to the throne of Castile. The late king, although known as Henry the Impotent, had in fact fathered a

daughter, Joanna, and she laid claim to the throne after marrying her uncle Alfonso of Portugal. The Castilian nobility, however, backed Henry's sister, Isabella.

In the fighting, the Portuguese fared badly at home, but they repeatedly out-fought the Spanish at sea. On the islands, too, they defeated the Spanish everywhere except in the Canaries. This state of affairs explains the terms of the peace treaty signed today at Alcacovas. Isabella, incidentally, is now queen of Castile.

Ferdinand and Isabella unite Spain

King Ferdinand II of Aragon.

Queen Isabella of Castile.

Castile, 1479

The crowns of Castile and Aragon are now united. Isabella of Castile and Ferdinand II of Aragon, who have been married for the last ten years, have joined their countries in what is effectively a federation, and many believe that a powerful new force has been created in today's Europe by this alliance of thrones.

The situation has come about with Ferdinand succeeding to the throne of his father, John II. Isabella on the other hand inherited Castile five years ago when her brother, Henry IV, died.

The couple have since successfully beaten off the Portuguese army of Alfonso V, who has been trying to claim the hand of Joanna,

Henry's daughter, and with it the Castilian crown. Ferdinand, aged 27, is fond of women, and of gold and jewels which he not only wears but also adorns the trappings of his horses. He showed great personal courage and endurance during the recent civil war struggles. Isabella, just a year younger, is intelligent, pious and possessed of a great sense of royal dignity.

It is evident that Castile is the dominant partner. Ferdinand is to live in Castile and is not to leave it without his wife's permission. Only Castilians are appointed to the Council of Castile, and Ferdinand is not allowed to wage war without Isabella's advice and, especially, her agreement.

Silver pavilion graces shogun's garden

Japan, 1483

The *shogun* (local ruler), Yoshimasa, has indulged his taste for fine architecture by building a magnificent pavilion at his retreat in a scenic area of Kyoto. The *Ginkaku*, or Silver Pavilion, stands on the site of an abandoned monastery.

It gets its name from the shogun's plan to cover it with silver leaf. There, worn out by a lifetime of war and strife, he practises the tea ceremony and welcomes men of taste with whom he discusses his collections of Sung paintings and porcelain. He has ordained that on his death his elegant residence be converted into a temple.

Yoshimasa's silver-plated residence.

Russian king defies demands of Mongols

Moscow, 1480

Ivan the Great has seen off a Tartar attack and declared the total independence of his state after the Horde's 200-year occupation. The punitive expedition to collect the customary tribute from Ivan was launched by Khan Akhmat, who had intended to join up with a simultaneous Lithuanian incursion.

The Lithuanians never arrived and there was no significant fighting on the banks of the river Ugra. Fed up with waiting, the khan decided to withdraw; it was on the way home that he was assassinated

by one of his political opponents. It may be that Muscovite rulers will still have to buy off or repel Tartar invaders but they will no longer accept the patent from the khans.

Ivan has also asserted his rights as titular prince of Novgorod, one of the oldest of Russian towns with wide authority over northern Russia. He has forced Novgorod to renounce relations with Poland and Lithuania. After an attempted revolt he removed 8,000 of the leading families to his own domain and replaced them with merchants from Muscovy.

Ivan III refuses the tribute demanded by the khan, by a 19th-century artist.

Fears for safety of princes in the tower

England, 1483

The two English boy princes, Edward V and Richard of York, have disappeared, and are widely believed to have been murdered on the orders of their uncle and successor Richard III.

The boys were put in the Tower of London before Richard announced his own claim to the throne in June. Rumours almost immediately began to circulate that they were dead. Some stories said they had been drowned in malmsey, stabbed, poisoned or smothered.

Belief in their deaths explains why Richard's opponents, who staged a rebellion this autumn, have had to find another claimant to the throne. Plans to restore Edward V have now been abandoned and the exiled Lancastrian Henry Tudor is the preferred candidate.

The Princes in the Tower, by Sir John Everett Millais (1829-96).

Central Africa, 1484. The Portuguese Diego Cao lands in Angola. Last year he explored the mouth of the river Zaire and set up a stone column marking his arrival.

Rome, 5 December 1484. Pope Innocent VIII issues a bull deploring the spread of witchcraft and heresy generally in Germany, and authorising the Dominican inquisitors to deal with it.

Flanders, June/July 1485. Maximilian takes Bruges and Ghent by siege. Although accepted by Holland, Zeeland and Hainault, Maximilian's claim to authority in the Low Countries as guardian of his son Philip had been rejected by Flanders and Brabant.

England, 22 August 1485. The victory of Henry Tudor (Henry VII) over Richard III at Bosworth establishes the Tudor dynasty.

Central Africa, 1485. Four Portuguese Catholic missionaries arrive in the Kongo kingdom *(Angola)*, south of the mouth of the Zaire river.

Germany, 1486. The Emperor Frederick III has his son Maximilian elected king of the Romans.

Spain, 1 May 1486. The Genoese seaman, Christopher Columbus, persuades Queen Isabella to sponsor his planned expedition to discover a western route to the Indies.

Mexico, 1487. The Great Temple of Tenochtitlan is inaugurated: 20,000 people are ritually sacrificed.

Spain, 1487. Ferdinand and Isabella take possession of Malaga, which until now has been an independent Moslem principality.

Central Europe, 1487. Jacob Fugger, from a rich merchant family in Augsburg, secures the right to mine silver in the Tyrol from Sigismund of the Tyrol.

Flanders, 1488. Maximilian, in Bruges to negotiate with disaffected tradesmen, is trapped by their rising. He is held captive for 11 weeks, and the cities are only brought to negotiate with him by the news that his father, the emperor, is advancing with an army. Maximilian is made to promise that he will give up his regency of the Low Countries.

South Africa, 1488. The Portuguese explorer, Bartholomew Dias, rounds the Cape of Good Hope.

Sailor rounds new Cape

Lisbon, December 1488

A remarkable feat of navigation has been recounted to King John II by the explorer Bartholomew Dias of Portugal, who has returned from a two-year voyage down the West coast of Africa.

Dias sailed so far south that the North Star vanished below the horizon. For 13 days a strong wind carried him out to sea and still further south. When at last he was able to turn back he found the lie of the land was to the east, not the south; Dias had discovered the way round Africa. The explorer continued on his new course to the east and, sighting native herdsmen with cows, went ashore. But Dias was unable to understand the language and the natives were so alarmed at the sight of the ships that they drove their animals inland. Dias has told the king that he named the great cape, with its table-like mountain, the Cape of Storms. But the king wishes it to be known as the Cape of Good Hope, because it gives promise of discovering a sea route to India.

Portuguese calculate latitude by the sun

Lisbon, 1484

The first European manual of navigation and nautical almanac has been prepared by a group of mathematical experts appointed by King John II of Portugal. The king was concerned that his navigators were embarking on long voyages without charts or sailing directions. The dead reckoning method of establishing a position by recording the distance and direction travelled is unreliable, and the North Star is not visible in southern waters.

The king told the mathematicians to devise a method of finding latitude by solar observation. The main problem was that the track followed by the sun in relation to the earth changes from day to day and from year to year. The experts studied a set of tables first worked out by the Jewish astronomer Abraham Zacuto of Salamanca, who had recorded the sun's declination for the years 1473-78.

A simplified version of Zacuto's

Model of a Portuguese caravel.

tables has been produced for seamen. But taking a reading of the sun's position and calculating what is called the "latitude" of a ship from that reading is complicated and a seaman must have a grasp of mathematics and astronomy.

Work of cabalistic magician is heretical

Rome, December 1486

A special commission called by Pope Innocent VIII has condemned as heretical part of the latest work of the brilliant 23-year-old philosopher, Pico della Mirandola. His *Conclusiones* comprise 900 propositions about God and man.

He takes a humanist view, writing that "nothing in the world can be found that is more worthy of admiration than man". He suggests Christ did not really descend into hell and that cabalistic magic is the best way of proving the divinity of Christ.

The son of a noble family from Ferrara, he began to study canon law at the age of ten in Bologna and philosophy two years later in Ferrara. He then moved to Perugia to study Hebrew and Arabic and was strongly influenced by Jewish scholars of the *Qabbalah*. He then went to the Sorbonne where he met many humanist philosophers.

Wars of Roses end at Bosworth Field

Henry VII (17th-century print).

England, 22 August 1485

As dawn broke over Redmoor this morning few could have guessed that by noon a new king and dynasty would occupy the throne of England.

On the surface, the odds were against the young exile, Henry Tudor, the heir to the Lancastrian cause, and heavily in favour of King Richard III and the white rose of York. Henry was a complete novice in battle, and led a force of 5,000 men, while the soldierly Richard headed over double that number.

But although Richard's army boasted distinguished commanders of the calibre of the duke of Norfolk, he was beset by men of wavering loyalty, such as the earl of Northumberland and Lord Stanley, who initially held back his troops.

Henry's army, led by the redoubtable earl of Oxford, was lighter and more manoeuvrable than Richard's, and contained many expert Welsh, Scottish and French soldiers. In the event, Oxford ably held his own against Norfolk until Richard, frustrated, decided to enter the fray in person at the head of a stupendous cavalry charge. Henry stood his ground, until Stanley finally joined the melee – on Henry's side. Richard, it seems, was forced into a swamp, unhorsed, and hacked to death by Welsh pikemen. His coronet was retrieved and, soon after, was placed on the head of the Tudor prince, henceforth known as King Henry VII.

Aztecs sacrifice 20,000

Mexico, 1487

In the most spectacular sacrificial display ever seen in the Aztec capital, Tenochtitlan, 20,000 people have lost their hearts to Huitzilopochtli, the war god.

The ceremony was supervised by Ahuitzotl, the ruler of the Aztecs. Two queues of 10,000 each, made up of captured rebels from northern Oaxaca, stood on either side of the sacrificial altar in the Great Temple, which Ahuitzotl has restored. Dressed as Huitzilopochtli he tore their hearts out by hand, one by one, and flung them into a gigantic urn where they were burnt to the war god. Exhausted, he retired and his ally, Nezahualpilli, took his place. When he collapsed from exhaustion Ahuitzotl's Aztec councillors continued the work. They retired and lesser notables took up the task in a ritual sacrifice dictated by the belief that only in this way would their god be propitiated.

Huitzilopochtli will not be short of hearts while Ahuitzotl rules. Ahuitzotl has led his army on con-

Aztec goddess of life and death.

quests throughout central America. Wherever he has conquered, his demands for tribute are so unlimited that the defeated have been forced to rebel, increasing the flow of hearts to Huitzilopochtli.

Book supports witch hunt in Rhineland

Rome, 1486

The publication of an encyclopaedia of witchcraft here confirms that the papacy is lending its support to the growing practice of persecuting and burning witches. For well over a century now Dominican friars have been burning witches, mainly in the villages of the Alps and the Pyrenees. But popes have mostly not seen witches as a real problem, with the exception of Pope John XXII, who lived in personal terror of witches and authorised an inquisition in 1326.

However, two years ago Pope Innocent VIII published a bull deploring the spread of witchcraft in Germany and authorising two Dominicans, Jakob Sprenger and Heinrich Kramer, to stamp it out. They have since been hard at work. Only last year the Como inquisitor burnt 41 witches who had confessed to sex with devils.

Sprenger and Kramer have now published *Malleus Maleficarum* (The Hammer of the Witches). It suggests that witches really do fly, that they can raise hailstorms and

"Witches", a 16th-century woodcut.

hurtful tempests and lightnings, cause sterility and make horses go mad under their riders. Witches are said to eat children, have sex with devils and engage in sexual and cannibalistic orgies. Voluminous evidence of these practices is provided, mostly obtained from torturing suspected witches.

Milanese genius is painter and engineer

Designs for war engines by Leonardo; note his right-to-left handwriting.

Milan, 1488

Now in his thirties, an Italian artist, scientist, philosopher and inventor, Leonardo da Vinci, has established himself as a supreme example of the Renaissance ideal of the multi-talented individual. There seems no end to his originality as a thinker – and skill as a craftsman and engineer.

In the six years that he has been living in Milan, Leonardo has accumulated sheet upon sheet of drawings and notes, penned in mirror writing that scans from right to left, the natural way for this left-handed genius.

In these copious notebooks are superb descriptive drawings of the natural world, from flowers in bloom to babies in the womb; advanced geometry and arithmetic;

and a prolific array of ingenious mechanical devices. Here can be found a multiple cross-bow gun; a contrivance for repelling enemy scaling ladders during a siege; even an armoured vehicle with firing guns.

For a Milanese castle, Leonardo has designed a forced-air central heating system and an arrangement for pumping water. He also sketches some apparatus to allow one to breathe underwater.

Many of his ideas cannot be realised with existing technology. From watching and drawing birds in flight, he has become fascinated by the possibility of a man-made flying machine and has a similar project for a flying device powered by revolving blade. Leonardo's genius has won him wide admiration.

China's Great Wall to be even greater

China, 1488

The Ming emperors are pressing on with their policy of rebuilding the Great Wall. This work, begun soon after the disastrous battle of Tu-mu in 1449 when the Ming army was slaughtered by the Mongols and the emperor captured, reflects Ming concern with the need for effective defences against the successive waves of barbarians from the north.

The original wall, built out of rammed earth by the Chin dynasty some 1700 years ago, had proved to be no real obstacle to the invaders and for much of its length had ero-

ded into mounds of grassy soil called "earth dragons" by the local people.

Now the Ming emperors, already renowned as great builders, have set armies of labourers to work on a wall which is truly great. When it is finished it will wind across northern China for 1400 miles.

Those parts already completed are faced with brick. The wall is 25 feet high, with a 12-feet wide cobbled road running along the top between guard houses. It seems likely to become one of the greatest man-made structures ever built.

Moslem Granada falls to Catholic kings

Granada, 2 January 1492
After a ten-year campaign Granada, the only remaining Moslem state in Spain, has fallen to the Castilian army. The surrender of the city is being hailed by Christians as the "most signal and blessed day there has ever been in Spain". Moslems are describing it as one of the most terrible catastrophes ever to befall Islam.

The war has been directed by Ferdinand and Isabella, the king and queen of Spain, with months of continual skirmishing by the Christian armies eventually wearing down the beleaguered Moslems. The victors are said to have been been extremely generous in victory and virtually all the Moslem petitions were granted. For three years they can emigrate freely, and are allowed to keep all arms except firearms. Their religion is to be free from interference and the Moslems will continue to enjoy their own communal life and maintain their judicial system and local officials.

Throughout Spain and in papal Rome bullfights are being held in celebration and people are rejoicing. Venice and other states are sending more or less sincere messages of congratulation.

All Jews are ordered out of Spain

German anti-Semitic propaganda: Jews ritually killing a Christian boy.

Spain, 30 March 1492
In a mass emigration reminiscent of the Biblical Exodus, the Jews are leaving Spain. But if their forefathers were eager to leave Egypt, these modern Hebrews are going reluctantly, forced to quit by today's edict of expulsion. The 150,000 strong community has just four months to be gone. After years of growing anti-Jewish feeling, the monarchy has decided to end its Jewish problem by expelling them.

Spain's Jews, benefiting for centuries from tolerant Arab rulers, are a highly assimilated group; they operate their own autonomous administrative sytem, the *aljama*, and congregate in special districts, the *juderia*.

Once an integral part of Spanish society and culture, the Jewish situation has declined since Catholic rulers replaced Arab ones. Urban anti-semitism has increased and the state has passed a series of punitive laws restricting Jewish activities. The Inquisition, founded in 1478, has made matters worse, denouncing them as blasphemers and usurers, and encouraging every form of intolerance.

Portuguese envoy arrives in Kongo

Kongo, 1491
A Portuguese embassy to Nazinga Nkuma, the king of the Kongo *(Angola)*, has arrived in Banza, the capital. Its aim is peaceful, to evangelize, not conquer. On Nazinga Nkuma's suggestion, priests, scholars and craftsmen will be left behind when the ambassadors leave.

The embassy is the result of seven years of tentative contact between Portugal and the Kongo. In 1483 Diego Cao, the navigator, came to the mouth of the river Congo, leaving four of his officers to make contact with the king of Kongo. The king already knew of their presence – his subjects had mistaken the Portuguese ships for whales. Diego Cao returned with missionaries in 1485, reaching Banza where they converted the crown prince to Christianity, baptising him Afonso.

Nazinga Nkuma's support for the embassy is essential for its success. The king of Kongo is not like other mortals. He is a *nzambi mpungu*, or superior spirit. Each king marries his sister, so that over generations the heir is descended only from the royal spirit and not from common mortals. There is little doubt that the Portuguese missionaries have their work cut out for them.

New maths signs are a major plus

Germany, 1489
An important development in mathematics has just been introduced in Germany by Johann Widmann. In a recent book Widmann uses the symbols "+" and "−" to denote the operations of addition and subtraction. In doing so, he has not only advanced the operational symbolism of the great Greek mathematician, Diophantus, and the Hindu scholars, but has also greatly simplified matters for fellow mathematicians.

Over the centuries a variety of signs and symbols have been employed, rather idiosyncratically, to denote adding, subtracting and other operations. These have often taken the form of abbreviated words.

Lorenzo de Medici, tyrant and arts patron, dies

Florence c.1490, with the cathedral and, to its right, the Signoria.

Florence, 9 May 1492

Lorenzo de Medici is dead at the age of 44 and the worlds of art and learning mourn the loss of their greatest patron, known everywhere simply as "The Magnificent". He began his rule at the age of 20, with his brother Giuliano, who was murdered by the Pazzi in 1478. Lorenzo showed his nerve and wisdom in pacifying Florence after the crisis and there were no more uprisings.

He was not only a patron of philosophers, he debated with them himself in the Platonic Academy which he maintained. He was the friend of writers like Ficino, the biographer of Plato, and his official poet, Angelo Poliziano, whose poems inspired Botticelli to paint *The Birth of Venus* and *Primavera*; Lorenzo himself was a leading lyric poet in vernacular Tuscan. He de-

lighted in carnivals, for which he wrote songs to be sung in the streets by his own Company of the Star.

Music delighted him – he was taught by the cathedral organist, Antonio Squarcialupi, who often wrote music for Lorenzo's lyrics. He loved antiquities, Greek and Roman busts, cameos, coins, which were collected for him in the Mediterranean. He welcomed scholars to his library of over 1,000 books.

He loved architecture, submitting his own design for the cathedral facade, and commissioned Filippino Lippi to decorate his villa and Andrea del Verrochio to sculpt busts of him and his brother. He also loved women, who found him attractive despite his harsh nasal voice and swarthy complexion. It was said of him: "It would be impossible to find a better tyrant."

Madonna and child, by Filippino Lippi (born c.1457), the son of another celebrated artist, Fra Filippo Lippi (1406-69), and a pupil of Botticelli. His work is full of breadth, strong colours and powerful movement.

A terracotta bust of Lorenzo de Medici by Andrea del Verrocchio.

"Venus and Mars", by Sandro Botticelli (b.1440), one of the group of great artists commissioned by Lorenzo.

The rise of the Ottomans

In 1453 the Ottoman Sultan Mehmet II achieved what Moslem rulers had striven for since the time of the Prophet Mohammed: the conquest of Constantinople, the capital of Islam's oldest foe, the Christian Byzantine empire. Under its new name of Istanbul the city became the capital of a new empire, which dominated the Near East and south-eastern Europe for half a millennium.

The origins of the Ottoman empire were extremely obscure. The Ottomans traced their ancestry to a nomad chief called Ertoghrul, the leader of a small band of about 200 Turcomans – one of the numerous nomadic tribes of Turks, of Asian origin and famous for their hardiness and military skills, which had come to occupy most of what is now Turkey. In 1289 Ertoghrul was granted a small fief around Eskishehir in north-western Turkey by the sultan of Konya, the ruler of the Seljuk tribe of Turks. The principality was small, but shared a common frontier with the declining Byzantine empire, a fact which Ertoghrul's son Osman exploited. In 1301 he had his first success against the Byzantines, and from then on Turks who wished to join the holy war against the infidel flocked to serve under the Ottomans, who assumed the role of champions of Islam.

The Ottomans drive westwards

It was natural that the small state should seek to expand westwards, occupying Byzantine territory, rather than attacking its Moslem neighbours to the east. At first the Ottomans by-passed Constantinople itself. In 1357, under Osman's successor Orkhan (1326-62), they crossed the Dardanelles and made their first European conquests. The decrepit empire was rent by endless futile civil wars, and the provincial garrisons felt isolated and betrayed by the emperors. Orkhan offered them new careers in his own army, a new religion and lower taxes; they flocked to join him. Rivals for the Byzantine throne even sought his aid, and the Emperor John Cantacuzenus gave Orkhan his daughter Theodora on the condition that she remained a Christian in the *harem*.

Sultan Murad I (1362-89) moved the capital from the western Turkish city of Bursa, capital since 1326, to the European town of Adrianople (Edirne) in 1366, closer to the frontier of Ottoman conquests. By 1400 the dynasty ruled modern Bulgaria and Albania and much of modern Greece, and Serbia had become a vassal state in 1389. The Christians of these areas could expect no help from the west, since, for all the talk of Christian unity in the face of the infidel Turks, the divisions between the Greek and Roman Churches remained fierce and bitter. The Hungarians and Italians would not help Orthodox Christians unless they accepted the authority of the pope. Many Orthodox Christians preferred the tolerant authority of the sultans to such Catholic arrogance. The Ottomans expanded in Turkey as well, though here, in 1402, they suffered their most important, albeit temporary, setback when the fearsome Mongol warlord Tamerlane defeated and executed Sultan Bayezid (1389-1402).

Zenith and decline

The fall of Constantinople in 1453 ushered in a century and a half of greatness. The conquests continued on all fronts; in the west, Serbia and, in 1526, Hungary were conquered, while in the Near East Syria and Egypt were taken in 1517 and Mesopotamia soon after. Modern Algeria and Tunisia were occupied by corsairs owing allegiance to the Ottomans, and both Rome and Vienna were threatened at different times. Indeed, the Ottoman war machine was the most formidable of its age. The new army of Janissaries, boys taken young from their Christian parents and raised as Moslem warriors, was both better trained and more dedicated than the rather amateur armies of the Christians. They were fully abreast of the latest martial technology and their artillery was formidable.

The high point of this Ottoman golden age was the reign of Suleiman the Magnificent (1520-1566), when culture flourished and the great Sinan designed mosques for Istanbul and Edirne which rivalled the finest works of Renaissance Europe.

After Suleiman's death decline followed swiftly, and the rot seems to have begun at the top with passionate family jealousies. Suleiman himself set a grim precedent when he ordered his able eldest son to be strangled before his very eyes. Thereafter near-paranoia seems to have ruled. Sultans kept their sons secluded in the famous "cage" in the harem of the Topkapi palace, whence they emerged to take control on the deaths of their fathers entirely innocent of the ways of the world. Small wonder that such men were unable to control so vast an empire or lead the army effectively. Lack of firm leadership soon led to military defeat and internal rebellion.

That the empire survived at all in the 17th century was largely due to the abilities of successive *grand viziers* (chief ministers) like those from the Koprulu family. The Ottoman empire had developed an extensive bureaucracy, and the civil servants who worked it could keep the system going even if the sultan was ineffectual. The empire had few outside enemies, the Persians to the east being occupied by their own problems and the Europeans too caught up in the Thirty Years War and subsequent conflicts to have eastern ambitions. Great trade routes no longer passed through the Near East, and the trade in silks and spices now went in Christian ships round the Cape of Good Hope. The Ottoman empire became increasingly poverty-stricken and backward, but its rulers and their Moslem subjects remained quietly convinced of their superiority over the western Christians. And with some justification: as late as 1683 they came close to capturing Vienna.

The 18th century saw little outward change. The appalling family violence of the previous century seems to have abated somewhat, and the sultans included the mild and civilised Ahmed III (1703-1730), a bibliophile and patron of the arts. But the outside world was changing. The Russians were extending their frontiers to the south, putting pressure on the Ottoman frontiers in the Balkans and the Caucasus. In 1795 Napoleon invaded Egypt, brutally demonstrating Ottoman feebleness.

Attempts at revival

Many people in the empire recognised this and did their best to create new institutions and new attitudes to cope with the outside pressures which now came thick and fast. The great reforming Sultan Mahmud II (1808-1839) founded new educational institutions to teach technical subjects and a new army based on western models. He was opposed by many conservatives. The powerful *ulema*, religious scholars, bitterly resented the implication that the Ottomans could learn anything from the infidel. The once formidable Janissaries had become state pensioners, an idle class, useless militarily but determined to protect their own privileges; only by a sudden and ruthless massacre in 1826 was the sultan able to break their power.

Later sultans continued his work with more or less effectiveness. Even Abdul Hamid II (1876-1909), famous in the west as "Abdul the Damned", made serious efforts to strengthen his power in the empire, aided by German military advisers and the telegraph to keep him in touch with the distant provinces. By the late 19th century the Ottoman empire was stronger and more efficient than at any time since the days of Suleiman the Magnificent. But other forces were at work which would undermine Ottoman power once and for all.

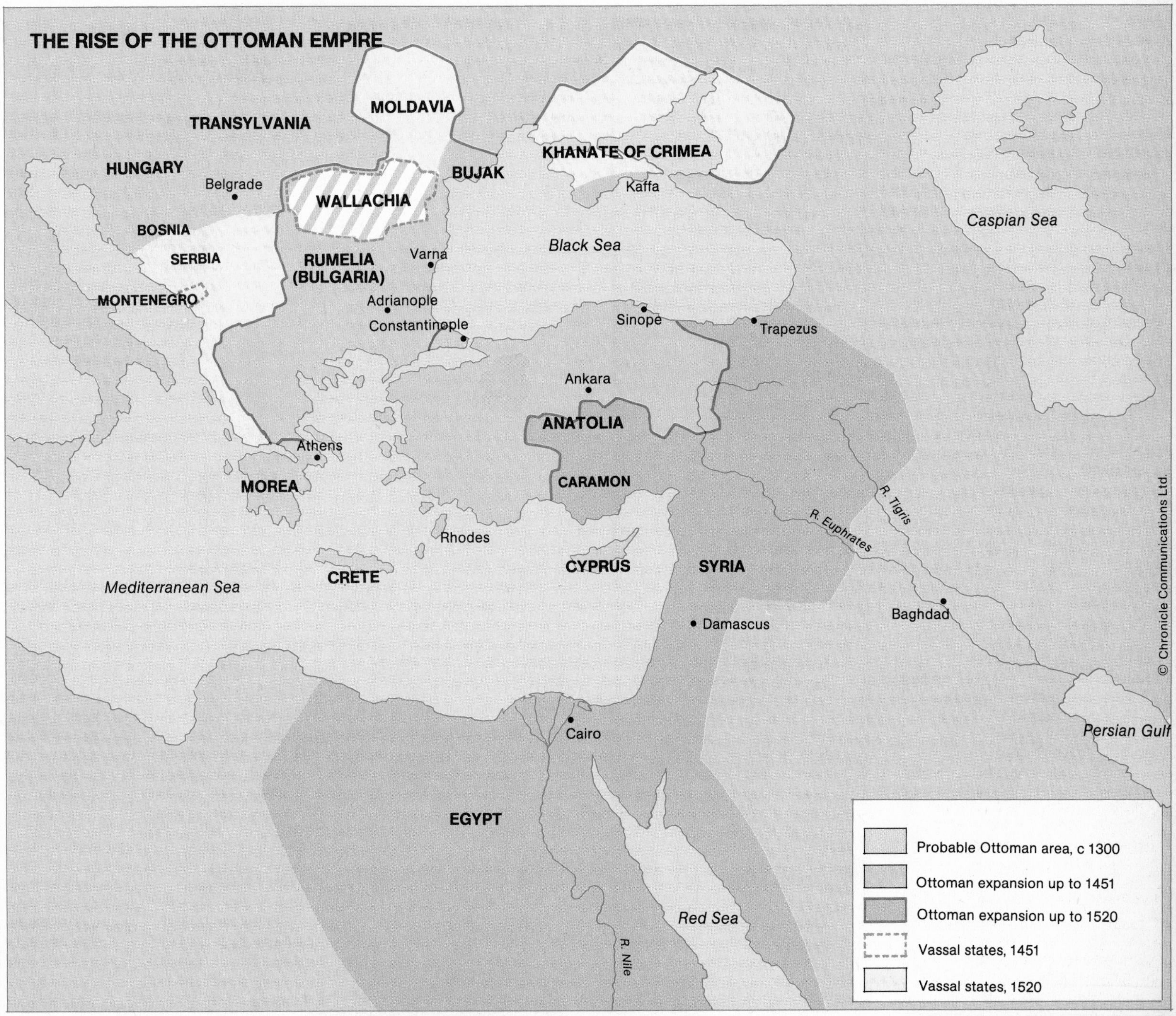

THE RISE OF THE OTTOMAN EMPIRE

TRANSYLVANIA

MOLDAVIA

HUNGARY

Belgrade

BUJAK

KHANATE OF CRIMEA

Kaffa

WALLACHIA

BOSNIA

Caspian Sea

SERBIA

RUMELIA
(BULGARIA)

Varna

Black Sea

MONTENEGRO

Adrianople

Constantinople

Sinope

Trapezus

Ankara

ANATOLIA

Athens

MOREA

CARAMON

R. Tigris

R. Euphrates

Rhodes

CYPRUS

SYRIA

CRETE

Mediterranean Sea

Damascus

Baghdad

Persian Gulf

Cairo

EGYPT

Red Sea

R. Nile

© Chronicle Communications Ltd.

	Probable Ottoman area, c 1300
	Ottoman expansion up to 1451
	Ottoman expansion up to 1520
	Vassal states, 1451
	Vassal states, 1520

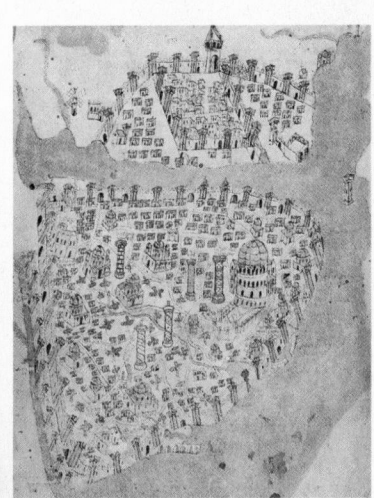

Constantinople: a plan dated 1422.

A 19th-century view of a Turkish family looking towards the Bosporus.

A palace fountain in Constantinople.

Armies with "French pox" infect Europe

A victim of the new pox, which many believe is a divine punishment.

Europe, 1494

A new, highly contagious disease has arrived in Europe, and cases have been recorded in France, Spain and Italy. Known as "the French pox", it attacks the genitals and according to experts is a punishment for sexual excess, gluttony, drunkenness and a generally dissolute life.

Transmitted through sexual intercourse, it appears as a sore on "the parts of shame" before eroding the palate and uvula, eating away the lips, nose or eyes, then weakening muscles and nerves before bringing its victim to an early and highly painful death. The origin of the pox is unknown – some talk of heavenly influence, others of small, winged worms – but it seems to have spread with increasing speed after the army of Charles VIII of France besieged Naples this year. The siege failed, but the army seems to have infected every country through which it has passed.

Several drugs have been used to combat the pox, but few have helped. The most successful treatment appears to be mercury ointment, already used as a cure for other skin diseases. So terrifying is the disease that numerous charlatans have emerged, all peddling their expensive, but useless, "cures".

Painter of elegant miniatures is dead

One of Bihzad's last works (1493).

Persia, 1494

Bihzad, one of the greatest of Persian painters, has died at the age of around 40. Orphaned early in life, he was brought up by the artist Mirak, and showed natural artistic talent early on. He achieved fame as a painter of miniatures, characterised by the complex and graceful harmony of their composition and by the wonderfully subtle use of the traditional flat, pure colours of Persian miniature painting.

No shortage of suspects in African ruler's murder

West Africa, 1492

Mystery continues to surround the alleged drowning of Sunni Ali, who turned Gao from a small kingdom into one of the largest states in West Africa in his 28-year reign. First allegations, suggesting that Sunni Ali died crossing a Niger tributary, are now thought to be false. New rumours suggest that Mohammed Ture, his nephew and a rival to Sunni Ali's son and successor Baro, was responsible for Ali's death.

There is, however, no shortage of suspects within the huge Songhai empire that Sunni Ali built up from a one-city state by major military conquest, ruthless determination and brilliant administration. Chief among the suspects is the Islamic community in Timbuktu, the scene of Sunni Ali's first conquest, whose mullahs were murdered for defying his authority.

The great mosque of Djenne in Mali was probably begun by a 14th-century Songhai ruler. Made of mud-brick, typical of Mali, it was rebuilt in 1909.

Columbus proves the world is round

Columbus, by Lorenzo Lotto.

West Indies, 12 October 1492

Christopher Columbus, who leads the royal Spanish expedition to pioneer a westward route to the Indies, stepped ashore today in a country inhabited by gentle, naked savages. Piously recognising the good fortune in making his long-awaited landfall, he has named this land *San Salvador* or "Saint of Salvation". For years Columbus has believed that the world is round; and today he appears to have proved his point to doubters – including some of his crew – who were convinced that it was flat.

It is 35 days since Columbus and his men last saw land as they sailed over the horizon from the Canaries. The admiral, from Genoa, is a navigator of genius and a shrewd master of men. For nine days he found strong winds to carry him westward. Then, as the ship slowed in a dense swamp of sinister yellow sea-

Columbus amid the oceans, an imaginative impression by a later engraver.

weed, the crew became increasingly nervous. The admiral fooled them into believing that they had not run as far west as they thought. As they picked up speed again, so did fears grow that the westerly bearing would take them over the edge of the world to their deaths in a giant abyss. At last, seeing large flocks of migrating birds, Columbus remembered that the Portuguese had discovered the Azores by studying such behaviour. So he changed course to south-west, to the birds' flight line. Only Columbus' calm confidence persuaded the crew to agree to two more days' exploration.

Columbus' fleet of three little ships had weighed anchor just be-

fore dawn at Palos in Spain, 71 days ago. His flagship, *Santa Maria*, is 85 feet long and displaces 100 tons; his escorts, *Pinta* and *Nina*, are about 55 tons. The crews have been scraped together from the back streets of Palos and the local prison.

In reality, this voyage began long before they sailed. Columbus, aged 41, first sought backing for his grand obsession in Portugal about eight years ago; then in France and England. He won Spanish support only after fighting the Moors for Spain and promising gold from his expedition to finance another holy war for Christendom. It is still unclear where San Salvador lies. Admiral Columbus believes that it is near Japan.

Spain and Portugal divide up the world

Tordesillas, Spain, 7 June 1494
Under the terms of a treaty signed here today, Spain and Portugal have divided between them all the new lands discovered in the recent voyages of exploration, and any others that may be discovered in the future.

It was Christopher Columbus who stirred things up with his stories about discovering a new world in the West, or maybe a new route to the Indies. Portugal's King John II, who was planning his own expedition to India, became alarmed, the more so when he learned that Ferdinand and Isabella had persuaded Pope Alexander VI to issue a series of bulls giving to Spain all the lands west of the Portuguese Azores discovered, or to be discovered, by Columbus.

John II opened direct negotiations with Ferdinand and Isabella and an imaginary demarcation line has been drawn down the western Atlantic. At this stage of discovery, no-one knows how much land does lie to the west; but Spain would seem to have the best of the deal.

Explorers in search for Prester John

Africa, 1494
The legend of Prester John, a Christian ruler somewhere in eastern Africa, has proved a powerful spur to Portuguese voyages of exploration in this continent. The legend is compounded by the keenness of the kings of Ethiopia to maintain contacts with the Christian west.

Two notable explorers, Pedro de Covilhao and Bartholomew Dias, left Lisbon in 1487 for Africa. While Dias sailed round the Cape of Good Hope, de Covilhao went overland in search of Prester John's mythical connection with the Indian spice trade. After travelling widely in the Levant, the Indian Ocean, the Persian Gulf, the Red Sea and the Gulf of Aden, de Covilhao has now arrived, via Zeila, in Ethiopia.

The Ethiopians are a Christian people. Male children are baptised after 40 days, females after 60. All then take communion.

Compass needle mystery has Columbus looking to the stars

Astrolabe for navigation (c.1300)

Mid-Atlantic, 1492
Four days out of Hiero, the most westerly of the Canary Islands, Christopher Columbus made an alarming discovery. The needle of his compass was pointing markedly west-of-north.

His crew, most of whom were anyway doubting the wisdom of this major expedition, were shaken. If they could not rely on the compass here in mid-ocean, what unimaginable disasters might strike them? Along the Atlantic coast of Europe, mariners have long since noticed that the compass points

slightly East of North. It is as if the earth's magnetic fields, instead of being fixed, are subject to fluctuation and variation.

More than ever the fleet of three caravels looks very vulnerable. These small ships, with their triangular lateen sails for tacking and catching light winds, and their squat, square sails for following winds, could be tested to their limits, and beyond. Only Columbus remains confident. His compass may not be trustworthy, but he can still navigate using the Pole Star as his guide.

John Cabot returns triumphant after discovery of Labrador

London, 6 August 1497

The Genoese navigator John Cabot has returned in triumph from an expedition across the Atlantic. Henry VII has given him £10 from the Privy Purse, and an annuity of £20. Cabot is planning a large expedition next year.

Though he is Genoese by birth and has Venetian citizenship, Cabot came to England about ten years ago to raise support for a transatlantic crossing, and settled in Bristol. Having set sail from there on 2 May, Cabot's ship *The Matthew* reached America on 24 June, at the coast of Labrador. There Cabot planted the Tudor banner and the standard of St Mark, in contravention of an agreement in 1494 to allow Spain a monopoly of voyages of discovery. The journey took Cabot less time than it had taken Columbus in 1493, and vindicated his decision to explore a more northerly crossing.

"The Cabot brothers leaving Bristol" by Ernest Board (1877-1934). A representative of the city bids farewell to the Genoese navigators before they board their ship, the mainsail of which is emblazoned with the royal coat of arms to show that their mission is officially approved by King Henry VII.

"Tabaco" pipe is good for your health, say American smokers

A later print of American natives smoking their pipes known as "tabacos".

Europe, 1496

Samples of a dried leaf whose fumes are inhaled when burnt are among some of the curiosities brought back from the West Indies by the explorer Christopher Columbus.

His crew were offered the "bewitching vegetable" by natives who use it in ceremonies and believe it possesses unique health-giving properties. According to Romano Pane, a monk travelling with Columbus, the natives dry the vegetable leaf and put it in a small slingshot-shaped pipe, known as a "tabaco". Its two ends are inserted into the nostrils, the leaf is set on fire and the smoke inhaled up the pipe. When exhaling, the smokers look like dragons breathing fire.

The leaf, which is chewable, can also be smoked rolled up tightly in a tube-shape. However, be careful: too much smoke inhaled this way can make you light-headed.

Teeth white, smiles brighter, thanks to Chinese invention

China, 1498

Since earliest times humans have probably wrestled with the irritating problem of food particles left lodged between the teeth. Traditionally, the answer has been some form of toothpick. Now, however, a new idea from China, the toothbrush, seems likely to do the job more effectively. At the same time it imparts a shine to the front surfaces of the teeth. The bristles are mounted at right angles to the handle, allowing one to manoeuvre into every crack and crevice.

Vasco da Gama arrives in India

A portrait of the navigator Vasco da Gama, from a Spanish manuscript.

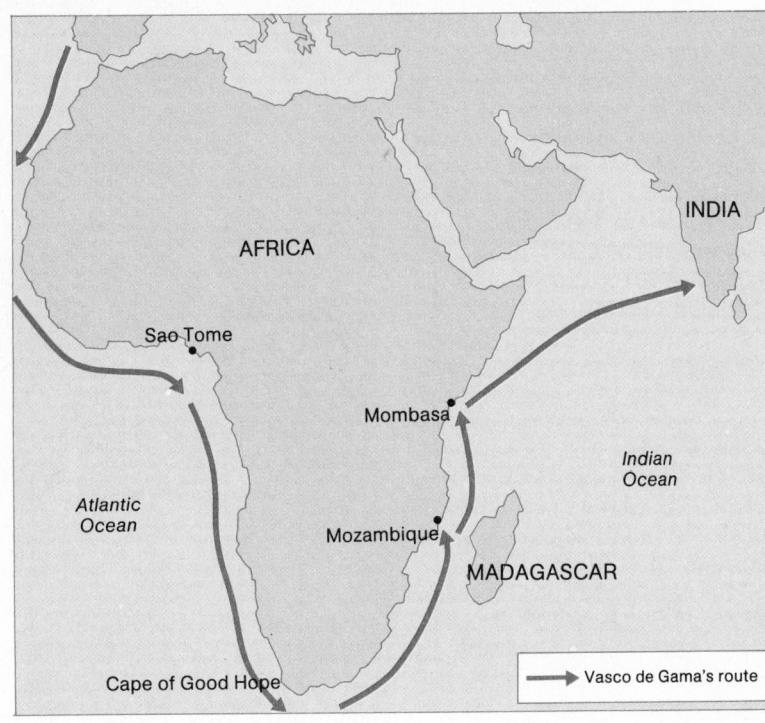

Vasco de Gama's route

India, 23 May 1498

Almost a year after setting sail from Lisbon, Vasco da Gama has arrived off Calicut, on the Malabar coast, thus becoming the first European to discover a sea route round the Cape of Good Hope to India. During the long voyage he encountered many difficulties and dangers that tested both his seamanship and his qualities as a leader.

Da Gama has four ships with 20 guns and 170 well-armed men, a wise precaution as it turned out, for the Moslem Arab traders, fearing the Christian Portuguese will challenge their monopoly of trade with the Hindus, are already seeking to set the *zamorin*, or king, of Calicut against the newcomers.

When da Gama went ashore he took presents for the king: hats, striped cloth, strings of coral and a case of wash hand-basins. The king scorned them, saying da Gama had claimed he had come from a rich country, but all he had brought were cheap trinkets.

After battling against hurricanes on its way round the Cape, da Gama's expedition met with Moslem hostility at almost every port of call in East Africa. At Mombasa, Moslems pretended to be Christians in order to get on board and prepare for an armed attack on the ships. Da Gama had to bombard Mozambique before he could obtain supplies of fresh water.

At Malindi, however, a friendly welcome awaited the Portuguese and they were able to recruit Ibu Majid, an experienced Gujarati seaman, who piloted them across the Indian Ocean. Da Gama plans to return to Lisbon with half a dozen Indians to show to King Manuel, who funded the expedition.

Pope denounced by "Black Friar"

Florence, 25 December 1497

After six months of silence following his excommunication last June, Girolamo Savonarola today openly defied the Pope. He celebrated Mass three times this morning in the Church of St Mark. For seven years now Florence has been under the spell of this preacher, known as the "Black Friar". He is a short, slender man with a hooked nose, deeply-lined brow and thick lips. But it is his burning grey-green eyes which mesmerise people.

He was born at Ferrara in 1452 and became a Dominican friar. When he became prior at St Mark's he was already known as a prophet. He railed against the corruption of church and secular leaders. He said the art of Florence was immoral and charged Leonardo da Vinci and Botticelli with sodomy, though they were acquitted.

On Good Friday 1492 he revealed his vision of the destruction of Florence by flashes of lightning in a dense black sky. His congregation trembled when he drew vivid pictures of "barbers armed with gigantic razors" invading the city.

In 1494, on a wave of popular frenzy and with the help of the French king, he drove out the ruling Medici family. He has made Florence a puritanical republic, burning "vanities" such as books and pictures. Botticelli has stopped painting nudes and Leonardo has moved to Milan.

Exhausted French army limps home after hollow Italian victory

A 19th-century view of the battle.

Italy, 6 July 1495

Exhausted, emaciated and riddled with disease, the army of Charles VIII is limping its way home to France today after being defeated at the battle of Fornovo. It is no more than a shattered shadow of the magnificent army which had paraded through Italy two years before. Both sides – French and Italian – are claiming victory; but if there was one, it was hollow indeed.

The young Charles had dreamed of conquering Naples, and after much dallying and womanising he crossed the Alps and made his way south. His entourage included 50,000 archers, crossbowmen and other footsoldiers, 36 huge cannon, several hundred prostitutes and his own baggage train of bedchamber, chapel, chamberlains, cooks, valets, ushers-at-arms, musicians, jesters, jousters and acrobats.

After much socialising along the route, Charles arrived at a castle near Naples. Heralds were sent forward demanding its surrender – only to return without ears or noses. Charles brought his big guns into play; a massacre followed and Naples fell.

But while the king disported himself there, a rare Swiss and Italian alliance was building up in the north; and it was this alliance that the French met at Fornovo on their return northwards.

Savonarola, by Fra Bartolomeo.

1498 (1498-1500)

Spain, 7 June 1498. Columbus leaves on his third voyage of exploration.

Portugal, 1498. All Jews are expelled.

France, 1499. Louis XII repudiates Jeanne of France and marries Anne of Brittany.

England/North America, 1499. Henry VII gives John Cabot a boat to sail to Cathay (northern China). The expedition reconnoitres the coastline from Newfoundland to New England. The boat returns in September without Cabot, who has died on the voyage.

Milan, 1499. Backed by the pope, Venice, Florence and the Swiss cantons, Louis XII of France claims his right of succession to the duchy of Milan. The French, led by the mercenary Trivulzio, seize Milan. The usurper Ludovico Sforza flees.

South America, 1499. The Italian navigator Amerigo Vespucci explores the north-east coastline.

South America, 1499. The Spaniard Yanez Pinzon explores the northern coast of South America from Cape San Augustin to the Orinoco.

Caribbean, September 1499. Columbus puts down a revolt by Spanish settlers and natives against his poor administration in Hispaniola.

Brazil, 1 January 1500. The Portuguese explorer Pedro Alvarez Cabral discovers the coast of Brazil.

East Africa, 1500. Portuguese trading posts are set up along the East African coast.

India, 1500. Cabral creates the first Portuguese trading posts on the west coast of India.

Milan, 1500. The Milanese rebel against the French commander, Trivulzio. Taking advantage of the revolt, Sforza attacks the French at Novara but is deserted by his troops, handed over to the enemy and sent to France as a prisoner.

Russia, 1500. Ivan III annexes Smolensk and Chernigov, thus pushing back the boundary with Lithuania.

North Atlantic, 1500. The Portuguese Gaspard Corte Real explores the southern coast of Labrador and the east coast of Greenland.

West Africa, 1500. Sheikh Masfarma ben Uthman writes a history of Bornu (northern Nigeria, Niger and Chad).

Spanish Inquisition continues despite death of Dominican friar

Toledo, 1498
Tomas de Torquemada, a Dominican friar and the president of the Spanish Inquisition for 12 years, is dead. But the inquisitions, here and in Seville and Barcelona, are still being vigorously prosecuted. They are spreading to many cities in Aragon, despite local protests. All told, several thousand people are thought to have been burnt at the stake in the last 20 years.

It was in 1478 that Spain's Catholic kings obtained the consent of Pope Sixtus IV to appoint inquisitors. The main target is *conversos* – Jewish people who have converted to Christianty. Many were forced to convert on pain of death, and so, unsurprisingly, are not very strong in their Christian faith.

The inquisition begins with edicts offering people a chance to confess their errors and also to denounce others. Only one informer is necessary for anyone to be charged. When anyone is convicted they are liable to be "relaxed", which means to be burnt alive; here

A 19th-century view of an "auto-da-fe", one of the Inquisition's show-trials.

more than 500 people have been "relaxed" and something like 5,000 have been "reconciled" by their confessions. Many of these have been sentenced to march for six Fridays to the cathedral, whipping themselves in the streets. Such penitents suffer heavy fines, are forbidden to wear anything but the coarsest clothes, and cannot ride horses or bear arms.

Sometimes they are forced to dress only in green, with cloth crosses on their clothes.

Garden is laid out for Zen Meditation

Japan, 1500
A garden of contemplation has been laid out in the grounds of the Zen Buddhist temple of Ryoan-ji in Kyoto, which is not only the capital but also the cultural heart of Japan. The temple was established by the warrior chief Katsumoto after a lifetime of fighting and its garden is a haven of tranquillity. It is oblong and contains 15 rocks of varying sizes arranged in an abstract composition on a bed of carefully raked white sand.

Stones in the garden of Ryoan-ji.

"The Trials of St Antony", by the Netherlandish painter Jerome (Hieronymus) van Aken, known as Bosch from his home town of s'Hertogenbosch. His paintings can be conventional, but some, like this one, are full of bizarre fantasy, with colourful and often horrific imagery.

Cabral claims Brazil for the Portuguese

Brazil, 23 April 1500

A vast territory lying south of the Equator has been claimed for the king of Portugal by the navigator Pedro Alvarez Cabral. He has called it *Vera Cruz*, or True Cross, but already it is becoming known as *Brazil*, after the red-coloured brazil wood which is abundant there.

Cabral had set out for India with a fleet of 13 ships. To avoid the known *doldrums* off the Guinea coast of Africa, he sailed far west and sighted an unfamiliar coastline, with a lofty, circular mountain in the background. Some men appeared on the beach – brown, naked and with bows and arrows.

Cabral's men captured two of them for inspection. They had their lower lips bored and sharpened bones inserted. Next day the natives brought their women to meet the white visitors. The women were also naked and painted with a red dye from the brazil tree.

As is usual on such voyages, Cabral had with him a number of convicts to be used for the more risky operations. He sent two of them to visit the village. They reported that the natives lived in large wooden huts, each with hammocks for 30 or more persons.

Cabral's men paid a number of visits to the land which they had found. Two of his ship's carpenters made a wooden cross which aroused great interest amongst the natives – not because of its shape, or what it represented, but because of the iron tools which the carpenters used. The locals used wedgeshaped stones to cut wood for themselves.

Cabral decided to show the natives the veneration which he and his men had for the Cross; they knelt before it and kissed it. On their final visit to the shore, when

Pedro Cabral (a 19th-century print).

the Portuguese landed to collect food and water, as many as 400 natives emerged to watch their new visitors. Some helped to carry wood to the boats and a few ate the food and wine which they were offered. Cabral is now sailing for India, but he will leave a few convicts to study the natives and their land.

Navigator Dias lost in Atlantic storm

Cape of Good Hope, May 1500

Disaster struck Cabral's fleet after it left the newly discovered land of Brazil and set sail across the South Atlantic for India. Cabral had sent one ship back to Portugal to announce his discovery of the new land and was leading the remainder of his fleet across the Atlantic when the tragedy happened.

As it was approaching the Cape of Good Hope, well south of the Tropic of Capricorn, a fierce storm blew up and four ships foundered with all hands, the rest being badly battered and scattered. Among those who perished was Bartholomew Dias, the great Portuguese navigator who, 12 years ago, became the first European to sail round this cape.

That historic voyage was to be the prelude to Vasco da Gama's epoch-making journey to India; in that, too, Dias played an important role. He supervised the construction and fitting-out of da Gama's fleet, and accompanied it on the first stages of its journey. The ships were three-masted, with two

A later picture of Dias (1450-1500).

square sails on the mainmasts and a triangular one on the mizzen. Much of the equipment Dias had recommended, such as a double set of sails and rigging, was novel at the time, but more recently has been taken for granted.

His brother, Diogo, was among the survivors of the storms which battered Cabral's fleet. Seven ships have managed to limp to a port in Mozambique for repairs.

Almost certainly it is the backup equipment which has enabled Cabral's battered ships to survive the storm that carried off Dias. While Cabral is at Mozambique, he hopes to make trade agreements which will further entrench Portuguese commercial interests in southern Africa. Trade has always been the spur to the great voyages of discovery undertaken by Portugal and its great rival, Spain, during the second half of this century. But the bravery and skill of men like Dias have also transformed the map of the world.

Portuguese "carracks" (a type of ship); attributed to Cornelius Anthonizoon.

Husband performs "Caesar" operation

Switzerland, 1500

Reports have reached the medical profession of an adventurous operation performed recently in Sigershauffen, Switzerland. Apparently a pregnant woman, Frau Nufer, was having considerable trouble delivering her child, possibly because of the baby's position or its size relative to her pelvis width.

Fearing for the health of both

mother and child, the husband, Jacob Nufer, took the bold step of cutting open the uterus to release the baby.

Legend has it that the great Roman, Julius Caesar, was delivered in this way. The Roman nobility, though, was usually attended by the best physicians and midwives. Jacob Nufer's occupation is that of a sow gelder.

Saxon woman playwright's work is found

Germany, 1500

There is much excitement in literary circles at the recent discovery of works by the tenth-century Saxon canoness Hroswitha of Gandersheim (c.935 to 972). Her writings include six Latin plays which establish her as the first known German woman writer and, more remarkably, the first European playwright since the classical age. Hroswitha's

plays (*Abraham, Callimachus, Dulcitius, Gallicanus, Pafnutius* and *Sapientia*) deal chiefly with Christian virgin martyrs, and include some graphic torture scenes similar to those in early accounts of the lives of the saints, as well as moving scenes of the conversion of prostitutes. Her other works include narrative poems and legends of the saints.

Spain, 1501. King Ferdinand issues directives to Nicolas de Ovando, his colonial governor in America, sanctioning the system of levying tribute payments from the Indians and using them as forced labour.

Mexico, 1502. Montezuma II becomes chief of the Aztecs.

Spain, 12 February 1502. A royal edict orders the expulsion from Castile of all Moors who have not been baptised as Christians.

Germany, April 1502. A peasants' rebellion breaks out in the bishopric of Speyer. It is known as the "Bundschuh" revolt, after the rebels' symbol of a laced boot.

Persia, 1502. The Shi'ite Shah Ismail founds the Safavid dynasty.

Spain, 20 January 1503. An office is established in Seville to supervise trade with the New World and, in particular, the expenses of Columbus.

Spain, 20 March 1503. The Saragossa Instruction sets out a series of measures intended to encourage the Indians in the New World to adopt a settled way of life and to spread the gospel among them.

Rome, 1 November 1503. Giuliano della Rovere, who takes the name Julius II, is the second pope to be elected in a year. He succeeds Pius III, who became pope on 18 August, on the death of Alexander VI.

East Africa, 1503. The Portuguese levy a tribute from the sultan of Zanzibar.

Balkans, 2 July 1504. Stephen (the Great), prince of Moldavia since 1457, dies. He secured possession of Bessarabia from the Ottomans and, in 1469, repelled a Mongol invasion.

Spain, 7 November 1504. Columbus returns from his fourth voyage, which began on 11 May 1502.

Spain, 26 November 1504. Isabella of Castile dies, leaving her daughter Joanna (the Mad) as heir to the throne of Castile, but effective power remains in the hands of Isabella's husband, Ferdinand.

Afghanistan, 1504. Babur, a descendant of Tamerlane from Turkestan, seizes Kabul.

Sudan, 1504. Funj kings, Moslems possibly of Bornu (*Nigerian*) origin, defeat and replace the Christian kings of Sennar between the Blue Nile and White Nile rivers.

Shi'ism becomes state religion in Persia

Persia, 1502

The conversion of the people of Persia to Shi'ism is being pursued with ruthless dedication. On the orders of Shah Ismail, the new Safavid ruler, Sunni dissenters are being executed.

Shah Ismail came to power last year after routing an Ak-Koyunlu force of 30,000 men at Sharur and marching into Tabriz. The Safavids are natives of Persia and claim to be the descendants of the Prophet Mohammed. Under Khwaja Ali, head of the order from 1391 to 1427, they moved away from Sunnism to militant Shi'ism, based on belief in a line of 12 infallible *imams*, from Ali to Mohammed. A succession of Safavid leaders were killed during the last century, but their propagandists, working from their base in Ardabil, east of Azerbaijan, kept alive a distinctive faith designed to attract non-Ottomans.

To assist the conversion of the Persian people, Shah Ismail has imported *ulama* from Arab lands, Bahrain, Hilla in Mesopotamia, and particularly from Jabal Amil, in Lebanon. Many leading Shi'ite theologians are of Amili origin, notably al-Karaki, the most important religious figure.

Michelangelo's David hewn from marble

Florence, 8 September 1504

A colossus of modern times, a 13-foot-high statue of David, naked, with his sling over his shoulder, by Michelangelo Buonarotti, has been set up in the Piazza della Signoria after a perilous journey of more than 200 yards, suspended by rope from a wooden frame which was winched along over planks.

The sculptor was in Rome, where he carved his widely admired *Pieta* for St Peter's, when he heard that a huge 18-foot block of marble lying in the works yard of the cathedral might be given to him to work on. It had been there since 1464, abandoned because of a gash in the marble. He calculated how to get his *David* out of the block by making a wax scale model. He let no one see it until it was finished.

Everyone is amazed at the faultless proportions and anatomical correctness on such a scale. He has been paid 4,000 crowns by the city, and *David* has established his reputation as a sculptor without rival.

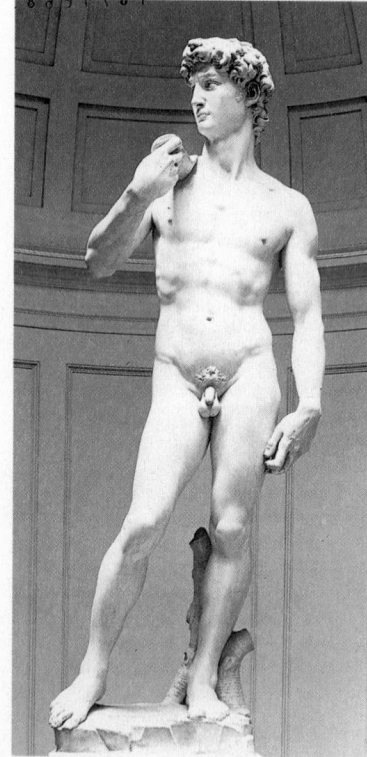

Michelangelo's new statue.

Time slows down when held in the hand

Nuremberg, 1502

Peter Henlein, a German locksmith, has invented a timepiece that can be carried in the hand. About four inches in diameter and three inches in depth, this pocket-size watch is made possible by another innovation, the coiled mainspring.

The flat mainspring is stressed when coiled. Winding it up stores energy in the curved metal. As the coil unwinds, this energy is transmitted to an oscillating section of the watch by means of a mechanism called a verge escapement, a notched gear wheel shaped like a crown, to produce a regular pulse.

Henlein's miniaturisation of the clock is not without its faults, the most serious being that the force of the mainspring is greater when it is fully wound. So time varies.

Explorer tells of cannibals in Brazil

Vespucci, from a 1673 book.

Spain, 1502

Amerigo Vespucci, the Florentine explorer, has returned from his voyage to the New World. Vespucci, whose expedition set off in 1499 to follow the trail of Christopher Columbus, has been sailing down the coast of Brazil to become the first European to see the Rio de la Plata.

Vespucci has written extensively of his experiences, telling of a veritable earthly paradise: a fertile land filled with fruits and wholesome vegetables, swarming with wild animals and exotic birds. But its native population, warlike cannibals who eat their enemies, have lives quite unlike our own.

"Having no laws and no religious faith they live according to nature. There is no possession of private property among them," he wrote. "They have no king, nor do they obey anyone. There is no administration of justice because in their code no-one rules."

They are a brutal people, he adds. The men pierce their lips and cheeks with bones to make themselves look more fierce. In war they slaughter without mercy, and "those who remain on the field bury all the dead of their own side, but they cut up and eat the bodies of their enemies". The survivors are taken as slaves who are frequently offered as sacrifices, providing ritual food for the cannibals.

Death of pope who flaunted his mistress

Rome, 18 August 1503

Romans are rejoicing today following the news of the death of Pope Alexander VI. Rodrigo Borgia was disliked because he was a Spaniard and a libertine. But he was hated because he was a first-rate administrator with enormous energy. He policed Rome and the countryside; he filled the papal treasury by stopping officials from diverting funds and he used the money to help his son, Cesare, to carve out a state in the Romagna, thereby angering nobles whose power he curbed.

Other popes before Alexander have departed from celibacy, but none has so flaunted his reputation as a great lover. He had a portrait of his chief mistress, dressed as the Virgin Mary, painted over the door of his bedchamber.

He publicly acknowledged his three bastards, two of whom have become notorious figures in their own right. His daughter, Lucrezia, had two husbands while still in her teens, although she probably did not have the excessive sex life that Roman gossips suggest. Cesare, his youngest son, must be fearing for his future.

Cesare is a head taller than most tall men, has massive shoulders and

Alexander VI, by Pintoricchio.

blazing blue eyes. He organised *corridas* so that he could show off by beheading a bull with one stroke of his sword. He was ruthless in supporting his father's aims. He lured enemies to the castle of Sinigaglia and had them murdered. He is also said to have had his brother and his sister's second husband killed.

Moscow breaks up the Golden Horde

Moscow, 1503

Muscovy is politically independent once more, thanks to Ivan III who has consistently refused to pay protection money to Genghis Khan's descendants.

The original Mongolian Golden Horde split into three autonomous *khanates* more than a century ago, but Ahmed, the leader of the core group still known as the Horde, demanded money as recently as 1480. Ivan outmanoeuvred him by negotiating a mutual defence treaty with the Crimean khan and by fighting hard. Ahmed Khan's advance on Moscow in 1472, unsupported by his Lithuanian ally, faded away. A similar assault in 1480 led to a battlefield stalemate after four days. Then Khan Ivak of Western Siberia hit Ahmed's camp and killed him. Muscovy is now ready to expand.

Gold and gilt metal-covered beaker made in the form of a fortress town (German, c.1500).

Portuguese punish king for "insolence"

Kilwa, East Africa, 24 July 1505

The Portuguese have inflicted terrible punishment on the African city-state of Kilwa for the insolence of its King Ibrahim and his failure to pay tribute. A German observer with the Portuguese fleet reports that "the heathen" were shot dead, houses were destroyed and "gold, silver, pearls, precious stones and costly clothes" were carried off.

Francisco de Almeida, the Portuguese commander, dropped anchor at Kilwa on his way to India, where he has been made the first viceroy. Ibrahim failed to welcome the Portuguese, offering the excuse that as he left his palace a black tom-cat had crossed his path, which was a bad omen. With that Almeida went on the attack and sacked Mombasa.

King Manuel of Portugal, having found the cost of equipping ships and providing funds for trading too heavy a burden, has made these into commercial operations. Italians and Germans are now partners in the India trade, which also encompasses raids on Moslem city-states in East Africa. The German who saw the sack of Kilwa says that King Manuel has ordered the building of a fort there.

German inventor of the globe is dead

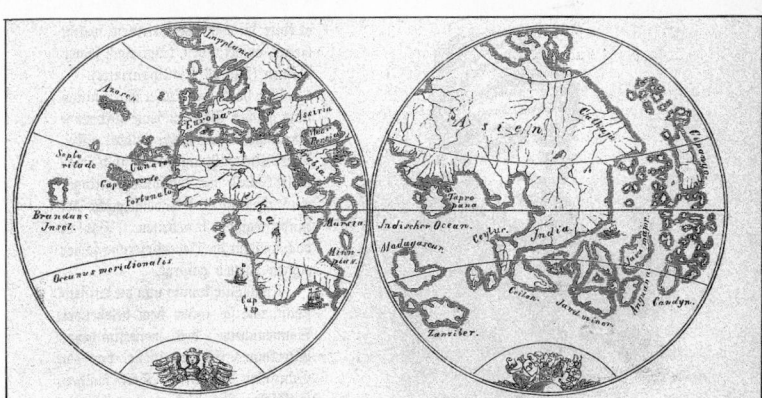

The two hemispheres, after the globe made by Martin Behaim in 1492.

Portugal, 29 July 1506

The great German map-maker Martin Behaim, who constructed the first known globe, has died in Lisbon at the age of 47.

Born into a family of merchants, Behaim spent most of his adult life in Portugal and the Azores. He kept company with all the explorers who came his way, and claimed to have accompanied the navigator Diego Cao on his expedition to Africa in 1485. Later he was captured by English pirates, and held prisoner for several years before being allowed to return to Portugal.

Behaim constructed his famous globe during a visit to Nuremberg in 1492. He drew the outlines of the continents in colour on a surface of fine parchment, probably copying extensively from other maps. The completed work summarised the geographical knowledge of the day.

This colourful tapestry, depicting "wild people" and fantastic animals, was made recently by a craftsman or craftswoman in Switzerland.

Durer studies in Venice and returns to paint Adam and Eve

The young Durer, by himself.

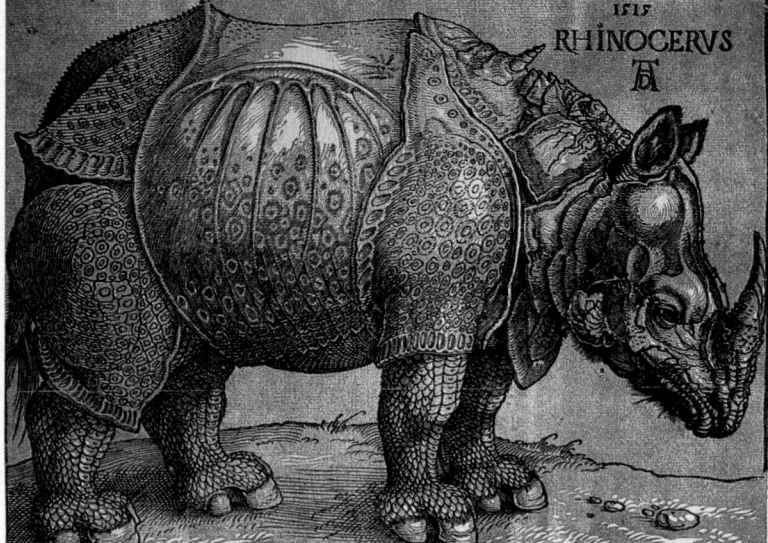

"The Rhinoceros", by Durer, a woodcut engraved from two blocks (1515).

Nuremberg, Germany, 1507
Albrecht Durer, the outstanding German painter and engraver who was born here to a Hungarian gold-smith, has lately returned from a two-year visit to Venice. Having gained a reputation with his popular woodcuts and copperplate engravings, such as *The Apocalypse*, he has turned to oil painting in the Italian manner.

While in Venice he painted a *Feast of the Rose Garlands*, which the doge came to see and which was admired by Giovanni Bellini, the aged Venetian master. Now back at home, he is attempting to render the ideal of human beauty in full length paintings of Adam and Eve – the first full-size nudes to be painted in Germany. These paint-ings are a contrast to his celebrated engraving of the couple, done a few years ago. Durer's powers of drawing, his studies of mathematics and his theory of art have won him the sort of fame which was unknown for a German artist before his time. People are beginning to speak of a renaissance in the north.

Venice monopolises Mediterranean trade

Carpaccio's "Lion of St Mark", an expression of Venice's civic pride.

Venice, 1507
The island city of Venice, founded more than a thousand years ago, has established itself as the most important centre of Mediterranean trade. Not only do its merchant ships bring in great wealth, but its navy ensures security from the attacks of greedy rivals.

Ideally positioned between western Europe and Asia, its merchants dominate every trade route. Its bankers, insurers and accountants are unrivalled and Venice stands proud, master of Europe's most commercially sophisticated area.

Portuguese discoveries in the New World have undoubtedly undermined Venetian power, but the expertise of traders and overall experience has ensured that continues to dominate the established Oriental routes.

The sought-after spice monopoly has been lost – American silver has given the Portuguese the funds to break it – but the new route round the Cape of Good Hope is simply too time-consuming. Spices do not keep. In any case, no one can rival the Venetian monopoly of Asia's luxury goods.

Indian sultan sinks Portuguese fleet

Bombay, 1508
A Portuguese fleet has been surprised and sunk off Chaul, on the west coast of India, by the Gujaratian and Egyptian navies. The Portuguese viceroy's son, Dom Lourenco, drowned in the battle.

The victory is a triumph for Mahmud Begara, the ageing sultan of Gujarat. A grandson of Ahmed Shah, founder of the state, he has ruled the country for 50 years, extending Gujarat's frontiers to their furthest limits. Tall and martial, with a beard that reaches his waist, he is as proficient at the negotiating table as on the battlefield. A strict Moslem, intolerant of other creeds, he protects himself from poison by daily absorbing small amounts into his system. He is now so impregnated, it is said, that flies die when they settle on him.

His victory has elated Moslems all over India and the Near East, who fear for Islam as it retreats before European expansionism.

Columbus' travels end

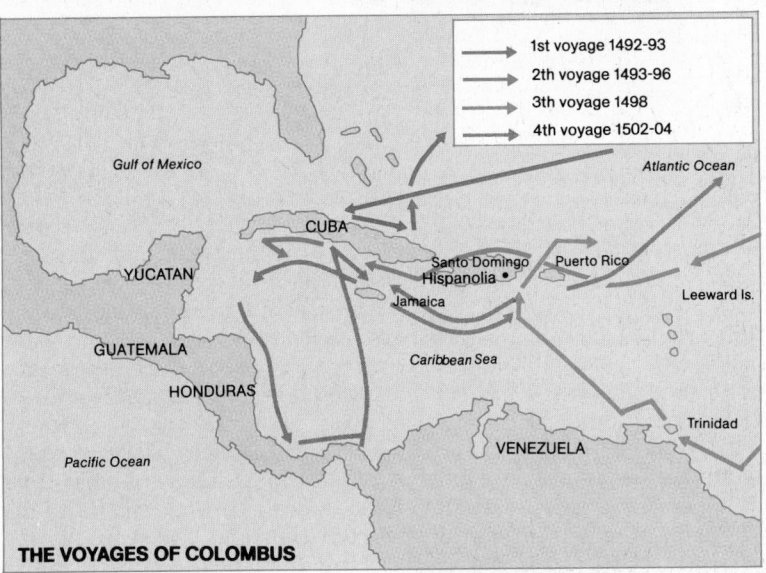

→	1st voyage 1492-93
→	2th voyage 1493-96
→	3th voyage 1498
→	4th voyage 1502-04

Gulf of Mexico

Atlantic Ocean

CUBA

YÚCATAN

Santo Domingo
Hispanolia •

Puerto Rico

Jamaica

Leeward Is.

GUATEMALA

Caribbean Sea

HONDURAS

Trinidad

Pacific Ocean

VENEZUELA

THE VOYAGES OF COLOMBUS

German map calls new world "America"

Lorraine, 1507
A map of the world has just been published which, for the first time, shows the New World to be a distinct continent between Europe and Asia.

It names this continent America, after the Italian explorer Amerigo Vespucci who claims to have discovered the mainland in 1497 – a year before Columbus arrived. In fact, all the indications are that the expedition took place two years later.

The cartographers, Martin Waldseemuller and Matthias Ringmann, seem to have accepted Vespucci's dubious version of events. The truth is, his achievements as an explorer do not compare with those of Columbus, whose log of his expedition is undisputedly genuine in every date recorded. However Vespucci's accounts of his voyages for Spain and Portugal have earned him a powerful reputation.

He certainly sighted land in several parts of central and south America. On his first expedition, under the leadership of Alonso de Ojeda, he discovered an Indian city built on water and named it Venezuela, or "Little Venice".

The irony of this new map is that – within a year of Columbus' death – it has given the principal credit for the discovery of America to a man whose principal talent seems to have been as a self-publicist.

Valladolid, Spain, 21 May 1506
The explorer Columbus died today aged 55, embittered, isolated and still convinced that what he had found in the west was the true Indies, not a place others describe as the "New World." His will, made yesterday, leaves his son the one-tenth share of the wealth generated by his discovery, as promised in his contract with King Ferdinand but still unpaid 14 years later.

Columbus was a great captain, but a poor coloniser. On his first voyage he deposited a small group of settlers at Hispaniola (*Santo Domingo*). All were soon killed by the natives. In September 1493 he sailed from Cadiz a second time, after only five months in Spain, with 17 ships and 1,200 potential settlers, and returned to the original site of Isabella. There was trouble as soon as the turbulent Spaniards got ashore. Columbus brought this under control and went exploring. He returned to discover his settlers at war with the Indians, who resented demands for food, women and gold. Columbus dealt with the problem by massacring natives. In spite of that, colourful complaints about him came to Madrid from the Spaniards. He would now be fighting on two fronts 3,000 miles apart. While he defended his political corner in Spain, his brother Bartolome built a new settlement, Santo Domingo, which became the empire's regional capital.

By now, with routes established, Spain needed Columbus less. His

Columbus at the Spanish court, by Eugene Deveria (1808-65).

third voyage ended in 1499, with his return to Spain in irons on the orders of Francisco de Bobadilla, his successor as governor. Columbus' offence was that he had suppressed another rebellion by hanging seven settlers in the street.

His last voyage ended four years ago, his ships beached and unseaworthy at Santa Gloria (*Jamaica*) and distress signals ignored for a year. Yet not even his worst enemy can diminish his achievements.

He charted about 60 islands, and landed on the shores of Venezuela. He found little gold but much else, including tobacco. His seamanship identified trade winds both ways across the ocean at different latitudes. He was thus, in a sense, the foreigner who put Spain on the map by making the map.

Spanish settlers make slaves of Indians

Hispaniola, West Indies, 1508
The fortunes of Spanish settlers, once threatened by their failure to find a major supply of gold here (*Santo Domingo*), have been boosted by a move away from the futile search for precious metal to the cultivation of a profitable cash crop: sugar cane. And they are benefiting from the exploitation of a valuable local commodity: Indian slaves.

Columbus introduced sugar to the Indies on his second voyage in 1493, but his main interest remained the discovery of gold in order to pay off his backers. Hispaniola simply had none to offer and, desperate for funds, Columbus imposed a gold tax, offering the natives copper bracelets for their valuables.

This scheme brought some revenue, but the island was no Eldorado. Today no one expects to find gold here, but the sugar crop is booming, fuelled by slaves working on huge, enclosed estates. Only dwindling manpower threatens profits: of the island's original 250,000 natives, the brutal work has killed off all but 60,000.

Spaniards force Peruvian natives to carry booty in this slightly later print.

Europe's century of discovery

In 1434 Portuguese seamen sailing south down the African coast first rounded Cape Bojador, which, with its treacherous currents, then marked the effective boundary of the known world. In the course of the next hundred years or so, the Portuguese rounded Africa and penetrated into the Indian Ocean, establishing trading posts in the East Indies. In the 1550s they acquired a base in China. Spain's activity, meanwhile, had been directed westward, and Spanish or Spanish-backed explorers had discovered the West Indies and South America. It was under Spanish patronage that Magellan found the westward passage around South America and his ships achieved the first circumnavigation of the world. North America was also explored, although more slowly.

This period, from roughly the mid 15th to the mid 16th centuries, saw what was probably the single greatest expansion of European awareness of the rest of the world. It was a growth in knowledge due solely to the efforts of the western Europeans themselves; the countries which they sought out had demonstrated no comparable desire to make contact with them and, on the whole, continued to show little interest in the west even after contact had been made.

Motives: wealth and wisdom

The European explorers and their patrons were not necessarily prompted by a disinterested desire for knowledge. Far from it: those who invested their capital in exploration naturally hoped for material gains. One major motive was the wish to tap the lucrative spice trade at its source in the Indies and cut out the Venetian middlemen who controlled existing routes, which brought spices overland through the Near East and then across the Mediterranean into Europe. Equally potent was the desire for gold. Portuguese exploration of the west coast of Africa was directed towards finding the gold-rich kingdom of Guinea, known to lie somewhere at the end of the great trans-Saharan trade routes. The 16th-century explorers of central America were driven by rumours of *El Dorado* (the gilded), the fabulous city of gold.

The prospect of financial gain was not, however, the only motive at work. The promotors of exploration also sought to make contact with Christian communities beyond Europe. When he set out for India, Vasco da Gama's declared objectives were Christians and spices, the former being a reference to the belief that the apostle Thomas had founded a church there. In a period when the western church was coming under increasing criticism for its worldliness and corruption, the discovery of such a community, isolated from developments elsewhere, seemed to offer a way of regaining contact with the apostolic roots of the church.

Even more compelling were stories of a priest-king, Prester John, who ruled a legendary kingdom in the heart of Africa. For 15th-century rulers of the Iberian peninsula, where the struggle against Islam was still continuing, an alliance with Prester John offered a chance of catching the Moslems of North Africa between two Christian fronts.

This crusading element could also shade into more radical millenarianism. It had been an undercurrent of mediaeval thinking that the end of the world, and the second coming of Christ, would not occur until all the world had been converted to Christianity. The discovery of new countries offered new fields for missionary activity, and Columbus, at least, saw his discoveries as a way of hastening the millennium.

The voyages of discovery thus did not entail a conscious break with attitudes current earlier in the middle ages. What the explorers hoped to find, and how they hoped to find it, was dependent on accepted views. Most geographers of the middle ages had taken it for granted that there were three major landmasses in the northern hemisphere: Europe, Africa and Asia. It followed that Asia, and its spices, could be reached not only by going eastwards, but also by sailing west from Europe. This was Columbus' intention, encouraged by a tendency among mediaeval writers to underestimate the circumference of the world, so that Asia seemed within relatively easy reach from the direction of Europe.

The greatest breakthrough

The discovery of a hitherto unsuspected continent between Europe and Asia was the most dramatic change in the mediaeval view of the world. It finally put paid to the belief that the southern hemisphere was inaccessible because it lay on the far side of a torrid zone where life was impossible. It also disproved the view of the ancient geographer Ptolemy (rediscovered by the west in the 15th century), that southern Africa joined Asia and that the Indian Ocean was accordingly landlocked.

In many cases the explorations filled in details of countries already known in part. Mediaeval Europeans had been gradually extending their knowledge of the rest of the world – contact with Islam, for instance, had led to a fuller awareness of some parts of Africa and Asia, and the travels of Marco Polo and his kinsmen to the court of Genghis Khan brought Cathay (China) into the consciousness of contemporaries – although that knowledge lost its value and became outdated once the collapse of the Mongol empire closed the routes used by the Polos.

Throughout the middle ages, individual European travellers went to see distant and unknown countries for themselves. Inevitably, however, the knowledge which resulted was patchy and inadequately integrated into a picture of the world as a whole. It was the improvements in the calculation of relative latitude, as well as the discoveries themselves, which make 16th-century maps by European cartographers so much more recognisable to modern observers.

Intellectual challenge

Although factual knowledge was becoming fuller, underlying assumptions changed more slowly. It was taken for granted in the middle ages that the world, created by God for man, could be read as a book of instruction, with visible reality symbolising deeper truths. This view of the world as a book did not change overnight. Although the new discoveries forced some adjustments, the explorers were simply providing more data upon which to moralise. Similarly, the voyages did not diminish credulity about the wonders to be found beyond the known world – if anything, they may have increased it. Even the effect on what might be called spiritual geography was not immediate. Jerusalem was finally ousted from its position as the literal centre of the world, but there was continuing belief in the Garden of Eden as a terrestrial paradise located in the extreme east of Asia. When, on his third voyage, Christoper Columbus reached the mouth of the Orinoco (in modern Venezuela), he identified it as one of the four great rivers which flowed out of Eden.

In the longer term, however, the discoveries did contribute to a shift in thinking. They endorsed the growing awareness among intellectuals that theory must be tested by experiment. They also made it obvious that modern people were, in some areas, far better informed than their predecessors had been, and that reliance on past authorities could therefore be intellectually suspect. In both respects, greater knowledge of the world foreshadowed the reassessment of the very nature of the universe which was to bring about a revolution in science over the following century.

Gerardus Mercator, seen (l.) with Iubocus Hondius, was the foremost cartographer of the 16th century, giving his name to a new projection for maps.

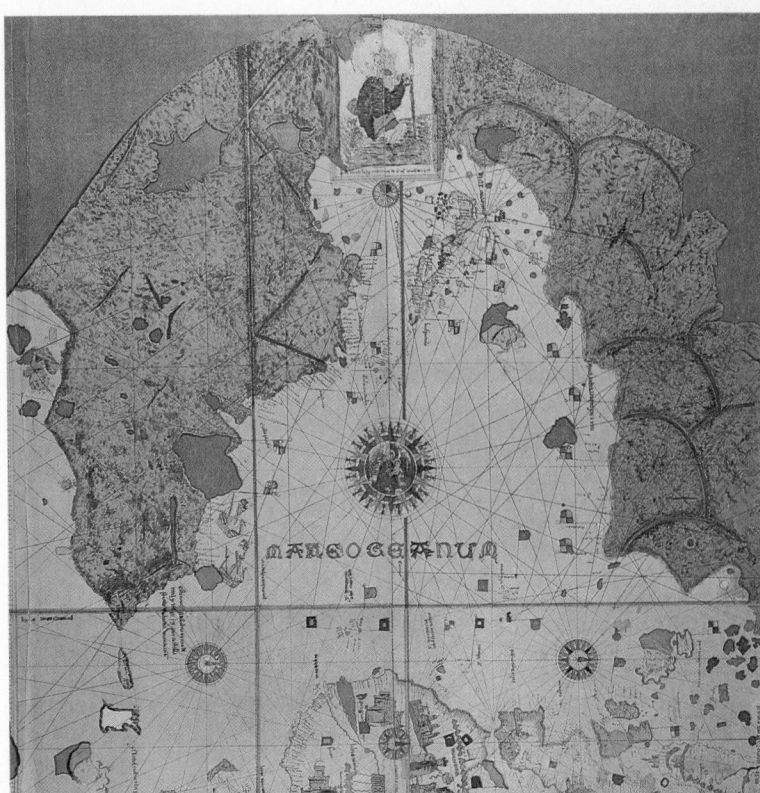

Fifteenth-century Portuguese explorers pioneered new routes south towards Africa and later into the Indian Ocean. This is a part of a chart prepared for Juan de la Cosa, at about 1500, after Vasco da Gama had rounded the Cape of Good Hope and reached India. This disproved the beliefs that southern Africa joined Asia and that the Indian Ocean was a landlocked sea.

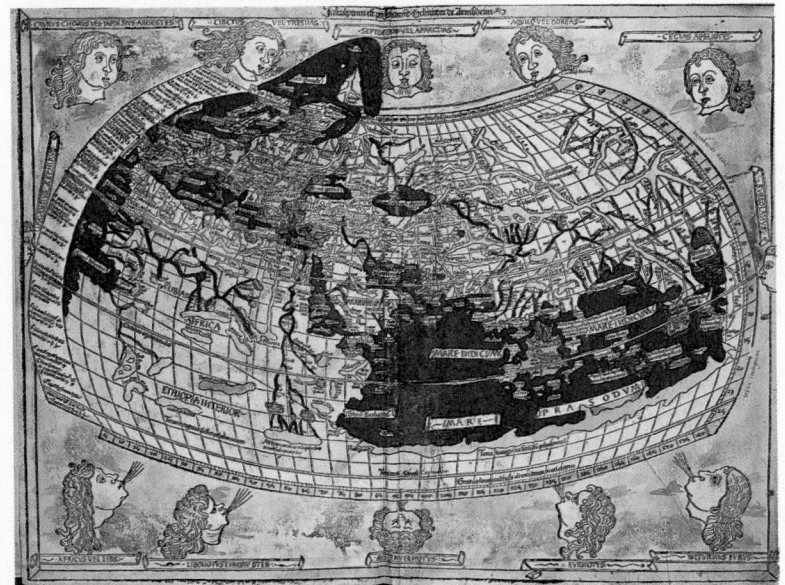

A 15th-century woodcut version of Ptolemy's second-century map: Ptolemy's work was rediscovered as 15th-century explorers ventured ever further.

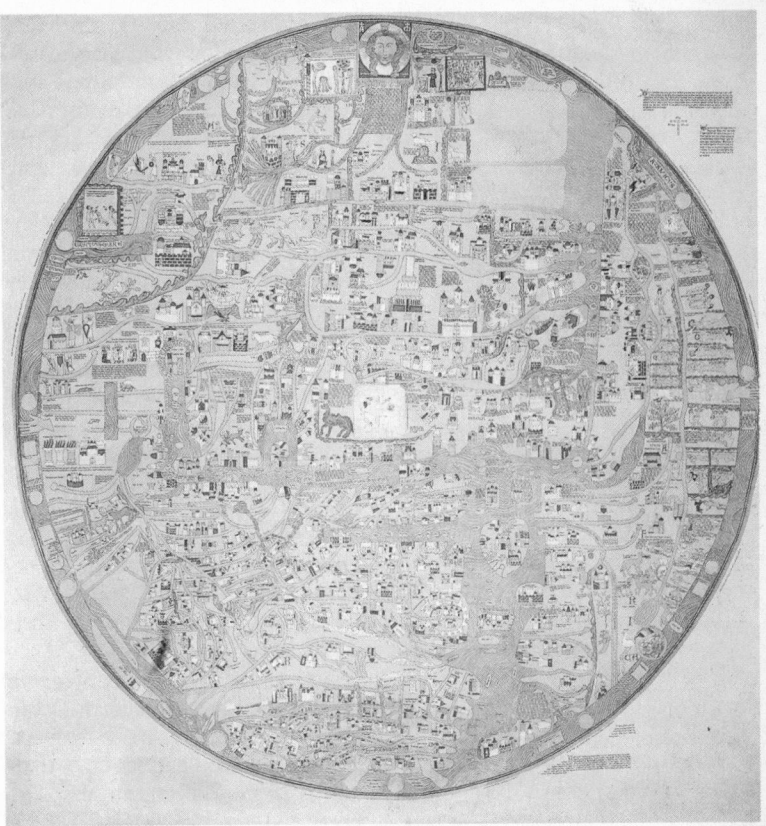

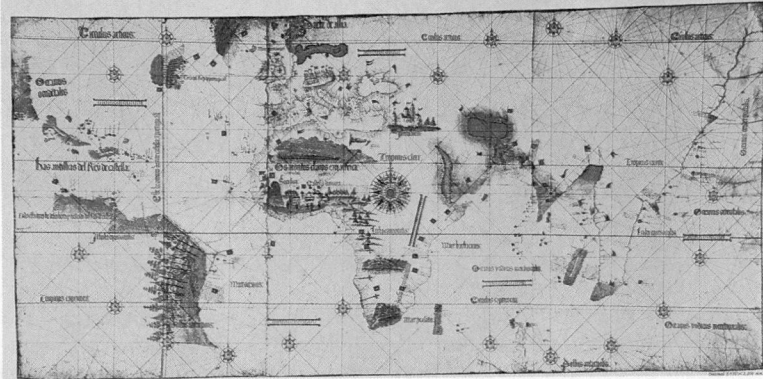

The Monumenta Cartographia map of 1502: the discovery of land between Europe and Asia dramatically changed the mediaeval view of the world.

Apart from Ptolemy in the second century, most early mapmakers concentrated on relatively local portrayals, as in this 13th-century Ebsdorf map.

Henry VII, victor of Bosworth Field, dies

England, 22 April 1509
Henry VII, final victor of the Wars of the Roses and head of the House of Tudor, is dead. Since ascending the throne after the defeat of Richard III at Bosworth Field in 1485, and thus ending 30 years of brutal and intermittent civil war, he has brought a period of much needed political stability to his realm.

Such stability has been hard won. Henry faced a number of pretenders to his throne – the most dangerous of which were Perkin Warbeck and Lambert Simnel – but by 1497 he had crushed every rival. Once established, Henry set about ruling his country. He sought to reduce the independence and factiousness of the powerful nobility, not by direct repression, but by building a broad-based body of support among the gentry and by tying the nobles to him financially, using bonds and recognisances. The country has benefited greatly from his reign, though much of the improvement

Henry VII: first Tudor monarch.

could be the natural result of internal peace. Henry has also earned a reputation as a just king, who used the legal system wisely.

However, his critics suggest that, especially in his later years, he used the law as much for his own ends as to dispense real justice. He is succeeded by his son who becomes Henry VIII.

Venice is crushed by papal alliance

Italy, 14 May 1509
The republic of Venice has suffered a shattering defeat at Agnadello, in northern Italy, by the armies of the League of Cambrai under King Louis XII of France.

The league, formed last year, was the brainchild of Julius II, the formidable Genoese pope, and was ostensibly set up as a "holy league" against Turks. But Julius had a more immediate use for the league, namely to recover for the papacy the towns of the Romagna region under Venetian rule. To this end he promised bits of Venetian land to most of the powers with territorial ambitions in Italy, including France, the empire, Spain, Hungary, Switzerland and some small Italian states.

But the pope's triumph may turn sour; in crushing Venice he has allowed more powerful states, such as France, to strengthen their footholds in northern Italy.

Eastern economy in decline as a new world beckons traders

Indian Ocean, 1510
The Mameluke dynasty which has ruled Arabia for more than a century, already weakened by a succession of incompetent, corrupt and degenerate sultans, is facing the new and potentially devastating threat of economic decline.

Arab traders have dominated the lucrative routes to the east ever since the eighth century, when they opened up contacts with India. Their ships sail across the Indian Ocean and their caravans bring the goods overland to the great cities of the eastern Mediterranean.

Now that monopoly is in jeopardy. Ever since the Portugese explorer Vasco da Gama discovered a new route to the Indies, sailing around the Cape of Good Hope, Portugal and other European nations have begun setting up their own trading posts.

Attacks on Moslem shipping in the Red Sea and the Indian Ocean have become increasingly frequent. The Portuguese have set up a trading post in Calicut, on the west coast of India. Sultan Qansawh al-Ghawri has threatened the pope with the destruction of Christian

A coloured print depicting Arab traders with camels at a desert port.

Holy Places, but the Europeans continue to establish themselves as the new spice merchants. Further European exploration has added to Arabia's difficulties, although the explorers have headed west rather than east. The discovery of the New World in 1492 has shifted the centre of world affairs to the west. The Mediterranean, the most westerly area of Arab power, has lost its central role.

Safavid artists redesign Persian carpets

A richly-woven Persian carpet showing a leopard attacking a gazelle.

Persia, c.1510
Persian carpet-weaving has recovered from its recent decline and is undergoing a complete revolution under the new Safavid rulers. Leading artists and weavers have gathered in large urban factories to create carpets quite unlike those produced by mediaeval artisans. Each city imposes its own style, but the overall emphasis is on new images. Animal and vegetable motifs predominate, often in combination. Some carpets show landscapes, their stylised contours reflecting current trends in painting.

First African slaves arrive in the Americas

Caribbean, 1510
Cuba is preparing for the first shipment of Negro slaves from Africa to overcome an acute shortage of labour among the native Indians. The Negro slaves from the Guinea coast are being sold to anxious colonists as being capable of doing the work of four Indians.

The importation of slaves plus moves to counter the decline in the Indian population – numbers have slumped in Hispaniola *(Santo Domingo)* alone from 300,000 to just 20,000 since 1492 – should stem settlers' fears that Spain is about to abandon the Americas.

Forthcoming Spanish legislation, prompted by visiting Dominicans appalled at Indian conditions, will regulate the practice of *encomienda*, where Indians are herded into camps for conversion to Christianity and used for forced labour.

Slaves, as depicted on the palace door at Ikere-Ekiti in Nigeria.

Strange breads bring on drugged stupor

Peasants are probably stupefied by a diet of mind-altering foodstuffs.

Europe, c.1510
Ideas are flourishing in studios and workshops, and the shape of the earth seems to change every moment. But how you see the world these days depends above all on what bread you eat.

A shortage of wheat grain means that herbs with odd side-effects are used for breadmaking. Darnel, a grass which causes disorientation, tiredness and nausea, and vetch, which leads to depression, are common adulterants. Poppy, inducing euphoria and sleep, is a common seasoning. Rye bread often contains lysergic acid, a powerful hallucinogen probably responsible for the convulsions and madness called St Vitus' dance. Most of western Europe's poor are in the grip of mind-altering foods such as these.

Japanese pirates pillage eastern Asia

China, c.1510
Japanese pirates, known to the Chinese as *wako*, are once again ravaging China's southern coast, landing to pillage the coastal villages. The pirate ships are often officered by Japanese, but crewed by Chinese, who cut off their pigtails and pretend to be Japanese.

These fake wako are mainly fishermen and sailors who have been deprived of a living by imperial edicts forbidding them to pursue their trades in the belief that if there were no flourishing coastal towns there would be nothing for the pirates to attack.

This absurd policy has created pirates who are more desperate than the Japanese and know where the treasure is hidden. China is not the only country to suffer from the depredations of the seawolves who hunt throughout the Asian seas.

Capital prospers under "benign" king

Vijayanagar, India, 1509
Within nine months of attaining the throne of Vijayanagar, Krishnadevaraya has repulsed an attack on the state by Sultan Mahmud of Bidar, leaving the sultan wounded, defeated an army of his rival, Yusuf Adil Khan, and advanced north into Gulbarga and Bidar. His military prowess, his mercy to his enemies and the benevolence of his rule suggest the beginning of a golden age for Vijayanagar.

Though Krishnadevaraya himself favours Vaishnavism, all Hindu sects are respected equally. Temples are being endowed, the poor are being fed, new lands are being irrigated, and Vijayanagar, the fabulously beautiful capital city, is attracting scholars from all over Hindu India.

1510 (1510-1511)

Italy, 24 February 1510. Pope Julius II lifts the excommunication of Venice, imposed last year, and turns against the king of France.

Switzerland, February 1510. Matthias Schiner, the cardinal bishop of Sion, dissuades the Swiss from forming an alliance with the French against the pope.

Florence, 17 May 1510. The Florentine painter Sandro Botticelli, a pupil of Fra Lippo Lippi, dies. Among his greatest works are *The Birth of Venus* and *Primavera*. He also painted superb portraits and illustrated Dante's *Divine Comedy* with pen drawings.

India, 1510. The Portuguese explorer Alfonso de Albuquerque seizes Goa.

Scotland, 1510. The Scottish theologian John Legrand argues in favour of the use of force to bring about the spiritual conquest of non-Christian races.

Spain, 1511. Diego Columbus, the son of Christopher, recovers the rights over his father's discoveries in America which were confiscated by the Spanish crown, thus restoring his family's fortunes.

North Africa, 1511. A Spanish force occupies the island of Penon, in the bay of Algiers.

Caribbean, 1511. The first African slaves arrive in the New World. This follows the granting of authorisation, in 1503, to Nicolas de Ovando, the Spanish governor of Hispaniola *(Santo Domingo)*, for the introduction to the island of African slaves.

Caribbean, 1511. The Dominican friar Antonio de Montesinos preaches a sermon to the colonists in Hispaniola questioning the religious principles of colonial ventures. He speaks out against the right of conquest, arguing that, because Indians are true men with souls, they should not be subject to enslavement.

Caribbean, 1511. Juan de Esquivel undertakes the conquest of Jamaica.

Caribbean, 1511. Led by Diego Velazquez, the Spanish take control of the island of Cuba by force.

France, 18 October 1511. The chronicler Philippe de Commynes, a former servant of Louis XI, dies. His *Memoires* recount the reigns of Louis XI and Charles VIII.

Warlike Pope set to drive out French

Rome, 5 October 1511

Pope Julius II has now recruited England under Henry VIII as a member of his "Holy League" against France. His main allies are Spain and Venice, but two years ago it was Venice that was the main enemy (for annexing papal provinces on the Adriatic) and France which was his ally. Now he has raised the cry to "clear the Barbarians out of Italy" – meaning the French under Louis XII. They have occupied Milan since 1499, when they captured it from the Sforzas.

A protracted war in Lombardy, the Romagna and the Veneto seems inevitable, now that the papal forces have been joined by Venetian and Spanish troops and Swiss mercenaries.

Julius' strategy is to re-establish the sovereignty of the papacy in all

Pope Julius II: warlike pontiff.

its ancient territories and end the foreign domination of Italy. He is a warlike pope. He is to direct the siege of the fortress of Mirandola in person, helmeted for battle.

Persian empire grows to rival Ottomans

Persia, 1511

The Shi'ite Shah Ismail, who first claimed rule over Persia ten years ago, has conquered Khurasan and killed the Ozbeg Mohammed Shaybani. He has also installed Babur, the descendant of Tamerlane who seized Kabul seven years ago, in Samarkand. As a result of these military successes the Safavid empire now extends from the river Tigris in the west to the river Oxus in the east, where the Ozbeg tribes roam. In the west, this new Persian empire now rivals Ottoman power.

Founded as a religious order by Safi al-Din in 1301, the Safavids established themselves in eastern Azerbaijan over the next 150 years, making alliances, then falling out, with the Ak-Koyunlu, who dominated Persia.

Although three Safavid leaders, Junayd, Haydar and Ali, all died at Ak-Koyunlu hands, Ali's son Ismail eluded them and lived in hiding before leading a successful revolution in 1500. The vital military factor in Shah Ismail's success was the loyalty of the fierce Turcoman tribesmen who became known as the Qizilbash. Having decisively beaten the AkKoyunlu army at Sharur in 1501, Shah Ismail dealt with the remainder at Hamadan in 1503, gaining control of central and

"Night attack", from the "Book of Victory", by the artist Nama Zafa.

southern Persia. In 1504 he subdued the Caspian provinces of Mazandaran and Gurgan, and captured Yazd. Next came the annexation of Diyar Bakr and the pacification of the western frontier. Baghdad was captured in 1508, and thus the conquest of south-western Persia was completed.

Qizilbash influence in government has been reduced by the dismissal of a Turcoman *wakil*, and his replacement by a Persian.

Erasmus censures male stupidity

Paris, 1511

Scholars at the Sorbonne are talking excitedly about a major new contribution to humanist thought. *Praise of Folly*, which has just been published here, is (despite its title) a profoundly serious work, which nevertheless sparkles with wit and imagination. It is written by a 44-year-old Dutchman, Desiderius Erasmus, who is already well known to several French scholars since he is a prolific letter writer.

The central character of *Praise of Folly* is Folly herself, a volatile and ever-changing woman. She delivers a series of homilies against the stupidities of all kinds of men. She even castigates crabbed scholars like Erasmus himself, but her most severe censure she reserves for worldly popes and hypocritical monks. She also shows a sense of humour. "Who would marry," she asks, "if they rationally anticipated the pains and problems?" She thinks a little folly helps to make the world go round.

Erasmus advocates a practical piety which is based on the human spirit rather than religious observances. He thinks that religion is too important to be left to the theologians. Men of letters can purify the scriptures by going back to the ancient sources. They can combine their learning with faith and so achieve mystic unity with God.

He is widely travelled. Recently he spent ten months in Venice as a proof-reader for the printer Aldo Manuzio. Before that he visited scholars in other parts of Italy and in Germany.

Erasmus of Rotterdam, by Durer.

Soft light of Venice produces brilliant paintings

"Concert Champetre", by Giorgio Giorgione, who died this year of plague.

A detail from "The Transfiguration", by Giovanni Bellini (born c.1430).

Venetian crystal reliquary, c.1500.

"Judith", by Giorgione.

"Colleoni", by Andrea Verrocchio.

A Chalcedony glass bottle.

Venice, c.1511

Venice, one of the richest of the Italian city states, is flowering with a renaissance like that of Florence 60 years ago. Venetian light, which is softer and more luminous because of its lagoon, affects the character of Venetian painting, which is mainly carried out in oil rather than fresco.

Giovanni Bellini, now in his eighties, is the doyen of Venetian painters. His work for the doge's palace was destroyed by fire, but his portraits of the doges, such as Doge Loredan, are celebrated for their richness of colour glowing as if from within. Bellini is so highly prized that when the Sultan Mohammed invited him to visit Constantinople, having seen some of his portraits belonging to the Venetian ambassador, the Senate would not

let Giovanni go. They sent instead his brother, Gentile, who painted the sultan's portrait.

Bellini has introduced a new soft and atmospheric quality to his background landscapes, especially in *The Agony in the Garden* where the hills and sky are suffused with the light of daybreak. He taught this to his pupil Giorgione, who came from Treviso and showed genius at an early age. Besides religious subjects Giorgione produced easel pictures, portraits and landscapes in rich, dark, suggestive colours that combine mystery and romanticism. A good musician, he often introduced music into his pictures, as in his *Concert Champetre*. He died this year of the plague, caught from a Venetian lady with whom he was in love.

One of his assistants, who was

also a pupil of Bellini, is Tiziano Vecellio, known as Titian, whose life-size portraits and landscapes with figures show the same romantic character.

Venice has also made a great advance in its long-established craft of glassmaking. The art of making crystal glass which is abso-

lutely clear has been perfected at factories on the island of Murano, where the glass-makers are concentrated by decree. Goblets of elegant lightness, bowls and dishes, many in exquisite colour and worked into bizarre shapes, are being exported all over Europe. The secret of the process is closely guarded.

"Blackmail" charges for St Peter's

Julius' dream for the Piazza di San Pietro: will it ever become real?

Rome, 1513
Pope Julius II, now aged 70, seems determined to go down in history as the man who caused St Peter's basilica to be rebuilt in the finest style of the age. He has already laid the cornerstone, but more money is needed to get the building under way. Nothing but the best is good enough for Julius, and he has been noted during his reign for his patronage of artists like Raphael and Michelangelo.

His financial stewardship is less admired than his taste in art, though. He is relying on the sale of indulgences and the tactics of his envoys in selling them amounts to emotional blackmail, according to his critics. It was Pope Sixtus IV who extended indulgences to loved ones assumed to be suffering from their sins in purgatory in 1476. This year, in efforts to extract money for the rebuilding, papal envoys have been depicting the voices of dead parents wailing in purgatory.

More scandalous still, money is being "diverted" before it reaches Rome. Prince Albert, the archbishop of both Mainz and Magdeburg, is the worst offender. He is deeply in debt to the great German banking house, the Fuggers of Augsburg. He is paying off his debts by selling indulgences.

Top Hebrew scholar faces heresy charge

Cologne, Germany, 1513
Johann Reuchlin, a noted Hebrew scholar, is to be brought before the court of the inquisition here. The main charge against him, according to the Rhineland inquisitor, Jakob van Hochstraten, is that his latest work, the pamphlet, *Augenspiegel*, is a work of heresy.

The story behind the trial goes back to 1509. In that year Johann Pfefferkorn, a converted Jew, with the help of the Cologne Dominicans, had obtained authorisation from the Emperor Maximilian to destroy all Hebrew books except the Bible. He was frustrated in this by the opposition of the archbishop of Mainz, helped by Reuchlin.

Pfefferkorn then vented his anger against Reuchlin, alleging in print that he had accepted bribes from Jews and that other scholars had written books which Reuchlin claimed as his own. *Augenspiegel*, which argues for the preservation of Jewish literature, was Reuchlin's stinging reply.

Despite the influence of the Cologne Dominicans and the draconian powers of the Inquisition courts, Reuchlin is not without hope. The archbishop of Mainz is still a powerful friend. He is also an internationally known scholar who is particularly respected in Italy.

He first became interested in Hebrew and the Jewish mystical texts of the *Qabbalah* when visiting Pico de la Mirandola in Florence. Reuchlin's most famous work, *On the Rudiments of Hebrew*, shows how the language is essential for Christian theology.

Florida is claimed for Spanish king

North America, 8 April 1513
Juan Ponce de Leon, the Spaniard whose quest for a fabled Fountain of Youth remains unsuccessful, has discovered a land which he has claimed for the king of Spain.

The new land is believed to be an island. Because of its abundance of flowers, and the proximity of the religious feast of Pasqua de Flores, de Leon has called the territory *Florida*, Spanish for "floral".

De Leon sailed with Christopher Columbus on his second voyage to the New World in 1493. He served on the island of Hispaniola and explored Puerto Rico in 1508, becoming the island's governor in 1509. He was later removed from office through a political dispute.

Governor de Leon: a later print.

Glories of Josquin and Flemish music

Flanders, c.1512
The current reputation of Flanders as a home of musical excellence is largely due to one man, Josquin des Prez, now in his seventies and almost universally praised as Europe's greatest composer. His music synthesises the polyphony of the Flanders masters Guillaume Dufay (c.1398-1474), Antoine Busnois (c.1430-1492), and, especially, his teacher, the great Johannes Ockeghem (c.1410-1497), with the more harmonic style of Italy, where, like his fellow Fleming, Heinrich Isaac, he is much in demand from major patrons.

Josquin's works include church masses, motets, and songs in German, French and Italian.

Portugal takes Malacca

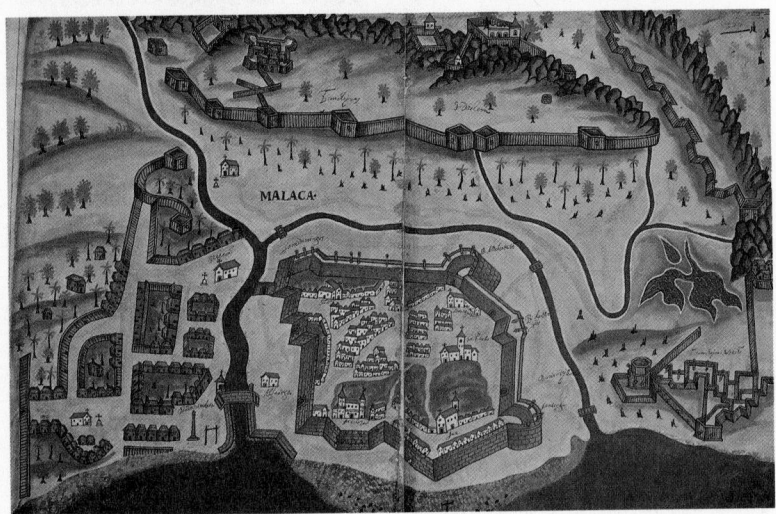

Malacca, whose capture could give Portugal control of the spice trade.

Malacca, 1511

Portugal's potential for dominating the lucrative spice trade with the east has been transformed by the operations of the brilliant naval strategist, Alfonso d'Albuquerque. With his capture of Malacca, which commands the passage from the Indian Ocean to the South China Sea, he has completed a string of naval bases and trading posts running from the Red Sea through Goa in India to the Far East.

The siege of Malacca severely strained his resources in men and ships. Because of the stiff resistance by the defenders and the problems caused by the monsoon he has been obliged to remain in the area for almost a year; during that time Goa, the city built on an island and the centre of a shipbuilding industry, which he captured only last year, almost fell to the Moslem sultan of Bijapur.

A Portuguese accountant who has been assigned to the newly established royal factory at Malacca reports: "Should anyone ask what advantage to his exchequer the king, our lord, can derive from Malacca, there is no doubt that – once the influence is finished that this ex-king of Malacca still exercises – the town is of such importance and profit that it seems to me it has no equal in the world."

The Portuguese are set to begin the regular shipment of Oriental spices to Lisbon. Cargoes will include pepper, cinammon, nutmeg and cloves.

Swiss foot-soldiers rout French at Novara

Novara, Italy, 6 June 1513

France suffered a new and crushing defeat in its struggle with Pope Leo X's Holy League today. Heavily mauled at last year's battle of Ravenna, when honours were declared even, French and Venetian forces have been routed at Novara, near Milan, where Swiss mercenaries under Cardinal Schiner took just an hour to put them to flight.

The defeat, which must surely put an end to French ambitions in Italy, has been compounded by the English invasion of northern France. Landing near Calais, they have already taken the towns of Therouanne and Tournai.

Leo X and nephews, by Raphael.

Spanish explorer discovers "South Sea"

Darien, Panama, 29 September 1513

Vasco Nunez de Balboa, the Spanish explorer, today became the first European to sight what he calls "the South Sea". Balboa and his men travelled from their base in Darien, near the Atlantic Ocean, heading west across the narrow isthmus in a gruelling 25-day journey across 45 miles of near-impenetrable jungle.

On reaching a mountain that overlooked the South Sea, Balboa climbed alone to its peak, where he prayed before calling on his men to join him. He has claimed the new sea, also known as the Pacific Ocean, for Spain.

As well as natural hazards, Balboa's 190 Spaniards and several hundred Indian slaves have had to fight off hostile natives. Armed with swords, crossbows and arquebuses, and led by a pack of bloodhounds, the expedition fought a

Balboa (a 19th-century engraving).

pitched battle against them. It was a bloody, unequal struggle, according to witnesses who tell how the big Spanish swords "hewed from one an arm, from another a leg and buttock, and the head from the body at one stroke".

Civil servant's guide to political power

Florence, 1513

In an attempt to regain favour with his former employers, a senior civil servant has written a remarkable study of political power, its uses and abuses. *The Prince*, by Niccolo Machiavelli, is the talk of Florentine political circles.

Machiavelli was 29 when he was appointed secretary to the Council of Ten, the second most important executive tier in the republic. The council handled wars (at a time when war was an almost permanent feature among the Italian city-states) and internal security. The post involved the secretary in frequent visits to Italian and foreign rulers, including the king of France, the pope and Cesare Borgia, upon whom many believe he based the prince in his book.

When the Medicis returned to Florence in 1512, Machiavelli lost his job and was exiled – urged by the Medicis to devote himself to writing a history of the republic. The secretary had walked the gilt-lined corridors of power, however, and still pined for high office; *The Prince* and three other books, including *Discourses*, are clearly designed to court favour with the Medicis. *The Prince* does not assume that princely rule is any bet-

A later impression of Machiavelli.

ter than popular "democratic" government, but it discusses at length the way in which princely power is gained and, more significantly, it analyses how power is preserved in the volatile climate of Italian politics.

The book does seem to have pleased the Medicis; however, many believe that Machiavelli's approach is too direct and blunt – and obvious in its intent.

1513 (1513-1515)

Satire mocks pleasure-seeking monks

Cologne, Germany, 1515

A brilliant new satire, *Epistolae Obscurorum Virorum* (Letters from Obscure Men), has appeared here. It is designed to help the Hebrew scholar Johann Reuchlin in his battle to escape from the clutches of the Inquisition. It is an amusing skit on the Dominican monks, deliberately written in vile Latin.

It is in the form of letters written to monks, teachers and theologians. The letter writer purports to be Ortvinus Gratius, a theologian of the University of Cologne who is one of the principal supporters of the Dominicans in their attempt to convict Reuchlin. The monks are portrayed as having more taste for earthly pleasures than for prayer. They love the wine of the Rhine more than that of the Mass. Their letters are long on coarse pleasantries and short on theological discussion. The title refers to *Letters from Illustrious Men*, written last year by humanists who support Reuchlin's cause.

There is little doubt here that the main author of the satire is Ulrich von Hutten. He comes from a wealthy Franconian noble family. He has never ceased to stress the warrior code of a nobleman of the Holy Roman empire. He is something of a hothead and has long had a reputation for ferocious anti-clericalism. Yet he is also a considerable scholar, having studied both Latin and Greek in Bologna, and is noted for the elegance and eloquence of his Latin poetry and prose.

America seen as two new continents

Europe, 1513

Following lengthy deliberations, cartographers and geographers in Europe have now reached agreement that the newly discovered lands west of the Atlantic Ocean are not in fact Asia.

A new edition of the *Geography* by the Egyptian expert Ptolemy – a popular source since its revival in 1405 – has been published, displaying the land mass as two distinct continents, situated between Europe and Asia.

Christopher Columbus was misled by the Romans' 1,400-year-old calculations, which are now known to have underestimated the circumference of the earth.

Builder of Portugal's Indies empire dies, a disappointed man

A later portrait of Albuquerque, whose service was ill-rewarded.

Goa, India, 16 December 1515

Portugal's greatest naval strategist, Alfonso d'Albuquerque, died at sea near here today, a deeply disappointed man. Despite great services to his country he fell victim to the intrigues of enemies at the Portuguese court. A few days ago he returned from the capture of Ormuz, at the mouth of the Persian Gulf, to be met at the entrance to Goa harbour by a vessel from Lisbon bearing a dispatch dismissing him as the king's viceroy in India. The blow almost certainly hastened his death. He was 62.

Albuquerque was 50 before he made his first expedition to the Indies, but he quickly perceived the need for secure bases, strategically placed to take account of sailing problems caused by seasonal wind and weather changes. Because of its small population – probably not more than a million and a half – Portugal has not been able to colonise the captured territories. Even the garrisons are partly manned by native recruits. Essentially, the system Albuquerque helped to create was to make the Portuguese middlemen in the trade between the east and Europe. It has become an immensely rewarding operation: a trading profit of 800 per cent was reported in 1512.

Priest campaigns against Spanish cruelty

Cuba, 1514

A Spanish missionary, the first priest to be ordained in the New World, has shocked his compatriots with a terrifying account of military atrocities committed during the conquest of Cuba. Bartolomeo de las Casas, who was a member of Panfilo de Narvaez' expedition in 1513, has revealed a nightmarish catalogue of torture and depravity.

His eye-witness report details the wholesale slaughter of the Indian population, sparing neither man, woman nor child. No cruelty seems to have been beyond the Spanish troops, who, as las Casas puts it, were overtaken by the Devil. Babies, torn from the breast, were smashed on rocks; others skewered on pikes. Adults, especially the nobility, were roasted alive on grid irons, or suspended from gibbets, with fires lit beneath them. Friendly Indians were butchered, while any who dared to resist were hunted without mercy by men and savage dogs.

Now las Casas has left Cuba and returned to Spain. He is publicising what he has seen, and is campaigning against the *encomienda* system, under which large estates exploit slave labour.

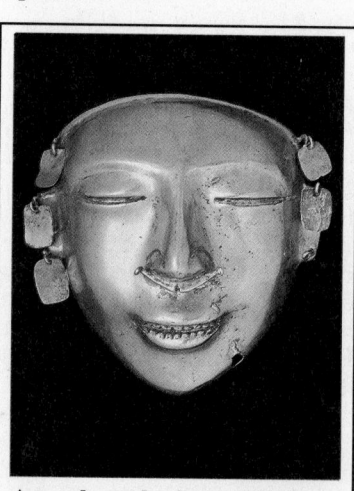

A mask made from gold by a skilled pre-conquest sculptor at Quimbaya in Colombia.

Michelangelo glorifies God and papacy in Rome

Pope Julius II, by Raphael, who has caught his brooding forcefulness.

Rome, 20 February 1513

Last month Pope Julius II was given a "Roman triumph" and hailed as "the liberator of Italy". Today he died and, like a prince, has a massive but unfinished tomb sculpted by Michelangelo awaiting him.

One of his first actions on being elected pope in 1503 was to send to Florence for Michelangelo, then 29, to design his tomb, and he resolved to rebuild St Peter's cathedral to make a worthy setting for it. His plan failed. Donato Bramante, who planned the great church, is not long for this world, and scarcely any of it is yet built – though Bramante's classical intentions can be seen in miniature in his Tempietto di San Pietro.

Michelangelo's progress on the tomb was halted by a quarrel. Refused admission to see Julius about obtaining the money he had paid for the marble, the proud sculptor left Rome for Florence and refused entreaties to return. When they were at length reconciled, in 1508, Julius asked him not to resume work on the lavish, three-storey tomb but to paint the ceiling of the Sistine Chapel, begun by Julius' uncle, Pope Sixtus IV. Michelangelo tried hard to escape the task, but Julius could not be defied.

After four years spent lying on his back, working alone behind locked doors, but constantly harassed by Julius demanding that he should work faster, Michelangelo completed his vast design. The ceil-

"The Creation of Adam", by Michelangelo, from the Sistine Chapel ceiling, unveiled last year.

A powerful portrait of Balthasar Castiglione, by Raphael.

ing, revealed last year, depicts God's creation of the world.

Meanwhile Raphael, Bramante's relative, is painting the pope's apartments with new frescoes and is to be the chief architect of St Peter's. His portrait of Julius II shows what a restless, fiery man was this patron of geniuses.

The Tempietto di San Pietro, by Donato Bramante (born 1444).

1515 (1515-1517)

Matthias Grunewald completes his Isenheim altarpiece

Isenheim, Germany, 1515
After three years of waiting, the hospital chapel at Isenheim has at last received its altarpiece, and this magnificent creation must stand as one of the contemporary world's finest artistic achievements.

Painted by Mathis Neithardt, known as Matthias Grunewald, the altarpiece has two sides. On weekdays it is a plague altar, devoted to the sick in the care of St Antony. On Sundays it is reversed to reveal four pictures, which can be varied by moveable panels, recounting the story of Christ's life.

Grunewald has been compared to Durer, but while Durer has been influenced by the Italian Renaissance, Grunewald remains rooted in the Middle Ages. The Isenheim Crucifixion, the centrepiece of the altar, stresses this attachment with the intensity of its religious feeling and the wealth of mystical symbolism that runs through the work.

"Nativity and Concert of Angels", by Matthias Grunewald (born 1455).

Sixteen-year-old Habsburg monarch adds Spain to his lands

A marble bas-relief panel from Charles V's palace in Granada in southern Spain, by Juan de Orea.

Spain, 13 March 1516
Charles of Habsburg, aged only 16, was crowned king of Spain today after making a sea voyage around the coast from Brussels. Charles succeeded to the throne on the death of his grandfather, Ferdinand II of Aragon.

The young king has inherited a troubled throne: at least one nobleman, Pedro Giron, is hinting at rebellion, and the young king's North African colonies have been lost in an insurrection. Fortunately, this son of Philip the Fair and Joanna the Mad comes to the throne with experience.

At the age of seven he became the titular ruler of the Netherlands, and was already learning Spanish and the customs of his faraway, future realm from a Spanish teacher, Luis de Vaca. His main teacher was Adrian of Utrecht, a devout ascetic. When Charles' father, Philip, died, Ferdinand locked the unfortunate Joanna away under close watch and assumed the regency. Another important influence in Charles' upbringing was Guillaume de Croy, the lord of Chievres, an ambitious nobleman who would take his bed into the young prince's room "so that he would have someone to talk to when he wakes up".

The young king shows much confidence. At 15 he told his people: "Be good and loyal subjects and I shall be a good prince to you."

French artillery smashes the Swiss

Marignano, 13 September 1515

Two years after the disaster of Novara the French have won a great victory at Marignano, in northern Italy, utterly defeating the Swiss and their leader, Cardinal Matthias Schiner. Now King Francis is marching his victorious troops towards Milan.

Francis has been determined to avenge Novara ever since he succeeded Louis XII earlier this year. An attempt to avoid a fight by offering bribes to the Swiss failed – French kings are renowned as bad payers. Forced to fight, he planned carefully. Treaties were negotiated with England, Venice and Austria, and an army of 40,000 French artillerymen and German light infantry was assembled.

After crossing the Alps and driving the Swiss back into Lombardy, Francis attempted a last-ditch negotiation at Gallarate on 8 September. He demanded the recognition of French claims to Lombardy and Milan and the withdrawal of the Swiss from Italy.

The talks failed and Cardinal Schiner declared: "I want to wash my hands and swim in French blood." Today the armies met at Marignano; the Swiss pikemen fought hard, but French artillery has sealed the victory.

King Francis on horseback, by Francois Clouet (born c.1510).

Ottoman sultan is now head of Islam

Constantinople, 1517

The destruction of the Egyptian Mameluke empire is complete, and the Ottoman sultan, Selim, has returned to Constantinople with the standard and cloak of the prophet. He is now the guardian of the holy places of Mecca, Medina and the pilgrim routes of the Hejaz, and can claim with justification to be the head of Islam.

Victory over the Persians at Chaldiran in 1514 was the first landmark of a period which has seen an extraordinary increase in Ottoman power. Diyar Bakr *(in Turkey)* was occupied the following year; the remaining eastern Anatolian cities over the next two years. Control of the high plateau of eastern Anatolia has given the Otto-

Selim beats the Persians (1514).

mans a natural rampart against invasions from the east, as well as the valuable silk routes between Tabriz, Aleppo and Bursa.

Meanwhile, the Mamelukes had entered into an uneasy alliance with the Ottomans, to defend themselves against the Portuguese who had destroyed their navy in the Red Sea in 1509.

When Selim invaded Mameluke land in 1516, the Prophet's descendants at Mecca and Kha'ir Beg in Aleppo were ready to go over to the Ottomans. The ageing Mameluke Sultan al-Ghawri nonetheless led his army to defeat at Marj Dabiq.

Tuman Bey proclaimed himself sultan in Cairo, but was defeated and hanged outside the city, leaving Selim master of Syria, Egypt and the Hejaz.

Thomas More writes "Utopia", his vision of the ideal city

Flanders, December 1516

Already it is known as the "golden little book" by the humanists for whom Thomas More, the scholarly lord chancellor of England, wrote it. *Utopia*, published this month at Louvain, is a shrewd, sometimes furious look at European society, an indictment of its harsh rulers, but also a guide – for that is how it is written – to an ideal civilisation.

Utopia is an island – More's title comes from the Greek for no place – somewhere off the New World. Its people are distanced from all the social ills of Europe and live a communal existence, sharing equally in their food, their government, clothes, houses, education and wars.

Only in their marital state is there no sharing. Thomas More is a strict monogamist, and Utopia is a deeply religious community, in which God rewards by an afterlife of immortality. Many see the book as little more than a fantasy, a humourless travelogue of a land which could only exist in the dreams of such an idealist. To some, though, the book is humorous in intent.

Thomas More is a greatly respected lawyer, an under-sheriff of the city of London, much loved by his fellow citizens who regard him as "the fairest of judges, the general patron of the poor". A man of simple tastes, he is noted for his gentle sense of fun and his interest in those around him. He was "born for friendship", according to one witness. More made his name as a writer with his condemnation of the usurper, Richard – "the pestilent serpent" – in a biography.

UTOPIAE INSVLAE FIGVRA

More's imaginary island of Utopia, somewhere off the New World, whose people live in communal harmony. Is it an idealist vision or a bitter satire on the selfish greed of the Old World?

Eastern spice: Asian sea trade

The mediaeval trade of Asia rested on several key products found in different parts of the region. From the east there came silk, porcelain, sandalwood and black pepper, which were exchanged for incense, thoroughbred horses, ivory, cotton textiles and metal goods coming from the west. Those items, and many others, travelled along two main routes: there was the caravan route along which camels, horses and mules journeyed from Damascus and Baghdad through the Persian cities of Hamadan and Nishapur to Bokhara and Samarkand in central Asia and thence across the Tarim Basin to the Great Wall of China. There was also the Indian Ocean route along which sailing vessels, dependent on the cyclical movement of monsoon winds, voyaged from the Red Sea and the Persian Gulf to India and the Straits of Malacca (between modern Malaya and Sumatra) and thence to the ports of China. During the 800 years up to the beginning of the 16th century the sea route became increasingly important.

Trade and Islam

From the seventh century the expansion of Islam brought new stimulus to the maritime trade of Asia. The rapid spread of Arab power in the first Islamic century led to the integration of Egypt, North Africa, Syria, Mesopotamia and Persia into a hugely powerful zone of consumption. At the same time those notable features of Islamic civilisation, great urban centres, emerged, their expanding demand for commodities and luxury goods spurring on the longdistance trade. Such developments were, of course, assisted by the capacity of Moslem rulers to protect merchant property, the care taken of commercial activity by Islamic law and the widespread ascendancy of the Arabic language. Up to the 16th century the expansion of this trade was inextricably linked to the steady integration of further areas – central Asia, the East African coast, India and South-East Asia – into an Islamic world system.

The growth of maritime trade led to the growth of notable port cities, for example, Kilwa on the East African coast, Aden at the mouth of the Red Sea, Siraf and later Suhar on the Persian Gulf, Daybul, Cambay and Calicut on the west coast of India, Palembang and later Malacca in South-East Asia, and Canton and Chuan-chou (Zaiton) in southern China. The ninth-century writer ibn Khurdadhbih describes, in his *Book of Roads and Provinces*, the routes followed by merchants from Siraf on their way to China; first they would call at Muscat or Suhar, then, depending on whether

fully laden or not, go to Daybul in Sind or straight to Kulam Mali in Malabar. After this they hazarded the cyclone belt of the Bay of Bengal as they headed for Kalah Bar in Malaya (probably Kedah), and then hugged the Indochinese coast, calling in at Hanoi before reaching Canton. The extent of the west Asian presence in China is suggested by the Arab historian Abu Zayd, who says that up to 120,000 Christians, Moslems, Jews and Zoroastrians were massacred when Canton was sacked by bandits in 878.

A century of change

As a result perhaps of such disturbances, and as a result too of Chinese determination to take some profit from their Indian Ocean commerce, the tenth century saw a transformation in the pattern of the long-distance trade. Merchants from the west no longer sailed all the way to China, but now stopped instead at Kalah Bar to exchange goods with merchants from further east. There is much evidence that, as China's coastal provinces developed during the Song and Yuan dynasties, there was a substantial growth in her seaborne trade. Marco Polo, who visited southern China towards the end of the 13th century, and the Arab writer ibn Battuta, who did so half a century later, were overwhelmed by the evidence of commercial wealth which they saw.

Important changes, too, were taking place at the other end of the trading area. The decline of the Mesopotamia-based Abbasid caliphate and the rise of the Egyptian Fatimid caliphs led to a shift in the destination of long-distance trade from Baghdad and Damascus to Alexandria and al-Fustat (Cairo). From the 11th century onwards Egypt and the Red Sea became the channel for an increasingly vigorous trade between the Mediterranean and the Indian Ocean, in spite of a papal ban on trade between Christians and Moslems. A recent and remarkable find, the Cairo Genizah papers, comprises the business records of Jewish merchants from 1000 to 1250, and reveals in intimate detail, for instance, trading activity linking Andalucia (Spain) and the Maghrib (Morocco) with India.

In the 15th century came a further important development with the emergence of Malacca as a great *entrepot*. Founded in 1401 at the narrowest point of the straits, it came by 1500 to be the mart where all the goods of the Asian trading region could be found. One Portuguese visitor reckoned that over 60 countries were represented at the port and over 80 languages spoken. The significance of the rise of Malacca, however, was not just com-

mercial. From the 13th century Islam had been slowly making its way in South-East Asia. For commercial reasons Malacca's rulers quickly found it convenient to adopt the faith. By 1500 their trading dominance had played an important part in establishing Islam as the major faith in much of South-East Asia.

A European intruder

In 1498 the arrival of the Portuguese in the Indian Ocean significantly altered the trade of the region. Hitherto it had been conducted in peace; the Portuguese were determined to use force to control it and in particular to take control of the fabled trade in spices to Europe. This trade which had once travelled through Alexandria and Venice was now to travel through Lisbon and Antwerp. Vasco da Gama's first voyage was quickly followed by a second, that of Pedro Cabral in 1500. Cabral informed the *zamorin* (ruler) of Calicut, the chief spice mart of the region, that he must expel all Moslems from his kingdom. Moreover, the Portuguese would seize all Arab ships and goods found at sea. On leaving Calicut with his 13 ships laden with pepper and spices, Cabral bombarded the port for two days. Thus were announced the new terms of Indian Ocean business. Within a few years the prices of oriental goods in Alexandria and Venice reached record heights.

By 1520 the extent of Portugal's achievement in the Indian Ocean and its plans for its exploitation were clear. It had captured Mozambique on the east coast of Africa (1507), Goa (1510) on the west coast of India, which was to become the headquarters of its Indian Ocean operations, Malacca (1511), which was the key to the trade of South-East and eastern Asia, and Hormuz (1515), which controlled the trade of the Persian Gulf. The Portuguese only failed before Aden (1513).

At the same time they had gone some way towards eliminating Moslem trade in the western Indian Ocean: they taxed Moslem traders by forcing them to buy naval passes. They had diverted the spice trade from the eastern Mediterranean to the Atlantic, and were beginning to build up an inter-port trade in the region which would come to embrace 50 forts and factories. Much of this early achievement must be attributed to the courage of Portuguese seaman and the leadership of Albuquerque, governor of the Indies from 1509 to his death in 1515. But it should also be noted that the great Asian land powers held naval affairs to be of little account. As long as trade still flowed the Portuguese could be tolerated.

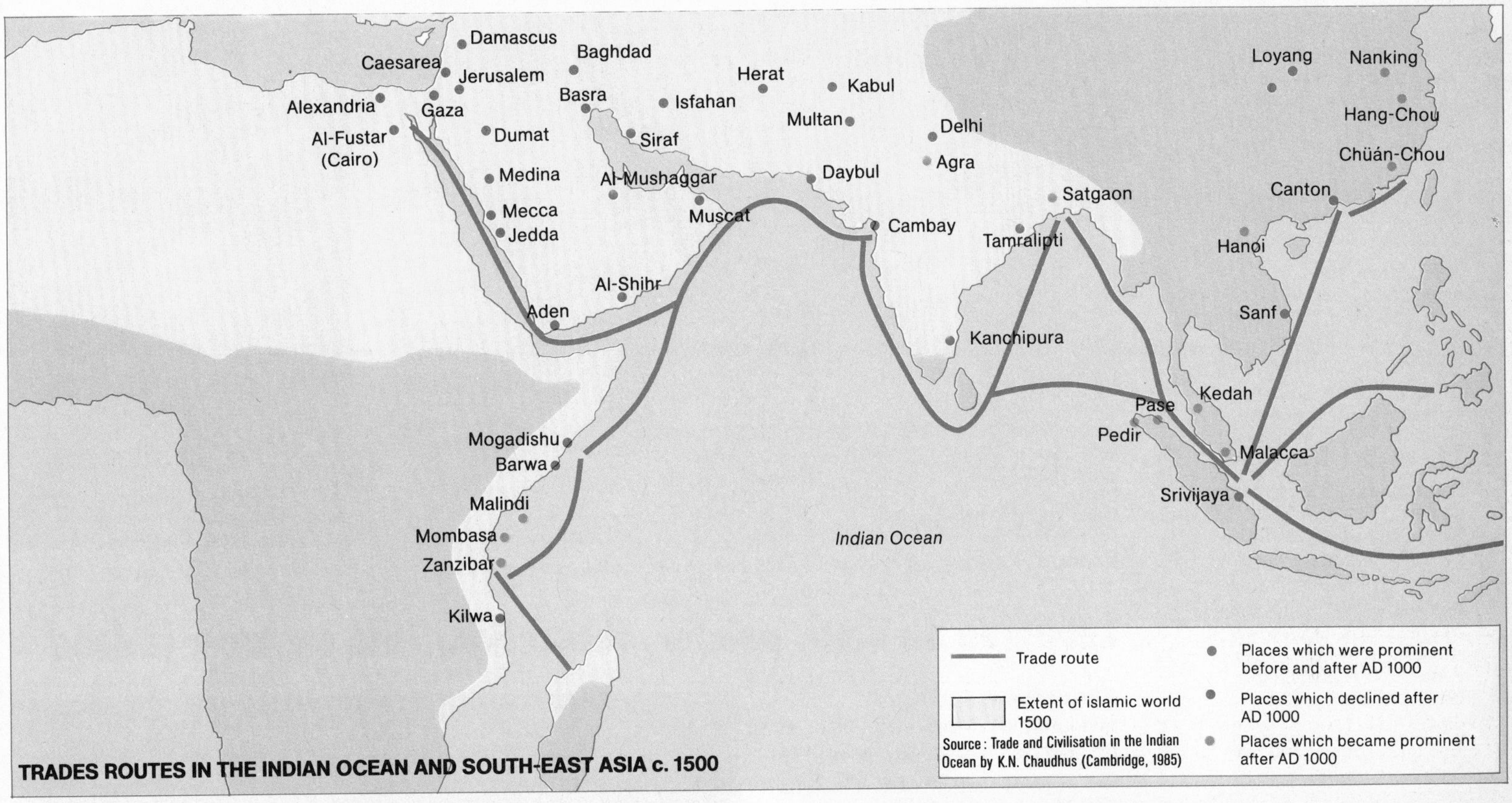

TRADES ROUTES IN THE INDIAN OCEAN AND SOUTH-EAST ASIA c. 1500

Damascus
Caesarea
Jerusalem
Baghdad
Herat
Alexandria
Gaza
Basra
Isfahan
Kabul
Al-Fustar (Cairo)
Dumat
Multan
Delhi
Siraf
Daybul
Agra
Medina
Al-Mushaggar
Mecca
Muscat
Jedda
Cambay
Satgaon
Al-Shihr
Tamralipti
Aden
Kanchipura
Loyang
Nanking
Hang-Chou
Chüan-Chou
Canton
Hanoi
Sanf
Mogadishu
Barwa
Malindi
Mombasa
Zanzibar
Kilwa
Pase
Pedir
Kedah
Malacca
Srivijaya
Indian Ocean

Trade route

Extent of islamic world 1500

Source : Trade and Civilisation in the Indian Ocean by K.N. Chaudhus (Cambridge, 1985)

Places which were prominent before and after AD 1000

Places which declined after AD 1000

Places which became prominent after AD 1000

Merchants hard at work knocking each others' prices down in an Indian port.

Indian ships announce their arrival: from an English manuscript c.1400.

From "The Book of Marvels": Beijing attracts travellers both rich and poor.

Natives gather pepper for export in the kingdom of Quilon, in southern India.

Germany, 31 October 1517. The Augustinian monk Martin Luther publishes 95 theses against the sale of indulgences granting the forgiveness of sins.

Portugal, 1517. The king of Portugal dispatches a first mission to Canton in China.

West Africa, 1517. The explorer Leo Africanus completes an expedition from Morocco to Timbuktu, Gao, Katsina, Kano and Lake Chad.

Mexico, 1517. A Spanish expedition led by Francisco Hernandez de Cordoba lands on the coast of Yucatan.

Netherlands, 1517. The Dutch humanist Erasmus founds at Louvain the College of Three Languages, to teach Latin, Greek and Hebrew.

England, 1517. English sailors complain to King Henry VIII about the growing number of French cod-fishermen in Newfoundland.

Switzerland, 1518. Zwingli receives the support of the Zurich authorities in his attempts to reform the church.

Netherlands, 1518. Erasmus publishes his *Colloquies*, strongly worded attacks on both the reformers and the religious orders.

Germany, 1518. At the diet of Augsburg, Luther refuses to retract his widely-circulated theses on indulgences.

North Africa, 1518. The Spaniards take Tlemcen, and the Barbary pirate Aruj al-Din Barbarossa is killed in the fighting.

Austria, 12 January 1519. Maximilian, Holy Roman emperor since 1493, dies at Wels Castle.

Panama, January 1519. Accused of involvement in a conspiracy, the Spanish explorer, Vasco Nunez de Balboa, is beheaded by order of his father-in-law, Pedro Arias Davila.

North Africa, 1519. The Barbary pirate Khayr al-Din Barbarossa repulses a Spanish offensive on Algiers from the nearby island of Penon.

Mexico, 24 April 1519. Envoys of the Aztec leader, Montezuma II attend the first Easter Mass to be celebrated in Central America.

France, 2 May 1519. Leonardo da Vinci, the Italian painter, sculptor, architect and engineer, dies.

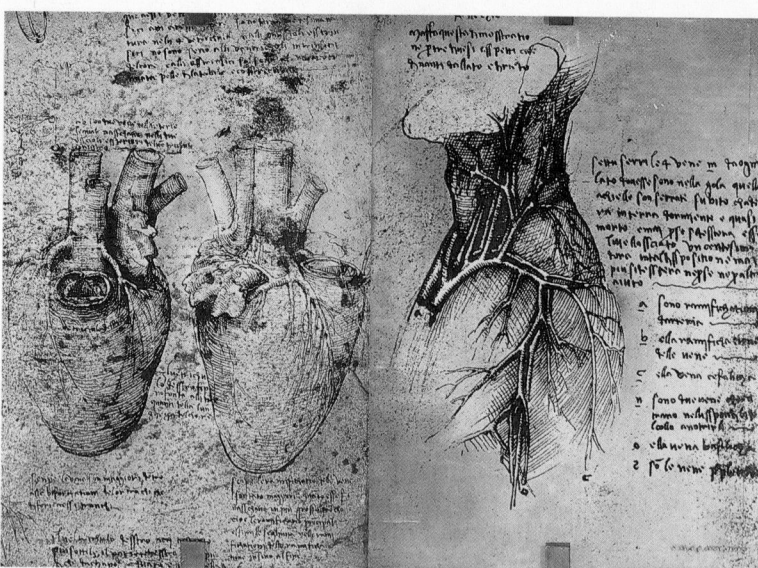 

Leonardo's anatomical drawings of the human heart and blood vessels.   *"La Gioconda", or "Mona Lisa".*

Leonardo da Vinci, painter, theoretician and engineer is dead

Cloux, France, 2 May 1519
Leonardo da Vinci died today at the age of 67. Some say he died in the arms of his last patron, King Francis of France, at whose court he has been an honoured guest for two years. Despite his magnificent achievements one of his last sayings was: "I have not laboured at my art as I should have done."

Leonardo's must be accounted the most curious mind which ever lived. His studies in the sciences as well as in the art of painting and drawing were encyclopaedic. His notebooks are said to be crammed with projects and studies for work, so much of which was left unfinished. Works that were finished have often not lasted because of the experimental methods he used.

Born illegitimate in Vinci in Tuscany, he educated himself and joined the studio of Verrocchio in Florence. At the age of 30 he left for Milan to serve the duke, Ludovico Sforza, as a fortifications engineer. At Milan he painted *The Virgin on the Rocks* and *The Last Supper* in the monastery of Santa Maria delle Grazie. This masterpiece, unfortunately, has already begun to peel.

The same happened to his battle picture for the Palazzo Vecchio in Florence, but not to the portrait of Mona (or Madonna) Lisa, wife of a Florentine merchant. He spent four years on its soft, blurred outlines attempting to paint the inner mystery of a human being. It is doubtful if he was satisfied, for when he went to France he took it with him.

"Portrait of a musician", identity unknown. Painting was just one of Leonardo's vast array of talents; he even learnt to write from left to right, which, because he was left-handed, he found more natural.

Luther nails revolt to castle door

Explorer beheaded on treason charge

Wittenberg, 31 October 1517
Martin Luther, a 34-year-old professor at the university in this pleasant little town on the banks of the Elbe, has issued a challenge to public debate on this, the eve of All Saints' Day. He has posted a list of 95 theses, mostly attacking the use of indulgences by the church, on the door of Wittenberg church. They are written in Latin and mix fine theological points with an emotional attack on the pope's men.

Luther was deeply shocked earlier this month when he saw the Dominican, Johannes Tetzel, travelling around Germany with a papal bull on a scarlet velvet cushion, auctioning indulgences like a common street pedlar. Even if the money is to be used to build the new Basilica of St Peter's in Rome, this does not justify suggesting to people that they can buy remission from their sins, according to Luther.

In one thesis he asserts that if the pope knew of his preacher's exactions he would rather have St Peter's reduced to ashes than "built with the skin, flesh and bones of his sheep". In another, he asserts that any Christian who is truly repentant is entitled to forgiveness, without any indulgences.

The 95 theses are not especially radical, or different from what many other critics of the church are saying. However, students who have been attending Luther's lectures over the last few years say that he is a most unusual man who is developing a radical theology which could easily bring him into head-on collision with the church.

Unusually for a scholar, he has no sophistication or cunning. He is open about his views and feelings. A big, tough man with disturbing eyes, he is immensely proud of his peasant blood. He is often vulgar, coarse and crude in his language and when he laughs it is long and loud and deeply. He sings tenor and plays the lute.

He was born in 1483, the son of a wealthy copper miner, in Eisleben, in Saxony. He studied nominalist philosophy at the University of Erfurt and after a dramatic experience in a thunderstorm decided to enter a convent of the Austin Friars. He studied St Augustine and fell in love with his work. In

Portrait by Lucas Cranach of the monk who has angered the Church.

A 19th century view of Luther nailing his theses to the church door.

Sale of indulgences, immediate cause of Luther's stand (19th century print).

1512, while living at Austin Friars house here, he became a doctor and professor of the university.

His lectures lay great stress on the epistles of St Paul and particularly his view that "the just shall live by faith". Luther argues that priests should not stand between men and the bible, and that faith is a gift from God. Unlike the humanists, he does not think that it can be gained by scholarship.

Panama, 1519
On the orders of his own father-in-law, the famous explorer and *conquistador* Vasco Nunez de Balboa, has been beheaded. Balboa's extraordinary career in Central America began seven years ago, when he fled from his creditors in Spain by stowing away to Santo Domingo.

Hearing from the natives of a gold-rich land washed by an unknown sea, he led 190 men into the swamps and rain-forested hills of the Panama isthmus. On 29 September 1513 he waded into the Pacific Ocean, his sword drawn in a gesture of conquest as the 67 survivors of the expedition sang the *Te Deum*. He had discovered the overland route between America's western and eastern seaboards.

The Spanish governor of Panama, Pedro Arias Davila, promptly betrothed his daughter to this bold adventurer. Father and son-in-law worked together on a series of lucrative gold hunts, but on their first disagreement Davila has had Balboa arrested and executed on a trumped-up conspiracy charge.

Vasco de Balboa: beheaded.

Death – and possible return – of Hindu critic of caste system

India, 1518
Disciples of the outspoken Hindu sage Kabir are claiming that he miraculously returned among them within hours of his death to settle a dispute about how they should pay final homage to him. True or false, the "miracle" is in keeping with Kabir's lifelong attempts to reconcile different views.

Adopted by a Moslem weaver after being abandoned by his Brahman widowed mother on a lotus leaf, Kabir worked tirelessly to reconcile Islam, in which he was brought up, with Hinduism, condemning religious sectarianism and the caste system. Readily accepted by both Islamic and Hindu worshippers, he preached the notion of a monotheistic religion stripped of idols. In Kabir's teachings God was one, whether he was called Rama or Allah.

Raphael's luminous "Madonna and Child with the Infant Baptist".

Papal court in mourning for Raphael

Rome, 6 April 1520

The papal court has been plunged into grief and mourning by the sudden, early death of Raphael, aged 37. He was friend as well as painter to two popes and was in charge of architectural and decorative work at the Vatican palace. He died of a fever on Good Friday, his birthday, having divided his possessions among his disciples.

Raphael Sanzio, the son of a painter in Urbino, studied so successfully with Perugino that people could not tell his work from that of his master. After studying the work of Leonardo and Michelangelo in Florence, he went to Rome where Julius II appointed him to decorate the Vatican apartments with great semi-circular frescoes, some of biblical scenes, some of classical antiquity, such as the philosophers of the *School of Athens*. He also drew the life-size cartoons for the tapestries to be woven for the Sistine Chapel. His secular portraits were as masterly as his serene Madonnas – that of Pope Julius was so lifelike

"St Michael and the Devil", c.1505.

that people trembled at it and that of Julius' successor, Leo X, was vividly alive. Leo sent Raphael's painting of St Michael casting out Satan to the king of France.

Lucrezia Borgia, a father's pawn, dies

Ferrara, 24 June 1519

Lucrezia Borgia, the duchess of Ferrara and daughter of Pope Alexander VI, has died, aged 39, after a life of family intrigue and several broken marriages. Though beautiful and intelligent, she was essentially a pawn in her father's many power games.

Betrothed at the age of 11 to the Spaniard Juan de Centelles, then to the more influential Don Gasparo, the count of Aversa, Lucrezia was eventually married two years later to Giovanni Sforza, the lord of Pesaro. At the age of 18 she left him to make a more politically favourable marriage to Alfonso d'Aragon, the duke of Bisceglie, with whom she fell in love. Two years later,

Never a free agent: the fair Lucretia.

when Pope Alexander was pursuing the French alliance, Alfonso became an embarrassment, and was murdered, probably on the orders of Cesare, Lucrezia's brother.

In 1499 Lucrezia was appointed governor of Spoleto, and later that year was able to buy for 80,000 ducats the castles of the Gaetani family, on the frontier between the Papal States and Naples, after they had been effectively confiscated by the pope. In 1500 Sermoneta was added to her dominions.

In 1501, after some debauched partying involving the pope, Cesare and Lucrezia, she was married for the last time to Alfonso d'Este, the duke of Ferrara. She had already fulfilled her dynastic function by having a son, Rodrigo.

New emperor is elected

Barcelona, 6 July 1519

It took the courier fewer than nine days to ride breakneck from Frankfurt across Europe to the gates of Barcelona to break the news to Charles of Spain that he had won a crucial election and would occupy the imperial throne of the Holy Roman emperor. Charles had successfully bribed the princes of Germany to cast their votes for him.

Few monarchs could move as swiftly as did Charles following the death of Maximilian of Austria in January. Within days of the news reaching the Spanish king, couriers were dispatched urgently to Germany to negotiate with the princes – all seven of whose votes were vital if Charles was to win. It was essential that he could get his bid in before his rivals.

Once the diplomatic work was under way, Charles wrote a courteous note to King Francis of France advising him of his intentions. The king's reply came quickly: "Sire, we are both courting the same lady." There were four candidates in this election: Charles,

Charles of Spain, now the emperor.

Francis, Henry VIII of England and Frederick (the Wise), the duke of Saxony. Charles was the favourite, particularly when it was known that he had borrowed freely from the Augsburg banking house of Fuggers, the biggest finance house in Europe (*see below*), who backed him in preference to Francis of France.

The bankers who won election for Charles

Augsburg, Germany, 1520

The Fuggers are king-makers; it was their money which bought Charles I of Spain the emperorship and, in return, he has given them the right to exploit silver and mercury deposits in his Central American colonies.

It was 150 years ago that Ulrich Fugger, a poor weaver, settled in Augsburg and set up a small textile business which expanded into an industry exporting fustian and buying Levantine cotton from Venice as well as dealing in spices. The industry was so successful that Ulrich was able to diversify into metals – obtaining, with a Polish partner, a monopoly of silver and copper mines in the Tyrol and much of the rest of eastern Europe.

Ulrich's financial ability was inherited by his sons who have built the House of Fugger into the most wealthy and powerful bank in Europe. Jacob Fugger II is known as "Jacob the Rich", and has the right to mint coinage in Rome as well as controlling the biggest trade net-

The Fuggers welcome the emperor.

work on the continent. Today's bankers are strictly entrepreneurial, with the Fuggers vying with their chief rivals, the Welsers – another German house – for more exploitation in the Americas, their agents acting more like *conquistadores* than businessmen. In the meantime, new and potentially even more powerful banks are developing in Italy, notably in Genoa.

Aztec king is captured

The conquest of Mexico: Cortes' army storms the town of Vera Cruz.

Mexico, November 1519

Since the arrival of a Spanish expeditionary force a few days ago, the emperor Montezuma has not been seen. The Spaniards, led by soldier-explorer Hernando Cortes, led Montezuma away after the two leaders had met in the Aztec capital of Tenochtitlan. Nine months of bloody conquest was over.

Cortes had made sure that there would be no retreat when he first landed here in quest of gold. He ordered his 700 men to burn their ships before marching inland to the high plateau of Mexico and Tenochtitlan. It was an ominous act: a decade ago Aztec seers had predicted fire in the night sky as a portent of doom.

After Cortes' sails came into sight Montezuma sent messengers with clothes fit for a god, but Cortes replied with a terrifying show of firepower. Soon he landed and took prisoners in a skirmish at Tabasco. These included a beautiful female slave named Marina, a natural linguist who quickly learned Spanish. Then, with armour, crossbows, firearms, cannon, and horses – all unknown in this country – Cortes burned a steady, bloody road uphill. His route was marked by a massacre at Cholula, but tribes long suppressed by the Aztecs flocked to support him.

Cortes found the capital a "well organised and most orderly" centre where 60,000 people trade goods daily. Alongside such order goes ritual human sacrifice, often of prisoners from tribal wars. The

Montezuma comes to meet Cortes.

premium placed upon live prisoners for sacrifice later limits the Aztecs' fighting efficiency. Montezuma met Cortes with wary courtesy, his slaves all sweeping the ground before him. Marina (now Cortes' common-law wife) translated.

Montezuma had long suspected that he was being pursued by a Spanish "god", and as the Spaniards gathered round Montezuma, stroking the emperor's arm curiously before taking him by the hand and leading him away, he must have realised that the god had caught up with him. Montezuma has not been seen in public since.

1520 (1520-1521)

Portugal becomes Europe's richest state

Shipyards and warehouses are built to cope with Lisbon's booming trade.

Portugal, c.1521
Suddenly, the king of a small country at the south-western corner of Europe has become the continent's wealthiest ruler. Sugar and spice, as well as gold from Guinea, have enabled Manuel of Portugal to build the magnificent monastery of St Jerome at Belem. Learning and artistic expression are being encouraged, and the king is subsidising the famous St Barbara College in Paris as a school for Portuguese students in France.

Sugar from Madeira is sold all over Europe, with England buying 20 tons a year. Spices from the east, shipped round the Cape, are likewise in great demand, since the growth of Turkish power in Anatolia has made the overland route unreliable for traders.

To manage his new-found wealth and his many commercial operations the king relies on Portugal's Jewish community, but now he is under pressure from Spain to expel all Jews. Manuel's stratagem is to tell the Jews that if they merely say that they have converted to Christianity they can stay on with no questions asked. One at least has refused and left; he is Abraham Zacuto, the mathematician whose

Great wealth means exotic windows.

calculations enabled Portugal to produce Europe's first navigation manual.

How long the king will remain a *cruzado* multi-millionaire is already a matter for speculation. The first pepper bought in the east for two cruzados for a quintal of 100lb sold in Lisbon for 80. The price has now dropped to 20. And the rising cost of the trading voyages is threatening to exceed returns.

Luther defies both pope and emperor

Worms, Germany, 18 April 1521
Friends of Martin Luther, the radical theologian from Wittenberg, fear for his life tonight. This evening he confronted the young emperor, Charles V, in the *Diet* of Worms, refusing to retract the views which led the pope to excommunicate him last January.

Luther's radical teaching challenges the papal claim to be the sole authority on the scriptures. He questions many of the rights of the priests and rejects the belief that bread and wine become the body and blood of Christ. He affirms Christians' personal right to faith.

The welcome of the German crowd here showed that he has touched a popular chord. The emperor fears that the revolutionary spirit may affect his power. Now that Luther has refused to retract, the diet will certainly denounce him and may even have him executed.

Catholicism adopts new ways in Kongo

Angola, 1521
Bishop Henrique, the son of King Afonso of the Kongo (Angola), has returned to his native land after 13 years in a Portuguese seminary. Portugal's contact with the Kongo goes back to 1482, when its intentions were peaceful, inspired by the desire to convert rather than conquer. Afonso became a Christian and took the throne from his usurping brother, and the Kongo became Portugal's colony.

Traders and opportunists arrived, vast areas have been depopulated by slave traders, white missionaries have behaved like rulers, and presumptions of European superiority have sullied relations between Kongolese and Portuguese. In spite of the hostility of both the Europeans and the indigenous pagans, Bishop Henrique is building a unique African Catholicism, incorporating numerous pagan elements. The Portuguese in Kongo, unable to manipulate it for their own benefit, call it heretical. However, Rome has rejected their accusations, seeing it as eccentric but orthodox.

Chivalry rules "Field of the Cloth of Gold"

A nineteenth-century view of the celebrated meeting of kings.

Guines, France, 24 June 1520
The events of the Field of the Cloth of Gold are over. Henry VIII of England and Francis of France have embraced and parted with tears in their eyes, swearing to build a chapel dedicated to Our Lady of Friendship on the spot where they met. It is not known what the political consequences of this meeting will be. The kings, attended only by their ministers, Wolsey and Bonnivet, met on 7 June and talked for several hours in a tent pitched between their two luxurious camps.

The substance of this talk remains secret, but the feeling in the English camp is that it would be better for Henry to ally himself with the Holy Roman emperor, Charles V rather than Francis. However, Francis owes Henry two million crowns because he is the guarantor of the French debt.

Everything about this encounter has smelt of money. The French pavilions were made of cloth of gold, thus giving the tournament field its name. Henry is said to have spent £15,000 – a seventh of his annual income. His tent was a two-storey palace of wood and glass. Henry appeared as Hercules; the knights jousted and fought on foot. There were banquets and dances. Chivalry ruled the field.

Explorer Magellan dies in tribal skirmish

Portuguese navigator Magellan, killed in the Philippines; from the Farnese palace in Caprarola.

Philippines, 27 April 1521
Having sailed three-quarters of the way round the world across seas hitherto unkown to Europeans, the intrepid navigator Ferdinand Magellan was killed today in a small-time tribal fight on an island in the Philippines. Earlier this month his ships dropped anchor off Cebu, where the local chief agreed to convert to Christianity and then asked Magellan to help him to conquer a tribe on the neighbouring island of Mactan. In fighting on the beach, Magellan was hit in the leg by a poisoned arrow and on his sword arm by a javelin; then, as he covered the retreat of his comrades, he was hacked to pieces with lances and scimitars.

Suleiman the Magnificent seizes Belgrade

Belgrade, August 1521
After a three-week siege Belgrade has fallen to the forces of the Ottoman sultan, Suleiman the Magnificent. The Danube is no longer a reliable line of defence, leaving both Serbia and Hungary exposed to the Ottoman advance.

With Charles V preoccupied by German problems and Luther's revolt, Hungary's pleas for help fell on deaf ears, and the defenders of Belgrade had no answer to the Ottoman mines and cannon bombardment from an island in the Danube.

When the city fell, the Hungarian inhabitants were massacred and the Serbs taken to Istanbul as prisoners. The Venetians are anxiously negotiating peace with Suleiman.

A Turkish view of the Belgrade siege.

Fierce fighting rocks capital of Aztecs

Tenochtitlan, Mexico, 1520
When Montezuma appeared on the roof of his palace with one of his lieutenants, telling his people not to resist the Spaniards, he was greeted with abuse followed by rocks and arrows. The emperor himself was now in irons. His people had scant sympathy for him; they were furious about the latest Spanish atrocity.

The Spaniards had told people to go to a temple courtyard for a religious festival. They then massacred them all without warning. This has unleashed general warfare in which the Mexicans, armed with bows, have besieged their own capital, cutting off the fresh water.

Cortes has been absent throughout, on a campaign to defeat a punitive Spanish column sent after him by the Cuban authorities. There is word that he has won this battle. He left control of the Aztecs to his deputy, Pedro de Alvarado.

A bloody scene as the Spaniards go into action against Montezuma's people.

1521 (1521-1523)

Aztec capital finally falls to the Spanish

A Spanish manuscript showing Montezuma wearing his royal Quezal feathers.

Tenochtitlan, Mexico, 1521
Since the siege of Tenochtitlan last year there has been general warfare in Mexico between Cortes and the Aztecs. Montezuma died in captivity and Cortes returned to lift the siege. As he led his people out, they were ambushed and many were killed. On their way to the coast they wiped out another village and left an epidemic of smallpox.

Now, almost a year later, Cortes has returned, probably with official Spanish blessing. This time there was tougher resistance. The Aztecs have exchanged formal war procedures for guerrilla tactics. This bitter campaign has been fought in boats across lakes and along canals, and ashore among city streets. Aztecs beheaded not only Spanish prisoners but their horses as well, displaying the heads of both on the same rack. After a long siege in which they were deprived of drinking water, the Aztecs surrendered their capital a second time. Now attempts will be made to convert them to Christianity.

Bitter German knights become bandits

Germany, April 1523
The revolt of the small-landowning German knights is over, their forces scattered at Landstuhl, their leaders fled. But a group of Franconian knights including Gotz von Berlichingen have become bandits, terrorising the country near Nuremberg.

Changes in the art of war, with growing emphasis on firearms and artillery, and the use of mercenaries deprived the knights of much of their power. Meanwhile the German princes have been building their political influence through councils and chancelleries.

Knights like Ulrich von Hutten and Franz von Sickingen tried to form a military arm for Luther's revolt against the church, but Luther rejected them.

Von Hutten, leader of the knights' rebellion, is a renowned humanist scholar; but he failed to enlist the support of Luther for a military revolt against the Roman church.

New religious sect retreats from world

Germany, c.1523
As the Lutheran Reformation takes hold, new prophets appear and new religious sects proliferate. The Anabaptists, an unworldly group, are proving more attractive than most.

Anabaptism appears to have started among the Zurich disciples of Zwingli, who had debated the validity of infant baptism. It also owes something to the radical ideas of Carlstadt and Munzer. Led by Conrad Grebel, Balthasar Hubmaier and Felix Mantz, the Anabaptists go further, insisting that only true adult believers should be baptised, and that they should renounce popish worship and political affairs and not bear arms.

The first coherent Anabaptist movements have grown up among the peasantry round Zurich, where they are effectively withdrawing into communities of saints.

Treaty of Moscow ends ten years' war

Moscow, 14 September 1522
The conflict over Lithuanian Smolensk officially ended today with an armistice conceding control of the town to the grand prince of Moscow, Vasily III. The five-year armistice treaty, signed in Moscow today, ends ten years of hostilities between the Muscovites and their Polish-Lithuanian enemies under Sigismund.

The treaty is a triumph for Prince Vasily. His forces – fighting alongside Lithuanian rebels led by Prince Mikhail Glinsky – only gained control of Smolensk eight years ago after two bloody but abortive previous attempts to take it.

Vasily, who styles himself "emperor", now plans to build up Smolensk, strategically placed on the banks of the Dnieper, as the pivot of his western defensive system. The treaty is also a diplomatic coup for Vasily. His defensive alliance in 1514 with Sigismund's western neighbour, the Holy Roman Emperor Maximilian, created papal concern about the conflict and brought pressure from Rome on Sigismund to settle.

Magellan's ship sails round world

Spain, 6 September 1522

Of the fleet of five vessels with which Ferdinand Magellan set sail from Seville three years ago, just one has returned; and of the 265 men aboard, only 15 have survived. But although their leader was not among them, the survivors, and their battered *Vittoria,* have made history by sailing round the world.

Magellan, who planned the expedition for Charles of Spain, was Portuguese, but fell out of favour in Lisbon after years of service in the Indies. He became a Spanish citizen and persuaded Charles that the Portuguese domination of the spice trade with the east, round the Cape of Good Hope, could be broken by ships sailing west to find a passage round South America.

Sailing south-west, Magellan steered clear of the coast of Brazil, where the Portuguese were established. He put in at the River Plate and further south, at Port St Julian. There the expedition encountered a race of primitive giants, whom Magellan named *Patagonians* (Big Feet). Mutiny broke out as the ships sailed deeper into unknown waters. Magellan crushed it and, as is customary, hanged the ringleaders. Further south, on 21 October, a year after leaving Seville, Magellan rounded what he called the Cape of the Eleven Thousand Virgins and found himself at the

A heavenly spirit guides Magellan's ship through the monster-infested seas.

eastern end of the long-sought passage. The channel ran through a maze of reefs, with snow-clad mountains on either side. He lost two ships, one wrecked by the violent winds, the other through desertion. After 38 days he passed a place which, from its many fires, he called Tierra del Fuego, and emerged into the Pacific Ocean. For 98 days the explorers sailed west, running out of food and water and being forced to eat rats.

When they made landfall in the Philippines and Magellan died in a tribal affray, the voyage was still only half completed. Command of the remnants of the fleet fell upon the Spanish navigator, Sebastian del Cano, who set sail with only two ships remaining. In the Moluccas, they traded their merchandise for spices; then, since nobody cared to face the dangers of Magellan's Straits again, they set out across waters where Portuguese merchantmen operated. One ship, the *Trinidad,* was soon seized. Del Cano took the other across the Indian Ocean and round the Cape to Seville and safety with the precious cargo.

Spain, 1522

It is a measure of the achievement of the late Ferdinand Magellan's fleet that when it set out on its epic voyage around the world three years ago there were those who believed that the journey would only take a few days.

Not only did people have no idea of the distance involved, but almost every aspect of the voyage was shrouded in ignorance. In mid-Pacific, for example, an attempt was made to measure the depths of the ocean for the first time. But after paying out a line to 1,300 feet they failed to reach the bottom.

His navigational aids weren't much more use. Although he took 21 quadrants, 18 sandglasses, 23 charts and 37 compass needles by the time he reached the Philippines he was over 3,000 miles away from where he thought he was.

On the plus side he was aided by current developments in naval technology. Ships are now heavier with three or four masts and a variety of square and lateen sails to take advantage of winds from all directions. There have also been improvements in the design of hulls which are built up on a wooden skeleton to which planking is attached, instead of filling-in a framework, making for greater strength and durability.

Leniency sets Spain on path to peace

Spain, 1523

Signs of stability are beginning to return to Spain after three years of civil unrest which severely undermined the authority of its king, the Holy Roman Emperor Charles V. His return to Spain with a general pardon, plus a decision not to withdraw privileges from cities that joined the rebels' *santa junta,* has eased tension.

At one point the Castilian rebels, protesting against both high taxes and top jobs going to Charles' foreign advisers, appeared to have control of Spain, with the revolt spreading to Catalonia and Andalucia. But their junta collapsed after a split between rebel leaders.

Luther translates Bible into German for the common people

Germany, September 1522

Martin Luther, who has been in refuge in the castle here since his denunciation by the *Diet* of Worms last year, has begun his most ambitious work. He is translating the Bible into German. In a few years' time Germans who do not understand Latin will be able to read the Bible and, thanks to the boom in new printing presses, they will be able to buy it relatively cheaply.

Although he is a university professor Luther has always written in plain language. He comes from peasant stock himself, and he makes sure that he is in tune with today's language by listening to the phrases the people use in the marketplace. His Bible is thrilling narrative, not dull theology.

The bottomless pit: woodcut from the first edition of Luther's Bible (1534).

Hero of Swedish independence made king

Sweden, 6 June 1523

The architect of Sweden's independence, Gustav Vasa, has been elected king of Sweden by the *Diet*, the Swedish parliament, in Stockholm today.

King Gustav, who for two years led the successful revolt against the king of Denmark, Christian II, now plans to take Sweden out of the Danish-controlled Kalmar Union which has united Norway, Sweden and Denmark for the last 144 years.

King Gustav is also planning to fill the power vacuum left in the Baltic by Denmark's defeat and its internal problems by building up a strong Swedish fleet of warships to protect its commercial interests.

Internally, King Gustav plans a series of far-reaching reforms to modernise the administration. Brought up at the court of Sten Sture, the old regent of Sweden, he has strong ideas on how the country can be governed more effectively. He plans, wherever possible, to replace nobles in local government with civil servants, answerable and loyal to the crown.

One early task will be to fill vacant bishoprics. The new king has Lutheran leanings and wants candidates who favour church reform. This will be hardest to impose in

A 1560 relief of King Gustav Vasa.

rural Sweden where Lutheranism is relatively unknown. Here the king, who raised his peasant army at Dalarna to fight the Danes, will be relying on popular support.

New history records daily life in Egypt

Egypt, 1524

An Egyptian historian, Mohammed ben Iyas, known as ibn Iyas, has published a massive history of his people, detailing the decline of the Mameluke dynasty and early years of rule by the Ottoman Turks.

Ibn Iyas' great work, which is entitled *Bada'i al zuhur fi waka'i al-duhur*, covers Egypt's past from the Pharoahs onwards. The early history is covered quite quickly, but from the Mamelukes onwards ibn Iyas adds more and more detail.

As an intimate of the Egyptian government ibn Iyas is able to offer eye-witness accounts of the more recent events. Among the wealth of fascinating material are his inside reports of court life, revelations of notorious scandals, biographies of the famous, and records of prices and market trends.

Celibate sect stirs church to reform

Italy, c.1524

The work which a new religious order called the Theatines does for the community is changing many ideas within the Church of Rome. The men who founded the new order, Gian Pietro Carafa and Gaetano di Thiene, are dedicated to the relief of human suffering. Formerly leaders of the Oratory of Divine Love, di Thiene and Carafa are attempting to persuade the church — by their own examples — to improve the training of clerics, and argue that priests should live in their parishes.

The Theatines' lives are made up of poverty, celibacy and work in schools, hospitals, orphanages and women's hostels. The puritanism of the order has bred a new kind of bishop to continue the reforms of these saintly founders.

Papacy is back in the Medici family

Rome, 19 November 1523

With a sigh of relief, the College of Cardinals has chosen Giulio de Medici to succeed Adrian VI as pope. He is the second member of his family to assume the papacy.

Adrian VI, who was of Flemish extraction, was an austere and spiritual man, whose pontificate lasted for less than two years. His successor, who has taken the name Clement VII, can be expected to resume the traditions of his cousin, Leo X, a notable patron of artists like Raphael and Michelangelo.

Clement VII, while he will hardly ignore his family interests, is understood to be keen to keep the papacy independent. He also wants to reform the Curia.

Clement VII, depicted by Raphael.

The perfect knight is killed in battle

Spain, 25 April 1524

Pierre du Terrail, the chevalier de Bayard, was known throughout Europe as an exemplar of chivalry and honour. Tonight he is dead — shot in the back by a Spanish *arquebusier* (infantryman armed with a gun) during a battle between his French troops and the imperial army. Refusing to leave the field, he was captured and died in enemy hands. This "fearless and blameless knight" appeared to many as an incarnation of the days of King Arthur's Camelot. He was a saintly figure who scorned money and material comforts and would never abuse a conquered enemy, and his tragic death is widely mourned.

Pizarro's mercenaries thwarted in Peru

What they wanted: ceremonial gold two-spouted huaco (water pot) from Peru.

Panama, 1524

The search for an empire on the South Sea coast by two prominent Spanish citizens of Panama is being temporarily abandoned after becoming bogged down in Peru. The expedition leaders are Francisco Pizarro, a soldier of fortune in the Indies since 1502, and his comrade, Diego de Almagro. The wealthy Pizarro was with Balboa when they discovered the South Sea.

Pizarro says that he will try again. The expedition includes a priest who represents the operation's banker together with a judge, 80 men and four horses.

Two years ago a Spanish sailor, Pascual de Andagoya, safely negotiated this mysterious coast as he searched for an exotic and fabulously rich tribe called the *Viru* or *Peru*.

Andagoya's ships now supply the new expedition, which is encamped at a place known as "Port of Hunger". Nothing of value has been found in the area, but Almagro has lost an eye in a skirmish with local Indians.

Although illiterate and a poor horseman, Pizarro is one of Panama's richest men, a middle-aged bachelor of simple habits. After a lifetime of jungle warfare he is bored without adventure.

His soldiers include some professional mercenaries, hardened by European campaigns, but most are the adventurous younger sons of Spain's grandees. In Spain, an ambitious youngsters will usually get ahead through sword-play or the "right" marriage. Pizaro's adventurous youngsters may find a shortage of suitable brides in the largely Indian inhabited mountains of Peru, however.

Warriors, from a Peruvian cloth.

Italian explores coasts of North America

America, 17 April 1524

Sailing under the French flag, the Italian explorer Giovanni da Verrazzano has landed in the New World (*at Cape Breton*). He first sighted land (*Cape Fear*) on 1 March, and has sailed some 200 miles up and down the coast. As well as seeking a passage through to the Pacific Ocean Verrazzano has explored the fertile terrain and made some contact with the native inhabitants who, he says, "are clad in feathers ... of diverse colours".

Among his discoveries, at the northernmost extent of his voyage, is "a very pleasant place, situated amongst certain little steep hills; from amidst the hills there runs down into the sea a great stream of water" (*New York*). This stream, which he has explored in a small boat, is easily navigable. Its mouth is "very deep, and from the sea to the mouth of same, with the tide, which we found to rise eight feet, any great vessel laden may pass up". Verrazzano began his voyage

Verrazzano, who found a deep river.

in the autumn of 1523. Of his four ships, two were lost in a storm. The survivors put into an English port for repairs, then proceeded along the coast of Spain, on which they made a profitable raid.

One ship took the booty back to France while Verrazzano went on to the New World in the other, *La Dauphine*.

Missionaries aim to speed second coming

Spain, 1523

An evangelistic team of Franciscan friars is expected to leave Spain in the next few months to found a Christian mission in Mexico. The proposal has the enthusiastic support of the Spanish king, Charles, and his people. Most devout Christians believe that the second coming cannot happen before the conversion or defeat of all pagans. In the recent past, Islamic heresy has been defeated in Iberia. Spain's discovery of the New World (and more pagans) is seen now as divine intervention. The theory is a particular favourite of the brown friars, who have chosen a team of men known as "The Twelve" to convert the Aztecs to a god of love.

A later image of a friar's attempt to convert an Aztec prince.

1524 (1524-1525)

Persia, 23 May 1524. Shah Ismail dies and is succeeded by his ten-year-old son, Tahmasp.

Egypt, 1524. A rebellion by Ahmed Pasha against Ottoman rule, established in Egypt in 1517, is put down.

Japan, 1524. Hojo Ujitsuna attacks and captures Edo castle. Followers of the Nichiren sect of Buddhism are expelled from Edo.

Germany, 1524. Led by the theologian Thomas Munzer, the peasants in southern Germany rise up and demand the abolition of feudal dues, serfdom and tithes.

Switzerland, 1524. The painter Hans Holbein the Elder dies.

Prussia, 8 April 1525. Albert von Brandenburg, the leader of the Teutonic Order, assumes the title "Duke of Prussia" and passes the first laws of the Protestant church, making Prussia a Protestant state.

Germany, 7 May 1525. The peasants' revolt is quelled. Thomas Munzer, its leader, is imprisoned and beheaded.

Germany, 19 July 1525. The Catholic princes of the north form the Dessau League to fight the Reformation.

Portugal, 21 August 1525. Estavao Gomes returns home after a year's exploration of the east coast of North America. He failed to find a clear waterway through to Asia.

Caribbean, 1525. The Welsers, an Augsburg banking family, establish a commercial and financial agency in Santo Domingo.

Spain, 1525. A conference at Badajoz confirms the 1494 treaty of Tordesillas, by which Spain and Portugal divided up the New World.

Spain, 1525. The last Spanish Moors, working on the great estates of the Valencian plains, are expelled.

Peru, 1525. On the death of the Inca emperor, Huayna Capac, the kingdom is divided between his two sons, Huascar and Atahualpa.

Germany, 30 December 1525. Jacob Fugger II (the Rich), financier to the Emperors Maximilian and Charles V, dies. Based largely on mining and the control of the copper market, the vast Fugger financial empire stretches from Lisbon in Portugal to Cracow in Poland and from the Baltic to the Mediterranean.

Revolt fired by Luther crushed by princes

One of the peasants' protests was against the alleged excesses of the Papacy.

Germany, 7 May 1525
The German peasant revolt has been crushed at Frankenhausen with the massacre of many thousands. German princes have been increasingly worried by the uprisings, which began last year in Bavaria and spread rapidly to Hesse, Franconia, Thuringia, Saxony and the Tyrol. The princes have acted determinedly and today one radical, Thomas Munzer, was beheaded.

The revolt was not a concerted movement so much as a series of local uprisings against oppression by princes, landlords and the church. It was inspired in part by Martin Luther's teachings and by radical Christian communities like the one set up at Allstedt in 1523 based on common ownership.

Some peasant leaders did get as far as drawing up a manifesto at Memmingen. It proposed the abolition of serfdom, the reduction of tithes and the right to choose and expel pastors. It was a programme radical enough to drive the princes to this month's repression.

Luther condemns peasants' uprising

Judgement and execution follow the bloodshed of the rebellion.

Germany, 1525
Martin Luther seems to have turned against the series of peasant uprisings which have been sweeping this country for more than a year. Luther's teachings have been one of the main causes of the revolts. Peasant leaders have been encouraged to call for the right to choose their own pastor, to oppose oppression by landlords and to win back former common land.

Luther supports many of their aims, but he was deeply shocked by a murder at Weinsberg, when peasants speared the count of Helfenstein in front of his wife and child. Luther has denounced them in a four-page tract, *Against the Murdering Thieving Hordes of Peasants*. "You cannot meet a rebel with reason," he wrote. "Your best answer is punch him in the face until he has a bloody nose."

Vasco da Gama, a fighter who won the Indies for Portugal, dies

India, 25 December 1524
Vasco da Gama, recalled from retirement by King John of Portugal to replace an incompetent viceroy in the Indies, died today at Calicut only three months after his arrival. He was 64.

After his epoch-making voyage to India round the Cape of Good Hope almost 30 years ago, da Gama spent five years engaged in trade and armed raids in the Indies. He put down rebellions with unbridled ferocity, on one occasion sailing from Calicut to Cochin "doing all the harm he could on the way to all he found at sea". He discovered the Seychelles Islands and, sailing as admiral of the Indian seas, he discovered and named the Admiralty Islands.

Retiring to Evora, the residence of the Portuguese court, he continued to advise the king on Indian affairs. He was created count of Vidigueira, with special privileges of civil and criminal jurisdiction and church patronage.

Da Gama was born in 1460, the year that Henry the Navigator died. It was Henry's enthusiasm for maritime exploration that gave Portugal the skills and experience vital for da Gama's expedition to discover the sea route to India. Da Gama had already proved himself as a young man fighting in the wars against Castile.

Vasco da Gama (16th century).

474

French king captured after Pavia disaster

Lannoy's use of the arquebus was the decisive factor in the battle of Pavia.

Italy, 24 February 1525
The French army has been utterly defeated at Pavia in Lombardy. King Francis had his horse shot from under him by an *arquebus* (a kind of gun) and tonight he is being held captive by Lannoy, the viceroy of Naples.

He has certainly lost his war with the Emperor Charles V for supremacy in Europe. The next logical step will be for Charles to force him into signing a humiliating peace treaty.

This disaster for the French began last autumn when Francis, with an army of French and Italian infantry, German and Swiss mercenaries, and a strong train of artillery, laid siege to Pavia.

At first the siege went well; the guns broke down the defences and the king's regiments stormed into

the breaches. But Antonio de Leyva, the Spanish governor of the town, had built new fortifications inside the walls, and the French were routed by the defenders.

They retreated to mount a classic siege throughout the winter. Francis, reinforced by Venetian troops, became sure of victory as the town ran short of food and ammunition.

But the imperial forces had been gathering at the nearby town of Lodi, and when they marched on Pavia earlier this month Francis found himself caught between the anvil of Pavia and the hammer of the attacking imperial army.

Pope Clement VII tried to mediate, but failed; battle was joined before first light this morning. At first the French guns gave Francis the advantage, but, believing in chivalry rather than guns, he ordered them to cease fire.

He then led his knights in a disorganised charge without waiting for the infantry. In the shambles that ensued 6,000 French died and their king, fighting on foot, his face bloodied, surrendered his sword.

King Francis: misguided chivalry led to his present captivity.

Pavia marks a change in the face of war

Europe, 1525
The firearms which killed King Francis' horse and destroyed the French army at the battle of Pavia are part of the revolution in military arms and strategy which is rapidly changing warfare in Europe as armies are modernised.

After Pavia, armoured cavalry can no longer be regarded as the rulers of the battlefield. The day of the knight in armour is over. New tactics are already being developed for mounted troops using the new carbines and horse pistols.

Perhaps the greatest changes can be seen in siege warfare where the *trace italienne*, a circuit of low, thick walls punctuated by square bastions, is replacing the high thin walls of the Middle Ages. These new defences, developed in the long-drawn-out Italian wars, are designed to absorb the punishment of the heavy siege guns which are now part of every successful army.

The adoption of this bastion defence is changing the entire pattern of warfare because the cities protected by this method can no longer be taken by the traditional methods of blowing a hole in the walls and pouring infantry through the breach. Now towns have to be encircled by siegeworks and batteries

No armour for this German soldier.

and starved or frightened into submission. Warfare is becoming more and more a matter of engineering and logistics.

At sea, too, the advent of the big gun has brought great changes. No longer do ships ram and board each other, but pound each other with formidable arrays of guns firing through ports in the ships' sides. The first such specialised gunship was built in England 12 years ago. It has set a pattern which all maritime nations must follow or face inevitable defeat.

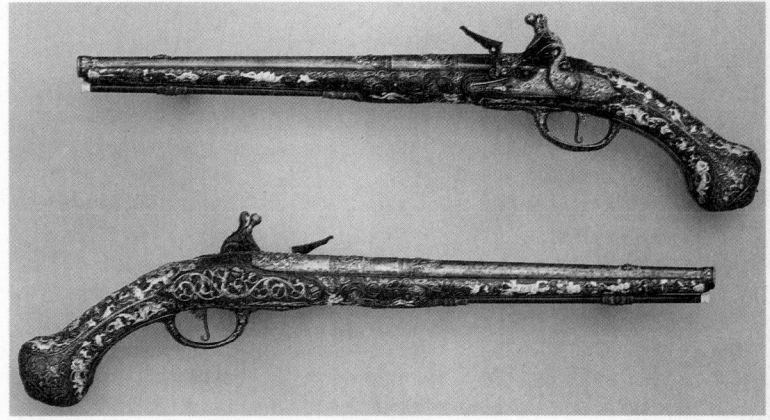

A pair of pistols: beautiful workmanship masks instruments of death.

Swiss rebel against church as a simple service replaces Mass

Zurich, 16 April 1525
This small Swiss town is now the focus of the breakaway movement from the church. Local magistrates have just banned the Roman Mass, and today the radical preacher Ulrich Zwingli held an alternative form of Holy Communion. It was

a service of great simplicity with neither music nor singing. Zwingli presided over a table laid with beakers and wooden vessels. He served the congregation first, himself afterwards.

Zwingli was inspired by the humanist Erasmus, and by Luther,

but he has proved more radical than either. Although an indifferent preacher with a weak voice, he has acquired a huge following. His tough-minded emphasis on simplicity and independence from Rome have a strong appeal for the mountain peoples of Switzerland.

Reformation: a logical consequence

In 1517 Luther produced his 95 theses criticising the established church and so, on the traditional interpretation, unleashed the Reformation. The reality was more complex. Criticism of the church had been gathering force for over a century before Luther. Some critics, notably the followers of John Wyclif (the Lollards) and Jan Hus, had been branded as heretics, but most had remained within the church, seeking change from inside. The restatement of the Catholic position, culminating in the Council of Trent (1545-63), was not simply a response to the Protestant attack, as the term "Counter-reformation" implies, but continued a process of self-examination which had begun long before Luther.

The gathering storm

Late-mediaeval criticism of the church had numerous strands. One of the most visible, because taken up on a political level, was a marked anti-papalism, growing out of the tensions generated by the great schism. Alongside this was a more general anti-clericalism, in part prompted by the acknowledged low standards of many of the parish clergy, but also possessing an ideological dimension. The tendency in the Middle Ages had been to reduce the role of the laity to that of passive consumer, unable to achieve salvation except through participation in rituals controlled by the church. By the 15th century this was producing something of a backlash among the more educated sections of society, in the form of greater emphasis on personal piety and private devotion. At the same time, closer study of the Bible was revealing the extent to which the simplicity of the apostolic church had been overlaid by later accretions, and prompting a desire to return to the ways of the primitive church.

Reformers within the church were also uneasy about various manifestations of popular religion. The cult of saints and their relics seemed to some commentators not only displeasing in itself (miracle stories often showed the saints in rather unseemly rivalry for the attention of supplicants, for instance), but to be drawing attention away from Christ. The strong magical element in such beliefs was also unpopular with purists, who, while not denying the power of God to work miracles, felt uncomfortable about attributing such powers to relics, let alone man-made images.

Luther was thus operating within a context where criticism of the church was commonplace, even, within limits, respectable. As with Wyclif in the 14th century, it was to be Luther's doctrinal views, rather than his criticism of the church as an institution, which in the end led him to be regarded as a heretic.

Luther: heir or heretic?

Luther himself never considered his ideas to be anti-Catholic. He justified his denial of transubstantiation (the doctrine that, at the moment of consecration by the priest, the bread and wine become the body and blood of Christ) as a return to earlier Christian teaching. Luther accepted the real presence of Christ, but argued that the bread and wine co-existed with the body and blood, just as hot iron holds fire. This divided him not only from the Catholics but from subsequent reformers, most of whom went further and insisted that the bread and wine were merely symbolic or commemorative.

In other respects, Luther could claim to be developing ideas which had been part of academic discussion throughout the Middle Ages. A central plank of his theology was his belief in justification by faith alone. For him, salvation was not something to be achieved through quality of life, expressed in good works and prayer, but through faith – and this was seen not as coming from the individual's own efforts, but rather as a free gift of divine grace. This did not, as the reformers were anxious to point out, end the need for charity as an expression of Christian virtue, but the implications of charity changed. The recipient of Protestant charity no longer had something of value (prayers for the salvation of the donor) to give in return, and the relationship of donor and recipient became less personal and less equal.

Justification by faith also had the effect of emphasising the power and divinity, rather than the suffering and humanity, of Christ – something implicit also in the doctrine of predestination, which was most fully developed by John Calvin and his followers. This taught that an individual's salvation, or otherwise, was foreknown to God and not a matter of human free will. Since everyone was either saved or damned, belief in predestination did away with the need for purgatory as a half-way house where sinners were cleansed of sin through suffering and made fit for heaven. The great late mediaeval edifice of prayers for the dead, designed to help souls through purgatory, was swept away.

Predestination had had its mediaeval apologists, and justification by faith could still command some Catholic sympathies as late as the mid 16th century, when Cardinal Pole left the Council of Trent rather than define his own views, which seem to have been close to Luther's. Another issue which initially spanned the doctrinal divide was the question of where authority resided. Most Protestant reformers took God's word revealed in the Bible as their religious blueprint. This approach was not necessarily fundamentalist, but it rejected any practices which seemed contrary to biblical teaching, even when sanctioned by long usage. But the Council of Trent ruled that scripture and tradition had equal validity, and in doing so turned its back on the humanist traditions of the 15th century.

A blurred divide

As this suggests, Protestant dissent did have an influence on the way in which Catholicism sought to define itself. Although in some areas the church tacitly accepted earlier criticism – as in its growing tendency to see the saints as examples to be followed, rather than great miracle-workers – elsewhere the identification of dissent with heresy led it to reject developments which might otherwise have been acceptable. An early example was the way in which the Lollard emphasis on Bible reading made vernacular translations of the Bible suspect, although the Council of Trent did not, in the event, outlaw them. The threat posed by heresy may also have made it easier for the papacy to reassert its supremacy: the decisions at Trent produced a long period of papal absolutism in matters of faith.

On some issues the Protestant and Catholic sides responded similarly. Both held similar views on witchcraft, for instance. The established Protestant churches also tended to be at least as intolerant of dissent as the Catholic Church. One manifestation of this was a rooted mistrust of mystics, whose claim to be in direct communion with God always seemed to threaten the church's authority. Even doctrinal divisions could still sometimes blur. In spite of Trent, the Catholic Church never became entirely monolithic and the Protestant churches were more dramatically divided. The sheer complexity of the theological issues must also have brought some unintentional confusions. An early example of the difficulties of definition was the Englishman Reginald Peacock, who wrote a major work against the Lollards, only to see it burnt by his clerical superiors for heresy. If scholars found the dividing line tricky to locate, the uneducated and inarticulate must have found it impossible. Even after reformers on both sides had accepted the need for an educated clergy able to instruct the laity, misbelief rather than disbelief remained a problem.

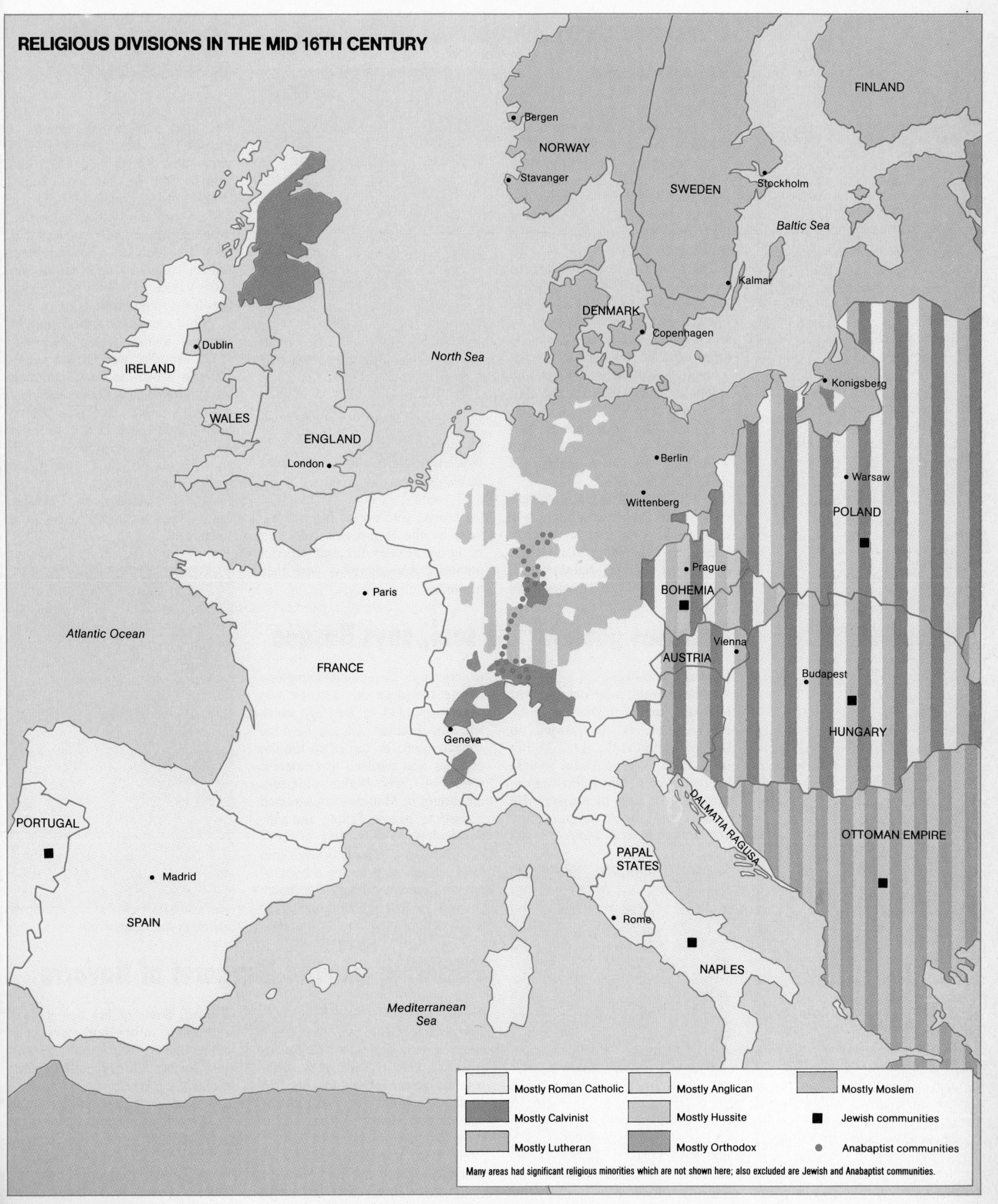

RELIGIOUS DIVISIONS IN THE MID 16TH CENTURY

FINLAND

Bergen

NORWAY

SWEDEN

Stockholm

Stavanger

Baltic Sea

Kalmar

DENMARK

Copenhagen

North Sea

Konigsberg

IRELAND

Dublin

WALES

ENGLAND

Berlin

Warsaw

London

Wittenberg

POLAND

Atlantic Ocean

Prague

BOHEMIA

Paris

Vienna

FRANCE

AUSTRIA

Budapest

HUNGARY

Geneva

PORTUGAL

PAPAL
STATES

OTTOMAN EMPIRE

Madrid

DALMATIA RAGUSA

SPAIN

Rome

NAPLES

Mediterranean
Sea

	Mostly Roman Catholic		Mostly Anglican		Mostly Moslem
	Mostly Calvinist		Mostly Hussite	■	Jewish communities
	Mostly Lutheran		Mostly Orthodox	●	Anabaptist communities

Many areas had significant religious minorities which are not shown here; also excluded are Jewish and Anabaptist communities.

Morocco, 1525. The Sadian dynasty, claiming descent from the Prophet's son-in-law Ali, establish their capital at Marrakesh.

Spain, 14 January 1526. Francis of France, held captive by Charles V for a year, signs the treaty of Madrid. He abandons Burgundy and gives up claims to Flanders, Artois and Tournai. He also renounces all claims to Italy and pardons the rebel high constable of Bourbon.

France, June 1526. King Francis, now released, declares the treaty of Madrid null and void.

Rome, June 1526. Pope Clement VII approves the founding of the Capuchin order by Matteo de Bascio, who aims to revive the Franciscan ideal of saintly poverty.

Caribbean, 26 July 1526. The Spaniard Lucas Vasquez de Ayllon leaves Santo Domingo with several hundred settlers to found a colony in Florida.

Hungary, November 1526. John Zapolyai of Transylvania has himself elected king of Hungary by a section of the nobility. The throne has been left vacant since the death of Lewis II at Mohacs.

Caribbean, November 1526. Settlers from the failed Florida colony organised by Lucas Vasquez de Ayllon return to Santo Domingo without their leader, who died on 18 October – one of the many to succumb on the expedition.

Germany, 1526. In response to the creation of the Catholic Dessau League, Philip, the landgrave of Hesse, and Johann of Saxony establish the League of Torgau. It is later joined by most of the Protestant states in the German empire.

Austria, 1526. In accordance with the 1515 treaty of Vienna, the Hungarian crown – in the absence of a direct heir – goes to Ferdinand, the grand duke of Austria and brother of Charles V. The hereditary territories of Austria and the states of Hungary and Bohemia are thus reunited under the Habsburgs.

France, 1526. Francis of France forms an alliance with the Ottoman sultan, Suleiman the Magnificent, against the Emperor Charles V.

Mexico, 1526. Dominican monks arrive in Mexico.

Ottomans crush Hungarians at Mohacs

Hungary, 29 August 1526
The flower of Hungarian manhood has been destroyed on the battlefield of Mohacs. After one of the bloodiest and most decisive battles of recent times, the young Hungarian king, Lewis II, lies dead with more than 20,000 of his troops, and Europe quivers before the armies of the Ottoman conqueror, Suleiman the Magnificent.

The Christian forces which tried to regroup after the fall of Belgrade in 1521 have since fallen apart. The French king, Francis, captured by the Habsburg emperor, Charles V, at the battle of Pavia in 1525, secretly wrote to propose an alliance with Suleiman. Meanwhile Charles failed to persuade the Protestant *diets* to grant aid for the defence of Hungary against the Turks until a few weeks ago – too late to prevent the slaughter at Mohacs.

Lewis's own forces were weakened by bitter rivalries. No effort was made to hold the line of the river Drava, and the Hungarian nobles rejected all delaying actions which might have enabled reinforcements

Suleiman's army at Mohacs.

to arrive. Successive frontal assaults by the Hungarians were met by heavy artillery fire and superior numbers. Any survivors were then massacred.

Exercises good for the soul, says Basque

Salamanca, 1526
Ignatius Loyola, who has returned to Spain from a pilgrimage to the Holy Land, is determined to become a priest at the age of 33. But he has had to leave Alcala because his regime of self-discipline was denounced to the Inquisition. He comes from a noble Basque family and began life as a soldier devoted

to chivalry. Defending Pamplona during the siege of 1521, he was badly wounded in the leg, which left him disabled. During his long convalescence he turned to the life of Jesus and resolved to become a soldier of Christ. Withdrawing to a monastery at Manresa, he subjected himself to prayer, fasting and self-flagellation, only agreeing to break off when his confessor ordered him to eat. He is now writing a book of spiritual exercises designed to break the will by contemplating the agonies of hell and the mercy of Christ.

Suffused with the fire of Divine love.

Suleiman, sultan and conqueror

Ottoman Empire, 1526
The rise of Ottoman power in Europe has been achieved with remarkable speed since Constantinople fell in 1453 to Sultan Mohammed II (ruled 1451-81). He had occupied southern Greece, most of Serbia and the Black Sea coast by 1461, and invaded other Balkan lands in 1463-4. In his war with Venice (1463-79) the Venetians lost several outposts.

Venice reasserted itself in the reign of Sultan Bayezid II (1481-1512). Another war ensued (1499-1503) in which the Turks raided as far as Vicenza and Venice lost more positions. Selim (1512-20) warred mainly in the Near East, but his son Suleiman took Belgrade in 1520, and Rhodes in 1522, and raided Austria and Hungary. After his victory at Mohacs, the Turkish army is just over 100 miles from Vienna.

Suleiman the Magnificent.

Glittering court of Margaret of Navarre

France, 1527
Margaret of Navarre, the king's sister, is establishing a brilliant intellectual court at Agen, at the Chateau de Nerac. Having lost her first husband, the duke of Alencon, she has married Henry d'Albret and is therefore queen of Navarre.

Her court is home to writers such as Dolet, Marot and Rabelais. She is a great writer of letters and a poet

of merit. Some of her best writing is contained in her short moral tales in the style of Boccaccio's *Decameron*, telling stories which often have erotic themes.

Perhaps more importantly, she is an advocate of religious liberty who gives shelter to clerics who question their church. Under her influence Nerac is becoming an important centre of French reformism.

Guns win priceless gem for Moghuls

Delhi, 21 April 1526

On the field of Panipat, to the north-west of Delhi, the Mongol or Moghul Emperor Babur has annihilated the Indian army of Ibrahim Lodi, the sultan of Delhi. Babur, descended from Genghis Khan and Tamerlane, has known fortune and failure. Thrice king of Ferghana (a tiny portion of Tamerlane's empire) and thrice deposed, he has been both beggar and emperor.

When Safavid power from Persia and Usbeg power from central Asia crushed the remnants of Tamerlane's empire, Babur rallied the Timurid princes and led them to conquests in Afganistan and Samarkand. In 1525 he turned on India, first taking control of the Punjab and then marching on Delhi.

The way was blocked at Panipat, by Sultan Ibrahim's army of 100,000 soldiers and 100 armoured elephants. Babur's army was hardly 12,000 strong. Protected behind a circular barricade of 700 carts, Babur opened up with his artillery, a weapon unknown to the Delhi army. The battle raged until noon, when the Indian army was sufficiently weakened for Babur to deliver the classic rear attack. "That mighty army," Babur later recalled, "in half a day was laid to dust."

With victory secure he sent his beloved son Humayun to Agra to secure the Indian treasury. Humayun returned with a diamond so large that its value would provide "two and a half days' food for the whole world", and offered it to Babur. With the extravagance of a man who has had everything and nothing, he waved it away dismissively. It is called the *Koh-i-Nor* diamond.

The emperor's army attacks a fortified town. From the "Baburnameh" (1590).

First bibles appear in English language

England, 1526

The first translation of the New Testament from its original Greek text into English has begun appearing in England a year after its publication at Worms, in Germany. Its author, William Tyndale, has been working on the project since 1522. The translation means that many more people, readers of English but not Greek, will be able to possess their own copy of the Scriptures.

Tyndale, who was serving as a tutor near Bristol, began his task as a reaction to the ignorance of the local priests and because he believed "that it was impossible to establish the lay people in any truth except when the Scripture were plainly laid before their eyes in their mother tongue, that they might see ... the meaning of the text".

A first-class linguist, Tyndale has drawn on the Greek Testament of Erasmus, published in 1516, for his translation. He has also made it clear, in his translation of certain critical words and passages, that he is seeking to strip away what he sees are the embellishments of Catholicism and lay bare the original text.

It is this rigorous attitude that sent him to Worms to complete his work. Encouraged by Martin Luther, he found a more congenial attitude there than in England. But that same attitude, relished by many readers, may well trouble the authorities.

From a later English Bible.

Moslems conquer Christian Nubia after a seven-year war

Nubia (Sudan), c.1527

The Christian culture of Nubia is dead. Churches where men and women worshipped for a thousand years are empty and crumbling, European travellers report. One, Reubeni, who has visited Soba, the capital of Alwa, found nothing save a few huts. Another, Alvarez, found nothing but ruins.

Christianity came to Nubia from Egypt in the sixth century, just as the two Nubian kingdoms of Maqurra (on the middle Nile) and Alwa (on the upper Nile) were emerging. It became the state religion but never took root amongst the masses. The services were in Greek and incomprehensible. Like Ethiopia, Nubia became isolated from the rest of Christendom by the advance of Islam, but lacked Ethiopia's mountains and sense of national identity. Maqurra fell to

Egypt in 1323, and Moslem traders, armies and tribes moved on Alwa.

While Alwa's northern frontiers fell to the Moslems, its southern frontiers crumbled to a new force from further up the Nile, the Funj. Seven years of war against Egypt, with the Funj first allying themselves with Alwa and then turning on it, were the final blow. Crushed by these various pressures the state has succumbed.

Albrecht Durer, artist and engraver, dies

Durer's "Melencolia" shows his mastery of the art of engraving.

Nuremberg, 1528
Albrecht Durer, who has died here at his home town at the age of 57, was regarded as the Leonardo of the north. A goldsmith's son, he became famous throughout Germany not only as an artist but for his treatises on optics and friendship with such men as Erasmus and Luther.

He met Erasmus on his visit to the Netherlands in 1521 and was disturbed that he did not support Luther openly. He wrote in his journal: "Oh, Erasmus of Rotterdam, where art thou? Defend the truth and earn a martyr's crown!" He drew his portrait in charcoal and Erasmus declared that there was nothing that Durer could not express without the use of colour.

Durer was the greatest master of engraving on wood and metal. He said: "Many a sketch made in a day on half a sheet of paper, or cut on a little piece of wood, has more and

"Lot and his daughters".

better art in it than some great work on which someone has laboured for a year." Some of his greatest works are engravings like *Melencolia* and *The Knight, Death and the Devil*, which he gave to Luther.

Features of perfect courtier delineated

Italy, 1528
A book of contemporary etiquette, defining every aspect of a gentleman's life and attitudes, has been published in Venice. As much as any similar compilation, *The Courtier*, by the writer Baldassare Castiglione, epitomises the thinking of modern cultured people.

Castiglione is himself an accomplished courtier, who has drawn on his own experiences in the service of Guidobaldo de Montefeltro, the duke of Urbino, for his work. He is also a veteran of the courts of Popes Leo X and Clement VII. His writing, which takes the form of instructive dialogues, has been further refined by his association with the Medicis and many other important figures.

The Courtier sets out the qualifications for good breeding. It is concerned with neither politics nor morals, but with the lifestyle of an elite, and portrays the cultured courtier as an idealised universal man or woman. It is not wholly original: Castiglione draws openly on Cicero, Plutarch and Livy, and on the opinions of friends such as the humanist Pietro Bembo and Giuliano de Medici.

Castiglione's campaign to remove affectation from well-bred living is having a profound effect on cultured society in Italy, and further afield in France and England.

Meditative soldier dies after revolt

China, 9 January 1529
Wang Yang-ming, the renowned philosopher who preached meditation and intuitive knowledge, has died at the age of 56. A soldier as well as thinker, he died while returning from quashing a revolt by bandits in Gwangxi province.

He made many enemies at court; at one time he was imprisoned, beaten with forty strokes and then banished on the orders of the powerful court eunuch Liu Jin. On his way to exile he found that Liu Jin's agents were following him. Fearing for his life, he left his clothing on a river bank and, tricking them into thinking he had drowned, escaped.

German troops sack and burn Rome

After the city falls, the mercenaries besiege the pope's stronghold.

Polemical engraving by Cranach.

Rome, 6-16 May 1527

Such is the fury of the 15,000 German mercenaries who are sacking Rome, looting, burning and raping in an orgy of destruction, that little can be left of what was once the finest city in the world. The Vatican has been occupied by Lutheran troops, its chapels used as stables and the Raphael paintings in the papal apartments covered with graffiti. As Rome is consumed by the rising flames, Pope Clement VII

has beseeched Charles V to call off the men who are destroying the city.

It is too late, however. The commanders of the armies sent to Italy had left before before the emperor and pope had signed a truce, and one of them (the commander of the Bourbon army) is dead. The other, Georg von Frunsberg, was badly wounded after telling his men: "I hope soon to make you all rich from the pickings of Rome." The result

was inevitable when his unpaid, starving and leaderless army came within sight of the city and its enormous wealth.

It is over a year since the formation of a Holy League by the Treaty of Cognac, under which Rome and Venice allied themselves with the pope to assist the French against Charles V. Few expected the Emperor to take such devastating action against the challenge to his growing power.

Medical row drives doctor from city

Basle, 1528

Dr Theophrastus Paracelsus, the town physician of Basle, has been expelled from the city following a dispute with the local magistrates, among them doctors opposed to his medical methods.

Paracelsus, whose real name is Theophrastus Bombastus von Hohenheim, was born the son of a physician, in 1493, in the Swiss canton of Schwyz. He went to Basle university at 16 and later studied alchemy and chemistry with the bishop of Wurzburg. He built up a huge store of facts and learnt medical practice at first hand, acquiring at the same time a deep distrust of traditional methods.

Two years ago he was made town physician at Basle. He taught at the university but, controversially, rejected the writings of earlier physicians such as Galen and Avicenna. Paracelsus also rejects the old notion of the "four humours" of the human body, the balance of which is said to determine illness. He prefers to think in terms of "outside agents" leading to disease, and argues that the body is really a complex chemical factory. To change the progress of a disease people need to change the body's chemical behaviour through specifically-aimed medicines.

However, Paracelsus' teachings, and his reputation for arrogance, have won him many enemies.

Theory seeks to explain why lean-faced men are quick to anger

The four humours: choleric (with lion), sanguine (with ape), phlegmatic (with sheep) and melancholic (with hog). Sound physical and mental health depends on a perfect balance of the humours. From the "Shepherd's Calendar".

Europe, c.1528

For centuries medicine has been dominated by the ancient theory of humours which, through the work of Paracelsus and others, is now coming under attack.

The theory is that the body is composed of four main fluids or humours: blood, phlegm, choler (yellow bile), and melancholy (black bile). In a healthy body, these fluids are in perfect balance; sickness results from losing that equilibrium. In other words, illness is an internal phenomenon.

The humours are also said to affect personality. If a person has an excess of melancholy, he or she will be of a gloomy disposition. Too much blood leads to a "sanguine" or positive character; phlegm is associated with passivity, and choler with quick temper. The humours are also said to influence appearance. Thus, the choleric man is lean faced and hairy.

Paracelsus wants to bring the principles of alchemy to medicine.

1529 (1529-1530)

Germany, 16 April 1529. After the second Diet of Speyer, 19 reformed states protest against the repeal of an imperial decree – passed in 1526, at the first Diet of Speyer – which allowed each prince to decide the religious allegiance of his state.

Spain, 22 April 1529. The treaty of Saragossa fixes the dividing line between the Portuguese and the Spanish in the Pacific Ocean at 17 degrees east of the Moluccas. The Portuguese have regained control of the archipelago in return for paying compensation to the Emperor Charles V.

India, 6 May 1529. Babur defeats the Afghan chiefs of Bihar and Bengal at the battle of Ghagra. His power now stretches from Kabul in the west to Bengal in the east.

Algeria, 27 May 1529. Khey ad-Din Barbarossa completes his conquest of Algeria in the name of the Ottoman sultan.

Spain, 29 June 1529. The Emperor Charles V and Pope Clement VII sign the treaty of Barcelona, settling their differences.

Spain, 26 July 1529. In Spain to secure the support of Charles V for his proposed expedition to Peru, Ferdinand Pizarro is granted the titles of governor and captain-general of the country he proposes to conquer.

France, 5 August 1529. Louise of Savoy, acting for Francis of France, and Margaret of Austria, representing her nephew Charles V, sign the peace of Cambrai, known as the *Paix des Dames*. Under the treaty, France renounces all its rights in Italy, Flanders and Artois and agrees to pay a ransom of two million crowns. Charles V renounces any claims to Burgundy.

England, 27 August 1529. Henry VIII also accedes to the treaty of Cambrai.

Hungary, 8 September 1529. The Ottoman Sultan Suleiman re-enters Buda and establishes John Zapolyai as the puppet king of Hungary.

Rome, October 1529. Under the influence of the Emperor Charles V, Catherine of Aragon's nephew, Pope Clement VII refuses to grant Henry VIII, the king of England, an annulment of his marriage to Catherine.

England, 17 October 1529. Angered by Thomas Wolsey's failure to secure from the pope an annulment of his marriage, Henry VIII strips him of the office of lord chancellor.

England, 25 October 1529. Thomas More replaces Wolsey as lord chancellor, becoming the first layman to hold the office in living memory. A fierce opponent of Luther he more recently became embroiled in controversy with the Protestant theologian William Tyndale who asserted royal supremacy over the church.

Germany, 1-4 November 1529. On the invitation of Philip of Hesse, the reformers of Wittenberg, Strasbourg and Zurich meet in Marburg to try to resolve the theological differences that divide the German Reformation. Luther, Melanchthon, Oecolampadius and Zwingli fail to reach agreement on the Eucharist.

Japan, 1529. Monks from the Tendai monasteries on Mount Hiei, north-west of Kyoto, sweep down on the city and massacre followers of the Nichiren sect of Buddhism.

England, 3 November 1529. The first Parliament for five years opens. The Commons put forward bills against abuses amongst the clergy and in the church courts.

Ethiopia, 1529. Under the leadership of Ahmad Gran, Moslems launch an attack on Ethiopia from the Red Sea. They win a battle at Shembura Kure and go on to conquer Shoa.

Italy, 24 February 1530. Charles V is crowned Holy Roman emperor by Pope Clement VII at Bologna. Elected on 28 June 1519, Charles was crowned emperor in France on 26 October 1520.

India, 1530. On the death of his father, Babur, Humayun becomes sultan of Delhi.

Brazil, 1530. The Portuguese begin to colonise Brazil.

Malta, 1530. Driven out of Rhodes in 1522 by the Turks, the Knights of St John of Jerusalem are given permission by the Emperor Charles V to settle on the island of Malta.

Silesia, 1530. Georg Bauer, known as Agricola, publishes a work of major importance in the field of mineralogy and mining techniques entitled *De Re Metallica*.

South-East Africa, 1530. Chikuyo, the Munhumutapa or king who has ruled the southern Zambezi escarpment for 30 years, is killed during a civil war.

Florence, 1530. The Medicis are restored to power in Florence by imperial troops.

Italy, 1530. Girolamo Fracastoro gives the name syphilis to the disease the Spanish call *bubas*, which may have been transported to Europe by sailors returning from the New World.

Last thoughts of first Moghul emperor

The dying emperor spends his last days with his son Humayun by his side.

Sakri, India, 1530

Babur, the descendant of Genghis Khan and Tamerlane the Great, who built an empire out of an impoverished central Asian princedom and conquered northern India, is dying. He sits alone in his garden, built to remind him of the pleasures of Kabul, writing his memoirs.

They go back to his childhood when, aged 11, he became king of Ferghana. Three times he lost and won that kingdom. He writes with sadness of tribesmen in 1519 who had never seen guns before, laughing at the noise and confronting them with obscene gestures before being massacred; but he has little sympathy for the supposedly sophisticated societies he conquered.

"Hindustan is a country that has few pleasures to recommend it. The people are not handsome. They have no idea of the charms of friendly society, of mixing frankly together, or of familiar intercourse. They have no genius, no comprehension of mind, no politeness of manner, no kindness of fellow feeling, no ingenuity or mechanical or artistic abilities, no knowledge of design or architecture, no horses, no flesh, no grapes, no melons, no ice, no decent food, baths, no candles, not even a candlestick."

Sometimes he puts aside his manuscript and, drawing hashish smoke into his lungs, allows the memories of bloody battlefields to metamorphose themselves into "wonderful fields of flowers".

He lists with loving detail the flora and fauna of his subject territories, describing parrots, rhinoceroses, the leaves of an apple tree and the changing colours of flocks of geese on the horizon.

His only sadness is his son's sickness. The holy men tell Babur that Humayun will only be cured if he gives up the most valuable thing he possesses. He thinks that this is the *Koh-i-Nor* diamond, not realising it is Babur himself. "What value is worldly wealth, and how can it redeem Humayun? I myself shall be his sacrifice." Babur sits alone in his garden and prepares to die.

Storms and disease end Vienna siege

Vienna, 15 October 1529

Europe can breathe again. The Ottoman armies, which have been encamped beneath the walls of Vienna for nearly three weeks, are heading back towards Belgrade. For once Suleiman has over-reached himself, although bad weather and disease have been the crucial factors rather than any feat of Christian arms.

Two years ago, while the Emperor Charles V was concentrating on his second war in France, his brother Ferdinand defeated the Hungarian nationalist Zapolyai and was crowned king of the part of Hungary that was still in Habsburg hands. Ferdinand was then rash enough to send an envoy to Suleiman demanding the return of fortresses taken by the Ottomans after their victory at Mohacs.

Suleiman, who was now committed to restoring Zapolyai to the Hungarian throne, embarked on his most ambitious campaign to date. His chief problem was to reach Vienna before winter. In the event, he lost a month battling through heavy storms, building bridges across rivers, and leading his troops through treacherous terrain of streams and marshes. Although he left Istanbul on 10 May, he did not arrive in Belgrade until mid-July, reaching Vienna on 27 September.

This time Ferdinand was prepared. In March the German Diet had

The emperor tramples the Ottomans underfoot, as Suleiman's forces retreat.

assembled in Innsbruck and voted 120,000 Rhenish guilders for defence against the Ottoman invader; in May, despite the opposition of Philip of Hesse and other Protestant princes, the Diet of Speyer had promised an army of 16,000 men and 4,000 cavalry. When the first Ottoman troops attacked, they were met by a garrison of seasoned veterans.

Suleiman needed a quick victory, but he did not get it. Wave after wave was beaten back, and no significant breach was ever made in the city walls. The Ottoman army lost horses and men from hunger and disease. Yesterday the sultan gave the order to retreat.

Turkish cruelty to Austrian captives.

Defiant princes are dubbed Protestants

Speyer, Germany, 1529

A letter of protest signed by six of Germany's Lutheran princes and the burghers of 14 cities has rejected the findings of the Catholic-dominated Diet of Speyer. The letter, *A Protestation*, for which the signatories have been dubbed "Protestants", is seen as a challenge to the authority of the emperor.

The letter states that "in matters which concern God's honour and salvation and the eternal life of souls, everyone must stand and give account before God for himself". Its message is almost identical to that of the diet three years ago which Charles V swore to overturn.

Church reformers seek to end split

Germany, 4 November 1529

Philip of Hesse has had only partial success in seeking to end the split in the church reform movement. To the amazement of many of their friends, he managed to persuade the two leaders, Martin Luther and Ulrich Zwingli, to meet him in the castle here. Even more surprisingly they signed the "Fifteen Marburg Articles" agreeing on all items of doctrine except the Eucharist.

However, the meeting between the two men was stormy. They remain deeply divided politically. Luther will not move against the emperor; Zwingli is keen for the Swiss to revolt.

Conquest of Peru given royal boost

Toledo, Spain, 26 July 1529

A royal warrant signed today allows the explorer Francisco Pizarro to return to a country which he found three years ago on the Pacific coast south of Panama. The queen's approval (or *capitulacion*) licenses Pizarro to "discover and conquer" Peru, of which he is now Spain's governor. Pizarro has brought back llamas, Peruvian boys to become interpreters, and various artefacts to prove that a highly developed culture exists. First contact with the natives shows them to be friendly. Pizarro's credibility was magnified by the presence at court of the hero of Mexico, Hernando Cortes.

Divorce row leads to Cardinal's fall

England, October 1529

The man who for the past 15 years has virtually controlled English domestic and foreign policy has been abruptly sacked as lord chancellor by Henry VIII. Thomas Wolsey, cardinal and papal envoy, failed to persuade Rome to allow the king to divorce Catherine of Aragon.

In 20 years of marriage, Catherine had one daughter, five infants who did not survive, and several miscarriages but was unable to produce a male heir. Henry is impatient and is also infatuated with the protestant Anne Boleyn, aged 18, who has a reputation as a flirt.

The king told Wolsey to get Pope Clement VII to annul the marriage to Catherine, who was the widow of Henry's elder brother Arthur. But an earlier pope had issued a special bull which over-rode objections to that marriage on the grounds of the closeness of the relationship. Also Henry's earlier liaison with Anne's elder sister Mary raises the question of a forbidden blood link. For the past two years Wolsey and Henry have been pressurising Rome and the pope has been procrastinating. Catherine is the aunt of the Emperor Charles V, who has the pope in his power after his troops occupied Rome. A furious Henry charged Wolsey with abuse of power and, stripping him of all offices, packed him off to York as archbishop; he is not expected to last.

King Henry VIII confers with his lord chancellor, Cardinal Thomas Wolsey; from a painting by Sir John Gilbert (1817-1897).

1530 (1530-1532)

Germany, 25 June 1530. At the Diet of Augsburg, the Lutherans deliver the *Confession*, a detailed statement of their faith prepared by Philip Melanchthon. It is designed to achieve reconciliation with the Catholic Church.

Antwerp, 13 July 1530. The painter Quentin Massys dies. His religious works were in the Flemish tradition of the last century, but his portraits reveal the influence of humanist idealism.

Rome, 8 October 1530. The city is flooded.

Bohemia, 5 January 1531. The Emperor Charles V secures the election of his younger brother Ferdinand as King of the Romans.

Hungary, 31 January 1531. John Zapolyai and Ferdinand of Habsburg, both of whom were crowned king of Hungary in 1526, reach a truce.

England, February 1531. The convocation of the church in England buy a pardon from Henry VIII for their "guilt" under the statute of praemunire (unlawfully exercising spiritual jurisdiction) and recognise him as their supreme head with major qualifications.

Germany, 27 February 1531. German Protestants form the League of Schmalkalden to resist the power of the emperor.

Ethiopia, 1531. Portugal sends troops to assist Ethiopia against the Moslems.

South-East Africa, 1531. The Portuguese begin to trade at the Moslem port of Sena on the lower Zambezi (*Mozambique*).

Florence, 1531. The Emperor Charles V marries his daughter Margaret of Parma to Alessandro de Medici and makes him duke of Florence.

France, 1531. Margaret of Navarre publishes a spiritual handbook entitled *The Mirror of the Sinful Soul*.

France, 1531. Francis of France forms an alliance with John Zapolyai, the king of Hungary.

Brazil, 1531. Martin Alfonso de Sousa, the leader of the first expedition to explore the interior of Brazil, dies during the journey.

Mexico, 1531. Hernando Cortes returns to New Spain as captain-general, having been removed from the governorship two years ago.

Netherlands, 1531. Charles V prohibits the adoption of Protestant doctrines in the Netherlands.

Switzerland, 11 October 1531. During the second civil war between the Protestants and the Catholics, the Protestants are defeated at Kappel. Ulrich Zwingli dies in the battle.

Germany, 24 October 1531. Bavaria, despite being Catholic, joins the League of Schmalkalden.

England, 29 November 1531. Thomas Wolsey, archbishop of York, dies at Leicester while travelling to London to answer a charge of treason.

Portugal, 17 December 1531. An inquisition is established.

England, 16 May 1532. Thomas More resigns as lord chancellor the day after a convocation of the English clergy agrees to seek royal consent before making any decisions.

Germany, 26 May 1532. Francis, the king of France, forges an alliance with Bavaria, Saxony and Hesse against the Habsburg Ferdinand.

Germany, 23 June 1532. The Emperor Charles V signs the peace of Nuremberg with the Protestant princes, who are granted freedom of worship in return for military aid against the Ottoman Turks.

Hungary, August 1532. Suleiman the Magnificent, the Ottoman sultan, who invaded Hungary in June, is defeated at Guns.

France, 1532. A treaty of union ends Brittany's independence.

France, 1532. The writer Francois Rabelais wins instant success with the publication of his first book, *Pantagruel*, a satire of a popular folk tale, which is condemned by the Sorbonne.

Scandinavia, 1532. Christian II of Denmark is taken prisoner after a failed attempt to conquer Norway.

Italy, 1532. *The Prince* by Niccolo Macchiavelli is published posthumously.

Italy, 1532. Ludovico Ariosto completes a revised edition of his epic poem *Orlando Furioso*.

England, 1532. The poetical works of Geoffrey Chaucer are published in a collected edition.

Netherlands, 1532. The painter Jan Gossart, known as Mabuse, dies at Breda. Following his visits to Florence, Rome and Venice, in 1508-9, he developed a passion for Italian art and developed its formal innovations, particularly in his secular works such as *Venus and Cupid* and *Danae*.

Crimea, 1532. Sahib Giray, khan of Kazan since 1523, founds the khanate of Crimea under Ottoman protection.

Protestants seek compromise with church

Augsburg, 25 June 1530

Lutheran Protestants today presented 28 articles of faith to the diet here in an attempt to avoid a split with the Catholic Church. The *Confession of Augsburg* bends over backwards to secure unity. The first 21 articles are points on which both groups are already agreed. The last seven deal with controversial issues like confession and the celibacy of priests, but leave them open as being "under discussion".

The confession is the work of Philip Melanchthon. Luther himself was unable to come since he is still an exile from the empire. While Melanchthon is a loyal disciple, and has not compromised on matters of essential doctrine, he is above all a pacifier who wants to avoid making common cause with the more rebellious Swiss.

The emperor, Charles V, is also keen to achieve unity. He wants the support of German Protestant princes to continue his struggle with the Turks, who last year laid siege to Vienna. Both sides here have been keen to compromise, but close observers see it as window-dressing.

The religious differences remain deep and, though Luther has continually made it clear that he will not go along with armed resistance to the emperor, his battle with the Catholic theologians is as fierce as ever. The Catholics are no less resolute and it can only be a matter of time before the split reopens.

The emperor Charles V rallies Germany's princes at the Diet of Augsburg.

League formed to defend Lutheran Church

Schmalkalden, 27 February 1531

Eight German princes and eleven cities today agreed to form themselves into a league to defend the reformist church of Martin Luther. It is to be called the League of Schmalkalden, after this little town which stands symbolically on the borders of Hesse and Saxony, two of the league's most powerful supporters.

Other members of the league include the duke of Brunswick and Luneburg and the cities of Strasbourg, Ulm, Lubeck, Bremen and Magdeburg. Today they affirmed that "on all occasions that any of us is attacked for the Word of God and the doctrine of the gospel or for any other thing connected therewith, all the others will come to his aid at once".

The princes have political reasons for wanting to resist the power of the emperor. But the key factor was the decision of the Diet of Augsburg last November – when the Catholic militants won the day – which insisted that Lutherans recognise the pope and threatened force if they did not. This united the more moderate Protestants like Luther with the Swiss, who have long been inclined to open revolt.

484

Ruler seized as Incas are massacred

New World Indian sees Virgin Mary

Lima, Peru, 1532

Over-confident with success in a bitter civil war against his brother, the Inca Atahualpa has gambled with his newly-won empire and lost it. His opponent in a bloody game of chance was Francisco Pizarro, a wily, if illiterate, veteran of many small wars. With only 150 soldiers, including 62 horsemen, and three months' march from any help, Pizarro should have been no match for thousands of Indian soldiers. That is what the Inca himself thought. Atahualpa, who is now a valuable hostage with a fortune in gold to be ransomed, admitted soon after his capture that his plan was to take the Spaniards unawares, sacrifice some of them to the sun god, and castrate the rest for service as eunuchs.

But Pizarro used surprise brilliantly. He occupied, peacefully, some long, low buildings round three sides of a square in the upland valley town of Cajamarca. He invited Atahualpa to meet him.

When the Inca came he was handed a Christian prayer book, which he threw down. Pizarro sprang his ambush: two hidden cannon blasted at point blank range into the packed Peruvian ranks, followed by a cavalry charge. Panic did the rest. Piz-

These sketches by Felipe Guaman Poma show the cruelty of the conquistadores. On the right, they are seen executing the Inca emperor Atahualpa.

arro led a squad which snatched Atahualpa from his litter while his soldiers butchered the survivors. In two hours, 7,000 Indians died and their leader became a captive.

Pizarro's march towards the Inca capital of Cuzco continues. Since the people of Cuzco were subjects of Atahualpa's defeated brother Huascar, they are potential allies, and Pizarro cleverly emulated his

former captain, Cortes, in conquering by exploiting a local civil war so as to divide and rule.

Pizarro's campaigning over thousands miles with a small force with no supply lines against apparently overwhelming odds is clearly paying dividends as the remnants of Atahualpa's army limps away from its own tribal territory ahead of the invaders.

Mexico, 13 December 1531

On the morning of 9 December, Juan Diego, an Indian and a devout Catholic, had a vision of the Virgin Mary. She told him to go to the Spanish bishop of Mexico and persuade him to build her a church on Tepeyacac Hill.

Not believing the Indian's story, the bishop refused. When Juan saw the Virgin again that afternoon he begged her to use a Spaniard for her mission. She just assured Juan of her love and concern for his people and asked him to persevere.

On 10 December Diego failed for the second time to convince the bishop. On his way home the Virgin told him to return the next day to collect proof for his story. But Juan's uncle caught the plague that day, 11 December, forcing Juan to stay at home.

On 12 December 1531, the Virgin cured Juan's uncle and simultaneously met Juan at Tepeyacac hill. There she ordered him to pick flowers and carry them to the bishop in his cloak. When Juan opened his cloak, the image of the Virgin was clearly to be seen on the lining and the bishop was finally persuaded to build the church.

Protestant reformer Zwingli dies in battle

Expanding Russia seeks more conquests

Switzerland, 11 October 1531

Ulrich Zwingli, the leader of the Swiss Reformation, has been killed in battle here. He was accompanying the army as a chaplain, but was caught up in the fighting. His body was quartered and burnt.

Zwingli symbolised the new unity of the reformist preachers with the lay power of the cities. In Zurich his reforms of the church service went side by side with a court, jointly administered by magistrates and church elders, which has made church attendance compulsory and punishes adultery.

The churches in Zurich and other Protestant cities, like Berne and Basle, have been freed of Catholic images and the Mass. In their places are a simple service and daily Bible readings. Zwingli blended his religious ideas with appeals to Swiss patriotism in his sermons. He launched the current war on the

Zwingli: patriotic Swiss preacher.

Catholic cantons, but failed to win enough support from other Protestant cities. Some were jealous of Zurich's prestige; others disliked Zwingli's attack on Swiss mercenaries, who are a major export earner for many cities.

Moscow, 1530

As a unified Muscovy continues to confront its Polish and Lithuanian neighbours in the west, its power has increased considerably under the energetic leadership of Vasily lll who is assiduously carrying on the work of his father, Ivan the Great, in building the country into a powerful political force in Europe.

Vasily began consolidating his father's work by annexing the two remaining Great Russian territories, Pskov and Ryazan, with little difficulty and no military effort. He appointed a civil servant to run Pskov. He also deprived 300 leading families of their estates, deported them to the interior, and replaced them by an equal number of families from Moscow.

Ryazan was taken over when its grand prince entered into secret negotiations with the Tartars. Determined to add to Ivan's gains in

Vasily: the heir to Ivan the Great.

Lithuanian Russia, Vasily invaded the territory and took Smolensk, the focal point of Muscovy's western defensive system. Vasily's problems on his eastern and southern borders have been eased by the failure of a Tartar invasion.

1532 (1532-1534)

England, 25 January 1533. King Henry VIII secretly marries Anne Boleyn.

England, 30 March 1533. The scholar Thomas Cranmer becomes archbishop of Canterbury. He takes the oath of allegiance to the pope protesting that he is doing so "for form's sake".

England, 1 June 1533. Shortly after the marriage of Henry VIII to Catherine of Aragon has been declared void by Thomas Cranmer – and the marriage to Anne Boleyn valid – the new queen is crowned at Westminster.

Hungary, 22 June 1533. A year after invading Hungary, Suleiman the Magnificent, the sultan of the Ottomans, signs a peace treaty with Ferdinand of Habsburg, the brother of the Emperor Charles V. Hungarian rule remains divided between Ferdinand and the Ottoman puppet John Zapolyai.

England, 11 July 1533. Henry VIII is excommunicated by Pope Clement VII.

Peru, 29 August 1533. On the orders of the governor, Francisco Pizarro, the Inca chief Atahualpa is executed, although he has already paid millions of pounds for his ransom.

Peru, 15 November 1533. Pizarro enters Cuzco.

Russia, 11 December 1533. At the age of three, Ivan IV succeeds his father, Vasily III.

Algeria, 1533. Suleiman the Magnificent appoints Khey ad-Din Barbarossa commander of Algiers with orders to cooperate with the French against the empire.

Germany, 1533. The radical religious sect known as the Anabaptists, which rejects infant baptism, takes power in Munster.

Persia, 13 July 1534. Ottoman armies capture Tabriz in north-western Persia.

North America, 24 July 1534. A French expedition under Jacques Cartier, patronised by King Francis, reaches the estuary of the River of Canada *(St Lawrence)* after a three-month journey from St Malo on the French coast.

North Africa, August 1534. Khey ad-Din Barbarossa wins back Tunis from its Moorish king, an ally of the Spanish.

Paris, 15 August 1534. The Spanish nobleman, ex-soldier and monk Ignatius Loyola vows to found a society in honour of Jesus Christ (the Society of Jesus). In 1521, after an intense religious experience which began his conversion, Loyola went on retreat to Montserrat, in Spain.

France, 5 September 1534. Jacques Cartier returns with furs to Normandy after exploring Prince Edward Island, Chaleur Bay and Gaspe Bay off North America.

North America, September 1534. Cabeza de Vaca, Estevanico (a slave) and two other survivors of the Panfilo de Narvaez expedition of 1527 escape after six years of Indian captivity in south-western North America.

England, November 1534. The Act the Supremacy separates the Church of England from Rome and declares the king to be its supreme head. The Act of Succession vests the succession in the children of Anne Boleyn; severe penalties are prescribed for anyone who opposes Henry VIII's marriage to her or its issue, and the king is given powers to demand an oath of allegiance to the act's provisions.

Baghdad, 31 December 1534. The Ottomans capture Baghdad.

Persia, 1534. Shah Tahmasp executes Husayn Khan, head of the Shamlu tribe, and assumes power in person.

England, 1534. Thomas Cromwell is made principle secretary.

Denmark, 1534. Christian III, a Protestant, becomes king of Denmark after defeating the Catholic supporters of his brother John in a civil war which broke out after the death of their father, Ferdinand, last year.

Florence, 1534. Leaving the Medicis' mortuary chapel at San Lorenzo unfinished, Michelangelo returns to Rome, where he has been commissioned to adorn the Sistine Chapel – whose ceiling he decorated over 20 years ago – with frescoes.

Germany, 1534. Francis of France signs the treaty of Augsburg, an alliance with the Protestant princes against Charles V.

Brazil, 1534. The ambitious scheme of John III, the king of Portugal, to divide the Brazilian coastline into 12 captaincies breaks down. It has been undermined by native attacks and by the reluctance of Portuguese noblemen to assume the necessary responsibilities.

Rome, 1534. On the death of Giulio de Medici (Clement VII), pope since 1523, Alexander Farnese is elected. He takes the name Paul III.

Peru, 1534. The Inca leader Manco Capac II leads an uprising against Pizarro.

Morocco, 1534. Abu Abdullah, the last Nasrid (Moslem) ruler of Granada, in Spain, dies at Fez.

The civilised home life of a Turk, depicted by Eugene Delacroix (1798-1863).

Private wealth, public squalor in the east

Near East, c.1533

The few occidentals who venture through the pirate-infested Mediterranean to what has become known as the "mysterious east" find a very different world awaiting them. Ancient cities like Cairo or Damascus still remain hidden behind their walls, their gates closed to the cries of the *hodja* calling the people to evening prayer from their minarets.

There are no wide streets, only narrow alleys with overhanging buildings which block out the sun; there are no wheeled vehicles, everything being carried on the backs of donkeys or humans. The visitor will find no town halls of the sort he is used to in Europe; the power lies in the sultan's citadel.

The cities are noisy throughout the day with the constant shouts of traders from their tiny booths in narrow covered markets. The visitor will find peace only in the mosques with their wide, cool, peaceful courts. House architecture, too, differs markedly from the west's. The visitor will see little but blank walls and shuttered windows. Elegance and decor are kept for the interior; much of family life takes place around shady courtyards.

Epic poet of bygone heroic age has died

Ferrara, Italy, 6 June 1533

Ludovico Ariosto, the author of the magnificent epic poem *Orlando Furioso*, has died aged 59. The poem, regarded by many as the finest of its era, was first published in 1516 and completed in 1532.

In Ariosto's words, his work celebrates "the ladies, the knights, the battles, the loves, the courtesies and the bold exploits" of a by-gone era: the heroic age of the *Chanson de Roland*, when French might dominated Europe and the noble Roland, Ariosto's Orlando, was a byword for chivalric perfection.

The poem is dedicated to the d'Este family who rule Ferrara and by whom Ariosto was employed as a diplomat, administrator and theatrical producer for 30 years.

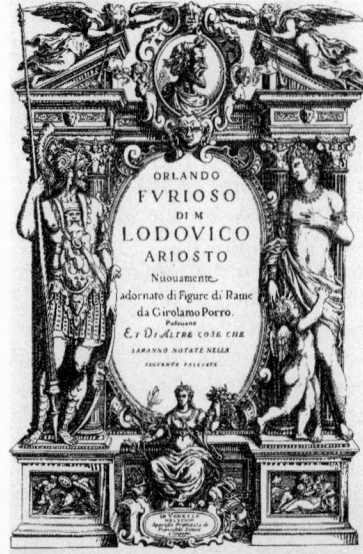

Cover of "Orlando's" 1583 edition.

King defies pope and marries mistress

England, July 1533
The king has had his way and has rid himself of Catherine in order to marry Anne Boleyn. The price has been the repudiation of papal authority in England. Assisted by his new first minister Thomas Cromwell, Henry persuaded parliament to pass a series of measures which make him head of the church in England and allow the archbishop of Canterbury to make all such dispensations as the pope has made in the past.

On the death of Archbishop Warham in January Henry appointed Thomas Cranmer, a favourite of Anne, to Canterbury. Cranmer, though for appearances' sake taking the oath of obedience to Rome, promptly declared Henry's marriage to Catherine invalid and blessed the marriage to Anne.

It was none too soon. Late last year Henry took Anne with him when he visited France's King Francis at Calais. Her suite of rooms adjoined Henry's. When they eventually got back to London Anne was pregnant. She was crowned queen last month and the birth is expected in September. In Rome, Pope Clement has excommunicated Henry.

The defeated pope slumps before Henry VIII (in bed) and Edward VI – from a satirical picture (undated) possibly commissioned by the King.

King becomes head of the English church

England, November 1534
The final break with Rome has been made by parliament. A Succession Act commands allegiance to Anne and her issue and makes it high treason to challenge the king's title to the throne or criticise the marriage. Another measure, the Act of Supremacy, makes the king the supreme head of the Church of England, with full powers to deal with heresies, errors and abuses. No more taxes are to be paid to Rome, and the laws against heresy have been amended to allow criticism of the Catholic Church. A Bible in English is to be published.

What began as a controversy over Henry's matrimonial problems has turned into a political revolution. Not only has England broken with the Catholic Church, but the king's need to carry public opinion with him has caused him increasingly to seek the support of parliament.

England's religious controversies have been taking place against a background of religious revolution in continental Europe. Martin Luther has been preaching against papal indulgences and calling for German control of the German church. In Zurich church reformation is going on; Sweden and Denmark have broken with the pope. But Henry has no fancy for such dissidence. His theology is strictly orthodox. He wrote a book denouncing Luther and his views and for this the pope gave him the title "Defender of the Faith".

Painter leaves family to work in England

London, 1533
Hans Holbein, the German portrait painter, is back in England, having abandoned his wife and children in Basle, where he normally works. He is busy painting German merchants and has done the portrait of Thomas Cromwell, the king's new favourite and chancellor.

On his previous visit as a young man, in 1526, Master Holbein was the guest of Sir Thomas More, to whom he had introductions from Erasmus, and who is now fallen from favour. His drawing of Sir Thomas among his family was sent to Erasmus, who wrote: "I should scarcely be able to see you better if I were with you."

The picture of *The Ambassadors* from France, standing full length with a strangely distorted skull in front of them, has impressed the king, so that he has begun to patronise the Augsburg-born painter. He has plans for a large mural at his palace at Whitehall, to show him, his parents, Henry VII and Elizabeth of York, and his queen in regal surroundings.

Christina of Denmark, by Holbein.

Anti-Catholic posters on king's palace

Paris, 18 October 1534
During the night placards violently criticising the Catholic Mass were posted in large numbers in Paris and several provincial towns. Some even appeared on the royal chateau at Blois.

The reaction this Sunday morning has been fierce. A wave of sectarian hatred has engulfed Paris. It is rumoured that the Protestants plan to murder the faithful at Mass. King Francis is expected to take harsh action against reformers.

French Protestant zealots tear down religious images and burn books.

1534 (1534-1536)

Mexico, 17 April 1535. Antonio de Mendoza is appointed the first viceroy of New Spain, assuming power in place of the governor and *audienca* of Mexico.

France, 19 May 1535. Inspired by stories of the wealthy kingdom of Saguenay, the French explorer Jacques Cartier sets out from Brittany on a second trip to North America.

Peru, June 1535. The Spaniard Francisco Pizarro founds the city of Lima.

Germany, June 1535. The town of Munster, the stronghold of the Anabaptists, is taken by an alliance of Protestant and Catholic troops and its inhabitants are massacred.

London, 6 July 1535. After 15 months' imprisonment in the Tower of London, Thomas More is beheaded for refusing to take the oath demanded by the 1534 Act of Succession. John Fisher, the bishop of Rochester, was executed last month for the same reason.

North Africa, July 1535. The Emperor Charles V captures Tunis from Barbarossa.

Canada, 2 October 1535. Having landed in Quebec a month ago, Jacques Cartier reaches a town which he names Montreal.

England, 1535. Henry VIII appoints a commission under his chief minister, Thomas Cromwell, to report on the state of the monasteries.

India, 1535. The Moghul emperor Humayun makes a brilliant raid into Gujarat, storming the fortress of Champener in person.

Spain, 1535. Hernando Pizarro, Francisco's half-brother, gives part of the booty taken from the Incas to Emperor Charles V. Francisco is made governor of New Castile and Diego de Almagro becomes governor of New Toledo.

Mexico, 1535. Spaniards establish a settlement called La Paz on an island off the west coast of Mexico *(Baja California)*. He names the bay between the island and the mainland Santa Cruz.

Mexico, 1535. Augustinian and Franciscan provinces are created in New Spain. The missionaries embark on a campaign against the exploitation of Indians.

South-East Africa, 1535. The Portuguese penetrate the Zambezi valley as far as the Moslem market at Tete. They took Sena, downstream, in 1531.

Milan, 1535. Following the death of Francesco Sforza II, the city is occupied by Charles V.

Britain, 1536. An Act of Union brings together Wales and England under one legal and administrative system. Henceforth Wales will send 24 members to parliament.

England, 1536. Catherine of Aragon, the first wife of Henry VIII, dies. Although she bore the king five children, only one of them, Princess Mary, who was born in 1516, survived infancy.

Switzerland, 21 May 1536. At a meeting of the city council in the cathedral, the Reformation is officially adopted in Geneva. This follows the return of the Protestant convert and reformer William Farel, who had twice been compelled to leave the city.

Switzerland, 1536. The French theologian John Calvin, who was converted to Protestantism several years ago, writes his *Institutes of the Christian Religion*, a full statement of his beliefs, which he dedicates to Francis, the king of France.

London, 19 June 1536. Anne Boleyn, the second wife of King Henry VIII, is beheaded in the Tower of London.

France, 6 July 1536. The explorer, Jacques Cartier lands at St Malo at the end of his second expedition to North America. He returns with none of the gold he expected to find after a harsh winter at Montreal during which 25 of his men died of scurvy.

Germany, 1536. Johann Faust, a physician, astrologer and magician, dies unexpectedly at Breisgau. It is rumoured that his strange disappearance was the work of the Devil.

Italy, 1536. The artist and architect Giulio Romano completes the decorative work on the Palazzo del Te for the Gonzaga dukes of Mantua.

Venice, 1536. Jacopo Sansovino is commissioned to build a library to house the valuable manuscripts rescued from the Turkish invasion by Cardinal Bassarion, as well as the manuscripts left to Venice by Petrarch.

Portugal, 1536. The dramatist Gil Vicente, author of *Auto de Visitacao* and creator of the Portuguese national theatre, dies.

France, 1536. Charles V's troops invade Provence, in pursuit of the army of King Francis, which has attempted to seize Piedmont. They are driven back by Anne of Montmorency, who applies scorched-earth tactics.

North Africa, 1536. The Berber corsair Khey ad-Din Barbarossa reoccupies Bizerta.

Rabelais creates the giant Gargantua

France, 1534
"At the moment of birth he did not yell Waa! Waa! as other children do, but shouted aloud Drink! Drink!" Thus reads the first appearance of the fictional giant Gargantua, the latest creation of the writer Francois Rabelais whose *Pantagruel*, another satirical celebration of gigantic and human appetites, appeared two years ago.

Rabelais is the physician of the municipal hospital at Lyons, and he writes "in moments of relaxation from the solace of the sick", publishing his books under a pseudonym – Alcofribas Nasier, an anagram of his own name.

Rabelais' work mixes fantastic tales with a fictional version of contemporary life. The giant represents everyday humanity, both good and bad, and either way a far cry from the idealised world demanded by the moralists. Above all, man's

A Rabelaisian vision of Pantagruel.

natural instincts are to be acknowledged. His motto *Fay ce que vouldras* (Do what you like) offers monastic life, with its rules and regulations, a direct challenge.

Sensual artist Correggio dies, aged 45

Correggio, near Parma, 1534
Antonio Allegri, known by the name of Correggio from this small town of his birth, has died here in his forties, having made the cathedral at nearby Parma one of the wonders of Italy with his paintings. The inside of the dome is a cloud of saints and angels, all seen from directly beneath, escorting the Virgin upwards into heaven. It is as though the dome is lifting off above the spectator's head. Correggio painted much in Parma and other Lombard towns such as Reggio and Bologna. In his last years he painted classical myths such as *Danae* and *Leda* with great sensuality.

Correggio's subtle blend of tones especially suits his pictures of women.

English king executes his second wife

London 19 June 1536
Anne Boleyn, the queen of England, was beheaded in the Tower of London today, a victim of court intrigues and her own arrogance. She used to mock the king, though whether she was guilty of adultery is highly doubtful. She gave Henry a daughter, Elizabeth, but this year she miscarried, and the king decided the marriage was damned. Awaiting execution Anne spoke of her "little neck".

Henry VIII and Anne Boleyn.

Charles V's troops murder 30,000 people

Gulf of Tunis, July 1535
An army of 60,000 allied troops led by Charles V has won a spectacular victory here, taking the city of Tunis and the port of La Goleta and capturing the bulk of Barbarossa's fleet of 80 galleys. Charles has allowed his soldiers five days of pillaging, and 30,000 inhabitants are reported to have been killed.

The emperor chose to invade after Barbarossa's fleet had ravaged southern Italy at the behest of the Turkish sultan. Spanish possession of Tunis would effectively cut off Barbarossa – "the master of Algiers" – from Constantinople. A combined fleet of Spanish and Genoan galleys sailed from Barcelona in April; only Charles and his two commanders, Admiral Andrea Doria and the marquis del Vasco, knew the destination. More ships joined the fleet at Sardinia with 22,000 German and Italian troops.

Charles' shock troops, the formidable *tercio*, were the first to land at La Goleta, followed by artillery and a detachment of cavalry. Barbarossa chose to remain behind the walls, trusting the extreme heat to wear down the enemy.

Allied progress was slow, with many of Charles's soldiers dying of dysentery. Barbarossa had not reckoned with the fire-power of the fleet and land-artillery who pounded the walls for five hours before the infantry broke through. Tunis fell more easily.

Discontent at exile of old African king

West Africa, 1536
Discontent is brewing in Gao, the capital of the vast Songhai empire, at the tyrannical rule of its monarch, Askia Bankouri.

His cruel predecessor, Musa, was assassinated amid general relief three years ago. In 1528 Musa had deposed his infirm and almost blind father, Askia Mohammed, who had founded the current Askia dynasty in 1493. Under Mohammed, peace, order and security reigned in the Songhai empire, and commerce and intellectual life flourished, as did Islam, neglected by his predecessor Sonni Ali, from whose son Mohammed seized the throne.

Mohammed's deposition was a sad affair for the old sovereign, but, given his infirmity, pragmatic for the state. Musa, at least, left him his dignity, whereas Bankouri, Mohammed's nephew, has caused much indignation by having the ex-monarch, now 93, exiled to an island in the river Niger. This is asking for trouble from the old man's other children and Bankouri's position is by no means secure.

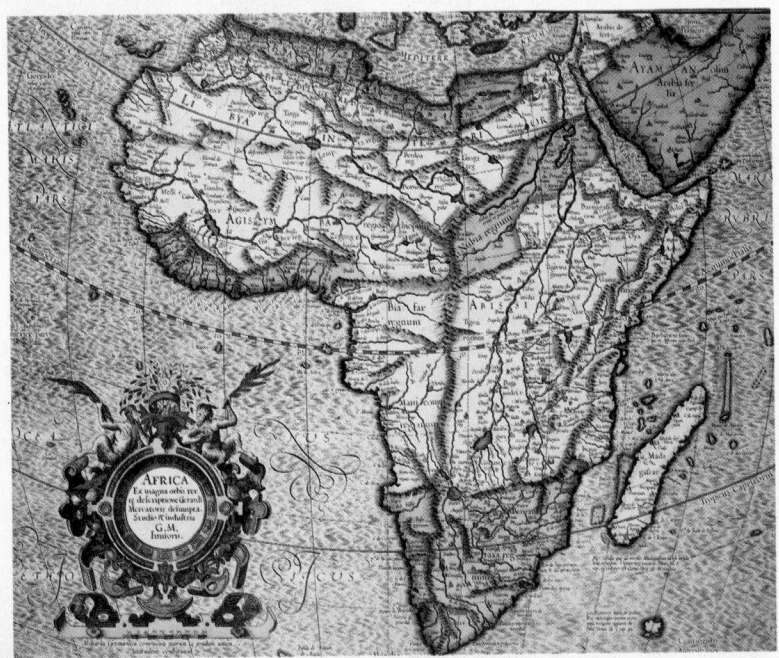

Africa, as shown in the 16th-century Mercator Atlas.

City of polygamy and world rebellion falls

Munster, Germany, 1 July 1535
Anabaptists throughout northern Europe are being forced into hiding as a tidal wave of disgust and repression sweeps Germany, Holland and Switzerland following the liberation of Munster, where Anabaptist revolutionaries had controlled the city for the last two years.

Munster's gates were reopened a week ago by the few citizens who had retained their sanity while millenarian fanatics practised polygamy, seized property, proclaimed world rebellion and threatened to kill anyone unbaptised.

Among the ringleaders seized was John of Leyden. Last August he dismissed the town council and proclaimed himself "King of New Zion" in Munster's marketplace. Leyden held the record for polygamy, taking 16 wives and using the Old Testament to justify his action. Among the 16 was the widow of Jan Matthys, the previous Anabaptist leader, killed last year when he and 20 men tried to take on forces besieging the city.

It was Matthys who ordered that no unbaptised adults should remain within the city. With the only choices being baptism or running the gauntlet of the siege troops, most chose to attend the baptisms in the town's square.

Among those killed last week was the preacher Bernard Rothmann. His questioning of the baptism of infants and promotion of a community of goods among Christians first won the townspeople to the Anabaptist cause two years ago, when some were elected to the city council long before their revolutionary tendencies became apparent.

Cartier searches for riches in Canada

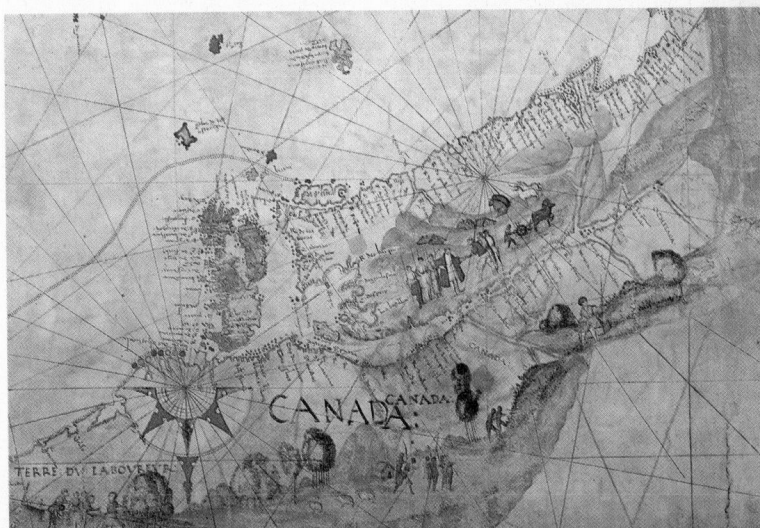

Cartier and his followers are shown in this contemporary map exploring the mouth of the St Lawrence river and having many other adventures.

St Malo, France, 6 July 1536
Jacques Cartier, the explorer, has returned from his second transatlantic expedition, having discovered the great River of Canada *(St Lawrence river)*, which he hopes will open up a huge expanse of North America. With him he has brought Donnaconna, an Iroquois chief, and ten other Iroquois.

It was the desire to find a passage to Asia, and perhaps some gold, which prompted King Francis to commission Cartier on an initial voyage in 1534, in the footsteps of the Florentine explorer Verrazzano. With three ships, Cartier made a circuit of the Labrador coast, and made friendly contact with the Indian natives, bringing two of Donnaconna's sons home with him. Last year he set off on his second voyage, taking the young Indians back. But as they penetrated further upriver, Cartier and his men fell foul of the harsh winter. Several died of scurvy while their ships were locked in ice. It was not until May that they could set sail for France.

South America, 1536. Sebastian de Belalcazar is appointed by Francisco Pizarro to organise the province of Quito. He founds the city of Popayan in the north.

South America, 1536. Pedro de Mendoza, the leader of a Spanish expedition founds the city of Santa Maria de Buenos Aires.

France, 14 July 1536. France and Portugal sign the naval treaty of Lyons against Spain.

England, 1536. Henry VIII crushes the "Pilgrimage of Grace", a religious and social rebellion in the northern counties, and orders the dissolution of the monasteries.

South America, 1536. Diego de Almagro, the governor of New Toledo, reaches Chile.

Rome, 2 June 1537. Pope Paul III issues a bull proclaiming Indians to be *veri homines* (real men and women with souls) and banning their enslavement.

England, 24 October 1537. Jane Seymour, the third wife of Henry VIII, dies.

Mexico, 1537. Antonio de Mendoza, the viceroy of New Spain, establishes the territorial limits of the estates distributed to the Spanish conquerors.

Peru, 1537. After rebelling against Pizarro and capturing Cuzco after a siege, Manco Capac II establishes a new Inca state at Vilcabamba.

Europe, 1537. The French and the Turks, who last year formed a military alliance, attack Charles V's forces in Italy and the Mediterranean.

Italy, 1537. Andreas Vesalius, a professor of anatomy at Padua, carries out dissections for the university.

Rome, 1537. Pope Paul III excommunicates the Catholic slave traders.

Hungary, 24 February 1538. Ferdinand of Habsburg and John Zapolyai, the two kings of Hungary, conclude the peace of Grosswardein.

Germany, 10 June 1538. The German Catholic princes form the League of Nuremberg to counteract the Protestant Schmalkaldic league.

France, 1538. By the truce of Nice, King Francis provisionally ends his conflict with the Emperor Charles V.

Europe, 1538. Pope Paul III, Charles V and the Venetian republic form a Holy League against the Turks.

Humans are saved or damned at birth

Basel, Switzerland, 1536
John Calvin, one of the foremost Protestant reformers, has published his personal testament of faith: *The Institutes of the Christian Religion*. Written during his stay in Strasbourg, its aim is to put an end to the divisions between the various strands of Protestantism. Its essential dogma is the omnipotence and omniscience of God.

While Martin Luther, Calvin's predecessor and in many ways his inspiration, concentrated on man and his sins, Calvin turns his attention to God and His awesome power. Calvin's worshippers must adore God; they must also show Him fear. As for sin, Calvin puts forward the doctrine of predestination. God has already chosen the elect: those who will go to heaven. No-one, however devout, can alter the divine decree. What determines whether one is chosen or damned cannot be explained. It is beyond human intelligence, but only the immoral would dare question it.

Man, to Calvin, is an insignificant creature dominated by the taint of original sin which followed the expulsion from Eden. Left alone man is incapable of good; unless he devotes himself to the abject adoration of God he is no more than a prey for every temptation. Only by submitting himself to divine omnipotence can he live a proper life. Such devotion may not lead him to heaven, but should satisfy his need to adore a greater being than his lowly self.

Protestant reformer Calvin stresses the awesome power of God.

"Danae", with Titian's characteristic rich colouring and energetic opulence.

Painter Titian reigns supreme in Europe

Venice, 1538
As a painter, Titian now has no rival in Venice and only one, Michelangelo, in the whole of Italy. He rarely leaves Venice, but this year has gone to Urbino where he is at work on a full-length Venus for the duke. The figure, a courtesan, not a goddess, looks the spectator boldly in the eye, with her little dog asleep beside her and her maids searching in her linen chest. For the duke of Ferrara, Titian painted the sensational *Bacchus and Ariadne*, in which Bacchus leaps through a rich landscape at the head of a train of satyrs and leopards. His portraits are in demand by the doges, the duke of Mantua and the emperor himself.

Humanist Erasmus has died in exile

Freiburg, Germany, 12 July 1536
Desiderius Erasmus, one of the few religious scholars who was as much loved by Catholics as by Protestants, has died here at the age of 69.

Erasmus inspired many to depart from the rigidities of the Roman Church with his emphasis on the value of education and his desire for a Christian renaissance. But he never wished for a complete split with Rome. He remained a Catholic and was recently exiled from Protestant Basle, where he had lived for many years. He believed that man could be helped to be good of his own free will, through diligent reading of the scriptures. His major work was a Greek edition of the New Testament, joined with a Latin translation, which was published in 1517 by his friend Froben, the famous printer.

Born in Rotterdam, Erasmus was widely travelled and corresponded with humanists everywhere, notably with John Colet and Thomas More, the leading English

The theologian and social thinker Erasmus, painted by Hans Holbein.

scholars. Although he was a monk for many years his real calling was scholarship. He once taught Greek at Cambridge. Many of his works, like *The Praise of Folly*, are as much critiques of contemporary social life as they are religious.

English king is seizing monastic wealth

Behaviour like this is the king's excuse to scrap monasteries altogether.

England, 1536
The son of a Putney brewer who is now Henry VIII's principle secretary has sent commissioners storming through England interrogating monks, nuns and friars and claiming to have uncovered "profound bawdry, drunken knaves" and whores in feather beds. Thomas Cromwell, a Protestant, often spoken of as a sacreligious ruffian, is seeking excuses for suppressing the monasteries and confiscating their assets. Monastic property is being put up for sale, the proceeds going to the king. Cromwell has boasted that he will make Henry the richest prince in Europe and he may well be right as the King's additional income from the sale of nearly 800 church properties has soared to around £90,000 a year. Most of them have been bought by

the gentry via the Court of Augmentations and already plans are in hand to turn many of them into private homes.

Abbots, monks and nuns are being given pensions, but many monks are seeking to supplement their incomes by becoming village priests, and this is causing much clerical unemployment. The dissolutions are said to be causing hardship because the distribution of alms has ceased. This may be one cause of the demonstrations, known as the Pilgrimage of Grace, which are taking place in the north. Others blame the unsettling effects of printing the Bible in English. When bibles were copied by monks with quills and parchment, few people ever read the sacred text. Now the monks have been bypassed by technology.

Ragged explorers were slaves of Indians

Mexico City, 1536
Some call it miraculous, others a sham, but the four emaciated men who have been brought into the city by a slaving party claim that they are all that survives of Panfilo de Narvaez' expedition of 1527, which attempted to penetrate the northern jungles.

Cabeza de Vaca, a Moor called Estevanico and two others allege that they alone escaped as 80 of their companions succumbed to

cannibalism and disease. Captured by the Indians, they spent the next six years working as bearers.

Finally they escaped and crossed the country working as *shamans* (quack doctors) They cured sick Indians and attracted large crowds, all desperate to hear the words of the "children of the sun".

Their travels took them all over Mexico, whose southern seacoast, they report, has "the best and all the most opulent countries".

Historian sees Italy as a single country

Florence, 1536
A former diplomat, and councillor to Pope Clement VII has published an important history of "Events in Italy from the Reign of Charles VIII to 1526". Francesco Guicciardini, who was born in Florence in 1483 and rose to become governor of Bologna, retired from public affairs three years ago. Since then he has been writing his History.

Guicciardini is no optimist: he sees man as a weakling, his life determined by chaotic and unforseeable events. The only hope lies in using one's intelligence, even if such efforts are often frustrated.

He despises princes, popes and people equally, although he has earned high honours working for the Medicis and the papacy.

What makes the History unique is its author's view of Italy as a single nation. Where other historians restrict themselves to studying Italy's various provinces, Guiccardini is the first historian to consider Italy as a whole. Wars and diplomacy are not divisive, but simply link one state to another.

Geneva banishes reformer Calvin

Geneva, July 1538
The Protestant reformers John Calvin and William Farel have been expelled from Geneva. The Swiss city may be considered by many as one of the citadels of the Reformed Church, but its council is still unwilling to accept the full force of the Reformation.

Farel, who makes up for his lack of learning with a fiery eloquence, arrived in the city in October 1532. After overcoming initial opposition from the Catholic hierarchy, he set about establishing Protestantism. The more the bishops attacked his preaching, the more the people flocked to hear it. On 21 May 1536 Farel's success was complete: the general council swore solemnly to live according to the word of God.

Calvin began preaching in Geneva in October 1536 and emphasised his own zeal for reform. In 1537 he joined Farel in demanding that every citizen swear to the Confession of Faith, on pain of banishment. The council rejected this reform and the two reformers have been banished themselves.

A new style for city halls in Flanders

The extraordinary town hall at Bruges, by William Callow (1812-1908).

Flanders, c.1537
A new style of architecture, combining the advances of the Italian Renaissance with traditional gothic flamboyance, is to be seen in a number of richly decorated new public

buildings in Flanders. Among the principal examples are the Palais de Justice at Michelen, the Stock Exchange at Antwerp and the city hall at Oudenaarde, which was completed in 1525.

The European Renaissance

When the artist Vasari produced his biographies of Italian artists in the mid 16th century, he arranged them in three groups, parallelling human growth. The first phase, corresponding to infancy, included artists such as Cimabue and Giotto. The second, adolescence, brought the work of Donatello and Brunelleschi. Maturity was reached with the work of Leonardo da Vinci, and, above all, Michelangelo. Implicit in the arrangement is the sense of a new artistic life. Like his contemporaries, Vasari took it for granted that Italy had led the way in a return to classical learning and values which constituted a break with the immediate past so radical as to deserve the title of *la rinascita*: the rebirth, or, in French, *Renaissance*.

A clean break with the past?

The image of rebirth has been immensely potent. It has led to the originally derogatory concept of the *middle ages*: the period between two high spots, the classical world and the Renaissance. Inherent in it is a cyclical view of history, with upswings and downswings; a concept which assumes that the period immediately before the Renaissance was one of decline and decay. Few historians would now accept that. Nor would most accept that the break with the past is as total, or as unheralded, as Vasari and others liked to believe. It does not belittle the achievements of the time to point out that they occurred within a context which was still, in many respects, recognisably "mediaeval", and that the mediaeval world itself had knowingly absorbed a range of classical influences.

The appeal to the past inherent in the Renaissance was in itself in one sense "mediaeval". The middle ages had strongly believed that the past was best, and that although contemporaries might excel the great men of the past, they did so because they had the benefit of their achievements. They were, in a popular image, dwarves on the shoulders of giants. It could be argued that the real shift in attitude only happened later, when people began to believe in the possibility of linear progress: that the future was necessarily better than the past.

Nevertheless, the Renaissance view of the past was in one important respect different from that of the middle ages. The humanists of the 15th century were aware that in studying the classical world they were exploring a society which was quite separate from their own. For mediaeval writers history was more usually seen in terms of the present. This was often true in a literal sense, with the past imagined in modern dress, as shown by mediaeval painting. The past was also valued primarily as a source of moral advice for the present, rather than in its own right.

As this suggests, the Renaissance did bring shifts of attitude, at least among the educated elite. They acquired a heightened sense of human potentialities. There was a sense that humanity could, if it chose, control its own destiny. The work of Niccolo Machiavelli emphasises man the political manipulator. Ambition, not in itself new, became rather more acceptable, even admirable. The eroticism fashionable in some literary circles is another manifestation of the view that it was up to individuals to take what they wanted out of life. This did not preclude a continuing sense of human transience and vulnerability, in fact the two were opposite sides of the same coin. Leonardo scribbled repeatedly in his later notebooks: "Was anything ever done?"

Sacred and secular

This emphasis on the individual and on individual achievements has been seen as a sign of a growing secularisation. Other aspects of the Renaissance support this picture. In the visual arts, the new genres of portraiture, still life and landscape, as well as a fashion for classical subjects, gradually began to erode the overwhelming predominance of religious themes, for instance. But the essential moral framework remained Christian. A few of the humanist scholars who immersed themselves in classical writings liked to claim that they were pagan rather than Christian, but the great majority saw their literary and philological skills as a means to reform the church rather than displace it. The period also kept the capacity for dramatic reassertions of Christian austerity, as in the famous bonfires of the vanities inspired by the preaching of Savonarola.

Alongside the rediscovery of the classical past ran a parallel rediscovery of astrological and magical texts; indeed the central assumption of cyclical ages is itself astrological. Few contemporaries would have disputed that, since the universe was a unity, the configuration of the heavens could be read as evidence of imminent happenings on earth. Similarly, an individual's character could be shaped by the stars at the moment of his birth. Since the unity of the universe was the work of God, astrology was not in itself considered un-Christian, although the church insisted that, given human free will, the stars could only predispose, not compel.

A number of Renaissance thinkers, however, were not prepared to be the playthings of the stars even to this extent. They believed that by using the techniques of natural magic, or words of power such as the Hebrew names of God, they could turn the power of the heavens to their own ends. This was the height of individualism, and some of the strongest claims for individual potentiality occur in the writings of the natural magicians such as Pico della Mirandola: "O highest and marvellous felicity of man. To him it is granted to have whatever he chooses, to be whatever he wills."

The natural magicians were careful to stress that their powers were essentially Christian. Mirandola, immediately before the passage quoted above, thanked God for his generosity in allowing man such freedom. The church was less convinced; but even so, the systems of natural magic can hardly be seen as "secular". Their emphasis on the inter-relationship of creation encouraged acceptance of an elaborate structure of mystical parallels and analogies, within which a mediaeval scholar would have been perfectly at home.

Symbols and reality

This was one manifestation of a continuing fondness for symbolism which needs to be set against claims that the Renaissance brought a new realism to art. Giotto and his successors worked steadily towards a solidity of representation which aimed to show things as "real" in the sense that they had apparent weight and substance. But Renaissance artists never just painted what was there. In painting a prince they were making a statement about the nature of rulers as well as mapping the face of an individual. They also continued, as the artists of the middle ages had done, to use images to make hidden, or semi-hidden statements by means of symbolism and metaphor. Although their work seems immediately accessible to the non-specialist, it was also, to that extent, avowedly elitist; something which is most obvious when the meaning has been lost, as with Botticelli's *Primavera*.

Italy was the birthplace of the Renaissance, but new techniques and attitudes soon spread. Artists such as Durer travelled to Italy to study. Italians took their skills elsewhere: Leonardo da Vinci ended his days at the French court. The result was not a universal culture; outside Italy, the Renaissance was inevitably influenced by national traditions. But, until the mid 17th century, Italy held its place as the supreme arbiter of European taste.

The elegant classicism of Sansovino's Library in Venice, by Canaletto.

The chateau of Chambord, a French Renaissance masterpiece, begun 1519.

Unidentified man, by Holbein (1497-1543), typical of his urbane realism.

"Salome", by Titian (c.1487-1576), almost impressionistic in its richness.

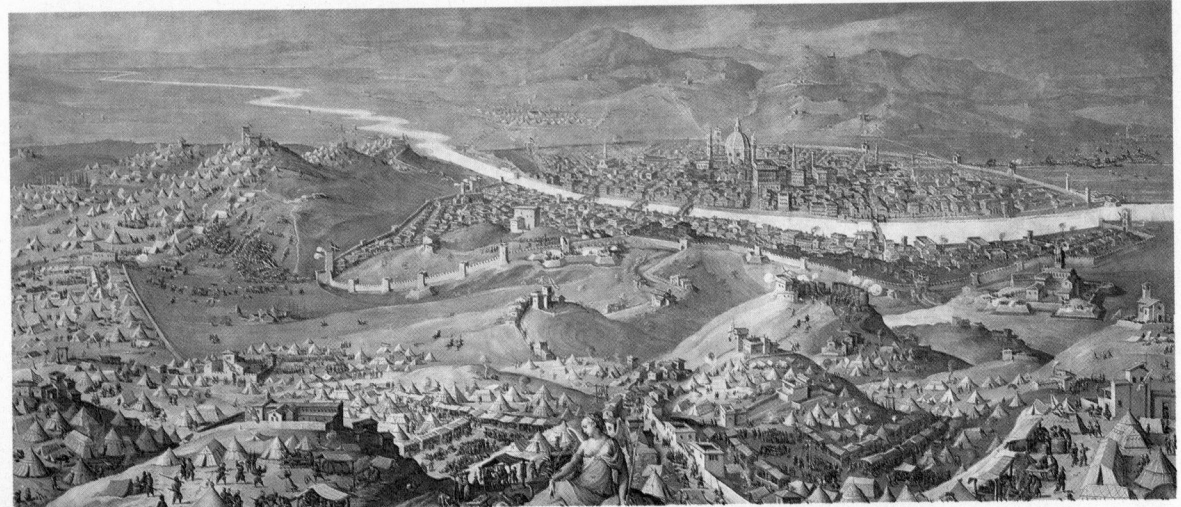

A view of Florence, a leading Renaissance city, by Giorgio Vasari, a major artist and commentator.

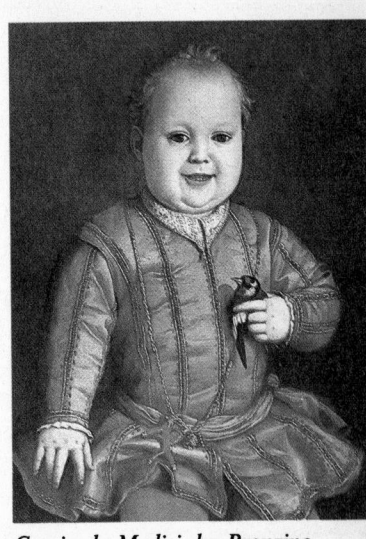

Garcia de Medici, by Bronzino.

Peru, July 1538. Diego de Almagro is executed on the orders of Pizarro.

Mediterranean, 1538. Supported by the French, the Ottomans try unsuccessfully to capture the island of Corfu from the Venetians.

Mediterranean, September 1538. The Ottomans defeat the Venetians and their allies under Andrea Doria at Prevesa, securing naval supremacy in the Mediterranean.

India, 1538. Khadim Suleiman Pasha, the Ottoman governor of Egypt, sends a fleet to attack India, but the Turks fail to take Diu in Gujarat and return home.

Arabia, 1538. With the surrender of Basra to the Turks, the Ottoman empire now reaches the Gulf.

Spain, 1 February 1539. The Emperor Charles V and Francis, the king of France, sign the treaty of Toledo.

Germany, 19 April 1539. The Emperor Charles V reaches a truce with the German Protestants at Frankfurt.

Florida, 30 May 1539. The Spanish explorer Hernando de Soto, coming from Cuba, lands 600 troops in search of gold.

Florida, 4 June 1539. Hernando de Soto finds Juan Ortiz, a survivor of the Panfilo de Narvaez voyage of 1527, living with the Indians.

New Mexico, June 1539. The Negro slave Estevanico is murdered by Zuni Indians. Father Marcos, his expedition leader, goes on to find the fabled Seven Golden Cities of Cibola. However, the villages do not contain gold; on the contrary, their Zuni inhabitants live in extreme poverty.

France, 10 August 1539. King Francis orders all legal decisions and documents to be drawn up from now on in French, not Latin. The same decree instructs priests to keep a record of all baptisms and deaths.

Mexico, 1539. Antonio de Mendoza, appointed viceroy of New Spain four years ago, establishes the first printing press in the New World, in Mexico City.

Flanders, 1539. The Emperor Charles V puts down a rebellion in Ghent and strips the town of its privileges. The townspeople had refused to pay taxes to finance the war with Francis of France and had called in vain on the French king for help.

Spain, 1539. Charles V orders the university of Salamanca to suspend all debates and to forbid the publication of all books on the right of conquest.

France, 1539. The edict of Villers Cotterets ends a paralysing strike of the printing industry in Paris and Lyons.

Italy, 27 January 1540. Angela de Medici, who founded the Ursuline order to educate young girls, dies at Brescia.

Mexico, February 1540. Francisco Vasquez de Coronado leaves New Spain with 400 Spaniards and 1,000 Indians on an expedition northwards to find the Seven Golden Cities of Cibola.

India, 17 May 1540. The Afghan chief Sher Khan defeats the Moghul Emperor Humayun at Kanauj. The emperor is forced to flee India and Sher Khan becomes *Sher Shah Suri*, ruler of northern India.

North America, 7 July 1540. Francisco Vasquez de Coronado conquers an Indian *pueblo* in south-western North America, believing it to be one of the Seven Golden Cities of Cibola.

England, 9 July 1540. Henry VIII divorces his fourth wife, Anne of Cleves, the choice of Thomas Cromwell, after only six months of marriage.

England, 28 July 1540. Henry VIII marries Catherine Howard.

London, 23 July 1540. Toppled and discredited by his enemies at court, Thomas Cromwell is beheaded on Tower Hill.

Hungary, July 1540. John Zapolyai, who declared himself king of Hungary in November 1526, dies and is succeeded by his son John Sigmund.

Italy, 28 August, 1540. The painter Francesco Mazzola, known as Parmigiano from his home town of Parma, dies at the age of 37, while still working on his *Madonna with the Long Neck*, which he began in 1534.

Paris, 30 August 1540. The humanist scholar Guillaume Bude dies. His vast learning encompassed languages (including Greek), mathematics, natural sciences, history and theology, and he founded both the College of the Three Languages and the library of Fontainebleau.

North America, August 1540. The Spaniard Hernando de Alvarado forges his way up the Rio Grande in south-western North America to the Indian village of Taos.

North America, August 1540. Hernando de Soto encounters Temple Mound Indian culture at Coosa *(Alabama)*.

Milan, 11 October 1540. The Emperor Charles V puts his son Philip in control of Milan.

Pizarro garrottes former partner in Peru

Diego de Almagro is garrotted and decapitated by Peru's governor Pizarro.

Cuzco, Peru, 1538
Governor Francisco Pizarro rejected pleas for clemency from his former friend and expedition partner, Diego de Almagro, before the 63-year-old Almagro was garrotted. The two men had always disputed the charter which made Pizarro governor. Almagro was also made governor of ill-defined territory beyond Pizarro's. Some years later an Inca rebellion besieged the mountain capital of Cuzco, defended by Pizarro's brothers. Almagro, returning with an embittered force from a fruitless search for gold in Chile, seized Cuzco himself. Internecine warfare followed.

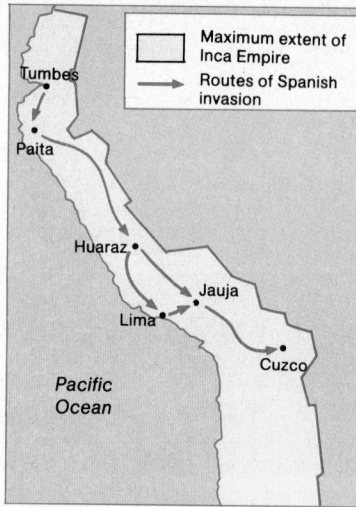

Poet founder of Sikh movement is dead

Punjab, India, 1539
Guru Nanak, poet, mystic and founder of a new faith which discounts both Islam and Hinduism has died.

In 1499, aged 30, Nanak experienced two days of mystical ecstasy. His conclusions are recorded in his *Adi-Granth*. The main emphasis of this religion lays in loving devotion to a wholly spiritual god by divine grace. He has called his followers *Sikhs* – the Punjabi for disciples. On emerging from his vision, the guru declared: "There is no real Hindu and no real Moslem."

Guru Nanak, who founded the Sikh religion after a mystical revelation.

Print makes big impression in Europe

One of Germany's printing presses.

A bible with Roman and Gothic type.

Europe, 1539
Fifteen years after the death of Gutenberg there are printing presses in operation in every country in western Christendom: from Sweden in the north to Sicily in the south, and from Spain in the west to Poland and Hungary in the east. The new technology has caught on rapidly and surely.

There have been developments of all kinds, both technical and aesthetic. Initially, the printers followed the old scribes in the type-faces which they used. But soon the possibilities opened up, with metal punch cutters being used to produce distinctive type styles, such as the Roman font which began to

supersede the traditional Gothic. Among the purely technical developments to assist the explosive spread of printing has been that of an oil-bound ink – attributed to Gutenberg himself – which clings closely to the metal type and produces a smudge-free impression.

Presses, too, are being improved all the time. The original Gutenberg press was modified so that the screw which forced the paper onto the linked type could be worked with a smaller amount of movement of the bar. This speeds up the printing of each individual sheet.

Few factors in this age of rapid technological advance have had more impact than printing.

Pope approves the Society of Jesus

Rome, 27 September 1540
A papal bull issued here today establishes a new religious order, the Society of Jesus, whose object is "the propagation of the faith". The order began in 1534 in Paris when Ignatius Loyola, a soldier turned priest, and six others took a vow to offer themselves to the pope to be sent wherever he wished to convert infidels, even the Turks.

The new order does not require its members to say the daily office together, like monks, but only to pray silently. Their essential vow is one of total obedience to the pope and to their superior, Loyola, who is to be elected general of the society. His *Spiritual Exercises* are the training for the life of a Jesuit.

Pope Paul III gives his papal bull to Ignatius Loyola, and so founds the Jesuit order.

Monks' treasures seized in royal purge

Monasteries must surrender all their treasures to Henry's commissioners.

England, 23 March 1540
The last of England's big monastic houses, Waltham Abbey in Essex, was seized by the crown today, bringing to a close a four-year campaign that has seen over 550 properties, with their treasure of plate and jewels, pass into the king's possession. The 370 smaller monasteries, which were the first to fall, brought Henry some £32,000 a year, and the 186 bigger ones, which followed, £100,000. But the king will not enjoy the whole of this income.

Henry is giving his supporters gifts of property and putting some other estates up for auction. Family fortunes are being founded on the suppression of the monasteries. A local squire in Sussex, William Cavendish, has already acquired three Hertfordshire manors and reckons that, with luck, he could become a duke in a few years' time. The appropriately-named Sir Richard Rich, who is helping to administer the seized properties, has himself acquired 59 manors, 31 rectories and 28 vicarages. Some of the new rich are founding colleges.

The suppression came about because Henry wanted to lay hands

The king also wants nuns' wealth.

on the wealth, but it is also true that, after his quarrel with Rome, the monasteries were an obstacle to the consolidation of his power over the church. As for the monks, they have lost more than their monasteries: mitred abbots no longer sit in the House of Lords.

Artificial limbs help crippled veterans

Paris, 1539
A French army surgeon, Ambroise Pare, has developed an innovation in medical treatment which gives new hope to those unfortunate enough to lose limbs on the battlefield and elsewhere. To replace amputated legs or arms, Pare is fitting ingenious mechanical devices which mimic the movements

of the natural limbs. He is not the first to attempt some kind of prosthesis for amputees, but his are the most sophisticated yet developed. One hand has a holder for a pen; another has fingers which move with the aid of tiny cog wheels.

Pare has already gained a reputation in the field for his treatment of gunshot wounds.

Flanders, 1540. After putting down a rebellion in the town last year, the Emperor Charles V demands that the aldermen and leaders of the guilds in Ghent come to beg his pardon with nooses around their necks. About 20 of them are executed.

Indian Ocean, 1540. Andriamanelo, the first Merina king of Madagascar, comes to the throne.

South-East Asia, 1540. The Portuguese start to trade with Cochinchina *(Vietnam)*.

Germany, c.1540. Maps published by the great cartographer Gerardus Mercator use the word America to describe the new lands discovered by Christopher Columbus – although it is now known that Amerigo Vespucci, after whom the lands were named, was wrongly described as his ship's captain.

France, 17 October 1540. King Francis entrusts the explorer Jacques Cartier with the task of "penetrating further into the country of Canada" in order to find a new route to China.

North America, 19 October 1540. The Spaniard Hernando de Soto is set upon by Choctaw Indians at Mabile *(Mobile, Alabama)*, who kill 18 of his party and injure 170. De Soto claims that his men have killed 2,800 Indians.

France, 14 November 1540. The Italian painter Rosso Fiorentino (Giovanni Battista di Jacopo) dies in Paris. Invited to France by the king in 1532, he supervised the building work on the chateau of Fontainebleau until his death.

North America, 1540. Priests accompanying Hernando de Soto on his expedition conduct the first recorded baptism in the New World: that of an Indian guide.

North America, December 1540. Lopez de Cardenas, an officer in the service of the Spaniard Francisco Vasquez de Coronado, discovers the Grand Canyon.

South America, 12 February 1541. Pedro de Valdivia, a lieutenant of Francisco Pizarro, founds the city of Santiago in Chile.

North America, March 1541. The Spanish suppress an Indian rebellion after a siege of *pueblos* at Tiguex.

North America, 8 May 1541. De Soto reaches a large river which he names Rio de Espiritu Santo *(the Mississippi)*.

Peru, 26 June 1541. Francisco Pizarro is assassinated in Lima. Diego el Monzo, the son of Almagro – executed by Pizarro's supporters three years ago – proclaims himself governor.

North America, 23 August 1541. Jacques Cartier lands near Quebec on his third voyage to Canada. His expedition has been commissioned to found a permanent settlement.

Austria, 24 September 1541. The Swiss alchemist and doctor Theophrastus Paracelsus dies in exile in Salzburg.

North America, 1541. Hernando de Soto completes a two-year expedition to explore the lands west of the Mississippi river.

Morocco, 1541. The Portuguese are driven out of Agadir by the Sadian rulers.

Rome, 1541. Ignatius Loyola is elected general of the Jesuits, the religious order which he created.

Hungary, 1541. Ferdinand of Habsburg, the king of Hungary and Bohemia, is defeated at Pest by the Turks, who seize Buda. Hungary becomes a Turkish province.

East Africa, 1541. Francis Xavier, the Spanish Jesuit and companion of Loyola, begins a mission to Mozambique, Malindi and Socotra.

North Africa, 1541. The Emperor Charles V launches an unsuccessful expedition against Algiers.

Hungary, 29 December 1541. Under the treaty of Gyalu, John Zapolyai's widow cedes Hungary to Ferdinand of Habsburg.

England, 13 February 1542. Catherine Howard, Henry VIII's fifth wife, is executed for immoralities committed before she married the king.

Mexico, April 1542. Francisco Vasquez de Coronado returns to Mexico after failing to find in the interior of North America either the fabled Seven Golden Cities of Cibola or another legendary land of fabulous riches called Quivira.

North America, April 1542. Jean Francois de Roberval arrives as governor of Canada at the settlement founded last year by Jacques Cartier, who has now returned to France.

North America, 21 May 1542. De Soto dies on the banks of the Mississippi river.

Rome, 22 May 1542. Pope Paul III summons a general council of the church to meet at the imperial city of Trent. Its purpose is to achieve the reformation of the church, the definition of dogma and the reunion of Christendom.

Europe, 1542. Prompted by the appointment two years ago of Charles V's son Philip to the control of Milan, Francis of France reopens hostilities with the emperor. Charles V has forged an anti-French alliance with Henry VIII of England.

New royal palaces reflect Italian styles

No need for fortifications: Francis' new gallery at Fontainebleau.

France/England, 1540

Spearheaded by the design for the new royal palace at Fontainebleau, an outburst of architectural activity is to be seen in France. Where nobles once built for defence, they are now building for beauty and for comfort. Led by King Francis, with his preference for Italian design, members of the aristocracy are turning their old castles into elegant modern palaces.

The king, who picked up his interest in Italian architecture during his recent campaigns, imported three Italians to work on Fontainebleau. Between them they formed what has been called "The School of Fontainebleau", and their ideas have spread across France, influencing many home-grown architects. And since Fontainebleau was completed, in 1528, the new architecture has spread beyond France to make its impression on builders across the rest of Europe.

Working with the ideas of the Italian Renaissance, architects have begun replacing the old thick walls, small windows and massive towers with elegant new structures which stress the modern role of a nobleman's home.

England, too, has a fine stately home in Hampton Court Palace, built by Cardinal Wolsey and presented by him to Henry VIII in 1526. Unlike many French castles, however, this great house has never been the scene of battle.

The battlements of Hampton Court, near London, are only for decoration.

Amazon named after its women warriors

A golden pectoral ornament of the Tolima culture, c.500-c.1500 AD.

South America, 24 August 1542
Spanish *conquistadores* have sailed the length of the great river which crosses this continent from the Atlantic to the Andes. They have named it the Amazon, after a gang of Indian women who attacked them with bows and arrows on their way homewards.

The 200-strong expedition was led by Gonzalo Pizarro, who set out on Christmas Day 1539 to find the legendary land of El Dorado. It was one of his men, Francisco de Orellana, who ventured onto the river to seek supplies. He built a boat, then sailed it with 57 men – facing danger on the way from Indians and strong rapids. Their journey lasted eight months, by which time Pizarro had returned to the river's mouth.

African slave-trade crosses Atlantic

Lisbon, c.1542
It is 108 years since the first slaves were bought by Portuguese traders from African slave dealers and sold in Lisbon. Ten years ago, 800 blacks went to Europe annually. A sharp increase in the trade to American colonies occurred as undermanned plantations sought more labour. The trade measures livestock by the *peca*, or one male slave in peak condition. Two women and a baby make the same unit. From low levels, the trade with America built up about ten years ago to 5,000 pecas from the Kongo alone.

The traffic gives Jesuit and Franciscan missions interesting problems. Africans fit for conversion, the argument goes, must have immortal souls. Having souls they are men, not beasts to be enslaved. Spain's colonial party cites Aristotle's dictum that natives are "slaves by nature".

Francesco Maria Mazzuola's painting of Antea La Bella shows what Italy's smart set is wearing: a silk gown with ruffles, heavy jewellery and fur accessories.

Pope steps up fight against Protestants

Determined: Titian's recent portrait of the pope and his nephews.

Rome, 21 July 1542
Pope Paul III has today set up a Roman inquisition. Six cardinals have been appointed as inquisitors-general, with powers to imprison on suspicion, to confiscate property and to execute the guilty. The move represents the triumph of the militant party, led by Cardinal Caraffa, which wants to put an end to the attempts of the moderates to conciliate Lutherans and Calvinists. According to Caraffa, "No man is to lower himself by showing toleration towards any sort of heretic, least of all a Calvinist." He wants a purge as fierce as that in Spain towards the end of the last century when many thousands of Jews were killed. Today's Protestants, however, are much more powerful and are likely to resist.

The weavers of Brussels produce finely-worked masterpieces of tapestry. Here, hunters, dogs and other beasts fill an exotic garden.

1542 (1542-1544)

Germany, 26 August 1542. Under the treaty of Nuremberg, the duchy of Lorraine becomes independent of the German empire.

Germany, September 1542. The German craftsman Peter Henlein dies at Nuremberg. He was responsible for inventing a spring to replace the weights in a clock, making possible the production of the first watch.

Peru, September 1542. Diego el Monzo Almagro is defeated at the battle of Chupas and condemned to death by Vaca de Castro, the representative of the Spanish crown.

North America, 28 September 1542. The Spanish explorer Juan Rodriguez Cabrillo enters a harbour *(San Diego)* on the Pacific coast. He is the first European in California.

Spain, 22 November 1542. New laws are passed in Burgos giving protection against enslavement to the Indians in America.

England, 24 November 1542. In a war provoked by Henry VIII's desire to control Scotland, the English inflict a defeat on the Scots at the battle of Solway Moss.

Scotland, 14 December 1542. James V of Scotland dies and is succeeded by his one-year-old daughter, Mary Stuart, whose mother, Mary of Guise, becomes regent.

Switzerland, 1542. Recalled to Geneva, from whence he was expelled three years ago, the Protestant reformer John Calvin begins to implement his original scheme for the creation of a godly government.

India, 1542. The Spanish Jesuit Francis Xavier arrives in Goa on a mission to spread the gospel.

North America, January 1543. Juan Rodriguez Cabrillo dies after exploring the western coast from lower California to the north for 1,000 miles *(Oregon)*.

Germany, 10 February 1543. Johann Mayer, known as Johann Eck, Luther's chief adversary, dies at Ingolstad. A humanist who hoped to see the revival of the Catholic church, Eck was responsible for having Luther excommunicated. He took part in the Diet of Augsburg in 1530 and, in 1537, published a Catholic version of the German translation of the Bible.

Mexico, 14 April 1543. Bartoleme Ferrelo, who took command of the Spanish fleet after the death of Cabrillo in January, returns after discovering and exploring a large bay area *(San Francisco)*.

England, 1 July 1543. England and Scotland sign the peace of Greenwich.

England, 15 July 1543. Henry VIII marries his sixth wife, Catherine Parr.

London, 29 November 1543. The German painter Hans Holbein the Younger dies at the age of 46, while at the height of his career. He settled in England in 1532 and was appointed painter to Henry VIII in 1536. He executed a series of portraits of the great Englishmen of his time.

Scotland, 11 December 1543. The Scottish Parliament repudiates the treaty of Greenwich.

Japan, 1543. A Portuguese ship is wrecked off Tanegashima island. Three matchlock guns on board are bought by the Japanese, who have not seen firearms since the aborted Mongol invasion in the 13th century.

France, 1543. The Berber corsair Khey ad-Din Barbarossa combines forces with the fleet of Francis, the king of France, to bombard, besiege and sack the imperial town of Nice.

England, 1543. Revising the *Bishop's Book* of 1537, which defended Catholic orthodoxy against Protestant innovation, the *King's Book* confirms statutes passed by parliament in May 1539. These maintain key elements of Catholic doctrine, such as the validity of monastic vows, and outlaw any further theological reform.

North America, 1543. Oil is found in the region *(in Texas)* for the first time, by the Spaniard Luis de Moscoso.

Italy, 14 April 1544. A French army defeats the imperial forces of Charles V at the battle of Ceresole, south of Turin.

Scotland, May 1544. The English invade Scotland and attack Edinburgh. They pillage the city but fail to gain a surrender from the Scots.

France, July 1544. In their war with France, the combined forces of the Emperor Charles V and Henry VIII of England take St Dizier and threaten Paris.

France, 14 September 1544. Henry VIII's forces take Boulogne.

France, 19 September 1544. In an effort to restore Catholic unity in Europe, King Francis and the Emperor Charles V sign the treaty of Crespy. Francis promises to support the emperor against the Protestants if they refuse to accept the decisions of the forthcoming Council of Trent; Francis' son will be married to a Habsburg princess.

King's physician was body-snatcher

Andreas Vesalius, the anatomist.

Basle, Switzerland, 1543
A superbly illustrated and printed work on human anatomy has rapidly become required reading among doctors throughout Europe. Called *De humani corporis fabrica libri septem*, this major event in medical publishing is the work of Andreas Vesalius, Charles V's physician, and the anatomical details are based on numerous dissections. Many of these were performed on corpses which had been exhumed or taken from gibbets while he was studying in France.

The book has already created controversy among doctors, who have mostly taken the work of the Greek anatomist, Galen, as definitive in this area. This new study corrects some 200 errors, but Vesalius' methods of obtaining bodies to dissect have offended many. Dissection of human bodies is officially forbidden in any case.

Suleiman assumes power as caliph

Constantinople, 1543
On the death of the last member of the Abbasid family, Suleiman, the Ottoman sultan, has assumed the title of *caliph* – successor to the Prophet Mohammed – which makes him the most powerful of the Moslem sovereigns. He has written to the sherif of Mecca, a direct descendant of the Prophet, to announce that God has put him in charge.

Suleiman's move has been accepted – with some reluctance – by the Islamic community. The sherif has written to the sultan accepting that, "by the grace of God", he does indeed occupy the throne of the sublime sultanate and the dignity of the grand caliphate. But he adds with some subtlety that it is Suleiman's conquests "that have made you first amongst all and the most senior of the sultans of Islam".

The new caliph, Suleiman.

Old adversaries' treaty has secret clause

Crespy, France, 19 September 1544
This small village was the scene today of the signing of a peace treaty between two great adversaries: the emperor, Charles V, and Francis, the king of France. Their countries have been at war for more than 20 years, but France has now agreed to join the emperor in his war against the Turks.

A marriage settlement has been agreed as part of the treaty. Francis' son, the duke of Orleans, is to marry either Charles' daughter, Mary, or Anne, the daughter of Ferdinand of Bohemia. In the first case, the dowry would be the Netherlands; in the second, Milan.

In the second part of the agreement, Francis has promised to help the emperor to reform the church and work towards bringing the German Protestants back into the Catholic fold – lending his army for the purpose if necessary. This part has been kept a close secret.

Earth may not be centre of universe

Nicolaus Copernicus, astronomer.

East Prussia, 24 May 1543
Today, a new book was brought to its author as he lay dying. The work in question promises to be a major contribution to the science of astronomy, and its author, Nicolaus Copernicus, has suggested a radically different way of seeing the universe and man's place in it.

In the six sections of *On the Revolution of the Heavenly Spheres*, Copernicus proposes a "heliocentric theory" of the universe. He claims that Earth is not, as the influential astronomer Ptolemy had proposed in the second century AD, the centre of all things. The planets do not revolve around us: Earth, like the other planets, revolves around the sun. Indeed, the text argues that even the sun itself is not the true centre of things; this

Revolutionary revolutions: the solar system makes Earth just another planet.

is some distance away. But the heliocentric theory still has a mathematical elegance and cogency that is lacking in Ptolemy and Aristotle.

If Earth is not the centre of the universe then nor, perhaps, are its inhabitants. We should begin to look at ourselves in a slightly different light, not as the trimphant epitome of creation.

Moreover, Copernicus' theory implies that the universe is much bigger than we thought. If Earth orbits the sun we should detect small periodic variations in the positions of the stars. The fact that

the stars seem to be static could mean that they are simply too distant for us to detect their variations. Some are saying that perhaps the universe is infinite, with stars going on for ever.

Another effect of the book is to change astronomers' views on falling bodies. In Aristotelian theory, the reason bodies fall to Earth is that Earth is the centre of the universe. Now that Copernicus has destroyed that idea, another explanation will have to be found for why a cannon ball or an autumn leaf falls to the ground.

Japan's "shoguns" get first shotguns

Japan, 1543
The gun has arrived in Japan. Two Portuguese adventurers, the first Europeans known to have landed in Japan, brought *arquebuses* with them, and when Tokitaka, the feudal lord of Tanegashima, saw them bring down a duck, he paid a fortune in gold for the guns.

Tokitaka handed them to his chief swordsmith, Yatsuita, and ordered him to copy them. Yatsuita, trading his daughter for lessons from the armourer of another Portuguese ship, has gone into mass production.

Turkish pirates capture and pillage Nice

Nice, France, 1543
Nice has been captured and sacked by the corsair Barbarossa. The town, the gateway to Italy, is on fire and the Turkish pirates are rampaging through the burning ruins, looting and raping. This destruction is in direct contravention of the terms of the surrender agreed when the governor capitulated to the joint French and Turkish forces. Now the French are blaming the Turks while the Turks blame the French.

This alliance against the forces of the Emperor Charles V has never been easy. Dubbed the "impious alliance" by Charles, it has brought

Barbarossa's fleet of 100 galleys to the ports of southern France and much unpopularity to King Francis. The corsair – "Chief of the Seas" – has set up his headquarters at Toulon where the inhabitants are humiliated by seeing Moslems pacing the decks of his ships while Christian slaves, Frenchmen among them, are chained to the galleys' oars and rowing benches. The Turks have taken to raiding French villages, carrying off peasants to replace rowers killed by the fever. Christian slaves are sold in the market place and the muezzin calls for Moslem prayer in Christian Toulon.

Explorer dies on Mississippi banks

Mexico, September 1542
The remnants of Hernando de Soto's expedition have landed in Mexico by the Panuco River. They are without their leader, who died on 21 May, aged 46, beside the "great muddy river" *(Mississippi)* that he discovered just over a year ago.

De Soto was an experienced Spanish soldier who made his name with Pizarro's expedition to Peru in 1524. Though he returned to Spain loaded with gold and silver, he grew restless. In 1538, with the blessing of King Charles, he set out from Spain with 600 troops, 200 horses and a pack of bloodhounds, bound for the Americas, once more in search of gold.

Landing on the west coast of Florida in May 1539, de Soto's well-armed force set about subduing the

De Soto: explorer and warrior who sailed the Mississipi last year.

natives, taking prisoners whether they were friendly or not. In August 1540, at Coosa *(Alabama)*, de Soto came across the Indians of the Temple Mound culture. Three months later he met and imprisoned Chief Tuscaloosa, who organised an ambush in which at least 18 Spaniards died, and de Soto claimed to have killed more than 2,000 Indians.

Pressing on through often inhospitable terrain, with hostile Indians, de Soto reached the great muddy river, and spent the next year exploring westwards. After his death, the 332 survivors built a raft and floated down to Mexico.

1544 (1544-1546)

England, 1544. Parliament recognises Mary and Elizabeth, the daughters of Henry VIII, as heirs to the throne of England in the event of the king's son, Edward, dying childless.

Peru, 1544. Blasco Nunez de Vela, appointed first viceroy of Peru last year by the Emperor Charles V, arrives in Lima.

Germany, 1544. Denmark and the Netherlands sign the treaty of Speyer, by which the Netherlands are granted full rights of trade and passage in the Baltic.

Germany, 1544. The first Jesuit college in Germany is founded in Cologne.

Denmark, 1544. A major witch-hunt results in the execution of 52 witches in Malmo, Koge and Jutland.

Mozambique, 1544. Portuguese trading posts are opened at the former Moslem port of Quelimane and at Maputo Bay *(Lourenco Marques)*.

Korea, 1544. Chungjong, who came to the throne of Korea in 1506 after a revolt against the cruel ruler Yonsangun, dies. During his reign he used the Confucian scholars in an attempt to curb the power of the great families, but the scholars were defeated.

Scotland, 25 February 1545. The English army receives a set-back at the hands of the Scots at Ancrum Moor.

Italy, 26 August 1545. Pietro Luigi Farnese, the son of Pope Paul III, establishes the duchy of Parma and Piacenza.

Scotland, September 1545. The English again invade Scotland.

France, September 1545. Hans Baldung Grien, the portraitist, engraver and painter of both religious and secular subjects, dies at Strasbourg.

Balkans, November 1545. The Emperor Charles V and Suleiman, the sultan of the Ottomans, reach a truce at Adrianople.

Italy, 13 December 1545. The general council summoned by Pope Paul III in May 1542 opens in the imperial city of Trent. It has been delayed by renewed fighting between France and the empire.

Mexico, 1545. The Spanish missionary Bartolomeo de las Casas takes up his duties as bishop of Chiapas, a position to which he was appointed two years ago. A champion of Indian rights, las Casas is given a hostile reception by the colonists.

India, 1545. Humayun, the Moghul emperor, captures Kandahar.

Germany, 18 February 1546. Martin Luther, dies at his native town of Eisleben.

Scotland, 1 March 1546. The reformer George Wishart, who preached the Lutheran doctrine of justification by faith, is burnt to death on the orders of Cardinal Beaton, the archbishop of St Andrew's.

South America, April 1546. The German explorers Philipp von Hutten and Bartholomew Welser are murdered by the Spanish at Coro.

Scotland, 29 May 1546. Cardinal Beaton, the archbishop of St Andrew's, who is responsible for a sustained persecution of Protestants, is assassinated by a band of conspirators who take possession of his castle. After the death of James V in 1542, Beaton produced a forged will, appointing himself and three others regents of the kingdom. He was arrested, but later became chancellor and promoted a pro-French policy.

France, 7 June 1546. Francis of France and Henry VIII of England sign the peace of Ardres, ending the conflict which began two years ago when Henry launched an invasion of France from Calais. Under the terms of the treaty, Boulogne is to remain in English hands for eight years.

Rome, 7 June 1546. Bent on crushing the independence of the German states and restoring the unity of the church, the Emperor Charles V makes a pact with Pope Paul III, who promises him money and troops in his fight against the Protestants.

Germany, 20 July 1546. Charles V, who has formed an alliance with Maurice of Saxony against the Schmalkalden League of German Protestant princes, outlaws Philip of Hesse and John Frederick, the elector of Saxony.

Paris, 3 August 1546. The printer Etienne Dolet, denounced for printing the works of the humanist reformers such as Erasmus and Melanchthon, is hanged and burnt at the stake for blasphemy, sedition and heresy.

Arabia, 1546. The Ottomans capture Yemen, the gateway to the Red Sea.

Mexico, 1546. The first extractions are made from the silver mine at Zacatecas.

Mexico, 1546. The Spanish gain control of the Maya region after crushing a serious revolt by the Maya people.

India, 1546. The Portuguese rout the Gujarati army at Diu.

Luther, who cracked Catholic unity, dies

Luther's enemies portrayed him as the instrument of, and crowned by, demons.

Eisleben, 18 February 1546
Martin Luther, the founder of the biggest new Protestant church, died here today in this small town in which he was born 63 years ago. His body was broken after years of overwork and illness. His mind, however, was as clear as a bell right to the end. And this man renowned for his violent temper died in a mood of total serenity.

His achievement was vast. Born of peasant stock, he was totally committed to the needs of the ordinary people. His training as a monk and his years as professor at Wittenberg did not diminish this dedication. His great works – a translation of the Bible, a mass, a book of hymns and one of catechisms – were not only written in German; they were written in plain language. Thanks to him, thousands of poor Germans can now read the scriptures. Luther's breach with the Catholic Church became total in 1521 when he was excommunicated. But the rebellious German princes helped him to establish the new church.

The former monk had a happy home life. He married a former nun, Katharina von Bora, in 1525, and fathered six children. Despite his scholarship he was often crude and vulgar and angry, but mostly in the cause of ordinary people, who he felt were exploited and oppressed by church and secular authorities.

He had many enemies. "Dear husband," Katharina once said to him, "you are too rude." "They teach me to be rude," was Luther's reply.

Massacre in France

Provence, France, 20 April 1545
A terrible massacre has been carried out against the Waldensian Protestants who live in this area. Villages have been pillaged, women have been burnt alive in a church, and men rounded up to slave in the galleys. It started with rumours that the Waldensians were plotting sedition, but it seems that the rumours were started deliberately by a local baron, Jean Meynier, who coveted the land of a Waldensian neighbour. The alarmed King Francis gave Meynier the task of stamping out the "sedition". This he has done with great cruelty. He has also seized the land which he coveted.

Smallpox epidemic

Mexico, 1545
An epidemic of smallpox, as devastating as Europe's Black Death, has devastated Mexico's Indian population. The Spaniards have suffered too, but it is the natives who have born the brunt of the disease. More than 800,000 have died.

Smallpox is just one of the diseases which have accompanied European exploration. Others include tetanus, leprosy, typhoid and a variety of intestinal, lung and venereal diseases.

The Indians seem to have no natural defences against these new illnesses which are threatening entire tribes with extinction.

Council to resist Protestant threat

In the chair: Pope Paul III.

The council looks set to confirm the rift between Protestants and Catholics.

Trent, 1546

A general council of the church is meeting in this small town beneath the Alps *(now in Italy)* to discuss Catholic doctrine and reform of the church, in the face of Lutheran ideas. It has been postponed for several years because of the emperor's wars with the French king, now settled. Trent was chosen because, while close to Italy, it lies within the Holy Roman empire and therefore meets the demand that the council should be on German soil.

Pope Paul III summoned the council with the object of debating the doctrinal controversies raised by Protestantism, which has been influential within the Catholic Church. But the Emperor Charles wishes to reconcile the Lutherans, who are dividing Germany, by reforming the church's practices, possibly even permitting the clergy to marry.

The council is being attended by 60 or more Catholic bishops (no Lutheran representatives have yet arrived). So far it has framed decrees which disdain any compromise with the Protestants. For example, it has just decreed that the scriptures are not, as Protestants claim, the only source of divine revelation. Apostolic tradition handed down by the church is also sacred.

The council is now debating the thorny question of justification by faith. There is much disagreement even among Catholics as to whether man may receive grace by his own efforts and good works or, as Luther maintains, by faith alone. There are many shades of opinion among the Augustinians, the Dominicans and the new Jesuit theologians, who stress that man may attract divine mercy by his own efforts. The council has already ruled against Luther's doctrine of original sin.

Silver vein reflects shepherd's fire

Cuzco, Peru, 1545

While searching for a stray llama, a Quechua Indian named Huallpa was recently stranded high on the slopes of a 14,000-foot mountain at Potosi, a few miles from here. When night fell, he lit a fire to keep warm and ward off evil spirits. Something shone back unnaturally in the firelight. It was a heavy seam of pure silver.

In Inca times a ruler put miners to work on the site to dig gold or silver to decorate Cuzco's sun temple. As they began digging, the hill stirred angrily. Work stopped. Now the Spanish *Conquistadores*, hearing of the find, are showing a keen interest in the "silver mountain".

Cannon ball kills Indian reformer

Central India, 1545

Sher Shah Suri, who crushed the Moghul empire in India, completely overhauled the empire's administration, and rebuilt Delhi, is dead' killed by a cannon ball while besieging Kalanjar, the Rajput stronghold.

Originally an Afghan, his grandfather came to India with Sultan Buhlulodi, and his father served Jamal Khan as a cavalry commander. Sher Shah himself served Babur, the Moghul emperor, and then Jalal Khan. Victorious in battle, he first ousted Jalal Khan from Lohani, and then ousted Babur's son, Humayun, from India, becoming emperor himself. Backed by an army of 150,000 horsemen he centralised administration, punished corruption, revalued the coinage and beautified Delhi. Immensely energetic, he followed his motto – "it behoves the great to be always active" – to his last days.

Pride of fleet sinks watched by king

Portsmouth, England, 1545

It was soon after dawn that a fishing boat brought the news that a French fleet had been sighted out in the channel. Portsmouth Harbour became the scene of hectic activity as the British prepared for action. King Henry VIII watched from the shore as his flagship, *Mary Rose*, newly delivered from the builders' yard and the pride of the Royal Navy was hastily loaded with new cannons and inspected the 400 bowmen in their leathern jackets as they went to their stations. The *Mary Rose* was warped out into the Solent where a stiff wind was blowing up from the Needles Channel. With her sails billowing and her crew scurrying over her decks as they readied themselves for action, she made a stirring sight for the King who watched from Spithead – until, with no warning, a strong gust of wind caused His flagship to heel suddenly. Her newly installed guns broke loose, crashing to her lee side. In less than a minute, *Mary Rose* had disappeared below the white-capped Solent.

As the Spanish conquistadors advance deeper into the rain forests of central America, they are sending reports of strange and wonderful beasts. Some, like scaly creatures with humanoid heads, are new discoveries.

1546 (1546-1548)

Italy, January 1547. Gian Luigi Fieschi drowns during a naval attack on Andrea Doria, the doge of Genoa. Fieschi had formed an alliance with Francis, the king of France, and Pietro Luigi Farnese, the duke of Parma and Piacenza, to overthrow the doge, who is supported by Charles V.

England, 21 January 1547. Henry Howard, the earl of Surrey, is executed on a charge of high treason. He was committed to the Tower of London last year after making a series of bitter speeches against the earl of Hertford, who superseded him in command of the English forces in France.

England, 28 January 1547. Henry VIII dies and is succeeded by his nine-year-old son Edward VI, whose mother was Henry's third wife, Jane Seymour.

England, 31 January 1547. Edward VI's uncle, the earl of Hertford, is appointed lord protector and duke of Somerset. He assumes control of the government.

Rome, 25 February 1547. The poetess Vittoria Colonna, marquess of Pescara, who wrote poems in the style of Petrarch, dies. She was the centre of a group of intellectuals and artists and was greatly admired by Michelangelo.

France, 31 March 1547. Francis, king of France since 1515, dies and is succeed by his son Henry II.

Germany, 24 April 1547. Charles V's forces defeat the Protestant League of Schmalkalden at the battle of Muhlberg. Philip of Hesse and John Frederick, the elector of Saxony, are taken prisoner.

Germany, 15 May 1547. Charles V gives control of the electorate of Saxony to Maurice of Saxony, who occupied the region at the end of last year.

Rome, 21 June 1547. The painter Sebastian del Piombo dies. After studying under Giovanni Bellini and Giorgione in Venice, he moved in 1510 to Rome, where he worked with Michelangelo. He painted his masterpiece *The Raising of Lazarus* in 1519.

Scotland, 31 July 1547. The reformer John Knox, a disciple of the Scottish Lutheran George Wishart, is captured by royalist forces at St Andrew's castle after a siege. The castle had been held by Protestants since the assassination of Cardinal Beaton last year.

Scotland, 10 September 1547. The duke of Somerset leads the English forces to a resounding victory over the Scots at Pinkie.

Spain, 2 December 1547. Hernando Cortes, the Spanish conqueror of Mexico, dies.

Russia, 1547. Ivan IV (the Terrible) is crowned first czar of Russia in Moscow. To counter the power of the aristocratic *boyars*, he establishes a special council composed of personally selected advisers.

Scotland, 1547. After his capture at St Andrew's in July, John Knox is exiled and condemned to the French galleys by the regent, Mary of Guise.

Italy, 1547. The Council of Trent is transferred to Bologna.

Afghanistan, 1547. Succession disputes among the successors to Sher Shah Suri have enabled Humayun to oust his Afghan supplanters and regain his Indian lands. He now captures Kabul.

England, 1547. At the instigation of the duke of Somerset, the statute of the Six Articles, a repressive decree of Catholic orthodoxy passed by Henry VIII in 1539, is repealed.

Rome, 1547. Commissioned to direct work on the building of St Peter's basilica, Michelangelo proposes the construction of a huge dome.

Mexico, 1547. Brother Andres de Olmo publishes the first Nahuatl grammar.

Netherlands, 26 June 1548. The administration of the Netherlands is made independent of the German empire.

Germany, 30 June 1548. At the Diet of Augsburg, Schmalkaldic League representatives reluctantly accept an interim agreement with Charles V which has a strongly Catholic bias.

Scotland, 1548. Mary Stuart, the seven-year-old queen of Scotland, is betrothed to Francis, the French dauphin.

England, 1548. The Venetian explorer Sebastian Cabot returns to England – from whence he launched his first expedition to America in 1509 – to seek backing for a project to find a north-west passage to Asia. Cabot has spent recent years in Spain, with whose support he explored the Rio de la Plata and established the first settlement at La Plata. In 1530 he brought gold and silver from the New World to Spain.

Poland, 1548. Sigismund II Augustus succeeds Sigismund I on the throne. His predecessor established serfdom in Poland. In a two-year war with Russia, which ended in 1536, Poland failed to regain Smolensk, lost to the Russians in 1514. Prussia remains a Polish fief.

Angola, 1548. Jesuits begin a mission in the Kongo.

Charles V takes Protestant prince captive

Muhlberg, Germany, 24 April 1547
The outnumbered army of Charles V won a critical battle here today, capturing Prince Frederick of Saxony, who founded the "Schmalkaldic League", a militant Protestant movement in Germany, with Philip of Hesse. Frederick has been sentenced to death after a trial conducted by Charles – although it seems that the death sentence is likely to be commuted to life imprisonment at the imperial pleasure.

This short war should have been won by the Protestants. At the outset, they dominated the Danube, capturing castle after castle as they advanced on the Tyrol. Their plan was to block the passes, ensuring that Italian troops could not get through to join the emperor's force. The plan failed, mainly through lack of organisation. Leading opponents of the emperor – Luther, Henry VIII, Barbarossa and Francis of France – were all dead. Charles' stature had never been higher in Europe and, as reinforcements arrived from the south, he began systematically to take German cities until his armies came to the banks of the Elbe.

Peru is still unruly

Lima, 1548
It is seven years since Francisco Pizarro, the governor of Peru, was assassinated, but the legacy of his murder still undermines attempts to govern Spain's richest colony. It was no accident that wealthy mine-owners, silver millionaires, had private armies to challenge Viceroy Vela, who was killed by them three years ago.

Like many leaders, Pizarro ignored intelligence about threats against him from a faction supporting a lost leader, Diego de Almagro, executed by the Pizarro clan in 1538. On Sunday morning 26 June 1541, the governor's palace at Lima was undefended when 20 of these dispossessed colonists smashed their way in. Pizarro, aged 63, killed one attacker, but was overpowered and killed.

Pastors may marry

Germany, 1548
Churchgoers throughout Germany are rejecting the traditional church service imposed by the settlement this year at Augsburg – the Emperor Charles V's attempt, after his Muhlberg victory, to turn the clock back to the pre-Lutheran era.

The emperor's only concessions to the Protestants – the right of clergy to marry and the use of the cup in the sacrament – are seen as inadequate by most worshippers. They dislike the restored Mass, and those few Catholic pastors willing to serve face open hostility – especially in northern Germany.

With Luther dead and his leading supporters in prison, the emperor had seen the Augsburg resolution as a golden opportunity to return his Protestant subjects to the Catholic fold.

Peking's Forbidden City: A fortress within the city of Peking and the site of the Emperors' Palaces from 1421. Most Chinese people were never allowed to enter the Gates of Heavenly Peace, or even walk near the walls.

Henry VIII dies at 56

England, 28 January 1547
Henry VIII, who died today aged 56, will be remembered for his six marriages and his momentous rupture with Rome, but in his 38-year reign there is much else to add to his reputation. Thomas Linacre, the physician, persuaded him to establish the College of Physicians. He counted Erasmus, the Renaissance scholar, among his friends. Sir Thomas More wrote his *Utopia* while in the king's service.

Henry was masterful and ruthless. He usually got his way in domestic affairs. In foreign affairs he was less successful, and in war with France in 1545 he had the humiliation of seeing his finest ship, the *Mary Rose,* keel over and sink with 500 men on board as 200 French ships were riding up the Solent. That war cost over £2 million and emptied the royal treasury.

His closest collaborators were liable to end up in the Tower. Sir Thomas More was executed for refusing to accept Henry's takeover of the church. Wolsey, sacked for failing to get the pope to sanction Henry's divorce from Catherine of Aragon, died before he could face trial. Thomas Cromwell, who masterminded the suppression of the monasteries, was also executed.

Admired, feared and much married.

Wives, too, were at risk. After Anne Boleyn's execution, Henry married Jane Seymour, who died after giving birth to a son, Edward. Of Anne of Cleves, the king said: "I liked her before I met her. Now I like her less." She was pensioned off and Henry married Catherine Howard, the duke of Norfolk's niece, who was beheaded for immorality. Henry's sixth bride, twice widowed before marrying him, is now a third-time widow.

Great King Francis dies

France, 31 March 1547
Francis, the great king of France, is dead. Aged 53, he was bold, dissolute, talented and unscrupulous, a typical Renaissance monarch. He was the patron of Rabelais; Cellini and Leonardo da Vinci worked at his court; and he built some of the finest chateaux on the Loire.

Despite his brilliance, however, he died a disappointed man. His four wars with the Emperor Charles V for supremacy in Europe ended with his relinquishing his claims to Naples, Flanders and Artois and losing Boulogne to Henry VIII of England, Charles' ally.

His persecution of the Protestants and the massacre of the Waldensians carried out in his name have also left sad marks on his reign, but no-one can deny his personal heroism on the battlefield where he spent much of his time.

He met Henry VIII on the Field of the Cloth of Gold, where these two larger-than-life kings not only conducted affairs of state but wres-

The late King Francis on horseback.

tled. Francis won. When news of Henry's death reached him at a ball two months ago, he laughed, but when he remembered that Henry had told him "we are both mortal" he grew more serious. That same night he developed a fever. He never recovered.

Ivan IV is the new "Caesar" of Russia

Russia, 16 January 1547
Ivan IV today had himself crowned at a ceremony in the Moscow Kremlin's Assumption cathedral. The new *czar*, which is the Russian form of Caesar, is 17 years of age. He succeeded to the throne when he was three, but the country has been ruled first by his mother, who is rumoured to have been poisoned by the *boyars*, the higher nobility, and then by a regency council.

Last year Ivan declared an end to boyar rule, and he has been taking advice on running Russia from the Metropolitan Archbishop Makary, who is the only man he appears to trust. He has plans to set up a two-chamber body, containing representatives of the gentry and merchants as well as nobles, to act to some extent as a check on the power of the boyar class. Ivan is the first czar to inherit all the Russias, and in

A woodcut of Russia's new czar.

theory at least enjoys undisputed sway over these territories. His reign could therefore be crucial to the development of a centralised and unified state in Muscovy.

Diane de Poitiers, the mistress of France's new king, Henry II, painted by Francois Clouet. His cryptic, intellectual style is currently in vogue.

1548 (1548-1551)

England, January 1549. The Act of Uniformity enforces the use of the moderate Protestant prayerbook, *The Book of Common Prayer*, drawn up by Thomas Cranmer.

Bohemia, 14 February 1549. Maximilian II, brother of the Emperor Charles V, is recognised as the future king of Bohemia.

Italy, 14 February 1549. The painter Giovanni Bazzi dies at Siena. A friend of Raphael, he is famed for his frescoes of the life of St Bernard at the monastery of Monte Olivieto Maggiore.

Switzerland, June 1549. John Calvin and the followers of Ulrich Zwingli reach agreement about the Eucharist.

Florida, 26 June 1549. Luis Cancer de Barbastro, a Dominican monk and veteran of missionary activity in Guatemala, is clubbed to death by Indians while praying in Tampa. He had sought to bring the peoples of Florida to obedience by peaceful means.

England, 9 August 1549. England declares war on France.

Italy, 13 September 1549. Pope Paul III closes the first session of the Council of Bologna (Council of Trent).

England, 14 October 1549. Having provoked aristocratic opposition, the duke of Somerset, the lord protector, is committed to the Tower of London.

France, 21 December 1549. Margaret of Navarre, the devotional writer and patron of the French reformers, dies.

Morocco, 1549. The Portuguese are driven out of Arzila, their last stronghold in Morocco.

England, 1549. Sparked by rising prices and the Act of Uniformity, social and religious rebellions break out in various parts of the country. The most serious are in Cornwall and Kett's rebellion in Norfolk.

Japan, 1549. The Jesuit Francis Xavier reaches Japan, and preaches Christianity in Kagoshima.

Brazil, 1549. Appointed the first governor of Brazil by John III, the king of Portugal, Tome de Sousa establishes a capital at Salvador da Bahia de Todos los Santos.

Rome, 7 February 1550. Paul III is succeeded as pope by Julius III, a Roman close to the Farnese family.

France, March 1550. France and England sign the treaty of Boulogne. The English surrender Boulogne for 400,000 crowns and the release of those Protestant Scots, including John Knox, captured by the French at the siege of St Andrew's castle in 1547.

Germany, October 1550. Maurice of Saxony, entrusted with the execution of the decree passed at the Diet of Augsburg two years ago, lays siege to Magdeburg, the centre of the Protestant opposition.

Scotland, 1550. After the signing of the treaty of Boulogne, English troops withdraw from Scotland.

Iceland, 1550. Bishop Arason, who has organised armed opposition to the introduction of Protestantism into Iceland, is condemned and executed by Frederick III, the king of Denmark.

Rome, 1550. A Jesuit college is founded in Rome.

Spain, 1550. Spanish explorers describe great wooden temple mounds built by Indians in south-eastern North America.

Florida, 1550. The Spanish bring the first beef cattle to North America.

West Africa, c.1550. The Nupe defeat the Yoruba of the Oyo kingdom *(in Nigeria)*.

West Africa, c.1550. The Manes invade the area of Sierra Leone.

Venice, c.1550. The Flemish composer Adriaan Willaert, the musical director at St Mark's church, is creating a brilliant synthesis of Italian melodic expressiveness and northern European polyphony to produce sumptuous choral sounds, often with instruments added.

Italy, January 1551. The second session of the Council of Trent opens.

Germany, 9 March 1551. Under a Habsburg family treaty, Charles V's son Philip is made the emperor's sole heir.

Austria, 19 July 1551. The treaty of Karlsburg reaffirms Ferdinand of Habsburg's rights to Hungary and Transylvania.

Italy, 1551. Henry II of France resumes the war against the Emperor Charles V and publicly disavows the Council of Trent.

Mexico, 1551. A new law bans Negroes from taking Indian mistresses or carrying firearms. Punishments include whipping, cutting off of ears and imprisonment.

England, 1551. Sir Thomas More's *Utopia* is translated from Latin into English.

Japan, 1551. The Spanish Jesuit Francis Xavier leaves for China after introducing Christianity into Japan. The Jesuit missionaries, two of whom stay behind to help to build up the nucleus of the new church, have come into conflict with the Buddhist priests.

King who kept Poland Catholic has died

Poland, 1 April 1548
Sigismund (the Old), the king who ruled Poland for more than 40 years, has died in Cracow at the age of 81. His reign is widely seen as marking a new peak of Polish civilisation, profoundly influenced by the Italian Renaissance.

Sigismund, who was blessed with a strong character and considerable political perception, governed Lithuania before becoming king in 1507. One of his first tasks was to bring in a programme of financial reforms. On the battlefield he defeated a Russian army under Vasily III. He imposed his rule on Wallachia, and also stamped his authority on East Prussia.

Sigismund was anxious to unite his realm in loyalty to Rome, and enforced strong measures against the Lutherans. He introduced death by burning for importing

Sigismund's monument at Wawel cathedral in Cracow.

heretical books and ordered all his subjects attending heretical universities abroad to return home. He also, briefly, brought in a similiar penalty for disobedience. But all such edicts were widely ignored.

Golden Age of Africa excites Europeans

Rome, 1550
An extraordinary book, *The History and Description of Africa and the Notable Things therein contained*, has just been published; it is an account of civilisations of which Europe had heard only rumours.

The author is equally extraordinary. Born in Grenada, a Spanish Moslem, he moved to Morocco, took the name *al-Fasi*, man of Fez, and travelled as far as central Asia and central Africa as a lawyer and accountant. Captured off Tunis by Christian corsairs, he was presented to Leo X in Rome, where he became known as Leo Africanus.

Twice he crossed the Sahara, passing the castle of salt, Teghaza, from where salt was taken to Black Africa and exchanged for gold. He travelled all over the decaying Malian and rising Songhai states.

What excited Europe above all else was his description of Timbuktu. Here was a "stately temple" and a "princely palace", where "the inhabitants are extremely rich" and "of a gentle and cheerful disposition". Here were libraries overflowing with priceless manuscripts, and "doctors, judges, priests and other learned men". Leo Africanus also wrote of "cottages built of chalk", but Europe was too blinded by the streets of gold to notice.

Czar Ivan attacks top Russian aristocracy

Russia, 27 February 1549
Ivan IV today opened a special assembly, known as the *Zemsky Sobor*, given the task of deciding important measures of state policy. This Assembly of the Land is made up of representatives of the *boyars* (the old nobility), the church, merchants, and the new nobility living in the towns and districts.

In a speech to the assembly Czar Ivan harked back to his youth when the boyars plotted against him and his family and dealt harshly with

the gentry and the peasants. He warned the boyars that they would be punished if they did not now obey his orders without question, and proposed setting up courts to hear complaints against them.

The czar has also introduced a new code dealing with court procedure and criminal laws. The code is known as the *Sudebnik*, and consists of 100 articles. Capital punishment is prescribed for everyone guilty of armed rebellion and conspiracy against the czar.

Spanish discuss morality of colonisation

Spanish colonists torturing Indian natives; from a later engraving.

Spain, 1550

Sixty years after Columbus landed in the New World and set off a chain of Spanish conquests, a debate is raging among Spanish intellectuals and colonialists. Their argument: is conquest, with its inevitable destruction of Indian culture, morally justified?

The Dominican Bartolomeo de las Casas has stated the case against the conquest, condemning the brutality of Spain's troops. In favour of conquest is Juan Gines de Sepulveda, who justifies Spain's actions by the Biblical text "Go out into the highways and hedges and compel them to come in".

To him the Indians are a barbaric race, certainly not Christians and barely human. "How can we doubt that these people — so uncivilised, contaminated with so many impieties and obscenities — have been justly conquered by such an excellent, pious and most just king?"

Renaissance artists recorded by Vasari

Florence, May 1550

A very popular book of biographies has just been published by Giorgio Vasari, the architect and painter, who was born in Arezzo. Its full title is *The Lives of the Most Excellent Italian Architects, Painters and Sculptors*.

Vasari studied under Michelangelo and became his friend, and the perfection attained by him is the climax of the book. Vasari has travelled Italy collecting memories, anecdotes and written memoirs to illustrate the rebirth of painting, from the time of Cimabue (who died in 1302) and Giotto to the present day. It is the first coherent book of art history and criticism, demonstrating the superiority of the artists of Tuscany.

New tools put nuts and bolts into work

Europe, c.1555

As technology develops, so too do the tools needed to promote it. Nuts and bolts are being used to fasten together materials. To tighten these two elements the spanner has been introduced. Both tools and fasteners are hand-made.

Another recent development is the screw fastener. For a long time pieces of furniture and other wooden objects have been held together by wooden joints. However, these are not adequate when metal has to be held fast to wood. Gunsmiths have found that a nail given a twist before being driven home will hold a gun mechanism tight to the stock. It seemed natural to fix the "screw" with a blade fitting into a slot on the nail head.

Jesuits protect natives from slave traders

A map of 1558, showing the first phase of the Spanish conquest.

Brazil, c.1551

Jesuit missionaries operating in Brazil have set new standards for the treatment of Indians in the colonies of the New World. While the conquerors have become notorious for their cruelty and exploitation of the native peoples, these missionaries go out of their way to improve the situation and treat the Indians as more than just slaves.

Ever since Manuel de Nobrega, the leader of Brazil's Portuguese Jesuits, founded the country's first archbishopric in the capital, Salvador de Bahia de Todos los Santos, and set up a Jesuit college at Sao Paolo, the order has been closely involved with the Indians.

The Catholic fathers live alongside the Indians, taking direct responsibility for their spiritual and economic welfare. Slavery is official policy, but, while they cannot stand in the way of the exploitation of Indians for work, they do attempt to curb the excesses of the overseers, and cut down on the regular slave raids into the interior.

Ironically, the natives have not responded to their benefactors by embracing their religion. Too many atrocities have been committed in the name of Christ for them to divorce the new faith from the savagery of colonisation which threatens to destroy entire cultures.

Thus the only way in which Christianity can be imposed is by the efforts of the colonial troops. Many more Indians have been converted at the point of a sword than have responded to the kindness of the Jesuits.

North Africa, 1551. The Ottomans capture Tripoli.

France, 15 January 1552. Henry II of France and Maurice of Saxony, who has turned against the emperor, sign the treaty of Chambord in opposition to Charles V. Henry promises to provide Maurice with troops and money in return for the formal possession of Metz, Toul and Verdun, which the French captured last year.

England, 22 January 1552. The duke of Somerset, the former lord protector, who played a leading part in the first half of Edward VI's reign, is executed. He was arrested by the duke of Northumberland and tried on trumped-up charges.

England, 24 February 1552. The privileges of the Hanseatic League in England are abolished.

England, March 1552. A new Act of Uniformity imposes an explicitly Protestant prayerbook.

Germany, May 1552. Maurice of Saxony takes Augsburg and almost captures Charles V at Innsbruck.

Germany, 2 August 1552. John Frederick, the elector of Saxony, and Philip of Hesse, taken prisoner by Charles V in 1546, are released.

Germany, 2 August 1552. The treaty of Passau, between Maurice of Saxony and Frederick of Habsburg, who is acting in the name of Charles V, revokes the Augsburg Interim of 1548 and promises religious freedom to the Protestant princes.

China, 3 December 1552. Francis Xavier, the "apostle of the Indies", dies of exhaustion near Canton.

Russia, 1552. Ivan the Terrible conquers the *khanate* of Kazan.

Persian Gulf, 1552. The Ottoman Red Sea fleet attacks the Portuguese stronghold of Hormuz but fails to capture it.

Spain, 1552. The Dominican friar Bartolomeo de las Casas publishes a book entitled *Brief Relations of the Destruction of the Indies*, attacking colonial practices in the New World.

Italy, 1552. The Italian anatomist Bartolommeo Eustachio makes important discoveries regarding the ear and the heart, identifying certain tubes and valves.

France, January 1553. Charles V fails to take Metz.

France, 9 April 1553. Francois Rabelais, whose utopian writings were condemned by Calvin and the doctors of the Sorbonne as licentious and dangerous, dies. His first book, *Pantagruel*, was an immediate success.

England, 1553. A new confession of faith, the Forty-two articles is introduced. It was drawn up by Thomas Cranmer, archbishop of Canterbury, and a committee of six to supplement the new Protestant prayerbook.

England, 6 July 1553. Edward VI dies, having assigned his crown to Lady Jane Grey, the daughter-in-law of the duke of Northumberland, who has her proclaimed queen.

Germany, 9 July 1553. Maurice of Saxony is mortally wounded at Sievershausen while defeating Albert of Brandenburg-Kulmbach.

Italy, 2 August 1553. French forces which have invaded Tuscany are defeated by an imperial army at the battle of Marciano.

England, 3 August 1553. Having thwarted Northumberland's plan to prevent her succession, Mary Tudor, the only surviving child of Henry VIII and Catherine of Aragon, enters London in triumph. She was recently proclaimed queen in Cambridge.

England, 22 August 1553. Arrested and tried for treason, the duke of Northumberland, is executed on the orders of Mary Tudor.

England, September 1553. Protestant bishops are arrested and Roman Catholic bishops restored.

Morocco, 23 September 1553. The Sadians defeat the last of their enemies and establish themselves as rulers of the entire country.

Germany, 16 October 1553. The German painter Lucas Cranach dies. He was closely associated with the reformers, many of whom were the subjects of his portraits. He also painted religious and classical scenes.

Switzerland, 27 October 1553. The Spanish theologian and physician Michael Servetus, who studied medicine in Paris and discovered the pulmonary circulation of the blood, is burnt for heresy. In his writings he denies the Trinity and the divinity of Christ.

Russia, 1553. The English seaman Richard Chancellor, chosen as "pilot-general" of Sir Hugh Willoughby's expedition in search of a north-eastern passage to India, reaches Archangel via the White Sea. He travels overland to Moscow, where he meets the czar.

Netherlands, 1554. Henry II of France invades the Netherlands.

England, February 1554. Sir Thomas Wyatt surrenders to government forces in London after leading a Protestant rebellion in Kent inspired by Queen Mary's proposed marriage to Philip of Spain.

Jesuit gains freedom to preach in Japan

Portuguese merchants accompanied by Jesuit missionaries arrive in Japan.

Japan, 21 November 1551

Francis Xavier, the Jesuit missionary, has sailed for Goa on a Portuguese ship after two years of preaching the gospel to the Japanese. The road was often hard for this son of noble Basque parents.

When Xavier stepped ashore on 15 August 1549 he was initially welcomed by the feudal prince of Satsuma and was given permission to preach in the prince's lands. He made some 150 converts, including the faithful Barnabas who became his servant and guard.

What Xavier did not appreciate was that the prince's indulgence stemmed from the belief that rich Portuguese ships would follow the priest. When they did not materialise the prince issued an edict in the summer of 1550 making it a capital offence for any of his subjects to become a Christian after that date.

Xavier and two companions then set out as wandering missionaries. Poorly clad and with no money, they made their way to the capital, Kyoto, in the bitter winter. Xavier was sometimes forced to hire himself out as a baggage carrier in order to eat. He persevered and, while unsuccessful in Kyoto, won many converts in other parts of Japan.

French troops take German bishoprics

Lorraine, April 1552

Henry II of France has taken up where his father failed and has successfully waged war against the Emperor Charles V. A 35,000-strong French army has marched into Germany, catching the prematurely-aged emperor by surprise and occupying the three bishoprics of Metz, Verdun and Toul which the French intend to annex.

This move is the result of a scheme proposed by Maurice of Saxony who, sensing that Charles' power was failing and the Habsburg family was losing its cohesion, entered into a defensive league with a number of other German princes and Henry in the treaty of Chambord three months ago.

Under the terms of this treaty Henry promised his new allies an army and in return was ceded the bishoprics. Charles did not recognise the importance of this conspiracy. He has been beaten and forced to flee across the Alps.

Ivan the Terrible defeats Mongols

Russia, 1552

In two well-conceived campaigns, supported by excellent artillery, Ivan the Terrible has dealt a devastating blow to the decaying power of the Tartars – Mongol invaders from the east. With a force of some 150,000 men, Ivan has captured Kazan, the Tartar capital on the Volga, after using gunpower to breach the walls. He followed this by conquering Astrakhan, another Mongol stronghold.

These actions have brought the whole Volga basin as far as the Caspian Sea into the Russian empire, thereby opening the way for Russian expansion beyond the Urals and as far as the Pacific Ocean. These new trade routes are also likely to appeal to foreign merchants. The exploits, which were due also in part to Ivan's major reforms of the army, have earned for him the name of *Grozny*, which can be translated as Dread, or Terrible.

Calvin condemns heretic to be burnt

Geneva, 27 October 1553
Michael Servetus, a fugitive from the Spanish Inquisition and author of *On the Errors of the Trinity* (1531), is to die at the stake, on the orders of Geneva's religious leader, John Calvin.

Geneva may be the home of the Reformed Church, but Servetus' attack on the Trinity was intolerable. Calvin's decision was allegedly taken on religious grounds only, but Servetus, a distinguished physician – he discovered pulmonary blood circulation – is one of his severest critics and Calvin had often stated that, were his rival to appear in Geneva, he would be dealt with harshly. Earlier this year Servetus arrived in the city as a refugee and began preaching.

An 18th-century print of Michael Servetus. His anti-trinitarian views brought on him the wrath of Catholic and Reformed Churches alike.

Cranach, Luther's portrait painter, dies

Cranach's "The Stag Hunt of Elector Frederick the Wise" shows his patron engaging in the sport of kings in a richly wooded landscape.

Weimar, Germany, 1553
Lucas Cranach, since Durer's death the leading German painter, has died here aged 81 in the company of his patron, the defeated elector of Saxony, John Frederick. His *Crucifixion* in Weimar church is his masterpiece. Fifty years ago he became court painter to the previous elector, Frederick the Wise, at Wittenberg, where Frederick had founded the famous university.

In later life Cranach was elected burgomaster of Wittenberg, where he and his three painter sons set up a busy workshop, patronised by rich merchants. He brought German landscape into religious painting. His *Rest on the Flight into Egypt* is like a northern forest scene, with angels flying out of the undergrowth. As a portrait painter equal to Durer, he did several portraits of his friend Martin Luther and of Germany's princes, and of the young Charles of Spain before he became emperor. In later years he turned to Venus as his subject and painted a series of erotic nude studies as well as hunting scenes. The most famous is the *Judgement of Paris*.

Harsh city rules silence the dance halls

Geneva, c.1552
The reformer John Calvin, once banished as a religious extremist, is now the unrivalled ruler of Geneva, a city he has re-created in the rigid image of his own Protestant orthodoxy. His *Ecclesiastical Ordinances*, first published in 1541, are fully accepted as the basis of government of both church and state.

The son of a lawyer, and a lawyer himself, Calvin relishes the practical details of government. And, as a religious zealot, he cannot conceive of a government that is anything but subject to the religion of its citizens. The Ordinances have as little time for free will as Calvinism itself, but, like the religion, are firmly stated, clearly laying down what is right and what is wrong. They demand strict moral order and unswerving religious conformism. Within the Genevan republic the laws of church and state are virtually inseparable. Citizenship depends on orthodoxy; perfect orthodoxy includes absolute respect for the state.The Ordinances are administered by several groups of officials, all appointed rather than elected. Pastors deal with religious orthodoxy and elders with public morals. The two groups meet at the weekly consistory and examine the state of Genevan morals. They may summon and punish any alleged sinner. Doctors, appointed by the pastors, deal with secular and spiritual education.

Apart from dealing with such major areas as the regulation of funerals and marriages the Ordinances take in even the trivia. Calvin believes firmly in individual piety. Thus every vestige of one's life must be controlled. Dancing is forbidden, as are the wearing of slashed breeches, the use of folk remedies and many everyday pastimes. The clergy are authorised to visit all parishioners annually, to ensure that they are living properly Christian lives. Yet although not all the rules are petty – Calvin has created an improved city code and sharp practice of every sort is punished – such measures are incidental, ultimately only the spiritual health of the citizens matters.

Dominican tells of destruction of Indians

Spain, 1552
A former colonialist turned Dominican monk has issued a savage condemnation of Spain's regime in the New World and demanded an end to the *encomienda* system, under which the native Indians are enslaved on the great estates.

Bartolomeo de las Casas once ran his own estate, but was so appalled by the excesses of the Spanish forces that he abandoned his holdings and began campaigning for colonial reform. Apart from attacking Spanish cruelty, he has also become an expert on the Indians, citing a mass of evidence to prove that their culture, while neither European nor Christian, is just as complex and sophisticated as their rulers'.

In 1542 he drafted the New Laws, demanding an end to slavery, and Charles V duly backed him up, suspending any new encomienda grants. But those who profited from the system rebelled and the new laws were repealed in 1546. The extraction of labour as a tribute remained forbidden. Now the colonialists may be forced to act them-

Mexican natives flee from the Spanish; from a contemporary drawing.

selves. The system generates huge products, but it consumes its own workforce. The brutality of the overseers and the ravages of "European" diseases are decimating the Indians. Soon there may be none left to exploit.

1554 (1554-1556)

London, 12 February 1554. Lady Jane Grey – proclaimed queen by her uncle, the duke of Northumberland, last year – is executed in the Tower of London.

England, 25 July 1554. Mary Tudor, the queen of England, marries Philip of Spain, the son and heir of Charles V.

Mexico, 22 September 1554. Francisco Vasquez de Coronado dies. He explored the south-west of North America in the hope of discovering a rich Indian civilisation similar to that of Mexico. He traced the Colorado and Rio Grande rivers and explored widely (*in Arizona, New Mexico, Texas, Oklahoma and Kansas*).

Arabia, 1554. The Ottomans capture Bahrain.

England, 1554. All the religious laws passed under Henry VIII and Edward VI are repealed by parliament. Roman Catholicism is re-established and the authority of the pope is recognised.

France, 1554. The Italian architect and sculptor Sebastiano Serlio dies at Fontainebleau, where he had been involved in work on the chateau. Serlio's architectural treatises helped to spread the ideas of Vitruvius, the Roman expert who flourished during the reign of Augustus, through Europe.

Rome, 1554. The Neapolitan Gian Pietro Caraffa is elected pope and takes the name Paul IV. He succeeds Marcellus II, who was in office for only 21 days. Caraffa is determined to stamp out heresy by any means.

London, 1554. Following Richard Chancellor's visit to Moscow, the Muscovy Company is formed to trade in furs and wood with Russia. The English are now in competition with the German merchants of the Hanseatic League, whose privileges were withdrawn in 1551.

Italy, 1554. Philip of Spain receives the kingdoms of Naples and Sicily and duchy of Milan from his father, Charles V.

Italy, 1554. The duchess of Ferrara, Renee d'Este, is imprisoned for heresy by her husband, the duke d'Este. Renee, the daughter of Louis XII of France, married the duke in 1528. Her support for the Reformation has grown too embarrassing even for the liberal court of France.

West Africa, 1554. Katsina (*in Nigeria*) regains its independence from Songhai.

Italy, April 1555. French forces occupying Siena surrender to an imperial army led by Cosimo de Medici, the duke of Florence, after a 15-month siege.

Scotland, May 1555. John Knox returns to Scotland from Geneva, where he was strongly influenced by Calvin. He begins to preach widely as an advocate of the Calvinist form of Christianity.

Germany, 3 October 1555. The Peace of Augsburg advocates that the religion of a prince should determine the faith of his subjects, thus sanctioning the existence of Lutheran states. It is decided that the imperial chamber should be composed of an equal number of Protestants and Catholics. Calvinists, however, are excluded from the agreement.

England, 16 October 1555. The Protestant bishops Nicholas Ridley and Hugh Latimer are burnt.

Europe, 25 October 1555. Charles V abdicates the sovereignty of the Netherlands to his son Philip.

Near East, 1555. The Ottomans and the Persians sign the peace of Amasya.

Germany, 1555. Philip of Spain renounces his claim to the German throne in favour of Maximilian, the son of Frederick of Habsburg.

Russia, 1555. The English navigator Richard Chancellor makes a second journey to Archangel and Moscow.

India, 1555. The Moghul emperor Humayun, who has recently recovered Kandahar with the help of the Persian Shah Ismail, reoccupies Delhi and Agra after defeating an Afghan claimant to the throne.

Cuba, 1555. The Spanish settlement at Havana is attacked by the French.

North America, 1555. A Basque privateering fleet led by Juan de Erauso and Perez de Hoa raids the French fort at St John's fishery in Newfoundland, capturing it for the Spanish.

South America, 1555. Durand de Villegagnon founds a French colony at Rio de Janeiro.

Ethiopia, 1555. The Emperor Galawdewos is victorious in the Ethiopian-Galla war.

China, 1555. Japanese pirates, who have already launched two attacks on China, besiege Nanjing.

Spain, 16 January 1556. Charles V hands over his remaining Spanish dominions in the Old and New Worlds to his son Philip.

Central Asia, 1556. The Russian army under Ivan IV seizes the *khanate* of Astrakhan, so reaching the Caspian Sea.

Scotland, 1556. Condemned to further exile, John Knox returns to Geneva.

Mary Tudor beheads Lady Jane Grey

Lady Jane Grey is urged to take the crown, by Giovanni Battista (1727-85).

London, 12 February 1554
Lady Jane Grey, queen of England in name only for nine days last year, was executed for treason in the Tower today with her husband.

The order for her execution came directly from Queen Mary Tudor – to whom she surrendered the crown – who feared that the Protestant noblewoman might serve as a rallying point for a rebellion against her own fierce Catholicism.

Jane Grey had successfully proclaimed herself monarch nine days after the duke of Northumberland, John Dudley, had named her, his protegee, as queen. Northumberland was executed immediately. Lady Jane, a granddaughter of Henry VIII, and her husband, Northumberland's son, might have remained alive, but last week 3,000 Kentishmen led by Sir Thomas Wyatt marched unsuccessfully on London to try to stop Queen Mary's marriage to Philip of Spain. Lady Jane had no direct connection with the revolt.

Picaresque novel seen as heretical

Burgos, Spain, 1554
A new sort of novel, known as *picaresque* from its celebration of a hero who is a *picaro*, or wandering rogue, has been published anonymously in Spain. Condemned as immoral, it has been placed on the Index. It is entitled *La Vida de Lazarillo de Tormes y sus Fortunas y Adversidades*.

The picaro is a common character in today's Spain. Often a veteran, he rejects hard work, living on his wits and chancing his luck with every new opportunity.

Reflecting a collapsing society, its citizens overcome by fatalism and a growing insecurity, the book has appalled the authorities, who particularly dislike its vigorous anti-clericalism.

The Frenchman Bernard Palissy has tried for sixteen years to crack the Italian secret of faenza enamel. Unlike the Italians, who favour a pewter solution, he uses a lead-based formula. This is a typical piece of his highly-decorated glazed rustic earthenware from the early 1550s.

Bishops burnt as Mary seeks birthright

England, 1555

Secret meetings of the new English Protestants are taking place in towns and villages in southern England as Catholic Mary's campaign of persecution spreads. Burnings at the stake began last February, the victims including four bishops, one of them a greatly respected friend of the poor, Nicholas Ridley.

Mary has persuaded parliament to abandon the independence of the English church and to submit to papal authority; accordingly, Pope Julius III has appointed Reginald Pole, an Englishman long resident in Italy, archbishop of Canterbury. He has revived the old Catholic services and sacked priests who, under the reforms of Henry VIII and Edward VI, were allowed to marry.

Some observers say that the queen is not directly responsible for the persecutions which have earned her the epithet "Bloody Mary"; still, she has a very personal reason for seeking to restore Catholic authority. When Henry's marriage to Catherine of Aragon was annulled, in spite of papal condemnation

The Catholic Queen Mary: made illegitimate by her father's actions.

of the action, Mary became a bastard; she was obliged to make an act of submission acknowledging Henry as "Supreme Head of the Church of England" and affirming that her mother's marriage had been "incestuous and unlawful". If she can restore papal authority over the English church her birth will become legitimate.

From Moorish potters in Spain comes the vivid ceramic technique called majolica, after the island of Majorca. Italian potteries, especially in the Florence area, soon learned how to do the same coloured ornamentation on white enamel. At first the Italians were content to copy the oriental designs favoured by the Moors. Nowadays the preference is for "istorati", illustrations of historical, biblical or mythological themes, such as this plate by F. Xanto from Urbino, showing Actaeon turned into a stag.

Dream dies at Augsburg

Augsburg, 3 October 1555

Catholics and Protestants, who have been meeting in the diet here since last February, today signed a peace treaty that ends the three-year war in Germany. It also represents a clear recognition by the Catholics of co-existence for the new Protestant churches throughout Europe and a recognition by the emperor of the powers and rights of the German princes.

The dream of the emperor, Charles V, was to bring the Protestants back into the Catholic Church and to secure imperial power over both Catholic and Protestant princes in Germany. At the beginning of this year, riven by gout and under attack from the Turks on his eastern flank, he finally admitted that his dream was impossible.

He raised his siege of Metz and nominated his brother, Ferdinand, to lead the Diet of Augsburg to find a compromise solution.

The principle established by the peace is *cuius regio, eius religio* (to each kingdom its own religion). In effect, it gives the princes power over the bodies and souls of their subjects. It does not give ordinary people their religious freedom, but at least they can move to adjoining states if their own prince does not permit their religion.

Charles V can also feel satisfied that the peace ensures the continuance of Catholicism in some German principalities. The Catholic princes, driven by different political motives, could never on their own have withstood the surging popularity of Lutheranism.

Local doctor reveals his world prophecies

Salon-de-Provence, 1 March 1555

A French country doctor, astrologer and self-styled prophet has published a book in which he claims to forsee the history of world events for the next 500 years. *Centuries*, by Michel de Nostradame, known as Nostradamus, is a collection of 1,000 quatrains. Each is filled with cryptic and mysterious references which, when deciphered, apparently set out the fate of mankind.

His prophecies are hard to interpret, but they include what readers see as coded references to many European monarchs. Other verses, often almost indecipherable, seem filled with death and disaster and allegedly deal in matters far beyond our own era. That some predictions have already proved accurate has led to *Centuries* being regarded with equal parts of respect and outright fear.

Although critics talk of the occult, and condemn Nostradamus as an agent of the Devil, the prophet, who admits to using deliberately difficult language, stresses his belief in God. All his work, he declares, "has been accomplished through divine power and inspiration".

Nonetheless, Nostradamus is said to have studied the mystical Jewish Qabbalah, the writings of the Sufis and classical Chaldean and Assyrian magic.

Nostradamus: prophet or crackpot?

Indians' Holy Book

Guatemala, 1555

A survivor of the 1524 Spanish assault on the Qiches tribe at Utatlan city has translated their holy book, *Popol Vuh*, into Roman script.

Until now the book, containing Toltec-Maya Indian theories of evolution, has only been decipherable by high caste members of the Qiches tribe. The *Popol Vuh* tells of past worlds – one where men were made of earth and another where they were made of maize gruel.

1556 (1556-1558)

India, 27 January 1556. The Moghul Emperor Humayan dies after falling from his library roof in Delhi. He is succeeded by his 13-year-old son Akbar.

France, 5 February 1556. Henry II of France and Philip of Spain sign the truce of Vaucelles.

England, 21 March 1556. Thomas Cranmer, the archbishop of Canterbury, is burnt at the stake in Oxford. The English reformer was imprisoned for heresy when Mary Tudor came to the throne.

England, 22 March 1556. Cardinal Reginald Pole, who was a candidate for the papacy in 1549, becomes archbishop of Canterbury.

Rome, 31 July 1556. Ignatius Loyola, the Basque nobleman and former soldier who founded the Society of Jesus, dies.

Spain, October 1556. Charles V resigns the empire to his brother Ferdinand and retires to a remote monastery at Yuste. He is succeeded as king of Spain by his son Philip II.

India, 5 November 1556. The Emperor Akbar defeats the Hindus at Panipat and secures control of the Moghul empire.

Scotland, 10 November 1556. The Englishman Richard Chancellor is drowned off Aberdeenshire on his return from a second voyage to Russia.

Germany, 17 November 1556. Ferdinand founds a military council to govern the German possessions of the Habsburgs.

Florence, 2 January 1557. The painter Jacopo Carrucci, one of the masters of mannerism, dies.

England, 7 June 1557. In support of Philip II of Spain, the husband of Queen Mary, England declares war on France. The war has been provoked by Pope Paul IV, a life-long enemy of Spain.

France, 10 August 1557. French troops, led by the constable, Montmorency, are defeated by the Spanish army of Emmanuel Philibert, the duke of Savoy, at St Quentin. Philip II of Spain promises to construct a magnificent building to commemorate the victory.

France, 1 September 1557. Jacques Cartier, who discovered Canada, dies at St Malo.

Scotland, 3 December 1557. The Protestants are united by a national covenant.

Portugal, 1557. John III, whose son John died in 1554, is succeeded as king of Portugal by his three-year-old grandson Sebastian. Sebastian's grandmother, Catherine of Habsburg, is appointed regent.

Netherlands, 1557. The world commercial centre of Antwerp faces a crisis. As a result of their war debts, the kings of France and Spain find it impossible either to pay the interest on their debts or to repay any borrowed money.

Morocco, 1557. Mohammad al-Mahdi, the effective founder of the Sadian kingdom, is assassinated. During his lifetime, the Sadians secured control of the whole of Morocco and moved their capital from Fez to Marrakesh, causing clashes with the Turks of Algiers.

Italy, 1557. Francis, the duke of Guise, launches an unsuccessful expedition to exercise his rights to the kingdom of Naples.

China, 1557. The Portuguese set up a trading post at Macao.

London, 1557. Sebastian Cabot, the Venetian explorer dies.

Newfoundland, 1557. With the help of an armed escort, the French recover St John's fishery, captured by a Basque fleet two years ago.

Germany, 1557. The first German novel is published: *Der Goldfaden*, by George Wickram.

Switzerland, 9 January 1558. Geneva becomes independent of Berne.

France, 20 January 1558. A French army under Francis, the duke of Guise, takes Calais from the English.

Germany, 14 March 1558. Ferdinand assumes the title of emperor without being crowned by the pope.

Russia, 4 April 1558. Ivan IV grants the merchant Grigory Stoganov the right to use and cultivate the lands in the area of the Kama river and its tributaries.

France, 24 April 1558. Mary, the queen of Scotland, the daughter of James V and Mary of Guise, marries the French dauphin, Francis.

France, 22 June 1558. The French take Thionville.

France, 13 July 1558. The French suffer a resounding defeat at Gravelines by the Spanish army, led by the count of Egmont.

Scotland, 1558. John Knox publishes his *First Blast of the Trumpet against the Monstrous Regiment of Women* attacking female monarchs.

Austria, 1558. The manufacture of firearms begins at Ferlach, Carinthia.

India, 1558. The Moghul Emperor Akbar conquers Gwalior.

Germany, 1558. The Hamburg Exchange is established.

Teenager Akbar wins the Moghul empire

India, 5 November 1556
On the battlefield of Panipat, 60 miles north of Delhi, 13-year-old Akbar, the son of Humayun and grandson of Babur, has gained the Moghul empire – thanks to Bairam Khan, his noble general and guardian.

Humayun regained the empire after the deaths of Sher Shah Suri and the latter's son, Islam Shah, but lived for only a few months to enjoy it before falling to his death down his library stairs.

Hemu, the capable and ambitious Hindu minister of the last Suri sultan, realizing the weakness of an empire ruled by a 13-year-old child, revolted. He took Agra and Delhi and proclaimed himself emperor, or *raja*, Vikramaditya.

Bairam Khan, with a smaller army, met Hemu's forces at Panipat, where Akbar's grandfather, Babur, had won his historic victory 30 years earlier. Victory appeared to be going to Hemu when he was struck by an arrow in the eye. His army, seeing him slumped on his famous war-elephant Hawai, fled. The unconscious Hemu was dragged before Akbar and Bairam and beheaded in front of the victorious Moghul troops. With a love of

The founders of the Moghul dynasty, (l. to r.) Babur, Timur and Humayun, with their chief attendants.

hunting a paramount factor in his makeup, Akbar shows few signs at this early age of beoming the kind of ruler which the Moghul empire – divided by internal strife and frequent rebellions – urgently needs.

Much will depend on the advice given to him by Bairam Khan in these next few formative years – and whether he will take it.

First among equals makes maths simpler

London, 1557
A book has just been published, written by an English physician and mathematician, Robert Recorde, which contains a welcome innovation in mathematical notation. In *The Whetstone of Witte*, Recorde proposes the use of the sign "=" to denote "equals". Hitherto mathematicians have been using verbal abbreviations and other short cuts to denote equality, but there has been no consistency. Now they can all employ the same notation. Recorde, a fellow of All Souls' College, Oxford, and the royal physician, also introduced algebra into England.

New empire rises south of the Sahara

Timbuktu, Africa, c.1556
The great empire of Mali is dying. A new empire, the Songhai empire, is taking its place in West Africa. The Malian empire proved too large for its rulers. Its decline was evident by 1433 when it was unable to defend Timbuktu from attack by Tuareg nomads. By 1512 Leo Africanus wrote of the king of Mali being so impoverished that he "cannot even give food to his family".

Over the decades the breakaway state of Songhai, under its ruler Sonni Ali, increased its power, taking Timbuktu from the Tuaregs in 1468. His successor, the philosopher-prince Askia, continued the conquests, extending Songhai's frontiers to the central Sahara in the north, Senegal in the west and Lake Chad in the east. Ten years ago the Songhai army invaded Mali again and, though it has withdrawn, Mali is but a shadow of its ancient glory.

Charles V's final retreat

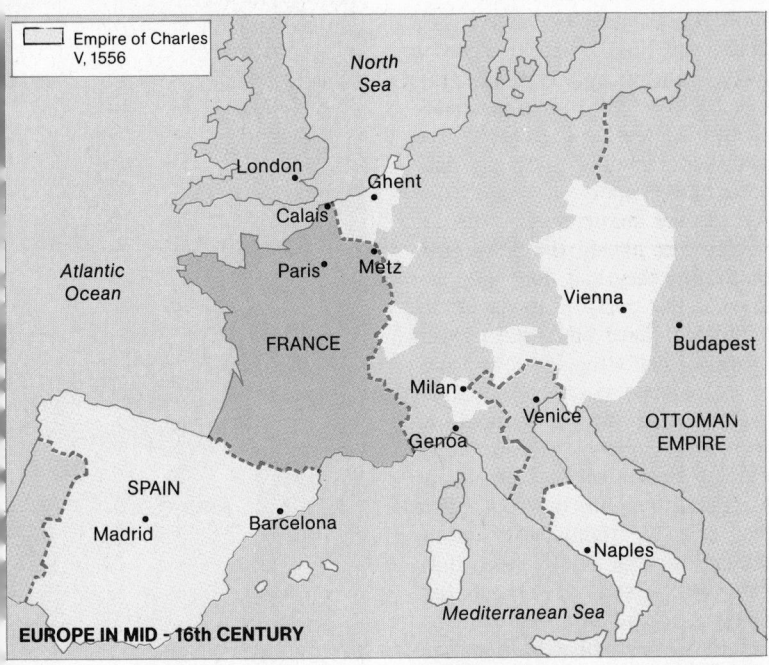

Empire of Charles V, 1556

EUROPE IN MID - 16th CENTURY

Brussels, 25 October 1556
Dressed entirely in black, except for the red collar of the Order of the Holy Fleece, Charles V, the Holy Roman emperor and king of Spain, Naples and the Netherlands, rode on a gentle mule into the castle here to announce that he had abdicated his empire and kingships and was retreating to a monastery. The 56-year-old emperor, broken in health, handed his kingdoms to his son, Philip, and the empire to his brother, Ferdinand. It was a moving occasion; and as the emperor, his voice breaking with the effort, asked for forgiveness for all past errors, the audience "could not restrain their tears and sobs".

As he drives across the continent to the monastery which he himself has designed, Charles will have much to reflect upon, particularly the state of the Europe which he has bequeathed. He was, by nature, a crusader, who lived for the ideal of a huge campaign to drive the Ottomans from the Holy Lands, yet spent much of his life in a defensive role as the forces of Suleiman the Magnificent continually threatened his realms. To achieve the true crusade he needed a united Europe; but Germany, at the very centre of his empire, was divided by Christian heresy, with its princes using the Reformation to fight for their own independence. Despite his pledge to "exterminate heresy

Charles V, by Van Dyck.

lest it should take root and overturn the state and the social order", Charles was prepared to compromise and accept the alliance of the Protestant princes when central Europe was threatened. Nonetheless, his principal bequest is a divided Germany which threatens to engulf the whole of Europe in a major war.

The man who bestrode Europe like a colossus, fighting brilliant battles and travelling huge distances as he sought to hold a great empire together, has one more achievement to reflect upon: it was in his name that Rome was destroyed.

Ignatius Loyola, founder of Jesuits, dies

Rome, 31 July 1556
Ignatius Loyola, the founder and first general of the Society of Jesus, died today, having seen its numbers swell from a handful in 1540 to over 1,000 members. Jesuits prepare themselves by following Loyola's rigorous *Spiritual Exercises*, published in 1548. Subjecting themselves to this ascetic discipline teaches them to master the will and learn total obedience to their superior and to the church. They have to be prepared to believe that what seems black to them is white if the church declares that it is.

One of Loyola's original brethren, Francis Xavier, left for the Indies with three companions in 1541 to carry out their original aim as missionaries. At home and across Europe the society has become a teaching order, starting with schools in the slums of Rome,

A later French portrait of Ignatius Loyola, Christian soldier supreme.

but now providing education for the best families at Jesuit colleges at the universities such as Padua and Rome. Jesuits are renowned for their teaching methods.

Bankruptcy looms in Spanish crisis

Spain, June 1557
Philip II of Spain has issued a decree suspending all payments from the Castilian treasury. All outstanding debts are to be consolidated into *juros* – annuities repaying loans out of revenue – at five per cent interest. Though Spain is not technically bankrupt, the move reflects the magnitude of the debts left by the Emperor Charles V.

In the early part of his reign, Charles was able to rely on Italy and the Netherlands to contribute to the fight against heresy in northern Europe, and campaigns against the Turks. But there was a tax revolt in Ghent in 1539, and by

1540 the Spanish viceroy warned that Naples, which had been heavily taxed since 1525, had been virtually bled dry.

The main source of revenue was Castile, followed by Aragon, the church and the South American colonies. But the cost of the emperor's campaigns meant constant new taxes, or other measures like the sale of indulgences by which noblemen became exempt from direct tax. The Cortes and the Spanish Council of Finance voted additional sums. Still Charles needed more, and he turned to German and Italian bankers, at increasingly exorbitant rates of interest.

The Spanish royal family, ostentatiously displaying their enormous wealth.

1558 (1558-1559)

Spain, 21 September 1558. Charles V, Holy Roman emperor between 1519 and 1555, dies. His reign was marked by almost constant wars with France, through which he gained control of Italy under the 1529 peace of Cambrai. Despite his tenacious struggle against the Protestant Schmalkaldic League, Protestantism in Germany won legal recognition under the peace of Augsburg, after Charles had been deserted by his powerful ally Maurice of Saxony.

England, 17 November 1558. Queen Mary, the daughter of Henry VIII and Catherine of Aragon, dies at the age of 42. Her five-year reign saw the restoration of Catholicism as the official state religion and brutal persecution of Protestant "heretics". Mary's half-sister Elizabeth, the daughter of Anne Boleyn, becomes queen.

England, 17 November 1558. Cardinal Reginald Pole, the archbishop of Canterbury, dies a mere 12 hours after Queen Mary, under whom he vigorously championed the restoration of Catholicism. His disapproval of Henry VIII's assumption of supremacy over the English church forced him to leave England in 1532. He was made a cardinal in 1536 and, after Mary's accession, returned to England as papal legate.

England, 20 November 1558. Queen Elizabeth appoints the statesman William Cecil to the post of her chief secretary of state.

Italy, 1558. Ramusio's *Delle Navigationi e Viaggi* is the first narrative of the North American voyages of discovery to be widely circulated in Europe.

Germany, 13 January 1559. The moderate Anabaptist leader Menno Simons dies. By imposing rigid discipline on the sect, he saved Anabaptism from extinction under persecution in northern Europe.

France, 3 April 1559. Philip II of Spain and Henry II of France sign the peace of Cateau-Cambresis, ending the long series of wars between the Habsburg and Valois dynasties. Under the terms of the treaty, France withdraws from Savoy and Piedmont but recovers Calais and retains Metz, Toul and Verdun. In Italy, Spain now controls Sicily, Sardinia, Naples, Milan and the coastal fortresses of Tuscany. The agreement is to be sealed by two dynastic marriages.

England, 8 May 1559. An Act of Supremacy defines Queen Elizabeth as the supreme governor of the Church of England and makes provision for a high commission for the correction of errors and abuses to be set up.

Mexico, 11 June 1559. The Spaniard Tristan de Luna y Arellano sets sail from Vera Cruz at the head of a 1,500-strong expedition, intending to establish a settlement on the gulf coast of Florida.

France, 10 July 1559. Henry II, the king of France, dies after being mortally wounded by Gabriel de Montgomery in a jousting tournament. He is succeeded by his 15-year-old son, Francis II, the husband of Mary Stuart, the queen of Scotland.

Florida, 14 August 1559. Spanish explorer de Luna enters a bay on the gulf coast *(Pensacola)*.

England, 1559. The learned theologian Matthew Parker is appointed archbishop of Canterbury. The Anglican service is reintroduced.

Scotland, 1559. Attempts by the regent, Mary of Guise, to suppress Protestant reformers provoke them into open rebellion.

Netherlands, 1559. Margaret of Parma, the sister of Philip II of Spain, becomes regent of the Netherlands.

Scandinavia, 1559. Frederick II, the son of Christian III, becomes king of Denmark and Norway. In alliance with his uncles, the dukes of Holstein, he conquers the peasants' republic of Ditmarsh, located between the Elbe and Eider rivers.

Rome, 1559. Pope Paul IV, who completed the organisation of the Roman Catholic Inquisition and issued a list of prohibited books, dies. He is succeeded by Giovanni Medici, who decides to take the name of Pius IV.

Near East, 1559. With the support of his father, Suleiman the Magnificent, the sultan of the Ottomans, Selim defeats his brother Bayezid at the battle of Konya. Bayezid and his five sons flee to Persia, where they are subsequently executed in return for a large payment made by Suleiman.

France, 1559. A French translation of Plutarch's *Lives* by the humanist Jacques Amyot is published.

Switzerland, 1559. John Calvin and the French Protestant reformer Theodore Beza, who has recently joined him in Geneva, found an academy for the teaching of Calvinist theology.

Germany, 1559. Under the direction of Matthias Flacius, the professor of theology at the newly-founded university of Jena, a group of Lutherans begins work on a church history entitled *The Magdeburg Centuries*.

France is humiliated at peace conference

Cambrai, France, 3 April 1559
The representatives of France, Spain and England today signed a treaty bringing an end to 60 years of warfare at the dilapidated chateau of Cateau-Cambresis. It is said that the only thing the delegates agreed upon was the discomfort of their quarters.

However much they disagreed politically, they had no option but to sign the treaty as both France and Spain have bankrupted themselves in their struggle for the mastery of Europe.

Under the terms, England acknowledges French possession of Calais. France also keeps Toul, Metz and Verdun, but it is Spain that emerges triumphant, winning the exclusion of France from Italy, the battleground of France and Spain for over half a century.

It is a treaty that is bound to cause bitterness among the French who have shed so much blood for so little. Already there is talk of France being humiliated.

Philip II of Spain, by Moro; Spain has won most from the treaty.

King is fatally wounded in tournament

France, 10 July 1559
Henry II has died in agony ten days after he was so terribly wounded at the tournament held to celebrate the Treaty of Cateau-Cambresis and the marriage of his daughter, Elizabeth, to Philip II of Spain.

His death is a story of foolhardiness. Although tired by several passages of arms he insisted on breaking another lance before retiring, and asked Gabriel de Montgomery to oppose him in the lists.

Montgomery begged to be excused and the queen told Henry that he was too tired to joust again. But Henry was adamant. The two men put on their helmets, galloped down the lists, clashed; Montgomery neglected to drop his broken lance and tonight France is ruled by a 15-year-old sickly boy.

Montgomery's lance spears Henry through his visor, shattering on impact.

Charles V dies in Spanish monastery

The Emperor Charles V at the convent of Yuste, by Alfred Elmore (1815-81).

Yuste, Spain, 21 September 1558
Charles V died today in the monastery in which he had lived out the last three years of his life in solitude. Rejecting a grand funeral, he will be buried in the chapel here under the high altar – "half my body to be placed underneath, the other half outside so that the priest will stand over my head and chest".

His last years were spent peacefully enough at Yuste, living in a small villa designed so that he could see the high altar in the monastery from his bed.

After the last rites had been administered, Charles asked for the crucifix which his wife had held on her deathbed and died to the sound of psalms.

Queen dies with Calais engraved on heart

England, 17 November 1558
Mary Tudor was England's first queen regnant. She ascended the throne five years ago with the intention of restoring papal authority over the English church; when she died today, aged 42, she had caused 300 men and women to be burnt at the stake for their Protestant faith.

She lacked experience of governing – her father, Henry VIII, had banished her from his court – and listened to her cousin, Charles V of Spain, who persuaded her to marry his son Philip. The union was unpopular and led to uprisings. When she thought she was pregnant she ordered thanksgiving services in London; but there was no child.

The Spanish connection led to war with France. At Calais the French mounted an unexpected assault on New Year's Day 1558, and captured the town. After 200 years, England's only foothold in Europe was lost. "When I am dead and opened," Mary said, "you shall

Mary, with Philip II of Spain.

find Calais engraved on my heart." Philip rarely visited England, yet once again, a few months before her death, Mary said she was pregnant. One of her courtiers sardonically observed that she had better hurry, as it was eight months since she had last seen her husband.

Ivan the Terrible invades Baltic states

Russia, 1558
Ivan the Terrible has sent his troops into Livonia in a lightning strike designed to secure the Baltic region for Muscovy and give it an outlet to the west. Ivan's troops have seized several large towns as well as the coastal fortress of Narva, but disputes in Moscow are beginning to destroy the army's momentum. At the same time the Livonian Order of Knights, still the area's main defence force, is managing to improve its military and diplomatic posture. Riga has put itself under the protection of the Poles, and Sweden and Denmark are looking poised to take over other areas of Estonia and Courland. Livonia is being partitioned.

Ivan may find that he has over-reached himself, but the Baltic area would have been a considerable prize. To a backward Russia, with a rudimentary agriculture and little industry, the Baltic and its ports, already important centres of international trade, offer the prospect of benefit from the more advanced countries of the west.

Adventurous goldsmith begins life story

The splendid salt-cellar which Benvenuto Cellini made in about 1540 for King Francis I of France. It is made of gold, enamel and ebony.

Florence, 1558
The goldsmith, sculptor, musician and soldier Benvenuto Cellini has begun what should be a colourful autobiography. Born in 1500, the tempestuous Cellini has served many leading dynasties as artist or soldier in these turbulent times, especially the Medicis in his native Florence. He worked first in Rome, producing jewellery, medals, coins and seals; he moved on to sculpture under the influence of Michelangelo and in around 1540 made the famous gold, ebony and enamel salt cellar for Francis I of France. Another famous sculpture is the Medicis' *Perseus*, made in 1553.

King who saved Ethiopia dies fighting

Ethiopia, 1559
Gelawdewos, who saved his empire first from Ottoman and Somali invaders, and then from Galla from the south, is dead, killed in battle consolidating his empire. His finest hour was in 1540. Almost all of Ethiopia was overrun by the Moslem armies of Almad ibn Ibrahim ("El Gran" – the left-handed). Nine out of ten Ethiopians had renounced their religion. He remained defiantly in the field; and when a Portuguese army sent to assist him was almost wiped out he continued to resist, until in 1543 he brought el Gran to battle at Weyna Dega and killed him.

Florida, 1559. De Luna founds a settlement on Mobile Bay (*Alabama*).

Paris, January 1560. The poet Joachim du Bellay dies of apoplexy at the age of 37. He was part of the group of poets known as the *Pleiade* and wrote its manifesto, *The Defence and Illustration of the French Language.*

France, March 1560. In what is known as the "conspiracy of Amboise", a group of Protestants launches an operation to capture the court and topple the Guise family. The Guises are warned, however, and the attempt fails. Several hundred Huguenots are executed and Louis de Bourbon, the duke of Conde, is imprisoned.

India, March 1560. The Moghul Emperor Akbar, now aged 17, dismisses the regent, Bairam Khan, and takes the reins of government into his own hands.

Germany, 19 April 1560. Philip Melanchthon, Luther's close associate, dies at Wittenberg. The main author of the 1530 Augsburg Confession, he was influenced by the humanism of Erasmus. Becoming spiritual leader of the Lutheran Church after Luther's death, he made great efforts to reconcile opposing factions among the reformers.

Sweden, 25 June 1560. Gustav Vasa – whose capture of Stockholm in 1523 drove the Danes from Sweden, thus ending the great Scandinavian union which had existed for 126 years – abdicates. He leaves the foundations of a strong Swedish army and navy and a more settled system of administration.

Scotland, June 1560. The Scottish Parliament accepts a Protestant confession of faith drafted by John Knox which forbids the saying of Mass and renounces the pope's authority in Scotland.

France, 2 July 1560. The Catholic statesman Michel de l'Hopital, who supports a policy of religious toleration towards the Huguenots, is appointed chancellor of France.

France, 6 December 1560. Francis II is succeeded as king of France by his ten-year-old brother Charles IX. The queen mother, Catherine de Medici, the widow of Henry II, becomes regent.

England, c.1560. The English navy is busy building ships on the pattern of Henry VIII's *Henry Grace a Dieu*, nicknamed the "Great Harry", the first four-masted vessel launched in England. The Great Harry is a symbol of the revolution in shipbuilding and navigation which has taken Europeans around the world.

France, 1560. The poet Maurice Sceve, a leader of the *ecole lyonnaise*, which laid the foundations for the *Pleiade* movement, dies.

Moscow, 1560. Construction of the cathedral of the Intercession of the Virgin (St Basil's cathedral) is completed.

Peru, 1560. The Dominican friar Domingo de Santo Tomas writes his *Gramatica y Arte de la lengua general del Peru* and a *Lexicon y Vocabulario*, enabling missionaries to study Quechua, the language of the native Andean peoples.

South-East Africa, 15 March 1561. Father da Silveira, the Portuguese Christian envoy to the Munhumutapa court, is killed at court – probably at the instigation of the Moslem imam.

Caribbean, 9 July 1561. Angel de Villafane and the remnants of the 1559 expedition of Tristan de Luna y Arellano return to Hispaniola (*Santo Domingo*) after failing to establish a colony at Pensacola Bay. Villafane took control of the expedition after de Luna was dismissed for poor leadership.

France, July 1561. Acting on the advice of Michel de l'Hopital, the regent Catherine de Medici sets up talks between the French Catholics and Protestants at Poissy. She consents to an edict giving the Huguenots qualifed toleration.

Scotland, 19 August 1561. Mary, queen of Scots, returns to Scotland following the death of her husband, Francis II of France, last year. The Scottish nobility is bitterly opposed to her Roman Catholicism.

Spain, 23 September 1561. Philip II gives orders that colonising efforts in Florida should be halted.

Netherlands, 1561. In compliance with an undertaking given to the regent, Margaret of Parma, in 1559, Spanish troops leave the Netherlands.

Netherlands, 1561. A papal bull is published proposing the creation of 14 new bishoprics in addition to the four existing ones. This alienates many nobles whose relatives are thus excluded from ecclesiastical sinecures.

Scotland, 1561. The reformer John Knox publishes his *Book of Discipline*, setting out a new Scottish church constitution based on the Calvinist model.

Italy, 1561. A *History of Italy* by the Florentine Francesco Guicciardini is published posthumously. The work completes his *History of Florence*, which was begun in 1508 but was still unfinished at his death.

Lutheran king of Sweden abdicates

Expansionist monarch Gustav Vasa, by Willem Boy (c.1557).

Stockholm, 25 June 1560
Sweden today achieved an orderly handover of power when King Gustav, who has done much to make Sweden a power in its own right, abdicated in favour of his son, Eric, after 43 years on the throne.

King Gustav, an elected monarch, ensured an hereditary succession for his son 15 years ago when he had laws passed establishing that the monarchy would pass through the male line.

The new king, Eric XIV, is expected to continue his father's policy of expanding Sweden's diplomatic and trade links with powers in western and central Europe.

Ever since King Gustav made Sweden independent of Denmark and took it out of the Kalmar Union, Sweden has been conscious that its sea and land routes to the west – the narrow strip of water known as the Oresund, and Norway – remain under Danish control and could ultimately jeopardise its independence.

Before his accession the then prince had already tried to forge one such diplomatic alliance with England by negotiating a marriage with its Queen Elizabeth.

Scottish Parliament bars Roman rituals

Edinburgh, June 1560
A decisive shift of power has taken place in Scotland and, linked as it is to the accession of Queen Elizabeth in England, promises to overturn the old pattern of relations with Europe. At a free Scottish Parliament meeting in Edinburgh, 100 lairds heard a confession of faith drafted by the Calvinist reformer John Knox. This document aims to embrace the "elect of all ages, realms, nations, Jews or Gentiles" and specifically rejects the rituals of Rome and abolishes the pope's authority in Scotland.

This new state of affairs came about after an English army fought alongside the Scots to drive out the French. Such an alliance would have been unthinkable as recently as two years ago, when Catholic Mary was on the throne of England. Even her successor Elizabeth was at first doubtful, not because of popish sympathies – far from it – but because of Knox's pamphlet delivering a blast against the "monstrous regiment" of woman. He has been busy explaining to the English that his fire had been aimed at the pro-French queen mother in Scotland, Mary of Lorraine, who married her daughter Mary to the French dauphin, Francis.

Knox spent two years in irons after being captured by the French. Released after English intervention, he fled to Geneva, where he was inspired by the teachings of Calvin to found the Scottish Kirk.

A later engraving of John Knox, the fiery anti-Catholic Scotsman.

Elizabeth I's church rejects papal power

A 16th-century manuscript illustration of Queen Elizabeth.

England, 1559

After months of parliamentary manoeuvring, and a shake-up of the Privy Council, Elizabeth's secretary of state, William Cecil, has achieved the religious settlement desired by his queen. The church is once more English and papal authority has been firmly repudiated.

Parliament assembled last February after Elizabeth's accession to the throne and in the wake of anti-Roman demonstrations in London and a Twelfth Night court masque, where asses were dressed as bishops. But Cecil's first bills were emasculated in the Lords. Another bill repealing Catholic Mary's heresy laws was also lost.

In the Privy Council, Cecil baited Catholic members until they walked out. He tackled parliament again and got his bills through by agreeing that Elizabeth should be the church's "supreme governor", not "supreme head". The bishops have rejected the settlement and been sacked. Married clergy are returning. Matthew Parker, who was chaplain to Elizabeth's mother, Anne Boleyn, has become archbishop of Canterbury.

French peace talks

France, September 1561

The most eminent Catholic and Calvinist theologians are meeting at Poissy at the instigation of the regent, Catherine de Medici, to try to settle the religious differences which are proving so dangerous to France. On one side there is the brilliant Jesuit, Diego Lainez, and on the other, Calvin's friend, Theodore Beza. But although the debate between these men should be memorable, the differences between both sides are so great there would seem to be little chance of reconciliation.

Catherine de Medici is French regent

France, 1560

Catherine de Medici, the widow of Henry II, has declared herself regent of France in the name of her ten-year-old son, Charles IX. This move puts her in a position of great power and equal danger.

It is an unusual situation for Catherine, for she was virtually ignored during the reign of her husband who was under the thumb of his mistress, Diane de Poitiers. During the short reign of her sickly elder son, Francis II, she was also unable to exert any influence because Francis, although only 16, was of age. Married to Mary, queen of Scots, he came under the control of the ultra-Catholic Guise faction led by Mary's uncles, the duke of Guise and the cardinal of Lorraine.

However, while Catherine may have little experience of power, there is no doubt about her passionate determination to preserve the French monarchy for her sons. Descended from a Florentine family of

King Francis II, reigned 1559-60.

popes on her father's side and from a noble French family on her mother's, she is a woman to be reckoned with. Her first priority is to gain time to allow a cooling of the religious passions of the Catholics and Protestants which are threatening to tear France apart.

The colourful domes of the great Russian orthodox cathedral of St. Basil, which was built in the last few years for Ivan, the czar of Russia. Standing next to "Red Square" in the centre of his capital, Moscow, it is a fittingly imposing monument to Ivan's autocratic rule; he is determined not to tolerate any opposition, especially from Russia's feudal aristocracy.

1561 (1561-1564)

Spain, 1561. Madrid becomes the capital of Spain.

France, January 1562. The edict of St Germain supersedes last year's July edict, again giving limited toleration to Huguenots (Protestants) but obliging them to practise their religion outside town walls. Parliament refuses to recognise or register the edict.

France, 8 February 1562. Jean Ribault leaves France at the head of a party of 150 French Huguenots intending to establish a colony in Florida.

France, March 1562. The massacre of an illegal Huguenot congregation at Vassy, by order of Francis, the duke of Guise, sets off a religious war.

Florida, 1 May 1562. Jean Ribault lands on the coast and discovers a waterway which he names the river of May *(St John's river).*

England, 20 September 1562. Queen Elizabeth signs a treaty at Hampton Court with the French Huguenot leader, Louis de Bourbon, the prince of Conde. Under the treaty the English will occupy Le Havre in return for aiding Conde's forces against Catholic troops; Elizabeth will leave Le Havre when Calais has been restored to England.

Venice, 17 December 1562. The Flemish composer Adrian Willaert, who had been chapel master at St Mark's for 35 years and founded a famous choir school, dies. His work synthesises Flemish, French and Italian styles.

West Africa, 1562. The Englishman John Hawkins begins the English slave trade across the Atlantic. He leaves Sierra Leone with a shipment of 300 slaves, sailing to Hispaniola *(Santo Domingo)* in the Caribbean.

Mexico, 1562. In Yucatan, Bishop Diego de Landa orders a large number of Maya manuscripts to be burnt.

Venice, 1562. The painter Paolo Veronese completes his decorations in the Villa Barbaro in Maser – greatly praised as an innovation in Venetian painting.

France, January 1563. The port of Le Havre, occupied by the English under a treaty signed with the prince of Conde last year, is seized by Catholic troops.

France, 19 March 1563. The peace of Amboise brings to an end the war of religion. Although the militant Catholic Francis, the duke of Guise, was assassinated last month and the English allies of the Huguenots defeated, limited toleration is once more granted to the Huguenots.

China, 1563. Ming generals finally manage to gain the upper hand over resurgent Japanese piracy along the south China coast.

Florence, 1563. Cosimo de Medici establishes the Accademia del Disegno, the first academy of art in Europe. Its members, who are governed by formal rules, are drawn mainly from the artists and sculptors of whom Cosimo is already an established patron.

Europe, c.1563. The term "Puritan" is used increasingly to stigmatise those English Protestants who want to purify the church further.

England, 1563. Jean Ribault visits the royal court, bringing his *Whole and True Discoverye of Terra Florida*, the first account of Florida published in English.

England, 1563. The "39" Articles of the Protestant Church of England are published.

England, 1563. The Statute of Artificers regulates trade and employment contracts and confers on justices of the peace the task of fixing wages in their county.

Spain, 1563. Juan Battista de Toledo begins work in the Escorial palace founded by Philip II of Spain outside Madrid.

Venice, 1563. Veronese paints the *Feast at Cana* for the Benedictine monks of San Giorgio Maggiore.

Russia, 1563. Ivan the Terrible orders the drowning of Jews in the Dvina river.

Scandinavia, 1563. The war of the Three Crowns breaks out between Sweden and Denmark; the latter is supported by Lubeck and Poland.

Paris, 1 January 1564. France adopts 1 January as the start of the year, in accordance with the Julian calendar. The New Year has been on 1 January for most civil purposes until now, but the official year, following a church decree issued 400 years ago, has begun on the day before Easter.

Italy, January 1564. The decrees of the Council of Trent are published. They reaffirm traditional Catholic theology, but propose radical reforms in church organisation, including the education of the clergy.

Netherlands, 22 January 1564. Antoine Granvelle, the adviser of Philip II of Spain and effective governor of the Netherlands since 1559, is recalled to Spain on account of growing unrest against Spanish domination and fierce lobbying against him in Madrid.

Rome, 18 February 1564. The sculptor and painter Michelangelo dies.

Council votes back pope

Trent, Italy, 4 December 1563

News of the severe, perhaps fatal, illness of Pope Pius IV has galvanised the Council of Trent here into action. A series of votes has been carried out rapidly in the last few days emphatically asserting the authority of the head of the Roman Catholic Church so much so that the delegate bishops here express their votes as propositions, which the pope has to approve in order for them to be effective.

The hopes of the reformers here, who hoped to have more power in the hands of the bishops, have been dashed. Pope Pius called the council, the third one here, in the hope of resolving the struggles between Catholics and Protestants, and particularly the bloody war between Catholics and Huguenots. His illness has strengthened the arm of the traditionalists who fear that any weakening in the face of the growing power of the Calvinists in France and the Lutherans in Germany will be fatal.

The council has asserted the importance of the Mass and the authority of tradition and of the bishops. It contradicts the Calvinist assertion of predestination and the idea that ordinary people can interpret the scriptures as well as the clergy. Some ground has been gained by the reformers. Bishops are to be urged to reside in their dioceses. The accumulation of wealth is prohibited. The ordinary clergy are to be properly trained. A new Bible, based on St Jerome's Latin version, is to be produced, which will be the ultimate authority.

The verdict reflects the views of the majority of the 200 delegates, who were Italian, Spanish and French. The Germans, where Protestantism is most powerful, were there as a tiny minority.

One in four dies as plague wracks London

London, 1563

What some call the sweating sickness, others the pestilence, and all know as plague, has hit London again. It is the sixth attack this century. In London more than 17,000 people, one quarter of the population, have died. Plague has become a fact of modern life, finding a welcome in the narrow streets of towns and cities. These "strange and unpredictable diseases which swarm among us", as one writer has it, defeat current medicine.

Every expert holds his own opinion and offers his own cure. The one general belief is that these epidemics reveal a general decline in the world. So random are the outbreaks, so varied those who perish and those who survive, that most observers are sure that the plague is God's work – his punishment for man's sins.

Silver gilt pomander of c.1580, made to carry perfumes to ward off disease.

Murder and rape in French religious wars

Renaissance genius Michelangelo dies

The execution of Huguenots: religious civil war seems inevitable in France.

France, 1562
Open warfare of the cruellest kind has broken out between the Catholics and the Huguenot followers of Calvin. Their quarrel has split the country from peasant to nobleman, with Gaspard de Coligny, the admiral of France, leading the Huguenots and the duke of Guise championing the Catholics.

Sadly, the bloodshed stems from an attempt at reconciliation by the regent, Catherine de Medici. After her seizure of power she stopped the persecution of the Calvinists and restored their leaders to influence at court, and in January 1562 her moderate chancellor, Michel de

l'Hopital, granted them a degree of freedom of worship. This served only to enrage the fiercely Catholic artisans in Paris and other towns. Led by nobles opposed to religious reform, they began to attack the Huguenots. On 1 March soldiers of the duke of Guise massacred a number of Huguenots as they prayed at Vassy.

The Protestant prince de Conde called the Huguenots to arms, and they retaliated by despoiling churches, murdering priests and raping nuns. They are now in possession of Lyons, Rouen and Orleans, but have been driven out of other towns with great slaughter.

"The Holy Family", by Michelangelo, a great artist, architect and sculptor.

Rome, 18 February 1564
The best all-round artist in Italy, probably the world, Michelangelo Buonarroti, has died at the age of 89. He told his friends on his deathbed that the works he left behind were his sons. His funeral will be in Rome, but Duke Cosimo de Medici plans a tomb for him in Florence.

Twenty years after he finished the ceiling of the Sistine Chapel for Julius II, Pope Clement VII asked him back to paint the wall behind the altar with his giant fresco of *The Last Judgement*, his mightiest composition, teeming with three-dimensional figures in dramatic poses. All his paintings, such as his circular *Holy Family*, are sculptural. His

last great frescoes, for a chapel of St Peter and St Paul adjoining the Sistine, were done in his seventies.

Besides having gifts as a poet, Michelangelo was a brilliant architect. He left the design and model for the unfinished dome for St Peter's and his plan for Rome's Capitoline Hill, the Campidoglio. His own dissatisfaction with his work as a sculptor caused him to leave many unfinished statues, like the *Pieta* on which he was working at his death. His friend, Giorgio Vasari, has told how frugally he lived and how he would sculpt through the night by the light of a candle he wore fixed to a paper helmet on his head.

Peace of Amboise follows duke's murder

Benin, 16th Century: A brass acquamanile in the shape of a leopard.

Amboise, France, 19 March 1563
An edict signed here today has ended the cruel religious war between Catholics and Protestants which has torn France apart for the last year. Catherine de Medici virtually imposed this peace after the murder of the Catholic leader, the duke of Guise, by a Huguenot gentleman a month ago. With the fierce duke removed from the scene, the regent

now has unchallenged control of Catholic forces, but, while she believes that France is a Catholic country, she is not a zealot.

There is doubt, however, as to whether this treaty will hold, for it leaves the Catholics angry at the concessions given to the Protestants, while the latter fear that the progress of the new faith has been curbed.

1564 (1564-1566)

Switzerland, 27 May 1564. John Calvin, one of the dominant figures of the Protestant Reformation, dies in Geneva. He is wrapped in a coarse shroud and buried without an address or a hymn.

Florida, 22 June 1564. The Frenchman Rene de Goulaine de Laudonniere lands at Matanzas inlet on the river of May *(St John's river)* with a party of 300 to set up the post of Fort Caroline.

Germany, 25 July 1564. On the death of Ferdinand, who inherited the Holy Roman empire after his brother Charles V abdicated in 1555, his son Maximilian II becomes emperor. Maximilian was named successor two years ago on the understanding that he would remain a Catholic.

Mediterranean, October 1564. The Flemish anatomist Andreas Vesalius dies of hunger and fatigue on an island in the Ionian Sea, where he had been thrown by a storm on a return journey from the Holy Land. Vesalius decided to make the pilgrimage after being accused of vivisection. His great work *De Humani Corporis Fabrica*, published in 1543, greatly advanced the science of biology.

Russia, January 1565. In an increasingly bloody reign of terror, Ivan the Terrible imposes his *oprichina*, a state within the state of Muscovy dominated by a private army called the *oprichniki*.

Brazil, 1 March 1565. A Portuguese colony is established at Rio de Janeiro.

Florida, May 1565. Beset by food shortages and mutinies since he set up Fort Caroline last year, Rene de Goulaine de Laudonniere attacks one of the villages of the Utina tribe. He holds its chief to ransom, hoping that the Indians will pay him with a supply of corn.

Spain, 29 June 1565. Pedro Menendez de Aviles leaves on a mission to Florida to break up the French colony of Fort Caroline.

Florida, 28 August 1565. Long overdue, Jean Ribault arrives at the colony of Fort Caroline with French reinforcements.

Florida, 28 August 1565. Pedro Menendez de Aviles enters the harbour defended by Fort Caroline, which he names San Agostin (St Augustine).

Florida, 13 September 1565. On the verge of attacking Menendez's Spanish settlement at San Agostin, Jean Ribault's fleet is scattered by a devastating storm.

Florida, 20 September 1565. Menendez wipes out the French at Fort Caroline.

Malta, September 1565. The siege of Malta by the Ottoman Turks is finally raised with the arrival of a Spanish relief fleet. The Knights of St John have withstood the Turks assaults since May.

Florida, November 1565. After renaming Fort Caroline as San Mateo, Menendez builds forts along the Indian river, with the help of 500 Negro slaves.

Angola, 1565. King Afonso II of Kongo is assassinated during mass.

India, 1565. Vijayanagar is captured and sacked after being defeated by the united forces of the five Dekhan sultanates at the battle of Talikota.

England, 1565. The English sailor John Hawkins returns from a slaving voyage to America with a shipload of tobacco. Last year he introduced the sweet potato from America into England.

Florida, 1565. Spanish settlers in San Agostin introduce the game of billiards into America.

Pacific, 1565. Arriving from Mexico, the Spaniard Legazpi settles in Cebu in the Philippines and establishes Spanish suzerainty there. He then embarks upon the conquest of the Visayas and the island of Luzon.

Flanders, 1565. Pieter Bruegel *(the Elder)* paints a series of five paintings entitled *The Seasons*.

England, 1565. A statute empowers the Royal College of Physicians in London to carry out dissections of the human body.

Rome, 7 January 1566. Following the death late last year of Pope Pius IV, the grand inquisitor Ghislieri is elected pope and takes the name Pius V.

Scotland, 9 March 1566. The Italian musician David Rizzio, who has become a favourite of Mary, queen of Scots, is murdered at Holyroodhouse in Edinburgh on the instigation of the queen's new husband, the earl of Darnley.

Netherlands, 2 April 1566. Backed up by Calvinist riots, two hundred noblemen petition the regent, Margaret of Parma, to demand the abolition of the Inquisition in the Netherlands. She promises to send a message to Philip II of Spain. The petitioners, led by William of Orange, Egmont and Admiral Hoorne, acquire the nickname of *les gueux*, "the beggars".

France, 25 April 1566. Louise Labe, the so-called "Belle Cordiere", dies. At the age of 16 she joined the royal army as a cavalryman under the name of Captain Loys. She used her knowledge of Greek, Latin, Italian and Spanish to write poetry.

"Children's games", a characteristically rustic, detailed and lively work.

Bruegel celebrates earthy peasant lives

Brussels, 1565
Pieter Bruegel, the genius of Flemish painting, has moved to Brussels from Antwerp and begun a series of detailed paintings of peasant life. He portrays people in a much earthier way than the Italians do, although he studied in Italy after becoming a master painter in the guild at Antwerp.

A brilliant draughtsman, he finds his subjects in the simple routines of haymaking, harvesting, children's games, birds-nesting or hunting in the snow. He likes to illustrate country proverbs, and to show man in harmony with nature.

He is just completing a painting of the myth of the Fall of Icarus in which a ploughman and a shepherd are quite unaware of the drowning man who had the presumption to fly. The *Adoration of the Magi* shows a rough stable crowded with peasant faces and a homely Joseph,

"The Adoration of the Magi".

listening to a peasant whispering in his ear. Bruegel has two painter sons, Pieter, who is nicknamed "Hell" because he paints devils, and Jan.

Leader's head puts Hindu army to flight

India, 23 January 1565
The Hindu empire of Vijayanagar has been utterly defeated and its ruler slain by the combined forces of four invading Moslem states at the battle of Talikota. The Hindu ruler, Ramaraja, a veteran warrior, called up a vast army of levies to meet the invasion and was confident of victory.

Thousands of men were involved on both sides along with war elephants and artillery. Ramaraja, in the centre, faced Husain, Nizam Shah of Ahmadnagar, while his brother Tirumala confronted the ruler of Bijapur, and his other brother, Venkatadri, fought the princes of Bijapur and Golkonda.

At first all went well for the Hindus, but a furious elephant rushed at Ramaraja's litter; his bearers dropped him; and he was captured and beheaded by Husain. His head was stuck on a long spear and at this gory sight his army fled.

Malta recaptured after falling to Turks

An assault on the Knights of St John during the Turks' failed siege.

Malta, September 1565
After one of the most heroic defensive actions in the history of warfare, the Turks have been repelled from Malta. It is a major setback for Suleiman's hopes of establishing control of the Mediterranean.

The Ottoman fleet having wrecked Philip II's navy and occupied Jerba in 1558, and Turkish corsairs having subsequently established control of most of the North African coast, there seemed little hope for Malta when Turkish ships converged on the island on 18 May. But in Suleiman's absence there

was division between Piale Pasha, the head of the navy, and Mustafa Pasha, the land commander. The Knights of St John fought with extraordinary courage, notably in holding the fortress of St Elmo for more than a month with only a few hundred men. When it fell only nine defenders remained alive, and they had claimed the life of Dragut, the leader of the Turkish corsairs.

When a Christian fleet from Sicily arrived to reinforce the Maltese, the Turks were too demoralised to continue. Only a quarter of their forces returned to Istanbul.

Enchanted garden of the duke of Orsini

Italy, 1565
The intellectual duke of Orsini has indulged his taste for the bizarre by having a *sacro bosco* (enchanted garden) laid out around his villa at Bomarzo in Tuscany. Rocks have been transformed into ogres, dragons, nymphs and mermaids, while architectural follies, such as a classical temple, litter the estate.

The architect of the duke's whim is the celebrated Ligorio, who designed the Villa d'Este at Tivoli in 1550 and has also worked at the Vatican for Pope Pius IV. He is one of a group of architects working chiefly in Rome and Tuscany who have achieved notable results in landscape gardening; others are Giovanni Lippi and da Vignola. The gardens at Bomarzo are very different from the sumptuous formality of the Villa d'Este; there, the natural environment is subjected to

An ogre's head at Bomarzo.

the rules of formal architectural symmetry. At the Villa Orsini, on the other hand, Ligorio's designs pay respect to the predominantly hilly natural setting.

Spanish wipe out a French settlement

A later, fanciful, impression of Ribault among the natives of Florida.

Florida, October 1565
The French settlement at Fort Caroline has been wiped out, and hundreds have been put to the sword by Spanish troops. The massacre is the culmination of several years of tension between the French and Spanish in the region, exacerbated by religious differences.

Captain Jean Ribault and 150 French Huguenots arrived in Florida in May 1562, but the settlers ran out of food and began to eat each other, and the survivors returned to France. In June last year, Rene de Goulaine de Laudonniere, the captain's second-in-command, established a new settlement at Fort Caroline, on the river of May.

This June, the Spanish commander Pedro Menendez de Aviles set out to destroy the French settlement before reinforcements could

arrive. Ribault returned with an auxiliary force on 28 August, just as Menendez entered the harbour, which he named San Agostin. On 13 September Ribault's attempt to attack the Spanish was foiled by a storm, and 200 men were shipwrecked, captured and massacred by the Spanish. Seven days later the Spanish army attacked Fort Caroline.

The attackers showed no mercy, slaughtering 132 people within an hour. Those who surrendered were killed too, including Ribault. Only a few Catholics and some women and children were spared. Menendez has written to his king, justifying the killings as "necessary to the service of God and your majesty". Some were hanged under a placard which read: "I do this not as to Frenchmen, but as to Lutherans."

King's wives hold the key to African gold

Mozambique, 1565
In spite of the assassination of its envoy, the Jesuit Goncola da Silveira, in 1561, by a conspiracy of the king of Munhumutapa and Arab traders, Portugal is continuing to secure its hold on the lower Zambezi area.

So far its occupation has been unprofitable. The gold that brought the Portuguese here remains continually just out of reach the gold traders moving inland whenever the Portuguese approach. Arab traders have allied themselves with the

indigenous people to exclude Portuguese traders; and the countryside is unable to feed the local population, let alone provide a surplus for Portugal. Portugal's strength is in its friendship with the king of Munhumutapa's chief wife, the *Mazarira*. Through her the Portuguese are finding a way into the African kingdom. She has moved into the Christian compound at Sena, and she calls herself the Portuguese colonists' "mother". Significantly, the Moslems are represented by the king's second wife.

1566 (1566-1568)

Florida, May 1566. The Spanish fend off an Indian attack on their newly established colony of San Agostin, but lose their supplies and most of their fort to a fire.

London, 7 June 1566. Sir Thomas Gresham lays the foundation stone of the Royal Exchange.

Netherlands, August 1566. A wave of religious iconoclasm hits Flanders, Ghent, Antwerp and the northern provinces. Calvinists attack hundreds of monasteries and churches. The revolt is rooted in hatred of the Inquisition and soaring grain prices.

Japan, 1566. Ieyasu, who formed an alliance with the powerful nobleman Oda Nobunaga in 1562, takes the surname Tokugawa.

Spain, 1566. Prompted by the church, Philip II of Spain takes repressive measures against the *Moriscos* (Moors converted to Christianity). They are forbidden to speak Arabic or to wear their traditional dress.

Netherlands, 1566. With the mediation of William of Orange, the regent, Margaret of Parma, signs a compromise agreement with the Calvinist rebels.

Aegean, 1566. The Turks take possession of the island of Chios.

Florida, 1566. The first Jesuit missionaries arrive in Florida.

France, 1566. The physician and astronomer Nostradamus dies. The publication in 1555 of his *Centuries*, a book of rhymed prophecies that were widely believed, brought him a large popular following.

Venice, 1566. Tintoretto paints a cycle of canvases on the life of St Mark for the Scuola Grande de San Rocco.

Scotland, 9 February 1567. Lord Darnley, husband of Queen Mary, is killed when his house is blown up by gunpowder.

Scotland, 15 May 1567. Mary, queen of Scots, marries the earl of Bothwell, who was acquitted in a mock trial on 12 April for the murder of Lord Darnley.

Scotland, 24 July 1567. Defeated by the Protestant nobility at Carberry Hill, and discredited by the murder of Darnley and her marriage to Bothwell, Mary, queen of Scots, is imprisoned and forced to abdicate in favour of her one-year-old son James VI.

France, 10 November 1567. The 74-year-old constable of Montmorency, one of France's highest nobles, dies during an attack by his Catholic troops on a Huguenot force under Louis de Bourbon, the prince of Conde, at St Denis near Paris.

Netherlands, 1567. Ferdinand, the duke of Alba, Philip II's commander in chief, is sent to the Netherlands to help to crush the Calvinist revolt. He orders the arrest of Counts Egmont and Hoorne, moderate noble leaders, and sets up a new court to try suspected rebels.

Netherlands, 1567. William of Orange, who opposes Philip II's policy of persecution of the Protestants and has tried to secure an agreement to ensure their religious freedom, is deprived of his office of *stadtholder* of Holland, Zeeland and Utrecht.

Japan, 1567. Oda Nobunaga puts down resistance from the Saito family and takes the town of Inabayama (Gifu).

Japan, 1567. The Daibutsuden, a large building in Nara housing the great statue of the Buddha, is burnt down in fighting.

Florida, 2 March 1568. An expedition led by Pardo returns to Santa Elena having charted a route to the Mississippi river.

France, 23 March 1568. Catherine de Medici signs the peace of Longjumeau with the Huguenots, ending the second French war of religion. The 1563 edict of Amboise, which was favourable to the Huguenots, is reimposed.

Florida, 3 May 1568. A French force led by the Catholic soldier Dominique de Corgues avenges the 1565 Spanish massacre of French Huguenots. Having slaughtered hundreds of Spaniards, they burn down the San Mateo fort.

England, 19 May 1568. Defeated by the Protestants at Longside, Mary, queen of Scots, escapes captivity and flees to England, where the Queen imprisons her.

Netherlands, 5 June 1568. Faced with continuing opposition from the province of Groningen, the duke of Alba, the new viceroy, orders the execution in Brussels of 20 noble leaders, including Egmont and Hoorne. He imposes crippling taxation on the rebel province.

Rome, 19 August 1568. Pope Pius V instructs the apostolic nuncio of Spain to set up a commission to deal with the problems of missionaries in America.

Sweden, 30 September 1568. Eric XIV, king of Sweden, is deposed after showing signs of madness. His brother John III becomes king.

Caribbean, 1568. On a slaving voyage to America, the English sailors John Hawkins and Francis Drake are trapped by the Spanish at San Juan de Ulua. Two English ships are lost in the attack.

Akbar trains his soldiers while hunting

"Akbar's remorse on the hunting field": a Moghul manuscript illustration.

Agra, India, 1567

The traditional military training of his Mongol forebears is being used by the ambitious 25-year-old Moghul Emperor Akbar. His army trains as it follows the emperor on his frequent hunting expeditions. It is lean, wholly mounted and capable of great feats of mobility.

Until recently Akbar seemed interested only in hunting, pleasure and military conquest. His dismissal of the worthy regent, Bairam, who had saved his empire, the undoubted enthusiam with which he flung Bairam's son, Adham Khan, over the palace battlements, his opportunist annexation of Malwa, and his designs on the Rajput states, supported this view.

Recently he has mellowed, however. He has become more cultured and his policies are showing tolerance and understanding.

Spanish execute Dutch resistance leader

Brussels, 5 June 1568

The count of Egmont, the former administrator of the Council of the Netherlands and subsequently leader of Dutch resistance to the rule of Spain, was executed today by order of the repressive Court of Unrest, the so-called "Council of Blood".

Egmont was appointed by Philip II in 1556, ruling jointly with the prince of Orange and Philip of Hoorne. In 1563, when Philip II decided to curb the Netherlands' autonomy and to bring the Spanish Inquisition to the country, all three resigned and began challenging Spain. Their stance made them symbols of Dutch resistance, but Egmont has paid the penalty.

Lamoral, count of Egmont.

Revered Suleiman dies

Istanbul, 6 September 1566
Suleiman the Magnificent, the ruler of the Ottoman empire for the past 46 years, is dead. He is succeeded by his eldest surviving son, the incompetent drunkard Selim, all potential rivals having been eliminated by intrigue or murder.

The most powerful influence in the second half of Suleiman's reign was Roxelana, a captive from Galicia who succeeded in replacing the sultan's favourite, Gulbehar, in his affections. After bearing Suleiman a child, Roxelana became in Moslem law his wife, as no sultan's concubine had been for two centuries. In 1541 she again broke new ground by moving, with her 100 ladies-in-waiting, dressmaker and slaves, into the Grand Seraglio, where the sultan governed.

Roxelana is thought to have had a hand in the execution of Suleiman's favourite adviser, Ibrahim. Then she secured the appointment as grand vizier of Rustem Pasha, who had married her daughter by the sultan, Mihrimah. Her next target was the removal of Mustafa, the son of Suleiman and Gulbehar and the sultan's preferred heir.

When Mustafa, the governor of Amasya, grew in reputation and in the affection of the Janissaries,

Suleiman at Qasr-i Shirin in Mesopotamia; C16th painting (detail).

Roxelana and Rustem persuaded Suleiman that he was plotting to overthrow him. Mustafa was murdered on Suleiman's orders.

Within three years Roxelana was dead, much mourned by Suleiman, and their two eldest sons, Selim and Bayezid, fought for the succession. When Selim won a battle at Konya in 1559, Bayezid fled to Persia. But Ottoman pressure persuaded the shah to hand him over to the sultan's executioner. Bayezid, like his half-brother, was strangled with a bowstring, as were his five sons, the youngest being aged only three.

Netherland rebels sack, loot churches

A church is ransacked by Calvinists: iconoclasm or simple looting?

Spanish Netherlands, 1566
A bad harvest and the increase in the price of bread have triggered a popular revolt, encouraged by Calvinists and other "heretics", against King Philip II of Spain.

Churches have been ransacked and gold and silver ornaments looted in villages throughout the Low Countries, as magistrates looked on helplessly. Years of smouldering resentment against the Inquisition – pursued with particular vigour in the Netherlands – erupted, to the alarm of Margaret of Parma, gover-

nor of the provinces since the departure of Philip to Spain in 1559.

As the rebellion gathered momentum, Margaret turned to Prince William of Orange, a shrewd negotiator, for help. An accord was signed which guaranteed suspension of persecution provided that the people laid down their arms and allowed Catholics to worship unmolested.

This is likely to be a fragile peace, however, as Margaret is using newly-arrived funds from Spain to build up an army.

Rising prices due to Spanish gold flood

Europe, 1568
The relentless and dramatic rise in the cost of living – up 1,000 per cent since the turn of the century – is due to the flood of gold and silver coming in from the New World, according to a French economist.

In a new monetarist treatise, quickly gaining wide acceptance, Jean Bodin points out that "the price of things 50 or 60 years ago was ten times less than at present". Recent research into the money supply shows that coinage in circulation is up by 60 per cent, nearly all of it accounted for by New World silver and gold bullion.

Bodin's theory challenges the conventional belief that food speculators and hoarders are to blame for price inflation by creating artificial scarcities.

British slave-trader escapes Spanish capture in West Indies

London, October 1568
Three English ships commanded by the slave trader John Hawkins have narrowly escaped a Spanish naval ambush in the West Indies. The incident, involving five English ships, has provoked an angry reaction in England, resulting in an undeclared state of war with Spain.

Hawkins, who escaped with his kinsman Francis Drake, is a popular and leading figure in the highly profitable trade of shipping slaves from West Africa to the Spanish West Indies, despite the ban imposed by Madrid. This voyage was Hawkins's third since 1562.

Two of Hawkins' ships were lost in the incident at San Juan de Ulua, which has angered the English crown. While Queen Elizabeth officially disapproves of slave trading, she is known to have invested privately in Hawkins' ventures.

A model of a late 16th-century English galleon, based on the plans of Mathew Baker in his "Elements of Shipwrightery" of c.1585, an important work on shipbuilding which includes many designs for ships.

India, 1568. The Moghul Emperor Akbar captures the fortress of Chitor. The Rajput women perform the rite of *jauhar* – immolating themselves on funeral pyres – to save themselves from dishonour.

Japan, 1568. The nobleman Omura Sumitada, who was baptised by the Jesuits in 1562, gives permission for foreign traders to establish posts at a small fishing village called Fukae *(Nagasaki)*.

Peru, 1568. Francisco de Toledo is appointed viceroy of Peru.

Pacific, 1568. The Spanish navigator Alvaro de Mendana explores the Solomon and Ellice islands.

Rome, 1568. Giacomo Barozzi de Vignola, who succeeded Michelangelo as chief architect of St Peter's in 1564, begins work on the church of Jesus. From 1550 to 1555 he built the Villa Giulia for Pope Julius III.

France, 1568. The economist Jean Bodin argues forcefully that there is a relationship between the influx of precious metals from the Americas and the current rise in European prices.

Spain, 1568. John of the Cross founds the first monastery of barefoot Carmelites. Teresa de Avila establishes the order of barefoot Carmelite nuns.

Spain, 1568. Led by Aben Humeya and Aben Aboo, the *Moriscos (Moors converted to Christianity)* in Granada rise up in protest against the campaign of intolerance towards them which began two years ago.

France, 13 March 1569. Royalist forces defeat the Huguenots at the battle of Jarnac. Louis de Bourbon, the prince of Conde, the Huguenot leader, is murdered while crossing the river Charente by the Catholic army of the king's brother, the duke of Anjou.

Poland, 1 July 1569. By the union of Lublin, the grand duchy of Livonia is formally united with Poland. The Jagiellon king, Sigismund II Augustus, now rules over a vast state stretching from the Baltic to the Dniester.

Brussels, 5 September 1569. Pieter Bruegel, the painter of often grotesque and carnivalesque scenes of country life, dies.

India, 1569. Akbar captures the fortress of Ranthambor, bringing independent Rajput power effectively to an end.

North America, 1569. Jesuits work among the Indians, hoping to establish permanent missions *(in Florida, Georgia and South Carolina)*.

Germany, 1569. The Flemish geographer Gerardus Mercator (Gerhard Kremer) publishes a map in the form of a cylindrical projection showing all the lines of longitude as parallel.

Russia, 1569. The Ottomans fail to take Astrakhan despite hauling their ships over land from the Don to the Volga. They retreat with heavy losses and the area remains under Russian control.

Florence, 1569. Cosimo de Medici becomes grand duke of Tuscany.

Scotland, 23 January 1570. James Stewart, the Protestant earl of Moray, who was appointed regent on the abdication of Mary, queen of Scots, is assassinated.

Rome, 25 February 1570. Pope Pius V issues the bull *Regnans in Excelsis* which excommunicates Elizabeth, the queen of England. The pope releases those subjects of Elizabeth who are still loyal to the Church of Rome from all duty of obedience to the English crown.

Moscow, 25 July 1570. Czar Ivan the Terrible attends the public executions of almost all his close advisers and ministers.

France, 8 August 1570. Charles IX signs the treaty of St Germain, ending the third war of religion. The treaty gives the Huguenots a large measure of religious toleration and the security of garrison towns.

Cyprus, August 1570. The Turks overrun Cyprus and expel the Venetian garrison from the island.

Portugal, 20 October 1570. Joao de Barros, author of *Decades*, a history of the Portuguese conquests overseas, dies.

Northern Europe, 2 November 1570. A tidal wave in the North Sea destroys sea walls from Holland to Jutland. Over a thousand people are killed.

Scandinavia, 13 December 1570. The peace of Stettin puts an end to the seven-year war of the Three Crowns between Denmark and Sweden by restoring the prewar frontiers.

South-East Africa, 1570. Portuguese slave trading on the Zambezi leads to the Zimba war among the Chewa to the north.

Spain, 1570. Don John of Austria, the illegitimate son of the Emperor Charles V, harshly suppresses the Morisco uprising.

Russia, 1570. To pre-empt moves by the feudal lords towards independence, Ivan the Terrible orders the savage destruction of Novgorod by the *oprichniki*.

Japan, 1570. Portuguese ships begin trading in Nagasaki.

Mercator publishes new map of world

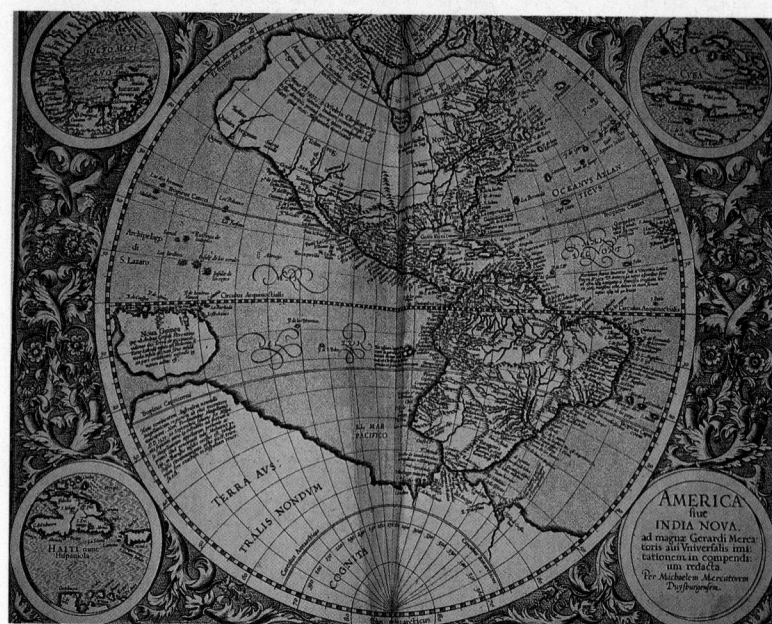

A 1631 map of the New World according to the great map-maker Mercator.

Duisberg, Germany, 1569
The first comprehensive map of the world has been published in Germany. Its designer, Gerhard Kremer, is a Dutch merchant who fled from the persecution of Protestants in the Netherlands.

Kremer, who is better known by the latinised name Gerardus Mercator (*mercator* means merchant) has developed an advanced system of cylindrical projection. This works outwards from the equator and permits the accurate placing of longitude, latitude, meridians and parallels.

Thus the map is invaluable to sailors, offering a degree of accuracy which has never before been available to navigators.

Spanish king halts Morisco rebellion

Granada, Spain, 1570
After a two-year war marked by appalling cruelties on both sides, Philip II of Spain has crushed the Morisco community of Granada. The Morisco revolt over the right to wear Moorish dress and maintain Moorish customs is at an end. A defeated and sullen population has been dispersed throughout Castile while 50,000 settlers have been brought to Andalucia to fill the gap. Philip's system of government was directly responsible for the outbreak of the revolt. The Moriscos had remained second-class subjects, exploited, hated and feared, and plagued by bandits of their own race. Philip refused to turn a blind eye to their Moorish customs and continue the slow process of assimilation. His half-brother Don John of Austria finally managed to crush them.

Tartar fears unite neighbour states

Lublin, 1 July 1569
Poland and Lithuania have allied themselves to form a vast multilingual union stretching from the Baltic to the Dniester. Under the Union of Lublin the two states have agreed to accept each others' religions and those of West Prussia and of Lithuania's dominions in White Russia and the Ukraine.

It is a remarkable achievement, as this union tolerates not only Jews but all types of Protestantism in officially Catholic Poland, while in Lithuania there is a majority of Orthodox Christians. One reason for the union is the danger to Lithuania from raids of the Crimea Tartars and from Muscovite imperialism. The Lithuanian nobility will now enjoy the enormous political, legal and economic privileges enjoyed by their Polish counterparts in the new union.

Duke crushes revolt in the Netherlands

Ferdinand, the duke of Alba.

Ghent, 5 June 1568
From the moment that 10,000 elite troops of the Spanish king marched through the streets of Ghent in ranks of five, followed by prostitutes in frilly dresses riding donkeys, and a host of camp followers, it was clear that the Calvinist insurrection was finally over. The new military governor of the Spanish Low Countries, the duke of Alba, has pledged himself to bring back the Inquisition and to establish a "new order" for Philip II.

From Alba's first arrival in the Netherlands, in August 1567, the behaviour of his troops underlined the ferocity with which the duke approached his task. Merchants were beaten up, and the population – even good Catholics – insulted in the streets as "traitors" and "heretics".

Alba's regime rapidly became a dictatorship. He humiliated the civil governor, Margaret of Parma, forcing her to demobilise the army which she had raised to counter an earlier rebellion two years ago, and assuming many of her powers until she left for Italy. A new and sinister form of inquisition – the "Council of Troubles" – was set up and organised the arrests of thousands in spring this year. More than 1,000 alleged heretics were executed and a further 8,000 stripped of their property. In the Calvinist city of Tournai 500 heretical books were seized and burned.

New Spain charts old Mexico history

Mexico, 1569
An impressive new book, almost an encyclopaedia of ancient Mexico, has been published in Spain. Eleven years in the writing, it is entitled *Historia General de las cosas de la Nueva Espana*, otherwise known as the *Calepino*. Its author, the Franciscan monk Bernardino de Sahagun, is being hailed as the foremost historian of the lands which are now known as New Spain.

Sahagun began his career as a missionary to the New World, and has devoted his career to the Colegio de Santiago Tlatelolco, which is dedicated to the education of young Indians.

In parallel to his religious undertakings, Sahagun has developed as an outstanding historian of the native tribes of Mexico. While his central task as a missionary is to wipe out native idolatry and replace it with Christian worship, his natural inclination has been to discover as much as possible about the Indians.

The fruits of these studies are contained in his *Historia*, a work that was begun with aim of giving his fellow-priests as wide as possible a knowledge of the culture with which they deal. It is not the first such history, but Sahagun's research methods make it the most authoritative. He is an expert in native crafts, the best of which he has seen himself, and native language, which he both reads and writes.

Learning local ways: one of de Soto's men who decided to stay in America.

Pope crowns Cosimo de Medici in Tuscany

Florence, 1569
Cosimo de Medici, who has been "head of the government and city of Florence" since 1537, and had established himself at the expense of the emperor Charles V as a major power in Italy, has taken a new title, indicative of his importance as a leader, civic reformer and connoisseur. As from today, when he was crowned by Pope Pius V, he will rule as the first archduke of Tuscany.

Cosimo's road to power has lain in his determination to free Florence from its domination by Charles V. In 1543, when Charles needed funds for his wars in France, he accepted a large payment from Cosimo to withdraw imperial troops from Medici territories. Since then Cosimo has been an independent ruler.

He wrote in 1545: "We are a ruler who accepts the authority of

Archduke Cosimo de Medici, painted in 1545 by Bronzino.

no one apart from God." His career has been concentrated on maintaining Tuscan autonomy. The state may not have expanded its boundaries, but it is far stronger than ever before.

Ancient Romans inspire Palladio's villas

Italy, 1570
This year has seen the appearance of a stimulating new work on architecture by the Venetian Andrea di Pietro, known as Palladio. Called the *Four Books of Architecture* it is inspired by the ancient Roman Vitruvius, whose work *De Architectura* Palladio helped to publish in 1556. Palladio describes how he sought out ancient Roman ruins "to find what the whole must have been, and give the design of them". The work is a guide to classical architecture, with sections on orders, materials, cities, churches, and houses (palaces and villas). He uses ancient buildings and his own work as examples.

The classically-inspired symmetry of Palladio can be seen in several fine palaces in the region near Venice, especially in the city of Vicenza. Symmetry is not always possible for Palladio's villas, though, because many of them are essentially grand farmhouses and require various outbuildings.

Classical symmetry: part of the Villa Capra at Vicenza, by Palladio.

1570 (1570-1572)

North America, c.1570. The Iroquois Indians in north-eastern North America form a league of tribes whose aim is to meet and settle their differences peacefully.

Brazil, 1570. A law is passed stating that only those Indians taken prisoner during the course of a "just war", or those suspected of cannibalism, may be enslaved.

Arabia, 1570. The Turks occupy Yemen.

Antwerp, 1570. The first geographical atlas, prepared by Abraham Ortelius, is published.

Spain, 1570. The Council of the Indies passes a law prohibiting *mestizos* (people who are half Indian and half European) from becoming notaries or *caciques* (local rulers).

Netherlands, 1570. The Emperor Maximilian II ennobles the Dutch musician Orlando di Lasso, the composer of many masses and motets. As well as church music, he has written a large number of secular works.

Rome, 1570. Pope Pius V issues instructions that Indians in America should be excluded from the jurisdiction of the Inquisition.

Venice, 1570. The Florentine sculptor and architect Jacopo Sansovino dies.

Palestine, c.1570. The town of Safed, on a mountain in upper Galilee, has become the centre of Jewish mysticism. At the end of last century the community was strengthened by an influx of refugees from Spain. The Sephardic element increased after the Ottoman conquest in 1516. The spiritual flowering of the town has been accompanied by material prosperity: there is a thriving weaving industry and trade in oil, honey, silk and spices.

North America, 2 February 1571. All eight members of a Jesuit mission in Virginia are murdered by Indians who had pretended to be their friends. The killers were led by Don Luis, an Indian who had been converted to Christianity, taken a Spanish name and been a guest at the court of Philip II.

Florence, 13 February 1571. The silversmith and sculptor Benvenuto Cellino, who is famous for his colourful autobiography, dies.

Mediterranean, 20 May 1571. Venice and Spain form a holy league with Pope Pius V to counter Ottoman expansion.

Mediterranean, September 1571. Don John of Austria and the navy of the Holy League defeat the Turks at the Battle of Lepanto, dealing a severe blow to Turkish naval power.

England, 1571. A Catholic plot – masterminded by the Italian banker Roberto Ridolfi, and supported by Spain – to murder Queen Elizabeth and replace her with Mary, queen of Scots, is discovered by William Cecil, Lord Burghley. In Ridolfi's absence abroad, the duke of Norfolk, one of the conspirators, is executed.

Japan, 1571. Oda Nobunaga destroys the rebellious Ikko sect, based near Osaka, and then razes the Enryakuji temple on Mount Hiei, home to a large number of soldier-monks.

Angola, 1571. Portuguese slave trading on the Angola coast leads to the Jaga war in the interior.

Hungary, 1571. Stephen Bathory becomes prince of Transylvania.

Rome, 1571. On the orders of Pope Pius V, an index of prohibited books is drawn up.

Philippines, 1571. The Spaniard Lopez de Legazpi founds the city of Manila.

Mexico, 1571. The Spanish instal an inquisitorial tribunal in Mexico.

Spain, 1571. A doctor called Nicolas Monardes publishes a book praising the medicinal value of tobacco.

England, March 1572. The *Gueux de mer* (Sea Beggars) – Calvinist rebels who fled from the duke of Alba's repression in their native Netherlands – are expelled from English ports. They have harried shipping between Spain and the Netherlands for three years.

Netherlands, 1 April 1572. The Sea Beggars under Guillaume de la Marck land in Holland and capture the small town of Briel.

Netherlands, April 1572. William of Orange returns to the province of Holland, where he is acknowledged as *stadholder* (local official).

Rome, 13 May 1572. Following the death of Pius V, Ugo Buoncompagni of Bologna is elected pope and takes the name Gregory XIII. Pius' six-year papacy marked a decisive stage in the implementation of the Counter-reformation developed at the Council of Trent, with the publication of the Catholic catechism in 1566, the breviary in 1568 and the missal in 1570.

Peru, May 1572. The Spanish capture Vilcabamba, the stronghold of the Inca rebels under Tupac Amaru.

India, 1572. The Moghul Emperor Akbar abolishes the *jizya* tax on non-Moslems.

Ivan the Terrible terrorises feudal lords

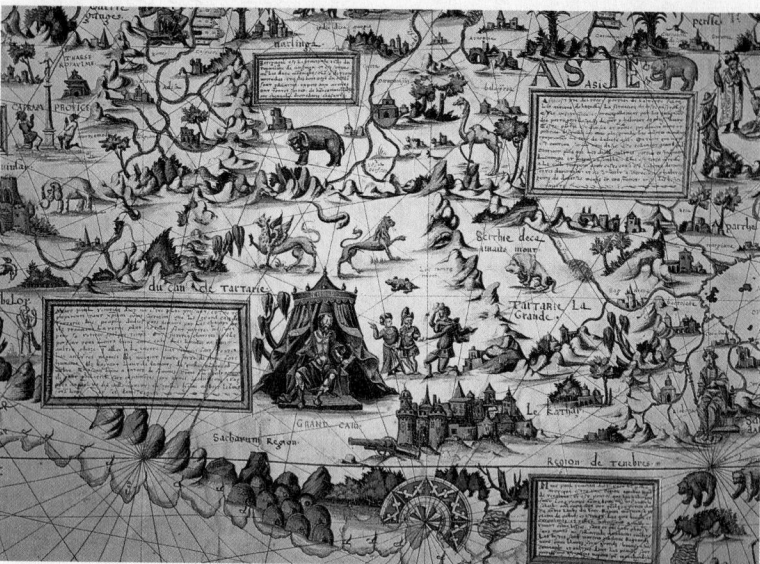

A map of Siberia and northern Asia, after Marco Polo's descriptions.

Russia, 1572

The eight-year reign of terror unleashed by Ivan the Terrible appears to have come to an end with the czar's decision to disband the *oprichnina*, the separate administration and court set up to do his bidding. Years of absurd denunciations, sudden arrests, executions and terror simply for the sake of terror have shattered Muscovite society.

Ivan established the *oprichnina* after a period of bloody infighting with the *boyars*, the aristocratic classes. Determined to eliminate all villains and traitors, and reaffirm his power and the servility of the peasants, he divided Muscovy into two distinct realms. The *oprichnina* was that part which came under his personal rule.

Its main instrument was a select corps of 6,000 oprichniki who wore black uniforms. Their badges were a dog's head and broom, symbols of their doglike devotion to the czar and their role in sweeping away treason from the state. Their atrocities reached their peak two years ago in the sacking of Novgorod after the town was suspected of seeking union with Poland. More than 60,000 people were killed – some by being pushed through holes in the ice – and the town devastated.

Index to censor books for heresy

Rome, 1571

Pope Pius V has formalised the censorship moves by recent popes in the Congregation of the Index, a tribunal of the Roman *curia* charged with examining books and ensuring that they do not contain any heretical ideas. Pius IV published a list of prohibited books in 1564, but it was Paul IV who brought in the first official Index in 1559. He not only banned middle-ofthe-road works, such as those of Erasmus, he prohibited any bible not in Latin. The puritanical zeal has even led to the painting – over of the nudes in Michelangelo's *Last Judgement* in the Sistine Chapel.

Rich gold and enamel ornaments of (from top) the fleece, two stallions and St Michael.

"Sea Beggars" challenge Spanish rule

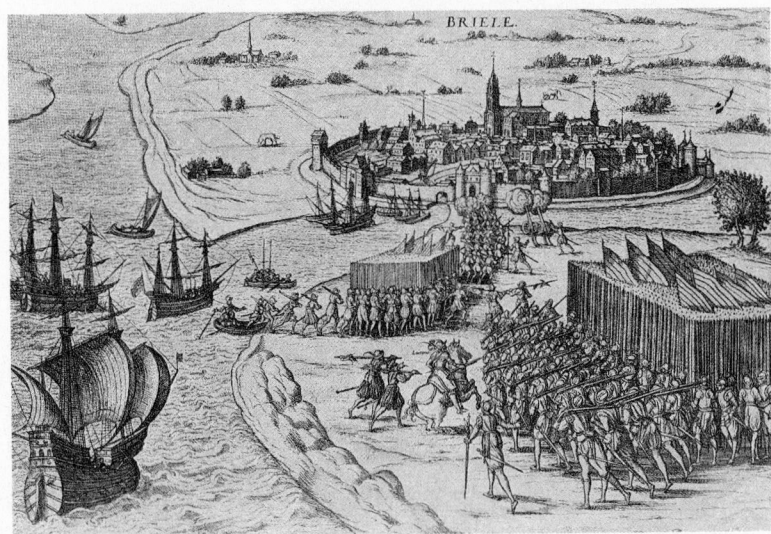

The capture from the Spaniards of Briel by the so-called "Sea Beggars".

Briel, Netherlands, 1 April 1572
A well-organised force of Netherlands privateers and foreign mercenaries – "the Sea Beggars" – has captured this small seaport and set up a bridgehead for the full-scale invasion of the Low Countries. The privateers were licensed by Prince William of Orange who has twice failed to invade the Netherlands.

Despite assurances of their peaceful intentions, the invaders have forced the mayor to swear allegiance and fortify his town against a Spanish counter-attack. Monasteries have been sacked and Catholic nobles removed from the town council. Prince William is counting on support from the artisan classes in their resentment at the hated "tenth penny" tax to be imposed by the tyranical duke of Alba to help a bankrupted Spain and pay his army in the Low Countries.

Bad harvests, famine, floods and mass unemployment have created an ideal climate for a second rebellion. Last month the streets of Ghent were littered with a parody of the Lord's Prayer addressed to the duke:

"Cursed father who in Brussels doth dwell,

"Cursed be thy name in Heaven and in Hell," it began.

The Sea Beggars originally planned to use Dover in England as the base for their operations, but Queen Elizabeth expelled them from the port.

New stock exchange founded in London

London, 1571
The Royal Exchange has been built at Cornhill in the City of London and inaugurated by the queen. It was founded by the businessman and royal agent Sir Thomas Gresham, who worked for many years raising loans in the Low Countries and exporting arms and other goods to Britain. He was a regular visitor to Antwerp's Stock Exchange, and wanted Britain to offer similar trading facilities.

The Royal Exchange is built over piazzas supported by marble pillars. The ground floor is reserved for wholesalers, with retail shops in the gallery above. Merchants are summoned to meetings by bells.

Gresham, by Sir Antonio Moro.

Christians smash Turks in holy war at sea

Christian and Turkish galley fleets clash at the Battle of Lepanto.

Mediterranean Sea, 7 September 1571
It was a spectacle that no survivor of this great sea battle will ever forget. Two great galleys, one flying the pennant of the crucified Christ, the other a huge flag with verses from the Koran, were being rowed directly at each other, gathering speed all the time as the galley-masters whipped their slaves to even greater efforts.

In *La Real*, the Spanish flagship, Don John of Austria drew his sword and braced himself for the inevitable head-on crash as Ali Pasha, the Turkish commander, ordered his men on the *Sultana* to prepare to board. The Cross was meeting the Crescent in what many believe will be the last great encounter between galley fleets.

It was the Turkish invasion of Cyprus by Selim II, Suleiman the Great's successor, that brought the combined fleets of Spain, Venice and Pope Pius V face-to-face with the larger Turkish fleet. Famagusta had fallen, and reports of unbelievable atrocities had incensed the Christians to a crusading fervour as they sailed from Messina.

Pasha's fleet was anchored in the gulf when the Christian fleet hove into sight. The Turks hesitated before moving out to attack in a crescent formation. It was then that *La Real* began her charge forward. The flagships struck so hard that they locked together. Fierce fighting continued for two hours with the fiery young Don John, the son of Charles V, leading his men on to the *Sultana's* foredeck and confronting Ali Pasha in person. The Turkish commander was killed by a bullet from an *arquebus*, his head struck off and presented to Don John.

The Turks have lost 230 galleys in this battle; the Christians, 16. News of the victory will bring great rejoicing throughout the west.

1572 (1572-1573)

Peru, May 1572. Tupac Amaru, the last of the Inca kings, is executed.

Paris, 24 August 1572. In Paris to celebrate the wedding of Marguerite of Valois, the daughter of Catherine de Medici, and the Bourbon Huguenot, Henry of Navarre, thousands of Huguenots are slaughtered with Catherine's connivance.

Paris, 24 August 1572. Among the victims of the massacre is the mathematician and logician Pierre de la Ramee, known as Petrus Ramus. A strong opponent of Aristotelianism, Ramus saw his work condemned by the Sorbonne.

Paris, August 1572. In the aftermath of the massacre, Henry of Navarre renounces the Protestant faith.

Paris, 22 September 1572. The painter Francois Clouet dies. Trained by his father, Jean Clouet, whom he succeeded as court painter, Francois painted four French kings: Francis I, Henry II, Francis II and Charles IX.

Scotland, 24 November 1572. John Knox, the father of the Scottish Reformation, dies in Edinburgh. He was forced to flee to Geneva, where he became a friend and disciple of John Calvin. The rebellion against the Catholic Mary, queen of Scots, in 1559 enabled him to return to Scotland.

Florence, 28 November 1572. The painter Agnolo di Cosimo, known as Bronzino, dies. A pupil of Pontormo, he became the official painter of the grand duchy of Tuscany in 1539. From the second generation of mannerists, he introduced a style of portraiture characterised by cold colours and an icy precision.

India, 1572. The forces of the Moghul Emperor Akbar overrun the fertile region of Gujarat.

Caribbean, 1572. The English sailor Francis Drake launches attacks on Spanish harbours and ambushes and loots Spanish ships.

France, 1572. Henri Etienne publishes his *Thesaurus Linguae Graecae* (Thesaurus of the Greek Language).

Spain, 1572. Sister Teresa of Avila writes the *Book of the Foundations*. She is the prioress at the convent of the Incarnation in Avila, where John of the Cross is the confessor of the Carmelites.

Peru, 1572. Extraction begins from the silver mine of Potosi. Francisco de Toledo, the viceroy, sets up a system by which the miners receive a collective payment in kind, usually of cloth, which is shared out among them by a chief.

Italy, 1572. Woodcuts of bananas and other American fruit trees seen for the first time in Europe appear in Girolamo Benzoni's *Historia del Mundo Nuovo*.

Istanbul, 7 March 1573. Venice concludes a peace with the Turks by which the doge of Venice recognises Turkish possession of Cyprus.

Poland, 11 May 1573. Henry of Anjou, the brother of Charles IX, the king of France, becomes the first elected king of Poland. His election was secured by his mother, Catherine de Medici. In Poland, Henry has to face a hostile nobility which wants to keep effective power.

Rome, 11 May 1573. The architect Giacomo Barozzi da Vignola dies.

Netherlands, December 1573. Recalled to Spain, the duke of Alba is succeeded as viceroy by Luis de Requesens y Zyniga. Brill, Enkhuisen, Flushing, Arnemuide, Veere, Holland and Zeeland are in the hands of the Sea Beggars.

Japan, 1573. The *shogun* Ashikaga Yoshiaki submits to the nobleman Oda Nobunaga, spelling the end of the Muromachi *shogunate*, which was founded in 1335.

South-East Africa, 1573. After punishing Mwenemutapa for the murder, in 1561, of the missionary Father da Silveira, a Portuguese expedition under Francisco Barreto withdraws from the Zambezi valley.

France, 1573. Catherine de Medici makes peace with the Protestants, ending the fourth war of religion, which broke out after the St Bartholomew's Day massacre.

Netherlands, 1573. The Spanish recapture Harlem from the rebels.

North Africa, 1573. The Spaniards, led by Don John of Austria, seize Tunis and Bizerta from the Berbers.

Brazil, 1573. After protests by the colonists at restrictions imposed by a 1570 law, new legislation makes slavery common practice.

England, 1573. Christopher Tye, the organist to the Chapel Royal and composer of some notable church music, dies.

Spain, 1573. Laws are passed barring territorial conquest in the Indies without royal sanction.

Spain, 1573. Sister Teresa of Avila writes her mystical handbook *The Way of Perfection*.

Argentina, 1573. The city of Cordoba is founded.

Venice, 1573. Tintoretto completes his painting of *The Battle of Lepanto* for the chamber of the grand council in the doges' palace.

Drake captures Spanish gold in Panama

London, 1573
Captain Francis Drake is said to be back from his latest raid on the Spanish Main with silver worth £40,000. The government seems pleased with the loot, but Drake must hide like a fugitive. The reason: London wants normal relations with Madrid. A triumphal reception for the man who recruited runaway slaves to ambush bullion convoys ashore at Panama last February is a major embarrassment. So Drake hides, perhaps in Ireland. But is he a pirate?

Neither he nor his queen feels bound by a trade treaty of 1494, blessed by the pope, which divides "Latin America" between Spain and Portugal. Queen Elizabeth licensed him as a privateer five years ago. Drake, a fervent Protestant, also has personal motives for his raids. Five years ago his ship *Judith* (50 tons) was part of an English fleet attacked by Spanish sailors while anchored in the Caribbean port of San Juan de Ulua. Drake limped back to England but never forgot Spanish treachery in betray-

A later engraving of Drake, whose deeds London covertly approves.

ing a local agreement to trade and not fight. He claimed compensation. When none was forthcoming, he recovered the damages himself, with interest. Since then he has become a legend. For his attack on Panama, he sailed last year with two ships which concealed three prefabricated pinnaces, which he reconstructed for raids on Nombre de Dios.

Church design reflects Catholic authority

Rome, 1571
Giacomo Barozzi da Vignola, who took over the direction of the building of St Peter's from Michelangelo, has produced a new design which is being adopted throughout the Catholic world. His impressive church of Jesus has been adopted by the Jesuits as the uniform standard for all churches.

The essence of the design is that it creates a huge space in the form of a Latin cross. There is an unbroken cornice supporting a lofty barrel vault. The nave is brightly lit by the cupola, in contrast to many existing churches where the light is very dim.

The buildings have been widely admired for their architectural splendour, but the reason for the design is theological rather than aesthetic. It reflects the determination of the papacy to resist reformist and Protestant tendencies and locate the Mass on the high altar.

The centrality of the Mass is reflected in the building. The altar is richly decorated with marble, stucco, fresco and gilded plaster, contrasting with the simple unad-

The front view of Giacomo Barozzi da Vignola's church of Jesus.

orned walls of the nave. The design allows a view of the brightly-lit altar by the maximum number of people. In the centre of it all the priest presides over this colourful ritual, exemplifying the authority of the church.

Massacre on St Bartholomew's Day

Coligny is wounded (l.) and assassinated (r.), precipitating the massacre.

Catherine de Medici: the instigator.

English composers are major force in European music

England, 1573

England has emerged alongside Italy in the front rank of modern European music. Robert White is a name to note among rising young talent, but 35-year-old Thomas Tallis is the most influential figure. He is seeking a royal licence to publish music with a gifted 30-year-old pupil, William Byrd, who, like Tallis, is a Gentleman of London's Chapel Royal. Tallis is regarded as one of Europe's finest composers, although his early work was more old-fashioned than that of Christopher Tye (c.1505-72) and lacked the festal qualities of John Taverner (c.1490-1545), who worked at the new Cardinal College (*now Christ Church*) in Oxford.

But the mature Tallis is master of most forms and styles, from masses and other church music in Latin and English to small-scale instrumental works. A member of the royal household from 1543, he was one of the first to write music for the new Anglican liturgy of 1547-53, and composed for the Catholic Queen Mary in 1553-58. One of his newest pieces is an astonishing motet, *Spem in alium*, written for 40 parts.

Paris, 24 August 1572

A most terrible massacre of Huguenots is taking place in Paris. It started just before dawn this morning, St Bartholomew's Day, when a band of Catholics burst into the house of Gaspard de Coligny, disembowelled him and threw him out of his bedroom window, still alive.

Coligny was the target of an assassin two days ago as he was leaving the Louvre, but the shot only wounded him. It seems that he was marked for death because of his influence over the young Charles IX. The king's mother, Catherine de Medici, fearing that Coligny was pushing the king into war with Spain, conspired with the Catholic leader, Henry of Guise, to have him removed.

When the attempt failed the king swore vengeance on the assassins so, in order to save herself, Catherine convinced him that the Huguenots were about to rebel and begged him to authorise the killing of their leaders by the Guises.

Many of the Huguenots were in Paris celebrating the marriage of their leader, Henry of Navarre, to the king's sister, Margaret. A list of those to be killed was drawn up, headed by Coligny. But once the killing started the people of Paris, apparently overcome by bloodlust, started a general massacre. It is still going on, with men, women and children being slaughtered in their hundreds. There are reports that the killing is spreading to other towns. Henry of Navarre has been spared, but he was arrested at dawn, taken to the king's chamber and forced to abjure Protestantism.

Last of the Incas beheaded in Cuzco

Cuzco, May 1572

Tupac Amaru, the last of the Incas, the hereditary sun-kings of Peru, is dead and his kingdom destroyed. Found guilty of opposing the Spanish colonisation of his country and of encouraging paganism, he has been beheaded.

His speedy and, to many eyes, unjust trial and sentence to death shocked Peru. Even the Spaniards appeared to regret the death of this unfortunate man, and many leading clergymen attempted in vain to gain him a reprieve. But Viceroy Francisco de Toledo, determined to stamp out the Incas' power, refused to reverse his decision.

Before his death the Inca, who had been converted to Christianity while in prison, denounced sun-worship and called on his followers to embrace Christ.

The last of the Inca kings, Tupac Amaru, is beheaded in Peru by the Spaniards.

Astronomer shocked by a starry surprise

Copenhagen, 1572

The Danish astronomer Tycho Brahe has sighted a new star in the heavens. On 11 November Brahe observed in the constellation of Cassiopeia a body more brilliant than Venus where no star was supposed to be.

He carried out further research and found that this novel object lies beyond the moon in the realm of what are believed to be "fixed" stars. The scientific community is both intrigued and disquieted by this. It means that the stars are not, as depicted by Aristotle, immutable and eternal. They can come and perhaps go. Together with the Copernican idea now taking hold, that Earth is not the centre of the cosmos, Brahe's sighting shakes still further the concept of celestial stability.

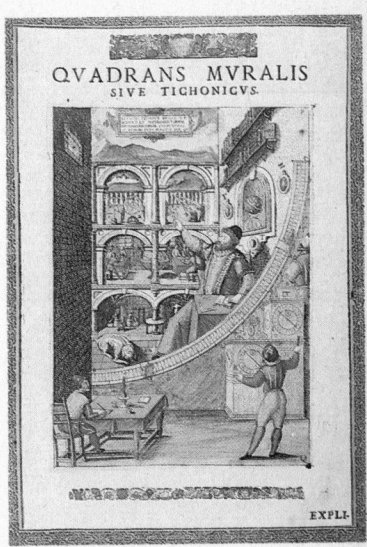

The pioneering Danish astronomer Tycho Brahe in his observatory, from his "Astronomiae Instauratae Mechanicae" of 1599.

1573 (1573-1575)

France, 1574. The duke of Alencon, the youngest son of Catherine de Medici, conspires to kidnap his brother, King Charles IX, but is betrayed by his fellow conspirators.

Mexico, 28 February 1574. On the orders of the Holy Office of the Inquisition, founded in New Spain three years ago, 60 people are scourged and sent to the galleys, seven are imprisoned, and two Englishmen and an Irishman are burnt for heresy.

Netherlands, April 1574. Luis de Requesens y Zuniga, who arrived in Brussels at the end of last year to replace the duke of Alba as governor of the Netherlands, defeats the Protestant rebels at Mook Heide.

France, 30 May 1574. Charles IX dies at the age of 24 after reigning for nearly 14 years. For the first ten years of his reign (1560-70) France was governed by his mother, Catherine de Medici, as regent. She remains a formidable influence. Charles is succeeded as king by his brother Henry III, who is to return from Poland where he was elected king last year.

Netherlands, June 1574. Requesens, the governor of the Netherlands, advises Philip II to grant a general pardon to the Protestant rebels and to abolish the hated "tenth penny" tax imposed by his predecessor, the duke of Alba.

Florence, 27 June 1574. The painter and writer Giorgio Vasari dies. His work includes frescoes for the Vatican of the *Life of Paul III* and the decoration of the Palazzo Vecchio and the Uffizi gallery in Florence. He wrote an account of *The Lives of the Most Eminent Italian Architects, Painters and Sculptors*.

Spain, 7 September 1574. Pedro Menendez de Aviles, who founded San Agostin, the first city in North America, dies in Santander.

Germany, 1574. With the Polish throne left vacant on the return of Henry III to France, the Emperor Maximilian II prepares to press his claims against Stephen Bathory, the prince of Transylvania.

Istanbul, 1574. Selim II, the sultan of the Ottomans, dies after a fall in a Turkish bath. A cultivated patron of arts and sciences despite being dubbed Selim the Drunkard, he largely retired to his harem after the defeat at Lepanto in 1571. State affairs were left to his grand vizier, Sokollu Mehmet. Selim is succeeded by Murad III.

Netherlands, 1574. The university of Leyden is founded.

North Africa, 1574. The Ottomans recapture Tunis and Bizerta and drive the Spanish out of La Goletta. Don John of Austria took Tunis for the Spanish in October last year with an expeditionary force of 20,000 men.

Spain, 1574. The "black code", a series of laws concerning the slavery of Africans in the Americas, is published.

Peru, 1574. A chair is created at the university of Lima for the study of Quechua, the language of the native Andean peoples.

Netherlands, February 1575. The Emperor Maximilian II mediates at a conference at Breda between the governor-general, Requesens, and Protestant representatives from Holland and Zeeland. Requesens agrees to withdraw Spanish troops and officials from the Netherlands.

Spain, 1575. The Spanish state goes bankrupt for the second time.

France, October 1575. Following the outbreak of the fifth war of religion, the Catholic forces under Henry, the duke of Guise, defeat the Protestants at the battle of Dormans.

Poland, 14 December 1575. Supported by the Turks, Stephen Bathory, the prince of Transylvania, is elected king of Poland.

France, 1575. The duke of Alencon forms an alliance against his brother, King Henry III, with the Bourbon Henry of Navarre.

Bohemia, 1575. Rudolf, the son of the Emperor Maximilian II, who was elected king of Hungary in 1572, becomes king of Bohemia.

Rome, 1575. The pope approves the foundation of the Institute of Oratory by Philip Neri.

Peru, 1575. Friar Cristobal de Molina compiles an anthology of *Tales and Ceremonies of the Incas*, a collection of Inca hymns.

Indian Ocean, 1575. Ralambo succeeds to the throne of the Merina kingdom in Madagascar.

Angola, 1575. The Portuguese found the city of Luanda.

England, 1575 Sir Humphrey Gilbert, the MP and explorer, publishes *Discourse to Prove a Passage by the North West to Cathay...* arguing for English colonisation of the far east.

Europe, 1575 The population of Paris is an estimated 300,000 people, compared with London's c.180,000 and Cologne's c.35,000.

Italy, 1575 An outbreak of the plague, which started in Sicily, travels north through the country and reaches as far as Milan.

Europeans face New World inquisitors

Mexico, 28 February 1574
Seventy Englishmen and an Irishman have been sentenced in the greatest trial by the Inquisition since it was officially set up in Spanish America in 1571. The men were all survivors of a slave-trading expedition to the Caribbean under Sir John Hawkins, who was forced to abandon them in 1568. After many tribulations they had mainly ended up as servants to Spanish colonists in Mexico City.

As potential "Lutheran" heretics the men were obvious targets for the zeal of the newly-arrived Inquisitors. They were questioned for months and eventually condemned at a public *auto-da-fe* (act of faith) for offences ranging from heresy to asserting that fornication before marriage was not a sin. Sixty-one men received from 100 to 300 lashes, followed by up to ten years as galley-slaves; seven were ordered to serve in monasteries for five years. Three men, including the Irishman, earned the honour of being the first people to be burnt as heretics in the New World.

Grand mosque at Edirne is completed

Six years in construction, the Selim mosque at Edirne is now complete.

Edirne, Turkey, 1575
The great mosque of Selim is complete, six years after building began. It is probably the finest architectural achievement of Sinan, who was also responsible for the Suleiman mosque in Istanbul.

The dominant feature of the building is the massive central dome. The interior is an octagonal baldachin built within a rectangular enclosure. Sinan may have got this idea from the octagonal mausoleum of Sultan Oljaitu Khodabandah Khan at Sultaniya, in Azerbaijan. The four symmetrical minarets emphasise the centrality of the design.

This magnificent mosque is a supreme expression of the spirit of reason which is sweeping through Ottoman art and architecture.

Polish nobles elect a Frenchman as king

A 1585 tapestry shows a French ballet in honour of Polish ambassadors.

Poland, 1573

In an extraordinary development a devious, egotistical and effeminate Frenchman, Henry of Anjou, has secured the crown of Poland. Henry, whose candidacy was put forward by his mother, Catherine de Medici, was voted king by a majority of some 40,000 Polish nobles and gentry assembled for the election on the Warsaw plain.

The event was precipitated by the death of Sigismund II Augustus, the son of Sigismund the Old. He had no heir, so with him disappear-ed the Jagiellon dynasty of Poland which had lasted some two centuries. Several footloose young princes ambitious for a crown and a piece of land they could call their own became interested, but by dint of propaganda and persuasion Catherine succeeded in building up a pro-French party among the Polish nobles. At the same time the powers of the Polish crown are being drastically reduced, and Poland is going to be governed by the Senate. Henry may lose interest in Polish power.

Rhyme Thyme comes for Britain's farmers

Suffolk, England, 1573

A Suffolk farmer, Thomas Tusser, has used his gift for verse to sow a rich harvest with the publication of a remarkable work, *Five hundred good points of Husbandry*. It is a book of rhymed proverbs, designed to help Tusser's fellow farmers

Cambridge University educated Tusser has already published his *One hundred good points* in prose, but the poems are more easily re-membered. He has advice for every season. When Spring comes, for instance:

Keep threshing for thresher till May be come in,
to have to be sure fresh chaff in thy bin;
And somewhere to scramble for hog and for hen,
and work, when it raineth, for loiter-ing me men.

And the farmer's wife is expected to make "the seede cake, the pasties and furmety pot". So thus ...

Good Ploughmen look weekly of cus-tome and right
for rostmeat on Sundays and Thurs-days at night:
Thus doing and keping such cus-tome and guise,
They call thee good huswife, they love thee likewise.

Spanish monarchy plunges into the red

Glory before profit: frescoes illuminate the royal library at the Escorial.

Spain, 1575

Imperial Spain, the dominant force in Europe and the New World for nearly a century, is bankrupt. For all its colonies, for all its power and prestige in Europe, years of costly wars – in the Netherlands, against England – have drained what was always a flimsy royal treasury in which apparent glory was set above hard-nosed practical planning.

Some would put the start of the problems as far back as the 1490s when first the Jews and then the Conversos were expelled, seriously depleting the country's merchant class, but the riches of the Americas have never been invested properly.

Philip II, who inherited from his father Charles V a country at the peak of its powers, is an accom-plished statesman, but he has let imperial interests override eco-nomic ones. The main consequence is that the Spanish crown cannot pay its troops in the Netherlands, so mercenaries frequently mutiny and thus military gains are lost.

Sultan dies after fall in Turkish bath

Istanbul, 1574

Selim the Drunkard is dead. After an undistinguished eight-year rule, the sultan met an ignominious death. He died of a fever after cracking his skull when falling down drunk in a Turkish bath. He is succeeded by his son Murad III.

Selim was short and fat, and no warrior. Nor did he have much appetite for affairs of state, which he left largely in the hands of Sokollu, his grand vizier. He whiled away his time drinking wine in the seraglio, surrounded by flatterers and cronies. Abroad, Ottoman prestige has been badly dented by the empire's defeat at Lepanto in 1571.

Selim II: from a book of poems.

Inflation and society in Europe

"The price of things 50 or 60 years ago was ten times less than at present" observed the French political philosopher Jean Bodin in 1568. Bodin's comment is exaggerated but it draws attention to the scale of the price rises that occurred during the 16th century and to the anxiety that they provoked. That anxiety was entirely justified, for inflation profoundly altered both the structure of society and the pattern of social relations in every part of Europe.

It has been calculated that if one represents the average price of a national "basket" of grains in England between 1450 and 1500 by an index value of 100, by the decades 1590-1609 it had risen to 575. A similar index constructed from French evidence reads 729 by the period 1600-20. Other commodities rose in price, though less dramatically. By 1600 industrial products had reached index values of 247 and 335 in England and France respectively. The pattern is repeated across Europe although it is less pronounced east of the Elbe.

Inflation: contemporary views

Although the general rate of inflation in the 16th century was rarely as high as two per cent a year, its impact was heightened because such price rises were without precedent and thus little understood. One influential explanation was put forward in 1566 by the French nobleman, the sieur de Malestroit, who argued that price rises were largely caused by the devaluation of the coinage. Monarchs in early modern Europe often raised revenue by calling in the coinage, melting it down and reminting it so that each coin contained less gold or silver. This could produce very healthy short-term profits for royal coffers. Thus King Henry VIII of England raised around £450,000 for his foreign wars by debasing the coinage, while between 1547 and 1551 the protectors who ruled during the minority of his son, Edward VI, raised a further £750,000 in the same way. However, such tampering with the coinage caused financial chaos and could provoke inflation because vendors increased their prices in order to obtain the same amount of precious metals for their wares. Certainly the coincidence of massive debasement with bad harvests in England under Edward VI was widely thought to have exacerbated price rises. Malestroit argued that if one calculated prices in gold and silver, not in the face value of the coinage, one would find an underlying stability of prices. There is some validity in Malestroit's argument, but it fails to provide a total explanation. Why did prices in England continue to rise after 1560 even though the coinage was not devalued by Queen Elizabeth or her successors?

Jean Bodin published a reply to Malestroit in 1568. His primary explanation for the price rises was the great increase in the precious metal circulating in Europe. (Monopolistic trading practices, dearth and noble extravagance were also, he claimed, contributory factors). Bodin was not entirely original in his views, but many historians have broadly agreed with his explanation. It has been argued that the around 300,000 lbs of gold and 16 million lbs of silver that flooded into Spain and thence all of Europe during the 16th century was the major cause of inflation and that the rate of price increase closely followed the rate at which bullion arrived from America. However, once again, problems arose: why did bread prices rise so much faster than prices of manufactured goods if the key factor in price rises was the influx of bullion?

More mouths to feed

Moreover, there is growing agreement among historians that both Bodin and Malestroit overlooked one vital factor – the dramatic growth in the European population during the period. From a large sample of parish registers it has been estimated that England's population grew from about 3,000,000 in 1550 to a peak of around 5,250,000 in 1650 before falling slightly in the second half of the 17th century. The kingdom of Naples contained around 255,000 households in 1505 and approximately 540,000 households in 1595. The total population of Europe grew from perhaps 61,600,000 in 1500 to around 78,000,000 in 1600.

Such an increase in numbers meant that there were many more mouths to feed and the agriculture of early modern Europe was sorely stretched to satisfy the demand. Production rose less rapidly than the population and this forced up prices, especially of bread, the staple diet of the poor. Wages did not keep pace with prices over the century and there is no doubt that the living standards of the poor fell dramatically as a result. In Valladolid in Spain, for example, wages rose less than 30 per cent between 1511 and 1550 while wheat and wine prices rose by 44 per cent and 64 per cent respectively.

Polarisation and hardship

Such circumstances offered opportunities for some. If one was able to produce a surplus of food for the market or otherwise maximise one's returns from land then there were ample opportunities for growing richer. If, however, small peasant producers could not grow enough to feed their families then they would sink into debt and frequently find themselves being driven from the land. In consequence 16th century Europe saw the development of sharper social polarisation, greater inequality and a growing class of landless or marginal poor, many of whom flocked to the rapidly expanding cities. In the Essex village of Terling, for instance, the percentage of poor cottagers and labourers grew from a quarter to half of the community between the 1520s and 1670s, while the percentage of middling villagers decreased markedly. In many villages across Europe historians have shown how a small group of landlords, including absentee town dwellers, came to own more and more of the farmland.

Consequently, the final decades of the 16th century and the early decades of the 17th marked a period of great hardship throughout most of Europe. There is evidence that the land in some parts of Europe, particularly in Mediterranean regions, was becoming exhausted and crop yields were falling as a result. Plague and harvest failure in Spain reduced the population from 8,000,000 to 6,500,000, while during the 1590s there were subsistence crises in many parts of northern England with people starving to death on the streets of Newcastle.

As a result of these harsher circumstances one can see a change in the demographic regime emerging in early 17th century Europe. By 1659 populations had stagnated or even declined. This was not caused by famine or plague, which rarely had any lasting impact on overall population, but largely by a rising age of marriage. In rural England between 1550 and 1599 the mean age for a woman to marry was just under 25; in the following half century it had risen to 26. In Bourg-en-Bresse in France during the 1560s the mean age was just over 20; by 1619 women were postponing marriage till the age of 22. Although such shifts might not appear dramatic, they significantly reduced the number of children a woman could conceive in her married life and thus the rate at which the population reproduced itself. It is probable that the later age of marriage occurred because it took longer for prospective couples to achieve a modest toehold in society and enough money to establish a household. In turn, this stabilisation of the population led to a modest increase in real wages in the second half of the 17th century. Thus the rise in prices touched both rich and poor, affecting not only their economic circumstances but also the pattern of their domestic lives.

"The fight between Carnival and Lent" by Pieter Bruegel the Elder (c.1515-1569) gives a graphic view of poverty in 16th century Europe.

"A beggar", by the Dutch artist Jan Adriaenszoon van Staveren (1625-1668).

"Feeding the hungry", by Cornelius Buys, the master of Alkmaar (died 1524).

Frenchman defends absolute monarchy

Angers, 1576

The new great debate in France after years of civil strife is whether the king, as the Royalist League have long claimed, should have absolute authority.

The leading protagonist for this view is one of France's most influential theoreticians, Jean Bodin, the Angers jurist, who has elaborated his notions of an absolute monarchy in his newly published treatise *Republique* (Six Books of the Commonwealth).

According to Bodin, no state can expect to exist satisfactorily without one single authority formulating, judging and enforcing the laws. Quoting Aristotle and Justinian, he claims that such authority can never be mixed, but has to be united in one person, the king.

In the last resort, Bodin holds, the king is responsible to God for carrying out his duties and administering justice fairly and responsibly. While Bodin does not subscribe to the notion that kings are always appointed by God, his critics claim that unscrupulous monarchs may attempt to misuse his ideas and suggest, they have a divine right to rule.

Plagues kill nine in ten Indians

Mexico, 1576

The number of Indian souls available to Christian salvation has shrunk. This is not because of the enthusiasm with which they have embraced the faith, but a result of epidemics whose appearance in Latin America coincided with the arrival of Europeans.

Colonists worried about native welfare have collated some frightening statistics about mortality in central Mexico. In 1519, there were an estimated 25.2 million Indians, whose life expectancy was good. Then smallpox arrived, followed by measles in 1529. By 1532 the population was down to below 17 million; by 1568 it had dropped below three million. Now a new plague, known as *matlazahuatl,* is wiping out Indians at a rate which could reduce numbers to six figures.

Titian, of the dark red canvases, dies

"The Death of Actaeon" by Titian: rich colours illuminate classical myths.

Venice, 27 August 1576

Venice is in mourning for its "prince among painters", Titian, who has died of the plague. No-one knows his exact age, but he was believed to be over 90. He will be buried in the church of the Frari (Franciscan friars) for which he painted the altar-piece of *The Assumption*, which glows with the red of rubies.

He became the most famous portrait painter in Europe. The dukes Sforza of Milan and Gonzaga of Mantua, Pope Paul III and the kings of France and Spain were among his sitters. Through his friend, the poet Pietro Aretino, he met the Emperor Charles V who sat for him often. He was paid 1,000 gold crowns for each portrait, appointed court painter and made a count. It is said that the emperor even picked up his brush when he dropped it.

Even Michelangelo admired the vibrance of Titian's colour. For Philip of Spain he painted many sumptuous scenes of classical myth with naked goddesses, such as *Diana and Actaeon*. In later years his brush-strokes grew bolder and he often used his fingers.

Titian's "Venus of Urbino" wonderfully expresses his ideal of female beauty.

Seeker after eternal life crowned emperor

Prague, 12 October 1576
The eccentric yet gifted Rudolf II of Habsburg, the archduke of Austria, king of Hungary and Bohemia and one of Europe's great patrons of the arts and sciences, was elected to the throne of the Holy Roman empire today. Despite his encouragement of the astrologers and alchemists – searching at his behest for the elixir for an eternal existence – Rudolf is committed, like Maximilian, his father, to the concept of a single religion.

Maximilian favoured Lutheranism, despite his Catholic upbringing. Rudolf, on the other hand, is a staunch Catholic, and his election has, to some extent, united Protestants – Lutherans, Ultraquists,

Calvinists and Bohemian Brethren – within his domain. Like his father before him, Rudolf chose to bend before the winds of change, especially under pressure from the wealthy Protestant nobles. The price of his election was acquiescence to the "Bohemian Confession", a document subscribed to by each of the Protestant churches.

For many, however, the state of the emperor's mind remains a major question mark when it comes to his rule of the empire. Although he has brought great scientists like Kepler to Prague, and commissioned work from artists of the stature of Bassano, Rudolf has likewise surrounded himself with charlatans in his quest for eternal life.

Europeans enjoy peppers and pineapples

Not just food, but art: a 17th-century painting of "Oriental Fruits".

Europe, c.1576
The dinner tables of European society now bear little resemblance to those of even a few decades ago, thanks to the introduction of new delicacies from the New World.

In England the pineapple, a tropical fruit first imported 22 years ago, has become a dessert favourite among top people. In their kitchens spices like red-hot chili peppers and flavourings such as vanilla have also become fashionable. On a less exotic level, maize, the corn grown as animal feed by Indians, is now

being successfully cultivated. Some foods are being re-exported, with the Spanish and Portuguese now cultivating American peanuts in parts of Asia.

But the food trade with the Americas is not all one way. Bananas, limes, lemons, oranges, olives, cabbages and lettuces are all being successfully grown in the New World. In the West Indies sugar cane is now a significant crop, while in Florida herds of Spanish cows and pigs are being raised to provide supplies of beef and pork.

Parisian Catholics turn against Huguenots

Paris, 1576
Henry, the duke of Guise, who is known as Henry the Scarred, has formed a Catholic league in Paris in reaction to the edict of Beaulieu which ended the latest round of religious civil war by granting favourable terms to the Huguenots.

These concessions have caused dismay among the Catholic zealots, and the league is receiving much support in the working class districts of Paris and among the fanatical lower orders of the clergy.

It has already become a major political force and Henry is the idol of the back streets of Paris. He has committed the league to the restoration of religious uniformity and has made demands on the new king, Henry III, which are a danger to royal authority.

The king, a foppish young man obsessed with the idea of death, who refused on religious grounds to negotiate a marriage with Queen Elizabeth of England, and helped to instigate the St Bartholomew's Day massacre, is trying to curb the league's power by taking over its leadership and declaring his hostility to the Huguenots.

Capital city built in honour of holy man

Fatehpur Sikri, central India, 1576
A new city has been built at Sikri by the Moghul Emperor Akbar. It is a city on a hill, and crowning the summit are the palace and mosque. The architecture is wholly Indian, drawing on Hindu and Moslem features.

Within Akbar's palace his audience chamber is imperial: Akbar on a pillar, his ministers sitting in a circular gallery, linked by four elegant bridges. His harem of five receding storeys is adorned with delicate stone screens from which ladies can see but not be seen.

It was built in honour of the holy man, Shaikh Salim Chishti, who prophesied the birth of Akbar's sons, Salim (Jahangir), Murad and Daniyal. Following Akbar's defeats of the Rajputs and Gujarat, he has prefixed the name Sikri with Fatehpur (meaning victorious).

Birth of Akbar's son Salim at Fatehpur in 1569, painted c.1590.

Imperial style: part of the palace of the women at Fatehpur Sikri.

1576 (1576-1579)

Persia, 1576. Shah Tahmasp dies after a reign of 52 years and is succeeded by his son Ismail II.

Florida, 1576. 287 colonists are evacuated from the northern settlement of Santa Elena following a siege by Indians.

Spain, 1576. Teresa de Avila is forbidden by the church to found any more Carmelite convents.

Italy, 1576. Dante's *La Vita Nuova* is published posthumously.

London, 1576. The first permanent public theatres, the Theatre and the Curtain, are opened in fields to the north of the city. The old monastery at Blackfriars is also adapted for performances.

Netherlands, November 1576. Spanish troops mutiny and take Antwerp, where they indulge in extortion and robbery.

Netherlands, 8 November 1576. By the pacification of Ghent, the 17 provinces of the Netherlands form a federation to maintain peace, to suppress propaganda against heretics and to keep Spanish and other foreign troops out of the country. Negotiations between William (the Silent), the leader of the rebels, and the states of Brabant were precipitated by the Spanish "fury" of Antwerp.

Florida, December 1576. Nicolas Strozzi, who was in command of a French privateer wrecked north of Santa Elena, tells the Indians that he is an enemy of Spain and builds a fort.

Spain, April 1577. Hernando de Miranda, the former governor of Florida, returns to Spain to face arrest. He is accused of stealing 6,000 ducats before fleeing from his post earlier in the year.

Florida, July 1577. Pedro Menendez Marques arrives in San Agostin to take over as governor and rebuild Santa Elena, which has been destroyed by the Indians.

Netherlands, 23 September 1577. William of Orange makes a triumphant entry into Brussels, where he is appointed lieutenant. Archduke Mathias of Habsburg is nominated governor.

England, October 1577. After a second voyage to America, the Englishman Martin Frobisher returns to Bristol with 200 tons of ore, which he mistakenly believes to be gold.

France, 1577. Marshal Blaise de Montluc, the governor of Aquitaine, dies aged 75. A soldier loyal to the Guise dynasty since the age of 16, Montluc is well known for his *Commentaries*, a work extolling the soldierly qualities of loyalties and uprightness.

Persia, 1577. Shah Ismail II dies and is succeeded by his brother Mohammed.

Ethiopia, 1577. Ethiopia conquers the sultanate of Harrar.

Rome, 1577. Giovanni Pierluigi da Palestrina, the master of music at St Peter's, is told by Pope Gregory XIII to restore the purity of Gregorian chant and to rid sacred music of anything which prevents the words being understood. This is in line with the decisions of the Council of Trent of 1545-63.

Spain, 1577. The painter Domenikos Theotokopoulos, who was born in Crete, moves to Toledo from Venice, where he is believed to have studied under Titian. He is given the name *El Greco* (the Greek).

England, 1577. Francis Drake leaves Portsmouth on a voyage to harass Spanish shipping along the Pacific coast of North America and to circumnavigate the globe.

Spain, September 1578. John of the Cross escapes from a monastery in Toledo where he has been imprisoned since 4 December 1577 by Carmelites hostile to his his proposals for reform. During his imprisonment he wrote 30 stanzas of a *Spiritual Canticle*.

South America, 5 December 1578. After sailing through the straits of Magellan, Francis Drake raids Valparaiso.

Caucasus, 1578. War breaks out between Ottoman Turkey and Safavid Persia as the Ottomans seek to dominate Georgia and other Caucasian principalities.

South-East Africa, 1578. The Portuguese sign a treaty with the Munhumutapa kingdom of the southern Zambezi area.

England, 1578. Martin Frobisher returns empty-handed from his third expedition to North America in search of gold and a passage to India through the northern ice.

France, 1578. Don John of Austria dies of typhus near Namur. After succeeding Requesens as governor of the Netherlands, he resorted to violence when his attempts at negotiation failed. He defeated the army of the estates-general at Gembloux and was last year declared an enemy of the Netherlands. He is succeeded as governor by Alexander Farnese.

Morocco, 1578. The Portuguese are utterly defeated by the Moroccans under Mulai Ahmed al-Mansur at Alcazar-el-Kebir.

Chile, 1578. Santiago is destroyed by an earthquake.

Spain, 1579. John of the Cross becomes rector of the college of Baeza in Andalucia.

Shah of Persia dies after 43-year reign

Persia, 1576
Shah Tahmasp of Persia has died after a 43-year reign. By avoiding pitched battles with the Ottoman army, and by taking decisive action when necessary against the Ozbegs in the east, Tahmasp has kept Persia's boundaries more or less intact, while keeping the peace at home. His two sons, Haydar and Ismail, are rivals for the succession.

In the south-west, Suleiman the Magnificent's forces captured Baghdad in 1534. In the northwest he captured the Safavid capital Tabriz in 1534 and again in 1548, but Tahmasp's scorched earth policy was effective and, after another campaign in 1554, the treaty of Amasya confirmed Ottoman rule over Mesopotamia, while Azerbaijan was to remain Persian. But Tahmasp took the sensible precaution of moving his capital from Tabriz to the more central Qazwin.

In the east, the tyranny of the Qizilbash prompted a section of the native population to seek the help of the Ozbeg ruler, Ubayd Allah, and seize Herat. But when the shah approached, the Ozbegs simply retreated. Khurasan was not threatened again during his reign.

During Tahmasp's rule, slaves from the Caucasus became integrated into the population, while tension between the Turkish military class – the Qizilbash tribesmen – and the Persian bureaucracy was kept well under control.

Frobisher seeks a "north-west passage"

Under fire: Frobisher and his men are attacked near Baffin Island.

London, 1577
The English explorer, Captain Martin Frobisher is preparing for his third voyage in 18 months to find the short, polar way from the North Atlantic to China which learned navigators are convinced must exist as a route known as the "north-west passage".

Last year he sailed into a strait in the far north-west beyond Greenland, convinced that Asia lay to starboard and America to port. He met Asiatic people called Eskimo, and found black ore which an Italian alchemist says conceals gold, although London's goldsmiths do not agree with him.

This year, in a voyage between May and September, Frobisher collected 200 tons of gold ore which the queen had locked up for safe-

Frobisher: seeking polar gold.

keeping in the Tower of London. As gold fever spreads, there is less interest in the route to Cathay, even though the keepers of the ore protest that they cannot find furnaces hot enough to transmute the ore into gold. Ore apart, the venture has collected only two bewildered Eskimo captives.

Women and children die in Spanish fury

Spanish soldiers portrayed waging brutal war in Harlem, in the Netherlands.

Ghent, 8 November 1576
As Spanish soldiers rampaged through the city of Antwerp, burning, killing and looting – leaving 8,000 dead and 1,000 houses destroyed – Catholic and Protestant leaders of the rebellious Habsburg Netherlands today signed a treaty to be known as the "Pacification of Ghent". Both sides aim to sink their religious differences in the face of the brutality of the Spanish military response to the revolt.

For the past four years, hatred of the Spanish has become universal in this country following the attempt to impose the "tenth penny" tax by Spain's governor, the duke of Alba, and the brutal treatment of rebellious towns during the war of 1572.

It was the mutiny four years ago by Spanish soldiers that brought the hatred to boiling point. Thousands of hardened veteran troops expelled their officers and formed their own revolutionary committees. Brutal excesses followed.

Nothing surpassed the brutality seen in Antwerp during the past few days. According to an English observer: "They spared neither age nor sex, time nor place, person nor country, profession nor religion, young nor old, rich nor poor, strong nor feeble, but, without any mercy, did tyrannously triumph."

Children have indeed been killed in their hundreds in Antwerp as what has become known as "The Spanish Fury" continues.

Crusade against Moors crushed in Africa

Morocco, 4 August 1578
King Sebastian of Portugal lies dead on the battlefield of Alcazar-el-Kebir ("Battle of Three Kings"). With him and 8,000 of his soldiers perish improbable dreams of a Christian crusade against the Moors of Africa.

From his early youth, the unstable Sebastian had an obsessive yearning to be Christ's captain against the infidel. In 1576 he found the pretext he needed, when Mulai Mohammed, the sharif of Fez, was deposed by an uncle who was backed by the Ottomans.

Although Philip II of Spain initially refused to help, Sebastian was determined, and in December 1576 asked for Philip's daughter's hand in marriage, and for galleys, men and supplies for a Moroccan campaign. He borrowed money wherever he could, and scraped to-

Sebastian: defeated holy warrior.

gether an army of adventurers and mercenaries from all over Europe. Out of touch with its fleet, as well as being overcome by the heat, Sebastian's army was outnumbered and crushed. About 15,000 Christians were captured.

Jewish protege of Sultan dies in Istanbul

Istanbul, 1579
Joseph Nasi, the duke of Naxos, has died in his belvedere palace, having established a Jewish community within the Ottoman court. Nasi was a Portuguese Jew who fled from the Inquisition in his own country, and travelled widely in Europe before finding refuge with the sultan, Suleiman the Magnificent, who valued his intelligence and financial expertise. When

Selim became sultan, he put Nasi in charge of Ottoman diplomacy, made him duke of Naxos and, in due course, gave him rights on Tiberias to establish a Jewish colony in Israel.

The first Jew to hold such a powerful position, Nasi became the sworn enemy of Spain and Venice, supporting the rebellion against the Spanish in the Low Countries, and taking Cyprus from the Venetians.

New house on London Bridge was originally built in Holland

London Bridge in the 17th century: a place to live as well as the capital's prime crossing point of the river Thames.

London, 1578
A new and unusual building has appeared among the shops and houses that line London Bridge. It is unusual because it was not built

there originally, but in Holland. It was brought over in sections and re-erected. This seems to be the first instance of a pre-fabricated building which makes its name –

"Nonsuch House" – particularly apt. It recalls the famous Nonsuch Palace, built in 1538 by Henry VIII, which was also architecturally unique.

Magnificent castle completed in Japan

Japan, 1579
The warlord Oda Nobunaga has built a magnificent castle at Azuchi, overlooking Lake Biwa. Erected as a barrier to invaders from the eastern provinces, it is not only a fortress but also a place of elegance which, as regards architecture, strength, wealth and grandeur, is the equal of anything in Europe. Surrounded by immensely strong stone walls, the castle itself is made entirely of wood and is richly painted in various colours. It is surrounded by exquisite houses decorated with gold, while beneath it a prosperous town is being built to serve the castle's defenders.

Netherlands, January 1579. The Union of Arras and the Union of Utrecht finalise the division of the former Netherlands. The United Provinces are formed.

North America, 17 June 1579. The English seaman Francis Drake, who has put in for repairs on the coast of California at a place he calls Drake's Bay *(San Francisco Bay),* claims the surrounding land for Queen Elizabeth. He names the territory New Albion because its white cliffs and summertime coolness remind him of England.

Florida, August 1579. Pedro Menendez Marques, the Spanish governor of San Agostin, attacks a group of Cusabo tribesmen, killing some 40 Frenchmen from Nicolas Strozzi's party, who are now scattered among the Indians.

Germany, 24 October 1579. Albert V (the Magnanimous), the duke of Bavaria, dies in Munich and is succeeded by William (the Pious), a strong supporter of the Jesuits.

Paris, December 1579. Guillaume du Bartas, a gentleman in the service of the king of Navarre, is enjoying great acclaim for his recent poetical work *La Sepmaine* (The Week), which describes the seven days of creation. It has already been translated into English, German and Spanish.

North America, 1579. Aboard his ship, the *Golden Hind,* docked in Drake's Bay, Francis Drake conducts Protestant services, the first in the New World.

India, 1579. The Emperor Akbar invites the Jesuits of the Portuguese colony of Goa to visit his court.

Madrid, 1579. The Theatre of the Cross is founded.

Rome, 1579. An English college is established for the education of priests and of English people who have remained faithful to the Church of Rome. Seminaries have been banned in England.

Ireland, 1579. The Spanish make an unsuccessful attempt to land in Ireland. The county of Munster rebels against English and Protestant domination.

Istanbul, 1579. The Grand Vizier Sokullo, who engineered the recapture of Tunis and Bizerta from the Spanish, dies. As the sultan, Selim, was preoccupied with pursuing his own pleasure, Sokollu had effectively controlled the Ottoman empire.

England, 1579. The Eastland Company is formed to trade with the Baltic.

Portugal, 1580. Philip II of Spain annexes Portugal, unifying the Iberian peninsula.

France, 13 February 1580. A group of burghers, ordered by Catherine de Medici to suppress a peasant revolt, murders Pommier, the leader of the rebel peasants who for a year have ruled the town of Romans, in the province of Dauphine, in protest at crushing taxes.

Portugal, 10 May 1580. Luis de Camoes, author of *The Lusiads,* an epic account of Portuguese adventures overseas, dies in Lisbon. He spent 17 years in India, the Far East and Africa.

Germany, 25 June 1580. The Formula of Concord agreed between John George, the elector of Brandenburg, Augustus of Saxony, the elector Palatine and 20 other princes, 24 counts and 38 cities brings together most of the German Lutherans.

Florida, 17 July 1580. While inquiring about Nicolas Strozzi at the mouth of St John's river, a French vessel under Gilberto Gil is trapped and destroyed by the Spanish.

Italy, 19 August 1580. The architect Andrea di Pietro, known as Palladio, dies.

England, 26 September 1580. Francis Drake returns to Plymouth at the end of his voyage to circumnavigate the globe.

France, 26 November 1580. The treaty of Fleix is signed by the duke of Anjou, leader of the Catholic forces, and the Protestant King Henry of Navarre. It ends the seventh French war of religion, which broke out last year, maintaining the previous balance between the two factions.

Poland, 1580. The leaders of Poland's Jewish communities create a "council of the four countries" – that is, the four Polish provinces. This new "parliament" will meet annually to discuss Jewish affairs.

India, 1580. The Moghul Emperor Akbar receives three Jesuit missionaries at his court. The Jesuits present him with a copy of the Polyglot Bible of Antwerp. The Flemish engravings introduce the artists in Akbar's court to Renaissance art and the laws of perspective.

Italy, 1580. *Gerusalemme Liberata* (Jerusalem Delivered) by Torquato Tasso is published while the author is in a mental asylum. The epic tells of the triumph of good over evil, symbolised by the capture of Jerusalem by the crusader Godfrey de Bouillon.

London, 1581. The Levant Company is formed to trade with Mediterranean countries.

Low countries divided by Union of Utrecht

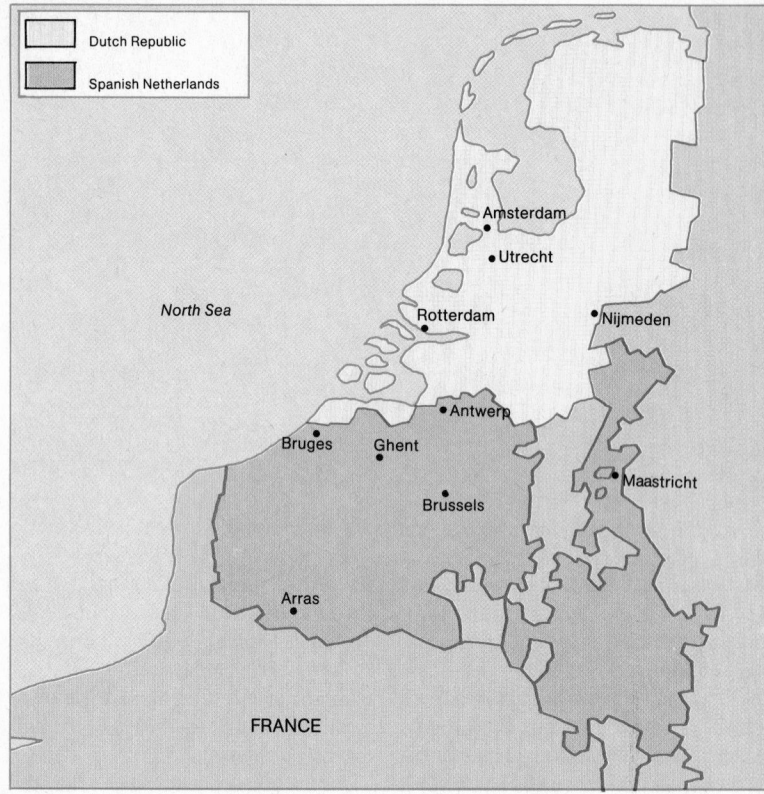

Dutch Republic

Spanish Netherlands

North Sea

Amsterdam
Utrecht
Rotterdam
Nijmeden
Antwerp
Bruges
Ghent
Maastricht
Brussels
Arras

FRANCE

Utrecht, 23 January 1579
Deputies from six provinces of the Habsburg Netherlands met here today to sign an historic agreement which pledges all of them to act together as allies in the event of war.

Even more significant in the treaty was their agreement that each province should be able to govern itself in its own way. For the first time, no mention of the Spanish king's name has been made; nor of the maintenance of the Catholic faith; nor of any question of reconciliation with Spain.

It is doubtful whether the Union of Utrecht will succeed in uniting the Low Countries, however. Earlier this month at Arras the Walloons, the Catholics in the south of the region, joined a union with the states of Hainaut and Artois and opened talks with the Spanish overlord, the duke of Parma, so a new Catholic powerbloc may emerge.

The effect of these separate agreements can only be to split a nation already deeply divided by religious beliefs at a time when Spain is facing new threats from the Turks in the Mediterranean. All hopes that the new Habsburg governor, Don John of Austria, might resolve matters have died with him in a new outbreak of plague.

Tract unites Lutherans against Calvinists

Dresden, Germany, 25 June 1580
James Andreae, the chancellor of the university of Tubingen, has produced a formidable tract of some 17,000 words designed to heal divisions in the Lutheran church. Published today on the jubilee of the Augsburg Confession, it is called the "Formula of Concord". It reaffirms the confession of 1530 as the heart of Lutheran doctrine, after the Bible and the three creeds. It is conciliatory in tone to

Catholic, but fiercely attacks Calvinist views of predestination as "all false, horrifying and blasphemous".

Since 1570 Calvinism has spread from Heidelberg to Rhineland, Westphalia and Nassau, the home of the Orange dynasty. Elector Palatine Ludwig has been trying to reverse the trend, and recently expelled over 500 Calvinist leaders. But in Germany they are still a bigger threat to Lutherans than Catholics.

Britain welcomes home pirate Drake

An Indian sets a parrot trap, drawn by one of Drake's companions.

Plymouth, England, 1580

After a three-year voyage which took him round the world by way of Capes Horn and Good Hope, Francis Drake is back in his native Devon, his ship and men intact, with enough Spanish treasure to reduce taxes for everyone. Spain has demanded his trial for piracy. With an inquiry into his conduct in train, rumours of knighthood are discouraged. Yet as the first captain to sail completely round the globe – Magellan died in the attempt – Drake is a popular, and probably an untouchable, hero.

In 1577, with the queen's backing, Drake sailed with three ships whose crews (along with Spanish intelligence) were misled into believing that they were bound for Alexandria. Instead they sailed west and were becalmed in the doldrums. There was talk of mutiny and at Port Julian, just north of the Magellan Straits, Drake executed

Drake's artist also saw slaves wash gold before handing it to a Spanish overseer.

his former confidant and fellow commander Thomas Doughty. The expedition's real target was now revealed as Spanish treasure along the Pacific coast.

Drake covered the 300 miles (480km) through the straits without a chart in just 16 days, often piloting the fleet himself in a small sailing boat. Then the fleet was hit by storms. One ship sank without trace; a second returned to England. Drake renamed his craft the *Golden Hind*, and rode out norther-

ly gales which lasted 52 days and drove him far south of Cape Horn. On 1 March 1579 his luck changed. With guns and sailors unmatched in the Pacific, he found the Spanish treasure ship *Cacafuego* and seized 26 tons of silver, 80 pounds of gold, 13 money chests and many jewels.

It was the first of many such operations. He sailed north, claimed "San Francisco" for England and crossed the Pacific in 68 days. His fame preceded him, through Spain's complaints.

Portugal, 1580

Philip of Spain has annexed Portugal to give his country a new Atlantic seaboard, a fleet to help to protect it, and a second empire stretching from Africa to Brazil, from Calicut to the Moluccas.

After two years of political and diplomatic manoeuvring and, finally, the dispatch of an army to his neighbour, Philip has convened the Cortes at Tomar and taken the oath to observe all the laws and customs of the realm. In turn he was recognised as the lawful king of Portugal.

Portugal's problems arose from King Sebastian's disastrous African crusade when his army was torn to shreds and most of the Portuguese

Philip II of Spain: adding Portugal and its empire to the vast Habsburg dominions spanning the world.

Italian earthquake sets lamps swinging and Galileo thinking

Pisa, Italy, 1581

A 17-year old medical student at Pisa university, named Galileo Galilei, was in the cathedral here when an earthquake rocked the town, causing the great hanging lamps above him to start swinging. Timing the oscillations by means of his own pulse, Galileo found that each lamp always completed an oscillation in a certain time – whatever the range of the swing – which has led him to believe that the regular rhythms he has discovered might be of use in some mechanical device.

Born in 1564, the son of a musician, Galileo looks as if he might abandon his proposed career as a physician in favour of theoretical and experimental science. Between medical lectures, he eavesdropped on a geometry lesson in progress at the university and became so excited by what he learned that he sought lessons under the famous teacher Ostilio Ricci.

His main problem is how to pay for it. He has precious little money to spend on extra tuition. Meanwhile he ponders the mystery of the swinging chandelier.

A later Italian statue of Galileo.

nobility were killed. His throne became vacant and was for a time occupied by his uncle, Cardinal Henry; it was then that Philip made a move.

He announced his claim to succession and, taking advantage of Portugal's bankruptcy, made available liberal supplies of Spanish silver to beat off the claims of his rivals. But because the Portuguese were, by tradition, anti-Spanish, Philip presented Lisbon with an ultimatum. When it was ignored he sent an army under the duke of Alba. For economic reasons Portugal at this moment needs a political connection with Spain, and it could bring benefits.

1581 (1581-1582)

Argentina, 1581. Buenos Aires, founded last year by the Spaniard Juan de Garay at the confluence of the Parna and Uruguay rivers, is starting to assume an air of permanence. A previous Spanish colony on the site in 1536 had to be disbanded after attacks by Indians.

France, 1581. Readers of Montaigne's *Essays,* published last year, debate his "scepticism" which leads him to describe all religion as an act of blind faith.

North America, 1581. The first English attempt at establishing a colony here, at Roanoke in Virginia, is reported to be proving successful.

Portugal, April 1581. Philip II, whose troops overran the country last summer on the death of Cardinal Henry, is declared king.

Netherlands, 26 July 1581. The Estates-General (parliament) of the Hague deposes Philip II as ruler of the seven provinces which formed the Union of Utrecht in 1579; by doing so, it declares both independence and war.

North America, 21 August 1581. Francisco Chamuscado, leading a voyage to the Pueblo area in south-western North America, claims it for Spain and gives it the name San Felipe del Nuevo Mexico.

Japan, 1581. Oda Nobunaga attacks Mount Koya, the head-quarters of the Shingon sect of Buddhism.

London, 1581. The English Jesuit Edmund Campion – considered one of the most remarkable members of the "English mission" – is arrested and executed. His fate illustrates the dilemma of those English Catholics who wish to remain loyal to both their faith and the crown.

France, 1581. Merchants from Dieppe, St Malo and Rouen unite to organise a fur-trading expedition up the St Lawrence river in Canada.

Netherlands, 1581. After being named king of the Netherlands by William of Orange, Francis of Valois, the brother of Henry III, attempts to regain Antwerp for the Calvinists.

Russia, February 1582. The Russians heroically resist the siege of Pskov by PolishLithuanian troops.

Rome, February 1582. To ensure that Easter falls on its proper date, Pope Gregory XIII decides to bring back the spring equinox to 21 March by removing ten days – those between 5 and 15 October – from this year's calendar.

Atlantic, 25 July 1582. Philip Strozzi, for whom his cousin Catherine de Medici had secretly promised to obtain the post of viceroy of Brazil, dies during a naval battle off the Azores. He was on his way to Portugal to support the claimaint to the throne in his fight against the Spaniards.

Russia, 10 August 1582. After 25 years of conflict, Russia makes peace with Poland and gives up its claims to the Baltic state of Livonia.

Spain, 4 October 1582. Teresa of Avila, who in 1562 re-established the ancient Carmelite rule for nunneries, dies.

Russia, 1582. A large group of Cossacks, led by Yermak Timo-feyevich, invade the Tartar *khanate* of Siberia and capture its capital, Kashlyk.

China, 1582. The statesman Zhang Juzheng dies. For the past ten years he has run the empire, on behalf of the Ming emperor, with a firm hand.

Japan, 1582. Oda Nobunaga, who has reunified the country under his control, is attacked by Akechi Mitsuhide and dies. Akechi subsequently loses a battle with Toyotomi Hideyoshi and is killed.

India, 1582. The Moghul Emperor Akbar attempts a synthesis of the great religions.

Italy, 1582. Giordano Bruno writes a philosophical treatise entitled *The Shadow of Ideas*, a work inspired by Neoplatonism.

China, 1582. The Italian Jesuit Matteo Ricci arrives in Macao and begins an intensive study of the Chinese language and civilisation.

Japan, 1582. Japan, which now has over 150,000 Christians, sends its first ambassador to the Vatican.

Netherlands, 1582. Alexander Farnese, who has been nominated governor of the Spanish Nether-lands by Philip II, takes Oudenaarde.

Spain, 1582. Philip II of Spain agrees to give financial support to the Holy League founded in France in 1576 by the duke of Guise in order to help defend the Roman Catholics against the Calvinists.

Europe, 1582. Richard Hakluyt's book *Divers Voyages* gives the English-speaking world a view of the American discoveries.

Istanbul, 1582. On the anniversary of the founding of the famous corps of footsoldiers known as the Janissaries, their recruitment and disciplinary rules are relaxed. In particular, the rule of celibacy is removed.

Church bans reminder of the Inquisition

Act of faith: a 17th-century English engraving of Inquisition "persuasion".

Madrid, 1581

Just over a century after it was founded by a papal bull of 1478, the Spanish Inquisition has found a critic from within the ranks of the Catholic leadership. Although he is a distinguished Jesuit, Juan de Mariana has had his book put on the index of banned works.

Prominent Catholics here do not like being reminded of the early history of this most unusual institution. Although it was set up by order of the pope it was responsible to the Spanish crown. Its first inquisitor-general, the rather sha-dowy figure of Thomas de Torque-mada, was a Dominican friar; but for most of the last century it has been run by Catholic lawyers rather th' monks.

In the last two decades of the fifteenth century the Inquisition did acquire a fiercesome reputation for the cruel persecution of "deviants" in general and Jews in particular. Some thousands of *Conversos* – Jewish converts to Christianity – were arrested, thrown into jail and sometimes tortured to extract confessions that they were still practising their old faith. They were encouraged to betray their friends and relations. Some thousands were burnt at the stake.

Those days are long past, however. In recent years only three or four people in the whole of Spain have been executed by the Inquisition, generally "Old Christians" who were neither Protestant nor Jewish but did not conform to pre-

Cruel past: sinners go to the stake.

vailing views. For instance, people brought before the tribunal have been charged witchcraft, marital misbehaviour and superstition. In rural areas the Inquisition has recently been handing out minor sentences for trivial offences like blaspheming while drunk or using love-potions to seduce the opposite sex. It has also been used to stamp out homosexuality.

If the Inquisition no longer strikes terror into people's hearts, it is still a powerful force restricting what goes into their minds. It has always been effective as a censor and now it has jumped on de Mariana for daring to remind us of its cruel past.

Akbar attempts to fuse great religions

Fatehpur Sikri, India, 1582
In his new city of Fatehpur Sikri, the illiterate Moghul emperor Akbar sits in his "house of worship" discussing religion with Sunnis, Shi'ites, Hindus, Zoroastrians and Christians. All seek unsuccessfully to monopolise his religious spirit, unaware of his fascination by comparative religion, or his intentions of synthesising the great religions, transforming himself into a deity and saving India from sectarianism.

At first Akbar invited only Moslems, but he was so disappointed by their bigotry that he has renounced orthodoxy and proclaimed his own infallibility. Orthodox Moslems are shocked, but since the failure of their rising in Afghanistan a year ago there is little that they can do. Portuguese Catholics are bitter. Three Jesuits (one a Persian convert from Islam, another a Spaniard and the third an Italian aristocrat) travelled to Akbar's court. They hoped to win him over with their bitter attacks on Islam, but

A portrait of Akbar held by his son Salim (Jahangir), painted c.1599.

Akbar espouses religious tolerance. The reason behind Akbar's policy is simple: India is divided by different faiths, and only by rising above religions will he be capable of uniting the continent.

Emperor discovers truth about his tutor

China, 1582
Zhang Juzheng, the most powerful man in China, has died suddenly, only nine days after being granted the title of "Grand Preceptor", an honour that has not been conferred for 200 years. Zhang started his rise to power as tutor to the infant emperor, Wan-li. Working hand in glove with the eunuch Feng Pao, the head of the palace staff, Zhang controlled every action which the emperor took.

Wan-li, who enjoyed the art of calligraphy, simply wrote in royal vermilion what his tutor told him to and took pleasure from his brush-work rather than understanding what the document said. Some attempts were made by court officials to protest to the emperor about Zhang's arrogance, but the protesters were accused of disrespect to the throne and cruelly beaten with jointed whipping clubs.

Zhang and Feng Pao grew fabulously rich through their corruption. When Zhang travelled he did so in a sedan chair, divided into a bedroom and a reception room, which was hauled by 32 bearers. Now he is dead and the emperor is at last learning the truth about his beloved tutor.

Ten days vanish with the new calendar

Rome, 15 October 1582
A new era for the Catholic world begins today. As authorised by a papal decree, the Julian calendar, established in 46BC, is to be replaced by a new method of calculation.

It will be named the Gregorian calendar, in honour of Pope Gregory XIII who instituted the reform. Experts have been demanding a replacement for the Julian system, under which calendar time gains one whole day every 128 years, for 300 years. The difference between official time and solar time is currently ten days.

The new system has cut these extra days by making 5 October into 15 October. Accuracy will be maintained by cutting three leap years every 400 years.

Cossack firearms defeat Siberian Tartars

Russian guns overcome the Tartars, by the 19th century artist Surikov.

Russia, 1582
The Siberian Tartars have been defeated by Muscovy, their troops unable to withstand withering firepower. Khan Kuchum has been captured and his capital overrun. Yet the organiser of the victory was not the czar but the Stroganovs, a family of immensely rich merchants, and the troops were not Russians but Cossack mercenaries under their ruler Yermak. The Cossacks are roving bands of warriors, as much brigands as regular soldiers. Yermak is a fitting leader, an imposing and energetic warrior whose employers, the Stroganovs, run the north-eastern corner of European Russia as virtually a private kingdom, making a vast fortune from salt and furs.

The larger the kingdom became, the more it has clashed with the Tartars and needed troops. Yermak's 1,500 Cossacks make an ideal private army.

Teresa, an ecstatic and mystic nun, dies

Albe de Tormes, 4 October 1582
Teresa of Avila, one of leading reformers of the monastic movement, has died. Her father was a Jewish convert and her mother a Castilian aristocrat. Teresa entered a Carmelite convent at the age of 21. She was shocked by the lack of piety she found, and determined to lead a return to the Palestinian Carmelite tradition of the hermit living in the desert. She first founded the convent of St Joseph of Avila, where she insisted that the main role of the nuns was to pray for souls in danger and intercede for others. Since 1567 she has founded many others, some with the help of John of the Cross, who shared her deep mysticism.

Her best known book is *Castillo Interior*, in which the castle is the soul, which has to go through seven rooms to attain purity. In the final room a divine union is achieved. In contrast with her severe puritanism, her writing is rich with the erotic and sensual experience of the

A book written by Teresa.

holy. Her asceticism, prayer and piety took her to a state of intensely physical ecstasy of a kind which lesser mortals associate with sexual love.

1582 (1582-1587)

England, 1582. Robert Browne, a separatist opposed to the Anglican liturgy, flees to Holland.

Netherlands, 1583. Dutch from the seven United Provinces occupy the mouth of the Scheldt, halting any seaborne trade with Antwerp.

North America, 5 August 1583. Claiming the right of first discovery, Sir Humphrey Gilbert takes possession of Newfoundland in the name of Queen Elizabeth.

China, 1583. Yunnan province is invaded by the Burmese.

Atlantic, 1583. On his return journey to England after annexing Newfoundland, Sir Humphrey Gilbert is drowned in a shipwreck.

North America, July 1584. An English expedition organised by Walter Raleigh lands on the south-eastern coast of North America and asserts English authority over an area some 1,800 nautical miles long. Raleigh, who has remained in England, has the permission of Queen Elizabeth to name the area Virginia after the virgin queen.

France, 10 August 1584. The duke of Alencon and Anjou, the younger brother of Henry III, dies, leaving the Valois line without a successor to the throne. According to the rules of succession, the crown should revert to Henry of Navarre, the duke of Bourbon and leader of the Protestants. However, Henry, the Catholic duke of Guise, also stakes a claim.

Milan, 1584. Cardinal Carlo Borromeo, archbishop of Milan, dies after reviving Catholicism in northern Italy.

Poland, 1584. The poet Jan Kochanowski, who translated the psalms, dies at Lublin. He travelled widely in Europe and met leading writers, including the great French poet Pierre de Ronsard. His works have earned him the status of a national poet in his native land.

Rome, 24 April 1585. Felice Peretti is elected pope following the death of Gregory XIII. He takes the name Sixtus V.

North America, 13 July 1585. A group of 108 English colonists, led by Sir Richard Grenville, reaches Roanoke Island. This is the second expedition to North America organised by Sir Walter Raleigh, who was knighted this year.

Netherlands, 17 August 1585 Antwerp capitulates to Alexander Farnese, duke of Parma, the governor of the Netherlands. Farnese has now secured the submission of the southern Netherlands, Flanders and Brabant to the Spanish crown.

Netherlands, August 1585. England concludes an alliance with the United Provinces the treaty of Nonsuch. Robert Dudley, the earl of Leicester, is sent by Queen Elizabeth at the head of an army to support the Netherlands in their war against the Spanish.

Rome, 9 September 1585. Pope Sixtus V deprives Henry of Navarre of his rights to the French crown.

Netherlands, 1 November 1585. Maurice of Nassau, the son of William of Orange, becomes governor of Holland, Zeeland and Utrecht.

France, 27 December 1585. The poet Pierre de Ronsard dies. His work, which was popular with the court of Henry II, reconciles sensuality with faith and enthusiasm for the classics with pride in the French language.

England, 1585. The composer Thomas Tallis dies.

Caribbean, 1 January 1586. Francis Drake, who left England on a new voyage to America last September, makes a surprise attack on the heavily fortified city of San Domingo in Hispaniola, forcing the governor to pay a large ransom.

South America, February 1586. Drake captures Cartagena on the Spanish main by a land and sea attack. He plunders the city and ransoms it for 110,000 ducats.

Virginia, May 1586. The English military leader Ralph Lane heads off an Indian attack, killing Wingina, an Indian chief from Roanoke Island.

Florida, 7 June 1586. Drake burns the Spanish city of San Agostin.

Virginia, 18 June 1586. Francis Drake leaves Roanoke Island on his return journey to England. He has taken aboard Ralph Lane and other surviving English settlers.

Virginia, August 1586. Sir Richard Grenville sets sail from Roanoke, leaving 20 settlers behind.

Japan, 1586. Toyotomi Hideyoshi takes the title of *kampaku* (civil dictator) and takes over the task begun by Oda Nobunaga of uniting Japan under his sway.

Spain, 1586. El Greco paints *The Burial of the Count of Orgaz* for the church of Santo Tome in Toledo. Its typically dramatic, almost feverish, forms and colours confirm his growing reputation.

India, 1586. The Emperor Akbar annexes the kingdom of Kashmir.

Florida, 1587. The Spanish evacuate the northern settlement of Santa Elena.

Protestant rights withdrawn in France

Nemours, France, 7 July 1585
The fearful Henry III has given in to intense Catholic pressure and, in an edict signed here today, has revoked all concessions to the Huguenots and proscribed the "pretended reformed religion".

This edict, which makes another war between the Catholics and Protestants inevitable, was the direct result of the death of the duke of Anjou, the last of the king's brothers. Without an heir, Henry was forced to recognise the Huguenot Henry of Navarre as heir to the throne. This was a shattering blow to the Catholics, and Henry the Scarred of Guise reformed the Catholic League, which had disbanded itself in 1576 rather than allow the king to become its leader.

The league quickly became politically and militarily powerful again. Its leaders replaced royalist commanders with their own men in many towns. The Guise faction then signed a treaty of alliance with King Philip II of Spain, and King Henry, recognising the threat to his throne, has caved in.

Warlord who unified Japan is murdered

Japan, 21 June 1582
Oda Nobunaga unifier of Japan, was treacherously murdered at dawn this morning at the monastery of Honnoji where he was staying while on his way from his castle at Azuchi to a distant battlefield.

Nobunaga was taken by surprise by a strong force of men belonging to Akechi Mitsuhide with whom he had no quarrel. He and his men fought as valiantly as they always did, but they were overwhelmed and killed. Some reports say that he committed suicide. The monastery was set ablaze and his body has not been recovered. He was 48.

Nobunaga was only 17 when he succeeded to his family's modest feudal barony. Disregarded and forced to fight for his land, he soon proved himself a ruthless warlord, killing his treacherous younger brother and swiftly achieving local ascendancy.

He then embarked on a career of conquest until he could rightly lay claim to being responsible for the reunification of Japan after a century of strife.

Poles elect a Swedish prince to throne

Poland, 19 August 1587
Once more the Polish and Lithuanian nobility have declined to consider a native king, and have opted for a Swede, Sigismund Vasa. The 21-year-old prince was elected by some 15,000 voters who preferred him to the Habsburg Archduke Maximilian. He succeeds Stephen Bathory who has reigned for ten years.

Bathory, who was a Transylvanian prince, will be a hard act to follow. A forceful personality and an experienced soldier, he had set back Moscow's hopes for an outlet to the Baltic and created a big Christian empire in eastern Europe. Yet even before his death it had become clear that the Poles would not support the almost limitless personal ambitions of their king.

Sigismund may find that he has the same problem as his predecessors, namely, failing to banish from his mind the thought of his native

Sigismund: crossing the Baltic.

country, and this could have a far-reaching effect on both domestic and foreign policy. The Polish king has various powers and prerogatives, but the greatest restriction on his authority is working through parliament.

The reforming czar who was a monster

Czar Ivan the Terrible: great reformer or deranged monster?

Moscow, 18 March 1584
Czar Ivan the Terrible, a great man who also happened to be a monster, has died at the age of 54 while preparing to play a game of chess. Because his attempted social revolution and his last 25 years of war have brought Muscovy to the verge of anarchy, special guards have surrounded the Kremlin. But the succession appears to have passed easily enough to his son, Fyodor Ivanovitch.

Ivan inherited the throne at the age of three, and when he was 13, in a fit of temper, he had his principal adviser torn apart by dogs. His first wife, one of the Romanovs, was chosen out of 1,500 virgins sent to Moscow from all over Russia. For some 13 years Ivan ruled with a group of good advisers from the clergy and the *boyars*, introducing a new code of law and reforming provincial government.

Ivan was a strong and successful ruler, and the most noteworthy thing about his reign was his policy of extending Muscovy's power and influence. By capturing Kazan and Astrakhan he pushed the borders of Russia eastwards, ambitiously looking towards Cathay and the Pacific. He was denied an outlet to the west by failing to seize the Baltic region, but nevertheless established diplomatic and commercial relations with England. He entered into long and curious negotiations for an English marriage, not shrinking from a union with Queen Elizabeth herself if that were possible. Ivan was almost deranged for the last 25 years of his life.

Spanish agent kills William of Orange

Delft, 10 July 1584
William, the prince of Orange and foremost leader of the Dutch revolt against Spain, was today assassinated by an agent of Philip II. He was shot dead by Balthazar Gerard, a Frenchman, who was posing as a Calvinist refugee.

William of Orange was born in 1533. The governor of Holland, Utrecht and Zeeland, he was appointed to the council of state in 1555 and resigned, with Count Egmont and Philip Hoorne, in 1563, protesting at Spain's growing influence. A Protestant since 1573, William quickly established himself as a leader of the growing revolt against Spain. After the Pacification of Ghent (8 November 1576) the country's seven northern, Protestant, provinces declared themselves the United Provinces of the Netherlands. William was appointed *stadholder*, or chief magistrate.

For a brief period William even won over the southern Catholic provinces, but the scheme collapsed when William's French ally deserted him and the Protestants preferred to stand alone. Until today, he ruled the north alone.

William of Orange holds up the head of the Dutch cow, succoured by Queen Elizabeth, as Philip II sits on it and the duke of Alba milks it.

Elizabeth beheads Mary, queen of Scots

England, 8 February 1587
Proclaiming her Catholicism to the end and raising her voice in Latin to drown the prayers of the English chaplain, Mary, queen of Scots was executed today at Fotheringhay in Northamptonshire. She had been found guilty of joining a conspiracy to murder Elizabeth and promote a Spanish invasion of England.

Mary was sentenced last October, but an anguished Elizabeth repeatedly refused to sign the death warrant. Mary spent almost 20 years as a political refugee in England after her intrigues, her marriages, and the murder of one husband by her next-in-line caused her to be driven from Scotland.

Queen Mary: the Catholic queen driven from her own country.

Poet's heroic death mourned by queen

Sir Philip Sidney: soldier and poet, famed for his selfless courage.

London, 5 November 1586
The queen, the court and the whole city are in deep mourning for Sir Philip Sidney, the poet and soldier, whose body was today brought back from the Netherlands and landed at Tower Hill. At the siege of Zutphen he charged recklessly with 500 English horsemen against 3,000 Spanish cavalry.

Struck in the thigh by a bullet, he managed to ride back to camp where he called for water. But seeing a dying foot-soldier brought in, he handed him the bottle, saying: "Thy necessity is yet greater than mine." After 26 days of suffering, he died of his wound, aged only 32. Elegies for him are being written by poets everywhere.

Decimals invented

Antwerp, 1585
A couple of small pamphlets have just been published with the titles *La Thiende* (The Tenth) and *La Disme* (The Decimal). In them a Flemish mathematician, called Simon Stevin, gives an easy-to-understand account of a system of fractions based on tenths. Stevin says the decimal system beats the present method of counting in twelves. He proposes his way should be in everyday use. Coins could be decimalised, and so, too, could weights and measures. His own career has been impressive. He rose from being a clerk to commissioner of Antwerp's public works.

1587 (1587-1588)

England, 8 February 1587. Mary, queen of Scots, is beheaded at Fotheringhay for complicity in the Babington plot. Its leader, Anthony Babington, and his five associates were executed last year. He had planned to assassinate Queen Elizabeth, free Mary from captivity and rally support among English Roman Catholics for a Spanish invasion force.

Spain, April 1587. Francis Drake attacks and pillages Cadiz and ravages the Spanish coast, destroying naval stores. The incident becomes known as "the Singeing of the King of Spain's Beard".

Virginia, 18 August 1587. The first English child is born in the New World. The daughter of Ananias and Ellinor Dare is named Virginia in honour of both the virgin queen of England and the fledgling colony.

Poland, 19 August 1587. Following the sudden death of Stephen Bathory at the end of last year, Sigismund III, the son of John of Sweden, is cjosen to be the king of Poland.

Virginia, 27 August 1587. Having arrived at Roanoke on 22 July, John White sails for Europe with supplies, leaving his 177 colonists behind. On landing at Roanoke, White's party found no trace of the colonists left behind by Richard Grenville.

England, August 1587. Robert Dudley, the earl of Leicester, returns to England after the failure of his expedition to the Netherlands to aid the Dutch in their revolt against Spain.

France, 20 October 1587. In the eighth war of religion, which began two years ago, Henry of Navarre defeats a Catholic army commanded by the duke of Joyeuse at Coutras. This latest Catholic-Huguenot conflict has developed into a struggle for the French succession between Henry of Guise, King Henry III and Henry of Navarre, known as the War of the Three Henries.

France, 24 October 1587. Henry of Guise forces the Swiss and German troops who are attempting to link up with Henry of Navarre's army at Vimory and Auneau to retreat.

South-East Africa, 1587. The second Zimba war breaks out among the Chewa peoples in Mozambique and Malawi, caused by Portuguese slave trading on the Zambezi.

Japan, 1587. Shimazu Yoshihisa surrenders to Toyotomi Hideyoshi, effectively bringing the whole of Kyushu under Hideyoshi's control.

Italy, 1587. Two banking houses, the Banco di Rialto in Venice and the Tavola in Messina, open.

North America, 1587. Searching for a north-west passage, the English navigator John Davis discovers a strait linking the Atlantic to the Baffin Sea.

Scandinavia, 4 April 1588. On the death of Frederick II, his 11-year-old son Christian IV becomes king of Denmark and Norway and duke of Schleswig-Holstein.

Venice, 19 April 1588. The painter Paolo Caliari, known as Veronese, dies. Veronese made a speciality of great ceremonial compositions with biblical themes, such as *The Marriage at Cana* and *The Feast in the House of Levi*. The latter caused him some trouble with the Inquisition, whose wrath he escaped by claiming the licence granted to poets and madmen.

Paris, 12 May 1588. King Henry III is forced to flee from Paris after Henry of Guise's triumphant entry into the city.

England, 10 September 1588. The Englishman Thomas Cavendish, who set sail from Portsmouth on 21 July 1586, returns home having become the third man to circumnavigate the globe.

England, 15 September 1588. The Spanish Armada – an attempted invasion of England by Philip II – is defeated by the English led by Lord Howard of Effingham.

Persia, 1 October 1588. The feeble Sultan Mohammed Shah, dominated by rival tribal leaders, hands over power to his 17-year-old son Abbas.

France, 23 December 1588. Henry, the duke of Guise, and his brother Cardinal Louis of Guise are assassinated at Blois on the orders of King Henry III.

France, December 1588. King Henry III forms an alliance with Henry of Navarre to defeat the Holy League.

Japan, 1588. Following an anti-Christian edict issued in 1587, some Christians are expelled from Nagasaki.

Rome, 1588. The papal curia is reformed.

Venice, 1588. Tintoretto completes his enormous cycle of paintings on the life of St Mark in the Scuola di San Rocco, begun in 1564.

Spain, 1588. Philip II authorises half-castes in America to become priests – provided that they are legitimate, which is rarely the case.

Spain, 1588. The first complete edition of the works of Teresa of Avila is published.

Court pleads with virgin Queen to marry

Queen Elizabeth: resolved to remain single, despite diplomatic dalliances.

England, 1588

Elizabeth's advisers have never tired of urging her to marry and produce an heir to the throne. Successive parliaments have beseeched God "to incline your Majesty's heart to marriage ... that we may see the fruit and child that may come thereof". Elizabeth accepts that she has a duty to marry, but her courtships have been no more than diplomatic quadrilles with French and Austrian princes.

More than once she has been heard to say that she would "live and die a virgin". London society gossip has it that a physical defect rules out marriage. Be that as it may, she uses her sex and good looks to manipulate her advisers. It is said the relationship between the queen and her secretary of state, William Cecil, is deeply emotional.

From the start, Elizabeth has had to overcome the handicap of being a woman in male-dominated Tudor society. A woman is expected to be an obedient and diligent wife. Sir William Fitzwilliam, the queen's lord deputy in Ireland, speaks of her in the most vulgar terms: "God's wounds, this it is to serve a base, bastard, pissing kitchen woman."

Christians ordered out of Japan

Japan, 25 July 1587

Hideyoshi, the Japanese strongman, has banned Christianity and ordered the Jesuits to leave the country within twenty days. This move has come as a terrible shock to the missionaries, for only yesterday he went on board a Portuguese ship to talk to the vice-provincial, Gaspar Coelho.

He appeared in a friendly mood, but then in the middle of the night a messenger woke Coelho with an angry denunciation from him, accusing the Jesuits of selling Japanese as slaves and smashing Buddhist images. He demanded a reply. Coelho did his best, but was unable to turn aside Hideyoshi's anger.

Two Portuguese priests, as depicted on a Japanese screen in c.1600.

Fireships smash the Spanish Armada

The Armada, possibly by Nicholas Hilliard: the smaller English ships wrought havoc among the Spaniards.

England, 15 September 1588

The ragged remnants of the Armada that was to have humbled the English lie skulking in the harbours of Spain and Portugal today after the most humiliating naval defeat in Spain's history. Outgunned by the English, panicked by their fireships and battered by a raging south-westerly, the scattered fleet sailed north, seeking to escape into the Atlantic round the Orkneys and Shetlands. The disaster would have been even greater had not the pursuing English ships been forced to turn back when they ran out of food and ammunition.

Philip of Spain had intended to teach England a lesson. His colonies and his ships had suffered for years from the raids of Francis Drake, John Hawkins and other English privateers. Whenever the Spanish ambassador protested, Elizabeth was non committal and the raids continued. When Elizabeth was told of a huge fleet building up in Philip's ports, she allowed Drake to launch a spoiling operation. With 23 warships he descended on Cadiz, guns blazing, and captured or destroyed 80 ships.

The Armada, commanded by the duke of Medina Sidona, set sail in May 1588, and was sighted in the English Channel on 20 July. During the night, with the Spanish anchored in close battle formation, the English slipped past to the Spanish rear. The Spanish outnumbered them by two to one, with some ships of 1,000 tons, packed

A map by Robert Adam showing the two fleets off the English coast.

with soldiers with great grappling irons. But the English ships, though small, were highly manoeuvrable and superior in long-range gunfire.

By darting in, releasing their broadsides and escaping before the heavier Spanish cannon could be brought to bear, the English created havoc among the enemy, although they could make no impact on the stout Spanish hulls.

All afternoon and during the night following, the Armada pushed up the Channel, with the English snapping at its flanks. Medina Sidona was expecting to rendezvous with reinforcements and landing craft from the Spanish Netherlands. They never made it. Patrols of rebel Dutch "sea beg-

gars" saw to that. After a week of running fights, Medina Sidona anchored off Calais. The English, standing off a mile distant, were ready with fireships, stacked with wood, pitch and explosives. They went in at midnight, the raging forest of fire causing panic aboard the Spanish galleons. Ships collided and sank as anchors were abandoned and cables severed.

Daybreak found the fearsome Armada broken up and drifting. Now the English struck repeatedly. Some ships were sunk, others ran on to sandbanks, the rest fled. All told, the Spanish lost 65 ships and upwards of 10,000 men. The English lost fewer than 100 men and not one ship.

French king flees Catholic barricades

Paris, 12 May 1588

Henry III, foiled by the citizens of Paris in his armed attempt to expel the duke of Guise, has been humiliated and forced to flee from the city. A confrontation between the king and the people has been inevitable ever since Guise defied the king's orders and entered the city at the beginning of the month. Rumours swept the streets: the king intended to kill the duke; he was planning another massacre, this time of Catholics; he had hired eight hangmen.

This morning the city woke to the sound of drums as the king's men, supported by the Swiss guards, took up strategic positions. Irate crowds gathered, erected barricades in the streets and stationed *arquebusiers* behind them.

A shot rang out near the Pont St Michel and 60 soldiers died in the ensuing fracas. Milling crowds surrounded groups of isolated troops. Most of these cut-off detachments surrendered to cheering crowds. By nightfall it was obvious that the king's coup had failed.

Sex and war find thoughtful outlet

France, June 1588

The *Essays* of Michel Eyquem, the seigneur of Montaigne, have acquired an avid readership since they appeared in 1580, and a fourth, expanded, edition has just come out. Montaigne was born in 1533 and brought up to speak Latin as his first tongue. After university he was a magistrate in Bordeaux until he sold his post – a common practice – and retired, at 37, to his estate.

Apart from visits abroad in 1580-1 and two terms as mayor of Bordeaux (1581-5), Montaigne has passed his time in his library, where he writes down what he protests are the first thoughts to come into his head. A serene, basically conservative scepticism and tolerance of human diversity lie at the heart of his often profound and always thought-provoking *Essays*. He covers life from sex to war, and concludes that wisdom begins with the study of oneself.

Japan, 1588. Toyotomi Hideyoshi institutes a "sword hunt" in order to disarm the peasantry.

France, 5 January 1589. Catherine de Medici dies at Blois. She was born in Florence in 1519 and became queen of France as wife of King Henry II in 1547. Mother of the next three kings – Francis II, Charles IX and Henry III – she dominated French politics from her regency (1560-70) for the young Charles IX until her death.

Moscow, January 1589. Job, the metropolitan of Moscow, is promoted to the newly created post of patriarch by Boris Godunov (who became regent for the incompetent Czar Fyodor after the death of Ivan the Terrible three years ago). The patriarch of Moscow is fifth in rank after that of Jerusalem.

Istanbul, January 1589. The independence of the Russian church is formally ratified by an ecumenical synod.

West Africa, March 1589. A Moroccan army under al-Mansur sets out across the Sahara to invade the kingdom of Songhai.

France, 3 April 1589. King Henry III and King Henry of Navarre are reconciled after sensitive negotiations.

Spain, July 1589. Pedro Menendez Marques persuades the Spanish authorities to agree to his plan to sail from Havana to Virginia and destroy the English settlement.

France, 2 August 1589. Henry III, the last Valois king, dies after being stabbed by Jacques Clement, a fanatical Dominican friar. The Protestant King Henry of Navarre becomes King Henry IV.

France, 21 September 1589. The duke of Mayenne, the brother of Henry of Guise and successor to him as the head of the Catholic League, is defeated at the battle of Arques by Henry IV.

Portugal, 1589. After a failed attempt to reconquer Portugal from the Azores in 1583, Antonio of Crato again lands in the country and marches on Lisbon. In spite of English support he is defeated by the Spaniards.

Portugal, 1589. English merchants are expelled from the kingdom.

Brazil, 1589. A supreme tribunal is created in the capital, Bahia, allowing some administrative arrangements to be transferred from Portugal to Brazil.

France, 14 March 1590. King Henry IV inflicts another defeat on the Catholic League under the duke of Mayenne, at Ivry.

Spain, April 1590. Antonio Perez, a former secretary of state and close adviser to Philip II, escapes from Madrid, where he has been confined for almost a decade, and finds refuge in Aragon. He was arrested in July 1579 after organising the murder of Juan de Escobedo, a councillor of Don John of Austria, who had been threatening to reveal Perez' involvement in political intrigue.

Mexico, 27 July 1590. Castana de Sosa sets out from Nueva Leon with 150 settlers in an unauthorised effort to establish a mining town in New Mexico.

France, September 1590. Alexander Farnese, the duke of Parma – who, as governor of the Spanish Netherlands, captured Antwerp in 1585 – forces King Henry IV to lift the siege of Paris.

France, 1590. Refusing to recognise Henry IV as king, the Catholic party declares the cardinal of Bourbon king under the name of Charles X.

West Africa, 1590. The second Jaga war breaks out in Zaire, caused by Portuguese slave trading on the Angola coast.

Japan, 1590. Toyotomi Hideyoshi completes the political unification of Japan under his rule. His powerful vassal Tokugawa Ieyasu moves his administrative and military base to Edo (*Tokyo*), a strategic position for the domination of the great plain of eastern Japan.

Rome, 1590. Pope Sixtus V, who has worked on the edition of the Vulgate known as the *Sixtus*, declares it the official text for the Catholic Bible. Produced by St Jerome in the fourth century AD, this translation of the Bible was recognised as authentic by the Council of Trent.

Italy, 1590. The composer Claudio Monteverdi publishes a collection of madrigals.

Portugal, 1590. Seeking to attack Spain, an English fleet under the leadership of Francis Drake and Sir John Norris makes an unsuccessful attempt to disembark at Lisbon.

Near East, 1590. Abbas, shah of Persia since 1587, concludes a peace treaty with the Ottoman sultan, Murad III, ending a war which began in 1578. Under the treaty the Turks acquire Georgia, Azerbaijan and Shirwan, thus extending their frontiers to the Caucasus and the Caspian.

India, 1590. Mohammed Quli Qutb Shah, the sultan of Golconda, founds the town of Hyderabad on the banks of the river Musi.

Japanese sword hunt disarms peasants

Hideyoshi: cracking down on civilian sword-bearers (painting on silk).

Japan, 1588
Hideyoshi, the regent of Japan, has ordered a "sword hunt" designed to confiscate the weapons held by civilians. He has cloaked the purpose of the hunt by claiming that the weapons are needed to provide the metal for the Great Image of the Buddha being built for the new Hokoji monastery in Kyoto.

The peasants whose weapons are taken are told their sacrifice will assure them of salvation. But the real reason is to disarm "peasants who keep needless weapons, do not pay their taxes and plot risings against landlords".

In fact, the order is two-edged. It disarms trouble-makers and distinguishes civilians from soldiers. It also provides a way to seize the weapons of the soldier-monks of the turbulent monasteries of Koyasan and Hieizan.

Queen's godson becomes closet inventor

England, 1589
Sir John Harington, the so-called "saucy godson" of Queen Elizabeth, has not wasted his time since his banishment from the court for telling risque stories in front of the ladies.

In the splendid mansion which he has built at Kelston, in Somerset, he has installed what is probably the world's first toilet which can be flushed from an overhead tank. Welcome though such an innovation must be, there is little hope that it will be widely adopted, as human waste will still have to be collected and disposed of manually.

In country districts it can be spread on the land, but in towns it presents a considerable problem. It has to go somewhere, and even a flushing toilet may create health hazards, especially if the waste seeps into rivers and ponds.

Fanatical monk stabs Henry III to death

Paris, 2 August 1589

Henry III, the last of the Valois kings of France, was stabbed to death today by Jacques Clement, a fanatical Dominican monk. So France's bloody religious wars claim one more noble victim. Last December the king had the duke of Guise and his brother, the cardinal of Guise, assassinated.

After these killings the Catholic League declared the Guises' brother, the duke of Mayenne, to be lieutenant-governor of the realm. But Henry will be succeeded by King Henry of Navarre, his ally against the Catholic League, who has a distant claim to the throne, and, more importantly, has his main rival, the ageing cardinal of Bourbon – the league's candidate for the throne – in custody.

The assassination of Henry III (centre), and the fate of his killer.

Starving Chinese grind stones for bread

China, 1588

Famine and pestilence are sweeping China, and whole provinces are being depopulated as villages are wiped out by hunger and the diseases that come with starvation and foul sanitary conditions.

Drought has brought such famine that people are eating goose droppings and cannibalism is rife. There are unbroken lines of beggars at the gruel kitchens. Children are being abandoned and infants killed. Some peasants, having stripped the countryside of anything growing, are grinding stones into flour.

With their resistance to disease lowered by hunger, the people are falling prey to the diseases that lurk in their filthy homes, especially in the towns where the houses crowd together surrounded by excrement and filth. Epidemics follow one upon the other. "Big Head" fever, in which the head and neck swell up, is currently rampant.

So many people are dying in the southern capital it is said that if you count a bean for every coffin going out of the south gate you will be counting by the pint. In Honan more than half the population has died.

The situation is made worse by the increase in banditry. Starving peasants have become robbers. The rice boats are being attacked on the rivers, and the soldiers sent against the robbers are themselves starving and living off the country. All these factors have led to a catastrophic decline in population.

Amsterdam is refugee capital of Europe

Amsterdam, c.1589

Amsterdam is fast establishing itself as the refugee capital of Europe. Religious toleration was written into the Union of Utrecht (1579), and in return for its generosity the city is gaining an unrivalled access to the world's most profitable trading networks.

Among the most conspicuous refugees are the Sephardic Jews, many of whom are successful merchants. Their forebears were expelled from Spain and then Portugal a century ago, and wandered abroad looking for a permanent.

Some moved to Moslem countries, where they were tolerated, while others preferred the new Protestant nations of Europe, where the Inquisition, which had spearheaded the persecution of the Jews, was not permitted. Their wealth, their business abilities and their wide-ranging contacts have made them very welcome settlers.

Tree-wielding peasants beat samurai

China, 17 January 1588

Qi Jiguang, the greatest of Ming generals, died today destitute and in disgrace. It was Qi who was given the task of clearing the coast of Japanese pirates who landed in their thousands from fleets of junks and even set up civil administrations complete with courts.

The Ming army had been neglected in the long years of peace. Its weapons were out of date, its supply system non-existent, and the troops had no idea of battlefield tactics. Faced by the fearsome Japanese *samurai* wielding two-edged razorsharp swords, they ran away.

Qi set about rebuilding the army. He recruited peasants for their strength and stolidity, and created a new concept of war. He formed them into squads consisting of lancers, javelin throwers, and strong-armed men carrying bamboo trees complete with their upper branches. Their function was to block the flashing swords of the samurai so that the lancers could deal with them. It was a tactic of

Samurai armour; the helmet dates from 1532, the rest from c.1750.

beautiful simplicity. Qi's "tree-men" defeated the pirates. Alas, he was implicated in the disgrace of Tutor Zhang and was dismissed by the Emperor Wan-li.

"Tolerant" empire thrives under Akbar

Fatehpur Sikri, Central India, 1589

After 33 years as the Moghul emperor, Akbar controls half of India. In battle his army has conquered the Rajputs, Gujarat, Bengal and Kashmir, and is still unbeaten. In his provincial capitals a streamlined bureaucracy collects taxes and rules with moderation. In his empire men of all religions, and of none, are treated with equal respect. His greatest triumph was first the defeat and then the co-option of the Rajputs, India's warriors, who are now the policemen of his empire.

Like his audience chamber in the palace at Fatehpur Sikri – where he sits on a central pillar surrounded by his ministers sitting in a circular gallery – his empire revolves around him. Having elevated himself into demi-god, with Sunni, Shi'ite and Hindu wives, he has succeeded in securing the loyalty of all his subjects. New cities are being built all over India. Akbar's own illiteracy does not stop him founding schools throughout his empire. Assisted by his ministers Raja Todar Mal and Shah Mansur, he has reformed the taxation system and

Akbar giving audience, from the work called "Akbarnama", c.1590.

established a new bureaucracy, with 33 grades; officials are being moved every two years so that they have an imperial, rather than a provincial, mentality and cannot develop a local following.

1590 (1590-1591)

Persia, 1590. Abbas, the shah of Persia, who is already responsible for the execution of many important tribal leaders, gives orders for his own father and brothers to be blinded.

Japan, 1590. More christian missionaries arrive in Japan with the returning envoys who were sent to Rome eight years ago.

Rome, 1590. The vast cupola of St Peter's basilica is completed to Michelangelo's designs.

Italy, 1590. The physician and mathematician Giovanni Battista Benedetti dies in Turin. Educated by the mathematician Tartaglia, Benedetti attacked Aristotelian dynamics, arguing that in a vacuum all things should fall at the same time.

Virginia, 17 August 1590. John White, the governor of Roanoke Island, returns to America from Europe to find the settlement mysteriously abandoned. One theory is that the colonists followed the Indians under Chief Manteo to the native village called Croatoan, which would be safer than the original settlement site.

Rome, 27 August 1590. Sixtus V, pope since 1585, dies. An energetic Franciscan of humble origins, he reorganised the papal curia and regularly visited bishops to make sure they were disciplined. In foreign policy he aimed to combat Protestantism and maintain the balance of the Catholic powers.

Rome, 1590. After the death of Sixtus V, two popes rapidly succeed each other on the throne of St Peter. The Roman Cestagna dies on 27 September, after reigning for only 13 days. He is followed by Sfondrati from Milan, who takes the name Gregory XIV.

Germany, 3 February 1591. The German Protestant princes form the League of Torgau to counter the Catholic threat.

Germany, 17 March 1591. The painter Jost Amman, who is also renowned for his wood engravings, is buried at Nuremberg.

West Africa, 25 April 1591. The troops of Ahmad al-Mansur, the sultan of Morocco, led by the Spanish renegade Jaudhar, launch a successful attempt to capture Timbuktu.

Russia, 15 May 1591. The epileptic czarevitch Dimitri Ivanovitch, son of Ivan the Terrible, is assassinated. The regent, Boris Godunov, is suspected of being behind the killing.

Mexico, August 1591. Arrested in New Mexico, Castana de Sosa is brought back to Mexico to face disobedience charges.

Spain, 23 August 1591. The writer and mystic Luis de Leon dies as he is about to be named vicar-general of the Augustinians in Castile. He entered the Augustinian order in 1544 and taught theology at Salamanca, where he was imprisoned by the Inquisition in 1572, accused of heresy. In his work *Of the names of Christ* he defined 13 descriptions attached to the name and person of Jesus.

Rome, August 1591. Pope Gregory XIV dies ten months after his election.

Spain, 1 November 1591. A law is passed integrating the Inca feudal system in Peru into the Spanish system of rule. The king of Spain and his viceroy become the successors of the Inca rulers.

Paris, 15 November 1591. Barnabe Brisson, the president of the Parliament of Paris, is executed by the populist League of Sixteen because he is suspected of being unsympathetic. The killing is part of a reign of terror recently initiated by the league.

Spain, 14 December 1591. The Spanish reformist monk Juan de Yepes, known as John of the Cross, dies at the convent of Ubeda. The author of mystical treatises, he also wrote poems, including the *Spiritual Canticle*, which count among the masterpieces of the age. Up to the end of his life he was a victim of betrayals and persecution.

South-East Asia, 1591. James Lancaster becomes the first Englishman to sail to the East Indies.

Italy, 1591. The Italian traveller Pigafetta publishes an account of customs in the Kongo kingdom (*Angola*) of central Africa.

Spain, 1591. In response to a rebellion over the affair of his adviser Antonio Perez, Philip II enters Aragon with an army and abolishes the province's constitutional privileges. Prosecuted for heresy by the Inquisition at Philip's instigation, Perez was freed by a rioting mob in Saragossa and has now fled the country.

Rome, 1591. Elected pope on the death of Gregory XIV, Facchinetti of Bologna, who took the name Innocent IX, reigns for only two months.

Rome, 1591. Pier Paolo Olivieri begins work on the nave of Sant' Andrea della Valle, a fine monument to the spirit of the Counter-reformation.

Japan, 1591. Sen no Rikyu, the celebrated tea-master who was formerly a favourite of Toyotomi Hideyoshi, is forced to commit suicide by Hideyoshi.

Vatican welcomes Japanese Jesuits

Rome, 1590
Four Japanese Jesuits have set sail for their homeland after spending nearly eight years in Rome. Well-born young men, they were warmly greeted by Philip II in Madrid, and Pope Gregory XIII welcomed them to Rome with a brilliant ceremony. Resplendent in Japanese costume, they rode in procession on fine horses to the Vatican where they kissed the pope's foot and were affectionately embraced by him.

Their mission was a great success for the Jesuits, who were granted the sole right to evangelise Japan. The young men were, however, delayed in their return because of the death of Gregory. It is feared that they may be sailing into danger, for Christianity may have fallen into disfavour during their long absence.

Death of pope who modernised Rome

Rome, 27 August 1590
Pope Sixtus V is dead. In his short reign of only five years he has transformed the appearance of this city. The jumble of old houses has been cleared to make space for broad avenues and squares with splendid vistas. He erected an obelisk in St Peter's Square and built a new aqueduct and many fountains.

He encouraged a revival of art with richly decorated frescoes and sculptures. He had a library and a new palace built in the Vatican. He encouraged cardinals and congregations to rebuild their own churches. He used art and architecture to encourage personal piety and religious mass emotion. He was also politically effective, and resisted the overwhelming power and ambition of Philip II of Spain.

Surgeon who soothed wounds of war dies

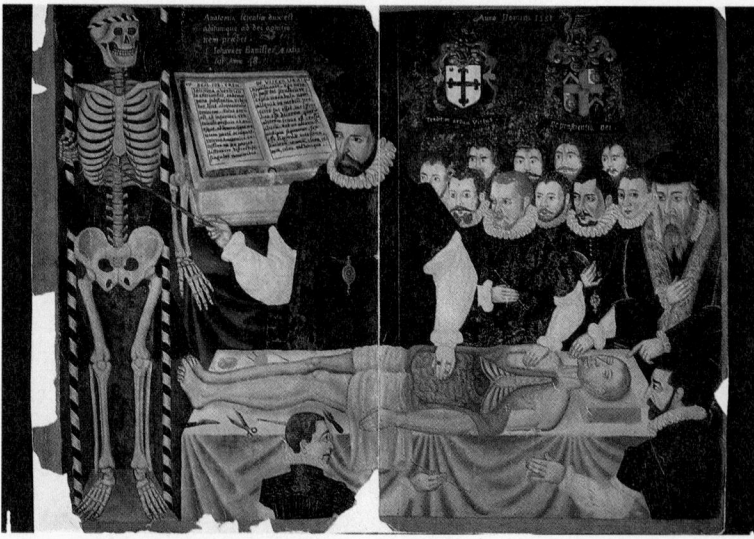

An anatomy lesson: Ambroise Pare has won wide respect for his techniques.

France, 20 December 1590
Ambroise Pare, one of the most enterprising and successful of modern surgeons, who has been credited with bringing surgery into a new era, has died in Paris at the age of 89.

A specialist in the treatment of wounds, he made many of his most far-reaching innovations on the battlefields of Europe. A master-surgeon at the age of 36, Pare followed his noble employers onto the battlefield. Here he developed new methods of treating wounds, setting bones and nursing men back to health. His most notable breakthrough was to treat wounds not by cauterising them in boiling oil, as had been traditional, but by tying off arteries and applying soothing lotions.

Between battles Pare kept a shop and wrote a book, *The Method of Treating Wounds*. He never read the classical physicians, but his surgical skills proved his excellence. He became a doctor of medicine in 1554, writing his thesis in French, not the usual Latin.

Raleigh's New World colony deserted

Virginia, New England, 1590

Three years ago, English pioneers on the windswept island of Roanoke (*off the coast of what is now North Carolina*) celebrated the birth of the first colonial baby. Since then she and 100 other souls of this little community have vanished, leaving no sign of violence and only one clue to what happened: the word "Croatoan" – the name of an Indian tribe – carved on a post at the entrance to the empty palisade.

The macabre disappearance of Roanoke colony was discovered on 17 August when John White, the governor, returned with two ships. The baby – named Virginia after the infant colony – was his granddaughter.

It is six years since a party of English sailors landed on the neighbouring mainland to claim possession of almost 2,000 miles of American coastline. They were led by Arthur Barlow and Philip Amadas commanding two ships which crossed the Atlantic before stopping at Puerto Rico and Florida.

They were made especially welcome at Roanoke, where Chief Wingina made gifts of meat, fish and other food. As Barlow put it: "We were entertained with all love and kindness and with as much bounty, after their manner, as they could possibly devise. We found the people most gentle, loving and faithful, void of all guile and treason, and such as lived after the manner of the Golden Age."

Two years later the explorer Walter Raleigh was knighted for his initial discovery of the territory, though he ran the Barlow expedition from England for political reasons. He also won royal permission to name the new territory on the eastern seaboard "Virginia" in honour of the "Virgin Queene".

In spite of repeated efforts, the colony has not fared well. Five years ago Sir Richard Greville put 108 settlers ashore without enough food. Their hunger led to hostility with the Indians. After a year, in June 1586, they were rescued by Drake. Greville put another 15 men ashore a few days later. A few months after that, when White put his 100 ashore, there was no sign of Greville's 15 settlers.

Woman and child, by John White.

Native chief, also by White, c.1585.

The native village of Pomiock, a watercolour by John White done in 1587.

Mysterious death of Ivan's last son

Moscow, 15 May 1591

One of Ivan the Terrible's two sons, the nine-year-old epileptic Dimitri, has been found murdered, his throat cut by a gang of hired killers. No arrests have been made, but rumours are widespread that the man responsible for the prince's death is the powerful aristocratic *boyar* Boris Godunov. Godunov has been effectively acting as regent for Czar Fyodor, the younger son of Ivan, an amiable and pious imbecile. Dimitri and his mother, Ivan's seventh and last wife, had been exiled to Uglitch where they may have served as a tool for disaffected boyars anxious to unseat Godunov. The boy was the logical successor to his brother, and this is behind the rumours that Godunov engineered the murder.

Blood flows freely in Angola anarchy

Angola, 1591

Angola is in anarchy. Coastal states are tearing each other apart on the instigation of Catholic missionaries. Portuguese adventurers are using slave warriors to carve out private kingdoms. There is famine, and a new European menace is penetrating deeper into the interior of central Africa: the Atlantic slave trade.

The horrors began in 1561 when Portugal tried to impose its own choice, Affonso, as king of the Kongo. There was a *coup d'etat*; Affonso's brother, Bernardo, took over and some Portuguese were killed. By 1566 Bernardo was dead and the weakened kingdom was invaded by the Jaga, a hard inland people, migrating in their thousands towards the Altantic. No one is in control and missionaries and traders raise mercenary armies. For 30 years the blood has not ceased to flow.

"Rich hill" spawns city of wantonness

Peru, 1591

Potosi, 28 years ago a miserable, windswept hamlet, has burgeoned into an "imperial city" of 130,000 people, bigger than Paris or Madrid. Twelve years ago Judge Matienzo noted the wantonness of the city, with its 34 casinos, 800 gamblers, 120 prostitutes and 14 dance academies as well as 36 lavish churches. The secret of Potosi's wealth is the local silver mountain, the *Cerro Rico*, or rich hill, from which tons of bullion are mined for Spain each year. Some streets are supposedly paved with silver bars and horses shod with the metal. But the mining environment is anything but luxurious: the thin air at an altitude of 14,000 feet, the bitter cold and the notorious roaring wind. The hard work is done almost exclusively by Indians, and the mine-owners are so politically powerful that some are even ready to challenge Madrid's representative in Peru. It is 45 years since Spain's first viceroy, Blasco Nunez Vela, died suppressing the mine-owners' first rebellion.

1591 (1591-1593)

Atlantic, 1591. A Spanish fleet defeats an English fleet off the Azores. Sir Richard Grenville is killed in the heroic fight of the *Revenge*.

England, 1591. The playwright William Shakespeare writes *Henry VI*, an historical drama in three parts, each consisting of five acts. Shakespeare takes his framework from the *Chronicles of England, Scotland and Ireland* by Raphael Holinshed, who died in 1580.

London, 1591. The publication of the second in a series of *Voyages* by Theodor de Bry is a huge success. The book features engravings of Florida Indians based on paintings by Jacques de Magne de Morgues, who lived with the French Huguenots at Fort Caroline until it was destroyed by the Spanish in 1565. He depicts monstrous reptiles, called alligators, and savages with tattoos all over their bodies. There are scenes of terrible executions and barbarous rites.

France, 1591. Francis Viete, a mathematician and privy counsellor to King Henry IV, publishes a treatise on algebra entitled *The Art of Analysis*. His is the first work to use letters to represent mathematical unknowns or indeterminates.

Ireland, 1591. Queen Elizabeth founds Trinity College, Dublin.

Rome, 30 January 1592. Cardinal Ippoliti Aldobrandini is elected pope in succession to Innocent IX and takes the name Clement VIII. He sets about amending the Vulgate Bible, promulgated two years ago by Pope Sixtus V, to produce a definitive version.

Italy, 13 February 1592. The painter Jacopo da Ponte, known as Bassano after his native town, dies. After moving to Venice over 40 years ago, he abandoned the forms and colours of mannerism and painted with a realism in which the effects of light predominate.

Florence, 22 April 1592. The sculptor and architect Bartolomeo Ammannati dies. He worked on the Pitti Palace and conceived the bridge of Santa Trinita and the fountain of Neptune on the Piazza delle Signorie.

France, 13 September 1592. Michel Eyquem de Montaigne dies. From a line of rich merchants, Montaigne studied law and became a member of the Bordeaux parliament. He was deeply affected by the death, in 1563, of his friend Etienne de la Boetie, with whom he was linked by a "marriage of souls". In 1571 he sold his parliamentary seat and retired to Montaigne in the Perigord, where he composed his *Essays*.

Sweden, 27 November 1592. John III, the king of Sweden, dies and is succeeded by his son Sigismund, king of Poland since 1587.

Italy, 3 December 1592. Alexander Farnese, the duke of Parma, who recovered the southern provinces of the Netherlands for the Spanish crown in 1579, dies.

West Africa, 1592. Djouder captures the Songhai capital, Gao.

Korea, 1592. When the government of Korea refuses Toyotomi Hideyoshi's trade terms, the Japanese leader invades Korea and battles with the Korean army with resounding initial successes. The Japanese General Konishi captures the castle at Pusan.

India, 1592. The Emperor Akbar's troops annex Orissa.

France, 1592. A violent peasant rebellion, known as the Revolt of the Croquants, breaks out in south-western France in protest at heavy taxes on the peasantry. It is met with savage repression.

Pacific, 1592. Juan de Fuca claims to have travelled through a north-west passage to the northern Pacific Ocean.

France, 6 February 1593. The classical scholar Jacques Amyot, tutor to the children of Henry II, dies. His translations of *Parallel Lives* and *Moral Works* introduced Plutarch to his contemporaries, in particular Montaigne.

Paris, February 1593. The estates-general, France's parliament, meets for the first time since 1576, under the auspices of the Catholic League, which holds Paris. The assembly – which has hitherto always met in Rheims – calls for a Catholic king of France.

England, 30 June 1593. The dramatist Christopher Marlowe dies in an argument in a tavern at Deptford near London at the age of 29. His rebellious and fevered spirit speaks through his tragedies: *Tamburlaine* (1587), a fierce indictment of ambition; *The Tragedy of Dr Faustus* (1588), in which he affirms his belief in supernatural forces; *The Jew of Malta* (1589), a denunciation of the power of money; and *Edward II* (1592), a tragedy of human impotence.

Milan, 11 July 1593. Giuseppe Arcimboldo, who was court painter to the Emperors Ferdinand and Rudolf II, dies. He is famous for his extraordinary compositions of vegetables, fruits and flowers arranged to resemble human forms.

France, 25 July 1593. King Henry IV abjures Protestantism and becomes a Roman Catholic.

Morocco seeks gold south of the Sahara

Timbuktu, 1592

Morocco, a major power after its army slaughtered 26,000 Portuguese at Alcazar el Kebir, has invaded Songhai. The 4,000-strong Moroccan army of Andalucian mercenaries and Christian renegades, with 8,000 camels, and arms supplied by Elizabeth of England, has crossed the Sahara. Twice it has defeated the Songhai army, first at Tondibi, near the capital Gao, then at Bamba near Timbuktu.

For Morocco's sultan, Mulai Ahmed al-Mansur (the Victorious), the goal is not territory but gold. The first task of his army was to occupy the mines at Taghaza, in the middle of the Sahara, where salt is hewed and traded for gold in Black Africa. On the Moroccans' approach the miners fled and the mine is now closed, a major blow to Moroccan ambition.

In spite of the victories the campaign is a failure. The occupiers are confronted by scorched earth, Gao is deserted, there is no gold to be found, and everywhere Moroccans are being harried by guerrillas.

Venetian Rialto bridge rebuilt in stone

Venice's Rialto bridge over the Grand Canal, by Canaletto (1697-1768).

Venice, 1591

The Rialto bridge, linking the banks of the Grand Canal at the Fondaco dei Tedeschi, has been completed. Functional rather than artistically pleasing, it is a single span, 52 yards long and 24 wide, with two rows of shops dividing it into three corridors.

When the decision was taken to replace the old wooden bridge with one made of stone, a competition was declared which attracted some of Italy's most distinguished architects. Designs were submitted by Michelangelo, Sansovino, Vignola, Scamozzi and Palladio before the job was entrusted to Antonio da Ponte, who had rebuilt the doges' palace.

Armoured ship smashes Japanese fleet

Korea, 1592

An iron-plated and turtle-backed ship developed here heralds a new phase in the history of marine warfare technology. This is the first ship to be build with an "armour" cladding of iron and it was recently used with spectacular success by Admiral Yi-sun-sin in his struggle against the Japanese. Japan's fleet was almost wiped out within a matter of days of the armoured ship's deployment.

The new warship presents a formidable sight, with rows of gleaming spikes, a battering ram at the prow and archery ports for firing arrows.

French king hears Mass for sake of Paris

Paris, 25 July 1593

King Henry IV of France today rejected Protestantim and was received into the Catholic religion. The ceremony took place in the basilica of St Denis and was witnessed by the archbishop of Beaune.

Then, having made his confession and heard Mass, he swore allegiance to the church, reiterated his renunciation of Protestantism, and received absolution. He left the basilica to the cheers of the Parisian crowd which sees in his transformation the promise of an end to the religious wars which have ravaged France for so long.

This is the second time that Henry has abjured his faith; the first time was during the St Bartholomew's Day massacre when he did so to save his life and afterwards recanted. This time it is with the hard-won knowledge that he would never be recognised as the

Henry IV: his rule spells an end to years of French religious strife.

true king of France without becoming a Catholic. As he looked down on the city from the hill of Montmartre today he said: "Paris is worth a Mass."

Galileo's thermometer is boon to science

Italy, 1592

The Italian scientist Galileo has invented a device for measuring temperature. It works on a principle known long ago to the Greeks of Alexandria – namely that air expands as it is heated.

Galileo's device has one important feature which sets it above previous attempts. It has a scale etched on it. The "thermometer" consists of a small glass bulb at the top of a thin glass tube containing water. As the air in the bulb is warmed it expands and pushes down on the water in the tube. The level then drops.

With this thermometer the fertile Galileo has given his fellow-scientists a truly scientific measuring instrument.

Galileo's thermometer (model).

Sex scenes arouse trouble for new novel

China, 1593

A long, complex, sophisticated and, some would say, pornographic novel is being passed round the literary world. It is titled *Jin Ping Mei*, or the Plum in the Golden Vase; its author hides his identity under the nom de plume of "The Laughing Scholar of Lan-ling". The book tells the story of a family caught up in the collapse of the Sung dynasty. It is enormously complicated and requires re-reading before its subtle allegories can be fully appreciated.

The anonymous author sets new standards in technical virtuosity, but his explicit descriptions of the sexual act may inhibit a proper critical assessment of his writing.

Queen takes hard line with parliament

England, 27 February 1593

After 35 years on the throne of England, Elizabeth has felt it necessary to remind MPs of her right to "assent to or dissent from anything done in parliament". She has also let it be known that she does not wish MPs to seek to override her in foreign and religious affairs.

The queen has taken action as two new statutes are about to come before MPs. One will heavily increase the fines for Catholics who refuse to attend Church of England services, as required by law; the other will make it a crime to attend Catholic assemblies for worship.

In recent years, Elizabeth, backed by her chief minister Lord Burghley, has found it increasingly difficult to get on with her parliaments. In 1558, on her accession, England was in turmoil after Mary's attempt to reimpose Roman authority over the English church; at the same time the threat of invasion and subjugation by Spain was looming.

There was a dire need for stability and unity, and Elizabeth

William Cecil, Lord Burghley, Elizabeth's secretary of state.

offered to provide them in co-operation with parliament which gave her support in return. The notion, emerging even under her father Henry VIII, that the sovereign power in the land was the "Monarch-in-Parliament" was strengthened. Now England's newly-prosperous middle classes are represented in parliament and asserting themselves.

Artist and practical joker dies at court

Man of vegetables: "Summer", from the school of Arcimboldo (1527-93).

Prague, 11 July 1593

Giuseppe Arcimboldo, the master of the revels of Emperor Rudolf and his trusted friend has died at court. He was also known especially for his deceptive portraits. He could paint a collection of books to look like the face of a librarian, and would make up portraits out of animals or a tree-trunk and its branches. He painted one portrait of the emperor himself entirely out of vegetables.

Arcimboldo came from Milan. Rudolf's court is a haven for eccentrics, astrologers and alchemists, as well as astronomers like Johann Kepler and Tycho Brahe.

Japan and the outside world

The arrival of Europeans in Japan in the mid 16th century was not greeted with hostility, nor was their later persecution the result merely of xenophobia. In fact, Japan was never as generally hostile to the outside world as is often believed, and closed its doors, on the whole, only when it felt its internal security or stability under threat. For instance, official relations between Japan and China were reestablished in 1401, having been at a standstill since the failed Chinese invasion attempts of the 13th century. Occasional exchanges of ambassadors took place until 1434, but subsequently lapsed, for the relationship meant different things to Japan and to China: the Ming court in China aimed to secure Japan's acceptance of Ming supremacy and its cooperation against piracy, while in Japan it was the potential for trade, particularly in luxury goods from China, that was the most compelling objective.

Broader horizons

The prospect of trade took the Japanese further afield in the 16th and early 17th centuries. Japanese settlements were established in the Philippines, the Malay Peninsula and Indochina. One of the largest settlements was in Siam (Thailand): a Japanese called Yamada Nagamasa (who died in 1633) even rose to high office as an adviser to the king in Ayuthia, the Siamese capital. These years of unaccustomed overseas expansion culminated in 1592 in the invasion of Korea under the Japanese leader Hideyoshi. Grand plans to conquer China ended in an ignominious withdrawal in 1598, but this marked Japan's first serious attempt to resist China's claims to hegemony in eastern Asia and to impose Japanese order on China, rather than vice-versa.

Japan's overseas contacts by this time were not, however, limited to its Asian neighbours. Relations with Europe had begun in 1542, when three Portuguese arrived in a Chinese junk at the island of Tanegashima, south of Kyushu. They were an immediate sensation owing to the miraculous equipment they had with them – muskets. They sold them for an exorbitant sum to the local warlord and, owing to the technical skills of Japanese swordsmiths, Japanese gunsmiths were at work within ten years producing their own, home-produced muskets, before long even improving on the imported models. At the battle of Nagashino in 1575 muskets proved their value for the first time to the Japanese, and thenceforward no credible army could be without a substantial body of musketeers.

The Portuguese vessels that came to Japan in the later 1540s brought missionaries and traders. The warlords of western Kyushu, the part of Japan closest to the Portuguese base of Macao, welcomed the traders for the guns and other artifacts they had to offer, and since the traders evidently respected the missionaries, they welcomed them as well. In 1549 St Francis Xavier reached Japan; he struggled with the Japanese language, made the acquaintance of several powerful figures, and left after two years. By 1570 there were some 20 Jesuit fathers in Japan and the Jesuit mission there was well established.

In the 1580s Hideyoshi treated the Jesuits with interest and friendship. He helped them to establish a church near the new castle which he had built at Osaka; he made no protests when some of his generals, his advisers and even his court ladies became Christians; he even indicated to a visiting senior Jesuit in 1586 that Japan could become a Christian country once China was in his grasp. There were already about 200,000 Christians in Japan and the number was continuing to rise.

The Christians under attack

In 1587 Hideyoshi suddenly and inexplicably ordered the expulsion of all missionaries. This edict was not enforced, though some Jesuits went into hiding, and Hideyoshi made it clear that he had no quarrel with the Portuguese merchants, but it was the beginning of the end. It seems likely that Hideyoshi had come to fear the political influence of Christianity: after all, although he had almost made himself master of Japan, the Jesuits would never be under his control. For the next decade Hideyoshi tolerated the Christian presence in Japan, but in 1597 he again took action: seven Spanish Franciscans and 19 of their Japanese followers were crucified at Nagasaki. Hideyoshi died in 1598, and for a couple of years the Christians enjoyed a respite.

In 1600 Dutch traders reached Japan along with an Englishman, Will Adams. The Dutch East India Company subsequently established a trading post in Japan, and Adams served Tokugawa Ieyasu, the new master of Japan, as an adviser on navigation and shipbuilding; before long there was even an English trading post in Japan, run by Richard Cocks, but he had difficulty in making a profit and it was abandoned in 1623. In 1611 and again in 1614 Ieyasu issued edicts for the extirpation of Christianity in Japan: churches were destroyed and high-ranking Japanese Christians were exiled to the Philippines. No foreign missionaries were put to death, however, and the traders continued to be welcome.

In the 1620s, under Ieyasu's successor as *shogun*, large numbers of Japanese Christians, and missionaries too, were executed, and in the 1630s a number of steps were taken to bring Japan's foreign relations under tighter control. Japanese ships were prohibited from making voyages abroad; Japanese who had lived abroad or who sought to go abroad were to be put to death; and all feudal lords were told to ensure that Christianity was not practised in their fiefs. In 1636, all foreigners were ordered to move to Deshima, a small island off Nagasaki, where they continued to trade under surveillance.

The Shimabara Revolt in western Kyushu in 1637-38 was taken by the shogun to be proof of the disloyalty of Japanese Christians, and led to the edict of 1639 prohibiting Portuguese vessels from approaching Japanese ports on pain of death. This threatened to curtail Portuguese trading activities, and a Portuguese mission from Macao reached Japan in 1640 in the hope of persuading the shogun to reconsider: the ship was burnt and 57 of the mission were beheaded. The remaining 13 were spared to carry the news back to Macao.

The rigour with which the Japanese government pursued the policies of excluding the Portuguese from contact with Japan and extirpating Christianity can be attributed to the overriding desire of the Tokugawa shoguns to establish an era of domestic stability after two centuries of internecine strife. Christianity was seen as a threat to that stability because of the divided loyalties of Japanese Christians, and the Shimabara Revolt seemed to provide confirmation of that threat.

Japan leaves the door open

However, Japan did not cut itself off entirely from the outside world. Contacts with Korea and the island kingdom of the Ryukus (south of Japan) were maintained and even used to bolster the legitimacy of the Tokugawa regime. Furthermore, the Dutch remained at Deshima from 1641 until the opening of Japan in the mid 19th century. Knowledge of Japan seeped through Deshima to the west, and the Dutch there were required to submit annual reports on European affairs. In the 18th century a school of learning developed in Japan called *Rangaku*, (Dutch studies), encompassing western science and medicine and any other branch of knowledge the Dutch in Nagasaki Bay could pass on. Japan was by no means as ignorant of the west as Commodore Perry and Admiral Putyatin expected when they arrived to end Japanese seclusion in 1853.

The bustling and prosperous city of Kyoto, the Japanese capital, in the early 17th-century, vividly depicted on a painted screen.

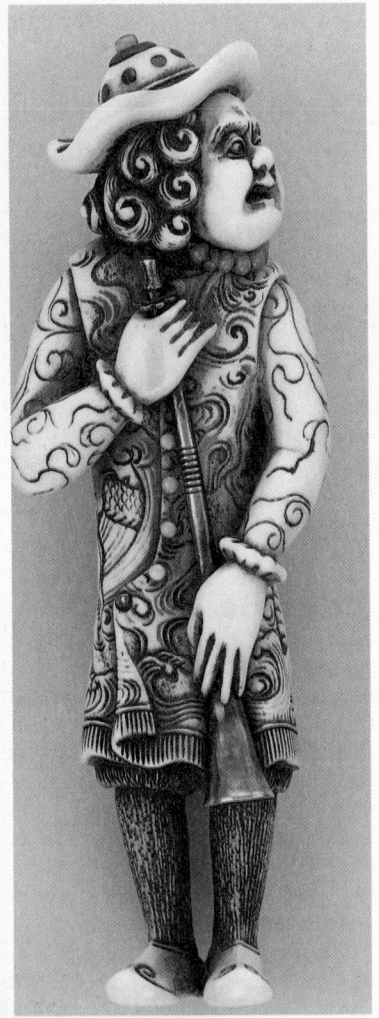

An ivory "netsuke", or toggle, of a Dutch musician in late 17th century dress. Kyoto school, 18th century.

Detail from a Japanese screen depicting Portuguese traders and Jesuit fathers. The Portuguese were the first Europeans to foster trade with Japan; three of them arrived on a Chinese junk on an island south of Kyushu in 1542 and sold their muskets to a local warlord. Other Europeans were to follow.

1593 (1593-1595)

Sweden, 1593. The Diet of Uppsala adopts the Augsburg Confession of 1530, imposing on King Sigismund the continuation of Lutheranism as the state religion.

North America, 1593. A Spanish expedition under Francisco de Levya Bonilla and Antonio Gutierez de Humana to find the "gold mines of Tindan" is massacred by Indians (*in Kansas*).

England, 1593. Parliament passes stringent new legislation aimed at curbing religious dissenters. Protestant separatists who establish self-governing congregations outside the Church of England are to be punished by prison terms as well as fines.

England, 1593. Charged with the authorship of the Marprelate tracts – extreme Puritan attacks on the Anglican bishops – John Penry is convicted of treason and hanged. Penry, a Welsh Puritan, had earlier written three treatises advocating a reform of the Anglican clergy.

England, 1593. Shakespeare writes *Richard III, Comedy of Errors* and a collection of erotic poems entitled *Venus and Adonis*.

Rome, 2 February 1594. Giovanni Pierluigi da Palestrina dies and his body is laid in St Peter's basilica. Summoned to Rome in 1551 by Pope Julius II to direct the choir of the Julian chapel, he was successively director of music at the St John Laterano and Great St Mary's churches, and from 1571, at St Peter's. He wrote over 100 masses and 600 motets.

Paris, 22 March 1594. Governor Brissac opens the gates of Paris to Henry IV. The opposition of the Catholic League, whose position was undermined by Henry's conversion to Catholicism last year, is on the brink of collapse.

Venice, 31 May 1594. The painter Jacopo di Robusti, known as Tintoretto, dies. He imitated Titian's use of colour and Michelangelo's drawing technique. A master of perspective, some of his most important work is in the Scuola di San Rocco.

Germany, 24 June 1594. The musician Orlando di Lasso dies. For a long time the master of chapel music at Munich, in the service of the duke of Bavaria, the "Divino Orlando" excelled in motets and songs, in which he combined Flemish and Italian musical traditions.

England, 22 November 1594. Martin Frobisher, the English explorer of North America, who attempted to discover a north-west passage to China, dies of a wound sustained at the siege of Crozon, near the French port of Brest.

Netherlands, 2 December 1594. The influential Flemish geographer and mathematician Gerardus Mercator (Gerhard Kremer) dies.

Central Asia, 1594. The Emperor Akbar's troops take control of Baluchistan and Makran, annexing them to the Moghul empire.

South-East Asia, 1594. The English navigator Sir James Lancaster, a soldier and merchant in the service of Portugal, returns to Europe after a three-year visit to the East Indies.

Netherlands, 1594. The province of Groningen joins the Union of Utrecht.

Hungary, 1594. In a renewed war with Hungary, the Ottoman Turks capture the fortress of Raab.

Florida, 1594. Father Baltasar Lopez holds a mass baptism of 80 Indians to encourage 13 new friars.

England, 1594. Shakespeare writes *Titus Andronicus* and a comedy entitled *The Taming of the Shrew*.

Mexico, 1594. The Mercedarian fathers, members of the Order of Mercy, arrive in Mexico.

Angola, 1594. The Portuguese Furtado de Mendoca is named governor of Sao Paolo of Luanda.

France, 1594. King Henry IV's mistress, Gabrielle d'Estrees, bears him an illegitimate son, Cesar of Bourbon, duke of Vendome.

France, 17 January 1595. Henry IV declares his intention to pursue the war against Spain, which is attempting to enforce the claims of a Spanish pretender to the French throne.

England, 21 February 1595. The Jesuit poet Robert Southwell is hanged for "treason" (i.e., being a Catholic priest) at Tyburn.

Rome, 25 April 1595. Summoned to Rome by Pope Clement VIII to be crowned poet laureate, Torquato Tasso dies at the monastery of Santo' Onofrio before the ceremony can take place. He is the author of the epic masterpiece *Gerusalemme Liberata*.

Rome, 26 May 1595. Philip Neri, the philanthropist and priest who moved to Rome from his native Florence in 1533, dies. In 1564 he founded the Congregation of the Oratory to rededicate the clergy to the service of lay society.

France, 5 June 1595. King Henry IV's army defeats the Spanish at the battle of Fontaine-Francaise and drives them out of Burgundy.

Ireland, 1595. Hugh O'Neill, the earl of Tyrone, who became leader of the O'Neill clan two years ago, has set himself up as the champion of the Catholics and approached Spain for help against the English.

The glowing tones of "St George and the Dragon", by Tintoretto.

Tintoretto, painter of grandeur, is dead

Venice, 31 May 1594

The largest canvas ever painted is the picture of *Paradise*, covering the entire wall of the council chamber in the doges' palace, 84 feet (25.6m) long and 34 feet (10.4m) high. The man who painted it (with assistants), Jacopo Robusti, died today aged 76. He was always known as Tintoretto. His father was a *tintero*, or dyer.

Tintoretto and Paolo Veronese were commissioned to decorate the ceilings and state rooms of the doges' palace with vast and glowing paintings showing the glory of Venice, the queen of the seas. As a youth Tintoretto was dismissed from Titian's workshop for disobedience, although some Titian admirers say it was out of jealousy. His paintings are mystical and often show vivid moments of drama, such as the snatching of the body of St Mark, Venice's patron saint, by night from Alexandria.

Tintoretto worked fast. He decorated the entire Scula di San Rocco in six years and often worked for nothing. He will be buried in the church where his *Last Judgment* 50 feet (15.2m) high, hangs.

Japanese invade Korea

Korea, 1593

The Japanese warlord Hideyoshi's invasion of Korea has become bogged down after a year of fighting and the Japanese army, having lost a third of its strength, is in danger of defeat. The well-prepared invasion opened with a landing at Pusan in May last year. It could have met disaster at the outset, for the Japanese navy failed to rendezvous with the troop convoys, but the Korean ships missed their opportunity to attack.

Troops poured ashore and broke the feeble defence of the Korean army, lopping off 8,000 heads in the first few days. The Japanese then captured Seoul, and the king of Korea fell back to Pyongyang while

the Japanese looted his capital. The strong Korean navy had recovered from its surprise, however, and started a damaging series of raids on the Japanese supply ships and troop-carriers. The Korean army's resistance stiffened and the passage of the Japanese through the countryside aroused fierce resistance among the peasants. Guerrilla bands hounded the invaders, more supply ships were sunk and the cruel winter set in. Yet it was the intervention of the Chinese in the early months of this year which proved the turning point. Marching in great strength across the Yalu, they have forced the invaders to evacuate Seoul. The signs are that Hideyoshi is ready to talk peace.

Himeji castle, one of Toyotomi Hideyoshi's strongholds, built in 1577.

Irish uprising threat alarms Elizabeth

Ireland, 30 June 1595

An Irish chief who was made earl of Tyrone for his devoted services to the English cause in Ireland was today officially proclaimed a traitor. It is now known that Hugh O'Neill has been smuggling arms into the country in preparation for an uprising against the introduction of Protestant ways. Another cause of anger among the Catholic Irish has been the arrival in Ulster of Scottish immigrants with their fiercely anti-Catholic Calvinism.

O'Neill, loudly professing loyalty to England, married the daughter of an aristocratic Anglo-Irish fam-

ily, though the union did not last. He was allowed to raise a force of 600 men, trained by the English. Each year the men were replaced by new recruits, so that when he launched the rebellion this year he had a force of 4,000 musketeers, 1,000 pikemen and 1,000 cavalry.

O'Neill has captured Enniskillen and Monaghan castles and appealed to Philip of Spain for help. But the English have blocked that and fought O'Neill to a stalemate. Now, schools are being opened and Trinity College has been founded – in the hope that education will pacify the Irish.

Europe loses two great masters of music

A musical duet: two of Europe's masters of music will be greatly missed.

Munich, 14 June 1594

In four months Europe has lost two of its towering musical geniuses. On February 2 Giovanni Pierluigi da Palestrina died; today saw the death of Orlando di Lassus.

Palestrina was born in the town of the same name, near Rome, in about 1525. He worked there until his bishop became Pope Julius III and made him head of music at the Julian Chapel in St Peter's (1551). A series of prestigious posts followed before Palestrina returned to St Peter's in 1571. A prolific composer of mainly sacred works (such as the famous *Papae Marcelli* mass), he was asked in 1577 to revise church plainchant following the Council of Trent's guidelines.

Lassus was born in Flanders in about 1530 and travelled widely. From 1553-55 he was head of music at St John Lateran in Rome (Palestrina succeeded him); he joined the duke of Bavaria's chapel in 1556, heading it from 1563 until his death. Less conservative than Palestrina, his huge output ranges from masses to raucous drinking-songs.

Polish king offered the Swedish throne

Stockholm, 17 November 1593

On the death of John III, the Swedish aristocrats have offered the crown to the king of Poland, Sigismund Vasa. The nobles, who have begun to think of themselves as the historic guardians of Sweden's laws and liberties, have nevertheless staked their claim to a major share in government.

Firmly Lutheran, they are determined to place a curb on Sigismund's Catholicism, as well as imposing new restrictions on the crown. Sigismund has already had to sign the Statutes of Kalmar which were designed to ensure that the union of the crowns should neither endanger the country's independence nor prejudice its faith.

"The horn of Venus", by English alchemist, geographer, mathematician and astronomer John Dee (born 1527). Once in prison for magic, Dee supports efforts to find the north-west passage.

1595 (1595-1596)

North America, 23 September 1595. Having decided that conversion of Indians is preferable to conquest, Spain divides south-eastern North America into mission provinces.

Sweden, October 1595. King Sigismund appoints his Protestant uncle Charles to rule Sweden jointly with the council in his absence from the country.

Hungary, October 1595. Shortly after losing the fortress of Esztergom, the Turkish forces are defeated by a Hungarian offensive, led by Sigismund Bathory, at Giurgiu.

Central Asia, 1595. The Emperor Akbar's troops annex Kandahar. All of India north of the Narbada river, as well as Kandahar, Kabul and Ghazna, now acknowledges Moghul supremacy.

Istanbul, 1595. Mehmet III succeeds Murad III as sultan of the Ottomans. On his accession to the throne he enforces the "law of fratricide", by which a new sultan is obliged to execute his brothers and their male children. Nineteen of Murad III's sons are killed.

Peru, 1595. Luis de Vlasco, the former viceroy of New Spain, is appointed viceroy of Peru.

England, 1595. Shakespeare writes the history play *Richard II* and the black comedy *The Merchant of Venice*.

Pacific, 1595. Having set out from Peru, the Spaniard Mendana de Neyra reaches the Marquesas islands, and then the island of Santa Cruz *(east of the Solomon islands)*, where he meets his death.

South-East Asia, 1595. The Dutch make a voyage round the Cape of Good Hope and across the Indian Ocean to Java. They begin to colonise the East Indies.

South America, 1595. The English navigator Sir Walter Raleigh explores the coast of Trinidad and sails up the Orinoco river.

France, January 1596. The duke of Mayenne, the leader of the Catholic League, surrenders to Henry IV.

Mexico, January 1596. Sebastian Rodriguez Cermeno returns to Mexico after a 22-month sea voyage up the Pacific coast.

Caribbean, January 1596. Sir Francis Drake, the English naval leader and privateer, dies.

France, April 1596. The Spanish capture Calais.

Spain, 1 July 1596. An English fleet under the earl of Essex, Lord Howard of Effingham and Francis Vere captures and sacks Cadiz.

Hungary, September 1596. The Turks, now under the personal leadership of the Ottoman Sultan Mehmet III, defeat the Hungarians at Erlau (*Eger*).

Ukraine, October 1596. The creation of the united Ruthenian church is ratified by the synod of Brest-Litovsk. After a year of negotiation, the Jesuits have managed to unite the Roman Catholic and Orthodox Churches of the Ukraine.

Hungary, October 1596. In spite of a mass desertion by the infantry, the Turks win an astonishing victory at Mezokeresztes. Sultan Mehmet III was personally responsible for turning the tide in the battle, in which 30,000 Hungarians and Germans are reported to have died.

Rome, 1596. Pope Clement VIII absolves Henry IV, the king of France, from his previous excommunication.

France, 1596. France forms an alliance with England and the Netherlands against the Spanish king.

East Africa, 1596. The Portuguese complete the building of Fort Jesus in Mombasa, Kenya.

North America, c.1596. The first wheeled vehicles – wagons, similar to German farm carts – appear in the New World. They are used to haul supplies as the Spanish continue to explore and settle the south-west.

Netherlands, 1596. Albert, the archduke of Austria, is appointed governor of the Netherlands. The third son of the Emperor Maximilian II, Albert was made a cardinal in 1577 and archbishop of Toledo in 1584. In 1594 he became viceroy of Portugal.

France, 1596. The political philosopher Jean Bodin, author of the *Republic* and the famous *Response to the Paradoxes of Malestroit*, dies. Bodin had argued that property and the family form the basis of society and that the best government is absolute monarchy.

England, 1596. *The Faerie Queen*, a seven-volume poem written by Edmund Spenser and dedicated to Queen Elizabeth, is published.

England, 1596. Shakespeare writes the comedy *A Midsummer Night's Dream* and a tragic love story entitled *Romeo and Juliet*.

Austria, 1596. Johann Kepler publishes his *Cosmographical Mystery*, in which he argues that there is a geometrical relationship between the distances of the planets from the sun which can be expressed numerically.

Hundreds burned in German witch hunts

"Witches' Sabbath" (detail), by Frans Francken the Younger (1581-1642).

German states, c.1595

The German states are convulsed with a new epidemic as pervasive, as widespread and as terrifying as the plague: the fear of witchcraft. Unlike the plague, this is a disease of the mind; but while no-one has yet discovered a cure for plague, there is a simple and often used remedy for witchcraft: death.

Germany has been torn by a series of witch-hunts, usually followed by a public trial and then, almost invariably, by the execution of the accused, whose confession has often been extracted through torture. Much of the hysteria has been inspired by the *Malleus Malificarum* (the Hammer of the Witches), a tract written by the Dominicans Institorus and Sprenger in 1487 and authorised by the pope. Its pages inflame many peasants, fearful of satanic attacks on their crops.

Between 1587 and 1593 the archbishop-elector of Trier burned 368 witches. On a single day in 1589, 133 witches were executed at the convent of Quedlinburg; the list is endless. Church dignitaries are the

Newes from Scotland, Declaring the Damnable life and death of Doctor Fian, a notable Sorcerer, who was burned at Edenbrough in Ianuary last. 1591.

Which Doctor was regester to the Diuell that sundry times preached at North Barrick Kirke, to a number of notorious Witches.

With the true examinations of the saide Doctor and Witches, as they vttered them in the presence of the Scottish King.

Discouering how they pretended to bewitch and drowne his Maiestie in the Sea comming from Denmarke, with such other wonderfull matters as the like hath not been heard of at any time.

Published according to the Scottish Coppie.

AT LONDON Printed for William Wright.

From James I's "Daemonologie".

most ferocious persecutors, but the secular powers are almost as keen. What has sparked off the witch-hunts is debatable. The *Malleus* is notably misogynistic, obsessed with female lust; the majority of the accused are women. The concept of the witches' "Sabbath" or "black mass" is also a potent image.

Gothic gives way to Elizabethan style

Jan Siberechts (1627-c.1700) painted this view of Longleat, built 1573.

England, c.1595
The architecture of England under Elizabeth has swept away the cobwebs of the late Tudor Gothic style, which by the middle of the century had become rather stagnant.

At the root of the new styles lies the continental Renaissance, but via Flanders and France rather than directly from Italy. In 1563 the Fleming Vredeman de Vries published a series of books in which the classical orders of building were extravagantly transformed and adorned with gables and strapwork. This style soon caught on throughout northern Europe, and under its influence English architecture began to acquire great originality, although Italian influence on large houses can be seen in the tendency to build symmetrical frontages. The arrangement of rooms internally is generally similar to that of earlier times, with the great chamber as the ceremonial heart of the house. Among the greatest of the new or rebuilt houses are Longleat (1573), Holdenby (begun 1577), Theobalds (altered 1580s) and Hardwick Hall (early 1590s).

Houses such as these reflect the weath of families prospering from rising prices, royal service and the dissolution of the monasteries. Despite the grandeur, English buildings have come under fire from some critics for being flimsy and two-

Wollaton Hall, Nottingham (1580-8).

dimensional compared with those of Henry VIII's day. Windows are, indeed, often flush with walls rather than set deeply into them, pilasters are preferred to columns, and buttresses are rare.

Threatened Portuguese build African base

East Africa, 1596
Shaken by repeated rebellions and the massacre of their small forces at trading stations on the East African coast, the Portuguese have started building a base on Mombasa Island. An Italian military architect has been commissioned, masons are coming from Goa, and labour is being recruited locally for a great castle to be called Fort Jesus.

But the work is proceeding slowly and costs are overrunning to such an extent that Lisbon has begun asking questions about where the money is going. An Augustinian prior and a judge have been appointed to a committee to handle funds, keep signed receipts and buy building materials.

The Portuguese have felt their position on the East African coast to be increasingly under threat after Turkish raiders appeared out of the Red Sea and sailed as far south as Mombasa, where the local ruler welcomed the Turks and turned on the Portuguese. When the Turks withdrew, the Portuguese sacked the town. The Turks returned again a few years later and the pattern of rebellion along the coast was repeat-

An African bronze, from Benin, of an armed Portuguese soldier.

ed, with only the king of Malindi still loyal to Portugal. That was when Lisbon finally gave heed to the appeals of the local Portuguese for a fortress to be built, with a 100-man garrison.

Death of Drake, England's great sailor

The Caribbean, 29 January 1596
A lead coffin containing the body of Sir Francis Drake, the scourge of the Spanish Main, was committed to the sea a few miles off Porto Bello, Panama, today. Drake was in his mid-fifties and died of dysentery. In April last year he had sailed from Plymouth (whose MP he had been for a time) on an ill-fated expedition with his old comrade-in-arms Sir John Hawkins. A fleet of 27 ships and 2,500 men could not be concealed from the Spanish enemy who was well prepared wherever the English struck. Hawkins died off Puerto Rico last November.

Sir Francis Drake (c.1585).

Armada disaster and internal revolts push Spain to bankruptcy

Madrid, 29 November 1596
Not for the first time Spain is bankrupt. The richest and most formidable power on earth, with a empire envied by allies and enemies, has admitted that the royal treasury has been drained and the nation's economy ruined. Official reasons given by Philip II for the situation are many. One is the series of wars, and particularly the decision to invade England. Wars have been especially costly, and have weakened the armed forces. Bad weather, poor management and heavy domestic spending have also played their parts as have revolts against the Spanish empire in the New World.

Florida, 1596. Over the past two years an estimated 1,500 natives have been converted to Christianity by Spanish Franciscan priests.

Atlantic, 1597. An English expedition to the Azores to intercept a Spanish treasure fleet, led by the earl of Essex ends in failure.

Arctic, 1597. The Dutch explorer Willem Barents dies while on his third voyage to search for a northeast passage to China.

Korea, 1597. The Japanese under Hideyoshi launch a further expedition against Korea, but are expelled by the Chinese.

Switzerland, 1597. The Dutch-born Jesuit Peter Canisius dies at Freiburg. An architect of the Counter-reformation in Germany, Canisius wrote a widely used catechism and founded 13 Jesuit communities.

North America, 1597. Simon Ferdinando, a Portuguese navigator working for the English crown, lands on the coast of Maine looking for treasure.

Spain, 1597. The Spanish lyric poet Fernando de Herrera dies in Seville. The best known of his *canciones* describes the 1571 Battle of Lepanto.

Central Asia, 1597. Abbas, the shah of Persia, drives back the Turkish Ozbegs beyond the Amudarja.

Russia, 1597. Czar Fyodor gives orders that fugitive serfs are to be subjected to ferocious punishments.

North America, 1597. The marquis of la Roche, elected lieutenantgeneral of Canada, founds a colony on Sable Island.

India, 1597. Abul Fazl, the Emperor Akbar's secretary, is hard at work on the *Akbarnama*, a book which is intended to be a comprehensive account of the emperor's reign.

England, 1597. Parliament passes an act allowing sentences of transportation to the colonies for convicted criminals.

England, 1597. Shakespeare writes *Henry IV*, an historical play in two parts, and a comedy entitled *The Merry Wives of Windsor*.

England, 1597. The lawyer and statesman Francis Bacon publishes a first volume of *Essays*.

Lucky victory saves Ottoman empire

Hungary, October 1596

In one fell swoop, Mehmet III, the Ottoman Sultan, has saved a huge swathe of territory for his empire. Threatened by a string of Hungarian military triumphs, his possessions in Macedonia, Bulgaria and Hungary have been secured by a remarkable victory on the Mezokeresztes plain.

It was a minor earthquake rather than any realisation of danger to his empire that moved the superstitious Sultan to battle. Urged on by his ministers, who feared a revolt by disgruntled janissaries, Mehmet took to the field. The capture of Erlau last month encouraged him to confront the Hungarian forces.

The battle started off badly, when early reverses caused the *sipahis* – the fief-holding backbone of Mehmet's army – simply to walk off the battlefield. The Sultan tried to follow them, but his generals held a council of war to persuade him to stay with the rest of his army. At this point, the overconfident Christians broke rank to plunder the Turkish camp. Mehmet's cavalry charged, killing over 30,000 German and Hungarian troops and taking enormous booty including a hundred cannons.

Mehmet is relieved. He wants to get back to Istanbul, where his mother, the Sultana Valide Baffo, holds the reins of power, keeping him happy with a steady supply of beautiful concubines.

Cowardly victor: Mehmet III.

Danish Astronomer records 777 stars

Denmark, 1597

No fewer than 777 stars have been logged by the Danish astronomer Tycho Brahe in a 20-year career of observing the heavens. Brahe, who was granted the island of Hven in south Denmark by the late King Frederick II to build his observatory, is now the world's foremost astronomer.

As well as noting the stars, he has vastly increased our knowledge of the moon, registered the refraction of light, and perfected a table of correction for the better identification of stars. It is through this table that he has been able to compile his own impressive catalogue of heavenly bodies.

Star gazer: Tycho Brahe (1586).

Dutch explorer dies in Arctic winter

Willem Barents' ship trapped in ice, from an account of the expedition.

Novaya Zemlya, 20 June 1597

An attempt to find a north-east passage to Asia has ended in the death in the Arctic of the Dutch explorer Willem Barents. This was his third attempt to find a route around the north of Russia to China, and the course that he chose took him in a more northerly direction than hitherto. He discovered Spitzbergen and Bear Island before his ship was trapped in ice-floes, forcing him and his men to spend the winter in the Arctic.

The historian of the expedition, Gerrit de Veer, has written a moving description of the men's ordeal by cold and hunger. When it was clear that they were trapped, they built a house from tree-roots. "It froze so hard, that as we put a nayle in our mouths, there would be ice thereon when we took it out again and make the bloud follow,"(*sic*) wrote de Veer.

They were attacked by polar bears and forced to eat foxes as their supplies ran out. They were nearly suffocated by smoke when snow covered their hut.

Despite the intense cold, the 16 survivors managed to celebrate the feast of the Epiphany. "For several days we had not drunke and so that night we made merrie and drunk to the three kings, and therewith had two pounds of meale whereof we made pancakes with oyle and everyman a white biskit which we sopt in wine," wrote de Veer (*sic*).

Akbar orders memoirs of his reign

Punjab, India, 1597

As the century draws to its close, Akbar, the great Moghul emperor, has ordered his historian, Abul Fazl, the son of the unorthodox Moslem mystic Sheikh Mubarak, to write an account of his reign.

None are as well qualified as Abul Fazl for the task. Like his brother Faizi, he is one of Akbar's closest advisers. He is a Moslem freethinker who, like his hero, is not afraid of religious intolerance, and is the proud owner of a library of 24,000 well-used books.

The two books which Abul Fazl is compiling, *The History of Akbar* and *The Laws of Akbar*, seem certain to be two of the most detailed books ever written about a great man.

Researching Akbar's biography Abul Fazl is talking to hundreds of witnesses. Akbar's aunt has recalled the Moghul empire at the time of Humayan, Akbar's father, who lost and regained an empire. Humayan's servants, Jauhar and Bayezid, have added their memories; Bayezid, old and suffering from a stroke is dictating his to Abul Fazl's clerk. Fifteen hundred pages are to be devoted to the minutest details of the emperor's life: what he drank, said and did each day, and which wife he slept with each night. Two clerks are with him wherever he goes, recording his actions for Abul Fazl. Abul Fazl's *Laws of Akbar* is equally weighty, recording the words of Akbar on subjects ranging from philosophy and etymology to cooking recipes and methods of oiling camels.

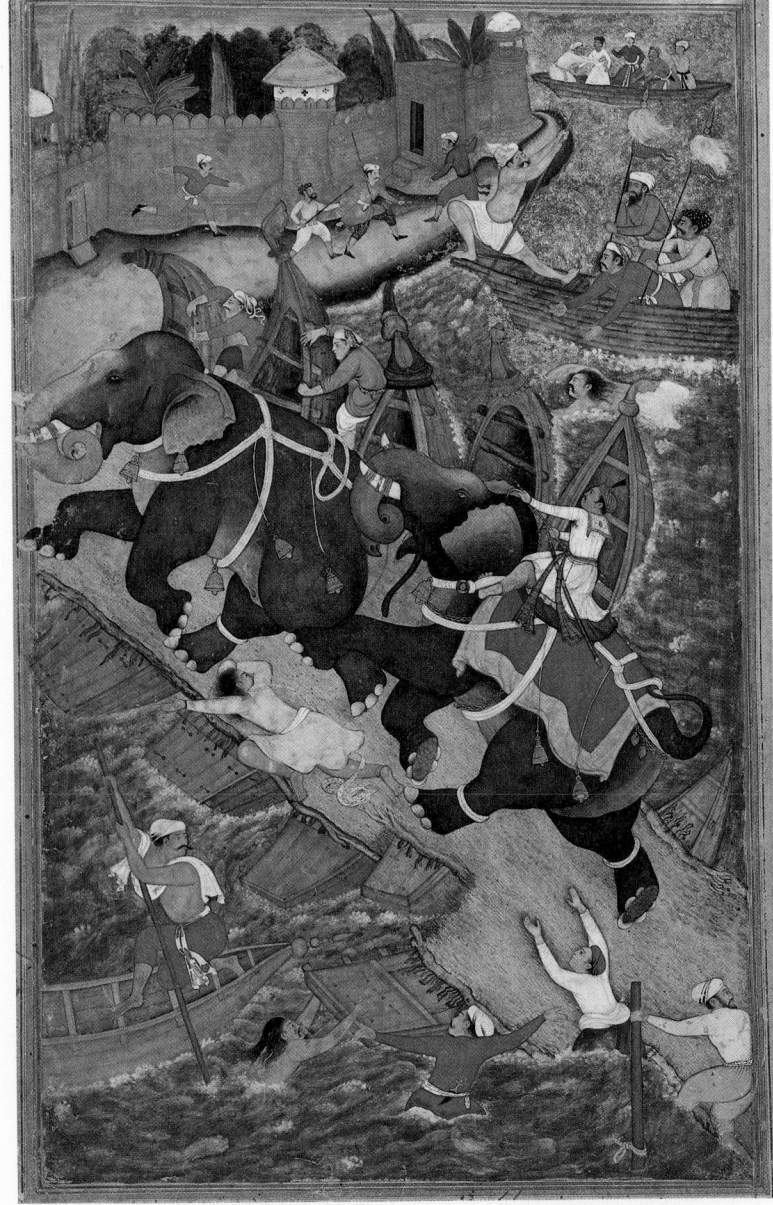

Elephants crossing a pontoon, from Abul Fazl's "The History of Akbar".

Theatres revived after plague threat

London, 1596

The London stage is returning to normal after the recent reopening of the city's theatres, closed in 1593 owing to a plague outbreak. One great figure absent from the revived theatrical scene is the playwright – and spy – Christopher Marlowe, who died in 1593, aged only 29. Apparently, Marlowe met three secret agents at Bull's tavern in Deptford, Kent; a quarrel led to a fight in which he was stabbed above the right eye, dying instantly.

The circles of dark and violent subterfuge in which Marlowe moved are reflected in some of his small output of seven plays, such as *The Jew of Malta*, *The Massacre at Paris* and *Doctor Faustus*.

Until about 50 years ago most plays were on religious themes, but there has since been a shift towards secular themes based on individuals and their motives, often drawn from classical legends, or history, such as Thomas Kyd's *Spanish Tragedy* (1589). The actor-playwright William Shakespeare has emerged as the leading light of the new English drama, working with the new Lord Chamberlain's Company at The Theatre, which was England's first public playhouse, built at Shoreditch in 1576.

Among works written since he came to London around five years ago from his native Stratford are *Henry VI* (in three parts), *Richard III*, *Romeo and Juliet* and *The Taming of the Shrew*.

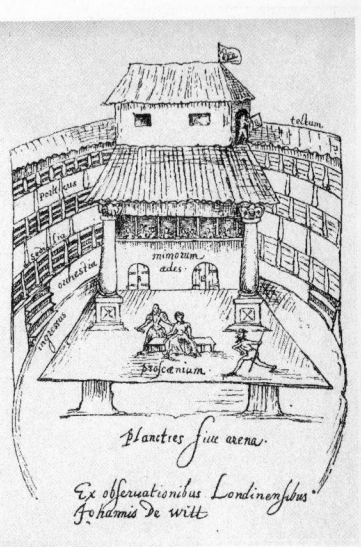

London's "Swan" Theatre (1596).

Portuguese merchants wary of Dutch rival in East Indies

Holland, 20 August 1597

A Dutch merchant, long resident in Lisbon, has arrived in Holland after a two-year voyage to the Far East Spice Islands that has left the Portuguese fearful for their monopoly of the eastern trade.

Cornelius van Houtman was for many years the prosperous carrier of pepper, nutmeg and other spices from Lisbon to countries of northern Europe. This came to an abrupt end when Philip of Spain claimed the crown of Portugal in 1580 and the two countries were united. He barred the Dutch from Portuguese trade because of their rebellion against his rule in the Netherlands. The Dutch thereupon resolved to get into the eastern trade on their own account.

Houtman was helped on his voyage by a book written by another Dutchman, who had served with the Portuguese East India fleet: Jan Huyghen van Linschoten. On 2 April 1595, Houtman sailed from Holland with four ships; a year later he dropped anchor at Bantam, Java, where the local Portuguese made him welcome. Very soon, though, they became hostile when they realised what the Dutch were about. Houtman outwitted them, persuaded the sultan of Bantam to sign a treaty, and departed with a cargo of spices.

The voyage home was marked by losses of ships and men, but Houtman's tales of rich trading opportunities have fired Amsterdam's merchants with enthusiasm and they are planning to found trading companies, described as *Van Ferne* (of the distant seas).

England, 1597. The first crop of domestically-grown tomatoes is produced and eaten.

Mexico, 8 January 1598. Don Juan de Onate sets out on an expedition to New Mexico with some 500 colonists.

Russia, 17 February 1598. Boris Godunov, the *boyar* of Tartar origin, is elected czar in succession to his brother-in-law Fyodor.

France, 13 April 1598. Henry IV, the king of France, promulgates the Edict of Nantes to promote "union, concord and tranquillity" between his Catholic and Huguenot subjects. The edict grants the Huguenots a large measure of religious freedom.

France, 2 May 1598. After three years of declared war, Henry IV signs the treaty of Vervins with Spain, ending Philip II's interference in France. Under the treaty – which is a setback for Habsburg ambitions – Spain keeps the provinces of Flanders, Artois and Charolais, but must leave Picardy.

England, 4 August 1598. William Cecil, chief adviser to Queen Elizabeth on both foreign and domestic matters since her accession in 1558, dies. He was created Baron Burghley in 1571 and lord high treasurer in 1572, and introduced important financial reforms. He built three magnificent mansions: Burghley House at Stamford, Theobalds in Hertfordshire and Cecil House in London.

Ireland, 15 August 1598. Two months after receiving a pardon for his rebellious activities from Elizabeth, the queen of England, Hugh O'Neill, the earl of Tyrone, leads an Irish force to victory over the English at the battle of Yellow Ford.

Madrid, 13 September 1598. Philip II, king of Spain since 1556, dies and is succeeded by his son Philip III.

Sweden, 25 September 1598. Having gained the supported of the Lutheran states against the members of the Swedish council, King Sigismund's uncle Charles inflicts a defeat on his Catholic nephew at Stangebro.

North America, 1598. The marquis de la Roche leaves France with 40 convicts to colonise Sable Island, off Nova Scotia.

Indian Ocean, 1598. The Dutch admiral Wijbrand van Warwijck takes possession of an island which he calls Mauritius, in honour of Maurice of Nassau.

Persia, 1598. Shah Abbas embarks upon an ambition scheme of urbanisation. He plans to make Isfahan one of the most beautiful cities in the world.

China, 1598. The Jesuit Matteo Ricci gains access to the imperial court at Beijing.

Japan, 1598. Toyotomi Hideyoshi, who proclaimed himself civil dictator in 1586, dies after entrusting his son and his dynasty to Tokugawa Ieyasu and four other of his senior councillors.

Korea, 1598. Following the death of Hideyoshi, Japanese troops withdraw from Korea.

West Africa, 1598. The Bambara people, from the Jenne region, overthrow the last of the kings of Mali and found the kingdom of Segu.

Anatolia, 1598. Jelali bands of brigands rise up against Ottoman authority.

England, 1598. Shakespeare writes two comedies: *Much Ado About Nothing* and *As You Like It*, and appears at the Curtain theatre, acting in his friend Ben Jonson's new play *Every Man in His Humour*.

England, 16 January 1599. The poet Edmund Spenser dies. He will be best remembered for his epic work *The Faerie Queen*, written for Queen Elizabeth, in which he sets out to show the ideal gentleman or courtier in action, and for his supreme marriage poem *Epithalamion*, which was written on the occasion of his second marriage.

England, September 1599. Appointed governor-general of Ireland earlier in the year, the earl of Essex returns to England in defiance of Queen Elizabeth's orders. He was sent to Ireland to put down the revolt led by Hugh O'Neill, the earl of Tyrone, with whom he has concluded a truce.

Sweden, November 1599. Sigismund III, king of Poland since 1587 and of Sweden since 1592, is deposed by the Riksdag (the Swedish parliament) because of growing opposition among his Lutheran subjects to his support for the Counter-reformation. His uncle Charles becomes regent.

Poland, 1599. Under the confederation of Vilna, the various branches of the church in Poland unite against the power of the Roman Church.

London, 1599. The actor Richard Burbage pulls down the Shoreditch Playhouse on the south bank of the Thames and begins to build in its place a roofless summer playhouse, the Globe, to seat 1,200 spectators. The Blackfriars theatre, on the north bank, also built by Burbage, is to remain as a winter playhouse. Among Burbage's partners in the new enterprise is the playwright William Shakespeare.

Henry masters France

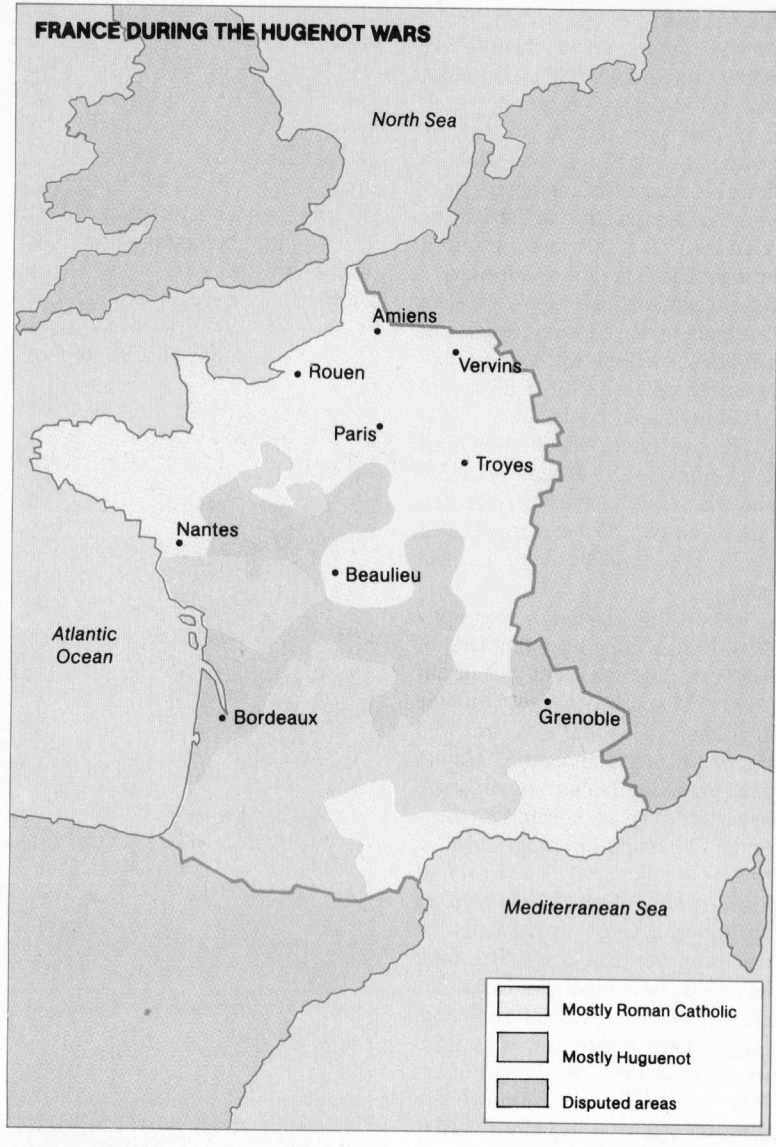

FRANCE DURING THE HUGENOT WARS

North Sea

Amiens
Rouen · · Vervins
Paris ·
· Troyes
Nantes ·
· Beaulieu
Atlantic Ocean
· Bordeaux
Grenoble ·

Mediterranean Sea

☐ Mostly Roman Catholic
☐ Mostly Huguenot
☐ Disputed areas

France, 1598

Henry IV can at last call himself king of France. The country is still plagued by brigands to whom warfare has become a way of life, and the religious quarrels are bound to persist, but he has at last brought the long agony of France to an end.

He has done it by diplomacy — his acceptance of the Catholic faith after being the champion of Protestantism for so long was a masterstroke. And he has done it on the battlefield, repelling the Spaniards and quelling the secessionist revolt in Brittany.

He has also won back the support of the Huguenots which he lost when he declared "Paris is worth a Mass". In April he signed the "perpetual and irrevocable" Edict of Nantes which granted Protestants freedom of conscience throughout the kingdom. The edict also restored their old places of worship to them and granted them permission to build new ones. They now have equal civic rights with the Catholics and are allowed access to all public posts.

A full amnesty is granted to all those who took up arms during the wars of religion, and 100 towns are assigned to the Huguenots as "towns of refuge".

The terms of the edict do not please many Catholics, but such is the war-weariness in France that they accepted the edict in return for peace. The following month the ailing King Philip of Spain signed the peace of Vervins and his army marched home. Now France truly belongs to Henry IV.

Irish rout English soldiers at Yellow Ford

Ireland, 15 August 1598
After years of skirmishes and truces between Irish rebels and English soldiers, the Irish have scored a decisive victory at Yellow Ford on the river Callan, near Armagh, Ulster. Last year the English planned a threefold attack on the rebels from Sligo to Westmeath. All three were repulsed and a truce was arranged to last until the middle of this year.

By then the Irish, led by Hugh O'Neill and Red Hugh O'Donnell, were ready. A small garrison on the river Blackwater was under siege and General Sir Nicholas Bagenal set out from Newry with a relief force of 4,000.

O'Neill's men, armed with muskets, sniped at Bagenal's flanks. The force became too scattered for the leading regiment to be given effective support. It was broken up and cut to pieces by cavalry. A rout was avoided, but only about 1,500 of the original 4,000 reached the safety of Armagh. It is a triumph for the Irish, but is certain to enrage Elizabeth who may decide to send more troops.

Boris Godunov elected czar of Russia

Moscow, 17 February 1598
Amid universal rejoicing, Boris Godunov has secured his own coronation as czar. With Fyodor's death the royal house of Russia has been extinguished.

By virtue of the power he has in fact been exercising Godunov was the favoured candidate, but before accepting the throne he insisted upon election by the *Zemsky Sobor*, or Assembly of the Land, drawn from the clergy, the *boyars*, the lesser nobility, officials and merchants.

Godunov is a boyar of Tartar origin who has practically ruled the country for the last 14 years while it has recovered from the disasters of the reign of Ivan the Terrible. He is quite illiterate, but this has not prevented him from directing all correspondence with heads of foreign states and looking like the man running Russia.

He began his career in Ivan's se-

Boris Godunov: ruler in effect, and now officially in name.

cret police, the *oprichnina*, and succeeded in marrying his sister Irene to Fyodor, thus making himself the new czar's brother-in-law, and indispensable.

Catholics crucified on hill in Nagasaki

Nagasaki, 5 February 1597
Twenty-six Christians have been martyred by being crucified upside down on a hill outside Nagasaki on the orders of the Japanese warlord, Hideyoshi. The execution of the seven Franciscans and 19 of their Japanese converts was carried out in the cruellest fashion.

They were condemned to death a month ago in Kyoto and, having first been mutilated, were dragged from city to city in degrading circumstances as a dreadful warning to the Japanese to have nothing further to do with Christianity. Hideyoshi has given no reason for the executions, although he has been surprised by the renewed strength of Christianity in Japan following the return of missionaries after he expelled them in 1587.

What is curious about the executions is that they involved only Franciscans; the strong Jesuit colony was not touched. There is some suspicion of court intrigue behind the martyrdoms. Certainly Christianity in Japan has been dealt a cruel blow.

Spain mourns Philip II

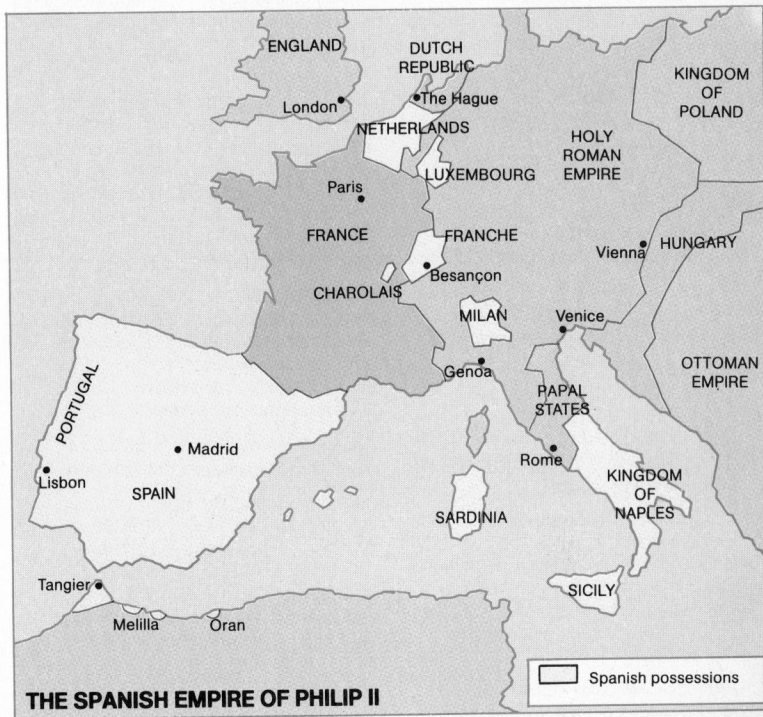

THE SPANISH EMPIRE OF PHILIP II

☐ Spanish possessions

Madrid, 13 September 1598
Philip II of Spain, who has ruled the world's most powerful country for more than 40 years, has died in ulcerous agony in his grim and gloomy Escorial palace outside Madrid. He was 71 and had spent the last few months preparing for his death, ordering black cloth for his own mourning draperies and rehearsing the ritual of extreme unction. Ceaseless prayers will be said in the huge basilica.

Under Philip, Spain became the richest and most formidable nation on earth, and he boasted of ruling the world from the Escorial with pen and paper. But Spain has been in trouble ever since he sent his "Invincible Armada" against the English in 1588. The bid to punish England for its support of Dutch Protestants fighting against Spanish rule, and for plundering Spanish possessions in Mexico and South America, came badly unstuck. Although Spain remained a major power after the defeat, its prestige had been seriously damaged and its naval supremacy lost.

Philip's achievements, however, were many. He and Don John of Austria broke the power of the Turks in the Mediterranean in 1571, and he conquered the Philippines in 1580. But the Netherlands, one of the most valuable possessions in the

Philip II: sad end to a reign.

empire, declared its independence in 1581 and a treaty with France shortly before Philip's death marked Spain's slow retreat from northern Europe.

Philip married Queen Mary I of England earlier in his reign, at a time when the English looked upon Spain as their greatest enemy, but deserted her shortly before she died. He regarded himself as a great champion of the Roman Catholic faith and supported the harsh measures of the Inquisition.

1599 (1599-1601)

Naples, 1599. The Dominican monk and Italian philosopher, Tommaso Campanella, is imprisoned for having attempted to stir up a revolution in the region of Calabria.

Spain, 1599. The first part of the picaresque novel of Mateo Aleman, *Guzman de Alfarache,* is published. It tells the life story of the eponymous hero, and represents a new type of long, many-episoded novel. It is instantly popular.

Scotland, 1599. In a treatise entitled *The True Laws of Free Monarchies,* James VI, the king of Scotland, defends the principle of absolute monarchy.

Spain, 1599. The Jesuit Juan de Mariana de la Reina writes *De Rege et Regis Institutione,* in which he justifies regicide and affirms popular sovereignty.

London, 1599. Shakespeare's English history *Henry V* is performed in the same year as his *Julius Caesar,* based on Plutarch's account of Caesar's murder on the Ides of March and the civil war that follow.

Rome, 17 February 1600. The philosopher Giordano Bruno is burnt to death as a heretic after a seven-year trial. Influenced by Neoplatonism, Stoicism and Epicureanism, he believed in a pantheistic system based on Copernican astronomy.

Japan, April 1600. The Englishman William Adams, a navigator in the service of the Dutch, reaches the Japanese port of Bungo. He is thrown into prison as a pirate at the instigation of jealous Portuguese traders.

Madrid, 14 October 1600. The theologian Luis de Molina dies. A disciple of St Thomas Aquinas, Molina is famed for his treatise of 1588 which opposes the Augustinian belief in the complete corruption of human liberty, asserting that free will is total and in accord with divine grace.

Japan, 21 October 1600. Tokugawa Ieyasu defeats his enemies in battle and affirms his position as Japan's most powerful warlord.

Spain, 5 November 1600. King Philip III notifies the Cuban governor Pedro de Valdes of his reservations about missionary and military efforts in Florida.

London, 31 December 1600. The East India Company – "The Governor and Company of Merchants of London trading into the East Indies" – is founded.

London, 1600. Ben Jonson's *Every Man Out of His Humour* is staged for the first time.

Uganda, 1600. The kingdom of Buganda (*near Lake Victoria*) defeats an attack by the neighbouring kingdom of Bunyoro.

France, 1600. After divorcing Margaret of Valois, King Henry IV of France marries Marie de Medici, the daughter of the grand duke of Tuscany and Archduchess Johanna of Austria. Henry's new alliance with the great Florentine banking family brings a massive dowry and should counter Spanish influence in Italy.

Barbados, 1600. A new spirit is being produced by the Spanish on their sugar plantations. They refine the sugar by-product molasses to make a cheap, deep brown alcohol with a unique taste (*rum*).

England, 1600. The population of England has reached four million.

Florence, 1600. The opera *Euridice* is composed by Jacopo Peri in honour of the marriage of Henry IV and Marie de Medici. The libretto, by Ottavio Rinuccini, is put to music again later in the year by Guilio Caccini. They are the first operas ever written.

Canada, 1600. The French found a fur-trading-post at Tadoussac, on the St Lawrence river.

Netherlands, 1600. Maurice of Nassau, the son of and successor to William of Orange, attempts to invade Spanish possessions in the south, having overcome the troops of Archduke Albert of Nieuport.

London, 1600. Shakespeare's new tragedy, *Hamlet,* about a reluctant young revenger caught in a web of intrigue and corruption in the Danish court of Elsinore, opens.

Italy, 1600. The *Rappresentazione di Anima e di Corpo* by the composer Emilio de Cavalieri is performed. It is the first dramatic oratorio.

England, 1600. William Gilbert, doctor to Queen Elizabeth, publishes *De Magnete,* the first treatise establishing a comprehensive theory of terrestrial magnetism. He compares the earth to a magnet and determines the existence of a magnetic field.

Central and South America, 1600. A law is passed in Spanish colonies forbidding whites to enter Indian villages without permission.

France, 1600. A new agricultural treatise by the Protestant Olivier de Serres is gaining influence, especially with the king. It recommends, among other things, crop rotation to make French agriculture more efficient after years of ruinous religious war.

Italy, 1601. A university is founded in Parma.

Portuguese naval mercenaries battle with Indians (late C16th drawing).

East meets west: a Goanese ivory carving of the Holy Trinity.

Goa: Portuguese jewel in the east

Goa, India, c.1600

It has been called Golden Goa – the settlement on India's west coast which is the focus of Portugal's seaborne commercial empire in Asia. Cottons from Gujarat up the coast are traded for pepper in Sumatra; the pepper buys Chinese goods and gold; the Chinese goods are exchanged for Japanese silver. Added to this network is the lucrative export of spices to Europe, also centred on Portuguese Goa.

The Portuguese are very much in the minority, both in Goa itself and as traders. In a population of about 75,000, about 3,000 are pure Portuguese, the rest being Indians, Africans and *Mastizos,* the offspring of Portuguese fathers and Indian women. Women are bought at slave markets; if they can sew, sing, dance and prove they are virgins, they can sell for 30 *cruzados* (a good horse fetches 500 cruzados).

Goa, a city of bazaars and narrow streets, is dominated by churches. The first printing press in Asia is here, and there is a royal hospital where European and Asian medicines come together. A patient will be bled with leeches and then prescribed cow's urine.

All Portuguese are traders, whatever their occupations: officials, including army and naval officers, settlers, even priests. Their activities are outside the official trading system, but they flourish despite opposition from the authorities. Yet Goa's prosperity may not continue much longer; the Dutch and the English are making their presence felt.

Scientific monk burnt alive for heresy

Rome, 17 February 1600

Giordano Bruno, who hoped above all to heal the splits between Protestants and Catholics and the church and science, was burnt alive today. He was first arrested by the Inquisition in Venice in 1592, but freed after he recanted the heresies of which he was accused. However, he withdrew his recantation, and just over a week ago he was expelled from the church as "an impenitent heretic" and sent to a secular court for punishment. Born in Nola, in 1548, he became a Dominican in 1565. He studied the ideas of Copernicus, who argued that the sun is the centre of the universe, not the earth as religious dogma believes. He hoped to reconcile Catholics and Protestants to the new idea of an infinite universe. The church, however, is not prepared to revise its beliefs.

English company to trade with the east

The East Indiamen set sail, hoping to extend Britain's far-flung trade empire.

London, 1 January 1600
Queen Elizabeth granted a charter of incorporation to the East India Company yesterday. This charter gives George Clifford, the earl of Cumberland, and 215 knights, aldermen and merchants the right to trade in the East Indies for 15 years.

The members of the Company have put up £72,000 to finance a large-scale trading expedition, and plans are ready to send out a fleet of five ships to Sumatra and Java to do business in the rich markets of the east. James Lancaster, who returned from a pioneering voyage to Sumatra, Malacca and Ceylon six years ago, has been appointed general of the fleet. John Davis, the great explorer of the Arctic seas, will be pilot-major. Their voyage promises to be in the tradition of the merchant venturers who have carried English trade around the world during the queen's reign.

Persia opens door to English guests

Persia, 1600
A remarkable alliance has developed between Shah Abbas of Persia and a group of English gentlemen adventurers led by the brothers Sir Anthony and Sir Robert Sherley.

Since the Sherleys reached Kazvin in 1598 with 26 followers, and presented gifts of jewels to the shah, they have achieved a favoured position at the Persian court. Sir Anthony returned to England last year as the shah's ambassador, and has been trying to win European support for an alliance against the Turks.

His brother Sir Robert, meanwhile, is putting his knowledge of artillery at the disposal of the Persian army, and helping to reorganise its regiments. As a result of the Sherleys' mission, special privileges have been granted to Christian merchants in Persia. They are free from customs' duties and religious interference.

Japanese military genius wins battle

Japan, 21 October 1600
Tokugawa Ieyasu has won a crushing victory over his enemies in a battle fought in the fog near the village of Sekigehara today. It was a close run thing, for when the fog cleared it could be seen that the forces of Ieyasu's rival for power, Ishida Mitsunari, commanded the high ground and threatened his rear.

Mitsunari had traitors in his ranks, however, and at the height of the battle these traitors, led by a general suborned by Ieyasu, changed sides. Mitsunari's army was routed by four in the afternoon. He has fled from the field where thousands of his men lie dead.

There is no doubt that Ieyasu, who has fought some 50 battles, is a cunning military genius. By winning he has also confirmed his position as the most powerful warlord in Japan. He has already sent out powerful forces in pursuit of his enemies. Their fate is certain.

Tobacco becomes a habit with Europeans

Europe, c.1600
Two products discovered in the New World are now beginning to have an impact on everyday life in Europe.

Tobacco taking – introduced by John Hawkins in 1566 – is now taken for granted. Pipe smokers include princes and peasants. Despite the price – three shillings an ounce – virtually every English pub now provides a communal pipe for its customers.

Less of an indulgence but fast becoming part of Europe's diet are potato tubers. These are now widely grown after being discovered in America, but not, as often claimed, by Sir Walter Raleigh in Virginia. He says he has never been there.

An Englishman experiences his first pipe; from a later painting.

Spanish horses fall into Apache hands

North American Plains, c.1600
Spanish settlers have begun to regret bitterly the day they let security slip and allowed Apache raiders to steal horses during attacks on settlements in the southwestern territories. Since then the Indians have been quick to appreciate the advantages of horsepower in riding and hunting and have started to breed their own horses from captured stock. Stealing horses is now one of their main reasons for raids on Spanish settlements. During the recent Pueblo uprising hundreds of horses were stolen. Some will be kept, but many will be traded for that other commodity the Spanish wish they had never introduced – the gun.

Horror looms out of the darkness. "The Medusa", by the Rome-based artist Michelangelo da Caravaggio, whose strongly-lit, natural looking, dramatic images represent a break with the prevailing mannerist style.

France, 17 January 1601. Following a French victory at Chambery, the treaty of Lyons ends a short war between France and Savoy. By the treaty France gains land near the Swiss frontier in return for Saluzzo and French lands beyond the Alps.

London, 25 February 1601. Robert Devereux, the second earl of Essex is beheaded after the failure of a plot he had hatched. Pretending to protect Queen Elizabeth from a Spanish conspiracy, and aided by his own supporters and those of James VI of Scotland, he had attempted to capture London and the Tower.

Prague, 24 October 1601. The astronomer Tycho Brahe dies. He set up an observatory in Prague with the help of the Emperor Rudolf II, and worked there with Johann Kepler. Brahe's greatest contribution to the science of astronomy was that he understood the need for constant observation of the skies and perfected instruments which enabled him to do this with accuracy. He did not believe in the Copernican theory of the universe, which puts the sun at the centre rather than the earth.

New Mexico, 24 November 1601. The governor of Mexico, Juan de Onate, returns to the capital, San Gabriel, after a six-month search for the fabled Quivira (*in Kansas*) – a legendary Indian ruler whose cities are said to be encrusted with gold and precious stones – to find the colony nearly deserted.

India, 1601. The Moghul Emperor Akbar has now absorbed the Dekhan kingdoms of Berar, Ahmadnagar and Khandesh into his kingdom.

London, 1601. Two new plays by William Shakespeare open in London: a comedy, *Twelfth Night*, celebrating the traditionally anarchic festival of 6 January, and *Troilus and Cressida*, a wryly comic tale of the lovesick man and his faithless lover.

Europe, 1601. Germany and France agree to co-operate in the establishment of a new postal service.

Germany, 1601. Many *badestuben* (brothels) are closed by the authorities in an attempt to halt the spread of venereal disease.

England, March 1602. Sir Walter Raleigh sends a final party in search of the Roanoake settlers in Virginia. Using a grant given to Raleigh in 1584, 225 settlers were brought to Roanoke Island between 1585 and 1587, but when the colony was visited again in 1591, no one was there. It is feared that they have died at the hands of Indians or Spaniards.

Rome, 11 March 1602. The composer Emilio di Cavalieri dies. He composed the first dramatic oratorio.

Netherlands, 20 March 1602. The Dutch East India Company is founded.

North America, 16 June 1602. The Englishman Captain Bartholomew Gosnold has given up his colonisation efforts in the north-east of the continent. He left Falmouth on 26 March and has discovered and named Cape Cod, after the fish he found there, and Martha's Vineyard, in honour of his daughter. He is now returning to England.

Paris, 29 July 1602. The duke of Biron is executed for conspiring with Spain and Savoy against the king, Henry IV.

Central America, 14 December 1602. The Spanish merchant and explorer Sebastian Vizcaino, leading an expedition to link up with the navigator Juan de Onate on the Pacific coast, directs his ships into the previously undiscovered Monterey Bay.

Beijing, 1602. The Italian Jesuit missionary Matteo Ricci visits Beijing for the second time and is given permission to stay.

Naples, 1602. Tommaso Campanella, an ex-Dominican friar who led an abortive revolution in southern Italy in 1600, writes *City of the Sun* in prison. It is a fantasy of the ideal city, ruled by priests through scientific magic.

Hungary, 1602. The Counter-reformation gathers force with the persecution of Protestants in Hungary and Bohemia.

South America, 1602. Dutch colonists found a settlement (*in Guiana*) near the estuary of the Essequibo river.

England, 1602. Sir Thomas Bodley opens the Bodleian Library in Oxford.

West Africa, 1603. Idris Aloma, the *mai* (king) of Bornu, dies. During a reign of 33 years he has won many campaigns, thanks to his use of Turkish firearms.

Persia, 1603. Shah Abbas of Persia retakes Tabriz from the Turks.

Canada, 1603. Colonisation of Sable Island has been abandoned. In 1597, 50 petty criminals and their guards were left on the island. They were sending sealskins and oil back to France. However, last year no word was received and when envoys returned to the colony they found that the guards had been killed and then the prisoners had turned on each other. Only 11 survived.

Oba Esigies returns from battle.   *Amufi dancers swing from a tree.*

Beautiful bronzes created at Benin court

Benin, West Africa, c.1601

Travellers have brought back tales of remarkably advanced bronze and ivory figures sculpted in the kingdom of Benin, in western Nigeria. The kingdom is ruled by the *oba*, who is believed locally to be the reincarnation of the founder of the dynasty in the 13th century.

Carved ivory is reserved for the oba's ornament, and carved tusks decorate the shrines of his ancestors. Ivory leopards, made from five tusks, each with inlaid copper discs as their spots, and bronze heads encased in ring-collars and fantastic helmets, have a style quite new to the European eye.

One traveller reports that at the burial of the oba he saw the grave surrounded by human heads on stakes, belonging to wives and servants who were to accompany the oba to the next world.

A bronze mask from Benin, of the type that has astonished western travellers.

Poor Law offers "whipping for the lazy"

Lazy, good-for-nothing scroungers? "Beggars" (1567) by Bruegel the Elder.

England, 1601

It is being said that parliament's latest bill to reform and extend the Poor Law will give England the best welfare system in Europe. Help for the poor is made a national responsibility, supervised by the Privy Council but administered locally by justices of the peace. The scheme is funded by the levying of rates on better-off households.

Claims that many poor do not want to work are often heard; the new law therefore provides for the whipping of vagrants and beggars, who will be returned to their home villages by the parish constable. Justices of the peace are required to obtain stocks of flax, hemp, wool, thread and other items in order to keep the unemployed usefully occupied. The house of correction awaits anyone who refuses to work.

Elizabeth's reign has been marked by genuine concern for the condition of the poor, partly because it is feared that population growth, economic recession and consequent poverty could lead to widespread unrest.

Wallachia collapses

Wallachia, Balkans, 1601

Michael the Brave, the prince of Wallachia, has been assassinated on the orders of the Habsburg emperor. With his death the independent state of Wallachia collapses.

For the past decade, Wallachia and the neighbouring states of Moldavia and Transylvania have played a crucial role in the balance of power between Austria, Turkey and Poland. No-one played a more delicate balancing act than Michael, who wanted to unite the three small states. He overran Transylvania in 1599, and Moldavia last year, purportedly in the emperor's name. But the emperor did not trust him.

Impostor hanged

Portugal, 7 September 1603

Another pretender to the throne of Portugal – claiming to be the foolhardy King Sebastian who was killed in battle 25 years ago – has been unmasked and executed. Marco Caltizzone, a Calabrian, appeared in Venice and was arrested on the orders of the Spanish ambassador. Like several other such "Sebastians" he was condemned to the galleys, but was later hanged.

The Sebastian phenomenon is the result of the Portuguese having to accept the Castilian king of Spain as their king. Sebastian was king for only a few months before being killed during a disastrous campaign against the Moors.

Dutch join race to trade with the east

Amsterdam, 20 March 1602

The various companies which have been engaging in cut-throat trading competition in the East Indies have today been formed into one corporation. It has been given a monopoly of Dutch trade and navigation east of the Cape of Good Hope and west of the Magellan Straits for an initial period of 21 years.

This Dutch East India Company has also been given sweeping powers. Governed by a court of 17 directors, drawn from the Dutch states, it can conclude treaties, wage defensive war, and build "fortresses and strongholds" in the East Indies. It has thus become a state within a state.

A warship of the Dutch East India Company. High, full-bottomed and manoeuvrable: a queen of the seas.

English navigator builds ships in Japan

Japan, 1601

Will Adams, a Kentish seafarer, is building ships of up to 100 tons for the warlord Ieyasu and teaching his men the skills of long-distance navigation. Adams arrived here as the pilot-major on board a Dutch ship, the *Liefde*, part of a squadron of five trading vessels which were also equipped to destroy their Spanish and Portuguese rivals.

A great storm struck the ships, the *Liefde* was crippled, and many of her crew died. She was towed into Kyushu with barely a score alive. And that was not the end of their privations, for they were denounced as pirates by Jesuit missionaries and threatened with crucifixion. Their lives were saved by Ieyasu, who sent for Adams. The Englishman reached Osaka in May last year along with the *Liefde's* cannons and ammunition which Ieyasu has since put to good use.

Will Adams shows some plans to his employer, the shogun Ieyasu.

Adams has been well treated and is happily employed in his shipbuilding work. It seems unlikely, however, that he will ever see the orchards of Kent again.

True and righteous warrior dies in Africa

Bornu, West Africa, 1603

Idris Aloma, the ruler of Bornu and one of the greatest generals of his generation, is dead. Ascending the throne in 1570, he rebuilt a weak and defenceless state, impoverished by famine, and founded a strong army equipped with firearms. His musketeers and camel-borne troops conquered the So people, the Tuareg and the people of Kano and Kanem, spreading Islam wherever they went. The state they created has surpassed the decaying Songhai empire and become the most powerful in Africa between the Niger and the Nile.

Idris was not only a warrior but also a diplomat and an administrator. Turkey and Morocco paid him their respects. "Truth and righteousness came into their own and shone in Bornu," wrote his chronicler, Ahmad ibn Fartua.

1603 (1603-1605)

Mexico, 21 March 1603. The *San Diego*, one of the navigator Sebastian Vizcaino's ships, returns to Mexico with the first full account of the Pacific coast of Central America.

England, 24 March 1603. Queen Elizabeth dies at Richmond having apparently named James VI of Scotland as her successor.

Canada, April 1603. The French explorer Samuel de Champlain lands in Canada on a mission to study conditions for a possible permanent settlement in New France.

Paris, 20 June 1603. King Henry IV officially reopens work on the Pont Neuf ("New Bridge"). Begun in 1578, building was interrupted by the French wars of religion.

Virginia, 29 July 1603. Bartholomew Gilbert is killed by Indians during a search for the Roanoke colonists, who were last seen in 1587.

India, 30 November 1603. Khwaja Mohammed Baqi Billah, a mystic who has done much to establish the Naqshbandi sufi order in India, has died.

France, 13 December 1603. The celebrated mathematician Francois Viete dies. He was the first person to use alphabetical symbols in algebra.

England, 1603. Puritans led by one Henry Jacob present the *Millenary Petition* (so-called because it was signed by a thousand clergymen) to King James on his first entry to England. It is a moderate plea for church reform, calling for the abandonment of "popish" religious ceremonies, such as the use of the ring in marriage and making the sign of the cross at baptism. The king promises to hold a conference at which it will be discussed.

France, 1603. King Henry IV authorises the Jesuits to resettle in his kingdom.

London, 1603. The city suffers a serious outbreak of the plague.

Morocco, 1603. Ahmed V, or Ahmed al-Mansur, dies. He came to power after his victory over Portuguese invaders in 1578, and was also known as the "Golden" or "Victorious". During his reign Morocco was unified and prospered. He made an alliance with England against Spain, subdued Mauritania, and took possession of the wealthy Songhai empire with its salt mines.

France, 1603. The first beaver skins arrive in the port of La Rochelle from Canada.

Istanbul, 1603. Sultan Mehmet III dies and is succeeded by Sultan Ahmed.

Japan, 1603. A female attendant at the Izumo shrine leads a theatrical performance on a dry river bed. The show includes dancing and comic sketches and is referred to by the audience as *Kabuki*, a term which refers to its unusual or shocking character.

Japan, 1603. Out of the general conflict that followed the death of the civil dictator and prime minister, Hideyoshi (in 1598), Tokugawa Ieyasu has emerged victorious and is now appointed *shogun*. He forms a *bakufu* (military government) in Edo and builds a castle there.

North America, June 1604. The French explorer Pierre du Guast, the sieur du Monts, founds the first French colony in the north-east region, on the St Croix river.

Netherlands, 20 September 1604. After a two-year siege, the Spanish retake Ostend from the Dutch. The Spanish Archduchess Isabella, imitating a chivalric tradition, had vowed that she would not change her blouse until Ostend fell.

Spain, 1604. Mateo Aleman follows up the hugely successful first volume of his gloomy picaresque novel *Guzman de Alfarache* (1599) with a second volume.

France, 1604. The edict of Paulette (after the financier Paulet), a decree of Henry IV, establishes a tax on the hereditary holding of offices, and so institutionalises the sale of government offices.

Rome, 1604. The painter Annibale Carracci puts the finishing touches to the decoration of the gallery in the Farnese palace.

London, 1604. King James describes the habit of tobacco-smoking as "vile and stinking" and "dangerous".

New Spain, 1604. The term "Mexican" appears in print for the first time in *La Gazetta Mexicana*, published by the creole Balbuena.

London, 1604. *Othello, or the Moor of Venice*, a tragedy by Shakespeare on the theme of sexual jealousy, is staged for the first time.

Italy, 1604. Over the past two years the Italian astronomer Galileo has discovered the laws of gravitation and oscillation.

England, 1604. King James dashes Puritan hopes that he would reform the church along lines suggested in last year's Millenary Petition. His only concession has been to authorise a new translation of the Bible.

Canada, 1605. Port Royal is established in Acadia (*Nova Scotia*).

Thousands die in Russian famine

Russia, 1603

Russia is in the grip of a terrible famine which has reduced men to eating grass and birch bark. Some reports talk of cannibalism. The famine is the result of a series of disastrously poor harvests, and it has completed the isolation of Czar Boris Godunov's regime. Whole village populations have disappeared, and a report says that at least 125,000 people have starved to death in Moscow alone.

Government decrees to deal with the problem have been of no avail. The famine has prompted widespread profiteering and a sharp increase in the price of bread. Czar Boris has ordered the distribution of grain to the most needy from the palace granaries. Other relief measures have included a vast building programme in Moscow.

Many landowners, unable to feed their peasants, have driven them from their estates. Another consequence has been the formation of marauding bands of homeless peasants who have been attacking the granaries of the merchants.

Sudden death of Czar Boris Godunov

Moscow, 13 April 1605

Czar Boris Godunov died suddenly today, either from a stroke or, as many suspect, from self-administered poison. He was 53 and had been the ruler of Russia almost since the death of Ivan the Terrible's weak son, Fyodor.

Boris was elected czar in 1598, and in many ways his rule at home and abroad followed the pattern set by Ivan. He was hostile to the *boyars* and more reliant on support from the lesser serving nobility. In foreign relations he pursued Ivan's aggressive policy.

His problems had mounted in recent years, however. To begin with, the land-owning nobles were never reconciled to his election as czar; and, for fear of being poisoned, he maintained six foreign doctors at his court. At the same time there has been famine, epidemics, and a revolt culminating in the appearance of a pretender, a "false Dimitri", named after Ivan's son whom Boris is alleged to have murdered. Even now, this pretender is marching on Moscow.

Mad Spanish knight tilts at windmills

Spain, 1605

A new book by the author Miguel de Cervantes is delighting readers all over his native Spain. The adventures of *Don Quixote de la Mancha* simultaneously poke fun at the traditional tales of chivalry and take a hard look at contemporary Spanish society.

The fictional Don Quixote is a keen consumer of just the sort of stories Cervantes mocks; indeed, too much romance has driven him mad. Accompanied by his squire Sancho Panza, whose earthy common sense contrasts with his master's fantasies, Quixote sets off on his ageing horse Rosinante to roam the world in search of adventure.

In his madness the most ordinary things appear romantic or terrifying. In true chivalric style he has his own fair lady, even if the girl he honours has no idea of his interest. Taking up his lance he tilts at what he thinks are giants, but in reality are only windmills. Quixote searches for fine ideals, but the

Title page of the 1612 English translation of Cervantes' masterpiece.

modern Spain in which he travels proves disappointing. Greed has replaced chivalry, and gold, looted from the New World, has taken the place of the knightly qualities he values.

English and Scottish thrones united

German maps stars of southern skies

England, 24 March 1603

When Queen Elizabeth died at Richmond early this morning, the crowns of England and Scotland became united under her successor, the Scottish King James VI. He will be known, by his wish, as James I of Great Britain – the most powerful Protestant sovereign in Europe.

Elizabeth succeeded to an England riven by religious divisions, at war with France, and heavily in debt to the bankers of Antwerp. After a reign of 45 years she has bequeathed to her successor an exchequer which, for all her parsimony, has been drained by rebellion in Ireland and support for the Protestant revolt against Spain in the Netherlands.

But in her long reign the arts flourished as never before: only last year Shakespeare's drama, *Hamlet*, was performed by the Lord Chamberlain's company of actors.

To her subjects Elizabeth was England personified. As she said before the Armada: "Let tyrants fear. I know I have the body of a weak and feeble woman, but I have the heart and stomach of a king, and a king of England too; and think foul scorn that any prince of Europe should dare invade the borders of my realm."

Her bad habits – swearing, beer-drinking and spitting – did not lose her the affection of those who served her. Her successor, the son of Mary, Queen of Scots, has been welcomed by the English, though some find his brusque manner and Scottish accent disconcerting; and they are none too pleased with his talk of the divine right of kings.

This portrait by Marcus Gheeraerts the Younger captures the stern face of Elizabeth, queen for 45 years.

Augsburg, Germany, 1603

Twelve new southern constellations have been mapped out in a groundbreaking astronomical atlas just published by Johann Bayer, a German amateur astronomer. Bayer's *Uranometria*, intended as a popular guide to the heavens, has already been greeted with so much acclaim that Augsburg's city council has decided to reward the 31-year-old bachelor with a 150-gulden honorarium. One of *Uranometria's* key features is the way it maps the stars without relying on verbal descriptions of their locations. Instead, stars are grouped according to their luminosity, with each type of star assigned a Greek letter; the brightest are designated as *alpha* stars.

Golden Temple at Amritsar completed

The Golden Temple at Amritsar: covered in gold leaf, it is the holiest Sikh shrine and represents a shining example of devotional architecture.

Amritsar, India, 1605

The Golden Temple, the great Sikh shrine at Amritsar in the Punjab, is complete. The Sikhs are the followers of Guru Nanak, the Punjabi mystic who rejected both Hindu and Moslem orthodoxies.

The Moghul emperor, Akbar, granted them Amritsar, a waterhole which they renamed the "pool of immortality". There, under the direction of their fourth *guru*, Ram Das, they have built a holy city. The city's architecture, a harmonious mixture of Moslem and Hindu styles, with exquisite ornamentation, centres on the "pool of immortality", surrounded by a finely carved marble balustrade. In the middle of the pool a causeway, also made of marble, leads to a small island.

Here stands the Golden Temple itself, its copper dome, walls and cupolas covered with gold foil that glistens in the Indian sun. The two-storey interior is as memorable as the exterior, displaying some of the most beautiful floral and geometrical motifs in India.

The Bolognese painter Annibale Carracci (born 1560) has recently completed this elaborate ceiling for the Farnese Palace in Rome. Rich in trompe l'oeil (optical illusion) reliefs and full of grand, heroic images, it is acclaimed as his greatest masterpiece so far, ranking with Raphael's frescoes for the papal apartments and Michelangelo's Sistine Chapel.

1605 (1605-1606)

Moscow, 10 June 1605. With Polish support, a Russian who has passed himself off as Prince Dimitri (the supposedly murdered son of Ivan IV) has himself crowned czar.

England, 17 July 1605. George Weymouth returns from the north-eastern coast of America (*Maine*) with glowing reports of agricultural development, notably barley and pea cultivation.

North America, 20 July 1605. The French cartographer and explorer Samuel de Champlain has reached Cape Cod on his second voyage of discovery in search of an ideal location for French settlement in the New World.

London, September 1605. *Eastward Ho* by Ben Jonson and others is published. It satirises the good publicity given to Virginia and the belief that the Roanoke colonists are still alive.

Geneva, 13 October 1605. Theodore Beza, the theologian, pastor and writer, dies. He succeeded Calvin as rector of the Academy of Geneva and wrote poetry, histories, treatises, pamphlets and even a tragedy *Abraham sacrifiant* (1553).

India, 17 October 1605. The Moghul Emperor Akbar the Great dies and is succeeded by Jahangir, his son.

London, 1605. Shakespeare's tragedy *Macbeth*, about the rise to power of a Scottish regicide and his ambitious wife, opens in London.

London, 1605. Ben Jonson's *Volpone, or the Fox*, a black comedy about a wily miser, is staged for the first time.

Germany, 1605. Two hundred and five people convicted of witchcraft have been burnt in the last two years at the abbey of Fulda. Prince Abbot Balthasar von Dernbach supervises the witch-hunts in the area, assisted by his minister Balthasar Ross.

Rome, 1605. Caravaggio's painting *The Death of the Madonna*, commissioned for the Santa Maria della Scala church in Trastevere, is rejected on the grounds of its indecency. The Madonna's body, swollen after death, is that of a poor woman.

America, c.1605. European diseases are decimating the American Indians. Smallpox, measles, dysentery, typhoid and tuberculosis are being passed to Indians at contact points on the coasts of both sub-continents and spread inland by trade and warfare. Alcohol is also reported to be having a disastrous effect on Indian communities.

South-East Asia, 1605. The English sailor John Davis is killed by pirates in the Malacca Straits. When searching for a sea route round the north coast of America in 1587, he discovered a strait linking (*the Baffin Sea to the Atlantic*) in 1592, during an expedition to the southern seas, he discovered islands known as the Malvinas (*Falkland Islands*).

South-East Asia, 1605. The Dutch capture Amboina and take the Moluccas from the Portuguese.

Florida, March 1606. Juan de la Cabezade de Altimirano is the first bishop to visit North America.

Venice, May 1606. Pope Paul V calls on the rulers of the Venetian state to abandon their policy of social and moral control, a power which they took from the church in 1582. They refuse and he places them under an edict.

Russia, 19 May 1606. Vasily Shuisky overthrows the "false Dimitri" to become czar.

Central Europe, 11 November 1606. The treaty of Zsitvatorok puts an end to several years of war between the Ottoman empire and the Habsburgs.

Canada, 14 November 1606. A French performance of *La Theatre de Neptune en la Nouvelle France* in Port Royal is one of the first plays staged in the New World.

England, 20 December 1606. The London Company dispatches the ships *Sarah Constant*, *Discovery* and *Goodspeed*, led by Captain Christopher Newport, to Virginia.

Portugal, 1606. A Dutch fleet blockades the river Tagus.

East Indies, 1606. A Spanish expedition returning from the Philippines recaptures part of the Moluccas from the Dutch. The Dutch attack Malacca with no success.

Germany, 1606. Matthias, the Emperor Rudolf II's brother, has himself recognised as heir.

England, 1606 The Virginia Company is given the task of colonising the area around Florida and Delaware, while the Plymouth Company is to colonise territory inland from Cape Cod Bay.

India, 1606. For two years the Spanish Jesuit Roberto de Nobilis has been preaching in the Dekhan region. He has learnt local dialects adopting the lifestyle of the Brahmins. His lifestyle arouses hostility in his fellow-missionaries.

London, 1606. Shakespeare's *Antony and Cleopatra*, a tale of ill-fated love between the Roman Antony and the queen of the Nile, opens in London.

Plot to blow up parliament is thwarted

The gunpowder plotters seen conspiring, captured and then hanged, drawn and quartered. Finally, their heads are set on poles as a warning to others.

London, November 1605

A Yorkshireman who served with the Spanish forces in the Netherlands after converting to Catholicism has been apprehended in the cellars under the Houses of Parliament with 20 barrels of gunpowder. Under severe torture, Guy Fawkes confessed to plotting to blow up the House of Lords when the king and queen, Prince Henry and members of both houses were assembled for the opening of parliament.

Fawkes at first refused to reveal his accomplices, but King James ordered the torture to continue indefinitely and Fawkes named Robert Catesby, a Warwickshire gentleman and a zealous Catholic, who had been involved in earlier plots against Elizabeth. Catesby and his fellow plotters were to have held a hunting party as a cover for a bid to kidnap the king's daughter Elizabeth once Fawkes had succeeded.

The conspiracy was exposed after Lord Monteagle, a Catholic peer who had declared his loyalty to the king, received an anonymous note urging him to find an excuse to stay away from the opening of Parliament on 5 November, because "God and man" would deliver "a terrible blow". Monteagle showed the note to Lord Salisbury, the king's chief minister, and the cellars were searched. Catesby and three others died resisting arrest. Six more, including Fawkes, await execution.

Breakaway sect plans to leave England

England, 1606

A new sect has emerged from amongst those who have rejected the Church of England but cannot accept orthodox Calvinism. Calling themselves the Baptists, they are led by a former Gainsborough preacher, John Smith, who in turn has broken away from the dissenting Separatists. Facing continuous persecution in England, the sect plans to emigrate to Amsterdam where tolerance is the norm.

Central to Smith's beliefs is his rejection of infant baptism. Since baptism is not simply "washing in water" but also "baptism of the Spirit, the confession of the mouth", how, he asks, can a baby appreciate its importance?

Instead Smith and a hard core of 32 followers believe that adult baptism is a more fitting ceremony. This has caused great controversy, as have the Baptists' refusal to read the Bible in anything but the original Hebrew or Greek and their rejection of the basic Calvinist doctrines of original sin and predestination.

Poisoning suspected in Akbar's death

Bullocks help one of Akbar's sieges.

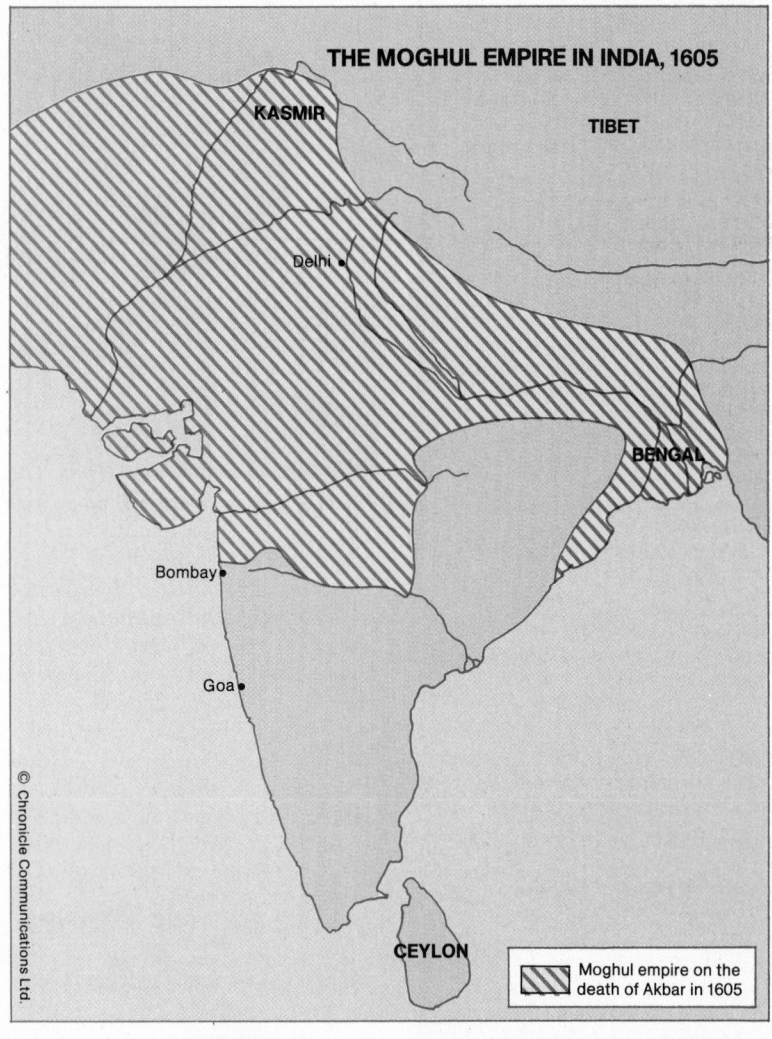

THE MOGHUL EMPIRE IN INDIA, 1605

KASMIR

TIBET

Delhi

BENGAL

Bombay

Goa

CEYLON

© Chronicle Communications Ltd

Moghul empire on the death of Akbar in 1605

Agra, India, 17 October 1605
Akbar, the greatest of all the Moghul emperors, is dead. He has suffered three weeks of diarrhoea and internal bleeding. Poison is suspected, though the suspects are too numerous to attempt to list.

Illiterate yet noble, capable of immense charm and violent rages, he was every inch an emperor. A Jesuit, who was proud to have been called his friend, described him as "vibrant like the sea reflected in the sun".

As a child he nearly lost his kingdom, but he never lost a battle, and as a man extended his empire by battle after battle until he ruled two-thirds of the subcontinent.

To administer this empire he reformed the bureaucracy, modernised the army and imported technology. He sought to stand above religion. Only in that way could he unite his Hindu, Moslem and Buddhist subjects.

He was both a deist and a mystic, who searched through the traditions of every religion known to him to find truth. He delighted in the fine arts, and in the evenings he loved to have books on history, geography, philosophy and theology read to him.

His only failure appears to have been in his family life. All three of his sons are said to be alcoholics, which bodes ill for India.

"Australia" found in southern seas

North Australia, August 1606
A Portuguese expedition under Luis Vaez Torres believes that it has found a new continent in the southern seas. Ironically the navigator Pero Fernandez de Quiros, whose conviction that there was a southern continent drove the three ships across the Pacific, never saw it. His own ship mutinied and sailed to Mexico. His name for the southern continent remains, however: *La Australia del Espiritu Santo*.

Torres, making his way to the Philippines after his Pacific voyage, may have glimpsed the north coast of Australia (*near Cape York*). Landing on some outlying islands, he found "corpulent and naked" black people and kidnapped some in the interests of research.

Only five months earlier a Dutch vessel, the *Duyfken* (Dove), had reported sailing down the western coast of New Guinea, where some of the crew were killed by "wild, cruel, black savages". It seems likely since Torres' report that New Guinea is the west of this new "Australian" continent.

The discovery of Australia has come as no surprise. There have been numerous rumours of its existence. Marco Polo learnt of it in the 13th century from Chinese traders.

In 1503 a French navigator, Binot Paulmyer, blown off course in the Indian Ocean, landed on a vast land which he was convinced was what is now called Australia. The Dutch historian and geographer Wytfliet estimated in 1597 that this undiscovered continent covered a fifth of the world's entire surface.

Francis Bacon looks at modern learning

England, 1605
A new book has been published by England's leading scientist, Francis Bacon. *The Advancement of Learning*, the first part of which appeared in 1603, is a highly elaborate survey and classification of the various types of knowledge. It is the first of Bacon's works to appear in English rather than Latin.

Bacon's aim is to redefine the whole basis of modern learning. He has divided knowledge into three parts – history, poetry and philosophy – and linked them to three faculties of the mind – memory, imagination and reasoning.

Rejecting the "empirics" – astrologers, magicians and others – who simply heap up unrelated facts, Bacon has attempted to set out what he calls "fixed laws". This system has, he claims, "levelled men's wits", and now anyone can use his laws to explain the occurrence of scientific events.

Habsburgs and Ottomans come to terms

Zsitvatorok, 11 November 1606
In an obscure town on the Hungarian frontier, the Ottoman and Habsburg empires have concluded a peace treaty that promises a new era of stability between two long-standing foes.

Whereas previous treaties have been "graciously accorded by the Sultan" to his "vanquished" rival, the Treaty of Zsitvatorok is between equals. Austria is no longer to pay an annual tribute. A final payment has been agreed, after which the ambassadors of the two great powers will exchange ceremonial gifts every three years.

With the exception of two newly-created provinces and the frontier fortresses of Erlau, Gran and Kanischa, Turkey renounces its claim to Hungarian land. Transylvania, whose prince, Stephen Bocskai, is a party to the treaty, gains considerable autonomy under Turkish rule. The treaty is signed for 20 years.

Rome, 1606. The painter Annibale Carracci is overcome by depression and abandons painting almost entirely.

Venice, April 1607. Denied practical support by France and Spain, Pope Paul V is reconciled with Venice, and withdraws the edict of May 1606, in which he objected to the government's control of the moral and social lives of the citizens, formerly the concern of the church.

England, 1 May 1607. *The Gift of God*, funded by Sir Ferdinando Gorges and commanded by George Popham, leaves on a voyage to North America.

Virginia, 24 May 1607. Captain Christopher Newport and 105 followers have founded the colony of Jamestown at the mouth of the James river on the coast of Virginia. They left England last December with 144 colonists.

North America, 15 June 1607. Colonists finish building James Fort in Jamestown, to defend themselves against attacks by the Spanish and Indians.

England, June 1607. Beggars and homeless people around Northampton tear down enclosures recently erected near the town, in protest against the loss of common land. Several protesters are killed; after the actions have been stopped, three people are hanged as an example to the rest.

North America, 14 August 1607. The Popham expedition reaches the Sagadahoc river in the north-east and prepares to settle.

New Mexico, August 1607. Juan de Onate resigns as first Spanish governor here, notifying the viceroy of New Spain that the colony will be abandoned if reinforcements do not arrive by next June.

France, 28 September 1607. Samuel de Champlain and colonists return from Port Royal (*in Nova Scotia*), abandoning the settlement there.

North America, September 1607. Newly-arrived Jamestown colonists have lived on sturgeon and sea crab all summer, and have buried at least 50 people in the last four months, lost to disease and starvation.

Russia, October 1607. A peasant uprising led by Bolotnikov, a former serf who had been captured by Tartars and sold as a slave to the Turks, is put down. Nobles who support the "false Dimitri", ousted by the current czar, initially joined the peasants, but, alarmed by the size of the movement, they betrayed Bolotnikov and he has been imprisoned.

North America, 10 December 1607. John Smith, a founder of the Jamestown colony, heads up Chickahominy river in search of food.

North America, 29 December 1607. Powhatan, the Indian chief, spares John Smith's life after the pleas of his daughter Pocahontas.

Italy, 1607. Monteverdi's opera *Orfeo* is performed in Mantua.

France, 1607. Honore d'Urfe publishes the first part of *L'Astree*, a novel on pastoral love.

Mexico, 1607. After the fourth serious flooding of Mexico City, the government is forced to think of a way of diverting the flood waters. The *desague* is built: an eight-mile long drainage canal, half tunnel and half open, which conducts the waters of the valley of Mexico through the mountains to the northwest of the city, into the Tula river, and then on into the Gulf of Mexico.

North America, 1607. The first ship built in the north-east of the continent by settlers, at George Popham's colony at the mouth of the Kennebec river, is christened the *Virginia*.

India, 1607. The Moghul Emperor Jahangir sends an envoy to meet the Portuguese viceroy in Goa.

England, 1607. *On the Value of the Colonies to England* by either Richard Hakluyt or Sir John Popham, is published.

Germany, 19 May 1608. The Protestant states form the Evangelical Union of Lutherans and Calvinists under the direction of the elector of Brandenburg.

Russia, 1 June 1608. A second "false Dimitri" attempts to usurp the throne, again supported by the Polish who besiege Moscow. He sets up a council in Tushino.

Canada, 7 July 1608. The first French settlement at Quebec is set up by Samuel de Champlain.

England, 1608. The English form an alliance with the United Provinces (*the Netherlands*) against Spain.

South America, 1608. The Jesuit state of Paraguay is founded.

London, 1608. Shakespeare's gory tragedy *Timon of Athens* and Thomas Middleton's lively comedy *A Mad World, My Masters* draw eager audiences.

Chile, 1608. A Spanish royal decree legalises the slavery of Chilean Indians.

Germany, 1609. Regular newspapers are published in Strasbourg and Wolfenbuttel.

Pretender czar killed after window leap

Left: the first counterfeit Dimitri. Right: the second, who waits in the wings.

Moscow, 19 May 1606
The pretender Dimitri, Russia's ruler since the death of Boris Godunov in 1605, has been killed and replaced in a revolt by the landowning *boyars*. Dimitri, known as "the false Dimitri" because he claimed to be the son of Czar Ivan IV — who is known to be dead — tried to escape by jumping from a Kremlin window, but broke his legs. His body was burnt and his ashes shot from a cannon. The pretender's downfall was precipitated by the arrival of his fiancee from Poland with her entourage. This angered Muscovites, who had backed Dimitri to get rid of Godunov, not to instal another czar, unless he was from their own ranks. There are now rumours that another pretender is being groomed for czardom.

Spain expels Moors who are Christians

Spain, 9 April 1609
The *Moriscos*, former Moslems who chose conversion to Christianity as the price of their residence in Spain, are to leave the country. King Philip III, bowing to pressure from his hostile subjects, signed the order for their expulsion today.

Much of the problem springs from the refusal of the Moriscos to assimilate fully into Spanish society. Some may genuinely believe in their new faith, and may have tried to give up their Moorish ways, but the majority of the 300,000-strong community remain essentially Arabs. Their language, society, clothes, customs and even their eating and drinking remain alien to native Spaniards. Few have truly abandoned the Koran. The Moriscos have been pressured to change their ways for a century, for with a large Moslem presence in North Africa, Arabs are seen as a major threat to national security. But still they resist integration.

Calvinists ally with Lutheran rivals

Germany, 19 May 1608
In a rare display of unity, the Protestant princes of Germany – both Calvinist and Lutherans – have formed a union at Anhausen and are now beginning to arm themselves against Catholic aggression following the Habsburg subjugation of the city of Donauworth. The monks there, whose monastery had survived the reformation, had been in conflict with the city's burghers.

The affair was minor, but it was worrying enough to infuriate the Protestant estates which regarded the action as a breach of the Peace of Augsburg. Their protests ended in a walk-out at the imperial diet of Ratisbon (Regensburg) in February this year. Although the new union's membership is confined to six princes – with Saxony and the north-west of Germany staying out – the historic rift between the Lutherans and Calvinists has been hard to hide even in a union of "peace-loving estates".

Earls' flight marks end of Gaelic Ireland

Ireland, 1608

Two fighting earls, Tyrone and Tyrconnel, by turns loyalists and rebels in Catholic Ireland's struggle with the English, have fled to the continent of Europe and been received at the gates of Rome by seven cardinals. The pope has placed a palace at their disposal, but back home they have been declared traitors and their lands in Ulster have been seized for settlement by Protestants from England and Scotland.

After defeat in battle and submission to the English, Tyrone, chief of the O'Neill clan, and Tyrconnel, of the O'Donnells, were pardoned by King James and restored to their lands. But they saw that feudal Ireland with its powerful Gaelic clan chiefs had been abolished and replaced by Englishstyle sheriffs and counties.

Tyrone, now in his mid-sixties, has been a triple renegade, first fighting with the English, then against them, and repeating the apostasy twice more before final defeat. He then found himself in a dispute over his feudal rights and the king invited him to put his case in London. Tyrone, fearing arrest, joined with Tyrconnel to hire a ship and escape abroad with their families and servants.

They planned to go to Spain, but were driven ashore in France. They were not wanted there and became refugees in the Spanish Netherlands. Unwelcome there, too, they went via Lorraine and Switzerland to Italy, finding refuge at last in Rome.

Netherlands and Spain sign truce

The Hague, 9 April 1609

After 40 years of rebellion and repression, Spain and the Netherlands have finally come to terms. A formal truce has been agreed here after months of negotiation, with envoys from England and France acting as mediators. The truce will last for 12 years but, because of the need to inform troops and ships outside Europe, it will be a year before it takes effect universally.

The truce represents a deal between Spain's governor, Archduke Albert, and his wife, the Infanta Isabella, in the south, and Maurice of Nassau, the leader of the States General of the United Provinces (the formal name for the separatist Netherlands government) in the north. The archduke tried desperately to secure a guarantee of an improvement in conditions for Catholics in the north. With their large merchant fleet, the Dutch, on the other hand, pressed for the right to trade with Spanish colonies.

A clause allows travel and trade between each other's countries, but "as for the places, cities, ports and harbours which he [King Philip III of Spain] holds outside these limits, the States and their subjects cannot engage in any business in them without the permission of the aforesaid king".

The sculptor Giovanni da Bologna, known as Giambologna, died in August 1608 at the age of 79. His "Rape of the Sabines" in Florence is hailed as the pinnacle of the "Mannerist" style, characterised by powerful figures set in contorted, dramatic poses full of motion and tension.

Shakespeare's sonnets are literary gems

London, 20 May 1609

The publication today by Thomas Thorpe of William Shakespeare's *Sonnets* has been long awaited. They were written at the time when the plague closed the theatres in 1593-4, and have been circulated privately among friends and intimates of the earl of Southampton, who was the poet's patron.

For the past ten years Shakespeare has been prominent at the Globe theatre on London's Bankside, where he is an actor and a shareholder in Richard Burbage's company, the King's Men, under royal patronage.

Shakespeare acts in his own plays – as Chorus in *Henry V* and Ghost in *Hamlet* – but his leading tragic roles are played by Burbage. Since 1602 they have presented *Hamlet, Prince of Denmark, Othello, Macbeth, King Lear, Antony and Cleopatra* and *Coriolanus*.

King James is very keen on plays, especially on *Macbeth*, which prophesies that his ancestor Banquo will father a line of kings, and deals with witchcraft, of which he has written. The old queen before him so liked the robust character of Falstaff in both parts of *Henry IV* and *Henry V* that she asked for another play to show him in love. This Shakespeare wrote, and presented on St George's Day under the title *The Merry Wives of Windsor*. The company has lately taken over the Blackfriars theatre, which is covered, for the winter seasons.

Portrait by miniaturist Nicholas Hilliard, possibly of Shakespeare.

"God's love for all" says Francois

Paris, 1609

Francois de Sales, the Bishop of Geneva, has published a new book in which he hopes to prove that the intimate love of God, often considered to be the province of priests and clergymen alone, is available to everyone who desires it.

De Sales was born in Savoy in 1567. Since then he has studied in Paris and Padua and has made his way through the church hierarchy to his present eminence.

Inspired by a visit to Paris in 1602, when he met the great representatives of French spirituality, Berulle and marie de l'Incarnation, de Sales has written his "Introduction a la vie devote" (Introduction to a life of devotion).

For de Sales the life of devotion is a life to which anyone may aspire. God does not love only His priests, but all of mankind. Wishing to offer a spiritual life to all, he has reconciled humanism with devotion.

An Indian bronze from Madras, showing the boy Krishna dancing on the snake Kaliya.

1609 (1609-1610)

London, 2 June 1609. The American province of Virginia is granted a new charter, extending its territory "from sea to sea".

France, 25 September 1609. Jacqueline Arnauld, the abbess of the convent of Port Royal, institutes strict enclosure – physical isolation from outsiders – as the first step to achieve a return to stricter monastic standards.

Netherlands, 9 April 1609. A 12-year truce is reached between the Netherlands and Spain, thanks to the mediation of Henry IV.

Bohemia, 9 July 1609. In a "Letter from the Crown", the Emperor Rudolf II grants Bohemia freedom of worship.

Germany, 10 July 1609. In response to the formation of the Protestant Evangelical Union, the Catholic states of the empire set up a league under the leadership of Maximilian of Bavaria.

Rome, 15 July 1609. The artist Annibale Carracci dies. Brought up to be a tailor, he rapidly established himself as a painter. He was influenced primarily by the works of Correggio and Raphael.

Bermuda, 25 July 1609. A hurricane hits a fleet headed for Jamestown, forcing the ship carrying Sir Thomas Gates and Sir Thomas Dale aground in Bermuda.

North America, 13 September 1609. In his second attempt to locate a passage to China, the English navigator Henry Hudson sails his ship, the *Half-Moon*, up the river near Manhattan island, (*the Hudson*) far enough to determine that it does not lead to the Orient. This is a great disappointment to Hudson.

Amsterdam, 1609. The Bank of Amsterdam is founded, modelled on the Rialto in Venice. It has a monopoly over currency exchange and is also a deposit bank. It makes large advances to the Indies Company, and booming sea trade from Dutch ports ensures good revenues.

Russia, 1609. The second "false Dimitri", known as the "bandit of Tushino", calls on Poland for help. The Polish king Sigismund Vasa besieges Smolensk.

Germany, 1609. Regular newspapers are published in Strasbourg and Wolfenbuttel.

England, 1609. Richard Hakluyt publishes *Virginia Richly Valued*, promoting the colony of Virginia.

Spain, 1609. Since the policy of forced conversion has failed, Philip III decides to drive out the *Moriscos* (nominally converted Moslems). They are sent to north-western Africa.

Canada, 1609. Samuel de Champlain sets out on an intrepid voyage of exploration covering the Ottawa river, Georgian Bay and Lake Ontario. He travels by canoe and, while expanding geographical knowledge to a great extent, he is also plunged into the middle of an internecine Indian war.

Spain, 1609. Garcilaso de la Vega, (the Inca) publishes his *Royal Commentaries relating the origins of the Incas*. He was the son of an Inca princess by one of the Spanish conquerors.

Prague, 1609. The German astronomer Johann Kepler provides evidence for the elliptical rotation of the planets round the sun in his *Astronomia Nova*.

Japan, 1609. The Ryuku islands (Okinawa) come under the control of the Shimazu family, the *daimyo* (feudal lords) of Satsuma.

Mexico, 1609. The *caciques* (Indian chiefs) stage an uprising.

Brazil, 1609. Jeronimo de Albuquerque discovers iron mines near the Rio Grande in the north-east of the country.

Beijing, 11 May 1610. The Jesuit Matteo Ricci, who founded the Catholic mission in China, has died.

Russia, July 1610. The Polish king's troops defeat Czar Vasily Shuisky, and proclaim the king's son, Ladislav IV Vasa, czar of Russia.

New Mexico, December 1610. The governor Pedro de Peralta has announced that the small village of Santa Fe is to be the new provincial capital. The first capital was San Gabriel, established in 1599, but Peralta has now decided that this site is too near hostile Indian territory for a governmental seat.

London, 1610. Shakespeare's play *Cymbeline*, based on a semi-historical British king, is staged for the first time.

Netherlands, 1610. The Dutch East India Company introduces the term "share".

London, 1610. Ben Jonson's low-life comedy *The Alchemist*, opens in London.

Madagascar, 1610. Ralambo, the ruler of the Merina kingdom, dies. During his 35-year reign he has greatly extended the kingdom by conquest.

Netherlands, 1610. Protestant theologians take up their positions against the states of Holland: in response to the "Remonstrances" of the Arminians (anti-Calvinists), the Gomarists (Calvinists) draw up their "Counter-Remonstrances".

Galileo's lens shows the way to the stars

Padua, Italy, 1610
Many important discoveries are being made by the Italian scientist Galileo Galilei using the newly-invented telescope. Galileo himself did not invent this remarkable instrument, but he has been responsible for its rapid development. First he built a telescope with a threefold magnifying power; next, 32 times magnification.

He has shown that there are mountains on the moon and he has revealed many stars invisible to the naked eye, proving, for instance, that the Milky Way is a large collection of stars.

When he turned his telescope towards the planet Jupiter, Galileo observed that it is accompanied by four satellites which he has called the "Medicean Stars".

The telescope through which Galileo discovered the four moons of Jupiter.

Young genius defends freedom of seas

Now the open sea is also subject to the pontifications of the lawyers.

The Netherlands, 1609
A one-time child prodigy has published, at the age of 26, a brilliant treatise defending the freedom of the seas. The Dutch theologian and lawyer Hugo Grotius was moved to write *De Mare Liberum* after being retained to defend the Dutch East India Company.

One of the company's captains had captured a rich Portuguese galleon in the Straits of Malacca. The right of a private company to take prizes was strongly disputed, especially by the Portuguese, who claimed that the eastern waters were their private property for trading purposes. Grotius set out to show that the high seas belonged to no one and could not be claimed by any country.

God, argued Grotius, wished human friendships to be engendered by mutual needs, one people supplying the needs of another; and the winds blow to make the oceans navigable. Grotius went to university at 12, accompanied a diplomatic mission to France at 15, at 17 was writing dramas in Latin, and at 20 was appointed historiographer by the States-General.

Jesuit who warned against Sodom dies

Beijing, 11 May 1610
Father Matteo Ricci, the Italian Jesuit who founded the Catholic mission in China and warned the Chinese of "the sins of Sodom", died here today. He arrived in China in 1583, having learnt to speak Chinese in Macao. He believed that if the church was to succeed in the east it would have to adapt to local customs, so he wore a mandarin's robe and took the Chinese name of Li-Mateo.

Ricci was a cartographer and clockmaker as well as a priest, and these skills, along with his profound knowledge of Chinese philosophy, won him permission to live in Beijing in 1601. From then until his death he made important converts and published a number of works which aroused much interest.

He translated the Ten Commandments and the Lord's Prayer into Chinese, and then published his great work, an explanation of Christian doctrine entitled *True Meaning of the Lord of Heaven*. In it he

Ricci, the Jesuit evangelist, with Li Paulus, his Chinese colleague.

fiercely attacked the "sins of Sodom" which many Chinese practise. "This kind of filthiness," he wrote, "is not even discussed by wise men in the west, for fear of defiling their own mouths." He is to be buried with great honour.

State extends "as far as eye can see"

Madagascar, 1610
Ralambo, the king of the Andriana, is spreading his domains through the mountains and forests of the Madagascan interior. He has renamed his ever-expanding country *Imerina*, meaning "as far as the eye can see".

Madagascar's cosmopolitan population of Africans, Arabs, Indians and Indonesians looks on him with favour. He has the strength to impose stability – and stability is good for trade.

As well as winning battles Ralambo has established an administration in his state, instituting a poll tax to finance his army, and increasing his country's wealth by raising the production of rice.

Warrior queen dies

Nigeria, 1610
Amina, the Hausa queen, has died after 34 years of a campaign to increase the size of her territory. Amina was 16 when she began the expansion of her ancestral lands, seeking to widen south and west her "empire" to include the mouth of the river Niger. Walled camps increased her military strength, and she was paid for her protection in eunuchs and food. She captured the northern cities of Kano and Katsina and added eastwest trade routes to those through the Sahara. Amina took a lover in every city she captured, but had each one beheaded next morning.

Basilica being built

Mexico, 1609
The construction of a magnificent vaulted basilica has begun near Mexico City, on Tepayac Hill. It will replace the church of the Indians which has housed the image of the Virgin of Guadelupe since 1555. The old adobe-built church marks the place where Juan Diego had a vision of the Virgin 122 years ago. The Holy Mother assured Diego of her love for Indians and sent him to ask the bishop of Mexico to build a church on the hill. Countless pilgrims have travelled there since, and by 1570 they had raised 8,000 *pesos* for the stone temple.

Britain mapped by historian John Speed

John Speed's map of Cornwall, in south-west England, is typical of his work: useful information and views surround a beautifully-drawn, accurate map.

England, 1610
The historian and cartographer John Speed is working on his *Theatre of the Empire of Great Britain*, which will bring together a series of 54 maps of different areas of England and Wales which have already appeared separately over the last four years.

It is the culmination of a career which began as a tailor in London. Speed was admitted to the Merchant Tailors' Company in 1580, but later built himself a house in Moorfields and devoted himself to the study of antiquity.

Speed's historical learning first brought him into contact with the poet Sir Fulke Greville, who became his patron. He also received help from scholars like Sir Robert Cotton and Sir Henry Spelman. Speed is also preparing a *History of Great Britain*, adding valuable material to the established history of the country.

The painter Caravaggio died on 18 July 1610, of malaria, having spent the last four years of his life as a fugitive, wanted for killing a man in a Rome brawl. His later works, such as "Martha Reproving Mary for her Vanity", have a stunning realism and an unusual contemplative stillness.

1610 (1610-1612)

Paris, 14 May 1610. King Henry IV is assassinated by a monk who believes in tyrannicide as a means of putting an end to policies which are against the interests of Catholicism.

North America, 24 May 1610. Sir Thomas Gates institutes "Laws Divine Morall and Martial", a harsh civil code, for Jamestown.

Italy, 18 July 1610. The artist Caravaggio dies of malaria in Porto Ercole aged 36, while waiting for permission from the pope to return to the Papal States. He fled in 1606 having killed an opponent in a duel.

Canada, 3 August 1610. The English navigator Henry Hudson discovers a great bay on the eastern coast of Canada (*Hudson's Bay*).

West Africa, 1610. The Dahomey kingdom is established.

German Empire, 1610. Count Tilly, a French courtier, is appointed Commander in Chief of the Catholic League, formed in 1609.

Virginia, 1610. During a winter of appalling hardship in Jamestown, a man is put to death for eating his wife's body.

France, 1610. Jean Beguin, a French scientist, publishes a chemical recipe book, *Tyrocinium Chymicum*.

Italy, 1610. Using the newly-invented telescope, Galileo observes the moons of Jupiter, and proves Kepler's theories about elliptical planetary rotation.

Portugal, 1610. The king of Portugal withdraws the freedom to trade from the "new Christians", or *Marranos*, converted Spanish Jews.

Rome, 1610. Carlo Borromeo, who was archbishop of Milan, and died in 1584, is canonised.

Paris, 26 January 1611. Maximilien de Bethune, the marquis of Sully, resigns as superintendent of finance and chief minister after disagreements with the regent, Marie de Medici. Concino Concini succeeds him.

Bohemia, 23 May 1611. The Holy Roman Emperor Rudolf II gives up the crown of Bohemia to his brother Matthias.

Virginia, May 1611. Colonists in Jamestown play bowls. This is the first game that settlers in the English colonies have found time for.

North America, 1611. The English navigator and explorer, Henry Hudson, his son and seven sailors are cast adrift in a rowing boat by his crew after a mutiny. They have little chance of survival.

Sweden, 30 October 1611. On the death of Charles IX, the Swedish nobles and the council declare the 16-year-old Gustavus II Adolphus of age, in exchange for a guarantee of their rights.

North America, 13 December 1611. The "Dale Code" codifies two years of harsh laws passed by Dale and others in Virginia.

Russia, 1611. As the Swedes enter Russia, the Poles, pressing home their advantage, occupy Moscow.

Spain, 1611. The Spanish composer Tomas Luis de Victoria dies. He was a profoundly devout man and wrote only religious music.

France, 1611. An assembly of reformed churches is held at Saumur.

Baltic, 1611. War breaks out between Denmark and Sweden. Christian IV of Denmark is determined to gain full power over the Baltic, and he already controls the Sound, without which it is landlocked. Gustavus Adolphus of Sweden has modernised his army, equipping it with units of reindeer-drawn sledges, in addition to the ski-ing units set up in 1567.

France, 1611. In a reversal of Henry IV's policy, Marie de Medici signs a pact with Spain promising that France will not interfere in internal affairs in the empire. To seal the pact, Louis XIII is betrothed to the Habsburg princess, Anne of Austria.

India, 1611. The Dutch found a trading post at Masulipatam on the central eastern coast.

Germany, 1611. The Merchant Adventurers, an English company dealing in foreign trade, sets up a branch in Hamburg.

Rome, 1611. The university of Rome is founded.

England, 1611. A new English translation of the Bible is published. It was authorised by King James in 1604, as a concession to the demands of Protestant clergy for reform.

Italy, 1611. The Italian theologian Marco de Dominis publishes a scientific explanation of the phenomenon of the rainbow.

London, 1611. Shakespeare's play *The Tempest* opens in London. It has a valedictory tone, with the hero, Prospero the magician, abandoning his magic, casting his wand and book of spells into the sea. He is attended to the last by his winged spirit Ariel, and plagued by his earthly servant, the half man, half beast, Caliban.

Germany, 13 June 1612. Matthias II is crowned Holy Roman emperor in succession to Rudolf II.

Monk assassinates "good King Henry"

Paris, 14 May 1610

Henry IV, the king of France, was stabbed to death this afternoon in the Rue de la Ferronnerie by Francois Ravaillac, a fanatical Catholic monk. The king, travelling by carriage from the Louvre to the Arsenal, had dismissed his bodyguard and was accompanied only by a few gentlemen when the carriage was halted in a traffic jam. The crazed assassin leapt onto a wheel and thrust his dagger twice into the king's chest.

The king cried out "I've been stabbed", then collapsed with blood pouring from his mouth. The carriage was then driven to the Louvre and doctors summoned, but Henry the Good was beyond their help. The assassin, a tall, red-haired man, who is believed to have acted because of Henry's proposed war against the Catholic Spanish and Austrian powers, is being examined to see if he belongs to a plot.

The news of Henry's death has caused consternation in Paris. He ruled wisely for over 20 years and

A later engraving of the triumphant Henry IV in ceremonial armour.

his concern for the common people was legendary. The crown now passes to his eight-year-old son, Louis XIII. The king had already made his wife, Marie de Medici, regent in preparation for his absence at war. Now she must rule for their son.

Monteverdi makes mark with Vespers

Italy, 1610

A magnificent set of church music published this year and dedicated to Pope Paul V has announced to the music world that it cannot afford to ignore its composer, 43-year-old Claudio Monteverdi.

Born at Cremona in 1567, Monteverdi has been *maestro di cappella* (head of music) at the court of Duke Vincenzo Gonzaga at Mantua since 1601. He has already aroused attention as an advocate of the new, expressive style of music known as the *seconda prattica* (second practice), and as a composer of two operas, *Orfeo* (1607) and *Arianna* (1608), which are the first to show the true potential of this new genre. He has also published five books of madrigals.

At the same time Monteverdi has also shown himself a master of the older style of music, or *prima prattica* (first practice) of Palestrina and earlier composers. Both styles are evident in the *Vespers*, a collection of pieces to be sung at the church's early evening service.

Immoral officials sacked in China

Beijing, 1611

This year's evaluation of the conduct and ability of civil servants has resulted in the sacking of a number of senior officials. So grave were the implications of the evaluation that the Emperor Wan li at first refused to release it, but enemies of the officials censured in the report leaked its details until they became common gossip.

Worse still, fake impeachment papers, spelling out the accusations against corrupt officials, were published in the *Beijing Gazette*, thus compelling the emperor to release the evaluation report.

Seven prominent officials were accused of notorious personal conduct. At the top of the list were Dang Binyin and Gu Zienzhun who were both put on the "inactive list".

This scandal must be seen in the context of the continuing struggle between the eunuch bureaucrats and the reforming Dunglin faction. The Dunglins would seem to have won this round.

Mutineers abandon Henry Hudson to icy waters in rowing boat

London, 1611

The veteran Arctic explorer Henry Hudson was cast adrift in a small boat in Arctic waters together with his teenage son, John, and seven loyal crew members by mutineers, it is being alleged in London. No sign of Hudson has been seen since, and it is almost certain that he and his party froze to death.

Members of the expedition to find a short route (or "North west passage") to the Spice Islands have returned to England. The circumstances of Hudson's loss during a mutiny aboard his ship *Discovery* are now under investigation while the survivors of the trip, drained by famine and sickness, wait in prison.

Hudson sailed from London on 17 April last year. By August he had crossed the Atlantic and found a narrow strait into a great bay which his admirers believe should now bear his name. He spent the next three months charting a watery "labyrinth without end", following creeks and leads that led nowhere. The *Discovery* was too far from open sea to escape the winter ice. On 1 November she was hauled ashore near Moose Fort.

Six months of bitter cold with little food and no work created conditions in which even the smallest quarrel loomed large. Hudson, like Columbus before him, was a remarkable navigator, but a poor leader with little understanding of

The explorer drifts across the Arctic wastes: a later painting by J Collier.

human nature. He was suspected of distributing rations unequally and favouring the more servile members of the crew. In a series of dangerous changes, he demoted his mate Juet, replaced him with Robert Bylot and, at the end of the winter, as they set sail again, demoted Bylot too. By now almost every man in the expedition was his enemy.

King wanted a duel

Stockholm, 16 October 1611

The autocratic and capricious king of Sweden, Charles IX, died here today, a broken old man of 63. His successor, the 16-year-old Gustavus II Adolphus, has inherited a country facing external threat and internal disintegration.

It is seven months since Charles provoked King Christian IV of Denmark into declaring war by Sweden's constant hostility towards Danish ships in the Baltic. Within weeks the Danes had taken the strategic stronghold of Kalmar – infuriating Charles so much that he challenged the Danish king to a duel, an offer scornfully rejected. One serious effect of war with the Danes could be to draw resources from Sweden's Russian front.

Jesuits protect Indians from slavery

Madrid, 1611

About 250,000 Guarani Indians in the Jesuit province of Paraguay will enjoy royal protection from the rigours of slavery thanks to a decree just signed by King Philip III. The lucky natives inhabit a sort of religious Utopia founded by the Order of Jesus seven years ago. All their material and spiritual needs are satisfied, except for the freedom to follow their former, disordered way of life in which work was not a favourite pastime. They now live in a twilight world where all are treated as children.

The Jesuits started their conversion of the Guarani in 1588. Since then the order has built 30 towns, always to the same pattern: a central grassed square is flanked by a

church with a tower and three longhouses containing apartments for 100 families or more. The Indians follow a regular day of work, song and prayer. Even the walk to the fields is a religious procession. Jesuits care for their charges like firm, but kindly, parents.

These self-sufficient communities, known as *reducciones*, are efficient enough to export surplus food and draw envious interest from Spanish colonisers dependent on slave labour and cruelty. In Peru's silver mines, for instance, Indians may not leave the workplace except to attend church on Sunday. In the reducciones property is held in common. The crop which the Jesuits harvest with greatest energy is the human soul.

Authorised version of Bible appears

London, 1611

Robert Barker, the king's printer, has at last brought out the new version of the Bible, authorised and backed by King James himself. It is a folio in black letter with a handsomely engraved title page signed by Cornelius Boel. But it is the majesty and music of the rhythm of the language which critics have been impressed by.

Fifty-four scholars based on the three centres of Oxford, Cambridge and Westminster have worked for seven years to produce the new translation, using much of the original Hebrew and Greek. Their work was reviewed by a committee of 12 before Thomas Bilson and Miles Smith then put the finishing touches to the final version. The unity of style achieved is most impressive. Nobody would guess that this was the work of a committee.

The impetus for the new bible came in January 1604 at a Hampton Court conference. The Bishops' Bible, published in 1568, has not been popular although it is used by many bishops. Many clergy and lay people favour the Geneva Bible. King James, however, thought there were seditious comments in the Geneva version, although he was anxious to have an English bible which was equally grand. He pushed the project ahead, even though many bishops were not very enthusiastic.

The handsome title page to Robert Barker's authorised Bible.

1612 (1612-1614)

Russia, 27 October 1612. The Russians have forced the invading Poles to capitulate. Incensed by Swedish and Polish advances into their lands, the Russian people have organised against them. Kuzma Minin, a merchant, appealed for money and set up a militia. People responded with great generosity and Minin appointed Prince Dimitri Pojarsky, a hero from the siege of Moscow, military leader. With the support of the *Cossacks*, he has finally achieved his aim.

Angola, 1612. The native men and women of Angola are being exported to Brazil as slaves by the Portuguese at a rate of more than 10,000 a year.

North America, 1612. The Dutch send the ships *Tiger* and *Fortune* to trade with Indians on Hudson's river. They build huts and establish a settlement.

Netherlands, 1612. The English Baptist leader John Smith writes *The Retraction of his Errors and the Confirmation of the Truth*, which affirms the beliefs for which he was exiled to the Netherlands but withdraws his condemnation of his opponents, which had been fierce and uncompromising.

Virginia, 1612. Settlers begin to cultivate tobacco plants.

Zaire, c.1612. Kibinda Ilunga, the founder of the Lunda kingdom in southern Zaire, has died.

Antwerp, 1612. Rubens paints his *Descent from the Cross* for Notre Dame cathedral.

India, 1612. The British East India Company defeats the Portuguese off the west coast of India and establishes its first factory at Surat.

Japan, 1612. The silver mint, called *Ginza*, is moved to Edo.

Germany, 1612. Jakob Boehme, a German theosophist and shoemaker, publishes his mystical *Aurora*. It comprises revelations and meditations on God, man and nature, and shows a remarkable familiarity with alchemical writings and the scriptures. It is condemned by the ecclesiastical authorities.

England, 1612. Henry, the prince of Wales, dies of a fever. The eldest son of King James, he was the hope of the English Protestant party because of his violent dislike of popery.

Germany, 1612. Hans Leo Hassler, a German composer, dies. He wrote choral and keyboard works.

South-East Asia, 1612. The East India Company establishes factories at Syriam (*near Rangoon*), Prome and Ava.

France, 11 January 1613. Workers in a sandpit in the Dauphine discover the skeleton of what is alleged to be a 30-foot tall man, the remains, it is thought, of the giant Theotobocus, a legendary Gallic king who fought the Romans.

Scandinavia, 20 January 1613. The peace of Knared ends the war between Sweden and Denmark. They have been fighting since 1611, but the Danish capture of Kalmar has turned the tide firmly in the Danish direction. Sweden gives up Finland, allows Danish merchants to enter Livonia, and gives Denmark Alvsborg as a surety.

Russia, 22 February 1613. Mikhail Romanov is elected czar.

Virginia, 1613. The governor of Virginia rents three acres of land to each colonist, abandoning unsuccessful collectivism.

Spain, 1613. Cervantes publishes his *Novelas Ejemplares*, a collection of short stories which includes amorous exploits and picaresque adventures.

South America, 1613. The Dutch settle in Paramaribo (*on the coast of Guiana*).

Japan, 1613. Date Masamune, the *daimyo* (feudal lord) of Sendai, dispatches a mission to Rome.

Canada, 1613. Samuel de Champlain, the French governor, sails up the Ottawa river and explores lakes Huron and Erie.

Canada, 1613. The Franciscan father Sagard begins to compile his French-Huron dictionary.

France, 1613. Publication of the *Voyages du Sieur Champlain, Saintongeois*, a "faithful Journal of the Observations and Discoveries of New France whilst seeking a northern route to China".

London, 1613. Sir Thomas Overbury is committed to the Tower for refusing a diplomatic appointment abroad. It is concluded that King James wished to put an end to Overbury's influence over Viscount Rochester, who is a favourite of the king's.

Mexico, 1613. Government troops attempt to storm a settlement of runaway slaves in the mountains. The community is led by Yanga, who has lived there for thirty years. Its guerrilla tactics outwit the troops, and the government agrees to treat with Yanga. He and his community remain free, having sworn to cause no more trouble and to help to turn in other runaways.

Spain, 7 April 1614. The Greek painter El Greco dies in Toledo.

Spanish Jesuit champions Indians' rights

Spanish "conquistadores" let their hounds tear native Indians to pieces.

Spain, 1612
A major split between church and state in Spain is threatened as a result of the writings of the Jesuit Francisco Suarez. Prompted by the conquest of America and the subjugation of the natives there, Suarez has championed Indian rights and challenged the divine right of kings.

In *Tractatus de legibus ac de legislatore*, the 64-year-old theologian and philosopher argues that all legislative as well as paternal power is derived from God, and that every law should be His law. Kings, he insists, do not have the same power, and he refutes the patriarchal theory of government. All states, Suarez argues, are the result of a social contract to which the people must give their consent. Indians should be treated no differently.

Suarez is a disciple of Luis Molina, the Jesuit professor of Evora. He adapted Molina's ideas on predestination and free will to the tricky subjects of grace and special election.

Believing that all men are born equal, with an absolutely sufficient grace, Suarez nonetheless argued that a certain elect were granted a special grace to whose influence they would willingly and infallibly yield. This allowed for popes, but not kings.

Musical prince who killed first wife dies

Italy, 8 September 1613
Carlo Gesualdo, the fiery prince of Venosa who had his wife murdered and yet wrote beautiful madrigals and motets, is dead. Gesualdo won notoriety when, in 1590, he caught his wife and her lover *in flagrante* and ordered their deaths. In 1593 he married Leonora d'Este at Ferrara; his musical talent blossomed into genius, and he wrote madrigals and sacred works famed for expressive melodies and unexpected, dissonant harmonies. Eventually he retired to his castle, sunk in melancholy – or remorse? – relieved only by music. He died there today, in his early fifties.

A fresco of Carlo Gesualdo.

Curiosity-collecting emperor is dead

Prague, 1612

Europe is poised for a Habsburg revival following the death this year of Rudolf II, regarded as the most eccentric and ineffective monarch ever to be crowned Holy Roman emperor. In recent years those close to the throne had manoeuvred to strip him of everything but his title. Even before Rudolf died, real power rested with his brother and successor as emperor Matthias, who last year forced Rudolf, aged 59, to abdicate as king of Bohemia in Matthias' favour. Four years ago Matthias awarded himself control of Austria, Hungary and Moravia.

This steady handover of power, fully supported by the rest of the Habsburg family, reflected growing concern about the creeping paralysis that had begun to grip Rudolf. Court circles said that he appeared increasingly shy and unstable, delayed taking decisions and sometimes seemed deranged. In affairs of state he was as likely to take advice from a valet as a minister.

Close friends, however, said that the criticism is unfair and that, after

Matthias: slowly taking control.

39 years as emperor, Rudolf was following his inclination towards the arts and science, preferring the company of artists and learned men like astronomers and alchemists to that of courtiers. Rudolf, who preferred Prague to Vienna, also has a passionate interest in things from other countries and built up one of the most outstanding collections of curiosities in Europe.

Protestants brought in to colonise Ulster

Ireland, 1613

The flight of the earls in 1607 has cleared the way for the systematic colonisation of Ulster by Protestants. Some half a million acres have now been thrown open to settlers, and estates of up to 3,000 acres are being granted to English and Scottish immigrants, who must undertake to build defensible houses. Native Irish who remained loyal to the English during the latest rebellion are also eligible for similar grants.

A parliament has assembled in Dublin to legalise these Ulster "plantations", and the City of London livery companies are now forming an Irish Society to raise capital for the exploitation of timber and fisheries in County Derry. A new city being built will be called Londonderry.

The London companies have undertaken to accept only English and Scots as tenants, but thousands of Irish remain on their holdings and there is little likelihood of their being removed. What is more, these industrious Irish peasants generally outbid the Scot or the Englishman when it comes to paying rent.

A new set of tables makes maths easier

Scotland, 1614

After 20 years of intensive work, the Scottish mathematician John Napier has published a revolutionary book. His 90 pages of tables, called *Mirifici logarithmorum canonis descriptio*, use a complex system of ratios to give "logarithmic" equivalents to numbers. To multiply two or more numbers, you simply look up their logarithms. Add them together and you arrive at the logarithm of the answer. The tables translate it back to the real number. Long division is done by subtracting the logarithms.

Napier's tables look set to be a best seller: astronomers, navigators and scientists are tackling ever more complicated sums.

Sixteen-year-old to rule deserted land

Moscow, 22 February 1613

Russia has put the recent troubles behind it and solved the dynastic problem by electing Mikhail Romanov as czar. He was chosen by the *Zemsky Sobor* – the Assembly of the Land – after much deliberation. The election is not altogether a break with the past for Ivan the Terrible's first wife, Anastasia, had been a member of the Romanov family.

Romanov, who is only 16, has received no training for the monarchy, having been brought up in a monastery. His father, a nobleman who has been patriarch of Moscow, will act as regent. Romanov will be crowned in the Kremlin with all his autocratic prerogatives intact. The Romanovs will ascend the throne amid rejoicing, but they are inheriting a deserted land. Half the villages of Russia are deserted of people and, because of the virtual collapse of authority, huge areas are vulnerable to wandering bandits. The treasury, too, is empty, and Romanov has asked another noble family for a loan in cash and kind – fish, salt and grain – to meet the urgent demands of his military and civil officials. And Poles and Swedes still occupy parts of Muscovy.

Passionate religious painter dies in Spain

Toledo, 7 April 1614

Ever since he first arrived in Spain, the painter Domenikos Theotokopoulos, who died today at 73, was known as El Greco, "the Greek". But he was also considered to be a Spanish Catholic religious painter of intense spiritual power.

He was born in Candia, on the island of Crete, and went to Venice to study painting under Titian. Later he met the dean of Toledo who offered him commissions in that city. El Greco arrived in 1567 and remained there for life, mainly painting for its churches. His altarpieces, with their elongated figures, harsh light and cool blues, are highly emotional.

Wide-eyed and beautiful: "Portrait of a Woman in a Fur Cape".

"Christ Driving the Money Changers from the Temple", c.1572.

1614 (1614-1616)

Virginia, 5 April 1614. An Indian princess, Pocahontas, is married to a Jamestown settler. The community hopes it will bring peace between them and the Indians.

France, 15 May 1614. The treaty of St Menehould brings a provisional end to the aristocratic uprising by the prince of Conde and other nobles which broke out in February. Marie de Medici, the queen mother, concedes honours and large pensions to the rebellious nobles in order to prevent an outbreak of civil war. She also agrees to the summoning of the Estates-General.

Amsterdam, 1 October 1614. Adriaen Block returns from North America with maps of the Manhattan coastline.

Germany, 12 November 1614. The treaty of Xanten puts an end to the Julich-Cleves war of succession, following the threat of French and English intervention. Johann Sigismund, the elector of Brandenburg, obtains Cleves and Ravensberg, consolidating his position in the north-east of Germany, while Philippe Louis, the count Palatine of Neubourg, annexes Julich and Berg.

France, 20 November 1614. Louis XIII is declared of age as king.

Russia, 1614. The czar, Mikhail Romanov, defeats the *Cossacks* at Rostokino.

Rome, 1614. Carlo Maderna completes the new facade of St Peter's.

Japan, 1614. The *shogun* Tokugawa Ieyasu issues an edict suppressing Christianity. The churches in Kyoto are to be destroyed and the missionaries are taken into custody. A total of 148 Japanese Christians, including the Christian *daimyo* (feudal lord) Takayama Ukon, are banished overseas, to Manila or to Macao. This action is taken mainly with the military in mind, for it is feared that Christianity will interfere with their loyalty to their overlords.

England 1614. King James asks MPs to grant him benevolences (free gifts to the crown). After the session, all those who spoke out against the king are arrested and thrown into the dungeons of the Tower.

Rome, 1614. The pope pronounces the beatification of St Teresa of Avila.

Denmark, 1614. The Danish East India Company is founded.

Brazil, 1614. The governor of Rio de Janeiro makes legal tender; it may be used to buy things or to pay taxes.

London, 1614. John Webster's revenge tragedy *The Duchess of Malfi* opens in London. The virtuous heroine marries beneath her to her steward, the only good man she can find in her court, but she cannot escape the designs of her wicked brothers.

England, 1614. The mathematician John Napier publishes a series of numbers known as Napierian logarithms.

Paris, 23 February 1615. The Estates-General is dissolved, having been in session since October 1614. It has gained no concessions on taxation from the monarchy.

New France, 28 July 1615. The French explorer Champlain, on his seventh voyage, finds a lake (*Lake Huron*), opening up an easier route inland for fur traders.

France, 1615. Antoine de Montchrestien, a dramatist and economist, writes a treatise on what he terms "political economy". As France, unlike Spain, has no gold supplies, he says it should encourage manufacturing to increase exports and add to gold stocks. He also advocates the creation of more French colonies.

Canada, 1615. Franciscans arrive in Quebec to start missionary work.

India, 1615. The English fleet defeats the Portuguese off Bombay.

France, 1615. In accordance with the provisions of the treaty of Fontainebleau, Louis XIII marries Anne of Austria.

South-East Asia, 1615. The Dutch seize the Moluccas from the Portuguese.

Paris, 1615. At the request of Marie de Medici, Salomon de Brosse begins to build the Luxembourg palace, which, in accordance with the wishes of the queen mother, is to be modelled on the Pitti Palace in Florence where she grew up.

England, 1615. The Merchant Adventurers are granted a monopoly on the export of cloth.

Southern Africa, 1615. Khoisan herders return to the Cape of Good Hope from England. They were taken there a year ago by traders in order to learn the language and culture.

France, May 1616. Conde, who led the aristocratic rebellion in 1614, joins the Royal Council and is entrusted with the government of Bourges.

France, November 1616. Richelieu is called to the King's Council and is made secretary of state for war and foreign affairs.

Lines of battle are drawn up in Europe

Germany, 1614

All Europe is holding its breath as the German princes – Catholics and Protestants alike – prepare for a war which threatens to engulf the whole continent. Battle-lines are now being drawn up and fortunes spent on equipping private armies throughout Germany.

In the mainly Protestant north, whole cities are being ringed with star-shaped walls, bastions and moats; in the Rhineland and Bavaria, great new fortresses pierce the skylines as Catholics brace themselves for war on a scale unprecedented in Europe. Germany, it seems, will be the battlefield should war break out.

Intense diplomatic activity has been taking place, particularly on the part of Prince Christian of Anhalt-Bernburg, the governor of the Protestant Palatinate, who has sought alliances with every other Protestant power to combat a growing Catholic revival since the beginning of this century. Approaches were made to England and France, with little success at first, but King James of England finally agreed to join an alliance with the Protestant Union of six princes and encouraged the union to make similar alliances with the Netherlands and Denmark.

With Louis XIII of France feeling more and more threatened now that the war between Spain and the rebel Dutch has been resumed, the great powers now face one another. On one side – though not necessarily Protestant – France, Holland, Denmark, Sweden, England and Russia in the north and several Italian states in the south are lined up against the Catholic houses of Habsburg and Poland, with Philip IV of Spain prepared to strike at heretics everywhere.

Japan's ruler dies as huge castle falls

Ieyasu's captain, Honda Tadamoto (in horned helmet), at the siege of Osaka.

Japan, 4 June 1615

The colossal fortress of Osaka has fallen to the army of the shogun Ieyasu after a cruel six-month siege, and tonight is burning out of control. Hideyori, the defender of the castle and son of the great dictator Hideyoshi, who built the castle, has commited suicide and his body has vanished in the flames.

Ieyasu, as usual, used cunning as well as force to achieve victory. He fostered dissension among the defenders until they accepted peace proposals in January. But as soon as the treaty was signed, he destroyed the castle's outer defences.

In May he resumed the siege and a desperate struggle ensued until two days ago when the defenders decided to fight a pitched battle outside the castle walls. The result can be seen in the flames. Ieyasu is now master of all Japan.

Englishman reports from Moghul court

Agra, India, 10 January 1615
Sir Thomas Roe, the first English ambassador to India, has been received by the Emperor Jahangir, the dissolute son of Akbar the Great. The Moghul court is magnificent, its daily ceremonies "as regular as a clock that strikes at set hours", according to Roe. At their first meeting Jahangir sat high under a canopy. Two attendants, standing on the heads of wooden elephants, fanned him. Roe refused to perform the standard obeisance of the Moghul court, but greeted Jahangir with a flourish, as he would an European monarch. Of the gifts Roe brought from King James, only two satisfied the emperor: a crate of alcohol and some English miniatures. A globe annoyed him, as he had not known how small the Moghul empire was compared to the rest of the world.

Roe, 35 years old and the Member of Parliament for Tamworth, left England in March 1614, arriving at Surat, on the west coast of India, on 26 September. He is not the first Englishman to be received at the Moghul court. Seven years earlier William Hawkins had negotiated with Jahangir on behalf of the East India Company. Speaking

A European at the Moghul court.

fluent Turkish, he was able to talk and drink with Jahangir, leaving a mixed impression of his countrymen behind him. Roe's mission, though, is likely to be beneficial to both sides. England is a naval power and trading nation. Jahangir requires protection from the Portuguese for his ships carrying pilgrims to Mecca; England requires factories and trading concessions.

Murder myths spark attacks on Jews

Frankfurt, 28 February 1616
Vincent Fettmilch, the leader of the attack on the city's Jewish ghetto two years ago, was beheaded today, with some of his followers, on the orders of the Emperor Matthias.

The attack, which was simply one more episode in a long history of anti-Semitic violence, was undoubtedly encouraged by charges of ritual murder which have plagued the Jews ever since they set up the Frankfurt ghetto in 1462. The

worst example of these charges, which the authorities accept as utterly unfounded, is to be seen in a painting at the city's Bruckenturm Gate. This depicts the supposed martyrdom at Jewish hands of one Simon of Trent in 1474.

Jewish leaders have petitioned for the removal of this painting, but the authorities refused. The mob, believing devoutly the blood libel, is not to lose its symbol, however much the Jews may suffer.

American Indian heroine meets James

London, 1616
An Indian princess has sat with the king of England, James, at a Ben Jonson masque, ten years after becoming a heroine by saving the life of an explorer, John Smith, and aiding the British colony at Jamestown, Virginia, with food and protection. In 1614 Pocahontas married John Rolf from Jamestown and was baptised Rebecca. Her father, the chief of the Algonquin people, had fought the settlers from the start. However, he approved what was obviously a love-match and left his enemies in peace.

Pocahontas pleads for Smith's life.

Comedy and horror lure crowds in London

London, 1 November 1614
Ben Jonson's chronicle of London low life, *Bartholomew Fair*, was performed yesterday with great success at the Hope theatre, and will be repeated tonight before the king at Whitehall. It is the latest hit on the London stage where comedy and a new style of horror plays are drawing enthusiastic audiences.

Jonson's new play is a comedy of knavery, where visitors to a fair at Smithfield are gulled of their money and belongings, whilst also exposing the hypocrisy of certain Puritans. Ben Jonson, once a bricklayer, began to succeed with his play *Every Man in his Humour*, in which Shakespeare acted. Jonson satirised human quirks further in *Volpone* and *The Alchemist*.

John Webster, whose *Duchess of Malfi* was first seen last year, is the poet of horror, providing new ingenuities with each new play. The duchess is killed for marrying her

steward after prolonged torments. She finds herself holding a severed hand in the dark. Vittoria, the whore of *The White Devil*, is stabbed to death, while her lover is poisoned by his own helmet and strangled by a "friar" pretending to give him the last rites. Other authors also dwell on horrors: in Cyril Tourneur's *The Revenger's Tragedy*, a lecherous duke is induced to kiss a poisoned skull and dies seeing his bastard copulating with his duchess. Shakespeare's *Titus Andronicus* has a scene where a mother finds that she has eaten her sons in a pie.

Authors often collaborate, so it is hard to be sure who is the author of many plays – Thomas Middleton, Cyril Tourneur, John Marston, George Chapman and Thomas Dekker, besides the ever-popular Beaumont and Fletcher, and even Shakespeare, have put their hands to many between them.

The architect Mohammed Aga has just completed the magnificent Blue Mosque in Istanbul for Ahmed, the Ottoman sultan, who is content to let his viziers rule while he concentrates on grand artistic projects.

1616 (1616-1618)

New France, 20 January 1616. Wounded in battle with the Iroquois, the French explorer Samuel de Champlain arrives to winter in Huron village.

Italy, February 1616. Galileo is placed under arrest by the Inquisition for his astronomical theories, the most significant of which reaffirms the Copernican concept of the universe, placing the sun, not Earth, at the centre.

Madrid, 23 April 1616. Cervantes, the creator of Don Quixote, dies.

England, 23 April 1616. William Shakespeare dies in his home town of Stratford-on-Avon, four years after returning there from London, where his plays were bringing him increasing fame and success.

Japan, 1 June 1616. The *shogun* Tokugawa Ieyasu dies of an illness. He is succeeded by his son Tokugawa Hidetada.

Arctic, 1616. The British navigator William Baffin, in his search for a north-west passage from the Atlantic to the Pacific, discovers a sound which leads into the Arctic Ocean, to which he gives his name. Following the lack of success of his expedition, Baffin concludes that there is no north-west passage.

South America, 1616. Willem Schouter and Jacob Lemaire discover a new route to the Pacific for Europeans, round a cape south of the Straits of Magellan, which they name Cape Horn.

Virginia, 1616. The population of the colony of Virginia is 351: 205 officials and workers on company land, 81 tenants and 65 women and children.

Brazil, 1616. The Portuguese expel the French from St Louis de Maragnan, ending French efforts to establish an Amazon colony.

South America, 1616. The Dutch found the colony of Guiana.

Istanbul, 1616. Sultan Ahmed's mosque, also known as the "Blue Mosque", is completed.

Poland, 1616. Protestant churches at Poznan are demolished.

Japan, 1616. All Japanese ports except Nagasaki and Hirado are closed to foreigners.

England, January 1617. King James makes his favourite George Villiers earl of Buckingham.

Russia, 9 March 1617. The treaty of Stolbovo ends the occupation of northern Russia by Swedish troops. Sweden also renounces plans for expansion towards the White Sea and in exchange the czar, Mikhail Romanov, gives up Russian access to the Baltic Sea and the towns conquered by Boris Godunov.

France, 24 April 1617. Concino Concini, the favourite of the regent Marie de Medici, is assassinated on the orders of the young Louis XIII, who installs his own favourite Luynes in his place. The queen mother is exiled to Blois, accompanied by Richelieu.

Virginia, May 1617. Captain John Rolfe returns to find that settlers have nearly deserted Jamestown to grow tobacco in the hinterlands.

Rome, 30 August 1617. The Peruvian Rosa de Lima is the first American saint to be canonised.

Lisbon, 25 September 1617. The Spanish Jesuit lawyer and theologian Francisco Suarez dies. At the request of Philip II, he was appointed to the first chair of theology at the university of Coimbra in 1597. His books include *Defensio Fidei* (1613), against King James of England.

Istanbul, 22 December 1617. Mustapha succeeds Sultan Ahmed as ruler of the Ottoman empire.

Virginia, 23 December 1617. The British set up a penal colony.

Spain, 1617. Spain reinforces its alliances against France by signing the treaty of Pavia with Savoy.

West Africa, 1617. The Dutch buy Goree Island, off Cape Verde, from the natives.

Netherlands, 1617. The Dutch mathematician Willebrord Snellius devises a technique of trigonometrical triangulation for surveying and cartography.

Japan, 1617. The ashes of shogun Tokugawa Ieyasu are transferred from Edo to the mausoleum of Nikko.

Geneva, 1617. The theologian John Calvin's collected works are published posthumously.

Germany, 1617. The composer Heinrich Schutz is made *kapellmeister* (head of music) of the elector of Saxony at Dresden.

Persia, 1618. The Ottomans recognise the reconquest of Persia by Shah Abbas.

Sweden, 1617. By the ordinance of Orebro, Catholicism is banned; the move is more aimed against those who want to restore Catholicism than an act of direct religious persecution.

England, 1617. King James makes poet and playwright Ben Jonson England's first "poet laureate".

Hudson's River, 1617. Dutch traders abandon the Fort Nassau settlement, set up in 1614.

Prague, 1617. The Emperor Matthias II makes his cousin Ferdinand king of Bohemia.

Emperor's men thrown through window

Prague, 23 May 1618

Three men were hurled through a window here tonight, giving a new word – "defenestration" – to the language. Two of the men, Martinitz and Slavata, were lieutenants of the Bohemian king, Ferdinand, a fanatical opponent of the Reformation. The third man was their secretary who made the unfortunate mistake of holding on to his employers while the mob vented their fury on them.

Feelings had been running high in the city since Ferdinand's governors refused permission for the building of two Lutheran churches. The Protestant leader, Count Thurn, called a meeting of nobles, gentry and burghers from all over the province, demanding death for the two men.

Martinitz went first, screaming "Jesu, Maria! Help!" as he crashed over the sill. Slavata fought hard and was knocked senseless. One of the rebels looked down from the window and shouted "By God, his

The Defenestration of Prague.

Mary has helped!". The victims had landed on a rubbish heap and Martinitz was already stirring. All three men survived. Martinitz has fled and Slavata is being cared for by the Countess Thurn.

Russians lose access to the Baltic Sea

Russia, 9 March 1617

British mediation and a loan have helped secure the peace of Stolbovo today between Russia and Sweden which could now end the years of desultory fighting. For a Russian indemnity of 20,000 silver roubles, Sweden has agreed to evacuate Novgorod and other areas of northern Russia and renounce its claim to the Russian throne. For its part, Sweden will retain the southern coast of Finland and its contact with its Estonian possessions; thus Muscovy is cut off from the Baltic and does not get back towns conquered by Boris Godunov before the Time of the Troubles. Czar Mikhail Romanov's big task now is to clear Russia of the Poles.

Royal Mosque built in Persian capital

Isfahan, 1617

The Royal Mosque, the *Masjid-i-Shah*, the most striking building in the magnificent new capital city of Shah Abbas of Persia, is complete. The mosque is on the south side of the Maydan, the great square at the centre of the city, reached by the wide straight avenue known as the Chahar Bagh. Like the whole city of Isfahan, 24 miles (38km) in circumference and home to a million people, it is an impressive example of imperial town planning. For all its grandeur, the Masjid-i-Shah's floral painted tiles are not as fine as the Timurid mosaics of the neighbouring Friday Mosque.

The clean, imposing lines of the Masjid-i-Shah in Isfahan.

Shakespeare shuffles off this mortal coil

England, 25 April 1616
William Shakespeare, the celebrated poet and dramatist, was buried today where he was christened, in Holy Trinity church, Stratford-upon-Avon. He died two days ago, on his 52nd birthday. His father, John Shakespeare, was an alderman of the town; his mother, Mary Arden, was a farmer's daughter from the village of Wilmcote. He went to the local grammar school.

Shakespeare first went to London in the late 1580s and soon made his name as an actor and playwright. After the death of Christopher Marlowe at just 29 in 1593 he emerged as the foremost of London's actor-playwrights, working from 1594 with the new Lord Chamberlain's Company. His "history" plays are mainly from this time. Following the great tragedies and comedies of his middle years, Shakespeare turned to fantastical romance, such as *The Tempest* (1611). The last play in which he had a hand was *King Henry VIII* of 1613.

From about 1610 Shakespeare, an amiable, honest and witty man,

William Shakespeare: an engraving from the title page of the 1623 edition of his complete works.

established himself as a man of standing in his native Stratford, where he had bought a house, New Place, in 1597 for £60. He is survived by his widow Ann and two daughters.

Poland to retain disputed province

Russia, 11 December 1618
After the failure of the offensive which brought Polish troops near to Moscow, the two countries have now agreed an armistice. Under the terms of the treaty, Poland will retain the provinces of Smolensk and Seversk. It will recognise the election of Mikhail Romanov to the throne of Russia, but it has not yet renounced a claim to that throne which stemmed originally from the "Time of Troubles" (1604-1613).

Poland had Smolensk in its possession at the end of the Troubles and used it as the base for the offensive earlier this year. At one point this caused serious concern to Czar Mikhail who has been grappling with a host of domestic problems which he inherited when he came to the throne five years ago. Somehow Moscow withstood the assault by the Polish forces. The Poles ran short of ammunition and provisions, and withdrew.

Galileo called before the Inquisition

Italy, 26 February 1616
Since 1613, Galileo has been under attack from the theological community for his advocacy of the claim by Copernicus that Earth goes round the sun. The Italian astronomer has observed variations in the way planets move in the sky which have convinced him that Copernicus was right to put the sun at the centre of the planets. The churchmen say that the Copernican system conflicts with holy scriptures,

and prefer the ideas of Ptolemy, which make Earth the centre of creation. Infuriated by Galileo's alleged impiety, and his success in communicating widely his novel ideas, his opponents have denounced him to the Inquisition.

Last year he was summoned to Rome and managed to clear his name, but failed to overturn the ruling that the teaching of Copernicanism should be suppressed. Today he was ordered to abandon his views.

Cervantes dies of sudden illness

Spain, 23 April 1616
Miguel de Cervantes Saavedra, the creator of Don Quixote and one of Spain's greatest writers, is dead. He had just completed his latest work, *Persiles y Sigismonde*, when he succumbed to a sudden, fatal illness.

Cervantes was born in 1547, in Alcala, to a noble but impoverished family. He left Spain at the age of 22 and enlisted in the army in Italy; wounded at the battle of Lepanto in 1571, he continued soldiering until in 1575 he was taken prisoner by the Turks. Despite many attempts at escape he spent five years in Algiers before he was ransomed and returned to Madrid. He began writing, but poverty forced him into a variety of temporary jobs.

His first book, *La Galataea*, appeared in 1585, but it was not until the publication of his masterpiece *Don Quixote* in 1605 that he experienced real success, although the playwright Lope de Vega was less than complimentary. So popular was *Don Quixote* that a "second part" appeared, written by an anonymous hack. Cervantes responded last year with a genuine sequel, as popular as the original.

Cervantes also wrote plays, in-

Miguel de Cervantes, whose death from a sudden illness will long be mourned by all the people of Spain.

cluding *La Numancia* and *Los tratos de Argel*. In 1613 he published a set of short stories, which he called *Exemplary novels*.

But it is for the adventures of *Don Quixote*, with its immortal characters of the Don and his squire Sancho Panza, that he will be best remembered.

A couple relax in a flower garden: a panel of earthenware tile-work decorated with coloured glazes, from a wall of a garden pavilion at Shah Abbas' magnificent royal palace at Isfahan in Persia. The city, an entirely new town, is wealthy enough to support the work of many artists who produce this characteristic style of delicate ornamentation on ceramics.

1618 (1618-1619)

England, 7 January 1618. The statesman Francis Bacon is appointed lord chancellor with the title Lord Verulam.

New England, April 1618. A smallpox epidemic is raging throughout New England, and spreading down the coast as far as Virginia. Indian tribes from the Penobscot River (*in Maine*) to Narrangansett Bay (*in Rhode Island*) are the hardest hit, and have lost up to 90 per cent of their population. At this rate, the disease could wipe out the Indians in the area within three years. One of the latest victims is Chief Powhatan, whose daughter Pocahontas, the wife of a colonist, died of the disease last year in a ship off Gravesend after visiting England.

Brussels, 28 September 1618. The first pawnshop is opened in the Catholic Netherlands. People of modest means can borrow money at a low rate of interest on leaving a security.

England, 29 October 1618. Sir Walter Raleigh is executed to appease Spain.

Virginia, 18 November 1618. The provincial governor, Argall, is recalled after crop failures and his public criticism of Virginia company officials. Sir George Yardley is appointed as the new governor.

Germany, 1618. Since 1611 the ecclesiastical officials of Ellwangen have had some 390 people burnt for witchcraft.

Virginia, 1618. The governor decrees that those who miss church will be jailed "lying neck and heels in the Corps of Gard the night following and be a slave the week following".

Bohemia, 1618. Count Thurn leads Bohemians in a revolt against the pro-Catholic policy of the regents in Prague.

Hungary, 1618. Archduke Ferdinand, made king of Bohemia in 1617, is crowned king of Hungary.

France, 1618. Richelieu is ordered into exile at Avignon for conspiring with the queen mother, Marie de Medici.

Spain, 1618. Lope de Vega publishes his play *Fuente Ovejuna* (Fountain of Rebels), about a fictional village of the same name.

Antwerp, 1618. Flemish artist Anthony van Dyck joins the city's guild of painters.

Brazil, 1618. The *regimento* system is set up: in accordance with the right of discovery, the ownership of mines will revert to the *descobridores*, the men who first discovered the veins of minerals.

Virginia, 1618. Headright laws offer 50 acres per colonist to each investor who pays the cost of the trans-Atlantic passage.

Virginia, 1618. Colonists begin to cultivate wheat.

England, 1618. King James issues a book in favour of games which may be played after church on Sundays. This enrages Puritans.

France, 9 February 1619. Accused of magic and atheism, Lucilio Vanini, who wrote as Giulio Cesare, is burnt alive in Toulouse. His rationalist and naturalist ideas had forced him to leave Naples for England, and England for France. In Paris, his *Amphitheatre of Divine Providence* (1615) and *Secrets of Nature* (1616) attracted the censorship of the Sorbonne.

Germany, 20 March 1619. Holy Roman Emperor Matthias II dies.

Virginia, 14 August 1619. The first general assembly in the provincial capital, Jamestown, has passed a series of stern laws against drinking, gambling, immorality, idleness and "excess in apparell". Settlers have been prohibited from planting mulberry trees, grapes and hemp, all of which could be used to produce intoxicants. Each city, borough or plantation is also required to educate the Indian children.

Bohemia, 26 August 1619. Bohemia has elected a new king, the Protestant Frederick V, the elector of the Palatinate, in preference to the Habsburg Ferdinand, whom the Bohemian estates had "accepted" as king in 1617.

Germany, 28 August 1619. Following the death of the Emperor Matthias II, his cousin Ferdinand, king of Hungary since 1618 and until two days ago king of Bohemia, is unanimously elected emperor as Ferdinand II. Since Bohemia refuses to take an oath of loyalty to the new emperor, he makes an alliance with Duke Maximilian of Bavaria and the Catholic League against Bohemia and the Palatinate.

Virginia, August 1619. A Dutch frigate lands 20 Africans, who are to be indentured servants in the port of Jamestown. This is the first cargo of its kind to arrive in a British North American colony. As the status of slave does not exist in law, the way is open for total exploitation of the labour force.

Virginia, 1619. Some 1,200 new settlers this year bring the population to over 3,000. The newcomers are "choice men, born and bred up to labour and industry", plus 90 women and 100 London slum children.

Indian emperor records animal behaviour

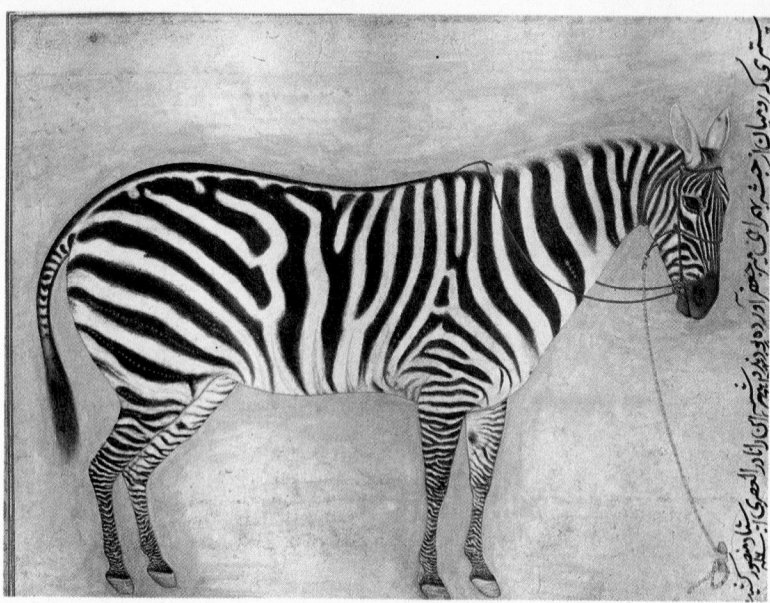

A miniature of a zebra, by Jahangir's favourite painter, Mansur.

Agra, India, 1618

Escaping from the cares of a vast empire and a domineering wife, Jahangir, the Moghul emperor, studies paintings, botany and zoology. Alternatively, at other times, he gets blind drunk. Such contrasts of behaviour run in the family.

Ascending the throne in 1605, after rebelling against his own father, the great Emperor Akbar, Jahangir expanded the empire into the Dekhan and Mewar, but reserved his real passion for nature.

Jahangir keeps a diary which records his love of the natural world. He delights in detailing the mating of two cranes, in dissecting a snake and discovering a rabbit in it, or in finding a meteorite while it was still hot and having swords made out of it.

He has surrounded himself with miniature painters, including the genius of that genre, Mansur, and ordered them to record the natural world around them. Their paintings of turkeys, peacocks, falcons and a hundred other exotic birds are exquisitely coloured and detailed.

A miniature of a dying man, by an unknown artist.

King orders execution of Walter Raleigh

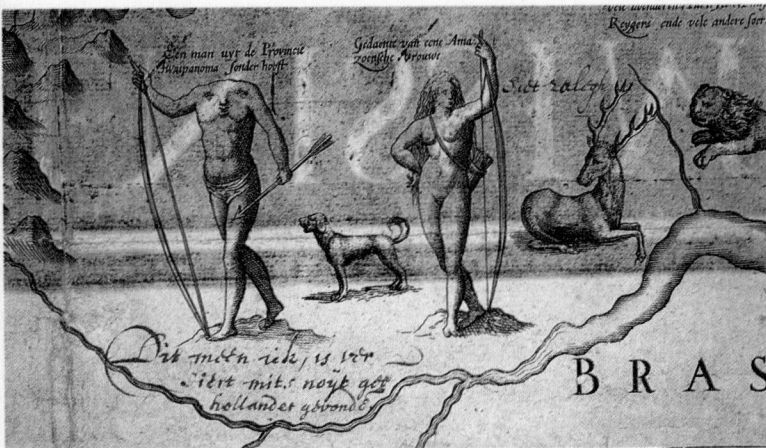

Men whose heads grow beneath their shoulders, as reported by Raleigh.

London, 29 October 1618
After the miserable fiasco of an expedition to South America in pursuit of El Dorado, Sir Walter Raleigh was executed today on the orders of the king. He was 66. He was sent to the Tower of London in 1603 after being accused of plotting against James, but a sentence of death was not carried out and he spent his time writing *A History of the World*.

Two years ago he obtained his liberty by persuading the king that he could find gold in the Orinoco country without clashing with the Spanish. After furious protests from Spain, Raleigh was told that trouble with the Spanish would cost him his life. He reckoned that if he

returned with rich booty he would be forgiven by a king in need of funds. But Raleigh fell ill and stayed at Trinidad while the expedition went ahead – and clashed with the Spanish. The dead included his son and several Spaniards; Raleigh returned home, doomed.

Previously, he had been Queen Elizabeth's favourite and she showered him with rewards, including his knighthood. But while he was at sea with an expedition to plunder Spanish galleons she recalled him for seducing one of her maids of honour. Raleigh was sent to the Tower and there married the lady. In the event he turned out to be a good husband and the couple had two sons.

Freethinker burned

France, 9 February 1619
Lucilio Vanini, an Italian freethinker, ex-Carmelite monk and wandering scholar, paid the price today for his unorthodox views. His tongue was cut out, he was strangled at the stake and then burnt to ashes, all on the orders of the Toulouse *Parlement*, which has been trying him since November.

Although faced with the executioner, Vanini proudly proclaimed his belief in a natural morality and his blasphemous view of miracles. He was born near Naples in 1585 and wrote under the name of Giulio Cesare. Many of his works, though admired by scholars from places like the Sorbonne, have been condemned to be burnt. His detractors, however, were not content until they had burnt the man as well.

Dutch statesman goes to block

Holland, 1619
Dutch statesman Jan van Oldenbarneveldt, 72, has been beheaded for treason after a trial on the orders of Prince Maurice of Nassau.

A moderate, Oldenbarneveldt helped secure the Union of Utrecht (1579), an alliance with England and France (1596) and a 12-year truce with Spain (1609). He ensured that Prince Maurice succeeded his murdered father, William the Silent, as stadholder, Dutch leader, in 1585. But the two fell out over the Arminian religious dispute. Maurice opposed the Arminians, who challenged Calvinist beliefs in predestination. Oldenbarneveldt supported the Arminians, and paid for his support with his life.

Blacks and women are sold in America

Jamestown, Virginia, 1619
A consignment of black servants described by Virginians as "twenty negars" has been landed and sold by the captain of a Dutch frigate. They are the first slaves to be delivered to North America, but their local status is unclear. The Normans abolished slavery in England more than six centuries ago. It is uncertain whether the same law

holds in a colony 3,000 miles away. Settlers who have acquired these negars believe that they have purchased them outright for life, whereas white servants are free of indentures after five years. In a separate transaction, 90 "willing maidens" were "sold with their consent" at the cost of bringing them here (120 pounds of tobacco) to become brides of settlers.

Black faces, seen in North America for the first time: painting by Van Dyck.

"Pure" Calvinists hammer dissenters

United Provinces, 29 May 1619
The Calvinist synod at Dordrecht has come down firmly in favour of the purest form of Calvinism, reaffirming the belief in absolute predestination.

Many of the followers of Arminius, who maintains God had not wanted Adam to fall from grace, have already been banished from the country. They had been ordered

not to preach while they waited their turn to be called before the synod, which began last November.

Prince Maurice of Orange, who called the synod, is against Arminius. The synod president is a stern Calvinist. Politics also played their part. In 1610 the Arminians published a "Remonstrance", which called for religious independence for the Dutch provinces.

Queen Marie leads rebellion against son

France, 1619
The scheming Marie de Medici has emerged from exile in Blois to lead an uprising against her son, Louis XIII. But her campaign has failed to win back the power she enjoyed as regent after the assassination nine years ago of her husband, Henry II.

Under the influence of her favourite, Concini, she had presided over a period of extravagant misrule. She appeased her nobles by granting them huge pensions, and reversed Henry's foreign policies, striking up alliances with Spain and Austria. But two years ago Louis finally resolved to free himself of his mother's influence. Concini was murdered and Marie was forced to withdraw from the court.

The flamboyant and ambitious Marie de Medici, on horseback, leads a rebellion against her own son; by Theodore Gericault (1791-1824).

Russia, 1619. Yeniseysk is founded, as capital of the region of the same name. It is at the heart of the gold-mining region and on the river Yenisei, Russia's eastern frontier.

France, 1619. Louis XIII recalls Richelieu from exile in Avignon to help defuse a rebellion by the queen mother, Marie de Medici.

Madrid, 1619. The Plaza Mayor is completed as part of plans to make Madrid a fitting capital for the Spanish empire. It is a large square, four-storeyed on all sides, with arcaded shops on the ground floor.

Germany, 1619. Johann Kepler, who has demonstrated the truth of the Copernican view of the universe, publishes his *Harmonices Mundi*.

South-East Asia, 1619. The Dutch build a fortress and a colony on the remains of the first settlement, dating from 1596. They call the colony Batavia *Djakarta* after an ancient district in holland.

South America, 1619. The London Amazon Company is created.

London, 1619. William Harvey announces his discovery of the circulation of the blood.

Virginia, 31 January 1620. Leaders of the colony write to the Virginia Company asking for more orphaned apprentices for employment.

France, 10 February 1620. Supporters of Marie de Medici, the queen mother, who has been exiled to Blois, are defeated by the king's troops at Ponts de Ce.

London, 29 June 1620. The crown bans tobacco growing in England, giving the Virginia Company a monopoly in exchange for tax of one shilling per pound of tobacco.

South Africa, July 1620. Two English officers, Captains Shillinge and Fitzherbert, erect the British flag on the shores of Table Bay in the name of King James. But they do not leave a colony to take possession of the Cape. The Cape of Good Hope is valued primarily as a stopping-off post for ships bound to India.

France, 10 August 1620. The king's chief minister, Richelieu, uses his diplomatic tact to persuade Marie de Medici to agree a peace treaty with her son Louis XIII.

England, 16 September 1620. A band of 35 religious dissenters sets sail in the *Mayflower* for Virginia, jubilant at the prospect of practising their brand of worship in the New World without official harrassment.

North America, 11 November 620. After a journey to find the mouth of Hudson's river is aborted because of bad weather, would-be settlers put in at Cape harbour.

North America, 21 November 1620. Leaders of the *Mayflower* expedition gathered in the ship's main cabin today to prepare a social contract designed to bolster unity. The document is meant to placate settlers angered by their arrival on land which has not been granted to them by charter. The "Mayflower Compact" establishes a civil body politic for the new colony that will set up "just and equal laws" based on church covenants.

Mexico, 1620. The population of Mexico has reached 1.2 million.

Netherlands, 1620. Simon Stevin, the mathematician, dies. He taught Maurice of Nassau, and was appointed by him to be engineer in charge of the dykes. He introduced the decimal system for money, weights and measures. Developing Archimedes' theory of physics, he established how to calculate the pressure exerted by a liquid on the sides of a container.

Southern Africa, 1620. The British colony of Saldanha Bay, near the Cape of Good Hope, fails.

England, 1620. Francis Bacon publishes his *Novum Organum*, a scientific treatise promoting his belief that scientific research should be conducted in the interests of humanity.

London, 1620. The poet, physician and musician Thomas Campion dies. He set Latin and English poems to music, as well as his own verses. He leaves several books of "ayres" for the voice, with lute accompaniment.

France, 1620. The province of Bearn becomes part of the kingdom of France. On the basis of a 1617 edict the king reinstates the Catholic religion, using military means to force Protestants to hand back former ecclesiastical property that they had secularised 50 years ago.

Virginia, 1620. The first public library is founded at the site of a proposed college in Henrico. Landowners donate the books for the library.

Japan, 1620. The imperial palace of Katsura is built in Kyoto, on the banks of the Katsura river which supplies the water for the ponds and streams in its gardens.

Rome, 28 January 1621. Pope Paul V dies. He is succeeded by the elderly Cardinal Alessandro Ludovisi from Bologna who will reign as Gregory XV.

Bohemian king has to flee after dinner

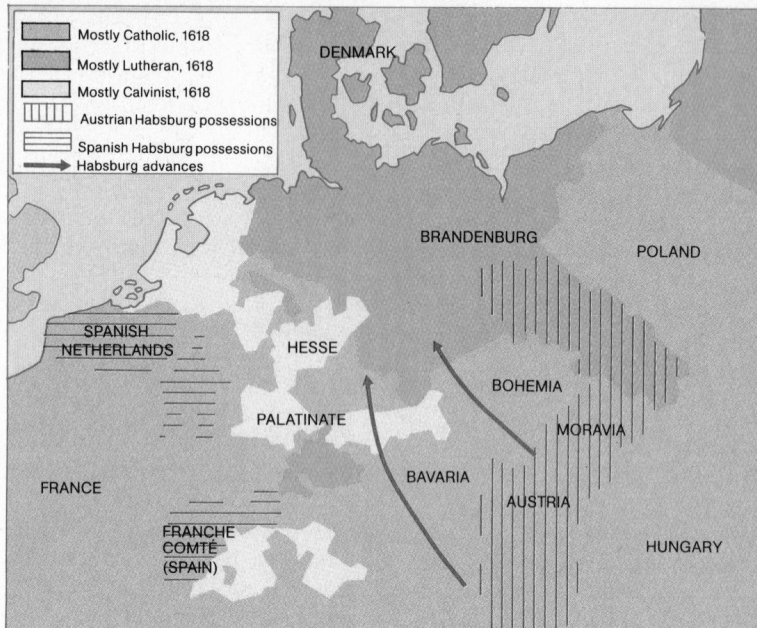

Mostly Catholic, 1618
Mostly Lutheran, 1618
Mostly Calvinist, 1618
Austrian Habsburg possessions
Spanish Habsburg possessions
Habsburg advances

DENMARK
BRANDENBURG
POLAND
SPANISH NETHERLANDS
HESSE
BOHEMIA
PALATINATE
MORAVIA
FRANCE
BAVARIA
AUSTRIA
HUNGARY
FRANCHE COMTÉ (SPAIN)

Prague, 8 November 1620
King Frederick of Bohemia and his queen were in high spirits at the dinner table tonight as they entertained the English ambassadors. Although the armies of the fanatically Catholic Emperor Ferdinand II had invaded his country from Austria, Frederick was confident that the enemy's forces were too weak with hunger or wracked with plague to fight. His own army occupied an unassailable position on the White Mountain near Prague.

After dinner, the king rode out to encourage his soldiers. However, he had not reached the city gates when he met the first fugitives. His army had been defeated: the emperor's banner flew over the White Moun-tain. Frederick's general, Anhalt, entered the city and told the king that the army had become mutinous during a lengthy artillery barrage, and many had refused to fight as they were overwhelmed by Bavarian and Spanish infantry.

As the citizens of Prague closed the gates against the invaders, the king and queen fled in such haste that they almost forgot their youngest prince, although they did remember most of the crown jewels.

Frederick's brief reign as king of Bohemia is over. He had become king in defiance of the emperor; whether the emperor will now allow him to revert to being Elector Palatine Frederick V remains to be seen.

Submarine tested

England, 1620
Cornelius Drebbel, a Dutchman, has just tested an underwater craft on the river Thames. Drebbel's vessels are made of wood with hulls of greased leather. Twelve oarsmen propel the vessels, their oars protruding through tight-fitting flaps covered in grease. The rowers breathe through hollow masts that project above the surface.

There is one snag to Drebbel's design. Under pressure the leather hull and oar openings are not completely watertight. The machine starts to take in water, and slowly but surely, it sinks.

Pope Paul V dies

Rome, 28 January 1621
Pope Paul V died of a stroke today only a few months after the great Catholic victory in the battle of the White Mountain in the war against the Protestants in Germany.

Born Camillo Borghese, in 1552, Paul has dominated the Catholic world in his 16-year reign. He excommunicated the doge of Venice because that state forbade the erection of religious buildings without the permission of Senate. He rebuked King James of England for demanding an oath of allegiance. He also completed the rebuilding of St Peter's.

MPs clash with the English king over punishment powers

Westminster, 18 December 1621

The House of Commons today delivered a sharp rebuff to the king after he had ordered MPs not to "meddle" in affairs of state and claimed the right to punish any MP who commits a "misdemeanour" in parliament. A Commons statement said that "the liberties, franchises, privileges and jurisdictions of parliament" are the birthright of the English people, and every MP must have "freedom from all impeachment and molestation (other than by censure of the House itself)".

James has repeatedly clashed with MPs, and for six years he tried to govern without parliament; but this left him short of funds. Earlier this year, faced with the prospect of

The king: rebuked by the Commons.

war in Europe, he resigned himself to another parliament. MPs were in a determined mood. They curbed the king's power to grant monopolies; they impeached Francis Bacon, the lord chancellor, for accepting bribes; and they set out new guidelines for enforcing the laws affecting religious worship. MPs wanted war with Catholic Spain; James did not, and told them not to meddle in these matters. They made a grant to support the Protestant cause in Europe. James shut down parliament and sent one MP to the Tower.

Winter to test "Mayflower" pilgrims

New England, November 1620

After a hazardous voyage across the Atlantic, the *Mayflower*, a 180-ton ship normally used to carry wine, has brought 120 anti-Catholic Puritans to the shores of what they have called "New England". The ship is moored in a harbour now dubbed "New Plymouth" which has become a refuge for the colony.

Danger has stalked the enterprise from the start. A year ago 35 English dissenters, who had lived in exile at Leyden, in Holland, for ten years, persuaded the Virginia Company to agree to a private plantation. They were to cross to England in the *Speedwell* to make convoy with the *Mayflower*, carrying another 66 settlers. After weeks of delay the *Speedwell* was unseaworthy. Everyone crowded aboard the *Mayflower* for a stormy six-week voyage scarred by disease and sudden death. Even as the settlers rowed ashore, Dorothy Bradford, the wife of one of their leaders, fell overboard and was drowned.

Some colonists made it clear that they would obey no law once they landed. The sense of impending lawlessness grew when storms drove the *Mayflower* north of her destination to Indian territory known as Massachusetts. The response of 41 of the settlers was to

A fresh start: a later American tapestry of the landing of the pilgrims.

draft their own "Mayflower Compact": a charter for civilisation rather than anarchy.

During the first days ashore, the fitter members carried the ailing majority and built temporary shelters near the beach. Miles Standish, a leading settler, led armed settlers on a reconnaissance of the area. They came under attack from local Indians after interfering with native graves, but frightened the attackers away with gunshot. With winter imminent the settlers must forage for food, including stores of Indian-grown corn. One useful source of food is a breed of bird entirely new to the settlers – the turkey.

England gets its world news on paper

England, 1621

The spread of information to the English public has been greatly increased with the publication this year of a number of newsbooks, or *corantos*, which offer short reports of events happening in a variety of places, often abroad.

These corantos, new editions of which appear every week, originated in Europe, where newsletters of this sort have been published in the Netherlands and Germany for the last couple of years.

Now the system has caught on in Britain, where the first such corantos detailed events in Europe's religious war. The king, under whose authority all printing is carried out, has licensed certain members of the Stationers' Company to issue such pamphlets on a regular basis.

A page of Dutch news pamphlet.

Spanish and Dutch renew trade war

Netherlands, 1621

The 12-year truce between Spain and the Netherlands has ended. A renewal of hostilities has become more or less inevitable in recent years as Dutch ships have grown in numbers, trading throughout much of the world and threatening Spain's trade monopoly with its colonial possessions. Apart from their success in trading, the Dutch have waged war with Spanish shipping and settlements on the Pacific.

A major argument at the Spanish court against continuing the truce was the damage that the Dutch were doing to American trade – the Netherlanders have established a "Fort Orange" on Hudson's river in North America. The last straw for the Spanish was the creation of the Dutch West India Company, formed to promote trade – and war – in South America.

1621 (1621-1622)

Germany, 15 February 1621. Michael Praetorius, a leading composer of music for the Lutheran church, dies at the age of 50.

New England, 22 March 1621. The English settlers who arrived in New England in November last year aboard the *Mayflower*, form an alliance with the chief of the Wampanoag Indians.

Madrid, 31 March 1621. King Philip III of Spain dies and is succeeded by his son, who becomes King Philip IV.

Germany, 14 April 1621. The Protestant Union, an alliance of Protestant princes, announces that it is to be dissolved.

New England, 1 June 1621. The *Mayflower* settlers are granted a royal patent, legalising their settlement at New Plymouth, outside Virginia, the area of their original patent.

Netherlands, 3 June 1621. The Dutch found the West India Company. It is granted a monopoly on trade and colonisation in North and South America for a period of 24 years.

Brussels, 13 July 1621. Archduke Albert dies without an heir. This marks the end of the fiction of an independent Catholic Netherlands. Policy towards the Dutch "rebels" is now controlled from Madrid where royal ministers are divided between "doves" and "hawks".

Virginia, July 1621. Sir Edwin Sandys tells colonists that the king has criticised the raising of tobacco in colonies, but settlers refuse to diversify.

Baltic, 16 September 1621. At the head of the most modern army in Europe, the Swedish king, Gustavus Adolphus, seizes Riga from the Poles.

Rome, 17 September 1621. The Catholic theologian Roberto Bellarmine dies. He was a Jesuit cardinal and leading figure in the Counter-Reformation.

England, 21 October 1621. The Privy Council orders all exports from colonies to have customs paid in England.

North America, 25 December 1621. The governor of New Plymouth prevents newcomers from playing cards.

France, December 1621. Albert de Luynes, the commander-in-chief of the king's forces laying siege to Montauban in Provence, has died, and Louis XIII, who is with the soldiers, has failed to secure the surrender of the Protestant town. Huguenots in the region began a rebellion in August.

Virginia, 1621. The first ironworks in the colonies are constructed at Falling Creek.

Angola, 1621. Nzinga, the sister of Ngola Mbandi, the king of Mbundu (*Angola*), is sent as an envoy to Portugal where she is baptised Anne Zingha.

Rome, 1621. The Italian sculptor Giovanni Bernini completes his *Rape of Proserpina*.

England, 1621. Robert Burton publishes *The Anatomy of Melancholy*, a strange book indebted to a huge range of classical and mediaeval writers.

France, 1621. The university of Strasbourg is founded.

Netherlands, 1621. The Dutch composer Jan Sweelinck dies at the age of 59. He composed mainly church music, especially settings of the Psalms, and works for the organ, and developed the fugue.

Alps, 1621. War breaks out between the Swiss League of Grisons and Spain over control of Valtellina.

Germany, 1621. Heidelberg university library is sacked by Count Tilly's Catholic troops.

Virginia, 1621. Elias Legardo settles in Virginia. He is the first Jewish colonial settler in North America.

Germany, 1621. Potatoes are planted in Germany for the first time. They have been brought over from America.

Japan, 1621. The Japanese are forbidden to board foreign vessels or to travel overseas, on pain of death.

London, 1621. John Fletcher's comedy *A Wild Goose Chase* is staged for the first time.

London, 1621. Francis Bacon, Lord Verulam, is accused of accepting bribes from suitors in his court. He is arraigned before fellow peers, fined and imprisoned in the Tower of London. He is also banished from parliament and the court.

Rome, 1621. The papal chancery adopts 1 January as the beginning of the year.

America, 1621. The Scottish settlement in Nova Scotia ("New Scotland") fails.

Germany, 1622. *Apologia pro Galileo*, written by the Italian philosopher Tommaso Campanella in 1616 while in prison, is published in Frankfurt. A defence of the revolutionary astronomer's work, it was first addressed to Galileo himself and Cardinal Bonifacio Gaetani. It is widely circulated here and in Holland.

Thanksgiving feast greets fine harvest

A Virginian Indian, by Hollar (1645).

New Plymouth, America, 1621
A year after landing, the Puritan settlement is at peace with the native Indian people thanks to a remarkable pair of English-speaking Indians of the Wampanoag tribe. One, named Tisquantum or "Squanto", was first taken to England in 1605 with Captain Waymouth's expedition.

Squanto recrossed the Atlantic in 1614 to help Captain John Smith, only to be sold as a slave to Spain by the English explorer Thomas Hunt. The Indian escaped and reached England before returning to Massachusetts two years ago.

There were many causes of conflict. Seven years ago some Wampanoags were taken as slaves in an endeavour to reverse the flow of such trade from east to west. There was also the inadvertent desecration of Indian graves when the Puritans first landed. All that seems to be forgotten as both communities come together for a week-long feast of thanksgiving for a bumper harvest of Indian corn. Among the delicacies served at the feast were venison and wild turkey.

Swedish king digs his way to Riga victory

King Gustavus Adolphus: Sweden's young king, popular for sharing the hardships of his troops.

Poland, 16 September 1621
The astonishing sight of their own king helping to dig assault trenches spurred the Swedish army to victory here today as Riga surrendered after a hard-fought siege. The youthful Swedish king, Gustavus Adolphus, ever at the forefront of his men, came close to death on at least one occasion as his troops advanced under a creeping artillery barrage and stormed the walls.

Two days ago the burghers of Riga parleyed, but angered Gustavus by describing him as "ruling prince in the kingdom of Sweden", rather than "king of Sweden" – their own king, Sigismund, has claimed the Swedish throne. This affront could have meant a full-scale sacking by the Swedish army; Gustavus relented, but is still claiming the city for Sweden.

Woman writes book on sexual equality

France, 1622
The writer Marie le Jars de Gournay has struck a new blow for women's rights with the publication of her book *Egalite des Hommes et des Femmes*. Already established as one of the first successful professional women writers and a staunch defender of women's liberty, de Gournay uses this book to attack the hypocrisy of society's attitude towards her sex. She has been treated with hostility and contempt because of her plain looks and her dogged refusal to play the submissive role expected of her.

The pope skilfully chooses new saints

Now a saint: Teresa of Avila.

Rome, 1622

Pope Gregory XV is proving a skilful politician. His choice of new saints shows careful attention for the temporal needs of the Catholic Church in its struggle against Protestantism, and the spiritual need to encourage the pious life.

Four prominent Jesuits, including their founder, Ignatius Loyola, are among the new saints. It is the Jesuits, above all, who have spearheaded the Catholic fight to regain the religious ground from the Reformation. But the pope has also canonised one of the greatest mystics, Teresa of Avila, who favoured the contemplative life.

Canonised: Jesuit founder Loyola.

An exquisitely-carved ivory dagger handle in the form of a camel's head; from the British Museum.

A European and his servants, seen through Moghul eyes: a fine example of the new spirit of realism.

Cross-fertilisation of cultures gave birth to this Moghul miniature of the "Nativity" (Bodleian Library).

Realistic and secular Moghul art flourishes under Jahangir

Delhi, 1622

Jahangir, the third Moghul emperor, is proving as great a patron of the arts as his father, Akbar the Great, who extended the empire of the descendants of Tamerlane throughout northern India and Kashmir.

Akbar gathered poets and painters around him, on the model of the Persian court. He recruited Hindu and Moslem painters and set them the task of illustrating the adventures of Amir Hamza, an uncle of the Prophet, in 1,400 painted pages, as well as the Hindu *Mahabharata*, the Book of Wars, in Persian translation.

Jahangir has encouraged portrait painting and pictures of his assembled courtiers as well as nature studies of animals and birds. He is a lover of nature and his favourite painter, Mansur, has produced exquisite paintings of zebras, wild goats, pheasants and turkey cocks. Jahangir has given Mansur the title of *Nadir al-Wasr* – the Wonder of the Age.

Jahangir prides himself on being able to look at any painting and tell immediately whose work it is. When one of his attendants was dying of opium addiction, Jahangir summoned his painters to record the man's emaciated appearance. He had himself painted embracing Shah Abbas of Persia; the Great Moghul is shown surrounded by an enormous gold halo, copied from his European paintings.

One of 1,400 illustrations for the "Romance of Amir Hamza" commissioned by Akbar and finished before 1582 in a mixture of Indian and Persian styles. The epic conflates the Prophet Mohammed's relation with a C9th Moslem hero; in this scene a giant is thrown down a well and beaten by gardeners.

Europe in turmoil, 1618-1648

Although the wars which convulsed Europe between 1618 and the Peace of Westphalia in 1648 have been dubbed "The Thirty Years War", this was not a term known to contemporaries. Coined in the 18th century by Frederick the Great and Schiller, this label suggests that the wars were rooted in the struggle for dominance within Germany. But the German civil war was only part of the story; while the German-speaking lands were the main battlefield, the rivalries and enmities which fuelled the warfare were truly international. If we are to regard the series of campaigns stretching from Bohemia to Denmark, and the overlapping wars in Mantua, Poland and the Netherlands, as a single struggle, then the common thread is the Habsburg dynasty and the common starting point is the year 1555.

A brewing conflict

At his abdication in 1555 Emperor Charles V had divided his lands and authority between the Spanish and the Austrian branches of the Habsburg family. His son, Philip II of Spain, retained Spain, Italy, and the Netherlands (which were in due course to rebel against his distant and autocratic rule). Meanwhile Philip's cousin in Vienna ruled over the Habsburgs' "hereditary lands" of Austria, Hungary and Bohemia, and enjoyed the title of Holy Roman emperor. Despite this title, Habsburg authority in the Germanspeaking lands of Europe was shaky. Germany was a patchwork of petty principalities, wealthy independent bishoprics and prosperous cities, over which the institutions of the Holy Roman empire provided a judicial and political umbrella. In theory the empire provided a forum for conciliation and a mechanism for joint action, such as repelling the Ottomans. The emperor himself was chosen by a college of "electors" made up of seven German princes: his power depended largely upon his own military and financial resources.

In 1555, in the aftermath of the emperor's abdication, the imperial Diet of Augsburg had drawn up a peace for Germany. This backward-looking settlement sought to freeze the German situation as it had been in 1552, an uneasy stalemate between the Catholic and Lutheran states.

As the minority faith, German Protestantism naturally sought to expand. It was Calvinism, rather than Lutheranism, which made the political running in Germany in the second half of the 16th century: but Calvinism had not been recognised by the Peace of Augsburg. Among Roman Catholics, meanwhile, the militancy of the Counter-reformation was beginning to make itself felt. The German princes also wanted to consolidate and concentrate their own power. Within their lands they tried to stifle independent and representative bodies, and outside them sought to overawe their neighbours, and to preserve their own freedom of action within the empire. Religion and ambition often coincided, as when the archbishop-elector of Cologne announced that he had become a Lutheran, was to marry a nun, and would convert his diocese into a secular hereditary possession. Naturally, he kept his electoral title.

By the beginning of the 17th century, three "parties" had emerged within the empire: the Counter-reformation Catholics, led jointly by Archduke Ferdinand of Styria (a Habsburg who became Holy Roman emperor in 1619) and his rival, Duke Maximilian of Bavaria; the moderate Lutherans, led by Elector John George of Saxony; and the Calvinists, who took a lead from Heidelberg, the seat of the electors of the Palatinate. Mutual distrust and antagonism thwarted imperial policies and institutions, and when the Protestant radicals formed a defensive union under Palatine leadership in 1608, the Catholics retorted with their own league led by Bavaria. Germany had become a tinderbox.

The other European powers took a keen interest. They naturally feared the potential power of the Habsburgs: Protestant nations were terrified by their fervent Catholicism; France feared encirclement; while the Dutch rebels were concerned with the strategic and mercantile importance of the Baltic and the Rhine valley. The rivalry between German princes and the contest between the princes and their imperial overlord were a standing invitation to interference. In 1614 war between the league and union over Julich-Cleves, a Rhineland principality, was narrowly averted by the mediation of France, England, Spain and the Dutch. War, when it finally did come, arose from a totally different quarter.

Rebellion and war

In 1618 the feudal aristocrats of Bohemia, many of whom were Lutherans, took exception to Ferdinand of Styria's heavy-handed policies of bureaucratic centralisation and religious uniformity. To make their point they threw two of the Habsburgs' Catholic councillors from a window in Prague's Hradshin palace (both survived). More significant than this "defenestration" was the deposition of Ferdinand as king of Bohemia and the choice of Frederick, the elector of the Palatinate, in his place.

Ferdinand was busy ensuring his election as emperor, and it was 1620 before he could finally deal with Bohemia. The Habsburgs mobilised all their European supporters: Spanish, Bavarian, Saxon and imperial armies dismembered Bohemia and the Palatinate, before crushing Frederick's armies outside Prague at the battle of the White Mountain (8 November 1620). By 1623 opposition to the Habsburgs and their allies had been overcome.

That the war in Germany flared into life again was mainly due to the Dutch. In 1621 a long truce between Spain and the Netherlands had expired. Spain's early military successes and its plan to occupy naval bases on the North Sea and Baltic coasts made it imperative for the Dutch to establish a second front against the Habsburgs, and they encouraged the illfated campaigns of Christian of Denmark. By 1628 the imperial generals Tilly and Wallenstein had chased the Danes back into their own land. However, these staggering imperial successes, the transfer of an electorship to Maximilian of Bavaria, and the Edict of Restitution of 1629, provoked a backlash.

Protestants fight back

German Protestant princes needed a counterweight to the Habsburgs. Gustavus Adolphus of Sweden was to be their Protestant champion. Unfortunately, he was also in the pay of the French: as Gustavus himself remarked, "all the wars of Europe are now blended into one". Only after his death (1632) did covert French support of the anti-Habsburg war become open French control, and finally, in 1635, open war. The German princes sought in vain to demilitarise Germany, hampered by their disunity and by the fact that much bigger players were now in the game. Led by Swedes, Scots and Italians, pursuing French, Dutch and Habsburg interests, the great armies criss-crossed Germany without hope of ever achieving a final victory.

The Peace of Westphalia (1648) took seven years to negotiate, and another five to implement; many related disputes were only finally resolved in 1660. Within Germany, a shift of power had taken place as the Austrian Habsburgs recognised the independence of the princes and began to see that their own future lay along the Danube rather than the Rhine. The exhausted Spanish Habsburgs recognised the sovereignty of the Netherlands. But almost more important than the details of the peace was the framework established for creating a European balance of power which would last to the treaty of Utrecht (1713) and beyond, perhaps even to the peace congresses of our own century.

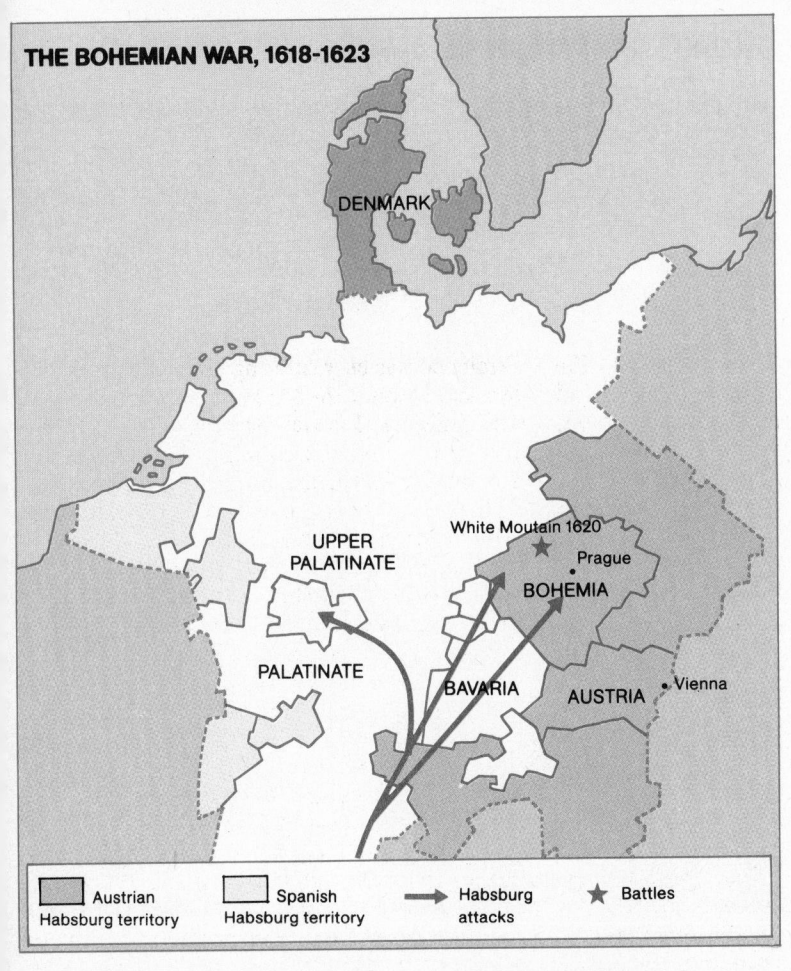

THE BOHEMIAN WAR, 1618-1623

UPPER PALATINATE

White Moutain 1620

Prague

BOHEMIA

PALATINATE

BAVARIA

AUSTRIA

Vienna

| | Austrian Habsburg territory | | Spanish Habsburg territory | → Habsburg attacks | ★ Battles |

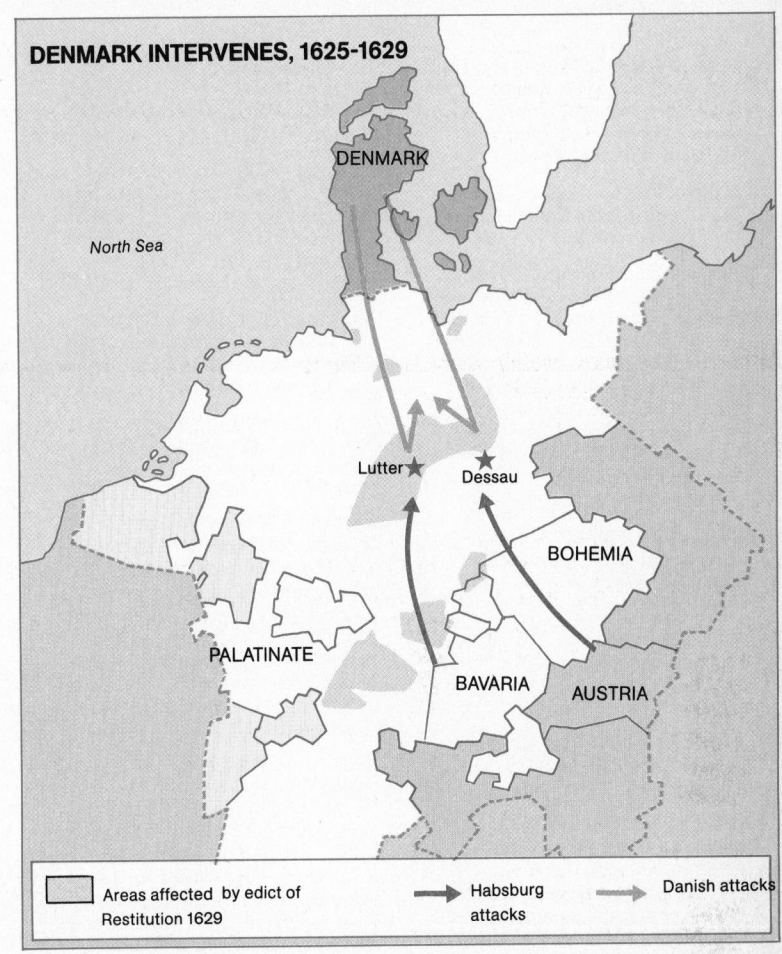

DENMARK INTERVENES, 1625-1629

DENMARK

North Sea

Lutter

Dessau

BOHEMIA

PALATINATE

BAVARIA

AUSTRIA

| | Areas affected by edict of Restitution 1629 | → Habsburg attacks | → Danish attacks |

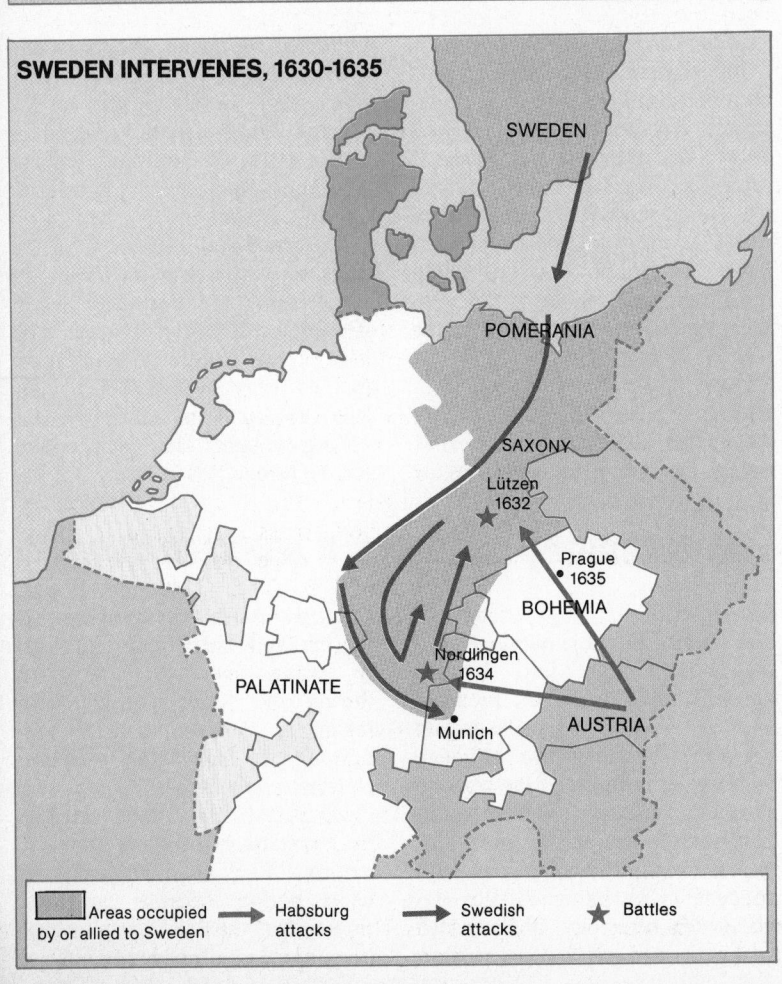

SWEDEN INTERVENES, 1630-1635

SWEDEN

POMERANIA

SAXONY

Lützen 1632

Prague 1635

BOHEMIA

Nördlingen 1634

PALATINATE

Munich

AUSTRIA

| | Areas occupied by or allied to Sweden | → Habsburg attacks | → Swedish attacks | ★ Battles |

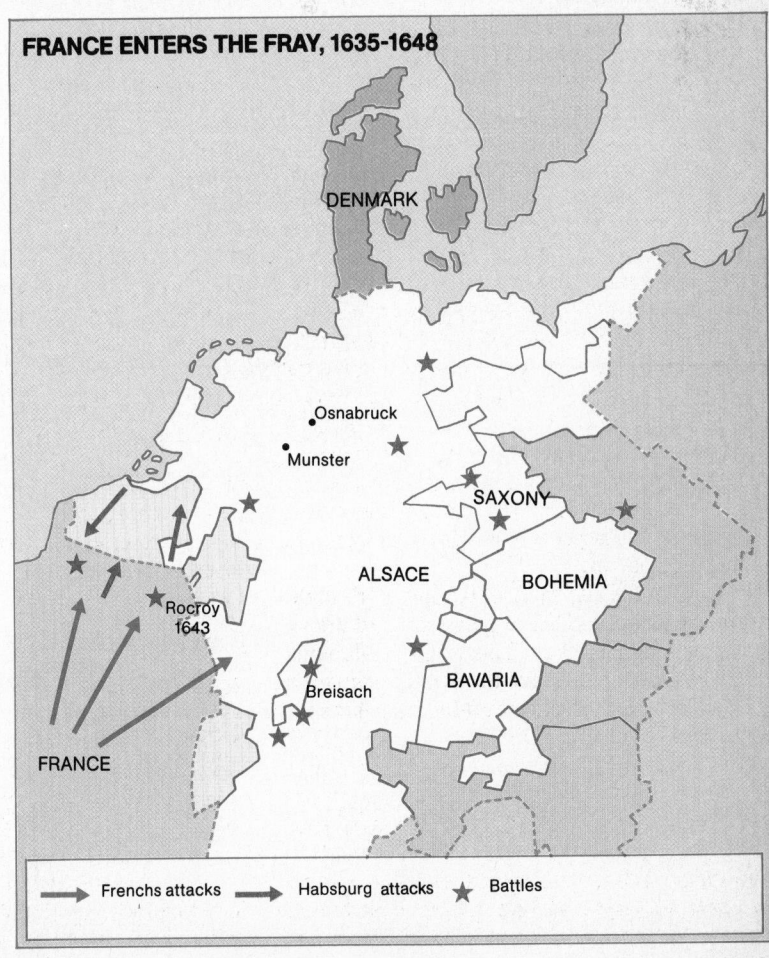

FRANCE ENTERS THE FRAY, 1635-1648

DENMARK

Osnabruck

Munster

SAXONY

ALSACE

BOHEMIA

Rocroy 1643

Breisach

BAVARIA

FRANCE

| → Frenchs attacks | → Habsburg attacks | ★ Battles |

1622 (1622-1623)

India, January 1622. The Moghul Emperor Jahangir's eldest son, the much-loved Prince Khusrau, who led an abortive rebellion against his father in 1606, has died.

London, February 1622. King James dissolves parliament after only two sessions.

Virginia, 22 March 1622. This morning an eight-year peace was shattered by an Indian attack in the James river area which has left 350 colonists dead in their fields and homes. The inhabitants of the port of Jamestown were saved by a warning from Chanco, an Indian who had converted to Christianity and was living on a settler's farm.

Istanbul, 20 May 1622. The 19-year old Ottoman Sultan Osman II is deposed and assassinated by his own guards.

Rome, 22 June 1622. The papal bull *Inscrutabili* founds the Congregation or College of Propaganda.

India, June 1622. The Moghul empire loses Kandahar to the Persians.

America, 5 September 1622. A hurricane has overrun a Spanish fleet bound from Havana to Cadiz, and sunk the prize galleon *Atocha*; 260 passengers were drowned and 200 million pesos went to the bottom with the ship.

France, 18 October 1622. After a hard campaign against the Protestants of southern France, Louis XIII lays siege to Montpellier and forces the duke of Rohan to agree to a peace which reaffirms the Edict of Nantes (a declaration of religious tolerance made at the end of the religious wars in 1598 by Henry IV), but forbids political meetings and leaves the Protestants with Montauban and La Rochelle as their only fortified strongholds.

France, 28 December 1622. Francois de Sales, the bishop of Geneva, a devotional writer and co-founder (with Jeanne de Chantal) of the Order of the Visitation of Our Lady (the Visitandines), dies at Lyons.

England, 30 December 1622. The Council for New England makes Robert Gorges lieutenant-general of New England, granting him 300 square miles on Boston Bay.

France, 1622. The talented French statesman Richelieu, the bishop of Lucon, is recalled to the Royal Council and appointed cardinal.

Netherlands, 1622. The marquis of Spinola, the commander of the Spanish forces, seizes the key fortress town of Bergen op Zoom from the Dutch.

Persian Gulf, 1622. Aided by the English, the Persian ruler Abbas drives the Portuguese out of Hormuz Island.

Hungary, 1622. A peace treaty is signed at Nikolsburg between the Holy Roman emperor and Gabor Bethlen of Transylvania. Bethlen renounces the title of king of Bohemia which he had since 1620.

Naples, 1622. Naples is thrown into turmoil by a series of social disturbances resulting from famine and economic problems.

Paris, 7 February 1623. France, Savoy and Venice sign the treaty of Paris, forming an alliance against Spain.

England, 4 July 1623. The composer William Byrd dies. He will be remembered as one of the greatest masters of polyphony of his day. He composed many works including madrigals, pieces for keyboard, songs and three masses. The masses, written for three, four or five voices, demonstrate the vitality of the art of counterpoint.

Rome, 6 August 1623. On the death of Pope Gregory XV, the Florentine Maffeo Barberini is elected and takes the name Pope Urban VIII. During Gregory's XV's reign, which lasted for two years and five months, the Catholic Counter-reformation made important gains: the spiritual reconquest of Bohemia after the military victory at White Mountain, and the foundation of the Congregation of Propaganda.

North America, 10 September 1623. Lumber and furs are the first cargo to leave New Plymouth for England, on a ship commanded by William Pierce.

North America, 13 December 1623. Colonists at New Plymouth today established the system of trial by 12-man jury in the American colonies. The system was originally instituted in the late 1100s by King Henry II to replace trial by combat or torture, which the defendant had to survive in order to be proved innocent.

Japan, 1623. The English trading station at Hirado is closed due to lack of profits.

New England, 1623. Captain John Mason of Hampshire has established the territory of New Hampshire from land granted to him by King James. Though it is now densely forested and inhabited by wild animals and Indians, Mason dreams of peopling it with farmers and adventurous aristocrats, and of making it an hereditary principality.

Spain, 1623. Diego Velasquez becomes court painter to King Philip IV.

Sultan Osman II is strangled, aged 19

Turkish Janissaries riding camels: a potent force for instability.

Istanbul, 20 May 1622

Sultan Osman II has been deposed and murdered by his own bodyguards, the Janissaries. Osman was 19 and had ruled for four years. It seems that the Janissaries heard of the sultan's plan to raise an alternative army with which to challenge their power. They broke into the harem and called for the reinstatement of the former sultan, the mad Mustapha.

According to various accounts, Dilaver Pasha, the grand vizier, was either executed on Osman's orders, to mollify the Janissaries, or murdered by them, along with the sultan's favourite, Hussein. After Osman had pleaded in vain for his life and throne, he was strangled on the orders of Sultana Valide, Mustapha's mother, who had taken effective control.

The greed and indiscipline of the Janissaries had been an increasing threat since the death of Sultan Ahmed in 1617. When Osman, who had rapidly succeeded Mustapha, led an army against Poland last year, he found the Janissaries unwilling to fight. They blamed him for the campaign's failure.

Tea ceremony intrigues a western guest

Macao, 1622

The western world is due to have a remarkable insight into the unknown way of life of the Japanese when 61-year-old Joao Rodrigues completes his memoirs. Although he is devoting much of the work to Japanese geography, history, politics, government and economy, he is also much concerned with etiquette – in particular the elaborate tea ceremony, about which he has written no fewer than four chapters. As a guest of several leading tea masters during his years in Japan, Rodrigues – exiled during the fierce anti-Christian regime in 1587 – had a rare opportunity to study the teahouses and the ceremony itself.

He stresses the importance that his hosts attached to conforming to nature: "Lack of artificiality is never boring, because experience shows that there is always something new to be found therein."

Christian martyrs beheaded in Japan

Franciscans executed by Hidetada.

Japan, 1622

The persecution of Christians is growing more cruel in Japan. While the last *shogun*, Ieyasu, banned Christianity but carried out no death sentences, his son and successor, Hidetada, is seeking out those Christian missionaries who have gone into hiding and executing them.

Some are beheaded, while others are hung upside down in pits. Great pressure is being put on Japanese who have converted to Christianity in order to make them recant. If they do not, they are tortured hideously and suffer drawn-out, agonising deaths.

This persecution has its roots not only in the opposition of militant Buddhism but also in the fear that the cross is the harbinger of the sword – that where missionaries go, soldiers will follow. It is the policy of the ruling Tokugawa family's military dictatorship to cut off Japan from the western world.

Dutch kill ten rival traders in the East

Indonesia, 1623

In an act of pure savagery, agents of the Dutch East India Company seized English traders at Amboina in Indonesia and tortured them before executing ten, along with ten Japanese and a Portuguese. They were accused of conspiring against the Dutch. Only three years ago, the Dutch gave the English permission to trade in spices at Amboina; they did so well that the Dutch saw their bid to monopolise the trade slipping away.

The perpetrators of the atrocity obviously felt they would be backed by the Dutch governor-general, Jan Pieterszoon Coen, who has acquired a reputation for unbridled ruthlessness since his appointment in 1619. When he founded the new colony at Batavia he razed the old Moslem town and drove out those whom he did not massacre.

Dutchmen torture an English trader.

Virginia's first settlers face disaster

Catastrophic colony: a map of Virginia, by John Smith, published in 1624.

London, 1623

The troubled Virginia Company headed by Sir Edwin Sandys seems doomed in the light of a recent Royal Commission report on the disasters which have killed around 3,000 settlers in 15 years.

The report provides King James with the pretext to revoke a charter of 1606, and declare Virginia as a royal province. The company's advocates claim that the king is more concerned about the colony's spirit of independence than its viability. Whatever the truth of that, the commission has found that people sent there in efforts to get a colony off the ground are "by sickness of body, famine and massacres dead" or "living in miserable, lamentable necessity".

Tragedies marking the history of the settlement include the failure by settlers to grow their own food despite fertile soil and a good climate. The settlers have been obliged to buy or extort grain, notably local corn, from the Indians. They have expressed their gratitude by killing Indians and burning their crops.

Virtually none of the settlers knew about agriculture before emigrating, though there were several goldsmiths in a territory without gold. Many were gentlemen, good administrators, but ignorant of farming. The working day, for most of them, is four hours. Intrigue and civil disorder provoked hangings and seven years of martial law.

There was just one successful crop, tobacco, which, in 1618, earned £50,000. But even this business suffered when King James denounced smoking as bad for the chest. Worse, the easy profit made from tobacco led to further neglect of basic foodstuffs. Pressure on the local Indians to supply corn at unfair terms provoked a massacre of 347 settlers by a native people who had previously been friendly.

Machine takes the pain out of calculation

Germany, 1623

Although the abacus has been in use for centuries, and William Oughtred's "slide-rule" is growing in popularity, a new step forward in calculation is likely to revolutionise mathematics.

The German Wilhelm Schickard has constructed an ingenious piece of wooden machinery capable of adding and subtracting automatically. Moreover, Schickard's calculating machine can also perform multiplication and division, albeit partly manually. The repercussions of such a device are profound. Human calculators who get tired and need to check their results are looking forward to using this invention.

William Byrd, master of madrigals, dies

England, 4 July 1623

William Byrd, one of Europe's greatest composers, has died at his Essex home, aged 80. Brought up in London, Byrd was taught by that other great master, Thomas Tallis (who died in 1585), and for a time the two men were joint organists of the Chapel Royal.

Byrd's huge output ranged from music for both the Anglican and Catholic churches to songs and instrumental music. He was particularly renowned for his masses and madrigals. These demonstrated a mastery of polyphony which gave him an unsurpassed reputation at home and abroad, is unsurpassed. One contemporary has called him "the father of British music".

1623 (1623-1626)

Paris, 1623. The free-thinker and Huguenot convert to Catholicism Theophile de Viau is sent to prison and his works are banned.

England, 1623. Thomas Weelkes, a famous composer of madrigals, dies aged about 50.

Persia, 1623. The Persian leader Shah Abbas takes Baghdad, Mosul and the whole of Mesopotamia from the Ottomans.

Rome, 1623. Pope Gregory XV clears the Jesuit Roberto de Nobili of corrupting the Catholic faith during his work in India. Nobili adopted local languages and customs and toned down some parts of the Christian message in deference to Hindu sensibilities.

Germany, 1623. The controversial German mystic Jakob Boehme, who came to the attention of the ecclesiastical authoritites in 1612, has published another book entitled *Mysterium Magnum*.

Switzerland, 1623. France withdraws from Valtellina.

Istanbul, 1623. Sultan Mustapha is deposed for a second time and replaced by Murad IV.

London, 1623. Edward Blount and Isaac Jaggard obtain a licence to publish 16 hitherto unprinted plays by Shakespeare on 8 November. Later in the year they publish a folio volume of nearly a thousand pages containing most of the original sixteen plays. Thirty-six pieces in all are brought together in the volume, and they are sold at £ 1 a copy. The plays are listed under three headings: "Comedies", "Histories" and "Tragedies".

Rome, 1623. The Polish poet Maciej Sarbiewski is crowned laureate by the pope.

India, 1623. Tulsi Das, the Hindu poet of the Rama cult, dies. He lived in Benares and will be best remembered for his version of *Ramayana*, the *Ramcharitmanas*.

Mexico, 15 January 1624. The people of Mexico hear at Mass that all churches are to be closed, and that their unpopular viceroy, Diego Carrillo de Mendoza y Pimentel, has been excommunicated as a heretic. A riot erupts and the viceregal palace is burnt and looted. It is the lower ranks of society, free negroes, Indians and *Mestizos*, who begin the riot.

Virginia, 5 March 1624. Class-based legislation is passed, exempting the upper classes from punishment by whipping.

France, 29 April 1624. Louis XIII appoints Cardinal Richelieu chief minister of the Royal Council.

Virginia, 24 May 1624. After years of unprofitable operation, Virginia's charter is revoked and it becomes a royal colony.

Rome, 1624. Pope Urban VIII, angered by tobacco imports from the American colonies, pledges to excommunicate all those who take snuff.

Japan, 1624. The Spanish are forbidden access to any part of the Japanese archipelago.

Caribbean, 1624. The first English settlers arrive in the West Indies, when Sir Thomas Warner occupies the island of St Christopher with a small group of followers.

Germany, 1624. Albrecht von Wallenstein is made duke of Friedland. A Catholic convert of noble Bohemian stock, he has a sizeable army which is now at the service of the emperor.

India, 1624. Bubonic plague, which has been raging through northern and western India for eight years, is at last dying down.

France, 1624. *Croquants* (peasants) in the province of Quercy, oppressed by heavy taxation and the ravages of continuing wars, rebel.

Brussels, 13 January 1625. The painter Jan Bruegel, known as "Velvet" Bruegel, dies. He is best known for his paintings of flowers and his allegorical scenes.

England, 27 March 1625. Prince Charles succeeds to the throne on the death of his father King James.

England, 5 June 1625. The composer Orlando Gibbons dies aged 42. He will be best remembered for his anthems and madrigals.

China, 1625. The first Manchu kings establish their capital at Mukden: their kingdom is a threat to the weakening Ming dynasty which rules China.

Canada, 1625. The Jesuits Lallemand and Brebeuf reach members of Quebec. Previously the Recollect order were the only missionaries operating in Canada.

West Indies, 1625. The Dutch seize San Juan, on Puerto Rico.

London, 1625. The city is ravaged by an attack of the plague.

China, 1625. Private academies throughout the empire are suppressed. They had become centres of opposition to the dominance of the eunuchs and their agents in the increasingly weak Ming dynasty.

North America, 1626. Salem is founded as the capital of Massachusetts.

Viceroy recalled after rioting in Mexico

A seventeenth-century view of Mexico City, by Cristobal de Villalpando.

Mexico, 1624

The viceroy of New Spain has been recalled to Madrid after 70 people died in food riots in which the vice-regal palace was burned and looted. The riots were sparked by food shortages after rumours swept the country that the authorities had artifically engineered the situation to force up prices and make a profit. Indians and *Mestizos* – people of mixed Spanish and Indian blood — rampaged through the city, setting fire to government property and destroying 280 shops and stalls before the viceroy's troops finally restored order.

The viceroy has been unpopular ever since he banished the popular archbishop of Mexico from the country after the prelate excommunicated him.

Dutchman writes on the right to war

France, 1625

Hugo Grotius, who gained an international reputation with his treatise on the freedom of the seas, has published another remarkable work, *De Jure Belli ac Pacis* (On the Law of War and Peace). Here he attempts to define relations between the new nation-states of Europe.

He argues that each nation is a sovereign power, subject to no higher authority, but that there is a law of nature, which is derived from custom and experience. To oppose that law is to cast aside the bulwark of peace. Yet a nation that sees its vital interests threatened is right to go to war. Grotius wrote his work in exile in France, where he fled after escaping from prison in Holland. He had published a plea for toleration in religious matters but this displeased the stadholder, Prince Maurice of Nassau.

English king turns down plea for help

Germany, 1623

Bavarian troops led by the imperial commander, the count of Tilly, have completely destroyed the duke of Brunswick's forces at Stadtlohn. Over 15,000 of Brunswick's 21,000 men were killed; now, with Heidelberg and Mannheim firmly in Tilly's hands, the entire northern Palatinate is under the control of the house of Habsburg. News of the defeat has reached the elector Palatine, Frederick V, who has abandoned further military ambitions and asked his father-in-law, King James of England, to mediate.

Although he has offered mediation before, James has turned down the request. His mind is on other things – notably his ambition of a "Spanish match" for his son Prince Charles. The prince has made a secret journey to Madrid to demand a speedy end to negotiations.

King looks to France for Catholic in-laws

The French bride: Henrietta Maria.

The English groom: king Charles.

Paris, 11 May 1625
Charles, the new king of England, has found himself a bride; Henrietta Maria, aged 16, the daughter of Henry IV of France, was married today in Paris, with a French duke acting as proxy for Charles. The terms of the match, initiated by the late King James, include ships for France and the suspension of England's laws against Catholics.

Charles' sister, Elizabeth, made a good Protestant match with the ill-fated Elector Palatine Frederick. To enhance his image as a European peacemaker, King James wanted a suitable Catholic bride for Charles.

Ships traded to win the hand of princess

Paris, 1625
King James of England and Cardinal Richelieu have come to an arrangement under which the English are to lease to the French a warship and seven merchant vessels for use against the rebellious Protestant Huguenots of La Rochelle. The deal, part of the terms of the marriage of James's son, Charles, to the French princess, Henrietta Maria, is not popular in Protestant Britain. But James dislikes those who rebel against kings.

"The Cheat with the Ace of Diamonds", by the French painter Georges de la Tour (born 1593), a master of dramatic lighting effects.

Spanish take crucial city in Netherlands

The key to Breda is handed over to the Spanish forces, ending the long siege.

Netherlands, 2 July 1625
The strategically vital town of Breda surrendered today after nearly a year of siege, and the armies of Spain are poised to overrun the entire Netherlands. Every attempt by English mercenaries – fighting under the banner of the prince of Orange – to break the Spanish siege has been foiled.

So desperate is the plight of the Dutch that their agents have begged France for assistance. Cardinal Richelieu, the French chief minister, has offered a subsidy of a million *livres* on condition that Dutch ships join in a blockade of the Huguenot fortress of La Rochelle which he is besieging. The irony of their navy fighting the Protestant Huguenots is causing great resentment among the Calvinist population of the Netherlands.

Olivares, the chief minister of King Philip IV, is anxious to revert to Philip II's policy of establishing Spanish rule and Catholic supremacy in Europe. The invasion of the Netherlands has created considerable strategic problems for him, however. Spain has to pay heavily to move her troops across Europe from Italy, while her depleted navy has to be deployed in protecting treasure ships in the Atlantic and escorting troopships to Genoa. This has left North Sea and Baltic ports open for Dutch shipping.

Dutch seize Brazilian capital from Spain

Brazil, 10 May 1624
The Dutch have been in revolt against Spanish rule for almost 60 years; now they have taken their fight across the Atlantic and seized the port of Bahia, the capital of Brazil. The Dutch are striking at other American possessions of Philip IV, the King of Spain and Portugal, in an attempt inflict maximum damage on the king's lucrative trade with the colonies.

, Had it not been for the rich rewards of trade in the East and West Indies, the Dutch war of independence would have ended years ago. When William of Orange raised the banner of revolt against Spain, only 20 towns with a total population of 75,000 joined him.

In the desperate struggle for survival the Dutch seized any opportunity to trade for profit. They ignored the claims of Spain and Portugal and dealt directly with the colonies. This trade became so large that the king could not make peace, because of what he would lose, and the Dutch would not, because of what they had gained.

1626 (1626-1628)

London, 20 February 1626. John Dowland, the lutenist and composer, was buried today. His early career was overshadowed by his failure to obtain a position in the Queen's Musick in 1594, though he was appointed court lutenist to Christian IV of Denmark in 1598. He finally gained a position in the English court in October 1612.

London, 9 April 1626. The statesman and philosopher Francis Bacon dies of a cold caught while stuffing a fowl with snow to observe the effects of cold in the preservation of meat.

Germany, 27 August 1626. The Danes are crushed by troops of the Catholic League led by Tilly and the imperial army under Wallenstein. This marks the end of Danish intervention in the European wars which have raged since 1618.

North America, September 1626. Following negotiations, a Dutch group led by Peter Minuit agrees to pay the Canarsee Indians the value of 60 *guilders*, or $24, in beads and trinkets, for the 22-square-mile island of Manhattan at the mouth of the river explored by Henry Hudson. The Indians were apparently not interested in being paid in gold or silver.

North America, 15 November 1626. The Pilgrim Fathers, who have settled in New Plymouth, buy out their London investors for £1,800.

Naples, 1626. The Spanish painter Jose de Ribera paints the *Drunken Silenus*.

France, 1626. Spurred on by his mistress, the duchess of Chevreuse, Henry de Chalais plots against Cardinal Richelieu. He is executed. Richelieu orders the destruction of all fortified castles, brings the nobles to heel and proclaims an edict forbidding duels.

France, 1626. Food shortages throughout northern France, cause much unrest. Exportation of wheat is forbidden in attempt to improve the situation.

Virginia, 1626. George Sandys, acting as the colony's treasurer, translates Ovid's *Metamorphoses*, the first literary work undertaken in America.

Paris, 1626. Cardinal Richelieu orders the construction of the buildings of the Sorbonne (*University of Paris*).

France, 1626. The poet Theophile de Viau dies at the age of 36.

Rome, 1626. The basilica of St Peter's is consecrated.

Prague, 1626. Adrian de Vries, the Dutch sculptor who worked with bronze, dies and is buried in Prague. He was frequently employed by General Wallenstein, the duke of Friedland and Mecklenburg.

Canada, 25 April 1627. Control of New France passes to the Company of New France (The Hundred Associates); it gains a fur monopoly and land from Florida to the Arctic.

Paris, 22 June 1627. The nobleman Francois de Montmorency Bouteville is beheaded for deliberately flouting King Louis XIII's year-old law banning duels.

Newfoundland, 23 July 1627. Sir George Calvert arrives to develop his 1622 land grant.

France, 27 October 1627. Cardinal Richelieu, Louis XIII's chief minister, lays siege to the Protestant stronghold of La Rochelle.

England, November 1627. King Charles, referring to the tobacco trade, says Virginia is "wholly built on smoke".

Iceland, 1627. Reykjavik, the capital of the island, is attacked by pirates.

China, 1627. Unrest amongst both the military and the peasants bodes ill for the Ming dynasty.

Virginia, 1627. More than 1,500 children who were kidnapped from the streets of London arrived in Virginia this year. It was under King James in 1619 that the practice of exporting orphans began, and since then criminals have been cashing in on this plentiful labour force.

India, 1627. Jahangir, the great Moghul emperor, dies.

Angola, 1627. The queen of Mbundu, Nzinga, is victorious in the year-old war against the Portuguese. She makes her sister queen of the Ndongo, who were previously allies of Portugal.

West Indies, 1627. English settlers arrive on the island of Barbados.

Bohemia, 1627. The kingdom becomes an hereditary possession of the Habsburgs. The Czech nobility emigrate in droves.

London, 1627. Francis Bacon's *New Atlantis*, a philosophical novel concerning the organisation of a city governed by scholars, is published posthumously.

Morocco, 1627. The death of Sultan Zaydan marks the end of the Sadian dynasty.

Virginia, 1627. Despite opposition from the pope and King James, tobacco exports total 500,000 pounds, up from 18,000 in 1617.

Spain to leave the crossroads of Europe

Switzerland, 5 March 1626

The treaty of Monzon between France, Spain and the papacy has settled the long-running dispute over the Alpine valley which has erupted into the forefront of European politics. The treaty restores the *status quo* of 1617 in the area. Spanish forts are to be destroyed, and France is to have the use of the passes in and out of Valtellina which is to be restored to the leaders of three associations of landlords known as the *Grisons*.

The Alpine valley involved lies to the south-east of the Swiss cantons, it has a population of only about 80,000, but has become a crossroads of European politics. Habsburg troops in Italy need a route across the Alps to the Netherlands and Germany, while France wants an Alpine route directly into the Habsburg backyard in Italy.

Chieftain dies of wounds invading China

China, 30 September 1626

Nurhaci, the chieftain of the Manchus, has died in his capital of Shenyang of wounds he received in his failed assault on the strategic Chinese town on Ning-yuan.

Nurhaci welded together the Manchu tribes, the latest of the invaders from the north. He overran the province of Liao-dong, which had formed part of the Chinese cultural area for some 2,000 years, and then prepared to attack the Ming heartland. Much of Nurhaci's military success stemmed from his invention of a system by which his soldiers fought not as tribes but under different coloured banners. He later expanded this system into the civilian administration. Unlike previous invaders from the north, Nurhaci also established himself as ruler of a viable monarchy before attempting his assault on China. This means that his death will not help the disintegrating Ming empire. He is being succeeded by his son, Abahai, a gifted general.

Disgraced eunuch leader hangs himself

China, 1627

Wei Zhong-sian, the most notorious of the eunuchs who have achieved great power under the Ming emperors, has hanged himself to escape the wrath of the new emperor, Zhu Yu-jian. Wei, after a criminal adolescence, voluntarily submitted to emasculation and spent the next 30 years working his way into a position of power in the palace. He succeeded in achieving such dominance over the sickly young Emperor Zhu Yu-jiao that he virtually ran China. When Zhu Yu-jiao died and was succeeded by the 17-year-old Zhu Yu-jian, the new emperor was deluged with accusations about the eunuch's behaviour.

Wei was ordered to leave the capital to take up a minor post. On the way he learned that the emperor had ordered his interrogation. He hanged himself in the city of Fucheng – but he has not been allowed to escape retribution. His body has been dug up, dismembered and put on display.

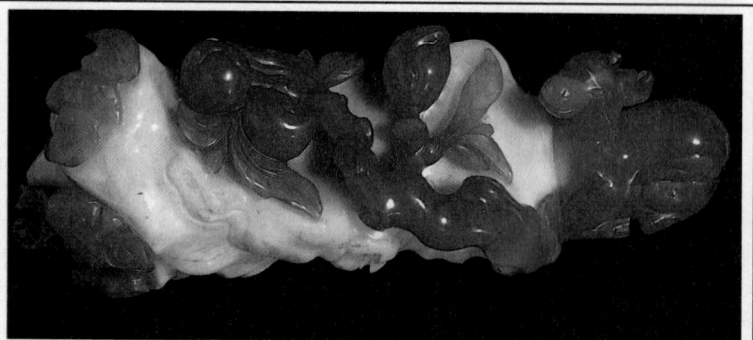

A carnelian and white quartz carving representing the female life force or "Yin" as dark red peaches, encircling its male counterpart or "Yang".

Moghul general bids to topple empress

Lion-hunting, one of the empress Nur Jahan's pastimes.

Agra, India, 1626

As Jahangir, the emperor of India, lies dying, and his wife, Nur Jahan (Light of the World), prepares to secure absolute power, she has tackled a coup mounted by the Moghul Mahabat Khan. His target was not the emperor, but Nur Jahan, who is as adept at killing rivals as she is at killing tigers.

Since 1611, when she married Jahangir, she has dominated the empire. She is the daughter of a Persian adventurer, once beautiful, now merely ambitious. As to her attitude to her husband, she "governs him and winds him up at her pleasure", according to the English ambassador Sir Thomas Roe. As Jahangir withdrew into the natural sciences, she ruled the empire through a triumvirate of herself, her father Itimad-uddaulah, and Jahangir's favourite son, Khurram.

After she had buried her father in a tomb more magnificent than Akbar's, she ran the empire single-handedly from the harem. Public business, reported Roe, "either sleeps or depends on her, who is more inaccessible than a goddess".

Recently she has been preparing for Jahangir's death. His oldest son, Khusrau, she assassinated. His favourite son, Khurram, she has provoked into rebellion. The next in line, the child princes Dara Shukoh and Aurangzeb, she has taken into her care. Mahabat Khan has been jockeying for position since Jahangir fell ill, so she was ready for this attempted coup.

Sexy theatre is sellout on and off stage

Kabuki is emerging from these rowdy popular song and dance performances.

Japan, 1628

Kabuki, a form of entertainment in which comic sketches are performed with dancing and singing, has become increasingly popular with the Japanese, taking the place of the traditional *No* drama which is considered too intellectual.

Okuni, a female attendant at the Shinto Izumo shrine, is generally given credit for developing *Kabuki* out of *No* in 1603 with a performance on the dry bed of the river Kamo-gawa in Kyoto. It was a great success largely because of its sensual dancing and erotic scenes.

It was given the name *Kabuki*, meaning unusual or shocking, and its performances became the scenes of uproar as spectators fought over the entertainers who were prostitutes as well as actresses.

The Tokugawa *shogunate* banned women from appearing in 1629 because it was feared they were corrupting the *samurai* warriors, but

A scene from a later Kabuki show.

their places were immediately taken by young men beautifully made up as women. The authorities remain unhappy about *Kabuki* because these young male entertainers are selling their sexual favours to their admirers, just like their female predecessors.

Austrians in revolt after mass hangings

Linz, Austria, 1627

Seventeen Austrian peasants have been led out of Frankenfeld castle and hanged. They have paid the Habsburg price for "heresy". The Austrian overlord did not like their rudeness to newly installed Italian Catholic priests in former Protestant churches.

The deaths have angered the Protestant population into revolt. Rebel peasants have put Linz under siege and are pleading for foreign aid. In the neighbouring Habsburg province of Bohemia, however, the Emperor Ferdinand II's avowed determination to "recatholicise" a reluctant Protestant population continues at a furious pace.

Calvinist ministers have been expelled; nobles face a choice between conversion and expulsion; and plans are afoot to proscribe Protestantism completely.

French troops keep Alpine route open

Mantua, Italy, October 1628

Spain has lost a bid to control a vital route through the Alps. A French task force has seen off Spanish troops in a military stand-off giving Charles of Gonzaga, the duke of Nevers, the decisive advantage in the struggle for control of Mantua and Montferrat.

The duke of Guastalla, who is backed by Spain's king Philip IV, is expected to leave his strongholds in Montferrat. France is surrounded by Habsburgs in Spain, the Netherlands and the Pyrenees. King Louis and his chief adviser Cardinal Richelieu count this victory as a step forward in their campaign to counteract their growing influence.

The Habsburgs have already established client states in Italy ruled by a member of their family, or failing that, a compliant aristocrat.

1628 (1628-1629)

North America, 7 April 1628. Jonas Michaelius arrives in New Amsterdam as the first Dutch Reformed minister in the colonies.

England, 23 August 1628. George Villiers, the Duke of Buckingham, is assassinated. He was the favourite of King James and then of Charles, and became one of the richest men in England through their favours. He also wielded enormous political influence which made him very unpopular.

North America, 8 September 1628. John Endecott, sailing for the New England Company, arrives with colonists in Salem, the capital of Massachusetts. He is to serve as governor of the colony.

Paris, 16 October 1628. The poet Francois de Malherbe dies. He was granted a pension by King Henry IV and wrote verses in many forms but with little originality.

France, 28 October 1628. After a fifteen-month siege the Huguenot town of La Rochelle surrenders to royal forces.

Virginia, October 1628. Lord Baltimore arrives in Virginia to form a colony. Being a Catholic, he refuses Anglican oaths.

West Indies, 1628. English settlers arrive on the island of Nevis.

France, 1628. A royal decree bars Protestants from settling in New France, sending Huguenots to English colonies.

North America, 1628. The New England Company is established, an English joint-stock venture to promote trade and colonisation in North America. The company is given a patent to land along the coast between the Merrimack and Charles rivers.

France, 1628. The first harbour with locks is built at Le Havre.

France, 1628. *Entretiens spirituels* by Francois de Sales is published posthumously. He was a highly respected bishop of Geneva.

New Hampshire, 1628. American settlers have found a new way of supplementing their meagre livelihoods: gun-running. Selling arms to natives is forbidden, but this has not stopped the new form of trade.

Madrid, 1628. The painter Rubens is sent by the Archduchess Isabel, on a diplomatic mission to Madrid, where he meets Velazquez.

Persia, 19 January 1629. Shah Abbas dies in Isfahan after a reign of 42 years. Of his five sons, two were murdered on their father's orders, two died of natural causes and the last was blinded on his father's orders. He is succeeded by his grandson, Shah Safi.

France, 28 June 1629. An edict of grace is signed, maintaining freedom of worship for Protestants, but depriving them of political privileges (right of assembly) and military privileges (places of safety). After the siege of La Rochelle (1627-1628), the war against the Protestants was carried into Languedoc. The towns were put down one after another.

Canada, 20 July 1629. The English adventurer Sir David Kirke has seized power in Quebec from the destitute French administration of Samuel de Champlain. Kirke had cut off supplies to the French colony, and by the time he reached Quebec the starving settlers were eager to surrender.

New Netherland, 10 September 1629. The Dutch West India Company is acting to colonise its holdings in the New World. A candidate who can round up 50 potential settlers and pay their passages, will be awarded a huge estate, given the title *patroon*, and enjoy privileges similar to those of a feudal baron. Settlers will live and work in conditions of near servitude, and the patroon will have jurisdiction over civil and criminal matters.

Mexico City, September 1629. The city is flooded, with up to six feet of water in some areas. One eye-witness, a Dominican friar, describes the scene as resembling a shipwreck rather than a city. Up to half the population has fled to higher ground outside the city or perished.

Germany, 1629. The Edict of Restitution, promulgated by the Emperor Ferdinand II, restores all ecclesiastical property to those who owned it in 1555. In this way the emperor hopes to recover all German lands lost to Protestantism during the previous 75 years.

North America, 1629. More and more Irish Catholic immigrants have been turning up as servants in the homes of settlers in Virginia, Maryland and Carolina. They are fleeing worsening persecution by the English in their homeland.

London, 1629. The Flemish painter Peter Paul Rubens is appointed envoy to King Charles, who knights him.

New Amsterdam, 1629. Jonas Bronk, a Danish immigrant, has bought 500 acres of land north of New Amsterdam from the Indians. He plans to lease land to farmers for three-year periods, to grow maize and tobacco. Locals are calling the Aquahungtives, Bronk's (*Bronx*) river.

London, 1629. A royal charter is granted to the Guild of Spectacle Makers.

King's ally Buckingham is assassinated

London, 1628
Charles has dissolved the third parliament of his reign, after a year of confrontations and evasions, and embarked on a high-risk strategy of trying to govern (and raise revenue) without parliament. At this crucial period he has lost the court favourite whose counsel has sustained him since his accession three years ago. George Villiers, the duke of Buckingham, was visiting the fleet at Portsmouth when a naval lieutenant who had been refused promotion rushed up and plunged a dagger into his chest. The killing caused rejoicing in the streets.

Charles stubbornly insists on the divine right of kings while practising deception and falsehood, so that he is wholly mistrusted by parliament. Short of money, he tried to pawn the crown jewels in Holland. When that failed he had to recall Parliament. But instead of voting funds for him, MPs raised constitutional questions and drew up a Petition of Right, forbidding taxation without consent of parlia-

Buckingham: focus for resentment.

ment, arbitrary imprisonment, martial law and compulsory billeting of troops in private homes. After much prevarication Charles accepted the petition and MPs grudgingly gave him money.

Dutch seize 80 tons of Spanish silver

Cuba, 10 September 1628
Spain's latest bullion cargo – 80 tons of silver and other treasures worth 12 million Dutch *guilders* – has been seized by a veteran seadog named Piet Heyn. Aged 51, Heyn commands a potent fleet formed to carry the Dutch-Spanish war across the Atlantic to colonies and shipping in the New World of the Americas.

Heyn picked up a straggler from a Spanish treasure fleet off Havana, which gave him the intelligence he sought about its movements. He then stalked the Spaniards who fled into a bay, and ran aground on a mud bank. The crews rowed ashore. Without a single shot or any casualty, Heyn moored nearby and crossed in his own cutter to take possession of his prize. He was also able to direct Spanish prisoners to the nearest plantation – ironically, where he had once been held prisoner. A former galley slave of Spain, Heyn treats captives with compassion. Madrid will be less kind to its defeated admiral.

Portugal puts down Mozambique revolt

Mozambique, 1629
After a bloody colonial war in which the Portuguese were nearly driven into the sea by the army of Nyambo Kapararidze, the king of Mozambique (Munhumutapa), the Portuguese have emerged victorious. The defeated Kapararidze has been replaced by a puppet ruler called Mavura, who has signed a treaty turning his kingdom into a Portuguese protectorate.

The war began in late 1628, when the new king, Kapararidze, resentful of Portuguese incursions into his territory, killed the Portuguese ambassador and sacked their trading posts at the instigation of Arab traders who feared competition would break up their monopoly. Four hundred Portuguese were killed before Kapararidze was defeated.

The Portuguese blame the Moslem traders for the conflict, unwilling to recognise the nationalism of the Mozambican populace. Anxious to give credibility to their own prejudices, their first order to the new king is to expel Arab traders.

Spain squanders wealth on a losing war

Harvey links heart with blood circulation

London, 1628

A small book of only 72 pages recording the results of experiments with animals by an English physician will undoubtedly become an instant medical classic. It is called *Exercitatio Anatomica de Motu Cordis et Sanguinis in Animalibus*, and its author is Dr William Harvey. In it he makes the bold assertion that the blood in our bodies is constantly on the move, driven by the heart, a natural pump.

For centuries the medical profession has believed the theory of Galen, that the function of the heart is that of a natural oven to keep the blood warm, and that blood was not driven in a circulatory system, like water through pipes, but subject to a kind of tidal ebb and flow. Harvey's treatise, though, demonstrates that the heart beats through muscular contraction, squeezing blood out of its interior into arteries through one-way valves. Then it returns the blood back to the heart through the veins. What comes back to the heart is indeed the same blood that left it earlier. It is recycled and not, as has been thought, freshly made.

Born in 1578 in Folkestone, the eldest of seven sons of the mayor of the Kentish town, William Harvey has had a distinguished career. After studies in Padua and the award of the fellowship of the College of Physicians, he has established himself as a brilliant teacher.

In Rubens' portrait of Philip IV, the New World holds out the king's helmet. The wealth of Spain's empire lines the pockets of mercenaries and arms dealers.

A later painting portrays Harvey demonstrating his theory to king Charles.

Spain, 1629

King Philip IV may well be the best horseman in Spain, but he is leaving policy to his closest adviser and favourite, Count Gaspar Olivares. Only four years ago Olivares was able to say "God is Spanish and fights for our nation these days" after a series of victories, including one over an English expeditionary force when it attempted an attack on Cadiz. Now he may not be feeling so optimistic.

The Spanish empire's foundations of sand are beginning to show, as the demoralising effect of a long-running and expensive war in the Netherlands begins to bite. The attempt to bring the Dutch Protestant rebels to heel goes back to the 1560s, with a short break between 1609 and 1621. It is now an almost intolerable strain on Spain's resources in manpower and money.

Spain depends on a steady flow of precious metal from the new world to pay its troops; its empire exists only to fund war. There was a big setback last year, when the Dutch captured an entire treasure fleet in the Caribbean. The proceeds enabled them to launch a major assault in the Netherlands. Meanwhile, Spanish troops mutinied because they not being paid, walking out of the forts as the Dutch took them over.

While Olivares' foreign policies and ostentatious patronage of the arts have helped propel the Spanish kingdom into penury, he has also proposed schemes to raise further income. Noting that Castile alone financed all Spain's wars and supported all her foreign dependencies, he tried to make Aragon, Portugal, Valencia and Catalonia bear their share of the military and financial burden by the "Union of Arms" in 1626. So far he has met outright defiance from the Catalans and limited co-operation from the rest.

Persian who drove out Ottomans dies

Kaswin, Persia, 1629

Shah Abbas, the outstanding ruler of the Safavid dynasty, has died. Having inherited a nation in thrall to the Ottomans, he leaves it 42 years later a powerfully centralised empire restored to the boundaries of Shah Ismail I, enjoying internal stability and a flourishing economy.

Born in Herat, where he survived the murderous intentions of his uncle, Ismail II, Abbas became shah in 1587 on the abdication of his father, Mohammed Khuda-banda. After a humiliating treaty with the Turks in 1590, he secured his borders against the Ozbegs. He eliminated potential opponents with extreme cruelty – he executed one son and blinded two others for plotting rebellion – or considerable skill, as with the diminishing of the power of Quizilbash tribesmen by forming new crack units of Caucasian slavewarriors. Victory at Sufiyan in 1605 was the greatest of his many triumphs over the Ottomans.

1629 (1629-1631)

Paris, 20 October 1629. The French theologian Cardinal Pierre de Berulle dies. He was the founder of the Congregation of the Oratory (1611), one of the new orders of the Counter-reformation movement.

France, 1629. Marillac, one of Richelieu's chief aides, draws up a series of internal reforms called the *Code Michaud*.

Netherlands, 1629. Albert Gerard is the first to use parentheses and other abbreviations in mathematics.

Australia, 1629. The Dutch sailor Francisco Pelsaert lands on north-western Australia after his ship, the *Batavia*, is wrecked on Morning Reef.

Mozambique, 1629. Munhumutapa state makes its fourth and most humiliating treaty yet with the Portuguese, having been defeated in battle.

Germany, 1629. 274 people convicted of witchcraft are executed in the prince-bishopric of Eichstatt.

Japan, 1629. Female entertainers are banned from appearing in *Kabuki* performances by the Tokugawa *shogunate*. Many of the performers are also prostitutes, and their erotic dancing leads to frequent fights in the audience.

Rome, 1629. The Italian architect Carlo Maderna dies.

Madrid, 1629. Velazquez paints *The Triumph of Bacchus*.

Angola, c.1629. The Portuguese plant the first American crops – maize and cassava – on the Angolan coast.

Massachusetts, 12 June 1630. The flagship of the Massachusetts Bay Company, the *Arbella*, docks in Salem, the first of 11 ships bearing 700 passengers, 60 horses and 40 cows. Led by John Winthrop, who immediately appoints himself governor of the new colony, they are devout Puritans who come to found a new colony and see America as their Promised Land.

Massachusetts, 7 September 1630. Governor John Winthrop and his assistants pass a resolution declaring that Trimontaine, on the Shawmut peninsula, "shall be called Boston". A resolution is passed that Boston will replace Salem as the colony's capital.

North America, 30 September 1630. John Billington is hanged for murder in New Plymouth – the first colonial execution.

Madrid, 5 November 1630. The treaty of Madrid formalises the peace of Susa between England and Spain.

Massachusetts, 9 November 1630. The first ferry route in the colonies opens, from Boston to Charlestown on the Charles River.

France, 10 November 1630. There is a trial of strength between the aggressive, warlike Cardinal Richelieu and Marillac, who is more concerned with domestic than foreign policy, and wishes above all else to keep the people happy by keeping taxes low. It appears at first that Louis XIII has capitulated to the Queen Mother and replaced Richelieu as his chief minister by Marillac. But later in the day the king announces that he will retain Richelieu. Marillac is arrested and Richelieu is left in political control, free to pursue his anti-Habsburg foreign policies.

Germany, 1630. Over the last two years some 124 people have been executed for witchcraft by the Teutonic Order at Mergentheim.

Naples, 1630. Travelling in Italy, Velazquez meets Jose de Ribera (known as the "little Spaniard"), the most prominent painter in the town, who has just finished the *Martyrdom of Saint Bartholomew*.

Geneva, 1630. Agrippa d'Aubigne, born in 1552, dies. He was a Huguenot soldier in the French wars and a poet and historian of note.

Germany, c.1630. In only eight years in the prince-bishopric of Wurzburg, Bishop Philipp Adolf von Ehrenberg has ordered the execution of some 900 people for witchcraft, including his own nephew, 19 priests and several young children.

Sweden, 1630. The king of Sweden, Gustavus Adolphus, invades Pomerania and Mecklenburg to counteract recent German military successes in Europe's long running wars.

Germany, 1630. The astronomer Christophe Scheiner, famous for his observations on sunspots, publishes *Rosa Ursina* in which he explains the apparent deformation of the sun when it sets and demonstrates that it turns on its axis.

Paris, 1630. The Luxembourg Palace, built by Salomon de Brosse for Marie de Medici and including a series of paintings of her life by Rubens, is completed after 15 years.

Denmark, 1630. Anders Christiensen Arrebo, the ex-bishop of Trondheim, who made his name with his translation of the Psalms in 1623, publishes the *Hexaemeron*, an epic work in Danish about the six days of creation.

Mozambique 1631. War breaks out again between Munhumutapa and the Portuguese.

A million feared dead in Italian plague

The survivors struggle to bury the plague dead outside the city walls.

Europe, c.1630

Bubonic plague has hit northern Italy with great ferocity, and the death-toll is rumoured to be approaching one million. Southern France is in the grip of a similar outbreak.

The latest affliction appears to have been brought into Milan by German troops invading Lombardy, perhaps also by French troops moving into Piedmont. The first victim in Milan was a German soldier. For the past three centuries Europe has been affected by plague every ten or 15 years, and doctors, of whom there are between one and ten per 10,000 inhabitants in most European cities, have found no remedy, apart from quarantine. Towns and cities are the worst hit, with poor people suffering the most. At the first hint of plague, the rich flee to the countryside.

Dutch to colonise Portuguese Brazil

Brazil, 1630

The Dutch have captured the sugar capital of Brazil, the port and islands of Recife, which are known as the Brazilian Venice. Though the Dutch were ousted from Bahia after only a year, they are set to get a firm grip on the Portuguese colony's north-eastern region, with its flourishing sugar plantations. Current production is running at some 10,000 tons a year. The Dutch are offering capital to Portuguese planters, and reorganising the slave trade with West Africa to ensure a regular labour supply. About 5,000 new slaves are needed each year.

The port is to be developed on the lines of Amsterdam, with canals and tall town houses. Architects, engineers and artists are coming from Holland. A policy of religious toleration has been introduced, allowing Calvinists, Catholics and Jews to practise their religions without interference.

Astronomer's laws are his monument

Prague, 1630

The German astronomer Johann Kepler, undoubtedly one of the most important scientists of recent years, has died at the age of 59. Kepler started studying theology, but switched to mathematics, teaching the subject at the university at Graz. In his work as assistant to the Danish astronomer Tycho Brahe, and later as astronomer to the emperor Rudolf II, he started to apply the principles of geometry to the movements of the planets, in particular Mars.

Kepler's three famous principles of planetary motion – the laws that govern the paths of planets around the sun – seem certain to ensure his place in astronomical history as they are already being referred to as Kepler's laws. He was an enthusiastic astronomer who spent many hours observing stars and comets, writing up in immense detail his results and theories.

Emperor sacks Wallenstein, the self-made warlord

Bohemia, 13 August 1630

In an extraordinary move, the emperor Frederick II has fired one of his most brilliant military commanders, Albrecht von Wallenstein, the duke of Friedland, and of Mecklenburg and self-styled "General of the Whole Imperial Fleet and Lord of the Ocean and Baltic Sea". The emperor was forced to sack him by pressure from German princes who fear both Wallenstein's power and the power that he created for the emperor.

Wallenstein, born into a minor noble family 47 years ago, is not merely a brilliant and mostly successful warlord; he is an enor-

A later engraving of Wallenstein.

mously wealthy magnate, the owner of the largest feudal network of land in Bohemia. His early financial success came about through marriage to a wealthy widow. Wallenstein used his wife's fortune and borrowed money to raise an army which he used to help to crush the Bohemian revolt against Habsburg rule headed by Elector Palatine Frederick V, the "winter king" of Bohemia 1619-20. In 1621 Wallenstein became governor of Bohemia and a warlord in his own right, making a fortune out of debasing the coinage and using the profits to buy 60 estates owned by executed and exiled Czech nobles. During the Danish war Wallenstein was made the imperial commander-in-chief, fighting campaigns in northern Germany and Austria.

Troops run amok as Magdeburg falls

Death's harvest: men hang from a tree like fruit in a scene of horror engraved by Jacques Callot in 1633.

Germany, 20 March 1631

The whole fury and savagery of war descended on the German town of Magdeburg today. Drunken soldiers of nine nations are reeling among the smouldering ruins, dragging captive women as they seek wine in charred cellars. Bodies are so numerous – estimated at 25,000 – that they are being thrown in wagonloads into the river Elbe. Only 5,000, mostly women, have survived.

Many believe that the people of Magdeburg brought disaster on themselves by refusing to help the Hessian commander, Dietrich von Falkenberg, to prepare his defence against the besieging army of the count of Tilly, the commander of the imperial forces. Even as Tilly began his final assault, they were pleading with the defenders to surrender.

The town fell to a two-pronged attack, and it was then that the

horror began. The conquering soldiers, largely Croats and Walloons, ran riot, murdering, raping and looting. A monk herded 500 women into the cathedral for safety. But there was worse to come. Gires – planned by von Falkenberg – spread across the town, fanned by a strong wind. Within minutes, Magdeburg was a roaring furnace burning soldiers and citizens to death without discrimination.

Holland: land of free expression and religious toleration

Holland, c.1630

"We refuse no honest persons ingress to come and have their residence in this city, provided that such persons behave themselves honestly and submit to all the laws." Thus ran a letter from the magistrates of Leyden, in Holland, to a group of English dissenters seeking refuge in their city, and there is no doubt that of all countries the Dutch republic is the most open and tolerant.

In a Europe torn by feuds and fighting, Holland embraces every variety of freedom. Refugees continue to pour into its cities, especially the capital, Amsterdam, in which 30 per cent of the 100,000 population are immigrants, notably those who have fled from the Catholic southern Netherlands.

Protestants of every country have set up their churches here, and political and intellectual refugees of every persuasion have found the freedom denied to them in their own countries. This influx brings

Enjoying Holland's freedom of ideas: child musicians, by Jan Molenaer.

many benefits. Holland can boast more newspapers than the rest of Europe put together; its universities, espcially that of Leyden, are centres of intellectual excellence; literature and painting are flourish-

ing. It is also Europe's trading centre, its wharves crammed with Baltic grain, English textiles, Indian silks and spices, German wine, Scandinavian timber and much more.

1631 (1631-1633)

France, 13 January 1631. Cardinal Richelieu, Louis XIII's chief minister, bent on an aggressive anti-Habsburg foreign policy, signs the treaty of Barwalde with the Lutheran Gustavus Adolphus of Sweden, who is about to plan to launch a military attack on the heartlands of Germany.

Paris, 30 May 1631. *La Gazette de France*, a weekly collection of news and the organ of royal power, is published for the first time by Theophraste Renaudot, under an exclusive royal privilege.

Amsterdam, June 1631. Spurred on by his recent successes, Rembrandt leaves Leyden for Amsterdam, a fashionable centre, where he intends to paint portraits.

Massachusetts, August 1631. The first American-built ship, the 30-ton sloop *Blessing of the Bay*, is launched in Boston harbour. Plentiful timber means that vessels can be built for half the price of those in England, and the colonists hope that this will be the beginning of a profitable new enterprise.

Germany, 17 September 1631. After the Protestant town of Madgeburg had been sacked by the troops of Tilly, the commander of the Catholic League, the elector of Saxony concludes an alliance with Gustavus Adolphus of Sweden, who crushes the Catholic troops at Breitenfeld.

Rome, 1631. Domenico Mazzochi's oratorio *Lamentations of Mary Magdalene* is performed for the first time.

France, 1631. The king's brother, Gaston d'Orleans, and his mother, Marie de Medici, rebel, refusing to be reconciled with the chief minister Cardinal Richelieu. The Queen Mother prefers to take refuge in the Low Countries thus beginning a war between mother and son.

France, 1631. The mathematician, Pierre Vernier invents the "scale" which bears his name and which facilitates the reading of graduations on a sextant. It is an improvement of a device invented by the Spaniard Pedro Nunez for the same purpose.

France, 1631. Pierre Gassendi makes the first observation of the passage of mercury across the sun's disc.

England, 1631. William Oughtred proposes the symbol x for multiplication.

England, 1631. *Love's Cruelty* by playwright James Shirley is first performed.

North America, 1631. Europeans found a settlement in Maryland.

Spain, 1631. The poet and scholar Francisco de Quevedo y Villegas publishes a highly successful expurgated version of his 1627 collection of moral satires, *Dreams*, which was condemned for ridiculing the Holy Scripture.

Amsterdam, 1631. The Czech educational reformer Jan Amos Comenius publishes *The Gates of Language Unlocked*, showing how language is best taught through real things and situations.

Antwerp, 1631. Rubens paints *The Artist with Helen Fourment in the garden*.

Toulouse, France, 30 October 1632. Henry of Montmorency, the governor of the Languedoc, is beheaded for having fomented a conspiracy with the queen mother, Marie de Medici, and Gaston d'Orleans, the king's brother.

New Netherlands, 6 December 1632. The whole colony of Swanadael has been wiped out because of a petty theft. In the autumn an Indian chief stole a Dutch coat of arms made of tin and made a pipe out of it. Settlers reported this to another tribe, who promptly presented them with the chief's head. His tribe took revenge by massacring all but one of the settlers.

Italy, 1632. Galileo publishes his *Dialogue on the the Two Chief World Systems*.

Japan, 1632. Following further executions at Nagasaki and Edo, a thorough search is launched for all remaining Christians in Japan.

Poland, 1632. The treaty of Altmark marks the annexation of the coast of Livonia by Sweden.

India, 1632. The Emperor Shahjahan orders the destruction of Hindu temples. In the Benares district alone, 76 are destroyed.

India, 1632. The Portuguese are forced out of Bengal.

India, 1632. More than a million people have died in a famine in the Dekhan, and some have only survived by cannibalism. The famine was caused by a drought in 1630-1 and excessive rains the following year. It is feared that a plague will follow.

Russia, 1632. One third of the Russian army is now constituted on western lines: troops are recruited locally and mercenaries engaged in the European Protestant countries are hired as officers.

India, 1632. The Emperor Shahjahan has begun the construction of the Taj Mahal in memory of his beloved wife, Mumtaz Mahal, who died last year bearing her fifteenth child.

Cathedral that took 120 years to finish

Bernini's baldacchino in St Peter's.

Rome, 1633
Over 120 years after Pope Julius laid the foundation stone of the new St Peter's, its interior is at last complete. The *baldacchino*, or canopy, marking the site of the supposed grave of St Peter has taken nine years to satisfy its designer, Gianlorenzo Bernini. It consists of four columns, twisted like barley sugar, but made of bronze, supporting an elaborate crown.

It stands at the crossing beneath the huge dome, originally designed by Bramante, but altered by Michelangelo and finished by Giacomo della Porta in 1590. The church was consecrated by Pope Urban VIII in 1626.

English poet nears his final stanza

London, 12 February 1631
A fervent congregation packed St Paul's Cathedral today to hear its dean, the courtly poet John Donne, preach his sermon "Death's Duel" – its subject was death and resurrection. Many felt that the dean's topic was all too personal: he is known to be ill, and it is feared that this could be his final address.

Although Donne's preaching has earned him the title "a second Augustine", it is for his poetry that he is best known. His first works, the *Satires and Elegies*, appeared in the 1590s. These were followed by the *Songs and Sonnets*, written after his marriage in 1601. The *Holy Sonnets*, inspired by the death of his wife, were written around 1610. The *Pseudo-Martyr*, attacking Catholic martyrs, was written in 1610, as was *Biathanatos*, a study of suicide.

John Donne, painted in c.1595.

Death toll mounts as Turk purges traitors

Istanbul, May 1632
The revolt of the Janissaries is over, and the young Sultan Murad IV is embarking on a ruthless purge of traitors. Rejeb Pasha, the Janissaries' choice as grand vizier, has been executed.

Anarchy among the military had been growing under the regency of Murad's mother, Sultana Valide, until there was a general revolt of Janissary garrisons last year. A few weeks ago a mutiny of the household troops brought terror to the Hippodrome for three days. To appease the bloodthirsty soldiers, Murad was obliged to sacrifice to the mob's vengeance his grand vizier, Hafiz Pasha, who was also his brother-in-law, the *mufti* and 15 other court officials.

But divisions grew among the Janissaries while Murad plotted his revenge. Having had the new grand vizier, Rejeb Pasha, strangled and beheaded by eunuchs, he persuaded *sipahis*, janissaries and judges to sign an oath of loyalty and co-operate in a purge on corruption and subversion. Murad is having all suspect traitors rounded up and executed.

Ethiopian leader turns against Rome

An Ethiopian Christ in judgement.

Gondar, Ethiopia, 1632

The dream of Susneyos, of modernising his empire in a generation, has failed. The emperor has abdicated and renounced his Catholicism. Susneyos came to the throne in 1607 with support from the descendants of Portuguese musketeers. Ethiopia, broken by Galla incursions and civil war, could not have been weaker. He proposed an alliance with Philip III of Spain to quash his enemies. In return for Spanish help, Susneyos made Catholicism the state religion.

With his brother, Si'la Christos, he swept tradition aside, imposing European methods of government and importing Jesuit missionaries. The Amhara majority rose up against forced conversion. Three rebellions failed to overthrow Susneyos and his European allies. A fourth has succeeded and forced Susneyos to abdicate. His son, Fasiladas, has become regent and has already promised to expel the Jesuits and restore coptic Christianity.

St George and the dragon.

Boston is capital of Puritan colony

Boston, Massachusetts, 1633

The rolling, wooded countryside of Massachusetts, a self-governing colony rings with the sound of axes to build chapels, homes and even some seagoing ships from an abundance of local timber. It is three years since the Suffolk landowner, John Winthrop, sailed here with the royal charter of government, followed by nearly 1,000 more English Puritans convinced that this rolling, fertile countryside must be the promised land of their Biblical dreams.

Soon after arriving in September, 1630 Winthrop and his assistants passed a resolution declaring that this particularly fine site on the Shawmut peninsula should be the place at which the settlers should build their seat of government. The frame of the governor's house has been moved here together with a church. The site is known by the local Indians as "living fountain" – after a local spring. Winthrop's council has renamed it "Boston" – after the Lincolnshire home town of two settlers, Lady Arabella and Isaac Johnson.

Winthrop's enthusiasm for the settlement is unbounded. "We shall be like a city upon a hill," he proclaimed. "The eyes of all people are on us."

Swedish king dies leading cavalry charge

The heavens open and the cherubs sigh for the late king Gustavus II Adolfus.

Germany, 6 November 1632

Sweden will mourn deeply the death today of the powerful leader who has turned this country from a feudal backwater into a major European power. King Gustavus II Adolphus was killed as he led a cavalry charge into victory in a battle against the forces of Albrecht von Wallenstein at Lutzen near Leipzig. He was only 37.

A huge man, blond and broad-shouldered, Gustavus displayed a remarkable charisma, particularly with the common people. He came to the throne at the age of 16, and it was at this time that he was bullied into signing a charter of accession which allowed only nobles to take high office. Working with his astute chancellor, Axel Oxenstierna, Gustavus was able to surmount this and proceeded to remodel his country in every department. Government was streamlined, its council sitting permanently as a cabinet, making decisions in his absence.

Gustavus was an outstanding statesman and a brilliant military commander. He ensured that his conscript army was paid regularly – a rarity in today's Europe, where most soldiers are expected to live off the land. He built up a large navy to challenge Denmark for the mastery of Baltic.

Artists' guild has admitted woman painter

Haarlem, 1633

A woman has been admitted to the painters' Guild of St Luke here, an extremely rare event. She is Judith Leyster, the daughter of a brewery owner, who showed great talent from an early age as a painter of domestic scenes, still life and portraits. She likes to paint people enjoying themselves, such as *The Serenade* depicting young lovers, *The Jolly Companions* in which a young woman pours wine for her young man who is playing the violin, or *The Jolly Toper*, a man laughing over his glass of wine.

Many of her subjects recall those of Franz Hals, whose pupil she was, and she is quite his equal. While her critics say she imitates him too closely, she has sued Hals for taking one of her apprentices for himself.

Judith Leyster's "Game of Cards": typical of her genre scenes, it shows ordinary people enjoying themselves, painted with warmth and affection.

Japan shuts out rest of the world

Japan, 1633

The persecution of Christians in Japan has been intensified with the issuing of an Exclusion Decree giving orders for the searching out of Christian converts, the arrest of missionaries working underground in Japan and the detention of others being smuggled into Japanese ports. This decree is believed to be aimed at Christianity not as a religion, but because it is the faith of potential invaders of Japan. The Tokugawa *shogunate* fears all foreign influences, and the decree not only attacks Christianity but cuts off Japan from the rest of the world. Nobody is allowed to leave, and all Japanese living abroad are to be put to death if they return.

1633 (1633-1635)

Virginia, 1 February 1633. The tobacco laws are codified, limiting production to reduce dependence on a single-crop economy.

Germany, 1633. During his ten year reign, Bishop Johann Georg II von Dornheim has had 600 people executed for witchcraft in the bishopric of Bamberg, including his own chancellor and one of the burgermeisters. Large numbers of those condemned were poor, elderly women, many of them widows.

Rome, 1633. Bernini finishes the *baldacchino* of St Peter's basilica.

Ontario, 1633. A white man is killed and eaten by the Huron Indians. It is not known whether he was cooked first.

France, 1633. Jacques Callot engraves *Les Miseres de la Guerre*, graphic scenes of suffering in the German wars.

France, 1633. Vincent de Paul and Louis de Marillac found the Order of the Daughters of Charity.

London, 1633. *'Tis pity she's a whore*, a tragedy by John Ford about incest between a brother and sister, is first performed.

India, 1633. The British establish a trading post in Bengal.

Russia, 1633. The Russians lay siege to the town of Smolensk, which is in Polish hands. They make little progress and the new Polish king, Wladyslaw, soon arrives to relieve the town. The king has also obtained the support of the Dnieper *Cossacks*, who have been disillusioned by Moscow's failure to come to their aid during a recent revolt.

Russia, February 1634. The leader of the Russian troops besieging the Polish town of Smolensk accepts an armistice from the Polish king, and the remaining 8,000 Russian men are permitted to retire.

Massachusetts, 4 March 1634. Samuel Cole opens the first tavern in Boston.

Germany, 5-6 September 1634. Imperial and Spanish troops under Archduke Ferdinand inflict a shattering defeat on the Swedes and other Protestant forces near the Bavarian town of Nordlingen. The victory ends Swedish influence in southern Germany.

France, 1634. *Sophonisbe* by Jean Mairet is performed. It is a tragedy which introduces the rule of the three "unities": of time, so that a play may not cover more time in the plot than it takes to perform; of place, so that it is confined to one place; and of action, so that nothing superfluous or irrelevant takes place.

North America, 1634. The French explorer Jean Nicolet crosses a great lake (*Lake Michigan*), wearing a Chinese robe, and enters what he thinks is the Orient. Instead he finds himself in the wilds of the north-west of the American continent, probably the first white man to set foot in the area.

Senegal, 1634. The French establish a settlement at St Louis.

France, 1634. Francois Mansart undertakes the rebuilding of the chateau at Blois, at the request of Gaston d'Orleans, the king's brother.

Spain, 1634. The painter Francisco de Zubaran is called to Madrid by Philip IV to assist in the decoration of the Buen Retiro, under the direction of Velazquez.

China, 1634. English traders establish a factory in Canton.

Japan, 1634. Deshima, a man-made island in Nagasaki harbour, is designated the only place in Japan where foreigners may live. The Dutch move there from Hirado.

North Sea, 1634. A tidal wave destroys Strand Island in the North Sea.

North America, 1634. Maryland is founded by Lord Baltimore.

Paris, 10 February 1635. King Louis XIII grants letters patent to a new French Academy, a group of educated men under Valentin Conrart, whose function, following Italian models, will be to give precise rules to the French language and to compile a dictionary.

France, 19 May 1635. Cardinal Richelieu intervenes in the great conflict in Europe by declaring war on the Habsburgs in Spain.

France, 1635. The French Company of American Islands is founded. The French occupy Guadeloupe.

Maryland, 1635. An Algonquin chief responds to the imposition of English law: "Since you are strangers here, you should rather conform to the customs of our country."

Spain, 1635. The playwright Lope de Vega dies. He is said to have written 1,500 plays, though no record survives of at least half of these. His popular plays were more notable for their entertainment value than their artistic merit.

England, 1635. Rubens finishes *The Apotheosis of James I* which adorns the ceiling of the great Banqueting House in Whitehall.

England, 1635. Anthony Van Dyck paints the *Equestrian Portrait of Charles I* and *Charles I hunting*.

Emperor has treacherous lord killed

Bohemia, 25 February 1634
An Irish captain, Walter Devereux, burst into the bedroom of Albrecht von Wallenstein in his fortress at Eger today and stabbed the famous warlord to death. The assassin was acting on orders from the Emperor Ferdinand II, who had learnt of Wallenstein's secret negotiations with the Swedes and other Protestant enemies.

Wallenstein was fired as imperial commander-in-chief in 1630 for behaving like an independent warlord, although he was recalled in 1632 to fight the Swedes. Latterly he had grown increasingly eccentric and megalomaniacal. He hated loud noises and would order the killing of every dog in any town in which he stopped. Servants –

Wallenstein is stabbed to death.

even officers – who talked loudly or shouted near him faced execution. Last month he demanded an oath from his colonels that they be loyal to him alone.

War engulfs Europe as France joins fray

Paris, 19 May 1635
After months of hesitation, Louis XIII finally declared war on Philip IV of Spain today – using the Spanish occupation of the fortress of Trier as his pretext. French intervention means that almost every country in Europe is involved in a complex war which shows no sign of abating even after 17 years.

The greatest fear of the French king's first minister, Cardinal Richelieu, is that the victory by the Emperor Ferdinand II over the Protestant princes of Germany at Nordlingen will lead to the revival of the late Emperor Charles V's dream of universal domination. This fear has involved France in considerable diplomatic activity for several years. In 1631 Richelieu came to the support of Sweden with a financial subsidy; he later succeeded in splitting the emperor's armies by forcing Spain to evacuate a critical transit point for its crack troops, the *tercios*.

The French have now occupied the whole of the duchy of Lorraine and established garrisons in Alsace. France has also signed treaties with Sweden and Holland.

Peacock throne brings misery to millions

Agra, 1635
Shah Jahan, who succeeded to the Moghul empire in 1627 after his father Jahangir's death, is accumulating the largest collection of jewels in the world. The cost in human misery and suffering is stupendous. Millions died in famines between 1630 and 1632 while Shah Jahan emptied his treasury to expand his collection.

His richest jewels are embedded in his "Peacock Throne", so large he can lie in it with ease. Its legs are of gold, and on the twelve pillars of its canopy are portrayed peacocks made of jewels, and trees bearing diamonds, emeralds and rubies on its branches.

Shahjahan sitting regally on the Peacock Throne.

Inquisition tries Galileo

Debate rages fiercely as Galileo's ideas are examined by the cardinals of the Inquisition. The defendant sits in the middle, underneath a huge cross.

Italy, 1633

Once more Galileo, the astronomer who has repeatedly voiced his opposition to the idea (favoured by the church) that the Earth is the centre of the universe, has fallen foul of the ecclesiastical authorities. This time he was called to Rome to stand trial for propounding his ideas in a book, published last year, called *Dialogue concerning the Two Chief World Systems*.

In this work Galileo criticised Aristotle's cosmology with its insistence on the notion that the universe has a central point – namely Earth. He also discussed at length the motion of stars, planets and falling bodies and commented on the periodic nature of sunspots, all of which are inconsistent with a stationary, pivotal Earth.

Sick and ageing, Galileo was forced by the pope to journey to Rome under "suspicion of heresy". After a protracted hearing on 21 June he was finally sentenced, having been found guilty by the Inquisition of teaching the banned Copernican doctrine. He was also ordered to recant, which he did in a carefully-worded formula renouncing his past errors. Although he should have been imprisoned, the pope has commuted his sentence to house arrest.

What has been on trial is not just the astronomical thoughts of one man, but a way of looking at the world that is bound to produce conflict. Galileo is a leading advocate

Observing the heavens: should you believe your eyes, or your priest?

of rational scientific thinking which is opposed to belief, superstition and supposition. For Galileo, numbers are supreme. "The Book of Nature", he contends, is written in mathematical characters. With that single sentence he shows himself to be a founding father of scientific experimental method.

The universe which he sees at the end of his telescope is vastly larger than had previously been conceived. This readiness to accept the value of observable phenomena is critical to the development of new ideas and theories, most of them very unpopular with the large conservative church authorities.

Founder urges French: "Settle Quebec"

Quebec, New France, 1635

Over 33 years after he first landed in Quebec, the French soldier-explorer Samuel de Champlain has returned to New France to continue work on the fulfilment of his dream of a flourishing France in the New World. This is de Champlain's first visit to Quebec since it was returned by the English three years ago, after they had forced de Champlain to surrender in 1629.

As the province's founder, one of de Champlain's earliest moves will be to strengthen the French presence by persuading more farmers to settle here. It was lack of settlers, he believes, that made Quebec vulnerable to the English, as French colonists prefer working with the Indians

Quebec's founder: de Champlain.

in the fur trade to working the land. Ironically, it was de Champlain's ability to co-operate successfully with the Indians that gave France a foothold in Quebec.

De Champlain's men, outnumbered by the Iroquois, wield their guns.

Statesman takes the helm of Sweden

Sweden, 1633

That Sweden's war effort has not collapsed since King Gustavus Adolphus' early death last year is largely due to one man: his brilliant chancellor Axel Oxenstierna, now effectively regent for the six-year-old Queen Christina.

Oxenstierna became chancellor – chief minister – in 1612. He negotiated peace with Sweden's Baltic neighbours, Denmark, Poland and Russia and, although he tried to prevent his king's entry into the current war, he supported him loyally in his campaigns. Under Gustavus and Oxenstierna Sweden's government and courts were modernised, its education, commerce and industry promoted and immigration encouraged.

A later portrait of Queen Christina.

1635 (1635-1636)

Prague, 30 May 1635. The Emperor Ferdinand II and John George, the elector of Saxony, sign a religious and political settlement known as the peace of Prague.

Armenia, July 1635. The Ottomans capture Yerevan from the Safavid Persians.

Canada, 25 December 1635. Samuel de Champlain, the explorer and founder of New France, dies in Quebec.

Japan, 1635. The *Sankin Kotai* system is introduced whereby all the *daimyo* (feudal lords) are compelled to live in Edo every alternate year, leaving their families there when they return to their provinces. This is to ensure continuing peace by preventing any individual family from building up excessive power.

Japan, 1635. The genre painter Kany Sanarku, the leader of the Kyoto Kano school of painting, dies. After a restless life, he took holy orders in Kyoto. He will be best remembered for his Chinese-style ink paintings.

Istanbul, 1635. The Druse *emir* Fakhr ed-Din and his three children are executed. He had tried to liberate Lebanon from Ottoman occupation.

Netherlands, 1635. The imperial soldier Ottavio Piccolomini, the duke of Amalfi, is sent to aid the Spaniards in the Netherlands to drive out the French. Piccolomini served in Wallenstein's army at Lutzen in 1632, then contributed to his commander's downfall and went on to distinguish himself in the imperial victory at Nordlingen.

England, 1635. In response to a book written by the Dutch philosopher Hugo Grotius in 1625, John Selden writes *Mare Clausum*, in which he claims domination of the seas for England.

China, 1635. A collection of scientific works entitled *Chongzhen Lishu*, jointly edited by Jesuit missionaries and Chinese scholars, is published.

North-central Africa, 1635. Abd el-Krim ben Jame seizes power from his father-in-law Dawud, the last Tunjur sultan in Wadai, and founds a Moslem sultanate in Chad.

Germany, 1635. The famous Jesuit theologian Friedrich von Spee dies. A courageous opponent of the procedure followed in witchcraft trials, he published in 1631 a critique of the subject entitled *Cautio Criminalis*. Von Spee was also a leading poet of his age. Inspired by the Spanish mysticism of John of the Cross, he wrote some fine church hymns and pastoral allegories.

Caribbean, 1635. The French explorers Olive and Duplessis land on Guadeloupe and claim the island for France.

North America, 1635. The charter of the Council for New England, founded in 1620, is returned to the English crown after repeated defiance of its authority by the New England settlers.

Arabia, 1636. The Ottoman Turks are driven out of Yemen by Zaydi *imams*, who establish an independent, theocratic state.

China, 1636. The Manchus, a new power in the north-east of China, adopt the Chinese dynastic name of Qing for their new state.

Netherlands, 1636. The university of Utrecht is founded.

Netherlands, 1636. Antoine van Dienem is appointed governor of the Dutch East Indies.

Ceylon, 1636. A treaty with the king of Kandy allows the Dutch to establish a presence in Ceylon (*Sri Lanka*).

Germany, 1636. After a visit to Venice, the German composer Heinrich Schutz composes his *Kleine geistliche Konzerte*.

Caribbean, 1636. The French take Martinique from the Spanish.

Japan, 1636. Tokugawa Iemitsu prohibits the construction of ocean-going vessels.

North America, 1636. The Puritan John Harvard founds the first American university, at Cambridge, Massachusetts.

North America, 1636. The Dutch are granted the first patents on Long Island.

Germany, 4 October 1636. The Swedes defeat the Saxons at the battle of Wittstock.

France, October 1636. Under the treaty of St Germain-en-Laye, Richelieu hires the services of the Protestant general Bernard of Saxe-Weimar, promising him the duchy of Alsace as a reward. Bernard led the Swedish army to victory at the battle of Lutzen in 1632, but was defeated by imperial forces two years later at Nordlingen.

Paris, December 1636. Pierre Corneille's tragedy *El Cid* is performed on stage for the first time, to great acclaim.

Paris, 1636. On the orders of Richelieu, the Cardinal palace is built and its garden laid out.

Paris, 1636. *Marianne* by Tristan l'Hermite is performed for the first time. A stirring portrayal of passion, its success matches that of *El Cid*.

Velazquez learns new techniques in Italy

Prince Balthasar Carlos on horseback, by Diego Velazquez, c.1635.

Madrid, 1635

A remarkable new picture, by Diego de Velazquez *The Surrender of Breda*, has been installed in the king's new palace of Buen Retiro. People are astonished by its sense of actuality, as if it had been painted on the spot. In fact, Velazquez relied on eye-witnesses.

Breda fell over ten years ago, and both the protagonists in the picture, the Spanish general Spinola and the defeated count of Nassau who is handing him the key to the town, are dead. Breda has since been re-captured by Dutch forces. After a visit to Italy, Velazquez changed to a less formal style of painting and began to employ warmer colouring. King Philip IV has delighted in Velazquez' work ever since he first sat for him when he was 18 and the painter 24.

Velazquez never wearies of using the king as his model. Their friendship is shown by the directness and honesty of the portraits. He has also begun to paint the king's son, Balthasar Carlos, who is only seven, on horseback.

Artist who served Chinese emperors dies

China, 1636

The great statesman and painter Dong Qichang has died aged 82 at his home in the city of Huating. An artist by training, he became renowned as perhaps China's greatest painter and calligrapher since Zhao Mengfu, who died in 1322.

But Dong also pursued a career in government, and in 1594 he became favourite tutor to the imperial heir Zhu Changle. But corrupt officials jealous of his position and integrity led him to retire twice; the second time a dispute over a concubine caused a riot and the burning of his home. At 76 he returned to the Ming court for the last time, retiring at 80 with the high office of president of the Board of Rites.

Arts blossom under authoritarian Charles

Three faces of Charles I, by Carlo Maratti (1625-1713) after van Dyck.

London, 1635

The art collection assembled by England's King Charles over the years is now said to be the finest in Europe. His agents have scoured the continent to bring him the works of Titian, Tintoretto, Raphael and a host of other painters. Poetry and music also enjoy the royal favour. Peter Paul Rubens, who is painting a picture of the king's father, James, ascending into heaven, says Charles is "the most art-loving prince in Europe".

The Rubens is one of three on the ceiling of the Banqueting Hall at Whitehall Palace. The other two portray James as the peacemaker and James linking the crowns of England and Scotland. After these,

Rubens will portray Charles as St George slaying the dragon.

While the king enjoys the role of connoisseur of the arts, however, the governance of England is in disarray as he tries to rule without parliament. He is becoming increasingly isolated from the people, making few public appearances, preferring to take part in masques in the Banqueting Hall.

Charles's favourite portrait is at Hampton Court. This 12-foot-high (3.7m) painting shows Charles on horseback, grasping a commander's baton, a long sword on the horse's flank. The king told van Dyck, the painter, that he wished to appear at least six feet tall. Charles is actually five feet four inches.

German war ends: Habsburgs are victors

Prague, 30 May 1635

The war that has devastated Germany came to an end today with the publication of a peace treaty signed by the two leading Protestant electors and Archduke Ferdinand, the emperor's son, who has assumed command of the imperial army. The House of Habsburg has emerged victorious, although the terms of the peace of Prague represent a marked scaling down of Ferdinand II's Catholic zeal.

Under the terms, the dukes of Saxony and Brandenburg retain the ecclesiastical lands which they held in 1627, but their armies will come under imperial command. Calvinists are specifically excluded from the treaty, however, and the

empire will continue to wage war on them. As other Lutheran states – Bavaria, Mainz, Cologne and Trier – hasten to add their signatures, the emperor can claim that all the major princes of the empire are united behind him.

It was the battle of Nordlingen, where a combined Austrian and Spanish force defeated the Swedish army, which brought about the ceasefire that led to the treaty.

The peace of Prague may have brought rejoicing to Germany, but other European powers – France and Holland in particular – will be less than joyful at the sight of a united Germany under their old adversary, Ferdinand and his armies.

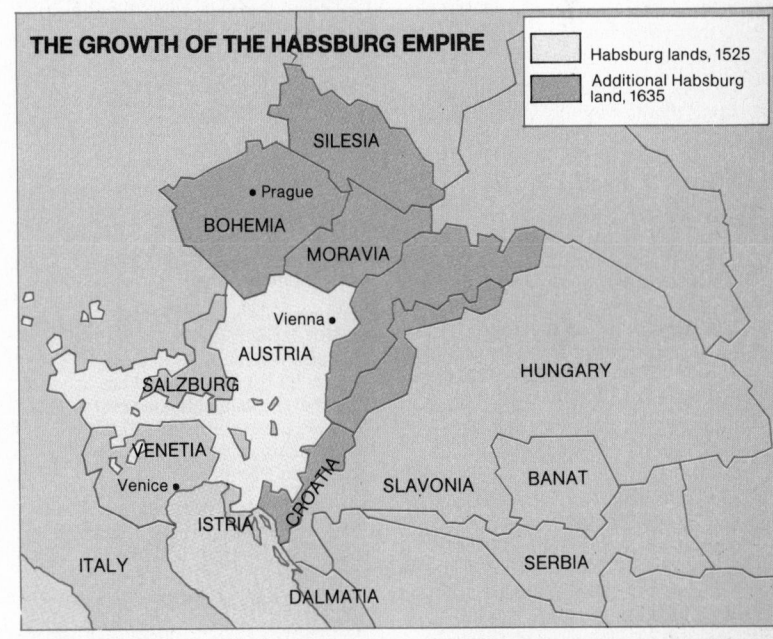

THE GROWTH OF THE HABSBURG EMPIRE

Habsburg lands, 1525
Additional Habsburg land, 1635

SILESIA
• Prague
BOHEMIA
MORAVIA
Vienna •
AUSTRIA
SALZBURG
HUNGARY
VENETIA
Venice •
CROATIA
SLAVONIA
BANAT
ISTRIA
ITALY
SERBIA
DALMATIA

Author who wrote a play a day is dead

De Vega (1562-1635): claimed he could write a play in a day.

Madrid, 1635

This year has seen the death of Spain's most prolific playwright, Lope de Vega, who claimed to have written 1,500 plays as well as six novels, several verse epics and hundreds of sonnets and ballads. His most famous play is *Fuente Ovejuna*, named after a village that rebelled against the Spanish king and queen under the leadership of a young woman.

Lope was notoriously unfaithful to his wife, and had five illegitimate children besides three

from his marriage. Despite this he was ordained as a priest and died a poor man, having given most of his large earnings to charity or the church. He claimed he could write a play in a day.

One of his hastily written pieces, *The Mayor of Zalamea*, was rewritten by Pedro Calderon de la Barca. In this play a peasant becomes mayor and defies the class conventions by ordering the execution of the nobleman who has raped his daughter – and is commended by the king for avenging her honour.

Calderon (born 1600): honour comes before class conventions.

1636 (1636-1637)

North America, 1636. Led by the Englishman Roger Williams, the first colonists settle on Rhode Island. A Puritan and champion of religious toleration, Williams, who emigrated to New England in 1630, suffered persecution and banishment for his beliefs. He escaped to the shores of Narragansett Bay and purchased land from the Indians which he has renamed Providence, to mark God's providence to him in his distress.

France, 1636. Following Richelieu's declaration of war on Spain last year, Spanish and Bavarian armies invade France, but are driven back.

Japan, 1636. Ornate buildings are constructed at Nikko to house the remains of Tokugama Ieyasu, the founder of the Tokugama *shogunate*, who died in 1616.

China, 1636. Dong Quichang, the painter and writer on aesthetics, dies. He introduced the distinction between the "northern" and "southern" schools in Chinese painting.

Canada, 1636. Jan de Brebeuf, a Jesuit missionary, observes Indians playing a game in which they propel a ball from a rawhide bag attached to a stick (*lacrosse*).

Germany, 15 February 1637. Ferdinand II, Holy Roman emperor since 1619 and staunch defender of Habsburg and Catholic interests during the great war in Europe, dies. He is succeeded by his son Ferdinand III, who became king of Hungary in 1626 and king of Bohemia in 1627.

North America, 5 June 1637. Supported by Indian allies, a Puritan force from the Connecticut river area attacks a Pequot village and slaughters 500 Pequot Indian men, women and children. The battle brings to an end several years of war between the settlers and the Pequot.

London, 23 July 1637. After a court battle, King Charles hands over the North American colony of Massachusetts to Sir Ferdinando Gorges, one of the founders of the Council of New England.

Scotland, 1637. Religious rebellion threatens, following attempts by King Charles and William Laud, the archbishop of Canterbury, to introduce the English prayerbook and Anglican church practices into Scotland.

France, 1637. An invading Spanish army in the south is repelled by French forces.

France, 1637. The peasant revolutionaries known as the *croquants* stage new uprisings in the regions of Perigord and Rouergue.

France, 1637. The philosopher Rene Descartes publishes his *Discours de la Methode*.

England, 1637. The parliamentarian John Hampden, a cousin of Oliver Cromwell, refuses to pay the assessment of "ship money" levied on his estate in Buckinghamshire. Ship money is a tax imposed by King Charles on maritime towns and shires to meet naval expenses. It was recently extended, however, to inland areas.

England, 1637. The dramatist Ben Jonson dies. He will be best remembered for his four theatrical masterpieces *Volpone*, *The Silent Woman*, *The Alchemist* and *Bartholomew Fair*.

England, 1637. The poet John Milton writes the pastoral elegy *Lycidas*. He is attacked for his outburst against the Laudian clergy.

Portugal, 1637. John, the duke of Braganza, is proclaimed king but, afraid of antagonising Spain, refuses to assume power.

Venice, 1637. The first public opera house, the Teatro San Cassiano, opens, sponsored by the Tron family.

Japan, 1637. Honami Koetsu, one of the most versatile artists of his day, dies. He was equally talented at painting, calligraphy, ceramics and gardening.

Germany, 1637. John Gerard, the English Jesuit missionary who became spiritual director of the English College in Rome, dies at Jena. After establishing several Catholic centres in England, he was imprisoned for three years and escaped to Europe in 1606.

West Africa, 1637. Thomas Lambert, the head of the Dieppe and Rouen Company, returns to the Senegal river. French slave traders become established in the country.

Vietnam, 1637. The Dutch arrive in Hanoi.

Korea, 1637. In response to outside threats, principally from the Manchus, the Korean Yi rulers decide to adopt a closed-border policy. From now on, any relationship with the outside world is punishable by death.

North America, 1637. The English offer a reward for every Indian killed – on production of the victim's scalp.

Brazil, 1637. The Dutchman Maurice of Nassau becomes governor of Brazil.

Netherlands, 1637. The tulip trade collapses after a boom last year which many observers feared had become excessive.

Herons and grass: a Japanese screen by the school of Towaraya Sotatsu.

Japanese calligrapher dies in exile

Japan, 1637
Honami Koetsu, the much admired calligraphist, has died at his village of craftsmen at Takagamine where he lived out his life in exile on the orders of the shogun, Ieyasu.

Koetsu, who came from a family of master swordsmiths, was himself trained in that warlike art before becoming fascinated by the tea ceremony and turning to the design of lacquer ware and ceramics. It was his calligraphy, however, which earned him most fame. Classical in style, his brushwork was soft, full, and sensuous, with a smooth, graceful line.

Some of his best work was done in cooperation with Towaraya Sotatsu, the brilliant designer of fans and screens. Sotatsu would paint a scroll and Koetsu would embellish his exquisite work with a beautifully written poem.

Secrets of Chinese industry revealed

China, 1637
Song Ying-xing, a civil servant from Fen-i district, has published *Tiangong kaiwu* (The Creations of Nature and Man), which explains the latest ideas in agricultural and industrial techniques. The author has taken advantage of the new climate of intellectual enquiry, and his work echoes the realism of contemporary artists, who are painting dogs and horses rather than mythical creatures. *Tiangong kaiwu* describes the growing of grain, manufacture of clothes, use of dyes, salt, sugar and oils, and metalworking techniques. Song Ying-xing writes also of ceramics, paper, ink, yeasts, pearls and gems.

The Gipsy Girl, a recent painting by the Flemish-born artist Frans Hals, who has become renowned for his fine, characterful portraits and rich, lively technique.

Descartes: it's the thought that counts

Paris, 1637

The French mathematician and philosopher Rene Descartes has published a major book, *Discours de la Methode*. It contains a phrase which encapsulates a radically new method of seeking after truth: "I think, therefore I am." Descartes is concerned to break with tradition in more ways than one. His book is written in clear, straightforward French, not Latin, the preferred language of philosophers until now.

Only the existence of the mind cannot be doubted, he argues. We have to begin here as a first principle, and in a framework of scepticism and logic build up to more complex truths. Reason, he argues, reigns supreme. The route to scientific truth is through testing, selecting and setting things in order; not simply accumulating knowledge, but systematising it. From his cornerstone of certainty, Descartes derives a number of basic philosophical ideas such as the existence of

An anonymous 17th-century French portrait of Rene Descartes.

God. No imperfect, finite human being, he argues, could have generated the idea of an infinite God. So God must have seeded the notion in us.

Poet who was witty – and fond of a drink

London, 9 August 1637

The funeral of Ben Jonson was held today in Westminster Abbey. King James appointed him to be the first Poet Laureate on a pension of £100, despite the offence the king took years ago at *Eastward Ho!*, which ridiculed his meanness.

Ben Jonson had great classical learning, ready wit and a tendency to drink too much Canary among his friends like Shakespeare, Beaumont and Fletcher. In the middle of a play like *Volpone*, castigating human folly, he was capable of such a lyric as "Drink to me only with thine Eyes". His tombstone bears the simple inscription: "O rare Ben Jonson".

"O rare Ben Jonson": great poet and observer of human foibles.

Spanish woman publishes horror stories

Spain, 1637

The novelist Maria de Zayas y Sofomayor has become the toast of Spain following the publication of her first collection of novels. The stories in *Novelas Amorosas y Exemplares* which have caught the public imagination are deliberately packed with horror and melodrama. All have happy endings and are built around the device of entertaining an elderly lady. The author, a noted scholar, is now working on an equally controversial sequel at her Saragossa home. This time, she says, the stories will have sad endings, but will continue to defend women against male claims of natural superiority and argue for a woman's right to be educated.

Invading allies only 50 miles from Paris

Paris, 8 August 1636

Wracked by internal strife – with peasants rebelling against high taxation – France has been invaded by the armies of Spain, Austria and Bavaria. Spanish troops, led by the count of Olivares, have crossed the border from Flanders and occupied the town of Corbie, 50 miles north of Paris, after an eight-day siege. The whole fate of France depends on the little village of St-Jean-de-Losne which is putting up stiff resistance to Olivares' army.

As advance units of the Bavarian cavalry arrive in the Parisian suburbs, Cardinal Richelieu – who is said to be on the point of a breakdown – is organising defences while King Louis XIII has ridden out at the head of his troops to meet the enemy at Senlis.

Tulip bulbs worth their weight in gold

A fool pays a vast sum for tulip bulbs in this satirical Dutch painting.

Netherlands, 1636

A new obsession has gripped the Dutch: tulipmania, the fanatical collecting and trading of the bulbs of a once-humble flower. In the frenzy of speculation that appears to have overtaken the entire country, single tulip bulbs can fetch 6,000 *florins* each. Critics, who fear the imminent collapse of this inflated market, call it *windhandel* – trading in the wind.

The tulip appeared in Europe around the mid 16th century, imported from Turkey by Ogier Ghislain, the Austrian ambassador. Since then the flower has become increasingly fashionable, although never on the current scale. Today's tulip is a prized commodity, its species classified in a strict hierarchy, its cultivators vying with each other to create ever more exotic varieties, and its buyers apparently undeterred by extravagant prices.

Today's frantic trading was triggered in 1634 when a market in tulip futures was opened to speculate on bulbs not yet reared. In a country devoted to trade, tulips represent the height of showy consumption and a chance to get rich quickly. In the rush to buy the rich pay in cash, the poor in kind; few seem immune from this lust to gamble on nature.

1637 (1637-1639)

Spain, 1637. A religious drama by the prolific Spanish dramatist Pedro Calderon de la Barca, *El Magico Prodigioso*, is performed.

England, 1637. The Puritan pamphleteer, William Prynne, imprisoned and mutilated for seditious writings in 1633, has what is left of his ears cut off in punishment for further publications which he has written while in prison.

Germany, 5 March 1638. France and Sweden sign a pact in Hamburg.

Scotland, March 1638. The Presbyterian opponents of King Charles' religious policy in Scotland sign a national covenant to preserve the purity of the gospel.

Netherlands, 6 May 1638. The theologian Cornelis Jansen, the archbishop of Ypres, dies. After a making a study of St Augustine he wrote *Augustinus*, challenging the doctrine of free will.

France, 14 May 1638. The *abbe* of St Cyran, a leading figure in the Counter-reformation in France, is imprisoned by Richelieu at Vincennes.

North America, 31 May 1638. Disillusioned by the autocratic rule of their leaders in Boston, a group of 100 Puritans, led by Thomas Hooker, a Congregationalist minister, establish a new settlement at Hartford, Connecticut.

Paris, 5 September 1638. Anne of Austria, the wife of King Louis XIII, gives birth to an heir to the throne after 23 years of marriage. He is given the name Louis.

Scotland, November 1638. A general assembly of the Scottish church abolishes the episcopate and defies King Charles' orders to disband.

Germany, 19 December 1638. Bernard of Saxe-Weimar, who has inflicted a defeated on the imperialist forces at Rheinfelden, takes Freiburg and the fortified town of Breisach.

Baghdad, 24 December 1638. The Ottomans under Murad IV recapture Baghdad from Safavid Persia.

Istanbul, 1638. Cyril Lucar, the patriarch of Istanbul, accused of inciting the *Cossacks* against Turkish rule, is put to death on the orders of Murad IV. Lucar's teaching is condemned by a church council at Istanbul because of his Calvinist sympathies.

West Africa, 1638. The French build a slave trading port at St Louis, on the mouth of the Senegal river.

Indian Ocean, 1638. The French take possession of the island of Reunion.

Japan, 1638. The fall of Hara castle brings to an end the Christian rebellion at Shimabara, which began last year. The Japanese are now armed with better guns than the armies of the west.

Japan, 1638. Christians are persecuted throughout Japan. The Japanese are banned from leaving Japan and the country is closed to foreigners. Only the Dutch and the Chinese are permitted to maintain trading posts under guard in a walled compound on the island of Deshima, in Nagasaki harbour.

Paris, 1638. Father Vincent de Paul sets up a charity for orphans, the latest in a series of charitable institutions which he has founded.

England, 1638. John Hampden, who last year refused to pay the "ship money" tax on his property, loses his case but wins a moral victory.

Italy, 1638. Nicolas Poussin paints *The Shepherds of Arcadia*.

North America, 1638. The Swedes and the Finns land in the Delaware estuary and lay the foundations of a colony (New Sweden), with a capital at Christiania.

North America, January 1639. The first printing press in America – at Cambridge, Massachusetts – issues its first volume. It is *Oath of a Free Man*, a broadside lambasting the vow of allegiance that colonists must swear to the English crown.

North America, 24 January 1639. Representatives from three Connecticut towns band together to write the Fundamental Orders, the first constitution in the New World. It establishes a general assembly, the office of governor and the right to tax. It guarantees the political rights of free men, but makes no mention of allegiance to the English crown.

North America, 3 March 1639. The college founded three years ago near the Charles river in Cambridge, Massachusetts, is named Harvard in honour of John Harvard, the Puritan minister who gave it half his fortune.

Near East, May 1639. The treaty of Qasr-i-Shirin establishes peace and a permanent frontier between the Ottoman empire and Safavid Persia. The Ottomans keep Baghdad, Shahrizur, Van and Kars, but renounce all claims to Azerbaijan.

France, 1639. The whole of Normandy is thrown into turmoil by a peasants' revolt.

New prayer book fuels unrest in Scotland

A 19th-century impression of a "Covenanters'" meeting in Edinburgh.

Edinburgh, 1638

The Scottish people have risen in fury over the attempt by King Charles to impose an English-style prayer book on them. Bishops fearing for their lives have fled to England and just one – the bishop of Brechin – read the new book in the kirk. He did so with loaded pistols pointed at his congregation.

Hundreds of thousands of people from all walks of life have subscribed to a "covenant with God" to resist to the death the attempt to destroy their Calvinist traditions. By imposing the prayer book the king hoped to bring Scottish forms of worship to in line with England's. But the people suspected a plot to restore the "popish Antichrist", especially as some detested rituals, including kneeling when taking communion, and oral confessions, have been reintroduced.

From the start of his reign the king has given offence to the Scots. He threatened the properties of the nobility by revoking all grants of crown lands made in the last 100 years. He ordered the Scottish Archbishop Spottiswood to wear an English surplice for his father's funeral. And Scottish visitors to his court are treated as uncultured roughs. The prayerbook provided the spark that has set off a firestorm of resentment at what Scots see as domination by London.

"Barefoot" peasants rebel in Normandy

France, 1639

A serious rebellion of the *nu pieds*, the barefoot peasants, has broken out in Normandy following the disastrous harvest which has brought hunger to this rich agricultural region. The peasants, enraged by the ever increasing demands of the taxes to pay for the war against Spain, have crushed tax collectors to death under carts with the cry of "Long live the king without the salt tax". Fearful that the urban poor will join the peasants, the authorities have closed many city gates.

Strong forces of the royal army have been ordered to the region, and the headsman's axe is already meting out exemplary punishments. But this seems to be a far more widespread and determined affair than the other peasant revolts which have plagued France for the past ten years, and will not be easily put down.

The peasants are demanding reductions in the new tax demands and amnesty for those taxes, they have been unable to pay because of the bad harvest. They are convinced that not their problems are the fault of the king, but stem solely from his administrators. They have a simple belief that once he is told of their trouble he will protect them against their oppressors. The king appears to have more weighty matters on his mind and is happy to leave the rebellion to his cunning chief minister, Cardinal Richelieu.

Calvinist tendency condemns patriarch

Istanbul, 27 June 1638

The Eastern Orthodox Church today lost one of its most outstanding theologians with the execution of Cyril Lucar, the patriarch of Istanbul. The 66-year-old patriarch was executed on the orders of Sultan Murad after he was accused of inciting the Cossacks to attack the Turkish government.

According to rumours sweeping Istanbul, the accusations were made by the patriarch's enemies, angered by his continuing support for the *Confessio Fidei* that reinterpreted traditional Eastern Orthodox faith in Calvinistic terms. During Lucar's 18 years as patriarch, Rome managed to have him removed from office three times, only to see him reinstated after intervention by Dutch and English envoys.

Lucar's affinity for the reformed churches and distaste for Rome date back to his attendance as a young man at the Synod of Brest-Litovsk in 1596. His pro-Calvinist teachings became famous after he presented his *Codex Alexandrinus* to Charles of England in 1628.

Turks win Baghdad after 15-year war

Baghdad, 1638

Baghdad, occupied for the past 15 years by the Persians, has been regained by the Turks, led personally by Sultan Murad IV. The capture follows a seven-month siege in which the defending Persians had vowed to fight until the last man.

The war between Persia and Turkey sprang from an internal struggle for power between the Ottoman rulers of Baghdad. The *pasha* and the army both claimed power and when, in 1621, a Janissary officer took over, displacing the pasha, he attempted to gain support from Persia to bolster up his position.

The Persians duly moved in, but when the Ottomans agreed to accept him, the Janissary rejected Persia, only to be assassinated, leaving Baghdad in Persian hands.

It has taken five campaigns – dogged by incompetence, bad weather and other commitments – to restore Baghdad to Turkey. Now the city is back in Turkish hands, although Yerevan, which fell to Persia in 1636, is to remain a Persian possession.

Italian-style piazza completed in London

Covent Garden: the piazza and market, painted by John Collet (1725-80).

London, 1638

Inigo Jones, the Surveyor to the Crown, has completed a *piazza* at Covent Garden, just north of the Strand. London's first example of town planning, it is laid out as "an estate for gentlemen" on behalf of its landlord, the earl of Bedford. It is a large square formed by uniform houses built over arcaded *loggias*, in the Italian manner. St Paul's church, like a classical temple of the Tuscan order, stands at one end of the piazza, where a fruit and vegetable market has been opened.

This is the latest of many innovations that Jones has carried out in the capital. The chief of these was the rebuilding of the king's Banqueting House in Whitehall on the Italian model of Andrea Palladio, inspired by Vitruvius' Roman treatise which Jones brought back from Italy. The scale is grandiose and the ceiling panels were commissioned by King Charles from Rubens, who sent them over from Antwerp in 1635. They depict the reign of his father, James, in Olympian style. In the same year Inigo Jones completed a house for the queen, Henrietta Maria, at Greenwich (east of London on the river Thames) in the style of a Palladian villa. Earlier he had built for her the Queen's Chapel in St James' Palace.

He has plans to rebuild Whitehall palace entirely, on as big a scale as Somerset House which he is building for the queen. He began as a stage designer, and his court masques introduced a proscenium arch, a revolving stage, flying scenery and costly costumes of cloth of silver and gold.

British open trading post in eastern India

Madras, August 1639

An English trading post has been established at Madraspattam on the east coast of India. Francis Day, the English merchant who acquired the land from the local ruler, is building warehouses, factories and a fort. The west coast of India has already opened up to English trade following the signing of the Anglo-Portugese treaty of Goa in 1635. With the opening of the east coast the London-registered East India Company will be in a position to expand its trade all over India.

Gujarati bedspread (detail), c.1600.

American settlers massacre whole Indian village in night raid

Connecticut, 5 June 1637

A force of New England settlers, drawn from Massachussetts and Connecticut and backed by their Indian allies, has destroyed a hostile Indian village in bloody revenge for years of raids and murders. Some 500 Pequot men, women and children have been slaughtered.

Such a confrontation was always inevitable as nearby Dutch and English settlements grew stronger and threatened the once-powerful Pequots.

While the tribe was able to defend its lucrative trade in shells and beads from Indian rivals, it proved too weak to drive away the settlers.

A number of murders of whites by the Pequot tribe have escalated the conflict over the past three years.

The most recent came last month when the Indians killed nine people. Last night's show of strength provided a bloody climax. It is unlikely that the Pequots will threaten the colonists again.

One of Jones' costume designs, for a torchbearer in a masque.

1639 (1639-1641)

France, 21 May 1639. The Italian utopian philosopher Tommaso Campanella dies in the Dominican monastery of St Honore, near Paris. Among his works is an imitation of Plato's *Republic* entitled *Civitas Solis*. Accused of heresy, Campanella was kept imprisoned in a Neapolitan dungeon for 27 years.

England, June 1639. The treaty of Berwick ends the short-lived Bishops' War between England and Scotland. Last year, Scottish nobility and clergy signed a covenant to defend the *kirk* against the imposition of a new prayerbook from London.

France, 18 July 1639. On the death of Bernard of Saxe-Weimar, his army and conquered territories are taken over by France.

Siberia, 1639. After crossing Siberia, a small group of Russians reaches the shores of the Pacific. In recent years the Russians have acquired vast territories in northern Asia. Attracted by easy profit, trappers and traders have moved eastwards, overwhelmed the natives and established Russian rule by building strategically located forts.

France, 1639. The mathematician Gerard Desargues publishes a book entitled *Brouillon Project*, which lays the foundations for analytical geometry.

France, 1639. The mathematician and physicist Blaise Pascal invents a calculating machine.

Spain, 1639. The painter Francisco de Zurbaran is asked to decorate the sacristy of the Hieronymite monastery of Guadeloupe. He is at present at work on a monumental altarpiece for the Carthusians monastery of Jerez de la Frontera.

Danzig, 1639. Martin Opitz von Boberfeld, who during his life was regarded as the greatest German poet, dies. The head of the Silesian school of poetry, he wrote a *Book of German Poetry*, in which he established rules for the "purity" of language, style, verse and rhyme.

Caribbean, 1639. Sugar cane is introduced into Martinique.

Angola, 1639. The Dutch seize the Kongo kingdom from the Portuguese.

Istanbul, February 1640. Ibrahim succeeds Murad IV, sultan of the Ottomans since 1623.

England, 13 April 1640. In order to raise supplies to resume the war against the Scots, King Charles convenes Parliament for the first time since 1629.

England, 4 May 1640. The "Short Parliament" is dissolved after refusing the king money.

Antwerp, 30 May 1640. The great Flemish painter Peter Paul Rubens dies. The dominant figure of contemporary art in northern Europe, Rubens produced over 1,200 works, characterised by dynamic energy, vigorous composition and brilliant colouring.

France, September 1640. *Augustinus*, the great work of Dutch theologian Cornelis Jansen, who died two years ago, is published by his friends.

England, October 1640. After several humiliating defeats of the English by the Scots, the treaty of Ripon ends the second Bishops' War. The Scots keep possession of Northumberland and Durham and are to be paid £ 850 a day until a new English parliament can work out final peace terms.

England, 3 November 1640. Fulfilling his obligations under the treaty of Ripon, King Charles again summons Parliament.

Japan, 1640. In a further step in the persecution of Christians, a board of enquiry called the Examination of Sects is established in Yedo.

Paris, 1640. *Cinna* and *Horace*, two plays by Pierre Corneille, author of *El Cid*, are staged for the first time.

Germany, 1640. Frederick William succeeds his father, George William, elector of Brandenburg since 1619.

India, 1640. The Moghul prince Dara Shikoh, the eldest son of Shahjahan, has the *Upanishads* translated into Persian. Dara Shikoh is deeply imbued with Sufi mysticism and consorts with Hindu philosophers and Christian fathers. His attitude to Islam offends his younger brothers, notably the devout Sunni Aurangzeb.

Rumania, 1640. Peter Moliva, a Moldavian scholar and the metropolitan of Kiev, founds the Basilian Academy, which is modelled on the academy at Kiev. Latin, Greek and the Slav languages are to be taught here, as well as rhetoric, philosophy and poetics.

Finland, 1640. The first Finnish university is founded at Turku by Per Brahe. Lectures are delivered in Finnish. This marks the emergence of an awareness of national identity.

Portugal, 1640. Richelieu supports a revolution which frees the Portuguese from Spanish domination. John IV (the Fortunate) is declared king and founds the Braganza dynasty.

Spain, 1641. An attempted rebellion takes place in Andalucia.

Mass beheadings are shogun's "lesson"

A 17th-century Japanese screen of a Portuguese carrack off Nagasaki.

Japan, 1640

The Japanese have beheaded 61 Portuguese in a ceremonial mass execution at Nagasaki. The Portuguese had arrived as a delegation from their base at Macao in order to plead for the lifting of the ban on trading with Japan.

However, they misjudged the temper of the *Bakufu* Curtain government which is convinced that the Portuguese were responsible for the uprising of the Christian peasantry at Shimabara two years ago. The *shogun* Iemitsu determined to teach the Portuguese a lesson they would not forget and ordered their execution. Thirteen seamen were spared and sent back to Macao to deliver the message.

Spain loses Portugal as Catalans rise up

Barcelona, 6 June 1641

Catalonia is in revolt against Madrid, and in Barcelona the mob have taken over and murdered the viceroy, Santa Coloma. The trouble has been coming on for some 20 years and poses a real problem for the Spanish leadership.

The blame lies in the failure of the count of Olivares to leave the Catalans alone. The principality has been pressed constantly to provide more men and money for the war against the encroaching French, and hatred of Madrid has steadily mounted. The viceroy was unequal to the task of keeping order and was caught and struck down trying to escape from the mob. In Spanish-dominated Portugal, the duke of Braganza has taken advantage of Olivares' preoccupation with the Catalans to enter Lisbon, declare himself King John IV and be crowned in Lisbon Cathedral.

Braganza's rule has been recognised by the Dutch, who have promised to send assistance, and by the French, whose fleet is anchored in the river Tagus. Olivares' only hope is a counter-revolution by an alliance of nobles and Jewish converts to christianity who have been refused any concessions by the Portuguese king for fear of offending the pope. The plot has been discovered, however, and most conspirators arrested.

Dutch rule sea-traders

A Dutch merchant family and a servant: painted cotton from near Madras.

Amsterdam, 1639

New and inexpensive cargo ships, navigational skills and aggressive exploitation of new markets have enabled the Dutch to expand their shipping trade to unprecedented heights world-wide and Amsterdam to become Europe's marine insurance capital.

The long-drawn-out war between the independent Dutch republic and Hapsburg Spain over the Spanish Netherlands has proved only a minor inconvenience. Both sides favour trading with the enemy. The Dutch levy port charges on ships sailing to Spanish territories and use the money to build warships. The Spanish need the grain and naval stores brought by the

Dutch from northern Europe. The Dutch have expanded their trading voyages far beyond European coastal waters to the Far East and the Americas. Dutch traders have appeared on the Hudson River, New York, and more trading posts have been established on the Wild Coast at the mouth of the Amazon. The Dutch dominate trade between Brazil and Europe.

Despite their wide-ranging operations the Dutch seem reluctant to establish colonies. Respectable Dutch women, it is said, will not emigrate to tropical countries, and Pieter Both, the governor-general of the East Indies, has advised Dutchmen in those parts to marry "heathen" women.

Japan bans westerners from its mainland

Dejima, Japan, 1641

Japan has now banned all westerners from its mainland in a bid to cut itself off from foreign influences which the shogunate blames for recent uprisings.

The only foreigners allowed to trade with Japan are the Dutch whose mainland trading post at Hirado has just been demolished.

Instead the Dutch have been given sole use of Dejima, the 130-acre man-made island in Nagasaki Harbour, originally built for the Portuguese before their expulsion two years ago. The only Japanese allowed on Dejima are male interpreters and courtesans. The Dutch are allowed entry to Japan only on ceremonial occasions.

Parliament plans to stand up to the king

London, 1640

For the second time this year Charles has been forced to call a parliament – and this time MPs are determined not to allow the king to ride rough-shod over them. When the first parliament for 11 years was called last April, Charles tactlessly told the Commons that they would be granted "all their just favours" provided that they voted to give him the money he needed.

The remark was greeted with a buzz of disapproval from MPs, who see their privileges as no more than constitutional rights. Charles did not get his money, and curtly dis-

solved parliament. But after appealing in vain to the kings of Spain and France, the pope and the City of London, he has been forced to meet MPs once again.

This time they have declared that parliament cannot be dissolved or prorogued without its own consent, and that parliament should meet at least once every three years. Other decisions include one to abolish the hated Star Chamber, which Charles used to punish his critics. It is a measure of the king's sorry plight that he has accepted decisions by MPs which, in effect, say that much of what he has done over the past 11 years has been illegal.

The Orthodox true Minifter,   the Seducer and falfe Prophet.

Pictures from a tract called "A Glasse for the Times", satirising the growing religious and political discontent in England under King Charles.

Expelled Puritans found new colony

Boston, Massachusetts, 1639

A decade after the Massachusetts charter was signed, the Promised Land has expelled its first dissidents. They believe that the Holy Spirit is within each individual, uninfluenced by church ministers. Some even claim that, now they are saved, they are without sin. The ruling Puritans assert that a real Christian must prove himself by religious observance. The breakaway party, led by Anne Hutchinson and others, has bought a large island (some call it "Rhode" island) to start a colony where no-one, except perhaps Catholics, will be unwelcome. It is not the first such

quarrel. Last year a Congregationalist minister, Thomas Hooker, went to Connecticut with 100 settlers including some influential merchants. Nearby in what they call "New Haven" are more ex-Bostonians, led away by the Reverend John Davenport from the alleged sinfulness of the New World's first Puritan settlement.

Yet another haven is Maryland, a settlement on the Potomac for Roman Catholics. The first patent was granted to Lord Baltimore (George Calvert) by King Charles. About 250 people, including two Jesuits, sailed from Cowes six years ago. Now there are 2,000.

1641 (1641-1642)

London, 12 May 1641. Impeached for high treason by the Long Parliament (summoned by the king after his defeat in the second Bishops' War), the earl of Strafford, King Charles' chief adviser, is executed.

France, June 1641. France and Portugal form an alliance against Spain.

Portugal, August 1641. Portugal signs a treaty of friendship and commerce with Sweden.

Ireland, October 1641. In protest against despotic treatment and Protestant immigration into Ulster, the Gaelic Irish rebel, slaughtering thousands of English settlers.

London, November 1641. John Pym and other leading Parliamentarians draw up a Grand Remonstrance for King Charles, detailing their position in the struggle against the king's authoritarian rule.

London, 9 December 1641. The great Flemish painter Sir Anthony van Dyck dies.

Massachusetts, December 1641. A woman and a man with "AD" clearly marked on their clothes, have been publically whipped for adultery. This is a relatively lenient punishment – the 1632 law making adultery punishable by death has only recently been abolished.

Naples, 1641. The painter Domenico Zampieri, commonly known as Domenichino, dies in Naples. Born in 1581, he was an assistant of Caracci at the Farnese palace in Rome, where he painted *Woman with a Unicorn.* His masterpiece, *The Last Communion of St Jerome,* hangs in the Vatican palace.

London, 1641. William Laud, the archbishop of Canterbury, is committed to the Tower of London after being impeached for treason by the Long Parliament.

London, 1641. The Star Chamber and the High Commission Court, pillars of the king's autocratic rule, are abolished by the Long Parliament.

Rumania, 1641. Prince Vasile Lupu sets up a printing press in the church of the Three Hierarchs at Jassy, the building of which was completed two years ago. From here the first book printed in Moldavia is issued.

Netherlands, 1641. Cardinal Don Ferdinand, *infante* and governor of the Dutch Netherlands, dies at the age of 32.

Italy, 1641. Claudio Monteverdi composes the opera *Il Ritorno d'Ulisse in Patria* (The Return of Ulysses to his Native Land).

Massachusetts, 1641. The general court of the Massachusetts Bay Colony establishes the *Body of Liberties,* a code of 100 laws.

Japan, 1641. The Japanese order Dutch traders to move from Hirado to the islet of Deshima in Nagasaki harbour, where they are virtually imprisoned and suffer many inconveniences and indignities.

Italy, 1641. Giacomo Torelli revolutionises theatrical tradition by introducing visible scene changes.

Russia, 1641. The Russians capture Azov.

Rome, 8 January 1642. The astronomer and philosopher Galilei Galileo dies. His contribution to science has been immense, including support for the Copernican theory of the universe, an explanation of the composition of the Milky Way, the discovery of Jupiter's satellites, observation of sunspots which enabled him to propose a theory of the sun's rotation and, just before he lost his sight, the discovery of the monthly and annual librations (apparent oscillations) of the moon.

New Netherland, 25 February 1642. Dutch settlers slaughter lower Hudson Valley Indians, who are seeking refuge from Mohawk attacks.

France, 12 September 1642. The marquis of Cinq Mars is beheaded for plotting to assassinate Cardinal Richelieu, the king's chief minister, and for making an illicit treaty with Spain.

France, 4 December 1642. On the death of Richelieu, Cardinal Jules Mazarin becomes chief minister.

Australasia, 1642. A Dutch navigator, Abel Tasman, discovers a large land mass (*New Zealand*) and a small island, Van Diemen's Land (*Tasmania*).

Massachusetts, 1642. An Englishman, Joseph Jencks, arrives in Lynn to set up iron and brass works.

Rome, 1642. Pope Urban VIII bans tobacco as a product of the devil which causes hallucinations and wayward behaviour, upsets relations between men and women and in the end destroys the fabric of society.

West Africa, 1642. The Dutch capture the Portuguese fort of Axim on the Gold Coast.

Rome, 1642. Monteverdi's opera *L'Incoronazione di Poppea* (The Coronation of Poppea) set in ancient Rome is instantly popular.

Few mourners for Cardinal Richelieu

Triple-headed portrait of Cardinal Richelieu by Philippe de Champaigne.

Paris, 4 December 1642
Cardinal Armand du Plessis, the great but unloved duke of Richelieu, died today. He was 57. It is said of him that he converted the absolutist theory of the French monarchy into reality. Although frail in health, he displayed an iron will in carrying out his autocratic policies on behalf of Louis XIII.

Born into a minor aristocratic family, he was destined for the army but gave up his military career to enter the church. Inheriting the family bishopric of Lucon, he prepared himself for politics by working to convert the Huguenots of La Rochelle before moving to Paris. There he began his devious but always logical acquisition of power. He cultivated the queen regent and her Italian favourite, Concini, and almost suffered the same fate as Concini when the young king had him murdered.

He worked his way back into royal favour by acting as mediator between the king and rebellious factions of nobles. Made a member of the Council of State in 1624, he rapidly unseated the chief minister and assumed the position of power which he enjoyed until today.

In his memoirs he said that he promised the king that he would "exalt his name among foreign nations". This he has done, but few are weeping for him today.

Inquisition tries leader of breakaway plot

Mexico, 1642
A minor Spanish nobleman, Don Guillen de Lampart, is being tried by the terrifying methods of the Inquisition. His alleged crime is a plot to declare New Spain an independent kingdom ruled by himself. This is the second time a plot of this sort has emerged from Mexico. An earlier author, some 76 years ago, was Martin Cortez, a member of the explorer's family.

De Lampart, who had suffered under harsh Spanish rule, came to Mexico only two years ago with plans to abolish taxes and slavery, restore the power of religious orders and protect the privileges of ruling colonial families.

Plans of Mexico, Mexico City, and Cuzco City, Peru, taken from Carl Nebel's "Voyage Pittoresque".

Irish rebels kill 10,000 British

Ireland, 1642

Irish rebels have massacred some 10,000 colonists in Ulster and driven the English from the province. With relations between king and parliament in England seemingly heading towards civil war, the Irish have seized their opportunity and a rebel parliament, known as the Catholic Confederacy, has met in Kilkenny.

The rebels have affirmed their loyalty to Charles, preferring him to the militantly Protestant parliament in London. Their demands include freedom of conscience, government by Catholic officials, and restitution of property seized on religious grounds. But the rebels are not united. Most are Anglo-Irish Catholics seeking to protect their religion, while the Old Irish are more interested in recovering confiscated property and preserving the rapidly vanishing Gaelic language and traditions.

Irish soldiers serving with the Spanish have returned home, with France providing arms and money to try to weaken England.

Portugal loses key port to the Dutch

Malacca, South-East Asia, 1641

For six years the Dutch have been blockading the Straits of Malacca, harrying Portuguese shipping, and now at last they have captured Malacca itself, the stronghold that dominates the straits. From the Persian Gulf to Japan the Dutch are picking off Portuguese coastal settlements in their bid to gain control of the lucrative trade in cloves, nutmegs, cinnamon and pepper.

In this struggle, the Dutch have the advantage of a stronger economic base at home to pay for better ships and better trained manpower. Portugal and the Netherlands have roughly equal populations (about 1,500,000), but the Portuguese have for the past 20 years been under Spanish domination and made to serve in the Spanish forces. Dutch commanders are trained professionals, whereas the Portuguese rely on aristocratic and generally incompetent *hidalgos*.

An era ends as Flemish masters die

Marchese Spinola, by van Dyck.

Endymion Porter by van Dyck.

"Samson and Delilah" painted by the Flemish master Peter Paul Rubens.

The Duque de Lerma by Rubens.

Rubens' "Descent from the Cross".

London, 9 December 1641

With the death of Sir Anthony van Dyck, following so soon upon the death of his master, Sir Peter Paul Rubens, in Antwerp last year, an era of supreme Flemish painting has ended. King Charles, who was their patron, knighted them both.

Van Dyck had been his court painter for nine years, painting over 30 portraits of Charles and his queen and especially beautiful studies of their children, full of spirituality along with elegance.

His house at Blackfriars, which the king used to visit by water for sittings, was kept in great style with his own musicians and fools. He was always richly dressed and fascinated women. His fiery English mistress, Margaret Lemon, in a jealous rage once tried to bite off his thumb to prevent his painting. Last year he married a lady-in-waiting.

Rubens lived in even grander style as a diplomat, fluent in six languages, travelling Europe. He was sent to Spain by Isabella, the regent of the Spanish Netherlands, and to England by Philip IV of Spain to negotiate a peace treaty with Charles. Charles, whom he called "the greatest connoisseur in Europe", bought much of his work, as did Philip and Marie de Medici, the queen mother of France, for her palace of the Luxembourg. His vast output of canvases, crowded with nymphs, satyrs and *putti* exhibiting the plumpest of flesh, was the product of a factory of assistants, who painted them from his sketches while he did the finishing touches. His energy was prodigious. "I have never feared to undertake any design however vast," he said. At 53 he gave up court life, retired to his chateau with a wife of 16 and painted landscapes.

1642 (1642-1643)

London, January 1642. King Charles tries to arrest five members of parliament, including John Pym, for treason, but fails.

Nottingham, England, 22 August 1642. The king's declaration of war on Parliament sets off a civil war between royalists (Cavaliers) and Puritans (Roundheads).

England, 1642. Under the command of Oliver Cromwell, six East Anglian counties raise a joint anti-royalist force – the nucleus from which a national parliamentary army could be formed.

Madrid, 14 January 1643. Philip IV dismisses his minister the count of Olivares, who is succeeded by his nephew Don Luis de Haro.

France, 14 May 1643. Louis XIII dies at St Germain. His will provides for a regency council consisting of his widow Anne, his brother Gaston of Orleans, the prince of Conde and Cardinal Jules Mazarin, who will govern during the minority of the four-year-old King Louis XIV.

Paris, 18 May 1643. Queen Anne, the widow of Louis XIII, is granted sole and absolute power as regent by the Paris parliament, overriding the late king's will.

Paris, June 1643. Jean Baptiste Poquelin (Moliere) gives up his law studies and founds the Illustre Theatre with Madelaine Bejart, her brothers Joseph and Louis, Tiberio Fiorelli, known as Scaramouche, and eight other actors.

England, 13 July 1643. The Roundheads (parliamentarians), led by Sir William Waller, are defeated by royalist troops under Lord Wilmot, in the battle of Roundway Down. The vanquished army loses all its ammunition and its cannons.

New Netherland, September 1643. The religious leader Anne Hutchinson is killed with her family in an Indian attack. She and her husband were expelled from the Massachusetts Bay colony by Governor John Winthrop because of their religious beliefs.

England, 25 September 1643. The English Solemn League and Covenant, a national oath to increase the pace of religious reform, guarantees Scottish support of the parliamentary cause in England. The Scots see it as a way to impose Presbyterianism in England and Ireland and to preserve the constitutional liberties won by the Scottish and English Parliaments.

New Haven, November 1643. The General Court, with local deputies, adopts the Frame of Government, with a legal system based on Mosaic law.

Venice, 29 November 1643. The revolutionary composer Claudio Monteverdi dies. He alarmed contemporary critics with his use of unprepared dissonances in madrigals, and went on to develop the new art of opera composition, writing his first, *Ariana*, in 1607. In 1632 Monteverdi became a priest and continued to compose.

Rome, 1643. The Italian composer Girolami Frescobaldi, the organist of St Peter's, dies. He travelled a great deal in the Low Countries and wrote mainly madrigals and pieces for the organ.

France, 1643. Serious rebellions break out in Rouergue, Auvergne and Dauphine. The export of wheat from Brittany and Normandy is banned because of famine in these regions.

England, 1643. Prince Rupert, a leading royalist commander and nephew of the king, captures Bristol. Rupert is the son of Frederick V, the elector Palatine, and Elizabeth of Bohemia (the sister of King Charles). He grew up in exile in the Netherlands and then became a soldier of fortune, enlisting in the royalist cause last year.

Ireland, 1643. James Butler, the duke of Ormonde, who has been put in charge of quelling the Irish rebellion, negotiates a truce.

Amsterdam, 1643. The painter Carel Fabritius leaves Rembrandt's workshop, where he has been a pupil since 1641. His master's influence is evident in Fabritius' recently completed *Raising of Lazarus*.

Amsterdam, 1643. Rembrandt paints a *Self-Portrait* which includes his wife Saskia, who died last year.

North America, 1643. The Puritan colonies of Plymouth, Massachusetts, Connecticut and Newhaven unite to form the dominion of New England.

North America, 1643. On the orders of General Kieft, the Dutch massacre the Algonquin Indians.

Chile, 1643. The city of Santiago is utterly destroyed by an earthquake.

Siberia, 1643. Russian pioneers reach the Amur river.

South Pacific, 1643. The Dutch navigator Tasman discovers the archipelago of Tonga and reaches Fiji and New Guinea.

England, 1643. The fiery Puritan John Milton publishes a pamphlet on *The Doctrine and Discipline of Divorce*. It is a passionate defence of divorce and follows the refusal of his wife, Mary Powell, the daughter of a royalist, to return to him after a visit to her family.

French score first victory for 100 years

The decisive battle of Rocroi, painted by Sauveur Le Conte.

France, 19 May 1643

The duke of Enghien crushed the Spanish army of the Netherlands at Rocroi today, driving its cavalry from the battlefield and slaughtering the *tercios*, the much-feared Spanish infantry.

The impulsive 23-year-old duke, first given the command by Richelieu, his uncle by marriage, played a daring game, leading his horsemen in an attack across the field to cut his way through the centre and drive Don Francisco de Melo's horsemen into the marshes. The tercios, as brave and skilful as ever, alone held their ground. They died where they stood. The importance of this battle cannot be over-estimated. It is France's first victory for many years, it has wiped out the cream of the Spanish army and, in Enghien, it has given France a brilliant new commander.

Attack on Jesuits alarms French court

France, 1643

A fierce debate on sacramental practices has opened in the Catholic church with the publication of a defence of the work of the Dutch theologian, Cornelis Jansen.

Written by Antoine Arnaud, it is called *On Frequent Communion* and argues for a return to greater personal holiness. It attacks the Jesuits for their casuistry and has attracted violent opposition from the Society of Jesus. The book is also causing disquiet at court because the rigorous morality of Jansenism reaches outside pure religious debate and extends uncomfortably into public life.

Pope Urban VIII: opposes Arnaud.

Tests show air is not so light after all

Italy, 1643

One of Galileo's pupils, Evangelista Toricelli, wanted to see what happened when a vaccuum was formed above mercury. He filled a long glass tube with mercury and sealed one end with his finger. When he removed his finger, the mercury fell slightly, leaving a column around 30 inches high.

Toricelli concluded that air pressing on the bowl was keeping the mercury up to a height which could be measured.

Civil war clouds loom over England

Strafford's trial and execution.

The royalist William Barnston.

THE
SOULDIERS
CATECHISME:

Compofed for the Parliaments
Armie.

Queſtion.
Hat Profeſſion are you of ?
Anſwer. I am a Chriſtian and
a fouldier.
Q. Is it lawfull for Chriſtians
to be fouldiers ?
A. Yea doubtleſſe : we have
Arguments enough to warrant it.
1. God calls himſelf a man of war, and Lord
of Hoſts.
2. Abraham had a Regiment of 318. Trained
men.
3. David was imployed in fighting the Lords
battels.
4. The Holy Ghoſt makes honourable mention of Davids Worthies.
A 2   5. God

A revolutionary catechism.

Tibet defies China with golden palace

Lhasa, Tibet, 1643
Perched on a mountain on the roof of the world stands the Palace of Potala, just completed by the fifth Dalai Lama. The Potala, its red mass and golden roofs sharply contrasting with the whiteness of the nearby buildings, is more than the Dalai Lama's winter palace. It is Tibet's largest monastery. Its lines speak a new Tibetan confidence, arrogantly and defiantly standing out on the mountaintop, contemptuous of Moghul and Chinese presumptions of control.

England, January 1642
The sands are fast running out for Charles. The king's long-running quarrel with parliament is pulling the country into a civil war that was unthinkable only a few months ago. Embroiled in military operations against Irish rebels, and with Scots enraged by an attempt to impose an English-style prayerbook on them, the king needs money badly. Parliament refuses to give him it until he has redressed their grievances.

Now he has tried to take action against the men he sees as ringleaders. He issued articles of impeachment against five members of

the Commons, including John Hampden, a rich landlord who refused to pay a tax he considered unjust, and John Pym, a squire from Somerset. The peers refused to arrest them. When Charles sent a serjeant-at-arms to make the arrests, the Commons procrastinated, saying they would consider the matter. Next day the king turned up with several hundred armed men. But the parliamentarians had taken refuge in the City of London. "The birds have flown," Charles said.

This "Long Parliament" assembled in November 1640 and has been in contention with the king ever

since, in an increasingly bitter atmosphere. Last May, the parliament found the earl of Strafford, Charles' chief adviser, guilty of treason. Later it issued a Grand Remonstrance setting out a long list of grievances, intending to curb the king's powers and increase those of the Commons.

Parliament has now passed a Bill to raise a militia and when necessary impose martial law. They have also voted to remove the bishops from the House of Lords. But there are signs that the Commons are wearying. Last autumn attendances began to dwindle and some votes have shown a fine balance of opinion. However, the king's abrasive style is alienating supporters.

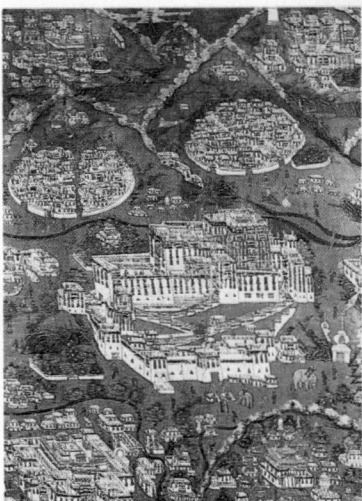

The Dalai Lama's palace at Lhasa.

Philip IV dismisses his right hand man

Madrid, 14 January 1643
The count of Olivares, Spain's dynamic chief minister for more than 20 years, has been dismissed – the victim of intrigues by a handful of disgruntled grandees. The count was the opposite number of the late Cardinal Richelieu, and for years the two men watched each other's every move on Europe's diplomatic chessboard.

Olivares' hectic routine has killed off four of his secretaries during his years in power as the favourite of Philip IV. His mistake was to commit Spain to foreign ventures – such as the bid to reconquer Holland – which were far beyond its powers. Moves to extend Madrid's power over Catalonia and Portugal also led to revolts.

Tibetan Buddhism's Mahakala, defender of the faith and fierce assailant of every unbeliever: a painted figure composed of clay, flour, paste and human bones.

Massacres in Brazil

Pernamboco, Brazil, 1643
Portuguese settlers, with the support of the Tupi Indians, have revolted against their Dutch masters. In a series of appalling massacres, the Indians on both sides are suffering much the worst casualties.

The revolt, led by the adventurer Joao Fernandes Vieira, was triggered by settlers' anger at the taxes of the West India Company, and the imposition of Calvinism.

Rebels trapped a Dutch detachment in a fort, released the commander, but killed 200 Indians. The cannibalistic Tapuia Indians, led by the Dutchman Jacob Rabe, have responded with wholesale butchery.

Oliver Cromwell, Puritan leader.

1643 (1643-1648)

Netherlands, 1643. The Dutch artist Adriaan van Ostade, known for his farmyard and low-life scenes, paints the *Slaughtered Pig*.

England, 1643. The Cavaliers (royalists) publish a newsheet, *Mercurius Aulicus*, in Oxford once a week. The Roundheads (parliamentarians) respond with the *Mercurius Britanicus*, published in London.

London, 24 March 1644. Roger Williams, pressed by the New England Confederation, gains a charter for Rhode Island.

England, 2 July 1644. Cromwell crushes the royalists at the battle of Marston Moor, near York, leaving some 4,000 dead, and taking 1,500 prisoners.

Rome, 15 September 1644. Pope Urban VIII dies. He condemned the *Augustinus* of Cornelis Jansen in 1640, and commissioned Bernini to work on the baldachin of St Peter's in 1633.

England, November 1644. The Puritan poet John Milton publishes a pamphlet on the freedom of the press entitled *Areopagetica*.

Germany, 1644. French forces under Turenne defeat the imperial army at Freiburg and capture Mainz and Worms.

Netherlands, 1644. The Flemish surgeon Jan Baptist van Helmont, who discovered carbon dioxide gas, dies. He also identified the role of the gastric juices in digestion.

Rhode Island, 1644. Roger Williams writes *The Bloudy Tenent of Persecution for Cause of Conscience* arguing for religious toleration; the book is burnt publicly in London.

Australia, 1644. The Dutch navigator Tasman compiles a map of the north and west coasts of Australia.

Angola, 1644. Dutch slave traders allied to Queen Nzinga of Angola take Luanda from the Portuguese.

Zimbabwe, 1644. The victors in the Torwa civil war move from Khami to a new hill capital at Danongome.

London, January 1645. William Laud, the archbishop of Canterbury, is executed. He sought to enforce an Anglican liturgy very close to Catholicism, provoking the rebellion of Puritans and Presbyterians.

New Netherlands, 9 August 1645. Settlers gain peace with Indians after the intervention of the Mohawks.

Austria, 1645. Formulated by Gyorgy Rakoczi, the peace of Linz guarantees the religious freedom of the Hungarians.

Paris, 1645. Pierre Gassendi is appointed a professor of the College of France. His doctrine of sensualism and materialism is opposed to influence of Descartes.

Rome, 1645. Athanasius Kircher, the German scientist who is working on deciphering the Coptic language and Egyptian hieroglyphics, invents a magic lantern.

Boston, 1645. The slave trade has become a profitable American industry, with ships regularly leaving Boston harbour for raids along the West African coast.

China, 1645. The German Jesuit Johann Schall becomes director of the institute of mathematics and astronomy in Beijing, contributing to the introduction of Catholicism.

South-East Africa, 1645. For the first time, the Portuguese take slaves from the Mozambique coast to Brazil.

England, June 1646. Oxford falls to the parliamentarians.

Massachusetts, 28 October 1646. John Eliot, a pastor, starts preaching to the Algonquin Indians in their own tongue.

Virginia, October 1646. Chief Necotowance agrees to acknowledge that Indian lands are held by courtesy of the British crown, ending a two-and-a-half year war.

New Netherland, December 1646. The Dutch West India Company's experiment in colonisation, the *patroon* system, fails. Settlers were offered huge areas of land and feudal rights over 50 people if they paid their passages. But it appears that the Dutch are not keen to sell themselves into servitude in a far-flung, uncivilised land.

Virginia, 1646. The colony's first law for the education of the poor is passed, providing for the apprenticeship of poor children.

Massachusetts, 26 May 1647. A new law bans Catholic priests from the colony; the penalty is banishment, or death for a second offence.

Central Asia, 1647. The Moghuls who last year captured the provinces of Balkh and Badakshan in northern Afghanistan from the Ozbegs, are forced to withdraw when their officers prove unwilling to serve in this harsh region and the Ozbegs receive Persian aid.

England, 1647. Convinced that he has been summoned by the Holy Spirit, a shoemaker named George Fox begins preaching. His followers reject the church.

Hungary, 1648. Rakowsky of Transylvania signs a peace treaty with the Habsburgs.

Cromwell routs king's army at Naseby

Royalist troops at Chester in 1646: a stained glass window of 1660.

Naseby, England, 14 June 1645
Charles' royalist forces suffered a crushing defeat today at the hands of the parliamentary army on the outskirts of the village of Naseby, Northamptonshire. The decisive factor was the iron discipline of the cavalry led by Oliver Cromwell.

At the outset the royalists showed their superiority and routed a squadron of parliamentary cavalry. They then made the mistake of setting off in pursuit. Cromwell seized his opportunity and proceeded to overwhelm the rest of the king's army. His Ironsides did not scatter in pursuit of fleeing troops, but remained on the battlefield to grind down the enemy. For practical purposes the war has ended in victory for the parliamentarians.

When, in 1642, Charles set out to achieve by force of arms what he had failed to do by intrigue and bluster, he had the loyalty of rural England. But parliament was backed by the towns, the City of London and, crucially, the navy, which closed the ports to the king and denied him supplies.

Tasman explores the South Seas

South Seas, 1644
Abel Janszoon Tasman, a captain of the Dutch East India Company, has returned from another voyage of exploration in the South Seas. He may not have discovered the fabulous Southern Continent, on which the Company hoped to find treasures equal to those of the new world, but his extensive explorations, notably the circumnavigation of the Southland, have revealed many new territories. Tasman first sighted the Southland on his earlier voyage of 1642-43, naming it Van Diemen's Land, and five days sailing to the east discovered another great island, which he called the Staten Landt.

Czar Alexis brings serfdom to Russia

Russia, 1648
A new and highly repressive civil code is being enacted in Russia. Following the worsening social unrest of the last few years Czar Alexis is preparing to come down hard on those who challenge his authority.

The code will establish the rights of merchants and the prerogatives of landowners. Nobles will be able to bequeath their property and peasants will be legally attached to the land which they cultivate.

Serfs will thus lose virtually all rights and will be no more than items of property, completely subject to the absolute rule of the landowner.

Emperor takes own life

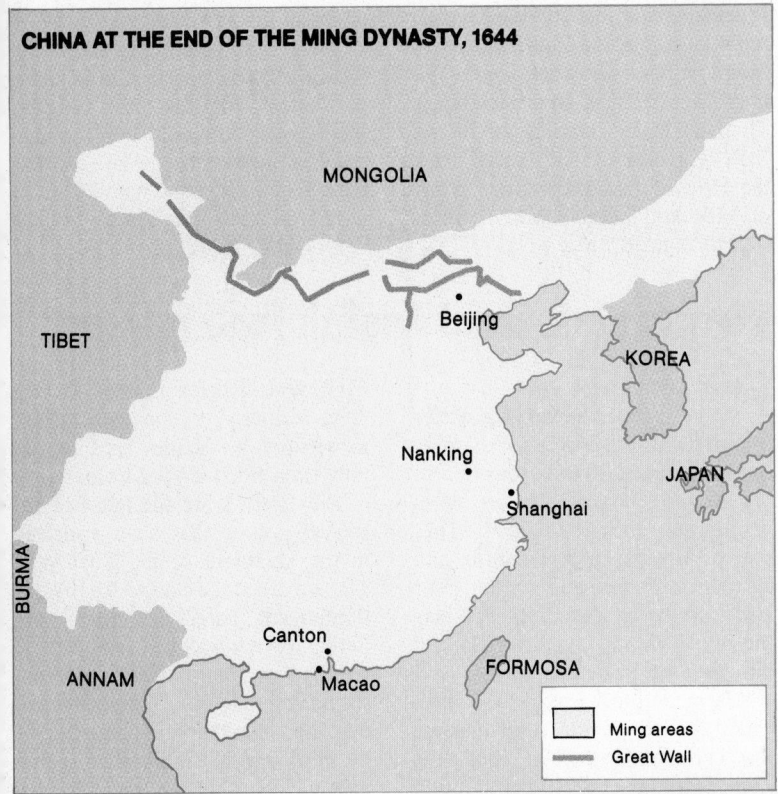

CHINA AT THE END OF THE MING DYNASTY, 1644

Ming areas
Great Wall

China, 25 April 1644
The Ming Chongzhen emperor hanged himself today in the pavilion of the Imperial Hat and Girdle department in the palace compound. His suicide followed the treachery of the eunuch Cao Huajun who opened the Zhangyi Men gate to the rebel forces of Li Zicheng.

Beijing now belongs to Li, and it seems that the long and glorious history of the Mings is at an end. It has, in fact, been crumbling for a number of years. Peasant uprisings caused by heavy taxation, the Manchu incursions and the breakdown of government were all bringing about the end of the dynasty.

The soldiers have been neither paid nor fed, for the imperial treasury and granaries are empty. Morale no longer exists, one general reporting that "when you whip one soldier, he stands up; but at the same time another is lying down".

In these circumstances it is hardly surprising that many of the emperor's generals and eunuchs have gone over to Li who has proclaimed himself emperor of a new dynasty, the Shun. The presence of these officials has enabled Li to take over the capital in an orderly fashion,

A Chinese Ming tapestry embroidered with peonies, phoenixes and rocks.

though most of his men are more interested in loot than in peaceful administration.

It is doubtful, however, if Li can sustain his claim to be emperor for very long. His motley army is unlikely to be a match for the well-disciplined forces of the Manchu general, Prince Dorgon, who is lurking just north of the Great Wall at Shanhaiguan.

A Ming general, Wu Sangui, is guarding the gate at Shanhaiguan. Li has promised him 40,000 *taels* to join his forces. Much depends on the decision.

Descartes thinks; the church worries

The philosopher Rene Descartes.

Paris, 1644
Rene Descartes has extended his reputation throughout Europe and produced more important works to spread his ideas. In his *Meditations* he developed the theme of doubt and scepticism. Indeed, he argued that there may be a great malignant demon which is deceiving humanity into believing things, in which case there is always the secure base of being sure that one does oneself exist.

Although *Meditations* may have enhanced Descartes' reputation, also lead him into dispute and controversy with the church. He has been accused of atheism. Undeterred, he has just brought out his *Principles of Philosophy*. In this book, ranging over physics, chemistry and physiology, he attempts to explain all physical phenomena through one system of mechanical principles. It is small wonder that some authorities are concerned about his rejection of the spiritual in favour of the scientific.

Fishermonger leads uprising in Naples

Naples, July 1647
The rebel who has brought the Spanish government of Naples to its knees is a 27-year-old street-smart illiterate fishmonger from Amalfi, Tommaso Aniello, better known to the crowds as Masaniello.

The new captain-general of the people, as a reluctant viceroy has proclaimed Masaniello, shot to fame on 16 July when he organised the strike in the Piazza del Mercato against the now abolished fruit tax. During the protest Masianello, who once served a jail sentence for smuggling, persuaded the 800-strong crowd to march on the palace, forcing the viceroy to flee. Masaniello's mentor behind the scenes, and the author of the escalating demands for reform, is the veteran radical Giulio Genoino, aged 70.

Masaniello urges on the crowds.

Danish greed loses supremacy in Baltic

The Baltic, 1645
Greed and envy on the part of the Danish king, Christian IV, have forced his country to bow to its Swedish neighbours. Christian had long coveted the German lands now being occupied by Sweden's mercenary armies, and he made the considerable mistake of increasing tolls for ships passing through the Danish Sound. Even though Sweden was exempt from such payments, Christian made life difficult for its ships and increased the toll for ships from any of Sweden's newly-acquired territories.

Two years ago Sweden withdrew an army from Moravia and attacked Denmark. While the Dutch fleet prepared to join them, Swedish troops took Jutland and Skane. Despite a hardfought naval campaign, Denmark can no longer view the Baltic as its private lake.

1648 (1648-1649)

Maryland, 21 January 1648. The first woman lawyer in the colonies, Margaret Brent, has been denied a vote in the Maryland Assembly. She has protested that proceedings were unlawfully conducted without her, since all landowners should be represented.

Netherlands, January 1648. The Dutch and the Spanish sign a peace treaty ending 80 years of war. The seven Dutch provinces are recognised as an independent nation by Spain, which surrenders its rights to the "generality lands" and closes the port of Antwerp.

Britain, March 1648. Royalist uprisings in Wales, Kent and Essex mark the start of a second phase of the Civil War. In December 1647 Charles gained the support of the Scots in return for an agreement to introduce Presbyterianism into England, and this has renewed his strength.

Massachusetts, 13 May 1648. Margaret Jones of Plymouth has been found guilty of witchcraft and sentenced to be hanged by the neck. She is said to have a "malignant touch", causing pain or vomiting, and to administer so-called medicines which brought people closer to death.

England, 19 August 1648. At the end of a two-day battle in Preston, an invading Scottish army led by the duke of Hamilton has been cut off from Scotland and put to flight in a series of running battles.

Paris, 26 August 1648. Parisians rise up in protest at the arrest of Councillor Broussel, who granted them their freedom. The royal family flees to St Germain. This "day of the barricades" marks the start of the so-called *Fronde* uprising (named after a game played by children in the streets of Paris).

England, 6 December 1648. Thomas Pride's purge of parliament arrests or excludes from the Commons, 140 MPs, leaving the "Rump Parliament".

Moscow, 1648. The people of Moscow revolt against heavy taxation.

Paris, 1648. The Royal Academy of Arts is founded.

Naples, 1648. Neapolitan partisans are finally suppressed by the viceroy Arcos and the fleet of Don John of Austria.

Massachusetts, 1648. Trade with the Canaries, Madeira and Spain begins to help the colony out of an economic depression.

Crete, 1648. The Ottoman Turks lay siege to Heraklion in a continuing war with Venice.

England, 1648. The royalist poet Robert Herrick, who was deprived of his living as a clergyman last year by the parliamentarians, publishes *Hesperides, or Works both Human and Divine*, containing many distinctly unpriestly verses.

Muscat, 1648. The Arabs capture Muscat from the Portuguese.

India, 1648. The imperial Moghul court, which was moved from Lahore to Agra in 1598, is now moved to Shahjahanabad (*Delhi*). The building of this new great capital, which includes the Red Fort and the great Friday Mosque, was begun in 1639.

Maryland, 1648. Richard Bennett leads 400-600 Virginians to form the Puritan outpost of Providence (*Annapolis*).

South Africa, 1648. Survivors from the Dutch ship *Haarlem*, which was wrecked in Table Bay last year, find the people and climate of the Cape of Good Hope hospitable.

Angola, 1648. Backed by reinforcements from Brazil, the Portuguese retake Luanda from the Dutch.

England, 1648. The nonconformist George Fox, who started preaching last year, founds the Society of Friends (the Quakers).

Paris, 1648. The painters Louis and Antoine le Nain die. Earlier this year they and their brother Mathieu were received into the French Academy. The subjects of their paintings are quite different from the mythological and allegorial topics currently in vogue. The le Nains paint scenes of humbler life, such as *Boys Playing Cards*, *The Forge* and *The Peasants' Meal*.

England, 1649. The Diggers, supporters of Gerard Winstanley, denounce property as a tool of slavery and propose a total transformation of society.

Istanbul, 1649. Sultan Ibrahim is deposed and murdered with the connivance of his mother. The seven-year-old Mehmet IV succeeds him.

North America, 1649. The Maryland Assembly passes an act permitting any form of Christian worship in the colony. This religious toleration and the fine position of the colony at the head of Chesapeake Bay attract numerous settlers.

Paris, 1649. Simon Vouet, court painter to king Louis XIII since 1627, dies. His almost classicist style has been enormously influential, and his studio has trained many young artists. His great rival was his former pupil Nicolas Poussin.

Parliament purged to stop deal with king

London, 6 December 1648

Members arriving at Westminster for a session of the Commons today found troops everywhere and a former drayman, now an army colonel, Thomas Pride, holding a list of MPs who were to be barred from the House. It appears that a group of MPs and militant army officers secretly agreed on a purge of parliament, in order to put a stop to negotiations with the king.

Since his defeat in the field, Charles has intrigued with soldiers, parliament and the Scots, hoping that dissension would fatally weaken his adversaries. The officers, backed by Oliver Cromwell, now have a "rump parliament" which will do their bidding.

Radical sects want English land reforms

England, 24 October 1649

A band of poor men carrying spades appeared on St George's Hill, Walton-on-Thames, one Sunday morning earlier this year and set about digging up the waste land. They sowed it with corn, parsnips and carrots, and appealed to the poor and starving to join them; they say the land belongs to the people and has been stolen by the squires.

Alarmed local property-owners called for troops and Lord Fairfax, the commander-in-chief, had the ringleaders arrested. They refused to take off their hats in his presence and one, Gerard Winstanley, said that any rights to common land claimed by lords of manors had ended with the king's defeat in the Civil War. Fairfax refused to take them seriously, but local landlords prosecuted Winstanley and he has now been fined £4 for trespass.

The Diggers are the latest of the radical groups that have appeared in the aftermath of the Civil War. The so-called Levellers, led by the flamboyant John Lilburne, want parliamentary reform, an end to monopolies and liberty of conscience in religion. Though the leaders are often men of substance, the Levellers appeal to folk of more modest means who lost their savings when they lent money to parliament for the war. Another sect, the Ranters, is said to go in for hard drinking and whoring in the name of the Holy Spirit and equality.

A 1647 satire on Levellers, who see all occupations as equal.

Conferences throughout Europe bring peace

Thirty years of war end at Westphalia

Munster, 24 October 1648

Three successive salvos crashed out from 70 cannons on the walls of this city today to announce that peace has come to a war-ravaged Europe after 30 years of bitter conflict in which almost every power became involved both on land and sea. It has taken three years of negotiation in two cities – Munster and Osnabruck – to bring about the signing of the Treaty of Westphalia.

With Swedish troops fighting in Prague – where the war started with a Protestant rebellion against the Catholic Habsburg empire – and the French army winning a succession of victories in Bavaria, Ferdinand III, the emperor, was forced to accede.

The treaty represents failure by the Habsburgs to turn Germany into a Catholic monarchy. It guarantees the full sovereignty of the German states and toleration for all three faiths – Catholicism, Lutheranism and Calvinism – except in the hereditary lands of the Habsburgs. By the terms of the treaty, the Habsburgs recognise the independence of Switzerland and the separation of the United Provinces of the Netherlands from Spain. France has acquired Alsace and other territories as reparation; Sweden has secured Pomerania, giving her dominance in the Baltic.

But now, even as the last shots are being fired in Bohemia, Europe is counting the dreadful cost of the "Thirty Years' War". Whole towns have been razed by siege and fire, some losing as many as 50 per cent of their population from plague borne by countless armies. Over 100,000 mercenary soldiers have to be paid and returned home lest they turn themselves into robber-bands adding even more torment to a war-weary Europe. The high cost of war is certain to cause massive tax demands on both nobles and peasants who are already threatening revolt. It is peace, certainly, but an uneasy peace that reigns in Europe.

Eighty years of war ended by a rumour

Munster, 1648

A rumour carefully planted by Spanish agents has brought about an end to 80 years of war between Spain and the Netherlands. With France making rapid headway in its campaign against Spain in the Low Countries, it was not difficult to persuade the wary Dutch that their French allies were negotiating a separate peace and planning to exchange Catalonia for the Netherlands. Despite strong opposition from the Calvinists of the north, a treaty was drawn up.

Spain – which was anxious to relieve itself of the Netherlands campaign in order to deal with France – has agreed complete independence for the United Provinces. It has also confirmed Dutch conquests in Flanders and Brabant and agreed the Netherlands, right to trade freely in the East and West Indies.

Frederick William, elector of Brandenburg, and his mother Elizabeth Charlotte, painted as "Solomon and Sheba" by Mathias Czwieczek. The elector has gained a number of bishorics under the Treaty of Westphalia.

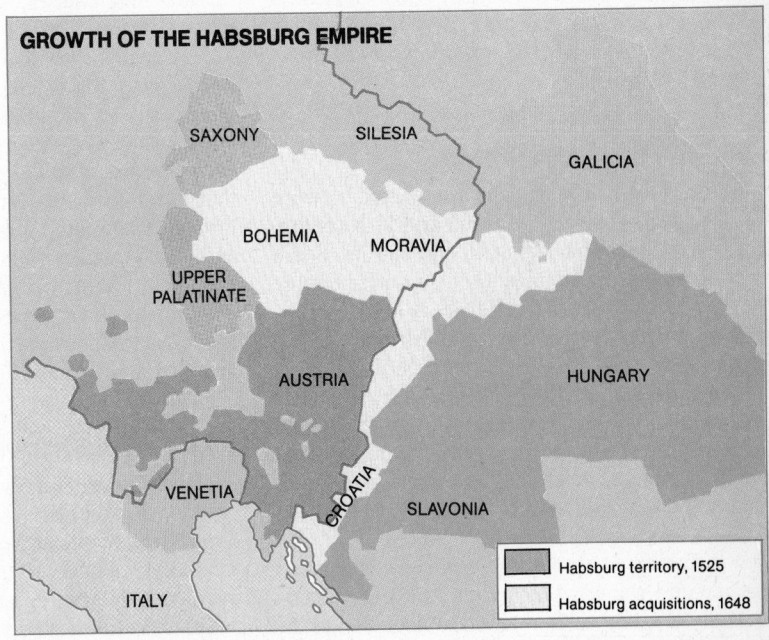

GROWTH OF THE HABSBURG EMPIRE

SAXONY
SILESIA
GALICIA
BOHEMIA
MORAVIA
UPPER PALATINATE
AUSTRIA
HUNGARY
VENETIA
CROATIA
SLAVONIA
ITALY

Habsburg territory, 1525
Habsburg acquisitions, 1648

Mad sultan imprisoned and assassinated

Istanbul, 8 August 1648

Ibrahim, the corrupt, worthless and mentally-ill brother of Murad IV, has become the second Ottoman sultan to be deposed and killed. The "mad sultan" was removed from the throne with the consent of his mother, Sultana Valide, then strangled by order of the grand vizier and the *mufti*. His seven-year-old son, Mehmed, has been proclaimed sultan. Ibrahim's mother saved his life when the dying sultan tried to have him killed in 1640. He was reared exclusively in the *seraglio*; weak, vain, greedy and cruel, he spent the next eight years indulging himself and his *harem*, and selling offices.

In 1644 Ibrahim ordered the execution of the grand vizier, Kara Mustapha, who had curbed his worst excesses. The expensive and ill-advised campaign against Venice, which began the next year, turned the Janissaries against him.

Ukrainian Cossacks rise up against Poles

The Ukraine, 1648

A complex conflict has built up in the Ukraine, or Little Russia, between the Poles, the Russians and the *Cossacks*, an intrepid brotherhood that lives for fighting. With fine impartiality the Cossacks have raided in their light vessels for the Holy Roman emperor as far as the coast of Anatolia, marched for the czar of Russia against Poland, and for Poland against Russia. The Cossacks have now risen against their Polish landlords. The revolt is being led by Bogdan Khmelnitski, a well-to-do Cossack who quarrelled with a member of the Polish nobililty over a girl.

Unable to obtain justice from the authorities, he raised the standard. Cossacks are flocking to support Khmelnitski and are being joined by thousands of Orthodox peasants who are banking on the Cossack soldiers freeing them from their Catholic landlords.

The Decline of Spain

By the middle of the 17th century, it had become apparent that Spain and Portugal, the first generation of "world powers", were being supplanted by their rivals. Towards the end of that century, for example, Spanish merchants were responsible for only 3.8 per cent of trade with Spanish America, while their French counterparts had 25 per cent, the Genoese 21 per cent, the Dutch 19 per cent and the English 11 per cent. In Europe, things were no better. Although Spain mounted impressive displays of military might in the 1620s and 1630s, it could only stand by helplessly as Louis XIV overran the Spanish Netherlands in 1667. Under the feeble Charles II (reigned 1665-1700), the monarchy which had dictated European politics since the time of the Emperor Charles V became the prize over which its neighbours quarrelled. The 17th century saw, in the words of one authority, "not a waning of the Hispanic world, but the recession of Spain within that world".

Spain: what went wrong?

Spain, to which Portugal was annexed between 1580 and 1640, mesmerised 16th and 17th-century Europe with its power, wealth and empire. Spain was an empire of empires: the Aragonese empire in the Mediterranean; the Habsburg lands in Burgundy and the Netherlands; the Portuguese possessions in Brazil, Indonesia and India; and, of course, Spanish America. With resources stretching from China to Peru, it was no wonder that Spain dominated the European stage, pursuing 80 years of war against Dutch rebels and interfering diplomatically and militarily from the Mediterranean to the Baltic.

Yet Spain had always had problems. It had few people and was hard hit by natural disasters, especially plague, and by human follies, such as the expulsion of the Moslems and the Jews. Its social ethos promoted a disdain for manual work, for commerce, and for other races – and although this arrogance allowed the conquistadores to sweep all before them in the New World, it was of little help in developing either Spain or its empire. The enterprising, the talented and the wealthy were not encouraged to build up the infrastructure of investment and commerce which would have enabled Spain to profit from its overseas empire: instead they chased glory by serving in the king's wars, or they carved out a future for themselves in Mexico, Chile or the Philippines. The domestic economy faltered as the crown declared repeated bankruptcies and devaluations of the coinage. Spain was a frontier society that had never really progressed.

The monarchy alone was what united Catalan to Castilian, Basque to Valencian. In the 1640s, with simultaneous revolts in Portugal and Catalonia, and plots and uprisings across Spain and Italy, the monarchy came close to falling apart. The cost of political survival had been the abandonment of the Netherlands and of a role in Europe.

The overseas empire had been a great boon to the Spanish, not least because it gave a second lease of life to the rapacious mentality of the Reconquista. True, the Spanish government tried to impose an administration which would reduce the American possessions to provinces of the mother country, but this was no match for the forces of exploitation, for land-hungry settlers, bigoted missionaries, unscrupulous traders and, indeed, a financially desperate monarchy. With hindsight it is clear that Spain should have developed a reciprocal commerce with her American colonies. But the colonies soon became self-sufficient and the amount of American silver arriving in Spain each year began to fall off. Contemporaries knew that silver from the New World flowed straight through Spain into the hands of Genoese, German and Dutch entrepreneurs who funded colonial trade and Spain's European wars. Since Europe could not produce goods for export to the East, much of the American silver eventually paid for spices and silks in Batavia (Java) and Macao.

Spain's competitors

The decline in Spain's international prestige and military capabilities was real enough, but her economic decline was an optical illusion: the Spanish economy had never risen. Spain was simply being overtaken by her more sophisticated rivals.

Spanish America was primarily a colonial empire, but the Portuguese and the Dutch also established maritime trading empires. A string of "factories" or trading posts on the coasts of Africa and India and in the East Indies enabled the Dutch and Portuguese to import silks, spices, pepper, coffee and tea – luxuries for which there was an insatiable European demand – without the trouble and expense of conquering and governing distant colonies. An alliance with an amenable local ruler, backed by the hint of force, was usually enough to establish a privileged trading position.

The Dutch became a colonial power in the early 17th century because they were fighting for survival at home against former Spanish overlords. A nation of seamen and traders, ever on the lookout for high returns on their investment to plough into the war effort, they saw that the richest pickings were in Brazil and the East, which just happened to be the most vulnerable flank of their Portuguese and Spanish enemies. The Dutch pioneered the use of the chartered trading company, an institution which spread the financial risks, kept government at arm's length, and operated according to strict commercial criteria. Ideally suited to the spice trade, the chartered company had limitations as a tool for building colonial empires. Bureaucracy proliferated, employees had no incentive to settle, and profit came before all else. The Dutch failure to colonise Brazil (1637-1654) – an attempt to displace the Portuguese from their sugar plantations – reveals their deficiencies as colonialists. The Portuguese returned to their plantations, and the Dutch went back to supplying them with slaves from West Africa.

Anglo-Dutch rivalry

In the second half of the 17th century, Europe's economy began to recover from a long recession. England was well placed to take advantage. Her plantations in the Caribbean and North America allowed her to share in the rewards of the booming Atlantic trade in sugar, tobacco and slaves. On the other side of the world, as the Dutch ousted the Portuguese from India and the East Indies, the English were close on their heels, attracted by the profits on the imports and by the carrying trade itself. The English adopted the methods and assumptions of their competitors. They believed that commercial growth depended upon acquiring new commodities from outside Europe, bringing them home in English ships, and re-exporting them to their European neighbours. Since it was assumed that the market for imported goods was finite – despite the abundant contrary evidence of growing consumption – the English and Dutch embarked on a series of wars for commercial and naval superiority (1654, 1664, 1672). In the 1660s, it looked as though the French were about to join in, but they then became distracted by European wars. The Dutch, too, found that war at home was draining them of funds and possibly undermining their shipping. It fell to the English, and to their East India Company, better funded and more energetic than its moribund Dutch counterpart, to reap the rewards of the next phase of Asian trade, in which India and the local "country" trade between East Africa, India and the Far East assumed major importance. It was only by the 1730s that France emerged as a formidable colonial and commercial rival to Britain.

618

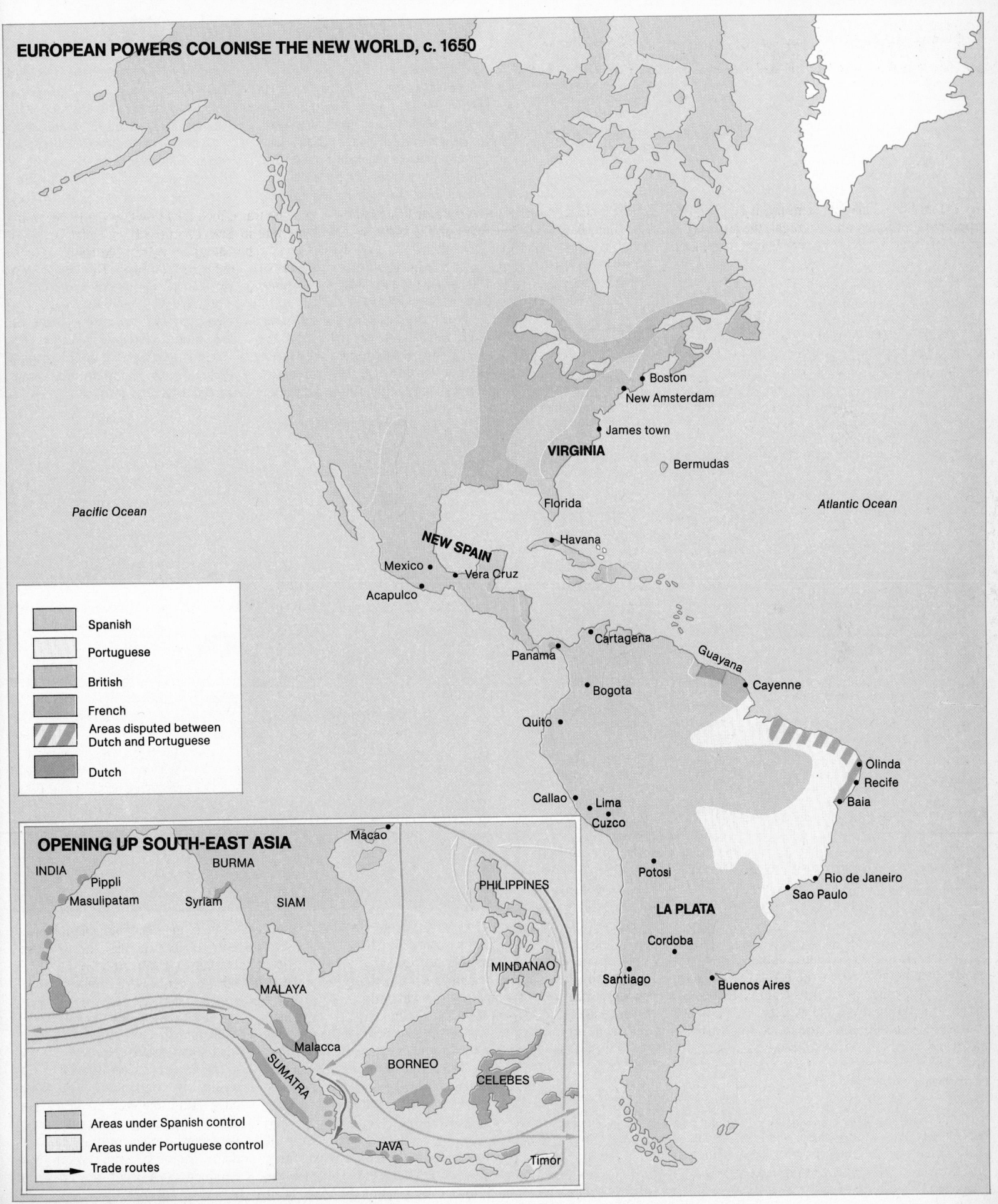

EUROPEAN POWERS COLONISE THE NEW WORLD, c. 1650

Pacific Ocean

Atlantic Ocean

Boston
New Amsterdam
James town
VIRGINIA
Bermudas
Florida
NEW SPAIN
Havana
Mexico
Vera Cruz
Acapulco

Spanish
Portuguese
British
French
Areas disputed between
Dutch and Portuguese
Dutch

Cartagena
Guayana
Panama
Cayenne
Bogota
Quito
Olinda
Recife
Callao
Lima
Baia
Cuzco
Potosi
Rio de Janeiro
Sao Paulo
LA PLATA
Cordoba
Santiago
Buenos Aires

OPENING UP SOUTH-EAST ASIA

Macao
INDIA
BURMA
Pippli
Masulipatam
Syriam
SIAM
PHILIPPINES
MALAYA
MINDANAO
Malacca
SUMATRA
BORNEO
CELEBES
JAVA
Timor

Areas under Spanish control
Areas under Portuguese control
Trade routes

London, 30 January 1649. King Charles is beheaded. He was brought to trial by the order of the Rump parliament – the MPs who remained after Pride's purge last year – and Thomas Pride signed his death warrant.

Paris, 11 March 1649. The peace of Rueil is signed between the *Frondeurs* (rebels) and the French government and court, bringing to an end the uprising that began last year.

England, March 1649. Parliament abolishes the monarchy and the House of Lords.

England, 19 May 1649. England is declared a "Commonwealth or Free State" by the Rump Parliament, with supreme authority vested in the House of Commons. The executive powers of the monarchy are now assumed by a Council of State composed of 40 members, 31 of whom are MPs.

Ireland, 11 September 1649. On the orders of Cromwell, 1,500 people are massacred at Drogheda. The victims include English royalists, civilians and Catholic priests. This policy of terror is designed to prevent the "effusion of blood" in the future.

England, 1649. John Milton writes *The Tenure of Kings and Magistrates* in defence of regicides and of the execution of King Charles and is appointed Latin secretary to the Council of State. He becomes official apologist of the Commonwealth.

Sweden, 1649. In Stockholm at the invitation of his pupil Queen Christina – a blue-stocking in mathematics – the French rationalist philosopher Rene Descartes publishes his *On the passions of the soul.*

Ukraine, 1649. Cossacks led by Kmelnitsky murder Jewish citizens.

France, 18 January 1650. The arrest of the prince of Conde, who is in conflict with the chief minister, Jules Mazarin, sets off a second *Fronde* uprising by the princes.

Sweden, 11 February 1650. The French philosopher Rene Descartes dies at Queen Christina's palace in Stockholm. At her request he had been rising at five o'clock every morning to give her lessons in philosophy, and the early morning cold gave him a fatal inflammation of the lungs. Descartes will always be associated with the proposition "I think, therefore I am".

Scotland, 3 September 1650. The English under Cromwell defeat a superior Scottish army under David Leslie at the battle of Dunbar. Scotland is subdued.

Connecticut, 29 September 1650. New Netherland governor Peter Stuyvesant signs a border pact with the New England Confederation recognising English claims to much of Long Island, Connecticut.

Netherlands, 6 November 1650. William II of Orange dies of smallpox. Despite the Peace of Westphalia, he had wanted to renew conflict with Spain and had attempted to intervene in the English Civil War on the side of the king, whose daughter Mary he had married in 1641. Towards the end of his life he lost the support of parliament because of his autocratic habits and over-aggressive foreign policies.

Scotland, 19 December 1650. Edinburgh Castle submits to Cromwell.

Michigan, 1650. French Jesuits abandon the last of the Huron missions following the destruction of the Huron population by Iroquois raids.

India, 1650. The British East India Company establishes a trading post at Hughli in Bengal.

India, 1650. A splendid temple to Shiva (the four-armed Hindu god of destruction) is built at Madurai. The Pearl Mosque is under construction at Agra.

Rome, 1650. Diego Velasquez paints the *Gardens of the Villa Medici*, a portrait of *Innocent X* and a nude entitled *Venus at her Mirror*.

Germany, 1650. At the Treaty of Nuremberg detailed negotiations between the Empire and Sweden follow the Peace of Westphalia which ended the Thirty Years War.

Angola, 1650. The Portuguese complete the recapture of the coast of Angola from the Dutch.

England, 1650. The English poet Phineas Fletcher dies. He will be remembered for *Purple Island, or the Isle of Man* which describes the human body as an island, founded on bones, with veins as rivers.

Germany, 1650. The Lutheran theologian Georg Calixtus publishes *Judicium de Controversiis* in an attempt to reconcile Lutherans with Calivinists.

Italy, 1650. The astronomers Fathers Riccioli and Grimaldi publish a map of the moon.

England, 1650. The mystic poet Henry Vaughan publishes *Silex Scintillans*, a collection of religious poems.

East Africa, 1650. The Portuguese are evicted from the Swahili ports on the East African coast by the sultan of Oman.

Moghul splendour in Indian cities

Delhi, 1649

A seventh city is being built in Delhi by the Great Moghul, Shah-jahan. It is called Shahjahanabad. It stands on the banks of the river Jumna and a beautiful boulevard, shaded by trees and cooled by water, runs through it. Dominating the city is the Red Fort, a palace, administrative centre, garrison and arsenal all in one building. The Jami Masjid (Friday Mosque) is at the highest point, and the gardens are the most exotic in India.

Work began, after consultations with astrologers, in 1638, and the Red Fort was finished last year. Every month stately pleasure domes and delightful gardens are completed. Shahjahanabad is not the only city built by the Moghuls; each emperor seems obsessed with leaving his mark on the landscape.

Akbar's own ceremonial capital was at Fatehpur Sikri, the home of the holy man Shaikh Salim Chishti, a few miles south of Delhi. Typically of its founder, it celebrated the best in Moslem and Hindu architecture. Equally typically, Akbar never checked the city's water supply and it was abandoned after 14 years. He built a second capital at Agra, downstream from Delhi on the Jumna. His son, Jahangir, preferred Lahore and built his capital there. Now Shahjahan's great capital outshines them all.

View across the courtyard of the mosque Jami Masjid at Shahjahanabad.

Tribes struggle for control of Morocco

Morocco, c.1650

The power of the Sa'di dynasty has waned, and several Berber tribes are vying for supremacy. Since the death of Mawlay Zaydan, in 1627, there has been a sultan of Morocco in name only.

In the Tafilalt, a new family of *sharifs* from the Hijaz is emerging much as the Sa'di did. These are the 'Alawi, who control the main trad-ing routes in the Sahara. But Mulay Mohammed, their sharif, has been unable to conquer Morocco.

In the Fez region, the Dila' fraternity its dominant. The Dila' have spent the last 20 years gradually increasing territory so that they now control central and northern Morocco, with Sultan Mohammed al-Asghar powerless to stop their advance.

Cardinal spirits boy-king out of capital

A later engraving of a Frondist haranguing his fellow-Parisians, urging them to revolt against what is being attacked as the tyranny of Cardinal Mazarin.

Paris, 6 January 1649
Cardinal Jules Mazarin, the chief minister of the crown, has been declared a public enemy by the Paris parliament after spiriting the boy-king, Louis XIV, and his mother, Anne of Austria, out of Paris in the early hours of this morning to escape the clutches of the *Fronde*.

This movement, named after a Parisian street-urchin game, has arisen from a combination of factors: a desire to limit the growing authority of the crown, the ambitions of discontented nobles, and the burden of taxation inflicted on the people by Richelieu and his successor, Mazarin. Trouble broke out last summer when, following the victory at Lens against the Spanish, the regency government felt strong enough to arrest three of its most distinguished critics in parliament.

Paris, as usual, took to the barricades and Mazarin was forced to give in to the demands of parliament to limit the power of the throne. The wily Italian had no intention of keeping his word, however, and made his move last night. He plans to join the duke of Enghien, the Grande Conde, at the head of the royal army to besiege Paris. Meanwhile, the Parisians shout "Murder, murder, murder Mazarin".

Angolan queen at peace with Portuguese

Angola, 1650
After 30 years of fighting between the Mbundu people and the Portugese, the Mbundu leader, Nzinga, the queen of Ndongo and Matamba, has made peace with Portugal.

Succeeding to the throne of Ndongo in 1623 after poisoning her brother, she led her army against the Portuguese, first in alliance with the Jaga people, and later – after she had been driven from Ndongo and re-established herself in Matamba – in alliance with the Dutch. Defiant and cunning, she stole her enemies' tactics, divided Dutch from Portuguese, and ruled both. The cost to Angola, however, has been dire. Tens of thousands have died, hundreds of thousands have been taken into slavery and whole kingdoms depopulated.

Afro-Portuguese salt cellar, c.1550.

King Charles beheaded

The ex-king meeting his fate, depicted by a slightly later German engraver.

London, 30 January 1649
At two o'clock this afternoon, King Charles stepped onto the scaffold outside the Banqueting Hall in Whitehall. He said that he wanted liberty and freedom for the people as much as anyone, but that "liberty and freedom consists in having of government ... not for having a share in government. A subject and a sovereign are clearly different things". Thereupon he set his head on the block, the hooded executioner brought the axe down and the crowd gave a great groan.

It is almost four years since the royalist forces were decisively defeated at Naseby. In that time the king manoeuvred and intrigued in the vain hope of escaping the consequences of that defeat. He sought the help of the Irish; he promised favours for Roman Catholics if they and the pope would help to restore the monarchy; and he gave himself up to the Scots, believing that they would protect him from the English. But the Scots were sceptical of his promises to establish Presbyterianism and handed him over to the English.

The Rump Parliament set up a High Court of Justice for the sole purpose of condemning Charles as "a tyrant, traitor, murderer and enemy of the people". While soldiers who had forced the trial shouted "Justice! Justice!" as Charles passed by, some of the crowd cried "God save the King!".

Expanding Russia fortifies Siberia

Russia, c.1649
The past ten years have seen a remarkable expansion of Russian territory. Ever since, in 1639, a small detachment reached the Pacific coast and established the city of Okhotsk, the whole of Siberia has fallen to Russian domination.

Most impressive are the series of fortifications that have been built across Siberia. These forts ensure Russia's control of the local population, though the further east one goes in this inhospitable land, the smaller that population becomes.

What populace there is can still be exploited, and Russian tax collectors venture deep into the area, even if few colonists are willing to join the natives of Siberia, eking out an existence on the chilly steppes. The *jassak*, a tax payable in furs, a staple of local trading, has augmented the government's coffers.

Siberia may be for the hardy, but its wealth is substantial and more than one fashionable Muscovite owes his family fortune to pioneering journeys into Russia's fruitful eastern territory.

1650 (1650-1652)

France, 1650. Pierre Corneille's *Andromede* is staged for the first time.

Netherlands, 1650. The Dutch poet Joost van den Vondel publishes a *Manuel of Dutch Poetry*. He is a wealthy Amsterdam hosier who writes verse in his spare time.

England, 1650. In his capacity as apologist for the Commonwealth, John Milton writes *Pro Populo Anglicano Defensio* (*In Defence of the English People*).

England, 1650. The non-conformist clergyman Richard Baxter publishes *The Saints' Everlasting Rest*.

England, 1650. England's first coffee house is opened, in Oxford.

England, c.1650. Tea is drunk for the first time in England.

Scotland, 1 January 1651. The executed king's eldest son is crowned Charles II at Scone.

Boston, July 1651. Two leading Baptists, considered ignorant and prejudiced by the city's religious leaders, are arrested for holding an unauthorised religious meeting. One of them, Obadiah Holmes, is whipped in the streets as a deterrent.

England, 3 September 1651. Cromwell defeats Charles II at Worcester.

London, 9 October 1651. Parliament passes a Navigation Act favouring English shipping in an attempt to break the Dutch hold on the carrying trade. Under the terms of the new legislation all goods imported to England must be carried in ships owned by Englishmen or colonials, with crews that are at least half composed of Englishmen.

Massachusetts, 14 October 1651. Laws are passed forbidding the poor to adopt excessive styles of dress.

England, 17 October 1651. The defeated Charles II escapes to France.

Boston, 25 December 1651. The General Court levies a five shilling fine on anyone caught "observing any such day as Christmas".

Paris, December 1651. The king's chief minister, Jules Mazarin, forced to flee from Paris after the city's parliament demanded his dismissal in February, returns to France with 7,000 troops recruited in Germany. He intends to put down the Fronde rebellion led by the prince of Conde.

Virginia, 1651. Anthony Johnson, a free Negro, imports five servants and forms a Negro community on the Pungoteague river.

Virginia, 12 March 1652. The royalist governor of the colony, Sir William Berkeley, submits to warships sent by the English parliament.

South Africa, 8 April 1652. A Dutch expedition to found a military settlement at Table Bay is met by two Khoisan herders who call themselves Harry and Donan and speak English.

Rhode Island, 18 May 1652. A law is passed banning slavery in the colonies, but it causes little stir and seems unlikely to be enforced.

England, 21 June 1652. One of the greatest architects of the day, Inigo Jones, has died. He leaves many varied monuments to his talents: he designed the Queen's House at Greenwich and the Banqueting House at Whitehall; he laid out Lincoln's Inn Fields and Covent Garden; he also staged Ben Jonson's masques for King James, and introduced movable scenery and the proscenium arch.

Massachusetts, 29 June 1652. Under Puritan leadership, convinced of its divine mission, the colony of Massachusetts defies parliament and declares itself an independent commonwealth.

France, 22 July 1652. The Fronde rebels under the prince of Conde narrowly defeat the chief minister Mazarin's loyalist forces at St Martin, near Paris.

Paris, 21 October 1652. On their entry into Paris, which has supported the monarchy against the Fronde rebels, the regent Queen Anne and 14-year-old Louis XIV receive a great welcome.

South-East Africa, 1652. Munhumutapa Manuza dies. Kazuruku Musapa succeeds after a member of the royal family who has become a Dominican declines the throne.

Spain, 1652. The inhabitants of Seville rise in revolt after a decade of economic depression caused by the collapse of American trade and aggravated by an outbreak of the plague in 1649.

France, 1652. The minuet – an elegant dance in three-four time – is all the rage amongst French aristocrats.

England, 1652. In an escalation of the conflict following last year's Navigation Act, England declares war on the Netherlands. The declaration follows an incident in which a Dutch fleet refused to be searched by the British. The Navigation Act was specifically designed to hamper booming Dutch sea trade, and trouble has been brewing ever since it was made law.

New English shipping rules anger Dutch

London, 9 October 1651

The worsening relations between England and the Netherlands received a further setback today with parliament's approval of protective legislation that challenges Dutch mercantile supremacy.

Under the new Navigation Act, goods from Asia, Africa and America can now only be imported into England by English ships. The Act also prohibits goods being imported via another country. This is being interpreted as a thinly-disguised attack on Amsterdam's status as Europe's leading port.

Behind the act lies growing concern in the Council of State and in the City at the state of the English economy, severely depressed for the last three years by plague and harvest failures.

A battle between the English and Dutch fleets, by Isaac Sailmaker.

Dutch seek to avoid absolute monarchy

The Hague, 12 January 1651

With the memory of the late Prince William II of Orange and his attempts to take them once more into a war with Spain still very fresh in their minds, the burghers of all the Netherlands are meeting here in a Grand Assembly to resolve the way in which their country should be governed. William died of smallpox last year at the age of 24, eight days before the birth of a son and heir. It was William II's determination to institute an absolute monarchy, plus concern for the future, that has brought about the constituent assembly of the states that make up the Netherlands.

William's close relationship with the House of Stuart had caused friction between the English Commonwealth and the republican-minded Dutch. To allay fears on both sides, commissioners were exchanged, much to William's fury. The prince's attempts to divide his country by encouraging the Calvinists in the north to join him with France in a campaign against the Spanish was another failure – leading to a royal tour in which the prince harangued officials in the 18 major towns of an unsympathetic Holland. Such was the hostility to this bullying that William, like his father-in-law King Charles, ordered the arrest of six deputies to the States-General. At the same time the city of Antwerp was put under siege by William's cousin, William Frederick, bringing the country close to civil war.

Nasty and brutish life seen by exile

Thomas Hobbes, philosopher of man's fundamental inhumanity.

Paris, 1651

Thomas Hobbes, an English writer living in exile in Paris, has published a new book of political philosophy which casts a grim light on human government.

Leviathan (meaning mortal god) supposes a society where human relations depend entirely on fear. Hobbes sees humanity as locked into a state of permanent war in which "the life of Man is solitary, poor, nasty, brutish and short".

Only the instinct for self-preservation, the fear of violent death, leads us to accept a form of social contract under which individuals give up their natural rights or liberties to society, in other words to the absolute power of the state, or Leviathan as he calls it.

For Hobbes the state is omnipotent and despotic. Its people have not delegated their power, but abandoned it completely.

Two powerful women enemies in France

Paris, 1652

Two passionate, clever and ruthless women who were once friends but are now bitter enemies are the talk of Paris. The first is the queen mother, Anne of Austria, and the other is a beautiful schemer, the duchesse of Chevreuse.

Once they schemed together in an attempt to assassinate Cardinal Richelieu. They failed. Then the queen was accused of treachery and the duchess was exiled. But even in exile she encouraged her admirers to intrigue against Richelieu.

The queen had to endure the cardinal's own schemes against her, following her indiscreet flirtation with the duke of Buckingham, so it might have been expected that when she came to power as regent, the duchess would be welcome at her court. Not so. Now the duchess opposes Mazarin, the queen mother's lover and chief minister, as fiercely as she fought Richelieu.

Dutch settle at the Cape of Good Hope

The Cape, 8 April 1652

A Dutch expeditionary force landed today at the Cape of Good Hope to start building a supply station for mariners making the long five-month voyage from Europe to the East Indies. They were surprised to be met by a couple of local herdsmen, called Harry and Donan, who spoke fluent English.

The Dutch East India Company, which is backing the expedition leader Jacob van Riebeck's team of 90, decided to establish this halfway point between Europe and the East after the crew of a shipwrecked Dutch freighter survived there four years ago by growing their own fruit and vegetables – thereby avoiding scurvy which accounts for many deaths on long voyages.

New light is thrown on life in the womb

England, 1651

William Harvey, the physician, has published the fruits of 35 years' research into animal reproduction in *De Generatione Animalium* (On the Generation of Animals). Harvey traces the development of chicken and deer embryos in unprecedented detail.

Harvey concludes that it is not, as has been thought, the mixture of semen and menstrual blood that produces a foetus, but the presence of an egg in the female which contains within itself the substance and power to develop into the animal. He advises midwives that the infant instinctively knows how to be born.

Veto brings political anarchy to Poland

Poland, 1652

At the very worst possible moment Poland is slipping into political anarchy after a deputy of the *Sejm* (parliament) exercised his veto as an individual for the first time. Wladyslaw Sicinski voiced his disagreement with the prolongation of the Sejm after a vote on increased taxes and because he wanted to go home.

The *liberum veto* gives every deputy the right to overturn legislation of which he does not approve. There is now continuous and irresponsible use of the veto at a time of external threats.

John V Casimir, king of Poland.

War, plague and famine ravaged Europe

Europe, c.1650

Three centuries after the Black Death decimated the population of Europe, many countries find themselves in crisis once more. The last century saw a satisfying upturn in the birth rate, with most populations easily making up for the losses of that disastrous era, but now for many nations the best that can be hoped is to resist a decline. Growth is out of the question.

Europe remains vulnerable to a triple threat: war, plague and famine. Some countries, such as England, have remained relatively unscathed. Others, such as Spain and the German states, have been devastated. This century has seen some of the worst plague attacks since the 14th century.

The Thirty Years War was a major factor in the near-destruction of much of the continent. Apart from battlefield deaths, the constant manoeuvring helped to spread disease and laid waste to vast tracts of farmland. Crops have been destroyed, and famine is on the increase. In a grim irony, Europe has passed on its problems to the New World, which it is exploiting, with 95 per cent of the native people killed off by plague.

Much of Europe may still be suffering after the ravages of the Thirty Years War, but this Norwegian family boasts no fewer than 14 children.

1652 (1652-1654)

Barbados, 1652. The governor complains of shortages due to a the parliamentary ban on foreign trade with colonies (Navigation Act).

West Africa, 1652. English royalists destroy a republican settlement on the Gambia river.

Paris, 3 February 1653. Cardinal Jules Mazarin returns to Paris after fleeing from the city two years ago because of the Fronde uprising.

London, 20 April 1653. Cromwell's soldiers throw out the Rump Parliament – MPs who have been governing since Pride's purge in 1648, and who declared the Commonwealth. Cromwell had come to see it as increasingly corrupt and ineffective.

Rome, 31 May 1653. Pope Innocent X condemns the five Jansenist propositions of Nicolas Cornet of the Sorbonne in Paris. Being a puritanical movement calling for moral and doctrinal reform, Jansenism inevitably angers the Roman Catholic authorities, and the pope in particular.

Switzerland, 8 June 1653. The latest in a series of peasant uprisings is violently put down near Berne. The year began with unrest in Lucerne, where peasants demanded reductions in taxes and mortgages and a more stable currency, and the rebellion has spread to neighbouring states.

Sweden, 30 July 1653. Gabriel Naude, the librarian to Cardinal Mazarin, dies while travelling to Stockholm, where he is being exiled because of the Fronde uprising. He is the first theoretician of library organisation and was librarian to Cardinal Richelieu before the latter was replaced by Mazarin. Naude collected some 40,000 books from all over Europe for the *Bibliotheque Mazarine*, and the library was open to all.

New France, 5 November 1653. The Iroquois League has signed a peace treaty with the French. The Iroquois have been waging war against neighbouring tribes for centuries, but most recently have nearly destroyed the Huron Indians, who have been forced to seek refuge with the French settlers.

London, 12 December 1653. The "Barebones Parliament" – which replaced the Rump Parliament – votes for its own dissolution. Composed of religious men hand picked by Cromwell and the Council of State, it was nicknamed after one of its members, Praise-God Barbon, a sectarian preacher. Alarmed by the intentions of the radical contingent, it is the conservative elements who vote to end the assembly.

London, 16 December 1653. Oliver Cromwell takes on dictatorial powers with the title of "lord protector". The writer John Milton becomes his secretary.

India, 1653. Three sieges of Kandahar, in 1649, 1652 and 1653, have cost the Moghul empire 120m *rupees*, more than half its annual income.

Netherlands, 1653. Johan de Witt becomes councillor pensionary of Holland.

Balkans, 1653. Peasant revolts break out in Croatia.

Hungary, 1653. Apaozai Csere Janos publishes his *Hungarian Encyclopaedia*.

India, 1653. The building of the Taj Mahal is completed.

North Sea, 1653. In the war following the Navigation Act, the English, led by George Monk, defeat the Dutch under Marten Tromp in a battle near Portland. Tromp is killed on the bridge of his ship.

China, 1653. The Dalai Lama holds an investiture for the Manchu dynasty in Beijing.

Russia, 18 January 1654. The Ukraine comes under Russian domination.

London, 15 April 1654. The peace of Westminster puts an end to the war between England and the Netherlands. The Navigation Act that caused the two-year war is retained and England asserts its supremacy over the seas.

Massachusetts, 3 May 1654. The first toll bridge in America is licensed to Richard Thurley at Newbury River. There is a charge for animals but not for humans.

New Amsterdam, 7 September 1654. A group of 23 Sephardic Jews arrives on board the *St Charles*, a French armed vessel. This follows an order given to the 5,000 Jews in Recife, Brazil, that they have three months in which to leave. The order was issued by the Portuguese who took Recife from the Dutch in January.

Maryland, 20 October 1654. Maryland's tolerant Act Concerning Religion, entitling Roman Catholics to the rights of man, has today been replaced by a law taken from the Cromwellian Instrument of Government which states that: "none who profess and exercise the popish religion ... can be protected in this province". The same spirit of intolerance is being fostered by Puritans in Massachusetts.

Germany, 1654. The German musician Samuel Scheidt, renowned for his compositions for the organ, dies.

Oliver Cromwell makes himself protector

London, 16 December 1653
England's outstanding general of the Civil War, Oliver Cromwell, donned a plain black suit today to signify his civilian status when he formally accepted the title of Lord Protector of England from the lord mayor and aldermen of the City of London. After accepting the Great Seal and the Sword of State, he returned to the Banqueting House at Whitehall and three salvos of shots were fired.

For four years the soldiers had struggled to solve the problem of government after the execution of Charles. Last April, Cromwell called in musketeers to send his fellow MPs packing. He formed a parliament of God-fearing men nominated by non conformists churches and army officers; this "Barebones Parliament" muddled along until last week, when it resigned. Now

Cromwell by the artist Edward Mascall, who worked c.1650-67.

the officers have produced an Instrument of Government; this provides for a lord protector, a council of state and an elected parliament.

Irish bishop puts a date to the Creation

Armagh, Ireland, 1654
The archbishop of Armagh, James Ussher, has been applying his considerable scholarship to establishing the date of Creation. After years of research that has involved totalling the ages of the Old Testament patriarchs, Ussher concludes that God created the world in the year 4004BC.

John Lightfoot, another scholar, is even more precise. He agrees with 4004BC and gives the date as 26 October – at 9.00am.

Sweden's scholarly queen has abdicated

Uppsala, Sweden, 16 June 1654
Queen Christina, infant monarch, European stateswoman and patron of Descartes, has abdicated the throne of Sweden, to the regret and consternation of her people. She is succeeded by Charles Gustav, her cousin, whom she was once determined to marry. Christina was the only child of Gustavus Adolphus and Princess Maria Eleanora of Brandenburg. She was six when her father died in 1632; until she came of age in 1644, Gustavus' great chancellor, Axel Oxenstierna, ruled as regent. She is an exceptionally gifted young woman, a linguist and a scholar.

In 1648 she was a signatory of the Treaty of Westphalia, which ended 30 years of European war, and confirmed Sweden control of the Baltic. She accelerated the sale of crown lands to pay for her armies, and played off the pea-

Queen Christina of Sweden: one of Europe's most influential rulers.

santry against the nobles ensuring Charles Gustav's succession. Her lack of freedom as monarch and a growing sympathy for Catholicism may be reasons for her abdication.

Cromwell gives Irish lands to veterans

Ireland, 1653
Cromwell has crushed the Irish rebels and simultaneously solved the problem of paying his soldiers by giving them grants of confiscated land. Those who fought against the English will lose two-thirds of their property; those who did not fight the English but simply failed to show proper regard for them lose one-third. Many landlords have been ordered to remove themselves to remote parts of western Ireland.

At the outset of his campaign to crush the ten-year uprising, Cromwell struck terror into the hearts of the Irish with his capture and sack of Drogheda. His call for the city to surrender and so avoid "an effusion of blood" was rejected. Two costly assaults were necessary before his Ironsides broke through, by which time Cromwell, in a raging fury, was ordering all the enemy to be put to the sword. The spectre of Drogheda's fate was such that other terrified garrisons could hardly wait to surrender and so avoid, as Cromwell put it, "the righteous judgment of God".

Patriarch of Moscow denounced as heretic

Two engraved Russian reliquary crosses picturing Christ and the saints.

Moscow, 1653
Thousands have been killed in a religious rift sparked by moves to change some traditions of the Orthodox Church. The changes have given rise to a new sect, known as the Old Believers, which has separated from the church. The new sect's leader, Avvakum, has been exiled to Siberia and thousands of his followers have been hanged.

Behind the reforms is the Muscovite patriarch Nikon, a peasant turned monk, who believes they are long overdue. The changes are small and largely involve the revision of the liturgy, including such details as the making of the sign of the cross with three fingers instead of with two and the use of the threefold "alleluia".

Nikon is a strongminded and tactless man who is backed by Czar Alexis and who has pursued his reforms with little concern for the simple-minded faithful. It was Avvakum's fierce denouncement of Nikon that led to his exile and the harsh repression by the czar.

An exquisite example of Iranian textile weaving, this silk cloth, with its design of figures in a garden, is from the Safavid era.

Taj Mahal is completed

Shahjahan's memorial to his favourite wife: built by the empire's finest craftsmen, the glorious Taj Mahal is a celebration of many national styles.

Agra, India, 1653
The Taj Mahal, emperor Shahjahan's dream in marble to his favourite wife, Mumtaz-i Mahal (Elect of the Palace), is complete. Building started in 1631, two years after Mumtaz-i Mahal died bearing her 14th child. Its designer, the Persian architect Ustad Isa Afandi, gathered together the finest craftsmen of the east. All who visit this magnificent, yet serene, edifice agree it is the greatest architectural masterpiece to emerge from the Moghul building boom.

It reflects the variety of culture in the vast Moghul empire. The architecture comes from Persia, the concept of the ornate garden tomb comes from Afghanistan, the decorative motifs from Shiraz, the dome from Turkey and the use of water as a mirror from Kashmir.

The mausoleum, consisting of three buildings including a mosque, stands with a garden to its south, and sheets of water for its domes and minarets to reflect in. Everything is symmetrical. At its centre is a two-storeyed cube topped by an onion-shaped dome and flanked by domed octagonal wings. Four minarets, surmounted by octagonal kiosks, rise from each corner.

Secret clause lets the Dutch off lightly

London, 15 April 1654
The peace of Westminster which was signed here today brings to an end the short war, fought almost entirely at sea, between England and Holland. Many critics believe that Oliver Cromwell has been too lenient with the Dutch, who have suffered heavily in loss of shipping and trade. Nevertheless the Netherlands will pay reparations for past damages and have agreed to salute English ships in English waters.

The reason for this leniency is contained in secret talks with Holland which have led to the Act of Seclusion under which the House of Orange is barred from the *Stadholderate* and thus unable to ally itself with Charles Stuart. This should ensure that the still-powerful Dutch navy is denied to the Stuarts.

1654 (1654-1656)

France, 1654. An exchange of letters between the scientists Pascal and Fermat gives rise to a theory of probability.

Boston, 1654. Joseph Jencks is commissioned to build the first fire engine in America.

Netherlands, 1654. The explosion of a gunpowder factory destroys a quarter of the town of Delft. Among the victims is Carel Fabritius, considered the most gifted of Rembrandt's pupils. He had just finished painting his *Self-Portrait*.

Maryland, 25 March 1655. Puritans jail Governor Stone after a military victory over Catholic forces.

New Amsterdam, 26 April 1655. The Dutch West India Company rules that Jews must be allowed to stay in the colony.

Boston, 23 May 1655. Joseph Jencks gets a commission to build an engine "for the more speedy cutting of grass".

North America, September 1655. Swedish rule in America comes to an abrupt end when the Dutch capture Fort Christina and retake Fort Casimir from the Swedes.

Morocco, 1655. The Sadi dynasty is overthrown.

Amsterdam, 1655. The architect Jacob van Campen completes the new town hall. It is a grand building in monumental style, with a wealth of decoration, very different from the restrained elegance of the town houses being built elsewhere in the city.

North America, 1655. Women's illiteracy rate in Massachusetts is put at 50 per cent; in New Netherland, 60 per cent and in Virginia, 75 per cent.

Holland, 1655. The Dutch physicist Christiaan Huygens discovers Saturn's fourth satellite and the true nature of its rings.

Paris, 1655. The College of France loses one of its masters: Pierre Gassendi dies. As a philosopher, he criticised the ideas of Rene Descartes and wrote on the moral theories of Epicurus. He was also at the forefront of the developing science of astronomy, counting Galileo and Kepler among his friends.

Sweden, 1655. Christina, the former queen of Sweden, officially becomes a Catholic.

Siberia, 1655. Russians settled in Albazino attempt to penetrate the forests of Manchuria, which are rich in fur-skinned animals.

Virginia, 10 March 1656. Suffrage is extended to all free men, regardless of their religion.

Virginia, 10 March 1656. A plan calls for the seizing of Indian children until conversion, and for a payment to chiefs of one cow for every eight wolves' heads brought in, to teach them about private property.

India, March 1656. The Moghul Aurangzeb is compelled to raise his siege of Golconda; nevertheless the Dekhan sultanate is forced to pay a considerable indemnity and to cede territory.

Boston, July 1656. The first Quakers to enter the colony, Mary Fisher and Ann Austin, are met with strip searches, jail and banishment.

New Haven, 23 July 1656. New Haven becomes the only colony in New England to reject trial by jury.

New Netherlands, 6 September 1656. The Mohawks ask the Dutch to stop selling rum to the Indians.

Maryland, 22 September 1656. The first all-woman jury acquits Judith Cathchpole of murdering her unborn child.

Rome, 16 October 1656. The papal bull *Ad Sacram* of Alexander VII renews the condemnation of the "five propositions" of Jansenism, a reformist, anti-papal creed.

Madrid, 1656. Diego Velazquez paints *Las Meninas* (The Maids of Honour).

Amsterdam, 1656. Rembrandt is declared bankrupt and all his goods are put up for sale.

Massachusetts, 1656. Harvard accepts the Copernican theory of the universe, which places the sun at the centre with Earth and the planets revolving around it.

The Hague, 1656. The prolific and talented Dutch painter Jan van Goyen dies. A landscape artist who perfected the art of conveying subtleties of atmosphere, he has had considerable influence on younger artists.

Sweden, 1656. The Bank of Sweden is founded.

Rome, 1656. The Academy of Painting is founded.

Rumania, 1656. The confederation of Rumanian countries – Wallachia, Moldavia and Transylvania – become an anti-Ottoman coalition.

England, 1656. The writer John Bunyan publishes a vigorous attack on Quakerism, *Some Gospel Truths Opened*.

Ottoman Empire, 1656. An aged Albanian, Koprulu Mehmed, is made grand vizier in Istanbul. He is charged with the re-organisation of the empire and the re-establishment of order.

Manchus push back Russians in Siberia

Czar Alexis Mikhailovitch: the inspiration of Russian expansion.

Siberia, 1655

The almost effortless Russian advance into eastern Siberia has been checked on the banks of the Amur by Manchu warriors despatched by Beijing to avenge the heavy Chinese defeat there three years ago.

The Manchus, then preoccupied with consolidating their conquest of China, failed at the first battle to send sufficient forces, believing that the aggressors troubling their Tartar kinsmen were just tribesmen from the north trying to settle centuries-old squabbles.

Beijing has since woken up to the Russian threat. However, its victory may be late to oust the Russians from their new bases further north along the Pacific.

Jamaica taken by English expedition

Jamaica, 1655

An English army has captured this island and is pursuing the remnants of the Spanish garrison into the jungle. The Spanish viceroy had surrendered before choosing to fight a guerrilla campaign inland. It was the Lord Protector, Oliver Cromwell, who sent the invasion force to the West Indies as part of his "Western design". The intention was to take Santo Domingo. That attempt was vigorously repulsed and the British went on to blunder into Jamaica. The two commanders have returned and been imprisoned in the Tower of London.

Rationalist Spinoza expelled by Jews

Amsterdam, 27 July 1656

Baruch Spinoza, the Jewish philosopher, has been expelled from his home in Amsterdam. His own community refuses to accept the strict rationalism of his beliefs.

Spinoza, a lensmaker by trade, combines orthodox Judaism with the teachings of Galileo and Descartes, to propose a world in which theology and philosophy, faith and reason, are completely separated. To him there is no way of reconciling modern science and the ancient Bible.

Baruch Spinoza: wondering Jew.

Princes act to quell revolt in Rumania

Rumania, 1655

A mutual support pact to guarantee political stability in Rumania has been signed by the region's three main princes, who control Moldavia, Wallachia and Transylvania.

The move is designed to stifle any future revolts and prevent a repeat of the recent disturbances. The princes are reported to be shocked by the strength of the recent peasants' revolt, which was only eventually crushed by brute force and exceptionally repressive measures involving the murder and mutilation of thousands. The authorities blame Serbian and Bulgarian mercenaries who were trying to avoid being treated as serfs by their landowners for starting the uprising.

Portuguese take back Recife from Dutch

Brazil, 1654
With the Dutch distracted by a two-year war against England, the Portuguese saw their chance of regaining the vast sugar-growing area of north-eastern Brazil taken by Dutch colonists almost a quarter of a century ago.

When the Portuguese fleet arrived off the city and port of Recife, the Dutch garrison and burghers, terrified of standing alone without relief from home, capitulated. The territory had been conquered by mercenaries of the Dutch West India Company; so many of these were English that an English Protestant chaplain was stationed in Recife.

Under Governor John Maurits the multi-racial, multi-cultural colony of Dutch and English Protestants, Portuguese Catholics, Jews, Mulattos and black slaves flourished. But after he returned to Holland the colony went into decline, Portuguese planters rebelled and Portuguese from elsewhere in Brazil joined in.

A demonstration of practically nothing

Von Guericke proves his point, as the horses fail to break the sphere.

Germany, 1654
The German experimental scientist Otto von Guericke has just amazed the imperial *Diet* with a flamboyant demontration. Von Guericke has been experimenting with vacuum pumps and studying the effects of atmospheric pressure.

He has had made two large brass hemispheres which fit snugly together to form a sphere. Before the assembled crowd he pumped air out of the hollow ball. Then he attached teams of eight horses to each side and signalled them to pull.

The strength of the horses failed to tear the hemispheres apart, showing that the atmosphere, while hating a vacuum, exerts considerable pressure.

Portrait painter Rembrandt is bankrupt

Rembrandt's "Scholar at a window": one of the master's later works.

Amsterdam, 1656
Rembrandt van Rijn, for long the most popular portrait painter in Amsterdam and one of the richest, has shocked the city by declaring himself bankrupt. His four-storey house, where he has lived and worked for 20 years, has been put in the name of his son Titus and is up for sale along with his art collection.

Rembrandt, who is 50, first made his name in the city with a group portrait commissioned by Dr Nicholas Tulp, the physician. He was painted giving one of his anatomy lessons, watched by a group of fascinated students. In 1642 he produced an even more dramatic portrait of the militia company of Captain Frans Banning-Cocq, *The Night Watch*. The 18 guards with their pikes are so shrouded in the shadow that Rembrandt loves that, instead of paying them 100 guilders each, it was agreed to vary the sum according to the degree of visibility of each man. Admirers say it makes other militia portraits "look like playing cards".

Of late Rembrandt has given up painting the burghers of Amsterdam for religious subjects and landscapes, and this "personal" work has lost him many patrons. His problems have been compounded by the cost of his collection.

His wife Saskia died in 1642 and under her will he may not marry again or he will forfeit her estate. His present companion, Hendrickje Stoffels, who was once his maid and has borne him a daughter, is taking charge of his affairs jointly with Titus.

Death of King John IV, who restored independence to Portugal

Lisbon, 6 November 1656
John IV, who regained Portugal's independence after 60 years under Spanish kings, died today, aged 53. In 1580, despite the claims of the House of Braganza, Philip II seized the Portuguese crown for himself. When John succeeded to the dukedom of Braganza in 1630 he set out, with the fervent support of the Portuguese people, to remove the injustice.

On his accession he declared war on Spain, although he was unable to commence military activity until he had found himself an army and navy. He pursued a vigorous diplomatic campaign to have himself recognised as king, which the pope, under Spanish influence, flatly refused. He married, in 1633, Louisa de Guzman, the sister of the Spanish duke of Medina Sidonia Their son, Alfonso, succeeds.

Rembrandt's self-portrait, painted late in life, reflects his sadness.

1656 (1656-1658)

Austria, 1656. The treaty of Konigsberg is forced on the Elector Frederick William of Brandenburg by Charles X of Sweden, following the latter's successful military campaigns last year which culminated in the invasion of Brandenburg. The treaty makes east Prussia into a fief of the Swedish crown and gives Sweden privileged access to the Prussian ports of Memel and Pillau and half the customs revenue. It is a step towards the fulfilment of Sweden's dream of Baltic domination.

Rhode Island, 20 May 1657. The colony becomes the third to defy the British ban on trade with the Dutch.

Massachusetts, 21 May 1657. The colony's governor for 30 years, William Bradford, is dead. He played a major part in the establishment of the colony and was re-elected as governor from 1621 for 30 years.

England, 25 May 1657. In the Humble Petition and Advice, parliament offers the title of, king to Oliver Cromwell, the Lord Protector. He refuses it.

India, August 1657. Over the past year the Moghul Aurangzeb has captured two fortresses in the Dekhan sultanate of Bijapur and ravaged much of the land. It is only by the intervention of his father, Shahjahan, that a complete conquest has been prevented.

England, 1657. John Bunyan, who wrote an attack on the Quakers last year, begins preaching in the Midlands. He rapidly gains a reputation as a powerful speaker and draws large, enthusiastic crowds.

Rhode Island, 1657. Rhode Island is becoming known for its religious tolerance and as a haven for dissenting Puritans, thanks to the efforts of Roger Williams. Williams has been arguing against the involvement of secular authorities in religious affairs since the publication of his book *The Bloudy Tenent of Persecution for the Cause of Conscience Discussed* in 1644. The book was publicly burnt in London on publication.

Aegean Sea, 1657. The Turks take the islands of Tenedos and Lemnos from the Venetians.

West Africa, 1657. The Swedes, who Carolusberg castle, a slave fort, on the Gold Coast two years ago, are driven out by Danes.

England, 1657. The Dutch physicist Christiaan Huygens invents the pendulum clock – using Galileo's observations on the behaviour of oscillating pendulums – and writes the first treatise on probability theory.

Paris, 1657. *Histoire Comique des Etats et Empires de la Lune* is published. The book the work of the fantasist and comic poet Cyrano de Bergerac, is bursting with ideas.

New Amsterdam, 25 January 1658. The governor, Peter Stuyvesant, has prohibited tennis-playing while religious services are being held. The neighbouring colony of Massachusetts has gone even further: during 1655 and 1656 colonists were punished for eavesdropping, scolding, meddling, naughty speeches, profane dancing, making love without the consent of the congregation, playing cards, pulling hair and pushing their wives.

India, 25 June 1658. Aurangzeb proclaims himself emperor of the Moghuls.

New Amsterdam, 12 August 1658. *Ratelwacht*, the first police force in the colony, is formed.

Montreal, August 1658. A French explorer and fur trader, Medard Chouart, the *sieur* des Groseilliers, his brother-in-law Pierre Esprit Radisson and a team of 31 set out from Trois Rivieres on the lower St Lawrence river to explore the southern shores of Lake Superior and the regions south and west of the lake. They hope to establish trading relations with Indians in the area.

South Africa, 1658. Dutch settlers at the Cape of Good Hope begin to import slaves from Madagascar and Java.

Sweden, 1658. The Bank of Sweden produces the first bank notes in the western world.

Maryland, 1658. Conflict between the rebellious Puritan population and the Lord Proprietor has ended with the reinstatement of Lord Baltimore and the restoration of the Religious Toleration Act, repealed by a rebel assembly after an uprising in 1655.

Netherlands, 1658. The naturalist Jan Swammerdam is the first to observe the activities of red blood corpuscles.

Spain, 1658. The Spanish Jesuit writer and philosopher Balthasar Gracian dies. He wrote several works setting out a system of practical ethics, but will be best remembered for his allegorical novel *El Criticon* – a savage's vision of civilisation.

Poland, 1658. The Counter-reformation triumphs, and Protestants are excluded from office.

Ceylon, 1658. The Dutch take Jaffnapatam, Portugal's last possession in Ceylon.

One in two Poles die of war and plague

Poland, 1657

Poland's Golden Age is over and the horrors of more recent history have a new name: "the Deluge". In a very short time invasion, war, plagues, slave raids and mass murders have reduced the population by almost half. Poland's king, John II Casimir, has had a lamentable nine years in power.

Much of the trouble has been due to Poland's neighbours invading the country. After the king failed to reach an agreement with the Cossacks they swore an oath of allegiance to czar Alexis, whose armies promptly invaded the country on two fronts. This alarmed the Swedes, who descended on Poland from Pomerania and Livonia. And these operations provoked the intervention first of Frederick William, the elector of Brandenburg, the heart of the Prussian kingdom, and then this year that of the prince of Transylvania.

The strains of the incessant war have led to all sorts of internal problems. The king has been in continual conflict with the *Sejm* (parliament) over money and constitutional issues. Apart from the sharp reduction in the population, many towns have been destroyed.

Scientist calculates where Jesuits err

Pascal: scientist and theologian.

France, 24 March 1657

A leading French mathematician, as gifted in science as he is in theology, has joined the battles between the Jesuits and the Jansenists of the convent of Port Royal. In 18 polemical letters, *Les provinciales*, Blaise Pascal, writing as "Louis de Montalte", has weighed in against the beliefs of the Jesuit fathers.

Unlike them, Pascal believes firmly that true faith will only appear to the morally upright. His letters blend his own faith, the sophistication of a man of the world and the learning of a genuine genius. He makes the most complex of theological questions seemingly simple, and has attracted a wide audience of "honest men" to whom he has revealed topics once reserved for specialists.

Europeans fight for spoils of Gold Coast

Gold Coast, West Africa, 1657

The Gold Coast is now a battleground between rival European powers. In the latest round the fortress of Carolusberg, which the Dutch took from the Portuguese in 1642, and the Swedes took from the Dutch in 1651, has now been taken by the Danes.

The black populace watches this extraordinary outburst of white tribalism with a defensive self-interest. Politics were simple until 1642. Portugal monopolised power. Now Portuguese, Dutch, Swedes, Danes, English, French and Germans fight for the wealth that can be gained from the gold, cloth, ivory, salt and slave trades.

The profits are enormous. The mines at Mina alone supply one tenth of the world's gold, while since the growth of sugar plantations in the New World there is now more profit from slaves than from gold. Slaves costing 45 *florins* are sold in the Americas for 210 florins. As Europeans fight each other on the coast, anarchy reigns in the interior. Firearms, swapped for gold and slaves, destroy traditional structures and kill thousands. The European powers, as if to protect themselves from the consequences of their own immorality, remain in their coastal forts. These forts frequently change hands and are now so numerous that in some places, like Accra, Komenda and Sekondi, they are even within gun-range of each other.

Saintly favoured son imprisons father

Shahjahan out riding with his son Dara, a favourite but a traitor too.

Aurangzeb, Shahjahan's "most worthy and most saintly son".

Delhi, 25 June 1658

The seemingly "most worthy and saintly" Aurangzeb, the third and favourite son of the Moghul emperor Shahjahan, has imprisoned his father and seized power. Inevitably there have been casualties: two brothers, a son and a nephew are dead. Such is the succession in the Moghul empire.

Shahjahan's illness, which precipitated the crisis, saw Aurangzeb in the Dekhan with a Moghul army. Recognising his three brothers as the three obstacles to the throne, he set out to eliminate them one by one. Unfortunately the three bro-

thers had the same ideas. The oldest, the liberal and honourable Dara, seized Delhi. The second, the dissolute and alcoholic Shuja, the governor of Bengal, went to war against him. The third, Murad, the governor of Gujarat, was tricked into an alliance with Aurangzeb.

Yet more unfortunate for the ambitious brothers, the shah recovered. Shuja continued his advance and was defeated by Dara, who in turn has been defeated by Aurangzeb. Murad has been kidnapped and has disappeared. Finally, Aurangzeb seized his father and imprisoned him in his *harem*.

Rome thrills to Borromini's architecture

Rome, 1657

Francesco Borromini, who worked as a stone carver at St Peter's when he first came to Rome, is winning a reputation as an architect equal to that of his great rival, Bernini. Pope Urban VIII was Bernini's patron. When he died, Innocent X turned to Borromini. Just as Bernini was given St Peter's interior, Borromini was given St John Lateran, which he decorated in Baroque style with giant pilasters and arches. His most original invention was shown in the church of St Charles at the Four Fountains whose walls seem to undulate beneath an oval dome. His St Agnes in the Piazza Navona faces Bernini's fountains.

Borromini's church of Santa Carlo.

Difficult sultan succumbs to Dutch bribes

Traders and natives pursue their business outside a colonial building.

Java, 1657

Despite recurrent difficulties with the sultan of the Mataram empire on Java, the Dutch, established in their fortified town of Batavia, have made no effort to subdue Mataram. Instead they seek to please Sultan Amangkurat by sending him costly gifts, and hope that the rice sup-

plies, on which they depend, will not be interrupted. The sultan rejected a Dutch suggestion that he should encourage overseas trade by his people, saying that they had nothing of their own, everything belonged to him, and it was going to stay that way. He says he is not interested in his people's welfare.

Anglo-French army routs Spaniards

Dunkirk, 25 June 1658

This city has today surrendered to a combined force of English and French troops under the command of Turenne. To the dismay of the French troops, who spilt much blood in the siege, it was promptly handed over to the English under the terms of an agreement between Mazarin and Cromwell.

Mazarin was anxious for English help in the war against Spain and Cromwell was under pressure to halt the attacks on England's east coast sea trade by Dunkirk privateers. The Cardinal was also impressed by the protector's effective army, who have restored England's military reputation in Europe.

The French have not done all the work, however. English troops took part in the rout of the Spanish at the battle of the Dunes 11 days ago. Only a small party of infantry is believed to have escaped.

An ornately-designed German powder flask of stagahorn here mounted in silver gilt.

1658 (1658-1660)

England, 3 September 1658. The Lord Protector, Oliver Cromwell, dies. He has ruled as a benevolent dictator since the dissolution of the Barebones Parliament in 1653, and last year refused the offer of the kingship from parliament.

England, 1658. The poet John Dryden publishes *Heroic Stanzas*, in quatrains, on the death of Oliver Cromwell.

India, 1659. After taking power, the Moghul Emperor Aurangzeb sets about re-establishing order.

Netherlands, 1659. The Dutch-Jewish philosopher and theologian Spinoza identifies God with nature in his *Short Treatise on God, Man and his Well-being*.

Paris, 1659. The first opera in the French language, *Pastorale*, is written by Abbe Pierre Perrin, the librettist, and Robert Cambert. Its performance marks the opening of the Royal Academy of Music in Paris.

Berlin, 1659. The Royal Library is founded.

India, 1659. Sivaji, the Maratha, kills the Moghul general, Afzal Khan, by ripping open his belly with a steel tiger's claw, while embracing him in welcome.

France, 1659. The peace of the Pyrenees is agreed – a Franco-Spanish agreement negotiated by Cardinal Mazarin and Don Luis de Haro, which finally brings the Franco-Spanish War to an end. The treaty is sealed with the arrangement of a marriage between the Spanish King Philip IV's daughter, Maria Theresa, and Louis XIV. The *infanta's* dowry will be paid in full only when she renounces all claims to the Spanish throne.

Italy, 1659. The Sicilian Francisco Procopio perfects the making of icecream.

Netherlands, 1659. The Dutch artist Jan Vermeer paints *Young Girl with Flute*.

England, May 1659. Six months after succeeding his father as lord protector, Richard Cromwell is dismissed by the recalled Rump Parliament, which was thrown out by Oliver Cromwell's troops in 1653. Lacking his father's charisma and will-power, Richard has shown little aptitude for this supremely powerful office.

France, 1659. The dramatist Pierre Corneille returns to the stage with his *Oedipe*.

China, 1659. Father Ferdinand Verbiest, a French missionary, sets out for Beijing.

Netherlands, 1659. A new drama by Joost van den Vondel, *Jephtha*, is performed.

Cambodia, 1659. The English factors of the East India Company's Cambodian factory are forced by an Annamite (*Vietnamese*) invasion to flee the country.

Virginia, 13 March 1660. A statute limits tax on the sale of slaves.

Massachusetts, 1 June 1660. The Quaker Mary Dyer is hanged in Boston. She escaped the noose last year through the intervention of her son, but then disobeyed the authorities by re-entering the colony to spread the doctrines of Quakerism. Unconvinced by her claim of a mission from God, the court ordered her execution.

France, 27 September 1660. The moral leader of the French church, Vincent de Paul, dies. At the age of 25 he was captured by pirates on a sea voyage and sold into slavery in Tunis. He escaped by persuading his master to return to the Christian faith, and landed back in France in 1607. He formed associations for helping the sick, and founded the Congregation of Priests of the Missions, which was sanctioned by Urban VIII in 1632.

England, 1 October 1660. The crown strengthens the Navigation Act, requiring that certain colonial goods are to be shipped only to Britain. Such measures are directed against the Dutch, but they inevitably limit colonial trading outlets and are resented by settlers struggling to establish their communities.

America, 1660. The Narrangansett Indian Passaconaway makes a death-bed speech: "Be careful how you quarrel with the English. Although you may do them much harm, yet assuredly you will all be destroyed and rooted off the earth if you do."

South Africa, 1660. In the Dutch-Khoisan war at the Cape of Good Hope, the Khoisan herders Harry and Donan, who greeted the Dutch settlers when they landed in 1652, are captured and imprisoned on Robben Island.

France, 1660. The artist Nicolas Poussin begins a cycle of paintings for the duke of Richelieu, the *Quatre Saisons* (Four Seasons).

Sweden, 1660. The Swedes mourn the death of Charles X in the course of a new campaign against Denmark. He is succeeded by his young son, Charles XI.

Copenhagen, 1660. Niels Stensen, the Danish anatomist, geologist and theologian, discovers that the heart is a muscle.

East Africa, 1660. The sultan of Oman, supported by the British, takes the port of Mombasa from the Portuguese.

Swedes besiege Danes

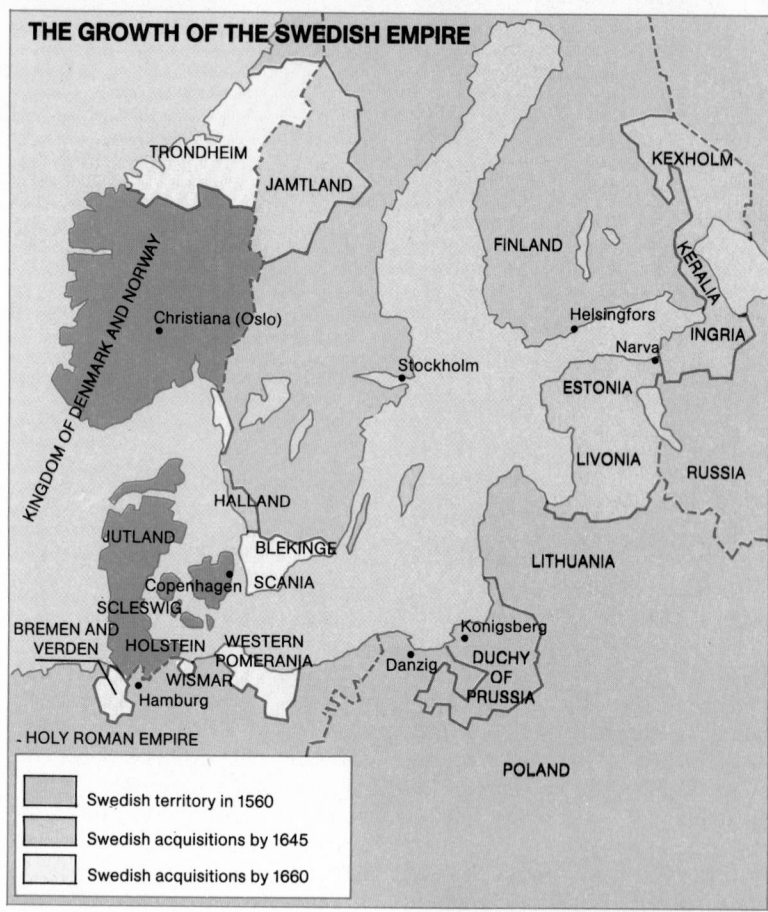

THE GROWTH OF THE SWEDISH EMPIRE

☐ Swedish territory in 1560

▧ Swedish acquisitions by 1645

☐ Swedish acquisitions by 1660

Copenhagen, February 1659

Helped by a Dutch fleet and led by their king, Frederick III, the people of Copenhagen are fighting hard against a Swedish besieging army. The Swedes invaded suddenly last year from the south, taking advantage of the frozen sea in an exceptionally cold winter to move rapidly from island to island, taking Jutland and Zealand before attacking an undefended capital.

The Danes sued for peace and the resulting treaty of Roskilde gave Sweden the islands of Skane, Halland and Blekinge – thus completing her peninsula north of the Baltic Sea – together with the islands of Bornholm and territories in Norway.

It was the aggressive Swedish king, Charles X, who launched this War of the North in 1655. Anxious to protect his empire against a Russian attack, he invaded Poland and took Warsaw.

During this campaign Denmark, encouraged by Holland and Austria, declared war on Sweden. Charles broke off the Polish cam-

Frederick III, leader of the Danes in their struggle against Sweden.

paign to turn on Denmark so suddenly. Now, despite the treaty, he has invaded again, determined to occupy the whole of Denmark. Only the courage of Copenhagen can save the Baltic Sea from becoming a "Swedish lake".

Cromwell, puritan and moralist, dies

The death mask of the Protector.

England, 3 September 1658

All through the night the Lord Protector was restless and he talked much of the grace of God. The last crisis came at three o'clock this Friday afternoon as he slipped into unconsciousness. Oliver Cromwell was in his 60th year and the fifth of his rule over England.

A stern Puritan and an inspiring general, he was respected and feared, but though the private expressions of grief have been many, in public there are none. Nor have the royalists raised their heads. John Thurloe, the head of Cromwell's intelligence service, writes: "There is not a dog that wags his tongue, so great a calm are we in."

Cromwell reshaped the Civil War's New Model Army into a professional force. He set up a militia organised in 12 districts, each under a major-general, to forestall conspiracies and enforce public morals. He wanted to curb drinking and to shut down theatres and whorehouses. He believed in the Bible as the true word of God, to which any man should have access.

The underlying problem of his rule was his dependence on the military and his lack of civilian support. His relations with parliament were uneasy. MPs wanted to be rid of the army, while he knew it was a necessity. They wanted a king, but his conscience could not accept a crown. He is succeeded by his son Richard; few expect him to last.

English to be biggest slavers vows prince

The British flag flies over Fort James at Accra: the Gold Coast is seen as a new source of wealth for the merchants of the expanding empire.

London, 3 October 1660

With the projected foundation of the Royal African Company by Prince Rupert and the equipping of an expedition to wrest control of the Gambia from foreigners, England's invisible earnings will be given a sharp boost. It is Prince Rupert's ambition for England to become the world's leading slave trading nation. The diarist Samuel Pepys, however, offered a share in the venture, politely declined.

Britain's interest in the Gambia began in 1588 when the exiled Portuguese pretender, Antonio, "granted" English merchants trade concessions in the Portuguese colony.

Prince Rupert's interest in the slave trade goes back to the Protectorate, when he led royalist privateers against English shipping on the West African coast. At the head of the Gambia, he was told, there were mountains of unprotected gold and nations of unexploited slaves. French, Dutch, Swedes and English jostle for access, whether their interest is in mining or slave trading, there is money to be made.

Franco-Spanish border fixed at Pyrenees

France, 7 November 1659

The Franco-Spanish war is at last at an end. After a series of meetings between Mazarin and de Haro on this island in the Bidassoa river, the peace of the Pyrenees was signed today much to the relief of Europe.

The war had reached a stage where Spain, its treasury empty, and shocked by the defeats of its much-vaunted army at Rocroi, Lens and Dunkirk, could fight no longer. The entry of England into the war, with the Ironsides ranged alongside France's increasingly confident army, was the last straw.

Among the most important of the 124 clauses of the treaty are those restoring Roussillon and Perpignan to France after a century and a half of Spanish rule, thus firmly fixing the Franco-Spanish border at the Pyrenees.

England is to have Dunkirk and Jamaica while the French will gain a series of fortresses in Flanders and Artois. In return the French are to restore Spain's ally, the duke of

Theodore van Thulden's allegorical view of the peace of the Pyrenees.

Lorraine, to most of his duchy. The treaty also stipulates an amnesty for the prince of Conde who, out of pride, fought for Spain. There is also to be a dynastic marriage. Louis XIV is to marry the Spanish princess, Maria Theresa, with a dowry of 500,000 *ecus*.

Quakers hanged on Boston common

Boston, Mass., 27 October 1659

Two members of the Quaker sect were hanged on Boston common today for preaching their non-violent doctrine in defiance of the Puritan government. A 200-strong guard held the crowd back with long pikes, while drummers drowned the condemned men's parting words. A third prisoner, a woman, was reprieved after being blindfolded with the noose about her neck, in response to her son's pleas. She is banished instead.

The Quakers – Will Robinson, Marmaduke Stevenson and Mary Dyer – have been repeatedly exiled from Massachusetts. They knew that all dissent in Boston is suppressed. Eight years ago, Baptists holding a service in a private house were raided by the sheriff. One of them was publicly whipped. The virus of Puritan intolerance, cultivated in England under Cromwell, has spread to suppress Catholicism in Catholic Maryland by force of arms. As in England, Catholics are fair game, their property pillaged freely.

Black-white line is an almond hedge

Cape Town, 6 April 1660

The 12-month South African guerrilla war between Khoisan pastoralists and Dutch settlers is over. The Dutch governor, van Riebeeck, opened peace negotiations today. The two sides are to be separated by a hedge of bitter almonds.

The settlement was founded in 1652 by the Dutch East India Company to provide victuals for their East Indies-bound ships. After five years van Riebeeck, a believer in free enterprise, encouraged company employees to set up their own farms. Africans who tried to thwart them were sent to Robben Island.

Conflict became inevitable: the Khoisans attacked outposts, burned crops and stampeded cattle. The overstretched whites have sued for peace. With the whites hoping to expand their colony and the blacks anxious to win back their land, however, the present compromise is unlikely to last.

England, 12 November 1660. John Bunyan, now a Baptist minister, is arrested for preaching other than in a parish church, a practice which local magistrates began to prosecute after the Restoration. He is imprisoned in Bedford county jail.

Copenhagen, 1660. The peace of Copenhagen ends the war between Sweden and Denmark. The Swedes restore the diocese of Trondheim to Norway, and Bornholm to Denmark, but retain Scania and other territories conquered since 1643 on their western borders.

England, 1660. The English political theorist James Harrington publishes his *Political Discourses*. Though a republican, he was a personal attendant of Charles I, and attended him to the scaffold.

Germany, 1660. Friedrich Staedtler founds a pencil factory in Nuremberg.

Germany, 1660. The peace of Oliva ends the war begun in 1655 by Sweden's attack on Poland. The Swedes gain no territory by the treaty, but keep Livonia, and John Casimir, the king of Poland, gives up his claim to the Swedish throne. The treaty also confirms the duchy of Brandenburg's sovereignty over the duchy of Prussia.

France, 1660. The French writer Paul Scarron dies. He earned his living from writing after contracting a disease which ultimately left him paralysed. He wrote sonnets, madrigals, epistles, and satires, but will be best remembered for his realistic novel *Le Roman Comique* (The Comic Novel) which was a reaction against the lengthy, flowery works of such writers as Mlle de Scudery and Honore d'Urfe.

France, 1660. Louis XIV of France marries Maria Teresa, *infanta* of Spain. The musician Francesco Cavalli, who studied under Monteverdi, composes the opera *Serse* in honour of the occasion.

England, 1660. The English writer James Howell publishes *Lexicon Tetraglotten*, an English, French, Italian and Spanish dictionary. Howell was a royalist spy between 1632 and 1642, and was imprisoned by the parliamentarians from 1642 to 1650. At the Restoration, the office of historiographer-royal was created for him.

Netherlands, 1660. Jacob Cats, the Dutch statesman and poet, dies aged 67. Known as "Father Cats", he served twice as ambassador to England, and has spent the last eight years of his life writing his autobiography.

England, 1660. James, the duke of York, becomes Lord High Admiral.

France, 23 April 1661. To fight against Jansenism – a puritanical movement calling for moral and doctrinal reform – a decree from the council orders all members of religious communities to sign a statement conforming to the papal condemnation of the five propositions in Jansen's *Augustinus*.

France, September 1661. Nicolas Fouquet, the superintendent of state finances, is arrested in Nantes at the instigation of Louis XIV. Jean-Baptiste Colbert, who worked for Mazarin until his death earlier this year, and has been agitating for Fouquet's arrest, replaces him.

Italy, 1661. The Italian physiologist Marcello Malpighi observes the flow of blood in the capillaries of a frog's lungs. He confirms William Harvey's theory of the circulation of blood.

Rhode Island, 1661. The Quakers hold their first annual meeting. Also known as the Society of Friends, this newly-emerged sect was founded by George Fox during the Puritan revolution in England. Fox taught that the essence of Christianity was the "inward light" in every man that needs no minister, sacraments or liturgy.

England, 1661. The Irish physicist and chemist Robert Boyle rejects Aristotle's theory of the elements. In his work *The Sceptical Chymist*, he defines simple and primitive bodies and complex bodies. As a physicist, he also improves von Guericke's pump, so that he can demonstrate the necessity of air in respiration and combustion.

Massachusetts, 1661. The first church for the Indians is founded by the pastor John Eliot who began preaching to the Indians in their own language 15 years ago. He also publishes the first bible in the colonies: the New Testament in the Algonquin language.

China, 1661. The Manchu dynasty, which was still being opposed around 1655 by the last Ming partisans, is now recognised throughout China. Shunzhi, the first Manchu ruler, succeeds in the normal way.

Amsterdam, 1661. The brilliant Dutch painter Rembrandt receives his most important commission to date, a gigantic canvas, roughly five and a half yards square: it is to be entitled the *Conspiracy of Claudius Civilus*.

India, 1661. The Portuguese cede the island of Bombay to Charles II as part of the dowry of his queen, Catherine of Braganza. With its fine natural harbour, Bombay has the potential to become a major port for the English, and is their first independent territory in India.

Traveller's gloomy impressions of India

Aurangzeb sits in state surrounded by his courtiers: reports from India tell of a tyrant who puts self-indulgent luxury above the national interest.

Delhi, India, 1660

As the Moghul empire empties its treasury in pursuit of architectural extravagance and aristocratic luxuries, the Indian peasantry, inevitably, pays the price.

The Indo-Persian city of Agra, the Red Fort at Delhi and the Taj Mahal may all be beautiful, but to a French traveller, Francois Bernier, employed in the Moghul court in the final years of Shahjahan and the early years of Aurangzeb, they epitomise tyranny.

It is a tyranny "often so excessive as to deprive the peasant and artisan of the necessaries of life, leaving them to die in misery and ex-haustion; a tyranny so excessive men and women prefer to be barren than witness their children die of starvation; a tyranny that drives the farmer from the land, into exile or military service."

Houses fall apart, irrigation canals fall in, there is no will to make repairs. "The country is ruined by the necessity of defraying the cost of the enormous court and army maintained to keep the people in subjection. No adequate idea can be given of how these people suffer. The cudgel and whip compel them to labour for the benefit of their rulers. Ruin and desolation overspread the land," he writes.

Chinese pirate makes base in Taiwan and evicts Dutch

Taiwan, 1661
Koxinga, the son of a Chinese pirate and a Japanese mother, has defeated the Dutch garrison on Taiwan and expelled the Dutch traders from the island.

Athough he was overwhelmingly superior in numbers, Koxinga was unable to storm Fort Zeelandia, a powerful fortress built with bricks imported from Holland. Exasperated by his failure, he wrote to the Dutch commander: "You Dutch people, a few thousand in number, how can you carry on war against us, who are so powerful by our numbers? Really, it is as if you were bereft of your senses."

Eventually he settled down to siege warfare and starved out the defenders. He showed mercy and allowed them to sail away with their possessions. He plans to use Taiwan as a base for an attack on the mainland in the hope of restoring the Mings.

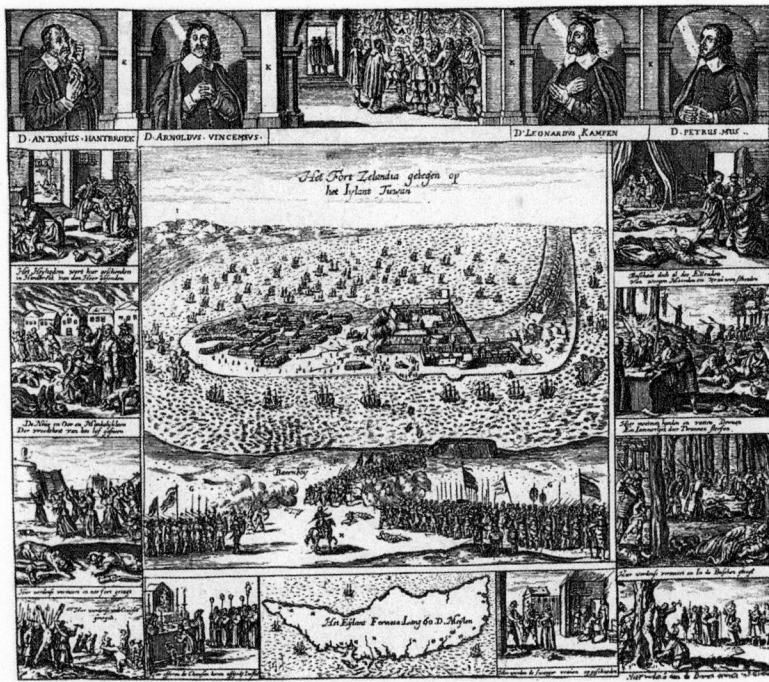

A map of the island of Taiwan, surrounded by pictures which tell the story of Holland's conquest of the island and the colonisation that followed.

Sea trade fuels war on shores of Baltic

Copenhagen, 1660
The conflict between Denmark and Sweden is over, at least for a while. The two countries have signed the Peace of Copenhagen, under which the Danes abandon claims to southern Sweden. This ends the war that began in 1658 with Sweden's attack on Denmark.

As the two countries glower at each other across the narrow sound which allows North Sea traffic to enter and leave the Baltic Sea, the eyes of the Europe are on Sweden and its domination of this inland sea. Charles X is dead, and, as his infant son Charles XI succeeds to the throne, Russia is looking for a foothold on the Baltic coast.

For all the wars that have plagued Europe, the Baltic, like that other inland sea, the Mediterranean, has been a vital route for seaborne trade, especially with the south. From the Levant come the wine, fruit and olive oil that cannot be produced in the north; and the north produces iron, copper and salt-herrings, a vital source of food. The Baltic also supplies the rest of Europe with grain, wood and other naval supplies in great demand. The economic and strategic importance of the Baltic also explains the support of other European states for Denmark when Sweden threatened its neighbour across the sound. The greatest support came from Holland. The Dutch, like other major trading nations, are always anxious lest the narrow, shallow sound which is the only entrance to the Baltic might fall under the control of only one nation.

Charles and the monarchy return to England by popular consent

"The Procession of Charles II" by Dirck Stoop: eleven years after his father was executed by Parliament, the people have called on Charles to restore the Stuart dynasty to its place at the head of English society.

England, 26 May 1660
After eleven years of rule by self-righteous factions in the shadow of the military, England has gained a form of government desired by the vast majority of citizens. Charles II, who landed at Dover today and made a festive journey to London, arrives not as a conqueror, but as a constitutional monarch. The Restoration is the restoration of parliamentary government.

Charles displayed unexpected shrewdness. Cromwell's death had left the nation rudderless. His son Richard was weak and soon gave up. By the end of last year it was recognised that the only solution was restoration. The question was: on what terms?

In Paris, Henrietta Maria, the queen mother, though a Catholic, was intriguing with Calvinists to gain control over her son. But Charles refused to visit her and instead issued a declaration at Breda to the English parliamentarians, saying that he supported liberty of conscience, a general amnesty for past deeds, full arrears of pay for all ranks in the army and full cooperation with parliament. Greatly relieved, MPs accepted these terms and proclaimed Charles king.

Serfs turn robbers under czar's new laws

Russia, 1660
A new danger faces travellers in rural Russia: the rapacious activities of robber bands of renegade serfs who survive by killing and theft. The upsurge of violence in the Russian countryside follows years of famine and plague. Observers also blame the tightening up of the laws on serfdom 12 years ago for making the situation worse.

Under the 1648 Code of Law enacted by Czar Alexis the time limits in which a lord could take legal proceedings to recover a fugitive peasant were abolished so that the right of recovery now lasts for a peasant's life. The code also extends the principle of binding a peasant to land to include the whole family, including sons and nephews. In the past the only person bound had been the head of the household. For heavily taxed peasants living on the edge of bankruptcy, the laws have closed off the last legal means of escape, suddenly making life as a fugitive an attractive alternative.

1661 (1661-1662)

France, 9 March 1661. Cardinal Mazarin, the king's prime minister, dies at Vincennes. Louis XIV confirms his wish to rule personally, without the assistance of a prime minister.

France, 1661. Philip, the duke of Orleans, marries Henrietta Anne, the sister of Charles II, the newly restored English king.

Russia, 1661. The peace of Kardis confirms the preliminary treaty made at Valiesar in 1659 which ended the Northern War between Russia and Sweden (1655-1660). The treaty restores the *status quo* between the two countries, with Russia surrendering all gains it has made in the Baltic provinces.

West Africa, 1661. The English capture Fort James in the Gambia and begin a rapid expansion of the slave trade.

Virginia, 1661. A law is passed which assumes that some Negroes must serve as slaves for life. Previously, Negroes were held for periods of indenture, as many white servants are. Last year the first law acknowledging slavery as an institution was passed, bringing in a tax on tobacco grown with the help of slaves imported by foreigners.

England, 1661. Matthew Locke, who composed the music for Charles II's coronation procession, is appointed composer-in-ordinary to the king.

Netherlands, 1661. The Dutch physicist Christiaan Huygens invents the manometer, an instrument for measuring pressure in gases and liquids.

India, 1661. There is widespread famine in India where there has been scarcely any rain since 1659.

Turkey, 1661. Koprulu Mehmed Koprulu, the grand vizier of Turkey, dies and is succeeded by his son Koprulu Fazil Ahmed.

London, 1661. Sir William d'Avenant, poet and dramatist, opens the Lincoln's Inn Theatre, with Shakespeare's *Hamlet* as the first production.

Tibet, 1661. Two Jesuit missionaries reach the Tibetan capital.

England, 1661. The Dutch artist Peter Lely is made court painter by Charles II. A man of broad sympathies, Lely has also worked for both Charles I and Oliver Cromwell.

France, 1662. Louis XIV, France's "Sun King", draws up plans for a magnificent palace to be built at Versailles, just outside Paris. The palace is to be a sumptuous new residence for the court; Charles Lebrun is the artistic adviser.

England, 1662. Elizabeth of Bohemia, the "Winter Queen", dies in England. The daughter of King James of England and his wife Anne of Denmark, Elizabeth married Frederick V, the elector Palatine, who was elected king of Bohemia in 1618. After the defeat of Bohemian forces at the battle of the White Mountain in 1620, the couple took refuge with Frederick's uncle, Maurice of Nassau. But Frederick died in 1632 and Elizabeth was only rescued from deepening poverty last year by Lord Craven, a former servant and friend, who invited her to England.

England, 1662. The English author Samuel Butler writes the first part of *Hudibras*, a satire on Puritanism which brings him instant popularity.

France, 1662. The dramatist Moliere's new comedy *L'Ecole des femmes* draws the crowds.

London, 1662. The Act of Uniformity is passed, stating that Church services are to be conducted in accordance with the revised prayer book. This is part of the Clarendon Code, a series of measures named after Charles II's chief minister, Edward Hyde, the first earl of Clarendon, aimed at reinstating Anglicanism as the official religion after the Restoration.

England, 1662. *Worthies of England* by the English antiquarian and divine Thomas Fuller, is published one year after his death by his son. It took 20 years to research and write. Fuller was a royalist who wrote several books in defence of the cause and was appointed chaplain to the king in 1660.

London, 1662. Charles II gives a royal charter to the Royal Society, founded to promote scientific knowledge. The society emerged from meetings of scientists and philosophers which were first held in 1645, and was formally established in 1660.

Paris, 1662. Francesco Cavalli's ballet opera *Ercole Amante* is performed in Paris.

England, 1662. An Act of Settlement is passed. A poor law, designed to curb vagrancy, it allows parish overseers to force homeless, unemployed people to return to their native parish.

England, 1662. The hearth tax is introduced, levied at the rate of two shillings per hearth fire. It is an attempt by the government to replace surviving feudal dues with a regular source of revenue, but it proves extremely unpopular.

France, 1662. The marquis de Louvois is appointed secretary of state and minister of war jointly with his father, Michel le Tellier.

Diarist pens attack on London pollution

London Bridge, from Visscher's map of London, originally printed in 1650.

London, 1661

Living in London is unhealthy, especially for the lungs, according to John Evelyn, English country gentleman, author and diarist.

Evelyn has been recording his impressions of places, people and contemporary events in Britain since he was 11. He has also travelled extensively in Europe. Few can match his erudition, and he is an influential figure in his country's cultural, political and religious life.

Now 41, and firmly in favour at the court of King Charles II, Evelyn is directing his energies into social issues. He has been active on a number of royal commissions and makes his views known on important issues of the day.

Pollution is a new crusade for his restless pen. There are, he complains, too many factories burning huge amounts of coal. He calls for various environmental countermeasures, such as the planting of shrubs and trees and the removal of industrial sites to beyond the city limits.

Unfortunately, Evelyn's plan for cleaner, sweeter air seems to be going unheeded. There is, as yet, no prospect of laws being passed to control pollution.

Danish king declares his power absolute

Copenhagen, January 1661

Faced by an angry aristocracy, but backed by the country's burghers and common people, Frederick III of Denmark has declared himself an absolute monarch, "above all human laws and knowing no other superior beings or judge over him ... save God alone".

The Swedish siege of Copenhagen is now two years old. Two days before it began, Frederick called his burghers together and announced far-reaching changes in their status. In the first place, they could control taxation. They could have access to offices of state hitherto reserved for nobility. And they could buy land on an equal footing with nobles who, at that point, were said to be "running like hares", desperate to save their fortunes from the Swedes. The city gates had to be closed to stop them leaving and the country was placed under temporary military control.

Iroquois struggle for fur monopoly

North America, c.1662

The Indian tribes of North America are locked into a relentless war for a highly lucrative prize: the profitable fur trade with France.

Since the start of this century the Huron Indians have built up their own "empire", in which for many years they had a virtual monopoly of the trade. This changed in 1640 when another tribe, the Iroquois, decided to challenge the Huron.

Taking advantage of the war in Europe between France and the Netherlands, the Iroquois enlisted Dutch aid and armaments and began a campaign against their rivals which has proved highly successful. Attempts by a band of missionaries to calm their hostility failed completely – the Iroquois massacred the agents of peace.

In 1649, still on the warpath, they began wiping out Huron villages, killing all in their path. The situation has only stablised with the arrival of Europeans of both sides, determined to end the bloodbath and restore normality.

Mazarin, France's second king, dies

Paris, 10 March 1661

Cardinal Mazarin, who has ruled France virtually as a monarch, died yesterday, and today the 22-year-old king Louis XIV assumed full power over his kingdom. There can be no doubt of his intentions, for he has already given his orders.

Today he told the chancellor: "I request and order you to seal no orders except by my command." And later, when the president of the Assembly of Clergy asked to whom he should apply for the settlement of business, the king replied: "To me, Monsieur the Archbishop, to me."

It is obvious that the king has learnt well under Mazarin and intends to put his lessons to good use in his rule of the powerful nation bequeathed him by Richelieu and Mazarin. His recognition of the debt that he owes to Mazarin, who may have secretly married his mother, is marked by his ordering full mourning for the dead minister.

Popes gild Rome in Baroque style

St Peter's throne, by Bernini: the focus of the great Roman basilica.

Rome, c.1662

Rome has been transformed into a city of elegant splendour under the last three Popes, Urban VIII, Innocent X and Alexander VII. Gianlorenzo Bernini, Europe's leading sculptor and architect, is now creating a new setting for St Peter's with a vast oval piazza surrounded by colonnades which encircle it, he says, "like the mother church embracing the world".

The balustrades above the 60-foot (18m) columns are lined with statues of saints like those on the main facade of St Peter's, which was completed in 1612 by Carlo Maderna, the pioneer of a new, highly decorative style. Inside the church, Bernini has completed an elaborate bronze throne of St Peter.

Bernini's sculpture is also beautifying the city with his fountains, like that of the Triton in the Piazza Barberini, and those in the Piazza Navona whose figures seem as alive as the water that courses among them. His *Ecstasy of St Teresa* in the Cornaro chapel illustrates the harmonious technique, showing the saint elevated at the moment of holy rapture.

This style, which some call "Baroque" (from the Spanish meaning "rough") is spreading throughout the whole of Italy. The Venetian republic has commissioned the church of Santa Maria della Salute to be built at the end of the Grand Canal in thanksgiving for Venice's deliverance from the plague of 1630.

"The Glory of the Barberinis": Cortona's ceiling at the Barberini Palace.

Bernini's "Ecstasy of St Teresa".

Charles II in marble, by Pelle.

Europe's Scientific Revolution

In the years spanned by the lives of Galileo (1564-1642) and Newton (1642-1727) European scientific thought flowered to produce some profound and far-reaching changes. This was the age in which the ascendancy of the physical sciences irreversibly challenged the mediaeval approach to knowledge, derived from long-established Aristotelian methods and notions. The very word science, from the Latin *scientia*, altered in meaning from simply "knowledge" to "systematically formulated knowledge, based on observation and experiment", to paraphrase the Oxford English Dictionary.

The British philosopher Bertrand Russell wrote thus of what he called this "century of genius": "Almost everything that distinguished the modern world from earlier centuries is attributable to science, which achieved its most spectacular triumphs in the 17th century". This was the era that produced, for example, Sir Isaac Newton, whose conception of the workings of the universe was to remain unchallenged until well into the 20th century when Einstein's theories began – after nearly 300 years – to steer thoughts in a different direction.

New values for old?

The 17th century saw the destruction of barriers to learning that had remained solid for many centuries. However, at the same time, the great innovators such as Galileo, Newton and Johannes Kepler (1571-1630) were able to marry their new-found knowledge and methods of inquiry to old beliefs, some of which would now be regarded as of an intellectually dubious nature. Often the very same scientist who declared the supremacy of observation and reasoning would adhere to such practices as alchemy, astrology and numerology.

Although the scientific view of the world called into question some basic tenets of orthodox religious beliefs, the two were not necessarily in direct conflict. Even Galileo, whose views on the structure of the universe brought him into direct confrontation with the established church, was not insisting that the destruction of the ancient concept of a cosmos centred on Earth – an idea mainly derived from the work of the Alexandrian geographer and mathematician Claudius Ptolemy (90-168) – meant that the Bible was wrong. He merely believed that it was open to interpretation and should not be taken literally.

Similarly, when during this period the study of geology and the discovery of ancient fossils put a question mark over the notion of a fairly recent Creation, the scientists involved were not being "irreligious". They did not question the fact that God made the world: they were just wondering how to reconcile their findings with the biblical stories. Moreover, many eminent men of science were also men of the cloth, and several fellows of England's Royal Society were bishops – even though the society was frequently attacked as being hostile to the church's teachings.

Not all those who rejected the authoritarian view of knowledge – that it was handed down and should not be questioned – necessarily espoused the new ideas that were becoming influential among scientists. Francis Bacon (1561-1626), for example, whose treatise *Advancement of learning* exerted immense influence throughout Europe, proclaimed a new scientific method. But, in reality, his intellectual roots were in the 16th century, with his dislike of the view of the universe propounded by Nicholas Copernicus (1473-1543) and his lack of interest in linking science and mathematics.

Impact of technology

An important driving force behind many of the new scientific ideas in the 17th century was the development of new technology. The growing needs of trade and navigation prompted an interest in astronomy, and that in turn gave impetus to the work of, among others, Newton, Kepler and Tycho Brahe (1546-1601). The manufacture of spectacles in Holland and Italy underpinned the invention of the telescope and microscope. The mining industry in Holland, Germany and Hungary produced a need for pumps to drain mines, which in turn led to the air pumps developed by Otto von Guericke (1602-86) and the research into gases of Robert Boyle (1627-91). The notion of a pump, too, inspired the famous work on the circulation of the blood, *On the workings of the heart* (1628), by William Harvey (1578-1657).

With the invention of new types of watermills, windmills, pumps, cranes and clocks, came a growing feeling that the universe might best be explained in mechanical terms: the older view of the world as a moral order was no longer quite so attractive. With the new technologies came discoveries that made former ways of looking at the world untenable; the telescope, for instance, led to many observations of stars and planets that were difficult to reconcile with an Aristotelian or Ptolemaic world picture. Things were becoming too complicated for existing theories. Alternative theories had to be found to fit the facts as they had been observed.

Another important trend in this period was the passion for quantitative measurements. Galileo invented the thermometer; Evangelista Toricelli (1608-47) the barometer; Edmund Gunter (1581-1626) the slide rule and Christiaan Huygens (1629-95) the pendulum clock. As a consequence of these developments, the physical world began to be described with increasing mathematical accuracy.

Proving the rules

What really distinguishes the science of this century, though, is the emphasis on experimentation. This is not to say that the Greek or mediaeval scholars never carried out experiments. They did, but not to any great extent; they preferred mental experiments to hands-on practice, with the result that they often failed to put their hypotheses and theories to the physical test. On the other hand, the philosophy of science which became increasingly prevalent in the 17th century was above all experimental. As Bacon wrote: "Nature, like a witness, reveals her secrets when put to torture."

One factor which certainly contributed to the spread of the new ideas on experimentation, observation and rational deduction was the formation of societies or academies. One of the earliest was the Roman *Academia dei Lincei* founded in 1601. Later in the century came the Royal Society in London (1662), which partly inspired the French *Academie des Sciences*, founded in 1666 by Colbert, Louis XIV's powerful finance minister. Not only did these bodies disseminate ideas internally but also forged links with other countries in Europe.

A new moral order

By the end of the century the "Scientific Revolution" was complete. It was no longer possible to regard the universe as a moral order of absolute values. Newtonian physics had replaced this with a notion of God as the Grand Designer, a great watchmaker whose cosmos was an immense, finely tuned machine running according to laws and principles that were being established through experiment and observation. Religion was not dead. But it now had to exist alongside an equally powerful set of values.

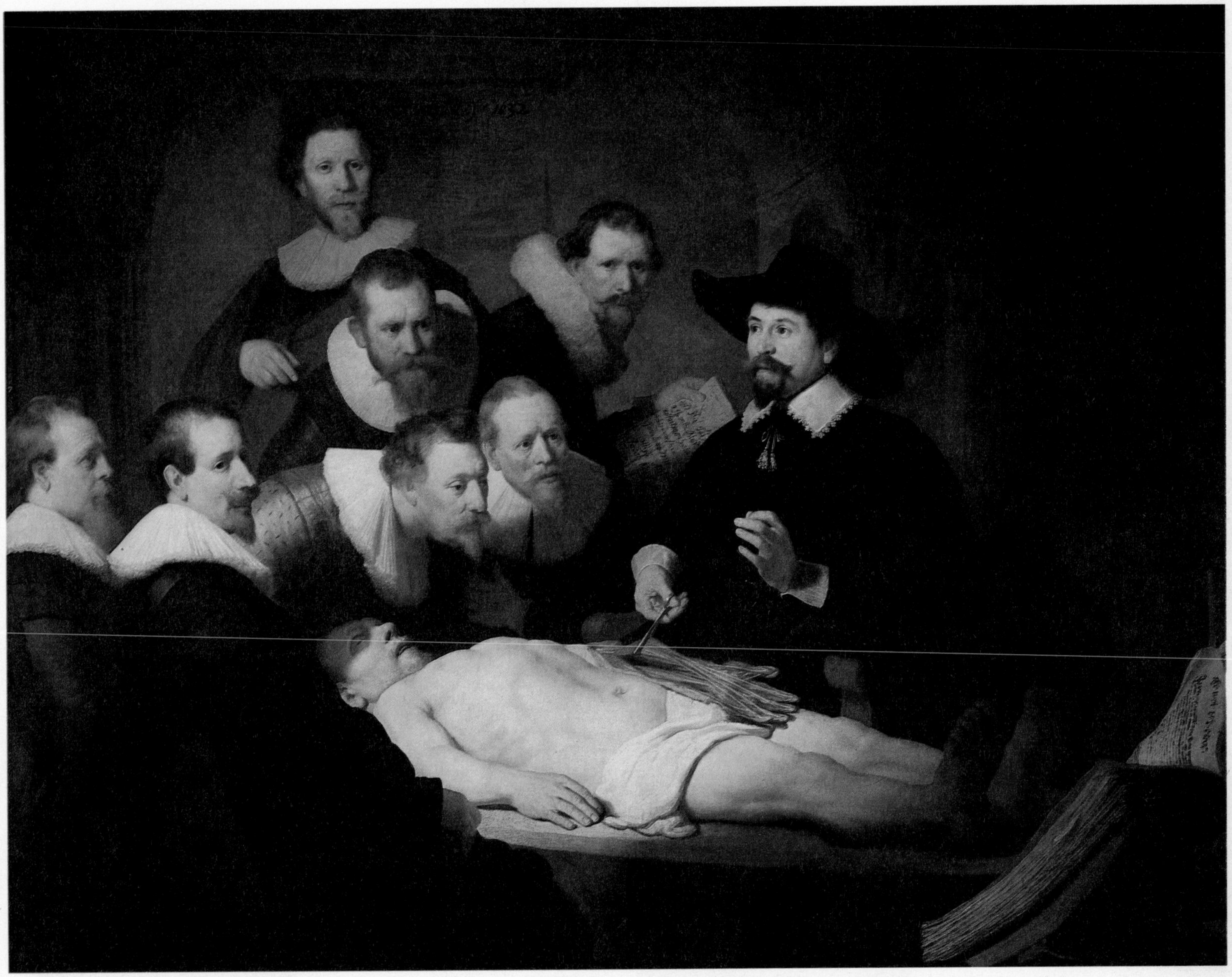

"Dr Tulp's anatomy lesson", by Rembrandt (1606-69). The human anatomy fascinated scientists like Harvey, who discovered blood circulation.

Italian microscope, of wood, cardboard and tooled leather, c.1675.

The world's first reflecting telescope, made by Sir Isaac Newton in 1671.

Copy of a 17th-century thermometer designed by scientists in Florence.

English clock of 1688, worked by pendulum rather than balance wheel.

1662 (1662-1664)

London, 3 May 1662. John Winthrop the Younger, the son of the first governor of Massachusetts, has been honoured by being made a fellow of the Royal Society, England's new scientific society. Winthrop has used his election to the society to gain access to the king, who has granted him a new charter uniting the colonies of Connecticut and New Haven.

Paris, 19 August 1662. The French mathematician, theologian and physicist Blaise Pascal dies aged 39. A passionate supporter of the predestinarian Jansenist movement, whose sister was one of the leading membe of the Jansenist Convent at Port Royal, Pascal wrote 18 anonymous pamphlets attacking the Jesuits, prime opponents of Jansenism. When he realised he was dying he asked to be moved to the hospital for incurables so that he could die there in the company of the poor.

England, 12 September 1662. Governor Berkeley of Virginia, in England seeking the revision of the Navigation Acts which severely restrict foreign trade with the colonies, gets a final denial to his appeal.

Amsterdam, 1662. Rembrandt paints *The Syndics*.

France, 1662. England cedes Dunkirk to France for a payment of £ 400,000.

Paris, 1662. Francois, the duke of la Rochefoucauld, publishes his *Memoires*. Destined for an army career, he was involved with the intrigues against Richelieu, which earned him a spell in the Bastille prison in 1637. Hostile to Mazarin, in 1648 he joined in the *Fronde* uprising. Now, re-admitted to favour, he commences a worldly life at court and in the salons.

Japan, 1662. The philosopher Yamaga Soko takes against his masters in a violent way and burns all the books he has written.

China, 1662. The Emperor Kangxi succeeds Shunzhi, who was the first Manchu ruler.

London, 24 March 1663. Charles II awards lands known as Carolina in North America to eight members of the nobility who assisted in his restoration. One of the fortunate is Lord Ashley, who, with the assistance of the philosopher John Locke, has devised a new form of government considered to be one of the most unusual colonial systems so far. It will grant nobility to any person in a position to buy 3,000 acres of land.

England, 8 July 1663. The crown grants Rhode Island a charter guaranteeing freedom of worship.

London, 27 July 1663. Parliament passes a second Navigation Act, requiring all goods for the colonies to travel in British ships from British ports. An extension of the 1651 act, it aims to make England and its colonies less dependent on foreign trade. It is unlikely that the new act will significantly curtail the flourishing smugglers' trade which has developed in response to the earlier restrictions.

Angola, December 1663. The princess dona Ana de Souza dies.

New Netherland, 1663. One Laurens Duyts is sentenced to be flogged and have his right ear cut off for selling his wife.

London, 1663. The Dutch physicist Christiaan Huygens becomes a member of the Royal Society.

North America, 1663. Witches are said to be attempting to undermine the new communities struggling to establish themselves in America. In Connecticut alone, ten offenders have been hanged for "familiarity with the Devil". Strangely, Rhode Island, which is criticised for religious tolerance by the Puritans, has escaped the witches' grasp.

London, 22 March 1664. Charles II has given large tracts of land, from the west of the Connecticut river to the east of Delaware Bay in North America, to his brother James, the duke of York. Much of the land has been claimed by the Dutch, but James has urged the king to help him conquer the New Netherlands, arguing that the continuing presence of Dutch colonists is inhibiting the enforcement of the Navigation Act, which promotes a British monopoly on colonial trade.

New Jersey, 24 June 1664. The area between the Hudson and Delaware rivers is named New Jersey in honour of the new proprietor, Sir George Carteret, the ex-governor of the Isle of Jersey.

Massachusetts, 23 July 1664. Wealthy non-church members get the right to vote.

New Netherlands, July 1664. The Dongan treaty makes the Iroquois subjects of the English king.

Madrid, 27 August 1664. Famous and sought-after in earlier years, the religious painter Francisco Zurbaran dies in poverty and neglect.

France, 1664. Armand de Rance reforms the Trappist order of monks in Soligny, instituting the rule of silence.

New Netherlands, 1664. Horse racing becomes the first organised sport in north America, as Governor Nicolls establishes the Newmarket course at Hempstead plains, Long Island.

Vengeful Russians terrorise Persians

Persia, 1664

In Mazandaran and the Ashurada peninula, by the shores of the Caspian Sea, the populace is living in terror of the notorious robber-baron Stenka Razin and his marauding Cossacks. Their raids have exacerbated Persian fear and loathing of their Russian neighbours.

The present troubles are the result of a diplomatic mission to the Persian court earlier in the year. The mission, which had 800 followers, was a pretext for Russian traders to evade duty on large quantities of merchandise which they had brought with them, and this aroused Persian resentment. When the Russian ambassadors were rudely treated, and one died, Czar Alexis Mikhailovitch sanctioned the Cossack raids in reprisal.

Star wars sentence Jesuit to execution

Looking at an eclipse in China.

Beijing, 1664

Adam Schall, a Jesuit missionary who has spent all his adult life in China, has been condemned to death by dismemberment after being found guilty of accusations made against him by a jealous Chinese astronomer whose calculations he proved to be wrong.

At one stage Schall, who wore the robes of a Chinese scholar and spoke perfect Chinese, was appointed director of the Bureau of Astronomy. But his influence faded, perhaps because he tried too persistently to convert the emperor and his foes. Other missionaries, who thought that he was too Chinese, and jealous Chinese astronomers began to undermine him in Rome and in Beijing.

The Chinese accused him of preparing a Christian revolution and he was found guilty. He is old and ill and it is unlikely that he will be executed, but his lifelong work is certain to be destroyed.

New prayerbook is a must for clergy

England, 1662

A new edition of the Book of Common Prayer, first composed in 1549 by the Protestant martyr Thomas Cranmer, has been issued. As part of the Act of Uniformity, which is designed to restore the Anglican Church to the status it enjoyed before the Commonwealth, the prayerbook is to be imposed on all congregations.

Any clergyman who has not accepted the revised Prayerbook by St Bartholemew's Day (24 August) will forfeit his living. It is expected that a number will still resist, but the bishops, outlawed by Cromwell and restored by King Charles, are determined to reinstitute their authority come what may.

Essays on women's equality published

England, 1662

Women's liberation is the subject of the duchess of Newcastle's latest book, *Orations of Diverse Persons*. The author, better known as the playwright and essayist Margaret Cavendish, concludes that women are the powerful sex, although their domination of men comes through the wiles of love.

Margaret Cavendish was born in 1624, the daughter of Sir Thomas Lucas. She spent two unhappy years at Charles I's court, and in 1645 married Newcastle, a royalist. While they lived in exile in Paris, she wrote poetry, her autobiography, and philosophy. She returned to England after the Restoration to gain a reputation as a popular writer and court eccentric.

Royal Society founded

Leading figures in science, philosophy and the arts are joining the Royal Society: Isaac Newton, Christopher Wren, Robert Boyle and John Locke.

London, 1662
Several groups of scientists have formed a society dedicated to the pursuit of learning. The principal group is that of John Wilkins, which dates back to Oxford in the 1650s and includes such luminaries as John Wallis the mathematician, the chemist and physicist Robert Boyle, the medical researcher Thomas Willis and the great polymath and architect Christopher Wren. These have been joined by people associated with Gresham College and a number of interested and influential royalists.

The society's principal aim is to act as a centre of intellectual debate and excellence, dedicated to scientific enterprise. This will mean, among other things, the financing of buildings, scientific instruments, laboratories and a library. The new Royal Society, as it has been named, levies an annual subscription on its members in order to maintain its independence and to publish a journal called *Philosophical Transactions*.

The society excludes such topics as theology and rhetoric and emphasises instead the "useful arts", such as the work of navigators and engineers, as well as academic scientists. Distinguished contemporary writers, Samuel Pepys among them, are beginning to subscribe. The meetings and lectures are lively and provide a focal point for the most eminent men to air their views, free from any government intervention. In France, a royal academy of sciences may be founded along similar lines.

Gas said to grow when it's on the boil

London, 1662
The Anglo-Irish chemist and physicist Robert Boyle has formulated an important law governing the compression and expansion of gases kept at constant temperatures. The law states that the pressure of a given quantity of gas varies inversely with its volume provided that the temperature is kept constant. Boyle, aged 35, has arrived at this formulation after numerous experiments at Oxford where he has been helped by the inventor Robert Hooke.

However, this is not Boyle's only achievement. He has also shown the crucial role of air in combustion, breathing, the circulation of the blood and the transmission of sound. His is a wide-ranging curiosity. He is concerned about the behaviour of gases and the nature of chemical substances, and also is investigating the freezing of water, the refractive properties of glass and the nature of electricity.

The apparatus used by Boyle and his colleague Robert Hooke.

"Great Elector" has firm hold on Prussia

Prussia, 1663
Frederick William is proving himself to be the "Great Elector" of Brandenburg, which has become the heart of the powerful Prussian kingdom. The elector (ruler) took over his country when he was only 20, and is energetically laying the foundations of what could prove to be military greatness for the region.

Frederick has dealt firmly with the *diet*, (parliament), and has taken on himself the responsibility of raising and collecting taxes. This money is being used to build a formidable standing army. He is also improving his country by encouraging industry, building canals and developing a postal system, and he is greatly interested in the arts.

Transvestite highway robber reveals all

London, 1662
Moll Cutpurse died in 1659, aged 75, leaving a full account of her criminal life. The book, published this year, tells how Mary Frith, the cobbler's daughter from the Barbican, became Moll, the famous highway robber.

Always armed and dressed as a man, Moll made an illicit fortune. Jailed only once, for robbing General Fairfax on Hounslow Heath, she escaped by paying a £2,000 bribe. Moll enraged her victims by opening a shop in Fleet Street where they had to pay to recover their own possessions.

Robber Moll in her usual costume.

Nuns of Port Royal defy Louis XIV

Port Royal, France, 26 August 1664
The nuns of the convent of Port Royal, the centre of Jansenist belief, are defying both their king and the pope and refusing to accept the "Formulaire", under which they are to renounce their beliefs. Some have signed the paper, but they have demanded an extra clause, stating the distinction between what they accept as law and what they actually believe.

As Jansenists, the sisters follow the teachings of St Augustine, with their stress on "original sin" and "irresistible grace".

Mother Agnes of Port Royal kneels to pray at the side of another sister.

1664 (1664-1665)

Hungary, 1 August 1664. A Turkish army is defeated at St Gotthard by French and German troops led by the imperial commander Montecuccoli. The battle is hailed as a triumph of Christianity over the infidel.

New Amsterdam, 5 September 1664. After several days of tense negotiation, the Dutch settlement of New Amsterdam has surrendered, without firing a shot, to British forces. The British move was ordered by King Charles II, and took the Dutch quite by surprise. Britain now controls ports from Virginia to Massachusetts, and will be better able to enforce the Navigation Act, which provides for a British monopoly on colonial trade.

Maryland, September 1664. In the latest of a series of laws dealing with slavery, marriages between white women and black men are declared a disgrace to the nation, and the children of such unions are ruled to be slaves.

Carolina, November 1664. Proprietors split the northern part of the colony into the counties of Albemarle and Clarendon.

France, 1664. The French East India Company is founded.

Netherlands, 1664. The Dutch artist Franz Hals paints the *Governors of the Old Men's Home at Haarlem*, a magnificent group portrait.

France, 12 January 1665. The French mathematician Pierre de Fermat dies at Toulouse. He made many discoveries in the theory of numbers, worked out a simple method of quadrating parabolas, and established a method of calculating probabilities.

New York, 11 March 1665. A new legal code is approved for the Dutch and English towns of New York, guaranteeing all Protestants the right to continue their religious observances unhindered.

Spain, 17 September 1665. King Philip IV has just died. Despite his many mistresses and his playboy reputation, it has been said that he laughed only three times in his life. Velazquez, who painted numerous portraits of him, was his only friend. He is succeeded by Charles II, a sickly four-year-old prince, under the regency of Marie-Anne.

Virginia, December 1665. Two actors, brought to trial for frivolity in the first play in the English colonies, *Ye Bare and Ye Cubb*, are acquitted, having performed much of the play to a delighted court.

America, 1665. There are about 75,000 English colonists in the New World, compared with 7,500 French settlers.

Angola, 1665. The Portuguese colonists based in Angola invade the Kongo, but are unable to subdue local resistance.

Paris, 1665. La Rochefoucauld publishes his *Maximes*, which cause a scandal on account of the decidedly pessimistic view of man that they reveal. They condemn the selfish motivation behind passions, feelings and social relationships: "Our virtues are often no more than disguised vices."

Japan, 1665. Yamaga Soko, a controversial leading scholar, publishes a short book, entitled *Essentials of the Sacred Teachings*, which questions accepted interpretations of Confucian thought. As an attack on the ideological foundation of the *shogunate*, the book is banned and Soko is banished from Edo and placed in the custody of the lord of Ako.

Indian Ocean, 1665. The French take Bourbon Island (*Reunion*).

Italy, 1665. The Italian Jesuit and physicist Francesco Grimaldi's *Physicomathesis de Lumine* demonstrating the diffraction of light, is published posthumously. He is also remembered for elaborating on the topography of the moon.

Rome, 1665. The French painter Nicolas Poussin dies in the city where he has spent most of his life. His work has made him a major figure in French classicism.

Portugal, 1665. The Spaniards are crushed at the battle of Montes Claros by the marquis of Marialva.

England, 1665. The scientist Isaac Newton conducts experiments with the force which attracts things to earth.

Netherlands, 1665. The Dutch are at war with Britain for the second time this decade. English attacks on Dutch slave traders in West Africa in 1663, and the taking of New Amsterdam (now renamed New York) last year, have provoked this renewed conflict.

Netherlands, 1665. The Dutch artist Jan Vermeer paints the *Lacemaker* and *Young Woman with Water Jug* in Delft.

England, 1665. The English chemist and physicist Robert Hooke discovers that plants "breathe" and that they contain living cells.

Ethiopia, 1665. Johannes succeeds King Fazilidas.

Italy, 1665. The Italian astronomer Giovanni Cassini determines the periods of Jupiter, Mars and Venus.

England, 1665. Peter Chamberlen, the court physician to Charles II, invents the midwifery forceps.

Spain's playboy king, Philip IV, is dead

Madrid, 17 September 1665

Philip IV, the king who preferred the theatre in Madrid to the theatre of world politics, died today after a 44-year reign during which his country gradually declined.

From the very beginning of his reign Philip handed over power to favourites, the count of Olivares in particular, preferring to spend his time in the company of actresses selected as companions by his agents. While the king thus dallied at court, Olivares committed Spain abroad to tasks beyond her strength and there were frequent setbacks. The Netherlands were never reconquered, Spain lost a war with France, and Catalonia and Portugal both revolted.

Philip, who was 60, had numerous mistresses, by whom he had at least 30 bastards, but the throne passes to his only legitimate son, Charles II, a sickly child.

Philip: mistresses and misfortune.

Priest is lowered into volcano for science

Kircher's picture of the fires that burn deep within the Earth's core.

Germany, 1665

Athanasius Kircher, the gifted and energetic German Jesuit priest and scholar, has had himself lowered into the crater of the volcano Vesuvius in order to observe its features and behaviour in the aftermath of an eruption.

Among his ideas is the notion that Earth has a fiery core. In his geological textbook *The Subterranean World*, Kircher describes our planet in terms of a furnace at the centre with many fire carrying channels spreading outwards to the surface. These are the sources of volcanoes and provide the heat for hot springs. Many people are attracted by these ideas of a hot, turbulent core to Earth. Kircher's book looks set to become a standard work of reference.

Executions boost Ottoman fortunes

Ottoman Empire, 1664
After two regicides and several decades of decline, the fortunes of the Ottoman empire have been restored largely through the efforts of successive grand viziers, members of the Koprulu family.

In 1656, after eight years of intrigue following the execution of Sultan Ibrahim, Sultana Turhan, the mother of the boy-sultan, Mehmed IV, called upon the 71-year-old Koprulu Mehmed, an Albanian-born former scullion who had risen to become a governor, to restore order as grand vizier. He accepted on condition that he was given almost absolute power.

Koprulu Mehmed renewed pride and discipline in the army, recaptured Tenedos and Lemnos from the Venetians, suppressed revolts, and had 35,000 executed during his five-year rule. He was succeeded three years ago at his palace, the Bab-i-Ali – now the effective seat of power – by his 26-year-old son, Fazil Ahmed, with the 20-year-old sultan's full consent.

A serpent goblet: a glass bowl surmounts a winged serpent.

Turks halted by Habsburg defences

Austria, 10 August 1664
The Turkish advance into Austria has been halted at St Gotthard, and peace agreed. This effectively renews the treaty of Zsitvatorok, with the Habsburgs paying money to the sultan, evacuating Transylvania and recognising the Ottoman vassal Apafy. The sultan also retains much of northern Hungary, and the newly-conquered stronghold of Neuhausel.

Habsburg incursions into Transylvania triggered this latest conflict three years ago, when Ottoman armies responded by invading Transylvania and Hungary. In June last year, Sultan Mehmed made a rare appearance at the head of his army before returning to the hunting field, leaving Koprulu Fazil Ahmed, his grand vizier, to march on, with the support of Tartars, Wallachians and disgruntled Hungarian peasants, to devastate the territories of Moravia and Silesia.

As Koprulu's armies advanced from Belgrade towards Vienna, the Habsburgs succeeded in persuading their Christian allies to come to their aid. With French and German support, the Austrian general Montecuccoli held the right bank of the Raab. At St Gotthard, French auxiliaries played a crucial role in repelling the superior numbers of the Ottomans, destroying most of their cannon and equipment. The Ottomans remained a threat, however, and Montecuccoli wanted peace.

English name New York

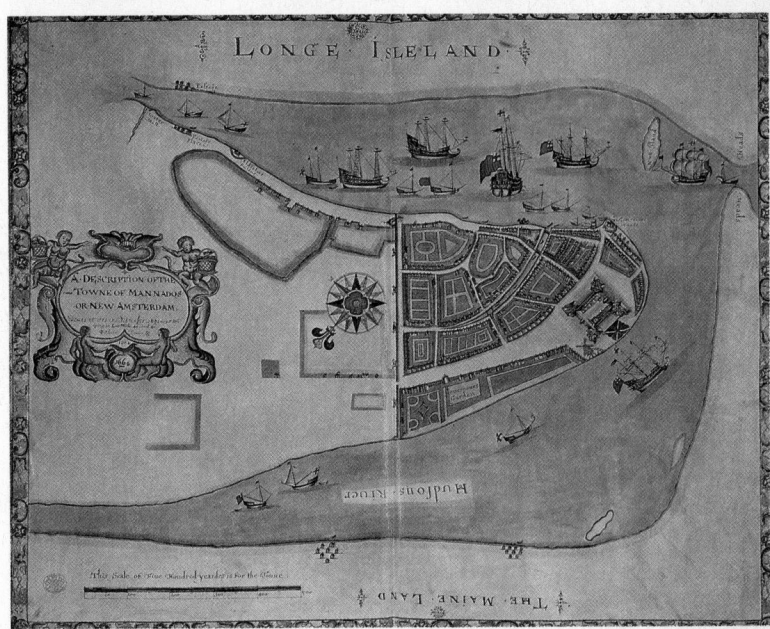

The most recent town plan of Manhattan, Long Island and New York.

Manhattan Island, 2 February 1665
Almost 40 years after the Canarsee Indians sold Manhattan Island to Dutch settlers for $24, the English have established themselves there and today renamed it "New York" after its new proprietor, the king's brother, the duke of York.

The Dutch paid for the island in beads to create a sanctuary for their farmers throughout New England, many under attack by Indians. With deep inlets, fresh water and fertile soil it is a natural fortress, but that was insufficient to keep out the British. A fleet armed with 120 guns and 500 experienced soldiers demanded surrender. Should Governor Peter Stuyvesant have stood his ground? He had just 20 cannon, 250 soldiers and many civilians pleading with him not to fight.

The English commander, Colonel Richard Nicholls, sent a letter promising to recognise human rights and trade with Holland. As tapers smouldered over the cannon, awaiting his order, Stuyvesant walked away saying "I would rather be carried to my grave". England's Charles II, needing a victory for the credibility of the restored monarchy, is reported to be overjoyed at this one.

Londoners flee from the city in panic as plague kills 100,000

London, 28 September 1665
The capital is in the grip of the worst attack of plague since the Black Death two centuries ago, with fears that the death toll could be as high as 100,000.

Official figures put last week's deaths from bubonic plague at 7,000 – the highest since the outbreak began. In July, deaths were averaging 200 a week.

Business has ground to a halt and most of the roads out of London are choked with traffic as people flee the city. Homes affected by the plague have warning red crosses daubed on the doors accompanied by the plea "Lord have mercy upon us". The commonest sound on the streets is the mournful toll of church bells announcing yet another funeral. With graveyards overflowing, corpses are now being laid on top of each other in large plague pits.

Treatment for the sick is almost non-existent because of a shortage of doctors and chemists. In Westminster all the doctors have been killed by the plague. Experts say that victims have only a one in ten chance of recovery. Symptoms usually include sores and enlarged glands, often in the groin. Patients generally run very high fevers accompanied by splitting headaches.

Counting the corpses in 1664.

1665 (1665-1667)

England, 1665. The Baptist John Bunyan writes *The Holy City* while serving a prison sentence, which began in 1660, for preaching other than in a parish church.

Paris, 20 January 1666. The queen mother is dead. The daughter of Philip III of Spain, she married Louis XIII in 1615. She took part in the plots against Richelieu and was accused of treason for having been in secret correspondence with her brother, the king of Spain. In 1648, on the death of Louis XIII, she became regent, and when her son Louis XIV took power in 1651 she retired to Val de Grace.

India, January 1666. The deposed Moghul Emperor Shahjahan dies. Since 1658 he had been confined by his son Aurangzeb in Agra fort from where he could gaze over the Taj Mahal where his beloved empress lies buried. Shahjahan himself was in revolt against his father from 1624 until he succeeded on his death in 1627.

Anatolia, May 1666. The religious leader Sabbatai Zevi, after a forced conversion to Islam, proclaims himself as the Messiah.

Paris, 4 June 1666. Moliere's *Le Misanthrope* (The Misanthropist) is performed.

Paris, June 1666. Louis XIV restricts the rights of the parliament in Paris.

Italy, 1666. The painter Giovanni Guercino dies in Bologna. He worked for Pope Gregory XV and has lived in Bologna since 1630.

France, 1666. The architect Francois Mansart dies. His buildings are characteristically sophisticated and luxurious; his first masterpiece was the Orleans wing of the *chateau* at Blois, which is unfortunately incomplete. Mansart was notoriously difficult to employ and was dismissed many times in the middle of a project by an infuriated employer. His most complete work is at Maison Lafitte, a country house near Paris.

India, 1666. Sivaji, the leader of the Marathas of western India, has fled in secret from the Emperor Aurangzeb's Moghul court in Agra. After various successful military operations against the Moghuls, Sivaji had been forced to submit and had come to Agra requesting only that Aurangzeb recognise him as an independent prince. When it became clear that the negotiations were not going his way, Sivaji took flight and has returned to his people, bent on revenge.

Spain, 1666. The painter Bartolome Murillo, a protege of Velazquez, finishes a series of 22 great figures of saints for the Capuchin convent.

Southern Africa, 1666. The Dutch take Saldanha Bay, near the Cape of Good Hope.

New Jersey, 1666. The governor, Philip Carteret, lures settlers from New Haven to New Jersey with land grants. Newly arrived colonists form settlements on the model of New England towns.

West Africa, 1666. The Gulf of Guinea is explored for the first time by the French.

Japan, 1666. The master of Japanese pottery, Kakiemon, dies.

Paris, 1666. The English scientist and mathematician, Isaac Newton, develops his differential calculus.

Paris, 1666. Louis XIV's chief minister, Jean-Baptiste Colbert, the marquis de Seignelay, founds the Royal Academy of Sciences.

Rome, 22 May 1667. Pope Alexander VII dies. For much of his rule he was in conflict with the French over the Gallican articles which asserted the king's independent power in temporal affairs. The situation deteriorated to such an extent that the French invaded the papal city of Avignon. Alexander will also be remembered for taking steps to suppress the radical Jansenist movement and employing Bernini to build the colonnade of St Peter's square. He is succeeded by Clement IX.

Virginia, 23 September 1667. A new law passed in Williamsburg bans slaves from obtaining freedom by converting to Christianity.

Paris, 17 November 1667. Jean Racine's tragedy *Andromache* is staged, and praised by Louis XIV.

Rome, 1667. The Italian architect Francesco Borromini commits suicide after finishing the facade of *St Charles of the Four Fountains*.

Lisbon, 1667. King Alfonso VI is deposed. His wife, the Princess of Savoy, has him replaced by his brother. Alfonso is imprisoned in the castle at Sintra, not far from Lisbon.

Germany, 1667. The composer Johann Froberger dies. He was court organist at Vienna for 20 years until 1657 and will be best remembered for his suites for the harpsichord.

Portugal, 1667. The writer Francisco Manuel de Melo dies. In 1640 he abandoned the Spanish language for Portuguese in honour of John, the duke of Braganza who became king of Portugal with the expulsion of Philip IV of Spain from the country. He will perhaps be better remembered for his critical works and his history of the Catalan wars than for his voluminous poetry.

New laws herald golden age for trade

International traders search for profits on Amsterdam's Stock Exchange.

London, c.1666

Bold new attitudes towards finance and commerce are being displayed by City magnates and their representatives in the Restoration parliament. With the granting to the East India Company of full liberty to export ingots to India, a free market in money has, in effect, been created, and a cherished pillar of financial rectitude has gone.

For years the nabobs have been complaining that the potential for trade is enormous but that restrictions on bullion experts have held it back. Now they will have all the funds they need.

It has long been held that the wealth of a nation depends on its possession of precious metals; their export should therefore be curbed, as should all avoidable imports of goods. Now with the emphasis on exploiting the new overseas colonies, bullion is seen as as much a commodity as any other.

Trade has been further boosted by the passing of the Navigation Act prohibiting the import of any goods carried in foreign ships. This has led to a big increase in the merchant marine and produced a formidable challenge to the Dutch domination of overseas commerce.

Despite the success of the Dutch and English East and West India Companies, which operate untrammelled by their home governments, there is no suggestion of free trade. Many still believe that there is a finite amount of world trade and that a country can only expand at the expense of others. Mercantile orthodoxy favours protectionism at home with colonies trading only with the mother country.

Indian textiles and Indian servants: the fruits of an expanding empire.

Fire devastates London

Londoners seek shelter on the river Thames: Stadler's aquatint of 1799.

London, 5 September 1666
At last, after four days and nights, the fire of London has been halted by the duke of York, who brought in naval gunpowder teams to blow up buildings in the path of the flames. Some 400 acres have been razed with 87 churches and over 13,000 houses destroyed. Miraculously, only nine lives were lost.

The fire started during last Sunday night in a baking house in Pudding Lane. When the parish watchman called out Sir Thomas Bloodworth, the lord mayor, he responded irritably: "Pish! A woman might piss it out." He went back to bed. But according to the diarist Samuel Pepys, next day he cried like a fainting woman: "Lord, what can I do? I am spent."

People were desperate to save their goods, even flinging them into the river. Houses were pulled down, but the flames leapt across the gaps. Pepys loaded his iron chests and bags of gold onto a cart and, riding in his nightgown, took

Firemen use hoses, pumps and leather buckets to battle the fire.

them with his wife to Woolwich. People are camping in fields outside the city, covering themselves with a few rags. The king has promised them bread and told them to ignore rumours of a foreign plot.

Polish king cedes Ukraine to Russia

Andrusovo, Russia, February 1667
A ten-year war between Russia and Poland is over, with the Polish king, John Casimir V, renouncing his claim to Smolensk, Kiev and a large part of the Ukraine on the left bank of the Dnieper. Lithuania remains in Polish hands. The settlement represents a belated victory for the Ukrainian Cossacks. A campaign against Polish domination from 1648 to 1656 was led by the Cossack Bogdan Khmelnitski, who abandoned the fickle Tartar alliance to put himself under Russian protection in 1654.

Cossack leads peasants' war in Russia

Russia, November 1667
Stenka Razin, the rebel Cossack chieftain to whom the peasantry are now flocking in ever-increasing numbers, has refused to submit in return for a pardon from the czar. Russia is on the verge of civil war.

For the past 20 years, peasants' revolts have broken out sporadically, in protest at price increases in salt and copper, food shortages and the tyranny of serfdom. While bandits roam the countryside, protected by the peasantry, the Cossacks have been plundering the czar's ships on the Volga. Last year the Cossack Vaska Us marched towards Moscow to appeal to the czar, collecting several thousand supporters. He returned after refusing to hand over the rebels.

Stenka Razin has now become the chief rebel, having raided ships, massacred nobles and officers and, in June, taken the fortress of Yaitsk, threatening Astrakhan.

Quaker woman writes treatise on religion

England, 1666
Margaret Fell, a devout widow and mother of nine, has written a book titled *Women's Speaking Justified, Proved and Knowed of the Scriptures*. It explains the revolutionary ideas she shares with her husband-to-be George Fox, the leader of the Society of Friends. Fell's campaign for religious freedom is based on Fox's doctrine that the Christian spirit in people has no need for church services conducted by paid ministers to sustain it.

Fell, who comes from an educated, land-owning family, helped Fox, a Leicestershire cobbler, to develop the political organisation of the Quakers. When Friends were sent to prison she pleaded with Charles II for their release, and in 1663 was sent there herself for refusing to take the Oath of Allegiance.

An uncomplimentary picture of a Quaker meeting by Heemskerk.

Japanese potter sold his ware to the west

Japan, 1666
Sakaida Kakiemon, a master potter, has died at the age of 70. His most oustanding achievement was the development of overglaze enamel-decorated porcelain, in particular the red enamel colour.

Kakiemon won local fame when he presented his gold, silver and coloured enamel to the lord of Nabeshima and became the first Japanese potter to sell his ware to Europeans. It is said that his name was originally Kizaemon, but he was renamed Kakiemon by a nobleman for whom he had made a porcelain ornament in the form of two persimmons, whose Japanese name is *kaki*.

A ceramic dog by Kakiemon, the epitome of the master's style.

1667 (1667-1669)

Netherlands, 31 July 1667. The peace of Breda ends the war between the English and Dutch. Trade laws are modified in favour of the Dutch who also gain possession of Surinam and re cognise English control over New York (which was New Amsterdam), New Jersey and Delaware.

London, 1667. The English chemist Robert Hooke proposes that the weather be recorded systematically.

London, 30 August 1667. Edward Hyde, the first earl of Clarendon, has been dismissed as lord chancellor by Charles II. He had been held largely responsible for the humiliating treaty of Breda signed in July, and this has brought about his downfall. Hyde has played a large part in the formation of colonial policy, favouring a strong crown in the face of colonial ambitions and supporting religious freedom.

Paris, 1667. A new magistracy is created in Paris, that of general lieutenant of the police. The duties are wide-ranging, including security, supervision of customs and censorship of books.

France, 1667. The marquise of Montespan becomes Louis XIV's mistress. Her husband the marquis is thrown into the Bastille.

Italy, 1667. Pietro-Antonio Cesti composes *Il Pomo d'Oro*.

Amsterdam, 1667. The painter Pieter de Hooch comes to live in Amsterdam after a stay in Delft where he met Fabritius and Vermeer. Influenced by the latter, his works reflect the intimacy of comfortable middle-class homes, with welcoming atmospheres.

Amsterdam, 1667. Johann de Witt passes the exclusion act which prevents the prince of Orange from becoming a stadholder (provincial governor).

Russia, 1667. The Cossack Stenka Razin leads a peasant uprising.

The Hague, 23 January 1668. During the War of Devolution, the Triple Alliance is formed between England, Holland and Sweden to defend the Netherlands against the ambitions of the French king, Louis XIV, who is pursuing a claim based on his wife's rights as Spanish *infanta*.

New England, 24 March 1668. Governor Edmund Andros takes personal control of colonial militias to quiet unrest.

Long Island, 25 March 1668. The first American trophy for horse racing is awarded to Captain Sylvester Salisbury.

France, 2 May 1668. The peace of Aix-la-Chapelle ends the War of Devolution.

Massachusetts, 27 May 1668. Thomas Gold, William Turner and John Farnum are the first Baptists to be expelled from the colony.

Maine, 6 July 1668. A convention at York accepts rule by Massachusetts, voting to send deputies to the General Court.

Poland, 16 September 1668. King John Casimir V abdicates. His reign has been one of the darkest periods in Poland's history, with foreign powers threatening partition, and internal strife amongst aristocratic factions.

England, 1668. The poet and essayist John Dryden publishes his *Essay of Dramatick Poesy* in which he attempts to reconcile the traditions of English drama with French classical taste.

North America, 1668. Father Jacques Marquette establishes the first colony in the northern plains.

Germany, 1668. Helvelius publishes his *Cometographia*, a systematic notation of all known comets.

Florida, 1668. The English buccaneer Robert Searles frees Henry Woodward from Spanish captivity.

Lisbon, 1668. The Spanish sign a peace treaty recognising Portuguese independence.

England, 17 August 1669. Three ships under Joseph West sail for Carolina via Barbados, funded by Carolina proprietors in their first sign of willingness to absorb the costs of settlement.

North America, 1669. Exploration of the north-west continues: several Jesuit missionaries have established permanent settlements and the explorer Robert Cavalier, the sieur de la Salle, has entered into friendly relations with the Iroquois. In Virginia, a German adventurer, Johann Lederer, has been granted a permit to explore westwards, and has made three journeys through the passes in the western region of the colony (*into the Blue Ridge Mountains and Kentucky*).

France, 1669. A Turkish ambassador to the court of Louis XIV starts a new trend: coffee-drinking. First drunk as a medicine, it is soon a social habit and is sold by street vendors and in shops and cafes. Both critics and enthusiasts cite the fact that it keeps the drinker awake.

Crete, 1669. The Venetians lose the Mediterranean island of Crete, their last colonial possession, to the Turks.

Massachusetts, 1669. The colony of Plymouth founds the first recorded Sunday School.

Dutch fleet in Thames threatens London

Dutch ships under admiral de Ruyter burn four ships of Britain's fleet as they lie at anchor in the Medway: this attack has badly damaged English pride.

London, 18 June 1667
The Dutch have humiliated the English by breaking through the Chatham defensive chain and sailing up the Thames to sink or burn four ships of the line and tow away the pride of the fleet, the *Royal Charles*.

The English went into the war two and a half years ago cheerfully confident that they could beat the Dutch by seizing their shipping. It did not work. Then England received two heavy blows: the Great Plague was followed by the Great Fire of London, and economic life was crippled. The fateful decision not to assemble a battle fleet for 1667 was taken. Now the price has been paid.

Blind Milton dictated "Paradise Lost"

Satan, Sin and Death: an 18th-century illustration to Paradise Lost.

London, 20 August 1667
John Milton's epic poem, *Paradise Lost*, has been published after much delay. In ten "books" it tells the story of the Fall of Adam and Eve in such a way as to "justify the ways of God to men". Milton has abandoned rhyme, but the sonorous power of his lines is greater than ever. For instance, Satan is thrown out of heaven "sheer o'er the crystal battlements, dropped from the zenith like a falling star".

Milton, who called Cromwell "our chief of men", served as Latin secretary to the Commonwealth, justified the execution of the king, and saw his pamphlets burned by the public hangman after the Restoration. Since 1652 he has been quite blind and depends on an amanuensis to take his dictation.

French give nationalist flavour to trade

Paris, 1667
Jean-Baptiste Colbert, the French chief minister, has taken another step on his nationalistic approach to finance. Having already carried out reforms giving Louis XIV power over the conduct of commerce, he has prepared a new tariff which will seriously affect the commerce of English and Dutch merchants who trade with France.

This draper's son has a hard-headed way of dealing with Louis' finances, and his ambition is to make France the wealthiest state in Europe. More money, he says, "will increase the power, the greatness and the affluence of the state".

He does not confine himself to fiscal matters. He seeks also to industrialise France and is putting state capital into many enterprises. Some concerns, especially those dealing with supplies for the army and navy, are being taken over com-

Colbert: his new tariffs will boost France but harm the rest of Europe.

pletely by the state. In all this activity Colbert is not neglecting his own finances. Like the late Cardinal Mazarin, his patron, he is amassing a huge personal fortune.

Japanese force ban on self-burning

Japan, 1668
The Japanese government has acted ruthlessly to stamp out the practise of *junshi*, or self-immolation, in which followers of a dead warlord burn themselves to death. This custom, which came about because it was said that a warrior could not serve two masters and must therefore end his own life when his lord

died, was banned five years ago; but it persisted.

Recently a *samurai* attached to the warlord Tadamasa committed junshi. Retribution has been swift. The samurai's two children have been executed and other relatives sent into exile. It is hoped that this exemplary punishment will finish junshi for ever.

Turks take Crete after 21-year siege

Dutch men-of-war and Turkish galleys mingle off Constantinople: Ottoman power has beaten Venice despite the republic's support from many allies.

Candia, Crete, 27 September 1669
After a 21-year siege, the capital of Crete has fallen to the Ottomans. Koprulu Fazil Ahmed, the grand vizier and supreme commander of the Turkish forces, led his troops into Candia to accept a formal surrender that was agreed 22 days ago.

Spain, Britain, France, the pope, Tuscan and Maltese seamen have

all supplied arms, men or provisions to the Venetian garrison. But as the Ottomans intensified their blockade, disagreements with the Venetian commander led to a withdrawal of European forces and made surrender inevitable. In return for Venice's evacuation of the island, the sultan is allowing it to retain some trading privileges.

Spanish Netherlands fall to French army

Flanders, 1667
A magnificent French army of 70,000 men, the best seen in Europe since Roman times, has advanced into Flanders, taking control of a dozen fortresses with hardly any resistance from the dispirited and outnumbered Spanish army. The

French are commanded by the able General Turenne, but Louis XIV is present in all his glory. It is his war, mounted to establish the rights of his Spanish queen and their son to their Spanish inheritance following the death of her father, the late Philip IV.

Born-again London is a thriving capital

London, 1669
Five years after the Great Plague and four after the Fire that burnt it out, London is flourishing as never before. Thriving trade, a burst of new building, improved civic amenities and, above all, an energetic citizenry are combining to make London one of Europe's most influential cities.

The Great Fire may have destroyed much of old London, but it has opened up opportunities for new, exciting development. The Guildhall has been rebuilt under the direction of Sir Christopher Wren, who is also designing a monument to the Fire. London is expanding

too. Leicester and Bloomsbury Squares have extended the "West End", while the aristocracy are flocking to St James.

The Fire spurred the growth of better public amenities. Building in brick, rather than wood, means that houses will be cleaner. New laws covering street-cleaning will help limit fresh plague attacks. Perhaps London's most outstanding novelty is the rash of coffee houses, where men gather to talk, to trade and to discuss affairs. The free flow of information to be sampled at every table are enabling the coffee houses to be seen as the best place outside the universities to improve one's learning.

One of the many new coffee houses which have been opening up all over London during the past ten years and which are rapidly becoming social and cultural centres. Here the patrons gather in warm and familiar surroundings to gossip, play cards, read the latest news and drink coffee.

1669 (1669-1670)

India, 18 April 1669. Aurangzeb, the Moghul emperor, gives orders that all recently constructed Hindu temples should be razed to the ground.

England, 31 May 1669. The naval administrator and politician Samuel Pepys makes the last entry in the diary that he began on 1 January 1660.

Amsterdam, 4 October 1669. The Dutch painter Rembrandt van Rijn dies in solitude and poverty, having defied the dictates of fashion to pursue his artistic genius. He survived both his son, Titus, and his mistress, Hendrickje Stoffels, with whom he lived after the death of his wife, Saskia. Among a huge volume of brilliant work, Rembrandt's series of self-portraits, spanning a period of 40 years, stand out as some of his greatest masterpieces.

Rome, 1669. The painter and architect Pietro da Cortona dies. He will be best remembered for his frescoes in the Barberini palace in Rome and the Pitti palace in Florence.

Germany, 1669. The German scientist Johann Becher publishes his *Physica Subterranea*, considering the Mosaic account of Creation in the light of contemporary scientific theories.

Germany, 1669. Hans Grimmelshausen publishes his novel *Simplicissimus*, depicting the sufferings of German peasants at the hands of lawless soldiers who overrun their country.

France, 1669. Jean-Baptiste Colbert, Louis XIV's chief financial adviser, known for the stringency of his protectionist measures, becomes secretary of state for the navy.

Germany, 1669. The German chemist Hennig Brand discovers the element phosphorus by chance while distilling a sample of urine.

Germany, 1669. The *Hanse* (an alliance of towns), which was virtually destroyed by the Thirty Years' War, is broken up. Its *diet* meets for the last time.

Poland, 1669. The rebellious French noble, the prince of Conde, has been defeated in his bid for the Polish throne, and cast aside in favour of the Lithuanian Michael Wisnowiecki.

North America, 1669. Robert Cavalier explores the mid-west; he is probably the first white man in this region.

India, 1669. Serious disturbances are caused near the imperial capital Delhi when large numbers of the Hindu Jat peasants rise up against Moghul rule.

Italy, 1669. The Italian physiologist Marcello Malpighi studies the lives and habits of silkworms.

Netherlands, 1669. The architect Pieter Post dies. The city of the Hague owes its town hall to him.

Copenhagen, 1669. The geologist Niels Stensen gives the first specific interpretation of the origin of fossil animals, thus setting out the basis for a chronological geology (stratigraphy). He teaches as an anatomist in Copenhagen.

Copenhagen, 1669. Erasmus Bertelsen Bartholin observes that Iceland spar crystals make rays of light that enter them divide (double refraction).

France, 17 February 1670. A Franco-Bavarian treaty is made for concerted action at the death of either of the monarchs Leopold of Germany or Charles II of Spain.

England, 26 May 1670. A treaty is signed in secret at Dover between Charles II and Louis XIV, ending hostilities between them. Henrietta Anne, the duchess of Orleans, the sister of the English king and sister-in-law of Louis XIV, persuaded Charles to sign the treaty, by which he promises to join a French attack on the Dutch, and to support French claims to the Spanish throne if the Spanish king dies childless. Louis promises money and troops for Charles' personal defence and financial aid during the war with the Dutch.

Spain, 18 July 1670. England and Spain sign the treaty of Madrid, by which the Spanish formally recognise English possessions in the West Indies.

Virginia, 13 October 1670. A law is passed ruling that Negroes who arrive in the colonies as Christians cannot be used as slaves.

Paris, 1670. The central body of the Palace of Versailles is completed.

The Hague, 1670. The Dutch-Jewish philosopher Spinoza publishes his *Tractatus* anonymously. The work promotes democracy as the most natural form of government and is unlikely to be welcomed by the authorities.

Virginia, 1670. Sir William Berkeley estimates that there are 2,000 Negro slaves and 6,000 white servants in an overall population of 40,000.

East Africa, 1670. Oman Arabs raid the east coast as far south as Mozambique.

New Jersey, 1670. An attempt at collecting quitrents – rents due on lands that were originally offered free to encourage settlers – sparks off a rebellion.

Isaac Newton kept his calculus secret

Cambridge, England, 1669

Although only 27 years of age, a Cambridge physicist and mathematician, Isaac Newton, has made some important discoveries. The son of a Lincolnshire yeoman, he recognised early on that he was suited to a life of learning and invention. Even as a student at Cambridge, Newton was quick to respond to the key ideas in contemporary science, being much influenced by Kepler, Galileo and Descartes. He began to think about matter as being composed of particles in motion being held together by various forces. In 1665 the university was closed by plague, giving Newton the opportunity to write up some of the many notes he had compiled. One outcome of this was an essay, *Of Colours*, which later became extended into Book One of *Opticks*.

He has published *On Analysis by Infinite Series*, describing what he terms "fluxions" a mathematical tool for analysing the slopes of curves and the areas bounded by them. Although the concept of fluxions, or calculus as it is also known, has been secret so far, there seems little doubt that from now on it will become widely adopted.

Thoughts on the agony of seeking faith

Paris, 1670

The fragmentary thoughts of the great mathematician and philosopher Blaise Pascal, who died four years ago at the age of 39, were discovered after his death and are now published, incomplete, under the title *Pensees*. They express in masterly language the agony of his search for faith, despite the doubts that his powerful intellect raised to torment him.

He was the son of an able mathematician who educated him personally. By the age of 11 he had worked out for himself most of Euclid's geometry, although his father had not yet taught it to him. He also specialised in the mathematics of probability. His experiments in fluid mechanics proved "Pascal's Principle", that the pressure in a liquid is everywhere equal. In 1641, when still a young man, he invented a calculating machine.

But in 1654 he had a revelation that led him to go into the Jansenite convent at Port Royal and join battle with the Jesuits in his *Lettres Provinciales*.

Miguel March's personification of the liberal arts: gathered in this painting are figures representing the vital branches of learning grammar, logic, rhetoric, music, geometry, arithmetic and astronomy.

Dutch painters tell the inside story

Spinoza's world is run on reason

The Hague, 1670
A new philosophical work, the *Tractatus Theologico-politicus* has been published anonymously in The Hague. Its author is thought to be Baruch Spinoza, the Jewish philosopher who in 1656 was exiled from Amsterdam when his own community rejected his rationalist philosophies.

The *Tractatus* aims to prove that states are based in natural rather than religious laws. Natural law guarantees every man his liberty. For security's sake, he has ceded some of that liberty to the state. This gives the ruler, whether the monarch or (as in Holland) the government, as guardian and interpreter of both civil and sacred law, his great powers. Spinoza accepts such power, but trusts authority to rule with justice and wisdom.

China produces exquisite silks

A picture, painted on silk, showing the process of silk manufacturing.

China, c.1670.
Technological advances have put the Chinese at the forefront of the world trade in silk. Shantung, Kwangtung and Chekiang are creating great wealth, and across China, silk is second only to tea in agricultural importance.

Intensive study of silk worms' behaviour has enabled the Chinese to regulate the worms' digestion and control their growth. When a cocoon is spun, the chrysalis is killed by steaming, the cocoon boiled before reeling, then threads spun by a machine worked by a single pedal.

Vermeer's "Girl reading a letter".

Delft, 1670
The small town of Delft has gained pre-eminence in Dutch painting. Since Rembrandt's death last year, the two leading Dutch painters both work here – Jan Vermeer and Pieter de Hooch. Both are famed for the richness and serenity of their rendering of domestic interiors of Dutch houses and scenes of domestic life going on within them. What is known as *genre* painting has been raised by them to fine art.

Vermeer was born in Delft and has never left his native town. Most of his pictures show the interior of the house on the main square where both he and his father have dealt in pictures and *objets d'art*. Music is a favourite subject – young women playing guitars, for instance – as is a woman standing at a window to examine a letter or a jewel. His paint gives a translucent glow to every object on the canvas and his colours, especially his blues, are of incomparable richness. His painting of Delft is bathed in a golden calm.

The rich Dutch merchants are enthusiastic picture collectors and this has led to widespread and varied styles of painting. Pieter de Hooch paints many scenes in courtyards or rooms with swaggering soldiers playing cards or drinking with women. Gerard Ter Borch shows the richness of women's apparel. But artists like Nicholas Maes and Gerard Dou have women peeling apples, plucking a duck or playing with children while Steen and Hals portray convivial, sometimes drunken, parties.

"The Beach at Egmond-aan-Zee": a painting by Salomon van Ruysdael.

"A Wijdship, a keep and other shipping": by Van de Velde the Younger.

Jan Vermeer's painting: "Christ in the house of Mary and Martha".

A painting of "The Backgammon Players" by Dirk Hals.

France, 1670. The French occupy Lorraine following the expulsion of the duke of Lorraine for his negotiations with the Dutch.

France, 1670. The astronomer Jan Picard determines the exact length of Earth's radius.

Rome, 1670. Clement X becomes pope in succession to Clement IX, the architect of the reconciliation between the Roman Church and the Jansenists known as the Clementine peace.

Italy, 1670. The Italian physiologist Giovanni Borelli tries to fly using artificial wings. Inspired by Cartesian mechanics, Borelli is the founder of the iatromechanism, which seeks to explain all bodily functions by physical laws.

West Africa, 1670. The French establish a trading post at Offa on the Dahomey coast.

New England, 1670. The English Hudson's Bay Company is formed.

France, 1671. France signs treaties of alliance or neutrality with several German states and the Emperor Leopold.

Hungary, 1671. Following the abolition of the constitution, Hungary becomes a province of Austria.

Angola, 1671. The kingdom of Ndongo is defeated at Ngola by the Portuguese, who annex it to form the Portuguese colony of Angola.

Central America, 1671. Having plundered Cuba, Portobello and Maracaibo, the English buccaneer Captain Henry Morgan sacks and loots the Spanish city of Panama.

Ukraine, October 1671. The Cossack *hetman* Peter Doroszenko is routed by the Poles, who occupy much of the Ukraine. Doroszenko has attempted to make alliances with the Crimean Tartars and the Ottomans to secure Cossack independence from both Poland and Russia.

London, 27 September 1672. The Royal African Company is granted a charter with a monopoly on the slave trade from Morocco to the Cape of Good Hope.

Poland, 18 October 1672. Following several defeats by the Ottomans – who were drawn into the conflict between the Poles and the Cossacks by the Polish occupation of the Ukraine – the Poles are forced to sign the treaty of Buczacz, by which they recognise Peter Dorszenko as sole hetman of the Cossacks and agree to become vassals of the sultan.

Paris, 1672. The German philosopher Wilhelm Leibniz visits Paris on a mission to persuade Louis XIV to conquer Egypt.

Netherlands, 1672. Having declared war on the Dutch, the French cross the Rhine and capture city after city. To halt the invasion the Dutch open dykes, causing extensive flooding.

England, 1672. In support of Louis XIV of France, King Charles II declares war on the Dutch.

New York, 1672. The Dutch regain control of New York from the English. The war of England and France against Holland crossed the Atlantic when 23 Dutch ships arrived in New York harbour on 7 August and attacked the garrison at Fort James.

Morocco, 1672. Mulay Ismail becomes sultan of the Alaouites and sets about uniting Morocco under his rule. He razes part of the old city of Meknes to build a complex of sumptuous palaces.

Netherlands, 1672. The painter Jan Steen returns from Delft to his native town of Leyden. One of the founders of the Leyden Guild, Steen excels at *genre* paintings of social and domestic scenes.

France, 1672. Louis XIV moves the French government from Paris to Versailles.

New Jersey, 1672. Colonists in Elizabethport opposed to the payment of the land taxes known as quitrents form an assembly.

New England, 1672. The Puritan poetess Anne Bradstreet, the first American woman writer, dies. Born in England, she sailed to New England with John Winthrop in 1630. Her first volume of poetry, published in England in 1650, was *The Tenth Muse lately sprung up in America.*

North America, 1 January 1673. A regular mounted mail service begins between New York and Boston. The mail is delivered by a "post road" along which men and horses are posted at intervals.

Paris, 21 February 1673. The great French comic dramatist Moliere is buried in secret.

North America, 11 September 1673. James Needham returns to Virginia after a four-month expedition to the lands to the west (*Tennessee*). He is the first Englishman to penetrate the area.

London, 1673. Parliament passes the Plantation Duty Act, imposing duties on any ship carrying certain products, such as sugar, cotton and tobacco, between colonial ports.

London, 1673. Parliament cuts off funds for England's war against Holland, forcing Charles II to drop the war, rescind religious liberties and accept the Test Act, which is designed to prevent Roman Catholics from holding office.

British slavers promise prompt delivery

London, 27 September 1672
Bulk deliveries of slaves from West Africa are being arranged by the Royal African Company, a new corporation which has just been granted monopoly rights under the English flag to collect slaves from an area that runs from Sallee on the Moroccan coast down to the Cape of Good Hope. With recently-raised capital of £100,000, Royal African promises prompt supply to those prepared to sign contracts for whole cargoes.

A slave between 12 and 40 years old "able to go over the ship's side unaided" will be supplied for £15 per head in Barbados, £16 in Nevis, £17 in Jamaica, and £18 in Virginia.

Swedish philosopher backs natural law

Lund, Sweden, 1672
Natural law, deduced by reason from the evidence of nature, is the true and immutable foundation of the state. Governments may rule, but only in so far as they pass laws that guarantee rights on the basis of this natural law. Thus the theory behind a new book, *On the law and nature of people*, written by the German jurist and philosopher Samuel Pufendorf, the professor of Natural Law at the university of Lund in Sweden. Humans are "social beings" with natural rights and freedoms. It is for governments to ensure that such rights are upheld, he argues.

Samuel Pufendorf: a believer that humans have "natural" rights.

Manchu rule means shaven heads for all

Peking, 1671
These are times of great change in China as the Manchu consolidate their hold over the country. As more and more Chinese come under Manchu rule they are being forced to wear their hair in the Manchu style, with heads shaven except for a pigtail hanging down the back of their necks.

To many loyal supporters of the deposed Mings this is a shameful sign of subservience and many are shaving the whole of their heads in the manner of Buddhist priests rather than submit to the attentions of the Manchu barbers.

Surprisingly, the young emperor, Kang-hsi, has allowed the Chinese to resume the practice of binding the feet of young children. On three previous occasions the Manchus had forbidden this strange and cruel practice which leaves women virtually unable to walk. They have now given in to Chinese pressure on this matter as part of the emperor's policy of placation. But he has ruled that the custom must be confined to the Chinese.

Mathematician gets into swing of things

Paris, 1673
The Dutch mathematician, astronomer and physicist Christiaan Huygens has become a founder member of the French Academy of Sciences. The Academy's funding will certainly help his wide-ranging and varied researches. While living in Paris he published a book, *Horologium Oscillatorium*, which deals with the mathematics of pendulum swing and the laws of centrifugal force. Concurrently Huygens has been working on pendulum mechanisms of various kinds. He designed the first practical pendulum clock in 1656, accurate to five minutes a day.

Orangemen murder diplomat brothers

The Hague, 20 August 1672
Johan de Witt, the Grand Pensionary of Holland, a leader of the United Provinces through their years of greatest glory, and his brother Cornelis have been murdered by a mob. Cornelis de Witt was in jail, accused of plotting against William of Orange; his brother was visiting him. As they spoke a mob of Orangemen broke in and literally tore the two to pieces.

Johan de Witt ruled Holland between the death of William II in 1650 and the coming of age of William III in February of this year. It has been a period of unparalleled prosperity, international trade and artistic and intellectual advance.

De Witt backed the merchants and artists, but he was equally devoted to maintaining his own power, scheming ruthlessly to defeat any opposition, notably that of the House of Orange, backed by the Catholic church, the poor and the rural landowners. When William came to power, de Witt was

Cornelis and Johan de Witt: two victims of their own ambitions.

reluctant to give up his authority. But the people, who fear his ties to Louis XIV, rallied to the Orange and showed the intensity of their belief today.

King's move sparks fear of popish plots

London, 1672
With England about to go to war with the Dutch yet again, the king has outraged public opinion by issuing a Declaration of Indulgence suspending all penal laws in religious matters. Ostensibly a gesture of toleration, the declaration is intended to favour Roman Catholics.

Charles' arbitrary suspension of statutes is greatly resented, especially as it is becoming known to ministers that the king has made a secret treaty with Louis XIV, promising to become a Catholic in return for French subsidies and troops to keep him on the throne. Parliament is at present in recess, but when MPs reassemble they are certain to force Charles to cancel his Declaration. In the public mind popery, France and arbitrary power are linked together.

King Charles II: his pro-Catholic bias has offended many subjects and parliament demands a climb-down.

French comedy playwright dies on stage

Jean-Baptiste Poquelin, who is also known as the playwright Moliere.

"Le Bourgeois Gentilhomme", one of Moliere's popular comedies.

Paris, 15 February 1673
Moliere, France's greatest comedian and playwright, died last night of a lung haemorrhage after collapsing on stage during his performance as the hypochondriac in his own *Le Malade Imaginaire*. He was 51. The king is mourning his favourite actor, but Moliere had many enemies at court and in the church who have suffered from his ridicule.

Moliere's real name was Jean-Baptiste Pocquelin. As a young man he joined the large theatrical family of Bejart to form *L'Illustre Theatre*. They failed in Paris and toured France for 13 years of varied fortunes, playing in tennis courts, with Moliere in the lead opposite Madeleine Bejart. In 1658 the King became their patron. They took over the Palais Royal theatre where Moliere created a series of great comedies. *Tartuffe* was banned for years. Moliere married Armande Bejart, a girl of 19 whom some critics alleged was his daughter.

Musical world mourns death of Schutz

Dirk Hals: "Elegant figures making music on a terrace by a lake".

Dresden, 6 November 1672
Heinrich Schutz, the first German composer to achieve international fame, has died at the age of 87. As a choirboy at Kassel, Schutz showed early talent, and in 1609 the local ruler gave him money to study music in Venice. Soon after his return, in 1613, he was seconded to

the elector of Saxony at Dresden, eventually becoming court *Kapellmeister* (head of music).

Schutz's powerfully expressive music is mostly for the church, and includes oratorical works like passions and motets. One of his few secular works is *Dafne* (1627), the first German opera.

Moghul India: seeds of decline

The long reign (1658-1707) of the Moghul Emperor Aurangzeb saw the zenith of Moghul power and prestige in India, and when he died at the age of 89 in 1707 the empire seemed more powerful than ever. He had pressed forward Moghul power in Burma and the Himalayan foothills; through his conquest of the Dekhan kingdoms of Bijapur and Golconda he had projected it to the Kaveri river in the south, further than the sway of Mohammed bin Tughluq had reached at the height of the Delhi sultanate. But half a century later Moghul power struggled to reach far beyond the walls of Delhi.

Growing weaknesses

The decline may seem rapid, but in fact throughout Aurangzeb's reign weaknesses became increasingly evident. One problem arose from the stresses caused by running a Moslem state in a primarily Hindu society. The Moghul empire rested on an alliance with its Hindu subjects, and its rulers had respected Hindu religious sensitivities. The Emperor Akbar abolished the *jizya* (the tax levied by holy law on unbelievers in Moslem territories), replaced the Islamic lunar calendar with a solar version, forbad Moslems to kill or eat the cow which Hindus revered, set aside the death penalty for apostasy and financed the places of worship of all faiths alive.

Such religious compromises brought protests from devout Moslems. Emperors from Akbar to Shah Jahan ignored these complaints, but Aurangzeb, possibly out of overweening confidence in his power and certainly out of personal prejudice, did not. Religious disabilites were reimposed on Hindus: from 1669 many temples were destroyed; from 1679 the *jizya* was levied again, even on those serving in the army; the lunar calendar was brought back. The emphasis on the Moghul state as the expression of partnership in a multi-confessional society was abandoned; it became, increasingly, an expression of Islamic domination. Hindus, not surprisingly, revolted, and they swelled a growing tide of resistance to Moghul power which also included peasants, Sikhs and Afghans. The most serious resistance, however, came from Hindu Marathas, a warrior elite, who, under their chief Shivaji, carved a state for themselves in the Dekhan in southern India, refusing either to be incorporated into the empire or to live peaceably with it.

A second problem was the breakdown of the imperial civil service, which was organised as a great military household answerable to the em-peror alone. The officers, called *mansabdars* or holders of commands (*mansabs*), were organised in 33 grades from a commander of ten to a commander of 5,000. They did not inherit their positions, progressing only by imperial favour; from among them the emperor chose his civil and military officers. Many *mansabdars* were foreigners from Persia and Central Asia although, in time, Indian warrior elites, notably the Hindu Rajputs, were incorporated into the system. All were assigned the revenues of specific lands, and encouraged to visit them, although payment itself came from the imperial treasury.

The imperial civil service worked well as long as Indian warrior elites were willing to collaborate and there was money to pay them. When the Marathas refused to come to terms with the empire, Aurangzeb went to the Dekhan to subdue them; he failed, and took to bribing them with high *mansabs*. But while the number of *mansabdars* grew, resources did not. The empire bestowed high value commands without the extra revenues to pay for them from newly conquered territories.

In consequence, the peasantry suffered as government demands increased, the army suffered because commanders were unable to raise required forces, morale suffered as they failed to win victories, and of course imperial authority suffered both at home and abroad.

Turmoil in the empire

On the death of Aurangzeb these problems came to a head. The *mansabdars* split into two factions, and imperial prestige disintegrated as nine emperors came and went between 1707 and 1719, some murdered, others mere puppets in the struggle for power. Central control slackened over the provinces. Provincial governors continued to pay obeisance to the emperor, but remitted revenue less frequently and began to build up their local bases instead. In 1724 Asaf Jah founded the dynasty of the Nizam in the Dekhan and Saadat Khan became ruler of Awadh; by 1740 Alivardi Khan, the governor of Bengal, no longer, in practice, recognised imperial sovereignty. By this time the Rohillas, Afghan tribesmen, had taken control of a rich tract between Awadh and the Ganges to the west. The Marathas emerged as the most considerable power in India. They recovered from their civil wars of the early years of the century to develop a first-class system of administration under the leadership of their *peshwas*, or hereditary chief ministers – the descendants of Shivaji were retained merely as figureheads. Evidence of the Marathas' new power came in 1720, when the Emperor Mohammed Shah allowed them to levy the *chauth*, or assessment of one fourth of the land revenue, over the whole Dekhan. Further evidence came in 1737 when, after mastering much of central India, Maratha forces appeared in the suburbs of Delhi. No greater demonstration could have been given of the decay at the heart of the Moghul system, and in 1739 Nadir Shah of Persia invaded India, brushed aside the imperial army and sacked Delhi, relieving its citizens of the accumulated wealth of over three centuries and its ruling family of its famed peacock throne.

An open door for Europeans

By the mid 18th century, therefore, the Moghuls exercised a shadowy authority in north-western India between the Indus and the Ganges, while their governors in Awadh, Bengal and the Dekhan were setting up as independent rulers. South of the Dekhan power was localised in petty kingdoms and the Marathas ruled a great swathe of central India from Gujarat in the west to Orissa in the east, and from Rajasthan in the north to Mysore in the south.

This was the political situation encountered by the British and French East India companies when the War of the Austrian Succession and Seven Years War brought Britain and France into direct conflict on the subcontinent. The British East India Company was an experienced mercantile corporation, boasting three great settlements in Bombay, Calcutta and Madras, all with networks of satellite trading stations. The population of these settlements was rising steadily, that of Madras being as much as 300,000. Trade prospered, particularly after the development of the China trade, and the company had access to capital in London and political support in Parliament. On the other hand, the French company was a state-run enterprise which had only begun to develop in a significant way after its reorganisation in 1723. It had one major settlement, Pondicherry, and initiatives depended on government policy. Between 1728 and 1740 French exports from India increased tenfold, but they were still less than half those of their British rival.

By 1765, when the Moghul emperor gave Clive and the British East India Company the right to manage the revenues of Bengal, Britain had clearly bested French efforts to gain supremacy in India. The British successes of these years heralded the greatest change in the course of Indian civilisation since the Moslem invasion of six centuries earlier.

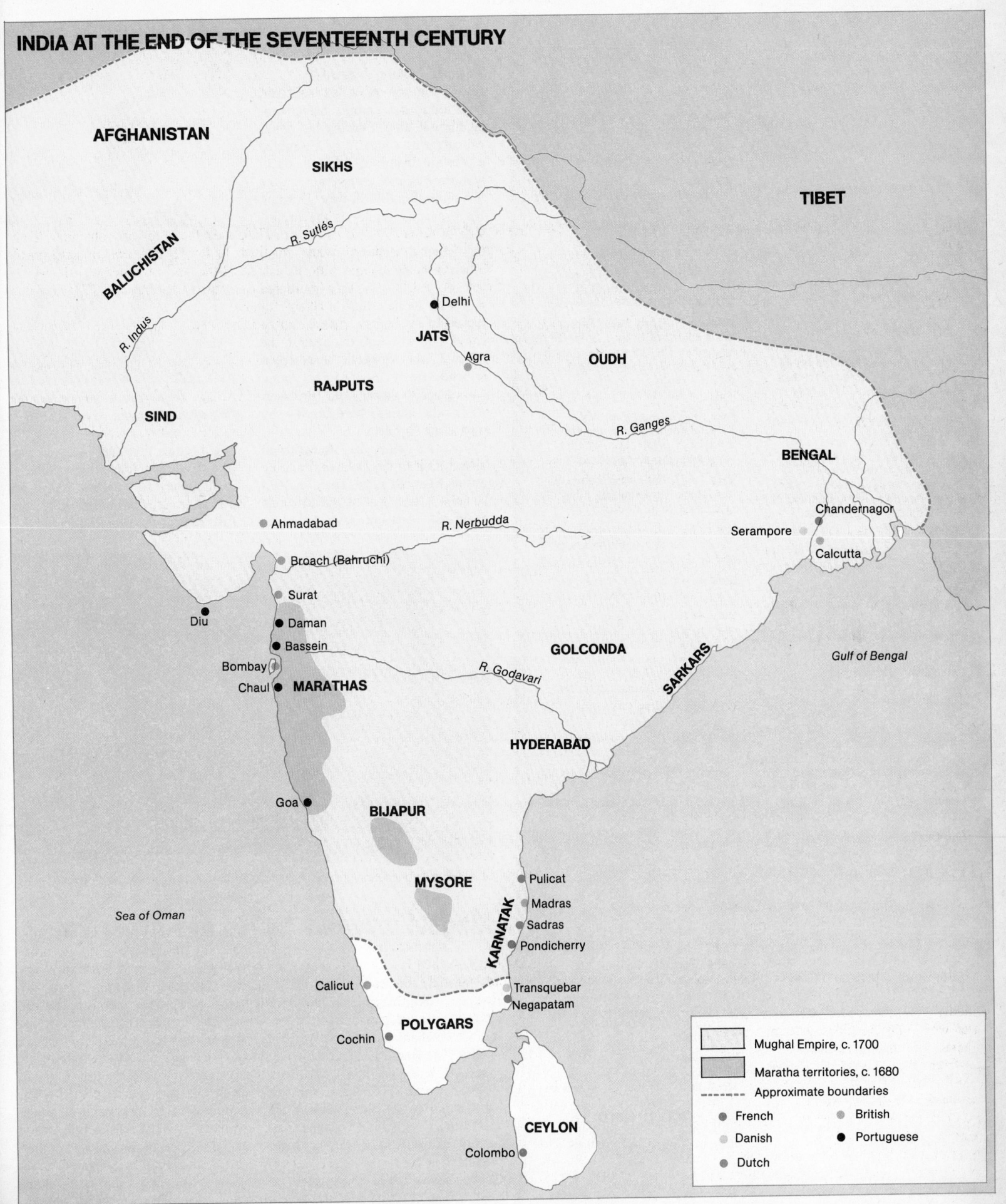

INDIA AT THE END OF THE SEVENTEENTH CENTURY

AFGHANISTAN

SIKHS

TIBET

BALUCHISTAN

R. Sutlés

R. Indus

Delhi

JATS

Agra

OUDH

RAJPUTS

SIND

R. Ganges

BENGAL

Ahmadabad

R. Nerbudda

Chandernagor

Serampore

Calcutta

Broach (Bahruchi)

Surat

Daman

Diu

Bassein

Bombay

GOLCONDA

SARKARS

Gulf of Bengal

Chaul

MARATHAS

R. Godavari

HYDERABAD

Goa

BIJAPUR

Sea of Oman

MYSORE

Pulicat

Madras

KARNATAK

Sadras

Pondicherry

Calicut

Transquebar

Negapatam

POLYGARS

Cochin

CEYLON

Colombo

	Mughal Empire, c. 1700
	Maratha territories, c. 1680
- - -	Approximate boundaries
● French	● British
● Danish	● Portuguese
● Dutch	

1673 (1673-1676)

Massachusetts, 1673. John Winslow is elected governor of Plymouth, becoming the first native-born colonial governor.

Poland, 20 May 1674. John Sobieski is elected king.

New Jersey, 13 June 1674. Philip Carteret, the governor of New Jersey, launches a campaign to enforce the payment of quitrents, the land taxes which have sparked a rebellion in the colony.

New York, 10 November 1674. All Dutch-held areas of New York are returned to English control by the treaty of Westminster. The Dutch regained the town on 9 August 1672 during the third Anglo-Dutch war.

Canada, 4 December 1674. The fur trader Louis Jolet and the Jesuit Father Jacques Marquette return to Montreal after a 2,500-mile journey exploring the basin of the great river that the Indians call the *Mississippi*.

New England, 1674. George Fox, the founder of the Society of Friends, returns to Rhode Island after a three-year expedition to spread Quaker beliefs in the colonies.

Spain, 1674. A second collection of novels by Maria de Zayas y Sofomayor is published posthumously. As a novelist she wrote sensational melodramatic tales; she also argued for education for women and was an admired playwright and poet.

Paris, 1674. The court and church painter Philippe de Champaigne dies. He painted the Sorbonne chapel, and leaves several portraits of Richelieu and Louis XIII. He was linked with the Jansenists after 1643, and his later serious and austere compositions led him to be considered the most eminent representative of French classicism.

Paris, 1674. Nicolas Boileau publishes *The Poetic Art*, which vigorously champions literary classicism.

Paris, 1674. The philosopher and theologian Nicolas Malebranche publishes *On the search after truth*. He is full of enthusiasm for Descartes' philosophy and develops Cartesianism in a religious sense, linking it with Augustinianism.

France, 1674. French troops conquer Franche-Comte.

India, 1674. Francois Martin founds Pondicherry for the French East India Company.

Iceland, 1674. Hallgrimur Petursson, one of the most important exponents of Icelandic religious poetry, dies.

England, 1674. The chemist John Mayow carries out an experiment placing a lighted candle inside a bell jar under water. In his *Tractatcus quinque Medico-Phisici*, he describes air as consisting of two elements, one inert, the other active. He is the inventor of a real technique for handling gases.

Bulgaria, 1674. Archbishop Peter Parchevitch dies. An ardent patriot who devoted his life to the liberation of his people, he travelled widely in Europe on missions to achieve this goal.

Germany, 28 June 1675. Frederick William, the great elector of Brandenburg, crushes the Swedes.

Germany, 27 July 1675. Turenne, the marshall of France, is killed at Sasbach while fighting the Italian leader Montecuccoli. Turenne recently reconquered Alsace at the battle of Turckheim.

India, 1675. Aurangzeb, the Moghul emperor, executes the ninth Sikh *guru*, Tegh Bahadur, for refusing to accept Islam.

Mali, 1675. Following the troubles in Macina, waves of migrating Fulani arrive in Hodh.

Spain, 1675. King Charles II reaches adulthood, but is sickly and uninterested in affairs of state.

London, 1675. The Greenwich Observatory is established.

Italy, 1675. The town of Messina rises up against the Spanish. Louis XIV sends a fleet which defeats the Spanish, but as soon as the French have left the Spanish return and institute cruel reprisals.

West Indies, 1675. After being knighted by Charles II, the buccaneer Sir Henry Morgan takes up the post of governor of Jamaica.

France, 1675. France comes into conflict with the pope over the previously accepted "king's right" to income from certain bishoprics between the death of one bishop and the appointment of the next.

Paris, 1675. While trying to calculate the speed of light, the Dane Ole Roemer observes eclipses of the satellites of Jupiter.

Netherlands, 1675. The painter Jan Vermeer dies at Delft.

Rome, 1675. The Spanish theologian Miguel de Molinos publishes his *Spiritual Guide*, advocating the suppression of all deliberate acts, giving birth to "quietism".

Massachusetts, 28 August 1676. Metacom, the chief of the Algonquin Wampanoags – known by the English as King Philip – is killed by English soldiers. His death ends a year of fighting between Indians and colonists.

Tax collector's son founds empire in India

Raigarh, India, 6 June 1674
Sivaji, the son of a tax collector, who founded a empire, has crowned himself king. Starting his political career as a bandit, he assembled a private army of Mawali backwoodsmen, and carved an empire for himself in north-west Dekhan. He proved a genius at the profession of arms. By 1657 he was raiding Moghul territory. When Afzal Khan was sent against him, he called for peace talks, then murdered him with hidden "tiger's claws" attached to his fingers. Aware that he could not win directly against the might of the Moghuls, he accepted a peace treaty in 1665, becoming Aurangzeb's vassal and prisoner. After nine months he escaped – by night and on horse.

For five years he strengthened his position in the Dekhan, building up his Maratha state. Then, in 1670 he was at war against the Moghuls again. So decadent have the Mog-

Sivaji: from tax collector to the first of the Maratha monarchs.

huls become that they prefer to pay him than fight him. Moghul blackmail money so enriches Sivaji can afford to crown himself king, the first king of the Maratha dynasty.

A Dekhan papier-mache box, painted, lacquered and fringed with ivory.

Moghul invaders halted at Khyber Pass

Kabul, 1676
A rebellion in Afghanistan led by Akmal Khan, the chief of the Afridis, has almost succeeded in separating Afghanistan from Moghul India. The first attempt to suppress the Afghanis failed in 1672, with 10,000 troops killed and tens of thousands of Afghanis joining the rebellion. A second Moghul attempt in early 1674 was similiarly defeated at the Karapa Pass. The defeats have forced Aurangzeb to come from Delhi and take overall command. In spite of his placing the operational command of his army under his most experienced officer, the Turkish general Aghar Khan, his army failed to open a way through the Khyber Pass.

Unable to defeat the Afghanis with the weapons of war, he has resorted to the weapons of peace: tribal chiefs have been bribed and religious divisions between Sunnites and Shi'ites inflamed. Now the rebels spend more time fighting each other than the enemy.

Knighted ex-pirate now governs Jamaica

Kingston, Jamaica, 1675

With the kind of pomp and ceremony that attends a royal occasion, a former buccaneer, Henry – now Sir Henry – Morgan, has taken up residence as lieutenant-governor of Jamaica. To the fury of Spain and the surprise of royalist society in London, Morgan was knighted last year by King Charles II and returned in style to the Caribbean where he had previously plundered with great success.

Morgan was born in Glamorgan in Wales in 1635 and went to America as a young man before he was given a command in a fleet led by the privateer Edward Mansfield, raiding Cuba, Nicaragua and settlements along the South American coast. When Mansfield was killed, Morgan took his place. In 1668 Morgan was commissioned by the governor of Jamaica to find out whether Spanish forces were planning to attack British possessions but exceeded his orders by sailing to Portobello in Panama and sacking the city.

There was no stopping Henry Morgan. He went on to attack and burn Maracaibo in Venezuela and crossed the isthmus to sack Panama City. News had not reached him at that point that peace had been made with Spain and that he was in disgrace. That was three years ago, but now, even in his high office, he is still involved in piracy.

Henry Morgan: the pirate chief who is now governor of Jamaica.

Morgan and his buccaneers attack the people of Maracaibo in 1669.

Frederick William crushes the Swedes

The Elector Frederick William of Brandenburg reviews his troops: his attack on Sweden is seen as one more step in his overall plan to unify Prussia.

Brandenburg, 28 June 1675

Frederick William, the elector of Brandenburg, has joined the war between France and Holland which is not only dominating politics in Europe but is also beginning to spread to the New World in the West Indies.

He has come a long way in the thirty-five years since he inherited a scattered group of lands ravaged by the battles of the Thirty Years' War. He consolidated them successfully, and is now a real force to reckon with. Supporting the Dutch, he has conquered their Swedish rivals at the battle of Fehrbellin and gone on to invade Bremen, Verden and Western Pomerania, Sweden's enclaves in north Germany. The elector's intervention may well have changed the course of the war. Observers note that the French seem to be less committed than previously while Frederick William will be encouraged in his greater plan – the unifying of Prussia.

Polish hero is to be the new king

Poland, 20 May 1674

John Sobieski, the architect of Poland's victories against the Turks, the Ukrainian Cossacks and the Swedes, has been elected king. Now Poland's national hero is its monarch too.

The election of a Polish king is a European concern, with all the major powers vying for influence. Sobieski had to defeat three other candidates, none of them Poles. Duke Charles of Lorraine represented Austrian interests, while the duke of Enghien and the prince of Neuberg both favoured France.

Sobieski himself has external sponsors. His marriage to Marie Casimire d'Arquien means that he has ties to Louis XIV, who wants to use Poland in his campaign against Austria. For the Poles what matters is that Sobieski, the victor of Chotin, the battle that smashed the Turks last year, is determined to resist any possibility of selling out their country. For the foreign ambassadors, each pressing his own country's interests, Sobieski is the strongest man available.

Greenwich observatory founded to help navigation at sea

London, 1675

The enterprise and vision of the astronomer John Flamsteed has now been rewarded. He has been arguing that there is a need to establish an observatory to determine the position of the moon and stars in order to give accurate information on longitude at sea for navigational purposes.

Such an observatory has now been built at Greenwich near the river Thames. Flamsteed has had to equip it with instruments, mostly at his own expense. His observatory houses graduated arcs traversed by telescopic lenses for measuring celestial angles, as well as more humble devices such as a quadrant and sextant. He is now at work on a new star catalogue.

Astronomers using a telescope and a sextant at the Greenwich Observatory, where researches should improve the accuracy of international navigation.

1676 (1676-1679)

Virginia, 26 October 1676. Nathaniel Bacon, the leader of an armed rebellion in the colony of Yorktown, dies. The revolt against the forces of Governor William Berkeley was sparked off by the governor's refusal to support Bacon's raids on the Indians.

Paris, 1676. Paul de Gondi, the cardinal de Retz, completes his *Memoirs*. This clergyman without a vocation demonstrated his political ambition as a party leader during the *Fronde* uprising. As a result of the part he played, he was obliged to give up the archbishopric of Paris.

Paris, 1676. Abbot Edme Mariotte studies the compressibility of gases and verifies the laws discovered by Boyle in 1661 expressing the inverse proportionality of volume and pressure at a constant temperature.

Paris, 1676. The artist and art theorist Abraham Bosse dies. A prolific engraver, Bosse was expelled from the Academy following a dispute with le Brun on the subject of perspective.

Ottoman Empire, 1676. Kara Mustapha succeeds his elder brother as grand vizier.

Massachusetts, 1676. The first coffee-house is licensed in Boston.

Paris, 1 January 1677. Racine's tragedy *Phedre* is staged for the first time.

Amsterdam, 21 February 1677. The Dutch-Jewish philosopher Baruch Spinoza dies of phthisis, aggravated by glass dust in his lungs from years of lens grinding. Expelled from the synagogue at the age of 24, he has led an independent life, in 1673 refusing a professorship of philosophy at Heidelberg University in order to retain that independence. The only work he published during his life (the *Tractatus*, 1670) was banned in 1674, by which time Spinoza's ideas on religion were regarded as dangerously subversive.

Virginia, 27 April 1677. Colonel Jeffreys succeeds William Berkeley as governor of Virginia and halts the executions of the followers of the rebel leader Nathaniel Bacon.

West Africa, 30 October 1677. The French take Goree.

England, 15 November 1677. Mary, the daughter of the duke of York and niece of Charles II, marries William of Orange. This marriage puts the seal on Anglo-Dutch rapprochement.

West Africa, 1677. The Dutch forts in Senegal are conquered by the French.

Netherlands, 1677. Spinoza's *Ethics* is published posthumously: it develops a metaphysical system along Euclidian lines from axioms, theorems and definitions. Only God is infinite; there is no notion of free will, we are "free" only in so far as we act in accordance with God.

Paris, 21 April 1678. Richard Simon, the author of a *Critical History of the Old Testament* which was recently published in Amsterdam, is condemned by Bossuet, the leader of the clergy.

England, November 1678. The country is in the grip of anti-Catholic hysteria following the unsolved murder last month of Sir Edmund Godfrey, who testified with Israel Tonge and Titus Oates that Jesuit priests were involved in a "popish plot" to assassinate king Charles II, put the Catholic James, duke of York on the throne and massacre Protestants. Oates may not be the most reliable witness. Expelled from school and colleges, he has also been dismissed from Holy Orders.

North America, 1678. The French explorer Robert Cavalier, the sieur de la Salle, and his chaplain, Father Louis Hennepin, are the first Europeans to see the Niagara Falls.

Paris, 1678. The Dutch mathematician Christiaan Huygens writes his *Treatise on light*.

England, 1678. The promising English composer Henry Purcell composes music for Shakespeare's *Timon of Athens*.

England, 1678. The Baptist preacher John Bunyan publishes his *Pilgrim's Progress*, an account of life as an allegorical journey with much vivid description and realistic narrative.

England, 1678. The poet laureate John Dryden writes a tragedy entitled *All For Love*. Although of Puritan origins, Dryden is now officially recognised.

Netherlands, 1678. Japanese *Chrysanthemums* are cultivated in Holland.

Netherlands, 5 February 1679. France signs a treaty at Nijmegen with the Holy Roman empire.

New England, 10 July 1679. The English crown claims New Hampshire as a royal colony.

India, 1679. Aurangzeb, the Moghul emperor, reimposes the *jizya* tax on non-Moslems, including those in his armies.

North America, 1679. The French explorer Cavalier de la Salle travels in an uncharted region in the northern central part of the continent (*Indiana*).

French playwright puts down pen at 38

This elaborate stage set is for the production of a play at Versailles.

Paris, 2 January 1677
The opening performance of *Phedre* last night at the hotel de Bourgogne was marred for its author, Jean Racine, by the presentation of a rival play of the same name by Pradon, performed by the *Troupe du Roi* backed by the duchess of Bouillon. Racine's play was recognised as a masterpiece, but he declares that he will write no more for the stage, although he is only 38. France's leading tragediennes are in mourning at the news.

Racine's tragedies observe the rules of Aristotle, confining them to one time and place and leaving all physical action to be described by messenger, as in *Phedre*, where the violent death of Hippolytus is the subject of the poetic Recit de Theramene. The only violence on stage is in the declaration of passion in strict metre.

Racine's older rival, Pierre Corneille, compressed the action of *Le*

A scene from Racine's "Iphigenia"; now the playwright has retired.

Cid into one day, but was still criticised for being too lax. Like Racine he wrote a *Berenice*, a work about the conflict between love and duty.

Huygens suggests light travels in waves

Europe, 1678
An important new scientific work by the Dutchman Christiaan Huygens is said to be near completion. It is titled *Traite de la Lumiere* (Treatise on Light) and contains the idea that light travels in waves.

There have been many theories about the nature of light. The ancient Greeks believed that it originated in objects being viewed. The Platonists believed that light was

the fusion of three rays of matter that originated in the sun.

Isaac Newton contends that light consists of minute particles of matter that emanate from luminous bodies such as stars and travel through space. The Dutch scientist contends that light consists of waves that travel through the ether at great speed, in straight lines and with vibrations at right angles to their direction of travel.

Victorious French impose peace treaty

"The Banquet of Peace": an allegorical rendering of the new treaty.

Nijmegen, 5 February 1679
The third Treaty of Nijmegen was signed here today, thus ending the European war which started with the French invasion of the Netherlands seven years ago. The victorious French, intoxicated with pride, are hailing their king as "Louis the Great".

The war has indeed ended on a victorious note for the French. They forced the Dutch to the conference table by capturing Ghent in a surprise attack a year ago, and under the treaty France acquires Franche-Comte from Spain and remains in control of Lorraine. There is also to be a rationalisation of the frontier in Flanders which gives Louis the "duelling-ground" advocated by the renowned military engineer, Vaubin.

So the French may well hail their hero king: but his victory is not as great as it seems. He embarked on this war to crush the Protestant Dutch and seize control of their maritime trade. The war started brilliantly for him, but then the Dutch cut their dykes and, under William of Orange, fought so bravely that Louis was anxious to make peace, his war aims unfulfilled.

Englishdissenterpublishespilgrim'stale

Bedford, 1678
A Baptist minister, whose faith has condemned him to more than a dozen years in jail has published a remarkable allegory of the true Christian life. A good deal was written in his prison cell.

The Pilgrim's Progress, by John Bunyan, lays out, in the form of a dream, the journey of Christian from the City of Destruction to the Celestial City. On his way he visits such places as Vanity Fair and the Slough of Despond, and meets Mr Worldly Wiseman, Giant Despair and many other characters.

Bunyan's work, equally popular among the learned and the uneducated, is notable for the clarity of its English, its vivid images and the author's sense of the world.

John Bunyan: a visionary writer.

Moslem zealots rebuffed in African war

Senegal, 1677
The Islamic *jihad* that has swept through the western Sahara since 1673 has collapsed. It began when Moslem zealots, led by the charismatic preacher Awbek ben Ashfaga, invaded Futa Toro and the Wolof states on the river Senegal and "liberated" the Zawaya, agriculturalists who were traditonally prey to the aggression of the Hassani, or warrior class.

Ashfaga assumed the title *Nasir al-Din* (Protector of the Faithful), proclaiming a heady mixture of anti-colonialism, social justice, and Islamic millennialism. Nasir al-Din's first task was to establish an Islamic state and collect the *zakat* (Islamic tax). The collection was his undoing.

Resenting Nasir al-Din's presumption in collecting a tax that only a *caliph* is permitted, many of the Zawaya revolted, and were quickly joined by Hassani opportunists under Hadi, the chief of the Trarza. Though Nasir al-Din thrice defeated them, he was killed in the third battle. Leaderless, the *jihad* is disintegrating, to the relief of established Islamic authority.

Church slams unorthodox bible scholar

Amsterdam, 21 April 1678
A new study of the Old Testament has appeared in Holland, and its author is already facing the wrath of the Catholic Church, which condemns it as impious.

A Critical History of the Old Testament, by the Catholic scholar and priest Richard Simon, submits the texts of Genesis and the Prophets to a searching historical and philological analysis. In it Simon has questioned the very bases of Roman Catholic faith. The church has always emphasised that freedom of research and critical analysis is incompatible with true faith when, like Simon's, it challenges current dogma.

Thus, although Simon's work was undertaken as part of the theological struggle against the Huguenots, it has been condemned by the French theologian Bossuet and placed amongst the forbidden books on the Index. Simon himself has been expelled from his order, the Oratorians.

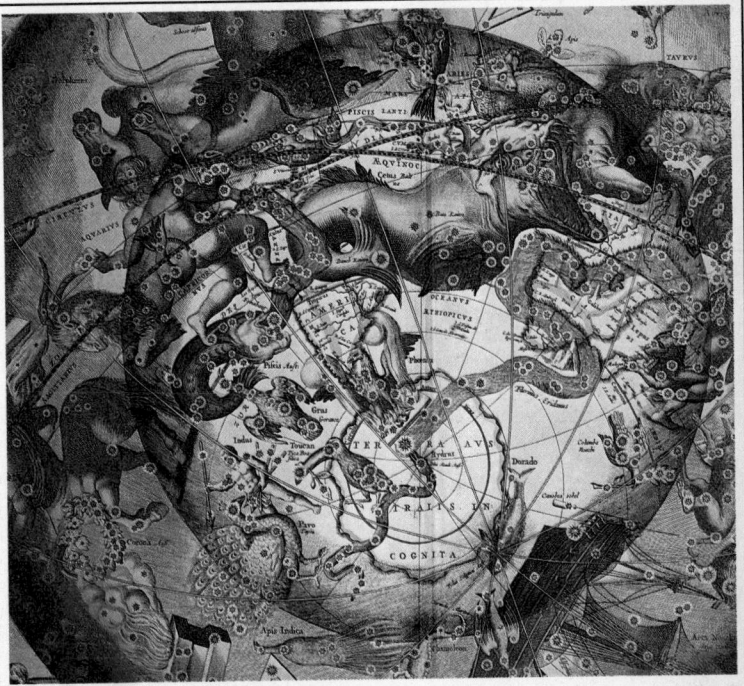

This illustrated astrological print, among the finest examples of celestial charts and featuring a number of the constellations superimposed upon a view of the globe, is one of 29 views of the heavens in the Harmonica Macrocosmica, a celestial atlas compiled by the monk Andreas Cellarius.

India, 1679. The Moghul Emperor Aurangzeb orders the destruction of many Hindu temples.

France, 1679. A study of the basic principles of differential calculus by the mathematician Pierre Fermat is published posthumously.

France, 1679. The Royal Academy of Painting is split by a dispute between the "Poussinists" and the "Rubenists". The latter oppose the rigidity of the Academy's official doctrine, which is based on the ideas of Nicholas Poussin.

Rome, 1679. Alessandro Scarlatti's opera *Gli Equivoci nell'Amore* is performed for the first time.

England, 1679. The astronomer Edmund Halley publishes his *Catalogus stellarum australium*, a catalogue of the stars in the southern hemisphere.

London, May 1679. In spite of King Charles II's opposition, the Act of Habeas Corpus is passed, making it impossible for anyone to be imprisoned without a court appearance.

China, 1679. The Chinese novelist and playwright Li Yu dies. The author of many popular and sometimes licentious novels, he was also a painter and decorative artist. He edited an encyclopaedia of Chinese painting and ran his own theatre company.

India, 1680. The death of Sivaji, the national hero of the Marathas, is followed by clashes between the Great Moghul Aurangzeb and the Marathas' allies the Rajputs.

London, May 1680. An Exclusion Bill, against the succession of James, the duke of York, is passed by the Commons but thrown out by the Lords.

New Mexico, 13 August 1680. The expulsion of the Spanish from Santa Fe by Indians under Chief Pope sets off a war.

England, 25 September 1680. The English satirist Samuel Butler, author of *Hudibras*, dies.

New England, September 1680. The province of New Hampshire is separated from Massachusetts by a Royal Commission.

London, 20 November 1680. John Culpeper, a customs officer from South Carolina, is acquitted of treason after leading the first popular uprising in America – in opposition to the imposition of English trade laws.

England, 30 November 1680. The Dutch painter Peter Lely, who settled in London in 1641 and was employed by Charles I, Cromwell and Charles II, dies. Among his finest works are 13 portraits of the English admirals who fought in the second Dutch war.

France, 1680. The French writer Francois La Rochefoucauld dies.

Paris, 1680. A new theatre, the Comedie Francaise, opens.

Indian Ocean, 1680. The last dodos in Mauritius are killed by English sailors. These large flightless birds were hunted for their meat and plumage.

West Africa, 1680. The Asante kingdom is founded on the Gold Coast.

Poland, 8 January 1681. The treaty of Radzin ends a war which began in 1678 when the Turks under Grand Vizier Kara Mustafa launched a campaign to expel the Russians and Poles from the Ukraine. By the treaty the Turks give up claims to the Ukraine.

England, March 1681. Charles II convenes a parliament in Oxford to debate the exclusion of his Catholic brother James, duke of York, from the succession. A compromise solution fails and the parliament is dissolved after a week.

France, 1681. The building of the canal du Midi, begun in 1664, is completed. The canal, which is more than 120 miles (192km) long, links the gulf of Gascony with the Mediterranean.

Netherlands, 1681. The genre and portrait painter Gerard Terborch dies in Deventer. He specialised in genteel interior scenes and his best compositions rival those of Vermeer.

Netherlands, 1681. Forced to flee France, the rationalist philosopher Pierre Bayle takes refuge in Holland and becomes professor of philosophy at Rotterdam. The son of a Calvinist minister, Bayle converted to Catholicism and then reconverted to Protestantism.

England, 1681. The theologian Thomas Burnet publishes his *Sacred History of the Earth*, developing his fantastic ideas on evolution.

France, 1681. The Benedictine monk Jean Mabillon publishes *De re diplomatica*, which lays the foundation for a science of diplomatics.

Madrid, 1681. The great Spanish dramatic poet Pedro Calderon de la Barca dies. His works include light comedies and many plays of religious inspiration.

China, 1681. The Ch'ing government gains firm control of China after a major civil war between semiautonomous "princes" in the south and south-east of the country.

India, 1681. Akbar, rebel son of the Great Moghul Aurangzeb, flees to the Dekhan. His father uses this as a pretext to invade the region.

Commons try to exclude Catholic heir

Two playing cards illustrating events in the plot against the Protestants.

London, 1680

With public opinion inflamed by lurid stories of popish plots to persecute Protestants and restore the Catholic religion, the House of Commons has set out to secure the exclusion of James, the duke of York, from succession to the throne. James, the brother of Charles II, was forced into exile after he converted to Catholicism and married Mary of Modena, a Catholic princess.

When Charles fell ill recently, James returned from Brussels and MPs made another attempt to push through an Exclusion Bill, only to be frustrated by the Lords. The Exclusionists, or Whigs as they have come to be called, represent the moneyed middle classes; but their willingness to encourage the London mobs in order to put pressure on the king has caused concern. Many Tory peers who were critical of James in the past now support him because they fear the Whigs are undermining the established order. Whigs denounce these Tories as "Papists in disguise".

On one important issue Charles has given way: he has accepted the Habeas Corpus Amendment Act, which makes it impossible for the Crown to imprison anyone without a court appearance.

French sell slaves in the West Indies

Paris, 1679

The French government has set up the "Compagnie francaise d'Afrique". The company's aim is to transport 16,000 slaves to the West Indies in eight years. Since Louis XIII authorised slave-trading in 1642 vast profits have been made providing labour for the coffee, tea and sugar plantations in the New World – in spite of a quarter of each shipment dying en route. The company's main competitor is the British owned Royal Africa Company, which has transported 40,000 slaves to the West Indies since 1674.

The dodo: the last of these large flightless birds has been killed in Mauritius by British sailors.

New high-speed pot piles on pressure

London, 1680
While working here at the Royal Society, the French physicist, Denis Papin, has invented what he calls a "New Digester". This is a cast-iron cooking pot with an air-tight lid which allows the liquids inside to boil at higher than normal temperatures. There is also a safety valve fitted in the lid. Food is cooked, by pressurised steam, in about a quarter of the normal time. The device helps to improve the texture and flavour of meat. He writes in a booklet: "The oldest and hardest Cow-Beef may be made as tender as young choice meat".

Denis Papin: a culinary pioneer.

Prince Akbar loses chance to oust father

Ajmir, India, 27 January 1681
The characteristic of disloyalty, which Aurangzeb, the fanatical Moghul emperor, used so effectively against his father Shahjahan, has been passed on to his favourite son, Akbar. When the Rajputs rebelled against the poll tax, Aurangzeb put Akbar in command of the Moghul army sent to subdue them. So incompetent was Akbar he was relieved of his command.

Smarting under the humiliation, and convinced his father's brutal policy against the Hindu Rajputs threatened the spirit of religious toleration he made an alliance with the Rajputs to overthrow his father. The Rajputs had clashed with Aurangzeb after the death last year of Sivaji, their prime Maratha ally.

Akbar's army, joined by the Rajputs, marched on Ajmir, where Aurangzeb resided. Aurangzeb resorted to the tactic he had used in Afghanistan: guile. He wrote a

Heroic Sivaji, painted c.1700.

letter to Akbar implying that father and son were leading the Rajputs into a trap and let it fall into the hands of the Rajputs. By morning Akbar's army had melted away.

Gold brings wealth to Asante kingdom

Ghana, West Africa, 1680
In the forests of West Africa, the Akan petty states are uniting. Rich from the gold and slave trades, supported by a strong army, amd cemented by a common religion, they have become a new regional power. They are the Asantes.

The new Asante kingdom is not based on tribes. It has modern institutions: tax collectors, judges and a bureaucracy. The Asante leader, Osei Tutu, who first

brought the Akan states together to free themselves of the domination of their neighbours, the Denkyira, is a first-rate general and politician.

The symbol of the state is the Golden Throne, which is said to have descended from the Asante god on to the lap of Osei Tutu. The Throne, or Stool, is only shown in public on important ceremonial occasions. It not only represents the unity of the Asante, but guarantees their well-being too.

Manchus wipe out Ming resistance

China, 1681
The Manchu emperor, Kangxi has defeated the rebellion of the Three Feudatories, killed its leader, Wu San-kuei, and finally established Manchu rule over the whole of mainland China.

The three feudatories were all former Ming generals who had gone over to the Manchus and put down Ming resistance in South China, where they set up powerful semi-independent states. They demanded huge amounts of money from the government and Wu, who had ordered the strangling of the last Ming emperor in the marketplace at Yunnan, was warlord of a formidable army.

They started their rebellion when Kangxi ordered them to disband their armies since there was no longer any threat from the Ming. But Wu, whose betrayal in opening up the Great Wall to the Manchus led to the downfall of the Ming, now betrayed the Manchus to restore what he had destroyed.

He very nearly succeeded, but a fatal hesitancy in his attack on Beijing allowed Kangxi to gather an army, relying on other former Ming generals who remained loyal to him. Wu was defeated and slain, his body chopped into many pieces. And now the Ch'ing dynasty of the Manchus rules all China.

Prince banned from fighting the French

The Netherlands, 1681
A bitter disagreement over foreign policy has arisen between William of Orange and the republic's state leaders. To protect the economy, they have stopped' him sending Dutch troops into Europe to quell French hostilities. William, the son-in-law of James, duke of York, who is heir to the English throne, became Dutch leader when John de Witt's regime was overthrown in 1672. For six years he led his country against French attack and occupation. He won limited hereditary power in 1675. An alliance with Spain, Germany and Britain helped him secure the Franco-Dutch Treaty in 1678.

Bernini, the Roman fountain designer, dies a disappointed man

Rome, 1680
Giovanni Bernini, who left such a mark on Rome with his colonnaded piazza in front of St Peter's, intended to make as a big an impact on Paris; but he has died disappointed in that ambition. In 1665 he was summoned to Paris by Louis XIV to submit designs for the eastern front of the Louvre. However, his flamboyantly curving facades were rejected by the king in favour of the French designers, Le Vau and Perrault. Bernini's last work was the tomb of Pope Alexander VII in St Peter's, where so much of the decoration was his.

Rome's glories: St Peter's, flanked by the Vatican and Bernini's Piazza.

1681 (1681-1683)

France, 1681. Following the occupation of Strasbourg by the armies of Louis XIV, the city is annexed to the French kingdom.

Russia, 1681. As Russia extends its boundaries eastwards, the Tartar lands in the Volga region are confiscated and there are forced conversions to Christianity.

Hungary, 1681. The treaty of Sopron between the Emperor Leopold and the Hungarian nobility restores the Hungarian constitution.

England, 1681. When his protector Lord Shaftesbury is imprisoned for high treason against the Stuarts, the philosopher John Locke, who had retreated to Oxford, is expelled from the university.

England, 1681. The poet John Dryden publishes a fine political satire entitled *Absalom and Achitophel*.

Zimbabwe, c.1681. Changamire Dombo, at the head of an army called the "Rozvi", coming from the eastern Zimbabwe plateau, conquers the Torwa of Butua and makes his capital at Danongombe.

Netherlands, 14 March 1682. The Dutch painter Jacob van Rysdael dies in Haarlem. He excelled in country landscapes and seascapes.

Spain, 3 April 1682. The Spanish painter Bartolome Esteban Murillo dies. He won fame for his cycle of paintings for the Franciscan monastery in Seville and in 1660 become first director of the Academy in Seville. He will be best remembered for his devotional pictures and his genre scenes of peasant children.

North America, 9 April 1682. Having travelled the length of the Mississippi river, the explorer Robert Cavelier, known as La Salle, formally claims possession of the entire Mississippi valley for France. He names the region Louisiana in honour of his king, Louis XIV.

Rome, 11 April 1682. Pope Innocent XI condemns the Declaration of the Four Articles – drawn up by Jacques Benigne Bossuet, the leader of the French clergy – which seeks to reconcile papal authority with Gallican independence.

Hungary, 1682. The Protestant nobleman Imre Tokoly, leader of the revolt against the Emperor Leopold in Hungary and Transylvania which began four years ago, is proclaimed king of Hungary by the Turks.

North America, 1682. Spaniards fleeing the New Mexican Pueblo revolt found the first settlement in Texas.

Ethiopia, 1682. Iyasu (the Great) comes the throne.

Paris, 1682. The English astronomer Edmund Halley observes a comet and plots its orbit.

England, November 1682. After trying unsuccessfully to organise a revolt of radical Whigs following his acquital from prison, the earl of Shaftesbury flees to Holland.

England, 1682. John Bunyan publishes a complex allegorical work entitled *The Holy War*.

England, 1682. Isaac Newton discovers the law of universal gravitation which identifies the nature of the earth's gravity and the pull of the heavenly bodies.

North America, 1682. The English Quaker William Penn founds Philadelphia and the colony of Pennsylvania.

Netherlands, 1682. The French philosopher Pierre Bayle publishes his *Thoughts on the comet* in Rotterdam. On the pretext of challenging superstition, he tackles great metaphysical and theological questions, separating the moral from the religious.

France, 1682. The court of Louis XIV is installed at Versailles.

France, 1682. The Huguenots are excluded from the commercial guilds, financial posts and from the house of the king.

Russia, 1682. Fyodor III dies childless and without naming a successor. The proclamation as czar, of Peter, nine-year-old son of Czar Alexis, is followed by a bloody revolt by the Moscow guard known as the Streltsy. Peter's half-brother Ivan is raised to the throne as co-czar and their elder sister Sophia is appointed regent.

Japan, 1682. The philosopher Yamazaki Ansai dies. Taking his inspiration from the Chinese philosophers of the Song dynasty, he founded thriving schools in Kyoto and Edo (*Tokyo*).

Germany, 1682. *Acta Eruditorum*, the first learned periodical in Germany, begins publication.

West Africa, 1682. Kaladian Coulibaly, king of Segu (*Mali*) since 1652, dies. He made his kingdom into a regional power, guaranteeing the independence of the Bambara.

England, 1683. The Republican politician Algernon Sidney is executed for his alleged involvement in the Rye House Plot against the Stuarts. The duke of Monmouth, illegitimate son of Charles II, also implicated in the plot, is forced into exile.

King's gift aids Quakers' holy experiment

Philadelphia, 31 October 1682
A few days ago the 300-ton *Welcome* arrived here from England. It is perhaps the twentieth ship bearing English Quaker refugees from religious persecution to arrive here in the past year. The difference is that this ship brought with it the 38-year-old English Quaker, William Penn, who is the absolute monarch of this town and the new colony of Pennsylvania which surrounds it.

Penn has been here before. Working with new idealistic settlers in West Jersey he recognised the possibilities. Back in England he used his political skills to persuade King Charles II to give him royal land here to repay debts of £16,000 owed to his father, Admiral Penn.

The Royal Charter of last March gave him absolute powers. But Penn intends this as a "holy experiment" in which "myself and my successors" have "no power of doing mischief" and ensuring that "the will of one man may not hin-

William Penn negotiates with the Indian natives of Pennsylvania.

der the good of a whole country". His cousin, William Markham, has built this town, and won the support of the 2,000 white settlers here with a democratic "frame of government". The Indians, too, have warmed to this Englishman, who is a devoted pacificist.

Soldiers force conversions in France

Poitiers, 1681
Thousands of Huguenots all over France are being forced to give up their Protestant religion. There has been steadily increasing pressure on them because of the wish of King Louis XIV and some of the Catholic bishops to have a unified France with one religion. The Edict of Nantes of 1598, which gave Huguenots religious freedom, is now being persistently ignored. This town, however, has led the way in Draconian measures. Marillac, the local *intendant*, is using the traditional police practice of quartering soldiers on unruly citizens. These "missionaries in boots" are extracting forcible conversions. But many Huguenots are wealthy merchants and they are emigrating rather than give in.

Louis XIV annexes town of Strasbourg

Strasbourg, 30 September 1681
The independent city of Strasbourg surrendered to Louis XIV's army today under threat of being put to the sword. The citizens, knowing Louis' reputation in these matters, had no option but to open the gates.

Strasbourg thus becomes the latest victim of the French policy of *reunion* under which Louis is using force beneath a cloak of legalism to take advantage of the confusion arising out of the Treaties of Westphalia and Nijmegen. All of Alsace, with the exception of Mulhouse, is now French.

A London lamplighter and his apprentice ply their daily trade.

Sun King's court moves to Versailles

Versailles, 6 May, 1682

King Louis XIV arrived today at his new chateau at Versailles with his family, ministers and court, and announced that from now onwards it would be the seat of French government. He has been making visits for years to inspect the building work that has transformed his father's hunting lodge into the largest palace in Europe.

In 1679 Jules Hardouin Mansart succeeded the original architect Louis le Vau, who had built the central block. He has added two great wings, the southern one for royal princes and their families, the northern one for the courtiers, many hundreds of whom are lodged in the building. With a block for 1,500 servants and stables for the Master of the Horse and the pages, the chateau is a small town with a population of over 2,000 people. There is a service of sedan chairs to carry them from one point to another.

Mansart's new Hall of Mirrors, of immense length, with a ceiling painted by Charles le Brun, is the main assembly point and the scene for the fetes and gambling parties that are a feature of court life. The gardens of formal terraces, ornamental basins of water lined with statuary and 1,500 fountains are the work of Andre le Notre. The tapestries and furnishings of the chateau are all designed by Le Brun

Lemonnier's painting of Louis XIV unveiling a new statue at Versailles.

and made at the Gobelins factory. The king insists on the strictest etiquette and punctuality throughout the royal day which is regulated by ceremonial – his *lever*, the procession to Mass, reception of ambassadors, his dining in public, his hunting in the afternoons and the evening entertainments, for which he may order the court to appear in new clothes. Many of the nobility fear that they may be ruined by the expense of court life.

Also in residence are Madame de Montespan, who has apartments next to his own, and his new favourite, Madame de Maitenon, who looked after the children whom she had by the king.

Mansart's "Galerie des Glaces" at Versailles, finished in 1684.

Whigs executed on charge of plotting to murder Charles

London, 1683

The so-called Rye House Plot has the makings of a re-run of the notorious Popish Plot fabricated by Titus Oates five years ago – but with the tables turned. Now it is the Whigs who are the victims of fanciful and often false evidence.

They are said to have plotted to assassinate Charles II and James as they passed Rumbold's Rye House on the London-to-Newmarket road. Prominent Whigs have been executed and others have fled.

Lord Shaftesbury, the former chancellor who intrigued against the Catholic James, escaped to Holland after being accused of treason and died there recently. He played a leading role in the persecution of Catholics after Oates, a sacked navy chaplain, claimed to have discovered a Popish Plot to assassinate Charles II and put James on the throne. Crowds roamed the streets of London threatening Catholics.

The latest purges are not limited to politicians. The City of London, a Whig stronghold, has lost its charter and universities are being brought to heel. John Locke, the philosopher, has left Oxford and fled to Holland, where he goes by the name of Dr Van der Linden, as he works on a book on human understanding.

Russian writer and priest dies at stake

Pustozersk, Russia, 1682

Avvakum, the leader of the a breakaway sect known as the "Old Believers", has been burnt at the stake after spending 15 years in a subterranean prison in the north of Russia. A talented but fanatical priest, he produced a string of sermons and treatises rejecting the influence of the Greek and Latin churches. Avvakum's movement has drawn large numbers of strictly Orthodox Russians, although it has been persecuted by the authorities. Whole groups of its members, even as many as 2,500, have turned to mass suicide by burning, a death preferable to eternal hellfire.

Celebrated landscape painter, Claude Lorrain, dies in Rome

Rome, 23 November, 1682

Claude Lorrain, the greatest of French landscape painters, died today in Rome where he lived and worked from the age of 13. He was 82 and famed for his mastery of light effects. He could even depict the rising or setting sun convincingly illuminating his landscapes.

Lorrain's real name was Gellee, but he was always known after his home province. Like his friend and compatriot Nicolas Poussin, who also spent his life in Rome, Claude liked to sketch direct from nature in the Campagna countryside outside Rome, littered with the remains of Roman architecture. But his ideal mythological landscapes were always imaginary.

Claude Lorraine's "Landscape with the arrival of Aeneas at Pallanteum".

1683 (1683-1685)

Pennsylvania, 23 June 1683. William Penn signs a treaty of peace and brotherhood with the Indians in his new colony.

Vienna, 13 July 1683. Having invaded Austria earlier in the year, the Turks lay siege to Vienna.

Paris, 6 September 1683. Jean Baptiste Colbert, Louis XIV's chief aide, dies. Active in all spheres of public life, Colbert sought to boost the economy by state intervention and to control state spending, but his oppressive taxes provoked public hatred.

Austria, 12 September 1683. A combined Austrian and Polish army, led by Charles of Lorraine and John III Sobieski of Poland, defeats the Turks at Kahlenberg.

New York, November 1683. A Charter of Liberties is enacted, banning taxation without consent.

Serbia, 25 December 1683. On the orders of Sultan Mehmet IV, the grand vizier Kara Mustafa, who led the disastrous Ottoman invasion of Austria, is strangled in Belgrade.

Versailles, 1683. Queen Marie Therese dies. Madame de Maitenon, Louis XIV's new favourite, marries the king in secret.

Iceland, 1683. An Icelandic translation of the Bible by Gudbrandur Thorlaksson is published.

Germany, 1683. The writer Daniel Caspar von Lohenstein, a master of German baroque drama, dies. He leaves unfinished an enormously long novel entitled *Arminius*.

Crimea, 1683. The Tartar chief Murat Giray is exiled by the Ottomans. He had attempted to impose a policy of independence in the Crimea and to replace the "divine law" of Islam with that of Genghis Khan.

West Africa, 1683. Merchants from Brandenburg establish a trading post on the Gold Coast.

China, 1683. Dutch merchants win the right to trade with Canton.

Taiwan, 1683. The Chinese seize the island of Taiwan, destroying the empire of Cheng Ching.

Portugal, 1683. Peter II becomes king of Portugal in succession to his brother Alfonso VI, during whose reign he was regent.

Netherlands, June 1684. A French army under Marshall Crequi seizes Luxembourg.

Germany, August 1684. The Emperor Leopold signs a 20-year truce with Louis XIV of France at Ratisbon, under which France retains control of Strasbourg and Luxembourg.

Paris, 30 September 1684. The tragedian Pierre Corneille, whose *Le Cid* took Paris by storm in 1636, dies.

Paris, 1684. *Nova Methodis pro Maximus et Minimus* by the German philosopher Gottfried Leibnitz, is published in French. In the essay the author sets forth the process which led him to create differential calculus.

South-East Africa, 1684. Changamire Dombo defeats the Portuguese at the battle of Maungwe.

Rome, 1684. Pope Innocent IX forms a Holy League with Venice, Austria and Poland against the Turks.

Netherlands, 1684. Pierre Bayle founds *Nouvelles de la Republique des Lettres*, a review of literary and intellectual life published in Rotterdam but reaching and reporting the whole European "republic of letters".

London, 1684. During an extraordinarily cold winter a "Frost Fair" is held on the frozen Thames. Streets of stalls are set up, meat is roasted on the spit; football, bowls, ninepins, throwing the cock, even foxhunting, are performed on the ice. A novel means of getting about is "sliding with skeetes" (skating).

Japan, 1684. The great Japanese writer Ihara Saikaku composes 23,400 *haikai* verses in a single day and night.

England, 16 February 1685. At the death of Charles II, his brother James II, the duke of York succeeds as the new king of England.

England, July 1685. Defeated by James II's army at Sedgemoor, the duke of Monmouth, illegitimate son of Charles II, is beheaded. Last month Monmouth, who was exiled two years ago after the Rye House Plot, landed at Lyme Regis in Dorset with a small band of men and denounced King James as an usurper.

England, September 1685. Judge George Jeffreys is appointed lord chancellor after presiding over the "bloody assizes" in which about 320 men implicated in the Monmouth rebellion were sentenced to death.

France, 18 October 1685. To force the all French to practise Roman Catholic religion, Louis XIV revokes the 1598 Edict of Nantes, which granted civil liberties and political powers to Protestants.

Scotland, 1685. A rebellion in Scotland on behalf of the duke of Monmouth fails and its leader, the earl of Argyll, is executed.

Emperor Kangxi's tour of Kiang Han in 1699: after Chai Ping Chan.

Enlightened rule of Manchurian emperor

Beijing, 1683
A golden age of culture is blooming under the enlightened reign of Emperor Kangxi. This reign has now lasted for 22 years and has been characterised by the emperor's policy of tolerance towards the Chinese gentry. Although this is partly a question of political prudence, to avert opposition, it also reflects the emperor's own cultural interests. He is a musician, poet, and calligrapher and has a keen interest in the sciences. His patronage has ensured that with the honourable exception of some Ming scholars who have exiled themselves in the south, most of the Chinese scholar officials have transferred their loyalty to the Manchus.

Louis XIV's wife founds poor-girls' school

France, 1684
A year after their secret marriage Francoise de Maitenon and King Louis XIV have founded a girls' school at St Cyr convent. Born in a debtors' prison in 1635, Francoise had a sobering affect on the King. She feared that if he did not mend his extravagant ways he would suffer divine retribution. Francoise met the king when she was nanny to his illegitimate children. When he legitimized them in 1673 he ordered her to bring them to the court and infuriated de Montespan and de Fontanges, his mistresses, when he gave Francoise the estate of Maitenon. After Queen Maria Theresa died, the king made her his morganatic wife.

The royal mistress in a suitably romantic setting: by Casper Netscher.

Protestant churches to be demolished following reversal of Edict of Nantes

Fontainebleau, 18 October 1685
King Louis XIV today revoked the Edict of Nantes, signed by his father in 1598, and granting religious and political freedom to the Huguenots. The move is only the logical extension of the policies of the past four years, during which the Edict has been ignored in practice. Louis is determined to stamp out Protestantism in France.

Nevertheless, today's Edict of Fontainebleau is even more severe than expected. Protestant worship is to be forbidden and the churches demolished. All citizens are being forced into Catholic baptism and marriage. Ministers who refuse to recant are being banished. At the same time the laity are being forbidden to emigrate. The latter measure reflects the king's concern about the economic effects on France of the massive emigration of Huguenots over the past four years. They include many wealthy merchants and skilled craftsmen and countries like England have welcomed their talents.

Many Catholics are rejoicing today. The Edict of Nantes did not abolish the fierce hatred existing between the two religious groups. Louis himself has been as much driven by the desire for political stability as for religious unity. The revolt at La Rochelle in 1628 had convinced him that Protestantism was a political threat to the monarchy while it existed.

Triumphant Catholic zealots demolish the Protestant temple at Charenton.

Luxembourg ceded to France by Spain

Luxembourg, August 1684
Luxembourg, which was occupied by the French army in June, has been ceded to France by Spain in a 20-year truce signed in a Dominican convent in Bavaria. Louis XIV has thus benefited again from the spoiling tactics of his army while the rest of Europe has been occupied with driving the Turks from the gates of Vienna.

The signatories to the Treaty of Ratisbon all had good reasons to sign: Spain because it had been thrashed by the French army; Emperor Leopold because he wished to pursue the Turks and; Louis because the treaty confirmed the gains made by his policy of *reunion*.

James II succeeds debauched Charles

London, 1685
After the amorous and dissolute Charles II, the new king, James II, presents himself as a model of rectitude and frugality. He has called an early parliament, but ensured a subservient one by ordering lord lieutenants to keep out Whigs and make sure Tories are elected.

The Whig cause has been damaged by inept rebellions mounted by the duke of Argyll and the duke of Monmouth, Charles II's illegitimate son. At the "Bloody Assizes" this year Judge Jeffreys sentenced 320 of Monmouth's supporters to be hanged, 841 to be sent as slaves to the plantations, and many more to be flogged.

Vienna siege is lifted

A panoramic view of the Turkish armies during their siege of Vienna.

Vienna, 12 September 1683
Vienna is saved. A 70,000-strong Christian army led by Charles, the duke of Lorraine and King John Sobieski of Poland has routed the vast Ottoman army that has been encamped around the city for the past eight weeks.

Six months ago, Kara Mustafa, the Turkish grand vizier, was in Adrianople, assembling an army of 200,000 men, purportedly to come to the aid of Tekeli in Hungary, and to capture the fortresses of Gyor and Komarom. The real target seems to have been Vienna. There was no effective opposition as Mustafa's forces marched towards Vienna. The siege began on 13 July, and although the Viennese had an advantage in artillery, and the 13,000-strong garrison resisted strongly, it could not have survived much longer.

But Kara Mustafa made fatal errors. He allowed the relief force to cross the Danube, and occupy the Kahlenberg Heights. He then tried to repel the attackers with cavalry alone, and did not commit his main force of janissaries until the initiative had been lost.

Duke of Lorraine defeats the Turks

The Duke of Lorraine, saviour of Vienna from the Ottoman forces.

Hungary, 1685
The Ottoman armies, once threatening Vienna itself, are being driven out of Hungary in a series of defeats inflicted by Imperial troops under Charles, the duke of Lorraine.

Turkish fortunes have been declining since the Ottomans were repulsed at Vienna in 1683. Now the armies of the Holy League, drawn from Venice, Poland, Malta, Tuscany and the papacy, are moving steadily across Hungary.

The Turks are not just suffering military setbacks. Morale in their empire is at an all-time low; the nobility are losing their lands, soldiers go unpaid and the poor have barely enough to eat.

1685 (1685-1688)

Germany, 8 November 1685. Frederick William, elector of Brandenburg, issues the Edict of Potsdam, offering French Huguenots refuge in Brandenburg.

France, 1685. A *code noir* is published defining slaves as chattels with no rights to ownership or justice – though they are allowed to rest on Sundays and be instructed in the Christian religion. The code also specifies punishments for slaves.

South Carolina, 1685. The renunciation of the Edict of Nantes spurs the migration of French Huguenots to South Carolina.

West Africa, 1685. King Wegbaja, who created the kingdom of Dahomey at Abomey, dies and is succeeded by his son Akaba.

South Africa, 1685. French Huguenots begin to settle at the Cape of Good Hope.

China, 1685. Louis XIV, king of France, sends five Jesuits to China, where they found a mission in Peking.

Hungary, 8 July 1686. The Austrians take Buda from the Turks and annex Hungary.

Russia, October 1686. Having joined Pope Innocent XI's Holy League and ensured the safety of Kiev by a treaty with Poland, Russia declares war on the Ottoman empire.

Germany, 1686. The Emperor Leopold breaks the 1684 truce of Ratisbon and joins the League of Augsburg, formed by Sweden and several German states to oppose Louis XIV of France.

India, 1686. The French found Chandernagore.

Bulgaria, 1686. An anti-Turkish conspiracy is uncovered at Tarnovo. The Turks destroy the town.

Moscow, 1686. The Russian painter and engraver Semion Fedorovitch Ouchakov dies. Famous for his decoration of churches, Ouchakov opened an icon workshop in Moscow.

Ireland, January 1687. Richard Talbot, earl of Tyrconnel, is appointed viceroy of Ireland.

North America, 19 March 1687. The French explorer La Salle is murdered by his own men while searching for the mouth of the Mississippi along the coast of the gulf of Mexico.

England, 14 April 1687. Having failed to persuade Parliament to repeal the 1673 Test Act, James II issues a Declaration of Indulgence, granting toleration to both Catholics and non-conformists.

Hungary, 12 August 1687. Charles of Lorraine defeats the Turks at the battle of Mohacs.

India, 1687. The Great Moghul Aurangzeb conquers and annexes the Deccan sultanate of Golconda.

Greece, 1687. The Venetians under Francesco Morosini, who have recently seized parts of Dalmatia and Morea, attack the Turks in Greece. They take Corinth and lay siege to Athens. The Parthenon, converted into a powder magazine by the Turks, is seriously damaged by a Venetian shell.

Istanbul, 1687. With the Ottoman empire in a state of complete anarchy, Sultan Mehmet IV is deposed by the Janissaries. He is succeeded by his younger brother Suleiman II.

England, 1687. The economist Sir William Petty, author of *Political Arithmetic*, a study of the value of comparative statistics, dies. Petty, who also wrote a *Treatise on Taxes* and invented a copying machine and a double-keeled boat, was one of the first members of the Royal Society.

Moscow, 1687. In a gesture of reconciliation between church leaders who are open to western ideas and those who think them dangerous, a Slavono-Greek-Latin academy is established.

Paris, 1687. Francois Fenelon writes his *Treatise on the Education of Girls*, in which he argues that a sound education depends on the fulfilment of a child's natural abilities.

Pennsylvania, 18 February 1688. The radical Protestant sect known as the Mennonites – which evolved out of the Anabaptist movement of last century – is the first religious group in the colonies to condemn slavery.

Hungary, 9 May 1688. The diet of Transylvania accedes to Habsburg domination.

England, 31 August 1688. John Bunyan, author of *The Pilgrim's Progress*, dies.

Serbia, 6 September 1688. Imperial troops defeat the Turks to take Belgrade.

Europe, 1688. Taking advantage of the Emperor Leopold's activities in the Balkans against the Turks, Louis XIV of France begins an undeclared war against the Holy Roman Empire. French forces capture the Palatinate, Trier, Mainz and Cologne and invade Franconia and Swabia.

Versailles, 1688. Jules Hardouin Mansart, chief architect to Louis XIV, constructs the Grand Trianon at the Palace of Versailles.

Emperor's son crowned king of Hungary

Buda, 9 December 1687

The Ottoman empire has suffered a major reverse at the hands of Emperor Leopold I's Habsburg army which has boldly fought its way across the plains to occupy much of Hungary and Transylvania in a campaign lasting more than four years.

The emperor's son, Joseph, was today crowned king of Hungary, putting Austria and Hungary under a Habsburg crown. This has been achieved despite the reluctance of the Magyars now freed of Turkish occupation.

The invasion of Hungary became inevitable when the Turkish army was defeated at Vienna, but remained in strength in Hungary. Leopold's diplomats succeeded in securing a truce with Louis XIV and arranging an alliance with Poland and Venice.

Japanese writer tells passionate stories

Diptych by Kitao Masanobu: "The Autographs of Yoshiwara Beauties".

Japan, 1686

The master of Japanese prose, Ihara Saikaku, has produced a sensational narrative, *Five Women of Pleasure*. It tells of the tragic lives of courtesans in five connected stories, all based on recent events.

Like his long narrative, *The Life of a Libertine*, it is a satire and has earned him the rebuke of the moralists. Ihara Saikaku originally practised as a poet. Now he is building up a survey of the way society lives today.

Prison critique puts midwife in the dock

London, England, 1687

Elizabeth Cellier, the Catholic midwife who was acquitted of "the Meal Tub plot" in June, is to be tried for her criticism of conditions inside Newgate prison. Many believe that the case has been trumped up to prevent her from being a witness in another case involving allegations of conspiracy to murder the king. Mrs Cellier, a pioneer of midwifery and obstetric skills, was first taken to Newgate after allegations that evidence of a conspiracy to prevent James' accession to the throne had been hidden in her meal tub.

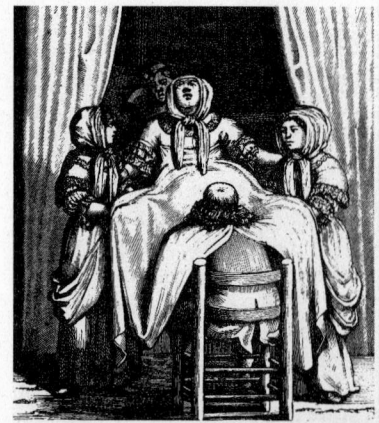

A midwife's profession: obstetrics.

The Universe attracts, says scientist

London, 1687
Two long, hard years of sustained writing effort have culminated in a new book from the mathematician and physicist, Isaac Newton, which is being proclaimed a masterpiece by those fellow-countrymen who are able to understand it. It is called *Philosophiae Naturalis Principia Mathematica*, The Mathematical Principles of Natural Philosophy and consists of three parts. The first part is devoted to the motions of bodies in an unresisting medium – such as planets in orbit round the sun; the second looks at bodies in resisting mediums such as fluids; the third applies these mechanical theories to astronomical problems, and demonstrates what the author calls "the frame of the System of the World".

In the *Principia*, Newton formulates a law of gravitation which is universally applicable. And he supports this gravitational theory with detailed and convincing mathematical proofs, including the use of the calculus. Newton also explicitly defines such concepts as force, momentum and mass and states three laws of motion.

Law one deals with inertia; a body stays at rest unless acted upon by forces. The second law states that the change of motion in a body is in proportion to the force acting on it, and is in a straight line. And the third law states that for every

Newton's reflecting telescope.

action in nature there is an equal and equivalent reaction.

However, it is the notion of a gravitational force that is capturing everyone's imagination. In Newton's universe, every single piece of matter, from a star to a feather, exerts a force on every other particle. This force is proportional to the product of their masses and inversely proportional to the square of the distance between them.

This universal gravitational law makes sense of the whole structure of the cosmos, and in doing so, produces a unified description of the earth and the heavens.

A microscope by Christopher Cock.

Isaac Newton: by Antonio Verrio.

A Chinese silver gilt teapot of the late 18th century, with bamboo-shaped spout. This was a rare piece made specifically for the European market.

Negro code to help French sugar slaves

France, 1685
France's negro slaves, whose labour creates the wealth the nation draws from her sugar plantations in the New World, are to be given some respite from the harsh conditions under which they work. The Negro Code is designed to offer them more humane treatment. For the first time they are to receive adequate food, as well as regular time off to cultivate their own crops. But the whip, source of so much cruelty, is to be retained.

Protestants wary of new tolerance by Catholic king

London, 14 April 1687
An ostensible act of reconciliation by James II has been received with great mistrust by his people. The King today issued a Declaration of Indulgence by which all penal laws in matters of religion are suspended. Prominent Dissenters are being released from prison and wooed. But James is a convinced Catholic and he is packing the Privy Council with Catholics. The chief commands of the army and navy have been given to Catholics, and they are being forced on universities. Even the royalist Lord Halifax is hostile. "You are being hugged now only that you may be better squeezed later," he warns English Protestants.

French poets clash over modern arts

Paris, 27 January 1687
The Academie Francaise was the scene of violent dispute between champions of ancient and modern literature today when Charles Perrault read his poem, *Le Siecle de Louis XIV*, which claims that the present age is producing greater literature and art than the age of Augustus or Pericles. He argues that present-day forms surpass the classics. But Nicholas Boileau, the critic and arbiter of French prose style, retorted that the Ancients were the only models to follow.

Charles Perrault: modern is best.

1688 (1688-1690)

France, 26 November 1688. Louis XIV declares war on the Netherlands.

England, 28 December 1688. Invited by seven English lords, William of Orange and his English wife Mary enter London, having landed in England last month. James II, meanwhile, has fled to France.

Ireland, 3 April 1689. After landing in Ireland with troops and money from France's King Louis XIV, James II is acknowledged as king by an Irish Parliament in Dublin.

New England, 19 April 1689. Emboldened by the news of William and Mary's victory in England, the residents of Boston oust their governor Edmund Andros and effectively break up the Dominion of New England.

London, 21 April 1689. William III and Mary II are crowned joint king and queen of England, Scotland and Ireland.

Europe, May 1689. England and the Netherlands join the League of Augsburg.

England, 17 May 1689. Following the decision by Louis XIV to send an expedition to aid James II in Ireland, England declares war on France.

London, 24 May 1689. Parliament passes the Act of Toleration, exempting Protestants dissenting from the Church of England from the penalties of certain laws, as long as they have sworn oaths of allegiance and supremacy. Roman Catholics are specifically excluded from such relief.

Germany, June 1689. The French forces wreak havoc and carry out massacres in the Palatinate.

Scotland, 27 July 1689. The Scottish Jacobites – supporters of the deposed James II – are defeated by government forces at the battle of Killiecrankie.

Ireland, 1 August 1689. A 15-week siege of Londonderry by James II's Irish-French army ends in failure. The Protestants of Londonderry have affirmed their allegiance to William and Mary.

Siberia, 6 September 1689. The Chinese and the Russians sign a treaty at Nerchinsk establishing the boundary between their two countries along the Argun and Gorbitsa rivers and the Stanovoi mountain range.

New York, 14 October 1689. Jacob Leisler, a German-born militia captain, leads a rebellion of supporters of William and Mary against a pro-Jacobite faction and sets up a provisional government.

Russia, 1689. Czar Peter (the Great), who has ruled jointly with his half-brother Ivan V since 1682, launches a successful coup and becomes sole ruler of Russia.

Germany, 1689. The forces of the Grand Alliance, as the Augsburg League has become known, recapture Mainz and Bonn from the French.

North America, 1689. The war of the Grand Alliance spreads to North America, where it is known as King William's war.

London, 1689. Thomas Sydenham, called the "Hippocrates of England", dies. Noted in particular for his invention of laudanum (a medicine with an opium base), Sydenham also wrote a treatise on gout.

Amsterdam, 1689. The Dutch landscape artist Meindert Hobbema paints a masterpiece entitled *The Lane at Middelharnis*.

Ireland, 1690. William III lands in Ireland with an Anglo-Dutch army.

Canada, 11 May 1690. In the first major engagement of King William's war, British troops from Massachusetts, led by Sir William Phips, seize Port Royal in Acadia (*Nova Scotia* and *New Brunswick*) from the French. Their main objective is to take Quebec.

Netherlands, 1 July 1690. Led by Marshal Luxembourg, the French defeat the forces of the Grand Alliance at Fleurus. In addition to England, the Netherlands and the Austrian Habsburgs, the alliance now includes Savoy, Sweden, Spain, the Holy Roman Empire. Bavaria, Saxony and the Palatinate.

England, 1690. French warships decisively defeat an Anglo-Dutch fleet at the battle of Beachy Head.

South-East Africa, 1690. Changamire Dombo's Rozvi army defeats Munhumutapa Nyakunembire.

West Africa, c.1690. The small Aja kingdom of Ouidah (*Whydah*) on the Dahomey coast has become a major port for European ships taking slaves across the Atlantic.

India, 1690. The English found a trading post at Calcutta.

London, 1690. The philosopher John Locke publishes his *Essay concerning Human Understanding* and a *Treatise on Civil Government*.

Paris, 1690. The publication of *Caracteres* by Jean de La Bruyere, a collection of character portraits of men and women of his time, wins the author great acclaim and a number of bitter enemies.

French terror tactics backfire in Germany

Paris, May 1689

A "Grand Alliance" has been formed to counter the war of aggression launched by Louis XIV against the Palatinate states in Germany. The atrocities carried out by French troops on his direct orders have roused hatred for the "Sun King" throughout Europe. Yet instead of forcing the German states to surrender, the burning of their towns has hardened their resolve and the spirit of German nationalism is burning brightly.

Louis started his war with limited objectives: to secure his sister-in-law's claims of succession in the Palatinate, force the appointment of his ally, the Prince of Furstenberg, as Archbishop-Elector of Cologne, and to prevent William of Orange ousting James II of Great Britain.

However, he also had limited resources; the building of Versailles had emptied his treasury. It would have to be a short war. Louis, contemptuous of the Germans, was sure they would quickly capitulate. But the valiant defence of Phillipsberg delayed his offensive and now his enemy, William of Orange, has been welcomed in London and the Grand Alliance formed.

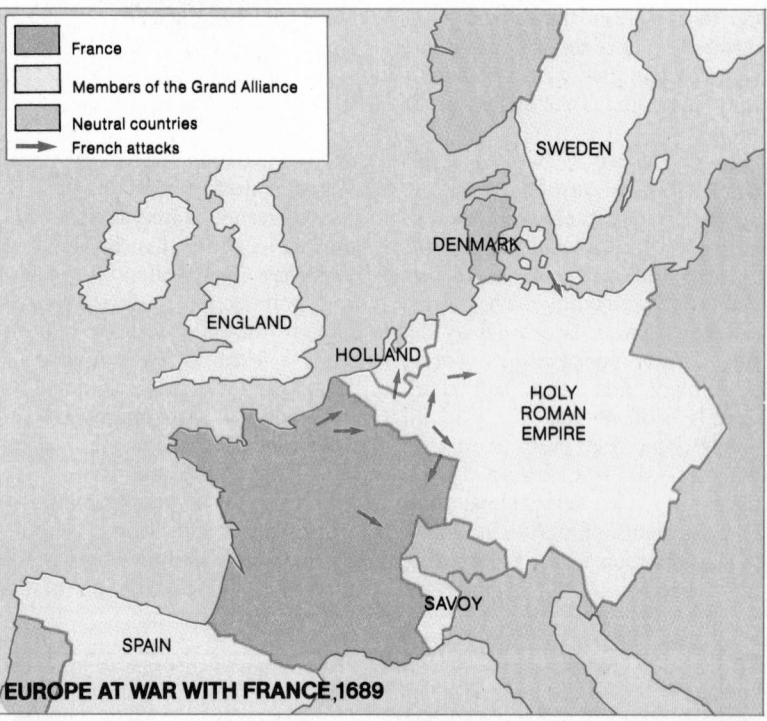

France
Members of the Grand Alliance
Neutral countries
French attacks

SWEDEN
DENMARK
ENGLAND
HOLLAND
HOLY ROMAN EMPIRE
SAVOY
SPAIN

EUROPE AT WAR WITH FRANCE, 1689

Ruler who united Prussia is dead

Konigsberg, Prussia, 1688

Frederick William, the Margrave of Brandenberg – but known universally as "The Great Elector" – has died, leaving a united and powerful Prussia. The country that Frederick inherited in 1640 was impoverished by the Thirty Years War, and yet, by shrewd diplomacy, the Elector gained territories, including East Pomerania, and turned a few hundred mercenaries into a standing army of 30,000 highly trained men which is the envy of his European neighbours.

Woman playwright was a former spy

London, 16 April, 1689

Aphra Behn, the first woman in England to be a professional writer, is to be honoured by burial in Westminster Abbey. Brought up in Surinam, her best-known work is the story of a West Indian slave, *Orinooko*, whom she knew personally. In 1668 Mrs Behn came to England and married a Dutch merchant who soon died. She went to Antwerp as a spy for the king, and then to prison for debt. As a widow she began writing, producing 17 plays, several novels and poems.

English exile their Catholic monarch

William of Orange rides into London

London, 28 December 1688
Leading a motley army of Dutch, Germans, French Huguenots, Swedes and Swiss – and reinforced by England's greatest general, John Churchill – William of Orange rode into London today to take over the crown with his English consort Mary. James II had fled and his feared and detested Lord Chancellor, Judge Jeffreys, has been picked up by a mob in east London and imprisoned in the Tower.

James caused dismay when he began putting Catholics in positions of power. Then he ordered his Declaration of Indulgence to be read in churches; seven bishops refused and were put in the Tower. With the birth of a son to James' wife, Mary, a Catholic succession was in prospect. The politicians sent for William and Mary.

William of Orange and Queen Mary accept Great Britain's Bill of Rights.

James II throws the Great Seal of Parliament into the river Thames.

New King agrees to protect freedoms

London, 22 January 1689
England's "Bloodless Revolution" reached its climax today when parliament formally invited William and Mary to become joint sovereigns. The invitation was accompanied by a Declaration of Rights, endorsed by the royal couple, which sets out constitutional guarantees to protect the freedom of the individual and the rights of parliament, in particular to vote taxes and raise an army. The Declaration will be converted into a Bill of Rights to be passed by parliament.

The group of MPs known as "Tories" (who at first had opposed the attempt to exclude James from the throne) joined with their Whig opponents to support his overthrow after being alienated by the arbitrary conduct of James. But some Tories were unhappy with the Whig insistence that James had abdicated and wanted a regency; others wanted Mary alone to be given the crown. But William would have no truck with a regency and Mary said she would not take the throne without her husband.

There is to be no systematic persecution of those who served the Stuart kings. A few are expected to go to gaol, but William insists that mercy can also be a demonstration of strength as well as weakness.

The City of London played a key role in smoothing the transition from the House of Stuart to the House of Orange. William called together members of the Lords, MPs from the time of Charles II, and City merchants to form a kind of pre-parliament convention.

Teenage Czar puts sister in nunnery

Russia, 1689
In a sudden coup, 16-year-old Czar Peter has taken over the country and forced his half-sister Sophia, the regent, to resign and retire to a convent. Her advisers have been arrested. Galitzin has been exiled and Chalitsky, head of the "streltsy" (the palace guard) has been put to death.

For the past seven years Peter has been ostensibly sharing power with his half-brother Ivan. He plotted the coup from a monastery where he had taken refuge, frightened that Sophia planned his execution to ensure Ivan's succession.

Now Peter has appointed a new regent – his mother – and until he reaches adulthood she will effectively rule Russia. Only one thing flaws the new situation: the excitement of events has given Peter what seems a permanent nervous and violent facial twitch.

Russia's new emperor, Czar Peter, who has taken over the country.

Turks rumoured to have poisoned prince

Romania, 1688
Turkish conspirators are suspected of poisoning Serban Cantacuzene, the popular prince of Walachia (*a region of Romania*) who has died suddenly, aged 48. Cantacuzene, a Turkish appointee, was about to march on Istanbul in a bid to drive his former masters back across the Bosporus and out of Europe.

The top-secret venture is believed to have had the moral, if not the practical support of the western powers. Cantacuzene, a cultured aristocrat of Greek descent, is being mourned in Walachia as a progressive leader. In his 11 years as hospador he started maize production, now the country's staple food. His cultural reforms designed to encourage the Romanian language included the creation of the Romanian school in Bucharest and the printing of the Romanian Bible.

Russia and China agree in Siberia

Siberia, 7 September 1689
The Russian and Chinese empires today signed a treaty at the Siberian frontier post of Nerchinsk bringing an end to 20 years of border fighting between Russian cossacks and the Manchu army.

The Russian military exploration of Siberia followed by traders eager to exploit the territory's riches was certain to provoke Chinese suspicion and the Manchus reacted violently to Russian incursion in territory they had already claimed. Four years ago the Manchus destroyed a Russian fort at Albazin on the Amur river and when it was rebuilt they laid siege to it again.

Under the terms of the treaty the boundaries between these two vast empires will lie along the Gorbitsa and Argun rivers thus recognising China's claim to the land north of the Amur.

1690 (1690-1695)

Ireland, 11 July 1690. William III defeats James II at the battle of the Boyne.

Serbia, 8 October 1690. Belgrade is retaken by the Turks.

New York, 26 May 1691. Jacob Leisler, leader of the popular uprising in support of William and Mary's accession to the English throne, is executed for treason.

Ireland, 12 July 1691. William III defeats the allied Irish and French at the battle of Aughrim.

New England, 17 October 1691. Maine and Plymouth are incorporated within Massachusetts.

Ireland, 1691. Limerick, the Jacobite headquarters, surrenders to William III's forces after successfully resisting two sieges. By the peace of Limerick, Catholics are granted a measure of religious toleration, and Jacobite soldiers and civilians remaining in Ireland are granted security of life and property.

Istanbul, 1691. Backed by the vizier Fazil Mustafa Koprulu, Ahmed II succeeds his brother Suleiman II as Ottoman sultan.

London, 1691. The navigator William Dampier publishes his *Voyage around the World*, in which he tells of his expeditions against Spanish trading posts in the Antilles and the Gulf of Mexico.

Scotland, 13 February 1692. On the orders of William III, nearly 40 members of the MacDonald clan are massacred at Glencoe for their Jacobite sympathies and their delay in taking an oath of allegiance.

Netherlands, 3 August 1692. Following their capture of Namur in June, the French forces under Marshal Luxembourg defeat the English at the battle of Steenkerke.

Massachusetts, 1692. Twenty people are executed in Salem for witchcraft.

France, 1692. The French are heavily defeated by a Grand Alliance fleet at La Hogue.

Mexico, 1692. Rioting breaks out in Mexico City, caused by food shortages.

Netherlands, 29 July 1693. The army of the Grand Alliance is crushed by French forces at the battle of Neerwinden.

Versailles, 15 September 1693. Louis XIV repudiates the 1682 Declaration of the Four Articles, which sought to reconcile papal authority with Gallican independence, and attempts to improve relations with the pope.

Germany, 1693. Louis XIV's forces inflict a defeat on Saxony, a member of the Grand Alliance.

New Mexico, 1693. Governor Ponce de Leon completes the reconquest of New Mexico for Spain.

Jamaica, 1693. The English found Kingston.

West Africa, 1693. The French admiral Tourville deals a severe blow to the English navy by capturing 100 ships, almost the entire Smyrna fleet, in the Gulf of Guinea off Lagos.

Japan, 1693. Ihara Saikaku, the great poet and writer of popular fiction, dies in Osaka at the age of 51. He composed hundreds of thousands of *haikai* verses and began a new genre of fiction known as "tales of the floating world".

South-East Africa, 1693. Changamire Dombo expels all the Portuguese from his Rozvi kingdom in Zimbabwe.

France, June 1694. After a desperate struggle with a superior Dutch fleet, the French naval commander Jean Bart recaptures a large flotilla of corn-ships and steers them safely into Dunkirk, breaking the English blockade.

Canada, 23 October 1694. American colonial forces led by Sir William Phips fail in their attempt to seize Quebec, the capital of New France, and withdraw after a two-week siege.

England, 28 December 1694. Queen Mary II dies.

Persia, 1694. Hussein, a devout Shia, becomes shah of Persia.

Aegean, 1694. A Venetian attack on the island of Chios is beaten off by the Turks.

London, 1694. The composer Henry Purcell publishes his *Te Deum for St Cecilia's Day* and *Timon of Athens*.

Paris, 1694. The French Academy publishes its *Dictionnaire*, prepared under the direction of the grammarian Claude Favre de Vaugelas.

Rumania, 1694. Constantin Brancovan founds the Academy of St Sava in Bucharest.

Prussia, 1694. The university of Halle opens. Its patron is the philosopher Christian Thomasius, a fervent patriot who desires to promote the German language in favour of Latin. Jacob Spener, head of the theology faculty, makes the new university a centre of "pietism", a movement opposed to the dogmatism of the established Lutheran church.

India, 1695. The Firangi Mahal school of Moslem learned and holy men is founded.

Exiled English King defeated in Ireland

James II flees after the Battle of the Boyne: painted by Gow in 1888.

Ireland, 1690
The Protestant William has scored a decisive victory over the exiled James II and his Irish, French and English Jacobites. When William arrived James' forces were well dug in on rising ground behind the river Boyne, the only defensive barrier between Belfast and Dublin.

William threw in his forces on 1 July, but kept the untried English regiments in reserve and attacked with his Germans, Danes, Dutch, French Huguenots and Finns. But when hand-to-hand struggles developed, the English were brought in and the Irish, French and Jacobites were broken. James lost 1,600 men killed, wounded or taken prisoner; William lost a third of that number.

Victory on the Boyne has been followed by a brilliant expedition led by John Churchill, who has brought all south-western Ireland under English control, with a swiftly mounted seaborne assault on Cork and Kinsale.

Life on other planets is a possibility

Holland, 1690
The Dutch scientist, Christiaan Huygens has just published his ideas on the wave nature of light in his *Traite de la lumiere,*(Treatise on Light). But his thoughts have also been taking a philosophical turn, as he contemplates the thought that life exists elsewhere in the universe. The earth is not the central body in the heavens, so why should we assume that we are privileged in being the only planet with life?

Huygens contends that there must be not just life, but other intelligent creatures like ourselves with high levels of intellect. He suggests that there are probably other worlds inhabited by plants and animals very like those on earth. He believes that the inhabitants are probably much like us.

Huygens: the Earth is not alone.

Bank of England formed

Financiers plan the national bank.

London, 1694

Faced with an urgent and recurring need for funds to continue the war with France, William III has adopted the novel idea of setting up a bank which will borrow from the public in order to make loans to the government. Although William takes public credit, the idea is thought to have been inspired by a suggestion of Lord Halifax. Magnates of the City have rushed to subscribe to the new institution, which is being called the Bank of England; the rate of interest, eight per cent, will be secured by trade and beer taxes.

In the past, much of the lending to the state was undertaken by the London goldsmiths, but their greed and appetite for speculation earned them the hostility of the City. Not surprisingly, the goldsmiths opposed the setting up of the Bank, as did the bishops in the House of Lords. The governmnent forced the measure through and within a few months of starting up, the Bank had lent the government the whole of its £1,200,000 authorised capital, though part of it had not been paid up. The shortfall was covered by issuing bills, which the Treasury accepted as cash and were paid out to creditors, who in turn cashed them later at the Bank. So a new phrase is coming into use: *The Bank of England promises to pay.*

So popular has the new institution become that the money was raised within a mere 12 days. There is no pressure to repay the loan, so long as the government continues to guarantee the interest.

The war with France has diverted capital from foreign trade into the manufacture of armaments, smelting and the mining of coal, copper and tin. Numerous joint stock companies have been set up to handle these enterprises.

Albanians throw out Turkish lords

Albania, 1690

Turkey is fast losing control of Albania, the latest Balkan outpost of the weakened Ottoman Empire to succumb to the rising tide of nationalism.

Albanian nationalist rebel forces have seized three key towns – Kamina, Vlore, and the citadel, Medun – as the country slides into open insurrection.

The basis of the fierce anti-Turkish resistance is an unusual coalition of urban Moslems and rural Christians. The Albanian uprising, coupled with the rebellion in neighbouring Montenegro, another Ottoman province, was sparked by the defeat of the Turkish sultan's armies at Vienna.

Banana tree poet had a light touch

Edo (Tokyo), Japan, 1694

Basho, the Zen master and greatest exponent of the poetic form known as the *haiku* has died in Japan. A major literary figure who taught others as well as displayed his own abilities, he leaves a community of 2,000 students.

"Basho" means banana tree and was the name adopted by the poet Matsuo Basho when he moved into a hut beside one to practise Zen and master the new art of the 17-syllable *haiku*.

He became a traveller, taking long journeys throughout Japan and writing travel notebooks in prose and poetry. He strove for "lightness". Now Japan mourns a literary giant.

Portuguese just hang on in Zimbabwe

A map of Sofala: one of the East African trading posts set up by Portugal.

Zambezi Valley, East Africa, 1695

Portuguese traders and settlers have survived the onslaught of Changamire Dombo of Zimbabwe, but only just. As the Portuguese barricaded Sena, their last surviving settlement on the Zambezi, news came that Dombo was dead, and his army had withdrawn. Few thoughful Portuguese are today blaming any but their own people for their predicament.

"The insolence of our people was the cause of these wars, for those who hold power and own African servants commit such excesses that from the scandalized kings and princes breaks forth these disas-ters," wrote the Portuguese viceroy. Dombo broke away from the Munhumutapa kingdom a generation earlier and it was then that he finally conquered the whole Zimbabwe plateau.

Controlling both the gold and ivory trade he grew rich enough to resist Portuguese pressures to come within their sphere of influence. Observing Portuguese attempts to expel the Moslem traders and dominate the region's commerce, and their economic exploitation of the Africans, Dombo was ready to go to war with Portugal. From the first battle in 1684 Dombo remained undefeated.

"Road on the Dyke" by Meindert Hobbema: a leading pupil of Jacob van Ruisdael. Hobbema's work, as popular in Britain as it is in Holland, concentrates on sunlit, summery representations of nature.

1695 (1695-1698)

France, 4 January 1695. On the death of Marshal Luxembourg, he is succeeded as commander of the French forces by the duke of Villeroi.

Istanbul, 27 January 1695. Mustafa II becomes Ottoman sultan on the death of Ahmed II.

Paris, 13 April 1695. The poet Jean de La Fontaine, author of brilliant collections of *Contes* and *Fables*, dies.

South-East Africa, 1695. Changamire Dombo dies after inflicting a further defeat on the Portuguese.

London, 1695. The architect Sir Christopher Wren designs a hospital for seamen at Greenwich.

London, 1695. *Love for Love,* a comedy by William Congreve, is produced for the first time.

England, April 1695. Censorship of the Press ends with the lapsing of the 1662 Licensing Act.

Brussels, August 1695. The French forces, led by the duke of Villeroi, lay siege to Brussels, which is in the hands of the Grand Alliance, and bombard the city.

Caucasus, 1695. Led by Peter the Great, the Russians lay siege to the Turkish-held city of Azov on the Don river. The siege fails and the Russians suffer heavy casualties.

Netherlands, 1695. Following the defeat of the French forces at the second battle of Namur, Louis XIV enters into secret negotiations with William III of Orange.

London, 10 April 1696. Parliament passes a Navigation Act to tighten its control over colonial trade.

France, 17 April 1696. Madame de Sevigny, famed for her writing of over 1,000 published letters reflecting the history of her time, dies of smallpox.

Caucasus, July 1696. At the second attempt the Russians capture the city of Azov from the Turks after mounting a blockade with their newly built fleet.

Germany, 6 October 1696. Savoy withdraws from the Grand Alliance.

London, 1696. The playwright and architect Sir John Vanbrugh presents his first comedy, *The Relapse.*

Poland, 27 June 1697. Frederick Augustus, elector of Saxony, is elected king of Poland and takes the name Augustus II.

Hungary, 11 September 1697. Imperial troops under the brilliant commander Eugene of Savoy defeat the Turks at the battle of Zenta.

Netherlands, 30 October 1697. The treaty of Ryswick ends the war between France and the Grand Alliance. Louis XIV recognises William III's right to the English throne. France gives up its territories gained in 1688 but retains Alsace and Strasbourg. The treaty also ends King William's War in the colonies, returning to England the territories on Hudson Bay that were seized by French forces.

France, February 1697. Francois Fenelon, who was made archbishop of Cambrai two years ago, publishes his *Explanations of the maxims of the saints.*

France, 1697. Charles Perrault publishes a collection of eight fairy tales entitled *Histoires ou Contes du temps passes.* They include "The Sleeping Beauty", "Red Riding Hood" and "Bluebeard".

Portugal, 1697. The Jesuit Antonio Veira dies. A vigorous opponent of slavery, he sailed up the rivers of Brazil spreading Christianity.

Sweden, 1697. Charles XI, who confiscated large areas of land belonging to the aristocracy and transformed Sweden into an absolute monarchy, dies and is succeeded as king by his son Charles XII.

Siberia, 1697. Continuing their expansion eastwards through the vast territories of Siberia, the Russians reach and conquer the Kamchatka peninsula.

Mongolia, 1697. Western Mongolia is conquered by the Chinese.

West Africa, 1697. Appointed director of the French Senegal Company, Andre Brue attempts to establish trading posts in the valley of the Senegal.

California, 1697. Spanish Jesuits found the first mission in California, at Loreta.

Moscow, 1698. Following a revolt by the Streltsy – the Praetorian guard composed of nobles that was founded by Ivan the Terrible – a thousand of their number are publicly put to death on the orders of Peter the Great.

Moscow, 1698. Peter the Great imposes the use of tobacco on his people.

Persia, 1698. Sent to Persia as a prisoner, the Afghan chieftain Mir Ways beomes a favourite of Shah Hussein.

Vietnam, 1698. The Cambodians evacuate Saigon.

Beijing, 1698. A newly constructed bridge is named after the explorer Marco Polo.

Penal laws oppress the Irish Catholics

Ireland, 1695

A form of racial and religious segregation is being introduced by the Protestant ascendancy in Ireland. The Catholic Irish are allowed to practise their religion, but they are not permitted to vote and are barred from the armed forces. A Protestant may not marry a Catholic and must produce a certificate of religious denomination before marriage. Catholics are not allowed to send their children abroad to be educated as Catholics.

Other measures include a ban on gambling in an attempt to prevent the upper classes losing the family fortunes. All of which measures passed by the minority at the expense of the majority may well satisfy Protestants, but are sure to exacerbate old enmities.

Brazil's gold makes the Portuguese rich

Brazil, 1697

Adventurers of all sorts, the unemployed from all over Brazil and from Portugal, and anyone with an eye to getting rich quick are flocking to the Minas Gerais region here. Gold has been discovered in the river beds and in alluvial deposits in the nearby hills. It is easy to extract and already a number of hopeful miners have made their fortunes. Villages have sprung up overnight and there are now several thousand inhabitants.

Meanwhile, Portugal is tightening its hold on the country. The excitement of finding gold has to be balanced with less romantic endeavours. The governor has just crushed the native black kingdom of Palmares which was threatening sugar and tobacco plantations.

Moghul soldiers are "padded dandies"

The court of Aurangzeb: fountains, elephants, soldiers and splendour.

Dekhan, India, 21 March 1695
The Moghul army of Aurangzeb would be totally unrecognisable to Babur, the empire's founder. Dynamism has given way to decadence; his soldiers, the descendants of the men who had built an empire from central Asia to southern India, are now said to be no more than "padded dandies".

This is the conclusion of Dr Gemelli Careri, a Neapolitan lawyer, received today at the Moghul court, while on a voyage round the world. The bureaucracy is corrupt, the army obese, and the peasants starve to pay for both, he says. The royal encampment has a circumference of 30 miles (48km). Within it are 250 markets and half-a-million soldiers, civil servants and camp followers.

In complete contrast is Aurangzeb himself. He received the Italian at ten o'clock, dressed in simple white cotton, with a white beard and olive skin, "slender and stooping with age". He alone, with his combination of weakness, cruelty and suspicion, holds the empire together; but he cannot live for ever, nor can his empire.

Rebel feminist poet in plague death

Mexico, 1695

The writer, Juana Ines de la Cruz has died at the age of 44 after nursing victims of the recent plague. Four years ago Juana re-affirmed her nun's vows after a row with the Church over her autobiography. In her book she criticises the Inquisition and argues for women's rights and education.

When Juana left the viceroy's court at 18 to join the Order of St Jerome her ambition was to pursue education and avoid marriage. During 21 years of convent life she wrote poems, ballads, comedies and sacramental plays. Juana collected 4,000 books which, until she sold them for charity, formed the largest library in South America.

Critical dictionary looks for tolerance

Holland, 1697

Pierre Bayle, a Huguenot exile from France, has produced a work that is being called "the sceptic's Bible". His *Historical and Critical Dictionary* attacks the dogmas and fallacies of past ages and argues for tolerance and detachment in its series of learned articles. Nothing, says Bayle, is certain and no one person has the monopoly of truth. He even claims that "the grounds of doubt are themselves doubtful." Thoughtful men everywhere are questioning the dogmas of religion and old superstitions, argues Bayle.

Bayle: doubt too is doubtful.

France gives up the right bank of Rhine

Dignatories assemble in Paris for the signing of the Peace of Ryswick.

Europe, 1697

With the Grand Alliance of England, Holland, Austria, Spain and Savoy clearly demoralised at the lack of a decisive victory, nine years of war against France has come to an end with the Peace of Ryswick. Although William of Orange's forces had been successful in taking Namur, fighting in the Spanish Netherlands had come to a stalemate. Peace would have been reached earlier had not Louis XIV been so stubborn in his refusal to recognise William as the king of England. Although he had worked hard to split the alliance, it was the cost of fighting on so many fronts that forced him to negotiate.

Under the terms of the treaty, Louis will relinquish his claims to Cologne and the right bank of the Rhine and restore Luxembourg, Mons, Courtrai and Barcelona to Spain; but he will retain Strasbourg and a few towns in Alsace. France will recognise William as king and withdraw support for the Stuarts.

Dom Perignon puts fizz in champagne

Champagne, 1698

France, home of great wines, has a new variety to enjoy: sparkling wine from the abbey of Hautvillers in Champagne. Champagne's "vin gris" is already well known, but the new fizzy version, a white wine made from black grapes, is quite original.

"Vin gris" often fermented in the bottle, thus turning slightly fizzy, but it took the skill of the the abbey's 60-year-old cellarer, Dom Pierre Perignon, to use this fermentation to create the new style of wine. Using a new blend of grapes, he has substituted cork stoppers for the old rag seal and uses strong English glass to withstand the pressure of the sparkling wine.

Purcell: writer of first English opera

London, 21 November 1695

Henry Purcell died today at only 36. Purcell was composing by the age of eight, and was organist of Westminster Abbey at 20. As well as church, ceremonial and chamber works he wrote theatre music, including *Dido and Aeneas*, the first true opera in English. He will be buried in Westminster Abbey.

Rome at odds with Jesuits over Chinese ancestor worship

Beijing, 1697

The success of the Jesuit mission to China is being threatened by a Vatican inquiry into the new line proposed by Monsignor Charles Maigrot, the vicar apostolic of Fukien. Four years ago he instructed his own missionaries to have nothing to do with the cult of Confucius and ancestor worship. Now he is seeking to get the Vatican to impose his views on all missions to China.

The Jesuits have been successful here by arguing that Confucian philosophy does not conflict with Christian laws. They have even lauded the *I Ching* as an excellent book of physics and morality. As a result Emperor Kangxi issued an edict of toleration of Christianity and even allowed a Jesuit house in this Forbidden City.

Oriental Christians are tortured cruelly by their unbelieving enemies.

Australia before the Europeans

The European conquest of Aboriginal Australia began in the 18th century, a mere 200 years ago, whereas archaeological discoveries clearly indicate that the continent of Australia has been occupied for over 40,000 years. Thus the human history of the continent is primarily a history of contemporary Aboriginal people. Until recently it was fashionable for European Australians to argue that Aboriginal people were an unchanging people in an unchanging landscape; it is now clear that both the landscape and ecology have changed dramatically and we are now more aware of the extraordinary richness and complexity of Aboriginal culture, and of the devastating impact of European conquest. Much that was important and unique has been lost forever.

Until recent years the vast bulk of research in Aboriginal history has been undertaken by non-Aboriginals, and has tended to focus on issues of greatest significance to European Australians. Aboriginal archaeology and anthropology have been seen as examples illustrating more general inquiries and not specifically concerned with writing the history of contemporary Aboriginal people. Historical accounts produced by Aboriginals themselves (until recent years mostly oral histories) have another story to tell. These accounts, for the most part, assume that Aboriginal people have always lived in Australia – that they are a product of the continent. Such histories celebrate a strong sense of cultural diversity and continuity which is the heritage of the Aboriginal peoples.

The first Australians

While it is widely accepted that the first Australians came from South East Asia, there is debate about the specifics of settlement and occupation. Was there a single migration or were there several, or many? Research indicates that until about 12,000 years ago Tasmania, Australia and New Guinea were linked to form a continent called Sahul. During the period from 12,000 BC to 6000 BC rising sea levels separated Tasmania and then New Guinea from the present Australian continent, flooding nearly all of the sites which would contain evidence of the earliest human occupation. They also increased open water distances between northern Australia and island South East Asia.

However, for the bulk of its human history northern Australia was a short sea voyage from island South East Asia. We now have no doubt that the first Australians did not arrive by accident. They had the means and the opportunity to return if they so chose. Furthermore, we have good reason to believe that immigration to Australia was pretty constant before 12,000 BC. Recent evidence from the Solomon Islands demonstrates the reality of a long sea voyage as long ago as 29,000 BC. These factors go a long way to breaking down a notion that Australia was cut off from the rest of the world for much of its human history, and there is increasing evidence that the physical form of contemporary Aboriginal people is the result of a complex process of variation from more than one founding population.

The changing environment

The climatic changes which led to rising sea levels also had major effects on the environment of Australia. It is difficult to generalise, but we can say that the broad divisions between arid, semi-arid, temperate and tropical areas of Australia have not been constant over the last 40,000 years and that there have been sometimes quite dramatic changes in rainfall, temperature and humidity within each of these zones. Human beings have had to cope with changing environments. For example, southern Tasmania was first occupied around 30,000 years ago, when the area was mostly grasslands. However, around 10,000 years ago rising temperatures and rainfall created an environment more favourable to temperate rain forests which restricted grassland areas and fauna which grazed on them, and at around this time human occupation of the area abruptly ceases. However, hidden behind these dramatic changes is a constant background of change in technology, subsistence and the ways in which sites were used. This story is repeated across the continent in all environmental zones.

During the 40,000 year human history of the continent we can reliably infer that change occurred in every facet of Aboriginal life – technology, art, subsistence and settlement strategies, and in social organisation. There is no good reason to believe that such changes were solely the product of environmental change. Indeed, we have every reason to believe that the Aboriginal people were a major force in shaping the Australian environment. For example, Aboriginal people co-existed for much of the last 30,000 years with now long extinct *megafauna* (large animals) – the *diprotodon*, the *macropus titan* (a relative of the grey kangaroo but double its weight) and the *thylacoleo* (a carnivorous phalangerid the size of a leopard) are just a few. We cannot be sure that Aboriginal people hunted these animals to extinction but it is reasonable to propose that the effects of human occupation were one cause of their demise. Aboriginal land management practices (particularly the regular burning of country) promoted changes in Australian flora. Fireadapted species, such as the eucalypts, came to dominate the environment.

Thus the Australian environment has been, in part, created by Aboriginal people, and they learned how to live in the great diversity of Australian environments. The range of plant foods exploited shows clear signs of increase over time, and technologies such as those developed for seed-grinding made it possible for populations to occupy permanently arid areas of the continent. Desert tribes were smaller, more mobile and less concentrated than tribes who inhabited more resource-rich areas.

Human networks

Even though the continent was sparsely populated there is clear archaeological and ethnographic evidence of long distance trade in a wide variety of commodities ranging from shells, stone and ochre to the narcotic *pituri*. Such material evidence of connection is only a small part of the story. Although we now understand more about how Aboriginal people comprehended their tribal areas through myth, dance and song, we have also begun to appreciate the ways in which myth and ritual bound diverse groups together over great distances. Aboriginal societies were far from cultural isolates. Indeed, it now seems clear that the Australian landscape was an intensely human place – its landforms, history and diverse populations must be understood in human terms.

The extraordinary resilience of Aboriginal society was badly shaken by the holocaust which followed the European conquest. Confronted by a society that placed no value on Aboriginal culture – to say nothing of Aboriginal lives – Aboriginal people were pushed to the edge of cultural extinction. Yet Aboriginal culture has survived and changed in its own terms. The fact of that survival has directly affected contemporary Australian society as well. It is now more widely understood that Aboriginal people have much to teach from their reverence for and knowledge of the land. They are beginning to force us to rethink our notions of the "primitive", and to take seriously the idea that although Aboriginal people did not develop agriculture or live in cities, they most emphatically developed social and cultural institutions which stand as a significant manifestation of the human spirit.

Aborigines hunting, by Guerard.

An aboriginal dance in Van Diemen's Land (Tasmania), by John Glover.

Carobaree, a ritual dance.

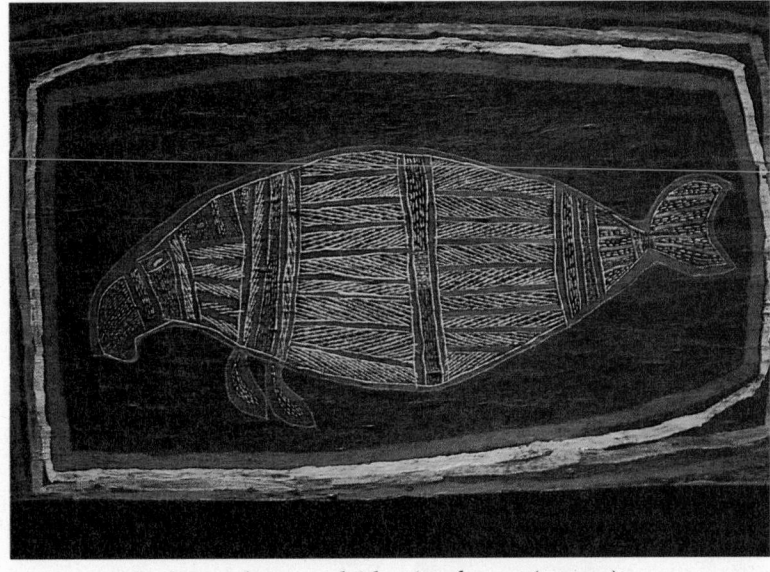

Aboriginal bark paintings of (left) animals, a tree and a human being, and (above) a dugong (sea-cow).

Aborigines watch as a European ship enters King George's Sound. Painting by De Sainson, 1830.

A painting on rock.

European values put aborigines at the bottom of society, seen here on the streets of Sydney in a painting by Augustus Earle, c.1830.

1698 (1698-1702)

Europe, 11 October 1698. France, England and the Netherlands sign a partition treaty to solve the problem of the Spanish succession after the impending death of the childless King Charles II. Under the treaty, Spanish possessions are to be divided between the dauphin, the electoral prince of Bavaria and the Archduke Charles, son of the Emperor Leopold.

New England, 1 January 1699. The Abenaki Indians and the Massachusetts colonists sign a treaty ending the conflict in New England.

Austria, 26 January 1699. The treaty of Karlowitz ends the war between Austria and the Turks which began in 1683. The Turks cede Transylvania and Hungary to the Austrians, Morea and Dalmatia to Venice and part of the Ukraine to Poland.

Russia, 20 December 1699. Peter the Great sets about reforming the Russian calendar. In August he banned traditional clothing, insisting that his subjects wear European dress.

East Africa, 1699. Fort Jesus (*Mombasa*) and Zanzibar are captured by Omani Arabs.

Philadelphia, 1699. The first clearly reported epidemic of yellow fever in the colonies kills one-sixth of the population.

Europe, 13 March 1700. Following the death of the Elector of Bavaria, a second partition treaty is signed to resolve the Spanish succession. The major share of the Spanish possessions is allocated to Archduke Charles.

Russia, 23 June 1700. Russia signs a truce with the Ottoman empire, halting the war which began in 1695. Russia gives up its Black Sea fleet but retains Azov.

Boston, 24 June 1700. Judge Samuel Sewall writes *The Selling of Joseph*, the first outright appeal for the abolition of slavery to appear in America.

England, 1 July 1700. The English dramatist and poet John Dryden dies. Among the works for which he will be best remembered are the play *All for Love* and the satirical poems *Absalom and Achitophel* and *MacFlecknoe*.

Denmark, 18 August 1700. Having invaded Denmark and captured Copenhagen, Charles XII of Sweden forces Frederick IV of Denmark to sign the peace of Travendal.

Spain, 2 October 1700. Charles II, king of Spain, draws up a will in favour of the Bourbon duke Philip of Anjou, the grandson of Louis XIV of France.

Spain, 1 November 1700. On the death of Charles II, Philip of Anjou comes to the throne as Philip V.

Baltic, November 1700. Charles XII of Sweden defeats the Russian forces besieging the city of Narva.

Boston, 1700. The port of Boston has become the most important colonial centre of the slave trade.

New England, 1700. The first Baptist association in the colonies is founded, on Rhode Island.

Indian Ocean, 1700. English pirates set up a base in Madagascar.

Germany, 18 January 1701. Frederick III, elector of Brandenburg, becomes king of Prussia.

Madrid, 19 February 1701. Philip V makes a ceremonial entry into Madrid.

England, 23 May 1701. Arrested in Boston on a charge of piracy and sent back to England for trial, the Englishman Captain William Kidd is hanged.

London, 12 June 1701. The Act of Establishment excludes Catholics from the English throne.

Michigan, 24 July 1701. Antoine de La Mothe Cadillac establishes a French fort at Detroit.

Netherlands, 7 September 1701. England, Austria and the Netherlands form an alliance against France. The allies are fearful of a union between Spain and France following the choice made by Charles II, the late king of Spain, of a Bourbon as his successor.

Poland, 1701. Having occupied Lithuania and Courland, Charles XII of Sweden invades Poland and seizes Warsaw and Cracow.

London, 11 March 1702. The *Daily Courant*, the first daily newspaper in the world, begins publication.

England, 19 March 1702. On the death of William III of Orange, Anne Stuart, sister of Mary, succeeds to the throne of England, Scotland and Ireland.

Europe, 4 May 1702. To stall the alliance of Spain and France, the Grand Alliance declares war on France.

France, 1702. French Protestants called Camisards – because of the white shirts they wear during night raids to promote recognition – rise up in revolt against persecution following the repeal of the Edict of Nantes in 1695. The Camisards' leaders are Jean Cavalier and Roland Laporte.

Denmark, 1702. King Frederick IV abolishes serfdom.

Catholics excluded from English throne

London, 1701
In a move with far-reaching implications, parliament has passed an Act of Settlement which bars Roman Catholics from the British throne. Any person who inherits the succession and subsequently converts to Rome or marries a Catholic will be declared incapacitated. So Catholics of the House of Orleans who married Stuart princesses are barred. The line of succession, after William and Mary, is her sister Anne and then the Electress Sophia of Hanover, the granddaughter of James I.

William rides high amid the gods.

Riding accident puts Anne on the throne

Anne: a 19th-century portrait.

London, 1702
King William III of England, and as William of Orange ruler of the Netherlands, died today after a fall from his horse while riding at Hampton Court. He will be succeeded by Anne, sister of the late Queen. His death comes only weeks after that of the exiled James II, whom he deposed in the "Glorious Revolution" of 1688.

The English confidently expect the new Queen to rule much as did William. The Dutch, under republican rule once more, face a less predictable future. William's unpopular favourites may well face a backlash, but it is hoped that Heinsius, the former chief minister, will maintain national stability.

Oman Arabs seize Madagascar port

Mombasa, East Africa, 1699
After a three-year siege by the Omanis and their East African allies, Portugal's garrison at Fort Jesus has surrendered. A few enclaves on the Zambezi and Mozambique coast are all that is left in Portuguese possession. Portuguese power had been declining since 1650 when she was evicted from the Arabian Gulf. On the East African coast the indigenous population led by the citystate of Pate, resentful of Portuguese efforts to dominate trade and impose Christianity, allied with Oman and revolted. Portugal's rivals, Holland and England, observe events with interest.

Piratical brethren terrorise Caribbean

Caribbean, 1700
A gang of pirates, known as The Brethren of the Coast, have established themselves in the islands of Jamaica and Hispaniola. Mutineers, escaped prisoners, the riff-raff of every colonial nation – they owe no allegiance to any law, except for that of plunder and gain.

Bloodthirsty and greedy in their dealings with the ships on which they prey, they have their own brutal code. Every man – there are no women – is considered equal. They vote on all matters of policy and share out the spoils and bounties. There are harsh punishments for those who defy the rules.

Czar goes to work in English shipyard

Czar Peter seeks experience among the labourers of the Deptford yard.

Deptford, London, 1698

For three months, workers in the shipyard here have enjoyed the sight of one of the most powerful men in the world wielding a saw or hammer or adze with the best of them. Russia's tall and vigorous czar, Peter the Great, is roving around Europe picking up knowledge and techniques for his drive to westernise his country.

He has become the first czar to cross his frontiers except on a military campaign and is accompanied by a "travelling embassy" of 250 – including priests, officials, dwarfs and bodyguards. After attending a debate in the House of Lords he said: "It is pleasant to learn how the sons of the fatherland tell the truth plainly to the king; we must learn that from the English."

In London Peter lodged in the home of the diarist John Evelyn with 15 other Russians and his coarse habits and drunken horseplay contributed to leaving behind £350 worth of damage to furniture and gardens. Peter also worked as a car-penter in Dutch shipyards and has visited the three Baltic provinces, Prussia, and France.

He has shown interest in government and political ideas, but it is ships, guns, lathes and coins that appear mostly to have caught his attention.

Cutting off their privileges: Czar Peter trims the Boyars' beards.

Seed drill implants fear of job losses

Berkshire, England, 1701

A machine just developed by the English farmer-inventor Jethro Tull of Berkshire has changed the agricultural practices of 10,000 years. No longer is there any need to scatter seed on prepared ground by hand, with all the haphazard-ness and waste that this implies. Tull has made a seed-sowing mac-hine that delivers the seeds to the soil in straight, even lines. These neat rows of seeds not only produce economies they also make it far easier to keep down the weeds bet-ween the growing crops.

Although this new device – and some of Tull's other practical ideas on farm management – seem to benefit the farmer, he is by no means universally popular. Farm labourers fear the machine will put them out of work. Some have even gone on strike against it.

Europe riven by wars

Swedes smash Allies: capture Warsaw

Warsaw, 1702

In a brilliantly fought campaign, the Swedish army of Charles XII has beaten an alliance of Denmark, Poland and Russia and captured Warsaw. The Polish King, Augus-tus II, has been deposed; Poland, now under a new ruler, Stanislas, has allied itself with Charles against Russia; and Sweden retains her mastery of the Baltic.

Denmark capitulated quickly after Copenhagen was put to siege in 1700; and then Charles led his small army of 10,000 men across Estonia to confront the Russians. Few expected the youthful Swedish king to show such military prow-ess; but he confirmed his schoolboy studies of his hero, Alexander the Great, with a spectacular victory at Narva against what seemed over-whelming odds.

King Charles XII of Sweden.

Fear of Franco-Spanish union sparks war

Europe, 1702

Had Charles II, the king of Spain, not died childless, Europe would probably have stayed at peace, but now the continent is braced for a major war – this time to stop France and Spain and its colonies uniting under one throne. Even while Charles was dying, every effort was being made to avoid con-flict; but because of the complic-ated series of marriages between the royal families, there was no clear contender for the throne.

France, Britain and Holland neg-otiated a treaty under which Span-ish possessions would be parti-tioned. Charles rejected this and made a will which made the dauph-in's second son, the duke of Anjou, the inheritor. With Charles's death, the French duke is now Philip V of Spain, and England and Holland have declared war.

Ships of the Anglo-Dutch navy destroy the Spanish treasure fleet at Vico.

1702 (1702-1707)

Florida, 1702. A British raid on the Spanish town of St Augustine sets an extension of the European war of the Spanish succession.

Portugal, 27 December 1703. The English diplomat John Methuen negotiates a trade treaty with Portugal.

Poland, 13 April 1703. The forces of Charles XII, king of Sweden, win a victory over the much larger army of Augustus II, king of Poland, at the battle of Pultusk.

Portugal, 1703. Portugal joins the Grand Alliance.

France, 1703. The military engineer Sebastien de Vauban imposes the use of the flintlock rifle by the French army and equips the soldiers with bayonets.

England, 1703. The philosopher Robert Hooke dies. He was the first to use a pendulum to determine the force of acceleration due to gravity.

Russia, 1703. Peter the Great founds St Petersburg.

Massachusetts, 29 February 1704. A French massacre of the Puritan colony at Deerfield intensifies the war, in which the French and their Indian allies have been attacking English settlements throughout New England.

Boston, 24 April 1704. A regular weekly newspaper, the *Boston News-Letter*, begins publication.

Poland, 12 July 1704. Following the deposition of Augustus II, Stanislas Leszczynski, the candidate of Charles XII of Sweden, comes to the throne.

Spain, July 1704. The English, led by John Churchill, duke of Marlborough, seize Gibraltar.

Germany, 13 August 1704. The forces of the Grand Alliance, led by the duke of Marlborough and Eugene of Savoy, defeat the French and the Bavarians at Blenheim.

Newfoundland, 29 August 1704. The English settlement at Bonavista on the east coast is taken by a French and Indian force.

England, 28 October 1704. The philosopher John Locke dies. A staunch defender of liberalism, he aroused the suspicions of the Stuarts and was forced into exile, in France and the Netherlands, until William III came to power.

England, 1704. Isaac Newton's treatise on *Opticks*, presenting his main discoveries concerning light and colour, is published.

Tunisia, 1705. Husayn ibn Ali, bey of the janissaries of Tunis, seizes power in Tunisia, under nominal Turkish sovereignty.

Japan, 1705. The Bakufu government accuses the house of Yodoya, the most prominent in Osaka, of ostentatious luxury and confiscates its entire wealth. In fact, the Yodoya has come to control the finances of many of the *daimyo* of Kyushu and western Honshu, whose huge debts to the Yodoya are cancelled by the confiscation.

England, 1705. The French-born English writer Bernard de Mandeville publishes his *Fable of the Bees*, a charter of utilitarianism in which he argues that the vices of individuals are of benefit to society.

England, 1705. Edmond Halley publishes his *Trajectory of Comets*.

England, 1705. The architect Sir John Vanbrugh builds Blenheim Palace in Oxfordshire.

Austria, 5 May 1705. Leopold, Holy Roman Emperor since 1658, dies and is succeeded by his son Joseph. Leopold tried to transform the Habsburg possessions into a modern state, strengthening the political institutions and re-organising the army and the finances. His struggle against the Turks led to the annexation of Hungary and Transylvania.

Spain, 14 October 1705. The English navy captures Barcelona.

Moscow, 1705. Peter the Great founds Moscow University.

Germany, 9 March 1706. The composer and organist Johann Pachelbel dies at Nuremberg. Highly regarded for the clarity of his polyphony and his well-structured harmonies, Pachelbel wrote motets, magnificats, chorals, variations and preludes.

Spain, 23 May 1706. The English raise a French siege of Barcelona.

Netherlands, 23 May 1706. The French under Villeroi are defeated by the English under Marlborough at Ramillies. The Spanish Netherlands falls to the English.

Spain, October 1706. Having entered Madrid earlier in the year, the Portuguese are driven out by Philip V of Spain.

North America, 1706. Juan de Uribarri claims a vast area in western North America for Spain (*Colorado*).

New Mexico, 1706. The governor of New Mexico, Francisco Cuervo y Valdes, founds an administrative centre for the lower Rio Grande area. He calls it Albuquerque after the viceroy of New Spain.

Persia, 1706. Shah Hussein builds a splendid temple called a *madrasah* at Isfahan.

Britain, 1 May 1707. Scotland is united with England by an Act of Union.

Astronomer claims that comets come back

London, 1705
Comets have been notoriously difficult to study because their appearance is so sudden and short-lived. They have also been surrounded throughout history by superstition and fear. Now, however, the distinguished English astronomer and polymath Edmond Halley has apparently succeeded in computing the motions of comets. He argues that these spectacular objects in the sky follow a regular pattern.

Basing his calculations on Newton's ideas in his remarkable new book, *Principia*, Halley concludes that comets travel in elliptical orbits. From this he goes on to suggest that the comets observed in 1531, 1607 and 1682 were, in fact, the same objects on their periodic journey through space. He further contends that sightings of a comet in 1305, 1380 and 1456 was again of this same body. Computing the

Edmond Halley at the age of 80.

orbit of this comet, he estimates that it will return to the vicinity of Earth in December 1758. Nobody will be completely convinced until and unless Halley's comet makes its predicted reappearance.

English inflict heavy losses on French

John Wooton's painting of Churchill's victory at the Battle of Blenheim.

Blenheim, 13 August 1704
John Churchill, the duke of Marlborough, today inflicted a crushing defeat on the French army, thereby decisively changing the balance of military power in the War of the Spanish Succession. The encounter took place near the Bavarian village of Blenheim, where French forces had assembled on their march to capture Vienna.

Churchill was far to the north in Holland, kept there by the Dutch who feared for their frontiers. They were duped by Churchill, who pretended he was preparing to campaign a few miles up the Rhine at Moselle. Instead, he made a lightning march to the Danube, hundreds of miles distant.

He was joined by Prince Eugene of Savoy and together they attacked the French and Bavarian forces. The enemy losses were 30,000 killed or captured with many more drowned in the Danube. British losses were 670 killed and 1,500 wounded.

England and Scotland are united

London, 1 May 1707

The discovery of 31 dead whales on the sands of Kirkcaldy is seen by many Scots as an evil omen for the union of the English and Scottish parliaments, which comes into effect today. But the opponents of union are far outnumbered by its supporters and those who do not care one way or the other. In the Edinburgh parliament debates some 40 members, a fifth of the House, did not bother to vote on the Union Treaty.

A crucial factor in winning over Scottish opinion was the decision by the London parliament to include in the Treaty a clause which safeguards the privileges of the Presbyterian Church. The Scots will also keep their own legal system. Last-ditch opposition to the Treaty comes from a faction of the Jacobite supporters of the Stuart claim to the English crown, which is widely seen as a lost cause.

Scottish supporters of union are looking forward to an economic boom for Glasgow, strategically

The Duke of Queensbury gives a copy of the Act of Union to Queen Anne.

placed to exploit the growing Atlantic trade. Scots are already moving south to take up jobs in England's developing industries and Highland regiments are being taken into the British army.

In London the union has been opposed by High Tories who are dismayed by the prospect of a phalanx of rough Scottish Presbyterians taking their seats in the English parliament. But for most English people today is a chance to enjoy an unexpected holiday as Queen Anne rode in state to St Paul's Cathedral for a ceremony of thanksgiving.

Hungarians resist Austrian rulers' bid to centralise power

Buda, Hungary, 1703

Sixteen years after their country was freed from Turkish occupation, Hungarian peasants have risen against heavy taxation which has been imposed by the Habsburg Empire. Every class has suffered, but the peasants feel themselves particularly hard done by. So fierce is the opposition that the Habsburg army is loth to move in the countryside, confining itself to garrisons and making only sporadic attempts to subdue the rebellion.

Two former Magyar exiles, Francis Rakoczi, a nobleman, and Nicholas Berczenyi have returned to lead the peasants. With much of his army occupied elsewhere, King Leopold is looking to wealthy Hungarian magnates for support.

An armed Hungarian warrior wearing his national costume.

Pamphlet attacks ribald comedies

London, 1707

The latest success of the London theatre, *The Beaux' Stratagem*, has made the name of the young Irish playwright, George Farquhar, following the success of his country comedy, *The Recruiting Officer*. But there has been a reaction against ribald comedies of aristocratic manners like Vanbrugh's *The Relapse* (1696) and William Congreve's *Love for Love* (1695), attacked by Jeremy Collier's pamphlet on stage immorality. Since *The Way of the World*, Congreve has given up the stage.

Mass suicide by Samurai warriors

Japan, February 1703

Forty-six samurai warriors have become heroes after committing ritual suicide. Their deaths were ordered by the shogun after they raided the home of court official Kira Yoshinaka whom they blamed for the forced suicide of their lord. They cut off Kira's head, presented it to their dead lord's grave and went willingly to their own deaths.

Farquhar's "Lord Foppington": pictured by Frith in the 19th-century.

Pope tries to alter Jesuit policy in China

China, 1704

Pope Clement XI has intervened in the bitter doctrinal quarrel between the Jesuits and the other Catholic missionaries in China. He has signed a decree, *Cum Deus Optimus*, in which he condemns the so-called Chinese rites of the Jesuits.

The quarrel arose over the Jesuit willingness to accommodate a measure of Confucian belief in the rites of their Chinese converts. The history of the Jesuits in China has been one of flexibility to the extent of accepting high office under the emperor and has long been the cause of anger among the other orders.

Charles Maigrot, the bishop of Fukien, has become the leader of the opposition to the Jesuits. He is proud of never having frequented the court, that "famous Babylon" and accuses the Jesuits of upholding idolatry in China. A papal legate has now been sent to China to investigate the Chinese rites.

Hungary, 1707. The Budapest parliament declares the fall of the Habsburgs and the independence of Hungary.

India, 1707. The great Moghul Aurangzeb dies at the age of 89, having secured control of most of the Indian peninsula. He is succeeded by Bahadur Shah.

France, 1707. *Dime royale*, an attack on the social and economic defects of France by Sebastien de Vauban, is condemned and banned on the orders of Louis XIV.

Britain, March 1708. James Edward Stewart, son of James II and pretender to the British throne, makes an unsuccessful attempt to land in Scotland.

Netherlands, 11 July 1708. The French are defeated at Oudenarde by Marlborough and Eugene of Savoy.

Newfoundland, 21 December 1708. French forces seize control of the eastern shore after winning a victory at St John's.

France, December 1708. After a five-month siege, the city of Lille falls to Grand Alliance forces under Eugene of Savoy.

Mediterranean, 1708. The English capture the islands of Sardinia and Minorca from the French.

India, 1708. The Sikh guru Govind Singh is assassinated.

Russia, 28 June 1709. Charles XII of Sweden, in alliance with the Cossack *hetman* Mazeppa, suffers a terrible defeat by the Russians at the battle of Poltava.

Netherlands, 11 September 1709. After inflicting heavy losses on the enemy, the French forces are defeated by Marlborough and Eugene of Savoy at Malplaquet.

Netherlands, 20 October 1709. Marlborough and Eugene of Savoy take Mons.

Afghanistan, 1709. The Ghilzai chieftain Mir Ways leads an uprising in Khandahar against the Safavid Persian rulers.

Poland, 1709. The Poles rise up against Stanislas Leszczynski, who flees, making way for the return of Augustus II.

Germany, 1709. Giovanni Maria Farina, a Cologne chemist and businessman, makes Eau de Cologne, following a recipe given him by a travelling merchant.

Turkey, 1709. Charles XII of Sweden seeks refuge in Turkey after his defeat at Poltava.

Venice, 1709. The German composer George Frederick Handel wins overnight fame following the triumphant production of his opera *Agrippina*.

Florence, 1709. Bartolomeo Cristofori, the famous maker of harpsichords, invents the pianoforte.

China, 1709. Emperor Kangxi requests the French Jesuits to draw a map of his empire.

Spain, 28 September 1710. Charles III Austrian King of Spain takes Madrid.

Turkey, 30 November 1710. At the instigation of Charles XII of Sweden, Turkey declares war on Russia.

Spain, 10 December 1710. The French defeat the Austrians at Villa Viciosa, forcing Charles III to abandon Madrid and making Philip V Spain's first Bourbon king.

Canada, 1710. A British expedition under Francis Nicholson captures the French stronghold of Port Royal in Acadia (*Nova Scotia* and *New Brunswick*).

Paris, 1710. An income tax known as the "tenth" is introduced.

England, 1710. The philosopher George Berkeley publishes an analysis of sense perceptions entitled *Treatise concerning the principles of human knowledge*.

London, 1710. Coffee-houses in London, which first appeared in the middle of the last century, now number about 2,000.

Vienna, 17 April 1711. On the death of the Emperor Joseph he is succeeded by Charles III, king of Spain, as Charles VI.

Boston, 25 June 1711. With the arrival of 64 British ships, carrying 5,000 troops and 6,000 seamen, preparations begin for an advance on Canada.

Russia, 21 July 1711. By the treaty of Pruth, ending the Russo-Turkish war which began last year, Russia is obliged to return Azov to the Turks.

Afghanistan, 1711. Mir Ways succeeds in defeating the Persian army sent to put down the Ghilzai rebellion and establishes the independence of the Afghan state.

Hungary, 1711. Denied support by France and Russia, the rebels agree peace terms with the Habsburgs.

Germany, 1711. Johann Bottger, who has discovered the secret of manufacturing hard Chinese porcelain, is put in charge of a new porcelain factory in Meissen.

Balkans, 1711. Supported by Venice and Russia, Danilo of Montenegro massacres the Moslems in his country and repels the Turks.

England, 1711. The South Sea Company is incorporated.

Crisis looms at Moghul emperor's death

A final portrait of India's emperor.

Ahmadnagar, India, 3 March 1707
Aurangzeb, the Emperor of India and last of the Great Moghuls, is dead. With him has died the dream of a strong and united India. A devout Moslem, who knew the Koran by heart, his very virtues turned out to be public vices. Out of his religious sincerity came religious intolerance. Hindus and Sikhs were persecuted. The Moghul's most powerful Hindu ally, the Rajputs, became alienated from the state.

His military victories (won more often by guile than by arms) over-extended his empire. His subjects were taxed to starvation to pay for his extravagant campaigns and equally extravagant court. Rarely a year went by without a revolt.

Chinese artist's revolt against tradition

Kiangsi, China, 1707
The painter, poet and calligrapher, Shitao, who renewed the art of Chinese landscape, is dead. He rebelled against the dogma that painters must imitate the style of the old masters and insisted that he would be true to the spirit of his age and his own personality. "Nowadays learned men are like withered bones and dead ashes," he said. "When I am asked if I paint in the style of the southern or the northern school, I say I do not know. I paint in my own style."

His atmospheric paintings show mountain peaks glimpsed through drifting clouds or lashing sheets of rain, rendered in pale washes with accents of dark ink brush-strokes which are allowed to spread and run.

Japanese art reflected the country's political isolation, developing in styles totally different to that of Europe where a more romantic style was flowering. These porcelain figures date from around the year 1700.

Russian winter beats Swedish invaders

Poltava, Russia, 1709

Few campaigns began with such promise for its leader – and none ended in such horror and humiliation. The vanquished invader is the king of Sweden, Charles XII, who has taken refuge in Turkey with the remnants of his once great army. The victors are Czar Peter's generals, who allowed the Swedish king and 10,000 troops to be lured into the depths of the worst winter that even Russia has known in living memory and weakened them to such extent that they were massively defeated at Poltava in June. Charles had not reckoned on a well-trained Russian army; nor on the Russian policy of burning foodstocks as they retreated, avoiding battle where possible. And he had not allowed for the Russian winter.

The Grand Vizier grants an audience to Swedish refugees in Turkey.

Great Sikh guru is killed by Afghan

Dekhan, India, November 1708

Govind Singh, the tenth of the Sikh-gurus, has been assassinated. There seems no doubt his killer, an Afghan, is in the pay of Bahadur Shah, the new Moghul emperor.

Guru Govind was more than a holy man. He was a general who militarized the Sikh movement, and a political leader, who first fought with Bahadur Shah, then turned against him. He will be most remembered as a religious reformer, who did more to shape the Sikh philosophy and identity than anyone since Nanak, who founded the movement 200 years ago.

African kingdoms growing slave rich

Gold Coast, 1708

As tens of thousands of Africans are being forcibly snatched from their villages and cruelly transported to America, the states of West Africa are growing rich from the slave trade.

None have done better than Abomey in Dahomey (Benin), situated between the Ouene and Mono rivers and controlling the slave ports of Allada and Ouidah. Its treasury overflows. It has a fast and efficient army, with many of the soldiers women. When it is not out on slave raids it is fighting the rival Oyo empire.

Marlborough turns tide against French

Netherlands, 11 September 1709

England's greatest general, the duke of Marlborough, today added another victory to his string of successes against the French. After a day's hard pounding at Malplaquet, near Mons, in the Southern Netherlands (Belgium), the French finally retreated. Some critics say the battle was indecisive, but most people believe that after Blenheim, Ramillies, Antwerp, Ostend, Menin and Oudenarde, the French have lost their appetite for doing battle with Marlborough. The duke's triumphs derive from his attention to detail, his care for his soldiers' welfare and his cool head in the heat of battle.

With St Paul's, Wren completes the rebuilding of London after great fire

The north-west view of Sir Christopher Wren's St Paul's cathedral.

London, 1711

The rebuilding of St Paul's cathedral is finished – 38 years after it began and 45 years after it was planned by Sir Christopher Wren when its mediaeval predecessor was destroyed in the Great Fire. Sir Christopher is now all but 80 years old and the last stone above the lantern was laid by his son. He has applied for his back salary of £200 a year; in 1697 parliament said he should be paid only half of it until the building was finished.

London has gained a masterpiece second only to Rome's St Peter's, which has the only larger dome in the world. Wren employed Grinling Gibbons to carve the stalls of the choir and the Huguenot, Jean Tijou, for the sanctuary's wrought-iron gates. But the inside of the dome, which he wanted in mosaic, is to be painted in monochrome by Sir James Thornhill. The cost of the building, £721,552 7s 7d, has been raised mainly by a tax on seacoal. Wren designed 51 of the city churches rebuilt after the Fire. Their towers and steeples surround the great dome with a skyline of architectural fantasy. Although Wren has designed other buildings, his plans for radiating streets and vistas came to nothing.

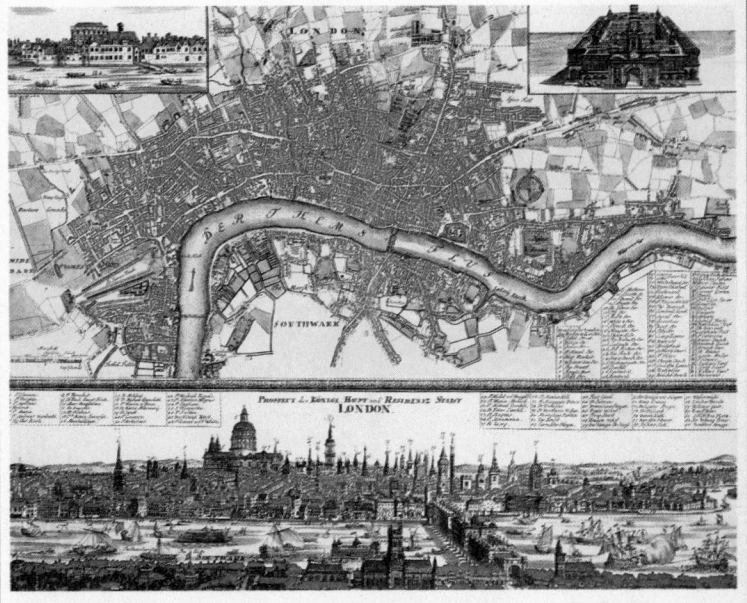

Homanns' map of London, including London Bridge and St Paul's.

1711 (1711-1715)

Carolina, 22 September 1711. Upset by a new wave of settlements, Indians attack colonists on the Roanoke and Chowan rivers, launching the Tuscarora war.

Ottoman Empire, 1711. The Ottoman government chooses a Greek phanariot (resident of Fanar, a suburb of Istanbul) to rule in Moldavia. The Ottomans are worried by Moldavian *rapprochement* with Russia, which is aimed at throwing off the Turkish yoke.

Pennsylvania, 7 June 1712. The assembly bans the importation of slaves into the colony.

New York, 4 July 1712. After one of the first slave uprisings in North America, 12 slaves are executed and six commit suicide before they can be brought to the gallows. Before the militia arrived to arrest them, the slaves killed nine whites.

Pennsylvania, 1712. The colony's Quaker founder, William Penn, suffers a severe stroke. His wife, Hannah, takes over the governing of the colony.

Baltic, 1712. Russians and Danes defeat the Swedes in the Baltic and Scandinavia. Since 1700, in what has become known as the Second Northern War, the Swedish king Charles XII has been fighting to preserve Swedish supremacy in the Baltic. However, after these most recent defeats, it looks as if Charles will be forced to sue for peace.

West Africa, 1712. The Bambara kingdom of Segu is founded upstream from Timbuktu. It is a non-Moslem state which challenges the declining Mali empire to the west.

North Carolina, 23 March 1713. Troops from North and South Carolina capture Fort Nohucke, a Tuscarora base, and force the Indians to negotiate. Fighting broke out in 1711 after the Indians devastated a settlement.

Britain, 26 March 1713. As part of the settlement in Queen Anne's war – the North American extension of the war of Spanish Succession – Britain gains *Asiento*, a contract allowing the South Sea Company to bring 4,800 Negro slaves per year into the Spanish colonies.

Netherlands, 11 April 1713. The treaty of Utrecht ends the war of the Spanish Succession. It confirms the permanent separation of the crowns of France and Spain and recognises Philip V as king of Spain.

Germany, 1713. Emperor Charles VI issues a "pragmatic sanction" settling the succession to the Habsburg lands on his daughter Maria Theresa.

Prussia, 1713. Frederick William succeeds his father Frederick on the throne of Prussia.

South Africa, 1713. The first smallpox epidemic spreads from the sailors at the Cape of Good Hope, killing Khoisan hunters and herders in great numbers.

Netherlands, 1713. Pierre Jurieu, the French Huguenot theologian and polemicist, dies in exile in Rotterdam. He led Calvinist resistance to the rule of Louis XIV.

Russia, 1713. Peter the Great has a naval base built at Tallin in Estonia.

Vietnam, 1713. In a continuing drive against Christianity, French missionaries are expelled from Tongking.

Germany, 6 March 1714. The Holy Roman Empire signs a treaty with France at Rastatt – one of several agreements concluding the war of the Spanish Succession.

Britain, 1 August 1714. On the death of Queen Anne without a direct heir, she is succeeded as monarch of Great Britain and Ireland by George, elector of Hanover since 1698 and great-grandson of James I of England.

Spain, 6 September 1714. King Philip V takes the Italian heiress Elizabeth Farnese as his second wife. The marriage is arranged by Giulio Alberoni, diplomatic agent of the duke of Parma, Elizabeth's father.

France, 1714. The famous keyboard instrumentalist Francois Couperin gives a series of ten concerts entitled *The Joined Tastes*. From a family of musicians, Couperin has been organist in the king's chapel since 1693.

Italy, 1714. The anatomist Bartolommeo Eustachio's *Tabulae anatomicae* is published posthumously. Eustachio died in 1574 and is famous for his discoveries concerning the heart and the ears.

Germany, 1714. The philosopher and mathematician Gottfried Liebniz publishes his *Monadologia*, according to which the universe is made up of "monads", divine mutually isolated creations. Each monad reflects the universe from its own point of view.

South Carolina, 15 April 1715. Yamassee Indians, goaded by Spanish agitation, kill hundreds of English settlers.

South Africa, 1715. Dutch burghers at the Cape of Good Hope elect their own commanders in an attempt to combat cattle rustling by Khoisan herders.

West African king dies courted by Europe

Ghana, West Africa, 1712

Osei Tutu, the founder of the Asante states, has been killed in an ambush. Thirty years ago he had been a penniless refugee, surviving on the largess of the nearby state of Akwamu. He died the ruler of a West African empire.

The Asantes' rulers are immigrants from the south, who settled in the forests only a generation ago. Under Osei Tutu, they forged themselves into a nation, their dominance assured after the defeat of their one-time overlords, the Denkyira, at Feyiase in 1701. Osei Tutu (aided by his powerful high priest, Okomfo Anokye) built an empire by combining war and diplomacy, cementing alliances with marriages, and enriching his people with profits from the gold and slave trades.

European powers, anxious to take a share in the wealth, courted him. Unable to buy slaves with gold (Asante has all the gold it needs), the Europeans bought slaves with guns, thus increasing the Asante's formidable power.

Within a year of Osei Tutu's victory over the Denkyira, Holland sent ambassadors to the Asante capital, Kumasi. Rival European powers, like Britain, unable to extract trading concessions from the Asante, impotently ally themselves with the Asantes' enemies.

Mask of an enemy slain in battle.

A horned and decorated helmet.

Boiling point is a matter of degrees

Holland, 1714

A German-born physicist, working in Holland, Daniel Fahrenheit has made a mercury thermometer that is more accurate than the alcohol-filled instruments currently in use. His thermometer has three fixed points. The lowest – 32 degrees – is the freezing point of a mixture of water, ice and salt. The highest is the boiling point of water at 212 degrees. In between is the temperature of human blood – 98.4 degrees. Fahrenheit is also interested in making precision meteorological instruments, such as barometers. And he discovered that water can remain liquid even below its freezing point and that it boils at different temperatures, according to atmospheric pressure.

British invasion of Canada fails

Quebec, 23 August 1711

Another British attempt to invade Canada has ended in a disaster which the locals here call the "magnificent fiasco". Nine British ships left Boston on July 30, but they got lost in the fog off Egg Island in the Gulf of St Lawrence. Eight of them were blown on to the rocks in a storm. Nearly 1,000 people lost their lives, including 35 women and some drummer boys. Admiral Walker and a few others survived on the remaining ship.

Perhaps Father de la Columbiere, the Montreal priest-in-charge, will be tempted into a repeat of his sermon after the last British effort 20 years ago. Then he claimed that Quebec had been saved by the Virgin Mary.

Treaty of Utrecht reshapes Europe

London, 1713
As the War of Spanish Succession drags to an end on the continent, British politicians are celebrating negotiations which have taken it out of the war. Under the terms of the Treaty of Utrecht, Britain has retained – from Spain – its hold on two great naval bases, Gibraltar and Minorca, and its position in the Mediterranean has been strengthened by a settlement which gives Naples and Reggio to its ally, the Emperor Charles VI. Britain has also gained – from France – sovereignty in Newfoundland, Hudson Bay and St Kitts as well as recognition of the Hanoverian succession in Britain.

The treaty confirms that Spain will be ruled by Philip V, although he has had to secede much of his empire, including Naples, Sardinia and the Netherlands (to Austria) and Sicily (to Savoy). He retains his colonial territories, although Britain has the monopoly of transporting negro slaves to them.

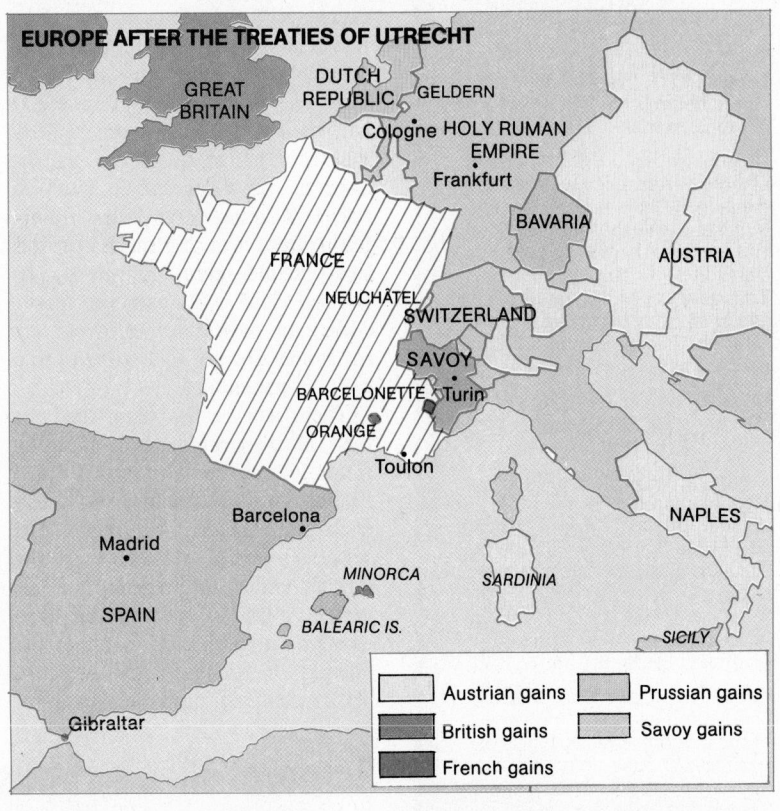

EUROPE AFTER THE TREATIES OF UTRECHT

GREAT BRITAIN — DUTCH REPUBLIC — GELDERN — Cologne — HOLY RUMAN EMPIRE — Frankfurt — BAVARIA — AUSTRIA — FRANCE — NEUCHÂTEL — SWITZERLAND — SAVOY — BARCELONETTE — Turin — ORANGE — Toulon — Barcelona — Madrid — NAPLES — MINORCA — SARDINIA — SPAIN — BALEARIC IS. — SICILY — Gibraltar

Austrian gains / Prussian gains / British gains / Savoy gains / French gains

New British king cannot speak English

England, 1714
George, the Elector of Hanover, has arrived in London to ascend the British throne, bringing with him two German mistresses, who will be made countesses. He speaks no English and he has a notoriously foul temper and nobody much cares for him, but at least he is a Protestant. Queen Anne, who died at Kensington on 1 August, detested the Hanoverians, but two days before her death she realised that, as the grandson of James I, George would succeed her. The alternative was a Stuart succession which would cause political turmoil – and be bad for business.

Claimant to British throne is defeated

Scotland, September 1715
A disaffected Scottish aristocrat, the Earl of Mar, known as Bobbing John because of his political vacillation, has organised a rebellion in an attempt to put James Stuart, the "Old Pretender", on the throne.

Stuart, the son of James II, believed the British were eager to welcome him, but when he arrived off the Devon coast, as Bolingbroke said, he was "refused even a night's lodging". He went on to Scotland, where 18 Scottish lords rallied to the cause, but English troops, with Dutch allies, put down the rebellion, and a disillusioned Stuart fled to France.

James Stuart: exiled to France.

Berkeley reduces objects to ideas

London, 1713
Few philosophers have made such an instant impact as George Berkeley, the young Irish theologian being introduced to London society by his countryman Jonathan Swift.

Berkeley's arrival coincides with publication of his latest work *Three Dialogues between Hylas and Philonous* in which he propounds his argument that the only things that are real are our ideas of what is presented to our senses.

A graduate of Trinity College Dublin – a haven for independent thinkers – Berkeley developed the metaphysical implications of his theory of perception with the publication three years ago of his *Treatise concerning the Principles of Human Knowledge*.

Berkeley's new principle – in which objects are reduced to ideas – does not mean to question their reality as everyday objects, but tries to bring out their token value. For Berkeley these ideas are part of a system in which God is the creative source.

Bull-baiting and cock fighting draw the crowds

England, 1711
Violent sports involving animals have become the norm in England and enthusiasts are flocking to enjoy the twin spectacles of cockfighting and bull-baiting.

The faint-hearted protest against what they see as the deliberate torture of dumb creatures, but most of the population, from high to low, see no harm in their entertainments.

Cock-fighting offers a chance for its followers to place a bet on one of the two competing birds. Placed in a pit surrounded with shouting spectators and armed with silver spurs they hack and gouge at each other until one is victorious. Wagers can reach twenty guineas and more.

Bull-baiting involves no betting, but simply the setting of dogs on a tethered bull to the amusement of those who watch. Around 30 dogs are used, attacking in twos and threes. Both dogs and bull are likely to be badly injured.

A violin by the master violinmaker Antonio Stradivari of Cremona: a pupil of Amati, his work is gaining an international reputation for unrivalled skill.

1715 (1715-1719)

France, September 1715. Following the death of Louis XIV and the accession of his five-year-old grandson, Louis XV, the regency is put in the hands of Philip of Orleans.

Massachusetts, 1715. Three years after the first sperm whale was killed at Nantucket, the whale-oil industry is booming. Nantucket has a fleet of six 30-ton whaling sloops that can cruise for six weeks at a time.

Lousiana, 6 June 1716. The first slaves are brought to French colonial territory in north America, in ships owned by the Company of the West.

Japan, 1716. The famous painter Ogata Koretomi, known as Ogata Korin, dies. Born into a wealthy merchant family, Korin's profligate lifestyle led him into financial difficulties and he was forced to take up painting as a profession. His works are marked by naturalism and an obvious talent for design.

Spain, 1716. The Italian Giulio Alberoni, favourite of King Philip V, becomes prime minister.

France, 1716. Francois Couperin, organist of the king's chapel, publishes *The Art of Playing the Harpsichord*, a treatise on keyboard technique.

Paris, May 1717. On a visit to Europe, Peter the Great of Russia proposes the marriage of his daughter Elizabeth Petrovna to Louis XV of France.

Paris, 4 August 1717. A friendship treaty is signed between Russia and France.

Spain, 1717. A Spanish army is sent to conquer Sardinia on the pretext that a Spanish citizen has been arrested in Italy.

New England, 1717. Colonial ships, now allowed to trade in the West Indies, begin bringing back French molasses, which they use to distil cheap rum in New England.

Vienna, 1717. The Schonbrunn Palace, built on the model of the Palace of Versailles, is completed. Intended as a place of leisure, its size and splendour serve to illustrate the magnificence of the imperial power.

Netherlands, 1717. A triple alliance, directed against Spain, is signed in The Hague by France, England and Holland. This is a response to Spanish expansionist ambitions: Philip V, as Louis XIV's grandson, wishes to gain the French crown, and his wife Elizabeth Farnese wants her children to inherit familial lands in Italy.

China, 1717. The painter and art theoretician Che-t'ao dies.

West Africa, 1717. Prussia sells its West African slave stations to the Dutch.

London, 1717. The Golden Lion coffee house is the first in London to admit women.

Austria, 21 July 1718. The treaty of Passarowitz, negotiated by the Emperor Charles VI and the Venetians with the Ottoman empire, ends the war begun by the Turks in 1714. Turkey cedes Temesvar to Charles, putting the whole of Hungary under Habsburg rule. The Turkish threat to Europe is effectively stamped out.

Pennsylvania, 30 July 1718. William Penn, the Quaker founder of the colony, dies.

Europe, 2 August 1718. The Holy Roman Empire joins the triple alliance formed by Britain, Holland and France against Spain last year. The new quadruple alliance aims to uphold the terms of the 1713 Treaty of Utrecht, which Philip V of Spain has violated by invading Sicily and Sardinia.

Europe, 24 August 1718. In the conflict following the drawing up of the quadruple alliance, Victor Amadeus of Savoy cedes the island of Sicily to Austria in exchange for Sardinia.

Virginia, 22 November 1718. The infamous pirate Edward Teach, known as Blackbeard because of an immense beard which he tied with ribbons, is killed by an English naval officer. A reward of £100 pounds had been offered by the government of Virginia for his capture.

Louisiana, November 1718. Governor Bienville founds a new city at the mouth of the Mississippi river, calling it New Orleans in honour of the French regent, the duke of Orleans.

Norway, 11 December 1718. Sweden's king, Charles XII, dies in battle at Frederikshald (*Halden*). He came to power in 1697 and has spent almost his entire reign engaged in the Second Northern War. Most recently he had been defeated by Russia and sued for peace, but then marched on Norway. He was killed by a musket shot fired from the fortress of Frederikshald.

Spain, 9 January 1719. In escalation of the conflict caused by the Spanish occupation of Sardinia and Sicily, and the drawing up of the quadruple alliance, Philip V of Spain declares war on France.

Prussia, 22 March 1719. Frederick William abolishes serfdom on crown property.

Dying Sun King was "punished by God"

St Germain, 1 September 1715

Louis XIV of France, the Sun King, died at St Germain en Laye at eight this morning. He would have been 77 in four days' time and had been king for 73 years. Suffering from gangrene of the leg, he knew he was dying and accepted his fate with courage and patience. Saying goodbye to his successor, his five-year-old great grandson, he advised him: "Remain at peace with your neighbours. I loved war too much. Do not follow me in that or in overspending."

There will be few tears shed for this hard-working, but haughty man. It was he who transformed France into an absolute monarchy declaring: *L'Etat, c'est moi* ("The state, it's me"). He came to the throne under the regency of his mother, Anne of Austria, and lived through dangerous times under the tutelage of Richelieu and Mazarin before claiming supreme power for

Louis poses as a Roman noble.

himself. The last years of this brilliant monarch have been darkened by defeat, a bankrupt economy and family deaths. He died believing he was being punished by God for the terror he had inflicted on Europe.

Emperor dies exhausted for China's sake

Beijing, 23 December 1717

The Emperor Kangxi called his many sons and his officials to the Eastern chamber of the Jianjing palace today and delivered a valedictory edict in preparation for his death. He said he would rather they listen to his words than those of an anonymous scholar.

The emperor, who is nearly 70 and has reigned for over 50 years, was in a reflective, sad mood, recalling the days of his youth when he was strong and talking about the burdens of ruling China: "Bowing down in service and wearing oneself out ... I exhaust myself for the country's sake."

He told them that the art of ruling was to be "always diligent and always careful, and maintain the balance between leniency and strictness, between principle and expediency ... that's all there is to it". Finally, he told them: "I've revealed my entrails and shown my guts, there's nothing left within me to reveal. I will say no more."

A scroll shows Emperor Kangxi inpsecting the construction of a dyke.

Turks lose Belgrade

Belgrade, 22 August 1717
Austrian forces today occupied the strategically important city of Belgrade, ending the Turkish military revival in the Balkans. As victorious troops of the Imperial House of Habsburg marched into the devastated city 60,000 Moslems, including 20,000 Turkish soldiers, were allowed to leave.

The Turks, who had supplies for another six months, decided to surrender after their relief force camped outside the city was slaughtered in a dawn raid a week ago by Imperialist troops led by Prince Eugene of Savoy.

The August 16 raid was a dramatic triumph for Prince Eugene who appeared to stand little chance of winning this battle. His siege army, ravaged by dysentery and raked by deadly artillery fire from the Turkish relief force on a plateau to the east, was thought to be trapped and on the verge of destruction. Prince Eugene left 10,000 men to watch Belgrade while, under cover of fog, 60,000 Imperial troops fortified by wine and beer overran the Turks.

In Vienna, Prince Eugene is now being hailed as the architect of the Imperial success. His victory against a much larger Turkish force in Hungary last year, plus the shrewd treaty with England to safeguard the empire's Italian flank from a Franco-Spanish attack, are now regarded as having laid foundations for the Imperial success.

Inefficient French seek German help

Louisiana, December 1719
French Louisiana, so inefficient that it must import its food from France, has recruited German farmers to raise agricultural output. The first of the new breed of colonists disembarked at Ship Island, near Biloxi last month.

The Germans are sturdy Rhinelanders and tough hill farmers from Switzerland, all hungry for land and sanctuary from Europe's endless wars. Formerly, only French settlers were accepted in Louisiana. Now the Germans are said to be "just the colonists we need", though they have much to learn.

A great german thinker is dead

Hanover, 14 November 1716
Gottfried Wilhelm Leibnitz, the German philosopher who dedicated his life to the spread of scientific discoveries for the benefit of all mankind, has died. He was 70.

To further his belief Leibnitz tried to construct a universal language and develop a system of logic through which any controversy could be solved. Central to his theories was the idea of "monads": indivisible substances on which all things are based.

Cristofori's "piano e forte" catches on

Two young ladies play a new tune.

Europe, c.1715
Musicians are taking an increasing interest in the instrument invented around 20 years ago by the Florentine keyboard maker Bartolomeo Cristofori (born 1655). He calls his invention a *gravicembalo col piano e forte* or "harpsichord with soft and loud"; it differs from normal harpsichords in that when the keys are pressed the strings are struck rather than plucked. The mechanism of what is becoming known as the "piano e forte" or "forte-piano" allows the struck string to resonate, giving the instrument a much greater range of loudness or softness.

Blood curdling rituals bind freemasons

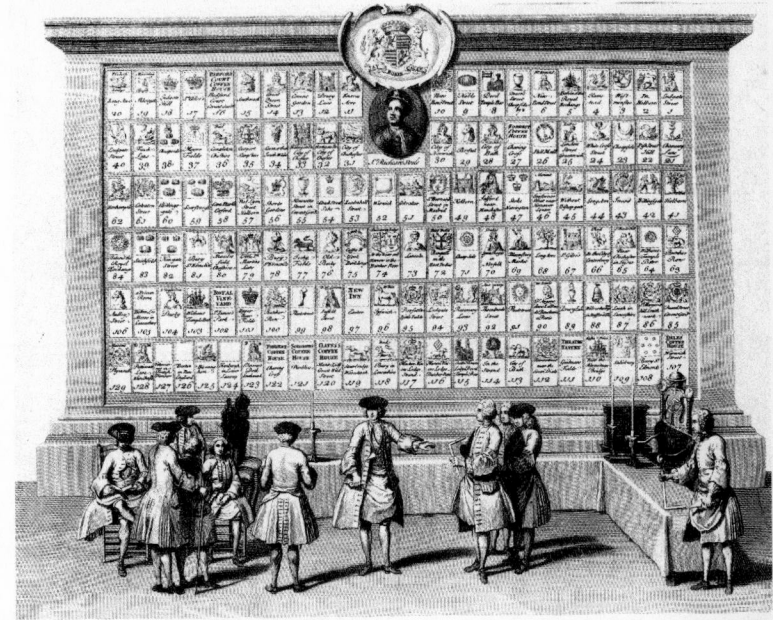
Masons meet under posters displaying the names of their many "lodges".

London, 4 June 1717
A secret society, which claims to date back to the beginning of time, has established itself in London. Freemasonry, as the society is known, has been growing for a number of years. Now the first Grand Lodge, or headquarters, has been set up at the Goose and Gridiron tavern in Covent Garden.

The Craft, as it is known, allegedly began with the sons of Adam, and its more immediate roots lie with Hiram, master-mason of Solomon's Temple, who it is said was killed for refusing to reveal masonic secrets. England's first freemasons, who appear to number around 1,300, were a trade guild like many others, and their lodges or local assemblies developed to meet the needs of workers whose jobs kept them moving from place to place.

Today's society includes few working masons. The old craft guild was gradually diluted by outsiders and now members join for the social and professional benefits. None the less freemasonry is highly secretive, with elaborate rituals, a blood-curdling initiation ceremony and a secret handclasp – the "Masonic Word" – by which members may recognise each other.

A view of the Schonbrunn Palace in Vienna: completed in 1717 the palace is designed as a place of enjoyment and relaxation, but its vast dimensions and superb furnishings make it a symbol of imperial might.

1719 (1719-1722)

South Carolina, November 1719. Colonists overthrow British proprietors.

Texas, 1720. Two years of hostilities between French and Spanish troops in Florida and Texas – caused by the war of the Quadruple Alliance in Europe – are over. Spanish possession of Texas has been confirmed.

Netherlands, 17 February 1720. Spain signs the treaty of The Hague with the Quadruple Alliance (Britain, Holland, France and the Holy Roman Empire), ending the war begun in 1718. Philip V of Spain agrees to evacuate Sardinia and Sicily, the invasions of which started the conflict. He exiles his chief minister Alberoni, whom he holds responsible for the war.

Sweden, 20 February 1720. Queen Ulrika Eleonora, Charles XII's younger sister, abdicates in favour of her consort, Frederick of Hesse-Kessel.

Paris, 24 March 1720. Banking establishments close in the wake of financial crisis.

West Africa, c.1720. Biton Mamari Kouloubali makes himself leader of the kingdom of Segu (*Mali*). Mamari was elected head of the *ton-den* brotherhood and began to conscript young Bambara into it destroying its previously egalitarian nature. He is establishing the *ton-den*, and himself, as the dominant powers in the community.

North America, 1720. Population of the British colonies now stands at 474,000. Boston is the largest city at 12,000; Philadelphia has an estimated 10,000 and New York some 7,000 inhabitants.

Central America, 1720. The English colony of Honduras is established.

Austria, 1720. The Pragmatic Sanction – issued by Emperor Charles V in 1713, settling succession to the Habsburg lands on his eldest daughter Maria Theresa – is slowly recognised by the Habsburg states.

Russia, 25 January 1721. The Holy Synod replaces the Patriarchate of Moscow and steps are taken against the sect of the Old Believers. They object to the 1667 revision of Russian church ritual and liturgy in accordance with Greek practice, and are regarded as schismatics by the Orthodox church.

Germany, 24 March 1721. The supremely talented musician Johann Sebastian Bach publishes the *Six Brandenburg Concertos*.

England, 3 April 1721. Following the collapse of the South Sea Scheme, the ambitious Whig politician Robert Walpole is made Chancellor of the Exchequer in the hope that he will restore financial order.

Rome, 8 May 1721. After the death of Clement XI on 19 March, Michelangelo dei Conti is elected pope and takes the name of Innocent XIII. He was secretary of state for Clement XI and has been elected after a long contentious conclave as a man of diplomatic tact and political acumen.

France, 18 July 1721. The painter Antoine Watteau dies of tuberculosis from which he had suffered all his life. Watteau will be best remembered for the palace-garden landscapes that form the typical background to many of his pictures.

Sweden, 30 August 1721. The peace of Nystad ends the Second Northern War – between Sweden and Russia – which began in 1700. Sweden cedes Livonia, Estonia, part of·Karelia and Ingermanland to Russia and retains Finland. This marks a considerable increase in Russian power in the Baltic.

Greenland, 1721. Led by the Norwegian minister Hans Egede, the Protestant mission of Godthaab is established with the aim of converting the Eskimos.

New Orleans, 1721. A group of women taken from a house of correction in France arrives to relieve the shortage of females in the colony. Many are married almost immediately after arrival, and the rest parcelled out to various French settlements to appease lonely bachelors.

Massachusetts, 1721. During an outbreak of smallpox Dr Zabdiel Boylston of Boston experiments with innoculation at the prompting of Reverend Cotton Mather. Mather heard of the technique from his African slave Onesimus. Opponents to innoculation believe it has caused the disease to spread more rapidly, though all but six of the 240 Boylston innoculated have survived.

France, 25 October 1722. Louis XV is crowned at Rheims.

Austria, 19 December 1722. Charles V creates the Ostend Company, an association of Flemish merchants trading with the east. This is a result of the transfer of the Spanish Netherlands to Austria under the Treaty of Utrecht of 1713. Both Britain and Holland object to the foundation of the Company seeing it as a threat to their own trading ventures.

Sweden's dream of Baltic power is dead

Stockholm, 21 January 1720
The last line of an epigram by the Swedish poet Carl Cederhielm says it all: "...and Sweden's clock has moved from XII to I..." he wrote as Sweden signed the Treaty of Stockholm, losing its empire and its control of the Baltic Sea. The "XII" referred to the late King Charles – killed while laying siege to Fredrikshald – whose impetuous advance into Russia in mid-winter impoverished his country, leaving it vulnerable. After the defeat of the Swedish army at Poltava, Prussia and Hanover joined the alliance of Denmark, Poland and Russia against Sweden. The greatest threat came from Russia whose raiding parties had already reached Stockholm.

This fear that created intense diplomatic activity, particularly by Britain – anxious to secure supplies of spars and hemp for her navy – and France, Sweden's long-time ally.

Sweden has lost her Baltic states to Prussia and Hanover and a once-great power has settled for a minor role on the world stage.

Tale of castaway Crusoe proves popular

London, 25 April, 1719
A book purporting to tell "The Strange Surprising Adventures of Robinson Crusoe of York, Mariner" is being read eagerly by people who take it to be a true account of shipwreck. It is only some half-dozen years since the Scottish castaway, Alexander Selkirk, got home after four years in solitude on the Pacific island of Juan Fernandez.

Robinson Crusoe claims to have exceeded this, having been marooned 28 years. But after 15 of these he discovered a creature he calls Friday to be sharing his island. Daniel Defoe, former editor of *The Review* and author of many political pamphlets, is the transcriber – or author? – of these remarkable adventures.

Daniel Defoe's Robinson Crusoe.

Letters from a Persian lost in Paris

A Persian prince out hawking.

Amsterdam, 1721
Letters have been published anonymously here and in Cologne purporting to be from a Persian living in Paris, satirizing French society. They are in fact the work of the Baron de Montesquieu.

The *Lettres Persanes* represent a correspondence between two brothers, Rica, in Venice, Usbek, in Paris, and their relatives in Isfahan. Usbek writes from Paris about his puzzlement at the role of that "magician", the Pope, and the political system which allows him such extraordinary influence.

Montesquieu, who is 32, is a member of the Academy of Science, and a writer of exceptional wit and perception.

Financial panic in Paris

"The Bubbler's Medley": a satirical print mocking the South Sea Bubble.

London, 1720

Financial scandals have erupted in London and Paris in the wake of an orgy of speculation by gullible investors tempted by promises of vast fortunes. The man who started it all is John Law, a Scottish exile who gained the confidence of the French Regent, the Duc d'Orleans. Law was allowed to launch a note-issuing Banque Royale, a trading company, the Compagnie des Indies, and to collect some land taxes. He promised to pay off the national debt by encouraging the public to exchange their government bonds for shares in his India company.

That gave ideas to Robert Harley, who had earlier founded the South Sea Company. Investors rushed to turn in their government bonds in exchange for South Sea stock. In six months the shares rose

from 150 to 1,000. John Windham, a Norfolk squire, wrote to his brother: "I grow rich so fast I like stock jobbing above all things."

All England seemed to join in. Hundreds of other companies were launched, with bizarre promises – to drain bogs in Ireland, to get gold from sea water, to collect hair for wig-making, to organise funerals. When the South Sea Company accused some of its rivals of dishonesty, the public lost confidence and began selling. Within weeks, South Sea shares had plunged to 180. Windham now wrote: "Almost all one knows or sees are upon the very Brink of Destruction."

The story was much the same in Paris. The India Company's shares slumped and panic-stricken Parisiens besieged the Banque Royale; but Law had fled.

Persian capital falls to the Afghans

Isfahan, 12 October 1722

Shah Sultan Husayn has surrendered the Persian capital to Afghan rebels after a seven-month siege, in which more than 80,000 people have died of famine.

The fall of Isfahan represents the collapse of the Safawid dynasty, defeated with remarkable ease by a modest tribal army, but crucially undermined by its own weaknesses. Since the death of Shah Abbas II in 1666, Persia has lacked a strong ruler.

Sultan Husayn, shah since 1694, is a weak man, dominated by mullahs whose determination to force Shi'ite Islam on a reluctant population has encouraged rebellion. Mahmud, the leader of the Sunnis of Afghanistan, now enjoys tenuous control of Persia.

Silk cloth: a youth drinking wine.

Spanish defeat at hands of Triple Alliance

Madrid, 26 January 1720

Guilio Alberoni, the devious cardinal of Madrid, was ordered out of Spain today – bringing to an end a short and bloody attempt to restore his country's Mediterranean empire and crush Habsburg power in Italy. British troops have occupied Vigo, Spanish troops are to

evacuate Sardinia and Sicily and Philip V has acceded to the Treaty of Utrecht.

Alberoni organised a futile attempt at invading England by the pretender, James III – foiled by storms off Finisterre – and also intrigued to start an abortive rebellion in Brittany.

Pacific island discovered on Easter day

Chile, 1722

Admiral Jacob Roggeveen, a Dutch navigator, has discovered a strange, lonely Pacific island inhabited by primitive sun worshippers. They call it "Rapa Nui" but Roggeveen,

noting the festival on which he landed there, has renamed it "Easter Island". As well as natives it is populated by hundreds of extraordinary statues, long-eared icons up to 32 feet (9.75m) tall.

The strange statues that have been found by Roggeveen on Easter Island.

1722 (1722-1727)

New England, 1722. The English parliament bans trade with Canada.

France, 22 February 1723. Louis XV comes of age.

Russia, 12 September 1723. The treaty of St Petersburg puts an end to the Russo-Persian war which began last year when Peter the Great, made anxious by a Turkish push towards the Caspian Sea, launched an offensive. By the treaty Russia gains control of the coastal areas between Derbent and Resht on the Caspian Sea and the shah receives a loan of Russian troops for domestic peace-keeping.

England, 2 October 1723. The English block Austrian trading activity by passing a law against trade with the Ostend Company of merchants.

Prussia, 10 October 1723. The treaty of Charlottenburg is signed between Britain and Prussia. Britain is seeking Prussian friendship in the face of the Emperor Charles VI's promotion of the Ostend Company.

Philadelphia, October 1723. Benjamin Franklin, 17-year-old publisher of an irreverent weekly, the *New England Courant*, leaves Boston for Philadelphia following a fight with his brother. Franklin writes satirical pieces under the pseudonym Silence Dogood.

West Africa, c.1723. King Agaja of the Dahomey kingdon at Abomey invades the kingdom of Allada. Allada, founded about 150 years ago, was once the most powerful kingdom of the Aja peoples.

Germany, 1724. Johann Sebastian Bach's *St John Passion* is performed on Good Friday in Leipzig.

Rome, 29 May 1724. The new pope, Benedict XIII, a very old man, allows Cardinal Niccolo Coscia to rule in his place.

London, 27 December 1724. Thomas Guy, a well-known philanthropist and bookseller, dies. Two years ago he began the construction of a new hospital on a site opposite St Thomas', and the building is now complete. His will provides for a vast number of people, both known and unknown to him, as well as leaving sufficient funds for the running of the new hospital.

Austria, 1724. Commercial differences between England and Austria are resolved. The Ostend Company of Flemish merchants is put into liquidation.

Louisana, 1724. The Black Code makes it legal for slave owners to cut off runaways' ears, hamstring and brand them. It also bars Jews and Catholics from the colony.

France, 1724. The famously talented keyboard instrumentalist Francois Couperin completes his second collection of *Royal Concerts*.

Russia, 8 February 1725. Peter the Great dies in St Petersburg. He is succeeded by his wife Catherine.

Spain, 2 March 1725. The architect Jose Benito de Churriguera dies. One of his finest works is the high altar in San Esteban, Salamanca.

Austria, 30 April 1725. Philip V of Spain and the Emperor Charles VI sign the treaty of Vienna ending Spanish and imperial adhesion to the Quadruple Alliance. Philip guarantees the Pragmatic Sanction – allowing for the succession of the emperor's daughter on his death – and receives a promise of support in the recovery of Gibraltar and Minorca, though this does not extend to military aid. Spain appears to have gained little, but the Spanish negotiator Ripperda's claims of secret clauses are worrying Britain and France.

France, 15 August 1725. Louis XV marries Maria Leszczynska, daughter of the deposed Polish king, Stanislav Leszczynski, by proxy in Strasbourg.

Naples, 22 October 1725. The composer Alessandro Scarlatti dies. He wrote many operas, among them – *The Triumph of Liberty* (1707), *Tigrone* (1715), *The Triumph of Honour* (1718) and *Griselda* (1721).

Netherlands, 1725. The composer Antonio Vivaldi publishes *The Four Seasons*.

Southern Africa, c.1725. Langa, the ancestor chief of Ngwane, Swazi and Hlubi nations, dies. Langa was tributary to the Tembe kingdom at Maputo Bay.

South America, 1725. Montevideo is founded.

Naples, 1725. The Italian philosopher Giambattista Vico publishes *Principles of a New Science*.

France, 12 June 1726. Louis XV's tutor, Fleury, becomes prime minister following the fall from grace of the duke of Bourbon. His dangerous foreign policies threatened to involve France in a war with Spain and Austria.

Russia, 16 August 1726. Russia becomes an ally of Austria and recognises the Pragmatic Sanction guaranteeing the succession of Emperor Charles VI's eldest daughter, Maria Theresa.

Ottoman Empire, 1727. The Ottomans and Persians form an alliance against Russia.

Czar Peter the Great's reforms: a commoner may rise to noble rank

Peter the Great's new palace of Petrodvorets in the city of St Petersburg.

St Petersburg, 24 January 1722
Czar Peter – "the Great" – has transformed Russia and set her on the path to becoming a great European power. His dazzling reforms over the past 30 years were capped today by the introduction of a "Table of Ranks" which will give the country a well-organised military and civil service. From now on a commoner can climb on merit to the highest positions.

Peter's other reforms include the abolition of the old *duma* of the Moscow aristocracy, the reorganisation of the government, and major financial changes including the introduction of a poll tax. His social revolution has included the shaven chin and the short coat of the western European – anyone appearing at the gates of a city wearing a long Russian robe is made to kneel while the coat is cut to the knee.

For most of his reign Russia has been at war and he has constructed a formidable military machine with an army of some 200,000 men. His most cherished project was the building of a fleet and Russia is now one of the sea powers of Europe. He is renowned for his cruelty but he has remodelled the calendar, simplified the alphabet, and founded the first Russian newspaper.

Czar Peter as a ship's carpenter.

King of Spain in sudden abdication shock

Spain, 10 January 1724
The courts of Europe are in a state of shock at the announcement by King Philip V of Spain that he has abdicated in favour of his eldest son, Louis. The move remained a well-kept secret, although Philip apparently had been planning it for more than three years. His motive is uncertain, but it is thought he has been concerned about the fits of depression that have been afflicting him. He was the first Bourbon king of Spain and under his autocratic rule, administration became more efficient, feudalism was destroyed and power was concentrated in the crown.

Regent dies after seven years of pleasure

Paris, 2 December 1723

Phillipe, the duke of Orleans, has died of apoplexy just nine months after giving up the regency of France when Louis XIV celebrated his thirteenth birthday and came of age. Phillipe, who did a deal with the *Parlement* to ensure he became Regent against the wishes of the late Louis XIV, had shown soldierly qualities in the war against Spain and could have had an outstanding career.

Instead, he gave himself over to pleasure. His rakish friends turned the seven years of his regency into a disorderly reaction against the sad, stiff austerity which characterised the last years of his uncle, Louis XIV's long reign.

The new young king: Louis XV, a teenage monarch for France.

Bering in the Arctic

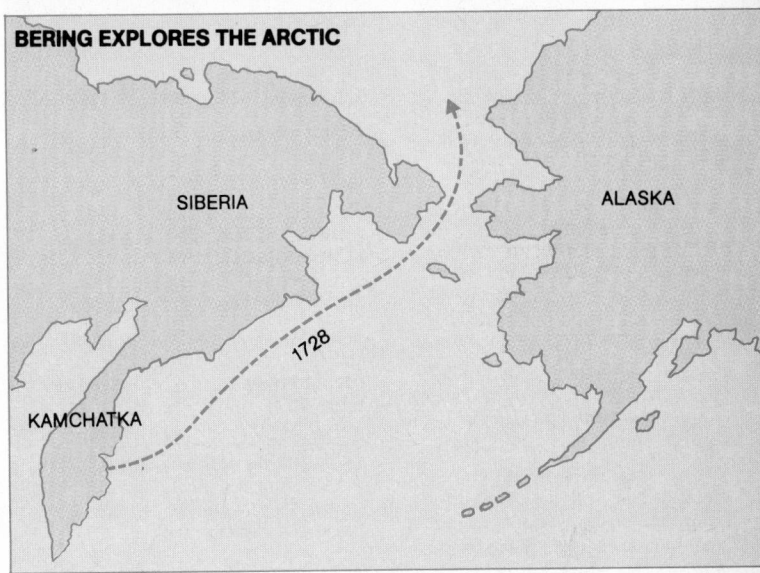

BERING EXPLORES THE ARCTIC

SIBERIA

ALASKA

1728

KAMCHATKA

Discoverer of life-giving forces has died

Holland, 1723

The death has been announced of Antoni Van Leeuwenhoek, the remarkable self-taught scientist who has done so much to advance the practice and technique of microscopy. In 1671, when Leeuwenhoek was 39 years old, he constructed a simple microscope, having ground the lens by hand himself. His crucial discovery was in 1674 when he found that the moving objects he saw through his microscopes were minute organisms such as bacteria and protozoa. In 1677 a medical student called Johan Ham told him that he had seen tiny animals in human seminal fluid. Leeuwenhoek identified these spermatozoa as a normal component of semen and went on to postulate that it is they that fertilise the egg.

Moscow, 1725

Vitus Bering, a Danish sailor exploring the oceans for Peter the Great, the czar of Russia, has discovered previously unknown straits separating Russia from the American continent. Czar Peter had commissioned Bering to find out exactly where Siberia meets with Alaska. Bering had already distinguished himself in the czar's service in the wars against Sweden.

Bering's small expedition set out last year, overland from St Petersburg to a small port in Kamchatka. There a ship was built and set out along the shore of the Kamchatka peninsula. The leader and his 33 men moved northwards up the Siberian coast towards the northeastern corner of Asia. Bering found that there is no strip of land between Siberia and America. His vessel passed through the straits into a new northen ocean before being forced to turn back.

Russia has three czars in two years

St Petersburg, 1727

In just two years Russia, the largest empire in the world, has had three rulers. After Peter the Great's death in 1725, power passed to his widow Catherine. Bawdy, kindly and a great brandy-drinker, she was also illiterate and left the affairs of state to Prince Alexander Menshikov, a close aide of the former czar.

Catherine has now died and has been succeeded by Peter the Great's 12-year-old grandson, also Peter, who is spending much of his time on extended hunting expeditions and precocious flirtation, not least with his voluptuous aunt, Elizabeth. Menshikov had secured the betrothal of his daughter to young Peter, but his overbearing ways upset his prospective son-in-law; he has been exiled to Siberia.

Polemicist Swift takes Gulliver to Lilliput and beyond

London, 28 October, 1726

A small book of *Travels into Several Remote Nations of the World* by a ship's captain, Lemuel Gulliver, is being eagerly bought and discussed with great amazement. Gulliver describes his voyages to *Lilliput*, an island off the Indies, where the people look human but are six-inches high, then to Brobdingnag, where they are as high as church steeples. He next finds himself taken up into a flying island called *Laputa* and finally reaches a land governed by horses of wisdom which employ as their beasts the *Yahoos*, who resemble gross and violent human creatures.

Wherever Gulliver goes to explain human civilisation, it is made to appear ridiculous, barbarous and disgusting and it is generally thought that the satirical Irish Dean, Dr Jonathan Swift, is the true author of these *Travels*.

Gulliver exhibited to the Brobdingnagians: a 19th-century illustration.

1727 (1727-1733)

Spain, March 1727. Spain breaks the terms of the treaty of Utrecht, invades Gibraltar and attacks the English.

London, 31 July 1727. Isaac Newton dies. Born on 4 January 1642, he became a mathematician, physicist and astronomer, and discovered the laws of universal gravitation.

Philadelphia, 1727. The satirist and polemicist Benjamin Franklin sets up a philosophy club called the Junto, the aim of which is the "sincere enquiry after truth". The club's main rule bars the use of dogmatic remarks.

London, 29 January 1728. John Gay's *Beggar's Opera* opens to an enthusiastic crowd in Lincoln's Inn Fields.

Spain, March 1728. In the conflict that began with the invasion of Gibraltar, Spain agrees to negotiate with England at the Pardo talks.

Germany, 23 December 1728. Prussia signs the treaty of Berlin with the Emperor Charles VI, guaranteeing the Pragmatic Sanction.

Madrid, 1728. The first masonic lodge in Madrid is presided over by the duke of Wharton, a Roman Catholic agent of the Pretender. The lodge is attended only by Englishmen.

Germany, 15 April 1729. Johann Sebastian Bach's *St Matthew's Passion* is performed on the evening of Good Friday, conducted by the composer.

Spain, 9 November 1729. In signing the treaty of Seville, Spain renounces its right to Gibraltar, which remains in English hands. All English economic privileges in the Spanish American colonies are retained.

Louisiana, 28 November 1729. Natchez Indians massacre most of the 300 French soldiers and settlers in Fort Rosalie, in the most vicious attack yet in the Louisiana colony. It was triggered by the demand that the Natchez give up their sacred burial ground and temple.

Russia, 29 January 1730. Peter II, czar since 1727, dies of smallpox and is succeeded by Anna Ivanova, daughter of Czar Ivan V. In 1728, Peter moved his court from St Petersburg to Moscow.

England 15 May 1730. Following the resignation of Lord Townshend, Robert Walpole becomes the sole minister in the English cabinet.

Louisana, December 1730. In retribution for last year's attack on Fort Rosalie, French soldiers take prisoner Sun, chief of the Natchez Indians.

Africa, 1730. The Portuguese finally lose Mombasa to the native power of the Omani.

Rhode Island, 1730. George Berkeley, Irish-born philosopher and Anglican minister, founds the Literary and Philosophical Society.

Pennsylvania, 1730. Benjamin Franklin publishes *A Witch Trial at Mount Holly*, satirising superstition of witchcraft.

Southern Africa, 1730. Tau, king of Rolong and son of Thibela, ruler of the unified Rolong kingdom north of the Orange river, dies.

Southern Africa, 1730. The Dutch abandon their trading post in Maputo Bay, which they have held since 1721.

Austria, 16 March 1731. On the signing of the second treaty of Vienna, Charles VI obtains England's recognition of the Pragmatic Sanction.

Austria, 22 July 1731. Spain gives its adherence to the Anglo-Austrian agreements and signs the third treaty of Vienna.

West Africa, 1731. The slave trading kingdom of Dahomey at Abomey, after defeats in battle, accepts the suzerainty of the Oyo empire (the Yoruba people).

Persia, 1731. Tasmasp II, shah for less than a year, is deposed by his brother-in-law Nadir Kuli. Tasmasp's eight-month-old son, Abbas, is elevated to the throne as a puppet.

Caribbean, 1731. Robert Jenkins, master of the *Rebecca*, sailing from Jamaica with sugar and other commodities for London, has his ear cut off by Spanish coast guards. After prolonged torture of Jenkins and his men, during which the Spaniards repeatedly asked for money, they sliced off his ear with a cutlass and told him to carry it home to the king.

Germany, 11 January 1732. The German Diet meets in Ratisbon (*Regensburg*) and guarantees the implementation of the Pragmatic Sanction which allows for the succession of Maria Theresa, Emperor Charles VI's daughter.

Pennsylvania, May 1732. The *Philadelphia Zeitung*, the first foreign language newspaper in British colonies, is published by Benjamin Franklin.

London, 7 December 1732. The Covent Garden theatre opens.

London, 1732. A law is passed prohibiting the export of American hats to England. Designed to protect English hat makers, the law is seen as another example of the so-called mercantile system which seems to benefit the mother country only.

Queen is power behind unpopular throne

London, 1727

Coffee house gossip has it that the power behind the throne of the new English king, George II, is Caroline, his cultured and determined wife. She likes to get away from her husband and spend time talking politics with Sir Robert Walpole, the prime minister. When George I died in June, in a carriage driving to Hanover, Caroline intervened to stop her husband sacking Walpole.

George II has been described as a humourless, choleric, conceited bore and womaniser. A man of routine and a penny-pincher (he counts his money, coin by coin, daily), he was banned from Court when he was prince of Wales after he quarrelled with his father over who should be godfather to his children. Now he threatens to ban his son Frederick from Court for intriguing with opposition politicians.

George II: Britain's new king, but as yet little loved by his peoples.

Encyclopaedia of 10,000 chapters finished

Beijing, 1728

A remarkable encyclopaedia of Chinese knowledge has just been published. Entitled "Collection of texts and illustrations old and new" it consists of no fewer than 10,000 chapters with a table of contents of 40 chapters and is so large only 64 copies have been printed. It was originally the work of the scholar Chen Menglei, who was brought back from exile by Emperor Kangxi and appointed tutor to Prince Yinzhe who became his patron and funded his work. When the emperor died, however, Chen again fell out of favour and the work was completed by Jiang Tingxi, a scholar who was appointed Grand Secretary this year.

"A scene from the Beggar's Opera" by William Hogarth: a painter and engraver, Hogarth is already well-known for his portraits, but he is fast establishing a new genre, that of what he calls "pictured morality".

Sultan's fall ends the "Tulip Period"

Russian friendship treaty with China

Istanbul, 1730
The abdication of Sultan Ahmed III and the execution of his Grand Vizier brings to an end the Tulip Age, in which the traditional Ottoman ethos of authority and militarism has given way to a more European culture exalting peace, beauty, literature and the arts.

Treaties in 1712 and 1713 secured the frontier with Russia, but gains by the Ottomans in Greece at Venetian expense were balanced by reverses in northern Europe; these culminated in the Treaty of Passarowitz in 1718, which gave Hungary and Serbia back to the Austrians.

The Sultan was now able to indulge his passion for building, music and books. He moved his summer court to the "Sweet Waters of Europe", at the head of the Golden Horn, where he diverted streams to make marble-lined canals, lakes, and fountains watering gardens. He built a summer palace at Sa'adabad, modelled on the French chateau of

Dancers and singers entertain sultan Ahmed III in a break from the hunt.

Marly. The high point of the year was the Tulip Fete, in the spring, when the Sultan would receive homage among spectacular tulip displays, multicoloured lamps and singing birds. Ahmet Nedim was the outstanding poet in a court where literature flourished, and artists were allowed to represent the human form.

A significant tool of the new enlightenment was a printing press brought from Paris by the Turkish ambassador in 1727.

Kyakhta, 14 June 1730
Russia and China have signed an important friendship and trading treaty in this border town south of Lake Baikal.

The new treaty confirms the boundaries agreed 41 years ago at Nerchinsk, when the Chinese Emperor Kangxi was mustering his forces on the border in response to Cossack incursions. Communication between the two nations had been non-existent until that point, when Jesuit priests installed in Beijing acted as intermediaries. The Russians, who had wanted to make the Amur river the frontier, agreed then not to venture beyond the Stanovoi mountains.

Today's pact, concluded in Latin, with official copies in Manchu and Russian, provides for regular merchant caravans to Peking. It also gives the Russians the opportunity to import textiles, tea, pottery, tobacco and ink from China, chiefly through Kyakhta.

Hand-picked debtors form a new colony

Corsican bandits rise up against Genoa

New England, 1732
England's thirteenth American colony has been founded by hand-picked debtors rescued from jail by their new governor, General James Oglethorpe MP. The general has acknowledged his royal charter by naming the colony "Georgia", after King George II. Its purpose is to remove debtors from prison and to create a buffer between hostile Spanish Florida and English Carolina. In Georgia, hard liquor and slavery are prohibited.

Genoa, 1729
The Genoan Republic has been shaken by a rebellion against the old order. For generations this maritime city state has been governed by a clique of top families ruling colonies with scant regard to local rights. Corsicans, for whom banditry is a "profession of honour", have united, surprisingly, to resist Genoan domination. Separated by sea from the mainland, they might yet be blockaded into submission.

Sealed alcohol is key to new thermometer

Compulsory military service in Prussia

France, 1730
Thermometers have been in use for about 100 years now, but so far they have not embodied scales that all scientists accept as universal. Fahrenheit's linear scale with its fixed points has attracted a lot of attention. But a Fahrenheit thermometer is only accurate if the diameter of the inside of the tube is perfectly regular along its length.

A French naturalist and physicist Rene Antoine Ferchault de Reamur has now attempted to meet this difficulty by constructing a hermetically-sealed thermometer using alcohol. In this a single degree of temperature is determined by volume as a fraction of the alcohol sealed in the tube.

Reamur and his assistant work on constructing the new thermometer.

Berlin, 1732
Frederick William I, the "Sergeant King", has introduced compulsory military service in Prussia, creating the fourth biggest army in Europe after the French, Russian and Austrian.

The permanent nucleus is provided by the peasantry. Every male is eligible for conscription from the age of 18. Each noble family sends one of its sons for training as an officer. Volunteers are recruited from abroad to swell the ranks.

The pride of the army is the infantry, under Prince Leopold of Anholt. It has become a model of discipline, marching with great precision and outdoing others with its rapidity of fire.

Prussia's "Sergeant King".

France, 10 October 1733. France declares war on Austria over the question of Polish succession following the death of Augustus II. Augustus III, supported by Austria, Saxony and Russia, has been elected in preference to Stanislav Leszczynski, the candidate supported by France.

France, 17 November 1733. The controller general, Orry, imposes the tenth emergency tax – repealed during the regency – to cover the cost of the war of declared on 10 October.

Japan, 1733. A large-scale food riot takes place in Edo (*Tokyo*) when some 1,700 people attack a rice store in protest against exorbitant prices. Such riots are becoming increasingly common, the earliest similar disturbance having occurred in Nagasaki in 1713.

Austria, 1 January 1734. The War of Polish Succession escalates when Emperor Charles, in an alliance with Russia and Saxony, declares war on France.

Poland, 9 March 1734. The Russians takes Danzig (*Gdansk*).

West Africa, 1734. The Sultan of Bornu becomes overlord of Kano following the war which began in 1731 in northern Nigeria.

France, 23 August 1735. Rameau has his opera *Les Indes galantes* performed.

France, 5 October 1735. France and Austria begin secret talks to settle the Polish question.

Germany 17 January 1736. The architect Matthaus Poppelmann (born in Herford in 1662) dies. He created the Zwinger complex in Dresden – one of the masterpieces of contemporary architecture in Saxony.

North America, 6 February 1736. The young Anglican preacher John Wesley lands in Georgia.

Austria, 12 February 1736. Maria Theresa of Austria, heir to the imperial throne by the provisions of the Pragmatic Sanction, marries Francois-Stephane of Lorraine.

Austria, 13 April 1736. Franco-Austrian talks on Poland and Lorraine are resumed following the conflict which broke out over the question of Polish succession in 1733. Augustus III is to remain on the Polish throne.

Austria, 21 April 1736. Prince Eugene of Savoy – a great general and military tactician – dies. He was commissioned by the Emperor Leopold and went on to a glorious military career, famously co-operating with the duke of Marlborough to win a decisive victory at Blenheim in 1704.

Netherlands, 16 September 1736. The German physicist Daniel Fahrenheit dies. Though not the first to use mercury as a thermometric substance, he is responsible for making mercury thermometers popular. He also devised the temperature scale using the temperatures of melting ice and salt, and the healthy human body, as his fixed points.

Ottoman Empire, 1736. Discovering that France is seeking Turkish aid in the war of Polish Succession, Russia declares war and sends troops into Turkish territory to the north of the Black Sea. The Ottomans inflict heavy losses on the invaders and force them to retreat to the Ukraine.

Austria, January 1737. Austria comes to the aid of her ally Russia, declaring war on the Ottoman empire.

Italy, 18 December 1737. The master violin maker Antonio Stradivarius dies in Cremona.

Scotland, 1737. A mob breaks into Edinburgh jail and hangs an English soldier, Captain Porteous. He was responsible for the shooting of several citizens six weeks ago at a riot which broke out following the execution of a popular smuggler called Wilson.

Austria, 2 May 1738. After three years of difficult negotiations, the fourth treaty of Vienna is signed, putting an end to the conflict caused by the question of Polish succession after the death of Augustus II.

Sweden, 1738. The "Hat" party is born during campaigning for the general election; they champion the French connection and advocate war with Russia. Their opponents, the "Caps" are led by Arvid Horn.

India, 20 March 1739. Nadir Shah of Persia occupies Delhi and takes possession of the Peacock throne.

Austria, 23 September 1739. Having lost Belgrade to the Turks, Austria enters into negotiations and signs the treaty of Belgrade.

Russia, 3 October 1739. Having lost the support of Austria, Russia decides to make peace with the Turks and relinquishes all her conquests except Azov by the treaty of Nissa. The three-year conflict is over.

England, 19 October 1739. England goes to war with Spain over borderlines in Florida and the mistreatment inflicted on British subjects. A British sailor, Robert Jenkins, attends a sitting of parliament exhibiting his ear which was cut off by Spanish coast guards. The conflict becomes known as "the war of Jenkin's ear".

Quarrels over the Polish throne

A snuffbox portrait of Stanislas Leszczynski: twice king, twice deposed.

Poland, 1733

After February's death of Augustus II, King of Poland since 1697 and elector of Saxony since 1694, the country, as ever the volatile centre of contesting international interests, has been plunged into a new crisis. The succession has excited new rivalries between the great powers, each backing its own candidate. The controversy remains limited to diplomatic manoeuvring, but the sabre-rattling may escalate into all-out war.

Affairs are further complicated by the nature of Augustus II's rule. By no means a clear-cut candidate himself, he was elected in 1697 against the interests of France, whose preference, the Prince of Conti, arrived too late in Danzig to put himself forward. Thus Augustus was duly elected, backed by the German sovereigns. The new king showed little interest in Poland, spending most of his time at the sumptuous electoral court of Dresden. In response to his lengthy absences the Swedes demanded a proper ruler and in 1704 forced the election of Stanislas Leszczynski. He ruled for five years until the Russians, who occupied Poland, deposed him and returned Augustus to the throne.

France, Spain, Sardinia, and the bulk of the Polish nobility all back the return of Leszczynski, now the father-in-law of Louis XV and he was elected in September. The election failed to last. Russia backs Augustus' son, as does Austria.

With the support of the the Lithuanian nobility, who are equally in favour of maintaining the ruling family, and judicious bribing of the electors, Leszczynski's victory has been annulled. Augustus III replaced him in October and Leszczynski has fled to Danzig.

Moghul empire mocked by its old enemy

Delhi, India 1737

Beyond the city walls a Marathan army – the Hindu enemy of the Moghuls – camps is at its leisure. So weak has the Moghul empire become that they have no effective army to march against them. For the Marathas of central India, it is merely a political demonstration; but for the Moghul monarch, Mohammed Shah, it is a personal humiliation. "I am resolved to tell the emperor the truth, to prove that I am yet in Hindustan, and to show him flames and Marathas at the gates of his capital," proclaimed the Maratha leader, Baji Rao Peshwa.

As Moghul power has declined, so Maratha power has grown. For years they fought a guerrilla war against the Moghul Empire. In 1720 Mohammed Shah, sought to co-opt them by giving them the tax revenues of the Dekhan province.

With their new wealth they became masters of Gujarat, Malwa and Bundelkhand; and Moghul armies sent against them have all been defeated. They are now the most powerful force in India.

Botanist Linnaeus classifies plants

Sweden, 1737

With the increase in world trade, new plants and animals are constantly being discovered, and with them comes the problem of how to classify the natural world. Carl von Linne – better known as Linnaeus – has for many years been working on a system of classification.

Linnaeus bases his classification on a so-called "binominal" system. That is, he puts organisms into both species and genera. And he has devised a way of temporarily classifying recently discovered plants and animals until they can be permanently arranged in the system. This year saw the publication of *Genera Plantarum*, said to be a milestone in systematic botany.

The Swedish naturalist Linnaeus.

Spanish slice off an English ear

Havana, 9 April 1739

The British trading brig, *Rebecca* was sailing past this Caribbean port today when a Spanish coastguard schooner ordered her to heave to.

The Spanish demanded heavy duties on *Rebecca's* cargo of sugar and rum. The British master, Robert Jenkins refused to pay. The Spanish tortured Jenkins and his crew. When Jenkins continued to refuse payment, the Spanish sliced off his ear with a cutlass, handed it to him and told him to give it to his King. An angry Jenkins is returning to England – where he will seek the ear of Prime Minister Walpole.

Nadir Shah, pictured as Persian troops destroy Moghul forces at Delhi.

Nadir Shah takes the Peacock Throne

Delhi, India, 20 March 1739

Nadir Shah, the most successful warrior Persia has ever produced, has entered Delhi in triumph. His entry, with the Moghul emperor Mohammed Shah a virtual prisoner, is the culmination of ten years of war. Born in 1688 in Kubkan, he first served the declining Safavid dynasty. He pacified Khurasan, defeated the Afghans who were occu-

pying central Iran, drove back the Ottomans, besieged Baghdad and conquered Transcaucasia.

On 8 March 1736 he crowned himself shah, then invaded Afghanistan. Three years later, after defeating the Moghuls at Karnal near Panipat, he controls Delhi. The Moghuls, weakened by attacks from their Hindu enemy, the Marathas, were no match for the Persians.

Russia intervenes in the Balkans

Belgrade, 23 September 1739

Russian soldiers have occupied the Walachian town of Iasi within hours of the signing of the new three-way Treaty of Belgrade between the Russian, Austrian and Turkish empires.

The Russian advance, seen as evidence of Czarina Anna Ivanovna's ambitions in the Balkans, came as Belgrade was rocked by a series of controlled explosions as departing Austrian troops demolished fortifications put up 22 years ago when they captured Belgrade.

The new Treaty – signed at six o'clock this morning after 34 days of intensive diplomatic negotiations – hands Belgrade back to the Turks and ends the latest conflict between the Austrian and Turkish empires. Ironically the conflict might never have started had Russia not invoked a military assistance agreement with Austria when Russian troops seized the Turkish town of Azov in the Crimea three years ago.

Under the new Treaty the Austrians lose all the gains made in 1718 and are forced back to the borders defined in the the Treaty of Carlowitz 40 years ago. Western Walachia, Serbia and Banat all return to Ottoman control. The fortress of Azov is to be razed to the ground and the area around it declared a neutral zone between Russia and Turkey.

Anglican priest John Wesley founds a "Methodist" movement

London, May 1739

This month sees the first anniversary of the conversion of a young Anglican priest, John Wesley, and people are talking of a new religious movement. Wesley recalls a specific time – a quarter to one – when he felt his "heart strangely warmed" by a feeling of contact with God. Since then he has moved around the country preaching in the open air to workers and peasants, rather as evangelist preachers such as Howell Harris are doing in Wales. Wesley and his brother Charles formed a Holy Club at Oxford in 1729. They were derisively called "Methodists" because of their studious and logical approach.

John Wesley, founder of Methodism, preaches from his father's tomb.

1739 (1739-1742)

England, 7 April 1739. The famous robber and smuggler Dick Turpin is executed; his body is seized by a mob and taken to York for burial. The son of an innkeeper, Turpin gained a name as a young man for atrocious robberies. Later he formed a partnership with the highwayman Tom King, whom he shot and killed by accident while trying to save him from arrest. Turpin was traced by clues left by the dying King.

England, 1739. The 28-year-old philosopher David Hume publishes his *Treatise on Human Nature.* Hume opposes the commonly accepted ideas on the absolute power of reason and follows John Locke and George Berkeley in claiming that knowledge comes from experience. This empiricist position finds little favour with his educated audience.

South America, 1739. The Spaniards establish New Granada as an independent viceroyalty, encompassing all territories between the Amazon and the Orinoco.

Colorado, 1739. French explorers Pierre and Paul Mallet arrive in New Orleans after a nine-month trek across the Great Plains during which they discovered a mountain range known to the Indians as the Rockies.

Netherlands, 1739. Francois Voltaire publishes the *Anti-Machiavelli*, written by Frederick of Prussia, in Amsterdam.

Massachusetts, January 1740. Some 50 slaves are hanged after the exposure of alleged plans for an insurrection.

Florida, January 1740. Governor Oglethorpe, taking advantage of the protection of some friendly Indians, invades Florida, capturing Forts Picolata and San Francisco de Pupo.

Prussia, 31 May 1740. Frederick William dies and is succeeded by his son Frederick II.

Russia, 17 October 1740. The empress Anna Ivanovna dies and is succeeded by Ivan IV.

Austria, 19 October 1740. The Emperor Charles VI dies. The succession rights of his daughter Maria Theresa, established by the 1718 Pragmatic Sanction, are challenged by Frederick II of Prussia.

Prussia, 16 December 1740. Frederick II invades Silesia starting yet another war in a Europe already beset by conflict.

Paris, 1740. The still-life and genre artist Jean Baptiste Chardin paints *Grace before a Meal.*

South Carolina, 1740. The assembly makes it illegal to teach Negroes to write or to hire them as scribes.

Britain, June 1741. The British prime minister Robert Walpole suffers an election setback as a result of opposition from the self-styled "patriots" to his foreign policy.

Vienna, 28 July 1741. The Italian violinist and composer Antonio Vivaldi dies. He won fame for the 12 concertos of *L'Estro Armonico,* which appeared in 1712. *The Seasons,* completed in 1725, was also enormously popular.

Sweden, August 1741. Sweden declares war on Russia, counting on support from France and intending to co-operate with the Russian czarevina Elizabeth, who is planning a coup d'etat in St Petersburg. The Swedes hope to take advantage of the fact that Russia is at war with Turkey.

Russia, 26 November 1741. In a palace rebellion, the czarevina Elizabeth overthrows Ivan VI and his mother, the regent Anne Leopoldovna. This puts an end to the German influence in Russia, which had been encouraged by the regent.

New York, 31 December 1741. Following a series of arson attacks in New York City, 29 slaves are executed – 11 are burned at the stake and 18 are hanged.

France, 1741. Maurice Quentin-Latour presents his *Portrait of the President of Rieux* to the Salon. Marivaux publishes his novel *The Life of Marianna.*

Pennsylvania, 1741. Scots-Irish presbyterian immigrants are arriving in the colonies in droves, driven out of the Irish province of Ulster by renewed religious persecution.

India, 1741. The Marathas threaten Pondicherry and Madras.

Germany, 24 January 1742. Charles Albert, elector of Bavaria is elected Holy Roman Emperor as Charles VII.

England, 25 January 1742. The astronomer Edmond Halley dies at Greenwich.

Britain, February 1742. Robert Walpole, Britain's first prime minister, resigns and is replaced by John Carteret.

Alaska, 9 August 1742. The remaining 31 members of Vitus Bering's expedition set off from their marooned ship on a timber raft, hoping to make it back to Russia. The Dutch navigator Bering, who was employed by the Russians to explore the lands east of Siberia, died of scurvy last year.

War drags on over imperial succession

Vienna, 1742

In the two years since Charles VI of Austria died, much of Europe has become embroiled in a ragged, sprawling war, in which almost everybody has changed sides at least once. Ostensibly the war concerns the Austrian succession; in fact, the dispute is seen as a chance to break up the Austrian empire.

For years Emperor Charles VI sought backing for something he called the Pragmatic Sanction; it was a decision to leave the crown to his daughter Maria Theresa. This did not suit Charles Albert of Bavaria; he claimed the throne because he had married a niece of Charles VI. Frederick of Prussia, seeing Maria Theresa preoccupied with the succession, marched into Silesia and offered to support her if she would cede the territory to him. Maria Theresa refused and sent her troops against him, only to have them shattered by the Prussians.

France then intervened with a plan. She would support Frederick provided he gave up part of his Silesian gains to Augustus of Saxony. The Bavarian Charles Albert would receive most of the Austrian empire, but Sardinia and Spain would share the spoils in Italy. France itself would get whatever it could take from the Dutch.

Britain and Hanover joined the war on the side of Maria Theresa, but took care not to offend Frederick in case he should decide to invade Hanover. Maria Theresa recruited an army from her Hungarian subjects and invaded Bohemia, where her rival, Charles Albert, had been proclaimed Austrian emperor in Prague.

Encouraged by Britain, who promised subsidies, she offered Frederick a deal. He was only too glad to accept; his troops were weary and his war chest was running out. Britain now offered to send a force to the Netherlands to join Austrian troops there and, with the Dutch, invade France. The Dutch refused to play. The war drags on.

Intellectual son replaces Prussian king

Berlin, 1740

The scholarly new king of Prussia, Frederick II, has brought a new style to the throne, in sharp contrast with his stern and soldierly father, Frederick William.

He is now free to indulge his taste for French literature and music composition at his home in Rheinsberg Castle. He has surrounded himself with intellectuals like Jordan of Geneva and devotes his free time to the study of Bayle and Racine. He exchanges letters with Voltaire and has published his first book, *The Anti-Machiavelli,* expressing the conviction that a King should serve his State.

Scholar king: Frederick II.

Dozens are slain in slave rebellion

Charleston, South Carolina, 1739

America has experienced its first slave revolt, a chilling affair which started when a group of blacks left their plantation to walk to Spanish Florida in search of freedom.

Embittered by years of harsh treatment, the rebels set out to kill every white man they met on the road. By the time they were finally surrounded, 21 people had been murdered. White settlers massacred the entire group of 44 men in revenge.

Soon other blacks revolted. At Stono River, a rebel called Cato and his men killed 30 whites. Slave-oriented South Carolina is getting nervous that the violent rebellion may continue to spread.

European music and art are flowering in harmony

Painting: visions of the grand and lowly

Canaletto's "Thames and the City of London from Richmond House".

Europe, 1742

One of Italy's most celebrated painters, Canaletto, moved to Rome this year from his native Venice with a reputation as one of the best of modern painters from one of the greatest centres of painting. Born Giovanni Antonio Canal in 1698, he is famed in particular for his views of Venice and other cities, highly atmospheric in their quiet colours and their exactness of detail and perspective.

Influenced by Canaletto, but more fanciful and impressionistic, are the townscapes of his fellow Venetian, Francesco Guardi (born 1712). Another Venetian, Pietro Longhi (born 1702), depicts everyday life with charm and attention to detail. The works of these men stand in contrast to the art of the most spectacular of Venetian painters, Gian Battista Tiepolo (born 1696). He combines panache and grandeur with vibrancy and an exquisite lightness of touch.

The elaborate pastoral fantasies of Antoine Watteau (1684-1721) are in contrast to the intimate realism of Jean-Baptiste Chardin (born 1699). Real life also provides subjects for England's William Hogarth (born 1697), who specialises in earthy social satire.

Watteau's "The Masked Party": typical of the artist's pastoral fantasies.

Music: the school of 1685 leads the field

Europe, 1742

"The sublime, the grand, and the tender, adapted to the most elevated, majestic and moving words". Thus wrote a Dublin music critic following the first performance of the oratorio *Messiah* by George Frederik Handel on 13 April this year. Handel was born in Saxony in 1685 and worked in Hamburg and Italy; he settled in London after his employer, the elector of Hanover, became King George I in 1714. He has written much for royal occasions, from the *Water Music* for a boating party to *Zadok the Priest* for George II's coronation in 1727. He has also written chamber music and about 40 Italian operas. Italian opera has become less popular recently, and Handel has turned to odes and oratorios such as *Alexander's Feast* (1736), *Israel in Egypt* (1739) and, of course, *Messiah*.

Of equally towering stature is another Saxon who has stayed closer to his roots. Also born in 1685, Johann Sebastian Bach has been head of music at Leipzig since 1723. His duties centre around the city's two main churches and his output includes motets, cantatas and two oratorio-like "passions", derived from the gospels of St John (1724) and St Matthew (1727). His instrumental music includes many organ works, and the six *Brandenburg Concertos* (c.1720).

Italian music is mourning the loss last year of Antonio Vivaldi (born 1678), the great Venetian priest-composer. He is renowned for his nearly 400 concertos, some of which Bach arranged and over half of which are for violin; his Op.8 includes the set known as *The Four Seasons*. Italy's greatest living composer is probably Domenico Scarlatti, a friend of Handel and also born in 1685. His father, Alessandro (1659-1725) was important for his operas; Domenico, composer at the Spanish court, is famed for his brilliant keyboard music.

Opera is the chief activity of the French composer Jean-Philippe Rameau (born 1683). He brings to his operas a wide range of moods and expressiveness together with richly coloured orchestration.

George Frederik Handel: oratorios, odes and music for royal occasions.

Alessandro Scarlatti: renowned for his operatic compositions.

Johann Sebastian Bach: cantatas, concertos and gospel passions.

The Agricultural Revolution

Around the year 1760 marked changes took place in agricultural methods and techniques in Britain; so marked, indeed, that it is tempting to call them "revolutionary". But most revolutions tend to happen quickly wheareas the seeds of Britain's agrarian change were sown at least a century earlier. Even though Britain was in the forefront of change the impact was patchy: large tracts of land in the north and west of the country were little affected until the 19th century.

The revolution was thus a leisurely affair. In the 17th century new crops and rotation planting systems had been introduced as scientific advances promoted new ideas and technologies. The central idea of land enclosures had been mooted as long ago as 1523 by Sir Anthony Fitzherbert in *Boke of Husbandrie* – the first farming textbook in English.

One cannot divorce the progress of agriculture from parallel developments taking place in industry. As manufacturing output increased, so did the demand for raw materials, such as leather, which came from the land. From farms, too, came the food to satisfy the demand from growing numbers of townsdwellers. Thus the potato, which had been discovered in the 16th century, first began to be grown on a grand scale in the open fields.

Another factor influencing the adoption of innovations in farming was a fall in prices of produce from the land, brought about by a string of good harvests. This forced farmers to seek out ways of improving their methods and raising efficiency in order to cut costs and get the most out of their land. Then, when the population began to rise around 1760, demand rose and with it, food prices. Again the effect on farmers was to stimulate them to increase efficiency.

New breed of entrepreneurs

There were changes, too, in the ownership of country property in Britain. Many traditional landowners sold off parts of their estates to the newly-rich merchants and businessmen who had the habit of making money. It was natural for these entrepreneurs to see the land as a vehicle for wealth generation and to adopt novel, profit-making methods to realise that aim. There was in any case a wealth of new ideas about farming itself: the use of root crops such as turnips, swedes and mangels, for example, which could be grown to feed livestock during the winter, hence obviating the need to slaughter animals in the autumn. This had been practised in Holland and parts of Germany, and had

percolated into Britain and other parts of Europe. The celebrated "Turnip" Townsend is probably the best advocate of the turnip on other grounds, too. It required little labour to produce good crops and helped break up the land during winter. Thus the lowly turnip changed both crop rotation and animal husbandry methods at a stroke.

New ideas about scientific stock-breeding were also in the air. Farmers began to see what might happen to the quality and quantity of their meat if they bred animals selectively, choosing only healthy males and females to generate their produce. As fresh meat became possible throughout the year with new root crops, farmers began to experiment more with different strains of animals. Robert Bakewell, for example, enjoyed considerable success with his New Leicester sheep and Dishley long-horn cattle, as did Thomas Coke with his sturdy strains of Southdown sheep.

A crucial change in agricultural practice was the way in which the land itself was divided into working units. At the beginning of the 18th century each English village or estate had three main fields, parcelled into small strips for individual farmers. It was a wasteful system. A good deal of land between strips was left unused because there had to be room for ploughing teams to turn; there were no barriers to deter wandering, hungry animals; there was no incentive for individuals to experiment or innovate; and much potentially valuable land was simply left unworked.

From 1750 onwards there was an increasing feeling that separate strips could be better exploited as compact, enclosed holdings. Landowners approached the British parliament in order to get Acts passed to legalise such moves. Not everyone welcomed the changes. The appearance of England was radically altered and bemoaned by such as John Clare, the ploughman poet of Cambridgeshire. Yet in time the enclosure movement was to give the English countryside – Scotland and Wales were less affected by the changes – what became its characteristic patchwork appearance of fields bordered by hedgerows. But as less efficient farmers began to suffer from the lower prices of larger producers and the loss of common land (an important source of firewood and animal food) enclosures were often fought fiercely.

On the other hand the new fields, allied to the Norfolk system of rotation between different uses in different years and longer leases, undoubtedly encouraged extensive improvements in the form of hedging and drainage. The change to a four-field system whereby each year a different crop was sown in each field – apart from one year left fallow

– made better use of the land, maximising its fertility and restoring the soil more quickly.

The introduction of new machinery, such as the seed drill of Jethro Tull and the Rotherham plough, together with improved hoeing, reaping and threshing devices also improved land use. Again, though, it was the more prosperous farmers who were able to benefit most from the new technology.

Model farm technology

Even so, the new technology was not introduced overnight. The Rotherham plough, which has been described as "the greatest improvement in plough design since the late Iron Age and Romano-British times", did not oust more traditional types of plough until the 1820s – 90 years after it was patented. Indeed, it was generally the case that, right to the end of the 18th century, a small subsistence farmer using long-practised craft skills would find his techniques adequate for his needs. As the poet Crabbe wrote:

Creatures no more enlivened than a clod,
But treading still as their dull fathers trod,
Who lived in times when not a man had seen
Corn sown by drill, or threshed by a machine.

Old habits then died hard. But the new ideas were being disseminated quite vigorously. Large landowners such as the Bedfords of Woburn held annual farming events such as sheep-shearing where visitors would hear speakers explaining the new breeding experiments or technological aids. Agricultural societies were formed to discuss the new methods, some publishing informative pamphlets and organising shows. Another important source of written information was Arthur Young, a former farmer who travelled extensively to visit farms and record what he saw. He helped to spread the word of change and so, fittingly, became the first Secretary of the Board of Agriculture when it was set up in 1793. Then there was the encouragement given in Britain by King George III, who earned the title "Farmer George" through his efforts with a model farm at Windsor.

Despite all these initiatives, the pace of change was not rapid. The 18th century farmer still extracted returns from his land which were low by modern standards. Yet the seeds for change had been sown; and without this revolution in agriculture it would have been impossible to feed the people who were to man the factories and mills of the industrial revolution still to come.

Hay-making: idealised image of 18th century farming in England.

Horsepower: "Farm Labourers Ploughing" by Gerricault (1791-1824).

Artistic licence: "A Leicester Sow" by W H Davis (1803-49).

Country-people leave their village.

Rural revolutionary: Jethro Tull.

Harbinger of change: cross-section of a wheat drill invented by Jethro Tull.

Samuel Palmer's "The Cornfield": a field enclosed by hedgerows.

1742 (1742-1745)

Ireland, 13 April 1742. The *Messiah* by the German-English composer George Frederick Handel is performed for the first time, in Dublin.

Germany, 11 June 1742. Maria Theresa of Austria and Frederick II of Prussia sign the peace of Breslau, which recognises Frederick's claim to Silesia.

Rome, 11 July 1742. A papal bull is issued condemning the actions of the Jesuits in China.

Peru, 1742. The Indians rise up in rebellion.

London, 1742. The poet Edward Young publishes his *Night Thoughts on Life, Death and Immortality*.

France, 29 January 1743. Cardinal Fleury dies. He became tutor to the future Louis XV in 1714 and replaced the duke of Bourbon as prime minister in 1726, at the age of 73. A convinced pacifist, Fleury supported the alliance with England. He brought France into the war of Polish succession only with the greatest reluctance.

Pennsylvania, January 1743. The printing magnate Benjamin Franklin sells his businesses to his partner, intending to devote his life to science, in particular the study of electricity.

Germany, 27 June 1743. An army of British infantry, led by King George II in person, destroy the French cavalry at Dettingen in Bavaria.

Sweden, 17 August 1743. By the treaty of Abo (*Turku*), Sweden cedes south-east Finland to Russia and accepts the Empress Elizabeth's choice of a successor: Adolf Frederick of Holstein-Gottorp. This ends a disastrous war with Russia in which Sweden had intended to help the empress take the throne. In the event, the Swedish army was hopelessly disorganised and Elizabeth herself seized power in a palace revolution.

France, 28 October 1743. Louis XV of France and Philip V of Spain forge a defensive and offensive alliance at Fontainebleau. This pact between the two Bourbon lines is known as the Second Family Compact.

New England, 1743. The American Philosophical Society is founded.

New Jersey, 1743. John Woolman, an itinerant Quaker clergyman, begins preaching about the evils of slavery.

Naples, 1744. The Italian philosopher Giambattista Vico, author of *Scienza Nova*, dies. He argued that the historical method is no less exact that the scientific.

London, 30 May 1744. The great satirical poet Alexander Pope dies. Among his masterpieces are *The Rape of the Lock* and the *Dunciad*.

Bohemia, September 1744. Having invaded Bohemia last month, Frederick II of Prussia takes Prague.

Paris, 8 December 1744. The beautiful and intelligent Madame de Pompadour comes into favour with King Louis XV.

East Africa, 1744. Mohammed ben Uthman al-Mazrui, who came to power as governor of Mombasa in 1739, declares himself independent from Oman.

Europe, 8 January 1745. England, Austria, Saxony and the Netherlands form an alliance against Russia.

Germany, January 1745. Charles Albert, elector of Bavaria, who was elected Holy Roman emperor in 1742 as Charles II, dies.

Germany, 22 April 1745. Maria Theresa of Austria and Maximilian Joseph, elector of Bavaria and son of the Emperor Charles VII, sign the peace of Fussen, restoring the status quo existing before the war of the Austrian Succession.

Netherlands, 11 May 1745. The French under Marshal Saxe defeat an Anglo-Dutch-Hanoverian army at the battle of Fontenoy.

Canada, 16 June 1745. After a six-week siege, the French fort of Louisbourg on Cape Breton Island falls to British colonial forces from New England. This intensifies hostilities in what is known as King George's war, an extension of the European war of the Austrian Succession.

New England, August 1745. The French and their Indian allies carry out a series of raids on English settlements.

Germany, 25 December 1745. By the treaty of Dresden, Frederick II of Prussia recognises Francis, duke of Lorraine and husband of Maria Theresa of Austria, as Holy Roman emperor. Frederick's control of Silesia is also recognised under the treaty.

England, December 1745. Having advanced as far south as Derby, Charles Edward Stuart, the young pretender, is forced to retreat.

England, 1745. The painter William Hogarth completes *Marriage a la Mode*. Like his earlier *Rake's Progress*, the work is a moral narrative – a series of scenes exposing the follies and vices of his age. This new genre is a departure from the small portrait groups, known as conversation pieces, which Hogarth favoured in the 1720s.

Enslaved Peruvians rise up against Spain

Peru, 1742

The native Indians of Peru, enslaved by their Spanish conquerors for the past two hundred years, have risen up in a rebellion. Slaves across the vice royalty have thrown away their shackles and united in a series of attacks on their hated masters.

The rebellion is led by Juan Santos, an Indian from the Huarochiri region. Taking up the old Inca tradition he has proclaimed himself emperor and taken the name Atahualpa II. This is a deliberate tribute to Atahualpa I, "the last of the Incas", whose execution by the Spaniards in 1533 inaugurated the enslavement and exploitation of his people. Over the past two centuries the once-thriving Indians have lost some nine-tenths of their population.

The brutality of their conquerors, the hardships they endure in the mines and the destruction brought by European diseases against which their bodies have no defence have all combined to destroy a once-proud civilization.

Santos' forces have proved surprisingly successful. Drawing on widespread support, his army has moved across the country's central plateau, defeating the Spanish in a number of battles. The Indians have reached Lima, the capital, where they are challenging the aristocracy, Spain's native allies.

Strict new faith attracts Arab rulers

Arabia, c.1744

The sheikh and emir of the Ibn Saud family of central Arabia have sworn reciprocal loyalty and adopted the fundamentalist Islamic doctrine of Wahhabism. They have created the first legally instituted Wahhabi state.

A jurist from Najd, Mohammed ibn Abd al-Wahhab, wanted to redefine Islam to make it distinct from Iranian Shi'ism and what was seen as the decadent Sunnism of the Ottomans. Insisting that faith must be inseparable from religious practice, he emphasises the absolute unity of Allah at the expense of all other forms of belief which might dilute the faith. The visiting of tombs and veneration of saints are therefore completely forbidden.

Wahhabism relies on the view of nature put forward in the Koran, and condemns any innovation that embroiders or departs from that original teaching. It is the ultimate fundamentalism, excluding any possibility of polytheism, and creating a uniquely Arab Moslem movement.

The renowned mirror room at the Amalienburg in Munich: this ornate, heavily decorated style, known as Rococo, was built by Francois Cuvillies; the stucco, a vital characteristic of the design, is by J B Zimmerman.

England's Prime Minister resigns

London, February 1742

Sir Robert Walpole, the Norfolk squire who who headed the British government for 20 years, has fought his last battle in the House of Commons – and lost. His opponents, failing to defeat him over his conduct of the war with Spain, manoeuvred to gain control of the Parliamentary Committee on Elections, a body which hears petitions for unseating MPs guilty of corrupt practices. When one of his supporters was voted down Walpole knew his days were numbered and resigned. Nominally a Whig, his practices seemed distant from principles of the Revolution of 1688.

Officially he was simply First Lord of the Treasury, but in time, as he gained the confidence of both the king and the House of Commons, he came to be known as Prime Minister. His reputation was established by his skilful handling of the the South Sea Bubble financial crisis. From then on, he clung to two principles: sound finance at home and freedom from the intrigues and wars on the continent.

When a sea captain, Robert Jenkins, told MPs how a Spanish officer had cut off his ear with a cutlass while searching his ship in 1739, public indignation boiled over and Walpole was forced to declare war on Spain.

Prime Minister Walpole addresses his cabinet: a picture by Joseph Goupy.

Papal Bull against Jesuit toleration of Chinese ways

Rome, 11 July 1742

Pope Benedict XIV has issued a stern papal bull *ex quo singulari* designed to put an end once and for all to the bitter Chinese Rites controversy. He has forbidden the Jesuits in China to continue with their policy of allowing their converts to include Confucian traditions in their Christian observances.

The Jesuits had ignored a previous attempt by Pope Clement XI to curb the practise of Chinese Rites under which they accepted ancestor worship and even domestic idols. But they cannot argue against this ruling.

It remains to be seen what effect it has on the Confucian-Christian symbiosis and the position of the Jesuits in China. The Jesuits fear with some justice that it will jeopardise not only their position but that of the whole Christian community in China.

The Chinese authorities are known to feel affronted by the pope's edict. The Jesuits had persuaded the emperor to issue a statement on the meaning on the rites which was in their favour. Now he has lost face and the results for the mission will certainly be embarrassing if not positively dangerous.

Poet and satirist Alexander Pope dies

London, 30 May 1744

The death has been announced of that master of the heroic couplet, the English poet and satirist, Alexander Pope. He was 56.

Pope was born into a Catholic family and was brought up in Windsor Forest without formal education. He moved in London's literary circles from the age of 15, and became friends with Tories like Swift, Oxford and Bolingbroke.

In the intensely political atmosphere of the time, Pope rapidly won recognition with his *Essay on Criticism* and his mock-epic *The Rape of the Lock*.

His translations of *The Iliad* and *The Odyssey* brought him financial stability. Later, in *The Dunciad*, he bitterly satirised the literary critics of the day.

The late Alexander Pope: master of wit, satire and the heroic couplet.

Irish and Scottish exodus to America

Philadelphia, c.1742

A flood of immigrants is arriving in the American colonies from the Irish province of Ulster. If present trends continue, they will be turning up at the rate of 10,000 a year by the end of the decade. Fortunately America has always offered a traditional refuge to the persecuted of other lands, whether on religious or political grounds.

Most of these newcomers are descendants of Presbyterians from lowland Scotland who settled in Ulster to safeguard English Protestant interests there. The renewal of religious persecution has meant that, increasingly, these so-called Scots-Irish are looking to the colonies as a refuge.

East India traders are braced for war

India, 1743

The tentacles of the European war have reached as far as India as British and French ready themselves to fight for national supremacy on the sub-continent. As news of the war arrived here last year, the British East India Company was much stronger commercially than its French equivalent, although it was prepared to accept a local agreement of neutrality. French and British fleets are in the vicinity, however, and fighting seems certain.

Both sides are courting Indian princes as allies, although French missionary zeal is not helping their cause. The British prefer to leave Hindu customs well alone and concern themselves solely with trade.

1745 (1745-1750)

Scotland, September 1745. Charles Edward Stuart, grandson of James II and pretender to the British throne, defeats a royalist army at the battle of Prestonpans. The "young pretender" – son of James Edward Stuart, the "old pretender" – landed in Scotland last year and rallied the Scottish nobles of the Highlands and other Jacobites against King George II.

Europe, 1745. Ewald von Kleist, a German, and the Dutchman Petrus van Musschenbroek independently invent the Leyden jar. This is a glass vessel, partially filled with water and with a nail projecting from a cork stopper, which can store electricity.

Scotland, 17 January 1746. Charles Edward Stuart, the young pretender, defeats the royalist forces at the battle of Falkirk.

Brussels, 21 February 1746. Following their defeat of the Austrian allies at Fontenoy last year, French troops occupy Brussels.

England, 1 April 1746. George Frederick Handel presents his oratorio *Judas Maccabeus*.

England, 27 April 1746. The pretender Charles Edward Stuart is defeated by King George II's army at the battle of Culloden and flees to France.

Austria, 2 June 1746. Austria forms an alliance with Russia against Prussia and the Ottomans.

Spain, 9 July 1746. On the death of Philip V, his son Ferdinand VI comes to the throne.

India, 20 October 1746. Following the spread the war of the Austrian Succession to India, Joseph Francois Dupleix, the French colonial governor, takes Madras.

France, 1746. The philosopher Etienne Condillac publishes an *Essay on the Origin of Human Knowledge*.

France, 1746. Denis Diderot's recently published *Philosophic Thoughts* is burnt by the parliament of Paris.

New Jersey, 1746. Princeton University is founded.

Persia, 10 June 1747. The Persian ruler Nadir Shah is assassinated at Fathabad. After defeating the Afghan invaders in 1729, Nadir restored Tahmasp to the throne and went on to defeat the Ottomans in the west. Proclaimed shah himself in 1736, Nadir conquered Afghanistan and launched a campaign against India which culminated in 1739 in the sack of Delhi.

Afghanistan, June 1747. After the death of Nadir Shah, Afghanistan becomes independent of Persia.

Netherlands, 2 July 1747. Marshal Saxe leads the French forces to victory over an Anglo-Dutch force under the duke of Cumberland at the battle of Lauffeld.

Netherlands, 16 September 1747. The capture of Bergen-op-Zoom consolidates the French occupation of Austrian Flanders.

Netherlands, 1747. The republic of the United Provinces is overthrown and the title of *stadtholder* (governor) is reinstated. William of Nassau, prince of Orange – grand-nephew of William III of England – is made hereditary *stadtholder*.

Beijing, 1747. The summer palace of the Emperor Qian Long is decorated and furnished in western style.

Pennsylvania, 26 August 1748. The first Lutheran synod is founded in the colonies, in Philadelphia.

France, 18 October 1748. The peace of Aix-la-Chapelle ends the war of the Austrian succession, giving general recognition to the Pragmatic Sanction and the Prussian conquest of Silesia.

England, 1748. The philosopher David Hume publishes his *Enquiry Concerning Human Understanding*.

France, 1748. The philosopher Julien Lamettrie publishes his materialistic work *The Man Machine*.

England, 1748. Samuel Richardson, author of *Pamela*, publishes the last part of his seven-volume novel *Clarissa*, again written in epistolary form. The novel is described as showing the "distresses that may attend the misconduct both of parents and children, in relation to marriage".

Pennsylvania, 1749. The university of Pennsylvania is founded in Philadelphia.

Canada, 1749. Some 2,500 settlers sent by Lord Halifax to consolidate the British hold on Nova Scotia found the town of Halifax.

France, 1749. Georges Louis Buffon publishes the first three volumes of a great *Natural History*, the prospectus of which he issued last year.

Spain, 1749. A lodge of freemasons is established at Cadiz, with over 800 members.

England, 1749. Henry Fielding publishes Tom Jones, a comic novel of manners designed, like his *Joseph Andrews*, as a reaction to the moral conventionality of Samuel Richardson.

France, 1750. The philosopher Jean-Jacques Rousseau publishes a *Discourse on the Sciences and the Arts*.

Lost Roman city emerging from grave

Later excavations reveal the city emerging from the ashes at Pompeii.

Naples, 1748
An entire city which suffocated to death in AD 79 under a pall of volcanic ash and sulphur fumes from Mount Vesuvius is being brought to light near Naples in a state of extraordinary preservation.

The excavations began on the orders of King Charles III. The ruins were revealed by tunnelling many years ago, but their scale was unknown. Streets of houses lie buried alongside two theatres, a forum, temples and baths. Skeletons of the inhabitants lie where they succumbed. An inscription has identified the site as Pompeii.

Wall painting of houses, Pompeii.

Slave-rich African state beaten in battle

A human head with ram's horns, made of carved wood, from the shrine of the King of Oyo, in eastern Yorubaland, Nigeria.

West Africa, 1747
Half a century of war between the states of Dahomey and Oyo is over, with Dahomey defeated. Dahomey was a state whose enormous wealth was derived from the slave trade with Europe.

First she took control of the hinterland and then of the coast, where tens of thousands were shipped to the New World. Oyo's strength was in her cavalry. Envious of Dahomey's wealth, she invaded the country in 1698, defeating all who confronted her.

Dahomey reverted to guerrilla warfare and threw out the invaders in the 1730s, only to be subjected to the Oyo cavalry again in 1738. After nine more years of guerrilla war, Dahomey has accepted defeat. None are more relieved than the slavers, who need a stable environment in which to conduct their business.

Bonnie Prince defeated

The Duke of Cumberland leading British troops to victory at Culloden.

Scotland, 1746
Disguised as a woman and with a price of £30,000 on his head, Bonnie Prince Charlie, the Young Pretender, is believed to be hiding in a cave in the Scottish Highlands after the defeat of his Jacobite force by British troops at Culloden. He intends to lie low until a French ship comes to his rescue.

When he arrived off Inverness-shire aboard a French brig last year, Scottish clan chiefs tried to persuade him to drop the idea of staging a rebellion to regain the English crown for the Stuarts. He went ahead and quickly raised a force of 2,000 men. He defeated a detachment of dragoons and, seizing Holyroodhouse, had himself proclaimed James VIII of Scotland.

Although the promised French assistance never arrived, he pushed on south. By the time he had reached Derby and looted the city, the English had put two new armies in the field. Then, as he retreated north, the desertions began.

Charles, still only 25, grew up believing the people of Scotland

Prince Charles Stuart, by Blanchet.

and England were ready to welcome a Stuart. But few of his supporters cared to run risks for him. The Highlanders who joined him at the start soon dropped out; for them, war was merely an excuse for brigandage. Charles, educated in Rome, speaks English, French and Italian, but his letters in English are barely literate.

Lead piping shown to damage your health

New York City, 1750
Lead piping in common use in plumbing, may be a health hazard according to an American doctor, Thomas Cadwalader, who has just published a work entitled "An Essay on the West-India Dry-Gripes".

In it, Cadwalader describes a case of gripes apparently brought on by a patient drinking rum. The rum had, it transpires, been distilled through lead pipes. Although Cadwalader himself does not attribute the poisoning to the lead, that is indeed the obvious inference. Lead is known to have toxic properties. Now these may be felt even through pipes such as those that bring us our water.

The peace treaty that pleases no one

Aix-la-Chapelle, 18 October 1748
The War of the Austrian Succession has at last been brought to an end with all the adversaries in a state of exhaustion. The war ended not with a great victory, but with the realisation that it could not be allowed to continue.

Under the terms of the treaty signed here today the courageous Maria Theresa was confirmed as the legitimate occupant of the Habsburg throne and her husband, Francis of Lorraine, was elected to the imperial throne.

In return, however, she has been forced reluctantly to abandon Silesia to King Frederick of Prussia. Frederick is, in fact, the only contestant in this land-grabbing war to be happy with the treaty. The others get less than they wanted.

England and France will exchange colonial outposts. France has agreed to evacuate the Austrian Netherlands, much to the disgust of Marshal Saxe who has spent so

Maria Theresa, Empress of Austria.

much time and trouble conquering them for Louis XV. Spain has failed to regain Gibraltar and Minorca from the English. The treaty has thus failed to settle the causes of Europe's bloody feuds.

Europe's cities: full of muck and money

Gin Lane, an unsavoury corner of London, by William Hogarth.

Europe, c.1750
Europe, for so long dominated by the countryside, a society of land-owners, farmers and peasants, is undergoing a radical change. The town has replaced the village as the centre of daily life for an increasing number of people, and the great cities are expanding as never before.

London and Paris, always important for their commerce, have developed into teeming urban centres, their growing populations each numbering half-a-million souls al-

ready. Such expansion is seen everywhere and while the cities still hold less people than the country, the urban minority is increasingly influential and important.

Thriving, energetic, never resting by day or night, the cities reflect the emergence of an affluent middle class whose lives are based not on land-owning but on trade. The old aristocrats appreciate the change and many have added a sumptuous town house to their rural acres.

Such luxury is restricted. The poor, abandoning their cottages for the city life, are crowded into insanitary tenements, crushed hugger-mugger along the narrow, dirty streets. Visionary architects are imposing more ordered design on city centres, with spacious boulevards and fine new buildings, but the masses remain trapped in squalor.

Cities are prosperous and an enterprising man may make his fortune, but they are dangerous too. Traffic threatens pedestrians by day and thieves lurk in the dark streets by night. London, where pavements offer refuge from the carts and coaches and where streetlights illuminate at least the major roads, has set an example to its peers.

Venice, 17 January 1750. The composer Tomaso Albinoni dies aged 79. He wrote operas, cantatas, sonatas, concertos and other works, characterised by distinct melodies.

Portugal, 31 July 1750. John V dies and is succeeded as king by his son Joseph Emanuel, who appoints Sebastiao Jose de Carvalho e Mello, marquis of Pombal, as his chief minister. Pombal immediately deprives the Inquisition of its rights.

India, 1750. By his victory at the battle of Tanjore, Joseph Dupleix, the French governor of Pondicherry, wins control of the Carnatic region in southern India.

London, c.1750. A works for the manufacture of bone china is established at Stratford-le-Bow.

Venice, 1750. The painter Giambattista Tiepolo completes his frescoed ceiling in the Palazzo Labia, the culmination of a series of works devoted to the story of Antony and Cleopatra.

Tibet, 1750. The Tibetans rebel against China.

Canada, 1750. British forces attempt to conquer Acadia (*Nova Scotia* and *New Brunswick*).

North America, c.1750. The population of the colonies passes the one-million mark.

Canada, January 1751. France and England conclude a provisional agreement over Acadia.

Britain, 20 March 1751. Frederick Louis, prince of Wales, dies.

India, November 1751. The French siege of Arcot, which was captured by Robert Clive in September with 210 men, is lifted after 53 days.

France, 1751. Voltaire publishes *Le Siecle de Louis XIV*.

England, 1751. The Englishman John Burton suggests that common puerperal or childbed fever may be caused by those who attend the patient. It is, he believes, their carelessness that produces the disease.

Denmark, 1751. Count Johann Bernstorff, the former Danish envoy in Germany and France, becomes foreign minister.

Germany, 1751. Johann Albrecht Bengel, the architect of the German Protestant evangelical movement known as pietism, dies.

Death comes to composer J S Bach

Leipzig, 28 July 1750
Earlier this month Johann Sebastian Bach, ill and blind despite two eye operations, began to dictate an organ piece, the last of a series he was revising. The 65-year-old composer decided to change the title to *Before thy Throne*. Days later he was dead.

Bach sometimes got into trouble when he put creative impulses before official duties. But few denied his genius; he was famed as Europe's greatest organist and only Handel matches his mastery of fugue and counterpoint. He wrote almost every type of music except opera, of which his employers, for the past 27 years the Protestant city of Leipzig, disapproved.

Bach's two wives (the first died in 1720), bore seven and 13 children respectively. His eldest sons, Wilhelm Friedemann (born 1710) and Carl Philipp Emanuel (born 1714) are both distinguished composers. Emanuel is harpsichordist to Frederick II of Prussia, whose chief relaxation is music (he plays the flute and composes). Three years ago J S Bach visited his son and family at Frederick's palace in Potsdam. As well as trying out a new "pianoforte" – he was unenthusiastic – Bach was given a theme by the king himself to improvise upon. The royal tune was used for a set of pieces dedicated to Frederick called a *Musical Offering*.

Maestro: Johann Sebastian Bach.

Military hero leaves nothing to chance

Punishments in the German army, an engraving by von Fleming, 1726.

Paris, 1750
That great soldier, Maurice, the Count of Saxony, better known as Marshal Saxe, has died, loaded with honours, at the age of 54. The natural son of Augustus II of Saxony and Countess Maria Aurora Konigsmark, he divided his life between equal pleasures: making war and making love. His long love affair with the actress Adrienne Lecouvreur was especially notorious.

Fighting under a number of flags, he eventually became Marshal General of France, capturing Prague and winning the Battle of Fontenoy for Louis XV. Saxe was a handsome man and a thinking soldier, leader of a new breed of commanders who revolutionised warfare. He called for the institution of universal military service and conscription to replace the old armies of the criminals and the dispossessed.

He also argued that no army should field more than 46,000 soldiers, for "multitudes serve only to perplex and embarrass" and he advocated the use of mobile units of infantry and cavalry. But, above all, he insisted that "war should be made so as to leave nothing to chance."

The Female Soldier parades on stage

London, 1750
Publicity for the biography, *The Female Soldier*, has drawn a big crowd to Sadlers Wells theatre to watch Hannah Snell perform military drill in full dress uniform.

In 1723 Snell, a single mother from Worcester, posed as a man and joined the Army to look for her sailor husband. After marching to Carlisle she deserted her foot regiment and joined a Marines' ship bound for India. When shot at Pondicherry by the French, she maintained her disguise by finding a woman to remove the bullet. On reaching Portugal, after more adventures in two more ships, she heard that her missing husband had been executed in Italy.

Brilliant victory for Clive in south India

India, 5 November 1751
After a 53-day siege, British-led troops have brilliantly beaten off a superior French-led force at Arcot, the capital of the Carnatic, India's south-eastern coastal region.

British and Indian troops led by Robert Clive, 26, seized Arcot on 12 September as part of the struggle for control of southern India between the British and French East India companies, which first flared up in 1744. So far, the French and their allies have had the upper hand, but their failure at Arcot has turned the tables. In the British camp the talk is only of Clive, the former East India Company clerk who only took up soldiery with the company's army three years ago.

The Encyclopaedia will explain existence

Paris, April 1751
The first volume of the *Encyclopedie*, or National Dictionary of the Arts, Sciences and Professions, appears this month. Published by Le Breton it will be sold by subscription and the complete work will comprise eight illustrated volumes, making up 280 books.

The original idea came from England, where Chambers' *Cyclopedia* appeared in 1723. The *Encyclopedie* was to be a simple translation but its editor-in-chief Denis Diderot, hired by the publishers whose scheme it is, rejected that idea.

Instead he has set out to create an entirely original work, a grand plan that, on completion, will provide a rational explanation for every aspect of existence.

Diderot is backed by two formidable men: Jean d'Alembert, one of France's most gifted mathematicians, and the wealthy, hardworking Louis de Jaucourt. He has also enlisted many leading intellec-

Denis Diderot, painted by Greuze.

tuals as contributors. Montesquieu writes on politics, Buffon on nature, Turgot on economics, d'Holbach on mathematics, while Voltaire and Rousseau will each write on philosophy.

Complaints box at shogun's castle gate

Eighteenth-century Japanese scroll showing a domestic scene, with animals.

Japan, 1751
The shogun Tokugawa Yoshimune who has controlled Japan for the last 29 years, has died at the age of 67. A forceful and capable man, he used the practical experience he gained as a feudal ruler drastically, but quietly, to redress some of the worst injustices of shogun rule.

One of his innovations was to put a *meyasubako*, a complaints box, at a gate of his castle in which the people could deposit suggestions for his personal attention, bypassing the bureaucracy.

He was a frugal man who wore plain clothes and lived on brown rice and vegetables. He had the luxurious apartment of the shogun torn down and lived in a bare anteroom. His spartan life helped him to understand his people's problems and formed the basis of his reforms.

Enclosures improve English farming in agricultural revolution

Catalogue of Fruits, Furber, 1732.

Britain, c.1750
Encouraged by various acts of Parliament, the enclosure system is taking hold of English farming. The system of open farms is giving way to enclosed fields. Small landowners are yielding reluctantly to larger estates, and there have been many complaints.

Enclosure is having profound effects on agricultural techniques. In the first place, farmers can now practise farming on a larger scale, introduce mechanisation and institute extensive land drainage schemes. They can also carry out a

Eighteenth-century drill plough, with seed and manure hopper.

certain amount of stock-breeding. And devote some of their time to scientific experiments with both plants and animals.

Using Jethro Tull's straight-line drilling of wheat and roots, allowing a horse-drawn hoe to cultivate the space between the rows, means that the spoil can be constantly tilled. Seed drills are now in widespread use. So, too, is the Rotherham triangular plough which replaces large teams of oxen attended by two horses and one man. There is also a great deal of attention being paid to the relationship between crop and animal. Rotating crops means that the two forms of

farming can be complementary.

Farmers are also having to respond to increasingly diverse demands from the market place. As industry develops so too does the need for raw materials: animal fats for soap; hides for leather goods; bones for glue. Only by turning to labour-saving devices and techniques can these demands be met. Truly we are witnessing the onset of a massive "agricultural revolution", although like any revolution, the changes are disturbing to many vested interests, not least the tenant farmers whose livelihoods have been sacrificed to the demands of a new world.

Temple of Heaven

Beijing, 1751
Work has been completed on restoring the Hall of Prayer for Good Harvests in the Temple of Heaven. The round hall, which rests on a triple-layered marble terrace, is 30 metres across and has a roof shaped in three cones covered by brilliant blue tiles. It is surmounted by a golden sphere. Perhaps the most remarkable fact about this beautiful building is that it is made entirely of wood, yet not one nail has been used in its construction.

It is here that the emperor comes to give homage to the heavens and to make sacrifices and pray for a good harvest. It is set in a large park forbidden to the people.

The Temple of Heaven, in Beijing.

1751 (1751-1754)

Paris, 1751. The Sorbonne condemns 14 propositions on evolution in Georges Buffon's *Natural History*. To avoid theological controversy, Buffon signs a declaration abandoning anything in his work that might be contrary to the account of Earth's origins given in Genesis.

Netherlands, 1751. On the death of the *stadtholder* William IV of Orange-Nassau, his widow Anne becomes regent for the three-year-old heir, William.

England, 1751. The philosopher David Hume publishes *An Enquiry Concerning the Principles of Morals*.

England, 1751. The poet Thomas Gray composes his *Elegy written in a Country Churchyard*.

England, 1751. The Scottish writer Tobias Smollett publishes a second novel, entitled *Peregrine Pickle*. His first novel, *Roderick Random*, appeared in 1748.

Paris, February 1752. The parliament of Paris condemns the *Encyclopedie*, edited by Denis Diderot, the first volume of which appeared last year.

Philadelphia, June 1752. In his book *Experiments and Observations in Electricity*, Benjamin Franklin concludes that lightning is identical with electricity produced by friction.

North America, July 1752. The French overrun the English trading post of Pickawillany in an effort to re-establish control over the Ohio river valley region.

India, July 1752. The English go on the attack. Robert Clive takes Trichinopoly and forces the French commander Bussy to evacuate Aurangabad.

India, 1752. Ahmed Shah Durrani, the ruler of Afghanistan, captures Lahore after a four-month siege.

Sudan, 1752. Abu al-Qasim, sultan of Darfur, dies in battle during a war with the sultanate of Kordofan, whose troops are led by the Funj general Abu al-Kaylak. The influence of the Darfur sultanate, which dates from the 1630s, stretches from Bornu around Lake Chad in the west to Kordofan near the Nile in the east.

South-East Africa, 1752. The Portuguese south-east African coastal settlements of Mozambique island, Zambezi prazos and Sofala are placed under the governor at Mozambique; they are no longer subordinate to the Portuguese colony of Goa in India.

Britain, 1752. The Gregorian calendar is adopted. The eleven days between 2 and 14 September are omitted.

Austria, January 1753. Count Anton Kaunitz, the former Austrian ambassador in Paris, is appointed chancellor by the Empress Maria Theresa.

London, June 1753. A conference is held with the aim of ending the Anglo-French conflict over India.

Paris, 25 August 1753. On becoming a member of the French Academy, the naturalist Georges Buffon delivers a *Discours sur le style*.

North America, 12 December 1753. George Washington, adjutant of Virginia, delivers an ultimatum to the French forces at Fort Le Boeuf, south of Lake Erie, reiterating Britain's claim to the entire Ohio river valley.

England, 1753. The home of John Kay, who invented the flying shuttle in 1733, is destroyed by a riot.

England, 1753. Samuel Richardson publishes a third novel, *Sir Charles Grandison*, which is designed to portray the perfect gentleman.

London, 1753. The British Museum is founded.

Britain, 6 March 1754. On the death of Henry Pelham, he is succeeded as prime minister by his brother Thomas, duke of Newcastle. Since November last year the brothers have headed the so-called "broad-bottomed" administration comprised of many political factions.

North America, 17 April 1754. The site of a British fort at the fork of the Allegheny and Monongahela rivers in the Ohio river valley is captured by the French. Militiamen under George Washington had been sent to build the fort by Robert Dinwiddie, governor of Virginia, in order to protect the region from French seizure.

New York, July 1754. At the Albany Congress, which brings together delegates from the 13 British colonies, Benjamin Franklin calls for the establishment of a common council of defence to fight the French and the Indians.

North America, 3 July 1754. British forces under George Washington are defeated by the French near Fort Necessity in the Ohio river valley.

Spain, 1754. Spain signs a concordat with Pope Benedict XIV by which the Spanish church becomes virtually independent of Rome and is placed under the control of the Spanish government.

England, 1754. The Society for the Encouragement of Arts, Manufacture and Commerce (*Royal Society of Arts*) is established.

Alexander and Campaspe in the Studio of Apelles, painting by Tiepolo.

Tiepolo's figures are floating in space

Wurzburg, Germany 1752

The flamboyant Venetian painter, Giovanni Battista Tiepolo, has been brought to Wurzburg to decorate the new residence of the Prince-Bishop. Amid its fantastic white and gold rococo interiors he has produced luminous frescoes of the life of the Turkish ruler Barbarossa. To decorate the great staircase he has brought together an amazingly heterogeneous gathering of the races, costumes, animals, plants and flowers of the known world, as well as crowds of gods and allegorical figures floating in space.

Tiepolo has already decorated many of the *palazzi* of Venice, Milan, Bergamo, Udine and villas at Vicenza, as well as painting single portraits. His *Alexander and Campaspe in the Studio of Apelles* is actually a picture of himself in his studio with his wife as his model.

Rioters attack shuttle inventor's house

Bury, England, 1753

Shuttle inventor John Kay has fled to Paris after making a narrow escape from a violent mob that stormed his home in Bury. The rioters blame Kay and his labour-saving invention, the flying shuttle, which has doubled mill operatives' output and halved manpower requirements, for putting jobs in jeopardy and making their work more monotonous.

Kay, who patented the shuttle 20 years ago, chose exile in France because he fears he can no longer get fair treatment in this country. He is disgruntled with mill owners who have refused to pay patent royalties and have banded together into a Shuttle Club to help pay the costs of numerous legal actions for patent infringement. Kay has won most of these cases, but has been ruined

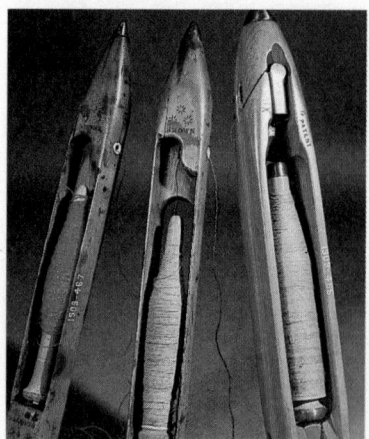

Flying shuttles. Kay's on right.

financially by legal costs. Kay claims to have many more inventions like the flying shuttle, but will not release them until the royalty situation is resolved.

Dalai Lama accepts authority of Beijing

Tibet, 1751
The Dalai Lama has been forced to acknowledge that he is the vassal of the Emperor of China after an abortive revolt by the Tibetans against Chinese rule. Two commissioners and many Chinese were killed in the revolt, but it was easily put down by a Chinese expedition.

Emperor Qianlong has heaped honours on the Dalai Lama, making him head, both spiritual and temporal, of Tibet and putting the Ministerial Council under his command; but there is no doubt who rules in Lhasa now.

A Tibetan bronze statuette of the supreme Adi-Buddha, with his female counterpart, the Sakti.

Royal approval for female "quack"

Germany, 1754
Germany's first woman medical doctor, Dorothea Erxleben, has graduated from Halle University with King Frederick's approval. Dr Erxleben, a widow of 39, interrupted her studies 12 years ago to nurse her father, get married and produce four children.

After being accused of practising "quack" medicine among the poor, she returned to University. Her book, *Rational Thoughts on Education of the Fair Sex* was published in 1749.

Franklin calls for union in America

Join, or Die. First American political cartoon. Pennsylvania Gazette, 1754.

Albany, New York, 10 July 1754
A call for the "voluntary union" of the 13 British colonies in North America was greeted enthusiastically today at a conference which included the chiefs of the six Iroquois nations. The proposal came from 48-year-old Benjamin Franklin, the proprietor of the *Pennsylvania Gazette*, whose plan is backed by the British government which sees the union as a way to control and pacify the Indians.

The new government would be administered by a president-general – to be appointed by the crown – and a general council of delegates from the colonies. It would have exclusive control of Indian affairs, regulating Indian trade and buying Indian land for the crown. It would also construct forts and pay troops to man them.

A less successful aspect of the conference was the dissatisfaction shown by the Indian delegates who complained about the removal of William Johnson, a representative of the crown who not only spoke several Indian languages but knew about their affairs and had their interests at heart.

"Machiavellian" chancellor for Empress

Vienna, January 1753
Prince Wenzel Anton von Kaunitz, a Machiavellian dandy with a wealth of cunning and ruthlessness hidden behind his fashionable frills and lace, has been appointed chancellor of Austria by the Empress Maria Theresa. Once destined for the church, this well-born aristocrat has served the empress well, first as minister to Turin, then in negotiating the Treaty of Aix-la-Chapelle and for the last three years as ambassador to Paris.

He became a close intimate of Madame de Pompadour, the mistress of Louis XV, and told a friend "I am here for only two things: for the interests of my queen, and these I serve well; for my pleasures, and on this score I need consult no one but myself...I have two persons to manage, the king and his mistress. I am getting along well with both".

Count Wenzel Anton von Kaunitz.

There are now signs that he will attempt to bring about a revolution in European diplomacy by persuading Maria Theresa that Prussia, not France, is Austria's enemy.

Outcry greets new calendar in Britain

London, 1752
The British Parliament has approved a switch from the Julian to the Gregorian calendar, but the people are furious. "Give us back our 11 days!" is the popular cry.

Since 1582, when Pope Gregory promulgated a new, more accurate calendar to replace that introduced by Julius Caesar in 45BC, Britain has lagged 11 days behind the Catholic and, later, Protestant countries which adopted the Gregorian year.

The change was the work of the astronomer, George Parker, earl of Macclesfield, and the bill was introduced in the House of Lords by Lord Chesterfield.

Franklin flies a kite in a thunderstorm

Franklin's experiment. Lithograph.

Philadelphia, 1752
During a recent thunderstorm Benjamin Franklin, the American statesman and inventor, flew a kite with a metal top. From this hung a key on a thread. As soon as lightning flashed in the sky, he held out his hand near the key and observed sparks streaming across to his fist and thence down his body to earth. He says that the damp thread had acted as a conductor of electricity.

Franklin believes that it may be possible to fix metal strips to buildings to conduct the flashes to earth, thus reducing and possibly even eliminating the risk of fire.

India, 1754. Joseph Dupleix, governor-general of the French possessions in India since 1741, is recalled to France after a brilliant colonial career. His departure leaves British prestige in India firmly established.

England, 1754. The novelist Henry Fielding dies. He will be best remembered for his epic novel *Tom Jones*, which appeared in 1749. Fielding began his writing career as a playwright, but in 1740, with the appearance of Samuel Richardson's *Pamela* – whose prudery and sentimentalism Fielding found highly amusing – he began a parody of the book. This became his first novel, *The Adventures of Joseph Andrews and his friend Mr Abraham Adams.*

Scotland, 1754. The Scottish philosopher David Hume begins publication of a monumental *History of England.*

France, 1754. The French philosopher Jean-Jacques Rousseau publishes his *Discourse Upon the Origin and Foundation of the Inequality Among Mankind.*

France, 1754. Pierre Louis Moreau de Maupertius, the mathematician and scholar, publishes his *Essai sur la Formation des Corps Organises*, where, for the first time, the idea of evolution of the species is stated in philosophical terms.

Moscow, 12 January 1755. The first Russian university opens in Moscow. The great scientist Mikhail Lomonosov played an important part in its founding.

Paris, 10 February 1755. The philosopher Baron de Montesquieu dies. His first great literary success was *Lettres Persanes*, published in 1721, which included a satire of French society. His most influential work was *De l'Esprit des Lois*, of which 22 editions were published in the two years following its first appearance in 1748.

England, 15 April 1755. Samuel Johnson's *Dictionary of the English Language* is published. The product of eight years' work, the *Dictionary*, which is both useful and entertaining, provides excellent definitions of the actual senses of words employed by the "best authors", without tracing their historical growth. Johnson believes that the English language reached almost its fullest development in the days of Shakespeare, Bacon and Spenser.

France, 26 May 1755. The bandit and outlaw Louis Mandrin is executed in Grenoble.

Britain, 8 July 1755. As their land dispute in North America intensifies, Britain breaks off diplomatic relations with France.

North America, July 1755. George Washington takes command of the British forces after their defeat by the French at the battle of the Wilderness, near Fort Duquesne (*Pittsburgh*). The British commander, Edward Braddock, was fatally wounded during the battle.

North America, 8 September 1755. British forces under William Johnson defeat the French and the Indians at the battle of Lake George.

Canada, 24 October 1755. A British expedition against French-held Fort Niagara ends in failure.

Lisbon, November 1755. More than 10,000 people die in an earthquake.

Canada, November 1755. The British admiral Edward Hawk takes possession of 300 French merchant ships.

South Africa, 1755. The first outbreak of smallpox in Cape Town spreads rapidly inland. Brought by sailors, it proves fatal to many Khoisan hunters and herders.

Corsica, 1755. The Corsican patriot Pasquale Paoli is appointed commander of an uprising against Genoese rule.

Canada, 1755. The British expel about 7,000 Acadians (*people from Nova Scotia and New Brunswick*) for refusing to take an oath of loyalty to Britain.

North America, 1755. The first regular passenger ship service begins between Britain and the colonies.

Burma, 1755. King Alaungpaya founds a new capital at Rangoon.

London, 16 January 1756. King George II and Frederick II of Prussia sign the treaty of Westminster, an agreement to secure the neutrality of the German states in the Anglo-French struggle developing in Europe.

India, 21 April 1756. Ali Vardi Khan, the ruler of Bengal, dies.

North America, 1756. A stage-coach line opens between Philadelphia and New York. By travelling at 18 hours a day, the distance can be covered in three days.

North America, 1756. The College of New Jersey is moved from Newark to Princeton.

Tunisia, 1756. Tunis is seized by troops led by the *bey* of Algiers.

France, 1756. The publication of Voltaire's *Essay on Universal History* confirms his reputation as a fine historian.

Quake brings fire and floods to Lisbon

An engraving of the Lisbon earthquake, from Le Monde Illustre.

Lisbon, November 1755
A terrible earthquake has devastated Lisbon, killing more than 10,000 people and reducing three-quarters of all buildings to heaps of rubble. Plans are already being drawn up for a completely new city to be designed by the military engineer Manuel de Maia. The earthquake struck Lisbon on All Saints' Day, when the churches were full, and lasted some nine minutes. One result was that the waters of the river Tagus receded, piled up and then came rolling back into the city to flood a huge area. This was followed by a great fire which raged for six days. Lisbon was a wealthy city with a population of about a quarter of a million.

Statue illustrates empiricist's theory

Paris, 1754
If you find a Parisian staring at a statue it is probably because he is musing over the latest philosophical theory put forward by the influential empiricist Etienne Bonnot, the abbot of Condillac.

Bonnot, in his recently published *Treatise des Sensations*, argues that the source of all our knowledge is our senses, which we transform into knowledge by the processes of attention, memory and reflection.

Take the statue. Bonnot invites readers to imagine it as first having only one sense, smell for example, and then another, perhaps taste, until it has all the senses. Try to imagine, he says, the statue's mental state at each stage. By combining the different sensations it would arrive at "judgements" in much the same way as humans reason, because the basis of our reasoning is our senses. This idea that reasoning is deductive challenges the traditional Cartesian view that man is endowed by God with knowledge of the basic principles of life.

Divine right's noble sceptic dies in Paris

France, 10 February 1755
The philosopher Baron de Montesquieu, renowned for his challenge to the divine right of kings, has died. Born in 1689, his most famous work *De l'Esprit des Lois* – The Spirit of Law – first appeared anonymously in 1748. Although banned by the Catholic Church, it ran through 22 editions in two years.

In his challenge to the divine right de Montesquieu based the authority of law on human reason, and argued that it varied from country to country according to differences in climate, religion, customs and past history. A constitution good for one nation may be bad for another.

He admired the constitution of Britain where he spent two years, believing that the English attitudes to religion, commerce and liberty are the result of their cold climate, which makes men impatient with tyranny. "Servitude always begins with sleepiness," wrote the baron, whose other work included satires of French society.

British routed by French in North America

North America, 13 July 1755
British attempts to end French expansion in North America have been dealt a serious blow with the latest French victory in the Ohio river valley, the focal point of recent Anglo-French clashes.

Early this month a British and colonial force was sent to recapture Fort Duquesne (*Pittsburgh*), a former British base which the French seized last year. On 9 July, seven miles south of the fort, French and Indian troops ambushed the British, killing or wounding almost two-thirds of the 1,000-strong force. The British commander, General Edward Braddock, was fatally wounded, and died today.

Command of the British forces has now fallen to Braddock's 23-year-old aide, Lieutenant-Colonel George Washington, who distinguished himself during the battle and retreat (he had two horses shot from under him and four bullet holes in his coat). Last year the governor of Virginia sparked off the present conflict when he sent Washington to scout and later eliminate French forts encroaching on land claimed by British colonies.

Cultured mistress enrages the people

Mme de Pompadour, by Boucher.

France, 1755
Public protest is building up the folly and extravagance of Louis XV and his beautiful mistress Madame de Pompadour. They are bleeding France's economy by their lavish spending on the arts, fine houses and court entertainments.

Pompadour seduced the King in 1745 when she appeared at the dauphin's marriage ball dressed as the goddess Diana. Lonely after the death of his favourite, the duchess of Chateauroux, the king rapidly installed Pompadour at Versailles. In September, that year he formally presented his new mistress to the queen.

Born Jeanne Poisson in 1721, the daughter of a clerk, and educated by her mother's lover, Pompadour is an intelligent woman, well-read, charming and musical. She became patron to Voltaire, Montesquieu and Rousseau, and is said to be unfailingly loyal to her family and friends who helped her to reach such an influential position.

France's Indian hero beaten by peace

Pondicherry, India, 1754
The marquis of Dupleix, the formidable governor of France's Indian enclave, has been sacrificed in the cause of European peace. Even his enemies, the British, admire his audacity. With meagre resources, he almost took control of southern India.

From 1742, when France and Britain went to war, he made up for his lack of French soldiers with astute diplomacy (turning Indian princes from overlords into dependants) and bold strategy, building up a trained Sepoy army and taking Madras in 1746. Britain recaptured it with reinforcements, but it was not until Robert Clive was given command of the British forces that Dupleix found himself against an opponent of equal skill. Clive's cap-

The Marquis of Dupleix.

ture in September 1751 of Arcot, which he held for 50 days, wrecked Dupleix' strategy. Unable to gain victory on the cheap, France has opted for peace.

Comfort and light: new priorities in French interior decor

Candelabrum, by Claude Duvivier.

Paris, 1754
The change from the style of Louis XIV to Louis XV is a change from the formal and stately to the elegant and human. It can be seen in the Place de la Concorde, laid out this year with modest facades and ornamental gardens by the royal architect, Jacques Ange Gabriel. The traditional formal gardens are giving way under English influence to a natural style, as at Bellevue.

In the salons, the centre of social

Louis XV's roll-top desk by J F Oeben, completed later by J H Riesener.

life, the taste is for amusing decoration, based on imaginary beasts, foliage, shepherdesses, *Chinoiserie* and *singerie* – decorative panels featuring monkeys. Chairs have become lighter and markedly more curved in appearance. They are also more comfortable. Tapestries take the paintings of artists such as Boucher as their subjects. In carpets the fashion is for the Savonnerie factory's medallions of flowers and acanthus leaves. A new type

of room is in vogue – the *boudoir*, where ladies receive friends while conducting their toilette at the dressing table.

There is a demand for *ebenistes* to provide veneers and marquetry and *ormolu* mounts at the corners and edges of furniture. Gilded bronze decorations riot over the curved surfaces of commodes. One of the most elaborate pieces is a bureau, now being constructed for Louis XV, by Jean Francois Oeben.

Versailles, 1 May 1756. The Austrian chancellor, Kaunitz, signs a treaty of alliance with France.

Mediterranean, June 1756. The British-held island of Minorca is taken by the French.

India, June 1756. Sirajuddaula, the new ruler of Bengal, captures Calcutta. Many of the British residents who surrender are allowed by Sirajuddaula's agents to die in a "black hole".

New England, 14 August 1756. Soon after arriving in America to command the French forces, Louis Montcalm de St Veran takes Fort Oswego from the British.

Germany, 29 August 1756. Frederick II of Prussia invades Saxony, setting off a war in Europe. Prussia is allied with Britain against Austria and France.

New England, 31 August 1756. The British at Fort William Henry surrender to Louis Montcalm.

Britain, November 1756. On the resignation of the duke of Newcastle as prime minister, William Pitt is appointed secretary of state and takes charge of the war against France.

Paris, 5 January 1757. Robert Francois Damiens makes an unsuccessful attempt to assassinate King Louis XV.

India, 28 January 1757. Ahmed Shah, the first king of Afghanistan, occupies Delhi and annexes the Punjab.

Austria, 2 February 1757. Austria, already allied with France, forms an offensive alliance with Russia against Prussia.

India, 22 June 1757. After retaking Calcutta and seizing the French station at Chandernagore, Robert Clive, leading the British East India Company's forces, defeats the ruler of Bengal's much larger army at Plassey, 100 miles up the Hooghly from Calcutta.

Bohemia, June 1757. After suffering a defeat by the Austrians at Kolin, the Prussians are forced to lift a siege of Prague and evacuate Bohemia, which they invaded earlier in the year.

Germany, 30 August 1757. Having invaded eastern Prussia, the Russians defeat the Prussians at Gross-Jagersdorf.

Germany, September 1757. The Swedes, who are in alliance with Austria, France and Russia, invade the province of Pomerania.

Germany, 16 October 1757. The Austrians reach Berlin.

Germany, 5 November 1757. The Prussians, led by Frederick II, defeat a Franco-Austrian force at Rossbach.

Germany, 6 December 1757. The Prussians inflict another defeat on the Austrians, at Leuthen.

Morocco, 1757. Mulay Mohammed III ben Abdullah comes to the throne and sets about re-establishing the economy and the army, which have been in disarray since the death of Mulay Ismail in 1727.

France, 1757. Denis Diderot presents a "bourgeois drama" entitled *The Test of Virtue*.

Germany, 23 June 1758. British and Hanoverian armies defeat the French at Krefeld.

New England, 8 July 1758. A British attack on Fort Carillon at Ticonderoga (in *New York state*) is foiled by the French.

Canada, 26 July 1758. British forces under James Wolfe capture Fort Louisbourg on Cape Breton Island from the French. The fort was taken by the British in 1745, but returned to the French three years later by the treaty of Aix-la-Chapelle.

Germany, 25 August 1758. The Prussians defeat an invading Russian force at the battle of Zorndorf.

Portugal, September 1758. A plot by a group of nobles against the king and Pombal, known as the conspiracy of the Tavora, is uncovered. Its leaders are tortured and executed.

North America, 25 November 1758. After losing Louisbourg and Fort Frontenac to the British, the French are forced to evacuate Fort Duquesne (*Pittsburgh*), which the British rename Fort Pitt.

Senegal, December 1758. Having taken St Louis from the French in April, the British seize the island of Goree.

India, 1758. The Maratha leader Raghunath Rao occupies Lahore.

France, 1758. Jean-Jacques Rousseau publishes his *Lettre a d'Alembert*.

Paris, 1758. *On the Mind*, a statement of militant atheism by the philosopher Claude Helvetius, is denounced by the Sorbonne and publicly burnt on the orders of the parliament of Paris.

India, 1759. Ahmed Shah Durrani, the king of Afghanistan, invades India for the second time.

England, 1759. The publication of *Rasselas, Prince of Abyssinia* by Samuel Johnson popularises the romantic view of Ethiopia.

London, 1759. The British Museum, which was founded six years ago, opens its doors to the public.

"Messiah" composer has died aged 74

London, 14 April 1759
George Frideric Handel, the towering figure in English musical life for over 30 years, died today. He will be buried in Westminster Abbey.

Handel, like Bach (whom he never met), was born in 1685 in eastern Germany; otherwise their careers ran different courses. For example, Bach remained in Germany, whereas Handel travelled to Italy and settled in England, becoming a British citizen in 1727. Bach wrote almost nothing for the stage; Handel composed about 40 operas and slightly fewer oratorios, including *Messiah* (1742).

Handel wrote much for royal occasions, such as the *Water Music* and music for the 1727 coronation. The story goes that George II was so moved by the *Hallelujah* chorus in *Messiah* that he stood up; the audience felt that it had to follow the king, and a tradition was born.

Handel's monument (1784).

Scarlatti, composer-royal, dies in Spain

Scarlatti; an anonymous portrait.

Madrid, 23 July 1757
Domenico Scarlatti has died aged 71. Born in Naples, he was the son of the composer Alessandro Scarlatti (1660-1725) and one of the great trio of composers (with Bach and Handel) born in 1685.

Scarlatti was made organist and composer to the Neapolitan court when just 15 years old. He worked at Rome from 1707 to 1719, and after a time in Sicily became composer to King John V of Portugal; he taught the king's gifted daughter and went with her to Spain when she married the Spanish crown prince in 1729. This fame rests on hundreds of keyboard sonatas, mainly written for the princess, which show a brilliant range of imagination and technique.

Swiss mathematician works on calculus

Berlin, 1755
Not only does the Swiss scientist Leonhard Euler find time to teach and carry out research at the university here, he also has written hundreds of books on topics as varied as artillery and ballistics, shipbuilding and navigation, astronomical orbits and many aspects of applied technology and engineering.

An important work is his recent *Institutiones Calculi Differentialis*, which shows him to be one of the most significant mathematical innovators after Isaac Newton. This book details Euler's many discoveries in the fields of both ordinary and partial differential equations which are useful in problems of mechanics.

New pact links France and Austria

Versailles, 1 May 1756

Chancellor Kaunitz of Austria succeeded today in bringing about what is being called a "diplomatic revolution" with the signing of a treaty between those traditional enemies, France and Austria.

The treaty is especially advantageous to the Austrians, for it contains an undertaking by each country to protect the other, with a promise of military aid, in the event of aggression and Austria is under threat from the Prussians.

Kaunitz must thank his friend Madame de Pompadour for her help in bringing off this coup by persuading her lover, King Louis, to end the old enmity. There were other potent forces at work as well, for this year has seen a dramatic upset in the alliances which have governed Europe for so long.

The Anglo-Austrian alliance has died because both countries were disillusioned with it. Britain had already signed a treaty with Russia, and in January the Hanoverian

Louis XV, the king of France.

King George II of Britain signed the convention of Westminster with Frederick of Prussia under which they agreed to guarantee the security of Silesia and Hanover.

With France and Britain already fighting in India and America, the Westminster treaty made Louis and

Frederick II, the king of Prussia.

his advisers much more receptive to the proposals from Vienna.

The Anglo-Prussian agreement has also disturbed the Russians and, despite the St Petersburg treaty, the indications are that they will now seek better relations with Austria and France.

Agriculture is key to national wealth

An allegory of a farmworker.

Paris, 1758

A nation's prosperity is solely dependent on its ability to increase its levels of agricultural production, according to a new group of Parisian economists, the Physiocrats.

Their leader, Dr François Quesnay, a physician with a passion for economics, has set out France's national income and expenditure in terms of agricultural goods in his new book *Tableau Economique*.

Quesnay, who regards agricultural production as the only true form of wealth creation, says that money is not true wealth and commerce is only a minor source of prosperity. His group, which takes its name from physiocracy – control by nature – wants the state to intervene less in agriculture, lower taxes and lift out-dated guild regulations which hamper production.

British Museum opens to the public

An engraving of the garden front of the British Museum, c.1800.

London, 1759

The British Museum has opened in Bloomsbury. It is to be a "general repository for all arts and sciences" and will be open "for public use to all posterity". It is Britain's first great public assembly of antiquities and will be administered by a number of trustees, drawn from the church and state.

The museum's exhibits are based upon the collections of Sir Hans Sloane, the physician and antiqua-

ry, and those of the first and second earls of Oxford. King George has donated the Old Royal Library, built up by successive monarchs over 300 years.

Plans for the museum began after Sloane's death in 1753. A lottery, provided for by the British Museum Act of 1753, raised £300,000 – sufficient to buy the Sloane and Oxford collections and to buy and then expand Montagu House in Great Russell Street to house them.

Reform is bringing Portugal up to date

Lisbon, 1759

The marquis of Pombal, Portugal's all-powerful prime minister, has set about dismantling the country's system of privilege and laying the foundations of a new order. Encouraged by King Joseph, he has introduced a remarkable series of reforms which have already earned him the nickname of the "Portuguese Richelieu".

Pombal has been particularly tough on the Jesuits, who had exercised control not only of the royal conscience and of the souls of the Brazilian Indians but also of education. He has expelled them and closed convents. His educational reforms intend to turn Coimbra into Portugal's greatest and richest university. Pombal is also working towards creating a wealthy mercantile class with, behind it, the phalanx of officials necessary to carry on administration and trade. Portugal's alliance with Britain has continued, despite resentment at London's stranglehold on the country's trade.

Japanese cobweb and insect design, hiramakie on black ro-iro.

1759 (1759-1761)

Paris, 8 March 1759. For the second time, the parliament of Paris condemns the *Encyclopedie* edited by Denis Diderot.

West Indies, 23 April 1759. The English seize Basse-Terre and Guadeloupe in the Antilles from the French.

Canada, 25 July 1759. British forces under the leadership of John Prideaux defeat the French at Fort Niagara; Prideaux is killed in the battle.

New England, 26 July 1759. Outnumbered French defenders blow up Fort Carillon at Ticonderoga and flee before an attacking British force.

Canada, 31 July 1759. In the face of a British attack on Crown Point, the French blow up Fort St Frederic.

Germany, 1 August 1759. British and Hanoverian armies defeat the French at battle of Minden.

Spain, 10 August 1759. On the death of Ferdinand VI, he is succeeded as king of Spain by his half-brother Charles III.

Prussia, 12 August 1759. The Austro-Russian coalition wins a resounding victory over Frederick II at Kunersdorf.

Portugal, September 1759. The marquis of Pombal, the prime minister of Portugal, gives orders for the Jesuits to be expelled from the country. This is a direct result of last year's Tavora conspiracy, in which some Jesuits were involved.

Canada, 18 September 1759. Quebec surrenders to the British after a battle which saw the deaths of both James Wolfe and Louis Montcalm, the British and French commanders.

France, 1759. Voltaire publishes a short story entitled *Candide*, a satire on the philosophy that "all is for the best in the best of all possible worlds".

India, 22 January 1760. British forces under Eyre Coote win a decisive victory over the French, led by the count of Lally, at Wandiwash in southern India.

South Carolina, 16 February 1760. Cherokee Indians held hostage at Fort St George are killed in revenge for Indian attacks on frontier settlements.

Netherlands, April 1760. Peace talks begun at The Hague to end the conflict between the European powers break down.

Quebec, 28 April 1760. French forces besieging Quebec defeat the British under James Murray in the second battle on the Plains of Abraham. The British retreat into the city.

Germany, 23 June 1760. The Austrians defeat the Prussians at Landshut.

South Carolina, 7 August 1760. The British garrison of Fort Loudon is overrun by Cherokee Indians after it was forced by starvation to surrender.

Germany, 15 August 1760. Frederick II defeats the Austrians at the battle of Liegnitz.

Quebec, 8 September 1760. The French surrender the city of Montreal to the British.

Britain, 25 October 1760. On the death of his grandfather George II, George III comes to the throne.

Germany, 3 November 1760. Following the Russian capture of Berlin, his capital, Frederick II of Prussia defeats the Austrians at battle of Torgau.

North America, 29 November 1760. Major Robert Rogers takes possession of Detroit on behalf of Britain.

North America, 1760. People of African descent are said to constitute 30 per cent of the population of the 13 British colonies in North America.

France, 1760. Jean-Jacques Rousseau publishes *Julie ou la Nouvelle Heloise.*

China, 1760. Canton becomes the only port in China authorised to trade with other countries.

Italy, 1760. The great comic dramatist Carlo Goldoni presents a new play entitled *The Tyrants.*

Scotland, 1760. The poet James Macpherson publishes *Ossian*, allegedly a collection of fragments of ancient poetry translated from the Gaelic. In fact, the author is Macpherson himself.

England, 1760. Josiah Wedgwood establishes a pottery works at Etruria in Staffordshire.

England, 1760. The Irish-born clergyman Laurence Sterne publishes the first two volumes of an eccentric novel entitled *Tristram Shandy.*

India, January 1761. The Moghul emperor and his Maratha allies are defeated by the Afghan leader, Ahmed Shah Durrani, at the battle of Panipat. There is no longer an Indian army able to resist British penetration seriously.

France, 8 June 1761. After the failure of peace talks with the French, the English capture Belle Ile sur Mer.

Britain, October 1761. William Pitt, finding himself isolated in the cabinet over war policy, resigns as secretary of state.

Royal desire for peace defeats Pitt

London, 1761
William Pitt, who came to power at the lowest ebb in Britan's fortunes and transformed the French war, has been forced to resign. He saw that Spain was about to join France and he wished to anticipate the blow with an ultimatum. But the king, George III, who said the war was "bloody and expensive", wanted peace and the Cabinet deserted Pitt.

Yet only months ago they were loud in his praise. Four years ago, a string of British defeats had culminated in the failure at Minorca, for which Admiral Byng was shot after a court-martial. Pitt shifted the war from Europe, where France was stronger, to the high seas and the colonies, where Britain had the advantage. The French were defeated by Wolfe in Canada, by Clive in India, and by Hawke and other admirals in the West Indies and West Africa.

Though Pitt is out of office, the Spanish will yet be faced with the consequences of his policies. The expeditionary forces which he raised are now poised to seize the Spanish colonies of the Philippines, Florida, Cuba and a string of islands in the Caribbean.

Chairing the member: an English scene by William Hogarth, c.1754.

Berlin burnt and pillaged by Russians

Berlin, 9 October 1760
A combined force of Russians and Austrians entered Berlin today, and the soldiers are busy pillaging the royal palaces of Charlottenburg and Schonhausen. The occupiers have also demanded the payment of a "war tribute" by the city.

The ordinary people, fearing for their lives, are cowering behind locked doors, but so far the enemy soldiers are too preoccupied with filling their knapsacks with royal treasures to undertake serious looting in the city.

It seems, in fact, that the Russians and Austrians are engaged in a secondary operation and are not here in great numbers. Rumours are spreading that King Frederick is already hurrying to the relief of the city with his formidable army.

However, while he will certainly be able to throw the invaders out of Berlin, the war is going badly for him. Prussia is exhausted by it, his soldiers have suffered great losses and much of his artillery has been captured or destroyed.

Frederick, renowned as a military leader, almost abandoned the fight last year after the Kunersdorf defeat. He contemplated suicide and wrote: "I believe everything is lost; I shall not survive the collapse of my fatherland." But he continues to fight and two months ago defeated the Austrians at Liegnitz.

Battle of Quebec: French expelled

Quebec, September 1759

In a carefully planned and brilliantly executed combined operation, British troops have scaled the allegedly "impossible" Heights of Abraham and driven the French and their allies from Quebec. Few thought that such an attack was possible, and the defenders of Quebec themselves were so confident that they made little effort to harass the British fleet under Vice-Admiral Charles Saunders as it weaved its way through the treacherous currents of the St Lawrence River – without the help of charts – with 8,500 war-seasoned soldiers. A previous British attack had ended in disaster 48 years before, and it was not until the British were encamped on the opposite bank that the French became concerned.

Even so, the French commander, marquis of Montcalm, remained confident that no army could scale the huge cliffs surrounding his city. He had not reckoned with James Wolfe, a youthful brigadier-general who had been chosen especially for this role. After weeks of deliberation, Wolfe chose to lead his men in a surprise attack involving a silent approach by flat-bottomed boats and a dangerous climb in darkness.

By dawn, the British Redcoats were lined up to attack. Montcalm chose to leave his fortress and attack at once, but British fire-power won the day. Montcalm and Wolfe were both mortally injured, but the dying Wolfe, hearing of his victory, said: "Now, God be praised, I will die in peace."

The death of General Montcalm near Quebec; an engraving by Watteau.

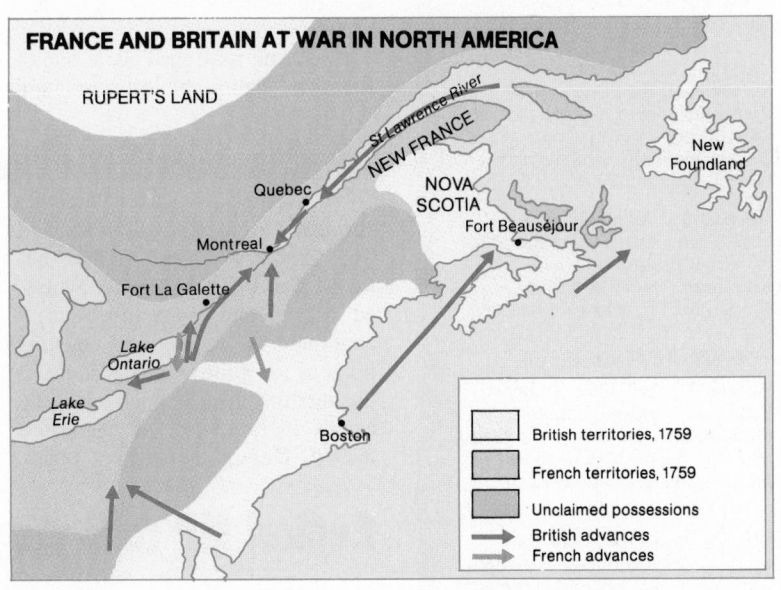

FRANCE AND BRITAIN AT WAR IN NORTH AMERICA

RUPERT'S LAND

St Lawrence River

NEW FRANCE

Quebec

Montreal

Fort La Galette

NOVA SCOTIA

Fort Beauséjour

New Foundland

Lake Ontario

Lake Erie

Boston

☐ British territories, 1759
▨ French territories, 1759
▨ Unclaimed possessions
→ British advances
→ French advances

Thousands die as Moslems defeat Hindus at Panipat

Panipat, India, 22 January 1761

After a terrible eight-hour battle, in which the fate of India lay in the balance, the Afghan army of Ahmed Shah Durrani has annihilated the Marathas.

Since 1748, when Nadir Shah of Persia died, apportioning to his son Durrani his eastern conquests, India has been a battleground between the Moslem Afghans and the Hindu Marathas, the Moghuls' allies. In October 1760 Durrani challenged the Marathas to battle. The Marathas opted for positional warfare, building a fortified camp at Panipat. It proved their undoing. The 300,000 soldiers and camp followers ran out of food and were forced to fight. Durrani, with only 80,000, staked everything on the outcome. "The Marathas are the thorn of Hindustan," he said. "By one effort we get this thorn out of our sides for ever."

For six hours the advantage was with the Hindus. An unexpected charge by Durrani's cavalry, in which the Maratha leader's son, Viswas Rao, was wounded, turned the tide. "As if by enchantment, the whole Marathan army turned their backs and fled at full speed, leaving the field of battle covered with heaps of dead," one eye-witness reported. As many as 200,000 Marathas may have perished in those eight frightful hours. But the blood-letting has weakened both sides, with the British poised to benefit.

Lay preachers raise question of dissension for Methodists

Bristol, England, 1760

John Wesley has taken a decisive stand against Methodists separating from the Church of England at the annual conference here. He led the conference in disavowing lay preachers who have been administering the sacraments and who have taken out licences as dissenting ministers to legalise their positions. He said that he would never ordain a separate ministry.

The pressure for separation has been building up for several years now. The strength of the Methodists is outside the church; initially it was in large outdoor meetings, but as the movement has grown around one hundred chapels have been built. Most of their meetings are deliberately held at different times from church services, but in many parishes the clergy remain hostile to Methodism.

Unlike Wesley, most Methodist preachers are tradesmen and craftsmen who have no loyalty to the established church. Only the immense prestige of Wesley has avoided a split.

John Wesley: wants to avoid split.

A brass altar made for a Benin king after 1750.

1761 (1761-1763)

Paris, 1761. The parliament of Paris condemns the Society of Jesus following a court case against the Jesuit priest Antoine de Valette, the leader of the order's French houses in South America.

Spain, 1761. Spain is drawn into the war of European powers by the so-called third Family Compact, which makes its foreign policy subservient to that of France. This treaty of mutual assistance involving all the ruling Bourbon dynasties was drawn up by the duke of Choiseul, Louis XV's chief minister.

India, 1761. British forces under Eyre Coote seize Pondicherry from the French.

England, 1761. The writer Samuel Richardson dies. His *Pamela*, which appeared in 1740, is regarded as the first modern novel.

Britain, 2 January 1762. Britain declares war on Spain.

Russia, 5 January 1762. The Czarina Elizabeth dies and is succeeded on the throne by her nephew Peter III, the maternal grandson of Peter the Great.

West Indies, 5 February 1762. Martinique, a major French base in the Lesser Antilles, surrenders to the British.

Germany, May 1762. Frederick II of Prussia signs a peace treaty with Sweden.

Britain, 29 May 1762. Lord Bute, a close adviser of George III and a believer in the supremacy of the royal prerogative, becomes prime minister.

Russia, July 1762. Peter III is assassinated with the complicity of his wife, Catherine, who succeeds him on the throne as Catherine II. During his brief reign, Peter gave his support to Frederick II, restoring eastern Prussia to him.

Germany, 21 July 1762. Frederick II defeats the Austrians at Berkersdorf in Silesia.

West Indies, 12 August 1762. The British capture Cuba from Spain after a two-month siege.

Philippines, 5 October 1762. A British fleet bombards and captures the Spanish-held city of Manila.

Austria, 5 October 1762. The opera *Orpheus and Eurydice* by Christoph Gluck is staged for the first time.

Austria, 24 November 1762. Austria signs a truce with Frederick II of Prussia.

North America, 3 December 1762. France cedes to Spain all lands west of the Mississippi – the territory known as Upper Louisiana.

Portugal, December 1762. With British support, the Portuguese repel an invasion by French and Spanish forces.

France, 1762. Charles Emmanuel of Savoy issues two edicts giving freedom to serfs.

France, 1762. Jean-Jacques Rousseau publishes *Le Contrat Social* (The Social Contract), which contains the opening sentence "Man is born free, yet everywhere he is in chains" and the slogan "liberty, equality, fraternity". He also publishes *Emile*, in novel form, which outrages church and state with its unorthodox views on monarchy and religion and causes him to flee into exile in Switzerland.

Versailles, 1762. The architect Jacques Ange Gabriel begins work on the Petit Trianon.

Rome, 1762. Construction of the Trevi fountain, the work of the architect Niccolo Salvi, is completed.

Paris, 10 February 1763. By the treaty of Paris, ending the Seven Years War, France loses all its North American territories, including Canada, except New Orleans and the islands of St Pierre, Miquelon, Guadeloupe and Martinique. Florida is ceded to Britain by Spain, which receives from Britain all conquests in Cuba.

Germany, 15 February 1763. Prussia and Austria sign the peace of Hubertusburg, by which Silesia is definitely ceded to Prussia. Frederick II fails to gain Saxony, however, which had been his objective in starting the war.

Britain, 23 April 1763. Today's issue of the anti-government newspaper *North Briton*, published by John Wilkes MP, includes insulting remarks about King George III.

Britain, April 1763. Lord Bute resigns after leading an extremely unpopular ministry and is replaced as prime minister by George Grenville.

North America, 7 May 1763. Pontiac, the chief of the Ottawa Indians, begins an all-out war on British garrisons in the region west of Niagara.

Lithuania, September 1763. Russian troops invade Polish territory.

Poland, 5 October 1763. Frederick Augustus II, the elector of Saxony and king of Poland, dies.

North America, October 1763. A large area on the Canadian border which is claimed by both New Hampshire and New York is given the name Verd-mont, meaning green mountain.

Illegal "Social Contract" is published

France, 1762
A new philosophical treatise – *Le Contrat Social* by Jean-Jacques Rousseau – has been published in Holland. Like others of Rousseau's works it is officially banned in France, but what is proving to be a major addition to our knowledge of human relations has been widely, if illicitly, circulated.

Le Contrat Social, Rousseau's political testimony, advocates universal justice through equality before the law, as well as a fairer distribution of wealth. He believes that government is essentially a contract between the rulers and the ruled.

Under the "general will" of the people, they consent to turn over power to their governors to be exercised for the common good. The community is greater than the individual, but as such the community is responsible for well-being of each citizen.

Rousseau, now aged 50, is one of France's leading philosophers and

Jean-Jacques Rousseau, the writer.

contributor to the *Encyclopedie*. His *Emile* also appeared this year, and his influential *Discourse on the origins of inequality* was published in 1755.

London scientist discovers hidden heat

London, 1762
The physicist Joseph Black has found that, if a thermometer is placed in a mixture of ice and water, it continues to register the melting point of ice while any ice remains in the mixture. The temperature only begins to rise when all the ice is melted. During the melting phase,

Black concludes, it is as if heat is passing steadily into the mixture of ice and water without affecting the thermometer. It is hidden or "latent" heat. Further experiments with latent heat show how this hidden form of energy may be measured. These findings may also aid the development of steam engines.

Radical MP calls the king a prostitute

John Wilkes, MP and journalist.

London, 23 April 1763
John Wilkes, the radical MP for Aylesbury, a member of the Hellfire Club and the publisher of the scurrilous anti-government newspaper – *North Briton*, has made his most outrageous attack on the government yet.

Today's edition of *North Briton*, number 45, contains outspoken criticisms not only of the prime minister, Lord Bute, but also of the king. Condemning Bute as incompetent, Wilkes, a fervent democrat, suggests that the king, by supporting him, has drawn the monarchy into "prostitution". This affront has reached far beyond its target and it seems impossible that Wilkes will go unpunished.

Coup d'etat brings Czarina Catherine to Russian throne

Catherine the Great of Russia.

St Petersburg, Russia, 1762
The Czarina, Catherine, has seized power in a *coup d'etat* staged by her lover, Gregori Orlov, a fiery lieutenant of the St Petersburg garrison, by whom she had a child last April. She was wildly cheered by the soldiery when she arrived in the capital. They kissed her hand and called her "little mother".

Four days after the coup her husband, Peter III, died in a scuffle during dinner. His guard, another Orlov brother, Alexis, says he cannot recall what happened. Peter was universally detested. After the death of his mother, Czarina Elizabeth, he continued drinking and whoring, while Catherine, in black, spent hours kneeling by the coffin. Peter offended the church by shouting and putting his tongue out at the priest during divine service. He took the soldiers out of the uniforms given to them by Peter the Great.

Mystic made Hindu-Moslem split deeper

Delhi, 1762
Shah Wali-Allah, the great Indian Moslem philosopher and mystic, has died. A man who sensed that he was living at the end of an age, he revitalised Islam in India.

His father, a religious official at the Moghul court, abandoned the luxury of court life and founded a religious school. Wali-Allah himself studied in Mecca. Troubled by the disorders of the times he evolved a new philosophy, based on Sunni Islam.

The worship of saints at shrines was to be given less emphasis. Moslems should become more exclusive, mixing less with Hindus, and should work to make their society more perfect in anticipation of the heavenly life to come. He leaves a stronger Moslem India behind.

Indians leave trail of death along the Canadian frontier

America, 7 May 1763
Four Indian tribes – the Shawnees, Delawares, Chippawas and Ottawa – have laid siege to the British stronghold of Fort Detroit in the Great Lakes region in an uprising by the native American people in which hundreds of British redcoats have lost their lives. The Indian leader, Pontiac, an Ottawa, has destroyed several British outposts and crushed expeditions with great ruthlessness.

It was a Delaware wise man calling for a return to the old Indian customs and a rejection of the white man who inspired the uprising of the tribes. Pontiac, concerned at the loss to his people of tribal lands and the valuable fur industry, brought the tribal chiefs together and announced a plan to drive the British out. He planned a surprise attack on Fort Detroit, but the plan was exposed, giving the British time to build new fortifications.

Chief Pontiac: a later engraving.

Paris treaty ends war

A contemporary cartoon of the signing of the Treaty of Paris, 1763.

Paris, 10 February 1763
Seven long, bloody and financially exhausting years of war ended today with the signing of the Treaty of Paris. Although it does not meet Pitt's demands, the treaty secures a great deal of land for Britain's burgeoning empire.

Among its provisions, France cedes Canada to Britian and relinquishes its Indian possessions except for Pondicherry and four small trading posts. Britain also gets Florida from Spain and, in compensation, France has given Spain the Louisiana territory west of the Mississippi.

Other provisions return Minorca to Britain, and there is an exchange of islands in the West Indies. Britain is to restore Havana and Manila to Spain and adjustments are made in African colonies.

The treaty, hammered out over two years of negotiations, should prove to be of great value to Britain but, while it is being received thankfully in France, it must surely mean the end of France's colonial ambitions in the New World.

Britain and France have also withdrawn from the war in Europe, and it is expected that Prussia and Austria will make peace within the next few days. The war will end in a triumph for Frederick of Prussia. So often near defeat, his right to Silesia now seems about to be recognised and he is confirmed as a hero in the eyes of the Germans.

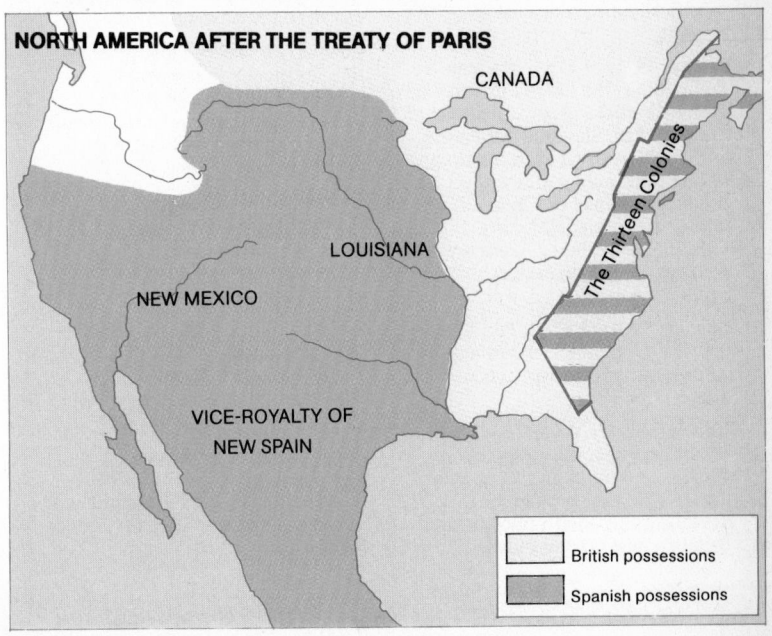

NORTH AMERICA AFTER THE TREATY OF PARIS

CANADA

The Thirteen Colonies

LOUISIANA

NEW MEXICO

VICE-ROYALTY OF NEW SPAIN

☐ British possessions
▨ Spanish possessions

1763 (1763-1765)

North America, November 1763. The Ottawa Chief Pontiac, who has inflicted several defeats on the British in the Great Lakes region, lifts a six-month siege of Fort Detroit after failing to gain French support for his rebellion.

North America, 1763. Two English surveyors, Charles Mason and Jeremiah Dixon, begin to survey a boundary line between the two colonies of Pennsylvania and Maryland.

North America, 1763. The British prohibit settlements in the entire region west of the Appalachian mountains.

New England, 1763. The Touro synagogue, the first major centre of Jewish culture in America, opens at Newport, Rhode Island.

Britain, 1763. Arrested on a general warrant of seditious libel, John Wilkes, the publisher of the newspaper *North Briton*, is discharged on the ground that his arrest infringes his privileges as a member of Parliament.

Russia, 1763. Catherine II appoints a commission to determine the future of the Russian nobility.

France, 1763. The group of French economic and political thinkers known as the Physiocrats begins publication of a newspaper entitled *La Gazette du Commerce*.

Iraq, 1763. The port of Bassora becomes the pivot of trade with Britain.

Britain, 19 January 1764. John Wilkes MP is expelled from the House of Commons and outlawed.

North America, February 1764. A French trading post is established at St Louis on the west bank of the Mississippi river, not far below the mouth of the Missouri.

London, 5 April 1764. Parliament passes a Sugar Act, its first law specifically aimed at raising revenue from the colonies.

France, 15 April 1764. Madame de Pompadour, the former mistress of Louis XV and a generous patron of the arts, dies. She used her charm and intelligence to exert a strong influence in public affairs, and her protege, the duke of Choiseul, rose to become foreign secretary. She founded the Military Academy and the royal porcelain factory at Sevres.

London, 19 April 1764. Parliament passes a Currency Act banning the colonies from printing paper money.

Boston, 24 May 1764. The lawyer James Otis denounces "taxation without representation" and calls for the colonies to unite in demonstrating their opposition to Britain's new tax measures.

Boston, August 1764. City merchants organise a boycott of luxury goods from Britain, inaugurating a policy of non-importation.

Poland, 6 September 1764. The pretender Stanislas Poniatowski, a favourite of Catherine II of Russia, becomes king of Poland.

India, 22 October 1764. The British defeat the Moghul emperor and the ruler of Oudh at Buxar, making themselves masters of Bengal, the richest province of India.

France, November 1764. King Louis XV officially dissolves the Jesuit order.

North America, November 1764. Allies of the Ottawa Indian Chief Pontiac reach a peace agreement with the British, but Pontiac himself is not among them.

Paris, 1764. Julie de Lespinasse opens a literary salon which attracts politicians, wits and artists.

England, 1764. The painter and engraver William Hogarth dies. One of his favourite subjects in later life was political caricature.

Russia, 1764. Catherine II orders further exploration of Alaska, the territory across the sea from the north-eastern tip of Siberia.

St Petersburg, 1764. The French architect Jean Baptiste Vallin de La Motte begins construction of Gostiny Dvor to house Catherine II's art collection.

Florida, 1764. The British farmer John Bartram discovers vast groves of wild oranges in Florida.

France, 1764. Voltaire publishes his *Dictionnaire Philosophique*.

Dresden, 1764. The German archaeologist Johann Joachim Winckelmann publishes *The Art of Antiquity*, in which he defends the return to the classical tradition.

London, 22 March 1765. In order to raise money in the colonies to support British troops stationed there, Parliament passes the Stamp Act, taxing stamps affixed to certain printed matter.

London, 24 March 1765. Parliament passes the Quartering Act, requiring the colonies to provide shelter and food for British soldiers and their horses.

Britain, 16 July 1765. Lord Grenville resigns and is replaced as prime minister by Lord Rockingham.

North America, 1765. The passage of the Stamp Act provokes widespread protests and riots in British colonies, and the campaign of non-importation of luxury goods from Britain is stepped up.

The Rake's Progress: Orgies, part of the series by William Hogarth.

London's sardonic chronicler is dead

London, 1764
William Hogarth, the engraver and painter, is dead. He was 67. Hogarth, the son of a modest but educated family, was an outstanding satirist of modern manners, using his art to create visual stories deliberately designed to have the same effect as a stage play.

Such series as *The Harlot's Progress* (1731), *The Rake's Progress* (1735) and *Marriage a la Mode* (1745) have made him the unrivalled, if sardonic, chronicler of fashionable London. *Gin Lane*, *Beer Street* and the *Four Stages of Cruelty* (all 1751) show the city's darker side with their depictions of poverty and decay.

A successful man who profoundly influenced his contemporaries, Hogarth was one of the first popular engravers to profit from his art. From 1735, in what was known as Hogarth's Act, artists held copyright in their own works, and piracy, from which Hogarth had suffered greatly, was made illegal.

Philosopher lobbies for justice and truth

Paris, 9 March 1765
Voltaire's influence and talent for satire has cleared the name of Jean Calas, executed three years ago for murdering his son Marc-Antoine.

Marc-Antoine was found dead in Jean's house in Toulouse. Rumour had it that the father, a staunch Calvinist, had killed the son because he intended to join the Catholic church. Jean insisted he was innocent, but was tortured on the wheel and executed in 1762.

Calas' sons brought the case to Voltaire's attention. He wrote a series of articles proving Marc-Antoine's suicide and the judges' pro-Catholic bias. The case was reopened and today the judges unanimously declared the case null and void.

Voltaire, the poet and philosopher.

Stamp tax inspires American rebellion

Boston, 25 August 1765

A mob sacked and burned the home of the Massachusetts governor, Thomas Hutchinson, tonight – furious at his support for the Stamp Act which has led to widespread opposition throughout the American colonies. In Boston, an effigy of the former prime minister, George Greville, hangs from the gallows, and serious rioting is reported in New York City.

The Stamp Act was imposed by Parliament to pay for British troops in North America. Like last year's Sugar Act – which gives British planters a monopoly of the American trade and restricts imports of foreign goods into the colonies – it has been denounced by speakers at public assemblies. The phrase "No taxation without representation", coined by James Otis, the Boston politician, is a familiar cry everywhere. With the British treasury running a high deficit following the Indian and French wars in America, the Stamp Act calls for revenue to be raised by affixing stamps to such printed matter as newspapers, pamphlets, legal documents like mortgages, deeds, licences and other items such as playing cards.

Parliamentary support for the act is by no means unanimous. The former prime minister, Pitt, believes that it was a mistake and that trade with the colonies is bound to suffer.

A Tory stamp agent is strung up on a liberty pole in an anti-Stamp Act demonstration in 1765; an engraving by John Trumbull, 1795.

Parisian salons turn from wit to politics

The first lecture at Madame Geoffrin's, on Voltaire, painted by Lemonnier.

Paris, c.1764

Literary and intellectual culture, always central to fashionable Parisian life, has established itself in a new world, that of the *salon*. Writers and artists once attended the royal court, but those days are gone. The new "monarchs" of the intellectual world are smart women, and the salons, held regularly in their own homes, are the new court.

Not only artists, writers and thinkers frequent the salons. Politicians mingle with the intellectuals, and eligible visiting foreigners are often invited.

The salons began some sixty years ago. At first they celebrated wit for its own sake, but these days the gatherings are more serious. Ladies such as Mlle de Lespinasse, Mme du Tencin and Mme Necker concentrate on politics. Mme du Deffand and Mme Geoffrin the "mother of the *Encyclopedie*", play host to the *philosophes*.

Voltaire's composer friend has died

Paris, 12 September 1764

The greatest French composer of the day, Jean-Philippe Rameau, died today, shortly before his 81st birthday. Born in Dijon, Rameau worked there as well as at Avignon, Clermont and Lyons before settling in Paris in 1722.

He soon became prominent as a musical theorist and composer of keyboard music and cantatas. In 1733 his first opera, *Hippolyte et Aricie*, caused excitement and some bewilderment by its unusual expressiveness and rich orchestral sounds, and it was for the stage that Rameau wrote much of his finest music.

Rameau was a friend of many of today's intellectuals, including Voltaire, and became more interested in musical theory in his later years. He was involved in several theoretical disputes, for example with Rousseau and Diderot.

Marquis calls for an end to torture

Italy, 1764

The guiding principles of law in most European countries have been challenged in a remarkable book by the 25-year-old marquis of Beccaria. *Of Crimes and Punishment* seems destined to become a seminal work, typical of the current trend for scientific enquiry.

Beccaria owes much to predecessors like Rousseau and Montesquieu, and he revels in the pure exercise of the intellect. Applying his rational analysis to contemporary law, he argues that executions, torture and retributive punishments are barbaric and useless.

Everyone should be equal before the law, argues Beccaria, and people should not suffer for their religious beliefs.

Although Beccaria is enthusiastically received by the Paris encyclopaedists, sceptics accuse him of trickery or plagiarism.

Archaeologist puts Greek art in vogue

Pompeian Room, Packington Hall.

Rome, 1764

A German cobbler's son is bringing order into the study of the art of the ancient world with a mighty reference work which seems set to stimulate the enthusiasm for all things Greek that is sweeping Europe

Johann Joachim Winckelmann arrived in Rome in 1755 as librarian to two cardinals. He visited Naples and the sites of Herculaneum and Paestum and managed to inspect the king's private collection amassed from these sites and from Pompeii. He has now published his *History of the Art of Antiquity* which classifies Egyptian, Persian, Etruscan and Greek art and sculpture. He writes rapturously of the Greek ideal of male beauty in sculpture as "noble and serene".

A rare and exquisite Famille Rose ox-head tureen, probably late 18th-century Qianlong porcelain. The top half of the head forms a detachable cover.

India, 12 August 1765. Robert Clive receives revenue authority over Bengal from the Moghul emperor.

Austria, 18 August 1765. The Emperor Francis dies and his wife, Maria Theresa, retires from public life. Their eldest son becomes emperor as Josef II.

France, December 1765. On the death of the dauphin, his son Louis becomes heir to the throne.

St Petersburg, 1765. The Russian scholar and writer Mikhail Lomonosov dies. Known for his work in chemistry, electricity, mechanics and history, Lomonosov was instrumental in the founding of Moscow university in 1755.

South Atlantic, 1765. A British colony is established on the western of the two main islands in the Malouines (*Falkland Islands*). The first permanent settlement in the islands was created last year by the French.

Austria, 1765. When the Emperor Josef II cedes to the state the large private fortune bequeathed to him by his father, his mother, Maria Theresa, reassumes power and makes Josef co-regent.

England, 1765. James Watt refines and improves the steam engine invented by Thomas Newcomen by making the first engine with a separate condenser.

Denmark, January 1766. Christian II succeeds his father, Frederick V, as king.

France, 23 February 1766. The former king of Poland, Stanislas Leczinsky, the father-in-law of Louis XV and duke of Lorraine since 1737, dies in a fire at his palace in Luneville. His death heralds the end of Lorraine's nominal independence; the duchy now comes under French control.

Versailles, 3 March 1766. The parliament of Paris, which had pledged its support to its counterpart in Brittany, backs down at the Seance de la Flagellation, presided over by Louis XV, which repudiates the Brittany parliament.

London, 4 March 1766. Parliament repeals last year's Stamp Act, the cause of bitter and violent opposition in the colonies.

Louisiana, 5 March 1766. Antonio de Ulloa, the first Spanish governor of Louisiana, arrives in New Orleans.

Spain, June 1766. Charles III makes the count of Aranda prime minister with the task of restoring order after uprisings against his Italian advisers allegedly perpetrated by the Jesuits.

Canada, 24 July 1766. The Ottawa chief, Pontiac, signs a peace agreement with William Johnson, the superintendent of Indian affairs, at Fort Ontario, ending his three-year rebellion.

London, August 1766. Charles Townshend becomes chancellor of the exchequer in a new ministry headed by Lord Grafton and Lord Chatham (William Pitt).

New York, 19 December 1766. Thomas Gage, the commander in chief of the British forces, closes the New York Assembly, which has resolutely refused to comply with the controversial Quartering Act.

France, 1766. Louis de Bougainville embarks on a voyage to circumnavigate the world.

Philadelphia, 1766. Benjamin Franklin invents bifocal spectacles.

Philadelphia, 1766. Southwark theatre, the first building in the colonies designed expressly for the staging of drama, opens.

France, 1766. Gribeauval, a military engineer, initiates a reform of the French artillery.

Russia, 1766. Catherine II confirms the privileges of the nobility.

Germany, 1766. Frederick II sets up the Bank of Berlin.

England, 1766. The Irish writer Oliver Goldsmith publishes his novel *The Vicar of Wakefield*.

England, 1766. The architect Robert Adam builds a Neoclassical hall at Luton Hoo, near Bedford.

Germany, 1766. Gotthold Lessing publishes *Laokoon*, a work of aesthetics concerning the relationship between poetry and painting.

St Petersburg, 1766. The French sculptor Etienne Falconet is commissioned by Catherine II to produce an equestrian statue of Peter the Great for St Petersburg.

India, February 1767. Robert Clive, the British governor of the East India Company, is recalled.

Spain, 27 February 1767. The new prime minister, Aranda, expels the Jesuits from the country.

London, June 1767. Parliament passes the Townshend Acts, spearheaded by Charles Townshend, the chancellor of the exchequer, imposing new taxes on the colonies and suspending the New York Assembly until it complies with the Quartering Act.

Russia, 1767. Catherine II gathers a great commission, composed of a representative of all social classes except the serfs, with the aim of drawing up a code of reforms.

Indians riot as Jesuits are ordered home

An engraving of Spanish settlers putting natives to work in the New World.

Mexico City, 25 June 1767

It is now a year to the day since the papal order expelling the Jesuits from New Spain (*Mexico*). Several hundred are still here, waiting for ships back to Europe. Others are coming in from outlying parts, surrounded by soldiers and mostly kept away from the towns.

The Jesuits had established a moral and intellectual leadership here which was popular with both the Creole elite and the Indians. Their expulsion has led to many Indian uprisings which have been brutally put down. Ringleaders have been shot and their heads placed on pikes. Others have been whipped for days on end.

The viceroy is now trying to get the Jesuits out as quietly as possible since every time they are seen the Indians flock to their carriages and kiss their hands.

Burmese invaders destroy Thai capital

Thailand, 1767

Ayutthaya, the Thai capital, has fallen to Burmese invaders after a bitter and bloody two-year siege. Until 1752 Burma embroiled in continual civil war was no threat to its neighbours. But King Alaungpaya united the country, extending its frontiers to their former limits.

Although his 1760 invasion failed, his son's 1764 invasion has succeeded. First he took Chieng-mai; the Thai army was predictably defeated, and now his troops control the capital city.

The ruins of Ayutthaya.

Composer dies, leaving 6,000 works

Hamburg, 25 June 1767

Georg Philipp Telemann has died aged 86. Born in Magdeburg, he could play four instruments by the age of ten and went on to become a universally acclaimed composer.

He wrote over 6,000 works – five times more than Bach – which range from opera to occasional music. Much of this vast output is rather superficial, but there are also hundreds of works of substance in Telemann's fluent, elegant style. From 1721 he worked mainly as music director of the city of Hamburg. He refused a similar post at Leipzig in 1723, and the job went to the city's third choice: J S Bach.

Emperor gives Clive power in Bengal

Clive receives the "diwani" of Bengal from the Moghul empire.

Bengal, India 1765

As the Moghul empire disintegrates and the French, British and a dozen Indian princes battle for the remains, Emperor Shah Alam has granted the British East India Company the *diwani* (revenue authority) of Bengal.

In 1756 the Moghul ruler of Bengal, where the British had established factories and trading posts, died. His grandson, Siraj-ud-Daula succeeded and went to war against the British and captured Calcutta, where 123 British prisoners died, incarcerated in the "Black Hole".

The company's administrator, Robert Clive, defeated first Siraj's allies, the French, and then Siraj, replacing him with the more pliable Mir Jafar. Clive left India in 1760.

Mir Jafar was soon overthrown by his son-in-law, the ambitious, able, and thoroughly anti-British, Mir Kasim, who hated the com-

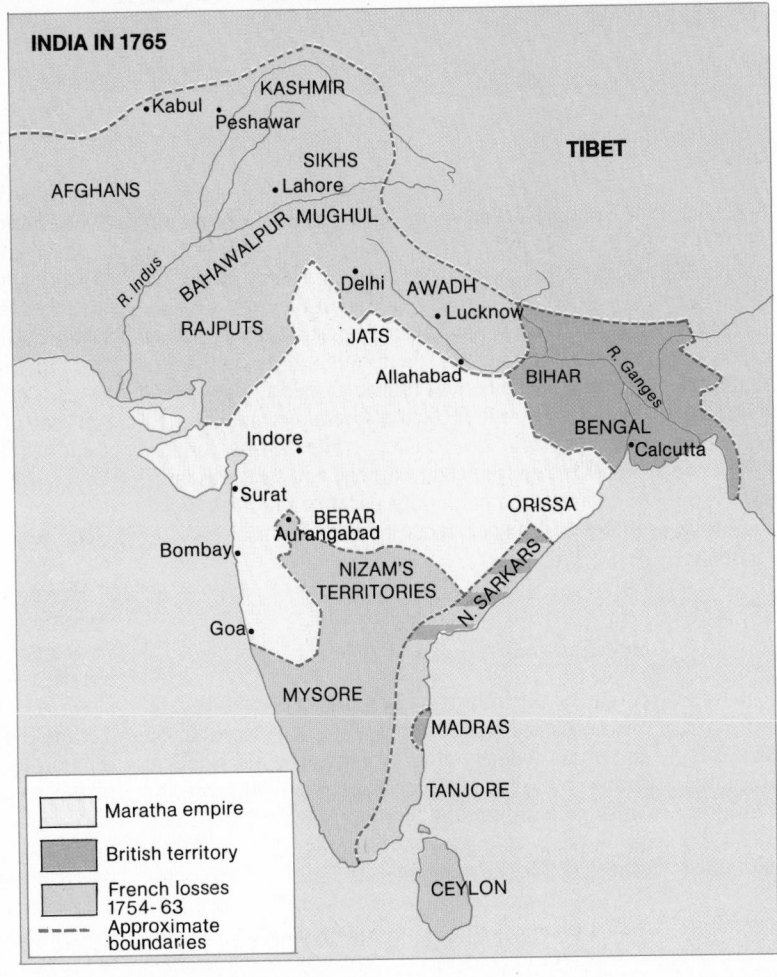

INDIA IN 1765

Kabul
KASHMIR
Peshawar
SIKHS
AFGHANS
Lahore
TIBET
R. Indus
BAHAWALPUR MUGHUL
Delhi
AWADH
RAJPUTS
Lucknow
JATS
Allahabad
BIHAR
R. Ganges
Indore
BENGAL
Calcutta
Surat
ORISSA
BERAR
Bombay
Aurangabad
N. SARKARS
NIZAM'S
TERRITORIES
Goa
MYSORE
MADRAS
TANJORE
CEYLON

Maratha empire

British territory

French losses 1754-63

- - - Approximate boundaries

pany for milking Bengal dry. War came in 1763 and Mir Kasim was beaten in five battles, the last of them at Baksar on 22 October 1764. Shah Alam, the Moghul emperor, wavered during the conflict, but with the British so victorious he came out in support of them.

In his new agreement, essentially a recognition of what is already a

fact of arms, the emperor has given to Clive and the company total authority in Bengal. The result, many fear, will be anarchy, corruption and extortion as never before.

Clive himself is extremely happy and sees no cause for alarm. Unlike so many he has yet to make his Indian fortune. The *diwani* of Bengal should change that.

Inflammable air is discovered in water

London, 1766

The English chemist Henry Cavendish has discovered what he calls "inflammable air". It is the gas that with oxygen forms water, hence the term "hydrogen" as it has been called. Cavendish has made this important discovery through meticulous experimentation and observation. He has taken dilute acids and studied their action on zinc, iron and tin. In this way he finds that he obtains his "inflammable air" – a gas that burns very readily.

Cavendish has also determined the density of this colourless, odourless and tasteless substance. He also finds that when air is decomposed into oxygen and nitrogen there is a small residue remaining and the air may contain other, inert gases, yet to be identified.

Equipment used by Cavendish.

Empress calls for a modernised Russia

St Petersburg, 1767

Greatly influenced by the liberal ideas currently spreading through western Europe, the Czarina or Empress Catherine has appointed a high-powered commission of 564 deputies to make recommendations for the modernisation of the Russian state. The commission has been furnished with a lengthy set of instructions written by Catherine herself.

The deputies represent landowners, burghers, administrators,

Cossacks and ethnic minorities (but not the church or serfs). They have been told to prepare a new code of laws, to recommend limiting landowners' powers over their serfs and to draw up a scheme for comprehensive education. Some western ideas, however, are not entirely to her taste. For instance, the English model for the division of powers into the executive, the legislature and the judiciary will be reworked and applied to make liberal despotism work more efficiently.

English in, French out, on German stage

Hamburg, 1767

A leading German drama critic, Gotthold Ephraim Lessing, has just produced a most successful comedy called *Minna von Barnhelm*. Lessing has frequently attacked the dominant influence of French classical dramatists in Germany and championed Shakespeare in their place as a model for less artificial drama. In this comedy there are real, living characters, Minna and her impossibly high-minded fiance, a Prussian officer with exaggerated

ideas of honour. She cures him of his pride by being equally standoffish and inhuman.

The Hamburgers want to make their theatre a national theatre and have entrusted Lessing with the task. His work *Hamburgische Dramaturgie* or commentaries on dramatic theory and opposition to the style of Corneille and Voltaire are increasing his reputation which began with *Laokoon*, a treatise on art and poetry, which he published last year.

The Industrial Revolution

There is no doubt that a true revolution took place in industry in the late 18th century, both in the massive increase in output of manufactured goods and in the technologies developed to keep the factory wheels turning ever more quickly.

Several theories have been put forward to explain this transformation of economic life, first in Britain and then elsewhere. One influential factor may have been the rise in population throughout the western world – generating a demand for more goods and services. Yet, although this population increase was general, industrialisation only took hold initially in Britain, France and Germany.

Capital: driving force

One key factor was the availability of large amounts of capital for investment. In Britain, the agricultural revolution begun in the early 18th century made the land much more profitable, and much of the extra profit was invested in industry. The Duke of Bridgewater (1736-1803), for example, put revenue from rents into coal mines, roads and canals.

Another source of capital was trade: merchants benefitting from links with the East and West Indies and the profitable slave trade, saw industry as a good home for their wealth. Cheap capital, rather than, as is often supposed, cheap labour, really drove the industrial investment boom.

The widespread and profound industrial changes which affected Britain, and later other countries, were characterised by the growth of large-scale manufacturing operational units, the deployment of extensive labour-saving mechanisation including the use of steam to oust animal and human muscle power, and the concentration of the workforce in and around factories. In late 18th century Britain, technological novelty and experiment became an everyday occurrence. Dr Samuel Johnson commented sarcastically that "the age is running mad after innovation".

Nowhere are these trends better exemplified than in the iron and cotton industries. Indeed it is here that Britain began to earn itself the title of "workshop of the world". In the iron industry, developments such as the puddling process of Henry Cort (1740-1800), which enabled the manufacture of wrought iron, and the Darby family's successful experiments with pig and cast iron, were rapidly converted into a steep increase in output in order to service many industrial applications for iron. Between 1740 and 1850 iron production in Britain alone rose from around 17,000 to 1.4 million tons annually.

Similarly, steel – iron with a small carbon content – became a growth industry as cheaper production processes developed by Henry Bessemer (1813-98) and others made manufacture less difficult. Railway engineers realised that steel was superior to iron for their rails, while in the expanding machine tool industry, special alloy steels were tested and perfected to enable machines to cut, drill and bore faster, while lasting longer. Another key application of iron and steel was military: armoured battleships cocooned in thick metal plates and bigger, more powerful guns.

King Cotton

The textile industry was well-established before the Industrial Revolution as Britain's second most important industry after farming. The old woollen industry was run along domestic lines with sorting, washing, carding and spinning being carried out in workers' cottages, using simple hand spinning wheels: "Every cottage had its wheel", it was said. This small-scale effort worked well because there was a plentiful supply of cottage labour.

It is easy to see why the scene was set for mechanisation and expansion in the newer cotton industry. For one thing, while various woollen workers' guilds opposed technological innovation in their own industry, there was no traditional labour force to raise similar objections in the newer cotton industry. What is more, the supply of cotton could easily be boosted quickly by sowing more fields in India and America, while lambs took time to mature.

A series of key technological advances pushed along this growth in the cotton industry. For example, James Hargreave's spinning jenny (1764) made for more rapid spinning; Richard Arkwright's water frame (1769) brought power to spinning, with machines that were too big to be housed in workers' homes, leading to factory-based mass production. John Kay's flying shuttle (1773) effectively doubled a weaver's output, and Edward Cartwright's steam power loom (1785-90), despite some initial worker opposition, increased the speed of the weaving process.

A measure of the impact of this new technology was British trade success abroad. In 1751 Britain's export of cotton goods was valued at £46,000; by 1800 this had risen to £5,400 000 and by 1861 to £46,800,000 – a thousandfold increase. This was not achieved though without setbacks and disadvantages. Much of the labour force in the "dark, satanic mills" was made up of young children, working in conditions that were injurious to their health and welfare. Mechanisation led to considerable adult unemployment, and fuelled great resentment. In Leicestershire in 1782, Ned Ludd destroyed some new machines, thus giving the opponents of change a name, *Luddites*. Between 1811 and 1818 they were responsible for a number of serious machine-breaking riots. Some Luddites were executed.

The revolution rolls on

However, once under way, the revolution extended into all areas of industry. Dyeing, for example, once a domestic occupation, was mechanised while shearing machines, introduced in the 1800s, ensured the demise of the manual cropper's trade. Technological advances helped to further coal production too, enabling mines to meet the demands of the new coke furnaces used for smelting.

As coal had been used in manufacturing and for domestic fuel since the time of Elizabeth I, many outcrops were exhausted by the 18th century. New deep shafts had to be sunk, in which gas and water would often accumulate. The introduction in 1712 of the pump invented by Thomas Newcomen (1663-1729), and of the steam pumping engines of James Watt (1736-1819) in 1776, enabled the colliery owners to maintain access to their precious seams.

Another important area of industrial expansion was pottery. Josiah Wedgwood (1730-95) not only made fine objects such as his famous Queen's Ware (1763) but also more humble items for wider consumption. The technique of slip moulding speeded up the drying process of wet clay; then came the introduction of "jigging" using a template to shape the clay. Both these methods moved the pottery industry towards mass production with cheap but attractive kitchen and tableware for the ordinary citizen. In 1750 a mechanised method of painting china using transfers came into use, thus making decorative goods widely available.

Driven by inventiveness and a desire for profit, and fuelled by the ready availability of capital, the Industrial Revolution advanced steadily, although it was not a spectacular, overnight phenomenon, and had some important social and political repercussions. Its transformation of working conditions sparked the formation of trade unions to protect the interests of the new factory-based workforce. In Britain the demands for a greater say in industry went hand in hand with calls for changes of another kind: the reform of the parliamentary system itself.

714

Cottage industry: spinning on a village green, near Colchester, c.1810.

Fiery furnace: Lymington iron works on Tyneside, by Thomas Allom, 1835.

Earth's riches: Cornishwomen break up ore at Dolcoath copper mine, c.1830.

Satanic mills: cannon foundry and boring mill at Madeley, Shropshire, 1788.

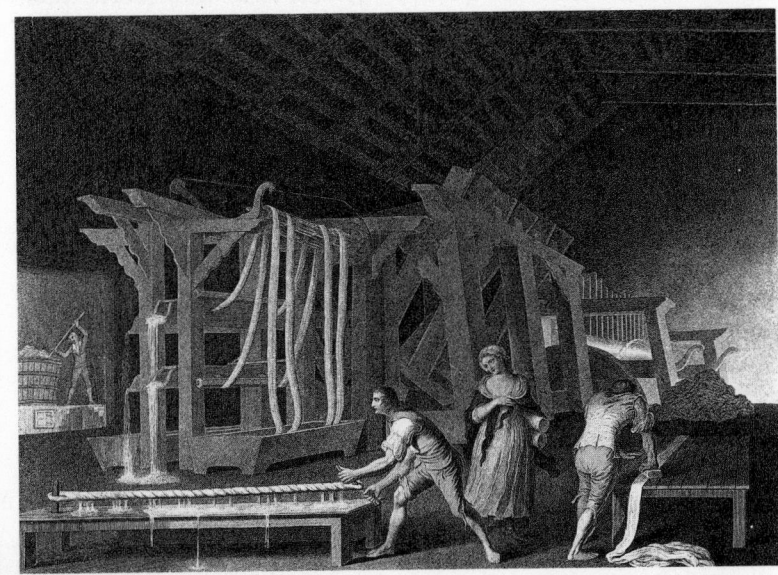

Hive of industry: bleach mill built "upon the newest..constructions", c.1780.

Arkwright's Water Frame of 1769.

Luddite in female disguise, 1812.

1767 (1767-1769)

New England, 28 October 1767. Boston leads a revival of the boycott of British goods.

Denmark, 1767. Christian VII, who was crowned king last year, extends his power over Schleswig and Holstein.

England, 1767. The chemist Joseph Priestley publishes the *History and Present State of Electricity*.

England, 1767. Laurence Sterne finishes *Tristram Shandy*, a long digressive comic novel which has been coming out in parts since 1760 and has delighted readers with its eccentricity and waywardness.

France, 1767. Georges Louis Leclerc Buffon publishes the last part of a 15-volume *Natural History*. The early volumes, which began to appear in 1749, caused a scandal by challenging certain ideas about the animal evolution.

Austria, 1767. The German musician Christoph Willibald von Gluck composes the opera *Alcestis*.

Austria, 1767. The Emperor Joseph II demands control over papal texts.

Boston, February 1768. Samuel Adams, the first American leader to deny the authority of the British Parliament over the colonies, calls for united action to oppose the Townshend Acts.

London, 10 May 1768. The imprisonment of the journalist John Wilkes as an outlaw provokes outbreaks of violence. Wilkes was recently returned to Parliament as member for Middlesex.

Corsica, 15 May 1768. By the treaty of Versailles, France purchases the island of Corsica from Genoa.

France, 16 September 1768. Rene-Nicolas de Maupeou is appointed chancellor in place of Guillaume de Lamoignon.

Boston, 1 October 1768. Lord Hillsborough, British secretary of state for the colonies, sends two regiments to Boston to quell unrest provoked by the Townshend Acts.

New Orleans, 28 October 1768. Germans and Acadians join French Creoles in an armed revolt aginst the Spanish governor, Antonio de Ulloa.

New York, 30 October 1768. Wesley Chapel, the first Methodist church in the colonies, is dedicated in New York City.

Istanbul, October 1768. Mustafa II, the Ottoman sultan, declares war on Russia, which has violated the 1711 treaty of Pruth by occupying Poland.

New York, 5 November 1768. William Johnson, the northern Indian commissioner, signs a treaty with the Iroquois Indians to acquire much of the land between the Tennessee and Ohio rivers for future settlement.

Poland, 1768. An organisation of Polish Catholic nobles, called the Confederation of Bar, is formed to oppose Russian influence and demands for religious and political equality for Protestants and Orthodox. When 20,000 Catholics and Jews are massacred in cold blood by advancing Russian armies, the rebels kill almost 200,000 people in three weeks.

Egypt, 1768. Having slaughtered the other beys two years ago, Ali Bey, leader of the Mamelukes since 1763, is proclaimed sultan.

Russia, 1768. The great commission convened by Catherine II is dismissed without having achieved any positive results.

Switzerland, 1768. The botanist Albrecht von Haller publishes the final part of his eight-volume *Physiological Elements of the Human Body*, which lays the bais for the new discipline of physiology.

Switzerland, 1768. Democratic stirrings in Geneva are embodied in a liberal edict limiting the power of the oligarchy is favour of the bourgeoisie.

Switzerland, 1768. The mathematician Leonhard Euler publishes his *Institiones calculi integralis*.

New England, 1768. The assembly of representatives in Massachusetts issues a petition in an attempt to organise a convention in Boston of all the colonies.

London, 1768. The Royal Academy of Arts is founded. The portrait painter Joshua Reynolds becomes its first president.

England, 1768. The English naval officer James Cook leaves Southampton aboard the *Endeavour* on a voyage to the Pacific.

England, 1768. Richard Arkwright perfects a spinning frame and sets up a mill in Nottingham driven by horses.

Spain, 1768. Charles III orders the distribution of common lands.

Corsica, 1769. After holding out against the French, who acquired Corsica from Genoa last year, the Corsican patriot Pasquale Paoli is overpowered and flees to England.

California, 1769. The Spanish begin to settle in California, establishing a mission at San Diego.

Canaletto dies in his beloved Venice

Venice, 20 April, 1768

The immortaliser of the architecture of Venice, the pearly light of its lagoon and the bustle of its canals is dead: Antonio Canal, known to the world as Canaletto.

He was born in Venice in 1697, near the Rialto, and began by painting scenery with his father for operas by Vivaldi. He grew up among the canals and builders' yards of backstage Venice, which he loved to paint, but it was the detailed and accurate views of the delicate architecture of St Mark's square and the Grand Canal which sold to the visiting noblemen doing the Grand Tour. An Englishman, Joseph Smith, banker, collector and English consul in the city, commissioned no fewer than 50 works for himself and many more for English visitors. In 1746 Canaletto went to England to paint the Thames and country houses, his only subjects other than his beloved Venice.

View towards St Mark's, one of Canaletto's many paintings of Venice.

Russian crackdown outrages the Poles

Poland, 1768

As many as 200,000 people have died in three weeks of bitter fighting which followed a Russian crackdown on Polish moves for greater political and religious freedom.

A tidal wave of anti-Russian anger swept Poland after the ruthless suppression of the *Seym* (parliament) by Russian grenadiers and the deportation of deputies and bishops. A group of squires had met in Bar, in the east, to proclaim a confederation of Catholic Christians to resist Orthodox Russia.

The Empress Catherine had one of her ex-lovers, Stanislaus Poniatowski, elected king while Russian troops stood by. But Stanislaus turned out to be a reformer and Prince Nikolai Repnin arrived from St Petersburg to impose Catherine's orders, followed by the Czarina's troops moved in. The latest bloodshed was sparked by a massacre of 20,000 Catholics and Jews.

Chemist publishes electrical history

Leeds, England, 1767

The British chemist Joseph Priestley, who combines scientific research with a ministry in the Presbyterian faith, has produced an important new book. *The History and Present State of Electricity, with Original Experiments* is really an extension of the author's deep interest in education. He wrote this book in order to encourage others to explore the nature of electricity.

He has for instance looked at the capacity of different substances to conduct electricity, ranging each in a table of comparative conductivity. He is the first researcher to notice the distinctive flash marks left when a spark discharges on a metal surface, or, as they are now called, "Priestley's Rings". His most remarkable discovery, however, owes something to Newton. Priestley has found that there is an inverse square law governing the force between electrical charges.

Radical Russian journal attacks serfdom

Moscow, 1769
A group of spirited young writers encouraged by Empress Catherine to launch literary journals on the model of Addison and Steele's *The Spectator* in England, seem to have got out of hand. Nikolai Novikov, who is 25, started *The Drone* and, despite his reputation as a moderate, promptly began attacking existing social conditions, including serfdom. The radical Aleksander Radishchev, a disciple of Rousseau, is writing a journal of a journey from St Petersburg to Moscow, in which he plans to attack both serfdom and autocracy. Novikov expects that his *Drone* will soon be banned.

Russian porcelain figures.

Corsican freedom fighter sent into exile

Tuscany, Italy, 1769
General Pasquale Paoli, the Corsican independence leader, and 300 of his supporters have landed in Tuscany after their crushing defeat by French forces.

The 44-year-old Paoli, who welded Corsica's warring clans into a nationalist front, is reported to be contemplating exile in England. A trained soldier and self-taught classicist, he admires the British system of government. Many of the institutions he set up during Corsica's brief independence were based on British models. For the French, who bought Corsica from the Genoese a year ago for two million livres, Paoli's choice of the traditional enemy, England, means that the threat of a nationalist revival cannot be ruled out.

English troops "show the flag" in Boston

British troops land at Boston, 1768. An engraving by Paul Revere.

Boston, 1 October, 1768
Watched by a sullen crowd, British troops landed in force here today and marched through the main street to the crash of drums and the sound of fifes. Men-of-war of the Royal Navy remained anchored offshore as the two infantry regiments – clearly determined on a show of strength – pitched their tents close to the centre of town.

Two other regiments have been ordered to Boston from Halifax by order of the secretary of state for the colonies after reports that the colony of Massachusetts, deeply resentful of the new Stamp Acts, was "teetering on the brink of anarchy". The disembarkation was made peacefully, however, and the army was greeted by Tory sympathisers and British officials who applauded General Thomas Gage, the commander of the British forces when he spoke of the "treasonable and desperate resolves" of the opposition leaders.

However, many moderate colonists view the billeting of troops on them in peacetime as a provocation.

London's greatest artists flock to join the Royal Academy

London, 10 December 1768
King George III today signed the founding document for the Royal Academy of Arts and declared himself its "patron, protector and supporter". Joshua Reynolds, who was elected its president, said: "One advantage, I venture to affirm, we shall have in our academy which no other nation can boast – we shall have nothing to unlearn."

He intends to give regular discourses on the Rules of Art to the students of the RA School, the first art school to be set up, in Somerset House. Beginning next year there will be an annual exhibition of the 50 Academicians' work. Among the founding RAs is Thomas Gainsborough, the Suffolk portrait painter, who has set up his studio in the fashionable world of Bath. Reynolds himself paints the cream of society in London at more than 100 guineas a portrait. Their rivalry is becoming acute. Reynolds has pointedly referred to Gainsborough as

Mrs Hartley, one of the greatest paintings of Sir Joshua Reynolds.

Jane, Lady Whichcote, painted by Thomas Gainsborough.

"the greatest landscape painter of the day".

Gainsborough often combines landscape with portrait painting, posing sitters against their country houses or out walking. Reynolds sticks to studio portraits in the grand manner, but excels at tender paintings of children. He wants to raise the status of painters and start a literary club with such distinguished members as Dr Johnson, Goldsmith, Boswell, Sheridan and David Garrick as members.

Outstanding atlas by Jesuits in China

China, 1769
The Jesuits, still pursuing a "flexible" attitude to their mission in China despite the disapproval of Rome, have produced an atlas of great accuracy. Called the "Qianlong Atlas" after the emperor, it is far superior to any European atlas.

From their arrival in China some 200 years ago, the Jesuits have been active in scientific work, especially astronomy and mathematics, seeing this as a way to lead the court towards Christianity.

This policy brought them into conflict with Chinese astronomers who became jealous when the Jesuits proved their calculations to be incorrect. But under the liberal patronage of the Manchu emperors Kangxi and now Qianlong, the Jesuits have prospered scientifically, even if such successes have not been accompanied by similar advances in their missionary work.

1769 (1769-1770)

North America, 20 April 1769. The Ottawa Chief Pontiac, who led a rebellion against the British from 1763 to 1766, is murdered by an Indian in Cahokia. It is rumoured that the British had him assassinated.

Rome, 17 May 1769. Giovanni Vicenzo Ganganelli is elected pope and takes the name Clement XIV. He succeeds Clement XIII, pope since 1758, who was elected through the efforts of the Jesuits but proved too weak to save them.

Virginia, May 1769. The House of Burgesses condemns the policies of London. Dissolved by the governor of Virginia, the House decides to boycott British merchandise.

Pacific, 17 June 1769. The English navigator James Cook observes the planet Venus from the island of Tahiti.

Pacific, September 1769. The Cook expedition circumnavigates New Zealand.

North Carolina, 7 November 1769. North Carolina joins South Carolina in adopting the Virginia Association's ban on trade with Britain pending the repeal of the Townshend Acts.

North America, 1769. The explorer Daniel Boone penetrates the fabled territory west of the Blue Mountains which the Iroquois Indians call Kentake (*Kentucky*).

Virginia, 1769. Thomas Jefferson, the scientist and free-thinker who was recently elected to the House of Burgesses, calls for the emancipation of slaves.

Ottoman Empire, 1769. Continuing their war against the Turks, which began last year, the Russians rout the main enemy army along the Dniester river and overrun Moldavia and Wallachia.

India, 1769. The French East India Company is dissolved.

Sweden, 1769. The "Hats" and the "Caps", the two major factions in the Stockholm government, come into conflict with King Adolphus Frederick.

North America, 1769. Virginia's boycott of British goods is joined by Maryland, South Carolina, North Carolina, Delaware and Connecticut.

France, 1769. Denis Diderot writes *D'Alembert's Dream*, a bold philosophical essay in which the author puts forward his materialist conception of the universe.

France, 1769. The French nobleman Louis Antoine de Bougainville completes a two-year voyage around the world. Seeking new lands for France, he explored Tahiti, Samoa and the New Hebrides.

London, 1769. John Wilkes – released after imprisonment as an outlaw last year – is twice re-elected as an MP, but Parliament, despite pro-Wilkes riots, declares his election void.

New York, 19 January 1770. A group of New Yorkers called the Sons of Liberty engage British troops in a pitched battle in New York city over British demands for compliance with the Quartering Act.

Britain, January 1770. Lord North, who is in favour of King George III wielding personal power, succeeds Lord Grafton as prime minister.

Boston, 5 March 1770. In what immediately becomes known as the Boston Massacre, British soldiers open fire on demonstrators, killing five.

London, 12 April 1770. Parliament repeals all the duties on the colonies imposed by Charles Townshend except the tea tax.

Pacific, 19 April 1770. The British expedition led by James Cook sights the east coast of Australia.

France, 16 May 1770. The dauphin Louis marries Marie Antoinette of Austria, the daughter of Maria Theresa.

Aegean, 6 July 1770. The entire Ottoman fleet is destroyed by the Russians at the battle of Cesme.

Ottoman Empire, August 1770. The Russians defeat a Turkish-Tartar army attempting to retake Moldavia and force it to retreat.

France, 7 December 1770. A disciplinary edict issued by Louis XV leads to the mass resignation of all members of the parliament of Paris, who are joined by certain members of the provincial parliaments.

Boston, 12 December 1770. The British soldiers responsible for the massacre in March are acquitted on murder charges.

France, 24 December 1770. Etienne Choiseul – who has controlled France's foreign policy, army and navy for over a decade since his appointment as foreign minister through the influence of Madame de Pompadour – falls from power. It is believed that his dismissal may have been caused by the hostility of Louis XV's new mistress Madame du Barry.

India, 1770. During a great famine in Bengal which began last year the population has been reduced from 29 million to 19 million.

Paris, 1770. The first public restaurant opens in Paris.

London, 1770. John Wilkes is elected lord mayor of London.

"Spinning Jenny" for the textile industry

Revolutionising the textile industry: Hargreaves' spinning jenny.

Yorkshire, England, 1769

The latest innovation in the textile industry comes from James Hargreaves who, for the past five years or so, has been working on his "spinning jenny". It consists of eight spindles – though this number will probably soon be increased to 16 and even more – all of which hold spinning yarn simultaneously. Thus, a single operator can handle far more thread than on a single spindle. Another inventor, Richard Arkwright, has just developed a water-powered loom called the water frame. Used in conjunction with Hargreaves' jenny, and other devices which are being developed, these technological innovations seem certain to transform working conditions and productivity in the textile industry.

Pragmatist North is new British premier

London, 1770

George III's new prime minister believes in letting sleeping dogs lie. An Old Etonian, Lord North is a classical scholar who did the grand tour after Oxford and speaks German, French and Italian. He has no new policies for home affairs, believing prudent housekeeping is all the country needs. Taxes will be held down because he fears that raising them would alarm the squires. In the Commons he intends to proceed with the measures that were in hand under his predecessor, the Duke of Grafton.

In foreign affairs he intends to stay out of Europe's quarrels; as to the colonies he will act with what is called quiet firmness. He is seeking a compromise with the Spanish, who have thrown the British out of the Falkland Islands. He has decided to retain the tea duty in the North American colonies and to present a Boston Ports bill.

A less than flattering cartoon of the Prime Minister, Lord North.

Russians destroy the Ottoman fleet

Mediterranean, July 1770

Military commentators are speaking of recent events in the eastern Mediterranean as a momentous turning point in the Ottoman empire's history. Two fleets of Russian warships, one commanded by a Scotsman, Admiral John Elphinstone, the other by a Russian, sailed from the Baltic down the Atlantic and into the Mediterranean, where they joined battle with the Turks off the island of Chios. In the engagement that followed, the Turkish fleet was annihilated.

On land, Russian armies have swept through the Turkish province of Moldavia and, with their capture of Bucharest, have been hailed by Christians as liberators from the Moslems.

The Turks said that they went to war because they were alarmed by Russian thrusts into Poland. But, in the wake of Russia's new successes, other great powers apart from the Turks are now wondering whether the ambitious and military-minded Empress Catherine will be content with her conquests.

Horror at German's mechanistic vision

London, 1770

Europe's religious and political establishment, including Voltaire, has been scandalised by the publication of the *System of Nature*, by the German-born writer Paul-Henri Dietrich, baron of Holbach.

The book has been published here under the pseudonym Mirabaud, because of French prejudice against the atheistic opinions of Holbach and his ally, Diderot. It is the most eloquent explanation yet of a godless, mechanistic philosophy of the world.

In *System of Nature*, Holbach argues that man is simply a physical being, organised to feel and think; that the soul is just the body considered relative to some of its functions; that morality is based on the need for reciprocal conduct to ensure social cohesion; and that evil arises simply from a mistaken vision of future happiness, which can be corrected by education.

Boucher's nude goddesses and cherubs delight French court

Spring, by Fragonard.

Autumn, by Fragonard.

Feminine voluptuousness: Diana After the Hunt, by Francois Boucher, with buxom, semi-naked women masquerading as goddesses appealing directly and unashamedly to the viewer's sensuality.

Sugary sexuality: Psyche crowning love, by Jean-Baptiste Greuze whose sentimental portrayals of young love have proved predictably popular.

Paris, 1770

French painting under Louis XV has shed many of its inhibitions. Francois Boucher, who died this year, appealed unashamedly to sensuality, filling his canvases with rosy-pink naked female forms disguised as goddesses, above all Venus – *The Birth of Venus, Venus after the Hunt, The Triumph of Venus* – invariably surrounded by cascades of fat-cheeked cherubs.

The lightness and artificiality of his charming compositions made ideal tapestries. He also made exquisite portraits of his discerning patron, the king's favourite, Madame de Pompadour.

Boucher's most brilliant pupil is Jean-Honore Fragonard, whose pictures idealise the life of pleasure

and high fashion at court, exemplified by the inviting pose of the young girls in *The Swing, The Stolen Kiss* or *The Stolen Shift* and other playfully erotic subjects, saved from giving offence by their charm.

Uninterested in today's fashionable world are France's two *genre* painters, Chardin and Greuze, both baptised Jean-Baptiste. Chardin, the master of still-life, loves to paint food, children at play and scenes of everyday life and domestic toil, giving his works a soft-edged serenity. Greuze's sweet, sugary paintings of slightly wanton-looking young girl models are highly popular.

Sublime serenity: Boy Playing Cards, painted by Chardin.

Denmark, 1770. With King Christian VII reduced to an imbecile condition by debauchery, his physician Johann Struensee – reputedly the lover of Queen Caroline Matilda – seizes power. Struensee replaces as leader Johann Bernstorff, who in 1767 negotiated with Catherine the Great of Russia a treaty whereby Denmark acquired the long-disputed lands of Holstein-Gottorp.

Greece, 1770. At the instigation of Russian agents, the inhabitants of the Peloponnese rise up against Ottoman rule. The revolt is put down by the Turks with Albanian support.

Austria, 1770. While peasant revolts rage in Bohemia, the Empress Maria Theresa publishes a new penal code.

North America, 1770. The campaign of non-importation of British goods is eased following the recent repeal of the Townshend duties.

England, 1770. The renowned portrait painter Thomas Gainsborough paints the *Blue Boy*.

England, 1770. The American-born artist Benjamin West paints *The Death of General Wolfe*, in which he defies precedent by depicting an event from recent history in contemporary costume.

South Atlantic, January 1771. Spain recognises British claims to a part of West Falkland in the Malvinas (Falkland Islands). A British colony was established on the islands in 1765, a year after the French founded the first settlement there. In 1766 Spain purchased the Malvinas from France and at first raised objections to the British colony.

Sweden, 12 February 1771. Gustavus III succeeds his father Adolphus Frederick as king.

North Carolina, May 1771. William Tryon, governor of North Carolina, puts down a group called the Regulators, who have been in rebellion against the Eastern elite in the colony since 1764.

England, July 1771. The poet Thomas Gray, author of the *Ode on a Distant Prospect of Eton College* and *Elegy in a Country Churchyard* dies. The latter was written at Stoke Poges, where his mother is buried and where he is to be buried beside her. In 1757, Gray refused the poet laureateship.

England, 17 August 1771. The Birmingham scientist Joseph Priestley discovers that oxygen is released from growing plants.

California, September 1771. Franciscans have founded three more permanent missions in California.

Scotland, 17 September 1771. The Scottish novelist Tobias Smollett dies. In 1741 he sailed as ship's surgeon on the expedition to Cartagena and described his experiences in the picaresque novel *Roderick Random*. This was followed by *Peregrine Pickle*, and *Humphrey Clinker*, which was published this year.

Crimea, 1771. Pursuing their war with the Turks, the Russians conquer the Crimea.

England, 1771. Captain James Cooke completes a voyage of exploration during which he circumnavigated New Zealand and took possession of the east coast of Australia for Britain. He returned home by way of Java and the Cape of Good Hope.

England, 1771. Richard Arkwright, the inventor of the spinning frame, opens England's first spinning factory, driven by water power, at Cromford in Derbyshire.

Scotland, 1771. A three-volume dictionary of arts and sciences edited by William Smellie and entitled the *Encyclopaedia Britannica* is published.

France, 1771. Nicolas Maupeou, who succeeded his father as chancellor of France in 1768, abolishes the parliaments and establishes new courts, incurring great unpopularity.

France, 1771. Gaspard Monge invents analytical geometry.

France, 1771. The chemist Antoine Lavoisier, a member of the French Academy, analyses the composition of the air.

Germany, 1771. Maximilian Joseph of Bavaria conducts a census of his kingdom's population.

Austria, 1771. Austria and the Turks sign a defence alliance against the Russians.

New England, 10 June 1772. Patriots led by Abraham Whipple seize and destroy the British customs boat *Gaspee* after it has run aground near Providence, Rhode Island.

England, 22 June 1772. During the case of James Somersett, a black slave – one of over 10,000 in England – who had escaped from his master, the lord chief justice Lord Mansfield declares that slavery is illegal on English soil.

Britain, July 1772. A crisis in the British banking system causes a reduction of credit in the colonies; as merchants begin selling off inventories, panic ensues.

St Petersburg, 5 August 1772. Russia, Prussia and Austria sign a treaty agreeing on the partition of Poland.

Poland stripped of a third of its lands

Poland, 5 August 1772
In a shameless act of brigandage, three East European monarchs have carved up the sovereign kingdom of Poland and seized one-third of its territory and about half its population.

Frederick II of Prussia had long coveted the wedge of territory known as West Prussia that separates Brandenburg from East Prussia. Catherine of Russia wants to see a weak Poland and to expand Russian power at the expense of Turkey. But Catherine's successes in the recent war with Turkey caused near panic in Austria.

Frederick calculated, rightly, that he could gain his ends by appealing to the greed of his fellow potentates. Catherine could take the slice of eastern Poland known as White Russia and calm Austrian fears by pulling out of the buffer territory of Danubian Turkey. The Austrians could have Silesia as a

Stanislaw Poniatowski: Poland's last king. Will there be another?

consolation prize for Frederick getting his hands on the most valuable of the spoils, economically and strategically: the maritime palatinate of West Prussia.

Radical reform of French judicial system

Paris, 23 February 1771
Chancellor Rene-Nicolas Maupeou has today introduced a radical reform of France's legal system which is being seen in many quarters, not least in the nobility, as an attack on the law itself.

The Paris parlement which is recognised as being too large, slow and costly, has been broken up with new courts established at a number of cities to hear the civil and criminal cases previously dealt with by the Paris parlement.

Paris itself is restricted to judging cases concerning the Crown and the peers of the realm. The reform also abolishes the right to buy and sell judicial posts and bans all charges on litigants. The argument now rages: is the reform an act of despotism or progress?

Japanese anatomy

Japan, 1771
Scholars have taken part in the first scientific dissection ever held in Japan. Normally such tasks are left to men of the *eta*, an unclean caste who work as butchers and tanners.

Armed with a Dutch book on anatomy, the scholars were allowed to attend the opening of the executed body of a notorious woman criminal, "Old Mother Green Tea".

They found that her organs were exactly as described in the book. One of the scholars, Sugita Gempaku, has written an account of the dissection in which he points out that the Chinese had no names for many of the body's parts. He is now translating the Dutch book.

A figure from Japanese mythology: Fudo the Immovable. Detail from bronze figure of the 18th century.

British map the Great Southern Continent

Captain Cook lands at the amazingly lush anchorage he calls Botany Bay.

Portsmouth, England, 1770
After three years' sailing round the world, HMS *Endeavour* has come home. The crew of sailors and scientists under Captain James Cook, searching for the Great Southern Continent, visited Tahiti, discovered New Zealand and mapped the east coast of Australia, the first Europeans to see it.

They reached Tahiti, via Cape Horn, in April 1769. There they found an innocent Arcadia, its people the epitome of Jean-Jacques Rousseau's *Noble Savage*. "Upon the whole," wrote Cook, "these people seem to enjoy liberty in its fullest extent." When the crew sailed off three months later, leaving behind a respect for private pro-

perty and several cases of venereal disease, the islanders begged them to stay.

From Tahiti the *Endeavour* sailed south, reaching New Zealand in September. Seven months later, on 19 April 1770, they sighted Australia. The crew's first hint of land had come three days earlier when they saw a butterfly.

Cook made his way up the eastern coast to a natural anchorage. "The country this morn rose in gentle sloping hills which had the appearance of the highest fertility, every hill seemed clothed with trees of no mean size," wrote Joseph Banks, the ship's scientist. So verdant is the coastline the crew call the anchorage Botany Bay.

Marathas install puppet emperor in Delhi

Delhi, 12 April 1771
Shah Alam, the Moghul emperor in exile under British protection in Allahabad, has been restored to the throne in Delhi. For this he must thank the Marathas and their leader, Mahadaji Sindhia, the king-maker of India.

Driven from his capital by Rohilla Afghans, Shah Alam lived for years on British promises of support, which came to nothing. Realising the British preferred a weak Moghul emperor in exile to a strong one in Delhi, he played the Marathan card, and played it well. The Marathas, who came from the

north-west quarter of the Dekhan Peninsula, are the warriors of India. Though defeated at Panipat in 1761, they have used the intervening decade to retrench. All those years they remained faithful to the emperor. When Shah Alam was threatened by revolts they crushed them. For the ruler in Allahabad they were a natural ally.

On 10 February the Marathas drove the Afghans out of Delhi and installed Shah Alam's son in temporary authority. Today, the emperor himself left Allahabad for Delhi, to the extreme discomfiture of the British.

An Indian prince entertains British officers at his house in Delhi. c.1820.

Columns of a young French genius revolutionise the art of war

France, 1771
The Count of Guibert, a military genius at the age of 28, has set out his revolutionary ideas in a book, the *Essai de Tactique* which seems destined to become the bible of officers who are pursuing new lines of military strategy.

Guibert, a fervent admirer of Frederick the Great, has produced what amounts to a formula for winning battles. He dismisses the old concept of the firing line as the main formation in battle and advocates the use of swift-moving columns.

These, he argues, will enable armies to manoeuvre freely on the battlefield instead of being tied to prepared positions. And, knowing his soldiers, he insists that their movements must be simple and

A villager is recruited into the army. Painting by Jean-Baptiste Greuze.

easily learnt. He believes such columns will inevitably defeat any troops that are formed into line and thus can only change their position slowly. He also advocates the use of

the column for its shock effect in attack. His proposals extend into all branches of warfare with new rules for cavalry, light infantry and even the baggage train.

Poor peasants' fury at ban on serfdom

Turin, 19 December 1771
Charles Emmanuel III has decided to make another attempt at abolishing serfdom in Savoy in a bid to improve the position of the rural classes and do away with feudalism. But the result is an outcry from his poorer peasants who have joined up with the nobles to oppose him.

For the second time in ten years he decreed that peasants could be released from Crown lands, and the nobles compensated through a fund raised from taxes and property sales. The idea has turned sour on Charles because the proposed changes will largely benefit the more prosperous peasants, the middle class and those who can afford to buy land.

1772 (1772-1773)

Denmark, 1772. Johann Friedrich Struensee is hung, drawn and quartered after the discovery of his affair with Caroline Matilda, the young queen. Struensee, who took power in Denmark in 1770 after obtaining the dismissal of the prime minister, Bernstorff, decreed the freedom of the Press, religious tolerance and the abolition of torture. His authoritarianism, however, won him numerous enemies.

India, 1772. The Englishman Warren Hastings, who has been a member of council in Calcutta and Madras, is appointed governor of Bengal.

England, 1772. James Cook embarks on a second voyage to the Pacific.

Scotland, 1772. The Scottish physician and botanist Daniel Rutherford establishes a distinction between "noxious air" (nitrogen) and carbon dioxide.

Russia, 1772. Catherine II abolishes the privileges of the Cossacks.

Portugal, 1772. The marquis of Pombal, the prime minister, introduces the teaching of exact sciences at the university of Coimbra. He has made important reforms in the army, agriculture and commerce.

France, 1772. *On Man* by the philosopher Claude Helvetius is published posthumously.

France, 1772. Denis Diderot publishes the *Supplement to Bougainville's Voyage*, the last section of the *Encyclopedie*.

Germany, 1772. The poet and dramatist Johann Wolfgang Goethe finishes his play *Gotz von Berlichingen*.

Germany, 1772. Christoph Martin Wieland publishes a political novel entitled *The Gilded Mirror*.

Sweden, 19 August 1772. Gustavus III, who became king of Sweden last year, destroys the rule of the parties in a bloodless military coup and re-establishes an absolute monarchy.

Mexico, 22 August 1772. The provinces of northern Mexico (including Texas) are separated from the rest of the country under a new authority as the Provincias Internas.

New England, 2 November 1772. In the face of a growing number of clashes between the English authorities and the settlers over the imposition of customs measures, radical Americans set up Committees of Correspondence.

Antarctica, 17 January 1773. Captain James Cook is the first person to cross the Antarctic Circle.

London, 10 May 1773. To keep the troubled East India Company afloat, Parliament passes the Tea Act. The Act allows the company to export tea directly to the colonies and keeps the Townshend duty of threepence a pound on tea.

London, 1 September 1773. Phillis Wheatley, a 20-year-old Negro slave from Boston, publishes a collection of poetry, *Poems on Various Subjects, Religious and Moral*, in London. The book had been rejected by American publishing houses.

Russia, September 1773. An army of Cossacks, led by Yemelyan Pugachev, besiege the towns of Orenburg and Kazan. Pugachev claims to be the deposed Czar Peter III, who was killed in the coup of 1762.

Istanbul, December 1773. Abdulhamid succeeds his father, Mustafa III, as sultan of the Ottomans.

Rumania, 1773. Attempts to end the Russo-Turkish war at the peace congress of Bucharest end in failure.

Rome, 1773. Pope Clement XIV suppresses the Jesuit order.

India, 1773. Under a Regulating Act the British Parliament attempts to control the East India Company. Warren Hastings is made governor-general with superintending authority over the presidencies of Madras and Bombay as well as Calcutta. The crown asserts the right to set up a supreme court in Calcutta.

Afghanistan, 1773. On the death of Ahmad Shah Durrani, he is succeeded by his son Timur Shah.

England, 1773. Robert Clive, suspected of embezzlement during his time in India, is acquitted on account of services rendered to the nation.

England, 1773. Work begins on the first iron bridge, at Coalbrookedale on the river Severn.

England, 1773. The brothers Robert and James Adam publish their *Works of Architecture*, the manifesto of the Neoclassical movement.

England, 1773. *She Stoops to Conquer* by Oliver Goldsmith is performed for the first time.

St Petersburg, 1773. The French writer Denis Diderot arrives in St Petersburg at the invitation of Catherine the Great.

Spain, 1773. The prime minister Pedro Aranda falls from power and is sent to France as ambassador.

Near East, 1773. Revolts in Egypt and Syria against Turkish rule are put down.

Spain pressurizes Pope to ban Jesuits

Rome, 21 July, 1773

Pope Clement XIV has issued a bull, *Dominus ac Remptor Noster*, abolishing the Society of Jesus. Clement was once a fervent admirer of the Jesuits and dedicated one of his first books to their founder. However, he has given in to the pressure from the kings of Spain and France. Vatican sources say that he sent a draft of the bull to the Spanish embassy for approval.

Their strongly argued theological views have sometimes made enemies for the Jesuits in Rome, but it is their activities overseas which have led to today's move. In China the row over the Chinese rites reflected fears that the Jesuits had gone too far in trying to secure *rapprochement* with Confucianism.

In New Spain (*Mexico*) their success brought their downfall. They had established an intellectual, moral and political leadership; they also won the admiration of

Pope Clement XIV, former admirer, now scourge of the Jesuits.

Creole leaders and the love of the Indians whose material lot they helped to better. This was all too much for the king of Spain who saw them as a threat to authority.

Four scientists all discover noxious air

Europe, 1772

A new gas, "phlogisticated" air, or "nitrogen", as it is generally called, has been "discovered" independentley by four chemists. A Scot, Daniel Rutherford, who calls it "noxious" air; a Swede, Carl Scheele; and two English chemists Joseph Priestly and Henry Cavendish. Rutherford's technique for isolating this gas is noteworthy. He obtains nitrogen by subtracting from air those components easily removed by combustion or respiration.

Island totem: this grotesque but powerful figure carved out of wood represents Ku, the war god of the Hawaiian islands.

Battle symbol: this feather image of Ku, also known as Kakailimokum is carried into battle to strike fear into the enemy.

Encyclopedia infuriates church and state

Turning the cloth for Gobelins Tapestries: illustration from Encyclopedie.

France, 1772

The *Encyclopedie*, promoter of the latest intellectual ideas, is coming under increasingly severe attacks from the Establishment here. The government resents its criticism of despotism and intolerance, the Roman Catholic church condemns its denial of organised religion.

The *Encyclopedie* has been forbidden to Catholic readers since it was placed on the Roman Index in 1759. Those who read or own it face automatic excommunication. Much of this hostility stems from the publication in 1758 of "On the Mind" by Claude-Adrien Helvetius, an enthusiastic encyclopedist. The book denied the existence of God and infuriated the authorities by stating that all men are equal. Unsurprisingly it has been banned and burnt.

ENCYCLOPÉDIE,
OU
DICTIONNAIRE RAISONNÉ
DES SCIENCES,
DES ARTS ET DES MÉTIERS,
PAR UNE SOCIÉTÉ DE GENS DE LETTRES.

Mis en ordre & publié par M. DIDEROT, de l'Académie Royale des Sciences & des Belles-Lettres de Prusse; & quant à la PARTIE MATHÉMATIQUE, par M. D'ALEMBERT, de l'Académie Royale des Sciences de Paris, de celle de Prusse, & de la Société Royale de Londres.

Tantùm series juncturaque pollet,
Tantùm de medio sumptis accedit honoris! HORAT.

TOME PREMIER.

A PARIS,
Chez BRIASSON, rue Saint Jacques, à la Science.
DAVID l'aîné, rue Saint Jacques, à la Plume d'or.
LE BRETON, Imprimeur ordinaire du Roy, rue de la Harpe.
DURAND, rue Saint Jacques, à Saint Landry, & au Griffon.

M. DCC. LI.
AVEC APPROBATION ET PRIVILÈGE DU ROY.

The Encyclopedie, of Diderot and d'Alembert. The title page.

Egyptian leader mortally wounded

Cairo, 8 May, 1773

Ali Bey, the increasingly autocratic ruler of Egypt since 1760, has died, a week after being wounded in a battle with rebels led by Abu'l-Dhahab. In a tempestuous reign, he was the first sheikh of the mamelukes, or former soldier-slaves, to challenge Ottoman authority. Installed as the premier bey in Egypt in 1760 by Abd al-Rahman Kahya, leader of the Qazdughliyya clan, Ali Bey began rapidly to eliminate opponents.

Abd al-Rahman Kahye was banished to the Hijaz, then Salih Bey exiled to Gaza. His commander Husayn Bey Kashkash deserted to Cairo, to build his own faction. Briefly isolated and banished to Syria, Ali Bey returned, reconciled with Salih Bey, to defeat his enemies. Kashkash and his ally Khalil Bey were defeated and put to death, then Salih Bey was assassinated.

Ali Bey put mamelukes in powerful posts instead of Ottomans. But when he attempted the conquest of Syria, he overreached himself, and his forces, led by Abu'l-Dhahab, rebuilt the Ottoman alliance.

East India Company gets opium monopoly

Calcutta, 1773

The British-owned East India Company has obtained a monopoly of the production and sale of opium in Bengal, where "Patna" and "Benares", the two most popular forms of opium in China, are grown.

British and Portuguese merchants have been exporting opium to China for 50 years. Until recently, however, profits were small. The East India Company used cotton as a staple to exchange for China tea, and cotton was where the profits were to be found.

Yet with ever-rising demand from the millions of customers, opium has taken over from cotton as the staple crop for export. Thousands of tons are shipped yearly to China. The Emperor of China may have banned opium, but the market remains. Shipping is left to "private traders", who run the contraband up the Canton River to Whampoa where it is distributed.

Workers in an opium den cut up balls of the drug to mix with tobacco.

American colonies defy British ruling

Boston, Mass., November 1772

Radical American colonists, infuriated by what they see as attacks on their liberties, are banding together to defy the British crown. Colonists in Massachusetts and Virginia, are forming "committees of correspondence", expressly designed to safeguard colonial rights.

The depth of feeling was made absolutely clear when a British schooner, commanded by lieutenant William Dudingstone, was burned to the waterline by American patriots after it had seized local fishing boats and their cargoes.

A furious British Government demanded that the culprits should be brought to England for trial, but the chief justice of Rhode Island, Stephen Hopkins, refused to sanction their arrest. Now the British have stated that colonial judges should be paid by the Crown and not dependent on colonial salaries.

Swedish sovereign stages coup d'etat

Stockholm, 19 August 1772

In less than an hour, Gustav III, backed by a handful of Guards officers of the Stockholm garrison, today staged a *coup d'etat* that has been hailed by cheering crowds as a blow for freedom. The king says he acted to establish himself as a constitutional monarch and to curb the extremes of Parliament.

When Gustav succeeded to the throne last year he sought to set up a government of national reconciliation between the rival parties: the self-proclaimed party of the people, the Caps – the pacifist "nightcaps" as their opponents dub them – and their opponents, the Hats, named for the tricorn hats worn by army officers. But the dominant Caps refused to co-operate, preferring to pursue extremist policies while the country's economy declined. Gustav had no option but to make his move.

1773 (1773-1775)

Boston, 16 December 1773. Patriots board three British tea ships anchored in Boston harbour, hack open all the tea chests and throw their contents into the harbour.

England, 4 April 1774. The playwright and novelist Oliver Goldsmith dies.

France, 10 May 1774. Louis XV dies and is succeeded as king by his grandson Louis XVI.

London, 20 May 1774. Parliament passes the Coercive Acts to punish the American colonists for their increasingly belligerent and anti-British behaviour. Among other things, the Acts close the port of Boston and reduce the power of the Massachusetts legislature.

London, 20 May 1774. Parliament passes the Quebec Act, enlarging the boundaries of Quebec to include French-speaking settlements (*in Ohio and Illinois*).

Ottoman Empire, June 1774. The Russians defeat the Turks in a battle near Shumla, almost wiping out the Turkish army.

London, 2 June 1774. Parliament reactivates the Quartering Act of 1765, requiring that all colonies provide housing for British troops.

France, 12 June 1774. Louis XVI ends the exile of the duke of Choiseul, a former minister of Louis XV famous for his reformist policies, which the king had condemned in 1770.

France, 20 July 1774. Louis XVI reshuffles his council, appointing the count of Maurepas minister of state and the count of Vergennes foreign secretary.

Russia, July 1774. The Cossack leader Yemelyan Pugachev captures Kazan, to which he laid siege last year.

Ottoman Empire, 16 July 1774. The Russians and the Turks sign the treaty of Kuchuk-Kainardji, ending their six-year war. Moldavia and Wallachia are returned to Turkish control and the Crimea becomes independent. Russia gains control of much of the northern Black Sea coast.

France, 13 September 1774. Turgot, the new controller of finances, urges the king to restore the free circulation of grain in the kingdom.

Russia, September 1774. The Cossack rebels led by Yemelyan Pugachev are decisively defeated by Catherine the Great's forces, ending their year-long revolt.

Philadelphia, 26 October 1774. A congress of colonial leaders criticises British influence in the colonies and affirms their right to "life, liberty and property".

Paris, 12 November 1774. Louis XIV recalls the magistrates who were exiled by Maupeou in 1771 and re-establishes parliament. Maupeou himself was dismissed as chancellor in August.

Virginia, 1 December 1774. George Washington signs the Fairfax Resolves, which bar the importation of slaves and threaten to halt all colonial exports to Britain.

New Hampshire, 14 December 1774. In the first military action by colonists against the forces of the crown, the lawyer John Sullivan and a group of militia capture Fort William and Mary and seize gunpowder and weapons.

Italy, 1774. The anatomist Anne Manzolini dies. She became professor of anatomy at the university of Bologna in 1760 and was an expert in making anatomical models from wax.

Italy, 1774. Charles III, king of the Two Sicilies, commissions Luigi Vanvitelli to build a palace at Caserta in Campania to rival that of Versailles.

Germany, 1774. Goethe's *The Sorrows of Young Werther* inspires a wave of hopeless passion among the book's admirers.

Austria, 1774. The physician Franz Mesmer uses hypnotism for therapeutic purposes. Immediately his name is perpetuated as the terms "mesmerism" and "mesmerise" are coined.

Austria, 1774. Maria Theresa grants religious tolerance to the non-Catholics of Hungary.

Austria, 1774. The composer Wolfgang Amadeus Mozart writes his *Mass in F Major*.

Paris, 1774. The German composer Gluck stages his first French opera *Iphigenia in Aulis* and the equally successful *Orpheus*.

France, 1774. The painter Jacques Louis David is awarded the Prix de Rome for his work *Artiochus et Stratonice*.

England, 1774. The German-born English astronomer William Herschel builds a great telescope.

England, 1775. Captain James Cook returns home after completing his second voyage of exploration. He circumnavigated Antarctica, discovered the South Sandwich Islands and annexed South Georgia, where he reported the presence of large herds of seals.

England, 1775. The engineer James Watt sells his first steam engine, to the industrialist John Wilkinson.

Brazil, 1775. The church of Notre Dame is constructed in Rio de Janeiro.

Cossack rebel betrayed and executed

Moscow, 21 January 1775
A disgruntled army deserter, who claimed to be the husband of the Empress Catherine and stirred up a peasant rebellion, has been captured, brought to Moscow in a cage and executed. At the start, the Cossack Emelian Pugachev had a price of 500 roubles on his head. Within weeks, as the rebels captured forts on the Volga and the Ural, and were joined by Moslem Bashkirs, the reward soared to 28,000 roubles. Pugachev was exploiting the genuine grievances of the serfs, whose conditions have worsened under Catherine. But his own Don Cossacks became disillusioned with him and handed him over to government forces.

Pugachev, the Russian Pretender, is brought to Moscow in a cage.

Chemists change old beliefs in England

Experiment with a Pump, painting by Joseph Wright (1734-97) of Derby.

England, 1775
Recent chemistry research is drastically altering many long-held beliefs. In England, Joseph Black has discovered that the air contained in some medical substances differs from that in the atmosphere. Henry Cavendish has studied "inflammable air" – hydrogen – which he adds to the two types of air or "gases" identified by Black.

But Joseph Priestley has identified and described seven individual gases: oxygen; hydrogen chloride; ammonia; nitric oxide; nitrous oxide; nitrogen peroxide and sulphur dioxide. Priestley's work gives a tremendous boost to the development of chemical investigation. Studies of oxygen, for example, show it greatly facilitates combustion.

Frenchman Henri Lavoisier's studies of water show it to be reducible to two gases. Water, then, is no longer a prime element.

These developments are accompanied by major breakthroughs in other scientific fields. Last year the German-born English astronomer William Herschel built a powerful new telescope, while this year Scottish engineer James Watt sold his first engine powered by steam to the industrialist John Wilkinson.

A tea party at Boston

Destruction of the tea cargoes in Boston harbour by colonists.

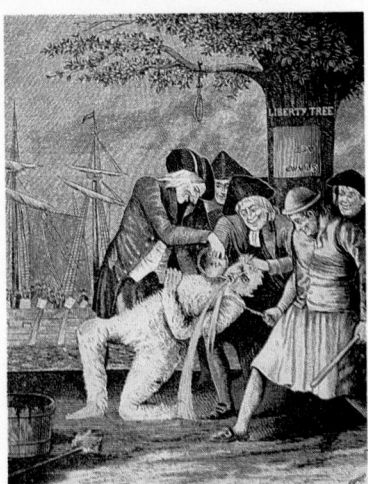

A Boston tax collector tarred and feathered. British cartoon, 1774.

Boston, Mass., 16 December 1773
Brandishing axes and whooping like Indians, their faces disguised with bronze paint, a thousand patriots ran from the Old South Meeting House here tonight and boarded three British ships loaded with tea. The crews were unharmed; but, within a matter of minutes, the *Dartmouth*, the *Eleanor* and the *Beaver* had been stripped of their cargo and hundreds of tea-chests had been emptied into the harbour.

As the sea-level fell, leaving the tea piled up on the beaches "like haystacks" – according to witnesses – no one can doubt that the tide of revolution is close at hand. As Bostonians wait for a British reaction, their leaders see this display of rebellion as the beginning of a major campaign for colonial freedom. Josiah Quincy, a patriot leader, saw it leading to "the most try-

ing and terrific struggle this country ever saw" and even the moderate John Adams clearly sees it as an epoch in history. "The people should never rise," he said, "without doing something to be remembered, something notable and striking. This destruction of the tea is so bold, so daring, so firm, intrepid and inflexible, and it must have important consequences."

As tidings of what is already becoming known as the "Boston Tea Party" spreads through the North American colonies and fast ships race to England with the news, war now seems inevitable with settlers and established colonists vowing never to pay British taxes.

The duty was imposed to capitalise on a massive "mountain" of tea which has piled up in London – threatening the East India Company with bankruptcy.

Colonists will ban tea and make war

Philadelphia, 5 September 1774
In a new act of defiance against the hated Tea Bill, delegates from all 13 colonies are meeting here today in what has already been dubbed a "continental congress" – called by the florid-faced and raucous rebel from Boston, Sam Adams. The delegates are meeting in secret, but is believed they will introduce measures to ban the consumption of tea throughout the colonies.

In several northern states, the "Sons of Liberty" are attempting to enforce an embargo of everything British. Some traders have been tarred and feathered; and others have had their homes burned. An ominous sign is the raising and training of independent companies of militiamen in every county. The colonies are preparing for war.

Turks humiliated in treaty with Russia

Ottoman empire, 16 July 1774
Russia's expansion at the expense of the Ottoman empire received a boost today when the Russians and Turks signed the treaty of Kuchuk-Kainardji, ending a six-year war between the two empires.

The treaty gives Russia lands and ports around the northern Black Sea coast, breaking the Turkish control of the sea. Russia has forced the Turks to recognise the independence of the Crimea, formerly controlled by the sultan, although he remains caliph (spiritual leader) of Crimean Moslems.

The Russians have also secured the right to build and protect an Orthodox church in Istanbul. This neatly furnishes them with a pretext for future interference in Turkish internal affairs.

Goethe inspires wave of suicides

Lotte and Werther. An illustration from Goethe's controversial novel.

Frankfurt, 1774
Every author yearns to write a book that will truly move the public but few can have achieved so frightening a success as has Johann Wolfgang Goethe, a young poet whose autobiographical novel, *The Sorrows of Young Werther*, has triggered a wave of suicides throughout Europe.

The story is simple: a sensitive artist, at odds with society, falls in love with a girl who is engaged to someone else. It ends tragically and

draws unshamedly on Goethe's own passion for Charlotte Buff, a friend's fiancee.

The mix of Werther's rejection of the pains of real life and his glorification of the mystical force of nature seems to have captured young Europe's imagination. Often the identification is harmless – teasets with scenes from the novel are highly popular, men ape Werther's blue coats and yellow breeches – but copying Werther's suicide sets a grimmer tone.

A tax of three pence a pound on her tea

There was an old lady lived over
    the sea,
And she was an Island Queen;
Her daughter lived off in a new
    country,
With an ocean of water between,
The old lady's pockets were full
    of gold,
And never contented was she,
So she called on her daughter to
    pay her a tax
Of three pence a pound on her tea
Of three pence a pound on her tea

The tea was conveyed to the
    daughter's door,
All down by the ocean's side;
And the bouncing girl poured out
    every pound
In the dark and boiling tide.
And then she called out to the
    Island Queen,
"Oh Mother, dear Mother,"
    quoth she,
"Your tea you may have when 'tis
    steeped enough,
But never a tax from me".

London, 9 February 1775. Parliament declares Massachusetts to be in a state of rebellion.

Massachusetts, 21 February 1775. As the conflict with Britain worsens, the committee of public safety votes to buy military equipment for 15,000 men.

Pennsylvania, February 1775. Thomas Paine, who arrived last year from England, at the urging of Benjamin Franklin, founds the *Pennsylvania Magazine*.

Paris, 23 February 1775. Beaumarchais' new comedy, *The Barber of Seville*, is a great success.

London, 22 March 1775. The statesman Edmund Burke makes a speech in the House of Commons urging the government to adopt a policy of reconciliation with America.

London, 13 April 1775. Lord North extends the New England Restraining Act to South Carolina, Virginia, Pennsylvania, Maryland and New Jersey. The act forbids trade with any country other than Britain and Ireland, and will be bitterly resented.

Massachusetts, 14 April 1775. General Gage gets orders to use force to implement coercive acts and halt colonial military build up.

Philadelphia, 14 April 1775. Benjamin Franklin and Dr Benjamin Rush form the Society for the Relief of Free Negroes Unlawfully Held in Bondage, the first colonial anti-slavery group.

Massachusetts, April 1775. Fighting breaks out between English and American troops – the Lexington massacre in Massachusetts is followed by more bloody outbreaks at Concord.

France, 28 April 1775. Jacques Necker, a Genevan banker, publishes a book on the grain trade and laws, attacking the finance minister Turgot's reformist policies.

North Carolina, 20 May 1775. Mecklenburg is the first colony to declare its independence.

Massachusetts, 12 June 1775. General Gage, imposing martial law, proclaims all armed colonists traitors and offers pardons to those who swear allegiance to the crown.

Massachusetts, 17 June 1775. British troops led by General William Howe defeat colonists at the battle of Bunker Hill. They take the stronghold overlooking the Charleston peninsula and Boston, but it is a costly victory.

Boston, 26 June 1775. George Washington of Virginia arrives to assume command of the continental army.

France, 21 July 1775. Malesherbes, whose remonstrances against royal abuses in 1771 led to banishment from court, but who was recalled with the accession of Louis XVI, is appointed secretary of state to the royal household.

London, 23 August 1775. King George III rejects an offer of peace, declaring that the colonies are in open rebellion against the crown.

Philadelphia, 13 October 1775. Congress bars Negroes from the continental army.

France, 27 October 1775. The count of St Germain, an ardent supporter of the enlightened Prussian king Frederick II's military strategy, is appointed secretary of state for war.

Virginia, 17 November 1775. Governor Dunmore offers freedom to slaves who join the loyalist army, thus losing the support of most planters, who see slaves as vital to their livelihood.

Massachusetts, 31 December 1775. Fearing the response to Lord Dunmore's offer to slaves, George Washington orders recruiting officers to accept free Negroes in the army.

Ethiopia, 1775. James Bruce returns to Britain from a pioneer British exploration of Ethiopia and the Blue Nile to contribute to cartography and trade intelligence of the area.

France, 1775. Bread shortages and a poor harvest, cause violent unrest to break out in the Champagne, Brie and Paris regions. This so-called "flour war" compromises finance minister Turgot's reform plans.

Austria, 1775. The Empress Maria Theresa's foreign policies ensure the Turkish surrender of the province of Bukovina, north of Transylvania. At home she issues a patent abolishing the corvee (tenants' obligation to work for landlords so many days a year) in Bohemia and the Austrian states.

Russia, 1775. Catherine II introduces major administrative reforms by which Russia is divided into 50 governments, which are then subdivided into districts. She gives assurances guaranteeing the freedom of trade and industry.

Palestine, 1775. Abul-Dhahab of Egypt invades Palestine on behalf of his Ottoman masters.

Lisbon, 1775. Lisbon's Comercio Square is opened, following the rebuilding of the Portuguese capital after the earthquake of 1755.

France, 1776. The marquis of Abbans experiments with a steam-powered boat on the river Saone.

Watt puts power of steam into industry

The steam-engine, important invention of James Watt, of Glasgow.

Birmingham, England, 1776

Steam-engine technology has made some crucial strides. The latest innovations come from James Watt, a former instrument maker in Glasgow University. When he was asked to repair a demonstration model of Thomas Newcomen's steam-pumping engine, Watt thought of ways in which this basic machine, first constructed in 1712 for use in the mines, could be improved.

One was the notion that the steam condenser could be kept separate from the cylinder, thereby lessening steam and fuel consumption.

In order to finance the development of his ideas, Watt has entered into a partnership with Matthew Boulton, owner of an engineering works at Soho near Birmingham.

From the outset, industrialists such as Cornish mine owners have been interested in using their engines for pumping purposes.

One effective innovation developed by Watt is the automatic regulator which maintains a constant speed in the engine shaft. In this way the straight-line pumping action of the piston is converted into a smooth and regular circular motion.

Spain rejigs South American policy

Peru, 1776

A new administrative system has been imposed on the viceroyalty of Peru by Spain. In an attempt to counter native independence movements in the New World, and to beat off British interests in the area, the new autonomous viceroyalty of La Plata has been created. Centred on Buenos Aires, the viceroyalty will be well equipped to protect the southern mainland. The estuary of the river Plata offers both access to the interior, and a port for ships patrolling the southern sea routes.

The new system is bound to benefit the economy and Buenos Aires, already a thriving centre, appears to be set upon a period of unprecedented prosperity.

The serene luxury of India's royalty is captured in this painting of a prince and his mistress.

War flares in America

The Battle of Bunker Hill, 17 June 1775. Painting by Charles McBarron.

Charlestown, Mass., 17 June 1775
British soldiers are in control of the key strategic hills overlooking the Charlestown peninsula and Boston, but their success has been bought at a high price. Some 1,000 British soldiers were killed in the battle for Bunker Hill – three times the casualties borne by the defeated Americans. And there is no sign that this British victory has quenched the spirit of the rebellious colonists.

It is barely three months since the first shot was fired in what has become the Americans' war for their independence from British rule. No one knows who fired that first shot. It could have been one of General Thomas Gage's British redcoats; or a "Minuteman" – a

greenjacketed American patriot. The Patriots had been warned that the British were marching by a Boston dentist and engraver, Paul Revere – a "Son of Liberty" whose society had been preparing for just such a British move for several months. A single lantern hanging in a church tower was the signal for Revere to ride the 20 miles to warn that the British were coming to seize a Patriot arsenal. The British redcoats were forced to retreat to Boston where they were then besieged. British plans to counter-attack by seizing the hills were discovered by the colonists who were waiting for the redcoats. British reinforcements eventually won the day, but the war is far from over.

Self-interest seen as the basis of wealth

London, 1776
A comprehensive analysis of the economic forces that shape society has been published by the Scottish academic Adam Smith. *An Inquiry into the Nature and Causes of the Wealth of Nations* suggests that economies are built on individual self-interest, and should not be constrained by the state.

Born in Kirkcaldy and Oxford-educated, Smith holds the chair of Moral Philosophy at Glasgow University. In 1763 he acted as tutor and companion to the Duke of Buccleuch on a continental tour. He studied European economies, and in Paris, met a group of thinkers and writers known as the Physiocrats, who see agriculture as the basis of all wealth. The *Wealth of Nations*, which has taken ten years to write, is the result.

In a work that is both learned and popular, Smith insists that peo-

Adam Smith, writer-philosopher.

ple conduct business to advance themselves. When they have the freedom to do this, the results are of general benefit. Capital gives rise to profit, which provides jobs.

Architectural revolution sweeps England

London, 1775
In their illustrated catalogue, *Works in Architecture of Robert and James Adam*, these Scottish brothers claim "to have brought about a kind of revolution in the whole system" of English architecture and decoration. In the year since it appeared it has been copied by decorators everywhere and has quite eclipsed the Palladian style.

An Adam house is conceived as a whole, its rooms of varying shapes with their plasterwork, mantelpieces, furniture, even doorknobs

and candlesticks contributing to the total effect. Externally the houses are adorned with stucco, for which the Adams hold a patent. Inside, the low-relief plasterwork is based on playful motifs such as griffins, sphinxes, swags, Grecian urns and coiled-leaf motifs on friezes and frames for mirrors and fireplaces.

The Adams style is seen at its best in London houses such as Ken Wood, Osterley Park, and Syon House. But their speculative Adelphi Terrace in the Strand nearly bankrupted them.

Scottish traveller returns from Ethiopia

Virgin and Child, painted on cloth. Eighteenth-century Coptic art from Gondar, in Ethiopia.

London, 1775
A Scottish laird, James Bruce, has arrived in London claiming to have discovered the source of the river Nile. Reaching the Ethiopian capital, Gondar, in 1769, he befriended Ras Michael, the power behind the throne, who flayed and stuffed his enemies. Bruce stayed two years, and visited Lake Tana, but travel was limited due to civil war.

"Africa is, indeed, coming into fashion," announced essayist and traveller Horace Walpole, but lexicographer Dr Samuel Johnson, whose opinion is always to be noted, thinks the man a fraud.

Carved and gilded pier glass, by Robert Adam. Osterley House, Middx.

Etruscan Room, by Robert Adam. Home House, Portman Sq, London.

1776 (1776-1777)

France, 1 March 1776. The French minister for foreign affairs, Charles Gravier, the count of Vergennes, advises his Spanish counterpart, Geronimo de Grimaldi, to support the American rebels against the English.

Boston, 26 March 1776. British troops and loyalist families evacuate Boston following the American capture of the strategic fortification of Dorchester Heights.

Denmark, April 1776. A provisional treaty of exchange is signed at Copenhagen. Russia cedes claims to Holstein.

France, 12 May 1776. Louis XVI dismisses Turgot.

New England, 7 June 1776. A vote on a resolution for independence is taken. It is carried by twelve colonies. New York is the only colony which does not vote.

Philadelphia, 4 July 1776. The American colonies declare themselves independent.

New York, 10 July 1776. Patriots and soldiers pull down a statue of George III in New York City in celebration of the declaration of independence on 4 July.

France, 19 August 1776. Louis XVI restores forced labour which was abolished by the ex-finance minister, Turgot.

Philadelphia, 9 September 1776. Congress resolves that the name of the colonies should be changed from United Colonies to United States.

Tanzania, 14 September 1776. The French make a treaty with the Kilwa sultanate to supply slaves for sugar plantations in Ile de France (*Mauritius*) and the Reunion islands.

United States, 3 October 1776. Congress borrows five million dollars to halt the rapid depreciation of paper currency, which is being printed to finance the revolution.

France, 22 October 1776. The bailiff Taboureau des Reaux becomes finance minister, in place of Turgot.

West Indies, 16 November 1776. Cannon fire on the Dutch island of St Eustatius is the first salute to the new American republic.

Paris, 31 December 1776. The American Benjamin Franklin arrives in Paris to negotiate for French aid for American rebels.

Naples, 1776. The chief minister, Bernardo Tannucci, who has been legal adviser to the crown for 20 years, is forced to retire. Tannucci reformed the brutal Neapolitan legal code and restricted the feudal privileges of the nobility.

Britain, 1776. Edward Gibbon publishes the first of what are planned to be several volumes of his *Decline and Fall of the Roman Empire*. Readers are scandalised by his treatment of Christianity as the chief cause of Rome's decline.

Senegal, 1776. The Tukulor chiefs seize power. They are led by Suleiman Bal who replaces the worship of local spirits with Islam.

Spain, 1776. Charles III appoints the reformist Floridablanca as his prime minister.

England, 1776. The explorer James Cook embarks on his third major voyage, hoping to find a north-west passage connecting the north Atlantic Ocean with the north Pacific Ocean.

London, 1776. The official royal architect, William Chambers, is commissioned to build Somerset House.

Vienna, 1776. The composer Wolfgang Amadeus Mozart composes his *Serenade in D* for the marriage of Elizabeth Haffner.

Central America, 1776. Guatemala Nueva (*New Guatemala*) is founded.

Paris, 1 January 1777. The *Journal de Paris*, the first French daily, hits the streets.

New Jersey, 3 January 1777. American troops under Washington defeat the British at Princeton.

Paris, 13 February 1777. The marquis de Sade is arrested. He was condemned to death in 1772 for various crimes, but escaped from prison before the sentence could be carried out.

Portugal, 24 February 1777. King Joseph dies and is succeeded by his daughter, Maria of Braganza. The prime minister, the marquis of Pombal, is dismissed by the queen mother, Marianna Victoria. Pombal used the power which he gained following his masterful handling of the 1755 earthquake disaster in Lisbon to reduce the tyranny of the church, expelling the Jesuits in 1759 and breaking the Inquisition.

Britain, February 1777. The Habeas Corpus Act, which says that people must be formally charged after they have been arrested, is suspended.

New England, 13 March 1777. Congress orders its European envoys to appeal to high-ranking foreign officers to send troops to reinforce the American army.

France, 29 June 1777. Following the dismissal of Taboureau des Reaux, Necker is made director general of finance.

Pamphlet hits at English king's cruelty

Philadelphia, 9 January 1776

Mad Tom, or The Man of Rights: Thomas Paine, in a 1791 cartoon.

The author of an anonymous pamphlet, *Common Sense*, which calls for complete independence of the American colonies from Britain is now known to be Thomas Paine, a former English customs officer and the editor of the *Pennsylvania Magazine*. More than 120,000 copies have been sold – although keeping the the price low to attract potential readers has left Paine in debt.

Common Sense is a powerful polemic against King George III – "the pride of tyrants" – who, says Paine, "trampled nature and conscience beneath his feet and by a steady and constitutional spirit of insolence and cruelty procured for himself an universal hatred. It is now the interest of America to provide for herself."

Paine argues that the longer the colonies wait for independence, the harder it will be to accomplish while politicians are divided.

"Let the names of Whig and Tory be extinct," writes Paine. "Let none other be heard among us, than those of a good citizen; an open and resolute friend; and a virtuous supporter of the Rights of Mankind, and of the Free and Independent States of America."

Austrian emperor abolishes torture

Vienna, Austria, 2 January 1776

A series of sweeping legal reforms including the abolition of the death penalty, torture and the crime of witchcraft was announced today by the Emperor Josef II.

The Habsburg emperor, elected last year, also announced the appointment of law reform commissions to bring in the changes and create new criminal and civil codes.

Until now Austrian law has been a mixture of Roman, Saxon and Swabian codes mixed with imperial edicts and overlaid with municipal and local laws. The Emperor Josef is keen to see changes that reflect the rationalist enlightenment spirit of the times and to abolish laws based on superstition and fanaticism. Along with witchcraft, intermarriage between Christians and non-Christians and apostasy – desertion of the faith – are to be abolished as crimes.

The emperor wants the commissions to abolish unnecessary torture such as the rack and breaking a man on the wheel, but to keep flogging, branding and the stocks. The reforms are expected to outlaw duelling and end class distinctions, with aristocrats liable to the same punishments as serfs.

French reformer ousted by aristocrats

Versailles, 12 May 1776

The struggle to set France on the road to reform received a major setback today with the dismissal of Robert Turgot as the king's comptroller-general after less than two years in office.

His removal is a major victory for the court establishment opposed to his reform package, the Six Edicts. Opposition centred on the proposed abolition of the *corvee*, the labour tax on the peasantry, and its replacement by a tax on all landowners without any exemption for the privileged classes. Also included in the package was a proposal to abolish tithes paid to the church. But Turgot's major achievements – opening up the grain trade and reducing state debt – are unlikely to be repealed.

728

American independence is declared

Philadelphia, 4 July 1776

In the words of John Adams, a delegate from Massachusetts, this was the "most memorable epoch in the history of America". He spoke as fellow delegates from 12 of the 13 colonies approved a moving document which declares these colonies independent from Great Britain. Only New York has abstained, but is expected to approve shortly.

The Declaration of Independence was drafted by a committee which included John Adams and Benjamin Franklin, and the text was written by a delegate from Virginia, Thomas Jefferson, chosen for his masterly prose style. "We hold these truths to be self-evident, that all men are created equal, that they are endowed by their creator with certain unalienable rights, that among these are life, liberty and the pursuit of happiness," it proclaims. It continues with a firm condemnation of King George III: "... the history of the present King of Great Britain is a history of repeated injuries and usurpations, all having in direct object the establishment of an absolute tyranny over these States," and goes on to outline injustices.

The declaration lists some 26 examples of British tyranny which range from the king's obstruction of justice to the cutting off of American trade with the rest of the world, the waging of war on the colonies and the quartering of armed troops on the colonial peoples. No one can

The Declaration of Independence, from the painting by John Trumbull.

doubt the power and sincerity of this document, least of all the British Parliament which has been "petitioned for redress in the most humble terms" yet "only answered by repeated injury". King George III is seen as "unfit to be the ruler of a free people".

And as the bells ring out in this town tonight and the king's statues are toppled to the ground, John Adams sums up the feeling of the people about this first day. "It ought to be solemnised with pomp and parade, with shows, games, sports, guns, bells, bonfires and illuminations, from one end of this continent to the other, from this day forward for ever more," he said.

Independence marchers: The Spirit of '76, painted by A M Willard.

Mercenary troops too drunk to fight

New Jersey, 26 December 1776

Hessian mercenary troops slept off the Christmas festivities today – unaware that an American division was preparing a "near-impossible" attack which involved the crossing by 2,400 men of the icy Delaware river in small boats in complete darkness. General George Washington, the American commander-in-chief, supervised the entire operation from the river bank. He had guessed well: the Hessian commander, Johann Rall, was sound asleep, dead drunk, when Washington's men stormed his camp and routed his men.

Rall had dismissed intelligence reports that the Americans might attack. "Let them come," he said. "We will go at them with bayonets."; but, before his men could fix their bayonets, they were overwhelmed. A hundred Hessians – including their commander – were killed and 900 taken prisoner.

"I have never seen Washington so determined as he is now," wrote one of his colonels. "The Americans are ready to suffer any hardship and die rather than give up their liberty."

For the Americans, it was a brilliant victory which may turn the entire course of the struggle. It was sweet revenge, too. Two weeks ago, General Washington was forced to retreat across the same river, pursued by Lord Cornwallis' twelve regiments.

Ruthless dictator Pombal spearheads major shake-up in Brazil

Brazil, 1777

"Energetic ... of iron will ... vindictive ... frightfully cruel": these are just some of the epithets chosen to describe the marquis of Pombal, Portugal's dictator in Brazil since 1751. Yet for all the fear and loathing he inspires, he is also an effective, respected ruler.

Backed by vigorous administrators, Pombal has revolutionised Brazilian government, crushing his opponents and ousting foreign interests, while vastly expanding the profits which Portugal takes from this wealthy colony.

Ruthlessly enforced fiscal policies have combined to reorganise public services, reform industry and agriculture, outlaw Jesuit influence and abolish slavery.

Play pits nature's storm and stress against reason's cold logic

Frankfurt am Main, 2 July 1777

Sturm und Drang (Storm and Stress) is the title of a new play by Friedrich Maximilian Klinger. Judging by its reception, when it stunned much of the first-might audience with its flouting of theatrical conventions, Klinger's title could not be more apt.

Ostensibly the tale of two Scottish families embroiled in the American War of Independence, the play celebrates the idea of "genius", setting the "storm and stress" of nature above the logic of reason.

Klinger rejects the sophistication of the Enlightenment, substituting the primitive energies of a rural culture, preferring the spontaneity of "natural man" to the artificial manners of his urban cousin.

General George Washington, the American commander-in-chief; a portrait after Charles Peale.

1777 (1777-1779)

New York, 7 July 1777. American troops give up Fort Ticonderoga, a huge complex of fortifications on Lake Champlain, to the British.

New England, 27 July 1777. The marquis of Lafayette arrives to help the rebels. He is accompanied by other European officers, including Kalb, a German in the service of the king of France.

New England, 26 September 1777. British troops launch a major offensive and capture Philadelphia.

New England, 17 October 1777. The British troops from Canada are defeated at Saratoga.

New England, 15 November 1777. Congress adopts the Articles of the Confederation, codifying the division of power between the states and the centralised government, and submits it for the approval of the States.

US, 23 December 1777. A plot to overthrow General Washington, the head of the continental army, is discovered, and the leader executed.

Germany, 30 December 1777. Maximilian III of Bavaria dies. He is succeeded by Charles Theodore, the elector Palatine.

Britain, 1777. The philanthropist John Howard publishes *The State of the Prisons in England and Wales*, calling for wholesale reform of the penal system.

France, 1777. The French chemist Antoine de Lavoisier perfects his theory of combustion.

Paris, 17 December 1777. Louis XVI recognises the independence of the American colonies and agrees to negotiate with them.

France, 6 February 1778. France signs a trade agreement with the United States by which it agrees to enter the war against Britain. The treaty is the result of lengthy negotiations led by Benjamin Franklin, who is now seen as the permanent ambassador at Versailles.

France, 30 May 1778. The writer and philosopher Voltaire dies at the age of 84.

New England, 28 June 1778. Retreating British troops are attacked from the rear at the battle of Monmouth, but the action is bungled by the American commander and only the arrival of Washington's main force prevents defeat. The British withdraw and arrive in New York by nightfall.

France, 2 July 1778. Jean-Jacques Rousseau, the Genevan political philosopher, dies insane after a sudden attack of thrombosis. Among his greatest works is the novel *Emile*, setting out his theories on education.

France, 10 July 1778. In support of the American rebels, Louis XVI declares war on England.

France, 31 July 1778. Denis Diderot dies of apoplexy. A prolific and radical writer, Diderot will be best remembered for the *Encyclopedie* which he edited, enlisting the greatest French writers to help him to transform Ephraim Chambers' original edition.

New England, August 1778. The French fleet gives up the idea of attacking New York and runs aground off Newport.

New England, 29 December 1778. The British take the American revolution southwards and capture Savannah, the capital of Georgia.

Paris, December 1778. King Louis XVI issues a loan of 80 million livres in an attempt to reduce the nation's deficit, which is being increased by France's aid to the rebels in America.

Paris, 1778. The composer Wolfgang Amadeus Mozart visits Paris and gives a performance of *Les Petits Riens*.

Britain, 1778. John Hunter, an Anglo-Scottish physician, establishes that tooth decay begins on the surface of teeth, not in the interior. He contends that decay is more likely at those sites where food particles are lodged.

South Africa, 1778. Governor von Plettenburg of the Dutch Cape Colony places a beacon on Fish river, and claims the river as the colony's eastern frontier. Dutch settlers known as Boers had been trying to set up cattle ranches in the area west of Fish river known as Suurveld (sour-grass country), already occupied by Khoisan and Xhosa cattle herders.

Italy, 1778. A new opera house, called La Scala, is inaugurated in Milan.

Bavaria, 1779. The crisis of the Bavarian succession, following the death of Maximilian II, escalates. Charles Theodore, the elector of the Palatinate, who succeeded as elector of Bavaria, ceded part of the territory to the Emperor Josef II in order to gain imperial recognition of his succession. This has angered Prussia and Saxony who have now invaded Bohemia in protest at Austrian expansion.

England, 1779. Thomas Chippendale, the well-known English cabinet-maker, dies. He is known for his use of the new wood, mahogany, in classically designed chairs, and for his much-consulted book of designs, *The Gentleman and Cabinet Maker's Directory*.

British troops defeated at Saratoga

"The Surrender of Burgoyne at Saratoga" (1817-1821) by John Trumbull.

Saratoga, 17 October 1777
Watched by its American opponents, a humiliated British army lined up in the town square here today to pile up its arms. General John Burgoyne solemnly handed his sword in surrender to a jubilant Horatio Gates, the American commander whose army had foiled constant British attempts to drive a wedge between the Patriot armies in the northern and middle states.

Gates had demanded an unconditional surrender, but agreed after negotiation to a "convention" which granted a free passage home for the British on their promise that they would not fight again on American soil.

The surrender was a gentlemanly affair. Towering over Gates, who looked up at the English general through thick pebble-lensed spectacles, Burgoyne said: "The fortune of war, General Gates, has made me your prisoner." Gates replied: "I shall always be ready to bear testimony that it has not been through any fault of your excellency."

In recent days, no less than seven British generals have been captured with 300 officers and nearly 6,000 men.

Swiss banker helps with French finances

Paris, June 1777
The wealthy Swiss banker Jacques Necker has been put in charge of the purse strings of France. King Louis XVI appointed the 45-year-old financier, whose fortune comes from speculation in East India Company shares, as his next comptroller-general on the advice of his chief courtier, Maurepas. It is felt to be time that France had a more stable financial policy; Necker will be the third finance minister in barely 18 months.

Necker, a prominent figure in French society, is a technician rather than a politician, and is unlikely to introduce any radical measures like Turgot's, although some administrative reforms are promised.

Jacques Necker, the Swiss banker who holds the French purse strings.

First iron bridge across the Severn

Shropshire, England, 1779
Work has been completed on the world's first cast-iron bridge. It has been built across the river Severn, in an industrial area of the English Midlands. The engineer responsible for the bridge is Abraham Darby, whose father and grandfather were both pioneers in the ironwork industry locally.

The new bridge has a span of almost 33 yards, and a rise of over 15 yards consisting of five huge cast-iron ribs. The weight of iron in the precisely engineered, interlocking structure is calculated as 378 tons, ten hundredweight.

Other engineers, inspired by Darby's example, are busy drawing up plans for similar projects in other parts of the country.

The iron bridge over the river Severn, at Coalbrookdale, in Shropshire.

Rebel genius was legend in own lifetime

Paris, 30 May 1778
One of the greatest Frenchmen of the century, Francois Marie Arouet, known to millions throughout Europe by his pen name "Monsieur de Voltaire", has died in Paris.

The prolific 84-year-old writer and philosopher, a legendary figure in his own lifetime, died – with an irony which he would have appreciated – as a result of his own triumph. Returning to Paris two weeks ago from self-imposed exile in Switzerland for the opening of his latest play, he was overwhelmed by the immense crowd that turned out to greet him. For two days Voltaire delightedly shook everyone's hand – a ceremony so exhausting that he never recovered from it.

Voltaire was a lifelong rebel against virtually every kind of authority, using his brilliant gifts as a writer, his enormous reputation and his wealth – earned from slave trade investments and army contracting – to wage constant war against injustice and oppression.

Dangerous, amusing and courageous, the friend of four kings, he was imprisoned twice in the Bastille and lived most of his life in exile.

Fossil studies show a new animal world

A Brazilian Red Curlew, from Buffon's "Histoire Naturelle".

France, 1778
The idea of a natural order of things, conforming neatly to biological classifications, has been challenged by Georges Buffon, the superintendent of the Paris observatory. Buffon believes that the study of fossils shows the properties and appearances of various species changing as a result of environmental conditions.

Buffon is the author of a 36-volume *Histoire Naturelle* which brings together the knowledge of astronomers, mathematicians, geologists and naturalists. In it he opposes Linnaeus' theories of classification and advocates organised study of the behaviour and reproduction of animals.

"Life and movement," writes Buffon, "instead of being a metaphysical degree of existence, are physical properties of matter." He believes observation of animals will establish the reasons for migration and other phenomena of the natural world.

Piranesi's macabre visions of Rome better than the reality

Rome, 9 November 1778
After a lifetime creating the dramatic architectural engravings of ancient Rome that are familiar throughout Europe, Giovanni Battista Piranesi has died, satisfied that his work will preserve for posterity the ruined splendours of his adopted city. Trained as an architect in Venice, he put his work into drawing buildings, not erecting them.

His first published etchings, *Carceri*, were of prisons. These vast, vaulted spaces, steeped in macabre gloom, were entirely imaginary, like so many of his architectural studies. His *Views of Rome, Ancient and Modern* seemed to show the ruins by moonlight and festoon them with sinister vegetation. Tourists, lured to Rome by his poetic visions in dramatic lighting, were often disappointed in the reality. However, his work appealed greatly to the new taste for the picturesque and romantic which is spreading fast.

The ruins of the Julia fountain, Rome; an engraving by the Venetian architect Giovanni Battista Piranesi.

America: liberty and law

Great Britain was riding high at the end of the Seven Years War in 1763. It had comprehensively defeated France in India, Canada and North America; its navy ruled the seven seas; its overseas trade and empire were booming. "Only the revolution which will occur some day in America will return England to that state of weakness in which Europe will have no more to fear of her", remarked the perceptive French minister Choiseul in 1765. As the American revolution unfolded in the years between 1763 and 1783, it was to reveal both the bankruptcy of British imperialism and the contradictions of the British constitution.

The power and prestige of Britain was underpinned by the possession of its American colonies, which were kept in economic and political subordination. Since the mid 17th century Britain had sought to regulate colonial trade in order to provide a ready market for British manufactures and, in return, a steady supply of raw materials – all to be transported in British ships. The colonies reaped many benefits, such as a monopoly market in Britain for Virginian tobacco and the protection of the Royal Navy, but there were drawbacks too, such as being at the mercy of English merchants and their prices.

Taxation without representation

However, in the 1760s, a significant shift occurred in British thinking towards the colonies: since money was short – the Seven Years War had raised the national debt from £70,000,000 to £130,000,000 and no more tax could be raised at home – the colonies were to become a source of revenue. It seemed only fair to the British that Americans should contribute to the costs of winning and keeping Canada, and of their own protection from the Indians, by paying taxes and customs dues.

The Sugar Act, Stamp Act, and the Declaratory Act, tactlessly drew attention to the colonies' political subordination. The royal proclamation of 1763, restricting the western expansion of the colonies, may have been to protect them from the Indians, but it was perceived as just one more example of British condescension towards the colonists. This patronising attitude was widespread: Benjamin Franklin noticed how "every man in England seems to consider himself as a piece of sovereign over America, and talks of *our subjects in the colonies*". But the colonies were used to running their own affairs: they often knew best what was both desirable and enforceable. Throughout the 1760s, a stream of young firebrands, like James Otis and Patrick Henry, asserted the independent claims of the colonies, claims

best summed up in the battlecry of 1765, "no taxation without representation".

British parliamentarians were not simply astonished that the colonies should take such exception to paying taxes, they were indignant at the rejection of their right to impose taxes. At bottom, the argument was about the British constitution, or rather about different interpretations of the constitution bequeathed by the Glorious Revolution which had ousted King James II in 1688. The spirit of 1688 was that government should be by consent. In Britain all men were taxed, but not one in 20 was directly represented in Parliament. There was no need, it was believed, because the whole nation and their interests were "virtually" represented in Parliament; this was fine while people were prepared to think of representation in terms of communities and interests, rather than of individuals.

Constitutional rights

Some Britons were already chafing at the unfairness of the system, and the Society of Supporters of a Bill of Rights, a pressure group for constitutional change, was formed. Progressive thinkers on both sides of the Atlantic agreed that – in the words of a young Virginian studying law in London – "the cause of America is the common cause of the realm ... both countries have the same complaint".

This complaint was the "corruption" of the constitution. The Whig tradition was deeply suspicious of the power of the crown or the executive, which would always seek to corrupt the free working of the constitution and raise up a "vile tyranny". This process seemed all too visible on both sides of the Atlantic, and to tax Americans without representation was, in the eyes of many, analogous to the sorry state of parliamentary representation in Britain. To many of the American rebels, their revolution was simply an attempt to assert the rights enshrined in the unwritten English constitution. But it also embodied a greater notion, a passion for liberty, that fugitive "hunted around the globe", whose last asylum was the free United States of America.

The course of the War of Independence did not, of course, depend upon such admirable but abstract principles. The seapower of France, especially in 1781, the generalship of George Washington, the determination of the rebels, and the lack of clear military objectives for the British did much to bring the mother country to defeat. But in a way the seven years of war were irrelevant to the fate of America. The British had already lost

the consent of those they governed there; they could not recapture the hearts and minds of the colonists by force. And the rebels were already committed to forging a new political identity for themselves.

We the people ...

This was no easy task. The 13 colonies had no common purpose beyond resisting British despotism. The Articles of Confederation had been sufficient alliance to win a war, but would it be enough to build a nation out of the colonies? It was clearly necessary for America to have some form of national government while the British, who still held the West Indies and Canada, waged an economic cold war against America, and the Spanish in Florida and Louisiana cast covetous eyes on the unoccupied territories of western America. The question of westward colonisation was pressing. However, relations between the states were far from easy, and the urgent need for a congress with real power was all too plain. Between 1787 and 1789 the new constitution agreed on at Philadelphia was ratified and the United States of America as we know it came into being. The constitution was not perfect, the conflict of interests between state and nation could never be resolved, but the independent constitutional role of the supreme court and the addition of a bill of rights – the first ten amendments – remedied many deficiencies. In the end, the American constitution was founded upon the principles of liberty and law, upon which the English constitution was also supposed to rest. In some ways America's constitution was a commentary on what the Americans believed that the English constitution should have been.

The war with the American colonies had been a great test for Britain; it had revealed her diplomatic isolation, involved her in yet another worldwide war, threatened her hold on India, and plunged her into domestic political crises. The conventions governing British political life were shaken. King George III did not retreat into the role of constitutional figurehead, as has sometimes been supposed, but there was a growing recognition of the legitimacy of organised political parties and of the part played by an opposition in the parliamentary system. And, of course, the theory of "virtual" representation had been dealt a fatal blow. The old paternalist constitution was a long time dying – "no taxation without representation" appeared on the banners of the protesters at Peterloo in 1819 – but the example of the American rebels led eventually to the parliamentary Reform Acts of the 19th century.

Thomas Paine (1737-1809).

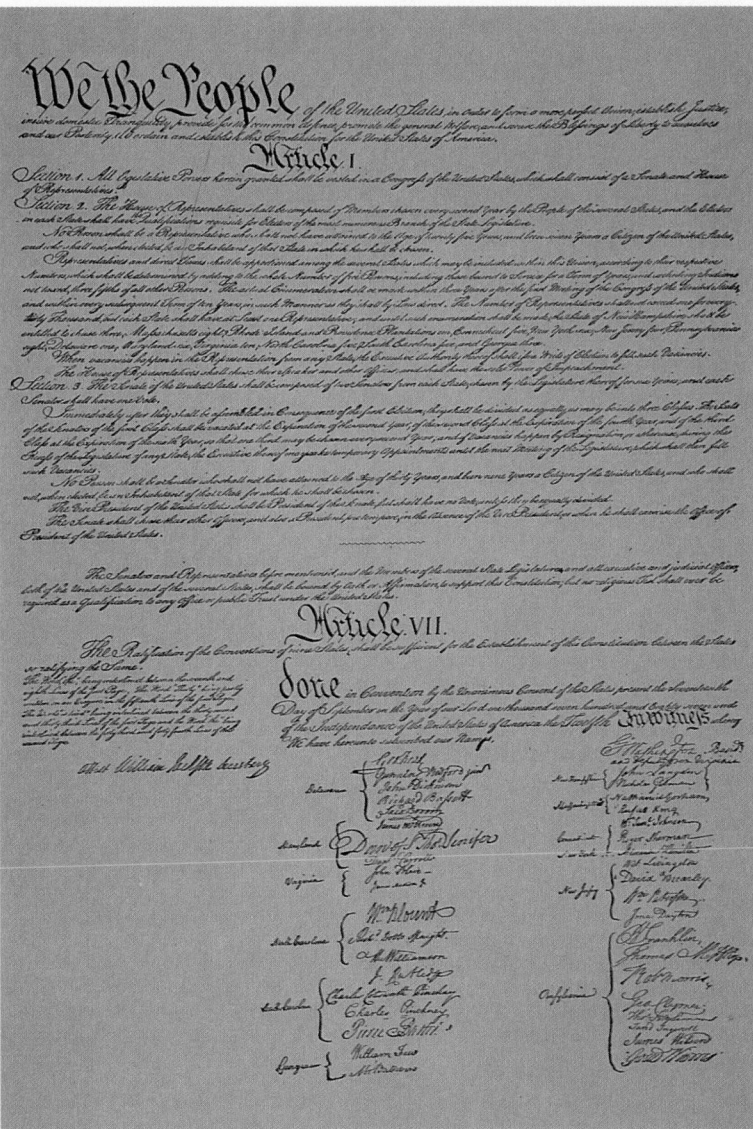

Part of the constitution of the United States, which was formulated in 1787.

George Washington (1732-99).

Thomas Jefferson (1743-1826).

Benjamin Franklin, (1706-90).

An impression of the British victory at Bunker Hill in June 1775.

As this cartoon implies, British naval prowess was not matched on land.

1779 (1779-1780)

England, 15 January 1779. The actor David Garrick dies aged 61. He retired as joint manager of the Drury Lane theatre three years ago. Since his debut as Richard III at Goodman's Fields in 1741 he has been acclaimed as the greatest actor ever. He "improved" many of Shakespeare's plays, cutting the duel in *Hamlet* to leave Laertes on the throne.

US, 25 February 1779. American troops recapture the fort at Vincennes, forcing the British to surrender.

France, February 1779. Lafayette returns from America and asks the king for more money for the revolutionaries.

Russia, 31 March 1779. Russia and Turkey sign a treaty by which they promise to take no military action in the Crimea.

Spain, 12 April 1779. By a secret treaty signed at Aranjuez, Spain is guaranteed a number of advantages if it joins with France in supporting the American rebels.

France, 27 April 1779. On the advice of Necker, the comptroller-general, a provincial assembly is created in the Dauphine to reduce the powers of the bailiffs and allow nobles to take part in regional administration.

Prussia, 13 May 1779. The treaty of Teschen, Silesia, ends the war of the Bavarian succession which started in 1778. The new king of Bavaria, Charles Theodore, placated Josef II by ceding lower Bavaria to Austria, whereupon Frederick II of Prussia invaded Bohemia, angered by the Austrian expansion. By the treaty, Austria relinquishes its claim to all but a narrow strip of Bavarian land along the Inn river, while Frederick II gives up his claim to Bohemia. The sovereignty of Charles Theodore, the elector of the Palatinate, is confirmed.

France, 10 August 1779. Louis XVI frees the last remaining serfs on royal land.

England, 23 September 1779. American privateers fighting for the cause of the American revolution capture a British warship, the *Serapis*, after a great naval battle off the English coast.

South Africa, 1779. The Orange river is traced from the southern African interior down to its mouth on the Atlantic by H J Wikar, a Swedish explorer. The Dutch settlers call the river "Orange" in honour of the ruling house of their native land, but the native Sotho people of the upper river call it *Ntshu*, meaning black, river.

Russia, 1779. A decree is issued to ensure freedom of enterprise.

England, 1779. By combining the spinning jenny and the water frame, the Lancashire weaver Samuel Crompton invents the spinning-mule. Making use of the spindle-carriage, this can produce thread suitable for making fine muslins which up to now have only been available as imports.

Netherlands, 1779. A deputation of Dutch settlers, calling themselves patriots and inspired by the American revolution, arrives in the Netherlands from Cape Town, vainly seeking representative government and a written constitution.

Paris, 1779. Christoph Willibald Gluck's new opera, *Iphigenie en Aulide*, is a great success.

Venice, 1779. The sculptor Antonio Canova produces *Daedalus and Icarus*, his first Neoclassical work.

West Africa, 1779. Britain abandons the Senegambia crown colony, withdrawing to the mouth of the Gambia river and leaving the wider Senegal area to the French.

Antilles, 1779. The British capture the island of St Lucia and force the French fleet led by Admiral d'Estaing to withdraw to Martinique.

France, January 1780. The finance minister, Necker, starts reforming the king's household in an attempt to improve the kingdom's disastrous financial situation.

Austria, 1780. The Empress Maria Theresa, who has ruled as co-regent with her son Josef II since 1765, dies. Her rule has been characterised by domestic reform, of the army, the church and the administration.

New Spain, 1780. Martial law (*estado de guerra*) is declared in New Spain (*Mexico*).

Britain, 1780. All colonial territories are placed under the secretary of state for war, and the post of secretary for colonies is abolished. This establishes a military administration pattern in place of the civilian, trade-orientated administration which existed previously.

Uganda, 1780. King Kyambugu of Buganda dies, having ruled since 1763. Under Kyambugu, Buganda has developed a strong economy based on bananas, and has strengthened its army in order to open up trade routes with the east coast through Kenya.

India, 1780. India's first newspaper, the *Bengal Gazette*, edited by James Hickey, is published.

Just and modest Persian ruler dies

Karim Khan Zand, the regent of Persia; a French engraving.

Shiraz, Persia, 1779
Karim Khan Zand, the regent of Persia and the country's undisputed ruler for 20 years, has died. Seeing himself as a representative of the people rather than the founder of a dynasty, he refused the title of "shah" (keeping the nominal shah in comfortable seclusion at Aba-deh), and called himself *wakil*, or regent.

Ignoring military adventures – making himself an exception among eastern potentates – he set a standard in justice and efficient administration unknown before his regency.

So anxious was Kharim Khan for his subjects to be happy that he paid musicians to play to them. He encouraged trade with the British, granting them a trading post at Bushire.

He made his capital in the city of Shiraz, where he built the magnificent mosque of Masjid-i Wakil.

Austrians mourn death of empress

Vienna, 29 November 1780
Maria Theresa, the Habsburg empress, archduchess of Austria and queen of Bohemia and Hungary, died today at the age of 63 after a long and tempestuous reign of 40 years.

Warm-hearted, pious and simple, the mother of 16 children by Francis of Lorraine, she was also an inspiring leader of her people in times of war. Her courage and tenacity in the war to secure her succession when she was only 23 won the hearts of her people and the admiration of the rest of Europe.

She worked on affairs of state, and especially on educational reforms, almost until the moment she died. Sitting up in a chair, she signed many documents and comforted her children who gathered round her. She refused sedatives, saying: "I wish to see death coming." All Austria mourns her passing.

Maria Theresa, empress of Austria for 40 years, in her maturity.

Louis XVI abolishes serfdom and torture

Paris, 1780
Legalised torture, known as "preliminary questioning", has been outlawed on the orders of King Louis XVI. This reform, a year after the king's decision to end serfdom – still thriving on feudal rural estates – convinces traditionalists at court that Louis must be watched. They see the king as unduly influenced by liberal thinkers such as Malesherbes, the chancellor, a censor who relaxed censorship. There are rumours that the next step will be equal rights for Protestants.

The liberals argue that the king is too timid towards opponents of liberalisation. The aristocrats, for all their rigidity, must accept the necessity for change.

Cook dies in Hawaii

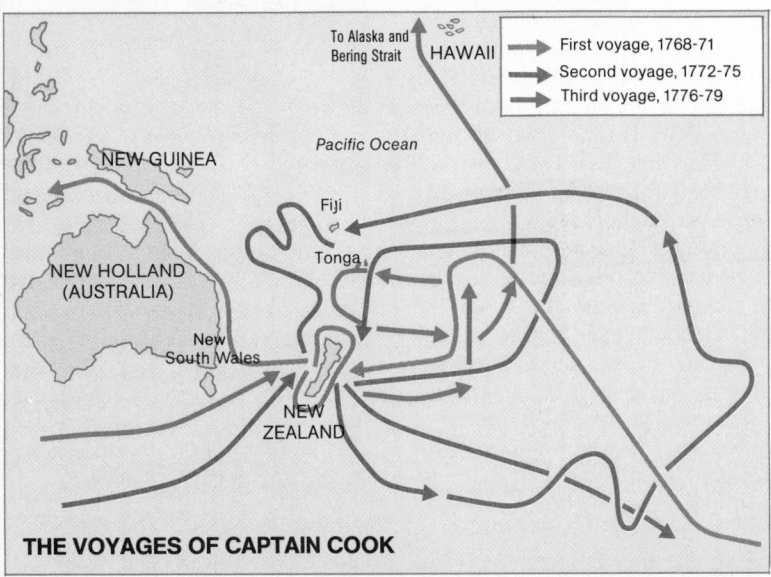

THE VOYAGES OF CAPTAIN COOK

First voyage, 1768-71
Second voyage, 1772-75
Third voyage, 1776-79

Night dance by women in Hapaee, from Hodges' "Journal of Captain Cook".

Hawaii, 14 February 1779
Captain James Cook, the bluff Yorkshire collier master who rose through the ranks in the Royal Navy and added an entire hemisphere to Europe's knowledge of the world, is dead. He has been killed in an unnecessary skirmish in Hawaii on his third great voyage of discovery in the Pacific Ocean.

On his first voyage he visited Tahiti, charted New Zealand and surveyed the eastern coast of Australia. On his second he reached Antarctica and discovered New Caledonia, and on his third he sailed to Alaska in search of the north-west passage between the Pacific and Atlantic.

Unable to find the passage, he made for Hawaii to survey and refit. The local people, who knew Cook from an earlier visit, had mixed feelings. A local chief was abused by sailors and Cook's ship's

Captain James Cook, the explorer.

cutter was stolen. Cook landed with 12 marines to take a hostage. The islanders, undeterred by firearms, which they had never experienced, attacked. Cook fell. The greatest explorer of the day lies dead.

Galvani's frogs and the body electric

Galvani's anatomical experiments; a contemporary copperplate engraving.

Rome, 1780
A strange and accidentally-produced effect has led to a fascinating theory about electricity in animal bodies. The 43-year-old Italian anatomist and physicist Luigi Galvani had laid out the spinal cord and lower limbs of a frog and was noting the responses which occurred when he applied a conductor from a static electricity machine. Galvani noticed that the frog's limbs would contract even when they were detached from the electricity machine. Indeed, they would twitch when some distance away from it.

From this Galvani suggests that an electric current passes through the frog itself when it is touched by a metal conductor. And the frog's nerves and muscles themselves seem to be charged with electricity of animal origin.

Conserve Mexico's past, urges Jesuit

Italy, 1780
A 59-year-old Jesuit priest, Clavijero, born in Mexico but exiled to Italy in 1767, has produced a major history of his country, the *Historia Antigua de Mexico*. Unlike previous historians, Clavijero has produced not simply a chronicle, but a wide-ranging study of many aspects of Mexican culture.

As a Jesuit, Clavijero is as keen to refute the beliefs of the Enlightenment as he is to chart Mexican history. As he puts it, the book's aim is "to serve my country and to restore to its true splendour the truth now obscured by the unbelievable rabble of modern writers."

In addition to religion, Clavijero is as fascinated by the physical side of Mexico as he is by its history and culture. He stresses the need for conservation, proposing a national museum and imploring his countrymen to preserve, while still possible, such remnants of Mexican architecture as have survived the Spanish conquest.

Home rule calls get louder in Ireland

Dublin, April 1780
Encouraged by mounting discontent among Protestants as well as in the Catholic majority in the country, Henry Grattan, the Irish nationalist leader, has moved a series of resolutions in the Dublin parliament calling for home rule for Ireland. The resolutions have been defeated by the dutiful backbenchers of the lord lieutenant, London's representative, but the feeling is widespread that something must be done to settle Irish affairs.

Grattan is a moderate, and loyal to the British connection, but he is in danger of being outflanked. Already, Irish magistrates are refusing to punish military deserters under the British Mutiny Act. The Irish have been greatly influenced by the defiant example of the American colonies, where many Irishmen have settled. At the same time, while they sympathise with the American rebels, Catholic and Protestant Irish are also volunteering to fight them.

1780 (1780-1781)

Russia, 28 February 1780. Czarina Catherine II appeals to European countries that are neutral in the American Revolution to unite against Britain in a league of armed neutrality. This is in protest at the fact that the British navy is attacking ships indiscriminately, whether they are involved in the conflict or not. The league threatens to declare war if this practice is not stopped.

Gibraltar, February 1780. The squadron of the British Admiral Rodney forces the Spaniards to lift their siege of Gibraltar.

France, 2 May 1780. Following Lafayette's latest departure for America, Louis XVI sends 6,000 men to New England under the command of Rochambeau to reinforce the revolutionary force.

Madrid, 11 May 1780. Negotiations begin between Spain and the American revolutionaries. France has been pressurising Spain to give support to the rebels' cause.

South Carolina, 12 May 1780. Five thousand American troops surrender Charleston to Major Benjamin Lincoln.

Russia, June 1780. Czarina Catherine II and the Emperor Josef II meet on the River Dnieper and then at St Petersburg to discuss new conquests in the Ottoman empire.

France, July 1780. The assembly of the clergy votes for a free donation of 30 million livres to help the nation's finances.

France, 24 August 1780. Louis XVI abolishes the "preliminary question", or torture, used to get suspects to confess.

France, 30 August 1780. Acting on the finance minister Necker's advice, the king announces a reorganisation of the prison system in a bid to improve conditions in jails.

India, September 1780. Under attack by the *nawab* (ruler) of Arcot – who is supported by the British – the Moslem ruler of Mysore, Haidar Ali, allies himself with the Marathas and retaliates fiercely. He launches an attack on the British coastal region of the Carnatic and the Marathas threaten Madras, where the East India Company has its headquarters. British soldiers relieve Madras and the Marathas withdraw to make a separate peace.

New England, October 1780. Considering himself unjustly treated, the American general Benedict Arnold betrays his country by giving the British the opportunity to capture West Point.

France, October 1780. Antoine de Sartine, the minister of the navy, is publicly disgraced after being accused by the finance minister, Necker, of being responsible for his ministry's vast debts of 20 million livres.

Britain, 20 November 1780. Britain declares war on Holland, one of the members of the League of Armed Neutrality. The Dutch had been supplying French and Spanish arms to the American rebels through their West Indian base.

France, 23 December 1780. The Upper Council is reshuffled as France battles with a deepening financial crisis.

New York, 1780. The Iroquois, who have occupied the valleys of the Mohawk river in central New York for generations, are devastated by American troops. In just over a month the Americans destroy their homes, barns, storehouses and cultivation. Most of the Indians flee. Washington ordered the offensive to discourage the Indians from attacking while the Americans are engaged in the war with Britain.

Mozambique, 1781. The Portuguese take the fort they call Lourenco Marques back from Austria, and resume control of Maputo Bay trade. This includes the slave trade from the southern Mozambique coast to Brazil, the French Indian Ocean islands and Arabia.

South Africa, 1781. The Suurveld war (eastern Cape frontier war) which began in 1779, ends. The war was provoked by Boer ranchers to take away land from the Khoisan and Xhosa peoples in the Suurveld area around Fish river. The conflict began with Boers shooting at Africans who scrambled for tobacco thrown on the ground before them – and it has been a success for the Boers.

Paris, 1781. The marquis of Condorcet, a brilliant mathematician and radical thinker, publishes his *Reflections on Negro Slavery*, contributing to the growing debate on the slave trade.

Austria, 1781. The Emperor Josef II publishes the Edict of Toleration for Protestants and Orthodox Christians.

England, 1781. Illiterate children in Gloucester are the first in the country to attend a Sunday school, established by the Christian educationalist Robert Raikes. They learn the catechism, and how to read and write.

India, 1781. The governor general, Warren Hastings, founds the Calcutta Madrassah, a college designed to foster Arabic studies.

Anti-Catholic rioters devastate London

London, June 1780

Almost 500 people have been killed or injured, five jails have been sacked and the prisoners let loose, and scores of houses have been burnt down in a week of anti-Catholic rioting led by the 29-year-old Lord George Gordon, MP for a pocket borough in Wiltshire and lately a fanatical Protestant.

He led a procession to parliament to protest against the repeal of anti-Catholic laws. Racing in and out of the House, one moment addressing MPs, the next haranguing the crowd, he created a frenzy of excitement. The crowd tore across London, plundering and burning. A distillery in Holborn was broken into and some rioters became so drunk that they fell into the buildings which they had fired.

At last the king and the Privy Council ordered troops to open fire.

The Gordon riots: crowds gather outside as Newgate prison burns.

Barristers from the Inns of Court joined coal-heavers and Bank of England clerks using bullets made from melted-down ink wells in suppressing the riot.

Sumo wrestling becomes public spectacle

Japan, 1780

The ancient sport of *sumo* wrestling, originally performed at shrines and temples as part of religious festivals, has become a public spectacle, with wrestlers taking part in competitions lasting for ten fine days, with rain stopping the bouts.

The wrestlers, who are paid for their performances, are easily recognised by their bulk which they use to force their opponents out of the small, circular ring. They are ranked according to their prowess and there is much ritual surrounding the short sharp bouts. The wrestlers arouse great passions among their followers, who include normally demure women as well as men. The *shogun* himself attends the bouts.

Wrestling positions, by Hokusai.

Land-hungry Boers massacre tribesmen

Cape Town, 6 June 1781

For the third time in three years, Xhosa Blacks have been massacred by Boers. The motive is land. Throughout the century Dutch *trekboers*, or frontiersmen, have expanded eastwards. Against the sedentary Khoisan they encountered little resistance, the Khoisan "selling" their land for liquor and tobacco, and being either driven off or turned into slaves. The Xhosa are more nomadic and present a more difficult problem.

The settlers have solved it by forming commandos under the dynamic Adriaan van Jaarsveld. The Dutch authorities in Cape Town are disgusted by his activities; van Jaarsveld usually asks the Blacks to leave the land before he shoots them.

100,000 African slaves a year traded for tobacco and rum

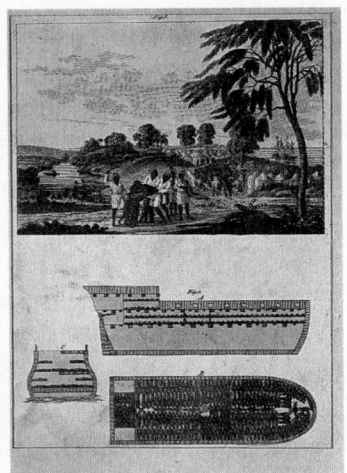

Slaves are captured and taken by ship (cross-sections).

Cruel treatment of slaves in the West Indies; an engraving by a British artist, representing a growing humanitarian backlash against slavery.

Atlantic Ocean, 1780
Among the crews of the slavers trading between Europe, Africa and the Americas, it is the infamous middle passage that is most dreaded. A ship puts in at Liverpool with a cargo of cotton, sugar or tobacco and, after loading a variety of trade goods, including textiles, hardware, spirits and trinkets, sets sail for West Africa. On the Gold Coast and the Niger delta, the African middleman waits with slaves from many sources. The ship's captain may spend up to two months bargaining with the local potentate. One king told a slaver that he found no demand for tankards, yellow beads and the like.

Once the deal has been made the shackled slaves are put on board, packed side-by-side and end-to-end like logs. Then begins the fearful journey across the Atlantic, the stench of bodies rising through the battened hatches, the cries of men, women and children making an unholy counterpoint to the creak and slap of mast and sail. At last, at Charleston or some such port in the New World, the slaves who have survived are unloaded and sold. Cotton, tobacco and other produce are loaded and the grim triangular voyage resumes. For Britain, France and other European countries it is a profitable trade. It extends from the southern states of North America, across the Caribbean and into Portuguese Brazil. Its apologists point out that the tropics are the white man's

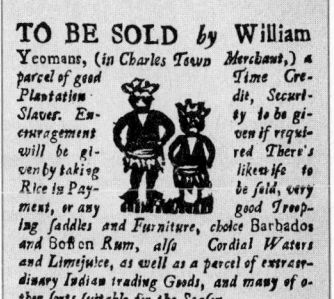

A notice of sale of slaves, from the "Charleston Gazette", 1744.

grave, the indigenous American Indian is dying from European diseases, and only the African can resist tropical diseases. Some 100,000 slaves are now shipped across the Atlantic each year, but criticism of the trade is mounting in England especially.

Marquis wins allies for colonists' cause

Philadephia, 1780
The marquis of Lafayette has returned from a brief visit to Paris where he succeeded in persuading the French government to send reinforcements of troops and ships to aid General George Washington's Patriot army. Lafayette, a 23-year-old enthusiast for the American War of Independence, came here in 1777 as a volunteer. He is a close friend of General Washington.

He fought at Brandywine, when Washington's army was outmanoeuvred by Howe's British divisions, and at Valley Forge, where the American army came close to total defeat during the worst winter in living memory. It was the plight of the troops that persuaded the aristocratic Frenchman to use his influence in Paris to aid Washington. With a French fleet threatening British reinforcements and Cornwallis' army hard pressed by General Greene's brilliant hit-and-run tactics, the advantage appears to have shifted to Washington.

New power rises to rule lands of Nile

Uganda, 1780
A new power is emerging in central Africa: Buganda. From their tiny state on the north-western edge of Lake Victoria the Baganda rose from total obscurity in the 17th century, conquering territory after territory. In the last 30 years, under their Kings Suna and Mutesa, the pace of conquest has increased. With the defeat of their main rivals, the Banyoro, and the annexation of the remnants of their Kitara empire, Buganda now dominates the lands at the source of the Nile.

One reason for their success has been the efficient centralisation of the state by King Suna, who replaced hereditary positions with royal appointments. Another is the effectiveness of the Buganda army.

Some observers, however, attribute every success to the fruitfulness of the banana, the Buganda staple diet. Baganda, they claim, have so much free time on their hands that they have little to do but go to war.

Passionate young Mozart makes a break for artistic freedom

Vienna, June 1781
Wolfgang Amadeus Mozart, the 25-year-old composer and former child prodigy, has been dismissed from the service of the prince-archbishop of Salzburg. He plans to earn his living as a freelance performer and composer in Vienna, abandoning the secure, if demeaning, world of noble patronage.

For Mozart, though, his position at Salzburg had become intolerable. From 1777 to 1779, on leave from Salzburg, he had travelled to Germany and Paris (where his mother died) in an unsuccessful attempt to

find a post suited to his huge talents. In March this year he was summoned to join his archbishop in Vienna at festivities for the new emperor, Josef II. Mozart was placed at table below the valets, and forbidden to play for the emperor.

Mozart's frustration came to a head and he asked for his discharge. He was refused, but on 9 June he saw the archbishop's chief steward and at last won his release, with, as he wrote to his father Leopold, "a kick up the backside." His Salzburg job will go to Michael Haydn, younger brother of Josef.

Wolfgang Amadeus Mozart.

1781 (1781-1782)

Paris, 19 January 1781. Continuing his major reform programme, Necker sets up the Hospital Administration.

West Indies, 3 February 1781. During the war declared by the British on the Dutch last year, the British capture the Dutch Island of St Eustatius.

Paris, 19 February 1781. Necker publishes his *Compte-rendu*, a report to the king for the year 1781. It shows the state of the kingdom's finances in detail and is a big success, even persuading the people that Necker has achieved a surplus. But financiers accuse the minister of cooking the books by leaving out arrears and the nation's special expenses.

United States, 2 March 1781. Maryland is the last state in the union to ratify the Articles of Confederation.

France, 19 May 1781. After having sought the position of minister of state in vain, Necker foresees his fall from grace and submits his resignation. His departure shakes financiers' confidence in the *Bourse* (the French stock exchange).

Russia, May 1781. An exchange of letters between Czarina Catherine II and the Emperor Josef II establishes a defensive alliance between their two countries against the Ottoman empire.

Prussia, May 1781. Prussia joins the League of Armed Neutrality formed by European countries that are not involved in the American revolution in order to protest against indiscriminate British naval attacks.

India, 1 July 1781. In the second Mysore war, Haidar Ali, the Moslem ruler of the southern Indian state of Mysore, is defeated at Porto Novo in the Carnatic by the British.

California, 4 September 1781. The Spanish name a tiny village near San Gabriel, Los Angeles.

North America, 19 October 1781. French and American allies defeat the British at Yorktown during the American War of Independence.

Austrian Netherlands, November 1781. The Emperor Josef II ends the "barrier" regime which was introduced at the time of the Treaty of Utrecht in 1713. He orders the destruction of all fortified towns in the Austrian Low Countries.

France, 1781. Jean-Jacques Rousseau's *Confessions* – a book of startling frankness – is published posthumously. Rousseau died insane in 1778. His last published works was *Lettres de la Montagne*, written in exile in Switzerland.

France, 22 October 1781. Louis Joseph, the son of Louis XVI and Marie Antoinette, is born.

London, 27 February 1782. Parliament rejects Lord North's ministry, voting to abandon further prosecution of the American war.

Ireland, March 1782. Legislative independence is granted to the Irish parliament following the plea by Henry Grattan at last month's Convention of Dungannon.

Britain, 19 March 1782. Lord Rockingham replaces Lord North, who resigned as prime minister on 11 March. William Pitt the Younger demands parliamentary reform.

Paris, 10 April 1782. Pierre Choderlos publishes *Les Liaisons Dangereuses*, which immediately causes a scandal.

West Indies, 12 April 1782. The British and the French fight a naval battle in the Saints Passage.

France, 7 May 1782. Peace negotiations are begun between France and Britain.

Vienna, 16 July 1782. Mozart's opera *Abduction from the Seraglio*, telling the tale of an escape from a Turkish harem, is performed for the first time.

Gibraltar, 13 September 1782. The British fortress in Gibraltar comes under attack by the French and Spanish, allies in the American War of Independence. Despite their new secret weapon – the floating battery – the allies are defeated and abandon ship, leaving many wounded men to burn to death in vessels pumped full of red-hot shot.

Prussia, 1782. The Academy of Berlin awards a prize to a treatise *On the Universality of the French Language* by Antoine Rivarol.

Russia, 1782. The architect Giacomo Quarenghi completes the theatre of the Hermitage at St Petersburg.

Britain, 1782. A bill introduced by the duke of Montrose repeals the 1747 act forbidding the wearing of Scottish kilts or other garments in England. The act was passed by the Hanoverian government in 1747 following the suppression of the Stuart rebellion.

India, 1782. Haidar Ali, the Moslem ruler of Mysore, dies while engaged in the second Mysore war with the British. His son Tipu Sahib takes command, but military aid promised by the French arrives too late and Mysore is defeated.

USA, 1782. Thomas Jefferson writes in his *Notes on Virginia* of the British empire: "The sun of her glory is fast descending the horizon."

Part-time astronomer spots new planet

Germany, 1782
A young German organist with a spare-time interest in mathematics and astronomy has just made an extraordinary discovery. On 13 March this year William Herschel was observing a small group of stars in the constellation of Gemini when he noticed that one of these "stars" had some peculiar features.

It has soon become apparent to astronomers that Herschel has seen a new planet in our solar system. Including Earth, there have been six known planets since ancient times. This new seventh one is the outermost planet so far – twice as far from the sun as Saturn. Now a suitable name is being sought for it. The favourite candidate is Uranus – the oldest of all the classical gods.

Herschel's telescope; an engraving.

Herschel is no novice astronomer. As an expert lens-grinder, who works with his sister Caroline, he has already built the largest telescope yet assembled.

36,000-volume anthology copied by hand

China, 1782
A mammoth book collection made up of 36,000 volumes has been completed on the orders of the Emperor Qianlong. The *Sigu Kuanshu*, or Complete Collection of the Four Treasuries of Literature, is so big that only seven hand-written copies have been made, and it is unlikely that it will be printed. There is a dark side to this huge project: its compilation was used to destroy thousands of "subversive" books and all favourable references to the Manchus have been cut out. Worse still, some authors have been executed and their families are being persecuted.

Author of hit play told to write no more

Mannheim, Germany 14 Jan 1782
A first play by a young army officer of 22, Friedrich von Schiller, had a huge success at the national theatre here last night. It is a revolutionary work.

Schiller was forced to become an army surgeon like his father by the tyrannical Duke Karl Eugen of Wurttemberg. He spent a reluctant four years at cadet school and as a surgeon in Stuttgart, writing his play which was published last year at his own expense. He attended the performance in Mannheim without leave. The duke has placed him under arrest and ordered him to write nothing but medical works in future.

The play, *Die Rauber* (The Robbers), is a fiery justification of rebellion against political tyranny in the strongest language. Schiller is one of the *Sturm und Drang* (Storm and Stress) writers, like Goethe. In

Friedrich von Schiller, the writer.

his tale of two brothers, it is the outlawed one, who leads a robber band in the forest, who turns out to be the noble idealist. Schiller plans to resign and flee to Mannheim.

Boy sailor tells of war

The battle of the Saints, 12 April 1782: a painting by Thomas Whitcombe.

Aboard HMS Goliath, 1782
A boy of 12, Midshipman Jimmy Gardner, one of several aboard British warships in action against the French during the American war, has described how he missed by inches a cannon ball that knocked the speaking trumpet out of the first lieutenant's hand. Another ball went through a fellow midshipman, pulling out his stomach, which stuck on the side of a launch. The ship's butcher tried to scrape it off, saying: "Who the devil would have thought the fellow's paunch would have stuck so?"

Another boy, aged 11, wrote to his mother after joining his shiat Spithead: "I am very happy and as comfortable as at home, and like it of all things. I have not yet gone higher than the maintop. Pray tell Patty I do not sleep in a hammock but a cot ..." This agreeable picture does not reflect the generality of life aboard ship. British crews are recruited from convicts and debtors, press-ganged or lured by bounties.

As one officer has written: "In a man-of-war, you have the collected filth of gaols. There is not a vice committed on shore, but is practised here."

British shipping technology is inferior to France's, though two recent inventions are now being copied by other countries: copper sheathing, which has reduced the fouling of ships' bottoms by weeds and barnacles, and the carronade, a short-barrelled large-calibre gun which is very effective at short range. Britain has now become the world's strongest naval power, with 174 ships of the line and 294 smaller vessels.

The Merry Ship's Crew: a cartoon satirising brutal naval discipline.

Britain loses America

American victory: the British surrender to George Washington at Yorktown.

Virginia, 19 October 1781
Charles Cornwallis, the portly British commander-in-chief, could not bring himself to watch the surrender of his army here at Yorktown today. He pleaded ill-health and sent a subordinate officer to hand his sword to the American victors. No-one doubts now that Britain must lose its 13 American colonies and that the Americans have gained their independence after five years of fighting.

As a band played a tune with the ironic – though appropriate – title of *The World Turned Upside Down*, American troops watched with quiet satisfaction as British soldiers marched out of their encampment, their bright red coats contrasting vividly with the victors' tattered clothing. Many of the British soldiers appeared to be drunk.

"Their step was irregular, and their ranks frequently broken," reported one American. "They were disorderly and unsoldierly." When ordered to surrender their weapons, many of the British soldiers started throwing their weapons on the pile with violence, as if to make them useless.

General George Washington, the American commander-in-chief, watched the surrender with his French ally the marquis of Lafayette, whose French and American troops had stormed British fortifications to find a "surprisingly weak and confused resistance". Washington, who had been planning an attack on New York, turned his army rapidly towards Yorktown when he learnt that French warships were off Chesapeake Bay, cutting off any chance of British reinforcements.

Kant says intuition comes before reason

Konigsberg, Germany, 1781
Immanuel Kant, the professor of mathematics at the university here, has produced a new book which promises to be the talk of philosophers all over Europe. He has grappled with the problem facing scientists ever since Descartes and Leibniz asserted the primacy of thinking over sensory experience.

Kant, in *Critique of Pure Reason*, suggests a synthesis between the analytical and the experimental. He suggests that theories are validated by reference to time and space, which are known only by intuition and sensory experience.

His father was a saddler and his early life was dominated by poverty and puritanism. He was destined for theology, but since joining the university in 1740 he has devoted himself to physics, mathematics and philosophy. He is only a little over five feet tall, has a deformed right shoulder and has never been further than 40 miles from here. He is widely read, however, and is a lively talker whom others travel a long way to hear.

1782 (1782-1784)

Ohio, 10 November 1782. American troops devastate the British-backed Shawnee Indians. One thousand Kentucky riflemen fire unremittingly on the Indians and destroy their food supply.

Paris, 30 November 1782. After several months of negotiations – from which the French are pointedly excluded – a preliminary peace treaty is drawn up to end the war between Britain and the United States.

Virginia, 1782. Legislation makes it legal for any man "to emancipate and set free his slaves".

Britain, 20 January 1783. Britain signs peace agreements with France and Spain, who allied against her in the American War of Independence.

London, 4 February 1783. Britain officially proclaims an end to the hostilities in America.

France, 23 February 1783. Ever deeper in financial crisis, Louis XVI creates a committee of finance. He appoints Charles Vergennes as its head.

Europe, February 1783. Spain, Sweden and Denmark recognise the independence of the United States of America.

Philadelphia, 11 April 1783. After receiving a copy of the provisional treaty on 13 March, Congress proclaims a formal end to hostilities with Britain.

Britain, April 1783. The Whig leader Charles Fox forms an alliance with Lord North, under whom he has previously refused to serve, in order to bring about the downfall of Shelburne's government. William Portland is prime minister.

Russia, 3 May 1783. Catherine II, thought of as an enlightened ruler by all of Europe, officially introduces serfdom in the Ukraine.

France, 4 June 1783. The Montgolfier brothers, Joseph Michel and Jacques Etienne, launch the first hot air balloon. Fascinated by the aeronautical ideas of a 14th-century Augustinian monk, Albert of Saxony, and the 17th-century Jesuit priest Francesco de Luna, they construct a balloon which takes off when a cauldron of paper is lit beneath it.

France, 3 September 1783. The Treaty of Paris formally ends the American Revolution. Britain recognises American independence, the Spanish regain Florida and Minorca from Britain, and France gets Senegal and Tobago. The United States are granted fishing rights off the British-Canadian coast, and they undertake to protect former loyalists.

Massachusetts, October 1783. A Negro woman is discharged from the army having served for three years under the name of Robert Shirtliffe.

Britain, 19 December 1783. Following the fall of the Fox-North alliance under Portland, which came to power in April, William Pitt the Younger becomes the youngest-ever prime minister at the age of 24.

USA, December 1783. It is estimated that up to 100,000 loyalists will have left the United States by the end of this year, following the defeat of the British. Some have returned to England, but the majority have settled in Nova Scotia and Canada, where land grants are being made available to the newly-arriving settlers.

Spain, 1783. The jurist and economist Pedro Campomans, the procurator of the Council of Castile since 1762, becomes president of the council.

Paris, 1783. Jean le Rond d'Alembert, the mathematician and philosopher, dies. With Diderot he was joint founder of the influential, but controversial, *Encyclopedie.*

New York, 1783. A 25-year-old graduate, Noah Webster, publishes *The American-Spelling Book,* the first acknowledgement that American spelling may differ from that which had been used previously by the English.

Angola, 1783. The Portuguese build a fort at Cabinda on the north side of the Congo river.

Maryland, 1783. The state prohibits the slave trade, which has now been banned in all northern US states.

Spain, 1783. The financier Francois de Cabarrus founds the San Carlos Bank.

Austria, 1783. Josef II continues the reorganisation of the church and takes action against the sects. He also makes a number of economic changes, abolishing private tolls and making the regulations for the sale of manufactured goods more flexible.

France, 1783. The chemist Antoine Laurent Lavoisier creates water from hydrogen and oxygen.

Prussia, 1783. The philosopher Immanuel Kant publishes *Prolegomena to any Future Metaphysic.*

Bohemia (*Czechoslovakia*kia), **1783.** Peasant revolts break out following land reforms.

Austria, 1783. Mozart completes his *Symphony in C Major.*

Pitt is prime minister at the age of 24

London, 19 December 1783
A young man whose health was so delicate as a child that he was educated at home has become Britain's prime minister at the age of 24. George III's appointment of William Pitt, only two years an MP, was ridiculed by the Commons as "a boyish prank". But the old politicians had discredited themselves with their intrigues and squabbles in the wake of the American war. Pitt, meanwhile, had relentlessly harried the old guard for incompetence and corruption. Why, he asked, was Lord North claiming £1,300 for stationery? Pitt intends to appeal to the country over the head of the Commons, which he says is unrepresentative.

The Bottomless Pitt; a cartoon of William Pitt the Younger, 1792.

Mob attacks the "patriots" in Holland

Holland, 1783
Sporadic riots and incitements to rebellion are commonplace in Dutch cities, as the *stadholder* (provincial governor) enlists the support of the mob against the militant "patriots" of the bourgeoisie.

An anonymous pamphlet published two years ago, entitled *To the Netherlands People,* is at the root of the present troubles. It urged people to take to the streets to protest about their grievances, to demand a free press, and to arm themselves. It was immediately banned by the government.

The pamphlet's author was Baron Joan Derk van der Capellen tot den Pol, a regent who sought to represent small traders, artisans, craftsmen, merchants and shopkeepers. Like other bourgeois agitators, he derided the government for social and moral decadence.

The "patriot regents" like van der Capellen enjoy the support of the Free Corps militia, while the stadholder relies on the mob's jealousy. Recently, mobs have attacked rich burghers and their homes, while the Free Corps has intensified policing in cities like Rotterdam.

Female black poet has died in America

Boston, Massachusetts, 1784
The Afro-American poet Phillis Wheatley, who encouraged her readers to trust in God, has died in poverty and debt. Phillis was eight when she arrived in Boston from Senegal. She was bought by the Wheatleys, a kind couple who gave her a good education.

In 1773 her book, *Poems on Various Subjects, Religious and Moral,* was published. Five years later, after a successful trip to England, Phillis' luck ran out. The Wheatleys died. She married badly, her husband went to prison, her children died and she lost touch with all her literary friends.

A posthumous study of Raja Goman Singh, ruler of Kotah in Rajasthan, who died in 1771. He is shown indulging in the sport of kings, shooting one of the lions which abound in Rajasthan.

United States of America recognised

A huge new base is planned in Crimea

Paris, 4 September 1783
Two years after the surrender of Cornwallis and his force of 7,000 soldiers at Yorktown, Virginia, the British have formally recognised the independence of 13 ex-colonies now known as the "United States of America". The new nation, which declared independence seven years ago, covers an area lying between British Canada and Spanish Florida, from the Atlantic to the Mississippi river.

This was a quarrel in which Britain had no friends except, at last, in secret diplomacy, its American "enemies". The French fleet helped to win the War of Independence from 1778 and provided a base for diplomacy to end the conflict. Spain, Holland and Russia all sided with the ragged rebels who routed a regular army. Peace talks began two years ago. The writer Benjamin Franklin – a friend of many British politicians – was prominent in the American team.

The Americans suspected that their claim to lands in the west, between the Allegheny mountains and the Mississippi river, would be blocked by French and Spanish ambitions. A separate pact was discreetly reached with London: Britain also did not wish to see Latin or French America grow. The agreement that Britain would support the States did not take immediate effect, but it strengthened the Americans' hand in relation to their allies. Yesterday's Treaty of Paris between France and Britain, confirmed the earlier arrangement between the States and Britain. The last sticking points were American debts to Britain, and assets taken from Americans loyal to England.

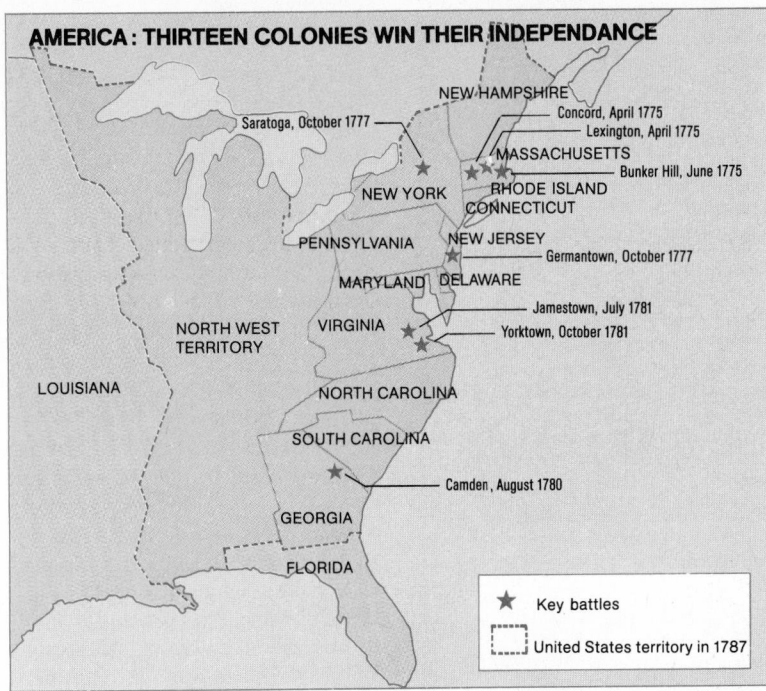

AMERICA: THIRTEEN COLONIES WIN THEIR INDEPENDENCE

Saratoga, October 1777
NEW HAMPSHIRE
Concord, April 1775
Lexington, April 1775
MASSACHUSETTS
Bunker Hill, June 1775
NEW YORK
RHODE ISLAND
CONNECTICUT
PENNSYLVANIA
NEW JERSEY
Germantown, October 1777
MARYLAND
DELAWARE
NORTH WEST TERRITORY
VIRGINIA
Jamestown, July 1781
Yorktown, October 1781
LOUISIANA
NORTH CAROLINA
SOUTH CAROLINA
Camden, August 1780
GEORGIA
FLORIDA

★ Key battles
⬚ United States territory in 1787

A Dutch cartoon displays Britain's misery in symbolic detail. Britain, in the form of a cow, stands helplessly while the American Congress chops off her horns. Holland gleefully milks her, while France and Spain wait to be fed. In the background, a British warship, rudderless and stripped of its guns, has run aground at Philadelphia while American militiamen sleep. At right, the royal British lion lies prostrate, oblivious to the monkey on its back and the Briton in mourning, praying for her rejuvenation.

Crimea, 1784
Czarina Catherine has commissioned huge new fortifications to be built in the Crimea, following her annexation of the territory. A vast base is planned, and will be named by combining the Russian forms of two words, the Latin *augustus* and the Greek *polis*: together they make the "Russified" name of Sevastopol.

The Crimea was formerly ruled by a feeble *khan*, nominally under Ottoman protection. The Czarina, who has long dreamed of a vast empire in the south, told her ex-lover and court favourite, Prince Grigori Potemkin, to settle the matter. He chose an outbreak of unrest, which he had probably instigated, as an excuse to intervene and humiliate the sultan of Turkey. A delighted Catherine has rewarded him with the gift of substantial estates in the region.

Catherine the Great, the Czarina of Russia, scourge of the Ottomans.

Army service brings freedom for slaves

Virginia, USA, 1782
Up to 10,000 negroes have won freedom from slavery in the past seven years by serving in the continental army or colonial militias. On practical as well as moral grounds, Thomas Jefferson has recently urged the state legislature to permit all slaveholders to free their slaves.

Most of the former slaves served as privates in the army or seamen in the navy. Many of them, according to Jefferson and those who favour freeing them, saw heavy combat and fought with conspicuous bravery. In the navy, they enjoyed greater freedom.

The records of one Connecticut regiment show 48 negroes adopting names befitting their new situation: names like Pomp and Jeffrey Liberty, Dick, Prinnis, Cuff, Ned and Jube Freedom.

Death for Peruvian hero and his family

Cuzco, Peru, 1783
A brief revolt against Spanish tyranny has ended with a macabre execution of the Inca leader Tupac Amaru II and his family in the main square of Cuzco. Tupac's wife and sons were tortured to death as he watched. His tongue was cut out; his limbs were pulled four ways by horses and he was then beheaded. Parts of the dismembered body were exhibited around the country. Tupac's "crime" was to insist that Spain kept laws promising protection for Indians.

Last year he appeared on a white horse to lead his rebellion. As thousands followed, he ordered the execution of a senior colonial official. He freed all slaves and abolished forced labour and taxation. As the Spanish plan the murder of all his relations, his cousin Diego has become the new rebel leader.

1784

Istanbul, 8 January 1784.
Vergennes, the French secretary of state for foreign affairs, intervenes to settle the long conflict over the Crimea between the Ottoman empire and Russia. Last year Russia took over the Crimea, claiming that it was simply restoring order. This enraged the Turks who signed a treaty with Russia in 1779 agreeing that neither side would take military action in the region. The Turks have now been persuaded to accept the inevitable.

France, 18 January 1784.
Appointed finance minister on 3 November 1783, Charles Alexandre de Calonne joins the council and is appointed minister of state.

New York, 22 February 1784.
Captain John Green sails for China on a voyage which marks the beginning of American trade with China.

India, 11 March 1784. Tipu Sahib, the sultan of Mysore and Haidar Ali's son, signs the treaty of Mangalore with the English, ending the second war of Mysore. Both parties surrender their respective conquests.

Britain, 25 March 1784. Following the rejection of William Pitt's bill on India – aimed at bringing the East India Company under government control – parliament is dissolved.

Maryland, 23 April 1784. A congressional land ordinance drafted by Thomas Jefferson names ten new states to be created from land ceded to the government by New York, Connecticut and Virginia.

Paris, 27 April 1784.
Beaumarchais' *The Marriage of Figaro* opens at the Comedie Francaise theatre. The play has been the talk of Paris for four years while the dramatist submitted it to censor after censor, repeatedly being refused permission for its performance. Louis XVI has condemned it as "unperformable" and ordered it to be banned – probably on account of its subversive morals, as it tells the tale of a handsome valet outwitting his master.

Britain, 18 May 1784. In the elections following the dissolving of parliament in March, Pitt is returned with an increased majority.

France, 20 May 1784. The peace of Versailles between England and Holland ends the hostilities that erupted when Britain discovered that the Dutch were supplying arms to American rebels. Holland cedes Negapatam on the south-east coast of India.

Paris, May 1784. After the performance of *The Marriage of Figaro*, Beaumarchais is the object of violent attacks and is incarcerated in Saint Lazare prison. However, he is released because of popular pressure after five days.

England, 13 August 1784. Pitt's India Act, which was passed soon after his re-election in May, becomes law. This effectively puts the East India Company under government control and amends the Regulating Act of 1773. This was intended to impose government control by making the post of governor general subject to a government-appointed council, but it proved unworkable, not least because of the independent behaviour of Warren Hastings the governor general, who is now being recalled to England.

Philadelphia, 21 September 1784. *Packet and Daily*, the first daily publication in America, appears on the streets.

Austrian Netherlands, 18 October 1784. The unilateral decision by the Emperor Josef II to reopen the river Escaut to traffic causes disagreement between Austria and Britain.

England, 13 December 1784. The lexicographer, poet and critic Samuel Johnson dies aged 75. He spent many years writing hack work for London's literary magazines to fend off encroaching poverty; but from 1762, a crown pension of £ 300 a year enabled him to take his place in high society and give free reign to his versatile genius. His remarkable dictionary, which took him eight years to compile, will probably be long remembered.

Paris, December 1784. Jacques Necker violently criticises the financial management and performance of his successor, Charles Calonne, in a treatise entitled *De L'Administration des Finances de la France*.

Austria, 1784. Josef II alters the ecclesiastical structure of his states and orders the destruction of theological works.

USA, 1784. Ethan Allen publishes publishes *Reason, the Only Oracle of Man* – believed to be the first anti-Christian book published in America.

Alaska, 1784. The Russians found their first colony in North America, on the island of Kodiak, in the Gulf of Alaska. Up to now the island has been inhabited only by a large number of bears and a small group of Eskimos – American observers are still puzzling over possible motives for the Russian settlement.

Vienna dominates Europe's musical scene

Chamber music is often played at private salons; 18th-cent. painting.

Vienna, 1784
In recent years Vienna has become widely regarded as the musical capital of Europe. The grand old man of Viennese music is Christoph Willibald Gluck, now 70, renowned throughout Europe as the man who reformed opera. In his operas, which include *Orfeo und Euridice* (1762), the Bohemian-born composer strove to make the music more relevant to the drama.

Gluck is now more or less retired, and Austria's senior active composer is Franz Joseph Haydn, aged 52, music director to Prince Esterhazy. Haydn has brought to the symphony and string quartet a range of inventiveness that has made him famous as far away as France, Spain and England.

A good friend of Haydn's, but 34 years his junior, is Wolfgang Amadeus Mozart. Mozart has become renowned for his piano playing,

Joseph Haydn, the composer, painted by Christian Ludwig Seehas.

usually in his own concertos. He is also writing string quartets, and is planning more operas following the success of *Die Entfuhrung aus dem Serail* two years ago.

Austrian ruler grants freedom of worship

Vienna, 1784
Freedom of worship is to be allowed in the Holy Roman empire as part of as wide-ranging shake-up of religious laws by the Emperor Josef II. His latest edict promoting religious tolerance grants freedom of conscience and worship to both the Protestant and Eastern Orthodox Churches. Civil marriage, divorce and freemasonry are to be recognised. Jews will no longer be barred from the university.

The Roman Catholic Church remains the official church, but now comes under state control with bishops expected to swear an oath of loyalty to the emperor. He will also be responsible for determining new religious laws, ceremonial procedures, and diocesan and parish boundaries. Priests will not be allowed to publish papal bulls without his consent. Monasteries which are not devoted to education, the care of children or the sick are to be closed. All pilgrimages and processions are banned.

The moves are part of a flood of reforms introduced by the emperor when he became sole ruler four years ago after his mother's death.

Treaty leaves Britain ruling the waves

London, 20 May 1784
The Royal Navy's victory over the French at the battle of the Saints two years ago gave Britain command of the sea, but was too late to save the American colonies. It has, however, enabled the British to gain advantages elsewhere.

When the Dutch made the hostile gesture of proclaiming armed neutrality during the American war, the British seized practically the whole of the Dutch merchant marine. In the peace treaty with the Dutch, signed today, Britain has annexed Negapatam, near Madras, and forced the Dutch to concede freedom of navigation in the Dutch East Indies.

These gains give Britain security of communications with India and beyond to Canton in China – vital to Britain's trade and prosperity in Asia. But some in Britain already have their eyes on the Dutch base in Ceylon.

Mesmer's magnetism falls out of favour

Salon and clients of Franz Mesmer, the doctor and alternative therapist.

Paris, 1784
The methods of Franz Mesmer, the German doctor who has become a favourite with fashionable society here, have been condemned by a committee of the Academy of Sciences. Mesmer works around a tub containing magnetised rods in fluid. The clients hold hands and the doctor presides dressed in lilac silk and waving an iron wand.

Such theatricality did not impress the committee, which included the American ambassador, Benjamin Franklin, no mean scientist himself. Members said that the animal magnetism, which Mesmer believes is the healing force, had no effect on them or other subjects.

They said that the convulsions experienced by his patients were produced by the imagination. Mesmer made his name in Vienna by curing a friend of Mozart's of blindness, but was forced to leave in 1778

Magic touch or animal magnetism? A caricature of Doctor Mesmer.

by rumours spread by rivals. The committee has now demolished his theory, but ex-patients still claim that the tub therapy made them feel much better.

Money problems rob puddler of payment

The iron forge at Broadlands, Hampshire; by Joseph Wright of Derby.

Britain, 1784
Henry Cort, a British inventor and industrialist, and creator of what he calls "puddling", a revolutionary new process for manufacturing quality cast iron, has lost his patents to this most valuable discovery. Beset by financial problems Cort has become unable to keep the process to himself. Now every ironmaster will be able to experiment with Cort's discovery.

Cort's loss is definitely the industry's gain. Despite years of gradual improvements in the manufacturing processes, cast iron has always remained too brittle. "Puddling" has changed that for good.

The technique involves refining pig iron over a coal fire, pouring the molten metal into a furnace to eliminate impurities, then making the molten metal into sheets.

Cort's method has three chief advantages. It uses coal, not expensive charcoal. It uses British pig iron and turns this into a substance that rivals high quality Swedish metal. And it makes iron in one continuous process from puddling – that is, melting and stirring – through to hammering and rolling.

Poor children sent to Sunday school

Gloucester, 1784
Two years ago Robert Raikes, the editor of the *Gloucester Journal*, hired four women and set up a Sunday school for 90 poor children. Now his supporters claim that there are no fewer than a quarter of a million children in such schools all over the country.

Raikes did not invent the Sunday school, but he has given it a new thrust and much publicity through his own paper and through his articles for *The Gentleman's Magazine*. An Anglican and a committed penal reformer, he sees the Sunday school as a means of teaching the illiterate to read and write in an age when many of the young are working in factories. "The aim of the Sunday School," he says, "is the reformation of Society."

Methodists have taken up the idea with enthusiasm. John Wesley called it "one of the noblest institutions which have been seen in Europe for some centuries". Mrs Sarah Trimmer, who has set up one of the best-known schools in Brentford, just north of London, has called upon all upper-class young ladies to come to the schools and exercise a civilising influence upon the children. She has written her own books to teach them, and *History of the Robins* is now a bestseller.

USA, 1784. The effects of an economic depression begin to be felt.

France, 7 January 1785. The Frenchman Jean Blanchard and the Englishman John Jeffries succeed in the first hot air balloon crossing of the Channel.

Paris, 14 April 1785. Calonne, the controller-general of finance, restructures the French India Company.

France, 17 July 1785. By order of the council, the importation of goods from Britain is strictly limited.

France, 1 August 1785. By agreement with the king, Jean Francois de la Perouse travels to the Pacific with the aim of developing the fur trade with China and Japan.

Paris, 8 November 1785. The treaty of Fontainebleau is signed under French supervision between the Emperor Joseph II and the Dutch. This settles a conflict which arose when the Habsburgs tried to open the Scheldt river to Austrian shipping, in contravention of the treaty of Munster (1648). The Dutch refused to give up their monopoly on the Scheldt trade and appealed to France for support. By the treaty Austria receives territory in Brabant and Limburg and complete control of the Scheldt above Sanftingen, plus 10 million florins in exchange for surrendering claims to Maastricht.

Britain, 1785. The reverend James Wilmot of Warwickshire claims that the dramatic works of William Shakespeare were actually written by Francis Bacon, Viscount St Albans.

Prussia, 1785. The philosopher Immanuel Kant publishes *Fundamental Principles of the Metaphysics of Ethics*.

Britain, 1785. Amid allegations of partiality and high-handedness, Warren Hastings, governor general of India, resigns his post and returns to Britain.

New York, 1785. The state makes slavery illegal.

Netherlands, 1785. The monopoly of the Dutch East India Company is ended.

Britain, 1785. The poet William Cowper publishes *The Task*, a work concerning nature and religion, written at the suggestion of Lady Austen.

France, 1785. The French astronomer Pierre Simon de Laplace advances a new theory on the rings around Saturn. He believes that there are many narrow rings or ringlets around the planet, and that each one is solid.

Paris, 1785. The painter Louis David's latest work, *Oath of the Horatii*, a classical piece inspired by the discovery of the ruins of Pompeii and Herculaneum, is highly praised in Paris. His austere rendering of the tragic tale from antiquity is heralded as a new manifestation of the classical school.

Virginia, 16 January 1786. The Council of Virginia guarantees religious freedom.

Vienna, 1786. Mozart's opera *The Marriage of Figaro* – based on the play by Beaumarchais – opens in Vienna. The story of the valet Figaro denying his master the feudal *droit de seigneur* of a night with his servant's new wife gives the piece a subversive flavour that delights the crowd.

Sweden, 1786. The chemist Carl Scheele dies in Stockholm. He discovered numerous acids and elements such as chlorine, oxygen, barium and manganese. In 1777 he demonstrated that the atmosphere consists mainly of two gases, one supporting combustion and the other preventing it.

Europe, 1786. The count of Mirabeau, the well-known soldier, returns from fighting in the American War of Independence and tours Europe.

Britain, 1786. The prime minister, William Pitt, introduces a new "sinking fund", into which a million pounds' worth of government revenue per year is to be paid to reduce the national debt. Walpole first established a sinking fund in 1717, but it was undermined when the money was used for other purposes. Pitt is appointing independent commissioners to ensure that his fund is put to its intended use.

Sicily, 1786. Marchese Domenico Caracciolo becomes the prime minister of Ferdinand IV of Naples, the king of the two Sicilies, and assumes the title of viceroy. His attempts at political and social reform on the island come up against the apathy of the central government and the opposition of the Sicilian nobility.

Sweden, 1786. King Gustavus III founds the Academy of Eighteen in Stockholm, based on the Prussian and French models. On his visits to Paris he attends meetings of the Academie Francaise, but he is more interested in art and literature than in the ideas of the philosophers.

Austria, 1786. The Emperor Joseph II issues a decree abolishing the guilds and continues his ecclesiastical reforms, advising the Catholic Church to conduct mass in the vernacular.

Hot air balloons take off all over Europe

Montgolfier's balloon takes off at Versailles in front of King Louis XVI.

London, 15 September 1784

Floating several hundred yards above the city, to the acclamation of the prince of Wales and 150,000 onlookers, Vincent Lunardi, the secretary to the Neapolitan ambassador, has become England's first human hot-air balloonist.

Lunardi's ascent, accompanied by a cat, a dog and a picnic hamper, was the latest adventure in a craze which has swept Europe in the past year. The first balloonists were the brothers Etienne and Joseph Montgolfier who, in June last year at Annonay, launched a canvas globe of glued paper filled with inflammable gas obtained by burning wet straw. The vessel rose 950 metres, and remained airborne for ten minutes.

Three months later, the Montgolfier brothers launched the first passengers when a rooster, a duck and a sheep took off in *Martial* in front of King Louis XVI and his court at Versailles. This craft, carrying almost two hundredweight more than its own weight, rose 480 metres and landed over a mile away. The rooster broke its skull, but the sheep survived to become part of Marie Antoinette's menagerie.

Vincent Lunardi's balloon, exhibited at the Pantheon in 1784.

Industry steams ahead

Britain, c.1786

In the decade since James Watt constructed his famous engine, industry has benefited enormously from the refinements in steam technology. Steam is proving to be the driving force of an industrial revolution. For the first time man has harnessed a reliable source of energy that relies neither on muscles nor on the wind.

Steam engines are suited to water pumping. This means that it is possible to mine deeper and deeper coal seams to extract the necessary fuel to power the factories that more and more can be seen as the prime source of national wealth. And it is steam power that drives the hoisting gear to lift the coal out of the ground.

Steam engines are being used in blast furnaces, too, where they produce a blast strong enough to burn coke instead of expensive and limited charcoal. This makes for all-year-round production, with the furnaces running continuously.

In other industrial processes steam has become indispensable. It drives spinning and weaving machines, paper mills, breweries and flour mills. Indeed, steam has made possible the development of industries such as these on a large scale. It has been the vehicle of mass production; the cottage industry is a thing of the past.

What is happening in Britain is

James Watt, the industrial pioneer who invented the steam engine.

that steam has changed industry from a wood and water occupation to a coal and iron enterprise. No longer is the muscle of the horse or the drive of the watermill or windmill enough to meet the growing needs of the manufacturer. An average windmill will only generate five or ten horsepower, the largest 30 horsepower. With steam those figures look trivial: 300 horsepower is not uncommon. Small wonder that Boulton and Watt alone are said to have manufactured around 500 steam engines. And there is no sign of any shortage of clients.

French chemist turns dry gas into water

Lavoisier with his combustion apparatus for converting gases into water.

France, 1785

The chemist Antoine Laurent Lavoisier has succeeded in burning substantial amounts of dry gases to obtain water, using a combustion apparatus. He concluded that the weight of the water was equal to the sum of the weights of the two gases from which it was made. He then went on to declare that water is not, as had been thought, a simple substance, but a mixture of gases, namely oxygen and hydrogen.

Lavoisier is acknowledged as foremost among today's chemists. Born into an aristocratic family in 1743, he made himself even richer by investing in a company that was used by the government to collect its taxes. He has used these profits to construct a large laboratory.

Like a number of scientists Lavoisier has considered the theories of combustion by "phlogiston", but this discovery, among other experiments, suggests they are false.

Astronomer foresees black stars in space

England, 1784

An English astronomer has calculated that a star as dense as the sun, but with a radius 500 times larger, would have sufficient gravity to stop light itself from being emitted and would thus be invisible. John Michell's theory argues that the velocity of light particles might be reduced by powerful gravitational fields so they could not travel through space.

Marie Antoinette: victim of a necklace

Paris, 1785

Queen Marie Antoinette has become involved in a extraordinary and complex affair over a diamond neckace consisting of 647 stones and worth a fortune. And, with her extravagant court expenditures already contributing to the French state's huge debt, it has done no good to her and her husband King Louis XVI's public standing.

The queen's passion for diamonds brought her into a scandal involving Cardinal Rohan, who was acquitted o all counts at his trial. The accusation that she was having a sexual relationship with the cardinal is unjust, but it has discredited the monarchy and increased its general unpopularity.

An extravagant and unpopular queen: Marie Antoinette.

Archery art: a Chinese painting on silk from the late 18 th-century.

1786 (1786-1787)

Morocco, 11 July 1786. Morocco agrees to stop attacking American ships in the Mediterranean for a payment of $10,000.

Egypt, July 1786. The Ottoman sultan, Abdul Hamid, sends an expeditionary force of 1,500 men to Alexandria. They occupy the delta and drive out the *bey*, who takes refuge in upper Egypt and starts a civil war. The sultan blames him for having signed an agreement with France in 1785 guaranteeing safe passage for merchandise travelling from Suez to Alexandria.

Savoy, 8 August 1786. Jacques Balmat and Dr Michel-Gabriel Baccard become the first to climb Mont Blanc.

Prussia, 17 August 1786. Frederick II (the Great), king of Prussia since 1740, dies and is succeeded by Frederick William II. Frederick the Great used his genius as a military commander to make Prussia into a great power. After coming to power he seized Silesia from Austria, and during the Seven Years War (1756-63) he prevented Austria, in alliance with Russia and France, from regaining the province. In 1772 he agreed a partition of Poland with Austria and Russia.

Versailles, 20 August 1786. In order to bypass parliamentary opposition, the French finance minister Charles Calonne advises King Louis XVI to convoke an assembly of notables to agree on a plan of financial reform, including more equitable taxation.

Germany, 25 August 1786. A group of German bishops who support the Holy Roman Emperor Josef II in his campaign to curtail papal influence draw up a document entitled the Punctuation of Ems, which amounts almost to a declaration of independence from the papacy.

Virginia, 9 September 1786. George Washington calls for the abolition of slavery.

Maryland, 11 September 1786. The Convention of Annapolis opens with the aim of revising the articles of confederation of 1776.

India, 12 September 1786. Lord Cornwallis – the British general who distinguished himself in the American Revolution, despite being compelled to surrender at Yorktown – is appointed governor general of India.

London, 26 September 1786. France and Britain sign a trade agreement.

Netherlands, 1786. The recently formed Dutch Patriot Party, which represents French influence, deprives the *stadholder* William V of the command of his army.

Massachusetts, 26 December 1786. Daniel Shays, a veteran of the revolutionary war, leads a rebellion of 1,200 farmers protesting about seizures of farms, livestock and household goods for non-payment of debts.

Italy, 1786. Leopold, the grand duke of Tuscany, brother of the Emperor Josef II, proposes a programme of ecclesiastical reform strongly influenced by Jansenism. The grand duke pursues his reformist policies by abolishing torture and the death sentence.

Paris, 1786. Supporters and opponents of a planned reform of the French judicial system clash after the Paris parliament sentences three peasants from Chaumont to death for murder.

France, 1786. The botanist Vilmorin introduces cultivation of sugar-beet to France.

Scotland, 1786. Robert Burns, an impoverished Scottish farmer, publishes *Poems Chiefly in the Scottish Dialect*, including the "Address to a Mouse".

Britain, 1786. The English naval officer Captain Arthur Phillip is put in command of a fleet whose purpose is to establish a penal settlement in Australia. He is also offered the governorship of New South Wales.

France, 11 January 1787. The signature of a Franco-Russian trade agreement opens up new opportunities for French traders in the Baltic and the Black Sea.

Japan, 1787. Matsudaira Sadanobu is appointed chief senior councillor and launches a far-reaching programme of bureaucratic reforms. He purges the government ranks of supporters of his predecessor Tanuma Ogitsugu.

Japan, 1787. Serious rice riots break out in Edo (*Tokyo*) following several years of famine and rising prices. Five thousand people go on the rampage, smashing rice shops and homes of rich merchants.

India, 1787. The East India Company signs a treaty whereby it gains substantial control over the revenues and the army of the ruler of the Carnatic region in southern India.

South-East Asia, 1787. Following the signature of a friendship treaty between Vietnam and France, Count Thomas de Conway, the French governor of Pondicherry, sends troops to Vietnam to restore King Nguyen Anh to the throne.

Scotland, 1787. The Scottish engineer William Symington patents an engine for road locomotion.

Mont Blanc conquered by Swiss hunter

Jacques Balmart and Michel-Gabriel Paccard, descending from Mont Blanc.

Chamonix, France, 1786
Two Frenchmen, a hunter and a doctor, have become the first climbers to reach the summit of Mont Blanc, at 15,782 feet the highest peak in Europe.

Not long ago mountains were thought unfit places for civilised people, who drew blinds on windows of carriages traversing Alpine passes. Lately the enthusiasm for nature of writers such as Rousseau and scientists including the Geneva naturalist de Saussure has changed popular opinion.

De Saussure offered a reward to the first person to reach the summit. The feat was accomplished jointly by Jacques Balmart and Michel-Gabriel Paccard.

Small farmers rebel at harsh debt laws

Massachusetts, 25 January 1787
Months of discontent boiled over into full-scale rebellion here today as an army of small farmers fought its way to the courthouse and federal arsenal at Springfield seeking weapons. The farmers were confronted by artillery and fled across the snow after one volley was fired. Their reluctant leader, Daniel Shays, has fled to Vermont, and militiamen are searching out his lieutenants, who face the death penalty.

The cause of the revolt was the harsh law of indebtedness. With trade at a near standstill and a heavy poll-tax imposed to pay off war-debts, the farmers, unable to sell their produce, faced eviction and prison as tradesmen demanded payment. The farmers' revolt has succeeded in creating public awareness, and new legislation is likely to exempt household goods and tools from seizure for debt.

Ottoman troops land in Egypt

Alexandria, Egypt, 1786
Ottoman troops have landed in Egypt to reassert Turkish control over the Mameluke *beys*, or princes, who rule in the sultan's name but act like independent sovereigns.

Since the death of Ali Bey the Great in 1773, Egypt has been ruled – or rather misruled – by two Mameluke strongmen, Murad Bey and Ibrahim Bey who not only oppress their subjects with high prices, famine and corruption, but hold their lives cheap. As one European resident remarked: "Death may prove the consequence of the slightest indiscretion".

Both Britain and France have interests in Egypt and the *beys'* foreign policy has been to play one off against the other. It is this independence in foreign affairs has given the Ottoman sultan, nominal master of the *beys*, one pretext for trying to reimpose his control over his unruly governors.

Frederick the Great dies

Potsdam, 17 August 1786

The flute-playing aesthete who became King Frederick the Great of Prussia loathed the sight of military uniform when he succeeded his father, Frederick William. Later he took to wearing a shabby blue tunic – torn with bullet holes and spattered with snuff – and it became his exclusive dress. He was wearing it when he took the military review in a rainstorm that led to his final illness. He died today, aged 74.

Frederick leaves a state that has become feared throughout Europe. Its territory has expanded from under 46,000 to over 71,000 square miles, and the population has grown from 2.2 to 5.8 million. It has a standing army of 200,000, strictly disciplined and ready for action in war and peace – Frederick thought nothing of attacking without a declaration of war. He kept some of his wars going with subsidies from the British.

Frederick's early interest in literature and music angered his father, and the boy learned to dissemble. At 21 he was married to Elizabeth, the duke of Brunswick's daughter. But

Frederick the Great: aesthete.

he hardly ever went near his wife, and there were no children. Almost certainly the marriage was not consummated.

A so-called "enlightened despot", Frederick abolished torture, except for mass murder, lese-majeste and treason. He cultivated Voltaire, although he annoyed him by asking him to rewrite bad poetry. Frederick kept a pair of whippets, which slept on his bed.

French struggle with looming bankruptcy

Paris, 20 August 1786

France is heading for bankruptcy unless a universal land tax, payable by everyone, is brought in immediately, the comptroller-general, Calonne, warned today as he introduced a package of reforms to save the French economy. His proposals include moves to protect free trade and creating provincial assemblies.

Since taking over in 1783 he has been alarmed by rising debt interest on loans taken out by his predecessor, Necker, and continuing court extravagance. National debt at £800 million now exceeds the annual budget of £550 million.

Alexandre de Calonne: financier.

Breech-loading gun invented in London

London, 1786

A London gunsmith, Henry Nock, is promoting his new invention, a development of the musket, known as the "breech-loader", which is bound to revolutionise weapons technology. By loading the musket through the breech the shot and powder can be put in quickly at the rear of the barrel, not dropped down through the bore, as has been the old, cumbersome method.

The musket has been in use for over 250 years, and in that time it has incorporated many improvements. There has been the introduction of lighter, more manageable weapons, and mechanisms such as the flintlock and wheellock have made firing more effective.

Mendelssohn, the "court Jew", has died

Berlin, 4 January 1786

Moses Mendelssohn, the philosopher who became known as "the German Socrates" and a leading figure in the Jewish community in Germany, has died. He was 56.

Mendelssohn was introduced to the court of Frederick II by the pro-Semitic playwright Gottfried Lessing, who used him as a model for his character "Nathan the Wise" in his play of that name.

Frederick freed Mendelssohn from the usual restrictions on Jewish life in 1763, from when, as the "court Jew", he was a leader of Germany's intelligentsia.

Moses Mendelssohn: philosopher.

Shogun blamed for famine and epidemics

Japan, 1786

Tanuma Ogitsugu, who rose up through the bureaucratic ranks to become chief official of the last two *shoguns*, has been stripped of office and disgraced by the powerful relatives of the new, infant, shogun.

Tanuma, a controversial figure who concentrated on increasing the profitability of the shogun's lands, is now being accused of everything that is wrong with Japan, including natural disasters, volcanic eruptions, famines and epidemics.

Catherine the Great's magnificent neo-classical palace at Tsarskoie Selo, built between 1786 and 1796. The empress herself preferred a more severe style, in keeping with her image as an absolute monarch, and had no hesitation in treating her architects like serfs.

Ukraine. The Emperor Josef II and Catherine II of Russia meet to discuss plans for the reconquest of Istanbul.

Versailles, 13 February. Charles Vergennes, the minister of foreign affairs, dies and is replaced by the count of Montmorin.

Versailles, 22 February. At the opening session of the Assembly of Notables, the finance minister, Calonne, admits that there is a national deficit estimated at 112 million livres (£ 800 million).

Versailles, 8 April. Calonne resigns under pressure from the Notables. He is replaced by Lomenie de Brienne.

Prague, 20 April. Ardent supporters of the papacy invade Prague cathedral and stone the insignia of Scipione dei Ricci, the councillor of Grand Duke Leopold of Tuscany, sounding the deathknell for Jansenist reform.

Italy, 23 April. Tuscan bishops meet to discuss the Jansenist theories put forward by Grand Duke Leopold and his adviser Scipione dei Ricci.

Britain, May. Warren Hastings, who was made the first governor general of India in 1774 and returned to England in 1785, is impeached for corruption.

USA, 25 May. A convention to draw up the constitution for the United States of America, presided over by George Washington, opens in Philadelphia.

Versailles, June. Lomenie de Brienne, the new French finance minister, replaces forced labour with a tax and allows the free circulation of grain.

Spain, 8 July. At the instigation of his minister Floridablanca, King Charles III decrees the setting up of a ministerial council known as a *junta*. This is an attempt to modernise central government by creating a link between separate ministerial departments.

USA, 13 July. Congress adopts the North-west treaty regulating future colonisation of the lands between the Ohio, the Great Lakes, the Appalachians and the Mississippi. It provides a framework for the incorporation of new states into the Union.

Paris, 30 July. After having demanded a meeting of the Estates-General, parliament refuses to approve a new land tax.

Ottoman Empire, 13 August. Following Catherine II's rejection of their ultimatum calling for an end to the Russian protectorate in the Crimea, the Ottomans declare war on Russia.

Versailles, 27 August. The council of ministers is reshuffled. The count of la Luzerne is appointed minister of the navy and the count of Brienne, Lomenie's brother, becomes minister of war.

Versailles, 30 August. Louis XVI decrees the parliament's exile.

Netherlands. The Prussians intervene to support the *stadholder* William V in his struggle with the Dutch Patriot Party.

Europe. Britain, Prussia and the Netherlands form an alliance against France and Austria.

Austria. The Emperor Josef II promulgates the Josephine code, guaranteeing the equality of all his subjects before the law.

England. *Thoughts and Sentiments on Slavery* by Ottobah Cugoana, a Fante freed slave living in England, is published. It calls on the British government to send its navy to the West Indies to suppress slave trading.

England. Following the pioneering anti-slavery work of Granville Sharp, the Committee for the Abolition of the Slave Trade is formed by the Rev Thomas Clarkson, with William Wilberforce as its parliamentary representative.

West Africa. Freed slave settlers from England land on the Sierra Leone estuary to found a "Province of Freedom". They elect James Weaver as their governor on the basis of a constitution drawn up by Granville Sharp.

Crimea. The Russian politician Grigori Potemkin, a favourite of Catherine II, erects sham villages to impress his monarch during a royal tour. Potemkin was responsible for annexing the Crimea in 1783 and developing a Black Sea fleet.

Prague. *Don Giovanni*, an opera by the Austrian composer Wolfgang Amadeus Mozart, is performed for the first time. Mozart's *The Marriage of Figaro* caused great excitement when it appeared last year.

Vienna. Christoph Willibald Gluck, the doyen of Viennese composers who spearheaded important reforms in the art of opera, dies. His greatest operatic success was *Iphigenie en Tauride*, which appeared in 1779.

Germany. The dramatist Johann Schiller completes a play in blank verse entitled *Don Carlos*. Parts of the play, along with many of Schiller's poems, first appeared in the author's own theatrical journal, which he began publishing two years ago.

Europe's youth takes to the East

A somewhat romanticised impression of the Ottoman sultan's harem.

Istanbul

The Grand Tour, the "finishing school" for the wealthy young men of Britain, has extended itself eastwards into the Orient.

Until a few years ago, the Grand Tour meant Italy and France. Better roads, a romantic youth and peace has opened up the Ottoman empire to rich young travellers.

Young men – and, increasingly, women – on tour now take in Greece, for a touch of antiquity, and sail through the Dardanelles to Istanbul, with its splendid Ottoman palaces. Here they buy their first Oriental prop, a *hookah*. From there – with the assistance of a local guide to interpret the many splendours of the east – the traveller rides at leisure through Anatolia to Aleppo, where he or she turns right for the Holy Land. Such places as Jerusalem, Bethlehem and Damascus are all available

Eunuch and Lady of the harem.

to the ambitious traveller. Such tours are now regarded as part of an education. Like the Arab geographers, the English regard travel as good for the character.

Colony of freed slaves founded in Africa

West Africa, 10 May

Three British transport ships have anchored on the Sierra Leone river. They are carrying 411 immigrants, four-fifths black men and one-fifth white women, sent to colonise the territory.

The colonists include freed slaves, negro loyalists, who supported Britain in the American War of Independence, and the black poor of London, former domestic servants and the victims of London society's frequent changes in fashion. They have called their settle-

ment Granville Town, after Granville Sharp, their patron.

The settlement comes as the morality of the slave trade is being increasingly questioned in Britain. The Rev John Newton, the rector of St Mary Woolnoth and a former slaver, and Ottobah Cugoana and Olaudah Equiano, former slaves, have just published their memoirs; and a committee has been formed in London, led by Thomas Clarkson, Granville Sharp, Samuel Hoare and William Wilberforce, to further the cause of abolition.

India corruption charges

Warren Hastings: castigated by the eloquence of the MP, Edmund Burke.

London, 3 April

Warren Hastings, the governor general of Bengal and effective ruler of British India, is to be impeached by parliament.

The 22 articles of impeachment – including violation of treaties, the sale of states, the stealing of treasure, fraud, corruption and judicial murder – were accepted after a brilliant speech by Edmund Burke, an MP who had himself invested heavily in the East India Company. Whigs are united against Hastings, while Tories are happy to sacrifice him for the well-being of the coalition government.

Hastings has many friends – the tens of thousands of Indians who benefited from his reforms – but none can influence events in the Commons. When Hastings took over as governor general of Bengal in 1772, the taxation system was oppressive and the administration corrupt, while fortunes were being made by company servants.

"We now arm you with full powers," the directors wrote to Hastings, "to make a complete reformation." Taxation was reformed. Customs duties were levied at a uniform rate for British and Indian, and the most corrupt of the Company's officials were dismissed.

In Hastings' favour were his energy, his ability to command and his personal honesty. Against him were his arrogance, his ability to make enemies and his high handedness. For every 10,000 Indians he won as friends, he made ten mem-

Hastings, by George Romney.

bers of the administration enemies. Amongst them none is more venomous than Sir Philip Francis, the former member of British India's ruling council who briefed Burke.

Giant "wonder boat" is made of iron

London

John Wilkinson, the English industrialist and ironmaster of Staffordshire, is well known for his innovative uses for iron. His latest venture is causing a sensation.

Wilkinson has built a 70-foot-long barge – called *Trial* – with an iron hull. The iron ship was designed specifically to transport the

heavy ordinance which Wilkinson is contracted to manufacture for the government. It breaks with centuries of traditional wood-based technology and opens up greater possibilities for both shipbuilding and the British iron industry.

Trial is not the very first iron-hulled boat, but it is by far the biggest.

Russian Czarina fooled by fake buildings

Crimea

Czarina Catherine the Great has made a triumphal progress down the river Dnieper, climaxing her voyage by opening Russia's new naval base at Sevastopol. Particularly gratifying were the many fine buildings along the river bank. But rumour has it that they are merely facades, set up by her lover and adviser Field-Marshal Potemkin, and will be dismantled later. Fakes

or not, the czarina was greeted in the Crimea by an old lover, Poniatowski, now king of Poland, and the Emperor Josef II of Austria.

A lengthy round of banquets and parades led up to the ceremonial opening of the new base, where 40 warships lay at anchor. A medal marking the journey shows the bust of Potemkin wearing Roman armour; on the reverse is a map of the route.

The royal sledge of Catherine the Great, the Czarina of Russia.

Ex-slave calls for trade not terror

London

A former slave has added his voice to the growing outcry against the slave trade in the West Indies. Ottobah Cugoano, a freed slave who has just published his memoirs, wants the British government to despatch a fleet to the West Indies immediately to stop slaving.

Cugoano, transported from Africa to America as a child and freed when he became a servant in England, is from the small but growing community of poor blacks who have joined forces with the anti-

slave trade campaigner Thomas Clarkson and his parliamentary spokesman, William Wilberforce.

Cugoano says that England will benefit if it stops treating Africans as a human merchandise and starts seeing them as potential customers.

A slave executed by the Dutch.

1787 (1787-1788)

Versailles, 4 September 1787. Louis XVI recalls parliament.

USA, 17 September 1787. The Philadelphia Convention publishes a constitution for the USA.

Versailles, 29 November 1787. Louis XVI promulgates an edict of tolerance, granting civil status to Protestants.

Australia, January 1788. A British fleet led by Captain Arthur Phillip arrives in Botany Bay and hoists the British flag at Port Jackson in Sydney cove. Apart from officials, marines and 579 convicts, the ships carry agricultural implements, seeds, animals and provisions.

Paris, January 1788. The mathematician Joseph Lagrange publishes his *Analytical Mechanics*, a vast synthesis of all the major advances in mechanics.

Versailles, 17 January 1788. Enraged by a charge of despotism, Louis XVI summons a delegation from the Paris parliament to explain its condemnation of the system of sealed orders, which allows the king arbitrarily to imprison unruly subjects.

Normandy, 20 January 1788. After a dispute over the abuse of justice, Normandy's parliament acquits three peasants from Chaumont who had been sentenced for a murder committed in 1783.

Paris, 20 January 1788. Antoine Rivarol publishes a *Little Almanac of Great Men*, a scathing satire of pillars of the establishment.

Paris, 29 January 1788. Parliament approves the king's decree granting civil status to Protestants, without guaranteeing either their freedom of religion or their access to office.

Paris, February 1788. Lomenie de Brienne, the finance minister, is suspected of an anti-parliamentary plot.

France, 17 February 1788. The painter Maurice Quentin de la Tour dies. He was a brilliant portraitist whose works include paintings of major figures of the court and the world of arts.

Paris, 19 February 1788. Abbot Gregoire, Jean Pierre Brissot and the marquis of Lafayette found the Society of Friends of the Blacks to fight against the slave trade.

Versailles, 19 February 1788. Summoned by Louis XVI, a delegation from the Brittany parliament is severely reprimanded for having given its support to the principle of the equality of all the nation's parliaments.

Paris, March 1788. Bernardin de St Pierre publishes another volume of his *Studies of Nature*; the first three volumes appeared in 1784.

Australia, 15 March 1788. In command of two frigates, *La Boussole* and *L'Astrolabe*, the Frenchman la Perouse sails east from Botany Bay for the last lap of his voyage around the world.

USA, 21 March 1788. Almost the entire city of New Orleans is destroyed by fire.

Versailles, 16 April 1788. Louis XVI ends the exile of his unruly cousin, the duke of Orleans, allowing him to return to Paris.

Paris, 16 April 1788. Georges Louis Buffon, author of a 36-volume *Natural History*, dies.

Versailles, 1 May 1788. On the orders of the lord chancellor, Lamoignon, parliament is stripped of all its legislative and judicial powers, which are given to two newly-formed bodies.

Paris, 8 May 1788. After barricading themselves inside the law courts for a night, the councillors Goislard de Montsabert and Duval d'Epremesnil, who had written parliamentary decrees criticising the reforms of the Brienne ministry, are arrested on the orders of Louis XVI.

France, 31 May 1788. Provincial parliaments revolt against judicial reforms.

Brittany, 3 June 1788. Magistrates in Rennes opposed to reforms win a reprieve from threatened exile after a riot in their support.

France, 7 June 1788. Street fighting erupts in Grenoble when royal troops try to break up an illegal meeting of magistrates, called to oppose Lamoignon's judicial reforms.

USA, 21 June 1788. The American constitution comes into force, ratified by nine states.

Finland, 21 June 1788. King Gustavus III of Sweden launches an invasion of Russian Finland without having declared war.

Paris, 28 June 1788. The German musician Jean Vogel, the composer of many famous operas, dies.

Black Sea, June 1788. The Russian Black Sea fleet, commanded by the American naval hero John Paul Jones, defeats the Ottomans in two naval battles near the mouth of the Dnieper river. Earlier in the year, the Russians repelled an Ottoman attempt to seize the Crimea and invaded Moldavia.

Paris, June 1788. *Voyage of the Young Anarcharsis to Greece* by Jean Jacques Barthelemy is published. Based on the fictitious journey of a young Scythian to the Athens of Demosthenes' day, the book brings the Orient and antiquity back into fashion.

French financial reforms blocked by fear

Paris, September 1787

As France plunges further into chaos with food riots on the streets, diehard conservatives appear to have won their campaign to prevent King Louis XVI's advisers bringing in reforms to save the French economy, now close to bankruptcy. Martial law has been imposed by troops under Marshal Biron in response to the riots and to wall posters lampooning the king and his ministers.

The sole glimmer of hope is that the Parisian parliament – exiled two months ago – has been recalled. It will support new loans, provided that the reform edicts are withdrawn and a meeting of the Estates-General – representatives of the clergy, nobility and bourgeoisie – is called.

The deal puts an end to the reforms first proposed by Calonne, comptroller-general, who resigned in April. His successor, Lomenie de Brienne, the archbishop of Toulouse, who opposed the reforms out of office, adopted them only to run into similar opposition from entrenched interests in the aristocracy and the provincial parliaments.

The Parisian rejection of the reform package is seen as a guarantee that other provincial parliaments will follow suit.

Congress plans to colonise Indian lands

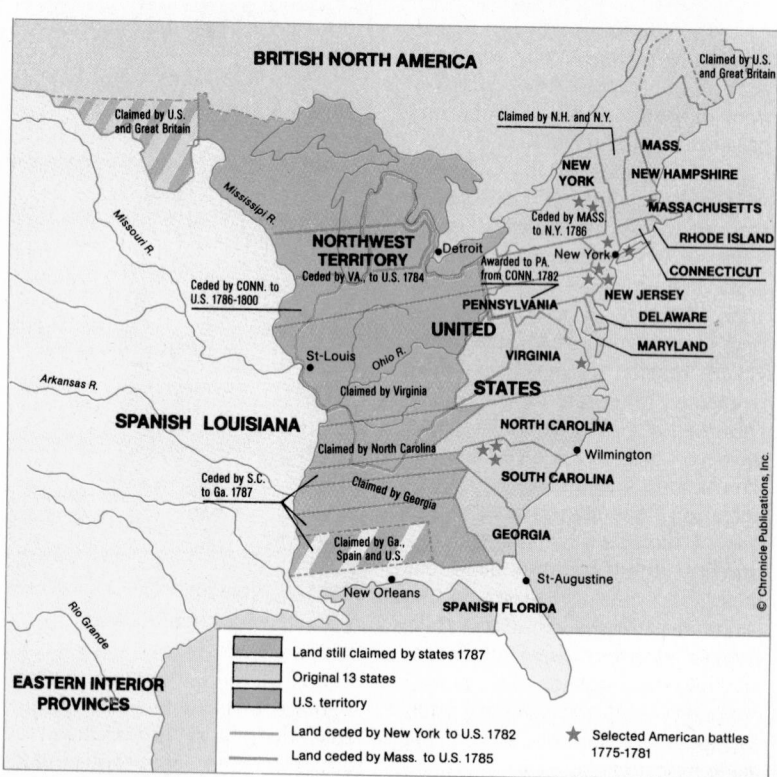

Washington, 1787

Only 11 years after the US declared itself free from colonial rule, the US Congress has approved a measure to extend its territory north-west by colonising former Indian territory. The US now comprises 13 former English colonies on the Atlantic coast. The new Northwest Ordinance provides for up to five new states across the Ohio.

Indian rights and land are protected from invasion unless Congress authorises a "just and lawful war"; yet the new governor is to create townships in places where "the Indian titles shall have been extinguished". The decree does not recognise the vital differences of perception of land ownership between the native population – who exist in a philosophical relationship with the land – and settlers who seek to own parts of it exclusively. Voters in the new territory must be adult, free males owning 200 acres. The governor has 1,000 acres of freehold land; judges have 500.

United States constitution approved

Philadelphia, 17 September 1787

Thirty-nine delegates, representing 12 of the 13 states, approved a constitution for the United States of America today and then adjourned, in the words of the chairman, George Washington, "to the City Tavern, dined together and took a cordial leave of each other". Delegates will take the draft document to their individual states for ratification, after which America will have one supreme law. Only tiny Rhode Island seems likely to dissent.

During weeks of what has been described as "occasionally tumultuous" debate, the major task facing the delegates was the framing of a federal system in which each state would be adequately represented.

Central to the constitution is the concept of the "separation of powers", designed as a system of checks and balances on the executive, the legislature and the judiciary.

All legislative power will be vested in a congress consisting of a senate and a house of representatives, the numbers of representatives based on the taxed popula-

George Washington accepts the Consititution of the United States.

tions of the various states. The legislatures of each state will elect two senators to the other house.

The role of the president will be crucial. He will serve for a four-year renewable term and have the right of veto, which Congress can annul by a two-thirds majority. He can be arraigned by the House of Representatives and judged by the Senate and removed from office on conviction for treason, bribery or other "crimes and misdemeanors".

Some southern states are worried that they will be at a numerical disadvantage, although it was a southern delegate, James Madison, who brought them round. "As we are laying the foundations for a great empire here," he told the conference, "we ought to take a permanent view of the subject."

"The Times" hits the London streets

London, 1 January 1788

In a bid to recapture readers, the fledgling *Daily Universal Register* was relaunched today as *The Times*. Its owner, the bookseller turned publisher John Walter, claims that the new title is more easily identified than the *Register*, which he says was easily confused with both the *Annual Register* and *Harris' Register of Covent Garden Ladies*. However, many readers believe that the change of title and the forthcoming redesign of the paper, scheduled for March, are intended to stave off competition from the *World and Fashionable Advertiser*, launched last year. *The Times* has added arts and literature coverage – the *Advertiser's* main features – to its normal diet of parliamentary and city news. Politically *The Times* promises it will have "two faces like Janus: with one it will smile on the friends of Old England, with the other it will frown upon her enemies".

The new face of "The Times".

Orange family back in Low Countries

Netherlands, 1787

William V of Orange is back in power, the Patriotic movement having fallen victim to powerful foreign alliances as well as its own internal weaknesses and contradictions.

For five years, the democratic Patriots have been gaining ground, winning control of town governments in Utrecht and Holland, with the support of the local Free Corps militia. But their support springs mainly from the lower middle-classes, disillusioned by Holland's economic decline compared with France and Britain. They have never won over the peasants, aristocrats or richest merchants.

The democrats' crucial mistake was to turn against the urban regents, who appealed to William for help. When his brother-in-law, the king of Prussia, lent an army, the "revolution" collapsed, and more than 5,000 eminent Patriots went into exile, many in France.

Cartwright's rival to the hand loom

Derbyshire, England, 1787

A visit by an English clergyman to a Derbyshire cotton mill has led to a new development in weaving technology. Edmund Cartwright, having looked round Richard Arkwright's spinning mills, has patented a machine for weaving.

Until now, the weaving process has been carried out on hand looms and has thus lagged behind other branches of the industry which are rapidly being mechanised.

Cartwright's new steam-driven loom, although needing further improvements, is operating in his own factory in Doncaster, Yorkshire. Unfortunately the power loom's future seems insecure. For one thing, Cartwright himself is reported to have money troubles which could slow down its development. And some people, particularly the weavers, remain unconvinced of the need for the change from manual to machine working.

Bach's son is dead

Hamburg, 14 December 1788

The pioneering composer Carl Philipp Emanuel Bach has died aged 74. The second son of J S Bach, he worked for the Prussian crown prince (later Frederick II) from 1738 until 1767, when Frederick, himself a flautist and composer, agreed to let him succeed Telemann (C P E Bach's godfather) as Hamburg's music director. In the city's less conservative atmosphere Bach wrote his most adventurous music, including keyboard works, oratorios and symphonies, often in a passionate, expressive style.

Fundamentalists threaten sultanate

Arabia, 1788

'Abd al-'Aziz has secured the recognition of his son Amir Saud as heir to his Arabian empire. Loyal to the rigorous Islamic fundamentalism of Mohammed ibn 'Abd al-Wahhab, the Saudis are a growing threat to Ottoman influence. The Wahhabi state was established in the Najd plateau over 40 years ago, annexed Riyadh in 1773, and gained control of Jabal Shammar last year. It now threatens the tribal territory of al-Ahsa in the east, the Hijaz to the west, and the Muntafiq on the fringe of Mesopotamia.

Paris, 6 July. Ten thousand troops are called out as unrest mounts in the poorer districts.

France, 13 July. A devastating tornado wipes out crops and causes severe damage to buildings across the country.

Paris, 15 July. Louis XVI jails 12 Breton deputies who protested to him about the judicial reforms ordered by the lord chancellor, Lamoignon, in May.

Paris, 19 July. Prices plunge on the Paris stock exchange.

South-East Asia, 20 July. Thomas de Conway, the governor of the French colony of Pondicherry, abandons plans to send troops to place King Nhuyen Anh back on the throne of Vietnam.

India, August. Tipu Sahib, the sultan of Mysore – who supports France's campaign to prevent Britain from dominating India – sends three ambassadors to France.

England, 2 August. The painter Thomas Gainsborough dies at the age of 61. As well as being a fine landscape artist, Gainsborough was a rival of Sir Joshua Reynolds as the most admired portrait painter of the age, notably for his portrait of the actress Sarah Siddons.

Versailles, 8 August. In an attempt to ward off economic crisis, Louis XVI decrees that the Estates-General will meet on 1 May 1789.

Versailles, 16 August. Having failed to persuade the financiers to provide new funds for the treasury, Lomenie de Brienne, the finance minister, declares the French state bankrupt.

Versailles, 25 August. In an attempt to save France from total economic collapse, Louis XVI recalls Jacques Necker, the Genevaborn Protestant banker, who was disgraced in 1783, to replace Brienne as finance minister.

Paris, 29 August. Eight people are killed in riots following the news of Brienne's resignation.

Paris, 12 September. The jailed Breton nobles, who have become symbolic victims of despotism and the abuse of royal power, are released at Necker's request.

USA, 13 September. New York is declared the federal capital of the USA and the seat of Congress.

The Hague, 15 September. An alliance signed by Britain, Prussia and the Netherlands on 13 August in Berlin is ratified.

Versailles, 19 September. Charles de Barentin becomes lord chancellor, replacing Lamoignon, who has been forced to resign.

Versailles, 23 September. Louis XVI announces that the judicial reforms have been dropped and the traditional roles of the parliaments restored.

Paris, 24 September. The parliament of Paris reassembles in triumph.

Poland, 6 October. The Polish *Diet*, which has effected important administrative reforms since being forced to accept the partition of Poland in 1772, decides to hold a four-year session.

Prussia, October. The Frenchman Jean Blanchard invents a flying ship equipped with six paddles hooked up to a hot-air balloon.

Spain, 14 December. Charles III, king of Spain since 1759, dies and is succeeded by his son Charles IV.

Australia. The British expedition led by Captain Arthur Phillip establishes an agricultural settlement at Parramatta, upriver from Sydney.

Prussia. King Frederick William II issues a "religious edict" abrogating all freedom of worship. The freedom of the press is also abolished.

Ottoman Empire. Continuing their war with the Ottomans, the Russians massacre the captured Turkish inhabitants of several towns in Moldavia and along the Black Sea.

Ottoman Empire. Ali of Teleben, an Albanian nobleman, seizes the town of Yanina and proclaims himself *pasha* of all Albanian territories.

Denmark. Serfdom is abolished.

England. The historian Edward Gibbon completes his *Decline and Fall of the Roman Empire.*

England. The philosopher Jeremy Bentham publishes his *Introduction to the principles of morals and legislation.*

England. The African Association is founded to promote a "legitimate" trade to replace the slave trade.

France. The astronomer Nicole-Reine Lepaute dies. From 1759 she was employed by Lalande, the director of the Paris observatory. Among her works are a monograph on the transit of Venus, published in 1761, and calculations for the sun, moon and planets.

Christianity aided Rome's breakdown

London
It is 24 years since Edward Gibbon, "musing on the ruins of the Capitol at Rome", had the idea of writing a history of the *Decline and Fall of the Roman Empire*. Now his great work, whose early volumes sold so quickly, has been completed with a fifth and sixth volume, with which the diminutive author (who is below five foot in height) has ended his labours.

They bring the history, which began in AD 180 with the death of Marcus Aurelius, down to 1453, the fall of Constantinople and the end of the Eastern empire, and includes Mohammed, Saladin, Genghis Khan and Tamerlane. Gibbon blames the decline of Rome on the loss of its old military virtues and the rise of Christianity. But this in turn helped to civilise the barbarian invaders. "We cannot determine to what height the human species may aspire in their advance towards perfection, but it may be presumed that no people will relapse into their original barbarism."

Human behaviour has universal laws

Konigsberg, East Prussia
Konigsberg's world-famous professor of philosophy, Immanuel Kant, has just published his second *Critique*, on moral philosophy. Seven years ago, in his *Critique of Pure Reason*, Kant argued that our knowledge of the physical world does not arise purely through sense-impressions, as David Hume, the Scottish sceptical philosopher, claimed. Experience is made possible by universal patterns or "categories" of space, time, unity and causality, all based on first principles and imposed on our perceptions by the mind.

Now, in the *Critique of Practical Reason*, Kant argues that our moral duties arise likewise from the mind and its awareness of being under obligation, a concept that he calls "the categorical imperative". Reason demands that we act in such a way that our maxims of conduct could serve as universal laws. Kant, a bachelor who has never left Konigsberg, lives to a strict time-table, beginning his studies at 5am.

Written rules for ancient game of cricket

Classy sport: a game of cricket at Kenfield Hall near Canterbury in Kent.

London
The game of cricket, long popular in English villages and recently taken up by the aristocracy, has been given a written set of rules by the Marylebone Cricket Club in London. Played with bats and balls (now of fixed size) on village greens, cricket satisfies the upper class passions for fresh air, exercise and gambling.

Typically, a prominent landowner will recruit villagers to do battle with rivals, and enjoy a wager on the result. British colonies are also learning the game.

King who brought Spain up to date dies

Madrid
The best king Spain has had for many decades, Charles III, has died after taking to his bed with a cold, which developed into high fever. He had ruled Spain for nearly 30 years with an enlightened policy of of material and cultural progress, and many of his reforms should prove to be of outstanding value.

Charles was the king of Naples and brother of the late Spanish king when he took over at the age of 43, after quickly renouncing his Italian kingdom for that of Spain. He proved to be a monarch who governed truly. Upright, inflexible, but at the same time reasonable, he carried out his kingly duties with mechanical exactitude.

His blind spot was that his foreign policy was often dictated by prejudice, such as the hatred of Great Britain which led him to take part unwisely in the American War of Independence, an adventure whose outcome might cause serious

King Charles III of Spain.

damage to the Spanish empire. Charles had also set his heart on taking Gibraltar from the British and laid siege to the rock, but he was unsuccessful. But under the Treaty of Versailles Spain won back Minorca and Florida.

People's vote in Estates-General raised

The Third Estate, burdened by the privileged clergy and aristocracy.

Versailles, 26 December
King Louis XVI has given in to the increasingly urgent demands of the bourgeoisie and has doubled the representation of the Third Estate at the meeting of the Estates-General planned for next May – the first time it will convene for 174 years.

The Third Estate, speaking for some 24 million people out of a total population of 25 million, will therefore equal the First Estate, the nobility, and the Second Estate, the clergy, when they discuss the urgent reforms needed to cope with France's desperate economic crisis.

The added power of the Third Estate may not, however, be reflected in the proceedings, for the king, at the urging of the nobility, has not so far agreed to holding joint debates or permitting a free vote.

English convict ship arrives in Australia

Sailors and marines from HMS Endeavour raise the flag at Sydney Cove.

Sydney, Australia, 26 January
A British convoy, including six transport ships carrying 730 convicts, has landed at Port Jackson. The commander, Arthur Phillip, describes the bay as "the finest harbour in the world". One cove, a quarter of a mile across and half a mile deep, he has called Sydney.

The convoy sailed from England 36 weeks ago. Before Phillip took command many convicts were suffering from smallpox and venereal disease. Although Phillip dramatically improved their conditions, 48 died during the passage.

Of the convicts, 570 were men and 160 women. The youngest was John Hudson, a nine-year-old chimney sweep. The oldest was Dorothy Handland, an 88-year-old rag dealer. Phillip was taking convicts to Australia because he refused to take slaves.

Their first landfall was six days ago at Botany Bay. Phillip found the bay unsuitable for colonisation and sailed round the coast to Sydney, where the second-in-command of the expedition, Captain John Hunter, described the land as resembling a deer park.

While the rest of the convoy waited in Botany Bay they encountered two French ships, commanded by la Perouse, on a world voyage. They also came upon Sydney's indigenous people who waved their fists at the intruders and shouted *"Warra-warra!"* – Go away!

Englishman reports on poverty in France

France
Reports of the misery of the French peasantry are reaching England via the pen of Arthur Young, a traveller and agriculturalist. They echo the dispatches of British diplomats, who sense revolution in the air.

Last year, Young wrote from the Dordogne of "many beggars ... country girls and women without shoes or stockings ... a poverty that strikes at the root of national prosperity". This year his travels took him through Brittany, where he saw primitive husbandry, wild people, mud houses and broken pavements. "Who is this Mons de Chateaubriand, the owner, that has nerves strung for a residence amidst such filth and poverty?" asked Young. In Montauban, he saw similar deprivation and misery.

On 17 April, from the British Embassy in Paris, one diplomat wrote to the Foreign Office of "disgrace and difficulties ... an entire revolution looked forward to with the greatest eagerness".

On 2 July, an envoy who had dismissed rumours of unrest two months earlier wrote: "The spirit of resistance is making hasty strides throughout the kingdom ... some of the regiments have already shown great reluctance to act against their fellow-citizens."

1789 ⇒

Poland, 19 January. The *Diet* suppresses the permanent council and takes over all its powers.

France, January. To avert a major famine, the finance minister Necker imports thousands of tons of grain and flour.

France, January. Electoral rules for the meeting of the Estates-General are published. Third Estate patriots in Brittany and Provence condemn them as unfair and demand equal representation with the other two orders (the nobles and the church).

Sweden, 20 February. King Gustavus III imposes an Act of Union and Security on the Riksdag, establishing despotism.

London, February. King George III regains his sanity after three months of madness, during which the Pitt government framed a bill providing for a regency regulated by Parliament.

Provence, February. Honore Gabriel Riqueti, the count of Mirabeau, is excluded from the order of the nobility after speaking out in favour of the Third Estate.

France, February. Pierre Lavoisier completes his *Elementary Treatise on Chemistry*.

USA, 4 March. The first Congress meets in New York.

Poland, March. The Diet imposes a tax of ten per cent on revenue from lands and 20 per cent on ecclesiastical property.

Istanbul, 7 April. Selim III succeeds his uncle Abdul Hamid as Ottoman sultan.

Pacific, 28 April. After a mutiny provoked by his harsh treatment, the British sailor William Bligh, the commander of the *Bounty*, is cast adrift near the Friendly Islands in a small open boat with 18 men.

USA, 30 April. George Washington is inaugurated as the first president of the USA.

France, April. Members of the Third Estate condemn the heavy tax burden on the poor and demand a constitution which would limit arbitrary royal power.

Paris, April. The Academy of Sciences publishes *Annals of Chemistry*, a compendium of major new discoveries in chemistry and related subjects.

Paris, 28 April. Three hundred people are killed when troops open fire on rioters at the Reveillon wallpaper factory. The riot started after news of a proposed pay cut at the factory.

Paris, 30 April. Two men sentenced to death for their part in the Reveillon riot are hanged.

Marseilles, 30 April. Rioters seize control of the city's three forts, killing one of their commanders.

Versailles, 5 May. The Estates-General is formally opened by Louis XVI.

Versailles, 11 May. Debate at the Estates-General is deadlocked by the Third Estate's refusal to comply with the proposed voting system.

Versailles, 22 May. The nobility follows the example of the clergy by giving up its fiscal privileges.

Prussia, May. The foreign minister, Herzberg, puts forward a plan to destroy Russian influence in Poland.

Austrian Netherlands, May. Weary of the rule of the Habsburg Emperor Josef II, Belgians call for a national monarchy.

Austria, May. The states of Styria and Carniola rise up against the Emperor Josef II.

France, 4 June. The dauphin Louis dies of consumption at the age of seven.

South-East Asia, 14 June. Captain William Bligh, cast adrift in April by his mutinous sailors on the *Bounty*, arrives at Timor, near Java, having sailed his small boat for more than 3,500 miles.

Versailles, 17 June. The Third Estate assembly changes its name to the National Assembly.

Austrian Netherlands, 18 June. Following the refusal of the Belgian states to pay taxes – to block increasingly unpopular decrees by the Emperor Josef II – Austrian troops occupy Brussels.

Versailles, 19 June. The chamber of the clergy votes for union with the Third Estate.

Versailles, 20 June. Following the closure of the Estates chamber by the king, the National Assembly deputies are sworn in at a meeting on the tennis courts of the Jeu de Paume.

Versailles, 27 June. Louis XVI caves in and calls on his "faithful clergy and loyal nobility" to meet jointly with the Third Estate. A group of 47 nobles joins the National Assembly.

Paris, 30 June. A mob attacks the Abbaye prison and frees a group of mutinous French Guards, who have allied with the lower middle classes.

Berlin. The composer Mozart visits Berlin in the hope of gaining a post at court. He is commissioned to write a series of string quartets for the Prussian king, who is a fine cellist.

Frenchmen compile lists of grievances

The French king, Louis XVI, distributing gifts amongst the poor.

France, March

Insufficient food, high taxes, an interfering government, overmighty noblemen and, priests who enrich themselves without labour – these are some of the complaints being listed in France's *Cahiers de doleances* or Books of Grievances.

The books were established by the Estates-General, France's legislative assembly, in 1484, and every tax-paying Frenchman over 25 is eligible to register his complaints with his parish assembly or, if a townsman, with his corporation. Once collected, the local lists are collated and the major points finally presented to the king.

This year's books centre on economics. The Third Estate deplores the heavy burden of taxes faced by the poorest citizens and condemns the activities of government tax collectors who are accused of systematic, gross corruption.

In the towns the professional guilds are under fire for their economic monopolies, while the rural

Marie Antoinette, Austrian-born queen of France, at Versailles.

areas concentrate on the nobility's maintenance of defunct feudal rights.

Most important of all are the political demands. The books call for a constitution limiting royal power and establishing equality and the rights to property and individual freedoms.

Radical reforms to boost taxes in Japan

Japan

A radical reform programme, known as the Kansei reforms, has been carried out by the *shogunate* in an attempt to rectify a huge drop in revenue and a steep rise in inflation. The reforms are not only economic. They are also aimed at the widespread bureaucratic corruption which is weakening the administration of the government. In the countryside, the reforms are aimed at restoring tax farming and the building up of rice reserves to cope with the series of famines and natural disasters which plagues the country. Monetary reform has also been carried out, with the reminting of silver coins and a revaluation of the gold currency.

French bourgeoisie demand to be heard

Ceremonial costumes of (l. to r.) clergy, nobility and commons.

Versailles, 5 May
The king is to address the Estates-General today when it meets for the first time since 1614. The people of France care little for the ceremony. They are demanding bread and reform from the Third Estate, which represent them in the legislature.

Much is expected of this meeting. The Books of Grievances, open to every Frenchman, are full and the members of the Third Estate, whose numbers have been doubled, are fully aware of the hopes resting on their shoulders.

Abbe Sieyes summed up these hopes in his pamphlet, *What is the Third Estate?* Answering his own question, he replied: "Everything," adding: "What does it ask? To be something."

All now rests on the king. Advised by his finance minister, the Swiss banker, Necker, he must today address himself to the aspirations of his people.

Washington elected first US president

New York City, 30 April
Looking tired and gaunt, George Washington took the oath of office as the first president of the United States today before a joint session of Congress and swore to "preserve, protect and defend the Constitution".

The 57-year-old Virginia land-owner was clearly over awed by the solemnity of the occasion. One senator said that the great war hero seemed "agitated and embarrassed more than he ever was by the levelled cannon or pointed musket".

Washington's election was never in doubt. Members of the electoral college were unanimous in casting their votes for the hero of Yorktown, and today, as he drove from his home at nearby Mount Vernon, his coach was surrounded by well-wishers whenever it stopped. Despite his large land-holdings, Washington is said to be "cash-poor" and needed to borrow money to pay the expenses of this inauguration. He took his oath wearing a simple

Washington, by James Peale (elder).

worsted suit and white silk stockings. The only trace of former military glory was his dress sword. One of his first executive decisions was to appoint the experienced Thomas Jefferson to take charge of foreign affairs. John Adams will be Washington's vice-president.

Third Estate swears oath in tennis court

Versailles, 20 June
The representatives of the Third Estate, and those members of the clergy who joined with them three days ago in proclaiming themselves the National Assembly, arrived at the Menus Plaisirs hall this morning only to find it locked against them on the king's orders, ostensibly for "cleaning".

Amid the ensuing uproar, Dr Joseph Guillotin, one of the deputies from Paris, suggested they should meet in the nearby tennis courts of the Jeu de Paume.

They hurried off to this large, bare building with its blue ceiling picked out with golden fleurs de lys and there, with a bench as a desk, they held their meeting while an enthusiastic crowd outside shouted

"Vive l'Assemblee!" At first there was talk of withdrawing to Paris to "seek the protection of the people", but Jean Joseph Mounier demanded that they must take an oath "never to separate and to meet whenever circumstances demand, until the Constitution of the Kingdom has been firmly established and consolidated".

The delegates went forward one by one to take the oath before the astronomer Jean-Sylvain Bailly, the elected senior member of the Third Estate.

Only one member, Martin d'Auch, refused to sign the oath and, despite cries of protest, was allowed to register his opposition "out of respect for the liberty which all members of the Assembly enjoy".

The Tennis Court Oath, painted by Jacques-Louis David (1748-1825).

Brazil's revolutionary "dentist" arrested

Minas Gerais, Brazil, 10 May
The Portuguese authorities have acted decisively to nip the conspiracy for an independent Brazil in the bud. Today they arrested all the key figures including the leader, Jose Joaquim da Silva, a sub-lieutenant of the dragoons. He is known as *Tiradentes* (the Dentist) because of his knowledge of dentistry.

The would-be revolutionaries were betrayed – although they had failed to agree about anything important. They include idealistic poets and priests who want a new republic as well as landlords and businessmen who are upset because Portugal has drained off the profit from the gold mines.

A Brazilian negro with a brightly coloured tropical bird.

1789 ⇒

Versailles, 9 July. The National Assembly declares itself the Constituent Assembly and sets about preparing a French constitution.

Paris, 12 July. Louis XVI's dismissal of Necker, the highly popular finance minister, fuels the violence in Paris, which is on fire after two days of non-stop rioting.

Paris, 14 July. The Bastille is seized by the people of Paris.

Paris, 15 July. The electors of Paris set up a "Commune" led by Bailly, who is elected mayor of Paris, and Lafayette, who becomes head of the National Guard.

Versailles, 16 July. Louis XVI recalls Necker.

Versailles, 16 July. The court nobility begins to emigrate from France.

Paris, 18 July. Camille Desmoulins publishes the first republican manifesto of the revolution, *La France Libre*.

Versailles, 20 July. Robespierre, a deputy from Arras, backs the revolutionaries.

Paris, 21 July. The Comedie Francaise is to reopen as the Theatre of the Nation.

Paris, 22 July. Bertier, the bailiff of Paris, and his father-in-law, the financier Foulon, are murdered by the mob.

New York City, 27 July. The department of foreign affairs, the first executive agency in the USA, is set up, with Thomas Jefferson at its head.

France, July. A "Great Fear" sweeps through the provinces and the revolution spreads to the provincial towns.

Paris, July. The botanist Antoine Laurent de Jussieu completes his *Genera Plantarum*, a classification of the vegetable world.

Versailles, August. The National Assembly is rocked by a provincial arson campaign and tax boycott.

Germany, August. Influenced by events in France, peasants in the Rhineland rise up in revolt against the nobles' privileges.

New York City, 2 August. A US war department is created, with Henry Knox at its head.

Versailles, 4 August. The Constituent Assembly abolishes the privileges of the nobility, destroying the social structures of the Ancien Regime.

Versailles, 26 August. The Constituent Assembly approves the final version of the Declaration of Human Rights.

France, 26 August. Miners in the Pyrenees rise up in protest against their working conditions.

Paris, August. Jacques Louis David completes his painting *Brutus*, a homage to republican self-sacrifice.

New York City, 2 September. A treasury department, headed by Alexander Hamilton, is created.

Orleans, 13 September. Guardsmen open fire on rioters trying to loot bakeries, killing 90.

Paris, 16 September. Jean-Paul Marat sets up a new newspaper, *L'Ami du Peuple*.

New York City, 24 September. Congress passes the Federal Judiciary Act, creating circuit courts, district courts and a Supreme Court.

New York City, 25 September. Congress proposes 12 amendments to the constitution known as the Bill of Rights.

New York City, 29 September. Congress votes to create a US army.

Paris, 7 October. After a march by the women of Paris to Versailles to demand bread, the royal family is forced to return to Paris, where they take refuge in the Tuileries.

Serbia, 9 October. Having invaded Serbia in the spring, Austrian troops defeat the Ottomans to take Belgrade.

Versailles, 10 October. Louis XVI is named "King of the French" by the Assembly.

Versailles, 10 October. The Paris deputy Joseph Guillotin, a professor of anatomy, says that the most humane way of carrying out a death sentence is decapitation by a single blow of the blade.

Paris, 12 October. The Constituent Assembly transfers from Versailles to Paris.

Paris, 21 October. The deputies impose martial law after the brutal killing of a baker accused of hoarding bread.

Austrian Netherlands, 24 October. The insurgents proclaim independence and strip the Emperor Josef II of his sovereignty over the country.

Germany, 24 October. The author Georges Francois Mareschal dies at Triesdorf in Bavaria. He was known as the "father of puns" for his habit of playing on the meaning of words.

Paris, 29 October. The Assembly approves a decree known as the "silver marc", by which only the rich will be allowed to vote.

Tension in Paris as king sends in troops

Versailles, July

Only a few days after bowing to the pressure of public opinion and summoning his "faithful clergy and loyal nobility" to meet jointly with the Third Estate, Louis XVI has ordered the old marshal de Broglie with 30,000 troops to "defend Paris from unrest". There is no doubt among the deputies of the Third Estate, however, that the king has declared war on them and means to put down their constitutional rebellion by using the army.

It is a move which is full of danger; there is great unrest in the provinces and Paris is as explosive as a powder keg.

French declare everyone has equal rights

Paris, 26 August

The Assembly has today approved the Declaration of the Rights of Man. This document, which states that "men are born and remain free and with equal rights", is based on the theories of the philosopher Rousseau and on the American Declaration of Independence.

It is not, however, merely a pious declaration, but aims to be a workable political document embodying the freedoms long denied to the French under the rule of the divine right of absolute monarchy. It specifies that the "free communication of thoughts is one of the most precious rights of man". From today the French may think, speak and write freely.

Not all the delegates are convinced of the wisdom of the declaration. One, Malouet argued: "Why should we carry men up to the top

Declaration of the Rights of Man.

of a mountain and thence show them the full extent of their rights, since we are forced to make them descend again, and assign them limits?"

Frank confession of insane French writer

Rousseau: confessing all.

Paris

"I desire to set before my fellows the likeness of a man in all the truth of nature, and that man myself." So wrote Jean-Jacques Rousseau at the opening of the *Confessions* which he began during his exile in England. The second volume has only now appeared, 11 years after he died insane.

In it the author of *The Social Contract* writes of his innermost feelings with unprecedented frankness. "I am not made like any of those I have seen. This is what I have done, what I have thought, what I was. I have told the good and the bad with equal frankness."

Rousseau confesses to his many passions for women – and theirs for him – to his cold decision to place his illegitimate children in a foundling hospital, and to friendships that ended in bitter quarrels, and reveals his continual suspicions of conspiracies against him. He ends with his books publicly burnt, his house stoned, himself expelled.

Parisian mob storms the Bastille

Feudal privileges to vanish in France

Paris, 14 July

The people of Paris today stormed the Bastille, the grim prison which was the symbol of absolute monarchy. The dramas started at dawn with the looting of the Invalides prison by the mob in search of arms to fight an expected attack by soldiers loyal to the king.

The mob found 32,000 rifles, but no ammunition. A rumour spread that ammunition was stored at the Bastille. The mob rushed there.

The prison was armed with cannon and guarded by 80 soldiers unfit for front-line duty reinforced by 30 Swiss Guards. The crowd, many of them furniture makers armed with their tools, milled around, frightened by the cannons.

A message was sent to the Assembly which despatched a delegation to negotiate with the Bastille's governor, Bernard de Launay. He promptly invited the envoys into the prison for lunch. When they did not return the mob became angry, believing they had been arrested.

A second delegation was then sent in, only to re-emerge to say that the governor refused to surrender. The spokesman added, however, that the cannon were unloaded and that de Launay had promised not to fire if they did not attack. But by now the crowd was in no mood to listen to reason.

The cry went up: " We want the Bastille! Down with the army!" The army in fact showed no desire to intervene, withdrawing to the Champ de Mars. Suddenly a group

A crude but vivid view of the siege by Cholat, who was in the crowd.

of youths climbed on to a perfumier's shop built against the prison wall and dropped into the courtyard. They let the drawbridge fall with a crash, killing one of the crowd. The mob rushed into the courtyard. There was a volley of shots. Men fell. A howl of rage went up and the fire was returned.

The fighting raged on into the afternoon until cannon were dragged through the streets to blow down the gates. De Launay surrendered before they could fire; his severed head was later paraded by the mob. There were only seven prisoners in the whole prison, but that was unimportant. An ancient symbol of royal tyranny had fallen.

A surrender note is pushed through.

Paris, 5 August

In an amazing all-night sitting the National Assembly has done away with the social structure and feudal rights of the old regime. The delegates had spent the day discussing with much trepidation the reports of turmoil in the provinces where peasants are revolting against their landlords. They seemed fearful, unable to make decisions.

Suddenly, at eight o'clock in the evening, the viscount of Noailles rose. The thing that drove peasants to sack country houses, he said, was the heavy burden of lordly rights and dues. They must be swept away.

The Assembly reacted with astonishment at first and then with wild enthusiasm. Everybody seemed to forget that Noailles was so poor that he was known as "Landless John" and had no rights to give away. It did not matter. A wild enthusiasm seized the Assembly, with delegates eager to give away not only their own rights but also those of other people.

The bishop of Chartres relinquished sporting rights at which the duke of Chatelet muttered: "Ah! The bishop is taking away my game; I'll take something from him." So he declared the end of tithes and was greeted with acclamation.

By eight o'clock this morning some 30 decrees had been made law. An astonishing social revolution had been accomplished in the course of one extraordinary night.

African kingdom that grew rich from trade in slaves and cloth

An Oyo chief from Eastern Yorubaland, Nigeria. Note the umbrella: a symbol of state.

West Africa

The West African slave state of Oyo *(south-western Nigeria)* is mourning the death of its ruler, Abiodun. He came to power 15 years ago by a *coup d'etat*, centralised the administration and weakened the Oyo oligarchies. Under him Oyo grew rich on trade in cloth, manufactured goods and slaves; Porto Novo, in particular, exported tens of thousands of the latter. Its revenues, like those of all the slave ports, went straight to Abiodun's exchequer. Oyo became widely known and the English moralist, Dr Samuel Johnson, pro-

nounced that it contained 6,600 towns and villages. How long this age of prosperity can continue is uncertain. The Oyo army is no longer the unbeatable force of a generation ago.

Wars and political upheavals in the north have made it difficult for its cavalry (the most powerful arm of the forces) to obtain mounts. The state has been increasingly relying on Dahomeyan soldiers to hold down insurrections. The revolt of the Egba people has still not been suppressed. Most significantly of all, an Oyo army was defeated by an army from Borgu in 1783.

The snakes of privilege are crushed.

1789 (1789-1790)

Black Sea, October 1789. The Russian general Suvorov takes Ochakov, the port at the mouth of the Bug, from the Ottomans.

France, 2 November 1789. All church property is nationalised.

Paris, 12 November 1789. The Assembly decrees that the towns and rural parishes will from now on have elected local councils.

Netherlands, 18 December 1789. Belgian patriots, who recently proclaimed the independence of Belgium, win a victory over the invading Austrians at Turnhout.

France, 1 December 1789. A mutiny of sailors in Toulon sets off a crisis in the French navy.

France, 13 December 1789. The National Guard is created.

France, 19 December 1789. Four hundred million francs' worth of government bonds, known as *assignats*, are issued to help to repay the national debt.

France, 24 December 1789. Protestants are given the vote on the same basis as Catholics.

North Pacific, 1789. A Spanish squadron lands at Nootka Sound, a small natural harbour (*off Vancouver Island*) in Canada, claiming it for Spain. A British trading settlement was established on the sound after its discovery by James Cook in 1778.

West Africa, 1789. The "Province of Freedom" formed two years ago in Sierra Leone collapses as settlers scatter after an attack by the local Temne ruler, "King Jimmy". The freed slaves had incautiously allied with local European slave traders against King Jimmy.

West Africa, 1789. King Abiodun, the great ruler of the Oyo state (*South-western Nigeria*) among the Yoruba people, dies. Oyo has never recovered from its defeat in 1783 by the army of Borgu from the north, and Abiodun's son Awole inherits a weakened kingdom.

India, 1789. Tipu Sahib, the sultan of Mysore, attacks Travancore, an ally of the East India Company in southern India.

USA, 1789. *The Power of Sympathy, or the Triumph of Nature* by William Hill – whose purpose is to "expose the dangerous consequences of seduction" – is the first novel published in the USA.

Ukraine, 1789. Polish nobles blame Russian infiltrators for new unrest among peasants in the Ukraine.

Paris, 21 January 1790. Dr Guillotin proposes a new method of execution: a machine designed to cut off the condemned person's head as painlessly as possible.

Paris, 25 January 1790. Maximilien de Robespierre's demand for universal suffrage is greeted by jeers in the Assembly.

Paris, 13 February 1790. The Assembly bans monastic vows and abolishes contemplative religious orders.

Paris, 19 February 1790. The marquis of Favras is hanged for his part in a plot to help the king escape and to kill Lafayette and Bailly.

Vienna, 20 February 1790. The Emperor Josef II, an embodiment of enlightened despotism, dies at the age of 48. He is succeeded by his brother Leopold, the grand duke of Tuscany.

Avignon, 22 February 1790. The papal consuls resign their positions in Avignon, ending the pope's secular power there. Tithes and feudal rights have already been abolished in the city.

France, 26 February 1790. France is divided into 83 departments.

Paris, 8 March 1790. The Assembly votes in favour of the continuation of slavery in France's colonies.

Paris, 15 March 1790. Jean Paul Rabaut St Etienne, a Protestant, is elected president of the Assembly.

Paris, 21 March 1790. Having banned sealed royal orders and ruled in favour of the equality of death duties, the Assembly abolishes the salt tax, dealing a final death-blow to the abuses of the Ancien Regime.

Paris, 31 March 1790. Robespierre is elected president of the Jacobin Club.

Algiers, 4 April 1790. A 100-year-old peace treaty between France and Algiers is renewed.

Paris, 7 April 1790. The publication of the *Red Book* listing gifts given by Louis XVI reveals that his secret expenses have totalled 228 million francs since the start of his reign. The destination of much of this money is unclear.

France, 17 April 1790. The government bonds known as assignats become legal tender.

Philadelphia, 21 April 1790. Twenty thousand people attend the funeral of the scientist and statesman Benjamin Franklin, who died on 17 April at the age of 84. The inventor of the life-saving lightning conductor, Franklin combined a fascination with new ideas and a determination to pursue Puritan aims to benefit the common good.

West Indies, 3 May 1790. Port Louis, the capital of Tobago, is destroyed by fire.

Satire bites as France allows free speech

From the shop floor to the streets, the press now shapes public opinion.

Paris, 1789
Political discussion is raging in France as never before, fuelled by a rash of new newspapers and political clubs, all dedicated to dissecting the ever-shifting world of governmental affairs and offering a mix of biting satire and hardhitting criticism.

The latest newspaper to appear is *L'Ami du Peuple*, published by Jean-Paul Marat, an ambitious radical whose book *Chains of Slavery* appeared in England in 1774 and who clashed with the authorities earlier this year for the anti-royalist content of his pamphlet *Offerings to the Motherland*.

But Marat is only the most recent of many. The new mood of open discussion emerged in July last year when the government relaxed its usual censorship, calling for the public to express opinions on the forthcoming meeting of the Estates-General.

Bastille Day celebrations in France

The Altar of the Fatherland (centre) is the focal point for the ceremony.

Paris, 14 July 1790
About 300,000 people flocked to the Champ de Mars today on the first anniversary of the storming of the Bastille for a ceremony dubbed "The Festival of Federation". Undaunted by torrential rain they watched as the king and others swore to maintain the constitution in a celebration of national unity.

Enlightened ruler whose reforms failed

Vienna, 20 February 1790

The emperor Josef II, the Habsburg empire's most ambitious reformer, died today a disappointed man as discontent, generated by his reforms, continued to spark protests and unrest throughout the Holy Roman empire. The emperor, who was 48, had been ill for some time.

During the last few months of his ten-year rule he had become aware of the growing resistance to his reforms, and anticipating his death had written his own epitaph: "Here lies Josef II, who was unfortunate in all his enterprises."

His brother Leopold, recalled from Tuscany, inherits most of these enterprises. One of his first moves will be to decide whether to end Austrian involvement in the unpopular Ottoman war, which has placed a heavy tax burden on Habsburg subjects. Josef's attempts to bring Hungary more directly under Viennese control has already been thwarted, and Leopold will have to accept coronation in Hungary.

Leopold is unlikely to undo other key reforms. The decision to make German the official language, despite its unpopularity in Hungary and Flanders, the abolition of most

Enlightened despot: the late Holy Roman Emperor Josef II.

monasteries, the narrowing of church power, naturally unpopular with prelates, and the introduction of the secret police, who are hated by civil servants, will all remain.

Ironically the Emperor Josef, a follower of the Enlightenment, believed that all his reforms would enhance the dignity of the individual and thus benefit his people.

French clergy's property is nationalised

Fate worse than death: caricature from 1789 on clergy's loss of property.

Paris, 22 July 1790

The king reluctantly promulgated the Civil Constitution of the Clergy today. Under this decree, passed after months of intense debate, the clergy's property will be nationalised, and the state will employ priests as it does civil servants.

The constitution also reorganises the geography of the church, cutting the number of dioceses from 139 to 83, with each diocese conforming to the map of the civil departments. The "profane and scandalous" Concordat with Rome has been abolished because, according to the politician the count of Mirabeau, it was concluded "between an immoral pope and a despot, without the knowledge of church or empire", in order to divide the rights and the gold of Frenchmen between two usurpers.

The pope, who was not consulted over the reforms, is unlikely to be pleased by the new constitution: it recognises his supremacy over the Roman Catholic church, but removes the French clergy from his jurisdiction.

No matter what it is, it won't go away

Paris, 1789

A new book by the French chemist Antoine Lavoisier contains many new ideas on the properties and behaviour of matter. Called an *Elementary Treatise on Chemistry*, it describes most of the discoveries of the age and is the first to provide a complete list of known elements.

Explicit reference is made to an important principle that others such as Black and Cavendish have stated implicitly. It is the Law of Conservation of Matter. In a passage on fermentation, Lavoisier declares that in the laboratory and in nature matter is always conserved: the same amount exists after a chemical process as before.

European's diaries tell of flourishing slave society in Surinam

London, 1790

When the Scottish-Dutch soldier John Stedman first stepped ashore in Dutch Guiana (*Surinam*) more than 20 years ago he saw "a beautiful negro maid". She was weighed down with chains. Her only other dress was "a rag round her loins which was like her skin cut and carved by the lash of the whip in the most shocking manner". The girl's crime was to fail to please her owner in a trivial domestic task.

Stedman fought an army of runaway slaves who began to massacre whites. Yet he never lost respect for "my brother the negro". After a life of adventure he has settled in England where he has written a journal of a five-year campaign against the rebels. It is an intimate account of a slave-owning society from within. Stedman is not opposed to slavery as such, only to the unnecessary excesses of those abusing the system. These include "overgrown widows, stale beauties

Skinning a snake in Dutch Guiana.

and over-aged maids" who torture young slave women to death. The jealousy is overtly sexual. Stedman claims that many of the white men in this and similar colonies are frequently exhausted by their relations

One casualty of a slave revolt.

with "uninhibited" black women. He also admires the skill and courage of blacks as jungle fighters. It is only with the aid of "slaves in red coats" (soldiers) that white rule survives.

France, 10 May. At Montauban, in the south, Catholics and aristocrats clash with Protestants and members of the National Guard, leaving five dead and 16 others injured. When 55 patriots are thrown into jail, Protestants begin to flee from the town.

Paris, 21 May. Paris is divided into 48 zones.

Paris, 22 May. A law is passed whereby the Assembly and the king will share the right to declare war.

France, 29 May. The patriots imprisoned at Montauban are freed.

West Indies, 9 June. Civil war breaks out in Martinique between white settlers and Blacks campaigning for equality.

Avignon, 12 June. Avignon breaks its ties with Vatican and seeks union with France.

France, 15 June. Called out in support of patriots, Protestant militiamen massacre about 300 Catholic "aristocrats" in Nimes.

Paris, 19 June. The Assembly passes a law abolishing the hereditary nobility.

Paris, 3 July. The marquis of Condorcet proposes giving civil rights to women.

Baltic, 9 July. Pursuing their war with Russia, which broke out two years ago, the Swedes win the great naval battle of Svensksund, sinking or capturing a third of the Russian fleet.

France, 12 July. The Assembly approves a Civil Constitution providing for the election of priests and bishops.

Paris, 14 July. A huge celebration of the Federation – a nationwide bond of mutual help and brotherhood, adopted by the Assembly on 7 June – is held on the Champ de Mars.

Paris, 23 July. A letter from Pope Pius VI dated 10 July condemns the proposed new Civil Constitution for the French church. It arrives the day after the king approves the proposals.

Lyons, 26 July. An attempt at a counter-revolution is put down by the National Guard.

Prussia, 27 July. Prussia and Austria sign the treaty of Reichenbach, giving Austria a free hand to take action against the Belgians.

Paris, 28 July. The Assembly refuses the Emperor Leopold II the right of passage over French territory to put down the Belgian insurrection, breaking the 1775 alliance between Vienna and Paris.

USA, 1 August. The first census taken in the USA reveals a propulation of nearly four million.

Sweden, 24 August. The treaty of Varala ends the war between Sweden and Russia and returns to the *status quo*.

Paris, 26 August. The Assembly refuses to help Spain in its conflict with Britain over Nootka Sound, breaking the "Family Compact" between the Bourbons of France and Spain.

France, 31 August. A revolt of soldiers in the Chateauvieux garrison at Nancy is put down with the loss of over 300 lives.

West Indies, August. An attempt by planters in Santo Domingo to win independence from France ends in failure.

Paris, 2 September. Forty-five thousand people march in protest at the massacre of mutineers in Nancy.

Paris, 4 September. Jacques Necker is forced to resign as finance minister.

France, 17 September. Sailors mutiny in the port of Brest.

North Pacific, October. Britain and Spain reach agreement on navigation of the North Pacific and the use of Nootka Sound, ending their year-long dispute.

England, October. The politician and philosopher Edmund Burke publishes his *Reflections on the Revolution in France*.

France, 21 October. The tricolour is chosen as the national flag of France.

Paris, 27 October. The Assembly adopts the decimal system for weights and measures.

Netherlands, 22 November. The Austrians start to reconquer the rebellious Belgian states.

Paris, 27 November. The Assembly forces priests to swear allegiance to the church's Civil Constitution.

The Hague, 10 December. Having completed the reconquest of the rebel Belgian states with his capture of Brussels a week ago, the Emperor Leopold II signs a treaty guaranteeing the restoration of Belgian national institutions.

Rhode Island, 21 December. Samuel Slater opens first cotton mill in the USA. The mill has 250 spindles powered by water and operated by children. Slater learnt textile manufacture as an apprentice to a partner of Richard Arkwright, inventor of the water frame.

Ottoman Empire, 22 December. The Russians take Ismail in Bessarabia (*Romania*).

"Canal mania" boosts English trade

The Grand Junction Canal disappears into a tunnel at Blisworth.

England, c.1790
The growing number of people who have lost patience with goods disappearing in the post, and who fear threats to the parcel service on the thief-infested roads, are turning to a safer alternative. The canal system, which will soon link most of the great navigable rivers, carries an increasing weight of general merchandise as well as the bulk loads of coal and timber associated with narrow boats. So popular are the new waterways that wits have coined a new phrase, "Canal Mania".

On one canal the general merchandise moved from Liverpool to Wigan between 1786 and 1787 increased from 3,836 tons to 4,610 tons. Almost 4,000 miles of waterway have been created over the last 30 years, costing £11 million.

But if canal transport is safe, it is slow compared with most land routes. Travelling from London to Glasgow, using successive teams of horses on improved roads, takes only 63 hours. Merchants use slow pack horses less and carriers' wagons more. Another innovation is the commercial traveller with his samples and order book instead of a complete consignment of goods for sale. Yet the high cost of Royal Mail services, often inflated by private tolls on what were public roads, means that modern times have not touched many communities. Some villages are unfamiliar with the potato, sugar and cotton.

Monarch sends impostor to pay tribute

Aman (Vietnam)
The Aman (*Vietnamese*) king, Nguyen Hue, has recognised Chinese suzerainty over his country by making the long journey to Beijing to present tribute to the emperor, Qianlong. Hue, who was invited to China "to come and be transformed", is being received favourably by the Chinese, following their traditional policy of managing tributary states on "an equal basis of benevolence". On learning that Hue was accompanied by his son, the emperor praised the son for his loyalty and made him crown prince. Yet there is a doubt about Hue's visit. It is said that, reluctant to leave his throne to the mercy of his enemies, he has sent a double to Beijing in his place.

Qianlong, the Emperor of China, who established suzerainty over Aman (Vietnam).

London orphans work in MP's mill

London

The new breed of man who is taking up the reins of power in Britain is epitomised by the arrival in the House of Commons of Robert Peel, the third son of a Lancashire mill-master, a self-made man and now head of one of the wealthiest "new money" families in the land.

The Peels were yeoman farmers settled near Blackburn and, like many of their kind, began to feel the pressures generated by large-scale agriculture and industrialisation. Robert's father mortaged their land and with a brother-in-law and a local publican opened a factory for calico printing, to which were later added spinning and weaving, operated by James Hargreaves' spinning jenny.

The enterprise prospered, but the local handloom weavers resented the new technology and wrecked the machines. The Peels moved to Burton-on-Trent and built three new mills and a canal. In response to a growing labour shortage in the region, the Peels hit on the novel idea of recruiting stray children found on the London streets and putting them to work in the mills. Robert, deciding to go into politics, bought himself a pocket borough at Tamworth, Staffordshire.

Revolution fever spreads to Geneva

Geneva

The poor townspeople and the peasants in rural Geneva have been infected with the new freedoms achieved across the border in France. They have now found a leader to press their new-found aspirations for political rights and a national assembly. Jacques Grenos is an aristocrat, but he developed an antagonism to his own class after his exile following the counter-revolution of 1782.

Before 1782 the bourgeois party which Grenos supported had been winning increasing power. In that year France, Zurich and Bern intervened to restore power to the aristocrats. Opponents were banished or went into voluntary exile.

Neither the townspeople nor the peasants have any political rights, and the former group have been increasingly disaffected since 1782 when efforts to improve their lot were reversed. Many of those who live in towns are educated and have been inspired by the French Revolution.

Grenos hopes to capitalise on this. He has a hard task. The aristocrats and the bourgeois are already seeking to compromise on some of their ancient disagreements and to unite against the new threat.

Burke stirs up anti-revolutionary feelings

A cartoonist's view of Burke's attack on revolutionary sympathisers.

London, October

The first denunciation of the French Revolution has come from Edmund Burke, the English Whig parliamentarian. His *Reflections on the Revolution in France*, just published, condemns its philosophical basis as false. Burke does not accept Rousseau's doctrine of a social contract or of the "natural rights" of man in a state of nature. The "real rights of men", he says, "apply only in a civil society ruled by law from which man obtains his right to justice and to his property, inheritance and the fruits of his industry. The state ought not to be considered as nothing better than a partnership agreement in a trade of pepper and coffee, calico and tobacco, to be taken up or dissolved by the fancy of the parties," as the French have torn up their constitution.

For Burke, human society evolves by a slow process like the British constitution, "adapted over the centuries to fit the nature of English society". Britain's "Glorious Revolution" of 100 years ago did not overturn the social order. Burke foresees that the consequences will be bloodshed, civil war and tyranny: "Some popular general will establish a military dictatorship in place of anarchy."

Russian gentleman's pamphlet on the evils of serfdom

The Grand Place, and its shops, in the centre of Moscow (in 1795).

St Petersburg

A wealthy Russian belonging to the landed gentry has been sentenced to death for sedition after he published a book recounting the evils of serfdom and proposing its gradual abolition. Alexander Radishchev was sent by the government to study at the university of Leipzig; on his return he became a civil servant. But the Pugachev revolt of 1773-4, in which landlords were massacred, made him aware of the sufferings of the Russian peasants.

In his book *Journey from St Petersburg to Moscow,* he argues that exploitation of the peasants discourages effort and holds down production. The peasant must work six days for his master and only on the seventh day can he plough land for himself. Such a system is counter-productive: "Everything we do for our own sake, everything we do without compulsion, we do carefully, industriously and well. On the other hand, all that we do not do for our own advantage we do carelessly and lazily." Radishchev's radical notions, though they have upset the czarina, may not prove fatal, after all; she is now talking of simply sending him to Siberia.

"The Zenith a French Glory": a British view of the Revolution.

The age of Enlightenment

The great intellectual and cultural awakening of the 18th century is known as the *Enlightenment* – but what was this light which was illuminating Europe?

It was "reason". All the various intellectuals, men of letters, scientists and administrators – both Catholic and Protestant, pious and atheistical – who saw themselves as "enlightened" shared this faith in the power of human reason. For the Enlightenment was no homogeneous movement, no party or platform, but rather a climate of opinion or even an attitude. It was the duty of these independent thinkers, "philosophers" as they called themselves, to subject their world and all its institutions to rational criticism, for nothing was beyond improvement and nothing which did not advance human happiness was justifiable. The dead hand of tradition and "superstition" had at last been lifted, and human dignity and free will had been rediscovered. When trying to define the Enlightenment in 1784, Kant wrote of humanity coming of age, throwing off its self-imposed tutelage, and taking full responsibility for its own freedom.

Natural law

The roots of this optimistic world view probably lay in the intellectual and scientific revolution of the 17th century, and the birth of a new philosophical scepticism which demanded that everything should be susceptible to proof in comprehensible terms. Soon the experimental scientists began to reveal the underlying laws of the physical world.

The philosophers of the Enlightenment were convinced that jurisprudence, morality and religion were no less dependent upon immutable laws than astronomy or physics, and they quickly set about eliciting the rules which made up natural law, natural ethics and natural religion.

Humanity guided by reason had an innate desire to do good and be happy: the apostles of the Enlightenment had little time for schemes where people spent their lives fulfilling the arbitrary commands of a stern God or for barbaric notions like original sin. Virtue was now to be its own reward.

The Enlightenment's war with Christianity was waged on several fronts. Against the church as an institution: its pomp and wealth; its "mediaeval" relics, such as monasticism; the miracles and "enthusiasm" by which it sustained superstition and "priestcraft"; and its control of the free expression of ideas through its grip on education and censorship. But the Enlightenment also questioned the very need for revealed religion. Anyone could infer the existence of a creator from reason and from the surrounding world. This "deism" was a natural and adequate religion: the God of the Old Testament, with all his rules and interfering, was replaced by a "cosmic watchmaker" who, having created the world, left it to run according to its own rules.

Such confidence in the inherent rationality of the world and of man led the *philosophes* to reject the social and political complexities of their own age. Just because 18th-century society was based on privilege and tradition did not mean that it should be. Individual rights and public utility were to be the criteria for social and political organisation: the object of government should be the greatest happiness of the greatest number. The leaders of the Enlightenment called for impartial justice, fair taxation, more education; they exposed intolerance, bigotry and abuses of power: but they were not really interested in dirtying their hands with the practicalities of reform. The Enlightenment can, perhaps, be seen at its best in the humane and rational approach of the marquis of Beccaria (1738-94) in his treatise on crime and punishment (1764).

Republic of letters

The cosmopolitan nature of the Enlightenment is one of its most striking features. The "republic of letters", established originally by Huguenot exiles and others in the Netherlands, became an international network for the exchange of ideas. Books and pamphlets were printed, translated, distributed – often in secret – across Europe. But the French were pre-eminent in this literary world. Since the days of Louis XIV, France had been the cultural leader of Europe. The French *philosophes* inherited this leadership, and made sure of their position through the success of authors like Voltaire and Diderot and of publications like the *Encyclopedie*.

The Enlightenment did not stand still however. The 18th century saw rapid changes in intellectual and aesthetic styles – as literary classicism came under attack from the "naturalistic" cult of "sensibility", and the Palladian style gave way to the Rococo in the arts – and a similar trend is apparent in the Enlightenment. For instance, Montesquieu and Rousseau, both of whom can be claimed for the Enlightenment, had almost nothing in common. Montesquieu, an admirer of the English constitution, propounded a constitutional arrangement in which monarchy would be limited by a virtuous aristocracy. But Rousseau argued in *The Social Contract* (1762) for a truly democratic society, claiming that supreme sovereignty rested with the "general will", which expressed the aspirations of all citizens. Neither had much experience of real politics.

The French "Economists" or "Physiocrats" were more down to earth. They hoped to solve France's economic ills in a free market for agricultural produce, for a while influencing ministers like Turgot. But autocracy and privilege were hard to reconcile with the freedom of enterprise and sanctity of property on which the Physiocrats pinned their hopes, and little enlightened reform was achieved.

Enlightened despots

The term "enlightened despotism" was first coined by de la Riviere, a Physiocrat, in 1767. Yet it was outside France that enlightened despotism came into its own – in Joseph II's Austria, Pombal's Portugal, Frederick the Great's Prussia, Catherine the Great's Russia and Grand Duke Leopold's Tuscany. In many of these countries a much closer connection existed between intellectuals and governments than it did in France. In the German states, for example, the Enlightenment was nurtured in the many state-controlled universities. The German tradition, exemplified by Thomasius and Wolff, created an ideology for autocrats, by arguing that absolutism was grounded in natural law.

These enlightened thinkers were, of course, economically dependent on their princes. It was only in France that the *philosophes* could make independent livings as writers. Censorship was more of an inconvenience than a gag, and writers were great figures, as Voltaire discovered on his return to Paris in 1778. Yet the Enlightenment and its values were the preserve of a small, self-consciously progressive circle. Side by side with the lofty thinkers of the Enlightenment, there flourished a darker world of inquisitors, religious zealots and slave traders. The elegant salons of 18th-century Paris existed amid mass poverty, squalor and corruption.

Some have seen the Enlightenment as embodying bourgeois values of individualism, merit, utility and rationality. But in 1789 it was the French nobility rather than the Third Estate who spoke with the authentic voice of the *philosophes*. True, the crucial documents of the Revolution, the Declaration of the Rights of Man and the 1791 Constitution, do espouse key Enlightenment values; but the revolutionaries quoted Montesquieu and Rousseau ceaselessly, without apparently recognising their contradictions. The often naive optimism of the Enlightenment was not to survive the Age of Revolutions.

Encyclopaedic genius: Diderot, by Carle van Loo (1705-65).

Garden of Eden, by Jacob Bouttats (c.1700). The Enlightenment questioned the Bible's account of creation.

People's man: Voltaire and peasants, perhaps by Huber.

Newton by William Blake (1757-1827), who sees him as serving a rationalistic, "prime mover", God.

Frederick the Great, c.1740.

Paris, December 1790. Louis XVI seeks help from Frederick William II of Prussia, asking him to set up a "European congress backed by armed forces".

Southern Africa, 1790. Zwide succeeds his father, Yaka, as chief of the militaristic Ndwandwe chiefdom, centred on the Pongola river. Once subjects of the Tembe kingdom at Maputo Bay, paying tribute in ivory and cattle, the Ndwandwe took advantage of the Tembe's involvement in civil war to build up power by attacking their neighbours.

Austria, 1790. Mozart completes a new opera, a sexual comedy entitled *Cosi fan tutte*. The opera was ordered by the late Emperor Josef II, to whom Mozart was chamber musician.

Paris, 13 January 1791. The Assembly introduces a universal tax on rent and property values.

France, 16 January 1791. A national police force known as the *gendarmerie* is created.

France, 20 January 1791. Talleyrand, who has taken the oath of allegiance to the church's civil constitution – of which he was the main author – is forced to resign as bishop of Autun.

France, January 1791. The requirement to swear allegiance to the church's civil constitution stirs up a widespread rebellion among priests.

France, 2 February 1791. The first bishops are elected under the new civil constitution.

Paris, 14 February 1791. The expedition to circumnavigate the globe led by the famous French explorer la Perouse is pronounced lost. Both his ships, *L'Astrolabe* and *La Boussole*, are believed to have sunk in the Pacific.

France, 19 February 1791. The king's aunts, Adelaide and Victoire, leave the country and seek refuge abroad.

Germany, 23 February 1791. The prince of Conde arrives in Worms to set up an army of exiles.

Philadelphia, 25 February 1791. President Washington signs a bill creating the Bank of the United States.

West Indies, 26 February 1791. The leaders of a Mulatto uprising in Santo Domingo are executed.

Paris, 28 February 1791. After putting down a people's uprising in Vincennes, Lafayette rushes back to Paris to disarm revolutionary plotters.

USA, 4 March 1791. Vermont becomes the 14th state of the Union.

London, 13 March 1791. Thomas Paine, a firm supporter of the French Revolution, publishes the second part of his *Rights of Man*, in which he rejects the arguments in Edmund Burke's *Reflections on the Revolution in France.*

Britain, 21 March 1791. Britain reaches an agreement with Prussia to oppose the expansionist ambitions of Russia.

Paris, 23 March 1791. Etta Palm, a Dutch champion of women's rights, sets up a group of women's clubs called the Confederation of the Friends of Truth. The Friends aim to give assistance to the poor, visit the sick and handicapped and take care of children's education.

Paris, 2 April 1791. Mirabeau, who has proved himself a highly influential force in the Assembly, dies. Poisoning is suspected.

Rome, 13 April 1791. Pope Pius VI threatens to suspend all priests who have sworn allegiance to the French church's civil constitution unless they recant within 40 days.

Paris, 18 April 1791. National Guardsmen prevent Louis XVI and his family from leaving Paris.

Poland, 3 May 1791. Stanislas II Augustus Poniatowski, the king of Poland, creates a constitution for his country providing for an hereditary monarchy and the separation of executive, legislative and judicial powers.

Paris, 16 May 1791. Maximilien de Robespierre, an increasingly influential figure on the extreme left of the Assembly, persuades the deputies to vote against seeking their own re-election.

Paris, 26 May 1791. The Assembly forces Louis XVI to hand over all the assets of the crown to the nation.

Paris, 30 May 1791. Robespierre calls for the abolition of the death penalty.

Paris, 1 June 1791. The Assembly abolishes all forms of torture.

Paris, 14 June 1791. The le Chapelier law bans strikes and abolishes all workers' associations.

France, 25 June 1791. The royal family return to Paris after their attempt to flee ended with the arrest at Varennes.

Paris, 25 June 1791. The Assembly temporarily suspends Louis XVI's powers.

France, 26 June 1791. News of the king's attempted escape sets off serious unrest in the Lyons region.

Brussels, 29 June 1791. The count of Provence, the brother of Louis XVI, arrives in Brussels after successfully fleeing from Paris.

William Blake: poet of revolutionary age

"Glad Days": from "Songs of Innocence" by William Blake.

Title page from William Blake's "Songs of Innocence".

London, 1790
William Blake, an engraver, of Poland Street, Soho, has invented a method of "illuminated printing" for his book of poems, *Songs of Innocence*. Words and images are combined on a single plate, resembling mediaeval illuminated manuscript. Each volume is finished by hand in full colour and no two are the same.

The poems concern man's childlike capacity for joy, spoiled by the "mind-forged manacles" put on him by society and religion. "How can the bird that is born for joy sit in a cage and sing?" Blake calls himself a "Son of Liberty" and openly wears the red revolutionary bonnet in the streets. He has written and printed, but not yet published, *The French Revolution*, a dramatised debate between king, nobles and commons.

His mystical work, *The Marriage of Heaven and Hell*, denies the separate existence of God and the soul of man. "The road of excess leads to the palace of wisdom", runs one of his "Proverbs of Hell".

"Semaphore" helps fast communication

Paris, 2 March 1791
A new system of rapid communication was unveiled today, and the transfer of information will never be the same again. Created by the engineer Claude Chappe, the optical telegraph is a truly revolutionary invention.

The device is simple: machines equipped with mobile arms are sited on towers built on open ground. The arms may be moved into 196 positions, 92 of which represent the signs used in transmitting a message. The system of signs is known as "semaphore".

The operator need only consult a codebook before sending information on to the next tower where it can be read by another operator, armed with a telescope, and duly passed on once more.

Armed for communication: Claude Chappe's original optical telegraph.

Paine's "Rights of Man" backs revolution

Thomas Paine, as seen by contemporary political cartoonist Cruikshank.

London, March 1791
Many writers have challenged Edmund Burke's anti-Revolution pamphlet, *Reflections on the Revolution in France*, but the most outspoken response has come from Thomas Paine, a Norfolk man who played a part in the American Revolution. *The Rights of Man* which he has written is dedicated to George Washington. It accuses Burke of "outrageous abuse on the French Revolution and the principles of liberty". Paine's tract explains the origins of the revolution in the ideas of Montesquieu, Rousseau and others and describes the Rights of Man as essentially that men are born free and equal in their rights to liberty, property, security and resistance of oppression.

"Man has no property in man," he says, "There is a dawn of reason rising on the world."

Slavery bill vetoed

London, 18 April 1791
After a speech of four hours in the House of Commons today, William Wilberforce moved that the import of African slaves into British colonies should be banned. He lost the vote by 163 to 88, but intends to keep the anti-slavery campaign going. Wilberforce, the son of a rich merchant family from Yorkshire, believes that his cause has been harmed by the abortive rebellion of slaves in the French colony of Santo Domingo, where many white slave owners have been killed.

Aztec art is dug up

Mexico, 1790
Drainage work in Mexico City has uncovered two massive pieces of pre-Spanish conquest Aztec sculpture. The first is already becoming known as the "Stone of the Sun", a circular object with an agonised face, tongue protruding. The second is an elaborate block weighing many tons, representing the goddess Quoatlicue or another named Teoyamiqui. The block has clawed feet and tusks. Both are housed in the university. The round stone might be a calendar.

Louis XVI's flight fails

Exposed: the fleeing French royal family is arrested at Varennes.

Varennes, 21 June 1791
The French royal family have been arrested at Varennes as they attempted to flee in disguise to Metz to join the army of the marquis of Bouille. The attempt was well planned by the count of Fersen, the Swedish officer who is believed to be the queen's lover. Dressed as a hackney driver, he smuggled the royal family out of the Tuileries.

They intended to head east towards the village of Pont de Sommeville where they would be met by the young duke of Choiseul and his hussars. But they were delayed and the villagers became suspicious of the soldiers, who had to hide in the woods and got lost.

The king, disguised as a valet, drove on and reached Varennes, 142 miles from Paris, where he was recognised by a horseman sent in search of him by Lafayette, the commander of the National Guard. The fugitives were escorted to the shop of the local prosecutor, a grocer named Sauce, where they were arrested. They are now on their way back to Paris.

Polish liberals oust Russia's old regime

Warsaw, 3 May 1791
Taking advantage of Russia's preoccupation with war with the Ottoman empire a group of Polish patriots today staged a *coup d'etat* to throw off the Russian yoke and introduce a new constitution to rid the country of its out-dated and anarchical customs. The patriots' leader, Hugo Kollontaj, acted when opponents of reform in the parliament were away.

Class distinctions are abolished and the special privileges of the gentry, including land ownership and access to state and church offices, are opened to townsmen. Plans are being made to abolish serfdom. But the Czarina Catherine is none too pleased at the course of events.

King splits Canada up into two parts

London, 19 June 1791
King George III today signed the Constitution Act, granting equal rights to the French and English inhabitants of Canada. The region is split into two provinces, each with its own representative assembly. In Quebec province there will be a huge French majority. French is recognised, with English, as the official language and full rights are granted to Roman Catholics.

Some see the measures as gratitude to the French for their loyalty during the American War of Independence. Others think that Britain has realised that British Canada cannot survive with a large disaffected French population in the north and a new republic to the south.

Pacific, June. The French navigator Etienne Marchand takes possession of the Marquesas Islands for France and renames them the Revolution Isles.

Paris, June. The publication of *The Spirit of the Revolution* by Louis Antoine de St Just, an ardent supporter of Robespierre, is a great success.

Italy, 6 July. At Padua, the Emperor Leopold II calls on the monarchs of Europe to join him in demanding the king of France's freedom.

England, 14 July. Celebrations to mark the anniversary of the fall of the Bastille cause a riot in Birmingham. A banquet given by the pro-liberal chemist Joseph Priestley is broken up by a mob incited by Anglican clergymen.

Paris, 15 July. The Assembly decrees that Louis XVI was not responsible for his own actions in fleeing and that he can only be put on trial after his abdication.

Paris, 16 July. Louis XVI is suspended from office until he agrees to ratify the constitution.

Paris, 16 July. A major split opens up in the Jacobin Club over the future of the monarchy.

Paris, 17 July. A republican demonstration on the Champ de Mars calling for the deposition of the king ends in bloodshed when the National Guard opens fire on the crowd, killing dozens.

Paris, 24 July. On the instigation of Robespierre, all Jacobins opposed to the principles of the Revolution – known as Feuillants – are expelled from the society.

Vienna, 25 July. Chancellor Kaunitz opens talks with Prussia aimed at setting up a European congress opposed to the French revolution.

Ottoman empire, 4 August. Austria and the Ottoman empire sign the peace of Sistova, by which Belgrade is returned to the Ottomans.

West Indies, 12 August. Black slaves on the island of Santo Domingo rise up against their white masters.

Prussia, 27 August. The Emperor Leopold II and Frederick William II of Prussia issue a joint declaration at Pillnitz in support of the French monarchy.

Paris, 8 September. The Salon opens at the Louvre palace. 247 artists, including 19 women, exhibit their works.

France, 9 September. Royalists take control of Arles and barricade themselves inside the town.

Paris, 14 September. Louis XVI solemnly swears his allegiance to the French constitution.

France, 14 September. Avignon and the papal state of the Comtat Venaissin are formally joined to France.

France, 27 September. Jews in France are granted French citizenship.

Paris, 30 September. During its final session, the Assembly decrees a general amnesty for all those sentenced for rioting since 1788.

Paris, September. The author Olympe de Gouges publishes a declaration of the rights of women.

Paris, 1 October. The National Legislative Assembly holds its first meeting. It comprises 745 deputies: on the right are 264 Feuillants; on the left 136 Jacobins, led by Condorcet and Brissot; and 345 independents.

Paris, 8 October. Lafayette resigns his post as commander of the National Guard in Paris.

Belfast, 14 October. The Protestant lawyer Theobald Wolfe Tone sets up the Belfast Society of United Irishmen, calling for the emancipation of Catholics – who are denied the right to vote – and parliamentary reform.

Avignon, 17 October. Sixty-one prisoners – arrested in August when the patriots took control of Avignon – are massacred in reprisal for the murder of the patriot secretary of the commune, Lescuyer.

West Indies, 19 October. An alliance is signed between the leaders of the Mulatto revolt in Santo Domingo and the royalist commanders who protect the white planters in west of the island.

Paris, October. The marquis de Sade publishes a work of fiction entitled *Justine or the Misfortunes of Virtue*, in which virtue is punished and vice triumphs. It was written during his imprisonment in the Bastille.

USA, 4 November. US troops under Arthur St Clair, the governor of the Northwest Territory, suffer a humiliating defeat in a battle with Ohio Indians under Chief Little Turtle.

France, 4 November. The marquis of Hericy and 84 other noblemen involved in a royalist plot are arrested in Caen.

India, 6 November. The French colony of Chandernagore promulgates its own constitution.

Dublin, 6 November. The Dublin Society of United Irishmen is set up.

Europeans intend to restore French king

Royal solidarity: the emperor, the king of Prussia and the elector of Saxony.

Pillnitz, Prussia, 27 August
The sovereigns of Europe, in a gesture of support for their cousin Louis XVI, have declared that royal authority should be restored in France.

Meeting at Pillnitz in Prussia, Leopold II of Austria and Frederick William II of Prussia have invited the rest of Europe's rulers to join in their attack on the revolutionary government.

The first response of France's Constituent Assembly was to prepare for war with Europe, but cooler heads have realised that the Declaration of Pillnitz is only a diplomatic move, designed to pressurise the Assembly and bolster the hopes of the French king.

Rebel slaves take part of Santo Domingo

Santo Domingo, 24 August
The black slaves of France's colony of Santo Domingo, "the pearl of the Antilles", have risen in a bloody revolt against their masters, the *grands blancs*, or rich plantation owners. A French expeditionary force is heading for the island.

Whites have died and the canefields have been burnt in the fertile Plaine du Nord area. The revolt has been directly inspired by the Revolution in France. In May the National Assembly decided to give the vote to the *gens de couleur*, the colony's Mulattoes and free Blacks. The planters, while demanding colonial autonomy, refused to comply, and a major controversy began.

Taking advantage of the confusion, some 100,000 of the island's half a million slaves chose to revolt

Toussaint-Louverture: rebel leader.

on 12 August. Driving the Whites from their plantations, they have destroyed the sugar and coffee crops and are currently in control of part of the island.

French revolution fires Irish rebels

Dublin, December

Wolfe Tone, a young Protestant lawyer fired by the ideas of the French Revolution, has helped to found a a society of United Irishmen to fight for social, political and economic rights for all Irish, Catholic and Protestant. Its supporters, largely Dublin and Belfast middle class, have been deeply impressed by the all-men-are-created-equal slogan of the Americans and the cries of "Liberty, Fraternity, Equality" heard in Paris.

London has been seeking to respond to Irish Catholic grievances. Catholics now hold the franchise on equal terms with the Protestants; they can serve on juries and be given junior commissioned ranks in the army. But the Anglo-Irish

An Irish rebel: a follower of the United Irishmen leader, Wolfe Tone.

governing class refuses to agree to complete equality for Catholics for fear of losing its ascendancy.

Whatever happens, the United Irishmen are not interested in mere reforms; they want complete independence for Ireland. They are allied with agrarian terrorists and Tone plans a secret trip to Paris to persuade the French to send troops to support an Irish rebellion. In response the Protestants in Ulster have formed an Orange Society to fight for their interests.

King signs constitution

The nation gives the king a constitution as clergy and nobles scrutinise it.

Paris, 4 September

King Louis XVI today approved France's first constitution. It was finally agreed yesterday after two years of work by the Assembly. The constitution embodies all the laws passed since that fateful day in 1789 when the Third Estate met in the royal tennis court at Versailles.

With his own hand Louis has, in fact, signed the death sentence of the absolute monarchy. France retains a monarchy, but it is a figurehead institution. The only power left to the king is to hold up for three years decrees issued by the

Assembly. He has become, in effect, a civil servant of the state, with a salary of 50 million livres. He has even had the right to declare war and conclude international treaties taken away from him.

Power now rests with the Legislative Assembly, made up of 745 deputies elected for two years by 50,000 electors who are themselves to be appointed by "active" citizens paying an annual tax equal to at least three days' work. The king, despite his reservations on the viability of the constitution, has agreed to accept it before the Assembly.

Mozart dies of a fever, aged only 35

Vienna, 5 December

Last December, Mozart saw Haydn off on his long journey to London; fearing that his elderly friend would not survive the trip he wept and said: "We shall never meet again!" His prophecy proved sadly right; but today it was Mozart who died, of a fever, aged only 35.

In spite of his early death, no musician can challenge Mozart's greatness. A child prodigy, he astonished audiences in Vienna, Paris and London; he wrote the first of his symphonies at nine and his first opera at 12. Frustrated by the limited opportunities of his native Salzburg, Mozart settled in Vienna in 1781, married in 1782 and gained a minor court post in 1787. Despite often living beyond his means and borrowing money, Mozart earned a good living from teaching and composing, especially piano concertos

Wolfgang Amadeus Mozart.

and operas (including *The Marriage of Figaro* (1786), *Don Giovanni* (1787) and *The Magic Flute* (1791)). He leaves a requiem mass unfinished.

Jews and actors better off in France

Paris

The social and economic impact of the Revolution is being felt in every aspect of life. Actors, Jews and Protestants now officially enjoy full civil rights, although some actors still find it difficult to get married in church, while Jews and Protestants still suffer from traditional prejudice.

Civil marriage has been introduced, and there is much agitation for a law allowing divorce. Socially, although gambling and the theatre are flourishing, people are more discreet in dress and manners.

The ending of feudal rights also ended feudal responsibilities, so another law had to be introduced for the state to take over the feeding of abandoned children, formerly the responsibility of the lord on whose land they were found. Perhaps the most popular of the reforms is the abolition of the "sealed orders" by which the king could consign anyone to prison.

Economically, abolition of both the salt tax and the Paris city toll has been heartily approved by the populace, but the cutting of the customs tariffs which have protected French industries has aroused much opposition.

Writer jailed for warning on Russia

Japan

The military commentator Hayashi Shihei has been arrested for publishing a book in which he warns of the dangers of a Russian invasion and advocates the development of Japan's northern defences.

He had great difficulty in raising the money to print the book and knew that it would cause trouble, for in the preface he wrote: "I realise that I have gone far beyond my station and that I shall not escape punishment. But it is his words and not the author which matter."

When his arrest was ordered for spreading false information and criticising official policies, he recited an epigram: "Will this head fly or won't it? Spring will soon be here." We shall see. Meanwhile he is locked up in Edo prison, awaiting trial.

1791 (1791-1792)

Paris, 11 November 1791. Using one of his few remaining powers, Louis XVI vetoes decrees ordering French emigres, including his own brother, to return to France.

China, 21 November 1791. The French navigator Etienne Marchand sets a new record for a crossing of the Pacific Ocean, completing the journey in 60 days.

Paris, 28 November 1791. Maximilien Robespierre is elected president of the Jacobin Club.

USA, 15 December 1791. Virginia is the tenth state to approve the ten amendments to the constitution known collectively as the Bill of Rights. As three-quarters of the states have now ratified the amendments, they become law.

Paris, 19 December 1791. Louis XVI vetoes a decree imposing punitive measures on priests who refuse to swear allegiance to the church's civil constitution.

Paris, 1791. The Dutch feminist Etta Palm leads a women's delegation to the Assembly and makes a speech calling for women's rights in education, politics, law and employment.

Japan, 1791. The famous author Santo Kyoden is sentenced to 50 days' house arrest in handcuffs for the publication of three risque books which have fallen foul of new censorship regulations. The books have been banned and the publisher heavily fined.

West Africa, 1791. Uthman dan Fodio – a scholar and poet in the Arabic and Fula languages, who has became an itinerant missionary preaching strict Islamic doctrine – is appointed tutor to the Gobir royal family in Niger. After taking up his new job, he has visions under the influence of Sufism and becomes an influential figure at the Gobir court.

West Africa, 1791. King Pepple of Bonny seizes control of slave trading at New Calabar (*Nigeria*) from his base in the Niger delta, establishing a prosperous coastal trade.

Australia, 1791. The third British fleet to arrive in Australia since 1788 increases the number of convicts and civilians in the new settlement at Sydney, putting extra pressure on supplies, already low as a result of crop failure from drought and inappropriate farming techniques.

England, 1791. The Sierra Leone Company is founded to promote "legitimate" trade to replace the slave trade in Sierra Leone.

England, 1791. The Scottish author James Boswell writes a biographical masterpiece entitled *Life of Samuel Johnson*.

Paris, January 1792. A split in the Jacobins between Robespierre and the Girondin party, led by Brissot – who favours war with the other European powers – is confirmed.

Ottoman Empire, 9 January 1792. The Ottomans sign a treaty with the Russians at Jassy ending their five-year war. Moldavia is returned to the Ottomans, but the Russians retain Ochakov and all the conquered lands between the Bug and Dniester rivers. Under the treaty Sultan Selim III also formally recognises the Russian annexation of the Crimea, achieved in 1783.

Paris, 24 January 1792. Five days of looting ends in a riot as the cost of living soars.

London, 25 January 1792. A political society modelled on the French Jacobins is set up. It is called the London Corresponding Society.

West Indies, 28 January 1792. The rebellious slaves in Santo Domingo launch an attack on the city of the Cap.

Vienna, 7 February 1792. Austria and Prussia sign a new military convention against France.

Vienna, 7 February 1792. The Italian composer Domenico Cimarosa presents his comic opera *The Secret Marriage* to great acclaim.

London, 23 February 1792. Sir Joshua Reynolds, the first president of the Royal Academy and one of the most brilliant portrait painters of his day, dies.

Strasbourg, 1 March 1792. Leopold II dies and is succeeded as emperor by his son Francis II.

Paris, 5 March 1792. The Sorbonne and the faculties of theology are banned.

Paris, 20 March 1792. The Legislative Assembly approves the use of the guillotine.

Paris, 23 March 1792 A ministry dominated by Girodins is formed.

Paris, 24 March 1792. Political rights are granted to free coloured men in the colonies.

Sweden, 29 March 1792. Gustavus III, king of Sweden since 1771, dies from wounds sustained in an attack by a nobleman, Ankaestrom, on 16 March at a masked ball. He was one of the firmest backers of the restoration of absolute monarchy in France.

USA, 2 April 1792. The first silver dollar is struck.

England, 1792. The chemist William Murdoch perfects a technique for the use of gas lighting.

Sloth, rudeness and high spirits recalled

London, 1791

Since the death of Dr Samuel Johnson seven years ago there has been a rush of memoirs about him. Now comes the long-awaited two-volume *Life of Johnson* by his Scots companion, James Boswell.

Boswell met Johnson in 1763 when the doctor was 54, his wife was dead, his *Dictionary* completed. He was already devoting most of his energy to conversation. Boswell made a habit of taking notes of Johnson's talk "of extra-ordinary vigour and vivacity" as soon as he left his presence.

In 1785 he published his journal of their entertaining *Tour to the Hebrides* when Johnson was 60, which had great success. He leaves out nothing – as well as the sayings, Johnson's slovenly dress, ungainly movements, uncouth eating habits, Lichfield accent, and mixture of melancholy, sloth, rudeness and high spirits contribute to an unforgettable likeness. "He will be seen as he really was," he writes.

Goldsmith, Boswell and Johnson at the Mitre Tavern, London.

Englishman offers to be French gaoler

London, 1791

An English philosopher has amiably offered to go to France, establish a model prison and himself be "gratuitously the gaoler thereof". He is Jeremy Bentham, the author of the newly published *Panopticon*, advocating penal reform.

Bentham was born in 1748; happy and hardworking, unmarried and unimaginative, his passions for friends, music and animals were extremely mild. In 1768 he came upon the formula "the greatest happiness of the greatest number". It has remained the rock of his philosophical principles. People, he believes, should not be punished on the basis of some principle of right or wrong; punishment should depend on the effects which both crime and punishment have on society: on "the greatest number".

States vote for Bill of Rights

Virginia, 15 December 1791

Ten vital amendments to the US Constitution, known as the Bill of Rights, have been ratified by three-quarters of the states and become law. Their acceptance is seen as a personal triumph for James Madison and his suporters, the anti-Federalists, who fear that the original constitution provides insufficient guarentees of rights of the states and individuals citizens against central government.

Eight of the amendments protect the rights of individuals: the first guaranteeing freedom of religion, speech, assembly and redress. The second gives citizens the right to bear arms. Others include the right to protection "against unreasonable searches and seizures", the "right to a speedy public trail" and "the right to trail by jury".

Sultan forced to cede Crimea to Russia

A cartoon expressing Europe's attentiveness to Russian expansion.

Jassy, 8 January 1792
After years of procrastination, the sultan of Ottoman has finally bowed to the inevitable and accepted Russia's annexation of the Crimea and suzerainty over Georgia.

Fearing that the Czarina Catherine was planning a partition of the Ottoman empire, the sultan declared war on Russia, but the Russians won victory after victory, culminating in the massacre of the Ottoman army at Mashin on 4 April last year; the outcome is the treaty of Jassy, signed today.

Catherine has vastly increased her territories on the Black Sea, thereby causing concern to the British, who see the weakening of the Ottoman positions in the region as a looming threat to British Mediterranean interests. Some observers claim that Catherine dreams of re-creating a Byzantine empire based on Istanbul.

War looms as new regime is sworn in

Paris, 23 March 1792
The Girondins, the group of moderates whose leaders were deputies for the Gironde, have brought about the downfall of the Feuillants' government, itself composed of moderate Jacobins, and have been summoned by the king to form a new administration.

Brissot, the Girondin leader, will not join the government: he needs to keep his seat in the Assembly. At stake is the question of war with Austria. The Girondins are in favour of war, but the situation has been thrown into confusion by the unexpected death of Leopold II of Austria, the brother of the queen.

It was Leopold who instigated the Declaration of Pillnitz inviting the European powers to join forces against the French revolutionaries. It seems now that the Girondins and the king are allied in their determination to go to war with the queen's relations.

Court martial for "Bounty" mutineers

Portsmouth, 1792
The court martial of the ten recaptured *Bounty* mutineers is set to commence on 12 August on board *HMS Duke* here. The ten, who face hanging if convicted, are charged with mutiny and desertion.

The prosecution witnesses will be led by the master of *HMS Bounty*, Captain William Bligh, who was cast adrift with 18 others in a 23-foot longboat on 28 April last year after the *Bounty* had anchored off the Friendly Isles.

In a remarkable feat of seamanship, Bligh's castaways, equipped with food but no maps, managed to sail 3,500 miles to Timor, in the Dutch West Indies, in just 47 days. Bligh and 12 survivors reached England late last year.

The ten mutineers were all captured on Tahiti. Another 12 and the ringleader, Fletcher Christian, plus three taken against their will, are missing, presumed to have settled somewhere in the South Seas.

The mutiny started after the *Bounty's* crew had spent six months in Tahiti collecting 1,000 breadfruit trees to ship to the West Indies. Some of the crew had formed attachments to Tahitian women and wanted to stay. The defence will argue that Bligh was a harsh and sadistic master.

Later portrayal of Bligh taking breadfruit trees aboard HMS Bounty.

Authoritarian Swedish king is killed

Stockholm, 29 March 1792
Sweden's formidable king for two decades, Gustavus III, died from his wounds today – two weeks after being shot while attending a masquerade at the opera. He was the victim of a plot conceived by his enemies who ranged from civil servants of noble birth to army officers cherishing grudges from Swedish defeats in wars against the Russians.

Gustavus, who was 46, spent a long period in France before coming to the throne, and one of his first acts was to impose a new constitution suppressing political parties and reducing the powers of the *Riksdag*, the Swedish parliament. He went on to rule as an enlightened despot. Gustavus introduced currency reform, reorganised Swedish defences and also tried, unsuccessfully, to tackle increasing alcoholism by cen-

Gustavus III, King of Sweden.

tralising all output of spirits in crown distilleries. But his war with Russia created huge inflation which fed the conspiracy on the part of his many enemies.

First silver dollar minted in America

Philadelphia, 2 April 1792
The newly independent United States of America now has its own coinage, the dollar. The first coins, bearing the head of an eagle, have been struck by the Philadelphia mint on the authority of the Bank of the United States, established by Congress last December.

Gold dollars have 24.75 grains of gold, and silver ones contain 371.25 grains of fine metal, roughly in line with the market ratio for the price of the two metals. However, sceptics warn that there could be difficult times ahead if the two metals fail to hold the same price ratio.

The "hard-money" men behind the US constitution prefer coins to paper money, which is easy to debase and has colonial overtones.

Europe, 20 April. Following Chancellor Kaunitz's refusal to dissolve the congress of European sovereigns, the French Legislative Assembly approves by a huge majority the king's proposal to declare war on Austria. Louis XVI's plan to attack his own nephew, the Emperor Francis II, violates the alliance that has linked France and Austria since 1756.

USA, 22 April. President Washington proclaims American neutrality in the war in Europe.

France, 29 April. The Jacobins regain control of Avignon.

New York City, 17 May. A group of 24 merchants and brokers creates the New York stock exchange, on Wall Street.

Poland, 18 May. Russian troops invade Poland.

Paris, 27 May. The Assembly orders the deportation of all priests who refuse to swear allegiance to the church's civil constitution.

Paris, 15 June. In a government reshuffle, moderate Feuillants take power at the expense of the Girondin group known as the Brissotins (followers of Brissot).

Paris, 20 June. A huge mob overruns the Tuileries during a march by the Brissotins to demand that the royal veto of the latest decrees be withdrawn and their ministers recalled.

Paris, 29 June. Lafayette makes an unsuccessful attempt to mobilise the National Guard to break up the Jacobin Club by force.

Germany, 14 July. At Koblenz, the duke of Brunswick, the commander-in-chief of the Prussian army, publishes a manifesto threatening Parisians with exemplary revenge if they do not submit to their monarch.

Poland, 24 July. By approving the confederation formed at Targowica by Polish nobles who support Russia, Stanislas II Augustus Poniatowski, the king of Poland, yields to Catherine II of Russia. This marks the death of the Polish constitution.

Paris, 10 August. The *sans-culottes* seize the Tuileries. The king is taken prisoner and suspended from office.

Paris, 11 August. A revolutionary commune is formed. Antoine Santerre is made head of the National Guard. The Assembly appoints a provisional executive council of six members, including Georges Danton and Jean Marie Roland, and calls a national convention.

Netherlands, 19 August. Lafayette is arrested by the Austrians. The fall of the Tuileries marked the final split between Lafayette and the revolution: the commander of the northern army was asked to hand over power to Dumouriez and chose to desert rather than face the guillotine, crossing the border into the Netherlands.

Paris, 25 August. Du Rozoy, the director of the *Gazette du Paris*, who had been charged with collecting funds for emigres and trying to start a civil war, is the first journalist to be guillotined. All monarchist newspapers have already been banned and their printing presses seized.

France, 26 August. The fortified town of Longwy surrenders to the Prussians.

Paris, 31 August. The Assembly cancels a decree, passed yesterday, that the rebel commune formed on 10 August is illegal.

France, 2 September. Verdun surrenders to the Prussians.

Paris, 2 September. More than 1,100 die as a wave of massacres spreads to the jails of Paris. Many of the killers are tradesmen living near the prisons and the majority of their victims are common criminals.

Paris, 5 September. The Paris deputies, including Robespierre and Danton, are elected to the National Convention.

Paris, 8 September. Bigot de Sainte Croix, the new foreign minister, orders the invasion of Savoy.

Paris, 17 September. The crown jewels are stolen.

Paris, 19 September. Thomas Paine arrives in Paris after fleeing from England, where he faces treason charges for views expressed in his *Rights of Man*, a defence of the French Revolution.

Paris, 20 September. The Assembly legalises divorce.

China. The British king, George III, sends Lord Macartney as a special envoy to the Qing court, but his mission to regularise diplomatic and commercial relations between the two countries achieves little success.

India. Ranjit Singh becomes king of the Sikhs at the age of 12.

Australia. Captain Arthur Phillip, the founder of the first British settlement in Australia in 1788, returns to England. Since the settlement was established, shortages of food and equipment, and conflicts among the settlers and between whites and aborigines, have been common.

The man who lost America saves India

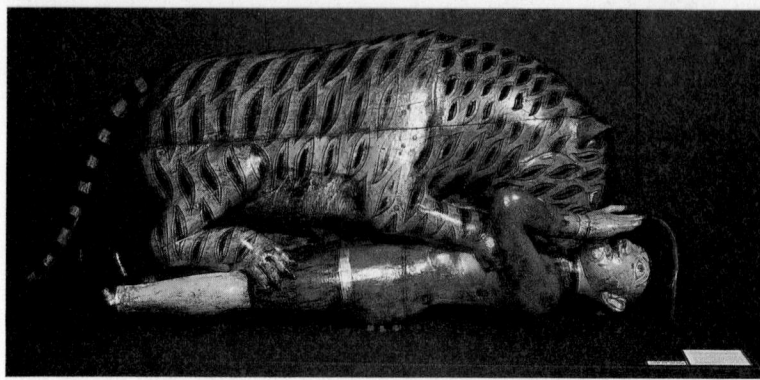

A mechanical growling tiger devouring a British redcoat, made for Tipu.

Southern India, 16 March
Charles, Lord Cornwallis, the man who lost British America, has saved British India. Tipu Sahib of Mysore, who fought three wars against the British, has surrendered. The victors, British, Maratha and Hyderabadi, are to take half his lands.

To the British, Tipu was a man without honour who milked his peasants dry and trained British boy hostages as Hindu dancing girls. Cornwallis' methods were the antithesis of Tipu's. In February 1791 he hanged nine British soldiers for looting. Tipu himself gives the appearance of accepting the terms; but already he has told his advisers he sees the arrangement as only temporary.

Guillotine sharpens up executioner's act

Paris, 25 April
The first execution to be carried out by the supposedly scientific means of the *guillotine* has been carried out on a convicted highwayman, Joseph Pelletier. A large crowd watched as the weighted blade, guided by upright runners, neatly removed the criminal's head.

Named after its inventor, the anatomist Dr Joseph Guillotin, who first demonstrated it to the Constituent Assembly in 1789, the aim of the machine is to replace archaic and brutal forms of execution with a quick, clean death.

In Guillotin's view the murderer, for all his or her criminality, is still a human being, and should be respected as such.

Dr Joseph Guillotin: humanitarian.

Scottish look-alike coast in Pacific

North Pacific, 20 July
Extract from a letter from a British seaman aboard *HMS Discovery* which is exploring the north-west American coast: "We have now reached a latitude level with Newfoundland, exploring the inlets between a large island and the mainland which is dominated by a huge range of snowcapped mountains covered with pine forests."

"Today we were visited by natives in canoes who traded otter skins and salmon for our buttons and beads. Captain Vancouver is due to meet the Spanish Commissioner here shortly to ensure there is no repetition of the Spanish seizing of our small post at Nootka Sound. This beautiful country reminds us of Scotland and looks ideal for British settlement."

Hardliners now firmly in control of revolution

Tuileries seized: king at mercy of mob

Paris: the revolutionary mob breaks into the royal wine cellar.

Paris, 20 June

This day, the anniversary of the Tennis Court Oath and the king's abortive flight to Varennes, has seen the most extraordinary events yet in the French Revolution.

A huge mob armed with all kinds of weapons first invaded the Assembly, where they demonstrated for three hours demanding the removal of the king's right of veto, and then marched on the Tuileries palace.

The people found the king in an anteroom whose door they smashed down with pikes. Then they made the man who was once their absolute ruler stand on a bench while they harangued him, chanting together "No aristocrats! No veto! No priests!".

They did little physical damage to the palace, but they humiliated the king, forcing him to put on that mark of revolutionary fervour, a Phrygian cap, and making him to toast his visitors. He did so, saying: "People of Paris, I drink to your health and to that of the French nation." But, despite his bravery, he is now powerless.

Red caps all the rage for revolutionaries

France

The true revolutionary is not just an activist, but a fashion-plate too. As the revolution advances, so too do its symbols, many of them manifested in the clothes one wears.

The red woollen "Phrygian" cap, symbolising the caps worn by ancient slaves, is especially popular, as are cockades in the national colours of red, white and blue.

Clothing that deliberately reverses aristocratic fashions is especially favoured. Many revolutionaries sport the baggy trousers or *sans-culottes* that mock the tight breeches of the nobility.

Voltaire is given a Phrygian cap.

Revolution threatened by foreign powers

Paris, 25 July

Fears of intervention by foreign powers in French affairs are growing following the publication in Germany, of a violently worded manifesto in which the duke of Brunswick threatens "exemplary punishment" to France if the slightest harm befalls the French royal family. Paris, he says, will be destroyed, and the revolutionaries punished "in a suitable manner".

The manifesto is believed to have been written not by the duke, but by a French emigre, the marquis of Limon. The threat follows the events of last month when the mob forced its way into the Tuileries palace and humiliated the king, forcing him to wear a Phrygian cap and drink to the French nation.

However, the manifesto has probably done more harm than good to the king at a time when there is an increasing clamour for him to be deposed. With his assertion that the

French soldiers rally to the Revolution: an opponent's view.

aim of the war is to "put an end to attacks against the throne", the duke has given ammunition to those who argue that the European powers are preparing to invade France in Louis' interests.

Priests and prisoners torn to pieces

A prisoner before a "court" of drunken revolutionaries, 2-3 September.

Paris, 4 September

For three days now the people of Paris have been swept up in bloody communal madness. Incensed by rumours of treason and fear of the advancing Prussian troops, groups of them are invading the prisons, dragging prisoners from their cells, subjecting them to travesties of trials and cruelly butchering them.

The original idea was to purge the nation of the priests and royalists who had not yet been put to death by the courts. But in the frenzy of killing, ordinary criminals are being hacked to death.

Today it was the turn of an almshouse containing prostitutes, madwomen and young orphaned girls. The killers, soaked in blood, spared none of them. At the Abbaye prison the queen's friend Madame de Lamballe was killed, and her head cut off and stuck on a pike. It was then paraded before the Temple where the king and queen are imprisoned.

France, 20 September. The French army under Kellerman defeats the Prussians under the duke of Brunswick at Valmy.

Paris, 21 September. At its first public meeting the National Convention decrees the abolition of the monarchy.

France, 22 September. The French republic is proclaimed. The Convention decides that all official rulings will from now on be dated from Year I of the French republic.

France, 24 September. Revolutionary troops march into Chambery, completing their conquest of Savoy.

USA, 29 September. Despite widespread protests in Pennsylvania and the South, President Washington says that he plans strictly to enforce the whisky excise tax introduced last year.

France, 29 September. Revolutionary troops take Nice.

Rhineland, 30 September. The French army of the Rhine, led by General Custine, seizes Speyer before making for Worms.

Germany, 5 October. French troops take Worms.

France, 7 October. The Austrians lift a siege of Lille.

Paris, 9 October. The Prussians leave Verdun.

Paris, 11 October. Santerre, the commander of the National Guard, resigns following a mutiny of guardsmen.

Germany, 21 October. The French army of the Rhine under Custine takes Mainz.

Germany, 23 October. The Society of German Friends of Liberty and Equality, modelled on the Jacobin Club, is established in Mainz.

Netherlands, 27 October. French forces led by General Dumouriez invade the Austrian Netherlands and march on Mons.

Switzerland, 30 October. French troops seize Basle. A republic is immediately proclaimed.

Netherlands, 6 November. The French under Dumouriez inflict a crushing defeat on the Austrians at Jemappes.

Netherlands, 14 November. Having entered Belgium on 27 October, defeated the Prussians at Jemappes and captured Mons, the French commander Dumouriez enters Brussels.

Spain, 22 November. Manuel Godoy, who recently replaced Aranda as prime minister, orders the arrest of French clergymen who have sought refuge in Spain.

France, 27 November. The former duchy of Saxony beomes the French department of Mont Blanc.

Netherlands, 28 November. A French army under General Miranda marches into Liege.

Netherlands, 29 November. The French take Antwerp.

France, 1 December. A revolt in the Beauce region is put down.

Germany, 2 December. The Prussians drive the French troops out of Frankfurt 40 days after they marched into the city.

Netherlands, 2 December. Namur surrenders to the French.

USA, 5 December. George Washington is re-elected president.

Netherlands, 7 December. French troops put down a demonstration in Brussels calling for the independence of Belgium.

Paris, 11 December. Louis XVI appears for the first time before the Convention, to hear the charges against him.

London, 13 December. Parliament votes to support William Pitt's war preparations against France.

West Indies, 13 December. The colonial assembly of Martinique declares war on the French republic.

Naples, 17 December. A French fleet arrives in Naples to force Ferdinand IV, the king of the Two Sicilies, to recognise the ambassador of the French republic.

Spain, 28 December. Spain offers to maintain its neutrality in the European war provided that the French royal family is freed.

West Indies, 29 December. An uprising in favour of the French republic breaks out in Guadeloupe.

Poland, December. The Prussians occupy the towns of Torun and Danzig, and Little Poland.

England. The exceptionally gifted singer Elizabeth Ann Sheridan, the first wife of the playwright Richard Brinsley Sheridan, dies.

Strasbourg. Rouget de Lisle writes the words and music for a *Chant de guerre pour l'armee du Rhin* (the *Marseillaise*).

West Africa. Freetown, Sierra Leone, is founded by 1,190 freed slaves who have landed from England.

England. *A Vindication of the Rights of Women* by Mary Wollstonecraft is published.

English workers read radical pamphlets

England

Inspired by the French Revolution, reformers in England have begun to publish pamphlets advocating manhood suffrage, annual parliaments, cheaper government and fairer land and legal systems.

Most influential is the Corresponding Society of London, led by a shoemaker, Thomas Hardy. It began with small meetings at the Bell Inn, near Covent Garden, often discussing ideas put forward in pamphlets from an intellectual elite calling themselves the Society for Constitutional Information. Whereas the latter charges its members five guineas a year, the Corresponding Society charges only a penny a week. Its numbers have grown since January from nine to 650, corresponding with groups in Manchester, Sheffield, Leeds and Norwich. In November it sent a delegation to the National Convention in Paris.

An "Address to the People" in August promised lower taxes, better education, prison reform and provision for the poor and old.

King promotes his queen's "companion"

Madrid

King Charles IV has appointed a new first secretary, the handsome duke of Alcudia, better known as Manual Godoy, who is also the queen's companion – and the Spanish people do not like it. Godoy, aged 35, has risen rapidly in military rank and government position over the past three years and was ennobled because he has enjoyed the protection of Maria Luisa.

This is a feature of aristocratic life in Madrid. Charles is said to be aware of the relationship and taking it for granted. But the lower classes of Madrid, as well as some of the nobles, are scandalised.

King Charles IV and Queen Maria Luisa of Spain.

Men furious at call for women's rights

England

Male opinion is up in arms following the publication of an essay which seriously questions the dominance of men in society. Challengingly entitled *A Vindication of the Rights of Women*, its author is 33-year-old Mary Wollstonecraft, a leading English radical.

She dismisses the notion, promoted by Rousseau, that women are inferior to men. She argues for equal opportunities in education and employment for women and men, and calls for female companionship with men on equal terms.

Mary was born near London of Irish parents; her father was a drunkard and wife-beater who squandered a fortune. She was largely self-taught and in 1782 started a school which failed. By 1790, while working for a London pub-

Radical: Mary Wollstonecraft.

lisher, she was part of a radical group which included Tom Paine. Her works include *Thoughts on the Education of Daughters* (1787) and an essay on the French Revolution.

French Revolution saved

The Battle of Valmy, where France's new army saved the revolution.

Valmy, France, 20 September
The French Revolution has been saved on a fog-shrouded plateau at Valmy where the duke of Brunswick's well-trained soldiers were turned back today by the untried army of the new France supported by cannons which once belonged to the king.

It is true that the Prussians were ravaged by dysentery, but as they marched towards Paris they expected to find a people ready to surrender. Instead they found 50,000 Frenchmen ready to stand and fight, roaring "Long live the na-

tion". It was not much of a battle, confined mostly to an exchange of cannon fire which killed 200 French and 300 Prussian soldiers, but the Prussians had no heart for it. "We won't be able to beat them here," said Brunswick, and ordered a humiliating retreat.

"You'll see how these little cocks will strut now," said one dispirited Prussian. "We have lost more than a battle." At the windmill headquarters of the victorious French generals, Dumouriez and Kellerman, the battle is being called the "miracle of Valmy".

Colony of freed slaves has second start

West Africa
A second group of black settlers has arrived at Sierra Leone. The colonists will take over this outpost of progress from the survivors of the first group of 411 colonists who arrived three years earlier and have been decimated by hunger, disease and war. The old colonists were idealistic. Their settlement was self-governing and they elected their own governor, Richard Weaver.

The new colonists are mostly from Nova Scotia and New Bruns-

wick, black slaves who escaped from American owners and came to England after the War of Independence. The settlement is no longer self-governing, but financed and controlled by the British-owned Sierra Leone Company.

The newcomers are as idealistic as the original colonists and, since the early attempts at agriculture have failed, they are concentrating on trade, hoping to prove to neighbouring African rulers that slavery is not the only profitable trade.

Russians breach Japanese seclusion

Japan
An expedition sent by Catherine the Great has arrived at Nemuro Bay, Hokkaido. Commanded by Adam Laxman, the Russians are using the return of a number of Japanese castaways as a pretext for their landing.

Laxman asked permission to travel to the capital, Edo, asking to be regarded as "neighbouring allies"

not as "antagonistic and infidel adversaries". Among the castaways he has brought home is Daikokuya Kodayu, who was blown onto the Aleutians ten years ago and was taken to St Petersburg where he had an audience with the czarina. It is doubtful that he will be as well received in Edo, for he has broken the *shogunate's* rule of seclusion forbidding anyone to leave Japan.

Royalty abolished and republic declared

Paris, 21 September
The monarchy was formally abolished at the first session of the National Convention meeting at the Manege in Paris today. There was some legalistic hesitation, but Collot d'Herbois, the leader of the Paris delegates, argued that it was a matter which could not be postponed "without being unfaithful to the wishes of the nation".

Another delegate then launched a virulent attack on the concept of royalty, demanding the destruction

of "this magic talisman ... kings are morally what monsters are physically". Although some preached caution, all objections were swept aside amid great excitement.

A decree was then passed unanimously declaring royalty abolished in France. There were scenes of great enthusiasm and couriers were despatched all over the country with the news. However, no mention was made of the establishment of a republic, which must now be inevitable.

Planting the Tree of Liberty: a painting by the le Sueur brothers.

France's long-trousered revolutionaries

Paris
To be called a *sans-culotte*, a man without breeches, used to be an insult in Paris. Now it is a name worn with pride by the extreme republicans and nobody dares to treat them with contempt.

Instead of breeches, they wear simple trousers held up by braces, short jackets called *carmagnoles*, a scarves at their open necks and the symbols of revolution, the red woollen Phrygian, or "liberty", caps on their heads. There are women sans-culottes who wear long skirts and are more fearsome than the men.

Both sexes are well armed with captured swords and most of them carry pikes, many of which have borne the heads of butchered aristocrats. They have abandoned all forms of polite behaviour, using *Citoyen* instead of *Monsieur* and have become a power in the streets of Paris.

A sans-culotte: one of the vanguard of the French Revolution.

Paris, 21 January. Louis XVI is guillotined.

France, 21 January. The county of Nice is annexed to France.

Poland, 23 January. Prussia and Russia agree on a second partition of Poland.

Ottoman Empire, January. The sultan, Selim III, introduces a new administrative regime and reorganises the Ottoman army on the European model.

Ireland, January. Catholics are given the vote.

France, 1 February. France declares war on Britain and the Netherlands.

France, 14 February. The principality of Monaco is annexed to France.

Indian Ocean, 25 February. An anti-royalist riot breaks out in Ile de France (*Mauritius*) following the proclamation of the French republic on the island.

Europe, February. Britain, Austria, Prussia, Spain, the Netherlands, Sardinia, Tuscany and Naples form a coalition against France.

Corsica, February. A conflict develops between Pascal Paoli, who seeks Corsican independence from France, and the Francophile Napoleon Bonaparte.

Netherlands, 5 March. Austrian troops crush the French to recapture Liege.

France, 7 March. France declares war on Spain.

France, 11 March. A rebellion against the republic breaks out in the Vendee.

Netherlands, 18 March. Having entered Breda on 25 February, the French commander Dumouriez is heavily defeated by the Austrians under Frederick of Saxe-Coburg at Neerwinden.

Germany, 20 March. French troops annex the German duchy of Zweibrucken.

France, 20 March. The rebellious Vendeans inflict a defeat on a French revolutionary army.

Europe, 25 March. By the treaty of London, Russia joins the coalition against France.

Netherlands, 4 April. Dumouriez, the commander-inchief of the French armies, defects to the Austrians.

Paris, 5 April. Elected president of the Jacobin Club, Jean-Paul Marat orders the arrest of counter-revolutionaries and the ousting of the main Girondin deputies.

Paris, 6 April. The Convention sets up a Committee of Public Safety.

West Indies, 14 April. The British seize control of Tobago.

West Indies, 14 April. A royalist rebellion in Santo Domingo is crushed by French republican troops.

France, 20 April. Spanish troops lay siege to Perpignan.

USA, 21 April. The US government officially proclaims its neutrality in the European conflict.

Paris, 23 April. The Convention decrees stringent new measures against priests who refuse to swear allegiance to the church's civil constitution.

Paris, 24 April. The revolutionary tribunal acquits Marat of despotism.

Paris, 24 April. The republican General Miranda is arrested because of his links with Dumouriez.

India, 27 April. The British orientalist Sir William Jones, who introduced eastern thought and literature, especially Sanskrit, to the west, dies in Calcutta.

France, 9 May. General Dampierre, the commander of the French army in northern France, is mortally wounded during an Austrian offensive at Valenciennes.

Paris, 10 May. Claire Lacombe sets up the Society of Revolutionary Republican Women.

North Atlantic, 24 May. The British recapture the archipelago of St Pierre and Miquelon off Newfoundland, dealing a blow to the French cod-fishing fleet.

France, 30 May. Girondins seize power from Jacobins in Lyons.

Paris, 2 June. After three days of street demonstrations, the moderate Girondins are ousted from the Convention by Jacobins.

France, 6 June. Marseilles, Nimes and Toulon rebel against the Convention.

France, 9 June. The royalist Vendean army captures Saumur.

West Indies, 20 June. The city of the Cap in Santo Domingo is destroyed after an attempted royalist uprising.

India, 24 June. A British squadron blockades Pondicherry.

Paris, 25 June. The extremist Enrages group, led by Jacques Roux, presents the Convention with a petition attacking the constitution.

France, 30 June. Saumur is recaptured by republican troops.

Cotton-cleaning machine does work of 50

Whitney's cotton gin: boosting production in America for British mills.

South Carolina
American production of cotton is set to increase dramatically thanks to a new invention which can clean in a day as much raw cotton as 50 men. Eli Whitney's saw-gin solves the problem of cleaning seeds from green seed cotton, the crop grown in the inland Carolinas by farmers keen to supply the fast-growing English cotton industry. Until Whitney unveiled his machine the whole process was done by hand.

Whitney, a Yale graduate who came south to teach mechanics, stands to make a fortune from his invention. The legislature of South Carolina has already bought the patent rights for statewide use for 50,000 dollars. Whitney shares royalties with the backer who put up the stake to build his first gin, so called from an archaic abbreviation of "engine".

The gin has a cylinder equipped with teeth projecting through strips of metal. These draw in the cotton fibre leaving the seeds behind. A second roller, fitted with brushes to free the teeth from the lint, revolves in the opposite direction. The gin can be powered by hand, by a horse or by water. Whitney got his idea for it after realising that there was a fortune to be made from automating the cleaning of cotton.

Counter-revolution begins in France

Vendee, France, 14 March
Counter-revolutionaries, under the charasmatic leadership of Jacques Cathelineau, a cart driver and door-to-door salesmen, have seized Chemille and are taking over the Vendee, (western France). The rebels talk of restoring the monarchy and the church, and are united by a religious vervour fed by the Church.

Today in the town's church the Abbot Barbotin, one of the most virulent opponents of the revolutionaries in Paris, came out of hiding and sung a Te Deum. The humble Cathelineau acted as his server. The capture of Chemille is not the peasant army's first victory. Two days ago they bested a republican force sent against them at Saint Florent. Cathelineau and his Catholic peasant followers have no doubt of the outcome of their revolt. When his

Cathelineau: counter-revolutionary.

wife – who has more doubt – pleaded with him to stay at home at support his family, he replied: "God, for whom I am going to fight, will take care of you".

French cut off the head of their king

Paris, 21 January

King Louis XVI of France went to the guillotine in the Place de la Revolution this morning. The blade fell on his neck and the royal head tumbled into the basket just before 10.30 on this cold, grey day.

Louis Capet, as he was called by his judges in the Assembly, met his death calmly. He left for the scaffold in a large green coach with his priest, Edgeworth de Firmont, and surrounded by a strong escort of National Guardsmen. Drummers marched in front of the carriage, beating loudly to drown any cries of support for the doomed monarch. But there was hardly a sound in Paris. Every shop was closed and there was a stillness in the city despite the curious crowds that hurried to the bloody spectacle.

The scaffold, where the executioner, Sansom, waited, was surrounded by armed men. No chance was taken of a Royalist rescue. As the coach arrived the king commended his priest to the guards: "Take care that after my death no insult be offered to him."

Sansom's assistants reached out to grab him. He shook them off and prepared himself for death, untying his neckcloth and opening his shirt. Then, despite his protests, his hands were tied. He climbed the steps on the arm of his priest and turned to address the crowd. Im-

Royal victim: the execution of Louis XVI at the Place de la Revolution.

mediately, the drums were ordered to beat, and only those close to him heard his last words: "I die innocent of all the crimes laid to my charge; I pardon those who have occasioned my death; and I pray to God that the blood you are going to shed may never be visited on France."

There was an awful silence as his severed head was shown to the crowd. A shout of *"Vive la République"* was then taken up by a thousand voices. Then there was silence again as the people realised what they had done. They had given the counter-revolutionaries their greatest martyr.

Regicide: Philippe Egalite, ex-duke of Orleans, by Cruikshank.

France discharges its women-at-arms

France

The women of France, who have fought with conspicuous bravery in the nation's cause, are to be deprived of their right to enlist in the army. Scandalised by the very idea of women as soldiers, the Convention has today decreed that women may no longer join up.

Many women enlisted in 1792, and such heroines as the young Fernig sisters, Reine Chapuy, Rose Bouillon and Catherine Pochetat have distinguished themselves with

Revolutionary women soldiers in France are now to be disbanded.

bravery the equal of any man's. Often dressed only in rags, they fought in the front ranks of such battles as Valmy and Jemappes.

To their fury, such valour counts for nothing now. All the deputies will offer in compensation are five *sous* for every league the women must travel to return home. Such tiny sums are unlikely to last very long, and many women fear a future in which they have neither job nor income. In any case, the women fought as much for glory as for cash, and they regret deeply being deprived of the excitement of military life. The world of family life holds little appeal to those for whom the army is a way of life.

Turkish sultan's "New Order" ignored

Ottoman Empire

A call for 12,000 volunteers to join the *Nizam-i-Jedid*, the New Order, of Sultan Selim III has been virtually ignored – an indication of the difficulty the sultan is having in carrying through his reforms.

In an effort to stem the decline in Ottoman power, Selim, with the support of 'Abdullah Effendi, the chief judge of the council, has reorganised his council, relieving the grand vizier of some administrative duties, and is reforming provincial government. Most crucially, he is trying to reform the army. With the help of European advisers, he has achieved better artillery training and equipment. But streamlining the Janissary corps is proving more difficult.

A Turkish Janissary, a major obstacle to reform.

Poland partitioned for the second time

Warsaw, 23 January

Czarina Catherine of Russia and the treacherous King Frederick William II of Prussia have agreed on a second partition of Poland. Catherine gets most of Lithuania and the western Ukraine (total population, three million). Prussia gets Danzig, Thorn and western Poland almost to the gates of Warsaw (total population, one million).

Frederick had signed a treaty agreeing to aid the Poles if Russia attacked. But when the blow fell, the Poles found that Frederick had gone over to the enemy. The Polish parliament, with Russian troops outside the building, have formally endorsed the annexation.

The French Revolution

The French Revolution is always with us, not simply in the sense that it created the forms and categories of our own political culture but also in the way that every generation of historians and thinkers has to engage with and argue over this "mythic" event. Above all else, the Revolution was founded upon, nourished by, and indistinguishable from its own mythologies.

A new order?

The myth from which all others flow is that the Revolution saw the birth of a new order, that 1789 was the year zero of a new world founded on equality. The Revolution of 1789 was born out of harvest failure and economic crisis, out of the conflict between the privileged and non-privileged estates – the aristocracy and the "patriots" – and out of fear of the peasantry and of the collapse of government: the goal of its leaders was "national regeneration", but their achievement was to sweep away the *ancien regime*. They abolished the old order in government – establishing the sovereignty of the nation, separation of powers, rule of law, representative government and individual rights – and in society – demolishing feudalism, venality and privilege. Destruction of the old order was one revolution, but establishing its successor was to require another.

By invoking the rights of the "people" and the sovereignty of the "nation", the bourgeois revolutionaries let the radical genie out of his bottle. How these men of '89 gave way to those of '92, how the Girondins were overtaken by the Jacobins and how the constitutional achievements of 1789 were swept away in the bloodshed of the storming of the Tuileries and the prison massacres, is a tale of distrust, recrimination and fear on all sides. It was a contest for the right to speak in the name of the "people".

The elite who had been brought to power in 1789 were the "notables" of French society, the noble and non-noble property owners, the "active citizens", who were to govern France under the constitutions of 1791 and 1795 and under the regimes of the 19th century. Their rivals were the advocates of greater egalitarianism, the bourgeois members of the Jacobin clubs and the *sans-culottes*, artisans and small property owners active in the politics of Paris. From the overthrow of the monarchy (August 1792) to the constitution of Year III (August 1795), France was under the "revolutionary government" of the Jacobins and *sans-culottes*.

It is significant that contemporaries used the term "revolutionary" to mean "provisional", the opposite of "constitutional". In this period a new form of politics was created. The Jacobin Club, with its meetings and control of the Constituent Assembly, laid down the model of direct democracy. The Jacobins appealed to the authority of Rousseau in support of their claim to embody the "general will" of the people and to have the right to force men to be free. It was and still is argued that the Terror was an inevitable and necessary phase of the Revolution. Yet the Jacobin Terror did not represent the predominance of any class, or any revolutionary vanguard, but rather the triumph of ideology and the liberation of the state to serve its own ends. As Marx pointed out, the Terror was succeeded in this role by the Revolutionary and Napeoleonic wars: permanent war replaced permanent revolution. By 1797 the armies saw themselves as the heirs of the *sans-culottes*, ready and willing to intervene in domestic politics if they believed that the purity of the Revolution was in jeopardy. The heritage of coup and counter-coup was the belief that the Revolution meant that force could be used if the principles of the revolution appeared under threat: a potent recipe for political instability.

Revolutionary rhetoric

"Liberty, fraternity and equality", the slogan of the Revolution, has a fine ring to it, but is it really any more than a pious platitude, another myth of the Revolution? The Declaration of the Rights of Man clearly defined liberty – the right to do anything that did not harm others or conflict with their liberty – but the Revolution soon curbed the freedoms of French citizens and imposed French "freedom" on other nations. Equality was envisaged in a strictly limited sense, that of equality of opportunity and before the law. There was no suggestion of equality of property and, apart from the rhetoric of 1793-94, little talk of equality of political rights.

Fraternity was, perhaps, the most hollow cry of the French Revolution. From 1789, the domestic opposition to Revolution was clear, consistent, and bloody. The reforms of 1789-91 did not benefit all groups in society; they did not even benefit all members of the Third Estate. The new individual political, religious and property rights clashed with a traditional regard for regional, corporate and communal privileges. Later, of course, the rising in the Vendee and the guerrilla war of the Chouans, peasant opposition to heavy taxes, falling agricultural prices, and the Revolution's policy towards the Catholic church brought civil war to France. But even among those who were loyal to the Revolution, the policies of the Terror could provoke armed resistance. It could be argued that the French Revolution took the course it did, including Terror and foreign war, largely because of its struggle against a widespread, popular and lasting counter-revolution.

Legacies

In material terms a decade of revolution and 23 years of war did France real harm: overseas trade, the most successful sector of her pre-1789 economy, was permanently damaged; there was no incentive to invest in anything other than land; meanwhile agriculture stagnated and unemployment soared. Specific groups, such as army officers, bureaucrats and war profiteers, gained from the Revolution. In general, however, no single social class emerged triumphant. Nobility and church returned, although shorn of much of their social and political power, and that amorphous class, the bourgeoisie, occupied a far more prominent social role than before 1789.

Above all, the Revolution of 1789-99 favoured those with money and property. The great transfer of land was from the church and nobles to the "notables", creating a powerful group with a vested interest in the Revolution and a strong desire to keep it under control. When their gains seemed in danger, they pushed the Revolution into the hands of Napoleon, a dictator who imposed stability.

The apparatus of the French state was one of the Revolution's greatest beneficiaries. Writing in the era of Napoleon III, the French historian de Tocqueville pointed out that the Revolution merely accelerated and consolidated a tendency of the *ancien regime* towards centralisation and bureaucracy: the Revolution and its successors espoused equality because it reduced resistance to the power of the state.

Although less tangible, the political legacy of the Revolution may be its most significant bequest. Thanks to the French Revolution, subjects of the monarch became citizens of the state; written constitutions have become the norm; we have a political vocabulary of "left" and "right", "terrorist", "conservative" and "revolutionary"; and we have an enduring belief in the identity and destiny of "nations". The Revolution has provided an inspiration for democracy and a model for totalitarianism. It shaped and expressed the egalitarianism which we take for granted, and it institutionalised and impersonalised repression. If, beneath all its mythology, the French Revolution was a paradox, then that is in keeping with modern political life.

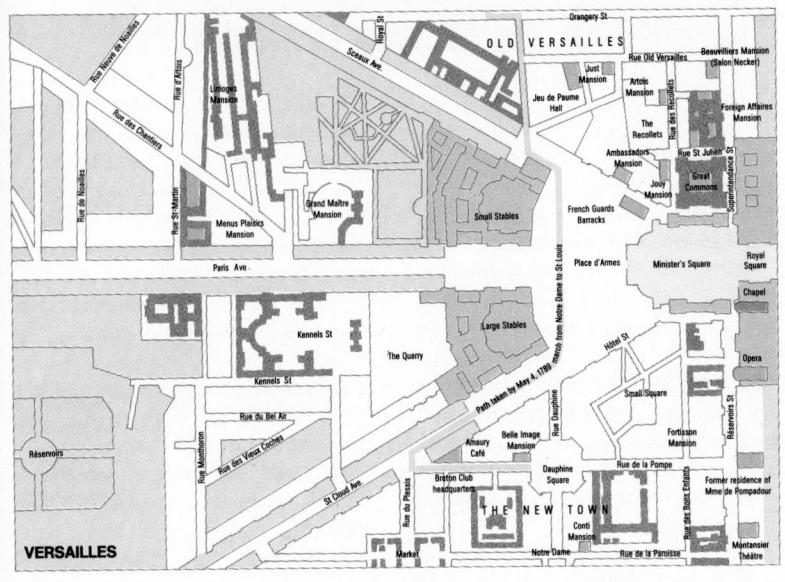

VERSAILLES

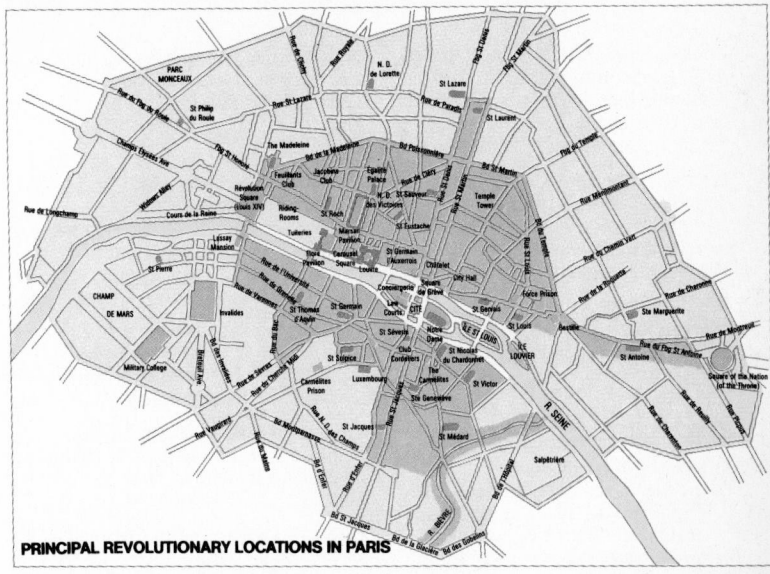

PRINCIPAL REVOLUTIONARY LOCATIONS IN PARIS

Ushant
June 2, 1794

Brest
Sept. 7, 1790

St-Brieuc
Oct. 27, 1799

Grandville
Nov. 14, 1793

Caen
June 14, 1793

Pacy-sur-Eure
July 21, 1793

Versailles
May 5, 1789
Opening of
Estates General

Paris

Amiens

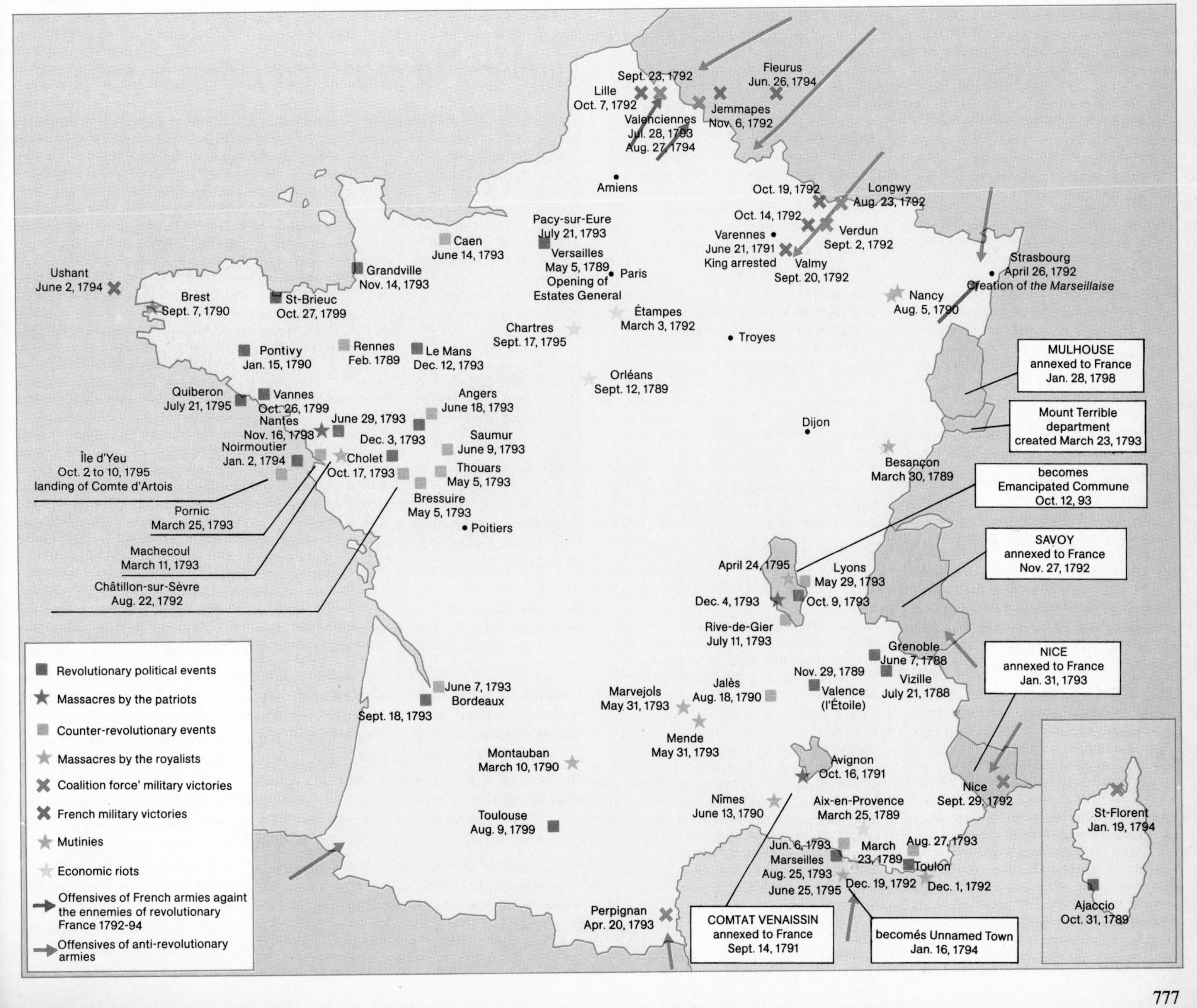

Lille
Oct. 7, 1792

Sept. 23, 1792

Fleurus
Jun. 26, 1794

Valenciennes
Jul. 28, 1793
Aug. 27, 1794

Jemmapes
Nov. 6, 1792

Oct. 19, 1792

Oct. 14, 1792

Longwy
Aug. 23, 1792

Varennes
June 21, 1791
King arrested

Verdun
Sept. 2, 1792

Valmy
Sept. 20, 1792

Strasbourg
April 26, 1792
Creation of *the Marseillaise*

Nancy
Aug. 5, 1790

Troyes

Chartres
Sept. 17, 1795

Étampes
March 3, 1792

Pontivy
Jan. 15, 1790

Rennes
Feb. 1789

Le Mans
Dec. 12, 1793

Orléans
Sept. 12, 1789

Quiberon
July 21, 1795

Vannes
Oct. 26, 1799

Nantes
Nov. 16, 1793

Angers
June 18, 1793

June 29, 1793

Saumur
June 9, 1793

Noirmoutier
Jan. 2, 1794

Cholet
Oct. 17, 1793

Dec. 3, 1793

Thouars
May 5, 1793

Île d'Yeu
Oct. 2 to 10, 1795
landing of Comte d'Artois

Bressuire
May 5, 1793

Poitiers

Pornic
March 25, 1793

Machecoul
March 11, 1793

Châtillon-sur-Sèvre
Aug. 22, 1792

Dijon

Besançon
March 30, 1789

MULHOUSE
annexed to France
Jan. 28, 1798

Mount Terrible
department
created March 23, 1793

becomes
Emancipated Commune
Oct. 12, 93

SAVOY
annexed to France
Nov. 27, 1792

NICE
annexed to France
Jan. 31, 1793

April 24, 1795

Lyons
May 29, 1793

Dec. 4, 1793

Oct. 9, 1793

Rive-de-Gier
July 11, 1793

Grenoble
June 7, 1788

Nov. 29, 1789

Vizille
July 21, 1788

Valence
(l'Étoile)

June 7, 1793
Bordeaux

Sept. 18, 1793

Jalès
Aug. 18, 1790

Marvejols
May 31, 1793

Mende
May 31, 1793

Montauban
March 10, 1790

Avignon
Oct. 16, 1791

Nice
Sept. 29, 1792

St-Florent
Jan. 19, 1794

Toulouse
Aug. 9, 1799

Nîmes
June 13, 1790

Aix-en-Provence
March 25, 1789

Jun. 6, 1793
Marseilles
Aug. 25, 1793
June 25, 1795

March
23, 1789

Aug. 27, 1793

Toulon
Dec. 1, 1792

Dec. 19, 1792

Ajaccio
Oct. 31, 1789

Perpignan
Apr. 20, 1793

COMTAT VENAISSIN
annexed to France
Sept. 14, 1791

becomés Unnamed Town
Jan. 16, 1794

Legend:
- Revolutionary political events
- ★ Massacres by the patriots
- Counter-revolutionary events
- ★ Massacres by the royalists
- ✕ Coalition force' military victories
- ✕ French military victories
- ★ Mutinies
- ★ Economic riots
- → Offensives of French armies against the enemies of revolutionary France 1792-94
- → Offensives of anti-revolutionary armies

France, June. Outlawed by Pascale Paoli last month, Napoleon Bonaparte and his family are exiled from Corsica and forced to seek refuge on the French mainland.

France, 1 July. The Convention dissolves Corsica's primary assembly and splits the island into two departments to reduce Pascale Paoli's influence.

India, 11 July. A British expeditionary force lands near Pondicherry, which is defended by French troops.

Paris, 13 July. Jean-Paul Marat is assassinated by Charlotte Corday.

France, 14 July. Jacques Cathelineau, the commander of the Catholic and royalist army of the Vendee, dies after being wounded during the siege of Nantes.

France, 16 July. Joseph Chalier, the leader of the Jacobins of Lyons, is executed.

Paris, 17 July. Pascale Paoli is declared a traitor to the French republic.

Paris, 17 July. Charlotte Corday is guillotined.

Paris, 22 July. Custine, the commander of the northern army, is arrested.

Germany, 23 July. The French garrison at Mainz capitulates to the Prussians and is allowed to leave the city.

Paris, 27 July. Robespierre becomes a member of the Committee of Public Safety.

France, 28 July. Valenciennes surrenders to the allied troops led by the duke of York.

Paris, 1 August. The Convention decrees the total "destruction" of the rebellious Vendee.

France, 14 August. Republican troops lay siege to Lyons.

India, 23 August. When news of the fall and execution of Louis XVI reaches Pondicherry, the French surrender the port to the British forces who have been besieging it since 24 June.

France, 25 August. Republican forces capture Marseilles.

France, 28 August. The Federalists of Provence hand Toulon over to the British.

Paris, 28 August. General Custine is guillotined.

West Indies, 29 August. Slavery is abolished in Santo Domingo.

Philadelphia, August. In the worst health disaster ever to strike an American city, over 4,000 have died in a epidemic of yellow fever.

Netherlands, 8 September. French troops under General Houchard defeat an AngloHanoverian army under the duke of York at Hondschoote.

Paris, 17 September. The Convention passes an "anti-suspect" law by which all enemies of the revolution will be arrested and held until the war is over.

USA, 18 September. In Washington DC, President Washington lays the foundation stone of the Capitol, the intended seat of the US government.

France, 9 October. The rebellious Jacobins in Lyons capitulate to the republican army after 60 days of fighting.

India, 10 October. Lord Cornwallis leaves India after greatly strengthening British administration in India. He has made a firm distinction between the commercial and administrative functions of the East India Company, Europeanised the administration and settled the revenue and land system of Bengal.

Paris, 10 October. An emergency government is formed.

France, 16 October. The French defeat the Austrians at Wattignies, forcing the Austrians to lift the siege of Maubeuge.

Paris, 16 October. Marie Antoinette is guillotined.

France, 17 October. The Catholic and royalist Vendean army is defeated by the republicans at Cholet.

France, 17 October. The French India Company goes into liquidation.

Paris, 31 October. Jacques Brissot and 20 other Girondins are guillotined.

Germany. Friedrich Schiller publishes a *History of the Thirty Years War*.

Germany. The philosopher Johann Gottfried Herder starts publishing his *Letters for the Advancement of Humanity*.

North America. Sir Alexander MacKenzie become the first white man to cross the North American continent, finishing his journey by canoeing down the Bella Coola river in Oregon territory to the Pacific.

Japan. Matsudaira Sadanobu resigns from the office of chief senior councillor, which he has held since 1787, and goes into retirement. His departure follows a clash with the emperor and growing disaffection with his authoritarian style.

Twenty-one moderates are executed

Paris, 31 October
It took five carts to bring the 21 moderate Girondin leaders to the scaffold today, and, even as they came close to the guillotine, they were singing the *Marseillaise*.

Many in the crowd wept, but there was no unrest. The Girondins knew all through their week-long trial before a revolutionary tribunal that their fate had been decided. To let them live would be an admission that a mistake had been made; and, such is the fear spreading through Paris, not one lawyer could be found to defend them.

The Girondins had been voted out of office in June when a mob of *sans-culottes* had threatened to over-run the Convention. Had it not been for legal difficulties, they would certainly have been executed long before now. The insurrection which brought about the arrest of the Girondins began late on 31 May when a secretly organised committee of Marat and the Montagnards called the people of Paris "to arms!".

Despite a powerful speech by the radical Jacobin Robespierre, the Convention resisted demands for a purge and immediate sentences. When members reassembled on the following morning, they found cannons levelled at the Palais National and troops preparing to arrest the "traitors".

Charlotte Corday stabs Marat in bath

Charlotte Corday is arrested after assassinating Jean-Paul Marat.

Paris, 13 July
Jean-Paul Marat, the founder of *L'Ami du Peuple*, deputy for Paris and sans-culotte supreme, is dead. Working as usual in his daily bath, where he nursed a persistent skin disease, he was stabbed to death by Charlotte Corday, the daughter of an impoverished aristocrat and a staunch royalist.

Corday appeared at Marat's apartment at 20, rue de Cordeliers, and gained admission to his rooms by claiming to have details of a group of Girondin conspirators in the Calvados.

As Marat listened to her story she pulled a kitchen knife from her bodice and stabbed him in the chest. He died almost immediately. Corday, who lives in Caen with her aunt, and is closely involved with the same Girondin whom she pretended to betray, arrived in Paris two days ago, determined to murder the man whom she saw as an enemy of the human race. She had planned to kill him at the Bastille Day parade, but, when the planned festivities were cancelled, was forced to attack him in his home.

When the police arrived on the scene she offered no resistance, but stood calmly at the window observing the mob which had gathered, and awaiting her arrest

Chinese reject western barbarians

Chinese Emperor Qianlong, meets the British ambassador, Lord Macartney.

All natives corrupt, says departing ruler

The Bengal Levee: Lord Cornwallis holding a reception in Calcutta.

Canton, October
Lord Macartney's mission to persuade the Chinese to lift trade restrictions on British merchants trading with Canton has failed.

The elaborate 95-man mission, costing £78,000, has been told that the celestial empire of the Emperor Qianlong, son of heaven, has not "the slightest need" for manufactured goods from England. The emperor has also rejected requests for a British ambassador – the first from the west – to be stationed at his court.

The East India Company, which financed the mission, hoped that a permanent ambassador could persuade the emperor to lift trade barriers. All exports from China, including high-demand items such as tea and silk, have to be paid for in silver. British exports to China bear high import duties plus the cost of bribes to officials.

The Macartney mission was politely received and the Irish peer was allowed into the imperial presence without having to knock his head nine times on the floor, as is customary. However, it was made clear that there was no place for a "barbarian from the western ocean", however eminent, in China.

Calcutta
After seven years as governor general of Bengal, Charles, Lord Cornwallis, is leaving India. He came here fresh from his surrender at Yorktown (for which, surprisingly, no one blamed him), and took on the job out of a sense of duty. He continued the reforms begun by Warren Hastings and completed the transformation of British India into the most powerful state in the sub-continent.

Unlike Clive or Hastings, his rank and reputation placed him above faction. Further, he had the supreme confidence of William Pitt, the British prime minister. Thus he was able to reform British India, essentially by separating the commercial elements of the Company from the administrative. Bribery is no longer normal practice.

In wars against Tipu Sahib he was applauded for his humanity and moral courage; but his "Europeanisation" of the civil service ("Every native in India, I verily believe, is corrupt") has caused much resentment, and his system of land taxation, creating a new revenue collecting class, the *zamindars*, is adding to the heavy weight of the already burdened peasantry.

A Georgian dandy or "macaroni": a victim of fashion from the tight buckled shoes and elaborate garters to the baroque wig and face-powder. By the end of the century men's fashions were more elaborate than women's.

The rise of Robespierre: a change in the mood of the revolution

Paris, 27 August
An ambitious young left-wing lawyer, Maximilien Robespierre, has been elected – "against my inclination" – to the Committee of Public Safety, a move which may well change the direction of the French Revolution. Robespierre, who is regarded by many as "incorruptible", had little influence at the Convention while it was dominated by the moderate Girondins; but now, invited to join the committee by left-wing friends, his political skills and deep respect for the law are certain to stand him in good stead at a time when lawlessness, with the sans-culottes mobilised throughout France, threatens to rip the country to shreds.

At first sight, 32-year-old Robespierre is not an engaging figure. He is small, thin and vain, with thick, carefully brushed hair and a pock-marked skin of a greenish pallor. He is a nervous man, highly strung, who bites his nails, pushes his tinted spectacles on to a bulging brow when he speaks and utters a rare, hollow laugh when required.

Robespierre has proved himself to be a hard-working and competitive advocate – although his soft voice usually failed him whenever as a deputy to the National Assembly, his left-wing views were shouted down. When he spoke to the masses, however, he was more successful. He wanted bigger audiences at the Assembly. "Under the eyes of so many witnesses, neither corruption, intrigue nor perfidy would dare show themselves," he claimed.

Maximilien Robespierre, the "uncorruptible" politician.

Paris, 3 November.
Olympe de Gouges, the feminist who once tried to defend Louis XVI, is executed.

Paris, 6 November.
Philippe of Orleans, the cousin of Louis XVI, is executed.

Paris, 8 November.
Madame Roland, the muse of the Girondins, is executed.

France, 10 November.
The Girondin Jean Marie Roland commits suicide in Rouen after his wife's death.

Paris, 16 November.
General Houchard is executed for having held talks with the enemy.

Paris, 18 November. The National Art Museum at the Louvre palace opens.

Paris, 24 November. The Convention approves the new revolutionary calendar.

New York, 25 November.
In one of a series of Negro uprisings, slaves in Albany, New York state, cause huge damage to the city by arson.

France, 30 November.
The French general Lazare Hoche is defeated by the Prussians at Kaiserlautern in Alsace as he attempts to break the siege of Laudau.

Paris, 4 December. A new war government takes office.

Paris, 5 December.
Camille Desmoulins launches a newspaper, *Le Vieux Cordelier*, to campaign against the Terror.

Paris, 8 December.
Madame du Barry, the former mistress of Louis XVI, is guillotined.

France, 12 December.
Republican troops under Marceau and Kleber crush the Vendeans at Le Mans.

France, 19 December.
French troops recapture Toulon from the British.

France, 24 December.
After a further defeat, at Savenay, the Vendean army is dispersed.

Paris, 25 December.
Robespierre gives his support to the Terror policy.

France, 26 December.
French troops under Lazare Hoche defeat the Austrians at Geisberg, relieving the threat to Strasbourg.

USA, 31 December.
Thomas Jefferson resigns as secretary of state and retires from public life.

New symbols for new names of the months: Ventose (l.) represents what used to be February, Thermidor (c.) is July and Frimaire (r.) is November; the months of the calendar are now symbolised by the climate and seasons.

Revolutionary calendar wipes out the past and renames months

France, 24 November
The revolution has brought many great changes, but none so far has touched the very time in which people live. Now that too must change. Today the Convention has initiated a new calendar, based on a scheme proposed by a committee including the mathematician Charles Romme and the dramatist Fabre d'Eglantine.

From today the traditional calendar – "a monument of slavery" – is to be abandoned. In its place comes a "natural" calendar. There will be 12 months, each of 30 days, with names reflecting changes in the climate – *Pluviose, Nivose* – or seasons – *Germinal, Floreal.* The five spare days, the *sans-culottides* will be holidays. Weeks, or *decadis*, will now last for ten days; days are renamed *primidi, duodi*, and so on Religious holidays are gone: there is no Christmas now, and saints' days will be renamed for plants, tools or animals.

Citizens of France are equal so long as they are not women

Paris, November
Olympe de Gouges and Manon Roland have mounted the scaffold, Theroigne de Mericourt has apparently lost her sanity and the Republican Women's clubs have been banned – this has been a devastating month for France's women, whose role in the Revolution has been as vital as that of any man.

Women's contribution to the revolution cannot be over-stressed. They included intellectuals like Roland, who dominated the Girondins, the feminist de Gouges, founder of the notorious Club des Tricoteuses, and the former courtesan Theroigne, whose Revolutionary Republican Women was only one of the clubs she founded.

Just as important were the anonymous market-women, fishwives and whores, who were among the most militant and implacable of the Revolution's pioneers. It was a woman, dressed fittingly as an Amazon, who led the atack on the Bastille. Equally momentous was the women's march on Versailles in October 1789. Demanding to know why the King had deserted his city in its crisis, they set in motion events that

Women patriots: their clubs, which preached revolution, have been banned.

ended in the King's execution. Of all the revolutionaries, the women of France have seemed least restrained, and it is this overthrowing of the ultimate law – of male superiority – that has led to this month's backlash.

"Woman is born free and her rights are the same as those of a man ... All citizens, be they men or women, must be equally eligible for all public offices, positions and jobs, according to their capacity and without any other criteria" – so said the *Declaration of the Rights of Women*, by Olympe de Gouges which was published in 1791.

Now, it seems, such feminism has outlived its usefulness. The Revolution still proclaims the "Rights of Man" but today it ignores those of women.

Jefferson resigns office

Virginia, 31 December
Thomas Jefferson, the author of the Declaration of Independence, has resigned as secretary of state and retired to his Virginia farm despite fervent pleas by the president. Jefferson, a former ambassador to Paris, is said to be disillusioned by Congress's refusal to impeach his arch-enemy, Alexander Hamilton, the secretary of the treasury, for financial impropriety.

The two men have been adversaries since the framing of the Constitution, Hamilton advocating a strong central government while Jefferson preferred to see greater power in the individual states.

Jefferson was a firm opponent of the "Hamiltonian System" under which the treasury assumed Revolutionary War debts, issued new bonds and established a Bank of the United States.

Although Jefferson has confided to his friend James Madison that "the motion of my blood no longer

Thomas Jefferson, one of the founding fathers of the USA.

keeps time with the tumult of the world", few believe that this distinguished reformer – for all that he owns slaves – will be able to resist a return to public life.

European monarchs unite against France

Europe, September
The whole of Europe has united against revolutionary France. With the signing of a treaty with Britain by Portugal – the last nation to join the counter-revolutionary Convention – the republic faces a ring of hostile monarchies.

Ever since the Declaration of Pillnitz in 1791, when Austria and Prussia called for an alliance against France, Europe's governments have been moving towards a

unanimous position. Co-ordinated by Britain's prime minister, Grenville, state after state has joined the Convention. Members now include Austria, Russia, Sardinia, Spain, Naples, Prussia and Portugal.

Nonetheless, the alliance remains flimsy at heart. Its members have called for France to restore the monarchy and return her conquests, but have signed no general agreement. There is no real leader, and each state thinks first of itself.

"Bombardment" of the crowned heads of Europe, fermenting the revolution.

Terror is firmly on the agenda in France

Sans-culottes, "refreshing after the fatigues of the day": an English view.

Paris
Suddenly, no-one is safe from the guillotine. A legalised reign of terror has set neighbour against neighbour, and no more than a hint, a whisper or a rumour of anti-revolutionary thought may bring a suspect to the guillotine. Revolutionary committees are working with extraordinary zeal to seek out those who, "by their behaviour, their relationships or what they have written have shown themselves to be supporters of tyranny". The entire city of Lyons has suffered under

draconian laws for not supporting the revolution. The guillotine was so busy there that firing squads were called in to shoot 59 "suspects". Here in Paris, the Protestant minister and ardent defender of religious freedom, Rabaut St Etienne, was beheaded for his moderation; so, too, was Olympe de Gouges, a feminist lawyer who had tried to defend Louis XVI. The Girondist poet Mme Roland looked at the statue overlooking the scaffold and said: "O Liberty, what crimes are committed in thy name!"

Wages and prices fixed in economic crisis

Paris, 29 September
The levels of prices and wages are to be fixed as part of an all-out attempt to tackle the economic crisis that is plaguing France.

Under the Convention's General Maximum Law, prices will be fixed by individual departments, and are to be pegged at no more than 30 per cent more than those of 1790, irrespective of inflation. Wages will be permitted to rise by up to 50 per cent of the 1790 levels.

The move follows a summer of agitation as the demands of a war economy channelled foodstuffs to the troops and the towns, robbing the peasants of what they feel is rightfully theirs. At the same time, the people of Paris had been demanding higher wages.

The French peasant: the success of the revolution depends on him; only stable prices can secure his support.

South Africa, 1793. The second Suurveld war, which began in 1789, comes to an end. The war was provoked by the Xhosa chief Ndlambe's attempt to regain control of Suurveld (*Eastern Cape Frontier*). Under the peace agreement, the Boers have to concede to Ndlambe, but they blame their Dutch magistrates for the defeat.

North Atlantic, 1793. A British attempt to colonise the Cape Verde Islands, begun last year, ends in failure.

Paris, 11 January 1794. Lamourette, bishop of Lyons since April 1791, who was taken prisoner by republican troops on 29 September 1793 during the siege of Lyons, is tried and guillotined.

Paris, 13 January 1794. The poet and musician Fabre d'Eglantine, a Dantonist opponent of the Terror, is arrested on charges of involvement in a financial scandal concerning the India Company, which compromises several prominent people. Fabre signed a fake decree ordering the liquidation of the company, to his own benefit.

France, 28 January 1794. Henri la Rochejaquelein, leader of the revolt in the Vendee, is killed by two isolated republican soldiers on a road near Nouaille in Maine et Loire.

France, January 1794. Republican troops under General Turreau embark on a systematic destruction of the Vendee region.

Paris, 4 February 1794. The Convention issues a decree abolishing slavery throughout the French colonies.

Paris, 10 February 1794. Jacques Roux, one of the leaders of the Enrages, the most extreme political group to emerge from the sansculottists, commits suicide in jail.

Mediterranean, 27 February 1794. Austria and Russia reach agreement on the sharing out of Venetian possessions in the Mediterranean.

Corsica, February 1794. Pascal Paoli, the patriotic leader who has now become governor of Corsica, seeks British help to maintain the autonomy of the Corsican republic, threatened by the Jacobin faction on the island. A nationalist assembly proclaims George III, the British king, as the island's sovereign.

Paris, 13 March 1794. Following a call for an insurrection by the extremist Cordeliers, Jacques Hebert, the editor of *Le Pere Duchesne* – who has come to dominate the Cordelier Club – and leading Hebertists are arrested.

West Indies, 23 March 1794. The British recapture Martinique, from which they were expelled last year by the French.

Poland, March 1794. Tadeusz Kosciuszko – who became leader of a group of exiled Polish patriots after the partition of Poland by Prussia and Russia last year – arrives in Krakow, wins the support of dissident Polish officers and proclaims a provisional constitution giving him dictatorial powers.

Paris, 24 March 1794. The extremist Jacques Hebert and leading Hebertists are guillotined for treason.

Paris, 27 March 1794. The *sans-culotte* "revolutionary army" is dissolved on the orders of the Convention.

Scandinavia, 27 March 1794. The Scandinavian states create a league of armed neutrality.

Paris, 28 March 1794. The Paris Commune is reorganised. The Hebertists are replaced by supporters of Robespierre.

France, 29 March 1794. Marie Jean Condorcet, the philosopher and mathematician who became president of the Legislative Assembly in 1792, is found dead in his cell in the town formerly known as Bourg la Reine. Condorcet, who was condemned for his Brissotin sympathies and went into hiding for several months before being recognised and arrested, is believed to have committed suicide.

Paris, 31 March 1794. Georges Jacques Danton and a group of his friends, including Camille Desmoulins, are arrested on charges of having connived with the foreign monarchs who are in league against the French republic. They are also accused of being accomplices of Fabre d'Eglantine in the India Company scandal.

Poland, 4 April 1794. At Raclawice, the Polish insurgents under the leadership of Tadeusz Kosciuszko inflict a defeat on a superior Russian army.

Indian Ocean, 1794. The Ile de France (*Mauritius*) ignores the French Convention's declaration of the abolition of slavery.

Southern Africa, 1794. The Maputo kingdom is victorious in the Tembe civil war, which has been raging around Maputo Bay for the past half-century. Maputo power, however, is limited to the bay and to trade with Portuguese ships, while the hinterland that stretches into South Africa (*Natal*) and Swaziland is left open to new militaristic powers, notably the Ndwandwe and Mthewa chiefdoms.

"Infernal columns" crush French revolt

Vendee, January 1794
General Turreau, the head of the Army of the West, calls it "a military stroll" but the peasants of the Vendee, whose revolt he is systematically wiping out, prefer another name: they call his troops, who pillage and massacre without restraint, the "infernal columns".

The revolt collapsed after last month's defeat at Savenay and many peasants were summarily executed by firing squads. Now Turreau, leading 12 columns of "Blue" troops, has set out to obliterate every remaining sign of resistance and impose a bloody "peace" on the area. His generals have been ordered to follow his scorched earth strategy without mercy.

"All brigands who are found with arms in their hands or are convicted of having taken up arms will be bayoneted to death. You will act in the same way with women, girls and children who are in the same category. All of the villages, towns, crops and everything else that can possibly burn will be consigned to the flames."

Total power of revolutionary government

Paris, 19 April 1794
Who governs France today? The answer is clear to everyone, the "Committee of Public Safety", in which almost total authority is invested. Headed by Robespierre, it has taken over responsibility for almost every political decision made in France. Although it is nominally answerable to the Convention, few delegates would dare to question the Committee, whose Revolutionary Tribunal is almost daily sending moderates to the guillotine.

The Committee has dismissed ministers, and its latest move is to order that all charged with conspiracy must be tried by the Paris Revolutionary Tribunal. It has given itself powers of arrest and has even formed its own police.

British gold driven off Indian warpath

Philadelphia, 19 November 1794
Britain is to withdraw its support for the Indians and to evacuate its posts in America's Northwest Territory by 1 June 1796. This is the central point in a treaty that has been negotiated between the two countries by the British prime minister, Grenville, and the US chief justice, John Jay.

Other provisions include the settling of outstanding US debts to Britain and the payment by the British of damages claimed by America.

Britain's encouragement of Indian attacks on American settlers, and its desire to make the territories into an Indian client state, has led to much bad feeling between the two countries. President Washington barely managed to stop Congress declaring war. Not until last August, when Major General Wayne roundly defeated the British-backed Indians at the battle of Fallen Timbers, destroyed their villages and built Fort Wayne, did Britain's government realise the need to change its policy. The more militant Americans still oppose a treaty, but war does seem to have been averted.

Animal forms not fixed, says radical

London, 1794
The English physician and radical freethinker Erasmus Darwin believes that animal species evolve over time. His new book *Zoonomia* posits a theory of evolution based on adaptability and competition.

Species, claims Darwin, evolve through both the inheritance of acquired characteristics and the preferential survival of those competing species that are best suited – or adapted – to the prevailing conditions.

Although he has yet to produce any convincing proof, Darwin contends that all life forms descend from a single source, and that all organisms are evolving to some higher level.

Revolution celebrated in arts and crafts

Post-revolutionary playing cards, without kings and queens.

A revolutionary tobacco box.

Racine replaces the King of Clubs.

Paris, 1794

Artists and craftsmen are serving the revolution by turning out images of its leaders and great events. Popular prints portray the Fall of the Bastille, or the execution of the king or Marie Antoinette. Female images of Liberty and the red Phrygian "Cap of Liberty" decorate plates, porcelain and snuff and tobacco boxes.

Jacques Louis David has been made official painter to the Convention (to which he is a deputy). He paints heroes and martyrs of the revolution, such as Joseph Bara, the boy who was killed for shouting "*Vive La République!*" instead of "*Vive le Roi!*", and the famous

Assassination of Marat. David had visited Marat, who worked in his bath because of a skin complaint, the day before Charlotte Corday killed him.

At the Louvre, now a museum, the erotic paintings of the royalist era by Boucher and Fragonard have been removed from public view. "Art must educate the people," rules David.

Since 1792 it is illegal to use royal insignia, so all packs of playing cards have been redesigned. The King, Queen and Jack are now symbolic figures, like *Prosperity*, *Modesty* and *Justice*, or are replaced by Racine, Voltaire and Rousseau.

Slavery abolished in all French territories

Paris, 4 February 1794

As the three black delegates from Santo Domingo watched from their seats in the Assembly, the Convention voted today to abolish slavery throughout the territories of the republic and to confer French citizenship on every former slave. Then the Domingans were led to the Tribunal where the president embraced them as the Convention rose in a standing ovation.

The abolition was proposed in Paris by the deputies Levasseur, Danton and Lacroix, but it was events in Santo Domingo that inspired the Convention's move.

In 1792, a year after the outbreak of the slave revolt, two civil commissioners – Sonthonax and Polverel – were sent to administer the island. In August 1793 they freed all of the 500,000 slaves. This humanitarian act had its political side. As long as the revolt continued it was impossible for France, at war with Spain and Britain, to defend its colony. Loyal freedmen were naturally better patriots than rebellious slaves. Now the Conven-

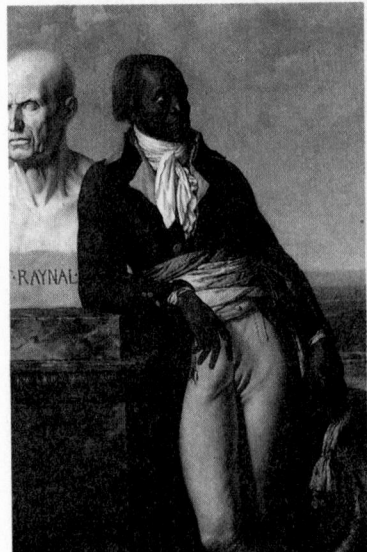

Belley: Saint Domingue's deputy.

tion hopes that France's example will stimulate Britain's slaves to rise in their turn, thus helping to undermine Britain's war effort. Danton, a fervent abolitionist, voiced his hopes for the effects of such an uprising. "Today," he declared, "Pitt died."

Republicans recapture city from British

Toulon, France, 19 December, 1793

Toulon, France's premier naval base, has been recaptured by the republicans. For three months it had been a royalist stronghold, and played host to the British fleet.

The Republican army's attack began five days ago. On the third day a young artillery captain called Bonaparte saw a weakness in the royalist Aiguillette redoubt. General Dugommier's forces stormed it. The

next day the British fleet sailed off, burning the French fleet on the way out. Today the republicans marched into the city.

Toulon went royalist in September after Toulon republicans had killed 17 people and been driven out of the city. The loss to the navy is enormous; ships, stores, arsenal and cargo vessels have been destroyed. The entire French fleet must be rebuilt.

The British fleet, under Admiral Hood, in Toulon harbour.

Paris, 5 April. Georges Jacques Danton and several of his supporters, including Camille Desmoulins, are guillotined.

Italy, 18 April. Napoleon Bonaparte, appointed a general in the French army in February, captures the port of Oneglia, a Piedmontese enclave on Genoan territory.

Poland, 19 April. Tadeusz Kosciuszko, the Polish rebel leader, enters Warsaw, which has been in revolt for two days against Russian occupation. The Russians withdraw from the city.

Netherlands, 19 April. Britain, Prussia and the Netherlands sign a treaty against France in The Hague.

Paris, 22 April. Chretien Malesherbes, a former minister under Louis XVI, is executed along with the Assembly members Thouret, le Chapelier and Duval d'Epremesnil.

Poland, 23 April. Kosciuszko enters Vilna, which was seized by the Jacobins yesterday.

France, 30 April. Landrecies in northern France surrenders to the Austrians.

Spain, 1 May. French troops enter Spanish Catalonia.

Paris, 7 May. On the insistence of Maximilien Robespierre, the Convention approves a decree recognising "the existence of a Supreme Being and the immortality of the soul".

Paris, 8 May. The famous chemist Antoine Lavoisier, who discovered the composition of water, is executed.

Paris, 10 May. Elisabeth, the sister of Louis XVI, is beheaded.

France, 17 May. General Moreau captures Tourcoing, opening up the route to Belgium for the French army.

Indian Ocean, 17 May. The British capture the island of Mahe from the French, securing control of the Seychelles archipelago.

Corsica, 22 May. British forces supporting Paoli Pascal capture Bastia.

Paris, 24 May. Robespierre survives an assassination attempt by Cecile Renault, a 25-year-old stationer's daughter. It is the second attack on his life in two days.

France, 29 March. The Austrians and the Piedmontese sign a mutual defence treaty at Valenciennes.

Spain, 31 May. The French invasion of Catalonia sparks off anti-French rioting.

Paris, 1 June. The Mars military academy is founded.

Paris, 4 June. Robespierre is unanimously elected president of the Convention.

West Indies, 4 June. British troops capture Port au Prince, the administrative capital of Santo Domingo, after a five-day siege.

West Indies, 7 June. After proclaiming the abolition of slavery, Victor Hugues, the envoy from the French Convention, recaptures Guadeloupe, which was taken by the British earlier in the year.

Paris, 8 June. Robespierre presides over the celebration of the Supreme Being held on the Champ de Mars.

Paris, 10 June. A law is passed establishing the regime known as the Great Terror. In future there will be no preliminary questioning of defendants or witnesses in trials if the revolutionary tribunal states it has enough factual or "moral" proof. Defence lawyers are banned and juries will have to choose between two verdicts: acquittal or death.

Poland, 15 June. The Prussian army defeats the French, who leave Warsaw.

Netherlands, 26 June. After seizing Charleroi, the French under General Jean Jourdan defeat the Austrians, led by Frederick of Saxe-Coburg, at Fleurus and force them to retreat.

Netherlands, 1 July. The French expel the Austrians from Ostend.

Brussels, 8 July. French troops capture Brussels.

France, 15 July. Landrecies, one of the last French strongholds to be held by the enemy, is liberated.

Paris, 27 July. The Convention orders the arrest of Robespierre and his followers. The Commune declares itself in revolt and hands them over.

Britain. The distinguished English silversmith Hester Bateman dies. On the death of her husband in 1760, she took over his work in gold and silver and registered her own hallmark. Her shop, which became very profitable, was known for its elegant domestic silver, especially coffee- and teapots, spoons and other tableware.

Britain. The novelist Mrs (Ann) Radcliffe publishes *The Mysteries of Udolfo*, a fantastic tale of horror, calculated to send shivers down her readers' genteel spines.

Supreme Being celebrated by Robespierre

The Festival of the Supreme Being: an idealised interpretation.

Paris, 8 June

Despite fears that revolutionary France would become an atheistical society, the entire country today celebrated what has been termed "The Supreme Being and Nature". From early morning, the residents of this city were decorating their houses with flowers and leaves and making their way through the Tuileries to join a procession led by Maximilien Robespierre himself, carrying an ear of wheat.

As the whole of France celebrates Robespierre's discovery of a supreme being, many are concerned about the Catholic undertones of the festival or fear that the "supreme being" they are feasting may turn out to be Robespierre himself.

Savage sentences stir Scots to fury

Scotland

Rumours of revolution are sweeping Scotland, where economic and political grievances have been fuelled by indignation at the savage sentences handed down to dissenters. Parliament has suspended *Habeas Corpus* to allow political suspects to be held without trial.

The most potent symbol of repression is the Scottish judge Lord Braxfield. Holding the constitution to be perfect, he has therefore found anyone proposing change to be an enemy of the state. Last year he sentenced Thomas Muir, a lawyer and the founder of Scottish Friends of the People, to 14 years' transportation for sedition, and the leading unitarian Thomas Palmer to seven years transportation.

While Palmer's pamphlet condemning the war with France is circulating, Muir is understood to be in Paris, forging links with Irish republicans.

Arrests after a secret convention in Edinburgh were followed by transportation and one death sentence – in contrast to the acquittal of alleged agitators in England on similar charges.

Revolutionary court guillotines Danton

Paris, 5 April
At his own request, the head of Georges Jacques Danton, once the favourite of the *Sans-culottes*, was held up to a hushed crowd here today. With his colleague, Camille Desmoulins, and other moderate "Indulgents", Danton was tried by a revolutionary court on charges of corruption and having former contacts with royalty. Most observers believe that the flimsy evidence produced was fabricated and that the court was acting under instructions from Robespierre.

Danton's eloquence was clearly swaying the crowd. The chairman took advantage of an interruption by him to order the defendants out of court, and the death sentence followed almost immediately. Danton was defiant to the end. "Take us to the guillotine now!" he shouted. Desmoulins pleaded with the crowd to save them.

The Indulgents' real offence was to speak out against the revolutionary committees, which they regard-

Georges Jacques Danton, executed for his eloquence and moderation.

ed as dictatorial, and to demand the return of the Convention. Such talk – especially by such popular figures as Danton – is regarded as treason by Robespierre.

Red and green never be seen together

London
Some people cannot distinguish between the colours red and green. They have a form of "colour blindness". One such individual is the British chemist and physicist John Dalton, who has just described the condition in some detail in *Extraordinary Facts Relating to the Vision of Colours*.

Being colour blind, however, has not incapacitated Dalton, who has made major contributions to the understanding of meteorology and the nature of gases. He is best known for his atomic theory – that all elements are really composed of indestructible atomic particles.

John Dalton, the scientist.

France's army invades Piedmont

Northern Italy, April
Faced by an alliance of European monarchs and fearing that Piedmont, lying in the foothills of the Alps between France and Italy, will be used as a base to attack France, the French have launched a military offensive "in support of Piedmont's revolutionaries".

The offensive was due to coincide with a Jacobin rising in Turin, Nice and the main towns, but the conspiracy has been discovered. Of the conspirators, 48 have been arrested, and three executed. Piedmont is anxiously soliciting a defence treaty with Austria. Such setbacks have not stopped the French, however, whose general, Bonaparte, has just captured Oneglia.

French get Austrian army on the run

The battle of Fleurus, where France stopped the Austrian army.

Fleurus, France, 26 June
As hot-air balloons hovered overhead and French generals rallied their men to ever-greater feats of valour, the Austrian army under the prince of Saxe-Coburg was forced to retreat today at the village of Fleurus, near the Belgian border. The 185,000-strong Austrian army had been pursuing a successful campaign through Belgium this summer until 13 May, when it was defeated at Tourcoing. Now the defeat at Fleurus should ensure that Saxe-Coburg's ambitions will be brought to a halt.

The battle raged for 14 hours, as 80,000 Frenchmen struggled to hold back the Austrians. Bravery apart, their victory was helped by a tactical blunder. At one crucial moment a simple flanking movement might have trapped the French, but it never came.

New Prussian code is aimed at radicals

Berlin
A definitive code of Prussian law, which has just come into effect, seeks to regulate the mutual relations of citizens and also their relations with the state. It lays down the powers of the king to levy taxes without seeking public consent. It re-defines the king's rights as duties. The lawyers who drafted the code wished to establish the judiciary as an independent mediator between the state and the people, but the king would have none of it.

The code defines the rights of citizens according to their estates: noblemen, burghers and peasants. The universities are free from censorship, but private citizens face severe penalties if they criticise political conditions and spread ideas likely to cause unrest. The monarchs of Europe are looking over their shoulders at France.

A Prussian officer.

1794 (1794-1795)

Paris, 28 July 1794. Robespierre and 21 of his companions are guillotined.

Paris, 2 August 1794. The painter David, once a fervent supporter of Robespierre, is arrested.

Paris, 2 August 1794. James Monroe, a Francophile and a partisan of the revolution, takes up his post as American ambassador in Paris.

France, 20 August 1794. Having been arrested on 9 August on suspicion of being a Robespierrist, General Bonaparte is released at the request of the commander-in-chief of the forces in the Alps and Italy in order to reinforce the Army of Italy's general staff.

USA, 20 August 1794. The revolutionary General "Mad Anthony" Wayne defeats the Ohio Indians at the battle of Fallen Timbers in the Northwest Territory, ending Indian resistance in the area.

Corsica, 21 August 1794. Bombarded by Captain Nelson's artillery at sea, and harassed on land by Pascal Paoli's Corsican nationalists, the French finally give the island up to the British.

Russia, 28 September 1794. The Anglo-Russian-Austrian alliance of St Petersburg is signed, directed against the French.

Poland, 10 October 1794. The Russian General Alexander Vasilyevich Suvorov crushes the rebel Polish army at Maciejowice. The injured Polish leader, Kosciuszko, is taken prisoner.

London, 17 October 1794. The British prime minister, William Pitt, cuts finances for Prussian troops. He holds Prussia responsible for the recent defeats suffered by antiFrench forces in Germany.

Germany, 23 October 1794. The French General Jourdan takes Koblenz.

Netherlands, 25 October 1794. Prussia denounces the treaty of the Hague, signed between Britain, Prussia and Holland in April, and withdraws its troops from the Netherlands.

Paris, 3 November 1794. After the intervention of the American ambassador James Monroe, Thomas Paine, the revolutionary writer who is an elected deputy of the Convention, is released from jail. He was imprisoned early this year having offended the Robespierre faction.

Poland, 4 November 1794. The rebel Polish army is beaten and massacred by the Russians at Praga.

London, 6 November 1794. Thomas Hardy, the leader of the radical Corresponding Society, who was charged with treason last month, is acquitted.

Poland, 9 November 1794. The Russians enter Warsaw, having successfully put down the Polish uprising led by Kosciuszko.

Britain, 11 November 1794. As part of a round of public order measures prompted by a fear of Jacobin activity, the British government suspends the ancient act of Habeas Corpus, which protects citizens against arbitrary arrest.

Philadelphia, November 1794. The uprising of the "whisky rebels" comes to an end. The dispute began in June when farmers in western Pennsylvania and throughout the Appalachians refused to pay the federal excise tax on whisky. The rebellion disintegrated when President Washington personally took the field with a force of 12,500 militiamen.

Paris, 26 December 1794. The painter David is granted a provisional release pending trial. He was imprisoned as an associate of Robespierre's.

Netherlands, 27 December 1794. Following the collapse of the treaty of The Hague, French forces invade Holland.

France, 31 December 1794. France signs an armistice with the Austrians.

Persia, 1794. The brutal and ambitious chieftain Aga Mohammed overthrows the Send dynasty, which has dominated Persia since 1750, and establishes the Kajar dynasty.

Paris, 1794. Claire Lacombe, known as "Red Rosa", is arrested while trying to leave Paris.

Germany, 1795. The writer Jean Paul Richter, who prefers to be known by his first names only, publishes a new novel, *Hesperus of Forty-five Days from the Post to the Dog*.

Britain, 1795. Having completed his composition of *The Marriage of Heaven and Hell*, the visionary poet William Blake goes on to write *The Book of Los*.

Nigeria, 1795. Sultan Agwaragi of Katsina defeats the sultan of Gobir, Bawa Jan Gwarzo, in battle near Kiawa and kills him.

Germany, 1795. The writer Friedrich Schiller – a trained army surgeon who is now honorary professor of history at the university of Jena – writes his *Letters concerning the aesthetic education of mankind*.

The Terror's creator dies

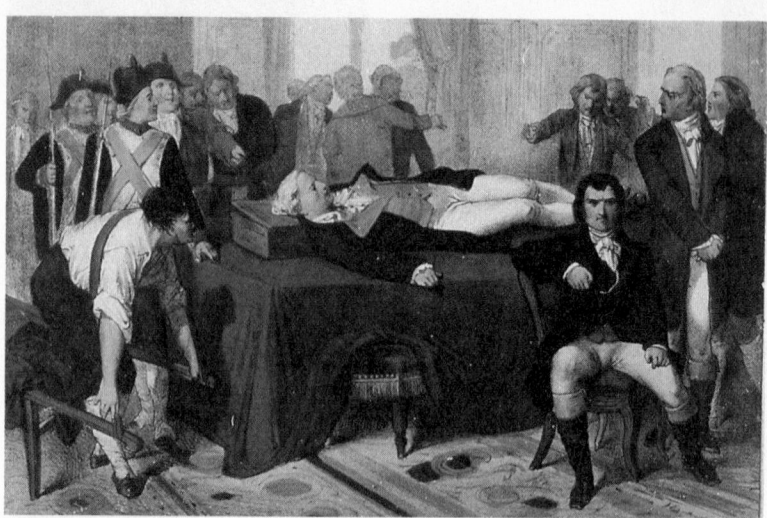

Robespierre, the "People's Friend", awaits the tumbril, his jaw broken.

Paris, 28 July 1794

Paris turned on the "incorruptible" Robespierre today, and jeered as the architect of terror and 21 of his allies were brought by tumbril to the guillotine which they had used so effectively to paralyse this country with fear.

Few expected such a dramatic turn in revolutionary events, but a conspiracy of deputies to the Convention – including many alleged supporters of the "tyrant Robespierre" – had been braced for this moment. They had filled the Convention with allies who cheered as Billaud Varenne, himself a member of the Committee of Public Safety, began a speech which turned many moderate supporters of Robespierre against their leader.

Fighting broke out in the Convention, and as Robespierre appealto the Montagnards for help, they turned their faces away from him. Finally, two deputies called for Robespierre's arrest, but such was his reputation that the ushers refused to take him and the others to the cells; nor would the turnkeys

Robespierre, the incorruptible.

lock them in that night. In an ensuing scuffle, Robespierre was shot in the chin and could only nod when the death sentence was passed on him. Robespierre and the others were free last night to turn Paris into a bloodbath, but, strangely, the army they mobilised was impotent to act.

Russia crushes patriotic Polish uprising

Warsaw, November 1794

Warsaw once again lies helpless beneath the Russian heel after a glorious and doomed eight-month uprising led by the Polish patriot Tadeusz Kosciuszko, a hero of victorious battles in the American and French revolutionary wars. Last April, when the Poles rose against

the second partition of their country, they drove the Russians from Warsaw and repulsed Frederick William of Prussia. Catherine sent in her greatest general, Alexander Suvorov, who overwhelmed the Polish forces and slaughtered 6,000 civilians trapped against the banks of the Vistula.

Bloody Terror is ended

Victims of the revolution, after the revolutionaries turned on their own.

Paris, August 1794
The reign of Terror is over. With Robespierre and his allies dead, the Convention is in control of the revolution once again and, as the prison gates are opened to release thousands of political detainees, France has begun a bizarre headcount of those who have perished since last September when the real Terror began.

No-one will ever know the exact numbers who were brought to the guillotine after summary trials by revolutionary tribunals, but at least 25,000 people were beheaded – most of them for alleged treason or rebellion – often on the flimsiest evidence. The merest hint of royalist sympathies or counter-revolutionary activity could bring a citizen before the dreaded tribunals. The Terror was an ideal opportunity for paying off old scores.

Paris recorded 2,639 executions. Outside the capital, it was the west of France and the Rhone Valley that suffered the most. In Loire Inferieure no fewer than 3,548 people were to face the guillotine's blade.

At the height of the Terror, the prison population of Paris alone soared to more than 8,000 and new prisons had to be opened to hold the flood of prisoners.

"Rosa" fires Paris

Paris, 1794
Claire Lacombe, known as "Red Rosa", has been arrested for inciting women's desire for suffrage. The 29-year-old actress, a heroine of the storming of the Tuileries two years ago, was leaving Paris for the theatre in Dunkirk when she was stopped by the National Guard and taken to the Bastille.

Rosa blatantly ignored Robespierre's ban on meetings of her Revolutionary Republican Women. Associated with the leftwing Enrages, the society was an organisation of women workers determined to petition for women's right to vote and participate in the Revolutionary Committee.

Scanty fashions all the rage in France

Paris, December 1794
It may be Paris in the depth of winter, but the capital's fashionable young women, barely clothed in draperies of sheer gauze, put many onlookers in mind of classical Athens.

Known as the "Wonderful Women", these exquisites, dedicated to the display of "insolent luxury amidst public wretchedness", wear their dresses with fans in the belts, purses at the bosoms and blond wigs on their heads. They are followed by their "handkerchief bearers", enraptured young men.

Radical chic: French "Incroyables".

French Revolution finds echoes in Europe

Europe, 1794
The French Revolution has galvanised Europe. Paris is the centre of political activity, attracting foreign intellectuals and publishing newspapers in English and French. But the Terror's victims have included the German Anacharsis Cloots, executed with the Hebertists, and the English radical Thomas Paine, in prison since December 1794.

British radicals are highly sympathetic, but the government remains vehemently anti-French. In Corsica the revolutionary ideas of Buonarotti have been rejected in favour of British rule by viceroy.

In the Habsburg empire there have been Jacobin conspiracies in Vienna and Hungary, but the Brabant revolution has been crushed. In Italy, Masonic lodges have become revolutionary cells, while in Holland rebels have linked up with invading French forces.

Cruelty of Persia's castrated monarch

Shah Aga Mohammed Khan.

Persia, 1794
Aga Mohammed, the *khan* of the Kajars, has completed the liquidation of the old Zand dynasty and cemented his reputation as the cruellest Persian ruler.

Castrated at the age of five by Adil Shah, Aga Mohammed, the eldest son of Mohammed Husein Khan, became the candidate for the throne of Persia on the death of Karim Khan, the regent, in 1779. After a prolonged struggle for power he took control, and in 1786 he moved the capital from Shiraz to Tehran, nearer his home base among the Kajar tribesmen.

He then set about subduing the southern half of the country, culminating in the destruction of Kerman, the headquarters of Lutf Ali Khan, the son of Kharim Khan and heir to the Zand dynasty.

Lutf Ali was wounded, captured, blinded and finally strangled in Tehran. The women of Kerman were raped, killed or sold into slavery. From the men Aga Mohammed demanded 20,000 pairs of eyes, which were duly delivered to him.

Hot Scot rocks are moving very slowly

Edinburgh, 1795
What is the nature of the forces that shape our earth? In a two-volume work, *Theory of the Earth*, published this year, the scientist James Hutton draws on extensive observations of the countryside of his native Scotland and sees features that lead him to claim that geological forces act extremely slowly over time. For example, Hutton says that stratified rocks were deposited as sediments of former seas. And if the strata are distorted from their regular horizontal layers, he says that this is because of movements in the earth's crust due to internal heat.

Brittany, 3 January. *Chouans* (royalists) and republicans agree to a ceasefire.

Russia, 3 January. Russia and Austria hold a secret meeting to draw up plans for the partition of Poland.

Amsterdam, 19 January. French forces led by General Pichegru enter Amsterdam after a vicious winter campaign. The *stadholder*, William V, flees as the Batavian patriots greet their "liberators".

Netherlands, 23 January. French republican forces take the entire Dutch fleet while it lies ice-bound off Texel.

France, 31 January. Violent rioting is sparked off in Rennes by food shortages. General Hoche calls in the army.

France, 3 February. Four *sans-culottes* are attacked by "reactionaries" in Lyons, marking a change in public mood towards the activists and their supporters.

France, 9 February. France and the grand duchy of Tuscany sign a peace treaty affirming Tuscany's neutrality.

France, 14 February. Joseph Fernex, a judge of the Revolutionary Committee who has been in prison since the overthrow of Robespierre, is killed and thrown into the river Rhone in broad daylight by "reactionaries".

France, 21 February. The convention approves a decree restoring freedom of worship.

Paris, 27 February. After clashes between "reactionaries" and Jacobins in the theatres, they are closed indefinitely.

Paris, 3 March. The *Bourse* (stock exchange) is reopened.

Paris, 25 March. Food stocks reach an all-time low. Only enough wheat for 115 days is left in the warehouses.

Paris, 1 April. A mob breaks into the convention screaming "We want bread!". But the protest fails to develop into a full-scale uprising, and the hungry men and women are rounded up by a unit of bayonet-wielding grenadiers. Martial law is declared.

Basel, 5 April. France and Prussia sign the treaty of Basle ending hostilities between the two countries.

Paris, 10 April. The Convention takes harsh measures following the protests of 1 April. It also takes the opportunity to root out *Thermidorians* (reformed Robespierrists) whom it suspects of trying to slow down the forces of reaction.

Paris, 12 April. Almost a year after his mysterious death in a prison cell, the philosopher Condorcet is honoured by the Assembly, though he died an outlaw.

Brittany, 20 April. The *Chouans* (royalists) agree to recognise the republic and not to take up arms against it again.

Paris, 26 April. Officially sanctioning the collapse of paper money, the Convention annuls the decree forbidding gold and silver trading.

France, 4 May. Thousands of rioters enter jails in Lyons and massacre 99 Jacobin prisoners.

France, 8 May. Hearing of his appointment in the west, General Bonaparte leaves for Paris in order to obtain a different posting.

France, 16 May. The French impose a treaty on The Hague, recognising the Batavian republic.

Budapest, 20 May. Ignac Martinovics, the head of the Jacobin movement in Hungary, is executed, dashing the hopes of Hungarian revolutionaries.

Paris, 23 May. After four days of rioting and violence, a *sans-culotte* uprising is suppressed. It began when rioters demonstrating against a severe bread shortage broke into the Conventiony. By yesterday the army had been called in and today the Saint Antoine district capitulated.

France, May. The White Terror, so called to differentiate it from Robespierre's Red Terror, sweeps across France, with all who are suspected as "terrorists" or political militants standing to lose their lives at the hands of the "reactionaries".

Marseilles, 5 June. Southern royalists calling themselves the Company of the Sun kill 700 defenceless "terrorists" in the prison of Saint Jean fort.

Luxembourg, 7 June. The duchy of Luxembourg, an Austrian possession for the last 82 years, surrenders to the French.

Paris, 8 June. The young *dauphin*, Louis, a prisoner in the Temple for three years, dies.

Paris, 15 June. General Napoleon Bonaparte has himself put on sick leave, having not received the posting he wanted from his superiors.

Paris, June. The writer Madame de Stael, daughter of the financier Necker, returns to Paris and reopens her salon. She declares herself a supporter of the republic.

Britain takes Cape Colony from the Dutch

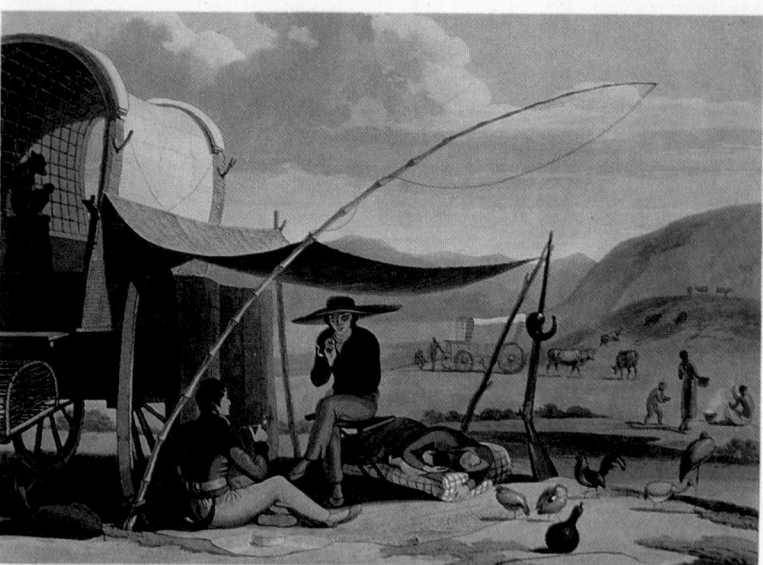

Boer farmers, who see themselves as Africans and resent the British presence.

Cape Town, South Africa
As the revolutionary Boers were declaring for liberty, equality and fraternity, British troops landed in Cape Town and took the colony from the Dutch. The British are now blockading the revolutionary republics into submission.

The Boer colony has been steadily expanding northwards, attacking and killing native Africans who got in the way. Holland opposed these methods. The Boers responded by driving out Dutch officials, sporting the revolutionary cockade and declaring republics.

It is unlikely, though, that the revolutionary ideas will benefit Africans. Indeed, one reason that the Boers declared their republics was to be able to attack their neighbours undisturbed.

France takes firm measure with measures

Paris
One of the important scientific outcomes of the French Revolution is the introduction of a new system of weights and measures. From now on there will be one system to replace the confusing variations from region to region. It will, it is declared, be a system "for all time, for all people".

The system is named *metric* after the Greek word for measure. The standard measure of length is the *metre*, which is one ten-millionth of the distance from the north pole to the equator. The system works in multiples of ten; thus, a *centimetre* is a hundredth of a metre, while a *millimetre* is a thousandth. The closest metric equivalent of the English mile is the *kilometre*. The new units of weight are based on the *gramme*, which is the weight of one cubic centimetre of water at a temperature of four degrees *centigrade* – another metric innovation to measure temperatures.

French propaganda prints herald the recently approved metric system; it is based on units of ten, to be universally applied "for all time, for all people" to calculate weights, volumes and distances in the new France.

Uprising in Paris put down by troops

Paris, 23 May

With the rallying cry of "Bread or Death!" thousands of revolutionary sans-culottes swarmed into the streets, smashing the gates of the Assembly, killing a deputy, Feraud, and brandishing his severed head on a pike before the president of the Convention, Boissy d'Anglas. Many rioters are women who spend hours queuing for the meagre bread ration of two ounces per person.

In the chaos that followed, Montagnard deputies formed themselves into an executive committee

A "sans-culotte" rioting for bread.

and, for a few hours, it seemed that the Robespierrists could be back in power. By nightfall, however, most of the sans-culottes had gone home, giving the Convention time to call in the regular army. As soldiers and insurgents faced each other today, the mob succeeded in freeing Feraud's killers. Nonetheless, as artillery faced the barricades, the sans-culottes were forced to surrender.

James Boswell, a British man of letters

London, 19 May

James Boswell, Dr Johnson's biographer, has died four years after publishing the long-awaited *Life*. It was an immediate success, and a second edition came out in 1793.

Boswell began keeping "an exact journal" from the age of 18 and put his best literary talents into it. He would often sit up all night recording his conversations as well as his sexual adventures. His irresistible good humour made him welcome amongst London's greatest wits – Goldsmith, Burke, Reynolds and Wilkes. His other works include an *Account of Corsica* and the famous *Tour to the Hebrides*.

New Dutch republic submits to France

French cavalry charging Dutch warships over the ice last winter.

The Hague, 16 May

The French republic has formally recognised the Batavian republic – the former United Provinces of Holland, which were occupied by French troops last year after the Dutch navy became trapped in ice.

The French move follows a popular uprising in the Provinces in which the stadholder (head of state) was driven out of office and a revolutionary constitution, based on the French model, adopted. The Dutch will pay dearly for their freedom, however. The new republic has to cede Dutch Flanders, Maastricht and Venlo to France, and pay 100 million florins as war compensation. It also accepts the installation of a French base at Flushing and has agreed to form an alliance with France against Austria and Germany.

The two republics may share revolutionary zeal, but there is no doubt who is the master.

Clay reclaims Wedgwood, master potter

Britain, 3 January

Josiah Wedgwood died today at Etruria, near Stoke-on-Trent, where he built what is now the biggest pottery in the world. He was 64. His success came after a difficult boyhood. The 13th son of a potter, he began work aged eight on the death of his father. He soon became an expert "thrower", but smallpox at 15 left him weak, so much so that his elder brother refused to take him into the firm. He concentrated on design and technique, producing the superb *Queen's Ware*, setting new higher quality standards, which made him world famous.

A Portland vase, by Wedgwood.

France approves a new constitution

Paris, 23 September

A new French constitution was ratified today after a referendum in which over a million French people voted in favour and fewer than 50,000 against. Only an eighth of the eligible population voted.

The constitution drops universal suffrage and replaces it with a two-tier system based on property ownership. Male taxpayers and army veterans of 21 or over and born in France – about five million people – will be eligible to vote in elections to local electoral assemblies in the French *departements*. The members of these assemblies – about 30,000 citizens – must be 25 or over with an income equal to 200 workdays a year. In the second tier of voting, the assemblies will elect members of a two-chamber national legislature. executive will consist of a five-man Directory with wide powers. The constitution contains many checks to block any attempt to set up a dictatorship.

Worker unrest now comes to England

London, 29 June

Fearful of an outbreak of rioting, the government today deployed a large force of cavalry and guards in Lambeth, south London, where a mass meeting was held to demand manhood suffrage and annual parliaments and to protest against "the cruel and unnecessary war" against revolutionary France. Some 10,000 people (the organisers say 100,000) endorsed a loyal address to the king before dispersing peacefully.

Many radical societies, inspired by events in France, have been formed in London and the provinces, but it is the hardship caused by war that has given the radical movement a sharper edge. Exports have collapsed and many workers are in dire straits. In Norwich, 25,000 of the city's 40,000 population are on poor relief.

Politics do not rule all hearts, though. One activist, Henry Redhead Yorke, was sent to prison for conspiracy; there he met and married the governor's daughter and abandoned his radical views.

Paris, 7 July 1795. At the Convention Thomas Paine defends the principle of universal suffrage which the deputies have decided to abandon in the next constitution.

France, 21 July 1795. Royalists are defeated at Quiberon, on the north-west coast. In alliance with the English, French emigres had planned an invasion of the mainland, but underestimated the powers of the republican army.

Basle, 22 July 1795. France and Spain sign a peace treaty following the fall of Bilbao and Vittoria.

Paris, 4 August 1795. The artist David is acquitted on charges relating to his friendship with Robespierre, who fell dramatically from a position of almost supreme power and was executed last year.

France, 15 August 1795. The Convention creates a new monetary unit, the *franc*.

Prussia, August 1795. Prussia joins the talks between Russia and Austria on the partition of Poland.

South Africa, 16 September 1795. Following the royal Dutch government's overthrow by France and the local Jacobins, the *stadholder*, William V, invites England to seize the Dutch colonial domain. England begins with Cape Town.

Netherlands, 29 September 1795. The government of the Batavian republic puts the stadholder William V on trial on a charge of high treason.

Paris, September 1795. The marquis de Sade publishes a new novel, *Aline and Valcour*, the story of an incestuous father thwarted by a double child swop, and of the dangers encountered by his virtuous wife during a voyage round the world.

Paris, 15 October 1795. An attempted armed takeover of the Convention by wealthy Parisians is put down, but only with heavy military intervention. From now on the Convention will have to take the army into account. One among the officers who attracted much attention was a young general, Napoleon Bonaparte.

Paris, 16 October 1795. Bonaparte is promoted to major-general.

Poland, 24 October 1795. The third partition of Poland is agreed between Russia, Prussia and Austria.

Paris, 31 October 1795. The Executive Directory, which replaces the Convention, is appointed. It consists of five Directors, nominated by the Council of Five Hundred and elected by the Council of Ancients.

Poland, 25 November 1795. King Stanislas abdicates following the partition of his country.

France, 17 December 1795. The British fleet, abandoned by the count of Artois, the pretender to the French throne, leaves the Ile d'Yeu.

Paris, 9 March 1796. Bonaparte marries Josephine de Beauharnais.

Santo Domingo, 31 March 1796. A coup by a mulatto general fails.

Italy, 11 April 1796. Bonaparte starts the Italian campaign at the head of 40,000 men.

Italy, 15 April 1796. The last Austrian corps in the Apennines surrenders at Dego.

Italy, 22 April 1796. Bonaparte wins the battles of Montenotte, Millesimo, Dego and Mondovi between 13 and 22 April.

Piedmont, 28 April 1796. Bonaparte concludes a treaty in Cherasco with the king of Piedmont and Sardinia. He has exceeded his instructions from Paris in the signing of this treaty.

Paris, 10 May 1796. A plot by the *Communes*, led by Francois Babeuf, to overthrow the Directory is uncovered and the leaders are arrested.

Italy, 10 May 1796. Bonaparte wins a brilliant victory against the Austrians at Lodi bridge.

Italy, 12 May 1796. Lombardian patriots rise up against the French and almost take Milan.

Milan, 15 May 1796. Bonaparte enters the Lombardian capital of Milan in triumph.

Paris, 15 May 1796. The treaty between France and Piedmont-Sardinia is signed, ceding Savoy and Nice to the French republic.

Italy, 23 May 1796. The people of Pavia massacre the French soldiers who sought refuge in the citadel.

USA, 1 June 1796. The Southwest Territory becomes the sixteenth state, known as Tennessee.

Italy, 5 June 1796. Bonaparte signs an armistice with the kingdom of Naples.

Italy, 23 June 1796. The pope, Pius VI, signs an armistice with Bonaparte in Bologna.

Elba, 9 July 1796. British forces take Elba as a Mediterranean base, having lost Leghorn to the French.

Philadelphia, 17 September 1796. President Washington makes his farewell address after 20 years as president.

Spain, 5 October 1796. Spain declares war on Britain.

Russia, 7 November 1796. Czarina Catherine II (the Great) dies.

French rout Austrians in battle for bridge

French troops crossing the river Alpone to take the Austrians from the rear.

Italy, 17 November 1796

The brilliant Napoleon Bonaparte, still only 27, scored another crushing victory in northern Italy today, where he has been campaigning since April. He as driven the Austrians back to Arcole after three days of heavy fighting for the bridge over the Alpone river.

The battle was brought about by the advance of the Austrian General Alvinczy and 50,000 troops transferred after the French retreat in Germany. At the beginning of the month he defeated the tired troops of Massena at Bassano, and then beat Augereau at Caldiso. Suddenly the whole French position in Italy was in danger. Napoleon met Alvinczy at Arcole, and both armies fought for two days over difficult, swampy ground until Napoleon showed his tactical genius by moving his men across the river on pontoon bridges and taking the Austrians in the rear.

Massena is now pursuing the Austrians through Arcole, and Augereau is harassing their flank. In three days of fighting the Austrians have lost 7,000 men and 11 cannons. The French have also taken heavy punishment, and sorely need rest and supplies. Bonaparte told them: "You have won battles without guns, crossed rivers without bridges, made forced marches without boots, encamped without food."

Theory links liberty with obeying laws

Jena, Germany, 1796

Man cannot achieve real freedom without a rational legal system, according to a new theory developed by the philosopher Johann Gottlieb Fichte, a disciple of Kant.

In his just-published *Foundation of the Study of Human Knowledge*, Fichte, a 34-year-old professor, explains that since man is forced to live in society, laws naturally arise from the social relationships that exist between men.

When these laws are guaranteed by the state then they form a protective framework that allows the individual to fulfil himself, argues Fichte. His new theory is a marked about-turn. Three years ago he was violently hostile to the state.

French astronomer makes stars clearer

Paris, 1796

The French mathematician, astronomer and physicist Pierre-Simon de Laplace has finally crowned his life's work on the structure and evolution of the solar system with a popular book.

Laplace's recently-published *Exposition du systeme du monde* is a beautifully written work on celestial mechanics. He is able to account for all the planets' deviations: why, for example, Jupiter's orbit seems continually to be getting smaller while that of Saturn is expanding. Another intriguing idea concerns planetary formation. The solar system, he argues, is formed out of a cooling, contracting mass of gas – the *nebula* hypothesis.

Despotic czarina leaves a stronger Russia

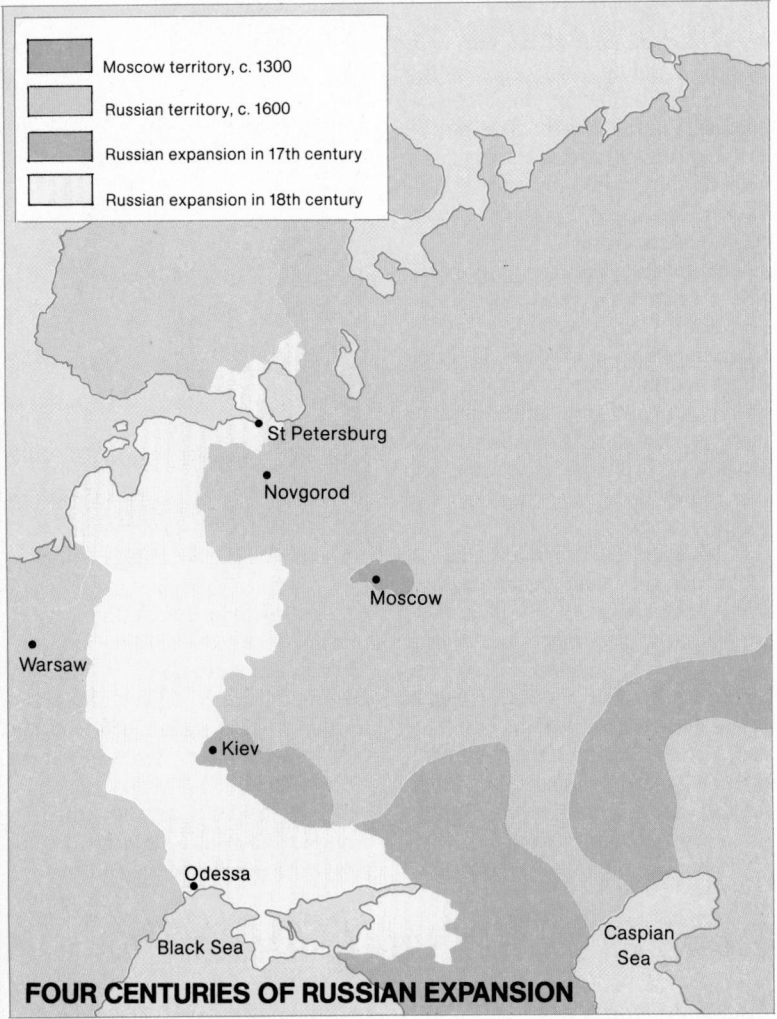

FOUR CENTURIES OF RUSSIAN EXPANSION

Legend:
- Moscow territory, c. 1300
- Russian territory, c. 1600
- Russian expansion in 17th century
- Russian expansion in 18th century

Map locations: St Petersburg, Novgorod, Moscow, Warsaw, Kiev, Odessa, Black Sea, Caspian Sea

Czarskoye Selo, 7 November 1796
Her court is riddled with corruption, scoundrels are promoted to the nobility, and injustice is rampant. Yet the czarina, who died today aged 67 at Czarskoye Selo (the Czar's Village), near St Petersburg, has become universally known as Catherine the Great.

She had not a drop of Russian blood. Born at Stettin, Pomerania, the daughter of the prince of Anhalt-Zerbst, she was taken to Russia at the age of 15 to become the bride of the mentally subnormal Grand Duke Peter. She endured 17 wretched years until, on Peter's succession to the throne, she arranged for his assassination by one of her lovers.

As czarina she was more Russian than the Russians whom she ruled. She said: "All I wish is that this country, in which God has cast me, should prosper." She said serfdom was against God's law, but under her serfdom flourished. She pushed the empire's boundaries to the Dniester in the west and the Black Sea in the south. In her will she advised her successors to avoid consulting "Germans of both sexes".

Robbie Burns, poet

Dumfries, Scotland, 21 July 1796
Scotland's bard, the poet Robert Burns, died today, aged 37, after months of failing health. Through hundreds of poems and folksongs, such as *Auld Lang Syne*, *The Highland Lassie* and the *Jolly Beggars*, he captured the soul of Scotland.

Yet Burns was 25 before he burst upon a startled world with a small book of poems that instantly sold out. The eldest son of a poor peasant farmer, Burns used the funds from his second book to buy a farm. Through contacts in Edinburgh society, which briefly lionised him, he obtained a job as an excise official in south-west Scotland.

Polish cake carved into three pieces

Warsaw, 1795
A bankrupt Englishman is the last foreign diplomat in Warsaw, the capital of a country that has ceased to exist. He has 300 refugees in the embassy and has written to London asking for money, but the British are too concerned about the victories of France's revolutionary armies to bother about a faraway land of which few people have heard. After crushing the Polish uprising last year, Russia, Prussia and Austria, which had twice before annexed large areas of Poland, decided to finish the job. The Prussians pushed their frontier further east to take in Warsaw; the Austrians seized the Cracow region; the Russians took the rest, which was greater than Prussian and Austrian gains combined. The three powers agreed to suppress the name of Poland "forever".

Lotus cult is focus for Chinese rebels

China, 1796
The White Lotus Society, an ascetic creed which believes that a "future Buddha" will usher in an era of peace and plenty, has risen in revolt against the government. Trouble has been brewing for some time, due to government oppression, and the White Lotus rebellion is spreading rapidly through the countryside.

The society is famous for driving the Mongols out of China in the 14th century, and its adherents have lost none of their ferocity in war. Its teachings are spread from village to village by missionaries and its members are protected by local defence associations. It is these which have taken up arms against rapacious local officials and, basing themselves in fortified mountain villages, are raiding valley towns for supplies and recruits.

Milkmaid clue to smallpox prevention

London, 1796
Smallpox – which has killed millions over the centuries – could be eradicated, thanks to the work of an English country doctor, Edward Jenner of Gloucestershire.

Jenner noticed while still a student that milkmaids who had contracted a disease called cowpox, which also causes blistering of cows' udders, did not catch smallpox. So now Jenner has taken some of the fluid from a cowpox blister and scratched it into the skin of an eight-year-old boy named James Phipps. A single blister rose up on the spot but, amazingly, young James has not caught smallpox even though he has been in close contact with other children suffering from the disease. Jenner has thus found a way of preparing the body in advance to cope with an infection.

The wonders of the smallpox vaccine, as seen by the Anti-Vaccine Society.

1796 (1796-1797)

Ireland, 24 December 1796. A storm breaks up the French fleet which was bound for Ireland to help the nationalists in their fight against the British.

Italy, 14 January 1797. Bonaparte crushes Alvinczy's army at Rivoli.

Italy, 16 January 1797. The main body of Provera's Austrian army surrenders to Bonaparte at La Favorite.

Italy, 20 January 1797. In accordance with a treaty signed with Bonaparte, the Polish general, Dobrowski, calls all Polish patriots to arms, to form a legion with him in Italy in support of the French.

Italy, 2 February 1797. Bonaparte takes Mantua from the Austrians, opening up the road to Vienna.

Italy, 9 February 1797. Bonaparte moves into the Vatican states and occupies Ancona, with a view to forcing Pius VI to negotiate.

Portugal, 14 February 1797. The Spanish fleet, which is allied to France, is defeated by the British just off the Cape of St Vincent.

Italy, 19 February 1797. Bonaparte signs the treaty of Tolentino with Pope Pius VI.

Paris, 2 March 1797. The Directory authorises vessels of war to board and seize neutral vessels, particularly if the ships involved are American.

England, 2 March 1797. Horace Walpole, who set the fashion for "Gothick" romance in *The Castle of Otranto*, dies. He lived in a "Gothick" castle which he had built at Strawberry Hill near London in reaction to the prevailing Classical style of country houses.

USA, 4 March 1797. Vice-president John Adams, elected president on 7 December to replace George Washington, is sworn in.

London, 18 March 1797. Chateaubriand brings out his *Historic Essay on Revolutions*, which is instantly popular among the emigres of the upper classes.

Paris, 20 March 1797. On the eve of the polls, the Directory passes a law requiring all voters to swear commitment to the republic and the constitution.

Italy, 27 March 1797. The constitution of the Cispadian republic is promulgated at Bologna.

Austria, 31 March 1797. Bonaparte makes peace proposals to Archduke Charles of Austria.

Paris, 4 April 1797. Election results show that the French people are now predominantly right-wing reactionaries rather than revolutionaries.

Austria, 7 April 1797. In the absence of news about the French campaign in Germany, Bonaparte signs an armistice with the Austrian envoys in Judenburg.

Britain, 15 April 1797. The British fleet mutinies at Spithead.

Verona, 17 April 1797. On Easter Sunday several hundred French soldiers are massacred by locals.

Verona, 27 April 1797. The revolt of the people of Verona and Venice, as a reaction against French taxes, is violently crushed and the *doge* removed from office.

Paris, 30 April 1797. The Directory ratifies the Leoben agreement between Austria and France, which Bonaparte signed on 18 April though he had no authority to do so.

Britain, 2 May 1797. The naval mutiny spreads from Spithead to the North Sea fleet.

Venice, 12 May 1797. The Grand Council replaces the doge by with a democratic republic.

Philadelphia, 15 May 1797. President Adams calls Congress into a special session, hoping to resolve the crisis with France.

India, 15 May 1797. An alliance between France and Mysore is made in Seringapatam.

Paris, 26 May 1797. The trial of Babeuf and his followers, for conspiracy to overthrown the government, comes to an end. Babeuf is sentenced to death.

Italy, 14 June 1797. A 22-man government appointed by Bonaparte takes up its duties in Genoa, marking the birth of the Ligurian republic.

Persia, 17 June 1797. The *shah*, Aga Mohammed, is assassinated. He is succeeded by his nephew Fath Ali.

Italy, 9 July 1797. The Cisalpine republic is founded in Milan, combining Lombardy and the Cispadian republic.

Britain, 9 July 1797. Edmund Burke, foremost political philosopher of the day, dies aged 68. He defended constitutional government against the French revolutionaries, but advocated conciliation with the American colonists before the War of Independence.

Mediterranean, 28 August 1797. The USA agrees to pay tribute to Tunis in an effort to halt piracy against American ships.

France, 22 September 1797. General Pichegru, convicted of treason because of his royalist sympathies, leaves France for Guyana where he is to be imprisoned.

Mutiny sweeps through British navy

London, 1797
In the darkest hour of the war, with Britain standing alone against the triumphant armies of revolutionary France, mutiny has broken out in the Royal Navy and is leaping from ship to ship, while the enemy's invasion fleet assembles in the Dutch naval base at Texel.

The trouble began at Spithead, near Portsmouth. The crew of the *Queen Charlotte,* the flagship of the Channel fleet, refused Lord Bridport's orders to put to sea and called for delegates from other ships to draw up demands. A petition to the House of Commons was prepared, demanding better pay (seamen's ten shillings a month has not been increased since the reign of Charles II), better food and better medical treatment. The men said that they would put to sea only if the enemy appeared. The authorities had ample warning of discontent below decks, but took no action. Now the men have found leaders among better-educated civilians recruited for the war, and London has hastily conceded the men's demands.

No sooner was the Spithead mu-

Richard Parker, the mutiny leader.

tiny settled than the North Sea fleet mutinied at the Nore, on the Thames Estuary. Led by Richard Parker, a former officer, the mutiny lasted for a month before being put down. Parker and 28 others were hanged.

These incidents are not isolated. Mutinies have also occurred in the navy's Mediterranean squadron.

Scotsman barters way to African river

Nigeria, 21 June 1796
By reaching the majestic Niger river at Segu, Mungo Park, a 24-year-old Scottish doctor, has discovered one of the secrets of mysterious Africa. He reports that the river is as broad as the Thames at Westminster and flows eastwards. He marked his discovery by drinking the river water and thanking God. Park is the first European to penetrate the West African interior; he has done it alone, and has learnt to live on native food and without western luxuries.

His instruments consisted of a pocket sextant, compass and thermometer. He paid for his food and shelter with beads, amber and tobacco, but was ultimately reduced to selling the buttons off his rags. His story should be a bestseller.

Park's first sight of what he called the "glittering" Niger (later portrayal).

Lucknow prospers under Asaf-ud-Daula

The royal family of Oudh, painted in Lucknow by Tilly Kettle, in foreground.

Lucknow, India, September 1797
Asaf-ud-Daula, the monarch of Oudh, is transforming Lucknow into the new cultural capital of northern India. Palaces, mosques and schools are being built. The finest poets, painters, musicians and architects of Moslem India have gathered here; so have travellers, adventurers, merchants and confidence tricksters.

Already Lucknow has surpassed Delhi in splendour, drawing into it such poets as Mirza Rafi, known as *Sauda*, Mir Taqi (*Mir*) and Mir Ghulam Hasan – the finest Indian and Persian poets of the age. Poets are not the only ones to be tempted by the wealth of Oudh. Shi'ite scho-

lars from Persia, painters from India and Europe, actors, musicians and Moghul princes flock to the city. Asaf-ud-Daula, who is bored by the bread-and-butter of statecraft, collects such people as other Indian princes collect jewels.

Yet behind the luxury and pomp of Lucknow there is little substance. The economy of Oudh is firmly in the hands of the British-owned East India Company. The more Asaf-ud-Daula has to rely on the military might of the British, and the more Oudh's treasury becomes indebted to the British, the more extravagantly Asaf-ud-Daula embellishes Lucknow, in splendid defiance.

Man demonstrates "parachute" device

Paris, 22 October 1797
From now on, stricken aeronauts whose hot-air balloons fail them will enjoy a way of escape, thanks to the pioneering efforts of the physicist Andre Jacques Garnerin, who today demonstrated his revolutionary *parachute* in the Monceau park.

Supported by one such device, made of 36 tapered strips of material sewn together to form a spherical "skullcap" eight metres in diameter, Garnerin dropped from a balloon 3,050 feet above the park. The folded parachute was attached to the gondola, and crowds watched as Garnerin cut the cord that attached him to the balloon and then, as the parachute unfolded above him, floated safely to earth.

Garnerin descends with his parachute above the environs of Paris.

France extends rule over Italian republics

Milan, 9 July 1797
Napoleon sat his horse for three hours in the burning sun today as the birth of his Cisalpine republic was celebrated in grand operatic – some would say musical comedy – style in the streets of Milan.

Cisalpine consists of two of his previous statelets, the Transpadian and Cispadian, and includes Modena, whose duke has been deposed. It follows Napoleon's policy of imposing his version of the French Revolution on states he has conquered on behalf of France. His victories and the flood of indemnities and loot he sends back to

Paris have made him enormously popular. There are those, however, who fear that the little general is becoming over-ambitious.

He has set up what can only be called a court at the chateau of Montebello, a few miles from Milan and he and his wife, Josephine, are behaving like royalty. They are surrounded by his family, his generals and brilliantly uniformed *aides de camp*.

Napoleon receives the nobility of Lombardy and the envoys of kings at his chateau. He basks in his glory and disposes of states like an emperor.

New republics, established by French arms, sprout throughout Italy.

Bonaparte's hand is seen in Paris coup

Paris, 4 September 1797
A *coup d'etat* led by the hulking General Augereau has swept away the royalist faction which, largely financed by the British, had made much ground in last spring's elections.

Primed with champagne, Augereau announced: "I have come here to kill the Royalists." When some of the deputies protested "in the

name of the law", one of his officers replied: "The sword is the law."

However, while Augereau is the very visible arm of the coup, there is little doubt that Bonaparte, safely out of the way in Italy, has a powerful hand in it. He despises Augereau, but uses him.

It was Bonaparte who wrote to the Directory: "If you need force, call on the armies!"

English missionary team arrives in Tahiti

Tahiti, 1797
Thirty-nine English missionaries have landed in Tahiti. The party of four ministers, carpenters, weavers, bricklayers and even shopkeepers is being financed by the Presbyterian London Missionary Society.

The near-Arcadian paradise that Captain Cook found has disappeared within a decade. Firearms, venereal diseases, rum and infanticide have decimated the population.

The staunch lower-middle-class Protestants who sailed halfway round the world on *The Duff* have no illusions about Arcadia. Guilt, hard work and public decency must be implanted in the islanders. The missionaries themselves observe such principles remorselesssly.

Ironically, they forgot to add a day when they passed the date line. Thus they observe a sober and silent sabbath every Saturday.

1797 (1797-1798)

Paris, 26 October 1797. The Directory ratifies the treaty of Campo Formio, signed by Bonaparte and the Austrians on 18 October.

USA, 4 November 1797. Congress agrees to pay a yearly tribute to Tripoli in a deal similar to that concluded last year with the *bey* of Algiers. This is the USA's only way of protecting its shipping.

Prussia, 16 November 1797. King Frederick William II dies and is succeeded by his son Frederick William III.

Germany, 1 December 1797. Bonaparte signs a convention with Austria at Rastatt, agreeing to a simultaneous evacuation of Mainz and Venice.

Paris, 12 January 1798. Bonaparte presents his plans for the invasion of England to the Directory.

Paris, 18 January 1798. Increasing pressure on British trade, the Directory passes a law authorising the seizure of any neutral vessel carrying British goods.

Switzerland, 24 January 1798. The people of Vaud, in the west, proclaim the republic of Leman, in defiance of authorities in Berne.

Rome, 15 February 1798. The republic of Rome is proclaimed by the French.

Rome, 24 February 1798. The French army rises up against its new chief, Berthier. The people of Rome seize the opportunity to revolt against the occupation.

Paris, 5 March 1798. Having shelved plans for the invasion of England, on Bonaparte's advice, the Directory accepts the idea of invading Egypt and puts Bonaparte in charge of the project.

Switzerland, 6 March 1798. French troops seize Berne, under the pretext of helping Vaudois patriots to remain independent.

Indian Ocean, 4 April 1798. French soldiers are under siege in their barracks in the Ile de France (*Mauritius*). Taking advantage of military unrest, the white and mulatto populations of the island have staged an uprising against slavery. The soldiers are trying to negotiate a surrender and are asking to be returned to France.

Switzerland, 12 April 1798. Deputies from 12 cantons proclaim a Swiss republic at Aarau.

Austria, 29 April 1798. Haydn's oratorio *The Creation* is first performed. Inspired by his hearing of Handel's oratorios in England, Haydn sets a text derived from Milton and James Thomson. It is scored for full orchestra, large choir and three soloists, and is a great success.

Caribbean, 2 May 1798. The black general Toussaint L'Ouverture forces the British forces to agree to evacuate the part of Santo Domingo still in their possession.

Ireland, 23 May 1798. Believing that a French invasion is imminent, the Irish nationalists rise up against British occupation.

Malta, 11 June 1798. The island surrenders to Bonaparte.

Ireland, 21 June 1798. British forces suppress an uprising by Irish patriots at Vinegar Hill near Wexford.

Egypt, 29 June 1798. The first French frigate to arrive at Alexandria learns that Nelson's fleet put in the previous day in search of the French.

Egypt, 1 July 1798. Napoleon Bonaparte takes Alexandria.

Egypt, 7 July 1798. Bonaparte's army begins its march towards Cairo.

Philadelphia, 11 July 1798. As the possibility of war with France grows, Congress passes the Sedition Act, aimed at curbing internal dissent. French negotiators are trying to intimidate the American envoys, and war at sea has already broken out, though it is undeclared. Under the Sedition Act American citizens may be imprisoned for obstructing the imposition of federal law or for seditious writings.

Russia, 21 July 1798. Czar Paul sends his army to help Austrian troops in their struggles with France.

France, 1798. The American engineer Robert Fulton invents the first submarine. He arrived in France two years ago and submitted his plans to the Directory. Now the *Nautilus* has taken to the water in a successful demonstration. However, naval officers are not convinced.

England, 1798. William Wordsworth and Samuel Taylor Coleridge publish the *Lyrical Ballads*, a joint collection of poetry. The volume marks a significant departure from current poetic conventions and is a celebration of the imagination and creative originality. Coleridge, in particular, reacts against the poetic dictates of the 18th century, revitalising his language by a skilful use of archaic diction, while Wordsworth is striving to transform everyday reality and to describe a mystical union of man with nature.

Austria, 1798. Ludwig van Beethoven presents his piano sonata, opus 13, known as the *Pathetique*.

Smuggler gangs bring home the brandy

Revenue men often ambush smugglers in the most picturesque surroundings.

England, c.1798

The coasts of Britain, from the North Sea round to Devon and Cornwall, are under siege from a widespread and highly successful variety of seaborne rogue: the smuggler, a breed that has grown in numbers and in profits over the last hundred years.

In 1782 the Customs Board reported ruefully on "the enormous increase of smuggling, the outrages with which it is carried on, the mischiefs it occasions to the country, the discouragement it creates to all fair traders, and the prodigious loss the Revenue sustains by it". There is no sign that the situation has improved.

Smuggling, the illegal duty-free importation of various goods – particularly rum, brandy and tea – all of which attract heavy taxes, began about a century ago. Faced with the sharp increases in duty that helped to finance the wars of William III, many of those living along the coasts saw the chance to make large profits by bringing in goods duty free.

Although the volume of goods smuggled in has certainly increased, the technique remains much the same. A ship anchors out at sea, dispatching a small boat to alert those waiting on shore. Once contact has been made, more small boats ferry the contraband ashore.

Smuggling is highly profitable. One Devonshire captain, Harry Carter, is said to make £1,000 profit a week. It also requires experts – even on a calm day, off-loading is a dangerous, skilful task, and smugglers are also outstanding seamen. The Revenue opposes the gangs as best it can, but its numbers are small, and few men will testify against hard-bitten smugglers who have no qualms in killing those who get in their way and who have many friends in high places.

Austria surrenders to Bonaparte in Italy

Campo Formio, 18 October 1797
Bonaparte has today signed a peace treaty with Austria after five months of hard bargaining. Given that the Austrians were driven to accept his proposals of peace by the threat his army posed to Vienna, they have come well out of the negotiations. Austria cedes Belgium to France, but no decision has been made about the left bank of the Rhine. Vienna also cedes Lombardy to the Cisalpine republic, receiving in return Venice and mainland territory as far as the Adige.

Bonaparte has behaved in his now customary high-handed fashion, for in giving up Venice he acted in contradiction to the government's orders. But he seems not to care for the politicians in Paris. A threat of resignation always brings

One image of Bonaparte.

them to heel. It is evident that he is prepared to trade territory – which he can always recapture – in return for fame in France as both conqueror and peacemaker.

Immoral and mystical Prussian king dies

Berlin, 16 November 1797
The imposing Brandenburg Gate in Berlin is a memorial not to King Frederick William II but to his first mistress, Wilhelmine Enke, the daughter of a horn-player in the royal orchestra, whom he took to his bed when she was 16. She it was who discovered the architect Langhans and won him royal support. When Frederick William died here today, aged 53, after a long illness, Wilhelmine was at his bedside.

After the disciplined regime of his uncle Frederick the Great, Frederick William's reign was a period of moral ambiguity. The arts flourished, and Immanuel Kant's *Critique of Pure Reason* was hailed as the masterpiece it is; but Kant was forbidden to write on Christianity. The king was recruited by the Rosi-

King Frederick William of Prussia.

crucians, who claimed to possess occult powers. Besides Wilhelmine, the king had many other mistresses and two royal and two morganatic marriages.

Lead balls reveal density of planet Earth

London, 1798
The latest achievement of the distinguished scientist Henry Cavendish is an experiment which claims to reveal the weight and density of the planet Earth itself. The "Cavendish Experiment" consists of a horizontal rod with a lead ball at either end, suspended in the centre from a fine wire or fibre.

Two large lead spheres are then moved near to the lead balls, producing a gravitational attraction.

This gravitational force is calculated from the amount the rod turns. From this figure Cavendish has sought to work out the mass of Earth. When divided by Earth's volume, this figure yields a value for Earth's density.

Temperature drives the ocean currents

United States, 1798
An American scientist, Benjamin Thompson, has shown in an essay, *On the Propagation of Heat in Fluids*, that water heated by the sun in northerly latitudes becomes denser and descends to the ocean bed. There it spreads out towards the equator and forms a counter-

current that drives back up from the tropics in a northerly direction. Thus water is constantly warming, cooling, rising and descending in a massive circulatory cycle. Thompson also argues that heat is transferred to and from the atmosphere with important consequences for climate as well as ocean currents.

Scientist claims animals do not evolve

Paris, 1798
An argument is brewing over the idea that life-forms on earth have evolved over time. Many biologists hold that view, but Georges Cuvier, a French zoologist and academician, has this year argued for the comparison of the features of one creature with those of another rather than the study of changes over a period of time. As a result of

his studies, Cuvier is convinced that the anatomical differences that characterise animals are evidence that evolution did, and does, *not* take place. Each animal species, says Cuvier, is so well coordinated in form and function that it could not survive any significant changes in its bodily makeup. This means, he claims, that each creature is now the same as when it was created.

Explorer's African trip ends in failure

Zambia, 18 October 1798
A gallant attempt by the Portuguese geographer Francisco Maria de Lacerda to cross the continent of Africa has failed. He has died, halfway through his journey, in the central African Lunda kingdom.

Since the British occupied Cape Town, Portugal has feared that they will expand north, driving a wedge between Portugal's colonies of Angola and Mozambique. Last year Portuguese traders made con-

tact with King Kazembe of Luanda. Lacerda, the governor of Mozambique's Rivers province, saw this as the opportunity to unite the two colonies. The expedition was a disaster. War, fever, dysentery and desertions took their toll, Lacerda dying today outside Kazembe's court. The survivors have been unable to make any agreement with Kazembe. One of Portugal's greatest explorers lies dead; his efforts have come to naught.

"The British Menagerie", a 1796 cartoon depicting the powers of Europe fed by Pitt with Britain's gold, including: 1, the Austrian leopard; 2, the Prussian eagle; 3, the (royal) French cock; 4, the Russian bear; 5, the Sardinian hedgehog; 8, the Neapolitan bat; 9, the Dutch frog; 10, the Swedish pig; 11, what the artist dubs the "whore of Babylon" – the Pope.

1798 (1798-1799)

Egypt, 23 July 1798. General Bonaparte enters Cairo which his troops occupied two days ago.

Egypt, 1 August 1798. The French navy is destroyed by Nelson at Aboukir. The French army is virtually imprisoned in Egypt.

France, 6 August 1798. Unaware that the Irish rebels have been defeated, a French expeditionary force sets sail for Ireland to help them in their fight against the British.

Ireland, 27 August 1798. After defeating several British contingents, the French General Humbert proclaims an Irish republic.

Malta, 2 September 1798. The Maltese people revolt against French occupation, forcing the French troops to take refuge in the citadel of Valetta.

Ottoman Empire, 9 September 1798. The Ottoman empire declares war on France because of its occupation of Egypt.

Ireland, 15 September 1798. The French force under General Humbert surrenders to General Cornwallis at Ballynamuck. This is the end of the attempted French invasion of Ireland.

Egypt, 22 October 1798. An uprising by the people of Cairo is brutally suppressed by French soldiers of occupation.

Caribbean, 22 October 1798. The black General Toussaint L'ouverture's supporters drive the French government's last agent off the island of Santo Domingo.

Mediterranean, 27 October 1798. Having taken the island of Zante on 25 October, the Russians now take Cephalonia. Of the other Ionian islands, only Corfu remains in French hands.

Luxembourg, 30 October 1798. A Belgian peasants' revolt against conscription into the French army is put down.

Greece, 5 November 1798. The Russo-Ottoman fleet begins a blockade of Corfu, which is held by the French.

Indian Ocean, 7 November 1798. The Ile de France (*Mauritius*) is in the hands of its settlers who have occupied the capital and dissolved the colonial assembly.

Ireland, 19 November 1798. In prison awaiting execution, the Irish nationalist leader Wolfe Tone commits suicide.

Italy, 22 November 1798. The Austrian-led Neapolitan army attacks the republic of Rome, defended by the French General Championnet.

Italy, 27 November 1798. The Neapolitan army of Ferdinand IV, the king of Naples and Sicily, who was forced to sign a peace treaty with France two years ago, occupies Rome.

Egypt, 7 December 1798. French troops capture Suez.

Rome, 14 December 1798. The French re-occupy the city after it is abandoned by the Neapolitans.

London, 29 December 1798. A second military alliance against France is formed by Britain, Austria, Russia, Naples and Portugal. The first coalition collapsed when the Austrians signed the treaty of Campo Formio with France. Now plans are being made to challenge France in the Netherlands, Italy and Brittany.

Mozambique, 1798. The Portuguese reoccupy the fort of Lourenco Marques at Maputo Bay and re-establish trade with the local Maputo kingdom in ivory and slaves.

Britain, 1798. Thomas Robert Malthus publishes his *Essay on the Principle of Population as it Affects the Future Improvements of Society* in which he asserts that populations inevitably increase more rapidly than food supplies.

Austria, 1798. Haydn composes his *Missa in Angustiis*, a brilliant, austerely powerful work. Shortly before its first performance the news arrived of Nelson's victory in Egypt; it has since been dubbed the *Nelson Mass*.

Italy, 23 January 1799. French troops take Naples after fierce street fighting.

Italy, 26 January 1799. As agreed with the French, the radicals of Naples proclaim the Parthenopian republic.

Botswana, 1799. Kora (Khoisan herders and hunters) from the south attack Kanye, the capital of the Ngwaketse kingdom, which is rich in hunting goods and cattle as well as copper. The Kora were leading Griqua and Boers north along the trade routes into the Kalahari. The attack is repulsed.

Philadelphia, 1799. In the first organised labour action in the United States, the Federal Society of Cordwainers (shoemakers) wins a nine-day strike.

Japan, 1799. Following unrest fomented by the Ainu people, the whole of Ezo (*Hokkaido*) is placed under the direct control of the *shogun* at Edo.

Germany, 1799. The well-known writer Friedrich Schiller concludes his dramatic trilogy *Wallenstein*, about the famous general of the Thirty Years War.

Population growth is threat to humans

England, 1798

The greatest threat to humanity, according to Thomas Malthus, the economist and Anglican minister, is the fact that population growth is bound to outstrip any increases in food production. The population of Europe has risen from from 66 million in 1700 to 180 million.

In his *Essay on the Principle of Population*, originally published anonymously, Malthus asserts: "Population, when unchecked, increases in a geometrical ratio. Subsistence increases only in an arithmetical ratio." He cites as an example the United States of America, where the population has doubled in 25 years. While that figure might go on doubling every 25 years, the food supply could not do more than increase by a similar amount each 25 years, he says.

Applying his theory to England, Malthus argues that the poor laws, which now provide £4,000,000 a year, tend to increase population

Thomas Robert Malthus.

without increasing the food for its support. "Dependent poverty ought to be held disgraceful," he writes, since it diminishes "both the power and will to save". Instead he advocates the abolition of parish laws, incentives for agriculture, and workhouses for those in distress.

New coalition formed against Bonaparte

A French cartoonist's view of the effects of British military expenditure. Britannia (l.) armed to the teeth and (r.) ruined as a result.

Europe, 1799

Since last December Britain has been putting together a formidable new coalition to fight France. Czar Paul of Russia has agreed to join the Anglo-Austrian alliance and is preparing to send an army into Italy to attack Bonaparte's puppet states.

The Russians have also promised to join Britain in an invasion of Holland and to send an expeditionary force to Brittany. In return the British have agreed to pay £225,000 plus £75,000 a month towards the costs of the war.

Turkey, Portugal and the kingdom of Naples and Sicily complete this second coalition. It is a considerable diplomatic and military achievement.

Bonaparte's army has conquered Egypt

The battle of the Pyramids, where Napoleon crushed the Egyptian Mamelukes.

Cairo, 21 July 1798
Bonaparte is the master of Egypt. His tired, thirsty men, grilled by the desert sun, today faced the glittering array of the Mameluke warriors and pummelled them into bloody defeat.

They met at Giza by the pyramids of the pharoahs. Some 50,000 men waited for the French. The entire Mameluke cavalry, mounted on the finest Arab horses, were drawn up on the left bank of the Nile, with the morning sunshine shining on their spears and jewelled scimitars.

Bonaparte ordered his divisions to form squares and place their can-

non at the corners. Then they waited for the enemy cavalry. On came the Mamelukes with the utmost courage. The guns tore great holes in their ranks and the volley fire of muskets tumbled horses and riders.

The carnage continued for most of the day until 2,000 Mamelukes lay on the battlefield. Murad, their leader, was gravely wounded. At last he gave the order to retreat and burnt his boats to prevent the French from pursuing him across the Nile. Tonight the desert is lit by fires as French soldiers strip the richly-clad bodies of the Mamelukes. And Cairo is Bonaparte's.

Nelson smashes French navy off Aboukir

Aboukir, Egypt, 1 August 1798
In an all night battle, the French Mediterranean Fleet has been almost completely destroyed by a British naval squadron commanded by Lord Nelson. Napoleon and his armies are literally trapped in Egypt.

Nelson had been searching for the French fleet since May, and found them at anchor. He formed his ships into two files, one led by HMS *Goliath* attacking the enemy centre, the other, with Nelson's *Vanguard* leading, savaging the French flanks. Five French ships were sunk with 4,000 men. Two were captured; and two frigates managed to escape.

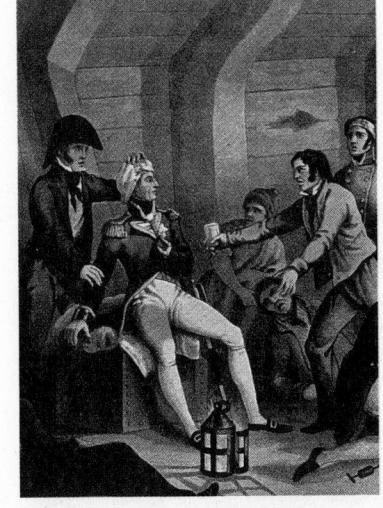

Nelson, wounded in the battle.

Parisians see looted Italian art treasures

The spoils of war arrive at the Festival of Arts and Sciences in Paris.

Paris, 28 July 1798
"To the victor the spoils" runs the saying, and a triumphant France, after winning its campaign in Italy, is showing itself a firm believer in the old proverb.

The fruits of two years' systematic ransacking of the art treasures of Italy were paraded through the Champ de Mars today, as part of the annual celebrations of the revolution. It was an exhibition worthy of a Roman triumph. Every piece has been selected by a seven-man artistic commission.

Some French artists have argued against the army's looting of so many treasures, but the crowds were ecstatic as 29 floats moved by, crammed with sculptures like the *Apollo Belvedere*, the *Laocoon* and the horses of St Mark's, and paintings that included Raphael's *Transfiguration* and Correggio's *Virgin with St Jerome*. Carriages packed with medals, books, precious manu-

Raphael's "Transfiguration".

scripts and much more were followed by loot of a different type: bears from Switzerland, lions and camels from Africa and other exotic beasts.

US Navy scores victory over the French

Nevis, West Indies, 9 February 1799
A US Navy frigate, the recently-commissioned *Constellation*, won a significant duel with the French *Insurgente* – giving the new and untried US Navy first blood in its sea war with France. In an engagement fought in gale force conditions, Captain Thomas Truxton was chasing the French ship which lost its maintop in a squall. The French ship tried to grapple with the *Constellation*, but Truxton held off and

raked her with gunfire until she struck her colours. A prize crew is bringing *Insurgente* into St Kitts with 173 prisoners.

Since the capture of one of its schooners by a French ship off Guadeloupe, the United States has stepped up its naval building programme, concentrating on fast frigates like the *Constellation*, one of five ships that patrol the Caribbean to protect American shipping from French interference.

India, 3 February. British troops enter Mysore in order to subjugate Tipu Sahib, with whom Bonaparte is trying to establish contact.

Egypt, 10 February. Bonaparte leaves Cairo for Syria, at the head of 13,000 men.

Palestine, 24 February. Bonaparte's army occupies Gaza.

Greece, 3 March. The last French garrison in the Ionian isles surrenders to Russo-Ottoman troops who have invaded the island of Corfu.

Palestine, 7 March. Napoleon captures Jaffa where his men massacre more than two thousand Albanian prisoners.

Germany, 25 March. French troops are defeated by Archduke Charles of Saxe-Weimar at Stokach.

Italy, 27 March. Austrian troops move into Verona having defeated the French at Legnano, near Milan.

Palestine, March. Soldiers in the French garrison at Jaffa are dying of bubonic plague at the rate of 30 a day.

Germany, 23 April. The conference at Rastatt between Austria and France collapses after a renewal of hostilities between the two countries. The conference was set up after the treaty of Campo Formio to supervise Prussian cession of lands on the left bank of the Rhine to France.

Italy, 29 April. The anti-French coalition army enters Milan.

India, 4 May. Tipu Sahib, the ruler of Mysore, dies fighting the British under the command of the governor, the marquis of Wellesley.

Palestine, 17 May. Bonaparte lifts the siege of Acre after failing to take the city.

France, 18 May. The great comic playwright Pierre de Beaumarchais dies of apoplexy. He returned to Paris in 1796 from exile in England and Holland, having lost his vast fortune in the revolution. The two plays which established him as a comic genius are *The Barber of Seville* and *The Marriage of Figaro*.

Spain, 5 June. The naturalist and explorer Alexander von Humboldt sets sail for America, planning to explore Venezuela, Colombia and Peru.

Paris, 18 June. The legislative councils force the resignation of the Directory as dissent grows among the elected deputies, triggered by the worsening military situation.

Britain, 12 July. The Combination Act is passed, forbidding the forming of an association by two or more people with the purpose of obtaining wage increases or improved conditions of work. The measure is prompted largely by fear of revolutionary ideas spreading from France.

Egypt, 17 July. Ottoman forces, convoyed by a British fleet, capture Aboukir from the French.

Egypt, 19 July. A stone bearing ancient Egyptian hieroglyphics and *demotic* (ancient Egyptian script) and Greek is found near the town of Rosetta on the west bank of the Bolbitic arm of the Nile. The discovery is greeted with great excitement by archaeologists who may be nearer to deciphering hieroglyphics.

Egypt, 25 July. Bonaparte defeats the Ottomans at Aboukir on his way back from Syria.

Italy, 30 July. The French garrison in Mantua surrenders to the Austrians.

France, August. Royalist uprisings break out across France.

Egypt, 23 August. Napoleon sails for France.

France, 29 August. Pope Pius VI dies in Valence.

Netherlands, 31 August. The fleet of the Batavian republic, moored at Texel, surrenders without a fight to General Abercrombie's British forces.

France, 15 September. Two hundred royalist leaders from Brittany, Anjou, Maine and the Vendee hold a council of war with a view to resuming hostilities against the French republic.

Netherlands, 19 September. The French repulse Anglo-Russian forces at Bergen in the continuing war over the Batavian republic.

France, 9 October. After avoiding a British squadron off Toulouse, Napoleon comes ashore at Saint Raphael.

Netherlands, 18 October. British and French generals sign an accord at Alkmaar concerning the withdrawal of Anglo-Russian troops from the Batavian republic.

Paris, 13 December. Having seized power in a military coup last month, Bonaparte has himself elected first consul.

Philadelphia, 14 December. The retired president, George Washington, dies. His last words are " 'tis well".

Austria. Haydn composes his *Theresienmesse* (Theresa Mass), named after the consort of the Emperor Francis II.

Chinese emperor dies; courtier follows

Kirghiz tribesmen present the Emperor Qianlong with a horse, by the Jesuit Castiglione, who painted for the court in a westernised Chinese style.

Beijing, 7 February
The Emperor Qianlong has died after ruling China for over 60 years. He officially retired three years ago in order not to rule longer than his grandfather, but it was a retirement in name only and he continued to exercise supreme power.

This meant that his favourite courtier, Heshen, also continued in power. Few men in China's long history have been as corrupt or as hated as Heshen. His power has been limited only by the emperor and there has been no limit to his greed.

His corruption has been one of the factors in the oppression and decay which marked the last years of Qianlong's rule. One of Heshen's favourite bribes was a pill made of a pearl encased in gold. He took one every morning believing they sharpened his powers of memory. There were always men ready to provide him with this luxurious tonic. But, although his behaviour was notor-

A robe of belonging to one of Qianlong's concubines.

ious, few officials dared to attempt to curb him, and those who did found themselves defeated by Heshen's cunning. His enemies bided their time. They knew that the heir to the throne, Jiaqing, hated Heshen. They were right. Heshen has been "allowed" to commit suicide and join his master in death.

Workers' associations banned in Britain

London
Beset by the continuing war with revolutionary France, the prime minister, William Pitt, and his cabinet have become alarmed at the growth of militancy and the spread of subversion among skilled workers. Pitt has responded with a series of tough measures.

He has cracked down on strikers with the Combination Act, which allows workers accused of forming trades unions to be given a summary trial by a justice of the peace.

Radical groups in what are known as Corresponding Societies in London and the provinces have been banned and their leaders arrested. Among them are cotton spinners, shoemakers, printers and clerks.

The press has also been curbed. The authorities must be given a copy of every issue of a newspaper together with particulars of the printer, publisher and proprietor. These measure follow a report by an MPs' committee investigating subversive activities.

George Washington, first president of US

Philadelphia, 14 December
The United States mourned its first president today. Courtrooms and churches were draped in black and citizens wore black crepe in memory of George Washington, who died today after a brief illness. Full mourning dress was worn in Congress and already plans are being made to build a "grand marble monument at a new city named after Washington under which, with the permission of his lady, the body of the general should be deposited".

George Washington came from a wealthy Virginia family and saw action in the French and Indian wars before leaving the British army with the rank of colonel. He was a strong political supporter of the independence movement and was elected commander-in-chief at the second Continental Congress. His principal task then was to mould 16,000 volunteers into a cohesive

General George Washington.

fighting force, which was finally victorious against the British. As president, he tried always to remain above political factions, but became identified with federalism.

Coup in Paris: Bonaparte seizes power

Bonaparte's coup of 9 November (18 Brumaire in the revolutionary calendar).

Paris, 9 November
Bonaparte has ousted the French government and the fate of the republic is now in his hands.

It was a *coup* that almost failed. Plotting with Emmanuel Sieyes, a member of the Directory who wanted the constitution overhauled, Napoleon, supported by his generals, yesterday had himself voted commander of the troops in Paris.

Today, however, he got a hostile reception from the neo-Jacobins in the legislature, the Council of Five Hundred, at Saint Cloud and was spat upon.

The scuffle saved the coup. It was claimed that he had been attacked with a knife. His soldiers, incensed, marched into the council chamber. And tonight Bonaparte, Sieyes and Duclos rule as consuls.

British kill their main Indian adversary

Tipu Sahib, the sultan of Mysore.

Southern India, 4 May
Tipu Sahib, the warrior of Mysore and bulwark of resistance to British expansion in India, has been killed. Since his defeat by Cornwallis in 1784, Tipu, the most powerful ruler in southern India, had been preparing for war. Britain's conflict with revolutionary France provided him with the opportunity. He planted a tree of liberty and made a secret alliance with France, whose army was in Egypt.

The British governor-general, the marquis of Wellesley, brought 4,000 reinforcements to India and

made a pre-emptive attack on Tipu, besieging his capital, Seringapatam. Today, assisted by the treachery of one of Tipu's commanders, he stormed the city with 5,000 troops. Tipu fought to the end, despite four wounds. "He had the appearance of dignity or perhaps sternness in his countenance, which denoted him above the common order of people," a British officer said. As for his tree of liberty, it has been hacked down.

Printing techniques take a leap forward

Europe
Literacy is on the march, and ever more books are in production. To meet the new demand, printing techniques, for many years little advanced from their 15th-century origins, have been developing fast. In

Germany Alois Senefelder has invented lithography, a method of printing pictures without engraving them first. In France the Didot family have created stereotypy, making it possible to keep and re-use typographic characters.

Postal service, the sole link to civilisation in some parts of the West, is expanding as fast as the frontier it serves. Mail carriers now travel on 16,000 miles of postal roads, a six-fold increase over the last 10 years. The postmen who began to appear on a full-time basis in 1794, are paid by the piece, generally two cents per letter.

How valuable was Napoleon's Legacy

The first historian to weigh the achievements of Napoleon was Napoleon himself. It was not the least of those achievements. Slowly dying in exile on St Helena, he used his time to construct an elaborate apologia. He wrote his memoirs; he talked freely to companions, knowing they would later publish; he composed a will rich in self-justification. In short, he re-invented himself for later generations.

"I die in the apostolic and roman religion in which I was born. My motto was: Everything for the French people. Every Frenchman could say in my reign – I shall be minister, grand officer, duke, count, baron, if I earn it – even king. The principles of equality, liberty, nationality never had a firmer friend: These truths will rule the world. They will be the creed ... This memorable era will be linked to my person because I have carried its torch and because persecution has now made me its Messiah."

The language is grandiose – such was the Napoleonic style – but the assertions should not be dismissed for that reason alone. Some claims (about his religious beliefs, for example) may be taken lightly as statements of fact. As statements of intent, however, they all demand attention.

Napoleon clearly wished to be remembered as Catholic, Revolutionary and Royalist – an odd mixture. His was a revolution in which any man could become King – a triumph of liberte if not egalite. He sought not to destroy the idea of noblesse but to renovate it, by detaching it from a notion of feudalism and attaching it to a notion of service to the state. Napoleon's self-portrait, in sum, presented a man who could reconcile opposites. Democracy and Freedom need not be traded for Authority and Order: all could be ensured by upholding the radical principles of careers open to talent, equality before the law, and the abolition of privilege.

A code with limited appeal

That Napoleon left a legacy to Europe is not to be doubted; that it was the one he claimed to be leaving is another matter. France herself was smaller in 1815 than she had been in 1789. Continuous warfare had cost her 500,000 men, a loss which seriously hampered future growth. The war was disruptive though not wholly without beneficial consequences. It stimulated industry – as did the blockade of English goods – in the north and east. On the other hand, the south and west suffered from losing the Mediterranean and Atlantic trade routes.

The administrative legacy was substantial, but needs to be given context. if Napoleon is to be remembered by the Civil Code which bears his name, he can be claimed as an egalitarian only in a limited sense. The Code was a charter for the propertied by the propertied; those without, owed little gratitude to it. It favoured employer over employee, landlord over tenant, husband over wife, parents over children. Even in its more radical aspects – for example, the requirement that land be divided equally between children – it was never universally honoured. Thus in some places it was actively resisted by the peasantry who, now fearing ruinous sub-division, had once thought to benefit from it.

As an exercise in juridical imperialism, however, it was highly successful. It was translated into Spanish and Portuguese; it accompanied the French armies into the Low countries; it influenced Italian, Romanian and Egyptian legislation; it was exported to Canada, Bolivia, Haiti and Japan. To this day, it forms the legal basis of the state of Louisiana. Not all countries were equally receptive to it. But in codifying the gains of a bourgeois revolution, Napoleon determined the political agenda for decades, particularly in Germany, Holland and Italy, where an articulate middle class was beginning to emerge.

A new vision of Europe

One of Napoleon's more intriguing claims was that he was the champion of European nationalism. Seen from distant St Helena, continental confusions became miraculously clear. He had always been, he said, in favour of Polish independence. German and Italian unification was only a matter of time; his Spanish policy (an admitted failure) had been intended to "regenerate" that country. "Europe thus divided into nationalities freely formed and free internally, peace between States would have become easier: the United States of Europe would become a possibility."

The United States of Europe became a reality in Napoleon's time, the only problem being that they were united against him. Similarly pugnacious was the assertion: "I wished to found a European system, a European code of Laws, a European judiciary : there would be but one people in Europe." This was hard (though not impossible) to reconcile with the vision of a continent divided into nationalities freely formed and free internally.

For all the special pleading, it is difficult not to be impressed by Napoleon's powers of prophecy. Isolated and dying in the South Atlantic, he seems to have foreseen the nation-state of the mid-19th century, the supra-national state of the mid-20th, and to have witnessed his hand in both.

Napoleon's legacy consisted of more than what he did; there was also the question of what he was. He had a nature which invited cult: energetic, wilful, courageous, possessed of powerful imagination. The Duke of Wellington held that "Napoleon was not a personality but a principle." Yet this was only half true: the personality was the principle. The Napoleon who crossed the Alps in David's famous portrait – handsome, decisive, an evident man of destiny – held strong romantic appeal. For Victor Hugo, the return of the emperor's body to Paris in 1840 was a fitting restoration. "The blessed poets shall kneel before you; the clouds which obscured your glory have passed, and nothing will ever dim its true lustre again".

The cult of strong leaders

Admiration is one thing, imitation another. Bonaparte made the "Great Man" fashionable, especially with those whose greatness was less apparent. His most conspicuous imitator was his nephew. "I believe," wrote the future Napoleon III from his prison in Ham, "that there are certain men who are born to serve as a means for the march of the human race ... I consider myself to be one of these." There were notable parallels: both achieved the highest office as upholders of a Republic; both became shortly afterwards emperors; both believed that decisive military victory would restore political fortunes; and both ultimately failed.

Thus to compare uncle and nephew is to flatter the latter by allowing that a comparison may be made. Yet it is also to condemn the former, whose political apologia required that there could be one as great as he to follow where he had led. Bonapartism – the cult of the strong leader who could reconcile both Freedom and Authority – made little sense without Bonaparte. Napoleon III revealed what Napoleon I concealed by posthumous propaganda: that Caesarism and Democracy are not compatible.

For a time it seemed as if the two might be compatible. "If I had succeeded, I should have been the greatest man known to history." A later age is more inclined to think that there was greatness in his failure. He was brought down by democracy and nationalism – the refusal of the French to heed his final call, the willlingness of the nations to do battle against him. Amidst the overblown claims of his exile years, one prosaic truth stood out. "A man is only a man. His power is nothing if circumstances are not favourable. Opinion is all important."

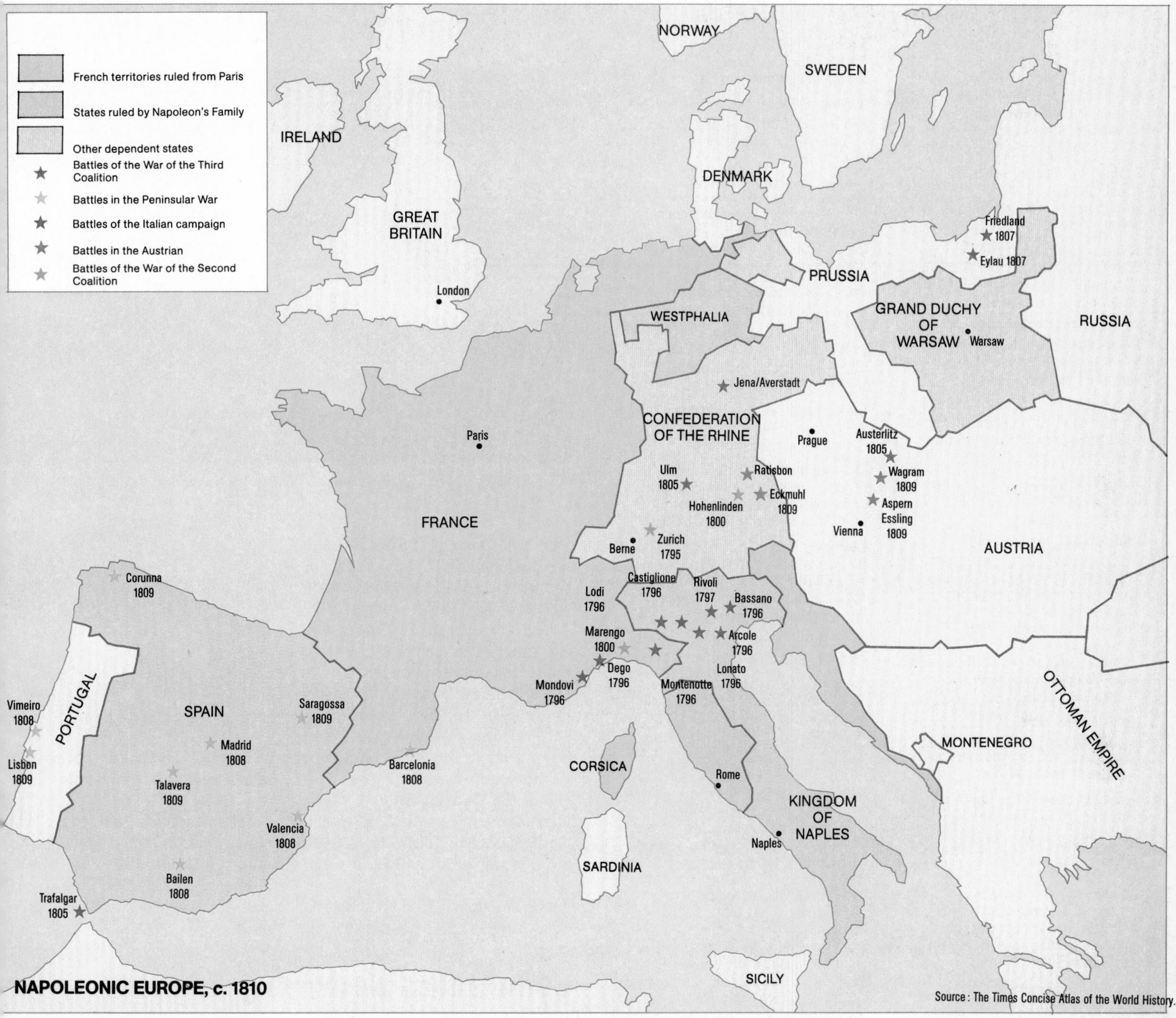

Legend

	French territories ruled from Paris
	States ruled by Napoleon's Family
	Other dependent states
★	Battles of the War of the Third Coalition
★	Battles in the Peninsular War
★	Battles of the Italian campaign
★	Battles in the Austrian
★	Battles of the War of the Second Coalition

NORWAY

SWEDEN

IRELAND

DENMARK

GREAT BRITAIN

London

PRUSSIA

Friedland 1807

Eylau 1807

WESTPHALIA

GRAND DUCHY OF WARSAW

Warsaw

RUSSIA

Jena/Averstadt

PARIS

CONFEDERATION OF THE RHINE

Prague

Austerlitz 1805

FRANCE

Ulm 1805

Ratisbon

Wagram 1809

Eckmuhl 1809

Hohenlinden 1800

Aspern Essling 1809

Berne

Zurich 1795

Vienna

AUSTRIA

Castiglione 1796

Rivoli 1797

Bassano 1796

Lodi 1796

Marengo 1800

Arcole 1796

OTTOMAN EMPIRE

Corunna 1809

Mondovi 1796

Dego 1796

Lonato 1796

Montenotte 1796

PORTUGAL

SPAIN

Saragossa 1809

MONTENEGRO

Vimeiro 1808

Madrid 1808

Barcelonia 1808

CORSICA

Rome

Lisbon 1809

Talavera 1809

Naples

KINGDOM OF NAPLES

Valencia 1808

Bailen 1808

SARDINIA

Trafalgar 1805

SICILY

NAPOLEONIC EUROPE, c. 1810

Source: The Times Concise Atlas of the World History.

Napoleon III (Bowes Museum).

Emperor of France: Napoleon is crowned in Notre Dame (Jacques David).

Napoleon crosses the Alps (David).

1799 (1799-1801)

Spain, 1799. The court painter Francisco Goya publishes *Los Caprichos*, a series of etchings which express his criticisms of a corrupt establishment. He withdraws them shortly after publication, fearing the Inquisition.

France, 1 February 1800. The new constitution, with Napoleon Bonaparte as first consul, is accepted by a referendum.

Brittany, 14 February 1800. The Chouan (*royalist*) leader Georges Cadoudal surrenders. The other leaders laid down their arms last month.

Rome, 14 March 1800. Pope Pius VII is elected to succeed Pius VI who died in 1799.

Egypt, 20 March 1800. Kleber, the French chief commander in Egypt, defeats the *grand vizier*, Ibrahim Bey, at Heliopolis.

Italy, 6 April 1800. The Austrians launch an offensive against the French.

Philadelphia, 7 May 1800. Congress divides the Northwest Territory into two parts, with the border between them running north from the junction of the Ohio and Kentucky rivers. The western part will be known as the Indiana Territory while the eastern sector keeps the name of the Northwest Territory.

Italy, 2 June 1800. Having crossed the St Bernard pass on 23 May, in response to the Austrian offensive, Bonaparte seizes Milan.

Egypt, 14 June 1800. The French commander, Kleber, is killed.

Italy, 17 June 1800. Having defeated the Austrians at Montebello and Marengo, Bonaparte signs an agreement by which the Austrian General Melas cedes the whole of Italy as far as the river Mincio to him. He then reconstitutes the Cisalpine republic.

Paris, 30 September 1800. The treaty of Morfontaine is signed, ending the undeclared but bloody naval war between American and France, waged mainly in the Indian Ocean. France will lift its embargo on American ships and the USA will return captured warships.

France, 1 October 1800. There are rumours that King Charles IV of Spain has signed a secret treaty with Bonaparte returning Louisiana to the French.

Virginia, 30 October 1800. The leaders of a planned slave revolt involving more than a thousand Negroes are hanged. Though the revolt was called off at the last minute, the conspiracy was betrayed to the authorities and more than 25 people are now dead.

Europe, 22 November 1800. Fighting breaks out again between the Austrians and the French.

Austria, 3 December 1800. The French General Moreau is victorious against the Austrians at Hohenlinden.

Europe, 16 December 1800. Russia, which had withdrawn from the field of battle in 1799, is the moving spirit behind a league of neutral Baltic nations which is anti-British in stance.

Paris, 24 December 1800. An attempt to assassinate Napoleon Bonaparte fails.

Philadelphia, 1800. William Young makes shoes designed specifically for the right and left feet.

India, 1800. The British compel the *nizam* of Hyderabad to accept the status of protectorate.

Washington DC, 1800. This year's census puts the nation's population at 5.3 million, an increase of more than 30 per cent in the last decade.

Germany, 1800. The poet who uses the pen name "Novalis" publishes verses called the *Hymns of the Night* in the final issue of the periodical *Athenaeum*.

India, 1800. Nana Fadnavis, the brilliant Maratha minister, dies.

Germany, 1800. The prolific dramatist and poet Johann Goethe publishes his *Ballads and Romances*.

South Africa, 1800. Dingiswayo seizes the chieftainship of the Mthethwa from his brother. The Mthethwa are a small clan on the Mfolozi river (*northern Natal*), but in Dingiswayo, who already has a considerable reputation as a hunter and warrior, is determined that his kingdom should rival the powerful Ndwandwe kingdom of King Zwide. Dingiswayo allies with the Maputo of Laurenco Marques (Maputo) against the Ndwandwe, with the aim of controlling ivory supplies from the interior to Portuguese ships.

Germany, 1800. The philosopher J G Fichte publishes *The Exclusive Commercial State*. Friedrich Schelling publishes his *System of Transcendental Idealism*.

Sierra Leone, 1800. Asante settlers arrive in Sierra Leone having been deported as rebels from Jamaica. They had been living independently in the mountain interior as freemen, and were known locally as *maroons*.

Washington DC, 4 March 1801. The House of Representatives chooses Thomas Jefferson as the new president and Aaron Burr as vice-president after the two men receive exactly the same number of votes in the electoral college.

British ready to buy all the tea in China

Filling tea chests in a British-owned factory on the Chinese coast.

Canton, China, c.1800

Tea from China has become the British national drink, accounting for five per cent of the average London worker's household budget. The British government also has a vested interest through 100 per cent excise duties on tea imports.

The tea trade is conducted entirely through the East India Company, which now invests £4 million a year in this one commodity. A triangular trading system involves the shipping from Calcutta to Canton, of raw Indian cotton, the profits from which are used to buy the tea, which is sold in London to help reduce the Company's increasing debts. This combination of consumer demand and economic

Tea in the garden: tea is now the most popular drink in Britain.

necessity ensures that trade with China continues, despite diplomatic ructions like the *kowtow* affair, in which British ambassadors were reluctant to bow before the emperor.

Volta makes electrifying discovery

Rome, 1800

The inventor Alessandro Volta has made an apparatus for producing a continuous flow of electricity – an electric "battery". The principle is that if two different metals are immersed in a solution of acid, alkali or salt, an electric current will flow along a wire linking the plates. Suitable metals, Volta finds, are zinc, copper or silver. If pairs of these are placed in layers with brine-soaked paper or flannel between each pair, then a "Voltaic pile" is created. Each pair or cell is linked to the next to produce a combined electrical output. Volta's equipment is the first method yet devised for giving a steady current.

Volta shows his battery to Bonaparte.

US president moves house to Washington

Washington DC, the new federal capital of the United States of America.

United States, 1800
On lush farmland close to the Potomac river, workmen are putting the final touches to a two-storeyed house that will shortly become the executive mansion for President John Adams and his wife Abigail, the "First Lady". Several hundred acres of the state of Maryland have been set aside for the building of a fine city which is to be the federal capital, in what is known as the District of Columbia, to be named "Washington". Congress approved the site – which will be free from partisan state pressures – and a distinguished French architect, Pierre Charles l'Enfant, has been commissioned to create a city with wide boulevards, fine buildings and wide vistas. More like Paris than Paris itself, some hope.

Dublin parliament votes to dissolve itself

Dublin, 5 February 1800
William Pitt reckons that he is well on the way to solving the Irish problem once and for all. As Britain's prime minister, he saw that there could be no peace so long as the Irish remained disaffected second class citizens in their own country. His policy of reconciliation took a big step forward today when the Dublin parliament resolved to dissolve itself and to unite with Westminster, as Scotland did a century ago.

To the Catholic majority in Ireland, Pitt argued, that since their emancipation would be seen as a threat to the Protestant ascendency, reform would always be blocked.

To the Protestants, he argued that union with Britain would make the Catholics a minority and therefore less of a threat to their position in Ireland.

These arguments were reinforced by a blatant appeal to the cupidity of the Protestants controlling the Dublin parliament.

MPs were promised peerages,

William Pitt, uniting the kingdom.

jobs and hard cash – £7,000 for each seat. As the debate continued, the son of Lord Cornwallis, the viceroy, was asked who would succeed his father as ruler of Ireland if the proposed union and Catholic emancipation were rejected. Mindful of French attempts to stir up revolution in Ireland, he replied "Bonaparte".

Pius VII signs concordat with Bonaparte

Two princes: Caesar's and God's.

Paris, 15 July 1801
A concordat was finally signed today by Pope Pius VII and Napoleon after prolonged and troublesome negotiations. It is popular with no-one. In the end it was imposed by the pope on a reluctant anti-Napoleonic church and by Napoleon on a reluctant anticlerical government.

The agreement recognises Catholicism as the religion of "the great majority" of the French people, but makes no claim for the restitution of church property. Its importance to Napoleon, who is cynical about religion, is that it restores religious peace to France.

Water splits in face of electric charge

London, 1800
Within weeks of Volta's invention of the electric cell, the new device has been put to use by two chemists, William Nicholson and Anthony Carlisle. They have made their own "battery" and, with it, separated water into its constituent gases, oxygen and hydrogen. When the leads from their battery were placed in water, the two scientists observed that they broke up the fluid by a process of "electrolysis". At the ends of the wire they noticed bubbles, indicating the liberation of the two gases.

Prolific Chinese go forth and multiply

The Pingzimen, one of the western gates into the Chinese capital, Beijing.

China, c.1800
The population of China is exploding at an alarming rate. In the century of internal peace that lasted until the outbreak of the White Lotus revolt four years ago, the population doubled from some 150 million to over 300 million. The increase continues, with natural disasters having little effect.

The result has been ever more pressure upon land even in the agriculturally marginal border regions. Refugees from poor harvests are moving into new areas and setting off intense competition for land, with consequent tensions. New kinds of economic and political growth are essential to absorb the fecund people of China.

France, 9 February 1801. The peace of Luneville puts an end to the war with Austria in Bonaparte's, favour. This leaves Britain as the only survivor of the second coalition against France.

Egypt, 6 March 1801. British troops land in Egypt, which is currently in the hands of the French.

Spain, 21 March 1801. France signs the treaty of Aranjuez with Spain. The duchy of Tuscany is transformed into the kingdom of Etruria and the American territory of Louisiana is returned to France.

Italy, 28 March 1801. France signs the treaty of Florence with King Ferdinand of Naples and Sicily. The island of Elba is ceded to France and the ports of the kingdom are closed to British trade. Otranto and Brindisi on the Adriatic are provisionally manned by a French garrison.

Denmark, 2 April 1801. The British bombard the port of Copenhagen, hastening the break-up of the neutral alliance against Britain. Its main moving spirit, Czar Paul of Russia, was assassinated on 23 March. He is succeeded by his son Alexander.

Tripoli (Libya), 14 May 1801. *Pasha* Yusuf Karamanli, declares war on the United States.

Tripoli, 17 July 1801. A US fleet arrives to blockade Tripoli, following Pasha Yusuf Karamanli's declaration of war in May when a demand for more tribute, to protect US ships from piracy, was refused.

Malta, 1 August 1801. The US schooner *Enterprise* captures the barbary corsair *Tripoli*, heaves its 14 guns into the sea and chops off its mast.

Egypt, 2 September 1801. The French under General Menou begin to leave Egypt following the arrival of British troops in March. France lost Cairo on 28 June and Alexandria on 30 August.

Spain, 29 September 1801. The treaty of Madrid puts an end to the "War of the Oranges" between Spain and Portugal. The Portuguese agree to French demands that they should not allow English naval vessels to enter their ports. Spain acquires the frontier town of Olivenza. During the fighting Britain has taken possession of Madeira and the Portuguese trading posts in India.

Netherlands, 6 October 1801. Bonaparte imposes a new constitution on Holland.

France, 8 October 1801. France signs a treaty with Russia, a culmination of the improvement in relations detectable since 1800.

New York, 16 November 1801. The *New York Evening Post*, published by Alexander Hamilton and John Jay, appears on the streets.

Japan, 1801. Ino Tadataka, an astronomer and surveyor, ordered by the *shogun* to undertake a geographical survey of the whole of Japan, heads north to start work in Ezo (Hokkaido).

India, 1801. Ranjit Singh, the leader of the Sikhs, defeats the Bhangis.

Britain, 1801. The first census shows a population of 10.4 million.

Persia, 1801. The British sign a trade treaty with the *shah*.

Germany, 1801. Friedrich Schiller's new play *The Maid of Orleans* opens.

USA, 1801. The American inventor Evans exhibits his steam-driven vehicle in the streets of Philadelphia.

Germany, 1801. Ludwig van Beethoven writes a sonata (Opus 27, number 2) which is nicknamed "Moonlight".

Germany, 1801. Inspired by William Herschel's discovery of a type of radiation beyond the red end of the spectrum (*infrared radiation*), the German John Ritter looks for something similar beyond the violet. He thus discovers ultraviolet radiation.

France, 18 January 1802. Bonaparte gets rid of all members of the Tribunate who are opposed to him.

Italy, 26 January 1802. Bonaparte is elected president of the Italian republic, the new name given to the Cisalpine republic.

France, 27 March 1802. Bonaparte signs the peace of Amiens.

France, 20 May 1802. Slavery and the slave trade are restored in the colonies.

France, 2 August 1802. Bonaparte is proclaimed consul for life by a plebiscite.

China, 1802. Over the last three years, during a revolt fomented by the secret White Lotus society, anti-Manchu supporters have been savagely repressed.

Mexico, 1802. Mexico's first archaeologist, Antonio de Leon y Gama, dies. He will be best remembered for his book describing the statue of Coatlicue, the mother goddess, and the Stone of the Sun, found in Mexico City during sewerage excavations.

Italy, 1802. The writer Ugo Foscolo publishes *The Last Letters of Jacopo Ortis*, an epistolary novel lamenting the Austrian occupation of Venice.

British navy opens Baltic to its shipping

The battle of Copenhagen, where Nelson sank the neutral Danish fleet.

Copenhagen, 2 April 1801

A defiant gesture by the British admiral, Horatio Nelson, has sunk the Danish fleet, ensuring that the Baltic Sea will remain open to British shipping.

Vice-admiral Nelson was leading a squadron through shoal waters under heavy fire from Danish shore batteries when signals went up from the commander-in-chief, Sir Hyde Parker, ordering him to withdraw. On the quarter-deck of *HMS Elephant*, Nelson said "Damn me if I do !" and placed his telescope to his blind eye. Although Nelson has gone ashore to explain his action to his "brother Danes", Britain is bound to suffer international disapprobation for this surprise attack on a neutral country, even one so blatantly pro-French.

Ailing king forces William Pitt to resign

London, 14 March 1801

After 17 years as Prime Minister, William Pitt has been forced to resign by the king's stubborn refusal to accept Catholic emancipation. His successor is Henry Addington, the speaker of the House of Commons, an old friend of Pitt's. He has said that he will work for peace with France and do nothing about Catholic emancipation. Pitt offered his resignation last month, but stayed on when George III was stricken by another bout of insanity, apparently brought on by the Irish question. Pitt, having achieved the union of the London and Dublin parliaments, had moved on to what he saw as the necassary sequel: Catholic emancipation. When this was put to the king he was enraged. Pitt says that he will never again raise the subject with the king.

Country united after 30 years of struggle

Hue, Annam (Vietnam), 1802

Nguyen Anh, the Emperor of Annam (*Vietnam*) has reunited his country after some 30 years of dynastic struggle and civil war. The emperor, who is a great organiser as well as a soldier, now rules from his palace in this pleasant city built astride the Perfumed River.

However, while Nguyen Anh rules Annam he has to recognise the suzerainty of China under the tributary system. For the Chinese it is an economical way of dealing with a border country without actually having to occupy it.

Another important influence on Nguyen Anh is that of the French missionary Pigneau de Behaine who helped the emperor in his struggle for power. Nguyen Anh has now given the French missionaries free rein to preach the Catholic gospel in his country.

People vote Napoleon Consul for Life

Britain critical of treaty with French

Amiens, 25 March 1802

The treaty signed here today by Britain and France has brought peace to the world, but at a cost not appreciated by most Britons. In the general exchange of territory Britain retains Ceylon and Trinidad but relinquishes Malta, the Cape and Egypt and most of its maritime conquests.

France, on the other hand, gives little except Naples and a guarantee of integrity for Portugal. What disturbs the British, however, is Bonaparte's refusal to lift the trade prohibitions imposed during the war; the Continent remains closed to British trade. There is much criticism of "this frail and deceptive truce" throughout Britain.

Czar Paul is killed in his bedchamber

Paul I, son of Catherine the Great.

St Petersburg, 23 March 1801

At two, o'clock this morning, after a night of carousing, a party of guards officers went over to the St Michael Palace and, breaking into the royal bedchamber, strangled the mentally unstable Czar Paul. One of the assassins, Nikolai Zubov, then awakened Paul's son, Alexander, to tell him that he was the new czar. Paul hated his mother Catherine, and decreed that no woman should ever again rule Russia. He went to war against France, then changed sides to ally himself with Bonaparte. He lost popular support by repealing Catherine's law exempting the free classes from corporal punishment.

Paris, 2 August 1802

The senate proclaimed Napoleon Bonaparte "Consul for Life" today following a plebiscite in which three and a half million Frenchmen voted in favour of the proposal and a mere eight thousand people voted against.

Napoleon (the name was used for the first time in the wording of the plebiscite) now assumes almost regal powers. A new constitution is about to be announced which will confer on him the royal prerogatives of pardoning the condemned and naming his own successor. Power will be further concentrated in his hands by the extension of the powers of the senate in which decrees will replace the debates of the other assemblies.

The overwhelming vote in favour of Napoleon certainly reflects the nostalgia for the past which is replacing the revolutionary fervour of the day ten years ago when the monarchy was abolished.

Sensing this reaction, Louis XVIII had written from exile asking Napoleon to restore the monarchy. He was sharply rebuffed. Napoleon replied: "You must not expect to return to France. It would mean marching over a hundred thousand corpses."

The concordat with Rome and the peace of Amiens increased Napoleon's own popularity, and he used it to "purify" the Tribunate and the Legislative Assembly by removing his opponents when their

Napoleon Bonaparte, voted by over three million Frenchmen "Consul for Life".

appointments came up for renewal. The senate, in a spirit of self-preservation, then voted to extend his term as first consul for a further ten years. It was not enough for Napoleon. He ordered the plebiscite which has made him Consul for Life. Curiously, and most significantly, many of the "No" votes were cast by the army.

Painting with light

London, 1802

Recently it was seen that certain compounds of silver nitrates can be used to preserve an image. Working with such light sensitive papers Thomas Wedgwood, the son of the famous English pottery innovator, and the chemist Humphrey Davy have now succeeded in taking light pictures or photographs. They have produced pictures of natural objects such as leaves and insect wings by putting them on chemically-treated paper and exposing them to sunlight. These images only last for a short time; they need further chemical treatment to "fix" them.

Goya's "La Maja Desnuda". Born in 1746, Goya spent his early years first in Zaragossa and then in Madrid, where he settled, after a tour of Italy, in 1775. In spite of his liberal and republican sympathies, he became a court painter in 1786, and the first court painter in 1786. Some of his finest paintings have been of the Spanish royal family. He hears no acclaim, however. A severe illness in 1792 has left him stone deaf.

1802 (1802-1803)

Italy, 11 September 1802. Piedmont is annexed by France.

Russia, 20 September 1802. The reformist Czar Alexander, who came to power last year, grants the senate legislative and judicial rights. Educated by the Swiss rationalist Jean Francois de Laharpe, he also grants an amnesty to all political prisoners and exiles.

Louisiana, 16 October 1802. In breach of the 1795 treaty of San Lorenzo – establishing the 31st parallel as a border between America and Spain in North America – Spain closes New Orleans to US cargo.

India, 31 December 1802. The Maratha Peshwa Baji Rao signs the treaty of Bassein with Lord Wellesley, giving the British mastery of central India.

USA, 1802. All states north of the Mason-Dixon line (between Pennsylvania and Delaware in the north and Maryland and West Virginia in the south) except for New Jersey have now passed anti-slavery laws calling for gradual emancipation.

Vienna, 1802. The composer Ludwig van Beethoven realises that he is going irreversibly deaf. However his new, second symphony reveals little of his personal anguish.

Switzerland, 19 February 1803. Bonaparte imposes the Act of Mediation which restores almost in full the thirteen cantons as they were before 1798, less Geneva and Mulhouse. Six new cantons are created. The constitution is a federal one, the cantons having a federal *diet* for external affairs.

USA, 1 March 1803. Ohio is the seventeenth state to join the union.

Britain, 15 March 1803. Britain contravenes the terms of the treaty of Amiens by demanding the right to remain on the island of Malta for ten years. By the treaty, signed on 25 March 1802 with Bonaparte, Britain agreed to give up all her overseas conquests.

France, 12 April 1803. The ban on workers' meetings is renewed. The same law sets up factory chambers to regulate trademarks.

France, 14 April 1803. The Bank of France is granted the privilege of issuing paper money for a period of 15 years, valid only in Paris.

Louisiana, 19 April 1803. The Spanish reopen New Orleans to American merchants.

Netherlands, 26 April 1803. In contravention of last year's treaty of Amiens, Bonaparte occupies Flushing and Dutch Brabant. Worried by this move, the British issue an ultimatum.

Netherlands, 12 May 1803. Napoleon withdraws from Flushing and Dutch Brabant.

France, 18 May 1803. Following Bonaparte's continued military activities in Italy, the Netherlands, Switzerland and Germany, the British government makes a formal break with the treaty of Amiens and declares war on France.

Germany, May 1803. The French General Mortier occupies the kingdom of Hanover, a personal possession of the king of England.

Europe, 5 June 1803. Czar Alexander proposes that he should mediate between the French and the British, but without success.

France, 20 June 1803. British imports are banned.

Ireland, 23 July 1803. Irish patriots rebel against union with Britain, which was established by law on 1 January 1801.

Caribbean, 29 August 1803. General Dessalines proclaims the independence of Haiti at the western end of the island of Santo Domingo.

Pittsburgh, 31 August 1803. Captain Meriwether Lewis leaves Pittsburgh on what is rumoured to be the first government-sponsored exploration of far western country.

India, 14 September 1803. General Lake, after defeating the Marathas beneath the city walls, captures Delhi for the British. The Maratha confederacy is the last remaining obstacle to the British East India Company's control of southern and eastern India.

India, 23 September 1803. Sir Arthur Wellesley achieves a notable victory over the Marathas at Assaye in the Dekhan.

Europe, 27 September 1803. France and the Helvetian republic sign a treaty of military alliance.

France, 2 December 1803. An army prepares itself to invade England at a camp in Boulogne.

USA, 20 December 1803. The United States buys the Louisiana territory from France.

Russia, 1803. Czar Alexander invades southern Georgia and occupies eastern Alaska.

Antilles, 1803. Britain occupies the islands of St Lucia and Tobago, and Dutch Guiana.

Brazil, 1803. Over the past 45 years, a total of 642,000 slaves have been taken from the ports of Luanda and Benguela on the Angolan coast to the Portuguese colony of Brazil.

Honolulu, 1803. Richard Cleveland and William Shaler introduce horses to the Hawaiian islands.

British factory workers helped by new law

The evils of child labour, as seen by the cartoonist, George Cruikshank.

London, 1802
In an unprecedented step to regulate life in the new factories the British Parliament is to introduce a ban on pauper apprentices working more than a 12-hour day.

The forthcoming Health and Morals of Apprentices Act follows growing concern that pauper children from London sent to work in mills and factories in the north are being exploited and made to work at night. Until now the factories that have sprung up to house the new cotton and wool processing machines have been unregulated. These factories have provided a welcome outlet for the London Poor Law authorities. By sending their charges north they have been able to claim that they have discharged successfully their duty of not allowing paupers, or their offspring, to become a burden on the parish rates.

However, reformers led by Sir Robert Peel, the bill's proposer, are concerned that this wholesale extension of Poor Law practice has meant that large numbers of children are now working in places without their parents or other relatives to supervise their physical or moral welfare.

Colours of rainbow can be measured

London, 1803
Light, says the English doctor and physicist Thomas Young, consists not of particles but of waves. This is the conclusion he arrives at after experimenting with light, proclaiming a principle of "interference". If light is shone onto a screen in which there are two pinholes set close to each other, the light beams produced will spread apart and overlap. In these areas of overlap, he says, there are bands of light and dark which are due to one wave interfering with the other, similar to the effect of two ripples merging on a pond. Young goes on to give an approximate wavelength to the seven colours in the spectrum: red, orange, yellow, green, blue, indigo, violet.

German cathedral sold to a butcher

Bavaria, Germany, 1803
Friesing cathedral has been sold to a butcher. Dozens of ecclesiastical states, prince-bishoprics, electorates and imperial abbeys, and hundreds of monasteries, have been secularised. All over Germany churches have been vandalised.

The Catholic Church is the biggest loser in Germany's reorganisation, agreed by the leaders of Germany's states meeting in Ratisbon.

The Ratisbon meeting was prompted by Napoleon's conquest of the left bank of the Rhine, which concentrated the mind of Germany's statesmen on the need to modernise. Prussia, Bavaria, Baden, Wurttemberg and HesseDarmstadt now dominate the informal cofederation.

US doubles its land area

Paris, 20 December 1803

The greatest land sale in history was concluded here today after months of negotiation between French and US diplomats. With the "Louisiana Purchase" the United States of America has literally doubled in size overnight – acquiring from France the whole of the Mississippi Valley as far as the Rocky Mountains, an area of 828,000 square miles. The price was high – 15 million dollars – but both the vendor, Napoleon Bonaparte, and the purchaser, the Congress of the United States, are delighted with the deal.

Napoleon wanted to sell this former Spanish territory. He had relinquished his former ambition (with Talleyrand) of creating a colonial empire in the West Indies and North America. US hostility to France was growing, and war with Britain seemed imminent.

President Jefferson wanted the land, and dispatched a special envoy, James Monroe, to assist in negotiations. Only Spain – concerned at the breaking of a French pledge never to sell the land – has objected. Whether the land-sale is constitutionally correct is a matter of doubt. Napoleon and Jefferson do not seem to be concerned.

Robert Livingstone, who bought Louisiana for the United States.

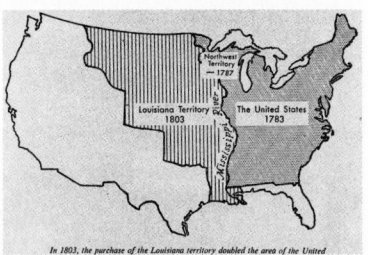

In 1803, the purchase of the Louisiana territory doubled the area of the United

The Mississippi river, once the frontier of the US, now divides it in two.

Irish rebellion against Britain fails

Lord Kilwarden, who was killed by Irish rebels led by Thomas Emmet.

Dublin, 24 July 1803

Late yesterday, Thomas Emmet donned his uniform of green coat, white breeches and cocked hat and led a chanting crowd of rebels to attack Dublin Castle. On the way they encountered Lord Kilwarden, the Lord Chief Justice and, dragging him from his carriage, stabbed and clubbed him to death with their pikes. But that act of brutality was the limit of the latest uprising against British rule, and Emmet has fled into the Wicklow mountains.

Emmet, the son of a physician to the British viceroy, is described in a Wanted notice as having "an ugly, sour countenance and dirty brown complexion". He studied at Trinity College, but soon fell under the influence of the United Irishmen who led the 1798 rebellion.

In Paris, Emmet met Napoleon and, believing that a French invasion of England was imminent, returned to Dublin to plan rebellion. But he was forced into premature action when his Patrick Street arms cache blew up. His movement was riddled with British spies.

New music hits Europe's capitals

Vienna, 1803

Joseph Haydn, Europe's greatest living composer, has had a visiting card printed with the first line of one of his songs: "Gone is all my strength, old and weak am I." Haydn, now 71, is exhausted by the effort of writing his great works of the last few years, which include six masses and two oratorios, *The Creation* (1798) and *The Seasons* (1801). This year he embarked on a string quartet, but so far has been unable to finish it.

At the same time, one of Haydn's ex-pupils, Ludwig van Beethoven, aged 32, has become renowned, though partly for his rebellious temperament. He moved from Bonn to Vienna in 1792 and made his name as a fine pianist and a composer of talent. Last year was a time of crisis for Beethoven, who realised that he was going deaf. But

Ailing genius, Joseph Haydn.

his second symphony, written at about that time, reveals little anguish, and he is now working on a third, which is on a grander scale than any previous symphony.

Slavery divides north and south in US

Virginia, 1802

The question of slavery is dominating every federal issue discussed in the United States today. It is 35 years since two surveyors, Charles Mason and Jeremiah Dixon, drew a line – at that time to define a border between Pennsylvania and Maryland – which has become a critical demarcation line between the slave-owning south and the liberal-minded northern states.

The knowledge that their brothers north of the Mason-Dixon line are free has been enough to foment a series of uprisings by slaves in several southern states. In North Carolina, 15 slaves have been executed after an alleged conspiracy to overthrow their masters.

Briton puts forward radical social theory

London, 1802

Jeremy Bentham, the philosopher and political writer, has put forward the idea that the object of all legislation should be "the greatest happiness for the greatest number". Bentham trained as a lawyer and has now become the exponent of utilitarianism in his *Introduction to the Principles of Morals and Legislation*. Bentham's conclusions are that mankind is governed by two sovereign motives, pain and pleasure, and the principle of utility recognises this state of affairs. The fame of the *principles* is spreading widely. He has been made a French citizen and his advice is respectfully received in many other countries of Europe and in America.

1803 (1803-1805)

Germany, 1803. The writer Johann von Herder dies. A friend to the young Goethe, Herder conveyed his own enthusiasm for folk-songs, ballads and the works of Shakespeare to a whole generation of writers who formed the *Sturm und Drang* movement, making a break with the age of reason and creating a new movement, the Romantic movement.

Britain, 1803. Henry Shrapnel's fragmentary shell, which he invented in 1784, is adopted by the British army.

Britain, 1803. The painter J M W Turner is elected the youngest Royal Academician at the age of 27. The son of a Covent Garden barber, he has been studying with the Royal Academy since the age of 14. This year he showed *Calais Pier*. Many dismiss his modern art as decadent and unrealistic.

Caribbean, January 1804. Haiti, occupying the western half of the island of Santo Domingo, becomes the first negro republic. It has declared itself independent after 11 years bitter fighting.

France, 28 February 1804. Following the discovery of a royalist plot to assassinate Napoleon Bonaparte, two senior officers, Generals Pichegru and Moreau are arrested.

Serbia, February 1804. Karageorges (Black George) leads a Serbian revolt against the Ottoman yoke.

France, 21 March 1804. Napoleon Bonaparte promulgates a civil code unifying legal practices across France. A compromise between the old regime and the egalitarian principles of the revolution, it protects the rights of property ownership above all else.

India, April 1804. War breaks out between the Maratha leader, Holkar, and the East India Company.

USA, 14 May 1804. The explorers Meriwether Lewis and William Clark set off on a journey to reach the Pacific.

New Jersey, 12 July 1804. The former treasury secretary, Alexander Hamilton, dies from wounds inflicted in a duel yesterday with political opponent Aaron Burr.

Austria, 10 August 1804. Fearing that the new modernised configuration of Germany, put into effect after the French occupation of the left bank of the Rhine, no longer guarantees his heir the title of emperor of the Holy Roman empire, Francis II proclaims himself hereditary emperor of Austria, with the name Francis I.

France, 16 September 1804. The physicist Joseph Gay-Lussac sets an altitude record of 22.942 feet (7.016 metres) during an ascent in a balloon with the aim of measuring the possible modifications of the composition of air.

Caribbean, October 1804. Jacques Dessalines, from Guinea, is proclaimed Emperor Jacques of Haiti following the declaration of independence in January.

France, 6 November 1804. A plebiscite ratifies the nomination of Bonaparte as hereditary emperor.

Europe, 6 November 1804. Austria and Russia sign a secret agreement against France.

Paris, 2 December 1804. Napoleon Bonaparte crowns himself emperor of France. He is known henceforth just as Napoleon.

Germany, 1804. Following Napoleon's coronation as emperor, Ludwig van Beethoven cancels the planned dedication of his *Third Symphony* and names it *Eroica*.

Denmark, 1804. King Frederick VI abolishes serfdom in his states.

Japan, 1804. Nicholas Rezanov, the Russian ambassador to Japan, reaches Nagasaki with the permit given to the Russian Lieutenant Adam Laxman in 1792 and requests permission to trade. After waiting six months, he is told that permission is not granted.

England, 1804. The poet William Blake publishes *Jerusalem*, a stirring religious and patriotic piece.

Chad, 1804. Uthman dan Fodio leads his people, the Fulani, in a *jihad* against the majority Hausa people and founds the Sokoto *caliphate* (holy war).

France, 1804. Charles Nicolas Appert publishes his process for the preserving of food which he invented in 1795.

England, 1804. Richard Trevithick constructs the first steam engine to run on a "railway", called the *Penn-y-Daran*.

China, 1804. The major rebellion stirred up by the White Lotus secret society in 1796 against the Manchu goverment is finally put down. The Qing dynasty survives but is much weakened.

Europe, 8 January 1805. France and Spain sign an agreement fixing the naval aid which the latter must supply to France in their joint war with Britain.

Italy, 17 March 1805. The Italian republic is established as the kingdom of Italy, with Napoleon as its sovereign. An hereditary kingdom, Italy nevertheless remains independent.

German artists and thinkers go romantic

Friedrich von Schelling: worshipping nature as the "world soul".

Weimar, 18 March 1804

Friedrich Schiller's drama *William Tell* was given here last night to great enthusiasm. It turns the story of the 14th-century Swiss patriot, who was forced to shoot an apple from his son's head, into the symbol of a people's struggle for freedom. It is theatrically more effective than Schiller's recent poetic historical dramas, *Wallenstein, Maria Stuart* and *The Maid of Orleans*.

Schiller is the object of veneration by Romantic poets, critics and philosophers who are creating a specifically German consciousness. They include Johann Fichte, who introduced the concept of the *ego*, or self-conscious self; Friedrich von Schelling, who deifies nature as the "world soul"; and Novalis, the Romantic poet.

The brothers von Schlegel jointly edit the influential *Athenaeum*. One of them, August, translates the plays of Shakespeare in such a way that they are now regarded as German classics. Clemens Brentano and Achim von Arnim are compiling authentic folkpoems to be called *Des Knaben Wunderhorn*. Ernst Hoffmann writes tales of the utmost fantasy. The Romantic cult is spreading all over Germany.

South American expedition is remarkable for seeking knowledge not conquests

Paris, 1804

A German explorer and scientist, Alexander von Humbold, has published a remarkable treatise based on his recent four-year adventure in South America. With the French naturalist Aime Bonpland he identified the convergence of the Amazon and Orinoco rivers, climbed the Peruvian Andes and studied an ocean current which seems certain to bear his name.

Scientific acumen accompanied physical boldness. His discoveries include the precise relationship between altitude and temperature; the influence of meteor showers; the use of isotherms in making maps, and measurement of the way the earth's magnetic field varies between the poles and the equator.

Some authorities already believe that Humboldt's great work – *Travels to the Equinoctial Regions of the New Continent during the years 1799 to 1804* – will lay the foundations for future physical geographic and meteorological re-

Humbold on the Orinoco river.

search. Yet before his voyage there was little to suggest that this assessor of mines in Berlin would be one of the new breed of explorers: people who do not pillage but acquire knowledge instead.

Napoleon crowns himself emperor

The emperor distributes eagles to his regiments on the Champ de Mars in Paris.

Paris, 2 December 1804
Napoleon crowned himself emperor of France in a magnificent ceremony in Notre Dame today. Pope Pius VII had been persuaded to conduct the ceremony, and he anointed the Corsican general; but Napoleon placed two golden laurel wreaths on his own head and then crowned his wife, Josephine.

This was not a spontaneous insult to the pope, as some spectators thought, but had been arranged with the *Curia* after long discus-sions about the ceremony. There can, however, be no misunderstandings about its meaning.

Charlemagne had also crowned himself. Napoleon sees himself in the same mould and the pope, the head of Catholic Christendom, had travelled from Rome to bless a self-made emperor.

It was in this fashion that monarchy returned to France almost 11 years after Louis XVI's gory head was shown to the crowd in the Place de la Revolution.

British supremacy is expanded in India

Calcutta, India, 1805
Lord Wellesley, the governor-general of Bengal and the man who turned the British presence in India into an empire, has been recalled. An energetic imperialist, his skills at defeating the French and their Indian allies by force, and the Indian princes by shackling them with treaties, are no longer required.

He arrived in India at a time of crisis. Bonaparte in Egypt threatened British India from without, and Tipu of Mysore from within. First Wellesley marched south, defeated Tipu and annexed the Carnatic. Next he turned on the lesser princes, provoking one against another, then "guaranteeing" the independence of both with troops.

Only in 1802 did he take on the still formidable Marathas. Exploiting divisions in the Maratha leadership, he imposed a treaty depriving

The English in the Orient.

them of their homeland. Then he provoked them to war; his brother Sir Arthur Wellesley defeated them at Assaye and Argaon. Thus is Britain building an empire here.

Americans launch night attack on Tripoli

Tripoli (Libya), 5 September 1804
A daring attack in February led by a young lieutenant, Stephen Decatur, succeeded in burning the captured US frigate *Philadelphia*, ensuring that it would never be used by the piratical *pasha* who has been holding *Philadelphia's* captain and crew hostage. The British admiral, Lord Nelson, described Decatur's action as "the most daring act of the age".

Decatur attacked by night; today, also under cover of darkness, Commodore Edward Preble took a leaf out of Sir Francis Drake's book and sent a fireboat, loaded with gunpowder, into Tripoli harbour to destroy the pasha's fleet after a day of bombardment. The ship was spotted by enemy gunners and blown up. It was to gain the release of the *Philadelphia's* captain and crew that Preble, aboard the 44-gun *Constitution*, has been battering Tripoli throughout the day. The United States has been paying substantial "protection money" to the pasha after attacks on US merchant shipping.

The burning US frigate "Philadelphia" lights up Tripoli harbour.

France unified by a single set of laws

Paris, 21 March 1804
A new legal framework, known to some as the "Napoleonic Code", has been approved after a four-year debate. Almost 16 years after the Revolution, the civil code gives France its first coherent set of laws concerning property, the family and individual freedom.

The code emerged from 84 wearing sessions of the State Council. The emperor presided at 36 of these, all concerned with the family and property. The authority of husbands and fathers is stronger, but the rights of illegitimate children are reduced. Women have no legal equality and colonial slavery is reintroduced. For men, however, the code enshrines the principle that all individuals are equal before the law; all enjoy freedom to work and to dissent from religious dogma.

Doctor knocks out wife for surgery

Japan, 1805
Hanaoka Seishu, a doctor in Kii province, has carried out an operation on a patient under a general anaesthetic for the first time in the history of medicine. His patient is his own wife and the operation, for breast cancer, is claimed to be a success.

The doctor has succeeded in preparing an anaesthetic substance after 20 years of experimentation. He calls it *mafutsusan*; it is a mixture of six crude drugs, including datura and aconite, listed in the traditional Chinese pharmacopoeia.

As he prepares to use his discovery in other operations, students are coming from all over the country to learn about his new techniques. His motto is: "Elucidate the principles of life, unite internal medicine with surgery."

1805 (1805-1806)

Europe, 11 April 1805. Britain and Russia sign an agreement of St Petersburg directed against France, thus inaugurating the third coalition. Sweden, already linked with Russia by an alliance signed in January, and the kingdom of Piedmont-Sardinia, are also members.

Virginia, 1 May 1805. A law is passed by the state leglislature requiring all freed slaves to leave the state, or risk either imprisonment or deportation.

Italy, 28 May 1805. Napoleon is crowned in Milan and appoints his stepson, Eugene de Beauharnais, as viceroy.

Tripoli, 4 June 1805. Yusuf Karamanli, *pasha* of Tripoli, signs a peace treaty with the United States ending the war which he declared in May 1801. He has been forced to surrender by the US fleet patrolling outside his harbour and by that fact that his rebellious brother Hamed has been installed, with US backing, in the eastern city of Derna.

Genoa, 10 June 1805. The Constitutional Assembly ratifies the annexation of Liguria to the French empire.

Ohio, 4 July 1805. A final treaty is between the United States government and the indigenous Indians for the purchase of Cleveland.

Louisiana, 25 July 1805. Leading US politician, Aaron Burr visits New Orleans as he allegedly develops plans to establish a country separate from the United States with New Orleans as its capital.

Europe, 9 August 1805. Austria joins Britain, Russia, Sweden and the kingdom of Piedmont-Sardinia in the third coalition against France.

Europe, 25 August 1805. Napoleon signs a treaty of alliance with Bavaria at Bogenhausen. In exchange for aid in the form of troops, the elector of Bavaria is maintained on the throne.

Bavaria, 8 October 1805. In a major battle the outnumbered French army of Napoleon defeats the invading Austrian army at Ulm and halt them.

Prussia, 3 November 1805. Coerced by Russia, Prussia joins the third coalition against France by a sectret treaty signed at Potsdam.

Pacific Ocean, 7 November 1805. The expedition led by Meriwether Lewis and William Clark has reached the Pacific coastline after a journey of nearly 4,000 miles which has taken 18 months. Many hope this will open a new era of westward expansion for the USA.

Austria, 14 November 1805. The French army enters the city of Vienna.

Austria, 2 December 1805. Napoleon defeats the combined Austrian and Russian armies at the battle of Austerlitz.

Austria, 26 December 1805. Austria signs the peace of Pressburg with France, abandoning the third coalition.

Italy, 27 December 1805. Napoleon proclaims the deposition of the House of Naples and forces the king to flee.

France, 31 December 1805. The republican calendar introduced after the French Revolution is abandoned in favour of the Gregorian one.

China, 1805. Several Roman Catholic priests are deported when a map of north China by the Italian priest Adeodato is discovered, ready to be sent to Rome.

Mexico, 1805. The first Mexican daily paper, *El Diario de Mexico*, is published.

France, 1805. Joseph Jacquard introduces the first weaving looms, thus enabling unskilled workers to produce beautiful and intricate patterns.

Britain, 23 January 1806. The prime minister, William Pitt, dies. The government is led by Lord Grenville and Charles James Fox.

France, 13 February 1806. Napoleon breaks with Pius VII after reservations expressed by the pope about the "imperial cathchism" which makes Napoleon "God's minister on earth".

Europe, 15 February 1806. The treaty of Paris is signed by France and Prussia, forcing the latter to accept the closing of its ports to British goods. Britain declares war on Prussia.

Spanish America, February 1806. The revolutionary Francisco Miranda – who has plans for a new great nation of South America – returns from Europe and attempts a coup in Venezuela which fails through lack of popular support.

San Francisco, 5 April 1806. Spanish authorities agree to sell supplies to Russian-American colonists who come down from Alaska in search of provisions. This is a complete reversal of policy and follows months of hard negotiating by the Russian representative, Nicholas Rezanov. He returns to his people not only with the agreement but also with a bride, the daughter of the Spanish commander of San Francisco.

French troops massing to invade England

Britain's answer to Napoleon's Grand Army, as George Cruikshank saw it.

Boulogne, August 1805
Napoleon is encamped here, waiting for Admiral Villeneuve to arrive with his fleet to cover the crossing of the Channel. Napoleon's orders are: "Let us be masters of the Straits for six hours, and we shall be masters of the world." He has assembled 2,343 ships and barges that can hold 167,590 men, but he will need calm weather over a number of tides before he can get his soldiers across, even without the attentions of the Royal Navy. He plans a lightning strike at London. But time is running out, and the only sails he can see are those of British frigates.

Explorers battle across Missouri to Pacific

Columbia River, 7 November 1805
After a hazardous 18-month journey across 4,000 miles of the unmapped plains, forests, mountains and deserts of North America, a United States government expedition is standing on the shores of the blue Pacific. The 28-man (and one woman) "Corps of Discovery" has been led by Captain Meriwether Lewis, President Jefferson's secretary and a veteran of several Indian wars, and Captain William Clark. Its mission is to survey the newly-purchased Louisiana territory.

Lewis and Clark on the Columbia.

The woman – who carried her baby son all the way – is a 16-year-old Shoshone Indian *squaw* called Sacajawea who is married to the expedition's interpreter, Toussaint Charbonneau. At one point, Sacajawea saved Lewis' life when he was threatened by an Indian chief.

The explorers left St Louis and journeyed up the Missouri River in six canoes and two longboats, sending back plant, animal and mineral specimens. They wintered in Dakota before crossing Montana, where they first saw the Rocky Mountains.

On the other side of the Continental Divide, they were met by Sacajawea's tribe who sold them horses for the long trek through the Bitterroot Mountains. The last leg of the journey, down the dangerous rapids of the Clearwater and Snake rivers in canoes, brought them to the Columbia river and the sea.

French lose at Trafalgar

The mortal wounding of Admiral Nelson, on the main deck of "HMS Victory".

Falmouth, 5 November 1805
The schooner *Pickle* sailed into the harbour here, bearing news of a great British naval victory off Cape Trafalgar. Twenty French and Spanish ships have been taken or sunk and Britain is safe from the invasion which Napoleon has been preparing. British joy will be tempered, however, by news of the death of Admiral Nelson, who was shot by a French sniper in the thick of the battle as his flagship, *HMS Victory*, came to grips with the French *Redoutable*.

The battle took place on 21 October. The combined fleets of France and Spain had been blockaded in Cadiz and it was a reluctant French admiral, Villeneuve, who sailed out on Napoleon's orders, hoping to avoid combat and unaware of the size of Nelson's fleet. Nelson divided his 27 ships into two columns to attack the rear of the enemy line, and as his fleet advanced in light winds, the admiral signalled: "England expects that every man will do his duty." Losses were heavy on both sides, but it was Nelson who carried the day.

Nelson's death will be mourned throughout Britain. His successes had made him one of the most popular men in the country with a public prepared to forgive his adulterous caperings with the voluptuous Emma, Lady Hamilton. His last words were: "Thank God I have done my duty."

French win at Austerlitz

Austerlitz, 2 December 1805
Napoleon crushed a numerically superior alliance of Russians and Austrians in a decisive battle here today, the first anniversary of his coronation as emperor of France.

Not for the first time, he started the battle in a precarious position. Outnumbered, he had to force a battle before the full weight of the allies could be brought to bear.

He pretended to retreat and gave an impression of weakness. Czar Alexander was taken in by this ruse and at daybreak advanced in extended line against the French massed behind the Goldbach brook, west of Austerlitz. The czar's plan was to turn the French right wing and cut off their retreat to Vienna. Napoleon allowed the allies to come on, with Davout holding fast on the right wing. The movement down the heights of Pratzen weakened the allies' centre where, suddenly, Napoleon ordered Soult to storm the heights.

There was a desperate fight between the Russian Imperial Guard and the French Guards until the Russians gave way. The allies were split in two and broke in utter rout, leaving 26,000 men dead and Napoleon as master of the battlefield.

Napoleon surveys the field of victory after the Russian and Austrian defeat.

Cape Town siezed

Cape Town, 10 January 1806
Cape Colony surrendered today to the invading British naval and military force led by Admiral Popham and Sir David Baird. There was little resistance from the meagre local forces assembled by the Dutch governor, General J W Janssens, who answers to Napoleon's puppet government in Holland.

The British first captured the Cape in 1795, but they found it a troublesome possession. The Boers and Xhosa Africans fought on the frontiers. The Boers, originally Dutch, had no love for the French, but they appeared to like the British even less. They rebelled in 1801 and in 1802 Britain gave up the Cape in the treaty of Amiens.

New ruler for Egypt

Cairo, 3 August 1805
Mohammed Ali, an Albanian former tobacco merchant, is the new ruler of Egypt. Khurshid Pasha, the former viceroy, has accepted the inevitable, and evacuated the citadel where he has been holding out since 14 May.

Seven years ago Mohammed Ali was recruited by the Ottomans to serve against Napoleon. At the head of a group of Albanian clansmen, he profited from the power struggle between Mamelukes and Ottomans. In 1803 he supported the Mamelukes, then last year switched to the Sultan's side. With Khurshid's administration accused of corruption, sultan Selim III turned to Ali to restore order.

Slave emperor of Caribbean state dies

Haiti, 1806
Jean-Jacques Dessalines, the slave who became emperor of Haiti, the Carribean's first independent state, has died. He was 48 years old. Born in Guinea, he came to the rich sugar-producing French colony of Haiti on a slave ship, and took the name of his owner, Dessalines, as his own.

When Haiti's free negroes, and then her slaves – their expectations inflated by the slogan *liberte, equalite et fraternite* – revolted in 1891 under Toussaint L'Ouverture, he rose to become second-in-command. For seven years the two men led the slave army, first against the French, then against the Spanish and British, defeating all of them. When Napoleon re-imposed slavery in 1800 and sent a military expedition to retake Haiti, L'Ouverture and Dessalines took to the field again. L'Ouverture was captured and died in a French prison in 1803 and Dessalines took control of the army. He renewed the war with vigour and cruelty, and drove the French Army from the country in October.

On 1 January 1804 he declared Haiti independent and then, on 8 October, he crowned himself emperor. Now unrestrained by the magnamnity and statesmanship of L'Ouverture, he gave his cruelty free reign. Hundreds were brutally killed and tortured. Indeed he proved so oppressive a tyrant that his leading general, Henri Christophe, ended up assassinating him. Christophe has now taken over control of the unhappy country.

1806 (1806-1807)

France, 10 May 1806. The university of France is founded.

Britain, 16 May 1806. Advised by Charles Fox, the foreign secretary, the cabinet decrees a blockade of the European coast from Brest to Hamburg.

Netherlands, 5 June 1806. The Batavian republic is established as the kingdom of Holland under Louis Bonaparte, the Emperor Napoleon's younger brother.

Germany, 12 July 1806. The confederation of the Rhine is established.

Germany, 1 August 1806. Napoleon gives notice to the Emperor Francis II of the end of the Holy Roman empire.

Germany, 6 August 1806. The Holy Roman Emperor Francis II accepts Napoleon's ultimatum and abdicates.

Spanish America, 12 August 1806. A British expeditionary force which took Buenos Aires in June, meeting little resistance, is forced to capitulate by a local army.

France, 22 August 1806. Jean Honore Fragonard, the painter of the erotic coquetry of the court of Louis XVI and Marie Antoinette, dies. He fell from favour with the revolution, was forced to give up his rooms in the Louvre and ended his days in poverty and obscurity.

London, 27 August 1806. US negotiators open talks with Lord Holland with a view to ending naval hostilities.

Britain, 13 September 1806. The death of the foreign secretary, Fox, interrupts Lord Yarmouth's mission, entrusted to him in March, to negotiate peace with France.

France, 21 November 1806. Napoleon promulgates the Berlin decree which declares the British Isles to be in a state of blockade and orders the confiscation of British merchandise in French territory, the imprisonment of British subjects, and the closure of all French ports to ships coming from Britain or British territories.

France, 10 December 1806. The Grand Sanhedrin, an official institution of the Jewish community, is created. This comes after the meeting of 111 representatives of the Jewish communities of France and Italy, which took place on 30 May in Paris. It marks the recognition of the French character of the empire's Jews.

Ottoman Empire, December 1806. Following a declaration of war by the Ottomans on Russia, the Russians occupy Baku, on the Caspian Sea.

Britain, 1806. Admiral Francis Beaufort perfects a graduated scale for measuring wind speed.

Haiti, 1806. The Emperor Jacques, who came to power two years ago, is assassinated following a rule of extreme barbarity during which he contrived the murder of almost the entire white population.

South Africa, 1806. Cape Colony is surrendered once again by Holland to Britain. The colony reverted to the Batavian republic (Napoleonic Holland) in 1803 under the treaty of Amiens of the previous year. After war resumed, the British first landed at Cape Town in July 1805, but have now returned in force.

India, 1806. Ranjit Singh, the Sikh leader, takes Lahore.

Paris, 4 January 1807. Napoleon visits the studio of the painter Louis David, who has just finished his monumental composition *The Coronation of the Emperor*, started on 21 December 1805.

London, 7 January 1807. Responding to the Emperor Napoleon's Berlin Decree, blockading the British Isles, a British order in council closes the coastal waters of France and its allies to all commercial shipping.

Britain, 25 March 1807. Parliament passes an act abolishing the slave trade. A resolution for the abolition of slavery was first brought before parliament in 1789.

Ottoman Empire, 25 May 1807. A revolt by the Janissaries (foot soldiers recruited from slaves) leads to the deposition of Selim III and to his replacement by Mustapha IV.

Russia, 25 June 1807. At the Tilsit convention Napoleon and the Russian Czar Alexander agree an end to hostilities between their two countries.

Spanish America, 5 July 1807. Having taken Montevideo on 3 February, the British fail in their attempt to re-take Buenos Aires.

Prussia, July 1807. The ministers Gneisenau and Scharnhorst reorganise the Prussian army.

England, 1807. Charles Lamb publishes his *Tales from Shakespeare*, written by him and his sister Mary. Lamb is guardian to his sister who stabbed their mother in a fit of insanity.

China, 1807. Robert Morrison, of the London Missionary Society, the first Protestant missionary to China, arrives in Guangzhou.

Japan, 1807. Russian ships attack Japanese settlements in the north in reprisal for the treatment of the expedition of the ambassador, Nicholas Rezanov, in 1804.

Utamaro, painter of the "floating world"

Utamaro's exquisite print "Lovers on a Balcony" from "Poems of the Pillow".

Edo (Tokyo), 31 October 1806
The death occurred today of the foremost painter of the "Floating World" school in Japan, Kitagawa Utamaro. His prints were published under such titles as *The Seven Beauties of the Gay Quarter, Ten Types of Feminine Demeanour* and *Women in Love*. His subjects were the famous beauties among the courtesans and tea-house girls of the Yoshiwara pleasure district.

He idealised the sitters, but subtle variations of detail conveyed feminine characteristics such as fickleness, conceit or petulance. In 1804 he portrayed the wife and concubines of *shogun* Toyotomi Hideyoshi and was imprisoned for "insult". He was kept in handcuffs for 50 days and painted no more.

Utamaro's "Three Girls Paddling".

New Reforms for beaten Prussia

Berlin, 1807
Shattered by Napoleon's defeat of his army at Jena, and with his kingdom cut to a mere half of its former size, Frederick William III of Prussia has turned to the outspoken and resolute Baron Heinrich von Stein for salvation.

Stein is pushing through a big reform programme, which includes the abolition of serfdom and all class distinctions in state employment. Local self-government will be introduced. Queen Louise, the real power behind the throne, is backing Scharnhorst and Gneisenau in reorganising the army.

Locals expel British from Buenos Aires

Buenos Aires, 1807
Creole irregulars defending their Argentian capital have inflicted two successive defeats on British invaders. In June last year British forces launched from South Africa a successful but unauthorised surprise attack with 1,200 men to seize a virtually undefended Buenos Aires. Two months later, a Frenchman led a locally-raised militia to defeat the invaders. On 3 February this year a new British expedition took Montevideo, then crossed the river Plate to reoccupy Buenos Aires. Again the invaders were trapped and disarmed.

US bans all trade with rest of world

Washington, 22 December 1807
After months of mercantile harassment by the British and French navies, the US Congress today voted to ban all trading with the rest of the world. No American ship can sail to any foreign port and all exports from America are prohibited. President Jefferson believes that these economic sanctions will force the British and French to rescind orders in council and decrees against neutral trade.

The US public is furious at what it terms the latest British outrage. The frigate USS *Chesapeake* refused an order to stop from *HMS Leopard* which opened fire without warning, killing 21 of her crew. Chesapeake's captain was forced to allow his ship to be boarded and three British seamen and a US citizen were impressed into the king's service.

British in Lisbon to harass French

Lisbon, 1 August 1808
A British military force led by Sir Arthur Wellesley has landed at Lisbon to help Portuguese and Spanish resistance to Napoleon. It has promptly routed the French Marshal Junot at Vimeiro. The action is seen as heralding the start of a Peninsula War which could tie down thousands of Napoleon's troops in the region.

The British landing must come as shock to the French leader, who has been counting on Spain to give him with ships, troops and cash. Spain had been forced to deny harbours to the British, and Portugal should have followed suit under threat of occupation. But Napoleon scattered his armies in attempts to capture and close Spanish-held ports, leaving Lisbon open to British ships and allowing Wellesley to land without opposition.

Importation of slaves in US is banned

Washington DC, 2 March 1807
The importation of slaves from Africa into the United States will be illegal from next January under an act passed by Congress today. Anyone who knowingly buys an illegally imported slave faces a penalty of $500, and equipping a ship for the slave trade is punishable with a $20,000 fine.

It was President Jefferson who insisted that the act should be placed in the statute book. The president has been a long-time opponent of slavery, and fought unsuccessfully with southern delegates to introduce anti-slavery statements in his first draft of the Declaration of Independence

There has been little opposition to the move. The United States has more than enough slaves at present. But what looks like a coming boom

Establishing ownership: branding.

in the cotton industry could create a substantial demand by the southern states. Some unscrupulous owners are already talking about "slave-breeding farms".

Locomotive inventor mounts London show

Richard Trevithick's "steam circus".

London, 1808
Richard Trevithick, the inventor of a locomotive steam engine, has exhibited his latest engine in London. The engine, known as the "catch-me-who-can", can be seen on the New Road as the centre piece of a "steam circus" on which the public may ride for a charge of a shilling.

Trevithick's first locomotive – known as "the puffing devil" – was completed in 1801 at his home town, Redruth, in Cornwall. A second followed in 1803, but the delicate engineering suffered on the rough roads, and his experiments in "steam-carriages" had to be abandoned. His first locomotive to run on tracks was completed in 1804. It could run at five miles per hour for nine and a half miles, pulling ten tons of iron, 70 men and five wagons. But this, too, was used mainly as a stationary machine. The problems were with the track; the engine was blameless.

Atoms all arranged on Dalton's table

London, 1808
The British scientist John Dalton has succeeded in devising chemical symbols for the various elements, such as oxygen and gold. He has drawn up a list of atomic weights and arranged them in a table. He has formulated the theory that a chemical combination of elements occurs according to certain laws governing the ratio of these atomic weights: the *Law of Multiple Proportions* and the *Law of Constant Composition*.

All these ideas are expounded in his *New System of Chemical Philosophy* which shows Dalton to be a unique thinker.

Napoleon blockades British commerce

George Cruikshank's view of the continental blockade; a starving Europe.

Paris, 1807
The "Continental System", Napoleon's boycott of British goods, is beginning to bite. When he issued his famous Berlin Decree last November, in which he declared "the British Isles are in a state of blockade" and British goods ordered to be seized, he was greeted with derision. Cartoons showed Boney blockading the moon.

Now, however, the treaty of Tilsit has forced Russia and Prussia into the system and their ports are closed to British trade. Napoleon is sure that his boycott will ruin Britain and force it to sue for peace.

He has told his brother, King Louis of Holland: "I mean to conquer the sea by land", and writes of Britain's vessels "laden with useless wealth wandering around the high seas, where they claim to rule as sole masters, seeking in vain ... for a port to receive them". The boycott has indeed had a serious effect on British trade this year, but such is the cunning of British smugglers and the greed of French officials that great holes are being torn in the blockade and Europe is overflowing with British goods.

Portugal, 30 August 1808. Having landed in Portugal at the beginning of the month, British troops force the French to surrender.

Algeria, 27 August 1808. The British bombard Algiers.

Europe, 14 October 1808. During their meeting at Erfurt which finishes today, Napoleon and the Russian Czar Alexander renew the treaty of Tilsit which both countries have broken since it was made last year.

Prussia, 24 November 1808. Napoleon obtains the dismissal of the minister Stein whom he suspects of organising an anti-French uprising.

Spain, 4 December 1808. Napoleon conquers Madrid, having put down the resistance in Somosierra last month.

Washington DC, 7 December 1808. James Madison is elected president in succession to Thomas Jefferson.

Vienna, 22 December 1808. Beethoven gives the first performance of his fifth and sixth symphonies, in a long, under-rehearsed and ill-received concert.

Serbia, December 1808. The popular leader Karageorges (Black George) is recognised as hereditary prince of the Serbs by an assembly of his people.

China, 1808. British forces occupy Macao.

Japan, 1808. Mamiya Rinzo explores Sakhalin and discovers that it is an island.

Britain, 1808. The Englishman Humphrey Davy uses the newly-invented voltaic pile to isolate barium. In this same year he also succeeds in isolating strontium, calcium, magnesium and boron.

India, 1808. Holkar, the Maratha leader, has become insane.

France, 28 January 1809. Having plotted against the emperor with Fouche, Talleyrand falls into disgrace. Stripped of every position he holds, he places himself at the service of Metternich, the Austrian ambassador to Paris.

Persia, 12 March 1809. Britain signs a treaty with Persia, forcing the French out of the country.

Europe, 10 April 1809. Austria declares war on France and her forces enter Bavaria.

India, April 1809. The treaty of Amritsar is signed. The British agree to give Ranjit Singh, the ruler of the Sikhs, a free hand to the west of the river Sutlej in return for his giving them a free hand to the east.

Portugal, 12 May 1809. The second British landing is led by Viscount Wellington.

New York, 8 June 1809. The revolutionary writer Thomas Paine dies. He was born in 1737 in England and came to America in 1774. After playing a leading role in the American Revolution, Paine became involved in French politics and was elected a deputy in the Convention. In an abrupt but not unusual fall from favour, Paine was imprisoned for 11 months, and then restored to his seat in the Convention. He eventually became disillusioned with French politics and returned to the US in 1802.

North America, 2 July 1809. The government of the Western Territory announces that the famous Shawnee Indian Chief Tecumseh and his brother (the Prophet) have launched a campaign to unite the 10,000 Indians who live in the area west of the Mississippi river. The aim of this confederation is to halt American expansion in their lands.

Washington DC, 9 August 1809. President Madison reinstates the embargo on British trade following Britain's refusal to revoke the orders in council that justify harassment of American shipping.

Rome, 20 August 1809. Pope Pius VII, who was arrested on 6 July on the orders of the emperor for having excommunicated him on 12 June, is moved to Savona from Grenoble.

Spain, 28 July 1809. An inconclusive battle is fought between the French and the Anglo-Spanish forces at Talavera.

Rome, 20 August 1809. General Malet organises his first plot against the Emperor Napoleon, which comes to nothing.

Netherlands, 30 September 1809. A British army that landed at Walcheren on 30 July is forced to set sail again.

Russia, 17 September 1809. The signing of the peace treaty of Hamina guarantees Russia's jurisdiction over Finland.

Britain, 1809. The painter Turner exhibits *London Seen from Greenwich*.

Spain, 1809. The novelist Alessandro Manzoni brings out *Urania*.

France, 1809. The scholar Lamarck edits his *Zoological Philosophy* in which he explains his theory about the origin and evolution of species.

Prussia, 1809. The *Tugendbund*, a cultural and scientific association directed against Napoleon, is dissolved by the king.

France honours artist of the revolution

David's vast canvas "The Sabine Women": three yards high and five yards wide.

Paris, 1808
Jacques Louis David, the artist most closely linked with the Revolution and now official painter to Napoleon, has been awarded the Legion of Honour. David's many admirers welcome this fitting tribute to the foremost painter of the last two decades.

David learnt his art in Italy and his style has a conspicuously classical bent, to be seen in such works as *The Oath of the Horatii*, the painting that brought him his first real celebrity in 1785, the propagandist *Victors Bringing to Brutus the Bodies of His Sons* (1789) and his masterpiece, *The Death of Marat* (1793).

With the fall of Robespierre in 1794 David himself faced trial, but escaped death despite a spell in jail. In 1799 his giant canvas *Les Sabines* attracted the attention of Bonaparte and David, an admirer, became a government painter once more. His latest painting is of Napoleon's coronation in 1804.

Haydn, master of symphony, dies

Vienna, 31 May 1809
As French armies bombarded the Austrian capital, Joseph Haydn died peacefully, today aged 77. Haydn wrote hundreds of fine works and will be revered as the person who brought the symphony and string quartet to the highest level of sophistication.

He wrote the last 12 of his over 100 symphonies for visits to London and crowned his career with six magnificent masses and two oratorios, including *The Creation*. "Papa" Haydn was a close friend of Mozart, and was devastated by his early death. Mozart summed him up perfectly: "There is no one who can do it all – to joke and to terrify, to evoke laughter and profound sentiment – and all equally well: except Joseph Haydn."

Family is dead in idealist's society

France, 1808
The family as we know it is dead. Instead, we should all live in co-operative groups of 100 families each, working together in agricultural communities.

Such is the view of Charles Fourier, the social reformer and mathematician. Fourier, whose theories appear in his book *Theory of Four Movements*, calls the philosophy *Fourierism*. The communities are *phalansteres*, a word combining *phalange*, meaning phalanx or tightly linked formation, with the final *ere* of *monastere*.

These communities are to share all profits, with the largest share going to the labourers. Women are to be completely equal, and it seems that free love will be taking the place of marriage.

Napoleon arrests insubordinate pope

Pius VII, the defiant pope.

Rome, 6 July 1809
Pope Pius VII and his secretary, Cardinal Pacca, were arrested today on the orders of the French general, Radet, and sent to Grenoble. This act is the result of the pope's continued defiance of Napoleon which dates from the emperor's coronation at which the pope officiated, but gained nothing.

Humiliated, he determined to make no more concessions. He refused to allow the Papal ports to become part of Napoleon's system of boycott against Britain. Napoleon replied by occupying Rome.

The pope shut himself up in his residence. Two months ago, when Napoleon annexed the Papal States to his empire, Pius issued a bull of excommunication against "the despoilers of the church".

He was careful not to name Napoleon, but when the emperor received the text of the bull shortly before the battle of Wagram, he wrote: "He is a madman who should be shut up. Arrest Pacca and other followers of the pope." It may be that he did not intend the pope to be arrested, but it is done now and Pius is to be interned.

Chinese writer tells of his floating life

China, 1809
Shen Fu, a government clerk of no great ability or status, has written a charming book which is enjoying a great success. Called *Six Records of a Floating Life*, it tells the story of his marriage to his childhood sweetheart, Yun.

It is essentially a love story although, in Chinese fashion, his married life is interspersed with affairs with courtesans and with his wife's attempts to find him a concubine. It explains much about Chinese married life to a western reader. Shen Fu emerges from the book as a dreamer, capable of crippling self-deception, forced by his education to be a scholar-administrator, but unable on a number of occasions to provide for his family.

He would have been better off if he had taken a higher-paid job with a more lowly status, but he could not bring himself to do this. This, his voyage through life, reflects only too accurately many of the ills plaguing China today.

The floating state: the emperor's gardens, Beijing, seen by William Alexander.

Retreating British thwart French in Spain

Corunna, where General Sir John Moore saved the British army in the Peninsula.

Paris, 17 January 1809
The failure of Marshal Soult to smash the redcoats at the Spanish port of Corunna and prevent them embarking has wrecked Napoleon's plans for the conquest of the Peninsula, and should give the shattered Spanish armies time to reorganise. After this failure to defeat the British army, Napoleon has put off his planned invasion of Portugal and Andalucia and left Madrid for Paris. The setback for France is all the more remarkable as Napoleon was in Madrid with some 75,000 men after accepting its surrender. He assumed that Sir John Moore, who replaced Sir Arthur Wellesley at the head of the British troops, would retreat to Lisbon, which the French had targeted for capture, and pursued him. Moore took 12 days to reach Corunna, making marches of 17 hours a day in rugged country covered with snow and cut up by torrents and defiles. But some 6,000 of his men dropped out, wearied by the perpetual marching and the absence of any battle.

At Corunna, as embarkation began, Moore pulled the army together and the infantry repulsed Marshal Soult's assault. Moore was hit by grape-shot while applauding his men going into action and died that night. As French guns on the heights re-opened fire on the harbour he was hastily buried in a grave dug by soldiers of the 9th Foot, with his cloak around him.

Unused organs wither, says scientist

Paris, 1809
The evolutionist Jean Baptiste Lamarck has given a clear statement of his views on how animals evolve. There are, he says, two basic laws governing the way organisms develop on their way to a higher stage. The first is that organs are improved with repeated use and weakened by disuse, even to the point of disappearing altogether. The giraffe owes its long neck to frequent stretching in order to eat from higher branches, and the snake has lost its presumed original four legs through lack of use. The second law is that these environmentally-determined changes acquired in an individual animal's lifetime are passed on to its offspring.

Jean Baptiste Lamarck: evolutionist.

1809 (1809-1811)

Europe, 14 October 1809. Austria signs the peace of Schonbrunn, ceding its Illyrian provinces to France.

Spanish America, 6 November 1809. The British are authorised to trade in Buenos Aires.

France, 16 December 1809. The Emperor Napoleon divorces Josephine on the grounds that she has not given him a son.

Britain, 1809. Walter Scott founds the *Quarterly Review*, designed to challenge Whig reformist doctrines.

Russia, 4 February 1810. Czar Alexander refuses Napoleon the hand of his sister Anna, aged 15.

Italy, 17 February 1810. France annexes the papal states.

Netherlands, 9 July 1810. Following the abdication of Louis Bonaparte, in disagreement with his brother about the usefulness of the blockade, the kingdom of Holland is annexed and divided into seven departments.

Mexico, 16 September 1810. A parish priest, Hidalgo, launches an appeal for Mexican independence.

Germany, September 1810. Courses begin at the university of Berlin, founded on 16 August 1809. Its first rector is the philosopher Fichte.

Washington DC, 27 October 1810. President Madison orders the annexation of the western part of West Florida following a rebellion of settlers in the area against the Spanish authorities. Troops are being sent to enforce the claim.

USA, 2 November 1810. President Madison, elected on 4 March 1809, re-establishes freedom of trade with France, having been assured that European ports will be opened to American shipping.

Sweden, 17 November 1810. Sweden declares war on Britain.

Indian Ocean, 3 December 1810. The British seize the islands of Reunion and Maurice following the battle of Grand Port in August. They undertake to respect the languages, laws and customs of the inhabitants.

Germany, 13 December 1810. The North Sea coastline of the duchy of Oldenburg is annexed by the French empire.

Britain, 15 December 1810. The writer Mrs Sarah Trimmer dies aged 69. A friend of Samuel Johnson, she was influential in setting up some of the earliest schools for the education of the poor. She published several educational books and also edited two magazines, *The Family Magazine* and *Guardian of Education*.

Russia, 31 December 1810. Czar Alexander breaks the Continental System of blockades, opening Russian ports to trade with neutral countries, and at the same time banning French imports in the Russian empire.

Britain, 1810. Walter Scott, a most popular writer of romantic verse, including *The Lay of the Last Minstrel* and *Marmion*, publishes *The Lady of the Lake*.

Germany, 1810. Franz Gall and Johann Spurzheim publish a four-volume work on the anatomy of the nervous system. They introduce the idea that various mental processes are localised in different regions of the brain. Gall also invents *phrenology*, a method of determining personality and intelligence by studying bumps on the skull.

Honolulu, 1810. The island of Hawaii is unified by King Kamhameha the Great.

Washington DC, 1810. The population of the US has risen by 36.4 per cent in the last decade, according to a census which puts the population at 7.2 million.

Madagascar, 1810. King Nampoina dies, having ruled since 1782. He is succeeded by King Radama.

Ghana, 1810. In retaliation against local traders who are allied with their enemies the Asante, the Fante people attack the coastal ports of Accra and Elmina.

France, 1810. Napoleon has Madame de Stael's manuscript *Concerning Germany* destroyed.

France, 1811. The banker James de Rothschild establishes a branch in Paris.

Venezuela, 1811. A congress proclaims Venezuela's independence and sets up a republican constitution. Simon Bolivar is a popular leader of the movement, as is the veteran revolutionary Francisco Miranda.

Indian Ocean, 1811. The British finally end French power in the area by taking the Seychelles, Mauritius and Madagascar.

China, 1811. A revolt by the Celestial Order (Tianlijiao) sect breaks out in the provinces of Shandong and the Hebei.

China, 1811. After the banning of Christian preaching in 1810, steps are taken against foreign missionaries and converted Chinese.

Haiti, 1811. Henri Christophe, an ex-slave, is crowned King Henri in the northern part of Haiti. The south falls to an educated Mulatto, Alexandre Pieton.

False freedom cloaks French occupations

Paris, 1810
The French Empire is at its zenith. Most of Europe lies under Napoleon's heel. Everywhere, liberty, equality and fraternity, the ideals of the revolution, have given way to repression of the cruellest nature.

A formidable secret police force, far more efficient than anything possessed by the beheaded "tyrant" Louis XVI, enforces a savage penal code in France. The old punishments of branding and the *carcan* or iron collar, have been revived. State prisons have just been re-established. A general controls the press. Napoleon's court is as lavish as that which was "swept away for ever" in 1793.

In the occupied territories, the fearsome effect of Napoleon's hegemony is even more obvious. His soldiers arrive preaching the "enlightened" law of the *Code Napoleon* and enforce it by the bayonet.

Such oppression breeds reaction. Spain will never forget the *dos de Mayo* when French soldiers slaugh-

Napoleon seen through British eyes.

tered the people of Madrid. Andreas Hofer, the Tyrolean patriot, has been executed, but remains a hero. Napoleon told his brother recently: "Abroad and at home, I reign through the fear I inspire."

Bags of rice bran get Japanese clean

A bath-house, or "uya", for Japanese women at Edo, the capital of Japan.

Japan, c.1810
Bath houses are becoming increasingly popular in Japan. There are 600 in the capital, Edo, alone. Originally these public establishments were places of ill-repute, more used for illicit sex than bathing, but they have developed into an important public service, as only the largest of town houses have bathrooms.

In the early days of the bath houses it was customary for men and women to bathe together, but decorum was ensured by the lack of lighting and the wearing of loin cloths by the men and underskirts by the women. Today, separate facilities are provided for each sex.

Soap is expensive, so bags of rice bran are used for the preliminary wash. Towels are strangely skimpy and bathers dress while still damp. The Japanese insist that this keeps them cool.

Metternich aims for new power balance

Vienna, 8 October 1809
Prince von Metternich has been appointed Austrian foreign minister by Francis in the hope that something can salvaged from the country's series of military defeats at the hands of Napoleon. The shrewd 36-year-old nobleman has served as Austrian minister in France and is thought to be a good judge of Napoleon and his plans.

Metternich is a committed anti-revolutionary. He was forced to flee three times himself before the advancing revolution – from Strasburg, then from Mainz, and from the Netherlands when Napoleon invaded. He has long been working for an effective alliance of Austria, Prussia and Britain to counter the French.

He failed to persuade Frederick William III of Prussia to join Austria in the 1805 war. But in his new position he will be well placed to achieve his aims.

Metternich: conservative diplomat.

Chinese pirate fleet led by women

Guangzhou, China, 20 April 1810
Zheng Yi Sao, the "dragon lady" of the South China Sea and leader of the area's feared confederation of pirates, surrendered today to governor-general Bai Ling. Zheng, a former prostitute, replaced her late husband Zheng Yi as pirate supremo when he died in 1807. For three years, backed by her lover and adopted son Zhang Bao, Zheng Yi Sao has dominated an empire of 1800 junks and 70,000 men and women. Her negotiating skills, as much as the fleet's unassailable power, have made her a great, if criminal, leader. It is those same skills that have created from her surrender a new victory. No pirate is to be punished – all will be pardoned – and Zheng and some of her senior commanders are to be given highranking positions in the state's military.

Canoe of silver for barbarian of genius

Madagascar, 1810
Despite the death of the Malagasy King Nampoina there is optimism here that the strong centralised kingdom which he created will survive. Nampoina (the Desired One) seized power from in 1783. He has been buried with high honours in a silver canoe. He was called by visiting Frenchmen a "barbarian of genius". He took land from the ruling families and redistributed it to the needy. He created a society where everyone worked. He used forced labour for public works and ensured that the lazy were beaten. He has carefully suppressed his other sons so that his favourite, Radama, is the unchallenged successor.

New Moslem ruler emerges in Nigeria

Nigeria, c.1811
Virtually the whole of northern Nigeria is now controlled by a strong Moslem ruler, Uthman dan Fodio. The last decade has seen an amazing transformation in the fortunes of the minority Fulani people at the expense of the Hausa majority. It has been achieved by Uthman, who is the son of an Imam, and also a religious teacher. But in 1802 the new Hausa king, Yunfa, banned the wearing of the turban and the veil in a bid to stop Moslem conversions. Uthman then had a series of visions urging him to restore the faith by *jihad* (holy war). He stirred the scattered Fulani leaders to combine in a successful war.

Independence movement born in Mexico

Mexico: cursed by the extremes of Spanish wealth and Indian poverty.

Mexico, 16 September 1810
Revolution has broken out here, inspired by the battlecry of the parish priest of the village of Dolores, a man demoted by his church but loved by his parishioners.

A follower of French philosophy, especially that of Rousseau, Father Miguel Hidalgo de Costilla has always sided with the underdogs of society, the Indians and the peasants. He has also been plotting against the authorities.

Hearing that the plot had been discovered and that the government was about to arrest him, Hidalgo chose this morning's sermon to act. After distributing weapons to his trusted supporters, he addressed a large crowd gathered at the church.

"My children, this day comes to us a new dispensation. Are you ready to receive it? Will you be free? Long live our Lady of Guadalupe, down with bad government! Death to the Spaniards!"

This *grito de Dolores*, or warcry of Dolores, set a great march in motion. It appears that as many as ten thousand Indians and a number of peasants have taken to the roads, a rag-tag but enthusiastic army. They have camped out for the night, but are heading for the city, their parish priest at their head.

Italian chemist describes nature of gases

Turin, Italy, 1811
A professor of physics at Turin university, Amadeo Avogadro, has proposed a new law governing the nature of gases. The hypothesis is that, under the same pressure and at the same temperature, equal volumes of different gases contain an equal number of molecules.

This is a controversial statement because it implies that atoms of the same element can become bound together in molecules – a completely novel concept.

How Russia became a power in Europe

The emergence of Russia as a Great Power was one of the most significant features of the 18th century. At the beginning of the century she was territorially vast, but politically and economically deficient. At its close, she had extended her boundaries, reformed her army, restructured her administration, and renovated her economy. The West knew little of Russia in 1700. By 1800 it knew enough to value her as an ally and fear her as a foe. In less than a century Russian leadership seemed transformed. Czar Peter I (known to history as Peter the Great) visited England in 1698 and stayed for three months at the house of John Evelyn, the diarist. The "house full of people and right nasty ...", reported one of Evelyn's servants. The czar and his party, all excessively fond of beer, caused £150 worth of damage to the building and the garden.

Yet 70 years on, his successor Catherine II cherished a reputation for *urbanitas*. She counted Voltaire among her correspondents (and Machiavelli among her reading). By 1776, the *Scots Magazine* was able to depict an indisputably great empire: "Russia enjoys her power, influence and glory, with a noble and splendid magnificence. All her affairs are conducted upon a great and extensive system, and all her acts are in a grand style. She sits supreme between Europe and Asia, and looks as if she intended to dictate to both." The prophecy was astute. Thirty-one years later, Alexander I and Napoleon met at Tilsit, the one matching the other in grandeur of vision. East and West were to be divided between them. From Finland to India, no territory was left unconsidered. "What is Europe?" the czar portentously asked the French ambassador. "Where is it, if it is not you and me?"

Expansion to north and south

The first Westerner was Czar Peter himself. However uncouth, he was far from empty-headed. Abroad, he pursued a policy of expansion; at home, one of thorough-going reform. At the beginning of his reign, Russia lacked access to the Black Sea, the Caspian and the Baltic. To remedy this, a stronger army and a much expanded navy were required. In 1696 Peter captured Azoz from the Turks, though was later forced to relinquish it after the war of 1700-1713. In 1700 he turned towards the Baltic, and for 21 years engaged Sweden in war to clear a path through Karelia, Ingria, Estonia and Livonia to the sea. The Treaty of Nystad (1721) ceded the eastern shores of the Baltic to Russia.

But even before the Northern War was concluded, Peter resumed his interest in the south. In 1722 he invaded Persian territory. The following year Persia abandoned the southern and western shores of the Caspian Sea in return for military aid. At his death in 1725, the Russian empire extended from the White Sea to the Caspian, from the Baltic to the Pacific Ocean.

This militarism generated domestic reform. An expanded army required finance; finance required efficient taxation; taxation presupposed and reinforced centralisation; and administration required administrators, a professional civil service. Armies and navies need weaponry, and thus a metallurgy industry. Not all of Peter's plans worked – inefficiency seemed endemic – but they laid the necessary basis of future development.

Sensual and cerebral appetites

The reigns of Peter and Catherine II are separated by nearly 40 years, but their contribution to Russian history is of a piece. Catherine, a German princess by birth but fiercely loyal to her adopted Russia, matched Peter in wilfulness and vision. Her culture may have contrasted with his coarseness, but she had sensual as well as cerebral appetites and did not stint in the satisfaction of both. Like Peter, she was land-hungry, desiring to extend the Russian border westwards and southwards. She coveted Courland, which lay between Russia and the Baltic. From 1763 she was able to control it by means of proxy rulers; after 1795 it was formally part of the empire.

Poland was next. Frederick the Great of Prussia had claimed in 1752 that Polish Prussia should be "eaten like an artichoke leaf by leaf ... now a town, now a district, until the whole has been eaten up". Many parts of the country were on Catherine's menu, too. In three partitions it was parcelled out among Russia, Prussia and Austria: the first (1772) to the equal benefit of all three, the second (1793) favouring Russia by ceding to her the Eastern Provinces, the third (1795) dividing the remainder of the country between them.

Not content with masterminding the disappearance of Poland Catherine had a plan, known as the "Greek Project", for the total dismemberment of the Ottoman Empire. This was originally the brainchild of a lover Prince Potemkin and followed the Treaty of Kuchuk-Kainarjii with the Ottomans in 1774 which strengthened Russian control over the Black Sea and the lower Danube. The project, which depended on the Austrians, did not succeed, but by the end of her reign Catherine had nonetheless acquired the Crimea, Ochakov, and the area between the River Dnestr and Bug from Turkey. In all she expanded the Russian empire by 200,000 square miles.

Catherine began as a liberal and ended as a reactionary. Her mystic and melancholy grandson Alexander I, czar from 1801 to 1825, began and remained an idealist, inconsistent only in the ideals he espoused: first, emancipation of the serfs, then his own enlightened despotism, finally a Holy Alliance of post-Napoleonic European powers to secure "the sacred rights of humanity".

His reign was dominated by his dealings with Napoleon. Russia declared war against France in 1804, but together with Austria was humiliated at Austerlitz in 1805. In 1807 defeat at the Battle of Friedland led to the Treaty of Tilsit, by which the czar promised to join the Continental System (blockade) against England and to recognize the Grand Duchy of Warsaw, in return for French permission to expand at the expense of Turkey and Sweden. Mutual dissatisfaction soon set in, however, culminating in the monumental French invasion of Russia in 1812.

Czar is triumphant in Paris

The Russian campaign was a disaster for Napoleon and a moment of revelation for Alexander: "Napoleon or I, I or Napoleon. We can no longer reign together!" This was belated wisdom, but he made the most of it. Napoleon was forced to retreat in disarray from Moscow and the czar pressed home his advantage by rallying Austria and Prussia to defeat France at the Battle of Leipzig (1813). Alexander triumphantly entered Paris in March 1814 – the first invading sovereign to do so since England's Henry V in 1420 – and beyond question Europe's most powerful ruler. The subsequent Congress of Vienna set the seal on a century of imperial Russian expansion and allowed her to keep her recent acquisitions – Finland, Bessarabia and most of Poland.

Peter the Great had visited the West as an oddity in 1698. Alexander came as its arbiter in 1815. The Congress of Vienna, and the Congress System which it inaugurated, thus marked Russia's emergence as a major Western power. It is a signal irony that as Alexander was posing as a liberator abroad, much remained to be liberated at home. For all the modernisation of the preceding century, he still inherited serfdom from his predecessor and passed it on to his successor. The empire may now have faced West, but the grip of the East remained strong.

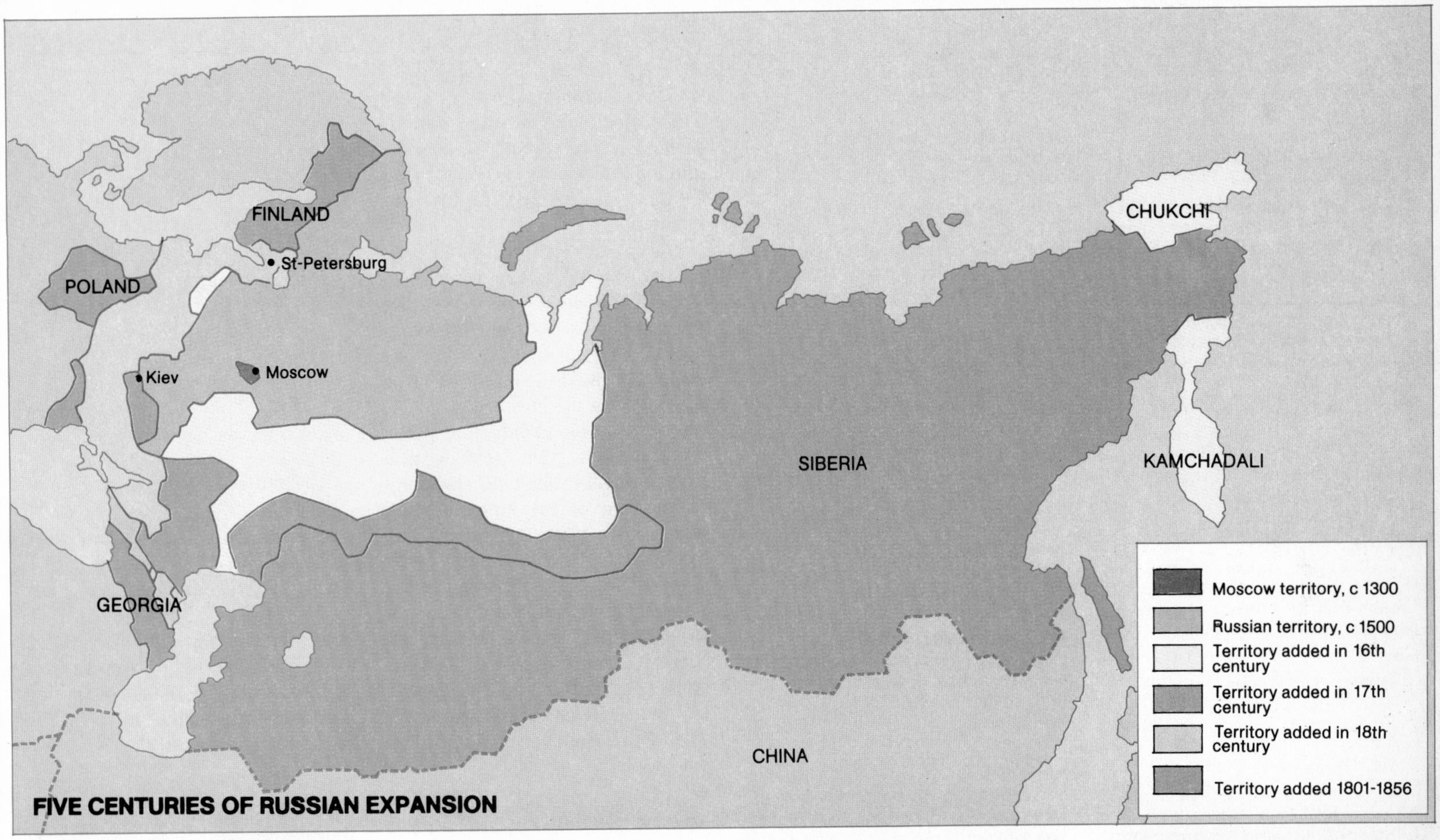

FINLAND

• St-Petersburg

POLAND

• Kiev   • Moscow

GEORGIA

SIBERIA

CHUKCHI

KAMCHADALI

CHINA

▧	Moscow territory, c 1300
▧	Russian territory, c 1500
□	Territory added in 16th century
▨	Territory added in 17th century
▨	Territory added in 18th century
▨	Territory added 1801-1856

FIVE CENTURIES OF RUSSIAN EXPANSION

Peter the Great (1672-1725).

Austerlitz, 1805: Russia and Austria surrender to Napoleon (r., white horse).

Catherine the Great (1729-96).

Alexander I (1777-1825).

Leipzig, 1813: Russia, Austria and Prussia turn the tables on France.

Napoleon (1769-1821).

1811 (1811-1812)

New Orleans, 10 January 1811. An uprising of over 400 slaves is put down. Sixty-six Negroes are either killed in the fighting or executed and their heads strung up along the road to the plantation where the uprising began.

Washington DC, 15 January 1811. In a secret session, Congress plans to annex Spanish East Florida.

USA, 2 February 1811. President Madison sends Britain an ultimatum, demanding that it revoke its orders in council of 1807 which justify British harassment of US shipping.

Briain, 5 February 1811. The Regency Act is passed, authorising George, the prince of Wales, to exercise the powers of regency in the place of his father, George III, who is insane.

Austria, 15 March 1811. The wave of financial speculation due to the Continental System of blockades, and inflation caused by soaring military expenditure, bankrupts the state.

Britain, 10 May 1811. With the country in the grip of economic crisis, the government is forced to adopt paper money as currency.

Virginia, 16 May 1811. Acting in response to instructions calling for the vindication of "the injured honor of our Navy", Commodore John Rodgers of the warship *President* attacks the British sloop *Little Belt* by night, killing nine and wounding 23.

Vienna, May 1811. Ludwig van Beethoven performs his fifth piano concerto, nicknamed *The Emperor*.

Spain, 28 June 1811. While the French commander Massena is defeated by Wellington at Fuentes de Onoro on 3 May, his compatriot Suchet takes the fortress of Tarragona.

Mexico, 30 July 1811. The parish priest Hidalgo, who called for Mexican independence last year, is executed, having been tried by the court of the Inquisition.

Prussia, 14 September 1811. By adopting an edict concerning the regularisation of relations between peasants and the nobility, Prussia abolishes the feudal system.

Europe, 17 October 1811. Prussia and Russia sign a military convention for joint action in the event of an invasion by France.

Washington DC, 4 November 1811. The 12th Congress convenes. It is Republican and dominated by a new breed of nationalistic, expansion-orientated "war-hawks".

Mississippi, 16 December 1811. A catastrophic earthquake hits the Mississippi valley.

Egypt, 1811. The Ottoman sultan concedes supreme authority in Egypt to Mohammed Ali, an Albanian tobacco merchant who entered Ottoman service leading Albanian troops in the war against the French.

Japan, 1811. Following the Russian raids of 1807, the Japanese capture the Russian LieutenantCommander Golovnin and his subordinates and take them to imprisonment in Matsumae.

Prussia, 24 February 1812. France and Prussia sign a military convention by which Prussia grants French troops all the quartering and provisioning facilities it needs on the way to Russia, as well as sending it a corps of 20,000 men.

Austria, 4 March 1812. Napoleon signs a military convention with Metternich similar to that concluded with Prussia. The Austrian corps is to be 30,000 strong.

Venezuela, 12 March 1812. An earthquake wreaks havoc in the capital, Caracas, and other republican territories. Royalist clergy proclaim the disaster as divine vengeance on the revolutionaries.

New Orleans, 4 April 1812. The territory of Orleans becomes the 18th state and will be known as Louisiana.

Finland, 9 April 1812. Russia and Sweden sign a treaty of alliance at Abo. Sweden cedes Finland to Russia and agrees to supply 30,000 men to co-operate with Russian forces. Russia agrees to help Sweden annex Norway.

France, 9 May 1812. Rejecting proposals by the Russian Czar Alexander questioning the policy of the continental blockade, Napoleon breaks relations with Russia.

Germany, 1812. The idealist philosopher Hegel publishes the first volume of his *Science of Logic*.

France, 1812. The naturalist Georges Cuvier publishes the first volume of *Researches on the Bones of Fossil Vertebrates*.

South Africa, 1812. During the fourth Cape Eastern Frontier War, the British under Colonel Graham support the land-hungry Boer ranchers and expel 22,000 Khoisan and Xhosa eastwards across Fish river. They then set up a line of forts along the river.

Mexico, 1812. Worried by the growing independence movement, the viceroy, Venegas, suspends ecclesiastical immunity, requisitions Mexico City University and the convents for quartering troops, and suspends the exemption from military service for students.

Regent replaces Britain's insane monarch

London, 5 February 1811
The prince of Wales was today appointed prince regent and effective king of England as his father, King George III, slipped further into madness.

Under the Regency Act – approved by a special commission because of the king's insanity – the prince regent's powers are severely limited. For the first 12 months he can make no long-lasting changes that the king might object to on his recovery. Consequently, the prince regent cannot grant peerages pensions, or deal in the king's property.

The care of the king has been entrusted to his wife, Queen Charlotte. The 73-year-old monarch, who lost his sight last year and has a history of mental illness, became so chronically depressed after the death of his favourite daughter Amelia last autumn that he was unable to transact official business. The 49-year-old prince regent is

Keeping up with the regent, a dedicated and time-consuming vocation.

the complete opposite of his father, with whom he clashed over his flamboyant lifestyle, his womanising, his excessive habits and his Whig politics.

Followers of "Ned Ludd" smash machines

Nottingham, 1811
They move about in bands at night, masked and sworn to secrecy, smashing up the new machinery which is taking over in the textile industry. Their leader is a mysterious Ned Ludd of Sherwood Forest, who has been likened to the legendary Robin Hood as a friend of the poor and discontented.

The hardships caused by the long war with France have been greatly increased by the new technology, which is displacing the old handicraft methods of producing stockings and lace. The high levels of productivity achieved by the new knitting frames have reduced the demand for labour, so even those craftsmen who keep their jobs suffer wage cuts.

The Luddites are well-organised and have public opinion on their side. They have been reported in action as far north as Yorkshire and Lancashire.

Grimm Brothers collect German folklore

The Young Giant and the Tailor.

Kassel, 1812
A book of folk-tales entitled *Kinder und Hausmarchen* has caused enormous interest in Germany. The tales have been collected mainly in this area by Jakob and Wilhelm Grimm. They contain no fairies, but plenty of magic, enchanted princes and princesses, witches and cruel stepmothers, stupid giants and helpful dwarfs. Some stories are similar to the eight published by Charles Perrault in Paris as *Tales of Mother Goose* in 1797. *Aschputtel* by the Grimms is Perrault's *Cinderella*, but he did not have *Snow-white* or *Rapunzel*.

American troops beat Shawnee Indians

Indiana, 7 November 1811
As European settlers continue to press westwards, a major confrontation with the native Indian people was inevitable. It came today at Tippecanoe where an army of 1,000 soldiers – said to be the equal in quality to the finest in the US – came face with the combined tribes of the Shawnee people.

Rebuffed in territorial demands by the governor, Harrison, the Indian leader, Tecumseh, rode to the south to unite the other tribes. Harrison chose to anticipate the chief and marched into Indian territory. The Shawnees attacked as soldiers slept and battle raged at close range – often hand-to-hand – throughout the night until a series of charges drove the Indians off. Harrison's men have marched on the Indian town of Prophetstown and razed it to the ground. Many believe that Harrison's victory was by no means as decisive as he would care to claim. The Shawnees were beaten, but not vanquished. It is believed that they were inspired by British agents.

US troops bayonet charge Shawnee Indians during the battle of Tippecanoe.

Things happen like this – probably

Paris, France, 1812
The French mathematician Pierre Simon de Laplace, has published a philosophical essay, *A Theoretical Analysis of Probabilities*.

Imagine this game of chance between two players. They each toss a coin. For every head, player A pays player B £1, and vice-versa for every tail. What is the probability that a player will be ruined?

Such questions have obsessed de Laplace for years. He has studied not only games of chance, like dice, cards and roulette wheels, but also the physical world.

Probability, de Laplace asserts, can be applied to the chances of having twins, the drift of smoke from a chimney, the eventual fate of the universe itself.

US declares war on Great Britain

Baltimore, 19 June 1812
American ships sailed from Chesapeake Bay today bearing giant flags proclaiming "Free Trade and Sailors' Rights". The United States of America is at war with its former colonial master, Great Britain. There are several reasons: the first is the frustration felt by the Americans at the trade restrictions imposed by Britain in retaliation for Napoleon's decree declaring Britain to be under blockade. The second is the way in which British ships are stopping American ships and "pressing" alleged British deserters, many of them US seamen, into service with the Royal Navy. Britain's relations with hostile Indians in the northwest of America are another factor.

Egyptian "pasha" destroys Mamelukes

Mohammed Ali's treacherous massacre of the Mameluke rebels in Cairo castle. By ending their threat to his rule, he can modernise Egypt.

Cairo, 1 March 1811
Leaders of the Mameluke dynasty were shot down here today in an act of treachery by Mohammed Ali, Egypt's ruler. Those who remained in their Upper Egypt homeland are being hunted down, and their homes destroyed.

Mohammed Ali, who always saw the Mamelukes as the single greatest threat to his rule, has avoided confrontation for several years, while taking comfort from a continuing feud between the two main houses of the Mamelukes, which sufficiently diverted their energies from taking over the throne.

The Egyptian leader is known for both his subtlety and his ruthlessness. He planned each of his moves. At first he appeared to be offering an olive branch when he invited the Mameluke leaders to a ceremony in Cairo's citadel to invest Ahmed Tusun Pasha, Mohammed Ali's son, as leader of an expedition against the Wahhabis in the Arabian peninsula. But the Egyptian ruler's assassins were waiting for them.

There followed a massacre, as Mohammed Ali's black slaves poured down bullets from the citadel's walls on the Albanian slaves, castrated in boyhood, who once served Egypt as her finest soldiers and now oppress her with their decadence.

Crazed businessman murders British PM

London, 11 May 1812
Towards five o'clock in the evening Spencer Perceval, the prime minister, was passing through the lobby of the House of Commons when a man rushed up brandishing a pistol. He fired one shot. The bullet struck Perceval in the breast and entered his heart. He died soon afterwards.

The assassin, it was learned, is a businessman, John Bellingham, who has been ruined by the war. It seems that for some time he has been besieging government offices vainly seeking redress. Though he is undoubtedly insane, he will be sentenced to death.

John Bellingham shoots Spencer Perceval in the House of Commons.

1812 (1812-1813)

Ottoman Empire, 28 May 1812. The Ottomans sign a peace treaty with Russia at Bucharest whereby Russia acquires Bessarabia (*Romania*) and the Ottoman-Russian border is set along the Pruth river.

Britain, 9 June 1812. Following the assassination of the prime minister, Spencer Perceval, Lord Liverpool forms a new ministry.

USA, 19 June 1812. Prompted by British interference with US shipping and the press-ganging of US sailors, the USA declares war on Britain.

Russia, 24 June 1812. Napoleon, at the head of the *Grand Armee*, crosses the Nieman and begins his invasion of Russia.

Poland, 28 June 1812. Napoleon captures Vilna, the capital of Russian Poland.

London, 29 June 1812. Mrs Sarah Siddons, the queen of the English stage, gives her last performance, as Lady Macbeth.

Sweden, 18 July 1812. Britain signs the treaty of Orebro, making peace with Russia and Sweden.

Spain, 22 July 1812. British forces under the duke of Wellington defeat the French at Salamanca.

Venezuela, 26 July 1812. Francisco Miranda the commander of the Venezuelan revolutionary army, surrenders to the Spanish, who have regained control of the country after the creation of an independent *junta* in 1810.

Spain, 12 August 1812. The British commander Wellington occupies Madrid, forcing Joseph Bonaparte, the king of Spain, to abandon the city.

Russia, 18 August 1812. Napoleon enters Smolensk.

North America, August 1812. General William Hull, the governor of Michigan, loses his battle plans to the British, who go on to capture Fort Detroit. Hull's campaign was intended as the first of two pincer movements designed to knock Canada out of the war.

Russia, 14 September 1812. Having forced the Russians to retreat after the battle of Borodino earlier in the month, Napoleon enters Moscow, which has been set on fire by its fleeing inhabitants.

Canada, 16 October 1812. British forces defeat US forces at Queenstown, near Niagara Falls. The Americans were attempting to cross the Niagara river and eliminate Canada from the war.

Russia, 18 October 1812. Murat, the king of the Two Sicilies, commanding Napoleon's cavalry, is defeated by Russia at Vinkovo.

Russia, 19 October 1812. After failing to persuade Czar Alexander to come to terms, Napoleon begins a retreat from Moscow.

Spain, 2 November 1812. Joseph Bonaparte reoccupies Madrid after the British fail to take Burgos, to which they laid siege in September.

Canada, 23 November 1812. Demoralised by a tactical error which resulted in two of their own columns fighting each other, the US forces abandon their Canada campaign and retreat to winter quarters in New York state.

Russia, 28 November 1812. The survivors of the *Grand Armee* cross the Beresina.

USA, 2 December 1812. James Madison is re-elected president.

Russia, 5 December 1812. Napoleon decides to return to Paris to put down a rumoured plot against him and raise a new army.

Prussia, 20 December 1812. The remnants of the *Grand Armee* reach eastern Prussia.

Lithuania, 30 December 1812. Having deserted the French after the catastrophic invasion of Russia, Prussia signs a treaty of neutrality with Russia at Tauroggen.

East Africa, 1812. The people of Lamu defeat the army of Mombasa and Pate at the battle of Shela. Lamu becomes independent of Pate.

Germany, 1812. The folklore experts Jakob and Wilhelm Grimm publish a volume of *Fairy Tales*.

England, 1812. Lord Byron publishes his *Childe Harold's Pilgrimage*, a poetical account of the author's grand tour of Europe.

Canada, 22 January 1813. British forces under Henry Proctor defeat a US contingent planning an attack on Fort Detroit.

France, 25 January 1813. Napoleon forces Pope Pius VII to sign a second concordat and sanction the 1809 French annexation of the papal states.

Austria, 30 January 1813. Austria signs an armistice treaty with Russia.

Prussia, 3 February 1813. Frederick William III of Prussia calls all his people to arms.

Poland, 18 February 1813. Czar Alexander enters Warsaw at the head of his army.

South America, 24 February 1813. The British ship *Peacock* is sunk by an American ship off the coast of Guiana.

Prussia, 27 February 1813. Frederick William III signs an offensive and defensive alliance with Russia at Kalisz.

Wellington captures Madrid for Britain

Madrid, 12 August 1812
Viscount Wellington is winning significant victories against the French and today entered Madrid with 28,000 troops to be greeted with great enthusiasm. Joseph Bonaparte, Napoleon's brother, has evacuated the Spanish capital, and everywhere in Spain guerrilla forces have taken new heart.

The British general's offensive to clear the Peninsula has gone on for more than a year. At Salamanca last month, a mass of British cavalry fell upon 40,000 French troops who were beaten in some 40 minutes. "There was no mistake," Wellington said. "Everything went as it should. There never was an army so beaten in so short a time."

The ripples of this first British and Spanish victory in open battle continue spreading. In Britain criticism of the long war is stilled. Wel-

The Peninsular War, seen in all its horrors, through the eyes of Goya.

lington may still find it impossible to corner the French army in the north of Spain. But the pattern of the campaign is now of a French withdrawal northwards, which would free much of southern Spain.

Lord Elgin's Greek marbles go on display

Part of the Parthenon frieze which was taken to Britain by Lord Elgin.

London, 1812
The British public is to be allowed to see the controversial Greek antiquities shipped back from Athens over the past decade by the Scottish peer Lord Elgin. With the arrival this year of the last 80 cases, the collection, which has been assembled in a private house in Park Lane, is now complete.

The removal of the marbles – priceless relics of the Parthenon and other ancient Hellenic monu-

ments – has cost Lord Elgin his reputation the former British ambassador to the Ottoman empire is now branded a vandal and a thief.

In his defence the art-loving peer claims that the Turkish authorities allowed him to remove parts of the monuments although he originally only sought permission for his draughtsmen to take casts and make drawings. Only when he saw the damage done by the Turks did he decided to remove them, he says.

Russian winter drives out Napoleon

Authoress exposes pride and prejudice

Russia, 29 November 1812

The remnants of Napoleon's *Grand Armee* crossed the Beresina yesterday with the rearguard holding off the Russians. Fifty thousand men got across before General Eble set fire to the two makeshift bridges which he had thrown across the river. He delayed destroying the bridges for two hours after his deadline, but thousands of stragglers were left behind to be killed or captured. The great army which crossed into Russia on 24 June is no more. Today its survivors face a new peril: the Russian winter.

Marshal Ney wrote a hurried letter to his wife in which he described the horrors of the French retreat. "The army marches covered in great snowflakes. The stragglers fall to the lances of the Cossacks. As for me, I cover the retreat. Behind files the army in broken ranks. It is a mob without purpose, famished, feverish.

"The Grand Army is surrounded by the Russians on the banks of the Beresina. It is necessary to construct a bridge. At the order of General Eble three hundred sappers hurl themselves into the icy water with a sublime devotion.

"The crossing begins and the Russian shells fall into the middle of this crowded mass, jostling and pushing – a dreadful sight. General Famine and General Winter, rather than the Russian bullets, have conquered the Grand Army."

The disintegration of the army started the moment that Napoleon ordered the retreat from burnt-out Moscow on 19 October. His army was still 100,000 strong, but it was encumbered by its loot, its sick and wounded – and its 600 guns.

There is no food. Bands of Cossacks and partisans cut down fora-

Invading Russia, the eternal problem, seen by cartoonist George Cruikshank.

The burning of Moscow by Russian patriotic incendiaries in September 1812.

ging parties unprotected by the cavalry whose horses have died. Thousands of men are killed in running battles. Ney's rearguard has 800 men left out of 8,000. Now men are staggering through the snow, dying where they fall. Only Napoleon still

eats well. He always has white bread, beef and mutton, and rice and beans or lentils, his favourite vegetables. He has Chambertin to drink and his linen is fresh. Even so, not one murmur is heard against him from the troops.

London, 29 January 1813

A new novel "by a Lady" entitled *Pride and Prejudice* (Egerton, 18 shillings) is attracting the attention of discriminating readers who believe it to be the work of the same Lady as *Sense and Sensibility*, published two years ago. Reviewers call it "a blend of instruction and moral entertainment".

It is the story of Elizabeth Bennet, one of the many daughters of a foolish, husband-hunting mother, and her gradual admission of love for the haughty, aristocratic Mr Darcy. The insight and tart precision of the character-drawing, especially of foolish or disagreeable people, such as Lady Catherine de Bourgh and the toady Mr Collins, cause some to call the nameless author the pioneer of "the modern novel", though others find her tame compared to romantic melodrama.

Some profess to know that the author is a spinster, Jane Austen, who lives in Hampshire.

Jane Austen, the 38-year-old who is said to be the anonymous author.

Russia and the Ottomans agree treaty

Bucharest, 28 May 1812

A peace of sorts has been reached in the six-year on-again, off-again war between Russia and the Ottoman. The treaty was signed here today after mediation by the British envoy, Stratford Canning.

The Russians had for years been clawing at the Ottoman empire's frontiers in Anatolia, but then in

1806, alarmed by growing French influence in the Balkans, they invaded the Rumanian principalities. They were not, however, left free to exploit their gains. Hearing of Napoleon's plans to invade Russia, Moscow hastily came to terms with the Ottomans, retaining Bessarabia, but surrendering the Principalities and Serbia.

Argentina fails to spread revolution

Buenos Airies, Argentina, 1812

Argentina has failed to spread its revolution to Uruguay, Paraguay and Bolivia. An army under Manuel Belgrano sent to liberate Paraguay has been defeated.

A Spanish colony since the 16th century, the Argentinians gained national confidence in 1806 and 1807 when they drove two British

expeditions out of the country. In 1810 the country refused to accept Napoleon's brother, Joseph Bonaparte, as king of Spain, and established a junta, dominated by Mariano Moreno and Manuel Belgrano. Morena is now dead and Belgrano defeated. For Argentinia's revolutionaries, who aim for a free continent, it is a bitter blow.

1813 ⇒

Sweden, 3 March. Britain signs a treaty with Sweden guaranteeing not to oppose the union of Norway with Sweden. Under the treaty Britain pays Sweden a subsidy in return for its providing the allies with an army of 30,000 men commanded by the regent, Prince Bernadotte.

Germany, 4 March. The Russians reach Berlin. The French garrison evacuates the city without a fight.

Germany, 18 March. Russian troops occupy Hamburg and, on the 27 March Dresden, the capital of Saxony.

Rome, 24 March. Pope Pius VII revokes the concordat signed with Napoleon in January at Fontainebleau.

Prussia, 27 March. King Frederick William III declares war on France.

North America, 15 April. US troops under James Wilkinson seize the Spanish-held city of Mobile (*in Alabama*).

Canada, 27 April. US troops capture York (*now Toronto*), the seat of government in Ontario, from the British.

Germany, 2 May. Napoleon defeats a Russian and Prussian army at Grossgorschen near Lutzen.

USA, 9 May. US troops under William Harrison break a ten-day British siege of Fort Meigs in Ohio.

Germany, 18 May. Swedish troops land in Pomerania.

Paris, 20 May. Panic breaks out on the stock exchange.

Germany, 20 May. Napoleon engages the allies at Bautzen.

USA, 27 May. US troops under Winfield Scott take control of Lake Ontario after dislodging the British from three forts in the area.

Germany, 4 June. Worn out by recent defeats, the allies sign a 40-day armistice with Napoleon at Pleischwitz. Despite heavy losses, Napoleon's troops have succeed in pushing the allied armies back to Silesia.

Spain, 12 June. Madrid is evacuated by the French.

Germany, 15 June. At Reichenbach, Britain signs conventions with Prussia and Russia, establishing a new coalition.

Spain, 21 June. French forces under Jourdan are defeated by the British under Wellington at the battle of Vittoria. Joseph Bonaparte, the king of Spain, flees to France.

Germany, 27 June. Russia, Prussia and Austria sign the treaty of Reichenbach, agreeing that the duchy of Warsaw should be abolished, the Illyrian provinces restored to Austria and French conquests in northern Germany relinquished. If France refuses to accept these terms, Austria will declare war.

India, 1 July. The East India Company's monopoly of trade in India is abolished.

Prague, 15 July. Representatives of Napoleon and the allies meet in Prague to discuss peace.

Austria, 12 August. Austria declares war on France.

Britain, 14 August. The US ship *Argus*, which has captured 27 ships in the Channel over the past few months, is taken and boarded by the British.

Germany, 17 August. Prussia, Russia and Sweden sign the protocol of Trachenberg, agreeing on an offensive against Napoleon.

Ottoman Empire, August. Taking advantage of the war in Europe, the Ottoman forces occupy Serbia and destroy the forces of Karageorges, the Serbian independence leader.

South America, August. While the Spanish are busy reconquering Chile, Simon Bolivar reoccupies Venezuela and its capital, Caracas.

Germany, 23 August. French forces under Oudinot are defeated at Gross-Beeren by the Swedes led by Prince Bernadotte.

Germany, 27 August. Napoleon defeats the main allied army under Schwarzenberg at Dresden.

Germany, 29 August. French forces under Macdonald are defeated by Blucher at Katzbach.

North America, 30 August. In revenge for white encroachment on their land, Creek Indians raid Fort Mims (*in Alabama*) and massacre over 500 whites.

Germany, 30 August. French forces under Vandamme are defeated by the allies at Kulm.

South Africa. A Griqua republic is proclaimed at Klaarwater (*Griquatown*) on the north side of the Orange river. The Griqua are people of Khoisan and Boer ancestry, who settled as horsemen, ranchers and hunters north of Cape Colony.

Italy. Gioacchino Rossini's opera *Tancred* opens in Venice to great acclaim.

England. Eight editions of *The Giaour*, a poem by Lord Byron, are sold out in a year.

Europe is now Napoleon's family business

Paris

Napoleon may be a great general and ruler of the "Grand Empire" but he is still a Corsican at heart and in family matters he behaves like one. His brothers and sisters expect to share in his good fortune and he has not disappointed them. He has loaded them with honours and turned the ruling of Europe into a family business.

He made his elder brother, Joseph, king of Naples in 1806 and, although Joseph proved highly inefficient, made him king of Spain instead two years later. The crown of Naples was simply transferred to Marshal Murat who had married Napoleon's sister, Caroline.

Another brother, Louis, was made king of Holland in 1806 after reluctantly marrying Hortense Beauharnais, Josephine's daughter by her first husband. But he only lasted for four years, Napoleon forcing him to abdicate when he objected to the ruinous effect of the Continental System (forbidding trade with Britain) on Holland.

Jerome, the youngest brother, was made king of Westphalia in 1807 and has pretensions to a military career. Only Lucien of the brothers has no title. He fled from Napoleon and is interned in England. Elisa, the most intelligent of the Bonaparte sisters, married Felix Bacciochi, an infantry captain, and was made princess of Lucca and Piombino in 1805 and duchess of Tuscany in 1809. Napoleon, it seems, is creating his own dynasty. But how long will it last?

Caroline Murat, the queen of Naples (left) and Elisa Bonaparte, (right), sister of Napoleon.

Lucien Bonaparte (left), and Joseph Bonaparte, the king of Spain (right), Napoleon's brothers.

Imperial ties: Jerome Bonaparte (left) and Louis Bonaparte (right).

James Gillray's Napoleon: a "little Corsican gardener" planting his garden.

Britain moves to curb the power of the East India Company

Calcutta, India

As the expansionist policy of Lord Wellesley is brought to a halt, the British government has drastically curtailed the powers of the East India Company and its *nabobs*, ending their monopoly of trade.

Reform is long overdue. The Company's policies are confusing and contradictory. In the south, Sir Thomas Munro is deliberately bypassing the indigenous aristocracy to better the lot of the cultivators. In the west, Mountstuart Elphinstone is strengthening the aristocracy and rejecting the "levelling" tendencies of Munro. In the north, the landlords are permitted to exploit the peasants at their will. Everywhere the peasants, unable to pay taxes with cash, are taking out mortgages on their land which they can never repay, creating a new landless class. Worse, the Company's treaties with one native prince after another, stationing troops in the prince's domains, are institutionalising misrule.

The last days of the nabobs, the English who made their fortune in India.

Italy trying to wriggle out from under the imperial thumb

Italy

There is turmoil throughout the country as the Italians attempt to escape from the collapsing "Grand Empire" of Napoleon. Austria, once more allied with Prussia, is threatening to invade, while the forces of Europe gather for a climactic battle in Germany.

The Italians are not inclined to die for Napoleon any more. They fought bravely in Russia, and less than one in eight survived the horrors of the retreat from Moscow.

Economically, the country is groaning under the system of tariffs imposed by the French. Imports of machinery have been discouraged so that Italy cannot compete with French manufacturers and serves only as a supplier of food.

The blockade has had a devastating effect on the ports. Genoa has been ruined. Milan is being swept by a wave of bankruptcies. And all the time the kingdom has to contribute two and a half million *lire* a month to the empire. As the war returns to Italian soil so the protests of the businessmen grow louder.

The church also has a quarrel with Napoleon for, despite his at-

A village in Italy, by Gianbattista Cimaroli: ruins, peasants and cattle.

tempts to appease the clerics, they will not forgive him for abducting the pope from Rome.

Then there is Marshal Murat, the king of Naples, the dashing cavalryman who is married to Napoleon's sister, Caroline. He is with Napoleon in Germany, but the emperor does not trust him – and with good cause, for he has already tried to make a deal with the allies to preserve his kingdom.

Above all there is the rising tide of nationalism and secret societies such as the *Carbonari* who are fighting for Italy's independence.

Wellington lances Napoleon's dream of Spanish glory

Spain, July

After five years of bloody conflict the Peninsular War appears to be over with the beaten French army continuing to retreat across the Pyrenees. This is the end of Napoleon's "Grand Design". The emperor's "Spanish ulcer" – Lord Wellington's military skill and constant guerrilla activity – has reversed his great achievements.

Wellington, the Anglo-Irish aristocrat who learned his skills in India, tied down vastly superior French forces. After victories he has often retreated, compelling the badly-mauled French to stagger along in pursuit until they finally arrived once again in front of care-

Lord Wellington: his soldiers referred to him as "Old Nosey".

fully prepared and disciplined defences. Wellington has been coordinating the activities of some 200,000 British and Spanish troops extending from Catalonia through central Spain to the Portuguese border. Wellington has benefitted from Spanish priests supplying him with intelligence about the French army. He said: "The French never did or said a single thing I did not know, and they never suspected it."

Thus last month he cornered the French at Vittoria. The enormous booty included five million dollars, of which only about $100,000 has reached Wellington's military chest. The campaign has a catastrophe for Napoleon, and now he faces a grand European alliance.

1813 (1813-1814)

Germany, 6 September 1813. While attempting to take Berlin, French forces under Marshal Ney are defeated by the Prussians under Bulow at Dennewitz.

Germany, 9 September 1813. Russia, Prussia and Austria sign the treaty of Teplitz, an alliance guaranteeing mutual assistance against Napoleon.

Canada, 10 September 1813. The British fleet on Lake Erie is destroyed by American warships.

Germany, 3 October 1813. Prussian troops cross the Elbe.

China, 8 October 1813. With the help of palace eunuchs, members of the millennial religious sects calling themselves the Eight Trigrams are thwarted in their attempt to seize the Forbidden City in Beijing. This violence coincides with disturbances in Shandong and Henan by associated sectarians.

France, 8 October 1813. Having liberated Spain from French occupation, British troops under Wellington invade southern France.

Germany, 8 October 1813. By the treaty of Ried, signed by Austria and Bavaria, Bavaria withdraws from the Confederation of the Rhine and joins the allies against Napoleon.

Germany, 19 October 1813. After defeating Napoleon in a three-day battle near Leipzig, the allies storm Leipzig, capturing the king of Saxony and forcing the king of Westphalia to flee.

Austria, October 1813. Driven out of Serbia by the Ottomans, Karageorges, the leader of the Serbian independence movement, takes refuge in Austria, where he is imprisoned.

Ottoman Empire, 28 October 1813. British troops occupy Ragusa (Dubrovnik).

North America, 3 November 1813. In retaliation for the attack by Creek Indians on Fort Mims in August, US troops destroy the Indian village of Tallushatchee in the Mississippi valley.

Mexico, 6 November 1813. Jose Maria Morelos proclaims Mexican independence from Spain at the congress of Chilpancingo.

Florida, 9 November 1813. US troops under Andrew Jackson kill almost 300 Indians in an attack on the village of Talladega.

Paris, 15 November 1813. Napoleon returns to Paris after seeing his meagre troops cross the Rhine between 2 and 4 November. Of an army 450,000-strong at the start of the autumn, there are no more than 50,000 survivors.

Netherlands, 15 November 1813. The Dutch rise up against the French, expelling French officials.

USA, 16 November 1813. The British announce a blockade of Long Island Sound, leaving only the New England coast open to shipping.

Germany, 1 December 1813. Napoleon rejects the peace terms offered by the allies at Frankfurt on 9 November.

France, 11 December 1813. By the treaty of Valencay, Napoleon recognises his prisoner Ferdinand VII as king of Spain and releases him.

USA, 17 December 1813. An embargo banning trade with Britain comes into effect. It is aimed at New England merchants who have been supplying the British in Canada.

North America, 23 December 1813. US troops under Ferdinand Claiborne take Escanachaha, the so-called "holy city" of the Creek nation, driving the death toll higher in the Indian war.

France, 31 December 1813. During New Year's Eve the Prussian forces under Blucher cross the Rhine, beginning the allied invasion of France.

Britain, 31 December 1813. The foreign secretary, Lord Castlereagh, is sent to Germany with full powers to give assistance to the allies.

Russia, 1813. Under the terms of the treaty of Gulistan, Russia receives control of the Caucasus region from Persia.

Colombia, 1813. Colombia declares itself independent of Spain.

Italy, 11 January 1814. The king of Naples, Joachim Murat, enters into an alliance with the Austrians – whom last year he crushed at Dresden – and decides to occupy central Italy.

Scandinavia, 14 January 1814. Under the treaty of Kiel, Bernadotte, the prince regent of Sweden and marshal of the northern armies against Napoleon, forces Denmark to surrender Norway to him.

France, 1 February 1814. After defeating Blucher at Brienne on 29 January, Napoleon is defeated at La Rothiere.

France, 14 February 1814. Napoleon wins his fourth victory in four days over Blucher, at Vauchamps.

France, February 1814. At the conference of Chatillon-sur-Seine, the allies offer to return France to its 1792 borders, but Napoleon rejects the proposal.

British outgunned by the US Navy

Lake Erie, USA, 10 September 1813
The Royal Navy suffered a humiliating defeat here today when a British fleet struck its colours in surrender to US warships after a long and bloody battle. British victory looked certain when the US flagship, *Lawrence*, hauled down her ensign, but two Royal Naval frigates, *Detroit* and *Queen Charlotte*, collided and became entangled, giving the Americans an easy target. With his masts shot away, it was the British captain's turn to admit defeat.

There will be grim faces when the news reaches the Admiralty in London. The Royal Navy has suffered a string of defeats in single ship actions, with superior US gunnery and seamanship playing a decisive role. The roles were reversed, however, off Cape Anne where *HMS Shannon* beat the equally matched *USS Chesapeake* in a classic duel at sea.

US Navy Commander Oliver Perry directs the battle from a rowing-boat.

Exiled hero fights way back to Venezuela

Caracas, October 1813
After leading 500 guerrillas on a forced march through jungle and swamps, the Venezuelan patriot Simon Bolivar has entered Caracas in triumph. With the flight of the Spanish garrison, Bolivar is hailed as "the Liberator" by the city where he was born 30 years ago.

The son of an affluent family, he studied revolution in Europe before practising it at home. Exiled to neighbouring Colombia after a failed coup last year, he rapidly became a general. As his latest success demonstrates, he is a master of irregular warfare.

What is still uncertain is how completely he will consolidate his hold on Venezuela. A Spanish attempt to restore the *status quo* is a near-certainty. If it should happen Venezuelan national solidarity would be severely tested.

Asteroid's orbit is calculated success

Germany, 1813
Karl Friedrich Gauss, one of the greatest mathematicians of all time, has shown his gratitude to the duke of Brunswick for giving him financial support for his higher studies by performing a remarkable calculation which has defeated all the other mathematicians of the day.

Astronomers had discovered the asteroid *Ceres* as it approached the sun, but had been quite unable to work out its orbit. Using his method of calculation, and only three observations, Gauss has been able to describe the asteroid's orbit and enable astronomers to locate *Ceres* with complete accuracy.

Allies defeat Napoleon

The battle of Leipzig, where Napoleon lost 60,000 out of his 190,000 men.

Leipzig, Saxony, 19 October 1813
Napoleon has been totally defeated in a battle which has raged for three days of slaughter. The French, 190,000 strong, faced 320,000 Russians, Prussians, Swedes and Austrians financed by Britain.

Despite the numerical advantage of the allies in this "Battle of the Nations", Napoleon had the best of the first day's fighting, but he lost too many men and waited in vain for the reinforcements to launch a decisive attack. He could have retreated then and saved his army, but chose to stay and fight it out. The turning point came when the Saxons, fighting as allies of the French, changed sides in the middle of the battle.

Yesterday the French were driven off the battlefield into the city. There was only one way of escape, the Lindenau bridge. The survivors poured across this today until it was blown up, the rearguard sacrificed. In the end it was a rout and Napoleon lost 60,000 men. The question being asked now is: how long can he continue the struggle?

Mexico declares it is independent

Chilpancingo, Mexico, 1814
After 300 years of smouldering resentment, Mexican nationalists have asserted their country's independence from Spain as Spain itself is relieved from domination by Napoleonic France. Although the new Spanish king, Ferdinand – who has been installed in place of Bonaparte's brother, Joseph – is acting like a dictator, his small army has failed to quell the Mexican insurgents.

Four years ago a priest, Father Miguel Hidalgo y Costilla, preached revolution to Indian peasants and fomented a wave of violence. Hidalgo was executed a year later, but his death inspired a new generation of Mexican patriots. Their new constitution creates a republic and abolishes class distinction as well as slavery.

House of Orange returns to Holland

The Hague, 2 December 1813
Orange cockades were everywhere to be seen today as the rule of the House of Orange was formally restored to this country. The prince, who landed at Scheveningen two days ago, was proclaimed William I, sovereign prince of the Netherlands. The end of French rule became inevitable after Napoleon's defeat at Leipzig. On 12 November Cossack troops moved in and the French military and officials began to leave. The people of Amsterdam revolted on 15 November and formed a provisional government, headed by a former official of King Louis Napoleon. Two days later the revolt spread here and the leaders, who had stood aloof from French rule, called for a return of the Orange dynasty. The prince was waiting in the wings.

Marquis dies but his "sadism" lives on

France, 2 December 1814
Donatien-Alphonse-Francois, the marquis de Sade, died today, still an inmate of the asylum at Charenton where he has been held for the past 13 years. He was 74 a philosopher, and erotic novelist, whose taste for pain as the basis of sexual pleasure will link his name with this particular sexual perversion.

Debt-ridden and dogged by scandals that arose from satisfying his sexual tastes, de Sade's life was typical of many aristocrats of the *ancien regime*. It was his writings that raised him above the commonplace debauchee.

His novels, a mix of philosophy and pornography, always emphasising the cruel side of sex, include *Justine* (1791) and *Juliette* (1798). Most notorious of all is thee *120 Days of Sodom* (1784), a catalogue of sexual excess, written while he was jailed in the Bastille. De Sade

The inventor of sadism: a later view.

had no illusions as to his character. All his portraits have been destroyed and in his will he hopes that "my memory will be effaced from the mind of men".

"Puffing billy" steams on smooth rails

Yorkshire, England, 1814
George Stephenson, the engineer, has just built his first locomotive at the Killingworth colliery in Yorkshire. The train is superior to others in many respects. Unlike existing colliery trains, it does not run on notched rails that engage in toothed wheels. Stephenson's rails are smooth, but they are effective even when the coal is being hauled up and down gradients.

It is more powerful than the existing engines designed by Richard Trevithick and John Blenkinsop. It had pulled a load of 30 tons of coal up an incline of one in 450 at a steady speed of four miles per hour. Its inventor is now working on improvements in the engine and boiler springing.

Stephenson has a vision of a country criss-crossed by these new "iron horses", or "puffing billies" as this first train is known, and is looking for financial support.

George Stephenson's "puffing billy", or "iron horse"; a later print.

1814 ⇒

France, 9 March. The four allied powers – Austria, Russia, Prussia and Britain – sign the treaty of Chaumont, negotiated by the British foreign secretary, Lord Castlereagh. Under the terms of the treaty, each ally will supply 150,000 troops to defeat Napoleon and Britain will provide a subsidy of £ 5 million.

France, 10 March. Napoleon is defeated by a combined allied army at the battle of Laon.

France, 12 March. Led by the duke of Wellington, British forces occupy Bordeaux.

France, 21 March. After failing to get the better of Blucher's troops, Napoleon is defeated at Arcis-sur-Aube by an Austrian army under the command of Schwarzenberg.

North America, 27 March. US troops under General Andrew Jackson inflict a crushing defeat on the Creek Indians at Horseshoe Bend (*in eastern Alabama*). More than 800 Indians lose their lives in the battle.

Paris, 30 March. Paris – encircled, poorly defended and flooded with refugees – surrenders to the allies.

Paris, 31 March. Czar Alexander and Frederick William III of Prussia enter Paris in triumph.

France, 6 April. Granted the sovereignty of the island of Elba and a pension from the French government, Napoleon abdicates at Fontainebleau. He is allowed to retain the title of emperor.

USA, 14 April. The Embargo and Non-Importation Acts, banning trade with Britain, are repealed.

Italy, 28 April. After rising up against the French earlier in the month, Milan is occupied by the Austrians.

France, 2 May. Having disembarked at Calais on 24 April, Louis XVIII issues the proclamation of St Ouen, making known his intention to govern as a constitutional monarch.

Paris, 3 May. Louis XVIII enters Paris.

Mediterranean, 4 May. Napoleon disembarks at Portoferraio on the island of Elba.

Spain, 4 May. King Ferdinand VII abolishes the 1812 constitution.

Norway, 17 May. A new constitution is adopted, providing for a single-chamber national assembly and denying the king an absolute veto and the right to dissolve parliament.

Italy, 20 May. Victor Emmanuel, the king of Piedmont, enters Turin.

Rome, 24 May. Pope Pius VII, who was exiled to France after Napoleon's annexation of the papal states, returns to Rome.

Paris, 30 May. The treaty of Paris returns France to its 1792 frontiers. It is agreed that the final settlement of Europe will be made at a congress to be held in Vienna.

France, 14 June. Louis XVIII grants a constitutional charter providing for an hereditary monarch, a chamber of peers nominated by the king and a chamber of elected deputies.

Canada, 5 July. US troops under Jacob Brown defeat a superior British force at Chippewa.

USA, 22 July. Five Indian tribes in Ohio make peace with the USA and declare war on the British.

Britain, 25 July. The engineer George Stephenson tests his first steam locomotive, at Killingworth colliery.

Canada, 25 July. British and US forces fight each other to a standstill at Lundy's Lane, in one of the bloodiest battles of their war which broke out in 1812.

North America, 9 August. By the treaty of Fort Jackson, ending the Creek war, the Creek Indians are forced to cede 23 million acres (*half of Alabama and part of southern Georgia*) to the whites.

USA, 25 August. The British capture and burn down much of Washington, DC, including the White House, causing President Madison to flee.

USA, 11 September. US forces led by Thomas Macdonough rout the British fleet on Lake Champlain.

USA, 13 September. British troops make an unsuccessful attack on Baltimore. During the battle, the American Francis Scott Key composes a patriotic song entitled "The Star-Spangled Banner".

New York City, October. *Fulton*, the world's first steam-engined warship, is launched.

Vienna, 1 November. A congress composed of representatives of almost all the countries of Europe opens.

Canada, 5 November. Having decided to abandon the Niagara frontier, the Americans blow up Fort Erie.

Florida, 7 November. Andrew Jackson attacks and captures Pensacola, defeating the Spanish and driving out a British force.

British army burns down the White House

Revenge for 1776: a British cartoon on the sack of Washington.

Washington, DC, 25 August

This fine capital city is a smouldering ruin tonight, burned by a British invading army which landed in Chesapeake Bay six days ago and marched unopposed to the banks of the Potomac river. The White House is a charred hulk, the House of Representatives and the Library of Congress totally gutted, as are many other fine buildings.

With only 500 militiamen to defend Washington against 4,000 infantrymen – fresh from campaigning in France – the militiamen had little chance. They assembled across the Bladensburg Bridge over the River Potomac, but fled in the face of a British assault supported by volleys of Gongrave rockets. President Madison, who had placed far too much confidence in the abilities of both his militia and himself, was forced to flee, but his wife, Dolly, watched the capital blazing from the safety of a friend's house in Virginia. She has rescued the life-sized portrait of George Washington and the original Declaration of Independence.

Napoleon's fall allows writer back

Paris

Now that Napoleon has abdicated, the political thinker and writer Germaine de Stael is back in Paris. The emperor banned her from her native France in 1804 after she turned her salon into a centre of opposition against him. As First Consul, in 1799, he snubbed the erudite de Stael by discarding her advice and opinions.

He could not stomach her view that ideas and feelings are inseparable and was infuriated by her romantic novelel *Delphine*. She was exiled at the age of 38, and spent some of the time under house arrest at her estate by Lake Geneva. There she always kept her salon open to Europeans wishing to plot against the emperor.

"Australia" is new name for new land

Sydney, Australia, 18 July

The Great Southern Continent has been given a name, *Terra Australis*. The man who named it, Captain Matthew Flinders, died today, 24 hours after the publication of his book *A Voyage to Terra Australis*.

Flinders, born in 1774, went to seas after reading *Robinson Crusoe* when young. In September 1795 he arrived at Port Jackson on the *Reliance*, and with the ship's surgeon, George Bass, began the first major survey of the continent's coast, continuing it in 1799 in command of first the *Norfolk* and then the *Investigator*. Captured by the French, he spent seven years as a prisoner in Mauritius. It broke his health, and it is a miracle that he lived long enough to complete his book.

Allies enter Paris and oust Napoleon

Turncoat diplomat finds new role

Paris, 6 April
Napoleon, faced with an impossible military situation and a revolt by his war-weary marshals, abdicated today at Fontainebleau Palace with the bitter comment: "You wish for repose. All right, you shall have it."

His downfall has been inevitable since his crushing defeat at the "Battle of the Nations" six months ago. He employed his military genius to inflict a series of stinging reverses on the allies as they advanced into France, but with each battle his army grew weaker. On 11 March he wrote: "The Young Guard melts away like snow." Murat abandoned him. Talleyrand betrayed him. His brother, Joseph, tried to organise an address from the Council of State and the National Guard in favour of peace.

Napoleon refused the first allied peace proposals, which would have allowed France to retain her "natural boundaries", sure that he could still defeat them. But as they advanced to Paris so their terms hardened. By 19 March they were demanding that France must accept its "prerevolutionary limits", a price which would have wiped out all the gains the revolution had made. Napoleon refused and decided on one last gamble. He left Paris uncovered, certain that its garrison and people could hold out for months, and withdrew to the east where he planned to attack the allied lines of communication, thus forcing them to withdraw. Unwisely he wrote about this plan to his wife. The courier carrying the letter to her was captured.

The first reaction of the allies on reading this letter was to pursue Napoleon, but Czar Alexander persuaded them to hurry on to Paris where Marmont and Mortier had

Russians in Paris, collecting souveniers of their travels in western Europe.

The Grand Army bids farewell to the "little corporal" who brought it glory.

barely 20,000 men to guard the capital. The French were beaten at La Fere-Champenoise on 25 March, and five days later fought the last battle at Montmartre. That night Marmont surrendered Paris. Napoleon talked of marching on the capital, but two days ago Ney told him: "The army will not march". Napoleon made one last effort to have his son recognised as his successor. But the victors refused. Tonight they have it; the senate has voted for the recall of Louis XVIII and Napoleon has been banished to Elba.

Paris
The elegant, crippled, devious Talleyrand has been made foreign minister by the restored Louis XVIII as a reward for his successful negotiations with the victorious allies. He is thus restored to the position in which he served Napoleon.

Napoleon had no illusions about him. On one famous occasion when Napoleon got wind of a plot between Talleyrand and Fouche, the police minister, the emperor berated him for half an hour, calling him a thief, a coward and a traitor.

Talleyrand remained impassive and the infuriated "Boney" taunted him with his lameness and his wife's affairs. Then, losing all control, he told him that he was nothing but "shit in a silk stocking". Talleyrand did nothing. When asked why, languidly replied: "I did think of doing so, but I was too lazy." He was, in fact, biding his time, and remained at Napoleon's court in the empty position of vice-grand elector.

He was already convinced that Napoleon was over-ambitious and destined for disaster, and made little secret of the fact that he was preparing for that day. His opportunity came with the allies' advance on Paris. It was he who persuaded the senate to depose the emperor. It was at his house that the czar stayed. And it was he who persuaded the czar to reinstate the Bourbons on the French throne.

The Treaty of Paris rolls back French border to pre-war lines

Paris, 30 May
Talleyrand has obtained relatively favourable peace terms from the victorious allies. In the Treaty of Paris signed today, France, as expected, must generally return to the frontiers of 1792 but will be allowed to keep certain areas of Belgium, Savoy, Alsace and the Rhineland. Britain will keep Malta, but will return

all France's captured overseas territories except Tobago, St Lucia and Mauritius. France will pay no indemnity and suffer no humiliation.

The treaty consists of six sections which contain a number of secret clauses. It is said that these entail the transfer of Norway to Bernadotte's rule and the takeover of Belgium by Holland. Northern Italy

will be shared by Austria and Piedmont. The treaty also calls for a congress to be held in Vienna "to establish a genuine and durable system to preserve the balance of power in Europe" on the basis of the Paris agreements.

France must be grateful indeed today for Talleyrand's diplomatic skills.

Talleyrand: the French diplomat who ended upon the winning side.

1814 (1814-1815)

USA, 13 December 1814. General Andrew Jackson, who made his reputation fighting Indians, proclaims martial law in New Orleans as British forces disembark at Lake Borne, 40 miles east of the city.

USA, 23 December 1814. Andrew Jackson halts a British advance on New Orleans.

Netherlands, 24 December 1814. British and US representatives sign a treaty in Ghent ending their war. Territory seized by Britain will be returned to the USA. It will take at least a month for the news to reach America.

Paraguay, 1814. Jose Francia becomes dictator of Paraguay, which declared its independence three years ago.

Rome, 1814. Pope Pius VII restores the Inquisition and the Jesuit order.

Denmark, 1814. The grammarian Kristian Rask writes a paper demonstrating the relationship between Icelandic and Slavonic languages and Greek and Latin. He is the first person to suggest the existence of an original Indo-European language.

Spain, 1814. Francisco Goya paints the *Dos de Mayo* and the *Tres de Mayo*, which celebrate the uprising of the citizens of Madrid against French occupation in 1808.

Britain, 1814. *Waverley*, a novel about the Jacobite rebellion of 1745, is a best-seller, but its authorship is a mystery.

London, 1814. The Marylebone Cricket Club plays its first match at Lord's cricket ground.

London, 1814. *The Times* is the first newspaper to be printed on steam presses.

London, 1814. Dulwich Picture Gallery, the first art collection accessible to the public, is opened.

Connecticut, 5 January 1815. Federalists from all over New England draw up the Hartford Convention, demanding several important changes to the US Constitution.

USA, 8 January 1815. The US forces under Andrew Jackson defeat the British at the battle of New Orleans.

USA, 11 February 1815. News of the treaty of Ghent, ending their war with Britain, finally reaches the Americans.

New Zealand, 24 February 1815. The Reverend Samuel Marsden is the first European to purchase land in New Zealand from the Nga-Puhi tribe. He intends use the land to establish a Church Missionary Society station.

France, 1 March 1815. Returning from Elba, Napoleon lands at Cannes with a force of 1,500 men and marches on Paris.

Mediterranean, 3 March 1815. Angered by the resumption of piracy in the Mediterranean, the US Congress authorises hostilities against the *bey* of Algiers.

Netherlands, 13 March 1815. Louis XVIII, the king of France, flees to Ghent.

Paris, 20 March 1815. Napoleon enters Paris.

Vienna, 25 March 1815. Britain, Austria, Prussia and Russia conclude a new alliance against Napoleon.

Austria, 10 April 1815. Austria declares war on Joachim Murat, the king of Naples, who has again given his support to Napoleon.

France, 23 April 1815. An act is passed re-establishing the constitutional charter granted by Louis XVIII last June, but making the chamber of peers hereditary.

Italy, 3 May 1815. Murat, the king of Naples, is defeated by an Austrian army at Tolentino.

Italy, 20 May 1815. Abandoned by his generals, who sign the Casa Lanza Convention with Britain and Austria, Murat leaves Naples and flees to France.

Prussia, 22 May 1815. King Frederick William III publishes an edict renewing the promises of the 1810 constitution.

France, 1 June 1815. Napoleon swears an oath of fidelity to the constitution.

Italy, 3 June 1815. Murat is replaced by the former king of Naples, Ferdinand IV.

Vienna, 9 June 1815. Britain, Russia, Prussia, Austria, France, Sweden and Portugal sign the Act of the Congress of Vienna, establishing a comprehensive peace in Europe.

Vienna, 9 June 1815. An act is passed creating a German confederation, comprising 39 states, to replace the old Holy Roman empire.

Netherlands, 9 June 1815. By the treaty of Vienna, Belgium and Holland are united to form the kingdom of the Netherlands.

Netherlands, 16 June 1815. Napoleon defeats the Prussians under Blucher at the battle of Ligny.

Egypt, 1815. A revolt by the Albanian regiments in Egypt compels the governor, Mohammed Ali, to flood Cairo. The revolt is suppressed and the mutinous troops sent to upper Egypt.

Imperial eagle returns to his empire

Paris, 20 March 1815

In astonishing scenes of enthusiasm Napoleon was today reinstalled in the Tuileries which Louis XVIII had left in a great hurry last night. It is a year since Paris capitulated to the allies and it has taken the emperor just three weeks to reach Paris after landing at Golfe Juan, Cannes, with a handful of men.

British fears that Elba was too close to the mainland as a place of confinement for Napoleon have now been realised. Yet, when he set out on his march north through the Alps, he gathered little support. It was not until he reached Grenoble and the soldiers posted to stop him fell in behind him that his return to glory seemed possible.

Regiments sent to oppose him went over to him. Marshal Ney, who had promised the king that he would take Napoleon to Paris in an iron cage, embraced him with all the old fervour.

Napoleon marched north, gathering men all the way, and today the "Eagle" returned to his eyrie. War with the allies must follow.

British army is repulsed at New Orleans

The death of Major-General Sir Edward Pakenham at New Orleans.

New Orleans, 8 January 1815

A hastily improvised rag-tag army of militiamen, volunteers, Negro troops and local French-led pirates has inflicted a massive defeat on 8,000 veteran British troops – and saved New Orleans. The fiery Major-general Andrew Jackson, a Tennessee lawyer and former commander of his state militia, was in a position to choose the killing field – a narrow strip of land which the British had to traverse. As the British commander, Major-General Sir Edward Pakenham, the duke of Wellington's brother-in-law, assembled his army, the Americans dug ditches, stacked cotton bales and placed artillery batteries to cover their flanks.

Wave after wave of red-coated infantrymen was repulsed with huge losses from the defenders' concentrated musket fire, grapeshot and cannon-balls. General Pakenham was killed as he tried to rally his troops; his second in command, General Gibbs, died later. More than 2,000 British troops died, against 45 Americans.

The art of the American Indians: the mask of a man from the north-western coast of America.

Map of Europe is redrawn in Vienna

The duke of Wellington, whose advance into France ended the war.

Vienna, 9 June 1815
The Congress of Vienna has remade Europe after the devastation inflicted by Napoleon. The "Final Act" signed today after nine months of negotiations confirms the territorial arrangements of the Treaty of Paris and, among other measures, creates a German confederation to replace the Holy Roman empire.

The Swiss Confederation is re-established with a guarantee of permanent neutrality. The legitimate dynasties are restored in Spain, Naples, Modena, Piedmont and Tuscany. Prussia benefits hugely, getting Posen, Danzig, a slice of Saxony, Westphalia and the former Swedish territories in Pomerania.

The congress also dealt with non-territorial matters, establishing the principle of free navigation on the Rhine and the Meuse, condemning but not abolishing the slave trade and extending the rights of the Jews. Another aspect of its work has been the establishment of an internationally recognised system of diplomacy in which ambassadorial precedence and the rights of diplomats are recognised.

It has been an exhausting time for the delegates, not only because of the amount of work they have accomplished but also because of the glittering social life surrounding the congress. Czar Alexander, convinced that he was responsible for the downfall of Napoleon, has been the dominant figure in the dazzling crowd of monarchs and statesmen.

EUROPE AFTER THE CONGRESS OF VIENNA, 1815

SWEDEN
DENMARK
GREAT BRITAIN
KINGDOM OF PRUSSIA
RUSSIAN EMPIRE
POLAND
BOHEMIA
FRANCE
BAVARIA
AUSTRIAN EMPIRE
SWITZERLAND
KINGDOM OF SARDINIA
WALLACHIA
SERBIA
TUSCANY
PAPAL STATES
KINGDOM OF SARDINIA
KINGDOM OF THE TWO SICILIES

Territories gained, 1815
Borders of the German Confederation

Emperor Francis of Austria has entertained 216 chiefs of mission and has been so lavish with his hospitality that his treasury has suffered severely.

His court's festival committee arranged a rich programme of events for his guests. There were balls, concerts, sleigh and skating parties, hunts, horse-shows and galas. There was a choice of dinner parties every night and the whole city was filled with diplomatic and sexual intrigue.

Most of the decisions have been taken by the four leading allies – Austria, Britain, Russia and Prus-sia – but Talleyrand has served his new master, King Louis, with great adroitness, weaving his way through the quarrels and the bargaining to France's advantage.

There was a considerable *frisson* when the news arrived of Napoleon's return from Elba. The congress reacted by declaring: "Napoleon Bonaparte has placed himself outside the pale of civil and social relations and, as the enemy and disturber of the peace of the world, has exposed himself to public indictment." Then the delegates went on dancing – as well as intriguing and settling the future of Europe.

Deep breaths greet the new stethoscope

Paris, 1815
A chance observation of a children's game has led to a revolution in medical diagnosis. The French physician, Rene Laennec, is said to have been walking in the courtyard of the Louvre when he saw some children bending over long hollow pieces of wood. Some were listening at one end while, at the other end, their friends were flicking pins to produce a tiny sound. From this Laennec went on to devise what he calls a *stethoscope* (from the Greek word meaning *chest*). It is simply a sheet of paper rolled into a tube and tied with a string. Placed on the chest, this concentrates and transmits the sounds made in a patient's lung. Now its inventor has made a wooden version of the device.

Boers rebel against British authority

Cape Town, South Africa, 1815
Although British troops have managed to suppress a rebellion by up-country Boer farmers, the final act – a bungled execution in which the hangman's rope broke – has not done much to help British prestige in the province. Britain is anxious to improve the lot of the black population; the Boers less so.

The insurrection originated in Britain's abolition of the slave trade in 1808, creating a labour shortage; the spread of the Boers into the interior; and the embracing of revolutionary ideals by white society after the French Revolution. The spark was the killing of Frederick Bezuidenhout, shot by British-officered Black Redcoats while resisting arrest.

Fortunately for Britain the rebels failed to gain the support of the majority of Boers, while the Blacks, inevitably, took the side of Britain. Even more fortunately, in spite of the disgraceful scenes at the execution, none but the most incorrigible see the rebels as martyrs.

Spain puts down American uprising

Mexico City, 1815
All over Spain's central and south American empire, her troops are putting down revolts. The wave of nationalist revolutions began in 1809 with an uprising in Chuquisaca, Bolivia, which was rapidly suppressed. Another in Chile led by Bernardo O'Higgins and Juan Martinez de Rozas was defeated by Spain, although a bloodless coup has gained independence for Paraguay.

The most serious revolt was in Mexico. A rebellion by Indians in 1810, led by a priest, Miguel Hidalgo, was crushed at Calderon Bridge in January 1811, and Hidalgo executed. A second revolt, led by another priest, Jose Maria Morelos, declared a republic and abolished slavery and judicial torture, before the Spanish under General de Iturbide broke through the rebel lines around Mexico City and defeated them. Morelos, like Hidalgo, has since been executed.

1815 (1815-1816)

Netherlands, 18 June 1815. Napoleon is decisively defeated by the British and the Prussians at the Battle of Waterloo.

Paris, 22 June 1815. Napoleon abdicates for the second time following the refusal of the parliamentary chambers to co-operate with him.

Algiers, 30 June 1815. Faced with a US threat to bomb Algiers, the *bey* agrees to cease piracy and release US prisoners.

Paris, 7 July 1815. The victorious allies enter Paris.

Paris, 8 July 1815. Louis XVIII returns to Paris.

France, 17 July 1815. After a futile attempt to escape to America, Napoleon surrenders to the British at Rochefort.

France, July 1815. Catholic royalists in southern France begin a campaign of reprisals, known as the White Terror, against supposed Bonapartists and revolutionaries; part of the garrison at Nimes is massacred.

North Africa, 5 August 1815. The US naval hero Stephen Decatur neutralises the Barbary pirates by persuading the bey of Tripoli to agree to similar terms to those accepted by the bey of Algiers.

Switzerland, 7 August 1815. The 22 cantons adopt a federal treaty which guarantees each of them its own constitution and territory. They are all authorised to sign agreements with foreign powers to supply contingents of troops.

France, 22 August 1815. The reactionary ultra-royalists win a large majority in the first parliamentary elections.

Netherlands, 24 August 1815. William, the new king of the Netherlands, grants a moderately liberal constitution.

Europe, 26 September 1815. On the instigation of Czar Alexander, Russia, Austria and Prussia sign a holy alliance, by which they agree to act towards each other and towards their subjects in accordance with Christian principles.

France, 26 September 1815. The duke of Richelieu, an opponent of the Ultra-royalists, is made prime minister and minister of foreign affairs.

France, 7 October 1815. Marshal Ney is condemned to death and shot for having left the service of the king and joined Napoleon's army.

South Atlantic, 17 October 1815. Napoleon arrives on the island of St Helena, where he has been banished by the allies.

Britain, 5 November 1815. Britain signs a treaty assuming a protectorate over the Ionian islands.

Paris, 20 November 1815. A second treaty of Paris puts an end to the war between France and the allies, reduces France to its 1789 frontiers and creates an organisation charged with the collective security of Europe.

Europe, 20 November 1815. Britain, Austria, Prussia and Russia renew their quadruple alliance, agreeing to maintain the exclusion of the Bonaparte dynasty from France for 20 years.

Poland, November 1815. The grand duchy of Warsaw – which was annexed to the Russian empire by the treaty of Vienna – is organised as the autonomous kingdom of Poland and given its own constitution by Czar Alexander.

South Africa, 1815. Five Boers are publicly hanged at Slagter's Nek, in the Eastern Cape Frontier, for rebellion against the British. The revolt was sparked by Boer anger at the British courts' willingness to hear cases brought by Khoisan labourers against their Boer masters. The Boers failed to get the Xhosa chiefdoms across the border to join them in their struggle.

Ottoman Empire, December 1815. Milos Obrenovic, a former pig farmer who made his fortune and led a rebellion, is recognised by the Ottomans as leader of the Serbs, for whom he obtains freedom of worship and a certain degree of autonomy.

Europe, 1815. The Holy Alliance formed in August is joined by most of the other European states, except Britain, the Ottoman empire and the papal states.

Scandinavia, 1815. Sweden and Norway ratify an act of union.

Germany, 1815. The German jurist Friedrich Karl von Savigny publishes his *History of Roman Law in the Middle Ages.*

Germany, 1815. The philosopher and critic Friedrich von Schlegel publishes a *History of Literature.*

China, 1815. Chinese officials execute the French missionary Jean Gabriel Taurin Dufresse.

China, 7 February 1816. The Chinese authorities at Changsha (*Hunan*) execute the Italian missionary Giovanni Lantrua of Triora.

Portugal, March 1816. John VI succeeds his mother, Maria of Braganza, on the throne. He has been emperor of Brazil since 1807, when he fled from Portugal to escape Napoleon's army.

Czar invokes religion in "Holy Alliance"

The czar, author of the "Holy Alliance": sacred truth or nonsense?

Paris, 26 September 1815
The Orthodox Czar Alexander, deeply influenced by the mystical beliefs of baroness von Krudener, has formed a holy alliance with his more conservative allies, the Lutheran king of Prussia and the Catholic emperor of Austria.

The three powers have agreed that "the precepts of Justice, Christian Charity and Peace must have an immediate influence on the Councils of Princes and guide all their steps".

The czar expects Europe's monarchs to join his alliance with the exception of the sultan – barred because he is not a Christian. The pope refuses to associate with heretics, and the prince regent has constitutional objections but agrees with their "sacred maxims".

Europe's statesmen, fearing the might of Russia and its influence on Europe, are less kind to the idea. Metternich calls it a "loud-sounding nothing", and according to Castlereagh it is "a piece of sublime mysticism and nonsense".

Britain's corn law halts grain imports

The price pf victory: high-priced corn, hungry bellies and popular discontent.

London, 23 March 1815
The free-traders have been defeated in the long-running controversy over the import of corn. In a move to protect the agriculture industry, Parliament has passed an act permitting the import of foreign corn free of duty only when the domestic price is 80 shillings a quarter.

A corn law passed in 1804 was seen as a selfish measure by landlords in Parliament to hold on to the high prices caused by war and bad harvests. But Napoleon's defeat and the end of the economic blockade, followed by good harvests, brought the price of home-grown corn tumbling down.

The economist the Rev Thomas Malthus, who recently argued that poverty is inevitable because populations increase faster than food supplies, supported protection because, he told MPs, Britain should not depend on foreign corn. Another economist, David Ricardo, spoke for free trade, saying that Britain should use its wealth and population to encourage enterprise and competition.

Crushing British victory at Waterloo

The Battle of Waterloo, where the duke of Wellington and his British Redcoats finally defeated Napoleon.

Waterloo, 18 June 1815
Napoleon has suffered a catastrophic defeat here today at the hands of the duke of Wellington (previously Sir Arthur Wellesley) and Blucher. The French army has been routed. Napoleon, defeated, and exhausted, has fled the field.

Wellington was dancing at the duchess of Richmond's ball in Brussels three nights ago when he realised that the French were about to attack. "Napoleon has humbugged me, by God!" he cried, and set his "infamous army" in motion.

Napoleon's plan was to destroy Blucher before turning on Wellington, but he succeeded only in delaying the Prussians. Wellington, on his horse, Copenhagen, coolly directed his soldiers in the face of the French cannonade.

The battle raged with terrible ferocity all day. One whole British regiment died to a man as it stood in square. Marshal Ney had five horses shot under him.

The end came late in the day when Napoleon at last unleashed the formidable Imperial Guard. The British infantry poured shot into them at close range. They wavered, broke and ran. At that moment Blucher arrived. The day was won but, as Wellington said, it was "a damned near run thing".

John VI is crowned king of Brazil

John VI, the new king of Brazil.

Brazil, January 1816
Dom Joao, the former prince regent of Portugal and head of the House of Braganza, has declared himself King John VI of Brazil and Portugal. The king and his family fled from Portugal in 1807, when Napoleon's French troops invaded.

The arrival of the royal family has been a great boon to Brazil. The economy has surged ahead, and cultural and intellectual links with Europe have been strengthened. A flood of immigrants, mainly professionals, continues to arrive. King John rules as an enlightened despot backed by Brazilian nobility.

Social and political order are guaranteed, although there is a growing movement for independence from Portugal.

Davy lights way for safer coalmines

London, 1815
Following a horrific disaster which killed 92 Durham miners, the leading scientist, Humphry Davy, has been asked to find a way of preventing lethal sparks which can turn a mass of "fire-damp" – methane gas – into a lethal underground explosion.

He has come up with a safety lamp in which the flame is enclosed in a wire-mesh cylinder to prevent the explosion of air and fire-damp mixture. The presence of fire-damp actually augments the flame in this gauze-covered lantern, thus warning of danger.

Napoleon settles into exile on the island of St Helena

St Helena, 1815
Napoleon, who was depressed by the volcanic mass of this island when he arrived on *HMS Northumberland* after his defeat at Waterloo, has settled into a pavilion in the garden of a house called "The Briars", the home of William Balcombe, the agent of the East India Company. As it will only house a few people he is relieved of the quarrelling antics of his mini-court, and his tedium is relieved by his friendship with Betsy, the 14-year-old tomboy daughter of the Balcombes. Napoleon, who grew up in a large and noisy family takes much pleasure in teaching Betsy French, and this odd couple enjoy a friendship uninhibited by ceremony. When he teased her about English roast beef she retaliated by producing a cartoon of a Frenchman with a frog jumping down his throat. She saddened Napoleon when she showed him an ingenious toy which made "Boney" climb a ladder and then fall onto St Helena. Her mother was furious and shut her in the cellar. Napoleon fed her sweets through her "prison" bars.

Such is the life of the former emperor in his own far-away prison. He refuses to accept official invitations because they are addressed to "General Bonaparte", but enjoys talking to the islanders on his long rides and walks.

Napoleon on "HMS Bellerophon", observed by crowds at Plymouth on his way to the island of St Helena.

India, 2 March 1816. Gurkha tribesmen in Nepal sign a peace treaty with the British, ending their year-long war.

South America, 9 July 1816. The United Provinces of Rio de la Plata (*Argentina*) declare independence.

Florida, 27 July 1816. Fort Apalachicola, which was occupied by runaway slaves after being abandoned by the British, is destroyed and 270 of its occupants killed after a ten-day siege by US troops.

China, 28 August 1816. A mission led by Lord Amherst, which left Britain on 8 February, arrives in Beijing.

France, 5 September 1816. King Louis XVIII dissolves the chamber of deputies, which has become too reactionary and independent, challenging his authority by opposing the initiatives of his chief minister, the duke of Richelieu.

France, 4 October 1816. Moderate royalists and liberals, supporters of Richelieu, win a majority over the Ultra-royalists in an election.

Germany, 5 November 1816. The *Diet* of the German Confederation, created by the 1815 treaty of Vienna, meets for the first time, at Frankfurt.

London, 2 December 1816. Rioting breaks out at Spa Fields during a mass meeting to promote demands for parliamentary reform.

USA, 4 December 1816. James Monroe, who served as secretary of state under his President, Madison, is elected to succeed him.

USA, 11 December 1816. Indiana becomes the 19th state in the union.

USA, 28 December 1816. The Presbyterian clergyman Robert Finley establishes the American Colonization Society, aimed at recolonising American Negroes in Africa.

India, 1816. The ruler of the Himalayan border state of Sikkim signs a treaty accepting British control of its relationship with other Indian states.

Japan, 1816. British ships reach the Ryukyu islands (*Okinawa*) and Uraga Bay near Edo (*Tokyo*) seeking trade. Their overtures are rebuffed, but increase the government's awareness of western pressures on Japan to open the country to foreign business.

Ghana, 1816. The Reverend Philip Quaque, the first Anglican African clergyman, dies. He was a key figure in the cultural development of the Anglo-African coastal elite of trading and professional families.

South-East Asia, 1816. The island of Java is restored to Dutch control.

Russia, 1816. A group of Russian Guards officers founds the Union of Salvation to promote the establishment of constitutional government and to abolish serfdom.

Netherlands, 1816. The British engineer John Cockerill takes over the factory founded by his father at Seraing, near Liege, in 1807, and starts to manufacture steam engines.

France, 1816. A new science of "comparative anatomy" is born with the publication of Georges Cuvier's book on classifying the animal kingdom. Cuvier is also a clever palaeontologist, able to "reconstruct" whole skeletons of long-dead animals from just a few bones.

Germany, 1816. The linguist Franz Bopp publishes a study of the *System of Conjugation in Sanskrit*, in which he seeks to trace the common origin of Sanskrit, Persian, Greek and Latin.

England, 1816. The anonymous author of *Pride and Prejudice* and *Mansfield Park* publishes another novel, *Emma*.

Ottoman Empire, 1817. Karageorges returns to Serbia from exile in Austria. Karageorges, the former leader of the Serbian independence movement, hopes to overthrow the increasingly unpopular Serbian leader, Milos Obrenovic, but is assassinated on the orders of his rival.

West Africa, 1817. Uthman dan Fodio, the scholar-warrior and instigator of the Islamic reformation of the Hausa states, dies.

Madagascar, 1817. Radama, the king of the Merina, who has embarked on a major expansion of his kingdom with the aim of dominating the whole island, signs a treaty of alliance with the British, who have promised military aid. The British see the Merina as effective agents for suppressing the slave trade from coastal areas into the Indian Ocean.

Hawaii, 1817. Russian fur traders who have abused the hospitality of the Hawaiian Islands for over a dozen years are banished by King Kamehameha.

USA, 1817. Construction begins on the Erie canal, designed to link the Great Lakes with the Atlantic.

Germany, 1817. Georg Hegel, who became professor of philosophy at Heidelberg university last year, publishes his *Encyclopaedia of the Philosophical Sciences*.

Unbending envoy wrecks trade prospects

Beijing, 29 August 1816
Lord Amherst's mission to Beijing, to establish better conditions for British traders in China, ended in farcical failure today.

The emperor Jiaqing agreed to receive Amherst only on condition that the English lord would perform the ritual of *kowtow*, kneeling three times and knocking his head on the ground nine times. But Amherst would only bend a knee, bow his head three times and repeat the performance three times.

This was accepted by the Chinese officials, who reported that the barbarian was learning how to *kowtow*. The emperor then agreed to an immediate audience. But when Amherst arrived, exhausted by his journey, and officials tried to hustle him to the palace, he insisted on resting and waiting for his credentials.

The emperor, told he was ill, reacted furiously: "China is the universal overlord. How can she willingly submit to this kind of insult and insolence?" Amherst's "tributes" have been rejected, his mission expelled.

The Chinese port of Canton, the entrepot for all trade coming into China.

Britain defeats Gurkhas, but only just

Nepal, 2 March 1816
The British army has won a decisive victory over Gurkha tribesmen – despite being pinned down for days in the Kathmandu Valley. It was an ill-deserved victory, however, with the war-seasoned British troops outnumbering the hill people by three to one. Only shrewd generalship by the British commander, Sir David Ochterlony, saved the day for Britain.

War became inevitable two years ago when Gurkhas seized the hill states of Simla, Garwhal and Kumaon and descended on British-controlled Oudh. Fighting began again last year with Ochterlony taking Kathmandu by an indirect approach. The fighting ability of the Gurkhas has gained much respect from the British, who see them as "good losers" and have allowed them semi-independence.

First black Anglican priest is dead

West Africa, 1816
Philip Quaque, Africa's first Anglican clergyman, has died aged 75. In his own terms, he was a failure. To the hundreds of Mulatto children whom he educated, he was an outstanding success. Sent to England to be educated and ordained, he returned to the Gold Coast with his English wife in 1765, fluent in Christian values but unable to speak his own language.

A victim of two cultures, only after his wife died and he "went native" did he find happiness – and a truly African Christianity.

France's King Louis XVIII dissolves the incredible chamber

Louis XVIII, burdened by the extremism of his own supporters.

Paris, 5 September 1816
King Louis has today signed a decree dissolving the Chamber of Deputies, an elected body of men so royalist that Louis himself called it "the Incredible Chamber".

The young and zealous royalists, elected under a widened franchise last year, have proved an embarrassment to the government, many of whom served under Napoleon. Swiftly getting themselves dubbed "the Ultra-royalists", they forced the government to accept a number of repressive measures.

Under this "White Terror" the army and the administration have been purged. Many who supported Napoleon during the "Hundred Days" have been exiled and some, like the gallant Marshal Ney, have been shot.

Louis has been forced to act against the royalists, but in doing so he has affirmed the power of the crown over the electorate.

England's romantic movement puts passion back into poetry

London, 1816
The last 12 months have been rich in Romantic poetry, with publications by Samuel Taylor Coleridge, Percy Bysshe Shelley and Lord Byron and the first sonnet of a 21-year-old newcomer, John Keats.

Coleridge first amazed his readers with the haunted vision of The Rime of the Ancient Mariner in 1798. The fragmentary poems he now publishes were written soon afterwards. Kubla Khan, considered his finest poem so far, was composed under the influence of opium and written down on waking – until interrupted half way through. The solitary remorseful wanderer is a favourite theme of the Romantics, and in Alastor (or the spirit of Solitude) Shelley hurls the Poet through ocean, precipice and torrent on a quest for the ideal that ends in death. Lord Byron, who has left the scandals which he caused in London society for further travels, has added a new canto to the autobiographical picturesque travelogue Childe Harold's Pilgrimage which made him famous overnight in 1812. In it he visits the field of last year's great battle, Waterloo. Keats' Romantic sonnet, On First Looking into Chapman's Homer, is in The Examiner, where Shelley's work first appeared.

Three poets of the English Romantic school: (left to right) John Keats, Percy Bysshe Shelley and Lord Byron.

Protesters stone British prince regent

London, 28 January 1817
As the prince regent was passing through St James' Park after the opening of parliament, he was stoned and greeted with a tirade of abuse. The Kendal Chronicle reports: "Gravel, stones, and other things were thrown at the Royal carriage," by the mob, "accompanied by the most foul, shocking, insulting and blasphemous language." Windows in the royal carriage were broken and there are reports that an air gun was fired at the prince.

Cabinet ministers are linking the attack to agitators who have been holding meetings in London and the provinces to demand votes for all men over 18, and no property qualifications for MPs, only "talent and virtue". During a meeting at Spa Fields, Clerkenwell, a mob broke into a gun shop, seized arms and went on to appeal to soldiers in the Tower of London to join the uprising. That "uprising", like the others, petered out. Now the government is using the outbreaks of discontent, caused by post-war hardships, as justification for a crackdown on dissent.

Briton expounds economic theory

London, 1817
David Ricardo, who made his fortune on the Stock Exchange and retired at the age of 27, has published a treatise on pay, profits and taxation in Britain in which he lays down the Iron Law of Wages, arguing that attempts to improve the real incomes of workers are bound to fail, because wages inevitably settle at about the subsistence level. In international trade he claims that exchange rates reflect values that would be accepted if trade were conducted by barter.

Ricardo, of Dutch-Jewish parents, broke with his family and adopted the Christian faith when he married a Quaker. He took up the study of economics after reading Adam Smith's Wealth of Nations. In his latest book, Ricardo says that taxes are not always paid by those on whom they are levied. A tax on farm produce, for example, falls on the consumer; a tax on wages is paid by the employer but the consumer pays the tax on profits.

Fundamentalist Islamic reformer who built up African empire

Nigeria, 1817
All over the savannalands of West Africa, Moslem fundamentalists are mourning the death of Uthman dan Fodio, the preacher and reformer, whose armies swept through Hausaland. Less fundamentalist Moslems are greeting his death with relief. Born into the devoutly Moslem Banu Al clan in 1754, from the age of 20 he called for reformation. All over the Hausa states he gathered disciples.

Faced with the hostility of the sultan of Gobir he proclaimed holy war in 1804, defeating Gobir four years later. Soon the green flag of Islam was flying all over Hausaland, and his son, Mohammed Bello was proclaimed the precursor of the Mahdi, the Expected One. By 1812 his state was so large that it was divided, his brother, Abdullah, administering the west, and his son the east, persecuting secularism and superstition everywhere. Content with his achievements he retired to a life of contemplation, writing over 100 theological works before his death.

1817 (1817-1818)

Britain, March 1817. In response to the riot at Spa Fields in London last year, a series of Coercion Acts are passed; these include the temporary suspension of habeas corpus and an extension of the 1798 act against seditious meetings.

Britain, March 1817. A delegation of Manchester spinners and weavers – called blanketeers on account of the blankets they carry – attempts to march to London to present its economic and political grievances to the prince regent. The march is halted by troops and its leaders are imprisoned.

Mexico, 5 April 1817. An expedition organised in Britain and the USA under Francisco Xavier Mina lands on the Gulf coast with the aim of overthrowing the royalist Spanish regime.

Maryland, 7 April 1817. Some 200 Negro slaves in Maryland riot, attacking Whites.

Germany, 18 October 1817. At the festival of Wartburg – organised by Jena university students to celebrate both the 300th anniversary of the Reformation and the battle of Leipzig – reactionary texts and military effigies are burnt. The university of Jena has become the centre of a liberal movement spearheaded by new student societies known as the *Burschenschaften*.

Ottoman Empire, 5 November 1817. Serbia is granted partial autonomy by the Ottomans.

Colombia, November 1817. Pola Salavarreta is captured and shot as a republican agent in the public square in Bogota. While working as a seamstress in the houses of Spanish royalist women, she passed on the information which she heard to Colombian rebels.

Mexico, 11 November 1817. Xavier Mina, defeated in his attempt to overthrow the royalist regime, is executed.

USA, 10 December 1817. Mississippi becomes the 20th state in the union.

USA, December 1817. A war starts in earnest between US troops and Seminole Indians, who last year refused to leave land between Georgia and Florida.

Australia, 1817. The Australian pioneer and wool merchant Elizabeth Macarthur retires from the management of Elizabeth Farm, the first great Australian estate. After taking over the business from her husband in 1809, she built up the merino flocks and travelled throughout Australia, expanding sales into the British market and establishing New South Wales as a major wool-producing area.

South America, 1817. Following his victories over the Spanish in Rio de la Plata (*Argentina*), General Jose de San Martin embarks on a campaign to liberate Chile.

England, 1817. The "romantic" poet John Keats publishes his first anthology of poems.

England, 1817. Lord Byron publishes his tragic poem *Manfred*.

Washington, DC, 1 January 1818. President Monroe gives the first public reception at the new White House, his official residence, rebuilt after being burnt down by the British in 1814.

New York City, 5 January 1818. The first regularly scheduled transatlantic service, between New York and Liverpool, begins.

Sweden, 5 February 1818. Jean-Baptiste Bernadotte, prince royal since 1810, succeeds Charles XIII as king, taking the name Charles XIV.

Florida, April 1818. Andrew Jackson, officially acting against the Seminole Indians, takes the Spanish fort of St Mark's, before capturing a Seminole stronghold in central Florida.

Germany, 26 May 1818. Bavaria adopts a constitution granting extensive powers to the king and nobility and giving the latter exclusive right of entry to the "first" chamber. A "second" chamber, more open to other classes, is created.

Prussia, 26 May 1818. A bill presented by the economist and councillor Karl Maaseen is adopted. It abolishes customs procedures within Prussia and lifts trade restrictions.

India, 2 June 1818. The Marathas are conquered by the British army and their empire is annexed to British India.

Florida, May 1818. Andrew Jackson recaptures the Spanish fort of Pensacola and sets up a military government.

India, June 1818. The Pindaris, freebooters who have ravaged much of central India since 1806, have finally been brought to heel.

Germany, 22 August 1818. Baden adopts a constitution similar to that of Bavaria.

USA, 23 August 1818. The first steamship service on the Great Lakes opens.

North America, 19 October 1818. Following the cession by Quapaw Indians of holdings in Arkansas to the USA, the Chickasaw Indians sell all their lands north of the southern boundary of Tennesseee to the government.

New architecture blooms in Britain

John Nash's Royal Pavilion in Brighton: built for the Prince Regent.

Cruikshank's mockery of Nash's architecture: "Nashional Taste".

London, 1818

A great new thoroughfare called Regent Street is being driven through the centre of London by the Prince Regent's architect and surveyor-general, John Nash. Now Nash is rebuilding the exterior of the Royal Pavilion in Brighton.

Regent Street will connect the prince's residence at Carlton House with Regent's Park (formerly Marylebone Park) which Nash is adorning with lakes and villas according to the principles of the new picturesque architecture.

He plans to surround the open space with terraces of houses sharing long stucco facades, which the tenants will be obliged to renew every year, named after royal titles, such as Cumberland, Hanover and York. A new Regent's Canal is being driven through the park. In the central part of Regent Street above Piccadilly Circus Nash has inserted a curve, known as the Quadrant, adorned with projecting colonnades, to break the straight line. At the top of the street he has placed the circular colonnade and spire of All Souls' church.

The Royal Pavilion at Brighton is even more spectacular. The Chinese-style interior is being kept, but the old neo-classical exterior is being completely transformed into a Moghul emperor's palace, with onion-shaped domes, tentshaped roofs, and pseudo-Moslem pinnacles and minarets.

A regent's extravaganza: the Music Room in the Royal Pavilion, Brighton.

Army of the mountains defeats Spanish

Chile, 12 February 1817

The "Army of the Andes", recruited by Jose de San Martin, the liberator of Argentina, and led by the Peruvian Bernardo O'Higgins, has struck a blow for Chilean independence. A surprise attack has routed the Spanish at Chacabuco. Now O'Higgins and his army are marching on Santiago.

The preparations for the advance go back to 1811 when San Martin established himself at Mendoza in western Argentinia and built an army. In 1814, after the disasterous battle of Ranagua re-established Spanish royalist authority in Chile, O'Higgins joined him.

The victory was as notable for its logistics as for the course of the battle itself. A force of 5,400 men marched 200 miles across mountain passes almost 13,000 feet (3,937 metres) above sea level. The crossing took a month, but the four

General Bernardo O'Higgins: hero of the "Army of the Andes".

columns met at exactly the appointed place and time. With that degree of precision, the success at Chacabuco was almost a foregone conclusion.

Mary Shelley's "Frankenstein" published

London, 1818

An extraordinary Gothic novel has appeared from the pen of Mary Wollstonecraft Shelley, the wife of the poet and daughter of the atheist William Godwin. *Frankenstein* is the story of a monster – man-made and mis-shapen – which turns on its creator when he gives it the the spark of life.

The tale was the result of a competition between the authoress, Shelley and their friend Lord Byron at Lake Geneva in 1816 for each to write a ghost story during a cold spell. The poets gave up when the weather improved, but Mrs Shelley completed hers which came to her one night in a trance.

"I saw the dull yellow eye of the creature open; it breathed hard."

Ottoman empire defeats the Wahhabis

Arabia, 1818

With the fall of the Saudi capital of Dariyya, the last of the Wahhabi fortresses has fallen to the Ottomans. The *emir*, Abdallah ibn Saud, has been executed in Istanbul. The campaign against the Wahhabi empire began in 1811 when an expedition set out from Cairo under Ahmed Tusun Pasha, the son of Mohammed Ali, Egypt's ruler. The aim was to reclaim control of

Mecca, Medina and the Hijaz, essential if the sultan was to be the true *caliph* and guardian of the sacred places of Islam. Tusun's forces recaptured Yanbu, Medina and Mecca, then agreed to a truce which ensured the free passage of pilgrims. When Tusun died in 1816, Ibrahim Pasha took over command, and advanced into the Saudi heartland of Najd until the last fortress fell.

British army defeats Maratha alliance

Bombay, 2 June 1818

After a six-month campaign by 100,000 British Indian troops, the Marathas have been crushed and their domains annexed. The final obstacle to British hegemony over India has been overcome.

The Marathas have plundered central India since 1812, even attacking the Bombay Presidency, or district. Lacking unity, they proved easy victims to Governor General Lord Hastings' tactics of "divide

and rule". Hastings' first move was diplomatic, isolating the most ambitious of the Maratha leaders, Sindia, by treaty. Next he broke the most anarchic elements, the Pindaris. Then he turned on the Maratha head, the *Pewsha*, provoking him into hostilities before he was ready. This left only the Pewsha's rival, Holkar, whose army he annihilated at Mahidpur on 21 December 1817. Britain is now truly master of India.

The household of an Indian monarch: courtiers, servants and hangers-on.

Parkinson names a nervous disease

London, 1817

The distressing disease known as "shaking palsy" which can affect both men and women in late adult life – and sometimes earlier – has been described in detail by the English surgeon James Parkinson. "Parkinson's Disease", as the condition is now being termed, is a relatively common malady, although no-one, including Parkinson himself, has been able to trace its cause.

It is certainly a nervous disorder. Over the course of ten to 20 years, an individual progressively acquires a number of striking symptoms. Body movements are a mixture of rigidity and tremor – *paralysis agitans*, to use the Latin name.

Ultimately, these symptoms become so severe that sufferers may lose balance frequently and fall over. Speech becomes poorly articulated and manual skills – such as writing – are gradually lost.

Atoms are weighed in Swedish kitchen

Stockholm, 1818

Atoms – nature's building blocks – are small. Typically an atom will measure no more than 300 millionths of an inch in diameter. This means that, if its nucleus or central particle, were the size of an orange, it would be half a mile across.

So it is remarkable that the Swedish chemist and academician, Jons Jacob Berzelius, has been able to determine the weights of different atoms. He has published a table of relative proportions and weights in which oxygen – with a value of 100 – is the standard. In addition, Berzelius had drawn up tables for the molecular weights of over 2,000 compounds which he has studied for over a decade.

His achievement is all the more noteworthy given his working conditions. He has made his discoveries in his spare time – improvising equipment from his own kitchen.

North America, 20 October 1818. Britain and the USA agree that the western border between Canada and the USA should be the 49th parallel.

Europe, 15 November 1818. The Quadruple Alliance between Britain, Russia, Austria and Prussia is renewed as a precaution against another possible revolution in France.

France, 30 November 1818. In accordance with an agreement reached at the congress of Aix-la-Chapelle earlier in the month, the last foreign troops leave France. The congress also settled the question of France's war indemnity payments and agreed to admit France to the alliance of European powers.

USA, 3 December 1818. Illinois, including Chicago, becomes the 21st state in the union.

France, December 1818. The prime minister, the duke of Richelieu, retires and is replaced by the marquis of Dessoles. Elie Decazes becomes minister of the interior.

South Africa, 1818. Faced with a threat to their capital in the Pongola valley, the Ndwandwe defeat the Mthethwa under the great warrior Dingiswayo at the battle of Mbuzi Hill. Dingiswayo is found demented in defeat and executed by the ruthless Ndwandwe leader Zwide. One of Dingiswayo's chiefs – Shaka of the Zulu clan – escapes back to his own people to build them up and fight another day.

Prague, 1818. The National Museum of Prague is founded.

Germany, 1818. The philosopher Arthur Schopenhauer publishes *The World as Will and Idea*.

Italy, 1818. The poet Giacomo Leopardi publishes *First Love*.

Germany, 20 January 1819. Karl von Stein founds the Society of Earlier German History.

North America, 22 February 1819. The US foreign minister, John Quincy Adams, signs a treaty with his Spanish counterpart, Luis de Onis, by which eastern Florida is ceded to the USA. The border of western Florida is fixed at the Mississippi.

Germany, 23 March 1819. The dramatist August Kotzebue is stabbed to death by a Jena student for having ridiculed the nationalist *Burschenschaft* movement and spying for the Czar of Russia.

Germany, April 1819. The economist Georg Friederich List founds an association of German industrialists to fight for the abolition of tariff barriers within the German Confederation.

Hawaii, 8 May 1819. Kamehameha, the Lonely One, the first chief of a united Hawaiian people, dies.

Bohemia, 1 August 1819. Prince Metternich and Karl Hardenberg, the chief ministers of Austria and Prussia, finalise the details of the secret convention of Teplitz, which introduces reactionary policies throughout the German Confederation.

Bohemia, August 1819. A series of decrees is issued at Carlsbad to check revolutionary and liberal movements in Germany.

USA, 14 December 1819. Alabama becomes the 22nd state of the union.

South-East Asia, 1819. The Englishman Sir Stamford Bingley Raffles occupies Singapore, which has been bought from the *rajah* of Johore by the East India Company.

South Africa, 1819. The British are victorious in the fifth Suurveld (*Eastern Cape Frontier*) war and imprison the enemy leader, the Xhosa prophet Makhanda, on Robben Island. After defeating the major chief of western Xhosa, Ngqika, Makhanda crossed into Cape Colony "to chase the white men to the sea that cast them up".

South Africa, 1819. The Zulus under Shaka defeat the Ndwandwe at the battle of Mhlatuze river and emerge as the dominant military power in the Natal region.

USA, 1819. Financial panic caused by runaway depreciation and speculation following the war of 1812 touches off a depression.

France, 1819. The adoption of the three *de Serre* laws relaxes restrictions on the press. Censorship and prior consent are abolished, the number of violation laws is reduced, and provision is made for any dispute concerning the press to be resolved by a jury.

France, 1819. The doctor Rene Laennec publishes his treatise *On Medical Auscultation*, describing the uses of the *stethoscope*, his invention.

Germany, 1819. Friedrich Jahn, who in 1811 founded the *Turnplatz*, the first open-air gymnasium, is arrested and the *Turnplatz* closed. Jahn played a leading part in the formation of the student patriotric societies known as the *Burschenschaften*, and is accused of being involved in subversive activities.

Scotland, 1819. The Scottish industrialists Thomas Hancock and Charles Macintosh perfect a process for manufacturing waterproof material.

United States takes over Spanish Florida

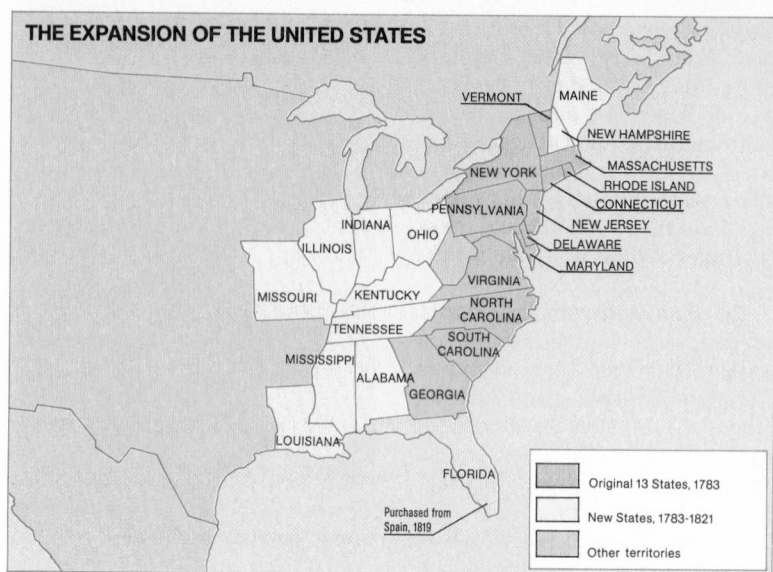

THE EXPANSION OF THE UNITED STATES

Original 13 States, 1783
New States, 1783-1821
Other territories

Washington DC, 22 February 1819
A private war fought by General Andrew Jackson, the hero of New Orleans, has brought all Florida under United States rule.

Congress has long claimed Florida as its own and today, in a treaty signed between the secretary of state John Quincy Adams, and his Spanish counterpart, Spain relinquishes claims to all its colonies east of the Mississippi. Jackson launched his invasion last year, after being ordered to suppress the Seminole Indians on the border. With an army of 1,000 men from his home state of Tennessee, supplemented by the Georgia militia and friendly Indians, Jackson pushed on southwards, executing several Indian chiefs and two white sympathisers, both British, before taking Pensacola and establishing military rule. Jackson faces a congressional inquiry, but few believe that he will be censured.

New alliance ties up Europe's loose ends

Aix-la-Chapelle, 21 Nov 1818
The Quadruple Alliance today completed its deliberations in the first congress of a series designed to discuss measures that would be "most salutary for the repose and prosperity of the nations and for maintaining the peace of Europe".

The congress tidied up much of the debris of the Napoleonic years. It agreed to Wellington's suggestion that the occupation troops should be withdrawn from France, and cut France's war indemnity. France is also to be admitted to the newly-constituted Quintuple Alliance. The congress also confirmed the decision taken at the Congress of Vienna extending the civil rights of German Jews, the slave trade was discussed and measures for Napoleon's security on St Helena, approved. Lord Castlereagh, Britain's foreign secretary, has played a major role in the congress, but there are signs that he is already

Louis XVIII: the main beneficiary of the Quadruple Alliance.

becoming disillusioned with the system of congresses, he has warned the others that Britain will not take part in interfering, unasked, in the internal affairs of other states.

African military genius expands empire

Southern Africa, 1819

The greatest military genius Africa has yet known, Shaka, the chief of the Zulus, is building an empire.

Shaka's childhood was a psychological disaster. The product of incest, he was driven with his mother from his home and hounded and despised by all who came into contact with him. Burning with revenge, he took to the profession of arms. He proved so brilliant that by 1816 he had returned to his Zulu clan as their chief. His genius lies in his attention to detail. He banned clumsy sandels so his barefoot army runs at 50 miles per day. Unaware of his two contemporary geniuses, he synthesised the Napoleonic column and the Wellingtonian square, creating horns, and can thus attack his enemies on three sides at once.

He has also introduced a new weapon, the short-handled stabbing spear, and a tough new shield made of cow-hide, to protect his soldiers from the long-handled throwing spears of his enemies.

Germany cracks down on revolutionaries

August von Kotzebue, the czar's spy, murdered by radical students.

Karlsbad, Bohemia, August 1819

Austria's Prince Metternich has persuaded ministers of the German states, meeting at Karlsbad, to adopt sweeping repressive powers to ban political meetings, impose press censorship and investigate the educational system.

The crackdown follows the stabbing to death by students of a minor author, Kotzebue, who topped up his income by sending the czar reports on student agitators. Student associations have been calling for a "true" German fatherland and protesting against foreign influences and Jews, who are now prominent in German literary circles. The students wear beards and long hair; they are confused romantics, but to the conservative Metternich they threaten revolution.

Red tide predicts Hawaiian king's death

Honolulu, 8 May 1819

Kamehameha ("the Lonely One"), who united the islands of Hawaii, died today. His death was predicted two days ago after an ominous red tide flowed into Honolulu harbour.

Innovative and ambitious, from his first contact with Europeans he was determined to exploit western technology to build his kingdom. "As savage a looking face as I ever saw" was how Cook's Lieutenant King described him, adding, "he was good natured & humourous, although his manner shewed somewhat an overbearing spirit".

Demanding payment for port facilities with firearms, and using renegade seamen as military advisers, he conquered one island after another. His greatest gift was patience. When his invasion fleet bound for Kauai was wrecked he spent 13 years rebuilding it before trying again. The threat was sufficient to secure Kauai's obedience.

The victory, without a shot fired, was his greatest triumph. "Endless is the good I leave you to enjoy" were his last words.

Spanish artist suffers black nightmares

Vision of age and death: Francisco Jose de Goya's "Old Women".

Madrid, December 1819

Francisco Goya, who has survived a dangerous illness, is covering the walls of his house, the *Quinta del Sordo* (Villa of the Deaf), with horrific "black paintings". One shows Death awaiting two old women, obscene in their youthful dresses and make-up. Another shows Saturn devouring his two sons. A third portrays Goya's rescue from his deathbed by his doctor. The doctor holds him upright to take a draught of medicine while, in the shadows ghoulish faces watch.

Goya's dark imagination dates from the illness that left him deaf in 1792. He went on to create his etchings *Los Caprichos* and *The Disasters of War*.

Scottish author's "Ivanhoe" starts trend for historical novels

Edinburgh, December 1819

A romantic novel of adventure, *Ivanhoe*, has sold out its first edition here within a fortnight. As with the *Waverley* novels, of which *The Bride of Lammermoor* is just out, no author is named. All are believed to be the work of the Edinburgh advocate Walter Scott, Scotland's most famous living poet since *The Lay of the Last Minstrel*. Novels like *Waverley*, *Rob Roy*, *The Heart of Midlothian* and *Old Mortality* show resemblances to Scott's historical poems. *Ivanhoe* leaves Jacobite Scotland for the mediaeval England of Richard the Lionheart, romance and chivalry.

1819 (1819-1820)

South America, 17 December 1819. At the congress of Angostura, the republic of Great Colombia – consisting of New Granada, Venezuela and Quito – is established. Simon Bolivar is made president and military dictator.

Britain, 1819. After the Peterloo Massacre, the government issues the Six Laws, banning any meeting of 50 or more people and any flag-bearing procession, authorising the arrest of anyone carrying a firearm and imposing a new tax on newspapers.

Spain, January 1820. A mutiny of troops in Cadiz sets off other revolts in northern Spain against King Ferdinand VII's anti-liberal policies and incompetent government.

Britain, 29 January 1820. George – prince regent since 1811, when his father, George III, was pronounced terminally insane – becomes king on his father's death.

New York, 6 February 1820. The ship *Mayflower of Liberia* leaves New York harbour for Sierra Leone in West Africa with 86 free Negroes aboard.

France, 14 February 1820. The duke of Berry, the nephew of the king, is assassinated by a fanatic. Elie Decazes is held indirectly responsible for the crime by the royalists and is forced to resign from the government.

China, 18 February 1820. Chinese officials at Wuchang strangle the French missionary Jean Francois Regis Clet.

Spain, 7 March 1820. To quell the mounting tide of revolt in Spain, King Ferdinand VII restores the constitution of 1812, which he abolished on coming to the throne in 1814.

USA, 9 March 1820. Congress passes the Land Act, paving the way for westward expansion by rich land speculators.

USA, 15 March 1820. Congress reaches a compromise on the slavery issue by admitting Maine to the union as a free state and Missouri as a slave state.

Europe, 28 March 1820. Louis XVIII of France and king William of the Netherlands sign a treaty fixing the frontier between their two countries at the 1790 border.

Hawaii, 30 March 1820. The first American missionaries arrive in Honolulu from New England.

Britain, 1 May 1820. The militant radicals involved in the Cato Street conspiracy to kill the prime minister and other members of the cabinet are executed. Their leader, Arthur Thistlewood, is suspected of being a police informer.

USA, 15 May 1820. Congress designates the slave trade a form of piracy.

Vienna, 24 May 1820. The Final Act of the Congress of Vienna is passed, authorising the German confederation to intervene in the affairs of member states threatened by internal unrest.

Germany, 20 July 1820. The German Confederation accepts the Final Act agreed at the Congress of Vienna.

Portugal, 29 August 1820. Encouraged by the revolution in Spain, the Portuguese army rebels at Oporto.

USA, 26 September 1820. The legendary frontiersman Daniel Boone dies.

USA, September 1820. Washington Irving publishes *The Sketch-book*, a collection of fanciful tales, including *Rip Van Winkle* and *The Legend of Sleepy Hollow*.

Germany, 19 November 1820. At the congress of Troppau, convened by Czar Alexander to discuss the rebellions in Spain, Portugal and Naples, Austria, Russia and Prussia sign the Troppau protocol, promising united action if national revolutions appear to threaten international order. Britain refuses to agree to the proposal.

USA, 6 December 1820. James Monroe is re-elected president in a landslide victory.

Portugal, 1820. The Portuguese rebels succeed in driving out the regency established in 1807 during King John VI's period in Brazil.

Africa, c.1820. Successful new crops are being introduced for cultivation on plantations – cloves into Zanzibar and cotton into Angola. Both crops are for export rather than local consumption, and their success depends on promoting the internal African slave trade for labour.

Africa, 1820. The Egyptian *pasha* Mohammed Ali conquers the Sudan and the region of Kordofan.

England, 1820. The poet Shelley publishes *Prometheus Unbound*.

England, 1820. Keats publishes a volume of odes and ballads which puts him in the first rank of contemporary poets.

Russia, 1820. Pushkin's romantic epic *Russlan and Ludmilla* is published.

France, 1820. Alphonse de Lamartine publishes his *Poetical Meditations*.

France, 1820. The doctors Pierre Joseph Pelletier and Joseph Bienaime Caventou discover quinine.

Simon Bolivar is "liberator" of Colombia

Colombia, 17 December 1819

Simon Bolivar, already liberator of his native Venezuela, has brought independence to another Spanish colony. The republic of Colombia, formerly a part of New Granada, was proclaimed today. A constitution has been adopted and Bolivar will be the first president.

Bolivar's plans for Colombia stalled in July 1817 when he was forced pitch camp on the island of Angostura on the Orinoco river. Faced by the ruthless Spanish general Morillo he was unable to advance his cause until he enrolled 6,000 English and Irish fighters, veterans of the war against Napoleon.

These troops, and Bolivar's promises of land and cattle, persuaded the llaneros, the people of the great plains. In February 1819 Bolivar was given dictatorial powers by a congress called at Angostura. He crossed the Andes in May and began a hard-hitting campaign. Caught by surprise, the Spanish lost a series of short, sharp battles until

Simon Bolivar, the "liberator" of Venezuela and Colombia.

the decisive encounter at Boyaca on 7 August. This victory opened the way to Bogota, Colombia's capital, and Bolivar entered the city three days later.

Mounted businessmen kill demonstrators

The Manchester Yeomanry in St Peter's Fields: their glorious "Peterloo".

Manchester, 16 August 1819

More than 60,000 men, women and children turned up at St Peter's Fields, Manchester, today to hear the pugnacious radical farmer, Henry Hunt, deliver a speech demanding parliamentary reform and repeal of the Corn Laws. The crowd was orderly – families had brought picnic lunches – but when Hunt began to speak a force of Manchester Yeomanry appeared. The mounted yeomanry are undisciplined local businessmen, and they were soon laying about right and left with their sabres, crying "Have at them!". Magistrates, fearful of radical gatherings, had issued warrants for Hunt's arrest. Nine men and two women were killed and 600 injured in what is already called the "Peterloo" massacre.

Farmer George, Britain's mad king, dies

Windsor, 29 January 1820

After the death of his favourite daughter Amelia, George III's insanity became permanent and when he died today at Windsor Castle, after years of seclusion, the 81-year-old king was blind as well as mad.

He had lived through a tumultuous period in Britain's history. An empire was lost in America, another was founded in India and Australia and, alone among the European powers, Britain had remained steadfast throughout the Napoleonic Wars. If the king's stubbornness lost the American colonies, it gave stiffening to the wars with France.

A conscientious, family-loving man, George was not much liked by his people when he came to the throne; but, as he became better known, affection grew. He liked going into the country and talking about such homely matters as making apple dumplings, so that he became known as Farmer George.

George III, the farmer king who lost one empire but gained others.

George asked Lord Bute "to save a great deal of trouble" and find him a wife. The marriage to Charlotte Sophia of Mecklenburg lasted for almost 60 years, until her death two years ago.

Uneasy deal over slave states in US

Washington, DC, 15 March 1820

After a noisy, rancorous all-night debate, Congress has accepted a compromise solution to the slavery argument which is threatening to tear these United States apart. Until now, slave and non-slave states have been equal in number, but, with the application by nonslave Maine for statehood, the balance will be upset.

The compromise was proposed by a senator from Illinois. It allows Maine to be admitted as a "free" state, with Missouri to join the union as a slave-state. It also calls for slavery to be totally prohibited north of a line in the Louisiana Purchase area.

Despite this uneasy agreement, the question of Missouri's admis-

A slave gang in chains, passing the Capitol in Washington, DC.

sion and the opposition to slavery by the northern states threaten to provoke a major political upheaval, with the political divisions between north and south ever widening.

Steamship crosses the Atlantic in 26 days

Liverpool, England, 20 June 1819

The steamship *Savannah* arrived here today – 27 days after she left Savannah, Georgia. Although she was aided by sail, *Savannah* is the first ship to cross the Atlantic partly by steam power. When she left her home port, dubious onlookers described her as a "steam coffin", but it is her captain, Moses Rogers, who has the last laugh.

Steam power has been harnessed to open up the vast open spaces of North America to exploration. The United States War Department has commissioned five steampowered paddle-boats to survey the Mis-

souri river. The first of these, the *Independence*, travelled 200 miles upstream to the settlement of Franklin in May to unload sugar, flour and whisky. Three other ships were less successful, their deep draughts unsuitable for the numerous Missouri mudbanks.

The most successful exploration trip was made by the *Western Engineer*, which has reached Council Bluffs with a team of leading US scientists and artists. *Western Engineer* is "dragon shaped" with a raised head that snorts steam and draws only 20 inches. She can travel at three miles per hour.

Plot to blow up the British cabinet foiled

Cato Street: the escape of the radical conspirators over the rooftops.

London, 23 February 1820

An estate agent turned revolutionary was seized today with a score of his followers and a cache of arms in a loft in Cato Street, off the Edgware Road. Arthur Thistlewood, last in the public eye when he called for an uprising at a Spa Fields meeting, came out of prison last year and set about plotting to blow up the cabinet while they took dinner

in Grosvenor Square. Thistlewood was greatly helped by a certain Mr Edwards, who provided pistols, grenades, powder and ball and gave the place and date of the dinner.

Edwards was really a police informer, so the "horrid conspiracy" was broken. Now the government claims its repressive measures have been justified and has called an election.

The steamship "Savannah", arriving at Liverpool after crossing the Atlantic.

Southern Africa, 1820. Southern Africa is thrown into turmoil by the great Mfecane wars. Since the defeat of the previously all-powerful Ndwandwe army by the Zulus at Mhlatuze last year, there has been a chain reaction of defeated armies fleeing and attacking rival chiefdoms. While the Zulus are subduing people to the south, remnants of the Ndwandwe army have formed raiding parties, know as *Ngoni*, as far as Maputo Bay in Mozambique.

Japan, 1820. Following increasing incursions by foreign ships into Japanese waters, a special commissioner is appointed to build up coastal defences, especially around Edo (*Tokyo*).

Russia, 1820. A mutiny by the Semonovsky regiment induces Czar Alexander to halt his programme of social and political reforms.

USA, 1820. The population of the USA reaches almost ten million.

China, 3 February 1821. Following the death of the Emperor Jiaqing last year, Daoguang comes to the throne.

Rome, 23 February, 1821 The poet John Keats has died of consumption, after the publication last year of *Ode to a Nightingale.*

Mexico, 24 February 1821. General Agustin de Iturbide proclaims Mexican independence, declaring that the government should be a constitutional monarchy under Ferdinand VII of Spain or another European king.

Greece, February 1821. Archbishop Germanos of Patras calls for a Greek uprising against the Ottomans.

Ottoman Empire, March 1821. The Greek nationalist leader Alexander Ypsilanti invades Moldavia with a battalion, seizes its capital, Jassy, and occupies Bucharest.

Italy, March 1821. An Austrian army overthrows the revolutionary government installed last July by Guglielmo Pepe and restores King Ferdinand to the throne.

Italy, March 1821. King Victor Emmanuel of Piedmont, who has refused to accept a constitution, is forced to abdicate in favour of his brother Charles Felix. In Charles Felix' absence, Charles Albert of Savoy becomes regent and proclaims the Spanish constitution.

Italy, 8 April 1821. A combined Austrian and Sardinian army defeats the Pietmontese army at the battle of Novara, returning Piedmont to Sardinian rule.

Greece, April 1821. The Ottomans begin a campaign of repression following a Greek massacre of Turks in the Peloponnese.

South Atlantic, 5 May 1821. Napoleon dies on the island of St Helena.

Germany, 12 May 1821. The congress of Laibach, which opened in July, comes to an end. In spite of British opposition, the congress authorised Austria to put down the rebellions in Naples and Piedmont.

Switzerland, May 1821. The cantons expel liberal Italians who had taken refuge in Switzerland after the defeat of their movements in Piedmont and Naples.

Berlin, 10 June 1821. The German composer Carl Maria von Weber triumphs with his opera *Der Freischutz.*

Ottoman Empire, 19 June 1821. Greek troops under Alexander Ypsilanti are heavily defeated by the Ottomans at the battle of Dragasani, west of Bucharest.

Florida, 17 July 1821. Andrew Jackson becomes governor of Florida.

Peru, July 1821. Peru declares itself independent of Spain.

Russia, 4 September 1821. Czar Alexander declares that Russian influence in North America extends as far south as Oregon and closes Alaskan waters to foreigners.

Central America, 15 September 1821. San Salvador proclaims its independence and becomes a member of the United Provinces of Central America.

China, 23 September 1821. Terranova, a sailor on the US ship *Emily*, is executed by the Chinese for the death of a Chinese.

Greece, 5 October 1821. Greek rebels capture Tripolitza, the main Turkish fort in the Peloponnese.

England, October 1821. Thomas de Quincey publishes his *Confessions of an English Opium Eater.*

China, 15 December 1821. A Chinese is killed in an attack on the landing party from *HMS Topaze* at Linding; the surrender of British sailors for punishment is refused.

Central America, December 1821. Panama declares itself independent of Spain and unites with Colombia.

Germany, 1821. The philosopher Georg Hegel publishes *The Philosophy of Right.*

USA, 1821. The USA's first natural gas well is tapped at Fredonia, New York state.

USA, 1821. The distinguished soldier Davy Crockett – who claims to have killed 105 bears in seven months in the western Tennessee wilderness – is elected as a state legislator in Tennessee.

John Constable's "The Hay Wain", a celebration of a rural idyll.

John Constable portrays idyll of rural life

London, 1821

John Constable is showing a large six-foot landscape at the Royal Academy summer exhibition at Somerset House this year. Entitled *"Landscape: Noon"*, it shows an empty hay wain fording the river Stour in Suffolk beside a lowly rural cottage. The scene is painted with freshness and captures the light of an overcast midday sky, but it has not been noticed as much as the fashionable "history" paintings that make up much of the exhibition, nor has it been sold. Constable spends the summer sketching in Suffolk around East Bergholt, where his father, a wealthy corn merchant, owned several mills.

Like J M W Turner, he was trained at the Royal Academy schools, but whereas Turner was elected an RA in 1802 at the age of only 26, Constable is still only an Associate at 45. He was married recently and moved to Hampstead where he turns his outdoor sketches into large easel paintings.

Britain tightens its grip on West Africa

West Africa, 15 January 1821

The West African enclave of the Gold Coast, formerly administered by British merchants, becomes a crown colony today.

The official reason is to provide Britain with a secure base for her anti-slavery patrols. The real reason is fear of growing French influence in Senegal, and the news that the USA will be establishing a home for liberated slaves (*in Liberia*). Britain, with a colony for former slaves in Sierra Leone, a second colony on the river Gambia, and numerous coastal trading forts, is determined to contain the new arrivals and dominate trade in the interior. Whether it will succeed, given both the competition from France and the USA and the cost, is open to question.

Secret societies in Neopolitan rising

Ferdinand, the king of Naples, a bulwark against reforms.

Naples, 2 July 1820
An unexpected revolt by two military garrisons outside Naples has put pressure on King Ferdinand to bring in constitutional reforms similar to the concessions made in Spain after the uprising there last January.

The rebel officers under General Pepe wanted the restored royal house limited to a constitutional monarchy, administrative reforms to lower taxes and a more vigorous attack on feudalism.

The officers from the Nola and Capua garrisons also resent serving under an Austrian commander. Many belong to the *Carbonari* – charcoal burners – the Masonic-style secret societies that now flourish in Italy. The Neapolitan Carbonari are mainly affluent republican sympathisers, but without any clearly defined leadership.

Asian poet dies

Annam (Vietnam), 1820
Nguyen Du, the author of the verse novel *The History of Kieu*, a celebration of filial piety, and the finest contemporary practitioner of classical Chinese poetry, has died. A mandarin, born in Ha-Tinh, he served the Le dynasty, but refused to serve the Tay-Son emperor and was exiled, when he wrote his most exquisite poetry. He returned to public office under Gia-Long, but in his heart remained a poet – the greatest Annam has produced.

Napoleon dies of boredom and ill-health

St Helena, 5 May 1821
Napoleon is dead. At two this afternoon he muttered: *"France. Armee. Tete d'armee. Josephine"*, and then fell into a coma. His household gathered round him and watched him die peacefully as the sun slipped into the sea.

He was 51 and had spent the last six years like a caged lion, suffering the petty indignities heaped on him by the British governor, Sir Hudson Lowe, who was ever fearful that "General Bonaparte" would escape. Napoleon took a certain delight in taunting Lowe, but as he grew ill Lowe's treatment of him became vindictive.

His approaching end became apparent last October when he fainted, and his vomiting and lack of appetite weakened him. He told his faithful court chamberlain Montholon: "There is no more oil in the

Napoleon: the British claim he died naturally, the French are unsure.

lamp." Now, the light of this military genius has gone out on a lump of volcanic rock far from the battlefields of Europe which he ruled with such mastery and the courts where he made and unmade kings.

George's embarrassing queen has died

London, 7 August 1821
She was a queen who was vilified, persecuted and humiliated by her husband, George IV; but she was loved by the people, and when she died today, aged 53, the City of London decided to pay tribute to her. But George said Caroline's cortege would not pass through the City, even if he had to call out the Life Guards to stop it.

When George first set eyes on Caroline of Brunswick he had to drink a dram of brandy to recover. They had one child and then separated. For the rest of her life he tried to prevent her seeing her daughter. He ordered the passage in the Prayer book which prays for "our Gracious Queen" to be removed. On coronation day last month, Caroline was barred from Westminster Abbey. The next even-

Caroline with an admirer, Bergami; her husband publicly vilified her.

ing she was taken ill at Drury Lane and died a week later. George is now free to dally with Lady Jersey and with Mrs Fitzherbert, whom he married secretly years ago.

Electric motor built by English inventor

London, 1821
The enthusiastic young scientist Michael Faraday has already been at the centre of important discoveries in the field of chemistry. Now, turning his attention to electricity, he is making practical use of two recent discoveries and has created an electric motor.

Oersted, a contemporary scientist, has discovered that a flow of electricity through a wire produces a magnetic field around it. Ampere too, has shown that this field is magnetic. Now Faraday has built a device – little more than a scientific toy at the moment – which uses electricity to produce rotary motion.

This impressive demonstration of electro-magnetic rotation is a tribute to the hands-on skill and intellectual power of Faraday, who was once laboratory assistant to the great Humphry Davy. Davy had been so impressed by Faraday's letter of application that he offered him the job on the spot – he had just fired Faraday's predecessor.

Faraday: scientist and inventor.

Greek independence movement born out of spontaneous revolts

Greece, 1821
The Ottoman empire's centuries-old domination of Greece is beginning to crumble as a spontaneous wave of nationalist revolts sweeps the country.

The signal for the uprising appears to have been a proclamation by the Metropolitan of Patras on 25 March that Greeks should no longer acknowledge Ottoman rule.

Among the first Ottoman strongholds to fall were the Morean fortresses, temporarily undermanned with most of the Ottoman garrison away in Albania trying to suppress the breakaway movement there. Key ports around the Greek coast are now in nationalist hands after attacks by Greek privateers. Among the islands held by the rebels are Psara and Spetsai – where a wealthy widow has paid to blockade the local gulf. In Hydra, as in many other parts of Greece, shipowners have organised and funded the revolt.

The "crushing" wars of a Zulu Bonaparte

Between 1818 and about 1840 a series of wars between various African states and chieftains raged across Southern Africa, changing its political structure for ever and opening it up to European penetration. Known as the *Mfecane* – which translates as "the crushing" – wars, they began when the Zulu in northern Natal began a chain reaction of battles and that reached as far north as Tanzania.

The spark for this expansion is usually attributed to one man – a Zulu chief called Shaka. An imposing figure over six feet tall with enormous energy and powers of organisation, Shaka is credited with social and military innovations which turned his small Zulu clan into a mighty empire within a handful of years.

He organised all the men of his nation into regiments according to their age and forbade them to marry until they were 40; taken from their homesteads, they had to live in one of 15 military camps dotted about the empire. He gave them short stabbing spears so that they would engage the enemy in close combat and long shields that could be locked together to present a "tortoise shell" against the enemy's throwing spears. He took away their sandals to toughen their feet and make them run fast; his warriors would jog from battle to battle and then sprint into close combat.

Shaka is also often credited with developing an effective new battle formation – the "chest and horns". The "horns" would feint at and finally enclose the enemy while the main "chest" advanced inexorably. He also abolished circumcision of the young men which weakened them and, perhaps more importantly, left the whole nation vulnerable to attack during the circumcision ritual when all other activities came to a halt.

Named after a stomach bug

Shaka is often compared with his rough contemporary Napoleon Bonaparte in that his influence spread across much of a continent. Yet he was a tragic, manic figure too, a sort of African Oedipus-cum-Bluebeard. He was the the illegitimate son of Senzangakhona, chief of the Zulu, who were at that time just another of the petty chiefdoms in the area. His mother Nandi is said to have explained away the first signs of her pregnancy around 1786 by saying she had *ishaka*, or stomach bug and hence her son's name. After a harsh childhood in exile, made worse by his illegitimacy, he returned home to kill his father and become chief of the Zulu. Later he was so fearful of ageing that he killed any wife that bore him a child. When his mother died

he became so unbalanced that he caused hundreds to be slaughtered.

Such anyway is the mythology surrounding this remarkable man. Realities, as sober historians are wont to point out, are likely to be more complex and less dramatic. It seems likely that a rapid rise in population combined with drought provided the urge for expansion to gain new pasturage for the cattle, rather than the megalomaniac visions of one man. Furthermore most of his supposed innovations can be attributed to earlier strategists and tactitians – with the possible exception of dispensing with sandals. This is not to deny his genius but to put it in context.

The "chest and horns" battle formation, for example can be traced back at least as early as the 1680's among the Rozvi of Zimbabwe. The ultimate origins of other Zulu innovations, notably the age-regiments and the religio-magical ceremonies of the nation can be traced to the Ronga kingdoms of Southern Mozambique in the 18th century. Shaka himself began his military career in the army of the Mthethwa, originally a vassal state of the Ronga which broke away to become independent in the late eighteenth century. Then led by the clever strategist and military leader Dingiswayo, the Mthethwa subordinated a number of the surrounding chiefdoms within a military confederacy.

Killed by his half-brother

The Mthethwa kingdom's major adversary was the Ndwandwe, who had earlier broken away from the Ronga and grown larger and stronger. They competed for cattle and followers, the Mthethwa supplying ivory to European traders in southern Mozambique while the Ndwandwe appear to have supplied slaves.

In 1818 the two nations met in battle; the Mthethwa were defeated and Dingiswayo was killed. But Shaka, who had headed one of the defeated regiments rallied the Mthethwa and, a year later beat the Ndwandwe — thereby inheriting Dingiswayo's confederacy which now became known as the Zulu after Shaka's own clan.

Fragments of the Ndwandwe called Ngoni were pushed north into the Transvaal, Mozambique, Zimbabwe and eventually Tanzania, attacking and destroying existing communities as they went. This was the beginning of the "crushing". By 1840 the old established states and ethnic identities all over the south-eastern quarter of Africa had been conquered and absorbed, either by the Zulu

themselves or by those who had fled, like the Ndwandwe, from the Zulu's military supremacy.

Shaka himself did not survive to see the immense consequences of his Zulu military revolution. He became increasingly violent and unpredictable, and terrified those around him by his sudden and arbitrary cruelty. He survived one assassination attempt only to be speared to death in broad daylight by his half-brother Dingane in 1828.

When the Europeans began to trek into the interior from the south in large numbers during the 1830's and 1840's they found a region dominated by Zulu-type kingdoms dotted strategically across the map. The Boer trekkers, as well as the British traders and missionaries who came in lesser numbers, fitted into the interstices of the strategic map, settling and making alliances with peoples opposed to the Zulu-type states. Some apologists for European settlement have claimed that the whites simply took over "empty lands" devastated by the *Mfecane* wars. However history, backed by the evidence of archaeology, shows that the lands between the Zulu-type states were not unoccupied but merely in a political and strategic vacuum.

Spears dominate the rifle

Zulu dominance was far from total however. A number of non-Zulu "shelter kingdoms" used their connection with European traders and missionaries to obtain guns and ammunition to resist the Zulu states whose supremacy rested on spear-power. One of the most successful of these was the Lesotho kingdom led by a cunning warrior and diplomat called Moshoeshoe. He built up a state in the foothills by a mixture of peaceful and warlike means. He raided for cattle but instead of using them for food and shields as the Zulu did he gave them to his followers to ensure their allegiance. Then with guns and horses traded from the Europeans he built up a powerful cavalry which enabled him to resist the advances of both the Boers and the Zulu.

But, remarkably, the Zulu spear-power remained in the ascendant until 1879 when it was overwhelmed by the superior technology of the repeating rifle – soon followed by the machine gun. In this context it should be noted that it was only a part of the Zulu army that was defeated by the Boers at Blood River in 1838. Zulu power was only finally broken, at great cost in men and materials, by the British at the Battle of Ulundi in 1879, when the humiliating British defeat at Isandhlwana earlier in the year was avenged.

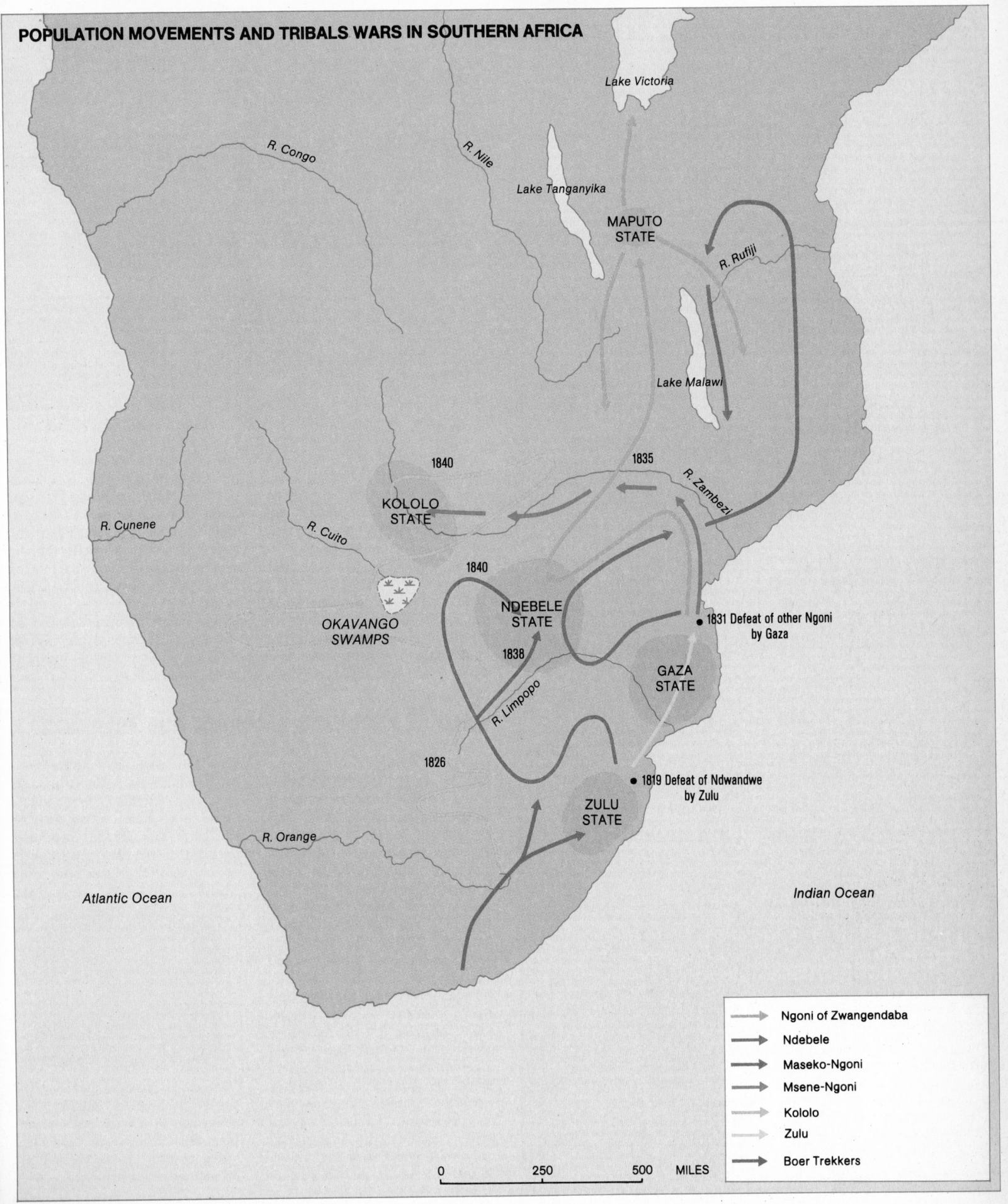

POPULATION MOVEMENTS AND TRIBALS WARS IN SOUTHERN AFRICA

R. Congo

R. Nile

Lake Victoria

Lake Tanganyika

MAPUTO
STATE

R. Rufiji

Lake Malawi

1840

1835

R. Zambezi

KOLOLO
STATE

R. Cunene

R. Cuito

1840

NDEBELE
STATE

● 1831 Defeat of other Ngoni
by Gaza

*OKAVANGO
SWAMPS*

1838

GAZA
STATE

R. Limpopo

1826

● 1819 Defeat of Ndwandwe
by Zulu

R. Orange

ZULU
STATE

Atlantic Ocean

Indian Ocean

→	Ngoni of Zwangendaba
→	Ndebele
→	Maseko-Ngoni
→	Msene-Ngoni
→	Kololo
→	Zulu
→	Boer Trekkers

0   250   500   MILES

Japan, 1821. Ino Tadataka's map of the whole of Japan, based on accurate surveying, is finally finished. It was begun on the *shogun's* orders in 1801 and completed after Tadataka's death in 1818 by his followers.

Greece, 13 January 1822. At Epidaurus, nationalist rebels proclaim the independence of Greece and draw up a constitution.

Aegean, April 1822. The Ottomans massacre thousands of Greek insurgents on the island of Chios.

South America, 24 May 1822. Antonio Jose de Sucre, a lieutenant of Simon Bolivar, defeats the Spanish royalist forces at the battle of Pichincha, securing the independence of Quito (*Ecuador*).

South America, 29 May 1822. The provinces of Quito unite with Colombia.

Mediterranean, 19 June 1822. A Ottoman fleet is destroyed by the Greeks under Constantine Kanaris.

Spain, 30 June 1822. King Ferdinand VII is taken prisoner by the rebels led by Rafael Riego.

Mexico, 21 July 1822. General Agustin de Iturbide has himself crowned emperor of Mexico.

Greece, July 1822. Following the invasion of Greece by a large Ottoman army, the Greek government flees to the islands.

Portugal, September 1822. A liberal constitution similar to Spain's is adopted.

Brazil, September 1822. Brazil declares its independence from Portugal.

Italy, 20 October 1822. A congress opens in Verona to discuss the revolutions in Spain, Greece, Italy and South America. It is attended by Austria, Prussia, France, Russia and Britain.

Brazil, October 1822. Dom Pedro, the son of King John VI of Portugal, is proclaimed emperor of Brazil.

USA, 12 December 1822. The USA grants formal recognition to Mexico's new revolutionary government, headed by Agustin de Iturbide. In June President Monroe extended diplomatic recognition to Great Colombia.

Italy, 14 December 1822. The congress of Verona closes. In spite of British opposition, France has been authorised to intervene militarily in Spain to quell revolt and restore Ferdinand VII to the throne.

Crete, 1822. A rebellion in Crete, set off last year by the Greek War of Independence, is brutally put down by the Ottomans, with the aid of Egyptian reinforcements.

South Africa, 1822. The Mfecane wars spread west over the Drakensberg mountain escarpment onto the South Africa plateau. The Khumalo, led by Mzilikazi, a brilliant young general, have fled from Zulu assaults to confront the Pedi peoples of the Transvaal, who name the attackers *Ndebele*. Another small army has fled from the Zulus to attack the Sotho peoples of South Africa and Lesotho, provoking the rise of numerous competing Sotho armies.

California, 1822. California becomes part of the republic of Mexico.

West Africa, 1822. Encouraged and financed by the American Colonization Society, a group of white clergymen and businessmen in the USA, the American Colonisation Society, freed African Americans found a small settlement on the West African coast. The new colony becomes known as Liberia.

Ottoman Empire, 1822. The city of Janina in north-west Greece capitulates to the Ottomans after a two-year siege. Its leader, Ali Pasha, is put to death.

Italy, 8 July 1828. The poet Percy Bysshe Shelley is drowned.

Russia, 1822. Pushkin's narrative poem *The Fountain of Bakhchisarai* is published.

Vienna, 1822. Franz Liszt, aged 11, makes his debut as a pianist.

USA, 23 January 1823. The USA gives formal recognition to Argentina and Chile.

Greece, January 1823. Having failed to take the key fortress of Missolonghi at the entrance to the Gulf of Corinth, the Ottomans are forced to withdraw.

Mexico, 19 March 1823. Agustin de Iturbide, who become emperor last year, is forced to abdicate following an uprising led by Antonio de Santa Anna.

Spain, April 1823. French forces led by Louis de Bourbon, the duke of Angouleme, cross the Pyrenees into Spain and march to Madrid. The rebels holding King Ferdinand VII are driven south to Cadiz, taking the king with them.

Prussia, 5 June 1823. Eight provincial assemblies in which the landed gentry hold the greatest powers are created. The reform is intended to reduce differences between the conservative, Protestant agricultural east and the more advanced, liberal and Catholic regimes in the west.

Britain, 1823. At a football game at Rugby school, William Ellis picks up the ball and runs with it, inventing a new game – rugby.

"Independence or death" cries emperor

Brazil, where the poor and barefoot take on the burden of independence.

Brazil, 12 October 1822
Dom Pedro, the 24-year-old son and heir to King John VI, today declared himself constitutional emperor of Brazil. He has been regent for the last 18 months, since his father finally gave in to demands that he return to Portugal.

Once seen as a dissolute young man, Pedro has come to symbolise the nation's hopes for independence in the face of Lisbon's efforts to reduce Brazil once again to the status of a dependent colony. He has refused an order to join his father in Lisbon, promising instead to remain in Rio de Janeiro. He has appointed a leading campaigner for independence as his chief adviser, and in May accepted the title of "Perpetual Protector and Defender of Brazil".

Last month Portugal annulled all his acts. His response was simple: "The hour has come! Independence or death!"

Hero of Peruvian freedom has resigned

Lima, Peru, 27 July 1822
Jose de San Martin, the figurehead of the struggle for South American independence, has resigned from his post as protector of Peru. Faced by increasing dissatisfaction he will quit politics and may well leave the country he fought so valiantly for.

San Martin entered Lima on 9 July 1821 and took the title "Protector of Peruvian Freedom". His brief rule has been precarious and unhappy. Of all South America's colonies, Peru, with its rigid class system bolstered by slave labour, was least ripe for a republican government. Indeed, San Martin suggested that a European prince should be imported to establish a monarchy. It appears that San Martin's decision was influenced by yesterday's meeting with Simon Bolivar, the Colombian leader and a fellow freemason, at Guayaquil. Whether San Martin had already chosen to resign, or if Bolivar's refusal to back his regime with cash or troops left him with no alternative, is debatable. Either way, he left the meeting abruptly, returning to Lima. There, declaring himself no longer useful, he resigned.

Tobacco is becoming fashionable again in England, despite the complaint by Dr Johnson over a generation ago that the habit far from creating placcid tranquility is anti-social and barbarous.

"Hands off", US warns Europe

Washington, DC, 2 December 1823
The United States has sent a "hands off" warning to any European country contemplating future colonisation anywhere in the Americas – North *or* South. The declaration, by President James Monroe in his annual message to Congress, follows a rumour, picked up in London by US diplomats, that European powers were planning the reconquest of the Spanish American republics which had declared their independence from Spain.

The "Monroe Doctrine" declares that the United States' political system is essentially different from those in Europe; and that any attempt by a European country to extend its influence in America will be regarded as dangerous to America's peace and security.

James Monroe: the fifth president of the United States, in Washington.

French fear Spain's radical government

A French Hussar officer: the perfect vehicle for counter-revolution.

Paris, 25 December 1822
The French government today declared its intention of acting alone to overturn the revolution in Spain. Chateaubriand, the impetuous foreign minister, is already planning to get together an army of 100,000 men to march on Madrid and restore King Ferdinand VII to power. Since the revolution of 1820 Spain has been governed by the so-called "jail birds", the persecuted liberals of the 1812 movement.

For the past year France, Russia, Austria and Britain have been squabbling with each other about what to do about Spain. All of them fear the spread of revolution to their monarchies. But Britain particularly will be furious if today's move leads to restoring Spanish power in South America.

US founds African home for freed slaves

Montserrado, West Africa, 1822
An advance party of freed American slaves is building the first homes for a settlement at the mouth of the Sewa river as part of a plan to establish a Negro homeland for ex-slaves and their descendants in West Africa. The ex-slaves are the first of 6,000 that the American Colonization Society hopes will settle here.

The settlement's director is a white American, Jehudi Ashmun, who started the society over five years ago to raise funds to buy slaves their freedom and pay for their passage to Africa. Contributions have come from the society's branches in every state, churches and state legislatures opposed to slavery. West Africa was chosen for the new homeland as the first generation American slaves are thought to have come from here.

A miniature mask, made by the Dan people near the Sewa river.

British foreign minister commits suicide

Robert Stewart, Lord Castlereagh.

England, 12 August 1822
Lord Castlereagh, Britain's foreign secretary, who was due to leave for a summit meeting of European powers at Verona, was found dead today at his country home in Kent. His health had been deteriorating for some time and his doctor, concerned about his patient's mental stability, had removed all the razors. A penknife, however, had been overlooked and with it Castlereagh cut his throat.

Castlereagh's greatest achievement was the peace settlement after the Napoleonic Wars and the creation of a concert of European powers through regular consultation. He opposed the Russian "doctrine" of military intervention to preserve the status quo.

Cannibals forgiven by African statesman

Cape Town, South Africa, 1822
As anarchy reigns in the no-man's-land between Shaka's Zulu empire in the north and the British empire in the south, one man, Moshoeshoe, the chief of the Mokoteli, stands firm in defence of civilised values.

Refugees, driven out by the two empires, are competing for land. One tribe after another – the Hlubi, the Khumalo, the Ngwaneni – achieved temporary dominance only to be crushed. The final horror is the emergence of the *makhwata* (lean ones), men so hungry that

they have taken to cannibalism. One victim was Moshoeshoe's own grandfather. With a magnanimity rarely equalled he has first defeated them and then – calling them the "living souls of my grandfather" – given them cattle to discourage their aweful practise.

Alas, Shaka, instead of saluting his statesmanship, sees him as a rival, and is sending his warriors to punish for him for his presumption in acting as peacemaker. There seems to be little chance of relief for the people of southern Africa.

Mr Macintosh invents a waterproof fabric

Manchester, 1823
The latest – and perhaps the most suitable – fashion being worn in Manchester is the Macintosh. It is a raincoat made of a layer of rubber sandwiched between two layers of cloth. The material was invented by Charles Macintosh, a chemist.

The material does have some disadvantages. It tends to become brittle in cold weather and can smell

pungently in the heat of summer. And the work-force in Macintosh's Manchester factory tends to be inept in making the material to the owner's prescription.

Macintosh, who began his working life in a counting house, has made several notable industrial contributions in the manufacture of dyes, bleaching powder and other commercial chemicals.

South Africa, June 1823. Sotho Mfecane raiders are defeated by the Tswana people at the battle of Dithakong. The Tswana victory stops the further invasion of Sebetweane's Kololo, who were rushing to join the attack, and turns the Kololo northwards to invade Botswana instead.

Central America, 1 July 1823. Guatemala, San Salvador, Nicaragua, Honduras and Costa Rica declare themselves sovereign states within the confederated United Provinces of Central America.

Britain, 14 July 1823. King Kamehameha II and Queen Kamamalu of the Hawaiian Islands die of measles during a visit to Britain.

Mexico, 20 August 1823. Mexico recognises the independence of the United Provinces of Central America.

Rome, 28 August 1823. Leo XII becomes pope in succession to Pius VII, who died a week ago.

Spain, 31 August 1823. The Spanish revolutionary forces under Rafael Riego are defeated by the French at the battle of Trocadero.

Spain, 23 September 1823. Cadiz falls to the French. Ferdinand VII, who was taken there by the rebels, is handed over to the victors and restored to the throne.

USA, 7 November 1823. John Quincy Adams, the US secretary of state, rejects a British offer to form an alliance to thwart possible intervention by the Holy Alliance in Latin America.

India, 1823. In spite of the failure of his mission to China, Lord Amherst is appointed governor general of India.

Britain, 1823. Robert Peel, the home secretary, institutes wide-ranging reforms of the criminal law and prison system.

France, 1823. Nicephore Niepce discovers the principle of photography.

South-East Asia, February 1824. Following the Burmese occupation of Assam and Manipur in north-eastern India, war breaks out between Britain and Burma.

USA, 17 April 1824. The USA signs a treaty with Russia settling their border dispute.

Burma, 11 May 1824. British naval forces under Sir Archibald Campbell seize Rangoon.

France, 6 June 1824. The foreign minister, Chateaubriand, is abruptly dismissed after a bitter disagreement with the prime minister, Villele, especially over the issue of Greece.

Britain, 6 June 1824. A law is passed recognising the right to strike.

Mexico, 19 July 1824. Returning secretly from exile, Agustin de Iturbide, the former president, is arrested and shot.

USA, 4 August 1824. The USA gives formal diplomatic recognition to the newly independent nation of Brazil.

France, 15 August 1824. Censorship is reimposed.

France, 16 September 1824. Louis XVIII dies and the count of Artois, his brother and the leader of the Ultra-royalists, succeeds him as Charles X.

Rhode Island, October 1824. A mob of more than 400 whites riots and attack Negro residents of Providence in a protest against their employment.

USA, 1 December 1824. No clear winner emerges from a bitterly fought presidential election.

Peru, December 1824. Following the defeat of the Spanish by independence fighters under Antonio de Sucre at the battle of Ayacucho, the Spanish are forced to agree to the withdrawal of the royalist troops remaining in Peru. Peruvian independence is secured.

North America, 1824. An expedition led by the explorer William Ashley discovers a huge salt lake west of the Rocky Mountains.

Greece, 1824. Mohammed Ali, the Albanian-born governor of Egypt, intervenes in the Greek War of Independence on the side of the Ottomans.

USA, 1824. An American invention makes it possible to harvest at three times the previous speed. Drawn by a two-horse team, Cyrus McCormick's reaper-harvester is an improvement on Patrick Bell's, which is pushed from behind.

California, 1824. The constitution of the United Mexican states is adopted, giving California territorial status.

Hawaii, 1824. The dowager Queen Kaahumanu becomes regent for her young brother Kauikeaouli.

France, 1824. The painter Delacroix exhibits *The Massacre at Shios* at the Paris Salon.

Vienna, 1824. Ludwig van Beethoven composes his ninth symphony.

London, 1824. The National Gallery opens.

Britain, 1824. The Society for the Prevention of Cruelty to Animals is founded.

British use steamboat to seize Rangoon

British troops storming one of Rangoon's principal stockades.

Rangoon, Burma, 11 May 1824
A task force of 11,000 British troops has captured Rangoon as a retaliatory first step against the king of Burma's invasion of the British Indian possession of Shahpuri in February.

The British commander-in-chief, Sir Archibald Campbell, is under orders from Lord Amherst, the governor general, to occupy all of Burma and depose the king. Sir Archibald, whose task force took Rangoon after a 400-mile river journey, plans to leave 3,500 men to garrison Rangoon before proceeding up the Irrawaddy to attack this mountainous kingdom's other main cities. However, the task force is locked in Rangoon until the end of the year as the monsoons, expected any day now, make the river impassable for six months. Included in the flotilla is the first steamboat to be used by Britain in war.

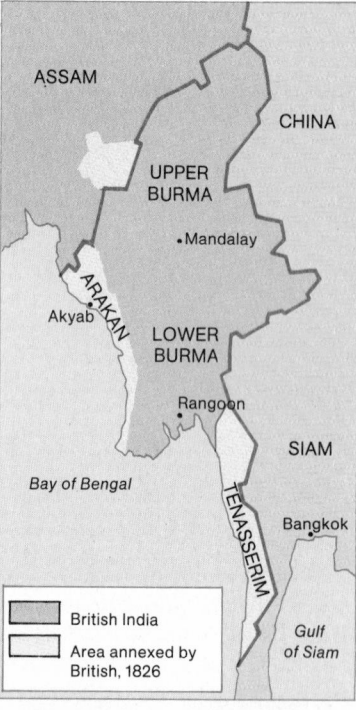

Steam engine study generates new law

Paris, 1824
A former officer, Sadi Carnot, has long been fascinated by scientific and technical ideas and turned his attention to improving the design of steam engines. France, he felt, was lagging behind in this area which has brought such wealth to Britain and the United States.

His interest is in the theoretical use of steam as a driving force. Now he has published an essay showing how the motive power of a steam engine is produced when the heat drops from the temperature in the boiler to the cooler condenser.

The efficiency of engines, Carnot concludes, depends on the temperatures of its hottest and coolest parts – and not on the energy source that drives the machine.

The "Carnot cycle", as it is called, is not therefore just about steam power, but abut energy movement in particular. His conclusions form a law of *thermodynamics*.

Britain recognises workers' right to strike

Britain, 1824

This year workers are once more allowed to form trades unions, and to strike, thanks to the repeal of the controversial Combination Laws of 1799 and 1800.

The change in the law was the result of a campaign by the activist Francis Place and the radical politician Joseph Hume. A parliamentary committee appointed to inquire into the Combination Laws was packed by Hume, and its recommendation for repeal was accepted by parliament. But Place was the inspiration. Unlike some of his associates, Place is not a political extremist, but a self-made businessman – refused work in 1793 after organising a strike – who has managed to support a wife and ten children from his tailor's shop.

He seeks reform, not revolution, and one of the keys to his success has been his ability to work with people from different classes, like Joseph Hume and the political economist J R McCulloch. Above all he has shown himself to be a brilliant manager of committees.

Cartoon politics: George IV, as Coriolanus, addresses the workers.

Louis XVIII, a good king of France

Paris, 16 September 1824

Louis XVIII, who died today after a long illness, leaves a strong, peaceful and prosperous France. This was quite an achievement for a man who was not a particularly strong personality and who came to power when France had suffered the shattering defeat of Waterloo.

Louis XVIII was the brother of Louis XVI, but he managed to escape the guillotine by fleeing to Brussels in 1791. As the revolution spread he moved first to Brunswick and then to Warsaw, until he finally went to England in 1807. In 1814, when the defeat of Napoleon seemed certain, he went to Ghent and made a shrewd compromise with the wily and opportunist French foreign minister, Talleyrand.

Talleyrand promised to restore the monarchy; Louis agreed to preserve the parliament.

Irish campaign for Catholic civil rights

Dublin, 10 May 1823

A 48-year-old Irish barrister, Daniel O'Connell, believes that he can pressure the British into granting full civic rights to Catholics by forming a mass movement based on an alliance between the Catholic middle class, the priesthood, peasants and moderate Protestants.

Earlier Catholic activist groups have been largely composed of lawyers, businessmen and landlords. With his Catholic Association, O'Connell intends to pitch his appeal right across the spectrum, from the rich, who will subscribe £1 a month or more, to the poorest, who will pay a penny a month. The funds will be used for both eduational purposes and political campaigning. O'Connell intends to take up Catholic grievances over rents, tithes, and the administration of justice.

Mexico is to become a federal republic

Mexico City, now the capital of Antonio de Santa Anna's new federal republic.

Mexico City, 1824

Mexico has declared itself a constitutional republic after 14 years of war and anarchy. The republic is to be federal, on US lines, and General Guadalupe Victoria has been appointed president.

Mexico gained its independence from Spain in 1821. The following year General Agustin de Iturbide, the Mexican conservative who had put down the radical nationalist revolt against Spain in 1815, seized power and declared himself emperor. His rule lasted for only ten months; then General Antonio de Santa Anna overthrew him and made way for the new republic.

Even then conflict amongst the Mexican republicans did not come to an end. Conservatives advocated a centralised state and radicals a federal state, each group identified with a different brand of freemasonry. The radicals appear to have won. To sooth the centralists' wounded feelings, President Victoria has recognised the special position of the Catholic Church, a key conservative demand.

Britain's Lord Byron becomes Greek hero

Byron, dressed as a Greek soldier.

Missolonghi, Greece, 19 April 1824

Lord Byron, who died of marsh fever here today, is being mourned as a national hero in Greece. He arrived in the Ionian islands last August and spent £4,000 on equipping a fleet to sail here to join the insurgents. In a poem written on his 36th birthday he foresaw his death.

Byron's poetry was mostly written in foreign lands. He first visited Greece on the Grand Tour when he was 22, and emulated Leander by swimming the Hellespont. From this eastern journey he produced the early cantos of *Childe Harold's Pilgrimage* and awoke "to find myself famous" as the archetypal Romantic figure, pale, sated with sensuality and suffering yet scornful of fate. After his marriage ended he left England in 1816 amid an aura of scandal. His years in Italy produced *Don Juan*, his long, relaxed, conversational poem.

His death removes the third English romantic poet abroad. Keats died in Rome in 1821, in his middle twenties, and Shelley was drowned the following year, aged 30.

1824 (1824-1826)

Australia, 1824. A penal colony is founded in Brisbane.

USA, 9 February 1825. John Quincy Adams, the former secretary of state, is elected president, ending a two-month impasse over the choice of the new head of state. The other main contender was Andrew Jackson.

Greece, February 1825. Egyptian troops led by Ibrahim Pasha, disembark in the Peloponnese and take the port of Pylos.

West Indies, 17 March 1825. The Spanish party on the island of Santo Domingo proclaims its independence in the name of the Dominican Republic.

France, 28 April 1825. The chamber of deputies adopts a law indemnifying emigres for loss of property damaged in the revolution.

Portugal, August 1825. Portugal recognises the independence of Brazil.

USA, 25 October 1825. The Erie Canal, linking the Great Lakes with New York City via the Hudson river, is completed.

Russia, 1 December 1825. Czar Alexander dies and there is confusion about the succession. His brother Constantine has secretly renounced his claims in favour of the youngest brother, Nicholas, who refuses to believe in the arrangement until he has secured a further renunciation.

USA, 12 December 1825. With the demise of the Federalist Party at the recent election, the rival Democratic-Republican Party splits into two factions in Congress.

USA, 25 December 1825. The USA signs a trade treaty with the Central American Federation.

Russia, 26 December 1825. The Northern Society – which is campaigning for representative government, the abolition of serfdom and social reforms – launches a disorganised revolt, which is immediately crushed by Nicholas, who has now accepted his succession as czar.

USA, December 1825. The Creek Indians sign a treaty ceding all their remaining land to the state of Georgia.

South America, 1825. Bolivia and Uruguay declare themselves independent of respectively, Peru and Brazil.

Japan, 1825. After further encroachments on the Japanese coast by British and American ships, the *shogun's* government issues an edict calling for the expulsion of all foreign ships from Japanese waters.

Caucasus, 1825. Persia rejects the 1813 treaty of Gulistan, which ceded the Caucasus region to Russia, and attempts to retake Georgia.

Sudan, 1825. Uthman Bey, the commander-in-chief of the Egyptian forces in Sudan, builds a citadel at Khartoum as the capital for Egyptian rule of the upper Nile.

India, 1825. A college is founded in Delhi to act as a channel for western learning in northern India.

England, 1825. *The Diary of Samuel Pepys*, which was left, with his library, to his Cambridge college, Magdalene, has been deciphered by John Smith and is published.

USA, 1825. Guided by visions, Joseph Smith publishes his *Book of Mormon* and founds the first Mormon church, at Fayette, New York state. He claims to be restoring the ancient, primitive Christian religion.

USA, 1825. On the death of her husband, Rebecca Webb Lukens takes over his boiler-plate mill in Pennsylvania, becoming the first woman manager in the iron industry.

France, 1825. Henri de Saint-Simon, the founder of a new system of social philosophy, dies. He argued for a reorganisation of society which would give the controlling share in government to industrialists and scientists instead of the military and property-owning classes.

Italy, 1825. Alessandro Manzoni publishes an historical novel entitled *I Promessi Sposi*, a Milanese story of the 17th century.

Denmark, 1825. The chemist Hans Christian Oersted isolates aluminium by reducing aluminium chloride with potassium.

South-East Asia, 1825. The aristocracy of the ancient kingdom of Java, led by Prince Diponegoro, rise up against the Dutch colonists.

Boston, 13 February 1826. The American Society for the Promotion of Temperance is formed.

India, February 1826. The British sign a peace treaty at Yandaboo with the king of Ava, bringing an end to a war that has raged since 1824. The Burmese cede the territories of Arakan and Tenasserim, agree to pay an indemnity of £ 1 million, conclude a commercial treaty and admit a British resident.

Portugal, 18 March 1826. King Pedro of Brazil inherits the Portuguese throne as Pedro IV on the death of his father, John VI.

Peruvians drive out Spanish rulers

Lima, Peru, 1825
The Spanish army in Peru has capitulated and 23,000 Spanish troops are to be withdrawn. The Spanish had little choice after their defeat by Antonio de Sucre at Ayacucho on 9 December. The independence of Peru is thus assured.

Peru had originally declared its independence in 1821, proclaimed by San Martin who asumed supreme authority. Factional quarrels weakened the new republic, San Martin was overthrown and Simon Bolivar took over the government. Taking advantage of the disorders, Spain counter-attacked.

Supported by Colombian reinforcements under de Sucre, Bolivar defeated the Spanish at Junin on 24 August 1824 and then returned to Lima. De Sucre took command and it was his army of 5,800 men that defeated the 9,300 Spanish troops at Ayacucho, ensuring their capitulation.

Antonio de Sucre: liberator of Peru.

Bolivia attains independence

Simon Bolivar, the scourge of Spain and now the liberator of Bolivia.

Bolivia, 1825
Another part of Spain's South American colonies has gained its independence. Upper Peru, among the most barren and remote areas of the continent, is to become the nation of Bolivia, named in honour of Simon Bolivar, the architect of South American freedom. Bolivar has also drawn up the Constitution.

For all its aspirations Bolivia is less a coherent state than a name. A vast territory of arid mountains and dense jungles, it lacks social, political or geographical cohesion. Its Indians are impoverished and the jungles virtually uninhabited. The ruling class lacks the ability to rule.

The former valuable trade route from Lima to Buenos Aires, which passed through the capital of La Paz, and in many ways justified the colony's existence, has been abandoned. Mining, once a vital industry, is no longer viable.

Sudan falls to brutal Egyptian invaders

Sudan, 1825
Mohammed Ali, the rough visionary who dragged Egypt into the 19th century with sheer willpower, has conquered the Sudan. Whether there is anything left there worth holding on to is debatable.

His motives are simple: to deny the Mameluke rebels (who previously effectively controlled all of Egypt) the sanctuary of Dongola, to milch the country of all the slaves and gold, and to divert his army from plotting at home. The army has obeyed his orders to the letter. Since they crossed the frontier in 1820, the brutality of the troops, commanded by Mohammed Ali's son, Ismail Pasha, has guaranteed Sudanese resistance. The Mamelukes of Dongola fled before him, but the Shayqiyya of the Nile fought and were massacred. Kordofan fell in 1821.

West African army defeats the British

Gold Coast, 22 January 1824
A British force has been wiped out by an Asante army under Osei Bonsu, with the British commander, Sir Charles MacCarthy, committing suicide. By coincidence, Osei Bonsu died of natural causes on the same day. The background to the British defeat is the refusal of the coastal Fante tribe to accept Asante domination. In this they were encouraged by the British who wrongly see Asantes as slave-traders and regard their hegemony as a threat to the standard policy of "divide and rule".

The major mistake of the British was to underestimate the strength of the Asantes under Osei Bonsu, who had ended the anarchy in the kingdom and centralised the state.

The defeat is the first serious defeat of a major colonial power by an indigenous African army. To recover their lost prestige, the British must now either mount a major expedition against the Asante or make peace.

A brass cast of an Asante family pounding "fu-fu", the staple diet in their region in Africa.

"Romantic" composer Weber dies at 39

London, 5 June 1826
German music has lost one of its pioneering figures with the death today from consumption of Carl Maria von Weber. He was 39. Weber, a cousin of Mozart's wife, championed a new emotional and "Romantic" style, which found its greatest expression in his German operas, especially *Der Freischutz* (1821) and *Euryanthe* (1823). The former won Weber international fame and he was invited to write an opera for London. He gave the first performance of this work, *Oberon*, at Covent Garden in June; it was a great success, but the effort dealt the final blow to Weber's health.

World's first steam railway is opened

The opening of George Stephenson's Stockton to Darlington railway.

England, 27 September 1825
There were scenes of wild enthusiasm here today when the Stockton to Darlington railway opened to traffic. It is the first railway in the world designed for steam locomotives. Parliament approved the building of the line in 1821, but it was only after the company acquired the services of a young engineer, George Stephenson, that the decision was made to go for steam.

Stephenson's locomotive weighs eight tons and can run at speeds of between 12 and 16 miles an hour. It is not only the engine that is crucial. Stephenson has found that even quite small hills can reduce hauling power by 50 per cent. So he surveyed the route himself. He also pushed for malleable iron rails, much more suitable for locomotives than the cast-iron used for most of the present crude tramways.

Ottoman sultan annihilates Janissaries

Istanbul, 16 June 1826
The Janissary corps, once the elite of the Ottoman army, but lately a corrupt, anarchic force posing the crucial obstacle to reform, has been annihilated by Sultan Mahmud II.

Unlike his ill-fated reforming predecessor Selim III, Mahmud secretly built up a new force, with powerful artillery, to resist the inevitable Janissary mutiny. When the Janissaries marched on the capital yesterday, Mahmud's guns moved them down outside the *seraglio*, then bombarded them to destruction when they sheltered in Istanbul's Hippodrome.

The slaughter complete, Mahmud has abolished the Janissary corps, destroyed its standard, and proscribed its name. Thus, the feudal Ottoman empire is dead.

The Janissaries: against reform.

Czar's troops stop December coup plot

St Petersburg, 18 December 1825
After a day of mutinous turmoil, with soldiers and sailors breaking ranks and shouting for political reforms, the new czar, Nicholas, is tonight personally interrogating the plotters, who include princes from famous families, the Obolenskis and the Trubetskis among them.

The plotters, inspired by the open societies of western Europe, had become disillusioned with the repressive Alexander, and after his death they refused to take the oath to Nicholas, who sat on his horse amid the surging mob, for several hours before giving the order to open fire. In southern Russia, a mutiny collapsed after the fiasco in the capital was reported.

Czar Nicholas, who had little difficulty crushing the Decembrists.

Brothers go to war

Lisbon, May 1826
Civil war has broken out here after a constitutional battle between two brothers. Before his death, King John VI of Portugal had recognised Brazil as an independent country. His eldest son, Pedro, ruled in Rio. Before he made his move, Pedro issued a parliamentary charter for Portugal and then renounced his throne in favour of his seven-year-old daughter, Maria – provided she married his brother, Dom Miguel, who would have to abide by the new constitution. Dom Miguel accepted the conditions – only to reject parliamentary government once he was in power.

1826 (1826-1828)

St Petersburg, 4 April 1826. Russia and Britain sign the protocol of St Petersburg, agreeing to mediate between the Ottomans and the Greeks with the aim of achieving complete autonomy for Greece under Ottoman suzerainty.

Greece, 23 April 1826. Missolonghi falls to Egyptian forces under Ibrahim Pasha.

USA, 26 April 1826. The USA signs a treaty of friendship and commerce with Denmark.

USA, 2 May 1826. The USA extends diplomatic recognition to Peru.

Portugal, 2 May 1826. Pedro IV waives the right of accession to Portuguese throne; Maria is to become queen provided she marries Dom Miguel, his brother.

Panama, June 1826. Simon Bolivar convenes a congress of Latin American states to promote continental cooperation, but only Peru, Colombia, Mexico and the Central American Confederation attend.

USA, 4 July 1826. On the 50th anniversary of the signing of the Declaration of Independence, two American founding fathers and former presidents, John Adams and Thomas Jefferson, die.

Caucasus, 26 September 1826. The Persian cavalry is routed by the Russians at the battle of Ganja as their war over possession of the Caucasus intensifies.

USA, 7 October 1826. The first railway in the USA opens at Quincy, Massachusetts.

California, 27 November 1826. An expedition led by the 25-year-old fur trapper Jedediah Smith reaches San Diego, becoming the first Americans to cross the south-western part of the continent.

South-East Asia, 1826. Penang, Malacca and Singapore are united to form the Straits Settlements.

Russia, 1826. Czar Nicholas re-establishes the Third Section, Russia's secret police, which was abolished by Alexander.

USA, 1826. James Fenimore Cooper, the first major US novelist, publishes *The Last of the Mohicans*, a frontier story set in America's recent past.

Peru, 26 January 1827. Peru ends union with Colombia and declares itself independent.

Switzerland, 12 February 1827. The Swiss educationalist Johann Pestalozzi dies. He argued that the development of human nature should depend upon natural laws and that all knowledge is acquired by observation.

New Orleans, February 1827. Students from Paris introduce a new *Mardi Gras* (Shrove Tuesday) celebration in New Orleans, supplementing the traditional masked balls.

Vienna, 26 March 1827. The composer Ludwig van Beethoven dies.

Greece, 11 April 1827. Ioannes Capo d'Istrias is elected president of the Greek national assembly.

Greece, 5 June 1827. Athens falls to the Ottomans.

London, 6 July 1827. France, Britain and Russia sign the treaty of London, threatening to use force if the Ottoman empire does not agree to an armistice with Greece.

Britain, 8 August 1827. George Canning, who succeeded Lord Liverpool as Tory prime minister in February, dies. During a political career spanning more than 30 years, Canning promoted liberal policies at home and abroad.

Ottoman Empire, August 1827. In response to a joint demand by France, Britain and Russia, the Ottomans refuse to accept an armistice in their war with Greece.

Mediterranean, 20 October 1827. British, French and Russian forces destroys the Ottoman-Egyptian fleet at the battle of Navarino.

China, 8 November 1827. The *Canton Register*, the first English-language newspaper in the Far East, begins publication in Guangzhou.

Armenia, 1827. Russia seizes Yerevan from Persia.

USA, 1827. Chief Red Bird, the leader of an Indian uprising against continued intrusion by whites into tribal lands in Michigan territory, is captured and held prisoner by Lewis Cass, the governor of Michigan, putting an end to the so-called Winnebago war.

England, 1827. In his *New System of Chemical Philosophy*, John Dalton presents the first formulation of atomic theory.

England, 1827. A fundamentalist Christian sect known as the Plymouth Brethren is founded.

Scotland, 1827. The poet and Edinburgh advocate Sir Walter Scott admits that he is the author of the extremely popular *Waverley* novels.

South Africa, 1828. In Cape Colony the British abolish the labour laws of 1809-23 which tie Khoisan (Hottentot) servants to European masters as "apprentices", creating a labour crisis for poorer, especially Boer, white farmers.

Owen's followers fail to live in Harmony

Indiana, 26 May 1827

An attempt to create an idealistic, socialist community in the United States ended in failure today when the British philanthropist Robert Owen admitted that his commune on the banks of the Wabash at Posey County was near to collapse from internal anarchy.

The Welsh-born, self-made mill-owner – whose humane treatment of his employees in Britain had made him noted as a reformer and educationalist – bought 30,000 acres of Indiana and founded a "model" village which he named New Harmony. Nine hundred disciples – many of them intellectuals – followed him there, pledging to make "an empire of good sense". All property was to be held in common and there was to be "absolute freedom of action for the individual" and equality of the sexes. Chores were to be shared. Owen did the baking; the community suffered communal indigestion. But Owen overlooked human greed and jealousy, and has lost four-fifths of his fortune.

Quadrille dancing at Owen's earlier community in New Lanark, Scotland.

World mourns Beethoven, giant of music

Vienna, 29 March 1827

Ten thousand mourners turned out today for the funeral of Ludwig van Beethoven, who died three days ago aged 56 after months of illness. Among the pallbearers was the composer Franz Schubert; a funeral oration was written by the poet Franz Grillparzer. The occasion was a tribute to the stature of the man who altered the face of music, from the symphonies, concertos, quartets and sonatas of the 1800s to the glorious *Missa Solemnis* (1823), the *Choral Symphony* (1824) with its huge setting of Schiller's *Ode to Joy*, and the extraordinary vision of his last string quartets (1825-26).

Beethoven had aristocratic patrons but, unlike his teacher Haydn, and Mozart, was never employed by the nobility. He helped to usher in a new age of the independent artist as a hero greater than anyone eminent by birth alone. It is wrong to say that he "improved" on his

Beethoven, for whom the act of composition was always a struggle.

predecessors, but he fashioned their musical legacy into something different, not "better", but more monumental, and more personally emotional.

Ottoman fleet destroyed

Navarino, 20 October 1827

The fragile peace in the Mediterranean was shattered today when the Ottoman and Egyptian fleets were destroyed by a combined fleet of British, French and Russian ships sent to guarantee Greek independence.

Over 50 Ottoman and Egyptian ships were sunk in the Bay of Navarino. They are reported to have opened fire first as the fleet sent by the three great powers entered the bay. The British, French and Russian ships were all at battle stations but under orders not to fire first.

Admiral Codrington, the fleet's commander, was told before he set sail to enforce "a pacific blockade" to maintain the uneasy armistice between the Greek nationalists and the Ottomans in the Peloponnese.

Why the admirals went beyond the spirit of the treaty agreed by the great powers in London last year not to take part in hostilities is certain to be the subject of an inquiry. In a pre-battle briefing Admiral Codrington is reported to have told his captains that, despite the treaty the British ambassador in Istanbul Stratford Canning, the brother of the late premier, believed that "cannon-shot would be the final arbiter" in settling Greek claims for independence.

The British lion watches as the Russian bear prepares to consume Turkey.

Ambitious Czar has his eyes on Armenia

St Petersburg, 1828

For Czar Nicholas, who began his reign by crushing an army mutiny, war with the sprawling Ottoman empire seemed a good way to keep his soldiers occupied. He has used the Greeks' struggle to throw off the Ottoman yoke as the pretext for going to war; but his ambitions extend from the Balkans to Asia.

In the Caucasus, at the eastern end of the Black Sea, Nicholas has just forced Persia to cede a substantial slice of Armenia, including Yerevan and the port of Baku. The czar is determined to seize the rest of Armenia from Turkey.

Meanwhile, he is consolidating Russia's grip on Siberia right through to the Bering Strait. A new governor-general has reorganised the administration, and agreements have been made with the United States and Britain settling the frontier of Alaska. Britain and France

A Persian warrior on horseback.

are none too pleased at Russia's expansionism, but there is little that they can do except seek to curb the czar's ambitions to seize a warm-water port in the Balkans.

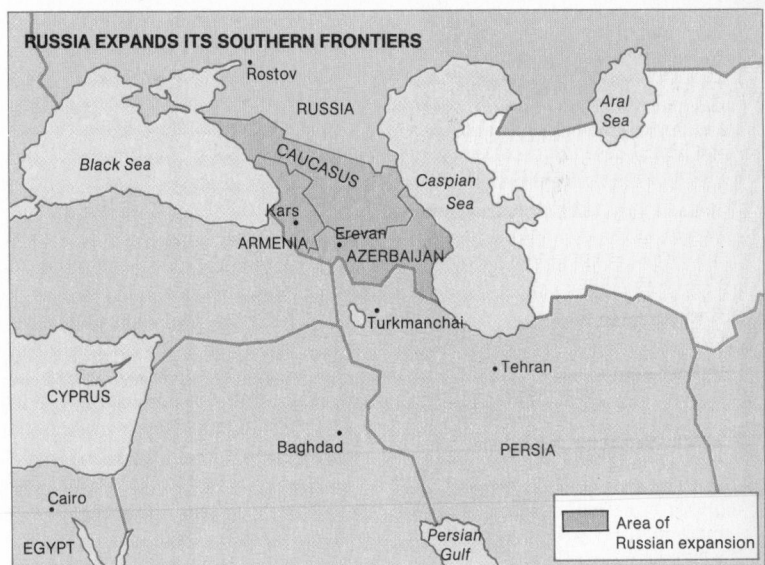

RUSSIA EXPANDS ITS SOUTHERN FRONTIERS

Rostov • RUSSIA
Aral Sea
Black Sea
CAUCASUS
Caspian Sea
Kars •
ARMENIA • Erevan
AZERBAIJAN
• Turkmanchai
• Tehran
CYPRUS
Baghdad •
PERSIA
Cairo •
Persian Gulf
EGYPT

Area of Russian expansion

Current laws for electricity found

Europe, 1827

In his book *The Galvanic Circuit* the German physicist George Ohm has introduced a new law concerning the law of electric currents. Ohm's Law says that the amount of current is directly proportional to the potential difference, or voltage, and inversely proportional to the resistance of the material through which it is flowing.

Meanwhile, in France, Jean-Jacques Ampere has discovered another law based on his observations of electric currents and magnetism. This gives a quantitative statement of the relationship between a magnetic field and the electric current that produces it.

Vital forces are put on the run by urea

Berlin, 1828

Although many people are clinging to the age-old belief that there is a "vital force" which distinguishes all matter taken from living creatures, science has now come up with an organic substance which has been synthesised from inorganic chemicals – a worrying development for the "vitalists".

The animal product is urea – the substance secreted in urine as an end-product of protein breakdown. Starting with ammonium cyanate, Friedrich Wohler, a chemistry teacher from the Berlin technical school, has succeeded in producing an entirely artificial synthetic version of the substance.

British PM quits after 15 years in office

London, February 1827

They said of Lord Liverpool, who has resigned as prime minister after a paralytic stroke, that he lacked vision but was a good chairman of committees. He entered the Commons when he was 20, waited a year before making his maiden speech, and became prime minister 21 years later, remaining in office for 15 years, a record exceeded only by Pitt and Walpole.

In the years of privation and unrest after the the Napoleonic Wars, Liverpool's government responded with repression, but public hostility was directed at his more colourful colleagues, Castlereagh and Sidmouth, rather than at him. He wanted to modify the Corn Laws, which were causing hardship.

Last December he began to feel that he could no longer face the burdens of office. "The government," he said, "hangs by a thread." He was married twice and has no children. Aged of 57, he lingers on, barely conscious.

1828 (1828-1829)

Britain, 25 January 1828. The duke of Wellington and Robert Peel form a Tory government.

Persia, 22 February 1828. Following the Russian capture of Tehran, Persia and Russia sign the treaty of Turkmanshai, ending their two-year war. Russia acquires part of Armenia, including Yereivan.

USA, 21 April 1828. *The American Dictionary of the English Language*, compiled by the editor and grammarian Noah Webster, is published.

Russia, 26 April 1828. In support of the Greek struggle for independence, Russia declares war on the Ottoman empire.

Washington, DC, 19 May 1828. President Adams signs a tariff bill imposing high duties on a wide range of manufactured goods.

Washington, DC, 24 May 1828. Congress passes the Reciprocity Act, calling for the elimination of discriminatory duties on goods imported from reciprocating nations.

Ottoman Empire, 8 June 1828. Pursuing their war with the Ottomans, the Russians cross the Danube.

Portugal, 30 June 1828. After removing his fiancee Maria II, the daughter of Pedro of Brazil, from the throne, Dom Miguel abolishes the liberal constitution and proclaims himself absolute monarch.

India, 4 July 1828. Lord William Bentinck, the well-known utilitarian, is appointed governor general of India.

Boston, 9 July 1828. The painter Gilbert Stuart, a brilliant portraitist of American leaders, dies.

Britain, July 1828. Although he is ineligible as a Catholic, the Irish politician Daniel O'Connell is triumphantly elected to the House of Commons at the expense of the liberal Protestant minister Fitzgerald. He goes to London, where he refuses to take the anti-papist oath of 1692, and his election is declared null and void.

Egypt, August 1828. The Egyptian pasha Mohammed Ali signs an agreement with Britain and France providing for the evacuation of Egyptian forces from Greece.

South Africa, 22 September 1828. The Zulu leader Shaka the Great is assassinated by his brothers Dingane and Mhlangane, who become joint kings. After his mother's death in 1827, Shaka became mentally unbalanced and started arbitrary executions. Zulu conquests reached a peak in the Natal area, with a double victory over the last Ndwandwe remnants in the north in 1826 and 1828.

Germany, 24 September 1828. Several German states found the commercial Union of Central Germany, after signing a customs agreement with Prussia and undertaking never to enter into any other such alliance.

Ottoman Empire, 12 October 1828. The Russians take Varna.

Vienna, 19 November 1828. The composer Franz Schubert dies.

USA, 3 December 1828. Backed by the fledgling Democratic Party, Andrew Jackson is elected president, defeating his long-time rival John Quincy Adams, the sitting president.

North America, 20 December 1828. Cherokee Indians cede their traditional lands in Arkansas territory to the USA and agree to migrate to lands west of the Mississippi river.

India, 1828. *Brahmo Samaj* is founded by Ram Mohan Roay in Calcutta. Its aim is to meet European criticisms of Hinduism by restoring Hindu worship to its early purity.

Madagascar, 1828. Queen Ranavalona becomes queen on the death of her husband, Radama.

Pacific, 1828. The French navigator Dumont d'Urville occupies the New Hebrides.

Canada, 1828. Nominated as a member of the council, the French-speaking deputy Papineau draws up a powerful protest document, known as the "ninety-two resolutions", aimed at the British government.

Britain, 1828. The weekly review *The Spectator* begins publication.

Britain, 1828. Thomas Carlyle's *Essay on Goethe* draws the attention of British readers to German literature.

Britain, 1828. Thomas Arnold is appointed head of Rugby school.

Germany, 1828. The architect Karl Friedrich Schinkel builds a museum of antiquities (*the Pergamon Museum*) in Berlin.

Germany, 1828. The *Memoirs* of the Italian adventurer Giovanni Casanova, who died in 1798, are published in many volumes.

London, 22 March 1829. At an ambassadorial conference, agreement is reached on the boundaries of an independent Greece.

Rome, 31 March 1829. Pius VIII becomes pope in succession to Leo XII, who died on 10 February. The new pope is opposed to the liberalism and the secret societies of Italian democrats.

London, 13 April 1829. The Catholic Emancipation Act becomes law.

Uruguay born of Argentina-Brazil rivalry

Uruguay, 1828
Territories along the eastern bank of the Rio de la Plata, formerly known in Brazil as the *banda oriental*, are to gain independent statehood. The new country is to be known as the republic of Uruguay.

The banda oriental has for many years been a focus of rivalries between Brazil and neighbouring Argentina, who took over the competition previously waged by their former colonial masters Portugal and Spain. Once part of the Spanish vice royalty of Rio de la Plata, the territory was annexed to Brazil by Portugal in 1776. When an Uruguayan independence movement emerged in 1825 it was funded by Argentina. Diplomatic rivalry developed into war and only mediation by Britain separated the rivals. Trade routes, threatened by the clash, were reopened and the disputed territory was removed from both spheres of influence as newly independent Uruguay, a buffer between two regional powers.

Schubert, master of the song, dies at 31

Vienna, 21 November 1828
Last year the composer Franz Schubert helped to bear the coffin at the funeral of his hero, Beethoven. No one could have imagined that today, less than two years later, Schubert himself would be laid to rest. He died two days ago, aged just 31, on the brink of great fame. He had been ill for some time.

Despite his early death, Schubert will surely be remembered for a long list of extraordinary masterpieces. His symphonies (especially the last two, one of which is incomplete) and chamber music wonderfully demonstrate his profound, lyrical expressiveness. But he was renowned in his lifetime above all for his vast output of over 600 songs, or *lieder*, which have established the *lied* as a major art form.

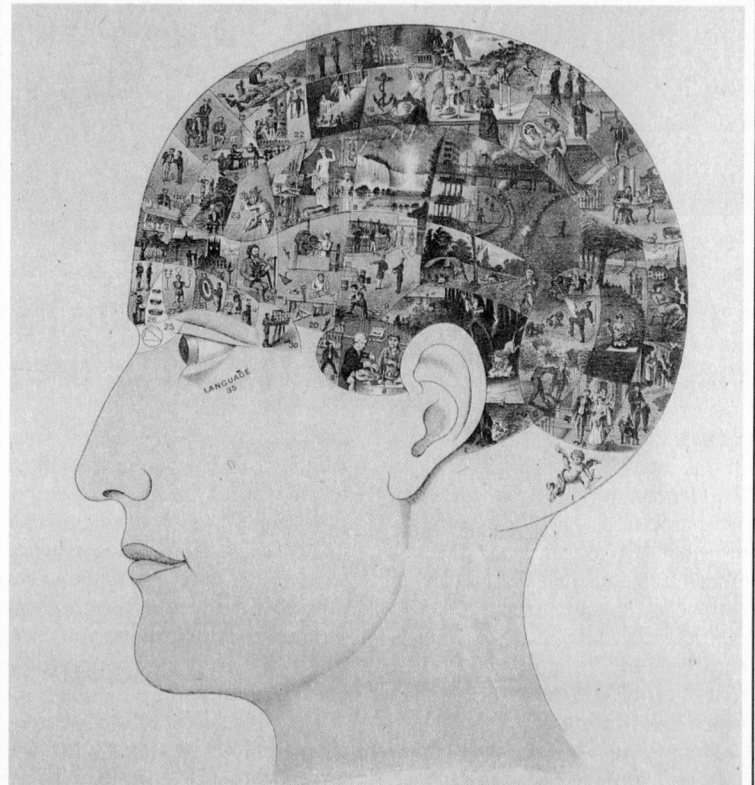

"Phrenology": the new science that claims to determine a man's morality, instincts, talents and intelligence by the shape of his head. It was invented by Franz Josef Gall, an Austrian living in Paris; his book "The Functions of the Brain", published in 1808, defined each part of the brain and established its potential. Criminologists find it fascinating.

British Catholics allowed to run for office

Fears of popery: Catholic clergy using the head of Robert Peel, a leading MP in the House of Commons, to batter down English Protestant institutions.

London, 13 April 1829
With the prime minister, the duke of Wellington, fighting every inch of the way against an evasive king and the intrigues of Protestant hard-liners, the Catholic Emancipation Bill has at long last become law. From today, Catholics can hold all public offices except those of regent, lord chancellor, and lord lieutenant of Ireland. It is being said that nobody but the "Iron Duke" could have done it.

After the success of O'Connell's Catholic Association in mobilising Irish opinion, the duke and his ally in the Commons, Robert Peel, agreed that emancipation was the only way of averting civil war in Ireland. The duke was ferociously attacked by the fanatical earl of Winchilsea, who accused him of introducing "popery into every department of the state". The duke responded with a challenge and they met in Battersea Fields one morning last month. The duke fired wide; the earl fired into the air and promptly apologised for his intemperate language.

Police force formed to stop city crime

London, 1829
Alarmed by the increase in crime in London, the British parliament has passed an act to create a police force for the metropolis. The measure was introduced by Robert Peel, the home secretary, who based his proposals on his experience of law enforcement in Ireland.

Though everyone agreed that the widespread robbery and violence called for tough action, Peel's plan has been attacked as an insidious attempt to enslave the people. But Peel claimed that an estimated one person in every 22 is involved in criminal activities. Besides, the new force will be answerable to parliament through him. But will the Peelers, as they are already being called, simply drive the criminals elsewhere?

Peeler and suspect: for many the police were seen more as a force for repression than protection.

US workers' movement grows in strength

New York, 1829
The newly-formed Workingmen's Party has polled 30 per cent of votes in the election here – confirming the emergence of a labour movement in the United States.

Craftsmen and artisans, alarmed at their declining status as *entrepreneurs* drove small shops out of business, were the impetus behind last year's creation of the Philadelphia Workingmen's Party. The "Workies" are campaigning for the reduction of the working day to ten hours, the abolition of imprisonment for debt, curbs on banks and other monopolies, free education for all, free public land, and liens on buildings to prevent cheating by corrupt contractors.

US bosses are alarmed by the involvement of foreigners like Robert Owen and Fanny Wright, whom they blame for the discontent.

German general's logic ends in total war

Berlin, 1829
A German general who fought at the Battle of Waterloo and with the Russians against Napoleon's *Grand Armee* has expounded the concept of total war in an analysis of the factors making for success in battle. In his massive work *Vom Kriege*, Karl von Clausewitz stresses the importance of chance and psychological factors, neither of which can be precisely calculated.

Strategy, therefore, should not be concerned solely with the enemy's armed forces, but should also embrace his resources and his will to fight. This means that enemy civilians and their property should be attacked. After all, he says, war is simply the continuation of diplomacy by other means.

Clausewitz, who comes from a family of Polish settlers in Prussia, joined the army at the age of 12 and saw his first battle a year later. He caught the eye of Gerhard von Scharnhorst, the director of the

Karl von Clausewitz, who served in the Prussian and Russian armies.

Berlin military academy, who introduced him at court; there Clausewitz met and married Countess Marie von Bruhl and later became *aide* to the crown prince.

Britain stamps on Indian widow-burners

Bengal, 1829
Suttee, the practice whereby a Hindu widow burns herself on her husband's funeral pyre, has been abolished in British India.

Evangelicals, utilitarians and other advocates of western values have applauded the decision. "Old India hands", who have a deep respect for Indian cultures, regard it as arrogant, insensitive and potentially dangerous. Typically, the administrative class feels caught in a dilemma: a dilemma as old as Pontius Pilate's.

The practice varies throughout Hindu India. In Bengal suttee is rarely voluntary and widows are dragged screaming to pyres by sons anxious to avoid supporting aged relatives. In the martial areas, suttee is not only voluntary but attains a certain savage nobility.

Every Englishman in India has his suttee horror story. Some, like Charles Harding of the Bengal civil service, risked riot to resue widows. Interestingly the best argument against suttee was put by Akbar the Great 200 years ago. "It is a strange commentary on the magnanimity of men that they should seek deliverance through the self-sacrifice of their wives," he said.

1829 (1829-1830)

Ottoman Empire, 11 June 1829. The Russians under General Diebitsch defeat the Ottomans at the battle of Kulevcha, opening up a route to the Balkan mountains.

France, 8 August 1829. King Charles X appoints the prince of Polignac, an Ultra-royalist, to replace his chief minister Martignac, a moderate, who was dismissed two days ago.

Ottoman Empire, 14 September 1829. Following Russian victories at Silistria and Adrianople, Sultan Mahmud II signs a peace treaty with Czar Nicholas at Adrianople. He recognises Greek independence and accepts the terms of the London agreements of November 1828 and March 1829, which established the borders of Greece. Russia receives Moldavia and Wallachia from Turkey.

Mexico, 2 December 1829. President Guerrero exempts Texas from the Mexican prohibition of slavery, revising a decree issued in September.

Argentina, 8 December 1829. The provincial leader and federalist Juan Manuel de Rosas becomes governor of Buenos Aires. Since independence in 1816, numerous rebellions in the provinces have reduced Argentina to a state of anarchy.

Maryland, 22 December 1829. The Baltimore and Ohio Railroad Company opens the first passenger railway line.

Netherlands, 1829. The two Belgian parties, the Catholics and the liberals, form a united front against King William, who is becoming increasingly autocratic. Angered by a concordat signed with the pope two years ago and by harsh press restrictions, the opposition demands non-intervention by the state in church affairs and freedom of education and the press.

France, 1829. The Paris professor Louis Braille, himself blind since the age of three, invents a reading system for the blind.

France, 1829. Victor Hugo publishes a collection of poems entitled *Les Orientales*.

Netherlands, 1829. The Belgian statistician and astronomer Adolphe Quetelet carries out the first statistical analysis of a census.

Berlin, 1829. On Good Friday, Felix Mendelssohn and the choirs of the Berlin Academy perform Johann Sebastian Bach's *St Matthew Passion*, which has lain forgotten for 100 years.

London, 1829. The first Boat Race between Oxford and Cambridge universities takes place on the Thames.

London, 1829. The first horse-drawn omnibuses appear on the streets of London.

Europe, 1829. A passion for the waltz, a dance which made its appearance at the end of the last century, spreads through Europe.

England, 7 January 1830. Sir Thomas Lawrence, the president of the Royal Academy and the leading portrait painter during the regency, dies.

London, 3 February 1830. At a London conference, Britain, France and Russian guarantee Greek independence.

Ottoman Empire, 5 February 1830. Milos Obrenovic has himself declared hereditary prince of Serbia.

Paris, 18 March 1830. Following criticism of his policies, Charles X dissolves the chamber of deputies.

Chile, 17 April 1830. The conservative party under Diego Portales, supported by the upper classes and the clergy, victorious in a civil war with the pro-democratic liberal party.

Colombia, April 1830. Following the separation of Venezuela and Quito (*Ecuador*) from Colombia, Simon Bolivar abdicates as dictator of Colombia.

Ecuador, 13 May 1830. The republic of Ecuador is created, with Juan Flores as president.

Washington, DC, 28 May 1830. The Indian Removal Act, giving Indians perpetual title to western lands, is passed.

Britain, 26 June 1830. On the death of George IV, he is succeeded as king by his brother William IV.

Algiers, 5 July 1830. A French expeditionary force captures Algiers and deposes the *bey*.

Uruguay, 18 July 1830. Uruguay adopts a liberal constitution.

USA, 1830. The latest census records the population of the USA as nearly 13 million.

France, 1830. The philosopher Auguste Comte begins publishing his *Course of Positive Philosophy*.

Italy, 1830. The French writer Stendhal (the pseudonym of Marie-Henri Beyle) publishes a novel entitled *Le Rouge et le Noir*.

England, 1830. The critic and essayist William Hazlitt, the author of *A View of the English Stage* and *The Spirit of the Age*, dies.

England, 1830. William Cobbett, a leader of the reform movement, publishes *Rural Rides*, a survey of England, in which he christens London "the Great Wen".

Treaty preserves Ottoman empire

Adrianople, 14 September 1829
The Ottoman empire, reeling from a succession of defeats at Russian hands, remains intact under the terms of a treaty concluded here today. The Russians, it seems, shrank from marching on Istanbul for fear of destroying the empire and precipitating a European war.

Under the treaty the Ottomans retain a nominal title over the Balkan principalities of Wallachia and Moldavia, which pay a fixed tribute. But Ottoman fortresses have been evacuated, their subjects withdrawn, and native governors appointed for life. Russian influence is now paramount in these areas.

In the wake of the Greeks' successful fight for independence, the treaty represents a major shift of power. Although the Ottomans can hardly complain, other European powers, notably Britain, are anxious at the growing power of Russia, which is perceived as a threat to Mediterranean interests.

Map swap brings torture and deaths

Japan, 30 December 1829
The German scientist Philipp von Siebold sailed from Japan today under orders never to return after being found guilty of exchanging forbidden maps with his Japanese friend. He was lucky to escape so lightly. His friend did not.

The case started a year ago when the ship which was to carry Siebold home was blown ashore and had to be unloaded. When the cargo was examined the prohibited articles were found; they pointed directly to the brilliant mapmaker Takahashi Kageyasu who was already under suspicion for his friendship with Siebold.

Takahashi was tortured, and when he died in prison after months of interrogation his body was pickled so that sentence could be passed on him. When he was found guilty, his head was chopped off. Siebold suffered terribly from the thought that he had brought such pain to his friend and attempted suicide. It is believed, however, that he has made copies of the maps.

Farewell to the clef by Rossini the chef

Gioacchino Rossini: composer of some of Italy's finest comic operas.

Paris, 1829
Gioacchino Rossini has announced that *William Tell*, recently premiered here to rapturous acclaim, will be the last work from his pen.

Rossini's 39 operas, renowned for their characterisation, brilliant, subtle scoring and winning melodies, are adored in Paris (his home since 1824), London and Vienna (Beethoven admired *The Barber of Seville* of 1816), but the hectic world of Italian opera has left Rossini, aged 37, exhausted. He can now pursue his other pleasures. Rossini is a celebrated gourmet and wit. A tenor, whose high notes he thought merely showy, called on him. "Tell him to leave his C sharp on the coat rack," he said.

A dance craze hits Europe, the waltz: a reaction to the formality of the 18th-century minuet.

Indian tribes exiled to western America

Washington, DC, 28 May 1830
America's native people – the Indian tribes who roamed the prairies and woodlands of this country long before the white man came – are likely to be swept westwards, away from the populated areas. Under the Indian Removal Act signed today by President Andrew Jackson, the tribes will receive perpetual title to lands in the west, financial assistance and a government guarantee of security.

Debate in Congress was fierce and lengthy. Many representatives thought the bill was inhumane.

A Creek Indian chief, promised land "as long as the grass grows".

Supporters claimed that it was the only way to save the Indians from extinction. For President Jackson the bill represents a singular personal triumph. He has never hidden his ambition to drive the Indians westwards. Last year, he urged the Creek tribe to cede its land and go west.

"Your white brothers will have no claim on the land and you can live on it, you and all your children, as long as the grass grows or the water runs in peace and plenty. It will be yours for ever," he told the chiefs. Indians are resentful as well as sceptical. They are aware that much of their tribal land covers valuable mineral deposits, and it will immediately leap in value as developers move in. Cherokees in Georgia are planning legal action to safeguard their gold.

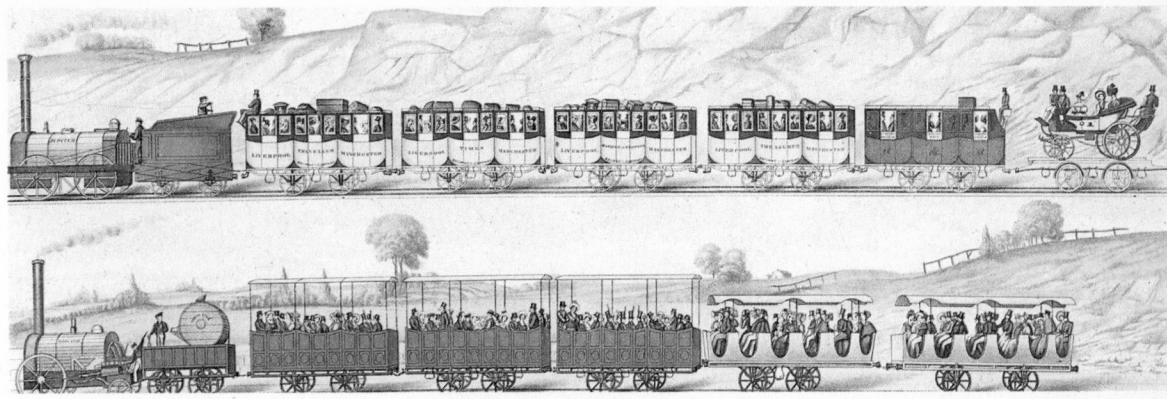

The "Jupiter" and the "North Star", two of the steam engines on the Liverpool to Manchester run.

Train accident kills top Tory as Britain goes mad about railways

Liverpool, 15 September 1830
William Huskisson, a Liverpool MP and former cabinet minister, died today after falling under a train making its inaugural run from Liverpool to Manchester on the first railway line built primarily to carry passengers.

The opening of the Liverpool and Manchester Railway is the latest development in an industry which promises to revolutionise transport. Enthusiasm for railways has grown steadily since the turn of the century. By 1812 there were 150 miles (240km) of track in South Wales alone, carrying coal; by 1821, 19 railway acts had been passed.

The man behind the railway boom is 49-year-old George Stephenson, engineer of the Stockton to Darlington Railway. This was opened in 1825 primarily to carry coal, but became the world's first steam railway to carry passengers. Stephenson is not only engineer of the Liverpool to Manchester line but designer of the "Rocket" engine which won a competition last year for the best steam locomotive. It

George Stephenson's famous Rocket.

was the "Rocket" that crushed Huskisson to death.

The accident occurred as Huskisson, a distinguished Tory reformer, was crossing the tracks after greeting the duke of Wellington who, as prime minister, insisted on his resignation from the cabinet two years ago. He lost his balance as he was clambering out of the path of the

George Stephenson, the engineer.

oncoming train.

His death may fuel safety fears, but new lines are planned from Bristol to London, Liverpool to Birmingham and Newcastle to Carlisle.

French expeditionary force siezes Algiers jewels collection

Algiers, 5 July 1830
A French expeditionary force today captured the fortress at Algiers giving France a much sought foothold in North Africa. In Paris the conquest may help to restore the fortunes of the embattled royalist Polignac ministry, which has been desperate for a foreign policy success as it goes to the polls.

French troops have also seized the priceless collection of jewels assembled by the now deposed *Dey* of Algiers.

Algiers: France's imperial rival, Britain, happily awaits the French defeat.

France, 26 July. King Charles X issues five ordinances limiting political and civil rights.

Paris, 29 July. Led by the marquis of Lafayette, liberals opposed to the king's ordinances seize Paris.

France, 2 August. Charles X abdicates.

France, 7 August. Louis Philippe, the Bourbon duke of Orleans, is proclaimed king of the French by the liberals.

Netherlands, August. Belgian resentment at forced union with the Dutch bursts into open rebellion in Brussels and throughout the provinces.

Netherlands, 4 October. A provisional government formed a week ago proclaims Belgian independence.

Netherlands, 27 October. The Dutch bombard the Belgian city of Antwerp.

USA, 5 October. Following diplomatic negotiations, President Jackson opens trade with the British West Indies.

London, 4 November. A conference of European powers to settle the Belgian question opens.

Britain, 16 November. The resignation of the duke of Wellington as prime minister ends nearly half a century of continuous Tory rule. He is replaced by the Whig leader, Earl Grey.

Poland, 29 November. Ten days after announcement of the mobilisation of young Poles in the Russian army to deal with the revolutionary threat in France and Belgium, an anti-Russian insurrection breaks out in Warsaw.

Britain, November. Violent riots by farmworkers in the south of England are harshly repressed by the army. "Bloody assizes" condemn nine workers to the gallows. Nearly 500 are deported and hundreds are imprisoned.

South America, 10 December. Simon Bolivar, the liberator of the Americas, dies.

North America, 13 December. Captain Black, a British naval officer, lands at Fort Astoria in Oregon and raises the Union Jack.

North America. The first wagon train to cross the Rocky Mountains, led by Jedediah Smith, reaches the Upper Wind river in Western Frontier territory.

Uprising calls upon king to abdicate

Paris at the barricades, where republicans and radicals have held their ground against royalist troops.

Paris, 30 July
The French capital is again in the grip of revolutionary fervour, with barricades on the streets and republicans claiming that King Charles will be forced to abdicate within days, and a republic proclaimed.

In the last 24 hours three regiments have deserted the king and joined rebel forces on the barricades as the three-day-old protest against a series of repressive decrees turns into open insurrection.

The 73-year-old king, the brother of Louis XVI, who was beheaded in the revolution, is thought to be preparing to flee to Scotland which he knows well. He was in exile there for 25 years until the restoration of the monarchy in 1815. His loss of control started at the beginning of July when the opposition won an overwhelming election victory against the reactionary Polignac ministry. The king's decision four days ago to stage a royal *coup d'etat* by disbanding the new radical and republican Chamber before it had even met and imposing censorship sparked off the uprising.

The insurgents – workers, students and petty bourgeois citizens alienated by the disbanding of the National Guard – split into two factions. One wants to replace King Charles by a republic, the other wants a limited constitutional monarchy with the duke of Orleans, Louis Philippe, as the new king.

Street fighting in Paris: a characteristic feature of the French Republican tradition since 1789.

Hero of South American liberation dies

Colombia, 10 December
Simon Bolivar, the patriot and revolutionary hero of South America's wars of independence, died today aged 47. He helped create Bolivia, Chile, Peru, Colombia and Venezuela, but has died a disillusioned man. "America," he said on his deathbed, "is ungovernable. Those who have served the revolution have ploughed the sea."

Born into a wealthy Creole family in Venezuela, Bolivar travelled widely in Europe and was influenced both by the French Revolution and by Napoleon, his lifelong hero. A self-proclaimed "man of destiny", he vowed in 1805 to liberate Venezuela from the Spanish. Despite exile and hardship he succeeded, and went on to help other colonies to gain statehood. Bolivar's tragedy was that having destroyed Spanish rule, he failed to replace it with an adequate form of government. The people proved less idealistic than their liberators and the champion of equality was forced by circumstances into despotism and dictatorship.

Burmese sacred goose, engraved in gold and studded with rubies.

Britons washed by tidal wave for reform

London

The general election, caused by the death of George IV in June, is taking place in a highly-charged atmosphere, with the threat of violence; just as the campaign opened, news came from France of the Paris mob bringing down the Bourbons and of the Citizen King, Louis Philippe ascending the throne.

At election meetings up and down the country, the people, egged on by radical agitators, are demanding parliamentary reform. They are calling for an extension of the vote, the abolition of "pocket boroughs" (controlled by single landowners) and "rotten boroughs" (controlled by a handful of voters) and an end to bribery at elections. Some even want a secret ballot.

When the new Commons meets, the Tories will have about 30 fewer seats. Tories and Whigs alike accept that electoral reform will have to be tackled. But if the Duke of Wellington remains prime minister he could prove an obstacle. It is said that he believes that reform would be pushed to such lengths as to rob the upper classes "of the political influence which they derive from their property – and possibly eventually of the property itself".

The dilemma of reform: four interpretations, from reactionary to radical.

Wagons cross Rockies

The first wagon train crosses the Rocky Mountains on its way west.

California, September

After an ordeal by bitter cold at high altitudes and scorching heat in the Californian desert, the first covered wagons have arrived here from the east. Although the settlers were close to starvation and few of the farm animals they brought with them survived the journey, this sun-rich western seaboard with its lush, fertile land has been opened to land traffic at last. Until now, travellers have either had to travel by land, risking disease and bandits in Panama or Mexico, or around Cape Horn at a huge cost.

The settlers used the southern route across the Continental Divide – using a route discovered by fur trappers in 1812, and plotted by Jedediah Smith, the legendary "mountain man" who lost an ear and was nearly killed by a savage grizzly bear when he came this way three years ago.

America is learning more and more about its vastness from adventurers like Smith and Jim Bridger, a fur trader who reported finding a huge salt lake west of the Rockies and Henry Ashley who is advertising for "mountain men" to travel to the source of the Missouri river and develop the fur trade.

The spectre of cholera haunts Europe

Europe

Cholera, unknown in Europe until 1817, is spreading westwards from Asia. Already Russian cities such as Moscow and St Petersburg have had their populations decimated – the majority of the victims from the urban poor.

In St Petersburg the epidemic caused panic among the wealthy, who fled the city. The fearful epidemic has now reached Poland, and is soon expected in western Europe.

European doctors, who wait for its arrival with trepidation, know no cure. Optimists speak of the benefits of bismuth, chlorine, quinine and steam baths. Experts are silent. Asians have suffered from cholera from at least the ninth century, when the symptoms were described in a Tibetan Sanskrit manuscript. In the common delta of the Ganges and Brahmaputra rivers thousands die every year from the disease.

What Europeans find particularly shocking are cholera's symptoms: debilitating dehydration caused by unstoppable diarrhea and vomiting. Cramp sets into muscles, the tongue becomes dry, the lips blue, the voice hoarse and the skin cold and clammy. In short, it should be a savage's, rather than a European's disease.

King Cholera, who has killed more people than any general could boast of and, like war, always discriminates against the poor and helpless.

1830 (1830-1832)

South-East Asia, 1830. Prince Diponegoro, the leader of an uprising against the Dutch colonists in Java, is captured and exiled to Macassar.

South-East Asia, 1830. Johannes van den Bosch, the Dutch governor general of the East Indies, institutes a system whereby the native population is forced to share one-fifth of its land and harvests with the government.

England, 1830. The scientist Michael Faraday discovers the phenomenon of electromagnetic induction.

Boston, Mass., 1 January 1831. William Lloyd Garrison publishes the first edition of a journal entitled *The Liberator*, calling for the complete and immediate emancipation of all the slaves in the USA.

London, 20 January 1831. The London conference of European powers signs a protocol delineating the boundaries of Belgium and Holland and establishing Belgium as a neutral state under the permanent guarantee of the powers.

Poland, January 1831. Following the Polish *diet's* proclamation of the end of the Russian succession to its throne, war breaks out between Poland and Russia.

Belgium, 3 February 1831. The duke of Nemours, the second son of Louis Philippe, rejects the offer of the Belgian throne under pressure from Britain.

Poland, 25 February 1831. The Poles halt the Russian advance at the battle of Grochow.

France, March 1831. The exiled Italian republican activist Giuseppe Mazzini founds a revolutionary society called Young Italy, with the aim of uniting Italy through a general uprising and elevating Italian patriotism by moral fervour.

Brazil, 7 April 1831. Under pressure from both the army and the people, the unpopular Emperor Pedro abdicates in favour of his five-year-old son.

India, 6 May 1831. The Sikh forces of Ranjit Singh suffer a defeat at Balakot in an attempt to establish a Moslem state by holy war in north-western India.

Poland, 26 May 1831. The Russians defeat the Poles under Jan Skrzynecki at the battle of Ostrolenska.

Belgium, 4 June 1831. The Belgians elect Leopold of Saxe-Coburg king, three months after the national congress had confered the regency on its president, Baron Erasme Surlet de Chokier.

Philadelphia, 11 June 1831. The Convention of the People of Colour, the first such convention ever for free Negroes, opens.

Netherlands, 26 June 1831. King William rejects the "Eighteen Articles" drawn up at the London conference to regulate the separation of Belgium and the Netherlands.

Virginia, 21 August 1831. The radical Negro preacher Nat Turner leads a band of slaves some large plantations, killing 55 whites.

Belgium, August 1831. Breaking off the armistice, King William of the Netherlands launches an invasion of Belgium but is obliged to retreat under pressure from the European powers.

Poland, September 1831. Russian forces seize Warsaw, crushing the Polish rebels with whom they have been at war since January.

Netherlands, 15 October 1831. King William refuses to accept the "Twenty-Four", Articles, drawn up by the London conference on terms more favourable to the Netherlands than previous proposals.

Britain, 31 October 1831. Two days of rioting in Bristol, caused by parliament's rejection of the Reform Bill, comes to an end.

India, October 1831. William Bentinck, the governor general of India, meets Ranjit Singh, the ruler of the Punjab, at Lahore, in order to sign a commercial treaty.

Southern Africa, 1831. Soshangane and his Shangane people, who have retreated north from the Zulu threat around Maputo Bay in Mozambique, win a civil war among the *Ngoni* on the Save river. Other *Ngoni* flee inland to launch raids on the Zimbabwe plateau, spreading the Mfecane wars towards the Zambezi.

USA, 1831. The physicist Joseph Henry invents the first electromagnetic motor and first telegraph.

New York City, 1831. Edgar Allan Poe, dismissed from West Point military academy for "gross neglect of duty" and "disobedience of orders", publishes his *Poems*.

New York City, 1831. Two Swiss cafe owners, John and Peter Delmonico, open a European-style dining room called a *restaurant*.

Paris, 1831. The Barbizon school of artists, who paint from nature, gives its first exhibition at the Paris Salon.

Italy, 22 February 1832. Louis Philippe sends French troops to the port of Ancona on the Adriatic to counter ever-increasing Austrian influence in the region.

Belgium wins independence from Dutch

Brussels, 20 December 1830
Three and a half million Belgian citizens rejoiced today as the Dutch King, William, conceded defeat and allowed them their independence. Resentment had smouldered for years since the treaty of 1815 which created the kingdom of the United Netherlands. The Belgians, who make up the majority of the population, were angered at the favouritism shown to the Dutch.

There were serious religious differences between the Catholic Belgians and their Protestant neighbours; when the cost of living soared, the Belgian workers, inspired by the July revolution in Paris, built barricades in the streets of Brussels. Although reluctant at first, the middle classes joined in. The demand was for administrative separation of the two provinces. King William refused and ordered Dutch troops into Brussels. Every attempt to repress the rebellion failed and, despite a plea from the Dutch king to the czar of Russia for assistance, the army has been forced to withdraw.

Divine revelation inspires new US church

Ohio, January 1831
Joseph Smith was only 15 and living in New York when the "revelation" came to him. He was woken, he said, by a vision of God, who told him that all existing religions were fraudulent and that Smith had been chosen to found the one true church. That was 17 years ago. Smith founded his church and faced persecution in New York. Now he and 70 of his followers, who call themselves Mormons, have arrived in the township of Kirtland to build a new Zion. Whether they will escape religious opposition – even here in the wilderness – is doubtful. They are hard-working, thrifty people who may find it hard to cope with the lawlessness of the west, in spite of the great trust they place in Smith's re-written Bible, the *Book of Mormon*.

Joseph Smith (right) and his brother Hyrum: founders of a new church.

European settlers kill Tasmanian natives

Tasmania, Australia, 1830
A new sport has become fashionable in Tasmania and is spreading through Australia: "Abo hunting". In Tasmania's largest "hunt" so far, a line of beaters spread across the island to push the Aborigines into the muzzles of huntsmen's guns. Bitter experience has made Aboriginal people wise to the tactics and, to the disappointment of the "sportsmen", only one was caught.

What good this will do to their longterm survival is uncertain. Many who escape the huntsmen succumb to smallpox, venereal diseases, alcoholism and hopelessness. The government discourages the practice. Indeed, Arthur Phillip, New South Wales' first governor, and lately, Tasmania's lieutenant-governor, Thomas Davey, have been threatening "Abo hunters" with the death penalty; but witnesses for the prosecution rarely come forward, and dead men cannot speak from the witness box.

Australia's attitude to the Aboriginal people is ambivalent. To the educated administrators they are a "noble savage", "mild and cheerful", according to Captain Cook, with "unusual grace and elegance" (said Sir George Grey). To the uneducated settlers they are vermin – to be subdued and slaughtered.

England: slow pace of reform brings riots

Riots in Bristol: Third Dragoon Guards charge protesters calling for reform.

London, 1831
Three attempts to push through an electoral reform bill have been frustrated by Tories and backwoodsmen peers, and protest meetings, leading to widespread riots, are taking place in provincial towns.

A mood of angry frustration began to build up late last year after the prime minister, the duke of Wellington, said that the present system was perfect and would not be changed. But the injustices have been repeatedly pointed out: some hamlets have two MPs, many industrial towns have none.

Wellington was defeated and Earl Grey formed a Whig ministry. The first reform bill was thrown out in April, the second in October and the third has run into stiff opposition in the House of Lords; Grey is talking of resigning. The situation may be saved, however, by the king. William IV is threatening to create an army of new peers ready to vote for the measure and override the opposition.

"Young Italy" founded by exiled patriot

Marseilles, 1831
Giuseppe Mazzini, the 26-year-old Italian who founded a secret society called the *Carbonari*, and has been exiuled for a year, has formed a new group with other expatriate Italians here. It is called *La Giovine Italia* (Young Italy) and aims for nothing less than the liberation of the Italian states and their unification into a free independent republic.

Mazzini is certainly bold and ambitious. He wrote an open letter to Charles Albert, the king of Piedmont, asking to be put at the head of a liberation movement, and for a new constitution and the expulsion of the Austrians from Lombardy.

The Young Italy group, which comprises people of all social classes, combines revolutionary tactics with an emphasis on education and belief in God, duty and sacrifice.

Giuseppe Mazzini, Italian patriot.

Mazzini is against both popes and kings, and thinks that Italy can only be saved and unified by a combined effort: the people and God working together.

Russia puts down chaotic Polish uprising

Warsaw, September 1831
After nine months of heroic but muddled rebellion, the Poles have once more been crushed by the Russians. Polish universities have been shut down and Polish students told to go to St Petersburg to study. Russian instead of Polish must be used in the administration.

The uprising began in the officers' training school and was soon joined by most army regiments and large numbers of civilians. But appeals for help from western governments went unanswered. Party squabbles broke out in the Polish parliament and when rioting erupted in Warsaw Russian troops were able to suppress the rebellion with little trouble. Some 10,000 Polish activists and intellectuals have fled to the West.

A Polish patriot, in an era when patriotism alone was not enough.

Bloody deaths end US slaves' rebellion

Virginia, USA, 11 November 1831
A huge crowd gathered in Jerusalem, Virginia today to watch the hanging of Nat Turner, a radical preacher and literate slave who was the leader of a slave revolt in which 57 white people were killed. Turner believed himself to be a divine instrument to lead his people out of bondage, and incited a group of fellow slaves to kill whites.

A posse of more than 2,000 armed men – together with troops and sailors – hunted the rebels down, killing many innocent black people in the process. Turner managed to escape and remained at large until his recapture. While he was at large he wrote an autobiography, *The Confessions of Nat Turner*, which has been edited and published in Baltimore. The rebellion

The capture of Nat Turner, the leader of the slave revolt.

has led to fears of a mass insurrection. Extra security is being imposed throughout the south, with many slaves finding themselves manacled at night.

Thesis and antithesis resolved for Hegel

Berlin, Prussia, 1831
Georg Wilhelm Friedrich Hegel, the most outstanding German philosopher since Kant, has died in a cholera epidemic.

His system of thought was summed up in his final work, the *Encyclopaedia of Philosophical Science*, covering logic, nature and mind. He claimed it included all knowledge. Hegel is best known for his "dialectical logic" in which thought proceeds from thesis to its denial, antithesis, and thence to synthesis, a combining of opposing ideas. This in turn provides a new thesis and the process starts again until it reaches an absolute, free of self-contradiction.

Hegel's political philosophy sees the state as a kind of super-individual with a reason and will superior to that of the people who compose it.

Latin American's sad fight for freedom

At the beginning of the ninetenth century the relationship between Spain and Portugal's colonies in Latin America and their masters was not unlike that between the American colonists and England thirty years earlier. Tied to a mother country for which many had no great affection there was a growing feeling that they would do much better socially and economically if they were to govern themselves.

The continent was divided up into five great viceroyalties: New Spain (Mexico with a bit of southwestern USA), New Granada (Columbia, Panama, Venezuela and Equador), Brazil and La Plata (Argentina, Bolivia, Chile, Paraguay and Uruguay). Lima was the administrative capital and there was considerable resentment at the centralised control it exercised, especially as geographically most of the other areas were far better placed to deal with the growing American and European markets directly.

This desire for independence crossed the racial and class boundaries, but did not in any way unite them. Each group had a different hopes for independence. The *creoles* (white Latin Americans) hoped for access to power and to greater profits from free trade; the *mestizos* (mixed race Latin Americans) desired a greater recognition of their place in society; while the Indians and African Americans aspired to emancipation from serfdom and slavery.

The American and French revolutions were obviously great sources of inspiration and a growing body of literature by writers like Voltaire and Rousseau was becoming available to justify insurrection against corrupt authority; the success of L'Ouverture's slave rebellion in Haiti also provided an encouraging model.

Bloodshed avoided in Brazil

The cleanest and quickest bid for independence was made by Brazil. On 7 September 1822 the heir to the throne of Portugal, Pedro, bowed to inevitable demands and declared Brazil independent in the *Grito de Ypiranga*.The following year he declared himself emperor of Brazil, thus sparing the country a great deal of bloodshed. For the rest of the continent freedom did not come so quickly or painlessly.

Ironically, a key event for the struggles in the rest of the continent concerned a dispute over royalty. In 1807 Napoleon exiled the Portuguese royal family to Brazil in and replaced the Bourbon King Ferdinand VII with his own brother Joseph Bonaparte as king of Spain in 1808. This provided a pretext for rebellion against Spanish authority while still claiming allegiance to the true Spanish throne.

In Mexico the first rallying call for independence came from the village priest Manuel Hidalgo. On 16 September 1810 he preached a sermon in his parish church that became known as the *Grito de Dolores* and expressed the mixture of religious and political ideas that characterised the Mexican rebellion, "Long Live Our Lady of Guadelupe, down with bad government, death to the Spaniards." Hidalgo's insurrection attracted wide support amongst the poor Indians and mestizos and for ten months he controlled the north of Mexico and came close to capturing Mexico City.

However, Hidalgo was inept as a military commander, his supporters were undisciplined and the rebellion failed when Hidalgo was captured and executed on 31 July 1811. Success only came when the movement gained the support of the creoles. Augustin Iturbide turned this changing situation to his own advantage and finally defeated the Spanish on 27 September 1821, declaring himself emperor of Mexico and New Spain.

Bolivar is saved by Haiti

The matter of Bonaparte's brother also sparked off the uprising in New Granada. In April 1810 the *cabildo* (council) of Caracas expelled the Bonapartist Captain-General and appointed a junta to rule in the name of the deposed Ferdinand VII. The main figure behind this move was Simon Bolivar, the son of a wealthy landowner who had married into the Spanish aristocracy and spent a considerable time travelling in Europe.

Despite failing to enlist the help of Britain he declared Venezuela independent on 5 July 1811. But then after some initial success his army was almost wiped out in a massive earthquake the following year. Undeterred he then raised an army in nearby Colombia and returned to Caracas where he was declared as Liberator and dictator.

By this time, however, Ferdinand VII had returned to the Spanish throne and was intent on suppressing the rebellions in Latin America. Bolivar was forced into exile, first in Jamaica where he wrote his major political statement on the politics and future of Latin America, *The Letter from Jamaica* and then in Haiti. In exchange for a promise that he would free the slaves, Bolivar was given help in mounting a new expeditionary force by the Haitian president, Alexandre Petion.

Bolivar returned to Venezuela and, with the help of European mercenaries and the independent cowboy-types, the *llaneros* gradually took control of the country. He then marched on Colombia and on 7 August 1819 was declared Liberator of Colombia in Bogota. Then in December 1819, having defeated the Spanish in Venezuela, he announced his impossibly grandiose intention to create the state of "Gran Colombia" uniting Venezuela, Colombia and Ecuador of which he was then elected President in 1821 at Cucuta.

Revolt that ploughed the sea

Further south in the vice-royalty of La Plata the struggle proceeded along similar lines with Bonaparte's brother sparking a declaration of independence in 1810. Here the military leader was San Martin, the son of a Spanish army officer and professional soldier who had fought for Spain in the Napoleonic wars. Over the next seven years he won territory piecemeal, until in February 1817 he crossed the Andes to liberate Chile and defeated the Spanish at the battle of Chacabuco. He then joined forces with the Chilean leader Bernardo O'Higgins and in 1820, with the assistance of the British mercenary Lord Cochrane, transported his forces by ship to the southern Peruvian port of Pisco for the victorious push against the royalist stronghold of Lima. The final defeat for Spain came at the battle of Ayacucho when Bolivar's general Antonio Jose de Sucre, defeated them and went on to create the state of Bolivia – named after Bolivar but which he ruled.

Although the independence movement in South America achieved its primary aim, none of the leaders enjoyed the fruits of victory. When the two Liberators, Bolivar and San Martin, finally met at Guayaquil in Ecuador the meeting was not a success and subsequently San Martin withdrew from all his posts. Bolivar then returned to try to hold together his creation of Gran Colombia, but it was a virtually impossible task and his health started to fail. Gran Colombia fell apart with the secession of Ecuador and Colombia in September 1830 and Bolivar joined San Martin to die in exile.

With the exception of the freeing of slaves in the Spanish-speaking countries, Latin American society was not greatly changed by independence. Power rested with the creoles, the mestizos remained poor and the Indians were still abused and treated as serfs while the control of Spain was soon replaced by the economic power of Britain and the United States. On his death bed in 1830 Bolivar wrote: "America is ungovernable. Those who have served the revolution have ploughed the sea."

POLITICAL INDEPENDENCE IN SOUTH AMERICA

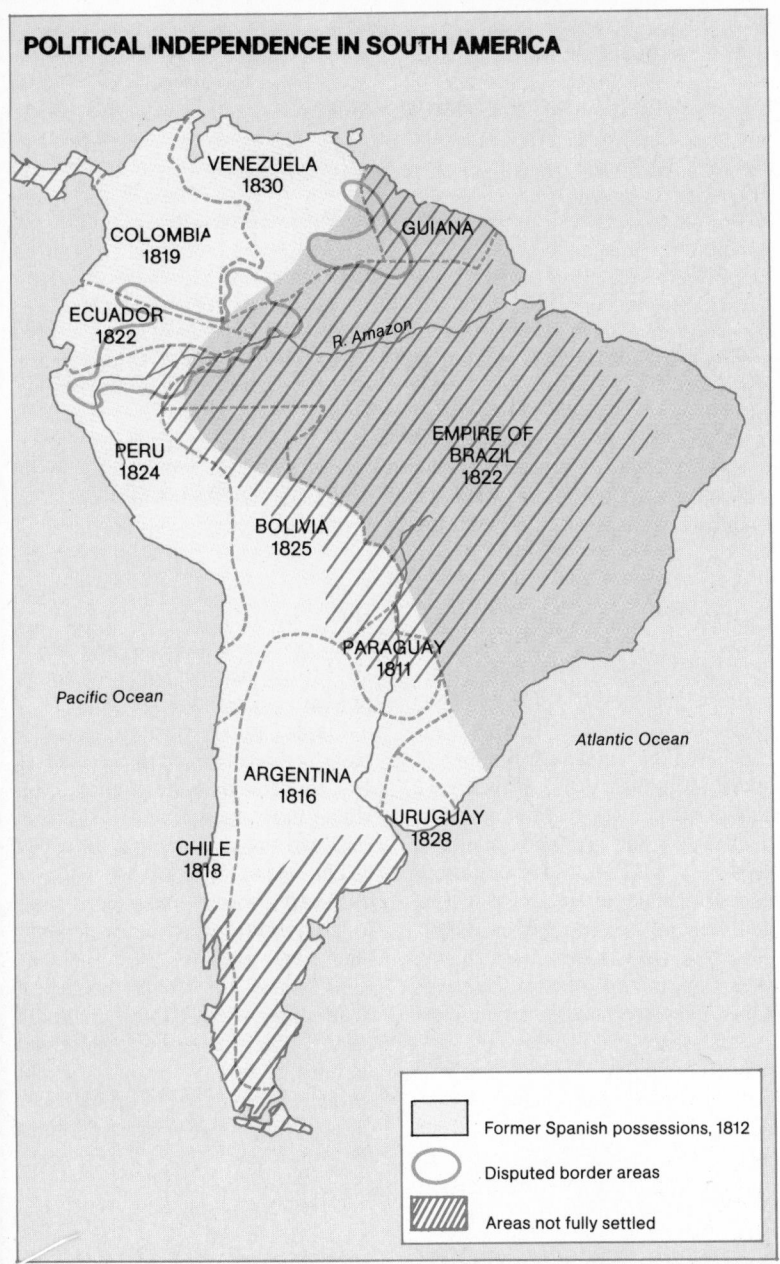

VENEZUELA 1830
COLOMBIA 1819
GUIANA
ECUADOR 1822
R. Amazon
PERU 1824
EMPIRE OF BRAZIL 1822
BOLIVIA 1825
PARAGUAY 1811
Pacific Ocean
Atlantic Ocean
ARGENTINA 1816
URUGUAY 1828
CHILE 1818

☐ Former Spanish possessions, 1812
⬭ Disputed border areas
▨ Areas not fully settled

Bolivar, liberator of Venezuela, Colombia, Peru and Ecuador.

The battle of Carabobo in April 1821, which ended Spanish rule in Venezuela. A detail of the ceiling in the Capitol building in Caracas.

Francia, Paraguay's first president.

Don Augustin de Iturbide.

Execution in 1867 of Maximilian, Mexico's last emperor, by Manet.

1832 (1832-1833)

USA, 25 January 1832. The immediate abolition of slavery is rejected by the Virginia Assembly.

Paris, 18 May 1832. The novel *Indiana* is published by George Sand, the pen name of Amandine Aurore Lucie Dupin. The 28-year-old Sand left her husband last year and came to Paris to make a living out of writing.

London, 4 June 1832. A bill of parliamentary reform is passed giving the vote to men of substantial property.

New York City, June 1832. Some 4,000 people die in a cholera epidemic.

Germany, 5 July 1832. Following the Hambach festival of South German Democrats, where revolt against Austrian rule was advocated, the government takes steps to curtail the freedom of the press and to limit the formation of unions and public meetings.

Minnesota, 13 July 1832. An expedition led by Henry Schoolcraft discovers the source of the Mississippi river.

Vienna, 22 July 1832. The duke of Reichstadt dies. Born the king of Rome, the son of the Emperor Napoleon I and Marie-Louise of Austria, he was known as Napoleon II during the hundred days between Napoleon I's escape from Elba and his defeat at Waterloo in June 1815.

Greece, 8 August 1832. The Greek national assembly elects Prince Otto, the second son of the king of Bavaria, king of Greece.

Norh America, August 1832. Chief Black Hawk and his tribe are massacred by US troops at the battle of Bad Axe, waged at the junction of the Mississippi and Bad Axe rivers (*in Michigan*).

North America, 21 September 1832. The Sauk Chief Keokuk, a rival of Chief Black Hawk who was defeated last month at the battle of Bad Axe, signs an agreement giving up his tribe's claims to lands east of the Mississippi river.

Britain, 21 September 1832. Sir Walter Scott, the most popular writer in Britain today, dies. As a poet he is best loved for *Marmion*, *Young Lochinvar* and *The Lay of the Last Minstrel*, but he will also be remembered for the *Waverley* novels.

Missouri, October 1832. The artist George Catlin returns from a voyage up the Missouri river with sensational pictures of Indian life. On a voyage of over 2,000 miles Catlin befriended Sioux and Mandan tribes and was rewarded by permission to record sacred rituals as well as daily life.

Washington, DC, 5 December 1832. President Jackson is re-elected.

Ottoman Empire, 21 December 1832. Russia offers military assistance to the Ottoman Sultan Mahmud II in his war with the *pasha* of Egypt, Mohammed Ali, whose troops have just taken control of Konya. Hostilities broke out earlier this year when the Ottomans refused to give Egypt Syria, which they had promised in return for military aid during the Greek War of Independence. The pasha's troops are now some 50 miles from Istanbul.

France, December 1832. Now that the Society of Friends of the People is being dissolved, another society closely linked to the working class, comprising three sections and recruiting about six thousand members, appears: the Society of the Rights of Man.

Algeria, 1832. Having been proclaimed *bey* by local chiefs, following his victories against the French, Abd al-Kader is now recognised as *emir* of Mascara.

London, 1832. William Wilkins designs the National Gallery in Trafalgar Square to house the Angerstein collection and other gifts.

Berlin, 22 March 1833. A customs treaty (*Zollverein*) is signed between Bavaria, Wurttemberg, Prussia and Hesse-Darmstadt, notably excluding Austria.

Texas, 3 April 1833. American settlers adjourn a three-day meeting, having agreed to make Texas independent of Mexico.

Germany, 4 April 1833. A liberal student uprising against Frankfurt police is brutally suppressed.

Piedmont, April 1833. The Italian radical Giuseppe Mazzini organises an anti-government plot which is discovered by the army. Mazzini's aim is the unification of Italy under a republican form of government. Following discovery of the plot, Mazzini flees and is sentenced to death in his absence.

Ottoman Empire, 4 May 1833. The treaty of Kutahya between the Ottoman Sultan Mahmud II and the Egyptian Pasha Mohammed Ali gives Egypt sovereignty over Syria and Cilicia and brings at least a temporary truce in the war between the two nations which began last year.

Britain, 15 May 1833. The actor Edmund Kean dies aged 45. Hailed by some as the greatest English actor since David Garrick, his delivery was described by the writer William Hazlitt as "like reading Shakespeare by flashes of lightning".

Twelve-hour day for Britain's teenagers

Children in a rope factory: in theory they will receive some education.

London, 1833

Tougher laws to prevent the exploitation of children in textile factories have been passed by the British Parliament. The new legislation closes loopholes in previous Factory Acts and limits the maximum number of hours that those aged between 12 and 18 can work to 12 hours a day.

The new act prohibits children aged nine to 13 from working more than nine hours a day and reaffirms the ban on under-nines working. No-one under 18 can work nights any longer, and one and a half hours have to be allowed in each day's shift for meal breaks.

The legislation does not apply to silk factories. Enforcement provisions in the new act allow four inspectors to be appointed to prevent employers evading the law.

Until now employers have been able blatantly to disregard the limits on ages and hours, safe in the knowledge that there was no one to present evidence against them.

Employers are also to be made more responsible for the welfare of any children in their employ, providing those aged nine to 13 with at least two hours' schooling a day.

The new legislation follows increased concern about conditions in the recently opened textile mills that now employ over 100,000. Lord Ashley, the son of the earl of Shaftesbury, decided to champion the act after visiting Lancashire and seeing so many young people severely crippled by working conditions that their distorted limbs looked "just like a crooked alphabet".

Success for symphony inspired by Italy

London, 14 May 1833

A London audience was last night delighted to hear the new *Italian Symphony* conducted by its composer, the 24-year-old German Felix Mendelssohn-Bartholdy.

Inspired by a trip to Italy two years ago, the symphony is the latest in a series of astonishingly mature and beautiful works by the young composer, who has been hailed as the greatest prodigy since Mozart. One was an octet for strings, written when Mendelssohn was just 16 and had already composed many apprentice works, including symphonies, operas and concertos. The octet was followed by the lovely overture to Shakespeare's *A Midsummer Night's Dream* the following year.

Felix Mendelssohn-Bartholdy: the young composer of mature music.

More Britons to vote

The Great Reform banquet at the Guildhall marks the passing of the Act.

London, 4 June 1832
Against a background of violent public disorders in London and the provinces, and under pressure from King William IV, the Lords today abandoned its stubborn opposition to parliamentary reform and passed an act that will give the vote to the small property owners and tenant farmers of middle classes. Now one in five adult males will have the vote – twice as many as before.

In declining rural areas, 56 "Rotten Boroughs" of fewer than 2,000 inhabitants have lost their representation entirely, and another 30 have lost one of their two MPs; their seats will be transferred to Manchester, Birmingham and other expanding industrial towns, some of which have been without MPs. The bill would have passed the Lords last year had it not been for the solid resistance of the 21 bishops.

In the long-running controversy over increased representation, Tories have accused Whigs of stirring up the people and risking revolution. The Whig cabinet, all but four of whose members are in the Lords, argues that prudent concessions to popular feeling are necessary in order to ensure stability and protect property.

Lord Grey's Whig cabinet resigned last month when King William refused to create 50 peers to get the bill passed; he stuck at 20 peers. But the Tories were unable to form a government and Grey was back within a week, with the king promising 50 peers. They were not needed; the Lords caved in.

Goethe's lovers inspire his poetry

Weimar, 22 March 1832
The great genius of German letters, Johann Wolfgang von Goethe, is dead. Poet, dramatist, scientist and court councillor to the duke of Weimar, he had been fully occupied in all these fields until his death at the age of 82, uttering as his last words "*Mehr licht!*" (more light).

It appears that he had finished his masterpiece, *Faust*, on which he had worked for most of his life. He published the first part in 1808 and its greatness was immediately recognised. The second part is his legacy.

Goethe's many love affairs inspired his outpouring of lyric poetry, the simplest and best Romantic poems in German, such as *Roslein*. His loves ranged from a parson's daughter to a society beauty, from a baron's wife to a humble village girl who bore him many children before he married her. Even in his seventies he was inspired by a new love, Ulrike von Leventzow, then 18. He is to be buried beside Schiller, his friend and rival.

Goethe: poet, dramatist, romantic.

Greatest happiness advocate has died

Bentham: the preserved body.

London, 1832
Jeremy Bentham, a leading English thinker behind legal, parliamentary and social reform advocated by a group of "Benthamites" including Edwin Chadwick, James Mill and the latter's son John Stuart Mill, has died, bequeathing his body to University College, London, which he founded "to provide higher education without religious bias".

His principle of "utility" was that men pursue pleasure and avoid pain and should be governed to produce "the greatest happiness of the greatest number". Trained as a lawyer, he advocated reform of the law, the penal system, public health, the Poor Law administration and suffrage. His plan for a model prison was rejected.

Papal bull condemns free-thinking press

Rome, 15 August 1832
Pope Gregory XVI has demolished the hopes of the new liberal Catholics in France led by Lamennais. In a papal bull, *Mirai Vos*, issued today he condemns the freedom of the press and other freedoms which Lamenais has been espousing in his Paris newspaper *L'Avenir*.

Under the slogan "God and liberty – unite them", Lamennais has been working for four freedoms: freedom of the press through the abolition of censorship; freedom of education through ending the monopoly of the state-controlled Napoleonic university; freedom of association for both workers and religious communities; and freedom of worship, including the right of individual churches to discipline their members.

He came to Rome in March to plead his cause in person, but the pope gave him only a 15-minute audience. Today the pope has declared that the church does not need reforming at all.

Spaniards rise up against heir to throne

Madrid, September 1833
Isabella has become queen of Spain and sparked off a savage civil war over the succession which threatens to ravage the countryside. She has succeeded her father Ferdinand VII against the wishes of the *Carlists*, a political group demanding that the throne is given to his brother Don Carlos. Isabella is backed by the liberals, the supporters of the democratic constitution that Ferdinand choose to repeal during a disastrous reign when Spain lost all her overseas possessions except Puerto Rica, Cuba, the Philippines, the island of Guam and a few outposts in Africa.

The sudden outbreak of a dynastic war among the semi-guerrilla Carlists, liberals and other groups is creating widespread disorder.

Ottoman Empire, 8 July 1833. The Ottomans sign the treaty of Unkiar-Skelessi with Russia, secretly granting Russian ships the right, in time of war, to close the Dardanelles straits.

London, July 1833. In order to enforce laws passed in 1802 and 1819 for the protection of child labour, an act is passed ensuring the appointment of factory inspectors.

New York City, 1 September 1833. Benjamin Day launches the *New York Sun* newspaper, price one cent. Packed with human interest stories and selling at a price that everyone can afford, the paper aims for a mass market. Editors of quality papers are sceptical about its chances of survival.

Washington, DC, 26 September 1833. President Jackson has government funds withdrawn from the Second Bank of the United States in the belief that it is controlled by his enemies in Congress and is out to oust him from office.

Spain, 29 September 1833. Civil war breaks out between the *Carlists* (supporters of Don Carlos, the pretender to the throne) and the supporters of Queen Isabella, who succeeded on her father's death.

Germany, September 1833. Russia, Prussia and Austria hold the semi-secret convention of Munchengratz, at which they agree concerted foreign policies. They support Don Carlos against Queen Isabella in Spain – France and Britain support the queen.

Britain, October 1833. Robert Owen presides over a conference of the *National Equitable Labour Exchange* which decides to set up a workers' trade union comprising all types of trade. The Union will be called the *National Consolidated Trades Union*.

Alabama, 13 December 1833. The people of Alabama witness the most spectacular part of a meteor shower that is visible across the North American continent. Known as the Leonid shower, it can be seen every year, but this year is the most dramatic so far on record.

Philadelphia, December 1833. Women led by Lucretia Mott found the Female Anti-Slavery Society, having discovered that women are banned from the American Anti-Slavery Society.

Mexico, 1833. General Santa Anna is elected president of the republic. Santa Anna supported General Iturbide, who was inspired by Napoleon's example to declare himself emperor in 1822, but was instrumental in his overthrow the following year.

Britain, 1833. A sermon given by the young John Keble, entitled *National Apostasy*, gives rise to the Oxford Movement which calls for the Church of England to reassert itself as a divine society with unquestioned authority. Members are disquieted by the liberalism they perceive in the 1829 Catholic Emancipation Act and the 1832 Reform Act.

South Atlantic, 1833. A British gunboat claims the Falkland islands as crown territory. In 1820, the Argentinians had claimed to succeed Spain in possession of the islands, which are also known as the Lalvinas, but Britain has now taken them without a fight.

Japan, 1833. Following the second poor harvest in a row there is famine throughout the country and the starving populace riots in several towns, smashing the houses of wealthy merchants.

Britain, 1833. The physicist Michael Faraday makes significant progress in his experiments aimed at the identification of electricity from different sources.

New York City, 1833. The Irish actor Tyrone Power makes his debut on the American stage.

Greece, 1833. Following the declaration of national independence last year, the Greek Church decides to sever its links with Istanbul.

Vatican, 1833. Pope Gregory XVI organises evangelistic missions to the South Sea Islands.

France, 1833. The historian Jules Michelet begins to publish the first volumes of his *Histoire de France*.

USA, 1833. Samuel Colt develops a new firearm – the revolver. This is a pistol with revolving chambers which allows several shots to be fired without reloading.

Germany, 1833. The physicist Carl Gauss invents the electromagnetic telegraph which is able to send messages over long distances by means of electric pulses passed along wires.

Honolulu, 1833. Kauikeaouli comes of age and is crowned King Kamehameha III.

Algeria, 26 February 1834. Without consulting the French government, General Desmichels signs a treaty with the *emir* of Mascara, Abd al-Kader, recognising him as commander of the faithful and his sovereignty over the *beylik* of Oran.

Savoy, February 1834. Revolutionary groups led by Giuseppe Mazzini and the Genoan Ramorino infiltrate the Annemasse area with the aim of seizing power, but they are soon dispersed by peasants.

Japanese artists Hokusai and Hiroshige make for Mount Fuji and Tokaido

Katsushika Hokusai's "Mount Fuji in clear weather", one of 36 views of the volcanic mountain by Japan's first painter to create landscape paintings.

Edo, Japan, 1833
Ando Hiroshige has completed his set of woodblock colour prints entitled *Fifty-Three Stages on the Tokaido*, the main highway between Edo and Kyoto, which his senior, Hokusai, also painted on a sketching journey made 20 years ago. These are considered Hiroshige's finest work to date.

Hiroshige inherited from his father the post of warden of the Edo fire brigade. He had to carry out these duties until he could pass them on to his own son and concentrate entirely on his own art. The pure landscape is a new departure in Japanese prints. Until now figure studies, of the girls of the pleasure district, or of actors or *Samurai*, have been preferred.

The great pioneer of landscape painting is Katsushika Hokusai, 30 years older than Hiroshige. Although over 70, he is now completing his most ambitious work, an illustrated book of *Thirty-Six Views of Mount Fuji*. He writes, "Of all I drew before the age of 70 there is nothing of any great note. At 73 I finally learned something of the true quality of birds, insects, fishes, grasses and trees. At 80 I shall have made some progress."

Hiroshige lacks Hokusai's versatility and his powerful realism, but he is admired for his relaxed human touch.

One of the stages on the Tokaido, the road between Edo and Kyoto, by Ando Hiroshige, a follower of the Japanese landscape painter Katsushika Hokusai.

Egypt asserts itself against Ottomans

Ottoman Empire, 3 May 1833
Mohammed Ali, the viceroy of Egypt, has consolidated the gains made by his son Ibrahim in campaigns against his Ottoman "masters". The convention of Kutahya confirms his acquisition of the *pashalik* of Acre, and he now controls Palestine, Syria and mountain passes on the Turkish frontier.

Hostilities began last year when the sultan, jealous of any overmighty vassal, declared Mohammed Ali an outlaw and sent an army against him. Ibrahim, having occupied Gaza, Jerusalem, Acre, Jaffa and Damascus, defeated the Ottoman army at Beilan, then, even more crushingly, at Konya in December.

With Ibrahim poised to attack Istanbul, the great powers inter-

Mohammed Ali: the ruler of Egypt.

vened. A Russian force of 6,000 landed in the Bosporus and, to ensure its withdrawal, the British and French persuaded the sultan to concede Mohammed Ali's demands.

Frenchman teaches the blind to read

Paris, 1833
Louis Braille, the blind inventor who teaches at the National Institute for Blind Children in Paris, is developing and improving his new form of writing which will enable blind people to read.

He first started working on this unseen writing in 1824, aged 15. He has even adapted it to musical notation. In 1829, when only 20 years old, he published a treatise announcing his invention. Now he is developing it with further elaborations. Already hundreds of blind children in Paris are learning to read books, and many are now capable of sitting standard academic examinations.

Braille himself was blinded at the age of three; yet he is an accomplished cellist and organist, as well as inventor.

A blind ballad seller in London.

From Bengal to Bristol: story of a genius

Bristol, 27 September 1833
Ram Moham Roy, the Indian utilitarian philosopher, has died. For a man dedicated to bridging east and west, who spoke ten languages, Stapleton, near Bristol, was as likely a deathplace as any other.

Born in 1770, he left his home in protest at a relation's death by *suttee* (widow-burning). Studying Buddhist, Hindu, Moslem, He-

brew, Greek and Christian texts, he devoted his life to the search for universal truths.

Nor were his concerns purely religious. He founded India's first newspaper (publishing Bengali, Persian and English editions), established secondary schools and rose to the highest position an Indian could hold in the Bengal Civil Service.

Oxford dons seek a different church

Oxford, England, 14 July 1833
In a sermon at St Mary's here today which kept the whole congregation wide awake, John Keble called for a radical transformation of the Church of England. He called for a revival of liturgical ceremonial, the introduction of religious communities, and a greater social awareness through the church establishing up settlements in poor areas.

All told, it represents a move back towards Catholicism which will produce fierce opposition. But Keble and two other fellows of Oxford's Oriel College, John Newman and Edward Pusey, are a determined group. More is likely to be heard of them.

Analytical engine is calculating marvel

England, 1833
There is a growing need for more and more calculations. Armies of clerks do them at present, but the English inventor Charles Babbage has the visionary idea of a machine for doing any calculations that its operator can specify.

It consists of thousands of cogs and gearwheels that form the heart of the "analytical engine", carrying out the arithmetical functions. In order to instruct the machine in what it has to do, there is a programme incorporated in a punched card. This technique has been used in the textile industry, in the Jacquard loom which has punched cards to vary the patterns.

London in 1833, looking west over Westminster, Chelsea, Kensington and Paddington, from the painter's platform on the roof of the Colosseum in Regent's Park. The market gardens of Shepherd's Bush and Chiswick beyond the suburbs of west London can be seen in the distance.

1834 ⇒

London, 22 April. Britain, Spain, France and Portugal form a quadruple alliance, prompted by last year's Munchengratz convention at which Russia, Prussia and Austria met. The four countries pledge to work together to guarantee Belgium's independence and to support Queen Isabella's claim to the Spanish throne against *Carlist* opposition. Meanwhile the civil war in Spain continues.

India, 6 May. Sikhs led by the Punjab ruler Ranjit Singh capture Peshawar, the Muslim city in north-west India.

Portugal, 24 May. King Miguel finally capitulates to his brother, Pedro, the emperor of Brazil, who restores his 15-yearold daughter Maria II da Gloria to her rightful position as queen of Portugal.

Washington, DC, 20 June. Congress passes a law making all land west of the Mississippi river – other than the states of Missouri and Louisiana and the Territory of Arkansas – Indian country.

New York City, 4 July. The Annual Convention of People of Color sets 4 July as a day of prayer and contemplation of the Negro condition.

China, 15 July. Following the recent abolition of the East India Company's trade monopoly, Lord Napier arrives at Macao as the first British chief superintendent of trade.

London, 1 August. Slavery is abolished throughout the British empire.

London, 2 August. The *South Australia Association* gains a charter to found a colony.

London, 14 August. The Poor Law Amendment Act is passed, establishing a system of workhouses.

China, 11 October. Lord Napier, the British chief superintendent of trade, who has failed in his negotiations with the Chinese, dies in Macao.

Philadelphia, October. A town meeting condemns race riots that erupted this summer in the city's Negro areas. The riots began when nearly 500 unemployed Whites entered the area intending to drive the Negroes out of town. Compensation will be paid to the Negro residents.

Britain, 27 December. The much-loved essayist and poet Charles Lamb dies. Writing under the pseudonym "Elia" he had his first success in 1807 with the *Tales from Shakespeare* which he wrote with his sister Mary.

Britain. The Whig prime minister, Lord Grey, resigns because of cabinet disagreements over his Irish policy. He is replaced by Robert Peel.

France. The prolific novelist Honore de Balzac publishes *Eugenie Grandet*.

South Africa. News of the British abolition of slavery reaches white Boer farmers in Cape Colony. Aghast at this loss of labour, many begin to move north in search of land outside British control.

London. The French wax-modeller Marie Tussaud establishes a permanent exhibition of her figures of famous people in Baker Street. A friend of Napoleon's ex-wife Josephine, Mme Tussaud emigrated to Britain in 1802.

Japan. A new senior councillor, Mizuno Tadakuni, is appointed and initiates reforms to cope with a financial crisis in the *shogun*'s government and the growing unrest caused by famine.

Britain. Six farm workers from the village of Tolpuddle in Dorset are sentenced to seven years' transportation to Australia for setting up a local trade union, a branch of the Friendly Society of Agricultural Labourers. The severity of the sentence causes huge public outcry and the six are hailed as the Tolpuddle Martyrs.

Persia. The Persian army seizes the town of Serakhs in Afghanistan while the British and Russians reach an agreement on the limits of their mutual zones of influence in the area.

Russia. Alexander Pushkin publishes a novella entitled *The Queen of Spades*.

Russia. Nikolai Gogol publishes *Taras Bulba*. This colourful and dramatic tale is a hymn to the Cossack people whose primitive, wild nature is exalted by Gogol.

Mexico. The president, General Santa Anna, launches a campaign to eliminate the vice-president, Gomez Farias, and assume a position of sole power.

Britain. The popular writer Bulwer Lytton publishes a new historical novel, *The Last Days of Pompeii*.

South Africa. Dutchspeaking Griqua hunting parties raid the Mfecane war areas to the north of their settlements for labour and cattle. They suffer a disastrous defeat at the hands of the Ndebele of Mzilikazi in the Pretoria region of the Transvaal, but do not give up their ambitions of northwards expansion.

Republican rising is crushed in France

Paris, April
Yet another insurrection against the Bourbon monarchy of Louis Philippe and his banking and factory-owning allies has been crushed. As usual the forces of "order" left their traditional trail of blood, killing hundreds of men, women and children in the Parisian working-class districts of the Cloitre Saint-Merri and Rue Transnonain.

This time the rebels were silk-workers from Paris and Lyons. Few save the leaders, such as Auguste Blanqui of the secret Society of the Rights of Man, are able to articulate their demands. Hungry men know more what they are opposing than what they want. The origins of the uprising are in the deplorable conditions of the French proletariat.

Trades unions are illegal, strikes forbidden, factory acts ignored and factory workers forced to carry the hated *livrets* (workbooks) listing all previous employers.

Further, the "July Revolution" of Louis Philippe, establishing a government committed to abolishing the peerage and extending the franchise, has created rising expectations among the poor that cannot be fulfilled: hence the piles of pathetic corpses in the Rue Transnonain.

Outcry greets harsh workhouse plans

Britain's new workhouses: "uninviting places of wholesome restraint".

London
Traditional poor law relief in Britain is to be abolished as a wages supplement and replaced by a system of workhouses, according to a new Poor Law report just published. The report, which proposes changes to the original Elizabethan legislation, has been condemned by every national newspaper as harsh and uncaring. Opponents fear that its central proposal – the establishment of workhouses – will destroy family life among the poor.

The report, which took two years to complete, advocates an end to the system of wage supplements and subsidies awarded to the low-paid according to family size. Instead, able-bodied men and women who want assistance will have to live and work in workhouses. According to one of the report's authors, these should be "uninviting places of wholesome restraint". A typical workhouse will separate husbands from wives and parents from children, restrict visitors and enforce silence at meal times. Tasks will include stonebreaking, bone-grinding and the hand-grinding of corn.

The report claims the workhouse will be preferable to the present system of outdoor relief which now costs over £8 million a year. This relief, however, will still be available to the old and the sick.

Slavery abolished in British colonies

New scheme unites Germany's states

London, 1 August

By today, Emancipation Day in the British empire, three-quarters of a million slaves have been set free. The man responsible for their emancipation, the philanthropist and campaigner Thomas Buxton, who took over the leadership of the Emancipation Party in the House of Commons from William Wilberforce in 1824, celebrated the success of his life's work quietly at his house in Spitalfields. Fellow campaigners presented him with two handsome pieces of plate.

The trade in slaves had been prohibited in Britain in 1807. Slowly and reluctantly other countries followed suit. Napoleon abolished the trade during the Hundred Days, but Bourbon France continued it until 1819. Spain abolished it in 1820 (getting £400,000 compensation from Britain), Portugal in 1830 (getting £300,000).

Inevitably the next stage was the abolition of slavery itself. The plantation-owners had dominated

Antigua: a plantation owner watches his black overseer supervising his slaves.

the unreformed parliaments before 1832, but with the passing of the Reform Act the emancipators had a sudden majority. Within a year the Emancipation Act was passed, with the slave-owners receiving £20 million in compensation.

Every slave in Britain's colonies is now free, although, to offset the dangers of a shortage of labour in the West Indies, field slaves will be "apprenticed" to their former masters until 1840 and domestic slaves until 1838.

Germany

Seventeen states, with a population of more than 20 million, have formed a customs union, the *Zollverein*, under Prussian leadership. The architects of the scheme hope that it will prepare the way for German leadership of the civilised world.

Prussia's economic development was hampered until recently by 67 different tariffs and 13 non-Prussian enclaves, each with a different fiscal system. When Prussia abolished internal customs duties in 1818, a number of small states opted to be absorbed. Other German states formed their own unions in 1828, but have now decided to come under the Prussian umbrella.

The *Zollverein* is the brainchild of the economist Friedrich List, who returned last year from exile in the United States. Although the maritime cities remain independent, the rest of Germany may be further unified by a railway system radiating from Berlin.

Grain harvester to revolutionise farming

Virginia, USA, 21 June

Cyrus Hall McCormick has invented an automatic grain-reaping machine, which will reduce labour and agricultural coats and multiple the US agricultural industry's productivity. Its components include a

reel to gather grain, a vibrating blade to cut it and a platform on which the cut grain is collected. His father, a blacksmith, had tried for years to make such a machine and Cyrus spent more time in his father's workshop than in school.

Midwifery advances in South America

Rio de Janeiro

New obstetrics practices from Europe are dramatically reducing the city's infant mortality rate. Marie Durocher, the first woman obstetrician to qualify in Rio, is using methods developed by midwives at La Maternite hospital in Paris and Geissen in Germany. She believes

in the minimum of intervention in normal childbirth, and takes full advantage of modern monitoring and measuring instruments. The fact that these improvements are coming from France and Germany, not from Britain, is largely due to their governments' sponsorship of midwifery training.

Tussaud's waxworks find London home

Madame Tussaud's waxworks.

London, December

Madame Marie Tussaud, the 73-year-old wax modeller, who attended the guillotine to take death masks from the severed heads during the French Revolution, is to establish a permanent exhibition site in Baker Street for her waxwork gallery of heroes, rogues, victims and confidence tricksters. Apprenticed to her uncle Dr Curtius, who owned a waxworks in the Palais Royal, Paris, she was imprisoned herself in the Revolution, but only for a short time. She came in England with her two children in 1800, and since then has been touring the country with her representations of Marie Antoinette, Napoleon, Sir Walter Scott and scores more.

The Palace of Westmister, the residence of English kings from Edward the Confessor to Henry VIII and seat of parliament, burning down in 1832.

1834 (1834-1835)

India, 1834. The British depose the *rajah* of Coorg because of his cruelty.

China, 1 January 1835. The *Society for the Diffusion of Useful Knowledge* meets for the first time. It is organised by foreign merchants and missionaries in Canton (Guangzhou).

Washington, DC, January 1835. Congress allocates surplus revenue as the government makes the final payment on the national debt.

Vienna, 2 March 1835. The Austrian Emperor Francis dies and is succeeded by his son Ferdinand in order to preserve the principle of hereditary succession. Mentally subnormal, Ferdinand is to be assisted by a regency council dominated by the conservative Prince Metternich.

Ottoman Empire, 24 March 1835. Sultan Mahmud II grants Britain complete freedom to trade in silk in Syria. But, following the Ottoman-Egyptian war which ended in 1833, Syria is now in the hands of Mohammed Ali, the *pasha* of Egypt, and he refuses to implement the arrangement.

USA, March 1835. The writer Edgar Allan Poe publishes a short story entitled *Berenice* in the *Southern Literary Messenger*.

London, 18 April 1835. William Lamb, Lord Melbourne, becomes prime minister following the resignation of Robert Peel.

Paris, 25 April 1835. France authorises the payment of American claims for damages incurred during the Napoleonic wars.

Belgium, 5 May 1835. The Brussels-Malines railway line is opened, providing the first passenger service in mainland Europe.

Algeria, 28 May 1835. The *emir* of Mascara, Abd al-Kader, attacks French troops in the Macta pass and defeats them.

France, 9 July 1835. The St Etienne-Lyons railway opens as a passenger service for the first time.

New York City, 25 August 1835. The popular *New York Sun* newspaper reaches a nationwide audience following the publication of an article claiming that vegetation grows on the moon.

USA, August 1835. The Anti-Slavery Society distributes 75,000 anti-slavery leaflets by mail to the south, to the fury of slave-owners.

Britain, 9 September 1835. The Municipal Corporations Act is passed, reforming city and town government in line with the shift in population brought on by industrial developments.

Italy, 26 September 1835. Donizetti's opera *Lucy of Lammermoor* is performed for the first time.

France, September 1835. The government takes steps to strengthen court procedures and punish offences committed by the press more severely in order to combat republicanism.

Mozambique, 19 November 1835. The Ngoni army of Zwangendaba crosses the Zambezi northwards during an eclipse of the sun. After four years of raiding on the Zimbabwe plateau, Zwangendaba is now taking his army north to spread the Mfecane wars to eastern Zambia and Malawi. He leaves some Ngoni raiders behind in Zimbabwe, notably those led by his niece Nyamazana.

Bavaria, 7 December 1835. The first German railway between Nuremberg and Furth passes into private ownership.

Texas, 20 December 1835. Leaders of the Texan secession movement issue a declaration of independence from the dictatorship of the Mexican President Santa Anna, and officially proclaim the creation of the republic of Texas. Full-scale civil war erupts.

Florida, 28 December 1835. Over one hundred US troops are massacred by Seminole Indians resisting attempts to drive them out of Florida.

New Orleans, December 1835. Residents ride in steam-driven streetcars on the New Orleans and Carrollton Railroad as the line puts its horses out to pasture.

Germany, 1835. Georg Buchner, a doctor and a poet, publishes a play based on the French Revolution entitled *The Death of Danton*.

France, 1835. The poet and dramatist Alfred de Musset writes *May Night* and publishes his *Confession of a Child of the Century*.

Britain, 1835. The young writer Charles Dickens publishes a collection of his journalistic pieces under the title *Sketches by Boz*, receiving £150 for the copyright.

Russia, 1835. Nikolai Gogol publishes his *Diary of a Madman*, inspired by the German Romantic movement.

Germany, 1835. The theologian and writer David Strauss publishes his *Life of Jesus* which is violently attacked by the religious authorities and involves him in legal proceedings. In it he interprets the New Testament as a product of communal Christian spirit rather than a divine revelation.

The noble savage, the object of Protestant endeavour: natives from New Guinea

Protestants come to save Samoans' souls

Samoa, 1835

The most important event on the island this year has been the arrival of the first Protestant missionary. The Rev Peter Turner, a Wesleyan, has already had substantial success in converting Tongans living here, and is beginning to make an impression on the native Samoans.

The Protestant missions can be dated back to the end of the 18th century when the London Missionary Society set up pioneering missions at Tonga and Tahiti. They did not stay long, but several other groups made efforts on other islands in the following years. The breakthrough came in 1811 when the Rev Samuel Marsden resumed the Tahitian mission. In 1814 he established the New Zealand mission at the Bay of the Islands.

Marsden had a genius for organisation. He treated missionary work as if it were a military campaign, dividing the South Seas into evangelistic compartments. He stopped the doctrinal differences of Church of England, Wesleyans and others splintering the efforts. How long the united effort will last is in doubt, however. Squabbles have recently broken out between the two missions on Tonga.

Poet who dreamed on opium has died

London, 25 July 1834

Samuel Taylor Coleridge, who died today, owed his high reputation in an age of poets to a single period of intense inspiration in 1797-98 in which he wrote *The Ancient Mariner, Kubla Khan* and *Christabel*. By 1802 he was mourning the loss of his poetic response to nature in an *Ode to Dejection*. It also ended his close collaboration with Wordsworth. Together they had rejected the artifice of 18th-century poetry in their joint book, *Lyrical Ballads*, which began the Romantic movement in poetry in 1798. Coleridge, who suffered endless financial problems, became a critic and journalist. He spent his life struggling against an addiction to opium, prescribed for rheumatic pain. Under its influence he "dreamed" of Xanadu.

Fall of Oyo empire splits West Africa

West Africa, 1835

The empire of Oyo, one of the great empires of West Africa, is breaking up. Its capital, Oyo, is deserted. The Oyo cavalry swept across the West African savannalands towards the end of the last century, and built a nation that grew rich from the slave trade.

Over a generations ago, under its ruler, Alafin, Oyo reached its zenith. From his death the state went into steady decline, weakened by internal discord and foreign invasions, mainly by the Fulani.

Driven from their lands the Oyo people moved south, colonising the forest lands of the Egda and the If peoples, where their distinctive double-ended *gangans*, or talking drums, have been adopted by the indigenous people.

Mr Gordon Bennett founds newspaper

New York City, 6 May 1835
A revolutionary new penny newspaper, the *New York Herald*, came onto the streets today and achieved instant success for its editor and proprietor, Gordon Bennett. The Scottish-born journalist has managed to launch the *Herald* despite lack of funds or party support.

The new paper owes its success to its comprehensive coverage of local news – presented in a piquant, highly individual style – and the fiercely independent editorials, most of them written by Bennett himself.

Gordon Bennett: newspaper owner.

Infernal machine fails to kill French king

Failed assassins: Fieschi, Morey and Pepin on their way to the guillotine.

Paris, 28 July 1835
King Louis Philippe narrowly escaped assassination on a Parisian boulevard today as a hail of bullets intended for him killed 18 bystanders and wounded many others. The assassination attempt happened on the Boulevard du Temples as the king and his sons were on their way to review troops. The king's sons all escaped unhurt. Among those who died were members of the court and some National Guardsmen.

Hundreds of bullets were fired at the king's party by an infernal machine, as police are calling it, devised by a republican sympathiser named as Giuseppe Maria Fieschi. The 45-year-old Corsican had rigged together 25 guns, linking their firing pins so that they could be fired simultaneously.

Police have also arrested two of Fieschi's alleged accomplices, Pierre Morey and Pierre Pepin, both members of the extreme republican group, the Society for the Rights of Man, which has advocated violence.

Fieschi, a smalltime crook who has served ten years for theft, made contact with the society recently. He claims to have worked as a secret agent for the government, infiltrating the Bonapartist movement under a false name.

Today's assassination attempt will almost certainly strengthen the hand of those in government who want to curb the incitements to violence that have appeared of late in the republican press.

Corporations take over British towns

London, 9 September 1835
The old rough and ready methods of running municipal affairs, by means of borough oligarchies or parish meetings, are being swept away and replaced by elected municipal councils. The Municipal Reform Act applies to two million people in 178 boroughs in the thriving industrial and commercial areas of the country.

The new councils will be elected on a much wider franchise than the parliamentary one. All rate-paying householders of three years' standing will have the vote; this effectively transfers municipal power from Tory lawyers, Anglican clergy and factotums of the aristocracy to shopkeepers, businessmen and Non-conformists. Some better-off members of the working class will become voters.

The new councils will take over the work of the Improvement Commissions which have been set up on the initiative of public-spirited citizens, who obtained their powers by private acts of parliament. The commissioners widen streets, improve water supplies and provide other amenities. In Manchester, the Police Commissioners have built a gas works and acquired fire engines. But critics of these "cursed improvements" say that the gas works should be sold to a private firm.

Romantic composer dies aged only 33

Paris, 23 September 1835
Once, playing through a piece of music to a friend, the Italian composer Vincenzo Bellini said: "If I could write one melody as beautiful as this, I would not mind dying young." Bellini did write many beautiful melodies, and today he died, of consumption, aged only 33.

Slight, languid and with swathes of curls, Bellini cut a romantic figure and attracted many admirers in Paris, where he spent a number of years. His operas, such as *Norma*, *I Puritani* and *La Sonnambula* allow the singers to display amazing feats of vocal acrobatics, but Bellini also pioneered an expressive, romantic style with rich, long, poetic melodies.

Vincenzo Bellini, the genius and consumptive, who died today aged 33.

Fairy story ends unhappily ever after

Copenhagen, 1835
A little book of *Tales Told for Children* has been published by Hans Christian Andersen, who began life as the son of a poor cobbler, tried to become an actor, and won himself an education at Copenhagen university and a royal pension on which he travelled around Europe. He has already published poems, plays and a novel.

His fairy stories include *The Tinderbox*, *The Princess and the Pea*, *Little Claus and Big Claus* and *Little Ida's Flowers*. They are founded on folk tales which he heard as a boy. He intends to publish many more. In spite of their frequently unhappy endings, these tales are in great demand.

Tommelise sitting desolately on a water lily leaf, from "Thumbelina".

1835 (1835-1836)

Argentina, 1835. Juan Manuel de Rosas, the governor of Buenos Aires, assumes dictatorial powers and embarks on a reign of terror.

Venezuela, 20 January 1836. The United States and Venezuela complete a treaty of peace, amity, commerce and navigation.

Algeria, 25 January 1836. In the long conflict between Algerians and French colonists, the French governor general, Clauzel, drives the resistance leader, *Emir* Abd al-Kader, out of the Tafna gorges.

Texas, 24 February 1836. Mexico's dictator, General Santa Anna, with 5,000 soldiers, lays siege to the fortified mission station, the Alamo, defended by 187 Texans.

Paris, 29 February 1836. Meyerbeer's opera *Les Huguenots* is performed for the first time.

Texas, 6 March 1836. The Alamo fort falls to Mexican troops.

Texas, 27 March 1836. The Mexican army massacres Texan rebels at Gohad.

Algeria, March 1836. The Algerian resistance leader Abd al-Kader occupies the capital, Mascara.

Texas, 21 April 1836. Texan troops led by General Sam Houston inflict a crushing defeat on the Mexicans at San Jacinto, taking General Santa Anna, prisoner.

Washington, DC, 26 May 1836. A resolution is passed stating that Congress has no authority over state slavery laws.

Arkansas, 15 June 1836. Arkansas becomes the 25th state of the USA.

London, 16 June 1836. The London Working Men's Association is founded.

Paris, 1 July 1836. Alfred de Musset publishes his play *Never Swear to Anything* in the magazine *La Revue des Deux Mondes*. It is a minor masterpiece on a light theme, full of freshness and youth, with a cast of worldly characters delightfully drawn from the society of his day.

Algeria, 6 July 1836. The French General Bugeaud wins a victory against Abd al-Kader's forces beside the Sikkak river.

Texas, September 1836. A referendum calls for annexation by the United States.

Texas, 22 October 1836. General Sam Houston is sworn in as president of the Texas republic.

Strasbourg, 30 October 1836. King Louis Philippe pardons Prince Louis Napoleon Bonaparte, following his attempt to persuade the local garrison to rebel against the government, and banishes him to America.

South Africa, 1836. Following the end of the sixth Eastern Cape Frontier War last year, Boers are disappointed when the British government hands back captured land to the Xhosa, with whom it makes friendship treaties. The Boers had joined the war in an attempt to gain land outside British domination following the abolition of slavery, but Christian missionaries had informed the government of the settlers' motives. The Boers are now *trekking* north to join hunters and raiders beyond the Orange and Vaal rivers.

Britain, 1836. Joanna Baillie, a 74-year-old Scottish poetess and dramatist, publishes a three-volume collection of her works.

USA, 1836. Oliver Wendell Holmes's *Poems* are published.

New York City, 1836. The New York Women's Anti-Slavery Society bans Negroes from membership.

USA, 1836. The radical writer Ralph Waldo Emerson publishes *Nature*, a collection of his lectures which develop the theory of the individual's potential for divinity.

Czechoslovakia, 1836. The historian Frantisek Palacky publishes his history of the Czech nation in Bohemia and Moldavia up to 1526.

France, 1836. The Schneider brothers, Eugene and Adolphe, buy the metalworking factory at Le Creusot, the royal foundry started by Louis XVI.

Germany, 1836. The League of the Just is founded, following in the steps of the League of the Reprobates, formed in Paris in 1832. It brings together apprentices and journeymen with the admirable aim of freeing Germany from oppression and humankind from slavery.

USA, 1836. James Madison, who was the fourth president of the USA, dies in Virginia.

Zimbabwe, 1836. The Rozvi kingdom, which has ruled Zimbabwe since about 1681, suffers a serious defeat at the hands of Nyamazana, a woman general who stayed behind after the main Ngoni force moved north last year. Nyamazana was determined to crush the Rozvi and she has lead an assault on the rocky citadel of Manyanga. Some say that she has had the last *mambo*, or king, Chirisamhuru II, skinned alive.

Britain, 1836. Parliament passes the Locomotive Act limiting the speed of all trains to five miles per hour, with a person carrying a red flag walking in front on the steam engine.

Boers "trek" out of South African cape

South Africa, 1836
A people is on the move. From all over Cape Colony wagons drawn by oxen, escorted by armed outriders, move north-eastwards. Ten thousand Boers are trekking to new lands beyond the reach of the British crown because they feel that they are being discriminated against. For a brief moment, inspired by the ideals of the French Revolution, they established republics, but Britain soon crushed them.

Complaints against Britain's utilitarian colonial policy are endless.

West Indian slave-owners, who are British, received full compensation for the emancipation of their slaves. Dutch Boer slave-owners received one-fifth. Land on which Boers had shed their blood is denied them and handed back to Blacks. British principles that all races should be treated as equal before the law have been twisted to favour the Blacks, it is said.

The road across the high *veldt* and over the Drakensberg Mountains is hard, and for the stubborn Boers it will seem very long indeed.

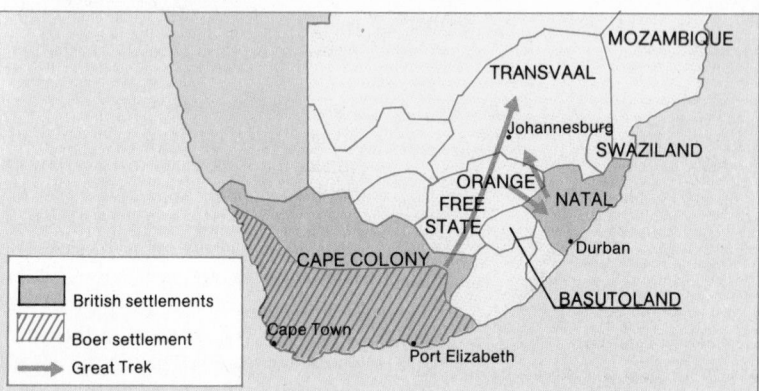

US president survives assassination bid

Washington, DC, 30 January 1835
A madman armed with two pistols took aim at President Andrew Jackson from a distance of six feet in the Capitol rotunda today. Both weapons misfired and Jackson was unhurt.

The fiery president is no stranger to gunplay. When he took office three years ago he was carrying two bullets in his body. One in his arm, the legacy of a gunfight 20 years earlier, was removed shortly after. The other, received from a duel over a gambling debt, stays lodged near his heart. Jackson killed his opponent, aiming deliberately at the groin.

This was the first-ever assassination attempt on a United States president in office. The assailant, a house painter called Richard Lawrence, claims to be the rightful heir to the British throne.

Despite Jackson's avowed hatred of the British and his controversial Indian policies, no political motive is suspected.

The Arc de Triomphe: Paris' great celebration of Napoleonic splendour.

Mexico takes Texan fort

The fall of the Alamo: a later, romanticised version of the Texans' battle.

San Antonio, Texas, 6 March 1836
After 12 days of bombardment, 5,000 Mexican troops stormed a former Spanish mission called the Alamo here today, taking no prisoners and slaughtering the 187 Texan defenders to the last man. The Mexican general, Antonio Lopez de Santa Anna, tonight gave orders to have the Texan bodies piled up and burned like cordwood as an example to other rebellious Texans – but already the call is echoing throughout the state of Texas "Remember the Alamo!".

Santa Anna, a vain, ambitious and devious blusterer, had marched into Texas when American settlers declared themselves independent and elected their own president, David Burnet. Surprised at the size of Santa Anna's army, the Texan Colonels William B Travis and James Bowie retreated to the Alamo – despite orders from their commander, the tough and doughty General Sam Houston, to withdraw from a defenceless position.

Once he had surrounded the mission, Santa Anna demanded an unconditional surrender from the Texans who replied with a single cannon shot.

The Mexican general hoisted a red flag – the traditional symbol that there would be no quarter given – and ate and drank well in a shady garden as his artillery pounded the mission into a ruin. Some reports suggest that more than 1,000 Mexican infantrymen were

killed or wounded when they finally advanced; but it took them less than an hour to massacre the defenders.

Colonel Travis lay dead, rifle in hand; Colonel Bowie – who had won fame from his exploits with the Bowie knife – was bayoneted to death; the body of Colonel Davy Crockett, the legendary frontiersman who had arrived in Texas only two weeks earlier, was found badly mutilated.

The only survivors were women who had sheltered in the sacristy below the mission. Santa Anna told one of them, Susanna Dickinson, a blacksmith's wife, to pass the message to other Texans that fighting was hopeless.

The Tennessee-born frontiersman Davy Crockett, with his hunting dogs.

British naturalist ends southern survey

London, 1836
HMS *Beagle*, a ten-gun brig of 235 tons, has reached port safely after completing a memorable five-year voyage of survey of South America and its islands under the command of Captain Robert Fitzroy.

One of the most remarkable aspects of the voyage of the *Beagle* was the work carried out by Charles Darwin, a young naturalist who sailed at the invitation of the captain and was on the ship's books for victuals, but got no pay.

He is well satisfied, however, by the wonders he has seen and by his collections of animals, birds and plants which are his to dispose of as he wishes.

He left England as an apprentice scientist and has returned a successful collector, an expert geologist and with a wide knowledge of nature acquired at first hand in many wild parts of the world. His letters home speak of being so excited by

Charles Darwin: naval naturalist.

his work he "could literally hardly sleep at nights". He was especially interested at the way in which related but different species inhabit the various islands of the Galapagos off the coast of Ecuador.

Algerians resist French expansion

Algeria, 28 May 1835
Algerian tribesmen, who united together to resist the French invaders in a holy war in November 1832, have defeated French troops in the Macta Pass. It is not their first victory, but Algerian victories are rare on the open battlefield. Their leader is the Emir, Adl-el-Kader, who has been fighting the French relentlessly since 1831. Since the French occupation of the coast he has continued the war in the interior, and refuses to surrender.

Editor calls for unity among Slaves

Zagreb, 1836
The literary review, *Danica Illirska* is no longer to be written in the Zagreb dialect, understood only by Croats, but in a language which can be read by Serbs as well. Its editor, Ljudevit Gaj, seees cultural rebirth as closely linked to a political awakening in south-east Europe. He has published a *Manifesto of the Illyrian Movement* in his review, calling on Southern Slavs to unite as Illyrians, to end their domination by other races.

No creed or church for writer's religion

Concord, Massachussetts, 1836
Ralph Waldo Emerson's book *Nature* has inspired his friends and disciples, such as Henry Thoreau, to form a discussion group, the Transcendental Club, which meets in Concord, a town founded by Emerson's ancestors.

Emerson gave up his ministry in the Unitarian Church four years ago, after a visit to England where he met and discoursed with Wordsworth, Coleridge and Thomas Carlyle. He finds God in nature,

and revelations of the divine in man's intuitions which transcend the experiences of the senses.

Transcendentalism is a religion without a creed or a church. Emerson teaches individual effort and a life of "plain living and high thinking". He writes: "A man should learn to detect and watch that gleam of light that flashes across his mind from within ... We are ashamed of that divine idea which each of us represents ... Trust thyself".

California, 3 November 1836. Californian rebels proclaim the territory's freedom from Mexico.

Austria, 6 November 1836. Charles X of France dies in exile at Gorz. His regime was toppled in 1830 in the *Trois Glorieuses* (three glorious days of revolution).

Britain, 7 November 1836. The British aeronaut Charles Green leaves London in the *Royal Vauxhall* balloon, crosses the channel and lands near Nassau in Germany after a journey covering 480 miles and lasting 18 hours.

Michigan, 26 January 1837. Michigan becomes the 26th state to join the union.

Washington, DC, 3 March 1837. On his last day in office, President Jackson recognises the Lone Star republic of Texas.

Japan, 27 March 1837. Oshio Heihachiro, a constable and philosopher in Osaka who led an abortive peasant uprising in protest against the lack of famine relief, commits suicide.

Britain, 20 June 1837. On the death of her uncle, William IV, Princess Victoria becomes queen of Great Britain and Ireland.

Britain, July 1837. The Birmingham Political Union, led by Thomas Attwood, the banker and MP, organises a demonstration that brings together 50,000 people in favour of a programme of political reform, demanding above all universal suffrage.

Washington, DC, 25 August 1837. The government notifies the republic of Texas that it will not be admitted to the union.

Dakota, August 1837. Fifteen thousand Indians in the Mandan, Hidatsa and Arikara tribes, who live on the Missouri river, die of smallpox. The epidemic is thought to have been started by an American Fur Company steamboat that came up the river in June.

New Mexico, 12 September 1837. Mexican troops crush the revolt that broke out on 25 August.

Washington, DC, 12 October 1837. Congress authorises the issue of $10 million in short-term government notes in an attempt to stem the financial panic that is sweeping the country.

Algeria, 13 October 1837. In the second war of Abd al-Kader, the town of Constantine is taken by General Valee, who guarantees French sovereignty over the province of Constantine.

Florida, 21 October 1837. Under a flag of truce and during peace talks, US troops seize the Indian Seminole Chief Osceola.

St Louis, 7 November 1837. Elijah Parish Lovejoy, the editor of the *St Louis Observer*, is killed by a pro-slavery mob. Lovejoy had been campaigning for the abolition of slavery for many years despite violent popular opposition.

South Africa, November 1837. After an eight-day running battle with Boers and Griqua people in the Marico plains, the Ndebele army strikes camp and marches northwards to find a new home.

Argentina, November 1837. Tenskwatawa, the "Shawnee Prophet", dies in exile. He spent his life working with his brother Tecumseh to unite Shawnee Indians against encroachment by white settlers of Indian lands.

Florida, 25 December 1837. US troops rout Seminole Indians at Lake Okeechobee.

Sicily, 1837. Riots break out in Messina, Syracuse and Catania due to rumours suggesting that cholera, which is claiming many victims, is being caused by poisonous powders distributed by the government.

Afghanistan, 1837. A British envoy, Alexander Burnes, conducts a "commercial mission" to Kabul as concern mounts about growing Russian influence in the area.

Switzerland, 1837. The Italian revolutionary Giuseppe Mazzini is prevented from leaving for Britain because of his political activities.

USA, 1837. In the autumn, Sioux Indians give up their traditional lands east of the Mississippi river.

Britain, 1837. The first measure favourable to the Irish Catholics is obtained by Daniel O'Connell, the Irish nationalist MP who was enabled to take his seat by the Roman Catholic Relief Act of 1829. From now on they will no longer have to pay a tithe to the Anglican Church.

Sierra Leone, 1837. The first groundnuts exported from Sierra Leone go down well with consumers in America and Europe, who call them peanuts.

Afghanistan, 1837. Moving in from India, the British prevent the Persians from occupying the town of Herat and the surrounding region.

Germany, 1837. The philosopher Georg Hegel's *Lessons on the Philosophy of History* is published posthumously.

Britain, 1837. The Scottish historian Thomas Carlyle publishes a *History of the French Revolution*.

Moscow, 1837. John Field, the Irish composer of nocturnes, dies in Moscow aged 55.

Macadamising engineer dies on the road

John McAdam: the "colossus" of the new transport era of turnpikes.

Dumfriesshire, 26 November 1836
John McAdam, who gave his name to a process of road improvement, has died on the road from Scotland, aged 80. He helped to develop the mailcoach network which has increased national prosperity.

A banker's son from Ayr, John McAdam bought an estate in Ayrshire where he was magistrate, deputy county lieutenant and road trustee, and constantly experimented with new road surfaces.

As agent for revictualling the navy in western ports in 1798, he transferred his Scottish experiments to Falmouth, and proved the effectiveness of a raised surface of broken stone, with drains on either side. After being made surveyor-general of Bristol roads in 1815, he wrote two books on road-building.

Parliament adopted his technique for road-surfacing in major towns, and in 1827 he became general surveyor of roads. His son James accepted the knighthood which his father had declined, and is now chief trustee and surveyor of metropolitan and turnpike roads.

Roads not controlled by trusts have been slow to improve, but that may change as a result of last year's General Highway Act, which gave parish ratepayers the right to appoint surveyors and levy rates.

The forge at Creusot in France, painted by Theodore Chasseriau. A century earlier, travellers like Defoe and Young had marvelled at the scale of the new industrial enterprises. By 1836 they had become the norm.

Getting the message gets easier – with Pitman's shorthand and Morse's code

Building telegraph lines in the USA.

Britain and US, 1836
A communications revolution is under way in Britain and the US as resourceful inventors devise speed-writing systems and ways of sending messages over long distances.

In Bath, Isaac Pitman, a former textile mill clerk turned school-teacher, has invented what he calls a Stenographic Sound Hand, based on the phonetic principle, or the sounds of vowels and consonants, rather than the conventional spelling of words.

Straight lines and shallow curves are used for consonants, and sounds are paired: a light slanted line stands for P and a heavier one for the deeper sound B. For vowels, dots and dashes are placed against the consonant strokes.

This invention enables speeches delivered at 50 words a minute and more to be written down.

In the US, Samuel Morse turned from portrait painting to telegraphy after a shipboard conversation on signalling gave him an idea, which he jotted down:
1) An apparatus to send signals by opening and closing an electric circuit;
2) A receiver to record the signals as dots and spaces on a tape;
3) A code to turn the dots and spaces into letters and numbers.

Morse spent a great deal of effort trying to turn this brilliantly simple idea into a complicated means by which the government could send messages in secret code.

When he realised that the dots and spaces could be heard as dots and dashes, he knew that he had hit on a revolutionary method of public communication.

In another area of communication inventions William Cooke and Charles Wheatstone are working in London on a "telegraph" system for sending signals by wires alongside railways.

"Little Magician" elected US president

Washington, DC, 7 December 1836
Martin van Buren, a New York lawyer known universally as "The Little Magician" – largely for his skill in political manipulation – was elected president of the United States today, the first president not to bear a British family name.

The former vice-president has pledged himself to support the policies of his predecessor, Andrew Jackson, although he is distrusted by both slave-states and abolitionists, having courted both.

It was as secretary of state that van Buren made his name as an outstanding negotiator. He brought about an end to the dispute between Britain and the United States over West Indian trade and secured a financial agreement with France.

Van Buren, the eighth US president.

British put down rebellions in Canada

York (Toronto), 14 December 1837
Although British troops have successfully quelled two rebellions that threatened to wreck this fast-growing colony, anti-government hostility continues to fester and there is an increasing danger of intervention by the United States.

The most serious uprising was led by Louis-Joseph Papineau, the Speaker of the Lower Canada Assembly, who has fled to the USA after agitating for an armed uprising. Twelve of his supporters have been executed. In Upper Canada, the second revolt was led by a Scottish-born journalist and political agitator, William Lyon Mackenzie, whose Radical Reformers were seeking a greater level of democracy in Canada. The uprising was put down quickly, although Mackenzie, with several followers, has established a government-in-exile in the USA.

London is placing high hopes in the newly-appointed governor general, the reformist Lord Durham, who is on his way here with "dictatorial powers".

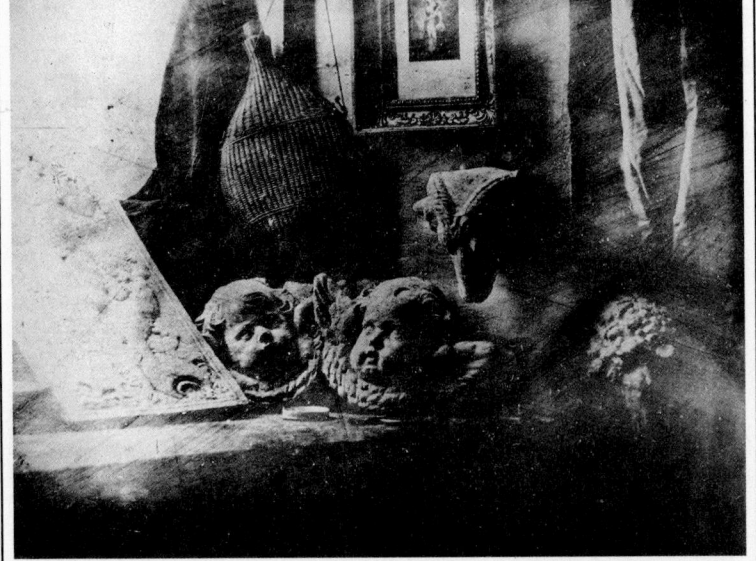

France, 1837: the earliest photographic image by Louis Daguerre, who has captured light and dark on copper plate and reproduced them.

Boer trekkers reach their promised land

Natal, South Africa, June 1837
Thousands of Boer *trekkers* have crossed the Drakensberg Mountains and settled in Natal. To the Dutch-speaking pioneers, coming out of the mountains, the rich and verdant pastures of Natal are like the Promised Land.

Here, in the no-man's-land between the British and Zulu empires, settlements are being built and the burgher democracy of the early Boers is being re-established. A constitution has been drawn up, and a governor, Piet Retief, has been elected. The state is to be known as the Free Province of New Holland.

Princess Victoria is new British queen

London, June 1837
With the death of William IV, the crown passes to his niece, Victoria, aged 18; she is without experience of public affairs, but is dutiful and self-possessed. At her first Privy Council meeting officials presented documents naming her Alexandrina Victoria. She told them to cross out the Alexandrina.

She then told her mother, Princess Victoria of Saxe-Coburg, that the latter no longer exercised any authority; she instructed her mother's secretary, Sir John Conroy, to stay out of London; and her uncle by marriage, Leopold of Belgium, was told to go home.

1837 (1837-1838)

Germany, 1837. Hanover becomes separate from Britain with the accession of Queen Victoria. Governed by Salic law, which forbids succession through the female line, Hanover is now ruled by Victoria's uncle, Ernest Augustus.

London, 1837. The architect Sir John Soane, who designed the Bank of England, dies aged 84. He bequeathes his house in Lincoln's Inn Fields to the nation.

Germany, 1837. The educationalist Friedrich Frobel sets up the first kindergarten in the world, at Blankenburg, in Thuringia.

Canada, 1837. The speaker of the Lower Canada Assembly, Louis-Joseph Papineau, leads a rebellion by French-Canadians against the proposed union of the British provinces of Upper and Lower Canada. A similar rebellion in Upper Canada is led by the Scottish journalist and political activist William Lyon Mackenzie.

Russia, 1837. The novelist and poet Alexander Pushkin dies of a wound received in a duel fought to defend his wife's honour. Unpopular and widely misunderstood in his liberal beliefs, Pushkin was forced into the duel by enemies at court. He leaves a large body of work, much of it influenced by Russian folktales.

England, 1837. The painter John Constable dies aged 61. He was highly acclaimed during his lifetime and will be remembered above all for his landscapes, among the best of which are *Valley Farm*, *Cornfield* and *Haywain*.

Austria, 6 January 1838. The first rail link, between Vienna and Wagram via Florisdorf, is opened.

South Africa, 6 February 1838. Having failed to obtain land by trickery from the Zulus, the Boer leader Piet Retief is executed as a witch by the chief Dingane.

China, 24 February 1838. The Medical Missionary Society is formally instituted.

Iowa, 4 July, 1838. The Territory of Iowa is established and Robert Lucas is appointed governor.

Ottoman Empire, 16 August 1838. The *Porte* (Ottoman government) signs a trade treaty with Britain which provides for the abolition of commercial monopolies throughout the empire, including Egypt. The Egyptian *pasha*, Mohammed Ali, who is hostile to this agreement, takes up arms.

Ohio, 30 October 1838. Oberlin College becomes the nation's first institution of higher education to admit women on an equal basis with men.

Britain, 1 November 1838. Lord Durham, the governor-general of British North America, returns home after mediating between English and French speakers.

China, 12 December 1838. A riot breaks out when British and American opium traders drive away Chinese officials intending to execute a native opium dealer in front of the foreign factories.

China, 31 December 1838. Lin Zexu is appointed imperial commissioner "to investigate and manage maritime affairs" and deal with the opium problem in the province of Canton (Guangzhou).

Canada, 1838. Robert Nelson, a survivor of the insurrection led by Papineau, decides to continue the armed struggle to the bitter end and declares himself president of the republic of Lower Canada. Having taken the town of Napierville, which he makes his provisional capital, he is forced to flee from the advance of the British army under John Colborne.

Mexico, 1838. King Louis Philippe demands 600,000 *pesos* from the Mexican republic in compensation for damage suffered by French nationals in Mexico. The demand is prompted by the complaint of a French pastrycook that his shop has been looted by Mexican soldiers. French ships take a fortress near Vera Cruz, and General Santa Anna comes out of retirement and joins the fighting with no authority. The conflict, which soon becomes known as the Pastry War, is settled when the president, Anastasio Bustamante, agrees to pay the compensation.

Philadelphia, 1838. The abolitionist Robert Purvis is made president of the now formally established Underground Railroad, a network of contacts which helps fugitive slaves to escape their owners.

USA, 1838. The writer James Fenimore Cooper turns to social criticism in his new work *The American Democrat*.

Italy, 1838. The French and Austrian expeditionary forces leave the cities of Ancona and Bologna in the papal states, to which they were summoned in 1832 to keep order.

Britain, 1838. The novelist Charles Dickens begins to publish a new work, *Nicholas Nickleby*, in serial form.

Guatemala, 1838. The government of Mariano Galvez falls from power. Galvez came to power in 1831 and has been responsible for introducing liberal reforms. Since 1837 the country has been affected by a cholera epidemic and has also had to contend with an Indian.

British steamships start Atlantic service

Isambard Kingdom Brunel's steamship "Great Western" crossing the Atlantic.

New York, 1838

The 703-ton *Sirius* has become the first ship to cross the Atlantic entirely under steam, and has beaten by a few hours the 15-day crossing record set recently by the *Great Western*. A transatlantic passenger service is now established.

The *Great Western*, a wooden paddle vessel 236 feet long and 35 feet wide, is far bigger than any previous steamship. Built by Paterson of Bristol, powered by Maudslay and Field, the brainchild of the great civil engineer Isambard Kingdom Brunel, the builder of bridges and railways, the *Great Western* has proved the viability of Brunel's theories on screw propulsion. The *Sirius* was of more modest origin – built for service in the Irish Sea. Chartered by the British and American Steam Navigation Company, she sailed from London to New York via Cork with 40 passengers. When fuel ran out just short of the American coast, the captain, determined not to resort to sail, insisted on feeding spars into the furnace. The vessel made it just in time to avert a mutiny.

The *Sirius* did, however, introduce one potentially important technical innovation: a condenser to recover fresh water used in the boiler.

Hindu thugs strangling a traveller: worshippers of Kali, the goddess of destruction, they would waylay travellers, steal from them and kill them according to ancient rites. They were not suppressed until 1837.

Briton writes with a social conscience

London, 1837
A new serial by the author of *The Posthumous Papers of the Pickwick Club*, which began last year and multiplied its sales a hundredfold, is appearing in monthly parts. The new novel, *Oliver Twist*, is the story of an orphan boy in a workhouse who falls into the company of criminals and pickpockets. It is shrouded in an atmosphere of evil far removed from the genial world of Mr Pickwick.

The hardships of Oliver reflect something of those of the author, Charles Dickens, in his own childhood, part of which he spent in a blacking factory while his father was in Marshalsea prison for debt.

Prolific author: Charles Dickens.

Convicts in Tasmania, Australia, made to walk 30 miles carrying 56lb weights.

Report claims convicts corrupted settlers

New South Wales, 1838
News of the evidence given before the House of Commons committee on the transportation of convicts is causing much anger here. Settlers, according to the evidence, have been "demoralised" and "corrupted" by transportation and the assignment of convict labour to free farmers. The settlers had prepared themselves for the end of the assignment system and, probably, of the increasingly unpopular dumping of Britain's unwanted convicts in Australia, but they had not expected to be insulted as well.

Much of the trouble stems from the fact that those convicts who will not or cannot work for the free colonists are held by the government in penal settlements where they are ruled by fear of the cat o' nine tails. In 1837 more than a quarter of a million lashes were laid on the bleeding backs of convicts. Another aspect of life in Australia which is causing much concern is the treatment of the Aboriginal population. Often hunted for sport, the Aborigines are being driven off their tribal lands and, when they resist, are herded into settlements where they exist on government handouts and die of drink and disease.

This is a great land, but much needs to be done before it can attract the free immigrants it so desperately needs.

The icy continent attracts explorers

London, 1838
The hitherto unexplored continent of ice which surrounds the south pole (*Antarctica*) is attracting expeditions from the United States, France and Britain. The interest is mainly scientific, though some of the voyages combine whaling and sealing with exploration.

Captain Cook's great voyage of 1774 destroyed myths about a southern continent which was actually habitable. Later James Weddell found an open sea route deep into the ice.

Liberal deals with rebels shock MPs

Canada, 1838
Despite the draconian powers which he has been given to put down Canadian rebellions, the new governor general, Lord Durham – "Radical Jack" – has shocked parliament and the prime minister by his liberal approach.

Lord Durham chose 24 June – Queen Victoria's coronation day – to announce an amnesty for all but 24 French-Canadian rebels. Until now, uprisings in the province have been dealt with harshly. In London, the prime minister, Lord Melbourne, has dissociated himself from Durham's moderation.

Peoples' charter demands change

London, 8 May 1838
Demands for "one man, one vote" elections, secret ballots and an end to conditions that prevent working men from becoming MPs have been put forward in a radical reforming People's Charter.

Also included in the six-point charter are demands for annual elections, equal electoral districts, salaries for MPs and abolition of the property qualification for parliamentary candidates.

The charter, published by the London Working Men's Association, has been endorsed by the radical Birmingham Union and the *Northern Star* newspaper.

Treaties have pushed America's Indians west across Mississippi

Western America, 1838
Already it is being called the "trail of tears" as thousands of American Indians are forcibly moved from eastern states to reservations in the far west. Under the Indian treaties, only successful Indian farmers are allowed to stay east of the Mississippi; the rest are being "persuaded" by chiefs, many of whom were made drunk by federal commissioners, to sign assents.

Numbers are being drastically reduced by disease and the Indians are being systematically robbed by officials. The survivors are so poor that they cannot hope to buy the equipment needed to till the soil in their new homelands, and starvation threatens.

Indian country: romanticised image of a Sioux Council by George Catlin.

1838 (1838-1839)

Germany, 1838. Mathias Jakob Schleiden, the professor of botany at Jena university, defines the cellular structure of vegetables.

France, 1838. The palaeontologist Boucher de Perthes discovers roughly-chipped flint instruments in the area around Abbeville.

USA, 1838. The American David Bruce builds the first automatic device for printing characters, at the rate of 100 per hour.

Pennsylvania, 12 January 1839. Anthracite coal is used for the first time in iron smelting.

Near East, 16 January 1839. The strategic important port of Aden is annexed to British India. This follows mistreatment of the crew of a wrecked British ship in 1837 and the sultan's failure to sell the town to the British as restitution, as his father had promised.

China, 24 March 1839. The commissioner Lin Zexu blockades foreign factories to force foreign merchants to surrender their opium stocks which are to be destroyed.

London, 19 April 1839. The treaty of London, signed by Britain, France, Prussia, Austria and Russia, finally guarantees the independence and neutrality of Belgium. It also closes the Scheldt river and establishes Luxembourg as an independent grand duchy.

Ottoman Empire, 24 June 1839. The sultan, Mahmud II, launches another offensive against Mohammed Ali, the *pasha* of Egypt.

Ottoman Empire, July 1839. Following the death of Sultan Mahmud II, his son Mahmud Abdul-Medjid succeeds to the throne.

London, 5 August 1839. News of the Chinese suppression of the opium trade at Canton (Guangzhou) reaches London.

China, 23 August 1839. In the continuing hostilities over the opium trade, British ships assemble off Hong Kong.

China, 4 September 1839. Following the evacuation of Canton by British traders, the destruction of confiscated opium, the stoppage of foreign trade as well as the denial of food and water to the British, British naval forces fire the first shots in the as yet undeclared Opium War.

London, 1 October 1839. The British government decides to send a punitive naval expedition to China.

China, 3 November 1839. British and Chinese forces clash near the Bogue forts at the mouth of the Pearl River.

Ottoman Empire, 3 November 1839. Sultan Mahmud Abdul-Medjid promulgates an imperial charter, the *Tanzimat*, which confirms the equality of all citizens of the empire, guarantees freedom and individual property and promises reforms of the tax system.

Algeria, 3 November 1839. Following an expedition by the French General Valee into the Hamza territory in October, the *emir*, Abd al-Kader, launches his horsemen against the Mitidja plantations and resumes hostilities with France.

Paris, 24 November 1839. The composer Hector Berlioz stages his opera *Romeo and Juliet*.

Russia, 1839. Czar Nicholas unites the Uniate Church with the Russian Orthodox Church.

Russia, 1839. A Russian military expedition in central Asia fails to take the oasis town of Khiva.

France, 1839. The republican theoretician Louis Blanc publishes a treatise, *The Organisation of Labour*, and founds *The Review of Progress*.

Britain, 1839. The painter J M W Turner presents the Royal Academy with five oil paintings including *The "Fighting Temeraire" Tugged to her Last Berth to be Broken Up*.

Philadelphia, 1839. Edgar Allan Poe publishes his first book of stories, *Tales of the Grotesque and Arabesque*, which lives up to its title.

Britain, 1839. Parliament passes the Infant Custody Act, giving divorced or separated mothers access to their children.

Mississippi, 1839. For the first time in the United States, women are given legal control over their property.

USA, 1839. The American Charles Page, a professor in Washington, builds the first electric locomotive.

Afghanistan, 1839. The British army deposes the emir of Kabul, Dost Mohammed Khan, and starts an Afghan war. The British are anxious about the growth of Russian influence in the area and intend to replace Dost Mohammed with a former emir who is more sympathetic to their wishes to protect the northern approaches to India.

Britain, 1839. The Anti-Corn Law League is established in Manchester by Richard Cobden and John Bright to petition for the repeal of duties on imported grain.

USA, 1839. Charles Goodyear discovers how to vulcanise rubber.

Boers kill 3,000 Zulu at Blood River

Natal, South Africa, 1838
A new leader skilful in war has emerged amongst the Boer *trekkers* of Natal: Andries Pretorius. For two years Boers have been settling in the Zulus' rich pastureland of Natal. Inevitably, the Zulu army of King Dingane came down on them. Piet Retief, the original leader, was killed, and the Boers were only saved by Pretorius who quickly raised a 500-man *commando* and stopped 10,000 Zulu at the Blood River, killing 3,000.

An austere nationalist, committed to Boer independence, Pretorius is expanding his commando, and fully expects to use it again.

Zulu soldiers: undefeated until now.

Sikh state mourn leader Ranjit Singh

Ranjit Singh: the great Sikh leader.

Amritsar, India, June 1839
The Sikhs are mourning the death of their *maharajah*, Ranjit Singh. Ranjit Singh has done more for the Sikh nation than any ruler for 200 years. Succeeding to power in Lahore in 1799, he defeated one rival after another, marching into Amritsar, the Sikhs' sacred capital, in 1802. Having united the Sikhs, he created a French-trained army and extended Sikh power to the borders of British India and Afghanistan.

"He is almost the first inquisitive Indian I have seen," one Frenchman who knew him wrote. "He asks a hundred thousand questions, about India, the British, Europe, Bonaparte, the world in general and the next."

Anti-Corn Law protest movement grows

Manchester, 1839
The "bread stealers" and "foot-pad aristocrats" in the British parliament have come under renewed attack in the wake of the recent bad harvests that have sent the price of corn soaring. The landowners, who have a majority in parliament, are resisting efforts to repeal the Corn Laws, which allow corn imports only when the price has reached a certain figure; at one time it was 80 shillings a quarter.

The renewed agitation has led to the launching of an anti-corn law league by a group of Lancashire manufacturers. The leading figures are Richard Cobden, who made his fortune as a calico printer, and John Bright, a Quaker textile manufacturer with powerful oratorical gifts. They rouse their audiences with a wealth of colourful abuse directed at landowners, because, as Cobden admits, people come to meetings not to learn, but to be "excited, flattered and pleased".

Free trade is the basis of the campaign. Imports of corn, it is argued, would be paid for by increased exports of textiles and other manufactured goods. But protectionists say that the campaigners want cheap bread in order to cut wages.

New breakthrough captures images

Paris, 19 August 1839

The French government today published details of a new invention, the *Daguerrotype*, by which exact images are produced through a lens on a copper plate by the action of light alone. With similar developments of *photogenic* images announced earlier this year in Britain, it appears that a major new art form is being born.

Louis Daguerre, a scene-painter who presents the Diorama in Paris, discovered the effect when tracing images thrown on a screen by a *camera obscura*. In 1837 he captured the interior view of his studio on a copper plate coated with silver iodide and exposed to the light through the lens. He sold the rights in the process to the government in return for a life annuity. His book on the process he uses is a bestseller. "One can make the most detailed views in a few minutes without any knowledge of chemistry," he claims.

In England, the Royal Society has awarded its gold medal to William Henry Fox Talbot, an English scientist who published an account of his alternative process of "photogenic drawing" earlier this year after hearing of Daguerre's experiments. He began experimenting because of his inability to draw the landscapes of his holiday travels. He discovered how to make paper sensitive to light by soaking it in silver chloride. On exposure to light this turns dark, creating a "negative" impression. From the negative he can make any number of positive prints. His results, though, are less sharply detailed than Daguerre's, and require people to sit still for many minutes.

A summer's afternoon at Lacock Abbey, by William Henry Fox Talbot, who experimented with photography because of his inability to draw landscapes.

The Tuileries and apartments of King Louis Philippe, by Louis Daguerre: the first photograph of Paris, taken from the left bank of the Seine.

British march into "soft" Afghanistan

Afghanistan, April 1839

The 5,000-strong British army that has just occupied Kandahar on its way to Kabul is finding that – so far – its invasion of Afghanistan is an easy matter.

There is little resistance; the 12,000 camp followers march without danger, and it will be months before winter.

The force, sent to instal the unpopular *Shah* Suja as emir and forestall Russian efforts to win influence in Afghanistan and thus threaten India, has the enthusiastic backing of Lords Palmerston and Melbourne and all but one of the British cabinet.

The exception is the duke of Wellington. The problem, the duke says, is not getting into Afghanistan; it is getting out.

Guns force British radicals to back off

London, July 1839

The threat of an armed working-class revolt and a general strike organised by the Chartists is now receding following army intervention. The credit for calling the Chartists' bluff is being given to the commander of the northern district, Sir Charles Napier.

His decision to opt for a show of force by stationing troops in key northern cities and then inviting Chartist leaders to a demonstration of how artillery fire could disperse a mob is thought to have dissuaded the Chartists from violence. Prior to the demonstration they had been advocating revolutionary tactics.

Jamaican riots bring down government

London, 1839

A rebellion by former slave-owning sugar planters in Jamaica has succeeded in temporarily bringing down the British government. Despite getting £20,000,000 in compensation following the abolition of slavery, the colonists are facing serious economic difficulties as world sugar prices fall. British demands for better conditions in Jamaica's Negro jails led to the island's legislature refusing to govern. With Tories in parliament refusing to support the suspension of the Jamaican constitution, the queen called on Robert Peel to form a new government.

Peel agreed, but insisted that some of the Whig ladies in the queen's household should be replaced by Tories. The young queen refused, and Lord Melbourne is back at 10 Downing Street.

Destruction of opium crop is ordered

Canton, June 1839

Lin Zexu, the imperial envoy sent to Canton to put an end to the opium trade, has ordered the destruction of 20,283 chests of opium worth 12 million dollars surrendered on his orders by British merchants.

The opium is to be destroyed in public, and trenches have already been dug so that the drug, imported from India, will drain away. The Chinese decision to stop the opium trade comes from the emperor who has been advised that the drug "utterly ruins the minds and morals of the people, it is a dreadful calamity". It is also draining wealth from the country, with huge profits in silver going to the merchants.

At the heart of the trouble, however, lies not only the opium trade but also the whole question of the opening up of China to the west.

Guatemala, 1839. The Indian leader Rafael Carrera seizes power. Last year the liberal government of Mariano Galvez fell following a revolt led by Carrera and the unrest caused by an epidemic of cholera.

Paris, 1839. Frederic Chopin publishes his 24 preludes, written last winter on the island of Majorca where he was staying with his lover, the novelist George Sand. They are dedicated to the piano-maker, Camille Pleyel, a friend of the composer.

Britain, 1839. Lord Durham, who served as governor general in Canada last year, publishes a report recommending that a firm stand be taken against the French-speakers and that Canada be given a responsible, independent government.

USA, 1839. Henry Wadsworth Longfellow's *Voices of the Night*, his first book of poems, is published and goes down well with the critics.

Germany, 1839. The Leipzig publisher and bookseller Karl Baedeker starts to publish travel guides for Europe.

London, 10 February 1840. Queen Victoria marries her first cousin, Prince Albert of Saxe-Coburg-Gotha.

Canada, 10 February 1840. Following the Durham report of 1938, in which union was recommended, an act is passed uniting the British provinces of Upper and Lower Canada.

France, 1 March 1840. The Soult administration resigns. It is replaced by a team headed by Adolphe Thiers.

Illinois, 10 May 1840. The Mormon leader Joseph Smith moves his band of followers to the Commerce Purchase in Illinois in order to escape the hostilities they experienced in Missouri.

China, June 1840. The formal beginning of the Opium War is declared.

Prussia, June 1840. On the death of Frederick William III, his son Frederick William IV succeeds to the throne. Welcomed by liberals for his "Romantic" reputation, he quickly disappoints them and comes under the influence of an effective, conservative court clique.

China, 5 July 1840. British naval forces bombard Dinghai on Zhoushan Island and occupy it.

China, 15 August 1840. The British plenipotentiary arrives at the Beihe in north China to force the Qing court in nearby Beijing into negotiations concerning the Opium War.

Connecticut, August 1840. A Spanish slave ship, the *Amistad*, arrives in Connecticut with 53 Africans in command. Slaves on board the ship rebelled while the ship was *en voyage* from one Cuban port to another, killing the captain and all but two of the crew. Spain is expected to demand extradition of the rebels.

China, 11 September 1840. Chinese officials strangle the French missionary Jean-Gabriel Perboyre at Wuchang.

China, 28 September 1840. Lin Zexu, the imperial commissioner whose hard line sparked off the opium war, is dismissed and replaced by Qishan.

Ottoman Empire, 6 October 1840. France, Britain and Russia enter the war between the Ottoman empire and Egypt on the side of the Ottomans. They occupy the Syro-Palestinian coastline to cut the Egyptian *pasha* Mohammed Ali, off from the route to Anatolia.

Netherlands, 10 October 1840. Following the abdication of King William, who refused to submit to the rules of the constitution, his son William II succeeds to the throne.

France, 29 October 1840. Adolphe Thiers resigns in the wake of the treaty of London which confirmed the existence of Belgium. He is replaced by Soult and Guizot, who has been ambassador to London since March.

Egypt, 4 November 1840. A British fleet bombards the ports of Beirut and Acre.

Washington, DC, 2 December 1840. William Henry Harrison is elected president of the United States, having won the hearts of the electorate with his "Log Cabin and Hard Cider" campaign emphasising his links with the common people.

Prussia, 4 December 1840. The Army adopts the artillery shell developed in 1836/7 by the gunsmith Nicholas Dreyse which combines the fuse, charge and projectile stages.

Paris, 15 December 1840. The ashes of the Emperor Napoleon I are buried at Les Invalides.

Britain, 1840. The Anglo-Canadian shipowner Samuel Cunard founds the first regular steamship line from Liverpool to Boston and New York.

Baltimore, 1840. Baltimore College of Dental Surgery, the first dental college in the country, is founded.

Britain, 1840. Sir Rowland Hill's proposals for a system of penny postage are implemented, despite bureaucratic opposition.

First commercial telegraph service

Wheatstone's telegraph receiver.

London, 1839

William IV has just granted a patent to William Fothegill Cooke and Professor Charles Wheatstone of King's College, London for an electric telegraph ("writing at a distance") system. It consists of fire wires connected to five needles, any two of which can be moved simultaneously to indicate a letter on a diagram. With electricity running along the wires, these signals are transmitted very quickly. The military will almost certainly take an interest in telegraphy, So, too, will the expanding railway networks.

Ndebele cross the Limpopo River

Zimbabwe, 1840

The army of the Ndebele has marched 300 miles (480km) north to the Zimbabwe grasslands since their defeat by white Boers trekkers in 1837. Their leader Mzilikazi, has gone further, taking a scouting party to survey the land as far as the Zambezi. Now he has returned to his Ndebele people and settled around Bulawayo.

After putting done a coup by one of his own generals, Kaliphi Gundwane, who had made Mzilikazi's own son king, he has strengthened his state by marrying Nyamazuma, the female general of the Ngoni people, who conquered the Bulawayo area just before the Ndebele arrived.

French king resists feeble coup effort

Boulogne, 6 August 1840

France has shrugged off the second attempted coup by Bonapartists in four years with its ringleader, Louis Napoleon, in jail today after staging an attempted invasion remarkable only for its ineptitude. Napoleon's latest attempt to emulate his late uncle and become leader of France started at 4.30 this morning and ended 210 minutes later with the 32-year-old pretender rescued by his capturers as he and five of his men half-drowned in the Boulogne surf. The death toll among the invaders is put at 45.

The 50-strong invasion force, dressed as members of the 40th Regiment, landed outside Boulogne after sailing overnight from London in the steamer *Edinburgh Castle*.

Napoleon intended to win over the Boulogne garrison while a sympathiser was in charge, rally the townspeople and then march on Paris to depose the king. Napoleon's plans misfired when his sympathiser was replaced on duty by a commander loyal to the king. Behind the invasion was the imminent arrival of the late emperor's ashes from St Helena. Napoleon is outraged that the regime which displaced his uncle is now making political capital from his remains.

Victoria and Albert: their seriousness after the extravagances of George III's sons made them popular with the people, though not with the aristocracy.

Britain claims New Zealand as colony

New Zealand, 6 February 1840
Captain Hobson of the Royal Navy today signed the Treaty of Waitangi with the Maori chiefs. Under this treaty New Zealand now becomes British, but the Maoris are guaranteed the rights to all their lands. If any of them wishes to sell this lands he must first offer them to the British government so that he will not be cheated. The Maoris are also promised full protection as British subjects.

Rarely has the annexation of a country been undertaken so reluctantly. The government's hand was forced by French plans to send settlers to New Zealand and by increasing concern at the treatment of the warlike but naive Maoris by landsharks, adventurers and escaped convicts from Australia.

These men have set up trading posts where they sell the Maoris guns and rotgut alcohol. One of their most profitable items of trade is preserved Maori heads which are sold at a high price in Europe. The

The signing of the Treaty of Waitangi, which annexed New Zealand to Britain.

situation has been further complicated by the formation of a private jointstock company headed by Gibbon Wakefield, who has already played a large part in the development of Canada and Australia. The government's orders to

Captain Hobson note that the annexation is "fraught with calamity to a numerous and independent people".

There are already signs that many Maoris object to the terms of the Treaty of Waitangi.

Canada is awarded independence by British statute

London, 23 July 1840
Canada is to be a self-governing union under a statute published by the British government today. The momentous decision follows the *Report on the Affairs of British North America* by Charles Buller, the chief secretary to the former governor general, Lord Durham.

The principal reason for the government's move is the fear of US expansion northwards, which is why responsibility for foreign affairs will remain with London.

The statute allows for the union of Lower and Upper Canada to be governed by a cabinet of colonists with a governor general as chief executive.

Buller's report recommended that the French-speaking Canadians should be harassed into abandoning their language – and that their minority status should be perpetuated.

Great powers recognise Egypt's new ruler

London, 15 July 1840
The great powers have recognised the right of Mohammed Ali and his heirs to the *pashalik* of Egypt. Only the French were not party to this agreement, and their support is encouraging Ali to insist on holding on to all his gains in Syria and Palestine. This latest concession to the Egyptian ruler, which further fragments the Ottoman empire, was

precipitated by another disastrous campaign by the sultan, whose forces invaded Syria last summer. Within a week the Ottomans were defeated at Nezib, and the sultan died before the news reached Istanbul. The appointment of a new *grand vizier* has prompted the Ottoman admiral, his political rival, to surrender his fleet to Mohammed Ali.

Mohammed Ali Pasha, with his French and British military advisers.

Property is theft says socialist

Paris, 1840
A new book, *What is Property?*, has caused a sensation. "Property", says its 31-year-old author, Pierre-Joseph Proudhon, "is theft." All over France men of property are demanding that it be banned.

Proudhon is no parlour socialist. The son of a drunken tavern keeper, he was herding cows in the Jura at the age of nine. The experience made a profound impression on him, and much of his vision of an ideal society comes from the Jura.

He won a scholarship to college, taught himself Latin, Greek and Hebrew, and came under the influence of the French utopian socialist Charles Fourier. A second scholarship took him to Paris where he has devoted the last two years to writing his book.

Men, he says, are dehumanised not merely by capitalism, but by large-scale production. He advocates a society of peasants and craftsmen, where the individual would remain in control of his own means of production and of his destiny.

Stamps devised as payment for mail

"Penny Black", the first postal stamp.

London, 1840
The reformer Rowland Hill has taken advantage of the evolving rail network and growing literacy to create a universal, cheap postal system in Britain. For just a penny a letter weighing half an ounce may be sent anywhere in the realm. Payment is by purchase from a post office of an adhesive tag bearing the queen's head (a "stamp") which is attached to the envelope.

1840 (1840-1841)

China, 1840. The mandarin Lin Zexu – dismissed when the harshness of his measures sparked off the Opium War – is recalled following British successes along the coasts of the province of Canton (Guangzhou). The war continues.

France, 1840. The essayist Alexis de Tocqueville publishes *Democracy in America*, a work of penetrating analysis that brings him almost instant fame.

USA, 1840. It is estimated that approximately 93 per cent of northern free Negroes are disenfranchised.

France, 1840. The historian Augustin Thierry brings out his *Accounts of Merovingian Times*, an evocative description of sixth-century Gaul.

USA, 1840. A census shows that the population has grown by a third over the last decade to just over 17 million.

Britain, 1840. The first episodes from a new novel, *The Old Curiosity Shop*, by the popular novelist Charles Dickens appear.

Germany, 1840. The chemist Justus von Liebig publishes *Organic Chemistry Applied to Agriculture and Physiology*, one of the earliest works of agricultural chemistry.

France, 7 January 1841. After three failures that affected him deeply, the writer Victor Hugo is elected a member of the Academie Francaise.

China, 20 January 1841. Following lengthy negotiations between British and Qing representatives concerning the conflict known as the Opium War, spurred on by a British attack on the Bogue forts, the draft convention of Chuanbi is concluded. Among other things, the Chinese negotiators agree to pay indemnities and cede the island of Hong Kong to Britain.

China, 29 January 1841. British ships occupy the Chinese island of Hong Kong and continue their attacks along the coast to Amoy, Ningbo and Shanghai, seeking to impose the lucrative opium trade on unwilling imperial authorities.

China, 25 February 1841. A proclamation is issued by the Chinese offering rewards for British heads.

China, 26 February 1841. British forces capture the Bogue batteries.

Washington, DC, 9 March 1841. The rebel slaves who seized a Spanish slave ship two years ago are freed by the Supreme Court, despite Spanish demands for extradition. They now plan to raise money to return to Africa.

Washington, DC, 4 April 1841. President William Harrison, aged 68, becomes the first US president to die in office, just a month after being sworn in. He developed pneumonia soon after a bitterly cold inauguration day on which he refused to wear a hat or overcoat, made a two-hour speech and went to three inauguration balls. Vice-president John Tyler becomes acting president.

Washington, DC, 9 April 1841. Acting president John Tyler is confirmed as president after appealing to Congress to grant him full powers. The US constitution is unclear on who succeeds presidents who die in office.

London, 30 April 1841. The British cabinet decides to dismiss Charles Elliot and appoint Colonel Sir Henry Pottinger as the new plenipotentiary to China.

USA, April 1841. Edgar Allan Poe's new book, *The Murders in the Rue Morgue*, makes a new kind of story popular – the detective story.

China, 27 May 1841. Local Qing officials agree to "ransom" the city of Canton (Guangzhou) with six million silver dollars. The rejection by both sides of the Chuanbi convention has led to renewed conflict, culminating in a full-scale attack by British forces under General Gough on Canton.

China, 30 May 1841. A massive force of rural dwellers attacks British forces near the village of Sanyuanli, just north of Canton. The villagers are incensed by the violent behaviour of the British troops who have been raping the local women and violating graves.

London, 13 July 1841. The Straits Convention is signed by the leading European powers. In a deal largely the work of Britain's foreign secretary, Lord Palmerston, the powers agree that the Bosporus and the Dardanelles should be closed to warships of all nations while the Ottoman empire is at peace.

Germany, 1841. The philosopher and moralist Ludwig Feuerbach publishes a radical book entitled *The Essence of Christianity* which sees religion merely as a consciousness of the infinite, and God merely as an outward projection of the human being's inner nature.

Germany, 1841. The economist Friedrich List publishes *The National System of Political Economy* arguing that tarriffs are essential during the shift from an agrarian to a manufacturing economy. The book is widely read and influential.

Treaty closes Dardanelles to all warships

The Dardanelles, 13 July 1841
The straits between the Aegean and the Sea of Marmara are closed to all foreign warships as long as the Ottoman empire is at peace, under the terms of the Straits Convention signed today by Britain, Russia, France, Austria and Prussia.

This agreement brings to an end an unusual arrangement between Russia and the Ottoman empire dating back to the treaty of Unkiar Skelessi in 1833. That treaty supposedly provided for mutual support in the event of an attack, but a secret clause absolved the Ottoman empire of the need to come to Russia's aid provided that the Dardanelles were closed to foreign warships, while allowing the Russians free passage from the Black Sea. Austria and Russia agreed later the same year to take common action to protect the Ottoman empire.

But Britain was suspicious of Czar Nicholas' intentions towards the declining Ottoman empire. "Russia ... perhaps thinks it better to take the place by sap than by storm," said Palmerston in March 1834.

Anxiety over the Ottoman empire's future was increased by its defeat in June 1839 by Mohammed Ali of Egypt at the battle of Nezib. France, Russia and Britain all compete with each other for influence. This latest treaty is of clearest benefit to Britain, which has acquired the protectorate of Aden.

Violinist with devilish reputation dies

Niccolo Paganini, the violin master.

Nice, 27 May 1840
There were things which Niccolo Paganini did on the violin which, so the rumour goes, only the Devil could have taught him. He would stop in mid-performance, cut three strings from his violin and perform amazing feats of musical wizardry on the remaining string. Tall, gaunt and forbidding, with a weakness for women and gambling, the Italian relished his devilish reputation. He amassed wealth and an army of toadies, but was generous to genuine admirers like Berlioz and Liszt. A romantic showman and virtuoso legend, Paganini died today of consumption. He was 58.

Charles Barry's new Houses of Parliament: originally a Classicist, he built the Travellers' Club in Pall Mall in Italianate style, and Parliament in Gothic style. Whatever the style, there was always grandeur of outline.

White men explore Australian interior

Australia, 7 July 1840

Edward Eyre, the pioneer of the overland droving routes for sheep and cattle, walked into Albany in Western Australia with his faithful Aborigine, Wylie, today at the end of a year-long journey of exploration from Adelaide across the Nullarbor Plain around the Great Australian Bight.

Eyre had been given up for dead and indeed came close to death from hunger and thirst. His friend and overseer, John Baxter, was murdered by two Aborigines who stole Eyre's water, leaving him to exist off dew mopped up with a sponge.

"Three days had passed since we left the last water," said Eyre, "six hundred miles had to be crossed before we could find help and I knew not one drop of water had been left us by the murderers."

The story of his expedition is typical of those men who are opening up this vast land. He tells of uncharted mountain ranges, of limitless inland seas too salty to drink, of privation and dying horse.

Sometimes Aborigines appeared out of the vast emptiness to help them to find water. At other times they gnawed the roots of eucalyptus trees to assuage their thirst. Ironically, Eyre and Wylie arrived in Albany in a rainstorm. Tonight Wylie is with his people and Eyre is celebrating with a hot brandy and a bath after a year of privation.

Fleet shells China as opium row grows

The British ship "Nemesis" bombarding Chinese junks in Anson's Bay.

China, 5 July 1840

British warships of the "Eastern Expedition" bombarded the island of Zhoushan at the entrance to Hangchow Bay today and landed troops to occupy the island. Tonight the British flag flies over the Chinese city of Dinghai. The origins of this "Opium War" can be traced to the Chinese seizure and destruction of 20,000 chests of opium belonging to British traders last year. Relations worsened when the British refused to hand over sailors who killed a Chinese peasant in a brawl.

The Chinese retaliated by ordering a boycott of British ships, and the traders retired to the barren island of Hong Kong where they have been living in conditions of some hardship. The proposal to send an expedition has not meet with universal approval. Gladstone argued in the House of Commons: "A war more unjust in its origin, a war more calculated to cover this country with permanent disgrace, I do not know.

The British flag is hoisted to protect an infamous traffic. "This war is about more than opium, however. It is designed to force China to open its ports to British ships with consular rights for the traders. Britain has gathered a considerable force to fight the war, with 4,000 British and Indian troops carried in a score of warships and transports led by the 74 gun *Wellesley*. The Chinese appear to have no answer to the firepower of the British guns and rockets.

Teetotaller starts a travel business

Loughborough, 5 July 1841

Thomas Cook, a wood-turner and pillar of the temperance movement, has chanced on a new scheme that could revolutionise the way that England takes its pleasures. Hoping to attract a large crowd to a temperance meeting in Loughborough, he arranged with the Midland Counties Railway to run a special excursion train from Leicester.

This was the first time such a "special" had been run for the public. So popular was Cook's idea, and so extensive the requests that he organise further trains, that he intends to expand his scheme.

Slaves who killed their captors freed

Washington, 9 March 1841

The trial of the African mutineer Cinque and his 52 fellow slaves ended here today. Swayed by the defence counsel, John Quincy Adams, the court found all the defendants not guilty and ordered their freedom. Two years ago the Negroes seized the Spanish slave ship on which they were held as it sailed around Cuba. They killed the captain and most of the crew before sailing north and landing in Connecticut. Spain has demanded their extradition, but today's verdict will make that impossible.

Sultan moves from Muscat to Africa

Zanzibar, 1840

Sayyid Said, sultan of Muscat, and head of a rich trading empire based on his sultanate in the Persian Gulf, is moving the centre of his operations to this East African island.

Africa has been Muscat's biggest growth area for 20 years. As Muscat trade grew, so did the number of Swahili ports under Muscat control. By 1837 the sultan had taken control of Mombasa and secured commercial treaties with Britain, France and the USA. The take over met with little resistance and is now accepted by both the local people and the foreign powers.

War breaks out again as Afghans resist British domination

Kabul, December 1841

As the first snowflakes float down on Kabul, the British army of occupation realises that all is not as it should be. There has been an insurrection in the city; British officials are being assassinated; worse, the elderly and gout-ridden British commander, General Elphinstone (who served bravely at Waterloo but has seen no active service since), is incapable of decisiveness.

Few worry, though. The camp, on low-lying ground overlooked by hills and two miles from the supply depot, is large enough for a racecourse and polo field, and everyone is expected to be thoroughly entertained over Christmas.

Afghan artillery dragged onto high ground to bombard the British camp.

1841 (1841-1842)

London, 28 August 1841. The Conservative leader Sir Robert Peel succeeds the Whig Lord (William) Melbourne as Prime Minister. This will be his second period in office. He has announced that his policy will be to reduce import duties in the cause of free trade.

Ohio, August 1841. Streets fight in Cincinnatti develop into a five-day anti-Negro riot.

China, August 1841. British forces, at war with China, who Britain is forcing to buy Indian cultivated opium, move along the coast, reoccupy Zhoushan island and enter the Yangze river. The troops are supported by a fleet of 16 warships.

Germany, 4 September 1841. The liberal democrat Hoffman von Fallersleben composes new words to the tune of Haydn's Austrian *Imperial Hymn*. The text, beginning *"Deutschland, Deutschland uber alles"* (Germany, Germany, above all), is a plea, not for German superiority, but for national unification.

Europe, 19 September 1841. The first railway line to cross a frontier is completed between Strasbourg and Basle.

USA, November 1841. As the conquest of the west continues, a group of 130 colonists crosses the Rocky mountains at South Pass and arrives at Walla Walla in Oregon after a 2,000-mile trek.

Afghanistan, December 1841. As attacks on occupying British troops mount, the puppet Afghan ruler, Shah Shuja al-Mulk, installed in Kabul is assassinated. His murder is followed by that of the British resident in Afghanistan, Sir Alexander Burnes.

Russia, 1841. M Y Lermontov, author of *A Hero of Our Time*, is killed in a duel.

South-East Asia, 1841. The sultan of Brunei, in northern Borneo, gives British interests influence over Sarawak, in return for support against enemy attacks. James Brooke, the British representative, becomes *rajah* of the region.

Germany, 1841. The philosopher Arthur Schopenhauer publishes *The Two Fundamental Problems of Ethics*.

Germany, 1841. At Leipzig, Felix Mendelssohn conducts the premiere of Robert Schumann's first symphony, the *Spring Symphony*.

Italy, 1841. The *Stabat Mater*, a sacred work by Gioacchino Rossini, is published. The first piece Rossini has produced since he retired in 1829, it was written before 1837, when he was in Paris.

Britain, 1841. The Miners' Association of Great Britain and Ireland is formed. It aims to represent and mobilise around 200,000 mineworkers.

Britain, 1841. The National Charter Association is created to press for the demands of the People's Charter through peaceful means. It has 282 branches by the end of the year.

Britain, 1841. The Scottish philosopher Thomas Carlyle publishes his *On Heroes and Hero-worship*.

London, 1841. The journalists Henry Mayhew and Mark Lemon launch a new satirical magazine, *Punch*.

Central America, 1841. The state of El Salvador declares its independence, effectively ending the Confederation of Central American States set up in 1823. Nicaragua and Costa Rica withdrew in 1838, followed in 1839 by Guatemala and Honduras.

USA, 1841. In a good year for American literature, the poet Henry Wadsworth Longfellow publishes his second book of poetry, *Ballads and Other Poems*; the novelist James Fenimore Cooper writes *The Deerslayer* and the radical Ralph Waldo Emerson publishes *Essays, First Series*.

West Africa, 1841. A large British force under a Royal Navy captain and a black African chaplain, Samuel Crowther, enters the Niger delta to set up an "African Civilisation Society" with missionary and commercial aims. The expedition is a failure owing to the many deaths from fever.

North Africa, 1841. A French expeditionary force under Thomas Bugeaud, which arrived in Algeria last year to launch a concerted campaign against Abd al-Kader, drives the Algerian resistance leader into Morocco, where he enlists Moroccan support.

Afghanistan, 6 January 1842. A 16,500-strong Anglo-Indian force under Lord Auckland is massacred while retreating from Kabul.

Britain, May 1842. Parliament rejects a new Chartist petition, for which Feargus O'Connor has collected three million signatures.

North America, 9 August 1842. The Webster-Ashburton treaty is signed by Britain and the USA, fixing the border between the state of Maine in the USA and New Brunswick in Canada.

China, 29 August 1842. Britain's opium war with China is over. Britain and China sign the treaty of Nanjing, ceding Hong Kong island to Britain and opening five ports to foreign trade.

Wagons cross Rockies via Oregon Trail

Settlers going west across the continent: a wagon train on the Oregon Trail.

Oregon Territory, November 1841
The lure of fertile valleys, ripe for grain harvests and orchards, the salmon-rich Columbia river and a warm moist climate has brought the first wagon train over the Rocky Mountains to Oregon Territory. This was no easy journey for the men, women and children who brought their covered wagons – "prairie schooners" – from the arid frontier states of Iowa and Missouri in search of wood, water and game.

The trail to Oregon is littered with furniture, discarded to lighten the load as the settlers blazed the trail westwards. Every night they parked their wagons in a ring against hostile Indians, and sang hymns to drown the howls of prairie wolves.

As they began the climb over the mountain range, the pioneers suffered terrible hardship from hunger as they left the known route and moved north. There was worse to come as they crossed the Wyoming Basin where alkali made the water almost undrinkable, killing many of the animals that accompanied the wagon train.

Even as they reached Oregon, the newcomers could not be sure whose country they were in. Britain and the United States are still discussing territorial rights and the border with Canada has yet to be resolved, with Britain threatening war if the United States annexes Oregon.

Sums are solved by calculating machine

England, 1842
Ada, Lady Lovelace, the mathematician has translated and annotated a paper by Menabrea on the *difference machine*, a machine that can think mathematically. Ada, the daughter of Lord Byron, the poet, has as good a grasp of symbolic logic as her friend and fellow mathematician, Charles Babbage, the inventor of the calculator.

Now the government is paying Babbage to develop an advanced "analytical engine" while Ada, who has a household and three children to support, works on a secret gambling system.

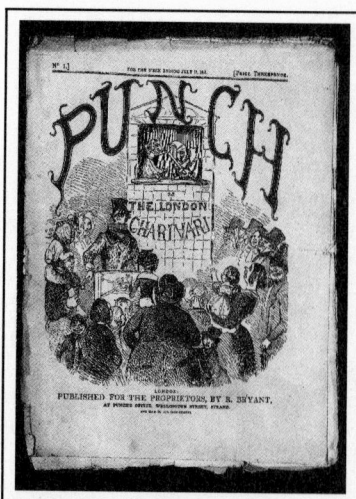

"Punch": the first issue of the satirical magazine published in 1841, disrespectful of authority and always banging its drum.

British guns force China to open up

China, 29 August 1842
The Opium War, which has lasted for two years of often intense fighting, ended today with the signing of the Treaty of Nanjing and complete success for the British. The treaty, forced on the Chinese after by the fall of Chin-kiang and the threat of a massive bombardment of Nanjing by British warships in the Yangze, opens with a call for "peace and friendship" between the two countries, but the terms are a total humiliation for the Chinese.

Over the next four years they must pay $21,000,000 which, includes the cost of the opium whose destruction started the war. More importantly the ports of Canton, Amoy, Foochow, Ningbo and Shanghai are to be opened to British trade and Britain will have consular rights in these ports. The island of Hong Kong is to be ceded "in perpetuity to Her Britannic Majesty, her heirs and successors". All British subjects and Chinese friends of Britain held in prison are to be released. This treaty promises to be a turning point in China's relations with the west. Curiously, no mention is made in it of the opium trade.

The signing of the Treaty of Nanjing, forced on China after the bombardment of the city by the Royal Navy.

US and Britain agree on Canadian border

Washington, 9 August 1842
The United States and Britain today signed a treaty settling several outstanding issues concerning the US-Canadian border.

The treaty agreed by Lord Ashburton and the US secretary of state, Daniel Webster, gives 5,000 square miles of disputed territory on the Maine border to the Canadian province of New Brunswick and 7,000 square miles to Maine. The treaty also settles how the border is mapped and marked.

Violent Chartist protests shake Britain

NOT SO *VERY* UNREASONABLE!!! EH?
The Charter: a special delivery.

London, 1842
Riots and strikes have broken out in northern England in protest against reductions in wages. The riots, which started in Lancashire when strikers pulled the plugs out of factory boilers, have now spread to Glasgow and the Midlands.

The authorities blame the Chartists for stirring up the unrest after their three-million-signature petition demanding universal suffrage was rejected by the Commons in May. In Staffordshire 54 Chartists have been sentenced to transportation. Among the agitators tried was the petition organiser, Feargus O'Connor, who was acquitted on a technicality.

British besieged by Boers trekkers in Port Natal

South Africa, June 1842
British troops, who marched into Port Natal (*Durban*) in May to cut off the inland Boer republic from the sea, are under siege. Two riders have broken through the Boer lines to call for reinforcements from Cape Colony.

Meanwhile Boer settlements, subject to the republic of Natalia, are proliferating in the interior. The Winburg colony, south of the Vaal river, and the Potchefstroom colony north of the Vaal, are typical representatives of the mixture of democracy and authoritarianism. Winburg is run by a democracy of white Boer men.

The governing body is the *volksraad*, people's council. Potchefstroom's system of government is the opposite. It is subject to the patriachy of Hendrik Potgieter. Women are silent, and Potgieter regularly defers his decisions to the Almighty.

Britain stages bloody retreat from Kabul

Afghanistan, January 1842
A lone rider is sighted by a British sentry at Jalalabad, on the road to Kabul. His name is Dr Bryden. He tells the horrified officers that he is the sole survivor of the expeditionary army sent into Afghanistan.

First the Afghans cut the British camp off from its supply depot two miles away; then they attacked it; the camp was indefensible and soon the British General Elphinstone was asking for terms. The Afghans gave him none, except to leave their country. So the 15,000 British soldiers began their retreat. Officers abandoned their men, thousands were slaughtered by Afghans, thousands more just lay down in the snow and died.

Afghans slaughtering British troops during the terrible retreat from Kabul.

St Petersburg, 9 December 1842. Mikhail Glinka's opera *Russlan and Ludmilla*, based on a story by Pushkin, is performed for the first time. It confirms Glinka's reputation as Russia's leading composer.

Britain, 1842. In the budget the prime minister, Robert Peel proposes lowering tariffs on about 450 types of merchandise. To compensate for the loss in revenue he plans to tax incomes of over £150 a year.

Britain, 1842. Lord Ashley's Mines Act, prohibiting the employment underground of women, girls, and children under ten years old, comes into force.

Ireland, 1842. The Irish poet Thomas Osborne Davis, with John Dillon and Charles Duffy, founds the *Nation*, the newspaper of the Young Ireland party. The paper aims "to direct the popular mind to the great end of nationality".

China, 1842. The scholar Wei Yuan publishes the *Shengwuji*, a work which stresses the need for military and political reform in China.

Serbia, 1842. Prince Michael Obrenovic, the son of Prince Milos Obrenovic and Serbia's ruling prince (under Ottoman suzerainty) since 1839, abdicates. The Serbian Senate sends for Alexander Karageorge, in exile in Russia, to replace him. The Ottomans accept the senate's choice, but insists that Karageorge is not an hereditary prince.

Russia, 1842. The novelist Nikolai Gogol publishes *Dead Souls*, a sombre portrayal of Russian life under serfdom.

Britain, 5 April 1843. Queen Victoria proclaims Hong Kong a British crown colony.

China, 26 June 1843. Britain and China sign a protocol to the Treaty of Nanjing which defines the legal status of merchandise.

Spain, July 1843. General Baldomero Espartero, who was made regent two years ago, is forced into exile as the result of an uprising backed by the former regent Maria Cristina. General Manuel Narvaez, the leader of the moderate faction, succeeds him. He plans to reinstate the Spanish monarchy with full powers.

France, 26 August 1843. The democratic newspaper *La Reforme* is founded.

Switzerland, August 1843. The anti-clerical majority in the Swiss Federal Diet approve the closure of all monasteries. The Catholic cantons of Lucerne, Freibourg and Zug appeal to France, Piedmont and Austria to help them to obtain a postponement of the decision.

Greece, September 1843. King Otto yields to popular demands for a Greek constitution.

France, September 1843. Queen Victoria of Britain visits France and meets King Louis Philippe.

China, 8 October 1843. Britain and China sign a diplomatic treaty determining the rights of British consuls and nationals on Chinese territory.

China, 17 November 1843. The port of Shanghai opens for foreign trade in accordance with the terms of the Treaty of Nanjing.

China, 1 December 1843. Opium smoking, the cause of the Opium War with Britain, is again banned by imperial edict.

South Africa, 1843. Britain declares the former Boer republic of Natalia to be the British colony of Natal, subject to the governor of Cape Colony. Some Boers remain, but most retreat across the Drakensberg Mountains to the Orange and Vaal countries of the plateau. The dream of the independent Boer state, with a sea coast and international recognition, is lost.

Italy, 1843. Vincenzo Gioberti publishes, in exile, a manifesto called *On the moral and political primacy of the Italians*. It calls for a united Italy under papal rule.

India, 1843. British troops under Sir Charles Napier and Sir Hugh Gough capture the Sind region after a campaign much lacking in strategy and skill.

St Petersburg, 1843. Czar Nicholas decides to send Admiral Putyatin to Japan in an attempt to open up the country. For financial reasons the expedition is postponed.

Afghanistan, 1843. Dost Mohammed is restored to the leadership of Afghanistan after the British defeat two years ago. Deposed and imprisoned by the British in 1839, he escaped and attempted to restore his regime, but was deported to India.

Milan, 1843. Giuseppe Verdi's new opera *I Lombardi*, set during the Crusades, is an immediate success. Its reception follows the success of the biblical opera *Nabucco*, which was premiered in Milan last year.

Britain, 1843. The political philosopher and utilitarian John Stuart Mill publishes his *Psychology as an independent science* and the *System of inductive and deductive logic*.

Britain, 1843. Michael Faraday establishes a general theory of electrolysis; his fellow physicist James Joule formulates the principle of the equivalence of forms of energy.

"The Fighting Temeraire" by J M W Turner, with clouds of scarlet.

Critic defends painter said to be mad

London, 15 May 1843

A passionate defence of the work of J M W Turner as superior to the Old Masters, *Modern Painters*, has been published by "A Graduate of Oxford". He has been identified as the precocious 24-year-old John Ruskin, the son of a sherry merchant who buys paintings for his son.

The violence of colour and vagueness of form in Turner's recent paintings has led some critics to suggest that he is mad. At last year's Royal Academy he exhibited a picture of a snowstorm at sea, noting: "The author was in this storm." He made the sailors lash him to the mast so that he could draw it. The painting shows a steamer in a vortex of churning foam and driving spray. It was dismissed by one critic as "soapsuds and whitewash".

Turner's painting of *The Fighting Temeraire*, a veteran ship of the Battle of Trafalgar being towed up the Thames by a steam tug under a symbolic sunset, was the sensation of the Royal Academy exhibition four years ago. "No man had hitherto painted clouds scarlet," writes Ruskin.

Greek king becomes constitutional ruler

Otto: now a constitutional monarch.

Greece, September 1843

A popular revolt has forced King Otto of Greece to agree to a constitutional monarchy, under which a Greek oligarchy will take the place of his own Bavarian line.

The second son of King Ludwig of Bavaria, Otto was made king of Greece by the great powers in 1832, and subsequently confirmed by the Greek National Assembly. He instituted a new legal code and organised a regular army, but he was a Roman Catholic in an Eastern Orthodox country, and his autocratic rule and high taxation made him unpopular.

When he failed in 1841 Crete from the Ottomans he lost the support of the British as well as that of his own people.

Britain extends its rule across three continents

Ireland: opponents of union arrested

Dublin, 1843
British authorities have strengthened their hold on Ireland.Following year of mass meetings in all of the Irish provinces outside Ulster, Daniel O'Connell and eight other nationalists have been arrested and charged with conspiracy to change the government, laws and constitution by "intimidation and the demonstration of great physical force".

Until the defeat of the Whig government two years ago, O'Connell and his colleagues, as Westminster MPs, sought reform by supporting the Whigs. When Peel's Tories took office, O'Connell went home to start a grass-roots campaign for repeal of the union with Britain. Within months the Repeal Association had organised over 40 mass meetings and was collecting £700 a week in subscriptions, with money coming from Irish communities in the United States. O'Connell became increasingly defiant; he talked of the association setting up its own courts of justice and a national assembly to form a *de facto* government.

The British in India, and their wives: Indians carying them ashore at Madras.

India: rough justice for annexed Sind

Karachi, India, 1843
Sind has joined British India. It has become a province. In February an agreement forced on the Sind leaders resulted in the British residency at Hyderabad being attacked. Anxious to impose his will, the British commander, Sir Hugh Gough, marched straight into Sind with 3,000 men and with will and firepower defeated a Sind army of 20,000 at Miani. Six *emirs* were captured. Only one, Sher Mohammed, held out until he was defeated in one of Gough's blind and furious battles.

In spite of cabinet disapproval of extensions of empire, Sind has been annexed. Amongst those most resentful are the *sepoys* (soldiers), who fear that all India will soon be British. Some, no longer entitled to overseas allowances for being in Sind, are refusing service there.

Natal taken; Hong Kong is now colony

London, December 1843
Satisfaction and dismay greet the imperial balance sheet this year. Believers in the "Forward Policy", who are to be found in the war office and the colonial office, are pleased to see new red spaces on the world map: Natal, in South Africa, and Hong Kong, off the southeastern coast of China.

Their opponents, who prefer influence to rule, regard colonies as a burdensome expense and see themselves as consolidators, are horrified. In neither case was annexation justified, they argue. In Natal a perfectly respectable Boer republic had been established and would have been left in peace if it had not been for the Evangelical lobby's claims that Blacks were being maltreated. In Hong Kong a useful military offshore base on the mouth of the Canton river, which had served well in the Opium War, has been turned into a colony. Further, the Anglo-Chinese agreement, signed at Nanjing, awarded Britain the expense of a colony and gave her rivals the benefit of the five new "Treaty Ports".

Law to stop British scandal of women and children in mines

London, 1842
Women, girls and children under ten are no longer to be allowed to work underground in coal mines following new legislation just approved by the British Parliament.

The Mines Act implements the principal recommendations of the commission appointed two years ago to investigate the scandal of conditions in Britain's coalmines. It found that children, sometimes as young as five, are employed underground to haul trucks in passages too narrow for men.

Others spend their entire day hunched down in dark, confined spaces operating ventilating shafts while women and girls are being harnessed like horse and made to pull coal trucks.

The new act provides for inspectors to enforce the law. It comes at a difficult time for Sir Robert Peel's new ministry, which is reluctant to alienate industrialists at a time of adverse trade figures.

Homeopathist dies, apothecaries' bane

Paris, 2 July 1843
Samuel Hahnemann, the founder of the controversial new medical practice of *homeopathy*, died here today aged 88. He was hounded by the medical establishment, particularly the apothecaries, and had to leave Leipzig, where he had studied medicine and done most of his formative work, in 1821. Patients, however, loved him and he secured the patronage of royalty. He then lived at Cothen as the guest of the archduke, before moving here in 1835.

Hahnemann's system is based on what he termed the "law of similars". Diseases can be cured by drugs which produce similar symptoms in the healthy, and only minute doses are needed, much less than those usually prescribed.

Children, some only five years old, hauling trucks in coalmines: now to be a thing of the past.

Britain, 1843. Charles Dickens publishes his novel *A Christmas Carol*.

Britain, 1843. The writer Thomas Macaulay, who achieved great popularity last year with *Lays of Ancient Rome*, publishes his collected *Critical and Historical Essays* in three volumes.

Britain, 1843. The weekly periodical *The Economist* begins publication.

Germany, 1843. Richard Wagner is given a conducting post at the Dresden opera following the success of *The Flying Dutchman*. However, it was less successful than his opera *Rienzi* of last year, possibly owing to its various structural innovations.

Denmark, 1843. The physicist Georg Ohm formulates the law of sonic vibrations.

China, 1843. Wei Yuan publishes his geography of foreign countries, *Haiguo Tuzhi*, in 50 chapters, providing a rather simplistic view of the non-Chinese world.

West Africa, 6 March 1844. The British governor of the Gold Coast (*Ghana*) forts, taken over from British traders last year, makes a "bond" with the various Fante states of the coast. It includes an alliance against other European powers on the coast and against inland Asante power, and gives Britain judicial rights over Fante people who come to the forts.

Sweden, 8 March 1844. Charles XIV, king since 1818, dies and is succeeded by his son, Oscar.

Spain, 13 May 1844. The regent Manuel Narvaez establishes a paramilitary police force called the *Guardia Civil*, aimed mainly at maintaining public order.

Washington, DC, 24 May 1844. The inventor Samuel Morse taps out the first telegraph message between two cities, to a friend in Baltimore, 40 miles away.

USA, 27 June 1844. Joseph Smith, the leader of the Mormon sect, and his brother Hyrum are killed by a mob in Carthage, Illinois, where they had been held on a charge of riot. This follows months of tension between the Mormons, who settled at Nauvoo, Illinois, in 1839, and locals who had come to resent and suspect Mormon political and economic power.

Prussia, June 1844. Weavers in Silesia rebel in protest at lower pay for hand-loom workers imposed by employers who have gone over to mechanical weaving. The revolt is bloodily suppressed.

Morocco, 1 July 1844. A French squadron under the duke of Joinville bombards Tangiers.

China, 3 July 1844. China and the USA sign the treaty of Wanghiya, giving US nationals similar rights to those granted to Britain by last year's protocol to the treaty of Nanjing. It also gives the USA access to the five ports now open to international trade.

Italy, 25 July 1844. The Bondiero brothers are shot for fomenting a revolt in Calabria.

USA, 8 August 1844. Brigham Young is chosen to head the Mormon church in succession to Joseph Smith.

Morocco, 14 August 1844. France's Marshal Bugeaud attacks and defeats the army of Abd al-Kader, the Algerian resistance leader, and his Moroccan supporters at the Isly river.

Morocco, 10 September 1844. France and Morocco sign the treaty of Tangiers, ending their conflict. France agrees to withdraw from Morocco.

Italy, 1844. King Charles Albert of Piedmont orders the foundation of teacher training colleges in a move to reduce the influence of the Jesuits. This is the latest in a series of liberal measures which began with the introduction of a civil code in 1837 and, two years later, a penal code establishing the principle of equality before the law.

Serbia, 1844. Prince Alexander Karageorge embarks upon a policy of land reform.

Japan, 1844. The *shogun* refuses a demand by King William II of the Netherlands that Japanese ports be opened to foreign vessels for trade and provisioning.

West Indies, 1844. The Dominican Republic secedes from Haiti.

Denmark, 1844 *The Concept of Anguish*, by the philosopher Soren Kierkegaard, appears. It follows the publication last year of *Either/Or, Fear and Trembling* and *Repetition*.

Germany, 1844. Heinrich Heine publishes *New Poems*, an anthology, and *Germany, Winter Story*.

Atlantic, 1844. The iron-hulled *Great Britain*, designed by the engineer Isambard Kingdom Brunel, becomes the largest steamship to cross the Atlantic.

Britain, 1844. The historian Thomas Carlyle publishes the essay *Past and Present*.

Britain, 1844. J M W Turner paints his dramatically atmospheric *Rain, Steam and Speed*.

Italy, 1844. Verdi's operas *Ernani*, based on Hugo, and *I due Foscari*, based on Byron, receive their first performances in Venice and Rome respectively.

Emperor's decree bans opium smoking

Imperial propaganda: a wife chops up her addicted husband's opium pipe.

China, 1 December 1843

The emperor has once again banned opium smoking in his unavailing struggle against the drug. It is doomed to have as little effect as his other measures, as his people have an insatiable appetite for it, an appetite which British traders are only too willing to feed.

The East India Company, anxious not to jeopardise its legal trade in tea, auctions its Indian opium to private traders in Calcutta. The "country traders" then ship the drug to China in specially built and heavily armed opium clippers.

Unloaded onto fortified receiving ships moored off the southern coast, the illicit cargoes are transferred to multi-oared "fast crabs" and "scrambling dragons" crewed by fierce Chinese pirates.

They run the opium past bribed officials and it is fed into the smuggling networks run by gangsters and secret societies like the *Triads*. The addicts are of all classes, but bureaucrats and soldiers seem especially vulnerable.

Commissioner Lin, whose burning of British traders' opium sparked the Opium War, has even written to Queen Victoria demanding that she ban the trade which, he said, "is repugnant to human feeling and at variance with the Way of Heaven". To no avail. The profitable trade goes on.

French book stars "Three Musketeers"

Alexandre Dumas: a relentless writer, after an idle and irregular youth.

Paris, 1844

The prolific Alexandre Dumas, who has already had ten years of success with his historical plays, has turned his hand to novels of adventure with *Les Trois Mousquetaires* and *Le Comte de Monte Cristo*. In the first, the three musketeers of the title, Athos, Porthos and Aramis, are joined by the young D'Artagnan in a series of adventures in the service of the queen, Anne of Austria, against Cardinal Richelieu, the mentor of King Louis XIII. Dumas has many collaborators – some say as many as 90 – who feed him with historical material for his newspaper serials or *feuilletons*. The output under his name includes four other books this year alone.

French guns defeat the Moroccan cavalry

Oujda, Morocco, 14 August 1844
French troops pacifying the Algerian-Moroccan border have crossed the frontier into independent Morocco and defeated the Moroccan cavalry in the Isly valley.

The decision to attack is certain to have repercussions in Paris where King Louis Philippe and his government had given the veteran campaigner, Marshal Bugeaud, express orders not to cross the Moroccan border.

French troops using scorched earth tactics have now advanced about 40 miles into Morocco, but do not appear to be following up

their victory with an advance on Fez, the capital. Marshal Bugeaud ordered his men to attack in the early hours of this morning after the duke of Joinville's fleet had shelled Moroccan ports yesterday.

Bugeaud's troops stormed across the valley of the Isly and engaged the Moroccan cavalry, which was forced to surrender by noon.

A post-battle statement by Marshal Bugeaud, who has made his men more mobile by lightening their equipment, celebrated the "glory of arms" and put the losses for each side at 800 Moroccans and 27 Frenchmen killed.

Britain creates new colonies in Africa

West Africa, c.1844
The European powers are turning the old bottlenecks of the Atlantic slave trade into colonies. Forts such as St Louis, Bissau, Christiansborg and Rufisque, each owned by a rival trading power, have become miniature city-states, producing a population of Mulattoes who act as middlemen between the European traders and the Africans in the interior. Until recently the boundaries of the city-states never went beyond the fort gates.

The Gold Coast typifies the development. The British, taking advantage of the fear that the coastal Fante people have of the neighbouring Asante empire, have formed a "bond" with the Fantes, extending British jurisdiction over 100 miles (160km) into the interior.

Mormon leader is murdered by mob

Carthage, Illinois, 27 June 1844
Mormon leader Joseph Smith and his brother Hyrum were dragged from their prison cell tonight by a mob of 200 and lynched – despite an assurance of safety by the state governor. The Mormon community had been split by a controversy over polygamy – which the Smiths sanction – and the brothers were jailed for destroying the offices and press of a rival Mormon newspaper, the *Expositor*, which opposed their views.

Martial law was declared when the crowd surrounding the jailhouse heard that the Smiths were about to be freed. The guards were powerless to hold off the mob whose leaders proclaimed that "as law could not reach them, powder and shot should".

Isambard Kingdom Brunel's "Great Britain": the most powerful ship afloat. Her launch on 19 July 1843 marked another first for Britain.

Cooperative and ten-hour movements help improve the lot of British workers

Workers of Lancashire unite: the dividend from the "Co-op" awaits you.

England, 21 December 1844
A group of unemployed workers in the Lancashire mill-town of Rochdale has hit upon an ingenious scheme for helping others while helping oneself. For the past six months members have been meeting in the Weavers' Arms and today they opened for business in a small shop in Toad (T'owd) Lane.

At present stocks are limited to a few essentials such as sacks of flour, but expansion is expected to be swift. Already, the Rochdale Pioneers, as they call themselves, have almost 50 members. Items are sold at regular market prices, but customers, who join the Pioneers for a shilling membership fee, receive a share or dividend of the profits. Thus thrift is encouraged and everyone is part of the business.

The idea of self-help is catching on among the working classes. In London, a drapery shop assistant is one of a dozen young men who have formed a club for the spiritual improvement of employees in the drapery and other trades. It is to be called the Young Men's Christian Association. The lot of the mill wor-

ker has greatly improved in recent years. The law now forbids anyone under 18 years to work more than twelve hours a day, and there is even talk of restricting teenagers to a ten-hour day.

Children under thirteen are already restricted to a 48-hour week and must attend school for two hours a day.

Frederick Engels: socialist thinker.

1844

China, 14 December 1844. The Qing court issues an edict relaxing a ban on the Catholic Church.

Germany, 1844. Mendelssohn's violin concerto in E minor is performed for the first time, in Leipzig, to great acclaim.

Brussels, 1 February 1845. The German political philosopher and dissident Karl Marx settles in the Belgian capital after being expelled from France.

USA, 4 March 1845. The Democrat James Polk is sworn in as 11th president following his landslide election victory last November. He is a supporter of further US expansion westwards.

New Zealand, 11 March 1845. Seven hundred Maoris led by their chief, Hone-Heke, burn the small town of Kororareka in protest at the settlement of Maori land by Europeans, in breach of the 1840 Treaty of Waitangi.

North America, 28 March 1845. Mexico severs relations with the USA following the US Senate's ratification of the annexation of Texas on 1 March.

Switzerland, 31 March 1845. Religious strife continues between anti-clerical radicals and the Catholic cantons. The radicals fail to seize the Catholic canton of Lucerne in their second organised attack in four months.

China, 25 July 1845. China grants Belgium equal trading rights with Britain, France and the USA.

Algeria, 8 September 1845. A French column surrenders at Sidi Brahim in the continuing Algerian war.

Germany, 21 October 1845. Wagner's new opera *Tannhauser* is given a mixed reception at its premiere.

Switzerland, 11 December 1845. In response to the armed band organised by the liberal cantons, the seven Catholic cantons – Uri, Schweitz, Unterwalden, Lucerne, Zug, Freiburg and Valais – form the *Sonderbund* to protect their interests.

Britain, 20 December 1845. Robert Peel returns to office as prime minister two weeks after resigning. This follows the failure of the Whig leader, Lord John Russell, to form a government, as invited to do after announcing his support for a repeal of the Corn Laws.

USA, 29 December 1845. Texas joins the United States of America and becomes the 38th state in the union.

India, December 1845. The British army in India embark on the conquest of Kashmir and the Punjab.

Britain, 1845. John Henry Newman, aged 44, a leading force in the Oxford Movement since 1833, converts to Roman Catholicism.

Britain, 1845. Parliament passes an law permitting Jews to stand for elections.

Britain, 1845. The politician and writer Benjamin Disraeli, the head of the "Young England" group of young Tories, publishes *Sybil*, his second political novel. His first, *Coningsby*, appeared last year.

Germany, 1845. Friedrich Engels publishes his *Condition of the Working Classes in England*.

Britain, 1845. The Scottish engineer R W Thompson patents an air-filled tyre for use on the *coupe*, a new two-seater convertible carriage for town use.

Poland, 1845. As part of their campaign for greater Russification, the Russians abolish the Polish penal code and impose the Russian one instead.

China, 1845. The boundaries of the British concession at Shanghai are fixed; Hong Kong becomes linked to Britain by a regular shipping line.

France, 1845. Prosper Merimee publishes the novel *Carmen*, set in Spain.

Peru, 1845. Ramon Castillo seizes power in a *coup d'etat* and establishes a reformist dictatorship.

USA, 1845. The author Edgar Allan Poe publishes his *Tales of Mystery and Imagination*.

Ireland, 1845. Blight strikes the potato, the staple food of the Irish countryside, making much of this year's crop inedible. The prospect of serious famine looms.

Sierra Leone, 1845. William Ferguson becomes Britain's first black colonial governor. Sierra Leone has a growing western-educated commercial, clerical and official class, and Forah Bay College, founded in 1827 for the education of clergymen, was Africa's first Christian college.

Germany, 1845. Robert Schumann's piano concerto in A minor appears. It is based on an earlier *Fantasy* written for his wife Clara, a fine composer and brilliant virtuoso pianist, in 1841.

India, January 1846. After several battles in a war with the Sikhs which began last year, the British break up the Sikh forces at Sobraon.

Madagascar, 1846. In protest at a government order making all foreigners subject to the native law, the French and British bombard Tamatave.

Maoris protest against foreign colonists

A Maori war dance; now the Maoris are really fighting, to protect their lands.

New Zealand, 11 March 1845

Hona-Heke, a Maori tribal chieftain, today led his warriors in an attack on the small town of Kororareka. The town was set on fire and a number of people were hurt in the fighting between Maoris and settlers. This attack, one of a number since the Treaty of Waitangi, five years ago, under which the Maoris ceded sovereignty but not land, is a direct result of Maori accusations that settlers are cheating them out of their birthrights. The settlers also have grounds for complaint because they fall foul of complicated tribal customs when they try to buy land from the Maoris. The situation is becoming increasingly dangerous, and the government will have to take strong action to prevent a bloodbath.

Religious fighting flares in Switzerland

Lucerne, December 1844

Theological debate has turned into armed clashes here in the last month or two. Earlier this year the Great Council of Lucerne invited the Jesuits to take all the theological teaching. This provoked an angry response from the Protestants which has now turned into actual fighting. Fuel to the flames of the old religious differences has been added by their new revolutionary fervour. Lucerne has now joined with six other Catholic cantons to form a defensive alliance called the *Sonderbund*.

Controversial composer stages new opera

Wagner: divisive genius.

Dresden, 21 October 1845

Excitement mixed with bewilderment greeted last night's premiere of the opera *Tannhauser* by Richard Wagner, at 33 the joint director of music at court here.

The work, set in the Middle Ages, is novel in that the music is more continuous and seamless than in operas based on the traditional pattern of arias and choruses – a departure already evident in his *Flying Dutchman* of two years ago. Wagner's music arouses either fanaticism or loathing, but he is used to controversy. In 1839 he had to slip out of Riga to avoid creditors, and he is involved in German patriotic movements. On top of this, he makes no secret of his contempt for Jews and all things Jewish.

Samurai preparing for war with West

Feudal Japan: soon to disappear.

Japan, 1844
Wide-ranging reforms instituted in the face of fierce opposition by Mizuno Tadakuni, the chief *shogunate* councillor, are changing the face of Japan. He has rooted out corrupt officials, and ordered the *samurai* to practise their martial arts in anticipation of an attack from western ships. He has also made urbanised peasants return to the land, to ensure food supplies, and has set about restoring the country's economy.

China relaxes ban on Catholic Church

China, 24 October 1844
The French, following British and US tactics in their determination to open up China to western trade, have today signed a treaty with the Chinese at Whampoa which will have far-reaching effects.

It opens up Chinese ports to French ships on a "most-favoured nation" basis, and gives France consular rights for its citizens, so Frenchmen will be above Chinese law, answerable to French law.

Where the Whampoa treaty differs from the British Nanjing treaty and the American Wanghiya treaty is in granting toleration of Roman Catholicism and giving the French the right to build Catholic churches in the treaty ports.

Potato blight forces Irish to seek refuge

Dublin, 1845
There have been over 20 largescale failures of the potato crop in Ireland in the past century, but this year's is without precedent. It has been caused by the blight which has ravaged crops in America appearing without warning in Britain and Ireland. The gravity of the situation can scarcely be exaggerated; over four million people in Ireland and two million in Britain live almost wholly on potatoes. Until well into July the Irish crop appeared to be very good. Then the hot, dry weather changed abruptly to chilling rain and fog. The first warning of trouble came from the Isle of Wight, which reported that potatoes were being destroyed by a mysterious distemper.

Before the authorities had quite grasped what was happening, Ireland was being devastated. When first lifted the potatoes appeared healthy, but within a few days they became a stinking putrefying mess. The scale of the famine has overwhelmed the authorities; the British have no machinery for dealing with disaster on such a scale. Besides, attitudes towards relief are much influenced by free trade notions, so that corn continues to be exported while the Irish starve.

Public works schemes have been hastily devised, and soon 750,000 people will be employed on relief

The potato famine: four million Irish people live purely on potatoes.

work, which means that some three million people are being supported by public funds. Even that is insufficient; Irish families are emigrating in tens of thousands, even though the voyage to America is almost as deadly as the famine – about one person in every six dies at sea. In their sufferings the Irish have, perhaps inevitably, blamed the disaster on "English oppression", a charge that has caused resentment in London where it is pointed out that the British government has provided more than £8 million for relief.

Texas joins rest of the United States

Washington, 29 December 1845
The vast republic of Texas became the 38th state in the union today – annexed peacefully after an almost unanimous vote in favour by its citizens. The ten-year-old republic has long been coveted by both the United States and Mexico, and an American diplomat, John Slidell, has been dispatched to Mexico City to smooth Mexican resentment. Texas was formerly a Mexican province and fought a bitter war before declaring its independence in 1836.

Since then the republic has lived through a series of upheavals. Its first president, Sam Houston, sought political stability, peaceful relations with the Indian tribes and ultimately to join the union.

His successor, Mirabeau Lamar, took a different policy line altogether. He saw Texas as a permanent republic and established diplomatic relations with Britain and France. Unlike Houston, Lamar saw the Indians as a threat and began a series of aggressive campaigns against them.

Houston was re-elected president of Texas three years ago and found the republic seriously in debt. Annexation became inevitable and it was Britain and France who acted as the intermediaries with Mexico.

Sikhs humbled as Britain sells off Kashmir for £1 million

A village in the Punjab, the Sikh heartland, still Sikh after the treaty.

Kashmir, 1846
Kashmir has been forcibly separated from the Sikh domain by the British and sold to the neighbouring *rajah* of Jammu for £1 million.

The Kashmir settlement is just part of the treaty which Britain is forcing on the Sikhs after defeating them at Sobraon in January. In addition the Sikhs are paying an indemnity to Britain of half a million pounds, half the price of Kashmir.

British moves against the Sikhs have been inevitable since 1839 when Ranjit Singh died and the Sikh territories degenerated into anarchy. For Britain the final straw came last December when Sikhs raiders attacked British troops. Now Britain is dictating the terms, which the Sikhs have no choice but to agree to.

Poland, March 1846. The Russians and the Austrians occupy the free republic of Cracow, ending a pro-independence revolt that began last month in nearby Galicia, the part of Poland that is under Austrian rule.

USA, March 1846. As tension grows between the USA and Mexico, President Polk orders the US army under Zachary Taylor to the Rio Grande river.

USA, 13 May 1846. The USA declares war on Mexico.

Britain, 25 June 1846. The highly unpopular Corn Laws, which imposed duties on imported grain, are repealed.

USA, 15 June 1846. Britain signs a treaty with the USA agreeing to end its joint occupation of Oregon Territory. All the land west of the Rocky Mountains and south of the 49th parallel now belongs to the USA.

Rome, 16 June 1846. Giovanni Maria Mastai Ferretti succeeds Gregory XVI as pope and takes the name of Pius IX.

Britain, 29 June 1846. Bitterly opposed to the repeal of the Corn Law, the protectionist wing of the Tory Party, led by Benjamin Disraeli, mount a revolt against Robert Peel's Tory government, forcing Peel to resign as prime minister.

California, 7 July 1846. A US navy squadron sails into Monterey and formally claims California for the USA.

Denmark, 8 July 1846. King Christian VIII lays claim, under the Danish succession law, to the independent duchies of Schleswig and Holstein.

Rome, 16 July 1846. Pope Pius IX orders an amnesty for political prisoners.

USA, 16 October 1846. The dentist William Morton carries out the first surgical operation under local anaesthetic, using sulphuric ether.

Spain, October 1846. The affair of the "Spanish marriages" severely damages Franco-British relations. Queen Isabella II marries her cousin Francis, the duke of Cadiz; her sister Louisa marries the duke of Montpensier, the son of Louis Philippe of France. Both marriages breaks agreements made between France and Britain, which has pressed the claim of another of Isabella's suitors, Prince Leopold of Saxe-Coburg.

Poland, 6 November 1846. Following the March uprising, the small republic of Cracow is annexed to Austrian-controlled Galicia, losing its independence.

Mexico, 16 November 1846. After defeating a large Mexican force at Monterey in September, General Zachary Taylor takes Saltillo.

California, 6 December 1846. A pro-Mexican revolt in California is put down by US troops.

Paris, 6 December 1846. Hector Berlioz cantata *The Damnation of Faust* is performed for the first time.

Panama, 12 December 1846. The USA and Colombia sign an agreement granting the USA transit rights on the narrow isthmus of Panama between the Atlantic and Pacific Oceans.

New Mexico, 25 December 1846. US troops defeat the Mexicans near Las Cruces, virtually completing the conquest of New Mexico.

USA, 28 December 1846. Iowa is admitted as the 29th non-slave state in the union.

Japan, 1846. Commodore Biddle arrives in Japan on an official mission from the US government. He enters Edo (*Tokyo*) Bay with two vessels and asks for the opening of trade relations between the USA and Japan. The Japanese refuse.

Portugal, 1846. Following the publication of a public health order ordering Portuguese peasants to be clean and decreeing that cemeteries must in future be sited outside large centres of population, peasants led by priests of the Minho region rise up and overthrow the dictatorial government of Costa Cabral.

Paris, 1846. A new brass reed-instrument known as a saxophone, one of a range of improved instruments invented by the Belgian Adolphe Saxe, makes its appearance.

California, 13 January 1847. The final surrender of pro-Mexico resisters in California to the US ends 25 years of Mexican rule.

France, 28 January 1847. During a period of severe depression and unemployment, disturbances break out among agricultural workers in central France, provoked by food shortages.

Canada, January 1847. Lord Elgin, a liberal and friend of Robert Peel, is made governor general of Canada. On his arrival, Queen Victoria announces an amnesty for those convicted all after the uprisings of 1837-38.

Prussia, 3 February 1847. King Frederick William IV convenes a new assembly which brings together delegates from all the Prussian provinces but is given no effective power over legislation or the budget.

Prime minister falls as free traders win

London, 25 June 1846
After a five-month debate in the House of Commons, the free-traders carried the day with a vote to repeal the hated Corn Laws. All duties on imported wheat, oats and barley are reduced to a nominal one shilling a quarter until full repeal in three years' time.

But within hours the protectionists had wreaked revenge on the prime minister, Sir Robert Peel. The Tory landowners on his own backbenches had never looked on Peel, a manufacturer's son, as a genuine Tory, and his conversion to free trade was taken as the ultimate betrayal. A bill to use coercion against Irish nationalists is coming up and the landowners, who had never been against coercion for Ireland, say they will vote against it.

Peel's decision to tackle the Corn Laws was given an added urgency last year, with the failure of the potato crop in Ireland. But he could not get the solid support of the cabinet and resigned last December. Within a fortnight he was again prime minister, the Whigs having been unable to agree among themselves as to who would be in the cabinet.

The fight was now within Peel's own party. Protectionists, who control a number of family seats in the Commons, gave orders for Peelites to resign. Peel argued that since repeal was necessary for the well-being of the people the party should support him – in vain. The landowners took their revenge – and split the Tory party.

Sir Robert Peel: the ex PM.

Sir Robert Peel's cheap bread shop.

New planet is found in the solar system

England, 1846
There is another planet in our solar system, discovered after something of a scientific race. The joint winners are the brilliant student John Couch Adams from Cambridge and the equally clever French astronomer Urbain Le Verrier. The planet has been named Neptune.

It all began years ago when astronomers noticed that there was something amiss in the orbit of the planet Uranus. It simply did not behave as it should, unless – and this was the intriguing thought – there were yet another planet further out producing perturbations and distortions in its motions. This prompted a lot of intense mathematical work to calculate the mass, distance and orbital velocity of this mysterious "planet X". Adams in Cambridge came up with an idea as to where the planet might be in 1845.

Simultaneously Le Verrier was independently arriving at the same position as Adams for the as yet unseen planet. He then contacted J G Galle at the Berlin Observatory who on 23 September of this year came up with the first sighting, less than one degree from the calculated, predicted position.

US and Mexico fight over California

Mexico, 13 May 1846

Although Congress in Washington only made a formal declaration of war today, full-scale fighting between the US army and Mexican troops has been under way on either side of the Rio Grande for several days. It was when the news reached Washington last night that Mexican forces had crossed the river and killed and captured US troopers that Congress went to war. "Mexico has ... shed American blood upon the American soil," declared the Democratic President James Knox Polk.

Despite his ringing denunciation of Mexico, few doubt that Polk has deliberately baited Mexico into conflict – with New Mexico and California as the prize. The US wants to buy both territories – with "money no object" for California – but the Mexicans have spurned offers and refused to talk money. The disputed Rio Grande was the excuse for the war, although Polk's justification is that Britain and

The battle of Palo Alto on 8 May: 2,200 US troops defeated 6,000 Mexicans.

France – both extending their Pacific ambitions – have covetous eyes on harbours in California.

As General Zachary Taylor – "Old Rough and Ready" – is reporting success by his 2,200 strong army against 6,000 Mexican troops massed on the border, the US is

divided over the declaration of war. Texas and the southern states are delighted and have furnished more than 49,000 volunteers. The original colonies are less eager and have supplied only 14,000 men. Abolitionists see this as a war of conquest by the slave lobby.

Faraday reveals electrical secrets

London, 1846

Having established himself as a leading experimentalist of the day with his development of the principle of the electric motor, Michael Faraday has now offered a further intriguing contribution to our understanding of the mysterious forms of energy that hold together all matter. In a Royal Institution lecture in London, Faraday discussed "Thoughts on Ray Vibrations" and described the magnetic and electrical forces holding together atoms, suggesting that these might serve to transmit light. Faraday seems to be suggesting that we might even unify all the forces of nature into just one.

Faraday, the inventor and scientist.

Nonsense verses set readers guessing

London, 1846

A new kind of verse is sweeping like wildfire through the adults of the country – the limerick:

There was an old man of Peru
Who watched his wife making a stew
Till one day, by mistake,
In a stove she did bake
That unfortunate man of Peru.

There are great numbers of Unfortunate Old Men, or Young Persons, in *A Book of Nonsense*, just published. Eccentric drawings il-

lustrate the plight of the Young Person of Crete (whose toilette was far from complete), the Young Lady (whose bonnet Came untied when the birds sate upon it). The author, on the title page tells us:

There was an old Derry down Derry,
Who loved to see little folks merry,
So he made them a book
And with laughter they shook
At the fun of that Derry down Derry.

French fugitive is hiding in London

London, 27 May 1846

Louis Napoleon, the nephew of Napoleon Bonaparte and claimant to the French throne, has been spotted in Piccadilly, having escaped from the chateau at Ham, near Amiens, where he has been imprisoned for the past six years.

He was seen by Lord Malmesbury, who reported the fact to a French Embassy attache at dinner this evening. "I never saw a man look so frightened," said Lord Malmesbury as the attache rushed out of the room.

Louis Napoleon is the son of Napoleon's brother, Louis Bonaparte of Holland, and Hortense Beauharnais, the emperor's stepdaughter. As a young man he travelled throughout Europe and lived in Italy, Bavaria, Switzerland and London. In 1836 and 1840 he failed in attempts to lead Bonapartist revolts against the July monarchy.

The government of Louis Philippe is understandably nervous about him, for the name of Napoleon still stirs the French.

War starts over axe in south Africa

South Africa, 1846

After ten years of uneasy peace, war between British and Xhosa has broken out once more on the Cape eastern frontier. The stealing of an axe by a Xhosa man, and a botched attempt by his comrades to rescue him, set off the war.

The British have kept the peace by making treaties with Xhosa chiefs across the frontier. But from 1844 British administrators began to bend before the pressure of white sheep farmers, seeking more land for expensive merino sheep imported from Europe.

There was an Old Man who said, "Hush! I perceive a young bird in this bush!"
When they said, "Is it small?" he replied, "Not at all!
It is four times as big as the bush!"

The old man who said "Hush!", from "A Book of Nonsense".

1847

Mexico, 23 February 1847. US troops under Zachary Taylor rout General Santa Anna's Mexican army at the battle of Buena Vista.

Mexico, 9 March 1847. In the first large-scale US amphibious operation, General Winfield Scott lands thousands of troops on the beaches south of Vera Cruz.

Mexico, 29 March 1847. US troops under Winfield Scott take possession of the Mexican stronghold at Vera Cruz.

Rome, March 1847. Pope Pius IX passes a liberal law on the press which entrusts censorship to a lay committee.

Mexico, 18 April 1847. US forces defeat a large Mexican army under Santa Anna at Cerro Gordo in one of the bloodiest battles of the war.

Washington, DC, 1 May 1847. The Smithsonian Institution for the increase and diffusion of learning, headed by the Princeton physicist Joseph Henry, is dedicated.

Philadelphia, 7 May 1847. The American Medical Association is founded.

Britain, 8 June 1847. An act is passed limiting the working day of women and children aged 13 to 18 to 10 hours.

Rome, June 1847. Pope Pius IX creates a council of ministers and a civil guard.

Britain, June 1847. In London, Karl Marx, Friedrich Engels and Stefan Born found the Communist League.

Utah, 24 July 1847. A group of Mormons led by Brigham Young founds a settlement on the banks of the Great Salt Lake.

Italy, August 1847. Austrian troops occupy the town of Ferrara in an attempt to check the introduction of liberal measures.

Germany, 12 September 1847. The radical and middle-class opposition, meeting at Offenburg, adopts a liberal and democratic reform programme which includes abolition of privileges, freedom of the press and equal voting rights.

Mexico City, 14 September 1847. A US army storms and captures Mexico City, putting an end to the Mexican war.

France, 19 September 1847. Francois Guizot becomes prime minister.

Morocco, 23 October 1847. Having lost the support of the sultan of Morocco, the Algerian resistance leader Abd al-Kader surrenders to the French.

Oregon, 29 November 1847. Cayuse Indians massacre 14 members of an Oregon mission.

Britain, 8 December 1847. An international convention of the Communist League adopts Karl Marx's principles of the overthrow of the middle classes and the dictatorship of the proletariat.

Italy, December 1847. Austrian troops are withdrawn from Ferrara.

Canada, December 1847. Following the victory of the reformists in a general election, Lord Elgin, the governor general, proclaims the birth of a parliamentary system.

Austria, 1847. The physician Ignaz Semmelweis discovers that the high mortality rate in newborn infants is due to infections.

South Africa, 1847. The British are victorious over the Xhosa people in the War of the Axe, which broke out last year as a result of moves by British sheep farmers to acquire more land.

West Africa, 1847. Liberia, the state founded by the American slave-trade abolitionists, proclaims its independence.

France, 1847. Reform "banquets" calling for measures such as universal suffrage and parliamentary reform are held throughout the country.

Britain, 1847. Among the new novels published this year are *Vanity Fair* by William Thackeray, *Wuthering Heights* by Emily Bronte, *Jane Eyre* by Charlotte Bronte and *Dombey and Son* by Charles Dickens.

Milan, 3 January 1848. Clashes occur during an anti-Austrian demonstration organised by the liberals.

India, 12 January 1848. The earl of Dalhousie, the young and gifted British minister, is appointed governor general of India.

Sicily, 12 January 1848. Following the outbreak of a revolutionary movement, Sicily proclaims a provisional independent government.

Paris, 14 January 1848. The prime minister, Guizot bans a reform banquet which was due to be held in Paris next month.

Denmark, 20 January 1848. Frederick VII succeeds his father, Christian VIII, as king.

Naples, 27 January 1848. The people of Naples rise up and demand a constitution.

Naples, 10 February 1848. King Ferdinand II promulgates a new constitution.

Tuscany, 17 February 1848. The duke of Tuscany promulgates a constitution.

Brighter future for surgery and childbirth

Massachusetts General Hospital: a tooth extracted under anaesthetic.

Boston, Massachusetts, 1847
Two recent advances in medical techniques hold out the hope that in future surgical operations will be almost painless and childbirth much safer. At Massachusetts General Hospital, in Boston, the US dentist William Morton has used the gas *ether* for the first general anaesthetic in the west; though some claim that the US surgeon Crawford Young has been using ether for anaesthesia for several years.

A patient had a neck tumour removed, and came round afterwards having felt no pain. So complete is the loss of sensation that Morton's technique could even be used for limb amputation.

Meanwhile, in Vienna, Dr Ignaz Semmelweiss, a Hungarian, has discovered the cause of puerperal or "childbed" fever, the scourge of maternity wards: careless students – careless because they come straight into the wards from the dissecting room without washing their hands. From now on, washing hands in a solution of chlorinated lime is the rule. Already mortality rates are plummeting.

Mendelssohn dies of a stroke at 38

Leipzig, 4 November 1847
Felix Mendelssohn-Bartholdy died today after his second stroke in six months, aged just 38. The grandson of the great Jewish philosopher Moses Mendelssohn and son of wealthy Lutheran converts, he always worked punishingly hard, rising at five in the morning and often working into the night.

Earlier this year he went on an exhausting concert tour of Britain, where the composer of the *Hebrides* overture, *Scottish Symphony* and music for *A Midsummer Night's Dream* was popular with public and royalty. Back in Germany he learnt of the death of his sister Fanny, herself a fine musician, and his health finally gave way.

Mendelssohn: popular composer.

Gold sends people rushing to California

Sutter's Mill, where the gold was found.

Los Angeles, February 1847
Six years after a prospector, Francisco Lopez, found traces of gold in the roots of a newly-dug onion, the world is waking to the news that there is gold in plenty in the streambeds of California. A gold rush is starting as farmers from across the country mortgage their property, clerks leave their desks – even ministers quit their pulpits – as they head for California.

The popular song is "I'm off for Sacramento with my washbowl on my knee". However, many believe that news of the gold finds is being deliberately fostered by a government anxious to encourage population growth in the Mexican-owned state.

Free Blacks declare their independence

Liberia, West Africa, 1847
A new state has been born: Liberia, a nation built by freed slaves. Founded by the United States as places to absorb both its surplus Black population and its freed slaves, the settlements of Liberia, Grand Bassa and Mississippi are aggressively colonial. Now, under the leadership of a prominent merchant, Joseph Roberts, they have proclaimed themselves a republic, but the United States has yet to recognise it.

Swiss army crushes Catholic alliance

Geneva, 29 November 1847
After a civil war lasting for less than a month, a defensive alliance of seven conservative Catholic cantons in Switzerland has been broken up. The defeated cantons, centred on Lake Lucerne, had reacted against the anti-clerical policies, including the closure of monasteries, of the radical federal government. The Swiss Catholics had powerful friends in France and Austria, but the federal government moved fast and the rebels surrendered within a month – too quickly for their allies to intervene. Jesuits, who allegedly organised the uprising, are being expelled.

US infantrymen storm Mexico City

Mexico City, 12 October 1847
After a day-long artillery bombardment, US infantrymen stormed the Mexican capital today: a major victory in the two year war over the sovereignty of Texas. Santa Anna, the Mexican commander, is in full flight with the remnants of his army, and General Winfield "Old Fuss and Feathers" Scott watched in full dress uniform as the union flag was hoisted over the National Palace. The battle cost more than 1,000 American lives.

New Indo-Chinese ruler faces threat

Annam (Vietnam), 1847
Tu Duc, the head of the Nguyen dynasty, has succeeded to the throne of Annam. He rules the biggest and most powerful state in the Indo-Chinese peninsula. Forces are gathering, however, which seem to be beyond his comprehension and threaten the survival of his regime. He has closed his mind to any modernisation and does not recognise the decline of Vietnamese influence in Cambodia. He also refuses to open up his country to western trade despite the clear indication of the Opium War in China that the west is prepared to open Asian markets by force.

Sharp social satires and romantic tales flourish in vintage era of English novels

(Left to right) Currer, Ellis and Acton Bell, alias the Brontes, with their alcoholic brother Branwell, who provided them with their best plots.

London, 21 December 1847
It has been an exciting year for novel readers in England. Early in the year William Makepeace Thackeray, already noticed for his *Punch* series on "The Snobs of England", began publication of *Vanity Fair*. Its monthly parts in yellow paper covers are keenly awaited for the latest doings of Miss Becky Sharp, clawing her way up the social ladder with "only herself and her own wits to trust to", or the latest tearful episode of her rival, "that little pink-faced chit", Miss Amelia Sedley. "Some people consider fairs immoral altogether: very likely they are right. Vanity Fair is not a moral place, certainly, nor a merry one, though very noisy," writes the author, who invites us to "step in for half an hour and look at the performances: some scenes of high life and some of very middling indeed".

This is far from the style of *Jane Eyre* by a new author, Currer Bell, whose reception in October has called for a second edition, published today. It tells the story of a plain and independent-minded governess, Jane Eyre, and her growing fascination for her employer, the dark tormented – and married – Mr Rochester.

Even more passions are unlocked in *Wuthering Heights*, set in the wild Yorkshire moors. The violence of Heathcliff makes havoc of other people's lives in an electric atmosphere described with great power by Ellis - Bell. It is published with *Agnes Grey*, a comparatively plain tale by Acton Bell. Some believe that all three Bells are the same author.

Tancred, the third novel of Mr Disraeli's trilogy, is a satire about religious issues, following *Coningsby*, which dealt with the ruling class, and *Sybil*, which contrasted England's "Two Nations", the rich and the poor, so feelingly.

William Makepeace Thackeray, a satirist on Victorian values.

Marx calls Europe's workers to revolt

1848, the year of revolution: barricades against a Baroque background at Michaelerplatz in Vienna, 26 May.

Brussels

An obscure German-Jewish journalist living in exile in Belgium has cooperated with a German textile manufacturer's son settled in England to publish a ringing call to working men to rise up in rebellion and smash the capitalist system.

Karl Marx' family converted to Christianity and he was sent to a Protestant high school in Trier; it was under police surveillance because it was suspected of employing liberal teachers. All his life Marx has never been short of adversaries, be they police spies or fellow socialists. Only when he met Friedrich Engels did he find a good friend – who could also relieve his poverty.

Last year Marx and Engels joined a secret society of exiled German workers, the League of the Just, for which they wrote a pamphlet. "All history has hitherto been a history of class struggles," this *Communist Manifesto* proclaimed. But now the proletariat has taken the stage for the final struggle to end the class system for ever. "Workers of the world, unite!" cry Marx and Engels. "You have nothing to lose but your chains."

The manifesto came out at the beginning of the year. Since then, revolution has erupted in France, Italy, Austria and Germany. These revolutionaries were not inspired by Marx and Engels; the authors believe that others will be.

Flames of revolution burn capitalist power bases

Italy: states expel Austrian rulers

Milan, March
Stirred by the news of revolution in Vienna and the flight of Prince Metternich, the people of Milan have risen in revolt against their hated Austrian masters. After five days of street fighting, the military governor, Marshal Radetsky, judging his force of 10,000 men to be too small to put down the rising, retreated to the Quadrilateral system of fortresses, last used in the Napoleonic Wars.

A provisional Italian government has been proclaimed, and now the people of Venice have risen, driven out the Austrians and proclaimed the republic of St Mark. As far south as Naples and Rome volunteers are clamouring to join the war and calling on the liberal Pope Pius IX to back them.

After some hesitation, Charles Albert, the king of Sardinia, who defused the revolutionary mood at home by granting a constitution, has been compelled by popular clamour to declare war on Austria. He has arrived at Cremona, in Lombardy, with 70,000 men, but his heart is not in it; too many of the Italian patriots are republicans and he fears revolution more than he detests Austria.

The Tuileries stormed: the art was saved, but the hall of state destroyed.

France: monarchy falls, republic declared

Paris, 24 February
The political storm that followed the government's ban on a "democratic banquet" planned by young radicals has blown up into full scale revolution and sent Louis Philippe, France's king for the past 18 years, fleeing into exile in England.

As the storm developed, the king sacked his prime minister, Francois Guizot, who had been resisting reforms. It was too late. Today the king escaped down the Champs Elysees as the Paris mob, armed with weapons seized from gunsmiths' shops, began pillaging his palace, before going on to take over the Prefecture of Police and the Post Office.

A brawling crowd which invaded the Chamber of Deputies was invited to agree to the formation of a provisional government. This "government" took over the Hotel de Ville and proclaimed a republic, with a promise to reduce working hours and guarantee jobs for the unemployed.

Germany makes U-turn on reforms

Berlin, 21 March
After a week of violent disorder in Berlin, with soldiers and citizens fighting running battles, the erratic King Frederick William IV has made a dramatic change of policy and assumed the role of reformer, promising a free press, a new Prussian constitution, a meeting of the *Landtag* to draw up an electoral law – and, boldest of all, a pan-German parliament.

This last move is a calculated appeal to German nationalist sentiment. The liberal movement in the German lands certainly demands curbs on arbitrary power and wants popular participation in government. But it also seeks the unification of the German people.

The king's action has set off a chain reaction of liberal promises in other German states. Much of the agitation is conducted by middle-class intellectuals and merchants. But a deepening economic crisis and widespread unemployment have pushed workers into action; as repression has eased, trade unions have appeared. In Berlin an attempt has been made, through the Central Committee of Working Men, to establish an all-German trade union centre.

Hungary: rebellion against Habsburgs

Hungary, 31 March
The Emperor Ferdinand has approved the March Laws, passed 16 days ago by the Hungarian *Diet*, which sweep away many feudal legacies and give substantial autonomy to a government in Budapest.

Rebellion against Habsburg rule in Hungary has been led by Lajos Kossuth, a radical patriotic pamphleteer released seven years ago from imprisonment for treason. Kossuth galvanised the diet earlier this month with his call for tax reform and national representation.

The Hungarian rebels have been peaceful, and have not sought separation from the Austrian empire.

Austria: riots oust Chancellor Metternich

Vienna, 13 March
Metternich, chancellor of Austria since 1821, has been forced to resign, the sacrificial victim of a reform movement which has taken its inspiration from the revolt in Paris and led to riots in Vienna and the provinces.

Pressure has built up rapidly in the past two weeks, with an industrial crisis in Vienna, petitions from students and the bourgeoisie, and intense political intrigue. Peaceful demonstrators have clashed with troops, and unrest is spreading.

Metternich's own vanity has been his downfall, since he has claimed personal responsibility for various decrees that have made him a symbol of repression.

Prince Metternich: diplomat.

England: collapse of Chartist idealism

London, 10 April
A threatened confrontation between the Chartists and the military was averted today when Chartist leaders decided not to lead a mass march on parliament to present their million-signature petition. The climb-down came after a surprisingly small crowd of Chartists had gathered on Kennington Common in south London.

The police, backed up by armed troops, warned the Chartists that the procession would not be allowed to reach Westminster. After speeches the crowd dispersed, and the petition was delivered by three black cabs.

Prague, 17 June. The Austrian General Alfred Windischgratz crushes a Czech uprising in Prague.

France, 24 June. The national workshops are disbanded by the assembly.

Paris, 26 June. Another revolt in Paris is bloodily put down by Louis Cavaignac.

Germany, 27 June. Heinrich von Gagern, the president of the German national assembly, orders the formation of a provisional central government.

Prague, 17 June. A pan-Slav congress, led by Frantisek Palacky, demands the transformation of the Austrian empire into a federation of peoples with equal rights.

Italy, 25 July. The Piedmontese army is defeated by the Austrians at Custoza.

Italy, 9 August. Piedmont signs an truce with Austria agreeing to abandon Lombardy and Venice.

Vienna, 12 August. The Emperor Ferdinand, who fled to Innsbruck on 17 May, returns to Vienna.

Italy, 26 August. Having continued to resist since the signing of the armistice, Giuseppe Garibaldi and his volunteers are defeated by the Austrians at Morazzone.

Scandinavia, 26 August. Denmark and Prussia sign a truce at Malmo, both agreeing to evacuate the duchies of Schleswig and Holstein.

Vienna, 7 September. The constituent assembly of Vienna, which opened on 22 July, abolishes serfdom.

Hungary, 24 September. Lajos Kossuth is proclaimed president of the committee for national defence.

Switzerland, September. A federal constitution is adopted, replacing the pact of 1815. An executive federal council and two legislative assemblies are created.

Persia, September. Mohammed, Shah of Persia since 1834, dies and is succeeded by his son Nasir al-Din.

Hungary, October. Joseph Jellacic, commander of the imperial forces operating against the Hungarians, is driven out of Hungary.

Vienna, 31 October. Prince Alfred Windischgratz forces Vienna to surrender after a third uprising.

Mexico cedes Texas and California to US

Don Pio Pico, the last Mexican governor of California, with his wife and nieces.

Vera Cruz, Mexico, 2 February
After over two years of fighting, in which nearly 13,000 US soldiers lost their lives, Mexico has finally collapsed. Under a treaty signed here today, Mexico surrenders Texas, New Mexico and California to the USA in return for a payment of $15 million. The acquisition of these territories increases the size of the USA by a third.

The Mexicans were anxious to save their own country from US occupation, and with their war chest empty they were desperate for the money. Although Generals Winfield "Old Fuss and Feathers" Scott and Zachary "Old Rough and Ready" Taylor are being hailed as the victors, the unsung hero is a State Department clerk, Nicholas Trist.

He was dispatched to Mexico by President Polk with orders to negotiate a peace. Months passed without progress. Polk ordered Trist to return, but the clerk ignored the order and went through the final battles with General Scott until the moment was right. Although at first sight Trist described Scott as "the greatest imbecile I have ever had anything to do with", the two ended the war as close friends.

Prussia in border war with Denmark

Schleswig and Holstein, April
Prussian troops have moved into the disputed duchies of Schleswig and Holstein and are fighting the Danish army on behalf of the rebellious German citizens, who wish to escape from the detested Danish rule.

The duchies have been a source of controversy for many years. Holstein's population is essentially German, and as such part of the German Confederation of States, but its hereditary ruler, the duke, is also king of Denmark. He also rules Schleswig, which is divided between Germans in the south and Danes in the north. Since it is not part of the Confederation, Denmark claims it as an absolute possession. The issue is further complicated by dynastic difficulties. The Danish crown passes through the female line, whereas the duchies themselves recognise only the Salic law, which demands male inheritance. Under this law the German dukes of Augustenburg claim that they have a greater right to rule.

Schleswig and Holstein have also become the focus of European interests. Prussia backs its German cousins, but Britain and France back Denmark, hoping to preserve the balance of power in the face of an expanding Germany.

Women fight for votes and equal status

Seneca Falls, 21 July
The first-ever all-women convention on women's rights ended here today with demands for universal suffrage and an end to religious and social discrimination against women. The convention – attended by 300 delegates who packed the Wesleyan chapel – was organised by the radical and feminist anti-slavery campaigners Lucrecia Mott and Elizabeth Stanton.

Basing their ideas on the Declaration of Independence, the delegates resolved to fight for the vote and to gain legal equality in marriage, education and work. Elizabeth Stanton worked on the Married Women's Property Act – allowing divorced women to keep some of their possessions – which was passed this year by New York.

Amelia Jenks Bloomer, wearing the costume named after her.

Call for state to regulate economy

London
A new book by the philosopher John Stuart Mill, *The Principles of Political Economy*, has cast a fresh light on Britain in the age of the "industrial revolution".

Mill, a former civil servant and politician, and the owner of the *London Review*, is a follower of Jeremy Bentham's "utilitarian" philosophy. He has also taken up and developed the economic ideas of Adam Smith, Ricardo and Malthus. A firm believer in social welfare, he suggests that economic policy should be dictated by government legislation. To ensure that this happens, he wishes to see government interference in an increasingly wide sphere of activities.

Revolutionaries face pro-establishment backlash

Italy: Austrian break-out defeats rebels

Italy, 25 July
The Italian nationalists, seeking to throw off their Austrian oppressors, reckoned without the 84-year-old Marshal Josef Radetsky. He has spent the last four months reorganising his forces in the Quadrilateral fortress complex hinged on Verona. He disregarded orders from Vienna to seek an armistice, ignored political concessions his government had made under British pressure, and two days ago came out fighting.

At the village of Custoza, 11 miles from Verona, he routed the army of King Charles Albert of Sardinia, who is now in full retreat. The outcome seems in little doubt. In a few days the king will be forced to surrender and Austrian rule will have been restored.

The Austrians charging at Custoza.

Germany: a constitutional assembly

Frankfurt, 18 May
The all-German parliament which has assembled here to draw up a constitution for a united Germany has over 200 lawyers and magistrates, 100 university teachers and one peasant. Its president, Baron Heinrich von Gagern from Hesse, favours Prussia's King Frederick as leader of the new Germany, with Austria and her emperor having only associate membership. Doubtless Frederick William would like to become *Kaiser* (Caesar), but he is not likely to accept, partly for fear of upsetting the Austrians, but also because his divine right will not allow him to accept a crown from commoners. Still, this gathering of middleclass intellectuals, assisted by the token peasant, will keep talking.

France: left-wingers are suppressed

Paris, 26 June
The radicals of the February revolution, who promised welfare services and jobs for all, have been crushed in four days of bloody battles in the streets of Paris. Some 10,000 people are believed to have died, and 3,000 more have since been shot without trial. Thousands more are to be transported.

After last April's elections, liberal republicans formed the majority in the assembly. Moderate socialists remained in the government, but the militants set out to exploit the workshops, which had been created to provide jobs for men thrown out of work by the economic crisis.

The workshops were soon overwhelmed by provincials streaming into Paris. In addition, the militants were using the workshops to recruit a revolutionary army. On Wednesday 21 June the workshops were shut down and the men told to go back to the provinces or join the army.

The workers of Paris took to the barricades. Alphonse Lamartine, the radical poet who headed the government, resigned after handing over to the minister of war, General Louis Cavaignac, who went into action with a ferocity that has sent shock waves across Europe

General Louis Cavaignac (left) crushing the Paris uprising.

and turned the tide of revolution into reaction. In London, the crushing of the radicals has been received with satisfaction by businessmen who had been alarmed at threats made by Lamartine and other ministers to nationalise the railways.

British investors are the biggest shareholders in the railways, but when they complained to Palmerston, the foreign secretary, he told them they must accept the risks of investing in foreign countries.

Austrian emperor flees democratic Vienna

Ferdinand I, the deeply uncharasmatic ex-emperor of Austria.

Vienna, 17 May
Popular pressure for democratic reform has persuaded the Emperor Ferdinand to flee to Innsbruck, having already conceded constituent power to an elected chamber. There has been a fundamental shift of power in European politics.

Metternich's resignation two months ago was followed by the emperor promising a constitution, freedom of the press and the formation of a council of ministers. Encouraged thereto by events in France, Italy and Germany, the imperial government granted Hungary an autonomous constitution, and published its own two weeks later. Eight days ago, all Austria's citizens were given the vote.

Ireland: Tipperary insurrection fails

Tipperary, 29 July
Irish hopes of a nationalist uprising have been dashed with the arrest of a second key figure in the radical Young Ireland movement. Police arrested William Smith O'Brien after a skirmish in a cabbage patch in Tipperary as he and his supporters protested against the sentencing of another Irish Confederation member, the journalist John Michel, to 14 years in prison and transportation for advocating a rent strike. The rebels, who planned to declare an Irish republic, expected more support from the peasantry whose main preoccupation is surviving the famine.

French colonies get the right to vote

St Louis, West Africa
In the Senegalese towns of St Louis and Goree, France's Mulatto people are celebrating. News has just come by ship that the republican government in Paris has given them the vote. From now on they will be returning a representative to the National Assembly, like any *departement* in mainland France.

Since the French Revolution the inhabitants have been *citoyens* in theory. Yet it was not until a few months ago, when the republicans took power in France, that slavery was abolished. Now the people will by law have the same rights as any other Frenchmen.

Revolt in Europe: victory or defeat?

The siege of Vienna in October before Austrian troops crushed the unrest.

Austria: emperor is forced to abdicate

Vienna, 2 December 1848
The Emperor Ferdinand has abdicated in favour of his 18-year-old nephew Franz Josef. The move was engineered by Prince Felix Schwarzenberg, who has become the most powerful man in Austria since the sudden resignation of the Austrian foreign minister and arch-conservative, Prince Metternich.

He is determined to put down the unrest, disorder and anarchy which has surfaced in Austria's imperial territories. The remnants of any radical dissent in this city were therefore ruthlessly stamped out by Prince Alfred Windischgratz, the Austrian military commander, when his troops marched in five weeks ago to end a siege of this city.

Schwarzenberg, a more moderate conservative than Metternich, has since formed a ministry of able men and presented a reconstruction programme to the *Reichstag*, which is still working towards the establishment of a federal, democratic constitution.

Italy: pope flees from the Vatican

Rome, 27 November 1848
Alarmed by the activities of revolutionary clubs and the spreading disorder in Rome, Pope Pius IX has fled to the seaport village of Gaeta, in the kingdom of Naples, where he is brooding on the assassination of Count Pellegrino Rossi, the man whom he chose to form a constitutional government, and having second thoughts about his support for reform in the papal states. A republic has been proclaimed in Rome; *Pio Nono*, as he is known, has appealed to Catholic monarchs to restore him to his temporal power in the eternal city.

Germany: emperor exiles assembly

Prussia, 5 December 1848
The king no longer fears the reformers, radicals and revolutionaries who have dominated the Prussian Assembly since it first met last May against a background of social unrest and the threat of insurrection. During the summer months the assembly was voting reforms right and left, and Frederick William IV did nothing. But when it set out to sack army officers considered to be hostile to democratic aspirations, the king sent the army onto the streets to crush dissent. Then he told the assembly to leave Berlin and meet in the provinces.

France: Bonaparte elected president

Paris, 11 December 1848
The year that opened with the overthrow of the monarchy and the proclamation of a republic is closing with the election of a prince-president who dreams of donning the mantle of his famous uncle and becoming emperor of a Bonapartist France.

During his years of exile, Prince Louis Napoleon gained the reputation of an adventurer and a political buffoon. He staged an abortive *coup* at Strasbourg and another at Boulogne, for which he was sentenced to life imprisonment. Having escaped to England, he returned to France last February and, despite the laws against Bonapartes in politics, was elected to the National Assembly. In the presidential election he was opposed by two left-wingers and a right-wing republican, General Louis Cavaignac. The leftwingers together received fewer than half a million votes. Cavaignac received a million and a half. But Louis Napoleon scooped up five and a half million, from workers and peasants as well as the bourgeoisie and upper-class conservatives, all of whom quite evidently judged him by his name rather than his achievements, which are non-existent.

Prince Louis Napoleon, who dreams of following in his uncle's footsteps.

America's master of macabre dies

Baltimore, USA, 3 October 1849
In an ending that could have come out of one of his own horror stories, the poet and storyteller Edgar Allan Poe died today, aged 40. Four days ago he was found drunk and delirious. He was taken to hospital, but never recovered.

Born in Boston and educated in England, he dropped out of university, rose to the rank of sergeant-major in the US Army, and was expelled from military school for deliberate neglect of duty. Already he had published his first poems.

He quickly gained success with his fantastic and frightening tales, but what money he made went on alcohol and opium. Impoverished and addicted, he attempted suicide last year. Now he has found the peace that he searched for through opium.

Famous composer dies an imbecile

Bergamo, 1848
Bergamo's most famous native composer, Gaetano Donizetti, has died aged only 51, paralysed and an imbecile. His first international success was the opera *L'Elisir d'Amore* in 1832, followed by *Lucia di Lammermoor*, whose virtuoso mad scene caused a sensation at Naples in 1835. In 1843 Paris acclaimed his *Don Pasquale*.

Gaetano Donizetti, who died mad: his late operas were failures.

The Sikhs become part of British India

Artillery shelling the Delhi gate at Multan, the heart of the Sikh revolt.

Amritsar, India, 21 February 1849
The powerful Sikh army has been shattered by the British at Gujerat. Since 1846, when British troops defeated the Sikhs and imposed a treaty on them, British policy has been to maintain the Sikh state as a buffer between Afghanistan and British India.

Complaining of British interference in their affairs, the Sikhs revolted again last year, this time in support of Diwan Mulraj, the governor of Multan, who killed two British officers sent to Multan to instal his rival.

In September a pro-British Sikh force under Sher Singh, sent to confront the rebels, went over to them. Then, on 10 October, the governor general of India, the earl of Dalhousie, declared: "Unwarned by precedent, uninfluenced by example, the Sikh nation has called for war, and on my word, they shall have it with a vengeance."

Command was given to Sir Hugh Gough, as energetic as he is unintelligent. Fortunately for the British soldiers they survived his disastrous generalship at two battles (at Ramnagar and Chillianwalla), and have now won the third at Gujerat.

The Sikh lands are no longer a buffer between Afghanistan and British India. The Sikhs can no longer claim to be the great warriors of India. By the fortunes of war, they are now part of British India.

Libreville, a city for freed French slaves

West Central Africa, 1849
As France takes on the work of suppressing the slave trade in its territories it is building a new city for freed slaves on the Atlantic coast and calling it Libreville.

Inland from Libreville, in the Gabon grasslands, there is anarchy as slave-traders and ivory-traders fight for the vast profits that are available, and firearms foment the ambitions of petty potentates. On the coast, however, protected by the frigates of France's anti-slavery patrol, all is in order, and France hopes that Libreville will soon grow into a major centre for French trade with Central Africa.

Austria opens war against Hungary

Hungary, 3 October 1848
After the euphoria of the spring revolution, Hungary is running into trouble. Beleaguered in the south by Slav armies, it now faces the wrath of the empire, which declared war in the aftermath of the murder of the imperial high commissioner by a Hungarian mob ten days ago.

Hungary's struggle for independence from the Austrians inspired nationalist movements among its neighbours Transylvania, Carinthia and Croatia, who all owe historical allegiance to the crown of St Stephen, but when these movements turned to the newly independent government in Budapest for recognition they were denied. In assemblies at Karlowitz, Blassendorf and Zagreb they proclaimed their autonomy and abolished feudal rights. Their declarations were endorsed by the government in Vienna. Hungary was isolated.

Lajos Kossuth, the Hungarian nationalist who inspired the *diet* in March, took charge of the recruitment of a Hungarian defence force, while across the frontier Josef Jellacic, a Croatian nobleman and general in the Austrian army, was given dictatorial powers by the Zagreb assembly. After its victory against the Italians the imperial government has repealed the March Hungarian independence laws.

Cholera linked to polluted water supply

God's gift of water: a London pump, supervised by "King Cholera".

London, 1849
Only now do we know what causes cholera – and it is not carried on the air. The English doctor John Snow contends that there is an infectious organism in polluted drinking water that carries the illness. Fatality rates are far higher in those areas supplied by water from parts of the Thames most contaminated by human waste.

This was convincingly demonstrated when the handle was removed from the water pump in Broad Street – a particularly cholera-prone corner of the city – and illness and death in the neighbourhood dropped dramatically. Snow argues for killing germs by boiling all drinking water.

Nationalism: the offspring of Empire

The phrase "French Revolution" is so familiar as not to cause a second thought, but in some ways it is a misnomer. "European Revolution" might be nearer the mark. The men of 1789 proclaimed universal principles – liberty, equality, fraternity – which by implication were not be be confined to one country but extended to all. Moreover, after 1792, when revolutionary war broke out, they had opportunity to put this belief into practice.

In November of that year, the Convention pledged "fraternity and aid to all peoples who wish to recover their liberty", a great rallying cry to patriotic movements all over Europe. Not all of them responded with comparable ardour, but in Italy, Belgium, Switzerland, and some German cities, "Sister Republics" were established along revolutionary lines. At first fitfully, then under Napoleon triumphantly, France waged a great war of freedom, acquiring a large continental empire in the process.

The consequence was paradoxical: an empire which was at once liberating and enslaving. France, having promised release from tyranny, herself became the power which subject nations sought to throw off. In Spain, in the Tyrol, in Russia, a new popular patriotism developed to resist this new domination. Thus when France was eventually defeated in 1815, the cause she had once sponsored ironically succeeded: a new nationalism, self-conscious, strident and eager for liberty, was beginning to become a factor in European affairs.

The Vienna settlement of 1815 reinforced nationalism not by acknowledging it but by ignoring it. The victorious powers – Austria, Russia, Germany, Britain – sought to weaken France and to establish a "Concert of Europe" (a new departure in diplomacy) to maintain the pre-1792 boundaries of Europe and to resist all liberal, democratic or nationalist threats. The "New Order", in short, was the "Old Order" of blessed, pre-revolutionary memory. This reactionary nostalgia was understandable but short-sighted.

Christ-like shedding of blood

Nationalism was a novelty: therein lay its threat and its appeal. The idea that political communities should be defined primarily by nation – as opposed to region or religion, city or empire – was new to the 19th century mind. For many, it was a thrilling discovery. Yet what constituted a nation? Shared history? Common language? Cultural convergence? Fear of the foreigner?

An enormous literature – philosophial, philological, poetic, propagandist – was devoted to the question. In truth, there were as many nationalisms as there were nations. Consider the Italian nationalism of Mazzini, shot through with confident liberalism. The nation, he said, was "the totality of citizens speaking the same language, associated together with equal civil and political rights in the common aim of bringing the forces of society ... progressively to greater perfection". Notice the secularism: it is no coincidence that the unification of Italy was won not with the help of the Pope but in spite of him.

Irish nationalism, by contrast, had close links with the Church. Catholicism and patriotism, though not synonymous, were hard to separate, and became increasingly so throughout the century. When Patrick Pearse led the abortive Easter Rising of 1916, he thought of his action as a Christ-like sacrifice, shedding blood for an unredeemed people. The religiosity overstated as it may have been, nonetheless came naturally.

Poland is ruthlessly crushed

German nationalism, was more romantic than religious. The idea of a "folk-nation", of a common language and culture to unify the separate German territories, of a dominant Germanic spirit based on a powerful state, were themes vigorously sounded by writers such as Herder, Fichte and Hegel. There was an economic component too. Friedrich List urged self-sufficiency and strong protective tariffs. The *Zollverein* (customs union), "one of the most important attributes of German nationality", should, he said, extend "over the whole coast from the mouth of the Rhine to the frontier of Poland, including Holland and Denmark". Here seems to be an echo of the Napoleonic era: hidden beneath the language of nationalism were designs essentially imperialistic.

The political agenda of such nationalism was clear: unification of the national territory in the case of Italy and Germany, self-government in the case of Ireland. Elsewhere, however, the picture was obscure. Nationalism in Eastern Europe was complicated by the sheer number of nationalities involved, and by the fact that the three imperial powers in the area – Russia, Austria, Turkey – had their different ways of dealing with subject peoples.

Compare Poland and Hungary, for example. A Polish nationalist revolt in 1863 was ruthlessly crushed by Russia, and a policy of "russification" was thereafter imposed in an attempt to obliterate Polish culture. Magyar nationalism, on the other hand was a sufficiently strong challenge to Austria that it had to be incorporated, not extirpated; the *Ausgleich* of 1867, whereby the Austria-Hungarian empire came into being, recognized that reality. The Ottoman Empire was, of the three, most at risk from nationalism: it was over-extended, backward in organisation, financially straitened, and contained a potentially explosive mixture of Christian and Moslem subjects. Its history in the 19th century was of protracted, apparently unstoppable, dissolution: Greek autonomy was recognized in 1829, independence three years later; Serbian autonomy was recognized in 1830, extended three years later.

Russia's relentless nibbling

Even positive developments had negative consequences. A series of reforms known as the *Tanzimat* between 1839 and 1876 designed to modernize and centralize the empire had the effect, among other things, of strengthening Moslem opposition to the sultan. Russia's defeat in the Crimean War, which might have eased pressure on Turkey, actually increased it by encouraging Western powers to look favourably on nationalist liberation movements in the Balkans.

It was here in the Balkans that the interests of the major European powers came most starkly into conflict in a very complicated fashion with Russia relentlessly nibbling at the territories of a weakened Turkey while the other powers supported one or the other, this nationalist movement and not that, as their individual strategies demanded.

It is paradoxical that the 19th century should have given to the world both the nation-state and a growth of empires. Sometimes indeed one reinforced the other. Witness the elaborate web of great power alliances before 1914. When Kaiser William II of Germany urged Moroccan independence in 1905, he was motivated by no great affection for North African nationalism but by a desire to weaken the *Entente Cordiale* (1904) between France – Germany's diplomatic rival – and Britain. Morocco was under French protection at the time. Much depended on striking the right balance: supporting nationalists in rival empires, crushing them ruthlessly in one's own. In 1914 the balance went disastrously awry. The era ended, as it had begun, with a Great War in which nationalist and imperialist factors – neatly personified by the Serbian nationalist assassin Gavrilo Princip and the imperial Archduke Franz Ferdinand of Austria – were inextricably combined.

The battle of Magenta, 1859, when the French and Italians beat the Austrians.

Funeral of the victims of the March revolution in Germany, 1848, by Menzel.

An army raid on a cafe used by "subversives", Berlin, 1848.

THE KINGS IN THEIR COCK-BOATS.

Europe's rulers tossed on a sea of revolt, a "punch" cartoon of 1848. Louis Philippe of France is already in the water.

An Italian nationalist song-sheet celebrating the uprisings of 1848-9.

The Bavarian Otto I, the first king of Greece, 1832-62.

The death of the Greek patriot leader Markos Botsaris, 1823.

Drawing attention to culture: Italian girl in local dress, 1840s.

The Italian nationalist writer Giuseppe Mazzini, 1805-72.

Hungary, 26 February. The Austrians under Windischgratz defeat the Hungarians at Kapolna.

Austria, 1 March. The Kremsier constitution, drawn up by the Austrian *Reichstag*, provides for a decentralised, federal form of government.

Austria, 4 March. The Austrian prime minister Felix Schwarzenberg promulgates his own constitution, providing for a highly centralised system.

Austria, 7 March. The Austrian Reichstag is dissolved.

Italy, 23 March. The Austrians under Marshal Radetsky crush the army of Charles Albert of Sardinia at Novara.

Italy, 24 March. Charles Albert of Sardinia abdicates in favour of the duke of Savoy, Victor Emmanuel II.

Germany, 27 March. Meeting at Frankfurt, the national assembly adopts a constitution which creates a federal state under an hereditary "Emperor of the Germans".

Germany, 4 April. Frederick William IV of Prussia, who was elected "Emperor of the Germans" on 28 March, rejects the imperial crown.

Hungary, 14 April. After retaking Budapest and defeating the Austrians at Godollo, the Hungarians hold a congress at Debrecen and declare Hungary independent of Austria.

Italy, 25 April. Asked by Pope Pius IX to intervene against the Roman republic, a French expeditionary force lands at Civitavecchia.

Rome, 30 April. The republican patriot and guerrilla leader Giuseppe Garibaldi repulses a French attack on Rome.

Russia, 1 May. The Russians and the Ottomans sign the convention of Balta-Liman, agreeing on joint supervision of the Danubian principalities for seven years.

Germany, 8 May. The Prussians suppress a revolt at Dresden.

New York City, 10 May. At least 20 die in anti-British riots provoked by Irish gangs.

Sicily, 15 May. Neapolitan troops enter Palermo, completing their reconquest of Sicily.

Italy, 25 May. Having subjugated Leghorn, the Austrians enter Florence.

Germany, 26 May. Prussia, Saxony and Hanover accept a draft constitution providing for a union of non-Habsburg Germany under the leadership of Prussia.

France, 26 May. The French National Assembly is dissolved.

Hungary, May. The Emperor Franz Josef appeals to Czar Nicholas for help in putting down the Hungarian insurrection.

Denmark, 5 June. A liberal constitution is introduced.

Germany, 18 June. The German National Assembly, which has moved to Stuttgart, is broken up by government troops.

Rome, 4 July. French troops under the command of General Oudinot occupy the city after a siege.

Germany, 23 July. Rebels in Baden capitulate to the Prussians.

Italy, 28 July. The Austrians restore Leopold, the grand duke of Tuscany, who fled to Gaeta in February.

Egypt, 2 August. Mohammed Ali, ruler of Egypt from 1805 to 1848, dies. Apart from his military successes, he laid the foundations of a modern administrative and educational system and revolutionised the Egyptian economy.

Italy, 6 August. Following the signature of the Vignale armistice by Victor Emmanuel II, the new king of Piedmont, Sardinia, the Austrians and the Piedmontese agree on the peace of Milan.

Hungary, 9 August. The Hungarians are defeated by a Russian army at Temesvar.

Hungary, 13 August. The Hungarian general Arthur von Gorgey surrenders to the Austrians at Vilagos.

China, 22 August. The Portuguese governor of Macao, Amaral, is assassinated because of his anti-Chinese policies.

Italy, 22 August. Venice surrenders to the Austrians.

Austria, 27 August. Austria rejects a Prussian scheme of union.

Baltimore, 7 October. The poet and horror-story writer Edgar Allan Poe dies at the age of 40.

Indian Ocean. French merchants on the island of Reunion, desperate for labour on the sugar estates, found a "free labour emigration scheme". This is a ploy to get slave labour from Zanzibar and East Africa without offending the French or British navies.

USA. Associated Press, a cooperative venture organised to distribute telegraphic news to the daily press, begins operation.

Gold rush prospectors flood California

Dreams of wealth and riches: panning for gold in northern California.

San Francisco, California
The greatest-ever gold rush is under way and this once peaceful sun-blessed state will never be the same again. Thousands of gold-hungry prospectors are flooding into California from all points of the globe following a major find by a Swiss settler, J A Sutter.

Within the US alone more than 80,000 people have headed west, and the nation's unexplored heartland is criss-crossed with trails. More still are sailing here via Cape Horn or crossing the Panama Isthmus. Others are arriving from Australia and China, and the harbour here is a forest of clipper masts as hundreds pour ashore clutching picks and pans and high hopes.

Fortunes are being made – so much so that Congress has agreed to the minting of a gold dollar and a $20 "double eagle". They are being lost, too, in the plethora of gambling houses which have mushroomed, along with saloons and brothels, in San Francisco which has grown from a village to a city of 25,000 in a few months. Traders are making the real fortunes, with apples fetching $5 each, eggs at $10 a dozen and a small whisky selling for a pinch of gold-dust.

Frenchman measures the speed of light

France
A French physicist has claimed this year that light travels at the speed of 186,000 miles – or 300,000 kilometres – a second. The true nature of light – that form of energy that makes visible those objects that produce or reflect it – has long been something of a mystery.

Current opinion seems to be in favour of a wave theory, though there are still those who cling to the notion that this energy consists of particles. Whatever light consists of, we do know that it travels extremely quickly – a flash of lightning is seen much earlier than the accompanying rumble of thunder – just how quickly has now been determined with some accuracy by the experiments of Armand Hyppolyte-Louis Fizeau. He already has another claim to fame: like Doppler, he has also explained the so-called "red shift" in light coming from stars.

Revolutions that came from nowhere

Chopin, pianist and composing genius

Europe
Now it's over, shaken statesmen and briefly triumphant revolutionaries alike are asking how it could have happened. At the start of 1848 Europe seemed stable and secure within the framework of the settlement bequeathed by the Congress of Vienna more than 30 years before. Yet within weeks the established order had been shaken to its foundations, pope and princes were fleeing in fear of their lives and revolutionary regimes were proclaiming liberal constitutions.

Then, as suddenly as it had erupted, the storm began to abate, authority recovered its nerve, and today the revolutionaries are on the run. But the *status quo ante* has not been completely restored. The constitutions that promised universal suffrage, a free press, the right to work and much else have generally been thrown aside, but monarchies are no longer quite so absolute, and the abolition of the feudal system by the revolutionary assemblies is a gain that reactionary forces dare not touch.

The revolutions were made not by the masses but by intellectuals inspired by the ideas of the French Revolution of 1789 and by nationalist aspirations. Their rhetoric terrified rulers haunted by the spectre of Jacobinism, but the fabric of society was not about to be torn apart. Extremists were were soon margin-

Giuseppe Garibaldi, who defended Rome against the besieging French.

The fall of revolutionary Rome: French troops enter the city.

alised and conservatives grasped the reins. In France, the republican constitution survives, but only just. Louis Napoleon is clearly plotting a *coup d'etat*.

In Hungary, the bid for independence from Austria under Lajos Kossuth, has been crushed with the help of Russian troops. In Vienna, the imbecile Emperor Ferdinand has been replaced by his 18-year-old nephew Franz Josef, the democratic *Reichstag* has been dissolved and a new constitution, with a limited franchise, proclaimed. But even this does not satisfy the prime minister, Prince Felix Schwarzenberg, who requires a centralised

state with ministers responsible not to the Reichstag but to the emperor. Austrian power is restored in Lombardy and Venetia, but in Piedmont Victor Emmanuel II remains a constitutional monarch. His kingdom has become the refuge for Italian patriots and liberals.

Elsewhere, political refugees choose England. Louis Philippe was followed by Prince Metternich, who has bought a house at Richmond. Now, Louis Blanc and other socialists have arrived. Lord Palmerston has told Blanc that he can use the state papers in the British Museum for his projected history of the French Revolution.

Paris, 17 October
Frederic Chopin, the great Polish composer who wrote almost exclusively for the piano, died today from consumption. He was 38, and had lived in Paris since first arriving there in 1831. The city took the great pianist, whose father was French, to its heart, and he made many influential friends. He wrote some of his best music while living with the woman novelist George Sand for nine years. Their traumatic break-up two years ago hastened his decline, as did his exhausting trip to Britain last year. He found the English hard to fathom. "What a queer lot," he wrote. "May God have pity on them."

Frederic Chopin, Polish composer.

Russia puts down Hungarian uprising

Budapest, 6 August
A Hungarian uprising was crushed by Russian troops at Temesvar today. The Russians acted on behalf of their ally Austria, which occupies much of Hungary. Responding to the spirit of independence that inflamed much of Europe last year, a lawyer, Lajos Kossuth, demanded a British-style constitution. This failed and he declared unilateral independence on 14 April. The uprising was defeated from within, by dissident Croats who aided Austria, as well as through external force. Kossuth is alive, but seems doomed to spend the rest of his life in exile.

Hokusai, versatile painter of Buddhas, landscapes and animals

Edo, Japan, 10 May
Katsushika Hokusai, who called himself "the old man mad about painting", has died at the age of 89, asking for "yet another decade".

In younger days he used to give public exhibitions of his powers, painting pictures of Buddhas and mythological figures in Zen temples which were over 2,000 square feet in size. His celebrated series, the *Thirty-Six Views of Mount Fuji*, includes the bold "breaking wave" which hangs suspended, frozen in motion, above the distant peak of Mount Fuji.

He wrote: "At the age of 90 I shall have penetrated even further the deeper meaning of things. At 100 I shall be truly marvellous."

"The wave", by Hokusai, a painter who sought "the deeper meaning of things".

Greece, January 1850. Britain orders a blockade of the Greek coast following an attack on Dom Pacifico, a Moorish Jew.

China, 9 March 1850. The Daoguang emperor's fourth son, Yizhu, ascends the throne in succession to his father, who died last month.

France, March 1850. A law – proposed by the liberal Catholic deputy Falloux – is passed extending the influence of the church over education by allowing state funds to be used for the foundation and continuance of church schools.

Italy, 9 April 1850. Giuseppe Siccardi, the minister of justice in Piedmont, Sardinia, introduces a law curbing the powers of the Catholic Church.

USA, 19 April 1850. The USA and Britain sign the Clayton-Bulwer treaty, which pledges both countries to a protective role in Central America and ensures the neutrality of the prospective Panama Isthmus canal.

Germany, April 1850. At Erfurt, an assembly of German states – excluding, among others, Saxony, Hanover, Wurttemberg and Bavaria – accepts the Prussian scheme for German union, which Austria strongly opposes.

Rome, April 1850. Pope Pius IX returns to Rome.

Palestine, 28 May 1850. France reaffirms its right to the Holy Places.

France, 31 May 1850. A new electoral law abolishes universal suffrage.

Germany, May 1850. The Austrian premier Felix Schwarzenberg revives the *diet* of Frankfurt and invites the German states to discuss a revision of the old German Confederation.

Berlin, 2 July 1850. Denmark and Prussia sign a peace treaty by which Prussia agrees to withdraw from Schleswig and Holstein.

USA, 10 July 1850. Millard Fillmore is sworn in as president following the death yesterday of Zachary Taylor.

Persia, 19 July 1850. Sayyid Ali Mohammed – known as the *Bab* (gateway) – the founder of *Babism*, a new Islamic mystical movement, is executed on the orders of *Shah* Nasir al-Din.

China, July 1850. Groups of pseudo-Christian God-Worshippers gather at Jintian, in Guangxi province, to stage a revolt.

Germany, 28 August 1850. Franz Liszt conducts the first performance of *Lohengrin*, an opera by his friend Richard Wagner. Wagner, who took an active part in the Dresden uprising of 1849, has fled fled Germany to escape arrest.

Australia, August 1850. The British parliament passes the Australian Colonies Government Act, giving the colonies self-government.

London, August 1850. At a conference in London, Denmark obtains a guarantee of its territorial integrity from the great European powers and from Sweden.

USA, 9 September 1850. California becomes the 31st state in the union.

Germany, September 1850. A revolt in Hesse-Cassel, supported by the Prussians, is opposed by the Austrians, bringing Prussia and Austria to the brink of war.

Italy, 11 October 1850. On the request of Victor Emmanuel II, Massimo d'Azeglio forms a government in Piedmont. Count Camillo Cavour is appointed minister of agriculture.

China, 22 November 1850. Lin Zexu, who was appointed imperial commissioner last month by the Qing court to deal with the God-Worshippers, dies.

Germany, 29 November 1850. By the convention of Olmutz, imposed by Austria, Prussia agrees to abandon the Erfurt Union and acknowledge Austrian superiority within the German Confederation.

West Africa, 1850. Denmark sells off its Gold Coast (*Ghana*) possessions to Britain and withdraws from African colonisation.

Britain, 1850. The pope decides to divide England into Roman Catholic dioceses and restore a regular Catholic hierarchy in the country.

Britain, 1850. Proposed by William Ewart, an act is passed authorising the establishment of public libraries.

Paris, 1850. Gustave Courbet attracts attention with his *The Stone Breakers* and *The Burial at Ornans* at the Paris Salon and sets himself up as the leader of the Realist school of painting.

USA, 1850. Nathaniel Hawthorne, known for his tales of Puritan life, publishes *The Scarlet Letter*, a novel of adultery set in 17th-century Boston. It is an instant bestseller.

Britain, 1851. The great English painter J M W Turner dies.

Rail revolution is transforming the world

Europe and North America, 1850

The spread of railways promises an economic and social revolution. In Britain, where the phenomenon began, an express train can travel the 175 miles from London to Exeter in less than seven hours – three times as quickly as a stagecoach, and at less cost.

Although a Jesuit missionary in Beijing built the first self-propelled steam vehicle at the end of the 17th century, it was the Stockton and Darlington Railway of 1825 which got British railways started. The Liverpool and Manchester in 1830 was followed in 1836 by the London and Greenwich, the first passenger service to London. By the time of the Great Western Railway in 1841, linking London and Bristol, there were more than 1,300 miles of track in Britain.

In continental Europe state planning made progress slower. By 1841, when the first international line, from Strasbourg to Basle, was completed, France had 350 miles of railway. In Austria and Germany the first steam railways began operating 15 years ago. Russia will be transformed by the 404-mile Moscow to St Petersburg link, now being built.

In the United States the Baltimore and Ohio Railroad in 1830 was the inspiration. By 1840 there were 2,800 miles of track. Here and in Canada the railroad is the means of opening up new territory.

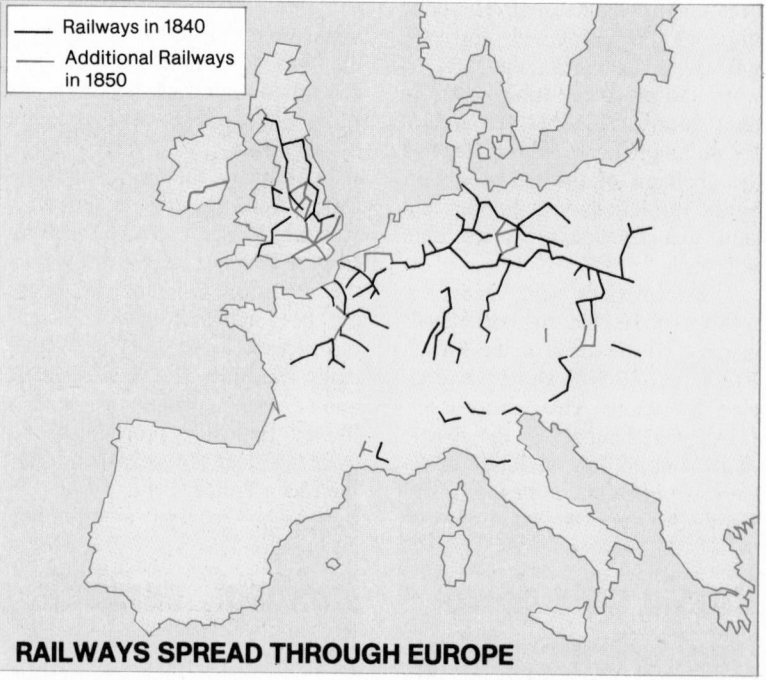

RAILWAYS SPREAD THROUGH EUROPE

Legend:
— Railways in 1840
— Additional Railways in 1850

Britain blockades Greece for dubious debt

Greece, 1850

As relations with France collapse, and an impotent but ostensibly independent Greek government is forced to look on, British ships are blockading the coast of Greece today. Yet this was no major international incident, rather a case of grossly inflated nationalism.

A Portuguese money-lender, one Dom Pacifico, had his house pillaged during a riot in Athens. Born in Gibraltar, he claims British citizenship and has demanded massive compensation from Greece and called on Britain to back his claim. The prime minister, Palmerston, already infuriated by Greece's failure to pay outstanding debts to far more credible British citizens, ordered the blockade. Although Russia and France are Britain's co-guarantors of Greek independence, he neglected to consult them.

Now Palmerston faces hostility at home and abroad. The opposition have capitalised on his blunder, while France, with whom he has reluctantly negotiated, has withdrawn its ambassador.

More colonies key to ending slavery

London, 1850
Ending the slave trade is proving to be more difficult than the philanthropic lobby in London had realised: no sooner has it been stopped in one place than it starts up again in another place.

The establishment of a separate administration for the Gold Coast, and the purchase from Denmark of her forts on the coast, was supposed to have effectively stopped the trade in the area. So it has. Instead the trade has increased in nearby Dahomey and Lagos, which are independent states. Indeed, the recent civil wars amongst the Yoruba has increased the supply of slaves. The only answer of the well-intentioned philanthropic gentlemen in London is to call for yet further colonial expansion.

Everything linked by new theory

Glasgow, Scotland, 1850
All theories dealing with matter and energy can be united into one theory of everything, according to William Thompson, Glasgow university's professor of physics. Thomson, who regards all forms of energy as interrelated, has formulated a second law governing the movement of heat – thermodynamics. At its simplest this states that heat cannot of itself pass from a cold body to a warm one; in other words the direction of naturally occurring processes is irreversible.

College is founded for women in London

London, 1849
With the opening this year of Queen's College, women finally have the opportunity of a university education. John Maurice, the principal, is for the first time training women to teach girls mathematics, classics and sport.

The well-known academic and Christian socialist shares his views on educational equality with Mrs E J Reid who has decided to open her house in Bedford Square for lectures to women. Two star students at Queen's are Frances Buss, who combines her studies with teaching at her mother's school, the North London Collegiate, and Dorothea Beale, who hopes to become head of Cheltenham Ladies College.

Funding for the new college came from the combined efforts of The Governesses' Benevolent Association and Miss Murray, one of Queen Victoria's maids of honour. They began raising money two years ago after the Taunton commission had criticised the education of girls as dreary and superficial.

Two literary giants close their books

London and Paris, 1850
Two great writers disappeared from the European literary scene this year. In England, William Wordsworth, the poet laureate, died aged 80. As a young man he was a revolutionary in politics and literature, throwing over artifice for simplicity.

In middle age his work deteriorated sadly, but his early poems, to daffodils, the rainbow, a daisy, cuckoo, skylark or the sleeping city of London, contain great passages and lines familiar to many.

In Paris, Honore de Balzac, who attempted to paint a complete picture of French society in his novel sequence *La Comedie Humaine*, died aged 51. His formidable energy turned out 85 novels in 20 years, inventing 2,000 characters.

Wordsworth, romantic reactionary.

Australians join in great rush for gold

Australian gold miners, the first finds were kept secret by the government.

Sydney, May 1851
A California-style gold rush has started in Australia after the discovery of the metal in New South Wales.

The town of Bathurst is besieged by treasure hunters with tools for digging and panning. The most gullible come with just a hoe, believing that two days' work in the Blue Mountains goldfields will make them rich for life.

The man who started the rush is Edward Hargraves, a veteran of the gold fever in California two years ago. He says the first clue was a similarity to the California terrain in the geological structure of the land around Summer Hill Creek. He said: "I took a panful of earth which I washed in the water hole. The first trial produced a small piece of gold. "Here it is," I exclaimed. Then I washed five panfuls in succession, obtaining gold from all but one."

Using the most basic of equipment, some prospectors are earning as much as £8 a day in the goldfields, and the government is considering the introduction of a strict licensing system.

Austria and Prussia avoid going to war

Olmutz, 29 November 1850
Prince Felix Schwarzenberg has won a major diplomatic victory for Austria here in the negotiations with the Prussians. Earlier this month both powers sent troops into Hesse and it appeared that a full-scale war was imminent. There was a strong lobby in Prussia which wanted to fight, but King Frederick William IV has opted for caution.

He decided that territorial gains in Hesse were not worth fighting for because of the danger of shattering the traditional conservative alliance of Austria and Prussia against liberal forces.

The Vulture, from "Birds" of America, by the American painter-naturalist, John James Audubon, who died in 1851.

China, January 1851. Hong Xiuquan, the leader of the God-worshippers, plans to declare himself heavenly king and set up a "heavenly kingdom of great peace" in Guangxi province.

Britain, February 1851. Lord John Russell, the prime minister, introduces an Ecclesiastical Titles Bill to curb attempts to restore a Catholic hierarchy in Britain.

Germany, March 1851. At a conference of German states in Dresden, it is decided to re-establish the German Confederation in its original form.

Spain, 16 March 1851. Spain signs a concordat with Pope Pius IX recognising the Catholic religion as the sole authorised faith and giving the church wide control over education and censorship.

Vietnam, 21 March 1851. Christian priests are put to death by the Emperor Tu Duc.

Britain, 6 April 1851. The Anglican prelate Henry Manning is converted to Roman Catholicism.

London, 1 May 1851. The Great Exhibition opens.

Portugal, 15 May 1851. On his return from England, where he went into exile in 1847, John Saldanha founds a monarchist party with the support of the middle classes.

Argentina, 25 May 1851. Jose Justo de Urquiza leads a rebellion against the authoritarian policies of his former ally, the absolute ruler Juan Manuel de Rosas.

Denmark, 5 June 1851. Frederick VII of Denmark, who has no heir, agrees with the Russian Czar Nicholas that he will choose a successor from a family which is loyal to Denmark and not suspected of having Prussian sympathies, namely the Sonderburg-Glucksburgs.

Uruguay, June 1851. Manuel Oribe, the leader of the *blanco* faction in Uruguay, which is supported by Rosas of Argentina, is forced to abandon an eight-year siege of Montevideo.

Australia, 1 July 1851. Victoria is separated from New South Wales and becomes a distinct colony.

Britain, 22 August 1851. A US yacht, *America*, wins a 60-mile race round the Isle of Wight to capture the Royal Yacht Squadron cup. The prize is dubbed the America's Cup.

Cuba, 1 September 1851. The Venezuelan-born Narciso Lopez is garrotted for leading an invasion force into Cuba with the aim of overthrowing the Spanish. Fifty others, mostly Americans, have also been executed for the revolt.

Germany, 7 September 1851. Prussia scores a diplomatic success by persuading Hanover, a city which has until now been a supporter of Austria, to become a member of the customs union.

China, 11 September 1851. The *Taipings* break out of the Qing military blockade and begin their march northwards into central China.

Ottoman Empire, October 1851. Czar Nicholas insists that Greek Orthodox monks must be allowed to maintain authority over the Holy Places in Palestine, bringing Russia into conflict with France over protection of the region.

France, 2 December 1851. Louis Napoleon Bonaparte, the president, overthrows the legislative assembly in a *coup d'etat* and dissolves the constitution.

France, 14 December 1851. In a plebiscite, French voters endorse Louis Napoleon's right to draw up a new constitution.

Britain, 19 December 1851. Lord Palmerston is dismissed as foreign secretary for recognising, without consulting his colleagues, the overthrow of the French republic by Louis Napoleon.

Austria, 31 December 1851. The abolition of the 1849 Austrian constitution leads to increased centralisation of imperial power.

USA, 1851. The painter John James Audubon – acclaimed for his dramatic pictures of birds and other wildlife – dies.

USA, 1851. A Young Men's Christian Association is founded for the first time in the United States in Cleveland, Ohio.

USA, 1851. The ex-whaler Hermann Melville publishes *Moby Dick*, a novel about a prolonged and obsessive hunt for a deadly great white whale.

Italy, 1851. Giuseppe Verdi's opera *Rigoletto* is performed for the first time.

Britain, 1851. William Newton and William Allen found the Amalgamated Society of Engineers. It soon has 11,000 members in Lancashire and the London area.

Britain, 1851. The critic and art theorist John Ruskin, a champion of the Pre-Raphaelites, publishes *The Stones of Venice*, in which he advocates a revival of the Gothic style.

Britain, 1852. William Holman Hunt, who co-founded the Pre-Raphaelite Brotherhood in 1848, paints *The Light of the World*.

London, 1852. Isambard Kingdom Brunel engineers Paddington railway station.

Bonaparte coup supported by plebiscite

Prince Louis Napoleon rides through Paris after his popular coup d'etat.

Paris, 19 December 1851

A huge majority of the people of France have endorsed by plebiscite the new constitution introduced by Louis Napoleon after his coup of 2 December. Leading republicans have been arrested.

Once elected president of the Second Republic in 1848 – after years of exile and failed attempts to claim the throne – Louis Napoleon was on a collision course with the assembly, with which he was obliged to share power. The constitution only granted the president a four-year term.

Although Louis approved conservative measures, including a limit on the franchise, to appease the majority in the assembly, he longed to put his own vision into practice. Last year he delivered a speech to the assembly outlining schemes for building railways, road, harbours and canals, for introducing agricultural machinery, establishing model farms, improving cultivation, cattlebreeding, sanitation, drains and street widening. He also proposed reintroducing universal suffrage.

Thwarted by the assembly, Louis appeared as the people's champion. Brief fighting in Paris and other cities was the only resistance to his assumption of power.

Slavery issue divides American states

New York, 1851

Bitter divisions over slavery surfaced again at the annual convention of the Anti-Slavery Society. At the heart of the debate was whether the United States should split in two with the pro-slavery southern states allowed to go their own way. Opposing this view, the Negro leader Frederick Douglass declared that the US constitition implied the eventual ending of slavery, and called for political action to end slavery in all states. Until now an uneasy peace has prevailed between northern and southern states. A series of bills last year covering slavery and other laws in new states such as California represented a temporary compromise.

THE LAND OF LIBERTY.

American hypocriscy, by "Punch".

Britain stars in "great exhibition"

London, 1 May 1851

Millions of visitors, including many from overseas, are expected to flock to the world's largest exhibition, which was opened today by Queen Victoria in London's Hyde Park.

Staged inside a giant iron and glass conservatory which has been dubbed the Crystal Palace, the Great Exhibition of the Works of Industry of all Nations is designed to pay tribute to the industrial advances that have given Britain unprecedented prosperity and economic mastery in the first half of this century.

The 13,000 exhibits from around the world are housed inside an 1,848-foot long, 408-foot-wide and 66-foot high glasshouse with 108-foot-high transepts. Designed by Joseph Paxton, the building won the Great Exhibition design competition against 254 international entries. It is an immensely magnified version of the Lily House at the duke of Devonshire's Chatsworth House, where Paxton was head gardener. The prefabricated structure took 17 weeks to erect and used a million feet of glass. The main focus of attention is the Machinery Court showing Jacquard looms, De La Rue's envelope machine and a pioneer reaping machine from America. The queen showed interest in the medalmaking machine and the electric telegraph, using the latter to send messages to Edinburgh and Manchester.

The Great Exhibition, at the Crystal Palace, Hyde Park; the world's largest exhibition, it has gathered together the "Works of Industry of all Nations".

Promises of heaven by teacher stir up rebellion in China

China, 25 September 1851

The followers of Hong Xiuquan, meeting in great numbers in the mountain town of Jintian, today announced that he had been chosen by God to be the heavenly king of their movement, the *Taiping tien-kuo* or heavenly kingdom of great peace.

Hong is a schoolteacher-mystic who, influenced by Protestant Christian tracts, believes himself to be the younger brother of Jesus Christ. Passionately dedicated to his beliefs, he has found zealous disciples among disaffected people in China. He appeals to all types, poor miners and charcoal burners, landlords and scholars, deserters from the increasingly corrupt army and peasants ruined by the inefficiency and greed of the Manchus.

The Taipings, as they call themselves, proclaim that "our heavenly king has received the Divine commission to exterminate the Manchus, to exterminate all idolaters generally, and to possess the the empire as its true sovereign".

Converts are flocking to join the Taipings who are now some 10,000 strong. Their discipline and dedication makes them a formidable enemy for the Manchu army, weakened as it is by opium smoking. They look for nothing less than a heavenly kingdom on earth.

Giuseppe Verdi, whose opera "Rigoletto" premiered in 1851.

Population soars in European countries

Europe, 1852

Figures released over the last two years show that populations in Europe have soared, despite emigration to the United States; the figures below are in millions.

Country	c.1800	c.1850
Austria	14.0	17.5
Britain	15.7	27.4
France	27.4	35.8
Germany	23.0	33.4
Hungary	5.0	13.2
Italy	17.2	24.4
Russia	40.0	68.5
Spain	10.5	15.5

Americans invent machines for sewing

USA, 1851

Spinning and weaving have been mechanised. Now it is the turn of sewing. Three American inventors have come up with a machine for sewing. Elias Howe from Boston has developed a machine that will sew seven times faster than by hand. Simultaneously Walter Hunt of New York and Isaac Merritt Singer, a mechanic from Pittsburgh, have been working on their own versions. Of them all, that of Singer is proving the most successful. This machine powered by a treadle, produces a lock stitch. A toothed wheel moves on the fabric between stitches, with a small foot-like presser holding it down.

Singer making final adjustments to his newly-invented sewing machine.

The Great Exhibition: Peak of British power?

The coincidence of the 1851 Great Exhibition with the half-century stimulated a national and international stocktaking. Polemicists of every disposition, sanguine and sceptical, reviewed past progress and speculated on future performance. In a speech at the Mansion House in London in 1851, Albert the Prince Consort declared: "We are living at a period of most wonderful transition, which tends rapidly to accomplish that great end to which indeed all history points – the realisation of the unity of mankind."

A few weeks later on 1 May his wife, Queen Victoria, officially opened a "Great Exhibition of the Works and Industry of all Nations" in Hyde Park designed to illustrate and exemplify just those sentiments. As the Edinburgh Review put it, the Exhibition's aim was to: "seize the living scroll of human progress, inscribed with every successive conquest of man's intellect". During the months that followed an estimated 6,000,000 people flocked to the newly-built Crystal Palace housing the Exhibition, representing no less than 17 per cent of the country's total population, many coming to London for the first time on the new railways. In box-office terms, the whole affair was a huge success.

The Great Exhibition arose from the feeling that Britain, which had led the way in industrialisation and, through free trade, became the "workshop of the world", needed a chance to show the world its products and inventions and to rank them alongside foreign competitors. There was also a political purpose in staging such an event. Britain, unlike Europe, was peaceful. A mighty fair dedicated to ingenuity and prosperity would tellingly underline this point, and show how the world's first industrial society, with over half the population living in towns of more than 2,500 people, was faring by not being hindered by internal strife or the necessity of diverting its energies into massive military spending.

Years ahead of its time

The Crystal Palace itself – re-erected after the Exhibition at Sydenham in South London where it was destroyed by fire in 1936 – was a remarkable structure. Designed in only 10 days by Joseph Paxton, a former chief gardener for the duke of Devonshire turned businessman, as the result of a casual conversation with his MP, it was, appropriately, a gigantic greenhouse nearly 2000 feet long and over 400 feet wide. Structurally it was years ahead of its time, using acres of glass for wall and roofing panels and a cast-iron skeleton, which was perfect for large scale prefabrication. Visually it created a futuristic panorama of glass enclosing some of the trees of the park as well as accommodating 25,000 visitors at a time.

The exhibition catalogue runs to hundreds of closely printed pages describing everything from telescopes to steel furnaces; pottery to firearms. The famous steam hammer invented by James Nasmyth in 1840 was on view, as were locomotives, sewing machines, musical instruments, kitchen appliances, photographic equipment and the rest. But it was in the metal industries perhaps that most important inventions were being introduced. Bessemer's new process for making steel patented in the year of the Exhibition, was represented along with the new screw gauges of Joseph Whitworth which helped not only to standardise the tool industry in Britain but also to unify engineering practices worldwide. On display too were precision made machine tools such as lathes, drills and saws, so necessary for the accurate mass-production of thousands and millions of identical items.

Britain sweeps the board

There were also products from abroad, including some pioneering gold prospector trays from the Californian fields and Colt's celebrated revolver. Alongside Wedgwood's fine pottery stood items from Sevres and Etruria. The printed fabrics from Manchester were complemented by exquisite black lace from Barcelona. These technological and industrial advances were judged by international juries, and great was the patriotic fervour generated by Britain sweeping the board with first prizes. Britain's creativity and resourcefulness was, apparently, unchallenged.

But, in reality, the upsurge of technological accomplishment had already peaked and was even on the downturn. Sixteen years later at the Paris Exhibition, Britain picked up no more than a handful of prizes. The euphoria of 1851 turned to shock, and one belief that emerged was that Britain was slipping behind because of the way it was educating its people for a working life in the technological age.

Indeed even before the Great Exhibition the *Economist* had warned that "the superiority of the United States to Britain is ultimately as certain as the next eclipse". For several decades after the Great Exhibition, however, the mood of buoyant self-confidence was sustained. The historian David Thomas describes the Exhibition as a kind of threshold to "the Golden Age of Victorianism", a period of prosperity for those who rated "industriousness, business efficiency and private enterprise as major virtues."

In absolute terms however, there was no economic decline looming for Britain either imminently or in the long term. The issue was whether Britain's relative economic growth was beginning to be overtaken by others, notably by the USA and Germany.

Underside of Victorian virtues

That some challenge would develop was inevitable as other nations became industrial and systematically exploited their mineral resources and reserves of manpower in larger domestic markets. Britain also perhaps suffered handicap from its early start, as the labour force was better organised to resist new patterns of work, existing technologies had to be preserved, and traditional markets preferred. It is also true that Britain's very success in maintaining political, economic and social stability tended to confirm conservative attitudes. But it would be wrong to assume that in the mid- or even late 19th century the eclipse of Britain's economic supremacy was plainly evident and that entrepreneurial failure was starkly exposed. Both wages and productivity in Britain were higher than in Germany, a reflection of the wider distribution of skills in its population.

The British economy was diversifying still; in shipping, in financial services, in the retail sector, and in emerging industries such as chemicals, transport and food-processing, there was impressive evidence of continued dynamism and innovation in Britain. In short it is hard to sustain the case that, before the 1914-18 war ushered in a changed international economic environment, British industrial supremacy was irretrievably broken.

But what is undeniably true is that there was a reverse side to the self-satisfied Victorian public face of virtue rewarded. There were also the poor of the great cities, whose everyday privations and miseries were minutely scrutinised by Henry Mayhew in *London Labour and the London Poor* (1851). This was the London of Dickens, whose Bleak House began to appear in instalments in 1852, in which grimy smoke and lowering fog curled round gaslamps on damp street corners. A rapidly increasing population, teeming in slum dwellings and carousing in seedy taverns, lay on the dark side of the glittering Great Exhibition.

The 1851 Great Exhibition: the biggest exhibit is the Crystal Palace.

The interior of the Crystal Palace, where 100,000 objects are displayed.

Henry Bessemer, man of steel.

Cyrus McCormick's reaping machine, exhibited at the Great Exhibition.

Prince Albert, patron of science.

Gobelins tapestries and Sevres porcelain at the Great Exhibition.

Britain's industrial might, displayed at the 1851 Great Exhibition.

1852

France, 14 January. A new constitution, providing for a senate, council of state and legislative assembly, is adopted.

South Africa, 17 January. At the Sand River convention, the British recognise the independence of the Transvaal Boers.

France, 22 January. Louis Napoleon issues a decree banning the Orleans family from France.

Argentina, 3 February. In alliance with Uruguay and Brazil, Justo de Urquiza defeats the dictator Juan Manuel de Rosas at the battle of Caseros.

France, 17 February. Press censorship is introduced.

Britain, 27 February. Lord Derby forms a Conservative minority government following the resignation of Lord John Russell, Whig premier since July 1846.

China, 28 April. Having broken the siege of Yongan, the rebel God-Worshippers known as the Taipings arrive at Guilin, the capital of Guangxi province.

Italy, 6 May. Leopold II, the grand duke of Tuscany, abolishes the Tuscan constitution.

London, 8 May. Britain, France, Russia, Austria, Prussia and Sweden sign a protocol confirming the agreement signed in Warsaw in 1851 between Denmark and Czar Nicholas guaranteeing the integrity of Denmark. Prince Christian von Glucksburg is to be the next king of Denmark.

China, 10 June. Feng Yunshan – the close friend, principal lieutenant and first convert of Hong Xiuquan, the leader of the God-Worshippers – is killed in battle at the age of 30.

France, July. The poet and novelist Theophile Gautier publishes a collection of poems entitled *Emaux et Camees*.

Channel Islands, August. Choosing to go into exile following Louis Napoleon's *coup*, the French writer Victor Hugo settles in Jersey.

Britain, 14 September. Arthur Wellesley, the duke of Wellington, the great soldier and statesman, dies.

France, 24 September. Henri Giffard makes the first flight in his newly invented steam-driven balloon.

USA, 2 November. The Democrat Franklin Pierce wins a landslide victory in the presidential election, defeating the Whig candidate, General Winfield Scott.

Italy, 4 November. Count Camillo Cavour becomes prime minister of Piedmont.

China, 12 November. Zhang Luoxing, the leader of a group of Nian bandits in northern China, starts an uprising in Bozhou.

France, 2 December. Louis Napoleon is proclaimed emperor as Napoleon III.

France, 9 December. The poet Charles Leconte de Lisle publishes his *Poemes Antiques*.

Britain, 29 December. Lord Aberdeen, the former foreign secretary, forms a Peelite-Whig coalition government. Aberdeen resigned with Peel over the Corn Laws in 1846 and succeeded him as leader of the Peelites.

Burma, December. Britain annexes the kingdom of Pegu in southern Burma, ending the second Anglo-Burmese war, which broke out in April.

New Zealand. A new constitution is promulgated, providing for the division of the country into six provinces, each to be governed by a superintendent and an elected district council.

Angola. Swahili traders from Zanzibar reach Benguela, having crossed the African continent.

USA. Henry Wells and William G Fargo, the founders of the American Express Company, which serves the eastern USA, establish a new company to provide a mail service in the western half of the country.

France. The physicist Leon Foucault invents the gyroscope, which, whatever its position, continues to move in the same direction. Foucault has also determined the speed of light and proved that by means of a freely suspended pendulum that the earth rotates.

France. The philosopher and sociologist Auguste Comte publishes his *Catechisme positiviste*.

France. Two new banks, the Credit Foncier and the Credit Mobilier, are founded.

Russia. The writer Ivan Turgenev publishes his *Sportsman's Sketches*, impressions of peasant life, which is interpreted by the government as an attack on serfdom.

Russia. The novelist and playwright Nikolai Gogol dies. He will be best remembered for his comic drama *The Inspector-General* and the novel *Dead Souls*.

Britain. Alfred Tennyson writes an *Ode on the Death of the Duke of Wellington*.

Britain. Karl Marx, the Hegelian philosopher publishes *The 18th Brumaire of Louis Napoleon Bonaparte*.

Wellington, England's soldier-statesman

Wellington's funeral car, epitomising the pomp he said he despised.

London, 14 September

The duke of Wellington, the victor of Waterloo and a former prime minister of Britain, died today, aged 83. He will be given a state funeral. For almost half a century "the Iron Duke" personified strength of will and public spirit. Although a rather delicate boy, whose greatest love was playing the violin, Arthur Wellesley, the third son of an Irish peer, became a disciplinarian who transformed the British army from, in his words, "the scum of the earth" into "worthy fellows". He served in India and distinguished himself in Spain before vanquishing Napoleon at Waterloo.

His new career in politics after Waterloo suffered from his trenchant opposition to electoral reform but it was impossible to form a Tory government without him. In 1848 he came out of retirement to organise a military force against the Chartists. In later life, his advice was still sought. The problem of birds fouling the Crystal Palace stumped all except him. "Sparrow hawks, Ma'am," he said to the queen. He was right – as usual.

After years working in the railway engine workshops at the Gare de l'Ouest, in Paris, Henri Giffard, an impoverished railway mechanic, makes the first flight over Paris in a balloon, watched by tens of thousands. The balloon is powered by a simple steam engine 18 feet (six metres) below the balloon. A triangular sails acts as a rudder. In spite of adverse and changing winds, Giffard is able to steer the machine with relative ease. Giffard is acclaimed by Paris and urged to build another. But the poor mechanic has been almost ruined by the cost of his invention, and claims that he has no hope of building again another such flying machine.

A Bonaparte is back on French throne

Paris, 2 December

A Bonaparte is once again emperor of France. With a flourish of glory reminiscent of his famous uncle, Louis Napoleon today elevated himself from president to emperor, restoring the house of Bonaparte after a 38-year interval.

The bachelor emperor, who styles himself Napoleon III on the grounds that Napoleon I had abdicated in favour of his son, now has to guarantee the hereditary succession that he persuaded Frenchmen to approve by an overwhelming majority in a referendum two weeks ago. The favourite to become the empress is Eugenie de Montijo, the daughter of a Spanish aristocrat who fought with the French.

The 44-year-old emperor is still largely an unknown quantity in the country which has just elected him. Since his return from exile four years ago he has out-manoeuvred his opponents, jailing thousands

Napoleon III, emulating his uncle.

while at the same time gaining massive popular support with his programme of tax and welfare reforms to benefit the French working man. Foreign anxieties about the return of a Bonaparte have been eased by his Bordeaux declaration that "the empire means peace".

"Uncle Tom's Cabin" rocks US slave trade

The book that moved a nation.

New York City

A small and simple book by a novice writer is stirring the conscience of America more than a thousand speeches by a thousand anti-slavery politicians. The book is called *Uncle Tom's Cabin, or, Life Among the Lowly*, and it is written by 39-year-old Harriet Beecher Stowe of Maine.

It is the story of a devoutly religious black slave who selflessly rescues a white child – but then finds himself sold to a sadistic master, Simon Legree, who is so unhinged by Tom's goodness that he has him flogged to death.

Uncle Tom first appeared as a serial in the *National Era* magazine, and has sold 300,000 copies as a book. The pro-slavery lobby has been forced to issue a reply, a collection of essays *In Defence of Slavery*.

Bon Marche, a French retailing revolution

Paris

The Bon Marche, a small shop in Paris, in recent years has greatly expanded the amount of goods it carries and looks set to change radically the way that Parisians do their shopping. The store's founder,

Aristide Boucicaut, has swept aside old restrictive practices and given shoppers wide choice under one roof, low and fixed prices, and the right to return goods. Staff have been encouraged by receiving commission on sales.

Row splits churches in Jesus' birthplace

Palestine, December

A dispute over the holy shrines of Bethlehem has brought Russia and France to the brink of war. Czar Nicholas has refused to recognise the Emperor Napoleon III's claim to have the right to protect Roman Catholics there, and has mobilised troops on the Danube and put the fleet at Sevastopol on stand-by.

For 100 years the Greek Orthodox Church, with Russian support, has argued its right to protect Christian shrines in Palestine. Now Napoleon, fresh from his success in restoring the pope to Rome, has pressured the Ottomans to recognise French rights over the Catholics in the area, and the French hold the key to the manger.

Russian satirist joins dead souls

Moscow

Nikolai Vasilievich Gogol, one of Russia's most popular novelist, dramatists and satirists, has died. A former civil servant and history lecturer, his *Inspector-General*, a satire on the corruption, vanity and ignorance of Russia's civil servants, came out in 1836, and his best-selling *Dead Souls*, a comedy on a small landowners attempts to gain compensation payments through the purchase of dead serfs, appeared the next year.

Like most of Russia's intelligensia, he left the country as soon as he could afford to, living in Rome from 1836 to 1846, before returning to Moscow as the grand old man of Russian literature.

Newspaper man is ruler of Piedmont

Count Cavour, the liberal statesman.

Turin, 4 November

Count Camillo Cavour, aged 42, is the new prime minister of Piedmont. He has widespread support from the anti-clerical left wing in parliament. At the same time because of his aristocratic connections and his diplomatic skills, he commands the respect of the conservatives. Political commentators here think that he is the ideal man to resolve the rumbling differences between King Victor Emmanuel and the parliament.

Cavour is a liberal by conviction. Because of that he abandoned his army career and visited Britain to study scientific farming and the parliamentary system. In 1847 he founded *Il Risorgimento,*, a newspaper which became a fierce advocate of a liberal but monarchical Italy. He entered politics two years later, and rapidly rose to cabinet rank.

Babis persecuted throughout Persia

Tehran, 15 September

A wave of persecution has broken on Shi'ite Islam's newest sect, the Babis, since four Babis failed to assassinate Shah Nasir al-Din as he went hunting a month ago. Today has been the bloodiest of all, with 28 senior Babi holy men killed, each assigned to a different class in the population, so that all Persia would have blood on their hands. Their fortitude in death probably

won more converts than ten years of proselytizing. The movement, which condemns Persia's political and religious establishments as corrupt, first appeared 50 years ago, but grew rapidly after 1842 when a 24-year-old Seyyid Ali Mohammed, proclaimed himself *Bab*, Gate to God. He was imprisoned in 1847 and executed in 1850, the movement still grows, mounting revolts in 1847, 1850 and this year.

Rome, 19 January. Giuseppe Verdi's opera *Il Trovatore* is performed for the first time.

France, 30 January. Napoleon III marries Eugenie Maria de Montijo, a Spanish countess.

Italy, 6 February. An uprising inspired by Giuseppe Mazzini in Milan, which is under the rule of the Austrian military dictator, Radetsky, ends in failure.

Germany, 19 February. Austria and Prussia sign a 12-year commercial treaty.

Russia, February. Russia proposes to Britain that the two countries share out what remains of the Ottoman empire.

Istanbul, February. Czar Nicholas sends his envoy, Alexander Menshikov, to Istanbul to secure concessions from the Ottomans in the matter of the Holy Places and conclude a treaty recognising a Russian protectorate over Orthodox churches in the Ottoman empire.

Balkans, 3 March. Having been forced to withdraw from Montenegro, which they invaded last year, the Ottomans sign a peace treaty with Prince Danilo of Montenegro. Danilo, who came to power last year on the death of his uncle, Prince-bishop Peter II, has embarked on a campaign to secularise the Montenegrin government.

China, 19 March. *Taiping* forces capture the large city of Nanjing on the lower Yangzi river.

Germany, 4 April. The customs union signed by the various German states is extended for a further 12 years. Austria remains excluded.

Netherlands, 20 April. The decision to introduce a Catholic hierarchy in the Calvinist Netherlands brings about the downfall of the liberal prime minister, Johann Rudolph Thorbeke.

China, May. Taiping forces launch an abortive expedition to capture the Qing capital of Beijing.

Istanbul, May. The Russian ambassador Menshikov returns home after failing to reach a settlement with the Ottomans on the issue of the Holy Places.

Mediterranean, June. After the failure of further diplomatic initiatives, fleets from France and Britain – which oppose Russia's position in the dispute over the Holy Places – assemble at Besika Bay off the Dardanelles.

Balkans, 2 July. Czar Nicholas sends his troops to invade the Danubian principalities of Moldavia and Wallachia.

Connecticut, 4 July. In a protest at the requirement that women cover their legs, Amelia Jenks Bloomer, an advocate of women's rights, gives a speech wearing a pair of Turkish-style pantaloons under a short skirt.

Japan, July. A US squadron under Commodore Matthew Perry arrives off Edo (*Tokyo*) and demands that Japan opens up for trade with the outside world.

Japan, 8 August. A Russian expedition under Putyatin arrives in Nagasaki harbour seeking to open trade relations with Japan.

China, 7 September. The "Small Sword" society, led by Liu Lichuan, occupies Shanghai.

Mediterranean, 23 September. The British fleet is ordered to Istanbul.

Ottoman Empire, 4 October. Following Russia's refusal to withdraw from the Danubian principalities, the Ottomans declares war on Russia.

Balkans, 23 October. Led by Omar Pasha, the Ottomans cross the Danube into Wallachia.

India. India's first railway, linking Bombay to Thana, opens.

Pacific. The island of New Caledonia, off eastern Australia, is annexed by the French.

West Africa. Britain gives its Gold Coast (*Ghana*) colony a legislative council.

New York City. The German-born piano-maker Heinrich Steinweg (Steinway) opens a piano factory.

New Orleans. Eleven thousand people die in a yellow fever epidemic.

France. Joseph Gobineau writes an *Essay on the Inequality of Human Races*, in which he develops his theory of the superiority of the Germanic race, on the basis of physical criteria.

Switzerland. The German composer Richard Wagner, in exile in Zurich, completes the text for *Nibelung's Ring*, a cycle of operas on the Nordic and Germanic sagas.

Germany. Franz Liszt, who has settled in Weimar, composes his sonata in B minor.

Italy. *La Dame aux Camellias*, a novel by Alexandre Dumas (*fils*), serves as the basis for Verdi's opera *La Traviata*, which is given its first performance in Venice this year.

Britain. Among this year's new novels are *Cranford* by Mrs Elizabeth Gaskell and *The Heir of Redclyffe* by Charlotte M Yonge.

Election breaks up painting brotherhood

Holman Hunt's "Our English Coast" (strayed sheep); Hunt shared a studio with Rossetti and was one of the founders of the brotherhood.

London

The election of John Millais as an associate of the Royal Academy has finally broken up the Pre-Raphaelite Brotherhood of controversial young rebel artists. Dante Gabriel Rossetti has declared that he will no longer exhibit. William Holman Hunt, the third founder, is leaving to paint in the Holy Land.

The brotherhood was founded in secret in 1848, when all three were students at the Royal Academy. They set aside tradition to paint directly and truthfully from nature, as Ruskin advocates. Pictures with the initials "PRB" appeared at the academy in 1849. In 1850 the aims of the group leaked out and the members abused for insulting the name of Raphael. Dickens, in his magazine *Household Words*, described Millais' painting of *Christ in the House of His Parents* as "a hideous, wrynecked, blubbering, redheaded boy" and his mother as looking like "a monster in the lowest gin-shop in Europe". Queen Victoria sent for the painting to see it for herself. Millais caused a sensation with his *Ophelia*, drowning beneath the willow tree. His model, Elizabeth Siddall, caught cold posing in a bath in his studio. This year *The Order of Release* had police protection.

Elizabeth Siddall, Millais' model for Ophelia: Siddall epitomised pre-Raphaelite beauty for the brotherhood, who saw her as their own Ophelia.

US threatens "shogun"

Captain Perry meeting representatives of the emperor on 14 July.

Japan, 8 July
Commodore Matthew Perry of the United States Navy today anchored his fleet of four ships in Edo (*Tokyo*) Bay almost within sight of the Japanese capital. The "black ships" which include the powerful steam frigates *Mississippi* and *Susquehanna*, have thrown the Japanese authorities into complete panic.

They have ordered Perry to take his ships to Nagasaki, the only port open to foreigners, but he has refused. He carries with him a letter from President Millard Fillmore and he intends to see that it is delivered to the seat of power. The letter requests that shipwrecked US sailors should be treated more kindly than they have been; that US ships should be allowed to coal and provision, and that one or more ports be opened to US trade.

The Japanese, mindful of the defeat of the Chinese in the Opium War with the British will be well aware of the threat behind these requests. They must fight, or end two and a half centuries of isolation.

Argentina split on new constitution

Argentina, 25 May
Argentina adopted a new constitution today, developed by last year's constitutional convention in Santa Fe, but Buenos Aires, the nation's most important province, is refusing to join the new confederation. Buenos Aires' independent stand is an extension of long-term rivalries. Under its governor, Rosas, the province has dominated the rest of Argentina since 1829 and Rosas himself has enjoyed an unprecedented degree of support from all sections of society.

Only the army showed itself dissatisfied and in May 1851 General Justo de Urquiza proclaimed a revolt against the "despot". Backed by Brazil, his forces defeated Rosas' troops at Caseros. Urquiza then set up the Santa Fe convention. Today's constitution is the result.

Russia furious at rebuff by Ottomans

Istanbul, May
Prince Menshikov, the Russian ambassador, has left the city in high dudgeon after the sultan rejected as "inadmissible" his demand that Russia be given a protectorate over all Orthodox Christians under Ottoman rule. The demand followed the French success last year in gaining control of the shrine at Bethlehem.

Before he departed, the Russian blamed the British ambassador, Lord Stratford de Redcliffe, for the Ottoman refusal. Stratford, no friend of the French, had no objection to the Russians supervising the Holy Places but he drew the line at the Russian further claim to have rights over any Christians in the Ottoman empire. An angry Menshikov accused Sratford of "trampling over the czar and his church."

Commandments delight Chinese rebel

Nanjing, April
Sir George Bonham, the governor of Hong Kong, has had an interview with Wei Changhui, the "northern king" of the Taiping rebels who have set up their Heavenly Capital in the city.

The interview went badly at first, with Wei lecturing Sir George on the need for the whole world to obey the Taiping leader, Hong Xuiquan, the "heavenly king." It took a turn for the better when Wei asked Sir George if he knew the "heavenly rules" and, with an inspired guess, the governor recited the Ten Commandments. Wei was delighted and cried: "The same as ourselves!" The mystical Hong, deeply influenced by the teachings of Protestant missionaries, has imposed an absolute discipline on Nanjing.

Opium, alcohol and tobacco are forbidden, and nobody is allowed to wear the Manchu pigtail. Prostitution has been outlawed and so has the crippling binding of women's feet. Rape is punishable by death and women are treated as the equals of men. It is the combination of such discipline with fervent faith which has allowed the Taipings to defeat the imperial armies.

Taiping rebels, who seized the Yochow arsenal and stormed Nanjing.

Bavarian sells brown jeans to US miners

San Francisco
At least one *entrepreneur* is making his fortune from the Californian gold rush. Levi Strauss, a Bavarian tailor, saw the miners' need for strong durable trousers and has created what have become known as "jeans" – from the French *genes* – made from durable twilled cotton with ample pockets for the miners' tools. The original jeans were brown in colour, but Strauss is experimenting with a blue indigo-based dye, a cheaper colouring – which might be appreciated by the less successful miners. Strauss is just one of many traders who are thriving in this boom city. Fresh fruit, chocolates and other luxuries sell at premium prices here and on the goldfields.

Gold miners at the Last Chance mine in California, wearing the Bavarian tailor Levi Strauss' new twilled cotton trousers nicknamed "jeans".

1853 (1853-1855)

Portugal, 15 November 1853. On the death of Queen Maria II, she is succeeded by her son Pedro V.

Black Sea, 30 November 1853. A Russian naval squadron bombards and destroys an Ottoman fleet at Sinope.

Black Sea, 3 January 1854. The British and French fleets enter the Black Sea to protect Ottoman coasts and shipping.

South Africa, 23 February 1854. At the convention of Bloemfontein, the British recognise the independence of the Orange Free State.

South Africa, February 1854. Following the British annexation of the territories north of the Orange river, inhabited by Africans and Boers, the Boer leader Andreas Pretorius instigates a revolt and forces the British back.

Europe, 12 March 1854. Britain and France form an alliance with the Ottoman empire.

Europe, 28 March 1854. Britain and France declare war on Russia.

Japan, 31 March 1854. The USA and Japan sign the treaty of Kanagawa, opening the ports of Shimoda and Hakodate to American trade.

Washington, DC, 31 March 1854. The USA and Britain sign a Reciprocity Treaty, agreeing on North American fishing rights and abolishing certain import duties.

Greece, 26 May 1854. Franco-British forces occupy the port of Piraeus to prevent the Greeks from joining Russia against the Turks.

USA, 30 May 1854. The Kansas-Nebraska Act, allowing settlers of the newly created territories of Kansas and Nebraska to choose between free land and slavery, is passed. The Missouri Compromise of 1820, which banned slavery north of the southern boundary line of Missouri, is repealed.

Austria, 14 June 1854. Austria, which has formed a defensive alliance with Prussia against Russia, signs a treaty with the Ottomans agreeing to occupy the principalities of Moldavia and Wallachia.

China, 17 June 1854. The "Red Turban" revolt breaks out in Guangdong province.

Spain, 28 June 1854. A liberal revolt led by Leopoldo O'Donnell and Balsomero Espartero overthrows the government and ousts the authoritarian Regent Maria Christina. Her daughter, Isabella, II, succeeds to the throne.

Egypt, July 1854. Abbas, khedive of Egypt, is murdered near Cairo.

Balkans, August 1854. The Russians evacuate Moldavia and Wallachia, which are occupied by the Austrians.

Crimea, 14 September 1854. Having abandoned the Black Sea port of Varna last week, the allies land at Eupatoria on the west coast of the Crimea.

Japan, 14 October 1854. Under the Nagasaki treaty, the British are awarded most-favoured-nation status and the right to refuel at Nagasaki and Hakodate.

Crimea, 20 September 1854. The allies defeat an inferior Russian force at the battle of Alma.

Crimea, 17 October 1854. The allies lay siege to the Russian naval base of Sevastopol.

Crimea, 25 October 1854. The allies win another victory over the Russians, at Balaclava.

Crimea, 5 November 1854. The Russians are defeated by the allies at the battle of Inkerman.

Egypt, 30 November 1854. The Frenchman Ferdinand de Lesseps obtains from Said Pasha a 99-year concession to build a canal linking the Red Sea to the Mediterranean.

USA, 1854. Kansas and Nebraska are admitted to the union.

USA, 1854. Two Boston gunsmiths, Horace Smith and Daniel Wesson, develop a new revolver.

USA, 1854. Groups opposed to the Kansas-Nebraska Act coalesce to form the Republican Party.

India, 1854. India's first cotton mill is established, in Bombay.

India, 1854. A new government-sponsored grant-in-aid system encourages a rapid growth in the number of Christian schools.

Angola, 1854. The British explorer David Livingstone arrives in Luanda after a journey from Bechuanaland (*Botswana*) and Cape Colony.

West Africa, 1854. For the first time, quinine is used successfully to treat malaria.

France, 1854. Gerard de Nerval publishes a collection of short stories entitled *Les Filles du feu*, with an appendix including the 12 sonnets *Les Chimeres*.

France, 1854. The French scientist Henri Sainte-Claire Deville synthesises aluminium for the first time.

Austria, 1854. The Semmering railway, the first mountain railway in the world, opens in eastern central Austria.

Britain, 1854. Lord Tennyson, the poet laureate, writes *The Charge of the Light Brigade*, a poem based on the battle of Balaclava.

Russia wipes out Ottoman war fleet

Turkey: Russia's Christmas meal?

Istanbul, 30 November 1853
The Ottomans have been at war with Russia for the past seven weeks, but they believed that they had an understanding that military operations during the winter would be strictly defensive. Today they discovered how mistaken they were. The Russians seized their chance, swooped on the Ottoman fleet in the Black Sea harbour of Sinope, on the north coast of Turkey, and annihilated it, drowning 4,000 Ottoman sailors. The attack has caused indignation in London; the government has ordered a naval squadron to join the French in a foray into the Black Sea.

Pacifist joins "underground railroad"

Concord, Massachussetts, 1854
The abolitionist lobby has found a major champion in Henry David Thoreau, one of America's most remarkable thinkers, who is writing and lecturing against slavery throughout the northern states – and working with others to help runaway slaves on what is known as the "underground railroad". Ten years ago the philosopher and poet forsook the urban life and built a one-roomed hut in the wood near Concord, vowing to live a life of complete self-sufficiency.

He described his experience in his book *Walden, or Life in the Woods*. His stay was interrupted when he was jailed for refusing to pay tax on the grounds that it supported the Mexican War and a government that allowed slavery.

Brazilians find railway is just the ticket

San Paulo, Brazil, 1854
Brazil's first railway has opened between nearby Guanabara Bay and the Serra do Mar. The milage is minute by North American standards, but its construction was an epic – thousands of labourers, most of them ex-slaves, hacking their way over mountains that have been called "a wall without gates", to the coffee plantations in the interior. The line does not only bring coffee to the coast, but people to the interior. New townships are growing all along the line.

Brazil's economy *is* coffee. Federal taxes vary as its prices goes up and down. Until now coffee has come to the coast by expensive mule trains. The railway, built with mostly British capital, will significantly lower production costs.

Virgin Mary free of original sin – pope

Rome, December 8, 1854
In a bull, *Ineffabilis Deus*, issued here today Pope Pius IX proclaimed the total sinlessness of the Virgin Mary. The bull declares: "From the first moment of her conception the Blessed Virgin Mary was, by the singular grace and privilege of Almighty God, and in view of the merits of Jesus Christ, Saviour of mankind, kept free from all stain of original sin." This finally ends a controversy which has raged for centuries. The idea of Mary as a sinless "new Eve" dates back to the seventh century.

In the 12th century the French theologians argued that since Mary was conceived in the natural way she could not be free of the stain of original sin. However, by the 16th century the doctrine of the Immaculate Conception was firmly established.

Blunder wipes out Light Brigade

Crimea, Russia, 25 October 1854
As night fell in Balaclava the British were both celebrating victory and mourning one of the most brave and foolhardy actions in their military history. As a result of a confusion over orders, a brigade of light cavalry charged one and a half miles (2.4km) down a narrow valley directly into the mouths of Russian guns with artillery batteries raking them from either side as well.

William Howard Russell, of *The Times* of London, has described the final moments thus: "They swept proudly past, glittering in the morning sun in all the pride and splendour of war ... At the distance of 1200 yards the whole line of the enemy belched forth, from thirty iron mouths, a flood of smoke and flame, through which hissed the deadly balls. Their flight was marked by instant gaps in our ranks, by dead men and horses, by steeds flying wounded or riderless across the plain."

Of the 607 who rode out, only 198 returned. Although the charge itself had no military value, the poorly provisioned British won the battle against much stronger Russian forces. It was the second victory since Britain, France, Turkey and Sardinia landed here six weeks ago to attack the giant Russian Black Sea naval base at Sebastopol.

It is a war that has happened almost by default. Lord Aberdeen, the British prime minister, wants to make peace as soon as possible, but he has in his cabinet a war party, led by Lord Palmerston and Lord John Russell, and in France's Napoleon III an ally who counts on military glory to bolster his regime.

The ostensible cause of the war was a dispute between Russia, France and the Ottomans about the rights of protection of Christian shrines in the Ottoman-controlled Holy Land. When the Ottomans refused Russia's demands Russia marched into Ottoman territories across the Danube. Britain was prompted to issue an ultimatum that the Czar withdraw – not out of concern for shrines but out of alarm at the prospect of a Russian occupation of Constantinople and a consequent threat to British communications with India.

Roger Fenton's photograph of British soldiers resting in the Crimea.

"The thin red line": the 93rd Sutherland Highlanders at Balaclava.

English nurse gives hope to the injured

Scutari, Crimea, 7 November 1854
A team of nurses led by Florence Nightingale has set to work with scrubbing brushes to clean up Scutari hospital. Doctors obstinately refused Nightingale's help until casualties from the battle of Inkerman spilled into their rat-infested corridors.

They resented interference from the trained outsider who was given £30,000 and a brief from Sidney Herbert, the secretary of state for war, to take complete charge of nursing British soldiers in the Crimea. By keeping army officials at bay and her nurses sober Florence turned Scutari into a highly effective hospital.

Nightingale, loaded with problems of administration and supply, always took her turn at nursing, and in the darkness of every night carried her lamp through the wards giving comfort and advice to her patients.

Florence Nightingale at Scutari.

Canal for Suez strip

Egypt, 1855
Work will begin shortly on a 100-mile (160-kilometre) canal connecting the Mediterranean at Port Said with the Red Sea at Suez. The canal will cut by almost a half the journey from London to Bombay. The accession of the pro-European Said Pasha to the throne of Egypt has created the opportunity for Ferdinand de Lesseps, a persuasive 49-year-old French viscount and engineer, to begin the ambitious project.

1855 (1855-1856)

Italy, 26 January 1855. Count Camillo Cavour, the prime minister of Piedmont, takes Piedmont into the Crimean War alongside the allies. He agrees to send 15,000 men to the Crimea.

Panama, 28 January 1855. The 47-mile Panama railway, linking the Atlantic and Pacific across the isthmus of Panama, is completed.

Britain, February 1855. Following the fall of Lord Aberdeen's coalition as a result of mis-management of the Crimean War, Lord Palmerston forms a Liberal administration.

Japan, February 1855. Russia and Japan sign a treaty of friendship at Shimoda.

Russia, 2 March 1855. On the death of Czar Nicholas, he is succeeded by his son Alexander II.

Afghanistan, 30 March 1855. Dost Mohammed of Afghanistan signs the treaty of Peshawar with Britain, ending 12 years of war.

Britain, 31 March 1855. The novelist Charlotte Bronte dies. She revealed in a note to the second edition of *Wuthering Heights* that its author, "Ellis Bell", was her sister Emily, "Acton Bell", the author of *Agnes Grey*, was her sister Anne and "Currer Bell", the author of *Jane Eyre*, was herself.

Paris, 14 May 1855. The Italian revolutionary Pianori is executed after attempting to assassinate Napoleon III.

Italy, 29 May 1855. Cavour abolishes all religious orders and convents in Piedmont which are not dedicated to preaching, education or helping the sick.

China, 31 May 1855. The Mongol prince Senggelinqin, the commander of the Qing imperial forces, captures the *Taiping* leader Li Kaifeng at Chiping in Shandong. This marks the end of the Taiping expedition to take Beijing.

USA, 4 July 1855. New York becomes the 13th state to ban the production or sale of alcoholic beverages.

Austria, 18 August 1855. The cardinal-archbishop of Vienna signs a concordat with the pope giving the Catholic church control of education, censorship and matrimonial law.

China, 7 September 1855. The Moslem leader Du Wenxin occupies the town of Dali in Yunnan province.

Crimea, 10 September 1855. Sevastopol, under siege for nearly a year, capitulates to the allies.

China, 24 September 1855. Zhang Xinmei of the Miao people rises in rebellion in Guizhou province.

Denmark, 11 November 1855. The philosopher Soren Kierkegaard dies. In his best known-work, *Concluding Unscientific Postscript*, he put forward the theory that subjectivity is truth. He attacked system-building in philosophy, arguing that existence is too varied to be incorporated into a particular system.

Hungary, 19 November 1855. The poet and playwright Michael Vorosmarty, who was inspired by popular folktales, dies. In 1840 he wrote the Hungarian national song *Szozat*, and he was a member of the 1848 national assembly.

Sweden, 21 November 1855. Sweden concludes a treaty of alliance with Britain and France against Russia.

Caucasus, 27 November 1855. The Russians take the town of Kars from the Ottomans after a siege.

Japan, December 1855. Much of Edo (*Tokyo*) is destroyed by the great Ansei earthquake. Many people lose their lives in the resulting fires.

Ethiopia, 1855. Ras Kass, who has reunified Gojjam, Begember, Tigrai and Shoa by conquest, crowns himself Emperor Tewodros (Theodore) II.

West Africa, 1855. The French annex Walo on the Senegal river, one of the Wallof kingdoms – the first inland colonial possession of a European power in West Africa.

India, 1855. India's first jute-spinning mill is set up, in Serampore.

Germany, 1855. Gustav Freytag publishes *Debit and Credit*, a monumental novel about German commercial life.

England, 1855. Robert Browning publishes *Men and Women*, a collection of love poems.

England, 1855. Herbert Spencer, the sociologist and philosopher of evolution, publishes his *Principles of Psychology*.

Britain, 1855. Following the abolition of the Stamp Tax on newspapers, London's first penny paper, the *Daily Telegraph and Courier*, begins publication.

Switzerland, 1855. Gottfried Keller publishes an educational novel entitled *Green Henry*.

Switzerland, 1855. The historian Jacob Burckhardt issues *Cicerone*, a guide to Italian art.

USA, 1855. Henry Wadsworth Longfellow completes *The Song of Hiawatha*, a narrative poem about a young Ojibway Indian.

USA, 1855. Walt Whitman publishes his first book of poems, *Leaves of Grass*.

Thundering waterfall named after queen

Stampeding buffalo at Victoria Falls: a romantic view by Thomas Baines.

Africa, 17 November 1855
A breathtaking waterfall at least 1,000 yards (914m) wide and 100 feet (30m) deep, and thought to be the largest in the world, has been reported in southern Africa by the explorer and missionary David Livingstone.

The 42-year-old Scot, keen to arouse British public interest in this previously unexplored area, has renamed the waterfall on the Zambezi "the Falls of Victoria" in honour of the queen. In doing so, he follows the precedent of his friend, Sebetwane, the leader of the Kololo, who renamed it Mosioatunya ("the smoke that thunders"). The original local name is Shongwenamutitma ("the boiling pot").

A native of the Zambezi by Baines.

Famine in China as Yellow River bursts

China, 1855
Thousands of people are starving to death in the terrible famine following the breaking of the banks of the Yellow River which is so appropriately named "China's Sorrow".

Over hundreds of years the peasants have built up the river banks until in places the river bed itself is above the level of the surrounding countryside, so that any break in the embankment floods large areas of the agricultural plain.

This latest break is so serious that the river has changed its course with devastating effects on millions of people, prompting much unrest.

Rioting miners are acquitted by court

Melbourne, 22 February 1855
Thirteen gold diggers have been acquitted of rioting and manslaughter after last December's fighting at the Eureka gold mine where 5 soldiers and 30 miners were killed. The diggers were demanding the right to the vote and to land ownership, and an end to their licence fee.

The diggers built defences, after taking over the town, "constructed of piles of slabs", according to one eyewitness. Troops cleared them with little difficulty. Now, by treating the rioters with leniency the government has averted a major radical confrontation.

Mexican ruler falls after years of strife

Mexico City, 1855
General Lopez de Santa Anna, Mexico's "president for life", has been deposed. He was ousted by a consortium of liberals who backed a liberal manifesto known as the Ayutla plan. He is to be replaced by General Juan Alvarez.

The story of Santa Anna is the story of modern Mexico. Born in 1797, he fought with Iturbide to rid Mexico of the Spanish, but overthrew him in 1822 to become president himself in 1833. Though he was forever losing battles he never accepted he had lost a war. Defeated by Texas rebels in 1836, he was imprisoned for eight months; defeated again by the French at Vera Cruz, he lost a leg; and twice defeated by the United States between 1846 and 1848, he became a symbol of Mexican independence. Twice president and twice exiled, he returned to his country from exile in Venezuala to take power again after the conservative revolution of 1853.

A courageous soldier rather than a thoughtful statesman, his political conservatism, presumption of royalty (he took on the title "His Most Supreme Highness") and financial recklessness alienated Mexico's liberals, who, led by the fiery Juan Alvarez, have overthrown him and sent him into exile for the third time. Liberals hope that his overthrow will open up the country to new ideas – and new liberties.

Fallen dictator: Santa Anna.

France and Britain capture Sevastopol

Corporal Philip Smith winning the Victoria Cross at Sevastopol.

Sevastopol, 10 September 1855
After a 12-month campaign marked by muddle, incompetence and querulousness on the part of all the military commanders, friend and foe alike, British and French forces have captured the Sevastopol naval base of the Russian Black Sea fleet. France's General Pelissier was so delighted he embraced General Sir James Simpson and kissed him. "It was a great occasion," Simpson said. "I couldna' resist him."

Many observers believe that the base should have been taken a year ago when the combined allied land and sea forces first arrived. The Russian commander, Menshikov, had failed to construct proper defence works, but French troops arrived late and British and French commanders disagreed over the timing of attacks. The British spent a bitter winter without adequate protection and on one occasion the Light Brigade attacked the wrong guns. For the final assault, Simpson sent his least experienced troops into action. Not surprisingly, Pelissier was relieved at the result.

Disease is spread by germs in the air

Paris, 1856
What actually causes disease to spread? For a long time now, the prevailing theory has been that poisonous vapours – miasmas – are to blame. But now a French chemist of humble origins and relatively little formal training has demonstrated that infection is the work of tiny living organisms.

Louis Pasteur has carried out many experiments on fermentation and on the putrefaction and souring of food. He concludes that germs in the air are responsible.

He has gone on to argue that disease, too, is caused by microorganisms. Agents such as bacteria are the mysterious carriers of infection.

Louis Pasteur, who discovered that the vehicles of infection are tiny living organisms called bacteria.

Piedmontese swell anti-Russian army

Turin, 26 January 1855
Piedmont-Sardinia is sending an expeditionary force of 15,000 men to help Britain in the Crimean War against the Russians. King Victor Emmanuel is hoping to get some military glory for himself from the move. He also hopes to distract attention from the real problems in Lombardy, where the Austrians have been confiscating the possessions of Piedmontese citizens.

The prime minister Cavour, is believed to be unhappy at the move. However, he is himself fighting to stay in office. He walks a tightrope, seeking to maintain the support of parliament, with its powerful liberals, without arousing too much anger amongst the conservatives who surround the king and would like to oust Cavour.

Heaven and Earth society is defeated

Shanghai, 17 February 1855
The army of the "Small Sword" secret society which has occupied Shanghai for the past two years was defeated today by imperial Chinese forces with the aid of French marines. The Small Sword leader, Liu Lichuan, a former interpreter for the British, part-doctor and part-sorcerer, was captured and immediately beheaded.

The Small Swords, one of the many societies of southern China, is a branch of the *Triads*, or Heaven and Earth Society, and draws its membership mainly from unemployed sailors and artisans.

Denouncing corrupt officials and harsh taxes, Liu's red-sashed fighters seized the walled city of Shanghai in September 1853, but carefully avoided the westerners' settlements outside the city.

The imperial forces caused the westerners more trouble than the Small Swords, and after an Englishwoman was insulted the celebrated Battle of Muddy Flat was fought between European volunteers, supported by British and US seamen, and the Chinese army. Most of the few casualties were caused when the British and Americans shot at each other.

1856 (1856-1857)

Japan, January 1856. Japan has now signed treaties of peace and friendship with the USA, Russia, Britain, France and the Netherlands.

Germany, 17 February 1856. Heinrich Heine, Germany's foremost lyric poet, dies.

Ottoman Empire, 19 Februry 1856. The Ottoman sultan, Abdul Mejid, issues a reform edict guaranteeing his Christian subjects security of life and property and the power to exercise freedom of conscience. The civil power of the heads of the Christian churches is abolished and civil offices are made open to all.

China, 28 February 1856. The Honghao rebellion, in Guizhou province led by Xu Tingjie, is put down.

China, 29 February 1856. The French Catholic missionary Auguste Chapdelaine, who has entered the country illegally, is beheaded.

Paris, 30 March 1856. Britain, France, Russia, the Ottoman empire, Piedmont, Austria and Prussia sign the treaty of Paris, ending the Crimean War and securing the neutrality of the Black Sea.

Europe, 15 April 1856. Austria, France and Britain agree to joint action in defence of Ottoman independence and integrity.

South Africa, 12 July 1856. Natal is made a British colony, after being part of Cape Colony.

Japan, August 1856. Townsend Harris arrives in Shimoda from the USA as the first foreign consul in Japan. He immediately encounters bureaucratic obstruction.

Switzerland, September 1856. An attempted royalist coup in the canton of Neuchatel, which proclaimed itself a republic in 1848, ends in failure.

Spain, 25 October 1856. The liberal Leopoldo O'Donnell, who replaced Baldomero Espartero as premier in July, is dismissed by Isabella II, who appoints Ramon Narvaez to head a more authoritarian regime.

China, October 1856. *Arrow*, a ship flying the British flag, is boarded at Guangzhou (*Canton*), by Chinese officers who arrest the entire crew on suspicion of piracy.

South-East Asia, October 1856. Siam (*Thailand*) signs a treaty with France which guarantees its frontiers.

Britain, 1 November 1856. In response to a Persian invasion of Afghanistan with the object of capturing Herat, Britain – which last year signed a treaty with the Afghans – declares war on Persia.

USA, 4 November 1856. At his fourth attempt James Buchanan, a Democrat, is victorious in the presidential election.

South Africa, December 1856. Western Transvaal Boers adopt US-style constitution for a South African Republic, with a capital at Pretoria. Eastern and northern Transvaalers still refuse to join.

India, 1856. The British annex the kingdom of Awadh in northern India. This is the most recent in a series of annexations since 1848, which has included the states of Satara, Jhansi and Nagpur.

Germany, 1856. At Neanderthal, near Dusseldorf, the remains of a *homo sapiens*, probably dating from 70,000 BC, are discovered.

Germany, 1856. The physicist Hermann von Helmholtz publishes his *Handbook of Physiological Optics*.

France, 1856. The political scientist and politician Alexis de Tocqueville publishes *The Old Regime and the Revolution*, in which he seeks to show the continuity of political behaviour and attitudes that makes post-revolutionary French society as prepared to accept despotism as that of the old regime.

Egypt, 1856. The first railway line in Africa, between Alexandria and Cairo, is inaugurated.

Britain, 1856. The first limited liability companies in Britain are formed.

Persia, January 1857. The British seize the port of Bushire on the Persian Gulf.

Vienna, 24 January 1857. A conference in Vienna introduces the silver standard in Austria and the countries of the customs union.

Greece, 28 February 1857. French and British naval forces end their occupation of the port of Piraeus, which began in May 1854.

China, 3 March 1857. Using the pretexts of the assassination of the French missionary Chapdelaine and the seizure of the *Arrow* last October, France and Britain declare war on China.

Balkans, March 1857. The Austrians evacuate Moldavia and Wallachia, and elections are held in the principalities to settle the question of their union. Widespread corruption results in a defeat for the unionists.

West Africa, 20 April 1857. Al-Hajj Umar, the Tukulor Moslem leader who in 1852 declared a *jihad* (holy war), continues his campaign of conquest by laying siege to the French fort of Medine built two years earlier on the Senegal river.

Bloodshed grows as Chinese rebels split

Nanjing, November 1856

The *Taiping* movement, the Heavenly Kingdom of Great Peace, which at one stage threatened to destroy the Qing dynasty, is tearing itself apart with a great bloodletting brought about by the rivalry between its leaders.

The killing started in September when Yang Xuijing, the "eastern king" who wielded power in Nanjing, made his bid to take over the movement from its founder, the "heavenly king", Hong Xiuquan who was growing increasingly remote from reality. Hong was not so remote that he could not smell out a plot and he summoned the other leaders to his aid. Yang and thousands of his followers were killed by the troops of Wei Changhui, the northern king. Then Shi Dagai, the "assistant king", and the Taipings' best general, fled in fear and his family was slaughtered. Wei then challenged for supreme leadership of the Taipings, but the heavenly king has had him executed and has sent his head, pickled in brine, to Shi Dagai.

A treaty to "civilise" Ottoman empire

Istanbul, 1856

A wide-ranging charter of reform for the Ottoman empire has been incorporated into the treaty of Paris. But Lord Stratford de Redcliffe, its chief instigator, is furious that the great powers have made no commitment to enforce it.

Carefully framed to ensure the empire's acceptance as a civilised western state, the charter emphasised the free and equal status of all Ottoman citizens, regardless of religion, race or language, for the purposes of taxation, education, the law and eligibility for public office. It also outlined financial and monetary measures, aid for commerce and agriculture, and the building of roads and canals.

But the parties to the treaty specifically refused "to interfere either collectively or individually in the relations of the sultan with his subjects or in the internal adminis-

Sultan Abdul Mejid: reformer.

tration of the empire". Lord Stratford de Redcliffe, who worked hard to convince the sultan of the need for reform, is now extremely sceptical about the charter's value.

US adventurer siezes power in Nicaragua

Granada, Nicaragua, May 1856

With a small mercenary army of no more than 250 men an American has seized this country and declared himself president. William Walker, a stocky, retiring man whose mild manner belies an adventurous past, has been recognised by the United States government.

This is the second attempt by Walker, a failed lawyer and journalist, to establish a puppet republic. His previous effort – in Lower California – ended in disaster. This time he has the backing of Cornelius Vanderbilt who plans to expand his transport empire here. Despite his mild manner, Walker appears to have impressed the Nicaraguan people as a man of action. One of his first moves this month was to make General Corral, the former dictator, his secretary for war. Soon after, Corral was led in front of a firing squad and shot for conspiring to take his country back.

Walker has grandiose plans for a trans-ocean canal and for the eventual unification of the whole of Central America. He also plans to introduce African slaves into his new and somewhat dubious "republic".

Crimean War ends with neutral Black Sea

Peace celebrations in London's Hyde Park mark the end of the Crimea war.

Paris, 30 March 1856
The Russian delegate to the Paris peace conference, Count Orlov, today agreed to the demilitarisation of the Black Sea as a prime condition for ending the Crimean War. The Czar will have to demolish four naval bases, including Sevastopol, and to withdraw his fleet from the area. Russia also renounced its claim to give protection to the Ottoman empire Christians. Lord Palmerston, who took over as British prime minister at a low point in the war, wished to impose even tougher terms on the Russians, but Napoleon III was trying to use the peace conference to liquidate the settlement imposed on France at the Congress of Vienna after Waterloo.

Palmerston decided that a relatively soft peace would be better than risking that. The queen was disappointed, but he told her that Britain could not continue the war alone.

French writer faces obscenity charges

Paris, 25 June 1857
Gustave Flaubert, one of France's rising literary stars, and a self-proclaimed "thinker and demoraliser", went on trial today. His new novel, *Madame Bovary,* was charged under French law as "an outrage against moral standards". But despite the prosecution's singling out of a number of passages as "immoral", the book as a whole was not found obscene and Flaubert has been acquitted.

The book is a study of the adulteries and eventual suicide of the wife of a provincial doctor. What shocks Flaubert's accusers is a plot that they claim belittles marriage at the expense of the charm of illicit love. In fact, Flaubert is more subtle. His book, with its attack on self-delusion, undermines not morality, but all human hope.

Kiwis "capable of ruling themselves"

New Zealand, 1856
New Zealand is to become self-governing. Already Canada, New South Wales, Victoria, South Australia and Tasmania are self-governing, as Britain realises that it can run its white empire far more efficiently through indirect rule, so long as Blacks cannot vote.

For half a century after Captain Cook's arrival, New Zealand had no status. For years the indigenous Maoris were persecuted by white settlers without any restraint; in 1836 there were even suggestions that France would take over the islands. In 1840 New Zealand was annexed to the crown, but the Maoris were still alienated and rebelled in 1845. It is their defeat that has made the steps to self-government so easy. There is no-one to protest.

Pro-slavery gang attacks abolitionists

Kansas Territory, 1856
As the fierce dispute between pro- and anti-slavers brings more and more bloodshed to Kansas, Governor Daniel Woodson – a pro-slaver – has declared the territory to be in a state of insurrection.

The blame for what has become a guerrilla war, with heavy casualties reported on both sides, is being laid at the door of John Brown, a fiery abolitionist from Connecticut, whose followers are alleged to have slaughtered five settlers on the Missouri border. Brown is crusading to keep Kansas from becoming a slave state. In retaliation, 300 pro-slavery men attacked Brown's stronghold at Osawatomie, but were driven off successfully by Brown and his 40 supporters.

John Brown: fiery abolitionist.

Xhosa slaughter cattle to fulfil prophecy

South Africa, October 1856
Cattle are being slaughtered by the thousand throughout Xhosaland following a 16-year-old's vision.

Nongquause, the 16-year-old, is the niece of the Xhosa's chief spiritual diviner. In her vision she was told that the Xhosa had to purify themselves: they had to kill all their cattle, cease planting crops and destroy all grain. Then the Xhosa dead would rise again, a great wind would sweep the white men into the sea, and food would become plentiful. News of the vision spread like wildfire. Thousands believe her.

The Xhosa have suffered one defeat after another at the hands of the white men. They are desperate, but they have been encouraged by rumours of British defeats on the Black Sea. Famine and depopulation are inevitable; this is a prospect which excites the land hunger of whites.

Syphilis kills Schumann in mental asylum

Bonn, 29 July 1856
Robert Schumann died today in a mental asylum near Bonn, where he had been placed at his own request four years ago. He was 46.

The man regarded as the champion of musical romanticism was tended at the end by his wife Clara, one of the greatest pianists of her day, and friends including Johannes Brahms, a talented young composer. Mental illness ran in the family, but Schumann probably caught syphilis before his marriage and over his last 15 years he grew increasingly withdrawn, unbalanced, and unable to work. Early in 1852 he had wild hallucinations of Hell and on 27 February he threw himself into the Rhine, celebrated in his *Rhenish Symphony*. He was rescued, but his mind was lost.

Robert Shumann and wife Clara: loyal to the final hours.

India, 10 May. *Sepoys* in the Bengal army at Meerut in northern India mutiny against their British officers.

India, 11 May. The Indian mutineers seize Delhi.

Switzerland, 26 May. Frederick IV of Prussia renounces his right of sovereignty over the canton of Neuchatel.

Britain, 25 June. Albert, the husband of Queen Victoria, is made prince consort.

Italy, 29 June. The patriot Giuseppe Mazzini, who has already provoked risings in Milan and Mantua, makes a vain attempt to mount a rebellion in Genoa.

Japan, June. The American consul Townsend Harris secures agreement from Japan on a trade treaty with the USA.

India, July. Over 200 Britons are massacred in Cawnpore.

Italy, 1 August. The republican lawyer Daniele Manin founds a national association for the unification of Italy under the king of Piedmont. Giuseppe Garibaldi is appointed vice-president.

Europe, August. France, Russia, Prussia and Piedmont break off diplomatic relations with the Ottoman empire over the issue of the union of Moldavia and Wallachia.

Tunisia, 10 September. In an effort to modernise Tunisia, the *bey*, Mohammed, grants a charter guaranteeing the equal treatment of Moslems and Jews.

India, 20 September. The British recapture Delhi.

India, 25 September. British forces under General Havelock arrive to relieve the British Residency in Lucknow, which has been under siege by mutineers since July.

Cochin China, (Vietnam), September. The French occupy Da Nang and Saigon.

Balkans, September. Following the annulment of the corrupt elections held in March, new elections in Moldavia and Wallachia result in a victory for the unionists.

Spain, 25 October. The liberal Leopoldo O'Donnell again replaces General Narvaez in power.

India. Universities are founded in Calcutta, Madras and Bombay.

US stock market bust follows boom

New York City, 8 August
The booming, bustling USA felt the first chill of economic depression today as one of the country's biggest finance houses, the Ohio Life Insurance and Trust Company, collapsed with huge liabilities. Most banks in this city have been forced to suspend all large payments.

As panic spread through the financial markets today, news came that several western railroads were plunging into bankruptcy, together with a number of other speculative enterprises. Over-speculation in railroad securities has led to the failure of 4,932 companies nationwide. Despite gloom on the New York Stock Exchange, America remains very much a boom country with Pennsylvania, at the heart of a coalfield 12 times larger than any in Europe, and vast agricultural production, fuelling an ever-expanding economy.

What makes a sun?

Kirchhoff: spectrum analyser.

Germany
A German scientist, Gustav Kirchhoff, has discovered a method of identifying the chemical composition of the sun, stars, and all the planets in the firmament.

After years of research he realised that when light passes through a gas or any heated material, only certain wavelengths are absorbed and emitted. Thus, by studying the spectrum of emissions, he can reveal its chemical composition.

Britain aids Afghans as Persians strike

Persian horseman: a mid 19th century hand-painted ceramic tile.

Persia, March
Persia, defeated by a British-Indian expedition led by Sir James Outram, has sued for peace. The second Persian campaign in Afghanistan in 20 years has ended, as before, with recognition of Afghan boundaries and the complete evacuation of Afghan territory. After 12 years of hostilities, the British and the Afghans made peace two years ago by the treaty of Peshawar. So when the Persians invaded Afghanistan in another attempt to capture Herat – they had tried in 1836, with Russian help – the British came to the Afghans' aid, just as they had done before. On 1 November last year, Britain declared war on Persia, and on 1 January seized the port of Bushire on the Persian gulf. The rapid end to the war gives Dost Mohammed the opportunity to try to unite Afghanistan, with its independent local rulers, under his kingship.

"The Gleaners", by Jean-Francois Millet. Born a peasant, he painted in poverty until exhibiting his first painting of rural life, "The Winnower", in 1848. He moved to Paris, became a friend of Theodore Rousseau, and continued painting serious and romantic rural scenes – including "The Bottlers" – celebrating the virtues of honest labour.

India rises up against "insensitive" British rulers

May: regiment mutinies and takes Delhi

Indian mutineers defending their position: a British caricature.

Delhi, 11 May

Thousands of Indian troops in Meerut have mutinied, killed their officers and marched on Delhi. Discontent has been growing in the Indian Army. Hindus resent the increasing dominance of Britain in India; Victorian military efficiency threatens the *caste* system and pay has not kept up with expectations. Nor is the discontent confined to the military; it can be found in the villages. Old India, with its priests and its princes, fears for its future in an entirely British India.

Two weeks ago, 85 men of the Third Cavalry regiment refused to handle new cartridges, which they claim contains cow and pig fat (thus offending both Hindus and Moslems). They were court martialled two days ago. The next day, while the European officers were attending church service, the convicted men's comrades rose in arms and liberated them.

Incredible as it sounds, the British had 24 hours' warning of the mutiny. Lieutenant Hugh Gough, warned by an Indian officer, told both his colonel and his brigadier, but such was their over-confidence that they "treated the communication with contempt, reproving me for listening to such idle words".

Joined by other regiments, the troops have captured Delhi, where they have killed every Briton they could find, and are holding the Moghul emperor prisoner.

September: British forces storm capital

Delhi, 21 September

Delhi has been retaken. The capital of India and heart of the Mutiny fell after a week's street fighting. It is being looted tonight.

Delhi was taken by the rebels on the second day of the Mutiny, the Sepoys proclaiming the somewhat uncomfortable Moghul emperor, Bahadur Shah, sovereign of India.

Delhi in the insurgents' hands directly threatened British India. The city meant more than prestige; it meant legitimacy. By June, troops had been gathered from Burma, the Punjab and southern India (which has remained quiet). A Sepoy army sent to intercept them was defeated at Badli-ki-Serai, and the British established themselves on a ridge to the north-west of the city. They were unable to surround Delhi, and there were times when it seemed they were being besieged.

On 14 September, strengthened by reinforcements, the British stormed the city. Two columns burst through breaches in the walls, a third flowed through the Kashmir

One against many: a British view.

gate, where four Victoria Crosses were earned during its blowing up. Twelve hundred British were killed. Street fighting, from one barricade to the next, continued for a week. Then, suddenly, resistance evaporated. Delhi is now in the hands of the British again; tonight it lies under a pall of smoke.

Britons chopped up and thrown down well

Cawnpore, India, 15 July

The mutilated bodies of 200 British men, women and children have been found in a well. The victims, discovered by General Havelock's column which came in to the city this morning, had been killed only last night. Sepoy riflemen refused to do the deed, which was done by the town's butchers instead.

Cawnpore joined the Mutiny on 4 June, its troops following Nana Sahib, a disaffected landlord. For three weeks, loyalists under 70-year-old General Hugh Wheeler held out against the mutineers. Most were massacred after surrendering. The survivors were the ones massacred yesterday. "The pavement was swimming in blood, and fragments of ladies' and children's dresses were floating on it," said one eyewitness.

The British are disgusted. Rumours, without foundation, that the women and children were raped before being butchered spread through the British Army. Indian prisoners cannot expect much mercy from the revengeful British.

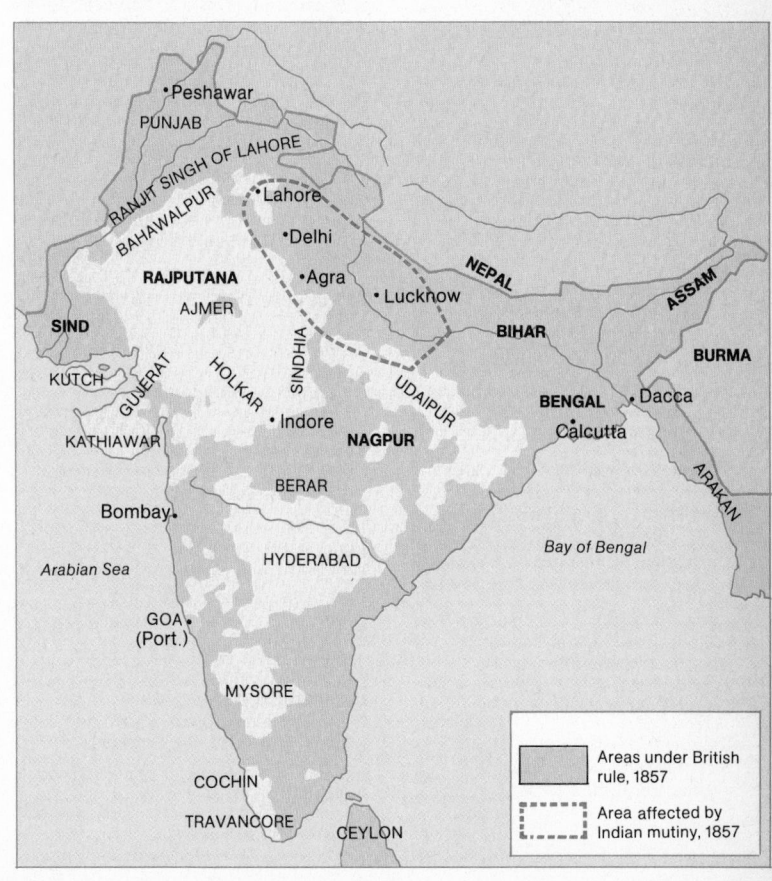

Map of India showing:

- Peshawar
- PUNJAB
- RANJIT SINGH OF LAHORE
- BAHAWALPUR
- Lahore
- Delhi
- NEPAL
- RAJPUTANA
- AJMER
- Agra
- Lucknow
- ASSAM
- SIND
- BIHAR
- KUTCH
- GUJERAT
- HOLKAR
- SINDHIA
- UDAIPUR
- BURMA
- BENGAL
- Dacca
- KATHIAWAR
- Indore
- NAGPUR
- Calcutta
- BERAR
- ARAKAN
- Bombay
- Arabian Sea
- HYDERABAD
- Bay of Bengal
- GOA (Port.)
- MYSORE
- COCHIN
- TRAVANCORE
- CEYLON

Legend:
- Areas under British rule, 1857
- Area affected by Indian mutiny, 1857

1857 (1857-1858)

Russia, 2 December 1857. Committees of aristocrats are set up with the aim of abolishing serfdom.

China, 29 December 1857. Guangzhou (*Canton*) falls to an Anglo-French force after heavy bombardment.

USA, 29 December 1857. William Walker, the renegade former leader of Nicaragua, is arrested and reprimanded for his exploits. Walker was extradited to the USA following his ejection by Central American troops after a failed attempt to regain power in Nicaragua.

Mexico, 1857. The adoption of a federal constitution and other political and religious reforms leads to a civil war between conservatives and liberals.

Spain, 1857. The Spanish heroine Agostina, known as *La Saragossa*, dies. She won fame for her bravery in the defence of Saragossa against the French invaders in 1808 and became a symbol of national pride, courage and liberty.

USA, 1857. The periodical *Atlantic Monthly* begins publication.

New York City, 1857. The first passenger elevator, invented by Elisha Otis, is installed in a New York department store.

France, 1857. Charles Baudelaire begins the Symbolist movement in France with his collection of poems *Les Fleurs du Mal*.

Britain, 1857. Anthony Trollope, a post office administrator, publishes *Barchester Towers*, a novel about the life and politics of a cathedral close.

Britain, 1857. Thomas Hughes publishes *Tom Brown's Schooldays*, a novel based on his experiences at Rugby school under the headmastership of Thomas Arnold.

London, 1857. The National Portrait Gallery is founded.

China, 19 January 1858. The forces of the "Sparks from the Lantern" sect, under Liu Yishun, take Sinan in Guizhou province, setting off the "White Signal" rebellion.

Britain, 25 February 1858. Lord Derby forms his second minority Conservative government following the Palmerston's resignation, defeated on a bill to increase the penalty for conspiracy to murder.

Paris, 13 March 1858. Felice Orsini, the leader of the Italian republican conspiracy to assassinate Napoleon III in January, is guillotined.

India, 21 March 1858. British forces lift the siege of Lucknow, ending the Indian Mutiny.

China, 31 March 1858. The Chinese agree to negotiate with the British and the French, who have ravaged Canton. They receive four envoys, including representatives from the USA and Russia.

India, 10 April 1858. Ye Mingchen, the governor general of the Chinese provinces of Guangzhou (*Canton*) and Guangxi, dies a prisoner in Calcutta. He was arrested by British and French forces in January after the fall of Guangzhou.

Mexico, 4 May 1858. The liberal government led by Benito Juarez establishes a capital at Vera Cruz. The conservatives, meanwhile, who control the army and are supported by the upper classes and the church, are ruling from Mexico City, under the leadership of Miguel Miramon.

USA, 11 May 1858. Minnesota becomes the 32nd state.

China, 20 May 1858. British and French forces attack and take the Dagu forts near Tianjin, in northern China, in order to force an agreement to the demands made on the Qing court by the foreign powers.

China, 28 May 1858. By the treaty of Aigun, China recognises the territory north of the Amur river as Russian.

Paris, May 1858. At a conference to discuss the future of the Balkan principalities, it is decided to create a common organisation to deal with the army, law and finance in Moldavia and Wallachia. While remaining under the suzerainty of the Ottomans, they are allowed to call themselves the United Principalities.

Algeria, 2 June 1858. The governor general is replaced by a French minister with responsibility for Algeria. The first occupant of this office is the emperor's cousin, Jerome Napoleon.

China, June 1858. The treaties of Tianjin (*Tientsin*) – signed with Russia, the USA, Britain and France – provide for aggressive expansion of foreign power in China.

Russia, 2 July 1858. Czar Alexander II gives orders for serfs working on the imperial lands to be freed.

India, 8 July 1858. Following the defeat of remaining rebel forces in central India, Lord Canning, the governor general, proclaims peace.

Japan, 29 July 1858. After much pressure Japan signs a treaty of commerce and friendship with the USA. The treaty opens Edo (*Tokyo*) and Osaka to foreign residents and permits freedom of worship.

Livingstone pleads for missions to Africa

Cambridge, October 1857

He is a short, a poor speaker and shy. His face is etched with exposure to the African sun. He speaks slowly with a Lanarkshire accent, frequently halting to find words as if unfamiliar with the English language after 16 years in the African bush. He is a man who positively hates publicity. But that is the one thing that David Livingstone, explorer extraordinary, cannot avoid. And he knows it. So with the same humble aplomb which won over African natives David Livingstone, who returned in December, is winning over English society, using his status as a national hero to raise funds for more missions to Africa.

The Livingstone message, addressed in private to the queen and to well-heeled audiences everywhere, is that Central Africa's salvation depends on three vital Cs – Civilisation, Commerce and Christianity. By direct trading and providing the cloth and guns that Central Africa wants Britain can end the Portuguese-run goods-for-slaves trade. The task of opening up the interior will last beyond Livingstone's lifetime, and he plans to appeal to Cambridge students to take up the missionary challenge.

Dr Livingstone reading the bible.

Benito Suarez, Mexico's new president

Mexico, October 1857

Benito Juarez was sworn in today as Mexico's new president, although he faces sustained opposition from an establishment backed by General Santa Anna.

The ceremony marks the climax of the 51-year-old populist's remarkable rise to power. Born into a poor Indian family, orphaned at the age of three, Juarez seemed condemned to a life of rural hardship. His chance employment as the servant of a Franciscan lay brother changed his life. He gained an education and by 1831 had begun work as a legal clerk. His practice concentrated on helping poor Indians, and the campaigning lawyer gradually evolved a substantial political power base.

He served in the national congress during the war with the United States and then, between 1847-52, as governor of Oaxaca. He proved an outstanding official, boosting the state economy and attacking corrupt officials.

Banished by Santa Anna in 1853, Juarez returned in 1855 to begin a new campaign that has climaxed in today's presidency.

The largest ship afloat: Isambard Kingdom Brunel's "Great Eastern", crossing the Atlantic Ocean on its maiden voyage to New York.

British reopen Opium War with China

China, January 1857
Hostilities have broken out again between Britain and China. The ostensible reason for the renewal of the Opium War, which was supposedly ended by the treaty in 1842, was the boarding of the British registered ship *Arrow* by Chinese officials who arrested the Chinese crew and are said to have hauled down the British ensign.

The facts of the incident remain obscure, but it roused British anger and – given Palmerston's belief that "such half-barbarian countries as China ... need a dressing down every ten years or so" – war became inevitable.

Relations with the Chinese, who believe that it is the British who are the barbarians, have been fragile ever since the Nanjing treaty was signed. The British have tried to capitalise on the trade concessions in the treaty, while the Chinese have done their best to prevent the despised intruders from gaining any further advantages.

Given this situation, it is not surprising that tensions have mounted in the treaty ports. There have been anti-foreign riots in Canton where European trading factories have been burnt down and threatening posters put up by secret societies.

One of these threatened: "If we do not completely exterminate you pigs and dogs, we will not be manly Chinese". With the British also displaying their contempt for the Chinese it was inevitable that war would erupt again.

A Chinese representation of British invaders – and Chinese resisting them.

Virgin Mary appears in Lourdes grotto

Lourdes, 15 February 1858
The small French town of Lourdes is eagerly discussing the claims of a 14-year-old peasant girl who says that for the last four days a lady "surrounded with light" has appeared before her in a cave.

Bernadette Soubirous, who referred to the vision as *Acquero* (The Thing), had gone into the grotto while her sister and another girl collected firewood. They returned to find her on her knees.

She told them: "I saw a young girl in white with a yellow rose on each foot. She was not bigger than me. She made a little bow and I saw a rosary hanging on her arm. She made the sign of the cross and was surrounded with light."

Artistic view of Bernadette's vision.

Assassin's bomb fails to kill Napoleon III

Italian republican Felice Orsini's attempted assassination of the emperor.

Paris, 14 January 1858
Emperor Napoleon and Empress Eugenie today escaped unhurt after an Italian assassin threw a bomb at their carriage as they drove to the Paris Opera. However, eight bystanders were killed and up to 100 people injured.

Police have named the assassin as Felice Orsini, an Italian republican sympathiser. He told them that he regarded the emperor as a traitor to the Italian cause. This is thought to be a reference to the emperor's support for the Italian *Carbonari*, which he supported as a private citizen. The emperor's uncle, Napoleon I, is still remembered in Italy as the country's liberator.

The attempted assassination has triggered a clampdown on republicans in France, with hundreds of arrests, and a wave of anti-British sentiment. A police raid has discovered papers showing that Orsini plotted the assassination with Italian republicans based in London, where they made the bomb.

Indian rebels surrender Lucknow fortress

Lucknow, India, 22 March 1858
British troops have entered Lucknow for the third time in a year. This city has been a weathercock of the Mutiny. For 87 days the residency had been under siege. Reinforcements came in September but were too few and the city endured three more weeks of fighting.

Even after the relief, Lucknow remained a rebel stronghold, and though one rebel centre after another fell to the British, the city remained with the *Sepoys*.

In the end the British, under Sir Colin Campbell, used 25,000 troops and 80 artillery pieces to subdue the Sepoy army. The collapse of the Sepoys yesterday, after two weeks fighting a battle of manoeuvre outside the city, took even the British generals by surprise.

Only *The Times'* correspondent, William Howard Russell, rose to the occasion, giving a first-hand account of the final assault.

"The Sepoys, dismayed by the fierce onslaught, abandoned their positions; and as they fled, with Brasyer's Sikhs and the Tenth regiment in fast pursuit, they rushed in such confusion through the detached houses that a universal panic was created. Some were shut up, or secreted themselves in recesses, and in the many mysterious apartments of an eastern palace; but all who were found in arms were shot down or bayoneted on the spot," he wrote.

With the final fall of Lucknow, the Indian Mutiny can now be said to be over, but not forgotten. The two sides have competed with each other in atrocities. The horrifying memories, on both sides, will be remembered in India for a long time to come.

Atlantic, 2 September 1858. The first transatlantic telegraph cable – running from the USA to Britain via Newfoundland – breaks down only 28 days after going into operation.

Prussia, October 1858. Frederick William IV, who has suffered a stroke, relinquishes power and his brother William becomes regent.

India, 1 November 1858. Queen Victoria is proclaimed ruler of India. The East India Company is abolished and the administration of India is transferred to the crown.

Prussia, 23 November 1858. The liberals win a majority in the elections to the Prussian ruling assembly.

Balkans, November 1858. The great European powers recognise the independence of Montenegro, which recently repulsed an Ottoman invasion.

Serbia, November 1858. Prince Alexander Karageorge, unpopular because of his servile policies towards Austria and his authoritarian internal rule, is deposed by the *diet*. He flees and takes refuge with the Ottomans.

Britain, 1858. Lionel de Rothschild becomes the first Jew to be admitted as an MP to the House of Commons. Although he was elected in 1847, and five times re-elected, he was not allowed to take his seat until the introduction of a new form of oath which omitted the words "on the truth faith of a Christian".

New York City, 1858. The Irish immigrant John Stephens founds an Irish revolutionary society whose members are known as the *Fenians* or the Brotherhood.

France, 1858. The *Bibliotheque Nationale* (National Library) opens.

Germany, 1858. The physicist Julius Plucker discovers cathode rays and the deflection produced upon them by magnetic fields.

London, 1858. The London news agency Reuter's acquires its first newspaper client, the London *Morning Advertiser*. Since its founding in 1851 by Paul Julius Reuter, a bank clerk, the Reuter's Telegraph Company has provided a commercial news service to banks, brokerage houses and leading business firms.

France, 19 January 1859. Following the secret meeting between Napoleon III and Count Cavour at Plombieres last July, France and Piedmont sign a treaty of alliance.

Serbia, January 1859. Following the deposition of Prince Alexander Karageorge, Milos Obrenovic, the 79-year-old former ruler of Serbia, is restored to power.

USA, 14 February 1859. Oregon becomes the USA's 33rd state.

Cochin China, (Vietnam), 17 February 1859. In revenge for the massacre of missionaries by the Emperor Annam Tu Duc, the French Admiral Rigault de Genouilly occupies Saigon.

Russia, 3 March 1859. Russia signs a secret treaty with France guaranteeing its neutrality in the event of an Austro-Franco war.

France, 17 April 1859. Napoleon III grants an amnesty for political prisoners.

China, 22 April 1859. Hong Rengan, the cousin of Hong Xiuquan, a leader of the God-Worshippers, arrives in Nanjing and sets out to introduce a reform package.

Egypt, 25 April 1859. Work begins on the building of the Suez Canal.

Italy, 26 April 1859. Count Cavour rejects an Austrian ultimatum to Piedmont to disarm.

Italy, 29 April 1859. Austrian troops invade Piedmont.

France, 3 May 1859. France declares war on Austria.

Italy, May 1859. Revolutions instigated by the National Society – which is campaigning for a unified Italy under the king of Piedmont – break out in Tuscany, Modena and Parma.

China, May 1859. Lan Chaogui and other members of the Incense Burners' League rebel at Daguan and Zhaotong in Yunnan province.

Italy, 4 June 1859. Piedmont and France crush Austria at Magenta.

Britain, 18 June 1859. Lord Palmerston forms his second Liberal ministry following the defeat of the Conservatives on an electoral reform bill.

Italy, 24 June 1859. The French and Piedmontese defeat the Austrians at Solferino.

China, 25 June 1859. British and French warships again attack the Dagu forts, but are defeated by the Chinese garrison. They are saved by the timely intervention of US naval forces.

Italy, June 1859. Rebellions break out in the papal states of Ravenna, Ferrara and Bologna.

USA, 1 July 1859. John Wise, an aeronaut, and three others are the first to transport mail by balloon. Their machine, *Atlantic*, covers the 812 miles between St Louis, Missouri, and Henderson, New York state, in 19 hours 40 minutes.

Italy, 11 July 1859. Napoleon III and Franz Josef of Austria reach peace terms at Villafranca.

Coach crosses US in 20 days non-stop

The Overland Mail Company's coach passing Mount Shasta, California.

Los Angeles, 7 October 1858
Caked with mud and dust, a stagecoach rattled into Los Angeles today – just 20 days after leaving St Louis over the longest stage route in the world. Carrying five passengers – including a *New York Herald* correspondent – and some letter mail, the coach ran day and night, non-stop (apart from changing horses) over 2,600 miles (4,160km) of deserts, plains and hostile Comanche Indian country.

The coach, which belongs to the new Overland Mail Company, was drawn by teams of six horses and is capable of covering more than 100 miles in 24 hours. Among the investors is William G Fargo, who is planning a national mail service.

Outrage greets book on human evolution

London, 30 November 1859
The reception of a book called *The Origin of Species*, published this week but already sold out, has been a mixture of amazement and violent rebuttal. In it Charles Darwin advances the theory that species evolve into other species by mutations from a common ancestor. The mechanism of "evolution" is by variations in individuals being selected by the pressures to survive in the environment: some variations flourish, others perish.

"Natural Selection" was the subject of two papers jointly delivered to the Linnaean Society last July by Darwin and Alfred Russel Wallace, who had arrived independently at the same conclusions.

Indian art: a fish seller and sweatmeat maker with their customers, by Shiva Dayal Lal, one of India's finest painters, from Patna, Bihar.

Secret deal on the liberation of Italy

Plombieres, 21 July 1858
Count Cavour, the prime minister of Piedmont-Sardinia, had a secret meeting with the Emperor Napoleon III here today. The emperor took time of from his numerous mistress and the two talked for several hours and then went for a three hour drive together in the Vosges forest. Napoleon took the reins himself.

Apparently Napoleon has agreed to help Piedmont to rid Italy of the Austrians. Cavour is planning to incite the people of Massa and Carrara to ask for the protection of Napoleon. This, they expect, will cause the duke of Modena to react aggressively with Austria's help. Then France can move its troops in to protect the people.

In return, Napoleon wants Nice and Savoy. An even bigger potential stumbling block is that he wants his cousin, Prince Napoleon, to marry Clotilde, the young daughter of King Victor Emmanuel, a suggestion which will not be welcome.

Women campaign to end US slavery

Men, women and children are auctioned in Charleston, South Carolina.

United States, 1859
Three years after the publication of Harriet Beecher Stowe's *Uncle Tom's Cabin*, women – former slaves among them – are in the forefront of the campaign for the abolition of slavery. Apart from lecturing throughout the country, often risking violence at the hands of fanatical pro-slavers, they are playing an important role in supporting the clandestine "underground railroad" to the north for runaway slaves.

Sojourner Truth was born a slave and belonged to several owners before she fled to New York where she wrote her autobiography, *The Narrative of Sojourner Truth*. Now she travels throughout the west, giving dramatic talks on slavery and the suffrage issue. Another former slave, Harriet Tubman, escaped when she was due to be sold to the deep south. She has helped more than 300 fugitives to reach the

Sojourner Truth: abolitionist.

northern states and Canada, using routes that are changed frequently and demanding strict discipline – often at pistol point – from the escapees.

Carnage as Austrians retreat in Italy

Solferino, 24 June 1859
The small northern Italian village of Solferino is tonight in French hands amid shocking scenes of carnage and suffering unrivalled since the Crimean War. Total casualties in the battle – the latest in the conflict between French-backed Piedmont and Austria – are estimated at over 40,000 after barely nine hours of fighting, much of it grim hand-to-hand combat.

With the Austrians retreating into the Quadrilateral, the impregnable defensive box formed by four fortified cities on the Mantuan plain, the conflict is at stalemate, with Piedmont no closer to gaining Lombardy or Venetia in its bid to unite Italy, which would relieve it of the need to cede Savoy to France under the deal agreed with Napoleon III. Many of the 22,500 Austrian casualties came as French shells rained relentlessly down on the town that Emperor Franz Josef,

A captured Austrian cavalryman.

aged 29, fighting his first battle, had selected as the starting point for a counter-offensive. Many of the 17,500 French casualties died as they charged *en masse* up the hill.

Self-help is solution for Samuel Smiles

London, 1859
The Industrial Revolution may be a matter of worry for many people, but the author and reformer Samuel Smiles has used it as the backdrop for his new book of social improvement, *Self-Help*.

Smiles, whose own jobs have included surgeon, newspaper editor and railway administrator, has produced a paean to industry, thrift and self-improvement. The individual is responsible for the success or failure of his own life; Smiles deplores "over-government".

Smiles has certainly touched a chord, even if his critics decry the book as the embodiment of smug middle-class individualism, claiming that such efforts are beyond society's many unfortunates.

Samuel Smiles: prophet of self-help.

Sydney is a cesspit, says British writer

New South Wales, October 1858
Parts of the city of Sydney are denounced by a sociologist as "social cesspools" of vice, misery and poverty, peopled by a "vicious and filthy humanity". The British-born William Jevons, writing in the *Sydney Morning Herald*, said that the muddy, narrow streets were devoid of gutters or sewers, and lined by dilapidated cottages with no sanitation. He asserted that both ground and air were poisoned by the cottagers' "foul drainings" which soaked into foundations and ran under other people's doors. He called on the council to clean up these slums.

Italy, 12 July 1859. Count Cavour resigns as prime minister of Piedmont in protest at the peace terms concluded yesterday by France and Austria.

Italy, August 1859. Parma, Modena, Tuscany and Romagna form a military alliance and demand union with Piedmont under King Victor Emmanuel.

Serbia, September 1859. On the death of Milos Obrenovic, he is replaced as Serbian leader by his son Michael.

China, October 1859. The rebel Incense Burners' League occupies Yunlian and Gaoxian in Sichuan province.

Switzerland, 11 November 1859. In confirmation of their preliminary negotiations at Villafranca in July, France and Piedmont sign a peace treaty with their defeated enemy, Austria, at Zurich. Lombardy is ceded to Piedmont.

Argentina, 11 November 1859. The city of Buenos Aires is compelled to rejoin the Argentine Federation, from which it broke away in 1853.

Britain, November 1859. Charles Darwin publishes his *Origin of Species by Means of Natural Selection.*

Australia, 1859. Queensland is established as a separate colony, with its capital at Brisbane.

India, 1859. The first power-loom is set up in India.

Massachusetts, 1859. The Massachusetts Institute of Technology is founded at Cambridge.

Russia, 1859. Ivan Goncharov publishes a novel on the delights of indolence entitled *Oblomov.*

Britain, 1859. John Stuart Mill publishes his essay *On Liberty*, stating the principle that individual freedom should be complete provided that it does not interfere with the liberty of others.

England, 1859. Karl Marx, in exile in London, publishes his *Critique of Political Economy*, putting forward a "materialist" interpretation of history.

Britain, 1859. Edward Fitzgerald publishes his verse translation of the *Rubaiyat of Omar Khayyam*, the mediaeval Persian poet and philosopher of resignation.

France, 1859. The naturalist Felix-Archimede Pouchet publishes *Heterogenie*, in which he gives details of his theory of the spontaneous generation of life from non-living matter.

France, 1859. Eugene Delacroix, the leader of the Romantic school of painting, completes his *Jacob and the Angel.*

France, 1859. Charles Gounod's opera *Faust* is performed for the first time. Among this year's other premieres is *Orpheus in the Underworld*, an operetta by Jacques Offenbach.

Germany, 1859. Richard Wagner completes his opera *Tristan and Isolde.*

USA, 10 January 1860. In the first big factory accident, 77 people are killed when a textile factory building collapses in Lawrence, Massachusetts.

Piedmont, 21 January 1860. Count Camillo Cavour becomes prime minister again, with the intention of uniting the duchies of Parma, Modena, Romagna and Tuscany. Referendums will be held in March.

Britain, 23 January 1860. Richard Cobden, one of the leaders of the movement to repeal the Corn Laws, negotiates a commercial treaty with France aimed at reducing customs duties on over 40 articles.

Prussia, February 1860. General Albert von Roon, who was appointed minister of war in December, puts forward proposals for reform of the army.

USA, 6 March 1860. The Republican politician Abraham Lincoln makes a campaign speech defending the right to strike.

Japan, 24 March 1860. Ii Naosuke, the *shogunal* councillor who signed the treaty of trade and friendship with the USA in 1858, is cut down and mortally wounded while on his way to an audience with the emperor. Anti-foreign extremists hold Ii Naosuke responsible for the current liberal foreign policy in Japan.

Italy, 24 March 1860. France signs a treaty with Piedmont at Turin. Piedmont is to annex central Italy, while France is promised Nice and Savoy.

Italy, March 1860. Tuscany, Parma, Modena and Romagna vote in favour of union with Piedmont.

Russia, 1860. The port of Vladivostok is founded on the coast of the Sea of Japan.

Russia, 1860. *The Tempest*, by Alexander Ostrovsky, Russia's leading playwright, is performed for the first time.

Britain, 1860. George Eliot (a pseudonym of Mary Ann Evans) publishes *The Mill on the Floss*, following the success of *Adam Bede* last year.

Britain, 1860. Wilkie Collins publishes *The Woman in White*, a new kind of novel – detective fiction.

First oil well yields 25 barrels per day

Pennsylvania, 28 August 1859
They have known about oil for the past 300 years in America. It seeped from the ground then, and was used firstly as a medicine to cure blindness, rheumatism, coughs, colds, sprains and baldness. In those early days it was skimmed from creeks in its crudest form and proved invaluable for lighting – even though it gave off a smelly, powerful odour. A chemist succeeded in distilling the crude oil into a satisfactory lighting fuel.

But it was in 1833 that the true value of oil as an industrial lubricant was realised, and there was a case for major exploitation. Edwin Drake, a former railroad conductor, has done exactly that, employing techniques used in drilling salt wells and boring down 69 feet to produce a steady flow of 25 barrels of oil daily which he is marketing for heating and lighting. With industry expanding rapidly, specu-

Drake (in top hat) and his oil well.

lators are watching Drake's operation with more than usual interest and, already, other prospectors are at work in the Allegheny valley and elsewhere.

English craze for everything mediaeval

James Archer's Death of Arthur, where neo-Gothic and pre-Raphaelite meet.

London, 1859
Alfred Tennyson, Britain's poet laureate since 1850, has published the first instalment of a long poem on the legend of King Arthur, *The Idylls of the King*. Since he wrote *Maud*, *In Memoriam* and *The Charge of the Light Brigade*, he is the most-read English poet of the time. He published *Morte d'Arthur* and *Sir Galahad* in 1842. Now he adds *The Coming of Arthur* and

other idylls. *The Holy Grail* and others are still to come. The Arthurian legend dominates literature. Matthew Arnold's *Tristram and Iseult* and William Morris' *Defence of Guenevere* have come out recently. Morris and Rossetti decorated the Oxford Union debating hall with Arthurian murals last year. Pugin's Gothic revival in architecture is part of the current mediaevalist craze.

Chinese rebels defeated

Shanghai, 19 August 1860

The *Taiping* rebel army has today been halted at the gates of Shanghai by a combined force of British, Indian and French troops. The Taipings, ravaging the land as they advanced, tried to buy off the "foreign devils" by offering them trading rights in their captured cities, but the British and French commanders promised the terrified inhabitants that they would protect the city against massacre and pillage, and they have kept their word.

This is a serious setback for the Taipings who had broken out of Nanjing under their brilliant new general, Li Xiucheng, the "loyal king", and shattered the besieging imperial army. Their long rebellion may now be sliding into defeat. The irony of today's clash is that in the north the British and French are preparing to advance on Beijing.

Taiping rebels under Li Xiucheng attacking Shanghai, by land and sea.

Peru grows wealthy on bird droppings

Peru, 1860

Peru, whose economy in recent years has been devastated by political upheaval, has found a new deliverer. But the agent of national wealth is not men, but birds, or, more precisely, bird-droppings.

Guano, as the Peruvians call it, has long been collected by the Indians, who gather it from the coast where it is deposited by millions of seabirds. They take it inland where it provides a rich fertiliser. Early colonisers, intent on gold, ignored this less romantic treasure, but recent scientific research has shown how very valuable guano is.

Now the Peruvian government has declared the exploitation of guano as a national monopoly. An extensive trade has been established with Europe, where the benefits of so rich a fertiliser are in great demand.

Fighter for slaves freedom hanged

Charleston, Virginia, 2 Dec 1859

Henry Wadsworth Longfellow summed up the feelings of many of his fellow-Americans. "This is sowing the wind to reap the whirlwind which will soon come," he said. He was referring to the hanging today of John Brown, a 59-year-old fanatical abolitionist, for treason, murder and conspiring with slaves.

Brown had planned to seize the arsenal at Harper's Ferry and turn the town into a base for an uprising by slaves. The plan succeeded, but the arsenal was recaptured soon afterwards by a force of marines led by Captain Robert E Lee. During his trial Brown refused to answer questions, saying that God had given him a mission to free slaves.

Many believe that John Brown was insane. The governor of Virginia has received 17 affidavits to that effect.

Japan's nationalists murder foreigners

Japan, 1860

Fanatical Japanese nationalists in the capital, Edo (*Tokyo*), have begun a campaign of assassination against foreigners. A Russian officer and two sailors were among the first to be killed. They were followed by two Dutchmen and Henry Heusken, the Dutch-born secretary and interpreter for Townsend Harris, the US consul.

Heusken, who had helped several foreign envoys in their negotiations with the Japanese authorities, was one of the most respected members of the foreign community. The presence of the increasing number of foreign diplomats in Edo has given the assassins a choice of targets, and their reign of terror has caused the envoys to absent themselves discreetly from the capital.

Only Townsend Harris, the US representative, a wealthy New York banker who gained his knowledge of the east by shipping cargo

A drunken foreign sailor served saki.

in his own boats, has stayed at his post. He has acquired considerable prestige among the Japanese by his courage in refusing to run away from the killers.

Gold transforms southeastern Australia

Victoria, Australia, 1860

Gold fever has gripped Victoria and transformed the colony's economy. In ten years the mines at Ballarat and Bendigo have produced eight million ounces, and the population of Victoria colony has risen from 77,345 to 540,322.

Thousands of new immigrants, have flocked to the fields. Many are from California, whence they have brought the latest mining skills. Others have come from Ireland and have brought radical and anti-British traditions with them. Another large group comes from Germany, and the thousands of Chinese cause deep resentment in the white working class.

The wave of people with their accompanying skills has created new industries in Victoria, while the new-found gold has provided much-needed capital. A decade ago the colony exported only sheep. Now it also exports gold.

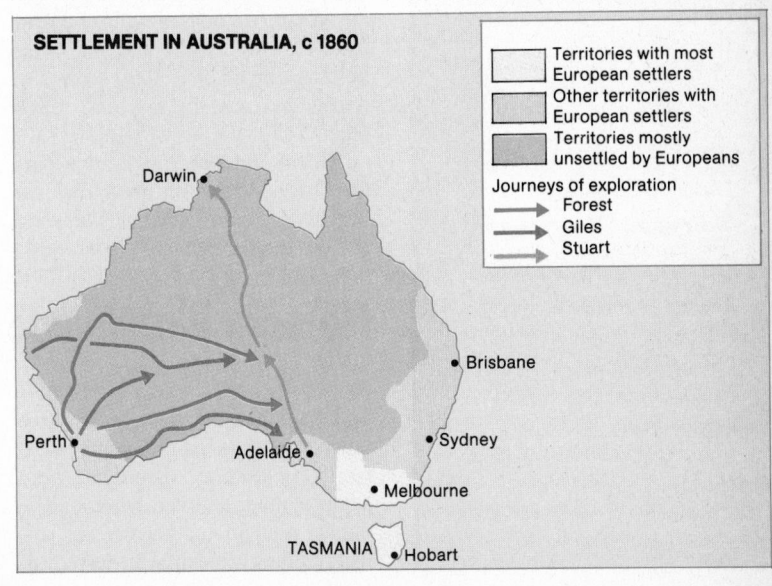

SETTLEMENT IN AUSTRALIA, c 1860

Territories with most European settlers
Other territories with European settlers
Territories mostly unsettled by Europeans
Journeys of exploration
→ Forest
→ Giles
→ Stuart

Darwin
Perth
Adelaide
Brisbane
Sydney
Melbourne
TASMANIA Hobart

Italy, 11 May. Garibaldi lands at Marsala in Sicily.

China, June. The American F T Ward enlists foreigners in a volunteer corps to defend Shanghai against *Taiping* rebels.

China, 19 August. British and French regular forces defeat Li Xiucheng's Taiping troops near Shanghai.

China, 21 August. Anglo-French forces take the Dagu forts in northern China, defeating the Qing defenders.

Honduras, 12 September. The American William Walker, the one-time ruler of Nicaragua, is executed by firing squad.

Italy, 18 September. Piedmontese troops move into the papal states to forestall Garibaldi. They defeat the papal troops at Castelfidardo.

Germany, 21 September. Arthur Schopenhauer, the most influential philosopher since Hegel, dies aged 72.

China, 21 September. Fighting continues in the second Opium War. AngloFrench forces defeat Qing troops at Baliqiao, on the road to Beijing.

China, 22 September. The Xianfeng Emperor flees from Beijing to Jehol.

Beijing, 13 October. Anglo-French troops occupy Beijing after several days spent looting the Summer Palace.

Beijing, 20 October. The Summer Palace is burnt to the ground.

Austria, 20 October. The October *Diploma* sets up a federal constitution for the empire. This is very unpopular with the Hungarians.

Beijing, 25 October. Following the signing of the Sino-British convention of Beijing yesterday, today the Sino-French convention is signed. The war is over.

Italy, 5 November. The papal states vote to unite with the Piedmontese monarchy.

Washington, DC, 6 November. Abraham Lincoln is elected president of the United States.

Beijing, 14 November. The emperor's brother, Prince Gong, signs the Sino-Russian convention, ceding land east of the Ussuri river to Russia.

USA, 20 December. South Carolina secedes from the union.

Postman gallops 2,000 miles in 11 days

Sacramento, Cal., 13 April

The first Pony Express clattered into town today bringing 49 letters and three newspapers posted in St Joseph, Missouri, 11 days ago. Hundreds cheered as young Tom Hamilton galloped up to the post office and handed over the mail satchel. The new mail service – which involves a run across 1,966 miles (3,145km) of desolate prairie with risks from hostile Indians and flash floods in the mountains – has been organised by the Central Overland Company which bought 500 horses and advertised for "skinny, expert riders willing to risk death daily". Each horse is galloped at speed for about 12 miles (19km) before the horseman changes mounts.

The first Pony Express rider arrives in California to a hero's welcome.

US customs amaze Japanese envoy

San Francisco, 18 May

The first Japanese envoys to the United States have seen many amazing sights since they arrived, but none has astonished them more than the scene they witnessed tonight after a dinner given for them Secretary of State Lewis Cass.

Vice-ambassador Muragaki recalls: "The music commenced and an officer in uniform with one arm round a lady's waist and the other holding one of hers, started moving round the room on his toes, many others following his example ...

"Our wonder at the strange performance became so great that we began to doubt whether we were not on another planet."

The Japanese envoys in Washington.

Thousand redshirt rebels in Sicily

Genoa, 6 May

The Italian republican and international revolutionary, Guiseppe Garibaldi, sailed from here today with a force of a thousand redshirts aboard two small steamers. They plan to liberate first Sicily and then Naples in the name of a united Italy. Garibaldi began gathering his force in the hope of stopping the ceding of his native Nice to France, but he realised that he could not get the support of Piedmont's King Victor Emmanuel. The king is likely to support his bid for a united Italy, however.

Giuseppe Garibaldi was born in 1807 and as a young man became a supporter of Mazzini's Young Italy movement. He was forced to flee to

Giuseppe Garibaldi in old age.

South America in 1834 and won military fame in battles against the Argentinians. In 1848 he returned to Italy and organised the defence of the Roman republic against the French. He was forced into a courageous retreat and exile. He has become the symbol of Italian liberation, and launched a guerrilla attack on Lake Como last year.

Florence Nightingale brings nurses and midwives more respect

England

The ambition of every respectable little girl nowadays, it seems, is to be like Florence Nightingale who has become a national heroine. The public, grateful for her care of soldiers in the Crimean War, have funded the Nightingale Nurse Training School at St Thomas' Hospital in London where a selected few will study, fully paid, for one year. Florence Nightingale has been dedicated to the reform of hospitals since she left her rich upper-class family to train as a nurse at Kaiserwerth Institute near Dusseldorf. Now aged 40, still full of determination, she plans to open another school next year. This time it will be for midwifery nurses at King's College Hospital, also in London.

Beijing falls to Allies

The Summer Palace, with the Bridge of Marble in the foreground, looted today.

Beijing, 6 October
The Franco-British expeditionary force has today captured Beijing, and tonight the troops are looting the fabulous Summer Palace of China's emperor.

Rarely can an army have captured so rich a prize. The emperor left behind all his treasure when he fled. There is so much that the French and British envoys, Baron Gros and Lord Elgin, have appointed commissioners from each army to divide up the spoils equally.

Lord Elgin chose the emperor's jade baton for Queen Victoria, and a similar one was found for the emperor of France. Every soldier is to get his share.

At first sentries kept the troops away from the 200 richly furnished buildings of the palace, but when the soldiers learnt that peasants had climbed the walls to steal what they could, they brushed the sentries aside and stormed the buildings.

English, French, Scots and Sikhs are staggering out of the palace, their arms filled with silks and brocades and their pockets with jewels. Some are cavorting in the gowns of the emperor's concubines.

They are smashing the furniture to get at the jewels set into the woodwork. Snuff boxes, pearl necklaces, and golden table sets are stuffed into sacks. One officer has acquired a priceless black jade chess set. Now we hear that Lord Elgin is considering burning the palace in revenge for the killing of 20 allied prisoners.

Lord Elgin's new Chinese marbles, a trinket from his travels.

Abraham Lincoln elected US president

Washington, 20 December
After a bitterly fought campaign, Abraham Lincoln, a former frontier shopkeeper and postmaster who became a successful lawyer in Illinois, was elected president today. The United States, already severely divided over the issues of slavery and the right of states to secede from the union, is braced for civil war. South Carolina has already seceded from the union, and six other southern states are threatening to follow suit before Lincoln takes office next year.

A tall, gangling conservative, noted for his dry wit and folksy wisdom, Lincoln won the election on an anti-slavery platform. "I believe this government cannot endure permanently, half slave and half free," he has said, although he admits freely that he sees no way of solving the problem. His only hope of saving national unity lies with more moderate southern leaders

Abraham Lincoln: 16th president.

like Jefferson Davis who are prepared to give the new administration a fair chance. The moderates are heavily outnumbered, however, by slave-owning planters.

China succumbs to British trade demands

Beijing, 24 October
Lord Elgin, escorted by British soldiers, marched through the deserted Chinese capital today to the Hall of Rites where the defeated Chinese, cowed by the burning of the Summer Palace, signed a treaty acceding to Britain's demands.

The terms are similar to those of the "treaty of peace, friendship and commerce" signed at Tianjin two years ago. It was the breaking of this treaty, when the Chinese refused to allow foreign diplomats to establish their embassies in Beijing, which led to the Anglo-French occupation of the capital. Under the terms 11 more ports, including Shanghai, the gateway to the Yangzi, are to be opened to foreign trade, and diplomats will be allowed to live in Beijing. China is also to pay an indemnity and cede part of Kowloon to Britain. Lord Elgin was met by 500 *mandarins* led by Prince Gong, half-brother of the emperor.

Bare-fist fighting is loser as marathon battle ends in stalemate

England, April
A bare-knuckled boxing match between the champions of England and the US ended in a draw this month after two hours and 20 minutes. Yet in one sense the marathon battle may yet prove conclusive: it seems increasingly likely that it will have been the last bout of its kind.

The possibly historic encounter occurred when Sayers, the English champion for the past three years, met Heenan, the best heavyweight in the United States, at Farnborough in Hampshire. The stakes were £200 a side. In a gruelling encounter, the much lighter Sayers suffered a torn tendon while his opponent was virtually blinded by facial swelling. Members of Parliament and famous authors watched the match, which was staged in secret because of police disapproval.

Bare-knuckled prize-fighting became an international sport 50 years ago, but now appals many of its original aristocratic promoters. Poorly-trained and ill-rewarded fighters often fall into penury and drunkenness. But the introduction of skintight gloves has helped to reduce injuries.

A pugilist, posing for the canvas.

1861

Prussia, 2 January. On the death of Frederick William IV, William succeeds to the throne.

USA, 8 February. Following the example of South Carolina, other slave states secede from the union and form the Confederate States of America.

Prussia, 8 February. The Progressive Party is set up with the aim of unifying Germany under Prussian leadership.

Italy, 18 February. Following the capture of Gaeta by Piedmontese troops four days ago, King Victor Emmanuel II of Sardinia is named "king of Italy". King Francis II of Naples takes refuge in Rome which is still held by France. Austria holds Venetia.

Austria, 26 February. The February Patent establishes a federal constitution.

Russia, 3 March. Serfs are emancipated by Alexander II as part of a programme of westernisation.

Washington, DC, 4 March. Lincoln is sworn in as president.

New Zealand, 19 March. An uneasy truce brings an end to fighting between the Maoris and British settlers sparked off in 1859 by a dispute over a land purchase near the Waitari river.

South Carolina, 14 April. Fort Sumter in Charleston port falls to Confederate troops.

Britain, 13 May. The government declares its neutrality in the American Civil War.

Italy, 6 June. Count Camillo di Cavour, the prime minister who worked to unify Italy, dies.

Ottoman Empire, 21 July. Sultan Abdul Mejid dies and is succeeded by Abdul Aziz.

Virginia, 21 July. The first thrust by union forces towards the confederate capital of Richmond is repulsed at Bull Run.

Washington, DC, 22 July. The senate passes the Crittenden Resolution, stating the war's main purpose as the preservation of the union, not the abolition of slavery.

Washington, DC, 5 August. President Lincoln makes the first nationwide income tax law, in an attempt to fund the civil war.

Washington, DC, 16 August. President Lincoln bars all commerce with the confederate states.

Austria, 21 August. Following the February Patent, establishing a federal constitution, the Hungarian *diet* is dissolved and replaced by Austrian imperial commissioners.

Tientsin, China, 2 September. A new commercial treaty is signed by representatives of China and Prussia, opening up China to further Prussian commercial penetration.

Frankfurt, 26 October. The German professor of physics, Johann Philipp Reiss, presents a telephone to the Society of Physics.

South Carolina, 7 November. Union cannons pounds confederate troops into submission in Port Royal, the second major victory for the union in a blockade of less than two months.

Portugal, 11 November. King Pedro V dies in a typhoid epidemic. He is succeeded by his brother Luis.

China, 2 December. Following the death of the Xianfeng emperor on 22 August, and the accession of Zaichun on 11 November, the two empresses dowager, Ci'an and Cixi, become regents.

Britain, 14 December. The prince consort, Albert, dies of typhoid, to the great sorrow of Queen Victoria.

Rumania, 23 December. The European powers recognise the principality of Rumania (Moldavia and Wallachia) which is ruled by Prince Alexander Cuza.

China, December. The *Shanghai xinbao* (New Shanghai Paper) is a new weekly.

Britain. The popular novelist Charles Dickens publishes the first episodes of *Great Expectations* in the journal *All the Year Round*. It is the story of Pip, a village boy, brought up by his overbearing sister and her gentle husband, Joe Gargery the blacksmith.

Nigeria. The British establish a protectorate over the port of Lagos.

Germany. Johannes Brahms composes his first piano concerto.

Britain. The feminist Maria Rye publishes the *Emigration of Educated Women* outlining her plans to find unemployed women positions in Australia and Canada.

France. The *velocipede* is invented – a two-wheeled vehicle which the rider sits astride and propels with his feet.

Madagascar. Queen Ranavalona's successor, Radama II, tries to impose a policy of westernisation, but comes up against opposition from the small elite that governs the country.

West Africa. The Tukulor leader, Al-Hajj Umar, who has been waging a *jihad* (holy war) since 1852, destroys and occupies the Bambara kingdom of Segu.

France extends rule in Cochin China

The emperor and his ministers.

Cochin China (Vietnam), 25 Feb
A French force of some 3,000 men under Admiral Charner has taken the forts guarding Saigon and relieved 900 French and Spanish troops blockaded in the city by 20,000 Annamese regulars commanded by General Nguyen Tri Phuong. There was some stiff fighting, but the French are now in command of the countryside in the vicinity of Saigon. They have thus extended their influence in Cochin China without setting out on any well planned imperialist venture.

Admiral Charner's orders were merely to relieve the garrison and consolidate the points already occupied by the French who were originally sent to Cochin China with some Spanish troops to protect persecuted Catholic missionaries. The appointment of M Chasseloup-Laubat as minister of marine and colonies may well bring a more aggressive approach to the spread of French influence in Cochin China, with a demand for French sovereignty over the newly-occupied south-east Asian territories.

Victor Emmanuel II, the first king of Italy

Garibaldi, fitting the king's boot.

Turin, 17 March
Victor Emmanuel, the king of Piedmont-Sardinia, was recognised as king of the new united Italy by the parliament here today. Victor Emmanuel – the cavalier king, as he is known – has been popular; but his position as monarch of all Italy is owed to the diplomatic and political skills of his prime minister Cavour. The critical events were last year. The success of Garibaldi's revolutionary army was ensured in the south and he was ready to march on Rome. He wanted a united republican Italy. Four days after Garibaldi's army entered Naples Cavour invaded the papal states, ostensibly to prevent revolution there.

There was no justification in law and Napoleon publicly condemned the act. Privately, though, Napoleon supported Cavour and sent only a small French force to Italy. After his military victory Cavour arranged plebiscites by secret ballot in Naples and Sicily which brought massive majorities for a united Italy under Victor Emmanuel.

Inbecile gives a clue to "map" of the brain

France, April
They called the patient "Tan". It was the only word that he knew. A surgeon, Pierre-Paul Broca, conducted a *post-mortem* which revealed that Tan's brain was degenerate in the frontal region. Broca believes that language seems to be placed in the frontal area of the brain; and presumably processes like movement, emotion and memory are situated elsewhere.

It's civil war in the US

Fort Sumter, Virginia, 15 April
With the high society of Charleston, the women in ball-gowns, their men in evening dress, watching from the waterfront, the first shots in this civil war two nights ago could well have been no more than a distant fireworks display. Few could accept that these were the first blasts of a conflict which threatens to rip the country apart.

With the confederacy of seven rebel southern states established under its president, Jefferson Davis, President Lincoln, determined to maintain the union, ordered union forces to relieve the federal garrison at Fort Sumter. But today, after a massive bombardment, the union commander surrendered and marched his men out with colours flying.

In Washington, President Lincoln called for 75,000 volunteers to fight forces "too powerful to be suppressed by the ordinary course of judicial proceedings". A senator summed it up as a "war of sentiment and opinion by one form of society against another form of society".

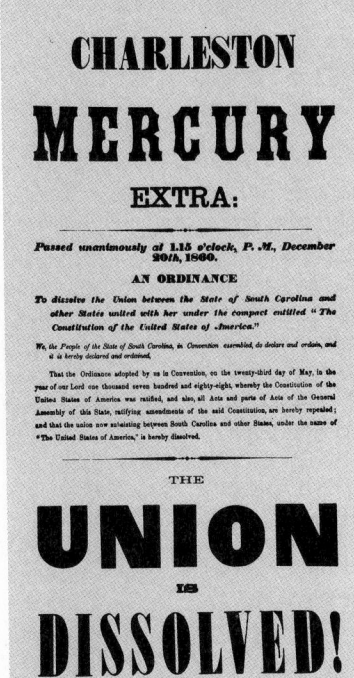

A South Carolina newspaper announces the first state to break from the Union last December, on the issue of slavery and state's rights.

Mexico promises to pay foreign debts

Mexico, 31 October
Representatives of the governments of Spain, France and Great Britain met in London today to sign an agreement under which they hope to regain the substantial loans each country has made to Mexico.

Under the convention of London the countries will occupy the Mexican coast until the debts, some of them 50 years old, are repaid in full. They will occupy the customs house at Vera Cruz and seize all customs receipts for themselves. There is no question of interfering in Mexican politics, or attempting to take over Mexican territory. They say: "The parties bind themselves not to seek for themselves any acquisition of territory, or any peculiar advantage, and not to impair the right of the Mexican nation to choose and freely to constitute the form of its own government."

Britain and Spain may well be sincere in their promises, but observers fear that France, whose president Louis Napoleon yearns to emulate his famous uncle, may have thoughts of actual conquest.

Czar Alexander frees twenty million serfs

St Petersburg, 3 March
For half a century Russia's leaders agreed that serfdom was evil – but that nothing could be done about it without risking the stability of society. When Alexander II came to the throne he said: "It is better to abolish serfdom from above than to wait until the serfs begin to liberate themselves from below." Today, the sixth anniversary of his accession, he issued an edict freeing 20 million serfs – one third of the population – and granting them the right to own the land they cultivate. But the serfs have to pay for their land, partly to the government and partly to their former landlord, so the effect of freedom may not be too great in practice.

Australian gold diggers attack Chinese

Victoria, 15 July
Three thousand goldminers, many armed, have driven thousands of Chinese immigrants from their camp at Lambing Flat, Victoria, Australia. And when police intervened, they threw them out as well.

There is a growing fear among uneducated whites that the large numbers of Chinese immigrants could undercut white labour. The first riot took place last December when 500 Chinese were driven out. The riots a fortnight ago were worse. The tiny police force stood by as Chinese gold diggers were burnt out of their homes. Yesterday the police finally moved and arrested three men for taking part in the attacks, or "roll-ups", as they are known locally. By evening the jail had been stormed, the three prisoners "liberated", and the ineffectual police force driven away. Needless to say there was not a Chinaman in sight in the camp.

The government's response has been remarkably speedy. In addition to the expected military column that is being assembled to restore order, the premier, Charles Cowper, has made it clear that he will be putting bills before parliament both to ensure gold diggers' safety standards and to limit Chinese immigration.

Nervous crown in new-look Indian policy

The ruins of the East India Company's India: skeletons of sepoys at Lucknow.

Delhi, India
The old paternal Englishman, with his *hookah*, his Indian mistress, and his languid Orientalism, no longer rules India. In a series of reforms following the suppression of the Mutiny, the old East India Company's governing powers have been taken over by the crown and the Indian Army has been reorganised.

The changeover from company to crown is hardly noticed. Little has changed except the letter-headings. Changes to the Indian Army have been more drastic. One third of the army (the Bengali regiments) took part in the Mutiny. The Company's European troops are to be disbanded. Every Indian brigade is to have a British battalion in it; Indian regiments are to be deprived of artillery.

Other changes have been somewhat less dramatic. Finances have been put in order without oppressing the peasantry. Indian princes have become more tightly bound to the crown, and Indians are being treated like subjects.

The Indian middle class, which remained loyal to Britain during the Mutiny, is taking on a greater role, but so great is the fear that the British now have of the Indians that the latter are being denied political responsibility.

Beating the barbarians at their own game

On 14 July 1853 Commodore Matthew Perry of the United States Navy set foot in Japan at the village of Kurihama. Behind him his flotilla of *Kurofune* "Black Ships" rode at anchor, emblematic of America's power. Perry, a confident and somewhat pompous man, was wearing his dress uniform and had two boys walking in front of him carrying two boxes wrapped in scarlet cloth. One contained his credentials, and the other protected a letter from President Millard Fillmore to the Emperor of Japan. Both were written on vellum and bound in blue silk velvet.

The letter, handed over to the emperor's representatives, Prince Idzu and Prince Iwami, in a scant half-hour ceremony, was direct by Japanese standards. It emphasised America's industrial strength and asked for: "friendship, commerce, a supply of coal and provisions, and protection for our shipwrecked people". It made clear that, "we are very much in earnest on this". The Shogunate government, which ruled in the name of the Emperor, was well aware of the meaning of this letter and when a Russian squadron dropped anchor in Nagasaki harbour a month later, it became obvious to the Japanese that their long period of deliberately imposed isolation from the non-Asian world was over.

The *Bakufu*, (literally "curtain-government") had brought down its bamboo barrier over 200 years before, cutting off all contact with the outside on pain of death, except for a handful of Dutch and Chinese merchants, strictly confined in Nagasaki. Christian missionaries and their converts had been killed, shipwrecked sailors harshly treated. The example of Western expansion in China was offered an awful warning. Both Russia and America had tried before to make contact. Catherine the Great had authorised the explorer Adam Laxman to visit Japan to open trade relations in 1792. He failed. Then in 1846 an American squadron under Commodore Biddle tried to put in at Yedo but it was closed. Now, with Russia pushing east across Siberia and American pushing west to acquire Oregon and California, Japan found itself caught between two irresistible powers.

Bamboo curtain swept aside

When Perry delivered his letter, there was still a strong feeling that he ought to be resisted. But Japan had no coastal guns and no fleet. On 31 March, 1854, the Treaty of Kanagawa was signed, opening the ports of Shimoda and Hakodate to American ships. Britain and Russia at once followed the United States in extracting similar treaties, with the Russians successfully claiming extra-territorial jurisdiction for its citizens. And so the bamboo curtain was swept aside and the feudal rule of the Shogun – literally the "barbarian-subduing great general" – brought to an end.

Now began the process of learning from the West, a task which the Japanese undertook so enthusiastically that half a century later they were able to inflict a great defeat on Russia and then, after another half century, were able to do battle with both Britain and America, losing because her rulers had forgotten Commodore Perry's lesson about America's industrial strength. But what the Japanese did accomplish in those two wars was to destroy for ever the myth of white superiority.

Before the process of learning could begin, however, Japan had to undergo a revolution. As one treaty followed another, giving the foreigners more and more rights until they became known as the "Unequal Treaties", so conservative opinion turned against the government. Arguing that the treaties had been signed without the emperor's approval, they accused the shogunate of treason and plotted its overthrow. Young, lower-ranking samurai known as *shishi* ("men of spirit"), whose motto was "Expel the Barbarians", murdered foreigners and, after the Harris Treaty of 1858 which extended America's trading privileges, assassinated leading officials of the shogunate. The emperor, asserting the imperial authority for the first time in 700 years, summoned the Shogun to court and ordered him to inform the foreign envoys that Japan would revert to the policy of seclusion.

Poorly-paid samurai rebel

The feudal lord of Choshu used coastal batteries to prevent foreign ships passing the Straits of Shimoneski and had his guns destroyed by a joint British-French-Dutch American naval expedition. The lord of Satsuma had his capital, Kagoshima, bombarded by a British squadron in revenge for the murder of an Englishman by some of his men. These were salutary lessons to the feudal lords and to the *shishi*, who were rapidly convinced of the futility of opposing western fire power. The government crumbled. The men around the 15-year-old Emperor Mutsuhito seized power and in 1868 the leaders of Chosu and Satsuma, who had felt the weight of western shellfire, induced the emperor to take the "Charter Oath", which contained the clause that "knowledge shall be sought all over the world". There then began that astonishing period in Japanese history known as the Meiji Period, in which Japan sucked in western knowledge and technology like a dry sponge in a bathtub.

It was not accomplished without bloodshed, however. In 1877, the Samurai – who had become civil servants paid by the government rather than their feudal lords – rebelled because they had no wars to fight and because their pay was so low. It took the government six months and the whole of the standing army of 32,000 to put down the rebellion. Nevertheless, its suppression demonstrated that such uprisings had no place in a Japan which had opened its doors to western knowledge. With that knowledge came political and social reform. Originally, efforts were made to model the Meiji government on the forms which had been current in the eighth century, seen as the golden age of imperial government. However, as the Japanese learned about the parliamentary democracies of the west, demands spread for a popular assembly and democratic rights, until the government was forced to announce that a parliament would be established in 1890.

Outraged by fancy dress

There was much culture shock as the Japanese went out into the world to learn and opened the country to western customs. A fancy dress ball held in Tokyo outraged the citizens, and brought severe criticism of prime minister Ito and his cabinet who attended the occasion. The sight of a leading statesman prancing round the dance floor holding a foreign woman dressed in a ridiculous costume was too much for even the most advanced citizen of Tokyo. This criticism marked a trend in Japanese thought away from the worship of all things western. In the 1890s the conviction began to take hold that Japan had sold it soul to the West and must once again endeavour to preserve its separate identity.

By then, however, a new army had been modelled on German methods, a new navy on the British. Industrialisation was proceeding at breathtaking speed to provide the arms and the ships and the base of a modern industrial society. A constitution based on the German model to give the executive the whip hand over the legislature had been introduced, and the first elections based on a limited male franchise were held in 1890. By 1900, fewer then 50 years after Commodore Perry had sailed his black ships into Japanese waters, Japan had become a western nation. Five years later Admiral Togo would destroy the Russian fleet at Tsushima.

Commodore Perry lands in Japan to treat with the emperor's representatives.

Traditional Japan, under seige by the West: the Japanese tea ceremony.

Traditional Japan: a contemporary photograph of a samurai warrior.

"Views of savage countries": the title of a print showing the Port of London as portrayed through the Japanese eyes of a noted artist, Yoshitora.

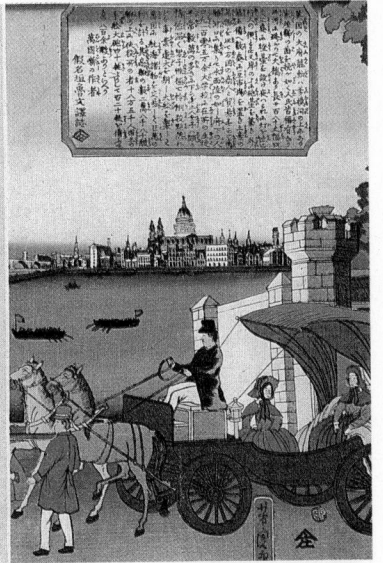

Mutsuhito, the crown prince, who came to the throne in 1867.

Modern Japan, where the old and the new jostle each other in the streets.

The penetration completed: barbarians at the Grand Hotel, Yokohama, 1907.

Blood and iron – the ultimate arbiters

Berlin, 24 September
Otto von Bismarck, the *junker's* son from Brandenburg, has become minister-president of Prussia with the task of rescuing the king from his quarrel with the liberal majority in the House of Deputies. The deputies rejected a bill put forward by King William to expand the army; when the king persisted, they threw out the budget.

Bismarck's solution is to tell the deputies that he does not need their vote in order to continue collecting taxes. The deputies strongly disagree, but there seems to be nothing that they can do about it – particularly since Bismarck has accused them of being wealthy aristocrats not representative of the people.

When he addressed the deputies' budget commission he largely disregarded finance and concentrated on foreign affairs. Speaking as the former Prussian envoy to the assembly of German states at Frankfurt, he said: "Germans do not look at Prussia's liberalism but at her power. Prussia must keep her

Bismarck: the "Iron Chancellor".

power together for the auspicious moment. The great questions of the age are not settled by speeches and majority votes, but by iron and blood."

A Chinese girl seated looking out of a window, by Lam Qua, who was trained in western painting styles by the Irish artist, George Chinnery, in China, lived in Hong Kong, and made his living selling Chinese scenes.

Les Miserables is a big hit in Paris

Paris, 30 June
The latest novel by Victor Hugo, published in Paris today, is an epic story of tortured conscience and remorse. Critics suggest that *Les Miserables* will be one of the author's major successes. In this densely plotted detective story, Jean Viljean, a thief dodging the police, moves to a small town, changes his name and reforms. He flourishes and becomes the mayor. Then he learns that a prisoner is on trial at the local assizes as the wanted criminal Viljean. He confesses after an anguished struggle with his conscience. Imprisoned, he escapes and is presumed dead. *Les Miserables* shows a huge range of genius.

Hugo: author and revolutionary.

Steeled for speed

Liverpool, England
Ships are increasingly benefitting from the latest technology which enables thin steel plates to be used in their design and manufacture. The first such vessel, a small paddle steamer, is now being built here; it is claimed that it will set new speed records when it goes into service next year. The *Banshee* is a 189-foot-long, 27-foot beam craft built by a Liverpool firm to ply between Dublin and North Wales, although its owners have not ruled out a trans-Atlantic voyage for their 16-knot steamer. Its 350-horsepower engine is being built by the Greenwich firm of John Penn.

French march on Mexico City is halted

A Mexican cattle herdsman: tough, independent and willing to fight.

Mexico, 5 May
Mexican troops led by General Ignacio Zaragoza have won a significant victory over invading French forces at Puebla. The French, under General Charles Latrille, had expected an easy, if not an unopposed, march from the coast to Mexico City. Their hopes have been severely confounded.

Far from the special *Te Deum* which Latrille had promised his troops that a grateful clergy would offer, the French were met at Puebla with a stern defence. Attacking recklessly, they used up half their ammunition within two hours. Zaragoza commanded his troops with a mix of caution and audacity and the French assault was repulsed with great success.

The day's decisive moment came when the youthful Brigadier-General Porfirio Diaz inspired his men to fight off a determined attack on the right flank.

US immigrants find haven of opportunity

The new railways are bringing thousands of hopeful immigrants out west.

New York City
Despite the civil war, great waves of immigrants are continuing to arrive in the United States. With the burgeoning steamship and railway companies in cut-throat competition for trade, it is possible today to get from Liverpool to New York and Chicago for as little as $35. "Agents", armed with enticingly adjectival pamphlets, are scouring Europe for potential customers.

The great bulk of newcomers are from the British Isles, many from the north of England and Scotland finding ready employment in the prospering armament factories in the north. With landlords "consolidating" small farms in Ireland and memories of the potato famine still fresh in their minds, it is the Irish who make up almost 80 per cent of immigrants.

For many, the lure is the fertile farm country of the west, and the Homestead Act, passed this year, offers every head of a family a 160-acre farm free of charge.

Death toll mounts in US

Union troops storming Confederate positions at the battle of Antietam.

Fredericksburg, 13 December
This once-pleasant town in Virginia, with its wide, tree-lined streets and white "colonial" houses is a smouldering ruin tonight after a day-long battle in which union troops failed to take a strategically important – though impregnable – ridge, Marye's Heights. Watching the bloody repulse of the doomed frontal attack by General Burnside's northern army, General Robert E Lee told an aide: "It is well that war is so terrible – we should grow too fond of it."

No-one can be fond of this war which is taking a terrible toll of human life as north and south are locked in mortal combat. At the end of it all, the battle of Marye's Heights may not prove to be significant; but it typifies the difference in military style between commanders. Heavily outnumbered, Lee, a cavalryman, relies on the manouvrability of his armies and his own capacity for quick thinking in battle. Union commanders like Burnside and Ulysses S Grant look to superior fire-power and text-book outflanking movements.

The casualty lists are horrific. In the battle of Antietam in September, no fewer than 23,500 soldiers were killed in one day of fighting in Maryland.

Garibaldi's men march to conquer Rome

Calabria, 28 August
Garibaldi has landed here in southern Italy with an army which he hopes will march to take over the papal states. He still dreams of establishing Rome as the capital of the new united Italy. Pope Pius IX is equally determined to stop him. He has refused to recognise the new Italian state and ordered Catholics not to vote in the parliamentary elections. King Victor Emmanuel has privately encouraged Garibaldi, but it is doubtful if he will help when it comes to the crunch. He depends on the support of France, and Napoleon III is unlikely to be prepared to risk challenging the authority of the pope.

Garibaldi: warrior and visionary.

1862 (1862-1863)

China, 1862. *Taiping* rebels approach Shanghai and come into conflict with Chinese regional armies, western-led forces such as the Ever-Victorious Army, and British and French regular forces garrisoned around Shanghai.

Virginia, 1862. The confederate army manufactures a balloon from silk dresses.

Austria, 1862. The musicologist Ludwig Kochel publishes a chronological catalogue of the musical works of Wolfgang Amadeus Mozart.

USA, 1862. John D Rockefeller invests $4,000 in his first oil refinery.

London, 1862. The Albert Memorial is designed by Gilbert Scott to be placed opposite the Royal Albert Hall, which is now being built.

Red Sea, 1862. As a response to the British presence in Aden, Napoleon III purchases Obock on the African coast of the Gulf of Aden.

France, 1862. Gustave Flaubert publishes *Salammbo*, an exotic tale somewhat buried in historical detail.

Nevada, 1862. Samuel Clemens becomes a reporter, using the pen name, "Mark Twain".

Paris, 1862. The actress Sarah Bernhardt makes her debut as Iphigenie with the Comedie Francaise.

Washington, DC, 1 January 1863. President Abraham Lincoln signs the Emancipation Act, proclaiming all slaves in the confederate states free.

Egypt, 30 January 1863. Ismail succeeds Said as khedive of Egypt.

Poland, February 1863. Polish nationalists rise up in revolt against Russian rule. The rebellion was prompted by a new law conscripting almost the entire young population of Poland.

Prussia, 8 February 1863. In order to combat the revolt in Poland, the Prussian prime minister, Otto von Bismarck, signs the convention of Alvensleben with Russia, which makes provision for reciprocal military assistance against the rebels.

Washington, DC, 3 March 1863. President Lincoln signs the Conscription Act, compelling US citizens to report for duty in the civil war, or pay $300. Thus he hopes to bolster the troops and top up the coffers.

Kansas, 3 March 1863. Congress provides for the forcible removal of all Indians from the state of Kansas.

China, 25 March 1863. Charles George Gordon takes over command of the Ever-Victorious Army following the death of F T Ward last September in battle near Shanghai with *Taiping* rebels.

Denmark, 30 March 1863. King Frederick VII separates Schleswig from Holstein and incorporates it into his states.

Greece, 30 March 1863. William, the prince of Denmark, is recognised as king of Greece.

Virginia, 10 May 1863. The confederate General Thomas Jonathan "Stonewall" Jackson, dies of wounds received in battle at Chancellorsville four days ago.

Mexico, May 1863. Mexican troops led by Jesus Gonzalez Ortega surrender Puebla after two months of resistance against French forces. Reinforcements have arrived from France since the Mexican victory in Puebla in 1861.

New Zealand, May 1863. Fighting between Maoris and British settlers breaks out in Taranaki. Conflict erupted in 1859 over a controversial land purchase and the 1861 truce has failed to maintain peace.

France, 1863. Alphonse Beau de Rochas, an engineer, perfects the theory of the four-stroke combustion engine.

Uganda, 1863. J H Speke and J Grant establish that the source of the river Nile is Lake Victoria.

Germany, 1863. The first socialist organisation – the German General Workers' Association – is formed under the influence of Ferdinand Lassalle who worked with Marx during the 1848-9 revolution trying to launch socialism in the Rhineland.

Russia, 1863. In the continuing programme of westernisation undertaken by Alexander II, academic freedom is restored to the universities and secondary education is made available to all who pass the necessary exams.

Britain, 1863. The scientist Thomas Andrews discovers a technique for liquefying gases.

India, 1863. Satyendra Nath Tagore is the first Indian to enter the Indian Civil Service.

Britain, 1863. The Football Association outlaws handling the ball, thus distinguishing soccer from rugby.

West Africa, 1863. The French establish a protectorate over the kingdom of Porto Novo in Dahomey.

Sierra Leone, 1863. The first elections to the legislative council are held.

America's slaves win their freedom

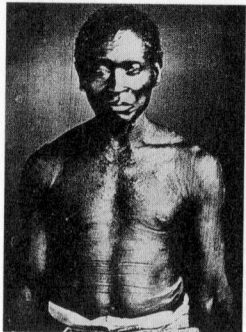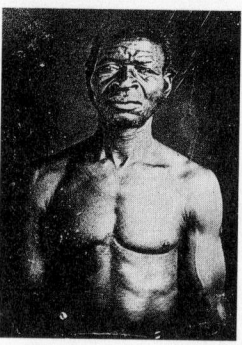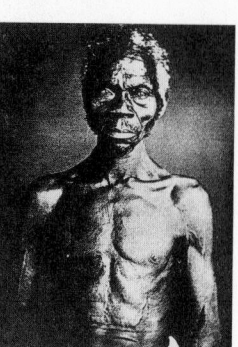

Three faces of slavery: an unknown slave; Renty (born in the Congo); and Jack (who was a slave driver from Guinea); all three from South Carolina.

Washington, 1 January 1863

Huge crowds of freed slaves and joyful abolitionists besieged newspaper offices as they awaited copies of the Emancipation Proclamation – freeing all slaves in the confederate states – which was signed today by President Lincoln. The proclamation honours a pledge made by the president last year. As free Negroes filled churches and held candle-lit vigils throughout the north, Lincoln said: "The old south must be destroyed and replaced by new propositions and ideas." The proclamation issue has dominated Lincoln's re-election campaign, with northern Democrats claiming that "two or three million semi-savages" would overrun the north. Already, two all-Negro army units are being formed.

Explorer crosses Australia, south to north

A township sends off an earlier expedition under Captain Sturt in 1844.

Melbourne, November 1862

A lone man, John King, has come from the outback with a harrowing tale. One of a party led by Robert O'Hara Burke and W J Wills that set out across Australia from south to north in August 1860, he is the only survivor.

Burke was impatient and overconfident. He set out with Wills, King, a man called Grey and a train of Afghani camels, not waiting for his baggage. They crossed the Great Dividing Range and followed the Flinders river to the Gulf of Carpentaria, which they reached in February 1861. The return was terrible; Grey died, and the surviving three arrived at their base camp at Cooper's Creek nearly dead. Brahe, a member of the expedition who had stayed four months at base, had left the camp only seven hours earlier.

The three trekked on across the Stoney Desert, making for Mount Hopeless, 150 miles away. Soon Wills and Burke were dead. King only lived to tell the tale because he was rescued by Aborigines.

Quality of happiness counts, says Mill

London, 1862
England's most celebrated philosopher, John Stuart Mill, was brought up by his father, James Mill, on Jeremy Bentham's principle that "the greatest happiness of the greatest number" should govern human affairs and legislation and refined it in *Utilitarianism*, published last year. Bentham did not distinguish between qualities of pleasure; Mill states: "It is better to be a human being dissatisfied than a pig satisfied. And better to

be Socrates dissatisfied than a fool satisfied." He argues that general rules of conduct should have priority over single acts; for example, keeping promises or telling the truth, even if at times it seems better not to.

Mill learnt Greek from the age of three, logic at 12 and political economy at 13. He published his *System of Logic*, treating inductive reasoning, in 1843 and his *Principles of Political Economy* in 1848. *On Liberty* followed in 1859.

Krupp uses new process for steelmaking

England, 1862
It is the American William Kelly who is credited with the technique of making steel by blowing air through or over the hot metal. But the English inventor Henry Bessemer is the first to find a method of cheap mass-production.

The Bessemer furnace or converter rapidly produces purified ingots – hardened by the right amount of carbon – in great quantity for use in forging or rolling mills. World steel production is soaring. Among

the customers for the Bessemer process is the German industrialist Alfred Krupp who is rolling massive ingots into armoured plate for naval vessels. Krupp, who built up his father's small iron forge into one of the biggest foundry in Europe, has been manufacturing armaments since 1847. Other applications include railway lines and locomotives and structural engineering.

Krupp's enormous output is making him a steel magnate of awesome proportions.

Outraged critics damn erotic French art

Paris, 1863
Edouard Manet's painting, *Dejeuner sur l'Herbe*, outraged the crowds at the Salon des Refuses after it was rejected by the Salon itself. People jeered at the indecency of a nude woman picnicking casually with men fully clothed in modern dress. "This is a young man's practical joke and not worth exhibiting ... Unfortunately the nude hasn't a decent figure and one cannot think of anything uglier than the man who has not even taken his cap off." Jean-Auguste Ingres, the

doyen of French classical painters, who is 83, is showing nudity on a far more lavish scale in his erotic fantasy, *The Turkish Bath* – indolent females abandoned to the music and incense of the bathhouse. This is the final version of a painting done for a Turkish count whose wife disliked it.

Eugene Delacroix, who died on 13 August, was Ingres' rival but shared his taste for the exotic. On a visit to North Africa he painted *Algerian Women* reclining in a harem.

Pain and pleasure: Delacroix's fantasy of the erotic and exotic Orient, which tells far more about the European psyche than about the Orient.

Profusion and pleasure: Ingres' Turkish bath, an Oriental fantasy.

Pastoralism and pleasure: Edouard Manet's Dejeuner sur l'Herbe, the picture that outraged Paris, and brought the erotic home.

1863 (1863-1864)

Virginia, 3 June 1863. Setting out with 75,000 confederate troops, General Robert E Lee begins a second attempt to invade the union states.

West Virginia, 20 June 1863. West Virginia is the 35th state to join the union.

Japan, 24 June 1863. After protracted negotiations, the government pays substantial indemnity for the murder of a British merchant last September and the threat of war is averted. But on the same day batteries in the Choshu domain near Shimonoseki open fire on a US ship.

Mississippi, 4 July 1863. Confederate forces under General Joseph Pemberton surrender unconditionally to federal troops which have besieged Vicksburg since May. Now that the union troops have control of this strategic town, the confederacy is effectively split in two.

Greece, 13 July 1863. Prince William of Denmark is recognised by Britain, France and Russia as King George of Greece.

Cambodia, 11 August 1863. The French establish a protectorate in Cambodia.

Japan, 15 August 1863. A British naval squadron bombards Kagoshima, the capital of the Satsuma domain, as punishment for the murder of Richardson last September.

Germany, 1 September 1863. A meeting of German princes in Frankfurt aimed at reforming the German Confederation breaks up following Prussia's refusal to co-operate.

Germany, 1 October 1863. The German *diet* decides to take federal action against Denmark following the Danish annexation of Schleswig earlier this year.

Washington, DC, 3 October 1863. President Lincoln declares the last Thursday in November a national holiday of thanksgiving.

France, 18 October 1863. A photographer by the name of Nadar takes the first aerial photographs from his balloon *The Giant*. But the trip ends in mishap near Hanover, with Nadar breaking a leg.

Ionian Sea, 14 November 1863. Britain cedes the Ionian Islands to Greece.

Denmark, 15 November 1863. Following the death of Frederick VII, who left no issue, Christian IX comes to the throne.

France, 23 November 1863. Louis Thiers forms a Third Party in opposition to Napoleon III.

China, November 1863. Li Hongzhang's Huai army attacks the *Taiping* stronghold of Suzhou, backed by General Gordon's Ever-Victorious Army.

China, 6 December 1863. Taiping leaders defending Suzhou (*Jiangsu*) handed the city over to the Qing military commander Cheng Xueqi two days ago on the understanding that they would be given high military commissions in the Qing army. But today Li Hongzhang and Cheng have had them executed instead. In view of this treachery, Gordon threatens to leave the Ever-Victorious Army.

Britain, 23 December 1863. William Makepeace Thackeray dies aged 52. The author of *Vanity Fair*, *Henry Esmond* and many other works, he was the country's most popular novelist after Charles Dickens.

Germany, 24 December 1863. Following the Danish annexation of Schleswig earlier this year, Saxon and Hanoverian forces move into Holstein.

France, 1863. The French theologian and philosopher Ernest Renan publishes his *Life of Jesus* in which he treats his subject as an ordinary man and scandalises the devout.

Russia, 13 January 1864. A law is passed which provides for the institution of *zemstvos* – regional assemblies elected by three bodies of electors the landowners, town-dwellers and the peasants.

China, January 1864. As part of a programme of military modernisation, Li Hongzhang orders the Scotsman S Halliday Macartney to purchase mechanical equipment for the Suzhou arsenal.

Virginia, 4 April 1864. Lieutenant-General Ulysses S Grant receives his commission to command the federal troops, and plans a consolidated strike against confederate troops in a bid to end the fighting.

Colorado, 1864. The gold rush dries up as many lodes run out.

Geneva, 1864. A multilateral agreement on the Red Cross – a voluntary relief society dedicated to the care of those wounded in war – is signed at the Geneva convention. This is largely the work of Henri Dunant, a Swiss humanitarian who organised emergency aid for French and Austrian wounded soldiers at the battle of Solferino in June 1859.

France, 1864. The engineer Pierre Martin perfects William Siemen's furnace – the new open-hearth process. He re-uses heat from the gases generated in the furnace to weld steel.

Underground railway opens in London

London, 10 January 1863
After three years of painstaking work, disturbing the growing network of sewers and gas mains, London now has the world's first underground railway. Aimed at relieving the city's congested roads, the line runs from Paddington to Farringdon Street. There are five intermediate stations, with Euston and King's Cross both being served.

The Metropolitan Railway was built by a method called "cut and cover". First, a trench was dug, often in an existing street then the side walls and arched roof were put into place. With the outside filled in, the street could be paved over once again.

Ordinary steam locomotives are being used. The railway company is trying to dispel public fears about breathing in sulphurous fumes by claiming that they are beneficial. There is, however, concern for the foundations of nearby houses.

The first underground passengers going to a banquet to celebrate the opening.

Mercenaries defeat the Chinese rebels

Soochow, December 1863
The Ever-Victorious Army, whipped into fighting shape by Major "Chinese" Gordon, has been in the vanguard of Viceroy Li Hongzhang's offensive, which has just led to the capture of this important city from the Taipings.

Originally commanded by an American adventurer, Fred Ward, who was killed in a reckless charge, the Ever-Victorious was taken over by another American, Burgevine, who, after a quarrel over money, deserted to the Taipings. In 1863 he later surrendered to the Imperial army and was expelled from China.

Major Gordon, authorised by the British Army to take service with the Chinese, then took command and turned it from an ill-disciplined mercenary force into a well-trained army of conscripts. At last living up to its name, it has won a series of victories against the Taipings. Viceroy Li thinks highly of Gordon: "What a sight to see this splendid Englishman fight."

New equations held to be "great guns"

London, 1863
In a direct line of descent from Faraday, Ampere and Thomson comes the brilliant work of James Clerk Maxwell. Maxwell's theory is that electric and magnetic fields are both aspects of one and the same force – electromagnetism. His superb mathematical equations take us one convincing step nearer to a unification of all the forces in nature. Maxwell himself holds them to be "great guns".

Important, too, are Maxwell's predictions that there are probably other forms of electromagnetic radiation at other wavelengths as yet undetected.

Confederates routed at Gettysburg

Lee: a compassionate commander.

Gettysburg, Penn., 3 July 1863

With battle-flags flying and the sun glinting on thousands of bayonets and swords, a mile-long battle line of confederate troops advanced over open terrain – to be torn to shreds by union shells and bullets. A few rebel soldiers reached the union lines only to be killed or captured. As survivors struggled back, their general, Robert E Lee kept repeating: "It's all my fault."

The bloodiest battle so far in this civil war is over and more than 40,000 bodies litter the cornfields and orchards around this small Pennsylvania township. The battle reached its crescendo today as both sides fought a massive artillery duel

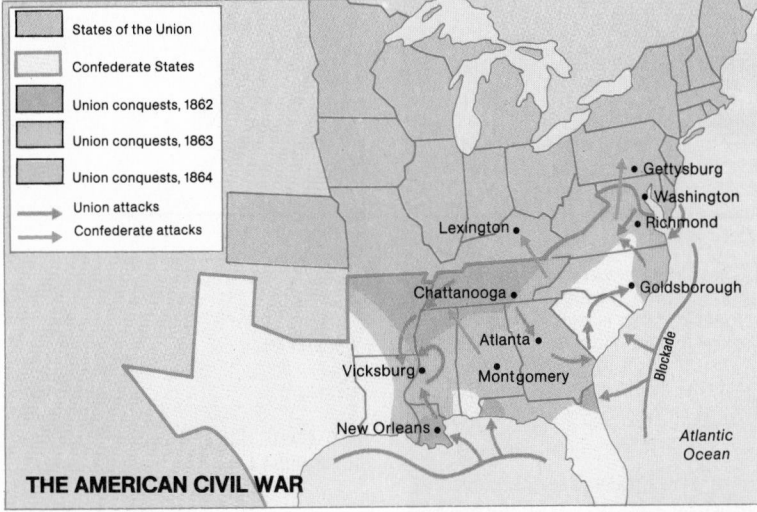

THE AMERICAN CIVIL WAR

States of the Union / Confederate States / Union conquests, 1862 / Union conquests, 1863 / Union conquests, 1864 / Union attacks / Confederate attacks

Gettysburg, Washington, Richmond, Lexington, Chattanooga, Goldsborough, Atlanta, Vicksburg, Montgomery, New Orleans, Blockade, Atlantic Ocean

which preceded Lee's attack. The union army has finally scored a major victory against General Lee whose superior tactics with inferior numbers have tormented the north since the war started.

Relying heavily on his tried and trusted colleague, General Thomas "Stonewall" Jackson – killed at the battle of Chancellorsville in May – Lee had won several critical engagements against the union. As Jackson succeeded in pinning down a superior force in the Shenandoah valley, Lee's army held back an attempt to capture the confederate capital, Richmond, and later forced the union to retreat back to Washington at the battle of Bull Run. More success followed at Fredericksburg, where the northern commander was forced to withdraw.

Lee's only real mistake was to invade Pennsylvania. The result was today's awesome debacle.

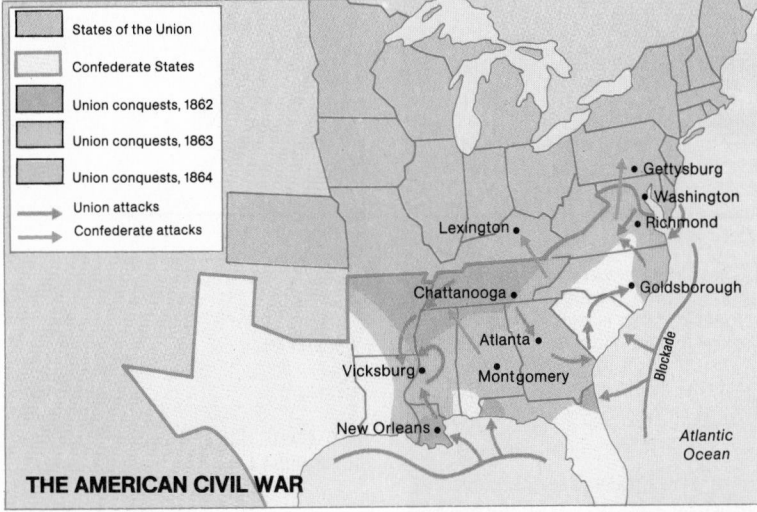

Union soldiers pose for the camera.

Government by and for the people, US president pledges

Gettysburg, 20 November 1863

Fifteen thousand people gathered on the site of the battlefield today to dedicate a cemetery for the nation's war dead today. They heard a thunderous two-hour oration by the scholar and lecturer Edward Everett, but, surprisingly, few of them caught many of the words spoken by President Lincoln who followed. And yet the *Chicago Tribune* – whose reporter took a shorthand note – has said that Lincoln's short address will "live among the annals of man".

The president reminded his audience of the very nature of this country. "Four score and seven years ago, our fathers brought forth upon this continent a new nation, coneived in liberty and dedicated to the proposition that all men are created equal," he began. "Now we are engaged in a great civil war, testing whether that nation – or any nation so conceived and so dedicated – can long endure."

In his high-pitched voice, Lincoln told the crowd "that the dead shall not have died in vain", and that "this Nation under God shall have a new birth of freedom and that government of the people, by the people and for the people shall not perish from the earth".

Leader of "superior" Moslem sect dies

Timbuktu, West Africa, 1864

Al-Hajj Umar, the warrior and religious leader, has been killed attempting to break out of Hamdullahi in Massina where he was besieged by Fulani and Tuareg rebels. He was 70 years old.

Umar, an imposing man of magnetic personality, was a fervent supporter of the Tijanniya sect of Sufism which claimed superiority over all other Moslems and promised its followers favoured treatment on the Day of Judgement. He

was imprisoned for his beliefs and exiled from a number of West African states, but acquired guns and warriors and grew powerful enough to launch a *jihad* (holy war) in which he fought the French and established the *Caliphate* of Tukolor.

Al-Hajj Umar comes from a line of Islamic reformers who have swept out of the Sahara, and established empires dedicated to reasserting the Koran, which have rarely lasted beyond the lifetime of the founder.

Four nations shell Japan back into world

Japan, September 1864

After bombarding Japanese defences on the Straits of Shimonoseki and Kagoshima, the navies of four countries have opened up Japan to foreign trade. The navies, from Britain, France, Holland and the USA, only acted after the emperor, against the advice of his *shogun* (chief minister), informed western diplomats that Japan would be reverting to her traditional policy of isolation. They refused to discuss the idea. After a day's bombardment, marines landed and spiked Jaspan's shore guns. On both land and sea Japanese tactics and equipment proved inadequate, and Japanese modernists are already urging Jaspan to learn from westerners, and beat them at their own game.

British, French and Germany "barbarians" arrive at Yokohama.

1864 (1864-1865)

Mexico, 10 April 1864. The Austrian Archduke Maximilian is appointed emperor of Mexico with the backing of the French army.

USA, 19 May 1864. Nathaniel Hawthorne, the leading American novelist and short story writer, dies aged 59. His most famous work is *The Scarlet Letter*, telling the tragic tale of a convicted adulteress forced to wear a symbol of her sin.

China, 31 May 1864. The Ever-Victorious Army, composed of foreign-trained soldiers fighting against the *Taiping* rebels, is disbanded.

China, 1 June 1864. The Taiping ruler and self-styled "younger brother of Jesus", Hong Xiuquan, kills himself.

China, 3 June 1864. A Moslem rebellion breaks out at Kucha, in Chinese Turkestan.

Washington, DC, 7 June 1864. The Republicans nominate President Lincoln for a second term.

China, 15 July 1864. A Moslem rebellion breaks out at Urumchi, in Chinese Turkestan, following which erupted last month at Kucha.

China, 19 July 1864. Nanjing has fallen to Hunan (imperial) forces which mounted a fierce attack on the Taiping-held city 14 days ago. Some 100,000 Taipings either commit suicide or are killed by Qing troops. This marks the end of the Taiping rebellion.

Alabama, 5 August 1864. A federal fleets take Mobile Bay for the union, despite the fact that the harbour is mined with torpedoes.

China, 7 August 1864. The Taiping commander Li Xiucheng is executed in Nanjing, aged 41, having written his own account of the Taiping rebellion for the imperial leader Zeng Guofan.

Italy, 15 September 1864. The French government signs a convention with the Italian minister Minghetti, planning the departure of French troops from Rome between now and 1866, the date by which the pope should have formed an army. The king of Italy, Victor Emmanuel II, undertakes not to interfere and to move the capital from Turin to Florence.

Spain, September 1864. The regent Queen Maria Christina, returns to Spain, after ten years in exile.

Virginia, 22 October 1864. Confederate troops are swept out of the Shenandoah valley.

China, 25 October 1864. Hong Tianguifu, the Taiping leader known as the Young Heavenly King, who escaped from Nanjing when it fell to imperial forces, is captured at Shicheng, Jiangxi.

Vienna, 30 October 1864. By the peace of Vienna, Denmark gives up Schleswig, Holstein and Lauenburg.

Washington, DC, 8 November 1864. President Abraham Lincoln is re-elected for a second term.

Atlanta, 16 November 1864. General Sherman wreaks havoc in confederate Atlanta, determined that it will no longer serve as a major supply centre for the confederacy.

China, 18 November 1864. Hong Tianguifu, the Taiping Young Heavenly King, is executed by lingering death ("death of a thousand cuts") in the provincial capital of Jiangxi. He was 15.

Georgia, 24 December 1864. General Sherman takes Savannah.

North Africa, 1864. The German soldier Gerhard Rohlfs explores the central Sahara.

Britain, 1864. John Henry Newman writes an *Apologia pro Vita Sua*, defending his conversion to the Church of Rome.

Britain, 1864. The poet Alfred Lord Tennyson publishes *Enoch Arden*.

Zambia, 1864. The Lozi people of the upper Zambezi flood-plain revolt against the rule of the Kololo – migrants from the south.

Nigeria, 1864. Ex-slave Samuel Crowther becomes the first black African Anglican bishop of the Niger river area.

China, January 1865. Buzurg Khan – a descendant of a former ruling house of Kashgar, – Ya'qub Beg, his chief of staff, and other Moslems enter Chinese Turkestan from Kokand. Buzurg Khan declares himself king of Kashgar.

China, January 1865. The Chinese government borrows £1,430,000 from Britain, beginning its national debt.

North Carolina, 22 February 1865. Wilmington, the last open confederate port, falls to union forces.

Washington, DC, 2 March 1865. President Lincoln rejects the confederate General Lee's plea for peace talks, demanding unconditional surrender.

China, March 1865. Tuoming declares himself "pure and true king" at Urumchi.

Ethiopia, 1865. The ambitious Christian Emperor Tewodros (Theodore) II, who came to the throne in 1855 after overthrowing the prince of Tigre, fails to capture and Amharic state of Shoa of King Menelik II.

Archduke crowned Mexico's king

Maximillian and his wife Charlotte.

Mexico, 10 April 1864

Maximilian, the archduke of Austria and brother of the Emperor Franz Josef, has been appointed emperor of Mexico. The move comes as part of France's attempt to establish a Catholic empire in the country and has been inspired by the ambitions of Napoleon III.

Maximilian was formerly the governor of Lombardy-Venetia, but was removed from office in 1859, blamed for Austria's failure to retain Lombardy against a Piedmontese-French attack. Since then he has lived in his castle at Trieste, busying himself with his hobby, botany.

Shy mathematician invents a wonderland

Oxford, 1865

Charles Lutwidge Dodgson, a brilliant if retiring lecturer in mathematics at Christ Church, Oxford, writing under the pseudonym "Lewis Carroll", has produced a new children's book which promises to delight every reader.

Alice's Adventures in Wonderland originated during a boat trip down the river Thames three years ago. To amuse the three Liddell children, the daughters of the Dean of Christ Church, Dodgson created "Alice", named for ten-year-old Alice Liddell, who so enjoyed the tale that she persuaded Dodgson to write it down. Now the shy don has published it as a book.

Alice and the White Knight.

Reactionary pope attacks liberal beliefs

Pope Pius IX: keeping rationalism pantheism and liberalism at bay.

Rome, 8 December 1864

Pope Pius IX today launched a two pronged attack on liberal and radical opinions which is quite astonishing in its comprehensive character. First there is the encyclical, *Quanta Cura*, an assertion of the distinction between true religion and false beliefs and a condemnation of socialism and communism. Then there is the *Syllabus Errorum*, or Syllabus of Errors.

The latter contains no fewer than 80 propositions. It condemns pantheism, naturalism and rationalism. It condemns those who deny the miracles. It condemns divorce and any interference in marriage by civil magistrates.

Southern city is destroyed in a firestorm

Union troops outside Petersburg, where they were thrown back last June.

Atlanta, Georgia, 15 Nov 1864
Puffing his ever-present cigar, General William Sherman, the eccentric union commander, watched tonight as his troops turned this city into an inferno. Determined to prevent Atlanta's further use as a confederate supply base, Sherman had tents, wagons and bedding piled up at the local railroad depot and put a torch to them. A firestorm ensued, destroying hotels, theatres, stores, fire stations and the local jail. Little of Atlanta remains.

It took five months of bitter fighting for Sherman to take Atlanta. He wasted no time in ordering the residents to evacuate the city. When civic leaders protested, he told them: "You might as well appeal against the thunderstorm as against the terrible hardships of war."

Though Sherman is idolised by his troops, his ruthlessness has

Sherman: authoritarian and cruel.

made him unpopular even in the north, where newspapers have questioned his sanity. He is a brilliant tactician, however, and highly regarded by President Lincoln.

Suicide of mystic rebel

Nanjing, June 1864
Hong Xiuquan, "heavenly king" of the Taiping rebels, at last realising that defeat was inevitable, has poisoned himself by eating gold leaf. He has been buried in the garden of his palace, and the trees above his grave are macabrely decorated with the bodies of his wives who have hanged themselves in grief at his death.

With death and disaster all around him, he retreated into unreality. He told his starving people they should eat "sweet dew" and, as his defeated troops retreated, he occupied himself with issuing decrees prescribing the method of execution to be imposed on those who did not use the word "heavenly" in documents. When the "loyal king" urged him to flee Nanjing, the "heavenly capital", he replied that he had nothing to fear because he was "the sole lord of ten thousand nations". When at last reality intruded he said that he had failed his heavenly Father and his brother, Jesus Christ, and swallowed his golden poison. This was the man who came near to toppling the Manchus from the throne of China, whose movement has maintained a separate kingdom for 15 years.

Meanwhile, the "loyal king", Li Xiucheng, is fighting on, desperately trying to drive the imperial forces from the walls of Nanjing. But miners are already burrowing under those walls. The end is very near, and a great slaughter is feared when the city falls.

Prussia beats Denmark in a land dispute

Gearing Prussia for total war: officers' wives making bandages.

Berlin, August 1864
Bismarck has had his first war. The duchies of Schleswig and Holstein are largely German, though they have been ruled since the Middle Ages by the king of Denmark as duke. On the death of the Danish king, a German, Frederick, the prince of Augustenburg, laid claim to the duchies and won the support of Prussia and the German states.

The dispute found the European powers in disarray. Russia was preoccupied with a Polish uprising. Napoleon III was fobbed off with vague promises of rearranging European frontiers in France's favour, Austria was coaxed into supporting a Prussian war against Denmark, and in Britain Palmerston was unable to persuade parliament to take a tough stand.

Bismarck seized his opportunity, sent in Prussian troops, which easily defeated Denmark, and forced the new King Christian to renounce his claim to the duchies. Bismarck's successful war has been applauded by many of his liberal critics in the House of Deputies.

Marx sets up international socialist club

London, 28 September 1864
The First International Workingmen's Association has been established by Karl Marx with the aim of coordinating the efforts of workers in various countries to achieve socialism.

The formation of the First International was prompted by two French delegates who wanted to marshal support for the Polish rebels. Many of the leading figures are foreign exiles settled in London, including Mikhail Bakunin, the Russian revolutionary anarchist, who does not share the pure socialist ideals of Marx and Engels.

Although conservatives are alarmed, the movement does not involve English trade unionists in any active commitment other than general sympathy with the socialist cause. Union officials take little part in meetings and, although there has been local terrorism, the larger associations have specifically repudiated the use of violent or criminal methods.

USA, 3 March. The Bureau of Freed Slaves is created to offer education, medical care and financial assistance to former slaves.

Virginia, 5 April. Union troops leave the confederate capital, Richmond, a smouldering ruin.

Virginia, 9 April. The confederate General Robert E Lee surrenders.

Washington, DC, 15 April. President Lincoln is killed by an assassin's bullet.

Virginia, 27 April. John Wilkes Booth, the accused assassin of President Lincoln, is shot dead.

Illinois, 4 May. The president is buried in Springfield, where he married and started his legal career.

Virginia, 22 May. Jefferson Davis, the former president of the defeated confederacy, is imprisoned, having been discovered disguised as a woman.

China, 4 July. Qing forces take Qianxi from the White Signal sect which has held the town since 1859.

Washington, DC, 8 July. Four of the conspirators convicted of President Lincoln's assassination are hanged today. Another three will serve life prison sentences.

China, 7 August. In the continuing Moslem rebellion in Chinese Turkestan, Ya'qub Beg captures the oasis towns of Kucha and Aksu and takes the ruler Burhanuddin prisoner.

Germany, 14 August. A convention signed at Gastein between Prussia and Austria allots Schleswig to Prussia and Holstein to Austria.

New Zealand, 2 September. Fighting stops between the British settlers and the *Kingitanga* – a Maori unity movement seeking to prevent individual chiefs selling land.

China, 7 September. Ya'qub Beg's rebel Moslem forces capture Kashgar, slaughtering some 4,000 Han Chinese. Ya'qub assumes the leadership of the Moslem rebellion in the Kashgar area.

Ireland, 15 September. The English authorities arrest *Fenian* leaders who are preparing an uprising.

London. William Booth founds a militarist Christian evangelist movement known as the Christian Revival Association.

Undertakers find doctor was a woman

London, 25 July
Who would have thought that Dr James Barry, a senior inspector-general and a very superior sort of man, would turn out to be a woman?

After her death this morning undertakers discovered Barry's 70-year-old female form hidden under copious nightclothes and blankets. It is thought that Barry – with her red hair and high cheekbones – was the granddaughter of a Scottish earl. It was her love for a military surgeon that made her join the army in male disguise – and the life certainly suited her.

She spent 45 years, from the age of 18, travelling the world and working her way up through the medical ranks, ending as a skilled physician at the top of her profession.

Austrian abbot discovers heredity laws

Austria
Watching an Austrian monk pottering in his monastery garden, one would hardly think that important scientific discoveries might be afoot. Gregor Mendel is no ordinary monk, however. He is a skilled and intelligent botanist and plant breeder who has been thinking hard about the way in which characteristics are passed on from one generation to another.

For his experiments he uses the humble garden pea. By crossbreeding different varieties, he can trace in the ensuing hybrids features such as height, colour, shape, flower position and pod forms.

From the data gleaned through these observations, Mendel has formulated certain laws governing patterns of inheritance, using statistical methods. Now this popular, devout man has given mathematical form to the shape of inheritance. And, perhaps, not only in plants.

Gregor Mendel, scientific monk.

When put to the test Mendelism may well be applicable to all biological organisms – humans included. So far, however, the scientific community wants nothing to do with Mendel's ideas.

British artist scales "unclimbable" peak

Whymper's party descend the peak.

Milan, Italy
A British party led by Edward Whymper, an artist, has conquered the Matterhorn, the mountain that towers 14,780 feet over Switzerland and Italy. The triumph was short-lived – four members fell to their deaths on the way down.

An 1861 entry in a hotel register reads "Edward Whymper – *en route* for the Matterhorn". He came to the Alps to sketch the scenery before developing an obsession with the peak which has defeated him on seven attempts. As the British party searches for its dead, a rival Italian team is still making an ascent of the mountain which many thought unclimbable.

Unplayable opera is a great success

Wagner: his work as loved as hated.

Munich
Tristan und Isolde, an opera or "music drama" by Richard Wagner, has been given an enthusiastic premiere here – at the second attempt.

In Vienna the piece was abandoned as unplayable after 77 rehearsals. Its chromatic harmonies have been compared to "a perfumed fog shot through with lightning". Nietzsche said: "Wagner's art is diseased; he has made music sick."

The opera is based on Arthurian legend. Tristan, conveying Isolde to marry King Mark, falls in love with her on the voyage. He dies at their reunion and Isolde literally dies of love in the concluding *Liebestod*. Wagner is believed to have been inspired by his love for Mathilde Wesendonck, the wife of his patron.

Tristan and Isolde prepare to die.

Confederates surrender

The surrender of General Robert E Lee at the Appomattox Court House.

Appomattox, Virginia, 9 April

General Robert E Lee shook hands with his opponent, General Ulysses S Grant, in the courtroom here today and formally surrendered his exhausted confederate army to the federal commander-in-chief. The civil war which set brother against brother in cruel, costly conflict and has taken more than half a million lives is effectively over.

The contrast between the two generals could not have been more marked. Lee was resplendent in his full-dress uniform as he sat and waited for the victor who arrived in a rumpled tunic, his mud-spattered trousers tucked into muddy books.

Lee and his 27,000 men had fought to the very end, trying to reach a railway which could take them south to unite with General Johnson in North Carolina. They were blocked by cavalry and infantry, and when Grant's well-fed army closed the trap, Lee sent a note asking for terms. Grant lived up to his nickname – gained in an earlier battle – of "Unconditional Surrender". Lee agreed, but told an *aide*: "I would rather die a thousand deaths."

Grant has allowed Lee's men to keep their small arms and horses and to be paroled without punishment – on condition that they do not take up arms again against the north.

As Lee stood waiting for his horse, he struck his fist repeatedly into his palm in despair as federal troops began to hand out rations to the army he had just surrendered. The confederate soldiers were beaten and starving; they wept as their general rode away.

US president murdered

Washington, DC, 15 April

The president of the United States, Abraham Lincoln, died early today from an assassin's bullet, fired as he watched a play in a Washington theatre last night. His secretary of state, William Seward, is critically ill from stab wounds received in a separate incident. Tonight, as a nationwide hunt is under way for Lincoln's assassin, John Wilkes Booth, a failed actor, police and federal agents are investigating the possibility that the president was the victim of a confederate conspiracy seeking revenge.

Just after 10 pm Booth entered Box Seven of Ford's Theatre and shot the president in the back of the head with a single bullet. The audience was laughing; few heard the shot. Slashing at an army officer who rushed him, Booth jumped on to the stage and shouted *Sic sem- per tyrannis!* (Thus always to tyrants) – "the South is avenged!" The President was carried to a cheap lodging house opposite the theatre, where a doctor said that he had been mortally wounded and could not possibly survive.

Before he went to watch the performance of *Our American Cousin* with Mrs Lincoln, the president told friends he had dreamt the previous night that he was moving with great rapidity towards a dark and undefined shore. It was a dream that he had dreamt on the eve of every major battle in the civil war. Earlier yesterday Booth, the son of a well-known actor, boasted in a bar that he would be the most famous man in America; as his victim lay mortally wounded, drifting rapidly towards that unknown shore, the US is preparing to mourn its 16th president.

Lincoln assassinated by John Wilkes Booth in Ford's Theatre, Washington.

Turkestan born as Russia wins Tashkent

Central Asia

Russia's expansion southwards has taken another step forward this year with the occupation of the great city of Tashkent in Turkestan and the addition of new frontier lands to the Romanov domains.

The Russian conquests stretch about 700 miles from the Aral Sea in the west to the Kirghiz mountains in the east, and are mainly at the expense of Kokhand, one of three states on the northern borders of Persia and Afghanistan. Russia's current thrust into central Asia began in around 1840, when its frontier was marked by the Ural river, 1,000 miles north of Tashkent. As well as hoping to expand their own influence, the Russians have been determined to counter British activity in the region, a resolve heightened since Russia's Crimean defeat. There are commercial motives, too: the civil war in America means that Turkestan is currently the only place from which Russian factories can obtain cotton.

Napoleon and Bismarck agree neutrality

Biarritz, France, 4 October

Bismarck has arrived at Biarritz to bathe in the invigorating waters of the Bay of Biscay – and to bamboozle Napoleon III into remaining neutral while Prussia goes to war with Austria over the Schleswig and Holstein duchies.

Just three months ago, Bismarck persuaded Austria to make a deal over the duchies: Austria would take over Holstein, with Prussia having Schleswig. The arrangement effectively isolated Austria because it was made behind the back of the German Assembly at Frankfurt.

Now Bismarck tells Napoleon that, if he stays neutral, Prussia will back his territorial ambitions; not with regard to German territory, of course, but to French-speaking parts of Belgium, perhaps. Nothing is being written down; they are statesmen and men of honour, surely. Napoleon's family are delighted with the wily Prussian. "A really great man," one observer says. "Full of *esprit*."

1865 (1865-1866)

China, 8 October 1865. The White Signal sect rebels take Guangshun and Dingfan (*Guizhou*).

Britain, 18 October 1865. Lord Palmerston dies.

Britain, October 1865. The practice of transporting criminals to Australia is abolished.

New Zealand, October 1865. Wellington is established as the capital of New Zealand.

Japan, November 1865. The *shogun*, Tyemochi, persuades the emperor to renew trading relations with the west.

Sweden, 7 December 1865. In a reform of the constitution, a two-chamber parliament is created, but the members will only be elected by ten per cent of the population.

Belgium, 10 December 1865. Leopold II succeeds his father Leopold.

Washington, DC, 18 December 1865. The 13th Amendment to the US Constitution abolishes slavery.

Hungary, December 1865. Austria incorporates Transylvania into Hungary.

Paris, 1865. Edouard Manet's painting *Olympia*, echoing Titian's *Venus* but showing a very worldly model in the same pose, causes a scandal at the Salon des Refuses where works rejected by the Salon of the Academy are exhibited.

Tennessee, 1865. A secret society is formed in Tennessee. Members, mostly Confederate veterans, ride at night in hooded white robes and there are fears that they intend to act against freed Negroes. However, the founders claim that the *Ku Klux Klan*, as it is known, is a harmless fraternity.

India, 1865. Bombay enjoys a cotton boom because of the US falling production during the civil war.

Paraguay, 1865. Under its ambitious dictator, President Francisco Solano Lopez, Paraguay is at war with a triple alliance composed of Brazil, Argentina and Uruguay following a dispute about Brazilian intervention in Uruguay last year.

Peru, 14 January 1866. Following last year's treaty ending the war with Spain, Peruvian resentment is such that General Mariano Ignacio Prado takes control and declares war once again.

Mexico, 12 February 1866. Invoking the Monroe Doctrine, (a US declaration warning European powers against further colonisation in the Americas) the USA calls for the withdrawal of French troops from Mexico.

Rumania, 24 February 1866. Wealthy landowners angered by land reforms overthrow their ruler, Prince Cuza. Bismarck and Napoleon III choose as his replacement Karl Friedrich, the cousin of the king of Prussia, who alters his name to Carol.

Chile, 31 March 1866. President Jose Joaquin Perez sides with Peru in the war against Spain.

New York City, 10 May 1866. At the first post-war meeting of the National Women's Rights Convention, a unanimous vote confirms the organisation of the American Equal Rights Association.

Egypt, 21 May 1866. The Ottoman sultan grants the right of primogeniture to Ismail of Egypt.

Germany, 8 June 1866. Prussia annexes Holstein, which came under Austrian rule by the convention of Gastein last year.

Austria, 12 June 1866. Austria signs a secret treaty with France as conflict with Prussia escalates.

Germany, 16 June 1866. Having declared the German Confederation dissolved two days ago, Prussia invades Saxony, Hanover and Hesse.

Italy, 20 June 1866. Prussia's ally, Italy, declares war on Austria.

Italy, 24 June 1866. The Austrian armies, led by Grand Duke Albert, defeat the Italian forces of Marquis Alfonso de la Marmora at the battle of Cuseozza.

Bohemia, 3 July 1866. Prussian troops defeat Austrians in Sadowa.

Austria, 4 July 1866. Austria cedes Venetia to Napoleon III.

Spain, 1866. General Juan Prim y Prats fails in his attempt to overthrow the government of Queen Isabella II.

Central Asia, 1866. The Russians continue the occupation of Chinese Turkestan (which began last year), and of Tashkent, the capital of the *khanate* of Kokand. They claim to be protecting themselves against the Moslem revolt in this area.

Rome, 1866. The Norwegian playwright Henrik Ibsen publishes *Brand*, an austerely puritan work.

England, 1866. Algernon Charles Swinburne publishes the first volume of *Poems and Ballads*.

Bohemia, 1866. The Bohemian composer Bedrich Smetana composes a new opera, *The Bartered Bride*.

Japan, 1866. Fukuzawa Yukichi publishes *Conditions in the West*, based on his own observations. The first edition of 150,000 is a sell-out.

"Pam" is dead after a mutton breakfast

London, 18 October 1865
Palmerston was staying at Brocket, his wife's house in Hertfordshire, when he was stricken by a violent fever. His doctors expected him to die in the night; remarkably, he appeared to recover and ate a hearty breakfast of mutton chops washed down with port. During the following night he became weak and died today at 10.45 am, two days before his 81st birthday.

When "Pam", as he was known, was born on 20 October 1784, the population of Britain was about nine million, of whom 80 per cent worked in agriculture; today it is 29 million, of whom 60 per cent work in industry.

He was secretary for war, foreign secretary and finally prime minister during an era when Britain was the richest and most powerful nation on earth. He encouraged reform abroad because he opposed absolutism; at home he opposed reform, believing that the British system, as it stood, was the best in the world.

Palmerston: British is best.

Victoria, who never liked him, wrote in her diary: "Strange and solemn to think of that strong, determined man – gone!" On the Stock Exchange Consols fell by a quarter per cent.

Fast-sailing clippers shrink the world

London, 6 September 1866
Thousands of Londoners lined the banks of the Thames today to watch the conclusion of a remarkable race by clippers bringing tea from China. Five of these great ships left Foochow in China within two days of each other last May. Three of them – *Taiping*, *Ariel* and *Sericaa* – arrived within two hours of each other. The other two are due within two days. This new breed of fast, elegant sailing-ship emerged from America, developed from privateers used in the slave trade, where speed was essential to outrun naval patrols.

Although American-built clippers like the *James Baines*, achieved remarkable records, British ships, with their streamlined hulls and huge sail areas, are putting up stiff competition in maritime trading.

A clipper on the tea-run from China: the fastest sailing ships afloat.

Prussia crushes Austria

Kaiser William, rallying his Prussian troops during the battle of Sadowa.

Sadowa, Bohemia, 3 July 1866

It was a decisive victory for Prussia and a personal triumph for the master of military strategy, Field Marshal Helmut von Moltke. In one day's fighting at Sadowa, 65 miles east of Prague, the Austrians lost 24,000 men killed or wounded and 13,000 taken prisoner. Prussian losses numbered 9,000.

This is the war that Bismarck has been looking for. He picked a quarrel with Austria over Schleswig-Holstein, and when the German princes backed Austria he took that as a declaration of war. Using the new railways, Moltke quickly deployed a main force of 250,000 men along a 270-mile (432km) front. The Prussians were equipped with the superior breech-loading rifle, while the Austrians still used the muzzle-loaded gun.

Thanks to Moltke, Prussia has defeated not only Austria but also her six German allies: Hanover, Nassau, Bavaria, Frankfurt, Hesse-Kassel and Saxony. Moltke has shaped the Prussian army into a formidable war machine, based on compulsory military service in peacetime. When war came, he had a huge reserve of trained men that he could call up.

Prussia takes control of her neighbours

Berlin, 1866

Austria's decisive defeat by the Prussian army in the Seven Weeks' War has changed the political map of Germany. The battle of Sadowa signified the end of Austrian dominance of the German states, but Bismarck, shrewdly judging that a humiliated Austria would attract sympathy, will be lenient.

The only territorial sacrifice demanded is the ceding of Venetia to Italy. The Italians made a poor showing in the field, but as useful allies of Prussia they have to be rewarded. Venetia represents an important step towards the unification of Italy.

Bismarck will not immediately exert to the full Prussia's newfound hegemony, but five of the six German states which sided with Austria in the war – Hanover, Nassau, Bavaria, Hesse-Kassel and Frankfurt – are being annexed. Saxony alone escapes.

Swede makes highly explosive discovery

Stockholm, 1866

The Swedish government has refused permission to Alfred Nobel to rebuild his factory after a serious explosion.

Some politicians have called him a "mad scientist", but Nobel, who was manufacturing liquid nitroglycerin, a powerful explosive compound, at the time of the blast which killed his brother and four workers, is persisting. He is determined to perfect his *dynamit* and make it safe to handle.

Negroes promised full civil rights

Washington, 6 April 1866

It took a civil war to achieve the historic Civil Rights Act which passed through Congress today. It means that Negroes and "anyone born in the United States" is a citizen of this country. The only exceptions are non-taxpaying American Indians.

Despite an attempt at a veto by President Andrew Johnson, the southern-born president who succeeded after Lincoln's assassination, the act gives people "of every race and color" all privileges to make contracts, hold property and testify in court.

Negroes may be equal in northern states; but a secret society, the Ku Klux Klan, dedicated to white supremacy, is thriving in the former rebel states. With other clandestine societies, the Klan ("the invisible empire of the south"), is conducting a terror campaign against "unruly" Negroes.

Back from Africa a slave ship captured

Havana, Cuba, 1866

A slave ship has been captured by Cuba. The slaves in it are to be returned to West Africa. With the Spanish authorities in Cuba and the newly-independent South American states acting against the slave-traders, and the United States executing captains of ships engaged in the trade, the Atlantic trade in human cargo can be said finally to be suppressed.

It has taken a long time. Since 1804, when the Danes declared the trade illegal, one country after another renounced it. The shipments did not come to an end, however, in spite of the Royal Navy's antislavery patrols. There were even larger profits to be made from the illegal trade than from the legal one and conditions on the voyages were far worse. Only British and US pressure on South America, the source of demand, has brought the trade in humans to an end.

Three and a half lines recipe for divorce

Love and marriage, a wood block print by the Japanese artist, Kiyonaga.

Japan, 1866

It takes just three and a half lines of writing for a man to divorce his wife in Japan. These lines, known as *mikudari-san*, are in a set form giving the woman permission to leave the house and to form any other liaison she wishes. The husband is supposed, legally, to refund her dowry, but usually there is little left. However, if she reports that she is pregnant within three months of being given her *mikudari-san* he must provide for the child.

It is typical of the relative status of men and women in Japan that women have no similar rights of divorce. All that they can do to escape from an unhappy marriage is take refuge in a temple.

1866 (1866-1867)

Britain, 1866. A committee presents the first petition for women's suffrage to parliament, through John Stuart Mill.

Russia, 1866. An attempt is made on the life of the czar, Alexander II. Fearful of the spread of atheism and socialism, he begins to slow down his programme of westernisation.

Crete, 1866. Christians on the island rebel against Ottoman rule when the *Porte* (Ottoman government) fails to implement promised reforms. The rebels force an entire Ottoman army to surrender on the plain of Apokoronas and in revenge the Ottomans attack a fortified monastery killing hundreds of refugees.

Russia, 1866. Fyodor Dostoyevsky publishes an epic novel, *Crime and Punishment*, which brings him instant popularity.

France, 17 January 1867. Jean Auguste Ingres, the foremost classical painter in France since David, dies aged 87.

Japan, 3 February 1867. The Emperor Komei dies. He is succeeded by his 15-year-old son Mutsuhito.

Germany, 24 February 1867. The parliament of the North German Confederation is opened. The crown of Prussia controls the league and represents the confederation internationally. An imperial *diet*, elected by universal male suffrage, will meet in Berlin to make federal laws. Count Bismarck becomes chancellor of the confederation.

Mexico, February 1867. French troops depart for France, without the Emperor Maximilian, who refuses to leave.

Paris, 1 April 1867. The Paris World Fair is opened. The occasion is marked by the demonstration of the first hydraulic lift by the engineer Edoux, and by the first viewing in the west of Japanese art.

Virginia, 11 May 1867. The former confederate president, Jefferson Davis, walks out of a courtroom a free man, after two years in prison. But he still faces charges of treason and involvement in the assassination of President Lincoln.

Luxembourg, 11 May 1867. The Luxembourg problem is settled by the treaty of London. Napoleon III had hoped to annex the grand duchy, which was under Dutch authority, as payment for services rendered to Bismarck and the Italians. However, in the face of the hostility of the other powers, he is forced to accept a collective guarantee of the independence and neutrality of the country.

Mexico, 19 June 1867. The Emperor Maximilian, placed on the Mexican throne, and then abandoned by Napoleon III, is seized by the republican President Benito Juarez' supporters and executed.

Canada, 1 July 1867. Four provinces have united to form the Canadian Federation: Quebec, Ontario, Nova Scotia and New Brunswick.

China, 5 July 1867. The revolt of the "night-bird bandits" (salt smugglers) erupts in Cangzhou, Yanshan, Bazhou and other parts of Zhili province.

China, 20 July 1867. Qing (imperial) troops in Guizhou under Can Yuying inflict a decisive defeat on the Miao rebels, killing 20,000 and capturing the former *Taiping* military commander Tao Xinchun.

Russia, 26 July 1867. Russia forms the governor-generalship of Turkestan, having moved into the area to prevent Moslem rebel incursions into their territory.

Europe, 1867. Europe suffers an economic crisis which is exacerbated by poor crops.

Crete, 1867. Ottoman troops leave, having destroyed property in the White Mountains in retaliation for the Cretan uprising last year.

Paraguay, 1867. Brazilian troops acting for the triple alliance of Brazil, Uruguay and Argentina, sack the Paraguayan capital of Asuncion. The Paraguayan leader Lopez, who declared war on Brazil in 1864, flees to the mountains with a guerrilla force.

India, 1867. A college designed to train Moslems to sustain Islamic society outside the framework of the colonial state has been founded at Deoband, north-east of Delhi.

Moscow, 1867. The Moscow Slavonic Ethnographic Exhibition is held, celebrating Russia's historic mission to free the Slavs from Ottoman and Habsburg domination. It is greeted with enthusiasm by the ruling classes.

France, 1867. Emile Zola publishes the novel *Therese Raquin* in the new "realist" style of fiction.

France, 1867. Gautier, Verlaine and Baudelaire form an association which calls itself *The Parnassians* to promote art for art's sake.

Norway, 1867. The first performance of *Peer Gynt* makes the reputation of the Norwegian playwright Henrik Ibsen.

Paris, 1867. The poet Charles Baudelaire, whose greatest work is the volume *Les Fleurs du Mal*, published in 1857, dies aged 46.

Britain gives Canada dominion status

London, 1 July 1867

Canada has moved one step further on the road to self-government following the passing of the British North American Act. Four Canadian provinces will become part of a federation to be called a "dominion". Although Britain will maintain control of foreign policy, the act effectively shows up its current lack of interest in colonial administration. As the provinces have matured over this century, they have tended to move away politically and economically from Britain. Canadians have not benefited from Britain's free trade policies and want to negotiate their own trade agreements. Hostility between English and French-speaking Canada has led to the belief that federation might help to harmonise relations.

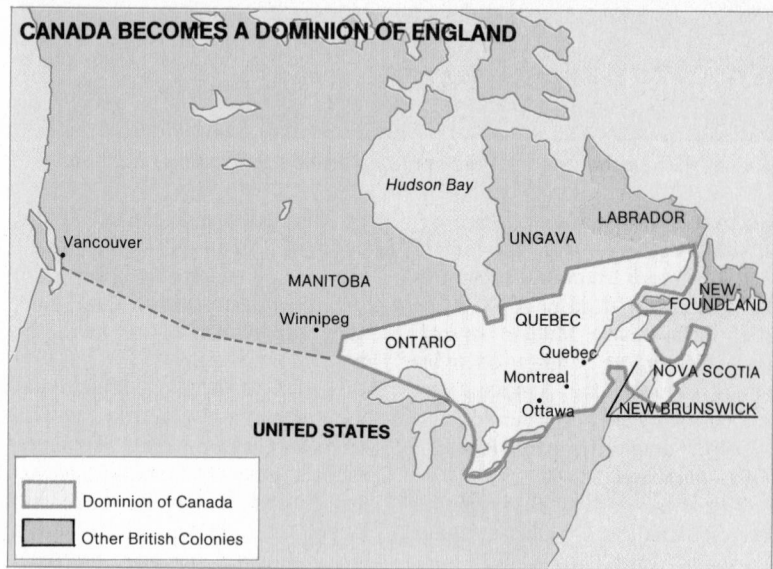

CANADA BECOMES A DOMINION OF ENGLAND

Hudson Bay · LABRADOR · Vancouver · UNGAVA · MANITOBA · NEW-FOUNDLAND · Winnipeg · QUEBEC · ONTARIO · Quebec · Montreal · NOVA SCOTIA · Ottawa · NEW BRUNSWICK · UNITED STATES

Dominion of Canada

Other British Colonies

Telegraph cable stretches across Atlantic

London, 27 July 1866

Communication with the United States is no longer subject to the hazards of a sea voyage, thanks to the successful laying of a transatlantic underwater cable. Since 1856 numerous attempts have failed, notably the 1857 effort which relayed the message "Glory to God in the highest, and on earth peace, good will to men". Shortly after, the cable broke. The electric telegraph was invented over 30 years ago with the need for a fast exchange of information about the movements of trains. Its potential was soon recognised by journalists. The service improved with Samuel Morse's code and the enterprise of Paul Reuter who set up the first international news agency in 1851 (using pigeon post where the lines were incomplete). In cities the telegraph ended the isolation of police precincts and fire brigades. The same medium informed the British public of the horrors in the Crimea. The 2,500-mile-long transatlantic

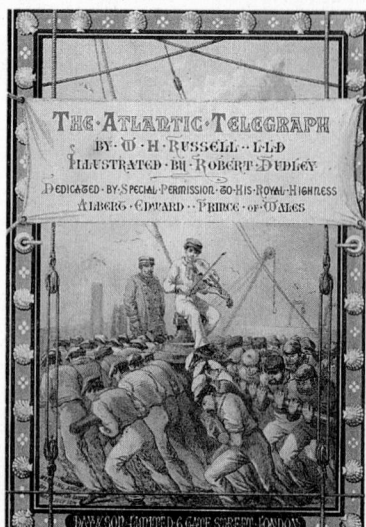

Cable ship weighing anchor.

cable, running from Newfoundland to Ireland, owes its success to the perseverance of C W Field, a one-time clerk who used his fortune, from paper distribution, and government grants from both sides of the Atlantic to fund the venture.

Mexican emperor killed

The ghost of the hapless Maximilian, playing Banquo to Napoleon's Macbeth, haunts the French emperor while the statesmen of Europe look on.

Querataro, Mexico, 19 June 1867
Maximilian, the emperor of Mexico, was executed today on the orders of the republican president, Benito Juarez. Maximilian was crowned three years ago, as a figurehead for Napoleon III's ambitions to establish a Catholic empire in Mexico. Now, abandoned by France, he has paid the penalty for Napoleon's imperial dreams.

Maximilian's brief rule, during which, surprisingly perhaps, he managed to set up a stable government, followed the invasion of Mexico by France, Spain and Britain, pursuing their debts. Spain and Britain abandoned the scheme, but France stayed, flouting the promises of the convention of London, which justified the invasion but denied any ideas of colonial expansion. Faced by increased pressure from the United States, Napoleon gave up his plans, and with them his emperor. Alone, the hapless Maximilian, an involuntary ruler at best, could only await his fate.

Hungary and Austria agree joint rule

Vienna, 15 March 1867
Austria and Hungary have buried the hatchet at last with the *Ausgleich* uniting the two countries under one monarch, with shared foreign, defence and financial commitments, but separate parliaments. The Slavs resent Hungary's privileged position.

The Austro-Hungarian *rapprochement* was made possible by the emergence of moderate Hungarian leaders like Deak and Andrassy. Deak in particular, though he held fast to the April Laws rescinded by the emperor and he had advocated passive resistance in the 1850s, always believed in Habsburg legitimacy. Since December 1864 he had been involved in covert negotiations instigated by the emperor Franz Josef.

A few months ago, Andrassy persuaded Franz Josef to drop federalism; the Saxon Count Beust joined the government, and the pro-Slav

Franz Joseph, emperor of Austra.

prime minister Belcredi resigned. Beust took over, secured a majority in the *Reichsrath*, and carried through the *Ausgleich*, which he hopes will modernise the empire.

Russia sells Alaskan wasteland to US

Washington, 9 April 1867
By a single vote, the United States Senate agreed today to buy Alaska from Russia for $7.2 million – so bringing to an end one of the most bitter campaigns to be fought by the government since the end of the war. Opponents of the measure claimed that the purchase of an "utterly useless land of perpetual snow" was an insane investment. Journalists have suggested that the vast expanse of land in the Arctic Circle should be named "Icebergia" or "Polaria".

For years William Seward, the secretary of the interior, has been urging Congress to buy the land, and, he claims that – at two cents an acre – the country has got a bargain on its hands. Alaska's furs, minerals and fisheries will be of "untold value" in future years, he says, and the territory is worth seven times what the US is paying for it.

US cartoon derides secretary of state, William Seward, for buying Alaska.

Lister's sterile surgery is a life-saver

Glasgow, 1867
Eleven-year-old James Greenlees fell while he was playing and broke his leg. It was a compound fracture, and when James was brought into the Royal Infirmary here, Professor Joseph Lister cleaned the wound thoroughly and swabbed it with a coal-tar product called carbolic acid. Six weeks later young James went home, his leg perfectly healed.

James is just one example cited by Lister in his frequent lectures of the need for cleanliness in surgery. Heavily influenced by the work on Louis Pasteur on germs and disease, the Scots surgeon has surprised his colleagues by his high rate of success in combating "hospital disease" – often fatal and generally caused by unclean surgical instruments and unsterile dressings. Many patients die unneccessarily – even though the original operation was a success – from blood poisoning which causes wounds to fester.

Although the introduction of his antiseptic system is likely to prove a major breakthrough in modern medicine, Lister is also well known for his research on blood coagulation and the various causes of inflammation.

1867 (1867-1868)

Britain, 15 August 1867. Parliament passes a Reform Act – spearheaded by Benjamin Disraeli, the chancellor of the exchequer – which adds nearly one million more voters to the electorate by enfranchising most male urban ratepayers.

China, 16 August 1867. Imperial Qing forces capture a stronghold of the Miao rebels near Weining.

Austria, August 1867. Napoleon III of France and Franz Josef of Austria meet in Salzburg with the aim of strengthening their ties against Prussia.

Britain, August 1867. Britain sends a military expedition to Ethiopia to force the emperor, Tewodros (Theodore) II, to release British officials held since 1864, when Britain failed to offer expected aid in escalating conflicts with the Turks. The mission is headed by Sir Robert Napier, commander-in-chief of the Bombay army.

Britain, September 1867. Karl Marx publishes the first volume of *Das Kapital*.

Austria, October 1867. The continuing dispute between Austria and Hungary is resolved by the *Augsleich* (Compromise), creating two theoretically separate countries under one monarch.

Italy, 3 November 1867. Giuseppe Garibaldi, who launched a march on Rome last month, is defeated by papal and French troops at the battle of Mentana. Garibaldi is captured, and Pope Pius IX is granted French support for a further three years.

Japan, 9 November 1867. The last *shogun*, Tokugawa Keiki, resigns in favour of the Meiji emperor Mutsuhito. Before his resignation he had become a virtual prisoner in his palace at Kyoto.

Austria, 1 December 1867. Johanns Brahms' *German Requiem* is performed for the first time.

New York City, 2 December 1867. The popular English novelist Charles Dickens gives readings around the city, drawing large crowds.

Britain, 13 December 1867. The Irish republican movement known as the *Fenian* Brotherhood launches a bombing campaign in London. Another attack in Manchester on 18 September, also ended in failure.

Austria, 21 December 1867. A new, more liberal, constitution is adopted.

New York City, December 1867. Cornelius Vanderbilt takes control of the New York Central Railroad by outmanoeuvring rival stock-holders.

Austria, 1867. Johann Strauss composes the *Blue Danube* waltz.

New York City, 1 January 1868. Susan B Anthony begins publication of a weekly Suffragist journal called *The Revolution*.

Japan, 3 January 1868. The Emperor Mutsuhito announces that the office of shogun has been abolished and assumes direct control of Japan.

China, 5 January 1868. The Eastern Nian rebels are annihilated by imperial Qing forces near Yangzhou and Lai Wenguang is captured.

China, 7 January 1868. The revolt of the "night-bird bandits", which began in July last year, is put down.

Britain, 25 February 1868. Ill induces the resignation of Lord Derby. He is succeeded as Conservative prime minister by Benjamin Disraeli.

Madagascar, March 1868. Rasoherina is succeeded as queen by Ranavalona II, who is married to Rainilaiarivony, the chief minister and effective ruler of the country.

Japan, 6 April 1868. The Charter Oath establishes the broad principles of the new government, including the convocation of an assembly and pursuit of knowledge in the interests of the nation.

Ethiopia, 13 April 1868. Following his defeat by the British under Sir Robert Napier at the battle of Aroge, the Emperor Tewodros (Theodore) II commits suicide.

USA, 26 May 1868. President Andrew Johnson is acquitted of all charges of impeachment.

Germany, 21 June 1868. Richard Wagner's comic opera *The Mastersingers of Nuremberg* is performed for the first time.

France, June 1868. Following the enactment of a liberal press law last month, the law governing public meetings is made less stringent.

Serbia, June 1868. Having rid the country of Ottoman troops, Prince Michael Obrenovic is murdered by conspirators seeking the restoration of Alexander Karageorgevitch. The assembly nominates his 14-year-old cousin Milan Obrenovic to succeed him, with Jovan Ristic as regent.

USA, June 1868. The first patent is granted for a typewriter.

USA, 25 July 1868. President Johnson signs an act officially creating the territory of Wyoming.

USA, 28 July 1868. A treaty is signed granting unrestricted Chinese immigration into the USA.

US president just escapes impeachment

Washington, 26 May 1868
By a single vote, the Senate failed to impeach the president of the United States today. Andrew Johnson, the man who succeeded after Lincoln's assassination, has continued to anger Congress by his refusal to accept the First Reconstruction Act which divided the southern states into military districts subject to military commanders.

The articles of impeachment were mostly concerned with Johnson's dismissal of his secretary of state, Edwin Stanton, but several dealt with speeches – said to be inflammatory – made by Johnson on a national tour. The most serious charge suggested that the president was involved in the conspiracy to murder Lincoln.

Johnson and a blindfolded Justice.

Garibaldi captured in bid to take Rome

Rome, November 1867
Garibaldi's irregular army was defeated for the second time this month and he himself has been captured. His dream of annexing the papal states for Italy and making Rome the capital has once again been frustrated.

After the first defeat he reconstituted his army and attacked at Mentana. However, the French had sent a large force to help the pope. They were equipped with a new rifle, the *chassepot*, which loads at the breach and has twice the range of a conventional rifle. They easily defeated Garibaldi. The once proud leader has been humiliated. No longer a threat, he will be allowed to return to Caprera.

Britain dithers over self-rule for blacks

Gold Coast (Ghana), 1868
The Gold Coast is 4,000 miles (6,400 kilometres) from London. Messages from London take a long time to get there, if they arrive at all. In 1865 a select committee of the House of Commons urged the British governor "to encourage in the natives the exercise of those qualities which may render it possible for us more and more to transfer to them the administration". Yet, three years later, after an indigenous Fante confederation had been formed for the express purpose of ruling themselves, the British administration is opposing it, doing all that it can to drive a wedge between the young intellectuals and the traditional chiefs.

New Russian novel tells of holy fool

St Petersburg, Russia, 1868
Fyodor Dostoyevsky, who had such success with his novel *Crime and Punishment* here two years ago, has followed it with another extraordinary story, *The Idiot*. Whereas the first was a psychological study of a nihilist and murderer, Raskolnikov, the hero of the second, Prince Myshkin, is of outstanding goodness, simplicity and moral radiance, drawing everyone to him. Yet his influence leads to tragedy and his return to idiocy. One of the stories Myshkin tells so compellingly is of the sensations of a man who lived through the last minutes leading up to his execution.

This is exactly what the author must have experienced when condemned to death as a dissident in 1849. Reprieved from the firing squad when all was ready, he was sent to hard labour in Siberia, about which he wrote the moving book *The House of the Dead*.

Teenage emperor's coup in Japan

Japan, 3 January 1868

The youthful Emperor Meiji, supported by the most powerful feudal lords of Japan, has today seized power from the shoguns who have ruled Japan for the last 700 years.

For all that time the emperors have been powerless, cut off from the world, their only function being to carry out certain religious rites while their country was ruled by the shoguns as hereditary *de facto* chief ministers.

The shoguns have been acknowledged as the real rulers of Japan by the great powers, and international negotiations have been conducted in their names and not those of the unknown men living in seclusion at Kyoto. Now all that has been changed by the proclamation "Restoration of Imperial Government". The great powers will now have to deal with the 16-year-old emperor and his advisers from the Chosu and Satsuma clans who have forced the resignation of the Tokugawa shogun, Keiki, whose family have been shoguns for 200 years.

Japan's relations with the west lie at the heart of this astonishing development. The failure of the shogunate can be traced back to the treaty made with Townsend Harris, the US consul, in 1858 which gave the Americans farreaching concessions.

In order to safeguard himself from criticism, the shogun took the

A village in Japan, still unprepared for the arrival of the outside world.

unprecedented step of asking the emperor to sign the treaty. This not only gave the impression that all treaties not signed by the emperor were invalid but, when he refused to sign the Harris treaty, sparked off fierce opposition to "the barbarians".

The Choshus and the Satsumas clashed with the western navies and were quickly defeated. However, their defeat convinced them of the impossibility of opposing western power, and by buying western arms and adopting western methods they have been able to overcome the demoralised shogunate. The way is now open for a new, western-influenced era in Japan.

Emperor Meiji, in his "hif" robes.

Workers will take over, says Marx

London, 14 September 1867

Capitalism will collapse from its own contradictions, and be followed by a dictatorship of the proletariat. This is historically inevitable, according to Karl Marx, a German-Jewish philosopher, newspaper columnist and member of numerous revolutionary movements, in his newly-published tome *Das Kapital*.

Marx was expelled from France and Germany for his revolutionary activities. For the last 18 years he has lived in London, spending many hours in the reading room of the British Museum. The most moving passages of *Das Kapital* are those setting out the facts of the misery experienced by the British working class.

Marx turns a lot of conventional thinking upside down. He argues that economic conditions determine men's thoughts, opposing Utopians who consider that great thoughts change social conditions. "The handmill gives you society with the feudal lord; the steammill, society with the industrial capitalist," he wrote in an earlier work.

Marx, with his friend Friedrich Engels, was the author of the *Communist Manifesto*. Its closing words – "the proletarians have nothing to lose but their chains. They have a world to win. Working men of all countries, unite!" – are intended to be a future rallying cry.

Irish bombs rock England, killing twelve

London, 13 December 1867

A barrel of gunpower was used to demolish the outer wall of Clerkenwell prison today in a bid by bombers to rescue an Irish prisoner. They not only brought down the wall but also wrecked a row of houses opposite, killed 12 people and injured 120 others. They failed to release their man.

The bombers are known to belong to the Fenian Brotherhood, a secret society named after a legendary band of warriors who roamed Ireland defending it against foreigners. The present-day Fenians, who were launched in the United States, have mounted a number of attacks on British property, usually without success.

ST. DRAGON AND THE GEORGE
Fenianism: a English view.

Secret society plans to topple the Sultan

Constantinople, 1867

A group of young middle-class intellectuals has formed a secret society to promote democracy. Through literature and journalism, the members hope to undermine the sultan's autocratic rule. The Young Turks, as they are called, became a coherent force two years ago at a picnic in the forest of Belgrade when they formed a "patriotic alliance" to pursue democratic ideals. Among their leaders are Ibrahim Shinasi, a poet and newspaper editor, Ziya Pasha, who has recently moved to Paris, and Namik Kemal, a radical essayist and devout Moslem.

Karl Marx: a scientific socialist.

1868 (1868-1869)

USA, 28 July 1868. The 14th Amendment to the constitution, giving full US citizenship to Negroes, is passed.

China, 16 August 1868. The western Nian bandits are wiped out by Qing troops near Chiping in Shandong province.

Austria, 22 August 1868. Annoyed at the minor role accorded the Czechs by the Austro-Hungarian *Augsleich*, or compromise, of last October, the Czech deputies withdraw from the parliament.

China, 22 August 1868. Some 10,000 people plunder and destroy the missionary residence of the China Inland Mission.

Spain, September 1868. Queen Isabella II is forced to flee to France after a liberal uprising.

San Francisco, 21 October 1868. An earthquake causes $3 million worth of damage.

Japan, October 1868. Edo is renamed Tokyo, and the new era is named *Meiji*.

USA, 3 November 1868. General Ulysses S Grant, a Republican who was in ultimate command of all union armies during the civil war, is elected president.

Japan, 6 November 1868. The last supporters of the Tokugawa family, led by Shogun Yoshinobu, are defeated at Wakamatsu.

USA, 6 November 1868. The Oglala Sioux Indians led by Chief Red Cloud sign a peace treaty with General William Sherman of the US government at Fort Laramie, Wyoming. The pact ends two years of fighting between gold miners and the Sioux.

China, 9 November 1868. A British naval force captures China's first naval steamship, the *Tianji*, construction of which was completed in July.

USA, 27 November 1868. The US Seventh Cavalry under George A Custer defeats a combined force of Arapaho and Cheyenne Indians led by Chief Black Kettle on the Washita river, east of the Texas Panhandle.

Britain, 9 December 1868. William Ewart Gladstone, who succeeded Earl Russell as Liberal leader last year, forms a ministry, following a Liberal general election victory.

China, December 1868. Ya'qub Beg, the leader of the independent Moslem state of Kashgaria, opens relations with Britain and Russia.

West Africa, 1868. The Fante confederation – an alliance of Fante rulers and the coastal trading/professional elite – is established to provide for defence and create a modern state.

Swaziland, 1868. King Mswati, the founder of the state of Swaziland, dies.

USA, 1868. *Little Women* by Louisa May Alcott – a novel about four teenage sisters growing up in a Victorian New England village – is a bestseller.

USA, 1868. The world's first railway dining car, invented by George Mortimer Pullman, comes into service.

Britain, 1868. The Trades Union Congress is founded.

Britain, 1868. Charles Darwin publishes *The variation of animals and plants under domestication*.

Britain, 1868. William Morris publishes *The Earthly Paradise*, a long poem based on Chaucer, alternating mediaeval tales with those of ancient Greece.

Britain, 1868. Wilkie Collins publishes *The Moonstone*, the first detective novel in English.

Germany, 1868. The historians Ranke, Sybel, Burckhardt and Mommsen publish *The Foundations of Historical Science*.

France, 1868. Edouard Manet paints a portrait of Emile Zola.

France, 20 February 1969. The poet Paul Verlaine publishes *Les fetes galantes*.

USA, 27 February 1869. The 15th Amendment, requiring all Southern states to allow Negroes to vote, is passed.

Japan, April 1869. The emperor moves from Kyoto to Tokyo and takes the old shogunal castle as his palace.

Europe, 10 May 1869. France signs a secret treaty against Prussia with Austria and Italy.

Spain, June 1869. A new constitution, providing for the continuance of monarchical government, is adopted. Francisco Serrano, the leader of last year's revolt, becomes regent, and Juan Prim is made chief minister.

Germany, 1869. Wilhelm Liebknecht founds the Social Democratic Workers' Party.

India, 1869. Mirza Asadullah, who wrote under the pseudonym "Ghalib", dies. He was the leading Urdu and Persian poet of the age and the last poet laureate of the Moghul emperors.

Britain, 1869. Robert Browning publishes an epic poem, *The Ring and the Book*, based on the story of a murder by an Italian count.

France, 1869. Jules Verne writes in instalments a story of an imaginary voyage in a steel submarine, *Twenty Thousand Leagues Under the Sea*.

Paraguay in ruins as its capital falls

Asuncion, Paraguay, January 1869
Asuncion, Paraguay's capital, has fallen to the armies of Brazil, Argentina and Uruguay. Though Paraguay's dictator-president, Francisco Lopez, escaped the Triple Alliance's encirclement of the city, his dream of a new South American empire lie smouldering in the sacked city. After four years of war Paraguay is almost destroyed. Nearly two-thirds of the adult population has died or disappeared, and most of the country is under enemy occupation.

The war started over Lopez' attempts to force a pro-Paraguayan president on Uruguay. Brazil intervened in support of the legitimate president, and Lopez declared war on it. Soon his megalomania dominated strategy. He declared war on Argentina for refusing to allow his troops passage through the country, and declared war on Uruguay just to add to his enemies.

Naturally Brazil, Argentina and Uruguay came together in a triple alliance, formed on 1 May 1865. A few months later Brazil's navy had sunk the Paraguayan navy in the Parana river. By 1867 the alliance's land forces under the Argentinian General Bartolome Mitre were advancing deep into Paraguay's territory. The country is now paying the price for its president's ambitions: almost total devastation.

Spain's rebel generals oust the queen

Spain, 28 September 1868
The defeat of the loyal government troops at Alcolea has compelled Queen Isabella to abandon her summer residence in the Basque country to seek refuge in France. Spain is now in the hands of rebel generals.

Corruption and inefficiency had undermined popular support for Isabella so that when a coalition of liberal generals and urban radicals led a rising, local revolutionary *juntas* lent a hand. Generals Francisco Serrano of the Liberal Union and Juan Prim of the Progresistas are committed to universal suffrage and a free press. All they need is a new monarch.

Isabella, the deposed queen of Spain, making way for liberalism.

Chinese army wipes out rebels in north

China, 16 August 1868
The Chinese imperial army has today wiped out the last of the Nian rebels who have plagued the northern part of the country for the past 15 years. During this period, while the best of the imperial forces were occupied with the *Taiping* rebellion, the peasant Nians, specialising in guerrilla warfare led by mobile cavalry, carried on a robbers' war against the authorities.

Commanded by a former salt smuggler, Zhang Luo-xing, and based on the White Lotus secret society, the Nians allied themselves to the Taipings and grew rich on ransom, plunder and protection rackets. They sheltered the remnants of the Taipings, but once the battlehardened imperial army had finished slaughtering the Taipings, the Nians' turn came.

Their cavalry was confined by massive dykes built round their base areas where the earth was "scorched" to deny them supplies. They managed to break out and split into two groups, but the eastern group was annihilated last January and the western group met its end at Shandong in a fierce battle today. This is not the end of China's troubles. There are uprisings among Moslems in Yunnan, the north-west and Turkestan.

King Ludwig builds castles in the air

Ludwig's fantasy, the Persian Peacock Throne at Linderhof Castle, Bavaria.

Munich, Bavaria, 1869
King Ludwig II has begun construction of Linderhof castle, modelled on the Trianon palace at Versailles. Like all his building projects, it is fantastic and costly. His most outlandish castle is to be Neuschwanstein, perched on a crag in the Bavarian mountains like a fairytale castle and decorated with scenes from Wagnerian operas.

Wagner is the king's other craze. He invited the composer to Munich when he ascended the throne at the age of 18, gave him a villa and a princely salary and offered to build him a theatre. But Wagner's interference in politics and his scandalous affair with Cosima von Bulow, the wife of the conductor and Liszt's daughter, caused Ludwig to banish him to Lake Lucerne.

Neuschwanstein: Ludwig's folly.

Russian count writes of war and peace

St Petersburg, 1869
The work that has occupied Count Leo Tolstoy for seven years is at last finished. *War and Peace* is the most ambitious and possibly the greatest novel yet written. It presents a gradually unfolding panorama of Russia from 1805 to 1814, depicting its struggle with Napoleon's armies and moving from defeat to deliverance.

Against this background the novel traces the fortunes of great families such as the Rostovs and Bolkonskys, and of peasants, of town and country, war and peace. Individuals like Natasha, Andrei and Pierre grow older and wiser through their experiences. The author believes that chance, not choice, determines human afffairs.

His vivid descriptions of battle and army life reflect his first-hand experience as a battery commander at the siege of Sevastopol during the Crimean War.

Leader's defeat ends Maori guerrilla war

New Zealand, 14 March 1869
With the defeat of the Maori guerrilla leader Titokowaru in the extreme south of South Island, the third Maori rebellion in 15 years appears to have been put down.

The rebellion was a blow to the governor, Sir George Grey, who had recognised the justice of the Maoris' claims to their land. In 1863 a militant Maori leader, Rewi Maniapoto, emerged, and urged Maoris to kill Europeans. On 15 April 1863 his followers killed eight British soldiers near New Plymouth in North Island. By June there was a fullscale war in North Island. On South Island the British disarmed all Maoris and demanded that they take an oath of allegiance or leave the British zone. Then they concentrated on North Island. Soon they had ten infantry regiments ploughing their way through the Maori lands.

Behind them came 3,000 armed settlers, recruited from the unemployed in the Australian goldfields to establish fortified settlements in the new lands.

By 1864 it looked as if they had won. Then the Maoris turned to guerrilla warfare, which spread through both islands. For five long years the two sides' atrocities have sapped the country. Now, with Titokowaru's defeat, peace may come to both peoples.

British trades unions split over report

British trades unions: the emblem of the London Society of Compositors.

Manchester, England, 1868
The first meeting of delegates from trade unions throughout Britain is being held here to decide a common front against a forthcoming Royal Commission report, which is likely to recommend only partial legalisation of unions.

The first Trades Union Congress is split between those who want to stay outside the law and the powerful London Trades Council which wants to accept the Royal Commission's minority report. It recommends legalising unions and making union activities legal provided that they are inside the common law. The issue is likely to be debated further at a second Trades Union Congress next year.

Elementary table

St Petersburg, Russia, 1869
Scientists have made notable attempts to classify elements. The latest system to date has been devised by a Russian chemist, Dimitri Ivanovich Mendeleyev, professor of chemistry at St Petersburg University for the last three years. In his periodic table all the elements are arranged in order of increasing atomic weights. Their properties are grouped so that, at a glance, the chemist can take in the nature of a given element, such as its hardness, colour and stability. One new element he discovered has even been named after him: "mendelevium".

Maori art: an ancestor's face, carved on a plank lining the inside of a tribal meeting house.

Scramble for South African gold and gems

Diamond mining: "white diggers" and black labourers near Klipdrift.

Southern Africa, 1869

Since diamonds were found near the lower Vaal river in 1867, and gold was found at Tati and Botswana this year, thousands of prospectors – many of them veterans of the Californian and Australian gold rushes – have streamed northwards across across the Vaal and Limpopo rivers in search of riches. The first diamonds were found around Hopetown; more were found near Klipdrift on the north bank of the Vaal. The area is claimed by the Boer republics (the Orange Free State and Transvaal), two African peoples (the Griquas and the Tlhapings) and the British. Gold came two years later the biggest find was at Tati, which is already dominated by one company, the London and Limpopo, which has its own steam engine. The prospectors call themselves "diggers", after the Australian term. They don't actually do any of the digging, though. That is done by the thousands of blacks who have migrated to the mines and form Africa's first industrial proletariat.

Drive for womens' rights grows in Britain

A woman's role: a post-Mill view.

England, 1869

John Stuart Mill, the political philosopher of Utilitarianism, has published a new book which should add to the current debate on women's rights. *The Subjection of Women*, heavily influenced by his late wife Harriet, demands the emancipation of women and acknowledges their complete equality with men.

Mill has been a consistent campaigner for feminism. During debates on the 1867 Reform Bill he claimed that the vote, even for a minority of women, would benefit all: "They would no longer be classed with children and lunatics, as incapable of taking care of themselves or others, and needing that everything should done for them."

Mill's efforts are part of a growing movement. This year's Married Women's Property Act has made it possible for women to own property. A women's suffrage committee was founded in 1866. The Ladies' Discussion Society, founded in 1865, is one of a number of such groups; and the *Englishwoman's Review* has since 1857 come out unequivocally for women's rights.

Morris designs for individual homes

Burne-Jones and William Morris.

London, 1869

A revolution in home decoration is being inspired by William Morris and his firm of craftsmen, Morris, Marshall, Faulkner and Co, which he founded with Dante Gabriel Rossetti, Edward Burne-Jones, Ford Madox Brown and the architect Philip Webb who designed the Red House in Bexleyheath, Kent, for Morris. It is dedicated to personal design, not mass production.

"Have nothing in your house that you do not know to be useful and believe to be beautiful," is the motto of Morris, an all-rounder who is a painter, glass-stainer and poet, the author of *The Earthly Paradise*. He has now begun designing wallpaper and tapestry.

Morris' "St Catherine", in silk.

US joined east to west

Promontory, Utah, 10 May 1869
As bands played and several thousand railwaymen cheered, the governor of California aimed a mighty sledgehammer blow at the ceremonial golden spike that finally completed the world's longest railroad. Governor Sandford missed, but nonetheless the telegraphs flashed the message to the whole of America that its east and west had been joined by 1,776 miles (2,841 kilometres) of steel track.

After three years of intensive stripping of forests, bridging, tunnelling and earth moving, the Union Pacific line has met the Central Pacific line here in Utah. The plan was for a decorous ceremony, with company directors, engineers and politicians attending from both directions. By the time that the Union Pacific train came roaring in three days late – it had become stuck in prairie floods – Promontory was inhabited almost exclusively by the working crews and their camp-followers – gamblers, whores, saloon-keepers and moneylenders. Both companies had every reason to race. The government was paying $16,000 for every mile of track they laid – more for mountainous areas.

The Central Pacific's and Union Pacific's chief engineers shake hands.

Britain severs Irish Church from state

Disraeli and "Victorian Morality" watch as Gladstone erodes the foundations of the Irish Church.

London, July 1869
Having been swept to power with a Commons majority of 112 for his Liberals, William Gladstone, the prime minister, seized his opportunity and produced a bill to sever the Church of Ireland's link with the state. The bill sailed through the Commons with what Disraeli called a mechanical majority, and even the peers have not dared to oppose it. Apparently the queen, at Gladstone's suggestion, told the archbishop of Canterbury that the bill ought not to be defeated.

The church claims descent from Ireland's patron saint Patrick, but since the time of Henry VIII it has been unpopular because of pressure to follow the reformed Church of England.

Canal opened at Suez

The thousands of labourers who excavated the Suez Canal watch its opening.

Suez, Egypt, 17 November 1869
Three months after the waters of the Mediterranean and the Red Sea met in the Bitter Lakes, a procession of vessels representing all the rulers of Europe is making its way along the Suez Canal which was opened officially today.

Built in spite of British opposition and costing the French-backed Suez Canal Company 400 million francs, 100 times its initial estimate, the 26-foot-deep canal has made use of several lakes to avoid the need for locks. There are bays every 16 miles (25.6 kilometres) for ships to pass. Work on the project, headed by Ferdinand de Lesseps, began over ten years ago. Until 1866, progress was slow with the use of forced labour, but speeded up when machinery took over.

In Britain there are many who fear that the canal will reduce its influence in the Near East and thus open up India, the lynchpin of the empire, to unwelcome outsiders. But commercial opinion largely favours the benefits that should ensue from the new sea passage.

Canada: rebels fear British immigrants

Ottawa, October 1869
A rebellion in western Canada has caught the government off guard and turned much of that remote region into a breakaway republic run by mixed-race (mainly French-Indian) rebels known as *Metis*.

The Metis were satisfied with the *laissez-faire* administration of the Hudson's Bay Company. Impending transfer of its territory to the federal state aroused fears of British immigration into a region to be renamed Manitoba. The rebels are led by a Montreal law student, Louis Riel, aged 25. They have now seized the big settlement of Fort Garry and want to negotiate acceptable terms for union with Canada. As tension mounts, force is as likely as diplomacy.

Berlioz, the titan of French music, dies

Paris, 8 March 1869
Hector Berlioz, the composer who could not play a single instrument properly but was one of music's most original geniuses, died today at the age of 65. Emotionally volatile, urbane, witty and extravagant, with deepset eyes, hooked nose and "an enormous umbrella of hair", the composer of the *Fantastic Symphony* and the massive *Requiem Mass* was a major figure in French musical life. But his own music was too advanced for Parisian taste – it was thought bizarre, or simply "wrong" – and he was forced to earn a living from journalism. He had a small, ardent following, though, and other great musicians, such as Wagner, recognised his unique and grand vision.

1870 (1870-1871)

France, 20 April 1870. A new liberal constitution, introduced by a decree of the senate, gives both the legislative assembly and the senate the right to initiate legislation and to amend bills proposed by the government.

India, April 1870. A political association known as the Poona Sarvajanik Sabha is founded in western India.

France, 8 May 1870. A plebiscite gives overwhelming endorsement to the constitutional changes proposed on 20 April.

China, 21 June 1870. A Chinese mob attacks a Roman Catholic orphanage in Tianjin accused of kidnapping and using children for devilish magic. Twenty-four foreigners are killed, including French and Belgian nuns, as well as the French consul.

Spain, 12 July 1870. Prince Leopold of Hohenzollern-Sigmaringen withdraws his acceptance of the Spanish throne, announced just over a week ago.

Prussia, 14 July 1870. Otto von Bismarck, the prime minister of Prussia, publishes a doctored version of the Ems telegram – a communication between himself and King William of Prussia about the Spanish succession – which is extremely insulting to the French.

France, 19 July 1870. France declares war on Prussia.

New York City, 24 July 1870. The first transcontinental through train arrives from San Francisco.

Britain, 1 August 1870. An Irish Land Act provides tenant farmers with compensation for eviction.

France, 18 August 1870. Prussian forces defeat the French at the battle of Gravelotte.

France, 1 September 1870. The French are decisively defeated by the Prussians at Sedan.

France, 2 September 1870. Napoleon III capitulates to the Prussians at Sedan.

Paris, 4 September 1870. A republic is proclaimed and a government of national defence formed.

Australia, 6 September 1870. The last British troops to serve in Australia are withdrawn.

Paris, 19 September 1870. The Prussians lay siege to Paris.

Rome, 20 September 1870. Taking advantage of the French defeat at Sedan, Italian forces enter Rome and expel the papal troops.

France, 28 September 1870. Strasbourg, under siege since August, surrenders to the Prussians.

Rome, 2 October 1870. In a plebiscite the papal states vote in favour of union with Italy. The capital of Italy is moved from Florence to Rome.

France, 27 October 1870. Metz surrenders to the Prussians.

Spain, 16 November 1870. Amadeus of Savoy, the son of Victor Emmanuel II of Italy, accepts the Spanish crown.

Germany, November 1870. The south German states of Wurttemberg and Bavaria ally with the North German Confederation, ensuring Prussian political hegemony.

USA, 12 December 1870. Joseph H Rainey becomes the first Negro member of the House of Representatives. The Rev Hiram R Revels became the first Negro member of the Senate in February.

Spain, 30 December 1870. The premier Juan Prim is assassinated.

Ireland, 1870. Isaac Butt, a Protestant lawyer from Dublin, sets up the Home Government Association, to spearhead the movement for Irish home rule.

Britain, 1870. An Education Act introduced by the Liberal MP William Forster makes elementary education available to all children between the ages of five and 13.

Venezuela, 1870. After a period of civil war, the liberal leader General Guzman Blanco wins power from the conservative federalists.

Central Africa, 1870. Swahili slave trader, Tippu Tib, sets himself up as ruler west of Lake Tanganyika.

Turkey, 1870. The German archaeologist Heinrich Schliemann begins excavations at Hissarlik, believed to be the site of Troy.

Britain, 1870. Dante Gabriel Rossetti publishes his *Poems* after the manuscript has been retrieved from the coffin of his wife, Lizzie (Elizabeth Siddall), where he placed it in grief at her death.

Paris, 8 January 1871. Prussian troops begin to bombard Paris.

France, 18 January 1871. William of Prussia is proclaimed German emperor (*kaiser*) at Versailles.

France, 28 January 1871. Beset by famine and surrounded by Prussian troops, Paris surrenders. During the siege, balloons were used to maintain contact with the rest of the country.

France, 26 February 1871. France and Prussia sign a preliminary peace treaty at Versailles.

France, February 1871. Elections are held for a national assembly which meets at Bordeaux and elects Louis Adolphe Thiers prime minister.

General is the pawn in China power game

Kashgar, China, 8 November 1870
The Turkic General Ya'qub Beg unified the many-headed Moslem revolt against Chinese repression today when he accepted the surrender of his rival, Tuoming, the self-appointed "pure and true king", at Urumchi in Chinese Turkestan. Now all the rebels will fight under Ya'qub Beg's banner.

This development takes place against a background of intense rivalry between Russia and Britain in this region. Czarist forces are continuing their advance into central Asia, and their probing towards the Indian frontier is causing the British much anxiety.

The British therefore look to Ya'qub Beg's newly-founded *emirate* of Kashgaria as a buffer state between India and Russia. Contact has been established between Ya'qub and Lord Mayo, the viceroy of India, who has sent a member of his staff to Kashgaria. So, without realising it, Ya'qub Beg is now a player in the "great game".

Pope declared source of infallible truths

Pius IX: the infallible pope.

Rome, 18 July 1870
The Vatican General Council meeting here today passed a major new constitutional dogma by an overwhelming majority. The dogma, *Pastor Aeternus*, declares that the pope, when he speaks as "Shepherd and Teacher of all Christians", enjoys infallibility in defining doctrine on faith and morals. His definitions are "unalterable in themselves and not by virtue of the assent of the church".

It represents a triumph for the conservative views of Pope Pius IX and a defeat for the liberal Catholic scholars, who have argued that history and science are disciplines in their own right, and that Catholics should learn from them. From now on the Vatican can be expected to be less tolerant of dissent.

Novelist's death hastened by overwork

Rochester, Kent, 9 June 1870
The sudden death has occurred of Charles Dickens at his home, Gadshill, which he bought in 1856, having coveted it as the son of a poor clerk in the navy yard at Chatham. He was 58; his death was hastened by his strenuous programme of public readings from his novels which he acted to the full.

Dickens first won recognition with his newspaper sketches of London life signed "Boz". He married his editor's daughter, Catherine Hogarth, but they separated after the birth of ten children. His readers waited eagerly for each part of his current novel. The death of Little Nell in *The Old Curiosity Shop* caused nationwide grief.

Charles Dickens at a public reading.

Germany crushes France at Sedan

Napoleon III surrenders to Kaiser William after the battle of Sedan.

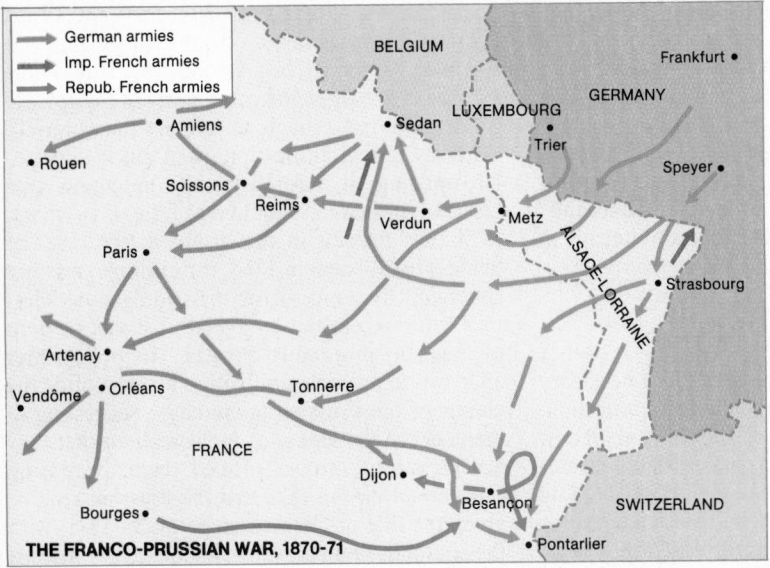

German armies
Imp. French armies
Repub. French armies

BELGIUM
LUXEMBOURG
GERMANY
Frankfurt
Amiens
Sedan
Trier
Rouen
Speyer
Soissons
Reims
Verdun
Metz
Paris
ALSACE-LORRAINE
Strasbourg
Artenay
Vendôme
Orléans
Tonnerre
FRANCE
Dijon
Besançon
SWITZERLAND
Bourges
Pontarlier

THE FRANCO-PRUSSIAN WAR, 1870-71

Sedan, 2 September 1870
A shattered Emperor Louis Napoleon, frequently in tears, surrendered his sword to William, kaiser (or king) of Prussia today after 44 days of warfare that have devastated France and confirmed newly-unified Germany as the most powerful new nation in Europe.

The beginning of the end came yesterday when Prussian troops encircled the emperor's relief force at Sedan as it tried to reach Metz, where the main French force has been penned in. The emperor, looking pale and dogged by illness, ended the squabbling among his generals and ordered the white flag to be raised. It was his reluctant acceptance that his 235,000-strong French army had been out-manoeuvred, outnumbered and outgunned by a 380,000-strong Prussian force. Only the hastily assembled National Guard now stands between the Prussians and Paris.

The surrender were negotiated this morning at a poignant meeting in a tiny weaver's cottage between the emperor and the architect of his downfall, the Prussian prime minister Bismarck, who has used the war to bring the Rhineland states into a German confederation.

It was Bismarck's decision to publish a provocative version of the Prussian response to French complaints over the nomination of a German prince for the Spanish throne that first inflamed French public opinion and forced a reluctant Napoleon to declare war, even though he knew that his army was weak. Tonight he is paying the price – as prisoner of the Prussians in the comfort of the royal apartments at Wilhelmshohe castle.

Germany proclaims empire in France

Versailles, 18 January 1871
Amidst the glittering splendour of Louis XIV's hall of mirrors in the Palace of Versailles, Bismarck today realised his long-cherished dream. His Prussian king, William, became emperor of a new German *reich*, and Bismarck himself became the first chancellor.

The *venue* for the ceremony was a humiliation for the French, but the choice had much to do with a desire to impress the numerous German princes, who had to be cajoled into joining the reich and giving up some of their petty privileges. The crushing defeat of France, and the capture of Napoleon III at Sedan, by Germans who had accepted the Prussian military system stirred German public opinion; the princes had to give way.

William, Europe's new emperor.

France declared a republic once more

Paris, 4 September 1870
France is once again a republic, with revolutionary crowds roaming the streets following the collapse of the 20-year-old second empire after Napoleon III's defeat by the Prussians at Sedan.

The new republic was declared today by the emperor's opponents in the legislative body, anxious to head off a revolutionary movement from the extreme left. A provisional government of national defence has also been established under the military governor of Paris to combat the Prussian threat. Meanwhile the Empress Eugenie and the prince imperial have fled to England.

The guilty men, French and Prussian: a Republican view.

Victor Emmanuel makes Rome his capital

Rome, 20 September 1870
The army of Victor Emmanuel II entered Rome today and declared its intention of making it the capital of Italy. Garibaldi made several attempts to take Rome with his people's army, the last being in 1867, but he was defeated by the French. Success this time had more to do with the absence of the French than with the prowess of the Italian army. Napoleon III withdrew his forces from Rome to help him in his war with the Prussians. Earlier this month the Prussians routed the French at Sedan and Napoleon was himself taken prisoner. For the first time Italy was free to move on the papal states without having to fight the French.

There was little resistance. The walls were shelled, and a breach made at Porta Pia. Only a few lives were lost.

Germany and Italy: two new nation-states

European diplomacy in the middle years of the 19th century was dominated by two events: the unification of Italy, which was completed in 1870 when Rome became the capital of the new state, and the unification of Germany, which was proclaimed with much ceremony at Versailles in 1871. Within a generation, the political map of Europe was redrawn. Austria, the former ruler of the Italian states, had been humbled, France humiliated, Germany had emerged as a strong nation-state, and Italy had shown that she was more than Metternich's "geographic expression". Moreover, it appeared that both countries had been unified in similar fashion: by a combination of diplomacy and war, by ardent nationalism, by inspired leadership, by enmity towards Austria. Indeed it seemed that each had a shared interest in the other's success. In April 1866 Italy allied with Prussia, and in 1870 Bismarck likened himself to Cavour, the former prime minister of Piedmont, claiming that the Franco-Prussian war was no different from the war against Austria which Cavour and Napoleon III had planned in 1859.

Yet German and Italian unification were significantly different processes. The states which emerged had little in common. The nationalisms they embodied were divergent. The legacies they bequeathed – in Italy, Mazzinian liberalism grafted on to Cavourian conservatism; in Germany, worship of the state as an end in itself – were far from compatible. What they share is paradoxical: that in neither case does "unification" adequately describe the manner in which they came into being.

The *Risorgimento*, or movement for Italian unification, reflected desires both for liberation and for liberalisation. Austria had to be expelled from Italy, but it was also necessary to replace her with a regime based on liberal principles. Three men embodied these aims. Giuseppe Mazzini, of the "Young Italy" party, was a radical, calling for "Union, Liberty and Independence! ... All aristocracy abolished: all privileges which do not depend on capacity, or actions, nullified. Public education encouraged without limit." Nothing could be achieved until the "barbarian had evacuated Italy".

The role of time and chance

Camillo Cavour, a more conservative figure, backed Mazzini. A pluralist, he argued for a free church, in a free state. In 1848 he wrote in his own journal *Il Risorgimento* of the need for a Piedmontese constitution and for a Piedmont-led war against Austria. Thus combining liberalism and

nationalism, he seemed entirely in keeping with the spirit of 1848. He opposed an alliance with France in any such war, on the ground that it would be "most shameful" to allow a new set of foreigners into the country to expel the existing set. If Cavour and Mazzini were politicians, Giuseppe Garibaldi was a soldier and a popular leader without peer, with advanced, if naive, social ideas and a strong anticlericalism. Without him, Italian unification could not have taken the form it did: a popular movement owing nothing to the support of the Catholic Church.

The patriotic confidence of the *Risorgimento* is impressive, but Italian unification was not inevitable. That achievement owed much to time and chance. Napoleon III's involvement in Cavour's war plans of 1859 could not have been predicted. Austria's tactical blunder – delivering an ultimatum to Piedmont to disarm just as other European powers were attempting to detach Napoleon from his new commitment – was a piece of great fortune for Cavour. Garibaldi's "March of the Thousand" (1860) to liberate Sicily and Naples by means of a popular uprising was a high-risk enterprise.

A politically cautious regime

The expulsion of the foreigner was a necessary but not sufficient condition for Italian unification. How united was the "unified" Italy? What kind of Italy was it? It was formed much in the image of Piedmont, the former home of the house of Savoy in north-west Italy. The new state was a constitutional monarchy, not, as Mazzini had hoped, a republic. Victor Emmanuel II of Sardinia-Piedmont became Victor Emmanuel I of Italy and the head of a politically cautious and socially conservative regime. The legal system owed much to the Napoleonic Code, a charter for the propertied in a patriarchal society. Less than 2 per cent of the population qualified for the new franchise: males over 25 paying at least 40 lire annually in taxes. Italian unification may have even enforced divisions between north and south, between the masses and the classes.

If it is an exaggeration to claim that Italian unification was, simply, "Piedmontisation", it is true that German unification was "Prussianisation". Such was the intention of its chief architect, Otto von Bismarck. Germany after 1848 was a welter of particularism, with every region enjoying considerable autonomy. It was the cornerstone of Bismarck's statecraft that Prussia should dominate them. He was not, however, avaricious: he would rather have had a "small Germany" (*Kleindeutsch*) which Prussia could easily control than a

"large Germany" (*Grossdeutsch*) which she could not. Again, it was Austria which lay in the way. Unlike Cavour, he had no "foreigners" to expel to achieve unification. Ironically, such was the logic of his *Kleindeutsch* intentions that the only people to be excluded from his unified state were German-speakers themselves – the 8,000,000 German Austrians who remained outside the empire proclaimed in 1871.

A man of "blood and iron"

The "Prussianisation" of the new Germany had significant cultural consequences. Bismarck made no claims to liberalism. His first speech as Prussian prime minister (1862) extolled not reason and argument but "blood and iron". The cynicisms of *real-politik* came easily to his lips. He was a militarist, though no military man himself. Whereas Italian unification owed much to popular uprising, it was Bismarck's intention that German unification should owe little, if anything, to it. His interest in the disputed territories of Schleswig-Holstein in 1864, for example, was not generated by concern for their indigenous German nationalism but by a wish that one or both of them be annexed to Prussia. His policy after 1866 was to promote unification by promoting the claims of the Prussian monarchy – suggesting to members of the House of Hohenzollern that they accept vacant thrones offered them, proposing (unsuccessfully) in 1870 that the Prussian king be given the title of German emperor. In 1871, with the southern German states joined in war against France but still chary of membership of an empire controlled by Prussia, he won them over not by arousing popular clamour but by making deals with the king of Bavaria and his fellow rulers. It was the German princes, not the people, who offered the imperial crown to William. Bismarck was an oddity: the creator of a nation-state who was no nationalist. In so far as nationalism was a form of popular self-expression, he was decidedly wary of it.

After 1871 European history had moved into a new phase. Regional self-interest had given way to the territorial unity of sovereign states. The centre of gravity had shifted from Paris to Berlin. France, after the disaster of Sedan, had become a republic, Italy had emerged as a constitutional monarchy, Germany a conservative and centralised empire, and Austria, after 1867, an imperial partner of Hungary. At the periphery was Britain, still industrially pre-eminent and with an expanding empire. This was the crucible in which Europe's future was formed.

GERMANY IN 1859

North Sea

DENMARK

Baltic Sea

POMERANIA

EAST PRUSSIA

HANOVER

NETHERLANDS

• Berlin

RUSSIA

BRANDENBURG

BELGIUM

WESTPHALIA

SAXONY

POLAND

Cologne •

SILESIA

BOHEMIA

FRANCE

BAVARIA

WURTTEMBURG

Munich •

SWITZERLAND

AUSTRIA

	Kingdom of Prussia
	Zollverein customs union

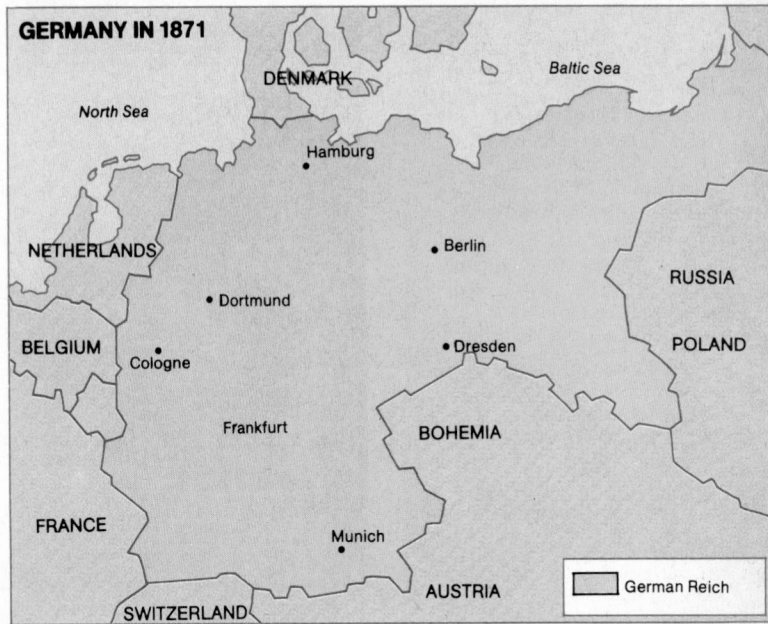

GERMANY IN 1871

DENMARK

Baltic Sea

North Sea

Hamburg •

NETHERLANDS

• Dortmund

• Berlin

RUSSIA

BELGIUM

Cologne •

• Dresden

POLAND

Frankfurt

BOHEMIA

FRANCE

Munich •

SWITZERLAND

AUSTRIA

	German Reich

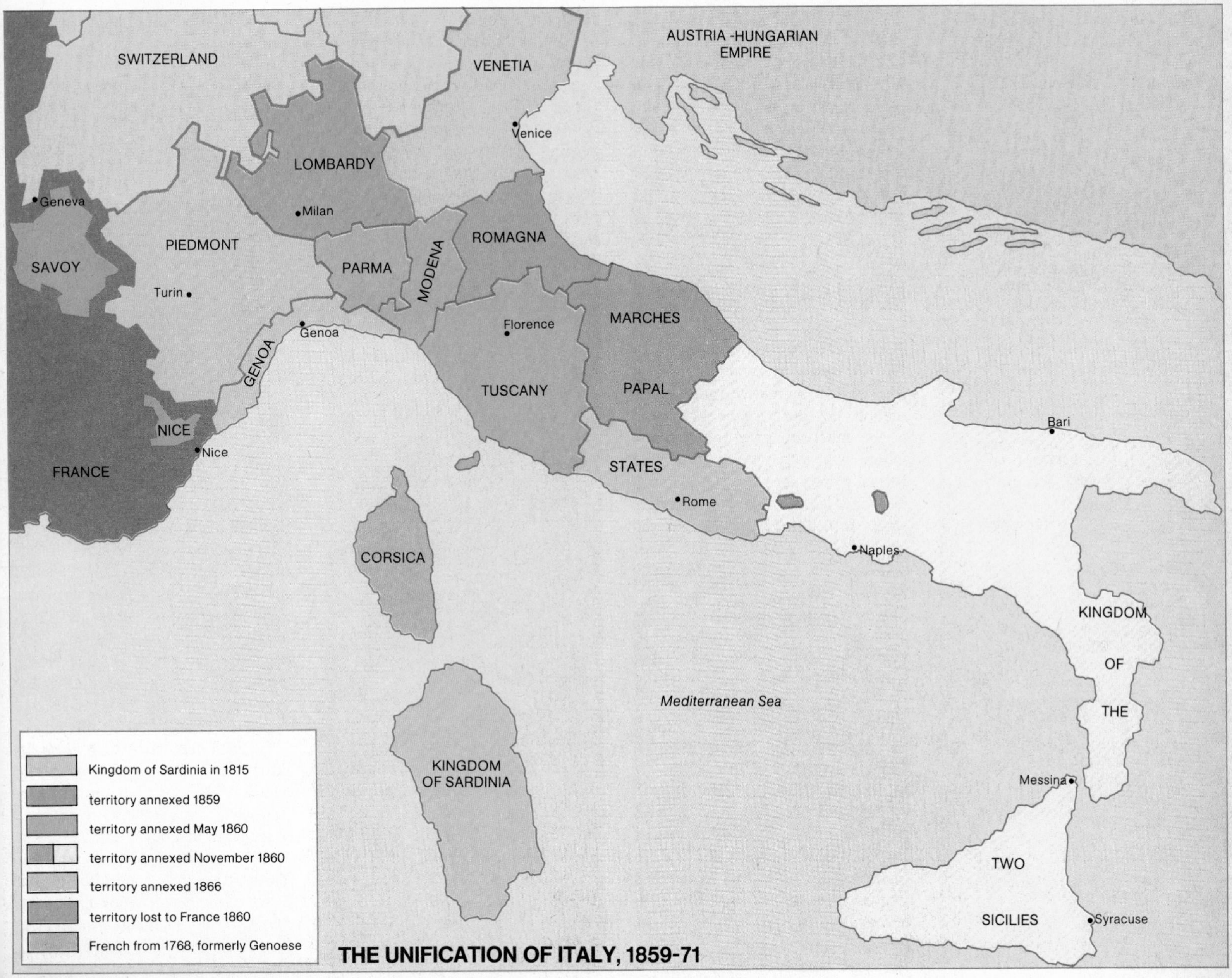

SWITZERLAND

AUSTRIA -HUNGARIAN
EMPIRE

VENETIA

LOMBARDY

Venice •

Geneva •

• Milan

PIEDMONT

ROMAGNA

SAVOY

PARMA

MODENA

MARCHES

Turin •

Florence •

GENOA

Genoa •

PAPAL

NICE

TUSCANY

STATES

Nice •

Bari •

FRANCE

Rome •

CORSICA

Naples •

KINGDOM

OF

Mediterranean Sea

THE

KINGDOM
OF SARDINIA

Messina •

	Kingdom of Sardinia in 1815
	territory annexed 1859
	territory annexed May 1860
	territory annexed November 1860
	territory annexed 1866
	territory lost to France 1860
	French from 1768, formerly Genoese

TWO

SICILIES

Syracuse •

THE UNIFICATION OF ITALY, 1859-71

US newsman discovers African explorer

"Dr Livingstone, I presume?" "You have brought me new life."

Uiji, Central Africa, 13 November
Britain's most famous explorer, David Livingstone, has been found alive at Ujiji in Central Africa after being feared dead for the past four years. An expedition led by a *New York Herald* journalist, Henry Morton Stanley, traced Dr Livingstone, frail and short of supplies, to the edge of Lake Tanganyika.

Mr Stanley's greeting: "Dr Livingstone, I presume?" were the first words the 58-year-old explorer has heard spoken by a white man for five years. Dr Livingstone told Mr Stanley: "You have brought me new life." The explorer insisted on hearing about major events that he has missed, including the Franco-Prussian War, the opening of the Suez Canal and the inauguration of the transatlantic telegraph.

Law makes Indian land prey to railroads

Washington, DC, 3 March
After decades of wrangling about the rights of the native Indian population and their legal relationship to the American government, legislation was introduced today that formally ends the idea that the Indians are inhabitants of a separate state. It has been thus since the British signed a treaty at Fort Stanwix in 1768 which recognised the "Indian Nation".

Under the Indian Appropriations Bill, all Indians will be considered as "individuals" and treated as such. They will be designated "wards" or government charges.

One reason for the new approach to the Indian problem is that the Indians do not have the same concept of sovereignty as "European" Americans. A chief may sign a treaty, but the extent of his authority is rarely agreed upon by his own people. And when Indians sign treaties, neither they nor the government knows for sure to whom the rules apply. Hence the "individuality" accorded these highly

Indians: now to be "individuals".

individual people. Little is said in the bill, however, about the rights of railroad owners to slice great parcels of land off the reservations. The new bill, indeed, allows the government freedom to do that with the stroke of a pen.

US party boss faces huge fraud charge

New York City, December
The law has finally caught up with William "Boss" Tweed, the corrupt czar of Tammany Hall – but not before he and his cronies had managed to salt away an estimated $100 million from bribes, graft and swindles on a gargantuan scale.

Tweed, a former saddler and bookkeeper, rose through the political ranks to become an alderman of the city and quickly showed a marked talent for corruption. He formed a ring of equally corrupt associates – who quickly became known as "the forty thieves" – and set out to use Tammany Hall, the

"Boss" Tweed, the corrupt giant.

headquarters of the state's Democratic Party, to become the virtual dictator of the party.

He secured membership of key boards and "placed" members of his ring in strategic positions where they could extort bribes and commissions from almost anyone who sought a city hall permit. Bogus citizenships were issued by the thousand – all at a cost – and rigged elections were the norm.

When Tweed tried to tighten his grip on New York with a new "city charter", the press, notably in cartoons by Thomas Nast in *Harper's Weekly*, turned its attention to the "forty thieves". The *New York Times* came into possession of evidence of the mass swindling. A committee of 70 eminent citizens was formed and even the corrupt police were forced to move.

Communards and French army tear Paris in half

Radicals proclaim commune in Paris

Paris, 28 March
It was quite a spectacle they put on outside the Hotel de Ville today. On a platform draped with scarlet cloth a group of men wearing red scarves stood to attention as units of the National Guard marched past. The parade came to a close with massive salvos of cannon-fire, and a man wearing a Phrygian cap, the symbol of revolution and liberty, began to speak, but his words were lost in the chants of *"Vive la Commune"*.

So the power of the people was asserted and the Commune of Paris proclaimed after a lost war. The marching and cheering and singing of the *Marseillaise* continued into the night. The National Guard, a locally-raised militia heavily infiltrated by left-wing elements, had made a poor showing during the four-month German siege of the city; now it was glowing with triumph. The government, led by Louis Adolphe Thiers and lodged at Versailles, was impotent. "I have not four men and a child," Thiers said when asked for reinforcements to crush the commune. The regular army has been reduced to a single division and the supposedly reliable elements of the National Guard have disintegrated.

Most of the *Communards* who took over the Hotel de Ville are writers, painters and assorted intellectuals, clerks and petty tradesmen, with a handful of workers. Vaguely inspired by slogans from France's past revolutions, they have no clear idea of what they want to achieve, other than somehow erasing the stain of defeat.

A month ago, National Guardsmen raided artillery parks in Paris and removed some 200 cannon to the heights of Montmartre. A detachment of regular troops sent to recover the guns arrived without horses to tow them away; was set on by Guardsmen and two generals were lynched. A wealthy Parisian woman, told that the Commune had banned night work for bakers, commented: "The Communards have decreed that Paris shall eat stale bread."

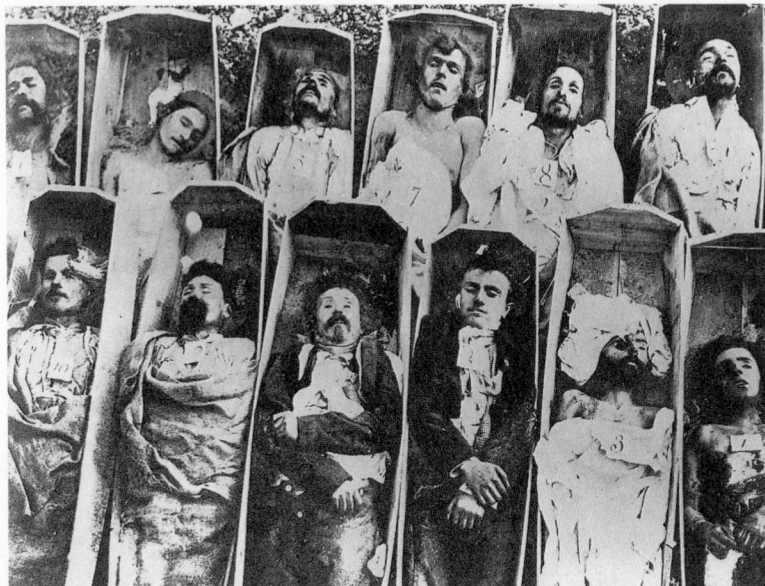

A few of the Communards who died in Paris. "They were madmen" said the painter Renoir, "but they had a flame within them that will never die."

Barricades at Port Maillot, stormed by Versailles troops early in the assault.

France concedes victory to the Prussians

Frankfurt, 10 May
A peace treaty formalising the end of hostilities between France and Germany was signed here today. It confirms the agreement reached by the two sides after Paris fell to Prussian troops in March.

Under the treaty France finally surrenders to Germany all of the border province of Alsace and most of neighbouring Lorraine. It was this demand that had prolonged the war. France also has to pay an indemnity of five billion francs to Germany, with a German army of occupation remaining in France un-

til the indemnity – equivalent to the amount Napoleon I imposed on Prussia in 1807 – is paid. The handing over of Alsace and Lorraine without a popular vote has led to a protest by the British prime minister Gladstone, who claims that the people should have been consulted.

The treaty, which places no limit on France's armed forces or foreign policy, reflects a strategic gamble on the part of Prussia's prime minister, Bismarck, who believes that France has already been sufficiently isolated and humbled by the catastrophic defeat at Sedan.

Paris commune is bloodily crushed

Paris, July
The commune is dead, drowned in blood. The communards, who had withstood Prussian and French besiegers for nine months, fought their last fight amid the graves and headstones of Pere Lachaise cemetery. Most communard prisoners taken are being shot. They expected no better.

The all-out assault on the city began by chance on 21 May, when one of the giant forts defending the western approach to the city was found to have been abandoned – which says much about the inefficiency and incompetence of the commune's leaders. Versailles troops poured in and during the following week, *La Semaine Sanglante*, Paris was taken, *boulevard* by *boulevard*, barricade by barricade, body by body.

The *forces d'ordre* came in through the predominately middle class west, where they were greeted as liberators. Soon they captured the city centre, though the *hotel de ville* and many other public buildings were burnt down by arsonists. South of the Seine the French army encountered strong resistence around Les Gobelins and the Jardin des Plantes. North, particularly in the working class areas, the resistence was even greater. Some of the most ferocious fighting came from Louise Michel's women's battalion around Place Blanche and Pigalle. Realising the French army's tactic of outflanking through the side streets, she had most of her battalion on her northern flank. Gradually the women retreated, the streets of Montmartre littered with their corpses, until they joined the men of Belleville for a last heroic stand in the cemetery.

Between 20,000 and 25,000 people were killed in fighting or are being executed in "retaliation" for the killing of the Archbishop of Paris. Whether these troops will be as successful in killing the myth of the commune in less certain. For Paris has become a place of horror and heroism – the stuff that legends are made of.

France, 31 August 1871. Louis Adolphe Thiers is elected president of the republic.

Japan, August 1871. Feudal domains are abolished and prefectures are created as the new units of local administration.

Brazil, 28 September 1871. The Rio Branco law, stipulating that children born to slaves are free, is passed.

Japan, 8 October 1871. The tenets of equality in taxation laws and compulsory, fee-paying education are laid down. A modern postal system is introduced.

Chicago, 9 October 1871. A great fire kills 300 people, makes 90,000 homeless and causes $200 million worth of damage.

Los Angeles, 24 October 1871. Nineteen Chinese are killed in anti-Chinese riots.

South Africa, 27 October 1871. Britain annexes the diamond region of Griqualand West.

Austria, October 1871. The Emperor Franz Josef rejects Bohemian demands for a position similar to that of Hungary in the Dual Monarchy.

France, 23 November 1871. The Chinese imperial commissioner, Chonghou, apologises to President Thiers for the Tianjin massacre of June 1870.

Germany, 4 December 1871. The *mark* becomes the unit of currency.

South Africa, 3 November 1871. Cape Colony takes over the government of Lesotho (Basutoland).

Europe, 1871. The Mont Cenis tunnel, the first great Alpine tunnel, connecting France and Italy, is completed.

France, 1871. Following the defeat of the Paris *Communards*, Elizabeth Dimitrieva, a Russian-French socialist who organised the Women's Union for the Defence of Paris as a branch of the Socialist International, escapes to Russia.

France, 1871. The electrical engineer Zenobe-Theophile Gramme gives a demonstration of his invention, the continuous-current dynamo.

Switzerland, 1871. The French mountaineer Henriette d'Angeville, the first woman to organise and undertake her own climb of Mont Blanc, dies in Lausanne.

Russia, 1871. Count Dimitri Tolstoy, the minister of education, reorganises the educational system in order to combat materialism and revive classical education.

USA, 1871. The National Association of Professional Baseball Players is founded.

Britain, 1871. James McNeil Whistler paints *Arrangement in Grey and Black – the Artist's Mother* and Sir John Millais exhibits *The Boyhood of Raleigh*.

Britain, 1871. Lewis Carroll publishes *Through the Looking Glass*, a sequel to *Alice in Wonderland*; and Edward Lear follows up his *Book of Nonsense* with *Nonsense Songs and Stories*.

Britain, 1871. Charles Darwin publishes *The Descent of Man*, which expounds his theory of natural selection.

London, 1871. Having left Paris because of the Franco-Prussian War, the French impressionist Claude Monet paints the Thames and its bridges.

Belgium, 25 January 1872. Henry, the count of Chambord, a claimant to the French throne, makes a speech in Antwerp rejecting a call for a "revolutionary monarchy" in France.

Bay of Bengal, 8 February 1872. Lord Mayo, the viceroy of India, is murdered by a Moslem fanatic while visiting a penal colony on the Andaman Islands.

West Africa, 6 April 1872. The British take over the Dutch forts in Gold Coast (*Ghana*).

China, 12 May 1872. The Miao rebellion is finally suppressed with the capture of its main leader, Zhang Xiumei.

Germany, 22 May 1872. The foundation stone is laid for the Bayreuth festival theatre in Bavaria, intended specifically for performances of Wagner's works.

Spain, May 1872. Don Carlos, a claimant to the throne, enters Navarre, but is driven back beyond the frontier by General Moriones.

France, May 1872. Marshal Bazaine, who surrendered to the Prussians at Metz, is sentenced to 20 years' imprisonment for treason.

France, June 1872. An agreement over war indemnities is signed with Germany at Versailles. They are to be paid in stages and the French government may settle the debt in advance and thus speed up the departure of Prussian troops.

Germany, 4 July 1872. A law is promulgated as part of the *Kulturkampf* banning all religious assemblies, particularly Jesuit ones.

Britain, 18 July 1872. The Ballot Act is passed providing for secret ballots at elections.

South Africa, July 1872. Thomas Burgers, a Dutch minister from the Cape, is Transvaal's new president.

Britain, 1872. Samuel Butler writes *Erewhon*, a Utopian satire on religious traditions and morals.

Telegraph to link Australia to the world

Adelaide, 23 November 1872

Australia's isolation from the rest of the world is about to end following the construction of an overland telegraph line linking south Australia with Darwin in the north. In November the new telegraph will be connected to a new undersea cable from Darwin to Java that will link Australia into the fast-growing transoceanic telegraph network.

The owners of the international cable, the British Australian Telegraph Company had made the completion of the Overland Telegraph a precondition of the Darwin-Java cable. The final join in the cable, nearly 2,000 miles (3,200 kilometres) long, was made today at Frew's Pond after work on the northern section of the line had been constantly interrupted by floods.

The route for the north-south cable which cost £120,000, follows that opened by John M'Dowall Stuart's third and successful nine-month expedition ten years ago when he became the first explorer to cross the Australian continent from sea to sea.

Ku Klux Klan, US racist club, suppressed

A Klan warning, directed as much at northern "carpet baggers" as Negroes.

Washington, August 1871

The civil war may have finished six years ago with slavery abolished, but many Negroes in the former slave states of the south remain in constant fear of the burning cross of the *Ku Klux Klan*, the hooded white terror organisation pledged to white supremacy. Former slaves who dare to tread the same sidewalk as white men are liable to be seized to face a secret court of hooded men and to be flogged – and often lynched from the nearest tree – if the "court" so decides.

In Florida alone, 153 Negroes were killed in a single parish this year; over 300 were murdered in the countryside near New Orleans.

Few doubt that the Klansmen are ardent former confederates, resentful in defeat and frustrated by the lack of subservient labour, and northerners have become increasingly angry at the idea that the south is robbing them of their success. The result is a bill before Congress which outlaws the Klan and other secret societies and allows for the suppression of violence by military force.

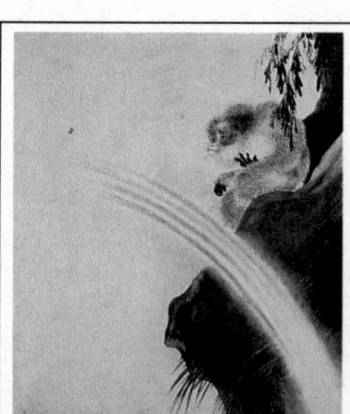

"Monkey and Rainbow", one of a series of exquisite and restrained watercolours by the 64-year-old Japanese artist Shibato Junzo Zeshin.

Bismarck launches attack on Catholics

Berlin, 14 May 1872
Bismarck has become embroiled in a struggle with the Roman Catholic Church – and found his own weapons turned against him. The conflict of beliefs, or *Kulturkampf*, stems from the Vatican Council of two years back, when it was decreed that when the pope speaks on matters of religious faith he is infallible and has to be obeyed by all Catholics. Distinguished German Catholics, some employed by state universities, objected; they were excommunicated and the Vatican called on the government to dismiss them.

Bismarck responded by pointing to the constitution, which guarantees civil and political rights irrespective of religious belief. Now he has published a set of laws which forbid the church to intervene in affairs of state, forbid the clergy to discuss politics in the pulpit and ex-

Bismarck: "Iron Chancellor".

clude the church from the state education system. The church is defending itself by pleading for the right to worship as conscience and reason dictate.

Indian nationalist has killed the viceroy

Port Blair, India, 8 February 1872
The viceroy of India, Lord Mayo, has been assassinated, struck down by a lone Indian nationalist while inspecting a penal settlement. A moderate conservative in the House of Commons, Mayo was conciliatory by nature. He disliked military intervention and sought to support rather than undermine states like

Afghanistan, which he saw as "outworks of our empire" against Russia.

He was a promoter of education for the Moslem people, and ally of the princes; but he failed to understand the increasing alienation of the urban middle class intelligentsia from British rule, and he has paid for it with his life.

French author looks into a bright future

One man's journey of imagination.

Paris, 1872
Lovers of "scientific" adventure have been eagerly reading *Le Temps* newspaper which carries regular instalments of Jules Verne's latest *voyage imaginaire*, entitled *Around the World in 80 Days*. This latest journey remains on the surface of the earth – or just above it – unlike his *Journey to the Centre of the Earth* or *Twenty Thousand Leagues under the Sea*.

It begins in London's Reform Club when a gentleman called Phileas Fogg makes a wager with his companions at the card table that he can circle the globe and be back in 80 days exactly. His stratagems include crossing the Alps in a balloon. Eighty days is of course an impossible time for such a voyage.

Marie Celeste mysteriously abandoned

Atlantic Ocean, 4 December 1872
She lay lifeless in the Atlantic swells, her sails flapping idly, and failed to respond to signals from the British freighter that spotted her. They made out her name as *Marie Celeste*, but saw no sign of life on her. The British crew were even more mystified when they boarded her and found her crewless. The cabin in her saloon was laid for tea. There was no sign of mayhem. Her cargo of 1,700 barrels of alcohol was intact.

The maritime world is completely baffled and theories abound in every seafarer's tavern. Some say the crew had got to the cargo, killed the captain in a drunken orgy and escaped on a southbound ship. Some talk of a sea-monster. Others think it was pirates ... but teetotal pirates? It seems unlikely that the mystery will ever be solved.

Verdi's Egyptian opera opens in Cairo

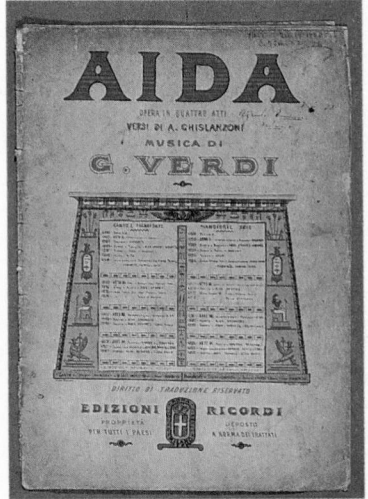

The libretto and music for Guiseppe Verdi's grand but taut opera, "Aida".

Cairo, 25 December 1871
The delayed first performance of Giuseppe Verdi's new opera, *Aida*, took place last night at the Italian Theatre, Cairo, built to mark the opening of the Suez Canal. It was to have opened the theatre last year, but the siege of Paris prevented the scenery arriving. The *khedive*, Ismail Pasha, Egypt's ruler, suggested the story.

The plot is about Aida, who is the slave of Amneris, the Pharaoh's daughter, and their rivalry for the love of Radames, the captain of the guard. The opera ends with Aida sharing the fate of Radames when he is entombed alive. "Celeste Aida" and the triumphal march are two of the opera's hits.

Edgar Degas' "Dance Studio at Rue le Peletier". Born in 1834 to a wealthy Parisian family, he studied at the Ecole des Beaux-Arts, learning his superb draughtsmanship from Jean Auguste Ingres. After three years in Rome he took to painting historical scenes, but after meeting Edouard Manet he began to paint contemporary themes, particularly ballet, the circus, cafes and horse races. He has been praised for his spontaneity, a quality which he rejects: "No art was ever less spontaneous than mine."

1872 (1872-1874)

Germany, September 1872. The emperors of Germany, Austria-Hungary and Russia form an alliance in Berlin.

USA, 5 November 1872. Ulysses S Grant is elected for a second term as president.

New York City, 19 November 1872. William "Boss" Tweed, the former head of Tammany Hall, the city's Democratic organisation, is jailed for fraud and corruption.

China, 26 December 1872. Du Wenxiu, the leader of the Moslem rebellion in Yunnan province, is executed, having surrendered to Qing troops at Dali.

South Africa, December 1872. Responsible government is established at Cape Colony, with John Molteno as the first prime minister.

Germany, 1872. The philosopher Friedrich Nietzsche publishes *The Birth of Tragedy*, dedicated to Richard Wagner, whose operas he regards as the true successors to Greek tragedy.

France, 1872. Georges Bizet composes the incidental music for Alphonse Daudet's play *L'Arlesienne*.

Hawaii, 8 January 1873. Prince William Lunalilo becomes the first elected monarch of Hawaii.

Britain, 9 January 1873. Napoleon III of France dies at Chislehurst, Kent, where he had withdrawn following his imprisonment at Wilhelmshohe, near Kassel, immediately after his surrender to the Prussians at Sedan.

Japan, January 1873. The imperial army is reorganised and modernised on European lines.

China, January 1873. Qing forces carry out a large-scale massacre of Moslems at Dali.

Spain, 11 February 1873. Amadeus abdicates after a two-year reign as king of Spain, and the first Spanish republic is proclaimed.

Southern Africa, 30 April 1873. The Scottish missionary and explorer David Livingstone dies near Lake Bangweulu (*in Zambia*). From the age of ten to 24 he had worked in a cotton factory. He was ordained under the London Missionary Society aged 27-years-old. He discovered Victoria Falls aged 41, and Lake Nyasa aged 46. He died aged 60.

France, 24 May 1873. President Thiers resigns and the right-wing monarchist candidate Marshal Marie Edme MacMahon is elected president.

China, 29 May 1873. The last remnants of the Yunnan Moslem rebellion are defeated.

Germany, May 1873. New laws against religious education bring seminaries under state control. The Catholic opposition takes shape, particularly in Silesia, Poland and the Rhineland, where ecclesiastical dignitaries are threatened with internment.

China, 29 June 1873. The US, British, Dutch, French, Japanese and Russian ministers are received in audience by the emperor and present their credentials.

Germany, 9 July 1873. The *Reichstag* passes a law which pegs the value of the *mark* to gold.

San Francisco, 1 August 1873. The first cable car service begins operation.

France, 16 September 1873. The last German troops leave France.

China, 12 November 1873. The Gansu Moslem rebellion ends with Zuo Zongtang's capture of Suzhou in Gansu province. His troops slaughter many thousands of Moslems.

Central Asia, 6 December 1873. Ya'qub Beg formally accepts the title of *emir khan* from the sultan of Turkey. From now on he is called Emir Mohammed Ya'qub Khan of Kashgaria.

Central Asia, 11 December 1873. Ya'qub of Kashgar receives Sir Douglas Forsyth, a British envoy sent from India, and expresses warm friendship for Britain.

USA, 14 December 1873. The Swiss-born naturalist Louis Agassiz, author of four volumes of a *Natural History of the United States*, dies at Cambridge, Massachusetts.

Bolivia, 1873. A peace treaty is signed at La Paz fixing the frontier between Chile and Argentina along the ridge of the Andes *cordillera*.

West Africa, 1873. Asante forces defeat the British at Assin Nyankumasi in the Gold Coast (*Ghana*).

Central Asia, 1873. The Russian General Skobelev captures the oasis of Khiva, the capital of the khanate of Khiva, to the south of the Aral Sea in Uzbekistan.

Brussels, 1873. The French poet Paul Verlaine is sentenced to two years' hard labour for shooting his friend and fellow-poet Arthur Rimbaud in the wrist. Rimbaud published this year a prose volume entitled *Une Saison en Enfer*.

France, 1873. The novelist Jules Verne publishes *Around the World in 80 Days*.

Britain, 1873. The Custody of Infants Acts is passed, extending the access of separated or divorced women to their children.

Bank failures and bad harvests hit US

New York, 1873
It has been a bad year for the United States of America. The country has been hit badly by not only natural disasters but also several man-made financial catastrophes. Drought has afflicted midwestern states, where unnaturally high rainfall in the 1860's brought illadvised settlement, and trains are being halted by the grease of millions of crushed grasshoppers on the tracks. In September, panic on the New York Stock Exchange left many ruined in its wake.

Over-speculation, believed to be at the root of the turmoil in New York, has also caused several national banks to collapse. As the demand for gold as a monetary unit goes up, the supply of the metal is now insufficient to meet the needs of the world's burgeoning economies.

Japan invaded Formosa to get at China

Formosa, October 1874
The Japanese are to withdraw the expeditionary force sent to Formosa (*Taiwan*) to punish the Formosans for the murder of 54 shipwrecked fishermen from the Ryukyu Islands four years ago. The truth of the matter is that the Japanese care little for the fate of the fishermen, but care a lot for ownership of the Ryukyus – foggy, remote islands which pay tribute to Beijing but fell under the control of a Japanese warlord 200 years ago. Now it seems that the Japanese have tricked the Chinese into acknowledging Japan's sovereignty over the islands, for, in order to stop the occupation of Formosa, the Chinese have agreed to indemnify Japan for the murder of the fishermen. They have bought off the Japanese, but have succeeded only in whetting Japan's appetite.

The new Remington typewriter, produced by the famous gunsmiths of New York state. The first practical typewriter was invented by Christopher Latham Sholes in 1867. His second model a year later wrote faster than a pen. It was still cumbersome, and it was not until he signed a contract with the Remington company that he was able to produce a machine for the mass market. Its components are a cylinder, with linespacing and carriage return mechanisms, and typebars so arranged as to strike the paper through an inked ribbon at a common centre. One of Remington's first customers for the machine is Mark Twain, the novelist.

Three emperors in pact

Three emperors: Czar Alexander, Kaiser William and Emperor Franz Joseph.

Berlin, 7 September 1872
After his victory in the Franco-Prussian war, Bismarck – rewarded by a grateful Kaiser William with the title of prince – looked for some means by which Germany could guard itself against a revanchist France. He has now persuaded Franz Josef of Austria and Alexander of Russia to affirm their solidarity with William in the preservation of peace in Europe. The fine-sounding *Dreikaiserbund* – the League of the Three Emperors – has yet to face its first test, but many observers believe this will have nothing to do with the French.

The real trouble spot is seen as the Balkans, where both Russia and Austria have long had designs on pieces of the increasingly feeble Ottoman empire. Bismarck could not remain indifferent to a big power struggle there.

Conscription swells European armies

Europe, c.1872
In much of Europe, with the exception of Britain, the professional armies which fought other people's wars for the last century are being diluted by conscripts. "National service", first introduced in Prussia in 1814, is now a fact of life for young men in France and Austria-Hungary and probably soon will be in Russia. Most states opt for a period of between one and three years in uniform, but the process is beset by doubts. The French President Louis Adolphe Thiers, with the *commune* in mind, describes it as "putting a rifle on the shoulder of every socialist". Yet the French working man, far from seeking a military life, dodges the draft in his thousands, occasionally using self-mutilation or assuming gender changes if other ploys fail. In Germany, fewer recruits are selected from politically unreliable states than from more conservative areas.

Despite such snags, the size of armies is growing apace. Some observers wonder if a part-civilian army will blur the distinction made between combatants and unarmed civilians in any future conflict.

A soldier's farewell to his family.

Spain's king quits; republic declared

Amadeus, who failed to establish himself as a constitutional monarch.

Madrid, 11 February 1873
Spain's unpopular King Amadeus has abdicated and the Cortes (parliament) has decided that the country must become a republic. Amadeus has reigned for four years, and throughout this time his regime has been beset by difficulties, largely caused by quarrelling among several political parties.

Over the last year ministry has succeeded ministry as parties split up, which has made stable government impossible. There has been non-stop opposition to any policy from the *Carlists*, culminating in another full-scale revolt which has effectively ended the democratic monarchy. Amadeus decided to step down after an attack on the army by the Radicals, and deputies voted in a republic.

Russian anarchist clashes with Marx

The Hague, Netherlands, 1872
Mikhail Bakunin, a turbulent, free-wheeling anarchist who for a quarter of a century has sought to ferment unrest in much of Europe, is no longer a member of the First International Workingmen's Association, the organisation created eight years ago by Karl Marx to coordinate socialist struggles.

Bakunin, an advocate of terrorism who claims that "the passion for destruction is also a constructive passion", was once a Russian army officer. He has been sentenced to death twice, and spent six years in a Russian prison before escaping – with such ease that suspicions that he was a czarist agent were rife – from exile in Siberia.

Marx, whose overriding concern is to set up mass socialist parties, has waged a vitriolic personal campaign aimed at reducing anarchist influence in the International. By meeting here, far from Bakunin's bastions of support in Spain, Italy and Switzerland, Marx' followers obtained Bakunin's expulsion.

Bakunin: prophet of anarchy.

"Blackbirding" – kidnapping of near-slave workers – banned

Brisbane, 1874
Ross Lewin, the greatest "blackbirder" of them all, is dead. He was shot in the back by a native as he walked towards his veranda. The native, whose cousin Lewin had shot for banana-stealing, had been hiding for three days in a coconut palm waiting for his opportunity. "Blackbirding" is the practice of recruiting South Sea Islanders, particularly the Kanakas, for work on the sugar plantations in Australia. The first 67 arrived on the schooner *Black Dog* in 1863. By 1867 Ross Lewin was advertising "the best and most serviceable natives to be had in the islands at £7 a head".

Ostensibly the natives were on contracts. Actually they were kidnapped and frequently brutally treated. Planters like Robert Towns argued that the Kanakas were well suited to the work and that he was avoiding "the inhumanity of driving to the exposed labour of field work the less tropically hardy European women and children". Public opinion and the law have now stopped the trade.

1874 (1874-1875)

Spain, January 1874. On the retirement of Emilio Castelar – made head of government last September during *Carlist* risings – a military *coup* puts Marshal Francisco Serrano back in power.

Vietnam, 31 January 1874. France signs a treaty with the Emperor Tu Duc which acknowledges a French protectorate over Cochin China.

Britain, February 1874. Following the defeat of Gladstone's Liberals in a general election, Disraeli forms his second Tory ministry.

Hawaii, 12 February 1874. On the death of King Lunalilo after one year's reign, rioting breaks out among islanders who support the claim to the throne of Queen Emma, the widow of King Kamehameha IV. The other claimant is Prince David Kalakaua, whom Lunalilo defeated in a bitter election fight for the crown.

Gold Coast (Ghana), 14 March 1874. After suffering a defeat by the British in January, the Asantehene, king of Asante, signs a treaty with British representatives at Cape Coast ending the Anglo-Asante war.

Japan, 13 April 1874. Eto de Hizen, a *samurai* of the Satsuma clan, is beheaded for rebelling against the imperial decision not to invade Korea, which had refused to receive missions from Japan.

Switzerland, April 1874. The Swiss Constitution is revised to increase the powers of the federal government, especially in military affairs. The principle of referendum is adopted for national legislation.

France, April 1874. The novelist Gustave Flaubert publishes *The Temptation of St Antony*.

Britain, 30 August 1874. The Factory Act limits the working week to 56.5 hours.

Switzerland, 9 October 1874. A treaty is signed in Berne by 22 countries establishing a Universal Postal Union.

Italy, October 1874. France recalls the ship *Orenoque*, which has been moored off Civitavecchia since 1870 ready to receive the pope should he be forced to leave Rome. The pope is waging an uncompromising battle against the Italian government and calling on Catholics not to participate in politics.

Pacific, October 1874. Britain annexes the Fiji Islands.

USA, 18 November 1874. The national Women's Christian Temperance Union is founded.

Spain, 29 December 1874. The *infante*, Don Alfonso, is declared king of Spain, ending the dictatorship of Francisco Serrano.

Sudan, 1874. General Charles Gordon succeeds Sir Samuel Baker as governor general of Sudan in the service of Egypt. Baker completed the conquest of the upper Nile region as far as Bunyoro (*Uganda*) and began the suppression of the slave trade.

Sudan, 1874. Zubair Pasha, a former slave-trader in the Sudan, conquers Darfur on behalf of the *khedive* of Egypt.

China, 1874. The rickshaw is introduced.

Germany, 1874. Wilhelm Wundt publishes his *Physiological Psychology*.

Spain, 1874. The writer Pedro Antonio de Alarcon publishes a short picaresque tale called *The Three-Cornered Hat*.

USA, 1874. Mark Twain publishes *The Gilded Age*, a novel satirising unbridled materialism.

China, January 1875. The Tongzhi emperor dies at the age of 18. The Empress Dowager Cixi (Ziaoqin) adopts her nephew Zaitian, the late emperor's cousin, and makes him successor to the throne. The two empress dowagers become co-regents for the second time.

France, 30 January 1875. France adopts a republican constitution under which legislative power will be exercised by two chambers: the Chamber of Deputies and the Senate. Executive power will reside with a president, elected for a period of seven years.

Rome, 5 February 1875. Pope Pius IX issues an encyclical denouncing Bismarck's laws and the *Kulturkampf*.

Germany, 6 February 1875. Civil marriage is made obligatory.

China, 21 February 1875. The murder of the British legation official Augustus Raymond Margary near the border with Burma by native bandits heightens Anglo-Chinese tensions.

China, 25 February 1875. The Guangxu emperor formally ascends the throne.

USA, 1 March 1875. Congress passes the Civil Rights Act, guaranteeing equal rights in transport, theatres and inns and on juries.

Hawaii, 18 March 1875. Hawaii signs a treaty giving exclusive trading rights with the islands to the USA.

China, 27 March 1875. The widow of the Tongzhi emperor, who died in January, commits suicide.

USA, 1875. Thomas Adams of Brooklyn, New York, manufactures the first chewing gum.

Rejected Paris painters put on show

Monet's impression of fog – "Try to forget what objects you have before you."

Paris, 15 April 1874
A group of artists who have been regularly rejected by the prestigious Salon, the arbitrator of taste, has put on its own exhibition as an independent group in a former photography studio on the Boulevard des Capucines. It is attracting incomprehension and ridicule. The group includes Claude Monet, Pierre-Auguste Renoir, Camille Pissarro, Edgar Degas and Paul Cezanne – 39 painters in all. Their aim is to capture light as it is directly perceived by the eye reflected from objects in particular conditions, rather than the objects themselves.

They use short brushstrokes of pure colour and high tone, even in shadows, that blend when seen from a distance. Claude Monet declares that he seeks to capture "the most fleeting effects". He paints from a boat on the Seine.

Outraged spectators object to the formlessness and vagueness of the paintings, which appear to be unfinished. Monet's *Impression: Sunrise* has been seized on by Louis Leroy, the critic of *Le Charivari*, to call the group "Impressionists" – a term of abuse. "Wallpaper in its embryonic state is more finished than that seascape," he writes.

Monet's impression of a poppy field – "Paint it as it looks to you."

British make peace with Asante ruler

West Africa, 14 February 1874
After two years of war, the British and the Asante have made peace. Technically, the British, under Sir Garnet Wolseley, won a battle, but neither side can claim to have won the war. At Fomena, Kofi Karikari, the Asante ruler, and Wolseley signed a peace treaty under which the Asante relinquish claims to the coastal states, which become British possessions.

War became inevitable after the Dutch evacuated their coastal forts. The Asante claimed one, Elmina, and the British took it. The Asante advanced and Wolseley's column of British and local troops marched to relieve it. The Asante withdrew, not because they were overawed by Wolseley, but because they were suffering from smallpox.

"The army of a civilised nation need not have been ashamed of a retreat conducted with such skill and such success," said Wolseley's

Cartoon entitled "The British Lion Aroused" shows how the Asante war was seen by a jingoistic press.

secretary, Mr H Brackenbury. Since then Wolseley has taken the Asante capital (which they did not defend), but failed to destroy their army.

Novelist politician back at Britain's helm

Benjamin Disraeli: 32 years an MP.

London, 18 February 1874
At 70, Benjamin Disraeli has found the time and the energy to carry on a romantic correspondence with two sisters, Lady Bradford and Lady Chesterfield, reorganise the Conservative Party, and win a resounding victory over his old adversary, Gladstone, to become prime minister for the second time.

Six years ago, when he first took office, he said: "I have climbed to the top of the greasy pole." He lasted only a matter of weeks and though he continued as Conservative leader he devoted far more time than his rivals' approved of to writing another novel, the three-volume political comedy *Lothair*.

Sultan bakrupt after a spending spree

Istanbul, October 1875
The Ottoman government's creditors are to receive only half the interest due to them, the remainder to be replaced over the next five years by bonds carrying five per cent interest. In other words, the *Porte* is bankrupt again.

Responsibility for the latest financial *debacle* rests squarely with Sultan Abdul Aziz, who, since

the death of Ali Pasha in 1871, has appointed six different *Grand Viziers* in three years and paid no attention to any of them. Returning from a European tour, he embarked on lavish palace entertainments and a massive programme of building warships and railroads. When state money ran out, he spent his own, and he repaid his loans by simply borrowing more.

"Editors" are hired just to go to jail

Japan, 1875
A struggle has developed in Japan between the Meiji government and the nation's press following the passing of a press law which gives the government extensive powers of control over the newspapers. Any editor criticising government policy is liable to a fine and imprisonment. The editors have retaliated by hiring "prison editors" whose sole function is to pay the fine and serve the jail sentence while the real editor produces the paper.

While this ploy is causing much amusement among the populace, the government is not amused and is already planning swingeing new laws which will entail the closing down of the papers as well as fines and jail for the "prison editors". The authorities also plan to make newspapers deposit large sums of money which will be forfeited whenever they break the law.

Turkestan falls to Russian invaders

Central Asia, 1874
Ya'qub Beg, ruler of Kashgar and a thorn in Russia's side for over 20 years, has yielded at last. Russia is now master of all Turkestan.

In 1852 Ya'qub Beg commanded the Khokand fortress of Ak-Mesjid against the invading Russians, and inflicted heavy losses on them before being bombarded into submission.

The past decade has seen a remorseless Russian advance into Turkestan. Since the fall of Tashkent in 1865, Bokhara has accepted Russian protection.

Ya'qub Bey, who founded the autocratic state of Kashgaria in eastern Turkestan, cultivated both the British and the Ottomans. He had coins minted in honour of the sultan, and an Ottoman military commission came to Kashgar to train Beg's army, secretly supplied with British arms.

Englishmen now ask: Anyone for tennis?

England, February 1874
A new game has been patented in England and its inventor, Major Wingfield, expects that this popular descendant of "real tennis" will establish itself as a firm favourite.

Lawn tennis, or *Sphairistike*, (from the Greek for playing ball), has been played before, but the major has set down formal rules. He first introduced the game last year, at a house party, and the rigours of its hour-glass shaped court proved no barrier to players of either sex. Indeed, heartier sportsmen have already condemned Sphairistike as too soft and social – for ladies only.

Tennis players, by Horace Cauty: a new ball-game for the middle classes.

1875 (1875-1876)

Germany, 8 April 1875. The publication in the Berlin *Post* of the article "Is War in Sight?", which expresses concern over recent French military measures, provokes panic in France.

Kentucky, 17 May 1875. The first Kentucky Derby – a horse race – is run at Louisville.

Germany, May 1875. Bismarck abolishes all Catholic orders and congregations.

Germany, May 1875. The Social Democratic Party is founded.

Germany, May 1875. Britain and Russian intervene to prevent war between France and Germany.

France, 3 June 1875. The composer Georges Bizet dies after the "failure" of his opera, *Carmen*, described by critics as obscene.

France, 16 July 1875. The new French Constitution is finalised.

Balkans, 29 July 1875. The peasants of the two mountain provinces of Bosnia and Herzegovina rebel against the Ottomans and put up resistance to the Ottoman army. The Bosnians wish to join Serbia, whereas the Herzegovinians prefer to be integrated into Montenegro.

Southeast Africa, July 1875. In an arbitration award, France assigns the southern shore of Delagoa Bay to Portugal, rejecting British claims.

Balkans, 16 September 1875. Following the uprising in Bosnia and Herzegovina, Bulgarian patriots under the leadership of Khristo Botev, the president of the revolutionary committee, trigger off a rebellion in Stara Zagora.

USA, 30 October 1875. Mary Baker Eddy publishes *Science and Health with Key to the Scriptures*, arguing that illness is illusory and laying the basis for Christian Science.

Egypt, 27 November 1875. Britain buys Suez Canal Company shares.

New York City, November 1875. The Russian theosophist Helena Petrovna Blavatsky founds the American branch of the Theosophical Society, whose beliefs are based on universal brotherhood.

Dakota, November 1875. War breaks out between the Sioux Indians of the Black Hills and white prospectors.

Russia, 1875. Count Leo Tolstoy publishes a new novel, *Anna Karenina*, about a sophisticated lady, unfulfilled by Russian polite society, who takes a lover, with tragic results. On the title page he put the quotation: "Vengeance is mine, I shall repay". His own marriage had never been happy.

Britain, 1875. The Public Health Act and the Artisans' Dwellings Act, which deals with the problems of housing the poor, are passed.

Hungary, 1875. Kalman Tisza forms the Liberal Party and becomes prime minister after the new party wins a large majority in an election.

Britain, 1875. The Conspiracy and Protection of Property Act legalises peaceful picketing.

Central Africa, 1875. The British explorer Verney Cameron is the first European to cross Africa from Zanzibar to Benguela in Angola.

Switzerland, 1875. The French geographer Elisee Reclus publishes the first volume of a vast *Universal Geography*.

France, 1875. The International Bureau of Weights and Measures in created.

India, 1875. Aligarh College is founded by Saiyid Ahmad Khan to build a bridge between Indian Moslems and western civilisation.

India, 1875. The *Arya Samaj* is founded by Swami Dayananda Saraswati to oppose Brahmanism and return Hinduism to the simplicity of Vedic ritual on the one hand and to oppose Islam and Christianity on the other.

New Zealand, 1875. New Zealand is brought under one government following the abolition of provincial councils.

East Africa, c.1875. The *kabaka* of Buganda, Mutesa reverses his pro-Islam policy, which he sees threatening his authority, and develops his policy of playing missionaries off against each other.

London, 1875. Sultan Sayyid Bargash of Zanzibar makes a state visit to London and meets Queen Victoria at Windsor.

Germany, January 1876. The imperial *Reichsbank* opens.

Korea, February 1876. Japan recognises Korean independence.

Italy, 25 March 1876. Led by Agostino Depretis, the progressive party forms a government and embarks on a far-reaching programme of reform.

USA, 1876. Mark Twain publishes *The Adventures of Tom Sawyer*, a novel based on his own childhood.

USA, 1876. John Harvey Kellogg, a Seventh Day Adventist, begins developing new types of flaked cereals. These, Kellogg claims, if included in a vegetarian diet, will help to curb sex drive.

USA, 1876. Henry J Heinz begins bottling and marketing tomato ketchup.

Horse buying stirs war scare in Berlin

Berlin, May 1875

Rumours that French agents are travelling through Germany buying up horses has set off a war scare in Berlin. Chancellor Bismarck has banned the export of horses, and the press is filled with excited articles asking whether war with France is imminent. It is widely known that France's rapid recovery from the defeat of 1871 has aroused fears in Germany that the old enemy might be plotting a war of revenge. This has led to suggestions in some quarters that Germany should launch a preventive war.

Some observers even suspect Bismarck himself of starting the war scare in order to stir up feeling against France.

Trucanini, Aboriginal queen, has died

Hobart, 11 May 1876

Huge crowds gathered in Hobart, Tasmania, today for the funeral of Trucanini, known as the Queen of the Aborigines, the last of her line. She was in her sixties.

Trucanini, 4ft 3in tall, saw her mother stabbed to death by white men; at 16 she was raped by white convicts. She took to hanging about work camps, selling herself for a handful of tea and sugar. Then she met a house-builder, a white man, whom she helped to record tribal customs. Last week she cried out "Rowra [the evil spirit] catch me!" and fell senseless. The coffin lowered into her grave was empty; fearing body-snatchers, the authorities buried her elsewhere.

Captain swims from England to France

Webb arriving to a hero's welcome at Calais, after swimming the Channel.

Calais, 25 August 1875

At 10.40 this morning, an Englishman, Captain Matthew Webb walked onto the beach here: the first man to have swum the English Channel. He had been in the water for 22 hours and had swum through the night a distance of 40 miles (64 kilometres). His body was covered by porpoise grease to keep out the cold. He was fed with cod-liver oil, beef-tea, brandy, coffee and strong old ale by accompanying boats.

Webb, now 27, learnt to swim in a local river when he was eight. He saved his brother from drowning a year later. Last year he won a medal for jumping overboard from a Cunard ship to try to save a seaman from drowning.

Britain snaps up shares in Suez Canal

Cairo, 27 November 1875
Britain has bought nearly half the shares in the Suez Canal for £4 million from the *khedive* (ruler) of Egypt. Disraeli, the British prime minister, is relieved to have prevented the French from wholly owning the canal. When the Suez Canal was built six years ago by French enterprise and French money, the then British prime minister, Gladstone, refused to take any interest. Now British ships account for four-fifths of the canal's traffic.

Twelve days ago Disraeli learned that the *khedive*, who held 177,000 of the 400,000 shares but was on the verge of bankruptcy, wanted to sell, or at least arrange a mortgage to a French syndicate. The British agent in Egypt asked for a suspension of negotiations while Lord Derby, the British foreign secretary, exerted pressure on his French opposite number, the duke

Tenniel's anti-Semitic view of Disraeli's purchase of the Suez Canal.

of Decazes. The French syndicate, without government help, pulled out, and Britain, with the financial help of Baron Lionel de Rothschild, was able to buy the shares.

Composer of Carmen dies as opera flops

France, 3 June 1875
Last night, an opera singer in Paris was stricken with such terrible foreboding that she fainted when she left the stage. The opera was *Carmen*, and its composer, Georges Bizet, was hours from death after a massive heart attack. He was 37.

Three months ago to the day, the Paris premiere of *Carmen*, Bizet's most mature work to date, caused a scandal at the Opera Comique. Its Spanish setting of thieves, gypsies and cigarmakers and its tragic ending were thought "obscene", its music "Wagnerian" and tuneless. Bizet was mortified. Never a very well man, he fell ill with quinsy, rheumatism and, finally, two heart attacks.

Painted in her finest role as Carmen is the opera singer Emma Calve.

Japan fakes military attack on Korea

Korea, 1876
Japan is determined to open up the "hermit kingdom" of Korea, just as Japan was opened up by the arrival of Commodore Perry's "black ships"; it is now using the same tactics of threat and bluff that the western powers used against it.

Rebuffed by the Koreans in their attempts to negotiate a treaty which would have destroyed Korea's isolation, the Japanese have sent warships to survey the Korean coast, braving the fire of coastal guns. At the same time they have warned the Koreans that the ships are preparing the way for the landing of an expeditionary force.

The bluff seems to have worked. The Chinese, who claim suzerainty over Korea and have been recently forced to agree to concessions in the Ryukyu Islands following the Japanese attack on Formosa, have told the Koreans to accept the Japanese diplomatic mission.

Yoshitaka's painting of the Japanese cabinet planing the invasion of Korea.

Germany's socialists unite in one group

Gotha, Germany, May 1875
Spurred on by Germany's galloping industrialisation and recent political unification, the two main strands of its rising workers' movement united with the foundation of the Social Democratic Party at a unity congress here this month.

The new party's programme combines the democratic socialist ideas of the late Ferdinand Lassalle with the revolutionary communist ideology of Karl Marx. Lassalle thought that workers could own the means of production after a fair electoral system was introduced. Marx believes that the state must be overthrown first. The party's demands include freedom of the press, adult enfranchisement, free and compulsory education and a single progressive income tax. It also seeks the prohibition of work on Sunday and "all forms of labour by women which are dangerous to health or morality".

August Bebel, German leftist leader.

"I promise liberal rule," says Mexico's new leader, Diaz

Mexico, November 1876
Mexico has a new leader. Porfirio Diaz, aged 46, has been elected president in a ballot that followed his army's occupation of Mexico City earlier this month. He promises to restore the liberal constitution of 1857.

Diaz was born in Oaxaca, the son of poor Indians. At the age of 17 he planned initially to enter the priesthood, but chose the army instead. After a year's service he turned to law and joined the Liberal movement. In 1855 he fought for Benito Juarez' guerrillas in the civil war against Santa Anna and then against the French invaders. In January 1861 he led Juarez' troops into Mexico City, ready to welcome his triumphant leader. Only when Diaz found Juarez disappointing as a ruler did the two fall out.

In 1871 Diaz attempted to defeat Juarez at the polls. Defeated himself, he led a rebellion; it failed, but after Juarez died in 1872 and was succeeded by Lerdo de Tejada, Diaz retreated to Texas, where he developed his plans to take power.

Balkans, June. The Ottomans embark on largescale massacres to put down a rebellion in Bulgaria.

Balkans, 30 June. Serbia declares war on the Ottomans.

Balkans, 1 July. Montenegro declares war on the Turks.

Bohemia, 8 July. Andrassy and Gorchakov, the Austrian and Russian foreign ministers, meet at Reichstadt to agree on the future of the Balkan states on the conclusion of the current conflict.

USA, 1 August. Colorado becomes the 38th state in the union.

Serbia, 9 August. Having invaded Serbia, the Turks defeat the Serbs at Aleksinac.

Ottoman Empire, 31 August. Abdul Hamid III becomes sultan following the deposition of Murat V, who succeeded Abdul Aziz, himself deposed in May by the *grand vizier* Midhat Pasha.

Serbia, 1 September. The Ottomans inflict another, decisive defeat on the Serbs at Aleksinac.

Brussels, 12 September. Leopold II of the Belgians forms the International African Association to coordinate the activities of European explorers in Central Africa.

Balkans, 31 October. Under pressure from Russia, the Ottomans agree to an armistice with Serbia and Montenegro.

Ottoman Empire, 23 December. Midhat Pasha, the grand vizier, introduces a liberal constitution.

India. Surendranath Banerjea founds the Indian Association, the leading Indian political association of Bengal.

China. The Shanghai Wusong railway, which was opened in April by Jardine Matheson & Co to serve the foreign mercantile community, is purchased by the Chinese authorities and dismantled.

Ethiopia. The Ethiopians inflict two defeats on the Egyptians near Gura, forcing Egypt to relinquish claims to the whole Nile basin up to Lake Victoria.

Germany. The engineer Nikolaus Otto builds an internal-combustion engine.

Germany. The Bayreuth theatre opens with the first complete performance of Richard Wagner's *Ring* cycle.

Call for help is heard down a wire

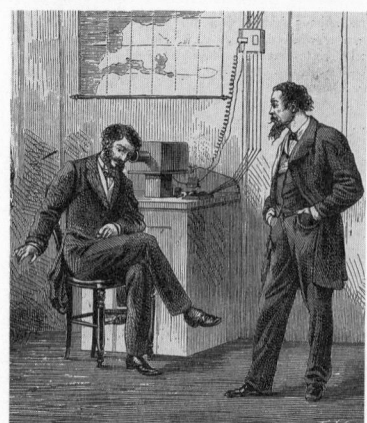

Bell: demonstrating his telephone.

Philadelphia

Alexander Graham Bell, the Scottish-American inventor and pioneer of mechanical methods of teaching deaf children, was about to test a new device which transmitted his voice over a distance along a wire. It was then that he spilt battery acid on his leg. He used his "electric speech machine" to call his assistant. "Watson, come here, I need you" were the first words to be spoken on what has quickly become known as the *telephone*.

The message is generated by a vibrating diaphragm that is activated by the voice to a receiver that amplifies the voice. It was developed from a form of deaf-aid.

Bell has demonstrated the system at the Centennial exhibition here, reciting "To be, or not to be" over 150 yards of wire to an excited emperor of Brazil who shouted "I hear! I hear!".

Born in Edinburgh, Bell was educated in London before emigrating to Canada and, later, the USA.

Bulgarian atrocities outrage the British

London, September

Though crippled by an attack of lumbago, Gladstone dashed off in four days a pamphlet, *The Bulgarian Horrors and the Question of the East*, which has become a runaway best seller. The Liberal opposition leader is incensed by the attitude of indifference adopted by Disraeli, the prime minister, towards the sufferings of the Bulgarians.

More than 12,000 men, women and children were massacred by Ottoman irregulars when the Bulgarians rose against their oppressors last May. Disraeli refused to intervene because, he said, Britain should support the Ottoman empire as a barrier to Russian ambitions in the eastern Mediterranean.

Gladstone, however, proclaims it to be a profoundly moral issue. The Ottomans are the "great anti-human species of humanity" who have violated "the purity of matron, of maiden and of child". He addressed a meeting at Blackheath in pouring rain and called on the

Punch's cartoon of Britain's "naivete" in allying with Russia in response to the Ottoman's atrocities.

Russians to drive the Ottomans out of Bulgaria. Referring to Disraeli, he told a friend that the Jews had always been against Christians. Disraeli, for his part, says that Gladstone is playing party politics and is worse than any Bulgarian horror.

Queensland's law bids to keep it white

Queensland, Australia

As thousands of Chinese labourers pour into northern Queensland, where gold has been discovered on the Palmer River, the government of Queensland has given in to the agitation for a "white Australia for white Australians". It has passed the Goldfields Amendment Bill imposing a heavy tax on Chinese immigrants to the minefields (repayable only when they leave), and a licence fee six times what white men pay. The Chinese government has protested and the gov-

ernor of Queensland has already said he will reject the bill on the grounds that it is offensive to British subjects.

The arrival of the Chinese has provoked a violent backlash from the white working class, who fear being undercut by cheap labour. Chinese labourers have been lynched (one unfortunate was nailed to a tree by his ears), and the goldmining centre of Cooktown – where Chinese outnumber white by seven to one – was burnt down by a white mob.

Scientist sees secrets of the mind by looking you in the face

Rome

Is there such a thing as the "criminal face"? Or "criminal build"? Is the wrongdoer, in fact, a product of the environment or of heredity?

Cesare Lombroso, the Italian anthropologist, is convinced not only that criminals are born with the "mark of Cain" but that it is possible to see criminality in their physical features. He believes that the criminal type has certain physical abnormalities or *stigmata*. These

might be seen, for example, in a certain pattern of lumps on the skull that mark out an individual as irredeemably immoral. Lombroso also cites such areas as nose and brow as important in criminal identification.

Not everyone likes Lombroso's ideas. Although his name is becoming widely known, his eccentric views are confined to a minority. Just what physical features have to do with a crime is not made clear.

Cesare Lombroso: criminologist.

972

Indians wipe out General Custer's troops

The last stand of Custer and 265 of the Seventh Cavalry at Little Big Horn.

Little Big Horn, Dakota, 25 June
The buckskin-clad General George A Custer expected to find no more than a handful of Sioux Indians as he led his force of 265 troopers of the Seventh Cavalry along the Little Big Horn river. Instead, as the cavalrymen rounded a bend, they found an entire army of Sioux, Cheyennes and Crows prepared to fight. With more Indians behind him, Custer had little choice but to raise his sword and order his men to charge. Within less than an hour, the general was dead and so was every one of his men. Custer's body was found on the pinnacle of a hill where he made his last stand, the flag of the Seventh Cavalry still flying over him.

So desperate was the army's plight that Custer's men shot their horses for cover and formed a

George Custer: the civil war hero.

square from which they took a heavy toll of the Indians. With no hope of relief, they were overwhelmed. Custer's force was a key element in a campaign to force the Indians to leave the plains and return to their reservations. They have been forced to leave the reservations by the threat of starvation.

Sultan agrees to liberty and equality

Istanbul, December
Abdul Hamid II has become the new sultan, subject to a constitution largely drawn up by the Young Ottomans, or Young Turks. His grand vizier is Midhat Pasha, one of the most influential advocates of liberty, equality and ministerial responsibility. Six months ago Sultan Abdul Aziz yielded to the demands of army and people, abdicating in favour of his nephew Murat V, backed by the democratic campaigners. But Murat proved mentally unstable, and Midhat was authorised to approach Abdul Hamid, Murat's younger brother.

The Ottoman sultan Abdul Hamid.

India has new empress

London, April
After a good deal of ill-tempered resistance from the Liberal opposition, Queen Victoria has received the title she greatly desired and is now empress of India. Some objected to the title because "emperor" supposedly has "bad associations" with Continental despots. But Disraeli told MPs that "the amplification of titles" was often necessary in order to catch "the imagination of nations". He said the title was being anxiously awaited by the people of India; it would demonstrate to the world Britain's commitment to India at a time when Russia had advanced to within a few days' march of the frontiers.

After the king of Prussia became the German *kaiser* (emperor), Victoria said to Lord Ponsonby, her secretary: "I am an empress and in common conversation am sometimes called empress of India. Why have I never officially assumed this title?" She argued that the title would once and for all settle ques-

"NEW CROWNS FOR OLD ONES!"

"New crowns for old ones", an anti-semitic jib at Disraeli by Tenniel.

tions of precedence with other European monarchs. Lord Ponsonby, discussing the question with his wife, quoted Dr Johnson, who had asked: "Who comes first, a louse or a flea?"

Triumph for Wagner at his own festival

Bayreuth theatre, Wagner's "total art work" for music, drama and dance.

Bayreuth, Bavaria, August
A huge banquet for 500 people has ended what has been called the musical event of the decade: the first performance together, over three days, of all four operas in Wagner's massive *Ring* epic, in the new opera house he has had built for his own works. It is a triumph for Wagner's unabashed belief in his own genius. Building on the opera house began years ago, with

money raised by subscription and by donations from the eccentric King Ludwig II of Bavaria, always willing to spend more than his ministers like on palaces and Wagner. The festival was attended by 4,000 people, including the emperors of Germany and Brazil as well as King Ludwig. Among the 60 correspondents were two from New York, reporting via the new transatlantic cable.

The Decline and Fall of the Ottoman Empire

In the history of empires, a special place should be reserved for the Turks. Theirs was no ordinary creation: it lasted longer and extended farther than many others perhaps better known. It was slow in the making, even slower in the breaking. It spanned the late 13th century, when the Ottoman dynasty extended control over land in Anatolia, to 1922, when Mustapha Kemal abolished the sultanate: wide-ranging, multi-cultural and prone to divisions. In 1453 the Ottomans captured Constantinople. In 1683 they almost captured Vienna. From Morocco to the Persian Gulf, from the Crimea to the eastern approaches of Vienna, its territorial hold was huge.

The failure to take Vienna was an ill omen: thereafter the empire waned. In 1792 the Ottomans had been at war with Russia and Austria for a total of 41 years; their losses included Hungary, Bessarabia, Podolya and the Crimea. The early 19th century promised no better. For decades the empire suffered the same pattern: reforms, revolts, retreats. A question inevitably arises: what enabled an empire, mainly unpopular and by the 19th century plainly in retreat, to survive as long as it did?

Primarily, the other powers wished to see it survive. British diplomacy required that Turkey be preserved against Russian expansionism, seen as threatening British India. Russia was interested in the fate of the empire, but in the role of a supposed protector of Orthodox (mainly Slav) Christians oppressed by the Turkish yoke. The other interested party was Austria-Hungary. If Turkey was the Sick Man of Europe, Austria-Hungary was the Avaricious Doctor: anxious (as another multi-racial empire) to see the patient survive, but not beyond coveting the estate should death prove inevitable.

The humiliation of Russia

The "Eastern Question" highlighted in the feelings of the subject peoples themselves. Balkan nationalism took three forms: the desire of Christians to be free of Islamic domination; resistance to Greek influences; and revived interest in Balkan history and culture. Given these stirrings, the European powers could probably best resist Russian aims not by propping up the decadent Ottomans, but by supporting subject peoples whose newfound nationalism owed little to Czarist sponsorship.

After the Crimean War several new elements demanded diplomatic consideration. Russia had been humiliated and she was reduced to preparing for eventual revenge. Austria was isolated, rightly suspected by both sides of infirmity of purpose. France seemed to emerge strengthened, but could still ill afford to offend Austria in Italy. Britain did best of all, securing the neutralisation of the Bosporus Straits. Turkey was obliged to declare equality of rights between Moslem and non-Moslem subjects throughout its territory. Yet the Treaty of Paris 1856, which ended the war, was clearly a holding operation, merely postponing the decisive struggle between Russian expansionism, Franco-British defensiveness, Ottoman inadequacy and revived nationalism.

Butchery of the Bulgars

The climax came in the years after 1875. Its causes were several. The empire had engaged in administrative reform without concomitant democratisation; now the power of the sultanate was enhanced to a point where it might be exercised with dangerous arbitrariness. Imperial finances remained parlous, the more so as credit virtually vanished after 1873, a year of downturn in the world's economies. Compounding this crisis were natural causes and nationalism – major floods in 1874, a rising by the Christian peasants of Bosnia and Herzegovina (July 1875) against Moslem overlordship. With its depleted treasury, the empire was hard pressed to quell this insurrection. When it spread to Bulgaria, fleetingly in September 1875, more seriously in May 1876, the methods of repression were of such barbarity as to earn the instant label "Bulgarian atrocities". Some 12,000 of the Bulgarian peasantry were butchered. "There is not a criminal in a European gaol," fumed the English statesman Gladstone, "there is not a cannibal in the South Sea islands whose indignation would not arise and overboil at that which had been done."

Turkey was now morally as well as financially bankrupt, but she remained strategically significant. British public opinion was substantially outraged by the news from the east, but Disraeli, the prime minister, persisted in making excuses. His pro-Turkish line was unfortunate yet predictable. The inflamed but endangered nationalism of the Balkans gave Russia the opening for which she had been waiting since the humiliation of the Treaty of Paris. An international conference at Constantinople (November 1876) to induce the Turks to reform proved futile: its anodyne proposals were rejected by the Porte. This provided the czar with a pretext for a war whose ostensible purpose was the protection of Slav Christians under Ottoman rule. It began in March 1877. Britain remained neutral, but the Turks resisted Russian advances at Plevna (July-December 1877), thereby easing the threat to Constantinople. With the collapse of Plevna, Russian victory was assured. Peace was concluded by the Treaty of San Stefano of March 1878.

Keep out of Constantinople

The treaty pleased none of the European powers. Neither Britain nor Austria-Hungary could accept a "big Bulgaria" stretching to the Aegean in the south and as far west as the Albanian border. It was equally objectionable to the non-Bulgar Slavs who would be incorporated therein. Russia also made substantial gains in Anatolia. With only slight simplification, Britain's policy towards Russia at this time echoed the words of a music hall refrain: "They shall not have Constantinople!" Russians approached Constantinople, the British fleet was dispatched to the Bosporus, and because Austria could block her line of retreat from the area, Russia agreed to return to the conference table at Berlin.

The Congress of Berlin (July 1878) was a rebuff for Russia, a triumph for Britain, a notable success for Austria-Hungary, and an important episode in the development of Balkan nationalism. "Big Bulgaria" was reduced to an autonomous province in the northern Balkans; Eastern Rumelia was formed south of Bulgaria; Serbian and Montenegrin independence was confirmed; Austria-Hungary was permitted to occupy Bosnia-Herzegovina, which nonetheless remained part of the Turkish Empire, and Britain occupied Cyprus. Russia was allowed to stay in the Caucasus. The other European lands lost by Turkey at San Stefano were restored.

Disraeli called it "peace with honour". There was little honour involved for the Ottomans, whose empire was once again obliged to reform itself under European supervision. Eastern Rumelia united with Bulgaria in 1885. Ottoman territories in Europe were now reduced to Macedonia, Albania and Thrace. Disraeli overstated his case. The Congress encouraged the nationalism it had sought to curb. Serbian nationalists sought the liberation of fellow Serbs still under Turkish or Austro-Hungarian rule. The effective transference of Bosnia-Herzegovina to Austria-Hungary simply shifted the focus of nationalist antipathy from one empire to another. The Austrians, fearing a fresh challenge to their authority, formally annexed the region in 1908. It took a much greater conflict than the phoney war of 1878 to divide up the moribund Ottoman Empire.

An impression of the Battle of Plevna just before the Turks surrendered.

OTTOMAN LOSSES IN THE BALKANS, c. 1890

AUSTRIA
Budapest
HUNGARY
TRANSYLVANIA
CROATIA
BANAT
RUSSIA
MOLDAVIA
WALLACHIA
ROMANIA
BOSNIA
Belgrade
Bucharest
Sarajevo
HERZEGOVINA
SERBIA
SANDJAK
BULGARIA
MONTENEGRO
Sofia
EASTERN ROUMELIA
ROUMELIA
Adrianople
ALBANIA
Constantinople
MACEDONIA
OTTOMAN EMPIRE
ITALY
Salonika
THESSALY
ANATOLIA
GREECE
Athens
Rhodes

▨	Ottoman Empire, 1890
—	Ottoman Empire, 1800
▨	New Nations
☐	Austrian acquisition
▨	Greek acquisition

SETTLING THE QUESTION.

"Mrs Europe" ready to smash the "overgrown sultan spider".

Turks hang Bulgarians charged with the mutilation of Moslems.

Russian camp at Yarem-Bouriga during the 1877-1878 war with Turkey.

Bombardment of the French battery at Sveaborg during Crimean War.

Delegates at the Congress of Paris in 1856 after the Crimean War.

975

1877 (1877-1878)

India, 1 January 1877. Queen Victoria is formally proclaimed queen-empress of India.

New York City, 4 January 1877. Cornelius Vanderbilt, who rose from poor agrarian roots to amass $100 million in shipping and railways, dies at the age of 83.

Balkans, 15 January 1877. Russia and Austria sign an agreement at Budapest whereby Austria agrees to remain neutral in a war between Russia and the Ottoman empire. The two powers reject the idea of a Slav state in the Balkans.

USA, 3 March 1877. Rutherford B Hayes, the Republican governor of Ohio, is elected president, his election confirmed by an electoral commission after disputed elections the previous November.

Ottoman Empire, 17 March 1877. The first session of parliament under the new constitution opens.

London, 31 March 1877. An international conference on the Balkans adopts a protocol demanding that the Ottomans introduce reforms which benefit the Ottoman Christians.

Russia, 24 April 1877. Following an Ottoman refusal to introduce reforms, Russia declares war on the Ottoman empire.

USA, 1 May 1877. President Hayes withdraws all federal troops from the south, ending what has become known as Radical Reconstruction in the aftermath of the civil war.

Nebraska, 6 May 1877. Chief Crazy Horse and his Sioux Indians give themselves up to US troops, abandoning claims to Nebraska.

France, May 1877. Following the crisis of *Seize Mai* (16 May), when President MacMahon forced Jules Simon, the republican prime minister, to resign, the duke of Broglie forms a pro-monarchist government.

Balkans, May 1877. Rumania enters the Russo-Ottoman war on the Russian side and proclaims its independence. Russian and Rumanian troops lay siege to the Bulgarian town of Plevna.

Boston, 1 August 1877. The Bell Telephone Company, headed by Alexander Graham Bell, is incorporated.

Australia, 20 August 1877. Sir Arthur Kennedy, the new governor of Queensland, gives his assent to a bill drastically cutting Chinese immigration into Queensland after the previous governor refused to pass it.

Britain, 23 August 1877. The Merchandise Marks Act obliges exporters to indicate the place of manufacture of their goods.

Utah, 29 August 1877 The Mormon leader Brigham Young dies.

France, October 1877. Despite losing a few seats to the monarchists, the republicans maintain a large majority in a general election and their share of the vote increases.

Caucasus, 18 November 1877. The Russians attack and capture the Ottoman fortress of Kars.

France, 13 December 1877. After two failed attempts by President MacMahon to sustain a royalist ministry, Jules Dufaure forms a republican government.

Balkans, December 1877. Ottoman forces at the Bulgarian town of Plevna, besieged by Russian and Rumanian troops since May, finally surrender.

Central Asia, 1877. Ya'qub Beg, who founded the independent state of Kashgaria in 1866, and sucessfully resisted Russia's ambitions in central Asia for years, is murdered. The Chinese have used the occassion to embark on the reconquest of Chinese Turkestan.

Paris, 1877. A sculpture, exhibited anonymously at the presigious Paris salon causes outrage. The naked figure of a young male is so lifelike that it is rumoured to have been cast from a living model. According to those who claim to know, the man responsible is a former mason, Auguste Rodin.

Italy, 1877. The Depretis government passes the Coppino Act, which makes elementary education free and compulsory for all.

France, 1877. The French inventor, Georges Leclanche, makes an electric battery.

Washington, DC, 1877. A new newspaper, the *Washington Post* appears in Washington.

Italy, 9 January 1878. King Victor Emmanuel II of Italy dies. He is succeeded to the throne by his son, Umberto.

Ottoman Empire, 31 January 1878. Having captured Plevna, Plovdiv and Adrianople, Russian troops are closing in on Istanbul. The Turks open truce negotiations at Adrianople.

Rome, 7 February 1878. Pope Pius IX dies and is succeeded by the cardinal, Gioacchino Pecci, who takes the name Leo XIII.

Ottoman Empire, 15 February 1878. A British fleet arrives at Istanbul in support of the faltering Ottoman empire. An earlier decision to send a fleet was reversed in January.

Judges free Russian populist agitators

Moscow, 23 January 1878

The sensational trial of 193 populist revolutionaries, most of them students, ended in anti-climax today when more than 100 of them were set free and the rest were given light sentences. In an earlier attempt to suppress the Populist movement, 770 people were arrested and 215 imprisoned, including Prince Peter Kropotkin.

Czar Alexander lost his enthusiasm for reform after university students from well-off families adopted the rhetoric of socialism and revolution and one of them made a clumsy attempt to assassinate him. Five years ago he ordered home all the young girls who had gone to Switzerland to study. They returned with heads full of anarchist notions and enthusiastically joined young men in donning peasant clothes and "going to the people" to spread revolution. More recently the activities of these young idealists has taken a sinister turn. It is believed that some have formed a secret terrorist society called the "People's Will".

Contraceptive campaigner acquitted

England, 1877

A couple who faced imprisonment and heavy fines for distributing a pamphlet giving instructions on family planning have been acquitted on appeal. Even so, the pamphlet was described as "indecent, lewd and obscene" when Annie Besant and Charles Bradlaugh faced the judges in court.

Due to publicity from the trial large numbers of the offending manual, *Fruits of Philosophy*, have sold to poor women desperate for relief from continual pregnancies. But the promotion of the revised edition of Dr Knowlton's book, first published in America in the 1840s, has brought nothing but hardship to Annie Besant.

Since her name has been linked to birth control she has been ostracised by society. She lost custody of her daughter because the judge feared that she might contaminate

Annie Besant: family planner.

the child with her ideas, and the suffragette movement gave her no support for fear of jeopardising its case for enfranchisement of women in Britain.

Machine can reproduce the human voice

Edison: phonograph inventor.

USA, 1877

Thomas Alva Edison, the inventor, advanced to a horn-shaped device and solemnly spoke five historic words. "Mary had a little lamb", he intoned. Edison rewound a foil-covered cylinder and placed a needle in a groove. The machine played his voice saying "Mary had a little lamb".

Edison's *phonograph* consists of a diaphragm attached to a stylus which etches the grooves. The cylinder is turned by hand. A second needle picks up the signal, and the recorded voice played back.

Samurai defence of rights fails

Japan, 24 September 1877
The *samurai* rebellion which erupted in Satsuma last January is over, crushed by the regular army, and its leader, Saigo Takamori, has committed suicide on the battlefield.

Saigo resigned from the government when it decided not to invade Korea, and became the leader of some 40,000 disaffected samurai frustrated at being deprived of a foreign war.

Their disaffection stems from the fact that these once fearsome warriors have been overtaken by the march of events, and their revolt was a last desperate effort to stave off the inevitable.

They had been forbidden to wear their distinctive dress or carry swords, and the new, western-style army threatened their status as a military elite.

What drove them to rebellion, however, was the financial hardship they were suffering because the government had assumed responsibility for their stipends – and cut them to the bone. They had become low grade civil servants.

Samurai, Japan's knights errant, defeated by firearms and technology.

Violent railroad strike paralyses US

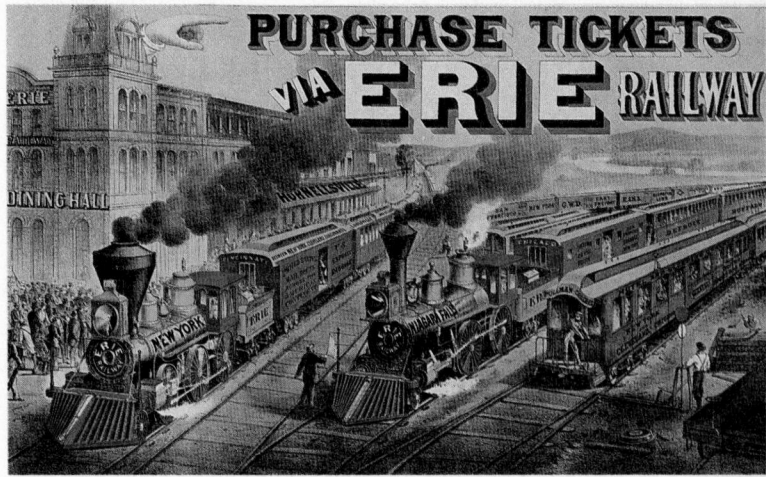

A poster for the Erie railway, famous for its "beautiful scenery".

Chicago, 26 July 1877
Nineteen people were killed here today when police and cavalry charged striking railwaymen. The growing violence follows the killing of nine men and boys in Baltimore last week when soldiers fired on a crowd marching on the railroad station. This first national strike by railway employees – angered by a ten per cent wage cut — has halted all throughline services and now threatens to bring the country's trade to a standstill.

In Pittsburgh, a mob set fire to the Pennsylvania Roailroad yards, burning some 2,000 carriages and trucks, a rail depot and a grain elevator.

Some observers are insisting that the strike is the work of foreign agitators and linked to what they regard as "communistic ideas". In some parts of Pennsylvania, the militia is reported to side openly with the strikers and has refused to move against them.

The strikers refute any political motive. They argue that a brakeman's rate of pay for a 12-hour-day is $1.75 and that this is the second wage-cut in four years.

Boer fury as British take over republic

South Africa, 12 April 1877
Britain has annexed the South African republic (Transvaal), to a wave of Boer resentment. The state treasury is bankrupt after false hopes of prosperity based on gold, and expensive warfare against the blacks. At the Sand River Convention in 1852 Britain recognised the republic. Now, claiming that the republic is unable to defend itself against its black neighbours, and that its existence constituted a danger to "Her Majesty's subjects and possessions in South Africa", it has torn up the treaty.

The Boers' response, taking their lead from the ousted president, Thomas Burgers, is non-violent resistance. One of Transvaal's most respected leaders, Paul Kruger, a veteran of the Boer treks, is going to London to present their case.

The British-born photographer Edward Muybridge's pioneer studies of limbs in motion, using a fast camera shutter, a revolutionary technique which he developed in the USA between 1872 and 1877.

Rome, 20 February 1878. Pope Leo XIII opens negotiations with the German government aimed at ending the *Kulturkampf*.

Ottoman Empire, 3 March 1878. Russia and the Ottomans sign the treaty of San Stefano, granting independence to Serbia, Montenegro and Rumania. Bulgaria becomes an autonomous state under Russian authority, and Bosnia and Herzegovina are granted reforms.

Germany, 24 May 1878. The *reichstag* rejects Bismarck's proposal to introduce repressive legislation following an attempt on the *kaiser's* life by a radical named Emil Hodel.

Germany, 2 June 1878. The kaiser is badly wounded in an assassination attempt, by another radical student, Karl Nobling.

Cyprus, 4 June 1878. Britain and the Ottoman empire sign a secret agreement by which Britain is allowed to occupy Cyprus in return for protecting the empire against Russian advances in Anatolia.

Germany, 30 June 1878. The Conservatives make substantial electoral gains at the expense of the National Liberals.

Germany, 13 July 1878. At the congress of Berlin, Britain, Russia, Austria, Germany, France, Italy and the Ottoman empire reach agreement on the future of the Balkan states superseding the terms of the treaty of San Stefano.

New York City, 15 October 1878. Thomas Alva Edison founds the Edison Electric Light Company.

Germany, 19 October 1878. Bismarck passes an anti-socialist law placing many restraints on socialist meetings and banning trade union activities.

London, 26 November 1878. The American artist James McNeill Whistler wins damages of one farthing in a libel action against the critic John Ruskin, who, on seeing *Nocturne in Black and Gold: The Falling Rocket*, accused Whistler of "flinging a pot of paint in the public's face".

USA, November 1878. An epidemic of yellow fever in the Gouth has claimed 14,000 lives.

Afghanistan, November 1878. Following the refusal of the *emir*, Sher Ali, to receive a British mission in Kabul, after a Russian one is received, the British invade Afghanistan.

China, 1878. The Qing reconquest of Chinese Turkestan is completed.

India, 1878. Over five million people have died of famine in the Dekhan area in the past two years.

Britain, 1878. The laws governing female and child labour are consolidated in the Factory Act.

Britain, 1878. Arthur Sullivan and W S Gilbert collaborate to produce the light opera *HMS Pinafore*.

Germany, 1878. The chemist Adolf von Baeyer successfully carries out the synthesis of indigo.

France, 1878. The first sleeping bag is made, commissioned by the Scottish writer Robert Louis Stevenson for his journey across the Cevennes mountains.

Madagascar, 1878. On establishing closer relations with Britain, Queen Ranavalona II seizes lands belonging to Jean Laborde, the French consul, and then occupies the Sambirano coast, which is under French protection.

France, 30 January 1879. Following large republican gains in elections to the senate, President MacMahon resigns and the conservative republican Jules Grevy is elected to succeed him.

Uganda, 17 February 1879. The White Fathers – the Society of Missionaries of Our Lady of Africa, which was founded in Algiers in 1868 – arrive in Entebbe.

East China Sea, 25 March 1879. Japan invades the kingdom of the Liuqiu (*Ryukyu*) Islands, hitherto a vassal of China.

Afghanistan, May 1879. By the treaty of Gandamak the emir of Afghanistan hands over territories to the British, permits the establishment of a British resident in Kabul and agrees to conduct foreign relations on British advice.

South Africa, 1 June 1879. Prince Louis Napoleon, the son of the former emperor, Napoleon III, dies in combat against the Zulu during an ambush.

Egypt, June 1879. Following the deterioration of relations between the French and British authorities, Ismail Pasha abdicates, to be succeeded by his son Tawfiq.

Belgium, 1 July 1879. The Liberal government brings primary education under state control.

Germany, 1879. The socialist August Bebel publishes the highly acclaimed *Women and Socialism*.

Paris, 1879. The first European telephone exchange is opened.

Russia, 1879. Tchaikovsky completes his opera *Eugene Onegin*.

India, 1879. Ghulam Ahmad of Qadian in Punjab begins preaching a heterodox form of the Moslem religion. His followers are known as the *Ahmadiyya*.

British outrage at Russo-Turkish treaty

Ottoman Empire, March 1878

The treaty of San Stefano on 3 March, which ended the war between Russia and the Ottoman empire, has aroused furious reaction from the other great powers. The chief bone of contention is the enlargement of a Russianised Bulgaria; it now includes much of Thrace and Macedonia, with ports in the Black Sea and the Aegean.

Russia, after aiding and abetting abortive risings against the Ottomans in Serbia and Montenegro, invaded the Ottoman empire last April, but met stiff resistance before the fortress of Plevna fell in December. British support for the Ottomans was equivocal until the Russians stood at the gates of Istanbul. The arrival of a British fleet in the Bosporus persuaded the czar to make peace. The terms of the treaty, in which the Ottomans made enormous concessions to Russia's Slav allies in Montenegro and Bulgaria, were such that the Ottomans may have believed all along that it would not last. Britain and Russia are on the brink of war.

Doll's bid for freedom causes scandal

Copenhagen, 29 December 1879

Shock and scandal surround the latest play by Henrik Ibsen, the Norwegian author of *Peer Gynt*, who lives abroad in Italy. Just published here and performed for the first time last night, *A Doll's House* ends with a bank manager's wife deserting her husband and children for no better reason than to assert her freedom.

"It's your fault that I have made nothing of my life," Nora tells Torwald, her husband, who has shown her every indulgence as his "little songbird", "little squirrel" or "little scatterbrain". She claims that he has made her into a doll, just as her father did. When he accuses her of failing in her sacred duty as a wife and mother she replies "I have another duty – to myself" and slams the door.

Ibsen: playwright of pessimism.

Pyschology is now a German science

Leipzig, Germany, 1879

Psychology has for centuries been less of a science than a philosophical pursuit. Wilhelm Wundt, a professor at the university here, is determined to change all that. He has set up the world's first psychological laboratory. He uses scientific methods to explore people and their attitudes; how they feel, generate ideas and experience sensations. His *The Principles of Physiological Psychology* conveys his belief that we will understand behaviour by seeing it as the outcome of the workings of the brain.

Sultan stamps on Ottoman assembly

Istanbul, January 1878

The Ottoman parliament, which is less than a year old, has been dissolved for the second time after bringing charges against three of the sultan's ministers in connection with the recently-concluded truce with Russia.

Although not free of official pressure, the elected parliament represents a cross-section of Christians, Jews, Turks and Arabs, and has proved willing to criticise the government. The sultan, however, seems autocratically inclined, and has banished dissenters.

Powers divide Balkans

The statesmen of Europe, dominated by Bismarck (centre), divide the Balkans.

Berlin, 13 July 1878

The dismemberment of the Ottoman empire was taken a stage further today when the Congress of Berlin gave the Caucasus to Russia, and Bosnia and Herzegovina to Austria, and confirmed Britain's right to occupy Cyprus. Bulgaria becomes an autonomous principality and Roumelia, including Macedonia and Albania, though still nominally Ottoman, is to have a Christian governor. The Russians have given an undertaking not to fortify Batum.

It could have been worse. Russia used the protection of Christians as a pretext for going to war against the Ottomans; the real motive was pan-Slav aggrandisement and the two-year conflict was ended last March by a treaty that created a Bulgaria which incorporated Macedonia and extended to the Aegean Sea. The Ottomans were required to pay a huge indemnity.

The treaty, signed at San Stefano, near Istanbul, caused misgivings in Austria, where the Bulgarian annexations were seen as a threat, and in Britain, which saw Bulgaria as offering Russia overland access to the Mediterranean. Thus Disraeli went to Berlin determined to rein in Russia's pan-Slav intrigues. He kept a special train waiting and, when Russia proved intransigent, threatened to quit. Bismarck, who was certain Disraeli was in earnest, put pressure on the Russians.

William Booth recruits Christian soldiers

A Salvation Army preacher among "fallen women" in Whitechapel.

London, 1878

Its motto is "Through Blood and Fire", its leaders are generals and its favourite hymn, trumpeted by bands that would not look out of place on the parade ground, is "Onward Christian Soldiers". The Salvation Army, founded this year in London's poor quarter of Whitechapel by a former Methodist minister, is showing that Jesus too needs his troops.

"General" William Booth, aged 49, opened the Christian Mission, the forerunner of the Army, in 1864. It preaches two ideas: that the unconverted face eternal damnation, and that the lot of society's poorest must be improved. The Army is devoted to both causes.

Bismarck curbs German Socialist Party

Berlin, 19 October 1878

Two attempts on the life of the kaiser in the space of one month have been seized on by Bismarck as pretexts for a determined assault on Germany's Socialist Party.

When a half-witted tinker from Leipzig attacked the kaiser, Bismarck blamed it on socialist ideas and presented the reichstag with a bill curbing socialist activities. It was voted down 251-57. A few days later a Dr Karl Nobling seriously wounded the kaiser.

This time Bismarck was ready. Neither of the would-be assassins had anything to do with the socialists, but Bismarck dissolved the reichstag and orchestrated a furious anti-socialist press campaign. He counted on killing two birds with his one stone. He hoped to win a conservative majority and rid himself of dependence on the liberals, and to demolish the socialist vote, which has risen from just over 100,000 to almost 500,000 in six years.

The election result was a disappointment. The socialists did lose a few seats, but the liberals remain powerful. Today, however, when the new reichstag met, liberals joined conservatives to pass the bill banning socialist meetings and publications.

Balkan deal crowns career of Disraeli

Disraeli's triumph after the Congress in Berlin: together Britain and Russia will share the Balkan element of a somewhat scrawny Turkey (Ottomans).

London, July 1878

Declaring that he had brought back "peace with honour", Disraeli drove past cheering crowds to today on his return from the Berlin Congress where his reception had been scarcely less enthusiastic, with Bismarck hailing him as *"Der alte Jude, das ist der Mann"*. (This old Jew, he's a real man.)

It was a remarkable achievement for a man from a Jewish family whose first success came with a novel describing the deep social divisions in Britain – *Two Nations*. He made three unsuccessful attempts to enter parliament before becoming an MP in 1837. A Tory reformer, he added a million town workers to the electorate in 1867 with the Reform Act while promoting empire abroad – making Victoria empress of India and buying into the Suez Canal which his great Liberal rival Gladstone consistently ignored.

His flamboyance in speech and dress made him a favourite of the queen, but, already an earl, he has refused a dukedom, saying he wants only the Garter. But at 73 his health is poor. In Berlin he was taken ill and was too sick to attend the farewell banquet.

South Africa, 4 July. British troops defeat the Zulus in the battle of Ulundi, later capturing their king, Cetewayo.

Germany, 4 August. A law is passed making Alsace Lorraine a *reichsland* (territory) of the empire.

Vienna, 12 August. A coalition cabinet, made up of Austrians, Czechs and Poles, is set up under the leadership of Edward von Taaffe.

Germany, 15 August. The Czar Alexander II sends a letter of complaint to Kaiser William about Bismarck's diplomacy during the Berlin Congress last year.

Ireland, 18 August. Michael Davitt founds the Irish Land League calling for the land to be returned to the Irish people. Charles Parnell, leader of the Irish party in the House of Commons is invited to be president.

Afghanistan, 3 September. Sir Pierre Cavagnari, the British envoy in Kabul, is murdered, disrupting the peace brought by the treaty of Gandamak in May.

China, 2 October. The Qing envoy Chonghou signs the treaty of Livadia, concerning Russia's return of the Ili region in Chinese Turkestan to China, without government approval. Russia annexed the area in 1871 during Moslem unrest.

Germany, 7 October. A dual alliance is formed with Austria following months of tension between Germany and Russia. The allies agree to come to each other's aid in the event of Russian aggression.

Chile, 8 October. The Peruvian iron-clad battleship *Huascar* is destroyed by the Chileans off Antofagasta in the conflict over nitrate-rich land in the Atacama desert which began earlier this year.

Idaho, October. War with the Indians in the north-west ends with the capture of 388 Indians.

Kabul, October. Following the murder of the British envoy in Kabul last month, the British move into the city forcing the *emir* Yakub Khan, to flee.

Peru, 17 December. Chilean troops take Lima.

Russia The author Fyodor Dostoyevsky publishes the first part of *The Brothers Karamazov*.

"Degenerate" painter of fleshy nudes wins social success

"Le Moulin de la Galette" by Renoir: he speaks of his "rainbow palette".

Renoir's "decomposing flesh".

Paris
For the first time a painting by Pierre Auguste Renoir has been hung at the Salon. It is a glamorous portrait of Madame Charpentier, the hostess of a celebrated literary salon, dressed by Worth, in her Japanese drawing room with her two pretty children. It is likely to win Renoir more commissions.

Until now he has exhibited with the Impressionists. At their first exhibition in 1874 he showed *La Loge*, in which the woman in the theatre box is dressed in striking black and white stripes, echoing her escort. "Black is the queen of colours," according to Renoir, who finds subtle tones within it. In 1876 he showed *Le Moulin de la Galette*, an animated panorama of the crowd under the trees at the Montmartre pleasure resort.

He has been sternly criticised for his nudes. "Try to explain to M Renoir that a woman's body is not a heap of decomposing flesh with green and mauve patches of putrefaction," sneered *Le Figaro*. He has also been called "degenerate".

"Black is the queen of colours."

Edison develops incandescent lightbulb

Edison's light bulb. Originally a railroad newsboy, he has invented an automatic telegraphy repeater, a megaphone and a phonograph.

New York City
When an electric current flows through wire it generates heat – and light. This has been known for a long time. In Newcastle, in England, Joseph Swan developed a filament lamp – but it has taken the inventive Thomas Edison to use the glowing wire principle to make an electric light-bulb that burns for at least 13 hours.

Spurred on by Swan's success, Edison has made a bulb that he plans to produce on a mass scale. It consists of a filament of sewing thread converted to carbon by baking – an arrangement the inventor finally came to after trying thousands of possible materials.

Edison is now experimenting with paper filaments and claiming precedence over Swan in his patent applications. A battle in the courts is likely to ensue.

Missionaries used as insurance policy

East Africa, 17 February
Five years ago Buganda seemed threatened by the Moslem *sultanate* of Zanzibar; its *kabaka* (king), Mutesa invited Moslem holy men to his court. Two years ago it felt threatened by Egypt. Mutesa invited Anglican missionaries from Britain. Now, feeling threatened by the penetration of British influence up the Nile, he has invited Catholic White Fathers, from France.

He keeps them all at court, always ensuring that no one group dominates, and uses them to offset the traditional power of the chiefs. "I am called Mutesa," he once said, "which means reformer, benefactor. I want history to say of me one day that if I had not been given that name at birth, posterity would give it to me at my death."

Zulus butcher Britons

King Cetewayo of the Zulus, who rejected Frere's ultimatums.

Napoleon III's son, the prince imperial, a British officer, killed by Zulus.

South Africa, 22 January
Zulu *impis* (regiments) have attacked the invading British army's main base at Isandhlwana, and killed 1,600 imperial troops, half of them British. Today's Zulu victory over white colonisers is triumph of African resistance.

War between the British and Zulu has been inevitable for two years, since the British governor-general Sir Bartle Frere took such a hostile attitude to the Zulus. Frere considered the Zulus' militarised society to be the most serious threat to the British empire in South Africa. Last summer he asked London for reinforcements, saying "the peace of South Africa for many years to come seems to me to depend on your taking steps to put a final end to Zulu preten-

sions". He was refused them. Ignoring the wishes of the British government he sent ultimatiums to the Zulu king, Cetewayo, demanding that he end the ban on marriages in his army – an action that would wreck the entire Zulu sociomilitary structure. Cetewayo refused.

So ten days ago Frere sent a column into Zululand under the command of Lord Chelmsford. The Zulus let it come deep into their territory, then lured the main force away by a feint. With astonishing speed the *impis* descended on the undefended camp.

The waggons had not even been *laagered* (formed into a defensive ring) – a mistake that no *Voortrekker* (Boer pioneer) would have made. British prestige has been severely dented.

Irish peasants boycott Captain Boycott

County Mayo, Ireland
Lord Erne's land agent, Captain Charles Cunningham Boycott, earned a reputation for ruthlessness in evicting tenants unable to pay. The usual response of a desperate people was rick-burning or cattle-maiming. But Charles Parnell, the Irish nationalist leader, said that anyone renting a farm from which a poor tenant had been evicted should be isolated "as if he were a leper of old". Everyone promptly refused to work for Boycott, deliver goods to him or buy his produce. In desperation, Boycott sent to Protestant Ulster for help, which only served to publicise his plight. Now others will be given the Boycott treatment.

"No rint" (rent), the agricultural equivalent of the industrial strike.

Boers assert their independence again

South Africa, 16 December
The Transvaal is in revolt. Today, the anniversary of the Boer stand against the Zulu at Blood River, a day packed with symbolism, the old Boer republic of Transvaal is reasserting its independence. Already Boers and British are fighting at Potchefstroom.

The last few years have seen a reawakening of Afrikaaner nationalism. Inspired by Calvinist revivalism and German nationalism, thinkers like Stephen du Toit and political leaders like Paul Kruger have

inspired men to dream of nationhood again. Most important of all, the Boers assert that southern Africa is their country and was built with their blood. "Weep Afrikaaners! Here lie your flesh and blood! Martyred in the cruellest fashion!" wrote du Toit in his *History of our land in the dialect of our people*, published two years ago.

In London the Liberal cabinet under Mr Gladstone – unlike Mr Disraeli's cabinet – want neither the cost of a colony nor the cost of a war.

China devastated by terrifying famine

Street scene in China: a travelling cook, a fortune-teller and a barber.

China
Millions of people are dying in one of the most terrible famines ever visited on this troubled country. So great is the people's hunger that cannibalism is rife. There has been drought for three years now. The crops have failed. The fields have turned to dust. Even the thatch from roofs has been eaten. Great stretches of farmland lie un-

ploughed, as bare as winter. The farmers are selling their daughters into prostitution and their sons into slavery. Disease rages everywhere.

Hundreds have become bandits and the government has reacted harshly, executing them by starvation in the "sorrow cage". Good work is being done by the missionaries, but the disaster is too vast. Hunger triumphs.

Austria signs defence deal with Germany

Vienna, 7 October
Austria's occupation of Bosnia and Herzegovina, endorsed at the Congress of Berlin last year, has become extremely unpopular, and Count Andrassy, the foreign minister, who wanted the occupation, is being forced to resign. His last act was the signing of the Dual Alliance with Bismarck of Germany. The

Austrians are anxious to preserve the *status quo* in Europe and see the alliance as protection against a Russian attack. As for Bismarck, he embraces Austria to prevent its being taken up by France, which he fears may be plotting war to avenge the defeat of 1871. All European powers, fearing war, are seeking "insurance" treaties.

1880 (1880-1881)

China, 19 February 1880. The court renounces the treaty of Livadia, concerning Russia's return of the Ili region in Chinese Turkestan, signed by the envoy Chonghou without government consent last year. China demands re-negotiation and mobilises an army along the Russian border.

Washington, DC, 8 March 1880. President Hayes declares that the United States will have jurisdiction over any canal built across the isthmus of Panama.

Paris, 27 March 1880. On the first day of its release, the publisher Charpentier sells 55,000 copies of Emile Zola's new novel *Nana*.

Britain, 15 April 1880. Following a Liberal election victory, William Gladstone takes over from Benjamin Disraeli, the Earl of Beaconsfield, as prime minister.

Tahiti, 29 June 1880. France annexes Tahiti.

Chile, June 1880. In the continuing war between Chile, Peru and Bolivia, disputing ownership of the nitrate-rich Atacama desert, Chile moves north and takes the towns of Arica and Tacna.

Morocco, 3 July 1880. The Madrid conference on Morocco ends having guaranteed all European powers in Morocco the status of most-favoured nation, thus establishing an open-door policy.

France, 11 July 1880. Amnesty is granted to the political prisoners sentenced for having taken part in the *commune* of 1871.

Germany, 14 July 1880. Chancellor Bismarck puts an end to the *Kulturkampf* – his anti-Catholic policy.

St Petersburg, 30 July 1880. A Chinese imperial commissioner, Zeng Jize, arrives to re-negotiate the treaty of Livadia.

Afghanistan, 1 August 1880. Sir Frederick Roberts frees the British garrison of Kandahar.

China, 12 August 1880. Chonghou, who signed the now annulled treaty of Livadia with Russia, without government authority, is released from jail where he had been awaiting decapitation.

France, 23 September 1880. Jules Ferry, the education minister in Charles de Freycinet's cabinet, succeeds him as prime minister.

Congo, 1 October 1880. The Afro-French explorer Pierre de Brazza-Savorgnan makes a treaty with the Kongo kingdom founding Brazzaville as the basis for a French colony.

North Africa, 1880. The French explorer Paul Flatters leads an expedition into the Sahara.

New Jersey, 2 November 1880. The suffragettes Susan B Anthony and Elizabeth Cady Stanton attempt to vote in the national election, but are stopped by a polling booth inspector.

Washington, DC, 2 November 1880. James A Garfield is elected Republican president.

New York City, 8 November 1880. The French actress Sarah Bernhardt makes her American debut.

Japan, December 1880. The liberal Itagaki Taisuke sets up the country's first political party.

Afghanistan, 1880. The conflict with Britain ends with the accession of Abdur Rahman Khan, the grandson of the kingdom's founder, Dost Mohammed, who supports British interests.

London, 1880. A newly-elected MP, Charles Bradlaugh, is banned from the House of Commons following controversy over his taking of the oath. An atheist, Bradlaugh initially refused to take the oath and though he later agreed to do so, conservatives objected that it would not bind him.

Sudan, 1880. The German explorer Wilhelm Junker sets off on an expedition to the Uele River.

USA, 1880. The author and soldier Lew Wallace's religious novel *Ben Hur* is a best seller.

Switzerland, 1880. Johanna Spyri publishes *Heidi* – a moving tale of a little girl forced to leave the mountains for the city.

Switzerland, 1880. The nine mile long St-Gotthard tunnel, linking the upper Reuss and Tessin valleys, is completed.

South Africa, December 1880. The Boers declare war on the British and drive them out of the Transvaal. The uprising is led by Petrus Joubert, Paul Kruger and Marthinus Pretorius.

USA, 1880. A census shows the population to have grown by more than 11.5 million in the past decade to 50 million.

St Petersburg, 31 January 1881. The funeral cortege of the novelist Fyodor Dostoyevsky, who died on 28 January, is followed by 30,000 people. His greatest works are *Crime and Punishment*, *The Idiot* and *The Brothers Karamazov*.

Paris, 10 February 1881. Jacques Offenbach's fanciful opera *The Tales of Hoffman* is produced posthumously.

Sahara, 16 February 1881. The French expedition of Paul Flatter's is massacred by Tuareg nomads.

British force lifts siege of Kandahar

Kandahar, 1 August 1880
The siege of the garrison at Kandahar was lifted today after a spectacular march by a relief force from Kabul which has routed the Afghan rebels and restored British authority in the southern part of Afghanistan.

The 10,000-strong relief force under General Sir Frederick Roberts covered the 313 miles (500km) in just 23 days, surprising the rebels under Ayub Khan, the son of the deposed pro-Russian *emir* of Kabul. Khan had laid siege to Kandahar after taking Maiwand in July.

Britain now plans to unite the province of Kandahar with Kabul under its new pro-British *emir*, Abdur Rahman. Kandahar's British-installed ruler, Sher Ali Khan is to retire to India.

Major White winning the VC today.

Cold meats get frosty welcome in England

London, February 1880
Housewives are giving a frosty welcome to the first supplies of chilled meat to arrive from Australia. Even though Australian frozen beef sells for less than threepence per pound, compared to as much as a shilling per pound for home-produced beef, many complain that refrigerated meat looks limp when it is thawed and is difficult to cook – a complaint levied against the first imports of chilled American beef six years ago. Traditional butchers are refusing to handle the imported beef saying that they do not want to be "hardbeef mashers". Importers are therefore setting up their own outlets, mainly on market stalls.

The resistance has surprised importers who see refrigeration as the key to bringing cheap and plentiful supplies of meat from South America and Australia without spoiling. The *Glasgow Herald* agricultural correspondent believes that some sections of the trade are side-stepping this hostility by passing off foreign meat as home-produce.

"Soul of French youth" freed from Jesuits

Jules Ferry: educating the French.

Paris, 30 March 1880
The French republican government today pushed through a new law expelling the Jesuits from France. The driving force behind it is Jules Ferry, the minister of public instructions, who is determined to build up a public education system which is free from church domination. His principal target is the Jesuits. "It is from them that we wish to tear away the soul of the youth of France," he said.

Ferry plans even more far-reaching reforms. He wants to make primary education free. He wants to open separate schools for girls and to introduce the teaching of technology and modern languages.

Kansas becomes first US state to go dry

Driving men to drink: US women's holy war against intemperance.

Kansas, 1880
Singing joyful hymns and waving banners of thanksgiving, thousands of long-suffering housewives marched through the towns and villages of Kansas today as the doors slammed shut on the state's saloons and hard drinking men came face-to-face with soft sarsaparilla.

After a lengthy and raucous campaign by the Women's National Christian Temperance Union and the Prohibition Party, Governor John St John has forced a bill through the state legislature outlawing the sale and consumption of alcohol. Until now, officials have refused to shut down illegal saloons – often for fear of physical reprisals by the drinkers within.

Prohibition represents a major victory for the women – angered by the high level of drunkenness and violence associated with alcohol – and indicates the new political muscle enjoyed by the temperance movement. They are certain now to make this a nationwide struggle, campaigning in every local, state and federal campaign, with the wealthy "booze lobby" bracing itself for the fight.

Argentinian troops crush Indian rebels

Patagonia, Argentina, 1880
Patagonia's Indians have been utterly crushed by Argentinian troops. Patagonia will now be opened for stock-raising, land speculation, railways and eventual colonisation by Argentina's newly-arrived Spanish, Italian and German immigrants.

For years the provinces south and west of Buenos Aires have been the victims of Indian raids, the Indians killing settlers' cattle with *bolas* (ropes with weights that entangle cattle's legs).

The campaign against them was organised by General Julio Argentino Roca, war minister until this year, and now president. He drew the Indians into the Rio Negro valley where, using modern military technology, he annihilated them.

Chinese negotiator may lose his head

China, March 1880
Chonghou, the Chinese statesman who so unwisely signed the treaty of Livadia with Russia without telling Beijing of its terms, has been sentenced to death by beheading while the government frantically tries to renegotiate the treaty and hotheads demand war with Russia.

Chonghou, a pleasant nobleman without too many brains, certainly allowed the Russians to foist terms on him which involved the cession of a large part of the strategic territory of Ili whose return he was supposed to negotiate.

However, execution seems an excessive punishment for diplomatic naivete, and pleas for his reprieve are arriving from all over the world. Even Queen Victoria has asked the dowager empress to spare him.

Ned Kelly, outlaw who wore steel armour

Melbourne, 11 November 1880
Edward "Ned" Kelly, Australia's most notorious bushranger, whose outlaw gang has terrorised the state of Victoria for the past two years, was hanged today at Melbourne jail. His last words were "Such is life". He was 25 years old.

Kelly came from an Irish convict family: his father had been transported to Tasmania in 1842. Scraping a living like most of his peers, he began his criminal career when he shot a certain Constable Fitzpatrick who had attempted to arrest his father for horse-stealing. It is also thought that Ned resented Fitzpatrick's pursuit of his sister and his ill-treatment of their mother. With three friends he fled to the bush, pursued by four policemen to Stringybark Creek. A shootout followed and the outlaw killed three policemen. A reward was offered for Kelly, alive or dead.

The gang's exploits polarised society. The upper classes condemned him as a killer, his fellow-poor saw him as a folk-hero, a latter-day

The last stand of Ned Kelly, the 25-year-old Australian bushranger.

Robin Hood determined to avenge the wrongs done to his family.

Kelly was captured on 28 June, after a gunfight in the town of Glenrowan. Then, even his home-made armour failed to save him, although he survived to face trial.

US book tells story of Indian sorrow

"Move on!": Harper's comment on the American Indians' lack of franchise.

New York City, 1881
A bitter indictment of the US government's treatment of the country's Indian population is stirring the consciences of thoughtful Americans. It comes in *A Century of Dishonour*, a ruthlessly researched book by Helen Hunt Jackson, a poet and storyteller, and tells a sad story of broken promises, cancelled treaties, enforced migration and countless massacres.

Although the native Americans lived in relative harmony with the white settlers for two centuries, it was the relentless push westwards across prairies and plains that brought death, disease and the white man's whiskey to these once-free people.

1881 (1881-1882)

St Petersburg, 24 February 1881. The treaty of St Petersburg is signed, replacing the treaty of Livadia. China regains a large strip of territory in Chinese Turkestan and Russia is granted the right to establish consulates in Turfan and Suzhou (*Gansu*).

Transvaal, 27 February 1881. British troops are defeated by the Boers at Majuba Hill, on the border of British Natal.

St Petersburg, 13 March 1881. Czar Alexander II is assassinated.

Russia, 28 March 1881. The composer Modest Petrovitch Mussorgsky dies of alcoholic epilepsy. He will be best remembered for his opera *Boris Godunov*, first performed at St Petersburg in 1874.

Russia, 3 April 1881. The revolutionary Sofya Perovskaya is hanged for her part in the assassination of the czar.

Ireland, 7 April 1881. The Land Act is passed, outlawing Michael Davitt's Irish Land League but accepting its programme. The new law is likely to meet opposition from both the English landowners and the Irish tenants.

Britain, 19 April 1881. On the death of Disraeli, Robert Gascoyne Cecil, Lord Salisbury, is chosen as leader of the Conservative Party.

Germany, 18 June 1881. The emperors of Germany, Austria and Russia sign a secret treaty guaranteeing the neutrality of the three signatories should one of them enter into conflict with a fourth power. A further agreement provides for Austria's annexation of Bosnia and Herzegovina.

Austria, 28 June 1881. A secret agreement is made with King Milan of Serbia, who undertakes to ban all Serbian propaganda in Austria in return for a vague promise that Austria will recognise his rights over the Vardar valley.

Greece, 2 July 1881. The Graco-Turkish commission, set up by the Berlin Congress to define the frontier between the two countries, accords to Greece the Volos, Larisa and Trikkala districts to the north. The town of Ioannina is restored to the Ottomans.

Washington, DC, 2 July 1881. President Garfield is seriously injured by an assassin's bullets.

New Mexico, 4 July 1881. The outlaw William H Bonney, alias Billy the Kid, is shot dead.

Canada, 20 July 1881. The Sioux Chief Sitting Bull, a fugitive for five years since he masterminded the massacre of General Custer and his men at Little Big Horn, gives himself up to the army.

Transvaal, 3 August 1881. At the Pretoria convention Britain recognises Transvaal's self-government.

New York City, 4 September 1881. The Edison electric lighting system for the city goes into operation as a generator serving 85 paying customers is switched on.

Boston, 22 October 1881. The Boston Symphony Orchestra gives its first concert.

Vienna, 8 December 1881. A fire breaks out in the opera house during a performance of Offenbach's *The Tales of Hoffman*. Four hundred spectators die.

Sudan, 1881. Mohammed Ahmed ibn Abdallah proclaims himself *al-Mahdi* (the expected guide) and calls for a holy war against the Europeans and the Egyptians.

Vietnam, 1881. France declares its sovereignty over Vietnam and sends troops down the Red River to occupy Tonkin in the north.

Colorado, 1881. The first geological survey of the Grand Canyon is completed.

Germany, 1881. Doctor Karl Eberth discovers the typhoid bacillus.

USA, 1881. The ethnologist Lewis Henry Morgan dies. He will be remembered as the founder of scientific anthropology, and for his work on kinship systems and theories of social evolution.

Berlin, 1881. The first electric tramway, invented by Werner von Siemens, opens in Berlin.

Central Africa (in Zaire), 1881. Henry Morton Stanley founds Leopoldville on the Congo river on behalf of the International African Association, a private company founded by King Leopold of the Belgians in 1876.

France, 1881. The chemist Louis Pasteur experiments with the anthrax vaccine on sheep.

Boston, 1881. Publishers are forced to withdraw the new edition of Walt Whitman's volume of poetry, *Leaves of Grass*, in response to charges of indecency.

France, 1881. The novelist Gustave Flaubert's *Bouvard and Pecuchet* is published posthumously.

South Africa, 1881. The gun war fought by Cape Colony in an attempt to disarm armed horsemen of Lesotho comes to an end. They will keep their guns but must register them and pay compensation.

Serbia, 6 January 1882. Milan of Serbia declares himself king.

Washington, DC, 25 February 1882. The Reapportionment Act expands the size of the House of Representatives from 293 to 325.

New goods are "puffed" by advertisers

Advertising hoardings at Charing Cross Railway Station in London.

Au Bon Marche: Parisian big store.

An advertisement for bustles, USA.

Sex and class, a new media tactic.

London and New York, c.1881
As ever more commodities emerge from the factories of the "industrial revolution", a new phenomenon is developing: advertising, designed to ensure that no potential customer misses the chance to buy. Manufacturers have used advertising for many years, but in the last decade the profession has moved far from the corrupt hucksterism that typified early practitioners.

The advertising agency, once no more than a wholesaler of newspaper space, now provides specialist services for the advertiser and has become a staple of modern commerce. Firms such as America's N W Ayer & Sons and J Walter Thompson, and their English peers, have revolutionised the way manufacturers are able to present their goods to the consuming world.

Health cures, new foods and inventions of every type are "puffed", as critics have it, by advertisements in newspapers or on hoardings in the streets. The new department stores – Whiteley's in London, Macy's in New York – are equally keen on touting their wares.

Shot US president dies

New York City, 20 September 1881
Less than a day after the death of President James Garfield from an assassin's bullet, his vice-president, Chester Alan Arthur, took the oath of office in the early hours of this morning.z

Garfield had been president for less than four months when, on 2 July, he was shot in the back and arm as he walked through a railroad waiting room in Washington. The president, who was rushed back to the White House, was heard to say as the shots were fired: "My God! What is this?"

His assailant, Charles Guiteau, a disappointed office seeker, will now face a murder charge, even though President Garfield eventually died of blood poisoning – possibly caused by the use of unsterile surgical instruments.

Arthur, who had originally supported President Grant for a third term, but fought on the Garfield ticket, represents the extreme right wing – the "Stalwarts" – of the Republican Party. He had been at odds with Garfield during the latter's short presidency.

These conservatives have been locked in a bitter feud with the "Half-breeds", moderate republicans who favour a conciliatory

Crowds outside the New York Herald office read the bulletins on Garfield's condition: "The president was somewhat restless and vomited several times during the night."

policy towards the south and a reformed civil service which bans "spoils of office". The Stalwarts face defeat. When holding the smoking pistol, the assassin is said to have shouted: "I am a Stalwart and now Arthur is president." Memories of Lincoln's murder are fresh in many minds.

Boers defeat the British at Majuba Hill

South Africa, 27 February 1881
A British force of 359 men has been annihilated by the Boers, with its commander, Sir George Colley, shot through the forehead.

The force, part of a 1,500-strong column, marched into the Transvaal after the country had declared itself a republic last December. There has long been tension between British and Boer settlers – and it has not been ended by the Great Boer Trek of the 1830's.

General Colley, a practitioner of the "forward" school of imperialism, had come to South Africa during the Zulu War, and was transferred to India where he was instrumental in sending British troops into Afghanistan after the destruction of the British legation in Kabul. In 1880 he was back in South Africa. Arrogant and over-confident, he suffered reverses at Laing's Neck

Highlanders fleeing Majuba Hill.

and Ingogo, but pressed on. Then, on Majuba Hill, where Colley had established himself, what was left of his force was overwhelmed. The British forces are now in a state of acute shock.

Russian czar murdered

St Petersburg, 13 March 1881
The czar was returning to the Winter Palace after a military parade when a bomb was thrown at his carriage. Uninjured, he stepped out and was standing in the road asking questions when another bomb was thrown, killing him.

Two years ago, members of a terrorist society known as the People's Will condemned Alexander II to death for failing to summon a constituent assembly. A terrorist got a job in the Winter Palace, smuggled dynamite in and kept it under his pillow. He blew up the room where the czar was to receive a Bulgarian prince. Neither was in the room. Other terrorists placed mines under railway tracks to blow up the royal train. They failed. Today's assassination would also have failed if the czar had not stood around asking questions.

After his death, the public (and the assassins) learnt that, before the military parade, the czar had agreed to reforms.

Alexander II, the assassinated czar, lying in state in the Winter Palace.

Tunisia becomes French protectorate

Tunisia, 12 May 1881
The treaty of Bardo has made Tunisia a French protectorate. The French invaded three weeks ago when the Tunisian first minister decided to sweep away various privileges which gave them effective economic control. French influence over Tunisian affairs, like Britain's dominance of Egypt, has increased as the Ottoman empire and its neighbouring powers have declined into actual, or effective, bankruptcy. However, the new treaty only gives France a veto over diplomatic manoeuvres. It leaves the government to Tunisia's own *bey* and his people.

China brings home its polluted students

China, 1882
The government has recalled its educational mission to the United States, and the students who were sent there to "learn the superior barbarian techniques to control the barbarians" are being treated more like outcasts than future leaders of a modernised China. They are housed in filthy lodgings in Shanghai and watched by the secret police. Their "crime" is that they have been exposed to excessive "spiritual pollution" by taking too enthusiastically to the American way of life.

Massachusetts, 24 March 1882. The poet Henry Wadsworth Longfellow dies aged 85. His best loved work is the *The Song of Hiawatha* which recounts Indian legends.

Missouri, 3 April 1882. The bank robber and train hijacker Jesse James is shot dead by a cousin seeking the $10,000 dollar reward offered by the authorities.

Indochina (Vietnam), 25 April 1882. Commander Henri Riviere seizes the citadel of Hanoi. This is seen as a serious act of provocation at a time when France and China are in the process of negotiating a common protectorate in the region.

New England, 27 April 1882. Ralph Waldo Emerson, essayist, poet and leading transcendentalist, dies. He first came to public attention with the publication of his essay *Nature* in 1836.

Ireland, 2 May 1882. An informal agreement is made at Kilmainham between the nationalist Charles Parnell and the British government. The government agrees to make further concessions to tenants, and Parnell is released from jail having promised to call a halt to the campaign of violent protest.

Ireland, 6 May 1882. On the evening of his arrival in Dublin, the new secretary of state for Ireland, Lord Frederick Cavendish, is assassinated in Phoenix Park, along with his assistant, Burke, by members of a secret society known as the Invincibles. The Kilmainham agreement is broken.

Italy, 20 May 1882. Italy joins the Austro-German alliance.

Washington, DC, 22 May 1882. The United States signs a treaty with Korea, recognising Korean independence from China, Russia and Japan.

Egypt, 11 July 1882. A British fleet bombards Alexandria in retribution for nationalist violence in which 50 Europeans have died.

Korea, 23 July 1882. A pro-Chinese conservative *coup d'etat* occurs in Korea, directed against Japanese influence. The *Taewongun*, (regent), Yi Si-eung, seizes power.

Germany, 26 July 1882. Richard Wagner's new opera *Parsifal* is performed in Bayreuth to great acclaim.

Washington, DC, 3 August 1882. Congress passes the Immigration Act to control the influx of foreign workers to the United States. In particular the new act bans convicts, lunatics and idiots from entering America and bans Chinese emigration for ten years.

Austria, 1 September 1882. The German National Association is founded. It calls for an aggressive pan-German policy and for workers to be incorporated into cooperatives.

New York City, 5 September 1882. Thirty thousand workers join the first Labor Day march.

New York City, 6 November 1882. The actress Lillie Langtry makes her debut on the American stage.

Boston, 11 December 1882. The Bijou theatre is lit with 650 bulbs as Gilbert and Sullivan's operetta *Iolanthe* becomes the first electrically illuminated theatrical production in the country.

Britain, 1882. The second Married Women's Property Act is passed, whereby women are allowed to own property in their own right after marriage. Previously all property passed to the husband.

Amsterdam, 1882. A Dutch doctor, Aletta Jacobs, establishes the world's first birth control clinic.

Italy, 1882. An independent workers' party is formed at the instigation of the Milan Workers' Circle.

India, 1882. The viceroy, Lord Ripon, forms a commission to examine the state of Indian education.

India, 1882. Bankim Chandra Chatterji's historical novel, *Anandamath* is published. It contains the hymn *Bande Mataram* (Hail to the Mother).

Germany, 1882. The composer Johannes Brahms completes his second piano concerto.

Egypt, January 1883. Britain unilaterally abolishes its joint rule with France over Egypt. The general consul for Great Britain now has almost unlimited power.

Tunisia, 11 February 1883. France sets up a general secretariat whose job is to control the *bey's* ministers.

France, 19 February 1883. Villiers de l'Isle-Adam publishes his *Cruel Tales*, short stories that show a significant debt to the American writer Edgar Allan Poe.

New York City, 26 March 1883. Mrs Alva Vanderbilt throws the world's most expensive party, spending $75,000 on food and entertainments at a costume ball.

South West Africa (Namibia), 24 April 1883. Germans settle the port of Angra Pequena which they rename Luderitz Bay.

Madagascar, May 1883. French warships blockade the island and occupy the port of Majunga. But the prime minister, Rainilaiarivony refuses to capitulate.

Chinese immigration barred for a decade

Red gentleman to yellow gentleman: "Pale face 'fraid you crowd him out, as he did me."

Whites welcome: going to America.

Washington, 1882
California needed cheap Chinese labour to dig its gold. It even imported shiploads of coolies to shift millions of tons of earth and rock to build its rail link to the east. Now – with 150,000 Chinese living in California alone – the white working class fear their labour will be undercut and have forced Congress to ban Chinese immigration for the next ten years.

Led by an Irish agitator, Denis Kearney, the anti-Chinese movement gathered strength during the '70s and was taken up by the Californian Workingmen's Party. The Chinese are accused of working long hours at low rates of pay with the clear intention of returning home with their savings. The reluctance of the Chinese to change their customs and adapt to western ways has created a serious outbreak of racial prejudice which is being fanned by the agitators.

The writer Robert Louis Stevenson has defended the Chinese workers. "They could work better and cheaper in half a hundred industries and hence there was no calumny too idle for the Caucasians to repeat and even to believe", he wrote in *Across the Plains*.

Scientist finds cause of tuberculosis

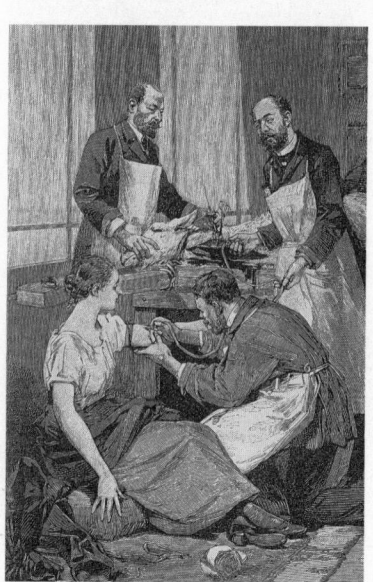

Robert Koch's treatment for tuberculosis, drawing blood from a goat and transferring it to the patient.

Berlin, 1882
It is seven years since Robert Koch identified the anthrax bacillus and performed what was thought to be a "miracle cure" on a dairy-maid for whom there had been no hope.

Now, with government support, Koch has established a laboratory in Berlin where he has succeeded in identifying another killer germ – the tubercle bacillus which causes the lung disease which has wiped out thousands, particularly in the kind of damp, airless slum conditions which have become endemic in industrial countries.

Although many medical traditionalists are prepared to scoff at this new science of "bacteriology", Koch and men like Louis Pasteur in Paris are convinced that it will make marked inroads in the treatment of illness.

No shortage of millionaires in America

Rockefeller, only 42 years old.

New York City, 2 January 1882
In an almost unprecedented atmosphere of secrecy and intrigue, control of the entire US oil industry has passed into the hands of just nine men. A "trust" agreement signed here makes John D Rockefeller the most powerful man in the United States outside the White House.

Rockefeller's Standard Oil already dominates the industry, and under this agreement shareholders have transferred their shares "in trust" to Rockefeller, his brother William and seven others – giving them power to create or dissolve corporations in any state and allocate funds of more than $70 million.

There is no shortage of millionaires in this free-wheeling, Devil-take-the-hindmost land. When the late Cornelius Vanderbilt sneezed, they said, New York shuddered; such was the power of the financial wizard who started life running a small sailing ferry between Manhattan and Staten Island and amassed $100 million from his railway and shipping empire.

Vanderbilt left the bulk of his money to his family. In contrast, Scots-born Andrew Carnegie, the steel magnate from Pittsburg, describes himself as a "distributor of wealth for the improvement of mankind" and will devote his fortune to education and scientific research.

Valhalla greets Jew-hating genius

Venice, 13 February 1883
Richard Wagner, the man who revolutionised European music, died today from a long-standing heart complaint. He was 69.

Wagner attracted either near-religious worship or near-animal loathing. But no-one disputes his profound influence on the whole language of music: harmony, form and orchestration have been transformed by the series of operas that ended last July with the mystical, sublime *Parsifal*, based, like many of his works, on Germanic legend.

Wagner was an outrageous egotist, even building an opera house for his own works. He knew he was a musical genius and thought he was a literary one too, writing his own libretti and churning out long, turgid tracts on many subjects. Jews, for example, he called "former cannibals, educated to be society's business leaders" who had corrupted "Aryan" purity.

Dreams and nightmares: Richard Wagner at home in the Villa Wahnfried.

Britain bombards Egypt

Conquerors of Egypt: Highlanders arrogantly posing by the Sphinx at Giza.

Egypt, 13 September 1882
The British expeditionary force under Sir Garnet Wolseley today met Arabi Pasha's army at Tel el-Kebir and totally defeated it, driving the Egyptians from the field and restoring the power of the spineless and pro-British ruler, the *Khedive* Tewfik.

The battle follows on the events of June when British ships bombarded Alexandria after the mob massacred 50 Europeans in the anarchy sweeping Egypt. The shelling led to riots and Arabi was transformed from a mutinous officer into a nationalist hero.

Fears for the safety of the Suez Canal and anger at the atrocities of the rebels led to the despatch of the expeditionary force to the Canal Zone. The soldiers have admirably fulfilled their mission, but their victory can only lead to increased British involvement in Egyptian affairs, a development not desired by the prime minister William Gladstone.

Hush-hush defence accord is signed

Berlin, 20 May 1882
The treaty signed today between Germany, Austria-Hungary and Italy is officially secret, but it has for some time been the subject of speculation in the chancelleries of Europe. It is an extension of an earlier secret treaty between Germany and Austria-Hungary.

The new pact is essentially a defensive alliance directed against France. The three powers are seeking to safeguard conquests made in recent years: Austria-Hungary's in the Balkans, Germany's in Alsace and Lorraine, and Italy's takeover of the papal states. Italy has another grievance against France: for occupying the Ottoman province of Tunis last year and declaring a protectorate.

Jews flee from Russian pogroms

St Petersburg, May 1882
The assassination of Alexander II last year was blamed on the Jews by people in high places with strongly anti-Semitic views, and the slander was given official endorsement by the new czar, Alexander III, who issued a *ukase* forbidding Jews to settle in rural areas, even within the permitted zone of residence, the Pale of Settlement.

The inevitable consequence has been a series of violent *pogroms* which have now lasted for over twelve months and taken the lives of many innocent Jews. Large numbers of Jews are being forced into ghettoes in Moscow and St Petersburg. Others are fleeing even further afield – to western Europe and the United States.

1883 (1883-1884)

New York, 25 May 1883. Brooklyn Bridge, designed by John A Roebling to link New York City and Brooklyn, is opened.

Tunisia, 8 June 1883. A convention specifies the details of the treaty of Bardo of 1881 which establishes a French protectorate over Tunis.

Madagascar, July 1883. Queen Ranavalona II dies and is succeeded by her cousin who becomes Queen Ranavalona III and also marries the country's prime minister Rainilaiarivony, himself a widower.

Indochina (Vietnam), 25 August 1883. While fighting continues with the French, a treaty is signed at Hue recognising Tonkin, Annam and Cochin China as French protectorates. This has been rejected by the Chinese, however, who regard the territory as a vassal state.

Indochina (Vietnam), 3 September 1883. Liu Yongfa's Chinese Black Flag irregulars and Vietnamese forces fight against the French in a bloody and costly battle near Hanoi.

Chile, 20 October 1883. The treaty of Ancon finally ends the war between Chile, Peru and Bolivia for land in the Atacama desert which is rich in nitrates. By the treaty Peru cedes Tarapaca to Chile and Chile also keeps Tacna and Arica for a period of ten years.

Vienna, 30 October 1883. Within the framework of the triple Alliance, Austria and Rumania sign their own secret alliance.

Germany, 1883. Johannes Brahms, the composer, completes his third symphony.

France, 1883. The artist Pierre Auguste Renoir completes his painting *Dancing in the Country*.

Bulgaria, 1883. The *sobranie* (upper parliamentary house) calls unanimously for Prince Alexander of Battenberg to restore the Turnovo constitution, which was suspended on 1 July 1881 when the prince was given full powers for seven years.

Wisconsin, 1883. James and William Horlick sell a new milk drink called Horlick's Malted Milk.

Spain, 1883. The architect Antonio Gaudi begins work on the church of the Holy Family in Barcelona.

USA, 1883. The growing influence of anarchism in the American workers' movement, brought over by European emmigres is illustrated by the formation of the revolutionary anarchist International Working People's Association in Chicago.

USA, 1883. In Chicago, William le Baron Jenney constructs the Home Insurance Building, the first "skyscraper" to have a facade which is disconnected from the building's skeleton.

Egypt, 1883. The fundementalist leader the *Mahdi* defeats the Egyptian army under General William Hicks and occupies Darfur and Bahr al Ghazal.

France, 1883. The French painter Edouard Manet dies. He hit the headlines in 1863 when his *Dejeuner sur l'herbe* caused a scandal when it was exhibited at the Salon des Refuses.

Switzerland, 1883. The Emancipation of Labour Group is founded by the Russian revolutionary Vera Zasulich.

India, 1883. The storm of protest raised by the European community in India against the Ilbert Bill of 1882, which proposes that Europeans should be open to trial by Indian judges, continues.

France, 19 January 1884. The French composer Jules Massenet meets fresh success with his new opera *Manon*.

Central Asia, 31 January 1884. Russian troops seize the town of Merv in Turkmenistan near the disputed area of Afghan border territory, alarming the British.

London, January 1884. A group of socialists founds the Fabian Society, named after the Roman general Fabius Cunctator who used delaying tactics to defeat his enemies.

Sudan, 18 February 1884. General Gordon, sent by the British government to evacuate Khartoum, decides to stay there.

Central Africa, February 1884. Britain signs a pact with Portugal over the control of the Congo estuary in an attempt to prevent King Leopold extending his empire in the region.

Washington, DC, 6 March 1884. Some 100 suffragists, led Susan B Anthony, present President Arthur with a demand that he voice public support for female suffrage.

Paris, 13 March 1884. A new Arab review, *The Indissoluble Link*, is published, aimed at thwarting British policy in the east by developing a pan-Arab, rather than pan-Islamic, consciousness.

France, 21 March 1884. The Waldeck-Rousseau law grants official status to professional and trades unions.

Chile, 4 April 1884. By the treaty of Valparaiso, Bolivia grants Chile the right to control Antofagasta including the Atacama desert.

Karl Marx, sower of socialist seeds, dies

London, 17 March 1883
Karl Marx, the revolutionary thinker who died on 14 March aged 64, was buried today at Highgate in London, where he has lived since his expulsions from Prussia and Paris in 1849. His friend and collaborator, Friedrich Engels, described him at the funeral as "the best-hated and most calumniated man of his time", but asserted that he died "mourned by millions of revolutionary fellow-workers".

Marx and Engels together drew up the *Communist Manifesto* in January 1848 for the Communist League of London, ending with its famous call to workers of all lands to unite. Later that year Marx took part in the revolutionary events in Cologne and made his only public speech at a street demonstration.

In London he, his wife Jenny and their children lived in poverty in two rooms in Soho while Marx studied economic history in the British Museum. He published *Das Kapi-*

Karl Marx: Hegelian philosopher.

tal, volume I, in 1867. He was the leading member of the First International Working Men's Association. Engels is editing the rest of *Das Kapital*.

Nietzsche's Zarathustra speaks out

Nietzsche: prophet of the superman.

Basle, Switzerland, 1883
Friedrich Nietzsche, the German philosopher who is a professor here, has published the first part of his major work of philosophical mysticism, *Also Sprach Zarathustra* (Thus Spake Zarathustra) in which he presents his idea of an *Ubermensch*: "I teach you the Superman. Man is something to be surpassed."

In a previous book he declared that "God is dead"; he considers that Christianity is played out and claims that "morality is the herd instinct in the individual". He shows the greatest contempt for the herd who, he fears, will trample individual excellence underfoot. Hence the idea of a race of Supermen, beyond good and evil.

Darkness at noon after volcano erupts

Krakatoa, Java, 28 August 1883
Over 30,000 people are feared dead after the volcano at Krakatoa erupted, triggering a tidal wave 120 feet (36.5 metres) high that has flooded homes in the nearby coastal towns of Java and Sumatra. Rescue efforts are being hampered by a thick cloud of black volcanic ash 17 miles (27 kilometres) high that has blotted out the sun and plunged the region into darkness for the last two and a half days. The volcano's most violent eruption yesterday could allegedly be heard 2,200 miles (3,520 kilometres) away in Australia.

Bolivia loses her coastline to Chile

South America, 1883

The War of the Pacific, waged between Chile and the allies Peru and Bolivia since 1879, is over and Chile has won. Chile has occupied much territory, including Lima, and defeated every allied campaign.

Under the peace Chile is to retain the mineral-rich areas it has seized from Peru, as well as the littoral that served as Bolivia's narrow connection to the sea. In return Chile will build a railway for the now land-locked Bolivians. The war began in 1879 following disagree-ments over national boundaries and the taxation by Bolivia of Chilean nitrate firms operated under Bolivian jurisdiction. When these taxes were raised and the Chileans refused to pay, the firms were seized. Chilean troops occupied the town of Antofagasta.

When Peru attempted to mediate the Chileans rejected its efforts, pointing out that Peru and Bolivia were allies under a treaty of 1873. Chile's demands that the treaty should be scrapped were ignored and war was declared.

Chilean gunners mounting heavy coastal guns during the War of the Pacific.

India worries over Russian advances

Persia, February 1884

The vaguely defined frontiers between Russia, Persia and Afghanistan to the east of the Caspian Sea have been causing concern in London and New Delhi, where officials fear continuing Russian pressure could pose a threat to India.

The Russians have just taken over a place called Merv and, though travellers say that it is no more than a mudhut village with an oasis, it is only 12 days' march from Herat in Afghanistan. The Indian government is urging London to get "a clear understanding" with the Russians as to the exact frontier line in the region. The Russians are proving evasive; worse still, they have forced the *shah* of Persia to accept a Cossack brigade to "defend" the frontier region.

Huckleberry Finn, tale of runaway boys

USA, 1884

The publication of *The Adventures of Huckleberry Finn* confirms the arrival of a major literary talent in Mark Twain, the pen name of Samuel Clemens, a lawyer's son. This latest book is a companion to *The Adventures of Tom Sawyer*, published nine years ago. Both tell of childhood adventures on the banks of the Mississippi, and are drawn from Twain's own life.

A journalist and travel writer, Twain has a growing international reputation. Four years ago he published *The Prince and the Pauper*, an adventure story that was also a socio-political allegory.

Buffalo Bill's Wild West

America's new mythology: a poster for William Cody's famous Wild West show.

Jesse James and the Younger gang.

Omaha, Nebraska, 17 May 1883

A new kind of circus came to town today – with gun-toting cowboys, heavily war-painted Red Indians, a herd of buffalo and a buckskin-clad sharpshooting colonel with shoulder-length hair by the name of Buffalo Bill. His real name is William Cody; he is a former cavalry scout, and his "Wild West Show" is aimed at re-creating America's pioneering days with fake gun-duels and stagecoach hold-ups.

Yet the show is not doing too well, perhaps because people in these parts don't really see why they should part with money when the real thing is still going on.

The west is still wild, with legendary heroes like Marshal Wyatt Earp, noted for his shootout at Tombstone's OK Corral in 1881 and Sheriff "Wild Bill" Hickok

William Bonney: "Billy the Kid".

who was shot in the back in a saloon clutching a poker hand 1876. The villains are equally legendary. The New York-born "Billy the Kid" (William Bonney) murdered 21 men before he was shot down in 1881; Jesse James, the bankrobber, was shot in the back in 1882 as he dusted a picture in his mother's home.

1884 (1884-1885)

South-West Africa, 24 April 1884. Bismarck cables Cape Town that South West Africa is now a German colony.

China, 11 May 1884. Li Hongzhang signs a convention in Tianjin with the French negotiator Fournier over Indochina (*Vietnam*). China agrees to recognise all past and future Franco-Vietnamese treaties, to open Yunnan and Guangxi to French trade and to withdraw its troops to the Chinese frontier.

New York City, 10 May 1884. Theodore Roosevelt, the 25-year-old legislator renowned for his attacks on government corruption, is retiring from politics following the sudden deaths of his wife and mother. He plans to hunt buffalo in Dakota.

Indochina, 23 June 1884. Unaware of the Li-Fournier convention, Chinese forces defeat the French at at Bacle and force them to retreat.

Equatorial Africa, 11 July 1884. Germans begin to sign up Cameroons chiefs as subjects.

Indochina, 12 July 1884. The French government sends an ultimatum to China demanding observation of the Li-Fournier convention and payment of an indemnity of 250 million francs. The *Zongli* Yamen refuses payment but withdraws Chinese troops from Indochina.

Formosa (Taiwan), 5 August 1884. French naval forces bombard Jilong because of the Chinese refusal to pay an indemnity for their non-observance of the Li-Fournier treaty.

China, 23 August 1884. French warships attack Fuzhou, sink or disable all seven warships of the Fujian fleet and destroy the French-built Fuzhou dockyard.

China, 26 October 1884. The court declares war on France.

Zurich, October 1884. Engels publishes *The Origin of the Family, Private Property and the State.*

Berlin, 15 November 1884. An international conference on the Congo question is organised by the German chancellor, Bismarck.

China, 17 November 1884. Chinese Turkestan is given provincial status, re-named Xinjiang (New Frontier).

Korea, 6 December 1884. Following a *coup d'etat* by pro-Japanese radicals three days ago, Yuan Shikai yesterday led some 2,000 Qing troops stationed in Seoul and Korean forces in an attack on the royal palace. The Japanese are defeated and withdraw from Seoul.

London, 1884. Maxim invents a new weapon, the machine gun.

France, 1884. The chemist Hilaire Bernigaud, the count of Chardonnet, patents artificial silk.

Bohemia, 1884. The composer Bedrich Smetana dies in an asylum. He is the founder of Czech nationalism in music.

London, 1884. The Reform Act introduced by Gladstone's government allows householders in the counties to vote and increases the total electorate from three to five million. By a separate act parliamentary seats are redistributed so that representation corresponds to population.

Central Africa (Zaire), 1884. Henry Morton Stanley leaves the Congo area 40 trading posts having set up on behalf of King Leopold of the Belgian's company, now called the International Association for the Congo.

Missouri, 1884. Mark Twain publishes *The Adventures of Huckleberry Finn*, the tale of an orphan and a runaway slave's journeys on the Mississippi River.

New York City, 1884. Lewis E Waterman has developed the first ink-storing pen fit for manufacture.

France, 1884. Divorce is reintroduced and can be obtained on the grounds of cruelty or injury. Financial maintenance and custody are to be awarded to the successful petitioner of a divorce. This gives women the means to keep their families which they have not previously enjoyed.

East Africa, 1884. The German Karl Peters founds the Society for German Colonisation and sets off on a journey along the coast of Tanganyika.

South Africa, 1884. The first black Southern African newspaper, *Imvo zabaNshundu* (The Voice of the Black People), is founded in Xhosa.

New York City, 1884. The surgeon William Stewart Halsted discovers that injected cocaine is an effective anaesthetic.

South Africa, 1884. The Tembu National Church, the first black church in Southern Africa, is founded.

Austria, 1884. The composer Anton Bruckner composes his seventh symphony which is a huge popular success.

East Africa, 17 February 1885. Germany establishes a protectorate over the Tanganyika coast.

Berlin, 25 February 1885. The Berlin Act is passed, summing up the agreements over West Africa at last year's Berlin's conference.

Horseless carriage frightens the cattle

Karl Benz' rival, Gottlieb Daimler, driven in his vehicle by his son, Adolf.

Mannheim, Germany, 1885

In the quiet and dusty lanes around this city, a noisy threat has emerged which could change the traditional, peaceful rural way of life for ever. At nearly eight miles (13 kilometres) an hour, young Karl Benz' "horseless carriage" is frightening the cattle and worrying the horse-trade.

The first such carriage, devised by Nicholas-Joseph Cugnot in 1769, was steam-driven, but Benz is exploiting petrol and has created an internal combustion engine with the pulling power of one horse. The engine has electric ignition and is sited at the rear of the vehicle. The machine is capable of variable forward speeds through a system of pulleys with power transmitted by means of a drive belt. The single front wheel makes for easier steering than on horse drawn vehicles, but it must be said that Benz' machine is not entirely reliable. It breaks down; knowing that rivals like Gottlieb Daimler are working on their own designs, Benz is anxious to ensure it does not.

Newsman exposes under age vice scandal

London, 1885

William Stead, the 36-year-old editor of the *Pall Mall Gazette* and self-appointed "trumpeter in ordinary of the Salvation Army", has published a horrifying revelation of Britain's white-slave trade. Now he faces a trial for publishing obscene material.

"A maiden tribute of modern Babylon" details a ghastly catalogue of degradation and exploitation. Stead mingled with prostitutes and took down their stories. Particularly shocking was his purchase for £5 of a girl of only thirteen.

Stead's pamphlet has excited much interest, even if his critics do dismiss him as a sex-obsessed puritan, an exploiter himself who uses sensation to sell his magazine.

Journalist as prisoner: a protest.

France blasts ships in surprise attack

Fuzhou, China, 23 August 1884
The French fleet which has been moored in the harbour here for over a month treacherously opened fire today, sinking 11 Chinese ships, destroying the dockyard which had been built with French help and killing some 3,000 people.

This attack follows the French bombardment of Jilong in Formosa earlier this month and is part of the French pressure on China to fulfil the terms of the Li-Fournier convention under which the Chinese agreed to withdraw from Annam (*northern Vietnam*) in exchange for a French promise not to invade South China. A clash between French troops and Chinese units not yet ordered to withdraw has given the French the opportunity to demand further concessions.

Germans expand African "empire"

Africa, 1884
German colonial expansion continues with the foundation of the Society for German Colonisation, by Karl Peters, a pastor's son. Peters is travelling along the East African coast persuading local chieftains to accept the society's protection.

Bismarck, the German chancellor, has encouraged merchants to found colonies. Adolf Luderitz, from Bremen, who acquired land round the bay of Angra Pequena in South West Africa. Britain recognised German South West Africa on 22 June, after Germeny made threats over Egypt.

In July, Togo and Cameroon, acquired by the Hamburg merchant and shipper Adolf Woermann, were also made German colonies.

Europe shares out Africa

The Congress of Berlin, where the nations of Europe cut the African cake.

Berlin, 26 February 1885
Delegates from 15 nations, meeting in Berlin with Bismarck in the chair, have agreed on the partition of Central and East Africa. Though Germany and France have gained substantial areas, by far the biggest prize has been taken, not by one country, but by one man: King Leopold II of the Belgians has been given possession of 900,000 square miles (2.3 million square kilometres) of the Congo basin.

Leopold used intrigue, bluff and downright humbug. Stanley, the explorer who has first-hand knowledge of the Congo, attended the conference as an adviser to the US delegation; in fact, he is in Leopold's employ. When delegates expressed doubt about giving in to him, Leopold threatened to abandon development of the Congo and wreck its settlements. At the same time, Leopold presented himself as a high-minded philanthropist who wanted to help the black man with his International Association for the Exploration and Civilisation of Central Africa.

But the decisive factor was Bismarck's determination to keep Britain out of the Congo basin. The British are not worried; when their options on various pieces of Africa have been closed they will control twice as much as that of France and Germany combined.

Chinese foil Japanese coup in Korea

Seoul, 6 December 1884
Chinese troops stationed in the Korean capital today seized the royal palace following an attempt by pro-Japanese radicals to mount a coup d'etat.

The coup was instigated by the Japanese minister to Korea, Takezoe Shinichiro, who led 200 Japanese soldiers in defence of the palace.

The coup failed and the Japanese were defeated.

It was a minor incident in terms of casualties, but it reflects Japan's determination to exert its growing power in Korea, for so long a Chinese vassal state. Korea's strategic geographic position between China and Japan is rapidly turning it into the cockpit of Asia.

Georges Seurat's "Bathers at Asnieres". Seurat seeks to go beyond the fleeting images of the Impressionists to a more timeless image, combining naturalism with formality. Earlier works had been exhibited in the Salon in 1883, but the Salon rejected Seurat's bathers the following year as superficial. Outraged fellow artists acclaim it as a masterpiece. Now Seurat is calling his minute brush-stokes, almost dots, "pointillism".

Congo is king's prize in African carve-up

Brussels, 1 August 1884
King Leopold II of Belgium formally proclaimed his "Congo Free State" today, following the concession to him by other European powers at Berlin last February.

His interest in the Congo dates from 1876, inspired by the travel narrative of H M Stanley, who described the river as "the great highway of commerce to broad Africa". Leopold recruited Stanley to open up the river basin for his company. In five years Stanley has founded 40 trading stations.

Under the Berlin agreement, the Congo basin is meant to be a free trade area, but Leopold has no intention of loosing his profitable monopoly of the highway.

Stanley, journalist and explorer.

The partition of Africa: a poisoned legacy

Europeans had held trading posts on the coasts of Africa since the sixteenth century, but they controlled very little African territory before the 1880s. However, by 1914 the map of Africa had been transformed into the colonies and territories which were to become the independent states of contemporary Africa. The process did not gather momentum until about 1885 yet was largely complete by the early 1890s, although the final details were ironed out after the First World War. Because of its remarkable rapidity, this partition is often called "the scramble for Africa".

The very fact that this "scramble" was so fast meant that the division of Africa into colonial territories remained a largely paper exercise until it was almost over. Conferences in Europe drew lines on maps, many of which were extremely inaccurate, based on diplomatic negotiations rather than any effective presence on the ground. The straight lines which mark the frontiers, not to mention the often ludicrous divisions of peoples and kingdoms between two or more colonies, testify to European ignorance of local realities.

A major impetus for this fresh burst of colonialism was economic. By the late nineteenth century, Britain was no longer alone in having developed an industrial economy, but was being challenged by the United States, France, Belgium, Holland and particularly the newly unified state of Germany. Competition for markets intensified as did international rivalry, however, as long as the economies continued to expand most felt that free trade offered the best opportunities for profit. On the whole, colonies had been felt to be needless encumbrances which brought little benefit, particularly when America – North and South – offered opportunities for investment and trade.

Protecting profit margins

This mood of optimism was shattered by the major depression which began in 1873. Falling profits, unemployment and social unrest began to challenge the economic orthodoxies of the earlier period. By the early 1880s some states were beginning to erect protective tariff barriers and others questioned whether they should not do so, if only in defence. In Africa, falling profits led to intense competition between traders, and between European firms and their African trading partners as each sought to protect their profit margins. In some cases, unrest in the coastal regions led European traders to call for intervention by their governments. When King Leopold of the Belgians was

seen to be interested in creating an empire for himself in central Africa, a conference was called to discuss trade in Africa. This conference was held in Berlin in 1884-5; although ostensibly to protect free trade in the area, it in fact fuelled an explosion of territorial claims.

Yet the economic crisis had political consequences as well. Poliical tension in Europe rose dramatically in the second half of the century; the rise of Prussia as a major military power, and the development of new political units in Italy and Germany altered the military balance of power, and threatened Britain's access to Asia. In this climate, sources of strategic raw materials became of crucial importance, adding to the pressures to move towards protectionism. The new states themselves unified by nationalist sentiment, and eager to reap the benefits enjoyed by countries such as Britain and France, began to look towards colonial possessions as a route to development. In France, groups also advocated imperial expansion as a means to reverse the humiliation of defeat by Prussia in 1870, and the uprising which followed it.

Technology and a new racism

There were other more long-term changes at work as well. Technological and medical developments in weaponry, communications and dealing with tropical diseases made the acquisition and administration of overseas territories a cheaper propostion than it had been at the beginning of the century. Such technological advances contributed to increasing racism and a belief in European superiority, reinforced in their turn by the quasi-scientific doctrines of social-Darwinism which saw the world in terms of survival of the fittest.

To justify its acquisition of territory, imperial propaganda encouraged the belief that the exploitation of other countries was a source of national pride, while total ignorance of Africa allowed the encouragement of fantasies of spectacular wealth which did not, in fact, materialise. This nationalism, harnessed to the new "scientific" racism, acted as a handy safety-valve for the growing class-conflict in Europe, where economic crisis had created social tensions which were increasingly expressed in the new socialist ideology which posed a threat to the interest of owners and managers of capital.

For a variety of reasons colonies had suddenly become a much more attractive proposition and the Berlin Conference, by outlining a procedure for making claims to territory in Africa, made

the threat of war over such claims recede. However, no country wanted to be left out, for fear that others would gain advantages which would strengthen further their economic and military position, so boundaries were drawn up rapidly without thought of administration or sober assessments of their value.

Short-lived colonial rule

It was only when the partition of Africa was nearly complete that it became necessary to discover what the newly gained territories actually contained. As the Europeans soon found, the process of conquering the land which was theirs on paper was a much more costly and drawn-out affair than the first stage had been. The African response to their new "masters" was mixed. For many they posed far less of a threat to local autonomy than existing local tensions, and leaders were happy to form alliances with Europeans against neighbouring states for as long as it served their needs; there was never a simple choice between collaboration and resistance.

The crunch came when the Europeans attempted to introduce such measures as taxes and forced labour. These often provoked wide-scale opposition including passive resistance, migration, protests, rebellion and military uprisings. Eventually all were forcibly repressed but some continued well into the 1920s and 1930s. Effective colonial rule was thus short-lived, at most lasting only 80 years and in a few areas spanning as little as 30 or 40 years.

Unplanned, haphazard and often inspired by nothing more than the desire to block a rival's claim, it is hardly surprising that the European African land-grab failed financially. Very soon the main concern of the occupying powers became to minimise costs, and the colonial economies were designed to raise revenue rather than with any thought of developing the territory. The political results for ultimately independent nation states were equally disastrous. Not only were they often defined by boundaries that had no basis in regional or political realities and which cut across economic regions, but in many cases European encouragement of old African kingdoms, often because they would administer areas more cheaply than whites, set up inevitable conflicts between them and the new nation states.

Although not all Africa's problems stem from the "scramble", its legacies – such as conflicting nationalisms, ethnic tension and economic isolation – are still major issues today.

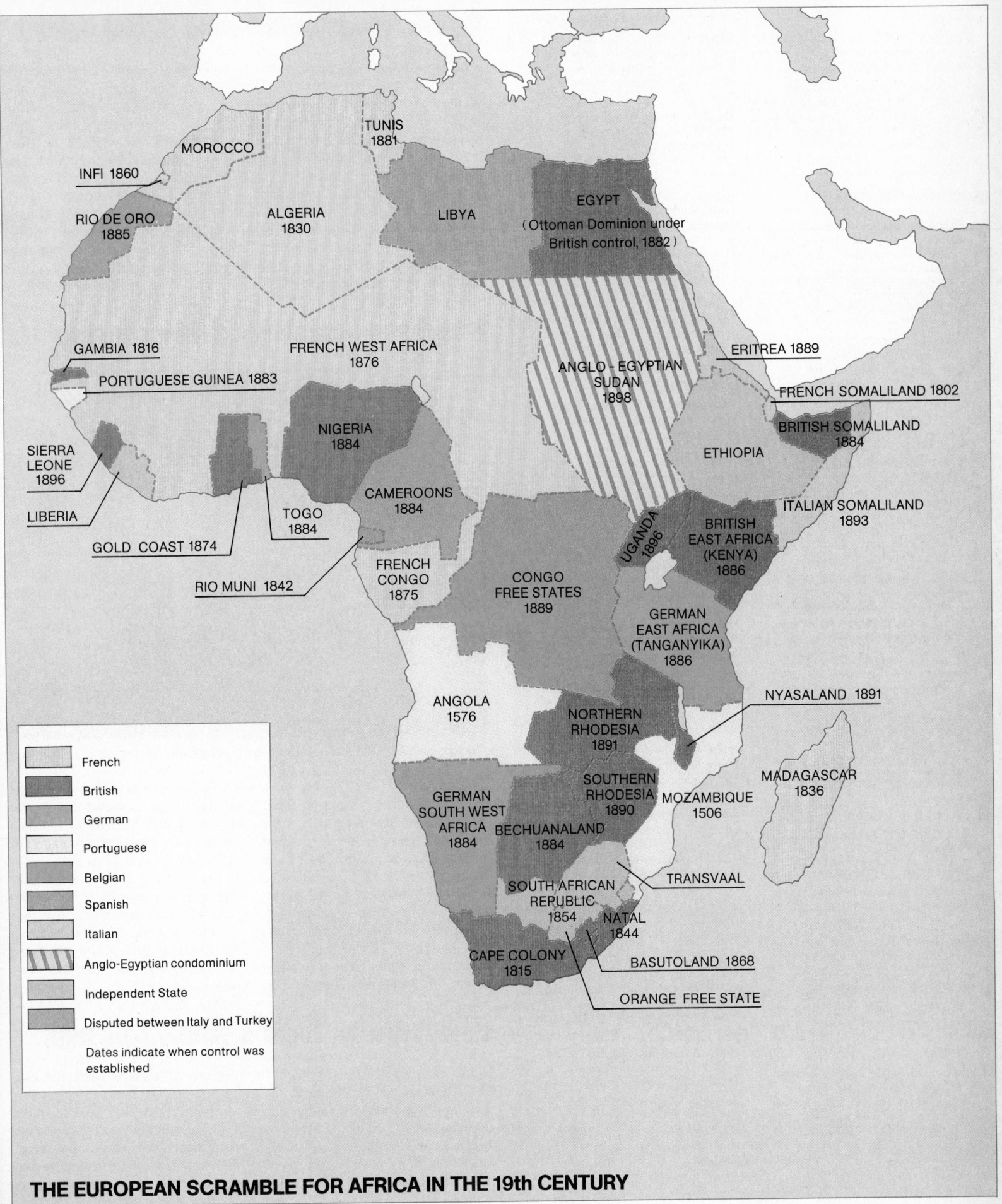

INFI 1860

MOROCCO

TUNIS
1881

RIO DE ORO
1885

ALGERIA
1830

LIBYA

EGYPT
(Ottoman Dominion under
British control, 1882)

GAMBIA 1816

FRENCH WEST AFRICA
1876

ERITREA 1889

PORTUGUESE GUINEA 1883

ANGLO - EGYPTIAN
SUDAN
1898

FRENCH SOMALILAND 1802

NIGERIA
1884

BRITISH SOMALILAND
1884

SIERRA
LEONE
1896

ETHIOPIA

LIBERIA

CAMEROONS
1884

ITALIAN SOMALILAND
1893

TOGO
1884

GOLD COAST 1874

UGANDA
1896

BRITISH
EAST AFRICA
(KENYA)
1886

RIO MUNI 1842

FRENCH
CONGO
1875

CONGO
FREE STATES
1889

GERMAN
EAST AFRICA
(TANGANYIKA)
1886

ANGOLA
1576

NYASALAND 1891

NORTHERN
RHODESIA
1891

MADAGASCAR
1836

GERMAN
SOUTH WEST
AFRICA
1884

SOUTHERN
RHODESIA
1890

MOZAMBIQUE
1506

BECHUANALAND
1884

TRANSVAAL

SOUTH AFRICAN
REPUBLIC
1854

NATAL
1844

CAPE COLONY
1815

BASUTOLAND 1868

ORANGE FREE STATE

French

British

German

Portuguese

Belgian

Spanish

Italian

Anglo-Egyptian condominium

Independent State

Disputed between Italy and Turkey

Dates indicate when control was
established

THE EUROPEAN SCRAMBLE FOR AFRICA IN THE 19th CENTURY

1885

Washington, DC, 4 March 1885. Grover Cleveland, Democrat, is inaugurated as president.

Indochina (Vietnam), 29 March 1885. Yesterday Qing troops under Feng Zicai attacked French forces at Langson on the Vietnamese side of the border, seriously wounding General Francois de Negrier. Today Langson has fallen to Feng.

Afghanistan, 30 March 1885. Russian troops inflict a crushing defeat on Afghan forces at Ak Teppe, despite orders not to fight. The British, Russians and Afghans are now seeking a settlement.

Paris, 30 March 1885. Jules Ferry's cabinet resigns following the loss of Langson to the Chinese.

Korea, 18 April 1885. The Sino-Japanese Li-Ito treaty is signed. Both powers withdraw their troops, which have been fighting since 1884, and undertake to work in concert in all new actions.

Central Africa (Zaire), 30 April 1885. Leopold II of the Belgians proclaims himself sovereign of the Congo Free State.

Paris, 1 June 1885. Victor Hugo, the famous novelist and poet who died on 22 May, is given a state funeral. His greatest work is without doubt *Les Miserables*.

Nigeria, 5 June 1885. Following the signature of the Anglo-Sokoto treaty on the first of this month, a British protectorate is established over the Niger districts.

China, 9 June 1885. The French minister Patenotre and Li Hongzhang sign the Sino-French treaty on Indochina in Tianjin. It reaffirms the French protectorate over Indochina and settles border and trade regulations.

New York City, 19 June 1885. The Statue of Liberty arrives from France.

Sudan, 22 June 1885. The religious leader the *Mahdi* (Mohammed Ahmad ben Abdullah) a *faqir* (fakir) from Dongola, dies. He proclaimed himself *al-Mahdi* (the expected guide) on 19 June 1881 and led his people in war against the British.

Washington, DC, 1 July 1885. The US cancels an 1871 treaty with Canada, terminating reciprocal fishing rights.

New York, 23 July 1885. Ulysses S Grant, the former president dies aged 63 leaving nothing but his memoirs.

Ireland, 14 August 1885. The new British government establishes close relations with Charles Parnell and passes the Land Act providing large state loans for Irish peasants to buy lands from the English landowners.

Bulgaria, 17 September 1885. A rebellion in eastern Rumelia allows Alexander of Battenberg, the prince of Bulgaria, to annex the region.

Southern Africa, 30 September 1885. The British divide the Bechuanaland protectorate (*Botswana*) from Bechuanaland colony.

Bulgaria, 17 November 1885. The Serbian army, with Russian support, invades Bulgaria following the announcement of its union with Rumelia. The Serbs are defeated at Slivnitsa, 25 miles outside Sofia.

Spain, 25 November 1885. On the death of Alfonso XII, his widow Maria Cristina comes to the throne in the name of the child she is carrying, due to be born in May.

Burma, November 1885. The British seize the capital, Mandalay.

Madagascar, 17 December 1885. By a treaty signed in Tamatave, France acquires the protectorate of Madagascar, which it is to represent in all foreign relations.

USA, 1885. Robert Louis Stevenson publishes *Dr Jekyll and Mr Hyde*, a chilling novel dealing with the question of evil.

Germany, 1885. The engineer Gottlieb Daimler invents the first motorcycle.

New Zealand, 1885. The American Mary Leavitt, an envoy of the Women's Christian Temperance Union of the United States, visits New Zealand and founds 15 branches of the organisation. In the US it has acquired a distinctly feminist character, concerning itself mainly with the issue of women's suffrage.

India, 1885. Bharatendu Harischandra, the father of modern Hindi, dies.

Paris, 1885. European vineyards are being destroyed by a plant louse called *phylloxera vasatrix*, brought over in American vines. The louse eats away at the roots of the vines and is devastating the European wine trade.

Germany, 1885. Johannes Brahms composes his fourth symphony, a tragic work whose unusual finale wins a mixed reception.

Washington, DC, 1885. The veterinarian Daniel Elmer Salmon describes salmonella bacteria which he believes causes food poisoning.

New York City, 1885. Gilbert and Sullivan's new musical *The Mikado* is given its American premiere, directed by Richard D'Oyly Carte.

Bulgaria, 3 March 1886. Bulgaria and Serbia sign the peace of Bucharest which maintains the *status quo* between the two countries.

British troops on the road to Mandalay

Rangoon, Burma, November 1885
An expeditionary force of 10,000 soldiers of the British Indian Army is marching up the Irrawaddy valley to head off French intervention in Upper Burma. Lower Burma, administered from Rangoon, is British as a result of campaigns in 1824 and 1852. Upper Burma, formerly a friendly independent state, is now ruled by young King Thibaw, who massacred 80 relatives on his coronation six years ago. Thibaw encouraged overtures by France, which itself occupies much of Indochina by force of arms, relying on Foreign Legion mercenaries. British traders in Rangoon protested about the likely loss of trade and influence. It is now likely that Upper Burma, a kingdom larger than Britain with a population of four million, will be brought under tighter control and possibly annexed. King Thibaw's army is no match for the British.

Frenchman inoculates child against rabies

Pasteur with English children whom he is inoculating against rabies.

Paris, 1885
A nine-year-old boy's life has been saved after he was bitten by a rabid dog. Until now rabies was regarded as incurable. Even though doctors had predicted certain death for the boy, Joseph Meister, he was taken to the surgery of Dr Louis Pasteur, a doctor who has been experimenting with a vaccine made from a weakened strain of rabies virus developed from dog saliva.

Young Joseph made an amazing recovery, and, within days, Dr Pasteur found his surgery besieged by crowds of optimistic victims of dog bites.

Pasteur, who pioneered the technique of heating milk to kill germs which is now named after him, has become something of a national hero after devising new methods for the treatment of anthrax and cholera.

Ramakrishna, India's saintly holy man

India, 1886
India is mourning the death at the age of 50 of Shri Ramakrishna, one of the saintliest of all its religious leaders.

The son of a village priest in Bengal, Ramakrishna went into his first mystical trance at the age of seven, and was installed as a priest in Calcutta with his brother when only 16. His utter devotion to the search for God brought him further mystical experiences, and, in due course, followers from the educated middle classes, who helped to propagate his simple, rustic holiness.

Guerrilla leader who fought French in Senegal is dead

Senegal, West Africa, 1886

Lat Dyor, the ruler of Kayor, who waged a four-year guerrilla war against the French in Senegal, has been killed. He fell in battle, dying with his men at N'Dekete.

He first became ruler of Kayor in 1862, but was driven out by French forces and fled to the Senegalese Moslem leader, Maba Diakhou Ba, who was fighting a holy war against the French. Lat Dyor became a Moslem and, when Diakhou died, led the resistance, until coming to terms with the French in 1871. He was reinstated king, and soon controlled all western Senegal.

When France began building a railway into the interior to open up the area for trade, groundnut cultivation and French administrators Lat Dyor recognised the danger to independent Africa and began a guerrilla war, tying down thousands of French troops.

Lat Dyor's death and defeat will not bring the war to an end – too many of his followers are still fighting – but it will take the railway further towards the river Niger.

Nationalist party is formed in India

Bombay, India, 28 December 1885

As British troops occupy Upper Burma, and the British empire takes control of more territory than ever before, Indian nationalists have met to form a new political movement. They are calling the movement the Indian National Congress. Since the founding of universities at Bombay, Calcutta and Madras in 1857, a middle class has emerged, resentful at being treated by Englishmen as racially inferior and being denied political responsibility. Congress' resolutions could not be more moderate: the British administration should be responsible to the House of Commons, and there should be elected representatives on the legislative councils and equality of opportunity in the Indian Civil Service. The British should watch them: over half of them are lawyers.

Dervishes spear Gordon in Khartoum

Khartoum, 26 January 1885

General Gordon is dead, killed by a Dervish spear today on the steps of his office and beheaded, while the relief force fights its way up the Nile against fierce opposition from the Mahdi's fanatics.

"Chinese" Gordon, who made his name fighting the *Taiping* rebels, had been sent to Khartoum to evacuate the Anglo-Egyptian forces from the Sudan where they were in danger of being overrun by the all-conquering forces of Mohammed Ahmad, hailed by his Moslem followers as the Mahdi or "divinely guided one".

Gordon, however, was a mystic and a puritan, as much a zealot as the Mahdi, and when he arrived in Khartoum he saw it as his duty to defeat the Dervishes

He asked for reinforcements from a government whose instructions expressly refused him a free hand. Gordon's will was pitted against Gladstone's determination not to be involved in fresh colonial adventures.

Lord Randolph Churchill took up Gordon's cause in the House of Commons as the Mahdi's forces closed on Khartoum. "Are they to remain indifferent," he asked, "to the fate of the one man on whom they have counted to extricate them from their dilemmas, to leave him to shift for himself, and not to make a single effort on his behalf?"

The public responded to the call. Gordon was a true British hero, a

An earlier British sucess against Mahdi forces at Tamanieb last year.

man of action who fought against slavery and for the children of the poor. Eventually, last September, the government gave in and General Sir Garnet Wolseley was sent to Cairo to raise a rescue force.

Ten thousand men were assembled with speed, but their progress against the Mahdi's forces along uncharted reaches of the Nile has been painfully slow. Sir Herbert Stewart took his Camel Corps in a dash across a loop in the Nile. He died in a desperate battle in which a British square was broken by the people they call "fuzzy wuzzies". But the survivors pressed on. They are within two days of Khartoum, but too late: Gordon is dead and the Mahdi is master of the Sudan.

The death of Gordon at Khartoum.

Waves in the ether

Germany, 1885

It was James Clerk Maxwell who, 20 years ago, put forward a theory that an unknown form of radiation exists that can travel at the speed of light through space. Now Heinrich Hertz, a German physicist, has demonstrated the existence of this radiation.

His experiment consists of a battery generating electric sparks between two metal balls. A yard or so away Hertz holds up a wire loop with two more metal balls at the ends, separated by a small gap. Whenever the first sparks appear, so do others which jump across the second "spark gap".

Henry James, promising young novelist

James, a middle-aged young man

London, 1886

A select public is appreciative of the subtle technique of Henry James, the American novelist who has adopted England as his home and lives off Piccadilly, dining out in London literary circles. His work contrasts European and US culture and attitudes, the Americans being shown as raw, innocent and narrow but possessing a free spirit and zest for life. The flirtatious heroine of *Daisy Miller* was declared to be "a libel on American womanhood". *Portrait of a Lady* also showed the American woman abroad, but *The Bostonians* returns to the society of James' youth.

1886 (1886-1887)

USA, 1 May 1886. Over 100,000 workers across the country strike for an eight-hour day.

Chicago, 5 May 1886. A bomb explodes on the fourth day of the general strike.

Bavaria, 10 June 1886. The minister of foreign affairs, Count Krafft von Crailsheim, dismisses Ludwig II, who has gone mad. The king's uncle, Leopold, is appointed prince regent.

Bavaria, 13 June 1886. The mad King Ludwig II drowns himself and his private doctor in the Starnberger See near Schloss Berg.

Greece, June 1886. The European powers organise a blockade of the Greek coast in order to prevent an attack on Turkey. Greece is demanding compensation for the Bulgarian union with eastern Rumelia, but the Ottomans are not co-operating.

London, 10 July 1886. A British royal charter is given to the Royal Niger Company to colonise Nigeria.

Burma, 24 July 1886. Following the British conquest of Upper Burma, the Chinese negotiator Yihuang and the British representative N O'Conor sign a convention relating to Burma and Tibet. China recognises British rule in Burma and Britain allows the continuation of Burmese tribute to China. Britain also agrees not to press the opening of Tibet.

Britain, 26 July 1886. William Gladstone is replaced by Lord Salisbury as prime minister, following his election defeat.

Arizona, 4 September 1886. The Apache leader Geronimo surrenders to General Nelson A Miles after a decade of guerrilla fighting designed to deter settlers in New Mexico and Arizona.

Bulgaria, 4 September 1886. Alexander of Battenberg, the prince of Bulgaria, abdicates, following the pro-Russian *coup d'etat* staged by the Sofia regiment last month.

South Africa, 20 September 1886. The city of Johannesburg is founded.

Germany, November 1886. Karl Benz patents the first motor car.

India, December 1886. Saiyid Ahmed Khan founds the Moslem Education conference, in part to prepare Moslems for life in a world dominated by the west and in part to prevent them from joining the Indian National Congress.

Atlanta, 1886. A pharmacist, Dr Pemberton, produces a non-alcoholic fizzy drink made from coca leaves, water and sugar, called Coca Cola.

London, 1886. A new speaker to the House of Commons, Peel, insists that Charles Bradlaugh, an admitted atheist MP who has been banned from the House of Commons since his election in 1880, be allowed to take his seat in the House.

Britain, 1886. A law is passed allowing women to assume sole guardianship of their children on the deaths of their husbands.

Germany, 14 January 1887. The *reichstag* is dissolved by Bismarck as a result of its refusal to vote for the military budget.

New Zealand, 20 January 1887. New Zealand annexes the Kermadec islands.

Honolulu, 20 January 1887. A renewal of the reciprocity treaty between the Hawaiian kingdom and the United States contains an amendment granting America exclusive rights to a coaling station in Pearl Harbor.

Washington, DC, 8 February 1887. An act is passed allowing the president to override Indian governments and sell traditional, communally-owned tribal lands to private owners.

Russia, 27 February 1887. The composer Alexander Borodin dies. He was the illegitimate son of a Georgian prince and was a notable scientist as well as a composer. One of the group of nationalist composers known as "the five", he leaves the unfinished opera *Prince Igor* which he has been working on since 1869.

Germany, 11 March 1887. Following the victory of the conservative cartel on 21 February, the second seven-year military law is passed.

London, 26 May 1887. A British royal charter is given to the Imperial British East Africa Company to colonise Kenya and Uganda.

Mediterranean, May 1887. Concerned about developments in the Balkans, Britain aims to stabilise relations with the Mediterranean countries and counter Russian designs on the area. Having exchanged secret letters with Italy guaranteeing the *status quo* in the Mediterranean and the Black Sea, Britain makes similar agreements with Austria and Spain.

London, 20 June 1887. Queen Victoria meets Annie Oakley, the famous American markswoman who can slice a playing card in two at thirty paces sideways on.

Honolulu, 7 July 1887. Revolution is threatened after King Kalakaua is identified as the ringleader in an opium bribery case.

The Irish question brings down Gladstone

London, 8 June 1886

The Irish question has brought down yet another British government. William Gladstone became prime minister only six months ago, with a 335-249 majority over the Conservatives, but dependent on Parnell's 86 Irish votes for an overall Commons majority.

Gladstone's Irish Home Rule Bill proposed a parliament and cabinet in Dublin, but with defence, foreign affairs, currency, customs and the post office remaining at Westminster. The bill was defeated 343-313, with almost a hundred Liberals deserting to the Conservatives. Influential Liberals had refused to join the cabinet because of the Irish issue. One was Lord Hartington, whose brother, Lord Frederick Cavendish, was murdered in Dublin in 1882.

Gladstone: three times PM.

Liszt, genius, showman, lover, is dead

Liszt, who gave piano concerts from the age of 12, with family and friends.

Bayreuth, Bavaria, 31 July 1886

Franz Liszt, the greatest pianist of his day and one of Europe's greatest musical pioneers, died today aged 74. In Paris, about 1830, he was impressed by Paganini's virtuoso fireworks and by the musical poetry of Chopin. Flamboyant, vain, often arrogant, but also generous and kindly, Liszt was a great showman. He was the first to give solo piano recitals and would appear in all his many medals, throwing his gloves to the floor and tossing back his mane of hair before lunging at the keyboard. He had a long affair with a married countess (one daughter later ran off with Wagner) and another with a Polish princess.

He worked for a time in Weimar, promoting advanced composers such as Wagner, Schumann and Berlioz as well as his own extraordinary, forward-looking works. In later life he took minor holy orders and lived mainly in his native Hungary, but travelled, composed and taught right up to his death.

Liberty enlightens the world at New York

"Give me your tired, poor, huddled masses yearning to breath free."

New York, 28 October 1886
An imposing 300-foot high statue commemorating the friendship between the peoples of France and the United States was dedicated today by President Cleveland on Liberty Island at the entrance to New York harbour.

The statue of a woman holding a torch in her raised right hand and holding a tablet with the date of 4 July 1776 in her left is the brain-child of the French historian Edouard de Laboulaye. He proposed it after the American Civil War and funds poured in from all over France. The 225-ton structure made of hand-hammered copper sheets on a steel frame was assembled in France and then dismantled and shipped to America.

Canadian-Pacific railway crosses country

Canada, 7 November 1886
Five years ahead of schedule Mr Donald A Smith drove in the last spike today, and the Canadian Pacific railway is finished. Taking in 25 million acres of land, and financed with a government loan of $25 million, this magnificent feat of civil engineering is seen as the centre-piece of Canada's development.

It has already been of use, even before all the track was fully linked. Three years ago half-breed settlers in the north-west, fearing the effect on their lives of the rapidly expanding immigrant population, staged a rebellion against the authorities in Ottawa.

They drove off a small force of police, but the militia, carried swiftly along the new tracks, crushed the rebels completely.

Settlers on the Canadian-Pacific.

Western fancy dress ball shocks Japanese

Tokyo, April 1887
A fancy dress ball held earlier this month in the *Rokumeikan*, the pavilion built in the western style by the government, has shocked Tokyo, and the prime minister, Ito and his cabinet are being severely criticised for attending the event.

Ito argues that the social functions held in the pavilion bring the Japanese and the foreign community into a closer understanding and will help in the negotiations for

the revision of Japan's unequal treaties with the west. However, while most Japanese will listen politely to western music and talks on cooking and dressmaking, the sight of a leading official wearing fancy dress and dancing with a foreign woman is deemed degrading.

Even the interest in all things western and the hope of revising the treaties does not compensate for such a severe assault on Japan's ingrained sensibilities.

US union clashes kill 13

An impression of events in Chicago just before the bomb was thrown.

Chicago, 1886
An anarchist bomb that killed seven police and strikers and injured 60 more has seriously damaged the US's fast-growing trade union movement. Fears of an international conspiracy are rife, and membership of the "Knights of Labour", which had reached 750,000 in five years, is dwindling rapidly.

At a time of comparative prosperity, the Knights and socialist unions struck for an eight-hour day. On 3 May police killed six strikers at a harvester factory. On the following day, an anarchist – a member of the "Black International" movement led by a German, Johann Most – threw the bomb. The perpetrator was never found; but a judge ruled that those who incited the bombing were equally guilty, and sentenced seven men to death. One committed suicide, four were executed and the other two had their sentences commuted.

Despite popular revulsion against the wholly innocent Knights of Labour, at least one trade union organisation appears to be gathering strength in the United States. The American Federation of Labour (AFL) which was founded this year in New York, is the brain-child of the London-born Samuel

Justice crushing the Chicago Seven, sentenced to death for incitement.

Gompers, a former worker in an insanitary East Side cigar factory. The AFL is determinedly divorced from independent political action and aims to become a national federation of craft unions contending for the immediate objective of shorter hours and better wages. It will rely on salaried organisers and its own labour press to keep solidarity among its workers and, unlike the idealistic "Knights", it accepts capitalism as a reality.

1887 (1887-1888)

China, September 1887. Towards the end of the month the Yellow River bursts its southern banks at Zhengzhou (Henan) causing disastrous flooding over a large area.

India, 1 October 1887. Baluchistan, an area crucial to the British north-west frontier, is declared British territory and united with India.

France, October 1887. In order to sanction its policy of alliance with Germany, France breaks the Franco-Italian trade agreement and begins a price war. It is intensified by the new Italian prime minister, Francesco Crispi, who was appointed on 1 August, a few days after the death of Agostino Depretis.

Louisiana, 23 November 1887. At least 20 Negro workers are killed by members of the sheriff's posse as more violence erupts in the sugar cane workers' strike in Thibodaux.

France, 2 December 1887. President Jules Grevy resigns following the discovery of an illicit trade in medals organised by his son-in-law. He is replaced by Marie-Francois Sadi Carnot.

Germany, 1887. The biologist August Weismann perfects the chromosome theory of heredity.

Nigeria, 1887. Britain establishes its protectorate over the country on the initiative of George Taubman Goldie, the founder of the Royal Nigeria Company.

USA, 1887. The physicist Albert Michelson repeats an experiment that he had already carried out in 1881 to prove that "absolute space" does not exist. As he finds no evidence of the motion of the earth relative to ether, he states that the speed of light is the same in any given space, whatever the speed of the light source, the observer or the length of the wave.

Italy, 1887. Giuseppe Verdi completes his opera *Otello*.

Russia, 1887. Tchaikovsky composes his ballet *Swan Lake*.

India, 1887. The Parsi magnate J N Tata opens his Empress cotton mill at Nagpur. This is a major step forward for the Indian textile industry.

Congo Free State (Zaire), 1887. Tippu Tib, a Swahili slave-merchant, is made governor of the Stanley Falls district on behalf of the Belgian king, Leopold II.

France, 1887. Tolbert Lanston invents the monotype, a typesetting machine.

East Africa, 1887. King Lobengula of the Ndebele signs a treaty of friendship with Transvaal Boers.

France, 1887. The engineer Gustave Zede draws up the plans for the "Gymnote", a submarine weighing 30 tons, which travels at a speed of five knots underwater and seven on the surface.

Germany, 9 March 1888. The Emperor William dies and his only son, the crown prince, succeeds him as Frederick III.

South-East Asia, 17 March 1888. Britain establishes a protectorate over Sarawak in the Malayan archipelago.

South-East Asia, 12 May 1888. Britain establishes a protectorate over North Borneo.

Brazil, 13 May 1888. Slavery is abolished, despite fierce resistance by the planters, thanks to the efforts of two societies founded in Rio de Janeiro in 1880, the *Sociedade Brasileira contra a Escradidao* and the *Associacao Central Emancipacionista*.

Germany, 15 June 1888. On the death of Frederick III at Potsdam after a three-month reign, his son succeeds as Emperor William II.

Britain, 1888. After founding the Scottish Miners' Union, the miner James Keir Hardie decides to stand for election, breaking away from the Liberals to found the Scottish Labour Party, which includes both radicals and socialists. His election manifesto gives priority to demands for an eight-hour day and the need for working-class MPs.

Italy, 1888. The Crispi government reforms local and departmental administration. From now on the presidents of the departmental assemblies and the mayors of the largest communes are to be chosen by election.

Greenland, 1888. The Norwegian explorer Fridtjof Nansen crosses Greenland from east to west.

China, 1888. Earthquakes in Zhili and Shandong, and floods in Henan, Shandong and Zhili, result in the deaths of some 3.5 million people.

East Africa, 1888. The British East Africa Company, headed by Sir William MacKinnon, is granted a charter to develop British territory in the region.

USA, 1888. George Eastman perfects the first Kodak camera.

USA, 1888. Gunpowder is replaced by guncotton or nitrocellulose, a new explosive which burns more slowly but releases more hot gases and so is more powerful.

USA, 1888. Congress adopts the Allotment Act which makes provision for the dividing up of Indian reservations.

London rocked by "Bloody Sunday" riots

London, 13 November 1887
Two people have been fatally wounded and over 100 injured around Trafalgar Square after police and troops clashed with protesters demanding the removal of the ban on open-air meetings in the square and the release of the MP William O'Brien, a leading figure in the Irish rent strike. Several hundred people have been arrested, including two MPs. The worst of the clashes came as the police, heavily outnumbered, staged baton charges to disperse demonstrators trying to get into the square from Holborn, the Strand and Parliament Street. Eventually troops on horseback cleared the square. Had they failed, a magistrate was ready to read the Riot Act. Blame for the incident is being aimed at the commissioner of police, Sir Charles Warren, who imposed the ban on meetings.

New work for the anti-Wagner brahmins

Brahms who symbolised tradition as opposed to radical Wagner.

Vienna, 1887
A concerto for violin and cello has ben completed this year by the great German composer Brahms. His supporters, known as Brahmins, regard him as the standard-bearer of traditional music against the iconoclasm of Wagner.

In 1853 when he was 20 Brahms met the composer Schuman who wrote in his diary, "Brahms to see me (a genius)". Born in Hamburg, where, as a ten-year-old prodigy, he played in dockland brothels to boost the family income, Brahms settled in Vienna in the mid 1860s. The *German Requiem* of 1868 made him famous, but awed by Beethoven's, Brahms waited until 1876 to write his first symphony. A series of masterpieces followed, including three more symphonies and the second piano concerto.

Light travels fast, report scientists

USA, 1887
Using a sensitive optical instrument – the Michelson interferometer – two American scientists have succeeded in doing what many scientists have thought impossible: measuring the speed of light. The instrument compares the paths of two light beams moving at right-angles towards each other.

The velocity of light is 186,329 miles (299,835 kilometres) per second, and this speed is constant and unchangeable throughout the universe.

Fellow scientists have described the discovery as "perhaps the most important negative finding in the history of science".

Bismarck stirs spy furore in Lorraine

Paris, 30 April 1887
When the police commissioner, Guillaume Schnaebele, was arrested by the Germans and accused of spying, the French detected the hand of their old enemy Bismarck, and hotheads in the government wanted to go to war. President Jules Grevy, however, sent the Germans evidence that Schnaebele had actually been invited to cross into the German territory of Lorraine and promised safe conduct. Today, after mounting tension and reports of German mobilisation, the Germans admitted that they had tricked Schnaebele, and, released him. The French believe that Bismarck was testing their nerve.

Victoria enjoys Jubilee

Queen Victoria accepting congratulations on her Jubilee from the court.

London, 1887
For the splendid Jubilee Thanksgiving Service in Westminster Abbey, attended by over 50 royal highnesses and hundreds of lesser potentates, Queen Victoria refused to wear a crown and robes of state. She insisted on a bonnet of white lace trimmed with diamonds.

After the service, during which the choir sang her husband's hymn, *Gotha*, 30,000 children gathered in Hyde Park and were given bun, milk and Jubilee mugs. In the East End, where she opened the People's Palace, the queen was puzzled by "a horrid noise". She was told it was "booing", but it was only from socialists and Irish. After weeks of parades, presentations and parties,

Victoria wrote in her diary: "Never, never, can I forget this brilliant year, so full of marvellous kindness, loyalty and devotion of so many millions."

She has seen her people fashion the greatest empire in the history of the world. She has given her name to an age when Britain became the world's workshop and the British the umpire of world affairs, building railways, populating remote lands, curbing savage potentates and bestowing the *Pax Britannica*.

As the year drew to a close, it became apparent that the queen would not be returning to the old seclusion, so disliked by her subjects, into which she had retreated after her husband Albert's death.

Rhodes diamond empire

Cecil Rhodes the empire-builder.

Between them, in no-man's-land, stood a third company, the French Company. Which ever of the two capitalists controlled the French Company would control Kimberley, and thus control the world's diamond market. With money advanced by Rothchild's Bank in London, Rhodes won.

Rhodes denies that his motive is greed. He needs the profits from the Kimberley diamonds to finance a white man's homeland in southern Africa, one to be as loyal to the diamonds in the crown as to those in the ground. Both Rhodes' colleagues and enemies are sceptical.

The Kimberley diamond mine, 400 feet (130 metres) deep. Once Kimberley was divided into small claim; now it is dominated by one man.

Kimberley, South Africa, 1887
Here, in the boom town that Anthony Trollope called "the ugliest place in the world", the bitterest financial battle in the history of Black Africa has been fought and won by the millionaire Cecil Rhodes. "Some people have a fancy for this, and some for that," the loser, Barney Barnato, told Rhodes. "You've a fancy for making an empire."

The rush for diamonds began after a rich find was made in an area of seven square miles in 1871. There were soon 3,600 small claims. Within 16 years the diamond field was dominated by two companies, Barney's Central Company and Cecil Rhodes' De Beers.

Nationalist music flourishes in Russia

Rimsky-Korsakov, who was a naval officer before turning to music.

Russia, 1888
Two new works by Nikolai Rimsky-Korsakov, *Capriccio Espagnol* and *Sheherezade*, prove how Russian nationalist music has flourished in recent decades. Glinka (1804-57) led the way, and his protege, Balakirev, now aged 51, led a group known as "The Five". The towering genius of Mussorgsky (1839-81), an alcoholic and ex-army officer, contrasted with the lyricism of Borodin (1833-87), the bastard son of a prince and also a great chemist. Rimsky, now aged 44, an ex-naval officer, and Cesar Cui, now aged 53, completed the quintet.

Bulgaria frustrates Russian intrigues

Bulgaria, 1887
Prince Ferdinand of Coburg has been elected ruler of Bulgaria, and recognised by Britain. His accession confirms Bulgaria's independence from Russia and the Ottoman empire. Since the Treaty of Berlin nine years ago, North and South Bulgaria have come together in a surge of nationalist pride, frustrating Russian intrigue, beating off a Serbian invasion and winning the acceptance of the Ottoman sultan.

When Russia kidnapped the Bulgarian Prince Alexander and tried to postpone elections, it only increased popular support for the rebel leader Stambulov, who has become an effective dictator.

Having ruled successfully in conjunction with the three regents appointed by Alexander as his successors, Stambulov has defied the Russians, who have broken off diplomatic relations. Sultan Abdul Hamid, in spite of Russian overtures, has refused to invoke his sovereign right of entry.

Britain now sees Bulgaria as a bulwark against Russian expansionism, hails Stambulov as the "Bulgarian Bismarck", and welcomes Ferdinand of Coburg, a relation of Queen Victoria.

1888 (1888-1889)

Britain, 6 August 1888. The Local Government Act establishes elected county councils.

Ottoman Empire, August 1888. A railway line is opened between Hungary and Istanbul.

Zimbabwe, 30 October 1888. Lobengula, the king of the Matabele, agrees to the Rudd Concession, which grants exclusive mineral rights in Matabeleland and Mashonaland to a syndicate headed by Cecil Rhodes.

Ottoman Empire. A German bank is granted the concession to start the Berlin-to-Baghdad railway.

Russia, October 1888. Russia acquires a large loan from France in order to finance industrial expansion.

USA, 6 November 1888. Benjamin Harrison, a Republican and the grandson of a former president, wins the presidential election, defeating Grover Cleveland, the present Democratic incumbent of the White House.

China, November 1888. The first railway in China, from Tanghshan to Tianjin, is opened.

East Africa, December 1888. The British agree to mount a naval blockade to help the Germans crush Moslem resistance on the German East African coast.

South Africa, 1888. Paul Kruger is re-elected president of the Transvaal.

Germany, 1888. The physicist Heinrich Hertz discovers electromagnetic waves.

Russia, 1888. The composer Tchaikovsky completes his fifth symphony.

France, 1888. The Dutch artist Vincent van Gogh moves to Arles, Provence, where he paints *Sunflowers*, *The Drawbridge*, *Yellow Chair and Pipe* and *The Cafe Terrace*.

West Africa, 10 January 1889. France declares a protectorate over the Ivory Coast.

France, 27 January 1889. General Georges Boulanger, the former war minister who has become the rallying force for disaffected radicals, fails in his attempt to provoke a "crisis" in Paris.

Austria, 30 January 1889. Archduke Rudolf, the liberal crown prince of the Austrian empire, commits suicide with his mistress, Marie Vetsera, at Mayerling. Archduke Franz Ferdinand, the emperor's nephew, becomes the heir.

Japan, 11 February 1889. A new constitution, which safeguards the powers of the emperor, is promulgated.

Britain, February 1889. Richard Pigott, an Irish journalist, admits forging politically damaging letter purporting to be from Charles Parnell, the leader of the Irish home rule group of MPs.

USA, 2 March 1889. Kansas becomes the first state to pass a law regulating trusts.

USA, 2 March 1889. Congress proclaims the entire Bering Sea, an important seal-breeding area, to be under US control.

Serbia, 6 March 1889. After a series of political mistakes and financial extravagances, Milan Obrenovic abdicates in favour of his 12-year-old son, Alexander.

Ethiopia, 10 March 1889. Following the death of John IV in battle against the Mahdists, Menelik, king of Shoa, proclaims himself emperor of Ethiopia.

USA, 1 May 1889. Asa Briggs Candler of Atlanta buys the rights to a local drink, Coca-Cola.

Britain, 31 May 1889. The Naval Defence Act is passed to meet the growing sea power of Russia and France.

Pennsylvania, 31 May 1889. Johnstown, in south-central Pennsylvania, is washed off the map by a flood. Deaths are estimated at about 2,000.

Germany, May 1889. Bismarck clashes with Kaiser William II over the handling of a strike of 90,000 miners in the Ruhr district. The chancellor wants to send in the army, but the kaiser is in favour of compromise.

Pacific, 14 June 1889. Following a conflict between Germany and the USA over the control of the Samoan Islands, Germany, the USA and Britain sign a treaty guaranteeing the independence and neutrality of the islands under the surveillance of the three powers, and the return of Chief Malietoa.

France, 17 July 1889. A law is passed banning multiple candidacies at elections.

London, 19 August 1889. A strike by 30,000 London dockers begins.

Germany, August 1889. The Social Democrats set up a miners' union.

South Africa, 1889. A chamber of mines is founded to provide a regular labour supply for the gold mines of Witwatersrand.

Britain, 1889. The Irish writer and socialist George Bernard Shaw edits a collection of *Fabian Essays* for the Fabian Society.

Ethiopia 1889. The Italians claim that the treaty of Ucciali with Emperor Menelik recognises Italian paramountcy over Ethiopia.

Thespian sex with servant causes outrage

Strindberg: accused of threatening the moral values of Swedish society.

Stockholm, 1888
A new play just published by August Strindberg, *Miss Julie*, the theme of which is a sexual liaison between a young lady of good birth and her father's valet, is causing the usual scandal that attaches to the author. Last year in *The Father* he dramatised the in-fighting of a marriage – thought to reflect his own to his actress wife, Siri von Essen, who is to play Miss Julie in a forthcoming production.

"No uglier, more revolting scene has ever been presented in a Danish theatre," was one Copenhagen review. Strindberg himself is the son of a housemaid and has written the story of his unhappy childhood in *A Servant's Son*.

Coca-Cola cures hysteria in the female

Atlanta, Georgia, 1889
Dr John Styth Pemberton, an Atlanta pharmacist, puzzled for weeks before coming up with a name for the fizzy drink which he had invented. It started life as "French wine of Coca – an ideal Nerve Tonic and Stimulant". Apart from being too long, it was hardly likely to attract thirsty teetotallers.

Pemberton repaired to his laboratory, removed the alcohol from the liquid and added caffeine-rich essence of cola nut. The resulting drink still did not go very well; despite claims that Pemberton's drink cures everything from head colds to "hysteria in the female", only 13 glasses a day were sold at the pharmacy as it competed with products like "Imperial Inca Cola" and "Coca Coffee".

It was Pemberton's book-keeper, Frank Robinson, who came up with the name. He called it "Coca-Cola" and designed a logo which was printed for the first time this year in the *Atlanta Journal*.

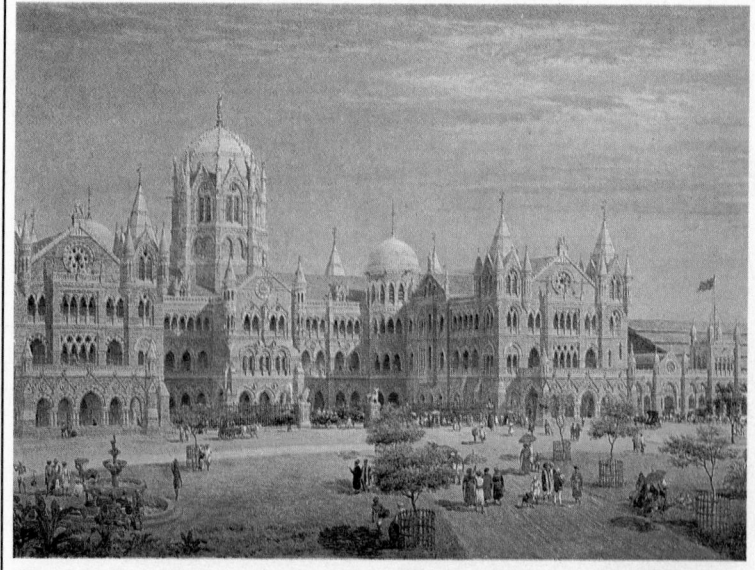

The British "raj" at its most vulgar and splendid: the Indian Peninsular Railway Terminus at Bombay, a brutal synthesis of Norman, Perpendicular and Moghul styles held together by cold steel. The terminus has been hailed as a symbol of the enduring quality of British rule in India.

Austria's archduke dies in suicide pact

Vienna, 30 January 1889
Archduke Rudolf, the crown prince of Austria, committed suicide today with his 17-year-old mistress, Baroness Marie Vetsara, at the hunting lodge of Mayerling.

Rudolf, unhappy in his arranged marriage to Stephanie, the daughter of the king of the Belgians, and unable to marry the lovely Marie, was also frustrated by his father's refusal to listen to his liberal plans for the future of the empire.

It is believed that his profound depression over these matters led to his shooting Marie and then turning the gun on himself. But already rumours are rife that he was murdered to prevent his succession to the throne.

Marie Vetsara, wearing the clothes that she always wore at Mayerling.

Scots writer seeks South Sea warmth

Robert Louis Stevenson and family, with islanders and a naval brass band.

Samoa, December 1889
Robert Louis Stevenson has arrived here after 18 months spent sailing across the South Sea by way of the Marquesas, Tahiti and the Gilbert Islands. With his American wife, Fanny, and his stepson, Lloyd Osbourne, he has decided to build a home among the forested hills. He is delighted with the islanders.

Stevenson has suffered from lung trouble, thought to be tuberculosis, since his youth in Edinburgh and has travelled frequently in search of a kinder climate. He is more famous in the US than in his own country. *Dr Jekyll and Mr Hyde*, his story exploring a man's double identity, one half good, the other evil, has had a great success on the New York stage. He returned to the subject of a man possessed by evil in *The Master of Ballantrae*, which he finished in Tahiti. His adventure stories *Treasure island* and *Kidnapped*, originally written as serials for a boys' paper, are now achieving popularity as novels.

Guns win mining rights

Bulawayo, 30 October 1888
Lobengula, the chief or king of the Matabele people, today signed an agreement with Cecil Rhodes' partner, Charles Rudd, giving mineral rights in Matabeleland and Mashonaland.

In return for this, Rudd has promised to give Lobengula 1,000 Martin-Henry breech-loading rifles, ammunition, a gunboat to patrol the Zambezi river and a monthly rent of $200.

This "Rudd Concession" is not all that it seems, however, for one of its terms grants the concessionaires "full power to do all things that they may deem necessary to win and procure the minerals". There seems little doubt that Rhodes will interpret that clause in the widest possible sense.

It means that Lobengula, who made the concession in the hope of preserving his land against the depredations of the aggressive colonialists, has, in fact, opened it up to them.

The chief was led into this decision by three of his senior chiefs who were bribed by the white men. He took their advice rather than that of the young men who wanted to fight any incursion by the would-be colonisers.

Lobengula certainly has no illusions about the British. He asks: "Did you ever see a chameleon catch a fly? The chameleon gets behind the fly and remains motionless for some time, then he advances very slowly and gently, first putting one leg and then another."

"At last, when well within reach, he darts his tongue and the fly disappears. England is the chameleon and I am that fly."

Cecil Rhodes: the empire-builder.

Lobengula: the king of the Matabele.

British footballers form players' league

London, September 1888
In a major expansion of the fixture list, football clubs in the north and midlands of England have decided to play matches under a league system. The new system is intended to generate more interest in the game and guarantee regular matches for the increasing number of professional players. Clubs in the league have agreed to play each other twice in the season, once at each ground, and have guaranteed – subject to penalties – to field their best teams in each match.

The additional games will allow clubs to spend more on players. Recently clubs have begun to pay wages and expenses to key players so that they can afford time off work to train for important games. The new league plans to be independent of the Football Association, the game's governing body.

1889 (1889-1890)

London, 14 September 1889. The London dock strike, which has ended today, has given rise to a widespread movement of international solidarity.

Washington, DC, 2 October 1889. The first International Conference of American States, organised by the secretary of state, James Blaine, opens.

Germany, 20 October 1889. Gerhardt Hauptmann presents his play *Before Dawn*, introducing a new theatrical realism into Germany.

South Africa, 29 October 1889. Britain grants a charter to the British South Africa Company, under Cecil Rhodes, to colonise Bechuanaland and other parts of southern Africa.

Istanbul, 29 October 1889. Britain, Germany, France, Austria, Spain, Italy, the Netherlands, Russia and the Ottoman empire sign a convention declaring the Suez Canal neutral and open to all ships in wartime as well as peacetime.

USA, 11 November 1889. The territories of Washington, Montana and North and South Dakota are admitted to the union as states.

Brazil, November 1889. following the deposition of the Emperor Pedro II in an army *coup*, a republic is proclaimed and a provisional government is set up.

Britain, 12 December 1889. Robert Browning, the author of *The Pied Piper of Hamelin* and *The Ring and the Book*, dies. In 1846 he married Elizabeth Barrett, whose *Sonnets* and *Aurora Leigh* were reckoned superior to her husband's work.

Chicago, December 1889. Construction of the Auditorium Building, designed by Louis Sullivan and Dankmar Adler, is completed. The ten-storey opera auditorium is topped by a 17-storey tower.

Sudan, 1889. The American explorer Henry Stanley leads an expedition to "rescue" Emin Pasha, the German-born governor of Egyptian Equatorial Sudan, reputed to be trapped in the province by enemies. The true purpose of the mission, largely financed by Leopold of the Belgians, is to stake a claim of an outlet to the upper Nile for the Congo state.

Crete, 1889. The Ottomans put down a Greek-backed rebellion in the island.

France, 1889. The company formed to build a canal through the isthmus of Panama, headed by Ferdinand de Lesseps, collapses as a result of corruption and mismanagement.

France, 1889. The philosopher Henri Bergson publishes *Time and Free Will: an Essay on the Immediate Data of Conscience*.

Italy, 1889. Gabriele d'Annunzio publishes *The Child of Pleasure*, the first volume of his *Romances of the Rose*.

Paris, 1889. Gustave Eiffel builds the Eiffel Tower.

Germany, 1889. The American markswoman Annie Oakley, touring Europe with the Buffalo Bill Wild West Show, proves her prowess by shooting a cigar from Kaiser William II's mouth.

USA, 31 January 1890. John Duke of North Carolina combines five of the largest tobacco manufacturers in the USA to form the American Tobacco Company.

USA, 18 February 1890. The National American Women's Suffrage Association is formed.

Germany, 20 February 1890. In the legislative elections, the Conservatives lose a third of their seats to the Liberals, the Social Democrats and, in particular, the Catholic Centre Party.

Germany, February 1890. In a growing rift between Bismarck and William II, the chancellor refuses to sign the kaiser's proclamation proposing an international conference on social questions.

Germany, 27 March 1890. Germany decides not to renew the Reinsurance Treaty concluded with Russia in June 1887. Under the treaty the two powers agreed to remain neutral in any conflict other than an Austro-Russian or Franco-German dispute.

Berlin, March 1890. The first international conference on job protection is held.

USA, 2 May 1890. The federal territory of Oklahoma, formerly known as the Indian Territory, is created.

Italy, 17 May 1890. The composer Pietro Mascagni wins fame with his one-act opera *Cavalleria Rusticana*.

Ethiopia, May 1890. The Italians proclaim a protectorate over the Red Sea coast (*Eritrea*).

Australia, 1890. Responsible government is established in Western Australia.

Germany, 1890. The bacteriologist Emil von Behring discovers the diphtheria and tetanus viruses.

Germany, 1890. The poet Stefan George founds a poetical journal called *Blatter fur die Kunst*.

Spain, 1890. Universal suffrage is adopted.

Armed uprising forces king to abdicate

Brazil, 16 November 1889
The 49-year rule of Pedro II, during which Brazil has enjoyed an unprecedented degree of stability and progress, is over. The emperor has abdicated following a military coup and will leave for Europe.

Pedro's rule has been characterised by his intelligence, backed by appointing excellent advisers. He balanced the country's warring interest groups and maintained good relations abroad. The economy prospered and Pedro helped to open up the country with railways and other forms of communication. For all his popularity, he became increasingly isolated from Brazil's most powerful groups: the army, which felt it would receive greater powers under a republic, and the emergent middle class. The turning point came with his abolition of slavery.

The landowners resented the lack of compensation, while the middle class wanted the process to go much faster. Pedro, ever liberal, refused to suppress his opponents: now they have chosen to usurp his power.

Satirical Mexican engravers beat censor

One of Poseda's lithographs depicting Mexico's tragedies, ironies and fantasies.

Mexico, 1889
Despite attempts by successive governments to censor them, Mexican artists are creating a lively tradition of satirical illustrations, best seen in the current crop of cheap new illustrated papers and popular broadsides known as *calaveras* and *corridas*.

Foremost among these satirists is Jose Guadalupe Posada, a 37-year-old lithographer whose work has been appearing since 1871. Posada mixes his undoubted graphical ability with telling satires on government and society, all of which are released by the Arroyo publishing house.

Capitalising on new technology, he has extended his skills to every type of printing and is responsible for the new technique of etching on zinc. Posada's output of illustrations easily exceeds 10,000.

Briton turns economics into a science

Cambridge, 1890
Alfred Marshall, the professor of political economy at the university here, has just published the first volume of a massive work, *Principles of Economics*, which goes a long way towards establishing economics as a science. Marshall's first discipline was mathematics and he was elected to a fellowship in that subject at St John's College in 1865. Two years later he began to apply his scientific mind to economics.

Marshall has introduced new concepts such as elasticity and welfare economics, and shows how they can be measured. He believes that the theory is now well established and that further progress will come from practical applications.

Popular French leader flees the country

Boulanger presents his credentials while assorted politicians dance to his tune.

Paris, 8 April 1889
General Georges Boulanger, with his blond beard and white horse, captured the imagination of many Frenchmen bored with grey politicians, but now he has fled to Belgium to avoid arrest on charges of attempting to overthrow the state.

Support for this former minister of war came from the discontented of all classes. He cultivated the private soldier and ignored the generals. He connived with every opposition party, accepting vast sums from the royalists while preaching radicalism. Even his vanity and ambition appealed to voters sickened by the scandals and squabbles that tarnish the reputations of more moderate politicians. He became "the man on the white horse" and, although the prime minister, Floquet, told him "at your age, General, Napoleon was dead" he posed a severe threat to the third republic. No longer. His flight must shatter his charisma and his power.

Eiffel's towering achievement stuns Paris

Paris, 1889
Parisians are divided over the world's tallest building, bestowed on their city to commemorate this year's centennial of the French Revolution. No-one doubts that the Eiffel Tower, the new 984-foot (289-metre)-high landmark alongside the Seine, is a unique technological masterpiece. It is its aesthetic value that is is in doubt. Artists and writers, including Dumas and Maupassant, have signed a protest comparing the tower to a "gigantic black factory chimney" and labelling it "a dishonour to the city".

The controversy has confirmed the wrought-iron open-latticework tower as the city's most popular tourist attraction. One of its main draws is the glass-cage lifts that travel on a curve on each of the four semicircular arches at the base.

Eiffel, with his engineer, above Paris.

Tourists benefit Gustave Eiffel, who designed the competition-winning monument. Under the rules he gets the profits from the tower for the next 20 years.

The white man rushes for Indian lands

Oklahoma, 22 April 1889
At noon precisely, a government official raised his gun and fired a single shot. The great race for land was on as thousands of settlers headed west into territory that was once home to 75,000 Indians. They swarmed over the border in covered wagons, carriages, hacks, on horseback, on bicycles and on foot.

It is estimated that more than 200,000 people had crossed over the state borders from Texas and Kansas by nightfall and that almost every one of the two million acres of the Oklahoma district had been claimed and settled.

President Harrison has finally succumbed to pressure from the US's "Boomers" – railroad executives and real-estate agents, together with farmers seeking their 160 acres of free land.

The idea of the land race was to ensure fair play. Law enforcement officers have been hard pressed to ensure that "sooners" who tried to beat the gun have not snatched up the prime plots.

Now, as neighbour fights neighbour over water-rights and rich "cattle barons" are using hired gunmen to oust homesteaders, many dreams are fast becoming nightmares for Oklahoma's new settlers, and the land is no more than a fading memory for the Indians who have moved on westwards.

Dockers' victory is union breakthrough

London, 14 September 1889
Striking dock workers today claimed victory in a month-long dispute after the employers conceded the strikers' main demand for sixpence an hour – the docker's tanner.

The strike victory is a major breakthrough for the new unionism espoused by the dockers' leaders Ben Tillett, John Burns and Tom Mann, all active socialists. Their strategy of persuading 10,000 men to come out together, ignore trade differences and take political action through marches and protests followed the pattern set by the gasworkers in their recent dispute.

Despite the damage to trade, the strike has had massive public support. Over £50,000 has been contributed to the strike fund, allowing the men to draw strike pay, while the employers have found

Marching for the docker's tanner.

blackleg labour scarce. Even the City has backed the dockers in their fight against casualisation, which is seen as unfairly penalising men who want to do an honest day's work.

Germans gain from Bismarck's social laws

Berlin, 22 June 1889
Bismarck's welfare programme for workers was completed today when the *reichstag* passed his bill to provide old age pensions and disability insurance. In the past six years accident and health insurance schemes have been established, with employers contributing one-third of the cost and employees two-thirds.

Initially, Bismarck wanted to set up a central government department to administer all welfare schemes, so that the workers would see who was really helping them and become loyal supporters of the *reich*, instead of falling prey to the socialists. But the Catholic Centre Party was opposed to the growth of big government, and the Liberals disliked welfare legislation because it smacked of socialism and undermined the self-reliance of the workers, so schemes are being administered at local level. Bismarck thinks that his welfare schemes have failed. The workers' lot may be eased, but they still support the socialists.

Berlin, 1 July 1890. Germany and Britain sign the Heligoland treaty, by which Germany gives up claims in East Africa, including Zanzibar, in return for the British island of Heligoland, off the Elbe estuary.

Washington, DC, 2 July 1890. The Sherman Anti-Trust Act, banning trade monopolies, is passed.

Brussels, 2 July 1890. An International Convention for the Suppression of the African Slave Trade is signed.

USA, 10 July 1890. Wyoming becomes the 44th state in the union.

South Africa, 17 July 1890. Cecil Rhodes becomes prime minister of Cape Colony.

France, 5 August 1890. Britain signs an agreement with France recognising Madagascar as a French protectorate, in exchange for the recognition of Zanzibar as a British protectorate. In West Africa, France gives up the lower Niger and retains the desert territories of the Sahara.

New York City, 6 August 1890. New York introduces a new form of capital punishment: the electric chair.

Mashonaland (Zimbabwe), 12 September 1890. The British South Africa Company founds the town of Salisbury (*Harare*), at the end of a pioneer march from South Africa.

Germany, 30 September 1890. The anti-socialist laws are revoked. The free unions combine to form the General Commission of German Unions.

Russia, 4 November 1890. Alexander Borodin's opera *Prince Igor* is performed for the first time.

Algeria, 12 November 1890. In an address to a gathering of naval officers, Cardinal Charles Lavigerie urges all French citizens to support the republican regime.

South Dakota, December 1890. The US Seventh Cavalry kills 153 Minneconjou Sioux at Wounded Knee.

Britain, December 1890. Charles Parnell is forced to resign as leader of the Irish party at Westminster after being cited as co-respondent in the O'Shea divorce case.

USA, 1890. The posthumous publication of Emily Dickinson's *Poems* wins her a reputation as the first lady of American verse. She died in 1886 after living as a recluse for 25 years and keeping her talent hidden throughout her life.

USA, 1890. The Harvard professor William James, the brother of the novelist Henry James, publishes *The Principles of Psychology*.

New York City, 1890. The McLeod American Pneumatic Company instals a system of air circulation which provides warmth in winter and cool air in summer.

New York City, 1890. The National Carbon Company markets the first commercial dry-cell batteries under the brand name "Ever Ready".

Britain, 1890. Construction is completed of a railway bridge – described by the poet and artist William Morris as "the supremest specimen of all ugliness" – across the Firth of Forth in Scotland. At 1,700 feet, its span is the longest so far in the world.

Britain, 1890. The mathematician John Venn produces a diagram which facilitates work on sets.

Hawaii, 29 January 1891. Following the death of her brother King Dalakaua, Princess Liliuokalani is proclaimed queen.

Brazil, 24 February 1891. A constitution similar to that of the USA is adopted.

New Orleans, 14 March 1891. A mob breaks into a New Orleans prison and executes 11 reputed Mafia members suspected of killing the city's police chief.

New York City, 4 April 1891. Edwin Booth, America's greatest actor, retires after a performance of Hamlet.

Ethiopia, 15 April 1891. Britain signs a second treaty with Italy, supplementing one signed last month, recognising borders of a would-be Italian protectorate over Ethiopia.

France, 1 May 1891. Troops open fire on a crowd of demonstrating workers at Fourmies, killing women and children.

Germany, 6 May 1891. The triple alliance between Germany, Austria and Italy is renewed.

China, 13 May 1891. In the belief that the missionaries were kidnapping children, a mob destroys the Catholic mission premises at Wuhu in Anhui province and attacks various Protestant missions.

Rome, 15 May 1891. Pope Leo XIII publishes an encyclical on the condition of workers, applying Christian principles to relations between capital and labour.

Zaire, May 1891. Fearing British annexation from the south, Belgian forces attack the Garenganze kingdom in the copper-rich province of Katanga.

Zimbabwe, 10 June 1891. Dr Leander Starr Jameson, a friend of Cecil Rhodes, becomes administrator of the British South Africa Company's territories.

Young kaiser dismisses old Bismarck

Berlin, 18 March 1890

When the crown prince became Kaiser William II at the age of 29 he said of his chancellor: "I shall let the old man snuffle on for six months, then I shall rule myself." In fact, Bismarck survived for a year and a half.

He treated the young kaiser with contempt, remaining at his country retreat, riding, reminiscing over enormous dinners about his past triumphs, and rarely visiting Berlin. He lost support in the *reichstag* and tried to inveigle William into staging a coup to govern without popularly-elected deputies. The kaiser, seeking popularity by backing labour reforms, said he would not start by shooting Germans. Bismarck invoked a "red scare", talking of strikes and civil war.

The end came when the kaiser called at the ministry for a frank talk and found Bismarck still in bed. William, a wilful young man, self-conscious because of his withered left arm, demanded the old man's resignation. Bismarck spent three days composing a letter full of self-justification. The new chancellor is Count von Caprivi.

"Dropping the Pilot", by John Tenniel.

Congress bans unfair trade agreements

"The Menace of the Hour": George Luks' protest at growing monopolies.

Washington, 2 July 1890

With more than 90 per cent of the US's oil industry in the hands of the Rockefeller family, and sugar, wheat and alcohol prices governed by equally mysterious "trusts", the US government was forced to act today against the monopolies and cartels which threaten the entire economic structure of the country.

A judge, Mr Justice Harlan, summed up the feelings of millions of Americans. "The nation had been rid of human slavery," he said, "but the conviction was universal that the country was in real danger from another kind of slavery, namely the slavery that would result from the aggregation of capital in the hands of a few." Today's Anti-Trust Act forbids "trusts" or similar conspiracies which restrain trade among the states, and declares attempts to monopolise commerce to be illegal. Whether or not the act will work is doubtful; some believe that it will help those who seek to evade the law.

Indians butchered at Wounded Knee

South Dakota, December 1890
The United States Seventh Cavalry has called it a battle, but few believe that the Sioux Chief Bigfoot's few half-starved braves were capable of serious resistance to heavily armed soldiers with artillery support. It was a massacre which left 153 Sioux, half of them women and children, dead in the Dakota snow.

It was a vision of an Indian holy man, Wovoka, which brought the rival Sioux tribes together. The holy man had predicted that if his people fasted and danced in a circle around a sacred tree, their dead brothers would rise again and lead them to good hunting grounds.

Worried that the Ghost Dance religion would bind tribes that had warred for centuries, the 5,000 cavalry moved into the reservation.

An attempt by Sioux police, loyal to the government, to arrest Chief Sitting Bull, a firm believer in the Ghost Dance, ended in the shooting of that veteran leader. Hearing of this, Chief Big Foot moved 350 of his people through the snow to their old camp on the Cheyenne river. The Sioux refused to hand over their weapons. The army opened fire with four cannons on a distant hillside, accounting for most of the women and children. Army casualties are said to be 25.

The burial of the dead, after another "victory" by the Seventh Cavalry.

Queen Victoria gives kaiser a mountain

Berlin, 1 July 1890
The colonial rivalry between Germany and Britain in East Africa and the naval rivalry between the two powers in the North Sea have been resolved. Britain is to have the island of Zanzibar and the East African interior north of it as far as the Congo; Germany is to have all the interior to the south, and the island of Heligoland in the North Sea.

As a special concession to Queen Victoria, the East African border will be additionally redrawn to give Germany Mount Kilimanjaro. The queen was anxious for this since the kaiser, her grandson William, had no mountains in Africa. The German chancellor, von Caprivi, is jubilant. In return for the loss of its economic influence in Zanzibar, Germany has gained a colony, a naval base, a possible ally against France and Russia – and an extinct volcano.

Van Gogh, beset by gloom, kills himself

The face of suffering: a self-portrait, after he had sliced off part of his ear.

Auvers-sur-Oise, 29 July 1890
A Dutch painter called Vincent van Gogh died here in France today, after shooting himself in the chest two days ago. He had been living under the supervision of Dr Paul Gachet, an amateur painter, after being released from a mental hospital at St Remy, Provence. His brother, Theo van Gogh, who is an art dealer with the firm of Goupil et Cie, reports his last words as "the sadness will never end".

A few days ago he completed an ominous painting of a wheatfield under threatening skies, in which lurid golden corn is overhung by blue cloud and black low-flying crows. In Arles, two winters ago, he shared a house with Paul Gauguin, another painter, but after a quarrel in which he threatened him with a razor, van Gogh cut off part of his own ear and nearly died as a result.

He showed two pictures at the Salon des Independants – *Irises* and *Starry Night* – causing bewilderment. He has only sold one painting – at a gallery in Brussels. A recent article in the *Mercure de France*, however, suggests that one day his mystical and original art may become fashionable, although it seems unlikely today.

Troops open fire on striking French miners, killing two children

Fourmies, 1 May 1891
Nine factory workers, including two children, died and about 60 more were injured today when French troops opened fire on strikers from the Sans Pareille factory in the streets of Fourmies. The incident, the most violent so far in the French workers' campaign for an eight-hour day, has sparked widespread protests among workers in northern France.

In many places the dead are already being honoured as martyrs in the worldwide workers' movement for a shorter working week. The killings are likely to harden support for left-wing candidates at the next general election. Among those standing is Paul Lafargue, Karl Marx' son-in-law.

1891 (1891-1892)

Mozambique, 1st June 1891. Portugal and Britain sign an agreement settling their territorial disputes around Lake Malawi.

Britain, June 1891. Edward, the prince of Wales, the eldest son of Queen Victoria, causes a scandal by appearing as a prosecution witness in the Tranby Croft case, about gambling irregularities. Edward, the leader of the rich and sophisticated "Marlborough House set", has been virtually excluded by his mother from royal political responsibilities.

Southern Africa, 31 July 1891. Britain declares territories north of the Zambezi, up to the Congo basin, to be within its sphere of influence.

Russia, July 1891. a French squadron visits Kronstadt, and France and Russia open negotiations on an alliance.

Russia, 27 August 1891. France and Russia sign an *entente* by which each power agrees to consult the other if threatened by outside aggression.

Chile, 19 September, 1891. Jose Manuel Balmaceda, who was elected president of Chile in 1886, commits suicide after the defeat of his forces in a civil war.

Brussels, 30 September 1891. General Georges Boulanger, who attempted to lead a radical uprising in Paris in 1889, commits suicide.

Germany, October 1891. The Social Democratic Party adopts a Marxist programme at its Erfurt conference.

Britain, October 1891. At their party conference in Newcastle, the Liberals adopt a new programme which, as well as Irish home rule, includes disestablishment of the Welsh and Scottish churches, extension of the Employers' Liability Act, restriction on working hours and the abolition of plural voting.

Germany, 14 December 1891. The illustrated magazine *Berliner Illustrierte* begins publication.

Congo (Zaire), 20 December 1891. Belgian Congo forces kill Msiri, the king of the Garenganze kingdom which controls the copper mines of Katanga.

China, December 1891. The government puts down an uprising in Manchuria by the Golden Elixir Sect which began last month. The rebels employed both anti-Qing and anti-foreign slogans and attacked foreign churches.

Russia, 1891. Work starts on the building of a Trans-Siberian railway which will link the Ural mountains with the port of Vladivostok.

Russia, 1891. Thousands of Jews are evicted from Moscow and forced into ghettoes.

USA, 1891. A new slide fastener known as a "zipper" is patented.

USA, 1891. Herman Melville, the author of *Moby Dick* and other classic novels, dies.

USA, 1891. William Burroughs is granted a patent for an "adding machine".

Germany, 1891. Frank Wedekind's play *The Awakening of Spring*, dealing with the sexual awakening of three adolescents, provokes a scandal.

Germany, 1891. Edmund Husserl publishes *The Philosophy of Arithmetic*.

Germany, 1891. The Norwegian playwright Henrik Ibsen completes his *Hedda Gabler*.

Britain, 1891. Oscar Wilde publishes a novel entitled *The Portrait of Dorian Gray*.

Britain, 1891. Arthur Conan Doyle publishes *The Adventures of Sherlock Holmes*.

Britain, 1891. The novelist Thomas Hardy publishes *Tess of the d'Urbervilles*.

France, 1891. Jean Rey and Jules Carpentier invent the periscope, making submarine navigation possible.

New York City, 1 January 1892. An office is opened on Ellis Island to cope with the vast flood of immigrants to the USA, many of them fleeing from political and racial persecution in Russia and Central Europe.

Egypt, 7 January 1892. Abbas Hilmi succeeds his father, the weak and pro-British Tewfik, as *khedive* of Egypt.

Germany, 1 February 1892. Georg von Caprivi, who succeeded Bismarck as chancellor, signs commercial treaties with Austria, Italy, Belgium and Switzerland.

Rome, 16 February 1892. Pope Leo XIII publishes an encyclical encouraging French Catholics to support the French republic.

Italy, 21 May 1892. The composer Ruggiero Leoncavallo presents his opera *I Pagliacci*.

Nebraska, 4 July 1892. The People's Party, formed as an alliance of farmers, holds its first national convention.

USA, July 1892. Federal troops are sent in to break up a miners' strike in Idaho, caused by a 15 per cent cut in wages.

Russia, 17 August 1892. Russia signs a military convention with France.

All the world is Sarah Bernhardt's stage

Paris, 1891
Sarah Bernhardt has set off on the most ambitious of her world tours, including South America and Australia in her itinerary. The French actress' first visit to London in 1879 with the Comedie Francaise was marked by her triumph as Racine's Phedre. Besides this role, audiences clamour to see her as Marguerite Gautier in *La Dame aux Camellias*, dramatised from his novel by Alexandre Dumas the younger.

In the last decade she has scored her greatest triumphs in melodramas written for her by Victorien Sardou: *Fedora*, *La Tosca* and last year *Cleopatre*.

Sarah Bernhardt, aged 33, in 1876.

Walt Whitman, bearded bard of US life

Whitman: the poet of the New World.

New York City, 26 March 1892
Few writers have managed to capture the exuberance of this fast-growing young country more than Walt Whitman, the poet, who died here today aged 73. Whitman had been a newspaperman until he published a set of mystical, sensual poems under the title *Leaves of Grass*. Although intellectuals like Thoreau and Emerson hailed it as a work of genius, the book fell like a lead weight from the press. Few readers could understand it, and many of those who could were shocked by the homosexual undertones. But in poems like *Song of the Broadaxe* Whitman expressed the United States as it is, vibrant and burgeoning.

Tempestuous poet dies after leg cut off

Marseilles, 10 November 1891
The death of Arthur Rimbaud here at the age of 37, after the amputation of a leg, brings his precocious and scandalous career to an end. He ran away from his birthplace, Charleville, to Paris at 15 and again at 16, when he stayed with the symbolist poet, Paul Verlaine. Later Verlaine left his wife to live with Rimbaud in London. Theirs was a stormy relationship and during one of Rimbaud's attempts to leave, Verlaine shot him, wounding him in the wrist, and was imprisoned. It was from this phase of his life that Rimbaud distilled his magical prose poems, *Les Illuminations*.

Arthur Rimbaud: an unpoetic death.

US sky "scraped" by lofty buildings

St Louis, Missouri, 1891

Louis Sullivan, an architect from Boston, has put up buildings as many as ten storeys high by using a new method of construction made possible by the use of special steel girders. The new Wainwright Building is supported by a frame of beams moulded in the shape of a capital "I" and made of Bessemer steel from Pittsburgh. In theory there is no limit to the height such buildings may reach in future, now that mechanical lifts are available.

Unlike architects who imitate the motifs of the classical styles, Sullivan has made the steel skeleton of his building manifest and refuses to disguise it with applied decoration. "Form follows function" is his dictum. It enables him to provide large uninterrupted floor areas and admit more light to the interior. Functionalism is the creed of a new generation of architects.

St Louis' new Wainwright Building.

Civilised world faces growing poverty

Newport, Rhode Island, 1891

In one world – the home of the Vanderbilt family in Newport – dinner guests were handed silver trowels and invited to dig in a sandbox for rubies and sapphires, and a man called Harry Lehr threw a party for 100 dogs, with stewed liver on the menu and diamond-studded collars as presents.

In the other world – the teeming, overcrowded tenements and foul dark alleys of the Lower East Side of New York City – children are working up to 16 hours a day in grimy sweat-shops.

Never has the contrast between monumental wealth and abject poverty been more stark. The great American dream has become a grey nightmare for millions. In Europe, too, the great industrial revolution may have created huge private wealth, but the accompanying public squalor and misery is a tragic feature of the Victorian era.

In New York, Jacob Riis, a Danish immigrant to America, has touched the conscience of New York's middle class with a book, *How the Other Half Lives,* in which he paints a grim picture of slum life. The tenements, he says, are "hotbeds of epidemics" and "nurseries of pauperism and crime" that breed "40,000 human wrecks" each year. It has had the same effect on the US's conscience as William Booth's *In Darkest England, and the Way Out* on the English conscience.

Despite the miserable conditions that await them, immigrants are pouring into New York at the rate of 3,000 a week; their numbers are swollen by disillusioned pioneers returning to the city after being bankrupted ("In God we trusted: in Kansas we busted") by mortgage

One of Jacob Riis' photographs portraying slum dwellers in New York City.

Public disinfectors, employed by local authorities in their war against lice and fleas among the urban poor.

Back-to-back slums in Yorkshire.

sharks and deflation. Across the Atlantic, the newly-formed London County Council is tackling the archaic system of sewage and reforming the education, housing and hospital systems; even so the *Pall Mall Gazette* reports that one in four Londoners is living in abject poverty; yet more immigrants arrive from eastern Europe each year.

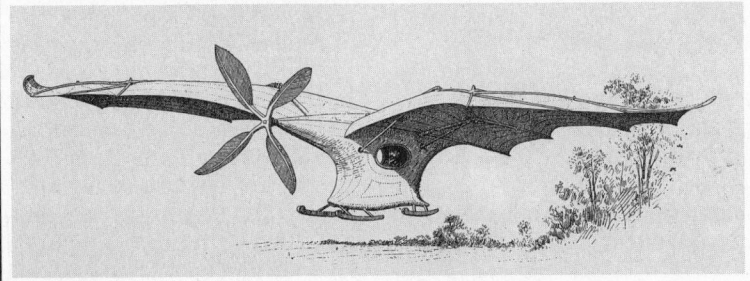

A flying machine, designed by Clement Ader and powered by a steam-driven propeller, has risen four feet above the ground and flown 180 feet. It weighs 150 pounds and is called "Eole" – the Greek god of the winds.

Social Democrats bring Marx to Germany

Erfurt, October 1891

After a heated debate at its Erfurt conference, the German Social Democratic Party adopted Karl Marx' doctrine of the class war and the transformation of society by the socialisation of the means of production and exchange. The conference, the first to be held in Germany since the lifting of Bismarck's anti-socialist laws, heard demands by young activists for the rejection of bourgeois parliamentary activity in favour of revolutionary campaigning in the streets. But moderates argued that the party must also appeal to the middle classes. August Bebel, the Prussian soldier's son who founded the party 21 years ago, said that they would fight for socialism inside and outside parliament.

Britain, 18 August 1892. William Ewart Gladstone forms his fourth Liberal government, following his defeat of Lord Salisbury's Tories in a general election.

Italy, August 1892. The Congress of Italian Workers splits into two factions, the socialists and the anarchists.

South Africa, September 1892. A railway from Cape Colony through the Orange Free State to Johannesburg is completed.

Russia, September 1892. Sergei de Witte is appointed minister of finance.

Britain, 6 October 1892. Alfred, Lord Tennyson, poet laureate since 1850, dies. Among his greatest works are *In Memoriam* and *The Idylls of the King*.

USA, 8 November 1892. The Democrat Grover Cleveland is re-elected president, defeating Benjamin Harrison for the Republicans.

France, November 1892. A parliamentary investigation begins into the collapse of the Panama Company in 1889 and the activities of Ferdinand de Lesseps and his associates.

West Africa, 3 December 1892. Following their occupation of the capital, Abomey, the French impose a protectorate on Dahomey (*Benin*).

Russia, 18 December 1892. Tchaikovsky's ballet *The Nutcracker* is performed for the first time.

Russia, 1892. Russia is devastated by a severe famine, which began last year.

Belgium, 1892. The play *Pelleas and Melisande* by Maurice Maeterlinck receives its premier.

Germany, 1892. Count Alfred von Schlieffen, the chief of the German general staff, devises a plan for offensive military action based on the premise that, in any future war, Germany would have to fight both France and Russia. The plan provides for a swift "knock-out blow" against France, while maintaining a defensive position against Russia.

Germany, 1892. The militant social democrat Clara Zetkin founds the socialist women's paper *Equality*.

Germany, 1892. The engineer Rudolf Diesel patents the first internal combustion engine.

Germany, 1892. The playwright Gerhardt Hauptmann, who won fame in 1889 with *Before Dawn*, causes another stir with his *The Weavers*, a compassionate dramatisation of the Silesian weavers' revolt of 1844.

India, 1892. The Indian Councils Act allows for the election of Indians to the provincial and central legislative councils of British India on a limited franchise.

Pacific, 1892. Britain proclaims a protectorate over the Gilbert and Ellice Islands.

New York City, 1892. Jose Marti founds the Cuban Revolutionary Party while in exile in the USA.

New York City, 1892. *Vogue* magazine begins publication.

New York City, 1892. Thomson-Houston Electric and Edison General Electric merge to form the General Electric Company.

Britain, 13 January 1893. The Independent Labour Party, founded by James Keir Hardie, who was elected to parliament last year, holds its first meeting.

Hawaii, January 1893. Queen Liliuokalani is deposed and the Hawaiian islands are declared a republic.

China, January 1893. Rebuilding of the Summer Palace, destroyed by the British in 1860, is completed.

Italy, 9 February 1893. Giuseppe Verdi's opera *Falstaff* receives its premiere.

USA, 27 March 1893. The American Bell Telephone Company makes the first long-distance telephone call – to its branch office in New York.

Germany, 1893. Germany signs trade treaties with Spain, Rumania and Serbia.

USA, 1893. The Anti-Saloon League is founded in Ohio to promote prohibition of alcohol.

USA, 1893. As a result of a stock-market crash, 600 banks, 74 railways and 15,000 commercial businesses collapse.

Chicago, 1893. Swami Vivekenada, who has founded a mission in India to preach the modern Hindu message of Ramakrishna, makes a great impact at the World Conference of Religions.

Chicago, 1893. The first self-service restaurant in the USA opens.

Britain, 1893. The idealist philosopher Francis Bradley publishes *Appearance and Reality*.

Italy, 1893. Giacomo Puccini's opera *Manon Lescaut* achieves a great success.

Britain, 1893. The Irish writer Oscar Wilde completes two plays, *Lady Windermere's Fan* and *Salome*, the latter in French.

Hundreds wounded in Japan poll violence

Japan, 15 February 1892
Twenty-five people have been killed and some 400 wounded in violence at today's general election, the bloodiest in Japan's history. The violence stems directly from the feudal lords' determination to retain power and to strengthen their representation in the *diet* at the expense of the popular parties.

The violence became inevitable when Shinagawa Yajiro, the ruthless home minister, ordered the police to support the government's candidates; where the voters could not be bribed, they were beaten.

Even these strongarm tactics do not seem to have been sufficient, however. The indications are that the popular parties have won.

Toulouse-Lautrec, artist of Paris clubland

Lautrec, by himself, "en Japonais": a fashionable Parisian fantasy.

Toulouse-Lautrec's poster of the Moulin Rouge star May Belfort.

Paris, 1893
Striking posters advertising the cabarets and dance halls of Montmartre appearing in Paris are the work of an equally striking and unusual artist, Henri de Toulouse-Lautrec, the scion of an ancient and noble family. His eccentric appearance – accidents to his legs in childhood have left him with the stature of a dwarf – is a familiar sight at the Moulin Rouge, the leading new resort of Montmartre night-life. He takes as his subjects the *declasse* cabaret performers and can-can dancers, such as La Goulue and Yvette Guilbert, Jane Avril, May Belfort and Aristide Bruant.

Toulouse-Lautrec shows them in the full vigour of their performances, making no concession to beauty. His bold use of line and space convey the *louche* atmosphere of Paris by night.

Britain's Egyptian puppet ruler has died

Cairo, Egypt, 1892
Few Egyptians are mourning the death of Tewfik, the *khedive*. The European powers' replacement for the deposed Ismail in 1879, he oversaw the steady eroding of Egypt's independence and the reduction of the once-proud country into a chattel of the British empire. Within months of his accession the European powers had secured complete control of Egypt's finances. When Egyptian officers led by a new kind of nationalist leader, Ahmed Arabi, rose in 1881 and formed a government, Tewfik appealed to Britain, which bombarded Alexandria, defeated Arabi at Tel el Kebir, occupied Egypt and imposed Sir Evelyn Baring as British consul-general and effective ruler of Egypt. The final destruction of its independence came in 1888, when the Suez Canal was "internationalised" under British control – without a protest from Tewfik.

A cloth cap in the House of Commons

Hardie: Britain's first socialist MP.

London, 3 August 1892
The new MP for the docklands constituency of West Ham shocked the frock-coated Tories and Liberals when he arrived at Westminster today in a two-horse brake to the strains of the *Marseillaise* played on a cornet. James Keir Hardie was wearing yellow tweed trousers, serge jacket and cloth cap.

Hardie was elected as an independent MP, but campaigned as a socialist and there is talk now of forming a Labour Party to champion the working-class cause.

Hardie started work in the mines at the age of ten, educated himself at night school, and, joining a trade union, campaigned for socialism for the workers.

Capitalism frightened by a shadow.

France destroys the Dahomey kingdom

West Africa, 17 November 1892
As France steadily extends its control over the interior of West Africa, French troops are marching into Abomey, the capital of Dahomey. Since French-led Senegalese troops came into the country in May, it has taken them six months to subject the kingdom. Five times the Dahomeyan army threw itself against them. It was a bitter and well-fought campaign, and many died on both sides.

The war was forced on Dahomey by France, which created "protectorates" amongst Dahomey's subject kingdoms, then provoked Dahomey into trying to reassert its control over them. Behanzin, the king of Dahomey, heard of the French declaration of war in April. His reply was defiant and digni-

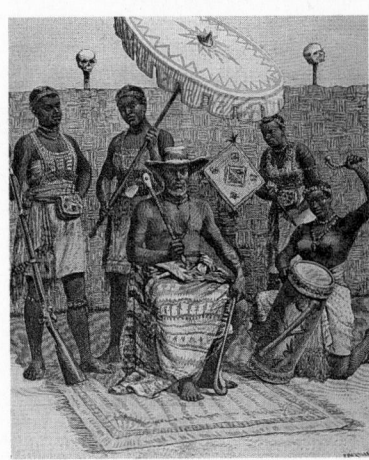
Behanzin, the king of Dahomey, who fought the French invaders with all the noblity of a "civilised" monarch.

fied: "I would like to know how many villages in France I, king of Dahomey, have destroyed."

France is determined to hold on to the kingdom, to provide its rapidly-growing empire in the interior with an outlet to the sea on the south coast of West Africa. That empire is expanding year by year. Since 1883, when French troops occupied Bamako on the river Niger, columns have been spreading out eastwards. Last year they reached Bissandugan, on the frontier of Guinea, Segou, further downstream on the Niger, and Nioro, on the edge of the Sahara desert. Their next stop, French officers boast, will be Timbuktu.

Private eyes break up US strike action

The Pinkerton Agency's ominous "private eye" logo and motto.

Pittsburgh, 1892
In the most violent strike in American history, armed and club-wielding private detectives fought a day-long battle with steel workers in Pittsburgh, leaving scores of dead and injured outside the gates of the Carnegie Company's Homestead works.

The detectives – industry's latest anti-strike weapon – belong to the company formed by Allan T Pinkerton, a civil war veteran. Although they were hired by the Carnegie Company's president, Henry Frick, heavy criticism is being aimed at Andrew Carnegie, the company's founder, who refused to talk to union officials and left for his native Scotland.

At a time when much of the industrial United States is being rocked by union activity, with the constant threat of strikes, the em-

Pinkerton (centre), Lincoln's exbodyguard and the founder of the firm.

ployment of "private armies" is seen as an ominous turn. In previous disputes, the police and national guard – and sometimes the army – have been called in, often with loss of life on both sides. In many cities, however, the police are demoralised by their poor payrates, and the volunteer national guardsmen are reluctant to fight.

Although many capitalists, like the banker Henry Clews, claim that strikes are treasonable, the unions insist that if capitalists can combine in so-called "trusts", labour should also be able to unite.

In 100 years the buffalo population of the US has been reduced from 20 million to 1,000. As recently as the mid 1860s there were 13 million. The slaughter began in earnest with the transcontinental railway boom, which started in 1867. Professional buffalo hunters, providing meat for railway construction workers, were followed by "sportsmen". In 1873 alone, three million were killed. Yet old Indians can still remember riding all day in a straight line, and never coming to the end of a herd of buffalo.

1893 (1893-1894)

Hawaii, 13 April 1893. US troops are ordered to leave Hawaiian soil, ending a protectorate established four months ago, when Queen Liliuokalani was deposed.

Serbia, 14 April 1893. Alexander, the son of Milan Obrenovic, who abdicated in 1889, stages a *coup d'etat* and abolishes the regency.

Belgium, 18 April 1893. Plural and universal male suffrage is introduced.

South Africa, 22 April 1893. Paul Kruger is re-elected president of the South African republic (Transvaal).

South Africa, 12 May 1893. Responsible government is introduced in Natal.

New York City, 24 May 1893. The Czech composer Antonin Dvorak completes his symphony *From the New World*.

Germany, 13 July 1893. A bill is passed substantially increasing the size of the German army and reducing military service in the infantry from three to two years.

Zimbabwe, July 1893. After a Matabele (*Ndebele*) raid on Mashona in the north of the country, troops of the British South Africa Company invade Matabeleland.

Greece, 6 August 1893. The Corinth canal opens.

Philadelphia, 31 August 1893. The anarchist Emma Goldman is arrested on a charge of incitement to riot.

USA, 18 September 1893. The Great Northern Railway, the northernmost transcontinental route operating between the Mississippi river and the Pacific Ocean, is completed.

Britain, September 1893. An Irish Home Rule Bill, introduced by Gladstone, is passed by the House of Commons but rejected by the House of Lords.

South-East Asia, 3 October 1893. Siam (*Thailand*) gives up all its territory east of the Mekong to France and recognises Laos as a French protectorate.

Austria, 29 October 1893. Count Eduard von Taaffe, the prime minister of Austria, resigns following the defeat of his bill providing for the introduction of universal manhood suffrage.

Russia, October 1893. Peter Tchaikovsky's sixth symphony, the *Pathetique*, is performed for the first time.

Zimbabwe, 4 November 1893. Having defeated the Matabele in battle, the British occupy Bulawayo, the capital of Matabeleland.

West Africa, 12 December 1893. Advancing down the Niger valley from Kayes in Senegal, the French take Timbuktu, the capital of Mali.

Russia, 27 December 1893. Russia and France reach an *entente* agreeing on mutual aid in the event of war with Germany.

Italy, 1893. The Italian Socialist Party is founded in Reggio nell'Emilia. In Sicily, the socialist leaders organise networks (*fasci*) of workers.

France, 4 January 1894. The French government ratifies the Franco-Russian military convention.

Germany, 10 February 1894. Germany signs a commercial treaty with Russia.

Africa, 15 March 1894. Germany and France sign a pact agreeing on their respective zones of influences in tropical Africa, around Cameroon and along the Chari river.

Korea, 17 March 1894. The nationalist *Tonghak* (Eastern Learning) rebellion breaks out. Chinese and Japanese troops are sent to Korea.

Britain, March 1894. Gladstone resigns as Liberal prime minister following the failure of his attempt to establish Irish home rule. He is succeeded by the Liberal imperialist Lord Roseberry.

East Africa, 11 Avril 1894. Britain declares a protectorate over Uganda.

Washington, DC, 1 May 1894. Jacob Coxey, who led a march of 100,000 jobless to the capital to demand economic reform, is arrested.

Armenia, 1894. In order to suppress a revolutionary movement for Armenian independence, the Ottoman Sultan Abdul Hamid II orders Turkish and Kurdish troops to embark on systematic massacres of Armenians.

Britain, 1894. Sir William Harcourt, the chancellor of the exchequer, introduces death duties.

Britain, 1894. Sidney and Beatrice Webb publish *The History of Trade Unionism*.

Britain, 1894. Rudyard Kipling publishes *The Jungle Book*, a collection of animal stories.

Germany, 1894. German landowners, angered by the concessions made to industry by the chancellor, Caprivi, at the expense of agriculture, form the Agrarian League.

Italy, 1894. Gabriele d'Annunzio publishes *Triumph of Death*, the third in his series of *Romances of the Rose*.

Prick with a needle cures many ills

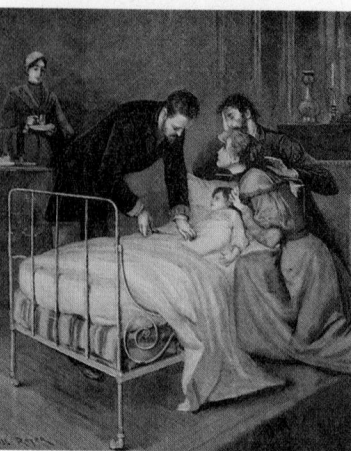

Dr Emile Roux, the bacteriologist, immunising against diphtheria.

London, 1894

Vaccines such as those developed by Jenner and Pasteur work by activating the body's natural defence mechanisms. A person is injected with a weakened or "attenuated" strain of what would otherwise be a dangerous, even deadly, microorganism. This stimulates the immune system to produce specialist blood cells to fight any future infection.

This principle is now being widely applied to protect people against all sorts of infections. Emile Roux, a French bacteriologist, together with the Swiss Alexandre Yersin, has shown that the symptoms of diphtheria, like those of tetanus, are due to a toxin produced by the diphtheria bacterium. Now a diphtheria antitoxin is likely to become available which will immunise the recipient against the disease.

Tchaikovsky dies, the rumours begin

St Petersburg, 6 November 1893

Nine days after the premiere of his anguished sixth symphony, Peter Ilyich Tchaikovsky has died after drinking unboiled water infected with cholera. He was 53.

That, at least, is the official story. But Tchaikovsky, the composer of six symphonies, four concertos and the ballets *Swan Lake*, *The Sleeping Beauty* and *The Nutcracker*, was at the height of his fame (which included receiving a doctorate from Cambridge university) and there were apparently fears in high places that his homosexuality would become public knowledge and embarrass the Russian court. There is talk that he was "tried" by a "court of honour" of his old school, found "guilty" of dishonourable conduct and "sentenced" to commit suicide.

Peter Tchaikovsky, the introspective composer and temperamental genius.

Australian journalist sets sail for Utopia

Australia, 16 July 1893

"Come together in all unselfishness, to trust each other and be free! To live simply, to work hardly, to win not the gold that poisons, but the home life that saves." Thus the stirring words of William Lane, the liberal journalist who has set sail with 220 followers, all trade unionists and teetotallers, to establish a settlement of "New Australia" in the South American land of Paraguay.

Lane began calling for volunteers to join him in the creation of an ideal commonwealth in 1889. An active unionist, he chose only those of like enthusiasms, each of whom had to put up £60 in cash. Given the high standards of his recruits, it seems that Lane's dream may well become fact. Critics regret only that so motivated a party should be removed from Australia, but Lane is convinced that his dreams would fail in "worn out" Australia.

"The world will be changed if we succeed," he says confidently. "And we shall succeed. We cannot help succeeding."

Panama bribes scandal rocks France

An excavator at work on the unsuccessful attempt to build the Panama Canal.

Paris, June 1893
Frenchmen with a little money to invest could not resist the Panama Canal project when they heard that Ferdinand de Lesseps, the genius of Suez, was the construction engineer. Millions of francs were borrowed from thousands of small savers for a 40-mile seaway to link the Atlantic and Pacific Oceans.

But Panama was not a sea-level Suez and de Lesseps had not reckoned with having to build locks. A combination of extravagance on a grand scale and shady financiers linked to shadier politicians led to bankruptcy in 1889. Although the government tried to hush up the scandal, it finally came into the open when de Lesseps and his associates went on trial for corruption; they were sentenced, but the sentence was "set aside". Work on the canal is to go ahead under new management. But prospects are not promising: in eight years, over 22,000 workers died from malaria and yellow fever.

Red planet is alive, claims astronomer

Arizona, 1894
Is there life on Mars? According to at least one wealthy astronomer, the red planet is populated by a race of intelligent beings. Percival Lowell, who has built his own observatory in Arizona specifically to study Mars, says that it is a drying, dying planet: its water resources are desperately scarce. So the Martians have built an intricate system of waterways to carry the precious liquid from the north and south poles.

Through the telescope one can see these "canals", though Lowell concedes that they may be belts of vegetation. He is not the first to suggest that there is life on Mars. Over a decade ago Schiaparelli also claimed the existence of canals, as did Secchi even earlier.

A celebration of life in the New World

New York, 17 December 1893
The Bohemian composer Antonin Dvorak scored a major triumph last night with the premiere of his new symphony, entitled *From the New World*, at Carnegie Hall.

In this work Dvorak says that he has tried to reproduce "the spirit of Negro and Indian melodies", and refers to the spirituals "Swing low, sweet chariot" and "Goin' home". Otherwise, however, this beautiful symphony is as Czech as Dvorak himself. Dvorak, aged 52, a butcher's son whose chief passion, next to music, is trains, came to public notice when Brahms recommended some of his piano pieces to a publisher in 1876. Dvorak never looked back, and last year he was invited to be head of a new National Conservatory of Music in New York.

Women get the vote in New Zealand

New Zealand, 19 September 1893
At 11.45 this morning the governor put his signature to the Electoral Act making this country the first to allow the female vote. A petition signed by a third of the women here persuaded the House of Representatives to pass the act, first mooted eight years ago by the Women's Christian Temperance Union. The head of the union's franchise department, Katharine Sheppard, had petitioned for the reform three times in the last three years. The number of women's signatures she collected rose each time by 10,000, until a record list of 31,872 names finally swayed the House. Despite an unscrupulous liquor trade lobby, New Zealand women won the first victory for the WCTU in its world suffrage campaign.

US takes over the Hawaiian islands

Honolulu, 17 January 1893
Grass-skirted Hawaiian islanders watched with bemusement today as US marines landed from the *USS Boston* and took up combat positions around the capital. Within hours, however, the marines, now garlanded with flowers, were relaxing under the Pacific sun with the local female populance, and the first stage of the annexation of Hawaii by the US was complete.

It is 40 years since Commander Matthew Perry predicted the rise of Japan as a world power and foresaw the need for a US base in the Far East; six years ago King Kamehameha III ceded Pearl Harbor on the island of Oahu to the United States government. The new ruler, Queen Liliuokalani, has been much concerned at American influence, and was looking for the return of autocracy. Her attitude, combined with pressure from sugar

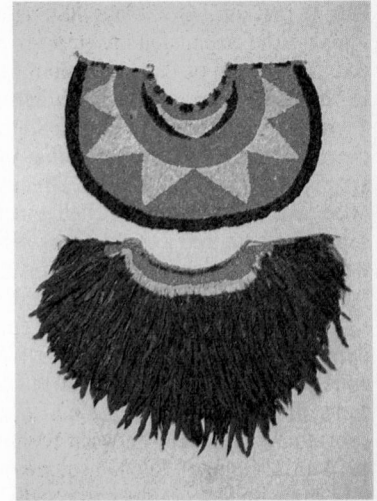

A traditional Hawaiian feather cape.

plantation owners on the islands to sell behind the newly-imposed US tariff wall, brought about demands for annexation. The queen has been deposed.

Norwegian paints his moment of torment

Munch's shrill "Scream", which has pierced Berlin's art establishment.

Berlin, 1893
Edvard Munch, the 30-year-old Norwegian painter, was ordered to remove his 50 paintings from an exhibition by the Berlin Artists' Union last year. As a result of the furore several of its members, headed by Max Liebermann, are leaving to form a Berlin *Sezession*.

Munch has an ambitious plan to assemble a "Frieze of Life" – paintings on the theme of "the poetry of life, love and death". One of these is *The Scream*, a lurid evocation of fear and horror. Munch was crossing a bridge by a *fjord* under the sunset when, he says: "I sensed a scream passing through nature. I seemed to hear the scream. I painted the clouds as actual blood."

Winners take all: the age of imperialism

Empire, claimed Rudyard Kipling, was "the White Man's Burden". Behind it lay not desire for conquest or lust for power, but a "heavy harness" of duty to bring law and civilisation to "sullen peoples". It was a yoke the White Man shouldered with especial enthusiasm between 1870 and 1914, the era, historians claim, of a "New Imperialism". During that time, two things dominated world diplomacy: the expansion of empires and the self-conscious speed of that expansion. Large stretches of the globe were annexed. Hitherto isolationist countries (Germany, the United States, Japan) acquired a taste for empires, joining countries (Britain, France, Russia) with an already well-developed taste and a still unsatisfied appetite for them. They also acquired a sense of urgency. If empires were to be won, they must be won fast. Thus the "scramble for Africa", which (predictably) produced a scrambled Africa – almost an entire continent parcelled out in the 20 years from 1880 on a principle not much more sophisticated than "first come, first served". The scale of absorption was enormous. Each year between the late 1870s and 1914 an average of 240,000 square miles of territory came under colonial control. At the outbreak of the Great War, the colonised world had a population of more than 560 million people. It was, moreover, a world not merely colonised but conquered. Indigenous resistance was quashed and structures of Government established.

A key to glory, a call to duty

All this took men, money, machines. It also took ideas. Without them, imperialism would have appeared mere caprice, a baseless belligerence. It needed a justification. The church militant was highly serviceable here. Missionaries (whose sincerity need not be disparaged) could only claim souls for Christ if their Governments also claimed territory. Culture, broadly defined, was adduced: it was the White Man's Burden to introduce native peoples to law and order, if not as yet, to democracy. Commerce too, seemed reason enough. Joseph Chamberlain, Britain's Colonial Secretary (1895-1903), believed that ties of trade could bind mother country and colonies in a closer, almost spiritual union. Finally, to possess an empire was a glory. Lord Curzon, erstwhile Viceroy of India, put it well. "In Empire," he wrote in 1908, "we have found not merely the key to glory and wealth, but the call to duty and the means of service to mankind". Imperialism had its passionate critics too, who noticed the disparity between the high-minded ideals of Empire and its high-handed methods. Beatrice Webb, the Fabian Socialist, deplored the "impossible combination" of "sentimental Christianity ... and blackguardism". The individualist liberal philosopher Herbert Spencer decried the enslavement of natives. Even a moderate Liberal such as Henry Campbell-Bannerman, a future British Prime Minister (1906-08), condemned the "methods of barbarism" (he was thinking of concentration camps) by which Britain had fought the Boer War, 1899-1902. The underlying assumption was that conquest brutalised the conqueror as much as the conquered. Militarism, anti-intellectualism, racial intolerance, greed: were these, critics of empire wondered, the real products of the new colonial era?

The highest stage of capitalism

It is important to set aside these arguments for and against imperialism to try to understand the phenomenon in a more profound way. What really lay behind it? According to the English economist J A Hobson, the explanation was to be found in the investment requirements of the capitalist class. In 1902 he argued that the wealthy sought outlets for their savings abroad because there was underconsumption of goods, and thus capital, at home. He proposed that fairer distribution of income would rectify this by boosting domestic consumption. Hobson was not a Marxist, but his views found an audience with Marx's disciples. Lenin borrowed from them in his *Imperialism: The Highest Stage of Capitalism* (1916), wherein he argued that capitalism had entered a new (and final) phase in the late 19th century. Increased wealth in fewer hands (monopoly capitalism, he called it) meant that the competitive urge had to express itself in imperial rivalry between the great monopoly capitalist nations, with their huge (and, he thought, self-destructive) demand for new raw materials and new markets.

Lenin's argument was sophisticated, but was it true? An alternative reading views imperialism not as the inevitable outcome of capitalism but as a deviation from it. J A Schumpeter, writing shortly after Lenin, proposed that for capitalist economics imperialism is irrational. Capitalism flourishes in peaceful times; it prefers free trade above all. Imperialism, on the other hand, causes wars and tariff controls. The explanation of the phenomenon was therefore to be sought in political terms: the desire of statesmen to win popular support, the residual militarism of a warrior class, and the need to provide employment for surplus administrators. Some of this has the ring of truth. In every country which practised imperialism, military success brought political benefit, military failure, political defeat. "Jingoism" – the word was coined at this time – is a potent political device.

Spoils of empire, roads to war

In the end the diversity of late 19th century imperialism eludes such general theories. Each empire had its own reasons for existence, and no two empires were exactly the same. There were national styles in imperialism as in other things. Russia was anxious to acquire warm water ports; Britain was keen to maintain the route to India; the United States wished to become the major power in the Caribbean and Latin America; France sought, as ever, "la gloire", hoping, no doubt, to obliterate the memory of Napoleon III by recreating the days of Napoleon I. All, having acquired empires, wished to protect them. Preservation of empire itself became a reason for imperialism.

This quality of self-protection was a necessary feature of empires, but it caused problems. Sometimes they grew too large, sometimes too great a distance separated centre and periphery. Most of all, it ensured conflict with other imperial powers. The colonial era is peppered with occasions which threatened war or, indeed, turned into it: the confrontation between Britain and France at Fashoda (1898) for control of the Nile; the "Agadir Incident" (1911) between Germany and France for control of Morocco; the war between the United States and Spain (1898); the Russo-Japanese War (1904-05); the Boer War (1899-1902). The inherent instability of large-scale territorial aggrandisement is obvious.

It was reasonable, therefore, for people to wonder how long imperial pretensions could be sustained without more serious conflict between the world powers. One way of interpreting the years prior to the outbreak of the Great War is to see in them a grim ineluctability: from international competition to international tension to international war. Certainly 1914 marked a definitive shift. After the war, the victorious powers sought to divide the spoils of empire, to resume the imperialism dramatically interrupted in 1914. But things could never be the same again. Independence movements in the 1920s increasingly challenged colonial authorities, and although it took another World War to bring about full-scale "decolonisation", the seeds were clearly sown in the years after 1918.

A somewhat prejudiced French view of the benevolence of British rule.

An equally prejudiced British view of the benevolence of British rule.

Rhodes, "making more blood in Africa than champagne in Kimberley".

The Foreign Legion in action, a French view of French colonialism.

Ruler of India, "at heaven's command", Lord Curzon with an Indian prince.

Colonialism as entertainment, dancing on the natives.

Saving the Colours, colonial wars before the Maxim gun.

The British lion, irritated, possessive, brutal, or just exhausted?

"And he calls himself a protector!", a French view on British colonialism.

1894 (1894-1895)

France, 24 June 1894. President Marie Francois Sadi-Carnot is fatally stabbed by Santo Caserio, an Italian anarchist.

France, 27 June 1894. Jean Casimir Perier is elected president of the French Republic.

Korea, June 1894. Troops from both China and Japan arrive in Korea in response to a plea for help from the monarchy, which is faced by a rebellion by the *Tonghak* society in the south of the country.

Hawaii, 4 July 1894. Having seized power, Judge Sanford B Dole proclaims the republic of Hawaii and issues a new constitution.

Ethiopia, 17 July 1894. The Italians take Kassala on the Eritrean/Sudanese border from the *Mahdists*.

France, 22 July 1894. The first automobile race takes place, between Paris and Rouen.

Korea, 23 July 1894. Japanese troops take over the Korean imperial palace, carry off Queen Min and her children to the Japanese legation, and attack the Chinese offices.

Korea, 25 July 1894. Japanese forces attack and sink the British steamer *Kowshing* carrying Chinese reinforcements to Korea.

Korea, 1 August 1894. War is formally declared between Japan and China.

USA, 27 August 1894. The Wilson-Gorman Tariff Act, introducing an income tax, becomes law.

South Africa, August 1894. Cecil Rhodes, newly-appointed minister of native affairs in the Cape government, introduces a "native policy" to attract Afrikaaner support in the Boer republics. It includes the removal of the right to vote from African landholders.

France, 15 October 1894. Captain Alfred Dreyfus, a Jewish army officer, is arrested for betraying military secrets to Germany.

Germany, 26 October 1894. Count von Caprivi is dismissed and replaced as chancellor by Prince Chlodwig von Hohenlohe-Schillingsfurst.

Russia, 1 November 1894. Alexander III dies and is succeeded as czar by his son Nicholas II.

China, 21 November 1894. Japan defeat China at Port Arthur (*Lushun*).

Washington, DC, 22 November 1894. The USA and Japan sign a commercial treaty.

Hawaii, 24 November 1894. Sun Yat-sen organises the Revive China Society in Honolulu.

Madagascar, 12 December 1894. Following increasing conflict between French settlers and the Hova government under the prime minister, Rainilairanivony, the French occupy Tamatava.

Chicago, 14 December 1894. Eugene Debs, the president of the American Railway Union, is jailed for six months for ignoring an injunction to end the Pullman railway strike, which began in July.

France, 1894. The sculptor Auguste Rodin completes his monumental group *The Burghers of Calais*.

France, 1894. Gustav Lanson publishes his *History of French Literature*.

France, 1894. The brothers Charles and Emile Pathe open the first French phonograph factory.

Hawaii, 16 January 1895. The former queen, Liliuokalani, believed to be plotting a violent overthrow of the republic, is jailed for treason.

France, 17 January 1895. Felix Faure is elected president following the resignation of Jean Casimir Perier.

China, 12 February 1895. Following a humiliating Chinese defeat on land and at sea by the Japanese at the battle of Weihaiwei, the Qing naval commander Ding Rucheng commits suicide.

Cuba, February 1895. Prompted by Spain's failure to carry out economic and political reforms, a newly formed revolutionary movement begins waging a guerrilla war against Spain with the aim of achieving Cuban independence.

Japan, 17 April 1895. China and Japan sign the peace treaty of Shimonoseki. China recognises the independence of Korea and cedes Formosa (*Taiwan*), the Pescadores Islands and the Liaodong peninsula to Japan.

Japan, 23 April 1895. Russia, France and Germany intervene in the settlement between China and Japan, forcing Japan to return the Liaodong peninsula to China.

Washington, DC, 20 May 1895. The Supreme Court rules that the income tax introduced last year is unconstitutional.

Germany, 21 June 1895. The Kiel Canal, connecting the Baltic with the North Sea, opens.

Madagascar, 1895. A French force of 15,000 troops under Jacques Duchesne lands at Majunga.

British gun down Matabele warriors

Zimbabwe, January 1894
Frederick Selous, the white hunter famous throughout Southern Africa, has written to his mother in England: "The campaign has gone through in the most wonderfully lucky way for our side." He was writing from Bulawayo, the *kraal* of the once-powerful Matabele chief, Lobengula, who has fled into the bush.

Dr Jameson, Cecil Rhodes' administrator of Mashonaland, had been looking for a pretext for war. His opportunity came with a raid by Lobengula's *impis* in July 1893 on Mashona people working for white settlers.

He seized the opportunity to declare war. British South Africa Company troops invaded from the west, while British government troops dawdled in the south. Bulawayo was seized and burnt. Mata-

Matabele warriors, mown down by the British South African Company.

beleland is now a white colony – and its land and cattle are being parcelled out among the settlers, thus strenthening further the hold of whites in Southern Africa.

Italian anarchist stabs French president

Lyons, 24 June 1894
President Sadi-Carnot was stabbed to death here today by a young Italian workman who cried "*Vive l'anarchie*" as he plunged a knife into the president's body.

M Carnot, visiting Lyons for the *Exposition*, had given orders for people to be allowed to approach his open carriage as he drove through the streets, so when his murderer pushed through the crowd with his knife hidden in a

newspaper the guards allowed him to pass, thinking that he carried a bouquet of flowers.

The assassin, a baker's apprentice called Santo Caserio, made no attempt to escape. He comes from Milan, the home of political turbulence, and belongs to a Swiss anarchist group called "Hearts of Oak", one of hundreds of anarchist groups that have sprung up in Europe, particularly in Italy and Spain, in this angry decade.

Seaside resort has a towering attraction

The new tower at Blackpool.

Blackpool, 18 September 1894
The Lancashire town of Blackpool has already established itself as a popular place for mill workers from northern England to celebrate their "Wakes Week" holiday by the sea. Today the town opened a new attraction, destined to bring even more holiday-makers to what is becoming a prime example of the new-style seaside resorts opened up by the railway boom.

The Blackpool Tower, a 500-foot (152-metre) replica of Paris' Eiffel Tower, is unrivalled in Britain and joins the town's three piers, music-halls, aquaria, ballrooms and this year's other addition, the Grand Theatre.

Irish wit jailed for his homosexuality

London, May 1895

Until this month Oscar Wilde was the toast of the stage, with his two wittiest comedies running simultaneously in London theatres. In January Charles Hawtrey opened in *An Ideal Husband* at the Theatre Royal, Haymarket; in February *The Importance of Being Earnest* was put on by George Alexander at the St James' to even greater admiration. All that is over.

Wilde's name has been removed from the theatres, posters and bills. After two sensational trials the portly poet and aesthete has been delivered to Reading jail to wear convict stripes for two years.

His dramatic downfall began with his friendship with Lord Alfred Douglas, the son of the Marquess of Queensberry; the latter accused Wilde of being a sodomite by inscribing the word (misspelt) on his card and pinning it up at his club. Wilde's suit for criminal libel collapsed and he was urged to flee the country by his friends. Instead he awaited arrest at the Cadogan hotel, confident that he would win.

The Importance of Being Earnest shows, he said, that we should treat trivial things seriously and serious things "with sincere and studied triviality". Well may he reflect on that during his two years of hard labour. "The truth is rarely pure and never simple," he also said. Never more so than in his case.

Wilde and Lord Alfred Douglas: a "sincere and studied triviality".

Japan the victor in anti-Chinese war

The battle of the Yalu estuary, where the Japanese navy sank the Chinese fleet, on 17 September 1894.

Japan, 17 April 1895

The Chinese statesman Li Hongzhang, nursing the wounds inflicted by a Japanese fanatic, today signed the treaty of Shimonoseki ending China's disastrous war with Japan.

The Japanese, who had destroyed the Chinese fleet and inflicted humiliating defeats on China's corrupt and badly-led army, were able to impose harsh conditions. China is to pay a huge indemnity and to cede the Pescadores Islands, Formosa and the Liaodong Peninsula to Japan. Four new treaty ports will be opened to Japanese trade and industry which will be exempt from Chinese taxation, and Korea's independence will be recognised by China but not by Japan. It was rivalry over Korea that led to the war. The immediate causes were the assassination of a pro-Japanese Korean politician in Shanghai and an uprising in Korea which gave the Japanese an excuse to send in troops. Hostilities opened without war being declared when the Japanese sank a Chinese troopship and machine-gunned the survivors.

Debussy's "Fawn" panned as formless

Paris, 1894

The 32-year-old composer Claude Debussy is at the centre of a musical controversy following the premiere this year of his symphonic poem *Prelude a l'apres midi d'un faune* (The afternoon of a fawn).

The work is a dreamy, highly evocative piece of a quite novel character. Its fluidity and sensuous orchestral sounds have led to it being derided by some critics as "formless" and "tuneless". It betrays Debussy's interest in the exotic and atmospheric gamelan music of the East Indies, which he heard at the Paris international exhibition of 1889.

Last year Debussy produced a string quartet which anticipates the style of the *Prelude*. He is working on an opera based on the recent play *Pelleas and Melisande* by the Belgian Maurice Maeterlinck.

French "spy" captain gets life sentence

France, 22 December 1894

Captain Alfred Dreyfus, an artillery officer attached to the general staff, was today found guilty of spying for Germany. He was sentenced to life imprisonment on Devil's Island off French Guiana.

This affair started when a French agent found evidence of treachery in the German embassy. Suspicion fell on Dreyfus. He was ordered to take a handwriting test; his hand shook and he was arrested.

He is an unlikely spy. Aged 33, he is nondescript in appearance, noteworthy only for the rimless *pince-nez* he effects. He is not liked by his fellow officers who find him a cold fish. But he has been punctilious in his duties, and he has no money troubles, as his father is a wealthy textile manufacturer.

He is, however, a Jew and therefore a natural target of suspicion for the militant Catholics who dominate the officer corps. There are

The degrading of the French Jew Alfred Dreyfus, convicted of spying.

already disturbing signs of an outbreak of anti-Semitism. But is Dreyfus guilty? There are worrying aspects to his court martial at which he protested his innocence. The evidence was thin and his lawyers were barred from the court.

1895 (1895-1896)

Britain, 25 June 1895. Following the fall of Lord Rosebery's Liberal government, Lord Salisbury forms his third ministry, a Conservative-Liberal Unionist coalition. Joseph Chamberlain is appointed colonial secretary.

Central America, June 1895. Nicaragua, Honduras and El Salvador conclude a treaty of union at Amapala.

South Africa, 8 July 1895. The opening of the Delagoa Bay railway – from Johannesburg and Pretoria to Maputo Bay – gives the Transvaal access to the sea independent of the British colonies.

Balkans, 15 July 1895. Stephen Stambulov, who was dismissed as Bulgarian prime minister last year, is murdered by Macedonian rebels.

China, 1 August 1895. The people of Gutian in Fujian province destroy churches and kill more than ten British and Australian missionaries, including women and children.

Britain, 5 August 1895. During a visit by Kaiser William II to Britain, Lord Salisbury, the prime minister, suggests the partition of the Ottoman empire as a solution to the troubles of the Near East.

USA, 26 August 1895. A hydroelectric plant, designed by Nikola Tesla and built by Westinghouse, opens at Niagara Falls.

Madagascar, 30 September 1895. Tananarive, the island's capital, surrenders to the French.

Madagascar, October 1895. France rejects an offer by Queen Ranavalona to accept a French protectorate over Madagascar on condition that she remains queen.

China, October 1895. Having launched an unsuccessful attempt at a revolution in Guangzhou, Sun Yat-sen flees to Hong Kong.

Germany, 5 November 1895. *Till Eulenspiegel* by Richard Strauss receives its premiere.

Germany, 27 November 1895. The Association of Industrialists is formed.

China, 30 November 1895. China concludes a secret treaty with Russia, allowing Russia to build the Trans-Siberian railway through Manchuria to the Russian Pacific port of Vladivostok.

South Africa, 29 December 1895. Leander Starr Jameson, an agent of the British South Africa Company, invades the Boer republic of Transvaal at the head of 470 men.

Ottoman Empire, December 1895. Britain intervenes to stop massacres of Armenians by Turks and Kurds.

China, 1895. Serious anti-Christian riots occur in Sichuan province.

Vienna, 1895. In collaboration with Joseph Breuner, Sigmund Freud publishes *Studies in Hysteria*.

France, 1895. French trade unionists combine to form the *Confederation Generale du Travail* (CGT).

France, 1895. Armand Peugeot perfects a petrol-driven engine and founds the Peugeot automobile company.

France, 1895. Emile Durkheim publishes *The Rules of Sociological Method*.

Britain, 1895. *The Time Machine*, a scientific novel by H G Wells, is a huge success.

Britain, 1895. Thomas Hardy completes his fourth novel, *Jude the Obscure*. It follows *The Return of the Native* (1878), *The Mayor of Casterbridge* (1886) and *Tess of the D'Urbervilles* (1891).

South Africa, 2 January 1896. Following his defeat yesterday by the Boers at Krugersdorp, Jameson surrenders at Doorn Kop.

Germany, 3 January 1896. Kaiser William II sends a telegram to Paul Kruger, the South African president, congratulating him on the suppression of Jameson. The telegram causes a storm of indignation in Britain, who sees in it an attempt by Germany to expand her influence in Africa.

USA, 4 January 1896. Utah becomes the 45th state in the union.

South Africa, 6 January 1896. Cecil Rhodes is forced to resign as prime minister of Cape Colony because of his implication in the Jameson raid.

South-East Asia, 15 January 1896. Britain and France sign an agreement on their respective spheres of influence in south-east Asia. Both countries guarantee the independence of Siam (*Thailand*) and the French protectorate over Laos is recognised.

Balkans, 19 February 1896. At the instigation of Nicholas II, the new czar of Russia, Ferdinand, the prince of Bulgaria, is recognised by the powers.

Crete, February 1896. A Christian rebellion against Ottoman rule breaks out in the island.

Ethiopia, 1 March 1896. The Italians are decisively defeated by the Ethiopians under Menelik at the battle of Adowa.

China, 27 March 1896. The Chinese diplomat Li Hongzhang leaves Shanghai on a goodwill tour of Russia, Germany, France, Britain and the USA.

Designer socialist against ugliness

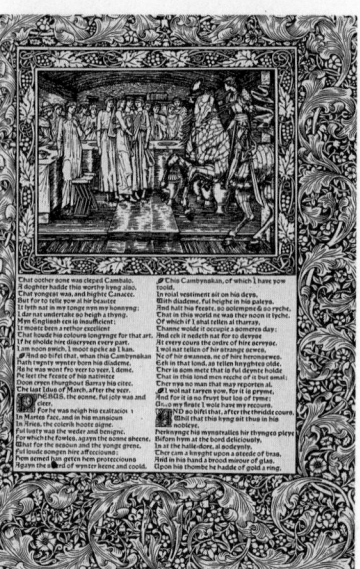

A page from William Morris' intricately-designed Kelmscott Chaucer.

London, 3 October 1896
William Morris, who spent his life resisting the materialism and ugliness of industrial society, died today and is to be buried at Kelmscott, Oxfordshire, which gave its name to his press. He devoted his last years to producing beautifully handprinted editions of classics, such as the Kelmscott Chaucer, in his own type fonts.

Morris and Co moved to Merton, Surrey, where it produces tapestries designed by Edward Burne-Jones. Since the 1880s Morris had preached socialism, founding the Socialist League. *News from Nowhere* described his vision of a rural Utopia. His regret was that working men could not afford his firm's goods.

William Morris' and Edward Burne-Jones' Merton Abbey tapestry.

X-rays to reveal the naked truth

Germany, 1895
A chance observation during a physics experiment has lead to an important discovery: a new form of radiation. The German scientist Wilhelm Roentgen calls it simply "X-rays". But whatever the rays' nature they have one astonishing property: they allow one to see through objects. While passing a current through a cathode tube, Roentgen noticed that rays were given off that passed through everyday materials such as paper, wood and aluminium.

This opens up an exciting prospect for doctors. Might it not be possible to use X-rays to see through flesh and study, say, broken bones?

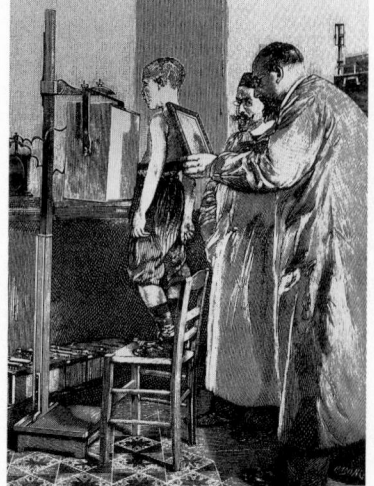

Preparing a patient for an X-ray.

Venezuela sparks international row

Washington, DC, 17 December 1895
Relations between the US and Britain have fallen to their lowest since the 1812 war following an ultimatum today by President Cleveland over the long-simmering British Guiana-Venezuela border dispute.

In a surprise move the president announced a US commission to decide the borderline. The US, he said, is prepared to impose the commission's findings on Britain by force if necessary. Venezuela recently granted a US syndicate concessionary rights over some of the disputed territory.

British hand seen in Transvaal raid

Dr Jameson, taken prisoner by the Boers after the failure of his uprising.

Johannesburg, January 1896
A foolhardy and criminal attempt to overthrow the Transvaal regime of Paul Kruger, the Boer leader, has been humiliatingly crushed by a force of Boer commandos.

The *Uitlanders* – foreign businessmen, engineers and speculators, drawn to Johannesburg by goldmining operations – have talked frequently of rebelling against Kruger's persecutions. At the end of last year, Dr Jameson, who works for Cecil Rhodes, decided to help things along by invading the Transvaal with 470 mounted men. The Uitlanders did not rebel and Jameson's men were taken prisoner. Did Rhodes, the mining tycoon who is prime minister of Cape Colony, know that Jameson was planning the raid? And did Joseph Chamberlain, the colonial secretary in London, also know? Despite denials, suspicion remains.

Shah is killed by Islamic extremist

Tehran, Persia, 1896
Naser al-Din, the *shah* of Persia, has been assassinated. He was shot at point-blank range by a man handing him a petition at the shrine of Shah Abdul-Azim, four miles (6.4 kilometres) south of Tehran.

For a decade the country has complained as the shah sold European companies concession after concession to finance his extravagances, accusing him of selling the country. A concession for a monopoly of the sale of tobacco provoked riots, but its cancellation left Persia with a debt of £3,500,000, for which the state's customs receipts were pledged.

The assassination is the work of Islamic fundamentalists, who have strong links with both Persia's *mullahs* and Jamal al-Din Afghani, the preacher and revolutionary who calls for pan-Islamic unity.

The assassination of Shah Naser al-Din by a pan-Islamic revolutionary.

Turks kill Armenians

Istanbul, 29 August 1896
The Ottoman authorities have re acted with the utmost ferocity to the seizure of the Ottoman bank in Istanbul by Armenian revolutionaries. At least 3,000 people have been massacred and killings are still taking place after three days.

The Armenians rose against Ottoman rule two years ago, hoping to attract attention to their plight and gain sympathy in Britain and elsewhere, as had happened to the Bulgarians when Ottoman massacres began. The uprising was put down with great brutality by Turkish troops and Kurdish irregulars.

Britain took the lead in setting up an inquiry into the apparent butchery and put pressure on the sultan to introduce reforms and reconcile the Armenians to Ottoman rule. The sultan has promised reforms, but has done nothing – or, worse, launched more massacres.

In October last year, he accepted a joint British-French-Russian plan and simultaneously began killing Armenians throughout Anatolia. About 200,000 people are be-

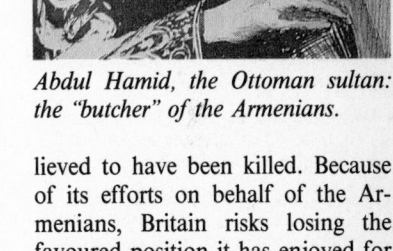

Abdul Hamid, the Ottoman sultan: the "butcher" of the Armenians.

lieved to have been killed. Because of its efforts on behalf of the Armenians, Britain risks losing the favoured position it has enjoyed for over 40 years at the sultan's court.

The Germans are already intriguing to take Britain's place, encouraging the sultan in his stubbornness and manoeuvring for railway concessions.

Three black kings see a white queen

Windsor, 20 November 1895
Three African kings – Khama, Sebele and Bathoen – met a single British queen today. At a reception at Windsor Castle, Queen Victoria presented each with a personally-inscribed Bible. The kings, all from Botswana, travelled here in an attempt to challenge Britain's decision to amalgamate their country with the British South Africa Company's territory.

They are paying their own way and, accompanied only by the Rev W C Willoughby of the London Missionary Society, have undertaken a substantial tour of the country. King Khama has proved a particularly effective orator whose impassioned delivery is in no way diminished by his interpreter.

The visit has proved popular, and public opinion is in the kings' favour. However Cecil Rhodes, the territory's founder, is determined to annex Botswana, and is working hard to this end.

Engels, salesman of communism, dies

London, 5 August 1895
Friedrich Engels, the immigrant businessman who, with the socialist Karl Marx, founded the political philosophy known as "Communism" is dead. He was 74.

While Marx was undoubtedly the better theoretician, Engels, with his experience in business as a partner in the Manchester textile firm of Ermen and Engels, was communism's exemplary salesman. Without his laudatory reviews, few readers would have noticed Marx' seminal work, *Das Kapital*.

Engels developed his political sensibilities in Germany where, in 1842, he discovered the radical theories of communism. He moved to England that year, believing that there he could best combine business with the pursuit of politics. He met Marx after submitting an article to his magazine, and in 1848 the two men crowned their relationship with the *Communist Manifesto*, the basis of their ideology.

British housewives are cooking with gas

Britain, c.1895
Gas for heating, lighting and cooking is becoming daily more popular. Economical and convenient, its use among all classes has rocketed since the invention of the gas mantle and the slot meter.

Although several large cities like London, Sheffield, Bristol, Liverpool and Newcastle are still dependent on private companies, more than 150 municipal authorities now control their own gas supplies. Having invested in gas, these corporations have checked the spread of

electricity by successfully lobbying for limits on operating licences.

On top of commercial and municipal use, the slot meter, pioneered in Liverpool, then London, has introduced tens of thousands of households to gas within the last three years.

Lighting, too, has been revolutionised by the Welsbach incandescent gas mantle, which intensifies lighting by passing a jet through a chemically treated fabric. Gas mantle sales have risen from 20,000 to 300,000 in two years.

1896 (1896-1897)

India, 15 April 1896. In a further example of growing nationalism in western India, the Maharashtrian leader, Tilak, launches a Shivaji festival, following his successful Ganpati festival a few years ago.

Ottoman Empire, April 1896. To pacify the Internal Macedonian Revolutionary Organisation, founded in 1893, the Ottoman Sultan Abdul Hamid II promises reforms in Macedonia.

Moscow, 3 June 1896. In Moscow for the coronation of Czar Nicholas II, the Chinese envoy Li Hongzhang signs a secret treaty of alliance with Russia.

Germany, 1 July 1896. A Civil Law Code is enacted by the *reichstag*.

Madagascar, 6 August 1896. Madagascar is proclaimed a French colony.

Canada, 12 August 1896. Gold is discovered on a creek off the Klondike river in Yakon Territory.

Zanzibar, August 1896. Sultan Khaled, who seized control of Zanzibar over the head of the British-favoured candidate Seyyid Hamoud, surrenders to the British after a bombardment of his palace. Seyyid Hamoud becomes sultan and recognises the British protectorate set up on 4 November 1890.

Sudan, 21 September 1896. Herbert Kitchener, who took control of the Anglo-Egyptian army in March with the object of reconquering the Sudan, seizes the town of Dongola.

Tunisia, 28 September 1896. France and Italy sign a convention by which Italy recognises the French protectorate over Tunisia and the status of Italian residents in Tunis is resolved.

Zimbabwe, 13 October 1896. Cecil Rhodes makes peace with the Matabele chiefs who revolted against his rule.

London, 23 October 1896. Kidnapped and detained in the Chinese legation in London, awaiting secret transfer back to China for execution, the Chinese revolutionary Sun Yat-sen is released through the intervention of his former teacher, Dr Cantlie.

Ethiopia, 26 October 1896. The Italians and the Ethiopians sign the treaty of Addis Ababa by which Italy recognises the independence of Ethiopia and retains only the colony of Eritrea.

USA, 3 November 1896. William McKinley, former Republican governor of Ohio, is elected president.

Persia, 1896. Following the assassination of *Shah* Nasir al-Din, he is succeeded by his son Muzaffar al-Din.

USA, 1896. *The Red Badge of Courage*, a second novel by Stephen Crane, about the American civil war, is published.

France, 1896. The Hungarian Jewish writer Theodor Herzl publishes *The Jewish State*, in which he advocates the formation of a Jewish state to solve the Jewish Question.

France, 1896. The physicist Henri Becquerel identifies the radioactivity of uranium.

Germany, 1896. The satirical newspaper *Simplicissimus* is founded by Albert Langen and the cartoonist Thomas Heine.

Spain, 1896. The novelist Vicente Blasco Ibanez publishes *Tierras Malditas*.

Britain, 1896. A new newspaper, the *Daily Mail*, begins publication.

New Orleans, 26 January 1897. Prostitution is legalised in an area on the edge of the French Quarter which is becoming known as "Storyville".

Crete, 10 February 1897. Following Crete's proclamation of union with Greece four days ago, the Greeks send ships and troops to the island.

Madagascar, 28 February 1897. The Malagasy monarchy is abolished.

Crete, 18 March 1897. The powers announce a blockade of the island.

Zanzibar, 6 April 1897. Sultan Seyyid Hamoud abolishes slavery.

Greece, 7 April 1897. War breaks out between Greece and the Ottoman empire.

St Petersburg, 30 April 1897. Russia and Austria reach an agreement to maintain the *status quo* in the Balkans.

Britain, 14 May 1897. The Italian physicist Guglielmo Marconi makes the first communication by wireless telegraphy.

Greece, 19 May 1897. Having suffered several defeats by the Ottomans and been forced to withdraw from Crete, the Greeks sign an armistice at Thessaly, ending their month-old war.

France, May 1897. The writer Andre Gide publishes *The Fruits of the Earth*.

Britain, 22 June 1897. Queen Victoria celebrates her Diamond Jubilee.

Germany, June 1897. Admiral Alfred von Tirpitz is appointed secretary of state for the navy.

Uganda, 6 July 1897. Following the arrest by the British of some of his chiefs, who were planning a revolt against Protestant power, *Kabaka* Mwanga flees.

Queen Victoria celebrates 60 years' reign

London, July 1897
The queen has taken up with great enthusiasm the suggestion by her colonial secretary, Joseph Chamberlain, that her Diamond Jubilee celebrations could be highlighted by a full-scale conference of prime ministers of all the colonies and representatives of India and the dependencies.

An informal gathering on these lines was held at the time of the Golden Jubilee. Now, ten years on, the imperial vision has gained a stronger hold on the public imagination, largely due to the efforts of Mr Chamberlain, who says that the empire must unite if it is to survive in the face of the growing power of Germany and other rivals. The colonial premiers applauded his call for closer political, military and commercial links, but, jealous of their own self-government, rejected his suggestion for a federal council for the empire.

Queen Victoria arrives at St Paul's Cathedral to celebrate her Diamond Jubilee.

Audiences flock to moving picture shows

New York City, Autumn 1896
People in the front row of a theatre here are ducking in their seats as a huge wave threatens to engulf them – but they stay dry. What they have been watching is the latest craze in entertainment.

It is the moving picture show, or "flickers", the result of almost simultaneous inventions by Thomas Edison in America and the Lumiere brothers, Auguste and Louis, in France. Several vaudeville theatres in New York are now equipped with the Edison "Vitascope" system and, between comedy turns, dancers and ballads, show hand-tinted scenes including an umbrella dance, a burlesque boxing match and that wave breaking on a New Jersey pier.

The Lumiere "Cinematograph" opened in June, showing six short films made by the brothers, and the American "Biograph" offers *Rip Van Winkle* and a spectacular railway journey shot in Wales. In Britain, enthusiastic "producers" centred in Hove, Sussex, are also making short "flickers".

Pere Ubu gives much calculated offence

Paris, 1896
Uproar engulfed the Theatre de l'Oeuvre at the premiere of *Ubu Roi*, a fantastic play by Alfred Jarry which offends all the traditional rules of playwriting and good taste. It centres on the grotesque character of Pere Ubu, bloated to pumpkinlike proportions and equally gross in his speech and behaviour.

He opens the play by advancing to the footlights and hissing a swear word in the audience's face. There are many more obscenities in this celebration of absurdity. Pere Ubu and his wife Mere Ubu lead a cast of unlikely characters such as the king and queen of Poland and a single person carrying a banner inscribed "Whole Polish Army".

"Big Sword" gang broken up after clash

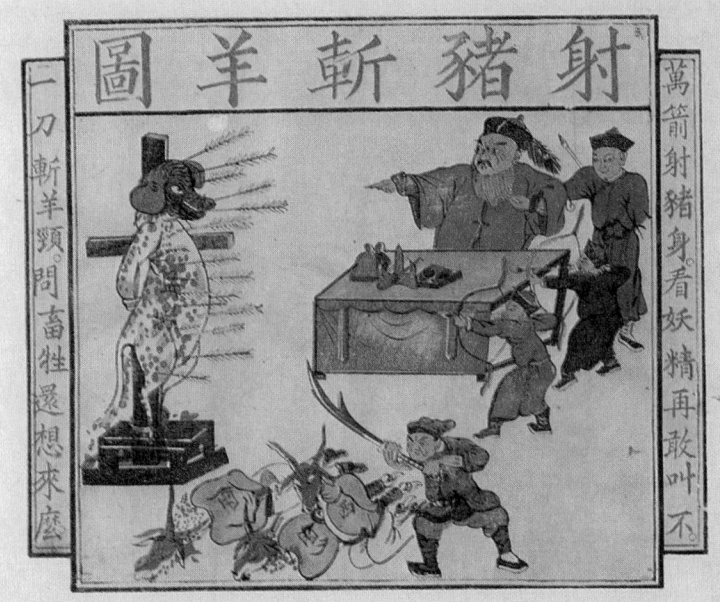

The crucifixion of Christ. The word "Jesus", in Chinese, means pig.

China, 1 July 1896

The troublesome Big Sword Society which has been raiding Catholic missions and the homes of their converts in Jiangsu was broken up by the authorities today. Thirteen members of the band led by Peng Guilin have been arrested following a clash between the society and troops cooperating with the local militia.

The origins of the Big Swords are lost in antiquity, but they emerged in the last few years as a self-protection organisation when troops were withdrawn from the coastal areas to fight in the Sino-Japanese war and banditry became rampant. The bandits were well-armed, so the Big Swords concentrated on learning martial arts and bolstered their fighting techniques with charms and incantations which were reputed to make them invulnerable to swords.

This combination of boxing skill and magic protection became known as the Armour of the Golden Bell. The Big Swords enjoyed considerable success against the bandits, but fell foul of the authorities when they turned on the Christians in a quarrel which had its origins in a feudal dispute over land.

German air pioneer dies in his own glider

Germany, 1896

Otto Lilienthal, one of the great pioneers of aviation, has made his last, tragic flight. News has come from Stolln, near Rhinow, in Germany, that his latest machine, a glider, has crashed, killing the man who had made over 2,000 flights.

Lilienthal had a passion for flying. He designed and flew monoplane and biplane gliders of all kinds, which he launched from an artificial hill near Lichterfelde. He also explored the possibilities – as Leonardo da Vinci had done centuries earlier – of aeroplanes with flapping wings. Lilienthal did much to popularise gliding as a European sport.

Otto Lilienthal flying in one of his unique gliders, near Lichterfelde.

Ethiopia routs Italians

Ethiopia, 1 March 1896

In the worst disaster to befall a European army in Africa, 100,000 Ethiopian troops have destroyed an Italian army at Adowa, in Tigre province, leaving over 7,000 dead.

The war was hardly necessary. But Crispi, the Italian prime minister, faced with economic depression and anarchy at home, was resolved on foreign conquest – and conquest on the cheap.

He despatched to Eritrea the elderly General Baratieri, a fellow veteran of Garibaldi's Thousand, to take charge of an inadequate army of 16,000. Recklessly provoking Ethiopia by occupying northern Tigre, Baratieri lingered in Tigre for a year, giving Menelik time to gether his army of 100,000 – 80,000 with Italian rifles.

Last night Menelik drew the Italians out of their prepared positions. Their advance was chaotic. Orders

Menelik, who has united Ethiopia, commanding his army at Adowa.

were misunderstood, brigades became separated, and one by one the Ethiopians wiped them out. The result will shock Europe. More Italians have died here than in the entire Italian *Risorgimento*.

Athens hosts the revived Olympic Games

The start of the Olympic 100 metre race, won by Burke (USA) in red shorts.

Athens, April 1896

After a gap of over 1,500 years the Olympic Games are being revived here in modern style. The original games were first held on the plains of Olympia, near here, in 776BC, in honour of the god Zeus. They included athletics, games and contests of choral poetry and dance. They were held every four years until AD393.

The new games focus on athletics and sports. They have been revived by Baron Pierre de Coubertin, a strong advocate of physical education in France. He began working on the idea in 1892 at a meeting of the French Athletic Sports Union. Two years later he won the unanimous support of an international athletics congress in Paris.

Coubertin is not just interested in physical prowess. He hopes that the big nations will fight each other in the games instead of rushing into wars of national prestige.

Boston, 1 September 1897. An underground railway system comes into operation.

China, 14 November 1897. Using the murder of two German Catholic missionaries in Shandong province on 1 November as a pretext, German naval forces occupy Kiaochow Bay, with a view to developing it and the village of Qingdao into a German naval base.

Spain, 25 November 1897. On the return to power of the liberal statesman Praxedes Sagasta, the Madrid government adopts a conciliatory attitude towards the rebels in Cuba.

Austria, 28 November 1897. Casimir von Badeni is forced to resign as president following his unpopular decision to give the Czech and Moravian languages equality with German for judicial and administrative purposes.

Istanbul, 4 December 1897. The Greeks and the Ottomans sign a peace treaty.

China, 15 December 1897. Russian warships enter Port Arthur (*Lushun*) on the Liaodong peninsula.

France, 28 December 1897. The playwright Edmond Rostand makes his name with *Cyrano de Bergerac*.

Sweden, 1897. The Swedish engineer Salomon Andree and his two companions are lost in attempt to cross the north polar region by balloon.

Egypt, 1897. Mohammed Abduk publishes his *Epistle*, a modern interpretation of Islam.

India, 1897. Serious risings break out on the North-West Frontier against British rule.

Switzerland, 1897. Theodor Herzl convenes the first Zionist Congress at Basle.

Britain, 1897. The physicist Joseph John Thomson discovers that atoms include very small, negatively-charged particles called electrons.

New York City, 1 January 1898. The boroughs of Brooklyn, Queen's, Richmond, Manhattan and the Bronx unite to form Greater New York.

Cuba, 15 February 1898. The US warship *Maine* blows up in Havana harbour – Spanish sabotage is suspected.

China, 6 March 1898. Germany signs a convention with China by which it acquires "leased territories".

India, 27 March 1898. The lawyer and educational reformer Saiyid Ahmed Khan, the greatest Indian Moslem of the century, dies.

Germany, 28 March 1898. An act is passed providing for a substantial expansion of the German navy.

USA, 25 April 1898. The USA declares war on Spain.

Germany, 30 April 1898. Admiral von Tirpitz founds the German Navy League.

Philippines, 1 May 1898. US forces under George Dewey destroy the Spanish fleet in Manila Bay.

Britain, 19 May 1898. The great Liberal statesman William Ewart Gladstone dies.

Italy, May 1898. Following a riot caused by the economic situation and the defeat in Ethiopia, a state of siege is proclaimed in Milan.

China, 1898. Britain obtains the New Territories of Hong Kong under a 99-year lease. In addition, Britain obtains Weihaiwei on the Shandong peninsula as a leased territory. France acquires Guangzhouwan in Guangdong province under a similar lease arrangement.

China, 1898. Devastating floods caused by breaks in the Yellow River banks in Shandong are followed by prolonged and severe drought in northern China. This conjunction of natural disasters and foreign aggression contributes to the rise of the violent, anti-foreign *Boxer* movement.

West Africa, 1898. Samori Toure, who retreated west in 1894 to set up a new Mandingo kingdom in the Ivory Coast/Gold Coast hinterland, is captured by the French and exiled to Gabon.

France, 1898. The sculptor Auguste Rodin unveils his *Monument to Balzac*.

France, 1898. The social scientist Emile Durkheim founds a learned journal called *L'Annee Sociologique*.

France, 1898. Oscar Wilde publishes *The Ballad of Reading Gaol* while living in Paris under the name of Sebastian Melmoth.

Britain, 1898. H G Wells publishes *The War of the Worlds*.

Spain, 1898. Miguel de Unamuno, Jose Ortegay Gasset and Jose Martinez Rui, known as Azorin, call for an intellectual and moral renaissance in Spain.

Moscow, 1898. Fyodor Chaliapin, the Russian bass, makes his first appearance as Boris Godunov.

USA, 1898. The novelist Henry James publishes *The Turn of the Screw*.

USA, 1898. Caleb Bradham of North Carolina begins marketing Pepsi-Cola.

J'Accuse! Emile Zola pleads for Dreyfus

Paris, 13 January 1898
The seething cauldron known as the Dreyfus Affair boiled over today with France's leading novelist, Emile Zola, publicly accusing the war office of judicial crime. In an open letter headlined *J'Accuse* in *L'Aurore*, Zola indicts the army general staff for anti-Semitism and for the way it has covered up the wrongful conviction for treason of Alfred Dreyfus, a Jewish officer, now serving life on Devil's Island.

Zola's attack, which may lead to his prosecution, was sparked by the latest farcical episode two days ago when Commandant Ferdinand Esterhazy was acquitted after requesting a court-martial. Esterhazy's handwriting was recently identified as that found on a note from a French officer to the military *attache* at the German embassy. Less than four years ago the handwriting was identified as Dreyfus' and led to his conviction. Georges Picquart, the intelligence chief who made the Esterhazy connection, has since been posted to Africa.

Zola: a sword for a pen.

Crete rises up against its Ottoman rulers

Crete, Summer 1897
After months of fighting between Christians and Moslems all over the island, Crete has won the approval of the great powers for its declaration of autonomy. Greek forces have left the island, but an Ottoman army remains.

Last September a package of reforms was agreed; since then Crete's Ottoman rulers have been dragging their feet, and the *Ethnike Hetaeria* secret society has been agitating for a Greek-led rebellion.

The arrival of a Greek expeditionary force in February brought renewed clashes and massacres, but an international fleet blockaded the coast while Greece and the Ottomans were forced to come to terms.

In 1896 gold nuggets were found in Yukon territory, on Klondike Creek, a tributary of the River Yukon in north-west Canada. Now miners are pouring up the Yukon trail from California. Typical of the adventurers is 20-year-old Jack London – runaway, sailor, socialist, drunk and tramp; hardly the sort of settler that Canada would wish to encourage.

Chinese lands grabbed

China, 15 December 1897
Chinese fears that their country will be "sliced up like a melon" by the great powers were justified today when the Russian fleet sailed into the ice-free naval base of Port Arthur on the Liaodong Peninsula. The Russians are using the pretext of protecting China, and forcing the Germans to withdraw from Kiaochow which they seized after the murders of two German missionaries.

The rivalry to slice the melon intensified after China's defeat in the war with Japan revealed all its weaknesses. Russia, France and Germany intervened when they learnt that Japan was to receive the Liaodong Peninsula under the treaty of Shimonoseki, and forced China to "retrocede" it. The powers have used threats, loans at exorbitant rates and huge bribes to obtain pieces of Chinese territory and trade. The Russians bribed Li Hongzhang, the emperor's envoy, with three million *roubles* to sign a deal enabling them to extend the

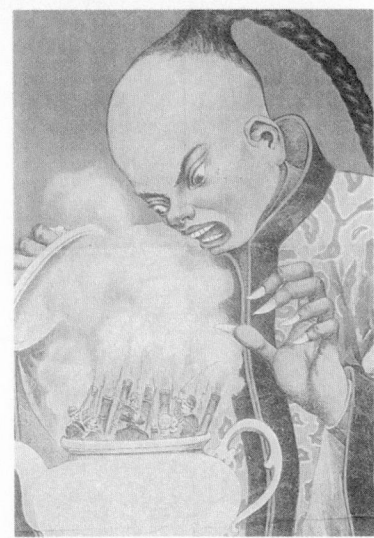

A Russian cartoon of Chinese reaction to increasing western penetration.

Trans-Siberian Railway through northern Manchuria, giving them a shorter route to Vladivostok. France has forced concessions in Indochina and Britain is enlarging its Hong Kong colony. Soon the melon will have no pips left.

FOREIGN POWERS IN CHINA

RUSSIA
OUTER MONGOLIA
MANCHURIA
XINJIANG
INNER MONGOLIA
Beijing
Port Arthur (Russ.)
KOREA
Weihai (Brit.)
SHANTUNG
Quingdao (Ger.)
TIBET
Shanghai
TAIWAN (Jap.)
Macao (Port.)
Hong Kong

Spheres of interest or influence

Russian	German
British	No dominant foreign influence
French	
Japanese	Foreign ports

"Decadent" artist dies a Roman Catholic

London, 1898
Aubrey Beardsley, the leading visual exponent of the "decadent" wing of *art nouveau* has died of consumption, aged 26. Daubed in his lifetime a force of evil, he died a convert to Roman Catholicism.

He stood for the new century which he never saw, and his graphic style questioned old assumptions

William de Morgan's peacock plate.

ISOLDE

Beardsley's magnetically evil Isolde.

and old philosophies. As his illustrations for the quarterly, *The Yellow Book* and *The Savoy*, he was not frightened to shock. His drawings for Oscar Wilde's banned play *Salome* caused scandal because of their eroticism, and this attained pornographic proportions in *Lysistrata*.

Like so many British artists he received more acclaim from abroad than from home. In Germany and Austria, where Gustav Klimt uses the *art nouveau* style, which they call *Jugendstil*, he is rated one who has captured the spirit of an age without god – though he found that God in the end.

A poster for Job cigarette papers.

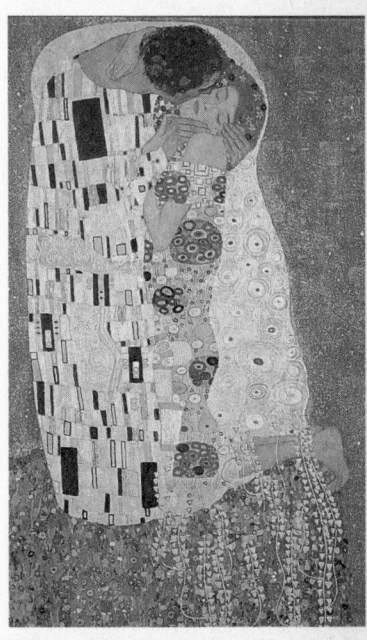

Gustav Klimt's painting "The Kiss".

World Zionist Congress spearheads push for a Jewish homeland

Switzerland, 31 August 1897
Leaders of the world's Jewish community met today in Basle to discuss their hopes for the establishment of a Jewish state in Palestine.

More than 200 delegates attended, embracing every variety of Jewish thought. They came primarily from the poorer communities of central and eastern Europe and Russia, where the Zionist dream has flourished most dramatically.

They heard the Zionist leader Theodor Herzl, the author of *The Jewish State* (1896), declare: "We want to lay the foundation stone for the house which will become the refuge of the Jewish nation."

The three-day congress then agreed the "Basle programme", stating: "Zionism aspires to create a publicly guaranteed homeland for the Jewish people in the land of Israel."

1898

China, 11 June. The Guangxu emperor issues a decree instigating a period of reform and self-strengthening.

Nigeria, 14 June. Britain and France conclude the Niger convention, settling one African dispute which is bringing them to the brink of war.

Pacific, 20 June. The US Navy seizes the island of Guam.

Sudan, 10 July. French troops under Jean-Baptiste Marchand occupy Fashoda on the Nile.

Cuba, 17 July. US forces capture Santiago.

Puerto Rico, 28 July. The island surrenders to the USA.

Hawaii, 12 August. The sovereignty of the republic of Hawaii is transferred to the USA.

Philippines, 13 August. Manila, the capital of the Philippines, falls to the US.

Europe, 30 August. Britain and Germany agree to share in a loan to the bankrupt Portuguese government, for which the Portuguese colonies in Africa will be treated as security.

Sudan, 2 September. Sir Herbert Kitchener leads the British to victory over the *Mahdists* at Omdurman and takes Khartoum.

Switzerland, 10 September. Elizabeth, the empress of Austria, is assassinated by the Italian anarchist Luigi Luccheni at Geneva.

Sudan, 19 September. British troops under Kitchener reach Fashoda.

China, 21 September. The Empress Dowager Cixi carries out a *coup d'e'etat* when a plot-by the emperor and the radical reformers against her is discovered. This ends the "Hundred Days" of reform.

Ottoman Empire, October. Kaiser William II visits Palestine and Syria and assures the Ottoman sultan, Abdul Hamid II, of his support.

Sudan, 3 November. Following an acute crisis in Anglo-French relations, the French evacuate Fashoda.

Crete, 6 November. The Ottomans evacuate the island.

Paris, 10 December. The USA and Spain sign a treaty ending their war in the Caribbean and the Pacific. The USA acquires Cuba, Puerto Rico, Guam and, for a $20 million indemnity, the Philippines.

Spain loses its colonies

The blowing-up of the "Maine" in Havana harbour, on 15 February.

Paris, 10 December
In March, a photographer sent to Cuba to take pictures of Cuban insurgents fighting for their liberty sent a cable to his editor. EVERYTHING QUIET STOP NO TROUBLE HERE, he reported.

The reply came from the publisher of the *New York Journal.* PLEASE REMAIN STOP YOU FURNISH THE PICTURES AND I WILL FURNISH THE WAR – HEARST. In three weeks the US was at war with Spain.

From the moment that Cuban colonists rose up against their masters in Madrid, William Randolph Hearst's *Journal* and its bitter rival, the *New York World* had been feeding and fomenting public feeling with stories of atrocities and brutality in Spanish concentration camps.

Despite the sincere reluctance of President McKinley, jingoism by Congress and people was a major factor in the declaration of war; when the *USS Maine* was blown up by a Spanish mine in Havana harbour with the loss of 252 men, the US was gripped by war hysteria. Washington's "hawks" had their

McKinley versus Alfonso of Spain.

way and Congress dispatched an ill-equipped invasion force to Cuba. The bellicose under-secretary for the navy, Theodore Roosevelt, made a name for himself, perhaps for foolhardiness, by leading his horseless "Rough Riders" in a near-suicidal charge up a hill at Santiago with 1,000 casualties.

A peace treaty was signed today. Spain has ceded Cuba, Puerto Rico, Guam and the Phillipines to the US for 20 million dollars. The secretary of state, John Hay, has called it "a splendid little war".

Married team finds glowing radium

Paris
Pierre and Marie Curie have identified the components of radium. The two scientists, Pierre Curie and Marie Sklodowska met in the spring of 1894 and were married the next year. For three years they have endured poverty to have time to develop their researches. Their first achievement was the discovery of a highly radioactive and dangerous element, which they called *polonium*, after Marie's native country, Poland. Since then the two scientists have continued their work and have now discovered another, more important, radioactive material in nature *–radium*. They detected it when they were extracting pure substances from ore. The Curies plan to study its radioactive properties in detail, including its effect on living tissue.

Britain wants pacts with US, Germany

Birmingham, Britain, 13 May
In a speech that has caused a sensation in foreign capitals, Joseph Chamberlain, the colonial secretary, told his Birmingham constituents that Britain could no longer live in splendid isolation, "envied by all and suspected by all". All the powerful states of Europe had made alliances and Britain must follow suit. He was critical of Russia for breaking its pledges of peace, saying: "Who sups with the devil must have a very long spoon."

Mr Chamberlain made it clear that he favoured pacts with Germany and the United States. His speech was received with derision in the German press, denounced in St Petersburg, scorned by his own prime minister, and welcomed only by some leading US journals.

Russian Seagull soars to dizzy heights after first flop

Moscow, 17 October
Anton Chekhov, who made his name with one-act farces, vowed that he would never write again for the stage after his first full-length play, *The Seagull*, was hissed in St Petersburg two years ago. Though

described as a comedy, it centres on a young would-be playwright, Konstantin, and a young would-be actress, Nina, both of whom come to unhappy ends.

The new Moscow Art Theatre, dedicated to natural acting by its

founder, Konstantin Stanislavsky, persuaded Chekhov to allow another production, which has triumphed as a new natural kind of drama. "There's no use being theatrical," Chekhov told his actors, "these are simple ordinary people."

Reforms crushed by Chinese empress

China, 21 September

The Empress Dowager Cixi, the power behind the young emperor's throne, moved ruthlessly today to stamp out the reform movement threatening to sweep aside the old, corrupt Manchu bureaucracy. The reformers, led by the scholar Kang Youwei, had gained the confidence of Emperor Guangxu in the crisis following China's defeat by Japan and the subsequent scramble for concessions by the great powers.

Kang Youwei urged the emperor "to adopt the purpose of Peter the Great of Russia as our purpose, and to take the Meiji Reform of Japan as the model for our reform".

Guangxu, impressed by the refor-

Cixi, China's dowager empress: the power behind the imperial throne.

mers' writings, summoned Kang to an audience on 11 June and began to issue decrees based on his proposals. In 103 days he issued 110 edicts ordering the remaking of China. This period is famous as the "Hundred Days of Reform".

The Manchu officials did their best to stem the flood; then, panicking, urged Cixi, "the Old Buddha", to take action. She, with all the accumulated cunning of 40 years in power in China, bided her time.

The moment came when the reformers, worried by their lack of military support, enlisted a sympathetic general, Yuan Shikai. But he betrayed them. Cixi staged a palace coup. The emperor has been made prisoner. Kang has fled. Six other reformers await execution.

Mahdists lose in Sudan

British Redcoats resist the first Mahdist attack of the battle, at 6.30am.

Khartoum, Sudan, 2 September

An Anglo-Egyptian force commanded by General Sir Herbert Kitchener today defeated a massive army of dervishes in a pitched battle outside Omdurman, killing at least 10,000. Of the 26,000 half-British and half-Egyptian army, only 500 have been killed. Gordon of Khartoum, the military misfit with passions for the bible and teenage boys, killed by dervishes 14 years ago, has been avenged.

The battle began when dervishes attacked the Anglo-Egyptian encampment at Egeiga, four miles from Khartoum. They fought with savage and noble courage, falling in lines to Kitchener's Maxim guns. Then Kitchener ordered a counterattack towards Omdurman and nearly lost the day when dervishes charged his rear. Only the equally noble and savage courage of the Sudanese Brigade saved the day. The battle ended in a cloud of dust, blinding all combatants, as the 21st Lancers – against all the rules of war – charged over open ground in a frontal attack on dervishes holding broken land. If the large dervish force there did not happen to be leaving (so the Lancers charged into nothing), they would have been slaughtered. As it was the dervish rearguard sniped off 25 per cent of them. Gordon would *not* have approved. He would probably have sent the Lancer's commander home. He would have disapproved even less of a young officer named Winston Churchill who claimed

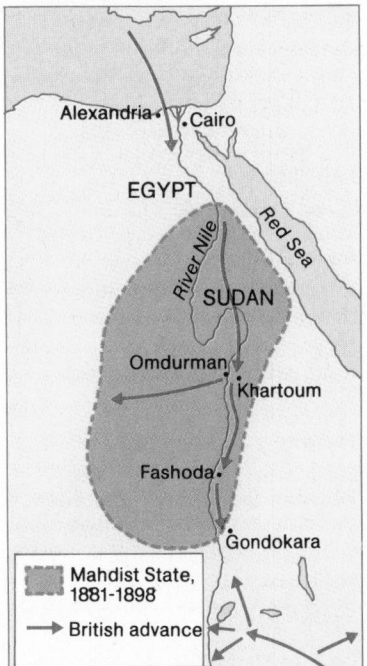

that he led the charge. He would have probably have had him shot. "I think we have given them a good dusting," said Kitchener, forgetting he was nearly overrun from behind.

French army forced out of Fashoda as Britain claims Nile

Southern Sudan, November

A French force of several hundred Senegalese troops under six white officers, are to evacuate their fort at Fashoda on the upper Nile. The French, under Captain Jean-Baptiste Marchand arrived there after an epic journey across the continent from Brazzaville, long after the dervishes had driven Britain out of the Sudan. The French came into a pagan area which the Moslem dervishes made no effort to occupy. Since then General Kitchener has defeated the Mahdists and advanced down the Nile, backed by an army of 25,000. Kitchener – who had no intention of allowing the headwaters of the Nile to go to a rival power – treated them with extreme courtesy, then hoisted the British and Egyptian flags and told them to clear off. The affair had the makings of a major international incident, but the French foreign minister, Theophile Delcasse, has accepted the local inbalance of power, averting a possible war.

Kitchener, as seen through French eyes: "the pacifier of Africa".

Matabeles revolt against Rhodes' dream

Zimbabwe, April 27

The revolts and risings by Africans which have rocked the white colony of "Rhodesia" for the past two years are over. The revolt of the old Ndebele kingdom was crushed in six months of 1896; but since then numerous small shona chief-

doms have risen. Now, with the execution of two priests who inspired the shona, the whites think they have crushed the spirit of rebellion. Nonetheless, the blacks hold the names of the two priests, Chimurensa and his female collegue, Nehanda, sacred.

1899 (1899–1900)

Sudan, 19 January 1899. Britian and Egypt establish condominium over Sudan.

Philippines, 4 February 1899. Fighting breaks out between US forces and Philippine rebels, who have proclaimed an independent republic.

France, 18 February 1899. Emile Loubet is elected president following the death of Felix Faure.

Sudan, 21 March 1899. Britain and France sign a convention ending the Fashoda crisis.

South Africa, 24 March 1899. *Uitlanders* (foreigners) attracted into the country by gold petition Queen Victoria to redress their numerous grievances.

Crete, March 1899. Prince George of Greece is appointed high commissioner of the island.

South Africa, 5 June 1899. Talks at Bloemfontein between Alfred Milner, the high commissioner in South Africa, and President Kruger break down over the issue of granting the vote to Uitlanders.

East Africa, 15 June 1899. By a victory at Isangi, east of Lake Kivu, Germany takes control of the lakeside kingdom of Rwanda.

The Hague, 29 July 1899. A peace conference attended by representatives from 26 states decides to set up a permanent international court of arbitration.

France, 7 August 1899. The guilt of Captain Alfred Dreyfus, condemned and deported for treason in 1894, is confirmed by a court martial at Rennes.

USA, 6 September 1899. The secretary of state, John Hay, embarks on an "open door" policy towards China, urging the European powers and Japan to respect the territorial integrity of China and pursue a policy of free trade with the country.

Somalia, September 1899. Mohammed ben Abdullah, a Somali chief known as the Mad *Mullah*, proclaims himself *mahdi* and declares a *jihad* (holy war) on the British and the Italians.

South Africa, 12 October 1899. War breaks out between the British and Boers from the Transvaal and Orange Free State.

South Africa, 15 October 1899. The Boers, who surrounded Mafeking two days ago, lay siege to Kimberley.

Moscow, 27 October 1899. *Uncle Vanya* by Anton Chekhov is performed for the first time, at the Art Theatre.

South Africa, 2 November 1899. The Boers under Piet Joubert lay siege to Ladysmith.

Washington, DC, 2 December 1899. The USA, Germany and Britain sign a treaty agreeing that the Pacific Samoan Islands will be divided between the USA and Germany.

South Africa, 11 December 1899. The Boers under Piet Cronje defeat the British at Magersfontein.

South Africa, 15 December 1899. British forces under Sir Redvers Buller are defeated by the Boers at the battle of Colenso.

Britain, 1899. Edward Elgar's *Enigma Variations* is performed for the first time.

Nigeria, 1 January 1900. Nigeria becomes a British protectorate.

New York City, 2 January 1900. The first electric omnibus goes into operation.

South Africa, 10 January 1900. Lord (Frederick) Roberts replaces Sir Redvers Buller as commander-in-chief of the British forces in South Africa, with Herbert Kitchener as his chief-of-staff.

Britain, 20 January 1900. The art critic and social theorist John Ruskin dies after years of insanity.

South Africa, 24 January 1900. The British under General Warren take Spion Kop.

Rome, January 1900. Giacomo Puccini's opera *Tosca* is performed for the first time.

Britain, 27 February 1900. British trade unions create the Labour Party.

South Africa, 27 February 1900. The Boer General Piet Cronje surrenders to the British at Paardeberg after suffering a defeat.

South Africa, 28 February 1900. Following their relief of Kimberley earlier in the month, the British relieve Ladysmith.

South Africa, 13 March 1900. British forces under Lord Roberts take Bloemfontein.

USA, 14 March 1900. The US dollar goes onto the gold standard.

Crete, 19 March 1900. The British archaeologist Sir Arthur Evans begins excavations at the palace of Knossos.

Brussels, 4 April 1900. Jean-Baptiste Sipido, a 16-year-old anarchist, attempts to assassinate the prince of Wales.

South Africa, 9 April 1900. The Boers defeat the British at Kroonstadt.

Paris, 14 April 1900. The World Exhibition opens.

Pacific, 19 May 1900. Britain annexes the Friendly Islands (*Tonga*).

Britain takes over control of Nigeria

A king receives his new masters.

Lagos, 1 January 1900

Britain's Colonial Office today gains control of all three parts of Nigeria. Since the Lagos colony was founded on the coast 40 years ago, British power has been moving inland. This power has been largely in the form of a private company, the Royal Niger Company, which was given the right to rule by the Crown in a charter of 1886. Now that the company has staked claims as far north as the Hausa (Fulani) kingdoms, the Colonial Office feels the time is ripe to take charge of administration and to leave the business of commerce and profit-making to the company. So from today, northern Nigeria joins southern Nigeria and Lagos under Whitehall control.

Ugandan kings deported to Seychelles

Kampala, Uganda, 1899
British officials have exiled the two most powerful local kings to the Seychelles in the hope of establishing peace in this country which has been scarred by wars for most of the last decade.

Although Britain established the protectorate of Uganda in 1894, old rivalries soon broke out. Mwanga is *kabaka*, or king, of the Baganda and Kabarega rules their traditional rivals, the Banyoro. As well as ancient tensions there are conflicts between Protestant and Catholic converts and with Moslems who have the support of many of Britain's Sudanese troops. Mwanga declared himself a Moslem in his final abortive bid for power.

US split over war in the Philippines

Armour from the Philippines.

Washington, DC, 24 Nov 1899
After nine months of fierce jungle fighting, US troops completed the capture of Luzon, the biggest island in the Philippines, today. But fighting is far from over for the Americans in a country which favours guerrilla warfare.

The Philippines were surrendered to the United States by Spain under last year's treaty of Paris. President McKinley has vowed to "uplift and Christianise" the Filipino people – despite the fact that they have been Christians for centuries.

The US is deeply divided over the war, with influential politicians of both parties joining with trade unionists and industrialists to campaign against what they see as "new imperialism". Mark Twain has suggested that "the Stars and Stripes should be replaced by the skull and crossbones".

France finally grants pardon to Dreyfus

Paris, 19 September 1899

Alfred Dreyfus, the Jewish officer who claims that he was wrongly convicted of espionage, was today formally pardoned by the French government in a bid to end the bitter controversy over injustice and anti-Semitism that continues to threaten France's political stability. The move is a major rebuff for the army and its allies in the church and on the right.

In June the army, faced with growing public pressure to acquit Dreyfus, staged a retrial, reconvicting the 40-year-old Jewish captain of treason and sentencing him to ten years. The decision, against the weight of evidence and with many officers blatantly perjuring themselves to cover up corruption at the original hearing, convinced the government that the army will never give Dreyfus a fair trial. Dreyfus now wants his name cleared of spying for Germany.

Zola stoking the flames, as seen by the Italian newspaper "Il Papagallo".

Priest finds Chinese treasure trove

Beijing, 2 July 1899

A Daoist priest has discovered an amazing array of Buddhist paintings and sculptures in caves at Dunhuang in Gansu. Dunhuang is at the eastern end of the Silk Road, one of the great trade routes that crossed central Asia. Manuscript evidence reveals that the first cave was carved in 366, and that over the next thousand years more than a thousand caves were cut into the hillside, stretching to an area of over 30 miles (48 kilometres).

The paintings show how the Chinese had mastered the Indian styles even at this early date. Figures of the Buddha dominate, showing him as a preacher and also in some of his early incarnations, such as a golden gazelle. Some of the ceilings pay homage to other religions as well, and one has Buddhist, Hindu and Daoist figures together.

The new finds are of immense importance to scholars because the ninth-century persecution led to the destruction of most Buddhist

One of the exquisite Chinese paintings found in the Dunhuang caves.

art in China. There are also full versions of Chinese texts of the Tang dynasty, which have hitherto been known to scholars only as fragments.

Boers score successes

Boer General Joubert with his staff occupying Newcastle in Natal.

Capetown, 16 December 1899

At the end of a black week for the British in South Africa, almost 2,000 men and 12 heavy guns have been lost in battles with the Boer forces. A despondent Sir Redvers Buller, the commander-in-chief who arrived with reinforcements from England, cabled the cabinet in London saying he wanted to surrender. He has been replaced by Lord Roberts.

The British were outnumbered when war began last October with the Boers invading Cape Colony; they had 15,000 regulars in South Africa, with 10,000 due from India, to face the Boers' 50,000 mounted infantry. The Boers were also superior in field tactics and the gather-ing of intelligence. Within weeks they had all the British forces besieged in Ladysmith, Kimberley and Mafeking.

This was when the Boers made a strategic mistake. If they had contained the British in the three towns and sent their main force into the Cape, they would have had virtually the whole country under their control and deprived the British of their supply port and naval base.

Instead, the Boers – who went to war to rid themselves of British influence in the Transvaal and Orange Free State – may be wasting their strength on mounting full-scale sieges. They have 10,000 men around strategically unimportant Mafeking, for instance.

Enigmatic theme in Elgar's variations

London, June 1899

The finest English composer since Purcell – that is the verdict on Edward Elgar since this month's premiere of his *Enigma Variations*. In this work a theme (Elgar says it "goes with" a well-known tune – hence the enigma) is varied 14 times, sketching his wife, friends and himself in music. Elgar, aged 42, is a Catholic organist's son from Worcestershire. In him the tree of British music, which has produced Arthur Sullivan, Hubert Parry and Charles Stanford, seems at last to have borne the fruits of greatness.

Class struggle is all, says Red Rosa

Berlin, 18 April 1899

Rosa Luxembourg, a 28-year-old Polish-born Marxist, emerged as a leading anti-revisionist force in the Social Democratic Party today.

Her vehement attack on Eduard Bernstein, who argues that the conditions of the workers have improved, so reforms must come from within the system, stressed that parliament is a bourgeois sham and reaffirmed the need for revolution.

"Bloody Rosa", who is German through a marriage of convenience, also emphasised the internationalist nature of Marxism.

South Africa, 20 May. The British relieve Mafeking.

China, 21 May. Russia annexes Manchuria.

South Africa, 29 May. Britain annexes the Orange Free State.

China, 17 June. In response to the growing *Boxer* threat, the allied troops of Britain, Germany, France, Russia, the USA, Italy, Austria and Japan capture the Dagu forts.

China, 20 June. Dong Fuxiang's Gansu troops and the Boxers begin attacks on the legations, churches and other foreign establishments.

Philippines, 21 June. Arthur MacArthur, the US military governor, grants an amnesty to the Filipino rebels.

Britain, 29 June. The *Dictionary of National Biography* is completed.

Paris, 19 July. The *Metro* underground railway opens.

Italy, 30 July. King Umberto is shot dead by an anarchist. Victor Emmanuel III succeeds.

USA, 10 August. The USA wins the first International Lawn Tennis Trophy, established by Dwight F Davis.

China, 14 August. The allies enter Beijing and end the siege of the legations.

Germany, 25 August. The philosopher Friedrich Nietzsche dies after 12 years of insanity.

South Africa, 1 September. The British annex the Boer republic of the Transvaal.

Britain, 17 October. Lord Salisbury's Tory government is re-elected.

Europe, 20 October. Britain and Germany sign a pact to continue the open-door policy towards China.

USA, 6 November. The Republican President William McKinley is re-elected.

Canada, 8 November. Liberals under Sir Wilfrid Laurier win the general election.

Britain, 22 November. Arthur Sullivan, the composer of the famous Savoy operas with librettos by W S Gilbert, dies.

Paris, 9 December. *Nocturnes* by Claude Debussy is performed for the first time.

Paris, 30 November. The Irish writer Oscar Wilde dies.

India. The famine and the epidemic of bubonic plague, which have ravaged India for the past four years, abate.

New century opens in optimistic glow

The "Dawn of the Century" march.

London, 1 January
The first chime of midnight echoed down the length of Whitehall and deafening cheers rocked Trafalgar Square as a hundred thousand raucous Londoners went joyfully crazy as they sang, danced and kissed their way into the new century.

They had good reason: had not the 19th century belonged to Britain? Had not the *Pax Britannica* brought peace and stability to huge areas of the world? And, after all, Britain had been both the strongest power on this globe economically and the most stable politically.

But as rockets crashed out and countless bands played *Auld Lang Syne*, it was a good time to reflect. Britain is truly *Great* Britain today, but how much longer can it wear that mantle? It is the head of a great empire – but a savage war in South Africa has done much to shatter what had become national complacency.

Economically, Britain is being overtaken by Germany and the United States – both of whom possess greater manpower and mineral resources.

The mood in the streets last night was one of sublime optimism. More thoughful Britons tempered that glow in the knowledge that Britain is slowing down, becoming smug, indeed. Where are the giants of the Industrial Revolution, men like Stephenson and Brunel, and the inventive geniuses like Arkwright? And could any wealthy and civilised nation truly rejoice and ignore the conditions of overcrowding and poverty that are only just beginning to touch middle-class consciences?

Doctor tells us what our dreams mean

Vienna, 14 October
"Dreams are most profound when they seem most crazy." So declares Sigmund Freud, the Austrian psychologist, in a major work just published, *Die Traumdeutung*, or "The Interpretation of Dreams".

Freud believes that dreams are "the royal road to the unconscious" and contain disguised symbols for the repressed desires of the dreamer censored to an acceptable form. He analyses universal dream imagery. Walls which one climbs represent a man or a woman, according to the smoothness of the surface. Parents appear disguised as kings and queens, birth is represented by water – falling into it, or saving someone from it – and death by setting out on a journey. The majority of images are sexual symbols.

Count flies up in a motorised balloon

Count von Zeppelin's airship, on its maiden flight over Lake Constance.

Friedrichshafen, 2 July
A ship that flies was launched into the sky over Lake Constance today. The 420-foot craft, "airship" *LZ1*, has been invented by Count Ferdinand Zeppelin, aged 62, who retired from the army ten years ago. Zeppelin made balloon ascents in 1863 as a military observer during the American Civil War. His craft is a cigar-shaped frame lifted by gas. A 16hp engine linked to two propellers makes it independent of wind and provides a top speed of 20 mph (32kph). A sliding weight on the keel adjusts pitch and two rudders ensure horizontal control. Crew and passengers occupy two chambers in the keel.

The craft has taken ten years to design. Some problems of control were evident during today's first outing from a floating hangar on the lake near Friedrichshafen. But Zeppelin will assuredly get public support and funding. The count's basic idea of lighter-than-air flight is more rational in the light of experience than plans to build a machine which must beat its own weight by forward speed and lift from wing surfaces.

Freud: exploring the unconscious.

Mafeking siege lifted

Long Tom, a Boer heavy gun, trained on the besieged British troops at Mafeking.

London, 20 May
As it happened, Queen Victoria was visiting Wellington College in Berkshire. As she drove up, a banner was raised in greeting, bearing the words "Queen of Mafeking". The whole school was "quite mad with delight", she recorded in her diary. As for Londoners, she said, the goings-on were "indescribable".

Throughout the land, the news of the relief of Mafeking, after a siege of 217 days, has been received with a wild excitement that betrays the sense of relief felt by the British people after months of military reverses. Now they hope that, with Lord Roberts, the hero of Afghanistan, in command in South Africa, the Boers are in for a drubbing.

Mafeking is a small town on the railway from Kimberley to Rhodesia. It is of no strategic importance in the war, but Colonel Robert Baden-Powell, the cavalry officer, the commander of the British force there, tied up a Boer force of 10,000 by holding out. He organised teams of sappers to dig trenches and throw up earthworks, and kept outposts in touch with his HQ by using the town's schoolboys as runners, whom he called Boy Scouts. He sent out messages telling the folk at home that morale was high among soldiers and citizens.

Not everyone has been impressed by Baden-Powell's heroics. Colonel Sir Herbert Plumer, who commands the Rhodesian detachment, has remarked that it is an odd sort of cavalry officer who, at the first whiff of battle, begins digging trenches and eating his horses.

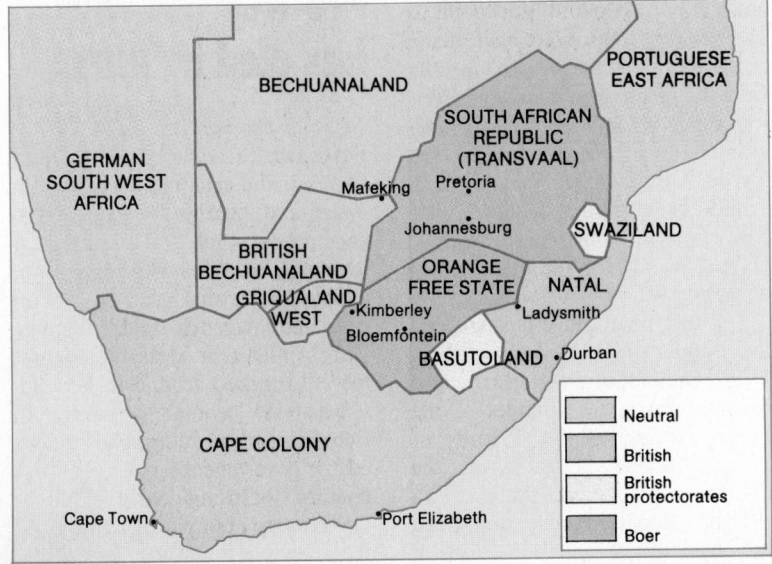

Allies march on Beijing

China, 14 August
The eight-nation allied relief force fought its way into Beijing in the early hours of this morning and lifted the siege of the legations, driving away the Boxers and the regular troops who have besieged the diplomatic quarter and the Beitang cathedral for the past two months.

The defenders have shown the utmost bravery, beating off repeated attacks while suffering from hunger and living in the most appalling conditions. It is unlikely, however, that they would have survived if it had not been for the restraining hand of Ronglu, the Chinese commander, who refused to allow the besiegers to use artillery which would have blown the legations apart.

Ronglu is convinced that the decision by Cixi, the empress dowager, to declare war on the "foreign devils" will prove disastrous for China. There seems little doubt that he is right. His army has vanished and Cixi, along with her nephew, the emperor – whom she keeps a captive – has fled, allegedly disguised as a peasant. Allied soldiers are already looting.

The trouble started with the wave of xenophobia which swept China after the defeat by Japan and the foreign scramble for concessions. From it emerged the society of Righteous and Harmonious Fists, who became known as the Boxers. Like their predecessors, the Big Swords, they practise martial arts and believe themselves immune from harm on the battlefield.

The explosion came last May when the Boxers massacred Chinese converts and isolated foreigners, burnt churches and destroyed the railway line between Beijing and Tientsin. Cixi was caught up in the tension. The German minister was murdered and foreign retribution became inevitable.

Allied troops battle against Boxers while relieving the legations at Beijing.

Theory says energy comes in tiny packets

Germany
A profound and disturbing idea has just been put forward that upsets the picture of the material world according to Isaac Newton that has been popular for centuries. The revolutionary theory comes from a 42-year-old German physicist, Max Planck. Planck, having studied a source of radiation known as a blackbody, has concluded that energy is emitted not in waves but in tiny packets, or *quanta*. Thus light consists of streams of packets called *photons*.

This new *quantum* theory explains phenomena such as absorption and radiation at the atomic level more convincingly than conventional theories. And Planck has also been able to describe quanta in precise mathematical terms.

Australia, 1 January. The Commonwealth of Australia comes into being.

Britain, 22 January. Queen Victoria dies and is succeeded by her son Edward VII.

Italy, 27 January. The composer Giuseppe Verdi dies.

Moscow, 31 January. Anton Chekhov's play *Three Sisters* is performed for the first time.

India, 12 February. The viceroy, Lord Curzon, creates the North-West Frontier province between Afghanistan and the Punjab.

Germany, 6 March. An anarchist makes an attempt on the life of Kaiser William II.

USA, 31 March. The first Mercedes motor car is built.

Venezuela, 9 August. Colombian troops invade Venezuela.

Detroit, 21 August. The Cadillac motor company is founded.

Britain, 4 September. In the Taff Vale railway case, the House of Lords rules that trade unions are liable for the financial losses of companies affected by industrial action.

China, 7 September. The *Boxer* Protocol is signed by China and the foreign powers, ending the Boxer rebellion.

France, 9 September. The painter Henri de Toulouse-Lautrec dies at the age of 36.

USA, 14 September. President William McKinley dies after being shot by an anarchist.

West Africa, 25 September. Britain annexes the Asante kingdom as part of the Gold Coast (*Ghana*).

China, 16 October. Russia signs a new agreement with China over Manchuria.

USA, 24 October. George Eastman sets up the Eastman Kodak camera company.

South Africa, October. Boer commandos invade Cape Colony, coming within 50 miles of Cape Town.

USA, 18 November. Britain and the USA sign the Hay-Pauncefote treaty, agreeing terms for a canal through Central America.

USA, 2 December. King Camp Gillette announces plans to market a disposable razor.

Britain, 11 December. Guglielmo Marconi sends the first wireless message across the Atlantic.

Polish anarchist assassinates president

President McKinley: a photograph taken 15 minutes before he was shot.

Washington, 14 September
President William McKinley, who established the United States as a world power with an overseas empire, died today after being shot by a Polish anarchist in Buffalo, New York. He is succeeded by the vice-president, Theodore Roosevelt, aged 42, already famous as a man of letters, soldier and statesman.

McKinley had served only six months of a second term; his administration has seen the highest tariffs in American history and the growth of expansionist policies. In 1898 Hawaii was annexed. In the Spanish-American War – when Roosevelt won glory commanding a volunteer force – the US acquired the Philippines, Puerto Rico and Guam.

"Teddy" Roosevelt becomes the youngest US president. Identified with the reform wing of the Republican Party, he sees his task as serving as the moral leader of the American people and safeguarding the nation against special interests.

Great minds deserve a prize, says Swede

Alfred Nobel, whose dynamite fortune will be used to further peace.

Oslo, 10 December
The first Nobel prizes were handed out today in Oslo and Stockholm to a handful of men who have made outstanding contributions in the fields of literature, chemistry, physics, medicine and peace. The cash awards have been funded by the Swede Alfred Nobel who made a fortune by inventing dynamite. His will stipulates that there will be annual awards for the great minds of the world.

The first peace prize is shared by the founder of the Red Cross, Jean Henri Dunant of Switzerland, and Frederic Passy, the founder of the French Society of the Friends of Peace. Another laureate was the discoverer of X-rays, the German Wilhelm Roentgen, who was given the physics prize.

Red radicals storm Russian cathedral

St Petersburg, 17 March
Mass was beginning in the great Kazan cathedral with its 96 Corinthian columns when several hundred students came tearing down the Nevsky Prospekt. They burst in, jeering and throwing stones at the precious *icon* of the Virgin of Kazan.

The students were eventually driven into the street, where they handed out leaflets calling for the overthrow of the czar. Two regiments of mounted Cossacks appeared and in a series of charges rounded up over 800 demonstrators.

Violent street demonstrations have occurred in Odessa, Kharkov and Kiev, and in Moscow, where the writer Leo Tolstoy joined factory workers and students in setting up barricades.

Cossacks clear Moscow barricades.

Pro-western writer has died in Japan

Japan, 3 February
Fukuzawa Yukichi, the Japanese *samurai* who renounced his warrior status and became a major influence on the spread of western ideas in Japan, has died at the age of 66.

Yukichi travelled widely in Europe and America and, adapting British utilitarian ideas to Japanese *mores*, attacked feudalism and advocated the people's possession of rights as well as duties. He supported the government's policy of "rich country – strong army", but he remains an example of enlightened thinking.

Australia becomes commonwealth

Melbourne, 1 January
After more than 50 years of debate and false starts the six separate states of Australia, including Tasmania, are united in a federal commonwealth constitution. Local pride and political jealousies repeatedly blocked moves towards unity, but external pressures did much to overcome parish-pump sentiment.

Notable among such pressures were fears from 1883 onward that Germany might colonise New Guinea and that France coveted the New Hebrides. Equally potent was the fear of Asian migration into Australia's remote northern territories. No unified defence policy existed for either contingency.

Even after the British Parliament had been presented with Australia's agreed proposals, Western Australia tried to amend them. There is still no agreement about the site for a federal capital except that it will be in New South Wales some 100 miles (160 kilometres) from Sydney. The first parliament, however, will meet in Melbourne later this year.

Australia proclaims whites-only policy

Australia
One of the first acts of the new Australian government has been to pass a law restricting the immigration of non-whites. The Federal Immigration Restriction Act prohibits the permanent settlement of any coloured person but allows students, officials and businessmen to enjoy temporary residence. Chinese immigration during the gold rush 50 years ago, which provoked riots, and a local shipping firm's attempt to replace white crews with cheap Chinese labour prompted the move.

There is also an underlying anxiety for Australia's cultural identity if massive immigration occurred from Asia or Polynesia. Some advocates of the new law think that a multiracial society would result in "mongrelisation", although white migration represents the genetically mixed stock of Celtic Ireland and Anglo-Saxon England. Aborigines are not discussed.

End of an era as Queen Victoria dies

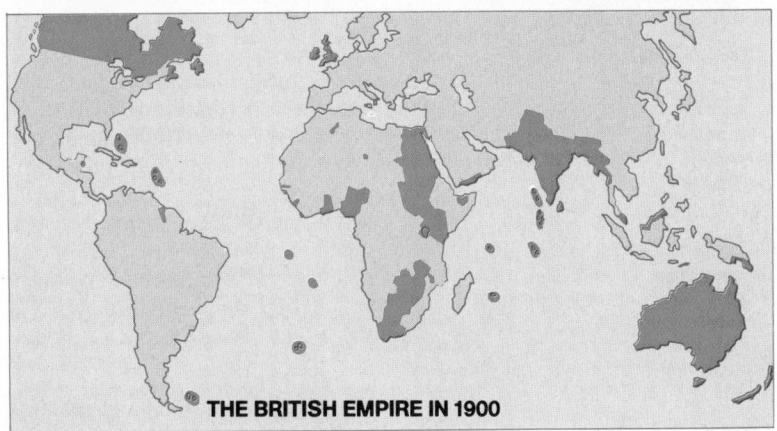

THE BRITISH EMPIRE IN 1900

Isle of Wight, Britain, 22 January
In recent months she left her chair only once without help, and then it was to pin a medal on a hospital patient. She was 81; her eyesight was failing and she suffered much from insomnia. The news filled her with sorrow. Her son Alfred ("poor, dear Affie") died, the king of Italy was assassinated, and a grandson, Prince Christian of Schleswig-Holstein, died of fever in South Africa. The war in South Africa overshadowed the last years of her eventful reign. Her 63 years on the throne had seen times of hardship and danger, but nothing quite like that war against a foe small in numbers but able to humiliate the greatest power on earth. It was like a portent. Victoria, the daughter of the impoverished duke of Kent, had seen her island people carry her power to the far corners of the world. They had made new countries, drawn new frontiers, and enjoyed wealth beyond the dreams of avarice. But now there were other runners in the race, bigger and potentially more powerful.

In the early years of her reign Victoria was supported by the dearly-loved Prince Albert, the husband from Germany. For many years she had mourned his death, but she had borne nine children

Victoria at her Diamond Jubilee.

and, as they married into other royal families, she became known as the "grandmother of Europe". This evening, soon after six o'clock, with her children and grandchildren at her bedside, her grandson the German kaiser among them, she passed into history.

Wireless message spans Atlantic Ocean

Guglielmo Marconi, whose messages in morse code can now cross the Atlantic.

Newfoundland, 11 December
Guglielmo Marconi, the 27-year-old Italian inventor, has finally confounded the sceptics who have sneered at his attempts at wireless transmission. At St John's here he has just received a message tapped out in morse code on the other side of the Atlantic in Poldhu, in Cornwall, England.

It is an even more impressive feat than his reports from mid-Atlantic on the yacht race two years ago. Marconi's invention owes a lot to the time he spent working in England, first with Sir Oliver Lodge and then with Sir William Preece, the chief engineer of the Post Office.

But it has been Marconi who pushed ahead with practical applications, first using balloons and kites to get his aerials to greater heights in order to transmit over huge distances.

Annie Oakley, the last of the great North America frontier myths, now in show business.

1902 (1902-1903)

London, 30 January 1902. Britain and Japan sign a treaty agreeing to respect each other's interests in China and Korea.

Berlin, 15 February 1902. The Berlin underground railway opens.

Spain, 20 February 1902. About 500 die in Barcelona strike clashes.

USA, 22 February 1902. The Yellow Fever Commission announces that the disease is carried by mosquitoes.

Britain, 26 February 1902. Lord Rosebery, the former Liberal prime minister, forms the Liberal League, splitting the Liberal Party.

Russia, February 1902. More than 30,000 students strike in protest at government attempts to curb the activities of student organisations.

South Africa, 26 March 1902. The British colonial statesman Cecil Rhodes dies.

USA, 7 April 1902. The Texas Oil Company (Texaco) is founded.

China, 8 April 1902. Russia signs a treaty with China over Manchuria, promising to withdraw its troops.

London, 9 April 1902. The Underground Electric Railways Company is incorporated.

Russia, 15 April 1902. Sipyagin, the head of the secret police, is killed by socialist revolutionaries.

Dublin, 16 April 1902. At a rally in Phoenix Park, 20,000 people protest at the British government's plans to impose tough new laws in Ireland.

Martinique, 8 May 1902. An eruption of Mount Pele wipes out the whole town of St Pierre.

London, 29 May 1902. The London School of Economics and Political Science opens.

Spain, 30 May 1902. King Alfonso XIII suspends the Madrid *Cortes* amid growing unrest.

South Africa, 31 May 1902. The Boers surrender to the British and sign the peace of Vereeniging, ending the Boer war and recognising British sovereignty.

Britain, 18 June 1902. The satirist Samuel Butler dies.

Europe, 23 June 1902. The triple alliance of Germany, Austria and Italy is renewed for 12 years.

USA, 28 June 1902. The USA pays France $40,000 for the rights to the Panama Canal.

Vienna, 29 June 1902. The French car maker Marcel Renault wins the first Paris-Vienna motor race.

USA, 1 July 1902. The Philippine Government Act, under which Filipinos will be ruled by a US presidential commission, is passed.

Russia, 3 July 1902. To avoid the spread of riots, in which thousands have already died, Czar Nicholas II offers talks with the people.

Britain, 12 July 1902. Arthur Balfour succeeds Lord Salisbury as Tory prime minister.

Venice, 14 July 1902. The campanile of St Mark's cathedral collapses.

Dublin, 1 September 1902. A state of emergency is declared.

South Africa, 17 September 1902. Martial law is lifted in Cape Colony.

Finland, 22 September 1902. Czar Nicholas abolishes nominal Finnish autonomy and appoints a Russian governor general.

France, 29 September 1902. The writer Emile Zola, the author of *Germinal* and *Therese Raquin* and valiant champion of Captain Dreyfus, dies.

Zimbabwe, 6 October 1902. A railway link between Bulawayo and Salisbury is completed.

Belgium, 15 November 1902. The anarchist Gennaro Rubino makes an attempt on the life of King Leopold II.

Germany, 22 November 1902. The steel magnate Friedrich Krupp, head of Germany's largest manufacturing firm and the richest man in the country, dies.

Vienna, 1 December 1902. Austria and Russia agree on joint supervision in Macedonia.

Venezuela, 9 December 1902. British and German warships seize the Venezuelan navy, demanding settlement of compensation claims arising from President Cipriano Castro's 1899 coup.

Egypt, 10 December 1902. The massive Nile dam at Aswan is completed.

Britain, 18 December 1902. The new Education Act puts elementary and secondary education in the hands of borough and county councils.

Britain, 1902. Beatrix Potter publishes *The Tale of Peter Rabbit.*

Britain, 1902. Among this year's new novels are *Anna of the Five Towns* by Arnold Bennett and *Heart of Darkness* by Joseph Conrad.

India, 1 January 1903. A mighty *durbar* is held in the old Moghul capital of Delhi to proclaim Edward VII king-emperor of India.

Central America, 22 January 1903. The US and Colombia sign a treaty to allow the construction of the Panama Canal.

British forces advance on Somali mullah

Somaliland, 24 February 1903
The notorious "mad *mullah*" who has been seeking to stir up rebellion in British Somaliland has fled across the border into Italian territory and a British flying column has taken up the hunt, accompanied by an Italian observer, Count Lovateli.

The mullah, Mohammed bin Abdullah, appeals to the credulity of the pastoral Somalis by telling them that he has supernatural powers. If they resist his demands then he returns with a raiding party to rob and kill. When he is on the run, as he is now; he is liable to vanish into the bush and lie low for months.

The British column includes detachments of the Punjab Mounted Infantry and the Camel Corps. A transport docked at the Indian Ocean port of Obbia recently with 600 camels, but many more are needed, and ports up and down the coast are been scoured for the animals at any price.

British writer speaks with imperial voice

Kipling: spokesman for (and critic of) Britain's empire in the east.

London, 1902
Rudyard Kipling, the poet of empire, has written more for children than for adults in recent years: this year the *Just So Stories*, telling how the camel got his hump and other matters, last year *Kim*, the brilliant evocation of British and native India as he knew it in boyhood. Before that came *Stalky and Co*, based on his schooldays, and in 1894-5 the two *Jungle Books*.

Kipling found himself famous at 25 for his *Plain Tales from the Hills* and *Barrack Room Ballads* – the lore of the private soldier east of Suez, who knew the road to Mandalay and the worth of Gunga Din.

A train arrives at a station platform – a symbol of expanding horizons and the modern world. Two brothers, Auguste and Louis Jean Lumiere, 33 years old and 31 years old, by taking one photograph after another extremely fast, and running the developed film through a projector at the same speed onto a screen, relive the movement of the train as it comes into the station. Many watching this extraordinary moving photography are impressed. Others find it jerky and say it gives them headaches. All agree it is quite unique. No one has seen anything like it before.

Slavery and atrocities revealed in Congo

London, 15 April 1903
Britain's consul in the Congo Free State, Roger Casement, is preparing an analysis of the barbarities inflicted on Blacks by the Belgian administration of King Leopold II.

Villagers are being intimidated by threats to their families into making arduous, dangerous trips into the forest to collect a high quota of raw, wild rubber. For this service they are paid nothing. While they are away for days at a time, working without food or shelter, becoming the prey of wild animals, their families are hostages to "sentinels" licensed to impose virtually any punishment for any "crime" they identify. Communities which do not deliver a set quota, or argue, are attacked by paramilitaries or regular troops who hack off the hands of dead victims.

King Leopold is blamed. He has dishonoured international guarantees, using the Congo as a personal estate a million miles square, to be squeezed for the last *sou*. Funds

King Leopold: the man accused of cruel exploitation in the Congo.

raised by such cruelty are used by the king to build increasingly preposterous buildings in Belgium, a modest nation which detests his architectural taste as much as his inhumanity.

Ford has vision of cheap cars for all

Ford in his first car, the quadricycle.

The price of the new mobility.

Detroit, 1903
Despite being turned down by the banking house of Morgan – which dismissed the idea of workers owning their own motor cars as "ridiculous" – a farmer's son, Henry Ford, has managed to raise $28,000 from local investors to rent a shed and build automobiles in Detroit. Although he has managed to sell seven models of his first design, an

eight-horsepower car with two cylinders, Ford has not lost sight of his dream – a low cost automobile available to all – and is seeking a strong cheap metal.

With more than 50 automobile companies already in production in America and others joining the race, Ford faces stiff competition. But not all of the others see a mass market as Henry Ford does.

US-backed rebels take power in Panama

Panama, 6 November 1903
A small group of railroad workers, barmen and militiamen, supported by the fire brigade and US adventurers, has overthrown Colombia's rule in the Panama Isthmus and proclaimed Panama a republic. To no great surprise, the US government, whose cruiser *Nashville* is lying off shore to deter Colombian troops from landing, has recognised the republic.

The *coup* was no more of a surprise than was the US state department's somewhat hasty recogni-

tion. Three months ago the Colombian Congress rejected a treaty for a canal to be built across the isthmus from the Atlantic to the Pacific, which would reduce the USA's shipping costs from the east coast to the west coast by millions of dollars. Needless to say, the new *junta* in Panama is extremely enthusiastic for the canal. Indeed the leader of the coup is none other than Philippe Jean Bunasu-Varilla, the canal's foremost advocate, who will be leaving for Washington in a few days to complete the arrangements.

Britain clinches Pacific deal with Japan

Tokyo, 30 January 1902
The Japanese government today welcomed the signing of the Anglo-Japanese alliance which recognises the special interests of Britain in China and Japan in Korea and provides for each country to safeguard the other's interests.

There is also a secret naval codicil which is believed to provide for an exchange of facilities and an agreement for both countries to maintain large naval forces in Far Eastern waters. Perhaps the most pleasing aspect of the treaty from the Japanese point of view is that Japan has become the ally of one of the most powerful European states.

The Anglo-Japanese agreement, seen from Paris: a debauched King Edward charmed by a "geisha" girl.

Britain blockades debtor Venezuela

Venezuela, 31 December 1902
The navies of Great Britain, Germany and Italy have set up a blockade of the coastline of Venezuela. Their action follows the refusal of Venezuela to compensate European nationals who have been injured in a recent series of rebellions. They are also acting to force Venezuela to repay its outstanding debts.

Britain's argument with Venezuela dates back to 1896, when both nations were involved in a major wrangle over the boundaries of British Guiana. Only the notably pro-Venezuelan stance of the US president, Cleveland, restrained the British. Now Venezuela has appealed to the new president, Roosevelt, but he is determined to keep out of the controversy.

African workers found churches

South Africa, 1903
New politico-religious movements are emerging amongst the black migrant labourers of South Africa. Identifying themselves as Africans rather than as members of tribes, they have established native congresses and black churches.

The native congresses associate themselves with the Pan-African movement in the New World. The black churches, which broke away from white Protestant missionary organisations, have united, calling themselves the Ethiopian Church (Ethiopia being the word for Africa in the Bible). They, too, have a black American link with the African Methodist Episcopal Church – the biggest black church in the USA.

1903 (1903-1904)

Washington, DC, 13 February 1903. Britain, Germany and Italy sign a treaty agreeing to lift the blockade of Venezuela.

Balkans, 23 February 1903. The Ottoman Sultan Abdul Hamid II accepts Russian and Austrian proposals for reforms in Macedonia, in order to quell a rebellion there.

USA, 3 March 1903. A bill is passed curbing immigration and banning "undesirables".

Russia, 12 March 1903. Czar Nicholas II issues a manifesto conceding important reforms, including the freedom of religion.

Nigeria, 15 March 1903. Following the fall of Kano last month, troops of the West African Frontier Force, led by British officers, take Sokoto. The sultan flees.

France, 18 March 1903. The religious orders are dissolved.

Finland, 26 March 1903. The czar appoints the Russian general Bobrikov virtual dictator of Finland.

Balkans, 14 April 1903. Bulgarians kill 165 people in a Moslem village near Monastir in Macedonia.

Balkans, 16 April 1903. In the latest act of Jewish persecution, peasants in Kishinev, in Bessarabia, massacre scores of Jews.

Britain, 21 May 1903. Joseph Chamberlain, the colonial secretary, founds the Tariff League to promote a preferential trading system within the empire.

Serbia, 11 June 1903. King Alexander and Queen Draga are murdered by disaffected army officers and Prince Peter Karageorgevich is proclaimed king.

Germany, 16 June 1903. The socialists make large gains in elections to the *reichstag*.

Britain, 17 July 1903. The American painter James McNeill Whistler dies.

France, 19 July 1903. Maurice Garin wins the first Tour de France bicycle race.

Rome, 20 July 1903. Pope Leo XIII, who worked throughout his 25-year reign to unite Christendom and reduce class warfare, dies.

Rome, 4 August 1903. Giuseppe Sarto, the patriarch of Venice, becomes Pope Pius X.

Switzerland, 19 August 1903. Delegates to the sixth Zionist Congress in Basle clash over proposals to set up a Jewish state in Uganda.

Britain, 22 August 1903. Lord Salisbury, who was Conservative prime minister three times, dies.

Britain, 17 September 1903. Joseph Chamberlain resigns as colonial secretary to have greater freedom to promote preferential trade with the empire.

USA, 21 September 1903. *Kit Carson*, the first Wild West movie, opens.

Balkans, September 1903. The Ottomans have massacred 50,000 Bulgarians in the region of Monastir.

Britain, 10 October 1903. Emmeline Pankhurst founds the Women's Social and Political Union.

Germany, 1 November 1903. The historian Theodor Mommsen dies.

France, 12 November 1903. The painter Camille Pissarro dies.

Russia, 17 November 1903. Vladimir Lenin splits the Social Democratic Labour Party, leading a majority breakaway group, the *Bolsheviks*.

Central America, November 1903. Panama declares itself independent of Colombia.

USA, 17 December 1903. Wilbur and Orville Wright fly a heavier-than-air flying machine at Kitty Hawk, North Carolina.

Korea, December 1903. Japan lands marines at Mok-Pho to deal with rioting Korean labourers.

South-West Africa, 11 January 1904. Rebellious Herero massacre 123 German soldiers and male settlers near Okahandja, the seat of the Herero chief, Samuel Maharero.

Moscow, 17 January 1904. *The Cherry Orchard*, a play by Anton Chekhov, receives its premiere.

Cuba, 5 February 1904. America ends its occupation of Cuba.

China, 8 February 1904. Provoked by Russian penetration of northern Korea and failure to withdraw from Manchuria, war breaks out between Japan and Russia with a Japanese attack on Port Arthur (*Lushun*).

Germany, 8 March 1904. The reichstag lifts its ban on Jesuits.

Tibet, 31 March 1904. British forces under Macdonald kill some 300 Tibetans attempting to halt a British mission to Tibet.

Europe, 8 April 1904. France and Britain sign an *entente cordiale* settling their colonial disputes in North Africa.

Britain, 22 April 1904. A bill is passed legalising peaceful picketing during strikes.

Britain, 26 April 1904. George Bernard Shaw's play *Candida* is performed for the first time.

Rivals wreck Madam Butterfly premiere

"Madam Butterfly": a tragic opera by Puccini on Japan, America, and the price paid when east meets west.

Milan, 18 February 1904
Jeering, whistling and general uproar greeted last night's premiere of the opera *Madam Butterfly* by the Italian composer Giacomo Puccini.

He has withdrawn the work, a tragic love tale set in Japan, for revision. However, the fiasco seems to have been caused by Puccini's rivals, who tried to ruin the first performance of his hugely successful *Tosca* in Rome four years ago.

Puccini, whose family have been musicians since 1712, is the greatest of the new generation of composers writing "realist" operas, often with contemporary, unheroic people and violent emotions on stage. He was born in 1858; his first big success was *La Boheme*, whose 1896 premiere was conducted by the brilliant young Italian, Arturo Toscanini.

Stockbroker who painted idyllic island life

Atuaha, Marquesas Is, 8 May 1903
Paul Gauguin, the French painter who has lived in the South Seas since 1891, died here today of syphilis, aged 54. He was under a prison sentence for defamation of the administration and the church. He gave up a successful stockbroking career on the Paris *Bourse* when he was 35 to concentrate on painting, at which he was self-taught.

He met Pissarro and Cezanne, and was influenced by the impressionists, before breaking from them. At 43 he finally abandoned his family and went to Tahiti in search of primitive culture.

Giving up naturalism completely, he aimed at expressing intense emotion with areas of deep, flat colour as in *The Watching Spirit of the Dead*, which shows his 13-year-old native wife who believed that such spirits entered houses in darkness. He exhibited in Paris in 1893 but sold little. He returned to Tahiti, moving to the Marquesas in 1901.

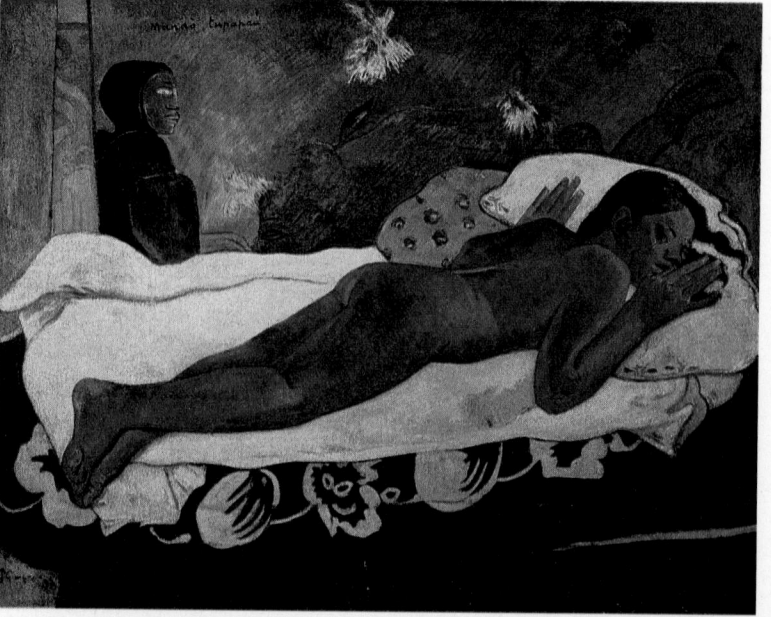

Paul Gauguin's painting "Manao Tupapau": the spirit of the dead keeps watch.

Turks kill 50,000 Bulgarian civilians

Sofia, Bulgaria, 8 September 1903
Another massacre of civilians by Ottomans has reportedly taken 50,000 Bulgarian lives. The worst butchery seems to have happened at the village of Monastir, politically part of Serbia but ethnically Bulgar and near the border with Bulgarian Macedonia. Women and children were among those slaughtered by a punitive expedition.

The reason for such savagery is a Bulgarian plan to launch a general uprising against Ottoman rule. The rebellion was due to start on 31 August, but the Ottomans got word of it and swamped Macedonia with 300,000 troops. The last similar event occurred in April 1876 when 12,000 Christian Bulgars were exterminated by the Islamic Ottoman government.

A week ago Macedonian terrorists blew up a Hungarian ship, killing 29 passengers and crew, in an apparent effort to internationalise the crisis provoked by Ottoman dic-

Ottoman troops killing Bulgarians.

tatorship. Such repression is perilous for the peace of Europe generally because of the number of great powers which may be drawn into defending client Balkan states.

"Bolsheviks" split Russian socialists

London, 17 November 1903
Vladimir Lenin, a Russian professional revolutionary, has emerged as leader of the *Bolshevik* group following the split at a congress today of the Russian Social Democratic Party. Lenin had found himself in a minority at the congress, but a walkout by a disgruntled group of Jewish Social Democrats played into his hands and gave him

a slight majority. The *Bolsheviks* (majority) are seeking to overturn Russia with a single centralised party of professional revolutionaries. The opposing *Mensheviks* (minority) are led by Yuly Martov and advocate a broad proletarian party. They also fear that Lenin favours the suppression of free intra-party debate and is in favour of a one-man dictatorship.

Marie Curie is first woman Nobel winner

Paris, 10 December 1903
Marie Curie, aged 33, has become the first female winner of the Nobel prize. She has won it jointly with her husband and a colleague for the discovery of radiation. But it was Madame Curie who did most of the pioneering work, discovering first *polonium* (named after her native Poland), then *radium*.

Her father was a teacher of physics in Warsaw, but after he lost his savings through bad investment she had to work as a governess and did not begin scientific work until she came here. She hopes that radiation will play an important part in the treatment of some diseases.

Marie Curie, Nobel prize winner and discoverer of polonium and radium.

Brothers take to the air

North Carolina, 17 December 1903
It lasted for only 12 seconds, and the fragile machine in which he rode rose a scant ten feet above the ground and covered barely 120 feet (37 metres) from start to finish, but today, on the sand dunes near Kitty Hawk, North Carolina, man has taken wings and made his first-ever powered flight.

The brothers Orville and Wilbur Wright, bicycle mechanics from Dayton, Ohio, have been moving steadily towards today's flights since 1899 when they began looking into hitherto unsuccessful attempts to fly. After experimenting with gliders they realised that the secret

lay in rigid, airworthy wings. After exhaustive testing of every part of their proposed flying machine, the Wrights came to Kitty Hawk. With Orville lying face down in a cradle slung beneath the wings, and the elder brother, Wilbur, running alongside, *Flyer I*, powered by its 12 mph engine, moved along the runners that supported it, and then, as the wind caught it, the flying machine gently rose upwards into the wind.

The Wrights made three further flights before their machine, called *Flyer*, was damaged by a sudden gust. The longest lasted for 59 seconds and covered 852 feet.

Orville Wright's first successful flight from Kitty Hawk, North Carolina.

Women form political pressure group

Manchester, 1903
Emmeline Pankhurst has formed a militant Women's Social and Political Union to rival the National Union of Women's Suffrage started six years ago by Millicent Fawcett. Pankhurst and her followers, many of whom are local women mill workers, impatient for the vote, feel that drastic action is now necessary to change electoral law in this country. "Action not Words" is their motto.

The first parliamentary debate on women's suffrage was over 36 years ago and, apart from Mrs Pankhurst's achievement of gaining the right for all women to participate in local elections, polite demonstrations of women's views have had no effect in getting them national voting power.

Emmeline Pankhurst: the leader of the new ultra-militant suffragettes.

1904 (1904-1905)

Bohemia, 1 May 1904. The Czech composer Antonin Dvorak dies.

Britain, 4 May 1904. Charles Rolls and Henry Royce sign an agreement to build motor cars.

Britain, 9 May 1904. The British explorer Sir Henry Stanley dies.

New York City, 15 June 1904. About 1,000 die when the paddle-steamer *General Slocum* catches fire in New York harbour.

South America, 15 June 1904. Britain and Brazil sign an arbitration convention to settle the disputed border of British Guiana.

Finland, 23 June 1904. The Russian governor general, Bobrikov, is assassinated.

China, 24 June 1904. Japanese forces inflict a major defeat on the Russians at Telissu.

Austria, 3 July 1904. The Hungarian-born Zionist Theodor Herzl dies.

Switzerland, 14 July 1904. Paul Kruger, four times president of the Transvaal republic, dies in exile in Geneva.

Russia, 15 July 1904. The playwright Anton Chekhov dies.

Russia, 28 July 1904. Viacheslav Plehve, the minister of the interior, is assassinated.

France, 29 July 1904. France severs diplomatic links with the Vatican.

Tibet, 4 August 1904. Following the arrival in Lhasa of British troops led by the explorer Francis Younghusband, the Dalai Lama flees to Urga.

France, 25 August 1904. The painter Henri Fantin-Latour dies.

Tibet, 7 September 1904. On behalf of Britain, Francis Younghusband signs a treaty with Tibet by which Tibet agrees not to cede territory to any foreign power.

Belgium, September 1904. Leopold II, the king of the Belgians, appoints an international commission to investigate conditions in the Congo Free State.

Morocco, 3 October 1904. France and Spain sign an agreement on Morocco by which the northern part of the country is recognised as a Spanish zone of influence.

North Sea, 22 October 1904. Ships of the Russian Baltic fleet torpedo and sink two British trawlers off the Dogger Bank.

New York City, 27 October 1904. The underground railway opens.

USA, 8 November 1904. The Republican Theodore Roosevelt is returned to power in the presidential election.

China, 5 December 1904. The Japanese destroy the Russian fleet at Port Arthur (*Lushun*).

Stockholm, 10 December 1904. The Russian physiologist Ivan Pavlov wins a Nobel prize for his work on the digestive system.

London, 13 December 1904. London's first electric underground train goes into operation.

Russia, 26 December 1904. Czar Nicholas II issues a decree offering liberal reforms, but warns that strikes and riots must stop.

Britain, 27 December 1904. James Barrie's play *Peter Pan* opens.

Russia, 1 January 1905. The Trans-Siberian railway officially opens.

China, 2 January 1905. The Russians surrender to the Japanese at Port Arthur.

St Petersburg, 22 January 1905. The czar's troops shoot dead more than 500 strikers on "Bloody Sunday".

USA, 7 February 1905. The states of Oklahoma and New Mexico are admitted to the union.

Russia, 13 February 1905. The Japanese lay siege to Vladivostok.

Moscow, 17 February 1905. Grand Duke Sergei, the uncle of Czar Nicholas II, is assassinated.

Russia, 9 March 1905. Found culpable by an international commission for the Dogger Bank incident, Russia agrees to pay Britain £65,000 compensation.

China, 10 March 1905. The Japanese defeat the Russians at Mukden after a ten-day battle.

France, 24 March 1905. Jules Verne, the inventor of the scientific novel, dies.

India, 4 April 1905. An earthquake in Lahore kills more than 10,000.

France, April 1905. The psychologist Alfred Binet invents intelligence tests.

Warsaw, 1 May 1905. Troops fire on May Day demonstrators, killing 100.

Switzerland, 6 May 1905. Seven eastern European socialist parties form a new group in Geneva.

Sea of Japan, 28 May 1905. The Japanese annihilate the Russian fleet in the strait of Tsushima.

Norway, 7 June 1905. Norway declares independence from Sweden.

Athens, 13 June 1905. The prime minister, Delyannis, is assassinated outside the Greek parliament.

Britain, June 1905. The Automobile Association is founded.

Irish writer is the toast of London stage

GBS, the Irish playwright, as seen in a later poster for "Great Catherine".

London, November, 1905
Major Barbara, the third play by George Bernard Shaw to be presented at the Court theatre this year, has confirmed his dominance among contemporary playwrights. In March his Irish comedy, *John Bull's Other Island*, made the king laugh so much that he broke his chair. In October came *Man and Superman*, introducing the Shavian philosophy of creative evolution.

Shaw had been better known as a journalist, critic and Fabian socialist than a playwright until Harley Granville-Barker began presenting seasons of his plays at the Court last year. *Major Barbara* contrasts different ways of dealing with poverty – "the worst of crimes".

Auguste Rodin: thinking man's sculptor

Rodin's "The Thinker", one of a series of sculptures for his "Gates of Hell".

Rodin's nude, the "Age of Bronze", the sculpture that so shocked.

Paris, 1904
France's greatest sculptor, Auguste Rodin, has unveiled a bronze entitled *Le Penseur* (The Thinker) which has all his power and ruggedness but less than his usual provocation. It is intended for the central position in his massive 20-foot (six-metre) *Gates of Hell*, which is planned to rival Ghiberti's *Gates of Paradise* in Florence.

Rodin's career began with an outcry at his *Age of Bronze*, exhibited in 1877, a figure that was so lifelike that it was rumoured to have been cast from a living model. There were some objections to his group

The Burghers of Calais from the town council which commissioned it, to his commemorative bust of Victor Hugo, and above all to his monument to Balzac, whose massive head was shown impressionistically emerging from the dressing-gown which he wore for writing. It was compared to "a toad in a sack".

In 1898 *The Kiss* was declared unfit for public exhibition at the Chicago World's Fair. Like *The Thinker*, this was intended for the *Gates of Hell* but executed as a separate sculpture.

Impressive Trans-Siberian railway opens

Siberia, 21 July 1904

The Trans-Siberian railway, a major new trading route linking Russia and China, has been completed. It is a feat of engineering and human endurance in one of the most inhospitable climates in the world.

The first stretch of the line was built in 1878 between Perm and Ekaterinburg, on the eastern slope of the Urals. This was extended to Tyumen, beside tributaries of the Ob, across the plains to Omsk, then Irkutsk, and round Lake Baikal to Chita and Vladivostok. The Chinese agreed in 1896 to extend the line across Manchuria.

Chiefly in order to bring tea, silk and cotton from China, and grain and cattle from Siberia, Russian workers braved temperatures as low as minus 85 degrees fahrenheit, and snowstorms.

Convicts who worked on the Trans-Siberian railway posing near Nertschinsk.

British army tangles with Tibetan troops

New Delhi, 6 May 1904

In the latest clash between a column of British-led Indian troops and Tibetan militia, at Gyangtse, on the road to Lhasa, 190 Tibetans died. The battle was similar to one in March, when 300 of the Dalai Lama's men were mown down by British Maxim guns and mountain artillery. The column fighting its way into Tibet is escorting Colonel Sir Francis Younghusband on his mission to persuade the Dalai Lama, a "living god", to stop supporting Russian intrigue on the north flank of India.

The Dalai Lama flees British troops.

Meddling kaiser provokes Morocco crisis

Tangier, Morocco, 31 March 1905

In a surprise visit, Kaiser William II has interrupted a Mediterranean cruise to speak up for Moroccan independence. His intervention will cause much consternation among the British, French and Spanish, who have privately agreed to the partition of Morocco. Germany has not previously declared any interest in Morocco, but Kaiser Willliam has been determined to increase his country's maritime influence. Now he proclaims "great and growing interests in Morocco", and insists that the sultan should be free to deal equally with all foreign powers.

Russian navy is crippled

The Russian flagship "Petro Pavlovsk", sunk by Japanese ships on 13 April.

Port Arthur, 9 February 1904

Russian and Japanese rivalry over Manchuria erupted into war here last night when the Japanese made a surprise attack on the Russian fleet lying at anchor in this heavily fortified naval stronghold.

As has become usual with the Japanese, they made no declaration of war but sent nine destroyers of Admiral Togo's main fleet at full speed under cover of darkness to launch their torpedoes at the fully-illuminated Russian ships whose officers were attending a ball given by the admiral's wife. Two of the destroyers collided on the way in, but the others executed a classic torpedo attack and escaped before the Russians could man their gun batteries. The Russians are lucky in that only three of the torpedoes exploded, but it is two of their best battleships, the *Czarevitch* and *Retvizan*, along with the cruiser *Pallada*, which have been hit and put out of action.

The Russians have always been convinced of their superiority over the Japanese "monkeys" and believe that they can beat them by "throwing our caps at them". It

The Japanese emperor as a hawk, with the Russian bear at his mercy.

will not be so easy. Togo is now cruising off Port Arthur in his modern ships, tempting the Russians to sally out to fight. It is an invitation that they may well refuse.

"Extermination" order shocks Germany

Namibia, November 1905

An insurrection by the Herero people in which 123 European colonists were killed last year has led to an unprecedented campaign of revenge by German troops.

Repression began immediately, with German soldiers driving 5,000 people into the desert where most of them died of thirst. For the German commander, Lothar von Trotha, negotiation with surviving Herero was out of the question. "Every Herero with or without a rifle, with or without cattle, shall be shot," he ordered, and he then signed his decree as "the great general of the most powerful emperor, von Trotha".

Von Trotha has been recalled after a national outcry, but three out of every four Hereros are dead.

Odessa, Russia, 3 July. Czarist troops kill 6,000 demonstrators to restore order in Odessa. Unrest, for long underground, is coming to the surface. A general strike is declared in St Petersburg.

South Africa, 4 July. Dutch-speaking Boers protest that the new electoral laws imposed by the British favour the English-speakers, and are an example of how Boers are discriminated against.

Russia, 8 July. The crew of the battleship *Potemkin* surrender to the Rumanians, who say they will not be extradited because the mutiny was a political act.

London, 10 July. Puccini's opera *Madame Butterfly* is performed for the first time in Britain at Covent Garden.

USA, 16 July. Commander Peary sets sail on his second expedition to the North Pole.

Finland, 24 July. The German Kaiser, Wilhelm II and Russia's Czar Nicholas II conclude the treaty of Bjoerkoe.

Russia, 31 July. The Russian governor of Sakhalin Island, off the Siberian coast, surrenders to Japanese forces.

German East Africa, July. Coastal peasants rebel, destroying cotton fields that German colonists forced them to plant.

Russia, 19 August. In a step towards constitutional monarchy, the Duma (a representative assembly) is established.

USA, 29 August. Russian and Japanese delegates agree peace terms. An armistice is arranged for August 31.

Russia, 2 September. The worst famine since 1891 is reported.

Central Asia, 5 September. Hundreds die in battles between Moslem Tartars and Christian Armenians.

USA, 5 September. The war fought in Korea and Manchuria between Russia and Japan ends today with the signing of a peace treaty at Portsmouth, New Hampshire.

London, 19 September. The Irish doctor, Thomas John Barnardo, who set up over 112 homes for deprived children, died today.

Stockholm, 25 September. The terms of Norway's independence from Sweden are announced.

USA, 5 October. The Wright brothers, Orville and Wilbur, make the longest flight yet of 38 minutes and three seconds.

Britain, 13 October. The greatest actor of the day, Sir Henry Irving, dies aged 67.

Britain, 14 October. The suffragettes Christabel Pankhurst and Annie Kenney opt to go to prison rather than pay a fine for assaulting a policeman at a political meeting in Manchester.

Sweden, 27 October. King Oscar II formally abdicates the crown of Norway.

Russia, 30 October. Czar Nicholas II issues an imperial manifesto that transforms the country from an absolute autocracy to a semi-constitutional monarchy in an attempt to quell mounting unrest.

London, 1 November. Police close George Bernard Shaw's new play, *Mrs Warren's Profession*, because of its portrayal of prostitution.

Russia, 8 November. 1,000 Jews are killed in a pogrom in Odessa when a mob of 50,000 goes on the rampage shooting and stabbing Jewish men, women and children.

Poland, 12 November. Martial law is declared in Russian-occupied Poland.

Norway, 18 November. Prince Charles of Denmark accepts the Norwegian throne, taking the name Haakon VII.

Vienna, 28 November. Universal suffrage is granted.

London, 5 December. Sir Henry Campbell-Bannerman, the Liberal leader, accepts King Edward VII's commission to form a new government following the resignation of Arthur Balfour, the Tory premier.

France, 6 December. A law is passed separating the state and the church.

Alaska, 6 December. The Norwegian explorer Roald Amundsen completes a two and a half year journey across the American Arctic coast from the Atlantic to the Pacific.

Russia, 7 December. Revolutionaries occupy the fortress at Kiev in the Ukraine.

Germany, 9 December. Richard Strauss's opera *Salome*, based on Oscar Wilde's play, has its first performance.

British East Africa (Kenya), 19 December. The Nandi resistance leader Koitalel is assassinated by a British officer in a drive to put down native opposition to colonisation.

Moscow, 30 December. Government forces crush an uprising by students and workers after a week of street fighting.

Austria, December. The publication of *Three Essays on the Theory of Sexuality* by the psycho-analyst Sigmund Freud sparks off fierce controversy.

"Fauvists" make artistic splash in Paris

Paris, 1 October

A room at the *Salon d'Automne* is astonishing visitors to the exhibition. Gathered in it are a group of painters who have freed colour from any connection with the way it occurs in life, applying it quite arbitrarily as decoration, straight from the tube.

A critic, Louis Vauxcelles, compared them to wild beasts – *Les Fauves* – and they have adopted the nickname. Their leader, Henri Matisse, shows a portrait of his wife with a green stripe down her nose. Andre Derain paints the trunks of trees bright crimson. Others in the group include Maurice Vlaminck, Georges Rouault, Georges Braque and Raoul Dufy.

Matisse, by Andre Derain: the two men are founders of Fauvism.

The vast soundscapes of modern music

Strauss and Salome: a satirical caricature of modern musical tastes.

Vienna

The monumental seventh symphony by Gustav Mahler was heard for the first time this year, and confirms that music is vaster, more complex and more emotionally charged than ever before. Wagner started it, and Bruckner, Richard Strauss (no relation of Johann) and Mahler have followed. The huge, noble symphonic canvases of the pious, unprepossessing, ill-tailored Professor Bruckner (who died in 1896) have been likened to cathedrals of sound. Strauss, 40, has recently turned more to opera after a string of brilliant, opulently scored orchestral pieces such as *Till Eulenspiegel*, *Don Juan* and *Don Quixote*. He caused a scandal with his "obscene" and "blasphemous" opera *Salome*, inspired by Oscar Wilde's work, last year. Mahler, 47, is the director of the Vienna Opera. But the genius once referred to as "that Jew" had to be baptised a catholic before he could gain the post in this anti-semitic city.

Russian navy wiped out

The Russian battleship Navarin, sunk by the Japanese fleet at Tsushima.

Tsushima, 28 May

The Russian Baltic Fleet has been annihilated in a single day after sailing for eight months halfway round the world to meet Admiral Togo's warships in the Straits of Tsushima.

The Russian fleet's voyage, planned to link up with the ships at Port Arthur and sweep the Japanese from the eastern seas, was a tale of misfortune. It opened fire on a British herring fleet in the North Sea in the belief that the fishing boats were Japanese torpedo boats.

Then it took so long, with its poorly trained crews laboriously refuelling from German-chartered colliers, that Port Arthur and its ships fell to the Japanese before Admiral Rozhdestvenski reached the eastern waters. He was ordered to sail for Vladivostok but this meant passing through the narrow straits between Korea and Japan, waters dominated by Admiral Togo's modern battle fleet.

The Russians, with their crews debilitated and their ships fouled by the long voyage, did not stand a chance. Ambushed by Togo, they

Russia is defeated: a moth-eaten bear and his Japanese keeper.

were battered and disorganised within an hour. The battleship *Oslyaba* was the first victim, followed by the flagship *Suvorov*. Then the *Alexander III* went down with all hands. Ship followed ship to the bottom until the survivors surrendered. A few small ships have got away, but the fleet and Russia's hopes of winning the war have been wiped out.

Navy mutineers throw officers overboard

Odessa, Russia, 27 June

Russian sailors have thrown their officers overboard and seized control of the battleship *Potemkin* in the most dramatic outbreak of unrest yet against the czar and his regime. The city of Odessa is in the grip of a general strike, with shootings and explosions.

The *Potemkin*, the most powerful battleship in the Black Sea, was keeping an eye on street rioters when one of the sailors complained about bad food, and was shot by the first lieutenant. The crew immediately mutinied. To cries of "liberty, liberty!" they threw the captain and several other officers overboard, and hoisted the red flag. The remaining eight officers joined the mutiny.

It appears that the crew of two torpedo boats may have joined in. A steamer laded with coal was seized and the fuel transferred to the *Potemkin*. The authorities are on the verge of panic, with no apparent means of controlling the Odessa populace who are in open revolt. Buildings along the waterfront are ablaze.

This latest revolt is by far the most serious yet, coming four days after Czar Nicholas repudiated his

Flattery at its most outrageous: "Liberty" kissing Czar Nicholas.

earlier promise to give Russia an elected assembly. In the wake of the catastrophic defeat of the Manchurian army by the Japanese at Mukden, there has been growing discontent over the war. Two provincial governors were assassinated last month before the Russian navy was annihilated by the Japanese at Tsushima.

The main squadron of Russia's Black Sea fleet is expected to steam to Odessa to crush the mutiny; but the fact that it happened at all suggests the Czarist regime's authority is now precarious indeed.

Physicist believes everything is relative

Germany

This year has seen the publication of several key papers by Dr Albert Einstein, the German physicist who, since the age of 12, has been determined to solve "the riddle of the world". He asserts that light consists of individual quanta – *photons* – that can behave both as

waves and particles. This is revolutionary stuff. So, too, is the view of mass and energy which we must regard as one and the same.

A further stunning idea is the concept of relativity. Embracing time, space and motion, this states that there are no absolute motions in the universe.

India's viceroy quits in defence quarrel

Delhi, India, 20 August

Lord Curzon, the viceroy of India, has resigned. A believer in the "forward" school of imperialism, his stewardship of India was brilliant, ostentatious and tactless. His pedestal was high, his fall is long.

His very arrogance ensured his fall. Not only did he alienate the army with his determination to protect the Indian peasantry from the brutality of the soldiery, but he alienated the commander-in-chief, Lord Kitchener. He blocked Kitchener's reforms and insisted on Kitchener's subordination to him. Kitchener refused to work under Curzon and offered his resignation. Curzon was powerful, but not popular, and had little chance against the hero of South Africa and the Sudan. In the end it was Curzon who resigned.

Though his foreign policy, which included crude displays of might in the Persian Gulf, displayed all the

Curzon: brilliant, but tactless.

arrogance of a world power unsure of its own supremacy, his internal reforms will not be forgotten. He changed the taxation laws for the benefit of the peasantry and protected cultivators from eviction for debt.

1906 (1906-1907)

London, 7 February 1906. The Liberals win a landslide victory in the general election. The Labour Representation Committee, led by James Keir Hardie, also makes substantial gains.

Tahiti, 8 February 1906. A typhoon kills over 10,000 people.

Britain, 10 February 1906. *HMS Dreadnought*, the most powerful warship in the world, is launched.

Rome, 11 February 1906. Pope Pius X condemns the separation of the French church from the state.

London, 12 February 1906. Keir Hardie is elected leader of the new Labour Party in the House of Commons.

Nigeria, 20 February 1906. British troops arrive to quell protests by the Tiv people against Moslem Hausa rule.

USA, 23 February 1906. Johann Koch of Chicago, alias "Bluebeard", who is said to have murdered at least one of his 50 wives, is executed.

Natal, 5 March 1906. British troops kill 60 Zulu in fierce clashes against the poll tax.

Finland, 7 March 1906. Suffrage is extended to all tax-paying men and women over 24.

Britain, 8 March 1906. A government publication out today states that the empire occupies one-fifth of the land-surface of the globe and has a population of 400,000,000.

Russia, 20 March 1906. Army officers are massacred in a mutiny in Sevastopol in the Crimea.

Paris, 22 March 1906. England win the first rugby international against France by 35 to eight.

New York, 28 March 1906. The State Meteorological Office says that the science of forecasting the weather is "within our grasp".

Spain, 31 March 1906. A conference on Morocco closes in Algeciras having upheld French hegemony under the sultan.

Italy, 7 April 1906. Mount Vesuvius erupts, destroying the town of Ottaiano.

Britain, 17 April 1906. The Labour Party calls for female suffrage.

France, 19 April 1906. The nobel prize-winning physicist Pierre Curie dies aged 47.

San Francisco, 18 April 1906. A major earthquake destroys most of the city.

Tibet, 27 April 1906. China reluctantly grants Britain control of Tibet, following the occupation of the capital Lhasa by British troops.

St Petersbury, 24 May 1906. Czar Nicholas II concedes universal suffrage but refuses to grant amnesty for political prisoners as suggested by the Duma.

Norway, 28 May 1906. The playwright Henrik Ibsen dies aged 78. Among his most controversial works are *A Doll's House*, *Ghosts* and *Hedda Gabler*.

Europe, 6 June 1906. Italy re-affirms its alliance with the Austro-Hungarian and German empires.

France, 27 June 1906. The first circuit motor race held at Le Mans is won by the Hungarian, Ferenc Szisz in a Renault.

London, 7 July 1906. Seven balloons take part in Britain's first hot-air balloon race.

France, 12 July 1906. Captain Alfred Dreyfus is rehabilitated having been publicly disgraced 11 years ago on charges of espionage and treason.

Guatemala, 20 July 1906. A treaty ends the war between Guatemala on the one side and El Salvador and Honduras on the other. Guatemala invaded both its neighbours in May but was defeated six days ago.

Russia, 21 July 1906. The Duma, is dissolved and martial law is declared.

Cuba, 28 September 1906. The American war secretary William Taft declares himself provisional governor of Cuba following the resignation of President Palma, under threat from rebel forces.

Russia, 2 November 1906. The Jewish revolutionary Leon Trotsky is exiled for life to Siberia.

Belgium, 9 November 1906. Prince Albert is declared successor to Leopold as king of the Congo.

Japan, 15 November 1906. The world's biggest battleship the *Satsuma* is launched.

South Africa, 12 December 1906. The Transvaal is given autonomy with white male suffrage.

New Hebrides, 1906. French and British residents agree to set up a joint administration.

China, 1 January 1907. Four million people are starving owing to heavy rains and crop failure.

German East Africa, 16 January 1907. The great rebel leader Abdallah Mapanda, who has been at the head of maji-maji (*magic water*) uprisings since July 1905 is run to ground by the Germans.

Tehran, 19 January 1907. Mohammed Ali Mirza is crowned Shah of Persia. He is intent on a programme of liberalisation.

Moslems form political league in India

Dacca, India, 31 December 1906
India's middle-class Moslems have scorned the predominantely Hindu Congress Party, and formed a Moslem League. Within a day of its foundation Congress leaders are calling it a British inspiration and accusing it of sectarianism. The League repeats Sir Syed Ahmed Khans' accusation: "The Congress is no more than civil war without the use of guns". However, the Moslem League is British-inspired.

Its paymaster, the Aga Khan, told Moslem leader Mohsinul-Mulk "not to move before finding out if the step has the full approval of the government privately".

Whether, as Congress says, it is simply a policy of divide and rule, is less certain. The new century has seen an upsurge in pan-Islamic consciousness, with India's Moslems identifying with Afghans, Turks and Egyptians. A moderate League could act as a safety-valve.

War secretary Taft sends troops into Cuba

Havana, Cuba, 6 October 1906
A thousand US troops have landed at Havana and will proceed to Camp Columbia tomorrow by trolley car. They are the first of 5,500 troops who will be coming in to suppress the liberal and anti-Yankee revolt of Jose Gomez at the request of ousted president Estrada Palma; though officially they will be in Cuba to supervise the disarming of both sides. Effective power in the country is now in the hands of US war secretary William Howard Taft, who declared himself provisional governor last week.

Painter who sought cone and sphere dies

Aix-en-Provence, 22 October 1906
Paul Cezanne has died at the age of 67 after being caught in a rainstorm on a painting expedition. He was just beginning to be recognised as one of the greatest modern French painters after a large exhibition devoted to his work two years ago.

In recent years his favourite subject has been Mont Sainte Victoire near here. Last year he finished his monumental *Grandes Baigneuses* after seven years' work. Cezanne's aim was to render space and volume ever more subtly through colour alone. Painters, he says, should "look for the cone, the sphere and the cylinder in nature".

He exhibited originally with the Impressionists, but he said that he wanted to make Impressionism "something solid and durable like the art of the museums". After the death of his banker father he became rich and lived as a recluse in the family mansion near Aix.

Cezanne's "Grandes Baigneuses": "something solid and durable", as he wanted.

Earthquake turns San Francisco to rubble

The ruins of San Francisco's Sacramento Street, looking towards the sea.

San Francisco, 19 April 1906
More than a thousand people are thought to have been killed in the massive earthquake which reduced downtown San Francisco to rubble yesterday. Shock waves are still hitting the city and an even bigger problem is the raging fires, which are now threatening the fashionable residential area of Nob Hill. Firemen are hampered by the destruction of the water mains in the first

tremor and are using dynamite to try to control the fire.

Thousands slept last night in the parks. Thousands more fled, filling all available ferries and trains. Sadly the lawless minority of this former gold-rush town tried to exploit the chaos. Martial law has been declared and the army has been moved in to help the police. Several looters have already been shot down on the streets.

Drooling dogs reveal our hidden reflexes

Moscow, 1907
A dog will lick its lips and salivate when presented with its bowl of food. It will salivate, too, if a bell is rung just before you hand it the bowl. It will even salivate on hearing the customary bell, even if you do not give it any food at all. These observations by the Russian medical researcher Ivan Pavlov have led to a new theory about what he calls "conditioned reflexes" – that is, conditioned is by a stimulus such as the bell.

Pavlov has done many experiments on the salivation of animals at feeding time and produced detailed descriptions of what stimulus produces the strongest and most durable effect. He has also investigated how these reflexes are acquired and how, sometimes, they appear to be lost.

Animals, Pavlov says, need to form conditioned relexes in order to survive in a changing, predictable

Ivan Pavlov: student of behaviour.

environment. His experiments are confined to dogs and monkeys, but there is no doubt in Pavlov's mind that humans, too, form these conditioned reflexes.

Russian parliament urges disobedience

Russia, 31 July 1906
Do not give a kopeck to the throne or a soldier to the army. That is the advice issued in the name of the Imperial Duma, Russia's first democratic institution, dissolved 10 days ago by Prime Minister Peter Stolypin.

It is just over two months since the Duma was opened by the Czar. Since then, unrest has continued, with a vicious pogrom aimed at the Jews, and mutinies among the soldiery.

The Duma, which had limited power over financial and other matters, was never respected by the government, and is now seen to have been a sop to an angry populace. When it was dissolved, nearly 200 leftist deputies fled to Finland to avoid the Russian police.

Today's manifesto from the Duma warns that it may not reassemble for at least seven months, during which time the government can be expected to act arbitrarily. Meanwhile, government concern centres on disaffection in the military, and security after the assassination of General Kozlov.

The opening session of the Russian Duma, dissolved ten days ago.

Iran capital rocked by revolution threat

Tehran, June 1906
The Iranian capital is in ferment. Most merchants and artisans are on strike, with bazaars closed and rioters running amok. A large number of the merchants and other protesters demanding legal reforms have taken sanctuary in Qum.

The prime minister's attempt to expel two influential preachers was the catalyst for this latest revolt. It

echoes the actions of a rebel group who took refuge in various sanctuaries last December in protest at the punishment of merchants accused of raising the price of sugar.

That earlier revolt was stalled when Shah Muzaffar-al-Din promised legal reforms. When nothing was done, there was a groundswell of unrest on which revolutionary secret societies could capitalise.

Landslide victory in British elections

David Lloyd George, one of the members of the new Liberal cabinet.

London, 7 February 1906
After ten years in opposition, the Liberals have scored a stunning election victory in Britain over the Conservatives. They have 375 seats to the Conservatives' 157. The growing strength of the six-year-old Labour Party is reflected in their 54 seats. Liberals and Labour made an electoral pact giving Labour a free run in what were considered winnable Conservative-held seats; in return, Labour would not contest Liberal seats.

The Conservatives went into the election deeply divided over tariff reform. But the vagaries of the electoral system worked against them. They polled over 2,460,000 votes, only about 100,000 behind the Liberals, but secured 218 fewer MPs. Over 500,000 votes went to Labour. But it is the Irish Nationalists who are heavily over-represented: for a mere 35,109 votes they have 83 MPs.

Washington, DC, 26 February 1907. President Roosevelt puts the American army in charge of building the Panama Canal.

London, 8 March 1907. Keir Hardie's Women's Enfranchisement bill is defeated.

Finland, 15 March 1907. The first women are elected to parliament.

South West Africa, 31 March 1907. The Germans end the state of emergency as all the Nama (*Hottentots*), except those led by Simon Koper, have been defeated.

Russia, 3 April 1907. Twenty million people are starving in the worst famine on record.

China, 15 April 1907. Japan hands Manchuria back to China under the terms of the treaty of Portsmouth which ended the Russo-Japanese war.

British East Africa, 16 May 1907. Nairobi is chosen as the capital of British East Africa (*Kenya*) because of its central location on the Mombasa-Uganda railway line.

London, 18 May 1907. Mrs Ramsay MacDonald chairs the Women's Labour League's first conference.

London, 10 June 1907. J M Synge's play *The Playboy of the Western World* is performed for the first time.

France, 10 June 1907. The cinematographers, Auguste and Louis Lumiere, invent a simple form of colour photography which they believe will make moving pictures in colour commonplace.

Russia, 16 June 1907. Russia's second Duma is dissolved with the prime minister Peter Stolypin accusing 55 socialist members of plotting against the czar.

South Africa, 1 July 1907. The Orange River colony gains autonomy as the Orange Free State.

Korea, 19 July 1907. The Emperor abdicates and is succeeded by the Crown Prince.

Casablanca, 4 August 1907. French troops arrive in Casablanca to avenge the murder of nine Europeans by Moorish extremists.

St Petersburg, 20 August 1907. The trial opens of the 18 revolutionaries accused of plotting to assassinate Czar Nicholas II.

Britain, 31 August 1907. An agreement with Russia is signed defining spheres of influence in Persia and policies in Tibet and Afghanistan.

Norway, 4 September 1907. The Norwegian composer Edvard Grieg dies aged 64. His piano concerto *Peer Gynt* is a classic.

The Hague, 7 September 1907. The peace conference, determining the conventions of war, rules that all powers must give notice of war.

India, 4 October 1907. Nationalist Riots rage in Calcutta following the visit of the Independent Labour Party MP Keir Hardie who accused the British government of running India "like the czar runs Russia".

Russia, 14 October 1907. A third Duma, or parliament – conservative, royalist and pro-Stolypin – meets.

The Hague, 18 October 1907. A secret proposal for an international court of justice, drawn up at the peace conference, is made public.

Brussels, 28 November 1907. King Leopold transfers the kingdom of the Congo up to the state.

London, 29 November 1907. King Edward VII appoints 87-year-old Florence Nightingale to the Order of Merit.

Sweden, 8 December 1907. King Oscar II dies and is replaced by Gustavus V.

Stockholm, 10 December 1907. Rudyard Kipling wins the Nobel prize for literature.

Natal, 12 December 1907. Dinizulu, king of the Zulu and rebel leader, surrenders to government troops.

Addis Ababa, 1907. The Emperor Menelik is paralysed by a stroke and Ras Tasamma becomes regent.

South Africa, 1907. White miners strike to preserve a job colour bar, reserving skilled jobs for whites only, after mines begin employing African and Chinese workers as operators of new mechanical drills.

Norway, 1907. Parliamentary suffrage is granted to women in a certain income bracket.

France, 1907. The philosopher Henri Bergson publishes his most significant work to date – *Creative Evolution*.

Transvaal, 30 January 1908. Mohandas Gandhi, the leader of the Indian protest against new laws requiring Asiatics to register, is released from prison.

Lisbon, 1 February 1908. King Carlos and Crown Prince Luiz are assassinated following last month's failed revolution. Don Manuel is to succeed the king.

Lisbon, 3 February 1908. The dictator Joao Franco and his cabinet resign following the king's assassination.

Russia, 8 February 1908. Czar Nicholas II orders troops to the Persian border following Turkish incursions into Persia.

Marxist writer's fame spreads to France

Paris, 1907
Literary circles in Paris are acclaiming a new talent, whose works have just been translated from their native Russian. Maxim Gorky (born Aleksei Peshkov) wrote his play *The Lower Depths* in 1902, and his novel *Mother* last year. Now both have appeared in France.

Gorky, whose pseudonym comes from the Russian word for "bitter", is deeply involved in his country's revolutionary movement. He has been a Marxist since 1899, and all his works, commencing with the short story *Chelkash* (1895), reflect his sympathies for Russia's exploited and poverty-stricken underclass. Now he is being compared to Tolstoy himself.

Maxim Gorky: revolutionary writer.

Spanish painter breaks all the rules

Picasso's "Les Demoiselles d'Avignon": new perspectives, new dimensions.

Paris, 3 July 1907
Pablo Picasso, a Spanish painter of 26 who moved to Paris in 1900 from Barcelona, has astonished his fellowpainters in Montmartre with his latest work, called *Les Demoiselles d'Avignon*.

It depicts three female figures posing like goddesses in an old master "Judgement of Paris" for two mystery spectators in African totem masks. The title refers to a brothel in Barcelona. The geometrical distortion of the forms, the multiple viewpoints and the flatness of the picture-plane made Guillaume Apollinaire declare: "It's a revolution!"

Women in court for staging votes protest

London, 14 February 1907
A record number of 57 suffragettes were sent to Holloway prison today after clashes with the police. Last night mounted officers rode into a deputation from the Women's Social and Political Union, on their way to parliament to demand the vote. A five-hour struggle ended with 15 women reaching the House of Commons. They, too, were arrested. In court, one defendant, Christabel Pankhurst said: "The women who asked for votes were in danger of their lives. We do not come here in any way to excuse our conduct. We feel yesterday was a great day for our movement."

The women had set up their own "parliament" in a London hall and the idea of the march was to present a petition to its all-male counterpart at Westminster. The women set off at dusk and were very soon under attack from mounted police.

Police expel demonstrating suffragettes from the Houses of Parliament.

Some had their clothes ripped and their bodies bruised, but still they fought their way through to the House of Commons where they tried to hold a meeting.

Transvaal Indians refuse to toe the line

Johannesburg, 22 March 1907
Transvaal's Indian community has chosen an unusual form of protest against a humiliating law which requires them to carry residence permits at all times.

Led by Mohandas Gandhi, a lawyer who has stated that "India's honour is in our keeping", they are practising *satyagraha* or non-violent non-cooperation. This means inviting, rather than causing, suffering in order to redress the wrongs

they are facing. Gandhi has been aware of South Africa's deep-rooted racism ever since he was thrown out of a first-class train compartment soon after arrival 13 years ago. Now he aims to "root out the disease and suffer hardships in the process".

With the Permit Offices due to open soon, Gandhi, who has chosen a self-sufficiency lifestyle on a farm near Durban, is preparing for the next phase of the confrontation.

The longest and most gruelling motor race ever held, from Beijing to Paris, ended on 10 August. The winner was Prince Borghese of Italy, who confronted on his 8,000 mile, 62-day journey – deserts, swamps, mountains, a bushfire, and a Belgian policeman who stopped him for speeding.

Indian congress suspended after clashes

Surat, India, 27 December 1907
The Congress Party of India was rent today by recriminations and violence. In the specially built pavilion in the French Gardens, decorated with scrolls and bunting, the 600 delegates have been fighting furiously with sticks, stones and fists. One British observer, Henry Newinson, said he had "caught glimpses of the Indian National Congress dissolving in chaos." The split is clear-cut between moderates and radicals. The Congress establishment leaders are middle class. They seek a franchise, but a limited franchise; they call for self-government, but set no date. They urge the "Indianisation" of the civil service to ensure their place in it.

The radicals despise such attitudes. Led by Bal Gangadhar Tilak, they want Congress to become a mass movement, fighting the British with civil disobedience to win their freedom.

Atlantic liners battle for speed record

The "Lusitania" arrives in New York after her record-breaking crossing.

Sandy Hook, 11 October 1907
The German-held record for the fastest-ever transatlantic crossing was cut by several hours today as the British luxury liner *Lusitania* steamed into Sandy Hook, New Jersey, after crossing from Queenstown, near Cork, in four days, 19 hours and 52 minutes.

The Cunard-owned *Lusitania*, carrying 1,200 passengers and 650 crew, averaged just over 24 knots, one knot faster than the previous record, held by the German-owned *Deutschland*.

British hopes are high that the record could be lowered further. Recent developments with turbines have produced speeds as high as 34.5 knots.

US clamps down on Japanese immigration

Washington, 24 February 1908
The Japanese government has formally agreed to limit emigration to the US. It reflects a stiffening in the US positon following the gentleman's agreement reached between President Theodore Roosevelt and the Japanese last year, to discourage "emigration of its subjects of the labouring classes". It was the influx of Chinese coolies following the Californian gold rush which finally caused the US to abandon its open-door immigration policy.

Immigration restrictions were introduced in 1882, 1890 and 1902, and as a result the Chinese population is falling from its peak of 107,000. The flood of Japanese immigrants is much more recent and in 1900 there were only 25,000 in the whole country.

1908 (1908-1909)

South West Africa, March 1908. The final battles of the German-Nama war are fought as Simon Koper retreats with his followers into the British territory of Bechuanaland (*Botswana*).

London, 12 April 1908. Herbert Asquith becomes the Liberal prime minister after the resignation of Sir Henry Campbell-Bannerman.

Algeria, 16 April 1908. The French Foreign Legion put Moorish bandits to flight following raids on French outposts on the border.

Washington, DC, 22 May 1908. The Wright brothers patent their "flying machine".

Uganda, 23 May 1908. 4,000 have died in famine in the Usoga region.

Russia, 21 June 1908. The Russian nationalist composer Nikolai Rimsky-Korsakov dies aged 64.

Turkey, 24 July 1908. The success of the Young Turks' revolution, which broke out on the 3rd July, forces Sultan Abdul Hamid II to restore the constitution.

Cuba, 1 August 1908. America supervises elections.

USA, 12 August 1908. Ford's first Model T is produced in Detroit – "a motor car for the multitude".

Morocco, 23 August 1908. The sultan, Abd-el Aziz, flees after his defeat by Mulai Hafid, who declares himself sultan.

Switzerland, 29 September 1908. The international conference on workers' protection bans night shifts for children under 14.

Bulgaria, 5 October 1908. Prince Ferdinand declares Bulgaria independent of Turkey.

Crete, 6 October 1908. Crete declares its independence from Turkey and union with Greece.

Balkans, 7 October 1908. Austria annexes Bosnia-Herzegovina. Though formally part of the Ottoman empire, the territory's predominantly Serbo-Croat population favour union with Serbia. Austria's unilateral move shocks other European powers.

Malta, 9 October 1908. The Royal Navy fleet sails for the Aegean as the Balkans crisis worsens.

London, 12 October 1908. Russia persuades Britain to participate in a congress on the Balkan situation.

London, 21 October 1908. The prime minister, Herbert Asquith, announces emergency measures to reduce unemployment.

London, 24 October 1908. The suffragettes Emmeline Pankhurst and her daughter Christabel are jailed after a sensational trial in which two cabinet ministers are called as witnesses for the defence.

Washington, DC, 3 November 1908. William Howard Taft, the republican candidate, is elected 27th president of the USA.

Australia, 12 November 1908. Andrew Fisher becomes the new Labour prime minister.

Balkans, 15 November 1908. Austria sends troops to the Serbian frontier.

Panama, 15 November 1908. The American President Roosevelt visits the city of Panama – the first president to travel abroad during his term of office.

Berlin, 17 November 1908. The kaiser endorses a retraction of his interview with *The Daily Telegraph* in which he expressed anti-British sentiments.

London, 28 November 1908. The Court of Appeal rules that unions cannot put their funds to political use. Many Labour MPs depend on sponsorship by the unions.

China, 2 December 1908. The child Emperor Puyi succeeds to the throne as Xuantong.

Vienna, 9 December 1908. Austria and Turkey resume talks aimed at easing the Balkan crisis.

Stockholm, 10 December 1908. Professor Ernest Rutherford wins a Nobel prize for his work on radioactivity and the atom.

Italy, 28 December 1908. The most violent earthquake ever recorded in Europe has devastated Messina.

Britain, 1908. Edward Elgar's first symphony is performed over 100 times.

Britain, 1908. Kenneth Grahame publishes a delightful children's book – *The Wind in the Willows*.

Britain, 1908. E M Forster publishes *A Room with a View*.

London, 1 January 1909. Astronomers sight what may be a planet beyond Neptune.

London, 1 January 1909. Men and women over 70 draw their first old-age pensions.

India, 5 January 1909. Hindus and Moslems riot in Calcutta.

Balkans, 12 January 1909. Turkey accepts Austria's offer of 2.5 million Turkish pounds for Bosnia-Herzegovina.

Cuba, 27 January 1909. The American governor leaves the island as Jose Gomez is sworn in as president of the republic.

Morocco, 9 February 1909. A Franco-German agreement recognises French hegemony.

Balkans, 24 February 1909. Serbia demands that Austria cede Bosnia-Herzegovina to it.

US temperance campaign shuts saloons

New York, 1 February 1909
Trouble is fermenting throughout the United States as war is waged on alcohol by an abstinent army of Prohibition campaigners.

The successes of the movement, with women at the helm, include a ban on saloons in 315 townships in New York state, 57 of Ohio's 66 counties and 48 towns in Colorado. In Tennessee it is now an offence to manufacture or sell liquor.

One temperance crusader is Mrs Carrie Nation who, with her 500-strong army, has organised raids on saloons leaving chaos behind. She has vowed not to rest while "there are yet some hell-holes here". The liquor lobby argues that Prohibition leads to fraud, secret drinking and drug abuse.

Carrie Nation waging intemperate war against alcohol in Kansas City.

Artists celebrate age of speed and steel

Paris, 1909
A new outrageous way of viewing the infant century has shocked Italy. "The splendour of the world has been enriched with a new form of beauty, the beauty of speed," says the *Futurist Manifesto of Poetry*, which was published in *Le Figaro* by Italian-born poet Filippo Marinetti.

The new technological century has presented new challenges, he writes. Painters and poets must reject both the stiffling oppression of tradition and the pessimism of the fin de siecle. The alternative is to be buried beneath the weight of history. "Set fire to the libraries! Flood the museums!" he urged in his manifesto. "An automobile, its bonnet writhing with metal tubes, is more beautiful than classical sculpture!"

Even in conventional society futurism is the vogue. Futurist histories foretelling the unlikely shape of things to come are published yearly – though none envisage a world quite like that of the dynamic Marinetti.

Elgar symphony gets a warm welcome

Elgar, the leading figure in the English musical renaissance.

Britain, 31 December 1908
The long-awaited first symphony by Sir Edward Elgar arrived this month to wild acclaim. Elgar is now at the height of his prestige, which began with the *Enigma Variations* in 1899. The oratorio *The Dream of Gerontius* followed, then the overture *Cockaigne*, an evocation of London, and four superb *Pomp and Circumstance* marches. King Edward VII suggested putting words to the great tune in No.1: "Land of Hope and Glory" is now almost a second national anthem. The oratorios *The Apostles* and *The Kingdom* and the lovely *Introduction* and *Allegro* are his other main works of Worcester man who was knighted in 1904.

Black boxer wins a world fight title

Jack Johnson (right), the new heavy-weight world champion.

Sydney, 4 December 1908

American fighter Jack Johnson made boxing history today when he knocked out reigning champion Tommy Burns to become the first black to hold the heavyweight championship of the world.

Texas-born Johnson's victory over Burns, a Canadian, returns the title to the USA after just two years. Americans have now held the title in all but four of its 26-year history. Johnson, aged 30, is the fifth American to become world champion.

For the giant nicknamed Li'l Artha, the championship is the key that should finally give him control of his career. He will no longer have to tolerate being discriminated against by America's white boxing establishment which has persistently denied him purses and opportunities since he turned pro 11 years ago.

Now the worried US boxing establishment is pinning its hopes on bringing former world champion James J Jeffries out of retirement to challenge Johnson as its "Great White Hope".

Nationalists turn to terror tactics

London, 1909

A new form of revolt has grown up in India: terrorism. Its roots are in the *thugees* who worshipped Kali, goddess of destruction, and in the European anarchist movements.

In their boldest move so far they have shot Sir Curzon Wyllie; here in the very heart of the empire. In spite of a spate of killings all over India, Lord Minto, the viceroy, is not going to be diverted from his policy of liberalisation, even though the London cabinet has vetoed his appointments of Indians on to the Viceroy's Council.

Empress dies and new era begins

China, 15 November 1908

The Empress Dowager Cixi who once claimed to have more power than Queen Victoria, died today of an attack of dysentery after eating a huge helping of her favourite dish of clotted cream and crab-apples. She was 73. Commonly known in her later years as the "Old Buddha", this remarkable woman began her long reign as the power behind the Qing throne as the beautiful young concubine of the Xianfeng emperor.

She was made empress when she bore him a son in 1856 and from that moment on has controlled the destinies of China. Ruthless and reactionary, she had kept the Guangxu Emperor, who was both her nephew and adopted son, prisoner ever since his flirtation with the reform movement ten years ago. He died the day before her and she just had time to designate a new Emperor, the two-year-old Puyi, whose weak and reactionary father, Prince Chun, will be regent.

Two sovereigns lying in state: the Empress Dowager and the emperor.

Kaiser's loose talk infuriates British

Berlin, 31 October 1908

Not for the first time, the kaiser's free-wheeling approach to foreign affairs has caused consternation in the chancellories of Europe; on this occasion, though, he has excelled himself. He chose to give an interview to a British newspaper in order to "have a go" at Britain.

He told *The Daily Telegraph* that during the Boer war, Germany, Russia and France held secret talks on finding a way to "humiliate England to the dust". He also claimed that most Germans of the middle and lower classes were "anti-British." German newspapers describe the interview as a "catastrophe". The chancellor, Prince von Bulow – to whom, under German rules, the interview had to be submitted – is being strongly criticised in the Press for allowing it to be published without him reading it first.

Leopold loses his heart of darkness

Congo, 15 November 1908

The Congo Free State has been nationalised by the Belgium government. King Leopold of the Belgiums, who personaly owns the colony, has received 50 million Belgium francs in compensation.

The take-over follows a ten year campaign by missionaries, traders and Mr Roger Casement, the British consul in Boma, the Free State capital, against the atrocities committed in King Leopold's name. Hostages are shot or mutilated when rubber quotas are not reached, villages are razed to make way for rubber plantations, forced labour has become the norm. According to Casement up to 100,000 natives are slaughtered yearly.

Leopold remains unaffected by the outcry. The atrocities are "sad, but one cannot accomplish a great work without doing some evil".

Parisian artists applaud a Sunday painter

Paris, May 1908

A banquet was given by Pablo Picasso in his studio at the *Bateau Lavoir*, Montmartre, in honour of Henri Rousseau, the primitive painter – known as *Le Douanier* because he was in the customs service until he retired to concentrate on painting. Self-taught, he used to exhibit at the *Salon des Independants* to general merriment. Now the meticulous and dreamlike clarity of his jungles, populated with tigers and monkeys have won the respect of the most *avant-garde* painter of the day. "We are the two greatest artists of the age, you in the Egyptian manner, I in the modern," said Picasso to Rousseau, who is extremely innocent.

Henri Rousseau's "Tropical storm with Tiger", making a virtue of naivity.

Balkans, 8 March 1909. The Balkans crisis worsens as Austria rejects Russian mediation in its dispute with Serbia.

Ireland, 24 March 1909. The Irish playwright, J M Synge dies aged 37. His greatest work is the comedy, *The Playboy of the Western World*.

Balkans, 28 March 1909. The European powers agree a formula for Serbia to renounce claims to Bosnia-Herzegovina.

North Pole, 6 April 1909. Commander Robert E Peary of the United States navy is the first person to reach the North Pole.

Britain, 10 April 1909. The poet and literary critic Algernon Charles Swinburne dies aged 72.

Persia, 10 April 1909. British forces land at Tabriz as fear of famine causes widespread unrest.

Bulgaria, 19 April 1909. Turkey recognises Bulgarian independence.

Ottoman Empire, 23 April 1909. Moslem fanatics backed by the sultan have massacred at least 30,000 Armenians in the last week.

Bulgaria, 27 April 1909. Germany, Austria and Italy recognise the independence of Bulgaria.

Ottoman Empire, 2 May 1909. The new Sultan Mehmet V promises liberty equality and justice.

Paris, 7 June 1909. France joins the arms race with a government announcement that it will spend £120 million on new ships.

South Africa, 12 June 1909. Natal votes for union with South Africa.

Congo (Zaire), 12 June 1909. Belgian and British troops clash over the border of Congo and Northern Rhodesia (*Zambia*).

Persia, 26 June 1909. Mohammed Ali Shah annuls a new law which promised elections and defers the promised constitution.

Persia, 13 July 1909. Nationalists opposed to the shah take Tehran.

Persia, 16 July 1909. The 12-year-old crown prince, Sultan Ahmed Mirza, is proclaimed shah.

Paris, 21 July 1909. The cabinet, led by Georges Clemenceau, resigns following a dramatic debate on the state of the navy.

Spain, 1 August 1909. An anti-government revolt in Catalonia leaves up to 1,000 dead.

Britain, 2 August 1909. Czar Nicholas II visits his uncle King Edward VII.

London, 7 September 1909. Lord Northcliffe, the owner of *The Times*, claims that Germany is preparing for war with Britain.

Geneva, 13 September 1909. The congress of Egyptian youth demands British withdrawal from Egypt.

Spain, 26 September 1909. The government announces that the Moors in Morocco have been defeated.

London, 28 September 1909. It is confirmed in the House of Commons that imprisoned suffragettes are being force fed.

Spain, 13 October 1909. The anarchist Francisco Ferrer is executed by a firing-squad following the *Semana Tragica* – a week of rioting of Barcelona.

Brussels, 28 October 1909. The government announces major liberal reforms in the Congo.

Hawaii, 14 November 1909. The American president, William Taft, announces that a naval base will be built at Pearl Harbor to protect America from a Japanese attack.

New York City, 28 November 1909. Sergei Rachmaninov gives the world premiere of his third piano concerto.

Russia, 29 November 1909. Maxim Gorky is expelled from the revolutionary party for his "bourgeois" high living on Capri.

London, 30 November 1909. The Lords reject Lloyd George's People's Budget. A general election will be held in the new year.

London, 3 December 1909. King Edward VII dissolves parliament. Taxes on beer, spirits, tobacco and cars are lifted because the budget has not been passed.

London, 7 December 1909. The The South Africa Act, bringing together the Cape of Good Hope, Natal, Transvaal and Orange River, is given royal assent, as promised by the British at the end of the Boer war.

London, 10 December 1909. The Liberal Herbert Asquith puts Irish home rule and abolition of the Lords' veto at the centre of the liberal election campaign.

Belgium, 17 December 1909. King Leopold II dies aged 74.

Nicaragua, 21 December 1909. Dr Jose Madriz is elected to succeed President Jose Zelaya who was ousted by Americans on the 16th.

Britain, 1909. H G Wells' *Ann Veronica*, the story of an independent woman, is banned by many libraries.

Africa, 15 January 1910. France reorganises French Congo as French Equatorial Africa.

Persia, 31 January 1910. Russia and Britain decide to intervene as political unrest sweeps the country.

"People's Budget" squeezes rich Britons

London, 29 April 1909

Britain was today presented with the most radical budget in its history and asked to pay for more dreadnoughts and the new old-age pensions. By introducing what he called the "People's Budget", David Lloyd George, the Chancellor of the Exchequer, stirred up a hornets' nest of opposition. But he described his policy as "Liberalism, not lunacy".

Among proposals for raising an extra £16 million in revenue is a new "supertax" of sixpence in the pound to be levied on the 10,000 people with incomes over £5,000 a year. The standard rate of tax on earned income stays at ninepence in the pound up to £2,000 and one shilling above that level. There will be increases in the "luxury" taxes on alcohol, tobacco and petrol.

The Budget was bitterly attacked by the Tory Opposition and it will be opposed in both Houses. The Opposition is arguing that the taxes will hit the propertied classes on whom, they claim, the prosperity of the country depends.

Conservative poster attacking Lloyd George's radical "People's budget".

Japanese Bismarck is assassinated

Harbin, 26 October 1909

Prince Ito Hirobumi, renowned as the "Japanese Bismarck", was assassinated here today, shot down by a Korean nationalist. He had given up his post as Japanese Minister-Resident in Korea earlier this month and had travelled to Harbin to reassure the Russians about Japan's intentions towards Korea.

Prince Ito, who was 72, visited England in secret in 1863 and returned the next year to mediate between Britain and Japan after the bombardment of Shimonoseki.

From then on he played a leading role in building Japan into a world power. He helped frame the constitution and became Japan's first Prime Minister. His final task was to bring Korea under Japanese control, a task for which he paid with his life.

Peary's Pole rival cooked the books

Copenhagen, 21 December 1909

A committee appointed by the university here today pronounced that it was Commander Robert Peary of the United States Navy who got to the North Pole first. He sailed to Greenland in the *Roosevelt* and got to the Pole last April after a 90-mile (144 kilometres) trek lasting 36 days. It was his sixth attempt. The committee dismissed the claim of Brooklyn doctor, Frederick Cook, who went with Peary on an earlier attempt. Cook said that he reached the Pole a year earlier accompanied by two Eskimos who testified that he had turned back while 20 miles (32 kilometres) from his target. The committee also ruled that Cook's documents lacked the vital observations proving that he had reached the precise geographical position of the Pole.

Frenchman flies across English Channel

Louis Bleriot, with admirers, and the plane in which he flew the Channel.

Dover, 25 July 1909
Louis Bleriot, the 37-year-old French aviator, made history today with a 43-minute flight from Sangatte, near Calais, to Dover Castle, and won the £1,000 prize offered by the *Daily Mail* to the first flyer to cross the English Channel, a feat previously the monopoly of the birds.

A French destroyer waited in mid-Channel, but Bleriot's flight, which has been put off for five days as he awaited for ideal weather con-

ditions, went without a hitch. His 24-horse power monoplane, its three-cylinder engine powering a single propeller, made a perfect flight at an average speed of 40 miles per hour (*64 kilometers per hour*).

His fellow-aviators warned Bleriot that cross-Channel winds could bring him down, but he remained confident that he could do it in his monoplane, convinced that a biplane could not have made so successful a flight.

Radio call captures suspected murderer

London, 31 July 1910
Nine years after Marconi demonstrated the use of wireless across the Atlantic, the system has been used to detain two much-wanted fugitives from justice. An American, Dr Harvey Crippen, has been arrested on board the liner *Montrose* off Canada for the murder of his wife, Bella, whose dismembered body was found in London. Two days after the discovery, Crippen and his mistress, Ethel le Neve, sailed for Quebec.

Miss le Neve was disguised as Crippen's "son" but the ship's master, Henry Kendall, got suspicious when he saw them holding hands. Kendall had read newspaper stories of the search for the pair and sent radio signals about his passengers to London. Chief Inspector Walter Dew of Scotland Yard then crossed the Atlantic on board the speedier *Laurentic* and boarded the Mont-

The arrest of Dr Harvey Crippen and Ethel le Neve on the "Montrose".

rose disguised as the St Lawrence pilot. When he was arrested, Crippen said: "Thank God it's all over. The suspense has been too great. I could not stand it any longer."

Young Turks topple tyrannical sultan

The sultan's palace is stormed by troops of the "Young Turks".

Istanbul, 27 April 1909
The tyranny of Abdul Hamid is over. The parliament he set up under pressure last summer has voted to depose him and instal his brother Mahmud Reshad.

An uprising by Islamic zealots supported by the Sultan has been suppressed, and a handful of troops in the palace garrison loyal to the Sultan overcome. The troops of the Young Turks, committed to the enactment of democratic reforms, are in control.

The seeds of the Sultan's downfall were sown in Paris in 1907 when the exiled reformers decided to build support in the army. They moved their headquarters to Salonica, and, led by Majors Niazi Bey and Enver Bey, recruited among dissident minorities in Macedonia and Armenia, and among the discontented troops in Arabia.

By last summer they had persuaded most of the Turkish army to pledge loyalty to the constitution that Abdul Hamid had introduced in 1876, suspended in 1878 and continued to flout ever since.

Ballet takes a step forward in Paris

Paris, 18 May 1909
The *Ballets Russes*, presented by Sergei Diaghilev at the Theatre du Chatelet, made a sensational debut last night, amazing an audience used to the conventions of Paris ballet by the free expressiveness of their dancing.

The excitement of the choreography by Michel Fokine in the Polovtsian dances from *Prince Igor* with the exotic decor of Alexandre Benois and rich costumes by Leon Bakst, above all the dazzling steps of Tamara Karsavina and Vaslav Nijinsky, the leading dancers, have never been combined before into a single spectacle like this.

Nijinsky, who danced the poet in *Les Sylphides* to the music of Chopin, was described by a critic as "the power of youth, drunk with rhythm, terrifying in his energy". "I do not follow fashion," said Diaghilev, "I create it."

Collector's item: the programme for Sergei Diaghilev's dazzling ballet.

Mark Twain, US storyteller supreme, dies

Redding, Conn., 21 April 1910
"Mark Twain" was the cry leadsmen used sounding the depth of the river when it was two fathoms deep when Samuel Clemens was a boy on the Mississippi. At the age of 18 he contributed humorous pieces to the *Hannibal Journal*, which he and his brother set up in Missouri. At 22 he learned from a steamboat captain

the trade of a Mississippi pilot. It was his reminiscences of his boyhood in the person of Tom Sawyer or Huckleberry Finn, that made him a national character, in drooping moustache and bowler hat, beloved for his pithy aphorisms. One was that "reports of my death have been greatly exaggerated" – not this time, alas.

British India: The Jewel in the Crown

When in 1911 the King-Emperor George V and the Queen-Empress Mary travelled to the imperial *durbar* (their audience with the Indian princes) at Delhi, Britain's Indian Empire was at its height. During the proceedings the monarch announced the removal of the imperial capital from Calcutta to Delhi, a dramatic stroke worthy of the Moghul emperors and Delhi sultans who had preceded him. Then, emphasizing that now they were truly rulers of India, the British began to build a brand new capital in Delhi beside the relics of Moghul Shahjahanabad.

This was the last truly untroubled imperial moment for the British in India. After sixty years of steady consolidation they now ruled over three hundred million people. There had been few external threats to their empire. One, in the northwest, came from Russia's advance into Central Asia; for much of the time they had adopted the wise policy of relying on Afghan desire for independence to be their assurance of security. A second came from French moves in southeast Asia; the British responded by annexing Upper Burma in 1886. A third, albeit somewhat imaginary, involved Russia's activities in Tibet; the British resolved it by means of a bloodthirsty and unsatisfactory expedition to Lhasa in 1904.

Inside their empire the British had set up the framework of a modern state. A system of administration came increasingly to reach down to each individual citizen. A system of law had been promulgated which in its penal and civil aspects at least, was common to all. As time went on more and more positions in government service were open only to those who could pass school and university examinations. On the other hand the British had set about building up the infrastructure of a modern economy.

A modern state established

By the early twentieth century they had developed the largest railway system in Asia. They had restored old irrigation systems and developed new ones. There were hydroelectric dams, harbourworks and bridges. There was also the considerable development of a system of higher education, although general education remained limited and illiteracy was widespread. The results of these and other developments were that famines were diminished and agriculture tended to become commercialised. Great plantation industries emerged in jute, cotton and tea, as did mining industries in coal and iron. The spread of these developments, it should be noted, was not even. The growth of infrastruc-

ture took place more rapidly than that of industry.

A survey of the benefits India brought Britain at this time underlines how valuable she was. India was the largest single purchaser of British exports, taking about ten per cent overall, and of these the major item was cotton piecegoods. India was also a favoured destination for British capital and ranged from fifth to second highest as an area of investment. Above all Indian taxes paid for a highly trained army of 250,000 men with establishments in Britain as well as in India; this army promoted the British imperial enterprise from China to Africa. It was not surprising that Indians complained of the drain of wealth which the British government imposed.

Victoria's special relationship

The army had not been needed within India after the Mutiny Uprising of 1857-58. These troubled years were followed by a substantial shake-up of policy. In 1858 the Crown had assumed full responsibility for India and in subsequent years a special relationship had developed between Queen Victoria and her subjects; it was one which she did much to cultivate. The Princes who controlled a third of India's territory were brought into a special and intimate relationship with the Crown which was underlined in all their dealings with government and exemplified at all great ceremonial occasions. The rural elites were similarly incorporated into the system of political control. In some areas, notably in north India, the British favoured large landowners; in others, for instance the Punjab and the Deccan, they favoured proprietary farmers. Whichever groups benefited, they received, in much the same way as the Princes, public marks of favour. Resting on the support of these "haves" of Indian society the British had not endeavoured to impose western ways on their Indian subjects, as they had done before the Mutiny. Indeed, they had taken to heart, to a degree at least, the criticism of their subjects and had begun to develop the means by which they might consult them in government, for instance, through legislative councils (from 1861), through municipal and district boards (from 1870s), and in elected provincial legislative councils which from 1909 contained good numbers of Indians although not quite enough to form majorities.

The growth of a new class

Not all Indians, by any means, were co-opted into the British system of political control. Notably,

there had developed a new class educated in government colleges, and sometimes in British universities too, who felt keenly the injustices both of their own situation and of India at large. A bad display of racialism in the early 1880s by Europeans who objected to being tried by Indian judges spurred them to found the Indian National Congress in 1885. The organisation won support from all over India; its annual meetings being celebrations of India's burgeoning sense of nationhood, its leaders, G K Gokhale, B G Tilak, S N Banerjea, national heroes. Its demands were limited: greater participation in the legislative councils, the Indianisation of the top ranks of the civil service, the abolition of tariffs on Indian cotton goods, the removal of all aspects of the colonial status of India's economy. Nevertheless, the way in which it pressed its case against the British had become increasingly vociferous. If some Congressmen were content to use the small arenas for political activity made available by the British, others were not. In the first decade of the twentieth century Congress divided into "moderates" and "extremists", the increasing use of direct action, and the emergence of revolutionary terrorism. The nationalist movement had come of age. But in doing so it had one great failure: it had not attracted significant numbers of Moslems to its ranks; they had formed their own organisation, the All-India Moslem League, in 1906.

At the time of the Coronation *durbar* in 1911 Congress was yet to demand the end of British rule. Within a decade this was an objective acknowledged both by the British and by Congress, although they differed radically over its timing. In 1917 the secretary of state for India announced that British policy was "the gradual development of self-governing institutions with a view to the progressive realisation of responsible government in India as an integral part of the British Empire." In 1921 Congress, in the midst of the greatest movement against British rule since the Mutiny Uprising, was calling for *swaraj* (freedom) within the year. The situation had been transformed by the Great War, which revealed how very dependent the British Empire was on its Indian subjects. The disturbed economic and political circumstances which followed it created ripe conditions for mass protest politics. Moreover, a remarkable leader had emerged to give shape to the new political opportunities, Mahatma Gandhi. He was to urge that India's pursuit of political freedom was not just a political but a moral goal. It should, therefore, be pursued without violence.

"A young civilian's toilet" (1844).

British India celebrating the elevation of their monarch, Queen Victoria, to Empress of India.

Running an empire, a member of the Indian Civil service, still in his twenties.

India's princes, "playing the game", a maharajah's tennis party in 1890.

Bridgebuilding in India, a British engineer directs its construction.

Climbing to the zenith, the "agony point" loop on the Darjeeling railway.

1910 (1910-1911)

Africa, 7 February 1910. Belgium, Britain and Germany fix the frontiers of Congo, Uganda and German East Africa respectively.

London, 14 February 1910. Tories and Liberals tie in the general election but the Liberals remain in power, supported by Labour MPs.

Tibet, 23 February 1910. The Dalai Lama flees to India as Chinese troops invade Lhasa. He returned from exile in Beijing only two months ago having fled in 1904 when British troops invaded.

Berlin, 6 March 1910. Socialists are shot and sabred during a suffrage demonstration.

China, 10 March 1910. Slavery is abolished.

Italy, 27 March 1910. Mount Etna erupts.

Australia, 13 April 1910. The Liberal prime minister Alfred Drakin loses to Andrew Fisher's Labour party in federal elections.

London, 14 April 1910. The House of Commons votes for bill to abolish the Lords' power to veto bills.

Ottoman Empire, 25 April 1910. Turkish troops battle with Albanian rebels.

London, 7 May 1910. King George V succeeds the throne following Edward VII's death from pneumonia yesterday.

London, 20 May 1910. Halley's comet today passes within 13 million miles of the earth.

London, 1 June 1910. Captain Robert Falcon Scott sets out on a journey to conquer the South Pole.

Russia, 3 June 1910. The Duma is to abolish Finnish autonomy.

Germany, 22 June 1910. Nobel prize winner, Dr Paul Ehrlich, puts forward a new drug for syphilis, known as salvarsan.

South Africa, 1 July 1910. The Union of South Africa, formed on 31 May, becomes a dominion of the British empire.

Far East, 4 July 1910. Russia acknowledges Japan's occupation of Korea in return for a free hand in Manchuria.

Ottoman Empire, 27 July 1910. Turkey threatens Greece with war if it accepts Cretan representatives in the Greek parliament.

London, 13 August 1910. The nursing pioneer Florence Nightingale dies aged 90.

New Jersey, 27 August 1910. Thomas Edison demonstrates talking motion pictures.

Balkans, 28 August 1910. Montenegro declares its full independence from the Ottoman empire under King Nicholas.

France, 2 September 1910. The painter Henri "le Douanier" Rousseau dies aged 76.

South Africa, 15 September 1910. Afrikaner nationalists win the first parliamentary elections.

South Africa, 19 September 1910. Although the prime minister Louis Botha loses his seat in the election, his National Party decide he should remain as leader.

Britain, 12 October 1910. Ralph Vaughan Williams' first symphony, "A Sea Symphony" is performed for the first time.

Portugal, 17 October 1910. The provisional government banishes the royal family and abolishes the nobility.

Britain, 20 October 1910. The liner Olympic is launched, the largest vessel afloat.

Switzerland, 30 October 1910. Henri Dunant, founder of the Red Cross, dies aged 82.

Portugal, 9 November 1910. The republic is recognised by Britain, France, Germany, Russia, Spain, Norway and Belgium.

Britain, 11 November 1910. The prime minister, Herbert Asquith, asks King George V to create enough liberal peers to allow the passage of the Lords reform bill.

London, 18 November 1910. Asquith the prime minister, announces that the king will dissolve parliament and this year's second general election will be held before Christmas.

London, 23 November 1910. Dr Crippen is hanged for the murder of his wife.

Germany, November 1910. A Russo-German convention is signed at Potsda.

Morocco, 3 December 1910. France takes the port of Agadir.

London, 20 December 1910. Liberals and Tories tie in the general election and the Liberal Herbert Asquith remains in power with the backing of 42 Labour MPs and 84 Irish nationalists.

Britain, 1910. Bertrand Russell and A N Whitehead publish Principia Mathematica.

Nicaragua, 2 January 1911. The American President Taft acknowledges the government of Jose Estrada and orders the withdrawal of troops.

Germany, 26 January 1911. Richard Strauss's new opera Der Rosenkavalier opens to great acclaim in Dresden.

Britain, 6 February 1911. The Labour Party elect Ramsay MacDonald as its chairman.

Spectacular Firebird sets Paris alight

The design for the second scene of Stravinsky's ballet "The Firebird".

Paris, 25 June 1910
Diaghilev's Russian Ballet has again astonished Paris with a spectacular new ballet to an old Russian fairy tale, *The Firebird*. Richly designed in oriental splendour by the painter, Natalia Goncharova, the Firebird wore a head-dress and costume of peacock feathers. Tamara Karsavina glided over the stage on point throughout. But the real sensation was the music, specially commissioned from a young Russian composer of 28, Igor Stravinsky.

A student of Rimsky-Korsakov, at whose country house the score was composed, he out-glitters even his master's music.

Eccentric Tolstoy dies in a railway station

Astopovo, Ryazan, 20 Nov 1910
Peasants are flocking to the little railway station at Astopovo, where the author Leo Tolstoy died today after a secret flight from his family estate at Yasnaya Polyana accompanied by his daughter Tatiana. At the age of 82 he was seeking to live as a hermit, free of land he inherited as a count but which made a mockery of his later beliefs.

After his conversion in 1879, related in *A Confession*, he rejected the Orthodox Church, which excommunicated him for his attacks in his last novel, *Resurrection*. He lived as a peasant working in the fields, but his wife, Sofya, refused to turn ascetic with him. He died refusing to see her.

Tolstoy, and his gipsy sister-in-law, Sasha, at his home, Yasnaya Polyana.

Fear of revolution returns to Mexico

Mexico, 18 November 1910
After thirty years of comparatively stable government under president Porfirio Diaz, Mexico is once again facing the convulsions of a revolution. Francesco Madero Jr, who calls himself a liberal and a reformer, today proclaimed an uprising against the authorities.

Earlier this year Madero challenged Diaz in the election. His reform platform faced a campaign filled with corruption and dirty tricks. Arrested at one stage for simply gathering a crowd, his defeat was ensured by systematic fraud at the polls.

Diaz himself, a former general, was seen as Mexico's saviour when he seized power in 1876. He did modernise his country, but his economic policies proved unpopular. He sided openly with the rich, neglecting the major problems of poverty and land reform.

After his defeat Madero retreated to San Antonio, Texas, where, on 7 October, he declared

Art and revolution, insurgent Mexicans call for land and liberty.

himself the provisional president. Although today's revolution seems somewhat muted – there has been but a single skirmish – Madero has gained important backers, notably Pancho Villa and Emiliano Zapata.

Suffragette hunger strikers force-fed

Liverpool, January 1910
Suffragettes on hunger strike in prison are being tortured by force feeding. Lady Constance Lytton, who is in Walton jail, under an assumed name, told visitors she was allowed only four days without food before doctors began this violent treatment on her.

Everyday she refuses to eat, a steel gag is pushed into her mouth and her jaws are fastened wide apart. A four-foot (1.2 metres) tube is pushed down her throat and liquidised food poured through it into her stomach. Her body promptly rejects the food making the whole cruel process pointless.

The Asquith Government is under pressure now to find a humane way of dealing with Mrs Pankhurst's militants. It wants to keep them alive, in or out of prison, without condoning their actions or giving way to their demands for female suffrage.

Suffragettes being force fed in prison.

Korea bows to new Japanese masters

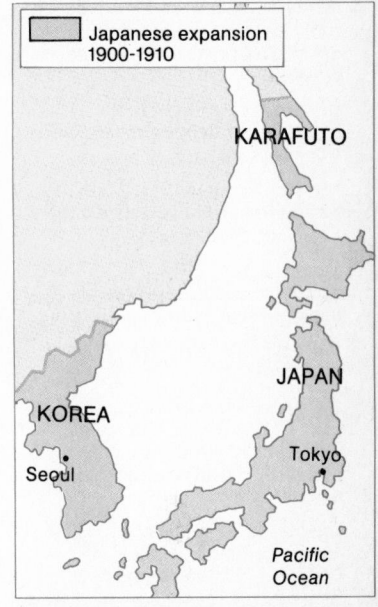

Japanese expansion 1900-1910

KARAFUTO

JAPAN

KOREA

Tokyo

Seoul

Pacific Ocean

Tokyo, 29 August 1910
Japan has achieved its ambition of annexing Korea. By a treaty made public today the Japanese have acquired sovereignty over Korea and its citizens are to be subject to Japanese law. The law is to be administered by the army and there is no doubt that it will make every effort to stamp out Korean nationalism.

It was an expression of this nationalism, the murder of Prince Ito, which led directly to the annexation. The Japanese installed Terauchi Masatake as minister-resident in Seoul and backed him with troops.

Terauchi rapidly assumed control of every aspect of Korean public life and the Korean king was at his mercy. Within a month Terauchi was able to agree to "Korea's request for annexation". The treaty was signed by Terauchi and the Korean king a week ago.

Revolutionaries oust Portuguese monarch

King Manuel's last Sunday as a monarch, before being toppled by a coup.

Lisbon, 4 October 1910
A republican-led coup has ended the short reign of Manuel II, who escaped from his bombarded palace today.

Coming to the throne less than three years ago, after his father and elder brother were assassinated by anarchists, Manuel sought political unity in Portugal by bringing all the main parties into government, but intense divisions between monarchists and republicans thwarted any prospect of success.

Although the coup had been anticipated, few of the troops brought in to defend the 19-year-old king proved reliable.

Italian army seizes Tripoli from the Turks

Tripoli, Libya, 20 October 1911
An Italian expeditionary force of 9,000 infantry landed here this morning. Four thousand more landed in Libya's second city, Benghazi, after a prolonged naval bombardment through the night.

The Turkish garrisons put up fierce resistance, though outnumbered and outgunned; and in Tripoli the army managed to escape into the desert, from where they are harassing the Italians. Since Italy's humiliating defeat by the Ethiopians at Adowa in 1896, it has coveted this Turkish colony, and in 1900 gained French recognition that it lay within its sphere of influence.

Three weeks ago Italy declared war on Turkey. Today's landings will raise Italian pride, and re-establish Italy as a colonial power after the disaster at Adowa.

Norway, 17 March 1911. Anna Rogstadt takes her seat as the country's first woman MP.

Morocco, 30 March 1911. The sultan asks for French help to put down the uprising that began last October.

Mexico, 15 April 1911. American troops begin fighting rebels led by Francisco Madero.

Mexico, 20 April 1911. Madero refuses to agree a ceasefire until President Diaz resigns.

Paris, 23 April 1911. The cabinet agrees to send reinforcements to put down the Moroccan uprising.

Portugal, 30 April 1911. Women get the vote.

London, 4 May 1911. Lloyd George reveals the Liberal government's insurance bill designed to deal with sickness and unemployment.

Austria, 18 May 1911. The great composer Gustav Mahler dies at the age of 50. He will be best remembered for the songsymphony *Das Lied von der Erde*.

Britain, 30 May 1911. The British writer and Sir Arthur Sullivan's librettist Sir William Schwenk Gilbert dies aged 75.

Mexico, 7 June 1911. A huge earthquake rocks Mexico City.

Britain, 14 June 1911. The seamen's union in Liverpool calls for a national strike.

Morocco, 16 June 1911. The French army occupies Fez.

Morocco, 1 July 1911. Kaiser Wilhelm II dispatches a German gunboat to the Moroccan port of Agadir, to the alarm of the French.

Balkans, 5 July 1911. 10,000 Montenegran troops have been mobilised on the Albanian border.

Lisbon, 5 July 1911. A revolt against the republic is put down after street fighting in the capital.

North Africa, 3 August 1911. Aeroplanes are put to military use when Italians reconnoitre Turkish lines near Tripoli.

London, 10 August 1911. The House of Lords gives up its right of veto, accepting the Liberal government's parliament bill. The bill follows a general election and a threat by King George V to create sufficient peers to pass it.

London, 18 August 1911. The Official Secrets Bill gets royal assent.

Paris, 22 August 1911. Leonardo da Vinci's masterpiece the *Mona Lisa* is stolen from the Louvre.

Portugal, 24 August 1911. Manoel Jose de Arriaga is elected first president of the republic.

China, 4 September 1911. Flooding along the Yangzi river kills 100,000 people.

Paris, 7 September 1911. The poet Guillaume Apollinaire is arrested, and later released, for the theft of the *Mona Lisa*.

Russia, 19 September 1911. Czar Nicholas II appoints Vladimir Kokovstev as premier in succession to Stolypin.

Berlin, 23 September 1911. France and Germany settle the Moroccan dispute.

Mexico, 2 October 1911. Francisco Madero is elected president.

Portugal, 3 October 1911. Royalists are beaten by republican troops in battle at Oporto.

Britain, 23 October 1911. Winston Churchill is appointed First Lord of the Admiralty.

Mexico City, 24 October 1911. Rebel supporters of Emiliano Zapato carry out raids around the capital.

North Africa, 1 November 1911. Italians carry out the first aerial bombing on Tanguira oasis in Tripolitania.

China, 2 November 1911. Hankou is burnt by imperial troops.

Egypt, 2 November 1911. Martial law is proclaimed following widespread Moslem unrest.

North Africa, 5 November 1911. Italy announces the annexation of Tripolitania, Libya and Cyrenaica.

China, 10 November 1911. Imperial troops massacre republicans at Nanjing.

Britain, 13 November 1911. Andrew Bonar Law becomes leader of the Tory party, succeeding Arthur James Balfour.

Russia, 6 December 1911. Mongolia is declared a Russian protectorate.

China, 6 December 1911. The regent Prince Chun resigns.

India, 12 December 1911. George V is crowned emperor of India and founds New Delhi to replace Calcutta as the Indian capital.

China, 29 December 1911. Dr Sun Yat-sen, leader of the Chinese revolution, becomes provisional president of the Chinese republic.

London, December 1911. The National Insurance Bill, providing for unemployment and sickness insurance, is passed.

Paris, 1911. Vaslav Nijinsky dances the lead role of Petrushka in Stravinsky's new ballet.

China, 1 January 1912. The republic of China is officially proclaimed.

Insurgents expel Mexico's hated dictator

Pancho Villa and his guerrilla officers, during the advance on Mexico City.

Mexico, 25 May 1911

Porfirio Diaz, the Mexican president since 1876, resigned today, victim of a popular revolution that has been brewing since last October, when the liberal reformer Francisco Madero declared him an "illegal" president, and called on the people to overthrow his rule.

Since then Madero and his allies, the guerrilla bands led by Emiliano Zapata and Pancho Villa, have advanced steadily towards power. Madero, temporarily exiled to Texas, first demanded an uprising on 20 November, but few Mexicans responded. The situation changed when on 14 February this year Madero returned to Mexico to take the head of the guerrilla forces. Sof-tened by years of power, Diaz's Federal troops could put up no real resistance to the uprising.

Aged generals, an ill-disciplined soldiery and an overall lack of strategy all combined to help the rebels. On 10 May the federal commander at Ciudad Juarez, where Madero had launched his first attacks, surrendered. From thereon the revolution gained momentum and the veteran president's support rapidly collapsed.

Diaz accepted a plan whereby he would resign and an interim president, who would immediately hold a general election, would be appointed. As guerrilla troops marched into Mexico City, Diaz was already en route for Paris.

Russian minister is murdered at opera

Kiev, 18 September 1911

Russia's premier, Peter Stolypin, died today after having been shot down at close range a week ago at the opera. Stolypin, who was 49, had made many enemies through his hard-line policies. The assassination was watched by Czar Nicholas II and his two daughters who were sitting in a box.

The assassin, Mordkha Bogrov is a socialist lawyer, as well as a police informer, and he entered the opera house without difficulty. He is also a Jew and there is considerable unease that the murder could create conditions for a retaliatory pogrom.

US senators to be directly elected

Washington, 12 June 1911

Proposals which will take America nearer the historic ideal of government by the people and for the people were agreed here today. They provide for the Senate, the upper house of the Congress, to be elected by direct popular vote.

At present the senators, two from each state, are chosen by a vote of each state's legislature. This means the choice is dominated by the local party machines which are in power at the time of the election every four years. If, as expected, the proposals pass into law, senators will be elected for six-year terms.

Five-year-old emperor losing power

Beijing, 30 October 1911

Revolution is sweeping across China and in a desperate attempt to stem the tide the reactionary but weak ruling Manchu clique headed by the Regent, Prince Chun, has today established a constitutional government and a cabinet of commoners. Acting in the name of his son, the five-year-old Emperor Puyi, the prince, who is incapable of handling the explosive political situation, has summoned the man he hates most, General Yuan Shi-kai, to be prime minister.

It was Yuan who betrayed Chun's reforming brother, the Guangxu emperor, and in revenge Chun had him removed from office in the most insulting manner, claiming that that he had a bad leg which made him hobble and so made it unseemly for him to to be seen at court.

Yuan retired to his estates but retained the loyalty of the troops of his well-trained Northern army and they will not move against the rebels without him. But he is returning Chun's insult, claiming that his leg is too bad for him to obey the Prince's summons.

He can be seen pottering about wearing a cotton smock and straw

Dr Sun Yat-sen and his wife, with pro-Republican officers of the Canton Army.

hat in the mild autumn weather. He fishes for carp, but his real quarry is power on his own terms and he seems likely to get it.

The rebellion which started prematurely when a store of explosives blew up in Hankou on 9 October, forcing the rebels into action, caught everyone by surprise. Dr Sun Yat-sen, the revolutionary leader, was in Denver on a fund-raising tour and learned of it from the American newspapers. The ex-

plosion enabled the government to arrest some of the rebel leaders, but the uprising took on a momentum of its own, with mutinous troops forcing unwilling officers to lead them.

Fanned by popular discontent, the movement is spreading rapidly through the western and southern provinces. Unless Yuan and his men march soon, there is little doubt that the long reign of the Manchus will be ended.

Norwegian beats Briton to South Pole

South Pole, 14 December 1911

Norway has won the race to the South Pole. In a message from Antarctica, explorer Roald Amundsen confirmed that his team had beaten their British challengers, led by Captain Robert Scott, in a competition that dates back to the beginning of the century.

"Everything went like a dance," said a jubilant Amundsen, although the 2,000-mile (3,200 kilometres) trek at a height of 10,000 feet (3,084 metres) above sea level, was full of hardships. Spurning the motorised transports used by the British, the Norwegians owe much of their success to the resilience of the dogs who pulled their sledges.

As for Scott, who has not been heard from since he set out for the Pole in November, Amundsen too knows nothing. However, he agrees that it is "extremely likely" that the British team will reach the Pole.

Captain Roald Amundsen, who beat the British team to the South Pole.

Riots ravage strike bound Britain

Liverpool, 8 August 1911

Violence flared in the streets of this seaport city today as the rest of the country was being brought to a virtual standstill by a nationwide strike. Two men were shot dead when troops opened fire on rioters; and police with military escorts are using armoured vehicles to patrol the city. Warships are anchored in the Mersey where a queue of merchant ships are waiting to unload.

Liverpool is badly affected; but more than 50,000 armed troops have arrived in London where the strike – by stevedores, railwaymen and other transport workers – is threatening a nationwide famine.

Labour leader Keir Hardie told strikers: "The masters show you no mercy. They starve you, they sweat you, they oppress you. Pay them back in their own coin."

Scientist sees huge power within the nucleus of an atom

Manchester, 1911

Ernest Rutherford, the outstanding physicist has shown that the atom is like a miniature solar system. At its centre is a nucleus around which revolve other particles – its "planets". Within these atomic nuclei are unimaginably powerful forces.

The nucleus occupies less than one thousand million millionth of the atomic volume. Helium nuclei cannot be deflected by powerful electric forces, yet they can be turned round by a thin gold foil. "It was," says Rutherford "as if you had fired a 15-inch shell at paper and it had bounced back."

US Democrat wins, thanks to split vote

Washington DC, 5 November 1912

Democrat candidate Woodrow Wilson, the former president of Princeton College and the man called "the schoolmaster in politics", has won the presidency with only 6.2 million votes. The win is a result of a split vote amongst his opponents, with Republican outgoing President Taft receiving 3.5 million votes, the former Republican president and now Progressive Party leader, Theodore Roosevelt, receiving four million votes, and the socialist Eugene Debs receiving almost a million votes.

Woodrow Wilson on the campaign trail, keeping to the rails.

1912 (1912-1913)

USA, 6 January 1912. New Mexico becomes the 47th state.

France, 13 January 1912. Raymond Poincare forms a coalition government.

South Pole, 17 January 1912. The British explorer Robert Scott reaches the south pole to discover that his Norwegian rival, Roald Amundsen, has beaten him to it.

Britain, 10 February 1912. Lord (Joseph) Lister, the pioneer of antiseptics, dies.

USA, 14 February 1912. Arizona becomes the 48th state.

China, 15 February 1912. Yuan Shikai takes over from Sun Yat-sen as provisional president of the republic of China.

USA, 28 February 1912. Albert Berry makes the world's first parachute jump from an aeroplane.

London, 7 March 1912. Henri Semiet makes the first Paris-London non-stop flight.

Morocco, 30 March 1912. By the treaty of Fez, Morocco becomes a French protectorate.

Britain, 13 April 1912. The Royal Flying Corps is set up.

Paris, 1 May 1912. L'Apres-midi d'un Faune, a ballet created by the Russian dancer Vaslav Nijinsky, receives its premiere.

Rhodes, 4 May 1912. The Italians occupy the Ottoman island.

Russia, 5 May 1912. The first issue of the Bolshevik newspaper Pravda appears.

Sweden, 14 May 1912. The playwright August Strindberg dies.

Balkans, 29 May 1912. Greece signs an anti-Ottoman alliance with Bulgaria.

Paris, 8 June 1912. The Ballets Russes give the first complete performance of Ravel's ballet Daphnis et Chloe.

Los Angeles, 8 June 1912. Carl Laemmie founds Universal Studios.

Balkans, 2 July 1912. Serbia joins the Greek-Bulgarian alliance against the Ottoman empire.

Britain, 22 July 1912. The admiralty recalls British warships from the Mediterranean to the North Sea to counter the growing German naval threat.

Europe, 1 August 1912. An air-mail service begins between London and Paris.

Albania, 3 August 1912. The Ottomans grant Albania limited autonomy.

Far East, 7 August 1912. Russia and Japan reach agreement on their spheres of influence in Mongolia and Manchuria.

Morocco, 11 August 1912. Sultan Mulai Hafid abdicates.

France, 14 August 1912. The composer Jules Massenet dies.

Britain, 1 September 1912. The composer Samuel Coleridge-Taylor dies.

USA, 23 September 1912. Mack Sennett releases the first Keystone Cops film.

Balkans, 8 October 1912. Montenegro declares war on the Ottoman empire.

Balkans, 14 October 1912. The Ottomans invade Serbia.

Switzerland, 18 October 1912. The Ottoman empire and Italy sign a treaty at Ouchy whereby the Ottomans cede Tripoli and Cyrenaica to Italy.

Turkey, 19 October 1912. The allied Balkan armies invade Turkey.

Balkans, 23 October 1912. The Greeks rout the Ottomans at Sarandaporos.

Germany, 25 October 1912. Richard Strauss' opera Ariadne auf Naxos receives its premiere.

Balkans, 1 November 1912. The Greeks occupy Samothrace.

Balkans, 8 November 1912. The Greeks capture Salonika.

Balkans, 18 November 1912. The Serbs take Monastir.

Morocco, 27 November 1912. France and Spain sign a treaty outlining their respective spheres of influence in Morocco.

Albania, 28 November 1912. Albania declares independence.

Balkans, 4 December 1912. The Ottomans conclude an armistice with Bulgaria and Serbia. Greece refrains from signing.

Europe, 5 December 1912. Germany, Austria and Italy renew their triple alliance for six years.

South Africa, 20 December 1912. Louis Botha forms a new cabinet.

Switzerland, 1912. Carl Gustav Jung publishes his Theory of Psychoanalysis.

Britain, 1912. George and Weedon Grossmith publish The Diary of a Nobody.

France, 17 January 1913. Raymond Poincare is elected president.

Turkey, 23 January 1913. The extreme nationalist Young Turks, led by Enver Bey, stage a coup d'etat, overthrowing the Ottoman grand vizier, Kiamil Pasha.

Britain, 31 January 1913. The House of Lords rejects a bill for Irish Home Rule.

Ottomans reel under Balkan offensive

Balkans, 31 October 1912

The Ottoman empire's centuries-old domination of the Balkans is coming to a violent and bloody end as the sultan's troops retreat in disorder, pursued by triumphant Bulgarian and Serbian forces. There are reports in the Bulgarian capital, Sofia, that the Ottoman minister of war, Nazim Pasha, has been shot and hundreds of officers are to be punished for their incompetence.

The Ottoman *debacle* comes only two weeks after the outbreak of hostilities. Serbia and Bulgaria have been spoiling for a fight for some time, and saw their chance when the sultan became embroiled in a fight with an Italian force in Libya. They sent a stiff note to Istanbul demanding immediate autonomy for Macedonia, which shares frontiers with Greece, Serbia and Bulgaria, and, counting on a less than satisfactory reply from the Ottomans, ordered a general mobilisation.

The sultan also mobilised and told his men that "not an inch of the sacred soil soaked with the blood of your ancestors" was to be given up to the enemy. The enemy, however, which consists of Bulgaria, Serbia, Greece and Montenegro – all once under Ottoman domination – considers the soil to

The Ottoman army in retreat, followed by Bulgarian troops.

belong to it. If it were simply a question of subject peoples fighting for their freedom, the rest of Europe would stand by and applaud. But the crumbling Ottoman empire offers rich pickings to tempt the great powers. More than once Russian czars have intrigued to lay their hands on Ottoman provinces, a process viewed with apprehension in the Austro-Hungarian capital of Vienna. Now the Italians, arriving late at the feast, are seeking to fashion an empire for themselves out of the Ottomans' North African provinces. They lost out to the French in Tunis, but have struck first in Libya.

Ulster loyalists rally to fight Home Rule

Edward Carson: a Unionist who is playing the "Orange card".

Belfast, 28 September 1912

While the Westminster parliament again discusses government plans to grant home rule to Ireland, the Protestant minority in the north of that country has put on a menacing show of armed force to back a "covenant" signed by 471,414 people. Seven days of marches and drum beats ended with a parade by riflemen who were addressed by their leader, Sir Edward Carson, the barrister who led the prosecution of the playwright Oscar Wilde for immoral practices in 1895. The Liberal government has other weighty opponents to Home Rule. F E Smith, the Conservative spokesman on Ireland, told the rally to use "permissible resistance" against the "technical law" on this issue. Many senior soldiers, including the influential Anglo-Irish General Sir Henry Wilson, agree.

Chinese emperor forced to resign

Beijing, 12 February 1912
The Manchu dynasty fell today after 267 years when the weeping Empress Dowager Longyu, the widow of the Guangxu emperor, read out an edict of abdication on behalf of the boy-emperor, Puyi.

The edict designates the strongman General Yuan Shikai as the new ruler of China and the republican leader, Dr Sun Yat-sen, has agreed to step down as president of the republic in favour of Yuan in order to avoid civil war.

It is a decision which Dr Sun may soon regret, for the general is cast in a dictatorial mould.

Puyi, his father and young brother.

"Unsinkable" liner sinks: 1,500 missing

The last moments of the "Titanic" in the Atlantic: an artist's impression.

Newfoundland, 15 April 1912
A frantic sea-search is under way in icy Atlantic waters for survivors of the supposedly "unsinkable" luxury liner *Titanic* which sank last night after hitting an iceberg. Of the 2,340 passengers and crew, more than 1,500 are believed to have perished – which makes this the greatest-ever sea disaster.

The *Titanic*, the pride of the White Star Line, was on her maiden voyage, and her captain was said to be aiming to break all records for an Atlantic crossing as he ignored iceberg warnings and ploughed at speed towards New York. Her designers claimed that she could never sink because she was built with 16 water-tight compartments; this is why she was equipped with a minimum of lifeboats. She sank within hours – and the first lifeboat to get away was almost empty and occupied by directors of the line and their friends.

Initial reports suggest that first-class passengers were given priority' and that many of those who went down with the *Titanic* were women and children immigrants on cheap "steerage" passages. There was heroism, too, from wealthy men, like John Jacob Astor who stayed behind after ensuring that his bride was safe in a lifeboat; and from the ship's band, which played hymns as the ship sank under it.

South Africa gets a national congress

South Africa, 12 January 1912
Representatives from dozens of provincial congresses and of South Africa's kings and tribal chiefs are meeting at Bloemfontein to unite in a South African native national congress. They are calling for better education, racial equality and national independence. The meeting was called by Pixley Seme, a New York- and Oxford-educated barrister, who pronounced: "The brighter day is rising upon Africa. Already I seem to see her chains dissolve, her desert plains red with harvest, her Abyssinia and her Zululand the seats of science and religion, reflecting the glory of the rising sun from the spires of her churches and universities."

Significantly, the day's meeting opened with prayers by a minister of the African Methodist Episcopal Church, which is strongly influenced by Negro Protestant churches in the USA. The new president, John Langalibalele Dube, was educated there and is a disciple of the ex-slave Booker T Washington. The vice-president, Walter Rubusana, the only black member of the Cape legislature, has a degree from McKinley university in the USA. These men are modernisers, not traditionalists – a novel threat to white power.

Continents drifting, says latest theory

Germany, 1912
The world's continents are constantly on the move, says the German geologist Aldred Wegener in his new theory of "Continental Drift". Once there was just one supercontinent on this planet; this broke up and the pieces slid around over millions of years until they took up their present positions. The rate is very slow: no quicker than human fingernails grow. This theory explains why the eastern coast of South America neatly fits that of western Africa. The Himalayas were formed by the Indian land-mass or "plate" driving up into the bottom end of Asia. Wegener has observed tiny continental movements we could all see.

World naval arms race speeds up

London, 22 July 1912
Britain is being asked to spend a record £45 million to build warships, including four dreadnoughts, eight cruisers, 20 destroyers and several submarines. The proposal comes from the first lord of the admiralty, Winston Churchill.

Meanwhile, British battleships are being withdrawn from the Mediterranean to patrol the North Sea. These moves follow the breakdown of talks with Germany to limit big shipbuilding programmes by both countries. The Germans have offered a mutual guarantee of neutrality to reduce the risk of war by accident, started by allies of either party. Britain, tied to France and Russia, says "No".

Decathlon star stripped of Olympic gold

Jim Thorpe: minor pro, major star.

Geneva, 27 January 1913
Jim Thorpe, whose stunning decathlon and pentathlon victories at last year's Stockholm Olympic Games won him the accolade of "the greatest athlete in the world", was today stripped of both his titles by the Olympic Committee.

Under the Olympic rules, no professional may compete in the strictly amateur games. When a newspaper revealed that Thorpe had received $25 a week to play minor league baseball in North Carolina, he was branded a professional and declared ineligible for olympic competition. Thorpe's name has been removed from the record books, even though the runners-up in both events have refused to claim his medals, in respect for a man more profesional than the amateurs.

How the Chinese empire died and rose again

When Puyi, the boy emperor of China, agreed to abdicate in February 1912, an institution was abolished which had endured for more than two millennia. It was the imperial dynastic system which had provided the cultural unity for the greatest, most populous and continuous civilisation on earth. The final dynasty of the rulers of "all under heaven" were the Qing, Manchus originally from north-eastern Asia, who had presided over a period of peace and prosperity from 1644.

However, by the end of the 18th century the interrelated problems of over-population, governmental corruption and inefficiency, social conflict between ethnic and economic groups, general lawlessness and the proliferation of anti-Manchu secret societies such as the Triads and heterodox millenarian sects of the White Lotus tradition, all combined to weaken greatly the hold of the central government. Control was further eroded by the devastating Opium Wars of 1839-42 and 1856-60 against the British, which demonstrated the Europeans' technical superiority to the surprise and terror of the Chinese. Subsequently, under the resulting "unequal treaties", the country was opened up to foreign trade and foreign ideas. But the greatest challenge to the Qing dynasty came from a number of internal revolts, the most violent of which was the Taiping rebellion (1850-1864) which nearly overthrew the dynasty, which claimed some 20 million lives and left the country devastated. Because it was only suppressed by relying on extensive assistance from the gentry, it brought about a significant shift of power from the centre to the periphery.

A concubine's rise to power

Attempts were made to deal with the crisis by adopting western technologies, but these were met with considerable conservative opposition and the central government was unable to co-ordinate them. These "self-strengthening" attempts also failed because of the opposition of Empress Dowager Cixi. A once low-ranking concubine, she rose to rule the country from 1861, and used her powerful personality and considerable political abilities to create a regime in which talent stagnated, and which was acutely short of competent and honest officials.

The inadequacies of self-strengthening were brutally exposed by the defeat at the hands of Japan (1894-95), and the punitive Treaty of Shimonoseki which followed. Taking advantage of China's weakness, the European powers then embarked on the "scramble for concessions", demanding territories and economic concessions. The threat posed by the Japanese and the Europeans gave rise to fears that the country was about to be "carved up like a melon". In response to such worries, and encouraged by radical reformers, the young Guangxu Emperor initiated the Hundred Days Reform in June 1898. However, the Empress Dowager, perceiving the reforms as a personal threat, brought them to a sudden end in the palace coup on 21 September.

Allies' terrible retribution

Intensely anti-foreign, the Empress encouraged the Boxers – bands of fanatical soldiers and peasants who blamed foreigners for China's plight – to expand and occupy Beijing in the summer of 1900. The foreign community was under seige for two months, and when the city was recaptured the allied European troops inflicted a terrible retribution on the hapless Chinese, insisting on the execution of high-ranking officials, looting and raping, and imposing an enormous punitive indemnity. After this, even the Court bowed to the need for reform.

In 1905 the Confucian civil service examinations, which had been the keystone of the imperial social order, were abolished. A modernised and educated officer corps was created, chambers of commerce were introduced and local assemblies for self-government were set up. However, in 1908 both the emperor and the empress dowager died in quick succession. Imperial power passed to a set of inept regents for the three-year old Puyi, who were trying to slow down the constitutional reforms and consolidate Manchu power. When it became apparent that the underlying intention of many of the government reforms was greater centralisation to prop up the ailing Qing dynasty, there was a hostile reactions from the local elites, who had lost faith in the central government at least a decade earlier.

Little by little gentry and merchant leaders, as well as foreign-trained army officers, had come to to give support to the small number of professional revolutionaries led by a western-educated doctor called Sun Yat-sen, who were fighting for democracy and greater social justice. The gentry, natural supporters of the government, were generally more concerned with gaining greater political and economic opportunities under a republic.

The outbreak of the revolution was not planned but accidental. On 9 November 1911, an explosion occurred in a revolutionary hide-out in Hankou's Russian concession. Fear of discovery of the people behind the revolutionary plot forced the rebels at Wuhan (i.e. the three cities of Hankou, Wuchang and Hanyang) to rise on the following day. The early successes of the revolutionaries at Wuhan encouraged other provinces and cities to rise and declare their independence. However, in most places it was the traditional elites, not the professional revolutionaries, who gained control.

War ravages the countryside

The imperial system ended on 12 February 1912, and the old warlord Yan Shikai, who had been recalled out of retirement by the regents in late 1911, emerged as the strong man of China. The settlement with the revolutionaries made him the republic's first president. But once in power, he quickly undermined and destroyed the new democratic institutions, using terror and military force against his opponents. However, he died the following year.

His power-base, the Beiyang Army, initially split into two factions and there followed a "warlord period" until 1928, with ever-shifting constellations of war-lord cliques and factions incessantly engaged in warfare, ravaging the countryside in the process. In order to finance their activities, the competing militarists and their civilian administrators extracted enormous revenues from the unfortunate inhabitants under their control, a process which was invariably accompanied by extortion, confiscation and looting. These chaotic conditions brought about a dramatic escalation of banditry and, in response, the proliferation of a variety of local self-defence forces, most notably the Red Spears.

Gradually, however, the cultural cohesion and national loyalty which, had focused on the emperor, began to coalesce around the Nationalist Party of Sun Yat-sen, reorganised in 1924. Having established a base in Guangzhou (Canton), the party started training an army with the help of Soviet advisers and the fledgling Chinese communist party. After Sun Yat-sen's death in 1925, control of the party passed to Chiang Kai-shek whose opposition to the communists culminated in the Shanghai purge of 1927. But the fragmentation and chaos of the previous 70 years was still not over. It was to be another generation – a time which included a bitter civil war between the nationalists and the communists as well as a Japanese invasion (19371945) – before Mao Zedong (Mao Tse-tung) united the country under the communists in 1949, and became the focus of popular loyalty, just as the old emperors had.

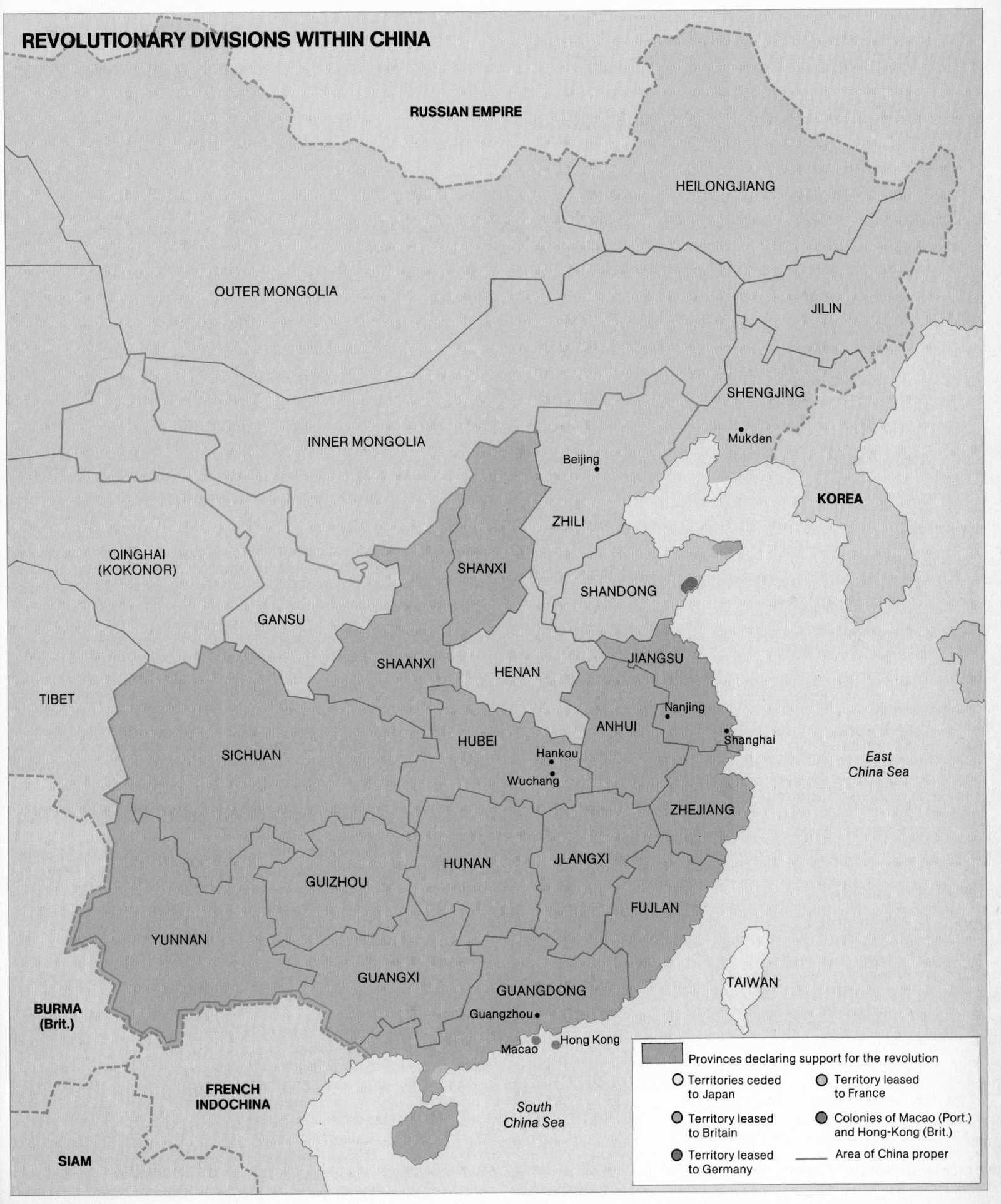

REVOLUTIONARY DIVISIONS WITHIN CHINA

RUSSIAN EMPIRE

HEILONGJIANG

OUTER MONGOLIA

JILIN

SHENGJING

• Mukden

INNER MONGOLIA

Beijing •

KOREA

ZHILI

QINGHAI
(KOKONOR)

SHANXI

SHANDONG

GANSU

SHAANXI

HENAN

JIANGSU

TIBET

Nanjing •

ANHUI

Shanghai •

SICHUAN

HUBEI

Hankou •

*East
China Sea*

Wuchang •

ZHEJIANG

JLANGXI

HUNAN

GUIZHOU

FUJLAN

YUNNAN

**BURMA
(Brit.)**

GUANGXI

GUANGDONG

TAIWAN

Guangzhou •

Macao • • Hong Kong

*South
China Sea*

**FRENCH
INDOCHINA**

SIAM

▨	Provinces declaring support for the revolution
○ Territories ceded to Japan	◉ Territory leased to France
◉ Territory leased to Britain	◉ Colonies of Macao (Port.) and Hong-Kong (Brit.)
◉ Territory leased to Germany	—— Area of China proper

1913 (1913-1914)

New York City, 2 February 1913. Grand Central Station, the world's largest railway station, opens.

Antarctic, 10 February 1913. The British explorer Robert Scott and two of his companions, who were attempting to return from the south pole, are found dead.

Mexico, 23 February 1913. Francisco Madero, who was deposed as president last week by Victoriano Huerta, is shot dead.

USA, 25 February 1913. Federal income tax is introduced.

Balkans, 6 March 1913. In a resumption of hostilities, the Greeks take Janina, capturing 32,000 Turks.

Australia, 12 March 1913. Canberra becomes the federal capital.

Greece, 20 March 1913. Following the assassination of King George, his eldest son Constantine, the duke of Sparta, becomes king.

Balkans, 26 March 1913. The allies take Adrianople after a 155-day siege.

Britain, 3 April 1913. The suffragette leader Emmeline Pankhurst is jailed for three years for inciting arson.

China, 8 April 1913. China's first parliament opens in Beijing.

USA, 14 April 1913. Dr Harry Plotz discovers a typhus vaccine.

Berlin, 18 April 1913. Professor Behring makes a new serum for diphtheria.

Balkans, 22 April 1913. Scutari falls to the Montenegrins after a six-month siege.

The Hague, 26 April 1913. The International Women's Peace Conference opens.

Paris, 29 May 1913. *The Rite of Spring*, a ballet by Igor Stravinsky, receives its premiere.

London, 30 May 1913. The Ottomans sign a peace treaty with the Balkan League, ending their war.

Germany, 6 June 1913. A bill is passed providing for a large increase in the German army.

Turkey, 11 June 1913. Mahmud Shevket Pasha, the new *grand vizier*, is assassinated.

Britain, 13 June 1913. David Lloyd George, the chancellor of the exchequer, and other ministers are exonerated of illegally dealing in shares of the Marconi company.

Balkans, 24 June 1913. Greece and Serbia break their alliance with Bulgaria over a border dispute.

Norway, 29 June 1913. Women get equal electoral rights to men.

Balkans, 30 June 1913. Bulgaria attacks Serbia and Greece.

Balkans, 1 July 1913. Greece and Serbia declare war on Bulgaria.

China, 8 July 1913. China agrees to grant Mongolian independence.

London, 8 July 1913. The suffragette Sylvia Pankhurst is sentenced to three months in jail.

Balkans, 11 July 1913. Rumania declares war on Bulgaria and invades.

London, 15 July 1913. The House of Lords again rejects an Irish Home Rule bill.

London, 16 July 1913. Robert Bridges becomes poet laureate.

Balkans, 10 August 1913. The treaty of Bucharest ends the second Balkan war.

China, 1 September 1913. A "second revolution", staged by the nationalist *Guomindang* and other forces in reaction to Yuan Shikai's anti-democratic forces, ends.

Balkans, 21 September 1913. Turkey and Bulgaria settle their frontier dispute; Turkey keeps Adrianople.

Tunis, 23 September 1913. Frenchman Roland Garros completes the first flight over the Mediterranean.

Panama, 10 October 1913. The Panama Canal is opened.

Mexico, 11 October 1913. President Huerta declares himself dictator.

Mexico, 15 November 1913. The rebel Pancho Villa takes Ciudad Juarez.

France, 1913. Marcel Proust publishes the first volume of a novel entitled *A la Recherche du Temps Perdu*.

France, 1913. Henri Alain Fournier publishes his novel *Le Grand Meaulnes*.

Britain, 1913. Parliament passes the "Cat and Mouse" Act, allowing the temporary release from prison of suffragette hunger-strikers whose health is in danger.

German East Africa, 2 February 1914. A 900-mile railway opens from Lake Tanganyika to Dar-es-Salaam.

Paris, 16 March 1914. Madame Caillaux, the wife of the French finance minister, shoots dead Gaston Calmette, the editor of *Le Figaro*, which has attacked her husband's plans to tax the rich.

London, 13 April 1914. *Pygmalion*, a play by George Bernard Shaw, receives its premiere.

Mexico, 21 April 1914. US troops opposed to President Huerta land and seize Vera Cruz.

Ford unveils moving car assembly line

Ford's Model T assembly line at Detriot: a completely new production process.

Detroit, 7 October 1913

Henry Ford, the one-time inventor whose automobiles are revolutionising the American way of life, has launched a new production process that is intended to alter the whole face of car manufacture and go a long way towards meeting the ever-expanding demand for new cars.

Ford's Model T, "the motor car for the multitude", appeared in 1908, the product of an "assembly line" using mass-produced precision parts. Now the car they call the "Tin Lizzie" will be put together on a 250-foot-long moving assembly line. Each worker will be assigned a specific task and will perform it over and over again as car after car rolls slowly by on the line.

It is estimated that the new system will mean that a new chassis can be assembled in just two man-hours, a huge increase over the former schedule of 14 man-hours. It will take only three man-hours to produce a complete new car; Ford aims to produce 250,000 next year.

Indian poet and teacher wins Nobel prize

Stockholm, 1 December 1913

The Nobel prize for literature has been awarded to the Indian poet Rabindranath Tagore – the first time that the prize has gone to an Asian. Educated India has gone wild with excitement at this recognition of Indian culture in the west. The poet said: "I shall never have any peace again."

Tagore comes from a cultured and talented Bengali family. He won fame at 20 with his first volume of Bengali poems. He also translates his poetry into English. Last year he published *Gitanjali* (Song Offerings) on the death of his wife and three children. He has founded a centre of Indian culture at Shantiniketan near Bolpur.

Indian poet: Rabindranath Tagore.

Treaty ends Balkan war

Bucharest, 10 August 1913
After their successful war against the Ottoman empire, the four Balkan allies, Bulgaria, Serbia, Greece and Montenegro, quarrelled among themselves over the spoils: Macedonia. Their brief war – Bulgaria against the others – came to an end today with a treaty signed in the Rumanian capital, Bucharest.

The Ottomans had surrendered Macedonia on the understanding that it would become a new and independent state, Albania. That did not suit Serbia and Montenegro. Serbia and Greece then plot-ted to carve up Macedonia between them and Bulgaria promptly attack-ed. Under the Bucharest treaty, al-most all the territory claimed by Bulgaria in Macedonia and Thrace goes to Serbia and Greece. Serbia and Montenegro are doubled in size and Rumania, which stopped the war by invading Bulgaria, helps it-self to a slice of Bulgarian territory.

In this murderous game of Bal-kan musical chairs, Serbia seems never to miss out. Diplomatic ob-servers fear that the Serbs will ask for even more and that there will be yet another crisis in Europe.

Macedonian rebels fighting the Ottomans, in control of the route to Salonika.

Mystery man assassinates king of Greece

Salonika, 18 March 1913
King George of Greece was assas-sinated here this afternoon. As the 68-year-old monarch took his reg-ular afternoon walk through the town where he has lived for the past five months, the assassin, Alexan-der Schinas, shot him through the heart. The king collapsed and died in the arms of an *aide*.

Schinas admits to no motive, and has revealed nothing about himself other than his name. His victim, who was within a few days of com-pleting 50 years as king, will be succeeded by his son, crown prince Constantine.

King George: assassin's victim.

US marines snatch Mexican seaport

Mexico, 21 April 1914
Three thousand United States ma-rines seized the port of Vera Cruz today. The seaborne attack has so far cost the marines four dead and twenty wounded; the Mexican gar-rison is believed to have lost at least 200 men.

The Americans have given no specific reason for the landing, but it is presumed that President Wil-son wishes to prevent supplies of arms from reaching General Huer-ta from Germany. Wilson opposes the Huerta regime, and backs in-stead the revolutionary forces that are fighting to unseat him.

"Rite of Spring" outrages audience

Paris, 30 May 1913
Bewilderment, shock, outrage: these were the reactions of the Paris audience at last night's premiere of the ballet *The Rite of Spring* by the Russian composer Igor Stravinsky. Stravinsky's supporters, led by Debussy, appealed for silence as the jeering and cat-calling greeted the pounding, discordant evocation of primaeval Russia. The uproar actu-ally started *before* the curtain rose on the production by Diaghilev's Ballets Russes. Stravinsky has al-ready provided Diaghilev with two works, *The Firebird* (1910) and *Petrushka* (1911).

Natal riots follow Gandhi jailing

South Africa, 25 November 1913
Two Indians were killed and 20 in-jured when Natal police fired into a crowd demonstrating against the jailing of Mohandas Gandhi, the British-educated lawyer who orga-nised an ambulance corps in the Boer War and who is leading the non-violent passive resistance cam-paign against racial inequality.

Gandhi refused to pay a fine for defying a law prohibiting Indians from Natal entering the Transvaal. He led 2,500 Indians into the Transvaal, where they were violent-ly arrested. Riots have been daily occurrences since then, but these are the first deaths.

Suffragette movement mourns its first martyr, Emily Davison

Britain, June 14 1913
A suffragette heroine was given a martyr's funeral today. Tens of thousands lined the streets of Lon-don to watch as militant women took Emily Davison to her last rest-ing place in her beloved Northum-berland. Flanked by a bodyguard of suffragettes dressed in white with black sashes, the coffin was drawn on an open carriage by four black horses and followed by vehicles bearing hundreds of wreaths from all over the world. The funeral pro-cession was over two miles long.

Miss Davison, who had been im-prisoned and force-fed on many occasions, died when she ran in front of the king's horse in the Derby horse race ten days ago.

Emily Davison, killed under King Edward's horse, Anmer, at the Derby.

Archduke's murder unsettles Europe

Sarajevo, Bosnia, 28 June

Archduke Franz Ferdinand, the heir to the Austro-Hungarian empire, and his morganatic wife, the duchess of Hohenburg, were assassinated here today by a Serbian nationalist. It was the 14th anniversary of their marriage.

The killer, Gavril Princip, darted out of the crowd as the car carrying the royal couple slowed to change direction. His first bullet struck the archduke in the neck, the second hit the duchess who had flung herself in front of her husband. She died almost immediately, the archduke ten minutes later. The murders were evidently part of a concerted plot. Earlier, the couple were on the way to the town hall of this capital of Bosnia when a bomb was thrown into their car. The archduke picked it up and threw it into the road where it exploded, wounding those in a following car.

The implications of this outrage are dangerous in the extreme. The killer, seized by the police, has told them that he wanted to take revenge for the oppression of the Serbian people. He is believed to have been helped by a secret society of Serbian officers known as the "Black Hand". There can be no doubt that the Austrians will make drastic demands on what the Austrian foreign minister, count von Berchtold, calls the "Serbian wasp's nest". But the Serbs, backed by Russia, are in no mood to be bullied by the Austrians.

An artist's impression of the assassination of Franz Ferdinand at Sarajevo.

Blacks protest over white land grab

London, 26 June

A black South African delegation, led by John Dube, the president of the South African Native National Congress, saw the colonial secretary, Lewis Harcourt, today. The delegation came to protest at the Native Land Act, passed last year. The act gives all but seven per cent of South Africa's land to Whites. Even in the poor and scattered "scheduled areas" Blacks may not actually own the land. Blacks living on white farms have to give 90 days labour to the farmer every year or be expelled to the reserve. In the Orange Free State, Africans are being defined "squatters" and driven to the reserves by force. The Blacks, with no economic base, are forced to work as migrant labourers.

The visit shows the confidence that the rapidly growing South African Native National Congress has acquired after campaigns against racial discrimination and landlessness and has been warmly welcomed by the British Labour Party. The colonial office has been less welcoming. Mr Harcourt, a Liberal, has told the delegates that they should be grateful for the act, since it stops the Whites taking *all* the land and the Blacks being reduced to the plight of their fellows in the Congo.

Ulster on the brink of war crisis

Belfast, 25 February

Civil war in Ireland seems imminent as an English-led Ulster Volunteer Force of 100,000 armed men puts on public shows of strength applauded by members of the establishment. In Tyrone, 12 infantry companies performed a tactical exercise under the eyes of their commander, Sir George Richardson. Such displays have not yet achieved their political aim – to frighten the British government into excluding Ulster from the Irish Home Rule Bill – but Sir George urges his men to attack more.

Europe stumbles into war as diplomats holiday

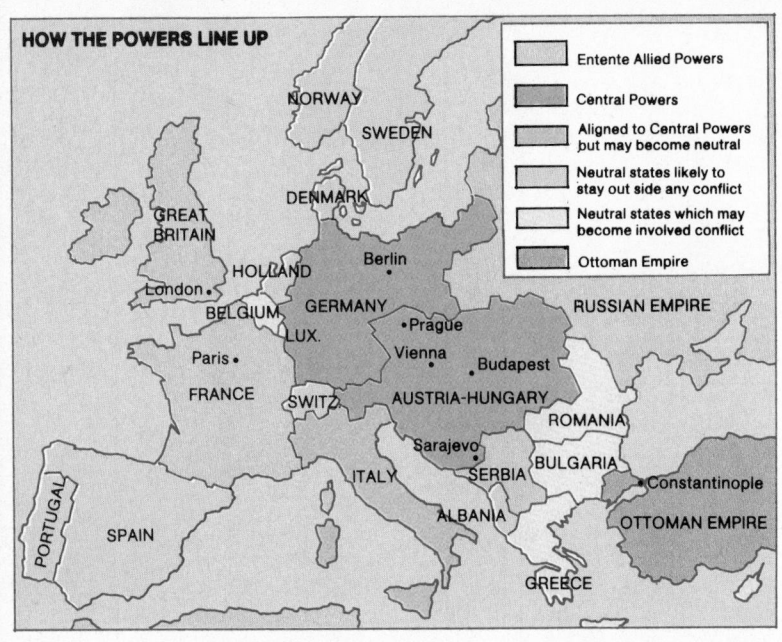

HOW THE POWERS LINE UP

- Entente Allied Powers
- Central Powers
- Aligned to Central Powers but may become neutral
- Neutral states likely to stay out side any conflict
- Neutral states which may become involved conflict
- Ottoman Empire

Volunteers from neutral USA rush to sign up in Paris for the duration.

Balkan crisis destroys precarious balance

London, 4 August
Britain declared war on Germany today and all the carefully constructed checks and balances of European diplomacy came tumbling down into catastrophe.

Few people foresaw the impending disaster. The German kaiser had talked of giving Austria full support, but had then left for his customary yachting holiday in Norway. General von Moltke, the German army commander, was taking the cure at a foreign *spa*. The French president was on a state visit to Russia. The Serbian prime minister was in the country, preparing an election campaign.

Austria's ultimatum to Serbia brought Russia in as Serbia's ally.

Germany came in as Austria's ally, and France as Russia's ally. Britain might well have stayed out of it had not Germany invaded Belgium in an attempt to outflank France.

Now – as the British foreign secretary, Sir Edward Grey, put it – the lamps have gone out all over Europe, while trains are moving millions of men to the two fronts. In the east, Russia has struck at East Prussia and Galicia; German and Austrian forces have answered with a thrust into Poland. In the west, von Moltke is drawing the French army into a "revolving door" that will take the Germans to Paris. The British Army is preparing to go to France. The shots at Sarajevo are echoing round the world.

THE BALANCE OF POWER

Standing armies and reserves at outbreak of war

(Chart showing: AUSTRIA HUNGARY ~3m, BRITISH EMPIRE ~1m, FRANCE ~4m, GERMANY ~4.5m, ITALY ~1.5m, RUSSIA ~5.5m; vertical axis 1m–7m)

Crowds cheer as volunteers rush to arms

London, 11 August
The tremendous enthusiasm which brought cheering crowds surging through London to sing the national anthem outside Buckingham Palace when war was declared has not abated.

Young men, anxious not to miss the war which is confidently expected to be over by Christmas, form long queues outside the recruiting offices. Farm boys, City workers, peers and dustmen are leaving their jobs to "serve King and Country".

There is a feeling of embarking on a great adventure amongst these young men. Many are schoolboys who give false ages. Friends join in groups, anxious to fight together. They think nothing of the hardships and dangers that they will face, and see war not only as a patriotic duty but also as a holiday from a humdrum workaday existence.

This same enthusiasm is being seen throughout the empire. Australia, Canada and New Zealand have offered to send contingents to the help of the Mother Country, and the men of the colonies are making their way in from remote outposts to join up.

Meanwhile, the professionals, the men of the Regular and Territorial Armies, marching in field uniform through the streets to join the British Expeditionary Force, are being given emotional farewells by their families and by total strangers who shower them with cigarettes and sweets.

Many of these men have seen the face of battle before, however, and their attitude is more workmanlike than emotional. Sir Edward Grey, the foreign secretary, is another professional who views the war realistically. "The lamps are going out all over Europe," he said to a friend. "We shall not see them lit again in our lifetime."

BRITONS

WANTS

YOU

JOIN YOUR COUNTRY'S ARMY!
GOD SAVE THE KING

Reproduced by permission of LONDON OPINION

Feeding the front line: a 1915 British Army recruiting poster.

Germany routs Russia at Tannenberg

Petrograd, 31 August

The myth of the Russian steamroller that was to flatten the German forces on the eastern front has been cruelly shattered in four days of fighting at Tannenberg, on the East Prussian border.

Some 300,000 men took part in the battle, with white-bloused Russian infantrymen being mown down as they charged German machine-gun posts. The German artillery was vastly superior to the Russians', and German supplies, brought up on the strategic railway system, simply overwhelmed the czarist forces. In the Russian capital, now renamed "Petrograd" to be rid of the Germanic St Petersburg, the defeat has been acknowledged with unusual candour.

The Russians sent two armies into East Prussia under the command of Generals Alexander Samsonov and Pavel Rennenkampf. Initially their advance went unchecked, but then two new generals took over the German defences – Erich von Ludendorff and Paul von Hindenburg, Prussian regular soldiers, born in Poznan. They adopted a plan submitted by a Colonel Max Hoffmann, based on his knowledge of a bitter feud between Rennenkampf and Samsonov.

The Germans concentrated their attacks on Samsonov's army at Tannenberg, taking 100,000 Russian prisoners. Rennenkampf made no move to come to the aid of his fellow general. Samsonov, after his crushing defeat, was filled with shame and shot himself. Soon it will be Rennenkampf's turn to face the Germans.

The czar with his army commander, Grand Duke Nicholas, in August 1914.

Russian prisoners of war, taken into Germany after the battle of Tannenberg.

British navy sinks four German cruisers off Falkland Islands

South Atlantic, 11 December

Britain once again rules the waves everywhere except the North Sea and the Baltic. The war at sea, which has been raging for three months now, took a decisive turn last night, with the German and British fleets concluding a running battle that has taken them a long way from home.

The decisive encounter was fought off the Falkland Islands, when under cover of nightfall, the two fleets came within six miles (9.6 kilometres) of each other. In a fierce battle the Royal Navy sank four of the finest German cruisers, the *Dresden*, the *Nurnberg*, the *Scharnhorst* and the *Gneisenau*, with no British losses. The Royal Navy is chasing the the remaining German light cruisers, hoping to turn victory into rout.

US officials here say that the government will be delighted. Although the US is officially neutral, it has been seriously worried by the spread of the sea war into Atlantic waters and by the fire-power of some modern cruisers. The victory will enable the Royal Navy to concentrate its resources on the battle in the North Sea. The picture is far less rosy there.

The German submarine fleet is still a constant danger to British ships, with its deadly torpedoes extracting a heavy toll. There is an additional hazard there from the mines which the Germans have laid extensively, using merchant ships as well as navy vessels.

Belgian defences yield to Hun attack

The war in Europe begins to involve each side's colonies

Belgian refugees, with what few possessions they can take, pouring westwards on the unarmed road of flight.

Belgium, 10 October

Antwerp capitulated to the Germans today after a gallant battle in which the Belgian army, only six divisions strong, was led with much bravery by King Albert. The effort of the Belgians, reinforced by a brigade of British marines and two brigades of naval volunteers sent by Mr Churchill, the First Lord of the Admiralty, has considerably upset the German Schlieffen Plan for the invasion of France.

A *sortie* by the king yesterday threatened the Germans' communications and forced them to deal with Antwerp before resuming their drive into France. They attacked Antwerp on 28 September, reducing its fortifications with huge siege guns until the garrison could no longer hold out.

King Albert and his government have sailed to England to carry on

the war, and the Belgian Field Army has escaped down the Flanders coast under the cover of two British divisions landed at Ostend and Zeebrugge in an attempt to save Antwerp. It is too late for that and Belgium must be considered lost to the enemy which invaded so treacherously. But the courage of "Little Belgium" lives on in Allied propaganda, which speaks of a war "in defence of small nations".

Africa and Asia, December

On 12 August Regimental Sergeant-Major Alhaji Grunshi, advancing into German Togoland, was the first British empire soldier to fire on a German. Two weeks later New Zealand troops occupied the German colony of Samoa in the Pacific.

Other campaigns outside Europe have not gone so well for Britain. A South African advance into German South-West Africa was dislocated by a rebellion of pro-German Boers. In German East Africa the British are unable to subdue Colonel von Lettow Vorbeck's Tanganyikan troops in spite of reinforcements from India. One Indian Army amphibious assault on the German port of Tanga was ignominiously repulsed by a swarm of bees.

The entry of the Ottoman empire into the war in November added new problems for Britain. William Wassmus, a German agent in Istanbul, has made contact with pan-Islamic revolutionaries and Indian nationalists, and is calling for a holy war against the British empire. Britain has made Egypt, constitutionally part of the Ottoman empire, a protectorate – to the disgust of Egyptian nationalists. Pro-Ottoman Senussi tribesmen are raiding its frontier from the safety of neutral Italian Libya. In south Arabia, Britons and Ottomans are unable to dislodge each other from Aden and Yemen respectively. In Somaliland Mohammed bin Abdullah, the so-called "Mad Mullah", has renewed his campaign against the British.

New machines rain death from the sky

Paris, 16 December

As the big battalions fight a war of attrition on the western front, aerial combat in the skies above – where individual fighter-pilots fight one-to-one battles under almost mediaeval rules of chivalry – is forcing strategists to reappraise their ideas of what is possible.

Initially only reconnaissance missions were flown, but soon airmen of both sides were using grenades and hand-held bombs against the men in the trenches. One aircraft

has already shot down another, and over Rheims yesterday a British pilot fired his revolver to dissuade a German aviator from dropping a bomb on the city. With an eye on the Germans' superior airship technology, strategists speculate as to what will happen if a Zeppelin bombs central London and whether it will cause mass panic. Another risk of what some call "air power" is the insertion behind the lines of spies and assassins. A picture is emerging of warfare without rules.

Optimism turns to jingoism in Britain

London, 31 December

They said that the war would be over by Christmas. But Christmas has come and gone and optimism has been replaced by jingoism as the stern-faced Lord Kitchener urges the country's youth to arms on thousands of posters. A popular music hall song tells young men "We don't want to lose you, but we think you ought to go", and recruiting centres offer the king's shilling (for signing up) and a shilling a day pay to volunteers. Britons at home

had their first taste of war this month when three German warships shelled Scarborough and other seaside towns in the northeast, killing 100 civilians and injuring a further 200.

Anti-German feeling is rife and hundreds of suspected "spies" have been rounded up under the emergency Defence of the Realm Act (DORA) which gives the authorities almost unlimited powers. London's Olympia exhibition centre has become a concentration camp.

1915 (1915-1916)

Italy, 13 January 1915. An earthquake kills 29,000 in central Italy.

North Sea, 24 January 1915. British warships sink the German battle cruiser *Blucher*.

China, January 1915. Seeking to extend its influence in China, Japan makes "21 demands" which severely undermine Chinese sovereignty.

Britain, 2 February 1915. The Germans announce a submarine blockade of the British Isles.

Germany, 1 March 1915. Britain begins a blockade of German ports.

New York City, March 1915. D W Griffith's epic film *The Birth of a Nation* opens.

Western Front, 5 April 1915. The French begin a broad offensive from the Meuse to the Moselle.

Western Front, 22 April 1915. The British launch a new offensive at Ypres.

London, 25 April 1915. Italy signs a secret treaty with Britain, France and Russia agreeing to enter the war on their side in return for territorial gains.

Turkey, 26 April 1915. Allied forces establish themselves along the Gallipoli peninsula.

Russia, 30 April 1915. The Germans invade the Russian Baltic provinces.

South-West Africa, 9 May 1915. German forces surrender to General Louis Botha's South Africans.

Italy, 23 May 1915. Italy declares war on Austria.

Britain, 25 May 1915. Herbert Asquith forms a wartime coalition.

Italy, 25 May 1915. The Austrians bomb Venice.

Eastern Front, 4 June 1915. Austro-German troops recapture Przemysl from the Russians.

Albania, 11 June 1915. Serbian troops invade Albania and take Tirana.

Eastern Front, 23 June 1915. The Austrians retake Lemberg, the capital of Galicia, which they lost to the Russians last year.

Eastern Front, 5 August 1915. The Austro-Germans take Warsaw.

Italy, 21 August 1915. Italy declares war on the Ottoman empire.

Eastern Front, 30 August 1915. The great Russian fortress of Brest-Litovsk falls to the Germans.

Poland, 1 September 1915. Following the partition of Poland by Germany and Austria, Josef Pilsudski forms a movement for a free Poland.

Petrograd, 5 September 1915. Czar Nicholas II takes personal command of the Russian army.

Bulgaria, 6 September 1915. Bulgaria signs a military convention with Germany and Austria.

Eastern Front, 19 September 1915. The Germans take Vilna.

Greece, 23 September 1915. King Constantine gives the order for the Greek army to mobilise in aid of Serbia against the Bulgarians.

Western Front, 26 September 1915. French and British troops launch two great offensives, in Champagne and Flanders.

Balkans, 8 October 1915. Russia opens hostilities against Bulgaria.

Serbia, 9 October 1915. Belgrade falls to the Austro-Germans.

Brussels, 12 October 1915. The British nurse Edith Cavell is executed by a German firing squad for treason.

Balkans, 14 October 1915. Bulgaria and Serbia declare war on one another.

Balkans, 16 October 1915. The allies blockade Bulgarian ports.

Europe, 19 October 1915. Russia and Italy follow Britain and France in declaring war on Bulgaria.

Britain, 23 October 1915. The great cricketer W G Grace dies.

Paris, 29 October 1915. The socialist Aristide Briand becomes prime minister after the resignation of Rene Viviani.

Paris, 14 November 1915. Tomas Masaryk, a leader of the Czech nationalist movement, issues a manifesto calling for the establishment of a Czech national council.

Germany, 12 December 1915. Hugo Junkers completes the first all-metal aeroplane.

Western Front, December 1915. Joseph Joffre is appointed commander of the French forces, Douglas Haig of the British forces.

Britain, 1915. Among this year's novels are *Victory* by Joseph Conrad and *Of Human Bondage* by W Somerset Maugham. The poet Rupert Brooke died on active service en route to the Dardanelles.

Germany, 1915. Albert Einstein propounds a new theory of gravity.

Central Asia, 17 January 1916. The Russians launch an offensive against the Ottomans.

Britain, 27 January 1916. Military conscription is introduced.

West Africa, 28 January 1916. British and Belgian troops take Yaounde, the capital of the German Cameroons.

Sub sinks "Lusitania"

The sinking of the "Lusitania", as seen by the German painter Claus Bergen.

Cork, 8 May 1915
More than 1,400 men, women and children are thought to have drowned yesterday when the *Lusitania* was torpedoed without warning by a German submarine. It happened within sight of the coast here, just eight miles (13 kilometres) off the Old Head of Kinsale. The liner was on the last stage of a return voyage from New York to Liverpool.

One passenger, Ernest Cowper, a Canadian journalist, actually saw the submarine's conning tower and the track of the first torpedo which struck at 2.12 pm. There was a loud explosion and pieces of the hull flew into the air. Seconds later came a second torpedo and the ship, one of Cunard's two finest ocean liners, sank in 21 minutes. There were 1,978 people on board. According to the survivors, at least five of those who drowned were women with babies in their arms.

Amongst the casualties were 128 Americans, including friends of President Woodrow Wilson and the millionaire yachtsman Alfred Vanderbilt.

The former president, Theodore Roosevelt, has already condemned the sinking as "an act of piracy". It will almost certainly lead to calls for President Wilson to abandon his policy of neutrality in the war. Today, however, the state department in Washington would go no further than to say that it viewed the incident "most seriously".

Japan issues "21 demands" to China

Beijing, 18 January 1915
The Japanese minister in Beijing has today presented 21 demands to President Yuan Shikai. The demands are so far-reaching and so severe that if Yuan accepts them China will become virtually a Japanese protectorate.

Notable among the demands are that China should cede Japan all German rights in Shandong; that Japan should supply weapons and advisers to the Chinese army, and that it should have have joint responsibility for the policing of important places in China.

Charlie Chaplin, the clown from Lambeth, in "The Tramp", which came to the cinemas in 1915.

Allies retreat from Gallipoli debacle

Australian infantry assaulting an Ottoman position at Gallipoli three days ago.

Turkey, 20 December 1915
The ill-fated attempt to force open the Dardanelles and capture Istanbul was abandoned today after ten months of bad luck and indecisiveness – and extraordinary heroism by Britons, Australians and New Zealanders who fought Ottoman troops, flies, fever, malaria, and the incompetence of their comman-

ders. It is sad to reflect that the most skilful operation of the whole campaign was the evacuation, carried out under the muzzles of the Ottoman guns without a life being lost.

The saddest thing of all is that the plan to knock the Ottoman empire out of the war might well have succeeded, but the landings were

not made until two months after the navy had first bombarded the Dardanelles forts and then lost six ships in a minefield. All the advantages of surprise were lost, so that when the troops did storm ashore they were mown down by the entrenched Ottoman troops. The tally for Gallipoli is 25,000 dead, 76,000 wounded, 13,000 missing and 96,000 sick.

Germany advances on eastern and Balkan fronts

Berlin, October 1915
The outstanding field commander in Germany's operations in eastern Europe is without question General August von Mackensen. After a string of victories in Poland and Galicia, he assumed command of a German-Austrian force on the Balkan front and has given the Serbs a severe drubbing. Belgrade was taken after fierce house-to-house fighting, and the railway through Greece to the port of Salonika has been cut, thus disrupting the Serbs' links with the Allied force recently landed there. Informed military observers expect Serbia to be overrun within weeks.

Von Mackensen commanded the force that captured the Russian fortress of Brest-Litovsk last August, after a 120-mile thrust from Warsaw in a month. It seems that the Russians' morale never recovered from the smashing defeats they suffered at Tannenberg and the Masurian Lakes early in the war. Von Mackensen was there, too.

Radicals take over Indian Congress

India, 1916
A year after the death of Gopal Krishna Gokhale, the father of Indian nationalism and India's "First Moderate", the Congress Party has been taken over by radicals. The arguments of 1907 between moderates and radicals are being rehashed, though this time a third force exists: a middle way, led by the Indian lawyer who led the civil disobedience campaign in South Africa, Mohandas Gandhi.

The death of Gokhale, a secular liberal who was trusted by Moslems, was the biggest blow that Congress has suffered. Even his radical opponent Bal Gangadhar Tilak praised him: "This diamond of India, this jewel of Maharashtra, this prince of workers, is taking eternal rest on the funeral grounds. Look at him and emulate him." Congress will become more militant under Tilak, taking advantage of Britain's wartime difficulties.

Poison gas: this war's horrific weapon

France, 22 April 1915
The Germans have introduced an horrific new weapon to the war. As dusk fell today Allied troops holding the line north of Ypres were enveloped in a swirling greenish-yellow cloud of poison gas released from the German trenches.

The gas, thought to be chlorine,

choked and blinded the defenders, and they were swiftly overrun by German troops wearing gas masks who tore a four-mile gap in the defences until they were stopped by soldiers untouched by the gas. Allied troops have no protection against this weapon, which spreads panic among the bravest.

German soldiers wearing gas masks await an attack near Chemin des Dames.

Botha rounds up the Boer rebels

South Africa, February 1915
The pro-German Boer rebellion, centred on the western Transvaal and led by five Afrikaner Boer War generals, has collapsed.

The rebellion was a disaster. One general was shot at a roadblock by policemen who thought that he was a bandit. Another was drowned swimming the Vaal river on his way to German South-West Africa after his commanddo unit had been scattered at Rustenburg. The third escaped to Mozambique while the fourth has been captured. The fifth was routed with his commando at Mushroom Valley in November. Altogether, 4,000 Boers have been taken prisoner.

Most Boers either support Britain or remain neutral. Indeed, the 40,000-strong South African army that is advancing into German South-West Africa is led by the rebel leaders' fellow ex-Boer War generals, Smuts and Botha.

1916 (1916-1917)

Western Front, 21 February 1916. The Germans launch a major assault on the Verdun forts.

Britain, 28 February 1916. The novelist Henry James dies.

Central Asia, 2 March 1916. The Russians take Bitlis in Turkestan.

Germany, 9 March 1916. Germany declares war on Portugal.

Europe, 9 March 1916. Britain and France sign the Sykes-Picot agreement, specifying plans for the future division of Asiatic Turkey.

Mexico, 31 March 1916. Sent in retaliation for Pancho Villa's raid into the USA, in which 18 Americans died, US troops under John Pershing rout Villa's forces.

Turkey, 14 April 1916. The Allies bomb Istanbul.

East Africa, 17 April 1916. The Boer leader Jan Smuts leads an anti-German drive from Kenya.

Dublin, 25 April 1916. A revolt breaks out against British rule.

Ottoman Empire, 29 April 1916. British troops surrender to the Ottomans at Kut-el-Amara in Iraq after a siege of 143 days.

Dublin, 12 May 1916. James Connolly is the last of the seven rebels who signed the proclamation of an Irish republic during the Easter Rising to be executed.

Britain, 6 June 1916. Lord Kitchener dies when the cruiser *HMS Hampshire* is sunk by a mine off the Orkney Islands.

China, 6 June 1916. President Yuan Shikai dies.

Arabia, 21 June 1916. Hussein, the *grand sherif* of Mecca, declares war on the Ottoman empire with the aim of achieving Arabia's independence from Britain.

Eastern Front, 23 June 1916. A Russian offensive under Alexei Brusilov has resulted in the capture of most of Galicia.

Western Front, 24 June 1916. The Germans begin a new Verdun offensive.

Western Front, 1 July 1916. The British and French launch a major offensive on the Somme.

Petrograd, 6 July 1916. Russia and Japan sign a peace treaty.

Dublin, 3 August 1916. The former diplomat Roger Casement, famous for exposing slavery in the Congo, is sentenced to death for his part in the Easter Rising.

Egypt, 5 August 1916. The British defeat the Ottomans in a naval battle off Port Said.

Persia, 7 August 1916. Persia forms an alliance with Britain and Russia.

Italian Front, 9 August 1916. Italian troops take Gorizia.

Germany, 24 August 1916. The socialist Karl Liebknecht is jailed for his part in peace protests.

Germany, 27 August 1916. Paul von Hindenburg becomes chief of the German general staff.

Italy, 27 August 1916. Italy declares war on Germany.

Balkans, 27 August 1916. Rumania declares war on Austria; Germany declares war on Rumania.

Balkans, 10 September 1916. The Allies launch an offensive in Salonika.

Western Front, September 1916. Tanks are used for the first time in battle, by the Allies on the Somme.

Prague, 16 September 1916. A provisional government of "Czechoslovakia" is recognised by France and Britain.

Balkans, 27 September 1916. Greece declares war on Bulgaria, which declared war on Rumania earlier in the month.

Greece, 9 October 1916. Spiridion Lambros takes over as prime minister.

Greece, 17 October 1916. Having occupied Athens, the Allies recognise the pro-Allied rebel government of Eleutherios Venizelos, opposed to Lambros.

Western Front, 24 October 1916. French troops break German lines along a four-mile front as the second battle of Verdun opens.

Berlin, 5 November 1916. The Central Powers, Germany and Austria, proclaim the independence of Poland.

USA, 7 November 1916. Jeannette Rankin of Montana becomes the first woman member of the United States Congress.

USA, 11 November 1916. Woodrow Wilson is re-elected president.

Austria, 21 November 1916. Franz Josef, ruler of the Austro-Hungarian empire since 1848, dies.

Vienna, 6 December 1916. The Czech nationalist Tomas Masaryk is sentenced to death for treason in his absence.

Britain, 7 December 1916. David Lloyd George succeeds Herbert Asquith as prime minister.

Petrograd, 30 December 1916. Gregory Rasputin, the infamous Siberian "seer" and "miracle worker", is murdered.

Petrograd, 9 January 1917. Dimitri Golitzin becomes prime minister, succeeding Alexander Trepov who resigned in the face of strikes, food shortages and anti-war protests.

No sex in women's battalion of death

Moscow, 1917
Although British women are playing a vital wartime role – as ambulance drivers, nurses and auxiliaries on the western front, and in industry at home – few have taken part in actual combat. With the formation of a "Women's Battalion of Death" in Russia, that situation may well be changed. The suffragette leader, Mrs Emmeline Pankhurst, who wants to negotiate women's war work in return for the vote, and is on a visit to Russia, is said to be "delighted" with the idea.

Two 1,000-strong battalions are being trained at a women's institute near here. Almost all the women are under 35 and represent most social groups. The army is providing male instructors.

Discipline is strict. Yashka Bochkareva, the commander, cashiered 80 girls in the first two days, and uses face-slapping to punish recruits who flirt with instructors. She has decreed that sex will be outlawed for the duration.

It was that last stricture that caused a mutiny. Incited by Bolsheviks, volunteers demanded a "soldiers' committee". Bochkareva has refused and is now left with only 300 of the original women.

Irish patriots stage uprising at Easter

Dublin, 1 May 1916
An Irish republican leader waited politely in a queue for stamps in the General Post Office here – before drawing a pistol and telling the startled counter-clerk that an Irish republic had been declared. Within hours Dublin was ablaze, as well-armed British troops – many of them Irish veterans from the war in France – blasted republican strongpoints, including the post office, with heavy artillery. It has taken a week to put down the insurrection – and Dubliners have jeered prisoners as they are being marched to internment. About 450 rebels are dead and 2,000 captured, with 100 soldiers dead or injured.

China challenges would-be emperor

Beijing, 6 June 1916
Yuan Shikai, the first president of the Chinese republic, died today at the age of 56 bitterly regretting that he had never achieved his ambition of proclaiming himself emperor and founding a new imperial dynasty. At first he denied this ambition, claiming in 1912: "Ignorant people are fabricating rumours to delude the masses, with alarming reminders of the story of Napoleon". Two years later, however, he announced the formation of a new Chinese empire. His plan was foiled by the men of his own Northern Army. They would have a dictator, but not an emperor and, revealed as a buffoon, he had to withdraw.

Thousands die in North Sea naval clash

London, 31 May 1916
Both the British and the German navies are claiming victory today in what sailors are already calling "the greatest naval battle in history", off Jutland. The Royal Navy, commanded by Lord Jellicoe ("the only man who could have lost the war in an afternoon") says it has driven the German fleet off the seas. But Berlin claims that British sea power has been destroyed.

Britain has lost seven ships and nearly 7,000 men, the Germans three ships and over 2,500 men, and have retreated to their ports. The sea is awash with bodies; one passing steamer counted over 500.

Action stations at Jutland.

Trench war deadlocked despite Somme bloodshed

British troops going "over the top" in one of the fruitless assaults in the Battle of the Somme in which half a million British troops died.

Western Front, 1 January 1917
The terrible slaughter of 1916 has been brought to an end by the onset of winter, with little accomplished. The Allies failed bloodily to make their "great breakout" on the Somme, despite the introduction of the tank, and lost over half a million men; 60,000 Britons perished on the first day alone at the Somme. The Germans also lost half a million, notably in the "mincing machine" of Verdun.

Now the men of both sides have again settled into the routine of the trenches where, except for snipers' bullets and random shells, they are reasonably safe. But the trenches have their own particular horrors. Hugely fat lice, killed by running a candle flame along the seams of a shirt, are everywhere. So are the rats which feed off the bodies of the dead. The trenches also breed their own diseases. There is trench foot,

a rotting of the foot caused by standing in deep mud and water; trench fever which spreads like wildfire; and a sickness which is only now being recognised as shellshock. Sufferers become hysterical and disorientated. Some refuse to obey orders; many have been courtmartialled for cowardice. Now they are treated with more sympathy.

The rest of the world is up in arms

London, 1 January 1917
The war is truly a world war. In East Africa, von Lettow Vorbeck continues his brilliant campaign against the British. In Egypt, British and Ottoman troops are entrenched in stalemate, fighting for control of the Suez Canal. In Mesopotamia, British troops are pushing up the

Tigris towards Baghdad after their defeat at Kut by the Ottomans in 1916. In Persia, William Wassmus, the German agent, leads a pan-Islamic army pledged to overthrow the pro-British government. Rarely are white troops to be seen: most of the fighting is done by and against brown-skinned people.

The trench dwellers lead a life of dirt, danger and monotony. From "stand-to" at dawn, their days follow a regular pattern of digging, wiring, and short periods keeping watch from the "firing step". The boredom is so intense that there is never any shortage of volunteers for raiding parties on the enemy lines. Small groups of men armed with

knives, clubs, sharpened entrenching tools and grenades slip through the barbed wire and go looking for trouble in no-man's-land.

Perhaps the moment that the men wait for most eagerly – apart from going to the rear – is mail call, when the letters arrive from home. Then these hardened, dirty soldiers find a quiet corner in the trench to read and reread those precious few lines from wives and sweethearts.

It is an extraordinary life: just a day's travel away from the delights of London, but it might just as well be on the moon. No-one who has served in the trenches will ever be the same again. Certainly, the soldier writing his letter home in the corner of a revetment will never be able to tell his story of fear and death, bravery and comradeship. Perhaps, paradoxically, that will be the task of the poets.

1917 (1917-1918)

Berlin, 1 February 1917. Germany announces a resumption of unrestricted submarine warfare.

Washington, DC, 2 March 1917. Congress passes the Jones Act, making Puerto Rico a US territory.

Ottoman Empire, 11 March 1917. The British enter Baghdad.

Petrograd, 12 March 1917. The *duma* ignores Czar Nicholas II's decree ordering its suspension and sets up a provisional government.

Russia, 16 March 1917. Czar Nicholas II abdicates.

Ottoman Empire, 27 March 1917. The Ottomans are heavily defeated by the British near Gaza.

USA, 1 April 1917. The ragtime musician Scott Joplin dies.

Washington, DC, 6 April 1917. President Wilson signs a declaration taking the USA into the war.

Western Front, 16 April 1917. Allied troops launch an offensive against the Germans manning the Hindenburg Line.

Petrograd, 17 April 1917. On his return to Russia with the other Bolshevik leaders, Vladimir Lenin publishes demands for the transfer of power to workers' *soviets*.

Western Front, 3 May 1917. The battle of Arras ends following the Canadian capture of Vimy ridge.

Italy, 3 June 1917. Italy declares Albania a protectorate.

Brazil, 4 June 1917. Brazil declares war on Germany and seizes all German ships in its ports.

Western Front, 8 June 1917. The British capture the Messines ridge.

Greece, 12 June 1917. The pro-German King Constantine, who has dismissed the pro-Allies Venizelos government, is forced to abdicate by the Allies.

Petrograd, 16 June 1917. The pan-Russian Congress of Soviets opens.

Western Front, 27 June 1917. The first US troops land in France.

Ukraine, 29 June 1917. The Ukraine declares its independence.

Berlin, 14 July 1917. Georg Michaelis succeeds Theobald von Bethmann-Hollweg as chancellor.

Finland, 14 July 1917. Finland proclaims its independence.

Russia, 16 July 1917. The provisional government crushes a *Bolshevik* uprising; its leader, Vladimir Lenin, flees.

Portugal, 17 July 1917. Pilgrims flock to Fatima, where visions of the Virgin Mary have been seen.

Petrograd, 22 July 1917. Alexander Kerensky is appointed prime minister.

Paris, 25 July 1917. Mata Hari, a glamorous Dutch dancer, is sentenced to death for spying.

China, 14 August 1917. War is declared on Germany and Austria.

Rome, 14 August 1917. After a failed peace bid last year, Pope Benedict XV sends another peace plan to the major powers.

Western Front, 20 August 1917. The French break the German lines at Verdun on an 11-mile front.

China, 10 September 1917. Sun Yat-sen sets up the republic of China military government in Guangzhou, in opposition to the Beijing government.

Petrograd, 15 September 1917. Kerensky proclaims Russia a republic.

Poland, 15 September 1917. Germany and Austria cede administrative and legislative power to the provisional government.

Russia, 17 September 1917. The Germans drive the Russians out of the Baltic port of Riga.

France, 26 September 1917. The painter Edgar Degas dies.

Western Front, 6 November 1917. Canadian troops capture the village of Passchendaele, ending the third battle of Ypres.

Petrograd, 7 November 1917. Kerensky and the provisional government are ousted in a Bolshevik coup.

Britain, 9 November 1917. Arthur Balfour, the foreign secretary, unveils plans for a Jewish national homeland in Palestine.

Russia, 16 November 1917. Bolshevik troops take Moscow.

France, 17 November 1917. The sculptor Auguste Rodin dies.

Palestine, 18 November 1917. British troops capture Jaffa.

USA, 7 December 1917. The USA declares war on Austria.

Portugal, 12 December 1917. Pro-German army officers under Sidonio Paes oust President Bernardino Machado in a *coup*.

Britain, 17 December 1917. Elizabeth Garrett Anderson, the first British woman doctor, dies.

Russia, 22 December 1917. The Bolsheviks open peace talks with Germany and Austria.

France, 14 January 1918. The ex-prime minister Joseph Caillaux, who advocated a negotiated peace with Germany, is jailed for treason.

Russia, 28 January 1918. Lenin creates a Red Army and the *Cheka*, a security police force.

US troops arrive to fight European war

US "doughboys" arriving in Britain on their way to the western front.

France, 27 June 1917
The first American troops to fight alongside the Allies were given a heroes' welcome as their ships tied up in French ports this morning.

Because of the submarine menace the troops' landing site had been kept a closely guarded secret, but by the time that the first US Marines had lined up to take their first salute on French soil a huge crowd had gathered to cheer them enthusiastically. With the arrival of each successive ship the crowd grew larger and the cheering louder in the brilliant summer sunshine.

The Marines are commanded by Major-General John Pershing, a much-decorated veteran of the Mexican and Filipino wars, who will be independent of the Anglo-French command. They are the vanguard of a US expeditionary force expected to number several hundred thousand men.

Apart from the Marines, an elite fighting force, many of the US troops to arrive will be conscripts fresh from training camp. Since the US entered the war 11 weeks ago urgent measures have been taken to augment their regular 128,000-strong army. Moves include the passing of the Selective Service Act, allowing all men aged between 21 and 30 to be drafted into the army.

Britain rejoices at Jerusalem capture

Jerusalem, 9 December 1917
The Ottoman commander of the Holy City has surrendered to General Edmund Allenby. The news has been welcomed by Jewish leaders and celebrated in London, where church bells rang out for the first time since war began.

The fall of Jerusalem is the culmination of an inspired campaign against the Ottomans which began nearly six weeks ago with the capture of Beersheba.

Guards have been placed over Christian holy places, and Moslems from the Indian Army are guarding Moslem shrines. Martial law is expected to be declared.

The power of the tank: a new weapon of war, but undervalued by traditional commanders.

Bolsheviks stage bloodless coup

Outside the Winter Palace: crowds scatter at the first burst of gunfire.

Revolutionary trio: Lenin, with Stalin and Trotsky alongside.

Petrograd, 7 November 1917
An ormolu mantelpiece clock in the Winter Palace stopped at ten minutes past two this morning. That was the moment when a party of "Red Guards", followed by an unruly mob, burst into the room and seized members of the provisional government. The cabinet ministers narrowly escaped being lynched by the mob before they were carted off to the Peter and Paul fortress. The total casualties in this seizure of power by a group of political conspirators known as Bolsheviks was three officer cadets wounded.

The leader of the Bolsheviks is a former law student, Vladimir Lenin, who only a few months ago was living in exile in Switzerland, virtually unknown outside the unholy circle of police agents and revolutionary visionaries. But the Germans knew him and sent him back to Russia in a sealed train: a troublemaker who they hoped would knock his country out of the war. That was after the February Revolution, when liberals and moderate socialists finally got rid of czarist autocracy following months of military defeats. In the euphoria of those days there was no sympathy for the Bolsheviks, and Lenin

fled to Finland to escape arrest. But the people were war-weary and hungry, and the provisional government, led by Alexander Kerensky, had only rhetoric to offer.

The coup was masterminded by Leon Trotsky, once Lenin's bitter critic but now his closest comrade. Trotsky got the Petrograd Soviet, or revolutionary assembly, to vote for action, and sent armed squads to take railway stations, the telephone exchange and other key points. When the cruiser *Aurora* came up the Neva and fired a blank shell outside the Winter Palace, it was pretty well all over.

Palestine should be homeland for Jews, say British rulers

Palestine, 9 November 1917
Palestine as a permanent homeland for the Jewish people is the declared aim of the British government. The foreign secretary, Arthur Balfour, has conveyed a declaration of intent to Baron Rothschild, the representative of the Zionists.

The War Cabinet, under David Lloyd George, believes that Zionist support will help the war effort, particularly the campaign against the Ottomans. Arabs outnumber Jews ten to one in the Holy Land, but, under leaders like Dr Chaim Weizmann, Zionists can be expected to try to build up their numbers.

Australian cavalry conquers Jericho

Jericho, 21 February 1918
Australian cavalry rode triumphantly through the rain into Jericho this morning. The Ottomans have lost their advance base for the defence of Palestine. Five miles (eight kilometres) from the river Jordan, Jericho is a strategically important supply route, linked to the Hedfaz railway. Now it can help the Allied forces under General Allenby in his advance north towards Syria.

U-boats blast US and neutral ships

Washington, 26 February 1917
News of the sinking of the Cunard liner *Laconia* reached Capitol Hill today at the very moment that Congress was debating measures to deal with the growing menace in the Atlantic of German submarines. Earlier this month a US ship, the *Housatonic*, was sunk, making a total of 134 neutral ships destroyed by the Germans in the last three weeks.

President Woodrow Wilson was asking Congress to authorise the arming of US vessels to "protect our ships and our people in their legitimate pursuits on the sea". Already the US Navy is mounting naval patrols in the Atlantic to protect US shipping.

Germany penetrates deep into Italy

Northern Italy, 31 October 1917
The Italian army has been shattered by a surprise German onslaught, and is retreating in disarray towards the Piave river, a mere 15 miles (24 kilometres) from Venice.

The Italian Second Army, which had held off the Austrians comfortably through 1916, and captured the stronghold of Monte Santo only two months ago, had seemed well entrenched in the mountains around Caporetto and Udine.

But a German gas attack, followed by a furious creeping barrage from artillery, made the Italians suddenly vulnerable. When German and Austrian troops made light of the rain and snow to punch through their most northerly postions, the defenders lost heart. Ita-

lian losses have been high, with 10,000 dead and 30,000 wounded.

Of greater strategic significance is the capture of nearly 300,000 troops, armour and ammunition, and the total collapse of morale. Throughout northern Italy, soldiers are throwing away their weapons and fleeing. Although military police have set up roadblocks, and field courts-martial are common, it is estimated that half a million may have deserted.

As German and Austrian forces advance from the mountains across the river Tagliamento, General Cadorna, the Italian commander-in-chief, has been obliged to retreat to the river Piave, where he is desperately trying to establish a new line of defence.

The home front: a British woman munitions worker filling shells. Industry has been surprised by female efficiency; some factories are more than twice as productive as when staffed by men.

Britain, 6 February. Married women over 30 win the vote.

Russia, 20 February. On the breakdown of peace talks, the Germans resume attacks on the Russians.

Estonia, 24 February. Estonia declares its independence.

Britain, 26 February. The Labour Party adopts a constitution aiming for common ownership and state control.

Russia, 3 March. Russia signs a peace treaty with Germany at Brest-Litovsk.

Russia, 5 March. The capital is moved from Petrograd to Moscow.

Western Front, 21 March. The Germans launch a great offensive on the Somme.

Western Front, 26 March. Ferdinand Foch is appointed commander-in-chief of the allied forces in France.

Britain, 1 April. The Royal Air Force is formed.

Far East, 6 April. US, British and Japanese troops land at Vladivostok.

Western Front, 23 April. British forces raid the Belgian port of Zeebrugge.

Rumania, 7 May. Rumania forms alliance with Germany and Austria.

Ireland, 19 May. Five hundred *Sinn Fein* members, including Eamon de Valera, are jailed.

Russia, 26 May. Armenia and Georgia declares independence.

Russia, 10 July. A provisional government of Siberia is set up.

Russia, 16 July. The former Czar Nicholas II and his family are massacred in a cellar at Ekaterinburg.

Western Front, 18 July. Allied forces launch a counter-offensive on the Marne.

Germany, 29 July. Germany severs diplomatic relations with the Ottoman empire.

Russia, 2 August. A British-led force lands at Archangel to support the White Russian opposition to the Bolsheviks.

Western Front, 8 August. The German line collapses as Allied forces go into action near Amiens.

USA, 15 August. The USA severs relations with Russia.

Western Front, 3 September. German forces begin a retreat to the Siegfried Line.

US launches post-war peace plan

Woodrow Wilson: 14 points for a brave new liberal world.

Washington, DC, 9 January
A liberal vision of a post-war world free of restrictions, enjoying open diplomacy and free trade and encouraging national self-determination was disclosed by President Wilson to Congress today.

The 14-point Wilson Plan, as it is being called, is based on proposals which the president put to the recent inter-Allied conference which failed to agree any post-war aims. Many of the points have also been put forward by a secret policy group in New York, known as the "Inquiry" and led by a young journalist, Walter Lippmann.

The president's aim in publishing the plan is to turn the German people against their government and push the Allied governments into granting liberal peace terms.

Specific proposals for post-war Europe include Germany evacuating occupied territories in Russia, Belgium and France as well as returning Alsace-Lorraine to France. The problem of the Balkan states, still ruled by the now politically unstable Habsburg and Ottoman empires, is solved by granting these states autonomous development. A novel feature of the plan is the formation of an association of nations to guarantee independence and national integrity.

Russia signs peace deal

Brest-Litovsk, 3 March
The four-month-old Bolshevik regime today put its seal on a peace treaty with Germany that requires Russia to give up 26 per cent of its population, 27 per cent of its own area, three-quarters of its iron and steel output 26 per cent of its rail network, and to surrender Poland and the Baltic states. The Ukraine becomes an independent state. And the Bolsheviks have agreed to pay 3,000 million *roubles* in reparations. The surrender has angered Russia's western allies, who will now be faced with massive German reinforcements brought from Russia to the western front. The *pince-nez*-wearing people's commissar for foreign affairs, Leon Trotsky, bamboozled the Germans for nine weeks with neither-war-nor-peace talk, hoping that revolution would spread to Germany.

That did not happen. German forces thrust deep into Russia and Lenin ordered peace at any price, before the Germans overthrew his shaky Bolshevik regime.

The Bolsheviks came to power last November with the popular slogan "Peace, land, bread – and all power to the *Soviets*". The people have now got their peace – and they must pay the price in land and bread.

Czar and household slaughtered in cellar

The czar and family at Czarskoe Selo before being taken to Ekaterinburg.

Ekaterinburg, 16 July
The deposed Czar Nicholas II and his family arrived in this small town in the Urals a few weeks ago when local Bolsheviks dragged them from a train that was taking them from Tobolsk to Ufa. Scarcely had they arrived in Ekaterinburg than the local Bolshevik-dominated soviet began expressing fears that they could be liberated by advancing anti-Bolshevik "White Guards" and Czechs.

The local branch of Lenin's secret police, the *Cheka*, took over guard duties at the house where the Romanovs were being held. Today the family were taken into the cellar, where the ex-czar, his wife, the invalid czarevitch and the four daughters were shot and bayoneted to death. And to make sure that nobody survived to bear witness, the family physician, valet, cook, parlourmaid and dog were killed. The bodies were burnt and thrown into a pit.

The Bolshevik leadership in Moscow has put it about that the massacre was a local decision; the truth, it seems, is that Moscow saw the Romanovs as a possible rallying force for anti-Bolshevik groups and let it be known that the liquidation of the family would not be unwelcome.

Allies smash through German lines

Western Front, 30 September
The German army is falling back all along the line under the hammering of 200 Allied divisions in the offensive launched at dawn four days ago. Von Ludendorff, the German commander, has described 8 August as the "black day of the German army", but today's news is even more significant.

The Germans, who came so close to success in the spring, are now avoiding battle wherever possible, making a stand only to cover the retreat as British, French and the fresh, confident Americans drive on from the Scheldt in the north to Sedan at the southern end of the western front.

King Albert's 28 Belgian divisions are in the forefront of the advance in Flanders, liberating their country which was occupied by the Germans in the first days of the war, four long years ago.

Tanks and planes are being used in large numbers and the stalemate of the trench lines has been broken. The British left wing is almost through the last defences of the Hindenburg Line, and the Allies will soon be where they have always wanted to be – in open country, fighting a war of mobility.

German morale is cracking everywhere, and all along the ruptured front pockets of soldiers are being found hiding in shellholes and ruined buildings. They offer no resistance, and are throwing down their weapons and equipment; every-

Autumn offensive: British troops move into no-man's-land near Bellicourt.

thing, in fact, except a small sack containing a few necessities – bread, soap and razor – for the prison camp. It is pointed out that many of these Germans belong to low-grade units; it is expected that Ludendorff, employing a system of elastic defence, will allow the Allied offensive to tire before putting in his reserve fighting divisions.

However, the evidence coming from the battlefield is of a German army emaciated by four years of bloodshed, and with its morale sapped by news of unrest at home, unable to cope with the fierce determination of the British and French and the keenness of the Americans.

That eagerness brings its own problems, for the Americans, with an untried war machine, and short of artillery, are apt to rush in where more experienced soldiers fear to tread. But they mean to win.

Civil war threatens Russian Bolsheviks

Moscow, 26 June
Lenin's Bolshevik regime is beset on all sides. In the south, General Anton Denikin has seized large parts of the Caucasus and the Ukraine; in the north, bands of anti-Bolsheviks roam at will; Czech former prisoners of war, now organised in the Czech Legion, have taken Omsk on the Trans-Siberian Railway. Over 100 British marines have landed at Murmansk to keep the port out of German hands. Trotsky, desperately seeking to create a Red Army, offers recruits 150 roubles (£2) a month.

British major helps to free Damascus from Turkish rule

Damascus, 1 October
Major T E Lawrence, known as Lawrence of Arabia, has led a triumphant Arab army into Damascus just ahead of General Allenby's army of Palestine. Horsemen cavort in the streets as the greatest city in the Arab world celebrates its liberation from the Ottoman yoke.

Alongside Lawrence is *Emir* Feisal, the son of *Sherif* Hussein, who now expects to be crowned king of Syria. Starting in the Hejaz several months ago, they have built an Arab army and led it across the desert, through skirmishes with Ottoman troops, Lawrence's tactical skill and Feisal's charismatic leadership proving a potent combination.

The only Ottoman troops left in the city now are the wounded, left behind in hospitals in appalling conditions. Although the tribesmen and Syrian townspeople have much to celebrate, there is concern at the possible breakdown of law and order. Allenby's first task will be to instal a military government in Damascus to prevent wholesale slaughter as a vengeful populace seeks out those who collaborated with the Ottomans. Thereafter, the French will take over Syria while Allenby moves on to join French forces in the advance on Beirut.

Number One Squadron of the new Royal Air Force, formed on 1 April.

Lawrence of Arabia: an incorrigible romantic in an unromantic war.

Armistice: Europe sighs with relief

Western Front, 15 November

Along the western front, from the Channel to the Swiss border, men are slowly becoming accustomed to an eerie, unfamiliar sound. It is the sound of silence. After four years and 14 weeks, the crash of artillery, the thump of the howitzer and the scream of the *minenwerfer* are no longer heard. Peace has come to a war-weary Europe, received with delirious relief by the victors and with bitterness by the defeated.

The end, when it came, took many by surprise. In mid October, Foch, the Allied commander, was asking for reinforcements for a November offensive and the Americans had their sights on campaigns in 1919. But behind the German lines there was a sense of desperation. Von Ludendorff, once the hero of the hour, was replaced by the levelheaded General Groener who told the kaiser either to shoot himself or abdicate.

By the end of last month, with their army reeling under the Allied blows, the Germans were in no position to haggle over the armistice terms. Shortly before dawn, in a railway carriage in the forest of Compiegne, Foch and the British Admiral Wemyss received a German delegation, including two generals and a Catholic politician. Six hours later, at 11am on the 11th day of the 11th month, the armistice took effect. The terms are hard,

The day the world stopped fighting: "The nightmare is over," said George V.

Germany surrendering 5,000 heavy guns, 30,000 machine guns, 2,000 warplanes, all its U-boats, 150,000 wagons and 5,000 trucks.

The German navy will be interned in British waters. The Allied blockade of Germany will remain in force to ensure that the Germans keep their word. When Germany first sought an armistice it undertook to end submarine warfare, but the U-boats continued to attack, sinking a transport, with the loss of 600 lives, and a British cruiser. In

Britain, the firing of "maroons" told people that peace had come and the whole country became, as one commentator said, "like a giant school let loose".

Boy Scouts cycled through the streets sounding the "all clear" on bugles. Factories shut down, munitions workers danced with servicemen, fireworks spluttered and paper boys raced along waving special editions. Wartime licensing laws were ignored and pubs stayed open until they ran out of beer.

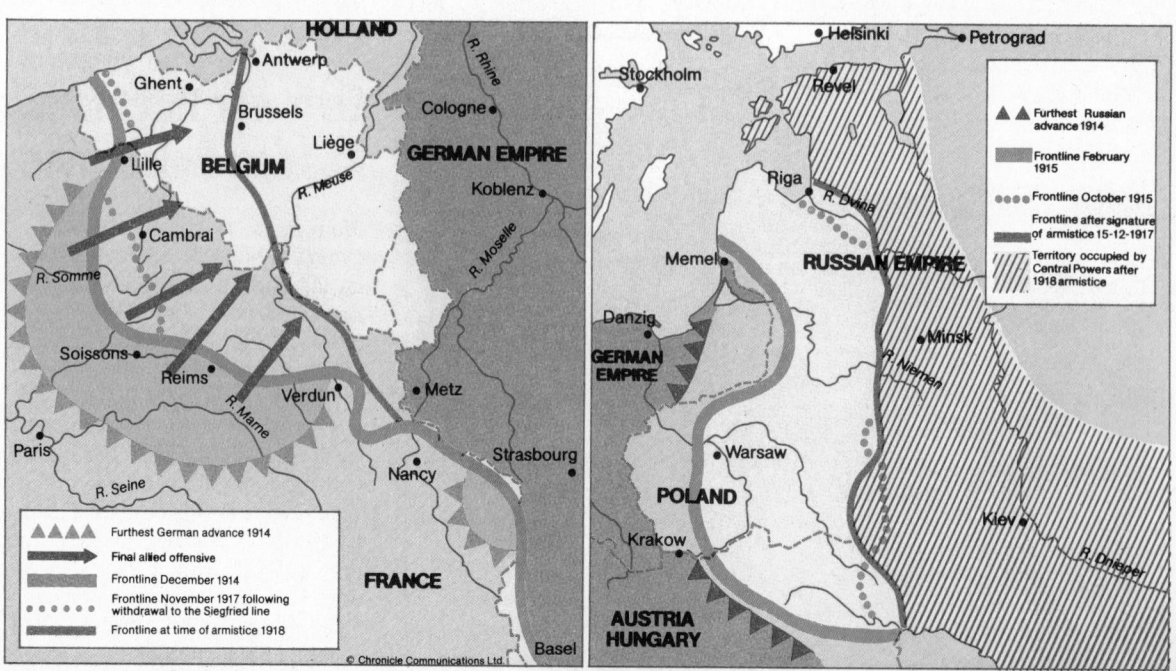

Defeated Germany plunges into chaos

Berlin, 30 November
The order and discipline for which the Germans were known, and even respected, throughout Europe vanished virtually overnight in the wake of defeat in war. The kaiser has fled to Holland, angry political agitators roam the streets, sailors have mutinied and dishevelled, disillusioned soldiers are seizing their command posts.

The Social Democrats are led by Friedrich Ebert, aged 47, a trade union boss and former saddlemaker who is attempting to restore order. Ebert told the *reichstag* that a republic had been proclaimed and that arms were being distributed to soldiers' and workers' councils. But he has appointed a tough-minded Socialist, Gustav Noske, as his minister of defence. Noske has gone to work with a loyal general, Wilhelm Groener, to form volunteer units of loyal anti-revolutionary soldiers.

Ebert and Noske are being fiercely denounced by extreme left-wingers like Karl Liebknecht and Rosa Luxembourg, who have formed the revolutionary Spartacus League and are calling for "a free socialist republic". In reaction to this left-wing ferment, far-right factions in the army are talking of "dealing" with such people as Liebknecht and Luxembourg.

Habsburg empire breaks into pieces

Vienna, 30 November
With the break-up of the Habsburg empire following the end of the World War, four "new" nations have come into being – Austria, Hungary, Czechoslovakia and one yet to be named. Their roots go back into Europe's pre-history.

Austria is now a republic and has kicked out Karl, the last Habsburg emperor. Czechoslovakia is led by the popular Tomas Masaryk. The Hungarians, or Magyars, who have enjoyed equality with Austria in the empire, have a government headed by the liberal aristocrat Michael Karolyi. The as yet unnamed country is a confederation of South Slavic peoples, including Serbs, and will be ruled by King Peter who led Serbia to victory.

Peace comes to the far-flung frontiers

Africa and Asia, 30 November
General von Lettow Vorbeck heard of the armistice on a bicycle, leading his undefeated 250 German and 1,750 African troops to invade Rhodesia. For four years they have held down over 130,000 Allied troops.

In Istanbul news of the armistice came after the Ottoman collapse in Palestine and Mesopotamia. General von Papen, the deputy commander in the Near East, was as shocked by the encouragement of soldiers' councils by his senior, von Sanders, as by the armistice.

Von Hentig, who for four years raised anti-British revolts in Persia, Afghanistan and China, heard the news in Shanghai. He is to be repatriated via the US, and thus will have circumnavigated the globe.

Spanish flu claims more lives than war

The World
The Great War is estimated to have claimed ten million lives. But a disastrous pandemic of a type of influenza called "Spanish flu" has already this year exceeded that figure. Doctors believe that the death-toll worldwide over the coming year could reach a staggering 20 million.

This virulent strain of influenza is itself dangerous, but it is the added risk of bacterial infection in the lungs which causes complications such as lethal pneumonia. So far, attempts to develop a vaccine to combat this mass epidemic have been unsuccessful.

The tag "Spanish Flu" may be a misnomer. No-one is sure where it originated. So far the greatest suffering has been in India and China where millions have already died. But now the menace is spreading to America and Europe.

Already in Britain the signs are being felt: absences from work are escalating and essential services such as the London central telegraph office are being hit as people sign off sick.

Ten million dead, a generation lost: world counts cost of its first total war

Paul Nash's "The Menin Road", as bitter a poem on canvas as Owen's on paper; with form, like no-man's-land reduced to its most naked.

31 December
"Blow out, you bugles, over the rich dead!" wrote Rupert Brooke, and Laurence Binyon echoed, in consolation: "They shall not grow old, as we that are left grow old." But that was said before the enormity of the casualties could be guessed at – over ten million dead, in war cemeteries lining the battlefields like serried battalions of crosses, or in unmarked graves at the bottom of the sea. In sheer total of dead, wounded and missing, Russia leads the list, followed by Germany and Austria-Hungary, France and then Britain and its empire with one million. Britain gave 767,000 dead and the empire 200,000 more.

The cost was a Lost Generation, and none were more aware of it than the writers on both sides. "What passing bells for these who die as cattle?" asked Wilfred Owen. Those who died, either in action or on active service, included Brooke, who came to stand for his generation cut off in the bud of promise, Edward Thomas, Isaac Rosenberg, and Owen, killed a week before the armistice on the western front. His poems, written in the trenches, begin with the words: "My subject is war and the pity of war. The poetry is in the pity."

Some of the survivors, like Siegfried Sassoon, have already make public the uncomfortable view that the lost generation had been sacrificed by incompetent commanders, careless of the lives of those who had to do the dying. Sassoon threw his Military Cross into the river Mersey in protest at the slaughter. His reward for such sanity was to be despatched to a mental hospital, diagnosed as shell-shocked.

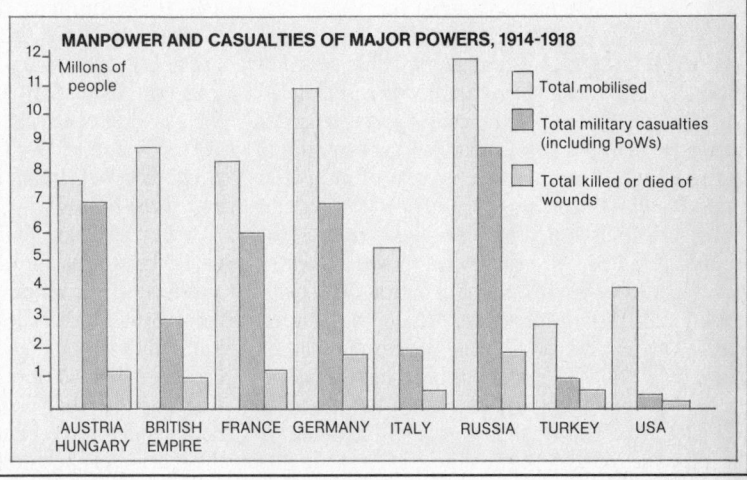

MANPOWER AND CASUALTIES OF MAJOR POWERS, 1914-1918

Millons of people

- Total mobilised
- Total military casualties (including PoWs)
- Total killed or died of wounds

AUSTRIA HUNGARY · BRITISH EMPIRE · FRANCE · GERMANY · ITALY · RUSSIA · TURKEY · USA

1914-1918: The Great Divide

The First World War marks the great divide of modern times. Like a vast geological fault it transformed a whole landscape. Nothing was untouched, from politics and economics to social relations and the arts. The previous century, after the turmoil of the Napoleonic Wars, had been relatively tranquil. Only the Crimean and Franco-Prussian wars were serious threats to the "Concert of Europe." Yet with dreadful suddenness that stability collapsed, never to return. The Austro-Hungarian and Ottoman empires fell. Bolshevism triumphed in Russia, the United States emerged as a world power. Dynasties vanished: the Romanovs, Habsburgs and Hohenzollerns evaporated. War itself was transformed. Men displayed more skill in killing (by means of tanks, poison gas, aerial bombardment) and in keeping alive (by improving surgery, perfecting anaesthesia, developing artificial limbs). It was also a uniquely articulate war. War poets like Wilfred Owen and Siegfried Sassoon proclaimed the wretchedness and stupidity of life in the trenches.

Europe was more triumphant than decadent in 1914. Its 450 million inhabitants constituted a quarter of the world's population. Rapid progress in health, hygiene and nutrition had increased life expectancy. Europe dominated world finance, industry and commerce. The United Kingdom, Germany and France were the largest lending nations: America the debtor. Europe controlled the major means of communication – shipping lines, press agencies, cable and wireless. She was responsible for three-quarters of the world's industrial production. By 1918, however, the world map had been utterly redrawn.

The first "total war" in history

Post-war nostalgia transfomed the period before the war into a golden age of unappreciated security, but the idea is plainly fanciful. Wars do not come from nowhere, as rain from an unclouded sky. The early years of the century saw tensions running high in Europe. Britain had a constitutional crisis in 1909-10, her worst-ever year of industrial unrest in 1911, the makings of a civil war in Ireland in 1912. Russia and Japan went to war in 1904, Germany and Britain nearly went to war at Agadir in 1911. In the Balkans, Serbian nationalism challenged Austrian imperialism. Only the United States seemed removed from developing diplomatic disputes. War may have been half-expected but it was something one could not take entirely seriously; so when it came it was still a shock. If the very fact of war was a shock, even more dis-

tressing was its nature. This was the first "total war" in history, a battle which engaged entire nations. The state assumed control as never before over individuals. "Your Country needs YOU", Lord Kitchener nagged from Britain's billboards. Moral intimidation was insufficient: conscription had to be introduced in Britain in 1916.

Factories, too, felt the change as entire economies had to be placed on a war-footing. Above all, with men away at war, women had to be pressed into service. This was a social revolution. That women could prosper in a man's world upset long-cherished notions of the proper ordering of the relations between the sexes. One result was that women in many countries were given the vote for the first time: in Denmark (1915), Netherlands and Russia (1917), Austria, Britain, Czechoslovakia, Poland and Sweden (1918), Germany and Luxembourg (1919), and in the United States (1920).

Sixty thousand dead in a day

The military strategy of the First World War has been justly reviled. It seemed almost wilfully designed to cause heavy loss of life. Two great sets of trenches – perhaps 25,000 miles of them in total – were established along the eastern borders of France. Attack the opposing trench at its strongest point, the thinking went, and should it fall the rest of the line would collapse in turn. The reality was different. When men "went over the top" in an attack, maximum loss of life generally gained minimum territory. It was pointless slaughter, which may have shown the folly of trench warfare but simply reinforced a desire to dig in.

The trenches themselves were dreadful places. Soldiers in both camps lived a troglodytic existence. In an unfamiliar world, men clung desperately to the idea of civilisation for which they were supposed to be fighting. Geoffrey Keynes, brother of the English economist, and distinguished in his own right as surgeon and bibliographer, recorded the startling contrasts of trench life. "As medical officer, I found to my astonishment that I was attended by a batman, a medical orderly, a groom, and three horses."

A key strategic assumption was that the war would be won in the west. So it turned out, but it was nearly lost in the east. Russia's stance, apart from Brussilov's offensive against the Austrians in the summer of 1916, was almost wholly defensive. An Allied attempt in 1915 to relieve the pressure by penetrating Turkish defences in the Dardanelles ended in the fiasco of Gallipoli. War tested the czarist regime and found it wanting. The poli-

tical system could not cope. In the last year of czardom there were four prime ministers, three war ministers, and three foreign minister. The army lacked ammunition and the populace food. Casualties were enormous, five and a half million in two and a half years.

Peace, bread and revolution

The February Revolution (1917) ended czarism but not the war. Lenin led the October Revolution of the same year with the latter intention. The Bolsheviks promised "peace, land, and bread" and by the treaty of Brest-Litovsk, signed with Germany in March 1918, they secured the first. Next, Lenin hoped for peace on all fronts, but his call to the European masses to follow the Russian lead had precisely the opposite effect. It horrified political leaders, who were able to renew the war effort by showing that war-weariness was simply disguised revolutionism. Bolshevism ended the war in the east, but it boosted belligerence in the west.

The immediate post-war years were dominated by demobilisation and the return of soldiers to civilian life. For many of them, it was a bitter revelation. The experience of the trenches had been the most significant event of their lives, yet many at home seemed strangely unmoved by it. Politicians promised a land "fit for heroes to live in"; but the pledge was soon discounted as economies buckled under the strain of re-adjusting from war to peace. In France, inflation destroyed the value of savings. In Italy and Germany, purchasing power fell by a quarter between 1913 and 1919. In Britain, industrial unrest marked the early 1920s. In Russia, the Bolsheviks refused to honour the debts of the Czarist regime, either to the Russians themselves or to foreign governments.

The social disruption of the war went far beyond the naive expectations of 1914. A whole generation of men was lost, and future generations were blighted as a result. Nine million people were killed and seventeen million were wounded, of whom a third became invalids. Four million women were widowed, twice as many children were orphaned. The absence of menfolk seriously hampered future population growth with the result that western European populations became more elderly. This had important economic consequences, as it meant, in effect, a relative shrinkage of the workforce. Not since the Black Death of the 14th century had Europe suffered such a human haemorrhage.

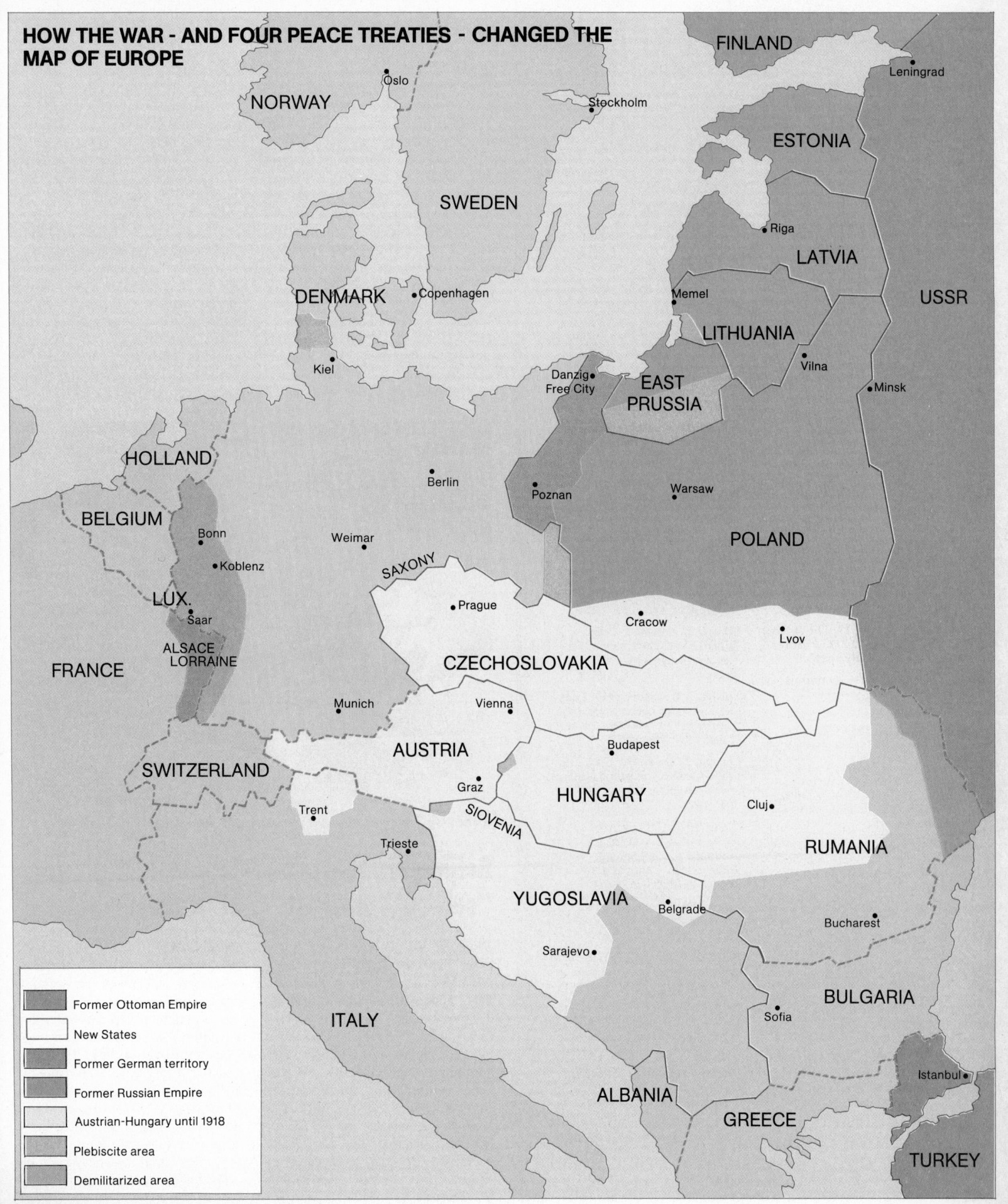

HOW THE WAR - AND FOUR PEACE TREATIES - CHANGED THE MAP OF EUROPE

NORWAY

Oslo

SWEDEN

Stockholm

FINLAND

Leningrad

ESTONIA

Riga

LATVIA

DENMARK

Copenhagen

USSR

Memel

LITHUANIA

Vilna

Kiel

Danzig
Free City

EAST
PRUSSIA

Minsk

HOLLAND

Berlin

Poznan

Warsaw

BELGIUM

Bonn

Weimar

POLAND

Koblenz

SAXONY

LUX.

Saar

Prague

Cracow

Lvov

ALSACE
LORRAINE

CZECHOSLOVAKIA

FRANCE

Munich

Vienna

SWITZERLAND

AUSTRIA

Budapest

Graz

Cluj

Trent

HUNGARY

SLOVENIA

RUMANIA

Trieste

YUGOSLAVIA

Belgrade

Bucharest

Sarajevo

ITALY

BULGARIA

Sofia

ALBANIA

Istanbul

GREECE

TURKEY

	Former Ottoman Empire
	New States
	Former German territory
	Former Russian Empire
	Austrian-Hungary until 1918
	Plebiscite area
	Demilitarized area

1919 (1919-1920)

London, 13 January 1919. Sir Satyendra Prassano Sinha becomes the first Indian peer and thus a member of the House of Lords.

Berlin, 16 January 1919. Rosa Luxembourg and Karl Liebknecht, the leaders of the Spartacist uprising, are murdered by German soldiers.

Versailles, 18 January 1919. Peace conference opens.

Dublin, 21 January 1919. An unofficial Irish "parliament", formed by 25 Westminster *Sinn Fein* MPs who refuse to attend the Commons, holds its first meeting.

Hungary, 20 February 1919. Bela Kun leads a communist revolt.

Germany, 22 February 1919. After the murder of the Bavarian prime minister, Kurt Eisner, a *soviet* republic is declared in Bavaria.

Russia, 3 March 1919. Bolshevik leaders establish the Communist International (Comintern) as a vehicle for world revolution.

Europe, 11 March 1919. The Allies reach agreement to supply famine-hit Germany with food relief.

Italy, 23 March 1919. Benito Mussolini founds a party, the Fasci di Combattimento, to fight both liberalism and communism.

Hungary, 26 March 1919. The former president Michael Karolyi is arrested by the communists.

Versailles, 4 April 1919. The Allies sign an agreement with Germany making Danzig a "free city".

Ireland, 5 April 1919. Eamon de Valera becomes Sinn Fein's president.

Mexico, 10 April 1919. The rebel leader Emiliano Zapata is killed by government troops.

Germany, 2 May 1919. Berlin government troops enter Munich to overthrow the fledgling soviet regime in Bavaria.

Afghanistan, 24 May 1919. Having defeated Afghan raiders in a clash on the Indian border, the British bomb Jalalabad and Kabul.

Lisbon, 27 May 1919. A US Navy NC4 seaplane completes the first-ever flight across the Atlantic.

Germany, 1 June 1919. A "Rhine republic" is proclaimed in several Rhineland cities.

Ireland, 15 June 1919. John Alcock and Arthur Brown complete the first non-stop flight across the Atlantic.

Britain, 21 June 1919. German sailors scuttle their captive fleet at Scapa Flow in the Orkneys.

Versailles, 28 June 1919. Germany and the Allies sign the Treaty of Versailles.

Britain, 13 July 1919. The British airship *R-34* completes the first two-way crossing of the Atlantic.

Germany, July 1919. A republic is declared at Weimar and a new constitution adopted.

Hungary, 4 August 1919. Rumanian troops enter Budapest, ending Bela Kun's 133-day-old communist republic.

Britain, 19 August 1919. A bill disestablishing the church in Wales becomes law.

Europe, 25 August 1919. The world's first scheduled international daily air service begins between London and Paris.

South Africa, 3 September 1919. Jan Smuts becomes prime minister following the death of Louis Botha.

France, 10 September 1919. Austria signs the treaty of St Germain with the Allies.

Ireland, 11 September 1919. The *Dail Eireann*, or Irish parliament, is declared illegal by the British government.

Italy, 23 September 1919. The poet-aviator Gabriele d'Annunzio occupies the city of Fiume.

Egypt, 19 November 1919. Britain grants Egypt a constitution.

Washington, DC, 19 November 1919. The US Senate votes against ratifying the Versailles Treaty.

France, 27 November 1919. Bulgaria signs the treaty of Neuilly, recognising the independence of Yugoslavia.

London, 1 December 1919. Lady (Nancy) Astor becomes the first woman MP to take her seat in the House of Commons.

London, 22 December 1919. David Lloyd George, the prime minister, announces plans for the partition of Ireland.

China, 1919. China refuses to sign the Treaty of Versailles, which has produced widespread anti-western sentiments in China and awakened interest in Marxism.

Britain, 1919. John Maynard Keynes publishes *The Economic Consequences of the Peace.*

Paris, 16 January 1920. The first meeting of the League of Nations is boycotted by the USA.

USA, 16 January 1920. The 18th amendment to the constitution, prohibiting the manufacture and sale of alcohol, comes into force.

Helsinki, 21 January 1920. The Baltic states decide to form a defensive alliance against Russia.

Paris, 24 January 1920. The death of the Italian painter Modigliani follows that of Renoir last year.

Berlin routs confused communist uprising

Berlin, 12 January 1919

The communist uprising in Berlin has been crushed by troops loyal to the government after a week of bitter street fighting.

The revolt by the Spartacists, who take their name from the last slaves to revolt against the Romans, began to collapse yesterday as 3,000 *Freikorps* men marched into the capital to reinforce the Freikorps forces already in the city, government troops and members of the Socialist People's Militia. By this morning the Spartacists, whose call to the workers to take up arms against the troops has been ignored, had faded away. The whereabouts of their leaders, the revolutionaries "Red Rosa" Luxembourg and Karl Liebknecht, a former *reichstag* deputy, is not known. They led the occupation of a number of public buildings after the government refused to bow to their demands for the formation of a true socialist republic – the same as the Bolsheviks have set up in Russia.

A Spartacist attempt to occupy the war office failed after the under-secretary of state told the leader of the raiding party that he needed proper written authority to do so. Much of the fighting has been confused, with men on both sides occupying barricades. Hundreds of bodies are still lying in the streets, according to eye-witnesses.

Right-wing Freikorps forces at the barricades behind newspaper bundles.

Beijing students in "sell-out" protest

Beijing, 4 May 1919

Some 3,000 student demonstrators assembled at the Gate of Heavenly Peace today to protest against the decision taken by the Allies at Versailles to give defeated Germany's rights in Shandong to Japan rather than return them to China. The students, believing that the minister of communications had sold out to the Japanese, sacked his house. Thirty-two were arrested, but the protest continues, drawing strength from the reformist faculty of Beijing university.

Eclipse test proves Einstein is right

London, 1919

A scientific expedition to the Gulf of Guinea has taken photographs during a total eclipse, verifying one of this century's most important scientific theories. The team was from the Royal Society of London and the theory is that of relativity, as propounded by Albert Einstein. According to Einstein, gravity is not, as Newton said, a force but a curved field in space-time. This can only be proved by measuring the deflection of starlight during a total eclipse of the sun.

League of Nations formed to stop war

Paris, 14 February, 1919
Delegates from 27 nations at the peace conference here today voted to set up a league of nations to try to prevent war. Much remains to be done before it becomes a reality, but today's vote demonstrates that the US president, Woodrow Wilson, is winning support for his belief that "the conscience of the world" is ready for such a move.

The league's charter is to be incorporated in the peace treaty with Germany being debated here. But there are still deep divisions between the hawks, like the French, who want to make Germany pay, and the doves, like Wilson, who argue for a "just peace".

An English scientist has split the atom

Manchester, 1919
Experiments at Manchester university by Professor Rutherford have culminated in a process for "splitting" atoms. Rutherford has fired alpha particles through hydrogen gas and dislodged their nuclei. He has also managed to knock hydrogen nuclei – H-particles – out of the elements boron, fluorine, sodium, aluminium and nitrogen.

Rutherford names these H-particles *protons*. They seem to be the indivisible building blocks of the nuclei of all elements.

Amritsar massacre stalls reform plans

Delhi, 1919
Emergency war regulations have been imposed by the British authorities and proposals for provincial self-government shelved. Britain's dilemma over India was sharpened in April when Gurkha troops, commanded by Brigadier Dyer, killed 379 unarmed demonstrators at Amritsar, the holy city of the Sikhs. Dyer's order to open fire has been condemned, but the emergency powers which prompted the demonstration have been toughened, diluting the impact of plans to "Indianise" the army and civil service.

Aviators pioneer new routes round world

Alcock and Brown's Vickers-Vimy biplane taking off from Newfoundland.

Australia, 10 December 1919
The flying Smith brothers arrived in Australia today and claimed the £10,000 prize offered by the Australian government for the first flight to arrive from Britain in under 30 days. Their trip brings to a climax a year of massive advances in international aviation.

In February fare-paying passengers were carried between London and Paris for the first time when a Farman F60 Goliath took three and a half hours to make the journey. A month later, on 27 March, the Atlantic was bridged by a US Navy NC4 seaplane, whose pilots Lieutenant-Commander Read and Lieutenant Stone flew 3,150 nautical miles in 44 hours. This involved three stages, the longest spanning the 1,200 miles between Newfoundland and the Azores.

On 15 June the Anglo-Irish team of Captain John Alcock and Lieutenant Arthur Whitten Brown went one step further. Despite atrocious weather conditions their Vickers-Vimy biplane flew the Atlantic non-stop, landing successfully in an Irish peat bog. They completed the 1,900-mile flight from Newfoundland in 16 hours and 12 minutes.

Aircraft are not the only means of airborne travel. The British airship *R-34* made the first two-way trip over the Atlantic in July. The leisurely *dirigible* took four days to reach New York, slightly longer than a fast liner.

Germany forced to pay cost of peace

Versailles, 28 June 1919
For five months the victors of the Great War had laboured to produce a peace settlement and for two months the vanquished had refused to accept the terms. Today, at ten minutes to four in the afternoon, the German delegation finally bowed to threats of military occupation and signed a peace treaty. The news was signalled by gunfire and greeted by cheers from crowds outside the Palace of Versailles.

The peace terms had caused anguish and division amongst the allies. The French had led those arguing for a tough line, urging that Germany be partitioned. Lloyd George, the British prime minister, had promised to "squeeze the German lemon until the pips squeak", but even he is now wondering whether the final terms might be too harsh. "We shall have to fight another war all over again at three times the cost," he said.

Under the treaty Germany has to make a provisional compensation payment of 20 billion gold marks – with further reparations to be decided later. Territory lived in by seven million people is to be surrendered; the Rhineland is to be demilitarized; and the Saar controlled by the new League of Nations. The German cabinet resigned and although majority of the National Assembly voted to accept the terms, the bitterness remains.

Dixieland jazzmen take syncopation to every nation

London, 7 April 1919
Jazz, now the rage in America, has arrived in Europe with the "Original Dixieland Jazz Band". Its tour has reached the London Palladium. Jazz began in New Orleans with its marching funeral bands and its "cornet kings". Many black musicians left the city with the closing of its red light district of Storyville two years ago. White jazz is known as "Dixieland", and the "ODJB" was formed by white New Orleans musicians in Chicago. It is led by Nick La Rocca, a cornettist and the composer of *Tiger Rag*, which nightly brings audiences to their feet stamping and clapping.

Nick La Rocca's all-white band, spreading jazz where black men fear to tread.

1920

Russia, 20 February. The Red Army captures Archangel.

Germany, 24 February. The National Socialist Workers' Party, led by Adolf Hitler, publishes a programme for a third *reich*.

Hungary, 29 February. The monarchy is restored, with Miklos Horthy as regent.

Syria, 8 March. Syria proclaims its independence from the Ottoman empire, with *Emir* Feisal, hero of the Arab Revolt, as king.

Turkey, 16 March. Allied troops occupy Istanbul.

Ireland, 26 March. Eight hundred special constables, the "Black and Tans", arrive from England to put down the republican revolt in the South of the country, where public order is rapidly deteriorating.

Budapest, 28 March. The Hungarian parliament is dissolved and the regent, Miklos Horthy, becomes dictator.

Germany, 6 April. French troops occupy Frankfurt.

Turkey, 23 April. Turkish nationalists set up a provisional government at Ankara, with Mustapha Kemal as president.

Ukraine, 7 May. Polish troops seize Kiev from the Red Army.

Persia, 19 May. The Red Army invades northern Persia.

Mexico, 22 May. President Venustiano Carranza is murdered by rebels under Rodolfo Herrera.

Czechoslovakia, 27 May. Tomas Masaryk is elected president; Eduard Benes is foreign minister.

Poland, 28 May. War is declared between Poland and Russia.

Spain, 1 June. The Spanish Communist Party is founded.

Versailles, 4 June. The treaty of Trianon cuts Hungary to a quarter of its former size.

Geneva, 13 June. The International Feminist Congress opens.

The Hague, 16 June. The League of Nations Permanent Court of Justice opens.

Mexico, 8 July. The guerrilla leader Pancho Villa surrenders to the Mexican government.

Syria, 24 July. A French expeditionary force occupies Damascus and the port of Aleppo. Emir Feisal, installed in Damascus by the British three months ago, flees.

London, 31 July. The Communist Party of Great Britain is founded.

France, 10 August. The Ottoman empire signs a peace treaty with the allies at Sevres, confirming the loss to it of 80 per cent of its land.

Geneva, 11 August. The first ecumenical conference is held, bringing together European, US and Eastern churches.

Poland, 16 August. As Russian troops close on Warsaw, US warships are sent to Danzig (*Gdansk*).

Poland, 23 August. With the support of British airmen, the Poles repel the Russian advance on Warsaw.

Near East, 1 September. France proclaims the creation of the state of Lebanon, with the seat of government at Beirut.

India, 10 September. The Indian National Congress votes to adopt Mohandas Gandhi's programme of non-violent non-cooperation with the Indian government.

Latvia, 6 October. Poland and Russia sign an armistice at Riga.

Britain, 7 October. The first 100 women are admitted to Oxford university to study for full degrees.

Russia, 14 October. The *Soviet* government recognises the independence of Finland.

Ireland, October. Riots erupt across the country following the death of the hunger striker Tomas MacSwiney, lord mayor of Cork.

USA, 2 November. Warren Harding, the Republican candidate, is elected president.

Geneva, 13 November. The first full session of the League of Nations opens, attended by 5,000 representatives from 41 countries worldwide.

Dublin, 21 November. Fourteen British officers and officials are killed in their beds by IRA members, setting off a day of violence and killing in Ireland.

Norway, 10 December. Woodrow Wilson, the former US president, is awarded the Nobel peace prize.

Ireland, 11 December. Martial law is declared.

Geneva, 15 December. China and Austria are admitted to the League of Nations.

Geneva, 18 December. Britain and France reach agreement on the frontiers of Syria and Palestine.

London, 23 December. The Government of Ireland Act, providing for the partition of Ireland between south and north, becomes law.

Italy, 31 December. Gabriele d'Annunzio hands over Fiume to Italy.

Somaliland, December. The Somali guerrilla leader Mohammed bin Abdullah (the "Mad *Mullah*") is killed by a chance bomb.

French troops occupy German Ruhr zone

A French tank in the streets of Frankfurt – "making the Germans pay".

Essen, Germany, 7 April
The risk of a dangerous international confrontation increased today when French troops were attacked by angry mobs as they advanced into the major cities of the Ruhr to counter a German breach of the Treaty of Versailles.

A number of people have been killed in skirmishes between German nationalists and French Moroccan soldiers. Student leaders are reported to have climbed onto motor cars to harangue the mobs.

The swift and decisive French move, which began with occupying Frankfurt yesterday, came after German forces had moved into the area in an attempt to block plans by armed communists to seize control of the industrial centre.

The German move, taking its troop levels in the neutral zone above the 40,000 threshold permitted by the Treaty of Versailles, has raised French fears that Germany plans to reoccupy the area. To defuse the situation the German government has sent a telegram to the Allies insisting that the communist threat in the area has become so serious that it could not wait any longer for permission to enter the Ruhr on a temporary basis.

America spurns the League of Nations

Washington, 19 March
President Woodrow Wilson's vision of a league of nations to end wars received a major setback today when the Senate refused to support US membership. Most of the opposition related to Article Ten, under which the US would have to go to war if another member were attacked. But there was also hostility to the voting rules which would give Britain and the dominions six votes.

There has been a long fight over the proposals. A Republican senator, Henry Cabot Lodge, had worked out a compromise solution acceptable to most senators, but Wilson, incapacitated by a stroke, refused to support it.

Mary Pickford, "the World's Sweetheart", founder of United Artists, with Douglas Fairbanks, Charlie Chaplin, D W Griffith.

Victorious allies redraw the map of the world as peace deals carve up empires

Sevres, France, 10 August

The final piece of the jigsaw of the post-war world was completed here today with former territories of the Ottoman empire divided amongst the victorious allies. Peace treaties earlier this year had already redrawn the map of Europe with that at St Germain creating Yugoslavia and Czechoslovakia; it also gave Galicia to Poland, Transylvania to Romania, and Istria, Trentino and South Tyrol to Italy. Agreement at Neuilly saw Greece and Yugoslavia acquire parts of Bulgaria. League of Nations mandates for the future of German colonies have also been agreed.

East Africa goes to Britain; most of the Cameroons to France, which shares Togoland with Britain; the Samoan Islands to New Zealand; and South-West Africa to South Africa. Germany itself was dealt with by the Treaty of Versailles in 1919 which gave territory to France, Denmark, Poland and Lithuania.

Russia's Red Army defeats the Whites

Moscow, 16 November

The bloody and chaotic civil war which has wracked Russia since the October Revolution is effectively over. Bolshevism has triumphed. The last of the "White" generals, Baron Wrangel – who supported the provisional government – has been beaten by Leon Trotsky's Red Army in the Crimea and evacuated with his men to Turkey.

The war has raged with varying fortunes since the winter of 1917-18. At one time communist rule was confined to an area similiar in size to that of the grand princes of Muscovy in the 15th century. The tide turned after Trotsky managed to whip the Red Army into shape, and Allied troops from Britain, Japan, the United States and some other countries had left. The Bolsheviks now control nearly all the former Russian empire with the exception of Poland, Finland, Bessarabia and the Baltic states.

The ultimate Red victory was due to the failure of the Whites to organise the peasants and to unify their aspirations. They also failed to work together. Lenin is now in charge of a poor, battered, starving, bankrupt country. Russia will need time to recover from its wounds.

Brave new world: Lenin addressing the Russian masses while Trotsky looks on.

US drinkers despair as prohibition bites

New York State troopers seizing booze, struggling to enforce the unenforceable.

Washington, DC, 16 January

The United States, the home of the mint julep, the gin sling and plain corn whiskey, has gone permanently on the wagon. And that's official. At one minute past midnight this morning the prohibition of the sale and consumption of alcohol became law, sanctioned under the Volstead Act, which was ratified in January 1919.

The temperance campaigners of the Anti-Saloon League, whose fight against the "demon drink" finds its roots in the sermonising of such 17th-century Puritan divines as Cotton Mather, and in the 19th-century campaigning of Carrie Nation, are jubilant. Their prime motivation has always been to preserve Christianity, even if the hardheaded businessmen whose votes in Congress actually made the law possible were more influenced by fears of the effect of too much liquor on their workforces. Stocks of alcohol have been seized, and a 1,500-strong body of enforcement agents is ensuring that the law sticks.

For those for whom drinking is no more than an admirable social pleasure, prohibition is one more example of the puritanism that has always been central to American life, running paradoxically hand-in-hand with a society that boasts of its devotion to freedom.

Gandhi formulates non-violent plan

Calcutta, September

The Indian National Congress has voted for Mohandas Gandhi's programme of non-cooperation with the British government. The programme, Gandhi told Congress, would win "complete responsible government" within a year.

Mr Gandhi's second victory is in persuading the predominately Hindu Congress Party to work with the Moslem *Khilafatist* movement. Indeed, Gandhi seems to be the only Indian leader capable of uniting the two communities.

An English concert is heard in Europe

Britain, 15 June

The voice of the singer Dame Nellie Melba was heard all over Europe by listeners who have wireless sets. Her voice could even be heard by radio enthusiasts in Newfoundland. It came from a concert promoted by the *Daily Mail* and broadcast by Marconi from its transmitter at Writtle, Chelmsford. The Marconi company obtained a licence for experimental broadcasts last year, but now there are complaints that the new medium should not be used merely for entertainment.

1921 (1921-1922)

Dublin, 22 January 1921. British tanks are sent into Dublin.

Russia, 5 February 1921. Anti-Soviet sailors mutiny at Kronstadt naval base outside Petrograd.

South Africa, 8 February 1921. Jan Smuts is elected prime minister.

Russia, 8 February 1921. Prince Peter Kropotkin, anarchist, dies.

Delhi, 9 February 1921. The new Indian Central Legislature opens.

Paris, 19 February 1921. France signs a military and economic pact with Poland.

Moscow, 26 February 1921. The Soviet government signs treaties respecting the territorial integrity of Persia and Afghanistan.

Germany, 8 March 1921. On account of Germany's failure to give a satisfactory response to demands for war reparations, Allied troops occupy Ruhr towns.

Moscow, 12 March 1921. Lenin announces that state planning of the economy will end and free enterprise will be permitted.

Russia, 17 March 1921. The anti-Bolshevik rebellion in Kronstadt is crushed by Red Army troops.

London, 17 March 1921. Marie Stopes opens Britain's first birth-control clinic.

Britain, 21 March 1921. Austen Chamberlain succeeds Andrew Bonar Law as Conservative leader.

China, 10 April 1921. Sun Yat-sen is elected president.

Sweden, 8 May 1921. Capital punishment is abolished.

Germany, 11 May 1921. Germany finally agrees to pay the war reparations demanded by the Allies.

Egypt, 23 May 1921. British troops are sent in to quell nationalist rioting in Alexandria.

Belfast, 22 June 1921. King George V opens the new Northern Ireland Parliament.

USA, 2 July 1921. President Harding signs a peace decree, formally ending the war with Germany and Austria.

China, 10 July 1921. Mongolia declares its independence as a people's republic, becoming the world's second communist state.

Ireland, 22 July 1921. Eamon de Valera, the president of *Sinn Fein*, agrees to a truce with the British government.

China, 23 July 1921. The first congress of the Chinese Communist Party is held in Shanghai.

Italy, 2 August 1921. The opera singer Enrico Caruso dies.

Ottoman Empire, 5 August 1921. Mustapha Kemal is appointed virtual ruler in the face of a Greek advance.

Baghdad, 23 August 1921. *Emir* Feisal is crowned king of Iraq.

India, 25 August 1921. Over 1,000 people die in riots on the Malabar coast.

Baltic, 22 September 1921. The Baltic states of Latvia, Lithuania and Estonia join the League of Nations.

Czechoslovakia, 26 September 1921. Eduard Benes becomes prime minister.

Berlin, 22 October 1921. The German government resigns as an economic crisis deepens.

Hungary, 25 October 1921. The ex-Emperor Karl is defeated in battle while attempting to regain the Hungarian throne.

Japan, 5 November 1921. Crown Prince Hirohito is made regent on the assassination of the prime minister, Takashi Hara Kei, the head of the first parliamentary government.

India, 17 November 1921. Riots break out in Bombay when Mohandas Gandhi, leader of the Indian Congress Party, burns foreign cloth during a visit by the prince of Wales.

Belfast, 21 November 1921. Troops are sent in to restore order as rioting breaks out in east Belfast.

Kabul, 22 November 1921. Britain signs a treaty recognising the independence of Afghanistan.

Ireland, 6 December 1921. An Anglo-Irish treaty is signed granting 26 counties of Ireland dominion status within the British empire as the Irish Free State.

Washington, DC, 13 December 1921. Britain, France, Japan and the USA sign a treaty aimed at controlling the naval build-up in the Pacific.

Britain, 1921. The novelist D H Lawrence publishes *Women in Love*, a sequel to *The Rainbow*, all copies of which were destroyed for obscenity in 1915.

Britain, 1921. Agatha Christie publishes her first detective novel, *The Mysterious Affair at Styles*.

South Atlantic, 5 January 1922. The British polar explorer Ernest Shackleton dies on the island of South Georgia.

Dublin, 21 January 1922. The *Dail Eireann* approves the treaty with Britain setting up the Irish Free State.

Rome, 22 January 1922. Pope Benedict XV dies.

Frontiers agreed in the Near East

Cairo, March 1921

The spoils of the Ottoman empire have finally been divided up, to the satisfaction of all save those who live there. At a conference chaired by the British colonial secretary, Mr Winston Churchill, and attended by such stars of British Near Eastern policy as T E Lawrence, Arnold Wilson, Sir Percy Cox and Miss Gertrude Bell, France's claims to Lebanon and Syria have been recognised. Iraq is to have Feisal (who led the Arab Revolt, and was expelled from Syria, where he had made himself monarch) as king; Palestine, with its mixture of Arabs, Christians and Jews, is to come under British control.

Whirling blades lift off helicopter

Paris, 18 February 1921

After a decade of experiments a gyroplane, or helicopter, has finally taken off. It is a triumph for its designer, Etienne Oehmichen, who has told the French Academy of Sciences how he built the machine with a light 25 hp motor, the whole structure weighing only 220 pounds (100 kilos). In theory, he says, an 8.5 hp motor can lift 297 pounds (135 kilos).

Other gyroplanes have been built, but they were powered by heavy and cumbersome motors and were only able to hover a few inches above the ground. Oehmichen can lift his machine; however, he has yet to stabilise it.

Italian Fascist chief calls himself "Duce"

Rome, 7 November 1921

A balding, heavily-jowled former editor, Benito Mussolini, declared himself *Il Duce* (the leader) of Italy's Fascists today and told businessmen that they could trust him and his followers to smash communism in the country.

Mussolini, a wartime corporal, has succeeded in uniting right-wing groups into a single force, and his blackshirted Fascists have been hired by businessmen to break up strikes and political meetings.

A one-time ardent socialist himself – he edited the party's paper, *Avanti*, before he was expelled – Mussolini formed his *Fasci di Combattimento* movement in Milan two years ago. Now it has 35 deputies in parliament.

Benito Mussolini: self-styled duce and bulwark against communism.

Spanish are driven from Morocco's Rif

Morocco, 19 September 1921

The Rif is declaring itself a republic. Since July, when 5,000 Rif tribesmen under Abd el Krim and his brother Mhamed inflicted a devastating defeat on a Spanish army at Anual, killing its general, Manuel Silvestre, the Spanish have been driven from all their Moroccan colony except for Tetuan, Chaoun and the coastal enclave of Melilla. The head of the new state is Abd el Krim himself, who has successfully united all the Rif clans against the Spanish. When the war is over he plans to hand over authority to Mhamed, his younger brother.

The el Krim brothers are no simple Berber tribesmen. Abd was educated at the university of Fez and has edited a Spanish Moroccan newspaper; Mhamed is a qualified engineer from the university of Madrid. Now they are Arab heroes, examples to all the oppressed people of the Moslem world, according to the Algerian writer Messali Hadj.

Bolsheviks appeal for aid as famine grips

Furlongs to furrows: a former racecourse is ploughed up to plant food.

Moscow, 4 August 1921
Russia is starving to death. No one can count the victims, but some seven million people may have died from hunger and disease since the Bolshevik Revolution. Vladimir Lenin, the Soviet leader, has admitted that not since 1891 has there been anything like it, and has appealed to the world community.

The worst-hit area is the huge Volga region east of Moscow where people are eating clay and twigs and cannibalism has appeared. Millions of peasants have slaughtered their starving cattle and are fleeing from the area and heading towards the towns to find food. Last year's

drought, which wiped out the harvest, is the immediate cause of the famine, but the effects of the revolution and the civil war have also played a part. There are peasant disturbances, banditry and highway robberies. Lenin has been forced to make a strategic retreat from Marxism and has introduced a "New Economic Policy" restoring private trade and ending the arbitrary seizure of food from the peasants. But it has come too late to deal with the famine.

The United States has responded to Lenin's appeal and 800,000 tons of food are on the way. Food trains should soon reach the Ukraine.

Britain agrees Irish Free State package

London, 7 December 1921
Irish aspirations have at last won expression in a treaty creating an Irish Free State. It incorporates all of Ireland except six northern counties which stay with the UK. This effort to satisfy conflicting wishes of the Catholic majority and the descendants of the Protestants who settled three centuries ago contains an important ambiguity. The partition line is subject to a boundary commission report. Also, a council of Ireland is to discuss eventual reunification, though in time the Catholic birthrate could yield a voting majority in the north.

Germany agrees to pay war reparations

Berlin, 11 May 1921
The risk of a major international crisis over Germany's war debt has been narrowly averted at the last minute today, with the German government agreeing to pay the unpopular war reparations in full.

With only a few hours to go before the expiry of an Allied ultimatum to pay or face reoccupation, right-wing ministers in the coalition government withdrew their threats to resign if reparations were paid. Their resignations would almost certainly have brought the

Weimar government down, precipitating a political crisis.

Anticipating a German refusal to pay, an advance Allied force of British, Belgian and French troops crossed the Ruhr eight weeks ago. The French government, which has spearheaded Allied demands that the Germans pay for war damage, has since mobilised its army for a further advance into the Ruhr.

Under the reparations deal Germany must pay £10 billion in gold over the next 42 years plus a 12.5 per cent tax levied on its exports.

Insulin brings new hope to diabetics

Toronto, Ontario, 1921
A cure for diabetes is in sight. Drs Frederick Banting and Charles Best, working in Toronto, Canada, have succeeded in isolating the natural chemical – insulin – in which diabetics are deficient. With too little or no insulin produced by the pancreas, a person cannot regulate the amount of glucose (sugar) in the blood.

Banting and Best have experimented with insulin production in laboratory animals, and the chemical which they have obtained has a pronounced therapeutic effect on diabetes in other animals.

US forced to set immigration quotas as unemployment soars

Washington, 19 May 1921
New immigration laws announced today lay down quotas limiting the yearly influx to three per cent of each nationality in the US in 1910. This ingenious proposal will favour groups from Britain, Ireland, Germany and Scandinavia, but severely restrict the newer waves from southern Europe and the Orient which have been flooding in much more recently.

Three groups have backed the measures. Organised labour is worried about unemployment; social reformers feel that the problem of the city slums will not be solved if tides of poor illiterates are not curbed; a third group thinks that any nonNordic race is inferior – it wants an absolute ban on Japanese immigration.

Immigration officers on Ellis Island sifting the tired and huddled masses.

Gandhi is jailed for sedition in India

Allahabad, India, 18 March 1922
Mohandas Gandhi, the Congress leader, has been sentenced to six years' imprisonment for sedition. Dressed in a simple loin-cloth and shawl, the British-trained barrister, the veteran of non-violent campaigns in both South Africa and India, pleaded guilty to all charges. Preaching disaffection, he told the judge, has "become almost a passion with me". He would "submit cheerfully to the highest penalty that could be inflicted".

He accepted responsibility for the violent riots in Malabar, Bombay and Chauri-Chaura, but would not renounce his policy of non-cooperation. Non-violence was the first and last article of his faith.

1922 (1922-1923)

Rome, 12 February 1922. Achille Ratti, the archbishop of Milan, is elected pope as Pius XI.

India, 13 February 1922. The Indian National Congress suspends its civil disobedience campaign.

The Hague, 15 February 1922. The Permanent International Court of Justice opens.

Italy, 5 March 1922. Fiume surrenders to the Fascists.

Egypt, 16 March 1922. Egypt formally declares independence under King Fuad.

China, May 1922. Peng Pai, a member of the Chinese Communist Party, begins to organise peasants for revolution in Haifeng, in Guangdong province.

Ireland, 16 June 1922. The pro-treaty party wins the first election in the Irish Free State.

London, 22 June 1922. Sir Henry Wilson, the former chief of the imperial general staff, is shot dead by IRA gunmen.

Berlin, 24 June 1922. Walther Rathenau, the foreign minister, is shot – extreme right-wing nationalists are suspected.

Dublin, 13 July 1922. The Irish Army Council is formed under the leadership of Michael Collins.

Ireland, 21 July 1922. Free State troops capture Waterford and Limerick from anti-Treaty rebels.

Paris, 24 July 1922. The League of Nations Council approves the British mandate in Palestine and the French mandate in Syria.

Italy, 4 August 1922. Mussolini's Fascists, who have already taken Bologna and the areas around Modena and Ferrara, take Milan.

Britain, 13 August 1922. Lord Northcliffe, the pioneer of popular newspapers, dies.

Ireland, 22 August 1922. The Irish nationalist leader Michael Collins is killed during an ambush in Cork. His death follows that of Arthur Griffith, the president of the *Dail Eireann*, last week.

Turkey, 29 August 1922. The Ottomans launch a major offensive against the Greeks to recover land lost after the Great War.

Balkans, August 1922. Rumania, Yugoslavia and Czechoslavakia sign a mutual defence agreement, establishing the "Little *Entente*".

Greece, 9 September 1922. The Greeks are ousted from Smyrna, ending their presence on the eastern Aegean seaboard.

Greece, 26 September 1922. Following the Greek defeat in Turkey, Constantine abdicates. He is succeeded by George II.

Turkey, 11 October 1922. The Ottomans and the Allies sign the treaty of Mudania, recognising Ottoman occupation of eastern Thrace.

London, 11 October 1922. Britain signs a treaty of alliance with Iraq.

Turkey, 15 October 1922. The Greeks sign the Mudania treaty and begin to evacuate Thrace.

Italy, 30 October 1922. Benito Mussolini becomes dictator.

Ottoman Empire, 1 November 1922. Mustapha Kemal abolishes the *sultanate*.

Berlin, 14 November 1922. Joseph Wirth resigns as chancellor over the economic crisis.

London, 14 November 1922. The newly-formed British Broadcasting Company makes its first regular news broadcast by wireless.

Britain, 16 November 1922. The Tories, led by Andrew Bonar Law, win an overall majority of 75 in a general election.

Britain, 21 November 1922. James Ramsay MacDonald is elected leader of the Labour Party.

Berlin, 22 November 1922. Wilhelm Cuno becomes chancellor.

Ottoman Empire, 24 November 1922. Ex-Sultan Abdul Majid II is installed as *caliph*.

Egypt, 26 November 1922. The archaeologists Howard Carter and the earl of Carnarvon uncover the treasures of the Pharoah Tutankhamun, buried 3,000 years ago, near Luxor.

Ireland, 5 December 1922. The Irish Free State is officially proclaimed.

Stockholm, 10 December 1922. The Danish physicist Niels Bohr wins the Nobel prize for physics for his work on atomic structure.

Russia, 30 December 1922. Soviet Russia is renamed the Union of Soviet Socialist Republics (USSR).

Paris, 1922. The bookseller Sylvia Beach brings out a limited edition of a novel by James Joyce entitled *Ulysses*, banned in the USA and Britain for obscenity.

China, 1 January 1923. The Haifeng Federation of Peasant Unions is inaugurated by Peng Pai.

Germany, 11 January 1923. In response to the German default in payment of reparations, French and Belgian troops occupy Essen.

China, 26 January 1923. A policy of cooperation (united front) between Chinese nationalists and communists is announced.

Germany, 27 January 1923. The National Socialist (*Nazi*) Party holds its first rally in Munich.

Broadcasting station opens in London

Lauritz Melchior, the Wagnerian tenor, broadcasting on 2LO from London.

London, 15 November 1922
The London broadcasting station, 2LO, went on the air yesterday for the first time as the British Broadcasting Company. A news bulletin was read by Arthur Burrows of the Marconi company from Marconi House in the Strand.

The Marconi company had been putting out weekly trial broadcasts since May, as had another station at Writtle, Chelmsford, run by Captain Peter Eckersley. Now the General Post Office (GPO) has decreed the formation of a single British Broadcasting Company as a consortium of wireless equipment manufacturers, to avoid the confusion that has arisen in America, where there are 500 rival stations. Today the BBC opens transmissions from Manchester and Birmingham. It hopes soon to broadcast for four hours a day, with news, talks and concerts.

John Reith, an engineer from Aberdeen, has been appointed general manager of the company, which is to be financed by the sale by the GPO of ten-shilling licences for the right to operate a receiver. For those who do not feel up to making their own crystal set, with "cat's whisker", the BBC offers sets at between £2 to £4, including headphones.

Beijing falls as war lords clash in China

Beijing, 28 April 1922
The Manchurian warlord Zhang Zuolin has been decisively beaten in battle today by his rival, Wu Peifu, and his army is retreating north in disorder leaving Wu Peifu firmly in control of Beijing.

In the chaos that rules in China this is more than just another fracas between warlords, for Wu Peifu is allied to Dr Sun Yat-sen who has returned from exile in Japan and set up his power base in the south, especially in the Guangzhou (Canton) area. An additional complication is that Zhang is paid by the Japanese while Wu Peifu is the pawn of Britain and the United States.

Modern art arrives in South America

Sao Paulo, Brazil, February 1922
A deliberately outrageous exhibition of contemporary Brazilian art has shock Brazil's conservatives. The exhibition is the centrepiece for Sao Paulo's Modern Art Week: a festival of art exhibitions, concerts and poetry readings – which few Brazilians understand. Many of the paintings – if they can be called that – are by women, for example Anita Malfatti and Tarsila do Amaral, who take their Dadaist and Cubist perspectives from Paris and their revolutionary politics from Mexico. Needless to say, thanks to the wealth of their parents, they can afford to visit both places.

Mussolini marches into power in Italy

Rome, 30 October 1922
Singing the anthem *Giovinezza* (*Youth*), 30,000 blackshirted members of Benito Mussolini's Fascist movement marched from Naples to Rome today to force the government to resign and make way for their leader as dictator of Italy. Soon afterwards *Il Duce* himself arrived in an open car provided by King Victor Emmanuel – who has long feared a communist revolution in Italy.

The weak government was helpless, especially when it became clear that the Fascists would hold the balance of power. The sight of so many young men in Fascist uniforms was enough to make deputies surrender.

"Blackshirts" have carried on a vicious street war with communists and socialists for the past three years; now their leader proposes to introduce a new electoral law which limits the voters' choice to Fascist candidates. He has already threatened a ruthless campaign to extinguish left-wing parties – several of whose leaders have already fled. Mussolini proposes a

Marching on Rome: Mussolini and his Fascist leaders – who came by car.

corporate state in which private enterprise and state-managed industry could co-exist, with labour courts taking the place of strikes and lock-outs.

He is also going to institute a welfare programme with old age pensions and holidays provided for workers, if they are Fascists. As Mussolini stood with the king on the balcony of the Quirinal palace tonight, he brandished the party symbol – an axe surrounded by a bundle of rods. It is called a *fasces* and was once carried before the magistrates of ancient Rome.

British coalition government breaks up

London, 19 October 1922
David Lloyd George, Britain's prime minister for the past six years, was driven to Buckingham Palace today to tender his resignation to the king. The coalition government collapsed when Tories, meeting in the Carlton Club, voted by 187 to 87 to withdraw support for the fiery Welshman, who had wanted a vote to prolong the coalition and instead found himself with one to end it.

With most of his cabinet resigning around him, Lloyd George had no alternative but to resign. His principal supporter is Austen Chamberlain, the leader of the Tory Party, but he, too, he has been ousted – disowned by his former supporters. Many Conservatives have long distrusted Lloyd George and his idiosyncratic style of government. Stanley Baldwin, the president of the board of trade, is an archenemy, and it was his speech at the Carlton Club that swayed many MPs and peers against the coalition. Lloyd George, he said, was

David Lloyd George, the Welsh wizard who is running out of party tricks.

threatening to split the Tory Party – just as he had almost wrecked the Liberals when he split with Asquith.

The king has invited Andrew Bonar Law to form a new government. He has agreed, but insists on a Tory vote of confidence.

Joyce and Eliot give new life to words

London, 1 October 1922
A new literary magazine, *The Criterion*, contains a long poem by its editor, the American T S Eliot (who works in a City bank), entitled *The Waste Land*. It has been greeted as "incomprehensible" and "a literary game" because of its many allusions to other poets, like Dante and Shakespeare, and to the *Upanishads* alongside Cockneyisms, the whole calling up a spiritual desert.

Another obscure publication this year is the novel *Ulysses*, banned from Britain and the US for "immorality" — 500 copies were destroyed by the US Post Office. Its author, James Joyce, is a Dubliner; he has lived abroad since 1904, but his book is impregnated with his native city. The events of the *Odyssey* are paralleled by the doings of Leopold Bloom on a single June day in 1904. The characters' thoughts occur in "interior monologues" like Mrs Bloom's long soliloquy which closes the book.

Family planning pioneer awarded libel damages

London, 1923
The ethics of sex education and contraception were brought into question during the recent nine-day libel case between Dr Marie Stopes and Dr Halliday Sutherland. She objected to his allegations that her birth control campaign encourages women's immorality and that she uses the poor as guinea pigs for her contraceptive experiments. Dr Stopes won and was awarded £100 in damages – despite a ruthless cross-examination by the defence and a summing-up from the judge which described as "obscene" her book *Married Love*. Her first clinic opened last year.

The birth control pioneer Marie Stopes and her three-month-old son.

Roentgen, X-ray pioneer, has died

Germany, 1923
The death has been announced, at the age of 77, of Wilhelm Roentgen, the German scientist and medical researcher who received the first Nobel prize for physics in 1901. Roentgen's name is synonymous with the now widespread use of so-called X-rays to examine the internal state of a body without the need for surgical intervention. These rays enable the doctor to study broken bones (which are denser than soft tissue) and patches of infection in the lungs, for instance.

1923 (1923-1924)

USSR, 9 March 1923. Vladimir Lenin retires from the Bolshevik leadership after a stroke.

India, 24 March 1923. The salt tax is restored.

Paris, 26 March 1923. The French actress Sarah Bernhardt dies.

Germany, 31 March 1923. Rioting Germans at the Krupps work at Essen in the French-occupied Ruhr are shot by French troops.

Paris, 13 April 1923. Madame Alfred Mortier is the first woman admitted to the Academie Francaise.

London, 28 April 1923. The Empire Stadium at Wembley stages its first sporting spectacular – the FA Cup Final.

Britain, 8 May 1923. Jack Hobbs, the Surrey and England batsman, scores his 100th century in first-class cricket.

Britain, 21 May 1923. Stanley Baldwin becomes Conservative prime minister on the resignation of Andrew Bonar Law.

France, 26 May 1923. The first 24-hour Le Mans Grand Prix is won by the Frenchmen Lagache and Leonard.

Britain, 7 June 1923. The Federation of British Industries is granted a royal charter.

Bulgaria, 9 June 1923. Alexander Stambouliski, the leader of the Peasant Party, is replaced as prime minister by Alexander Zankoff in an army *coup d'etat*.

Germany, 22 June 1923. The *mark* is trading at 622,000 to the pound sterling, having lost nearly half its remaining value since the start of the month.

Britain, 6 July 1923. Suzanne Lenglen of France wins the ladies' singles tennis championship at Wimbledon for the fifth successive year.

London, 18 July 1923. The Matrimonial Causes Bill, allowing wives to divorce their husbands for adultery, becomes law.

Mexico, 20 July 1923. Pancho Villa, the revolutionary turned rancher, is shot dead by gunmen.

Switzerland, 24 July 1923. Turkey, Greece and the Allies sign the treaty of Lausanne, whereby Armenia and territories in the Aegean lost after the Great War are restored to Turkey.

USA, 2 August 1923. Vice-president Calvin Coolidge succeeds to the presidency following the sudden death of Warren Harding.

Berlin, 12 August 1923. Chancellor Cuno resigns as the German economy collapses. Gustav Stresemann takes over.

Spain, 13 September 1923. Army officers led by Miguel Primo de Rivera and backed by King Alfonso XIII seize power.

Geneva, 10 September 1923. The Irish Free State is admitted to the League of Nations.

Germany, 26 September 1923. President Friedrich Ebert declares a state of emergency throughout the country.

Palestine, 29 September 1923. The British mandate officially begins.

Germany, 30 September 1923. Dr von Karr, the newly appointed dictator of Bavaria, imposes martial law on the province.

Rhodesia, 10 October 1923. Rhodesia (*Zimbabwe*), previously British South African Company administered, becomes a self-governing British colony.

Turkey, 12 October 1923. The Turkish capital is moved from Istanbul to Ankara.

Germany, 13 October 1923. With the approval of the *reichstag*, the government assumes dictatorial powers.

Germany, 20 October 1923. Bavaria breaks off relations with the *reich*.

Germany, 21 October 1923. A republic is declared in the Rhineland.

Germany, 27 October 1923. French troops occupy the Rhineland areas of Bonn and Wiesbaden.

Turkey, 29 October 1923. Mustapha Kemal proclaims Turkey a republic and himself its first president.

USA, October 1923. Albert Fall, the secretary of the interior, is implicated in the Teapot Dome oilfield-leasing scandal.

Berlin, 15 November 1923. A loaf of bread costs 200 billion marks.

Britain, 25 November 1923. The first transatlantic wireless broadcast to the USA is made.

Berlin, 29 November 1923. Dr Wilhelm Marx succeeds Stresemann as chancellor.

Stockholm, 10 December 1923. The Irish poet W B Yeats wins the Nobel prize for literature.

Britain, 11 December 1923. A general election results in a hung parliament.

Germany, 9 January 1924. Herr Heinz, the leader of the "Rhineland republic", is assassinated.

China, 20 January 1924. The first congress of the *Guomindang* (Nationalist Party) approves the "united front" of communists and nationalists.

Earthquake razes Tokyo

Tokyo in ruins, following the worst earthquake that Japan has ever experienced.

Tokyo, 1 September 1923
The Japanese capital, Tokyo, was devastated today by the worse earthquake that Japan has ever experienced. Half a million of Tokyo's houses have been destroyed, a million of its people made homeless, and 132,807 killed.

Towns and cities for hundreds of miles around have been levelled, including Yokohama, while the Fukuro, Chiyo and Takimi rivers have burst their banks, bringing the total number of dead to over 300,000, with 2.5 million homeless. In Tokyo – where martial law has been declared – and Yokohama essential services such as water and hospitals no longer exist, and there are fears of cholera and starvation.

Ku Klux Klan claims a million members

Baltimore, 30 June 1923
The Ku Klux Klan, notorious for its white hoods and flaming torches carried through the night to harass Negroes, Jews, Catholics and even any foreigners, now claims one million members. Its strength lies in the south; it was founded after the Negro slaves won their freedom in the civil war. It soon degenerated into anti-Negro terrorism and was disbanded in 1869. Revived in 1915, it has gradually widened its targets to include anyone who is not white and Protestant. The new imperial wizard is a dentist, Hiram Evans, who even opposes foreign alliances.

A Ku Klux Klan get-together in Georgia, articulating "poor white" fears.

Germany groans under crippling inflation

Clerks picking up their firms' wages from a Berlin bank in laundry baskets.

Berlin, 15 November 1923
In a desperate effort to rescue the country from raging inflation, the *Reichsbank* has invented a new German mark. It is to be called a *rentenmark* and will be tied to the country's real estate. Each rentenmark will be worth a trillion existing marks.

Since the beginning of the year inflation has spiralled out of control. In January a loaf of bread cost 250 marks – still high, compared with 63 *pfennigs* in 1918 – and by July it had reached 3,465. By this month the cost of the loaf had soared to 201,000,000,000 marks. A US dollar is worth four trillion marks

– if you can find anyone who will sell a dollar. The pound sterling buys 20 trillion marks.

In effect, German money is now worthless; barter is increasingly being adopted for trading goods and services, and middle-class families who kept their wealth in banks have been wiped out.

The government cannot escape blame. When French and Belgian troops occupied the Ruhr in order to enforce war reparations, the Germans encouraged resistance and printed marks in limitless numbers to finance the fight, though industry was crippled and unable to produce the wealth.

Chinese gang seize 300 train hostages

China, 6 May 1923
Bandits swooped on the luxurious "Blue Express" at Lincheng last night. They killed an American who resisted, derailed the train, and then marched some 300 hostages, including a number of wealthy foreigners, to their impregnable hideout on top of Mount Baozigu.

The bandits, numbering around 1,000, are ex-soldiers from the disbanded army of a defeated warlord. They made an extraordinary sight hustling their captives away. They had looted the train, even taking mattresses from the sleeping berths. One man had a brassiere tied round his waist, using the cups to carry his loot. Their demands are awaited.

National hero leads Turkish republic

Turkey, 29 October 1923
Turkey, once the figurehead of the Ottoman empire, was proclaimed a republic today. Mustapha Kemal, under whose astute military leadership the Turks successfully expelled a Greek invasion, and who fought successfully for Turkish territory at the Lausanne conference, is to be the first president.

The Ottoman empire, which backed Germany in the Great War, was deprived of 80 per cent of its possessions in 1920. In his unyielding struggle to hold on to territories in which Turks formed a majority, the new president established himself as a national hero. His new post comes as a fitting reward.

Greece deposes its king, democratically

Athens, 25 March 1924
King George II of Greece was deposed today, voted out of office by the nation's parliament. Few were surprised: so unpopular was the — king that he was forced to flee into exile last year, making his home in Rumania, the country of his wife, Queen Elizabeth.

George is the fourth successive Greek monarch to gain and then prematurely lose power since 1913, when George I was assassinated. The pro-German Constantine was forced to abdicate in 1917, and

Alexander died of a monkey bite. Monarchy as an institution may well not survive in Greece. The people are determinedly republican at the moment, and crowds celebrated in the streets as they heard the news of George's deposition.

A referendum on the monarchy will follow soon, and the whole population will be given the chance to decide whether it wants yet more kings. Given the current mood, it seems unlikely. In the meantime Admiral Konduriotis is acting as regent.

Agitator starts revolution in beer cellar

Munich, 12 November 1923
A gang of men wearing brown shirts burst into a *bierkeller* (beercellar) here today. Its leader, a man with a toothbrush moustache, leapt on to a chair and fired a shot into the air. "The national revolution has begun!" he shouted.

The man has been identified as Adolf Hitler, the leader of the National Socialist (or *Nazi*) Party which is demanding dictatorship for the whole of Germany. In his harangue to an eager crowd Hitler called on people to march with him to Berlin.

He produced as his star supporter a somewhat reluctant Field-Marshal Erich von Ludendorff, the war hero.

Hitler, on parade before his bierkeller coup, with his "flag of blood".

"Element Mecanique" by Fernand Leger: an example of the abstract art which is developing, of which Pablo Picasso is a leading proponent.

Moscow, 22 January 1924. A council is appointed to succeed Lenin: Gregory Zinoviev, Leon Kamenev and Joseph Stalin.

USSR, 26 January 1924. Petrograd is renamed Leningrad.

Rome, 27 January 1924. Mussolini signs a pact with Yugoslavia, annexing the free city of Fiume.

Rome, 27 January 1924. Mussolini dissolves the chamber of deputies.

Britain, 1 February 1924. Britain recognises the USSR.

India, 4 February 1924. Mohandas Gandhi is released from prison.

Italy, 7 February 1924. Italy recognises the USSR.

New York City, 12 February 1924. *Rhapsody in Blue* for jazz band and piano, by George Gershwin, is performed for the first time.

Ankara, 3 March 1924. Mustapha Kemal, Turkey's secular nationalist leader, who saved Turkey from Greek invasion, abolishes the *caliphate*.

Cairo, 15 March 1924. The first Egyptian parliament is opened.

Washington, DC, 28 March 1924. Harry Daugherty, the attorney-general, resigns in the Teapot Dome oilfield-leasing scandal.

Britain, March 1924. The airline Imperial Airways begins operation.

Germany, 1 April 1924. Adolf Hitler is jailed for five years for his abortive Munich beer-hall *putsch*.

Hollywood, USA, 16 April 1924. The new Metro-Goldwyn-Mayer film corporation is formed by merger.

Germany, 16 April 1924. Germany agrees to a new war reparations plan, drawn up by the American banker Charles Dawes.

Italy, 17 April 1924. Mussolini's fascist party wins a sweeping electoral victory.

Britain, 23 April 1924. King George V opens the British Empire Exhibition at Wembley Stadium.

April, 24 April 1924. Britain recognises the Greek republic.

India, April 1924. An epidemic of plague has claimed 25,000 victims.

Berlin, 6 June 1924. The *reichstag* votes in favour of the Dawes plan.

France, 13 June 1924. Gaston Doumergue is elected president.

South Africa, 17 June 1924. Jan Smuts loses his seat as nationalists win the general election.

Paris, July 1924. At the Olympic Games, Harold Abrahams and Eric Liddell triumph for Britain; while Paavo Nurmi, the "Flying Finn", wins five golds.

Germany, 17 August 1924. Following the signature by Germany and the Allies of the protocol on German war reparations, French and Belgian troops withdraw from the Ruhr.

USSR, 16 September 1924. The government quells a revolt in the southern republic of Georgia.

Britain, 9 October 1924. The minority Labour government falls after losing a vote of censure.

France, 12 October 1924. The author Anatole France dies.

Arabia, 20 October 1924. Having forced the abdication of Hussein, king of the Arabs since 1916, Wahabi forces under ibn Saud enter Mecca.

London, 24 October 1924. The foreign office publishes the "Zinoviev letter", allegedly from Moscow, urging a revolution in Britain.

France, 28 October 1924. France recognises the USSR.

Britain, 31 October 1924. The Tories win a huge victory in a general election following the scare over the Zinoviev letter.

USA, 4 November 1924. Calvin Coolidge is returned to the presidency.

Rome, 12 November 1924. Mussolini opens Italy's new one-chamber parliament.

Cairo, 19 November 1924. Sir Lee Stack, the governor general of the Sudan, is shot dead by Egyptians.

Cairo, 24 November 1924. Zaghlol Pasha resigns as prime minister after refusing to apologise to Britain for the death of Stack.

Moscow, 26 November 1924. A special session of the Communist Party called by Stalin, Zinoviev and Kamenev denounces Trotsky.

Germany, 20 December 1924. Adolf Hitler is freed on parole after serving just eight months of his jail term for treason.

Albania, 24 December 1924. Albania is declared a republic.

Britain, 1924. The novelist E M Forster publishes *A Passage to India*.

Norway, 1 January 1925. The capital, Christiania, is renamed Oslo.

Rome, 5 January 1925. Having assumed full dictatorial powers, Mussolini forms a new cabinet.

Germany, 15 January 1925. Hans Luther, an independent, becomes chancellor.

Turkey, 30 January 1925. Constantine II, the Greek Orthodox patriarch, is expelled from Istanbul.

Socialist government comes to Britain

Ramsay MacDonald, the new Labour prime minister, with his supporters.

London, 22 January 1924
James Ramsay MacDonald, a weaver's son from Scotland, emerged through the gates of Buckingham Palace today as the first Labour prime minister of Great Britain. MacDonald will head a minority government which will depend on Liberal MPs for support. Few believe that any of Labour's socialist policies can be implemented.

MacDonald has named mass unemployment as his government's principal target. An ambitious slum-clearance and house-building programme will also be introduced.

The new prime minister has been forced to deliver powerful lectures to left-wingers in the Labour Party, many of whom were prepared to oppose his decision to accept power on these terms. Some of them were demanding salary cuts for cabinet members. MacDonald dismissed the notion. He had good reason to: unlike previous prime ministers, he and his family are poor, and when the MacDonalds moved into 10 Downing Street tonight they had no more than a few scraps of furniture. "We are camping out in one room while the country's destiny is being decided in the cabinet room next door," his daughter told friends. The ministry of works is helping out.

Gandhi goes on a hunger strike

Allahabad, 18 September 1924
Mohandas Gandhi, serving six years' imprisonment for sedition, is to fast for 21 days. He calls the fast "an effective prayer to Hindus and Moslems not to commit suicide".

The announcement comes after days of communal rioting between the two communities. Hundreds have been killed and driven from their homes. Even as he spoke, Moslems and Hindus were being killed in Kohat. A pacifist and believer in universal toleration, he speaks sadly of his "unbearable hopelessness".

Big socialist murals brighten Mexico

Mexico City, 1924
The public buildings of Mexico City are being transformed by the Mexican artist Diego Rivera, lately returned from painting in Paris. A massive man, over six feet, weighing 21 stone, he works on a massive scale in fresco. His murals commissioned for the new ministry of education cover over 1,900 square yards with scenes of peasants and revolutionaries. His best-known mural, *The Distribution of Land to the Peasants*, is inspired, like all his work, by passionate Socialism.

Lenin, Soviet Russia's founder, dies

Moscow, 21 January 1924
The middle-class lawyer who made a revolution on behalf of workers and peasants died today after a series of debilitating strokes. Vladimir Ilyich Ulyanov, who called himself Lenin, was 54.

His death sets the stage for a power struggle in the six-year-old Soviet state. Leon Trotsky, the spellbinding visionary who created the Red Army, is mistrusted for his very brilliance. The Communist Party general secretary, Joseph Stalin, seems certain to make a bid for power, even though Lenin warned against his bullying ways.

Lenin, the third of five sons of a schools' director in Simbirsk, on the Volga, took up revolution after his brother Alexander was executed for his part in the attempted assassination of Czar Alexander III. Exiled to Siberia for subversive activities, Lenin met and married Krupskaya, an idealistic social worker. They lived abroad for much of their life. In London, Lenin spent his time studying in the British Museum library. After the 1917 seizure of power, he nationalised all business and industry, shops, banks and agriculture. In the summer of 1921, when the Russian economy had ground to a halt, Lenin produced the New Economic Policy, allowing private trade in goods and farm produce; rationing was abandoned and workers were paid by results. He denied that he was giving up socialism. "It's two steps forward, one step back," he said.

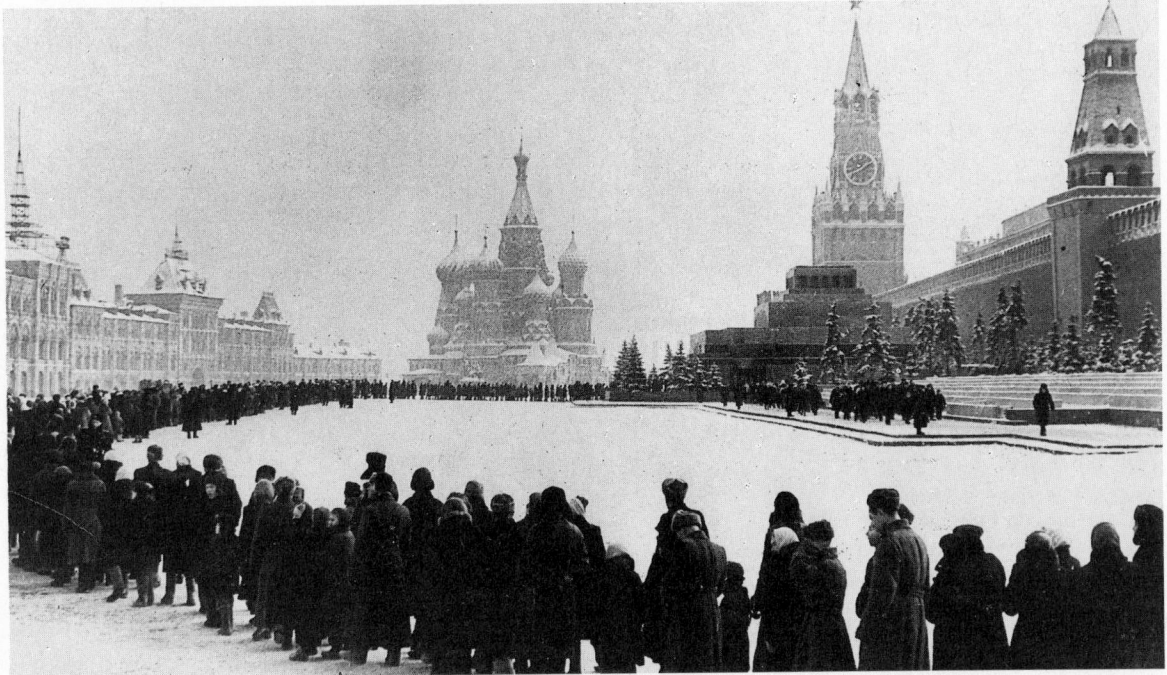
Russians queuing for hours outside the Kremlin, to file past the body of Lenin, the father of the Russian revolution.

China's nationalists seek Russian help

China, 20 January 1924
Sun Yat-sen's Nationalist Party, or *Guomindang*, opened its first congress at Guangzhou (Canton) today. Dr Sun, disappointed by the warlords and refused support by the western powers, has turned to the Soviet Union for help.

The Bolsheviks have sent one of their top agents, Michael Borodin, to advise Dr Sun, and such is his influence that he is reputed to have drafted the Guomindang's constitution. Among the moves agreed is that the Chinese Communist Party will join the Nationalists to form a "united front".

Winter sports get Olympic treatment

Chamonix, 31 January 1924
The first series of winter sports competitions sanctioned by the International Olympic Committee finished here, in this French Alpine resort, today.

So great was the opposition to the committee's decision that the week-long contests have yet to be given the official title of "Olympic Games", but every sport drew top-class performances from the competing teams. Sportsmen, and a few women, from 18 nations took part, notably the Norwegian Thorlief Haug, the master of cross-country ski-ing, and the Finn Clas Thunberg, an outstanding skater.

Italian Fascists kill Socialist opponent

Rome, 10 June 1924
Few people dare to speak their minds freely in Mussolini's Italy. One man did last week: a deputy in the Chamber, Giacomo Matteotti, who denounced the Fascists and the atmosphere of terror in which they conducted the elections. He gave details of the extent of the frauds used to obtain huge Fascist majorities, and demanded that the elections be declared void. At the end of a passionate speech he told deputies: "And now get ready for my funeral." He knew. He was abducted in the street today, and is assumed to have been murdered.

Britain plans naval base in Far East

Singapore, 19 March 1925
Britain is to reinforce its network of strategic links with the empire with the establishment of a major new naval base at Singapore.

The proposed £400,000 base, incorporating a huge floating dock seized from Germany, will serve as a vital supply and maintenance centre for the Royal Navy in the Far East, securing vital links with Hong Kong and other British possessions in the Pacific.

Many MPs, led by the Labour Party leader Ramsay MacDonald, are concerned that Japan will see the new base as a threat.

Soldier's tale is a musical milestone

Vienna, 1925
Alban Berg, the Austrian composer, has opened new musical horizons with his latest opera *Wozzeck*, premiered this year in Berlin. The three-act tale of a soldier's downfall shows just how expressive the new "dissonant" music can be. It is a powerful work, with styles ranging from cafe music to crunching counterpoint, and passages harking back to Mahler. Berg, like his fellow-Austrian Anton von Webern, is an old pupil of Arnold Schoenberg, the man who pioneered "atonal" music – music without keys – in 1908.

Ski-jumping from Tullin Tarns during the first winter Olympic Games.

Germany, 14 February 1925. The state of emergency and ban on the *Nazi* Party is lifted in Bavaria.

Austria, 2 March 1925. A new currency is introduced, the *schilling*.

China, 12 March 1925. On the death of Sun Yat-sen, Chiang Kai-shek becomes leader of the *Guomindang* (Nationalist Party).

Austria, 30 March 1925. Rudolf Steiner, the founder of "anthroposophy", dies.

Australia, 8 April 1925. The government announces a scheme to encourage large-scale immigration.

Britain, 14 April 1925. The American-born painter John Singer Sargent dies.

Turkey, 16 April 1925. A Kurdish uprising against the government of Mustapha Kemal is quelled.

Morocco, 23 April 1925. Troops of the rebel Rif leader Abd el Krim enter French Morocco.

Germany, 25 April 1925. Paul von Hindenburg becomes Germany's first directly elected president.

Britain, 28 April 1925. Winston Churchill, chancellor, puts Britain on the gold standard.

Britain, 30 April 1925. The Distillers whisky group is formed.

Paris, April 1925. The Exposition des Arts Decoratifs reflects the growing popularity of "Art Deco".

Cyprus, 1 May 1925. The island becomes a British colony.

South Africa, 8 May 1925. Afrikaans is made an official language of the Union.

China, 30 May 1925. British police kill demonstrators protesting at working conditions in Japanese-owned factories in Shanghai's international settlement.

Detroit, 6 June 1925. Walter P Chrysler founds the Chrysler Motor Company.

Greece, 25 June 1925. General Theodoros Pangalos seizes power in a *coup d'etat*.

South Africa, 29 June 1925. A law is passed further excluding Blacks, Coloureds (people of mixed race) and Indians from all skilled jobs.

China, June 1925. The "30 May incident" leads to protests in Hankou and Guangzhou – foreign troops kill more demonstrators.

China, 1 July 1925. The Nationalists begin a "northern expedition" to reunify China.

Britain, 31 July 1925. The government agrees to pay a subsidy to coal-mine owners in order to end a month-long strike in the pits.

Washington, DC, 8 August 1925. The first national congress of the Ku Klux Klan opens.

Britain, 18 August 1925. The Surrey batsman Jack Hobbs surpasses W G Grace's record of 126 centuries in top-class cricket.

Rome, 20 August 1925. Rome's first underground rail line opens.

China, 7 September 1925. Anti-British rioters are shot in Shanghai.

Switzerland, 16 October 1925. Germany signs a mutual security pact with Britain, France, Belgium and Italy at Locarno. The pact also affirms the postwar frontiers set out in the Versailles Treaty and accepts Rhineland demilitarisation.

Paris, 28 October 1925. Paul Painleve forms a left-wing cabinet.

Persia, 31 October 1925. Reza Khan deposes *Shah* Ahmed Mirza, ending the Kajar dynasty.

USSR, 6 November 1925. Kliment Voroshilov is chosen to succeed Trotsky as head of the Red Army.

Germany, 9 November 1925. The Nazi *Schutzstaffel* (Protection Squad), or SS, is founded.

Paris, 14 November 1925. The first Surrealist exhibition opens. Artists exhibiting include Max Ernst, Paul Klee, Joan Miro and Picasso.

Paris, 28 November 1925. Following the resignation of Paul Painleve, Aristide Briand forms his eighth ministry.

London, 3 December 1925. Stanley Baldwin, the prime minister, signs an agreement fixing the frontier between Northern Ireland and the Irish Free State.

Stockholm, 10 December 1925. The Irish writer G B Shaw wins the Nobel prize for literature.

California, 12 December 1925. The first "motel" in the USA opens in San Luis Obispo.

USSR, 21 December 1925. *Battleship Potemkin*, a film by Sergei Eisenstein, opens.

Britain, 1925. The "Charleston", the dance that scandalised America, takes Britain by storm.

London, 1925. A surgeon, Henry Souttar, performs the first surgical operation inside the heart.

Germany, 6 January 1926. The airline *Lufthansa* is founded.

Paris, 12 January 1926. The Pasteur Institute announces the discovery of an anti-tetanus serum.

Berlin, 10 January 1926. Fritz Lang's film *Metropolis* opens.

Germany, 30 January 1926. British troops end a seven-year occupation of the Rhineland.

Three million dead in Chinese famine

China, 1925

Famine, the perennial scourge of China, is once again ravaging this vast country which is in turn both bountiful and cruel. This year it is Szechuan's turn to suffer. The crops have failed in the rich plain along the capricious Yangzi, and some three million people have already starved to death.

The villages present dreadful scenes, with bodies lying unburied in the streets, torn by dogs and crows and, sometimes, with pieces hacked off them by starving relatives turned cannibal. Many once prosperous communities are deserted. Their inhabitants have fled in a great migration to the virgin lands of Manchuria in search of food and security – for it is not only the failure of their crops which has brought death to them, but also the anarchy which covers the land.

Rival armies march across the fields, destroying, looting and killing. Peasants turned brigands take what is left. The misery of the innocent people is heartbreaking to see.

Genesis view triumphs in "monkey trial"

Scopes arriving at the Tennessee court room with Clarence Darrow (right).

Dayton, Tennessee, 21 July 1925

The "monkey trial", which has brought the world's press crowding into the tiny courtroom here, ended today with victory for the religious fundamentalists. A biology teacher, John Scopes, was found guilty of teaching evolution in a state school and fined $100. He is expected to appeal to the state's supreme court.

Scopes was accused of violating a law passed by the Tennessee legislature earlier this year banning the teaching of theories denying the divine creation of man as told in the Bible. The indictment charged that he "did teach thereof that man has descended from a lower order of animals".

The trial was a battle royal. Prosecuting was William Jennings Bryan, a spell-binding orator and former Democratic candidate for president. Leading for the defence was Clarence Darrow of Chicago, one of the finest lawyers in the country. Outside the court hundreds of fundamentalists cheered, sang hymns and prayed for a favourable verdict.

Bryan ridiculed Darwin's theory of human descent from monkeys. Darrow challenged him. "The creation might have been going on for a long time?" he asked. "It might have continued for millions of years," Bryan admitted. But the judge stressed that the schoolroom was the place in which to teach discipline, restraint and character, not to violate the laws. At one point he himself read the creation story from Genesis. On another occasion he adjourned the court after gales of laughter had greeted Bryan's attempts to advocate biblical truth.

Trotsky falls from grace

Commissar of War, Leon Trotsky, addressing Red soldiers before being ousted.

Moscow, 16 January 1925
Leon Trotsky, who played a leading role in organising and carrying out the Bolshevik Revolution, has been ousted from leadership in the Soviet Communist Party by Joseph Stalin, his deadly rival. Trotsky has been sacked as commissar for war and is effectively under house arrest. The *Cheka* security police, which are under Stalin's control, have rounded up hundreds of Trotsky's allies and bundled them off into exile in remote areas of Russia.

Trotsky's position in the ruling *Politburo* has been growing steadily weaker since the death of Lenin last year, and he is the first major victim of the power struggle that followed.

It is inconceivable that he will ever be able to make a comeback.

Trotsky, an intellectual who has lived most of his life outside Russia, has emerged as too individualistic and restless to be a good politician. He has certainly proved himself to be no match at all for Stalin, the Georgian who became the party secretary in 1922 and had consolidated his grasp on the party apparatus before Lenin's death.

In the inter-party struggle Stalin cleverly allied himself with the leading Bolsheviks Zinoviev and Kamenev to defeat Trotsky, using the slogan of "building socialism at first in one country" to counter Trotsky's call for "permanent revolution".

Hitler tells his tale in "Mein Kampf"

Munich, Germany, 1925
Adolf Hitler, whose *putsch* with Field-Marshal von Ludendorff ended ignominiously in 1923, has written a book. Most was written in the Landsberg fortress, dictated to his cellmate Rudolph Hess.

It is not easy to read. Like James Joyce's *Ulysses*, it needs to be read twice. Hitler writes of the cleansing nature of war, blames Germany's defeat on Jews and communists, and glorifies Germany's ancient myths. The book is called *Four and a Half Years of Struggle against Lies, Stupidity and Cowardice*. Friends suggested he shorten the title to *Mein Kampf* (My Struggle).

Ibn Saud proclaims rule from Riyadh

Mecca, 8 January 1926
All the *sheikhs*, merchant princes and *imams* of the Hejaz gathered in the Grand Mosque today to witness a ceremony honouring Abdul Aziz ibn Saud as king of the Hejaz – which he proposes to rename Saudi Arabia.

Having set out from exile in Kuwait 24 years ago to capture his home city of Riyadh, ibn Saud reached the pinnacle of power last month when he arrived in Jeddah in triumph to accept the city's surrender. His traditional enemy, Hussein, the sheikh of Mecca, had already abdicated, and was followed into exile by his son Ali.

Jazz Age inhabits a nightmare castle and a sanatorium with art deco style

Novelists of the 1920s: F Scott Fitzgerald, Franz Kafka and E M Forster.

The distinctive tone of the Twenties can now be heard in its literature. F Scott Fitzgerald has become a symbol of what he christened "the Jazz Age", which "raced along under its own power served by great filling stations full of money". *The Great Gatsby* is about an American dream soured by money. A fellow American, Ernest Hemingway, has cultivated the style of a camera shutter, deliberately withholding warmth in his his novel of Americans in Europe, *The Sun Also Rises*.

The European novel has also changed. Works of Franz Kafka, an insurance official in Prague, have been published posthumously against his instructions. They take their readers into a waking nightmare in *The Trial* and *The Castle*, symbols of an alienating and hostile system. Thomas Mann has set *The Magic Mountain* in a sanatorium, his characters decaying as the world outside goes mad.

In *A Passage to India*, the English novelist E M Forster has discomfited many by describing Anglo-Indian relations very differently from Kipling. The new voice of Virginia Woolf seeks to capture consciousness, inner and outer, in a myriad of facets, *Mrs Dalloway* being her boldest experiment so far.

In the visual arts, too, there is a distinctive Twenties style, christened "Art Deco", or International Style. France's ultra-modern architect Le Corbusier designed the Pavilion of New Spirit for the 1925 Paris Exhibition, a year that saw two major exhibitions characterising the era, the Exposition des Arts Decoratifs, celebrating Art Deco, and an extraordinary exhibition of the new surrealism.

A dining room in the Art Deco style: note the curved "ocean liner" lines, the rich and luxurious colours, and the Pharaonic-Hollywood ambience.

1926 (1926-1927)

Geneva, 13 March 1926. Germany is refused a permanent place on the League of Nations council.

Britain, 13 March 1926. Alan Cobham ends a 16,000-mile return flight from London to Cape Town.

Italy, 7 April 1926. Benito Mussolini survives a third attempt on his life.

India, 24 April 1926. The first Hindu-Moslem riots for many years breaks out in Calcutta.

Berlin, 24 April 1926. Germany signs a friendship treaty with the USSR.

Persia, 25 April 1926. Ali Reza Khan Pahlavi is crowned *shah*.

Britain, 1 May 1926. A national coal strike over proposed pay cuts and longer working hours begins.

India, 2 May 1926. Indian women are granted the right to stand for election to public office.

Britain, 3 May 1926. The first general strike in British history begins after the Trades Union Congress votes to back the miners.

Britain, 12 May 1926. The TUC calls off the general strike.

Poland, 13 May 1926. Josef Pilsudski takes control after leading a military *coup*.

Alaska, 13 May 1926. An international team of flyers completes the first-ever trip over the north pole in a airship.

Germany, 17 May 1926. The Center Party candidate Wilhelm Marx becomes chancellor again.

Britain, 20 May 1926. The miners resolve to fight on alone.

Morocco, 26 May 1926. The rebel leader Abd el Krim surrenders to a French-led force.

Portugal, 28 May 1926. General Manuel Gomes da Costa seizes power in a *coup d'etat*.

London, 8 June 1926. The soprano Nellie Melba gives her farewell performance at Covent Garden.

Geneva, 10 June 1926. Brazil leaves the League of Nations.

Britain, 25 June 1926. The American Bobby Jones becomes the first amateur since 1897 to win the Open Golf Championship.

Canada, 28 June 1926. The Liberal prime minister William Mackenzie King and his cabinet resign in the wake of a customs scandal.

Portugal, 9 July. General de Costa, who seized power in May, is overthrown by General Carmona.

Britain, 6 August 1926. Gertrude Ederle from the USA becomes the first woman ever to swim the Channel, cutting more than two hours off the record time.

Greece, 22 August 1926. A coup led by Georgios Condylis overthrows the regime of Theodoros Pangalos.

USA, 23 August 1926. The Italian-born film star Rudolf Valentino dies.

Germany, 29 August 1926. A *Nazi* Party rally is held at Nuremberg.

Spain, 7 September 1926. Spain leaves the League of Nations after being denied a permanent seat on the council.

Geneva, 8 September 1926. The League of Nations votes to admit Germany as a member.

Canada, 25 September 1926. Mackenzie King's Liberals are returned to power in an election.

London, 1 October 1926. Alan Cobham completes a record 28,000-mile round trip to Australia by air.

Italy, 7 October 1926. The Fascist Party is decreed the party of the state. Mussolini assumes total power and bans all opposition.

Britain, 14 October 1926. A A Milne publishes *Winnie-the-Pooh*, a book for children.

Moscow, 23 October 1926. Leon Trotsky and Gregory Zinoviev are expelled from the Communist Party central committee.

USA, 31 October 1926. The Hungarian-born escape artist Harry Houdini dies.

Britain, 2 November 1926. Imperial Chemical Industries (ICI) is formed.

South-East Asia, 12 November 1926. Nationalists in the island of Java launch a rebellion against Dutch rule.

Britain, 19 November 1926. Miners end their six-month pit strike, agreeing to work longer hours.

Italy, 15 December 1926. The Roman *fasces*, the symbol of authority and origin of the word "fascist", is adopted as the national emblem.

Japan, 25 December 1926. Hirohito ascends the throne on the death of his father, the Emperor Yoshihito.

Dublin, 1926. A fight breaks out on stage during a performance of Sean O'Casey's *The Plough and the Stars*, about the Easter Rising.

Britain, 1 January 1927. The British Broadcasting Corporation comes into being.

India, 8 January 1927. The first scheduled London-Delhi flight arrives.

Britain, 4 February 1927. Malcolm Campbell sets a world land-speed record of 174.224 mph in his car, *Bluebird*.

Old empire turns into commonwealth

London, 20 November 1926
The greatest empire that there has ever been today acquired an extra title. An imperial conference in London, taking note of the self-reliance acquired by the self-governing dominions during the war, decided that Canada, Australia, New Zealand, South Africa and Newfoundland should have equal status with Britain as members of the British Commonwealth of Nations. Each dominion will acknowledge George V as its king. His title is now "George V, by the Grace of God, of Great Britain, Ireland and the British Dominions beyond the Seas, King, Defender of the Faith, Emperor of India".

The empire, including colonies and protectorates in Africa, the South Pacific and the South Atlantic, represents one-fifth of the land area of the entire globe. The first colony was Newfoundland, acquired in 1583.

Moralists attack degenerate new fashions

Causing a flap: Charlestoning.

Causing more flaps: Oxford bags.

Rome, 1926
Catholic bishops in Italy are banning scantily-dressed women from church and criticising women's new involvement in sport as "incompatible" with a woman's dignity.

Outrage at women's fashions and manners is not confined to bishops. Traditionalists claim that women's morals decline as their hemlines rise. Many find men's fashions no less ridiculous, particularly the acres of flannel called "Oxford bags" which young men wear.

Not so George Bernard Shaw. In England he is encouraging wearers of short, light dresses, saying that they are for "real human beings" rather than "upholstered Victorian angels". But doctors warn that fashion slaves of the current Art Deco-style boyish look are weakening their health by obsessive dieting. Others believe that dances like the "Charleston" can cause complications in future childbirth.

The trend for rich modern women to live frivolous lives of parties and wild American dancing puts them at risk, too. Dr J S Russell told the institute of hygiene this year that women are turning to drink and drugs in a desperate bid to cope with their hectic lives.

Strike paralyses Britain's industry

England, 20 May 1926
Despite a resolution by the Trades Union Congress to call off the general strike which has threatened to paralyse the country, Britain's miners – feeling "deserted" by their brother trades unionists – vowed at a delegate conference to continue industrial action; but the national strike has failed.

The trades unions had neither the will nor the cash to support it, particularly when 5,500 trains were running – many of them driven by eager volunteers – and troops were unloading food at London Docks and delivering it throughout London.

Many believed that the general strike would be a signal for violent social upheaval, but there was little sign of this during the nine days in which only one newspaper was published – the *British Gazette*, edited by Winston Churchill – and the BBC fought off attempts at government control of its news.

Some trains were derailed, and public vehicles were driven off the road in Glasgow where looting took place. For thousands of undergraduates and railway enthusiasts, it was a time to put on official armbands and drive trains, buses and lorries, breaking the law with abandon.

Moving images are sent by wireless

Baird with the two ventriloquist's dolls were the first images to be televised.

London, 27 January 1926
The transmission of moving images by wireless was demonstrated in London today by John Logie Baird, a Scottish engineer of 38. He calls the process "television".

Before an audience at the Royal Institution he managed to project flickering and indistinct pictures of two ventriloquist's dolls on to a screen with the aid of an electrical camera which converts the image into electronic signals. These are transmitted by wireless and recreated through a cathode-ray tube by a 240-line scanning process.

The result is far from equal to film images on a cinema screen, but Mr Baird, who gave up his job with a Clyde Valley electric power company in order to concentrate on his research, believes that one day there will be a television screen in every home.

Savage race riots break out in India

Calcutta, 24 April 1926
The brief unity of Hindus and Moslems that Gandhi brought about after the war is over. Gandhi's dream of the two communities united in the struggle for nationhood is spattered with blood. Already 151 have died here in the worst communal riots within memory. Many of the bodies are horribly mutilated. The rioting started over a rumour – that two Moslems had been beaten to death by Hindus – which turned out to be untrue.

Rockets penetrate upper atmosphere

USA, c.1926
The rocket is emerging as a scientific tool for exploring space, and the father of modern rocketry is undoubtedly the American professor of physics at Clark university, Robert Goddard.

Goddard's rockets are designed to study the upper atmosphere about a mile above Earth. From the Russian Tsiolkovsky, Goddard borrowed the idea of multi-stage vehicles which discard successive spent-fuel units. He is experimenting with a variety of solid and liquid fuels.

Final blink for once-reviled eye of "Impressionist" founder

Giverny, Normandy, 6 Dec 1926
Claude Monet has died, aged 86, at the house where he had lived for 40 years, with its garden and lilyponds which he so often painted.

He was the first "Impressionist" – the name was derived from one of his works, *Impression – Sunrise* – and the last survivor of the group that exhibited to incomprehension and ridicule from 1874 to 1886. His huge output includes series of paintings done under varying light conditions of haystacks, poplars, Rouen cathedral, the steamy Gare St Lazare, and the Thames. Monet worked on several paintings at once, changing them with the weather. "My strong point is knowing when to stop," he said. "Only an eye," Cezanne said of him, "but my God, what an eye!"

Monet's "Gare St Lazare", painted shortly before his battle with blindness.

Revolt threatens to engulf Austria

Vienna, 15 July 1927
Eighty-nine people have died in rioting that engulfed Austria's capital, Vienna, today. As armed police fired on crowds of workers, the ministry of justice was set on fire and many shops were looted and burnt. The trouble began when three members of the right-wing *Kampfer* party were acquitted of last January's murder of two communists, killed during a political *fracas*. Left-wing orators urged the revenge murders of judges, juries and the middle class. The enraged masses duly took to the streets.

The *Volkswehr* reserve, called out by Chancellor Siegel, refused to defend law and order, but the police proved loyal to the authorities.

1927 (1927-1928)

Paris, 6 February 1927. Yehudi Menuhin, a ten-year-old violinist of Russian-Jewish parentage, causes a sensation with his playing.

Lisbon, 9 February 1927. Antonio Carmona, who seized power in a *coup* last year, puts down an attempted revolution.

China, 21 March 1927. The victorious Nationalist army of Chiang Kai-shek enters Shanghai.

Britain, 26 March 1927. The Gaumont-British Film Corporation is founded.

Florida, 29 March 1927. A Briton, Henry Segrave, sets a new world land-speed record of 203.841 mph.

Paris, 7 April 1927. Abel Gance's film *Napoleon* has its premiere.

Cardiff, 21 April 1927. The National Museum of Wales opens.

China, April 1927. Chiang Kai-shek carries out a coup against left-wing elements, killing trade union activists and communists, leading to the break-up of the united front. The communists are driven into the rural areas.

Canberra, 9 May 1927. The new Australian Parliament House is opened by the duke of York.

Saudi Arabia, 20 May 1927. Britain signs the treaty of Jeddah, recognising the independence of Saudi Arabia.

Britain, 24 May 1927. Britain severs diplomatic relations with the USSR amid accusations of espionage and subversion throughout the British empire.

Czechoslovakia, 27 May 1927. Tomas Masaryk is re-elected president.

South-East Asia, 4 June 1927. Ahmed Sukarno founds the Indonesian Nationalist Party.

USSR, 9 June 1927. The Russians execute 20 people accused of being British spies.

Britain, 14 June 1927. The writer Jerome K Jerome, the author of *Three Men in a Boat*, dies.

Britain, 23 June 1927. Parliament passes the Trade Disputes Act, making sympathetic strikes illegal.

Britain, 30 June 1927. The US teams wins the first Ryder Cup professional golf tournament.

Dublin, 10 July 1927. Kevin O'Higgins, the vice-president of the Irish Free State, is shot dead.

Vienna, 15 July 1927. Government troops put down communist riots and strikes provoked by the acquittal of nationalists for political murder.

Romania, 21 July 1927. Prince Mihai, aged five, succeed King Ferdinand.

China, August 1927. Ye Ting and He Long lead a communist uprising in Nanchang, in Jiangxi province, holding the city for a few days.

France, 14 September 1927. The American dancer Isadora Duncan is strangled when her shawl is caught in a car wheel.

Geneva, 15 September 1927. Canada is elected to the League of Nations council.

Germany, 16 September 1927. President von Hindenburg repudiates German responsibility for the Great War.

China, 19 September 1927. The "autumn harvest uprising" which began earlier in the month, under the leadership of Mao Zedong (Tse-tung), suffers a serious defeat.

Ireland, 20 September 1927. President William Cosgrave wins his second Irish Free State general election in three months with an effective majority of six.

Moscow, 1 October 1927. The USSR signs a non-aggression pact with Persia.

Iraq, 15 October 1927. Iraq's first oil strike is made at Kirkuk.

Norway, 17 October 1927. The first Labour government is elected.

China, October 1927. Remnants of Mao's uprising move to the Jinggang mountains in Jiangxi province and set up the first revolutionary base there.

France, 18 November 1927. Jules Rimet, the head of the International Football Association, announces the creation of a "World Cup".

London, 23 November 1927. Stanley Baldwin, the prime minister, refuses to meet 200 unemployed miners who have walked from the Rhondda Valley.

Berlin, 23 November 1927. Germany and Poland sign a trade pact.

Britain, 25 November 1927. A commission is set up to study the working of the constitution granted to India after the Great War.

China, 15 December 1927. Russians are expelled from Shanghai following an attempted communist coup in Guangzhou.

London, 15 December 1927. The House of Commons rejects a revised Book of Common Prayer.

New York City, December 1927. Florenz Ziegfeld's *Showboat* opens, with music by Jerome Kern.

London, 6 January 1928. Fourteen people die as the Thames bursts its banks, flooding low-lying areas including the palace of Westminster.

Talking movies enthral cinema audiences

Al Jolson in "The Jazz Singer", the first "talkie" that cinema-goers have heard.

New York, 6 October 1927
The first spoken voice in a feature film, that of Al Jolson in *The Jazz Singer*, brought the audience to its feet applauding when it was shown today. In the middle of a night club sequence, Jolson suddenly spoke: "Wait a minute, wait a minute," he said. "You ain't heard nothin' yet!" In another part of the film he sits at the piano exchanging lines with his mother between verses of *Blue Skies*.

Jolson had ad-libbed during the shooting of the two music sequences and the producers left it in. Synchronised music in film has been possible since Warner Brothers bought the "Vitaphone" system last year, using it first with John Barrymore's *Don Juan*, but no-one had spoken spontaneously to audiences before in a realistic way. Crowds are flocking to hear it.

Fox have been developing a rival sound system called "Movietone" for shorts since early this year. In June they showed the reception for Charles Lindbergh by President Coolidge and a speech by Mussolini. These had such effect that Fox are setting up Movietone News to make regular sound newsreels.

The industry is faced with costly reinvestment in sound studios and theatres, and many predict that sound will only be popular briefly. Charlie Chaplin discounts it.

Pioneer of African education has died

New York, 30 July 1927
James Kwegyir Aggrey, Africa's most influental scholar and educationalist, died here today aged 52. Born in the Gold Coast and educated in missionary schools, he sailed to the USA in 1898, attended Livingstone college in North Carolina, stayed on the faculty, and studied at Columbia university, New York. In 1920 and again in 1924 he toured Africa for the Phelps-Stokes commissions into African education. His great work on the history of Africa remains incomplete.

Scientists ask what can the matter be

Germany, 1927
The German Werner Heisenberg has just developed his "Uncertainty Principle" – that there is no certainty in the way an electron revolves around the atomic nucleus. Its path is totally unpredictable.

Another uncomfortable notion has been put forward by Paul Dirac in Cambridge. He reckons that the negatively-charged electron has a positive equivalent – a "positron". Thus, here is a particle with an "anti-particle" having directly opposite properties.

Left purged in China

Generalissimo Chiang Kai-shek addresses the "People's Political Council".

China, 12 April 1927
General Chiang Kai-shek, who took over the Nationalist movement on the death of Sun Yat-sen two years ago, carried out a bloody purge of leftists in Shanghai today. He pre-empted Communist moves to take over the movement by hiring Du Yuesheng, a powerful gangster. Du's gunmen, disguised as workmen, raided the homes of Communists and took them away to be executed while Nationalist army units disarmed the Commu-

nist military force, the Workers' Inspection Corps, and shot its leaders. There was further bloodshed when machine guns opened fire on people demonstrating outside Chiang's headquarters.

While all this was going on Chiang was in Nanjing where he had gone to supervise a similar purge of leftists in preparation for establishing a new conservative-dominated Nationalist government there. He intends to destroy the Communists.

Bushwhackers get their own flying doctor

Queensland, Australia, 1928
A unique new medical service aimed at getting doctors to the most remote parts of the Australian bush has already saved several lives and is to be extended throughout the country. Since May, Dr St Vincent Walsh and his pilot have flown thousands of miles in their de Havilland aircraft, touching down on hastily improvised airstrips and

caring for a variety of medical and surgical problems – including childbirth.

The service is the brainchild of John Flynn, the superintendent of the Queensland Presbyterian Mission, who borrowed the plane from a local flying club and arranged for the installation of "pedal-powered" wireless sets in distant mission stations.

Frenchman ends his search for times past

Paris, 1927
Although he died five years ago, still hard at work revising his immense novel, even Marcel Proust's search for "lost time" has come to an end this year with the publication of the last part of *A la Recherche du Temps Perdu*, entitled *Le Temps Retrouve* – Time Recap-

tured. No recluse ever devoted his life more singly to a work of art, working by night in his corklined apartment, conjuring out of memory a whole lifetime spent among the *Beau Monde* – artists, hostesses, courtesans. "The true paradises," he writes, "are the paradises one has lost."

Solo flyer crosses Atlantic at 110 mph

Paris, 21 May 1927
Charles Lindbergh has touched down at Le Bourget airport after a solo flight of 3,600 miles across the Atlantic. His Ryan NYP monoplane, the *Spirit of St Louis*, was greeted by a crowd of 100,000. Backed by a consortium of St Louis businessmen, and regarded as an outsider, he took off from Roosevelt Field, Long Island, at dawn yesterday. Thousands watched him fly northwest to Newfoundland and then, at 7.15pm, west across the ocean. He came in to Paris 27 hours later. He is a shy midwesterner, now richer by $25,000 prize money; the main question he was asked was how he answered calls of nature. The reply: into a bottle.

Crowds greet the "Spirit of St Louis" at Croydon Airport on 29 May.

Stalin sends his opponents into exile

Moscow, 16 January 1928
Joseph Stalin has cracked down on his defeated political rivals and sent many of them into exile in Siberia. His security police, the *OGPU*, have rounded up some 30 leading Bolsheviks, including Leon Trotsky and Stalin's closest allies among them, Zinoviev and Kamenev. His chief opponents have been banished for alleged "counter-revolution." His triumph over his former com-

rades, whom he has consistently outmanoeuvred, is nearly complete.

The crackdown comes at a time of grave social crisis which Trotsky, among others, had predicted. With the short-fall in the government's purchases of peasants' grain, there are several cities and towns facing famine. Meanwhile there are virtually no consumer goods to be had in the nation's shops, and Soviet exports are negligible.

Duke Ellington (centre), jazz's foremost composer and the bestknown black American jazz player in the US, with his 11-piece band. The Duke has now taken up residence at Harlem's Cotton Club, and his music is being played on the wireless and phonograph all over the United States.

1928 (1928-1929)

Britain, 15 February 1928. The *Oxford English Dictionary* is completed after 70 years' work.

Near East, 20 February 1928. Britain recognises the independence of Transjordan.

Near East, 3 March 1928. British planes strafe Wahabi tribesmen from Saudi Arabia who have launched a huge raid aimed at Kuwait and the Iraq frontier.

Malta, 12 March 1928. The British colony of Malta becomes a dominion.

China, March 1928. Anticommunist forces destroy the Haifeng and Lufeng soviet governments set up in Guangdong province by Peng Pai.

China, 7 April 1928. Nationalist troops launch an offensive with the ultimate aim of capturing Beijing.

Turkey, 9 April 1928. Islam is abolished as the state religion.

China, 3 May 1928. Seeking to impede Chiang Kai-shek's drive for national reunification, Japanese forces clash with Nationalists at Ji'nan in Shandong province.

London, 7 May. Women over 21 win equal suffrage in British elections.

China, 11 May 1928. The Japanese win control of the stricken provincial capital of Shandong after three days of savage fighting.

New York City, 16 May 1928. Share prices plunge as panic selling hits Wall Street.

China, 4 June 1928. Fearing that he is no longer willing to be a Japanese puppet, the Japanese murder the warlord Zhang Zuolin.

China, 8 June 1928. Beijing is taken by Nationalists, who have set up a government in Nanjing.

Germany, 28 June 1928. The Socialist Hermann Muller succeeds Wilhelm Marx as chancellor.

China, 28 June 1928. The name of the old capital is changed from Beijing (northern capital) to Beiping (northern peace).

Mexico City, 17 July 1928. President Alvaro Obregon is assassinated at a lunch to celebrate his election earlier this month.

Egypt, 19 July 1928. Having dismissed the prime minister, Nahas Pasha, King Fuad ends parliamentary government in Egypt and makes himself dictator.

Japan, 22 July 1928. Japan breaks off relations with China.

Britain, 27 July 1928. Randall Davidson resigns as archbishop of Canterbury following the House of Commons' second rejection of the revised Book of Common Prayer.

Yugoslavia, 1 August 1928. Croatian deputies set up a separatist parliament in Zagreb.

Albania, 25 August 1928. President Ahmed Zog declares Albania a kingdom and himself king.

Paris, 27 August 1928. Delegates of 15 nations sign the Kellogg-Briand pact, outlawing war.

Berlin, 31 August 1928. Bertolt Brecht's *Threepenny Opera* is performed for the first time.

Moscow, 6 September 1928. The USSR signs the Kellogg-Briand pact.

Rome, 20 September 1928. The Grand Fascist Council becomes the supreme legislative body in Italy.

USSR, 1 October 1928. Joseph Stalin issues a five-year economic plan to industrialise the USSR.

China, 6 October 1928. A new Chinese constitution is promulgated. Chiang Kai-shek becomes president of the republic.

USA, 6 November 1928. The Republican Herbert C Hoover is elected president.

Japan, 10 November 1928. The 27-year-old Emperor Hirohito is crowned.

Paris, 11 November 1928. Raymond Poincare forms a cabinet which excludes Radical Socialists.

Mexico, 30 November 1928. Emilio Portes Gil is sworn in as president.

Russia, November 1928. Stalin continues to arrest and exile hundreds of Trotsky's supporters.

Afghanistan, 17 December 1928. King Amanullah and Queen Suriya take refuge in a fort outside Kabul as a revolt against reform breaks out in the capital and Jalalabad.

China, 20 December 1928. Britain signs a tariff pact with China, recognising Chiang Kai-shek.

Britain, 1928. The novelist Evelyn Waugh publishes *Decline and Fall*.

Yugoslavia, 6 January 1929. King Alexander dissolves parliament, abolishes the constitution and establishes a dictatorship.

Afghanistan, 14 January 1929. King Amanullah abdicates in favour of his brother Inayatullah.

Moscow, 16 January 1929. Nikolai Bukharin resigns as head of the Comintern.

Afghanistan, 17 January 1929. King Inayatullah abdicates in favour of the rebel chief Bacha-i-Sachao, who leads a coup.

USSR, 23 January 1929. The OGPU, the secret police, arrest 400 Trotskyists for an alleged plot to start a civil war.

Stalin prescribes five-year economic plan

Moscow, 1 October 1928

Joseph Stalin's first Five-Year Plan went into operation today hurling the whole of the USSR into a gigantic struggle to build socialism. Over the next few years Stalin intends to transform the face of the nation and lay the foundations of a modern industrial society very quickly. A country standing only a decade earlier on the brink of dissolution is about to be put in the very forefront of world economic development.

The plan is a six-volume work which has taken two years' study. Class A industries – coal, iron, oil, steel and machine-building – are scheduled to triple their output. Class B industries, which turn out consumer goods, are to double their output. The plan is to be achieved through the ruthless accumulation of capital, the ploughing back of surplus and the limitation of personal consumption and amenities. A major programme of heavy industrial development, with huge ironworks, blast furnaces, oil refineries and tractor factories, is planned. The

Stalin, the Bolshevik whom Lenin so distrusted, transforming the USSR.

plan goes hand in hand with a revolution in the countryside – the collectivisation of agriculture, which could easily prove to be the biggest event in all Russian history.

The key question is: will the USSR's mainly peasant population put its back into the plan?

Woman says she is late czar's daughter

New York City, 6 February 1928

A mysterious young woman, calling herself Anastasia Chaikovsky and claiming to be the youngest daughter of the murdered Russian czar, reached New York today.

Mrs Chaikovsky held a press conference on the liner *Berengaria* and told reporters that she is here to have her jaw reset – it was broken by a Bolshevik soldier, she said. She was welcomed by the son of the czar's doctor, who was killed in the cellar with the royal family. Mr Gleb Botkin greeted her grandly as "Your Highness" and declared that she was certainly the grand duchess with whom he had played as a child. He denied that the public were being hoaxed. Rumours have persisted of survivors from the Bolshevik carnage at Ekaterinburg in 1918, and of the crown jewels' continued existence. Even so, Anastasia will not find it easy to prove her claim to royal blood.

Mouse called Mickey steams into action

New York, 19 September 1928

A mouse with big boots and ears like black ping-pong bats made his bow today in *Steamboat Willie*, the first animated cartoon to have a sound track. His perky and impudent voice was supplied by his creator, Walt Disney, who hurriedly added voices at the last moment to keep abreast of feature films. The drawing is the work of his animator partner, Ubbe Iwerks. Disney's wife supplied the name "Mickey". The idea was Disney's.

A star is born: Mickey Mouse at the helm in "Steamboat Willie".

Chiang launches attack

China, 7 April 1928
General Chiang Kai-shek has launched a massive assault on the northern warlords. The objectives of this Northern Expedition, first planned by the late Sun Yat-sen, are to drive the warlords out of Beijing, crush their power and unite China under a Nationalist government.

Chiang, who returned to lead the Nationalists recently after a tactical "retirement", commands an army of nearly a million men against the smaller but still formidable forces of the Japanese puppet, Zhang Zuolin. One of the dangers that Chiang faces is of Japanese intervention on behalf of their client warlord. It is difficult to gauge how the offensive is progressing, for Chiang has refused to allow foreign observers to accompany his troops, no doubt to conceal his secrets from Japan.

While Chiang concentrates his efforts on the warlords, his other enemies, the Communists, are retreating to the mountains to lick their wounds following the debacle of the "Autumn Harvest" uprising.

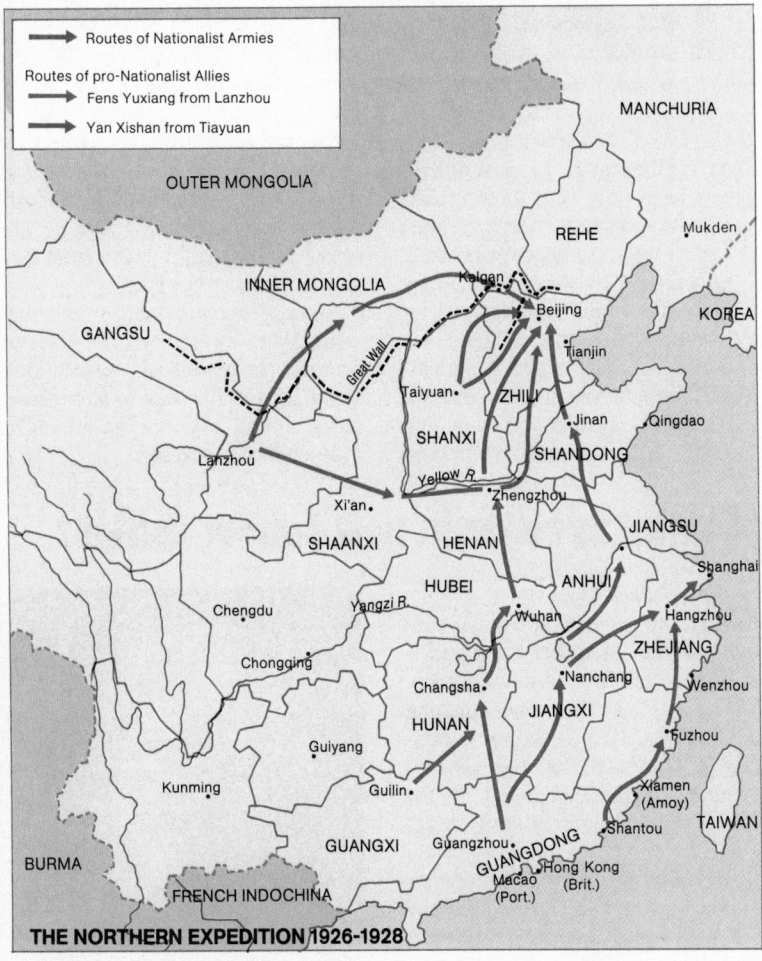

THE NORTHERN EXPEDITION 1926-1928

Routes of Nationalist Armies
Routes of pro-Nationalist Allies
Fens Yuxiang from Lanzhou
Yan Xishan from Tiayuan

Free India report is for Hindus only

New Delhi, 15 August 1928
As India steadily becomes less governable, a report is out drafting the constitutional framework of a free India. The report, by the Congress leader, Motilal Nehru, calls for universal suffrage, a two-chamber parliament and dominion status. Unfortunately it represents the aspirations of only one community, the Hindu majority. For a moment, in 1927, it looked as if Hindus and Moslems would agree to a proposed constitution, but any concession to one community was rejected by the other. The old cycle of minority Moslem and majority Hindu fears has triumphed once again.

Mouldy dish may be health breakthrough

London, 30 September 1928
A substance that appears to kill bacteria responsible for many human infectious illnesses has been discovered, by a combination of chance and shrewd observation, by a British scientist. Professor Alexander Fleming of Queen Mary's hospital in London seems to have stumbled on an important find with many potential applications.

He had left a dish of staphylococcus bacteria on his laboratory bench. When he looked at it next, a mould had contaminated the sample. However, around the mould were patches that were completely clear of staphylococcus. The inference is that the mould – which Fleming later identified as *Penicillium notatum* – kills other kinds of infectious micro-organisms too, so this could form the basis for new kinds of "antibiotic" agents.

However, the germ-killing agent has to be isolated. Then it has to be cleared for use on humans. This may take several years.

Brisbane welcomes cross-Pacific flyer

Brisbane, Australia, 9 June 1928
Half the population of Brisbane welcomed Charles Kingsford Smith and his co-pilot, C T P Ulm, after their 7,000-mile (11,200-kilometre) non-stop flight in a Fokker tri-motored aircraft, the *Southern Cross*, from California across the Pacific. The 83-hour journey is the longest flight ever made over water.

"Smithy" served in the Royal Flying Corps in the Great War, winning the Military Cross, and then took up stunt-flying. In 1927 "Smithy" and Ulm made a round-Australia flight in less than half the previous record time, giving the two the experience needed for their epic trans-Pacific flight.

Violins open up on Valentine's Day

Chicago, 14 February 1929
Chicago shuddered today as news spread of one of the worst-ever outbreaks of homicidal gangland warfare. In what seems to have been a premeditated attack, seven members of George "Bugsy" Moran's gang, assembled in a garage at 2122 N Clark Street, were machine-gunned to death by five assailants, all dressed as police officers.

Investigators attribute the killings, which the press have christened "the St Valentine's Day Massacre" and which stem from rivalry over the lucrative market in bootleg liquor, to the gang of Al "Scarface" Capone, who is fighting for supremacy among Chicago's mobsters.

Mexican president killed by fanatic

Mexico City, July 1928
Alvaro Obregon, who first served as Mexico's president from 1920 to 1924, following one of the bloodiest decades in his country's history, is dead. He was assassinated today by a religious fanatic, just weeks after he was re-elected to the presidency. It was hoped that he might continue his successful social and economic reforms. A follower of Madero's revolution of 1911, Obregon, then a general, had led the troops of Mexico's north-west. He challenged Huerta's *coup d'etat* of 1913, siding instead with the "first chief" Carranza. When in 1920 Carranza denied him a spell as president, Obregon organised his own coup.

Hirohito aged 27, Japan's emperor in the steps of his "heavenly and imperial ancestors".

1929 (1929-1930)

Vatican, 11 February 1929. The Vatican state comes into being.

Germany, 15 February 1929. Over three million are now out of work.

Paris, 21 February 1929. The exiled Leon Trotsky, Stalin's most feared opponent, is refused asylum.

Beiping (Beijing), 2 March 1929. Martial law is declared after a mutiny is crushed among Nationalist troops.

Washington, DC, 4 March 1929. Herbert Hoover is inaugurated as president.

Mexico, 8 March 1929. Catholic rebels take the town of Juarez.

France, 20 March 1929. The French commander Marshal Ferdinand Foch dies aged 68.

Italy, 25 March 1929. Mussolini's "single party" government claims it has won 99 per cent of the votes in the general election.

Germany, 4 April 1929. The engineer Carl Benz, the builder of the first internal-combustion motor car, dies aged 84.

USA, 6 April 1929. President Hoover sends warplanes to the Arizona-Mexico border following the deaths of American troops in cross-fire between Mexican rebels and government troops.

Monte Carlo, 14 April 1929. The first Monaco Grand Prix is won by Williams of Britain in a Bugatti.

Rome, 20 April 1929. King Victor Emmanuel III and Mussolini open the first all-Fascist parliament.

Berlin, 3 May 1929. The city is declared to be in a state of siege as civil unrest escalates.

Bombay, 5 May 1929. A curfew is imposed in a bid to quell new Hindu-Moslem riots.

London, 10 May 1929. King George V dissolves parliament and election campaigning begins.

USA, 16 May 1929. The Academy of Motion Picture Arts and Sciences gives its first awards.

India, 27 May 1929. The nationalist Pandit Nehru calls for rebellion if India does not get dominion status by the year's end.

Britain, 31 May 1929. Thirteen women are elected as MPs. The Tories win most votes but Labour most seats.

London, 7 June 1929. Ramsay MacDonald forms Britain's second Labour government.

China, 13 June 1929. Soviet troops cross into China in retaliation for raids on Russian consulates.

Tokyo, 26 June 1929. The government ratifies the Kellogg-Briand pact banning war, the last of the signatories to do so.

Britain, 11 July 1929. Leon Trotsky is refused asylum.

Russia, 17 July 1929. Russia breaks off relations with China and begins to mobilise on the border.

Italy, 19 August 1929. Sergei Diaghilev, the founder of the Ballets Russes, dies aged 57.

India, 21 August 1929. Mahatma Gandhi is elected president of the Indian National Congress, but refuses to accept the post.

Jerusalem, 25 August 1929. The British declare martial law as Arabs and Jews continue fighting.

Geneva, 5 September 1929. Aristide Briand, the French prime minister, proposes a united states of Europe.

China, 9 September 1929. Heavy fighting between Chinese and Soviet troops is reported along the Manchurian border.

South America, 16 September 1929. Bolivia and Paraguay sign a peace treaty to end their ten-month-old border dispute.

Berlin, 22 September 1929. Communists and Nazis are involved in armed street confrontations.

Belgrade, 3 October 1929. Yugoslavia is declared the official name of the Kingdom of Serbs, Croats and Slovenes.

Kabul, 17 October 1929. The Afghan national assembly elects the rebel leader Nadir Khan king.

New York City, 24 October 1929. The stock exchange crashes.

Germany, 8 December 1929. Hitler's *Nazi*, or National Socialist, Party, wins Bavarian municipal elections.

Lahore, 22 December 1929. The All-India National Congress demands independence.

Russia, 22 December 1929. The Sino-Soviet border dispute over the eastern railway ends with both sides agreeing to withdraw troops.

Cairo, 11 January 1930. A new Egyptian parliament opens after 18 months of rule by royal decree. The majority of the deputies are nationalists, supporting the Waft party.

China, 13 January 1930. Two million have died of starvation and famine threatens millions more.

Spain, 29 January 1930. The dictator General Primo de Rivera resigns.

London, 31 January 1930. The Five Power Naval Conference, between Britain, the US, Italy, France and Japan, aimed at curbing the arms race, opens.

Stalin declares all farms are collectives

Soviet peasants making a "spontaneous" demonstration against kulaks.

Soviet Union, 5 January 1930
Tens of thousands of government agents have been sent to the countryside to persuade rich peasants, or *kulaks*, to join collective farms.

Encouraged by the initial success of collective farms, and spurred on by the threat of famine, Stalin has decided that the nation's agriculture should be turned into a cooperative system. Under the scheme, every poor farmer who turns his land over to collective ownership will be allowed to own a house, garden, stable and one car for his family. He will also be allowed to keep any income from the sale of garden vegetables.

Stalin's reconstruction of the country's agricultural system promises to be a social revolution. It will also enable him to strengthen party control over the traditionally independent peasantry.

Woman minister in new Labour cabinet

London, 7 June 1929
Britain is to get its first woman cabinet minister. Margaret Bondfield is to become minister of labour, a key job in the light of the lengthening dole queues. Hers is the most exciting appointment in the government list announced today by the Labour Party leader, Ramsay MacDonald.

This is only Britain's second Labour government, and like the first one it has no overall majority in the House of Commons, so MacDonald is concerned to present a moderate image. Most appointments go to those on the right of the party, and left-wing socialist measures are unlikely.

On foreign affairs, moves to resume diplomatic relations with the Soviets are in train and there will be vigorous pursuit of disarmament. The government will be helped because the Conservatives and Liberals hate each other more than

Ramsay MacDonald: the Labour PM courting a moderate image.

they hate Labour. Another first was chalked up by the new prime minister. He presented his new team in front of film cameras invited into the Downing Street garden.

Financial panic as Wall Street dives

New York's Wall Street on the morning of the Great Crash.

A victim of the Crash: "Brother can you spare me a thousand dimes?"

New York City, 24 October 1929
The show-business weekly *Variety* summed it up in a headline. WALL STREET LAYS AN EGG, it proclaimed, as millions of shares became worthless in a matter of hours and panic-stricken brokers fought each other at the Stock Exchange counters. Their orders were to "sell at any price" – but there were few prepared to buy worthless pieces of paper today.

President Hoover's belief that the participation by millions of small investors – farmers, bus drivers, road-sweepers, chorus girls and housewives among them – was "the final triumph over poverty" has been proved disastrously wrong. Soon after Wall Street opened for trade this morning, brisk selling caused the value of shares to fall. With the ticker tapes unable to cope with the volume of traffic, they fell further, and as worried investors throughout the country add their orders to sell, the market plummeted until at 11.30 it was in total chaos.

As leading bankers held an emergency meeting today at the offices of J P Morgan and Co, the market rallied at the hope of intervention. The bankers' injection of $25 million into the market did ease matters, but not for the thousands of small investors who fought with riot police as they struggled to get to their brokers and sell.

The bankers tried hard to soothe and smooth things over. "A minor adjustment," said one. "A little distress selling," declared another. Eleven suicides in New York alone tell another story.

New plan to rejig German war debts

The Hague, 8 June 1929
Financial reparations imposed on Germany to compensate the Allies for debts incurred to the USA during the Great War seem to have been rescheduled. Under a provisional agreement, Germany is no longer required to reconstruct France's war-damaged provinces.

The Young Plan, named after its American author Owen Young, removes controls over the German economy. Nevertheless, Germany must repay £1.65 billion over the next 40 years, including £2 million a year which Britain still insists must be repaid to cover its American debt. Militant Germans, including the Nazis, are demonstrating against such payments.

Germany – chained and bound by the fetters of the Young Plan.

Fairbanks presents first Academy Awards

Hollywood, 16 May 1929
The film industry's first awards for outstanding achievement by actors, directors, producers and technicians were presented last night. The award is symbolised by a 12inch (0.3-metre) -tall model of a naked man plated in gold. The awards were given by the Academy of Motion Picture Arts and Sciences formed in 1927 by producers like Louis B Mayer of MGM as "an alliance of the creative elite of Hollywood".

The academy president, Douglas Fairbanks jnr, gave statuettes to Janet Gaynor and Emil Jannings, the directors Frank Borsage and Lewis Milestone, the screenwriter Ben Hecht and the producer Jack Warner. The awards will be annual.

Janet Gaynor

Janet Gaynor: first award-winner.

Britain keeps order in Palestine riots

Palestine, 31 August 1929
British troops stepped in today as Arabs and Jews continued to clash in the sultry summer heat. Outbreaks of rioting have been suppressed for the moment, but a large force of Arabs is said to be massing across the Syrian border. Spotter aircraft are shadowing their movements. The worst riots came in Safed last Thursday, when armed Arabs killed eight Jews and then burnt whole streets of houses. The cause of the riots is unknown, although many see it as stemming from Arab hostility to Jewish access to the Wailing Wall, a Jewish monument isolated in the heart of Arab Jerusalem.

Fascist-papal pact

Vatican City, 11 February 1929
The Vatican state came into being at noon with a treaty designed to end the church's six decades of hostility with the Italian state.

The 27-point agreement, signed by Mussolini and Cardinal Gaspari, Pope Pius XI's representative, emphasises the sanctity of marriage, recognises Roman Catholicism as the state religion and makes Catholic education obligatory in schools.

The Vatican, which gets a 1,750 million *lire* lump sum settlement, is guaranteed certain civil immunities and promised specific services by the state.

1930 (1930-1931)

USA, 18 February 1930. A new planet discovered beyond Neptune by the astronomer Clyde Tombaugh is named Pluto.

London, 22 February 1930. Press baron Lord Beaverbrook launches the United Empire Party to promote imperial preference.

Russia, 24 February 1930. A report claims that 40 *kulaks* (rich peasants) a day are being murdered by Stalin's agents.

Italy, 2 March 1930. The controversial novelist D H Lawrence, author of *Sons and Lovers* and *Women in Love* dies of tuberculosis at the age of 44.

Britain, 19 March 1930. Arthur James Balfour, the conservative prime minister from 1902-05, dies.

Britain, 21 April 1930. Robert Bridges, poet laureate since 1913, dies aged 85.

London, 21 April 1930. The London Naval Treaty, limiting the great powers' navies, is signed.

China, 23 April 1930. The nationalist General Chiang Kai-shek battles with the northern warlord General Yan Xishan.

Britain, 9 May 1930. John Masefield is appointed poet laureate.

South Africa, 19 May 1930. White women are given the vote.

London, 22 May 1930. Talks between Labour and Liberal leaders over electoral reform break down. The informal pact between the two parties is over.

London, 29 May 1930. The BBC forms its own permanent symphony orchestra under the directorship of Adrian Boult.

India, 31 May 1930. New measures are introduced to curb civil disobedience, following the arrest of Gandhi on 5 May and the consequent civil unrest.

Baghdad, 30 June 1930. Britain recognises Iraqi independence.

Germany, 30 June 1930. France pulls the last of its troops out of the Rhineland, five years before the date set by the Versailles Treaty.

Britain, 7 July 1930. The writer Sir Arthur Conan Doyle, the creator of Sherlock Holmes, dies aged 81.

China, 10 July 1930. Communist armies unite to attack Hankow.

Egypt, 22 July 1930. British battleships sail for Egypt to deal with nationalist anti-British riots.

Uruguay, 30 July 1930. Uruguay win football's first World Cup.

London, 7 August 1930. Two million people are unemployed.

Central Asia, 12 August 1930. The Turkish and Persian armies launch an offensive on Kurdish rebels.

Australia, 18 August 1930. The two halves of the new Sydney Harbour Bridge are joined.

Peru, 25 August 1930. President Augusto Leguia resigns after a coup.

Beiping (Beijing), 2 September 1930. General Yen Hsi-chan forms a rebel government.

Argentina, 6 September 1930. The radical president Hipolito Irigoyen is overthrown by army officers led by General Uriburu.

Germany, 15 September 1930. The *Nazi* leader Adolf Hitler is barred as an Austrian citizen from taking his seat in the *reichstag*.

Athens, 5 October 1930. A congress between the Balkan states opens, aimed at promoting cooperation.

Berlin, 13 October 1930. There is uproar in the reichstag when Nazi deputies turn up in uniform, which is illegal for civilians.

France, 16 October 1930. A line of defences known as the Maginot Line is to be built along France's frontier with Germany.

Ankara, 30 October 1930. Turkey and Greece sign a treaty of friendship.

Brazil, 1 November 1930. President Vargas dissolves the congress.

Addis Ababa, 2 November 1930. Ras Tafari is crowned Emperor Haile Selassie of Ethiopia.

China, 5 November 1930. An "encirclement campaign" by Nationalist government forces against areas of Hunan, Hubei and Jiangxi begins.

Austria, 9 November 1930. The Socialists are victorious in elections to the Austrian parliament.

Japan, 14 November 1930. The prime minister, Hamagushi, is shot dead by a right-wing militant.

Germany, 30 November 1930. The Nazis are victorious in municipal elections in Bremen.

Iraq, 6 January 1931. A royal palace dating from 550BC is found at the site of the city of Ur.

London, 23 January 1931. The Russian ballerina Anna Pavlova dies aged 49.

London, 26 January 1931. Winston Churchill resigns from Baldwin's shadow cabinet after disagreeing with the policy of conciliation with Indian nationalism.

India, 26 January 1931. Mahatma Gandhi, the Indian nationalist leader, is released from prison.

Woman flies from England to Australia

Darwin, Australia, 24 April 1930
Record crowds were here this afternoon to cheer the arrival of Amy Johnson. At 3.55 pm, after circling the aerodrome, she landed her plane smoothly to become the first woman ever to fly solo from England to Australia.

Amy Johnson's adventure began with crossing the English Channel in thick fog. Violent storms twice made her lose control of her de Havilland Moth and forced her to land – once in a Near Eastern Desert, and again between Java and Sourabaya. She finished her epic journey in 19 days, despite delays in Rangoon and Bangkok to repair damage to the plane.

Amy Johnson, on the Tiger Moth that took her to Australia.

British report recommends federal India

London, 23 June 1930
The Simon Commission has recommended a federal India. Such a federation, the former Liberal home secretary believes, will safeguard the many different Indias: Hindu India, Moslem India, Sikh India, Anglo-India and the India of the princes. State elections (outside the princely states) will be direct federal elections will be indirect. That Britain is prepared to consider self-rule for India is seen as a victory for one man, though like the rest of the Congress Party he boycotted the commission: "this one-time Inner Temple lawyer, now turned seditious fakir", as the report's bitterest critic, Winston Churchill, calls Gandhi.

Plan for Palestine angers the Zionists

Palestine, 20 October 1930
Zionist leaders today condemned Britain's latest plan for Palestine as a charter for the control of immigration to what the world's Jews still see as their "promised land". Dr Chaim Weizmann, the president of the Jewish Agency, has threatened to resign in protest against the terms of the White Paper. Ramsay MacDonald, the British prime minister, claims the plan will give more self-government to both Jews and Arabs. He says that in accordance with the League of Nations' mandate, it favours neither group. Zionists contend that the plan reverses the Balfour Declaration of 1917, in which Jews were promised a national home in Palestine.

Twin threat to power of Chiang Kai-shek

China, 23 April 1930
Two powerful challenges, from the right and the left, emerged this week to challenge General Chiang Kai-shek's long struggle to bring the whole of China under the rule of his Nationalist Party.

The aggressive northern warlord Yan Xishan has mounted a surprise "punitive expedition" and driven Chiang's men back to the southern bank of the Yellow River. Nationalist sources, however, claim that the warlord's advance has been halted and that Chiang is preparing a counter-offensive.

A far more serious long-term threat to Nationalist rule is posed by the growing power of the Communists. Bloodily and treacherously purged from the Nationalist party, they have retreated to a base in Jiangxi province where they have established a communist state and built up an army of 10,000 dedicated men and women.

Gandhi marches in defiance of salt laws

Dandi, India, 6 April 1930
Mahatma Gandhi has reached the sea, after a 300-mile (480-kilometre), 25-day journey from his *ashram* near Ahmedabad. Thousands followed him, prepared to defy the British salt tax and "break the mournful monotony of compulsory peace that is choking the heart of the nation for want of free vent". To India's millions of nationalists the salt tax of one *rupee* per 82 pounds (40 kilos) is an effective poll tax, burdening the poorest, and a symbol of foreign oppression.

At 5.30 this morning Gandhi walked down to the shore and symbolically picked up a piece of crystallised seasalt, thus breaking the salt laws. His thousands of followers did likewise. They had wanted to work the saltflats, encrusted with salt at every high tide, but the police forestalled them by stirring the

Defying the salt laws: Gandhi and his followers on the road to Dandi.

salt deposits in the mud. Many have been arrested, including Ram Das, Gandhi's son, charged with selling salt illegally. So far no policeman has dared arrest the father.

Army coup in Brazil ousts ruling clique

Rio de Janeiro, 26 October 1930
The Brazilian *coup d'etat* was formally completed today with the appointment of Dr Gertuilo Vargas as new provisional president.

He was chosen by a *junta* of army officers who overthrew the government of President Luis and his elected successor, Dr Julio Prestes, during a three-week uprising which enjoyed some popular support. The greatest number of casualties – 27 dead – occurred when the revolutionaries shot at a German liner as it left Rio.

The old regime had held power for 40 years. Its sudden disappearance has taken foreign governments by surprise. The US, a staunch supporter of the Luis regime, now wonders whether the change threatens a lucrative export market for American goods as well as its primary source of coffee.

Dr Vargas, Brazil's new strongman.

Stars are twinkling in daylight (by radio)

United States, 1931
A new kind of astronomy has been born with a "radio-telescope" developed by the American Karl Jansky. Working at the Bell Telephone laboratories, Jansky has discovered that the stars in our galaxy – the Milky Way – emit not only light

but radio waves. He has studied this radiation emanating from the constellation of Sagittarius, towards the centre of the galaxy.

This is an important development because it enables astronomers to observe the heavens in broad daylight.

Hitler is runner-up in German elections

Young Nazis "encouraging" support during the election campaign.

Berlin, 15 September 1930
The unexpected success of extreme right-wing National Socialist candidates in the Reichstag elections sent shock waves through the Berlin *Bourse* today, with shares falling as much as 20 points. The Nazis, as they are known, gained 107 seats to become the second largest party after the Socialists. In the old Reichstag they had only 12 deputies. Their vote went up from 800,000 in 1928 to 6,409,000, only 2,000,000 behind the Socialists.

Adolf Hitler, the Nazi leader, played on voters' fears of economic chaos and social disorder. The world economic crisis has meant soaring unemployment and widespread hardship, and the powerful Communist Party has instigated violent street demonstrations in the hope of starting revolution. In the election campaign, Hitler made furious speeches denouncing Jews and Bolsheviks as the cause of the nation's problems and promising to make Germany great again.

Weimar star Marlene Dietrich, breaking into the English-speaking market with Josef von Sternberg's cinematic masterpiece, "The Blue Angel".

1931 (1931-1932)

Spain, 18 February 1931. Martial law is re-imposed as King Alfonso struggles to retain power.

Germany, 24 February 1931. Almost five million people are unemployed.

London, 28 February 1931. Oswald Mosley forms the New Party, dedicated to parliamentary reform.

Washington, DC, 3 March 1931. "The Star Spangled Banner" becomes the US national anthem.

India, 4 March 1931. The viceroy agrees to end the government's salt monopoly in return for an end to civil disobedience.

London, 16 March 1931. The minority Labour government is defeated in the Commons over a clause in the Electoral Reform Bill.

Spain, 12 April 1931. Election results show that republicans have swept the polls in most cities.

Spain, 14 April 1931. King Alfonso XIII abdicates.

Turkey, 20 April 1931. The Republican People's Party of Mustapha Kemal wins by a landslide in the national elections.

China, 30 April 1931. Rebels under General Chen Jitang split with Chiang Kai-shek and take control of Guangzhou (*Canton*).

New York City, 1 May 1931. President Hoover opens the 1,245 foot, 120-floor Empire State Building.

Vienna, 11 May 1931. The bankruptcy of Credit-Anstalt begins European financial collapse.

Rome, 31 May 1931. The pope denounces Mussolini's Fascists following attacks on priests and church property.

Chicago, 12 June 1931. Al Capone and 68 henchmen are charged with breach of prohibition laws.

China, 17 June 1931. The British arrest Nguyen Ai Quoc, also known as Ho Chi Minh, founder of the Indochinese Communist Party.

Washington, DC, 22 June 1931. The President Herbert Hoover proposes that all war debts should be suspended for a year, in order to revitalise world trade.

Germany, 13 July 1931. All banks close until 5 August following the collapse of the *Danatbank*.

China, 17 July 1931. Rebels launch a drive on Tientsin.

London, 22 July 1931. Britain, the US and France renew recent credits for Germany for three months, to help Germany through financial difficulties.

China, 3 August 1931. Hundreds die when a dam on the river Yangzi bursts during a typhoon.

Cuba, 10 August 1931. President Machado declares martial law to quell a rebellion.

China, 18 September 1931. Japanese troops occupy Shenyang in Manchuria.

London, 24 August 1931. An all-party national government is formed to cope with the financial emergency that defeated the Labour government. Ramsay MacDonald remains prime minister.

Belgrade, 2 September 1931. King Alexander ends his dictatorship.

Austria, 13 September 1931. A *coup d'etat* by the Fascist Heimwehr (*national guard*) fails.

London, 15 September 1931. Gandhi demands Indian independence at a conference.

London, 23 September 1931. The Stock Exchange re-opens after closing for two days when Britain abandoned the gold standard.

Copenhagen, 28 September 1931. Denmark abandons the gold standard. Norway, Sweden and Egypt did so yesterday.

London, 6 October 1931. A general election is called for 27 October.

Britain, 28 October 1931. The National government stays in power after the largest election landslide in history.

China, 7 November 1931. The Chinese Soviet Republic is established, with Ruijin (*Jiangxi*) as its capital.

Germany, 15 November 1931. The *Nazi* Party wins elections in the state of Hesse.

China, 27 November 1931. Mao Zedong is appointed chairman of the central executive committee of the Chinese Soviet Republic.

London, 1 December 1931. The conference on India ends in failure.

Spain, 10 December 1931. Senor Nicetor Alcala Zamora is elected as Spain's first constitutional president by the national assembly. Manuel Azana is prime minister.

Tokyo, 11 December 1931. Japan abandons the gold standard.

India, 4 January 1932. Gandhi is arrested and the Indian National Congress outlawed.

China, 31 January 1932. Japanese forces take Shanghai in the war that began with the invasion of Manchuria.

China, 19 February 1932. The Japanese government has established a puppet regime in occupied Manchuria.

Berlin, 25 February 1932. Hitler is granted German citizenship.

Pound devalued as Britain faces crisis

London, 20 September 1931
The pound is poised to take a nose-dive on the foreign exchanges to-morrow after the government's shock announcement that it is abandoning the gold standard because of heavy pressure on the nation's gold reserves. A 30 per cent devaluation is expected to take the pound from $4.86 to around $3.50.

The National government, for-med a month ago by Ramsay Mac-Donald, the Labour prime minister, promised then to take all necessary steps to restore confidence in ster-ling. But the cuts in unemployment pay and other economies proved inadequate in the face of the financial crisis sweeping the world.

The Labour government collap-sed when the cabinet could not agree on spending cuts. The king asked MacDonald to head an all-party cabinet; he has four Labour ministers, four Tory and two Liberal. But Labour back-benchers, almost to a man, have denounced him as a traitor.

"Poison" fears for wonder racehorse

San Francisco, April 1932
Forensic scientists are to examine the stomach contents of Phar Lap, after an autopsy has revealed that the champion Australian racehorse may have been poisoned.

A close check is also being made on all visitors to Phar Lap's stable at Menlo Park outside San Francisco where the horse collapsed and died after making a sensational de-but in America two weeks ago.

Phar Lap was resting at the stables while a contract was being negotiated with Hollywood's MGM studio for the racehorse to star in a series of short films.

America, like Australia, had taken Phar Lap to its heart after the horse had won Mexico's prestige *Agua Caliente* Handicap after giving the leaders ten lengths' start before storming to the front with half a mile to go. In Australia, where flags are flying at half-mast for Phar Lap, newspaper placards are carrying the news with the words "He's Dead".

Devastating quake hits New Zealand

The morning after: the British Insurance Company's offices in Napier.

Hawke's Bay, 3 February 1932
At least 256 people have died and thousands have been injured and made homeless by an earthquake that struck Hawke's Bay's two main centres, Napier and Hastings, early today. A fire that followed the 'quake swept through both towns and also destroyed several other centres. The force of the earth-quake – New Zealand's worst – has destroyed landmarks, with chunks of coastline falling into the sea. Napier's Bluff Hill, a sub-stantial suburban promontory, has crumbled and disintegrated.

A wide stretch of water, Ahuriri Lagoon, has been emptied by the 'quake's upthrust, creating 9,000 acres of land in a day.

Republicans force out Spanish king

Alfonso XIII, Spain's unlucky monarch, deposed by the republicans.

Madrid, 14 April 1931

With the abdication today of King Alfonso, Spain has been declared a republic and is again thrown into political turmoil. The king's downfall follows the collapse last year of the military dictatorship of General Miguel Primo de Rivera and last week's elections when the republicans swept the polls in most Spanish cities and won a huge majority in the *Cortes* (parliament).

As they celebrated victory the Republicans made it clear that it was a question of either the king's abdication or civil war. In a dramatic ceremony in the Royal Palace he signed a renunciation document, and then stood up and told the country's leading politicians: "I believe I have conscientiously served my country. Such has been my intention. At this moment I feel more a Spaniard than ever."

During his reign King Alfonso has survived several attempts on his life by anarchists, including a bomb attack on his wedding day when he was driving with his bride in an open carriage. In 1923 the army seized control with his full approval and he counted the brilliant General Primo de Rivera as his friend.

The general's resignation led to some fierce street battles between the police and students throughout Spain, and the veteran General Berenguer, appointed prime minister to see through the crisis, was unable to fill his cabinet.

Atoms smashed to pieces by scientists

Cambridge, 1932

With a £1,000 grant from their university and the backing of Lord Rutherford, two Cambridge physicists have built a machine for smashing atoms.

John Cockroft and a young Irishman, Ernest Walton, have designed and constructed a machine for accelerating elementary particles up to high speeds, using the kicking force of 800,000 volts of electricity.

In April this year, they trained a high energy beam of protons – constituents of the atomic nucleus – on to a target of lithium and transmuted the lithium atoms into those of helium. This is the first time such a transformation has been achieved.

Royal Navy mutiny against pay cuts

Scotland, 30 September 1931

The Royal Navy has mutinied. The mutiny – involving 12,000 naval ratings on 15 ships of the Atlantic Fleet at their Invergordon base on the Cromarty Firth – is the seamen's response to the government's tough new measures to combat the international crisis and prevent the country "living beyond its means". These include the 25 per cent cut in servicemen's pay which sparked off the mutiny.

The mutineers, led by Able Seaman Len Wincott, occupied a shore canteen and held a mass meeting on a nearby recreation field. The atmosphere, however, is closer to a peaceful strike than a mutiny. Though there are firearms on the ships, the ratings have not broken into the magazines, and the only violence has been an officer being hit on the head by a beer glass. The men have now returned to their ships, singing "The more we are together, the merrier we will be".

Protests against the economic measures are not confined to the navy. Government employees, who will all suffer cuts, have been marching the streets in protest all month. Reaction amongst the unemployed has been even stronger, with rioters in the streets demanding a full restoration of the "dole".

Japanese launch attack in Manchuria

Manchuria, 18 September 1931

Japanese troops, sent to Manchuria to guard the South Manchurian railway which Japan has turned into a huge military-industrial complex, today launched a surprise attack on the Chinese garrison at Mukden. The local Japanese commander used the pretext of a bomb explosion on the railway line to attack the Chinese garrison. He seems to have acted on his own initiative.

Between 70 and 80 Chinese soldiers have been killed, and the city has been overrun without any resistance being offered. The governor of Manchuria apparently ordered his men not to shoot because he believes that the attack is designed to provoke an incident which will provide the Japanese with an excuse to seize Manchuria. To outsiders, however, it appears that the ultranationalist Japanese officer corps intends to annex Man-

Might and money: Japanese militarism, suckled by Japanese capitalism.

churia as the first stage in the occupation of all China, with or without pretext. General Chiang Kai-shek is understood to be placing his faith in an appeal to the League of Nations rather than fight the Japanese.

Light goes out for legendary inventor

Edison: the inventor of the lightbulb, phonograph and ticker-tape machine.

New Jersey, 21 October 1931

America dipped its lights for a minute tonight in honour of the man who gave it the electric light-bulb. Thomas Alva Edison, perhaps the most prolific inventor in history, has died at the age of 84. His was an extraordinary career, a huge catalogue of nearly 1,300 inventions. His energy was equally tireless. "To stop is to rust," he once said – 3,500 crammed notebooks bear testimony. To him the world owes the lightbulb, the phonograph, ticker-tape machines and much of the technology of moving pictures. He gave this insight into the workings of the creative mind: "Genius," he said, "is one per cent inspiration and 99 per cent perspiration."

Huxley's vision of a Brave New World

London, 1932

Critics are hailing *Brave New World*, a vision of the future as a sanitised playground for carefully indoctrinated inhuman beings, as one of the most important novels since the Great War.

Aldous Huxley, the grandson of the scientist T H Huxley and author of satires on contemporary life, envisages a Utopia in which babies are fertilised in laboratory bottles, children are made to conform by "sleep-learning", sterile adults indulge in safe promiscuous sex and a mildly stimulating drug called "soma" is passed around at parties. The "Feelies" have overtaken the movies. The burden of the nightmare is that the idea of human progress through scientific advance will turn out to be an illusion.

1932 (1932-1933)

China, 9 Marhc 1932. Puyi, the last emperor of China, is installed as head of the Japanese puppet state of Manchukuo (*Manchuria*.

Australia, 18 March 1932. Sydney Harbour Bridge is opened, the world's longest single-span bridge.

Ireland, 29 March 1932. Eamon de Valera, the hard-line republican leader of the *Fianna Fail* Party, will head the new government.

Germany, 10 April 1932. Paul von Hindenburg wins the presidency against Adolf Hitler after a second ballot to secure a majority.

Berlin, 24 April 1932. The *Nazis* lead in four state elections. In the Prussian state parliament their seats rise from six to 162.

China, 5 May 1932. Japanese troops withdraw from Shanghai after an armistice is signed.

France, 6 May 1932. President Paul Doumer is assassinated.

Japan, 15 May 1932. Militarists assassinate the prime minister Ki Inukai.

Austria, 20 May 1932. Engelbert Dollfuss, the Christian Socialist leader, is appointed chancellor to succeed Karl Buresch who failed to form a government.

Athens, 25 May 1932. A new government is formed with as prime minister, Andreas Papanastasiou following the resignation of Eleutherios Venizelos on 21 May.

Berlin, 31 May 1932. President Hindenburg invites Franz von Papen to form a government.

Berlin, 1 June 1932. Franz von Papen forms a cabinet that excludes the Nazis.

Bangkok, 29 June 1932. The Siamese army seizes power in a *coup* against the monarchy.

USA, 2 July 1932. Franklin D Roosevelt wins the Democratic nomination for president.

Lisbon, 5 July 1932. Antonio de Oliveira Salazar is appointed fascist prime minister.

Switzerland, 9 July 1932. The allies vote to ease Germany's economic crisis by suspending the repayments of war debts.

Switzerland, 11 July 1932. The World Bank calls for a return to the gold standard.

Berlin, 26 July 1932. The war minister, Kurt von Schleicher, says that Germany is ready to rearm.

Germany, 31 July 1932. The National Socialists (Nazis) are now the biggest party in the *reichstag* following the general election, but without an overall majority.

Berlin, 13 August 1932. Adolf Hitler refuses to serve as vice-chancellor under von Papen.

Berlin, 30 August 1932. The Nazi Hermann Goering is elected president of the reichstag.

Madrid, 9 September 1932. The government acknowledges the autonomy of Catalonia.

India, 24 September 1932. The Poona Pact is signed, extending the voting rights of Untouchables. Gandhi, who has risked unpopularity for supporting the Untouchables' cause, ends his prison fast.

Britain, 28 September 1932. Four Liberal ministers resign in protest against the National government's trade policies.

China, 6 October 1932. With the help of Germany military advisers, Chiang Kai-shek launches a campaign to isolate rebel territories held by both the warlords and the Red Army.

USSR, 9 October 1932. Joseph Stalin expels two leading Bolsheviks, Gregori Zinoviev and Leon Kamenev, from the Communist Party and exiles them to Siberia.

Berlin, 14 October 1932. The government unveils plans for direct presidential rule in the state of Prussia.

Berlin, 16 October 1932. Albert Einstein puts the earth's age at ten billion years.

London, 30 October 1932. Hunger marchers, protesting at unemployment, fight pitched street battles with police.

USA, 8 November 1932. Franklin D Roosevelt defeats the sitting republican president, Herbert Hoover, in the presidential elections.

Berlin, 17 November 1932. The prime minister von Papen resigns after failing to form a government.

Berlin, 21 November 1932. Hitler refuses the chancellorship if it means combining with other parties as Hindenburg wants.

Germany, 24 November 1932. The Nationalists take seats from the Nazis in the election.

Berlin, 2 December 1932. General Kurt von Schleicher is appointed chancellor.

Britain, 25 December 1932. King George V makes the first royal Christmas Day broadcast to the empire.

Dublin, 2 January 1933. The *Dail* is dissolved; de Valera calls an election for 24 January.

Berlin, 28 January 1933. Amidst growing violence General von Schleicher resigns as chancellor.

Martial law in Spain as anarchy brews

Madrid, 10 January 1933
Spain is rapidly descending into violent anarchy and the government is poised to declare martial law. The trouble is being caused by the Anarchists, who have been joined by the Anarcho-Syndicalists and the Communists, and a general strike is in the offing.

In the southern provinces where the turmoil is at its worst there is already undeclared martial law. A number of people in Seville have been wounded in exchanges of gunfire, and there have been several bomb explosions. In Barcelona bombs have killed five people in the last few days. An Anarcho-Syndicalist manifesto has called on opponents of the government to disrupt telephone, telegraph and railway lines. Given the situation, the prime minister, Manual Azana, is not expected to survive in office.

Australian leader is forced from office

Sydney, 13 May 1932
In an unprecedented constitutional move, John Lang, the prime minister of the Australian state of New South Wales, has been dismissed by state governor, Sir Philip Game. Lang, a militant socialist, led the 1925-27 Labour government of New South Wales, which restored the 44-hour week, introduced free secondary education brought in child endowment and widows' pensions. Re-elected in 1930 he promised to be equally radical, but his plan to limit the effects of the Depression by withholding interest on British loans provoked strong opposition. The strongest comes from the neo-Fascist New Guard, who have promised to stamp out "the bushfire of Langism".

India: favour for one alienates other

New Delhi, India, 16 August 1932
Electoral arrangements for the provincial legislatures of India have just been published. It is known as the "Communal Award", but it appears only one community has got any awards – the Moslems, who now have control of Bengal and Punjab. The new provincial legislatures are Britain's main hope for legitimacy as the pro-Congress Hindu majority continues its policy of non-cooperation. But fear by Moslems of Hindus, and fear by Britain of Congress, have weighed the reforms in the Moslems' favour.

Indeed, the Moslems and the princes are the only allies Britain has left in India, but the more it relies upon them, the more militant the Hindu majority becomes.

"King Kong", Hollywood's version of "Beauty and the Beast": the story of a prehistoric monster, captured, displayed and humiliated, yet refusing to submit to the outrages inflicted on him – until face to face with Beauty.

Japan quits the League

Japan's Manchurian candidate, Puyi, ready to serve his masters.

Japan, 25 February 1933
Japan withdrew from the League of Nations this afternoon in response to a vote condemning the invasion of Manchuria. The league unanimously resolved that the Japanese should evacuate Manchuria and allow an autonomous government to be set up.

The split has been on the cards ever since Japanese troops attacked the Chinese garrison at Mukden in September 1931. American mediation secured a temporary cease-fire, but within a few weeks the Japanese had advanced again and captured Shanghai. British, Italian and

Wondering why? A victim of Japanese bombing and his daughter.

French forces became involved, in an attempt to protect foreign nationals.

Having installed Puyi, the last emperor of China, as head of the puppet state of Manchuria, Japan pursued its war with China, claiming that the Nationalist government of Chiang Kai-shek had no sovereign rights over the area.

"Japan has left the League of Nations with a heavy heart," said Mr Matsuoka, the chief Japanese delegate, who was outvoted 42-1, with the Siamese abstaining. Dr Yen, the Chinese delegate, thanked the league for its "courageous verdict".

Dark days of Depression

London: hunger marchers from the north, charged by mounted police.

The World, 1932
In Britain, ironically enough, they are singing "The sun has got his hat on" as the country lurches into deep industrial depression. In America, where unemployed executives and skilled workers begged on street corners, the smash hit song is more to the point. "Buddy, can you spare a dime?" it asks.

Throughout the western world unemployment has soared. More than two million Britons are out of work, relying on the "dole" money of 29s 3d a week to live. The industrial north is hardest hit, with factories, mills and docks lying idle.

Although men have marched to London from Lancashire to protest, and food riots have taken place in London, Bristol and Liverpool, the bulk of unemployed appear to have accepted their lot with sullen stoicism. They have even accepted a means test, allowing a tribunal to cut their meagre dole on the slightest suspicion of extra earnings.

In America, some 14 million are

USA: an unemployed man, fighting the stigma of the unemployable.

unemployed and a young British student, Alistair Cooke, has written of well-dressed men who had told their wives they were looking for night work, begging for dimes.

American hopes are pinned on a presidential candidate, Franklin Roosevelt. Britain has discarded a much-divided Labour government; in Germany, five million unemployed look to Adolf Hitler's Nazi party to solve their problems.

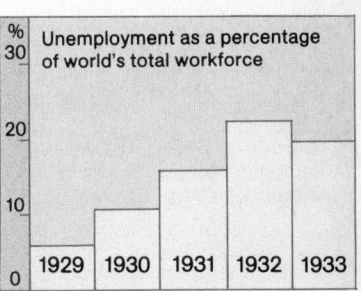

Stalin purges close colleagues of Lenin

Moscow, 9 October 1932
Joseph Stalin has stepped up his purge of the Old Bolsheviks and has expelled two close colleagues of Lenin from the Communist party. Lev Kamenev and Gregory Zinoviev, who shared power with Stalin after Lenin's death have lost their party cards and been sent into exile in Siberia. Nearly 20 other leading Communist officials have also been caught up in the crackdown. They have all been accused of trying to restore capitalism, and more significantly, of receiving documents from a "counter-revolutionary group". This is seen as a reference to a journal written by the exiled Leon Trotsky, whose strident criticisms of Stalin's authoritarian rule could produce a ferocious backlash.

Zinoviev, chairman of the Communist International – ousted.

"Bodyline" bowling is just not cricket

Adelaide, January 1933
A total break in cricket relations between England and Australia is now threatened, following a cabled demand by Australia's Cricket Board of Control to the MCC for a ban on bodyline bowling, which has marred the first three Tests.

The potentially dangerous technique, developed by England's Harold Larwood, of bowling very fast short-pitched deliveries on the leg side is a "menace" and "unsportsmanlike", the Australian board says. It warns that "unless stopped at once it is likely to upset friendly relations existing between Australia and England".

Australian tempers flared during the latest Test at Adelaide when rising balls from Larwood knocked out one Australian batsman and thumped the Australian captain, Billy Woodfull, close to the heart.

New York is shocked by Marxist mural

Diego de Rivera: a detail from his mural "The city of Tenochtitlan".

New York, 13 May
A mural by the Mexican revolutionary painter, Diego Rivera, for the Rockefeller Center has so shocked New York Society that Nelson Rockefeller has destroyed it. Called *Man at the Crossroads*, it is provocatively Marxist, with portraits of Marx, Lenin and Trotsky.

Mexico's muralists emerged from the Mexican revolution. "The Revolution revealed Mexico to us," said the painter Octavio Paz. "Or better, it gave us eyes to see it." Mexico had a long Indian tradition of mural painting. Rivera saw his first Indian murals at Chichen Itza, in the temple of the Jaguars, on his return to Mexico after a successful career as a Cubist painter in Paris. Soon, like his fellow revolutionaries, he was heavily romanticising Mexico's Indians, seeing them as Mexico's proletariat.

With his fellow revolutionary muralists, Hose Orozco and David Siqueiros – *Los Tres Grandes* – he daubed Mexico City in bright murals, depicting man at the centre of an Indian universe. One, Orozco's *Christ destroying his cross*, was so defaced by angry Catholics that it had to be repainted. Rivera's early murals, such as his *Creation*, were allegorical. It was not until 1926 that they took on the political and epic qualities that have so outraged New York Society.

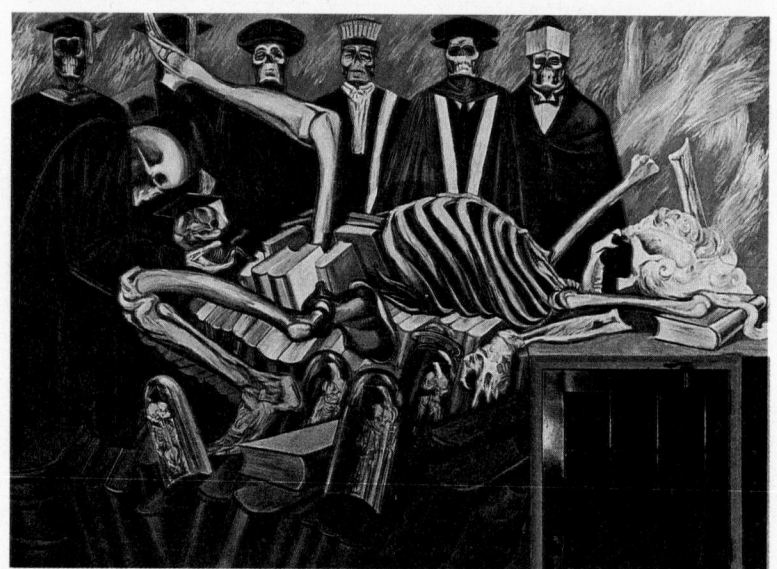

Marxist Hose Clement Orozco's mural: "Gods of the Modern World".

FDR: 100 days of war on Depression

Washington, 16 June
No one really believed that this shy, crippled patrician, the very epitome of American wealth, could take hold of the failing economy of this country and shake it so violently. President Franklin Delano Roosevelt has done just that.

Today he persuaded the US Congress to pass an act – the National Industrial Recovery Act – which would have been thought unthinkable in a capitalist society six months ago before he became President. The act gives him power not merely to control industry, but to bring unions and bosses together, shorten working hours, fix wages and regulate production.

Roosevelt made it clear he was prepared to adopt near-dictatorial powers to save the country. He closed the banks, allowing federal

"What we need is another pump": a comment on the New Deal.

aid only to the efficient; now he is bailing out farmers and homeowners who are behind with their mortgages. Three billion dollars being ploughed into public works programmes throughout the states. The Tennessee Valley Authority will bring water and forests to the dustbowl; and a civilian "conservation corps" will employ young people to plant trees. A million new jobs will be created.

Unlike others, this president confides in the people in regular "fireside chats" on the radio which are listened to by millions. With supreme confidence, he has repealed prohibition laws. "I think this would be a good time for a beer," he told Congress; back at work, Americans drank his health.

Terror and oppression launch Hitler's new age

Hitler becomes chancellor in new coalition

Berlin, 30 January

Adolf Hitler, a rabble-rousing Jew-baiting demagogue who has never held public office, today became chancellor of Germany. President Paul von Hindenburg, who had earlier dismissed Hitler as "that Bavarian corporal" who would make the country a dictatorship, finally gave way to pressures from bankers, high army officers and right-wing politicians, who were crying for order and discipline.

Three chancellors in as many years failed to secure a stable majority in the reichstag and were obliged to rule by presidential decree, while unemployment soared to six million and Hitler's Nazis and Communists fought bloody street battles.

The right-wing Nationalists in the cabinet, including Franz von Papen, the vice-chancellor, are confident they will soon tame Hitler and his wild men in brown uniforms with swastika armbands. Others are not so sure. Hitler's

Hitler at a Brownshirt rally.

speeches, in which he denounces Jews, Bolsheviks, capitalists and the Versailles peace treaty, bring his audiences to their feet baying "*Sieg Heil! Sieg Heil!*" and stabbing the air with Nazi salutes.

Reichstag is funeral pyre of democracy

Berlin, 28 February

All legal guarantees of personal liberty, freedom of speech and the right of assembly were wiped out today by an official decree issued in the wake of last night's devastating reichstag fire. For many Berliners the gutted, smoke-blackened building represents the funeral pyre of German democracy.

The fire has been blamed on a simple-minded Dutch Communist, Marinus van der Lubbe, who was picked up by police in the reichstag grounds. But some observers accuse the Nazis of having a hand in the affair. Certainly Adolf Hitler, who became chancellor a month ago, seems delighted. "This is a God-given signal," he cried as he watched the building burn.

Within hours he had pressured President Hindenburg into giving him dictatorial powers. Now he no longer needs the votes of the deputies in the reichstag, where his Nazis did not have a majority. In the run-up to the election, to be

The forces of order surveying Germany's gutted democracy.

held next month, Nazi Storm Troopers, now enrolled as special police, are arresting socialists and communists and suppressing opposition newspapers. The radio has become a Nazi propaganda vehicle controlled by Dr Goebbels.

Germany is swept by a wave of tyranny

Nazi students feeding a bonfire of liberal and intellectual "vanities".

Berlin, 23 March

Against a background of mounting Nazi violence throughout Germany, the reichstag today voted to give Hitler, rather than the president, full powers to rule by decree. In spite of the intimidation practised during the election campaign, the Nazis, with 17,277,180 votes (44 per cent) failed to gain a reichstag majority. Hitler solved the problem by having Communist and Socialist deputies arrested.

The Nazi campaign of terror against Jews is being stepped up. Jewish-owned shops are being shut down, Jewish professors are being thrown out of universities, and school textbooks are to be rewritten

to include "racial science". A three-times-married mother of 11 children, Gertrud Scholtz-Klink, has been appointed National Women's Leader to mobilise German women to serve the state.

Officials of trade unions and employers' organisations are being sacked and replaced by Nazis. The Boy Scouts are being dissolved and replaced by a Hitler Youth organisation run by the anti-Semite Baldur von Schirach.

Translated – "I am a Jew but I will never complain about the Nazis."

"Urban debauchery," by Otto Dix, one of first artists to flee from Hitler.

1934 (1934-1935)

Germany, 10 January 1934. The alleged Reichstag arsonist Marinus van der Lubbe is guillotined.

Britain, 21 January 1934. The British Union of Fascists, led by Sir Oswald Mosley, holds its biggest rally ever in Birmingham.

Berlin, 26 January 1934. Germany signs a ten-year non-aggression pact with Poland.

Belgium, 17 February 1934. King Albert dies in a climbing accident near Namur; his son succeeds as Leopold III.

Austria, 17 February 1934. A Socialist uprising is bloodily suppressed.

Nicaragua, 22 February 1934. National Guardsmen gun down General Augusto Sandino.

Britain, 23 February 1934. Sir Edward Elgar, Master of the King's Musick since 1924, dies aged 76.

China, 28 February 1934. The ex-emperor Puyi accepts the throne of Japanese-occupied Manchukuo (*Manchuria*).

Madrid, 25 April 1934. Martial law is declared as the government resigns.

Rome, 29 April 1934. The Italian parliament votes to remove its last remaining powers.

Vienna, 30 April 1934. The Chancellor Engelbert Dollfuss is made dictator of a rump parliament which then votes itself out of existence.

Near East, 6 May 1934. Saudi Arabian forces capture the Yemeni city of Hodeida.

Saudi Arabia, 13 May 1934. Saudi Arabia signs a truce with Yemen in Jeddah.

Bulgaria, 19 May 1934. Fascists seize power in a coup aided by King Boris.

Louisiana, 23 May 1934. The famous outlaws Bonnie and Clyde are killed in a police ambush.

Czechoslovakia, 24 May 1934. Tomas Mazaryk is elected president for the fourth time.

Britain, 25 May 1934. The composer Gustav Holst, who made his name with the suite *The Planets*, dies aged 59.

Eastern Europe, 8 June 1934. Poland, Rumania and the USSR sign a pact guaranteeing their present frontiers.

Saudi Arabia, 27 June 1934. King ibn Saud and the Imam of Yemen sign a peace treaty to end the "Desert War".

Germany, 30 June 1934. In the "Night of the Long Knives" Hitler purges the Fascist Party.

Berlin, 3 July 1934. The Vice-chancellor von Papen, resigns.

Berlin, 13 July 1934. Hitler justifies the "Night of the Long Knives", claiming that the SA were plotting to overthrow him.

Germany, 13 July 1934. Heinrich Himmler is appointed head of the concentration camps.

Vienna, 26 July 1934. The government orders the round-up of Austrian Nazis following the murder of Chancellor Dollfuss.

Vienna, 29 July 1934. Dr Kurt von Schuschnigg is appointed chancellor.

Berlin, 2 August 1934. Hitler assumes the title "Fuhrer" on the death of Hindenburg.

Germany, 4 September 1934. 750,000 attend the opening of the Nazi party conference.

Spain, 8 October 1934. Martial law is declared following a bid to declare Catalonia independent.

Yugoslavia, 11 October 1934. Anti-Italian and anti-Hungarian riots follow the assassination of King Alexander in Marseilles two days ago. His ten-year-old son Peter will succeed.

Ankara, 25 November 1934. Mustapha Kemal tells Turks to adopt a surname by 1 January 1935. His will be *"Ataturk"*, Father of The Turks.

Egypt, 30 November 1934. A royal decree annuls the constitution and dissolves the Egyptian parliament.

USSR, 1 December 1934. Stalin's aide Sergei Kirov is murdered.

Ethiopia, 5 December 1934. Ethiopian and Italian troops clash at Wal-Wal, over 20 miles inside southeastern Ethiopia.

Turkey, 14 December 1934. Women get the vote.

Tehran, 27 December 1934. The government declares that Persia will now be known as Iran.

USSR, 29 December 1934. More than 100 people have been executed following the murder of Stalin's aide Sergei Kirov.

North Africa, 1 January 1935. The Italian colonies of Cyrenaica, Tripoli and Fezzan are merged under the name of Libya.

Africa, 15 January 1935. Mussolini unites Eritrea and Somaliland as Italian East Africa.

Rome, 24 January 1935. Mussolini dismisses the entire cabinet.

Italy, 23 February 1935. Troops set sail for Ethiopia as the border dispute over the Italian post at Wal-Wal inside Ethiopia escalates.

Purge follows murder of Stalin associate

One of Stalin's party "purge committees", rooting out "Trotskyists".

Leningrad, December 1934
The bloody reprisals following the murder of Sergei Kirov, a rising star in the Communist Party, have led to speculation that Joseph Stalin is once again embarking on a policy of terror.

More than 100 people have been hastily implicated, tried and executed. Zinoviev and Kamenev, former comrades of Lenin, have been sent into internal exile. However, it is rumoured that Stalin himself ordered the assassination, carried out by an obscure dissident.

Stalin claimed recently there was "nothing to prove and no one left to beat"; the civil war against the peasants was over and most of the industrial targets of the first Five-Year Plan had been met. However, this month's events suggest he has declared war on the party that gave him his ladder to power.

Encircled Chinese communists break out

China, 16 October 1934
China's Communists under their general, the ex-warlord, ex-opium addict Zhu De, have began to break out of their Jiangxi Soviet Republic through Chiang Kai-shek's encircling forces. Columns of troops, carrying rifles, hoes and sowing machines, pour westwards. Chiang, who failed to take Jiangxi by storm in four campaigns, has adopted new tactics, surrounding the Red enclave with a network of barbed wire and blockhouses. Nearly half a million men and 400 modern aircraft have been used against the communists, and the innocent peasants caught up in this ruthless war have suffered terribly.

One 10,000-strong force under Fang Zhihmin tried to break out earlier this summer but it was wiped out and Fang's head was put on display in Nanchang. Now Zhu De and his political mentor Mao Zedong have set out with 80,000

On the march: Mao Zedong, political mentor of China's Reds.

troops, accompanied by 20,000 non-combatants, to march eastwards to safety, although no one knows where. All that is certain is that it will be a very long march.

Long knives buried in Brownshirt backs

Munich, 30 June 1934

Lurid stories of perversion and debauchery are being passed on after the massacre, in the early hours this morning, of hundreds – some say thousands – of senior Nazi Storm Troopers. Among the dead is Ernst Roehm, one of Hitler's closest comrades from the earliest days of the National Socialist Party. He was dragged from his bed and shot in a lakeside hotel outside Munich. In another room, Obergruppenfuhrer

Edmund Heines was found in bed with a youth. Hitler was on hand to make sure no one was overlooked. Hitler claims he has foiled a plot to overthrow him, but the more generally accepted story is that the army threatened to take over unless he got rid of his Brownshirt thugs and stopped talk of socialist revolution. Whatever the truth, the "Night of the Long Knives", has crushed the Brownshirts and established the supremacy of the Blackshirts, or SS.

Unrest in Spain as Catalonians rebel

Half a million demonstrating in Barcelona for a "free Catalonia".

Madrid, 8 October 1934

Despite martial law fierce fighting is taking place throughout Spain as workers stage a series of strikes and riots with Catalonia bidding to set up its own government. The trouble has been triggered by the new right-wing government in Madrid introducing three ministers from the staunchly Catholic "Popular Action".

In Catalonia the situation was relieved with the arrival by sea from Morocco of a battalion of the Span-

ish Foreign Legion which marched from the harbour to the sound of bugles and drums. Rifle and machine-gun fire can be heard from many quarters of Madrid. The army garrison has been mobilised to relieve the exhausted civil guard. The home of the prime minister, Lerroux, has been fired at.

Some 8,000 monarchist officers who were retired at the time of the abdication of King Alfonso have been invited over the radio to resume service with the colours.

Briton invents aeroplane tracking device

Slough, England, 1935

A new device for tracking enemy aircraft has been developed at a government research station here. It bounces radio off flying objects.

"Radar" is the brainchild of Robert Watson-Watt and his colleague, A F Wilkins, who recalled a Post

Office engineer reporting in 1931 that passing aircraft distorted radio reception.

The idea was put to the test on 26 February when a BBC transmitter at Daventry detected a bomber at 10,000 feet from a distance of eight miles (13 kilometres).

Austrian dictator dies in failed Nazi coup

Homage to Dollfuss, his coffin guarded by members of his old regiment.

Vienna, 25 July 1934

Over 150 Austrian Nazis are under arrest tonight after an unsuccessful coup d'etat, during which the Chancellor, Engelbert Dollfuss, was shot in the throat and left for four hours to bleed to death in his office. It is widely believed that Hitler was behind the plot.

The Nazi gang, dressed in army and police uniforms, broke into the Chancellery around noon. When it was apparent the coup was going to fail, they took other ministers as hostages and tried to negotiate safe conduct to the German border. A promise was given and then retrac-

ted when it was found that Dollfuss was dead. Three police and two Nazis died in a three-hour battle for the radio station

Six months ago, Dollfuss, a devout Catholic and violently anti-socialist, used the army to crush the Schutzbund, the socialist defence force established in the big housing estates outside Vienna. The workers held out for five days. Dollfuss suspended the constitution and intended ruling by decree in order to check the growing strength of the Austrian Nazis. He sought the backing of Mussolini in resisting German pressures.

Last Chinese emperor is Manchuria's first

Manchuria, 1 March 1934

Puyi, once the boy emperor of China, now the puppet of Japan, was installed today as emperor of conquered Manchuria, renamed Manchukuo by the Japanese.

The ceremony took place amid scenes of high nostalgia. The streets were thronged with bemedalled soldiers, Mongol horsemen, painted geishas and Lama priests. Chinese nobles paid homage in splendid robes hidden since the revolution.

At his first court Puyi, now using the title Kangte, announced: "The empire of Japan, in the name of righteousness and justice, assisted the establishment of this state. Armed hostilities have ceased. The country is bathed in the radiance of the sun and moon."

Puyi: last emperor no more.

1935

Bangkok, 2 March. King Prajadhipok abdicates when his government rejects plans for more democracy in Siam.

Switzerland, 7 March. Nine-year-old Prince Ananda, now in Europe, is crowned king of Siam.

USSR, 9 March. Nikita Khrushchev is elected chief of the Communist party.

Berlin, 11 March. The German air force, or *Luftwaffe* is officially created in a proclamation by Hermann Goering.

Greece, 12 March. The former president Eleutherios Venizelos fails in an attempted coup.

Britain, 18 March. Britain protests at Germany's introduction of conscription.

Moscow, 31 March. Anthony Eden, the Lord Privy Seal, meets Maxim Litvinov, the Soviet foreign minister for talks on the international situation.

Danzig, 7 April. The Nazi party wins 60 per cent of the vote in the free city.

Italy, 14 April. France, Britain and Italy agree to form a united front against German rearmament.

Geneva, 17 April. The League of Nations condemns Hitler's reintroduction of conscription.

Paris, 2 May. France and the USSR sign a mutual defence pact in case of attack.

Britain, 19 May. The soldier and writer Colonel Thomas Edward Lawrence dies aged 46 in a motor bicycle accident.

London, 22 May. The government announces plans to treble the size of the air force in the next two years.

Rome, 24 May. Pope Pius XI condemns the Nazi sterilisation of 56,244 "inferior" German citizens.

Paris, 4 June. Pierre Laval becomes prime minister.

Britain, 7 June. Stanley Baldwin becomes prime minister again following the resignation of Ramsay MacDonald for health reasons.

Argentina, 12 June. Bolivia and Paraguay sign an armistice to end their three-year-old war over the disputed Chaco area.

Paris, 19 June. French anger mounts following the Anglo-German naval deal signed yesterday which allows Germany to build up its navy again, albeit limited to one third of the tonnage of the Royal Navy.

Moscow, 9 July. Engineers on the underground railway discover Ivan the Terrible's torture chamber.

Britain, 29 July. T E Lawrence's *Seven Pillars of Wisdom* is published posthumously.

Washington, DC, 14 August. President Roosevelt signs the Social Security Bill, introducing welfare for the old, sick and unemployed.

Germany, 15 August. On Hitler's orders the *swastika* becomes the national flag.

Ethiopia, 25 August. The country is put on a war footing in anticipation of an Italian invasion.

Mexico, 1 September. It is announced that women workers are to be given the vote.

Utah, 3 September. Sir Malcolm Campbell sets a new land speed record of 301.337 mph.

Philippines, 15 September. Manuel Quezon is elected president in the first elections since the US granted a new constitution.

Ethiopia, 3 October. Mussolini's Fascist troops march into Ethiopia.

Britain, 8 October. Clement Richard Attlee is elected stop-gap leader of the Labour party.

Ethiopia, 8 November. The Italians complete their occupation of Tigre province, seizing the provincial capital, Makale.

Britain, 16 November. The National government, now Tory in all but name, is back in power with a huge majority.

Italy, 18 November. Economic sanctions are imposed on Italy by the League of Nations.

Greece, 25 November. King George II returns to his country after 12 years in exile, restored to his throne by a referendum.

China, 26 November. Japanese troops march into Beiping (*Beijing*) to support a coup in Tokyo which has set up the so-called autonomous state of Hebei province in the north.

Cairo, 12 December. King Fuad restores Egypt's 1923 parliamentary constitution.

Czechoslovakia, 18 December. Eduard Benes, the chosen successor to Masaryk, who resigned four days ago because of old age, is elected president.

Britain, 18 December. Sir Samuel Hoare, the foreign secretary, resigns following an agreement he made with the French prime minister, Pierre Laval to appease Mussolini. The prime minister, Stanley Baldwin, demanded apology or resignation.

London, 22 December. Anthony Eden is appointed foreign secretary.

Mao's troops end long march into history

China, 20 October

At the end of a march which has lasted a year and covered 6,000 miles (9,600 kilometres) the battered, emaciated survivors of the Communists' First Front Army have at last reached the comparative safety of Yan'an in the wilds of northwest China.

The long march has already become a legend. The Communists, forced out of their "soviet state" of Jiangxi, have passed through 11 provinces, crossed 18 mountain ranges and 24 major rivers and broken through ten encircling armies. They fought all the way. Of the 100,000 that set out only 10,000 footsore survivors have reached safety.

There are many stories of bravery against impossible odds, none more remarkable than that of the 30 volunteers who captured the Luding bridge over the Dadu river

gorge in the teeth of murderous machine-gun fire. The march has established Mao Zedong as the undisputed leader of the China's communists. He awaits the arrival of stragglers from other communist forces and plans to rebuild the Red Army on the battle-hardened, dedicated cadres of the Long March.

China caves in to Japanese ultimatum

Japanese soldiers being blessed by the emperor before departing for China.

China, 18 June

The government of China caved in today to a Japanese ultimatum and agreed to remove a division of troops from the north and to dismiss Song Zheyuan, the governor of Chahar and one of the few Chinese commanders to put up a successful resistance to the Japanese during the aggression of 1933.

The Chiang Kai-shek government has also agreed to replace loyalist government officials with puppets who can be trusted to do the bidding of the Japanese. The excuse for this humiliating agreement was the arrest of three Japanese secret agents. The Japanese pretended outrage at this treatment of their "civilian officials" and demanded a more "friendly" attitude from the Chinese.

Chiang, busy fighting the Communists, was forced to give in, but he will lose much political and military influence in northern China.

Britain to increase spending on arms

London, 4 March

In a major reversal of rearmament policy Britain today announced new expansion plans for its army, navy and air force. The plans, in a defence white paper, are to demonstrate that Britain does not take lightly Germany's continuing rearmament.

The white paper calls for an enlarged fleet, improved defences for warships against air attack, more aircraft for the RAF and new coastal and anti-aircraft defences. The emphasis on air defence follows fears that Britain is an easy target for cross-Channel air raids.

Explaining the government's policy shift Stanley Baldwin said: "Our attempt to lead the world towards disarmament by unilateral example has failed." German rearmament now threatened to put peace at peril. Despite claims by Germany's leaders that they wanted peace, Britain could not ignore the way Germany's forces are constantly being mobilised, he added.

Britain's new stance on the eve of an important Anglo-German meeting in Berlin is a victory for those in the government who believe in the healing effects of the drums of war now beginning to sound more loudly across Europe. At the Berlin meeting they want Hitler left in no doubt about how strongly Britain feels about German rearmament.

A Conservative poster for the National Government in the 1935 British general election.

Fascist troops march into Ethiopia

Ethiopia, 3 October

Mussolini's Fascist troops marched into Ethiopia today – and as the war-drums called Emperor Haile Selassie's people to fight, the League of Nations in Geneva was facing its greatest test since it was formed in 1919. Mussolini has long coveted Ethiopia, the only independent black state to survive the scramble for Africa, which inflicted such a humiliating defeat on Italy at Adowa in 1896, which he is determined to avenge.

Although the Ethiopians are resisting strongly, in spite of being attacked by gas, the real question is whether or not the league has any teeth to counter aggression. Ethiopia has cabled the league, claiming that the first bombs on the country struck a hospital bearing the Red Cross. Neither Britain nor France – the most interested of the world powers – seem anxious to intervene. Between them, they can close the Suez Canal to Italian troopships, but France is treatybound with Italy not to oppose the invasion, and Britain's Foreign Secretary, Sir Samuel Hoare, does not want to alienate Mussolini and drive him into the arms of Hitler. Although many Members of Parliament are pleading for sanctions against Italy, he has made it clear that he will seek a "breathing space" before taking steps.

For millions of Britons who have enjoyed a sweltering summer, events in Ethiopia are little more than a sideshow; the US, impotent because it is outside the League, can do nothing except except express outrage. But some observers see ominous overtones as a well-armed European power vents its power

Hoping for another Adowa, Ethiopia's army awaits the Italian invader.

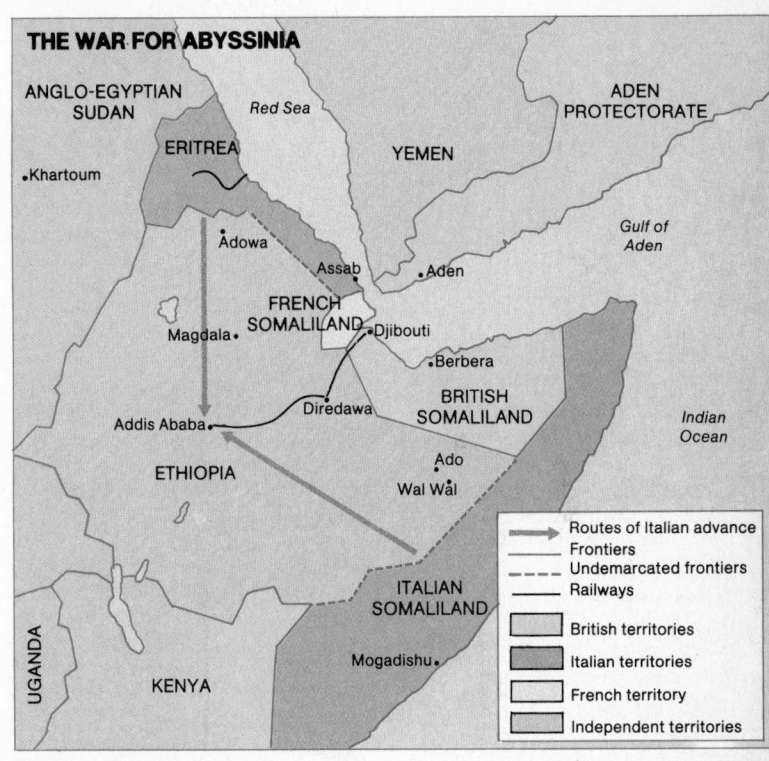

THE WAR FOR ABYSSINIA

ANGLO-EGYPTIAN SUDAN

Red Sea

ADEN PROTECTORATE

ERITREA

•Khartoum

YEMEN

Gulf of Aden

•Àdowa

Assab

•Aden

FRENCH SOMALILAND

Magdala•

•Djibouti

•Berbera

Addis Ababa•

Diredawa

BRITISH SOMALILAND

Indian Ocean

ETHIOPIA

Ado•

Wal Wàl

UGANDA

ITALIAN SOMALILAND

Mogadishu•

KENYA

→ Routes of Italian advance
— Frontiers
--- Undemarcated frontiers
— Railways

British territories
Italian territories
French territory
Independent territories

against a near-primitive African nation. In every town and village in Italy, 40 million people were ordered to gather to listen to Mussolini defy any move by the League of Nations. "We will answer with our discipline and our abstemiousness and our spirit of sacrifice," he told his captive radio audience.

War between Bolivia and Paraguay claims 35,000 victims

Paraguay, 12 June

Urged on by the United States and a confederation of five South American states, the warring nations of Bolivia and Paraguay accepted a truce here today, bringing to a halt the three-year long Chaco War.

The war, which has claimed 35,000 victims, has been fought over the ownership of the *Chaco Boreal*, a wasteland of some 100,000 square miles west of the

Paraguay river, the subject of a dispute between Paraguay and Bolivia since 1825.

Bolivia, deprived of its coastal territories since the war of the Pacific, wanted to use the Chaco as a shipping route for its oil exports. It also hoped to exploit the oil reserves of the Chaco itself.

Bolivian troops invaded in 1928, but a Pan-American conference averted outright war. Skirmishes con-

tinued until 1932 when Paraguay launched a major offensive, and formally declared war in May 1933. The Bolivian army, larger and better trained, fought back successfully, but in 1934 the Paraguayan offensive reversed the position, capturing much Bolivian land.

This tit-for-tat sequence came to an end today when the two sides, wearied by war, accepted the ceasefire.

1936 (1936-1937)

Britain, 21 January 1936. Edward VIII is proclaimed king following the death of his father George V yesterday.

India, 8 February 1936. Jawaharlal Nehru is elected president of the Indian National Congress.

Paraguay, 18 February 1936. President Eusebio Ayala resigns following yesterday's coup by military rebels.

Washington, DC, 29 February 1936. President Roosevelt signs the second neutrality bill, banning loans to countries at war.

Rhineland, 7 March 1936. German troops march into the Rhineland, in defiance of the treaties of Versailles and Locarno.

Paraguay, 11 March 1936. Paraguay sets up America's first Fascist regime.

South Africa, 7 April 1936. The Native Representation Act bans blacks from office but lets them elect three whites to represent them.

Madrid, 17 April 1936. The parliament dismisses President Zamora for trying to dissolve it unconstitutionally.

Egypt, 28 April 1936. King Fuad dies and is succeeded by the 16-year-old Prince Farouk.

Addis Ababa, 5 May 1936. The Ethiopian capital falls to Italian troops.

Spain, 10 May 1936. The *Cortes* elects Manuel Azana president in succession to the ousted Zamora.

Bolivia, 17 May 1936. President Tejada Sorzano is ousted in a coup.

Belgium, 24 May 1936. The *Rexists*, Belgian Fascists, win 21 seats in the general election.

France, 8 June 1936. Within five days of sweeping to power as leader of a socialist popular front coalition, Leon Blum ends the strikes that have crippled France.

Palestine, 21 June 1936. British planes go into action against Palestinian Arabs who have ambushed British troops.

Spanish Morocco, 17 July 1936. General Franco heads an uprising against the government in Melilla.

Spain, 19 July 1936. General Franco lands in Cadiz heading rebel Spanish foreign legionnaries.

Spain, 24 July 1936. The government appeals for foreign help in the civil war.

Berlin, 1 August 1936. Adolf Hitler opens the Berlin Olympics.

Spain, 19 August 1936. The writer Federico Garcia Lorca dies shortly after his arrest, aged 37.

Egypt, 26 August 1936. An Anglo-Egyptian treaty ends the British protectorate over Egypt and gives Britain control of the Suez Canal for 20 years.

Spain, 29 August 1936. Following the rebels' capture of Badajoz, Spain is divided in half, with the nationalists holding the southwest and the north and the government controlling Madrid.

Spain, 17 September 1936. Franco's troops take Maqueda, between Toledo and Madrid.

Spain, 28 September 1936. Franco is made head of the rebel forces.

London, 11 October 1936. 100,000 people barricade East London streets to prevent a march of Oswald Mosley's Fascists.

Baghdad, 29 October 1936. Pro-western Iraqi Kemalists come to power in an army coup.

Spain, 29 October 1936. Republican troops south of Madrid hold Franco's forces at bay.

Rome, 1 November 1936. Mussolini announces the anti-communist Axis with Germany, urging Britain and France to join.

USA, 3 November 1936. President Roosevelt is elected for a second term.

Spain, 7 November 1936. The government flees to Valencia.

Spain, 18 November 1936. Hitler and Mussolini recognise Franco's provisional government in Burgos.

Berlin, 25 November 1936. Germany and Japan sign an agreement to protect world civilisation from the Bolshevik menace.

Spain, 1 December 1936. 5,000 Germans land at Cadiz to join Franco's rebels.

Britain, 11 December 1936. Edward VIII makes his abdication speech.

Britain, 12 December 1936. Prince Albert is proclaimed king as George VI.

Britain, 1936. Among the great writers who died this year are Rudyard Kipling, A E Housman and G K Chesterton.

Britain, 1 January 1937. The Public Order Act comes into force banning political uniforms and sounding the death-knell for Oswald Mosley's British Union of Fascists.

Berlin, 7 January 1937. Hitler agrees to support a non-intervention pact on Spain if all other powers do likewise.

Moscow, 17 January 1937. The USSR refuses to halt aid to the republican rebels in Spain.

Colonialism in Africa: contrasting views

On the top of the pile: French colonialism, through German eyes.

THE EMPIRE STANDS FOR PEACE

WE ALL WANT PEACE FOR OURSELVES AND OUR CHILDREN, SO DO THE FATHERS AND MOTHERS OF EVERY COUNTRY IN THE EMPIRE OVERSEAS.

The best guarantee of peace we can give the world is a united and prosperous British Empire. Every man and woman can help to provide that guarantee by buying Empire produce.

● ASK FIRST FOR HOME PRODUCE
● ASK NEXT FOR THE PRODUCE OF THE EMPIRE OVERSEAS

Write for a copy of the leaflet 'Why should we buy from the Empire?', obtainable, post free, from the Empire Marketing Board, Westminster, S.W.1 — an official body, on which all the three political parties are represented.

On top of the world: British colonialism, through British eyes.

Southern Africa, January 1936
As arrangements are made for Britain's African colonies to join in the celebrations for the accession of King Edward VIII, there are sharp differences of opinion about whether colonial rule is benefiting or exploiting the native populations. Men like Sir Charles Rey, the UK's resident commissioner in Bechuanaland, fume at what he calls "the rotten socialist dogs at home" for misguidedly claiming that the military brutally overawe the natives. Instead, as the accession celebrations approach, he revels in the idea of "wild savages and civilised beings, drawn together at the insistance of a single white officer in common loyalty to the head of this vast Empire of ours".

A less rosy view, supporting the idea that Africa is being raped by Europe, is taken by Major Trevor, director of public works in Northern Rhodesia for 40 years, who claims that "the only reason that takes any white man, other than a traveller or missionary, to a tropical dependency is to exploit cheap land, cheap labour and new mines".

Negro upstages Nazis at Berlin Games

Jesse Owens: leaping into history.

Berlin, 16 August 1936
The Black American athletics star Jesse Owens has shattered two worldclass sprint records – and the Nazi regime's hopes of turning the 11th Olympic Games into a showcase for its dogma of Aryan supremacy. Owens, who won four gold medals in the 100 metres, 200 metres, 400-metres relay and the long jump, was the undisputed star of the games which closed today with a host of records by 5,000 athletes from 53 nations. Just as notable was Owens' upstaging of the Nazi leader Adolf Hitler who had intended to greet winners. The thought of publicly congratulating a Negro was too humiliating, and after Owens' second win Hitler stormed out of the stadium.

Show trial purge of 17 "Trotskyists"

Moscow, 29 January 1937
Joseph Stalin, bidding to extend his phenomenal power over the Soviet people, scored a notable success today with death sentences meted out to 13 of the 17 party members on trial for treason and lengthy prison terms for the others.

The trial was little more than an obscene farce with ludicrous confessions abounding. The accused readily admitted to plotting with the exiled Leon Trotsky against Stalin.

In the custody of the *NKVD*, Stalin's secret police, they had been processed through a mixture of ill-treatment, threats for the safety of their families and pleas for party loyalty.

Crisis in Palestine as riots continue

Palestine, 25 May 1936
A force of 300 Arabs attacked the Jewish colony of Mesha last night, writing another, bloodier than ever chapter in the story of murder and rioting that has dominated recent Palestinian history.

In six weeks of civil strife between Arabs and Jews 11 people have died and 50 have been wounded. Both sides blame Britain. Jews are demanding that the authorities suppress Arab violence, Arabs wish to see an end to Jewish immigration and land-buying.

Trouble has flared in Gaza and a general strike has been called in Nablus by Arab leaders. A curfew has been established in a number of places.

Civil war erupts in Spain

Defending the republic Spanish men and women: rally to the call.

Madrid, 31 July 1936
Spain is in the grip of bloody civil war with the shaky Republican government being challenged by Nationalist rebels centred on the army. The war is being waged with utmost ferocity and atrocities are being carried out by both sides.

The war erupted a fortnight ago when the army rose against the new government of Jose Giral, a leftwing Republican, who promised to step up revolutionary experiments in collectivisation. General Franco, one of the rebel leaders, warned Madrid in a telegram sent from the headquarters of his African army in Morocco: "The Spanish Restoration Movement will triumph very shortly, and we will demand explanations of your conduct."

Franco will have difficulty ferrying his men across the Straits of Gibraltar and he has turned to Italy and Germany for help. At the same time, however, several areas have already fallen to the rebels, mainly around the conservative towns of Leon and Old Castile.

This is a deeply rooted and complex conflict involving struggles between workers and employers, landowners and peasants, catholics and secularists, regionalists and centralists. It might also be seen as an ideological class war between the forces of reform and reaction.

The Nationalists appear to share the single basic aim of smashing the Republic, whereas the Republicans are divided between those fighting to defend the constitution, and those who see the war as a launchpad for social revolution.

King quits, putting love before duty

London, 11 December 1936
Broadcasting from Windsor Castle tonight, King Edward VIII announced his abdication of the throne, a burden he found impossible to carry, he said, "without the help and support of the woman I love". He added: "The decision has been mine and mine alone. The other person most concerned has tried to persuade me to take a different course."

The king's wish to marry the twice-divorced Mrs Simpson (born Wallis Warfield of Baltimore) has been the talk of European and American Press for two years. But Britain has only just learned of it because of self-censorship by Fleet Street. Tomorrow Albert, duke of York, will be proclaimed King George VI in his brother's place.

"On your bike": a pro-king demonstrator moved on in Whitehall.

Right-wing army coup bid fails in Tokyo

Tokyo, 29 February 1936
The attempt by a group of young right-wing officers to overthrow the government which has paralysed Tokyo for the last four days has collapsed with the surrender of its leader, Captain Teruzo Ando.

Troops led by the ultra-nationalist officers occupied the government quarter while teams of assassins murdered leading politicians who were thought to be too liberal. They had intended to kill the prime minister but were foiled by the Imperial Guard. While there is relief that the attempted coup has failed there is much worry here that the plotters represent a strong element in the army and navy.

It is composed of politically active junior officers who belong to a secret society called the *Sakura-kai* or Cherry Society, who advocate the uncompromising worship of the emperor, military conquests and the domination of the Pacific.

Chinese leader mysteriously kidnapped

China, 12 December 1936
The Chinese Generalissimo Chiang Kai-shek was kidnapped today, the "Double Twelfth", at Xian, headquarters of the "Young Marshal", Zhang Xueliang, The town was woken by the sound of a furiously beaten gong and gunfire as troops of Zhang's Northeastern army rounded up Chiang's staff.

Chiang himself escaped in his pyjamas, but was captured on a nearby mountainside. His feet were bleeding so he was carried down on the back of his captor, Sun Mingchiu, commander of Chang's bodyguard. The generalissimo is now housed in "new quarters" at Zhang's own headquarters.

This mysterious incident has its origins in Chiang's determination to continue fighting the communists against the wishes of Zhang and a number of other generals who want him to lead a united China in war against the Japanese.

1937 (1937-1938)

Spain, 8 February 1937. Malaga falls to Franco, aided by 15,000 Italians.

Spain, 22 February 1937. Britain, France, Germany, Italy, Portugal and the USSR agree to a cordon around Spain to enforce the arms ban agreed on the 16 February.

China, 23 February 1937. Chiang Kai-shek, the head of the Chinese government, rejects Communist suggestions that they and the Nationalists should join forces to fight against the Japanese invaders.

Spain, 26 February 1937. Portugal and the USSR withdraw from the Spanish cordon pact.

India, 1 April 1937. The Indian constitution comes into being under the Government of India Act. Burma is separated.

Spain, 27 April 1937. Guernica is destroyed by the German air force.

Washington, DC, 7 May 1937. An enquiry begins into the Hindenburg disaster.

London, 12 May 1937. King George VI and Queen Elizabeth are crowned.

Spain, 16 May 1937. The prime minister Largo Caballero resigns.

Spain, 18 May 1937. Franco is checked at Guadalajara.

Britain, 28 May 1937. Neville Chamberlain becomes prime minister following Stanley Baldwin's retirement.

Spain, 31 May 1937. Italy and Germany withdraw from the Spanish non-intervention cordon.

France, 3 June 1937. The ex-king Edward VIII, now the duke of Windsor, marries Mrs Simpson.

USSR, 12 June 1937. Eight top generals are executed as Stalin's purge extends to the Red Army.

Spain, 19 June 1937. Bilbao falls to Franco's rebels.

Paris, 21 June 1937. Leon Blum's Popular Front ministry resigns.

London, 7 July 1937. The British government announces plans to partition Palestine.

China, 7 July 1937. Japanese soldiers in night manoeuvres outside their designated area attack Wanping at the southern end of the bridge near Beiping (*Beijing*).

Eire, 21 July 1937. Eamon de Valera is re-elected president.

Germany, 1 August 1937. A new concentration camp has been opened at Buchenwald.

China, 8 August 1937. The Japanese occupy Beiping (*Beijing*).

Baghdad, 12 August 1937. General Bakr Sidki Pasha, Iraq's dictator, is assassinated.

China, 14 August 1937. Hundreds are reported dead in a Japanese bombing raid on Shanghai.

Germany, 5 September 1937. The biggest-ever Nazi rally marks the opening of the Nazi congress in Nuremberg.

China, 25 September 1937. The Japanese bomb the Chinese Nationalist capital Nanjing.

Geneva, 28 September 1937. The League of Nations condemns the Japanese invasion of China.

China, 25 September 1937. Chinese troops defeat the Japanese at Pingxingguan (*Shanxi*).

China, 29 September 1937. Chiang Kai-shek, the Chinese leader, comes to an agreement with his Communist rival Mao Zedong in the face of the full-scale Japanese assault on their country.

Palestine, 20 October 1937. The British authorities limit Jewish immigration.

Spain, 21 October 1937. Gijon, the last Republican stronghold in northern Spain, surrenders to Franco.

Moscow, 21 October 1937. Sixty two are executed in Stalin's latest purges.

Italy, 6 November 1937. Italy joins the anti-communist pact between Germany and Japan.

China, 9 November 1937. The Japanese take Shanghai.

Spain, 28 November 1937. Franco tells the government to surrender by 12 December or face a massive offensive.

China, 7 December 1937. The Japanese launch a general attack on Nanjing; bitter fighting follows.

Java, 10 December 1937. Parts of the skull of one of humankind's ancestors is discovered.

Geneva, 11 December 1937. Italy leaves the League of Nations.

China, 13 December 1937. The Japanese army occupies Nanjing.

Spain, 21 December 1937. Republicans capture Franco's stronghold of Teruel.

Dublin, 29 December 1937. The new constitution comes into force; the republic is called Eire.

London, 6 January 1938. Sigmund Freud arrives in London, fleeing from Nazi persecution.

Rumania, 10 February 1938. King Carol ousts the anti-Semitic prime minister, Octavian Goga, and becomes a dictator.

London, 21 February 1938. Anthony Eden resigns as foreign secretary in protest against Chamberlain's appeasement.

Jewish state is planned for Palestine

Palestine, 7 July 1937
In the face of what they call the "irreconcilable conflict" between Jews and Arabs, the British authorities have succumbed to years of community violence with a plan, finally, to partition Palestine. In a white paper Britain proposes dividing the country into three: two-thirds to remain Arab, the remainder to be the promised national homeland for the Jews. Zionist leaders are unimpressed.

The Holy Cities of Jerusalem, Bethlehem and Nazareth are to be placed under permanent British control. Trans-Jordan will receive a £2 million grant, and Arab land-owners will be compensated.

The British lion, in the mud of conflicting promises to Arabs and Jews.

Mexico takes over all US oil firms

Mexico, 18 March 1938
Mexico has today nationalised 17 American and British oil companies, with assets worth $450 million. The seizure follows a government report, bitterly contested by the oil firms, that the companies must pay some $40 million in wages and compensation, as demanded by unions. President Cardenas is a nationalist and trade unionist and his action stems less from a desire to rid Mexico of foreign capitalists than to ensure that those capitalists treat their workers fairly. The oil magnates' refusal to acknowledge the demands of the Syndicate of Petroleum Workers triggered today's move. A last-ditch attempt to compromise with the government failed to halt the expropriation.

Freud is shrunk by female shrink

USA, 1937
The German psychoanalyst Karen Horney has published a strong attack on the founding father of the psychoanalytic movement. In her new book, *The Neurotic Personality of Our Time*, Horney – a leftwing, socially orientated analyst – claims that the industrial civilisation of contemporary America is to blame for the problems and anxieties that beset men, women and children today. This is a direct attack on the orthodox Freudian line that biological givens lie at the core of neuroses. Though Horney trained with the Berlin Psychoanalytic Institute, she began criticising Freud for antifeminism early in her career. This latest book is bound to step up the conflict.

The Spanish painter Pablo Picasso's "Guernica", his angry memorial to the small Basque town destroyed by German bombs in a calculated experiment of terror. Though the town was wrecked, the oak tree, under which the Basque parliament has met since the Middle Ages, has survived.

Japanese seize Nanjing

Nanjing, 13 December 1937
The Japanese marched into Nanjing today and immediately began an orgy of brutality and wanton destruction. Defeated Chinese troops who try to surrender are being slaughtered, women are dragged from their homes to be raped and murdered, the city is being sacked and burnt.

Foreigners gathered in the international safety zone are trying to help the thousands of destitute Chinese who are seeking sanctuary in the zone. Other refugees are trying to flee across the river and many are drowning as the overcrowded junks capsize and sink.

The end in Nanjing was signalled last night when, after months of brave resistance, the Chinese army broke and began to stream in disorder through the city under heavy aerial and artillery bombardment.

All organisation broke down when it became known that General Tang had fled. The soldiers threw away their rifles and there were appalling scenes of panic.

Chinese troops marching towards the front along the Great Wall of China.

Then, at 11 this morning, the Japanese arrived. The planes which had been bombing the city dropped leaflets saying the Japanese were the real friends of the Chinese. And the killing began.

"Nylon" points way to tomorrow's world

United States, 1937
It has been a golden year for America's inventors. A former chemistry teacher, Wallace Carothers, has made an artificial silk – superior to cellulose-based rayon – by combining two chemicals. He calls the result "nylon", although it is not yet being marketed. In Chicago, Chester Carlson has developed a system, of dry copying or "herography" which replaces the wet chemical system and will allow machines to do the job at the push of a button. And finally the "Polaroid" camera – the brainchild of Edwin Land – now makes it possible to produce a positive print without taking the negative out of the camera.

The Promenade Deck Cabin Lounge on the "Queen Mary", the most luxurious ship afloat. The flagship of the Cunard Line, the 80,733-ton super liner is taking 1,840 passengers across the Atlantic on each voyage.

The horrors of Guernica

Spain, 27 April 1937
German bombers, sent by Hitler to help Franco's Fascist forces against the Republicans, destroyed the Basque town of Guernica yesterday in one of the most horrific military actions since the 1914-18 war. Thousands of innocent civilians perished.

It was market day in Guernica, and the square was crowded with shoppers when a squadron of Heinkel 1-11 and Junker 52 bombers, escorted by fighter-planes, appeared and jettisoned high explosives on the town.

Incendiary bombs then set it on fire, while the fighters machine-gunned survivors.

Noel Monks, a British reporter, arrived soon after the bombing and helped collect burned bodies. He described the scene: "Some of the soldiers were sobbing like children. There were flames and smoke and grit, and the smell of burning human flesh was nauseating. Houses were collapsing into the inferno. In the Plaza, surrounded almost by a wall of fire, were about 100 refugees. They were weeping and wailing and rocking to and fro."

"It was impossible to go down many of the streets, because they were walls of flame. Debris was piled high. I could see shadowy forms, some large, some just ashes. I moved round to the back of the Plaza among survivors. They had the same story to tell, aeroplanes, bullets, bombs, fire."

Guernica was a communications centre, with a munitions factory. But the bombing was random.

"Hindenburg" explodes in a ball of flame

The "Hindenburg" crashes down in a ball of flame and exploding gas.

New Jersey, 6 May 1937
The *Hindenburg*, the pride of the German airship fleet and veteran of ten successful transatlantic trips, exploded in a ball of flame as she came into land in New Jersey tonight. As horrified crowds watched the mighty *dirigible* was reduced within minutes to a tangle of white-hot metal, a fiery grave for 35 passengers and crew.

The cause of the disaster has yet to be ascertained, but it is thought that static electricity, the product of a thunderstorm that had already held up her landing for 12 hours, somehow ignited the hydrogen gas that kept the airship aloft.

The horror of the explosion was made even more graphic by an eye-witness broadcast by Herb Morrison, a reporter for Chicago's WLS radio. Expecting a routine landing, Morrison, collapsing in tears, told his audience of "smoke and flames, and oh, the humanity ...".

1938 (1938-1939)

Vienna, 11 March 1938. Chancellor Schuschnigg resigns and the pro-Nazi Artur Seyss-Inquart succeeds. German troops invade on his invitation.

Vienna, 13 March 1938. The *Anschluss*, Germany's annexation of Austria, is declared.

Vienna, 14 March 1938. Vienna gives Hitler a tumultuous welcome.

Moscow, 15 March 1938. Another show trial ends in the execution of 18 top-ranking Soviet figures, including Nikolai Bukharin.

London, 24 March 1938. The Prime Minister Chamberlain, announces that Britain will fight for France and Belgium.

London, 1 April 1938. Britain and the US abandon the London naval treaty to allow for the building of battleships.

Spain, 3 April 1938. Franco takes Lerida, a major town in Catalonia.

Vienna, 6 April 1938. Leading Jewish figures are sent to Dachau concentration camp.

Vienna, 7 April 1938. The Nazis seize Rothschild's bank; Baron Rothschild is arrested.

China, 7 April 1938. The Chinese claim victory in the battle of Taierzhuang (*Shandong*) against the Japanese.

Austria, 10 April 1938. A plebiscite indicates that 99.75 per cent are in favour of Hitler's annexation of Austria.

Spain, 19 April 1938. After successive victories in Catalonia, Franco broadcasts an appeal for surrender.

Dublin, 21 April 1938. Douglas Hyde is elected Eire's first president.

Eire, 25 April 1938. Under the Anglo-Irish agreement Eire wins big financial and defence concessions.

London, 29 April 1938. Top-level Anglo-French talks end with a vague promise to defend Czechoslovakia.

Rome, 4 May 1938. The Vatican recognises Franco as leader of Spain.

Prague, 20 May 1938. The government orders 400,000 troops to the Austro-German border.

Britain, 1 June 1938. The Bren gun comes into service.

China, 7 June 1938. *Guomindang* (Nationalist) troops burst the dykes of the Yellow River at Huayuankou to prevent the southward move of Japanese forces. The river floods disastrously.

China, 8 June 1938. The Japanese have been bombing Guangzhou (*Canton*) mercilessly for 10 days.

Germany, 17 August 1938. Austria's former leaders, including Schuschnigg, are being held in Dachau concentration camp.

Prague, 28 August 1938. The *Sudeten* (Nazi) party begins talks with President Benes.

Prague, 6 September 1938. Benes offers self-government to the Sudetenland.

Prague, 21 September 1938. The government agrees to Anglo-French plans to cede the Sudetenland to Germany; Czechs protest.

Germany, 30 September 1938. A solution to the Czechoslovakian crisis is announced following talks between Chamberlain, Daladier, Hitler and Mussolini. Sudetenland will be ceded to Germany.

Czechoslovakia, 1 October 1938. German troops march into the Sudetenland as Teschen, in Czech Silesia, is annexed by Poland.

Prague, 5 October 1938. President Benes resigns.

Budapest, 13 October 1938. Tension mounts amid calls for the annexation of southern parts of Czechoslovakia.

London, 19 October 1938. New plans for Palestine abandon the idea of partition.

China, 21 October 1938. Guangzhou falls to the Japanese; fire spreads throughout the entire city.

Budapest, 23 October 1938. Hungary rejects Czech proposals for ceding Czechoslovak areas.

Britain, 31 October 1938. Orson Welles' vivid radio production *War of the Worlds* causes widespread panic because of its realism.

Czechoslovakia, 2 November 1938. Following "arbitration" by Hitler, Hungary annexes the southern parts of Slovakia and Ruthenia.

Germany, 9 November 1938. Jews across the country are subjected to violent attacks.

Ankara, 11 November 1938. Ismet Onu succeeds Kemal Ataturk, who died yesterday, as president of Turkey.

Paris, 6 December 1938. France and Germany sign a pact on the inviolability of their present frontiers.

Tokyo, 4 January 1939. The fascist Baron Hiranuma becomes prime minister.

Cairo, 20 January 1939. King Farouk is declared the *caliph* (spiritual leader) of Islam.

Trek is celebrated by the Afrikaners

South Africa, 16 December 1938
On raised ground, near the banks of Blood River, the Afrikaners are celebrating the centenary of the Great *Trek*. No one speaks English; many wear uniforms modelled on Europe's fascist movements. The Great Trek is not the only anniversary today. Five years ago, to the day, South African police used tear-gas for the first time on blacks.

Since 1925, when segregation first became government policy, to protect the wages of "civilised labour", there has been considerable separation of the races – made easier by the disintegration of the main black union, the Industrial and Commercial Workers' Union, in 1928. The Afrikaners at Blood River have a lot to celebrate.

Leading Islamic philosopher dies

Karachi, 21 April 1938
Sir Mohammed Iqbal, the greatest Urdu poet and one of the world's leading Moslem philosophers, is dead. Born at Sialkot in the Punjab in 1873 he studied in Lahore, Cambridge and Germany. Although influenced by Nietzsche and Bergson he never lost his devotion to the great Moslem thinkers. He wrote in Persian as well so that more Moslems could read him.

He emphasised the innate greatness of the human self and argued that this could be best developed if the community were organised on a righteous basis. As president of the All-India League in 1930 he proposed a separate state for the northwestern part of India where Moslems are in a majority.

Britain builds its first "jet" engine

England, 1939
It is ten years since Frank Whittle, a young graduate from the RAF's Cranwell College, suggested that aircraft might be driven not by propellers but by jet propulsion. Only now has he been able to build a prototype of such an engine. Air enters at the front and is compressed and heated up. Then fuel is injected into the compressed air and ignited. The result is a tremendous backward thrust of expanding gases that pushes the whole assembly forwards like a rocket.

Whittle is not the first to apply the jet engine in a real aircraft. The German engineer, Dr Hans von Ohain, has used one to power a Heinkel He 178.

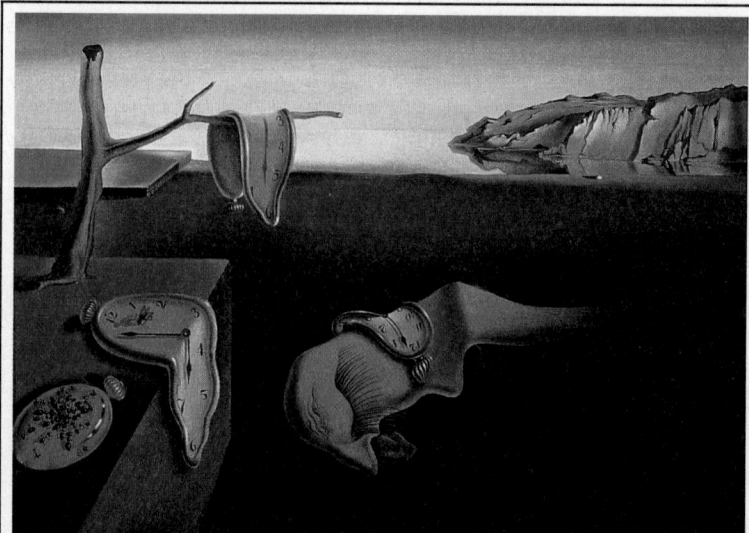

"Persistence of Memory", by Salvador Dali, who was expelled from the ranks of Europe's Surrealists for his support of Franco in the Spanish Civil War. The accusation was unjust. His instinct was not to support Fascism, but to ignore it – and other forms of uncomfortable reality – and retreat into an inner hallucinatory world. His reaction to the controversy has been to retreat further, producing mannered, almost

Austria joins the Reich

Austria on "Anschluss Day" Viennese women greeting a lost countryman.

Vienna, 14 March 1938

A forest of Nazi salutes stabbed the air as a triumphant Adolf Hitler rode into Vienna today accompanied by goose-stepping soldiers and tanks. Young girls threw flowers into his car, older folk wept with joy and church bells pealed.

At six o'clock he took the salute from the balcony of the Hotel Imperial and withdrew. The crowd continued to cheer with such a frenzy of enthusiasm that he reappeared and cried: "The German nation will never again be rent apart." Thus Hitler returned to his native land and the city where he had lived in poverty and obscurity.

The fall of Austria became inevitable when Hitler persuaded Mussolini to join the Axis pact and abandon support for Vienna. Last February, Hitler took the Austrian Chancellor, Kurt von Schuschnigg, to his Berchtesgaden retreat and shouted and raved at him for hours on end.

Schuschnigg refused to agree to the *Anschluss* (union) Hitler demanded and returned to Vienna to announce a plebiscite on Austrian independence. Hitler demanded Schuschnigg's resignation and the chancellor was replaced by the Austrian Nazi, Artur SeyssInquart, who duly invited German troops to prevent "disorders".

Tonight, Hitler was given an extravagant reception such as few Habsburg emperors can have enjoyed. Nazi supporters were brought in from as far away as Czechoslovakia to swell the crowds. The union of Germany and Austria was forbidden by the peace treaties which Hitler has contemptuously brushed aside. By bluster and bullying he has created a Greater Germany of 74 million people.

Now "the great spring cleaning", as the Nazi newspapers are calling the planned *pogrom*, begins. Jewish judges are marked down for dismissal, Jewish shops will be placarded and theatres and music halls purged of Jews, among them Max Reinhardt and Richard Tauber. Jews are being made to scrub the pavements while Nazis with whips stand over them.

"Planting the Rice", a painting by the Balinese artist G A Oka.

Hitler in Czechoslovakia

Sudentenland: German Czechs also greeting their fellow-countrymen.

Sudetenland, 5 October 1938

"Thus we begin our march into the great German future," Hitler cried as he crossed the frontier to take possession of his latest conquest, the Sudeten border areas of Czechoslovakia, claimed as German-speaking. So they may be, but they also include natural and man-made defences vital for Czechoslovakia's security.

The summer-long crisis, orchestrated by Hitler, with his puppet, Konrad Henlein, in Sudetenland spreading disorder, reached its climax a week ago, when the British and French leaders, Neville Chamberlain and Edouard Daladier, flew to Munich to agree with Hitler and Mussolini on the dismemberment of Czechoslovakia.

Earlier this year, the Czechs were prepared to fight; after all they had a treaty with the French. But the French were defeatist and Chamberlain was ready to make almost any concession to appease Hitler, whom he believed to be a man of his word. The Czechs were pressured into making compromises; but with each step Hitler demanded more.

Chamberlain came home waving a paper bearing Hitler's signature, and saying: "I believe it is peace for our time." He was wildly cheered. Then misgivings began to be felt. A far-away country, as Chamberlain called it, has been sacrificed to a ruthless dictator, whose appetite for conquest seems to grow with each success. Many believe, with Winston Churchill, that Hitler will soon strike again.

Night of violence against Germany's Jews

Germany, 9 November 1938

Exultant Nazis are calling it *Kristallnacht* (Crystal Night), a testimony to the millions of marks worth of broken glass that litter Germany's streets, following the worst outbreak yet of anti-Jewish violence. In a day's orgy of looting, arson and assault, hundreds of synagogues were burnt, shops smashed and thousands of Jews beaten.

According to Dr Goebbels, the minister of propaganda, the outburst came as a spontaneous reaction to the assassination two days ago of a German diplomat in Paris, killed by a young Polish Jew.

Anti-Semitism is a central tenet of Nazi ideology, and under the Nuremberg laws of 1935 the once assimilated Jews, who saw themselves as no less German than their compatriots, have been systematically deprived of their rights and jobs; but today's excesses are quite unprecedented. Nazi storm troopers have always attacked the Jews, but today they were joined by middle-class folk who cheered as "the sub-humans" were beaten.

Barcelona is Franco's latest prize

"The Angel of Peace ... of the Fascists!": a Republican poster.

Spanish Republicans behind a barricade in Barcelona, waiting for the Fascists.

Barcelona, 26 January

General Franco's attack on the bastion of Republicanism, Catalonia, has led to another Nationalist triumph. His troops entered Barcelona today and met with only sporadic resistance. Two exhausted Republican armies are crossing into France where they will be interned.

Franco's troops, among them the feared Moors, were greeted by crowds emerging from the underground stations where they sought refuge from bombing raids carried out by the Italian air force. Many of them gave the Fascist salute and carried portraits of the Nationalist leader.

The fundamental weakness and exhaustion, both moral and material, of the Republican forces has been clearly exposed over the last six months. Following the offensive which cut the Republic in two, the Nationalists, heavily reinforced and regularly supplied by Hitler and Mussolini, have won a series of victories. On the other hand a notable weakness of the Republican army has been its inability, from political causes, to launch offensives in the enemy's rear or to organise the type of guerrilla operations which would have held up Franco's troop movements.

The fall of Madrid cannot be delayed for much longer, and with it the Spanish Civil War will be over. At least 300,000 Spaniards have been killed during the hostilities. And Franco's prisons are filling up quickly.

The massive force of atomic fission

Germany

There is colossal power locked in the nucleus of the atom. Now, it seems, it may be possible to release that force by the process of nuclear fission. The German physicists Otto Hahn and Fritz Strassman have bombarded the element uranium with a stream of neutrons. They have found that the element barium is produced.

According to two other scientists, Otto Frisch and Lise Meitner, this means that the uranium atoms' nuclei have been split apart producing new elements with less mass than the original uranium and releasing enormous energy in the process. Properly harnessed, fission could mean energy unlimited.

"Gone with the Wind", the Hollywood box-office success of 1939, in which audiences escaped from the fear of a possible war with the romance of a past one.

Menzies takes over as Australian PM

Canberra, Australia, 24 April

Robert Menzies, a nationalist and an avowedly anti-communist politician, is the new Australian Prime Minister. He is 44. At six foot four inches tall, the United Australia Party leader has a reputation for toughness and has opted to end coalition government by excluding members of the rival Country Party from office.

The main planks of his policy are social insurance and the build-up of defence against Japan's military might. He intends to set up new ministries for both these areas. Bob Menzies has already served as attorney-general and deputy prime minister. He was a barrister before entering politics.

Swastika flies in Prague

German occupation troops on their first day in Prague – very much in control.

Prague, 15 March
The long agony of Czechoslovakia's dying democracy finally ended today when Adolf Hitler entered Prague with detachments of his jackbooted *Wehrmacht*. He was greeted with boos and hisses and tears as he rode up to the Hradzin Castle, ancient palace of Bohemian kings and latterly the residence of the state president.

Only six months ago, when the Czechs ceded Sudetenland to Germany, Hitler declared he had no further territorial claims; but two days ago he presented Prague with a series of demands:

*Complete independence for Slovakia and Ruthenia;

*Formation of a new Czech government favourable to Germany;

*Payments of gold and foreign exchange to Germany.

The demands were preceded by disorders stage-managed by German agents. German papers carried headlines: "Bloody Terror of the Czechs against Germans and Czechs creates an Intolerable Situation."

Gathering war clouds loom over Europe

London, August
Events are unfolding with bewildering speed as Europe races towards a second great war. First there was Ethiopia, of which Mussolini said that with so few Italian casualties "victory had come too cheap". Then there were the Rhineland, Austria, Sudetenland and Czechoslovakia. And all that time Spain was bleeding to death. Now Germany, having made a pact with one dictator, Mussolini, has made a second with Stalin (*see below*).

Signing of the pact has triggered mobilisation orders everywhere. In Poland, men up to the age of 40 have been ordered to report to barracks. France has called up reservists and requisitioned the railways. In Britain, as mobilisation papers went out, the admiralty issued orders closing the Mediterranean and the Baltic to British shipping. Germany has become an armed camp.

Laying the foundations of the state.

Troops are everywhere and heavy trucks, motor cycles and civilian aircraft have been requisitioned. In Berlin, Western embassies are destroying secret papers.

Hitler and Stalin in non-aggression pact

Moscow, 23 August
Western hopes that a war in Europe can still be averted were shattered today by the news that Germany and the Soviet Union have signed a non-aggression pact. The treaty between Stalin and Hitler, who have been sworn enemies for the past six years, virtually guarantees Hitler that Germany can now use military force to claim territory from Poland without fear of intervention by Russia.

It is apparent that Stalin has been in secret negotiation with Hitler and his foreign minister, von Ribbentrop, for some time, even though an Anglo-French military mission is about to arrive in Moscow for talks to discourage German aggression against Poland.

The Hitler-Stalin pact comes into force at once and is to be ratified "in the shortest possible time". The two sides agree not to use force against one another or join hostile alliances with other powers. The pact makes German military action more likely, with the army continuing to requisition vehicles.

Jews entering Palestine face British curbs

Palestine, July
Europe's Jews are desperate to flee spreading Nazi persecution, but British bureaucrats are equally determined to resist their cries for help. As tens of thousands of Jewish refugees make their way to Palestine, the colonial secretary, Malcolm MacDonald, stated today that from October this year immigration will be suspended for six months. The flood of Jews, he claims, is fanning the flames of Arab revolt and must be suppressed. He denied that the government was indifferent to the refugee situation, saying that 75,000 immigrants would be allowed into Palestine over a five-year period, but stressed that one country could not take in every Jew. He especially condemned organised attempts to outwit the law. Some 8,000 "illegals" have tried to smuggle themselves into Palestine since May. Jewish leaders refuse to bend. In May some 10,000 Jewish women marched through Jerusalem, protesting any limits on immigration and condemning Britain's efforts as "a fatal error" and refusing to accept this "breach of faith".

Profiting from the deluge: Joseph Stalin, a dictator's dictator.

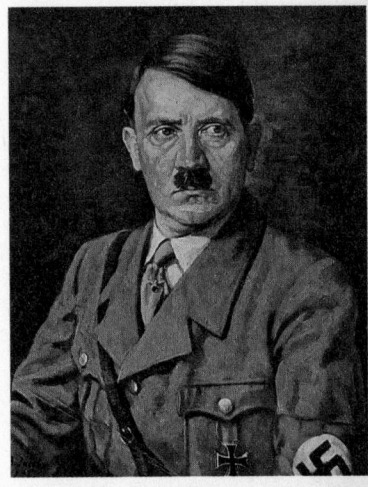

Investing in the deluge: Adolf Hitler, a dictator's role model.

1939 (1939-1940)

Poland, 1 September 1939. German troops invade at 5.45 am.

London and Paris, 3 September 1939. War is declared.

London, 4 September 1939. Winston Churchill is First Lord of the Admiralty again.

Germany, 4 September 1939. French troops cross the border into the Saarland.

Washington, DC, 5 September 1939. President Roosevelt declares US neutrality.

Poland, 17 September 1939. Soviet troops invade.

Warsaw, 29 September 1939. Polish troops evacuate as the city surrenders to the Wehrmacht.

Moscow, 11 October 1939. The USSR signs a pact ceding the former Polish city of Vilna to Lithuania.

France, 12 October 1939. British troops are now here in strength.

Britain, 16 October 1939. The battleship *Royal Oak* is sunk in her home base of Scapa Flow by a German torpedo.

Ankara, 19 October 1939. Turkey signs a mutual assistance pact with France and Britain.

Berlin, 24 October 1939. Hitler's month-long peace offer to the Allies comes to an end; the fighting continues.

London, 30 October 1939. The government publicises the horrors of Nazi concentration camps.

USA, 4 November 1939. President Roosevelt announces that he will amend the Neutrality Bill, which will allow Britain and France to buy arms from the US.

Germany, 8 November 1939. A bomb goes off shortly after Hitler has made his traditional speech on the anniversary of the abortive 1923 *putsch*.

Britain, 13 November 1939. The first bombs are dropped on British soil, on the Shetlands.

Moscow, 28 November 1939. Stalin renounces the Finno-Soviet non-aggression pact.

Finland, 30 November 1939. Soviet planes bomb Helsinki and Viipuri.

Montevideo, 17 December 1939. The German battleship *Graf Spee* is scuttled after being chased by British warships into the River Plate.

Moscow, 23 December 1939. Stalin sacks General Meretzkov, in charge of the war against Finland, as Finnish successes continue.

London, 1 January 1940. Two million 19- to 27-year-olds are called up.

France, 6 January 1940. The Germans gain ground in a fierce onslaught along a 120-mile front north of Paris.

Finland, 1 February 1940. The Soviet army launches an attack in Karelia.

Britain, 7 February 1940. Two IRA men are hanged.

Britain, 11 February 1940. John Buchan, Lord Tweedsmuir, the governor general of Canada, and author of great adventure stories such as *The Thirty-nine Steps* dies aged 64.

Finland, 13 February 1940. The biggest battle so far in the winter war between the USSR and Finland is waged. Finland appeals for international aid.

Finland, 16 February 1940. Soviet troops pierce the Mannerheim Line of Finnish defence.

Tibet, 22 February 1940. The new five-year-old Dalai Lama is enthroned.

Norway, 26 February 1940. More than 300 British prisoners of war are rescued from a German tanker hiding in a Norwegian *fjord*.

The Hague, 8 March 1940. Martial law is declared throughout the Netherlands because of the German threat.

Finland, 13 March 1940. Finland signs a peace treaty with the USSR, surrendering a large part of the territory.

USA, 16 March 1940. The mission of Roosevelt's envoy Sumner Welles, to see if peace negotiations in Europe were possible, has ended in failure.

Paris, 22 March 1940. Paul Reynard becomes prime minister following the resignation of Edouard Daladier yesterday.

Poland, 27 March 1940. Heinrich Himmler orders the construction of a concentration camp at Auschwitz, near Cracow.

Holland, 2 April 1940. Dutch troops are put on full alert along the German frontier.

Norway, 9 April 1940. A full-scale German invasion of Norway begins. Denmark has already been overrun.

Norway, 30 April 1940. The Germans claim they have advanced and taken the towns of Dombaas and Stoeren. Meanwhile, British and French troops hit back, particularly in the north.

Norway, 2 May 1940. The Allies withdraw their troops south of Trondheim.

Denmark, 9 May 1940. Britain occupies Iceland and the Faroe islands.

India's Moslems call for separate state

Lahore, India, 23 March 1940
The Moslems of India are opting for a separate state. At the Moslem League conference, held here today, they accepted the principle of "autonomous and sovereign" Moslem states.

For India's Moslem leader, the brilliant lawyer Mohammed Ali Jinnah, it is a bitter victory. In the 1910s he had been in the Congress Party, an admirer of the moderate Congress leader Gopal Gokhale (who called him a potential ambassador of Hindu-Moslem unity), and a member of the imperial Legislative Council.

But as Congress turned more to mass agitation, and inevitably became more Hindu, he felt alienated. He went into self-imposed exile in England, and has only recently returned – the leader from across the water.

Thousands of Indian Moslems share his sense of alienation. Moslems note with apprehension the steadily increasing communal violence, and the complaints of Moslems in Hindu-dominated areas that provincial Congress governments favour Hindus over Moslems. They resent Congress' assumption to speak for all Indians.

Mohammed Jinnah, the Indian Moslem barrister from Lincoln's Inn.

"Congress leaders may cry as much as they like that Congress is a national body," said Mr Jinnah. "But I say it is not true. The Congress is nothing but a Hindu body."

Most significant of all, the call for Moslem states is fitting in with the growing aspirations of the people of the north-west and the north-east, where the majority are Moslems opposed to British rule and opposed to Hindu rule, and feel they have nowhere else to go.

The Home Front: the Women's Royal Voluntary Service, boosting the war economy by collecting pots and pans which the ministry of information in Britain said could be turned into Spitfires and Hurricanes. Soon there were saucepan mountains. The sacrifice proved useless and many a saucepan mountain remains unlevelled. There is easily enough scrap metal without depriving housewives of their kitchen equipment. But with individuals reduced to four ounces of butter, 12 ounces of sugar, four ounces of ham and three and a half ounces of bacon, there is not a great deal of use for kitchen equipment – unless you like offal and brawn.

Europe is again at war

London, 30 September 1939

Poland lies shattered, partitioned yet again by her more powerful neighbours. As Polish forces were reeling under the hammer blows of the *Wehrmacht*, Stalin sent Red Army troops to occupy eastern Poland. The treacherous significance of the Nazi-Soviet Pact thus became clear.

Soon after dawn on 1 September, 1.25 million German troops, with six armoured divisions and eight motorised divisions, swept into Poland. The *Luftwaffe* knocked out the Polish railway system and shot the air force out of the sky. By Day Three – when Britain and France declared war – the Germans had cut the Polish Corridor and by Day Eight were at the gates of Warsaw. The city endured two weeks of terror bombing before surrendering.

An estimated 60,000 Poles have been killed, 200,000 wounded and 700,000 taken prisoner. The Polish government has fled to Rumania. Hitler has proved that the static trench warfare of 1914-18 is a thing of the past. The English language has acquired a new and terrifying word – *blitzkrieg,* meaning lightning war. In London, after some

A stab in the back: Soviet armoured cars invading Poland from the East.

uncertainty, the British Government declared war on Sunday, 3 September at 11am. The French followed at 5pm. A joint statement said the two governments would avoid bombing civilians. In Washington, President Roosevelt announced US neutrality, ordering an embargo on the shipment of arms to countries at war.

Hitler orders U-boats to hit neutral ships

London, 20 February 1940

Unarmed merchant ships of all nations are potential targets for U-boat torpedoes as a result of Hitler's latest order to his submarine captains to open fire "without question" on neutral shipping in the waters around Britain.

Since war began five months ago most neutral ships passing through the Dover Strait call at British ports for a cargo check. They are granted a certificate stating they are not carrying prohibited cargo to Germany. Hitler wishes to take control of all neutral shipping, forcing uninvolved nations to divert exports from the two Allies, France and Britain, to Germany.

Norway, Sweden, Denmark and the Netherlands are all anxious. Norway's foreign minister recently revealed that 50 Norwegian merchant ships had been sunk since the conflict started, although Norway is not a participant. In every case

A German U-boat on the hunt for allied shipping in the Atlantic.

the attack was made by a German submarine or aircraft. Observers note that no US ship has been hit, perhaps because of memories of the *Lusitania* in May 1915.

Germans overrun Denmark and Norway

German troops landing on the coast in Norway, where they have taken Oslo.

Oslo, 9 April 1940

The Germans have stolen a march on the British in the race to take control of Norwegian home waters. Royal Navy warships were preparing to sow mines in the area, in order to prevent Germany using the ports and fjords, when they ran into a German flotilla. The Germans had already occupied Denmark, with only token resistance from the Royal Guard.

Last night, German warships moved on the Norwegian capital, Oslo, and were attacked by shore batteries. Hitler's newest cruiser, *Blucher,* was sunk, with the loss of 1,000 men. The city was taken by airborne troops. Norway's King Haakon and his government have

escaped to a village in the interior. Using a low-powered local radio, the king broadcast mobilisation orders.

Though the Norwegians insist they will put up a determined resistance, the Germans seem already too well established to be dislodged. They successfully put seven divisions ashore within 48 hours and now hold all the main ports. British forces have only a toehold ashore in the far north.

The Germans have installed their puppet in Oslo. Major Vikdun Quisling, a Nazi sympathiser whose name has instantly become a synonym for traitor, made a radio broadcast calling for resistance to Germany to cease.

British troops boost French defences

France, 12 October 1939

The British "Tommy" has returned to France where, like his father in the Great War, he still regards it as effeminate to speak French with a correct accent. Some 158,000 men of the British Expeditionary Force, with 25,000 vehicles, have been ferried across the Channel to take their place alongside the French army under General Gamelin.

The troops' movements are considered a great achievement. A small team of war office planners, helped by just seven clerks and typists, worked out every detail of the complicated movements.

Secret routes were taken across Britain to prevent air attacks on the road convoys. The men moved in small groups, concealed by day and travelling by night. There was not a single casualty.

The RAF, equipped with Blenheim and Battle bombers and Hurricane fighters, has been operating from French airfields for some weeks, carrying out reconnaissance flights over the German lines.

The war secretary, Leslie Hore-Belisha, told the Commons that troops were also being sent to the Near East to reinforce British interests there.

Low Countries invaded

Amsterdam, 10 May

German forces went into action before dawn today, after heavy bombing of airfields, railways and military strong-points in Holland and Belgium. Along a 150-mile (240-kilometer) front, troops moved forward, seizing key positions before the defenders could react.

In spite of numerous intelligence reports of the presence of at least 28 German divisions in the frontier areas, the Dutch and the Belgians refused to undertake resolute defensive measures, co-ordinated with the Allies, for fear of offending Hitler.

"After our country, with scrupulous conscientiousness, had observed strict neutrality, Germany made a sudden attack on our territory without warning," Holland's Queen Wilhelmina said in a broadcast. She called on her people to fight to the last. Both she and King Leopold of the Belgians are counting on the Allies to come to their aid. Under the Anglo-French contingency plan, a force will advance into Belgium to join up with the

The remains of a bridge in France, destroyed to delay the Germans.

Belgians within two days. That may be too late. The Eban Emael fortress on the Liege front has fallen and the Belgian army shows signs of disintegrating. The Dutch are in no better shape. The great port of Rotterdam is about to surrender after a pulverising bombardment killed 800 people.

Stalin strikes at the Baltic republics

Lithuania, 17 June

The Soviet Red Army is marching into neighbouring Baltic republics on the pretext that there is a conspiracy among these tiny countries to attack Russia. No doubt this is part of the same policy which has just defeated Finland, in spite of her gallant resistence.

The first of the little states to come under pressure is Lithuania. More than 200 Soviet tanks crossed the frontier yesterday and soon reached the capital Kaunas. As Red Army troops seized key points in the city, Russian administrators arrived by air.

The invasion is entirely unopposed. Reports reaching Stockholm suggest that Stalin has committed 500,000 men to the operation. The Lithuanian government accepted an ultimatum alleging a conspiracy before the President, Dr Smetona, with other ministers and their families sought sanctuary in Sweden or Germany.

Now the peoples of Latvia and Estonia wonder how long their freedom will last. The position of German minorities is of special interest. A Nazi-Soviet treaty signed last August makes it unlikely that the Germans will oppose what is happening so long as Hitler's expansion encounters no Soviet opposition. But 35,000 Lithuanian Germans want to go home.

Plucky Finns resisting the USSR: now it is the Baltic republics' turn.

Italians advance in British Somaliland

Somaliland, 7 August

Italian troops crossed over the border from Ethiopia into British Somaliland three days ago and are now advancing in three columns. They captured Hargeisa and Zeila despite resistance by the Camel Corps. The Italians have tanks, artillery, machine-guns and aircraft. It was the brutal annexation of Ethiopia in 1936 which first alerted Britain to the danger from Mussolini's Italy. However, the prime minister, Neville Chamberlain, believed that he could reason with the dictator. Two years later he concluded the Anglo-Italian agreement which he said paved the way for future co-operation.

Trotsky killed after ice-pick assault

Mexico City, 21 August

Stalin's rival Leon Trotsky was assassinated today in his closely guarded refuge near Mexico City. The killer, an enigmatic journalist with five aliases, is almost certainly one of a team of assassins who have stalked Trotsky ever since he was sentenced to death in his absence at a Moscow show trial. Last May Trotsky's bodyguard fought off 30 men with machine-guns who missed their target. The latest killer came to consult Trotsky about an article. On a sunny day he carried an ice-axe concealed under a raincoat. The guards did not notice.

Leon Trotsky, a victim of Stalin and martyr for permanant revolution.

British evacuate France

The ones who never made it: British and French troops led to PoW camps.

Germans enter Paris: France humiliated

Paris, 14 June

Victorious German troops are marching up the Champs Elysees less than a month after invading France. The French government, which evacuated Paris four days ago, has moved from Tours to Bordeaux, with little prospect of avoiding total surrender within a matter of days.

Parisians stand on the pavements to drink in their national humiliation. Not since 1871 have they been obliged to bow the knee to German conquerors.

The Germans said they would treat Paris as non-belligerent if it surrendered at once. The French wanted to retain outlying areas, but capitulated when threatened with further bombardment. The first German motor-cyclists rode into the capital soon after 7am, followed by cameramen, radio technicians and announcers, who are now recording the march past in the Place de la Concorde.

Roads to the south are clogged by up to two million refugees pushing carts loaded with their belongings. German dive-bombers are attacking them sporadically, and machine-gunning the columns.

The French High Command says Paris was surrendered for purely military reasons, and still publicly insists that the fight must continue. Germany claims the Armee de Paris has been routed.

While Churchill, the new British leader, has been discussing strategy with General Weygand, the Allied commander-in-chief, French politicians are talking of surrender.

German troops marching in triumph through Place de la Concorde in Paris.

Chinese Communists fight the Japanese

China, 30 August

Mao Zedong's Red Army, striking from its northern vastness at the Japanese, is inflicting heavy casualties and has paralysed their railway communications.

The attack, called the Hundred Regiments campaign, took the Japanese by surprise for, departing from the usual communist practice of waging guerrilla war and avoiding large scale contact, it involves the whole of the Eighth Route Army of nearly half a million men.

These soldiers, trained in the mountains of Shensi, are dedicated fighters, able to exist on a handful of dried rice and, led by peasant guides, can cross difficult terrain at great speed. With no aircraft, little artillery and no mechanical transport, they rely on the local population for food, shelter, and porters. According to Peng Te-huai, "the people are the sea, while the guerrillas are the fish swimming in it".

They fight with rifles, bayonets and grenades, but their main weapon is their determination to defeat the Japanese, a weapon sadly missing from the Nationalist armoury. There are signs, however, that the Japanese are recovering from their surprise and are ready to strike back.

They have already initiated a brutal "Three-all" campaign in which they "kill all, burn all, destroy all". It is being carried out with great cruelty.

Dunkirk, 4 June

The beaches of Dunkirk are littered with the wreckage of war and the bodies of those who did not make it to the ships. But 338,226 men of the British Expeditionary Force, together with many French and Belgians, have been brought to England and safety.

When the French front was turned by a German thrust around Sedan, and King Leopold ordered the Belgian army to lay down its weapons, the British position became untenable and Lord Gort, the British commander-in-chief, pulled his men back to Dunkirk under relentless German air attacks and through thousands of fleeing refugees. It was thought at one time that no more than 45,000 could be saved.

As the days passed, the number built up. The Luftwaffe continued the dive-bombing of the beaches, but the German armour which had been pressing forward suddenly stopped outside Dunkirk, apparently unwilling to risk an advance through the coastal marshes.

Lying off Dunkirk was a huge fleet – destroyers, ferries, fishing vessels and even river cruisers. Anyone who had a ship and could cross the Channel was roped in for the great rescue. The troops formed lines from the beach out to sea, where they were hauled on board and taken to south coast ports.

Seven French destroyers went down under Luftwaffe attacks and scores of other ships have been lost. But the Royal Navy continued to shepherd the little ships back and forth. Operation Dynamo, as the heroic rescue operation was called, cannot be presented as a military victory, but it has made sure that the British and their army will live to fight another day.

1940 (1940-1941)

Bucharest, 6 September 1940. King Carol is made to abdicate in favour of his son Michael after his pro-German prime minister resigns.

Egypt, 12 September 1940. Italian troops advance from Libya.

Japan, 27 September 1940. Japan signs a ten-year pact with Germany and Italy.

London, 30 September 1940. Hitler's long-awaited *blitz* on London has started.

Helsinki, 1 October 1940. Finland signs a military and economic treaty with Germany.

Rumania, 7 October 1940. German and Italian troops invade.

Bucharest, 12 October 1940. The city is occupied by Axis troops.

New York City, 21 October 1940. Ernest Hemingway's novel *For Whom the Bell Tolls* is published.

Spain, 24 October 1940. Hitler fails to persuade Franco or Petain to join the war against Britain.

Greece, 28 October 1940. Italy invades Greece.

USA, 5 November 1940. President Franklin D Roosevelt is re-elected for a record third term.

London, 7 November 1940. Britain, Australia and the US agree on defence co-operation in the Pacific.

Britain, 14 November 1940. Coventry is devastated by the worst air raid of the war.

Warsaw, 15 November 1940. 350,000 Jews are now confined to a ghetto.

Budapest, 20 November 1940. Hungary joins the Axis.

Greece, 22 November 1940. The Greeks put the Italian invaders to flight in a great victory at Koritza.

Bratislava, 24 November 1940. Slovakia joins the Axis.

North Africa, 9 December 1940. British troops launch an attack on Italians in the Western Desert.

London, 29 December 1940. In the biggest air raid of the war, the *Luftwaffe* razed one-third of the City, including the Barbican. St Paul's survives amid the flames.

Libya, 5 January 1941. The Italian garrison of Bardia falls after a two day assault by Commonwealth troops commanded by the brilliant unconventional Irish-born generals, O'Connor and Dorman-Smith.

Britain, 6 January 1941. One of flying's heroines, Amy Johnson, is drowned when her plane ditches in the Thames estuary.

Britain, 8 January 1941. Boy Scouts founder and Boer war hero, Lord Robert Baden-Powell.

Switzerland, 13 January 1941. The Irish author James Joyce dies in Zurich aged 58. His greatest work was undoubtedly the novel *Ulysses*.

Libya, 30 January 1941. Derna falls to General Wavell's troops after a fierce three-day battle.

Libya, 7 February 1941. British and Commonwealth troops take Benghazi.

North Africa, 14 February 1941. The advance guard of Rommel's Afrika Korps arrive in Tripoli.

Sofia, 14 February 1941. Bulgaria accepts German occupation.

Sudan, 16 February 1941. The last Italian troops are expelled.

Sofia, 17 February 1941. Bulgaria and Turkey sign a non-aggression pact under German pressure.

Berlin, 19 February 1941. Hitler warns Greece to end the war with Italy or face Germany fighting with the Italians.

North Africa, 25 February 1941. Mogadishu, the Italian-held port of Somaliland, falls to the British.

Sofia, 1 March 1941. Bulgaria joins the Axis.

Ankara, 4 March 1941. Turkey refuses to join the Axis.

Ethiopia, 6 March 1941. Haile Selassie's troops capture the Italian stronghold of Burye.

Belgrade, 25 March 1941. Prince Paul, the Yugoslav regent, signs a pact with the Axis.

Sofia, 26 March 1941. The pro-German government is ousted.

Britain, 28 March 1941. The novelist Virginia Woolf commits suicide aged 69.

Eritrea, 1 April 1941. Allied troops take the capital Asmara four days after storming Keren.

Libya, 3 April 1941. British-led troops evacuate Benghazi in the face of Rommel's advances.

Iraq, 4 April 1941. The ex-prime minister, Rashid Ali, an Axis supporter, seizes power.

Yugoslavia, 6 April 1941. Axis troops invade.

Ethiopia, 6 April 1941. Allies occupy Addis Ababa, the capital of Ethiopia.

Greenland, 10 April 1941. The US sends forces to Greenland to protect arms supply lines from America to Britain.

USSR, 13 April 1941. Stalin signs a neutrality pact with Japan.

Yugoslavia, 17 April 1941. Yugoslavia falls to German forces.

Athens, 26 April 1941. The Germans march into Athens.

Commonwealth forces capture Tobruk

British Bren-gun carriers advancing into Italian Libya, on their way to Tobruk.

Libya, 22 January 1941

The port of Tobruk has fallen to British and Australian forces. General Wavell's Western Desert Force has taken more than 100,000 Italian prisoners, and looks set to advance on Benghazi.

The RAF started bombing Italian bases in Libya three weeks ago, and on 5 January Bardia was captured with 25,000 men and six generals. The Italians have continued to suffer heavy bombardment by land, sea and air. At Tobruk, Italian resistance melted in the face of infantry, tanks and Bren guns. British and Australian forces arrived simultaneously.

Allied armies take Ethiopian capital

Addis Ababa, 6 April 1941

Allied forces including including British, Indian and South African troops and local guerrillas have liberated the Ethiopian capital after a three-month campaign. Plans are now in hand for the Emperor Haile Selassie to re-enter Addis on 5 May, the fifth anniversary of Italy's invasion. Defeat for Italy became certain after British forces took Keren in the north and Harar in the southeast, and converged onto the centre, Addis Ababa.

Britain appeals for more women workers

England, 1941

Womanpower for the war effort – that is now the call from Britain's minister of labour, Ernest Bevin, as he announced the first steps in a massive mobilisation plan. The registration of 20 and 21-year-old women will begin next month with the aim of filling vital jobs in industry and farming together with the auxiliary services.

Women are desperately needed to get shell-filling factories working round the clock and to take over all kinds of other jobs to free men for active service. As yet, married women with young children are exempt, but those who are able do war work locally will be backed up by a huge expansion in day and night nurseries.

Turning ploughshares into swords.

Germans bombs begin London blitz

London, 30 September 1940
As Britain awaits an invasion, London is now the front line in the war the Britain is fighting virtually alone. Every night for three weeks London has been pounded by bombs, tens of thousands of the population sheltering deep underground in tube stations. The bombs first fell in the Docks and East End, now they are moving westwards. Even Buckingham Palace has been hit. Six days ago King George VI introduced the George Cross, in recognition of the heroism of London's firemen.

In Kent and Sussex, inadequately armed troops and even worse armed "Home Guard" militiamen, can see the fires of London as they prepare to resist invasion. For three months they watched dogfights above them as the RAF and the Luftwaffe fought for control of the skies over southern England. It was not planes that either side were short of, but pilots; and with baled out British pilots returning to their airfields, and baled out Germans going into POW camps, the RAF won the battle.

On 5 September Hitler switched tactics, vowing to turn London into rubble in retaliation for a RAF raid on Berlin. Three days later his bombers came. "Leisurely enormous mushrooms of black and brown smoke shot with crimson climbed into the sunlit sky," a Londoner recalls. "There they hung, and slowly expanded, for there was no wind, and the great fires below fed more smoke into them as the hours passed."

RAF bombing crew: even during the Blitz the RAF was bombing German cities.

The Blitz: London wakes up to the debris of another night's bombing.

Churchill's finest hour: "Let us brace ourselves to our duty."

Japanese join the Nazi-Fascist Axis

Tokyo, 27 September 1940
Although Japan has been politically and militarily linked with Nazi Germany and Fascist Italy for over five years, a formal alliance was signed today which will send tremors through the Soviet Union and the United States.

The wording of the pact tries to assuage the Soviets who are uncomfortably situated between the three powers. For the Americans there is an unmistakable warning that entry into the war on behalf of the Allies will also entail a war in the Pacific.

Britain and USA forge Atlantic Charter

Newfoundland, 14 August 1941
When Britain's newest battleship, the *Prince of Wales*, set sail last week, it was a well-kept secret that Winston Churchill was on board. The purpose of his voyage was to meet Franklin D Roosevelt, ostensibly on a fishing trip, and the outcome is an agreement which brings the United States one step closer to war.

The Atlantic Charter states that neither country has any territorial claims to make and proposes that aggressor nations be disarmed. In the presence of their military chiefs the two leaders discussed Japanese encroachments in the Pacific where both nations have colonies.

The president's support for the Allied cause is no secret. Last December he proudly proclaimed the United States was the "arsenal of democracy". True to his word a "lend-lease" pact was signed this March, deferring British payment for American arms until the end of hostilities.

However, all Roosevelt's efforts at bringing the United States into the war have thus far been thwarted by Congress.

Balkan blitzkrieg smashes Yugoslav and Greek forces

Cairo, 17 April 1941
Late tonight British headquarters here was making no attempt to disguise the seriousness of the situation in the Balkans. Yugoslavia has fallen and Greece is now in grave danger. Just before midnight the German High Command said: "All the Yugoslav armed forces which had not been disarmed before, laid down their arms unconditionally at nine o'clock tonight."

German troops are already crossing the border into Greece to join up with their compatriots who have been pressing hard against the Greek, British and Australian troops. So far the lines are intact, despite very heavy fighting.

The Nazis are clearly throwing their entire weight into the attack. There are at least ten divisions supported by hundreds of Stukas and Messerschmitts which are raining bombs on the allied lines. RAF bombers are pounding the German supply lines. But Greece is now surrounded. German troops are well-established on the Bulgarian frontier and Albania is in the hands of Italy. Now Yugoslavia has fallen, the allied forces have nowhere to retreat except the sea.

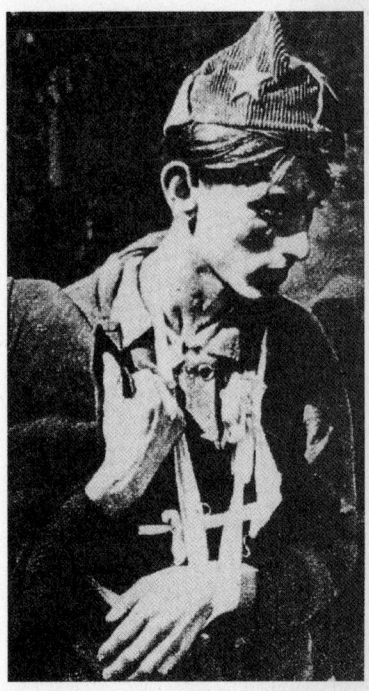

Resisting the Nazi occupiers: a wounded Yugoslavian partisan.

South-East Asia reels under the lightning advance of Japan

Hong Kong, 25 December

Three weeks after the attack on Pearl Harbor (*see right*), Hong Kong fell to Japan today. After a seven-day battle, 6,000 troops will surrender at noon tomorrow.

News of the fall of Hong Kong was announced in a communique that spoke of "a great fight against overwhelming odds", but failed to mention to incompetence of commanders who ignored warnings that the Japanese would swim the straits. It could not have come at a worse time for a British public which was still recovering from the news that Britain's two greatest battleships, the *Repulse* and the *Prince of Wales*, had entered hostile waters without aircraft cover and had been sunk by Japanese dive-bombers in the South China Sea.

In Malaya, crack Japanese divisions have landed and are advancing towards Singapore, where the British are confident they can stop them at their "impregnable" fortress. More are pushing their way northwards and eastwards into Burma, and towards India.

American forces, still shocked by the news from Pearl Harbor, put up fierce resistance before they lost Wake Island and Guam, though the soldiers' courage was ill-served by an inadequate leadership. The Japanese army has landed in strength on the Philippines and are steadily advancing. General Douglas MacArthur, the US commander, is in retreat with 150,000 US and Filipino forces.

Few doubt that the principal Japanese goals are India and Australia, and the creation of a new empire.

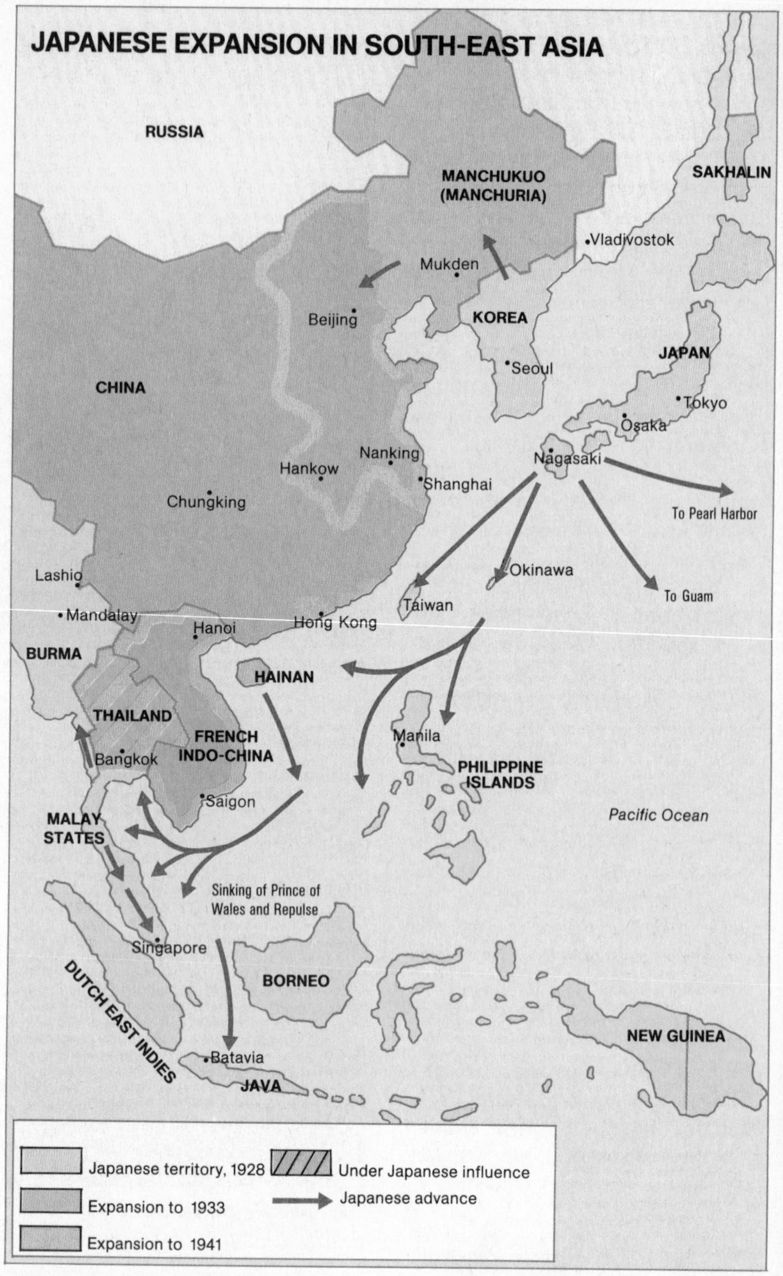

JAPANESE EXPANSION IN SOUTH-EAST ASIA

Legend:
- Japanese territory, 1928
- Expansion to 1933
- Expansion to 1941
- Under Japanese influence
- Japanese advance

USA takes Iceland

Iceland, 7 July

American forces have landed in Iceland to help Britain prevent it being attacked by the Germans. An independent country, but with no means of defending itself, Iceland was occupied without bloodshed by a British force early last year.

President Roosevelt, announcing the move in Washington today, said that he had sent a marine brigade to Iceland. The marines will release British troops from the 20,000-strong garrison. The British government welcomed the US action.

Allies occupy Iran

Iran, 25 August

British and Soviet troops marched into Iran today, encountering little opposition. The operation, a shameless infringement of Iran's neutrality, claims to have pre-empted a coup by the Germans who had built up a strong Fifth Column. British air troops were dropped on the oilfields to protect Britons and prevent sabotage, while British and Indian troops and armour crossed the border at Khanikin. At the same time Soviet troops moved in from the north capturing Tabriz.

Divers reclaim gold

New Zealand, 8 December

The trans-Pacific liner, *Niagara*, sunk in 70 fathoms by a German mine last year, has yielded her cargo of bullion to the Australian diving brothers J and W Johnstone.

Working at extreme depths in conditions made hazardous by storms and mines which twice threatened to destroy the salvage ship *Claymore*, the Johnstones have raised 555 ingots, valued at £2,379,000 – 94 per cent of the shipment sent by Britain to the USA to pay for American weapons.

Hitler invades the USSR

USA joins the Allies

Russia, 30 June
German *panzers* are smashing into Russia in the greatest blitzkrieg yet seen. Hundreds of tanks supported by clouds of Stukas are rolling across the Russian plains. The Red Army units guarding the frontier have been destroyed. Minsk, over halfway to Moscow, has fallen.

The Germans claim that two Russian armies have been surrounded and "would be forced to capitulate in a few days or be annihilated". The Red Army was clearly caught unprepared by the German onslaught at dawn on 22 June, despite clear indications that Hitler was about to break his infamous non-aggression pact with Stalin.

The Germans had massed 100 divisions and, together with their Finnish and Rumanian allies, rolled over the 1,800-mile (2,880-kilometre) border from the Arctic Circle to the Black Sea.

In Britain Mr Churchill told the Commons: "I gave clear and precise warnings to Stalin of what was coming. I can only hope these warnings did not fall unheeded". He

A Cossack tradition, Soviet cavalryman using his dead horse as cover.

promised Russia "whatever help we can; we have offered any technical or economic assistance in our power". He went on: "We are resolved to destroy Hitler and every vestige of the Nazi regime. From this nothing will turn us. We will never parley, never."

Soviets repel Nazi advance on Moscow

Russia, 12 December
The Red Army has turned on the German invaders and inflicted a series of smashing defeats on Hitler's panzers who, unprepared for a winter war, are suffering heavy casualties from "General Frost".

Following the recapture of Rostov in the south, General Zhukov has counter-attacked and routed the Germans halted before Moscow, recapturing Solechnaya Gora, 40 miles (64 kilometres) north-west of the capital, the closest the Nazi spearhead came to Moscow.

According to last night's communique, more than 400 towns and villages have been retaken in five days' fighting. Some 30,000 Germans have been killed and nearly 700 tanks captured or destroyed.

The Russians claim that "German plans for surrounding and capturing Moscow have ended in utter fiasco". Jubilant Russians, warmly clad in white camouflage uniforms are pursuing the frozen Germans through the snow as fresh divisions from Siberia enter the battle. The

German soldiers, getting their first harsh taste of a Russian winter.

front has undergone a remarkable change since Marshal Timoshenko's great southern counterstroke a fortnight ago. Now the Red Army holds the initiative everywhere. For the first time the Nazis are on the defensive.

The twisted wreckage of the USS Arizona in Pearl Harbor after the attack.

Pearl Harbor, 7 December
Soon after dawn today, wave after wave of Japanese warplanes began to bomb America's major Pacific base. Pearl Harbor was taken entirely by surprise and within two hours the Japanese had destroyed five battleships, 14 smaller craft and 200 aircraft. At least 2,400 people, many of them civilians, were killed. Although the US Navy has suffered a major disaster, Japan's bombers failed to find and hit America's all-important aircraftcarriers, both of which were away on manoeuvres.

However, Japanese planes have attacked US bases in the Philippines, on Wake Island and Guam in the middle of the Pacific. The Japanese had obviously planned the operation carefully. Twelve days ago, six aircraft-carriers left the Kurile Islands in total secrecy and headed for Honolulu. The first bombs fell even as Japanese diplo-

How the news broke: Pearl Harbor ends two decades of isolationism.

mats were meeting with the US Government in Washington. Congress will meet to declare war in emergency session tomorrow – to the infinite relief of Britain.

Bismarck, pride of German fleet, is sunk

Atlantic, 27 May
The Royal Navy avenged *HMS Hood* today and sent the *Bismarck* to the bottom of the sea after a three-day hunt to the death.

The *Bismarck*, reputed to be the world's most powerful warship, broke out from the North Sea to harry the convoy lanes, but was in-

tercepted by the *Hood* and the *Prince of Wales*. One of her shells penetrated the *Hood's* magazine and she blew up.

Bismarck was wounded in the encounter and Swordfish aircraft damaged her steering, enabling the navy to catch her and deluge her with shells and torpedoes.

1942

Philippines, 2 January. Japanese troops take Manila.

India, 15 January. Gandhi names Pandit Nehru as his successor.

Germany, 20 January. Officials learn of Reinhard Heydrich's "final solution" – to exterminate the 11 million Jews in Europe.

Singapore, 31 January. The Japanese lay siege to the island.

Norway, 1 February. Vidkun Quisling is appointed puppet prime minister by the Germans.

Singapore, 9 February. Japanese forces land on the island.

South East Asia, 14 February. The Japanese invade Sumatra.

Singapore, 15 February. Singapore surrenders to the Japanese.

Burma, 22 February. Civilians are evacuated from Rangoon – battles rage 80 miles northeast of the city.

South East Asia, 8 March. Java capitulates to the Japanese.

Germany, 26 March. The Nazis begin the deportation of Jews to Auschwitz concentration camp.

Germany, 28 March. The RAF begins a round-the-clock offensive on German munitions factories.

India, 29 March. The British reveal a plan for Indian independence after the war.

India, 7 April. The Indian National Congress Working Committee rejects British plans for India.

Tokyo, 18 April. US planes bomb Tokyo.

Yugoslavia, 3 May. German reinforcements arrive to fight Tito's partisans.

Libya, 27 May. Rommel's *panzer* divisions launch a long-expected offensive in the desert.

Czechoslovakia, 31 May. Czech partisans assassinate Gestapo leader Heydrich.

Mexico City, 1 June. Mexico declares war on the Axis.

Pacific, 7 June. The Japanese withdraw after four days of serious fighting around Midway Island.

Australia, 8 June. The Japanese shell Sydney and Newcastle.

Libya, 21 June. Tobruk falls to Rommel's troops; 25,000 Allied soldiers are taken prisoner.

USA, 25 June. Major General Dwight Eisenhower is given command of all US forces in Europe.

Egypt, 25 June. Axis forces threaten Cairo.

USSR, 29 June. The Germans launch an offensive at Kursk, south of Moscow.

USSR, 1 July. Sevastopol falls to the Germans after a nine-month siege.

USSR, 6 August. The Germans advance on Stalingrad.

North Africa, 6 August. General Bernard Montgomery becomes commander of the Eighth Army.

Pacific, 7 August. US marines land on the Solomon Islands.

New Delhi, 9 August. Gandhi and other Congress leaders are arrested.

France, 19 August. Allied forces go ashore at Dieppe to gain experience of an amphibious attack against coastal positions.

Brazil, 22 August. Brazil declares war on Germany and Italy.

Egypt, 30 August. Rommel launches a new offensive in Egypt.

Warsaw, 2 September. German SS troops "clear" the Jewish ghetto of 50,000 people.

USSR, 6 September. The Germans take the major Black Sea base of Novorossiisk.

Germany, 10 September. The RAF drop 100,000 bombs on Dusseldorf in under an hour.

USSR, 11 September. The Germans drive a wedge through Soviet positions in Stalingrad.

Madagascar, 23 September. The British capture the island's capital of Antananarivo.

New Guinea, 27 September. The Japanese pull back in the face of the advancing Allies.

Egypt, 30 September. The Eighth Army seizes key German positions near El Alamein in a dawn raid.

Britain, 24 October. A giant task force led by General Eisenhower leaves for North Africa.

Egypt, 30 October. Montgomery is victorious at El Alamein.

Yugoslavia, 3 November. The Bosnian capital of Bihacs falls to Tito's partisans.

North Africa, 7 November. Allied troops land in Vichy-French North Africa.

North Africa, 8 November. Rommel retreats into Libya.

France, 11 November. The Axis invades Vichy France.

USSR, 26 November. Soviet troops smash through German lines in Stalingrad.

France, 27 November. The French fleet is scuttled hours after the Germans move into Toulon.

Burma, 19 December. British troops advance down the Malay peninsula pushing the Japanese back into Burma.

Chinese peasants beat Japanese veterans

China, January
Nationalist troops have scored a remarkable victory over the Japanese in a bloody ten-day battle for the city of Changsha, the capital of Hunan province. The over-confident Japanese, who had neglected to bring up their heavy guns, were driven off by the raw, young Chinese soldiers – peasants fighting for their own homes and land.

They had waited all winter for the Japanese to attack, planting vegetables in their dug-outs to relieve the boredom. But when the attack came, they fought like veterans under the command of the respected Colonel Li.

His success proves that under efficient officers who care for their men, the Chinese soldier is the equal of any. Certainly these youths in their light-blue padded uniforms inflicted a terrible beating on the Japanese and gave the Nationalist cause a much-needed boost.

Congressmen jailed after Quit India vote

New Delhi, 9 August
Within hours of Mahatma Gandhi and 50 other Congress leaders being arrested by the British authorities, India is experiencing its biggest civil commotions since the Mutiny. The move came only 12 hours after Congress passed a motion demanding Britain "quit India", and launched a mass civil disobedience campaign. It deeply wounded the British psyche. To British administrators and pro-British Indians, particularly those whose soldiers are retreating in the face of Japanese advances in Burma, it is akin to treason. In Bombay, where pro-Congress crowds took over the streets, police fired on rioters, killing five. At Shiva-Ji Park, where Gandhi was to address a meeting, 20,000 people took to the rampage. In Patna and Bihar the administration has completely lost control. Behind the riot is the Indians' disappointment at Sir Stafford Cripps' proposals for self-go-

Gandhi, the "Mahatma" or Living Soul of India: now confined in jail.

vernment. Big expectations were raised, but his proposals were so watered down by Churchill that they were "a postdated cheque on a crashing bank", as Gandhi put it.

"Casablanca": war means goodbyes for Bogart and Bergman.

The Nazi Spring offensive is blunted

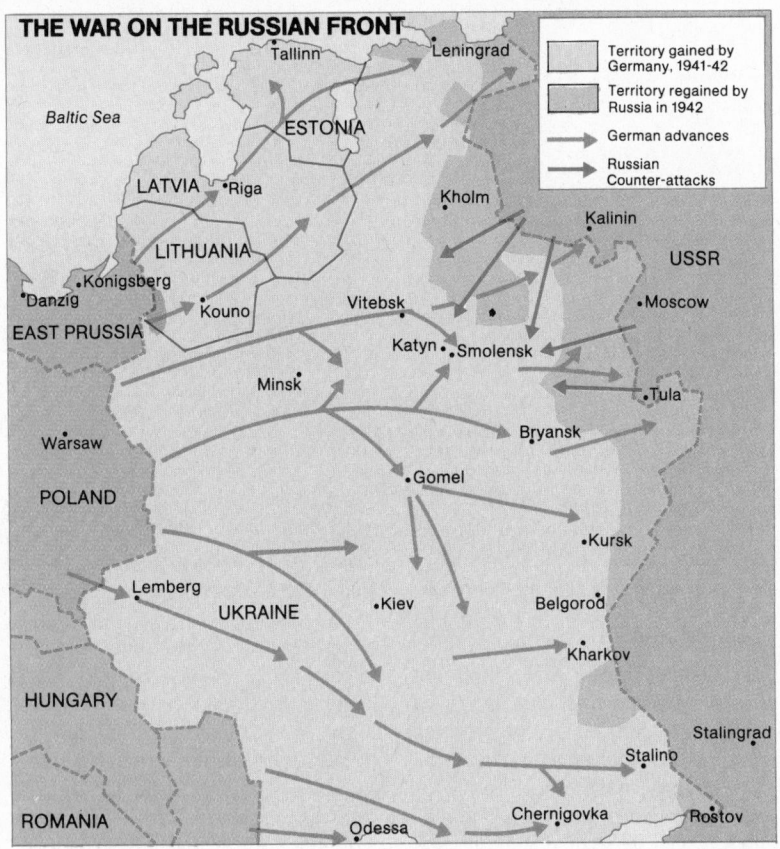

THE WAR ON THE RUSSIAN FRONT

Legend:
- Territory gained by Germany, 1941-42
- Territory regained by Russia in 1942
- German advances
- Russian Counter-attacks

Map locations: Baltic Sea, Tallinn, Leningrad, ESTONIA, Riga, LATVIA, Kholm, Kalinin, LITHUANIA, Königsberg, Danzig, Kouno, Vitebsk, USSR, Moscow, EAST PRUSSIA, Katyn, Smolensk, Minsk, Tula, Warsaw, Bryansk, POLAND, Gomel, Kursk, Lemberg, Kiev, Belgorod, UKRAINE, Kharkov, HUNGARY, Stalingrad, Stalino, ROMANIA, Odessa, Chernigovka, Rostov

Russia, 31 May

A tremendous battle is raging for the Donetz river crossings south of Kharkov, with the armies of General von Bock and Marshal Timoshenko locked in fierce hand-to-hand fighting. Both sides are pouring in men and tanks and guns. Swirling air battles fill the sky over the front as dive-bombers from both sides pound their enemy.

A Russian dispatch from the Kharkov front speaks of 14 waves of massed German tanks being hurled back. Among the German losses were 500 of their latest tanks. The fighting is part of Hitler's much-talked-about spring offensive which opened on 12 May with an onslaught on the Soviet lines on the Kerch peninsula in the Crimea.

Much of the offensive's impact was blunted, however, when the Russians pre-empted the development of the main German thrust by striking towards Kharkov and inflicting heavy casualties on the Germans still holed up in their winter positions. The battle rages. The outcome is still uncertain.

British put Japanese to flight in Burma

Burma, 19 December

For the first time since Burma was overrun by the Japanese almost a year ago, British and Indian troops are fighting back – and advancing at a remarkable pace through difficult jungle terrain along the Mayu Peninsula on the Bay of Bengal.

First reports suggest that the 14th Indian Division under Major General W L Lloyd are meeting little resistance as they thrust down either side of the Mayu Range of mountains. The little port of Maungdaw has been recaptured and a Punjabi patrol has made contact with the enemy. British generals believe the recapture of Burma is now a distinct possibility.

After the bombing of Pearl Harbor and the fall of Singapore, it is the Japanese who are on the defensive. With massive support from three carriers, the Americans landed successfully on the Solomon Islands and are advancing inland against near-suicidal Japanese resistance.

US Navy trounces Japanese at Midway

The USS Enterprise, waiting to launch its torpedo bombers during the battle.

Pacific, 7 June

In one of the greatest battles ever to be fought at sea, the US Navy wreaked revenge for its Pearl Harbor debacle today, sinking four large Japanese aircraft-carriers, and badly damaging three battleships off Midway Island. As the Japanese Imperial fleet withdraws, American commanders are hoping that the battle will be seen as a turning point in the war.

Unaware that American intelligence had succeeded in "cracking" their battle codes, the Japanese were taken completely by surprise when American dive-bombers flew out of the sun, raining their bombs on carrier decks packed with aircraft. As more dive-bombers savaged the battleships, torpedoes succeeded in turning the carriers into floating infernos.

The significance of Midway has not been lost on either side. It was a battle won by aircraft-carriers. America lost the carrier *Yorktown* and 147 aircraft. The Japanese have only one large carrier left with its others under repair. America has three in service with a further 28 under construction.

El Alamein: Monty hits Germans for six

Egypt, 30 October

The Eighth Army has punched deep into the Afrika Korps positions at El Alamein, in what looks sure to be the crucial battle of the desert war. After ten months in which Rommel's brilliant generalship has won battles against superior numbers, the "Desert Fox" seems at last to be on the run.

The Allied commander General Bernard Montgomery, who promised to hit the Afrika Korps for six, now has a two-to-one advantage in men, and a greater edge in armaments. Although the German lines are five miles deep, and heavily mined, intelligence estimates that they are reduced to a mere 90 tanks against the Eighth Army's 800. Half of Rommel's 100,000 soldiers and 600 planes are Italian, lowly rated by friend and foe alike. Mont-

Monty: leading from the front.

gomery has about 800 planes. The Axis reserves are now committed to the battle, and against such superior numbers and armaments, they can only postpone defeat.

1943

Brutal Nazi pogrom in the Warsaw ghetto

Warsaw Jews, lined up by SS troops, destined for the concentration camps.

Warsaw, 19 April

As German, Polish and Ukrainian troops move relentlessly through its shattered streets, destroying every building and shooting down anyone they can see, the Jews of the Warsaw ghetto are behaving in a way unknown in years of seemingly passive acceptance of Nazi persecution: they are fighting back.

The SS General Jurgen Stroop promised Hitler that the ghetto would be easy to crush. Unarmed, starving, their numbers decimated by years of isolation, Warsaw's Jews seemed to pose no threat – 50,000 were massacred last year. Yet, with courage born of desperation, the survivors are making the Nazis fight for every inch. Millions of Jews have been deported to concentration camps as Germany's conquest of Europe has expanded. For whatever reason, none has resisted. Until now. They will not win, they cannot win, but these "sub-humans and cowards", as the Nazi Stroop dismisses them, are proving a real stumbling block to the "Master Race".

Allies take 110,000 Germans in Africa

North Africa, 12 May

German and Italian resistance is over. Allied forces have taken 110,000 Germans and 40,000 Italians prisoner. It was the arrival of 140,000 American troops last November that clinched the victory.

One by one African landmarks have been falling to a pincer movement by Montgomery's Eighth Army in the south and east, and Eisenhower's forces in the west. Forced back on to the promontory of Tunis, Rommel evacuated four weeks ago, and on 7 May the Allied forces entered Tunis to a rapturous welcome.

General Jurgen von Armin, captured in Cap Bon with his entire staff by a British reconnaissance patrol, signed the surrender.

Communists purify their diluted party

China, 15 August

Cables ordering the screening of *cadres* have today been sent by the Central Committee of the Chinese Communist Party to all party organisations. This is part of the "Rectification Movement" which was started last year in order to cope with the problems caused by the huge expansion of the party.

Many new members have been recruited in the "liberated areas" and there has been some diffusion of the party's ideals. The screening ordered today is designed to stamp out corruption and reinforce the proletarian nature of the party's ideology and political programme.

It will also enable Mao Zedong to strengthen his grip on the party leadership.

Italy is out of the war

Italy, 8 September

A secret meeting between Dwight Eisenhower, the Allied commander, and Marshal Pietro Badoglio, the prime minister of Italy since the fall of Mussolini in July, has resulted in the unconditional surrender of Germany's ally. The news was broadcast this evening by Eisenhower.

Less than an hour earlier, Berlin radio was reporting "solid resistance" by Italian and German troops to the British invasion of southern Italy, and it seems the surrender has taken the Germans by surprise. In Corsica, the Italian garrison is reported to have overpowered its former allies. All ships, trains and vehicles carrying German troops are now liable to be halted on the orders of the Italian government.

Three weeks ago, Messina, the last fortress in Sicily, fell to combined British and American forces after a grim struggle which left the city in ruins. Long-range guns began to pound the mainland, and five days ago the first Allied troops

George Patton, the aggressive and charismatic US general, in Sicily.

landed opposite Messina. At the same time, Badoglio had embarked on his secret talks with the Allies in Rome. Italians, whose dislike of their German occupiers has become more and more blatant, have been laying down their arms *en masse*. They are now being invited to take them up again – this time against their former allies.

RAF and US bombs pulverise Hamburg

The aftermath of saturation bombing: the heart of Hamburg lies in ruins.

London, 3 August

Over seven square miles of Hamburg have been "wiped off the map", the British air ministry claimed today, after eight days of round-the-clock bombing with more than 10,000 tons of bombs dropped on Germany's second largest city. The non-stop air raid with the RAF attacking by night and the US Air Force by day is part of new terror-bombing tactics. Civilian casualties are put as high as 200,000 killed. The raids have systematically destroyed the city's factories, shipyards and U-boat bases.

Russians win Stalingrad

Russia and her ally – snow; sappers clear barbed wire for a Soviet advance.

Russia, 31 January

The Battle of Stalingrad is over. Field-Marshal von Paulus today surrendered the pitiful remains of his once-proud Sixth Army to a Red Army lieutenant in the basement of what had been Stalingrad's largest department store.

The lieutenant told him: "Well, that finishes it". Von Paulus replied with "a miserable look." Fifteen other German generals surrendered at the same time. A small pocket of Germans is still holding out in the northern part of this totally devastated city, but for them, too, the war will soon be over.

Some 300,000 Germans have been killed or died of starvation and cold since the Russians broke the Rumanians and encircled the Sixth Army last November with 100,000 dying in the ferocious hand-to-hand fighting in the city's ruins.

Von Paulus twice refused to surrender although his situation was hopeless. Goering's promises to fly in 500 tons of food, fuel and ammunition a day proved empty. Since December the Germans have been eating what was left of the Rumanian cavalry division's horses. Hitler forbade surrender and made von Paulus a field-marshal because no German marshal had ever surrendered. "Sixth Army will hold its positions to the last man," he ordered. Today the new field-marshal refused to obey his *Fuhrer's* orders any longer.

Atlantic war: U-boats are on the run

London, May

The Allies have dramatically turned the tide in the war against U-boats in the Atlantic putting enemy submarines on the run.

Improved submarine detection techniques, including sonar radar, and the deployment of extra escort ships and aircraft-carriers from North Africa have swung the balance in favour of surface vessels with fewer German commanders prepared to venture out into the Atlantic. Last month eight U-boats were sunk in one attack on an Allied convoy.

At the same time Allied losses were down last month to just 18,000 tons of shipping sunk compared with a monthly average loss of 650,000 tons last year.

A German U-boat leaving port to join in the battle of the Atlantic.

New York City, 1 January. DNA is discovered by Oswald T Avery.

Berlin, 4 January. Hitler orders the mobilisation of all children over the age of ten.

USSR, 19 January. The Russians smash the German siege of Leningrad.

Italy, 22 January. Allied troops make a surprise landing at Anzio, 30 miles south of Rome.

Pacific, 29 January. The world's biggest warship, the *USS Missouri*, is launched.

France, 1 February. The Forces Francaises de l'Interieur (*FFI*) is created, unifying all Resistance movements.

New York City, 1 February. The Dutch artist Piet Mondrian dies aged 71.

Pacific, 4 February. US warships shell the Japanese home island of Paramishu.

France, 13 February. The Allies drop weapons for the Resistance in Haute-Savoie.

Tokyo, 21 February. Hideki Tojo becomes chief of staff of the Japanese army.

Helsinki, 24 February. The Finnish prime minister announces that his country is ready to make peace.

London, 26 February. The Polish government rejects the Curzon Line, reached by the USSR and Germany in 1939 as its eastern frontier.

Pacific, 29 February. American troops land at Los Negros in the Admiralty Islands in a new assault on Japanese territory.

Britain, 3 March. The RAF admits it is dropping new 12,000-pound bombs in its latest raids on German cities.

Britain, 12 March. All travel between Britain and Ireland is banned to prevent invasion plans from being passed to pro-German spies in Ireland.

Hungary, 18 March. The Germans begin to occupy the country.

Burma, 19 March. It is revealed that Allied troops have been landed by glider 200 miles behind Japanese lines.

Eastern Europe, 22 March. The Germans continue their march into Hungary; German troops cross into Slovakia.

Rumania, 2 April. The Russians cross the Rumanian border.

Hungary, 5 April. The Germans begin deporting Jews.

Berlin, 7 April. Hitler suspends all laws and makes Goebbels dictator of the city.

France, 9 April. General Charles de Gaulle becomes commander-in-chief of the Free French forces.

USSR, 13 April. The Soviet army take Simferopol.

Germany, 20 April. The RAF sets a new record for a single raid, dropping 4,500 tons of bombs for Hitler's 55th birthday.

Paris, 20 April. Petain visits the city for the first time since the fall of France.

Pacific, 24 April. The Japanese evacuate New Guinea as US troops land.

Britain, April. Britain becomes one big armed camp as Eisenhower oversees Allied preparations for the invasion of Europe.

Moscow, 1 May. Stalin tells Bulgaria, Rumania and Hungary to declare war on Germany.

London, 8 May. The exiled Czech government signs a convention to allow the Soviet army to liberate the country.

USSR, 9 May. The Soviet army takes Sevastopol, winning control of the whole Crimea.

France, 15 May. Field-Marshal Erwin Rommel attempts to cut occupied France off from neutral countries to stop information being passed out to the Allies.

Italy, 18 May. British and Polish troops capture Monte Cassino.

Italy, 23 May. The Allies begin an offensive from Anzio.

Yugoslavia, 25 May. Tito escapes to the hills as Germans capture his Bosnian headquarters.

London, 28 May. MPs hear that 47 Allied airmen have been shot in a mass escape bid from *Stalag Luft III* in Silesia.

Eire, 1 June. De Valera's *Fianna Fail* wins an overall majority.

Algiers, 3 June. General de Gaulle announces a provisional French government to take over from Vichy when France is liberated.

Rome, 4 June. The Allies take Rome.

Rome, 5 June. Victor Emmanuel III resigns, Crown Prince Umberto becomes acting head of state.

France, 6 June. Allied forces begin landing in Normandy – the invasion of Europe has begun.

Rome, 9 June. Ex-prime minister, Ivanoe Bonomi, is chosen to head a provisional government.

France, 10 June. German troops obliterate a whole village in reprisal for the killing of an SS officer.

Japan, 15 June. US planes bomb the Japanese mainland.

Allies liberate Rome

US General Mark Clark, commander of the Fifth Army, in St Peter's Square.

Rome, 4 June

Cheering crowds, throwing flowers and handing round bottles of wine, celebrate the arrival of American and British troops as the Allies march into Rome. President Roosevelt declared jubilantly: "The first Axis capital is in our hands. One up and two to go."

Apart from the occasional German sniper, there has been little fighting in Rome itself, and Allied planes command the skies, harassing retreating German columns.

The city's historic sites remain undamaged. Hitler's orders to blow up the Tiber bridges were ignored.

But for the Allied victors, it has been a grim struggle since American and British troops landed at Anzio in January. Faced with crack German troops commanding the road to Rome from the fortress of Monte Cassino, they suffered heavy losses before Monte Cassino fell ten days ago, enabling the Anzio forces to link with the Fifth Army, advancing from the south.

British jungle fighters glide into Burma

Burma, 24 March

Britain's "forgotten army" – the "Chindit" jungle fighters who are fighting the Japanese at their own game in Burma – mourned an outstanding leader today. General Orde Wingate, their brilliant yet eccentric commander, has been killed in an air crash. "Gideon" Wingate, a loner who has been compared to Lawrence of Arabia, spurned military orthodoxy, particularly in jungle fighting, and relied on surprise as his principal tactic.

Wingate pioneered the use of gliders to land troops behind the Japanese lines. Five days ago, details of one of the most daring operations of the war were revealed. Gliders landed men, mules and a bulldozer behind the Chin Hills where they built a strategically vital airstrip.

Burma: "the forgotten war".

Allied troops take Normandy beaches

Japanese launch big attack on China

An endless column of US vehicles drives through the village of Isigny on the way to the front at St Lo.

GIs in La Haye du Puits in Normandy, on the sixth day of the invasion.

Normandy, 6 June

In the biggest combined land, sea and air operation of all time, British, American and Canadian forces have landed on the Normandy beaches at more than a dozen points along a hundred miles of coast. The Germans appear to have been caught off their guard. Allied air reconnaissance has shown that the strongest German defences are concentrated in the Pas de Calais, and that a powerful armoured force there has not been moved.

The massive operation began with heavy aerial bombardment of German coastal batteries and the sweeping of mines from the invasion route. A seaborne force of several thousand ships, brought from widely scattered British ports, converged on the invasion coast soon after 5am. Battleships far out to sea and destroyers closer inland pounded the German defences. Engineers demolished beach obstacles and the fighting men came up behind them with tanks and self-propelled artillery.

The question that has yet to be settled is whether the Allies can bring in reinforcements faster by sea than the Germans can by land. The land-based forces would have the advantage, but for the work of the RAF and the US Air Force in knocking out railways, bridges, radar stations and supply columns. Only at night can the Germans risk large-scale movement of men and

supplies. In the House of Commons tonight, Mr Churchill told MPs that the invasion "is proceeding in a thoroughly satisfactory manner. Many dangers and difficulties which appeared extremely formidable are now behind us." Shipping

losses have been less than feared and the resistance of enemy batteries has been greatly weakened by Allied bombing. At the end of this momentous D-Day, as it was known, Allied forces had penetrated several miles inland.

China, April

The Japanese have opened their first large-scale campaign in China since the end of 1938. In the intervening years an informal truce has been established between units of the Nationalists and the Japanese with much money being made in trade between the two armies.

That cosy arrangement has now been swept away as the Japanese, most of their merchant shipping sunk, attempt to establish a land link with their armies in South-East Asia.

They are also determined to wipe out the airfields from which the Americans have begun bombing the heart of the Japanese war machine. These airfields are poorly protected on the ground and are proving easy targets for the Japanese.

Their assault, codenamed *Ichigo*, has shocked the Chinese. The Nationalist army in Hunan has been routed and the Americans are abandoning their bases, flying their aircraft to safety but destroying huge amounts of equipment.

Russian army drives Germans out of Crimea in bitter attack

Russia, 16 April

The Red Army is sweeping the Germans out of the Crimea. The remnants of nine German and Romanian divisions, once more than 100,000 strong, are being harried through the streets of Sevastopol and in the open country around those other nineteenth century battlefields, Inkerman and Balaclava.

It is only five days since the Russians opened their campaign to recapture the Crimea with three armoured thrusts, their tanks smashing into the German defences across the neck of the peninsula.

The Black Sea port of Odessa fell almost immediately, followed by Kerch, the easternmost town in the Crimea, and the vital railway junction of Dzankhoi. The capture of Odessa was the climax of a 13-mile (21-kilometre) drive which left 5,500 Germans dead and hundreds of tanks destroyed. Now Yalta on the south coast has been taken and the Germans are desperately trying to organise a "Dunkirk" to save their troops pinned against the sea

The last of the German troops leaving Zhitomir, before the Red Army advance.

by the Russian tanks and dive-bombers. The Crimean victories are being celebrated with salvoes of gunfire. Stalin has issued an Order of the Day urging the army not to allow any German to escape: "The arrogant invaders run like rats, the

ground hot beneath their feet. Destroy their ships. Shoot down their planes. Don't allow a single enemy to escape retribution."

Some 118,000 of the "rats" have already been killed as the Soviets gather for the last push.

1944 (1944-1945)

USSR, 3 July 1944. Minsk, the last big German base on Soviet soil, falls to the Russians.

Lithuania, 13 July 1944. The capital, Vilna, is captured by the Russians as they advance through the Baltic states.

Berlin, 21 July 1944. Troops pour into the city following an attempt on Hitler's life yesterday.

France, 31 July 1944. The pilot and writer Antoine de Saint-Exupery is declared missing.

France, 31 July 1944. The Allies drive the Germans from Normandy.

Berlin, 2 August 1944. Germany breaks off relations with Turkey.

Berlin, 8 August 1944. Officers convicted of attempting to assassinate Hitler are executed by being strangled with piano wire.

France, 15 August 1944. A massive Allied force lands on a coastal strip from Nice to Marseilles.

Germany, 17 August 1944. The Russians reach the East Prussian frontier.

Britain, 19 August 1944. The conductor Sir Henry Wood dies aged 75.

Bucharest, 25 August 1944. Following King Michael's armistice with the USSR on 23 August, Rumania declares war on Germany.

Paris, 25 August 1944. General de Gaulle enters liberated Paris.

Poland, 27 August 1944. Polish and Soviet officials show the Press the Maidenek concentration camp.

Rumania, 31 August 1944. Russians and Rumanians have taken the Ploesti oilfields, which have been supplying Germany with one-third of its military oil.

Belgium, 4 September 1944. The Allies capture Brussels and Antwerp and cross into Holland.

Sofia, 6 September 1944. Bulgaria declares war on Germany.

Germany, 11 September 1944. The US First Army under General Omar Bradley leads the Allies on to German soil.

Helsinki, 19 September 1944. Finland signs an armistice with the USSR.

Estonia, 22 September 1944. The Russians capture the capital, Tallinn.

Athens, 14 October 1944. British troops march into Athens.

Germany, 14 October 1944. Erwin Rommel takes poison rather than be executed for conspiracy against Hitler's life. Hitler had promised him a hero's funeral if he committed suicide.

Czechoslovakia, 18 October 1944. The Russians enter the country.

Germany, 18 October 1944. Hitler orders the formation of a home guard in anticipation of the invasion of Germany.

Philippines, 20 October 1944. General MacArthur lands on the central Philippine island of Leyte.

Germany, 20 October 1944. Aachen surrenders to the Allies.

Belgrade, 20 October 1944. Tito's Partisans and the Red Army take Belgrade.

Paris, 28 October 1944. De Gaulle orders the Resistance to disarm.

Hungary, 5 November 1944. Soviet tanks enter Budapest.

Washington, DC, 7 November 1944. President Franklin Delano Roosevelt wins an unprecedented fourth term in office.

Belgium, 28 November 1944. The first Allied convoy sails into the port of Antwerp.

Hungary, 29 November 1944. The Russians cross the Danube and pierce the German defences in the south of the country.

Germany, 6 December 1944. Twenty million people are reported to be homeless after Allied bombing.

Moscow, 10 December 1944. De Gaulle and Stalin sign a treaty of alliance.

Paris, 13 December 1944. The Russian artist Wassily Kandinsky dies aged 78.

Indochina, 22 December 1944. Vo Nguyen Giap forms the Vietnamese People's Army.

Britain, 1944. The poet T S Eliot completes his *Four Quartets*.

Budapest, 13 January 1945. The city is now in Russian hands.

Warsaw, 17 January 1945. Soviet and Polish troops take the city.

Budapest, 21 January 1945. Hungary declares war on Germany.

Poland, 27 January 1945. The Red Army takes Auschwitz.

Germany, 31 January 1945. Soviet troops cross the river Oder north of Frankfurt, 40 miles from Berlin.

Philippines, 1 February 1945. US troops advance 25 miles into Japanese-held territory and free over 500 prisoners of war.

Philippines, 6 February 1945. MacArthur announces the capture of Manila and the liberation of 5,000 prisoners.

Cairo, 24 February 1945. The prime minister, Ahmed Maher Pasha, is shot dead after reading Egypt's declaration of war on Germany and Japan.

German flying bombs devastate London

London, 19 June 1944
For the past week the Germans' secret weapon, the V1 or "Flying Bomb", has been unleashed on London and its south-east approaches at a rate of 100 a day. The flying bombs, nicknamed "doodlebugs", look like pilotless planes with a primitive rocket engine at the rear and carry nearly a ton of explosive.

Launched from the Pas de Calais with enough petrol to reach London, they stall when the fuel runs out and nose-dive silently for 15 seconds to earth. Their low altitude prevents anti-aircraft guns from ranging on them. Yesterday one hit the Guards Chapel during a service killing 119 people.

RAF fighter pilots are desperately seeking new methods to counter this high-speed menace in what has become known as "bomb alley" over Kent and Sussex.

London's second Blitz: searching for survivors after a "doodlebug" blast.

American warships land in Philippines

Philippines, 21 October 1944
"I shall return", vowed General Douglas MacArthur when Japan ejected him from the Philippines in 1941. He has kept his pledge and strode up a beach at Leyte today to watch his invasion force of 250,000 fighting to retake the islands, while thousands of Japanese reinforcements have been killed in a massive naval battle offshore.

Two divisions of the Japanese navy, including a carrier, several cruisers and destroyers, have been destroyed, and American torpedoes have accounted for numerous troopships. A jubilant MacArthur said: "The Japanese navy has suffered its most crushing defeat of the war."

As American troops fight their way back across the Pacific – island by island – and British and Commonwealth armies are beating the Japanese in jungle warfare, a fearsome new weapon has appeared in the Pacific war: the *kamikaze*

MacArthur: "I have returned."

(divine wind) bomber. Dressed in ceremonial robes, these pilots fly their aircraft directly at the decks of American ships where their impact bombs do the most damage.

Paris falls to the Allies

De Gaulle and "la France", marching triumphantly down the Champs Elysees.

Paris, 25 August 1944
Paris was liberated today by the combined efforts of the resistance and the free French forces. By this evening the Germans had capitulated and General de Gaulle himself was able to march down the Champs Elysees and address his countrymen: "I wish simply and from the bottom of my heart to say, *Vive Paris!*"

It was all made possible by General Eisenhower who ordered the Allied armies sweeping through northern France to encircle Paris, not invade it. He then contacted the resistance. Loyal police then took over the Ile de la Cite and the Prefecture and fighting broke out on the streets with the resistance attacking key German positions.

Last night the French Second Armoured Division, under General Jacques Leclerc entered the city. By this morning effective German resistance had collapsed and General Dietrich von Choltitz surrendered, defying an order from Hitler to destroy Paris. Tonight a few Parisians are out for revenge, beating up collaborators and trying to lynch German officers. But most are celebrating, beside themselves with joy now the *swastika* has been hauled down.

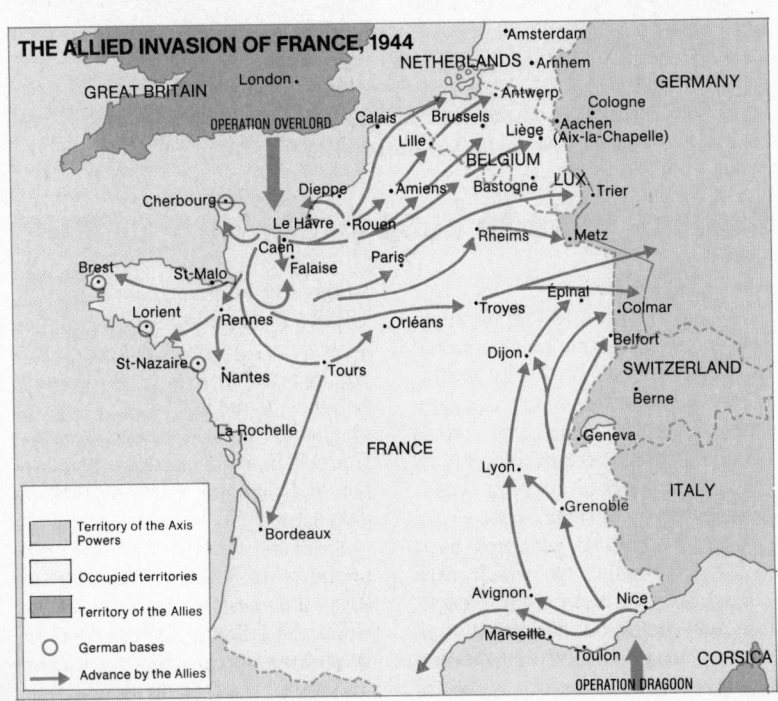

THE ALLIED INVASION OF FRANCE, 1944

GREAT BRITAIN — London
OPERATION OVERLORD

NETHERLANDS — Amsterdam, Arnhem
Antwerp
GERMANY
Calais, Brussels, Cologne
Lille, Liège, Aachen (Aix-la-Chapelle)
BELGIUM
Dieppe, Amiens, Bastogne, LUX, Trier
Cherbourg
Le Havre, Rouen, Rheims, Metz
Caen, Paris
Brest, St-Malo, Falaise
Lorient, Rennes, Orléans, Troyes, Épinal, Colmar
St-Nazaire, Nantes, Tours, Dijon, Belfort
La Rochelle, SWITZERLAND, Berne
FRANCE, Lyon, Geneva
ITALY
Bordeaux, Grenoble
Avignon, Nice
Marseille
Toulon, CORSICA
OPERATION DRAGOON

- Territory of the Axis Powers
- Occupied territories
- Territory of the Allies
- German bases
- Advance by the Allies

Allied air raids reduce Dresden to rubble

Dresden, 14 February 1945
The civilian death toll from 24 hours of Allied air raids on Dresden may be as high as 130,000. Total casualties in the devastated city are thought to be 400,000.

The raids by 800 RAF Lancasters and 400 US Air Force heavy bombers have provoked widespread criticism. Dresden, once comparable to Florence for its wealth of fine art and architecture, was thought to be safe from attack, even though it is an industrial centre providing communications for German forces on the Eastern Front. Its population of almost a million is above its peacetime level.

Most of the raids' criticism is aimed at the head of RAF Bomber Command, Air Chief Marshal Sir Arthur Harris. He is accused of clinging to his increasingly controversial theory that terror bombing by itself can destroy the enemy's will to fight. Other senior Allied officers say bomber resources would be better deployed stepping up attacks on enemy communication and oil installations.

Naked city: the remains of Dresden after a firestorm which killed 130,000.

Allies agree shape of post-war world

Yalta, 12 February 1945
Germany is to be forced into unconditional surrender and then partitioned into four zones, according to an agreement revealed here tonight. For the last eight days Churchill, Roosevelt and Stalin have been meeting to plan the final stages of the war and to carve out their post-war areas of influence.

Allied sources are worried that President Roosevelt has been primarily concerned about an invasion plan for Japan. Certainly, Stalin, flushed with recent great Soviet victories, has gone a long way towards winning acceptance for his domination of eastern Europe. And he gets the huge area of eastern Germany, which surrounds Berlin, where a joint control commission is to be established.

Partisans help the British win Athens

Athens, 14 October 1944
The entry of British troops, side by side with Greek Partisans, today brought relief to this strife-torn and poverty-stricken capital. Vast crowds celebrated the end of three and a half years of occupation by the Axis powers.

As the Germans withdrew up the Peloponnese earlier this month, the British landed at Patra on the Gulf of Corinth. Finding little opposition they set their sights for Athens. Colonel Earl Jellicoe headed the motley army's arrival in the city.

They have found a hungry population dispossessed of almost all they had. They are also quite aware that the murderous rivalry of socialist and ultra-right wing resistance groups is not going to disappear with the Nazis' departure.

Burma, 5 March. The British take the Japanese base of Meiktila, cutting Burma in two.

Indochina, 10 March. Tran Kim declares the independence of Vietnam.

Indochina, 11 March. Cambodia declares its independence.

Britain, 26 March. The politician and social reformer Lloyd George dies aged 82.

Germany, 30 March. The Russians take Danzig and cross from Hungary into Austria.

Pacific, 7 April. The US Navy sinks Japan's biggest battleship, the *Yamamoto*.

USA, 12 April. The American statesman Franklin Delano Roosevelt, president four times, dies aged 63. Harry S Truman is sworn in as president.

Vienna, 13 April. Vienna is liberated.

Poland, 15 April. Allied troops liberate the concentration camp at Bergen-Belsen.

Germany, 17 April. US troops liberate Buchenwald.

Germany, 20 April. Nuremberg, the scene of huge Nazi rallies, falls to the Allies on Hitler's 56th birthday.

Italy, 28 April. Mussolini is executed.

Germany, 30 April. US troops liberate Dachau.

Berlin, 30 April. Hitler shoots himself.

Europe, 2 May. All the one million German troops in Italy and Austria surrender.

Burma, 3 May. The British 14th Army takes Rangoon.

Berlin, 8 May. Field-Marshal Keitel signs Germany's final act of capitulation.

Prague, 10 May. Prague is the last European capital to be liberated.

Germany, 23 May. Himmler kills himself in British custody.

Britain, 23 May. The Coalition government resigns; there will be a general election on 5 July.

Berlin, 5 June. Allied supreme commanders sign a pact for the occupation of Germany.

USA, 16 July. The first atomic bomb tests take place in the New Mexico desert.

Britain, 26 July. Labour wins a landslide election victory.

Electronic computer sums everything up

Pennsylvania, December
It weighs 30 tons, occupies 1,500 square feet of floor space and contains more than 18,000 thermionic valves. It is the world's first general-purpose computing device.

It was originally intended to calculate gunnery tables, but came too late to contribute to the war effort.

Even so, it can perform 5,000 additions or subtractions in a second and revolutionises computation of all kinds, scientific and commercial. It has a drawback. The valves tend to get very hot, so it cannot work continuously for long periods.

War sparks African nationalist trend

Manchester, 19 October
Here in the unlikely setting of Chorlton town hall, 200 black delegates, representing almost every black colony in the British empire have called for a promise from Britain of eventual independence, as France made at Brazzaville a year ego. From Kenya's Jomo Kenyatta, who opened the Fifth Pan-African Congress's first session, through speakers like Kwame Nkrumah of the Gold Coast, there is a new spirit of optimism. The anti-imperialist USA is the dominant world power. Empire-building is past history – in the west at least.

Britons vote for a socialist future

London, 26 July
Labour has won an historic landslide victory in the British general election. For the first time it has an overall majority with 393 seats compared with 213 for the Conservatives and 34 for others. The party won on a detailed programme of public ownership of key industries and huge social reforms. Winston Churchill, the cigarsmoking wartime leader, has been rejected, even by the armed forces vote. Taking over is the pipesmoking Clement Attlee, who said: "We are facing a new era. We can deliver the goods."

Partisans kill Mussolini and his mistress

Milan, 28 April
The bodies of Benito Mussolini and his mistress, Clara Petacci, hanging upside down in the Piazza Loretto here, provide a grisly monument to European Fascism.

As Italian Partisans were rounding up Nazi sympathisers, the former dictator and a few confederates were discovered hiding in a convoy of eight cars. *Il Duce* emerged from beneath a pile of coats to plead for mercy from his captors.

After a brief trial presided over by the Communist leader Cino Moscatelli, Mussolini and those with him were machine-gunned to death. He had been on the run since his rescue by German parachutists from an Italian prison in September 1943.

Although some of those with him, notably the Fascist bosses Carlo Scorza and Alessandro Pavolini, shouted "Long Live Italy" as they died, Mussolini is said to have gone to death as if in a daze. It was an ignominious end for the man who ruled Italy for more than two decades.

The end of Fascism: the bodies of Mussolini and his mistress in Milan.

Nations unite to keep peace forever more

New York, 26 June
The United Nations Organisation, proposed at a 46-nation conference in San Francisco in April, became a reality today when the delegates from 50 states signed the World Security Charter, establishing an international peace-keeping force contributed by all members.

The UN will be governed by a General Assembly in which each nation has one vote. Major decisions will require a two-thirds majority. There will be a Security Council of 11 members, five of whom will be permanent – the US, USSR, Britain, France and China. A secretary-general and secretariat will be based in New York, an International Court of Justice in the Hague and an Economic and Social Council in Paris. London will host the first General Assembly session next January.

Speakers declare that the new organisation will be more effective than the League of Nations, to which the US and Soviet Union did not belong. "It provides for a peace with teeth," said General Smuts.

Allies march into Berlin

Nazi death camp horror

The horror of it all: corpses of concentration camp victims at Buchenwald.

The red flag flies triumphantly over the battered "reichstag" in Berlin.

Berlin, April 30

The Third *Reich* was consumed by the flames of its own mythology today as Red Army tanks and Allied guns pounded Berlin into dust. Below the streets even the architect of the myth of German superiority, Adolf Hitler, was obliged to acknowledge his defeat. In his bunker he dictated a banal message blaming his own army as well as a Jewish-Bolshevik conspiracy for his failure. Then he shot himself.

For other Germans there was no simple, final solution of that sort. With the Russians in control of a third of Berlin, the city was in a state of panic. Soldiers discarded weapons and deserted, only to be shot or hanged on the street by roaming bands of SS fanatics who attached to the bodies the slogan "We betrayed the Fuhrer". Low-flying Russian biplanes machine gunned queues of people desperate for bread. Once-elegant streets were littered with rotting corpses from which anything of value, including boots, were removed. It was not the romantic twilight of the gods described by Goebbels in his address to the party faithful in Berlin, exulting in "total war". Some Berliners believe the Russians have sent a Mongolian horde to exact revenge and now pray they will be defeated by the western allies. Meanwhile, on the Elbe, Russian and American soldiers shook hands.

Mother and child in ruined Berlin.

Buchenwald: the living and dead.

Russia to occupy half German territory

USSR, 6 June

About half the total territory of Germany is to come under Russian control after the war, according to information published today by Moscow papers.

With the War now over, Russian citizens were treated to a detailed description of the future shape of the map of Germany despite the rule of secrecy adopted by the European Advisory Council responsible for defining the zones of occupation. The Soviet zone will extend far west of its present position. In some areas US troops will have to pull back more than 150 miles (240 kilometres).

The shattered capital, Berlin, will be within the Russian zone, but is to be divided into four parts, occupied separately by Russia, America, France and Britain, with a joint control commission.

In London officials merely commented that current zones of occupation were never expected to be the basis of post-war Europe.

Poland, 30 April

On the day on which Adolf Hitler put paid to his "Thousand Year Reich" with his own suicide, allied troops have begun to uncover the grimmest testimony to the madness of his 12-year rule. Barely able to believe their eyes, soldiers are entering the concentration camps in which millions of Jews, Poles, gypsies, homosexuals, communists and many others have been systematically put to death.

Named after the villages or towns near which they were built – Belsen, Auschwitz, Buchenwald – the camps are 20th-century charnel houses where emaciated, diseased survivors, themselves barely alive, wander between huge piles of naked rotting corpses. Their rescuers are fighting to save them, but their best efforts are often doomed. Of the 40,000 survivors at Belsen, 600 die every day, victims of starvation, typhoid and tuberculosis.

Tales of unimaginable cruelties, of scarcely credible depravity are emerging, but what is most terrifying about the camps is, in some perverse way, their ordinariness. Nazi efficiency permeated the entire war, and these camps are no exception. They are literally factories of death, where the living, brought by cattle truck from every corner of Europe, were transformed, often within hours of their arrival, into corpses to be stripped and burned.

Nazi murderers put on trial by victors at Nuremberg

Nuremberg, 20 November
Hitler's old associates were today brought to the Palace of Justice at Nuremberg, scene of the Fuhrer's rallies, to answer to the world for their crimes before a tribunal of British, American, Russian and French judges.

In the dock are Goering, Hess, Ribbentrop, Keitel, Doenitz, von Papen, Streicher, and a dozen others, men who spread terror through Europe but today are just grey, nervous, nondescript. They are accused of waging a war of aggression, violating the laws and customs of warfare and crimes against humanity.

Justice Jackson, the chief US prosecutor, said that "the wrongs we seek to condemn and punish have been so calculated, so malignant and so devastating that civilisation cannot tolerate them being ignored."

He said the court faced a grave responsibility but that all the evidence of "greed, duplicity and torture" would be taken from "books and records which the defendants kept with their Teutonic passion for thoroughness".

Syria and Lebanon win their freedom

Near East, 13 December
French and British troops are to evacuate Syria and the Lebanon, whose freedom at last seems guaranteed. The Levant states were granted independence by France in 1941, but the British moved in soon afterwards.

Today's agreement, announced in the House of Commons by the foreign secretary, Ernest Bevin, marks the end of three months of negotiations with his opposite number, Georges Bidault. Bevin has had to convince the French that British intervention was aimed purely against the pro-Nazi Vichy government, and not intended to usurp long-standing French influence in the area.

With both countries committed to the United Nations, the principle seems settled. Details will be finalised next week in Beirut.

Colonel takes reins of power in Argentina

Buenos Aires, 17 October
Military leaders here have finally decided to hand over power to the Colonel who has become the idol of the labouring classes, Juan Peron. Only eight days ago they arrested Peron to thwart his ambitions. But the body of union support he built up while secretary of labour and social welfare came to his aid. The so-called "shirtless ones" took to the streets in processions and rioting. Peron is now near his dream of a populist government based on the support of workers, army officers and the police.

The students and teachers will not be pleased. A week ago they were marching on the streets shouting "Death to Peron".

Allied unity lies in tatters after Potsdam

Stalin, Truman and Churchill before the start of the Potsdam conference.

Potsdam, 31 July
The victorious political leaders of the Allies have failed to agree a post-war future for Europe. Meeting at Potsdam, Attlee (who succeeded Churchill after the British general election) and Truman have disagreed with Stalin about where Germany's new frontiers should be drawn. Britain and America object to Poland, with Russian encouragement, seizing huge areas of Germany. Stalin's refusal to accept free elections in eastern European countries or ease restrictions on western officials in those countries has angered the western leaders.

The casualties of war		
	Military	Civilian
British		
Commonwealth	452,000	60,000
China	3,500,000	10,000,000
France	250,000	360,000
Poland	120,000	5,300,000
United States	295,000	
USSR	13,600,000	7,700,000
Other Allies	370,000	1,940,000
Germany	3,250,000	3,810,000
Japan	1,700,000	3,600,000
Other Axis powers	980,000	917,000

The numbers killed in the war: the price of victory and defeat.

Britain pledges independence for India

London, 19 September
India will have its independence, "at the earliest possible date," Mr Attlee broadcast to India today, appealing to Indians to settle their differences and decide their own destiny. In this he has the solid support of his viceroy, Lord Wavell, who released Gandhi from prison in May 1944. Whether Indians will resolve their differences in time is less certain. Moslems and now Sikhs demand states separate from the Hindu majority.

Atom bomb wipes out Japanese city

Mushroom cloud hangs over future

Hiroshima after the Bomb: survivors spoke of a noiseless flash and a light brighter than a thousand suns.

Japan, September

It took two billion dollars, a workforce of 100,000 and several years to develop the atomic bomb. British and American scientists involved in what was code-named the "Manhattan Project" knew they were in a race with German nuclear experts; it was a German who discovered soon before the war that a form of uranium – 235 – could be split into roughly equal halves with the release of energy in a chain reaction. Allied scientists used this knowledge to produce the atomic bombs.

An entire city of 70,000 people was built in the New Mexico Desert around Los Alamos. Most workers did not know what they were making; and the first test bomb was exploded on a pylon so deep in the desert that few were present to assess its power.

The bombs that fell on Japan took less than four seconds to obliterate the hearts of two big cities and kill so many people; but the "mushroom" clouds that followed may kill many more. A new word – "fallout" – has entered the English language; and the radioactivity contained in those clouds will remain in the atmosphere, possibly for years. Scientists have created a monumental force and ended a great war; but they are the first to admit that they do not know a great deal about the effects of "fall-out" on this planet.

Japan, 9 August

The people of Hiroshima had been told to expect an air-raid. Many had spent restless nights in shelters; and, as they emerged into the bright sunlight, they watched a small parachute descending from a lone B-29 bomber flying high over the city. For many, it was to be the last thing they saw.

At precisely 8.15 on 6 August, a nuclear chain reaction in the bomb carried by that parachute built up a temperature of several million degrees centigrade. In 0.1 millisecond, a fireball of 300,000 degrees Celsius was created and expanded to 250 yards in diameter one second after the bomb had been detonated. Hiroshima had been the target of the first atomic bomb. And apart from a handful of substantial buildings, a city centre has been wiped from the face of the earth. A third of the population of 300,000 are dead, many of them killed mercifully outright by the blast; more by

the firestorm that ripped through the city fanned by fierce man-made winds; and thousands are dying daily from the effects of deadly radiation burns. As stunned survivors stumble hopelessly through the flattened remains of this once-prosperous shipbuilding city, the world has learned of the huge flash – "brighter than the sun", said a US Navy captain who witnessed the bombing from the air – and the mushroom cloud that followed, reaching 23,000 feet into the sky.

The aircraft that dropped the bomb was named *Enola Gay* – after the pilot's mother. The captain, Paul W Tibbets, reported that the blast hurled it around in the air even from a distance of ten miles.

In Washington, President Harry S Truman has demanded the immediate surrender of Japan; and, as though to emphasise the power that the Allies now have, a further bomb was dropped today on Nagasaki killing 40,000 people and

creating similar devastation to that of Hiroshima. President Truman has repeated his demand, threatening more A-bombs on a Japan which must be close to collapse.

VE Day in London, after over 2,000 days of war. By midday Whitehall and the Mall were packed with people chanting "We want the king", while all over Britain people drank, danced and thanked God it was over.

After the Bomb: living in the nuclear shadow

After Hiroshima and Nagasaki, nothing was ever the same again. Not all historical turning-points are recognised as such at the time, but there can be no dispute that the use of the atomic bomb in August 1945 changed the world more dramatically than any single event which preceded it. It was not simply the extent of the devastation; for the first time human beings had discovered, and unleashed, a force capable of destroying life on Earth.

In the perspective of a book which began its detailed chronicle when humans first emerged, the nuclear watershed seems an appropriate point to pause and take stock. *Chronicle of the World* therefore ends with a series of essays on the post-war years; these do not attempt to summarise the events of particular decades, but seek to identify major trends which have stretched across the years since 1945 and to put them into some perspective. The essays are complemented by very brief summaries of the main political events of those years. A fuller and detailed story of the years since 1945 is told in our companion volume, *Chronicle of the 20th Century*. Subsequent developments are also covered in the national histories of each country which begin on page 1147.

1946

Albania, 11 Jan. Proclamation of communist people's republic.
London, 30 Jan. Inaugural session of UN General Assembly.
Hungary, 1 Feb. Republic set up.
USA, 5 March. Churchill warns of "iron curtain" across Europe.
Vietnam, 6 March. France recognises communist republic.
Jordan, 25 May. Kingdom created.
Argentina, 4 June. Peron president.
Italy, 10 June. Republic declared.
Pacific, 1 July. First US atomic test over Bikini atoll.
Philippines, 4 July. Republic set up.
China, 19 Aug. Civil war resumes.
Germany, 16 Oct. Ten top Nazis executed at Nuremberg.
Japan, 3 Nov. New constitution.
Vietnam, Dec. Hostilities open between French and Ho Chi Minh.

1947

Paris, 10 Feb. Italy, Rumania, Hungary, Bulgaria and Finland sign peace treaties.
India, Feb. Mountbatten viceroy.
Netherlands, 25 March. Indonesian independence recognised.
Britain, 3 June. Plans announced for partition of India and Pakistan.
USA, 5 June. Marshall offers aid plan for European recovery.
India, 10 July. Jinnah appointed first governor general of Pakistan.
Burma, 19 July. Prime minister U Aung San assassinated.
India, 15 Aug. India and Pakistan become separate British dominions.
Europe, 1 Nov. Benelux customs union becomes effective.
USA, 30 Nov. UN votes to partition Palestine.
Italy, 22 Dec. New constitution.
Rumania, 30 Dec. King Michael abdicates; republic declared.

1948

Burma, 4 Jan. Union of Burma becomes independent republic.
India, 30 Jan. Gandhi assassinated.
Ceylon, 4 Feb. Ceylon becomes self-governing British dominion.
Czechoslovakia, 27 Feb. Communists under Gottwald seize power.
Brussels, 17 March. France, Benelux and Britain sign 50-year pact.
Europe, 16 April. Organisation for Economic Cooperation set up.
Israel, 14 May. New state created.
Berlin, 30 June. Western Allies start airlift to beat Soviet blockade.
Britain, 5 July. National Health Service comes into being.
South Korea, 15 Aug. Republic proclaimed.
North Korea, 9 Sept. Independent communist republic proclaimed.
India, 17 Sept. Rebellion crushed in kingdom of Hyderabad.

1949

Kashmir, 1 Jan. India and Pakistan agree truce in war over Kashmir.
Moscow, 25 Jan. Comecon set up.
USA, 4 April. NATO founded.
Ireland, 18 April. Republic created.
India, 27 April. Republic created.
London, May. Council of Europe established.
Berlin, 12 May. Blockade ends.
Germany, 23 May. Federal Republic (West Germany) established.
South Africa, June. Apartheid programme put into effect.
Middle East, July. Truce ends war between Israel and Arab League.
USSR, Sept. First A-bomb tested.
China, 1 Oct. Mao proclaims communist people's republic.
Germany, 12 Oct. Democratic Republic (East Germany) formed.
Formosa, 8 Dec. Chinese nationalists set up government-in-exile.
Australia, 17 Dec. Menzies PM.

1950

Vietnam, 31 Jan. USSR recognises Ho Chi Minh regime.
USA, 9 Feb. Joseph McCarthy launches anti-communist crusade.
Vietnam, 7 Feb. Britain and USA recognise Bao Dai's Saigon regime.
Moscow, 15 Feb. USSR and China sign 30-year alliance.
Formosa, 1 March. Chiang Kai-shek proclaimed president of nationalist China.
Jordan, 24 April. King Abdullah annexes Arab Palestine.
France, 9 May. Schuman proposes plan for integration of western European coal and steel industries.
Korea, 25 June. North Koreans invade South Korea.
Indonesia, 14 Aug. Republic set up.
Korea, 28 Nov. Chinese enter war.
Tibet, 25 Dec. Dalai Lama flees in wake of Chinese invasion.

1951

USA, 28 Jan. Atomic bomb tested in Nevada desert.
USA, 30 March. Rosenbergs, atom spies, sentenced to death.
Europe, 18 April. European Coal and Steel Treaty signed.
Iran, 2 May. PM Mossadegh nationalises oil industry.
London, 4 May. Festival of Britain.
Pacific, 12 May. US hydrogen bomb tested on Eniwetok atoll.
Britain, 7 June. Burgess and Maclean, Soviet agents, defect.
Jerusalem, 20 July. King Abdullah of Jordan shot dead.
USA, 8 Sept. Japan signs Second World War peace treaty.
Egypt, 19 Oct. British troops seize Suez Canal zone after Egyptian abrogation of 1936 treaty.
Libya, 24 Dec. Independent kingdom established.

1952

Britain, 8 Feb. George VI dies. Elizabeth II succeeds.
Cuba, 10 March. Batista overthrows president and seizes power.
Gold Coast, 21 March. Kwame Nkrumah is first PM elected in sub-Saharan Africa.
Paris, 27 May. European Defence Community created.
South Africa, 26 June. Non-violent anti-apartheid campaign begins.
Berlin, 1 June. Soviet "iron curtain" isolates West Berlin.
Egypt, 26 July. King Farouk ousted in army coup led by Neguib.
Jordan, 11 Aug. Hussein king.
Ethiopia, 15 Sept. Eritrea united with Ethiopia.
Kenya, 21 Oct. British troops sent in to deal with Mau Mau terrorists.
Australia, 3 Oct. First British A-bomb test, off Monte Bello islands.
USA, 5 Nov. Eisenhower elected.

Left to right: President Truman, Mao Zedong and Chancellor Adenauer.

The post-war world: culture undermines ideology

The single most striking aspect of the cultural life of the human race since the end of the Second World War is the way in which every society of the world has become conscious of all the others. As a result people all around the world now have the expectation that the quality of their lives should improve. Previous generations had no such expectations, and this change has not only accelerated political and economic movements but has consistently confounded all attempts to predict its effects.

New means of transportation and communication have brought about a shift of consciousness in even the poorest and most inaccessible parts of the world. Simultaneously, in thousands of cities it has become possible to purchase the same cars, household goods and gadgetry, clothing, drinks, perfumes – hundreds of items of everyday and luxury goods.

This phenomenon has spread far beyond the rapidly growing urban elites into the villages and *favellas*. The Hilton Hotel is found even in the communist world; the hit tunes of the record industry reach Beijing and Caracas. An international style in architecture has emerged which tends to override climatic and ideological divides; the characteristic building of the era is the airport. Marshall McLuhan's prediction of a "global village" has come to pass.

One source of a sense of community for the "village" is television, which has also accelerated these developments. Universal in developed societies by the 1960s, it spread throughout the Third World in the 1970s. New ways of sending signals and switching signals arrived with the development of the computer and its miniaturisations. Telephones became universal in prosperous countries, especially with the use of satellites. Cable television started to spread from America in the 1980s.

The "village" looks set to become even more tight-knit as distance become increasingly irrelevant in determining the cost of communication. By the end of the century most of the globe will probably have access to a variety of channels, many emanating from foreign countries. Distinguishing between

A crowd of thousands crams Wembley to hear rockstars sing for the hungry.

the medium and the message – *pace* McLuhan – just what comes down those channels has already become an issue.

Until 1970 global media output was dominated by the US, a fact which became a source of resentment in many countries; parts of Asia and Africa began to fight back and built film industries to provide images and stories rooted in their own culture. South America became the home of a vibrant new literary culture; Japan and the Soviet Union opened their vast cultural heritage to the world through technological success in one case and political influence in

half of the century, began to lessen, though not to disappear.

However, future historians may well decide that it was human relationships that were the most profoundly changed by all the developments of the post-war years. Cheap and reliable forms of contraception, developed in the 1950s, made it possible for both sexes to decide when sexual relationships should lead to procreation, and this rapidly enabled women, not only in western societies, to enter careers previously reserved for men and to delay the years of childbearing. Women also came to demand and play an ever greater role in economic and

groups to demand that their quality of life should improve too. The disabled, the homosexual, the unemployed, teenagers, the elderly and, in particular, the ethnic minorities which grew up in the aftermath of postwar population migrations all came to demand the removal of political, legal and simply social constraints.

The force of these movements, amplified by the media, was felt across the north/south and east/west divides. The class divisions which had lain at the heart of 19th- and early 20th-century culture came to be overlaid, perhaps even superseded, by the antagonisms generated by people in search of social justice.

The sense of individuals having a right to happiness has inevitably affected the family. Contraception has meant that marriage has ceased to be a defining institution in the setting-up of households, increasing the numbers of new households and altering the kinds of housing needed. While population growth in Europe and North America has levelled off, elsewhere it has multiplied, and from a world total of two billion in 1945 it is heading for five or six billion only 55 years later.

Each of the decades has earned its own character. The 1940s were an age of austerity and recovery, the 1950s of consumer advancement and the beginnings of a powerful teenage culture, which came to the fore in the world of the 1960s when teenage styles in dress, hair and music, all coloured by a movement of protest against the Hbomb and the Vietnam War, were expressed in the pervasive, rhythmic music of the Beatles and the Rolling Stones.

The 1970s were an age of recoil from what had gone before and became an era in which culture – advertising, in particular – expressed the need for individual self-realisation through possessions and self-care. The 1980s have been a period in which personal economic satisfaction has come to dominate culture as much as economics, and the realisation of it confronts governments of socialist as much as capitalist beliefs. It has become the age of privatisation, of the ideology of the market.

"The global village has come to pass"

the other. Pakistan, India, China, and the Philippines have all developed film industries as great as Hollywood, although none has the volume that has enabled the US vision to continue dominating the world's eyes.

But the overpowering US presence is not limited to images. In popular music it reigns supreme, sometimes sharing the crown with Britain; however, here again several other countries, in Africa, South America and the Caribbean, have successfully injected their own unique sounds and rhythms into the mix. In music, as in art, the rigid division between highbrow and lowbrow culture, crucial in the first

cultural life, though to a lesser extent in the political sphere.

The women's movement in the 1970s played an important role in raising the determination of women to cease playing a subordinate role, but this took different forms in different countries, the Islamic world especially insisting on maintaining the traditional sense of sexual conduct. The right of a woman to decide whether, or not to terminate a pregnancy became a major political issue; in some countries abortion became almost a form of contraception, in others it remained, legally, a measure of last resort. Women's "liberation", in fact, became the model for many other

The post-war world: European empires retreat

At the end of the Second World War, the European powers, directly or indirectly, ruled virtually all of Africa and the Middle East, plus south and south-east Asia. Russia and the USA had *de facto* empires of differing kinds, economic and political, but these, too, were formed in the European mould.

In the 30 years after the world war, all these empires vanished. All that remains of five centuries of imperialism are a few inconsequential islands and peninsulas. There is one exception: the Russian empire, now called the Soviet Union, the last and greatest of the empires, still stretches from the Elbe to the Pacific, although that is now showing the same fissiparous tendencies that beset the rest 30 or 40 years ago.

An era that began with the conquests of the 15th and 16th centuries has come to an end. In the catalogue of world empires it did not last for long. The French only completed the conquest of Chad in the 1930s, and the British empire in East and Central Africa lasted less than a lifetime.

Europe did not lay down "the white man's burden" by choice, but of necessity. The western European empires were brought down by a combination of changing circumstances, all of them unfavourable, and surrendered with varying degrees of dignity.

The most important of the changes was the refusal of the subject peoples to continue to tolerate their inferior status. Whatever the conditions in 19th-century Asia or Africa, by the middle of the 20th century no people in the world willingly accepted being ruled by foreign-

a small force of Boers armed with guns defeated the whole Zulu army armed with spears. Three thousand Zulus were shot dead; three Boers were wounded. Now the balance has changed.

The spread of guns throughout the world supplied colonial rebels everywhere with the means to fight the empires. The French and, later, the Americans, in Indochina and the Portuguese or Rhodesians in Africa, were better armed – but

"No longer an honour for sons to die"

ers. They had learnt that such a disposition was not in the natural order of things (and in the Far East had observed the ease with which for a time the Japanese had defeated the French, British and Dutch). In every colony, even the most backward, there was now a class of educated people which took the lead in demanding independence.

Their political ambitions were supported by the technological evolution of the modern world. Britain conquered India with the musket and Africa with the Maxim gun. At the Battle of Blood River in 1838,

the rebels were more numerous and their motivation was far greater. The American and Soviet empires, which both saw themselves as liberators rather than imperialists, failed to heed the writing on the wall. They were the last two powers to be defeated by this inexorable arithmetic – in Vietnam and Afghanistan. The *Mujahedeen*, like the *Viet Cong* and the African rebels before them, could inflict more casualties upon the empire than the empire could bear.

Lastly, in Europe itself, political and social changes, conceived dur-

ing the Second World War, wiped out centuries of imperial propaganda. The weakness of conservative parties after 1945, the spread of education and the rise of the mass media, which reported all the horrors of imperial wars, lost the empires public support they had previously enjoyed. The political classes calculated the real economic costs of empire, while people no longer considered it an honour to send their sons to die for it.

Governments that did not bow to the wind of change were replaced: the Fourth French Republic in 1958 and the Portuguese regime in 1975 were both overthrown largely because of public animosity to colonial wars.

In the widest sense, history was repeating itself. The 20th-century empires went the way of the 18th and 19th- century British, Spanish and Portuguese empires in the Americas, though European politicians preferred to recall the decline of the Roman empire. The empires had become too big for the imperial powers' economies to sustain, and were defeated by political developments in the colonies, a loss of political will at home, and a transfer of

---

1953

Yugoslavia, 14 Jan. Tito president.
USSR, 5 March. Stalin dies.
Kenya, 8 April. Kenyatta jailed.
Nepal, 29 May. Hillary and Tensing climb Mount Everest.
East Berlin, 17 June. Soviet tanks crush anti-communist uprising.
Korea, 27 July. Armistice signed.
Rhodesia, 1 Aug. Federation of Rhodesia and Nyasaland created.
Iran, 22 Aug. Shah restored after military coup ousts Mossadegh.
Saudi Arabia, 9 Nov. Ibn Saud dies.
Vietnam, 29 Nov. French take Dien Bien Phu.
USSR, 23 Dec. Beria executed.

1954

USSR, 20 March. Khrushchev becomes first secretary of the party.
Kenya, 24 April. Security forces launch big drive against Mau Mau.
Vietnam, 8 May. Dien Bien Phu

falls to the Viet Minh after siege.
Geneva, 20 July. Cambodian independence from France confirmed.
Geneva, 21 July. Armistice divides Vietnam into North and South.
France, 30 Aug. France rejects European Defence Community.
Manila, 8 Sept. South-East Asia Collective Defence Treaty signed.
Egypt, 19 Oct. Britain agrees to withdraw troops from Suez Canal.
Iran, 21 Oct. International agreement concluded on Iranian oil.
Paris, 23 Oct. NATO votes to end occupation of West Germany and form Western European Union.

Egyptian President Nasser (l.) and Soviet leader Khrushchev.

1955

USSR, 8 Feb. Bulganin replaces Malenkov as prime minister.
Baghdad, 18 Feb. Turkey and Iraq sign defensive pact.
Britain, 5 April. Eden PM.
Java, April. Bandung conference of Asian and African states.
Warsaw, 14 May. Warsaw Pact signed.
Vienna, 15 May. Austrian sovereignty restored.
Argentina, 19 Sept. Peron ousted.
South Vietnam, 26 Oct. Ngo Dinh Diem proclaims a republic.
Cyprus, 28 Nov. State of emergency declared to fight EOKA terrorism.

1956

Sudan, 1 Jan. Independence.
Cyprus, 9 March. Makarios exiled.
USSR, 18 March. Khrushchev denounces Stalin.
Pakistan, 23 March. New constitu-

tion; Islamic republic proclaimed.
France, March. Independence of Morocco and Tunisia recognised.
Egypt, 26 July. Nasser nationalises Suez Canal.
Poland, 21 Oct. Gomulka PM.
Egypt, 29 Oct. Israelis invade.
Egypt, 31 Oct. Anglo-French forces bombard Suez.
Hungary, 5 Nov. Anti-communist revolution crushed by Soviet tanks.
Egypt, 6 Nov. Allies seize Canal.
Egypt, 8 Nov. UN orders ceasefire.

1957

West Germany, 1 Jan. Saar incorporated into Federal Republic.
Britain, 10 Jan. Macmillan PM.
Ghana, 6 March. Independence.
Rome, 25 March. Treaty of Rome creates EEC.
Canada, 17 June. Diefenbaker forms Conservative cabinet.
USSR, 3 July. Khrushchev foils Molotov coup.
Tunisia, 25 July. Republic.

military technology had eliminated the overwhelming advantages of the empires.

The speed and manner of leaving varied. Belgium abandoned the Congo (now Zaire) at the first sign of trouble. The French fought bitterly for Indochina and Algeria, but converted the rest of their African possessions into independent states which remained bound by financial chains to Paris. The British hung on doggedly in India until 1947 when Gandhi and Nehru finally pushed them out, but put up a fruitless resistance for several years in Cyprus, Egypt and Aden.

The Dutch put up a short fight after the Second World War in the East Indies, but were defeated. The Portuguese resisted in Guinea, Angola and Mozambique in the nastiest of colonial wars in Africa. White settlers in Rhodesia finally admitted defeat in 1980 (the country became Zimbabwe), and in 1989 South Africa began the process of giving Namibia its independence. Portugal's experience in Africa, the French (and American) experience in Indochina and the developing troubles in the Soviet Union show the inevitable consequence of trying to maintain an empire.

What is the balance sheet? In Africa, the powers imposed preposterous frontiers upon the continent

Afghanistan's Mujahedeen look down on a Russian army of occupation.

and did not succeed in creating viable states within them. The Somalis are divided between five nations, for instance. Civil wars in Zaire, Angola, Chad, Nigeria, Mozambique, Uganda, Ethiopia and Sudan have killed millions.

The colonial legacy certainly contributed to these disasters, most conspicuously, perhaps, in Angola, where Portugal abandoned the country to anarchy, and Sudan, where Britain forced the Arab north and the African south into an impossible union. The British left a

more positive legacy in India, where the world's largest democracy survives on a basis of British parliamentary tradition, law and language. Most of former French Africa continues to benefit from a close relationship with France, but the disasters in Indochina are to a large extent a direct consequence of France's refusal to give way gracefully in 1946.

The former imperial powers have all profited immensely escaping from their burdens. Germany and Japan are the most conspicuous ex-

amples of the advantages of abandoning imperial delusions, but France, Britain, Belgium and the Netherlands have all done well out of decolonisation; Portugal, if not thriving, is now at least spared the immense cost of a colonial war. All these countries (except Portugal) conduct far more trade with their former colonies than before, and have none of the expenses (though France continues to aid its former colonies generously). Colonies are no longer a source of dispute between the powers. India, the Dutch East Indies, the Belgian Congo and a few other colonies were once most profitable, but by the end of the colonial era the costs far exceeded the benefits.

The imperial urge occasionally reappears (as it did in Britain and Argentina in their dispute over the Falklands in 1982) and is still potent in Washington, where the US is trying to assert its control over Central America, and in Moscow, where the Russians have yet to grasp that their empire is one main cause of their poverty.

Perhaps one of the most lasting consequences of the European empires is that they brought every part of the globe into contact with the modern world, forcing the advantages and miseries of the 20th century onto everybody.

Malaya, 31 Aug. Federation of Malaya attains independence.
Arkansas, 25 Sept. US troops sent to Little Rock to maintain government's desegregation policy.
USSR, 4 Oct. Sputnik I launched.

1958

USA, 1 Feb. First US satellite.
Cairo, 1 Feb. Egypt and Syria form United Arab Republic.
USSR, 27 March. Khrushchev becomes supreme Soviet leader.
Britain, 7 April. First CND march from London to Aldermaston.
Algeria, 13 May. French nationalists launch rebellion.
Iraq, 14 July. King Feisal assassinated; republic proclaimed.
South Africa, 2 Sept. Verwoerd becomes prime minister.
London, 9 Sept. Notting Hill riots.
Rome, 28 Oct. Roncalli succeeds Pius XII as Pope John XXIII.
France, 21 Dec. De Gaulle elected first president of Fifth Republic.

1959

Cuba, 3 Jan. Castro seizes power.
USA, 3 Jan. Alaska 49th state.
London, 19 Feb. Britain, Greece and Turkey agree plan for independence of Cyprus.
Tibet, March. Dalai Lama flees from Chinese invaders.
Singapore, 3 June. New constitution creates self-governing state.
Canada, June. St Lawrence seaway links Great Lakes with Atlantic.
USA, 21 Aug. Hawaii 50th state.
Stockholm, 20 Nov. European Free Trade Association formed.
Cyprus, 14 Dec. Makarios elected president.

1960

Cape Town, 3 Feb. Macmillan makes "wind of change" speech.
South Africa, 21 March. Police kill 56 black Africans at Sharpeville.
South Korea, 27 April. Synghman

Rhee resigns as president.
USSR, 1 May. U-2, US reconnaissance plane, shot down.
Congo, 30 June. Belgian Congo becomes independent.
Somalia, 1 July. Republic created.
Ghana, 1 July. Republic created.
Congo, 11 July. Katanga declares independence under Tshombe.
Ceylon, 21 July. Sirimavo Bandaranaike is world's first woman PM.
Cyprus, 16 Aug. Republic created.
Congo, 14 Sept. Army seizes control under Mobuto.
Nigeria, 1 Oct. Independence.
USA, 9 Nov. Kennedy president.

1961

Britain, 30 Jan. Contraceptive pill goes on sale.
Congo, 13 Feb. Lumumba, former PM, dies mysteriously.
USSR, 12 April. Yuri Gagarin becomes first man in space.
Cuba, 19 April. Anti-Castro Cuban exiles invade at Bay of Pigs.

Algeria, 26 April. Army revolt collapses.
South Africa, 31 May. Republic created; leaves Commonwealth.
Kenya, 21 Aug. Kenyatta freed.
Berlin, Aug. Berlin Wall rises.
Congo, 13 Sept. UN forces crush Katangan rebels.
Northern Rhodesia, 18 Sept. Dag Hammarskjold dies in air crash.
Europe, 30 Sept. OECD formed.
Tanganyika, 9 Dec. Independence.
Jerusalem, 15 Dec. Ex-Nazi Adolf Eichmann sentenced to death.
India, 19 Dec. India annexes Goa from Portuguese.

National heroes: General de Gaulle (l.) and Cuban leader Fidel Castro.

The post-war world: science unravels code of life

Just as high explosives played a crucial role in the "chemists' war" of 1914-18, so radar and the atomic bomb largely settled the "physicists' war" of 1939-45. As a result, government support for scientific research continued apace during the 1950s and even increased in some countries.

The 1960s, however, saw stirrings of public and political disenchantment. Science and technology seemed to be out of control and began to be blamed for everything from pollution to the proliferation of military technology – seen in a peculiarly forceful way in the use of defoliant chemicals to destroy jungle and crops in Vietnam.

The combination of this disrepute and the need to retard the growth of research budgets, aggravated by world recession, brought increasing difficulties for scientists in the 1970s. The outcome has been that during the 1980s science funding has levelled off in most countries. Governments today increasingly insist that more research provide value for money and be applied to identifiable practical ends; curiosity-orientated "pure science" is contracting. At the same time, public opinion surveys reflect a widespread view of science as both a major contributor to human wellbeing and a source of potentially harmful developments.

The period since 1945 has seen several key developments in science. They include the emergence of potent antibiotics to combat many previously incurable infections; the invention of the transistor and the silicon chip, with their successive impacts on the

"Sheep can make drugs in their milk"

sophistication and miniaturisation of microelectronics; the evolution of "expert systems" through which computers can simulate, and even improve on, human expertise; and a space programme that has annexed the moon, revolutionised communications through artificial satellites, and given us new categories of information about our planet through remote sensing.

There is, however, one scientific development that eclipses even these triumphs. The emergence of molecular biology was largely the work of a group of researchers at the Cavendish Laboratory, Cambridge, England, during the early 1950s. Francis Crick and his American colleague Jim Watson tackled one of the central questions of biology: what was the structure of DNA – the genetic blueprint at the heart of every living cell – and how did it fulfil its function of transmitting hereditary characteristics?

By building stick and ball models which incorporated all the different clues as to the three-dimensional shape of the DNA molecule, particularly those obtained by Maurice Wilkins' team in London by X-ray diffraction, Crick and Watson had solved the problem. In 1953 they announced that the shape was that of a double helix and that the genetic "messages" were stored in coded form as sequences of proteins. The sequences were copied during cell division when the two strands of the helix separated and acquired new complementary partners.

In 1962 Watson, Crick and Wilkins received the Nobel prize for medicine. Aso in that *annus mirabilis* for British science, the Nobel prize for chemistry went to two other Cambridge scientists, Max Perutz and John Kendrew. They were honoured for their work in unravelling the structures of the second class of substances upon which life depends – proteins. Like DNA, proteins are composed of sequences of building blocks, but their three-dimensional structures are even more complex. After a decade of painstaking work, Perutz and Kendrew succeeded in showing that X-ray diffraction could be used to discern the structure of proteins such as myoglobin.

In the years after these two momentous breakthroughs, molecular biologists charted many more aspects of the living cell, particularly the nature of the genetic code and the way in which coded messages in DNA are translated into the structures of proteins. Then, in 1970-3, US scientists found that they could insert into bacteria genes that they had removed from other bacteria – or even from animal or plant cells. This was the origin of genetic engineering, by which genes are spliced from one organism to another with extraordinary precision. Some 20

1962

USA, 20 Feb. John Glenn completes first US orbit of the earth.
Laos, 10 May. US Marines sent in to oppose communist Pathet Lao.
Algeria, 3 July. France recognises Algerian independence.
USA, 10 July. Telstar satellite (transatlantic television) launched.
West Indies, Aug. Jamaica, Trinidad and Tobago win independence.
Uganda, 9 Oct. Independence.
USSR, 28 Oct. Khrushchev agrees to dismantle Soviet missile bases in Cuba, ending crisis with USA.
Tanganyika, 9 Dec. Republic established, with Nyerere as president.

1963

Brussels, 14 Jan. De Gaulle vetoes Britain's entry to EEC.
Congo, 15 Jan. Katanga surrenders to UN forces.
Central Africa, 29 March. Central African Federation collapses.
Canada, 22 April. Pearson PM.
London, 5 June. Profumo resigns.
USSR, 16 June. Valentina Tereshkova is first woman in space.
Rome, 21 June. Paul VI pope.
Moscow, 8 Aug. Britain, USSR and USA sign nuclear test-ban treaty.
Nigeria, 1 Oct. Republic set up.
West Germany, 16 Oct. Erhard succeeds Adenauer as chancellor.
Britain, 18 Oct. Home PM.
Britain, Oct. Beatlemania arrives.
Dallas, 22 Nov. Kennedy shot dead; Johnson president.
Kenya, 12 Dec. Independence.

Kenya's prime minister Kenyatta: J F Kennedy, mourned by the world.

1964

India, 27 May. Nehru dies.
S. Rhodesia, 13 April. Smith PM.
Tanzania, 27 April. Tanganyika and Zanzibar united as Tanzania.
South Africa, 14 June. Mandela jailed for life.
USA, 2 July. Civil Rights Act.
Malawi, 6 July. Independence.
North Vietnam, 4 Aug. USA starts retaliatory bombing.
USA, 5 Aug. Congress approves "all necessary action" in Vietnam.
USSR, 15 Oct. Khrushchev out.
Britain, 16 Oct. Wilson PM.
Zambia, 24 Oct. Independence.
Kenya, 12 Dec. Republic created.

1965

Britain, 24 Jan. Churchill dies.
South Vietnam, March. Johnson sends in US Marines.
Alabama, March. Luther King leads civil rights march.

Dominican Republic, 30 April. US troops aid new junta after coup.
Algeria, 20 June. Boumedienne ousts Ben Bella.
South Vietnam, 29 June. US troops take first offensive action.
Singapore, 9 Aug. Secedes from Federation of Malaysia (1963).
Los Angeles, 13 Aug. Watts riots.
Kashmir, 22 Sept. India and Pakistan halt undeclared war.
Philippines, 9 Nov. Marcos elected.
Rhodesia, 11 Nov. UDI issued. Smith regime declared illegal.

1966

Nigeria, 16 Jan. Balewa assassinated in coup; Nzugwa takes power.
India, 19 Jan. Indira Gandhi PM.
Australia, 20 Jan. Holt succeeds Menzies as prime minister.
Ghana, 24 Feb. Nkrumah ousted.
USSR, 8 April. Brezhnev becomes general secretary.
South-East Asia, 11 Aug. Malaysia and Indonesia end three-year war.

years after the announcement of the double helix – a product of basic curiosity-orientated research – practical benefits seemed likely. Soon, genetic engineers had begun to fabricate microbes for a wide range of applications in industry, agriculture and medicine. Insulin for diabetics, for example, used to be extracted laboriously from the pancreases of sheep and pigs. Now it is being manufactured more conveniently by growing cultures of bacteria into which an insulin gene has been inserted. Human growth hormone is made in the same way.

Genetic manipulation has revitalised biotechnology. It is being used to incorporate qualities such as drought resistance into plants. "Transgenic animals", such as sheep producing pharmaceuticals in their milk, are another possibility. But the capacity to splice genes, particularly those most unlikely to come together in nature, has also triggered apprehensions about possible hazards.

Scientists themselves were the first to voice this concern, in the early 1970s, but now tend to argue that their initial fears were unjustified. Also, guidelines and laws have been put in place to ensure that such experiments are conducted safely in contained facilities. Today, opposition towards genetic

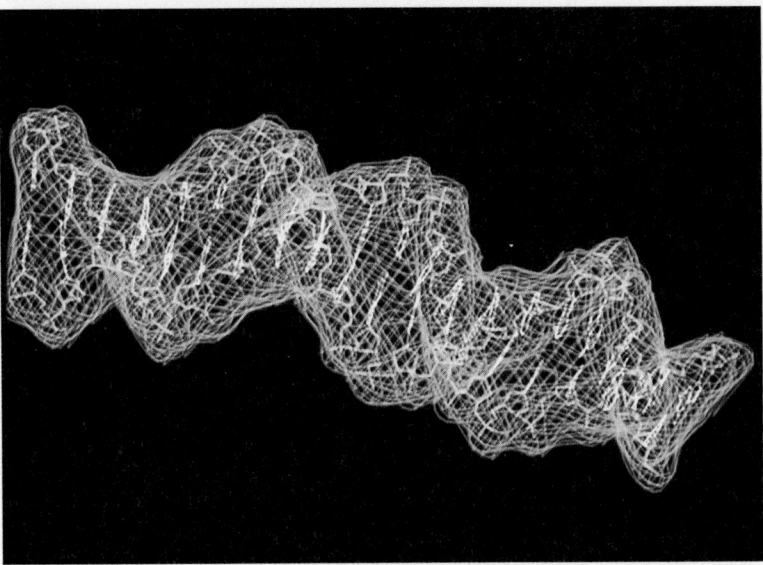

Colourful computer graphics representation of part of the DNA molecule.

engineering comes largely from individual activists in the USA and from political lobbies such as the Greens in Europe.

There is particular concern about organisms (such as insecticidal microbes and highyielding plants) that will not be contained within laboratories but will be released into the environment for agricultural, medical, and pollution control purposes. Although many potential benefits can be foreseen from the deliberate dissemination of engineered organisms, the impossibility

of recalling them should anything go wrong makes regulatory agencies cautious about permitting such work. Another source of both high promise and growing unease is the application of genetic engineering to human beings.

In principle, tomorrow's doctors could use "gene therapy" to ameliorate hereditary disease – by, for example, inserting into a patient's cells normal genes to replace the malfunctioning ones responsible for sickle cell anaemia. More immediate is the prospect of combining

genetic screening with *in vitro* fertilisation (the procedure heralded by the birth of the world's first test tube baby in 1978) to ensure that only embryos not carrying defective genes are implanted into women.

These techniques have enormous potential – especially when combined with information expected from the proposed comprehensive map showing every one of the genes on the human chromosomes. But they could also be mis-use if, for instance, applied not to genes of medical significance, but to those related to traits deemed desirable or undesirable for other reasons.

Ultimately the use made of genetic engineering will depend upon a delicate interplay between the momentum of research, the skills of the regulatory agencies, and the persuasive powers of both opponents and advocates.

The same factors seem likely to determine what happens in other areas of science. In contrast to their relatively monastic existence before the last war, when scientists were largely accountable only to themselves or their peers, scientists today are subject to many other pressures – not least to produce fast results, cut costs and measure their work by its practical application – which in the long run can only harm science.

China, 13 Aug. Mao Zedong proclaims cultural revolution.
South Africa, 6 Sept. Verwoerd assassinated.
South Africa, 13 Sept. Vorster PM.
Ireland, 9 Nov. Lynch PM.

1967

Greece, 21 April. Colonels under Papadopoulos take power in coup.
France, 16 May. De Gaulle again vetoes British EEC membership.
Nigeria, 30 May. Biafra secedes under Ojukwu, starting civil war.
Middle East, 10 June. Israel victorious in six-day war against Arabs.
Uganda, 8 Sept. Republic created.
Bolivia, 9 Oct. Guevara shot dead.
South Yemen, 30 Nov. British withdraw; people's republic formed.
Cape Town, 3 Dec. Barnard performs first heart transplant.
Greece, 13 Dec. Constantine XIII flees.
Australia, 17 Dec. PM Holt accidentally drowns; Gorton succeeds.

1968

South Vietnam, 30 Jan. Viet Cong launch great Tet offensive.
Memphis, 9 April. Martin Luther King assassinated.
Canada, 20 April. Trudeau PM.
France, May. Student riots and workers' strikes cause "month of the barricades".
Los Angeles, 6 June. Robert Kennedy fatally wounded.
Czechoslovakia, 20 Aug. Warsaw Pact invasion overthrows Dubcek.
USA, 1 Nov. Johnson orders end to bombing of North Vietnam.
USA, 6 Nov. Nixon president.
USA, 27 Dec. First moon orbit.

1969

Kenya, 1 Jan. British Asians deprived of trading licences.
Cairo, 3 Feb. Yassir Arafat becomes PLO leader.
Israel, 7 March. Golda Meir PM.

Northern Ireland, 20 April. Troops sent in to guard key installations.
France, 15 June. Pompidou succeeds de Gaulle as president.
Nigeria, 30 June. Red Cross relief flights to Biafra banned.
21 July. US astronauts Armstrong and Aldrin make first moon walk.
Northern Ireland, 15 Aug. More British troops arrive.
Libya, 1 Sept. King Idris ousted; Gadaffi takes power.
Hanoi, 3 Sept. Ho Chi Minh dies.
USA, 15 Oct. Millions protest at US involvement in Vietnam War.
West Germany, 21 Oct. Brandt becomes chancellor.

1970

Nigeria, 12 Jan. Biafra surrenders to the federal government.
Rhodesia, 2 March. Smith declares a republic.
Cambodia, 18 March. Sihanouk ousted by Lon Nol in army coup.
Cambodia, 30 April. US troops sent

in to attack communist bases.
Britain, 19 June. Heath PM.
Moscow, 12 Aug. USSR and West Germany sign friendship treaty.
Jordan, 12 Sept. Palestinians blow up three hijacked planes.
Cairo, 27 Sept. PLO agrees to evacuate strongholds in Jordan.
Egypt, 28 Sept. Nasser dies.
Egypt, 5 Oct. Sadat president.
Fiji, 10 Oct. Independence.
Canada, 16 Oct. State of insurrection proclaimed in Quebec.
France, 9 Nov. De Gaulle dies.
Poland, 20 Dec. Gomulka resigns after riots; Gierek succeeds.

Ousted Czech leader Dubcek (l.) and American astronaut Neil Armstrong.

The post-war world: religion's death exaggerated

Religion seemed to be in general decline after the end of the war. Communism, avowedly atheist, appeared to be the wave of the future in the poorer parts of the globe. Church attendance had dropped rapidly in many of the rich Christian nations as faith in the ultimate goodness of God was undermined by two world wars.

Although the Moslem state of Pakistan was carved out of India amid inter-communal slaughter in 1947, religion played a minor role in most of the independence movements that freed the European colonies in Africa and Asia. In the Middle East, Islam took a back seat to Arab nationalism.

Religion had largely ceased to be part of the mainstream western thought, art or music. On a moral plane, it found it difficult to preserve its authority and to reverse the huge growth in divorce, illegitimacy and abortion. Its imperatives seemed increasingly irrelevant in secular, consumer-orientated societies.

Nevertheless, the argument that religion is losing its importance in the modern and materialistic world has always been fragile. Two of the states created immediately after the war, Pakistan and Israel, were both religiously inspired. The arrest of scores of priests in eastern Europe in the 1940s failed to root out the religious sense. Cardinal Mindszenty was one of the first figures to be released by the Hungarian rebels in the anti-Communist uprising of 1956. In the United States, secular and urbanised and thus theoretically vulnerable, religion has shown

"Jesus Christ is outlasting Karl Marx"

no sign of succumbing to modernity. Indeed, in their use of mass media, the television evangelists made full use of modern technology, even if remaining susceptible, in a series of sex scandals, to the old temptations of the flesh.

More Americans were going to church and synagogue in the 1980s than in the 1930s – 40 per cent against 37 per cent – and all but three in a hundred said that they believed in God. That figure has remained constant since 1947.

Constant, too, have been conflicts with religious roots. The partition of India resulted in several million deaths in Hindu-Moslem rioting and was followed by recurrent fighting between India and Pakistan. Sikh extremism resulted in the assassination of the Indian prime minister, Indira Gandhi, after troops had assaulted the Sikhs' Golden Temple in Amritsar. Israel has fought three wars with a distinctly religious flavour against her Moslem neighbours. The centuries-old conflict between Moslems and Christians, which for a long time was seen as the threat to Europe, has been at least partly responsible for a string of civil wars in the Third World.

The conflict in Nigeria pitted northern Moslems against separatist Christian Biafrans. The pattern of fighting between southern Christians and northern Moslems extends to Chad, where the Libyan leader Colonel Gadaffi was continuing to supply northern rebels at the end of the 1980s; to Uganda, where the dictator Idi Amin relied on northern troops during his reign of terror; and to the Sudan, where the introduction of Islamic law has been bitterly resented by southern Christians.

Meanwhile in Europe itself there has been a marked improvement in relations between those other two equally virulent enemies – the Catholics and the Protestants. The archbishop of Canterbury visited Pope Paul VI in 1966. The Anglican and Roman Catholic churches ended a 400-year-old dispute when they agreed in 1971 on a definition of the essential meaning of the Eucharist. However, these improved relations have failed to check the sectarian violence that re-emerged in Northern Ireland after 1969.

Islamic fundamentalism emerged as a major force with the overthrow of the shah and the rejection of westernised society in Iran. Over a decade, Ayatollah Khomeini transformed Iran into a rigorous — clerical state, in which dissent was ruthlessly suppressed as blasphemy and the United States treated as "the Great Satan".

The potent images of black-garbed Islamic revolutionaries, veiled women and hostage-taking in Lebanon were backed up by actions such as the seizure of the US

1971

Uganda, 25 Jan. Amin deposes Obote and seizes power.
Pakistan, 26 March. Civil war over independence of Bangladesh starts.
Haiti, 21 April. Jean-Claude Duvalier succeeds father, Francois.
East Germany, 3 May. Honecker succeeds Ulbricht.
30 July. Apollo 15 moon landing.
Northern Ireland, Aug. Riots follow introduction of internment.
Pakistan, 17 Dec. Defeat by India in war; Bangladesh independent.
Pakistan, 20 Dec. Bhutto succeeds Yahya Khan as president.
USA, 21 Dec. Waldheim UN chief.

1972

Ghana, 13 Jan. Acheampong seizes power in coup, ousting Busia.
Brussels, 22 Jan. Britain, Norway, Denmark, Ireland sign EEC treaty.
China, Feb. Nixon visits.

Northern Ireland, 25 March. Direct rule from Westminster imposed.
Ceylon, 22 May. Becomes republic as Sri Lanka.
Moscow, 29 May. Brezhnev and Nixon sign SALT I.
Uganda, 6 Aug. Amin expels British Asians.
South Vietnam, 11 Aug. US combat troops withdrawn.
Munich, 5 Sept. Arab guerrillas storm Israeli Olympic compound.
USA, 7 Nov. Nixon re-elected.
Australia, 2 Dec. Whitlam PM.
North Vietnam, 30 Dec. Intensive US bombing of Hanoi halted.

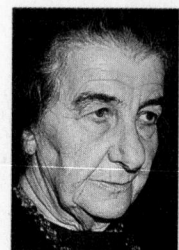

Israeli Prime Minister Golda Meir (l.) and disgraced President Nixon.

1973

Europe, 1 Jan. Britain, Denmark and Ireland join EEC.
Paris, 23 Jan. Vietnam peace agreement signed.
USA, 30 Jan. Watergate burglars convicted.
Chile, 11 Sept. Allende killed in military coup.
Sinai, 6 Oct. Egypt launches Yom Kippur War.
Egypt, 11 Nov. Egypt and Israel sign ceasefire agreement.
Spain, 20 Dec. PM Carrero Blanco killed by bomb.
Middle East, 23 Dec. OPEC quadruples price of oil.

1974

Britain, 6 March. Wilson forms minority Labour government.
Israel, 26 April. Rabin PM.
West Germany, 16 May. Schmidt replaces Brandt as chancellor.

France, 19 May. Giscard president.
Northern Ireland, 28 May. Power-sharing executive toppled.
Argentina, 1 July. Peron dies.
Cyprus, 20 July. Turks invade after overthrow of Makarios.
USA, 8 Aug. Nixon resigns over Watergate; Ford president.
Ethiopia, 12 Sept. Selassie deposed.
Britain, 11 Oct. Labour wins election with tiny majority.
Greece, 17 Nov. Karamanlis PM; rule of colonels ends.

1975

Saudi Arabia, 25 March. Faisal assassinated; Khalid king.
Cambodia, 17 April. Phnom Penh falls to Khmer Rouge.
South Vietnam, 31 April. Saigon surrenders, ending Vietnam War.
Helsinki, 1 Aug. Human rights pact signed.
Lebanon, Aug. Civil war breaks out between Christians and Moslems.
Australia, 11 Nov. Whitlam fired.

diplomats in Tehran, which led to President Carter's downfall, and, in 1989, the death sentence on the English writer, Salman Rushdie, which illustrated just how great the gulf between the two societies was.

A quieter revolution has been the achievement of religion in its long contest with communism. The creation of Christian Democrat parties in western Europe immediately after the war, notably in West Germany and Italy, was an important factor in resisting communist pressure. More recently, Moslem *Mujahedeen* guerrillas in Afghanistan forced the Soviet Army to pull out of the country a decade after the 1979 invasion. Although the charter of the Soviet Communist Party continues to oblige all its members to "lead a resolute struggle against the survival of religion", the party has softened its attitude.

Three-quarters of a century after the Communists came to power, at least 70 million Russians still adhere to their thousand-year-old Christian beliefs. Moslem awareness in Soviet Central Asia is stirring. The number of priests in the Soviet Union, which had been reduced to fewer than 500 by the end of the war, had recovered to 6,000 in 1989. Only the Russian Orthodox Church is legal, however, and the four million Catholics in the

Overcome by grief, the Iranian nation mourns Ayatollah Khomeini in 1989.

Ukraine still worship secretly. The Catholic Church remains a focal point of loyalty in Poland, where the murder of Father Popieluszko by security police in 1984 underlined the shakiness of the communist regime.

The election in 1978 of John Paul II, the first non-Italian pope for 456 years and the first Polish pope ever, had a deep impact. The Lutheran Church is steadily expanding its influence in East Germany. Throughout the 1980s, the signs have been that Christ is outlasting

Karl Marx. However in Europe, its old heartland, Christianity is stagnating, although there were signs that the decline in worship had halted by 1987.

In Britain, the two-million-strong Moslem congregation now outnumbers the Methodists. The *rapprochement* between Protestants and Catholics is threatened by the ordination of women priests. The first woman priest was ordained in the US in 1977. What growth there is tends to be split between highly traditional groups, resentful of such

changes as the new liturgy, and revivalist evangelical movements. Elsewhere, conversion is booming.

The emphasis of the religion is shifting from the old, rich nations of the north to the south, materially poorer but with rapidly expanding populations. African Christians now number 250 million. In Asia, the present 150 million Christians are expected to number 225 million in ten years. In South Korea, the proportion of Christians rose from 16 per cent in the mid-1970s to 25 per cent by the time of the Seoul Olympics in 1988. Evangelists set themselves a target of 80 per cent by the end of the millennium.

In Asia and Africa, Christianity is associated with progress, technology and a better material life, almost the opposite to the traditional European view. In Latin America, it is often thought of in radical political terms, as a liberating force from landowners and the military.

The Catholic ban on all forms of artificial contraception, confirmed by Pope Paul VI's encyclical *Humanae Vitae* in 1968 and the continuing arguments over abortion, shows that religion continues to clash with secular and political morality. But rumours of its death have proved to be exaggerated; the Bible continues to be the global bestseller.

Spain, 22 Nov. Monarchy restored following death of Franco.
Angola, 24 Nov. Civil war starts.
Britain, 29 Dec. Sex Discrimina-
Australia, 13 Nov. Fraser PM.
Britain, 29 Dec. Sex Discrimina-

1976

Angola, Feb. Cuba-backed MPLA gains control of nation's key points.
Argentina, 29 March. Videla president after deposing Isabel Peron.
Britain, 5 April. Callaghan PM.
Portugal, 25 April. Soares PM.
Lebanon, 16 May. 30th ceasefire in 13-month civil war collapses.
South Africa, June. Soweto riots.
Uganda, 3 July. Israelis free hostages in Entebbe raid.
Mexico, 4 July. Portillo president.
Northern Ireland, 7 Aug. Women's peace movement launched.
China, 9 Sept. Mao Zedong dies.
USA, 2 Nov. Carter president.
Canada, 15 Nov. *Parti Quebecois* wins Quebec provincial election.

1977

Czechoslovakia, 8 Jan. Charter 77.
India, 22 March. Indira Gandhi resigns as PM after election defeat.
India, 24 March. Desai PM.
Israel, 18 May. Begin becomes PM.
Spain, 15 June. Suarez wins first general election since 1936.
USSR, June. Brezhnev president.
Pakistan, 5 July. Bhutto overthrown and arrested by Zia.
South Africa, 12 Sept. Biko dies.
Israel, Nov. Sadat talks to Knesset.
Rhodesia, 24 Nov. Smith accepts principle of black majority rule.
South Vietnam, Dec. Exodus of Vietnamese boat people has begun.

1978

Afghanistan, 27 April. President Daoud killed in army coup.
Rome, 9 May. Former PM Moro killed by Red Brigades.
Britain, 26 July. World's first test-

tube baby born.
Kenya, 22 Aug. Kenyatta dies.
Iran, 8 Sept. Martial law.
USA, 18 Sept. Sadat and Begin sign Camp David agreement.
South Africa, 28 Sept. Botha PM.
Rome, 30 Sept. Pope John Paul dies after a month in office.
Kenya, 10 Oct. Moi president.
Rome, 16 Oct. Karol Wojtyla becomes first non-Italian pope for 450 years, as John Paul II.
Iran, 10 Dec. Millions march in protest against the shah.
Oslo, 10 Dec. Begin and Sadat share Nobel peace prize.

1979

Cambodia, 8 Jan. Vietnamese take Phnom Penh; Khmer Rouge falls.
Iran, 1 Feb. Ayatollah Khomeini returns following exile of shah.
USA, 26 March. Israel and Egypt sign peace treaty.
USA, 29 March. Accident at Three Mile Island nuclear power station.

Rhodesia, 29 May. Muzorewa becomes Rhodesia's first black PM.
Cambodia, April. Vietnamese reveal Pol Pot's mass graves.
Pakistan, 4 April. Bhutto executed.
Uganda, 11 April. Amin ousted.
Britain, 4 May. Thatcher PM.
Vienna, 18 June. SALT II signed.
Nicaragua, 20 July. Somoza resigns; Sandinistas take power.
Ireland, 27 Aug. Mountbatten killed by IRA bomb.
Tehran, 4 Nov. Nearly 100 US embassy staff taken hostage.
Afghanistan, 27 Dec. Soviet troops invade.

Two leaders, two visions: Iran's Khomeini and Britain's Thatcher.

The post-war world: nuclear powers in stalemate

In 1945, the United States stood higher than the greatest empires of history. It had a monopoly of atomic weapons and, with its allies in the United Nations, a near-monopoly of economic and military power which offered a bright hope of lasting world peace.

That was not to be. The story of global politics since 1945 is the story of how American dominance was first challenged by the Soviet Union and then gave way to an uneasy competitive truce between five super powers, the United States, the Soviet Union, Europe, China and Japan.

With the single exception of the Korean War, the fear of nuclear weapons deterred overt conflict between these five and kept the peace in Europe. But the rest of the world now became the theatre for almost continual warfare. The ostensible causes of the 100 or so wars which have ravaged the Third World varied – some were anti-colonial, others were inspired by ancient religious or ethnic rivalries – but most of them, whatever their origin, became surrogates for the unresolved ideological and political contest between the two grand alliances led by the United States and the Soviet Union.

But by the mid-1960s the sheer size of the military budgets involved had gradually eroded the relative dominance of the US and the USSR, while Japan and Europe – the latter built around Germany, the other defeated power of 1945 – began economically to overhaul the two superpowers. Immediately after 1945, Stalin had used the Red Army to impose communist dic-

"The potent genie of nationalism"

tatorships on eastern Europe; he then tried to subvert western Europe, but was deterred by the collective security arrangements of NATO, which had been set up in 1949 and were guaranteed by US nuclear power.

That year the Soviet Union acquired its own atomic bomb and the Chinese Communists won power. For the next decade it seemed quite possible that Russia and China together would surround and eventually overwhelm the west, all the more so because between 1946 and 1960 the British, French and Dutch empires in Asia and Africa were largely dismantled.

In 1956, however, a shift occurred in the communists' global strategy, following a meeting at Bandung in Indonesia of the leaders of the newly independent countries at Bandung in Indonesia who proclaimed their nations "non-aligned" as between East and West. The Soviet leadership under Khrushchev saw this as an opportunity. It had concluded that western Europe, under the American guarantee, could not be taken by assault, but now believed that it might be taken by siege if Third World supplies of oil and raw materials were cut off.

Under Kennedy the US set out to respond to this redefined threat. That meant rearming to face three levels of war: nuclear war, conventional war and counter-insurgency. In the Cuban missile crisis of 1962, the United States seemed to have called Khrushchev's bluff and survived a challenge at the strategic level. But Kennedy also committed the US to combating insurgencies in many parts of the world, most critically in south-east Asia where, by 1968, his successor Lyndon Johnson, eventually had 500,000 US troops bogged down in a war that was unwinnable in the field and unpopular back home.

By 1972 President Nixon, Johnson's successor, and his adviser on national security, Dr Kissinger, needed a way out of the Vietnam war, and so, in a bold diplomatic stroke, opened relations with China, which had returned to its traditionally hostile relationship with Russia ten years earlier.

In the meantime, both Western Europe and the United States had been severely affected by the abrupt rise in the oil price caused by the Arab oil boycott in 1973, which led to a decade of slow growth, inflation and consequent social conflicts in most parts of the world. These troubles were an opportunity for the Soviet leader, Leonid Brezhnev. He enunciated the "Brezhnev doctrine" that the Soviet Union would support liberation movements in Third World countries; it did so in Angola, the Horn of Africa, South Yemen and Afghanistan. At the

---

1980

Iran, 25 Jan. Bani-Sadr president.
Zimbabwe, 18 April. Becomes independent, with Mugabe as PM.
Iran, 25 April. US attempt to rescue hostages ends in fiasco.
Yugoslavia, 4 May. Tito dies.
London, 5 May. SAS storm Iranian embassy to free hostages.
Canada, 20 May. Quebec votes against leaving Canada.
India, 23 June. Sanjay Gandhi killed in plane crash.
China, 7 Sept. Zhao Ziyang PM.
Poland, 22 Sept. Solidarity founded.
Iran, 24 Sept. War with Iraq starts.
USA, 4 Nov. Reagan president.

1981

Iran, 21 Jan. US hostages freed.
China, 25 Jan. "Gang of Four", including Mao's widow, sentenced.
Poland, 9 Feb. Jaruzelski PM.
Spain, 23 Feb. Army coup fails.

Britain, 26 March. SDP launched.
USA, 30 March. Reagan survives assassination attempt.
London, 4 April. Brixton riots.
USA, 12 April. First space shuttle.
France, 10 May. Mitterrand elected president.
Rome, 13 May. Pope John Paul II survives assassination attempt.
Iran, 22 June. Bani-Sadr deposed.
Ireland, 30 June. Fitzgerald PM.
Britain, July. City riots.
Egypt, 6 Oct. Sadat assassinated.
Egypt, 10 Nov. Mubarak president.
Poland, 15 Dec. Martial law.
Argentina, Dec. Galtieri president.

Fellow countrymen: Poland's Pope John Paul II (l.) and Lech Walesa.

1982

Falklands, 2 April. Argentinians launch invasion.
Sinai, 25 April. Israel withdraws.
Saudi Arabia, 13 June. Fahd king.
Falklands, 14 June. Argentinians surrender to British.
Beirut, 31 Aug. Israel ousts PLO.
Lebanon, 17 Sept. Massacres in Palestinian refugee camps.
Lebanon, Sept. Gemayel president.
West Germany, 1 Oct. Kohl chancellor.
Poland, 8 Oct. Solidarity outlawed.
Spain, 28 Oct. Gonzalez PM.
USSR, 12 Nov. Andropov succeeds Brezhnev.

1983

Australia, 11 March. Hawke PM.
Portugal, 25 April. Soares PM.
Syria, 26 June. Arafat expelled.
Sri Lanka, July. Racial violence involving Tamils mounts.

Philippines, 21 Aug. Aquino killed.
USSR, 1 Sept. Korean airliner shot down, killing 269.
Israel, 10 Oct. Shamir PM.
Europe, 22 Oct. Anti-nuclear protests in several capitals.
Beirut, 23 Oct. *Shia kamikaze* raids kill 299 US and French troops.
Grenada, 26 Oct. US troops invade.
Argentina, 10 Dec. Alfonsin first civilian president for eight years.
Lebanon, 20 Dec. PLO evacuates Tripoli, last Lebanese stronghold.

1984

USSR, 13 Feb. Chernenko leader.
Lebanon, Feb. Western peace-keeping force starts withdrawal.
Britain, 12 March. Pit strike starts.
USA, 23 April. AIDS virus found.
India, 6 June. Troops storm Sikh Golden Temple in Amritsar.
Canada, 4 Sept. Mulroney PM.
Israel, 14 Sept. Peres PM.
Britain, 12 Oct. IRA bomb at Tory conference kills five.→

same time, while America limped through the 1970s, economically depressed, the limits of its power dramatically illustrated by Vietnam and the Iranian hostages fiasco, the Japanese economy took off. Forbidden from substantial spending on defence, Japan expanded its exports and moved up the technological ladder – from textiles and bicycles to watches, cameras and cars, and finally to robots and computers. The guarantor of Japan's defence, as well as that of Europe and the newly industrialised "little tigers" of Asia (Taiwan, Korea, Hong Kong, Thailand and Singapore), was the United States.

Despite this already massive military budget, in 1981 the new American president, Ronald Reagan, initially planned to build up American forces still further while all but cutting off arms control contacts with the Russians. His strategy was to force the Soviet Union into an arms race it could not afford. After 1985 it became clear that the US could not afford it either and Reagan dramatically changed his posture and signed substantial arms control agreements with Moscow. By then, however, there had been even more dramatic political changes in Soviet Russia. Brezhnev died in 1983. His two elderly successors were replaced in 1985 by a

One man's defiance in Beijing was televised to millions worldwide.

younger and far more dynamic leader, Mikhail Gorbachev, and it was with him that Reagan was able to conclude agreements on reducing nuclear weapons.

Though Gorbachev presented himself as a Leninist, his twin watchwords were *glasnost* – openness, or publicity – and *perestroika* – restructuring, or reform. He admitted that the Soviet Union was in economic crisis, caused in part by the effort to compete militarily with the United States. He allowed the Supreme Soviet and other ins-

titutions greater freedom and encouraged frankness, even about the Soviet past, as well as cutting armaments. By 1989, however, there was little sign of perestroika curing the ailments of the Soviet economy, and widespread signs of unrest, violence and even separatism in the Baltic and Moslem regions of the Russian empire suggested he had unleashed the potent genie of nationalism which the Soviet Union had previously kept bottled up.

When George Bush became president in 1989 the recognition by

both nuclear superpowers that the cost of the arms race was insupportable paved the way for some dramatic rethinking of global nuclear strategy. In 1945 the first masters of nuclear power thought that it enabled them to impose their will. By the late 1980s it was clear that nuclear weapons had forced a stalemate between the nuclear powers, while war, banished from the heartland of superpower conflict, smouldered on the borderlands.

While each of the five superpower blocs exhibits its own signs of stress – European divisions over defence and the perennial American problem of race – it now seems that it is the two once apparently monolithic communist superpowers which are the most vulnerable. By 1989, as nationalism flared in the Soviet Union, the pressures generated by economic liberalism and political repression in China suddenly burst into the "democracy movement". Then came the tanks. And once again, as in Budapest and Prague, Saigon and Santiago, the world witnessed the three leading characteristics of the politics of the 20th century: the universal power of the communicated image; the shameless ruthlessness of power; and the defiant courage with which individuals will fight and die for freedom.

Ethiopia, Oct. Western countries start airlift to relieve famine.
India, 31 Oct. Mrs Gandhi assassinated; Rajiv Gandhi succeeds.
India, 3 Dec. Bhopal gas leak.
China, 19 Dec. Hong Kong treaty.

1985

Nicaragua, Jan. Ortega president.
Spain, 4 Feb. Gibraltar siege ends.
Britain, 3 March. Pit strike ends.
USSR, 11 March. Gorbachev succeeds Chernenko.
Albania, 11 April. Hoxha dies.
Bangladesh, 25 May. Cyclone and tidal wave kill over 10,000.
Belgium, 29 May. Heysel disaster.
New Zealand, 10 July. Greenpeace ship *Rainbow Warrior* blown up.
13 July. "Live Aid" concerts.
South Africa, 20 July. State of emergency imposed in 36 areas.
Mexico, 19 Sept. Earthquake.
Columbia, 13 Nov. Volcanic eruption kills 20,000.
Geneva, Nov. USA-USSR summit.

1986

USA, 28 Jan. Space shuttle explodes on take-off.
Haiti, 7 Feb. "Baby Doc" ousted.
Philippines, 25 Feb. Marcos forced to flee by Corazon Aquino.
Stockholm, 28 Feb. Palme killed.
Libya, 15 April. US air strike.
USSR, 30 April. Chernobyl fire.
Austria, 8 June. Waldheim elected president.
South Africa, 12 June. Nationwide state of emergency.
Iceland, Oct. USA-USSR summit.
USA, 30 Nov. North sacked in "Irangate" row.
USSR, 23 Dec. Sakharov freed.

1987

Beirut, Jan. Waite taken hostage.
USSR, Jan. Gorbachev launches *perestroika* and *glasnost*.
China, 16 Jan. Zhao Ziyang becomes party leader.

Ireland, 10 March. Haughey PM for third time.
Lebanon, 8 April. Syrian troops end siege of refugee camps.
Britain, 12 June. Thatcher re-elected PM for third term.
France, 3 July. Barbie sentenced.
Mecca, 30 July. Rioting Iranian zealots killed.
Britain, 16 Oct. Hurricane.
Oct. World stock markets crash.
USA, 8 Dec. Gorbachev and Reagan sign INF treaty.

1988

Gaza/West Bank, Jan. Palestinian uprising intensifies.
USSR, 2 March. Army sent in to quell unrest in Azerbaijan.
Gibraltar, 6 March. Three IRA members gunned down by SAS.
North Sea, 6 July. Piper Alpha oil-rig fire kills over 150.
Gulf, 20 Aug. Truce between Iran and Iraq halts eight-year war.
Bangladesh, Sept. 20 million are re-

ported to be homeless in floods.
USA, 8 Nov. Bush president.
Belgrade, 19 Nov. A million Serbs demonstrate in Kosovo protest.
Pakistan, 30 Nov. Benazir Bhutto becomes PM.
USSR, Nov. Georgia and Estonia join drive for national freedom.
USSR, 7 Dec. Gorbachev cuts Red Army by ten per cent.
Armenia, 7 Dec. Earthquake.
Scotland, 21 Dec. Lockerbie crash.
New York, 22 Dec. Withdrawal of Cuban troops from Angola agreed.
Pakistan, 31 Dec. India and Pakistan sign nuclear treaty.

Seeking world sympathy: Yassir Arafat (l.) and Mikhail Gorbachev.

The number one best-seller: the Book of the Century

Chronicle of the 20th Century is the perfect companion volume to Chronicle of the World with over 1,350 pages, 3,000 photographs and more than one million words. The events which have shaped the most dramatic century the world has ever known are recaptured in a style that has won critical acclaim and broken sales records around the world. More than three million copies have already been bought in different national editions. For anyone wanting more detailed coverage of the 20th Century than provided by the broader panoramic vision of Chronicle of the World, this is the book to buy.

The Nations of the World

The key feature of *Chronicle of the World* is that it tells the story of mankind and the world chronologically. Thus, developments in one continent or culture are reported alongside contemporary events elsewhere. In the pages that follow, however, we complement this global approach by summarising the histories of today's independent nations of the world from their origin to the present day. In doing so, we concentrate on their political development in terms of discovery, settlement, political structures and wars rather than their economic or cultural history.

The histories vary in detail, although not necessarily on grounds of the size of a nation. For many Third World countries there are few reliable historical records to cover the earliest centuries, particularly those before European settlers arrived. To some extent the histories also concentrate on developments in the 20th century, not only for subjective reasons such as presumed reader interest but also because the detailed coverage of events in this book ends at 1945.

The articles are arranged in alphabetical order and each traces the chronological development of the nation to which it belongs whilst also evoking the peoples and cultures beyond the present national frontiers whose influence can be seen in all or part of the present day state. Proper names and place names have been spelt to coincide with current usage and aim to respect the versions accepted in the country concerned. Thus, for China, we use Beijing and Mao Zedong rather than the still more familiar Peking or Mao Tse-tung. The general information which forms the head of the article on each country is made up of the following: the geographical location; the national flag; the letter or letters used to identify the nationality of motor vehicles (for example CH in the case of Switzerland); the surface area; the total population and the population of the capital (according to the most recent estimate or census before this book went to press); the main international organisations of which each nation is a member (see key on page 1241 at the end of this section); the official language or languages; the principal religions practised with estimates of their approximate percentages (although data often conflicts).

This general information is concluded by the date at which the nation in question acquired independence or, alternatively, the date at which the constitution validating its current system of government came into force.

The "homelands" set up 1971 by South Africa (Bophuthatswana, Ciskei, Transkei and Venda) have not been described as sovereign states as they have not yet been recognised by the international community.

Subsequent developments in the history of each nation are summarised in the yearbooks published by Chronicle companies around the world.

Afghanistan

AFG
Central Asia
251,773 sq.mi
Pop: 18.1 m
UN

Capital: Kabul (pop: 1.2 m)
Official languages: Pashto, Dari (Persian)
Religions: Sunni Moslems (74 per cent), Shi'ite Moslems (24 per cent)
System of govt: People's republic since 27 April 1978

For the entire course of its history Afghanistan has been a disputed territory. Occupied by Persian tribes in c.1500 BC, the country was conquered by Cyrus II the Great, king of Persia, in the sixth century BC. Alexander the Great occupied it during his Asian campaign of 329-327 BC. Following his death the region came under the rule of sovereigns of Greek and other origins. The Arabs brought Islam to the country in the seventh century and no local dynasty gained power until the Ghaznavids in 962. The Mongol Timur (Tamerlane) subjugated Afghanistan in 1381. The 16th and 17th centuries saw the north of the country under the domination of Turkish sovereigns and the south under that of the Persian Safavids. A new period of independence began in 1747 with the foundation of the Durrani dynasty by the Emir Ahmad Khan. The Afghan capital, Kabul, was occupied by the British in 1839, who feared Russian interference from the north. Britain's attempt to interfere in Afghanistan was a disaster, and the Anglo-Afghan peace treaty of 1879 guaranteed Afghan autonomy. The Peace of Rawalpindi of 1919 and the friendship treaty of 1921 finally settled Afghan independence. Amanollah proclaimed himself king in 1926, but his westernising reforms earned him the hostility of the religious and conservative opposition and he was overthrown in 1929. The country became a member of the League of Nations in 1934 under the reign of Zahir Shah. Prince Mohammed Daud, prime minister from 1953-63 and later president, followed a prudent policy of cooperation with the USSR, proclaiming a republic in July 1973 and forcing Zahir Shah into exile. Daud was removed from power by a military coup on 27 April 1978. The government formed by a revolutionary council was immediately recognised by the USSR and the two countries concluded a 20 year peace agreement in August 1978. The popular rising of September 1979 which left tens of thousands of dead was ended on 27 December 1979 by the intervention of Soviet troops acting in the name of the 1978 "protection" treaty. Despite the hostile reaction of the Moslem world, UN resolutions of protest and western boycotts (especially the 1980 Moscow Olympics boycott and 1980-81 US grain embargo) the USSR continued to back Afghan government forces in a bitter war against Afghan guerrillas. However, Gorbachev committed the USSR to withdrawal and the last Soviet troops left early in 1989. But the struggle continues between the Afghan guerrillas and the government of President Najibulah.

Albania

AL
South East Europe
11,101 sq mi
Pop: 3.2 m
UN

Capital: Tirana (pop: 206,000)
Official language: Albanian
Religion: Forbidden
System of govt: People's socialist republic proclaimed 11 January 1946

Albanians have a long history of resisting invaders, from the Romans onwards. Their national hero is the 15th century Skanderbeg, son of a prince and born a Moslem. He renounced the faith at the age of 40 and spent 20 years fighting the Turks, allied at various times with the pope, the Venetians, Naples and the Hungarians. After his death the Turks took over; uprisings continued for the next 150 years until the Ottoman empire was forced to acknowledge Albanian independence.

In 1924 the former prime minister Ahmed-i-Zog seized power and made himself King Zog in 1928. He fled when Mussolini sent Italian troops into the country on Good Friday in 1939. During the Second World War Albania created a successful underground resistance movement. French-educated Enver Hoxha emerged in 1941 as founder of the Albanian Communist party and leader of the partisans fighting the Axis occupying forces. Italy left the war in 1943 and by 1944 the partisans had the Germans in retreat. Hoxha was in effective control of the country in 1944 and proclaimed a people's republic in January 1946.

The Stalinist Hoxha maintained a comradely relationship with Tito's Yugoslavia; but this became hostile when Tito fell out with Stalin. Destalinisation in the USSR in the mid-1950s led Hoxha to turn his fire on his former Soviet allies, accusing Khrushchev of deserting socialism. This left Albania with only Mao Zedong's China as a friend and supporter. Even China fell out of favour when the Chinese and the Americans began talking to each other after the Vietnam war. In Hoxha's judgement Stalin and Mao Zedong had been the only ones true to the cause.

Religion was abolished in 1960, when Hoxha decreed "the death of God" and turned mosques and churches into warehouses or museums of atheism. Hoxha's wartime comrade-in-arms, Mehmet Shehu, prime minister since 1954, died in 1981, reportedly having committed suicide; other reports had him shot dead at a cabinet meeting. Hoxha died in 1985, after leading Albania for 40 years. He was succeeded by Ramiz Alia. Recently tourism and contact with foreign countries, such as Greece, have increased – but slowly.

Algeria

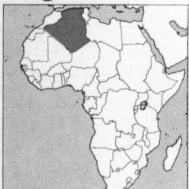

DZ
North Africa
919,595 sq. mi
Pop: 20.5 m
UN, AL, OAU,
OPEC

Capital: Algiers (pop: 2.5 m)
Official language: Arabic
Religion: Sunni Moslem
System of govt: Democratic people's republic; independence proclaimed 3 July 1962

The central Maghreb (*Algeria and Morocco*) was the site for the establishment of Phoenician harbour bases from c.1500 BC onwards. After the foundation of Carthage (*Tunisia*) by the Tyreans (814-813 BC) the Carthaginians became the masters of the coast of Numidia (*Algeria*). After the destruction of Carthage (146 BC) and the defeat of the Numidian King Jugurtha (105BC) the Romans extended their rule to Numidia with Caesar's victory at Thapsus (46 BC). The romanisation of the country brought great prosperity, with agriculture in particular thriving. The Roman period was brought to a close by the invasion of the Vandals (429), who were expelled by Byzantine forces under Belisarius in 533.

In 647 the Arabs invaded, and in 720 succeeded in subjugating the Maghreb, despite Berber resistance. The recognition of the sovereignty of the Abbasid Arab caliphs by the Hammadid dynasty in Bougie at the end of the 11th century led the Fatimids to provoke the Bedouin Banu Hilal tribe to invade the region. The Arab nomads drove the Berbers back in the mountains. At the end of the 12th century the Maghreb enjoyed a period of temporary unity secured by Abd al-Mumin, the first caliph of the Almohad dynasty, the conqueror of Ifriqiyah (*Tunisia*) and a number of ports held by the Normans. The arrival of Turkish corsairs in 1514 conferred a degree of unity on Algeria by placing it under the protectorate of the Ottoman sultan. These pirates built up the wealth of the Algerian ports, despite European attempts at intervention. The replacement of the pasha of Algiers, who was appointed by the Ottoman sultan, in 1711 saw Algeria attain a certain degree of autonomy.

The French occupation

France's intervention in Algeria in 1830 was a result of the exploitation of a private financial dispute dating back to 1798 to divert attention from domestic political problems. Algiers fell on 5 July. The revolt of Abdel Kader, the emir of Mascara, and the bey of Constantine in 1832 led to a renewal of hostilities in 1835, and in 1837 France was forced to recognise Abdel Kader's sovereignty over the whole country with the exception of the ports. In 1839 Abdel Kader declared war on France, which had decided on the total conquest of Algeria. Abdel Kader continued the struggle until he was forced to surrender in 1847. The Second Empire organised the colonisation of Algeria. Emperor Napoleon III's visit to Algeria in September 1860 was, however, to persuade him to put a halt to the policy of colonisation, although this was then continued by the Compagnie Genevoise at Sétif. Further conquest was facilitated by the Franco-British accord of 1890. Nationalist movements were founded after the First World War by Ali Abdel Kader and Messali Hajj and Ferhat Abbas founded the UPA (Algerian Popular Union) in 1938.

After the allied landing in 1942 Algeria became the capital of Free France until the liberation of Paris. The failure to grant the autonomy promised at the 1944 Brazzaville Conference led to insurrections in 1945 and the adoption of severe repressive measures. A clandestine nationalist revolutionary movement (CRUA) was formed in April 1954 by Hussein Ait Ahmed, Ahmed Ben Bella and Mohammed Khider and rebellion broke out in October of the same year. The French declared a state of emergency in August 1955 and order was only re-established in the cities early in 1957. Shaken by the Algerian crisis, the French government recalled General de Gaulle to power in June 1958. He proclaimed Algeria's right to self-determination, and, in spite of expatriate French hostility, announced negotiations with the FLN (National Liberation Front, created in 1955) in June 1960. The announcement of negotiations at Evian was followed by a revolt of a section of the French army in April 1961, the failure of which resulted in the formation of the OAS (Secret Army Organisation) which adopted terrorist methods, including attacks on de Gaulle's life.

Independent Algeria

Algeria became independent in July 1962 following a referendum, and Ben Bella emerged victorious as head of government in September 1962. He was overthrown by the military in 1965 and remained in prison until 1979.

A revolutionary council was set up under the leadership of Colonel Houari Boumedienne, who adopted a new constitution following a referendum held in 1976. Boumedienne died in 1978 and was succeeded by Colonel Chadli Ben Djedid in February 1979.

Algeria sent a contingent to the 1973 Egyptian-Israeli war and opposed the peace initiative of Egypt's President Sadat in 1977. Relations with Morocco were strained by Algeria's support for the anti-Moroccan Polisario Front in the Western Sahara.

Algeria has had to cope with economic problems resulting from a runaway birth rate and inadequate agricultural production.

Andorra

AND
South West
Europe
180 sq. mi
Pop: 48,800

Capital: Andorra-la-Vella
(pop: 15,600)

Official language: Catalan
Religion: Catholic (94 per cent)
System of govt: Principality, governed since 1278 by France and Spain

The political system of the principality of Andorra dates from an accord entered into in 1278 between the count of Foix and the Spanish bishop of Urgel. This placed the principality under the suzerainty of two co-princes. The rights of the counts of Foix passed to France in 1608. In 1806 Napoleon I installed a permanent representative in Andorra.

The rights of the bishop of Urgel are in effect exercised by the civil governor of the province of Lerida. The Andorran general council (parliament) met for the first time in 1868, its members then being elected for a period of four years by the heads of the 625 families having the right to vote. The council exploited the imprecision of the constitution to assume ever greater powers. The first official visit of a French co-prince, General de Gaulle, took place in 1967. Universal suffrage was introduced in 1970 and a firm constitution established in 1981, after the first meeting of the two co-princes. A prime minister, Oscardo Ribas Reig, was elected for the first time in 1982. He undertook a huge reform of Andorran institutions. The Andorran prime minister now possesses de facto the powers of a head of state. Having lost its attraction as a financial haven following legislation in 1983, inexpensive Andorra now derives most of its income from tourism.

Angola

South West
Africa
481,351 sq. mi
Pop: 8.75 m
UN, OAU

Capital: Luanda (pop: 1.13 m)
Official language: Portuguese
Religions: Christian (65 per cent), traditional beliefs (34 per cent)
System of govt: People's socialist republic since 11 November 1975

In 1483 Diego Cao, the Portuguese navigator, landed at the mouth of the river Zaire or Congo and founded the colony of Sao Salvador (Mbanza). The king of the Kongo people, Nzinga Nkuwu, who at that time reigned over northern Angola, had himself baptised and his successors pursued a policy of co-operation with the Portuguese, who limited their activities to the coastal region. In 1576 the Portuguese commenced the conquest of the interior of the country following the foundation of the port of Sao Paolo Luanda. They named the port's hinterland "Angola" after the local chieftain, the Ngola. The Portuguese set up a trade in slaves from Angola to their settlements in Brazil. A Dutch contingent which landed in 1641 was expelled by Portuguese troops drafted in from Brazil in 1648. Portugal soon became engaged in a row with the king of the Kongo over the sovereignty of Luanda and forced the Kongo to recognise its overlordship.

The kingdom of the Kongo eventually disappeared but the Portuguese continued to use the country as a source of slaves for Brazil. The slave trade was banned in 1836, but persisted until 1869, when it was replaced by forced labour until 1910.

The Portuguese remained based principally along the Angolan coast until the end of the 19th century, when other colonial powers began the "Scramble for Africa" and finally prompted the Portuguese authorities into fixing their colony's eastern boundaries. The present frontiers of Angola, together with Portuguese sovereignty, were universally recognised by the international African Conference held at Berlin in 1884-85.

The Portuguese encountered opposition from Angolan tribes in the first half of the 20th century. In 1951 Angola was given the status of an overseas province of Portugal.

The fight for independence
In 1954 the UPA (Union of Angolan Peoples) was formed, which provoked a nationalist revolt in the north of the

country in 1961. The Marxist rival to the UPA, the MPLA (Angolan People's Liberation Movement), was established by Mario de Andrade and Agostinho Neto in 1956, although it was obliged to retreat to neighbouring Congo-Brazzaville (French Congo) after the 1961 uprising. The UPA took refuge in Leopoldsville (Kinshasa), the Zairean capital.

Angola obtained limited autonomy in 1964. In 1965 the UPA became the FNLA (National Front for the Liberation of Angola) which splintered to create UNITA (National Union for the Total Independence of Angola) under

the leadership of Jonas Savimbi.

The ensuing guerrilla war saw the deployment of 55,000 Portuguese troops in Angola by 1973. Angola's right to independence was recognised by Portugal's President Antonio de Spinola in June 1974 and the various independence movements united to form a provisional government in January 1975. Backed by Portugal, now in a state of revolution after the overthrow of the Portuguese military dictatorship, the MPLA ousted UNITA and the FNLA from Luanda and declared independence in 1975. Agostinho Neto was elected as Angola's first president.

These moves against the opposition sparked off Angola's civil war. Aided by Cuba and the USSR, the MPLA took control of the country in February 1976. UNITA, based in the south-east of the country, was supported by South Africa in its conflict with the MPLA government.

Agostinho Neto died in 1979 and his successor, Eduardo dos Santos, made efforts to end the guerrilla war. In August 1988 a ceasefire was agreed between South Africa, Cuba and Angola, pending talks on foreign withdrawal. Talks also ensued between Angola's warring parties.

Antigua and Barbuda

Caribbean
171 sq. mi
Pop: 82,400
UN, OAS,
CARICOM, CW

Capital: Saint John's
(pop: 30,000)
Official language: English
Religion: Anglican (87 per cent)

System of govt: Constitutional monarchy; independent 1 November 1981

Antigua, a small island in the Antilles, was discovered by Christopher Columbus in 1493 on his second voyage to the Americas. He named the island after the church of Santa Maria de la Antigua of Seville in Spain.

In 1632 Antigua, Barbuda and the volcanic island of Redonda were occupied and colonised by the British. Antigua provided the Royal Navy with an important base during the various Anglo-French wars of the 17th and

18th centuries. The French only once succeeded in occupying Antigua, which they did briefly in 1666.

Work on the port of English Harbour was completed in 1764. During the revolutionary and Napoleonic wars Lord Nelson and his fleet stayed there on a number of occasions.

The island's slaves were officially liberated in 1834. In 1871 Antigua joined the British League of the Leeward Isles which was dissolved in 1951. Antigua and Barbuda had already acquired a certain degree of autonomy when, in 1953, it joined the Federation of the

West Indies. This grouping comprised, besides Antigua and Barbuda, Barbados, Trinidad and Tobago, Jamaica, St. Christopher and Nevis as well as the Windward Isles (Dominica, Saint Lucia, Saint Vincent and Grenada).

In 1967 Antigua and Barbuda was granted the status of a state associated to Britain. In 1981 it acquired independence as a member of the Commonwealth, with Queen Elizabeth II as head of state. Tourism is Antigua and Barbuda's principal source of revenue, amounting to half of the gross national product.

Argentina

RA
South America
1,073,358 sq mi
Pop: 31.5 m
UN, LAIA, OAS

Capital: Buenos Aires (pop: 3.32 m)
Official language: Spanish
Religion: Catholic (90 per cent)
System of govt: Republic; independence proclaimed 9 July 1816

Before the arrival of Europeans the oldest human traces in what is now Argentina go back to c.14,000 BC, at least 16,000 years after humans first crossed from Asia to America. They were hunter-gatherers in the north-west and south, in Patagonia and Tierra del Fuego. Their hunting way of life continued after other parts of America had developed agriculture, and was still the basis of subsistence when the first Europeans arrived.

The Spaniard Juan Diaz de Solis was the first European to explore the Argentine coast and he discovered the Rio de la Plata. Buenos Aires, which was founded in 1536 by Pedro de Mendoza, was abandoned five years later and re-

taken by the native population. Buenos Aires was restored in 1580 by Juan de Garay after the creation of other main towns.

Colonisation and independence
Argentina's economic prosperity was slow in arriving and a significant economy arose only after Spain's formation, in 1776, of the vice-royalty of La Plata (the River Plate), which comprised the region of modern Argentina, Uruguay, Paraguay and Bolivia. In 1778 Spain abolished trading limits, boosting economic activity.

After the failure of Britain's attempt to gain a foothold in Argentina during the Napoleonic Wars (1806-1807), the growing independence movement erupted in open revolt against Spain in 1810. On 25 May 1810 the Spanish viceroy was deposed, a junta was elected in Buenos Aires and a national government of La Plata took charge of the national insurrection. As the struggles progressed Paraguay, Uruguay and Bolivia also broke away from the old vice-royalty of La Plata.

La Plata was the only South American colony to escape reconquest in the short term. On 9 July 1816 the Congress of Tucaman proclaimed the independence of South America. Argentinian troops helped win independence for Chile (1818) and Peru (1821).

Following the declaration of independence, the urban middle classes demanded a strong, central government. But the estate owners, stockbreeders and provincial governors preferred federal government with a weaker centre. The federalists triumphed in 1827 and Juan Manuel de Rosas imposed a merciless dictatorship on the merchants of Buenos Aires. He was overthrown in 1852, but the civil war dragged on until 1880. At around this time the colonisation of Patagonia began in earnest, along with the extermination of most of its native inhabitants. This colonisation was facilitated by the construction, from 1856, of a railway.

Immigration from Europe accelerated in the late 19th century, and cereals and stockbreeding established themselves as Argentina's primary economic activities, especially after the introduction of refrigerator ships made beef exports possible. Under the presidency of Hipolito Yrigoyen (1916-22 and 1928-30) the country experienced a real economic boom, which was unfortunately ended by the world economic crisis of 1929.

Political unrest followed, and the civil government was overthrown by the army in 1930 and in 1943, the second time because of army hostility to Argentina's entry into the war on the side of the Allies.

The Peronist era
A populist member of the 1943 military government, General Juan Peron, was sacked in 1945 but recalled in 1946 after huge demonstrations in his favour by his underprivileged followers, the *Descamisados* (Shirtless Ones). His Justice Front party won the ensuing election with 56 per cent of the votes, and Peron's populist policies were backed by the trade unions and middle classes, as well as by his popular wife Eva Duarte ("Evita") before her early death in 1952. But social reform drained the economy, and Argentina fell into serious crisis. Facing church hostility because of an attempt to liberalise divorce laws, Peron was overthrown in September 1955 by a coup and fled to Spain.

Military and civilian governments
The military regime gave way in 1958 to President Arturo Frondizi's civilian government, but neither he nor his successors, Jose Maria Guido (1962-63) and Arturo Ilia (1963-66), were able to return Argentina to political and economic stability. The coup of June 1966 abolished the civil institutions. A third junta, led by Alejandro Lanusse, took over in March 1971 and prepared for the return to civilian government. The Peronist Hector Campora was elected president in May 1973. Returned from exile, Peron himself was re-elected in

October. Peron died on 1 July 1974 and was succeeded by his third wife, Isabel, who, unable to solve the country's internal problems, was overthrown by a coup in March 1976.

A new junta: human rights and war

The junta formed by the commanders of the three branches of the military, led by General Jorge Videla, restored some health to the Argentine economy, partly through new trade links with the USSR. But the junta's rule was discredited by the persecution and elimination of thousands of its opponents, the *Desaparecidos* (Disappeared Ones). In March 1981 Videla was replaced by General Roberto Viola and then, in December, by General Leopoldo Galtieri.

To divert attention from his domestic problems, Galtieri provoked Britain's last colonial war in early 1982 by invading the Falkland Islands, a British colony of 2,000 people known to the Argentinians as the Malvinas Islands, which had long been the subject of dispute between the two countries. The Argentine defeat in June by the British led to the fall of Galtieri and his replacement by former General Reynaldo Bignone.

The return to democracy

After seven years of discredited dictatorship Argentina returned to civilian rule with the election of Raul Alfonsin and his Radical Union party in October 1983. The new government faced a much deteriorated economy and a tense political climate resulting from the trial of those responsible for the organised terror of the military junta. Revolts by sections of the army took place more than once under Alfonsin's administration. An IMF-inspired austerity plan was put in place to tackle Argentina's inflation and economic problems. But the crisis was not solved by the plan, and elections of 14 May 1989 were won by the flamboyant Peronist Carlos Menem.

Australia

AUS
Oceania
2,966,200 sq. mi
Pop: 16.2 m
UN, ANZUS,
CW, OECD

Capital: Canberra (pop: 267,000)
Official language: English
Religion: Christian (76 per cent)
System of govt: Federal constitutional monarchy since 1 January 1901

Australia's first inhabitants, the ancestors of modern Aboriginal people, probably originated in Asia. They headed for the continent via the islands of south-east Asia some 50,000 years ago. It is estimated that by 1788 (the start of the European conquest) there were approximately 750,000 Aboriginals in Australia, leading a wide variety of hunter-gatherer lifestyles in all parts of the continent. These people celebrated their relationships with each other and with the land through a complex and vivid culture. Aboriginal myth, song, dance, music and art are especially noteworthy. Traditional Aboriginal society has suffered greatly during 200 years of European conquest through disease, neglect or plain murder. Few Aboriginal people still live a traditional lifestyle, although in recent years numbers choosing this way of life for at least part of the year have been increasing. The first European to set foot in Australia was the Portuguese Godinho de Eredia in 1601. Explorations after this time were fostered first by the Dutch through the voyages of Abel Tasman (after whom Tasmania is named) and others, and then by the English. In 1770 Captain James Cook claimed the east coast of Australia (which he named New South Wales) for Britain.

The British in Australia

In January 1788 Captain Phillip established the convict colony of Sydney in New South Wales. Penal immigration from Britain – "transportation" was the sentence for a wide range of offences, many of which now seem extraordinarily trivial – was prompted partly by the loss of penal outlets in the American colonies, and continued until 1853. From 1793 penal arrivals were joined by the first free settlers. In its first decade the colony struggled for survival with agricultural activities primarily devoted to supplying Sydney and its outlying settlements. However, after this time the export of wool and other pastoral products began to figure more prominently in the local economy. The exploration of the coasts progressed more quickly than that of the hinterland. The Blue Mountains to the east of Sydney were not crossed until 1813. Nonetheless during the next 50 years virtually all of the continent had been explored, often at a great cost in human lives. In 1851 a series of gold discoveries were made, first in New South Wales and later in Victoria, which sparked off a flood of immigration. The population of Australia reached the million mark in 1861.

Economic expansion, based on the export of primary products, continued strongly until the late 1870s when it slipped into recession. The social unrest which followed was instrumental in the foundation of the Australian Labour Party in 1891.

Australia becomes a federal state

From 1850 Britain had granted each of its Australian colonies a large measure of autonomy. In the last decades of the 19th century negotiations aimed at achieving a federation of the colonies were begun. A draft constitution for a federal Australia was approved by referendum and by the British parliament and the nation came into being in 1901. Melbourne was the capital until 1927 when government was transferred to the new city of Canberra.

In 1907 Australia obtained the status of a dominion within the British Empire. The country's political orientation up to the First World War was the result of a compromise between Liberal and Labour. Under this the protectionist policies of the Liberals were supported by Labour in exchange for a revision of social and labour law. A more notorious aspect of pre-war politics was the "White Australia" policy. The Immigration Restriction Bill of 1901, which prohibited the immigration of non-whites, was prompted by the European Australians' fear of being swamped by Asians.

In the First World War 330,000 Australians fought for Britain as part of the Australia and New Zealand Army Corps (ANZAC), and of these 59,000 were killed. They were engaged in the Dardanelles – the Gallipoli disaster of 1915 is particularly remembered – and in Flanders as well as in the Pacific, where they conquered German New Guinea.

The world economic crisis of 1929 was a severe blow to Australia, which was still dependent on the export of its wool. Gaining power in 1929, Labour was scarcely able to improve the situation; by 1933 one third of the working population was unemployed. Worried by the rapid expansion of Japanese power in the Pacific from the 1920s onwards, Australia aligned itself more closely with the USA and established a professional army, conscription having been abolished in 1929. Despite Australia's pacifist policies an expeditionary force was sent to Europe in September 1939 to fight alongside the Allies. Japan's entry into the war in December 1941 turned Australia and its possessions in the Pacific into a new front-line. Saved by the Battle of the Coral Sea, Australia was later to serve as the launchpad for the allied reconquest of the Pacific.

Post-war Australia

One of the founder members of the UN in 1945, Australia received a mandate to govern New Guinea. The Liberals under Robert Menzies, prime minister from 1939-41 under the banner of the United Australia Party founded by his predecessor J A Lyons, won the 1949 elections from the Labour Party, which had carried out an interventionist economic policy since 1945. Menzies stayed in power until 1966. Under the post-war Liberal government Australia enjoyed considerable economic expansion, aided by a policy which welcomed foreign investment, and reopened the country for immigration (100,000 people per year between 1945 and 1972) and the return to a liberal economy (denationalisation). At the same time Liberal policy was aligning itself more and more with the USA. From 1966 to 1972 an Australian corps served in the Vietnam war.

Labour's return to power in 1972 heralded a change in Australian foreign policy. The prime minister, Gough Whitlam, sealed diplomatic relations with communist China and then with North Vietnam in 1973. In September 1975 Papua New Guinea was granted independence.

In November 1975 the governor general, Sir John Kerr, the queen's representative, sparked a constitutional crisis by sacking Whitlam over his handling of the ailing economy. London distanced itself from Kerr's unprecedented action, which gave a boost to growing Australian republicanism.

Whitlam's successor was the Liberal Malcolm Fraser, who won a large majority in the December 1975 elections. Continuing economic problems and disputes within the Liberal and National Party coalition brought about Fraser's defeat by the Labour Party, now led by Bob Hawke, in March 1983. Hawke re-emphasised Australia's commitment to the ANZUS (Australia, New Zealand and the USA) defence alliance while being sharply critical of French nuclear and colonial policies in the Pacific. Economic relations with Japan and South East Asia achieved a new prominence during this period. Indeed, under Hawke, Australia has moved closer to Asia and played an active role in attempts to achieve a settlement of the conflict in Cambodia, for example. White Australians celebrated the bicentenary of their nation in 1988. However, Australia's Aboriginal peoples are still struggling to achieve equity and justice within Australian society at large. This struggle recently received sharper focus by the appointment of a royal commission into black deaths in police custody. The White Australia policy may be dead, but the goals of universal land rights for Aboriginals, and the normalisation of relations between white and black Australia through a treaty, are still a long way off.

Austria

A
Central Europe
32,376 sq. mi
Pop: 7.56 m
UN, EFTA, OECD

Capital: Vienna (pop: 1.49 m)
Official language: German
Religion: Catholic (84 per cent)
System of govt: Federal parliamentary republic; second republic recognised 15 May 1955

The Alpine regions have been occupied by humans since the palaeolithic era (600,000 BC-10,000 BC). The so-called Hallstatt civilisation developed on what is present-day Austria between 800 BC and 400 BC.

The Romans first arrived in the region, at that time populated by Celts, in approximately 15 BC, and annexed it as the province of Noricum. In the fifth century the area was threatened by Germanic tribes arriving from the north, especially the Lombards. These were followed by Slavonic tribes and the Asiatic Avars who arrived from the east and settled in Austria in around 570. They were defeated by Charlemagne, king of the Franks, who annexed the country in 803. The region became part of the Magyar (Hungarian) domains in 907, until conquered by the Holy Roman Emperor Otto I after his victory over the Magyars at Lechfeld in 955. The easternmost part of the country acquired the name of *Ostarrichi*, (eastern domain, in Latin *Austria*). The Margrave Luitpold I of Babenburg annexed the region in 976. Babenburg domination lasted until 1246 when the last king of the dynasty met his death in battle against the Hungarians. Ottokar II, king of Bohemia, conquered Austria in 1251.

The rule of the Habsburgs

Rudolph I of Habsburg defeated Ottokar II at the battle of Marchfeld in 1278. In the following two centuries well-engineered marriages and successions ensured Habsburg mastery of all the south-east German territories except Bavaria. Austrian prosperity flourished thanks to its trade and its mines of salt and metal. The marriage in 1477 of Maximilian I of Habsburg to Mary of Burgundy, the daughter of Duke Charles the Bold, gave the Habsburgs the Netherlands and Franche-Comte. Another marriage assured the dynasty of Spain. When Charles V was elected Holy Roman Emperor in 1519 his domains stretched from America to Asia. In 1521 he entrusted Austria to his brother Ferdinand I whose marriage added Bohemia, Moravia, eastern Hungary and Croatia to his pos-

sessions. The Habsburg inheritance was now divided between the two lines of Austria and Spain. On Charles V's abdication in 1556, Ferdinand I assumed the Holy Roman imperial mantle while Charles's son Philip II inherited the Spanish empire.

Austrian ascendancy

Roman Catholic Austria spearheaded the counter-reformation: the emperor suppressed Lutheranism in the Austrian states and in Bohemia, which had made a bid for independence in 1618, and which was annexed by Ferdinand II after the Battle of the White Mountain in 1620. These events marked the start of the Thirty Years War (1618-48), the long struggle for central European domination largely fought on German soil.

Later in the century Austria faced a new threat from the Ottoman empire, a long-standing enemy to the east. In 1683 the Turks besieged Vienna in their last deep thrust into central Europe. They were repulsed by imperial troops with the crucial aid of King John Sobieski of Poland. By the peace of Karlowitz in 1699 Austria was confirmed as ruler of the former Ottoman lands of Hungary, Slovenia and Transylvania. When the Habsburg King Charles II of Spain died without issue in 1700 he named as his heir the Bourbon duke of Anjou, grandson of Louis XIV of France, who came to the throne as Philip V. The Austrian Habsburgs were not about to let the Spanish empire pass to their old dynastic enemies without a fight, and the War of the Spanish Succession erupted in 1702. The treaty of Rastatt in 1714 finally deprived the Habsburgs of Spain and her colonies. Austria was compensated with the former Spanish Netherlands, the province of Milan, Naples and Sardinia.

Maria Theresa and Josef II

Emperor Charles VI (ruled 1711-40) had no male heir. Under Salic law only males could inherit, so he secured the exceptional succession of his daughter Maria Theresa with the "Pragmatic Sanction". On his death some major European powers withdrew their guarantee of Maria Theresa's right to succeed and the War of the Austrian Succession (1740-48) ensued. The support of England and the Netherlands enabled her to consolidate her position although she lost Silesia to Prussia.

On the empress's death in 1780 her son Josef II, co-ruler and Holy Roman Emperor since 1764, succeeded her. He was to pursue the enlightened despotism of Maria Theresa, but many of his reforms met stiff opposition and had to be abandoned before his death in 1790.

Austria and Napoleon I

Bonaparte's armies penetrated into Austria in 1797 and Vienna fell in 1805. The treaty of Pressburg in 1805 forced

Austria to cede Dalmatia to France, Venice and Istria to Italy and Vorarlberg to Bavaria. The Emperor Francis II adopted the title of Emperor Francis I of Austria in 1804, as the dissolution of the Holy Roman empire seemed inevitable. It was formally abolished by Napoleon in 1806. Between 1813 and 1815 Austria entered into a coalition with Prussia and Russia aimed at the defeat of Napoleon. On Napoleon's defeat (1814) victors gathered at the Congress of Vienna (interrupted by Napoleon's return in 1815) to determine the new European order, under the presidency of the Austrian chancellor, Prince von Metternich. The congress restored the Austrian frontiers of 1805. Metternich conducted diplomatic relations with the leading European powers, following a highly conservative policy which harshly repressed any attack on monarchic absolutism.

From the Congress of Vienna to 1918

The series of social and nationalist movements which erupted in 1848 forced Metternich to flee to Britain. Emperor Ferdinand had to abdicate and his nephew Franz Josef I ascended the throne. The new emperor faced an alliance between France and Piedmont which expelled Austria from Piedmont after inflicting defeats at Magenta and Solferino (1859). A humiliating defeat by Prussia at Sadowa in July 1866 ended Austrian leadership of German affairs, which became dominated by Berlin.

Franz Josef (1848-1916) turned to his own domains, establishing the dual monarchy in February 1867 in response to Hungarian nationalist demands. Under this arrangement Franz Josef was jointly emperor of Austria and king of Hungary. But the Balkan nationalities and relations with Balkan states remained a problem, aggravated by the annexation of Bosnia-Herzegovina in 1908 and the first Balkan War (1912). Finally, on 28 June 1914, the heir to the Austrian throne, the Archduke Franz Ferdinand, and his wife, were assassinated in Bosnia by a Serbian nationalist; war with Serbia followed into which all the major powers were soon drawn. Defeats occurred shortly after the First World War began, against Russia and Serbia. The Italian front opened in 1915 while imperial troops invaded neighbouring Poland and Serbia. On the death of Franz Josef (21 November 1916) his nephew, the Archduke Charles, became emperor. Negotiations which he held with the Allies in 1917 for a separate peace failed. In October 1918 Charles promised to transform the empire into a federal state. Instead the empire disintegrated.

The emperor, without actually abdicating, renounced all participation in the affairs of state on 13 November 1918. The dual monarchy was dissolved and Austria was reduced to its German-

speaking territories. An Austrian republic was proclaimed, led by social democrat Karl Renner.

The first republic

Austria was forbidden to merge with Germany for fear of creating a potentially over-powerful German state. Austria was obliged to remain independent and the first general elections in 1919 were won by the social democrats, who were succeeded in October 1920 by the Christian socialists.

Tensions between minority Slavs and the German-speaking population, city dwellers and country conservatives, led to the formation of numerous paramilitary leagues such as the nationalist militias (Heimwehren). Chancellor Engelbert Dollfuss, who came to power in 1932, introduced a Fascist-style authoritarian regime after the dissolution of parliament and the banning of both the communist and Nazi parties in 1933. Dollfuss was assassinated by Nazis during an attempted coup in July 1934 which saw Mussolini send troops to the Austrian border. The regime, however, remained alive under Kurt Schuschnigg until Austria was annexed by Hitler in March 1938, a move widely welcomed by the public despite official protests.

Austria since 1945

The eastern part of Austria was occupied by Soviet troops in March 1945. and a second republic was proclaimed by a provisional government under the veteran Karl Renner. In July 1945 Austria was divided into four Allied occupation zones, and elections in November were won by the Austrian Peoples' Party. Karl Renner was elected president, an office he held until his death in 1950.

The Allied occupation was ended by the international treaty of May 1955, under which Austria had to observe strict neutrality. Austria was admitted to the UN in 1955 and to the Council of Europe and European Free Trade Association (EFTA) in 1960. The country's reputation as an international mediator grew under the successive governments of the socialist Chancellor Bruno Kreisky between 1970 and 1983, when he handed over to Fred Sinowatz at the head of a socialist-liberal coalition government. Since then Austrian political life has been dogged by a succession of scandals and problems in the country's normally prosperous economy, especially in the state sector.

Sinowatz was succeeded by Franz Vranitzky in 1986. In the same year Austria was the focus of worldwide controversy following claims that former UN secretary-general Kurt Waldheim, a candidate for president, had lied about his war record as an officer in the German army. Waldheim was elected president in June 1986, and survived in office despite national and international pressure for his resignation.

Bahamas

BS
Central America
5,353 sq. mi
Pop: 245,000
UN, CARICOM,
OAS, CW

Capital: Nassau (pop: 135,000)
Official language: English
Religion: Christian (90 per cent)
System of govt: Constitutional monarchy; independent since 10 July 1973

The Bahamas were the first part of the New World sighted by Christopher Columbus, who sailed into view of the island of San Salvador on 12 October 1492. Having failed to find gold there, the Spanish satisfied themselves with deporting the Indian populations (Arawaks) to the island of San Domingo where they were put to work as slaves in the mountain mines. The 20,000 to 40,000 inhabitants of the Bahamas were deported over the course of only a few years, so the British found the islands totally uninhabited on their arrival in 1629. The first British governor was appointed in 1671. The islands were long a base for pirates and freebooters such as Blackbeard, until the early 18th century when Britain ordered the governor to stop their activities. The Bahamas, from this time a British crown colony, were defended against the Americans (1776) and the Spanish (1782-83). American victory in the War of Independence saw an influx of British loyalists to the islands. The slaves were given their freedom in 1834. An elected legislative assembly was created in 1841.

In the 1920s US rum smugglers used the Bahamas as a base during the Prohibition era. The islands were given an autonomous constitution in 1964, and the first black head of government was Lynden O Pindling, elected in 1968 and still in power in 1989 despite allegations of corruption aimed at him and his government. Full independence came in 1973.

Tourism and overseas companies attracted by the liberal tax system constitute the archipelago's main sources of income, although fishing, mainly for lobster, remains an important activity. The poverty of the soil and the lack of heavy industry have combined to focus the economy of the Bahamas on tourism and finance.

Bahrain

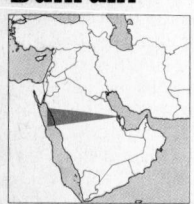

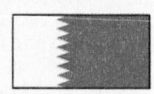

BRN
Near East
265.5 sq. mi
Pop: 481,000
UN, AL, GCC

Capital: Manama (pop: 147,000)
Official language: Arabic
Religion: Moslem (85 per cent)
System of govt: Emirate; independent since 15 August 1971

Some 3,000 years ago the archipelago of Bahrain was probably a site of commercial importance between Sumer and the Indus valley, a theory supported by the discovery of a number of palaeolithic and neolithic sites containing the ruins of temples dating from c.2500 BC.

Further proof of Bahrain's commercial role at this time has been furnished by the discovery of a prehistoric city yielding numerous pottery artefacts, especially round seals comparable to those produced around the same time in Sumer and the Indus.

Bahrain was occupied by Arabs in the seventh century. The Portuguese were in charge between 1515 and 1612, after which, until 1782, it was subjected to Persian domination. The Arab Khalifa dynasty, originally from Kuwait and in power from 1783, turned to Britain in the 19th century for aid in maintaining sovereignty against its neighbours. After making Bahrain a protectorate in 1867, Britain started the first petroleum exploration in the Persian Gulf in 1932.

The emirate, the residence of the British governor of the Gulf until 1958, was evacuated by British troops after the proclamation of independence in 1971.

The first parliamentary elections following the introduction of universal suffrage were held in 1973 and saw the left making considerable gains. The conflict which exploded in late 1974 between Emir Isa ibn Salman al Khalifa and parliament over security legislation led to the dissolution of parliament on 27 August 1975. Since then the constitution has been suspended and power has been monopolised by the emir and his family. Bahrain has been a member of the Arab League since 1971.

Bahrain's economy is based both on the production and refinement of oil and on the country's role as an international financial centre. Bahrain possesses an advanced social welfare system, including free health care and is liberal in its attitude towards education and the role of women.

One of the greatest problems confronting Bahrain is its rapid rate of population growth (ten per cent a year), due mainly to high levels of immigration, chiefly from other Gulf countries and the Indian sub-continent.

Bangladesh

BD
Southern Asia
55,598 sq. mi
Pop: 105.3 m
UN, CW

Capital: Dhaka (pop: 4.47 m)
Official language: Bengali
Religion: Moslem (86 per cent)
System of govt: Presidential people's republic since 26 March 1971

The eastern part of Bengal was annexed in 360 by the Gupta kingdom. The principal religion of the country remained Buddhism up until the Moslem conquest of 1202. Between 1576 and 1740 Bengal formed part of the Moghul empire. Dhaka, the present-day capital of Bangladesh, was the capital of eastern Bengal between 1608 and 1639 and then between 1660 and 1704. A number of powers (Britain, Holland and Portugal) possessed trading posts in the area.

Britain and France were the chief European nations with ambitions in Bengal in the mid-18th century. There was resistance to Britain's presence in the region, including a rebellion against the British East India Company in 1756 in which nearly 150 Britons were held in the notorious "Black Hole of Calcutta", a tiny cell. Twenty-three prisoners survived (although the number imprisoned is now thought to have been greatly exaggerated). In 1765 Robert Clive and the East India Company were charged with the administration of the country by the Moghul Emperor Shah Alam. A devastating famine wiped out a third of the population of Bengal in 1770, and relief was badly organised. The province received a British governor-general in 1774.

After the Indian Mutiny in 1857, Bengal became a directly ruled part of British India. Plans to partition it in 1905 met with local hostility and fuelled Indian nationalism; partition was scrapped in 1911.

When the British withdrew from India in 1947, eastern Bengal, with its Moslem majority, was attached to Pakistan. The two parts of Pakistan (separated by 950 miles) were in truth united only by Islam. The population of East Pakistan disliked being politically subordinated to a West Pakistan which was less densely populated and economically less stable. Separatist agitation broke out in 1968 and came to a head in 1971. The refusal on the part of President Yahya Khan to convoke the East Pakistani parliament following the election victory of the separatist Mujibur Rahman led to the explosion of the troubles in the spring of 1971. Imprisoned, Rahman was not released until December 1971 by the new Pakistani leader, Zulfikar Ali Bhutto.

The fighting in East Pakistan had led to the flight of many thousands of Bengalis to India. War broke out between India and Pakistan. Following the capitulation of Pakistan, Mujibur Rahman was able to return to what was now declared to be the new state of Bangladesh (January 1972). In the elections of 1973 he led his party, the Awami League, to an overwhelming victory. After the introduction of the state of emergency in December 1974 he abolished the parliamentary system and became president at the head of the country's only party. Rahman was killed during an army coup of 15 August 1975 and Bangladesh became an Islamic republic under General Ziaur Rahman.

Ziaur Rahman was assassinated during a failed coup of May 1981. After a period of civilian government the military regained power on 24 March 1982. The new president, General Hussain Ershad, introduced martial law and dissolved parliament. He assumed the presidency in December 1983 and was re-elected in October 1986.

Bangladesh is desperately poor, with few natural resources, and its agriculture, which enjoys exceptional climatic conditions (as many as three crops per year) is not enough to support a population increasing by two million a year. The economy and people face the constant threat of natural disaster. Thousands died in a tidal wave in 1970, and in September 1988 nearly 2,000 people died and 29 million were left homeless in floods. A cyclone killed at least 1,500 three months later.

Barbados

BDS
Caribbean
166 sq. mi
Pop: 254,000
UN, CW,
CARICOM, OAS

Capital: Bridgetown (pop: 7,500)
Official language: English
Religion: Anglican (70 per cent)

System of govt: Constitutional monarchy; independent since 30 November 1966

Barbados was discovered by the Portuguese in 1536. By the time the first British settlers arrived in 1627 the majority of the Indian population had already been deported into slavery by the Spanish. The British brought with them African slaves whom they put to work in the cultivation of sugar cane. In 1639 the inhabitants of the oldest British colony in the Caribbean were granted autonomous government. The slaves were freed between 1834 and 1838.

In more recent times, the fall in the price of sugar in 1937 caused the local population to revolt. The fundamental social and economic reforms which followed culminated in the granting of the to vote to blacks in 1950. Between the years 1958 and 1962 Barbados was a member of the Federation of the West Indies, formed by the British territories of the Antilles. Errol Barrow, head of the Democratic Labour Party and prime minister from 1961, remained head of government after independence was granted in 1966. In 1976 his party was defeated by the Barbados Labour Party led by John Adams, who was succeeded in 1985 by Bernard St John. Sugar cane, plantations of which cover 50 per cent of Barbados, still provides the majority of the country's revenue (80 per cent). Barbados possesses one of the world's highest population densities (1,500 per square mile). Tourism and the petroleum industry are contributing to economic growth.

Belau

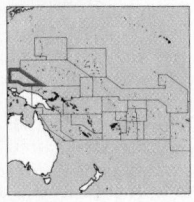

Oceania
188 sq. mi
Pop: 15,000

Capital: Koror (pop: 8,000)
Official languages: Micronesian, English

Religions: Protestant, Catholic
System of govt: Republic associated to the United States; independent since 1 January 1981

The island of Belau is the principal island in an archipelago of the same name, which is part of the Caroline Islands, the main archipelago of Micronesia. It is situated to the south of the Mariana islands and east of the Marshall islands. The Belau archipelago comprises 200 volcanic or coral islands which are, for the most part, uninhabited. Discovered by the Spanish navigator Villalobos in 1543, the archipelago was also visited during the 16th century by the Portuguese and then by the English. The Spanish did not officially claim the archipelago until 1875. They were to retain it until 1899, when the German empire purchased the islands, only to lose them after the First World War to Japan, who obtained them under a League of Nations mandate. Japan was master of the archipelago from 1919 to 1945. Strategically important to Nato, the islands were placed under US administration by the 1947 Trusteeship. The archipelago obtained semi-independence and became a republic on 1 January 1981. The Belau population declared itself in favour of maintaining its status of free association with the USA by a 60 per cent majority in the 1983 referendum. The USA remains in charge of the archipelago's defence. The Belau economy is based mainly on the export of fish and shellfish. Haruo Remeliik has been president of the republic and head of the Belau government since 1981.

Belgium

B
Western Europe
11,778 sq. mi
Pop: 9.86 m
UN, EC,
NATO, OECD

Capital: Brussels (pop: 976,000)
Official languages: French, Dutch, German
Religion: Catholic (92 per cent)
System of govt: Constitutional monarchy; independence proclaimed on 4 October 1830

Before it was conquered by Julius Caesar (57-51 BC), Gallia Belgica (Belgic Gaul) was inhabited by Celtic tribes and extended from the Seine to the Rhine. The area was divided between the Frankish and Lotharingian kingdoms by the Treaty of Verdun in 843. In the 13th and 14th centuries textile production allowed the southern Netherlandish towns of Bruges, Ghent and Ypres, under French sovereignty, to enjoy considerable economic prosperity.

The Habsburgs

With the marriage (1477) of the future Emperor Maximilian I to Mary of Burgundy, daughter and heiress of Charles the Bold, the Habsburgs gained control of the Burgundian inheritance. Crowned emperor in 1519, Maximilian's son Charles V tried to bring about the unification of the 17 provinces of Burgundy (including present-day Belgium, the Netherlands and Luxembourg). After his abdication in 1556 the Spanish Habsburg line inherited the provinces in the Low Countries.

In the late 16th and early 17th centuries the Protestant north of the Spanish Netherlands (the United Provinces, modern Netherlands) rebelled, and in 1648 Spain renounced the Netherlands by the Peace of Westphalia. Spain retained possession of the southern Low Countries (Belgium).

The Spanish Netherlands were a target for Louis XIV's expansionist policies (1638-1715) and a prize at stake in the War of the Spanish Succession (1701-13). The French took control of Artois (1659), Flanders (1668) and the French Hainault (1678).

The Peace of Utrecht of 1713 returned control of the southern Low Countries to the Austrian Habsburgs. The War of the Austrian Succession led to the occupation of the now Austrian Netherlands by the French (1744-1748).

The reforms of the Emperor Josef II provoked the revolt of Brabant in 1789-1790. The "United Belgian States" proclaimed independence in January 1790. France annexed the province during the revolutionary wars, which Austria recognised under the treaty of Campo Formio in 1797.

Following Napoleon's defeat in 1814-15, the Congress of Vienna merged Belgium with the former United Provinces to form the United Kingdom of Holland.

Independent Belgium

In 1828 the Liberals and Catholics jointly opposed King William I, whose policies favoured the northern Protestant provinces and who attempted to impose Dutch as the official language in the French-speaking south of Belgium. Encouraged by the success of the July revolution in France, Brussels revolted in August 1830. Independence was proclaimed on 4 October 1830 after Dutch troops had withdrawn from the country with the exception of Antwerp. A conference of European powers met in London and recognised the new Belgian state on 20 January 1831, guaranteeing its independence. Leopold of Saxe-Coburg, an uncle of Britain's Queen Victoria, became first king of the Belgians.

Politics in the new kingdom were dominated by rivalry between Catholics and Liberals on the questions of education and the linguistic opposition of French-speaking Walloons and Dutch-speaking Flemings. Religious education was made obligatory in 1895 and Dutch was accorded the same status as French three years later, in 1898. The personal property of Leopold II since 1885, the Congo sparked a quarrel between Belgium and France, Britain and Germany, mainly over Leopold's misrule of the territory. The conflict was finally brought to an end in 1908 when Leopold ceded the rights to the Congo to the Belgian government.

Two World Wars

The German invasion of neutral Belgium in 1914 caught the country unawares at a time of economic prosperity. The country was overrun despite the opposition of Albert I (king since 1909) and the suspension of all political rivalries. For most of the war Belgium was subjected to German administration. The west of the country continued to fight under the king. The Treaty of Versailles ceded Eupen and Malmedy to Belgium, and Belgium joined France in the occupation of the Ruhr in 1923. The language quarrel was defused in 1923 by the introduction of Dutch as an administrative language. Leopold III succeeded in 1934 following the accidental death of Albert I. Like many countries, Belgium had a quasi-Fascist movement, the Rexists, who were active during the 1930s. Neutral Belgium was invaded by Germany on 10 May 1940. The government fled to London, whence Hubert Pierlot directed Belgian resistance. King Leopold III was held prisoner in the palace of Laeken. Lib-

Belize

erated by the Allies in September 1944, Belgium was governed until 1950 by Leopold III's brother, Prince Charles, who assumed the regency while the future of Leopold was decided.

Since 1945

Belgium, the only country in Europe at the end of the war to be a creditor of the USA, which had made intensive use of the port of Antwerp, turned towards its industrial recovery in a political climate dominated by Paul Henri Spaak. The kingdom joined the UN

in 1945.The Christian democratic government elected in 1950 recalled King Leopold III who had returned from Germany in 1945 and was suspected of collaboration. A socialist-inspired general strike in 1951 procured his abdication in favour of his son, Baudouin I. Following the agreement of a customs' union with the the Netherlands and Luxembourg (Benelux, 1948), Belgium was in favour of the creation of a western European union. It joined Nato in 1948, the Council of Europe in 1949 and the EC and EURATOM in 1957.

The independence of the Congo came into effect on 30 June 1960 after intense international and UN pressure. Under 1970 constitutional reforms four linguistic regions were formed (Dutch, French, German and Brussels – French and Dutch although it is 80 per cent French-speaking) and three partly autonomous regions (Flanders, Wallonia and Brussels).

Regionalistion was the key policy of the government of the Christian socialist Leo Tindemans (1974-1978), which has also confronted economic difficul-

ties in the wake of the oil crisis. A coalition of Christian socialists and Liberals under Wilfried Martens (1981) introduced austerity measures, leading to a civil service strike in September 1983. The resignation of six Liberal ministers after the Heysel stadium riot, when English football fans were involved in trouble that led to 41 deaths in May 1985, resulted in early elections on 13 October. The coalition attained a majority and Martens remained prime minister. He was re-elected on 13 December 1987.

Belize

BH
Central America
8,866 sq. mi
Pop: 176,000
UN, CARICOM, CW

Capital: Belmopan (pop: 4,500)
Official language: English
Religions: Catholic (61 per cent), Anglican (13 per cent), Methodist (13 per cent)

System of govt: Constitutional monarchy; independence gained 21 September 1981

The territory of present-day Belize is situated at the heart of what was the Maya empire right up until its destruction by Hernan Cortes in 1524. French and English pirates fought over the region in the 17th century. Britain dispatched a superintendent there before colonising it in 1862 and making it a crown colony – British Honduras – in 1871. From that time onwards neighbouring Guatemala exploited the imprecision of the 1859 border treaty

(which opened the door to differing interpretations) to claim sovereignty over the territory. It was this longstanding claim of Guatemala which provoked military incidents in 1972, 1975 and 1977.

Since 1960 Belize's government has been in the hands of the People's United Party (PUP) which was granted some degree of autonomy in 1964. On the initiative of Prime Minister George Price the country took the name Belize in 1970. Movement towards full autonomy under the British crown, which was to succeed in 1976, was held up by the territorial claims of Mexico and

Guatemala. Following agreement between Britain and Guatemala and resolutions passed by the UN in 1975 and 1980, Belize won full sovereignty in 1981. A contingent of British troops remains stationed in Belize at the government's request. The country, which is very poor, is regularly devastated by natural disasters (recently, in 1931, 1961, 1978 and 1980). The main economic resource of Belize, whose name comes from a Maya word signifying "troubled water", is its plantations where sugar cane and lemon trees have now replaced the previously dominant cultivation of rare wood essences.

Benin

DY
West Africa
43,483 sq. mi
Pop: 4.3 m
UN, OAS,

Capital: Porto-Novo (pop: 208,000)
Official language: French
Religions: Traditional beliefs (61 per cent), Christian (22 per cent),

Moslem (15 per cent)
System of govt: People's republic; independence gained 1 August 1960

The Fon kingdom of Dahomey (or Dan Homé) was founded around the year 1625 by a prince of the royal family of the Allada, which reigned over the kingdom of the same name founded in 1575 by the Aja tribe. Agaja, the king of Dahomey (1708-32), annexed the kingdom of Allada in 1724 and then that of Ouidah in 1727. For a century Dahomey was to be a tributary of the Oyo kingdom by which it was defeated in

1730. The country's principal resource at the time was the selling of slaves, which was officially encouraged by the authorities of the kingdom. Dahomey was freed from the grip of the Oyo kingdom by Gezo (1818-58) who signed a treaty of friendship with France in 1851. His successor, King Glegle, opposed the French after the establishment of the protectorate of Porto-Novo in 1883. The French settlements in the Bight of Benin, created in 1883, were to become, in 1894, the colony of Dahomey. In 1956 Dahomey was granted internal autonomy and then in 1960

it gained independence. The first president, Hubert Maga, was confronted with serious economic difficulties and General Soglo seized power in 1963 and again in 1965. A number of attempts at democracy failed and a new army regime seized power in October 1972. A Marxist-Leninist revolutionary council was set up by General Mathieu Kérékou. In November 1975 Dahomey took on the name of the mediaeval kingdom of Benin.

The country has been governed since then by one party, the only contestant in elections in November 1979.

Bhutan

Southern Asia
18,000 sq. mi
Pop: 1.3 m
UN

Capital: Thimphu (pop: 15,000)
Official language: Dzongkha (Tibetan dialect)
Religions: Buddhist, Hinduism

System of govt: Constitutional monarchy

The history of Bhutan (Drug Yul or, in Dzongkha, "land of the dragon"), situated in the south-east of the Himalayan high plateau, has been moulded by religion and by the cross-border relations with India and Tibet. Under Tibetan domination since the ninth century, the country won its independence in 1557 under the reign of the Lama Shabdung I. At the end of the 19th century temporal power fell into the hands of the governor of Tongsa, a mem-

ber of the Wangchuk family, whilst Bhutan came under Anglo-Indian domination in 1865. Theocratic rule ended in 1907 when Ugyen Wangchuk was proclaimed king with British support. Britain assumed control of the country's external relations in 1910. This power was transferred to India in 1949. Since 1953 a national assembly (Tsogdu) has existed whose decisions, since 1968, the king has no longer been able to veto. Since this date the king has also had to obtain the confidence of the assembly's representatives every three years. The Chinese annexation of Tibet

in 1959 led to the arrival in Bhutan of large numbers of refugees. King Jigme Dorji Wangchuk (died 1972) broke off relations with China and Tibet in 1960. The refugee problem led in 1976 to an attempted coup by Tibetans.

King Jigme Singye Wangchuk, ruler since 1972, has favoured opening the country to tourism. Bhutan has been in the UN since 1971 and has attempted to free itself from India both in its foreign policy and by the creation of a national currency. Lamaism continues to play an important role in the life of the country.

Bolivia

BOL
South America
424,165 sq. mi
Pop: 6.4 m
UN, LAIA, OAS

Judicial Capital: Sucre (pop: 86,000); **Administrative Capital:** La Paz (pop: 992,000)
Official languages: Spanish, Quechua, Aymara
Religion: Catholic (94 per cent)
System of govt: Republic; independence proclaimed 6 August 1825

The kingdom of Tihuanaco grew between 600 BC and 1200 on the high plateau of the central Andes. The city of Tihuanaco formed the cultural and economic centre of an immense region comprising the depression of Lake Titicaca and a vast coastal territory of the Pacific. The kingdom's centralised organisation broke down around the year 800 and in 1460 the Inca Pahacutec was rapidly able to subjugate the various Aymaran and Quechuan tribes.

Present-day Bolivia and Peru were part of the Spanish vice-royalty following the destruction of the Inca empire by the *conquistadors* in the 1530s. Sucre (Chuqisaca), the present constitutional capital, was founded in 1538 and La Paz, the seat of the Bolivian government, in 1548. Upper Peru – Bolivia – was to assume considerable importance following the discovery of the Potosi silver mines in 1544.

Modern Bolivia, Paraguay, Uruguay and Argentina were united in 1776 under the Spanish vice-royalty of La Plata. An Indian revolt in 1781 failed, and Upper Peru remained loyalist in the face of Argentinian aggression right up to 1824.

In 1825 the armies of Simon Bolivar, the great liberator, commanded by General Sucre, wrested the country from Spain. The new republic of Upper Peru adopted the name of its first president, Bolivar.

Independence

General Santa Cruz, whose dictatorship was imposed in 1829, failed in his attempt to form a Peruvian-Bolivian confederation following the intervention of Chile and defeat at Yungay (1839). The downtrodden Indians revolted again in 1870-1871 and a state of near-anarchy persisted until 1880. The speculative development of quinine, nitrate (guano), silver and tin (from 1890 onwards) saw Bolivia being systematically exploited. Allied to Peru in the "Nitrate War" with Chile, Bolivia lost the province of Atacama in 1879 and with it its access to the sea.

The Liberals were carried to power by the civil war of 1898-1899. Peace was signed with Chile in 1904, whilst Bolivia lost the Acre region in the wake of the 1903-1904 war with Brazil. Trading in tin, which was monopolised by a few individuals, and mineral production reached their peak in 1920 following the Republican party's rise to power and increased US investment.

The disparities between the rich mineral regions and the agricultural remainder of the country were aggravated by the world economic crisis of 1929. The economy was completely shattered by the Chaco War of 1932-1935 against Paraguay. The country lost most of the Chaco province and, with it, access to the rivers flowing into the Atlantic. The military dictatorship which took power after the war attempted to redeem the situation, nationalising the American company Standard Oil and setting up mineworkers' trade unions. New parties, however, such as the Nationalist Revolutionary Movement (MNR) were able to channel the feelings of discontent. The 1952 revolution which followed the stabilising of the price of tin with the USA in 1951 brought MNR to power under Victor Paz Estenssoro.

Dictatorship and democracy

MNR social reforms, including the restitution of Indian lands, were accepted by the USA, but provoked an army coup in 1964. The military regime survived in the face of opposition movements and a Castroist guerrilla war led by Che Guevara, who was killed in 1967. Removed from power in the elections of 1978, General Hugo Banzer Suarez was succeeded by General Pedro Asbun. Three coups and three more generals followed before civilian rule was restored in 1982. Elected president in October, the head of the Democratic and Popular Union (UDP), Siles Suazo, was unable to come to terms with the financial crisis facing Bolivia. A general strike in March 1985 won wage rises of 350 per cent in the face of 8,216 per cent inflation. The elections of August 1985 were won by veteran MNR leader Victor Paz Estenssoro. A policy of financial and economic rigour was introduced but, despite its mineral wealth – Bolivia is a leading producer of metals – the country remains in serious economic difficulties.

Botswana

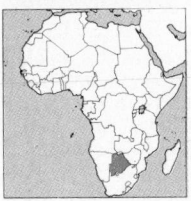
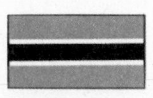

RB
Southern Africa
600,372 km2
Pop. 1.16 mill.
UN, CW, OAU

Capital: Gaborone (pop. 96,000)
Official languages: English, Tswana (Bantu)

Religions: Traditional beliefs (50 per cent), Christian
System of govt: Republic.
Independence obtained 30 September 1966.

In the late 19th century the Tswana tribes were being encroached upon by the Matabele, Bantu tribes living on the edge of the Kalahari desert. The Tswana looked to Britain. The protectorate of Bechuanaland, created in 1885, also established a buffer against the Germans in South-West Africa.

Bechuanaland became independent as Botswana in 1966, formed from the union of the former protectorate and two areas of Cape Province in South Africa. The first president was Seretse Khama, son of a tribal chief, who had been forced into exile after marrying a Briton and who had not been readmitted to the country until he renounced his position of tribal head in 1956. Khama's Botswana Democratic party won the 1969 elections. Botswana accepts refugees from South Africa and denounces apartheid, but has economic links with South Africa, on which it depends for export routes. The BDP won elections in 1974 and 1979. A new currency, the pula, was created in 1977 in order to replace the South African rand. On the death of Seretse Khama in July 1980, parliament elected the vice-president Quett Masire as his successor (re-elected in 1984). Since June 1985 there have been South African incursions against suspected African National Congress bases. Botswana appealed for international aid in 1987, its sixth successive year of drought.

Brazil

BR
South America
3,286,487 sq. mi
Pop: 141.3 m
UN, LAIA, OAS

Capital: Brasilia (pop: 1.57 m)
Official language: Portuguese
Religion: Catholic (89 per cent)
System of govt: Federal republic; independence proclaimed 7 September 1822

The first evidence of human settlement in Brazil goes back to approximately 8000 BC. The subsequent development of the country is based on the difference between the south and the Amazon basin in the north.

The first European to reach Brazil was the Spaniard Vicente Yanez Pinzon in January 1500. A few months later, in April, the Portuguese Pedro Cabral arrived in Brazil, which he claimed for Portugal on 3rd May 1500. At that time the new territories were called Vera Cruz (True Cross) and were allotted to Portugal by the Treaty of Tordesillas in 1494. The Portuguese claims, however, were not recognised by Spain until 1522. In the 16th century colonisation was limited to isolated settlements, in particular in the north-east, where the importation of African slaves permitted the cultivation of sugar cane from 1532 onwards. Brazil was divided by the king of Portugal into 13 fiefdoms, each under a "captain". In 1548 King John III sent a governor to Brazil to hold together the 13 captaincies.

Colonial growth

From 1554 Jesuit missions from Sao Paolo started the conversion of the Indians to Christianity. The French attempted to establish settlements between 1555 and 1615.

Dutch settlements at Bahia and Pernambouc were destroyed following the revolt of Portuguese settlers in 1654. The exploration of the interior of the country was prompted by the discovery of gold veins in the Minas Gerais (1694) and the Mato Grosso (1718) as well as by the discovery of diamond mines in 1699. Mining laid a heavy burden on the Indian population which was persecuted and reduced to slavery. This led in its turn to the neglect of agricultural production on the great plantations, the *fazendas*. Rio de Janeiro, which enjoyed a more favourable position for mineral trading, replaced Bahia as capital in 1763.

Stockbreeding increased at the end of the 18th century. Colonisation continued from the north-east and the south, with settlers coming from the Azores. The Anglo-Portuguese Methuen Treaty (1703) granted Britain exclusive trade rights with Brazil and led to French intervention in 1711.

The conflict with Spain for possession of the southern territories ended in 1777 by treaty. Spain was given the lands of the Jesuit missions (Uruguay) from which the Portuguese had been ejected by the Jesuit-provoked Indian revolt of 1750.

Despite the growth of the Brazilian economy which had seen the introduction of various new crops (rice, tobacco and plants producing dye, cotton, cocoa), the appearance of a revolutionary movement at the end of the 18th century brought to light the exploitation of mixed-race people. Brazilian nationalism was further strengthened by the arrival of the Portuguese royal family in Rio in 1808 when Portugal had been occupied by Napoleonic troops. King John VI remained in Brazil until 1821. In January 1815 Brazil became a kingdom associated to Portugal. The reorganisation of Brazil faced internal opposition and by the country's economic dependence on Britain which was strengthened by a treaty of 1810.' Returning to Portugal after the revolution of 1820, John VI left the regency of Brazil to his son Dom Pedro. He accepted the proclamation of independence of September 1822 and became emperor of Brazil under the name Pedro I in October.

From empire to republic

Threatened by a British contingent, Portuguese troops withdrew in 1823. When, in 1826, Pedro I announced his intention of returning to Lisbon to succeed his father as king of Portugal, a riot forced him to abdicate in favour of his son Pedro, five. Emperor Pedro II, ruler from 1840 after a regency, promoted economic expansion, especially the cultivation of coffee, adopted from Guyana. He granted universal suffrage, abolished slavery and secularised the civil service, but was also authoritarian. This fact provoked a military-led revolution (the army had grown in power since the war with Paraguay of 1865-70) and the proclamation of a republic in November 1889.

The federal republic of Brazil

The constitution of 1891 established a secularised, federal and democratic state. In fact power was largely dependent on a propertied oligarchy. The expanding cultivation of coffee advanced the state of Sao Paolo to the detriment of the north-east, prompting an overproduction crisis in 1906. Exploration of the Amazon basin was also continuing. In 1914 Brazil was the most powerful country in Latin America with its economy, in particular wheat and rubber production, benefiting from the First World War which it entered on the side of the Allies. The disappearance of Brazil's monopoly of rubber production with the emergence of competition in south-east Asia, the world economic crisis of 1929 and the dramatic fall in the price of coffee in 1930 led to a serious recession whose political consequence was the rise of Getulio Vargas, whose dictatorship was backed by a plebiscite in 1937. His regime relied on the support of the middle class and the poor against the great landowners and brought the policy of the *Estado Novo* (New State) into being. In 1942 Brazil sent a contingent of 25,000 troops to fight alongside the Allies. Vargas was overthrown in October 1945 by a group of generals and a new democratic constitution was adopted in 1946. A populist movement carried Vargas back to power in 1951. His policies became more radical and faced violent opposition, resulting in his suicide in August 1954. His successors pursued his policy of independence from US control. They also favoured decentralisation to the federal states. In 1960 a new capital, Brasilia, was officially founded, the building of which placed heavy strains on the national economy. A former member of the opposition, President Janio Quadros, elected in 1960, ceded to military pressure and resigned in August 1961 as a result of his overtures to the Eastern Bloc and the Third World. His successor, Joao Goulart, was deposed by a coup in April 1964.

Dictatorship and democracy.

The new regime suppressed political parties, founding an official party, ARENA (National Renewal Alliance). Social disparities were worsened by the ambitious policy of industrial expansion pursued by the generals.

The first free elections since 1965 were held in November 1982 in the wake of the liberal policies introduced by President Figueirido in 1979. The introduction of universal suffrage for the presidential elections of January 1985 was suppressed by the military. Demonstrations in Rio de Janeiro and Sao Paolo in April 1985 led to a state of emergency. In January 1986, however, the candidate of the social democrats (formed from the old ARENA) was defeated at the presidential elections by Tancredo Neves. Seriously ill, Neves died on 21 April 1986. Vice-president José Sarney succeeded him and ushered in the return to democracy with a massive austerity plan and fundamental agricultural reform.

The economy remains in bad shape and serious poverty and unemployment persist. Brazil is under increasing pressure to curb the destruction of the Amazon rain forests, which is proceeding at an alarming rate.

Brunei

BRU
South East Asia
2,226 sq. mi
Pop: 241,000
UN, CW,
ASEAN

Capital: Bandar Seri Begawan (pop: 55,000)
Official language: Malay
Religion: Moslem (63 per cent)
System of govt: Sultanate; independent since 1 January 1984

Brunei was an important port 1,000 years ago, and a mission to the emperor of China left Brunei in 977. Islam arrived in the early 16th century and the kingdom became a sultanate.

After helping the sultan of Brunei put down a rebellion, the British adventurer James Brooke received powers of government over Sarawak in 1841. Brunei became a British protectorate in 1888. The extraction of oil started properly after 1929. The sultanate was granted internal autonomy in 1959, and plans for joining the Malaysian Federation were dropped in 1963 after a revolt. The present sultan, Sir Muda Hassan al Bolkiah, was crowned in 1968. Oil-wealthy Brunei became fully independent in 1984. The sultan supports a British army contingent of Gurkhas.

Bulgaria

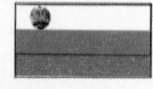

BG
South East
Europe
42,823 sq. mi
Pop: 8.98 m
UN, COMECON,
WP

Capital: Sofia (pop: 1.1 m)
Offical language: Bulgarian
Religions: Atheist (64 per cent), Orthodox, Moslem
System of govt: People's socialist republic since 15 September 1946

The Bulgarian people are a mixture of Slavs and Bulgars, a Turkic tribe from central Asia. They settled between the Danube and and the Balkans in around 650 and briefly established an empire that stretched from the Adriatic to the Aegean. During this time they were converted to Christianity and adopted the Cyrillic alphabet, reputedly invented by the Greek missionaries Cyril and Methodius in around 870. By 1000 the Bulgarians had been conquered by the Byzantines – the Emperor Basil II (976-1025) was notoriously known as "Slayer of Bulgars" – and although there were later periods of independence the nation's story is essentially one of domination by more powerful neighbours.

It became a tributary of Serbia before passing into the Ottoman empire. The treaty of San Stefano in March 1878 ended a war between Turkey and Russia and created a new, large Bulgarian state, ostensibly independent but effectively under Russian aegis. This was not acceptable to other major powers and the new Bulgaria was superseded by the terms of the Congress of Berlin in June 1878, signed by Russia, Turkey, Austria, Germany, Britain, France and Italy, creating a smaller, autonomous Bulgaria and a semi-independent Eastern Roumelia.

In 1908 the German Prince Ferdinand of Saxe-Coburg-Gotha, a relation of Queen Victoria of Britain, declared himself czar, and Bulgaria independent. A successful war followed against the Ottomans, then a disastrous one against its Balkan neighbours just before the First World War.

Bulgaria was an ally of the Central Powers, Germany and Austria, in the war. The inter-war years saw a succession of coups and dictatorships that reached a climax with the still unexplained death of King Boris II in August 1943.

Bulgaria was occupied by German troops from early 1941, but the country claimed neutrality in the Nazis' war with the USSR. It was a neutrality Moscow did not accept and in 1944 declared war. The Bulgarians asked for an armistice and two days later declared war on Germany. Soviet troops entered the country and a communist-led coalition of political parties formed the Fatherland Front. Non-communists soon fell, or were forced out of the coalition. The dominant figure was Georgi

Dimitrov, the communist leader whose defiance of the Nazis in the Reichstag fire trials in 1933 had made him a hero in communist circles and beyond. Though imprisoned by the Nazis there was apparently an understanding with Moscow and he was released and allowed to travel to the USSR, where he remained during the war.

Bulgaria thus emerged from the war as a close and far from unwilling ally of the USSR. The country's significance within the East European bloc of Soviet satellites stems from the part played by its leaders in aggravating Moscow's quarrel with Tito and precipitating the Stalinist show trials of East European leaders in the early 1950s.

Dimitrov was known as a Moscow man, to be distinguished from the local communists, such as Traicho Kostov, who had fought in the underground against the Nazis. But Dimitrov was also in favour of a Southern Slav or even a Balkan federation and in January 1948 the Soviet communist party newspaper *Pravda* denounced him for a speech he had made advocating such a Balkan federation.

This was a time when Stalin's quarrel with Tito was gathering momentum. Moscow had already begun the purge of satellite communist parties. The Bulgarian politburo of 14 members, only four of which were Moscow men, was replaced by a seven-member body, five from Moscow. Dimitrov was called to Moscow and when he returned he had abandoned his talk of a Balkan federation. A few months later he went to Moscow again, on the pretext of needing treatment for diabetes; there he died. He may have died from natural causes, but his removal from the scene was a necessary part of Stalin's bid to assert his power over the satellites. His rival in the Bulgarian party, Kostov, was given a show trial, in which Tito's "treachery" was exposed at length, before being shot.

The extensive purges of the Bulgarian party, which lasted until the early 1960s, eventually left the pliable Todor Zhivkov in power. He could be counted on to follow the Moscow line, whatever it happened to be. In time the Bulgarian party became rather a family affair for the Zhivkovs, with his daughter taking over culture, the son moving up and other relatives finding jobs for themselves.

Zhivkov was linked to a bizarre and notorious murder in London in September 1978. Georgi Markov was a Bulgarian author who had made a name for himself in his own country and had found favour with Zhivkov during a brief period of cultural thaw. When the ice age returned he left the country and eventually came to London, where he joined the BBC Bulgarian Service. He also broadcast for the West German Deutsche Welle and the American-funded Radio Free Europe. On these channels he began broadcasting his impressions of life at the top as he had experienced it with Zhivkov and his associates.

On 7 September he was crossing London's Waterloo Bridge, after leaving the BBC, when he felt a sharp sting in the back of his thigh and turned to see a man bent down to retrieve an umbrella. The man apologised and hurried away. The next day Markov's body was racked by raging fever and he told his wife he believed he had been poisoned. He had, in fact, received several warnings to stop his broadcasts or face death. At the hospital his fears were dismissed. He died four days after the attack. British police forensic experts found a hollowed-out pellet in Markov's leg. They said it had contained ricin, a poison with no known antidote. The assumption was that the poison and the method of administering it had been developed in Moscow. Several days after Markov's death a lieutenant general in Bulgaria's security service made a speech in which he expressed "the deepest gratitude to our Soviet comrades-in-arms of the KGB for their constant help and comradely assistance".

The Bulgarian regime has won further notoriety over its treatment of its big Turkish minority. Bulgaria began a campaign of forced assimilation which came to a head in the late 1980s. Turkish Bulgarians were forbidden to speak Turkish or to practise Islam and were forced to adopt Bulgarian names. Offenders or protesters were beaten, imprisoned and, reportedly, even killed, while others were expelled or encouraged to leave, often at a few hours notice. In 1989 the number of Turks crossing the border into neighbouring Turkey became a flood, and in June the two countries withdrew ambassadors. Bulgaria denies claims it is breaching its Turks' basic human rights and insists those leaving Bulgaria are emigrants, not refugees. But the persecution looks as if it may backfire, as Bulgaria is drained of valuable human resources, especially in the agricultural south.

Burkina Faso (Upper Volta)

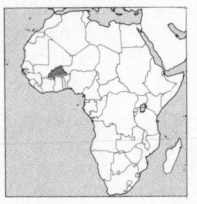
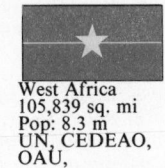

West Africa
105,839 sq. mi
Pop: 8.3 m
UN, CEDEAO, OAU,

Capital: Ouagadougou (pop: 385,000)
Official language: French
Religions: Traditional beliefs (65 per cent), Moslem, Christian
System of govt: Republic since 5 August 1960

The Mossi people from Dagomba arrived in what is now Burkina Faso during the 11th century, and in c.1200 Ouedraogo, grandson of the king of Dagomba, founded the kingdoms of Ouagadougou and Yatenga. Nassegue, *naba* (king) of Yatenga, captured Timbuktu in the 15th century, but his successor was defeated in 1483 by the Songhais.

The kingdoms were self-sufficient, although some salt was imported and cotton exported. A Moslem community, the Yarsees, grew up, descended from Islamic merchants who had settled in the towns. In the 17th century a neighbouring state arose, centred on Bodo-Dioulasso, into which the Mossi were integrated. In the 18th century Yatenga successfully resisted the eastward drive of the Bambara. The first European missions appeared in around 1890. In 1895 a French mission signed a treaty with the *naba* of Yatenga. In 1896 another mission expelled the ruler of Ouagadougou. French troops occupied the country in 1897. Upper Volta was separated from Upper Senegal-Niger in 1919 then divided between Sudan, the Ivory Coast and Niger until reunification in 1947. It became independent in 1960.

From 1946 politics was dominated by the RDA (African Democratic Assembly). Discontent led to a coup in January 1966 under Sangoule Lamizana. After a period of democracy (1971-75) Lamizana regained power, but was overthrown in November 1980. A coup took place in 1982 and one in August 1983 brought Thomas Sankara to power. In 1984 Upper Volta changed its name to Burkina Faso (Land of Dignity). A border conflict with Mali was settled by treaty in 1975, but re-erupted in 1985 over the supposed mineral wealth of the Aguacher desert. A ceasefire was signed on 30 December. Sankara was overthrown on 15 October 1987 in a military coup which led to a broad coalition.

Burma

BUR
South East Asia
261,228 sq. mi
Pop: 39.2 m
UN

Capital: Rangoon (pop: 2.4 m)
Official language: Burmese
Religion: Buddhist (85 per cent)
System of govt: Socialist republic; independent since 4 January 1948

A Burmese-Tibetan people, the Pyus, settled in the what is now Burma at the beginning of the first century. Buddhism was introduced to the region by King Anawrahta in the 11th century. The Burmese kingdom of Pagan, founded in the 9th century, subjugated the kingdom of the Mons in the south. The arrival of the Mongol hordes under Kublai Khan signalled the destruction of Pagan (1287). The fragmented country was not reunited until the reign of Alaungpaya, in 1752. The Alaungpaya dynasty cultivated the arts. King Bodawpaya (1782-1819) started work on an enormous pagoda in Mingin although this remained unfinished. The Konbaung dynasty, founded by Bodawpaya, continued to expand the empire until 1885 when the dynasty was overthrown by the British, who had first appeared in Burma as far back as 1612.

Three wars (1824-26, 1852-53, 1885) enabled the British to turn Burma into a province of their Indian empire in 1886. Following the recommendations of the Simon Commission on the future of British India, Burma was separated from India in 1937. A nationalist party, the Thakin, founded in 1929 by Aung San and U Nu, played an increasing role in Burmese affairs. Progress towards autonomy was interrupted in 1942 by the Japanese occupation. The first head of government, Aung San, was assassinated in July 1947 and replaced by U Nu, who took the country to independence in January 1948. Faced with rebellions among the Karen and Kachin peoples and by a guerrilla war led by the Communist Party, the democratic government was overthrown in a military coup in September 1958. The prime minister, General Ne Win, was replaced by U Nu who returned to power after the elections of February 1960. The plan for regional autonomy was approved by parliament in 1961, but the military seized power again in 1962. Ne Win set up a centralised socialist structure. In

Burundi

1964 the Burmese Socialist Party Programme (BSPP) became the country's sole party. The economy took a downturn, leading to numerous revolts led by the pro-Chinese "White Flag" communist party which set up an anti-government resistance. Anti-Chinese demonstrations in Rangoon in June 1967 led

to a rupture in relations with China, although Sino-Burmese economic co-operation was re-established in 1970. The funeral of U Thant, Burma's former un secretary general, was the scene of renewed rioting in December 1974 which led to the proclamation of martial law.

Persecution of Rohingya Moslems

led in 1978 to the dramatic flight of 200,000 people to Pakistan, later to be repatriated in 1979 after the intervention of the UN. General Ne Win stepped down from presidency of in 1981 but remained in control of the BSPP. He was replaced by U San Yu. In March 1984 clashes with resis-

tance movements for regional independence led to an incident with Thailand after Burmese troops crossed the frontier whilst pursuing Karen rebels. During the summer of 1988 pro-democracy riots in Burma led to bloody suppression and the declaration of martial law on 3 August.

Burundi

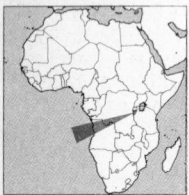

RU
East Africa
10,759 sq. mi
Pop: 5 m
UN, OAU

Capital: Bujumbura (pop: 141,000)
Official languages: Kirundi, French

Religions: Catholic (60 per cent), traditional beliefs
System of govt: Republic since 28 November 1966

According to tradition the kingdom of Burundi was founded in the 17th century by Ntare Rushatsi. The country acquired roughly its present frontiers under the reign of Ntare IV Rugamba (c.1796-1852). The kingdom was weakened by the struggles between King Mwezi Gisabo (c.1852-1908) and his

brothers and by the threat posed by Zanzibar in around 1880. The German conquest started in 1896 and Mwezi was subjugated in 1903. After the First World War Rwanda-Burundi came under Belgian mandate, renewed by the UN in 1946. Burundi became independent on 1 July 1962. The moderate premier, Peter Ngendandunwe, was murdered in January 1965.

King Mwambusa was dethroned by his son, Charles Ndizeye, in July 1966. He was deposed in turn by his premier,

Colonel Michael Micombero, a Tutsi, who declared a republic in November 1966. Tension between Burundi's two tribal groups, the Hutu and the Tutsi, has erupted more than once into bloodshed. The Hutu revolt of April 1972 led to the massacre of more than 100,000 Hutus. Some 50,000 fled to Tanzania and Rwanda. Micombero, a Tutsi, was overthrown in November 1976 by Colonel Jean-Baptiste Bagaza. More Hutu-Tutsi troubles in 1988 reportedly led to thousands of deaths.

Cambodia (Kampuchea)

K
South East Asia
69,898 sq. mi
Pop: 7.6 m
UN

Capital: Phnom Penh (pop: 600,000)
Official language: Khmer
Religions: Buddhist (88 per cent), Moslem (2 per cent)
System of govt: People's republic since January 1979

At the beginning of the first century the Malayo-Polynesian kingdom of Funan appeared in the valley and delta of the river Mekong. This state dominated South East Asia until the middle of the 6th century, when it was conquered by the Khmers who had been settling to the north of Funan since the third

century. The Khmer empire reached its height under Suryavarman II (1113-c.1144) who built Angkor Vat.

Outside threats and colonialism
The Champa kingdom seized and ransacked Angkor several years later (1177). Siam was a growing threat to the declining power of the Khmers. Angkor fell in 1431 and the Khmer sovereigns established their capital near present-day Phnom Penh. From then on until the 19th century the history of Cambodia was dominated by its struggle against Siam and Annam (Vietnam), its two most powerful neighbours, who progressively stripped it of most of its territories.

In 1863 King Norodom (ruled 1859-1904) placed the country under the protectorate of France whose intervention in 1867 forced Siam to recognise Cambodia's "sovereignty". Harsh colonial rule provoked uprisings in 1884 which French troops quelled in 1887. In March 1945 King Norodom Si-

hanouk, backed by the Japanese, proclaimed independence. Following the defeat of Japan, France would only concede limited autonomy, until the 1954 Geneva Convention recognised Cambodia's independence.

Independence
In 1955 Sihanouk abdicated and became prime minister at the head of the People's Socialist Party. Sihanouk's policy of neutrality was followed by mistrust of the USA, which backed the territorial claims of its South Vietnamese ally. Sihanouk was overthrown in March 1970 by the US-backed General Lon Nol and founded a government in exile in Beijing.

Pol Pot's terror and after
Backed by China, a "National Liberation Army" threw out Lon Nol's regime in 1975 and replaced it in April with a reign of terror under Pol Pot's Khmer Rouge, which cost the lives of an estimated one million people. Half

the population vanished between 1975 and 1978. The economy was ruined. The Vietnamese invasion put an end to the Khmer Rouge regime on 10 January 1979. The People's Republic of Kampuchea was proclaimed a few days later. The Vietnamese made Heng Samrin president and the real position of power, minister of defence and head of the Communist Party, was given to Pen Sovan. The Khmer Rouge began a protracted guerrilla war against the Vietnamese, along with the National Liberation Front of Kampuchea, which was united under Sihanouk in 1982. Pol Pot's probably enforced withdrawal from the head of the Khmer Rouge in September 1985 opened the possibility of negotiations. Vietnam vowed in 1985 to withdraw all troops from Kampuchea by 1990, bringing hope of an end to the conflict. Vietnam speeded up troop withdrawals after January 1989 and talks took place between the opposing parties. In 1989 Kampuchea re-adopted the name of Cambodia.

Cameroon

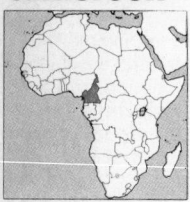

Central Africa
179,558 sq. mi
Pop: 10.7 m
UN, OAU

Capital: Yaoundé (pop: 583,000)
Official languages: French, English

Religions: Traditional beliefs (51 per cent), Moslem
System of govt: Republic; independent since 1 January 1960

The Sao people occupied the north-east of present day Cameroon. The Tikar people appeared in the 16th century and a kingdom of Tikar origin became dominant in c.1700. The north was conquered in 1806 by Ousmane dan Fodio, founder of an Moslem kingdom in the north of present-day Nigeria.

The first European to visit Cameroon had been the Portuguese Fernando Po in 1472. Local tribesmen acted as middlemen in the slave and ivory trades. The British set up missions and trading posts at the end of the 18th century and Germans intervened in the region from 1860 onwards. The coastal territory was annexed by Germany in 1884. The Franco-German Treaty of 1911 extended Cameroon as far as the Congo. In 1919 the League of Nations put the country under British and French

mandates. French Cameroon became independent in 1960, and in 1961 the south of British Cameroon joined the new state, while the north remained part of Nigeria. Ahmadou Ahidjou remained president from 1961 until his retirement in 1982. He was succeeded by his premier, Paul Biya. An attempted coup in April 1984 led to severe repression.

The Cameroon economy, based on cocoa, coffee, wood and oil, is one of Africa's most stable.

Canada

CDN
North America
3,553,357 sq. mi
Pop: 25.3 m
UN, NATO,
OECD, CW

Capital: Ottawa (pop: 819,000)
Official languages: English, French
Religions: Catholic (46 per cent),
Protestant (41 per cent)
System of govt: Constitutional
monarchy; independent since 1931

The territory of present-day Canada was originally peopled by Indian tribes which spread from the Pacific towards the Atlantic. Norsemen from Greenland were the first Europeans to reach Canada, in the 11th century.

Exploration and settlement

Around 1500 a number of European navigators arrived there while searching for a route to the Indies. In 1524 the Italian Verrazzano, sent by King Francis of France, gave the country the name of "New France"

Jacques Cartier landed in the "land of Canada" in 1534 and gave the country its present name (from *kanata*, the Huron-Iroquois word for settlement). He sailed up the St Lawrence river as far as the future sites of the cities of Montreal and Quebec during his second voyage of 1535-36. A first attempt at colonisation failed as did Cartier's third expedition (1541-42) on which he was accompanied by 20 farm workers.

The geographer on the expedition which arrived in 1603 was Samuel de Champlain, who founded Quebec in 1608. In 1627 Cardinal Richelieu created the Company of the Hundred Associates which took possession of the country and was responsible for colonisation, a task entrusted to Champlain. Captured by the English in 1629, Quebec was recaptured in 1632. Quebec's sole resource was the fur trade and its inhabitants were exposed to Iroquois attacks.

In 1663 Louis XIV added Canada to the French crown. Emigrants were sent to accelerate what was proving to be a problematic colonisation. The population rose from 2,000 in 1660 to 10,000 in 1680 as settlers spread along the St Lawrence river. British settlement began in 1668 with the birth of "The Company of Adventurers of England trading into Hudson's Bay", set up by Frenchmen Medart Chouart des Groseilliers and Pierre Radisson under the patronage of Prince Rupert, cousin of King Charles II of England. The renamed Hudson's Bay Company received a charter from King Charles in 1670 granting it exclusive fur trading rights, and claimed the land surrounding the Hudson's Bay as Rupert's Land in honour of Prince Rupert. English and Indian attacks on French Quebec were repulsed. The Treaty of Ryswick (1697) guaranteed the colony's survival and the Iroquois signed a peace treaty in 1701.

Britain became the leading power in North America when it gained Acadia (later Nova Scotia), Hudson's Bay, and Newfoundland from France in the Treaty of Utrecht in 1713.

From 1750 New France, with its population of a mere 70,000 and low immigration, became a prime objective for Britain whose colonies numbered 1,500,000 inhabitants.

Three years later General Montcalm resisted an English attack. Defeated on the plains of Abraham in 1759, he met his death in battle at almost the same time as his British adversary General Wolfe. New France capitulated at Montreal on 8 September 1760 and was definitively ceded to Britain by the Treaty of Paris in 1763. This period saw extensive colonisation of Acadia, renamed Nova Scotia. When the Acadian population refused to serve against the French in 1755 Britain's governor had some 6,000 Acadians taken prisoner and deported to the American colonies. The other Acadians, numbering some 16,000, were able to escape.

British domination

The French Canadians of the new British province of Quebec were allowed to practise both their language and their religion freely. French law was reinstated in June 1774 and the British governor was assisted by a legislative council which included French Canadians.

Canada was attacked by rebel American troops when the British colonies in America revolted, and Quebec militiamen of French origin aided the British victory over Montgomery's American troops in 1775. Around 40,000 American loyalists fled to Canada after US independence was recognised in 1783, seeking to remain under British rule. The Constitutional Act (1791) divided the Canadian provinces into Upper and Lower (French) Canada.

The Anglo-American war of 1812-14 saw Canada confronted by American troops who evacuated the country after the Treaty of Ghent ended the war. A large influx of British immigrants in the early 19th century aided the development of agriculture and small-scale industry. Gradually, popular pressure for active representation in government grew, and conservative resistance ignited the popular movement in Upper Canada. In March 1837 MacKenzie marched on Toronto. Sparked off by Papineau and his "patriots", revolution exploded in Lower Canada where 120,000 French catholics were dominated by 10,000 British protestants. After the suppression of the revolts the provinces, renamed United Canada, were united in 1840. State government was soon set up in the coastal Canadian provinces: Nova Scotia (1848), Prince Edward Island (1851) and in New Brunswick (1852).

Canadian agriculture boomed as the price of wheat doubled in the wake of the Crimean War (1854). Industry was also boosted by a trade agreement signed with the USA in the same year. However, the following economic crisis led to the idea of a federation of the five provinces. The British Parliament passed a law federating four of them, which came into force on 1 July 1867.

The Canadian Confederation

The British America Act, Canada's constitution, created four provinces: Quebec, Ontario, New Brunswick and Nova Scotia. The province of Manitoba was formed in 1870 from the territories attached to the Hudson Bay Company, whose territorial rights, including Rupert's Land, had been sold to the Dominion of Canada in 1869.

The territories to the west of the Rocky mountains, claimed by Vancouver since 1792, joined the confederation in 1871 as British Columbia. Prince Edward Island followed it in 1873. The Conservative governments in power until 1896 oversaw a growth in the economy, and Wilfred Laurier's Liberals (1896-1911) strengthened Canada's political autonomy.

The rapid growth in the population continued (5,700,000 to 7,200,000 from 1901-11) and two new provinces, Alberta and Saskatchewan, were created in 1905.

During the First World War, it sent a sizeable military contingent of 600,000 men, mostly volunteers, to fight alongside other British Empire troops.

The elections of 1921 (the first in which women participated) brought the Liberal party to power. The Conservatives returned to power in 1930.

Canada and independence

Canada, in accordance with the 1931 Statute of Westminster, became a completely self-governing dominion, on an equal footing with Britain, with George V as head of state.

Economic agreements with Britain and the USA were renewed in 1938 by another Liberal government, which also signed a mutual military defence pact with its US neighbour in August 1940. Canada's declaration of war on Germany was the first such declaration in its independent history.

The Liberal party under Louis Saint-Laurent remained in office from 1948 to 1957, and then returned to power after the fall of John George Diefenbaker's Conservative administration (June 1957-February 1963).

Newfoundland became a Canadian province in 1949. The Canadian Parliament adopted a new national flag in December 1964.

French separatism

The independence from Ottawa of the French-speaking Quebec province was extended by the Union Nationale government of Maurice Duplessis and then by the Liberal administration of Jean Lesage (1960-66). De Gaulle's evocation of a "free Quebec" during his visit of July 1967 deepened divisions.

The Liberal party triumphed in the federal elections of 25 June 1968, and Pierre Trudeau became prime minister. In Quebec, Robert Bourassa's Liberal party won provincial elections in April 1970, in which Rene Levesque's separatist Parti Quebecois gained only seven seats.

However, the separatist movement became a priority issue on the national agenda when, in October 1970, the Quebec Liberation Front (FLQ) kidnapped Quebec labour and immigration minister Pierre Laporte and a British diplomat. Trudeau outlawed the FLQ, declared a state of "insurrection" in the province and invoked war emergency powers. Laporte's murdered body was found two days later; the diplomat was released unharmed in December.

The Liberals won another victory in the Quebec elections of 1973. In the face of separatist unrest in Quebec, labour problems culminating in a nationwide general strike (14 October 1976) and the election of Rene Levesque in Quebec in November 1976, Trudeau was rebuffed at the elections of May 1979. The head of the minority government, Conservative Joe Clarke, resigned in December 1979. Trudeau returned to power after the Liberals' decisive victory at the general election in February 1980.

A referendum called in Quebec in May 1980 rejected the "sovereignty-association" plan proposed by Rene Levesque, who was re-elected Quebec premier in April 1981. A constitutional amendment, approved by London in March 1982, was rejected by Quebec. An accord, agreed by the provincial premiers and Prime Minister Brian Mulroney in April 1987 and finalised in Ottawa in June, defined the terms on which the Quebec provincial government would agree to the 1982 amendments to the constitution.

Trudeau resigned in June 1984 and was succeeded as Liberal party leader John Turner. The Conservatives under Brian Mulroney won elections in September.

Canada's economy began to recover a measure of growth. A series of scandals forced three Conservative ministers to resign in 1985. However, in November 1988, the Conservative government of Brian Mulroney was re-elected, on a platform endorsing a historic free trade agreement which he had negotiated with the USA.

Cap Verde

Cape Verde Islands

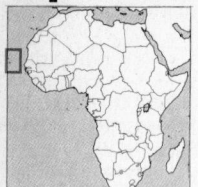

East Atlantic
4,033 km2
Pop. 319,000
UN, CEDEAO,
OAU

Capital: Praia (pop. 49,000)
Official language: Portuguese
Religion: Catholic (90 per cent)

System of govt: Republic.
Independence proclaimed 5 July 1975

The 15 volcanic islands off Cape Verde in West Africa were discovered in 1456 by the Portuguese Cada Mosta and Usodimare. Portuguese traders settled in the islands from 1462 onwards, dominating the native inhabitants. An important port of call, Cape Verde was officially made into a Portuguese colony by the Treaty of Tordesillas (1494). Cape Verde developed into a centre of the slave trade and the islands' econ-

omy was ruined by the abolition of slavery in 1870. Portuguese sovereignty was confirmed by the Berlin conference on the Congo (1884-85). Separatist activity grew in the 1970's, led by the African Party for the Independence of Guinea and Cape Verde (PAIGC), founded by Amilcar Cabral. The struggle against the Portuguese, restricted at first to the colony of Portuguese Guinea (later Guinea-Bissau) on the continent of Africa, spread to the islands. The movement declared the islands' independence in July 1975. Plans for union

with Guinea-Bissau were abrogated by the November 1980 coup in Guinea which ended in the expulsion of a number of Cape Verdean leaders. Shortly afterwards the national assembly adopted the archipelago's first constitution.

In 1981 the PAIGC became the African Party for the Independence of Cape Verde (PAICV). Aristides Pereira has led Cape Verde since independence in 1975, pursuing increasingly moderate socialist policies. One of the chief problems he faces is the islands' over-population.

Central African Republic

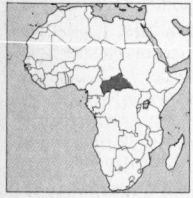

RCA
Central Africa
240,324 sq. mi
Pop: 2.7 m
UN, OAU

Capital: Bangui (pop: 187,000)
Official language: French
Religions: Christian (50 per cent), Traditional beliefs (24 per cent), Moslem (15 per cent)
System of govt: Republic since 1 December 1958.

The oldest populations of the present-day Central African Republic were the Pygmies, Babingas and Bantu tribes. The three Banda kingdoms were created at the beginning of the 19th century. For several centuries the coun-

try had been the object of intense slave hunting, which became more acute in the 19th century. Once established in the Congo basin the French embarked upon the conquest of the north of the region in 1885. Bangui was founded in 1889. After the failure of the Marchand mission (1898), France had to leave the Nile basin and the Bahr al-Ghazal. Oubangui-Chari became a colony in 1905 and, with the Congo and Chad, formed French Equatorial Africa. The frenzied exploitation of the country by concession-holding companies sparked off a number of uprisings which a military expeditionary force could not bring to an end until 1911. In 1946 the colony became an overseas territory within the French Union.

In 1956 it obtained internal autonomy, on 1 December 1958, it was proclaimed the Central African Republic (CAR). Official independence was acquired in 1960. The party in power since independence, MESAN, became

the sole party in 1962. In December 1965 Colonel Jean-Bedel Bokassa overthrew the regime of his cousin, President David Dacko. Bokassa installed a ruthless dictatorship and made himself life president in 1972, and carried out merciless repression of opponents. The republic became a monarchy in December 1976 and Bokassa had himself crowned, Napoleon-style, emperor of Central Africa in 1977. Bokassa had severed all diplomatic relations with China in 1966. Having separated Zaire and Chad, the Central African Republic drew closer to Gabon and the Congo, joining the Central African Customs and Economic Union (UDEAC). The opposition in exile joined together in a common front in 1979. While he was away in Libya, Bokassa was overthrown by David Dacko with French support. Dacko immediately reinstated the republic, but he allowed very few of the political representatives of the opposition in exile a place in his govern-

ment. He won the presidential elections of March 1981 with over half the vote. A new military coup, however, forced him to cede his place on 1 September to the army chief of Staff, General Andre Kolingba. In 1982 a military coup, supported by the Central African People's Liberation Movement (MLPC), failed. On the first anniversary of his coup, Kolingba announced the gradual return to democratic rule in three years. The political opposition remained, nevertheless, in exile, mainly in France. In 1983 the former rector of the university of Bangui was accused of conspiracy and condemned to five years imprisonment and ten years privation of his civil rights. In August 1983 he was pardoned as part of an amnesty granted to 64 political prisoners. In September 1985 President Kolingba appointed a civilian dominated cabinet. In a referendum in November 1986 voters approved the establishment of a one party state, with Kolingba at its head.

Chad

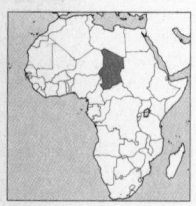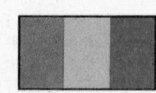

Central Africa
495,752 sq. mi
Pop: 4.79 m
UN, OAU

Capital: N'Djamena
Official languages: French, Arabic
Religions: Moslem (52 per cent), traditional beliefs (43 per cent), Christian
System of govt: Republic; independence proclaimed 11 August 1960

Rock carvings found in the region of Lake Chad date back to the Neolithic era, and so came after the phase of desert formation which began around 7000 BC. The Kanem kingdom was founded in the 9th century by the dy-

nasty of the Sefawa who were of nomadic origin. Having been converted to Islam, Kanem was defeated in the 13th century by the Bulalas of Bahr el-Ghazal. The Sefawa took refuge in Bornu and then reconquered Kanem in the 16th century.

The sultanate of Bagirmi was conquered between 1892 and 1894 by the adventurer Rabeh and was integrated into his vast kingdom, which extended as far as Darfour in the east, Kanem and Ouaddaï in the north, Adamaoua in the south, and beyond Lake Chad in the west.

After eliminating some French settlers, Rabeh was defeated and killed in April 1900. The territory of Chad was gradually conquered and formed part of French Equatorial Africa.

On the invasion of France in 1940, Chad was the first French colony to back de Gaulle's Free France, in August 1940, and served as a base for operations in Libya until the Axis de-

feat in North Africa in 1943. In 1958 Chad obtained autonomy as a republic within the French Community. The republic remained integrated into the French Community after its accession to independence in August 1960. The first president of Chad was Francois Tombalbaye, head of the Chadian Progressive Party (PPT), elected in April 1962. The republic tried to forge economic links in Africa and with Europe. In 1967 Tombalbaye had to face a pro-Libyan rebellion in the Moslem north, which was supported by Libya. After French intervention (1969), the rebels regrouped in Sudan. Tombalbaye split with Tripoli in 1971, and two years later a Colonel Gaddafi-inspired coup brought General Felix Malloum to power. The French had to leave the country. Libyan preparations for a new campaign led the government to conclude a cease-fire agreement with the Moslem rebels. Their leader, Hissene Habre, became prime minister. Fight-

ing broke out again, however, the following year, and President Malloum went into exile in Nigeria.

The new president, Goukouni Oueddei, a Moslem, was unable to put an end to the troubles, and Hissene Habre seized N'Djamena in June 1982. Oueddei took refuge in Algeria and formed a government in exile. In June 1983 the rebels took Faya Largeau, which led to the immediate granting of American aid and assistance to Hissene Habre. France intervened in August 1983 and fighting ceased. In September 1984 the French and Libyans agreed to a withdrawal of forces, with Libyans, however, remaining stationed in the north. In November the Chad reconciliation conference at Brazzaville broke down. A new rebel offensive began in February 1986, but was stopped by French air power on 16 February. Both sides pledge to respect a cease-fire in late 1987 and Chad restored relations with Libya in October 1988.

Chile

RCH
South America
284,520 sq. mi
Pop: 12.07 mill
UN, LAIA, OAS

Capital: Santiago (pop: 4.8 mill.)
Official language: Spanish
Religions: Catholic (80 per cent),
Protestant
System of govt: Republic; independence proclaimed 1 January 1818.

The Atacama region in the north of present-day Chile has yielded traces of human occupation as early as c.12,000 BC, in particular at the site of San Vicente de Tagua-Tagua. Numerous remains testifying to human presence as long ago as 8000 BC, can also be found in southern Chile. In the centre of the country the ceramics of El Molle, produced up until the sixth century, have created remarkable containers in a variety of shapes, both human and animal. The principal people of ancient Chile, the Araucans, were gradually conquered, first by the Incas in around 1480 and then by the Spanish, beginning when Diego de Almagro ventured from Peru in 1535. A second expedition under Pizarro in 1540, enabled Pedro de Valdivia to push the Araucans back south of the river Bio-Bio. He founded Santiago in 1541 and Concepcion in 1550. A widespread Araucan revolt followed. In 1557 the revolt led by Lautaro and Cautipolican ended in the Battle of Mataquito and in 1598 the Spanish were pushed back to the far side of the Bio-Bio.

The river was recognised as the frontier in 1726, by a treaty, in effect, guaranteeing the independence of the Araucans. However, widespread revolts took place until 1773 and pockets of Indian resistance survived until the end of the 19th century. British and Dutch set-tlements on the Chilean coast between 1587 and 1623 were unable to withstand Araucan harassment and proved to be shortlived. This climate of insecurity prevented Chile's development as a colonial economy, and between 1544 and 1778 the country remained simply the province of "New Estremadura" in the Spanish vice-royalty of Peru. At the beginning of the 18th century the major ports of Concepcion and Valparaiso were controlled by French shipowners and served as ports of call on the way to the greater riches of Peru. Chilean development did not get underway until after 1778 when Spain established a captaincy-general and opened up free trade relations with the country. The economy was based on agriculture, organised by the great *haciendas* (estates) belonging to wealthy landowners, with most produce being exported to Peru. The system of *encomienda*, abolished in 1790, organised the exploitation of the native work force. Britain's growing role in Chile (Valparaiso was a major base for British ships) along with the occupation of Spain by Napoleon, (1808) precipitated the country into a struggle for independence.

Chilean independence

The government assembly formed at Santiago in September 1810 demanded sovereign rights and proclaimed Chile open to international trade (1811). An army of Chilean insurgents was defeated by colonial troops sent from Peru at Rancagua in 1814. The insurgent leader, Bernardo O'Higgins, joined José San Martin's independent troops in Argentina and the two re-entered Chile in February 1817 and defeated the loyalists at Chacabuco. The proclamation of the Chilean Republic soon followed. The south was liberated after the battle of the river Maipo (5 April 1818). After the dictatorship of O'Higgins (1817-23) and Freire (1823-26) a conservative constitution was established in May 1833. Spain officially recognised Chilean independence in 1844. The war against Spain and Peru of 1866 was followed by the Pacific War of 1879. The conflict, which had erupted over the nitrate wealth of the Atacama desert, ended with Chile triumphing first over Peru (1883) and then over Bolivia (1884), the latter losing its access to the sea. Chile retained the province of Tarapaca and the town of Arica. Economic growth through mineral wealth and the emergence of a power-hungry middle class led to revolution in 1891 from which parliamentary power emerged stronger than before. Conflict with Argentina over the proposed Andean frontier was resolved in 1904 after mediation by King Edward VII of Britain.

Attempted social reform

Thanks to its mineral wealth, Chile profited from shortages elsewhere during the First World War. The post-war crisis brought Arturo Allesandri, leader of the Liberal Alliance party, to power. He was overthrown by a coup, then returned to power by another army faction in 1925. Seeing his reformist policies blocked by the Chilean congress, Allesandri imposed presidential rule. Far-reaching social reforms were introduced. From 1938-52 Chile was governed by the Popular Front.

Chile was the only country in South America in which communists participated in government, until the Chilean Communist party was banned in 1948. Chile's raw material wealth helped it to another period of economic expansion during the Second World War.

By the end of his term President Carlos Ibanez del Campo (1952-58) had not managed to end a new economic crisis which had brought with it high levels of inflation and unemployment. Defeating the socialist candidate, Salvador Allende, at the elections, the conservative Jorge Allesandri pursued a policy of economic austerity from 1958 to 1964 which was supported by the USA. At the elections of November 1964 Allende was defeated once again, this time by the Christian democrat Eduardo Frei. His plan of "revolution in freedom", of agricultural reform and taking con-trol of the mining industry, at that time entirely in the hands of US companies, did not bring the expected results. None of the candidates could win an outright majority at the elections in September 1970, and Allende, the candidate of the Popular Unity party, was designated president by the Chilean Congress in October. The mines and a number of banks were nationalised and the great plantations transformed into co-operatives.

But economic crisis followed initial euphoria; foreign credits disappeared and unrest and strikes shook the country. Allende was forced into a number of ministerial reshuffles and had to ask the military into his government. The drastic fall in the world price of copper and the increasing paralysis of the economy (in which, as it was revealed shortly afterwards, the American CIA played some part), led to the coup of 11 September 1973 during which Allende was assassinated.

Military dictatorship

The military junta, led by General Augusto Pinochet, banned all political activity, dissolved the parliament and instituted a policy of brutality towards its opponents.

Pinochet returned the economy to private capital. The economic situation was stabilised in 1979 at the cost of severe austerity measures.

A referendum in 1980 gave Pinochet another eight years of power. From 1983 a popular movement, spurred on by the renewed instability of Chile's economic position, openly opposed the power of the junta which introduced special powers for the "Supreme Head of the Nation", General Pinochet. A total of seventeen demonstrators (government figures) were killed in anti-Pinochet rallies in August 1983.

Pinochet, confident of victory, asked for eight more years of rule at the end of his present term in a plebiscite in October 1988. He lost the vote, and a general election to find a successor was scheduled for 14 December 1989.

China

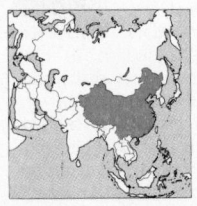

TJ
Asia
3,682,131 sq. mi
Pop: 1,100,000 m
UN

Capital: Beijing (pop: 5.9 m)
Official language: Chinese
Religions: Confucianism, Taoism, Buddhism; Christianity, Islam.
System of govt: People's republic, proclaimed 1 October 1949

The discoveries made in China from 1920 onwards have made it possible to identify some of the earliest known human remains, in particular the most archaic type of *homo erectus* found to date, from about 600,000 years ago. It was found in 1964 in Shaanxi, at Lantian.

The early historic period was typified, from c.4000 BC to c.1000 BC, by painted pottery ("Yangshao" culture in Henan and Gansu). A bronze-based civilisation probably appeared in Henan between 2000 BC and 1000 BC, as shown by the bronze foundries discovered in Zhengzhou, the first Shang capital of Henan.

The Shang dynasty (c.1766-c.1100 BC)

After the legendary Xia dynasty, the first documented Chinese dynasty was that of the Shang who spread to their last capital at Anyang (Henan) and along the middle and lower course of the Yellow River. During their rule bronze-based art attained a remarkable degree of mastery.

The Zhou dynasty (c.1100-221 BC)

The Shang dynasty was overthrown in 1122 BC by Wu, leader of the western principality of Zhou in the river Wei valley. Political change was accompanied by a religious upheaval. The idea of "virtue" was seen as the foundation of the sovereign's ability to govern. The Zhou capital remained at Hao on the Wei until 771 BC when the invasion of nomads from the north forced them to move to Luoyang (Henan).

The "Springs and Autumns" period of the eastern Zhou (771-481 BC) saw the feudal system extended. The numerous small city-states of the centre were surrounded by larger, semi-barbarian states, five of which were to play an increasingly important role: the Qin (Shanxi), Jin (Shanxi), Qi (Shandong), Chu (Hubei) and Song (Henan). In the state of Lu (Shandong) Confucius (551-479 BC) spread his teaching of the virtue of the higher man, based on the

China

idea of harmony, which was transmitted in writing in the "Lunyu". The final period of the Zhou, known as the time of "Warring States" (481-221 BC) saw the start of a widespread war of annexation and two of the seven principalities, the Qin and the Zhou, emerged, enlarged from the conflicts. The armies of the king of Qin gradually won the whole of China.

The Qin Dynasty (221-206 BC)
The conquest of the land of Qi by the Qin prince in 221 BC marked the birth of the Qin dynasty. King Zheng of Qin had himself proclaimed emperor of China (after his death known as *Shi Huangdi*, First Emperor) and ordered the construction of a "Great Wall" to protect the empire against the Xiongnu (sometimes identified with the Huns of European history). Qin Shi Huangdi abolished the reign of the feudal principalities and unified the empire. Administration was centralised and strengthened. The struggle against the old social order led to the persecution of the Confucians and the destruction of classical books. Writing, weights and measures were standardised. On the death of Qin Shi Huangdi (210 BC) the country was shaken by a number of rebellions and a rich peasant, Liu Bang, succeeded in mounting the throne in 202 BC, thus founding the Han dynasty.

The Han dynasty (206 BC-220 AD)
Liu Bang, known to history by his temple name Han Gaozu (d. 195 BC), restored the unity of the empire. It was under the Emperor Wudi, who reigned from 140 BC to 87 BC that Confucianism was rehabilitated. Civil servants were chosen on a competitive basis and the mandarinate appeared. The empire's territorial expansion continued. The Xiongnu were defeated in 119 BC, giving China mastery of the Silk Route and enabling it to annex vast territories in the south. China imposed its rule in parts of Vietnam and Korea and advanced as far as the Pamirs in Central Asia. After the reign of the usurper Wang Mang (9-23) the Han dynasty re-established itself in the wake of the "Red Eyebrows" revolt.

Guang Wudi was crowned in 23 AD. The capital then moved from Chang'an (Shaanxi) to Luoyang (Henan). The nomads were pacified at the beginning of the first century at the same time as the first Buddhist communities made their appearance in the Chinese capital. Trade, science and the arts were all at their height. The revolt of the Taoist-inspired "Yellow Turbans" broke out in 184 and the empire was subsequently shared between the three generals who suppressed it.

The barbarian invasions (220-581)
After the fall of the dynasty China was divided into three kingdoms, Wei in the north, Shu Han in the Sichuan and Wu in the south. The Xi Jin dynasty was founded at Wei in 265 by

the prince Sima Yan and in 280 it succeeded in restoring a fragile unity to China. This, however, could not survive the invasion of the northern barbarians. The Emperor Xi Jing was captured in 311. The dynasty took refuge in Nanjing in the south. The Xianbi (Tabgatch) invaded the north of China in 349 and founded the kingdom of the northern Wei which was to survive until 507. A series of dynasties followed in the south with Buddhism establishing itself in Wei (386) and in Nanjing (502).

The Sui Dynasty (581-618)
The Sui dynasty annexed the kingdoms of the south and re-established the supremacy of the emperor against the Turkish kingdoms in Central Asia. It was, however, defeated in Korea and the Turks attacked the north, the Emperor Yangdi (died 617) being taken prisoner.

The Tang dynasty (618-906)
China recovered its power and its prosperity under the reign of Taizong (Li Shimin) (627-649). The tea trade was flourishing, the use of currency had become widespread, and printing had been invented. Buddhism once more enjoyed royal favour, in particular after the journey of the monk Xuanzang to India (629). On the death of Gaozong, son of Taizong, in 683, the throne was usurped by the Empress Wu Zetian (died 705). The great poets Du Fu, Li Bo wrote in the reign of Xuanzong (712-55), in whose reign Chinese influence spread across Central Asia. Conditions for peasants, oppressed and overtaxed, worsened before the last Tang emperor was overthrown in 907.

The Song dynasty (960-1279)
In 960, after a period of anarchy, Zhao Kuangyin founded the Song dynasty and conquered, by 979, all the Chinese kingdoms with the exception of the Liao or Qitan (Khitan) kingdom around modern Beijing. Political stability was restored and trade flourished. The years after 1000 saw the appearance of inventions such as the compass, gunpowder and moveable printing type. In 1115 the kingdom of the Jin dynasty was founded in the north, forcing the Song to move their capital from Kaifeng to Hangzhou in 1127. Mongol invaders led by Genghiz Khan and his successors finally crushed the Jin in 1234. The Song Empire disappeared when its capital was captured by the Mongol Kublai Khan in 1276.

The Yuan dynasty (1280-1368)
Kublai Khan was proclaimed emperor of China in 1280 and founded the Yuan dynasty with its capital at Khanbalik (Beijing). It was at Khanbalik that Kublai received the Venetian Marco Polo on his first journey in 1275. Mongol attempts to revive the devastated empire failed in the face of the growing peasant poverty and un-

rest, which became a nationwide rebellion after the Yellow River flooded in 1351. The "Red Turbans" revolt, supported by the privileged classes, ended in the fall of the Yuan dynasty in 1368.

The Ming dynasty (1368-1644)
A peasant, Zhu Yuanzhang, seized power and founded the Ming dynasty adopting the name of Hongwu (died 1398). The most opulent reign of the dynasty (1403-24) was that of the Yongle emperor who endowed his capital, Beijing, with most of the splendid palaces still to be seen today. However, the restoration of agriculture and irrigation works was of little use to the peasants, exploited by a new class of civil servant. Another problem was Japanese piracy.

Portugal was permitted to found the first European commercial settlement in China at Macao in 1557. The first Jesuit missionaries arrived in 1582. Towards the end of the reign of Emperor Wanli (1573-1619) the first league of Manchu tribes was formed. The first of the Manchus' kingdoms, with its capital at Mukden (Shenyang), became a rival, north east of the empire.

The Qing dynasty (1644-1912)
Called in to help put down a rebellion, the Manchus refused to leave Beijing and their new king, Shunzhi, was declared emperor. Under the Kangxi reign (1662-1722), the Jesuits enjoyed their period of greatest influence. A treaty with Russia in 1689 established the northern frontier between the two empires. Taiwan was annexed in 1683 and in 1696 a protectorate was established over Mongolia. A first expedition to Tibet in the same year failed, but the country was annexed in 1720.

The reconstruction of Ming palaces in Beijing and the embellishment of the city with parks and palaces was continued under Qianlong (1736-96). By Qianlong's death the Chinese empire had reached its greatest epoch. But decay soon set in; the "White Lotus" revolts (ended 1804) and the uprisings of the Heavenly Reason society (1813), endangered the emperor himself. The only trade routes open to the west were now Guangzhou (Canton), from which the British exported tea and silk, and Macao, a Portuguese settlement.

Guangzhou became a key market for opium coming from British India, but the trade was banned in 1839. The British response to the ban led to the the Opium War of 1841-42, ending in the treaty of Nanjing (Nanking) which ceded Hong Kong to Britain as well as various trade concessions.

European penetration (1844-94)
Chinese military weakness, exposed in the first Opium War, led to the signing of further trade agreements with France and the USA. A second Opium War broke out in 1856 with Europeans and Americans intervening in 1858 and 1860. The Chinese armies

were defeated at Baliqiao near Beijing; the capital was ransacked and the summer palace set on fire. China conceded numerous trade advantages to the western powers. In 1864 the empire suppressed the pseudo-Christian Taiping rebellion, led by failed scholar Hong Xiuquan. Foreign influence grew under the Tongzhi (died 1874) and the Guangxu emperors. They renounced suzerainty over Amman (Vietnam) and Tonking after war with France (1884-85).

End of the Qing dynasty (1894-1911)
Japan gained the Liaodong peninsula and Taiwan, in the wake of the first Sino-Japanese war (1894-95). Worried by this, France, Russia and Germany obliged Japan to give back Liaodong. The foreign powers established spheres of interest and lease territories along the coast, as well as economic concessions in mining and railway building. China thus became a theatre for imperialist competition.

In 1898 the former regent, Empress Dowager Cixi, reacted against radical reforms, staged a coup and took the Guangxu emperor prisoner. A popular anti-foreign revolt followed, organised by the Yihetuan secret society (Boxers) and encouraged by court conservatives. Many foreigners were killed. Eight-nation allied intervention put an end to the Boxer Rebellion in 1900. A huge punitive indemnity was imposed on China in 1901. Western domination grew, and with it discontent with the dynasty. On the death of Cixi and Guangxu in 1908 three-year-old Puyi became emperor.

Revolution and republic
The Guomindang (Nationalist party), founded by Sun Yat-sen, was behind the revolutionary uprising which broke out in the Yangzi valley on 10 October 1911. The success of republican ideas was assured on 29 December when Sun Yat-sen was elected provisional president of the republic by an assembly of provincial delegates. Yuan Shikai became president of the republic in 1912 after the abdication of the last emperor on 12 February. In 1915 Japan tried to impose a protectorate over China after Germany's leasehold in Shandong province. On the death in 1916 of Yuan Shikai, who had failed to become emperor himself, China was plunged into over a decade of civil war among a multitude of militarists (warlordism). In the south Sun Yat-sen established a rival republican regime at Guangzhou (Canton). The intellectual and revolutionary 4 May movement (1915-23) was led by men such as Li Dazhao and Chen Duxiu, who founded the Chinese communist party in 1921. In 1924 Sun Yat-sen's Guomindang was reorganised with the support of the USSR. The party split upon the death of Sun Yat-sen (1925). The military commander Chiang Kai-chek gained control of the Guomindang in

1926 and embarked on the "Northern Expedition" to unify the country. His attack on the communists forced them underground in 1927. The Chinese Soviet Republic was proclaimed in Jiangxi in 1931 as the Japanese invaded Manchuria, turning it into a satellite state under China's last emperor, Puyi. After a prolonged attack by nationalist troops the communists were forced to leave Jiangxi in 1934. They reached Shaanxi in 1935 after the Long March. The Japanese invasion of 1937 brought about a "united front" of nationalist and communist resistance. The struggle between the two factions was resumed in 1946 after Japan had been defeated. The communist People's Liberation Army, supported by the peasant masses, the moderates and the USSR, advanced from the north and eventually triumphed in 1949. Chiang Kai-chek took refuge in Taiwan on 8 December after the People's Republic of China had been proclaimed by Mao Zedong (Tse-tung) on 1 October.

The People's Republic after 1949

A treaty of friendship and alliance was signed with the USSR in 1950. Chinese collectivisation was based on the Soviet example. Tibet was annexed in 1951. China intervened militarily in the Korean War (1950-53) on the side of North Korea and then lent support to the Vietminh in Indochina. To overcome opposition Mao Zedong launched

the "Hundred Flowers" campaign in 1956 and then the revolutionary "Great Leap Forward" in 1958. The break with the "revisionist" USSR in 1960 accelerated the progressive decline in the economy. The rivalry between Mao and the head of state, Liu Shaoqi, broke out with the launching of the "Cultural revolution" in 1966. Mao reorganised and purged the party, relying on the destructive "Red Guard" youth. Order was more or less restored with the intervention of the People's Liberation Army. Liu was stripped of office in 1968.

The predominance of centrist politics, represented by Zhou Enlai (Chou En-lai), was affirmed by the visit of US President Nixon in 1972 and the signing of a first treaty with Japan in 1974 following the normalisation of relations in 1972. Deng Xiaoping pursued a policy of moderation following his return to the leadership of the party in 1973. This modernist, moderate policy was opposed to the radical movement led by Mao's wife Jiang Qing and the "Shanghai group" who took control of the party's politburo at the end of 1975. On the death of Zhou Enlai in early February 1976, Hua Guofeng became prime minister and Deng Xiaoping was stripped of his functions.

Mao died on 9 September 1976 and Hua Guofeng arranged for the arrest of radicals of the "Gang of Four" along with Jiang Qing (condemned to death

but reprieved in 1981).

Mao's ideas have been called into question as of 1978 and Deng Xiao ping was rehabilitated. Relations with Vietnam became strained after the Vietnamese invasion of Cambodia where the Khmer Rouge enjoyed Chinese support.

Deng Xiaoping's visit to the United States in 1979 signalled a radical change in Chinese foreign policy. The policy of "demaoification" was accentuated. Hua Guofeng was removed in 1980 and was replaced as general secretary of the party by Hu Yaobang, an ally of Deng Xiaoping. Zhao Ziyang became prime minister and Liu Shaoqi was rehabilitated. Reorganisation of the army has continued while priority has been accorded to economic development, with more private enterprise being allowed in 1984.

In 1983 the assembly elected a president of the republic, Li Xiannan, for the first time since Liu Shaoqi was stripped of office in 1968. Rapprochement with the USA has accelerated since President Reagan's visit to China in April 1984, signing an agreement on nuclear co-operation in the civilian domain. In September 1984 China and Britain signed an accord to ensure the smooth handover of Hong Kong in 1997, guaranteeing its present economic system for 50 years. Queen Elizabeth visited China in 1986.

In a victory for conservatives, Hu

Yaobang was replaced as party leader in 1986 after failing to prevent six weeks of student demonstrations for greater political freedom. His successor Zhao Ziyang formally became general secretary when Deng "retired" in November 1987.

Anti-Chinese unrest in Tibet was violently suppressed in 1988. The death of disgraced reformist Hu Yaobang in early 1989 sparked massive student-led demonstrations, especially in Beijing, for more democracy. The students peacefully occupied the centre of the city, embarrassing the government during the historic visit in May of Soviet President Gorbachev, the first by a Soviet leader since Khrushchev. Students and workers halted efforts by prime minister Li Peng, acting on the ailing Deng's authority, to send troops into the city until the night of 3 June, when tougher units cleared the demonstrators in an orgy of bloodshed.

Thousands are reported to have died on that night and in the ensuing crackdown against demonstrators and sympathisers all over China. Zhao Ziyang, who had shown sympathy to the students, followed his predecessor into disgrace.

The widespread foreign outrage at the massacre has hit China's diplomatic and trade relations and severely blackened Deng's "reformist" image. Political change now appears unlikely before his death.

Colombia

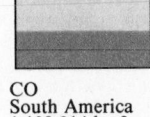

CO
South America
1,138,914 km2
Pop. 28.65 mill.
UN, LAIA, OAS

Capital: Bogota (Pop. 3.97 mill.)
Official language: Spanish
Religion: Catholic (95 per cent)
System of govt: Republic since the constitution of 1886

The colonial period

The first European to reach the coast of Colombia was the Spaniard Alonso de Ojeda in 1499. At that time a great centre of Indian culture still existed in Colombia, that of the Muiscas on the high eastern plateau. In the following years voyages to Colombia increased and Bacata (Bogota), founded in 1538, rapidly became an important trade centre. New Granada, created by Spain in 1547, included the territories of present-day Colombia, Panama, Ecuador and Venezuela. The principal wealth of New Granada was agricultural. Great estates exploited the In-

dian work force and later black slaves brought to Colombia. Attached to the Spanish viceroyalty of Peru until 1717, New Granada became an autonomous viceroyalty after 1739 with Bogota as its capital. The growing creole consciousness led to the revolt of Socorro in 1781. Demands for independence also grew, and a junta was formed at Bogota in July 1810. The federation of the provinces of New Granada declared independence a year later. The ensuing struggle was led by Simon Bolivar.

Independence

Bolivar's victory at Boyaca in 1819 led to the proclamation of the republic of Gran Colombia, made up of Colombia and Venezuela followed by Panama and Ecuador in 1821-22. Venezuela and Ecuador seceded in 1830. From then on the republic of New Granada (Colombia and Panama) was torn by the opposition of federalist liberals and centralist conservatives, which threw the country into civil war in 1854 and led to dictatorship. On their return to power in 1863 the liberals gave the "United States of Colombia" a federalist constitution. Another civil war erupted in 1876, and the new republic of Colombia was born in 1886, when the conservatives gave the country a centralist con-

stitution, for the most part still in force today. The federalists organised a number of uprisings, in particular the "War of a Thousand Days" (1899-1903).

The 20th Century

Colombia possessed a very poorly developed transport system and an economy essentially based on coffee. The independence of Panama, which was backed by the USA, ended Colombia's-control of trade between the Atlantic and Pacific oceans. US compensation, along with the political stability brought by the government of General Rafael Reyes (1904-09), made a programme of economic development possible. However, most sectors of the economy (coffee, bananas and, from 1925, oil), remained in the hands of US companies. The 1929 world economic crisis struck Colombia hard, and the liberals returned to power. Under Alfonso Lopez Pumarejo (1934-38) they introduced a programme of social and anti-clerical reforms. Lopez was again in power from 1942-45.

The liberal tendency became more radical after the war under the influence of Jorge Eliecer Gaitan, who was assassinated in April 1948. This event caused an insurrection which heralded a period of civil war. Nearly 200,000

died by 1953. The coup led by General Rojas Pinilla in June 1953 interrupted the violence. Pinilla sought election in 1957 but was confronted by strikes and a "National Front" of liberals and conservatives. Thereafter power switched regularly between the two parties. The conservative Belisario Betancur was elected president in August 1982.

Since 1948 Colombia has been the scene of a Cuban-inspired guerrilla war, fuelled by the poverty of the peasants. The "Revolutionary Armed Forces of Colombia" (FARC) were created in 1966, whilst the pro-Sandinista urban guerrilla movement "M 19" was behind incidents such as the seizure of hostages at the embassy of the Dominican Republic in 1980. In 1984 President Betancur entered into negotiations with the guerrillas, resulting in the suspension of hostilities by the FARC, which became the legal Patriotic Union Party in March 1985. But the "M 19" group denounced the cease-fire in June 1985, and in November took 300 people hostage at the Bogota law courts. Over 100 people, including many senior judges and 35 terrorists, died when government troops stormed the courts. Colombia also faces problems of drug trafficking and a precarious economy.

Comoros

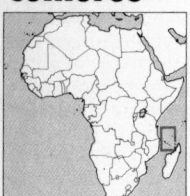

F
Indian Ocean
719 sq. mi
Pop: 422,000
UN, OAU

Capital: Moroni (pop: 17,000)
Official languages: French, Arabic
Religion: Moslem (95 per cent)

System of govt: Islamic federal republic; independent since 6 July 1975

The Comoros are an archipelago of four islands, Mayotte, Ngazidja (Grand Comoros), Moili (Mohéli) and Ndzouani (Anjouan). Visited from the 11th century onwards by Arab navigators, the archipelago was also to be frequented by Persians who arrived from Chiraz in the 15th century. Rival sultanates were founded here by Madagascans and Arabs. Mayotte became the first of the islands to be attached to the French island of Reunion in 1843. The others followed in 1886. The archipelago became a French colony in 1912, and was attached administratively to the neighbouring French possession of Madagascar until 1946, when the Comoros obtained autonomy.

After becoming an overseas territory following the referendum of 1958, the Comoros started to demand their independence from 1972 onwards. In a referendum in December 1974, a large majority voted in favour of independence. An architect of independence, Ahmed Abdallah, issued a declaration of independence on 6 July 1975, but was overthrown a few days later by a military coup. From then on Ali Soilih installed a neo-socialist dictatorship until the return of Ahmed Abdallah after a coup in May 1978. He was elected president at the end of the year, following the adoption of the constitution of the new federal and Islamic Republic of the Comoros.

In January 1985 Ahmed Abdallah also became head of the government of the Comoros. Comoros exports of aromatic plants account for 70 per cent of the raw materials used by the French perfume industry.

Congo

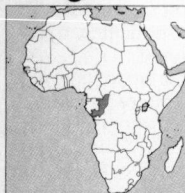

RCB
Central Africa
132,046 sq. mi
Pop: 2.18 m
UN, OAU

Capital: Brazzaville (pop: 600,000)
Official language: French
Religions: Christian (50 percent), traditional beliefs (42 per cent)
System of govt: People's republic since January 1970; independent since 15 August 1960

According to 16th century Portuguese reports the kingdoms of the Savannah to the north of the Congo were dominated by the Tyo (or Teke) kingdom. The Teke king, or Makoko, refrained from intervening in the tribal structure of the various ethnic groups. The kingdom enjoyed a monopoly in the trading of slaves, replaced in the 19th century by the exploitation of ivory. French presence in the Congo, which began with the explorations of Savorgnan de Brazza in 1875, was affirmed by the Makoko treaty of 1880. The Congo became a colony in 1866, gaining administrative autonomy in 1903. The government of French Equatorial Africa established its headquarters at Brazzaville in 1910. Oppressive colonial government led to a number of uprisings, some of which disrupted building of the Congo-Ocean railway between 1923 and 1934.

Matswanaism, a movement founded by André Matswa, sustained the agitation right up until his death in prison in 1942. The Congo became an overseas territory of the French Union in 1946. At this time the political life of the Congo was dominated by three individuals: Jean Félix Tchicaya, head of the Congo Progressive party (PPC) and a member of the African Democratic assembly (RDA); the socialist J Opangault, and the priest Fulbert Youlou who founded the Democratic Union for the Defence of African Interests. Self-determination was approved by referendum in 1958 and Youlou was elected president in November 1959.

The republic of the Congo became fully independent on 15 August 1960. Youlou was forced to resign after the strikes and riots of August 1963. In response to the unrest the new government, under Massamba-Débat, established one party, the National Revolutionary Movement (MNR) and moved further to the left, strengthening the country's links with the USSR, China and Cuba. A coup attempt by Marien Ngouabi failed in June 1966. The 1968 crisis forced Massamba-Débat to cede to Ngouabi's National Revolutionary council. Ngouabi was elected president in January 1969. A year later Congo became the People's Republic of the Congo.

The sole party, the Congo Workers' Party (PCT), which had replaced the MNR, faced a number of attempts to destabilise the country and Ngouabi was assassinated in 1977. Massamba-Débat, who was accused of the murder, was executed with six others on 25 March.

In February 1979 President Joachim Yhombi-Opango was expelled from the PCT and was replaced by Colonel Denis Sassou Nguesso, who continued in power in 1989. A new constitution in July 1979 reaffirmed the government's socialist leanings and the domination of the PCT. Economic co-operation with capitalist countries, such as France, has continued more or less undisturbed.

Costa Rica

CR
Central America
19,730 sq. mi
Pop: 2.8 m
UN, CARICOM, OAS

Capital: San Jose (pop: 241,000)
Official language: Spanish
Religion: Catholic (95 per cent)
System of govt: Republic; independence obtained 15 September 1821

The east coast of Costa Rica, between the empires of the Aztecs and Mayas and that of the Incas, was discovered by Europeans when Christopher Columbus landed in 1502 during his fourth voyage to the Americas. Twenty years later the Spanish explorer Davila took an expedition into the centre of the country. Military conquest, however, did not start until 1561. In 1563 Juan de Coronado founded the town of Cartago, which remained Costa Rica's capital until 1823.

A number of Indian rebellions took place throughout the colonial period, in particular in the Talamanca region, notably in 1709. A part of the Spanish "captaincy" of Guatemala, Costa Rica's main income was derived from the raising of mules to carry goods between the Atlantic and Pacific Ocean through Panama. On its independence in 1821 Costa Rica was integrated into the Mexican empire. From 1823 it constituted an independent state in the Central American Confederation, and abolished slavery.

The federation broke up in 1838 and Costa Rica proclaimed independence as a republic on 3 August 1848. Coffee-growing predominated under the government of Braulio Carillo (1835-42), and the first banana concession on the Atlantic coast was awarded to the US United Fruit Company. Costa Rica's political life was disturbed only by a border conflict with Nicaragua, resolved in 1899. Under the presidency of Gonzales Flores (1914-17), the state began to intervene in an economy hitherto previously dominated by US companies. The dictatorship of General Tinoco (1917-19) brought Costa Rica's liberal development to a temporary end. An old border wrangle with Panama was settled by a treaty in 1944. The victory of the liberal Otilio Ulate in the presidential elections of 1948 led to a military coup. The civil war which followed saw the victory of the "Caribbean Legion" under Jose Figueres Ferrer, who succeeded President Ulate in November 1953.

The events of 1948 had led to the adoption of a new constitution on 7 November 1949. Costa Rica renounced the possession of military forces, but still maintained an armed civil guard. The presidency of Figueres lasted until 1958, and was marked by a number of serious border incidents with Nicaragua and, at home, by a reformist but resolutely anti-communist policy. The powerful United Fruit Company agreed to operate in a way more beneficial to the country. Figueres' National Liberation Party still managed to dominate Costa Rican political life with the re-election of Figueres himself in 1970, Daniel Oduber in 1974 and Luis Alberto Monge in 1982. From 1984 Costa Rica was indirectly involved in the Nicaraguan conflict with the US-backed "Contras" setting up bases on its territory. Oscar Arias Sanchez, who was elected president in 1986, won the Nobel Peace Prize in 1987 for his key role in a peace plan aimed at ending wars in Nicaragua and El Salvador. Colombian drug gangs moved into Costa Rica in 1987, prompting some citizens to hire bodyguards.

Cuba

C
Caribbean
44,206 sq. mi
Pop: 10.3 m
UN, COMECON,
OAS (observer)

Capital: Havana (pop: 2.1 m)
Official language: Spanish
Religion: Catholic (85 per cent)
System of govt: Socialist republic since
1 January 1959

Spanish domination

The eastern coast of Cuba was among the first parts of the New World known to Europeans; it was discovered by Christopher Columbus during his first voyage in 1492. The island was conquered in 1511-13 by Diego Velasquez. The native population of around 50,000 was rapidly decimated.

In 1519 the *conquistador* Cortes used Cuba as a springboard for the Spanish conquest of Mexico. The colony developed very rapidly with stock-breeding, ink-producing plants and tobacco being its primary resources. What remained of the indigenous population were forced to work in huge plantations, and their numbers had sunk to 5,000 by 1544. The introduction of sugar cane around Santiago in 1548 was the signal for the import of vast numbers of African slaves. The population of the island passed 50,000 again in 1700.

During the 17th and 18th centuries Cuba was a coveted prize for pirates and the European powers. The British occupied Havana in 1762-63, and then liberated it in exchange for Florida. Having obtained the right to trade with Spain in 1765, the Cubans profited from the collapse of the economy of the nearby French colony of Santo Domingo.

The mainly black Cuban population grew from 150,000 in 1763 to 1,300,000 in 1860. At the start of the 19th century the growth in the number of slaves led to rebel movements. Numerous US attempts to acquire the island failed. The 1868 uprising under the anti-slavery Carlos de Cespedes began the "Ten Years' War" against the Spanish. At the peace of Zanjon in 1878, which ended the rebellion, Spain agreed to a package of reforms and a degree of autonomy. Slavery was abolished in 1880. A new uprising in 1895 under the leadership of the poet Jose Marti, led to the proclamation of a republic. The brutal repression of the insurrection led to US intervention. War was sparked off by the accidental blowing up of the US battleship *Maine* in the harbour of Havana in February 1898. Defeated, Spain renounced Cuba under the Treaty of Paris in December that year. A military government was imposed in Cuba by the US, which had considerable interests in the island, particularly in the sugar plantations.

Independence

Cuba became independent on 1 January 1899. The US withdrew its troops in 1902 and granted favourable trade and tariff terms to Cuban products in exchange for the establishment of a protectorate over the island and the ceding of two naval bases. Tomas Estrada Palma, the first president of Cuba from 1902, ran for president again at the elections of 1906. The liberal uprisings under Jose Miguel Gomez led to renewed US intervention in 1906 and 1917. Links with the US were strengthened with the introduction of parity between the dollar and the peso in 1914. The economic crisis which descended on the island after the First World War resulted in the dictatorship of General Machado (1925-33). A coup, in which Sergeant Fulgencio Batista played a leading role, put an end to the dictatorship. Anti-US feeling came to a head and the US renounced its right of intervention in 1934. Cuban political life was dominated by the now General Batista, although he was only officially in power from 1940-44, and again from March 1952. Opposition to the Batista regime's misrule grew in many quarters. A revolt involving the seizure of the Moncada barracks at Santiago in July 1953 was put down and its leader, Fidel Castro Ruz, was arrested. Castro was granted an amnesty and took refuge in Mexico. In December 1956 he landed in the east of the island with a number of followers, including Che Guevara. They managed to go underground in the Sierra Maestra where Castro organised a rural guerrilla war. The insurgents' push at Christmas 1958 overthrew Batista's dictatorship, and the Socialist Republic of Cuba was proclaimed on 1 January 1959.

Castro's revolution

The major problem facing Cuba was the near-monopoly of sugar cane cultivation enjoyed by US companies. Sugar refineries and then oil refineries were nationalised in 1959. Soviet support for Cuba led to the imposition of a US embargo on Cuban products from October 1960. A US-backed invasion by Cuban exiles ended in fiasco at the Bay of Pigs in April 1961 and helped to strengthen Castro's position.

The stationing of Soviet missiles in Cuba led to the outbreak of a serious international crisis in October 1962, which ended largely owing to the firm stance taken by President Kennedy. The missiles were removed. Cuban socialism became more radical, leading to a new wave of emigration in 1970; by then 600,000 Cubans had left since the revolution. Cuba supported revolutionary movements in Central America but, despite an improvement in relations with the US after 1977, the regime remained largely isolated and predominantly reliant on Soviet support.

Despite a degree of social and economic success the increasing concentration of power in Castro's hands led to the departure of some 100,000 Cubans in 1980. Castro appeared to pass some of his power over to his brother Raul, vice-president and head of the army, who was received in the USSR by Mikhail Gorbachev at the funeral of Konstantin Chernenko in March 1985. In April 1989 Gorbachev in turn visited Cuba, where he had a series of meetings with Fidel Castro and addressed the Cuban National Assembly. Cuba agreed to withdraw its 37,000 troops – its largest overseas commitment – from Angola in 1988 as part of a UN-sponsored peace plan for the region.

In mid-1989 the regime was shaken by a scandal involving General Arnaldo Ochoa, a national hero who led Cuban forces in Angola, and who admitted helping Colombian cocaine traffickers smuggle drugs to the US.

Cyprus

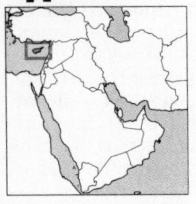

CY
East
Mediterranean
3,572 sq. mi
Pop: 665,000
UN, CW,

Capital: Nicosia (pop: 164,000)
Official languages: Greek, Turkish
Religions: Orthodox (78 per cent),
Moslem (18 per cent)
System of govt: Republic;
independent since 14 December 1959

Inhabited since c.6500 BC, Cyprus developed its trade with the Aegean Sea between 2000 BC and 1000 BC, when it was primarily an exporter of copper (the word derives from the island's name) and wood. The island developed its own culture and from c.1500 BC possessed a system of writing which has not yet been deciphered. Devastated by seafaring peoples in the century after c.1300 BC, Cyprus became the home of numerous Mycenaean refugees and enjoyed great economic prosperity in c.1200 BC-1100 BC. After a period of decline which followed a number of earthquakes Cyprus became a crossroads of peoples from c.900 BC onwards, with Greek and Egyptian influences predominating. Cypriot kingdoms were dominated by Assyria, then by Egypt, the Persians (525-332 BC) and then by the Hellenic Egyptian dynasty of the Ptolemies.

Cyprus became a Roman province in 58 BC. In the late 600s the island was split between the Arabs and the Byzantine empire, successors to the Eastern Roman empire. After being conquered by King Richard the Lionheart of England during the third crusade (1189-92), Cyprus was sold to Guy de Lusignan and became a kingdom in 1197. The order of Teutonic Knights settled there in the 13th century. Prosperous Cyprus was taken by Venice in 1489. Cyprus was conquered from the Venetians by the Ottoman empire in 1571 and Turkish domination lasted until 1878, when the Congress of Berlin gave Britain the right to administer the island under Ottoman sovereignty. Annexed in 1914 when Turkey entered the war alongside Germany, Cyprus became a British colony in 1925. In the 1950's Britain faced a terrorist campaign conducted by EOKA (National Organisation of Cypriot Struggle), under the leadership of Colonel Grivas, who backed *Enosis* (Union with Greece). In the face of resistance from the island's Turkish minority, Cyprus became independent in February 1959. Britain kept military bases in Cyprus. The first president of the republic was Archbishop Makarios, who ruled with a Turkish vice-president, Fazil Kucuk, both men being elected at the end of 1959. But tension between the two communities worsened. Re-elected in 1973, Makarios was overthrown in July 1974 by a coup. A pro-*Enosis* regime was formed, and forces from Turkey landed on 20 July, occupying the north of the island. The northern Greek population was forced to flee to the south of the island. In February 1975 Turkish Cypriots declared the independence of the Turkish part of the island under the leadership of Rauf Denktash.

Spyros Kiprianou succeeded Makarios, who had returned to Cyprus in triumph at the end of 1974, as Greek Cypriot president on the archbishop's death in August 1977. Kyprianou was defeated in elections in February 1988, which were won by the independent candidate George Vassiliou. Negotiations on the future of the Turkish republic, which is recognised only by Turkey, are continuing under UN auspices and a draft plan for the island was scheduled for the autumn of 1989.

Czechoslovakia

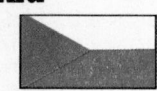

CS
Central Europe
49,383 sq. mi
Pop: 15.4 m
UN, WP,
COMECON

Capital: Prague (pop: 1.19 m)
Official languages: Czech, Slovak
Religions: Catholic (70 per cent),
Protestant
System of govt: Socialist federal
republic since 28 October 1968

Origins of the republic

The republic emerged from the ruins of the Austro-Hungarian empire, and comprises Slovakia and the Czech lands of Bohemia, Moravia and Czech Silesia. Though relatively well-developed, with prosperous industries, the state was, from the start, essentially an artificial one. Almost a quarter of the population were Germans, Magyars and Ruthenians. Czechs and Slovaks, two-thirds of the population, were mutually antagonistic, the Czechs being the more advanced economically.

In the 1930s, Hitler used the German minority to mount a furious nationalist campaign aimed at breaking up the state. This he achieved in 1939. Bohemia and Moravia were made "protectorates" – in effect, annexed – and the rump of the republic, Slovakia, became nominally independent.

Communist coup

At the end of the Second World War the country was restored to its prewar borders, except that the USSR annexed Ruthenia and 2.4 million Germans were expelled, followed by half a million Hungarians. In Prague a coalition government, with Communists in the interior ministry and other key positions, was installed in Prague. The last pre-war president, Eduard Benes, a follower of Tomas Masaryk, the founder of Czechoslovakia, became president, and Masaryk's son became foreign minister. The Moscow communist Klement Gottwald became premier.

In 1947 three non-communist cabinet ministers received parcel bombs (which failed) and the cabinet, by a majority vote, called for an investigation into the (communist-controlled) security police. Gottwald refused to act on the decision. The non-communist ministers resigned, expecting thereby to force an election.

Instead, in early 1948, the communists stage-managed a series of public rallies calling for a people's government. Communist-controlled police occupied Prague's main thoroughfares. A new communist-socialist cabinet was formed after the socialists had (as in East Germany and elsewhere) been dra-

gooned into a "unity" pact with the communists.

Twelve non-communist members of the cabinet resigned and a new cabinet was "approved" by the ill President Benes. Jan Masaryk was allowed to remain as foreign minister, presumably to give the regime international credibility.

But in March Masaryk fell from a window of his office in Prague. It was said that he committed suicide; many believe he was pushed. With the death of the ailing President Benes, aged 64, in September, the coup was complete and Czechoslovakia joined the Soviet bloc.

Early history of the region

The Slavs began to settle in Bohemia, Moravia and Slovakia in the sixth century. According to tradition one of the settlers' leaders was Cech, who gave his name to the Czechs, and one of his descendants married a ploughman named Przemysl, who gave his name to Prague.

Bohemia was the scene of bitter religious struggles between Catholics and reformers, led by Jan Huss, inspired by the Englishman John Wyclif. In 1402 Huss was rector of Prague University and became preacher in the Bethlehem Chapel, a foundation for preaching in the Czech language. When the university condemned the teachings of Wyclif, he came to his defence. When a papal bull ordered the burning of Wyclif's books, Huss went on preaching about Wyclif and was excommunicated. He was forced into exile and then, with a guarantee of safe conduct from the Emperor Sigismund, he attended the Council of Constance, which had been called to deal with divisions within the catholic church. There, Huss was seized and burned at the stake. In Prague, mobs stormed the town hall and prison; freed Hussite prisoners and threw two Catholic councillors out of the window – Prague's first defenestration.

Pope Martin V ordered a crusade against supporters of Huss in 1420. Since the Bohemian and Moravian noblemen had sworn to continue Huss' work, doubtless for nationalistic reasons, war was inevitable. Hussite forces devastated Bavaria, Franconia, Silesia and Brandenburg before a peace was agreed in 1436. The Czechs got themselves a king, which was what they had been seeking. In the 17th century, under the Habsburgs, the Czechs rebelled again after the emperor failed to keep his promise to preserve their religious liberties. Once again, pro-government councillors were thrown out of the window of the Hradcany castle. The officials survived, but the train of events, including the Bohemian estates' election in 1618 of the Elector Palatine Frederick as king, in defiance of the Habsburgs, who had come to regard

Bohemia as a hereditary fief, sparked the series of central European conflicts known as the Thirty Years War. The emperor crushed Frederick, the "Winter King", at the battle of the White Mountain in 1620, and Czech nationalism was effectively crushed until the 19th century, when population growth and industrialisation restored the people's self-confidence.

The Habsburgs' nervousness about the Czechs was demonstrated at the outbreak of the First World War, when a state of emergency was proclaimed in the Czech lands, and remained in force until the empire collapsed in 1918.

The Prague Spring and after

In early January 1968, a behind-the-scenes struggle within the Czechoslovak Communist party ended, with the ousting as leader of the pro-Moscow stalwart Antonin Novotny. He was replaced by Alexander Dubcek, a reputed liberal. Dubcek, a party official since the war and the first Slovak to lead the party, promised economic reforms and a loosening of the government's hold on freedom of expression. Thus began the few months of relative freedom known since as the "Prague Spring".

In March Dubcek relaxed press censorship and arrested the former head of the secret police. Novotny, who had earlier threatened to use the army to cling to power, resigned as president on 22 March. The media began to report real news, including the uncovering of corruption in high places, criticism of housing conditions, low wages and stifling bureaucracy.

Dubcek insisted that Czechoslovakia remained a loyal ally of the USSR, but tensions between Prague and Moscow increased, and in early May Soviet bloc tanks and troops began to move up through Poland and East Germany to the Czech border. Fears of an invasion were heightened by reports of a hastily-called meeting between eastern bloc leaders – except the Czechoslovaks and Romanians – but on 17 May the Soviet premier Kosygin arrived in Prague for talks to heal the rift between Prague and Moscow.

Five Warsaw Pact states met in Warsaw on 15 July to discuss the situation in Czechoslovakia. On 18 July Dubcek pledged to continue his "socialism with a human face" and insisted there would be "no retreat" from the new "democratic process". He was invited, on 22 July, to hold "friendly bilateral talks" with Brezhnev and east bloc leaders in eastern Czechoslovakia. The talks ended on 30 July with little agreement. In the meantime over 1,000 Soviet tanks and 75,000 eastern bloc troops had amassed on the Czech frontier. Brezhnev claimed that US spies were active in Czechoslovakia and that they were preparing a West German invasion. He insisted that Warsaw Pact forces should be allowed into the coun-

try to "protect" it against such an eventuality.

Dubcek fired Soviet anger when the Yugoslav leader Marshal Tito arrived on an official visit to Prague on 9 August. Dubcek signed a 20-year pact with Romania, another independent-minded (but internally repressive) communist state, on 16 August. Five days later Warsaw Pact tanks rolled over the Czechoslovak border, accompanied by several hundred thousand troops, intent on ending the liberties of the Prague Spring. Citizens in Prague attempted to defy the tanks with guns, sticks or their bare hands. Soviet officers took away Dubcek and other leaders. The national assembly was occupied and the government news agency shut down.

A one-hour general strike was called in protest on 23 August. Dubcek and his premier, Cernik, held extended talks with Soviet leaders on 24 August. Despite continuing protests in the following few months, including the dramatic suicide of Jan Palach in January 1969 in protest at the Soviet invasion, the Prague Spring was clearly over. Czechoslovak leaders, under orders from Soviet officials, reinstalled censorship and restored party oppression. Dubcek and other reformers and their supporters were sacked or arrested in April 1969. Dubcek was eventually made ambassador to Turkey in December 1969, but was sacked from that post and finally expelled from the party in June 1970. The new party leader, Gustav Husak, vowed to sweep away "all that stands between Czechoslovakia and the Soviet Union".

In January 1977, 240 intellectuals set up a group called "Charter 77" to monitor Czechoslovakia's implementation of democratic rights in according to an international accord signed at Helsinki. On 9 January several figures in the group were arrested, and the leader, Jan Potocka, died after police interrogation on 13 March, prompting western protests.

Intolerance of dissent continued into the late 1980s, despite Gorbachev's reforms in the USSR, which have encouraged political reform in neighbouring Hungary and Poland, which had both seen liberal movements put down in 1956.

In December 1987 Husak was replaced as party leader by Milos Jakes, but remained head of state. Demonstrations in 1988 to mark the 20th anniversary of the Soviet invasion were met with the familiar pattern of repression and arrests. In October 1988, however, a small hint of possible change appeared when, for the first time in decades, the government sanctioned celebrations to mark the 70th anniversary of the republic. And, in November, the government allowed Alexander Dubcek, a forestry official in eastern Slovakia since 1970, to travel to Bologna to pick up an honorary degree.

Denmark

DK
Northern Europe
16,631 sq. mi
Pop: 5.1 m
UN, EC, NATO,

Capital: Copenhagen (pop 469,000)
Official language: Danish
Religion: Lutheran (97 per cent)
System of govt: Constitutional monarchy, according to the constitution of 5 June 1953

The northwards expansion of Charlemagne's empire brought a confrontation between the Franks and the Danes under Godfred. In 811 the river Eider was established as the boundary, although attempts at Frankish invasion continued during the political fragmentation of Denmark which followed the death of Himming (812).

Expansion overseas

Over the next 200 years the Danes, who were gifted shipbuilders, set out on a series of expeditions to northern Europe, first raiding and then settling in north west France and eastern England. In the 10th century a new dynasty, founded by Gorm the Old (died c.950) began the process of reunification of Denmark.

Gorm's work was continued by his son, Harald Blaatand (Bluetooth, who died c.986) who extended the kingdom to Norway and Pomerania. The Christianisation of Denmark also commenced in his reign. The Viking voyages took them to Greenland (c.982), and then to North America (c.1000). After Sven I "Forkbeard" (died 1014) had completed the conquest of England, his successor Knut (Canute) the Great (died 1035) reigned over a vast kingdom which was to split up on his death.

A great Nordic power

Valdemar I the Great (1157-82) created the conditions for a strong centralised monarchy, supported by the feudal aristocracy and the church. He started the expansion of the kingdom along the Baltic, conquering the island of Rugen and a number of bases on the Pomeranian coast. Copenhagen was founded in 1165. The reign of Valdemar II the Victorious (1202-41) can be considered as the high point of mediaeval Denmark. Trade flourished (especially herring, fishing, horse breeding) and laws were codified. The Baltic coast was conquered as far as Estonia, where the town of Reval was founded in 1219.

However, the defeat of a Danish invasion of Holstein in 1227 heralded a troubled era marked by the decline of royal power in the face of the nobility and the increasing influence of the Germans.

The Danish monarchy recovered under Valdemar IV Atterdag (1340-75), who defeated the Swedes and the cities of the Hanseatic League. His success prompted a coalition of his enemies, and in 1370, by the Treaty of Stralsund, the Hanse regained major commercial privileges.

Valdemar's real successor was his daughter Margaret, who ruled as regent for her young son Olaf. In 1380 she also became regent of Norway on the death of her husband Haakon VI. In 1397 she brought about the union of the two kingdoms with Sweden, in the Union of Kalmar, encouraged by shared hostility to Germany. The union survived until 1523 when Gustavus Vasa was proclaimed king of Sweden.

The loss of supremacy

The 200 years which followed were marked by repeated conflicts with Sweden. These troubles were not to stop until after the death of Charles XII of Sweden and the Peace of Frederiksborg in 1720. Denmark regained its prosperity under Christian VI (1730-46), Frederick V (1746-66), Christian VII (1766-1808), and trade flourished, with the establishment of links with the West Indies and Asia.

A well-managed policy of neutrality contributed to economic growth. Christian VII's minister Johann Friedrich Struensee introduced far-reaching social reforms such as the abolition of serfdom, the recognition of individual and press freedoms and religious tolerance. However, Struensee was overthrown and executed in 1772. His policies were pursued in a more moderate form after Andreas Peter Bernstorff's liberal coup d'etat of 1784.

The 19th century and two world wars

Denmark, which maintained neutrality until 1800, entered into conflict with Britain which bombarded Copenhagen, (1801, 1807) and destroyed Denmark's fleet. Allied to France, Denmark lost Norway by the Treaty of Kiel (1814), but in exchange Frederick VI (regent since 1784 and king from 1808 to 1839), received the German duchies Schleswig and Holstein.

The reign of Christian VIII (1839-48), which started with the granting of a constitution, was peaceful and prosperous, although troubled towards its close by the growth of German agitation in the duchies. His successor, Frederick VII (1848-63), was confronted by an uprising in the duchies on the promulgation in 1852 of a democratic constitution. In the same year, the Conference of London decided to declare Christian of Glucksburg (Christian IX, 1863-1906) as Frederick VII's successor. In 1863, shortly before Frederick's death, his nephew William was chosen by the Greeks to become their king. He adopted the name George I.

Prussia was determined to take possession of Schleswig-Holstein and, in an alliance with Austria, attacked Denmark in 1864. The War of the Duchies was ended by the Treaty of Vienna later that year, with Denmark losing the three duchies of Schleswig, Holstein and Lauenburg as well as the city of Kiel. In all it lost a third of its territory, although mainly German-speaking areas.

A two-chamber parliament was instituted in 1866. The liberal and social evolution of the monarchy continued. Pension funds were introduced in 1891, and health and unemployment funds in 1892. A first moderate left-wing government was convened by the king in 1901. Dynastic relations with other royal families had been cemented when two princesses married, respectively, Britain's prince of Wales (later Edward VII) and Russia's crown prince (later Nicholas II). In 1920 the League of Nations decided to return northern Holstein to Denmark, which had remained neutral during the First World War. The social democrat government of Thorvald Stauning met the economic crisis of 1929 with the introduction of progressive new social laws. The German invasion of 9 April 1940, contravening a non-aggression pact, forced the government to accept Nazi occupation. A domestic resistance movement arose, however, invoked from London by Christmas Moller. King Christian X (1912-47) was put under house arrest. The government resigned on 29 August 1943 and the Danish fleet scuttled itself.

Denmark after 1945

The constitutional monarchy was restored after the war, and Frederick IX became king in 1949. Iceland had proclaimed its independence in 1944. The Faroe Islands were granted autonomy in 1948 (union with Denmark was confirmed by the elections of 1955) and Greenland became a Danish province in 1953 (internal autonomy took effect as of 1979). After accepting the aid offered by the Marshall Plan in 1948, Denmark joined NATO in 1949. The 1953 constitution instituted a single-chamber parliament, the Folketing. On the Nordic Council since 1951, Denmark joined the European Free Trade Association (EFTA) in 1960, and signed an agreement for co-operation between the Nordic states in Helsinki in 1962. Denmark's entry into the EEC, which took effect in 1973, was the subject of considerable political debate, resulting from the wide-ranging structural economic changes it necessitated. Power since 1960 has been in the hands of coalitions of social democrats, liberals and conservatives, which have adhered to the welfare state policies which have burdened Denmark with a considerable budget deficit.

Margaret II, Denmark's first queen since 1412, succeeded her father Frederick IX on 14 January 1972.

Djibouti

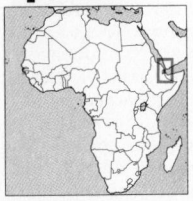

East Africa
23,000 km2
Pop. 470.000
UN, AL, OAU

Capital: Djibouti (pop. 200,000)
Official languages: French, Arabic
Religion: Sunni Moslem (94 per cent)
System of govt: Republic. Independent since 27 June 1977.

From the ninth century sultanates grew up out of the Islamic territories of the Afars, at the entry to the Red Sea. They were progressively pushed back by the Issas, Somali tribes.

Occupied initially by Arab and Portuguese merchants, the territory of the Afars and the Issas (Djibouti) saw the establishment of a first French post at Obock in 1862, later a naval base. Agreements were concluded with the Afar and Issa chiefs in 1884. The protectorate of Djibouti was created in 1888 and in 1896 took the name of French Somaliland.

Djibouti gained autonomy in July 1957. Serious rioting broke out in 1966 after the visit of General de Gaulle. The pro-French Afars clashed with the Issas, who favoured union with the former British Somaliland. A referendum in March 1967 confirmed Djibouti's attachment to France. In the same year Djibouti became the Afars and Issas, and the Afar leader Ali Aref became head of government in 1968. In 1972 the African People's Independence League (LPAI) was formed and joined Hassan Gouled Aptidon's Issa independence movement. Aptidon became president of Djibouti, declared a republic in June 1977 and admitted to the Arab League in September. Hassan Gouled Aptidon was re-elected in June 1981.

Dominica

Dominica

WD
Caribbean
290 sq. mi
Pop: 87,000
UN, CARI-
COM, OAS

Capital: Roseau (pop: 8,300)
Official language: English
Religion: Catholic (76 per cent)
System of govt: Republic;
independent since 3 November 1978

Columbus was the first European to reach Dominica, on Sunday 3 November 1493 (*Dies Dominica* is Latin for Sunday – hence the island's name). The Europeans met with fierce resistance from the natives, whose natural environment of forests and mountains enabled them to escape total extermination. The last descendants of the original Caribbean population today number about 500 people, living in a reserve created by the British in 1903. In the 18th century Britain and France each sought to occupy the island. The Treaty of Aix-la-Chapelle in 1748 accorded the island neutral status and French settlers began to arrive soon after. Britain occupied the island in 1759 during the Seven Years War, and the Treaty of Paris of 1763, which ended the war, acknowledged Britain's sovereignty over Do-

minica. But the struggle for sovereignty continued right up until the Napoleonic Wars, with the British emerging as victors. The descendants of a large black slave workforce for the island's plantations, form the majority of Dominica's population. The island became a British crown colony in 1898, obtained autonomy in 1956 and became independent on 3 November 1978. Dominica chose to be a republic.

The island's first Labour administration had to cope with financial scandal and the catastrophe caused by Hurricane David in August 1979. The island's first general elections in June 1980 were won by the conservative Dominica Freedom Party under Mary Eugenia Charles, who thereby became the first female head of government in the Caribbean region. The first president of Dominica was Aurelius Marie, succeeded in 1984 by Clarence Seignoret. Eugenia Charles was one of the motivators of the invasion of the neighbouring island of Grenada by US and Caribbean troops in October 1983.

Charles' problems include poverty (living standards are lower than some neighbouring states), illiteracy (30 per cent) and a high birth rate (2.7 per cent annually). The island suffers from overpopulation, and has seen a high level of emigration in recent years. Dominica's economy depends on agriculture, primarily cocoa, bananas and citrus fruit, which were badly hit by the 1979 hurricane.

Dominican Republic

DOM
Caribbean
18,700 sq. mi
Pop: 6.7 m
UN, OAS

Capital: Santo Domingo (pop. 1.5 m)
Official language: Spanish
Religion: Catholic (93 per cent)
System of govt: Republic; independence proclaimed 27 February 1844.

The Dominican Republic occupies the eastern part of the island of Hispaniola, with Haiti as its neighbour to the west. The Amerindian Arawaks from Venezuela colonised the island in c.700 AD and introduced agriculture. The island was discovered by Europeans when Christopher Columbus landed in 1492, and European colonisation began the following year.

The Indian population was exterminated and replaced by black slaves. The French conquered the island in 1695 but only retained the western part (Haiti) after the Treaty of Ryswick in 1697. In 1795 Spain ceded her territories to revolutionary France, but an uprising of Spanish-speaking creoles expelled the French in 1808. In 1821 the Haitians reconquered the present-day Dominican Republic from the Spanish. Dominican independence was proclaimed in 1844.

Spain managed to reimpose her presence on the island between 1861 and 1865. Once having recovered independence, the republic remained politically unstable. In exchange for a loan of $20,000,000, the USA assumed control of Dominican national finances from 1907 to 1940. US troops were stationed in the republic from 1916 until 1924.

The Trujillo dictatorship
Rafael Leonidas Trujillo, head of the US-formed army, seized control of the country in a coup in 1930. He and his family took possession of the country and exploited it until 1962. Trujillo, who at first enjoyed USA support, became one of the richest men in the world.

Washington turned against the dictator under pressure from protests from South American states. Although Trujillo had entrusted his powers to his brother Hector in 1952, the first free elections were not held until 20 years later. On 30 May 1961 Trujillo was assassinated, and the ensuing civil war forced his family to flee the country.

Civil War and democracy
The Dominican Revolutionary party (PRD) candidate, Juan Bosch, won the elections of 20 December 1962. He was overthrown by a coup on 25 September 1963. His successor, Reid Cabral, the head of the military junta, was overthrown in his turn on 24 April 1965 by supporters of Bosch. With the support of some of the South American countries, US troops intervened on 28 April, and on 19 May imposed a cease-fire in the civil war.

The elections of June 1966 were won by the conservative, Joaquin Balaguer, who also won the May 1970 elections, despite calls by the PRD for a boycott. Balaguer was re-elected for the second time in 1974, but the 1978 elections were won by the PRD.

The leader of the PRD since Bosch's retirement in 1973, Antonio Guzman Fernandez, became president. Constitutional guarantees were re-established. Salvador Jorge Blanco, also a PRD member, became president in August 1982.

Essentially an exporter of primary agricultural goods (sugar, coffee, cocoa), the Dominican economy is highly dependent on its oil imports. In 1986 the blind Balaguer, 80, was re-elected for his third term as president and in 1987 and 1988 the continuing IMF-inspired programme of economic austerity instituted in 1984 led to a wave of strikes and considerable industrial unrest.

Ecuador

EC
South America
104,505 sq. mi
Pop: 9.9 m
UN, LAIA,
OAS

Capital: Quito (pop: 1.1 m)
Official language: Spanish
Religion: Catholic (92 per cent)
System of govt: Republic;
independence proclaimed 11 May 1830

What is now Ecuador was among the first South American territories to be inhabited. Remains of cultures going back to 8000 BC have been found at El Inga. The country was dominated by an independent kingdom up until the beginning of the 15th century. The high plateau was conquered by the Incas under Tupac Yupanqui between 1463 and 1471, with the coastal territory being annexed in 1493.

Spanish colonisation
Weakened by internal struggles, the Inca empire in Ecuador fell to the Spanish between 1531 and 1533. The last Inca general, Atahualpa Yupanqui, was defeated by the conquistador Sebastian de Belalcazar in 1534, who in the same year founded San Francisco de Quito and Santiago de Guayaquil, the centres of Spanish colonisation. After becoming the *audiencia* of Quito in 1563, Ecuador was integrated first into the Spanish vice-royalty of Peru and then, in 1739, into the vice-royalty of New Granada. The "Quito school" of painting was later to acquire a considerable reputation.

Independence
The long struggle for independence began with the conspiracy of 10 August 1809, and ended with the battle of Pichincha (24 May 1822). General Sucre's victory here also marked the triumph of the patriots. Ecuador, inspired by Simon Bolivar, joined the republic of Gran Colombia which, however, did not survive the ensuing wars with Peru.

Ecuador proclaimed itself an independent republic on 11 May 1830. Political conflict plagued the country from the rule of the first president, General Juan Jose Flores (1830-34), right up to the authoritarian regime of Gabriel Garcia Moreno in 1861. Moreno was assassinated in 1875. Under the influence of religious extremism, Ecuador became the "Republic of the Sacred Heart". The liberals in the coastal towns gained in influence as the international market continued to consume Ecuador's exports, especially cocoa. A decline in exports shifted the centre of economic activity to the high plateau, and furthered the influence of the conservatives. A rapprochement between Ecuador's two geographical regions was made easier at the start of the 20th century, by the creation of a network of railways and roads. Internally divided and threatened by its neighbours, Ecuador has lost nearly two-thirds of its territory since the beginning of the 20th century to Brazil and Colombia (1904 and 1916), and to Peru (1942). The Galapagos islands were annexed by the USA.

The era of Velasco

Jose Maria Velasco Ibarra, an independent with a large popular following, was elected president for the first time in 1934. His attempts to resolve the country's social problems by introducing reforms were thwarted by conservative and military opponents, who overthrew him on a number of occasions. Velasco Ibarra was elected president five times (1934-35, 1944-47, 1952-56, 1960-61, 1968-72) and on only one occasion was his rule not interrupted by a military coup. After his final term, in 1972, Velasco Ibarra was forced into exile in Argentina.

Military domination

The "nationalist, military and revolutionary" junta under the leadership of Guillermo Rodriguez Lara (1972-76) introduced diverse nationalist and reformist policies aimed at overturning the country's traditional politico-economic structures. The coup of January 1976, led by Vice-Admiral Poveda Urbano, brought with it no modification of these policies. The new regime promised a return to democracy and presented a draft constitution on January 1978, which attempted to give the right to vote to the illiterates and greater social rights.

The return to democracy

The free elections of 29 April 1979 were won by Jaime Roldos, the Christian Democratic candidate of the Popular Democracy party (DP). Quarrels within the DP, a conflict with parliament, and an armed conflict with Peru over oil-rich lands between the Maranon and Putomayo rivers (1981), made it impossible for President Roldos to implement his reforms before his accidental death on 24 May 1984. He was succeeded by Vice-President Osvaldo Hurtado Larrea. The border conflict with Peru continued. The fall in the price of oil after 1981, and the drop in demand for other exports worsened Ecuador's mounting catalogue of economic problems. The conservative Leon Febres Cordero, elected president in May 1984, introduced a policy of economic liberalisation which opened Ecuador to foreign capital. He also attempted to solve the ever-present social problems of a country with 50 per cent unemployment. In January 1987 the president was taken prisoner by rebellious troops, but later released.

Ecuador's relations with the USA became strained in July 1987, when the Ecuadorian congress ordered a contingent of US troops working on a road to leave the country. On 10 August 1988 President Febres was succeeded by Rodrigo Borja Cevallos of the centre-left Democratic Left party.

Egypt

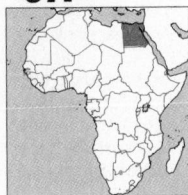

ET
North Africa
386,900 sq. mi
Pop: 52 m
UN, AL, OAU, OPEC

Capital: Cairo (pop: 6.3 m)
Official language: Arabic
Religions: Moslem (94 per cent), Coptic Christian
System of govt: Republic since 18 June 1953

Although it was in the region of Khartoum, in the south of Egypt, that the neolithic era was to leave its richest legacy of rock carving and incised pottery, it was Narmer in the north who brought about the first unification of the kingdoms of Upper and Lower Egypt in c.3200 BC. The basis of the agricultural economy and of a centralised administration was already present during this period. The "Old Kingdom" reached its apogee in c.2780 BC under the reign of Djoser, for whom the architect Imhotep built the stepped pyramid at Saqqarah. The pharaohs who followed Djoser, including Cheops, Chephren and Mycerinus, built huge pyramids which still dominate the desert around Giza. From 2134 BC Egypt enjoyed renewed splendour under the "Middle Kingdom". Egypt's rulers subjugated Nubia, the Sinai Peninsula and southern Palestine. In c.1650 BC Egypt fell under the domination of the Hyksos, a foreign people who had themselves been displaced by Indo-European migrations. The "New Kingdom" was born when the Pharaoh Amosis repelled the Hyksos in 1551 BC. Under Thutmose I (1505 BC-1494 BC) Egypt became the leading power in the Mediterranean. Egypt's imperialist expansion was halted after 1364 BC by Amenhotep IV, who became Akhenaten after replacing the cult of Amun by the monotheistic cult of Aton. After falling prey to anarchy, the empire lost many provinces and was not to recover its stability until the reign of Rameses II (died 1224 BC), who revived the great tradition of monumental architecture. The conquest of Egypt in 525 BC by Cyrus II the Great, founder of the Persian empire, heralded the decline of monarchical power. Egypt became a satrapy (province) over which Persian domination was to continue until the country was conquered by Alexander the Great in 332 BC. On his death in 323 BC one of his generals, Ptolemy Soter, founded a pharaonic dynasty under the name of Ptolemy I Soter. His descendants retained the throne for 300 years until Cleopatra was defeated by the Romans in 30 BC. Rome turned Egypt into an imperial province.

Dawn of the Islamic era

On the division of the Roman empire in 395 AD, Egypt was part of the Eastern Roman empire. The country was wrested from the Byzantines by the Arabs in 642 and its destiny became linked to that of the caliphs of Islam. In 868 a mercenary contingent, the Mamelukes, was organised, who made it possible for the Tulunid dynasty to take control of the country until 905. Conquered by the Shi'ite Fatimid dynasty in 969, Egypt once more fell under the Mamelukes' control in 1250 until they were defeated by the Ottoman Sultan Selim at Aleppo in 1516 and Egypt became part of the Ottoman empire. The Mamelukes, however, continued to exercise a certain amount of influence in the country.

French ambitions in Egypt grew in the 1790s. The Mamelukes were defeated at the pyramids by Bonaparte in July 1798 during a French campaign which eventually ended with the capitulation of the French army to the British and Turks in August 1801. In 1805 a Turkish officer, Mohammed Ali, was recognised as pasha (governor) of Egypt by the sultan, after massacring many hundreds of Mamelukes and introducing a number of reforms of western inspiration. Egypt regained a measure of prosperity under Mohammed Ali's successors Said (1854-63) and Ismail (1863-79). The Suez concession granted to Ferdinand de Lesseps by Said in 1856 made possible the building of the canal, which was inaugurated in November 1869. Railways were also built under French impetus.

British domination

Disturbed by the growth of French influence in Egypt, Britain repurchased the bankrupt Ismail's Suez Canal shares in 1879 and took control of the Egyptian administration alongside France. A nationalist rising led to British intervention in 1881, ostensibly to protect the canal. Egypt was placed under the authority of a British governor general. An Anglo-Egyptian administration ran the Sudan to the south.

In 1914 Britain made Egypt a protectorate. The country demanded its independence in 1918 and the nationalist Wafd party was organised itself. The troubles led the British to renounce the protectorate in 1922, retaining however, the control of the armies and the Suez Canal. Egypt became a monarchy under its first king, Fuad I (1922-36).

Independence

Continuing hostility to the British presence led to full independence on 26 August 1936, subject to the British military occupation of the Suez Canal zone continuing for 20 years. The defeat of the Arab countries in the war against the new state of Israel (1948-49) led to problems in Egypt and King Farouk (1937-52) called Nahhas Pasha, Wafd leader since 1927, to lead the government. Nationalist agitation continued to grow and led to Farouk's deposition in 1952.

The Egyptian republic

In power from July 1952, General Neguib suppressed political parties and proclaimed a republic in June 1953. Neguib was replaced in November by Colonel Gamal Abdel Nasser, the real power behind the revolution. The announcement of the nationalisation of the Suez Canal in July 1956 led to Anglo-French intervention. Britain and France withdrew in November after UN and super-power pressure made it clear that old-style imperialism was not wanted.

In 1967 Colonel Nasser closed the Tiran strait, Israel's access to the Gulf of Aqaba. Despite Egypt's defeat in the ensuing Six Day War (June 1967), Nasser's power was strengthened by Soviet aid. On his death in September 1970 he was succeeded by Anwar el-Sadat.

Peace with Israel

The 1973 war with Israel ended in a ceasefire. A rapprochement with the USA made talks with Israel possible through US mediation. Sadat's visit to Jerusalem in November 1977 ended in the signing of a peace treaty in Washington in March 1979, and Israeli prime minister Menahem Begin became the first Israeli leader to visit Egypt the same year. Sadat's policy of reconciliation with Israel led to Egypt's isolation from its Arab neighbours, expulsion from the Arab League and inspired the assassins who killed him in October 1981. Vice-President Hosni Mubarak succeeded him, pledging to continue the peace process with Israel. The Israelis pulled out of Sinai in April 1982 in accordance with the peace treaty.

Mubarak has been faced with a resurgence of Islamic fundamentalism and the necessity of reintegrating Egypt into the Arab world.

El Salvador

El Salvador

ES
Central America
8,236 sq. mi
Pop: 5.4 m
UN, OAS,
SELA

Capital: San Salvador (pop: 459,000)
Official language: Spanish
Religion: Catholic (91 per cent)
System of govt: Republic;
independence proclaimed 15 September 1821

The first inhabitants of El Salvador were forced to flee the region around the year 100 by the eruption of the volcano Ilopango, a number of the emigrants making their way to the Maya territories. The recolonisation of the country did not get under way until approximately the year 1000 with the arrival of the Pipil from Mexico.

Spanish colonisation

The Spanish started the conquest of the country in 1524. After bitter fighting the indigenous people were defeated in 1547. The country was divided into three provinces attached to the Spanish *audiencia* (jurisdiction) of Guatemala. Creole uprisings in 1811 and 1814 were suppressed by the Spanish. After the proclamation of Central American independence (1821), Guatemala's decision to join the Mexican empire led to the forming of an autonomous government in El Salvador.

Independence and El Salvador

On 1 April 1823 El Salvador was integrated into the Central American Federation while retaining its autonomy. The first president of the federation was the El Salvadorean M J Arce. A constitutional wrangle led to the secession of Guatemala and the breaking up of the federation in 1839. The republic of El Salvador, named in 1841, continued to agitate for a Central American Federation. A union of Guatemala, Nicaragua and Honduras lasted from 1842 to 1847.

The second half of the 19th century saw a continuation of the struggle between liberals and conservatives. Real political power, however, remained in the hands of the rich landowning families and plantation owners. The world economic crisis of 1929 hit coffee production, and a peasant uprising in 1931 was put down by General Maximiliano Hernandez Martinez, who had overthrown the civilian President Arturo Araujo. The repression continued into 1932, accounting for more that 10,000 deaths.

General Martinez' retirement, forced by a general strike in 1944, brought in its wake a rapid succession of governments until 1949. With his Revolutionary Party of Democratic Union (PRUD), founded in 1950, Colonel Oscar Osorio brought El Salvador some political stability until 1956. His successor, Colonel Jose Lemus, was overthrown in 1960 by a leftwing military junta.

The following year a rightwing junta, supported by the USA, seized power. Julio Carballo, candidate of the National Conciliation party (PCN), the successor to the PRUD, was elected president. He was succeeded after elections in 1967 by Fidel Hernandez, the PCN candidate who was supported by the landowners and the military. After invading Honduras on 14 July 1969 during the "Football War", El Salvador was forced to withdraw its troops a month later in the face of pressure from the Organisation of American States.

Civil war

Arturo Molina's victory in the fraudulent 1972 elections was followed by an attempted coup staged by the opposition. The year 1974 saw the beginnings of a long and bloody guerrilla war between guerrila groups and the armed forces, with some appalling savagery on both sides. Army-backed rightwing assassination squads became particularly notorious direct.

In March 1980, under General Humberto Romero's junta, in power since a coup in 1979, Oscar Romero, archbishop of San Salvador and an outspoken government critic, was assassinated while saying mass. His murder led to the uniting of the opposition under the banner of the Democratic Revolutionary Front (FDR).

Supported by the US, the Christian democrat Jose Napoleon Duarte, who came to power since December 1980, declared martial law in October 1981. He was re-elected in May 1984, after having lost the March 1982 elections to a rightwing coalition, and initiated peace negotiations with the main guerrilla movements (FDR and the Faribundo Marti Front for National Liberation, FMLN). Despite this, the armed struggle between the government and the guerrillas has continued and is estimated to have claimed over 70,000 lives.

Duarte was terminally ill with cancer, and in March 1989 a new presidential election was held. The rightwing Arena Party candidate, Alfredo Christiani, was elected as of June 1 1989. Coffee remains the product which contributes most to the country's economy. Forty per cent of the nation's revenue passes into the hands of the rich landowners, five per cent of the population. The country is the most densely populated in Central America.

Equatorial Guinea

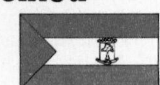

West Africa
10,831 sq. mi
Pop: 328,000
UN, OAU

Capital: Malabo (pop: 37,000)
Official languages: Spanish
Religion: Catholic (88 per cent)

System of govt: Republic; independence obtained 12 October 1968.

In 1471 the Portuguese discovered the islands off central West Africa which subsequently took on the name of their discoverer, Fernando Po (now Bioko). The islands became Spanish after the Treaty of Pardo (1778) along with the coastal territories owned by the Portuguese. The islands were occupied by Britain from 1827 to 1845, with Spain re-establishing sovereignty in 1843. The territory became a Spanish colony in 1858 with the arrival of the first governor sent by Madrid, and in 1885 it took on the name Spanish Guinea. Conflicts grew between Spain and France over the continental territories until the 1900 Treaty of Paris, when Spain had to agree to limit her continental possessions to Rio Muni (present-day Mbini). The colony became a Spanish province in 1959 with Spanish citizenship being bestowed on her inhabitants.

The colony obtained internal autonomy on 1 January 1964 and the republic was proclaimed on 12 October 1968 after a constitutional referendum. Spanish military intervention was necessary in February 1968 for the evacuation of Spanish citizens.

Macias Nguema's brutal dictatorship led to the exodus of a third of the Guinean population, and the loss of 40,000 lives. The departure of Spain forced Nguema to call upon the USSR and China for aid. Nguema was executed in 1979 and Colonel Teodoro Obiang Nguema Mbasogo's junta renewed economic relations with Spain and the West.

Ethiopia

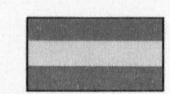

ETH
North East Africa
471,800 sq. mi
Pop: 45.9 m
UN, OAU

Capital: Addis Ababa (pop: 1.4 m)
Official languages: Amharic
Religions: Coptic Christian (52 per cent), Moslem (31 per cent)

System of govt: Socialist people's republic since 12 September 1974

Ethiopian tradition tells of the descent of the emperors of Aksum from Menelik I, himself a descendant of Solomon and the queen of Sheba who are said to have founded the kingdom of Abyssinia (Ethiopia) in c.1000 BC. The rulers of the dynasty assumed the title (until 1974) of Negus (*Negusa Nagast*, King of Kings) and "Lion of Judea". The kingdom of Aksum reached its zenith under the Emperor Azana (300-50), who furthered the spread of Christianity. The arrival of the Arabs in 642 put an end to Aksum's supremacy. The Zagwe Dynasty and King Lalibela reintroduced Christianity in the 12th century. It was not until 1270 with the arrival of Yekuno Amlak that a dynasty descended from Solomon regained the Ethiopian throne. The centre of political power moved to the south, to Tegoulet in the Shoa region.

Centuries later the Ethiopian kingdom of Amhara was only able to protect itself against the Moslem populations by calling upon the assistance of Portuguese mercenaries. A Jesuit attempt to convert the people led to an uprising in 1622.

Emperor Fasiladas (1632-67), whose capital was at Gondar, forbade catholic preachers to enter Ethiopia.

The European colonial powers attempted to settle in Ethiopia during the 19th century. The British intervention in 1868 caused the downfall of the Emperor Tewodros II (1855-68), who had usurped the throne. The French settled in Obock (1881) and in Djibouti (1885) in response to settlements established by the Italians. The Italian attempt to conquer the territory in 1896 failed in the face of the troops of Emperor Menelik II (1889-1907), who crushed General Baratieri's forces at Adoua on 1 March. The emperor established his capital at Addis Ababa and attempted to modernise the country and its infrastructure. A series of military campaigns enabled him to extend his territories.

Thus it was that Ethiopia, known to Europeans as Abyssinia, was one of only two states in Africa (the other was Liberia) to remain independent of European colonial control. Until, that is, the Italian dictator Mussolini decided it should form part of his Fascist empire.

Italian invasion and after

Emperor Menelik's nephew, Ras Tafari, ascended the throne in 1930 and took the name of Haile Selassie. In late September and early October 1935 Mussolini engineered a border dispute with Ethiopia and ordered an invasion of the country from Italian-occupied Somaliland and Eritrea. Italy's Fascist troops moved into the country – although not without some fierce resistance put up by the under-equipped Ethiopian troops. A pact between the British and French foreign ministers, who agreed to let Italy keep the most fertile parts of Ethiopia it had conquered, was scrapped after an outcry that led to the resignation of Britain's foreign secretary. Haile Selassie fled to neighbouring French Somaliland (Djibouti) three days before the fall of Addis Ababa in May 1936. He took refuge in London until the country was liberated by Anglo-French troops in 1941.

The emperor reorganised the administrative structure and granted a liberal constitution in 1955. The Organisation for African Unity (OAU) was created in Addis Ababa in 1963 and established its headquarters there.

The first free elections in Ethiopia were held in 1967. Economic crisis and famine led to the overthrow of the monarchy in a coup in 1974. Nationalisation and radical agrarian reform were introduced. The ageing Haile Selassie, held under house arrest since the coup, died in August 1975. The junta's internal problems led to Haile Mariam Mengistu's rise to power in February 1977.

A conflict with neighbouring Somalia in 1978 was followed by renewed troubles in 1982. The country, which is supported by other socialist states, was severely afflicted by a drought claiming hundreds of thousands of victims, as well as by wars in the Ogaden (until 1978), Eritrea and Tigre. The European Community (EC) was among those who granted huge amounts of famine aid in 1984, and the Live Aid appeal launched by Irish rock singer Bob Geldof in 1985 raised over 50,000,000 pounds for famine relief.

Colonel Mengistu reverted to civilian rule in 1987, with himself as president under a new republican constitution. Famine, locusts and malaria plagued the country in 1988, when the government introduced new agricultural reforms to help the country's precarious economy.

Fiji

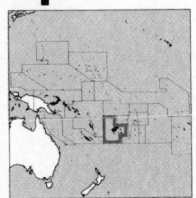

FJI
Oceania
7,076 sq. mi
Pop: 715,000
UN

Capital: Suva (pop: 75,000)
Official languages: English
Religions: Christian (51 per cent), Hindu (39 per cent)
System of govt: Republic proclaimed 7 October 1987

Fiji's population is probably descended from Polynesians who were the first inhabitants of the islands in c.1500 BC. This population was then joined by Melanesians arriving from the west. Dutchman Abel Tasman was the first European to sight the north coast of Fiji, in 1643. The first European to observe the south was the Englishman, James Cook, in 1774.

The British did not establish themselves on the commercially unprepossessing archipelago until the start of the 19th century. In 1858 Prince Cakobao, with the military support of the king of Tonga, formed an independent Fijian kingdom. A treaty of friendship signed with Britain on 10 October 1874 made Fiji a British colony.

From 1879 the Melano-Polynesian population declined as the immigrant population of Indian sugar plantation workers and their descendants expanded, eventually accounting for 50 per cent of Fiji's inhabitants. Trouble between the two communities erupted in confrontations in December 1959.

In 1970 Fiji gained independence, remaining part of the Commonwealth. It was led by Prime Minister Ratu Sir Kamisese Kapaiwai Tuimacilau Mara. On April 12 1987, Tuimacilau Mara was defeated in a general election by Dr Timoci Bavadra, an ethnic Fijian, heading a coalition of the left. There was a majority of Indians in Bavadra's government, a fact which was unacceptable to the ethnic Fijian Lieutenant Colonel Sitiveni Rabuka, who staged a coup. On October 7 1987 Rabuka declared a republic. Fiji left the Commonwealth. On December Rabuka returned the country to civilian rule. Former Governor General Ratu (Chief) Sir Penaia Genilau was appointed president and Ratu Sir Kamisese Mara prime minister. Many Indians left in the wake of the coup and their continued exclusion from a role in the country's affairs, deprives Fiji of valuable human resources.

Finland

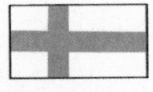

SF
Northern
Europe
117,615 sq. mi
Pop: 4.9 m
UN, NC, OECD

Capital: Helsinki (pop: 487,000)
Official languages: Finnish, Swedish
Religion: Lutheran (91.5 per cent)
System of govt: Republic; independent since 6 December 1917

Finland's original Finno-Ugric population, related to the Hungarians, came from the territories bordered by the Volga and the Urals. Missionaries were active in the area in the 12th century, followed by Swedish settlers. The territorial expansion of the Swedish settlers led to a number of wars with Russia between 1555 and 1617. The Reformation was introduced into the country by Bishop Pietari Sarkilahti in 1527 and in 1581 Finland was designated a grand duchy of Sweden. Swedish wars with Russia (1713-21, 1741-43) led to Finland's loss of Karelia.

Finland was acknowledged as being within the Russian sphere of influence under the short-lived Franco-Russian alliance of 1807, signed by Czar Alexander I and Napoleon. Russian troops occupied Finland in 1808 and the country was declared a Russian grand duchy in 1809, although the czar retained the former Swedish constitution.

The policy of russification, including the imposition of the Russian language, announced in February 1899 by Czar Nicholas II, led to an uprising to support Finnish demands for autonomy. The troubles eventually led to the assassination of the Russian governor of Finland, Bobrikov, in 1904, and the czar withdrew the measures in 1905.

The Finnish parliament declared independence from Russia, which was in the throes of revolution, on 6 December 1917. But Russian troops remained stationed in the country, and the Bolshevik Red Army subsequently engaged in a war against a German-backed Finnish civil guard. The Finns won and a constitution was adopted on 21 June 1919.

The 23 inter-war governments were unable to solve either serious economic problems or the rivalry between populations of Swedish and Finnish origin. Despite a non-aggression treaty with Stalin in 1932, the USSR invaded Finland on 30 November 1939 following an ultimatum to the Finns to give up Karelia, which Stalin claimed he needed for the defence of Leningrad. The Finns were no push-over, however, with a brilliantly organised defence line (Mannerheim Line) and skilled ski troops who ran rings round the Red Army in Finland's forests. When Finland capitulated, in March 1940, it was only through sheer weight of Soviet numbers (as many as a million Soviet troops died). Finland lost a tenth of its territory, principally in Karelia, to the USSR. The perceived weakness of the Red Army had dire consequences for the USSR, which was invaded by Hitler in June 1941. Finland allied with Nazi Germany against the USSR in 1941, but abandoned the alliance in September 1944.

Under the Treaty of Paris (1947) Finland lost Karelia, the mining district of Petsamo and the port of Porkkala on the Baltic to the USSR. It regained the port in 1956 after an improvement in relations with the USSR following the death of Stalin; a friendship and non-aggression treaty had already been signed in 1948, which has been renewed without interruption since.

A well-managed policy of neutrality was maintained under the presidencies of Juho Paasakivi (1946-56) and of Urho Kekkonen (1956-82). Trade and economic agreements were signed with both COMECON and the EEC in 1973. Helsinki has become a favoured venue for international talks, such as the Strategic Arms Limitation Talks (SALT) of the late 1970s and early 1980s and the Conference of Security and Co-operation in Europe (1973-75). The social democrat Mauno Koivisto has led Finland since 1982. He was re-elected for a second six-year term as president on 1 March 1988.

France

France

F
Western Europe
211,968 sq. mi
Pop: 55.5 m
UN, EC,
OECD, NATO
(special
status)

Capital: Paris (pop: 2.2 m)
Official language: French
Religion: Catholic (90 per cent)
System of govt: Republic, according to the constitution of 28 September 1958

The earliest traces of human occupation discovered in France date back 400,000 years. The Celts appeared in c.700 BC. The first clear stage in the development of what was then called "Gaul" came when Julius Caesar conquered this land on behalf of the Romans between 58 BC and 51 BC. The Romans started to withdraw from the region in the 3rd century in the face of invasions of Germanic tribes, the Alamanni and the Franks. The Franks reunified Gaul under the reign of Clovis (486-511). By the death of Charlemagne in 814 the Frankish kingdom extended well beyond the frontiers of present-day France. It was divided after the reign of Louis I (the Pious, 814-840) by the Treaty of Verdun (843). Charles II (the Bald) obtained a territory bounded in the east by the Scheldt-Saône Meuse line which foreshadowed the extent of the future France. But the Carolingian dynasty was unable to impose its monarchical power in the face of the great feudal lords.

The confirmation of royal power

This situation changed in 987 after the accession to the throne of Hugh Capet, elected by an assembly of feudal lords. The founder of the Capetian dynasty imposed the principle of hereditary succession which bequeathed the throne to his son Robert II. The rapprochement between the pope and the monarchy allowed the latter to impose a gradually more centralised power. Later kings continued the process, and also made territorial gains. In the 14th century, French rulers were able to take advantage of the proximity of the pope, who moved to Avignon in 1309 and remained there until 1376. The Capetian dynasty ended, after 300 years on the throne, with Charles IV in 1328. An age of internal and external troubles dawned which was not to end until Louis XI ascended the throne in 1461.

The Hundred Years War

Salic law (barring the accession of women) meant that the Capetians, who had left only daughters, were succeeded by the Valois, a younger branch of the same house. However, the rights of Philip VI, the first Valois king (1328-

50), were contested by Edward III, king of England and grandson of Philip the Fair, through his mother. The Hundred Years War started in 1337. The English troops inflicted a number of crushing defeats on the French forces: Crecy (1346) and Poitiers, where John the Good was taken prisoner (1356). France also suffered internal disputes between the Armagnacs, led by the duke of Orleans, and the duke of Burgundy. In 1419 the Burgundions concluded an alliance with the English king, Henry V, who had defeated the French at Agincourt in 1415. Henry V married Catherine, daughter of Charles VI, in 1420 and became heir to the French throne following the Treaty of Troyes in the same year. But Henry V died two months before Charles VI in 1422 and his son, Henry VI, still a minor, was proclaimed king of France. England was unable to consolidate its position, however, and by 1453 had lost all its territories in France except Calais.

The Renaissance

When he ascended the throne in 1461 Louis XI became master of a kingdom enjoying healthy finances and possessing a powerful army. He and his successors continued the process of absorbing autonomous regions: Anjou, Provence, parts of Burgundy and Brittany. Kings from Charles VIII onwards were also drawn into Italian affairs, an involvement which produced a major victory for Francis I at Marignano (1515) and a decisive defeat at Pavia ten years later. The concordat concluded with Pope Leo X in 1516 at Boulogne made the Catholic Church one of the pillars of the French monarchy. During the final ten years of his reign Francis I struggled against the spread of the Reformation. John Calvin had to flee from Paris in 1534. The religious conflicts were far worse under Francis I's successors.

The wars of religion

An attack on the Huguenots (French Protestants) organised by the Catholic house of Guise at Vassy in March 1562 marked the start of the wars of religion, which were to continue until 1598. The reconciliation beginning to take shape between King Charles IX and the leader of the Huguenots, Admiral Coligny, came to a brutal end on Saint Bartholemew's eve in 1572 when Paris' protestant population was massacred by catholics.

The war was resumed with increased ferocity after the assassination of Henry III in 1589. The accession to the throne of the leader of the Huguenot party, Henry of Navarre, was the only avenue of reconciliation. Henry IV was converted to catholicism on 25 July 1593 at Saint Denis and guaranteed freedom of confession in the Edict of Nantes in 1598. Henry was assassinated in 1610, leaving an under-age heir. Royal authority was restored under the successive ministers of Louis XIII, Cardinal

Richelieu and Mazarin. When Louis XIV made the government of France his personal responsibility in 1661, after the death of Mazarin, he inherited a country with secure frontiers, a well-functioning administration, healthy finances and a well-organised army.

The age of the Sun King

Louis XIV (1643-1715) took to its limit the idea of absolute monarchy. His methods of government, the style of his reign, his court and his palace became the model for the European sovereigns of the day. With the aid of his minister Jean-Baptiste Colbert, Louis presided over a surge in trade and industry. Economic growth, however, was compromised by the wars fought in the search for supremacy in Europe. The financial situation continued to deteriorate under Louis XV (1715-74) and Louis XVI (1774-92). The increasing national debt led to a heavier tax burden falling on peasants and artisans. In 1763 the Peace of Paris put an end to the Seven Years War which had broken out in 1756. Under it France surrendered Canada to England, losing at the same time its status as a great colonial power. The financial crisis forced Louis XVI to convoke the Estates General – France's parliament – for the first time since 1614.

The Revolution

The Estates General met at Versailles on 5 May 1789. Faced with the impossibility of achieving reform, the third estate, calling itself the National Assembly, pledged to formulate a constitution. The capture of the Bastille on 14 July demonstrated anti-monarchical feeling and marked the start of the revolution. The National Assembly abolished a number of the nobility's privileges, but on the whole it remained favourable to the monarchy. The failure of the king's attempt to escape with his family and his return to Paris in June 1791 intensified the revolutionary climate. An unsuccessful war against Prussia further fuelled political radicalism. A republic was proclaimed on 22 September 1792 and Louis XVI was executed the following year. The Terror ended with the overthrow of Robespierre in July 1794. A new constitution, the third, was established and a Directory of five members took over the leadership of government in 1795. General Napoleon Bonaparte, who had returned in triumph after his victories in Italy against Austria and Sardinia, launched a coup d'etat against the Directory in November 1799 and replaced it with a Consulate in which he assumed the office of first consul.

The Napoleonic age

The new constitution established by Bonaparte in 1799 was followed by far-reaching social and administrative forms. At the same time Bonaparte was recording a number of important suc-

cesses abroad. The Peace of Luneville was signed with Austria (France regained Italian territories lost in 1799) and the Peace of Amiens was signed the following year (1802). Britain at this point was isolated in opposition to Bonaparte.

Bonaparte crowned himself emperor in 1804 in the presence of the pope. The retention of elected assemblies did not prevent the reign from developing in a monarchical fashion. The centralisation of the administration, the placing of the judiciary under state supervision and the existence of an omnipresent police force guaranteed the emperor's power. However, Emperor Napoleon faced economic problems exacerbated by the Continental System, intended as a boycott of Britain, which ruined maritime trade. War continued against coalition after coalition of European powers, all of which were held together, despite defeats, by Britain's naval supremacy. The fourth coalition was defeated in 1807 and the fifth in 1809 (Wagram). At its height, the empire extended from the North Sea to the Adriatic and numbered 130 departments. In 1812 the tide began to turn with Napoleon's retreat from Russia. Napoleon capitulated and abdicated on 6 April 1814. The first Treaty of Paris (30 May 1814) signed by the representatives of the restored monarchy restricted France to her 1792 frontiers. But the restoration of the privileges of the emigre nobility and the church aroused deep discontent in France and this was exploited by Napoleon who returned from exile on the island of Elba in March 1815 and reached Paris after a triumphal progress. Louis XVIII, brother of Louis XVI and the new king of France, was forced to flee. Napoleon's hundred day adventure was ended by a new European coalition on the battlefield of Waterloo in Belgium. Napoleon abdicated for the second time four days later, on 22 June 1815. He died in 1821 in British captivity on the island of Saint Helena. The second Treaty of Paris (20 November 1815) stripped the country of further territories.

Restoration and republic

Louis XVIII granted the country a constitutional charter: two chambers were to be elected by restricted suffrage. On the death of Louis XVIII in 1824 the throne passed to his brother Charles X, whose return to authoritarian monarchy provoked the outbreak of revolution in 1830. Charles X was forced to abdicate in favour of Louis-Philippe of Orleans, the "bourgeois king". The rapid expansion of industrialisation created new social tensions and an urban proletariat.

Workers' revolts broke out throughout the country and the troubles were further aggravated by the econnomic crisis of the 1840s. The banning of a reformist banquet in Paris sparked off a new revolution, and brought about the abdication of Louis-Philippe on 24 February 1848. The Second Republic was proclaimed and socialists and republicans joined in a government which introduced national workshops to enable the unemployed to find immediate work. The closure of the workshops after the victory of the moderate republicans in June provoked a workers' uprising in Paris which was bloodily put down. The nephew of Emperor Napoleon I, Prince Louis Napoleon Bonaparte, was elected president on 10 December 1848.

The Second Empire
The coup of 2 December 1851 left Louis Napoleon Bonaparte in sole control. The president was proclaimed emperor on 2 December 1852 after the re-establishment of the French empire had been approved by a large majority in a plebiscite. Seen from abroad the reign of Napoleon III appeared to be marked by success: in foreign affairs he presided over the Crimean war against Russia (1853-56), the conquest of new territories in North Africa and the foundation of colonial power in Indochina.

On the domestic front the universal exhibitions of Paris in 1855 and 1867 gave the impression of a politically stable France. However, the failure of the Mexican expedition after the execution (1867) of the Emperor Maximilian of Mexico, who had been supported by the French, revealed the fragility of the regime. In 1870 war broke out between France and Prussia over a conflict of diplomatic prestige: the candidature of a German prince for the Spanish throne.

The Third Republic
Defeat at Sedan on 2 September 1870 brought about the abdication of the emperor followed by the proclamation of the Third Republic in Paris. Armistice negotiations with Prussia – shortly afterwards proclaimed the German empire at Versailles – began on 28 January 1871. Named head of government after the February elections, Adolphe Thiers signed the peace at Frankfurt-am-Main on 10 May 1871. France lost Alsace and

Lorraine and had to pay war damages of five billion francs. The Paris Commune also fell in May. This attempt to constitute a socialist state was crushed by government troops from Versailles. More that 20,000 partisans of the Commune were killed. For parties of the left this defeat initiated a brief period of exclusion from French political life. From then on the struggle for power took place between the conservative grand bourgeoisie and convinced republicans. French monarchism still remained strong, but shortly after the war of the pretender the refusal to recognise the tricolour as national flag more or less ended hopes of a restoration of the kingdom.

Liberal reforms were introduced as of the 1880s. The question of the secularisation of schools remained a subject of intense debate. The Dreyfus affair, in which a Jewish officer was wrongly imprisoned for spying, shook public opinion and led to irreconcilable opposition between the supporters of left and right. France was only able to survive the shock of the First World War by mustering all the resources of the nation. The German offensive was halted by Joffre and Gallieni at the Marne (September 1914) and the war then dragged on in the trenches. After the 1916 German offensive had been pushed back at Verdun, the entry of the USA into the war allowed the Allies to go on the attack. The sure grip which Clemenceau brought to the affairs of state secured the political unity indispensable for victory. Alsace and Lorraine were recovered after the negotiations of the Treaty of Versailles in 1919. France between the wars experienced a continuous deterioration of her economic problems and a persistent financial crisis. The left, which had split into communists and socialists in 1920, allied itself to the radicals in 1936 and won the elections in May. The government formed by Leon Blum after the victory of the Popular Front introduced a package of new social laws. Blum's cabinet was forced to resign in 1938 following divisions in the Popular Front and pressure from the right. The new government formed by Edouard

Daladier declared war on Hitler's Germany after it had invaded Poland on 3 September 1939. The French army fell very soon after the beginning of the German offensive on 10 May 1940. Marshal Philippe Petain, France's First World War hero who became head of a puppet "French State", signed an armistice with Germany. French underground resistance movements were united in May 1943 when a Free French army (FFL) was reformed in England and in Africa. The FFL took part in the battles to liberate France after the landing of the allied forces in June 1944. The FFL's leader was General de Gaulle, a junior minister in the last Daladier cabinet. De Gaulle headed the French Committee for National Liberation, which was created in Algiers in June 1943, which formed a provisional government after the entry of the Allies into Paris on 25 August 1944.

The Fourth Republic
General de Gaulle, who was unable to push through his views on the constitution which was to be established, resigned from his post of premier after the elections of October 1945. The Fourth Republic was born when the constitution was approved by referendum on 13 October 1946. At a time when economic growth seemed to be re-establishing itself in the wake of the aid brought by the Marshall Plan, the new republic was shaken by colonial crises. France withdrew from Indochina after the defeat of Dien Bien Phu in 1954. The Anglo-French Suez expedition, which was intended to protect the interests of the two old colonial powers in Egypt, failed at the end of 1956 in the face of opposition from the USA and the USSR.

The political crisis reached its height after the uprising in Algeria in May 1958. De Gaulle alone seemed capable of mastering the situation.

The Fifth Republic
The constitution of the Fifth Republic, intended to prevent the ministerial instability which had characterised the Fourth Republic, was adopted following the referendum of 28 September

1958. The president recovered significant institutional powers and de Gaulle set about realising his vast plans for economic and social recovery. Algeria was granted independence in 1962. De Gaulle presented France with an autonomous nuclear capability intended to guarantee its independence from the USA and which in turn led to greater rapprochement between France and its German neighbour.

De Gaulle faced student and worker unrest and strong political opposition in May 1968, and eventually resigned after losing a constitutional referendum in April 1969. He died shortly thereafter. Gaullist politics, hostile to an extended Common Market (created in 1957), continued to evolve under the presidency of Georges Pompidou. On Pompidou's death in 1974 the Independent Republican Valery Giscard d'Estaing was elected president. He was confronted by the economic crisis induced by the monetary and oil crises. The coalition of the right and the centre united under the president, was able to win the general election of 1978, but in May 1981 the presidency fell to the candidate of the union of the socialist and communist left, Francois Mitterrand. The left also triumphed in the June elections. A policy of social reform and nationalisation was introduced into an unfavourable economic climate.

The electorate showed itself to be unenthusiastic about such committed policies and gave victory to a coalition of the right at the March 1986 elections to the national assembly. This sharing of executive power between a president and prime minister of opposing parties was new to the Fifth Republic. The socialist President Mitterrand found himself presiding over an administration headed by the right-wing prime minister Jacques Chirac. Mitterrand was re-elected president on 8 May 1988. In June 1988 new elections resulting from a hung parliament led to the appointment of the socialist Michel Rocard as prime minister.

In 1989 the 200th anniversary of the storming of the Bastille was celebrated with great ceremony as western leaders met for an economic summit in Paris.

Gabon

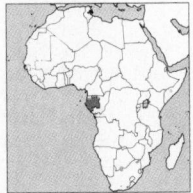
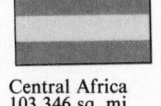

Central Africa
103,346 sq. mi
Pop: 1.2 m
UN, OAU, OPEC

Capital: Libreville (pop: 250,000)
Official language: French
Religion: Christian (75 per cent)

System of govt: Republic; independence obtained 17 August 1960

Gabon's early history remains largely unknown until the Portuguese arrived in c.1470. The two main reasons for the European presence in Gabon remained, until the 18th century, trade in both slaves and ivory. Trade, conducted by the Portuguese, the English, the Dutch, the French and the Spanish, was confined to posts along the coast.

In an attempt to end the slave trade the French founded Fort Aumale

on the estuary of the river Gabon in 1839, and concluded treaties of protectorship with the Mpongwe kings Denis and Louis. It was close to this fort that the French founded Libreville ("free town") in 1839, and offered refuge to freed slaves arriving from the Congo. Gabon was annexed by France in 1885 and became a colony in 1886. Pierre Savorgnan de Brazza was named government commissioner for Gabon and neighbouring French Congo. The Fang peoples pushed back the Mpongwes and reached the Atlantic coast in

about 1900. The country was made part of French Equatorial Africa in 1910, although it was not pacified until 1929. Leon M'ba became the first president of Gabon in 1961. He was overthrown in February 1964 by a coup incited by Jean Aubame, the leader of the banned opposition. French troops enabled M'Ba to regain control. On his death in November 1967 he was succeeded by Omar Bongo, supported by the country's only party, the Gabonese Democratic Party (PDG), created in 1967. Bongo was last re-elected in 1986.

Gambia

Gambia

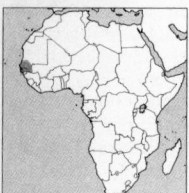
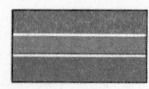

WAG
West Africa
4,127 sq. mi
Pop: 787,000
UN, CW, OAU

Capital: Banjul (pop: 44,000)
Official language: English
Religion: Moslem (95 per cent)
System of govt: Republic; independence obtained 18 February 1965

The country extends along the course of the river Gambia, an area subjugated by the Ghana empire in the 10th and 11th centuries before falling under the influence of the Mali empire until the 15th century. The Portuguese reconnoitred the Gambia in 1447 and established trading posts there. They were closely followed by the English who imposed their supremacy from 1589 onwards.

Over the following centuries the European powers fiercely contested the ascendancy over the estuary of the river Gambia which constituted an ideal base for expeditions into the interior of the continent. This rivalry continued between Britain and France after the Portuguese, Spanish and Dutch had been expelled from the area. The island of St James, close to the south bank of the estuary, served as a base for British expansion which continued up the course of the river Gambia.

True colonisation did not start until after the town of Bathurst (Banjul) had been founded in 1816 on St Mary's Island, a refuge for freed slaves. The island obtained colonial status in 1843, and retained this after a protectorate had been established over the whole of the Gambia in 1888. Gambia gained its independence on 18 February 1965, remaining a part of the Commonwealth. A republic was proclaimed on 24 April 1970 by Sir Dawda Kairaba Jawara, head of Gambia's principal party, the People's Progress Party (PPP), who was elected president.

Gambia's co-operation with neighbouring Senegal intensified during the 1970s after President Senghor's visit in April 1967. A serious crisis broke out at the end of October 1980 when the Senegalese army was called on to intervene against an uprising. In July 1981 Jawara was deposed in a coup while in London for a royal wedding. The coup was ended a week later by the intervention of Britain's crack troops, the SAS. A loose union of Gambia and Senegal, the confederation of Senegambia, was officially born on 1 February 1982. The Senegalese President Abdou Diouf and Sir Dawda Jawara became respectively president and vice-president of the new federation.

In October 1988 the two countries set up a free trade zone.

German Democratic Republic

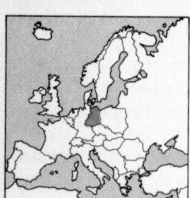

DDR
Central Europe
41,827 sq. mi
Pop: 16.64 m
UN, COMECON, WP

Capital: East Berlin (pop: 1.2 m)
Official language: German
Religions: Protestant (47 per cent), catholic (7 per cent), unaffiliated and other (46 per cent)
System of govt: Socialist republic, proclaimed 7 October 1949

With the defeat of the Nazis in 1945, Germany was divided by the Allies into four zones of occupation: British in the north, French in the centre, US in the south, and Soviet in the east. The capital, though isolated inside the Soviet zone, was likewise divided between the four powers.

The declared intention was eventually to reunite the country; military commandants of the four powers met each month in Berlin to discuss administrative problems. It had been decided by the Allies at the Potsdam conference that, for the time being, central German administrative departments should be established to handle finance, transport, communications, foreign trade and industry. These never came into operation.

Dissension between the USSR and the western Allies, caused only partly by the German question, led to the increasing isolation of the Soviet zone from the three western ones.

Divided Germany

Currency reform carried out in the west, in an attempt to bring raging inflation under control, was not accepted by the USSR, which by now was preparing to set up a regime to its own taste in the east. Otto Grotewohl, a social democrat who had served in the Brunswick state government before the Nazi takeover, was pressed by the Russians to arrange a fusion of the Berlin social democrats and the communists. Grotewohl dithered. The Russians stepped up the pressure with a mixture of flattery and threats. Social democrats were drafted into meetings by Russian officers, who asked for resolutions to be passed calling for fusion with the communists. Social democrats who failed to put up their hands were detained for all-night interrogation.

As for Grotewohl, he was told that a socialist-communist unity party would help to persuade the Soviet government that Germany would not be a threat to peace.

Grotewohl was then offered palatial offices for the new party in East Berlin. He called a meeting of the social democrats' executive, which voted against fusion with the communists. After Grotewohl had spoken for an hour or more, another vote was taken and this time it was in favour of the fusion. The Socialist Unity Party was born and the Russians made Grotewohl prime minister, with the communist Pieck as president.

According to emigres who fled to the West, the Russians made sure Grotewohl understood who was master by presenting him with photos of himself in an embarrassingly intimate embrace with his confidential secretary (provided by the Communist Party.) Grotewohl remained premier for more than a decade.

In 1948, the USSR began interfering with land communications between west Berlin and west Germany. By June the land blockade was complete and it was evident Moscow's purpose was to force the western Allies out of Berlin. From Moscow's point of view Berlin was a western bridgehead in the east; it not only offered Germans visible comparison between life in the west and life under socialist rule, but it also offered an easy way of escape for east Germans, who needed only to board the underground railway.

One link with the west remained: air. The United States and Britain mounted a massive airlift of food, fuel and raw materials to West Berlin. The USSR, clearly unwilling to risk action that might have precipitated war, did not seek to interfere with the flights, and by May 1949, almost a year after the blockade had been imposed, the Soviets made contact with the western Allies at the United Nations and it was lifted. The USSR redrew the eastern frontier of Germany, annexing for itself the northern area of East Prussia. The rest of East Prussia, and territory east of the rivers Oder and Neisse, was transferred to Poland. The German Democratic Republic was formally proclaimed in October 1949, following the creation of the Federal Republic in the west in May of that year.

The death of Stalin in March 1953 had an unsettling effect on the Soviet bloc. This event, coupled with food shortages in East Germany and a directive to workers to increase output by ten per cent, led to anti-Soviet riots in June 1953. They were put down by Soviet tanks.

The tide of East Germans seeking refuge in the West continued unabated and was proving a serious drain on the East German economy. The population had been 17,000,000 soon after the war ended, and people were fleeing at the rate of some 200,000 a year. In one year alone (1960) 700 doctors, 142 professors and 2,000 school teachers fled. By 1961, a total of 2,600,000 had fled, and even today the population has not recovered to the 1946 level.

On Sunday 13 August 1961 the East Germans suddenly appeared at the sector boundary in Berlin and began constructing a barricade of barbed wire and breeze blocks. This was only partly effective in preventing escapes to the west and work on strengthening the wall continued over the years. In time it became two walls with a wide strip of dead ground, strewn with mines, between. Watch towers with searchlights were erected at intervals. Would-be escapers were shot and dragged back into East Berlin.

From the outset, West German governments had refused to recognise the East German regime as a legitimate government, though special terms of trade favourable to the East were operating. In 1969, the social democrats Willy Brandt (a former mayor of West Berlin) became chancellor in Bonn and proceeded to implement a policy of openness to the east (*Ostpolitik*). The East German leader Willi Stoph met Brandt in 1970 and by 1972 a treaty normalising relations between the two states was signed. The agreement paved the way for the admission of the two Germanys to the UN.

Willy Brandt's purpose in seeking an understanding with the East Germans was to persuade them to make contacts between East and West easier. The East Germans did agree to allow elderly people to visit the West and to allow West Germans to visit the East, but some obstacles remained. Every visitor to the East was required to purchase a fixed sum of East German marks for each day's visit. Even so, West Germany continues to provide the East with substantial interest-free credits for trade.

East Germany's leader, Erich Honnecker, made a historic visit to West Germany in September 1987, but hopes for Soviet-style reforms remain unfulfilled.

In November 1988 East Germany banned Soviet magazines it considered "too daring". Soviet President Gorbachev visited in 1989.

German Federal Republic

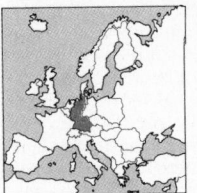

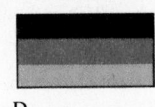

D
Central Europe
96,025 sq. mi
Pop: 61.14 m
UN, EC,
NATO, OECD

Capital: Bonn (pop: 291,000)
Official language: German
Religions: Catholic (49 per cent),
Protestant (45 per cent)
System of govt: Federal republic,
proclaimed 23 May 1949

In the fifth century BC Celtic tribes settled on the eastern Rhine. In the second century BC these were driven back southwards by Germanic tribes arriving from the north. Caesar led two expeditions across the Rhine in 55 BC and 53 BC, but the province of Gaul as created in 51 BC had the Rhine as its boundary. From 12 BC onwards, the Romans launched a series of attacks into Germany, although their defeat in the forest of Teutoburg in year 9 forced them to abandon their plan to conquer the whole of "Germania". The fortified Rhine frontier was to be abandoned in c.260, although the Rhine itself was maintained as a frontier.

The birth of the German kingdom

The large-scale migration which occurred at the time of the decline of the Roman empire saw the arrival of a number of Germanic tribes between the Baltic coast and the Alps. Spreading from Gaul, the Frankish kingdom established its supremacy in the region under Clovis and his successors.

Charlemagne (768-814), crowned by the pope as Western Roman emperor in Rome in 800, subjugated Gaul and the Frankish regions of the lower and the middle Rhine, Thuringia, Alamannia, Bavaria and Saxony. After the death of Charlemagne his empire was divided a number of times between his descendants.

Despite these divisions the idea of a unified Frankish kingdom lived on until the line of the eastern Carolingians died out in 911. When Henry I (died 936) was elected king in 919 the eastern Frankish kingdom assumed the name of "German kingdom" for the first time. It was in the reign (936-973) of Henry's son, Otto I (the Great), that royal power in Germany started to develop.

The German empire

Threatened by revolt, Otto I aligned himself with the church in order to establish his domination. His victory over the Magyars at the Lechfeld in 955 secured the empire's eastern frontier. Otto's second Italian campaign saw him crowned as emperor at Rome in 962, thus signalling his desire for hegemony over the west. Italy was to play a deci-

sive role in German politics during the middle ages. German princes fiercely defended their independence. The pope, too, frequently proved to be a difficult partner as Henry IV of the Salian dynasty (who assumed power in 1024) discovered, when in 1077 he was forced to submit to Gregory VII who had excommunicated him. Their quarrel, over the right of investiture, was continued by their successors and not resolved until the Concordat of Worms in 1122. This gave the German sovereign the right of intervention in the nomination of German bishops but simultaneously strengthened the influence of the princes and the independence of the bishops.

Hohenstaufen and Habsburg

In an attempt to secure his influence in Germany and Italy, the second of the Hohenstaufen emperors, Frederick I (Barbarossa, 1152-90), both reinforced the independence of the German crown from the pope and consolidated his Italian territories when his son married the heiress to Sicily. After the death of his father during the crusades in 1190, Henry VI carried the power of the Hohenstaufens to its apogee. His premature death in 1197 plunged the empire into serious crisis. Frederick II, the last king of significance of the Staufen dynasty, acceded to the throne. His interest in Italy strengthened the influence of the German princes. In 1257 the seven electors (princes who chose the king of Germany) elected two kings to the German crown: Richard, the earl of Cornwall and Alfonso X of Castille. Neither of these, however, was able to impose his influence and the country underwent a period of unrest which lasted until the reign of Rudolph I of Habsburg (1273-91). Habsburg hegemony was not, however, assured until the 15th century. The reign of Frederick III (1440-93), which followed the domination of the house of Luxemburg-Bohemia (1346-1438), marked the start of the Habsburgs' domination of the Holy Roman empire, a hold which was not to be broken until 1806. The power of the German royal house was limited by its method of election. Claimants to the throne had to assure themselves of the goodwill of the princes. German towns witnessed the growth of a self-assured bourgeoisie, whose power was formalised in powerful guilds and, in the north, in the Hanse league of trade towns. Powerful merchant families such as the Fuggers and Welsers were able to rise to a high level of political influence thanks to their role as bankers. Charles V of Habsburg owed his election to the German throne in 1519 to loans from the house of Fugger.

Reformation and Counter-reformation

The rapid propagation from 1517 onwards of the 95 theses formulated by

the monk Martin Luther at Wittenburg marked the start of a reform movement which was soon to endanger the unity of the empire. Luther's criticism of the church's failings were echoed throughout Germany, and the peasants saw in the new doctrines the signal to revolt for their liberty. This revolt was crushed in 1525. A temporary end was put to the conflict between catholic and reformist princes with the Peace of Augsburg in 1555. Lutheranism was recognised as a religion and the faith of the subjects was to be that of their master. The counter-reformation led by the pope and the Habsburgs partially checked the growth of the reformist faith.

Religious conflicts, exacerbated by a struggle for the imperial throne, triggered the Thirty Years War (1618-48). Germany was devastated and a third of the population of the empire left dead. At the Peace of Westphalia in 1648 the empire was finally deprived of Switzerland, the Netherlands, the territories of the Baltic coast of Pomerania, Alsace and Lorraine.

With the Thirty Years War the fiction of the Holy Roman empire as a political entity ceased to be.

The end of the Holy Roman Empire

Following the defeat of the Ottomans before Vienna (1683), Austria was gradually to establish itself as an independent great power. Although officially the Habsburgs still reigned over the Holy Roman empire, the princes had become increasingly powerful: the elector of Saxony became king of Poland in 1697, while the elector of Hanover acceded to the English throne in 1714. The Elector Frederick William (1640-88) turned Brandenburg-Prussia into the dominant power in northern Germany, a position further strengthened under Frederick II the Great (1740-86). Opposition between Prussia and Austria first manifested itself in the Seven Years War (1756-63) and continued to mark German politics during the 19th century. The conflict was not settled until the Seven Weeks War in 1866, when Prussia defeated Austria at Sadowa.

By this stage the Holy Roman empire was long dead, dissolved by Napoleon in 1806 and replaced by the French satellite Confederation of the Rhine. The last Holy Roman emperor, Francis II, abdicated and became Emperor Francis I of Austria.

At the Congress of Vienna in 1815, the 1,700 or so states of varying sizes which had existed before 1803 were largely absorbed by bigger states. The German states formed themselves into the loosely-bound German Confederation. The creation of a German economic zone, the Customs Union, under Prussian leadership in 1834, was not joined by Austria but still constituted an important step towards unification. The unification and democratic move-

ment had already brought about the adoption of constitutions in the various states in central and southern Germany in the 1820s. This movement provided a channel for significant manifestations of popular feeling. The revolution in France of February 1848 was followed in March by revolutionary risings in Germany. The German National Assembly was formed in Frankfurt in May 1848. A constitution was proposed by parliament in the spring of 1849 but the king of Prussia, Frederick William IV, was successful in suppressing democratic uprisings in Saxony, Baden and the Palatinate.

Prussian domination

Otto von Bismarck became premier of Prussia in 1862. He took Schleswig-Holstein from Denmark in 1864 and defeated Austria in 1866, an event which put an end to the German Confederation and replaced it in 1867 with the North German Confederation. This grouped together 22 states, the three Hanseatic cities and the free cities north of the river Main, under Prussian tutelage. The Franco-Prussian War of 1870 and the victory over Napoleon III by a Prussian-led "alliance" of German states made the realisation of German unity possible. The German empire was born on 18 January 1871 when southern German states joined the North German Confederation. The Prussian king, William I, became the first German emperor. Although the empire had a parliament, from which the socialists had been excluded, the imperial chancellor was responsible only to the emperor (kaiser). Bismarck was dismissed in 1890 at a time when the Kaiser William II (ruled 1888-1918) was pursuing increasingly personal and imperialist policies. A treaty signed by Bismarck with Russia was denounced in 1890. A huge programme of naval expenditure begun in 1898 was to lead to a race for naval supremacy with Britain. By 1914 the Triple Alliance of Germany, Austria-Hungary and Italy faced the Triple Entente of Britain, Russia and France. The brewing showdown boiled over into four years of terrible conflict.

The First World War and after

The defeat of November 1918 had cost Germany nearly two million lives. The country was intact (Allied troops never crossed the German frontier in the war) but profoundly demoralised. By the end of September 1918 dissatisfaction and weariness had drawn the social democrats into the government of the chancellor, Prince Max of Baden. Once it had become clear, in the face of revolutionary unrest, that the monarchy could not be saved, Prince Max propagated the news of William II's abdication and transferred power to the social democrats. Under the terms of the Treaty of Versailles signed on the 28 June 1919 Germany lost Alsace and

Lorraine, numerous territories in the east as well as all its overseas colonies. There were communist uprisings in Berlin, Bremen and Bavaria in 1919. The workers' parties, however, failed to achieve the hoped-for majority in the elections of January 1919. The socialist party (SPD) was forced to enter into a coalition with moderate partie. This "Weimar coalition" lost its majority the following year. Only in Prussia was the SPD able to win a ruling majority. In 1923 France occupied the Ruhr to "compensate" for the non-payment of war reparations. Germany's precarious economy collapsed in the face of runaway inflation which wiped out savings of many citizens. Between 1924 and 1929 the republic enjoyed a brief period of economic and political stability but the world-wide depression along with unemployment, which rose to 6,000,000 in 1932, plunged it back into crisis marked by the rise of right-wing extremist movements, especially the National Socialists (Nazis) under Adolf Hitler. From 1930 onwards the chancellor acted without the support of the Reichstag, Germany's parliament, and enjoyed only the confidence of the president, since 1925 the ageing war veteran Marshal von Hindenburg. Attempts to keep the increasingly well-represented Nazis from power broke down, and on 30 January 1933 Hindenburg asked Hitler to form a new government.

Nazi terror and war

Hitler wasted no time in clamping down on opponents (aided by the propaganda coup given by the Reichstag fire within weeks of his rise to power, for which a communist was tried) and the Jews, whom the Nazis blamed for the ills of "pure" Germans.

By the end of the Second World War more than six million Jews had perished through what turned, in 1942, into a policy of systematic extermination. German cultural pride was perverted into ideas of racial superiority. Dictators were not a new phenomenon,

but Hitler's regime was unprecedented in its ideological brutality, surpassing even that of the ridiculous but ruthless Mussolini in Italy. In March 1933 the first concentration camp opened and the Nazis became the only permitted party. Hitler eliminating potential internal rivals in 1934 and became *Fuhrer* (Leader) on the death of Hindenburg in August. A boycott of Jewish businesses began almost immediately after the Nazis came to power and in July decrees were passed aimed at sterilising "unpure" Germans (such as the handicapped). A wave of Jewish emigration soon got under way. In September 1935 the Nuremberg Decrees banned Jews from public life and virtually all professions.

Hitler set about tearing up the Treaty of Versailles, for example by the reoccupation of the Rhineland in 1936, and by rearmament.

Austria was annexed in 1938, the hapless Czechoslovakia in 1938-39. The offensive against Poland launched on 1 September 1939 triggered the second world conflagration in a quarter century.

An attempt on Hitler's life in Munich in November 1939 failed, but the event (which killed seven) was eagerly used as anti-Allied propaganda. Hitler declared all shipping was fair game for the German navy, a move which met with protests from Holland, Belgium, Norway and Denmark, but all opposition was silenced when the Germans invaded all four countries in April and May 1940.

A British Expeditionary Force was expelled from Dunkirk in June as the Germans swarmed across France, and the French surrendered on 22 June. Britain now faced air attack and potential invasion on its own against Germany and Italy, which now joined the war. The Blitz of 1940-41 caused much damage and loss of life in Britain's cities, but the country held out until Hitler broke his word with Stalin and attacked the USSR in June 1941. Hitler thrust deep into the USSR, but he was

now fighting on two fronts. In December the USA declared war on Japan, but not Germany, after the bombing of Pearl Harbor in December 1941. However, Hitler, long angered by open US aid to the British, declared war on the vast resources of wealth and manpower of the USA, thereby, as Churchill said, making his defeat almost certain.

So it proved. Hitler was caught between the combined weight of Britain and its empire, the USA and the USSR. It took nearly four years, but, eventually, Germany capitulated. Hitler committed suicide on 30 April; other German leaders lived to answer for the Nazi nightmare, which ended on 7 May 1945.

Again the human cost was staggering (especially in the USSR and China) and again Germany lost, but this time it was invaded and divided, its cities devastated.

Occupied Germany

The four victorious powers partitioned Germany into four zones, although in practice there were two, western and eastern. The original intention was for Germany to be reunified, but as the Cold War set in this was not to be. The Federal Republic of Germany was established on 23 May 1949 from the western zones, with its capital at the small and uncontroversial city of Bonn. A rival German Democratic Republic emerged in the Soviet zone on 7 October. (See separate entry, page 1174)

The Federal Republic

Konrad Adenauer's CDU (Christian democrats) won the first election in West Germany in August 1949. He formed a coalition government which co-operated closely with the western powers. In 1951 West Germany was a founder member of the European Coal and Steel Community, one of the forerunners of the Common Market, which was created in 1957. The republic became a member of the Council of Europe in 1951 and joined NATO in 1955. The process of reconstruction of the

war-shattered economy in the 1950s and 1960s was such a spectacular success that it has been called an "economic miracle". But confidence in Adenauer's government began to wane after the construction of the Berlin Wall in August 1961. The ageing Adenauer stood down as chancellor after the conclusion of the Franco-German treaty of friendship in January 1963. His successor, Ludwig Erhard, was able to retain power only until November 1966, when for the first time social democrats were represented in government, led by christian democrat Chancellor Kurt Kiesinger (CDU) from 1966. A social democrat and liberal coalition came to power in September 1969, headed by ex-mayor of West Berlin Willy Brandt. It was during his period of government that a "new policy towards the East" (*Ostpolitik*")appeared, aiming at a normalisation of relations with the eastern Europe in general and East Germany in particular. Brandt resigned over a spy scandal in 1974. His successor, Helmut Schmidt, faced economic uncertainty owing to the oil crisis.

Terrorist attacks, in particular those by the Baader-Meinhof gang, were a headache throughout much of 1970s and early 1980s. Unemployment and NATO plans to station more nuclear weapons on German soil partly led to a split in the governing coalition in September 1982. In October 1982 CDU leader Helmut Kohl took over from Schmidt in a centre-right coalition re-elected in March 1983.

West Germany is strategically placed both within NATO and the EC. It has strong and active peace and environmentalist movement. Chancellor Kohl was re-elected in January 1987; economics and east-west relations remain key issues. Kohl has continued the thaw in relations with the east of his predecessors, as exemplified by the visit of East German leader Erich Honecker in September 1987 and the meeting of Kohl and Gorbachev in Moscow in October 1988. Gorbachev paid a well-received return visit in June 1989.

Ghana

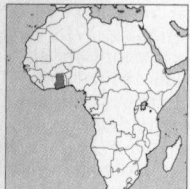

GH
West Africa
92,010 sq. mi
Pop: 12.4 m
UN, CW,
CEDEAO, OAU

Capital: Accra (pop: 859,000)
Official language: English
Religions: Christian (52 per cent), traditional beliefs (30 per cent), Moslem (13 per cent)
System of govt: Republic; independent since 6 March 1957

Osai Tutu (1695-1731), ruler of the Asante, a tribe belonging to the Akan people, founded a kingdom in the region of present-day Ghana and fixed his capital at Koumassi. The Asante reached the coast where they took up contact with European traders.

Trade developed on a bartering basis with the Asante providing gold and ivory, thus earning their territory the name of "Gold Coast".

The Portuguese had been the first Europeans to reach the coast of Ghana in 1471 and established the fortified, trading post of Sao Jorge da Mina there in 1482. They were expelled by the Dutch in 1637 at a time when a number of maritime powers were attempting

to settle in the territory. Trading posts catering for the slave trade were established all the way along the Gold Coast until the abolition of the slave trade in 1807.

Britain took over the Gold Coast's affairs after it became a colony in 1821. In 1874 it became a British protectorate, but the Asante territories would only be conquered after years of bitter fighting. The UGCC (United Gold Coast Convention), founded in 1947, demanded independence. US-educated Kwame Nkrumah left the UGCC and created the Convention People's party (CPP) in 1949.

The CPP's goal was not simply independence, but also the removal of

the power of the tribal chiefs which would enable them to surmount tribal opposition. The CPP swept to a triumphant victory in the 1951 elections. Nkrumah formed Gold Coast's first autonomous government in August 1956. On 6 March 1957 Gold Coast became the first European colony in Africa to gain independence, taking the ancient name of Ghana.

The republic

The republic was proclaimed in July 1960 and Nkrumah was elected president. His dictatorial regime was marked by an ambitious pan-africanism. The nationalisation of the economy fuelled a rapid growth in the national debt which damaged the president's popularity. Nkrumah was overthrown by a coup in February 1966 while he was in China. The new government, the National Liberation Council, pursued a policy of openness towards the west. Normal political life was resumed in 1969 and the leader of the Progressive Party, Dr Kofi Busia, became prime minister after August elections. Nkrumah's CCP was banned and the privileged links which his regime had established with China and the Soviet bloc were severed. But the civilian regime was also unable to resolve the country's economic difficulties.

A new military coup in 1972 carried Colonel Ignatius Kutu Acheampong to power until his resignation in July 1978. Captain Jerry Rawlings led another coup in June 1979. Generals Acheampong and Akuffo, then head of state, were executed for corruption. Elections, which were held as promised on 18 June, were won by the National People's party (NPP) under Dr Hilla Limann who became president.

The corruption and mismanagement of the country which ensued led to a new coup by Captain Rawlings in December 1981, and the banning of political parties. In March 1984 the Rawlings regime suppressed an attempted coup allegedly supported by the neighbouring states of Togo and the Ivory Coast.

The frontier with the Ivory Coast was reopened in May 1984. In 1988 student unrest led to the temporary closure of three universities.

Greece

GR
South East
Europe
50,949 sq. mi
Pop: 10 m
UN, EC,
NATO, OECD

Capital: Athens (pop: 885,000)
Official language: Greek
Religion: Greek orthodox (98 per cent)
System of govt: Republic since 7 June 1975

It was in Crete and Mycenae that Greek history and culture were born. A people probably originating from Asia Minor reached Crete around 7000 BC. The Cretan culture saw outstanding development between 2600 BC and 2000 BC and evidence of its influence is confirmed by the commercial contacts between Crete and distant regions of the Mediterranean and by the foundation of the first palaces after 2000 BC. Five of these palaces have been discovered: Knossos, Kato, Zakros, Mallia, Phaistos and Hagia Triada. The vast palace installations constituted the centre of religious, political and economic life in the Cretan regions. The island was ravaged by several earthquakes around 1700 BC and the palaces were reduced to ashes. They were reconstructed, even larger and more embellished, by the Minoans, so-called (by the archaeologist Arthur Evans) after the legendary King Minos. Their commercial power spread and around 1600 BC the zenith of Cretan civilisation was reached. The Minoans had commercial trading posts in Aegina, Cos, Cythera, Melos, Rhodes, Thera and Miletus. The last of the great palaces were burnt down for unknown reasons around 1400 BC and the Minoan civilisation disappeared to be replaced by the Mycenaean civilisation. From 1400 BC the Mycenaeans, named after their largest city, Mycenae in the Peloponnese, dominated the south of Greece.

They were in Crete from 1450 BC, absorbing its cultural influences and supplanting Crete as a maritime power. The tombs of the Mycenaean princes, exhumed in the 19th century by the German Heinrich Schliemann, revealed the wealth of the warrior city, whose culture, however, never managed to attain the finesse or elegance of the Minoan culture. The centres of Mycenaean power on the Greek mainland were, apart from Mycenae itself, Pylus, Thebes, Tiryns, Athens, Iolcos and Orchomenus.

By about 1300 BC Mycenaean hegemony was complete, but a century later it ceased. It was crushed in c.1100 BC and the greater part of Greece fell under the domination of the Dorians, invading from the north and north-west and colonising most of central Greece as well as the north and north-east of the Peloponnese.

The classical era
The traditions of the Mycenaean world survived most strongly on the mainland of Attica, where the Ionians held only the coastal strip. Over-population was forcing the latter to colonise new areas from the eighth century BC onwards. Among settlements founded in the next two centuries were the ports of Byzantium, Syracuse, Marseilles, Naples and Nice. The Greek micro-states and their colonies were usually governed either autocratically by tyrants or oligarchically by dominant families. This epoch saw the birth of the Homeric epics and the Olympic Games, the first of which were held in Olympia in 776 BC, events which contributed towards the forging of a growing feeling of community among the Greek states. The rise of the Persian kingdom of Cyrus II the Great from the middle of the sixth century BC saw the Greeks faced with a dangerous rival for the first time. By the end of the sixth century the Persians had established a colossal empire and ruled over the Greek cities in Asia Minor which had fallen after prolonged combat. Around 500 BC a desperate revolt broke out in the Ionian Greek cities in Asia Minor but was crushed. Miletus was destroyed in 494 BC. But the parent cities then entered the combat. Athens rushed reinforcements to the Ionian colonies and in 490 BC the Athenians carried off a decisive victory at Marathon against the Persians of Darius I. Ten years later under Xerxes I the Persians again took up the assault of Greece. The Spartans, renowned for their bravery and tactical genius, tried in vain to hold back the Persian army at Thermopylae. The latter, however, was vanquished by Greek forces in the naval battle of Salamis in 480 and on land at Plataea in 479. The key role played by Athens in the struggle against the Persians helped it to become the most important city in Greece. The city, and Greek culture, attained their apogee under the democrat Pericles (461 BC-429 BC). It was also under his government that the Acropolis acquired its classical physiognomy (c.440 BC). Athens was a rich and magnificent city, its democratic system allowed every citizen a voice in government, its intellectual influence was considerable; the masterpieces of Greek tragedy were performed there. The hegemony of Athens soon attracted hostility from its neighbouring cities, and Athens was attacked during the Peloponnesian War (431 BC-404 BC) by a league of cities led by Corinth. Athens' maritime supremacy was equalled only on land by the almost invincible Sparta, its great rival. It seemed impossible that the end of the war could be decided by battle, but then Athens was hit by plague in 429 BC, Pericles himself succumbing. His successors continued the war, but without his political talent. Peace was concluded in 421 BC on the basis of the status quo, but hostilities soon broke out again. Spartan victory was complete in 405, the Athenian fleet was destroyed and Sparta took over the leadership of Greece. However, the Spartans owed their victory to an agreement with the Persians, who had granted them generous subsidies in return for the deliverance of the Greek towns in Asia Minor. The Spartans reneged on their promises and lost their supremacy during the course of the troubles that broke out in Asia Minor and mainland Greece. After having been beaten by the Theban Epaminondas at Leuctra in 371 BC, Sparta was finally defeated in 362 BC by the second Peloponnesian League.

Macedonian supremacy
Rivalry and war continued, preparing the way for the conquest of the country by King Philip II of Macedonia (382 BC-336 BC). His use of wedge-shaped formations of heavy cavalry gave him victory at Chaeronea in 338 BC and the doors of Greece lay open to him. Philip's son, Alexander the Great, continued his work of conquering Asia Minor, defeating the armies of King Cyrus III at Issus in 333 BC and then at Gaugamela in 331 BC. Having mastered the Persian empire, Alexander the Great turned towards the east and conquered as far as the Indus. His death in 323 BC left the vast empire to be disputed by his generals, the Diadochi (Successors), who founded dynasties of their own across the Alexandrine territories. Ptolemy I, Antigonus I, Lysimachus I, Seleucus I and Cassander I all took on the title of king in 306-305 BC and tried to reconstitute Alexander's empire at the expense of their rivals. Only three dynasties survived after the Wars of the Diadochi, in Macedonia until 168 BC, Egypt until 30 BC and the Near East (the Seleucids) until c.30 BC. The reign of the Greek minorities in these areas furthered the extension of Greek culture in the eastern Mediterranean and Near East.

The Antigonids, in power in Macedonia since 276 BC, maintained their hegemony in Greece.

The Roman and Byzantine eras
From the beginning of her expansion around the start of the 3rd century BC, Rome was interested in Macedonia and Greece. Rome intervened first of all against Macedonia which was defeated by Flamininus at Cynoscephalae in 197 BC. The Roman victory against Perseus, son of Philip V of Macedonia, in 168 BC during the third Macedonian War, enabled Rome to annex the kingdom which from then on was divided into four Roman provinces. Free in principle but nevertheless subjected to Roman political control, Greece joined with Macedonia for the revolt of 149-148 BC, which was crushed by the Romans. Corinth was destroyed in 146 BC. Greece was integrated with Macedonia into a single Roman province, the province of Macedonia, created in 148 BC. The attempt by Mithradates to liberate Asia Minor and Greece (88-84 BC) ended in failure and Athens was taken by Sulla after a difficult siege. Exhausted after the civil wars in which she had supported Caesar's rival, Pompey, Greece became an autonomous province, Achaea, under the Roman Emperor Augustus (died 14), with Corinth as her capital. The Emperor Constantine the Great (ruled 306-37) founded the city of Constantinople on the site of the ancient city of Byzantium as a new Christian capital

Grenada

for the empire. After the fall of the Western Roman empire, Constantinople remained the capital of the Eastern Roman, or Byzantine, empire.

As time went by and Roman imperialist ideas lost ground, Greek culture imposed itself across the Byzantine empire, especially as its outer territories were whittled away by various invaders. After the great barbarian invasions of the fourth and fifth centuries, Byzantine Greece was to suffer several more invasions. The Arabs conquered Crete in 826 (retaken in 961); the Bulgars were defeated at Thermopylae in 996; and the Normans ravaged Epirus, Euboea and Attica during the 11th century. Constantinople, the capital of the Byzantine empire, was taken by the Venetians during the crusades to the Holy Land in 1204. Western Europeans, culturally severed from Greece since the final split between Roman catholicism and Greek orthodoxy in the 11th century, became the masters of Greece. The empire was in terminal decline, although the emperors were restored in 1261.

Ottoman domination

Constantinople was captured by the Ottomans in 1453. The crusader states and Greece gradually fell under the control of the Ottoman sultanate. Having been in Venetian hands since 1212, a large part of Crete was, in its turn, conquered by the Ottomans in 1669. Greece was allowed to keep its language and religion in return for loyalty to to its new masters. Numerous Greek artists and scholars sought refuge in Italy, where they gave added momentum with a growing interest in Hellenic art and culture, or Russia, where Byzantine religion had already been transplanted. By an ironic quirk of history, the Greeks acquired an ever greater freedom of trade during the course of the wars between the European powers and the Ottoman empire, eventually taking over from the Venetians in the eastern Mediterranean from the 17th century onwards.

Independence

Greece gained the support of Russia under Catherine the Great, who in 1770 encouraged a revolt in the Peloponnese as part of her own moves against the Turks. Greece also benefitted from a strong current of European sympathy from the beginning of the 19th century. Insurrection broke out in March 1821 and a Greek congress presided over by Alexandros Mavrokordato proclaimed independence in January 1822. The Turkish reprisal was fierce; after two years of bloody combat Greece was retaken by the troops of Mohammed Ali, Pasha of Egypt. Greece was saved by the intervention of the European powers against Turkey in 1827 then by that of Czar Nicholas I in 1828. Greece regained her liberty and was proclaimed a hereditary monarchy by the first London Conference in February 1830.

Modern Greece

The authoritarian regime of King Otto I, who tried to abolish the constitution, caused him to be overthrown in 1862. William of Denmark, brother of Britain's future Queen Alexandra, succeeded him under the name of George I. He ruled until his murder in 1913. Greece, which maintained its neutrality at the beginning of the First World War, joined with the Allies in June 1917 and, obtained southern Albania, then Smyrna (Izmir) in Asia Minor and western Thrace under the treaties of Neuilly and Sevres. The war which broke out with Turkey ended in the defeat of the Greeks at the hands of the troops of Mustapha Kemal, and Smyrna and Thrace were restored to Turkey. The Peace of Lausanne (1923) fixed the border between Greece and Turkey and it has remained unchanged since that date. More than a million Greeks had to emigrate from Asia Minor into European Greece. A republic was proclaimed on 25 March 1924 after the electoral victory of the followers of Eleutherios Venizelos. But the country sank into a state of anarchy and the republic was abolished after the military coup d'etat of March 1935. King George II was recalled by a plebiscite and returned from exile in November 1935. A few months later (4 August 1936) a new coup staged by General Ioannis Metaxas permitted the installation of a new military dictatorship which lasted until the Italian invasion of 1940. Occupied by Axis troops until 1944, Greece was liberated by British troops. A civil war broke out in 1946 between the old communist resistance, which refused to be allied with the royalists, and the legal government which was supported by Britain and then by America.

The government was not able to put down the insurrection until 1950. A modification to the constitution made Greece a constitutional monarchy in 1952. Constantine II succeeded to the throne in 1964 on the death of his father, Paul I, who had been in power since 1947. The following year the king dismissed the prime minister, Georgios Papandreou, accusing him of wanting to increase civil control over the military. The question of union between Cyprus and Greece (Enosis) shook successive governments. The USSR sided with the Turks over the question of the island.

Military dictatorship

In April 1967 a group of officers overturned the civilian government and installed a predominantly military government which swore a loyal oath to the king. Repressive measures aimed at the parties of the left were immediately applied. The government of Constantine Kollias had to withdraw Greek troops from Cyprus in the face of Turkish political pressure. King Constantine, who attempted a counter-coup in December 1967, had to leave Greece and took refuge in Rome with his family. Colonel Papadopoulos took over the government. The constitution promulgated in 1968 established the principle of army pre-eminence in the state. Political opposition was silenced within the country. Opposition in exile, although divided, was unified in the Stockholm Accord of April 1969. A wave of purges affected the trade unions, the church, the administration and even the army. Freedom of the press was suspended in 1970. An attempt at liberalisation in 1971 preceded US recognition. Papadopoulos concentrated power more and more in his own hands and took total control after March 1972. Fearing the return of the king, he proclaimed a republic on 1 June 1973 and became head of state after a referendum in 29 July. An uprising of Athenian students on 14 November 1973 was violently suppressed. Papadopoulos was overthrown a few days later by General Phaedon Gizikis, who further intensified the repression. The aggravation of tension in Cyprus gave rise to the recall of the civilian government, constituted by the former prime minister, Constantine Karamanlis.

The return to democracy

Elections in November 1974 were won by the "New Democratic" Party of Karamanlis. In 1975 a referendum voted in favour of the abolition of the monarchy and King Constantine left for exile in Britain. The new republic opened negotiations to resolve the Cyprus question.

The year of 1981 saw Greek entry into the EC as well as an electoral victory for the socialist party (PASOK). The prime minister, Andreas Papandreou, distanced himself from NATO and the USA, who were accused of showing favour to Turkey to the detriment of Greece.

The election of Christos Sartzetakis as president in March 1985, and its victory in June elections, constituted a double victory for PASOK.

Sex and corruption scandals severely dented the popularity of the Papandreou government, and following inconclusive elections in June 1989, Papandreou was forced to give way to a "clean government" coalition of conservatives and communists.

Grenada

WG
Caribbean
120 sq. mi
Pop: 104,000
UN, CW,
CARICOM,
OAS

Capital: St George's (pop: 30,000)
Official language: English
Religions: Catholic (64 per cent), Protestant (34 per cent)

System of govt: Constitutional monarchy; independence obtained 7 February 1974

The island of Grenada was discovered in 1498 by Christopher Columbus who named it Concepcion. Acquired by the Martinique government in 1650 and then by the French West India Company in 1665, Grenada was colonised under the control of the French crown from 1674. Plantations of cotton, coffee and cocoa were developed. As the indigenous population had been decimated, the workforce was provided by black slaves, brought across the Atlantic from West Africa. Britain, which captured the island from France in 1762, gained complete possession of Grenada after the Treaty of Versailles in 1783, which ended the American War of Independence. Three years previously, the island had been recaptured by the French. From 1958 to 1962, Grenada belonged to the West Indies Federation, a pre-independence grouping of Britain's colonial possessions in the Caribbean. The island obtained internal autonomy in 1960, and then independence within the Commonwealth in 1974.

The regime of Prime Minister Eric Gairy was overthrown on 13 March 1979 by Maurice Bishop's New Jewel Movement. Bishop's overthrow by the army on 20 October 1983 led to the the intervention of US and Caribbean troops five days later, on the grounds that Cuban troops stationed on the island posed a threat. Another reason put forward by President Ronald Reagan was the danger to US citizens on the island; either way, the mission was an easy way of warning nearby states of the perils of allowing communism close to the USA. The USA vetoed a UN resolution "deeply deploring" the invasion. Bishop turned out to have been murdered in the coup that overthrew him. Herbert Blaize, head of the New National party, won elections in December 1984 and has been in power since.

Guatemala

GCA
Central America
42,042 sq. mi
Pop: 8.4 m
UN, OAS,
LAES

Capital: Guatemala City (pop: 1.3 m)
Official language: Spanish
Religions: Catholic (75 per cent),
Protestant (25 per cent)

System of govt: Republic;
independent from Spain since 1821

The first inhabitants of Guatemala were the hunters dating back to c.10,000 BC. The first villages appeared after 2000 BC on the Pacific. The period 250-950 saw the blossoming of Maya culture. After the fall of the Teotihuacan and Toltec empires by c.1200, several kingdoms were founded by northern warriors, who ruled the highlands until the Spanish arrived in February 1524.

Guatemala, part of the vice-royalty of Mexico, united Chiapas, Guatemala, Honduras, El Salvador, Nicaragua and Costa Rica from 1570 until 1821.

Guatemala gained independence in 1821 and split from Mexico in 1823. It was a member of the Central American Confederation from November 1824 to 1839. Rafael Carrera established a dictatorship which lasted until 1865. Civil war erupted, won by the liberal Rufino Barrios (1873-85). Civil war flared after 1885, and a pattern of dictatorships and growing US influence set in right up to the 1960s.

In 1965 Guatemala gained a civilian president, but power remained with the army. Rival terror groups conducted a guerrilla war from 1961 which led to the proclamation of a state of siege in 1970.

A coup in March 1982 brought General Efrain Montt to power until another coup in 1983. The far right won elections in June 1984, but, under international pressure for its appalling human rights record, called new elections in late 1985, when Christian democrat Vinicio Cerezo was elected president. But coup attempts occurred in June and December 1987, and May 1988.

Guinea (Republic of)

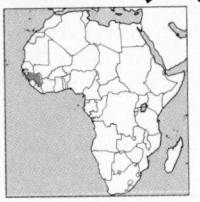
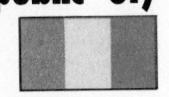

West Africa
94,926 sq. mi
Pop: 6.4 m
UN, OAU

Capital: Conakry (pop: 763,000)
Official language: French
Religions: Moslem (69 per cent),
traditional beliefs (30 per cent)

System of govt: Socialist republic, proclaimed 2 October 1958

The territory of the present-day republic of Guinea belonged to the kingdom of Mandingo which, from the third to the ninth centuries was vassal to the great empire of Ghana. The coastal regions were charted in 1445 by Portuguese navigators.

The French followed the Portuguese in Guinea and developed their interests in the early 19th century. The coastal trading posts on the southern rivers were placed under Senegalese administration from 1859. The country became a French colony in 1891, was given the name French Guinea in 1893, and was integrated into French West Africa in 1895. The mountainous regions to the south managed to resist French occupation until King Samory Toure was defeated in 1898.

Until the Second World War the country's economy was dominated by banana plantations and remained poor. The mining of bauxite and iron began after 1945. Guinea became independent in September 1958 under the leadership of Sekou Toure, grandson of Samory Toure. Supported by the socialist countries, Guinea gradually isolated itself from France and its moderate neighbours. Sekou Toure was re-elected three times. He placed the port and airport at Conakry at the disposal of the USSR and Cuba during the Angolan War from 1974, and pursued authoritarian policies until his death in March 1984, when the military took power and declared it would restore democracy. The new president, Brigadier Lansana Conte, thwarted a coup in July 1985. Conte remained in power in 1989, pursuing a policy of non-alignment.

Guinea Bissau

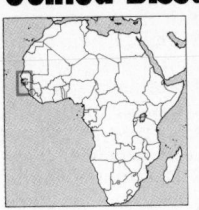

West Africa
13,948 sq. mi
Pop: 912,000
UN, OAU

Capital: Bissau (pop: 109,000)

Official language: Portuguese
Religions: Traditional beliefs (65 per cent), Moslem
System of govt: Republic; independence proclaimed 24 September 1973

The first European to see the coast of present day Guinea-Bissau was the Portuguese Nuno Tristao in 1446. The country quickly became an important centre for the slave trade. Guinea-Bissau became a Portuguese province in 1879, a colony in 1927 and then a province again in 1951. Bissau, founded in the 17th century, became the country's capital in 1941. Amilcar Cabral founded the African Party of Independence for Guinea and the Cape Verde Islands (PAIGC) in 1956. A guerrilla movement was based in neighbouring Guinea after it became independent in 1963. Cabral was assassinated in Guinea in January, 1973. Independence was proclaimed in September 1973, and was accepted by Lisbon in August 1974. Luis de Almeida Cabral, brother of Amilcar Cabral, became the first president of Guinea-Bissau. He was toppled by a coup in November 1980, and a junta was set up under Joao Vieira, who became secretary-general of the PAIGC. After elections in March 1984, the junta was replaced by a council of state, also led by Vieira.

Guyana

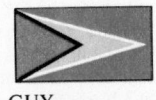

GUY
South America
83,000 sq. mi
Pop: 750,000
UN, CARI-
COM, CW

Capital: Georgetown (pop: 185,000)
Official language: English
Religions: Christian (57 per cent),
Hindu (33 per cent)
System of govt: Republic; independent since 12 October 1968

Situated on the north-eastern coast of South America, what is now Guyana was discovered by Christopher Columbus in 1498. He reached the Orinoco river but did not establish any settlement. Other Spanish explorers in 1517 and 1584 preceded Walter Raleigh in his search for El Dorado (1595).

But the Spanish found the country to be of little interest and left the Dutch, English and French to settle there from the 16th century onwards. Towards the middle of the 17th century the English were expelled by the French and Dutch, but the British returned a century later, in 1796, and occupied the Dutch territories of Guyana. Pushed back for a while, the British became definitive masters of the country in 1814. The Dutch territory was divided between the two powers.

Guyana became a British colony in 1831. The abolition of slavery in 1833 led to the arrival, by 1917, of several hundreds of thousands of families originating from India. This Indian population was to play a crucial role in Guyana's history. The conflict which flared up in the second half of the 20th century between the planters and Dr Jagan's Progressive party led to serious political problems.

Guyana obtained internal autonomy in August 1961, and became completely independent on 26 May 1966. Political life was dominated by two opposing parties: the People's National Congress (PNC), representing the black population, and the increasingly influential People's Progressive Party (PPP), representing the Indian population. Lindon Forbes Burnham was elected first president of the country in 1980. He died in August 1985 and was replaced by the prime minister, Hugh Desmond Hoyte, whose successor in government was Hamilton Green.

Since 1986 the government has faced the problem of refugees who have fled from neighbouring Surinam, following unrest there.

Haiti

Haiti

RH
Central America
10,700 sq. mi
Pop: 5.5 m
UN, OAS, LAES

Capital: Port-au-Prince (pop: 450,000)
Official language: French
Religions: Catholic (80 per cent),
Protestant (10 per cent)
System of govt: Republic;
independent since 1 January 1804

It was in December 1492 that Christopher Columbus discovered the island of Hispaniola, the west of which is occupied by modern Haiti.

The extermination of the indigenous Arawak populations led to the importation of a black slave work force at the beginning of the 16th century. The gradual occupation of the western part of the island, by French pirates and buc-

caneers from the start of the 17th century, was recognised by Spain after the Treaty of Ryswick (1697), which endowed France with the western third of the island. The wealth of the colony came from the cultivation of sugar cane and then coffee (from 1726).

The black leader Toussaint Louverture, who had led an uprising in 1791, installed a dictatorship and proclaimed independence in 1801. An expedition sent by Bonaparte put an end to the secession and Louverture was deported to France, where he died. The French were expelled from the island in 1803 by Jean-Jacques Dessalines, and Santo Domingo returned to its former name, Haiti.

The Spanish reconquered the island in 1808. In the south and west Alexander James founded a black republic, while in the north Henri Christophe established a kingdom where he conducted a reign of terror under the name of Henri I until his suicide in 1820. The country was then reunified by Jean-Pierre Boyer, who went on to conquer the Spanish part of Haiti, two years af-

ter its declaration of independence as Santo Domingo in 1821. A year after Boyer's death in 1843, the eastern part of the island seceded and became the Dominican Republic.

Faustin Soulouque made himself the Emperor Faustin I in 1849, persecuted the mulattos (mixed race) and made voodoo the state religion.

After his overthrow in 1859, a republic was again proclaimed. The US military intervened in Haiti in 1915 after the assassination of President Vilbrun Guillaume Sam (26 July). Even when the USA quit the island in 1934 it retained control of the administration of finances.

After several dictatorships, the general elections of 22 September 1957 gave the leadership to Dr François Duvalier ("Papa Doc"), who represented the landowners, the middle classes and the army. He had himself nominated as life president in April 1964 and installed a dictatorship, excluding the until then dominant mulattos from government.

His son and heir, Jean-Claude

Duvalier ("Baby Doc") became life president of the republic of Haiti at the age of 19 on his father's death in 1971. After a half-hearted attempt at liberalisation, partly under US pressure, he adopted the authoritarianism of his father. During the regime of Baby Doc, supported by the brutal special police, the "Tontons Macoutes", approximately a million Haitians departed from the country, fleeing from repression and famine. The unrest exploded on 28 November 1985, after the murder of demonstrators by police, and spread across the whole country. Jean-Claude Duvalier left Haiti suddenly on 7 February 1986 in the face of popular pressure.

The military junta led by General Henri Namphy held elections on 17 January 1988 under a new constitution, which were won after a very low turnout by Leslie Manigat. However, on 19 June Manigat and his government were ousted by Namphy, who again set up a military government. In September 1988, General Prosper Avril ousted Namphy.

Honduras

Central America
43,277 sq. mi
Pop: 4.65 m
UN, OAS

Capital: Tegucigalpa (pop: 571,000)
Official language: Spanish
Religion: Catholic (96 per cent)
System of govt: Republic;
independent since 1821

Traces of a civilisation dating back to c.2000 BC, and similar to that of the north of Central America, have been found in the north-east of present-day Honduras. The ruins of the Mayan city of Copan testify to the level of civilisation reached in the west by c.600 BC.

Columbus first set foot on continental American soil at Cape Honduras on 14 August 1502. Attracted by the country's wealth of precious metals, European colonisation started in 1524 and with it the eradication of the indigenous populations.

Honduras, which became a Spanish colony in 1525, was attached to the captaincy-general of Guatemala be-

tween 1539 and 1821. The country became independent in 1821 and formed part of the Mexican empire until 1823, before joining the Central American Confederation. The country became a republic in 1838, and underwent great political instability for the rest of the century.

The post-1911 period saw frequent US intervention in support of the interests of the United Fruit Company. The first general strike in the banana plantations took place in 1954. El Salvador occupied the country in 1969, following the expulsion of several thousand illegal immigrants. A peace treaty was finally signed on 30 October 1980.

A coup in 1978 brought General Policarpo Paz Garcia to power. His democratisation led to a Liberal Party victory at elections in November 1981. The liberal Dr Roberto Suazo Cordova was elected president in January 1982.

US-Nicaraguan tension in November 1984 led to the arrival of US paratroopers in Honduras. The Liberal Party again won elections in November 1985 and a new liberal president, Jose Azcona del Hoyo, took office on 27 January 1986. In March 1988 Honduras accused Nicaragua of invading, causing a build-up of US troops. Hurricane Joan caused devastation in October 1988.

Hungary

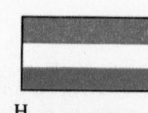

H
Central Europe
35,911 sq. mi
Pop: 10.6 m
UN, COMECON,
WP

Capital: Budapest (pop: 2.07 m)
Official language: Hungarian
Religions: Catholic (60 per cent),
Protestant and others (20 per cent)
System of govt: People's republic
since 20 August 1949

The Hungarian language is related in Europe only to Finnish. They both be-

long to the Finno-Ugrian family, which diverged so long ago that the relationship between Finnish and Hungarian is now barely recognisable.

Early history

The Magyars, as the first Hungarians were called, began arriving in their present homeland on the fertile plains bisected by the Danube 1,000 years ago. Long before then, they had begun their migration from somewhere beyond the Ural mountains, settling for a time in the Caucasus and along the Volga. They are believed to have been driven westwards during the invasions of the Huns. Before the Magyars, Hungary had been settled by Celtic tribes and conquered by the Romans. Known as Pannonia, it lay on

the extreme edge of the empire. As Roman power declined, Goths, Lombards and other Germanic peoples appeared. One of these groups defeated the Huns and founded a kingdom in Pannonia. The first Magyars in Europe were led by a certain Arpad, who went on to mount raiding expeditions into Moravia, Germany and Italy. The Magyars were finally stopped by the German king, Otto the Great, at Lechfeld in 955. But the Arpad dynasty survived for 400 years until 1301. The Hungarians converted to Christianity in the tenth century, turning to Rome rather than Constantinople's orthodox church.

The Hungarian kingdom

It was the Arpad Istvan (Stephen) I who brought the clan chieftains un-

der control, and established church and state on a firm foundation during his rule (997 to 1038). Pope Sylvester II expressed his appreciation by bestowing on Stephen the title Apostle of Hungary, and awarding him a crown that permitted him to assume the title of king of Hungary. To this day the crown of St Stephen is a precious national treasure, and Hungarian catholics celebrate his feast day.

Stephen's successors annexed Transylvania, Slovenia and Croatia, and in 1058 secured from the Holy Roman empire full renunciation of all claims to sovereignty over Hungary. Turko-Mongol invasions of Transylvania began in the 13th century. The Hungarians sought help from the Teutonic Knights, a military religious order dating from the crusades. Once they were in Hungary, it took the Hungarians more than ten years to get rid of them.

In the 14th century Hungary was conquered by Louis the Great of the House of Anjou, whose family came originally from western France. Louis conquered Serbia, Bosnia, and Bulgaria, and united Hungary and Poland under his rule. A century later the growing power of the Ottoman Turks was signalled by the defeat of the king of Hungary and Poland, Vladislav Jagiello, by Sultan Murad II. Within a few years the Ottomans had taken Constantinople (1453), closing the long history of the Byzantine empire, and raising the curtain on the Ottoman empire that was to last almost 400 years until the early 20th century.

Sultan Suleiman the Magnificent defeated the Hungarians in 1526, reaching but failing to take Vienna. This was a turning point in Hungarian history. Hungary's king, Louis II, died in the battle and, since he had left no heir, the crown of St Stephen was taken by the Austrian Archduke Ferdinand.

Habsburgs and Ottomans

Disaffected Hungarians chose a rival king, Janos Zapolya, magnate of Transylvania, who made an alliance with the Ottomans and conquered the greater part of Ferdinand's kingdoms. But then Hungary was absorbed into the Ottoman Empire. In 1699 the Habsburgs succeeded in driving the Ottomans out and Hungary, Slovenia and parts of Croatia were incorporated into the Austrian domains.

Rebellious Hungarians gave the Habsburgs a great deal of trouble, until they finally granted Hungary a constitution and accepted the Hungarian nobility's claim to privileges. But German was imposed as the language of the state and, because of the devastation caused by the war and Ottoman occupation, the Hungarians found themselves a minority in their own country.

In 1848, the year of revolutions in Europe, the Hungarians, under Lajos Petofi and Lajos Kossuth, rose in revolt. Briefly, a Hungarian republic appeared, only to be crushed by the Austrians with the help of the Russians. The dual monarchy (two countries, one monarch) set up by Emperor Franz Josef (ruled 1848-1916) was proclaimed in 1867, in response to Hungarian feelings after Austria had been weakened by defeat at the hands of Prussia in 1866.

Independence and regency

With the collapse of the Habsburg empire at the end of the First World War, Hungary's independence was proclaimed on 16 November 1918 and the political quarrelling began. The liberal Count Michael Karolyi formed a government, but the socialists threw in their lot with the communists.

On 21 March 1919, the communists under Bela Kun seized power, proclaimed the dictatorship of the proletariat, and launched a wave of repression. The regime was virtually starved out by the refusal of the peasants to deliver food. Kun sent his "Red Legions" against Czechoslovakia and Romania. When the Romanians defeated the legions Kun fled on 1 August, his regime having survived just over 100 days.

Miklos Horthy, an admiral in the old Austro-Hungarian navy, became "regent". He ended the conflicts with other successor states of the empire, by surrendering Transylvania and other territories hitherto claimed as Hungarian. Horthy defeated the Habsburg ex-Emperor Charles. Moved by expediency and perhaps also conviction, Horthy pursued a policy of appeasement towards Fascist Italy, Nazi Germany and authoritarian Austria. He took Hungary into the Second World War as an ally of Germany.

War and communism

Soviet forces occupied Hungary in April 1945. In accordance with understandings reached by the Allies at Yalta, a provisional government of non-fascist parties was formed. The communist ministers were represented by a small minority.

Behind the scenes, though, Stalin's agents were helping the communists to organise a police force outside government control. The socialists were brought under pressure to form a united party with the communists; this became the Hungarian Socialist Workers' Party.

The first elections were held late in 1945. The Peasants' Party polled 57 per cent of the vote and formed the first freely-elected government. But the key post of minister of the interior was taken by the communist Laszlo Rajk. The communists were also allowed to organise the frontier guards. Even so, Hungary seemed to be settling down.

But towards the end of 1946, army officers and diplomats were arrested and accused of conspiring against the government. Members of the Peasant's Party were arrested and tortured to make confessions. In mid-1948 new, rigged elections were held, which were won by the Socialist Workers' Party.

The regime tackled the last bastion of resistance, the Roman Catholic church, in 1949. The Hungarian primate, Cardinal Jozsef Mindszenty was arrested, and tortured into confessing a host of crimes. He was given life imprisonment. A few months later the People's Republic of Hungary was proclaimed.

Show trials and uprising

The 1950s saw a succession of show trials in Eastern bloc countries as Stalin sought to eradicate "Titoism". The premier, Matthias Rakosi, used the purge to liquidate Laszlo Rajk, the minister of the interior.

The ferment in eastern Europe that followed Stalin's death in 1953, and Khrushchev's denunciation of Stalin's "excesses", erupted in violent revolution in Hungary. In 1956 the regime virtually disintegrated. Imre Nagy, previously purged for alleged Titoist sympathies, returned to power, promised a multi-party system, released Cardinal Mindszenty and called for Hungary's withdrawal from the Warsaw Pact.

The USSR put down the uprising with a massive force of tanks, artillery and infantrymen. Janos Kadar, another communist who had been purged and imprisoned by Rakosi, was installed as premier. After an initial cleaning-up period, during which hundreds of "traitors" disappeared, Kadar pursued relatively liberal policies.

Imre Nagy sought asylum in the Yugoslav embassy. He remained there for over a year, eventually emerging when the Kadar regime gave him a promise of safe conduct. He was never seen again. In 1989 the general committee of the Hungarian party formally determined that Nagy had been executed after "a fabricated political trial". Cardinal Mindszenty took refuge in the US embassy and refused to leave until 1971, when the Vatican and the Hungarian government reached an understanding.

Kadar and democracy

Kadar remained in power for over 30 years, a period that saw the acceptance of a limited market economy, removal of state subsidies on most products, and increased trade with the west. Liberals were encouraged by Gorbachev's reforms in the USSR. Kadar was replaced in May 1988 by the reformer Karoly Grosz. Kadar died in early July 1989, only hours before the final rehabilitation of Imre Nagy, who with other 1956 leaders had been reburied in June. As Grosz was edged out for being too dilatory over reform, a senior figure in the Hungarian Socialist Workers' party, Imre Pozsgay, called for a multi-party system. President Bush visited, free elections seemed certain by 1990, and even plans for EC membership began to be discussed.

Iceland

IS
Northern Europe
39,758 sq. mi
Pop: 247,000 m
UN, EFTA, NATO, OECD, Nordic Council

Capital: Reykjavik (pop: 93,000)
Official language: Icelandic
Religion: Lutheran (96 per cent)
System of govt: Republic; independence proclaimed 17 June 1944

Irish hermits settled in Iceland in the early ninth century. They were supplanted from c.875 when Norwegian settlers began to arrive. They established an assembly of free men, the Althing, ancestor of the modern Icelandic parliament, and the oldest parliament in the world. Iceland, which was converted to Christianity in c.1000, joined the Norwegian kingdom in 1262, and then became Danish after the union of Denmark and Norway in 1397.

Iceland lost two thirds of its population during a plague outbreak (1402-04). The island was devastated again in the 18th century by a smallpox epidemic, and a number of volcanic eruptions.

Nationalist demands grew, especially in the 19th century, with the result that Denmark was forced to grant Iceland restricted autonomy in 1874. In 1918 Iceland became an independent state under the king of Denmark. The island became an independent republic following the plebiscite of 23 May 1944.

A conflict with Britain, the so-called "Cod War", broke out in 1958 when Iceland decided to extend her territorial waters from three to 12 nautical miles. The new limit was recognised by Britain in 1961 but, a new fishing conflict broke out in 1972 after Iceland's territorial waters were extended to 50 miles, an act which affected a number of European countries.

Reykjavik severed diplomatic relations with Britain in February 1976 before an agreement ended the conflict in June.

Leftist parties won elections in 1978. In August 1982 social democrats withdrew from a centre-left government, led by Gunnar Thoroddsen, which lost its majority in August 1982. A new centre-right government was formed by Steingrimur Hermannsson, the leader of the Agrarian party, after the elections brought forward to April 1983. Vigdis Finnbogadottir became the first woman president in June 1980, and was re-elected in July 1984 and June 1988. Following the general election of April 1987, protracted negotiations resulted in a coalition government under Thorsteinn Palsson, which introduced tough austerity measures including a wage freeze, new taxes and currency devaluations.

India

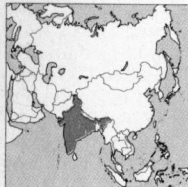 

IND
Southern Asia
1,222,713 sq. mi
Pop: 783 m
UN, CW

Capital: New Delhi (pop: 6.2 m)
Official languages: Hindi, English
Religions: Hindu (82 per cent),
Moslem (11 per cent)
System of govt: Federal republic;
independence gained 15 August 1947

The first villages of the Indian subcontinent probably appeared in the 4th millennium BC in the Indus basin. It was this region that saw the flourishing of the Harappa civilisation, which possessed a written language as early as 2000 BC. The Harappa civilisation is believed to have ended at the same time as less advanced Indo-European (Aryan) nomadic tribes entered India from the north, and in the east of the Ganges valley in c.2000 BC, implying a conquest. The Aryans gave birth to a civilisation which used Sanskrit as its language, although excavations of Harappa sites indicate the Aryans may have adopted some cultural aspects of their predecessors.

The structure of this society was evidently extremely hierarchical and, with its warrior, preacher and peasant castes, it prefigured the Indian caste system. The subjugated, dark-skinned, indigenous peoples formed a separate caste of their own.

In c.1000 BC the *Rig Veda*, a collection of more than 1,000 sacrificial verses, was assembled for the first time. Although it was not written down until after 1300 AD, the holiness of the verses meant that it had to be memorised perfectly, and it was probably transmitted almost exactly intact. It is an invaluable source for early Aryan culture in India.

By the seventh century BC, when the first hard facts about early Indian history begin to emerge, the cultural focus shifted to the Ganges valley from the Punjab, as Aryan culture spread eastwards. By 600 BC there were 16 kingdoms in northern India, and writing – a skill last known to the Harappans – developed.

In the sixth century Siddhartha Gautama, a high-caste warrior prince in the northern Ganges area, abandoned luxury for asceticism and contemplation. His doctrines began to spread and he became known as Buddha (enlightened one). Although Buddhism never supplanted Hinduism in India, where it became a minority religion, it eventually became the most widespread religion in east Asia.

The Maurya dynasty

Alexander the Great crossed the Indus between 327 BC and 325 BC, but pursued his conquest no further before his death in 323 BC. Shortly afterwards, in c. 320 BC, Chandragupta founded the first Indian empire and the Maurya dynasty. His grandson Piyadasi, whose surname was Asoka, had his Buddhist-influenced edicts inscribed throughout the empire. The empire broke up on Asoka's death and was divided into autonomous principalities. Scythian tribes entered India from the first century BC onwards. These were followed by the Kushana who, under the reign of King Kanishka, succeeded in establishing their own empire in Central Asia based at Benares (c.50), following a brief period of Parthian domination.

The beginning of the fourth century saw the rise of the Gupta dynasty which managed to impose its rule over the whole of northern India. Gupta domination went hand in hand with a flowering of Sanskrit literature. Their reign was ended by the arrival of the Hephthalite Huns in c.500. The north of India broke up into a collection of small rival kingdoms.

Arrival of Islam

The first Moslem conquest in India took place in 712. The Arabs under Mohammed ibn al-Qasim settled in the Sind. Mahmud of Ghazni conquered extensive territories in the north-west around the year 1000. But no lasting Moslem settlement could be established, until after the capture of Delhi by a lieutenant of the Sultan Mohammed of Ghur, Qutb al-Din Aibak, in 1192. Aibak proclaimed himself independent of the sultan and founded the sultanate of Delhi which was expanded southwards by his successors. The Moslem empire crumbled at the beginning of the 14th century. Famine led to a rebellion of the Indian populations against the sultanate which finally fell to the Mongols under Tamerlane in 1398. Small Moslem states were formed throughout the country.

In the 15th century European navigators first reached India. The Portuguese Vasco da Gama sighted the western coast at Calicut in 1498, and the Portuguese seized Goa in 1510.

A descendant of Tamerlane, Babur, founded the Moghul dynasty in 1526. It was under his grandson, Akbar (ruled 1556-1605), that the Moghul empire enjoyed its greatest extent and unity. Akbar succeeded in unifying Afghanistan, Kashmir and northern India in one empire.

Akbar's toleration of the Hindus led to peaceful co-existence of the Moslems and Hindus within the Moghul empire. The decline of the empire during the 18th century after the death of Emperor Aurangzeb (ruled 1658-1707), led to the rise of a number of Hindu and Moslem states hostile to one another. However, the Moghul empire lingered in name until after the Indian Mutiny of 1857, when the British exiled the last of the Moghul emperors to Burma, where he died in 1858.

European colonisation of India

The British followed the Portuguese into India, with the East India Company setting up trading posts at Surat, Madras, Bombay and Calcutta. The rival French East India Company was created in 1664, and the French settled in Madras and then Pondicherry (1674), which was taken by the Dutch before being returned in 1699. In 1744 Anglo-French rivalry came to a head in the Carnatic, the south-eastern coastal region. Hostilities broke out anew in 1751, and again during the Seven Years War (1756-63), which left the British as the unrivalled European power on the subcontinent.

The East India Company, whose own troops were commanded by the brilliant Robert Clive, became formal rulers of Bengal in 1764.

The British introduced a system of joint crown and company control in British India in 1784. Wider British domination was imposed after the defeat of the Gurkhas in Nepal (though the British met with such fierce resistance they decided to recruit Gurkhas for their own army) in 1816 and the Marathas in 1818. Sind was annexed in 1843 and the Sikh kingdom of the Punjab in 1849. In 1857 sepoys, native soldiers in the service of the East India Company, mutinied over the introduction of new cartridges allegedly greased with animal fat which, for religious reasons, they refused to handle. The rebel sepoys had won the support of a number of Indian princes, who saw an opportunity to regain their independence. The mutiny was crushed by British and loyal Indian troops after 14 months of fighting.

The mutiny led to a shake up of British administration. The East India Company was relieved of control, and India was directly subjected to the British crown in 1858. A viceroy held direct authority over two-thirds of India, and indirect authority over more than 500 principalities.

Queen Victoria was proclaimed empress of India in 1876. The government of British India had its seat at Calcutta, although this was moved to Delhi in 1911.

The introduction of the British legal and administrative system put an end to slavery and traditional customs such as the burning of widows, but Britain chose on the whole not to interfere with traditional Indian society. The territorial rights of princes were respected and they were allowed to govern their own lands (containing one-fifth of all Indians) unhindered under British supervision.

Growing national feeling

A group of middle class intellectuals – some of them British – founded the Indian National Congress in 1885. This followed an attempt by the viceroy to give Indians and Europeans equal treatment before the courts – a reform modified after an outcry among British residents.

At this stage, the Congress sought only to allow Indian opinion to be heard by those in power. It was not until two decades later that full independence began to be a declared aim.

Britain first came up against Indian nationalism over the partition of Bengal in 1905. Hindus protested at the creation of East Bengal, with a principally Moslem population, under a governor who favoured Moslems. The governor was dismissed, and Moslem resentment was fuelled. A Moslem League was created in 1906, widening the gap between the two communities.

Britain had allowed Indians to be represented on the viceroy's council in 1892 and conceded further rights in 1909. It abandoned the partition of Bengal in 1911, a victory for Hindu opinion against the Moslems.

But Britain also shifted the capital of British India from Bengal to Delhi, the old Moghul capital, in the same year. It was at Delhi that George V, the only reigning British monarch to visit India, was crowned emperor with great splendour at the 1911 durbar.

Gandhi's struggle for freedom

Unrest continued until 1914 and the First World War, in which many Indians served Britain loyally. In 1917 Britain said it favoured steady progress towards home rule, but fell short of offering dominion status (independent association under the crown), demanded by some nationalists.

Reforms in 1918 were also disappointing, and new conspiracy laws in 1919, prompted by fears of Bolshevism, provoked the first acts of Indian civil disobedience. At their forefront was Mohandas Gandhi, a lawyer who had worked for Indians in South Africa. His intention was for passive protest only, but the death of some Britons during a general strike in the Punjab in April 1919, led a British commander to fire on crowds in Amritsar, killing 400 demonstrators.

The massacre changed Gandhi's attitude, which up till then had been a conviction that it was possible to work together with the British. He demanded complete independence for India. Under the inspiration of Gandhi, Congress became a party of the masses. One of Gandhi's closest collaborators, Jawaharlal Nehru, became president of Congress in 1929.

Side by side with the growth of this mass nationalist movement, the British devolved more power on Indians in the Montagu-Chelmsford reforms of 1920, and the 1935 Government of India Act, giving Indians autonomy in provincial government.

Despite the principal of non-violence (Ahimsa) preached by Gandhi the unrest continued to claim victims, especially in clashes between Moslems and Hindus. In the final period of the independence movement, Mohammed Ali Jinnah's Moslem League distanced itself from the Congress party and demanded the creation of an independent Moslem state.

The Labour government in power from 1945 in Britain negotiated for an autonomous, united India but failed. The last British viceroy, Lord Louis Mountbatten, oversaw the transition to independence of two new dominions, India and Moslem Pakistan, on 15 August 1947. Mountbatten and Jinnah became governor-generals of India and Pakistan respectively.

There were high hopes that partition would put an end to the state of near civil war which existed between the Hindu and Moslem communities.

Independent India

But independence only saw an escalation of the civil war, with fighting between Hindus and Moslems claiming 600,000 lives in the Punjab alone. Fourteen million people fled in both directions along the exodus route across the India-Pakistan frontier. The large number of Hindu refugees arriving from Pakistan, added to the problems India already faced over the conflict for Kashmir. An great emotional blow to the new state came when Gandhi was assassinated on 30 January 1948, by a fanatical Hindu.

The Indian princely states were integrated into the Indian Union, whose first constitution came into effect on 26 January 1950. India became a federal republic with Nehru as its prime minister. His first objectives were the modernisation of the country and the abolition of the caste system.

New industry sprang up while rural structures remained bound by traditional methods. Internationally Nehru pursued a policy of non-alignment until the border conflict with China which erupted in 1962. India, defeated militarily, sought new allies. A mutual aerial defence pact was signed with Britain and the USA in 1963.

Nehru died in May 1964. His successor, Lal Bahadur Shastri, was confronted by a new crisis with Pakistan, concerning the former principality of Kashmir. Soviet mediation helped end the conflict after the Tashkent Conference in January 1966. Soviet influence in India continued to grow. A 20-year friendship treaty was signed in August 1971, followed, in November 1973, by an agreement on economic co-operation.

From Indira to Rajiv Gandhi

Jawarhalal Nehru's daughter, Indira Gandhi, succeeded Shastri as the head of government in January 1966. Overcoming major differences within the Congress party, she won elections in 1967 and 1971. India went to war with Pakistan in December 1971 following a number of armed clashes. Indian troops entered East Pakistan in support of the Hindu minority.

The war ended on 16 December, but not before it had brought about the creation of the new republic of Bangladesh from East Pakistan. During the hostilities 10 million Hindus fled from Pakistan to India, a circumstance which weighed heavily on the Indian economy.

Indira Gandhi's popularity continued to fall as criticism of her regime increased. She proclaimed a state of emergency in 1975, and the government was granted special powers, with press censorship being introduced. Up to 100,000 people were imprisoned. The emergency provisions were relaxed in 1977, shortly before the announcement of new elections.

Congress suffered a severe electoral defeat in March 1977, at the hands of the Janata coalition created by Morarji Desai on 20 January, the day after his release from prison. Morarji Desai became prime minister, but his government was quickly weakened by factional conflict within the Janata coalition. He also aimed at an increased level of literacy. The Congress Party, which had been divided since the elections, split in January 1978, as did Janata in July 1979. Morarji Desai resigned on 15 July 1979 and was replaced by Charan Singh. The elections of January 1980 returned Gandhi to power but she had, however, lost the support of a section of Congress. In September the government once more took special powers to overcome troubles in a number of states. Sectarian unrest in Assam escalated at regional elections in February 1983, leaving over 3,500 dead.

The conflict which had pitted Hindus and Sikhs against one another in the Punjab for two years culminated on 5 June 1984 with the Indian army's attack on the Golden Temple in Amritsar which had been occupied by Sikh extremists; 650 Sikhs and soldiers were killed. Indira Gandhi was subsequently assassinated by one of her Sikh guards on 31 October 1984. A wave of violence broke out against the Sikh minority throughout the country and Sikh army units rebelled.

The new prime minister, Rajiv Gandhi, succeeded his mother a few hours after her assassination; the elections of December 1984 gave Congress its greatest electoral victory since Indian independence. He pursued a policy of religious pacification. In 1985 elections were organised in the Punjab, which had been placed under the control of the government in New Delhi since June 1984. Despite the defeat of Congress, a Sikh chief minister was sworn in on 29 September and the state recovered its autonomy. Other troubles flared in Gujerat over anti-caste laws.

Gandhi's first foreign visit was to Moscow in May 1985. The USSR remained India's principal supplier of industrial installations. A few days later Gandhi was received in Washington where he concluded a contract for the delivery of high technology material. Gandhi has kept India a non-aligned country, although relations with the USSR have remained close, with Gorbachev visiting New Delhi in November 1986 and Gandhi Moscow in July 1987. At home, in addition to the problems of continuing Sikh extremism and relations with Pakistan, India was faced in 1987 by the disaster of widespread drought, the worst in a century.

However, relations with Pakistan have improved since the election of Benazir Bhutto as Pakistani premier in 1988.

Indonesia

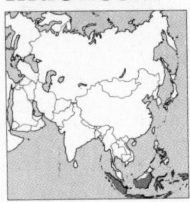
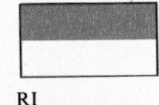

RI
South East Asia
741,098 sq. mi
Pop: 172.2 m
UN, ASEAN, OPEC

Capital: Jakarta (pop: 6.5 m)
Official language: Indonesian
Religions: Moslem (88 per cent), Christian (9 per cent)
System of govt: Republic; independence obtained 27 December 1949

Indonesia is formed by 13,700 islands, the most important of which are Sumatra, Java, Bali and the archipelagos of the Celebes and Sunda. Borneo and New Guinea belong in part to Indonesia.

Indonesia was populated by a series of Malayo-Polynesian peoples from 2000 BC onwards. These inhabitants have left shrines on stepped terraces on which pyramids were built. They produced and worked bronze and iron.

The region, which up until the seventh century was a collection of small kingdoms, then witnessed the birth of a major kingdom in the south of Sumatra, the Buddhist kingdom of Srivijaya. Its influence extended to Java and the Malaysian peninsula and perhaps even as far as Cambodia and Sri Lanka.

From the tenth century the Srivijayan kings' supremacy was challenged by the Singisara kings of the eastern part of Java, especially Airlanga (1039-49). The power of the Singisara kingdom was strengthened after Airlanga's death. Kertanagra (1268-92), the last ruler of the Singisara kingdom, instigated an expedition to China, at that time dominated by the Mongol Emperor Kublai Khan. The failure of the Mongol expedition enabled Kertanagra's nephew, Raden Vijaya, to found the maritime empire of Majapahit, a rival to the Srivijaya kingdom over which it finally triumphed in 1377.

Between 1522 and 1525 Majapahit succeeded in exercising its domination over the greater part of present-day Indonesia. The fall of the Majapahit empire was due to the continuing growth of Malacca, which was developing into the major centre of commerce in South East Asia, and to the arrival of Islam, brought by Indian and Persian merchants. The empire crumbled at the beginning of the 16th century and Buddhism and Hinduism declined throughout the whole of Indonesia.

European penetration

The Portuguese had learnt from Indian merchants the origin of the spices which they prized so much and which up till then had been practically monopolised by Arab traders. Albuquerque seized Malacca on the Malay peninsula in 1511 and this was followed by the creation of the first fortified trading posts on the northern coast of Sumatra. Further settlements followed at Timor and in the Moluccas.

Following Spain's annexation of Portugal (1580), the Dutch arrived in Indonesia to find the spices which they were no longer able to buy from Lisbon and established themselves in western Java in 1596. The Dutch East India Company was created in 1602. The Portuguese gradually lost their trading posts to the Dutch, who also removed the English from Indonesia. Spice plantations were established in the Lesser Moluccas and in Java, colonised after the defeat of the sultanate of Mataram. The Dutch governed the areas they either possessed or exploited through treaties from Batavia on the northern coast of Java, the centre of Dutch trade from Persia to Japan.

The Dutch East India Company began to lose money in the early 18th century. The decline was undetected for many decades because of the company's failure, and inability, to keep adequate accounts. Thus while goods from the East Indies, production of which was often controlled ruthlessly to the company's advantage, always sold for a profit in Europe, little record was kept of the enormous outlay required for building and maintaining ships, forts and trading posts. Bankrupt, the company was dissolved in 1800.

During the French Revolution the Netherlands became the French satellite state of the Batavian Republic, allied to France from 1795. It lost Dutch colonial territory in the East Indies to Britain, which occupied the Moluccas and then Batavia (1811).

Dutch colonisation did not properly get under way until after the restitution of the Dutch colonies to the new kingdom of the Netherlands in 1816.

The colonial administrative and economic system, including forced cultivation of export crops, led to a series of revolts on Sumatra (1817-37) and on the other islands. Colonial policy was not liberalised until after 1870 when the native population was allowed to cultivate essential foodstuffs. Colonisation did not reach Borneo until after 1900.

The movement for independence

A nationalist movement grew from the start of the 20th century with a number of independence parties being founded. The Budi Otoma, a moderate party, was founded by intellectuals in May 1908. The Sarekat Islam, a national religious movement was founded by Moslem traders in 1911. These were opposed by the more radical parties created after 1920, the Communist Party of Indonesia (1920) and the Indonesian National Party founded in 1927 by Dr Ahmed Sukarno. The demands made by the nationalists were obstinately refused by the Dutch colonial authorities.

The Dutch East Indies were occupied in 1942 by the Japanese, who freed the nationalist leaders and were supported by them in their turn. An independent republic was proclaimed in August 1945 following the Japanese surrender. Sukarno took over the leadership of the new state. The Dutch recog-

nised the new republic, but wanted to limit it to Java alone. Dutch troops were sent in and fighting continued until October 1946. An agreement created the Netherlands-Indonesia Union in November 1946.

The Netherlands intervened again on the territory of the republic of Indonesia in 1947 and 1948. When the UN Security Council decreed an end to hostilities the Netherlands was forced to abandon its sovereignty over Indonesia, except western New Guinea (which joined Indonesia in 1969).

In accordance with the Conference of The Hague of August 1949, the Dutch transferred complete and unconditional sovereignty on 27 December 1949. Dr Sukarno became president of the sixteen states making up the United States of Indonesia.

The republic of Indonesia

The opposition of a number of islands to the centralisation of power in Java was marked by a series of uprisings. The provisional constitution of 1950 was drawn up in response to the problems caused by making Indonesia a unified republic. The first parliamentary elections saw the victory of Sukarno's Nationalist Party.

Uprisings continued after the president's proclamation of what he called a "directed democracy" in February 1957. Martial law was proclaimed and an emergency government was formed, while the rebels established a revolutionary government in Padang (Sumatra).

Dr Sukarno was named life president

in 1963. His rule was backed on an assembly which, until 1965, comprised only members of the ruling party.

Dr Sukarno was confronted by a serious economic crisis and pursued an anti-western policy in foreign affairs whilst tightening his links with the USSR and China. After a coup d'etat led by the chief of the presidential guard, General Kemusu Suharto intervened in Jakarta in an attempt to stabilise the situation. An anti-communist campaign spread across Indonesia with communists and alleged communists being massacred.

The violence was the cause of some 50,000 deaths. The head of the Communist Party (PKI), Aidit, was arrested and executed in November. President Sukarno, who was still in power, gave way before the army and on 11 March 1966 was forced to sign a declaration placing complete power in the hands of General Suharto.

Suharto's presidency

Suharto became what was termed "caretaker president" on 20 February 1967. Dr Sukarno was placed under house arrest and died on 21 June 1970. Foreign affairs underwent a transformation. Relations with socialist countries were frozen. Conflicts with neighbouring Malaysia and Singapore were settled and Indonesia retook its seat at the UN. The Association of South East Asian Nations (ASEAN) was created in 1967, with Indonesia as a founder member. Despite considerable economic advances the country's foreign debt continued to grow.

The 1971 elections saw Suharto's official Golkar party obtaining a large majority. At the same time the Indonesian military exerted considerable influence in civilian administrative and economic affairs. The regime was relaxed with a number of political prisoners being freed.

The declaration of independence by the Portuguese colony of East Timor led to its invasion by Indonesian troops in December 1975 and its attachment to Indonesia in July 1976 as the country's 27th province. Tens of thousands of victims are thought to have fallen prey to guerrilla warfare, repression and famine between independence and annexation.

Golkar again won the elections of May 1977 and Suharto was re-elected in March 1978, a double process which was repeated in May 1982 and March 1983. Traditional areas of unrest continued to pose problems: anti-Chinese agitation and rivalries within the army.

The repression in East Timor and the prosecution of the guerrilla war led to an agreement between Indonesia and Papua New Guinea in October 1984 designed to seal their common frontier. A controversial plan to move 65 million people from the overcrowded island of Java to other parts of Indonesia by the end of the century was announced at the end of 1984.

In elections on 23 April 1987, the Golkar party again won an overwhelming victory, while at presidential elections on 10 March 1988 Suharto, the sole candidate, was re-elected for a fifth five-year term as president, prime minister and defence minister.

Iran

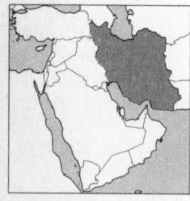

IR
Near East
634,724 sq. mi
Pop: 49.9 m
UN, OPEC

Capital: Tehran (pop: 6 m)
Official language: Persian
Religion: Moslem (96 per cent)
System of govt: Islamic republic since 1 April 1979

The first prehistoric agrarian cultures appeared on the Iranian high plateau after c.7000 BC. The working of copper and then other metals made its appearance after 5000 BC, and opened the door to trade with the Indus and Mesopotamia.

As the civilisation of Mesopotamia evolved, a civilisation with its own system of writing, and the structure of a proto-state was developing from 3500 BC onwards in Susiana. The appearance of a new culture, probably Aryan

(Indo-European) in origin, after 2000 BC permitted the flowering of a number of brilliant regional cultures dominated by a warrior aristocracy.

The Medes and the Persians, divided into a number of small kingdoms, were subjugated by their neighbours, the Assyrians, the Scythians and the Elamites from Zagros. The kingdom of Elam was destroyed by the Assyrians in 646 BC, before Assyria in its turn succumbed to the Babylonians and the Medes in 612 BC. The Medes extended their kingdom westwards beyond Iran as far as the river Halys.

The Persian empire

It was in 559 BC that Cyrus II of the Achaemenian dynasty seized the kingdom of the Medes, which was ruled over by King Astyages. Under Cyrus' reign the Persian empire conquered Assyria, Asia Minor and Babylon. Cyrus' son, Cambyses (550 BC-522 BC) continued to extend the empire by conquering Egypt. It was under Darius I (522-486 BC), however, that the empire reached its greatest extent, reaching the Danube in the west, the Jaxartes (Syr Darya) in the north, the Indus

in the east, and taking in Egypt in the south. The attempted conquest of continental Greece by Darius I and his successor, Xerxes I (486-465 BC) failed first at the hands of the Athenians at Marathon (490 BC), and then the Greeks at Salamis (480 BC) and Plataea (479 BC).

From the Seleucids to the Sassanids

The Achaemenian empire was finally overcome after the victory of Alexander the Great over Darius III in 331 BC. After Alexander's death in 323 BC, his empire was divided among his generals, one of whom, Seleucus, founded the Seleucid dynasty in Persia. Parthian tribes coming from the north east invaded the Iranian high plateau in c.250 BC. One of their leaders, Arsaces, founded the dynasty of the Arsacids (247 BC), which defeated the Seleucids after 150 years of fighting. The Arsacid empire reached its greatest extent under Mithradates I (171-138 BC) who conquered Bactria and parts of India.

The Romans struggled in vain to overcome the Arsacids, and the Emperor Augustus (died 14) was forced to recognise the Euphrates as the limit of

Roman conquest. It was left to the Persian Sassanid dynasty to overcome the Parthian kings. King Ardashir defeated the last Arsacid, Artaban V, in 224. The Sassanids restored the Persian frontiers of the Achaemenians, despite a number of Roman expeditions.

Islam arrives

The Arabs put an end to the Sassanid dynasty in 637 under the Umayyad Caliph Umar. Persia's religion, Zoroastrianism, was supplanted by Islam.

A rebellion which spread from Khorasan and was led by Abu Moslem, put an end to the Umayyad caliphate in 750. The leadership of the caliphate was taken over by Abu al-Abbas who established his capital at Baghdad and founded the Abbasid dynasty.

Turkish tribes spread into Persia towards the end of the tenth century. A Turko-Persian kingdom was founded in Anatolia (the sultanate of Rum). Subjected to pressure from the crusades and the Latin states of the east the Seljuk Turks were forced to retreat on all fronts. They were defeated in 1194 by the Persian Turks of Khorazmia allied to the Kara Khitan Mongols.

The Mongols of Genghis Khan occupied the whole of Persia in 1227, after having crushed Khorazmia and Kara Khitan in 1220. The caliphate of Bagdhad was destroyed in 1258. The Mongol thrust towards the south was halted by the Mamelukes of Egypt in 1258. Mongol domination declined and the Persian dynasties were able to regain their independence, until the arrival in 1360 of Tamerlane's Turko-Mongol hordes. But his immense empire was not to survive him.

From the Safavids to the Qajars

The Safavid dynasty established itself in Azerbaijan. The Safavid Shah Ismail assumed the title of shah of Persia in 1502 after defeating Turkoman tribes. The Safavids restored the unity of Persia, but were opposed by the Ottoman sultanate which won Kurdistan in 1514, followed by Mesopotamia, Georgia and Azerbaijan.

Safavid Persia reached the pinnacle of its power under the reign of Abbas I (1587-1629), who temporarily reconquered a number of territories from the Ottomans. He re-established order and reopened trade routes and embellished his splendid capital, Isfahan.

Safavid domination ended in 1722, after the capture of Isfahan by the Sunni Moslem Afghans of the Emir Mir Mahmud from Kandahar.

Eight years later, Nadir Shah entered Isfahan at the head of a band from Khorasan. Within a few years he had expelled the Afghans, reconquered Mesopotamia, Azerbaijan and Armenia from the Ottomans and the Caspian provinces from Russia. In 1738 he entered India where he defeated the Moghul emperor at Panipat (1738).

Nadir Shah was assassinated in 1747 and his empire broke up. In 1786 Agha Mohammed Khan proclaimed himself king in Tehran, which became the capital of Persia, after he had united the Turko-Mongol Qajar tribes. He was as-sassinated in 1797 before he had been able to reconstitute the empire.

In the 19th century Persia became the object of European power struggles, mostly involving Britain and Russia. In 1907 Shah Muzzafar al-Din conceded a French-mediated colonial agreement, dividing Persia into zones of British and Russian influence. After the nationalist revolution of 1909 the 11-year-old child who ascended the throne, Ahmad, was unable to oppose the foreign presence.

The Pahlavis

The head of the Persian cossack regiment, Reza Khan, staged a coup d'etat on 21 February 1921. He signed a treaty with the USSR in which it renounced all claims to Persia.

Reza Khan, who became prime minister in 1923, had himself proclaimed king in 1925, and was crowned under the name Reza Shah Pahlavi in April 1926. In 1933 the shah negotiated a new agreement with the Anglo-Persian Oil Company which was more favourable to Persia. Persia, which had pursued a policy of rapprochement with Germany, was occupied by Britain and the USSR in 1941. Reza Shah was forced to abdicate in favour of his son, Mohammed Reza Shah Pahlavi.

US influence in Persia (known internationally by its native name, Iran, from 1940) grew considerably during the Second World War.

At the end of the war a nationalist riot carried Mohammed Mossadegh to power. He nationalised Iranian oil and pursued an anti-British policy. The shah sacked him in August 1953, but was then himself forced into exile by a popular uprising. Backed by the USA the shah returned a few days later and had Mossadegh arrested.

In 1961 the shah embarked on a vast programme of economic and social reforms financed by Iran's oil revenue. But his modernisation programme, and the westernised style of his regime met opposition from the country's Shi'ite Moslem clergy.

The shah, who was crowned emperor in 1967, came up against stiffer opposition in the 1970s, which was not pacified by the promise of a political amnesty and a partial relaxation of press censorship. The mullahs and ayatollahs, Shi'ite preachers and dignitaries, called for mass demonstrations which were brutally suppressed by the Savak, the Shah's secret police.

But the opposition prevailed and the shah was forced into exile on 16 January 1979.

The Islamic Republic

The spiritual leader of the Shi'ite community, Ayatollah Khomeini, who had been in exile since 1963, returned to Tehran in triumph on 1 February 1979. Mehdi Bazargan was named as the leader of the provisional revolutionary government by Khomeini's Islamic Revolutionary Council. Revolutionary tribunals were convened, and former followers of the shah were summarily tried and executed.

The seizing and holding hostage of the US embassy in Tehran by "students" in November 1979, plunged the country into a serious crisis with the USA. A military operation organised by the USA in April 1980 to free the hostages failed. The hostages were freed in January 1981, on the day President Carter left office.

The regime became more severe in the face of pressures both at home, such as religious infighting and the attempted secession of the Kurdish minority, and abroad, such as the Iraqi offensive at Khizestan in September 1980, which heralded the start of a bloody eight-year Gulf War between Iran and Iraq. The suppression of the political opposition from 1981-84 is thought to have claimed 40,000 victims, according to the left-wing People's Mujaheddin (Combatants) organisation.

The regime, whose power was by then well consolidated, moderated its more extreme measures. The head of state, Sayyed Ali Khameini, elected in 1981, was re-elected in August 1985. In November 1985 the Ayatollah Hussein Ali Montazari was designated as successor to the then 85-year-old Ayatollah Khomeini. Despite the mounting human and economic cost of the Gulf War, Iran refused to discuss an end to hostilities. Iranian offensives in 1986 and 1987 failed to achieve a land breakthrough.

Iran's economy deteriorated – oil production was badly hit – and splits were appearing within the regime on the issue of the war and on the succession to Ayatollah Khomeini.

Iranian and Iraqi attacks on neutral shipping in the Gulf led to an international outcry, and the presence in the area of naval protection from various countries, especially the USA. The tragic climax of Gulf tensions came in July 1988, when the US navy shot down what it said it believed was a "hostile" aircraft. Nearly 250 died on what turned out to be an Iranian civil airliner.

On 18 July 1988 Iran accepted a UN ceasefire resolution, which came into effect on 20 August, ending the costly and fruitless war. In February 1989 a new crisis erupted between Iran and the west when Ayatollah Khomeini exhorted the Moslem world to arrange the assassination of the British author Salman Rushdie, in protest of the publication of his allegorical novel *The Satanic Verses*, which allegedly insulted Islam.

Ayatollah Khomeini died on 4 June 1989. President Khameini and parliamentary Speaker Rafsanjani emerged as the regime's leading figures, following Ayatollah Montazeri's withdrawal from the leadership contest shortly before Khomeini's death.

Iraq

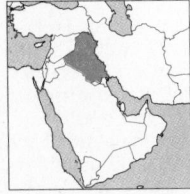

IRQ
Near East
167,925 sq. mi
Pop: 14.6 m
UN, AL, OPEC

Capital: Baghdad (pop: 3.4 m)
Official language: Arabic
Religion: Moslem (96 per cent)
System of govt: Socialist republic since 14 July 1958

The first great civilisation appeared after 4000 BC in Mesopotamia, the region between the rivers Tigris and the Euphrates. The Sumerians, who arrived in southern Mesopotamia after 3000 BC, established a number of powerful cities, Ur, Uruk, Lagash and Kish. The Semite king, Sargon, put an end to Sumerian domination in c.2334 BC, and founded the kingdom of Akkad in the north.

The kingdom broke up after Sargon's death (2279 BC), and Mesopotamia was not reunified until 1700 BC under the Babylonian king, Hammurabi.

The Assyrian kingdom developed between 1300 BC and 1200 BC along the upper reaches of the Tigris and became the leading military power in southwest Asia. Assyrian hegemony reached its high point under King Assurbanipal (669-627 BC), whose power spread as far as Egypt.

The Assyrian Empire was defeated in 612 BC by the Babylonians under Nebuchadnezzar II and the Medes. The last Babylonian kingdom survived only a century. It was conquered in 539 by the Persian King Cyrus II (the Great).

Mesopotamia, which was conquered by Alexander the Great in 331 BC, fell under Parthian domination in the second century BC. In the years which followed the country was devastated by continual wars between the Romans, who were attempting to expand beyond the Euphrates, firstly with the Parthians and then with the Sassanids.

Arabs in Mesopotamia

Mesopotamia was conquered by the Arabs in 637. In 762 Baghdad replaced Damascus as the seat of the Moslem caliphate.

Mesopotamia was subjugated by the Mongols between 1258 and 1534, before being annexed by the Ottoman empire. It remained an Ottoman province until the beginning of the 20th century.

After the Ottoman empire had crumbled at the end of the First World War, the British, who had taken Baghdad in March 1917, were given a mandate to govern a new Mesopotamian state, Iraq, by the League of Nations. The Hashemite Emir Faisal ibn Hussein was crowned king of Iraq in 1921. The British had no particular desire to remain in Iraq beyond the expiry of the mandate in 1932, but they were anxious to ensure the continued flow of oil from Iraqi oil wells, and retained a military and air force presence in the new independent kingdom.

Independent Iraq

Iraq became a member of the Arab

League and of the UN in 1945, and took part in the unsuccessful Arab war against the new state of Israel two years later.

The monarchy was overthrown by a coup staged by General Kassem on 7 July 1958. King Faisal II was assassinated and a republic proclaimed on 14 July.

General Kassem's regime provoked major unrest on a number of occasions. This was aggravated by the conflict with the Kurds which broke out in the north-east of the country in 1961. The Kurds, who represent the largest minority group in Iraq, succeeded in obtaining a degree of autonomy in 1970.

General Kassem was overthrown on 8 February 1963 and later executed.

Colonel Abdul Salam Aref and his pro-Nasser followers took power. A further coup carried General Ahmad Hassan al-Bakr to power, in the wake of the Arab defeat in the Six Day War against Israel in 1967.

The nationalist Ba'ath party has remained in power since 1967 and has pursued pan-Arab policies. An agreement on oil production was signed with the USSR in 1969, followed by a treaty of friendship in 1972.

After the 1978 Camp David agreement between Egypt and Israel, Iraq assumed leadership of the Arab opposition to Israel and signed a "Charter for United Action" with Syria. General al-Bakr resigned all his powers in July 1979 and was succeeded as leader of the

Ba'ath party and head of state by Saddam Hussein.

The Islamic revolution in neighbouring Iran was seen by Iraq as an opportunity to revive an Iraqi claim to the strategic Shatt al-'Arab waterway and the oil-rich province of Khizestan.

The Iraqis attacked Iran in September 1980, sparking the eight-year Gulf War. A wave of anti-Iranian and anti-Shi'ite purges was organised in Iraq, where the population belongs mainly to the Sunni sect.

After initial successes the Iraqi army, which enjoyed massive financial backing from moderate Arab states, was checked and then pushed back behind the Iraqi border. Years of near stalemate followed, with neither side fully

in a position to win the upper hand.

The war, which was the cause of a massive loss of human life, was also responsible for a catastrophic decline in oil exports. International efforts to end the fighting were embodied in a UN resolution in July 1987. Iran agreed to a ceasefire, which came into effect on 20 August 1988.

Kurdish agitation has continued and has met with a brutal response from the Iraqi government. In March 1988 5,000 Kurds died in one village after a poison gas attack by Iraqi forces, in breach of international conventions. Iraq strenuously denied such claims. In August 1988 150,000 Kurds fled to Turkey. In October the US Senate voted to impose sanctions on Iraq.

Ireland (Republic of)

IRL
Western Europe
26,600 sq. mi
Pop: 3.54 m
UN, EC, OECD

Capital: Dublin (pop: 502,000)
Official languages: Irish (Gaelic), English
Religion: Catholic (94 per cent)
System of govt: Republic; independence obtained 6 December 1921

It was between 500 and 200 BC that a Celtic people, the Gaels, settled in Ireland, pushing back the indigenous populations. Five major kingdoms were formed at a very early stage: Ulster, Leinster, Munster, Connacht and Meath. The conversion of Ireland to Christianity is traditionally associated with St Patrick (d. 461), although there is evidence of earlier missionary activity.

A Norse attack

Ireland was first attacked by the Norwegians in 795, and the early raids were followed by permanent settlement. In 838 the Vikings took Dublin, and occupied Waterford in 914, and Limerick in 920. Further Norse conquest was halted by their defeat at Clontarf (1014) by Brian, king of Munster and high king of Ireland. Brian died in battle, and a period of internal rivalry followed. In 1166 the king of Leinster appealed to Henry II of England for help, and was allowed to raise men. Richard de Clare, the earl of Pembroke ("Strongbow") landed at Waterford in 1170, and captured it and Dublin. His success led Henry II to fear the formation of an independent Norman state, and in 1171 he crossed to Ireland to assert his own overlordship. English influence, however, remained weak ex-

cept within the Pale – the area around Dublin.

English interference

This did not prevent number of mediaeval English kings sending expeditions to Ireland in an attempt to enforce their authority. Henry VIII tried in vain to impose church reform in 1541. Anti-English rebellions were violently put down, catholic land was confiscated and the plantation (colonisation) of especially the north of the island (Ulster) was undertaken by protestants from Scotland and England. An Irish rebellion which began in 1641 was savagely crushed in 1649-50 by Oliver Cromwell. Cromwell suppressed all Irish resistance – the massacre of Drogheda (September 1649) was one particularly brutal episode – and continued the dispossession of catholics.

After the deposition of James II of England in 1689, James used the support of Irish catholics in an attempt to regain his throne. His troops, which had French backing, were defeated by William III at the battle of the Boyne in 1690. The end of the war in the following year left the protestant interest dominant, and a range of social and political restrictions were placed on catholics. Internal tensions were intensified by the threat of French invasion in 1796, and in 1801 Pitt decided to resolve the Irish question by an act of union. The (all protestant) Irish parliament was dissolved, and Ireland was to be represented instead at the Westminster parliament. However, Irish catholics did not gain the right to vote until 1829.

Growing nationalism

The nationalist movement continued to grow throughout the 19th century, as resentment of absentee landlords and apparent British neglect grew. In the mid-1840s up to one million Irish people died in a terrible potato famine, and millions more emigrated, especially to

the USA and Britain. Ireland, in fact, was the only country in western Europe where the population (c. eight million in 1840), fell during the 19th century – and that by almost half, mostly before 1850.

The agitation of groups such as the Fenians and the widespread sympathy behind anti-British acts, spurred Gladstone's Liberal government of 1868-74 into action. A Land Act gave Irish tenants some protection against summary eviction and the Anglican church, whose hegemony over catholics was a major cause of resentment, was disestablished in Ireland (1871). Gladstone introduced a first home rule (autonomy) bill in 1886, but it was defeated. A second home rule bill was rejected by the House of Lords. A third, in 1912, could only be delayed by the now reformed Lords, and became law in 1914, but was postponed by the war.

As nationalist opposition continued both within and outside parliament, a new factor came to the fore: the refusal of protestant Ulster to become part of an independent, catholic Ireland.

Home rule was interrupted by the First World War, in which many Irish fought. Extreme nationalists staged an uprising at Easter in 1916. It was suppressed and many of its leaders executed for treason. In 1919 Sinn Fein (Ourselves Alone) party nationalists set up an illegal independent parliament (Dail), and an Irish Republican Army, (IRA).

Two years of virtually open warfare between Britain and the IRA followed, with acts of savagery on both sides.

In 1921 elections to two Irish parliaments – one for Ulster – were held and the (southern) Irish Free State was recognised by London in 1921. Michael Collins headed the state's government until his assassination in 1922. William Cosgrave took over until 1932.

The six counties of the north, however, remained attached to London. Some republicans refused to accept the div-

ision and the movement split in 1922. A bloody civil war broke out (1922-23). Eamon de Valera, who as leader, premier and president dominated Irish politics for 60 years until his death at 92 in 1975, won the 1932 elections with his Fianna Fail (Soldiers of Destiny) republican party founded in 1926. The loyal oath to the British crown was abolished in 1932. In 1937 a republican constitution was adopted and the Irish Free State was renamed Eire, although this was not recognised by London until 1945.

De Valera left office in 1948, the year Eire officially became the Irish Republic and withdrew from the Commonwealth. He returned as premier from 1951-54 and 1957-59. Ireland joined the EC in 1973. The troubles in Northern Ireland dominated relations with Britain from their outbreak in 1969. Jack Lynch's Fianna Fail left office in 1973 after 16 years in power. A Fine Gael (conservative) and Labour coalition under Liam Cosgrave became the first Irish government to recognise Northern Ireland as part of Britain. Fianna Fail returned to power in 1977, and Fine Gael's Dr Garrett Fitz Gerald became prime minister in 1981, in an alliance with the Labour Party. The coalition collapsed and Fianna Fail returned to power briefly under Charles Haughey in 1982. FitzGerald returned to power when Haughey's government collapsed after only a few months.

A major breakthrough on Northern Ireland came when FitzGerald and Mrs Margaret Thatcher signed the Anglo-Irish Agreement in November 1985, which allowed the republic a consultative role in the affairs of Ulster. However, this agreement produced a hardening of the political oppositions in Northern Ireland. Violence and tensions continue. Haughey became premier in 1987 and again, in a coalition with the small Progressive Democratic Party, in July 1989, after elections failed to give him a majority.

Israel

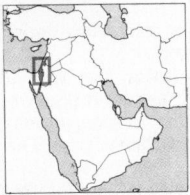

IL
Near East
8,017 sq. mi
Pop: 4.05 m
UN

Capital: Jerusalem (pop: 457,000)
Official language: Hebrew
Religions: Jewish (83 per cent), Moslem (13 per cent)
System of govt: Republic; independence proclaimed 14 May 1948

Early history of the Jewish people

According to the Bible, Abraham led the first Hebrew-speaking people to settle in Canaan (probably c.1800 BC), a land roughly covering the area of modern Israel.

The Hebrews were freed from slavery in Egypt by Moses (c.1220 BC), and took 40 years to return to Canaan. In this period the cult of the god Yahweh (Jehovah) developed, from whom, according to the Old Testament, Moses is said to have received the Ten Commandments on Mount Sinai. The Tables of the Law became the basis of the Jewish religion, the alliance of the Hebrews with Yahweh symbolised by the Ark of the Covenant.

In Canaan the Hebrews kept their former tribal structure. It was not until the reign of Saul in 1020 BC that the Israelite tribes united against the Philistines and the Ammonites.

Saul's successor, David (1004-965 BC), conquered Jerusalem and made it the capital of his kingdom.

Israel reached a high point of its culture and power under David's son, Solomon (965-932 BC), who established a strong, centralised regime, and built up a fleet and a powerful army as well as giving Jerusalem a temple and a palace. On his death the kingdom split and was beset by internal wars (931-587 BC).

Jerusalem was the capital of the kingdom of Judah in the south while the kingdom of Israel (931-722 BC), in the north, eventually established its capital at Sumaria, founded by King Omri (885-874 BC). The northern kingdom was conquered in 722 BC by the Assyrians under King Sargon, and the elite of Israel's population was deported to Mesopotamia. Judah was conquered 135 years later by the Babylonian King Nebuchadnezzar II. Jerusalem was destroyed and the Israelites were deported to Babylon. The "Babylonian captivity" continued until 539 BC when the city fell to the Persian king, Cyrus II (the Great), who authorised the return of the Jews to Judah and the reconstruction of the temple of Jerusalem.

During the centuries which followed Israel was dominated in turn by the Persians, the Macedonians, the Egyptian Ptolemies and the Seleucids. Foreign domination ended in 167 BC after the rebellion of the Maccabaeans, named after their leader, Judas Maccabaeus. The Maccabaean dynasty was overthrown by the Romans in 63 BC. Judaea, or Palestine, was then governed by kings dependent on Rome. It was under the reign of one of these kings, Herod Antipas, that Jesus of Nazareth lived in the first 30 or so years of the first century.

The anti-Roman revolt which broke out in 66 led to the destruction of Jerusalem in 70 by the future emperor Titus. The Romans also put down major revolts between 132 and 135.

Large numbers of Jews fled or were deported from Palestine, and many established Jewish communities in Europe, where they were treated over the centuries usually with suspicion and often violent intolerance. It is this phenomenon which is usually referred to as the Diaspora, or dispersion.

After the division of the Roman empire in 395, Palestine became part of the Eastern Roman, or Byzantine, empire. Palestine, conquered by Moslem Arabs in 636, was attacked by various waves of European Christian crusaders in the middle ages. In 1099 some of the crusaders founded the kingdom of Jerusalem, a state which survived until 1291. In 1518 Palestine was conquered by the Ottomans and remained part of their empire for 400 years.

The Zionist Movement

The first Zionist Congress met in Basle in August 1897 as a result of the efforts of the Hungarian Jewish journalist, Theodor Herzl. Jewish nationalists demanded "the establishment for the Jewish people of a home in Palestine". Some 60,000 Jews emigrated to Palestine between 1882 and 1914. Palestine was conquered by the British during the First World War and they were given a League of Nations mandate to govern the territory between 1918 and 1948. The British foreign secretary, Arthur Balfour, had already guaranteed the establishment of a national home for the Jews in the "Balfour Declaration" of 1917, on condition that the rights of existing populations were not harmed. This declaration, however, stood in contradiction to the promise already given to Arab leaders to form Palestine into an independent Palestinian Arab state. Trouble seemed inevitable.

Jewish immigration to Palestine accelerated during the 1930s, especially from Nazi Germany. After the Second World War various British and UN plans aimed at dividing Palestine into an Arab state and a Jewish state proved to be impracticable.

The founding of the state of Israel

Before the British withdrew various Jewish guerrilla groups had become active in the territory, conducting a terror campaign against the British troops stationed in Palestine. On 14 May 1948, a few hours before the expiry of the British mandate in Palestine, the Jewish National Council proclaimed the State of Israel. David Ben Gurion headed the first Israeli government. A parliament (Knesset) was set up in January 1949 and a first president, Chaim Weizmann, the successor of Theodor Herzl as leader of the Zionist movement, was appointed in February.

The state was declared open to Jews worldwide on 15 May 1948. Two days later Arab, Egyptian and Syrian troops attacked Israel which, however, halted the offensive and counter-attacked in July 1948, nearly doubling its territory in the process. The majority of Israel's Arab neighbours signed an armistice at the end of 1948.

A UN resolution passed in 1949 attempted to resolve the problem of the flood of refugee Palestinian Arabs from Israel – a huge exodus of up to 900,000 people, which had started in 1948.

Tension between Israel and the Arab world, accentuated by the Suez crisis, led Israel to take the initiative in a new war with Egypt on 29 October 1956. The rout of Egyptian troops permitted Israel to occupy Gaza and the Sinai from which it withdrew in 1958 in the face of UN pressure. Israel, however, still retained the port of Eilat in the Gulf of Aqaba, which gave the country access to the Red Sea.

Israeli political life was dominated by the Israel Workers' Party (later the Israel Labour Party) and the Conservative Coalition. The Workers' Party split in 1965, but remained in power in the face of a coalition between the conservative Herut and the Liberal parties.

At about the same time tension was growing within the Israeli population. The Jewish majority from Asia and Africa demanded posts which up until then had been filled by European Jews.

While the economy was shaken by serious crisis from 1965 onwards, the blockade of Eilat by Egypt on 23 May 1967 ignited the Six Day War (or third Arab-Israeli war) at the end of which Israel occupied Sinai, Gaza, the west bank of the Jordan, east Jerusalem and the Syrian Golan heights.

On 6 October 1973, on the Jewish festival of Yom Kippur, Egypt and Syria launched a surprise offensive which was pushed back by Israel only after heavy initial losses.

A ceasefire was signed on 24 October after the prime minister Mrs Golda Meir had been replaced by General Yitzhak Rabin. A peaceful Israeli withdrawal from occupied Egypt took place in January and February 1974.

The head of the conservative Likud Party, Menahem Begin, became prime minister in May 1977. Difficult negotiations led to an Israeli-Egyptian rapprochement, on the initiative of Egypt's President Sadat and through the mediation of US President Carter.

The process ended with the Camp David agreement signed by Begin and Sadat in 1978, and then by the Washington peace treaty of March 1979. Israel pledged to withdraw its troops from the Sinai (which it did by April 1982) while Egypt opened the Suez canal to Israeli shipping.

Jerusalem was proclaimed the capital of Israel by the Knesset in 1980. The majority of foreign countries, however, refused to recognise it as such and kept their embassies in Tel Aviv.

Israeli troops invaded Lebanon in June 1982 with the aim of expelling the Palestinian Liberation Organisation (PLO), the main military and political group representing Palestinian Arabs. The Palestinians withdrew under international supervision.

The war in Lebanon placed a heavy burden on the Israeli economy, with inflation already at over 150 per cent. Begin stepped down in September 1983, sparking a political crisis resolved by the formation of a centre-right coalition government under Yitzhak Shamir in October.

Shamir gave way in September 1984 to a Labour-Likud coalition under Shimon Peres, whose Labour party had become the largest party in the Knesset.

Peres' problems included daunting 400 per cent inflation, the withdrawal of Israeli troops from Lebanon, and continued Israeli settlements on the West Bank. The process of stabilisation of Israeli-Arab relations, which included a rapprochement between Israel and Jordan, was halted by an Israeli air attack on the PLO headquarters in Tunis in October 1985.

The last Israeli forces were withdrawn from Lebanon in June 1985. The gravity of the economic crisis led to price increases, devaluations of the currency, and the creation of a new unit of currency (shekel) in September 1985. Peres had some success in tackling inflation, bringing it down to less than 20 per cent before Peres handed over, as agreed, to his coalition partner, Shamir, in October 1986.

In foreign affairs, 1986 and 1987 saw little real progress towards an Arab-Israeli peace settlement. From the end of 1987 the situation was exacerbated by a Palestinian uprising on the West Bank, and in the Gaza Strip. The Israeli army was widely criticised for its excessive force used in suppressing the unrest.

Efforts towards a peace settlement have continued, with the possibility of dialogue growing closer. But hardline Jewish opposition to any accommodation of Palestinian aspirations remains, and the uprising (*intifada*) continues.

In 1988, Israel and the USSR established contacts for the first time since they had been broken off during the 1967 Six Day War.

Italy

Italy

I
Southern Europe
116,319 sq. mi
Pop: 57.2 m
UN, EC, NATO,
OECD

Capital: Rome (pop: 2.8 m)
Official language: Italian
Religion: Catholic (99 per cent)
System of govt: Republic since 2 June 1946

Italy was first inhabited as a result of the progressive penetration of a number of peoples arriving from the north, the east (Illyrians) and the south. The Etruscans appeared on the west coast of the peninsula towards the end of the eighth century BC, and rapidly extended their sphere of influence to the Apennines and then to the plain of the Po without, however, ever reaching the Adriatic coast. At the same time as the Etruscans, the Greeks were establishing their first colonies in the south east, from the gulf of Taranto to the Campania. The Etruscans, threatened by the expansion of the Greek colonies, allied themselves with the Carthaginians to whom they allowed the control of Sicily and Sardinia following the defeat of Massalia's Greek fleet at Alalia in Corsica (c.540 BC).

The Etruscan drive southwards was halted at Cumae (524 BC). The Celts invaded Italy during the fifth century BC, overrunning the Etruscan domains and penetrating as far as Rome in the fourth century BC. Rome, in the area called Latium, was founded traditionally in 753 BC, and ruled by Etruscan kings until 510 BC. It profited from the decline of Etruscan power; between 400 BC and 200 BC, Rome gradually conquered the Italian peninsula, its language, Latin, supplanting those of the Etruscans and other Italian peoples.

Roman expansion in the south of Italy was opposed by Carthaginian (or Punic) power. War broke out between Rome and Carthage in 264 BC and continued until 146 BC when the great African city was destroyed. After Sicily, the Romans subjugated the Celtic tribes in the Po valley in 222 BC, and pursued the conquest of the Balkan peninsula.

The expansion of the Roman empire continued for a number of centuries, which saw the conquest of vast territories around the Mediterranean. A number of civil wars broke out in Rome between 133 BC and 59 BC, until Caius Julius Caesar was nominated life dictator by the Roman Senate. It was the effective end of the Roman republic.

Caesar was murdered in 44 BC and a power struggle was won by his great nephew and heir, Octavius. He assumed the name of Augustus in 27 BC and be-

came the first Roman emperor (imperator). His reign (he died in 14) ushered in a period of peace and general prosperity, which continued for two centuries. The decline of Rome started after 200 with the reign of the first soldier emperors.

The empire exhausted itself in an economic crisis and conflicts on its far-flung borders. A series of barbarian invasions took place from 250 onwards, with Gothic tribes coming from the Black Sea region in the east and Frankish and Alamanni tribes crossing the Rhine in the north, while the new Persian kingdom of the Sassanids scored notable successes in Asia Minor.

The emperor Diocletian succeeded in reviving the finances of the empire with a general tax reform in 284. He attempted to make the immense empire more easily governable by dividing its administration into two parts. Christianity became the official religion of the empire under Constantine (324-37), who made the city of Byzantium (rebuilt and renamed Constantinople after him) his chief residence in preference to Rome.

The Roman empire finally split into an eastern and a western part on the death of Theodosius I (395). The last ruler of the Western Roman empire, Romulus Augustulus, was deposed in 476 by the German chieftain Odoacer, who was in turn overthrown by the leader of the Visigoths, Theodoric, in 493.

The Eastern Roman emperor Justinian succeeded in reconquering large tracts of Italy, including Rome and Ravenna, and a number of strips of coastal territory. Here the empire maintained itself until the middle of the sixth century.

At the same time a Germanic Lombard kingdom was being formed in the north, with its capital at Pavia and comprising the duchies of Spoleto and Benevento; the growing influence of the papacy permitted Pope Gregory the Great (590-604) to turn the Holy See into a major centre of political power.

In 774 the Lombard kingdom was conquered by Charlemagne, the king of the Franks. On Christmas Day in 800, Charlemagne was crowned Western Roman Emperor by Pope Leo III. Neither Charlemagne nor his successors were able to maintain sovereignty in Italy. The Saracens conquered much of Sicily in 827. The Normans later settled there and founded, under King Roger I, the Norman kingdom of Sicily.

The German King Otto I had himself crowned emperor in Rome by Pope John XII in 962, an act which marked the birth of the Holy Roman Empire and bound together Germany and Italy.

The growth of the cities

Mediaeval Italy was a heavily urbanised land. Although the cities generally recognised a feudal overlord, many were effectively independent. While the

cities were growing, so too was the rivalry between popes and emperor for political and spiritual supremacy over the peninsula. In 1162 the emperor, and king of Germany, Frederick I (Barbarossa), destroyed Milan, which had assumed the leadership of the Lombard League.

Ten years later the cities of northern Italy rose again against Barbarossa, who was forced to concede a number of rights. Barbarossa's grandson Frederick II, heir to Sicily, was crowned emperor in 1220.

The power of the northern and central Italian states continued to grow during the 14th century. The Florence of the Medicis won itself a leading role in Europe with its production of fabrics and banking activities. Milan, renowned for its wools and silks, controlled the passage through the Alps and with it, access to the commercial markets of western and northern Europe. Venice, whose first *doge* (duke) was elected in 697, drew its wealth from maritime trade.

The commercial wealth of these cities fuelled the Renaissance. It also paid for the mercenary armies which kept their regional authority intact. Florence controlled the whole of Tuscany; Milan and Venice struggled for supremacy on the plain of the Po; Naples, conquered in 1442 by King Alfonso of Aragon, and Sicily remained feudal states. The five powers of Italy – Florence, Milan, Venice, Naples and Sicily – allied themselves in 1454 to the Papal States to form the Italian League. This, they hoped, would constitute a power of sufficient political significance to temper the aspirations of their European neighbours.

Foreign domination and Risorgimento

For more than half a century Italy was the scene of conflict between the big European powers, which spread to the rest of Europe after the election of Charles V as Holy Roman emperor (1519). The king of France, Charles VII, claimed the throne of Naples in 1481, invoking the right of succession of the house of Anjou. He entered Italy in September 1494. The French success led the pope to create the Holy League in which he was joined by Austria and Spain. The French were defeated at Naples in July 1496.

The kingdom of Naples was retaken by Louis XII in 1501 when it was divided with Spain. A new coalition assembled by the pope forced Louis XII to abandon Milan in 1513. Francis I reconquered the province in 1515.

Spain imposed its domination over Italy in 1559. The sovereignty of the Spanish Habsburgs lasted until the accession of a French Bourbon sparked the War of the Spanish Succession in 1713.

After the war the Spanish lands in Italy passed to the Austrian Habsburgs, who ushered in a more peaceful period.

"Enlightenment" thinking was put into practice, for example, in Tuscany under Grand Duke Leopold.

The French revolution met with a sympathetic reception from Italian intellectuals, easing the French annexation of parts of northern Italy. The balance of power in Italy shifted completely after Bonaparte's successful Italian campaign. After the conquest of Lombardy (1796), the Treaty of Campoformio in 1797 left only the newly defunct republic of Venice to Austria. Republics were created in Lombardy, Rome, Genoa and Naples. Napoleon was crowned king of Italy in 1805 and annexed Rome in 1807. Pope Pius VII was arrested and sent into exile.

Austria reacquired its sovereignty in Italy from 1814 onwards with three states (Naples, the Papal States and the kingdom of Piedmont-Sardinia) retaining their independence.

The liberal opposition to Habsburg rule started to regroup in the principal Italian cities. A revolution broke out in Naples in 1820, at the instigation of the Carbonari secret society, and this spread to Turin in Lombardy. Austrian troops intervened and put down the revolt.

New uprisings broke out in northern Italy in 1831, but these were soon repressed. A true national revolution was not to be ignited until 1848, after two years of serious economic crisis. Milan rose against Austria in January. Sicily followed suit in February. Revolts in Paris and Vienna were a signal for the movement to spread across the whole of Italy. King Charles Albert of Piedmont responded to the Lombard call. Lacking international support he was defeated by the Austrians at Custozza in July and then at Novara in March 1849, and abdicated.

Austrian domination aroused pan-Italian nationalism in Italy. The leaders of this *Risorgimento* (Resurgence) were Mazzini, Cavour (the premier of Piedmont) and Garibaldi (a guerrilla leader); they recognised that Italian unification could only be attained with foreign intervention and accordingly allied themselves with France. In 1859 Napoleon III sent an army whose victories at Magenta and Solferino forced the Austrians to withdraw from Lombardy. At the same time Garibaldi, with British backing, conquered Sicily and Naples at the head of his "Thousand Redshirts".

King Victor Emanuel II of Piedmont became the first king of Italy on 14 March 1861. Venice and Rome, where the pope had maintained his authority under French protection since 1849, remained independent. Venice was annexed by Victor Emanuel II in 1866 after the Prussian defeat of Austria in a different conflict.

The French had to withdraw from Rome during the Franco-Prussian war (1870-71) and the city was taken by Italian troops on 20 September 1870. Victor Emanuel II made his official entry into Rome on 31 December 1870, and the city became the capital of the Italian kingdom. However, some areas (Trento and Trieste) remained under Austrian sovereignty.

Nationhood and Fascism
The alliance with the French, whose colonial interests in Africa were at odds with Italian ambitions in Ethiopia and Tunisia, was abandoned in 1881. The new king of Italy, Umberto I, concluded the Triple Alliance with Germany and Austria in May 1882.

The severing of commercial relations with France added to the poverty and economic problems within the kingdom and sparked off rebellions in Sicily and Milan (1898). Socialists and Christian Democrats were repressed. Umberto I was assassinated by an anarchist on 29 July 1900.

Victor Emanuel III acceded to the throne just as Giovanni Giolitti's government was taking office. Giolitti was to remain prime minister until 1914, and his period of government saw an improvement in relations with France, a revival of economic activity and the instigation of liberal political reforms.

Politically divided, Italy entered the war against the Central Powers in 1915-16. The ill-prepared Italians were defeated at Caporetto (24 October 1917) before regaining the offensive with the help of the other Allies.

After the war and the break up of the Habsburg empire, Italy expanded to the north and north-east gaining the predominantly German-speaking South Tyrol in addition to Trieste, Istria and a number of territories in Dalmatia with a predominantly Slav population. Dis-contented, Italy was beset by a serious economic and political crisis.

The founding of the "Italian combat squads" by the former socialist journalist Benito Mussolini in March 1919 was followed in 1921 by the establishment of the Italian Communist Party by Gramschi and Togliatti. The rapid growth in support for the communists led the great landowners and industrialists to support Mussolini's new Fascist party (named after its symbol, the *fascio*, a sign of authority in ancient Rome) to which the king entrusted the government following the "March on Rome" of October 1922.

Mussolini's arrival in power was at first welcomed as an end to anarchy. It was only gradually that he moved towards an official dictatorship, which was announced in 1925.

Mussolini, the *Duce* (Leader), abolished most liberal freedoms in the late 1920s and early 1930s. Opposition parties were banned in 1926 (the leader of the socialists, Matteotti, had been murdered in 1924) and women barred from public office the same year. He also clamped down on secret societies such as the freemasons and the Mafia, and reached an accord with the pope in 1929. He embarked upon winning Italy an empire to add to Libya, taken from the Turks in 1911-12, and Italian Somaliland. Mussolini chose suitably vulnerable targets: Ethiopia (1935) and Albania (1939).

In the late 1930s Mussolini moved closer to Nazi Germany, left the League of Nations (which had condemned the invasion of Ethiopia) and signed the "Pact of Steel" with Hitler in May 1939. At about this time the Fascists also began to persecute Italian Jews.

In the war Italian troops, supported by Germany, suffered a number of setbacks in Greece and North Africa from 1940 onwards and were unable to prevent the Allied landings in Sicily in July 1943.

The king and a new government had Mussolini arrested and concluded an armistice with the Allies. Most of Italy, however, remained in the hands of German troops who freed Mussolini and fiercely opposed the Allies, whose advance was supported by the Italian partisans. Rome was not liberated until 4 June 1944. Mussolini was arrested by the resistance and shot dead near Como on 28 April 1945.

Republican Italy
King Victor Emanuel III abdicated on 9 May 1946 in favour of his son, Umberto II. On 2 June 1946 a referendum came down in favour of abolishing the monarchy, and Umberto went into exile.

Italy gained a new republican constitution on 1 January 1948. The Christian Democrats, who won an absolute majority at the 1948 elections, lost it again in 1953 and were forced to form a series of short-lived coalition governments opposed by a growing communist Party as well as neo-Fascist and far-left extremist movements. Social unrest, political scandal and ministerial crises resulting from the scope of indispensable social and economic reforms, were all reasons for the parties of the centre and the right to reach a compromise with the communists in July 1977.

The "historic compromise" with the communists was abandoned after the kidnapping and assassination of Aldo Moro, the Christian Democrat former premier, from March to May 1978. Moro's killers were the Red Brigade, the most prominent of the numerous armed revolutionary terrorist groups then operating in Italy.

The wave of extremist terrorism culminated in August 1980 with a bomb attack on the railway station at Bologna, which killed 80 people, and for which right-wing extremists claimed responsibility. In July 1981 the Republican Party's Giovanni Spadolini became the first head of government not to come from the ranks of the Christian Democrats. His government fell in November 1982 over economic policy. After the elections of 26 June 1983, which saw a fall in the Christian democrat vote, a new coalition government was formed by the socialist Bettino Craxi. Despite a number of scandals Craxi was able to celebrate the longest tenure of office of any Italian premier since 1945 (two years three months) on 14 November 1985. Craxi's government no doubt owed its stability to the country's improved economic performance, with inflation falling from 20 per cent in 1984 to 8.8 per cent in 1985. Craxi remained in power until the general election of 14 June 1987, with the Italian economy continuing to improve. A new coalition government under the Christian Democrat Giovanni Gona took office in July 1987, but was forced to resign in March 1988 after suffering repeated defeats over its budget proposals. In April 1988 the Christian Democrat Ciriaco de Mita was sworn in as leader of Italy's 48th post-war government.

Ivory Coast

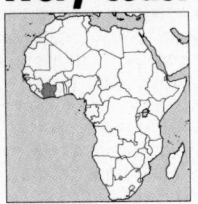

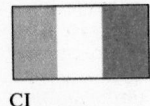

CI
West Africa
124,503 sq. mi
Pop: 11.1 m
UN, OAU

Capital: Abidjan (pop: 2 m)
Official language: French
Religions: Traditional beliefs (65 per cent), Moslem (23 per cent)
System of govt: Republic; independent since 7 August 1960

The shores of the Ivory Coast were known by Portuguese navigators from the 14th century although their inaccessibility meant that the first settlement was only founded there in 1687, by the French, at Assinia. It was abandoned in 1705.

Two new posts were established in 1842, Assinia and Grand Bassam, bases for the exploration of the interior.

Once the slave trade had been abolished palm oil became the principal economic resource, which remained relatively quiet until 1886, when the territories became protectorates. The occupation of the coast between Grand Lahou and Cavally was accomplished peacefully by 1889.

Ivory Coast became part of French Equatorial Africa in 1889, and a colony in its own right in March 1893. The conquest of the interior of the country met with determined resistance, in particular from the Guro and Baule peoples. In the north, Chief Somore Toure bitterly opposed the conquest up until his arrest in 1898. Resistance continued throughout the First World War. Ivory Coast then underwent rapid economic development based on the cultivation of coffee and cocoa, and the exploitation of palm products and timber.

The period between the two World Wars saw the undertaking of large-scale construction work such as the development of the port of Abidjan and the digging of the Vridi canal, completed in 1950, and the construction of the Abidjan to Bobo-Dioulasso railway.

Ivory Coast became a republic in December 1958. In 1960 the country obtained full independence under the impetus of Felix Houphouet-Boigny, founder in 1946 of the Ivory Coast section of the African Democratic Assembly (RDA) and a member of the French government between 1956 and 1959.

As soon as it was independent, Ivory Coast became the centre of an association which included the former French colonies of Upper Volta, Niger and Dahomey. Houphouet-Boigny attempted to achieve a grouping of African states hostile to socialism. Tension developed in 1966 between the Ivory Coast and Guinea which had given shelter to the deposed president of Ghana, Kwame Nkrumah. The visit of the Senegalese President Senghor to Abidjan in 1971 saw the start of a process of rapprochement with Senegal.

Houphouet-Boigny has been consistently re-elected president without a break since the country's independence. His political base is Ivory Coast's sole party, the Parti Democratique de Cote d'Ivoire (Ivory Coast Democratic Party, PDCI).

Political opposition appears badly organised. The Ivory Coast communist party has been banned since 1963 and student unrest disappeared after 1970.

Abidjan, the capital of Ivory Coast since 1934, was replaced in 1983 by Yamoussoukro, but the move to the new capital has not yet been implemented.

The economy of the Ivory Coast, one of the healthiest in Africa, is predominantly based on agriculture, which accounts for one-third of the nation's income, but supports 75 per cent of the country's population.

Ivory Coast is the world's largest producer of cocoa and the third largest of coffee. Palm oil and wood are also important. The country possesses few mineral resources but oil has been discovered. Hydro-electric potential has been partially exploited. Ivory Coast's trade balance shows a clear surplus.

Jamaica

Jamaica

JA
Caribbean
4,411 sq. mi
Pop: 2.35 m
UN, OAS, CW,
CARICOM

Capital: Kingston (pop: 104,000)
Official language: English
Religions: Protestant (70 per cent),
Catholic (9 per cent)
System of govt: Constitutional
monarchy; independent since 6 August
1962.

Jamaica, one of the Greater Antilles, was discovered in 1494 by Christopher Columbus, who took possession of it for Spain. The Spanish settlers developed sugar cane plantations on the island they called Xaymaca, with the indigenous Arawaks providing the workforce. The treatment inflicted on the Arawaks was such that the Spanish soon had to import slaves from Africa.

In 1655 Oliver Cromwell sent an expedition to Jamaica under orders to expel the Spanish and occupy the island. After the Spanish had left in 1660, Jamaica obtained a constitution and an elected popular assembly in 1662.

In the 1670 Treaty of Madrid, Spain recognised English sovereignty over the island. Jamaica became a trading centre for English contraband on its way to Spanish America, and then for the slave trade when Britain obtained a monopoly under the 1713 Treaty of Utrecht.

In the 1730s fighting broke out against black rebels, who sought refuge in the central mountains. The struggle continued until 1739 when the British governor guaranteed the rebels autonomy over their own territories. The island's economy, drawing its wealth from the exportation of sugar, indigo and cocoa, reached its apogee in the middle of the 18th century.

The abolition of slavery in 1833 and the fall in sugar prices brought ruin to many plantations. After the revolt at Morant Bay the island became a crown colony in 1865 and was placed under direct administration from London. During the renewed calm of the following decades major foreign companies, such as the US United Fruit Company, established themselves on the island to exploit Jamaica's bananas and sugar.

Jamaican nationalism came into being during the 1940s under the impetus of the trade unionist Alexander Bustamante and his cousin, the lawyer Norman Manley. In 1953 a constitution came into force which opened the way to autonomy, and in 1961 Jamaica left the West Indies Federation, a loose grouping of British Caribbean territories, after the victory of Bustamente's Labour Party.

Independent Jamaica

Jamaica became independent within the Commonwealth on 6 August 1962. The Jamaica Labour Party stayed in power under Bustamante until 1967, and then under Hugh Shearer until 1972. The victory of the socialist People's National Party led by Michael Manley (son of Norman Manley) in the 1972 general election brought the socialists into power.

In 1973 Jamaica joined Barbados, Guyana and Trinidad and Tobago to form CARICOM, the Caribbean economic community.

By the late 1970s the left-wing Manley government faced a serious economic and political crisis after the imposition of a tax on bauxite exports had caused a reduction by almost half in mining operations.

Gross national product had fallen by a quarter since 1972, and 35 per cent of the workforce was unemployed.

The general election of October 1980 brought Labour (conservatives) back to power under Edward Seaga, who favoured a free market economy. Seaga, who enjoyed greater support than his predecessor from the USA, tried to implement the passage from an essentially rural economy to an industrial economy based on the mining of bauxite, which represented 70 per cent of income from exports. The economy, however, remained heavily encumbered by foreign debt.

In 1985 the Seaga government had to face serious social troubles starting with bloody riots in January after a rise in fuel prices, followed by a general strike in June.

The Seaga government promoted the island's tourism which, according to official figures, brought Jamaica almost half of its foreign currency revenue. It has also been estimated that the illegal traffic in marijuana was worth $200 million in 1984. However, by 1985 a recession in international bauxite and aluminium markets had further contributed to the deterioration in the Jamaican economy which had occurred since Labour had come to power.

These continuing economic and financial difficulties led to an increase in support for the opposition People's National Party, which had refused to contest the 1983 elections. At the elections held on 9 February 1989 the ruling Labour Party was overwhelmingly defeated and the People's National Party leader Michael Manley was once again sworn in as prime minister. His manifesto was more moderate in tone than that of his previous government, aiming at national reconciliation of the country.

Japan

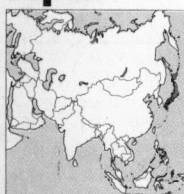
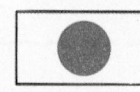

J
Far East
145,874 sq. mi
Pop: 122 m
UN, OECD

Capital: Tokyo (pop: 8.35 m)
Official language: Japanese
Religions: Buddhist, Shintoist
System of govt: Constitutional
monarchy since 3 May 1947

The islands of Japan, the principle ones being (from north to south) Hokkaido, Honshu, Shikoku and Kyushu, were populated before the eighth millenium BC by peoples originating mainly from the northern Asiatic continent. The late mesolithic culture (Jomon period) was succeeded by the Yayoi culture (tomb culture) from the third century BC. The Yayoi, probably originating from southern China, brought with them the technique of rice cultivation along with bronze and iron metal working.

The same epoch saw the appearance of the Ainus from Siberia in the north who mixed with the Jomon. The Yayoi were organised into agricultural communities dominated by a high priest. Korean warriors who appeared in the south of Japan at the end of the third century, were easily able to impose their domination over the rural Yayoi populations.

The Yayoi were regrouped into clans whose importance continued to grow during the conquests which followed, until kingdoms were formed which perpetuated the traditional rivalries. The "aristocrats", many of whom were of Korean origin, had themselves buried in great earth mounds. The Yamato clan, whose domination spread from around Nora, claimed hegemony and gave their king the title of tenno (emperor). Japan's legendary first emperor was Jimmu Tenno (660-585 BC).

Legends surrounding the early emperors are known from two works, the Kojiki and the Nihon-shoki, both compiled later (around 715 AD).

Japan until the shogunates

Japan made its first appearance in recorded history with the introduction of Buddhism into the imperial court in 538. The favour accorded to Buddhism by the Yamato and their allies led them into war against the Shinto clans, Shinto being the indigenous culture. The Buddhists finally gained the upper hand in 587.

A legal code was promulgated at the end of Empress Suiko's reign (593-628). The Nakatomi clan, which imposed its supremacy in 645, extended the Chinese model to Japan's social life with the Taika code, which was replaced in 711 by the Taiho code, reforming the distribution of land and the legal system. A year later the imperial court chose Nara, which became a major centre for the Buddhist religion, as its permanent residence. In 741 the Emperor Shomu ordered the construction of Buddhist temples across the whole of Japan.

The Emperor Kammu tried to put an end to the considerable influence of the Buddhist monks of Nara by constructing a new capital at Heiankyo (Kyoto), inaugurated in 794. The return of the Japanese Buddhist monks, Saicho and Kukai, from China in 806 marked the beginning of a cultural upheaval from which emerged a new Japanese system of writing and a new religious doctrine, combining Buddhist, Confucian, Taoist and Shintoist influences.

The reign of the Fujiwara clan, who held the title *kampaku* (regent), was a peaceful period favouring the development of an outstanding Japanese culture and the penetration of Buddhism, previously reserved only for an elite, into the populace. In c.950 the Taira and Minamoto clans emerged as powerful military forces in the provinces and threatened the position of the Fujiwara, who by then had divided into rival factions. The Taira and Minamoto then clashed openly and, after an initial battle in Kyoto itself which gave victory to the Taira in 1060, an incessant struggle developed between them, which threw the country into misery, famine and lawlessness.

The deciding battle took place near Shimonoseki in 1185. The Taira fleet was destroyed and Yoritomo, head of the Minamoto clan, turned on the Fujiwara whose Honshu territories he conquered in 1189. Relying on the support of a feudal system based on the pre-eminence of the samurai warriors, Yoritomo gradually extended his powers across the whole of Japan. The tenno lost all power and Minamoto no Yoritomo adopted the title *shogun* (military dictator). The whole of the ruined country rallied round the most powerful warlord in Japan.

The reign of the shoguns

On the death of Yoritomo the Hojo clan imposed their supremacy and took over the military government (*bakufu*) which Yoritomo had formed at Kamakura. The shoguns were then chosen from the imperial family but it was the

Hojo who were the true masters of the bakufu.

In 1266 the Chinese Emperor Kublai Khan declared his intention of invading Japan. Coastal defences were established in the north of Kyushu. The attack by the Mongol and Korean fleet, 30,000 men strong, took place in 1274, but the would-be invaders were forced to retreat. The bakufu had prayers of thanks offered to the gods throughout Japan, and the following year emissaries from Kublai were executed. The bakufu had a powerful fleet constructed as well as a stone wall on the north coast of Kyushu. Two Mongol and Korean fleets, numbering more than 140,000 men, succeeded in setting foot on two points of Kyushu.

A typhoon destroyed part of the enemy fleets, causing the immediate departure of part of the Mongol army. The rest were massacred by the samurai. The end of samurai mobilisation on the death of Kublai Khan in 1294 meant ruin for many of them. For the merchants, however, enriched by the war, it meant the cheap acquisition of land even though the bakufu had banned its sale.

With the aid of a Minamoto rebel, Ashikaga Takauji, and the general uprising of the lords against the bakufu, the Emperor Go-Daigo (Daigo II) succeeded in destroying Kamakura in 1333 and restored imperial power. Ashikaga Takauji had himself named shogun by Go-Daigo, and installed a regime in Kyoto. Civil war broke out during which Kyoto was captured and destroyed four times, and did not end until 1392 when the Ashikaga shoguns finally imposed their authority over the emperor.

In the face of the threat from the Wako pirates, Japan, China and Korea renewed amicable relations from 1400 onwards. However, Japan fell prey to bandits; Samurai brigands and peasants driven by famine formed bands of pillagers. It was in this atmosphere that the civil war of the "Onin era" broke out in 1467, with a confrontation in the Kyoto valley between 160,000 men belonging to several clans disputing the succession to the shogunate. An aimless war spread across the country, and in 1486 the peasants revolted to put an end to the war between the lords, the *daimyo*.

Effective control from the centre was now at an end, for both the emperor and the shogun were powerless and the territory of each daimyo was to all interests and purposes an independent kingdom. After the shipwreck of Portuguese sailors with muskets on the island of Tanegashima, south of Kyushu, in the mid-16th century, the use of firearms spread across the whole of Japan, and Portuguese merchants came to trade with Japan a few years later.

A minor lord from the north, Oda Nobunaga, succeeded in uniting Japan in 1580. He was overthrown in 1582 and was succeeded by one of his generals, Toyotomi Hideyoshi, who in 1590 defeated the last of the independent daimyo, and made them build him an enormous palace-castle at Osaka. The expedition which he sent to Korea in 1592 and reinforced with 100,000 men in 1597 ended in disaster in 1598.

On Hideyoshi's death, a second general of Oda Nobunaga, Tokugawa Ieyasu, took over as shogun and established his capital at Edo (Tokyo). The work of Ieyasu, who died in 1616, was considerable. Renewed amicable relations with China and relations with Europe allowed Japanese maritime and commercial growth to flourish, whilst Ieyasu endowed the country with a stable government. The reigns of his son and his grandson, Tokugawa Iemitsu (1624-51), were marked by the persecution of Christian priests and the total closure of all Japanese ports to foreigners, except to the Chinese and Dutch, who were allowed access to part of the port of Nagasaki.

Even Japanese ships had to carry a special authorisation in order to be able to travel abroad. Merchants and urban dwellers grew more important in the 17th century, as the political power of the daimyo could not match their economic power.

Crippled by taxes and threatened by famine, the peasants revolted a number of times between 1735 and 1773. Russian ships began to appear at Hokkaido in 1792. At the beginning of the 19th century foreign powers began to show their impatience with the closure of the Japanese ports. The Russian Admiral Rezanov waited for six months in the port of Nagasaki for an invitation to Edo which never arrived. In 1808 an English vessel threatened to bombard Nagasaki when it was refused permission to restock its supplies of food and water. In 1825 the Shogun Ienari ordered the destruction of all foreign vessels anchored in Japanese ports.

The opening of the Japanese ports was finally obtained by force when the American, Commodore Perry, who had brought a message from the president of the USA in 1853, returned the following year to get a reply accompanied by four battleships. The indignation aroused by the accords with the "barbarians" led to an uprising in parts of the country in 1858. After several incidents and the capture of the port of Shimonoseki by an international expedition in 1863, a revolt by the emperor's partisans defeated the bakufu, and the last of the Tokugawa shoguns had to submit to the emperor in 1867. Emperor Mutsuhitu assumed power in 1868 and transferred his capital to Edo, renaming it Tokyo. Thus began the Meiji era.

The Meiji and Taisho eras

Major reforms were undertaken by the Emperor Mutsuhito, in the spirit of the Meiji ("illumined reign") era. Japan's administrative and social structures were radically reorganised, the peasants becoming legal owners of the land, which could now be bought and sold freely again (1871). Universities were set up; the samurai lost their ancient privileges; the government was westernised and free trade with the outside world was established (1873). It took the imperial army, created from conscripts in 1871, just a short while to succeed in putting down the rebellion, which had been led by Saigo Takamori and others unhappy about the loss of samurai privileges. The imperial council was replaced in 1885 by a cabinet based on the western model, and presided over by Prince Ito Hirobumi. The process of westernisation was undertaken in all the provinces, and on 11 February 1889 a constitution was created providing for the setting up of a two-chamber parliament; the modernisation of the judicial system, army and navy; the introduction of compulsory military service; and the process of industrialisation, which had begun with railways in 1870.

The invasion of China by Japanese troops in 1894, resulted in total military and diplomatic victory with the Peace of Shimonoseki in 1895 sanctioning a heavy Japanese presence in Korea. An alliance with the western countries emerged when Japan cooperated in the suppression of the Boxer Rebellion in China (1900), with the 1902 alliance between Japan and Britain being above all directed against Russia. After Czar Nicholas II had sent troops into Manchuria, Japan attacked the Russian fleet stationed at Port Arthur, and sent an army into Korea and to Liaodong (1904).

Russia's capitulation at Port Arthur and then the destruction of the Russian Baltic relief fleet in the Strait of Tsushima, enabled the Japanese troops to occupy Manchuria and Korea. Russia also had to cede the southern half of the island of Sakhalin to Japan.

In 1910 Japan annexed Korea. Resources drawn from the protectorates of China and Korea after Japan's two war victories, gave the Japanese economy an enormous boost. A year before Mutsuhito's death in 1912, the militarists had gained the upper hand over the liberals.

Mutsuhito's death marked the end of the Meiji era and he was succeeded by his son Yoshihito (Taisho Tenno). Japan, governed by Admiral Yamamoto, entered into war against Germany in 1914 alongside the Allies, but was particularly interested in China, who had to give way to the Japanese ultimatum of 1915. After the Russian Revolution, Japanese troops penetrated Siberia (1918). Japan received, for her modest part in the war, the German concessions in China and the North Pacific.

The Korean nationalist uprising, led by Syngman Rhee, was bloodily put down by the Japanese army in 1919. The death of Emperor Yoshihito in 1926, and his son Hirohito's accession to the throne, put an end to a reign whose final years had been marked by the cataclysmic earthquake which had destroyed Tokyo and Yokohama in 1923, and by a return, in politics, to tradition and xenophobia.

The reign of Hirohito

The new emperor chose to call his reign the *Showa* (Brilliant Peace) era. Solidly established in power, the militarists decided to extend the Japanese presence in China by force.

Manchuria was invaded, apparently against the emperor's advice, in 1931. Forced by US pressure to retreat from China, Japan made Manchuria into a puppet state, Manchukuo, placing at its head the last emperor of China, Puyi.

The assassination of prime minister Inukai put an effective end to parliamentary rule in 1932. In 1934 Japan, which had invaded the north of China, denounced the international agreements on disarmament which it had earlier ratified. In 1935 the USSR had to cede the eastern Chinese railway network to Japan.

Coming to power in 1936, the ultra-nationalists intensified the imperialist war against China. Japan's advance accelerated despite the resistance of Chinese communists and nationalists, and in 1937 the Japanese created a Chinese puppet government in Nanjing headed by Wang Jingwei, a general of the Guomindang opposed to Chiang Kai-chek.

In 1938 the nationalist troops withdrew to Chongqing, while the communist troops succeeded in putting a partial stop to the Japanese advance. The German defeat of France in 1940 allowed Japan to deliver an ultimatum to the French governor-general of Indochina, demanding free passage for Japanese troops. Directed by Konoye Fumumaro, the nationalists continued their policy of aggression and gave support to Thailand's claims to Cambodia; they demanded the oil reserves in the Dutch East Indies; and, finally, concluded a pact with the Axis powers on 27 September 1940.

Japan signed a non-aggression pact with Stalin in 1941 while relations with Washington became strained after the USA blocked Japanese credit.

Konoye had to resign under pressure from the militarists, and General Tojo took over at the head of government. The end of 1941 saw the US entry into the war against Japan, after the surprise attack on the US Pacific fleet at Pearl Harbor in Hawaii on 7 December. By 1942 Japan had overrun most of the Far East and western Pacific. Hong Kong had fallen in December 1941, and Manila fell on 2 January 1942. The first US action was on 18 April, when Tokyo was bombed. The US counter-offensive in the Pacific began with the naval defeat of the Japanese at the Midway islands in June 1942. In 1943 US forces were in New Guinea and the Solomon islands. The British counter-offensive in Burma began in the same year. In 1944 Japan had lost nearly all the Pacific islands it had invaded.

Jordan

General Tojo resigned and was replaced by the equally militarist Koiso Kuniaki. The battle of Leyte enabled the US to recapture the Philippines and from then on the Japanese high command had to resort to suicide (kamikaze) missions. US troops landed on the island of Okinawa south of Japan on 1 April 1945 while the bombing of urban areas intensified. Although their oil supplies were almost exhausted, the Japanese continued fighting.

The emperor, and Koiso's successor, Admiral Suzuki Kantaro, tried, in vain, to make peace through the USSR. Japanese resistance was crushed when the first, and only, atomic bombs used in anger annihilated Hiroshima on 6 August and Nagasaki on 9 August.

The USSR declared war on Japan on 8 August. On 14 August Emperor Hirohito decided on unconditional surrender. The official surrender took place on 14 September aboard the US battleship, Missouri, and was accepted for the Allies by the US General MacArthur. He was charged with the military administration of occupied Japan.

As many as 1,800,000 Japanese died in the war; 40 per cent of Japanese towns were been reduced to rubble; Japan lost all her foreign territories; its economy was ruined. Konoye committed suicide in 1945, but Tojo and 700 other senior figures were tried and condemned to death as war criminals in 1946. But not the emperor: recent research suggests that even if Hirohito had not been as powerless as he and others claimed in the face of the militarists who ran the government, the USA feared that putting him on trial would spark a revolt. He was, after all, regarded as divine.

The new Japanese constitution, instigated by MacArthur, came into force in 1947 and made Japan a constitutional monarchy on the British model. Hirohito renounced his divinity. A general policy of reform was put into place and the Japanese population was introduced to the ideas of democracy.

There was a succession of socialist governments in Japan until 1952. The Korean War (1950-51), which saw thousands of western troops based in Japan, brought new life to the lethargic Japanese economy. Japan regained its sovereignty on 28 April 1952, while still being forbidden from forming an army.

Japan's integration into the western world began in 1954 with the signing of a mutual aid agreement with the USA. At the same time Japan's economy became the fastest growing economy in the world (1960-64). The Liberal democrat Eisaku Sato managed to stay in power from 1964 until 1972 in spite of pressure from the left, linked with anti-Americanism, particularly prevalent at the time of the Vietnam War. The oil crisis of December 1973 hit Japan's economy, leading the government to introduce a state of emergency.

The normalisation of relations with China led to the signing of a treaty of friendship between the two powers on 12 August 1978. In power from November 1982, the Liberal Democrat prime minister Yasuhiro Nakasone had to call the early general elections (18 December 1983), after the former prime minister (1972-74) Kakuei Tanaka had been accused of involvement in financial scandals connected with the US aircraft company Lockheed.

In 1984 Japan undertook the huge policy of reconciliation with the rest of Asia, which culminated with the president of South Korea visiting Japan in November. In the same year Japan recorded a huge trade surplus, over 50 per cent greater than that of the previous year.

In 1985 Japanese political life was dominated by the question of whether Nakasone's period in office should extend beyond the end of his term in autumn 1986, and the size of the proposed military budget for the period 1986-90, which was projected to exceed one per cent of the GNP for the first time since the Second World War. The imbalance in foreign trade in Japan's favour continued to be a problem affecting economic relations with other states.

In the July 1986 elections the Liberal Democrats did well, and Nakasone's term of office was extended for a year. The government adopted measures to expand domestic demand and the increased military budget was agreed. As a result of a leadership struggle in 1987 within the Liberal Democrats, Noboru Takeshita became party president in October and was elected prime minister by the Japanese Diet (parliament) in November.

On 7 January 1989 the 87-year-old Emperor Hirohito died after 62 years on the throne, the longest-reigning ruler in recorded Japanese history. As he lay dying, controversy surrounding his role in Japan's militaristic and imperialistic period before 1945 was renewed. He was succeeded by his 55-year-old son, Crown Prince Akihito, whose accession ushered in a new era, Heisei (Attained Peace).

In May 1989 Takeshita's government was beset by accusations of influence-peddling and bribery, and he was forced to offer his resignation. His successor, Sosuke Uno, was in trouble within weeks after a former geisha claimed he had paid her for sex. The Liberal democrats did badly in Tokyo elections in early July, and it seemed as if their decades-long hold on power might be loosened.

Jordan

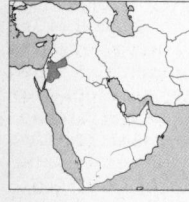

HKJ
Near East
34,443 sq. mi
Pop: 2.67 m
UN, AL

Capital: Amman (pop: 1.1 m)
Official language: Arabic
Religion: Moslem (93 per cent)
System of govt: Constitutional monarchy since 24 January 1949

Present-day Jordan, named after the river it straddles, was for several thousand years under the successive domination of foreign kingdoms: Egypt, Assyria, Babylon, Persia and Macedonia. An indigenous kingdom, however, the kingdom of the Nabataeans, existed between the fourth century BC and its occupation by Rome in 106. Its capital, Petra, hewn from solid rock in the south of the country, is an impressive remnant from this period. Nabataean wealth came mainly from trade in the precious incense from Yemen which the Nabataeans sold throughout the Roman empire. Occupied by the Romans in 106, Nabataean territory was conquered by Moslem Arabs in the seventh century. Under the authority of the crusader kingdom of Jerusalem for a brief period, Jordan was integrated into the kingdom of the Egyptian Mamelukes in 1187. Defeated by the Ottoman Turks in 1517, the Mamelukes abandoned Jordan, which remained under the authority of the sultan of Turkey until the First World War.

Following the defeat of Turkey, Jordan was put under the British League of Nations mandate for Palestine in 1922. It was separated to constitute the autonomous emirate of Transjordan with Abdullah bin Husain at its head. On 22 March 1946 the British granted independence to the emirate which became the kingdom of Transjordan. When the British mandate in Palestine expired, in 1948, the proclamation of the state of Israel provoked the first Arab-Israeli war. King Abdullah occupied east Jerusalem and the territories to the west of the river Jordan. In 1949 the country was renamed, after its ruling dynasty, the Hashemite Kingdom of Jordan.

Assassinated on 20 June 1949, King Abdullah was succeeded by his son Talal, and then on 11 August 1952 by his grandson Hussein. Jordan under premier Nabulsi severed relations with Britain over Suez (1956) and moved closer to the pro-Soviet Egypt and Syria.

Later King Hussein secured closer ties with Saudi Arabia and the USA, but relations with Nasser's Egypt were severed in December 1966. At this time 800,000 Palestinian refugees lived on the West Bank. Their revolt against the regime at the end of 1966 led to Hussein's closure of the PLO bureau in Jerusalem.

On 5 June 1967 Israeli troops occupied the whole of the West Bank in the Six Days War, taking six per cent of Jordan's area but 30 per cent of its fertile land.

Unrest among Palestinian refugeess in Jordan led to confrontation with the Jordanian army in 13 February 1970. After a compromise, the Jordanian army went on the offensive against the Palestinian camps in June. The crisis culminated in pro-Palestinian Syrian troops entering Jordan in September. They withdrew after the Cairo Conference (27 September).

In July 1971 the last of the Palestinian camps were cleared and the PLO moved to Lebanon.

Jordanian sovereignty over the West Bank and east Jerusalem, both occupied by Israel, was transferred by Hussein to the PLO in October 1974.

A new civil war broke out in September 1977 (Black September) after Jordan's signing of the Arab-Israeli ceasefire agreements. Hussein refused to join the Egypt-Israeli peace treaty of March 1979, because this failed to recognise the rights of the Palestinians to self-determination.

Relations with pro-Iranian Syria became strained after the outbreak of the Iran-Iraq Gulf War in 1980. A Jordanian-US plan to give the occupied West Bank autonomy within a confederation with Jordan was rejected by the PLO, which continued to demand a Palestinian state.

In April 1983 Hussein announced an end to his efforts towards a peace initiative in the Near East. Jordan renewed relations with Egypt in 1984, whilst severing relations with Libya. The aggravation of Arab-Israeli tension after the bombing of the PLO headquarters in Tunis and the hijack of the Italian liner Achille Lauro in October 1985, again ended Jordanian plans to call an international conference on the region.

At the Arab League summit held in Amman on 8 November 1987, Hussein again reviewed plans for an international peace conference on the Near East, but this was opposed by the Israeli prime minister Yitzhak Shamir, who wanted to exclude the PLO from any conference. On 31 July 1988, King Hussein reaffirmed that Jordan would renounce its claims to sovereignty over the Israeli-occupied West Bank, in favour of the Palestinians.

Kenya

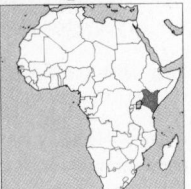

EAK
East Africa
224,960 sq. mi
Pop: 20.3 m
UN, CW, OAU

Capital: Nairobi (pop: 1.16 m)
Official languages: Swahili, English
Religions: Christian (73 per cent), traditional beliefs (19 per cent)
System of govt: Republic; independent since 12 December 1963

There were cattle herders in what is now Kenya 7,000 years ago; agriculture was introduced in the thousand years after 1000 BC from Ethiopia. The migrations which followed were to distribute the region's Bantu peoples (amongst them the Kikuyu), as well as the Kalenjin and (by 1600) the Turkana and the Sambura.

The Masai occupied the centre of Kenya between Lake Victoria and the Indian Ocean. Arab merchants founded a number of trading posts for ivory, gold, copper, and slaves along the coastline of present-day Kenya during the seventh and eighth centuries at Lamu, Malindi and Mombasa. The Arab posts fell into the hands of Portuguese traders who followed Vasco da Gama's landing on the Kenya coast in 1498. It was not until 1729 that the Arabs regained their former territories and expelled the Portuguese. The sultans of Oman conquered Zanzibar and the coast of Kenya between 1737 and 1784.

At the beginning of the 19th century the European powers began to interest themselves in Kenya. After German preachers had made their way far into the country for the first time in 1844, the British founded their first trading post. The Imperial British East Africa Company obtained a British royal charter for the exploitation of Kenya and Uganda as well as Zanzibar, which was an independent sultanate.

From 1895 these territories were administered directly from London and the construction of a railway was undertaken from the port of Mombasa to neighbouring Uganda. These undertakings led to the arrival of a large Indian work force and numerous Europeans, who settled, principally, in the fertile high plateau areas. In the years after becoming a crown colony in 1920, Kenya became the scene of increasingly violent confrontations between the differing population groups. The Indians demanded social and political equality and the British settlers demanded their own self-government.

Black African aspirations were co-ordinated from 1921 by welfare societies such as the Kiyuku Central Association (KCA), which was founded by Joseph Kangethe in 1924. Under the leadership of Jomo Kenyatta, the Mau-Mau campaigns of the Kikuyu broke out between 1952 and 1956.

The terror campaign of the Mau-Mau and the British crackdown and reprisals, led to the deaths of 63 Europeans and 11,503 Kiyuku. Kenyatta was arrested and imprisoned.

Over 25,000 Mau-Mau were arrested and interned in camps. The state of emergency which had been imposed during the troubles was not lifted until 1960.

Freed from jail in 1961, Jomo Kenyatta founded the Kenya African National Union (KANU).

KANU won pre-independence elections in May 1963 against its main rival, Ronald Ngala's Kenyan African Democratic Union (KADU). Complete independence was gained on 12 December 1963, Kenya opting to remain within the Commonwealth.

Kenyatta became the first president of Kenya, which was declared a republic on 12 December 1964, the first anniversary of independence. Politically Kenya was aligned with the west.

Attempts to create an East African Community with Tanzania and Uganda failed. The Africanisation of the country was undertaken rapidly; numerous Europeans and Indians left in 1968 after their possessions had been expropriated. Internal political opposition was eliminated after the assassination of Tom Mboya, Kenyatta's heir, in July 1969.

The KANU became the sole party, and the leader of its dissident left-wing (Kenyan Peoples Union), was arrested. (He was expelled from the KANU in 1981 after serving a long sentence.)

Although the Kenyan economy is essentially agricultural, the country possesses the most highly developed industry in East Africa. Dependent on oil, the country has developed a national energy policy favouring the development of hydro-electricity.

Vice-President Daniel Arap Moi became head of the party and president on Jomo Kenyatta's death on 22 August 1978.

The regime became more severe and the one-party system was instituted in officially in June 1982. An attempted coup followed in August, but the one-party regime has remained despite some continuing opposition and unrest. President Arap Moi was re-elected unopposed first in August 1983 and then in February 1988, having been nominated two days earlier as the unopposed candidate of KANU. In 1984 Kenya had the highest birth rate in the world (4.1 per cent), and it has been estimated that the population will reach over 36 million by 2000.

Kiribati

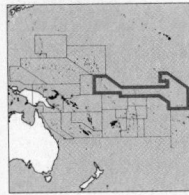

Oceania
276.9 sq. mi
Pop: 61,000
UN, CW

Capital: Bairiki (pop: 22,000)
Official language: English
Religions: Protestant (51 per cent), catholic (30 per cent)
System of govt: Republic; independent since 12 July 1979

Kiribati consists of 28 islands and atolls spread across a large area of the Pacific Ocean. The main island groups were discovered by Europeans from the late 16th to late 18th centuries, but Europeans did not settle on the archipelagos until the 19th century. The Gilbert Islands, the Ellice Islands (now Vanuatu) and the Line islands were declared a British protectorate in 1892, and a crown colony in 1916, extended in 1937 to include the Phoenix islands. The two main archipelagos were partly occupied by Japan at the beginning of the Second World War, but reconquered by US forces in 1943. Kiribati came into being in 1979 and has been governed since independence mainly by Ieremia Tabai. His ten ministers represent clans rather than parties.

Korea (North)

Far East
46,540 sq. mi
Pop: 21.3 m

Capital: Pyongyang (pop: 1.5 m)
Official language: Korean
Religion: Non-religious (67 per cent)
System of govt: People's republic, proclaimed 9 September 1948

The part of Korea situated to the north of the 38th parallel was occupied by Soviet troops following the defeat of Japan. Kim Il-Sung, secretary of the Korean Communist party in 1945, became general secretary of the Korean Workers' Party, an amalgamation of the communists and the Democratic Party, in 1946. Fundamental Marxist reforms were undertaken. In 1947 Kim Il-Sung became leader of the government elected by the people's assembly (parliament), itself the product of a convention of people's committees which met in February 1947.

On 25 June 1950 North Korea invaded South Korea, sparking the Korean War, in which North Korea was backed by the Chinese and the South by a large UN force of US, British and other western troops. By October 1950, initial UN successes had nearly rolled the communists back to the Chinese border, until a Chinese counter-attack almost completely overran the South by January 1951. The war dragged on until peace talks at Panmunjom were concluded on 27 July 1953 with the establishing of the 38th parallel as the frontier between the two countries.

Chinese troops withdrew in 1958. The North Korean economy, shattered by the war, had practically recovered by 1961. After distancing itself from the USSR from 1956, when Khrushchev denounced Stalin, Korea drew closer to China and from 1966 tried to hold a balance between its two powerful neighbours.

In December 1972 Kim Il-Sung relinquished his position of premier and became head of state. At the same time a new constitution reinforced the Workers' Party's dominant role in Korea. The country's admission as an observer at the UN in June 1973 facilitated its opening up to the international community, and it established economic links with Japan.

It was also in 1973, after communications with South Korea had been re-established, that Kim Il-Sung vowed to refrain from any attempted invasion of his southern neighbour.

The division of Korea, however, has remained the country's main political problem. Tension between the two Koreas has been regularly awakened by, for example, naval espionage by US warships or the driving of tunnels by the North into the demilitarised zone, discovered in 1974 and 1975. A US offer of tripartite negotiations on

Korea (South)

reunification was rejected by North Korea in 1979.

In 1983, Kim Il-Sung's son, Kim Jong-Il, emerged as the country's second most influential person, and seemed destined to succeed his father, even though China showed little enthusiasm for this hereditary succession.

In its attempt to avoid too restrictive a dependence on China, North Korea, the country with the most powerful economy in communist Asia, laid the foundations for a rapprochement with the USSR when Kim Il-Sung visited Moscow in May 1984, the first such visit for 20 years.

North Korea sent 100,000 tons of cement, and large quantities of rice and textiles to South Korea following the catastrophic flooding of September 1984 which left more than 200,000 people homeless. This initial gesture of appeasement in the relations between the two Koreas was followed the next

month by an offer to revive negotiations with the Red Cross, which would allow families separated for 30 years to meet once more.

Talks were also held with the Seoul government aimed at sharing the 1988 Olympic Games, due to be in Seoul, but no agreement was reached in time.

Korea (South)

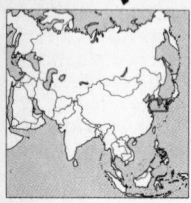

ROK
Far East
38,232 sq. mi
Pop: 41.8 m

Capital: Seoul (pop: 10 m)
Official language: Korean
Religions: Buddhism (48 per cent), Christian (44 per cent)
System of govt: Republic since 15 August 1948

Korea before 1945

Korean legends tell of the founding of the country of Choson in the Tae-dong basin by Tangun, the son of a she-bear which metamorphosed into a woman. The Chinese took control of Korea in the first century BC after defeating the dynasty probably founded by the Chinese Kija in 1122 BC.

Chinese garrisons disappeared in the first century and were replaced by three local dynasties. The northern kingdom of Koguryo, centred on Pyongyang was defeated by the Silla kingdom in the south east which, allied to the Chinese, then conquered the south-western kingdom of Paekche, allied to the Japanese in 668. The Korean peninsula was unified by the Silla kingdom in 735.

Chinese influence in Korea also saw the growth of Buddhism and Confucianism. The Silla kingdom, with its

capital at Kyongju, disappeared in 935 when it was attacked by the Khitans in the north, after the Koryo dynasty was founded in 918 in the south. The Khitan threat was not finally ended until 1019.

The capital of Kae-Song was taken by the Mongols in 1231. When the Mongol Yuan dynasty of Chinese emperors fell in 1368 their Ming successors were unable to prevent the rebel Yi Song-Gye (1355-1408) from founding in 1392 the Korean Yi dynasty based at Seoul, which survived until 1910.

In 1582 Portuguese sailors reached the Korean coast. The Japanese invasion of 1592 failed in the face of the determination of Admiral Yi Sun-Shin. The Japanese withdrew in 1598.

After conquering China, the Manchu dynasty dominated Korea from 1637. European influence did not start to make itself felt until the 18th century. Catholicism was proscribed in 1786. Having succeeded in making inroads to Korea in the 19th century, the westerners were driven back by the regent Taewon in 1864. French and US displays of power brought about the fall of Taewon in 1873. A reformist tendency, supported by Japan, led to the opening of the country between 1876 and 1886. In 1895 Japan overcame Chinese suzerainty in Korea, which sought a fruitless alliance with Russia. Japan annexed Korea in 1910.

The reign of terror imposed by Japan led to a mass uprising in 1919. The more liberal Japanese policies introduced after 1920 accompanied an at-

tempt to eliminate Korean culture.

The USSR declared war on Japan on 8 August 1945 and invaded Korea. Liberated after the Japanese surrender, Korea was divided into two as a result of the presence of Soviet and US troops on either side of the 38th parallel. Superpower hostility led to the birth of the southern Republic of Korea on 15 August 1948 under Syngman Rhee and of the People's Republic of Korea under Kim Il-Sung on 9 September 1948.

The Korean War and after

North Korean troops invaded the South on 25 June 1950. On 27 June the UN called on member states to support South Korea. US divisions stationed in Japan intervened on 30 June, under the command of US General MacArthur. Peace talks opened in Panmunjom in 1951 and ended in July 1953 with agreement on keeping the pre-war frontier along the 38th parallel.

South Korea's economy was shattered by the war and rebuilding began soon after hostilities ended. The authoritarian regime of Syngman Rhee provoked the March 1960 uprising which led to his overthrow. A military junta seized power in May 1961, headed from July by General Park Chung-Hee.

Park was elected president in December 1963. A treaty normalising relations with Japan was signed in Seoul in February 1965. In 1967 the government, formed by the Democratic Republican party, ordered the arrest of some members of a new democratic party created in February by Yun Po-

Son. Park won the presidential elections of the same year, his party gaining a sizeable majority at fraudulent general elections. Park won a third mandate in April 1971, which although unconstitutional had been approved by referendum in 1969.

A non-aggression deal with the government of North Korea was signed in July 1972. Repression of the opposition toughened and the main opposition leader, Kim Dae-Chung, was arrested in 1974. Re-elected in 1978, Park was assassinated in October 1979.

Hopes of liberalisation were short-lived as the army regained power, and General Chun Du-Hwan was named head of state in August 1980. The new constitution of October 1980 reinforced the authoritarian power structure.

Closer ties with Japan were given substance by President Chun's visit to Tokyo in September 1984. The choice of Seoul to host the 1988 Olympics, forced the South Korean regime into making apparently liberal concessions in the face of opposition unrest.

In September 1985 a visitor exchange between South and North Korea indicated a further relaxation of relations between the two states. The question of holding the 1988 Olympic Games jointly was proposed, but no agreement was reached between the two countries before the games took place.

Following allegations of corruption, Chun was forced to step down before the games. Ex-General Roh Tae-Woo was subsequently elected president, taking advantage of a divided opposition.

Kuwait

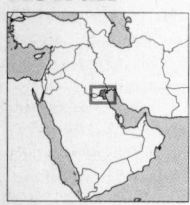

KWT
Near East
6,880 sq. mi
Pop: 1.87 m
UN, AL, GCC, OPEC

Capital: Kuwait (pop: 400,000)
Official language: Arabic
Religion: Moslem (91 per cent)
System of govt: Constitutional monarchy (emirate); independent since 19 June 1961

In the 16th century the Portuguese settled temporarily in Kuwait. The city of Kuwait was founded in the 17th century and expanded rapidly, becoming the capital of an emirate under Sheikh Sabbah in 1756. In 1776 the capture of Basra by the Persians diverted the trade route to India towards Kuwait, which thus became attractive to the British. Britain backed the shaikh of Kuwait when he supported the exiled Abd al-Rahman ibn Saud from Riyadh against the Ottoman empire in 1895. In 1899 Sheikh Mubarak bin Sabbah agreed to a British protectorate.

The first oil field was discovered in 1938 and Anglo-US companies start-

ed drilling for oil in 1946. Kuwait became one of the richest and most important Arab oil producers. The 1899 treaty of protectorate was annulled in 1961, but Sheikh Abdullah as-Salam al-Sabbah again received British support against Iraqi territorial claims. Following a modernising and democratic path since 1961, Kuwait faced a political crisis in 1976 which led to the dissolution of the national assembly.

Democratic liberties were restored by the new emir, Sheikh Jabir al-Ahmad as-Sabbah and elections took place in February 1981. Kuwait and the other Arab countries stood together in their oil policies and in regard to Israel, but

Kuwait had to contend with border conflicts with Iraq, the border being closed since 1981.

The February 1985 elections showed declining support for Shi'ite fundamentalism and perceptible progress on the part of the Arab left. However pro-Iranian Shi'ite Moslem terrorists were responsible for the world's longest hijack ordeal when a Kuwaiti airliner was held for almost three weeks in April 1988. Tension between Iran and Kuwait continued both in 1987 and 1988, due to Iranian attacks on Kuwaiti tankers in the Gulf. This resulted in the US Navy escorting Kuwaiti tankers which were allowed to fly the US flag.

Laos

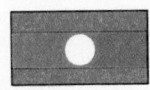

LAO
South East Asia
91,400 sq. mi
Pop: 3.7 m
UN

Capital: Vientiane (pop: 200,000)
Official language: Lao
Religion: Buddhism (85 per cent)
System of govt: People's republic since 2 December 1975

Until the 13th century Laos belonged to the Indo-Khmer kingdom of Cambodia. At the end of the 13th century the Thai kingdom of Sukhotai occupied the country as far as Luang Prabang and Vientiane (Vieng Chan). The first independent Laotian kingdom of Lan Chang was formed in 1353 by King Fa Ngum who favoured the introduction of Buddhism. Occupied for some years by Annam (Vietnam), Laos regained sovereignty under King Phothisarath (1520-c.1548). The Emerald Buddha, which he brought with him from Lan Na, was installed at Vientiane, the new capital, in 1563.

The first Europeans reached Laos in 1641 during the reign of Suliyavongsa (1637-94) whose death was the beginning of a period of division which lasted two centuries.

In 1707 three kingdoms came into being around Vientiane, Luang Prabang and the new Champassak. Siam (Thailand) occupied the whole of the country in 1827. In the first half of the 19th century, however, the Annam empire, rival of the Thais, extended its sphere of influence into the north west of the Khmer country. A French expedition reached Laos in 1861. Un Kham, the new king of Luang Prabang, asked for French aid against Siam, which was forced to give up the left bank of the Mekong and recognise the French protectorate over the Lao states in 1893, and then again in 1902 and 1904 under the reign of Zakarine (1895-1904). His son Sisavang Vong reigned until 1959, first as king of Luang Prabang and then of independent Laos after 1947.

Laos was integrated into French Indochina in 1917. The Japanese who occupied the country during the Second World War pushed the king into proclaiming independence on 8 April 1945. Sisavang Vong had to abdicate and the Alo Issara government was proclaimed by nationalists linked with the Viet-

minh. Vientiane was taken back by the French in April 1946 and Laos became autonomous the same year, then independent within the French Union on 19 July 1949.

Nationalist Pathet Lao troops, with Vietminh troops, occupied the north of Laos after the French defeat in the Indochina War (1953). The Vietminh left the country after the Geneva Conference of July 1954, and the US and Thailand immediately reinforced their presence in Vientiane.

A coalition government formed by the moderate Prince Suvanna Phuma and the left-wing Prince Suphanuvong broke down into renewed civil war in 1959. The Pathet Lao seized control of half the country until the ceasefire of 11 May 1961. A new coalition government was constituted in June 1962 following a 14-power Geneva conference.

A US-backed right-wing coup overthrew the government on 19 April 1964 and US bombing began in the zones controlled by the Pathet Lao, vital to North Vietnam in escalating Vietnam conflict.

Pathet Lao troops crossed the 1961 ceasefire line in 1970. Talks, resumed in 1972, led to a peace treaty in February 1973. US and Thai troops pulled out (although the USA retained a mis-

sion in Vientiane) and a new coalition regime was set up on 5 April 1974, led once more by the Princes Suvanna Phuma and Suphanuvong.

The fall of Saigon in South Vietnam caused instability in Laos which enabled revolutionary committees to seize control of the country's assembly. A national congress abolished the Laotian monarchy on 2 December 1975 and Suphanuvong became president of the Lao People's Democratic Republic. Kaysone Phomvihane, head of the Lao People's Revolutionary Party (PPRL) became prime minister.

A guerrilla war pursued by right-wing insurgents and the Miao "secret army" led to the exodus of more than 100,000 people by 1977. Socialist policies continued and links with Vietnam were reinforced, particularly after the fall of the Khmer Rouge in Cambodia.

Chinese-backed guerrillas presented no threat to the regime's progressive liberalisation policy (including the release of 10,000 political prisoners in 1979) nor to the reconstruction of the essentially agrarian economy. A ceasefire was agreed in February 1988 after a further series of border clashes with neighbouring Thailand had caused the deaths of hundreds of troops on both sides.

Lebanon

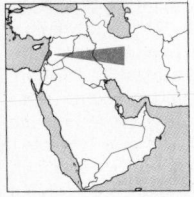

RL
Near East
4,036 sq. mi
Pop: 2.76 m
UN, AL

Capital: Beirut (pop: 700,000)
Offical Language: Arabic
Religions: Moslem (53 per cent), Christian (40 per cent)
System of govt: Republic; independent since 23 December 1945

The territory of present-day Lebanon was dominated by Phoenicians, Assyrians, Persians and Greeks before being conquered by the Romans in 67 BC. After being converted to Christianity in the first century, Lebanon remained so for the most part after the Moslem conquest in the seventh century.

The emirs of Lebanon preserved a large degree of autonomy under the Ottoman empire (1515-1920). The 1840 revolt against the regime of the Egyptian Mohammad Ali, who had conquered the country in 1831, marked the first surge of Lebanese nationalism. As a result of the uprising Lebanon was split into two districts, Druze (a Moslem sect) and Maronite (a Christian sect).

In 1860 a civil war broke out after a massacre of Maronites by Druze, in which France intervened in August 1860. France negotiated international accords in 1861 and 1864 guaranteeing autonomy to the country.

In 1920 France obtained a League of Nations mandate to run Lebanon; a 1926 constitution made Lebanon a parliamentary republic under French supervision.

While Christians found Europeans acceptable, pro-Syrian Arab nationalism grew among the Moslems. The communities founded their first militias in 1936. Independence was recognised in 1941 by General de Gaulle's delegate, General Catroux, but, owing to the war, could not take effect until 1 January 1944. However, the presence of French and British troops provoked serious unrest in 1944 and 1945, and Paris and London agreed to withdraw forces in December 1945. Relations with France relaxed, but tension rose with neighbouring Syria, leading to a breakdown in economic ties in 1950.

The civil wars

Moslem opposition grew to the pro-western policies of Camille Chamoun, in power since 1952 aided by Pierre Gemayel's Phalangist militia. Civil war broke out in 1958 and led to the intervention of US troops. The government of Rachid Karame, composed of Christians and Sunni Moslems, restored

national unity and devoted itself to industrialisation and modernising the country.

The PLO set up bases in Lebanon, however. The Israeli attack on Beirut Airport in December 1968 aggravated the conflict between the pro and anti-Palestinian factions. The new government formed by Karame in January 1969 affirmed its support for the Palestinians, but placed them under a measure of control. Riots in April brought down the government. The Palestinian problem again led to Karame's resignation in October 1970.

President Suleiman Franjiyeh, who was in power from August 1970, maintained a policy of balance between the west and the Arab countries. This policy was upset when an Israeli commando unit killed a number of Palestinian leaders in Beirut on 9 and 10 April 1973. After the ensuing combat between the Lebanese army and the Palestinians (2-17 May) Syria and Iraq severed their relations with Lebanon.

The situation was aggravated by Israeli and Palestinian attacks in 1974-75, which successive governments were powerless to stop. A Christian militia attack on Palestinians in Beirut in April 1975 unleashed a civil war as Palestinians and left-wing Lebanese groups battled against right-wing Phalangist militias. Rachid Karame's return to power in May did not alter the situation.

The intervention of Syrian troops in

May 1976 against the Palestinians and Kamal Jumblatt's Lebanese National Movement provoked the meeting of an Arab conference at Cairo on 25 October 1976. An Arab peace-keeping force largely composed of Syrian troops was to guarantee a general ceasefire, but violent clashes broke out again in southern Lebanon between Phalangists and Palestinians.

A reversal of alliances after 1977 saw Syria aligned with the Palestinians and the Lebanese left against the Israeli-backed Phalangists. Israel's invasion of southern Lebanon in March 1978 provoked the intervention of an interim UN peace-keeping force. Israel withdrew in June while keeping control of the Lebanese border territory through the Christian militias.

Violent struggle continued between Syria and the National Lebanese Party and between the Israelis and the Palestinians in the south until Israel invaded Lebanon in June 1982, in spite of the presence of the UN peace-keeping force. The Israelis surrounded Beirut on 3 July. An international agreement enabled the Palestinians and the Arab peace-keeping force to leave by sea by 1 September.

The Israelis invaded Moslem West Beirut after the assassination on 14 September of President Bashir Gemayel (elected 23 August), head of the Christian Phalangist militia. On 16 and 17 September several hundred Palestinians in the Sabra and Shatila refugee camps were massacred as the Israeli troops looked on.

A Shi'ite militia group claimed responsibility for separate suicide bomb attacks on 23 October 1983 in which 241 US and 58 French soldiers in the UN force were killed. The US withdrew from the force as a result.

Replacing his assassinated brother, Amin Gemayel was elected president on 21 September 1982. He negotiated a treaty for the withdrawal of Israeli troops in May 1983, while in the mountains east and south east of Beirut, the Druze, supported by Syria, and the Phalangists engaged in open warfare. In April 1984, when fighting broke out for the first time in Tripoli between rival Moslem militias, Rachid Karame formed a government of unity and national reconciliation.

In 1985 western hostages were taken by various groups. Despite the withdrawal of Israeli troops in June, all attempts to bring peace to Lebanon were doomed to failure. In December 1985 a peace agreement was signed between the leaders of the Moslem Druze and Amal and the Christian militias, but its terms were not carried out because of the overthrow of the Moslem leadership which signed it. Clashes between factions continued, with Syrian troops acting as a peace-keeping force.

The murder of Karame in June 1987 and death at 87 of Camille Chamoun in August were setbacks to hopes of peace and fighting has continued on and off between rival guerrilla factions. Israeli forces also made periodic incursions into southern Lebanon. Hostages taken in this same bleak year included Terry Waite, on a peace mission for the archbishop of Canterbury. Over 20 westerners were still held, probably in Beirut, in 1989. The turmoil continued into 1989, with more hostage taking and the near collapse of government following the failure to find a replacement for President Gemayel when his term expired in September 1988.

Lesotho

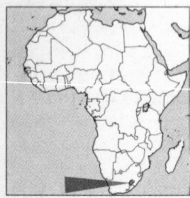

LS
Southern Africa
11,720 sq. mi
Pop: 1.4 m
UN, CW, OAU

Capital: Maseru (pop: 288,000)
Official language: English, Sesotho
Religions: Protestant, Catholic
System of govt: Constitutional monarchy; independent since 4 October 1966

The mountains of Lesotho were occupied by Khoisan hunters, among whom Sotho farmers began to settle, spreading from the Vaal river in the north after about 1500. The tribal wars of 1822 led to the growth of two rival Sotho states in the area of Lesotho – the Tlokoa of Sikonyela, and the Mokoteli of Moshoeshoe. Moshoeshoe finally defeated Sikonyela and united Lesotho by 1853, but was faced by an aggressive Boer settler republic – the Orange Free State. After a series of wars, Moshoeshoe accepted British jurisdiction in 1868. The new protectorate of Basutoland was annexed to the (British) Cape Colony in 1871, but became a separate colony again in 1884.

Basutoland's national council, which was chaired by the king, was founded in 1903, and given increased powers in 1944 and 1960. In 1966, the country, surrounded by and economically dependent on South Africa, became the independent kingdom of Lesotho.

When it became clear that the opposition had won the elections of 1970, the prime minister, Chief Leabua, seized power. He deposed King Moshoeshoe II, but restored him in December because of the threat of civil war. Guerrilla actions in January 1974 led to repression of the main opposition party. A nominated national assembly was established in April 1974. Meanwhile Leabua's deference to South Africa was replaced by defiance to improve his international image. He was overthrown in January 1986, after a South African blockade. The king, aided by a military and a ministerial council, now wields all executive authority.

Liberia

LB
West Africa
42,989 sq. mi
Pop: 2.3 m
UN, OAU

Capital: Monrovia (pop: 425,000)
Offical language: English
Religions: Traditional beliefs (70 per cent), Moslem (20 per cent)
System of govt: Republic;

founded 26 July 1847

In 1816 the American Colonisation Society was formed in the USA to enable black slaves to move to Africa. The society bought land at the mouth of the Mesurado river on the Pepper Coast, visited by European traders since its sighting by the Portuguese in the 15th century, and the island of Providence. From 1822 it began to send former slaves there. Liberia became a republic in 1847 with a US-inspired constitution and named its capital, Monrovia, after US President James Monroe. Liberia fused with the similar settlement of Maryland in 1857 and was recognised by the USA in 1861. It numbered some 22,000 former slaves by 1900. Economically it remained highly dependent on the US enterprises which supported it.

Integration of English-speaking, non-tribal US blacks into the indigenous population was difficult, and the native inhabitants were pushed into the interior. Exploitation of the interior began after 1925 when the US Firestone Company developed the huge rubber plantations which remained Liberia's chief source of exports until 1961 when it was overtaken by iron ore.

The American-Liberians were a privileged class and President William Tubman (in office 1944-71) tried to create a fairer balance between the two populations, as did his successor, William Tolbert. In April 1980, however, Tolbert was killed during a coup which put power in the hands of a "People's Redemption Council", led by Sergeant Major Samuel Doe. Doe was elected president on 15 October 1985 for a seven-year term. A month later, an attempted coup failed and its leaders were executed on 15 November. A new constitution approved in July 1984 came into force in January 1986.

Libya

LAR
North Africa
679,358 sq. mi
Pop: 3.9 m
UN, AL, OAU, OPEC

Capital: Tripoli (pop: 858,000)
Official language: Arabic
Religion: Moslem (97 per cent)
System of govt: People's republic; independent since 24 December 1951

In the ninth century BC the Phoenicians founded three cities in part of what is now Libya, whence the later name Tripolitania, "country of three cities". Cyrenaica, now eastern Libya, was later colonised by the Greeks and fell under Roman domination in 74 BC. Both areas were subsequently organised into provinces called Tripolitania and Libya Superior. The fifth century Vandal invasion put an end to Roman sovereignty in the west of the region.

The Eastern Roman, or Byzantine empire, reconquered Tripolitania from the Vandals in 536, but were chased out in their turn by the Arabs in 643. Cyrenaica and Tripolitania remained separate and, except for in the hinterland, were not properly colonised by the Arabs until the 11th century.

After being conquered by the Normans for a brief period (1145-80), the two provinces became briefly Spanish in 1510 and were then subjugated by the Ottoman empire in 1551.

The Islamic Sanusi brotherhood effectively took over Ottoman Cyrenaica in 1843. Although Libya became an Italian protectorate after the 1911 invasion, the Italians could not defeat the Sanusi until 1934. Fascist Italy annexed Tripolitania, Fezzan and Cyrenaica, which were organised under the name of Libya.

After the Second World War Libya was temporarily placed under Franco-British administration. Becoming independent after a UN decision in 1951, Libya became a monarchy, with the Sanusi leader ascending the throne under the name Idris I. The king conducted a nationalist policy which aimed at the evacuation of all British and US troops stationed in Libya.

Idris' conservative internal politics provoked a military coup on 1 September 1969. A republic was proclaimed by a revolutionary council led by a young Colonel Gaddafi. The evacuation of British and US bases (December 1979) was followed by the nationalisation of oil companies and of the other principal economic sectors of the country.

Colonel Gaddafi's powers were increased and his Zawara speech of 16 April 1973 defined the principles of the "cultural revolution" which he intended to bring about. The shari'ah, the law of the Koran, was to become predominant again and people's committees were to be charged with controlling the life of the country at all levels.

In April 1974 Gaddafi transferred all his official functions, except that of president, to Commander Jallud. A new constitution was promulgated in March 1977, which founded the Libyan people's republic and gave the most important political role to the Libyan People's Congress. The leaders of the revolutionary council, including Gaddafi and Jallud, gave way to people from the Arab Socialist Union and from the congress. Abdul Ati al-Obeidi took over the presidency of the secretariat general of the congress and Jadallah Azzuz at-Talhi took over as president of the Libyan People's General Committee. Gaddafi, though, remained the key figure. In 1971 Libya, Syria and Egypt formed a federation of Arab republics. In 1974 Libya turned to the USSR which furnished her with a huge supply of armaments from 1975 in great disproportion to the needs of the country. Libya gave direct support to African and Near East revolutionaries as well as to the Palestinian resistance movements. Close Soviet-Libyan ties led to the USA toughening its stance towards Gaddafi. American nationals and companies were advised to leave Libya in 1981.

Ideas of federation with Egypt, more or less defunct since quarrels in 1974, came to an end after Egypt's peace treaty with Israel in 1977.

Similarly relations with Tunisia, with which Gaddafi had signed a unification treaty in 1974, underwent several crises, such as the attack on the Tunisian town of Gafsa in January 1980. Libya supported the Polisario Front against Morocco in the western Sahara, and Iran in the war against Iraq; it claimed the Aïr region from Niger and occupied the Aozou strip in northern Chad in 1973. Libyan troops, who were supposed to withdraw from Chad after the two states had reached an agreement on 17 June 1980, remained stationed in the north of the country and supported another offensive by Chad rebels in June 1983. The rebels faced French intervention.

Economic difficulties faced by Libya because of a drop in oil exports led to the expulsion of almost 70,000 foreign workers, mainly Arab, in 1985. Tension with the USA, aggravated by alleged Libyan involvement in a number of terrorist attacks, led to the Gulf of Sidra confrontation on 24 March 1986, when US and Libyan aircraft clashed, and the bombing of Tripoli on 14 April, which killed several civilians, including one of Gaddafi's daughters.

In the summer of 1987 Libya suffered military reverses in Chad against a Chadian army supplied with equipment by the USA. Tension between Libya and the USA has continued, culminating on 4 January 1989 in an incident when two US fighters shot down two Libyan jets over the Mediterranean, amid US accusations that Libya was planning production of chemical weapons at a plant near Rabra, south of Tripoli.

Liechtenstein

FL
Central Europe
61.8 sq. mi
Pop: 27,714
EFTA,

Capital: Vaduz (pop: 4,900)
Official language: German
Religions: Catholic (87 per cent), Protestant (8 per cent)

System of govt: Constitutional monarchy (principality)

A part of the Roman Alpine province of Rhaetia, the territory of present-day Liechtenstein was invaded in the fifth century by the Germanic Alamanni, from whom the population descends. The lordship of Vaduz later separated itself from Rhaetia, which had became a dukedom under Charlemagne. Vaduz was integrated into the Holy Roman empire in 1396, and was attached to the lordship of Schellenberg in 1434.

Liechtenstein's prince bought Schellenberg in 1699, and then the county of Vaduz from the count of Hohenhembs in 1712. Liechtenstein was elevated to the status of an imperial principality by the Holy Roman emperor in 1719. Liechtenstein joined the Confederation of the Rhine on the empire's abolition in 1806, and then linked itself to Austria through a monetary and customs union in 1852, and to Switzerland in 1921 through a postal and monetary union. The 1924 customs union with the Swiss enabled Liechtenstein to increase its foreign currency revenue by 27 per cent, without having to undertake any customs administration. Economically Liechtenstein is closely bound to Switzerland. It possesses its own industry, but the main attraction to foreign enterprises are its financial and tax advantages. In 1984, after a 46-year reign, Prince Franz Joseph II transferred his powers to his son, Prince Franz Adam. A month earlier, in July, women had obtained the right to vote.

Since the constitution of 1921 the state has been a constitutional monarchy. The prince has a right of veto in parliament, which, in turn can appeal to the people by means of a referendum.

Luxembourg

L
Western Europe
998 sq. mi
Pop: 368,000
UN, EC, NATO, OECD, Benelux

Capital: Luxembourg (pop: 77,500)
Official languages: French, German, Letzeburgesch
Religion: Catholic (95 per cent)
System of govt: Constitutional monarchy (grand duchy); independent since 11 May 1867

At the time of the Roman conquest, the area was inhabited by the Treveri, a Belgic tribe. It later became part of Charlemagne's empire; after the partition of the empire it became, in 963, an independent lordship under Siegfried, son of a count from the Moselle, who built the castle of Luetzelburg. One of his descendants, Conrad, took the title Count of Luxembourg in c.1060.

The male line of the Luetzelburgs died out in 1136, and the domain was returned to the counts of Namur and then, through marriage, to Walram of Limburg in 1214. The latter's great grandson was elected king of Germany under the name of Henry VII in 1308 and his son, John I the Blind, became king of Bohemia. Luxembourg lost its importance when the reigning German family stopped living there.

In 1354 the son of John I, Charles IV, the Holy Roman emperor and king of Bohemia, gave Luxembourg the status of an independent duchy which he entrusted to his brother, Wenceslas, who joined the duchy with Brabant in 1355, and died without heir in 1388. His nephew Wenceslas, son of Charles IV and king of Germany, inherited Luxembourg which passed to Jobst of Moravia in 1388, and then to Duke Anthony of Brabant and Limburg in 1411. In 1443 Duke Anthony's wife, Elizabeth of Gorlitz, sold her rights to the duchy to Duke Philip the Good of Burgundy, and the Habsburgs inherited Luxembourg along with Burgundy in 1477. The Spanish Habsburgs received it in 1555 and incorporated it into the Spanish Netherlands, though it remained within the Holy Roman empire's sphere of influence. The south of the duchy became French in 1659, and the remainder of its territory was claimed by Austria in 1714. Revolutionary France absorbed the rest in 1795.

The 1815 Congress of Vienna restored territorial integrity to Luxembourg, which became a grand duchy and a member of the German League, but was administered by the king of the Netherlands. In 1831 the larger part of the country was absorbed into the new state of Belgium, William I retaining the eastern part. From 1839 this, the grand duchy, was administered separately. It joined the German customs union in 1843. When the German League was dissolved in 1866 Napoleon III of France attempted to acquire Luxembourg. It became an independent and neutral under the Treaty of London (May 1867). Sovereignty was vested in the Dutch house of Orange-Nassau.

From the 1870s, metallurgy became one of Luxembourg's main economic activities. The male line of the Orange-Nassau dynasty died out in 1890, and sovereignty over the grand duchy returned to the Walramian branch of the Nassaus. Luxembourg was occupied during the First World War by Germany.

In 1919 the grand duchess, Marie-Adelaide, who was known to have pro-German feelings, had to abdicate in favour of her sister Charlotte, who gave the country a democratic constitution.

The German invasion of 1940 forced the grand duchess to seek refuge in Britain. After the Second World War Luxembourg joined Benelux in 1947 and NATO in 1949. Luxembourg was one of the six countries which formed the core of the future EEC in 1950.

A centre-left coalition under Jacques Santer has held power since 1984. Jean, the grand duke, succeeded when his mother abdicated in November 1964. Iron and steel accounts for most exports, which go mainly to EC nations.

Madagascar

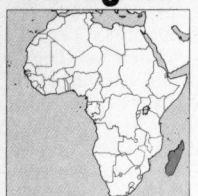

RM
Indian Ocean
587.041 km2
pop: 10.6 mill
UN, OAU

Capital: Antananaviro (pop: 622,000)
Official languages: French, Malagasy
Religions: Christian (51 per cent); traditional beliefs (47 per cent)
System of govt: Republic; independent since 14 October 1958

The first people to arrive on Madagascar probably came from east Africa. Malayo-Polynesian people reached the island after 1000 BC (the Malagasy language is related to Indonesian).

Arab merchants established trading posts on the north-west coast in the tenth century. More Arabs settled in the south in the 13th century, and created the kingdom of Anteimoro. At the same time the Merina, of Indonesian origin, were settling in the centre.

In the 16th century the Portuguese carried out raids on the Moslem settlements. In 1643 the French founded Fort Dauphin in the south-east, abandoned in 1674. In c.1700 the only Europeans to frequent the island were pirates, who established bases there for their raids in the Indian Ocean.

Among the kingdoms in Madagascar between 1500 and 1800, the kingdom of Imerina was constituted around its capital, Tananarive, by c.1600. In the 18th century it split into four kingdoms reunited in 1797 by King Andrianampoinimerina (1787-1810). King Radama I, who succeeded him, subjugated most of the island and invited in European specialists and missionaries. His widow, Ranavalona I (1828-61) resumed isolationism but her successors took up the modernisation of the country. French expansionism sparked off a war with the Merina people. Madagascar became a French protectorate in 1890. The French conquest was completed in 1898 but the colonial period was marked by violent uprisings. A revolt in 1947 caused 11,000 deaths.

Independence was obtained in October 1958. Philibert Tsiranana was president until October 1972, when student protest against cooperation with France in May 1972 provoked a military takeover. The democratic republic of Madagascar was proclaimed on 31 December 1975.

Captain Didier Ratsiraka took over as president, and socialist reforms were set in motion. He was re-elected for a further seven years on 7 November 1982. In November 1988 he promised elections in 1989.

Malawi

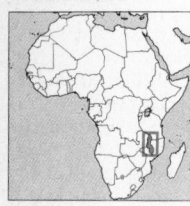

MW
East Africa
36,325 sq. mi
Pop: 7.5 m
UN, CW, OAU

Capital: Lilongwe (pop: 175,000)
Official languages: English, Chichewa
Religions: Christian (64 per cent); traditional beliefs (19 per cent) Moslem (16 per cent)
System of govt: Republic since 6 July 1966

The country around Lake Malawi has been occupied by Iron Age farmers until the last few centuries BC. Further migrations between about the 12th and 15th centuries brought highland rulers from the direction of modern Zaire to live among the lowland people around the lake.

The Maravi kingdom flourished in the centre and south of what is now Malawi, from around 1480 until the middle of the 17th century. The agricultural societies around the lake prospered until they were undermined by the slave trade in the 18th century. Portuguese and Arab slave merchants took a heavy toll on human life.

Swahili traders from the east coast penetrated northern Malawi between 1830 and 1860 and became an important aristocracy there. European influence was increased towards the end of the 19th century, especially after the publicity given to the Scottish explorer David Livingstone's travels in the country between 1859 and 1863.

The British set up a protectorate over Malawi in 1891 and put an end to the slave trade with the aid of Indian troops in 1895. Malawi became a British colony and was given the name Nyasaland.

The colonial administration directed the development of the country's agriculture to the production of goods for export. Such controls and the decision to join Nyasaland to the Central African Federation, with Northern and Southern Rhodesia (1953-63) provoked violent rural protests. Militant nationalism led to riots in 1959, and a new constitution in 1960, and independence in 1964.

Nyasaland became Malawi and then a republic in 1966, opting to remain in the Commonwealth. President Hastings Kamuzu Banda has held office and supreme authority over parliament and people as prime minister and head of state since then. He was reputed to be nearly 90 in 1989. The construction of a new capital, Lilongwe, inaugurated in 1975, was largely financed by South Africa.

Malawi is the only African state to have full ties with Pretoria, a fact which has led to diplomatic tension with other black states. Nevertheless, in 1988 the Malawian and South African governments declared their intention to increase mutual co-operation.

Malaysia

MAL
South East Asia
329,749 km2
Pop: 16.5 mill.
UN, ASEAN, CW

Capital: Kuala Lumpur (pop: 1.1 mill.)
Official language: Malay (Bahasa)
Religions: Moslem (52 per cent), Christian, Buddhist
System of govt: Constitutional monarchy since 16 September 1963

Before 4000 BC the Malay peninsula saw the development of a number of neolithic civilisations. An Indo-Malayan culture succeeded a highly developed bronze culture in the second century. For over 1000 years the peninsula remained under strong Indian influences, with as many as 30 independent states appearing on the west coast, alternately dominated by Ayuthia (Thailand), the Khmer kingdoms, Sumatra or Java.

In c.1400 Prince Paramesvara from Sumatra failed to make Tumasik (Singapore) independent of Ayuthia and fled to the town of Malacca. Under the protection of the Chinese empire, which sought to contain Ayuthia's expansion, he succeeded in making this small fishing town into a commercial and political centre of a powerful state. Shortly before his death he was converted to Islam which began to spread across the peninsula and became the cultural link for a highly heterogeneous population.

Malacca fell to the Portuguese in 1511, and to the Dutch in 1641 after an eight year siege. The city never fully recovered as a trading centre, the Dutch concentrating their activities in Java.

In 1786 the British East India Company leased Penang island from the sultan of Kedah. British possession of Province Wellesley, opposite Penang, came in 1800. In 1795 the Dutch placed Malacca under the protective custody of Britain to prevent it from falling into French hands.

In 1824 it was permanently transferred to the British East India Company. In 1819-24 Stamford Raffles acquired the right for the company to establish a trading station on the island of Singapore which rapidly developed into a major entrepot. In 1826 the company's peninsular possessions combined to form the Straits Settlements, for which the British government assumed direct responsibility in 1867.

From about this time the British intervened more vigorously in the neighbouring tin-area sultanates. In 1874 a protectorate was established over some of the sultanates, hitherto vassals of Siam, which in 1896 became the Federated Malay States. Siam gave up its rights to four other states in 1909 and they, with Johore, accepted British control, but preferred to be unfederated.

Japanese occupation of the Malay peninsula from 1941-45 gave rise to both nationalism and inter-racial antagonisms. In 1948 the British established a Federation of Malaya which did not, however, include Singapore on account of its predominantly Chinese population. In order to deal with the ensuing uprising by Chinese communists, an "emergency" was declared, which was to last until 1960. In 1957 the federation became independent. In 1963 an enlarged Federation of Malaysia was formed, consisting of Malaya and the former British colonies of Singapore, Sarawak and North Borneo (Sabah). Singapore withdrew in 1965 and became an independent republic.

Tunku Abdul Rahman was the first prime minister of the Federation of Malaysia. The king is elected for five years from the nine sultans of the Malay states. Mathathir bin Mohammad has been prime minister since 1981, and Sultan Mahmood Iskandar of Johore was elected king in 1984.

Maldives

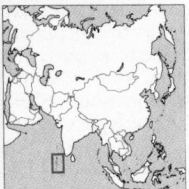

Indian Ocean
115 sq. mi
Pop: 195,000
UN, CW

Capital: Male (pop: 46,000)
Official language: Divehi
Religion: Moslem (98 per cent)

System of govt: Republic; independent since 26 July 1965

The Maldives, 19 atolls grouped together over a thousand islands, were populated towards the sixth century by people from Sri Lanka. The first settlers on the islands were Buddhists. The introduction of Islam in 12th century led to Buddhism finally being abandoned in 1153. The Portuguese attempted to colonise in 1558 and conquered Male, but were expelled by the natives in 1573. The Maldives were subsequently frequented by pirates and appealed to the Dutch in Sri Lanka to defend them. The Dutch installed a protectorate in 1645, which the British took over in 1796. A formal protectorate was only established in 1887 after an agreement with the islands' ruling Didi dynasty. A democratic constitution came into effect in 1932 and the monarchy became elective. Proclaimed in 1953, the republic was abolished the same year. The southernmost islands attempted to break away, but were reintegrated into the sultanate after British mediation.

On independence in 1965, the Maldives granted the British the use of an air base on the tiny island of Gan until 1986. The Maldives again became a republic on 11 November 1968, with several islands effectively independent of the central government. President Amir Ibrahim Nasir dismissed the Maldives' premier and governed alone until his resignation in 1978. He was replaced by Maumoon Abdul Gayoom, re-elected in 1983 and 1988. A failed coup shortly after the 1988 election was blamed on "invading mercenaries".

Mali

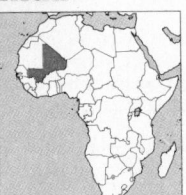

MM
West Africa
478,832 sq. mi
Pop: 8.3 m
UN, OAU

Capital: Bamako (pop: 600,000)
Official language: French
Religions: Moslem (90 per cent), traditional beliefs (9 per cent)
System of govt: Republic; independent since 20 June 1960

The Ghana empire appeared in the area of modern Mali after 400 and reached its zenith in the eighth century. Ghana profited from Saharan trade, with salt from the north being exchanged for gold and ivory from the south. In c.700 the Arabs completed the conquest of North Africa, their commerce spreading Arab and Moslem culture deep into black Africa. In the 11th century the Ghana empire collapsed under the attacks launched by Almoravid Berbers. The Mali empire, was formed in c.1000, when it freed itself from Ghana. It imposed its supremacy in western Africa right up until the 16th century. In the 15th century the subjugated peoples revolted, with Gao rebelling in 1400 and the Tuaregs seizing Timbuktu, a cultural and commercial centre for several centuries, in 1431. The Wolof and Mossi in the north of present-day Burkina Faso also won independence.

The Mali empire lost its supremacy in 1550, and the ascendancy of the Songhai empire began in Gao and along the middle reaches of the Niger. The Songhai had at their disposal a permanent army and a well-organised administration. They had long since mastered the most important communication route for commerce, the river Niger, and drew from it their economic wealth. Gao, however, was conquered by Morocco in 1591. An army of 4,000 men equipped with firearms seized the most important towns of Gao, Timbuktu and Djenne, and established a military kingdom which lasted until the 18th century. Saharan trade, however, in the hands of nomadic tribes, evaded the Moroccans. The Tuareg exacted a tribute from them and took Timbuktu in 1770. The Moslem empire of the Peuls in Masina succeeded the empire of the Bambaras at the start of the 19th century, but was unable to resist French conquest.

The French occupied Timbuktu in 1893 and Tuareg resistance continued until around 1920. During this period French sovereignty was exercised indirectly through nominated chiefs. The country, known as French Sudan, was poor and sparsely populated.

The country, associated with Senegal in the Federation of Mali, joined the French Community in 1959. The federation broke down a year later; French Sudan became fully independent and took the ancient name Mali.

President Modibo Keita was overthrown in a coup in November 1968. A Military Committee of National Liberation took power, presided over by Lieutenant Moussa Traore. He established a one (socialist-oriented) party state. In February 1981 economic difficulties led General Traore to undertake the liberalisation of the economy. A border conflict between Mali and Upper Volta (Burkina Faso) from 1974 sparked off a brief war at the end of 1985. In 1988, on the 20th anniversary of his coming to power, General Traore released 240 political prisoners and said the country's problems were now economic rather than political.

Malta

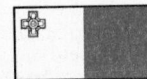

M
Mediterranean
121.9 sq. mi
Pop: 345,000
UN, CW,

Capital: Valletta (pop: 9,300)
Official languages: Maltese, English
Religion: Catholic (98 per cent)
System of govt: Republic; independent since 21 September 1964

The megalithic culture which developed in Malta was one of first in the Mediterranean. Temples were built on the island after 3000 BC. Possibly a Phoenician colony in c.1000 BC, Malta became a Carthaginian possession in the sixth century BC. It was taken by the Romans in 218 BC. According to tradition the apostle Paul was shipwrecked on the Maltese coast in 60, an event which began the island's conversion to Christianity. On the division of the Roman empire in 395, Malta was assigned to the Eastern Roman empire based at Constantinople.

In the fifth century Malta fell to the Germanic Vandals, who were chased out by the Ostrogoths in 498. The Eastern Roman empire succeeded in to reconquering Malta in 533.

The island was conquered by the Moslem emir of Kairouwan (in modern Tunisia) in 870, and remained in Moslem hands until taken by the Norman King Roger of Sicily in 1091.

Malta eventually passed to the Habsburgs, and in 1530 the island was given as a fiefdom by the Emperor Charles V to the order of the Knights of St John (Hospitallers), who had been expelled from Rhodes. The knights made Malta a fortified base for their struggle against the Ottoman empire.

In 1798 the order, renamed the Order of the Knights of Malta, was expelled by Napoleon Bonaparte. French rule was unpopular and rebellion broke out in the same year.

The rebels appealed for British help, and in 1800 the French were chased out by Anglo-Neapolitan troops. Malta became a British colony after the 1814 Treaty of Paris. Britain made the island a naval base, but had to face opposition from the population, and the introduction of English as the administrative language in the 1880s provoked an uprising. Discontent remained below the surface; a constitution granted in 1887 was suspended in 1903. Similarly the constitution of 1921, granting limited autonomy, was suspended in 1930. Malta regained its autonomy in 1939. In World War II the island became a crucial Allied base and was effectively besieged by the Axis powers for three years. Britain's King George VI awarded Malta the George Cross for its resilience during the siege.

Malta became autonomous again in 1947. Dominic ("Dom") Mintoff, the head of the Maltese Labour Party, was prime minister from 1955 to 1958, in which year he resigned over Britain's decision to cut aid. The governor of Malta ruled directly until autonomy was restored in 1961. Malta became fully independent in 1964, opting to remain in the Commonwealth.

A rift with Britain occurred in 1967, when Maltese premier Borg Olivier ordered British forces to leave Malta. Mintoff was again in power from 1971 until his resignation in December 1984. Carmelo Bonnici succeeded him and came into conflict with the catholic church, a row eventually settled with the church agreeing to phase out fees in its schools. Elections in May 1987 resulted in victory for the Nationalist Party, ending 16 years of Labour rule. The new prime minister, Eddie Fenech Adami, adopted a programme of economic liberalisation. The principle of Maltese neutrality based on a policy of non-alignment was embodied in the constitution.

Mauritania

Mauritania

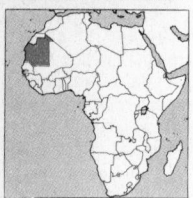

RIM
North West Africa
398,000 sq. mi
Pop: 1.87 m
UNO, AL, OAU

Capital: Nouakchott (pop: 350,000)
Official languages: Arabic, French
Religion: Moslem (99 per cent)
System of govt: Republic; independent since 20 November 1958

The desert regions of present-day Mauritania harbour rock paintings dating back to the Neolithic era. The first indigenous populations were pushed back after 3000 BC by invading Berber nomads from the north.

Like Morocco, Mauritania was covered in forest until Roman occupation. The Arabic conquest in the seventh century converted the Berbers to Islam, and the mixed Arabic-Berber people, the Moors, now make up 80 per cent of the Mauritanian population. In the 11th century the Moorish Almoravid dynasty extended its domination into Morocco and Spain and as far as the Niger. The Almoravid empire collapsed in 1147. The north, where the population consisted mainly of independent nomads, remained linked to Morocco while the south was integrated into the Mali kingdom. The centuries which followed were marked by a constant struggle between the Mali and the Arabs, who progressed towards the south at the end of the 13th century. The fighting culminated in the Shar Buba War (1644-77).

The Portuguese had settled on the coast near Cap Blanc in 1448. Arguin, where they had constructed a fortress, attracted Spanish, British, Dutch and French traders, in search of "gum arabic" in particular.

The French, established in Senegal since the 18th century, concluded their first treaties of protectorate with the desert tribes in 1858. They laid claim to Mauritania from 1904 but had to confront a Moorish revolt the following year. A colony in 1920, Mauritania was integrated into French West Africa, but was not pacified until 1934.

Mauritania became an autonomous republic on 28 November 1958 under the presidency of Moktar Ould Daddah. Full independence was attained in 1960 and a new capital, Nouakchott, was founded. Co-operation agreements with France were denounced in 1973 and iron mines were nationalised.

The Polisario Front, which aimed to achieve an independent Western Sahara (Spanish Sahara before Spain left in November 1975) conducted a guerrilla war against Mauritania, which claimed the territory. Mauritania renounced all claims to Western Sahara in August 1979.

Daddah was overthrown by a military coup in July 1978. Named prime minister in May 1979, Colonel Mohammed Ould Haydalla seized complete power in January 1980. Haydalla's regime, accused of corruption and wastefulness, was itself overthrown in December 1984 and Colonel Maaouya Ould Sidi Ahmed Taia became head of state. Controversy arose in November 1988 when a jailed former health minister died in prison in the capital Nouakchott.

Mauritania, much affected by the encroachment of the desert, depends on foreign aid for 90 per cent of its food.

Mauritius

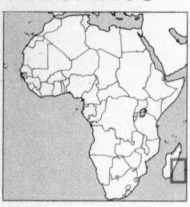

MS
Indian Ocean
2045 km2
Pop: 1,054,000
UN, CW

Capital: Port Louis (pop: 138,000)
Official language: English
Religions: Hindu (51 per cent), Christian (30 per cent), Moslem (13 per cent)
System of govt: Constitutional monarchy; independent since 12 March 1968

The island and archipelago of Mauritius were known to Arab and African navigators in the tenth century. The first Europeans to arrive there were Portuguese, who landed on the island in 1510. In 1598 Mauritius was given its name by the Dutch, who took possession of the island for the Dutch East India Company.

Dutch attempts to colonise the island in 1638-58 and 1664-1710 were unsuccessful, and their presence there was replaced by that of pirates. Mauritius, named Ile de France by the French in 1715, was occupied by the French East India Company in 1721. Port Louis, fitted out as a naval base, became the capital of Mauritius. The island came directly under the French crown in 1767 and enjoyed considerable commercial and economic growth.

Britain took possession of Mauritius in 1814. A large work force of Indian origin was brought in for the cultivation of sugar cane. Various modifications to a 1947 constitution were not enough to appease the nationalist agitation, and Britain granted independence after the victory of Seewoosagur Ramgoolam's Independence Party in the 1967 elections.

In June 1982 the opposition came to power, led by Aneerood Jugnauth. Although the official language is English, a French creole dialect is the everyday language for many of the island's inhabitants.

Mexico

MEX
Central America
756,198 sq. mi
Pop: 81.3 m
UN, OAS, LAES

Capital: Mexico City (pop: 12.9 m)
Official language: Spanish
Religion: Catholic (95 per cent)
System of govt: Republic; independence proclaimed February 1821

What is now Mexico was inhabited as far back as 20,000 BC. Several civilisations developed in Mexico while the rest of the continent lived in the stone age. The Olmecs, whose zenith was from c.1100-400 BC, were master sculptors, leaving both minuscule jade figurines and granite statues several yards high. They were the first people on the continent to build pyramid temples. Around 400-200 AD they were succeeded by the Teotihuacan civilisation, while at the same time the Maya and Zapotec civilisations were also developing. Important towns appeared and an aristocracy emerged within the rival empires. By c.400 Teotihuacan controlled almost all of Central America. The empire collapsed in c.650 after the invasion of the Mixtecs from the north. Major climactic changes also contributed to the fall of these civilisations.

Mayas and Aztecs

The Maya civilisation, which had developed architecture, astronomy and mathematics to a high degree, enjoyed its apogee from the seventh to the tenth centuries, then abandoned its territories at the end of this period for reasons which remain inexplicable. From c.900 to c.1200 the Maya were succeeded by the Toltecs. These two peoples also constructed cities, great cultural and economic centres, and extended their commercial relations far and wide. Favoured by the climate, agriculture prospered and skilled crafts flourished, covering all the needs of the population and allowing exports. Large deposits of metal-bearing rock were exploited, gold above all being used for religious purposes.

The Aztecs were originally nomads who came from the north in c.1200. The Aztec empire had as its capital Tenochtitlan, the residence of the Aztec sovereigns, which was founded in 1385, and Aztec power truly established itself from c.1430 onwards, dominating the greater part of Mexico. Priests played a highly important role in the state, with human sacrifice being demanded for the preservation of the sun and of the empire.

The Spanish conquest

Francisco Fernandez reached Mexico in 1517, and Hernan Cortes landed there in 1519.

The Spanish were received by the Indians as "white gods", but turned out to be less than benign. They all but wiped out the Aztec aritocracy in 1520, and captured and assassinated the Aztec Emperor Montezuma II in 1521, after first obtaining colossal ransoms in gold for his liberation. In 1521 the whole of Mexico was conquered with the exception of the Yucatan peninsula, which held out until 1547.

Mexico became the vice-royalty of New Spain, which was feudally governed and exploited for three centuries. The indigenous population was for the most part exterminated, the remainder reduced to slavery, and the cities of the great local civilisations were abandoned.

Independent Mexico

At the end of the 18th century revolutionary ideas found voice in Mexico with the creoles demanding independence. King Charles III of Spain liberalised his regime, but the troubles began again under his successor Charles IV, with the lesser clergy allying itself to the revolutionary movement. The Spanish revolution of 1820 unleashed a revolution in Mexico, which declared independence in 1821.

Agustin de Iturbide was proclaimed emperor of Mexico in 1822, and the former Spanish captaincy general of

1200

Guatemala became part of the Mexican empire, which comprised the whole of Central America except Panama.

The federation was broken up in 1823 when General Santa Anna took power and proclaimed a republic. The first Mexican constitution came into being in 1824. After the 1836 declaration of independence by the North American settlers in Texas, Mexico lost almost half of its territory (Texas, New Mexico, California) in the 1846-48 war with the USA. Santa Anna remained in power until 1855.

The radical Benito Juarez became president in 1858, and was opposed by conservatives. The French Emperor Napoleon III intervened and had the Archduke Maximilian of Austria pro-claimed emperor. The dictatorial Maximilian was overthrown and executed by Juarez' supporters in 1867.

Porfirio Diaz installed a dictatorship in 1876 which lasted until 1911. Civil war broke out in 1910, led by Francisco Madero, and ended in 1917 with the victory of President Venustiano Carranza's revolutionaries over the peasant uprisings of Pancho Villa and Emiliano Zapata. The revolutionary constitution which then came into being made Mexico a republic, led from 1928 by presidents from the Party of Institutional Revolution (from 1944 named the National Revolutionary Party).

Agrarian reform came to a close in 1936 at the end of a civil war which had been provoked by the revolutionary government's harsh anti-clericalism.

Mexico nationalised all oil companies in 1938, but its industrial policy following the Second World War was marked by an opening to foreign investment.

The arrival in power of Luis Echeverria (1970-76) marked a new turn to the left. New agrarian reforms were undertaken and the copper mines were nationalised. The discovery of new oil fields under Jose Lopez Portillos's presidency (1976-82) was not enough to stabilise the troubled Mexican economy. After the nationalisation of the banks and the introduction of exchange controls in September 1982, the new president, Miguel de la Madrid, elected in December, had to bring in austerity measures which led to mass protests in 1987. Part of the country's economic trouble was attributed to unforeseeable events: the massive earthquake which largely devastated Mexico City in 1985, and the sharp drop in world oil prices.

In 1987 inflation in Mexico ran at an average of 140 per cent. De la Madrid was succeeded in December 1988, after a close-run and controversial election, by President Carlos Salinas of the National Revolutionary Party, which had been in power for the last 60 years. Drugs and illegal immigration caused friction between Mexico and the USA. George Bush, the US president-elect, met Salinas in November 1988, after the US granted $3.5 billion to Mexico in October.

Monaco

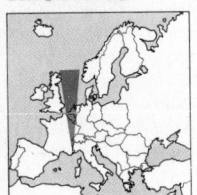

MC
Southern Europe
481 acres
Pop: 27,000

Capital: Monaco (pop: 1400)
Official language: French

Religion: Catholic (95 per cent)
System of govt: Constitutional monarchy (principality) since 1911

The Monegasque city was founded in the fifth century BC by the Phoenicians. It was annexed by Marseilles in the first century and by the Genoese in 1191. The lordship and its castle, which had been built in 1215, were conquered in 1297 by Francis Grimaldi, but Grimaldi sovereignty was not imposed until 1419. The Grimaldis allied themselves with France, except from 1524 to 1641 when they were under the protection of Spain. The Grimaldi male line died out in 1731 with Prince Antoine I, but his son-in-law, Count Goyon-Matignon, took on the name. The French National Convention annexed the principality and its French territories in January 1793. After the restoration of the Grimaldis in 1814, Sardinia imposed a protectorate.

The development of gambling establishments allowed the abolition of taxes in 1869 and the building of the Monte Carlo casino in 1879. A constitution granted in 1911 stated that Monaco would become an autonomous state under French protectorate if the Grimaldi lineage were to die out. Prince Louis II had no legal heir, but his brother-in-law adopted the name Grimaldi and his son, Louis' nephew, succeeded Louis II as Rainier III in 1949. In 1956 the prince married the US actress, Grace Kelly (died 1982). In 1962 he liberalised the constitution.

Mongolia

Northern Asia
605,022 sq. mi
Pop: 1.98 m
UN, COMECON

Capital: Ulan Bator (pop: 488,000)
Official language: Khalkha Mongol
Religion: Tibetan Buddhism
System of govt: People's republic, proclaimed 26 November 1924

The Chinese chronicles of the second millennium BC are the first to mention Mongol tribes. The Mongols, Tungus and Huns were nomadic mounted peoples who moved across vast areas with their herds. In the fourth century BC the Huns founded an extensive empire whose organisation was based on tribal structures. Fighting with China lasted for centuries. The Hun empire divided, with some southern tribes submitting to China and several northern tribes starting on a migration to the west. They reached Europe, united by Attila, in the fifth century. The territories abandoned by the Huns in Central Asia were occupied by Turco-Mongol peoples.

In the eighth century the Altaic tribe of Avars took the road to Europe in its turn, but was vanquished and dispersed in Bulgaria by Charlemagne. In the seventh century the Turco-Mongol peoples in the north had freed themselves from Chinese domination and made themselves masters of all Mongolia, all the while becoming less nomadic. The Mongol lords had fortified palaces constructed and an aristocracy developed. Cultural and political relations with China were forged.

In the tenth century the Khitan tribe affirmed its domination over Mongolia, the north of China and Manchuria, but was chased out by the Jurchens, a Tungus tribe allied to the Tartars, in c.1120. Pushed back to the west, the Khitans became dominant in the steppes to the east of the Aral Sea.

In 1206 the Mongol leader Temujin (c.1162-1227) succeeded in unifying the Mongol tribes by a skilful policy of alliances which exploited tribal rivalries. He took the title "Genghis Khan" (Great Conqueror) and invaded the north of China in 1207. He entered Beijing in 1215. By his death, in 1227, the Mongols reigned over much of Asia as far as the west of Persia. His sons continued the conquest, annexing the Jurchen kingdom in 1234 and Korea in 1236. The Russian principalities, Poland and Hungary, were devastated by the 1236-42 campaign led by Temujin's grandson, Batu, head of the Golden Horde.

Kublai Khan subjugated China in 1279, founding the Yuan dynasty, and Tibet in 1293. The three main khanates were subsequently either absorbed in the conquered populations or were defeated. China was reconquered by the Ming in 1367 and the Golden Horde was crushed by Muscovite princes in 1380. The rise of the Manchus began in the 15th century. They subjugated Inner Mongolia, long integrated into China, between 1628 and 1636, then Outer Mongolia in 1691.

After the 1911 Chinese revolution, Outer Mongolia proclaimed its independence on 1 January 1912. Russia, which wished to establish control over the country, intervened militarily. An accord reached in 1915 with Russia and China guaranteed autonomy to Mongolia. After the Russian Revolution the Chinese reoccupied Outer Mongolia, renouncing the agreement of 1915. In 1921 the Soviet Red Army invaded Outer Mongolia, a base for Japanese-backed anti-Bolshevik armies. The conquest ended in July 1921 and a treaty of friendship was signed with the USSR. A pro-Soviet government was formed, but the Jegtsundamba Hutukhtu (head of the Buddhist hierarchy) continued as a constitutional monarch. When the Hutukhtu died in 1924, the People's Republic of Mongolia, the world's second communist state, was proclaimed.

The communist leader, Choibalsang, took over as head of government and a Grand Khural (Supreme Soviet) was instituted. The radical transformation of the country, which started in 1921, continued.

Soviet aid made it possible to contain the Japanese invasion of Inner Mongolia in 1935 and prevent invasion of the Mongolian republic in August 1939. Independence and the republic were confirmed by referendum in 1945 and recognised by China in 1946. Mongolia became a member of COMECON in 1962, and further reinforced ties with Moscow by signing a new friendship treaty in 1965. Yumjaagiun Tsedenbal succeeded Choibalsang in 1952 and stayed in power until his dismissal in August 1984. The Moscow-educated Jambyn Batmonh succeeded him. In 1987 the USSR withdrew about 10,000 troops from Mongolia; about 65,000 Soviet military personnel remain in the country.

Morocco

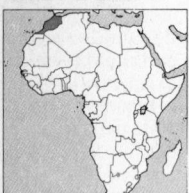

MA
North Africa
177,116 sq. mi
Pop: 23.6 m
UN, AL

Capital: Rabat (pop: 841,000)
Official language: Arabic
Religion: Moslem (98 per cent)
System of govt: Constitutional monarchy; independent since 7 April 1956

Traces of human presence in modern Morocco go back as far as the Palaeolithic era, and Neolithic cave drawings have been discovered high up in the Atlas Mountains.

In c.1000 BC Morocco was a fertile, wooded area and its inhabitants were farmers. The Phoenicians, whose trade routes ran along the Moroccan coast, established trading posts there in the second millennium BC. Rome ousted the Carthaginians and in 40 BC Morocco and the west of present-day Algeria were made the province of Mauritania Tingitana. Nomadic Berbers escaped Roman domination and raided the Roman settlements.

The desert expanded rapidly at this time, but Roman deforestation continued. Today only a third of Morocco is arable.

In the fifth century the Vandals invaded the country and established a kingdom. In the sixth century Morocco fell under Byzantine domination.

Islam and imperialism

Moslem Arabs conquered Morocco in 708. Converted to Islam, the Berbers nevertheless remained fiercely independent. Berber uprisings in 740 could not be overcome by the caliph, and in 789, King Idris I founded a kingdom with Fez as its capital.

In the tenth century the caliphs of Cordoba entered Morocco to counter Fatimid expansion. The Almoravid and Almohad dynasties ruled Morocco until 1269, when the Berbers conquered Marrakesh, whic was then the Almohad capital.

The Watassid dynasty managed to impose its domination between 1420 and 1554, a time when Portuguese and Spanish merchants settled in the coastal regions. The Portuguese were expelled for the most part in 1578.

European influence in Morocco grew from the 18th century onwards, its sultans ratifying commercial treaties with Britain and France. French hegemony in the sultanate was affirmed by the Franco-British entente of 1904.

In 1911 Germany sent a gunboat to Agadir to protest about French policy in Morocco, and the ensuing international crisis resulted in the setting up of a French protectorate over Morocco in 1912, with Germany's commercial interests guaranteed, while Spain obtained the Rif territories and Tangiers was placed under a multi-national administration.

The Rif uprisings which began in 1919 were led by its emir, Abd el-Krim (1884-1963), who defeated the Spanish in 1921. After the revolt spread to French Morocco, France intervened and Abd el-Krim surrendered in 1926.

Nationalist and Islamic agitation gathered pace after the First World War, aggravated by European immigration. Sultan Mohammed V headed the nationalist movement from 1944, and both Spanish and French Morocco became one independent kingdom in 1956.

Independence

King Hassan II has governed Morocco since 1961. He introduced a constitution in 1962 and another more democratic one in 1972.

In 1975 Morocco claimed Western Sahara when the Spanish left, bringing confrontation with the nationalist Polisario Front. Morocco left the UN over its unrecognised claim in 1984.

Food riots in January 1984 caused at least 100 deaths. Morocco hoped that a treaty of union with Libya in August 1984 would end Libyan support for the Polisario Front. However, the confrontation continued and relations with Libya did not improve when, in July 1986, King Hassan invited the Israeli premier, Shimon Peres, for talks in Morocco. Hassan cancelled the treaty with Libya the following month. He patched up a 12-year rift with Algeria over Western Sahara in May 1988. Fighting between Morocco and the Polisario Front has continued and, despite both sides provisionally accepting a UN peace plan on 30 August 1988, heavy fighting broke out again a few weeks later.

Mozambique

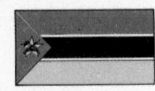

South East Africa
308,642 sq. mi
Pop: 14.5 m
UN, OAU

Capital: Maputo (pop: 882,000)
Official language: Portuguese
Religions: Traditional beliefs (60 per cent), Christian (30 per cent), Moslem (10 per cent)
System of govt: People's republic; independent since 25 June 1975

Iron Age farming extended as far south as Maputo Bay by the second century. By the eighth century Arab and Persian merchants were visiting the ports regularly to barter for gold and copper. During the course of the next two centuries the Sofala coast became an important area for the gold trade. Nearly 40 trading posts were founded between the 11th and 15th centuries, with tracks linking the coast to the interior of the continent, including present-day Zimbabwe, Zambia and Malawi.

The Portuguese navigator, Vasco de Gama, reached Mozambique in 1498 and less than eight years later the Portuguese had seized all the important ports on the East African coast, including the ports of the Sofala coast and Mozambique island. These acquisitions allowed the Portuguese to dominate the gold, ivory and slave trades between Africa, Arabia and India.

However, the interior of the country was only conquered in the 19th century and Mozambique was not given definitive borders until 1912. The exploitation of the country's resources was confined to the huge concessions granted to private companies. The construction of railways was of crucial importance, particularly to the British whose interior colonies, such as Rhodesia, needed to be linked to the coast.

In 1951 Mozambique became a Portuguese overseas province, while nationalist movements were also beginning to develop. Three independence movements coalesced in 1962 to constitute the Mozambique Liberation Front (FRELIMO), of which Eduardo Mondlane was leader. Initially moderate, the organisation moved to the left.

From 1964 FRELIMO soldiers engaged in guerrilla activities against the Portuguese authorities, especially in the north of the country. Supported by Tanzania, the guerrillas made important military gains. In 1970 the Portuguese attempted a vast offensive in order to regain control of affairs. But in 1972 military failure forced Lisbon to grant Mozambique autonomy. Mozambique obtained internal autonomy on 1 January 1973, and the fall of the dictatorship in Portugal accelerated the process of independence which was acquired in 1975. The People's Republic of Mozambique was proclaimed, with the president of FRELIMO, Samora Machel, becoming the new republic's first president. FRELIMO changed its name to Partido de Vanguarda (Vanguard Party) and became the sole party of the country. The nationalisation of industry and a programme of agrarian reforms were set in place.

Mozambican foreign policy included the ratification of a friendship pact with the USSR, with which Mozambique established close relations, and support for guerrilla movements fighting the white minority government of neighbouring Rhodesia.

The suppression of a white opposition uprising in Mozambique led to the mass exodus of Portuguese expatriates, causing an economic vacuum which forced the government to enter into closer economic relations with South Africa.

From 1975 the government's collectivisation of agriculture was opposed by peasant resistance. An anti-government guerrilla war waged by the Mozambican National Resistance movement (RENAMO), which was supported by South Africa, began to escalate in 1979. At the same time Mozambique, with advisers from Cuba and other socialist countries, supported the ANC in its struggle against the South African regime. In 1984 Mozambique and its neighbour South Africa signed a series of bilateral agreements, including a non-aggression pact under which both countries agreed that their territories would not be used as bases from which guerrilla attacks could be launched against the other.

Despite this accord, the continuing struggle between the government and the RENAMO in Angola and the activities of the ANC in South Africa have led to accusations by both sides that this agreement was being breached. In 1987 President Machel was killed in an air crash and his successor, Joaquim Chissano, claimed he had been murdered. Chissano met US President Reagan in October, amid signs that the USA might put pressure on Pretoria to halt its support for RENAMO. In 1988 some western nations accused the movement of massacring civilians.

The Mozambican-South African deal has remained, and in September 1988 South African President Botha visited Maputo for talks with Chissano. Both countries committed themselves to reinforcing the bilateral accord. In the meantime, Britain is among western nations giving military advice to the Maputo government.

In June the government moved to normalise relations with the church, and pledged to return all church property nationalised after 1975.

Another visitor in September 1988 was Pope John Paul II, who called for an end to the bloody guerrilla confrontation that was ruining the country's economy.

Namibia

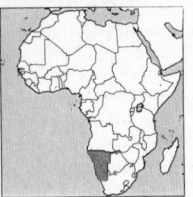

South West Africa
318,261 sq. mi
Pop: 1.19 m

Capital: Windhoek (pop: 110,000)
Official languages: Afrikaans, English, German
Religion: Lutheran (51 per cent), Catholic (19 per cent),

traditional beliefs
System of govt: State illegally occupied by South Africa since 27 October 1966

The first European landings in Namibia, formerly South-West Africa, were those of Diogo Cao in 1484 and Bartolomeu Diaz in 1488, but colonisation did not begin until the 19th century. In 1878 Britain declared Walvis Bay a crown colony. A German trader purchased the Luderitz Bay, and the Germans established a protectorate there in 1884. Germany took direct control of the colony from 1892. From 1904 German troops were involved in a brutal two-year war against the Herero people.

German South West Africa was conquered in 1915 by South Africa, which gained a League of Nations mandate in 1920. It refused to return the mandate to the UN after the Second World War. From 1950, the International Court of Justice condemned Pretoria's de facto annexation. The UN decision of October 1966 to revoke the mandate was rejected by Pretoria, which threatened to use force against any attempt by the UN to enforce its resolution. However, in 1973, after negotiations with the UN, a multi-racial advisory council was appointed and in April 1978 South Africa accepted a plan for UN-supervised elections. The elections for a constituent assembly were boycotted by the nationalist South West African People's Organisation (SWAPO) and most internal political parties.

In June 1985 South Africa agreed to talks with the UN on Namibian independence and the withdrawal of South African troops. In January 1989 the UN set 1 April for a ceasefire between South Africa and SWAPO. UN troops arrived to oversee moves to independence, which proceeded despite clashes between SWAPO and South African forces.

Nauru

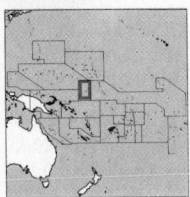

Oceania
8 sq. mi
Pop: 8,000

Capital: Yaren (pop: 4,000)
Official language: English, Nauruan

Religion: Mainly Protestant
System of govt: Republic; independent since 31 January 1968

The small atoll of Nauru was first settled by Micronesian groups. There was also a Melanesian influence, from the Solomon Islands. The islands consisted of 12 districts, each of them under a tribal chief.

The first European to visit Nauru as John Fearne, in 1798, although a more permanent European presence began only in c.1830, when Nauru served as a supply point for whalers. In 1888 Nauru was annexed by Germany into its Marshal Islands protectorate. From around 1898, British firms were allowed to exploit Nauru's phosphate reserves, the highest-grade in the world.

Captured by Australians during the First World War, Nauru was governed by Australia, New Zealand and Britain under a League of Nations mandate after the war. Phosphate mining continued, and the island eventually reached agreement with the three ruling powers to receive a share of the profits.

Nauru fell to the Japanese in 1942. Australia retook Nauru in 1945, and the UN gave the former ruling powers a new mandate.

The independent Republic of Nauru came into being on 31 January 1968. Hammer de Roburt was president from 1968-76, and again from 1978. A trust has been set up to assist the prosperous economy when the phosphate runs out in around 1990.

Nepal

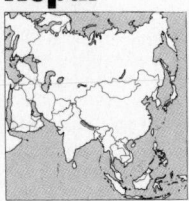

Southern Asia
56,827 sq. mi
Pop: 17.5 m
UN

Capital: Kathmandu (pop: 235,000)
Official language: Nepali (Pahari)

Religions: Hindu (89 per cent), Buddhist (5 per cent)
System of govt: Constitutional monarchy since February 1951

Classical Indian writings indicate that Nepal had contacts with the Ganges valley from the sixth century BC. Buddhism was born in Nepal at Lumbini in 563 BC.

The first peoples of Nepal were Mongols who were joined by Tibetans and Indians. From the fourth to the eighth centuries Nepal was a part of the Gupta kingdom. It became the main spiritual and commercial centre between central and southern Asia. The Mallava dynasty ruled from the tenth to the 18th centuries. In 1450 dynastic rows split the kingdom into three.

The Gurkha principality conquered the whole of Nepal in 1769. The young or weak kings who sat on the throne between 1775 and 1832 were unable to govern; the Thapa family held real power from 1806 to 1837, and the Rana family did so between 1846 and 1951.

The expansion of Nepal was curbed by war with China in 1792 and the British in 1814-16. The latter war reduced Nepal to its present boundaries, and led to the first recruitment of Gurkhas into the British army.

King Tribhuvan Bir Bikram's 1951 coup removed the Ranas and was succeeded by his son, Mahendra, in 1955. His grandson, Birendra, succeeded in 1972. The king retains most executive power.

Netherlands

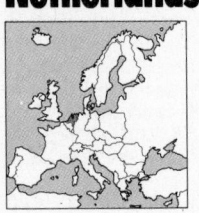
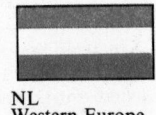

NL
Western Europe
15,770 sq. mi
Pop: 14.6 m
UN, EC,
NATO, OECD

Capital: Amsterdam (pop: 679,000)
Official language: Dutch
Religions: Catholic (40 per cent), Protestant (31 per cent)
System of govt: Constitutional monarchy since 1848

Traces of the first cultures in what is the present-day Netherlands are megalithic. The Bronze Age began in c.1600 BC, and its transition to the Iron Age happened around 650 BC. When Julius Caesar conquered the Gauls (57 BC) the area of the present-day Netherlands was inhabited by Germanic tribes: the Batavians in the south, and the Frisians in the north. These tribes revolted on several occasions despite alliances concluded with the Romans. When the Romans pulled out in the fifth century, power passed to the Salian (western) Franks.

The Carolingian rulers, who originated from the lands between the Rhine and the Meuse, encouraged the growth of Christianity in the country.

Charlemagne (768-814) divided the administration of his kingdom into several counties, the counts of which were subject to imperial control. When the Frankish empire was divided from 843, the territories south of the river Scheldt returned to the eastern Frankish kingdom, and the territories known as the Netherlands went to Lotharingia (Lorraine), which in 925 also rejoined the eastern Frankish kingdom.

As imperial power weakened, several counties increased their autonomy, particularly those of Holland and Flanders. The counts even constituted a threat to the king of France, Philip Augustus (1180-1223).

The rise of the burghers

In the 13th century the growth of the towns, and North Sea ports in particular, was quite remarkable. The Flemish towns were important centres of commerce between England and the Baltic; their renowned cloth was exported across the whole of Europe, and they won charters from their lords and formed town councils.

The counts of Flanders sought alliance with France in their struggle to assert their authority over these increasingly independent towns. In 1302 the Flemish craftsmen inflicted a decisive defeat on the French at Courtrai, but in a later rebellious uprising against the count of Flanders the Flemish troops were beaten at Rozebeke (1382).

The count of Mâle managed to regain supremacy over Flanders and his only daughter, Marguerite, married Philip the Bold, duke of Burgundy, who then inherited Flanders on the count's death in 1384.

Foreign domination

The successors of Philip the Bold, and particularly his grandson Philip the Good (1419-67), extended their territories in the Netherlands by purchase, marriage or treaty. Philip the Good thus acquired the counties of Holland and Zeeland in 1433. The last duke of Burgundy, Charles the Bold, took effective control of Liege in 1468 and annexed Guelders in 1473. His daughter Mary promised the Dutch States General to respect the "great privileges" of the cities of the Netherlands. Mary of Burgundy, however, married the Austrian archduke and future Holy Roman emperor, Maximilian of Habsburg, who proceeded to re-establish imperial authority in the Netherlands, which included present-day Belgium.

The Emperor Charles V brought the number of Dutch provinces to 17, annexing Frisia, Groningen and Guelders between 1524 and 1543. He passed on sovereignty over the Netherlands to his son, Philip II of Spain, in 1555.

The Reformation had prospered in the Netherlands but Philip II, a strict catholic, pursued the merciless repression of Dutch Calvinist protestantism, which fanned the flames of open revolt in the Dutch provinces.

The struggle for independence

The seven protestant provinces in the north, Guelders, Holland, Zeeland, Utrecht, Frisia, Overijssel and Groningen, united in 1579 at Utrecht and started the Ten Years War with Spain, supported by the southern provinces of the Netherlands. The seven provinces proclaimed independence from Spain and their union in the "Republic of the United Netherlands" in 1581, under the leadership of stadholder (ruler) William

the Silent, prince of Orange, who was assassinated in 1584.

The stadholder Frederick Henry of Nassau (1625-47) enabled the union to regain its principal towns from the Spanish, recognised the Dutch republic by the Treaty of Munster in 1648. The loyalist provinces of the south remained in Habsburg hands.

Colonial power

In the 17th century the new republic of the United Provinces saw considerable economic and cultural growth. A Dutch East India Company was set up in 1602 and a West India Company in 1614. A stock exchange was established at Amsterdam in 1609. Dutch settlements also multiplied in America.

The maritime and colonial power of the United Provinces led to increasing tension with England which erupted into war in 1652. Two other maritime wars followed, in 1665 and 1674, with the Dutch emerging victorious from both.

From 1793 to 1795 the Netherlands were a theatre for revolutionary confrontations in the wake of the French revolution. In 1795 the Netherlands were conquered by the French, who made them the Batavian Republic. In 1806 this gave way to the new kingdom of Holland whose throne was given by Napoleon to his brother Louis.

The kingdom was annexed by France in 1810, but regained its independence after Napoleon's defeat in 1815. The former ruling house of Orange returned as sovereigns of the United Kingdom of the Netherlands.

A Belgian revolt against the Dutch king, William I, began in Brussels on 25 August 1830, and its extension into the Catholic provinces forced Dutch troops to withdraw from Belgium which proclaimed its independence on 4 October 1830. The kingdom of Belgium was not recognised by William I until 1838. He abdicated in 1840 in favour of his son, William II.

After the serious economic crisis and poverty which hit the country between

1845 and 1848 the new king assembled a commission charged with revising the constitution, extending parliamentary and ministerial powers. The country's industrial and commercial activity flourished at the end of the 19th century, aided by the development of the great ports of Amsterdam and Rotterdam. Religious problems, such as the question of sectarian schools dominated political life, often paralysing governmental activity (the question was not to resolved until 1920).

The world wars

By 1913 the proliferating number of political parties made the formation of a stable government virtually impossible, and Queen Wilhelmina (1890-1948) formed an extra-parliamentary government. The Netherlands maintained its neutrality during the First World War which led, however, to economic hardships. The former German kaiser lived in the Netherlands in exile after the war. After the failure of the socialist-communist revolution led by Troelstra in 1919, a coalition government was set up under premier Ruys de Beerenbrouck. He remained in office until 1926 and was premier again from 1929-33.

In the 1930s the Netherlands welcomed large numbers of Jews and political refugees from Nazi Germany. Hitler's troops invaded the Netherlands on 10 May 1940 and Nazi repression cost the lives of 100,000 citizens. The queen and government fled the Netherlands and spent the war in London, where they supported a Dutch resistance movement, which was backed by a number of general strikes (in 1941 and 1943). The country regained its freedom on 5 May 1945.

After 1945

The elderly Wilhelmina abdicated in 1948 in favour of her daughter, Juliana. Apart from the Dutch Antilles in the Caribbean, all the colonies of the Netherlands obtained independence shortly after the war, although some,

such as Indonesia, were given up somewhat reluctantly.

A Dutch Commonwealth-like union was created with Indonesia, Surinam and the Dutch Antilles, from which Indonesia withdrew in 1956, with the Netherlands keeping sovereignty over Irian. The loss of the colonies was offset by the continuing world importance of the Dutch ports.

The Netherlands dropped its long-standing neutrality in 1949 and became a member of NATO in 1957, joining the Common Market the same year. Since liberation, the two main political parties have been the catholic People's Party and the socialist Labour Party, which was in power until 1958. After the 1963 elections the catholics held office until 1971.

The socialists took power again in 1973, remaining in office until a centre-right coalition government was formed in 1977.

In April 1980 Queen Juliana abdicated in favour of her daughter Beatrix.

After his victory in the elections of September 1982 Rudolph (Ruud) Lubbers formed a centre-right government. His government faced controversy over decisions in autumn 1985 to take part in the USA's "Star Wars" strategic defence initiative (SDI), and to accept US cruise missiles, despite popular and opposition protests. In the event, however, the US-Soviet treaty on short and medium-range nuclear weapons signed by Reagan and Gorbachev in December 1987, prevented the arrival of the missiles.

Another problem was high unemployment (15 per cent), one of the highest levels in Europe, despite an improving economy.

Re-elected in May 1986, the Lubbers coalition introduced austerity measures, including spending cuts and tax increases, which were continued into 1987-88. They aimed to boost economic recovery, which was only moderate, while unemployment decreased more slowly than forecast.

New Zealand

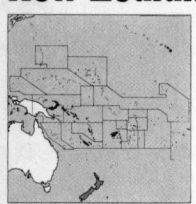

NZ
Oceania
103,736 sq. mi
Pop: 3.2 m
UN, CW, OECD

Capital: Wellington (pop: 134,000)
Official language: English
Religion: Mainly Christian
System of govt: Constitutional monarchy; independent since 1931

The Maoris, a Polynesian people, ar-

rived in New Zealand by about 1300. The Dutchman Abel Tasman was the first European to visit the islands, in 1642. However, the Dutch did not proceed to colonise the island. James Cook, was the next European to visit New Zealand when he landed there in 1769 on his search for the legendary "Great South Land". He charted both islands with great accuracy, and remained in New Zealand water until 1770. The first European colonists, some of whom were escaped convicts from New South Wales, began settling coastal areas of New Zealand from 1792. Their principal activities were whaling, seal hunting and stock breeding.

US, British and French whalers were

based in the North and South islands, but more highly organised colonisation was begun from 1839 by the New Zealand Association, which tried to buy land in advance of annexation.

In 1838 London had decided to annex New Zealand: the North Island would be annexed by right of cession, and the South Island by right of discovery. In 1841 Britain named William Hobson as governor; he had previously negotiated with the Maoris since 1839. Under the 1840 "treaty" of Waitangi with northern chiefs the Maori ceded sovereignty to the crown in return for protection and guaranteed possession of their lands, agreeing to sell land only to the crown.

In the 1840s the rate of colonisation alarmed the Maori, who raided and obstructed new settlements. Peace was finally achieved by force in 1846 and lasted until 1860; Maori troubles did not cease until 1870; British reprisal policies meant the loss of the best Maori land in the following 40 years.

In the 1840s the colonists also attacked the personal rule of the Governor George Grey (1845-53) and demanded representation. An initial constitution was granted in 1852 and the first New Zealand General Assembly (consisting of the governor, a crown-appointed council and House of Representatives) met two years later, with the Maoris having four seats. The new provinces had their own administrations abolished in 1876.

A huge flood of immigrants headed for the islands after the discovery of gold at Otago in 1861 and the population of New Zealand reached half a million by 1880.

An economic slump hit New Zealand from the 1870s to about 1895. Political life really got under way when the Liberals were in power from 1891-1912, especially under the energetic premier Richard Seddon (1893-1906). They introduced numerous social reforms and the women of New Zealand were the first in the world to obtain the right to vote, in 1893.

New Zealand fought for Britain in both the First and Second World War in ANZAC (Australia and New Zealand Army Corps) contingents. In addition, Britain enjoyed benefits from New Zealand wool and foodstuffs.

In 1919 New Zealand gained a mandate over the former German colony of Western Samoa. Despite joining the League of Nations under the Reform Party premier William Massey (1912-25), New Zealand was unenthusiastic about independence, despite the 1931 Statute of Westminster, which it did not enforce until 1947.

New Zealand's attachment to Britain was shown by the rapidity with which it went to war in 1939. Troops were sent to Europe, as they had been in the First World War, but after 1941 New Zealand itself was directly threatened by the Japanese and New Zealand forces were in action in the Pacific. However, New Zealand forces fought under US, not British command, and it was the USA, not Britain, which defended the country from Japan. New Zealand's unswerving loyalty to Britain was inevitably strained.

After the Second World War New Zealand loosened its bonds with the Commonwealth in order secure closer military and economic links with the USA and the states of South East Asia, by joining the ANZUS (Australia, New Zealand and the United States) defence pact in 1951 and sending troops to the Vietnam and Korean wars.

Western Samoa became an independent state in 1962. Diplomatic tension with France over nuclear testing in the Pacific reached crisis point between 1972 and 1974. The conservatives took power in 1975.

The Labour Party (formed 1916, first in power 1935-49) won the elections of July 1984 under David Lange, and was returned to power with an increased majority in August 1987. Lange's hostility to nuclear arms led to serious tension with France, particularly over the sinking in Auckland harbour of the *Rainbow Warrior*, flagship of Greenpeace, the environmentalist group, by French secret agents in July 1985. One Greenpeace crew member died. *Rainbow* Warrior had been about to sail to protest against forthcoming French nuclear weapons tests in the Pacific, to which New Zealand also objected.

Lange's rejection of nuclear weapons, especially from 1987, was popular until recently, when public concern over the rift with the USA began to shift opinion away from Labour. Lange banned US warships from visiting New Zealand ports when the US government refused to say whether or not they were carrying nuclear weapons, a move which effectively ended New Zealand's participation in ANZUS.

Nicaragua

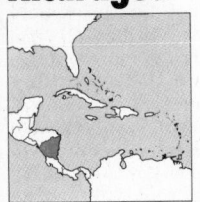

NIC
Central America
50,193 sq. mi
Pop: 3.14 m
UN, OAS, LAES

Capital: Managua (pop: 682,000)
Official language: Spanish
Religions: Catholic (87 per cent), Protestant
System of govt: Republic; independent since 1838

Little is known about the proto-historic period of present-day Nicaragua. An agricultural population lived here in c.1500 BC and produced ceramic objects. A people from Mexico in c.1000 later settled in the south-west. Also from the north, the Nicarao succeeded them in 1500, settled in the region of Lake Managua and disappeared completely a few years later. Around the year 1000, another culture in the east erected stone statues of up to 13 feet (four metres) in height.

In 1502 Columbus reached what is now Nicaragua. The Spanish conquest, however, started in the south from the Pacific coast. There was rivalry between the Spanish conquerors and they also faced native uprisings from indigenous peoples reduced to slavery. From c.1530 gold and cocoa made the towns rich. In c.1650 Nicaragua suffered from pirates. Later, the Spanish were also confronted with the growing influence of the British, present on the east coast from 1740.

Nicaragua proclaimed its independence in 1821 and joined the Mexican empire. Independence was proclaimed for a second time in 1823 when Nicaragua joined the Central American Federation. The country became truly independent in 1838, but her troubles continued, with indigenous uprisings and a British occupation of the Mosquito Coast until 1860.

In 1885 the country's liberal hired an American adventurer, William Walker, who conquered Nicaragua with his private army. Walker proclaimed himself president in 1886, but was thrown out by the conservatives a year later. The dictator Jose Santos Zelaya took power in 1893 and promoted the development of railways and coffee plantations.

Zelaya's policy of aggression towards his neighbours and the USA caused his downfall in 1909, in a civil war which continued until the intervention of the USA in 1912. The USA occupied the country until 1933, with one brief interruption.

Cesar Augustino Sandino, head of the guerrilla movement against US occupation, was murdered in 1934. With US support, Anastasio Somoza Garcia, head of the national guard, became sole candidate in the presidential elections of 1936. He remained in power until his assassination in 1956. His son, Luis Somoza Debayle, succeeded him, and another family member, Anastasio Somoza Debayle, won the presidency in 1967 elections, which were marked by unrest and political murders. In 1972, the year that an earthquake devastated Managua and killed 10,000, Somoza abrogated the constitution. Sandinista guerrillas, named after Cesar Sandino, forced him to leave the country, half of which he personally owned, in July 1979. Thus ended the brutal Somoza dynasty of dictators.

The Sandinistas' socialist policies led to the threat of intervention by the USA, which supported right-wing guerrillas (Contras). The Sandinistas, led by Daniel Ortega, progressively hardened its attitude towards liberals and censored the press. In response to critics elections were held, which the Sandinistas won, and the junta was dissolved in January 1985. However, the war between the Sandinista government and the US-backed right-wing rebels has continued. On 9 January 1987 President Ortega signed a new constitution, but immediately reimposed a state of emergency, which was followed by an intensification of the civil war. Despite peace and ceasefire negotiations during 1988, the war has still not been brought to an end, although the US Congress has blocked support for the Contras.

Niger

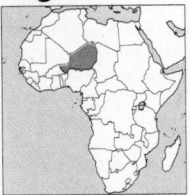
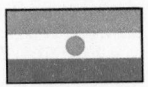

RN
West Africa
489,189 sq. mi
Pop: 6.9 m
UNO, CEAO, OAU

Capital: Niamey (pop: 399,000)
Official language: French
Religion: Moslem (97 per cent)
System of govt: Republic; independent since 3 August 1960

Around 5000 BC Saharan farmers began moving southwards as the Sahara gradually dried out. The Hausa arrived in the west of present-day Niger in the 12th century and set up a number of rival kingdoms, which, in the 16th century, fell under the domination of the Moslem Songhai empire. After the collapse of the Songhai empire (1591), a Songhai state was established at Diamare. The country fell under Peul domination in the 19th century. The black populations and the Tuaregs were in continual conflict in the north. French colonial troops occupied Niger in 1890. In 1899 the west of Niger was attached to the French territories of Upper Senegal-Niger and the rest of the country to Dahomey. In the north the fighting with the Tuaregs continued until 1906. A new revolt, led by the Sanusiyyah, was put down in 1916. The region became a French colony in 1922, and Niamey became its capital in 1926. The last of the northern rebellions was finally quashed in 1932.

Niger became independent in 1958 with Hamani Diori elected president on 9 November. The new Niger Progressive Party became Niger's only party, and Hamani was re-elected in 1965 and 1970.

Niger suffered both from drought and high-level corruption. Lieutenant-Colonel Seyni Kountche, seized power in April 1974. Political parties were banned and parliament dissolved. The regime relaxed after 1976 and became more liberal from 1980. Since 1986 the USA has been providing military and financial aid. Kountche died on 10 November 1987 and was succeeded by his cousin, Colonel Ali Saibou.

Nigeria

Nigeria

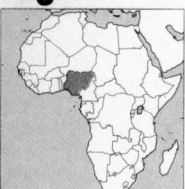

WAN
West Africa
356,667 sq. mi
Pop: 100 m
UN, ECOWAS,
CW, OAU, OPEC

Capital: Lagos (pop: 1.1 m)
Official language: English
Religions: Moslem (45 per cent),
Christian (38 per cent), traditional
beliefs (15 per cent)
System of govt: Federal republic;
independent since 1 October 1960

The first known civilisation within the territory of present-day Nigeria was that of Nok on the Bauchi Plateau between 500 BC and 200.

From the seventh to the 11th centuries, after considerable intermixing of populations, tribes established themselves – the Hausas in the north and the Yorubas in the south-west – while the native populations were pushed out onto the Jos Plateau or into the eastern swamp forests.

When the Islamicisation of present-day Nigeria began in 1085 AD, the Hausa states of Kano, Katsino and Zaria had already organised themselves (since around the year 1000) into significant centres of trade and craft. In the 13th century the Kanem-Bornu kingdom spread towards the north-east of Nigeria from the central Sudanic belt. This expansion continued westwards until the 16th century.

From the 14th century, the nomadic warrior Fulani people had established itself in the Hausa regions, and had acquired considerable influence. At the start of the 19th century, under their leader, Usman dan Fodio, they undertook the systematic conquest of the Hausa kingdoms.

In the south west the Yorubas had established several kingdoms and principalities from the 11th century onwards, the main ones being Oyo and Benin. The religious centre of the Yoruba civilisation was at Ife, where art and sculpture reached its apogee in the 14th century.

The coasts of Benin were visited by the Portuguese from 1472, and trading relations were established from 1486. The slave trade was in full swing during the 17th and 18th centuries. The Yoruba kingdoms were conquered and converted to Islam by the Fulani in 1811.

British colonisation

After destroying the Portuguese settlements in 1553, the English had exclusive control of the slave trade in the Gulf of Biafra until the 19th century. The first British consul, charged with exploring inland and controlling the slave trade, was appointed at the island of Fernando Po in 1849. Lagos was occupied in 1851 and became a colony, enlarged by several coastal annexations, in 1861.

The British Royal Niger Company, created in 1879, swiftly supplanted all foreign rivals, particularly the French. The company had been charged with exploiting all the territories placed under British protectorate, from Lagos to Cameroon, and continued to expand towards the river Niger in the north.

In 1897 an agreement with France fixed the borders between British and French areas. The northern and southern territories were officially declared protectorates in 1900, and in 1914 they were joined under the name of the colony of Nigeria. The Moslem north of the country continued to be administered by indigenous sovereigns under British control, most of the commercial interests being grouped together on the coast.

After the First World War a nationalist movement developed, particularly amongst the Ibo people eastern Nigeria. The first Nigerian political party however, was not founded until 1944 by Nnamdi Azikiwe. The 1945 and 1951 constitutions confirmed the participation of elected Africans in government. After negotiations, which were complicated by tribal problems, the eastern and western parts of Nigeria obtained self-government on 8 August 1957 and the north in March 1959. Nigeria, divided into three distinct political regions, obtained full independence from Britain on 1 October 1960.

After independence

Nigeria's first governor-general was Dr Azikiwe, the head of the Northern People's Congress, while Sir Abubakar Tafawa Balewa, a Hausa Moslem from the north and in power since the 1959 elections, became federal prime minister. A republic was proclaimed in October 1963, although Nigeria remained in the Commonwealth.

Regional political rivalries considerably slowed the development of the national economy. However, this was aided by the existence of oil deposits around Port Harcourt which had been exploited since 1958.

A group of Ibo officers from the east under Major Chukwuma Nzuga overthrew President Azikiwe on 15 January 1966, and over 50 politicians and officers were killed, including Tafawa Balewa. Many of the dead were northern Moslems, and the long-standing rivalry between the Moslem Hausa and Christian Ibo looked set to boil over into conflict. A Hausa faction took power in a counter-coup in July and installed Lieutenant Colonel Yakubu Gowon as federal leader.

A massacre of the Ibo, which had begun in the north of the country at the start of the year, continued after the coup, and upwards of 1,000 people are believed to have died by October. In the event as many as 30,000 were killed. On 27 May 1967, Colonel Gowon announced the abolition of the three regions and the creation of 12 federal states. The Ibo leader Colonel Odumegwu Ojukwu, military governor of the oil-rich eastern region, rejected the planned division and proclaimed the secession of the Ibo state of Biafra two days later, claiming that the Ibo no longer believed that their lives and property were safe under federal rule. Of Nigeria's 50 million or so population, around 12 million lived in the eastern region, not all of them Ibo.

On 6 July a civil war broke out which lasted until 21 January 1970, when Biafra capitulated to federal forces. General Ojukwu sought asylum in Ivory Coast. The war had cost one and a half million lives, many through appalling famine caused partly by the Nigerian government's interference in Red Cross relief flights from June 1969.

Twelve federal states, grouped into three main regions, were created within the federation. Gowon, now a general, instigated the country's reconstruction and reconciliation, but was overthrown on 29 July 1975 by the Hausa General Murtala Ramat Mohammed, who created seven new federal states. He was assassinated on 13 February 1976, and the Supreme Military Council designated General Olusegun Obasanjo as his successor. A plan for the return to civilian government was proposed, the state of emergency was lifted and political parties were again authorised in 1978. A new Nigerian constitution came into force after the elections of 11 August 1979, which were won by the National Party of Nigeria, whose head, Shehu Shagari, became president. Despite the grave economic crisis and fall in exports which followed OPEC's decision to raise oil prices, Shagari was re-elected in August 1983. Accusations of electoral fraud provoked another coup on 1 October and brought General Mohammed Buhari to power. Bahari was overthrown in August 1985 by General Ibrahim Babangida, who dissolved Buhari's secret police and freed political prisoners. The new government promised a liberalisation of the regime, announcing in July 1987 that Nigeria would return to civilian rule in 1992.

Norway

N
Northern Europe
125,181 sq. mi
Pop: 4.18 m
UN, EFTA,
NATO, OECD

Capital: Oslo (pop: 450,000)
Official language: Norwegian
Religion: Protestant (88 per cent)
System of govt: Constitutional monarchy; independent since 7 June 1905

In the first centuries AD Norway was peopled by Lapps in the north and Germanic Scandinavians in the south and south-west. Scandinavian society was based on the land-owning farmer, who was master of a small community of slaves, villeins (feudal serfs) and freemen. Each valley of farmers elected a leader.

The age of the Vikings started in the ninth century, with poor farmers colonising the Faroe, Orkney and Shetland islands. The landowners traded with the British Isles and then pillaged and occupied the north of Scotland, the Isle of Man, the Hebrides and a number of Irish ports. Exiled lords at the head of groups of Norsemen colonised Greenland and Iceland.

According to tradition, King Harald I Harfaagre (Fairhair) brought about the unification of Norway at the battle of Stavanger in c.900. On his death his sons divided the kingdom and the south was conquered by the Danes. Unity was re-established under Olaf Tryggvesson (995-1000), who founded his capital at Nidaros and encouraged the spread of Christianity.

His successor, Olaf II Haraldsson, was killed in 1030 at the Battle of Stiklestad by the Danes under Canute (Knut) the Great, king of Denmark and England, whose son Sven took the Norwegian throne.

Sven was expelled by the Norwegians in 1035 and replaced by Magnus (1035-47), the son of St Olaf. The Viking conquests continued under Harald Hardraade (1047-66), the founder of Christiania (Oslo), and the Norwegians departed on crusades under King Sigurd (1103-30). On Sigurd's death royal power weakened in favour of the church and the nobility.

Magnus IV Erlingsson was the first king of Norway to be crowned (1163). His successor, Sverre Sigurdsson (1180-1202) reduced the opposition of the church and nobility. His work was continued by his grandson, King Haakon Haakonsson (1217-63), who regained a great number of the islands which had been lost during previous reigns:

the Orkneys, Shetlands, Greenland and Iceland. He died during a campaign against the king of Scotland.

Haakon's successor, King Magnus Lagaboetir (the Lawmender) (1263-80), had to cede the Hebrides and the Isle of Man to Scotland. Magnus VI (1319-43) had to concede feudal privileges to the aristocracy and the higher clergy, and little by little Norwegian society became organised on feudal lines. Norway's kings also encouraged the arrival of German merchants.

The Hanse secured privileges in 1294 which enabled them to become complete masters of Norwegian trade and economy by the end of the 13th century. The country lost almost two-thirds of its population in the great plague of 1349.

The Scandinavian union

The short-lived reign of Haakon V Magnusson (1299-1319), son of Magnus VI, who had already ruled Norway and Sweden, brought Denmark into the union. The marriage of King Haakon VI, who inherited Sweden in 1359, to Margaret, daughter of King Valdemar IV Atterdag of Denmark, allowed the union of the three Scandinavian kingdoms. Regent of Denmark in 1375 and regent of Norway and Sweden on the death of King Haakon VI (1380), Margaret had her great-nephew, Eric of Pomerania, recognised as sovereign of the three kingdoms, formalised in the Union of Kalmar (1397). The union was not to the benefit of Norway, which lost several islands and was put under Danish rule. Norway was pulled into Danish wars against Sweden, which regained its independence in 1524. The only noticeable effect of the decline in Denmark's power was the loss of Norwegian regions to Sweden: Jamtland in 1645, Bohuslan and Trondheim in 1658.

A number of agrarian reforms, the birth of an entirely Norwegian commerce and the appearance of an intellectual elite encouraged the development of a national consciousness during the the 17th and 18th centuries. Under the Treaty of Kiel (January 1814), Bernadotte, regent of Sweden, regained Norway from Denmark. But Norway rejected the treaty and claimed the right to determine its own sovereignty.

The Swedish invasion of 1815 did not prevent Norway from retaining its liberal constitution adopted in 1814. This constitution, modelled on US, French and Spanish democracies, entrusted the greatest part of the power to an elected parliament, the Storting, the king having only delaying powers. By 1900 Norway again found prosperity, its merchant navy being the third largest in the world.

Independent Norway

The Storting pronounced the deposition of King Oscar II on 7 June 1905. Sweden accepted Norwegian independence and the Storting chose Prince Charles of Denmark as king and he became Haakon VII.

Norway was very early to have full manhood suffrage (1898) and the vote for women (1913), and remained neutral throughout the First World War, thus bringing about a rapid growth in her economy. Having already lost Iceland and the Faroe islands in 1814, Norway abandoned Greenland to Denmark in 1933.

Despite her neutrality, Norway was invaded by German troops on 9 April 1940: Norwegian and Allied forces resisted until 9 June 1940, the king and government having left for London on 7 June. After the war Norway's Nazi puppet leader, Vidkun Quisling, was executed for treason (August 1945).

In power before the war (1935), the Labour Party maintained its majority until 1965. Offshore oil production began in 1971. In a referendum in 1972 the Norwegians pronounced themselves against entry into the EEC, and in 1976 a referendum showed a large majority against the abolition of the monarchy.

The Oxford-educated King Olaf V has reigned since Haakon VII's death in 1957. The Conservatives returned to power in 1981 and their coalition returned to power in September 1985. On 1 May 1986 it was succeeded by a minority Labour government under Norway's first woman prime minister, Gro Harlem Brundtland.

Oman

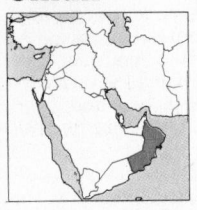
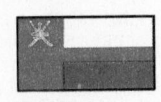

Near East
82,030 sq. mi
Pop: 1.3 m
UN, AL, GCC

Capital: Muscat (pop: 50,000)
Official language: Arabic
Religions: Moslem (86 per cent), Hindu (13 per cent)

System of govt: Monarchy (sultanate)

Oman was converted to Islam in c.630, and remained under the authority of the first Moslem caliphs until the end of the seventh century. The Kharijite sect of the Ibadiyyah then seized power and Oman became de facto an independent imamate in the ninth century.

From the 13th to the 16th centuries, the coastal regions and towns remained under the domination of Hormuz until it was conquered by the Portuguese in 1509. The town of Muscat became one of the most important Portuguese fortified towns.

The sultan of Oman expelled the Portuguese in 1650 and also seized their East African territories to the north of Mozambique.

Oman became one of the most important powers in the Indian Ocean and reached its apogee during the first half of the 19th century. The sultan's residence was moved to Zanzibar after its conquest in 1840. The fall of the sultanate of Muscat and Oman began after the loss of Zanzibar in 1856, as conflicts over inheritance and succession weakened the sultanate. The British imposed a protectorate in 1891.

The discovery of oil fields provoked a conflict with neighbouring Saudi Arabia in 1949, but oil drilling did not really get under way until 1967. Sultan Sa'id bin Taimur had to abdicate after the coup instigated by his son, Qabus bin Sa'id on 23 July 1970, from which date Muscat and Oman has been called simply Oman.

The last British troops pulled out in 1977. Oman gave its approval to the Camp David Arab-Israeli agreement by signing a treaty of co-operation with the USA in 1980.

Pakistan

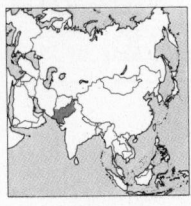

PAK
Southern Asia
310,403 sq. mi
Pop: 96 m
UN

Capital: Islamabad (pop: 201,000)
Official languages: Urdu, English
Religion: Moslem (96 per cent)
System of govt: Islamic federal republic since 29 February 1956

The Indus valley provided shelter for one of the oldest civilisations of humanity. The Indus civilisation appeared in the 3rd millenium BC and was succeeded in the second millenium BC by several civilisations, particularly the one known from one of its principle sites as Harappa.

Nomadic Indo-Europeans (Aryans) invaded the region some time after 2000 BC. Alexander the Great conquered the rich valley in 327 BC.

The Sind kingdom was conquered in 712 by the Moslems and the whole of northern India fell under their domination during the 11th and 12th centuries. The power of the Moslem sultans collapsed in 1398 after the Mongols of Tamerlane had captured Delhi. Several small kingdoms and principalities were formed from the sultanate. In 1526 Babu, a descendant of Tamerlane, founded the Moghul empire, which was able to maintain significant power until the 18th century.

The British conquest

The British East India Company was founded in 1600 and became a major power in Indian politics when the Moghul emperor gave it the right in 1765 to collect revenue in Bengal; this effectively ceded control of the region to the company and its chief employee, Robert Clive.

It was the climax of a 30-year struggle in eastern and south-eastern India between the British and French East India companies, which saw the British emerge as the unrivalled foreign power on the sub-continent.

By 1818 the British were confirmed as the paramount power in the land and in the 1840s they first set foot on the territory of present-day Pakistan in Sind and the Punjab.

The last of the Moghul emperors was deposed in 1857 after acting as the figurehead of the rebels in the Indian Mutiny against the British, which was only suppressed with difficulty. Out of the failure of the uprising there grew a determination to build bridges between India's Moslems and Hindus on the one hand and British rule and western civilisation on the other.

This determination was focused in the Aligarh movement, which, at the turn of the 20th century, urged upon Moslems a political development separate from that of Hindu-based Indian nationalism and the Indian National Congress.

In 1906, following the controversial British division of Bengal to give its Moslems a greater say, which was opposed by Hindus (and eventually rescinded in 1912), this separate Moslem movement became enshrined in the All-India Moslem League. In 1909 separate electorates for Moslems were granted within the constitutional framework being developed under British rule.

In 1940 the League, led by Mohammad Ali Jinnah demanded the foundation of Pakistan, independent states for Moslems in the east (Bengal) and west of India.

Independence and division

With India's independence in 1947, the British accepted the creation of an autonomous Moslem state. Jinnah became governor-general of the dominion of Pakistan. The drawing of the Indo-Pakistani borders led to the exodus of seven million Hindus to India and of about the same number of Moslems to Pakistan.

However, Pakistan itself was divided into two regions, separated by 1,000 miles, with East Pakistan lying to the east of India and sharing a border from Burma.

A conflict over sovereignty in the northern state of Kashmir sparked off two Indo-Pakistani conflicts in 1947 and 1965. The ceasefire agreement of 1965 maintained the status quo, Kashmir's division into one Pakistani zone and one Indian zone. The problems resulting from Pakistan's division led to the proclamation of independence in

1971 of the eastern half which took the name Bangladesh.

The war between the two Pakistans came to an end in December 1971 when the Indian army intervened and forced the East Pakistan army to capitulate. India recognised Bangladesh on 6 December 1971. Later in the month the prime minister, General Yahya Khan, resigned. He was replaced by Zulfikar Ali Bhutto, hitherto foreign affairs minister and head of the Pakistan People's Party.

A new Pakistani constitution came into force on 12 April 1973, which gave Pakistan the status of federal republic. Pakistan officially recognised the republic of Bangladesh in 1974 and the two countries renewed diplomatic ties a year later.

Bhutto was accused of rigging his party's election victory in March 1977; he admitted there had been irregularities, but they probably would not have affected the result. But unrest grew and Bhutto declared martial law in major cities. The army stepped in and Bhutto was overthrown on 4 July 1977 by a

military coup supported by conservative circles and Islamic fundamentalists. The army chief of staff, General Zia ul-Haq, became president of Pakistan in September 1978 and established a military dictatorship. The regime pursued a policy of Islamicisation; the Koran was proclaimed as being the supreme law of Pakistan on 10 February 1979.

Bhutto was executed for corruption on 4 April 1979, despite international pleas for clemency. All political activity was banned and the provisional constitution of 24 March 1981 proclaimed the supremacy of military tribunals over all other forms of jurisdiction. The Soviet invasion of Afghanistan (1979) led to a massive influx of Afghan refugees into Pakistan, but also to an increase in US aid.

A December 1984 referendum on the policy of Islamicisation enabled Zia to remain in power for five more years. The constitutional amendment which came into force on 3 March 1985, further extended his powers at the expense of the prime minister. On 24 March, as

a result of elections held the previous month (in which most opposition parties were banned), Zia's nominee Mohammad Khan Junejo was made prime minister with a vote of confidence from the new national assembly.

Martial law was lifted on 30 December 1985, and in this atmosphere of improved freedom the Pakistan People's Party, led by Bhutto's daughter Benazir, unsuccessfully contested local elections held in November 1987. On 29 May 1988 the national assembly was dissolved by Zia who announced new elections.

However, on 17 August 1988 Zia was killed – almost certainly assassinated – in an air crash, and a state of emergency was declared. Ghulam Ishaq Khan became acting president pending elections, which were held as planned on November 16. The Pakistan People's Party won the elections and Benazir Bhutto became Pakistan's first woman prime minister. Ghulam Ishaq Khan remains as president. Relations with India have improved since Benazir Bhutto came to power.

Panama

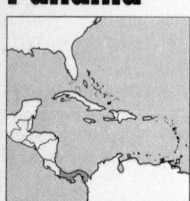

PA
Central America
29,208 sq. mi
Pop: 2.27 m
UN, OAS, LAES

Capital: Panama City (pop: 439,000)
Official language: Spanish
Religion: Catholic (93 per cent)
System of govt: Republic; independent since 3 November 1903

Traces of fishing activity, of which the oldest date back as far as c.4800 BC, have been found around the Gulf of Parita. Tombs discovered at Venado Beach prove the existence of a developed culture around 500 whose reli-

gious rituals entailed considerable human sacrifice. The cultures which coexisted from 800 to 1525 bear witness to a high level of skill in the art of ceramics and the working of gold.

The Spanish, who first set foot in Panama in 1501, found an indigenous population of Chibcha people. The first Spanish settlement, Santa Maria la Antigua (1510), was the point of departure for Vasco Nunez de Balboa in 1513, when he made the first crossing of the American isthmus. Between 1516 and 1520 the majority of the indigenous peoples were subjugated by Gaspar de Espinosa. Panama town, founded in 1519, was rebuilt on a different site in 1673 after being destroyed in 1671 by the English pirate Henry Morgan.

Panama was attached to the viceroyalty of New Grenada on its creation in 1739, and then to Gran Colombia, which became independent in 1819.

After attempts at secession, Panama became a mere Colombian province in 1886. The French failed to assure Panamanian autonomy in 1889, after Ferdinand de Lesseps had created a company charged with digging a Central American canal. In 1902 Colombia rejected a US plan to give the proposed canal special status, and Panama declared independence in a US-backed uprising of November 1903.

The new republic of Panama ratified the canal treaty proposed by the USA, and the canal zone was leased to them for an unlimited period at $250,000 dollars per month, with a $10 million advance. Work started on the canal in 1906 and it was opened in 1914.

Panama's 1904 constitution gave the USA the right of intervention in Panama, which it made use of in 1908, 1912 and 1918. Colombia did not recognise Panamanian sovereignty until 1921.

In 1936 the USA made concessions, although these did not call into question its sovereignty over the canal zone. The USA recognised Panama's sovereignty over the canal zone in 1960 and again in 1977, but this is not to come into full effect until 2000.

The military have determined the political life of Panama ever since the 1968 coup against President Arnulfo Arias, when General Torrijos came to power. He remained in office until his death in 1982. He was succeeded by Ricardo de la Espriella in 1982. Eric Arturo Delvalle took office as head of state and premier in 1985. In February 1988 he was replaced by Manuel Solis Palma after a failed attempt to remove army chief General Manuel Noriega, Panama's strongman. Internal opposition and US economic sanctions had failed to dislodge Noriega, wanted in the USA for drug trafficking, by 1989.

Papua New Guinea

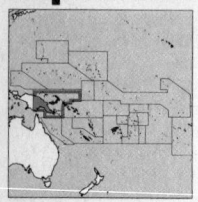

PNG
Oceania
178,259 sq. mi
Pop: 3.5 m
UN, CW

Capital: Port Moresby (pop: 145,000)
Official language: English
Religions: Christian (62 per cent), traditional beliefs (38 per cent)

System of govt: Constitutional monarchy; independent since 16 September 1975

The island of New Guinea was probably first inhabited at the same time as Australia, around 50,000 years ago. The first traces of sedentary inhabitants and agriculture date back to 7000 BC. The original population was composed of over 700 tribes of Papuans and Melanesians.

Portuguese sailors were the first Europeans to visit the island, in 1526. The highlands of New Guinea, how-

ever, were not penetrated until the 1930s. The first attempt at colonisation was carried out by the British in 1793 in West Irian (Irian Jaya). The Dutch claimed this western portion of the island in 1828.

Present-day Papua New Guinea, in the east, was explored in 1870 by the Briton John Moresby, after whom Port Moresby is named. European planters began agricultural exploitation around 1880.

In 1884 Britain annexed the southeast of the island and the Germans annexed the north eastern part in 1889.

From 1906 British New Guinea was administered by Australia, which obtained a mandate over the former German territory in 1921.

From 1942 to 1945 the Japanese partially occupied the two eastern regions, but were defeated by the US and Australia. In 1946 the regions were unified. Papua New Guinea obtained independence in 1975, with Britain's queen as head of state. Elections are held every five years. In July 1988 premier Paias Wingti was ousted by opposition leader Rabbie Namaliu, with whom he said he would cooperate.

Paraguay

PY
South America
157,047 sq. mi
Pop: 3.9 m
UN, LAIA,
OAS, LAES

Capital: Asuncion (pop: 729,000)
Official languages: Spanish, Guarani
Religion: Catholic (93 per cent)
System of govt: Republic; independent since 14 May 1811

The first human inhabitants of present-day Paraguay were the Guarani people who settled there around 8000 BC. Unlike other Andean states, Paraguay shows little trace of ancient civilisations.

Spanish were the first Europeans to reach the country, in 1525. They conquered the territory in 1535-36 and an expedition founded the capital, Asuncion, in 1537.

In 1609 Governor Hernando Arias de Saavedra, born in Asuncion, encour-aged the establishment of a Jesuit mission to evangelise the Guarani. The Jesuits set up a model state. They gathered the indigenous people into vast communities in reserves, which enjoyed great administrative and economic autonomy, while still being nominally under the authority of the Spanish governor. Thirty establishments of this kind were set up by the missionaries. Besides religious education, the Guarani learned new skills and agricultural techniques as well as developing a certain political awareness.

The Jesuit state rapidly succeeded in attaining real economic prosperity despite being exposed to continuous attacks. In 1641 an army of missionaries beat back a troop of Brazilian slave hunters who regularly carried out raids into Paraguay. Warrior tribes from the uncharted territories of Gran Chaco made frequent incursions, sometimes as far as Asuncion. Instability was further aggravated by an unceasing conflict between spiritual and temporal authorities.

In 1750 Spain ceded all her territories to the east of Uruguay to Portugal. The Jesuits, however, refused to give up their independence and opposed the two colonial powers. This led to the Guarani war in 1753, which was intended to prevent Paraguay's annexation by Brazil. The Jesuits were finally expelled in 1768. The missionary establishments were destroyed and the Guarani dispersed into the virgin territory of the forest.

In 1776 Paraguay was integrated into the Spanish vice-royalty of the River Plate, and submitted to the Spanish civil administration of Buenos Aires. When Argentina proclaimed its independence on 25 May 1810, Paraguay seceded, but was invaded by Argentine troops on 4 December. Argentina was defeated on on 19 January 1811, and was unable to oppose the proclamation of Paraguayan independence on 14 May 1811.

The dictatorship of Jose Gaspar Rodriguez de Francia from 1814 until his death in 1840 marked a period of diplomatic isolation for Paraguay.

Francia's successors turned the state into an apparatus for military dictatorship. Paraguay attempted to exploit the civil war which had broken out in Uruguay in 1862 in order to gain access to the sea. This attempt failed, and Paraguay and Bolivia remain South America's only two landlocked states. A new conflict which broke out in 1864 against Brazil, Argentina and Uruguay ended in crushing defeat for Paraguay in 1870. The population dropped from 1.1 million to 300,000 of whom only 30,000 were men. In 1932 war broke out against Bolivia over the Chaco region, which Paraguay won in 1935.

Paraguay has since been governed by dictators. General Alfredo Stroessner, supported by the USA and Brazil, governed the country from 1954. He was re-elected for an eighth five-year term of office in February 1988, in elections marred by allegations of fraud. His dictatorship had lasted for 34 years, the longest in Latin America, when on 3 February 1989, he was overthrown in a violent coup led by General Andres Rodriguez. Rodriguez, second in command of the armed forces and a former close ally of Stroessner, was sworn in immediately as interim president, announcing that there would be presidential and congressional elections on 1 May, with himself standing as official presidential candidate of the ruling Colorado Party.

Peru

PE
South America
496,222 sq. mi
Pop: 20.7 m
UN, LAIA,
OAS, LAES

Capital: Lima (pop: 5.3 m)
Official languages: Spanish, Quechua
Religion: Catholic (92 per cent)
System of govt: Republic; independent since 28 July 1821

Finds of stone tools, the first signs of human activity in Peru, date back 26,000 years BC. Agriculture and stock breeding became widespread in c.8000 BC, and the first temples appeared between 2500 BC and 1800 BC. The first developed civilisation was that of the Chavin, who worshipped cats, in c.1000 BC. Among Peru's cultures from c.200 BC, the Mochicha civilisation (c.200 BC-c.800) was a highly skilled society which constructed fortifications, temples and sophisticated irrigation systems. Sea fishing provided an abundant source of nourishment.

From c.600 the Huari-Tiahuanaco civilisation dominated other Peruvian cultures, reaching its peak around 800. It disappeared for reasons which remain uncertain, whether through natural disaster, war or religious causes.

The south of Peru, the centre of the Huari culture, remained sparsely pop-ulated until the arrival of the Incas. The unification of Peruvian cultures, which had been achieved by both the Huaris and the Chavin, disintegrated again, with a number of local cultures developing. One of them, the Chimu culture, gradually extended its influence throughout the 12th century. The Chimu empire did not form a political unit, but comprised a collection of relatively independent city states. The heart of the Chimu territory was in the desert regions to the north of Peru, with a succession of towns in the coastal oasis valleys.

The Chimu perfected the sophisticated techniques of irrigated terrace cultivation, as well as developing a remarkable network of roads.

The Inca empire

The Inca civilisation appeared on the central high plateaus of Peru, where they founded their capital, Cuzco, in the 12th century. They began their conquest of neighbouring territories at the start of the 15th century. They conquered the Chimu empire, which was too dependent on its oasis-valleys to put up any real resistance. The Inca empire was at its largest around 1530, extending along the western coast of South America, from modern Ecuador to the centre of modern Chile, taking in vast areas of modern Argentina and Bolivia. Unlike the Chimu empire, which had no central power base, the Inca empire had a rigorous, centralised structure. The Inca reigned over a population of around 12 million people speak-ing 20 languages. The history of the Inca, who did not use a writing system, is relatively well known through the oral tradition recorded by the Spanish. The Incas used *quipus*, knotted cords, for their administration; the knots were coloured, each colour representing a number.

Inca communications were particularly efficient; the Incas made use of the great Huari and Chimu roads, improving and enlarging them. A system of couriers kept the Incas informed of events in the most distant corners of their empire and enabled them to exercise control over all their subjects. The Inca owned all land farmed by serfs, and agricultural produce was distributed according to the needs of each community. If any of its members were in need because of illness or bad harvest, then, as long as they were not in debt, the means of survival and starting anew were given to them. On the other hand, the severest punishments were meted out to anyone who misused imperial goods.

The Spanish conquest

After a century of supremacy, the Inca empire was brutally smashed at its height. From bases in Panama the *conquistador* Francisco Pizarro conducted expeditions, reaching Tumbes in 1527, where he took possession of the northern coastal regions. Named governor of Peru in 1529, he did not actually seize the country until 1532, when, on 24 September, he set off at the head of an expedition into the interior, reach-ing Cajamarca, home of the Inca leader Atahualpa, on 15 November.

The empire at this time was in the throes of a civil war, in which the Spanish interfered, cunningly negotiating with both sides and exacerbating their differences. On 16 November the Spanish sent an ambassador to the mistrustful Atahualpa, reassuring him that they would recognise him as legitimate emperor. Atahualpa was betrayed and taken prisoner. Despite his agreeing to be baptised and the payment of an enormous ransom, Atuahalpa was killed by poison a few months later.

In order to crush the Inca partisans, the Spanish allied themselves to his old adversaries. When Atahualpa's half-brother, the Inca Huascar, realised the danger presented by those who had offered him the throne, he rallied the last of his troops, but his revolt was crushed.

Fighting soon broke out among the conquistadors and Pizarro was killed in 1541. The first Spanish viceroy, appointed in 1544, promulgated a law limiting the ownership of conquered land. The colonists, under Pizarro's son, rose up against the viceroy and conquered the whole of western South America and Panama, but were defeated in 1548. Peru was pacified in 1572, after the defeat of the last Incas who had taken refuge in the mountains of Vilcabamba.

Peru remained a Spanish vice-royalty in 1821, its gold providing a major contribution to the financing of Spanish enterprises. Reduced to slavery, hundreds of thousands of indigenous people died in the mines in the mountains and the aboriginal culture was systematically destroyed.

Independence

The struggle for independence spread from other Latin American countries. Jose de San Martin entered Peru at the head of Argentine and Chilean troops in 1820, and proclaimed independence in 1821. Simon Bolivar crushed the Spanish at Ayacucho in 1824. Peru was annexed to Bolivia from 1836-39 and thereafter Spain did not recognise independence until after several attempts at reconquest (1862-66).

In 1879 a war over the Atacama desert nitrate deposits broke out with Chile and Bolivia, which annexed several areas in 1883.

The dictatorship set up by Augusto Leguia y Salcedo in 1908 lasted, with a few interruptions, until 1930, when it was ended by a military coup. The military took power again three years after the 1945 elections. After a further coup in 1968, the return to democracy was begun in 1978.

President Alan Garcia, who has been in power since 28 July 1985, faced a threat from the Maoist terrorist group known as *Sendero Luminoso* (Shining Path), and from the army, although his social democratic government's main problem was the economic crisis. An emergency economic programme was set up, comprising a twofold rise in the minimum wage, a freeze in the price of essential commodities, and an 18 per cent rise in the average salary. Peru refused to apply policies recommended by the IMF and has decided to pay off only ten per cent of the interest on its foreign debts a year.

However, despite some expansion in 1986 and 1987, President Garcia was forced in 1988 to implement new austerity programmes. In November 1988 inflation was running at over 1,100 per cent. In the same month, a nationwide wave of strikes forced the government to revoke a controversial decree limiting salaries. A state of emergency against the Shining Path guerrillas continued in force, with the armed forces on a war footing.

Philippines

RP
South East Asia
115,831 sq. mi
Pop: 57.35 m
UN, ASEAN

Capital: Manila (pop: 1.63 m)
Official language: Tagalog (Pilipino)
Religion: Catholic (83 per cent), Protestant (9 per cent), Moslem (5 per cent)
System of govt: Republic; independent since 4 July 1946

In c.1000 BC the Philippines, a group of over 7,000 islands, were gradually peopled by southern Asiatic populations. These Malayo-Polynesian immigrants pushed the original Negrito inhabitants into the interior. The new tribes had hardly any contact with each other, nor were they ever assembled in a single culture. The islands remained isolated from mainland Asia, although Chinese traders had established bases there since the first millenium BC. Contact with the Malay peninsula took place later, but neither Buddhism nor Hinduism made inroads into the Philippines.

Most of the islands' inhabitants were still nomadic hunter-gatherers until the arrival of Moslems from Brunei, who began the spread of Islam in the 15th century. Two sultanates appeared in the middle of the 16th century.

This evolution was interrupted by the arrival of the Europeans. The Portuguese navigator, Fernao de Magalhaes, landed in the Philippines in 1521 and took possession of them in the name of Spain. They were later named after King Philip II. The first permanent Spanish settlement was founded at Cebu in 1565.

Manila, on the island of Luzon, was founded in 1571. By 1600 the Spanish controlled most of Luzon and the north of the island of Mindanao. The mountainous regions, with their difficult terrain, long remained unconquered.

Spanish domination was contested by several other maritime powers; a Dutch fleet was defeated at Corregidor in 1646 and Britain occupied the Philippines from 1762-64. An important commercial centre between Europe and the Americas, the Philippines were controlled by the Spanish for a long time, with galleons still sailing regularly from Spain to Acapulco via the islands in 1811.

The Spanish monopoly gradually disappeared and foreign merchants were able to trade freely in Manila in the 1830s. New life was breathed into the Philippines' commercial activity with the opening of the Suez Canal in 1869. Filipino nationalist movements began to appear in the late 19th century, and uprisings broke out in 1872 and 1896.

When the Spanish-US war broke out in 1898, the Philippines sided with the USA, having received assurances that they would become independent. But independence hopes were dashed when Spain ceded the islands to the United States in the 1898 Treaty of Paris. A guerrilla resistance movement led by Emilio Aguinaldo was defeated in 1901.

A Philippine parliament was elected in 1902, its powers being extended in 1916. Autonomy was granted in 1934 and independence promised for 1946. Manuel Quezon became president of the autonomous Philippines in 1935.

Occupied by the Japanese in 1941, the Philippines were reconquered by US forces in May 1945. Independence was gained in 1946. The treaty signed in 1947, which guaranteed military bases to the USA for 99 years, was modified in 1959 and limited to 25 years but subsequently extended. In 1950 guerrilla warfare, corruption and a disastrous economic situation forced the Philippine government to return full responsibility for economic affairs to the USA. Extensive reforms were set in motion.

Ferdinand Marcos was elected president in 1965, afterwhich he and his wife, Imelda, instituted a particularly corrupt and brutal dictatorship.

Benigno Aquino, the main opposition leader, was assassinated on his return from exile in August 1983. Marcos' claim that he had won patently fraudulent elections in February 1986 triggered an uprising which brought Aquino's widow, Corazon, to power.

Marcos, who was himself implicated in Aquino's death, was forced to flee the Philippines on 25 February 1986. He and his wife Imelda, exiled in Hawaii, later faced charges in the USA of illegal business deals involving billions of pounds of Filipino state money siphoned off into their private fortune.

On 2 February 1987 a new constitution was approved, restoring a strong presidency together with a two-house congress, but Corazon (Cory) Aquino faces a still unstable political situation, with opposition from right-wing army elements and leftwing guerrillas. An aid and military deal with the USA was signed in October 1988.

Poland

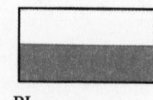

PL
Eastern Europe
120,727 sq. mi
Pop: 37.7 m
UN, COMECON, WP

Capital: Warsaw (pop: 1.65 m)
Official language: Polish
Religion: Catholic (95 per cent)
System of govt: People's republic since 22 July 1952

Poland is one of the most ancient of Europe's nation-states. Slav tribes began to settle on the territory of modern Poland in the ninth century BC, and an aristocracy emerged from the seventh century. The first historical Polish sovereign, Mieszko I of the Piast dynasty, ruled from 960-92. Mieszko was converted to Christianity and extended his kingdom to include Pomerania and Slav tribes on the Elbe and in Silesia. In 1018 Boleslaw I the Brave annexed Lusatia, Moravia, Slovakia and parts of Bohemia. In 1025 he became the first king of Poland.

The kingdom was partly devastated by invading Tartars in 1241. German colonisation of western lands reached a peak between 1200 and 1400. The Teutonic Knights established a state based at Torun, but were beaten in 1331, although they gained Pomerania. Jagiello, the grand duke of Lithuania, married Queen Jadwiga of Poland in 1384 and became King Wladyslaw II of a powerful Polish-Lithuanian state. The Teutonic Knights were defeated at Tannenberg in 1410 and again in 1466, giving Poland access to the Baltic. In 1525 the Teutonic state was put under Polish sovereignty as the duchy of Prussia and Kurland and Livonia were annexed in 1561.

The male Jagiello line died out in 1572, whereafter the Polish monarch was elected by the aristocracy. Other European powers interfered in successive elections and Poland, together with its monarchy, grew progressively weaker. In the 17th century Poland was often under attack from Sweden and Russia in particular.

Until the 18th century Poland's independence was secure, however. But it has no natural, defensible frontiers, and when Frederick the Great began to shape the power of Prussia and Catherine the Great set Russia on the path of aggrandisement, Poland's fate was sealed. Four times in the past 200 years the country has been partitioned between Germany and Russia, most recently in 1939 after the pact between Hitler and Stalin.

Modern Poland

Only twice in those two centuries has Poland achieved its independence: in 1807-14, when Napoleon briefly neutralised Russia and Prussia; and after 1918, when Germany had been defeated in war and Russia was in the throes of revolution.

The first president of Poland was the pianist-politician Ignac Paderewski, who led the new republic briefly and then the war-hero Marshal Joszef Pilsudski dominated Polish politics until his death in 1935.

After the Soviet-German occupation in 1939, the Poles set up a government-in-exile, first in Paris and then in London, under General Wladyslaw Sikorski. Poles abroad, and those who escaped from Poland, joined a Polish brigade, raised by the British. The exiled government also organised an underground resistance – the Home Army – in Poland itself.

German arrests and deportations in western Poland had been matched by the USSR in eastern Poland, with the systematic deportation of politicians, professors, teachers, writers, intellectuals, military officers – all, in fact, who could be thought of as natural leaders.

Because of Moscow's desperate situation after the Nazi attack on the USSR, and because Britain at that time was the only country able to provide military aid, the British were able to pressure Moscow into releasing the many thousands of deported Poles. A great many left the USSR and joined the army in exile; but, equally, many were missing and unaccounted for.

The explanation, or part of it, was provided when the German army in the USSR stumbled on a mass grave in the forest of Katyn. The Germans offered to allow an independent Red Cross investigation and invited other independent observers. In support of

their charge that the massacre had been carried out by officers of the Soviet secret police, the Germans produced documents found on the bodies. These, allegedly, demonstrated that the killings must have taken place in 1940 – that is, before the Germans invaded.

For its part, Moscow not only denied the charges, but claimed the affair had somehow been cooked up by the Germans in connivance with the exiled Poles. At all events, Stalin broke off relations with the Poles in London and soon afterwards a different set of Poles, claiming to represent Poles at home, appeared in Moscow.

After General Sikorski died in a still unexplained air crash in 1943 the Polish leadership was divided and often at odds, particularly in formulating policy towards the USSR. In these circumstances, the Home Army staged an uprising against the Germans in 1944 when Soviet troops appeared on the Vistula at the gates of Warsaw. For weeks, while the Poles battled with the Germans, the Russians remained immobile.

At this stage the Moscow Poles appeared, to form a provisional government at Lublin. The London Poles were invited to join. A few, after much hesitation, accepted the invitation, though trust was noticeably lacking. Soviet occupying authorities issued an invitation to representatives of the Polish underground to meet Soviet officers under guarantee of safety. When the Poles accepted they were arrested, taken to Moscow, put on trial and executed. However, at least one survived and reached the west several years later to tell his story.

Poland was not treated with quite

the repression that marked Moscow's intervention in, say, Romania. A great deal of rebuilding was undertaken, in devastated Warsaw especially, and an attempt was made to reach an understanding with the catholic church. The USSR recognised Poland as its most difficult problem in asserting its hegemony in Eastern Europe and they responded to repeated Polish expressions of defiance with a caution lacking in their treatment of the other satellites.

In 1956, while Soviet tanks were sent into Hungary, the Poles were allowed to deal with the Poznan bread riots, although a Polish general with a Soviet career background was put in command of the Polish armed forces. Further unrest in 1970 led to the removal of Wladyslaw Gomulka, the leader who had taken over after 1956.

In 1980 Gomulka's successor, Eduard Gierek, was removed after the strikes in the Gdansk shipyards led to the formation of an independent trade union body, Solidarity.

The election of a Polish pope in 1978 played its part in raising Polish spirits and encouraged them, once again, to challenge the communist domination of society. But the organisers of Solidarity took care to avoid provoking the USSR. There was no challenge to the USSR relationship, and as far as possible civic disorder was avoided – until the declaration of martial law in December 1981 and the banning of Solidarity by the country's new leader, General Wojciech Jaruzelski. The authorities broke up Solidarity demonstrations, and the murder by secret policemen of the popular opposition priest Father Popieluszko in October 1984 fanned Solidarity support.

Central to the government's problems was the dire state of the economy. In the 1970s Poland had attempted to borrow itself out of trouble with loans from the west. When these became too much of a burden and no more were available, the underlying causes of economic failure – inefficiency, lack of workforce motivation, market distortion by subsidies – had to be faced. When the government tried to remove subsidies, workers went on strike. The population as a whole refused to cooperate in austerity measures for as long as Solidarity remained banned and repression continued.

Seven and a half years after the declaration of martial law, Jaruzelski's men were sitting round the table with Solidarity representatives and planning to hold elections in which Solidarity candidates would be allowed to stand for a third of seats in the Polish lower house and all seats in the Polish Senate. Jaruzelski publicly acknowledged that his "path to reform", as he called it, "was made possible largely by the change in the leadership in Moscow".

In June 1989 Solidarity roundly humiliated the communists in the elections, winning all but a tiny handful of seats open to them. US President Bush praised reform efforts on a visit in early July 1989, but offered less financial aid than Poland expected. In a separate move, Jaruzelski, admitting his unpopularity, announced in early July that he would not stand in the election of an executive president on 19 July. However, he was persuaded to change his mind in the interests of stability. With Solidarity voting against him or abstaining, the reformed Polish parliament voted Jaruzelski in – by a single vote.

Portugal

P
Western Europe
35,553 sq. mi
Pop: 10.3 m
UN, EFTA, EC, NATO, OECD

Capital: Lisbon (pop: 827,000)
Official language: Portuguese
Religion: Catholic (97 per cent)
System of govt: Republic since 1910

Present-day Portugal has been inhabited since the Neolithic era. Relations with the Mediterranean cultures began around 500 BC and Phoenician, Carthaginian and Greek merchants frequented the Portuguese coast.

Roman conquest began in 154 BC. In the south the Lusitanians, a Celtic tribe, put up fierce resistance to the Roman legions until the assassination of their chief, Viriathus, in 139 BC. The peoples

of Portugal were not completely subdued until the reign of Augustus, when their territories were formed into the province of Lusitania.

In 406 the Germanic tribes crossed the Roman Rhine frontier, and the tribe of the Suevi passed through Gaul into Portugal where they founded a kingdom. The Visigoths, who had founded a kingdom in Spain, conquered the Suevi territories in 469. When the Iberian peninsula fell under Moslem domination Portugal became part of the emirate of Cordoba. In the extreme northwest of the Iberian peninsula a number of Christian kingdoms (Asturia, Leon) managed to hold their own and became the point of departure for the Reconquista, the reconquest of the peninsula from the Moors.

King Alfonso VI of Castile and Leon gave Portugal to his son-in-law, Henry of Burgundy, in 1095. Portugal was again occupied by the Moors in the late 12th century, but was gradually reconquered in the 13th, becoming at the same time increasingly independent

of Castilian sovereignty.

In 1297 King Denis I (1279-1325) secured a treaty with the kingdom of Castile recognising Portuguese possession of the Algarve. Portugal's economy and culture flourished under King Denis. The first Portuguese university was founded in Lisbon in 1290, and the construction of a large fleet quickly extended Portugal's trade. In 1385 the house of Burgundy was supplanted on the throne by the related house of Avis after many years of fighting.

John I (1385-1433) reinforced Portugal's merchant fleet while Lisbon became one of the most important centres of trade in Europe. The capture of the rich Moroccan trading town of Ceuta (1415) opened the gates to the African continent. Henry the Navigator, son of John I, organised systematic reconnaissance expeditions, and his maritime policies were continued by John II (1481-95) whose main aim was to find a sea route to India. It was three years after his death before it was discovered by Vasco de Gama. More

and more colonies were gained: Goa, Malacca, Macao, Brazil, Mozambique, Angola. Riches poured into Portugal; but this fortune was not used to develop the Portuguese economy. On the contrary, the creation and development of a craft industry were prevented and Portugal, like Spain, neglected to lay the foundations for a flourishing economy, preferring short-term gain.

The last king of the Avis dynasty, Henry, died in 1580. King Philip II of Spain proceeded to annexe Portugal, which was governed by the Spanish kings until 1640, when growing Portuguese demands for independence led to the establishment of the Braganza dynasty, in the person of John IV. Spain finally recognised Portugal's independence in 1688.

The 1703 Methuen trade treaty with Britain boosted Portugal's wine industry, and the country regained great economic prosperity under the reign of John V (1707-50).

In 1822 John VI was forced by the Portuguese parliament to accept a constitution. Parliament remained under the strict control of the monarchy, however, and the Republican Party grew rapidly from 1870 onwards. In 1910 the monarchy was overthrown and a republic proclaimed.

Portugal's political and economic situation remained unstable until the dictator, Antonio Salazar de Oliveira, arrived in power in 1928. He died in 1970

and his successor, Marcelo Caetano, was ousted in a coup in April 1974. General Spinola, Portugal's new leader, was forced out by a growing democracy movement in September 1974 and staged a failed coup in March 1975. In April 1975 Mario Soares' Socialist Party won Portugal's first free elections for nearly half a century, and a new constitution was adopted in 1976.

Meanwhile, after the overthrow of the dictatorship in 1974, Portugal had rapidly wound up what remained of its old overseas empire: Guinea-Bissau (September 1974), Mozambique (June 1975), Cape Verde Islands (July 1975), Angola (November 1975). East Timor was invaded by Indonesia in December 1975. Portugal has agreed to hand Macao back to China in 1999.

The defeat of the socialists in October 1985 led to the formation of a minority social democratic government headed by Anibal Cavaco Silva. An agreement to join the EC was signed on 12 June 1985. On 19 July 1987 Cavaco Silva's government was re-elected with a substantial majority.

In August 1988 a blaze destroyed much of the historic centre of Lisbon.

Qatar

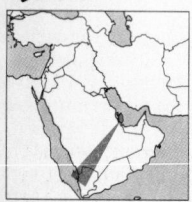
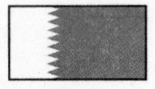

Q
Near East
4,247 sq. mi
Pop: 315,000
UN, AL, GCC, OPEC

Capital: Doha (pop: 229,000)
Official language: Arabic
Religion: Moslem (95 per cent)
System of govt: Monarchy (emirate);

independent since 1 September 1971

After being the prize in a centuries-long struggle between the Persians and the Arabs, Qatar's independent history begins in the 18th century when the al-Thani family emigrated from Arabia to settle on the Qatar peninsula.

The British controlled the coastal areas of the Persian Gulf from the mid-19th century, and supported the rise to power of the al-Thani, who undertook not to allow any other powers to instal themselves in Qatar.

In 1868 Britain and Qatar signed

treaties of a protectorate, which were renewed in 1916.

When Britain announced its intention of pulling out of the Persian Gulf in 1968, it conducted negotiations aimed at the formation of an independent federation of Arab emirates. Qatar, however, preferred to go it alone, and gained independence on 1 September 1971. In power since 1970, Sheik Khalifa bin Hamad al-Thani became prime minister of independent Qatar and ratified a new treaty of co-operation with Britain two days later. Qatar was admitted to the Arab League and the UN.

On 22 February 1972 the Emir Ahmad bin Ali al-Thani was overthrown in a coup by Sheik Khalifa, his cousin, who enjoyed the support of the royal family. The new emir pursued a policy of modernisation and, in 1974, took control of oil companies established in Qatar. Wealth from oil and natural gas (exploited since 1949) has encouraged the arrival in Qatar of a large foreign workforce, in particular from Iran and Pakistan, which now represents 80 per cent of Qatar's population. In August 1988 drilling began off Qatar in possibly the world's largest natural gas field.

Romania

RO
South East Europe
237,500 km2
Pop: 23 mill.
UN, COMECON, WP

Capital: Bucharest (pop: 1.57 mill.)
Official language: Romanian
Religion: Romanian Orthodox (80 per cent)
System of govt: People's republic since 30 December 1947

In the 40 years since the end of the Second World War, Romania under its communist leaders has been seen in the west first as a repellent, almost sadistically repressive, political dictatorship, then as relatively enlightened and determined to demonstrate its independence of Moscow, and latterly as an odious family tyranny denounced even by its (still just) communist neighbour, Hungary, and viewed with misgivings by the Soviet leader, Mikhail Gorbachev.

The Romanians are exceptional in south-eastern Europe in speaking a language descended from Latin. But it may be questioned whether they can claim to be a distinct nation, after 2,000 years of being overrun by Thracians, Cimmerians, Scythians, Sarmatians, Celts, Romans, Goths, Huns, Slavs, Magyars, Saxons and Turks.

What cannot be doubted is the distinction bestowed on the Romanians

by their Latin language in a part of Europe dominated by Slav and Magyar tongues. This, perhaps, helps to explain why in the midst of so many racial strains, and having only a short history as a nation-state, Romanians, even communist ones, can be somewhat xenophobic.

The land that is now Romania was annexed to the Roman empire at the time of the Emperor Trajan in 106 as the province of Dacia. In 271 the Romans abandoned Dacia to the invading Goths, who stayed for two centuries until displaced by Huns.

The Avars invaded in the sixth century and maintained their domination for two centuries. At the same time, during the sixth and seventh centuries, the Slavs arrived the region.

From the tenth to the 13th centuries modern Romania was divided into a number of principalities. Transylvania was invaded by Magyars (Hungarians) in the tenth and 11th centuries, then became home to Saxons who had been recruited by the Magyars. A number of autonomous principalities appeared in the 14th century, including Wallachia (1310) and Moldavia (1353).

Transylvania was conquered by the Ottoman Turks in 1541, but retained a degree of autonomy. Wallachia and Moldavia were not occupied, but were obliged to pay tribute to the Ottomans. Resistance to Ottoman rule was put up by the Wallachian princes Mircea the Great (1386-1418) and Vlad Dracul or Dracula (c.1460-76), known, from his preferred method of dealing with prisoners, as The Impaler. The Moldavian

prince, Stephen the Great (1457-1504) also put up a fight and in 1598 Wallachia's Prince Michael the Brave expelled the Ottomans completely.

Wallachia annexed Transylvania in 1599 and Moldavia in 1600. The Habsburgs attempted to impose sovereignty, and the three united principalities turned to the Ottomans.

Transylvania finally fell under the domination of the Austrian Habsburgs in 1691. In 1774 the Russians, in a treaty with the Turks, gained spiritual protectorship over the Orthodox Christians in Wallachia and Moldavia. Russia eventually occupied the principalities (1828-36) but handed them back to the Ottomans after the Russian defeat in the Crimean War (1856). A Romanian uprising in 1848 had been crushed by the combined might of the three dominant powers, Austria, Russia and the Ottomans.

In 1858 the main interested powers, including Britain and France, signed the Treaty of Paris at the end of talks to decide the future of the two principalities, nominally under Turkish rule. The treaty provided for elections of separate princes and parliaments in each country, but for joint bodies to deal with finance, law and the armed forces.

In 1859 the two parliaments chose a single candidate for their thrones, Alexander Cuza.

In December 1861 Alexander Cuza united Moldavia and Wallachia under the name Romania, and declared independence in 1877, which was recognised by the 1878 Congress of Berlin.

Romania fought a Balkan war to gain

territory and joined the First World War for the same reason. In the peace settlement it was awarded Transylvania with its largely Romanian-speaking population. Hungary was to seize the territory in the Second World War, with Romania securing its return afterwards.

Politics in the interwar years were for the most part a tale of violence, corruption and assassination. The 1930s saw the growth of the fascist Iron Guard, led by premier Ion Antonescu, who overthrew King Carol II and installed Carol's son, Michael, as a facade for his dictatorship.

Antonescu took Romania into the Second World War alongside Nazi Germany, and was executed when the communists came to power.

There were few communists in Romania; most estimates put the membership at 2,000 at the end of the war. But in the early years Soviet troops were there to ensure the transition to a socialist republic. Banking and such industry as existed were nationalised, the land collectivised and opposition parties suppressed.

The first communist leaders, Ana Pauker and Vasile Luca, were Soviet-trained and, judging from their names, probably not even Romanian. Gheorghe Gheorghiu-Dej came out on top after a series of purges.

This was the beginning of the "Romanian way" – an assertion of independence from Moscow, and it continued under Gheorghiu-Dej's successor, Nicolae Ceausescu. Close ties with China and Yugoslavia were established at a time when Moscow was quarrelling bitterly with these two countries. Next, friendly relations were established with Western Europe, the USA and even Israel. Romania refused to take part in the Soviet-led invasion of Czechoslovakia to crush the liberal movement (the Prague Spring) of 1968.

More recently, Romania's reputation has plummeted as Ceausescu's megalomania has invaded almost all walks of Romanian life: gigantic palaces were ordered in Bucharest and gargantuan agro-industrial complexes in the countryside, at a time when lighting and heating, even in Bucharest, were scarce.

By 1989 one third of the historic centre of Bucharest had been destroyed to make way for Ceausescu's Roman empire-inspired apartment blocks for the party elite and a presidential palace for himself. The inhabitants of 8,000 villages were due to be relocated in the grim agro-industrial complexes and their villages razed. Mercifully, Romania's poverty has meant that so far only a handful of villages, mainly near Bucharest, have suffered this fate.

The fact that many villagers scheduled for uprooting, especially in Transylvania, are Hungarian-speakers has brought angry protests from the Hungarian government, which, with other countries, has accused the Romanians of cultural genocide. Refugee centres in Hungary have been set up to deal with the hundreds of ethnic Hungarians fleeing from Romania every year. Early in 1989 the Romanians began to erect barbed wire fencing and machine-gun posts along its border with Hungary, but they were later removed after vigorous protest from Budapest.

Romania's ethnic Saxon (German) community also lives in earmarked villages, mainly in eastern Romania. West Germany has agreed to take in many of these people, a move which prompted Ceausescu to say that Romania's main exports are "oil and Germans".

Ceausescu has further isolated himself from his people by appointing members of his family to key positions. In mid 1989 Romania succeeded in paying off all its foreign debt, an achievement attained principally by exporting almost any product that can be sold. As a result shortages of even basic commodities are frequently chronic.

Romanian industry is hampered by central control so excessive that production targets of state companies have to be personally approved by Ceausescu himself.

Rwanda

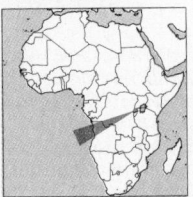

RWA
East Africa
26,338 km2
Pop: 6.4 mill.
UN, OAU

Capital: Kigali (pop: 156,000)
Official languages: French, Kinyarwanda
Religions: Catholic (56 per cent), traditional beliefs (23 per cent), protestant (12 per cent), Moslem (9 per cent)
System of govt: Republic; independent since 1 July 1962

Present-day Rwanda (or Ruanda) has been densely settled by farming people for millenia, but its history is conventially traced from the appearance of the Banyiginya dynasty in the 14th century. Their state, larger than modern Rwanda, was divided into districts, each one governed by a representative from each of the two main ethnic groups, the Hutu and the Tutsi. A Hutu was responsible for the land and a Tutsi for the cattle. Hutu agriculturalists are to this day the dominant class.

Rwanda came under German rule in 1899. After the First World War, in 1919, Belgium obtained a League of Nations mandate over Ruanda-Urundi. The king's authority over the chieftains gradually disappeared, King Mutsinga being deposed in 1931 and replaced by his son, Mutara III. The 1952 elections ended to the Tutsi's advantage and they then removed the Hutu from key posts. The Hutu seized power on King Mutara's death in 1959, and the Tutsi elite had to flee. Rwanda-Urundi split from the Belgian Congo in 1960 and became two independent republics, Rwanda and Burundi, on 1 July 1961. Anti-Tutsi reaction continued until a coup by General Juvenal Abyarimana in July 1973.

A new constitution was adopted by referendum on 17 December 1978 and Abyarimana was elected president on 24 December. He has pursued policies of national reconciliation and international non-alignment. He was re-elected in 1983 and again in December 1988.

Saharawi Democratic Republic (Western Sahara)

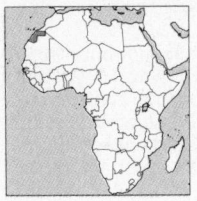

DARS
North Africa
266,000 km2
Pop: 181,000
OAU

Capital: El Aaiun
Official language: Arabic
Religion: Moslem (99 per cent)

System of govt: Republic, proclaimed 27 February 1976

Western Sahara has been inhabited by people since prehistoric times. From the fourth century BC the Phoenicians established trading posts on the coasts. The Romans also came into contact with the Saharan peoples. In the middle ages the country was conquered by the Berbers, who were subjugated in 640 by Moslem Arabs. In 1346 the Portuguese landed on the coasts. Then Western Sahara became a Spanish protectorate in 1884.

When Spain decided to pull out in 1974, Mauritania and Morocco planned to share the former Spanish Sahara. However, they encountered resistance from the Polisario Front which was created in May 1973 and supported by Algeria. In November 1975 Morocco annexed the phosphate-rich Saguia El Hamra region. The Polisario Front declared the independence of the Sahara in February 1976 and conducted a war of liberation against Mauritania and Morocco.

The UN and OAU recognised Saharan independence. After a number of Moroccan and French interventions, a peace accord was signed with Mauritania in August 1979. Morocco reacted with a counter offensive and the construction of a 1100km long wall.

On 31 August 1984 Morocco reached an accord with Libya which deprived the Polisario Front of an important source of support. The OAU invited Polisario to the November 1984 OAU conference in Ethiopia. Morocco left the OAU in protest at this move.

Saint Kitts and Nevis

Caribbean
267 km2
Pop: 47,000
UN, CW, CARICOM

Capital: Basseterre (pop: 15,000)
Official language: English
Religions: Catholic, protestant
System of govt: Constitutional monarchy; independent 19 September 1983.

Saint Kitts (or Saint Christopher) was visited by Europeans for the first time, along with neighbouring Nevis in the Lesser Antilles, when Columbus landed in 1493.

English colonists settled on St Kitts from 1623, and the island constituted the first lasting colonial settlement in the West Indies.

The French arrived two years later and the island was divided between the two powers. Plantations of sugar cane and cotton were the main economic activity on St Kitts and on Nevis, where a colony had also been successfully established in 1628.

France recognised British rule over both islands under the 1783 Treaty of Versailles.

In 1882 the island of Anguilla was annexed and administratively attached to Saint Kitts and Nevis. From 27 February 1967 the three islands formed an independent state associated with Britain and remained within the Commonwealth. Considering themselves to have been wronged by the agreement, the population of Anguilla proclaimed independence in May 1967.

Britain intervened on the island in 1969, re-establishing its sovereignty in 1971. In 1976 Anguilla obtained an autonomous constitution but remained integrated with Saint Kitts and Nevis, before dissociating itself again in 1980, remaining dependent on Britain since then. Saint Kitts and Nevis acceded to independence on 19 September 1983, and was then admitted to the UN. Queen Elizabeth II remains the islands' head of state. Since 1980 the prime minister has been Kennedy Alphonse Simmonds.

Saint Lucia

Saint Lucia

WL
Caribbean
616 km2
Pop: 138,000
UN, OAS, CW,
CARICOM

Capital: Castries (pop: 52,000)
Official language: English
Religions: Catholic (90 per cent),
protestant (10 per cent)
System of govt: Constitutional
monarchy; independent since 22

February 1979.

The island of Saint Lucia is one of the Lesser Antilles, to the south of Martinique. It was discovered, probably on Saint Lucia's Day (18 June), in 1502 by Christopher Columbus on his fourth voyage to the New World.

The two attempts made by English colonists to settle on the island in 1605 and 1638 both failed in the face of fear of the indigenous population, who believed that the white men were gifts from the gods and worthy of consumption in cannibalistic rituals.

The French succeeded in settling on the island in 1650. During the vari-ous Anglo-French wars of the 18th and early 19th centuries the island changed hands a number of times, falling definitively under British sovereignty in 1814 after Napoleon's defeat.

French influence, however, is still marked, the majority of the population being catholic, and French was for a long time the most commonly spoken language.

The British developed large single-crop plantations of banana, sugar cane, citrus fruit and cocoa, for which they imported large numbers of black slave workers from West Africa. One consequence of the influx of slaves is that the majority of the island's present-day population is black or of mixed race.

In 1967 the colony obtained internal autonomy, with Britain retaining control of foreign policy and defence. Saint Lucia's independence within the Commonwealth was gained on 22 February 1979, and the island was admitted to the UN shortly afterwards.

Since May 1982 John Compton has been the island's head of government. The island was involved in a row with other Caribbean Community members in July 1988 when it, and some other states, could not agree on suspending Haiti's observer status within the community. Saint Lucia lives mainly from agriculture and tourism.

Saint Vincent and the Grenadines

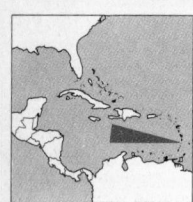

WV
Caribbean
389 km2
Pop: 112,000
UN, OAS,
CARICOM, CW

Capital: Kingstown (pop: 33,600)
Official language: English
Religions: Protestant (77 per cent),
catholic (19 per cent)

System of govt: Constitutional monarchy; independent since 27 October 1979.

The island of Saint Vincent was discovered in 1493 by Christopher Columbus. Several British, French and Dutch attempts at colonisation failed in the face of resistance by the indigenous Caribbean population. It was not until 1763 that the British were able to establish a permanent settlement.

The French recognised British rule over the island in the 1783 Treaty of Versailles, but in 1795 the French lent their support to an indigenous uprising which the British managed to suppress. The Caribbean population was deported to Islas de la Bahia off Honduras. In 1817 a new uprising led to another deportation, this time to Roatan.

The abolition of slavery in 1834 severely affected the island's economy, dependent as it was on plantations of banana and coconut worked by slaves. From 1846 Portuguese colonists came in to replace the slave work force, followed by Indians after 1861.

In 1969 Saint Vincent obtained the status of state associated to Britain, then on 27 October 1979 became independent within the Commonwealth.

Saint Vincent is volcanic with the volcano of La Soufriere in the north of the main island. Its eruption in 1902 killed 2,000 people, and the eruption in 1978 destroyed all the banana plantations. Saint Vincent comprises the island of Saint Vincent itself, along with some of the Grenadine islands in the Lesser Antilles. Since 1984 the prime minister has been James Mitchell of the New Democratic Party (NDP), which defeated Robert Milton's Labour Party in the elections of July 1984.

Samoa (Western)

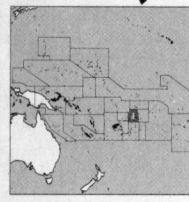

WS
Oceania
2831 km2
Pop: 163,000
UN, CW

Capital: Apia (pop: 33,000)
Official languages: Samoan, English
Religions: Protestant (75 per cent),
catholic (23 per cent)

System of govt: Constitutional monarchy; independent since 1 January 1962.

The Polynesian people of the Samoan islands are of ancient origin. The first European to visit was a Dutchman, in 1772. Visited by Bougainville in 1768, the Samoas were converted to Christianity by the London Missionary Society from 1830. US, British and German traders were interested in the islands as a port of call on the Pacific route to China. In 1889 the USA established a naval base at Pago Pago. The islands were administered jointly by the three powers, but continual conflicts led to their partition in 1898. The USA obtained the eastern Samoas, and the islands to the west went to Germany. Britain received Tonga and part of the Solomon islands in compensation.

Eastern Samoa is still under US rule today. The German islands, occupied by New Zealand in 1914, were placed under New Zealand mandate by the League of Nations in 1920 and in 1947 came under UN trusteeship. Western Samoa, which comprises two main islands, Savai'i and Upolu, obtained independence on 1 January 1962, becoming a member of the Commonwealth in 1970 and of the UN in 1976. Under the 1962 constitution the state remains based on the highly hierarchical tribal structure of the Polynesian population. When Malietoa Tanumafili II, the last of the two elected chiefs, dies, his successor will be elected for a duration of five years by a parliament representing village chiefs. Many Western Samoans seek work in the US Samoas, where the standard of living is much higher. The main exports are copra and cocoa, with fishing also making a considerable contribution to the economy.

San Marino

RSM
Southern Europe
24.1 sq. mi
Pop: 22,000

Capital: San Marino (pop: 4,500)

Official language: Italian
Religion: Catholic
System of govt: Republic since 1569 constitution

According to tradition, a fourth century Christian hermit, Marinus, sought refuge on Mount Titano to the south of Rimini. The small community which had assembled grew into a secular town which had to fortify itself against Norman and Saracen attacks. San Marino was first mentioned in 755.

In the 13th century San Marino took the title of "republic" and freed itself from Vatican rule. Its borders were fixed in 1462. The 1569 constitution established a Grand Council of 60 – 20 each representing the nobility, burghers and farmers. San Marino's independence was recognised by Rome in 1549. The republic's independence was also recognised in 1797 by Bonaparte, and by the Congress of Vienna in 1815. It signed treaties of friendship with unified Italy in 1862, 1897, 1939, 1953 and 1971. San Marino remained neutral in World War II .The Italy-San Marino border is not subject to any control and most of San Marino's civil servants are Italian.

The Grand Council is elected every four years, and is presided over by two regents who govern alternately for six months. The country lives mainly from tourism.

Sao Tome and Principe

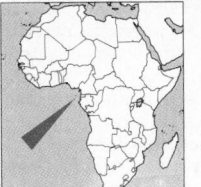

East Atlantic
387 sq. mi
Pop: 112,000
UN, OAU

Capital: Sao Tome (pop: 34,000)
Official language: Portuguese
Religions: Catholic (80 per cent), protestant
System of govt: Republic; independent since July 1975

When the island of Sao Tome, off West Africa, was first sighted by Europeans in 1471, by Joao de Santarem and Pedro Escobar, it was probably uninhabited. From 1475 it became a colony of prisoners, Jews in exile and slaves drawn from the neighbouring African coasts. Huge plantations were created, the largest of which now covers ten per cent of the island's surface.

After sugar cane production had seen considerable development in Brazil at the end of the 16th century, the island's sugar cane plantations were joined by cocoa and coffee plantations. Plantations of palm were also of importance, producing copra and palm oil.

At the beginning of the 18th century Sao Tome played an important part in the slave trade. Slaves were captured by slave hunters on the western coast of Africa, especially along the old "Slave Coast", which corresponds to the present-day states of Togo, Benin and Nigeria. On this Slave Coast the captives were purchased by European slaving merchants and taken to the island of Sao Tome, from where escape was virtually impossible.

The abolition of slavery put an end to this human commerce in 1876. The island's economy, hitherto dependent on slave labour, adapted by increasing its coffee and cocoa plantations, which were cultivated by a smaller, paid workforce. The small number of crops produced on Sao Tome forced the island to import most essential commodities.

Uprisings against the island's Portuguese overlords occurred frequently throughout Sao Tome's colonial history and in 1953 a revolt by the plantation workers was brutally suppressed by Portuguese troops.

Sao Tome and neighbouring Principe obtained internal autonomy in 1973, and independence was granted by the socialist government of Mario Soares in July 1975, following the fall of the dictatorship in Portugal.

The country has been ruled since becoming independent from Portugal by Manuel Pinto da Costa, who nationalised the islands' plantations shortly after independence. A coup attempt in March 1988 was crushed by the army, and two of President Pinto da Costa's opponents were killed.

Saudi Arabia

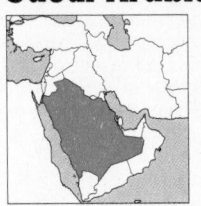

Near East
849,400 sq. mi
Pop: 11.5 m
UN, AL, GCC, OPEC

Capital: Riyadh (pop: 1.31 m)
Official language: Arabic
Religion: Moslem (99 per cent)
System of govt: Monarchy, founded in 1932

The Arabian peninsula was of relatively little world importance before the birth of Islam. It was inhabited by pagan tribes, along with some Jews and Christians, although its traders travelled as far as India and Africa.

Mohammed was born in Mecca, site of the Ka'aba stone, pagan Arabia's most holy shrine, towards the end of the sixth century. The Moslem calendar starts in the Christian year 622, the year Mohammed and a group of his followers were forced by citizens opposed to his monotheistic teachings to leave Mecca for the city of Yathrib (since known as Medina, Town of the Prophet), about 200 miles (320 kilometres) to the north. From Medina, Mohammed was able to unite the different, often rival, tribes of Arabia and weld them into a power of national proportions united by a new religion – Islam.

At his death in 632 Mohammed left behind a country unified both politically and in religion. Those who took over his mantle as leaders of Islam, the caliphs (from the Arabic for successor), subjugated the Near East and North Africa, followed in the eighth century by Spain. An Islamic conquest of western Europe was halted by the victories of Charles Martel, king of the Franks, at Poitiers and Tours in 732; however, it seems unlikely that the Arabs wanted to settle in the cold northern lands.

Central Asia was islamicised in the tenth century and Moslem domination in India started in the 11th century. The rules of Moslem society have been based, right up to the present day, on the code formulated in the Koran, the holy book of Islam.

The Saudi Arabian constitution

In the 16th century most of Arabia was subjugated by the Ottoman empire. Mohammed ibn al-Wahhad, founder of the Islamic sect of the Wahhabiyah at the beginning of the 18th century, brought about a return to the original purity of Islam and inspired the tribes of Arabia with the enthusiasm necessary for the reconquest of the interior of the Arabian peninsula.

The movement was defeated in 1818 by Mohammed Ali at the head of a force of Ottoman troops. From his base in Kuwait the Emir Abd al-Aziz ibn Sa'ud launched his attempt to reconquer the Wahhabi kingdom in 1902. He unified the central Arabian tribes and took Mecca in 1924, threatening both Syria and Iraq. During the First World War the Arabian national movement was supported against the Ottoman empire by the British, especially under Colonel T.E. Lawrence (Lawrence of Arabia). Ibn Sa'ud was proclaimed king of the Arabian regions of Nejd and Hejaz in 1926, and his kingdom was renamed Saudi Arabia in 1932.

The kingdom of Saudi Arabia

The king of Saudi Arabia was an absolute monarch. His power was hereditary and limited only by the customary rights of the tribes. Legislation was considered of relevance only in those spheres of social life which are not determined by the Koran. The country's first oil deposits were discovered in 1930 and drilling was begun in 1933 by Standard Oil of California. From 1935 onwards the concession produced regular yields.

Shortly before his death Ibn Sa'ud instituted a council of ministers composed of members of the royal family. He was succeeded by his son Sa'ud ibn Abd al-Aziz. In 1958 the decline of the economy, ever more linked to the USA, caused Sa'ud to stand down in favour of his brother Feisal, prime minister and former viceroy of Hejaz. More open to western ways, Feisal undertook the building of the kingdom's first schools and hospitals and embraced austerity with deflationary policies.

These policies, together with the opposition provoked by the continuing conflict with Colonel Nasser's Egypt, led to King Feisal's overthrow in 1960. Called back to power following the overthrow of his successor King Sa'ud on 2 November 1964, Feisal pledged economic support to a number of Arab states following the June 1967 war with Israel.

The conflict with Nasser, ostensibly over North Yemen but really a struggle for the role of leader of the Arab world, was settled at the Khartoum Conference on 1 September 1967. In June 1968 Saudi Arabia, Libya and Kuwait combined to form an inter-Arab petroleum organisation.

A border conflict broke out with the People's Republic of South Yemen in 1969. Shortly before, there was an attempt to assassinate Feisal. He was eventually assassinated by one of his nephews on 25 March 1975. The country, which benefited from the windfall of two consecutive years of oil price rises (Saudi Arabia boasts 30 per cent of the world's oil reserves), was able to put its fortune to good use whilst still holding fast to the rigour of its Islamic values.

Feisal was succeeded by his brother Fahd ibn Musaid Khan and then by his half-brother, Fahd, in June 1982. The crown prince was the commander of the national guard, Abdallah ibn Abdal-Aziz. Despite moments of tension, such as the oil embargo of 1973-74 and the Camp David accords between Egypt and Israel of September 1978, relations between the USA and Saudi Arabia have been very close, based on economic cooperation resulting from considerable Saudi investment in the USA, and military cooperation, strengthened by the 1974 accords, the outbreak of the Iran-Iraq conflict and the Soviet invasion of Afghanistan.

The kingdom's attitude towards Israel and Egypt has toughened since the signing of the Israeli-Egyptian peace treaty in March 1979. Saudi Arabia was party to decisions taken relating to Egypt, including breaking off diplomatic relations in March 1979, by the United Front of Arab states founded in Baghdad in November 1978.

Otherwise Saudi Arabia has played a moderating role in the Near East where it has guaranteed the security of the Arabian Gulf and the Red Sea in the face of regional pressures. This role, however, along with the country's position at the heart of OPEC, were challenged by the pressure for Moslem union which followed the attack on the Great Mosque at Mecca in November 1979, where 244 people were killed. Sixty-three of the "rebels" were beheaded on 9 January 1980. On 18 June 1985 the first Saudi to travel in space, Prince Salam al-Saudi, went into orbit aboard the US space shuttle "Discovery".

In August 1987 demonstrations by Iranian "pilgrims" at Mecca degenerated into bloody violence in which 400 people were killed. Saudi Arabia accused Iran of plotting to have the Ayatollah Khomeini proclaimed spiritual leader of Islam, to which the Iranians responded by blockading the Saudi embassy in Tehran, killing a diplomat. In April 1988 Saudi Arabia broke off relations with Iran.

Senegal

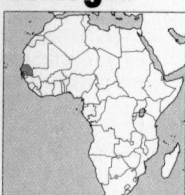

SN
West Africa
75,750 sq. mi
Pop: 6.7 m
UN, OAU

Capital: Dakar (pop: 550,000)
Official languages: French
Religion: Moslem (91 per cent)
System of govt: Republic; independent since 20 August 1960

During the ninth century populations along the river Senegal rapidly succumbed to the thrust of the Moslem Moors. The Ghana empire probably exerted its influence on the south-eastern regions, the kingdoms of Tekrur and Namandirou.

In the north, the Djolof kingdom developed after its foundation at the beginning of the 14th century. Several years before the fall of the Djolofs (around 1549) a kingdom developed in the Senegal valley, founded by Koli Tengella, who was of Peul-Mandingo origin. This kingdom continued its expansion into the 18th century.

From 1460 Portuguese traders established a number of trading posts on the coast. The Dutch landed at Goree in 1617 while the Senegal delta was visited by the British and the French, who founded Saint-Louis, a centre of the slave trade, in 1659. The French controlled Goree from 1677 until it and Saint-Louis were seized by Britain in 1758.

The colonial era

France regained possession of Senegal under the Treaty of Vienna in 1816 and soon abolished the slave trade. The Tukulur Confederation, established in 1776 in Lower Senegal, remained independent until 1854, when it was defeated by French troops. French influence extended north against the Moors, and south as far as Casamance, which was only pacified at the start of the 20th century. The boundaries of present-day Senegal were set in 1890. Dakar was founded in 1857 and became the headquarters of all French West Africa in 1895.

The autonomous republic of Senegal was founded in 1958 and joined with French Sudan in 1959 to form the federation of Mali within the French Community. When the federation was dissolved Senegal became independent, and Leopold Senghor became its first president in September 1960.

Since independence

In 1962 Senghor had the prime minister, Mamadou Dia, arrested. A new constitution in 1963 transformed the country into a one-party republic with a sole party, the Democratic Socialist Party (PSD). The office of head of government was combined with that of head of state. This system was abandoned in 1970 and Abdou Diouf was appointed prime minister. Re-elected in 1973, Leopold Sedar Senghor granted an amnesty to a number of political prisoners, among them Mamadou Dia.

The prime ministership was strengthened in 1976 by a new constitutional reform, inaugurating a period of liberalisation. The PSD changed its name to the Senegal Socialist Party (PSS) in 1977. Certain authorised political parties as well as the PSS were permitted to contest Senegal's first free elections in 1978. Senghor won, with 82 per cent of the vote.

Senghor resigned on 1 January 1981 and was succeeded by Abdou Diouf. An attempted coup at Banjul in neighbouring Gambia led to renewed Senegalese intervention in Gambia and then the creation, on 17 December 1981, of the Confederation of Senegambia. This was presided over by Diouf and brought about the military, economic and monetary union of the two states. The union came into force in February 1982 and had to face numerous difficulties. Diouf's position was reinforced by the 1983 elections.

Senegal had to come to terms with separatist movements in Casamance. Abroad, Senegal entered into good relations with the western countries. The process of political liberalisation has also continued. There are now 16 recognised political parties, six of which contested the general election in February 1988 when Diouf was again elected.

Seychelles

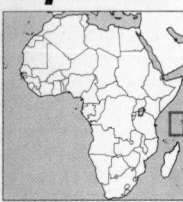
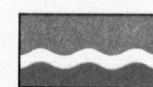

SY
Indian Ocean
175 sq. mi
Pop: 65,000
UN, CW, OAU

Capital: Victoria (pop: 24,000)
Official languages: Creole, English, French
Religions: Catholic (90 per cent), Anglican (8 per cent)
System of govt: Republic; independent since 29 June 1976

The Seychelles, a group of 85 islands, lies to the north of Madagascar in the Indian Ocean. They were known by the year 851 to Arab merchants, who visited them regularly until they were seen by the Portuguese in 1502.

In the early 1740s they were reconnoitred by a Frenchman, who named them after Jean Sechelles, the French minister of finance. They were annexed by France in 1756. The first colonists did not arrive until 1770. They introduced the cultivation of spices.

The Seychelles were occupied by the British in 1811 and officially passed into their control in 1814. The islands' flourishing economy collapsed in 1822 after the abolition of the slave trade.

Cotton plantations, previously worked by slaves, were replaced by cocoa plantations, and prosperity returned, thanks to copra, cinnamon and vanilla. The Seychelles, governed jointly with Mauritius, were directly ruled as a separate crown colony from 1903.

When the USA had to close down a satellite observation station in Zanzibar in 1964, Britain authorised its transfer to the Seychelles island of Mahe. In 1965 several islands of the Seychelles were leased to the USA as a strategic military zone for 50 years. Internal autonomy (1970) was followed by full independence on 29 June 1976, after an agreement between the two main political parties, the Seychelles Democratic Party (SDP) led by James Mancham, and the Seychelles People's United Party (SPUP) led by France-Albert Rene.

Mancham was elected president but was overthrown by Rene, the prime minister, in June 1977. The SPUP became the Seychelles People's Progressive Front (SPPF) and installed a single party system and a new socialist constitution came into force. President Rene was re-elected in 1979 and managed to survive both a coup attempt in November 1981 and a mutiny in August 1982. President Albert Rene was re-elected for a further five years on 1984. Tourism is the Seychelles' principle source of income.

Sierra Leone

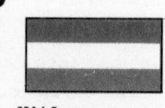

WAL
West Africa
27,925 sq. mi
Pop: 3.8 m
UN, CW, OAU

Capital: Freetown (pop: 470,000)
Official language: English
Religions: Traditional beliefs (50 per cent), Moslem (39 per cent), Christian (8 per cent)
System of govt: Republic; independent since 27 April 1961

From the 12th to the 16th centuries present-day Sierra Leone was dominated by the great Sudanic kingdoms of west and north-west Africa.

In 1447 the coasts of present-day Sierra Leone were reconnoitred by the Portuguese navigator Alvaro Fernandez, and in 1463 another Portuguese, Pedro et Cinto, named the country Sierra Leone (Lion Mountain) from the shape of the promontory at present-day Freetown.

A century after the Portuguese had arrived, the interior of the country was invaded by warriors of Mande origin, the Manes among others, who began to sell their captives to European slave traders.

The British first established a trading post in 1651, and in 1787 agreed to allow freed slaves from the USA and the West Indies to settle along the coast of the Sierra Leone estuary under the aegis of the Abolition Society. This society was a philanthropic group founded that year by William Wilberforce and Thomas Clarkson and was dedicated to the abolition of the slave trade, which it was largely responsible for achieving in 1807.

A settlement called Free Town was established in 1787-88 and the Sierra Leone Company was formed in 1791. Blacks from New England arrived in 1792, and creoles from Jamaica in 1800. British commercial establishments had existed on the coast since the 17th century, and the Freetown peninsula became a naval base.

Sierra Leone was declared a British crown colony in 1808. The British then conquered the islands off Freetown and most of the hinterland, which they placed under protectorate in 1896.

A revolt which broke out in 1898 against the descendants of the creoles and the British was severely suppressed. The 1947 constitution gave the protectorate twice as much representation as the colony, thus provoking anger from the creoles. The leaders of the protectorate founded the Sierra Leone's People's Party, led by Milton Margai.

Internal autonomy was granted in 1958 and Sierra Leone gained full independence within the Commonwealth in 1961. The SLPP and Albert Margai, Milton's brother, were defeated in the 1967 elections by the All People's Congress (APC), led by Siaka Stevens. Stevens was almost immediately afterwards removed from power by a mili-

tary coup, but was returned to power by another coup in 1968.

In 1971 Stevens became the first president of the republic of Sierra Leone and was re-elected in 1973. A constitutional reform turned Sierra Leone into a one-party state, the APC being the sole party, with the offices of head of state and of government combined.

The 1982 elections gave rise to outbreaks of bloody violence, while the principal trade union organisation was dissolved. On 28 November 1985 President Siaka Probyn Stevens retired, at 80 years of age, after having appointed General Joseph Momoh as his successor. Momoh declared a wish to combat the harmful influence of "immoral" pri-

vate entrepreneurs. His nomination to head of state and government was approved by a 99 per cent vote in a national referendum.

In May 1988 Siaka Probyn Stevens died aged 83. Joseph Momoh declared in October 1988 that his government would not tolerate anti-government "subversion".

Singapore

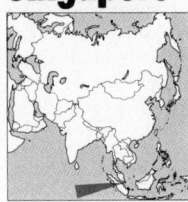

SGP
South East Asia
238.7 sq. mi
Pop: 2.6 m
UN, ASEAN, CW

Capital: Singapore (pop: 2.6 m)
Official languages: Chinese, Tamil
Religions: Buddhist (majority), Taoist, Confucian, Moslem, Christian
System of govt: Republic; independent since 9 August 1965

The city of Singapore (in Malay, Tumasik, "City of Lions"), on an island at the foot of the Malay peninsula, was already an important commercial city in the 13th century. It was destroyed by the Javanese in 1365 and remained

uninhabited for a long time afterwards.

Portuguese traders established settlements there in 1511. Sir Stamford Raffles (1781-1826), a distinguished orientalist, botanist and zoologist and an official of the British East India Company, persuaded the company to acquire Singapore island, then almost uninhabited, from its Malay owners in 1819. In effect, he refounded Singapore, and had a commercial trading post constructed on the site of the old city. Singapore became incorporated into the Straits Settlements (Singapore, Penang, Malacca and Labuan) in 1824, in which year Raffles retired because of ill health.

Rapid immigration and the swift development of portal installations, along with the island's geographical position, made it the principal port of the region from 1832, as well as an important British strategic base, despite Britain's acquisition of Hong Kong on the China coast in 1841.

The city grew still further after the invention of steamships and the opening of the Suez Canal in 1869.

From February 1942 until September 1945 the island was occupied by the Japanese. Once more under British rule, Singapore was detached from the other Straits Settlements in 1946 and became a crown colony. The colony was granted partial self-government in 1955 and full self-government in 1959. In the same year elections were won by the People's Action Party (PAP), led by the lawyer Lee Kuan Yew, and Singapore joined the Malaysian Federation on 16 September 1963.

Singapore, whose population is 75 per cent Chinese, withdrew from the Malaysian Federation and regained its independence on 9 August 1965. Although Lee readily protected the minority Malay population of Singapore, he had been apprehensive of Malayan domination within the federation.

Having become a major industrial, financial and commercial centre, Singapore emerged as an important shipping port. Since independence power has been in the hands of prime minister Lee Kuan Yew who has held the post continuously since June 1959.

Singapore's relations with the USA took a turn for the worse in May 1988 when the island accused a US diplomat of "gross interference" in its domestic affairs. In July premier Lee proposed that an international panel resolve the row.

Lee's rule came under increasing international criticism for its authoritarian character. Nonetheless, in the elections of 3 September 1988 his People's Action Party returned for its eighth consecutive term of office with just over 60 per cent of the vote. Lee, in power for nearly 30 years, promised to retire from office in late September, some time after his 65th birthday.

Solomon Islands

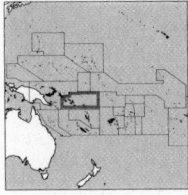

Oceania
10,640 sq. mi
Pop: 291,000
UN, CW

Capital: Honiara (pop: 30,000)

Official language: English
Religions: Protestant (76 per cent), Catholic (16 per cent)
System of govt: Constitutional monarchy; independent since 7 July 1978

The Solomon Islands, once thought to be the source of King Solomon's gold, were inhabited by Melanesians before they were visited in 1568 by Spanish navigator Alvaro de Mendana de Neyra.

The islands were not colonised by Europeans until the late 18th century. Missionaries and merchants frequented the islands in the 19th century, and the Melanesian natives were subjected to frequent raids by slave hunters. The northern islands were declared a German protectorate in 1885.

Except for Buka and Bougainville, they were exchanged in 1893 with Britain for Western Samoa. In 1900 British rule was confirmed.

After the First World War Buka and Bougainville were placed under an Australian mandate. The Solomons were occupied by Japan in 1942, but reconquered by US forces 14 months later. The Solomons gained internal self-government in 1976. Full independence came on 7 July 1978.

Sir Peter Kenilorea took over as premier in October 1984. He resigned in late 1987 to be succeeded in 1988 by deputy premier Ezekiel Alebua.

Somalia

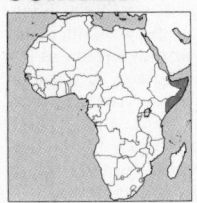

SP
North East Africa
246,201 sq. mi.
Pop: 6.1 m
UN, AL, OAU

Capital: Mogadishu (pop: 1 m)
Offical Language: Somali
Religion: Moslem (99 per cent)
System of govt: Republic; independent

since 26 June 1960

From c.1500 BC the horn of Africa, present-day Somalia, was known to the Egyptians, Phoenicians and Greeks as the "land of incense". Nomadic Somali herders arrived from the south of the Arabian peninsula from the tenth to the 14th centuries.

From the tenth century the Somali ports of Berbera, Mait and Zeila traded with Arab and Persian merchants. The country was divided into small sultanates following the arrival of Islam. Adal, the most important, fell under

the domination of Christian Abyssinia (Ethiopia) in 1420. It was reconquered in 1542 by the Somali national hero, Ahmed ibn Ibrahim Al-Gurey.

From 1874 to 1884 Egypt occupied areas including Zeila and Berbera, until the British placed northern Somalia under a protectorate in 1887.

From 1889 Italy signed a number of treaties of protectorate, gaining several ports including Mogadishu. Italian Somaliland became a colony in 1905 and, after Mussolini's invasion of Abyssinia in 1935, annexed several Abyssinian territories. In 1941 Somalia was recon-

quered by the British. Britain governed the two Somalilands until they became independent as one state in 1960.

The military took over in 1969, and in 1976 Somalia became a socialist republic. The border war with Ethiopia (1977-78) led the USSR to sever relations with Somalia, where the conflict caused a serious economic crisis. The border dispute has continued, although hostilities ceased after a meeting between President Ziyad Barre and President Haile Mengistu of Ethiopia on 19 March 1988. Drought and locusts have also plagued the country.

South Africa

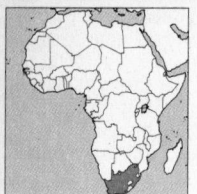

ZA
Southern Africa
433,678 sq. mi
Pop: 23.38 m
UN

Capital: Pretoria (pop: 822,900)
Official languages: Afrikaans, English
Religions: Catholic, Moslem, protestant, traditional beliefs
System of govt: Republic; independence effective from 1931

There is evidence in South Africa of the earliest human beings next to those found in Kenya and Ethiopia. Evidence of Khoisan hunters and gatherers dates back many millenia.

Some Khoisan converted to herding sheep and cattle in the last few centuries BC. Agriculture and Iron Age culture came to South Africa in the first few centuries, and were well established in the Transvaal by 500 and as far south as the Transkei probably by 1000.

African states, based on wealth in cattle and from mining or hunting, rose to power in the Transvaal around 1500 and in Natal around 1800. European colonisation of the Cape of Good Hope was begun by Dutch settlers in 1652; they were strengthened in numbers by French Huguenots (protestants) after the revocation in 1685 of the Edict of Nantes (which had guaranteed their freedom of worship) in France. The Cape Colony expanded through a series of frontier wars with Khoisan and Xhosa peoples, and was captured from the Dutch by the British first in 1795-1803 and finally in 1806.

The Boer Trek and the Boer War

Angered by the abolition of slavery by the British in 1833, many Dutch Boers (Dutch for farmers) abandoned the Cape to trek (migrate) to Natal. The battle of Blood River in 1838 checked the power of the Zulu kingdom and opened up Natal to the Boers. Natal was conquered by the British in 1843, but the British conceded the independence of Boer states in the interior (Transvaal and Orange) from 1852-54.

The annexation of the Transvaal by Britain in 1877 preceded Britain's defeat of the Transvaal's Pedi and Zulu enemies in 1879, and by successful Boer rebellion regained Transvaal independence in 1881. The discovery of diamonds at Kimberly in the 1870s and of gold in the Transvaal during the 1880s led to the immigration of British *uitlanders* (foreigners) into the interior, and to the rise of powerful uitlander mining magnates such as Cecil Rhodes.

The new wealth of the Transvaal, where the city of Johannesburg was founded on the gold mines in 1887, led Cecil Rhodes, who in 1890 became prime minister of Cape Colony, to attempt to seize Transvaal. The failure of the "Jameson Raid" led the uitlanders and the British to provoke a war against the Boers in October 1899.

European opinion aligned itself in the main on the side of the Boers. The Boers lost the war, but won the peace negotiations in 1902 with the Treaty of Vareeniging, which removed their independence but guaranteed their rights as white men over all blacks. The union of the South African colonies (the Cape, Natal, Orange and Transvaal) was completed in 1910. London was to name a governor-general in Pretoria whilst a prime minister represented the political majority of white voters in the union. (From 1931 onwards the governor general was named by the politicians in Pretoria). The first prime minister was Louis Botha, and Boers dominated the union's political life from the start.

From 1914 to the republic

War was declared on the Germans in August 1914 and German South-West Africa (now Namibia) was conquered in 1915. The "colour bar", keeping black workers out of skilled jobs, was reinforced after 1922 following a strike called by white mine workers demanding a wage ten times higher than that earned by the black workers. The National Party continued to develop its racial segregation doctrines and put these into action from 1933, two years after the Statute of Westminster made South Africa a completely autonomous dominion under the British crown.

Segregationist pressure increased in the wake of the Second World War with further measures against Africans, Indians and "coloured" (mixed race) people. At the same time the policy of territorial annexation in southern Africa continued. The apartheid policies pursued by the purified National Party, in power since 1948, were intensified and marked by the suppression of the "defiance campaign" launched by Albert John Luthuli's African National Congress in 1952. In March 1960 South African police shot dead 56 demonstrators – protesting against hated "pass laws" requiring blacks to carry identity cards – at Sharpeville in Transvaal, sparking outrage around the world and especially within the Commonwealth. On 31 May 1961 the Union of South Africa became a republic and cut political links with the Commonwealth.

Isolation

South Africa defied condemnation in the UN, in the Organisation for African Unity, and boycott measures advocated in the west. The intensification of apartheid matched a growth in South Africa's military power.

South Africa's answer to majority rule and independence in other parts of Africa was to convert its "Bantustan" African reserves into "independent" black states after 1976. In reality these policies simply had the effect of stripping the blacks in these "homelands" of the rights of citizenship in South Africa as a whole.

The independence from Portugal of Angola and Mozambique in 1975 saw an intensification of South Africa's military engagements both inside and outside its borders, particularly in southern Angola and in Namibia, illegally occupied since South Africa's UN mandate ran out in 1966. Independence for Namibia only seemed likely when Pretoria accepted a UN regional peace plan in November 1988.

The bloodshed of the Soweto riots in June 1976 was just one episode in the long series of rioting and deaths resulting from the policies of apartheid pursued, with minor moderations, by P W Botha from 1978 onwards in the face of ineffective international pressure. Fresh rioting in the black townships followed the promulgation of the new constitution in 1984 which raised P W Botha to the office of state president, but which granted no representation to the black community. The unrest this caused led to the declaration of a state of emergency in 1985 and this situation still continued in 1988, with sweeping curbs on the press. In 1989 Botha was forced to give way to the slightly more reformist F W De Klerck as National Party leader, but insisted on remaining president until elections in the autumn.

The apartheid problem remains unresolved and a major source of national and international tension. It has been complicated by a right-wing backlash even to the limited reforms of apartheid already introduced. The far right Conservative Party is now the main opposition party in the white-dominated parliament, and groups such as the neo-Nazi Afrikaner Resistance Movement (AWB) have been responsible for violence aginst anti-apartheid campaigners. One group, the White Liberation Front, was the first pro-apartheid organisation to be banned after a member shot dead three blacks in November 1988. The ANC leader Nelson Mandela was moved to a low security prison in November 1988, but despite pressure for his release he has remained in jail. On 18 July 1989 Mandela, 71, celebrated his 26th birthday in capitivity.

Spain

E
South West Europe
194,884 sq. mi
Pop: 38.8 m
UN, EC,
NATO, OECD

Capital: Madrid (pop: 3.1 m)
Official language: Spanish
Religion: Catholic (99 per cent)
System of govt: Constitutional monarchy since December 1978

The civilisations of Altamira and the Levante testify to the fact that the Iberian peninsula has been inhabited since palaeolithic times. According to tradition Iberians, who arrived from Africa, peopled the region during the neolithic era.

Ancient Spain

The Spanish coast was involved in Mediterranean trade from the c.1000 BC. Greeks and Phoenicians searched the area for metals, in particular tin. Phoenician and Punic (Carthaginian) trading posts were established on the southern coast at Cadiz and Alicante. The Greeks established trading settlements and later permanent colonies, including Emporion on the coast of Catalonia. Whilst the eastern civilisations were imposing their influence on the coastal regions, the territories of the interior were gradually being penetrated by the Celts. Carthage undertook the conquest of Spain after the defeat of Carthage in the first Punic War against Rome. Hamilcar Barca, who died in 229 BC at Elche, was the conqueror of the country as far as Barcelona, which he founded. Hannibal's capture of Sagunto, which was allied to Rome, sparked off the second Punic War in 219 BC. Scipio Africanus conquered the whole of Carthaginian Spain for Rome in 206 BC.

Roman subjugation of Spain proved to be an arduous undertaking and the north of the peninsula was not pacified until 19 BC. Spain was the scene of many rebellions, including those of Sertorius (died 72 BC), the sons of Pompey (until 44 BC), and of Galba in 68. It was also the birthplace of a number of Roman emperors such as Trajan and Hadrian and the writers Seneca and Martial. Under Diocletian at the end of the third century Spain was composed of five provinces: Lusitania, Bethica, Galicia and Asturia, Tarragona and Carthaginia and, finally, Mauretania (Morocco). Christianity, which made its appearance in the second century, took a firm hold of the country in the fourth century. Under the Romans all Spain was latinised, except for the defiant Basque region in the north.

Early mediaeval and Islamic Spain

Peace was maintained longer in the peninsula, with the sea and the Pyrenees as natural barriers, than elsewhere in the empire, and it was not invaded by barbarians until the fifth century. Despite Roman attempts to reconquer the territory, the Germanic Vandals settled in Bethica and then invaded Africa under Gaiseric (428-35).

The Alans, the Suevi and the Visigoths settled across the whole of the country. The Visigoths who had originally settled in Aquitaine subjugated the whole of Spain in 585. Their domination lasted for two centuries. Leovigild (573-86) unified the administration and centralised royal power but the ethnic and cultural differences between the Visigoths and Hispano-Romans remained. The conversion of King Reccared (587) opened an era of religious domination with the church councils of Toledo electing kings up until the Arab conquest, which began in 711.

After King Roderick had been defeated at Guadalete (19-26 July 711), Arabs (Moors) under Tariq ibn Ziyad took only two years to subjugate the whole of Spain. Spain became an emirate under Musa ibn Nusayr, governor of the Maghrib (Morocco and Algeria), which was a dependency of the Islamic caliphate. The independent emirate of Cordoba was founded in 756 by the last survivor of the overthrown Umayyad dynasty of caliphs, Abd al-Rahman I. Cordoba entered a cultural and economic golden age and preserved its independence until 1031.

Spaniards accepted the Moors and large numbers of them were converted to Islam. At the same time, a class of urban Spaniards, the Mozarabs (from the Arabic for "arabicised") took on Arab culture while remaining Christian. The north-west and north of Spain, however, escaped Arab domination. The Carolingian Franks attempted to establish authority over Spain between the Pyrenees and the Ebro (785-811). The first Christian kingdom to appear was that of Navarre (852). Others, Leon, Castile and Aragon, were formed around 1000. In the 11th century Moslem Spain split up into some 20 states or taifas. The rivalries between them were exploited by one warlord, known as El Cid, who briefly carved out a state at Valencia at the end of the 11th century.

The capture of Toledo by Alfonso VI of Castile in 1085 appeared decisive, but the following year he was defeated by the North African Almoravids, newly arrived in Spain, and the Christian reconquest (*Reconquista*) received a setback. The arrival of the Almohad dynasty at the end of the 12th century provoked a coalition of Spanish rulers who, aided by crusaders from elsewhere in Europe, crushed the Almohads at Las Navas de Toloso in 1212. The last Moslem kingdom, Granada, held out until 1492, when it was defeated jointly by Isabella of Castile (1474-1504) and Ferdinand of Aragon (1479-1516).

Spain as a great sea power

Castile disputed the mastery of the seas with Portugal, but the papal Treaty of Tordesillas (1494) divided the world into Spanish and Portuguese spheres of interest. Two years earlier Christopher Columbus, under the patronage of Castile-Aragon, had been the first European since the Vikings (who had not stayed) to see the Americas. Conquest and exploitation of the "New World" soon got under way, and colonial affairs were organised officially from 1503.

Joan the Mad, the daughter of Isabella and Ferdinand, was deposed from the Castilian throne by her son Charles I who proclaimed the union of the two kingdoms and was crowned in 1516. Charles I was elected Holy Roman emperor under the name Charles V after the death of his grandfather, Maximilian of Habsburg. More German than Spanish, the emperor pursued an ambitious policy in Europe, especially in his rivalry with the king of France, Francis I. These policies were financed by the gold of the New World.

When Charles V abdicated in 1556 his domains were divided, Charles's son Philip inheriting Spain and its empire as Philip II (1556-98). Spain became the leading cultural, economic and military power in Europe. In 1580 Philip took the vacant throne of Portugal. The destruction of the "Invincible Armada" in 1588 by the English was a severe blow.

Philip II faced rebellion towards the end of his reign in the Protestant northern Spanish Netherlands, which Philip IV (1621-65) recognised in 1648. Philip IV also faced growing French might and had to accept the marriage of the infanta Maria Theresa to Louis XIV. Uprisings in Catalonia, Portugal (independent from 1640) and Naples and Sicily shook the monarchy between 1640 and 1646.

Philip was succeeded by the ailing Charles II (1665-1700), who died childless and bequeathed his throne to his great-nephew, the grandson of Louis XIV, who became Philip V (1700-46). Spain thus passed from the Habsburgs to their dynastic arch-rivals, the Bourbons, and the Austrian Habsburgs did not take this lying down. The ensuing War of the Spanish Succession (1702-12) saw the Bourbons keep the Spanish throne, but lands in Italy and the Low Countries passed to the Austrians.

The reign of Philip V's younger son, Charles III (1759-88), was marked by the acquisition of Louisiana, compensation for the loss of Florida to Britain after the Seven Years War (1763). Florida returned to Spain in 1783 after the American War of Independence, during which the Spanish fought against the British.

An "enlightened despot", Charles III (1759-88) embarked on the recovery and modernisation of the Spanish economy. He expelled the Jesuits in 1767 and curbed the Inquisition. Charles IV (1788-08) was dominated by Manuel de Godoy, the favourite of Queen Maria Luisa.

In the Revolutionary and Napoleonic Wars Charles allied Spain to France (1796) and suffered the destruction of his fleet by Nelson at Trafalgar in 1805. In 1808 Charles IV and his son were deposed by Napoleon who placed his brother Joseph on the Spanish throne. This prompted a war of independence against the French, in which British intervention proved decisive. The Bourbons were restored in 1813.

Spain's domestic problems encouraged revolutionary independence movements in South America led by figures such as Bolivar, San Martin and Iturbide. Under Ferdinand VII (1813-33) Spain's colonial empire in America virtually ceased to exist.

Meanwhile, Ferdinand VII's domestic rule had provoked a revolt in 1820 which forced him to reinvoke the liberal constitution established in 1812 by the Cadiz parliament. His position was restored by the arrival of a French expeditionary force in 1823.

There was a succession crisis on Ferdinand VII's death. Don Carlos, his brother, claimed the throne against Ferdinand's daughter, Isabella. Although Carlos' supporters (Carlists) were defeated in 1839, Isabella did not to ascend the throne until after 1843. A military plot deposed her in 1868 and put an end to a period of political instability.

A regency chose a relation of the king of Prussia for the vacant throne, dropped in favour of Amadeus of Savoy (1870-73). A republic was proclaimed in February 1873, but a decree of December 1874 restored the monarchy and placed a Bourbon, Alfonso XII, on the throne. He was confronted by a new revolt by Carlists in 1876 and died in 1885, leaving the regency to his wife Maria Christina.

Spain lost Cuba, Puerto Rico and the Philippines after a war with the USA in 1898. Alfonso XIII instituted a personal reign in 1902; many cabinets followed one another and premier Eduardo Dato, was assassinated in 1921. Spain faced rebellion in Morocco while Catalonia demanded autonomy.

The age of the dictators

General Miguel Primo de Rivera, captain-general of Catalonia, staged a coup in 1923. Parliament was dissolved and the constitution abrogated. All but one party were banned in 1925.

Rivera was forced to resign in 1930, the same year that an alliance of conservatives and socialists allied with the aim of toppling the monarchy. Municipal elections in 1931 gave victory to the Republicans in the large cities, and a republic was proclaimed on 14 April 1931. Alfonso XIII left Spain, and the Republicans won an overwhelming victory at ensuing general elections. Alcala Zamora formed a coalition government, followed by governments tending more and more to the right. The years 1931-36 saw growing unrest throughout the country. The Front Popular, a union of the left, won the elections of February 1936, and Manuel Azana formed a government. A military rebellion broke out in Moroccan garrisons in 1936 and spreading to Spain led to the outbreak of civil war. General Francisco Franco, the leader of the military revolt, was proclaimed *generalissimo* and head of Spain's national anti-republican government. The nationalists received direct aid from Fascist Italy and Nazi Germany, who used the conflict as a cynical test of their warpower. The Republicans were supported by "international brigades" of volunteers, mainly from western democracies.

The ferocious civil war ended on 1 April 1939 with the victory of Franco. His government, to the dismay of its former Axis allies, declared its neutrality at the outbreak of the Second World War. The principal of monarchic succession to Franco's regime was approved in 1947. International recognition of the regime began in 1953 with a concordat with the pope and an economic and military agreement with the USA. Spain joined the UN in 1955.

Monarchy and democracy

General Franco died on 20 November 1975 and Juan Carlos of Bourbon-Parma, his successor and grandson of Alfonso VIII, was proclaimed king of Spain. Spain divested itself of Spanish Sahara almost immediately. In 1977 the first free general election since 1936 was one by Adolfo Suarez's Union of the Democratic Centre. In 1978 a new constitution made Juan Carlos a constitutional monarch. He remained a stabilising figure, and he was praised for his resolve in thwarting an attempted coup by Francoist officers in 1981. The Socialist Party under Felipe Gonzalez Marquez won the 1982 election. Regional autonomy, rescinded by Franco, has been restored to the Basque country, where an independence movement has been spearheaded by the terrorist group ETA (Euzkadi ta Azkatasuna, Basque Country and Freedom) and the Basque National Party (PNV), which rejected ETA violence in 1985.

Spain joined NATO in 1981 (a move approved by referendum in 1986) and the EC in 1986. In June 1986 Gonzalez was re-elected. An eight-year defence pact with the USA was signed in December 1988.

Differences still remain with Britain over Gibraltar. Spain reopened the land border in 1982 after 13 years, and talks continue. But Mrs Thatcher's visit to Spain in 1988, the first by a British prime minister, strengthened otherwise good Anglo-Spanish ties.

Sri Lanka

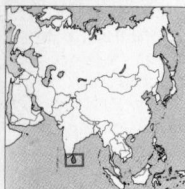

CL
Southern Asia
25,332 sq. mi
Pop: 16.3 m
UN, CW,
Colombo Plan

Capital: Colombo (pop: 643,000)
Official language: Sinhala
Religions: Buddhist (70 per cent), Hindu (14 per cent), Christian (7 per cent), Moslem (7 per cent)
System of govt: Republic; independent since 4 February 1948

The first traces of human habitation found on the island date back to 10,000 BC. The first inhabitants of Ceylon were the Veddas, of which there are only 2,000 today. During the fifth century BC they were pushed back by the Sinhalas, Aryans from the north of India, led by Prince Vijaya. The Tamils, from the south of India, also settled on the island during the following centuries, and hostility between the Sinhalese and the Tamils has provoked constant conflict. Ceylon was unified by King Devanampiya Tissa (250-210 BC), who made Anuradhapura his capital and introduced Buddhism.

Ceylon was known to Greek merchants who named it Taprobane. Sinhalese supremacy was re-established in 100 BC. A Sinhalese dynasty reigned until the island was conquered in 993 by the Chola King Rajaraja. Sinhalese resistance succeeded in expelling the occupiers in 1070 and Prince Vijayabahu established a new capital at Polonnaruwa. Under the reign of Parakramabahu I (1153-86), however, the ruin of the Sinhalese kingdom began, its populations having to retreat before Tamil invaders from the Indian subcontinent.

The Tamils intensified their penetration in the 12th century and founded probably the first independent Tamil kingdom, in the north of the island in 1234. The capital of the Sinhalese kingdom was moved to Kandy.

In 1410 Chinese invaders captured the Sinhalese king, Vira Alakeshvara. His successor, Parakramabahu VI, reconquered the whole of Ceylon in 1415, but the Sinhalese kingdom broke up on his death in 1467. During the 16th century the north and western coastal area were conquered by the Portuguese, who had landed at Colombo in 1505 and traded in spices. In 1656 the Portuguese were expelled by the Kandy kings, supported by the Dutch. The Sinhalese had withdrawn into the interior of the country, abandoning the coasts to the Dutch, who were expelled in 1796 by the British.

The arrival of the British, who took Kandy in 1815, made a huge difference to Ceylon's economy. Tea plantations were developed, and a large Tamil work force was imported from India. Colonisation met with several revolts, however, notably in 1818 and 1848.

After rapid development of the nationalist movement at the start of the 20th century, the Congress Party won universal suffrage in 1919, and Ceylon was granted internal self-government in 1931. Differences within the Congress Party led to the appearance of a number of parties: the Socialist Party in 1935, the Communist Party in 1943 and the United National Party (UNP) in 1946.

Independence was gained in February 1948. The first government was formed by the pro-western UNP leader Solomon Bandaranaike, who left the UNP in 1951 to found the nationalist left-wing Sri Lanka Freedom Party (SLFP), which won the elections of 1956. Bandaranaike was assassinated in 1959 by a Buddhist extremist, while Tamil opposition to the introduction of Sinhala as the official language provoked violent troubles. Solomon Bandaranaike's widow, Sirimavo, assumed the leadership of government and became the first woman prime minister in the world in 1960. But the failure of her nationalist economic policy and her policy of non-alignment were confirmed in March 1965 elections. Dudley Senanayake, head of the UNP, replaced her and conducted a more liberal policy, supported by the west. Tamil was also recognised as a national language.

In 1970 Mrs Bandarinaike returned to power in a left-wing coalition, which included the communists. Radical measures, such as nationalisation, preceded great economic difficulties. In 1971 she reacted to social unrest by introducing repressive measures which cost several thousand lives.

In the Commonwealth since independence, Ceylon proclaimed a republic in 1972 and changed its name to Sri Lanka. The UNP was reorganised under a new president, Junius Jayawardene and won the 1977 elections by an overwhelming majority. The SLFP obtained fewer votes than the Tamil party, the Tamil United Liberation Front (TULF). A new French-style constitution came into force on 7 September 1978, making Jayawardene executive president.

In 1979 a number of public figures, amongst them Mrs Bandaranaike, were accused of abuse of authority and were stripped of civil rights for seven years. Decentralisation was introduced to appease Tamil feeling. Economic policy became more liberal, with free zones being created around the capital, Colombo. Jayawardene was re-elected in October 1982.

Ethnic violence, which had started again in 1980 and 1981, became considerably worse in 1983. Over 360 people were killed after Tamil separatists attacked the police. Several hundred prisoners were summarily executed in prison. The TULF was banned. The Tamils, who account for 20 per cent of the Sri Lankan population, live mainly in the north and east of the island. They demanded the creation of an independent state, the Tamil Eelam. On India's initiative negotiations were undertaken between the government and the Tamils, but these broke down in August 1985. The spread of violence continued to grow throughout the year, culminating in several massacres and this situation escalated further in 1986 and 1987 so that by the middle of 1987 some 6,000 lives had been lost.

Jayawardene and India's prime minister, Rajiv Gandhi, arranged a ceasefire by the Tamil guerrillas and the merging of the northern and eastern provinces. Indian troops were sent in to help implement the agreements. Because of continuing violence most of these troops had not been withdrawn by the end of 1988.

On 2 January 1989 Ranasinghe Premadasa, until then prime minister, replaced Jayawardene as president. Tension grew between Sri Lanka and India in July when India expressed reluctance to withdraw its forces in the face of renewed unrest on the island.

Sudan

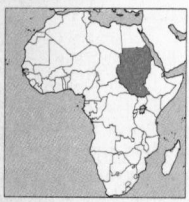
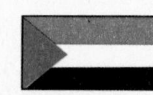

North East Africa
967,500 sq. mi
Pop: 21.5 m
UN, AL, OAU

Capital: Khartoum (pop: 476,000)
Official language: Arabic
Religions: Moslem (70 per cent), traditional beliefs (20 per cent), Christian (8 per cent)
System of govt: Republic; independent since January 1956

During the Egyptian Middle Kingdom (c.2000 BC) Nubia, present-day Sudan, was colonised by the Egyptians as far as the fourth Nile cataract. Nubian tribes had to pay tribute to the Pharaohs. In the eighth century BC the Kush kingdom appeared, whose capital was Meroe (Napata) and the Kush kings dominated Egypt from 750-663 BC.

In the first century the Kush succumbed to attacks from the Romans and from the Semitic tribes of Aksum. Three kingdoms came out of Meroe – Nobatia, Makuria and Alwa – and were converted to Christianity in the sixth century.

Moslem Bedouin Arab tribes penetrated into Sudan from the seventh century onwards. After the invasion of 852, the northern kingdoms had to pay a tribute to the Arabs.

Little is known about the period until the 19th century when in 1820 Mehmet Ali, the Ottoman governor of Egypt, began the conquest of the north of Sudan. In 1821 he founded a new capital, Khartoum. The south of the country was conquered in 1874 by the Egyptian khedive, Ismail Pasha.

In 1881 Muhammad Ahmad ibn Abd Allah proclaimed himself Mahdi (a sort of Moslem messiah). He led the revolt against Egypt and their British advisers, taking Khartoum after a siege in 1885 in which the British commander, General Gordon, was killed.

The rebels continued their struggle after the Mahdi's death the same year, and resisted Anglo-Egyptian troops until the capture of Khartoum by forces led by Kitchener in 1898. The failure of a French expedition in 1898 left Sudan in the hands of Britain and Egypt.

Kitchener was given the office of governor-general. From 1889 the country was officially administered as an Anglo-Egyptian condominium, but the British governor-general appointed all the civil and military authorities.

In 1951 the Egyptian King Farouk briefly became king of Sudan. Following Farouk's overthrow the independence of the Sudan was proclaimed after a referendum under the auspices of Colonel Nasser in 1956. A bloody civil war immediately broke out between Arab Moslem tribes in the north and the black Christian tribes in the south. After a coup in 1969 general Jaafar al-Nemery came to power, and a peace treaty was signed with the separatists in the south in 1972. In 1973 a new constitution was established, reinforcing the personal power of General Nemery. A coup attempt in July 1976 failed after the intervention of the Egyptian army.

Aid agreements were signed with the Egyptians in October 1976 and January 1977. Nemery was re-elected in April 1977 and, after another attempted coup in August 1979, carried out a purge of the leadership of the official party, the Sudanese Socialist Union. The civil war, which had been resolved in 1972 by the granting of a degree of autonomy in the south, was sparked again by its division into three regions in 1983.

After the proclamation of Islamic law in September, fighting intensified. Relations with Egypt, deteriorating since 1979, declined sharply at the end of the year, with Sudan ordering general mobilisation. Tension with Libya, internal unrest, economic crisis, famine in the south (threatening six million people) and civil war led to Nemery's overthrow in April 1985. A junta presided over by the former minister for defence, Abd al-Rahman Hassan Suvar al-Dahab, promised a return to democracy and installed a temporary government.

Yet all Sudan's problems remained: the catastrophic economic situation, the question of islamicisation and the civil war in the south, led by John Garang, head of the Sudan People's Liberation Army.

Elections were held in April 1986 and a new coalition government was formed led by Sadiq al-Mahdi who, because of the worsening economic situation and failure to end the civil war, declared a 12-month state of emergency in July 1987. After resigning in March 1988, Sadqid al-Mahdi was re-elected in April 1988 as head of a more broadly-based coalition.

Surinam

SME
South America
63,250 sq. mi
Pop: 490,000
UN, OAS, LAES

Capital: Paramaribo (pop: 103,000)
Official language: Dutch
Religions: Hindu (27 per cent), Catholic (22 per cent), Moslem (19 per cent)
System of govt: Republic; independent since 25 November 1975

Surinam was first visited by Europeans (Spaniards) in 1499, but the first attempts to settle there were not made until the first half of the 17th century and then by the Dutch, British and French. The first lasting settlement was founded on the river Surinam in 1651 by the Englishman Hugh Willoughby.

The colony ws recognised, in 1662, by King Charles II of Britain, and was reinforced by the arrival of new Jewish settlers (Marranos). In the Treaty of Breda in 1667 the Dutch obtained Surinam (Dutch Guiana) in exchange for New Amsterdam (New York). The Dutch developed the colony's plantations (sugar cane), drawing on a slave workforce which revolted on a number of occasions.

In 1815 the Congress of Vienna officially confirmed Dutch sovereignty. Before the abolition of slavery (1863) a large workforce of Chinese, Indians and Indonesians began to arrive. The exploitation of bauxite, a principal resource, began in 1938. Self-government, in 1954, brought successively the Conservative, Hindu and Creole Parties to power, later followed by the Progressive Party, whose leader, Henck Arron, undertook the independence negotiations with Holland 1975.

Arron remained prime minister until February 1980, when he was overturned by a military coup. A junta took power, suspended the constitution and proclaimed a state of emergency after an attempted counter-coup in August 1980. Sergeant (later Colonel) Desi Bouterse held the reins of power and became president in 1982. The regime imposed tougher measures after an attempted pro-democracy coup in March 1983. Holland suspended her economic aid (a third of Surinam's national budget) in 1983, leading Surinam to sign an accord with Brazil, which agreed to grant economic and military aid.

On 1 January 1985 a national assembly was appointed to draft a new constitution, and in general elections on 25 November 1987 opposition parties won a landslide victory over the NDP party of Colonel Bouterse, whose military rule had lasted seven years. On 25 January 1988 a civilian Mr Ramsevak Shankar was sworn in as president.

Swaziland

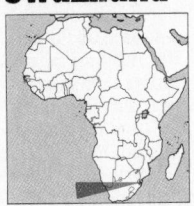

SD
Southern Africa
6,705 sq. mi
Pop: 676,000
UN, CW, OAU

Capital: Mbabane (pop: 30,000)
Official language: English, Siswati
Religions: Traditional beliefs (57 per cent), Christian (43 per cent)
System of govt: Monarchy; independent since 6 September 1968

The ruling dynasty of the Swazi can be traced back to the 16th century. Chief Dlamani and his son, Ngwane, who succeeded around 1760, were the founders of the ruling Dlamani clan and of the Ngwane (Swazi) nation. Until 1819 Ngwane became subjects of the Ndwandwe kingdom, then paid tribute to the Zulu before winning independence under kings Sobhuza I (1815-39) and Mswati (1840-68). The people of Mswati became known as "Ama Swazi" to the Zulu, and the country as "Swaziland" in English. The Swazi still refer to their country as "Ka Ngwane".

The Swazi became allies of the Boers, and subsequently of the British, against hostile Zulu and Pedi kingdoms. The Boer republic of the Transvaal imposed its "protection" on Swaziland through a series of Anglo-Boer conventions from 1890-94. The British formally took control in 1906, and Swaziland continued as a British enclave closely integrated with the Transvaal.

Under the rule of Sobhuza II (1899-1982, but effectively from 1921), the Swazi pursued a long campaign to regain land from white settlers.

There were national elections in 1967 prior to independence in 1968. Radical politicians threatened the monopoly of his party in 1972 elections and King Sobhuza abolished parliament in 1973. A form of parliament was revived in 1978, but absolute power was still with the king and his councils. Sobhuza died in August 1982, and a period of factional struggles followed in these councils. In April 1986 the second youngest of Sobhuza II's 60 sons was inaugurated as King Mswati II.

Sweden

S
Northern Europe
173,731 sq. mi
Pop: 8.35 m
UN, EFTA, NC, OECD

Capital: Stockholm (pop: 659,000)
Official language: Swedish
Religion: Protestant (93 per cent)
System of govt: Constitutional monarchy since the constitution of 1 January 1975

To many outsiders Sweden is the one country where equality and efficiency have learned to live together and produced a land of well-educated, well paid and contented workers who have abjured the messy, inefficient, embittered them-and-us industrial practices of so many other countries. Swedes, certainly do enjoy a high standard of living; they do have a number of highly successful manufacturing firms; and the Swedish bargaining system and provisions for industrial democracy do generally work.

Not always, though. In the early 1980s, Sweden shared with other developed countries the consequences of the world-wide recession and soaring oil prices. Inflatory pressures mounted and austerity measures led to strikes, even the civil service stopped work.

By the late 1980s, Sweden was adopting many of the politics which had been associated with Britain's experience in the past decade. Exchange controls were being abolished, the country's financial system was being deregulated, and the emphasis of taxation was being shifted from income to goods and services. The national collective bargaining system for wages was being broken down into localised bargaining units. And, for good measure in a country that has had a socialist government – with one six-year break – for over half a century, share ownership was being encouraged.

These developments have come in the wake of publicly expressed anxieties about Sweden's economic future. By international standards, unit labour costs are high and productivity is low. Its industrial record rests on a limited number of multi-nationals which make most of their profits overseas.

Sweden's achievement has been to create a significant industrial base in a country with a small population and high levels of emigration in the 19th century. Energy sources are limited – at one time Sweden was importing more than seven million tons of British coal annually – but the iron ore deposits are among the richest in the world. Though industrial development began in the mid-19th century (the first railway line was opened in 1851) only 15 per cent of the work force was engaged in industry by the end of the century.

The first trade unions appeared in about 1870 and the Social Democratic Party was founded in 1889. Adult male

Sweden

suffrage, though with a property qualification, was introduced in 1909; the vote was extended to women in 1921. A state pension scheme dates from 1913 and the eight-hour day from 1921.

In 1921 the first Social Democratic government was formed, but not until the 1930s did the party become accepted as the natural party of government. Four decades later, Olof Palme, the socialist prime minister, stirred controversy with his hostility to America over the Vietnam War, as did his party's high-taxation policies when Ingmar Bergman, the producer, was arrested on the film set for being in arrears with his tax payments.

Palme was defeated in the 1976 election, but returned to power in 1982. On Thursday 20 February 1986 he was shot dead in a Stockholm street after leaving a cinema. The subsequent police inquiry was marked by muddle, dissimulation and mutual recriminations. Eventually a Stockholm drug addict was brought to trial for the murder – on mainly circumstantial evidence – in the summer of 1989.

Early history

Traces of neolithic human habitation dating back to 4000 BC have been found in Sweden. The use of copper appeared around 1800 BC and was connected with the Mediterranean amber trade. Modern Swedes are descended from the Germanic tribes that came to Scandinavia in the years after the first century BC. The Roman historian Tacitus knew of a Svear people and by the fourth century the Svears had conquered small Gothic kingdoms in the south of what is now Sweden and founded their own kingdom, Svearike (hence *Sverige*, what the Swedes call Sweden). The kingdom was divided up into more or less autonomous regions, each with its own *thing*, an assembly of free men, which debated matters of public concern. The political centre of Svearike was Uppsala, but its chief commercial centre was Birka. The kingdom became unified in c.1100 after the conquest of the islands of Gotland and Oland.

Christian missionaries had arrived in the ninth century and Christianity spread rapidly after the baptism of King Olaf (c.944-c.1021). Fighting continued, however, between heathen and Christians until the church became more rigorously organised with the foundation of the archbishopric of Uppsala in 1164.

In 1156 King Erik IX (the Saint) undertook a crusade to neighbouring Finland, which he conquered a year later. The church gained important privileges as its influence strengthened while, in the economic sphere, German influence (via the Baltic port of Lubeck) became dominant by 1200.

From 1250 to the union of Kalmar

In 1250 Jarl Birger, the brother-in-law of King Erik Eriksson, founded the Folkung dynasty, and had one of his sons elected king. Exhausted by the struggles between the opposing dynasties of Erik, Swerker and Stenkil during the preceding centuries, Sweden now remained united under a single dynasty for the next century.

Jarl Birger, acting as regent for his son until 1266, ensured Swedish rule in over Finland and renewed friendly relations with Denmark and Norway. He established the capital at Stockholm, where he set up a powerful administration. He unified the land laws and encouraged the growth of commerce, supported by the towns of the Hanseatic trade league around the Baltic and further south in Germany.

Swedish territory was at its most extensive in the middle ages under Magnus VII Ericsson (1319-63), who inherited the Norwegian crown. When he tried to reinforce royal authority over the feudal lords, they aligned themselves with Duke Albert of Mecklenburg, who overthrew the Folkung line in 1364.

In that year the last of the Folkung had married (1364) Queen Margaret I of Denmark, who, on his deposition, became regent of Norway. She sent Danish troops to intervene in Sweden in 1369 and took the usurper Albert of Mecklenburg as a prisoner. Queen Margaret became regent of Sweden, thereby uniting the four mainland Scandinavian peoples – Swedes, Danes, Norwegians and Finns – under one sovereign for the first time. Margaret chose Eric of Pomerania, her great-nephew, as heir, and had him proclaimed king of Norway in 1389, then king of Denmark and Sweden in 1396. Representatives of Sweden, Denmark and Norway approved her policies, and formed the Union of Kalmar in 1397.

Swedish nationalism

A movement born within the nobility in the 15th century demanded a national monarchy. King Christian I of Oldenburg had already been named king of Sweden by the Danes in 1448, but in 1471 his troops were defeated at Brunkeberg by Swedish troops under Sten Sture the Elder. Sweden obtained greater autonomy, within the Union of Kalmar.

King Christian II of Denmark tried to reassert his authority in Sweden and his army defeated Sten Sture at Lake Esunden in 1520. King of Denmark and Norway since 1515, he was crowned king of Sweden in March 1520, an event which sparked immediate discontent among Swedes. Christian II's response was the massacre of Swedish notables known as the "Stockholm Bloodbath" in November 1520.

Gustavus Vasa escaped the atrocity and took over the leadership of a popular uprising against the Danes, which was joined by the nobility. In 1523 the Danish rulers were expelled and the

Union of Kalmar dissolved. Gustavus Vasa was proclaimed King Gustavus I of an independent Sweden. During his reign (1523-60) he introduced the Reformation to Sweden (1527), no doubt mainly out of conviction but also, perhaps, because it gave him a fine excuse to confiscate catholic church property. He used it to pay off debts to the wealthy Hanseatic city of Lubeck, which had given valuable aid against the Danes, and, of greater long-term significance, to build the fleet which helped Sweden forge a Baltic empire.

The early Vasas

Gustavus I abdicated shortly before his death in 1560 in favour of his son, Eric XIV (1560-68). The first attempt to establish Swedish supremacy in the Baltic, during Eric's reign, failed. The Scandinavian Seven Years War broke out in 1563 over Denmark's retention of the Swedish crown in its coat of arms; Denmark, Lubeck and Poland seized Gotland from Sweden and forced Eric to recognise freedom of trade in the Baltic.

Eric was succeeded by his brother, John III (1568-92), who married Polish royalty and whose son, Sigismund, was king of Poland before inheriting Sweden in 1592. He swore the right oaths, but was seen as an unpalatable (and largely absentee) catholic, and the Swedish *Riksdag* (parliament) dethroned him in 1599. His relation and former Swedish regent became Charles IX in 1604, and prosecuted generally successful wars against the Poles, the Danes and the Russians before dying in 1611. On his death the nobles and Riksdag declared a 17-year-old royal youth of age and gave him the throne. In return King Gustavus II Adolphus agreed to guarantee their privileges.

The Baltic: a "Swedish lake"

Gustavus II Adolphus made Sweden a great power abroad and, with the aid of his brilliant chancellor, Axel Oxenstierna, a highly efficient and prosperous one at home. By the time he died at the Battle of Lutzen in 1632 he had almost made the Baltic Sweden's fiefdom – a Swedish lake, as one commentator said – and a lot more besides. He obtained eastern Karelia and Ingria from Russia in 1617 and wrested Livonia from Poland in 1621. In 1630 Sweden intervened in Pomerania (a region along the southern shore of the Baltic) and became embroiled in the struggle for supremacy in Central Europe later known called the Thirty Years War (1618-48). Protestant Sweden confronted the Catholic League led by the Habsburg emperor.

The French, keen at the prospect of Sweden thrashing their old enemies the Habsburgs, subsidised Gustavus's war effort from 1631. Sweden and its allies trounced the Catholic League at Breitenfeld in north Germany (September 1631) and plunged even deeper into

German territory. The protestant army came off best at Lutzen in November 1632, but lost Gustavus, killed at the head of his troops. He was only 38.

Gustavus was succeeded by his six year old daughter Christina, for whom Oxenstierna acted as regent until 1644. He conducted Swedish policy for the rest of the war until the Peace of Westphalia confirmed Sweden as the greatest power in the Baltic. Danish claims to supremacy had been laid to rest by a pact in 1645.

Zenith and decline

The remarkable Christina came of age at 18 and her interest in state affairs quickly gave way to a passion for learning and the arts. She gathered round her musicians, poets and scholars. Descartes visited her. She refused to marry and in 1654, when she was 28, she became a catholic, abdicated and went to live in Rome.

Christina's cousin Charles X Gustav became king in 1654-60, and he fought the First Northern War to safeguard Swedish supremacy in the Baltic; Poland, Russia, Denmark and Brandenburg were involved. Sweden conquered Denmark (1658) and Poland (1660), but Charles XI (1660-97) was beaten by Brandenburg in 1675. However, Brandenburg restored Swedish land in 1679.

Charles XII (1697-1718) sparked off another Northern War by marching into Russia with the aim of seizing Moscow. He was humiliated at Poltava by the Russians in 1709 and took refuge with the sultan in Constantinople until 1713, leaving Russia, Brandenburg-Prussia and Poland to turn on his empire. The Peace of Nystad, three years after Charles' death, deprived Sweden of nearly all its empire between Denmark and Finland. Charles, a follower of (with hindsight) sinister theories of Nordic superiority, dealt the monarchy's prestige a severe blow, and the Riksdag imposed a constitution on his successor in 1720 which curtailed his absolute power.

Gustavus III (1771-92) restored absolute royal power in a coup (1772). He opened up public office to non-nobles, but the days of Swedish royal absolutism were really over, and Gustavus was assassinated in 1792.

The Napoleonic wars gave Sweden a king from France. Jean Baptiste Jules Bernadotte was a lawyer's son from Pau, who became a successful soldier in the revolutionary wars. Under the Emperor Napoleon he became a marshal of France. The ageing King Charles XIII of Sweden, who was childless, adopted him and Bernadotte was elected crown prince. Then when Charles XIV became king he allied Sweden with the British and Russians against his former commander Napoleon and helped to defeat him at the Battle of Leipzig in 1813. He also annexed Norway, which remained under the Swedish crown until 1905.

Switzerland

CH
Central Europe
15,943 sq. mi
Pop: 6.53 m
EFTA, OECD

Capital: Berne (pop: 138,000)
Official languages: German, French, Italian, Romansch
Religions: Catholic (48 per cent), protestant (44 per cent)
System of govt: Federal republic since 29 May 1874

The oldest sites to have been occupied by humans, in caves in the Alps and the Jura, date back to around 50,000 BC, the palaeolithic era. Neolithic civilisations left traces of lakeside settlements. The Celts began to settle in the territory of present-day Switzerland in the eighth century BC, driven from the north by Germanic tribes. The Celtic tribe of the Helvetii settled in central Switzerland, and pushed southwards, coming into contact with Julius Caesar, who defeated them at Bibracte in 58 BC.

Withdrawing to the Alps, the Helvetii gradually became more open to Latin culture. After the Rhaetians of eastern Helvetia had been subjugated, the region was divided into two, the provinces of Rhaetia and Celtic Gaul. A number of settlements of varying importance appeared during Roman domination, including Geneva, Lousanna (Lausanne) and Basilia (Basle). A route across the St Bernard Pass was opened in 47 AD.

The barbarian migrations, which led to Rome's downfall, brought several Germanic tribes to Helvetia. In 443 the Roman general, Flavius Aetius, installed the Burgundians in Savoy, and charged them with halting the progression of the Alamanni, who managed to settle in the centre of Helvetia in the sixth century.

Shortly after the country had been conquered by the Franks in the sixth century, Christianity appeared for the first time in Switzerland and monasteries were founded at Saint Gall (612), and Reichenau (724) on Lake Constance. These became important centres of cultural influence.

After the Frankish empire was divided into three, in 843, eastern Helvetia and Rhaetia were attached to the Eastern Frankish kingdom. When the Holy Roman Emperor Konrad II inherited Burgundy in 1033 Helvetia was completely integrated into the German empire.

Swiss independence

From the 11th century feudal states were set up by the counts of Zähringen, Kyburg and Savoy, and by the Habsburgs (originally from Aargau). At the same time dependencies were developing around the monastries and bishoprics, the two most important being Berne and Freiburg, which appeared in the 12th century. The towns and lords engaged in incessant fighting, while the rural communities associated with the towns tried to obtain privileges from the emperor, the overlord of the region. When the last of the Zähringen dynasty died, the towns of Zürich, Berne and Solothurn obtained their freedom. Uri purchased its emancipation from the empire in 1231, followed by Schwyz (the area which gave the country its name) and Unterwalden, and later Obwald. The two most important centres in the struggle for independence, which was directed above all against the Habsburgs, were Berne and Zürich.

After the death of Emperor Rudolph I, who made himself master of central Switzerland, the forest cantons of Schwyz, Uri and Unterwald took the "Oath of Rütli" in 1291 and joined in the "Everlasting League", thus laying the foundations for the Helvetican Confederation. They adopted a policy of mutual defence and established a shared legal system. The victory of the three cantons at Morgarten on 15 November 1315, against an Austrian army led by Duke Leopold I, enabled them to renew their 1291 federal charter, to which was added the unification of the cantons' foreign policy.

The alliance was extended to include the cantons of Lucerne, Zürich, Zug, Glarus and Berne (1332-53), thus forming the "Confederation of the Eight Original Cantons". In 1386 at the Battle of Sempach, the Confederation, allied to a number of Swabian and Rhine towns, crushed the Habsburg army led by Duke Leopold III, who died in the battle.

The expansion of the confederation

In spite of internal dissensions, the confederation became a major force in the 15th century. It allied with Louis XI of France against Charles the Bold, the duke of Burgundy, who was killed at Nancy in a battle against the confederation. Internal disagreement over foreign policy prevented the confederation taking full advantage of this success, although the important role played by the Swiss in the destruction of the Burgundian state increased their military reputation, the first Swiss Guard being recruited by the pope in 1506.

It also aided their struggles for independence. The cantons had ceased participating in the imperial diets from 1471, having their own assemblies to take care of their affairs, and the struggle for independence intensified in 1495 when the imperial Diet of Worms decided on a policy of legal and political unification. War broke out with the empire when Constance aligned itself with the Swabian League, a union of the nobility and the south-western cities of the empire. In 1499 the emperor Maximilian I was forced to recognise the confederation's *de facto* independence by the Peace of Basel. This guaranteed the confederation's freedom from the empire's tax and legal systems, although the empire did not officially recognise Swiss independence until 1648, in the Treaty of Westphalia.

The participation of Swiss mercenaries in the Italian wars led the confederation to try to play a political role there at the beginning of the 16th century. In 1513 the Swiss defeated the French and Venetians at Novara. The growth of Swiss power however, was halted by the defeat at Marignano (1515) at the hands of Francis I of France. This was a period which saw the augmentation of the confederation by the addition of Freiburg, Solothurn, Basle, Schaffhausen and Appenzell, to form a confederation of 13 cantons, without a central government, and also including several associated regions such as St Gall and the Upper Valais. The delegates from the cantons debated questions of mutual interest in their diets.

The Reformation

Huldrich Zwingli's radical reformist Programme of Reform was adopted in Zürich in 1523 and quickly spread to several other cantons. The expansion of the Reformation led to conflict between the catholic and protestant cantons. Zwingli was killed at the Battle of Kappel (1531), after which the cantons' denominational division was recognised, each canton choosing its own religion. That other great religious reform movement of the 16th century, Calvinism, started in Geneva, where it was adopted in 1541. In 1566 the second Helvetic Confession reconciled the teachings of Zwingli and Calvin.

Constitution of the federal state

During the 17th and 18th centuries political power developed in different ways within individual cantons. The Lurban Patriciate moulded the political framework of the cantons of Berne, Lucerne, Solothurn and Freiburg, while trade and craft interests dominated in Zürich, Basle, Schaffhausen and St Gall. Conflict between urban and rural cantons erupted at the same time as the French Revolution, with uprisings in Lower Valais and Vaud in 1789.

The revolutionary party was victorious at Geneva and Basle in 1792. The Helvetian Republic was proclaimed after the entry of French troops in 1798, and was granted its first constitution, reformed by Napoleon, who promulgated the "Act of Mediation" in 1803. The Congress of Vienna (1815) guaranteed Switzerland "eternal neutrality" and a new constitution, the Federal Pact, was promulgated the same year, recognising the autonomy of the cantons.

After the July Revolution in France in 1830, pressure for a more liberal constitution developed within most of the cantons. The liberals tried to set up a state, in which institutions were based on the sovereignty of the people and the equality before the law of all citizens. In 1831 12 cantons overthrew their aristocracy and an indecisive struggle between conservatives and liberals continued for a number of years. In 1845 the conservative catholic cantons formed the Sonderbund (Separate Federation), a "protective association", which was defeated and dissolved in 1847. The new constitution of 1848 endowed the Swiss with central federal institutions and, for the most part, still remains in force today. A federal council of seven was charged with overseeing Swiss foreign relations, post, coinage, customs and the army. Two legislative assemblies were created, the National Council (lower house), elected by manhood suffrage, and the States' Council, made up of representatives of the various cantons, elected according to the local practice.

Modern Switzerland

In 1856 the confederation had to face its first test, with an attempted royalist coup from the canton of Neuchâtel. The insurgents' aim was to restore the sovereignty of the king of Prussia, Frederick William IV, who was also prince of Neuchatel. The attempt failed, and Prussia suffered a severe diplomatic setback when it had to renounce all claims to Neuchatel. Switzerland established a policy of armed neutrality supported by friendly economic and diplomatic relations with most other states.

The founding of the Red Cross at Geneva in 1863, followed by the creation of other international institutions, gave Switzerland an international vocation. In 1874, for example, 22 nations signed an international postal treaty, which in 1878 became the International Postal Union.

Swiss neutrality was respected during both World Wars. Geneva became the seat of the League of Nations, and then of many institutions of the UN. Switzerland is not in the UN, claiming that membership could compromise Swiss neutrality, if, for example, the UN gave a vote of censure on another country.

On 31 January 1874 a modified federal constitution came into force, which recognised nine cantons and six semicantons. A movement demanding autonomy for the Jura, attached to the canton of Berne since 1815, developed in the 1960s, after the Jura Assembly lost a 1959 referendum on self-determination. It was not until June 1974 that a new referendum permitted the creation of the 23rd canton of Jura. The new canton was officially created on 1 January 1979. The office of Swiss president is held for one year at a time.

Syria

Syria

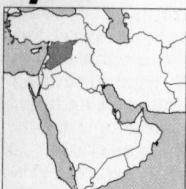

SYR
Near East
71,498 sq. mi
Pop: 10.96 m
UN, AL

Capital: Damascus (pop: 1.29 m)
Official language: Arabic
Religions: Moslem (90 per cent),
Christian (10 per cent)
System of govt: Republic; independent
since April 1946

The oldest remains which have been found in Syria date from the palaeolithic era (c.800,000 BC). Despite enjoying a strategic geographical situation between Mesopotamia, Anatolia and the Mediterranean, which, in antiquity, would have been a key commercial position, it was not until the 20th century that the territory of Syria evolved into an autonomous state.

After being invaded by the kingdom of Akkad, the Egyptians, the Hittites, the Assyrians, the Babylonians and the Persians, Syria was integrated into the Macedonian empire by Alexander the Great in 333-332 BC. After Alexander's death, the country was divided and belonged, for the most part, to the kingdom of the Seleucids, the dynasty founded in the Near East and Mesopotamia by Alexander's general, Seleucus (from 301 BC). The region was conquered in 63 BC by the Romans.

Integrated into the Eastern Roman (Byzantine) empire in 395, Syria was conquered by the Arabs (633-40), and then by the Ottoman Turks in 1516.

Ottoman domination of Syria collapsed during the First World War; in 1916, France and Britain divided the Ottoman Near East into zones of influence under the secret Sykes-Picot accord. The British obtained Mesopotamia, Jordan and Palestine, while the French gained Syria (including modern Lebanon).

The Ottoman front was broken at Jaffa in the Palestinian war and the British fought alongside Arab troops as far as Aleppo, Damascus and Beirut. In March 1920 the Syrian National Congress proclaimed the independence of Syria, including the Lebanon and Palestine, and named as king the Emir Faisal, son of Hussein, the king of Hejaz (a region of the Arabian peninsula).

Faisal, however, was expelled in July 1920 by the French, who had obtained a League of Nations mandate over Syria at the Conference of San Remo. In 1925 a national uprising which broke out in the Jebel ed Druz region led to brutal repression which was not to come to an end until 1927.

Democratic institutions were gradually introduced by the French, and a Syrian delegation to Paris in 1936 obtained Syria's accession to independence. This was set to take place after a three-year probationary period, although the accord was not ratified by the French parliament.

The authorisation given by the puppet Vichy French government for the German airforce to use Syrian air bases – to support Iraq against the British – led to the intervention of British and Free French troops in June 1941. Syrian independence was proclaimed formally on 1 January 1944, but the country continued to be occupied by an Anglo-French condominium until April 1946, when French troops departed under pressure from the British.

The initial years of Syrian independence were marked by the alternation of dictatorships and coups. The socialists of the Arab nationalist Ba'ath Party encouraged the agreement of a union between the republics of Syria and Egypt within the United Arab Republic (UAR), on 1 February 1958, which was to be placed under the presidency of the Egyptian leader Colonel Nasser. The UAR broke up in September 1961 following a military uprising in Syria.

The Ba'ath Party took power after a military coup in 1963. The Marxist wing of the party carried out another coup in 1966, bringing Nureddin al-Atassi to the presiidency. He was overthrown in 1970 by General Hafiz al-Assad, commander-in-chief of the Syrian Air Force, who represented the pragmatist wing of the Ba'ath Party.

Assad was confirmed as head of state by a referendum in 1971. A new constitution was prepared by the People's Assembly, and came into force in January 1973. It did not proclaim Islam as the state religion, a decision which was met with hostility in Sunni Moslem circles, including such groups as the Islamic Brotherhood. Syria became officially a people's democratic Arab republic.

Having already intervened against Israel in the Arab-Israeli War of May 1948 and the Six Days War of June 1967, Syrian troops intervened again in the Yom Kippur War in October 1973.

After initial successes in the Golan Heights, the Syrian army had to retreat, but continued to harass the Israeli army until the agreement of 31 May 1974 gave Syria half of the territories occupied by Israel since 1967.

Relations with Egypt became tense after the intervention of Syrian-Arab troops in the Lebanese civil war in 1976. Syria was at this time dependent on Libya, with whom an accord of union (which was never implemented) was drawn up in 1980, and on the USSR, which signed a treaty of friendship and co-operation.

After the failure of an attempt to assassinate President Assad in June 1980, several hundred of the prisoners in the Palmyra prison were slaughtered. An uprising at the town of Hama, in February 1982, was suppressed after several weeks fighting, with thousands of victims.

The military support Syria granted to Iran in the Iran-Iraq war from 1980 onwards caused relations with neighbouring Jordan to deteriorate. Occupying the north and east of the Lebanon after Israeli intervention in 1982, Syria refused to ratify the Lebanon-Israeli agreement of 1983, and continued to support Palestinians in Lebanon, even after the expulsion of the PLO leader, Yassir Arafat, in June 1983.

The deterioration of the situation in Lebanon, and the bombing of Syrian positions by the US in November 1983, led to a reaffirmation of USSR support for Assad, who ordered general mobilisation. Syria opposed the stabilising of Israeli-Lebanese relations and supported the Moslem Lebanese opposition (such as the Amal militia) to President Gemayel.

In February 1985 President Assad was re-elected for the third time (official figures gave him 99.97 per cent of the vote), and pursued policies which gave Syria a key role in the Middle East conflict, and an important role as a mediator in negotiating the fate of a number of western hostages in the Lebanon.

In February 1988 thousands of Syrian troops were sent into Beirut. In September of that year the US renewed relations with Syria after it closed the offices of the Palestinian extremist Abu Nidal. In 1989 Syria still played a major military and political role in strife-torn Lebanon, as pro and anti-Syrian groups clashed in and around Beirut. Syrian influence in Lebanon led to a political stalemate when a successor could not be found to the outgoing President Gemayel.

Taiwan (Formosa)

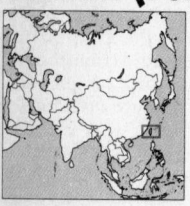

RC
Far East
13,969 sq. mi
Pop: 19.3 m

Capital: Taipei (pop: 2.5 m)
Official language: Chinese
Religions: Buddhism (50 per cent),
Confucianism, Taoism
System of govt: Republic; proclaimed
1 March 1950

Originally inhabited by a population of Malayo-Polynesians, the island of Taiwan was not appreciably populated by Chinese before the 17th century. In the 16th century Portuguese sailors gave it the name Ilha Formosa (Beautiful Isle). The Dutch set up trading stations and built forts in 1624. They were dislodged by the Chinese pirate and Ming loyalist Zheng Chenggong (or "Koxinga") in 1662. His principality was taken by Qing forces in 1683 and incorporated into the Chinese empire.

In the 18th century Chinese immigration accelerated; by the middle of the 19th century the aboriginal inhabitants had been displaced from the western lowlands. Taiwan was administered as part of Fujian until 1886 when it became a separate province. The French occupied Jilong during the Sino-French War in 1884. As a result of the Sino-Japanese War, Taiwan was ceded to Japan in 1895.

The Cairo Declaration of December 1943 envisaged the return of Taiwan to China. Upon the Japanese surrender in August 1945, the Nationalist Chinese government proclaimed sovereignty over the island. In 1949 it became the refuge for Chiang Kai-shek (Jiang Jieshi) and his Nationalist troops after the People's Republic of China had been proclaimed by Mao's communists on the mainland. On 8 December 1949 the provisional government of the Republic of China was established, with Taipei as capital. In a peace treaty between Japan and the western powers Japan renounced all rights to Taiwan.

Chiang Kai-shek, who was still aiming at the reconquest of mainland China, got substantial military aid from the USA, especially under the mutual security pact signed in 1954. In 1971 the Republic of China was forced to give up its seat in the UN in favour of the People's Republic of China. As a consequence, Taiwan's diplomatic isolation grew progressively.

On Chiang Kai-shek's death in 1975, his son Chiang Ching-kuo (Jiang Jingguo) succeeded him as head of the Guomindang (Nationalist Party) and in 1978 as president of Taiwan. He died in January 1988 and was succeeded by Taiwan-born Vice-President Lee Teng-hui. Martial law was lifted after 38 years in 1987. While Taiwan is beginning to enjoy unofficial trade links with the mainland, its principal economic partners are still Japan and the USA.

Tanzania

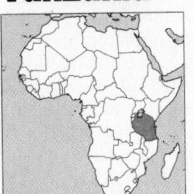

EAT
East Africa
364,886 sq. mi
Pop: 23.2 m
UN, CW, OAU

Capital: Dodoma (pop: 47,700)
Official languages: Kiswahili, English
Religions: Christian (40 per cent), Traditional beliefs (30 per cent), Moslem (30 per cent),
System of govt: Federal republic; independent since 9 December 1961

Tanzania bears traces of human habitation which count among the oldest yet discovered, going back some three million years. The Tanzanian coast, with its islands of Zanzibar, Pemba, Mafia and Kilwa, also traded with Arabia and India from the early centuries of the present era.

Zanzibar and mainland coastal ports were colonised in the seventh century by Arabs from southern Arabia and the Persian Gulf. Founded at the end of the tenth century, the town of Kilwa subjugated the other coastal towns and became the capital of an African sultanate, which also gained the territory of present-day Mozambique in the 13th century. The meeting of the Arab and African cultures resulted in the coastal Bantu language, Swahili.

In 1498 Portuguese explorer Vasco de Gama first visited the coast of Zanzibar. In 1503 the Portuguese conquered Zanzibar, but were pushed back by the Arabs in 1652. In 1741 Ahmad ibn Said, the imam of Muscat, founded a dynasty which reigned in Zanzibar until 1964.

From the mid-19th century European colonial powers extended their grip from Zanzibar to Tanganyika. In 1885 the German East Africa Company acquired the mainland known as Tanganyika, and obtained the coastal zone of Tanganyika from the sultan of Zanzibar in 1888. Germany installed a protectorate over the area in 1891, after an accord (1890) with Britain, which gained Zanzibar.

After the First World War the German colony was divided between three countries: Portugal, which got possession of a band of territory in the south; Belgium, which obtained a mandate over Rwanda-Urundi; Britain, which got most of the former German territory (Tanganyika), and retained it after 1945, with the task of preparing it for independence.

A nationalist movement led to the formation, in 1945, of the Tanganyika African National Union, headed by Julius Kambarage Nyerere. Independence within the Commonwealth was acquired in 1961, and Julius Nyerere became first prime minister, and then president following the proclamation of a republic in December 1962.

The sultanate of Zanzibar became independent in its turn on 10 December 1963, and became a republic after a revolution against the sultan led by Marxist-inspired nationalists. Zanzibar was united with Tanganyika in April 1964, and the new state, headed by Nyerere, took on its present name, Tanzania (from TANganyika and ZANzibar). Nyerere instituted a socialist programme of development and social cohesion (ujamaa) from 1967.

The TANU and the Zanzibar Afro-Shirazi Party fused in 1977 to become the revolutionary Party of Tanzania (Chama Cha Mapinduzi or CCM).

In 1972 a border war broke out between Tanzania and its East African neighbour Uganda, led by the recently installed dictator Idi Amin. The two countries eventually settled the dispute through Somali mediation.

Relations between Tanzania and the brutal buffoon Amin were never serene, and the Ugandan leader's declaration, in November 1978, that he was going to annex a large tract of Tanzania proved the last straw. In early 1979 Tanzanian troops and the Tanzanian-backed Uganda Liberation Front crossed the border and closed in on the Ugandan capital, Kampala. Libyan troops arrived to back Amin, but Amin had fled by the end of the month.

Nyerere retired from office at the elections of October 1985, and was succeeded by Ali Hassan Mwinyi, former head of the Zanzibar government. In November 1988 Mwinyi reached a deal with the IMF in which the organisation would back stringent austerity measures to cope with the country's troubled economy.

In the early 1980s it was decided that the state institutions of Tanzania, one of Africa's most stable countries, should gradually move from Dar-es-Salaam to a new capital city. Among the first to move has been the Tanzanian parliament, which now sits either in the new city, Dodoma, or Dar-es-Salaam. Dodoma, which is being constructed with foreign aid, will probably be finished by the mid-1990s.

Thailand

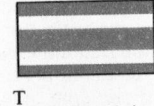

T
South East Asia
198,456 sq. mi
Pop: 53.7 m
UN, ASEAN

Capital: Bangkok (pop: 5.3 m)
Official language: Thai
Religion: Buddhism (95 per cent)
System of govt: Constitutional monarchy since constitution of 22 October 1976

Archaeological remains of an ancient and densely populated habitation have been found on the territory of present-day Thailand. The first mention of the region, named Suvannabhumi (Land of Gold), appeared in Buddhist texts dating back to about 250 BC. Dvaravati, a large kingdom of the Mons, seems to have exerted a major influence until the arrival of Thai tribes in the eighth century. From the south of China (though not of Chinese origin), and entering the country through the Menam Basin, these tribes subjugated the Mons and the Khmers and founded the kingdom of Sukhothai in the 13th century.

In c.1350 the rivalry between the different Thai principalities gave way to the creation of the kingdom of Siam (the Syam Thai people), with the prince of Uthong being crowned under the name Ramadhipati, who established his capital at Ayuthia, on an island in the Menam River. The Ayuthia kingdom seized Angkor (1431), putting an end to Khmer power, took possession of the Sukhothai kingdom, and extended its domination as far as Cambodia and Malaya.

After coming into conflict with the Burmese, Siam was conquered in 1569. Siamese independence was recovered in 1592 by Naresuen. The first treaties with European powers were signed in 1518 with the Portuguese. The Spanish, Dutch and English followed. In 1686, the French obtained trading rights and the right to station their troops in the region, thanks to negotiations undertaken by a wily Greek adventurer, Constantine Phaulkon, who was entrusted with the superintendence of Thai foreign trade by King Narayana (1657-88).

The king's death marked the beginnings of a nationalist reaction, and the country was closed to Europeans until the start of the 19th century, especially to missionaries whose activities clashed with Buddhist beliefs.

Despite being dominated by rivalry with the kingdom of Annam (Vietnam) in Laos and Cambodia, and by another Burmese offensive (1759), the first half of the 18th century was marked by a lively growth in the Thai economy and culture. Ayuthia was seized and destroyed in 1767, but was rapidly reconquered under the half-Chinese bandit leader General Taksin, who subsequently usurped control and established his new capital at Thonburi (Bangkok).

Restoration of Thai power

General Chakri had to return from Cambodia, where he had re-established Thai domination, in order to sort out the chaos caused by King Taksin, who had gone insane. General Chakri himself crowned king of Siam under the name Rama I and reaffirmed the capital as Bangkok (1782). Thailand's present-day king, Bhumipol Adulyadej, belongs to the Chakri dynasty founded by Rama I.

The desire of King Rama IV (Mong Kut) to open his country to the western powers led to the signing of a trade agreement with Britain in 1855, followed by identical treaties with, among others, France, the USA and Prussia. This policy enabled Siam to be the only south-east Asian country to remain fully independent of European colonial powers.

Rama V carried out major reforms before 1910, such as the modernisation along western lines of state institutions, and the abolition of slavery and servitude. Anglo-French rivalry protected Siam from colonial imperialism, although Siam did have to concede the towns of Vientiane, Luang Prabang, Battambang and Siem Reap to France in 1893, and then the four Malayan states of Kedah, Perlis, Kelantan and Trengganu to Britain in 1909.

Modern Thailand

A group of intellectuals and officers educated in the west, led by the lawyer Pridi Phanamyong, took control of the government in 1932 and forced King Rama VII (1925-35) to accept a constitution in preparation for the gradual introduction of universal suffrage. The king abdicated in 1935, when his successor, Ananda Mahidol, was ten years old. A regency council took power, and was gradually more and more dominated by the army. Major Pibun Songgram, in power since 1938, established a nationalist policy, and from 1939 Siam became known officially as Thailand.

Supported by Japan during the Second World War, Pibun attempted to constitute a Greater Thailand, at the expense of French and British territories. In 1944 he was overthrown by a resistance movement led by Pridi Phanamyong, who turned the country into a democracy. Pibun, however, carried out a coup in 1947 and set up a military dictatorship while retaining the monarchy. Political parties and trade unions were banned in 1952. Under the dictatorship the influence of the USA replaced that of Britain, with the 1950 accord permitting the USA to establish military bases on Thai soil and allowing

US companies to exploit the country's resources. In 1954 Thailand became a member of the South East Asian Treaty Organistion (SEATO), an eastern version of NATO.

After Pibun's overthrow in 1957 the country remained governed by the military, who employed repression and the retention of a state of emergency until 1973. The military supported US policy in Vietnam and was predictably opposed to Thai communist movements.

A brief period of democracy, with all agreements with the USA being renounced, was ended by a coup in 1976. General Prem Tinsulanond arrived in power as prime minister in February 1980. The general was able to maintain power despite considerable political tension both at home, leading to the dissolution of the Thai National Assembly in March 1983, and confrontations with Vietnamese troops on the Cambodian border.

Yet another attempted military coup was unsuccessful in September 1985. General Tinsulanond was again chosen to head the government after the elections held in July 1986, his third successive term as prime minister, but after the election held in July 1988 declined an invitation to serve again. He was succeeded by Major General Chatichai, the first prime minister to sit in the Thai House of Representatives as an MP since the coup of 1976.

Togo

TG
West Africa
21,925 sq. mi
Pop: 3.15 m
UN, OAU

Capital: Lome (pop: 366,000)
Official language: French
Religions: Traditional beliefs (46 per cent), Christian (37 per cent), Moslem (17 per cent)
System of govt: Republic; independent since 27 April 1960

Around 1470 the coast of Togo was first visited by the Portuguese. Later Togo was visited almost exclusively by slave traders, replaced by palm oil traders in the 19th century until, in 1884, the German explorer Gustav Nachtigal signed protectorate treaties with tribal chiefs, and named the country Togo after a small village. By 1901 all present-day Togo was under German domination.

In 1919 Britain obtained a mandate for western Togo and France eastern Togo (modern Togo). In 1946 the UN entrusted both parts to France, until a 1956 referendum joined part of the country to the British Gold Coast (Ghana).

Togo became independent in 1960. The first president was Sylvanus Olympio, killed in a coup in January 1963. His successor, Nicholas Grunitzky, installed a democratic regime, itself overthrown in January 1967. In April 1967 Lieutenant-Colonel Gnassingbe Eyadema took power and suspended the constitution. In 1969 a single party was created, and Eyadema confirmed in office in January 1972. The country's prowestern policy was not changed. A policy of africanisation was set up (1974) and the phosphate industry was nationalised.

The 1967 state of emergency was lifted in December 1979 after a new constitution had been ratified. In January 1983 Eyadema announced that a plot by Olympio's banished sons had been thwarted. Another coup attempt failed in September 1986. In December 1986 Eyadema, the only candidate, won a new seven-year term.

Tonga

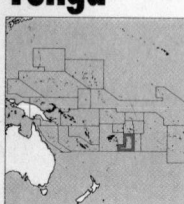

Oceania
289 sq. mi
Pop: 96,000
CW

Capital: Nuku'alofa (pop: 28,800)
Official languages: Tongan, English
Religions: Protestant (81 per cent), Catholic (16 per cent)
System of govt: Constitutional monarchy; independent since 4 June 1970

The ancestors of the first Polynesian inhabitants of Tonga were probably navigators coming from Samoa about a thousand years ago.

There are around 150 islands on the coral and volcanic archipelago and the origins of some of their ruling dynasties date back to the ninth and tenth centuries. The first Europeans to set foot on the Tongan archipelago were the Dutch; Le Maire arrived in 1616 and then Tasman in 1643.

The British navigator James Cook, who landed there in 1773 and 1777, gave the archipelago the name Friendly Islands from the reception he received. Methodists from the London Missionary Society landed in Tonga for the first time in 1797, but their mission came to nothing. However, in 1831 Tonga's Chief Taufa'ahau Tupou was baptised and brought unity to the Tonga islands with British support. He had himself crowned King George Tupou I.

In 1875 parliamentary and governmental institutions were put into place. Tonga became a British protectorate in 1900, reinforced by a 1905 accord and extended in scope in 1959. Queen Salote Tupou III (1918-65) was succeeded by her son, Taufa'ahau Tupou IV. In 1970 Tonga became an independent constitutional monarchy within the Commonwealth. Fatafehi Tu'ipelehake, brother of the king, has been prime minister since 1970. Tonga lives mainly off agriculture, especially the production of yams and taro, and the export of copra. Its main trading partners are the Netherlands and Australia.

Trinidad and Tobago

TT
Caribbean
1,978 sq. mi
Pop: 1.22 m
UN, OAS, CW, CARICOM

Capital: Port of Spain (pop: 59,000)
Official language: English
Religions: Catholic (32 per cent), protestant (28 per cent), Hindu (25 per cent)
System of govt: Republic; independent since 31 August 1962

In July 1498 Christopher Columbus was the first European to visit the two islands now known as Trinidad and Tobago. The islands were declared Spanish territory in 1532, whereafter, like numerous other islands of the Lesser Antilles, they served mainly as a hideout for pirates.

In 1763 the British seized Tobago from Spain, followed by Trinidad in 1797. The growth of the islands' economy began with the arrival of French settlers from Haiti and colonisation by the British, which allowed sugar plantations to be developed.

Oil was discovered in 1866, and today hydro-carbon exploitation is the main sector of the Trinidad and Tobago economy. The abolition of slavery in 1838 led to a large influx of foreign workers, mostly Indians, who now represent 40 per cent of the population.

Trinidad and Tobago were united as a British crown colony in 1888. In 1941 the USA obtained a 99-year lease for naval and air bases. Most of the British colonies in the West Indies, among them Trinidad and Tobago, Barbados, Jamaica and the Windward and Leeward islands, were joined together in 1958 to form the West Indies Federation, which Britain intended to grant independence as a single state. But local differences led to its eventual dissolution in 1962.

At the time of independence in August 1962, power was held by Dr Eric Williams, a member of the People's National Movement, representing the black community. In southern Trinidad a number of refineries were installed, treating mainly Venezuelan oil. In 1970 there was an unsuccessful uprising by the Black Panthers, who were joined by part of the civil guard. Trinidad and Tobago became a republic after a new constitution came into force in 1976.

Eric Williams died in 1981 and was succeeded as premier by George Chambers of the same party. Relations with Barbados and Jamaica, already strained since the Caribbean economic war of spring 1983, deteriorated badly after the US invasion of Grenada, which was strongly condemned by Trinidad and Tobago.

In elections held in December 1986, a new party, National Alliance for Reconstruction (NAR), formed from four opposition parties, won a landslide victory and its leader Arthur Robinson replaced George Chambers as prime minister. In the autumn of 1988 the deteriorating economy led the government to dismiss 25,000 of its 60,000 employees.

Tunisia

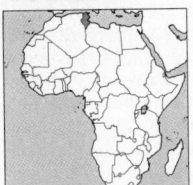

TN
North Africa
59,664 sq. mi
Pop: 7.63 m
UN, AL, OAU

Capital: Tunis (pop: 596,000)
Official language: Arabic
Religion: Moslem (99 per cent)
System of govt: Republic; independent since 20 March 1956

The first Phoenician settlements on the Tunisian coast date back to c.1100 BC. In 814 BC the colonists of the Phoenician town of Tyre founded a settlement, Carthage (New Town), on the peninsula off present-day Tunis.

Carthage became one of the most important ports of transit for Phoenician sailors en route to Spain. Carthage and its empire were destroyed by the Romans at the end of the Third Punic (Carthaginian) War, in 146 BC. The then highly fertile region, integrated into the province of Africa, became the "granary of the Roman empire".

Carthage was conquered in 439 by Gaiserich, who made it the capital of the Vandal kingdom. His fleet briefly managed to dominate the whole of the Mediterranean. The Byzantine general Belisarius destroyed the Vandal kingdom in 534 and present-day Tunisia was integrated into the Eastern Roman (Byzantine) empire.

Arab and Ottoman domination

The Arabs conquered the country and destroyed Carthage, the last Byzantine bastion in Africa, in 698. Native Berber tribes put up fierce resistance to the Arab conquest until their subjugation in the ninth century, and from then on there were no further obstacles to the Arabic islamicisation of the country.

In 800 Ibrahim ibn al-Aghlab established the Arab dynasty of the Aghlabids, who established their capital at Kairouan in the centre of Tunisia and were able to extend their ascendancy in Ifriqiyah (Tunisia, from the Latin name Africa) despite its attachment to the caliphate of Baghdad. A succession of dynasties followed: the Fatimids from the mid-tenth century, the Almohads (the mid-12th century) and the Hafsids (start of the 13th century).

The Ottomans conquered the country in 1547 and placed a pasha at its head, while power was exercised by the military chiefs, the beys and the deys. The bey dynasty of the Husainids was founded in 1705 by Husain ibn Ali and continued to reign until 1957. From the early 18th century Ottoman sovereignty was only superficial.

During the 19th century Tunisia became more and more dependent on Europe, the beys having recourse to loans from European banks for their reforms, including modernisation of the army, education and the introduction of a constitution (1861).

Corruption and the extravagance at court led to the kingdom's bankruptcy in 1869 and a joint Franco-Italian commission was charged with its financial administration.

After Britain had recognised French interests in Tunisia through the 1878 Congress of Berlin, France forced the bey, Muhammad al-Sadiq, to entrust the responsibility for Tunisian foreign policy to France (1881). In 1883 the country became a French protectorate. The bey officially remained head of state, but the French resident held true power.

The first Tunisian nationalist organisation appeared in 1907 with the Young Tunisian Party. In 1920 the liberal and constitutional Destour Party was created. It split under the influence of Habib Bourguiba, who created the radically separatist Neo-Destourian Party in 1934.

Independent Tunisia

Bourguiba came to power in April 1956, shortly after independence, and proclaimed a republic in July 1956. He removed the last bey, Mohammed VIII al-Amin. After a phase of collectivist economic planning in the 1960s, a return to liberal policy was initiated by the 1969 peasant revolts. A border conflict with Algeria was ended after the signing of a treaty of friendship and co-operation between the two states in 1983.

Huge rises in the price of bread and the withdrawal of subsidies for essential goods provoked violent troubles in January 1984, which resulted in a number of deaths. The expulsion of 20,000 Tunisian workers from Libya and threats by Colonel Gadaffi led to the severing of diplomatic ties between Tunis and Tripoli.

Habib Achour, the leader of the principal trade union, was arrested in August 1985. Bourguiba, who had been life president since 1975, resumed control of the country's affairs.

Tunisian's prime minister, Mohammad Mzali, was replaced by Rachid Sfar in July 1986 and the latter in turn by General Ben Ali in October 1987. Under the Tunisian constitution General Ben Ali, in his position as prime minister, became heir to the presidency and in November 1987 he became president after quietly removing from office, with government support, the increasingly infirm and senile 84-year-old Bourguiba who had led the country since independence.

Turkey

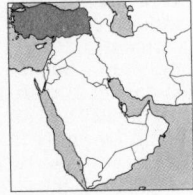

TR
Near East
300,947 sq. mi
Pop: 47.28 m
UN, NATO, OECD

Capital: Ankara (pop: 2.23 m)
Official language: Turkish
Religion: Moslem (98 per cent)
System of govt: Republic; proclaimed 29 October 1923

The town of Catal Huyuk in southern Anatolia, is one of the oldest cities in the world. The people who lived there in the seventh and sixth millenia BC left remains of a highly developed neolithic civilisation.

During the Indo-European (Aryan) migrations at the start of the second millenium BC, the Hittites settled in Anatolia, and their king, Labarnas I, founded the first Hittite empire, establishing his capital at Kussara. His son, Hattusilis I, transferred the Hittite capital to Hattusa (Bogazkoy) and conducted campaigns as far as Syria.

In around 1440 BC the new Hittite empire was founded and reached its peak under the reign of Suppiluliumas I in the 14th century BC when he conquered the whole of Asia Minor and the kingdom of the Mittani on the Euphrates, pushing back the Syrian rulers. Around 1200 BC the Hittite empire gave way under the attack of the so-called "sea peoples".

In 738 BC the Phrygians established a powerful kingdom in Asia Minor. In 680 BC their capital, Gordion, fell into the hands of the Lydians. In 658 BC the Greek city of Megara founded the colony of Byzantium (later Constantinople, and today Istanbul), on the western bank of the Bosphorus. This Greek city, which had been remarkably well equipped as a port since high antiquity, was to play a key role in trade with the Black Sea and Mediterranean regions and came to dominate the strategic passage from Europe into Asia.

The greater part of the territory of present-day Turkey fell under Persian domination in the fourth century BC, and, shortly afterwards, under Macedonian domination, becoming a Roman province in the second century BC.

Byzantine domination

In 330 the Roman emperor, Constantine the Great, chose Byzantium (which had been renamed Constantinople after him in 326) as the imperial residence for his Christian empire, and embellished it as befitted an imperial city.

Byzantine spiritual and intellectual influence was extended ever further. A number of church councils assembled in the city, which was a Christian spiritual centre. Byzantium reached its apogee under the reign of Justinian the Great (527-65). He attempted to restore the world power of the Roman empire and his civil law code was the foundation of the Roman law used in many countries.

Justinian, who built the magnificent church of Hagia Sophia in Constantinople, partially restored Roman power in the former western empire, especially in Africa and Italy.

One of Justinian's successors, Emperor Heraclius I, definitively made the Eastern empire a Greek and not a Latin one, making Greek the official language of the Byzantine empire. He also succeeded in restoring imperial authority in the face of threats from the Avars, the Sassanids and from internal religious quarrels. In 627 the Persians were defeated at Nineveh, and Heraclius arrived a year later at Ctesiphon, precipitating the fall of the Sassanid empire.

In 717 Leo III the Isaurian forced the Emperor Theodosius III to abdicate, and founded Syrian (Isaurian) imperial power. In 730 Leo III, an iconoclast (image breaker), promulgated an edict against religious images, which he declared sacrilegious. The iconoclastic dispute foreshadowed the division of the church. The Greek church began to move further away from the Roman catholic church in the west, which approved of religious images.

The Turks made their first recorded appearance in history in 552 when they destroyed a kingdom in eastern Central Asia. In 1055 the Seljuk tribe of Turks seized Mesopotamia from the caliphs. The Seljuk sultan, Alp Arslan, nephew of the dynasty's founder, crushed the Byzantine Emperor Romanos IV Diogenes at the Battle of Manzikert in 1071. Thereafter eastern Anatolia fell into the hands of the Seljuks.

The Seljuk sultanate fell at the end of the 13th century to the advancing Mongols. The Turkish tribes were dispersed around Anatolia.

Birth of the Ottoman empire

The Ottomans, a tribe related to the Oghuz, fled from Khorasan before the Mongols and took refuge in Asia Minor. Their chief, Ertogrul, and then his son, Osman I Ghazi (1280-1326), turned the Mongol invasion to their advantage. The Seljuk empire was thrown into disarray in the face of the Mongols and the Ottomans were able to conquer

Turkey

territories in Anatolia, to which they added conquests from the Byzantines.

On the death of the last of the Seljuk sultans in 1302, Osman I had himself proclaimed bey of the independent Ottoman emirate. In 1354 the Ottomans took Gallipoli, which provided them with the route into Europe.

In 1365 Adrianople (Edirne) became the Ottoman capital under the reign of Murad I, who officially took the title of sultan. In 1371 Constantinople was subjected to payment of a tribute, in 1388 the Bulgarians were subjugated and, a year later, the Serbians were crushed at Kosovo.

The sultan was assassinated at the end of the battle. He was succeeded by his son, Bayezid I. The siege of Constantinople undertaken by Bayezid failed after intervention by the Mongols of Timur Lang (Tamerlane) in 1396.

Vanquished by Tamerlane, the Ottoman empire revived, and Mehmed II (1444-81), grandson of Bayezid, seized Constantinople, by then a rather run down and depopulated city, in 1453; this finally killed off the decrepit Byzantine empire, the oldest enemy of Islam and the ultimate prize of Moslem conquerors. Constantinople (known as Istanbul to the Turks) instantly became the capital of the Ottoman empire.

The Ottomans advanced into the Balkans, occupying Bosnia in 1463 and Herzegovina in 1483. The Peloponnese (southern Greece) was completely occupied in 1460 and the kingdom of Trebizond, the last Greek Christian bastion in Asia Minor, was conquered in 1461.

In 1511 the sultan was overthrown by the Janissaries, the Ottomans' crack troops, after a religious revolt in Anatolia. His son, Selim I (1512-20), defeated the Mamelukes who ruled Egypt and annexed their kingdom and domains from Syria to Egypt. The Persian Safavid king was also driven back and Selim annexed Azerbaijan. After his conquest of Mecca, Medina and other holy Islamic sites of the Hejaz (modern Saudi Arabia), Selim I took the title of caliph (spiritual leader of Islam) in 1516.

The Ottoman empire attained the zenith of its power and cultural influence in the reign of Suleiman the Magnificent (1520-66). In 1522 Suleiman expelled the Knights of St John from Rhodes and turned his efforts towards Europe. Belgrade was taken in 1521 and in 1526 Suleiman crushed King Louis II of Hungary and Bohemia at the Battle of Mohacs, then laid siege to Vienna in 1529. Conquests were also pursued in Asia, where Armenia and Mesopotamia were taken, and in Persia and North Africa, where Algeria fell into the hands of the sultanate in 1529. On the death of Suleiman the Magnificent in 1566 the empire had reached its greatest extent, apart from a short-lived advance in Europe a century later.

The Christian Mediterranean powers united under the leadership of Don Juan of Austria and destroyed the Turkish fleet at the Battle of Lepanto (1571). The Ottomans thus lost their former maritime supremacy and their defeat was followed by a serious political and military crisis, the military complaining that its share of the spoils of war was insufficient. The Ottoman economy also fell into crisis after the sea route to India removed Asia Minor's key position for trade between Europe and India, and the price of silver had fallen following silver imports from America.

The empire, however, did undergo a new phase of expansion under the reign of Mehmed IV, with the conquest of Transylvania and part of Hungary, in 1664, a loss which Austria was forced to recognise. After 25 years of war against Venice, Crete was conquered in 1669, and the sultan again laid siege to Vienna in 1683. A Polish-German army under John Sobieski liberated Vienna and pushed the Ottomans back towards Hungary. In 1687 they were crushed at Mohacs by the Austrians, who recaptured Transylvania. Imperial troops continued their advance into Hungary where they expelled the sultan's troops.

The end of political expansion

The failure of the siege of Vienna in 1683 and the defeat at Mohacs marked the definitive halt of Ottoman expansion into western Europe. The Janissaries overthrew Mehmed IV and put Suleiman III in power. In the 1699 Peace of Karlowitz the Turks recognised new Austrian victories, and the Habsburgs formally obtained Hungary, Transylvania, and major areas of Slovenia and Croatia, and thus became the leading central European power.

The Ottomans were thrown back into south-eastern Europe. Prince Eugene of Savoy took Belgrade in 1717, and in 1718 the Sublime Porte (as the sultan's court and government was called) had to abandon the Temesvar, northern Bosnia and northern Serbia, Belgrade and Lesser Wallachia to Austria.

From the end of the 17th century, the other growing rival to the Ottoman empire was Russia, whose fleet, supported by the British, destroyed the Turkish fleet at Cesme in 1770, the most serious Ottoman defeat since Lepanto. Under the 1774 Peace of Kuchuk Kainarji, Catherine the Great won Russia's Azov and the Black Sea coast between the Dniester and Bug rivers, as well as suzerainty over the khanate of Crimea. At the same time, she won for herself the protectorship of all eastern orthodox Christians in the Ottomans' lands, giving the Russians a ready-made pretext for future interference in Ottoman affairs.

Sultan Selim III tried in vain to halt the empire's decline by installing an administrative and financial system based on the French model. Yet he was unable to prevent further foreign encroachment on Ottoman interests. In 1799 Britain achieved a long-desired objective – the right of free passage through the Dardanelles – and France attained the same right in 1802 under the Peace of Amiens.

The Young Turk Revolution

In 1865 a secret society was formed, comprising young officers and intellectuals. The "Young Ottomans" demanded the installation of a constitutional monarchy, the expulsion of foreign influences and the development of industry. They obtained from Sultan Abdülhamid II (1876-1909) the granting of a constitution in 1876, which was then suspended two years later. The Young Ottomans were succeeded by the Young Turks who sparked off a revolution in 1908. Abdülhamid II had to restore the constitution, guarantee amnesty for political prisoners, lift censorship and dismiss political reactionaries from important posts. The Empire became a constitutional monarchy and in 1909, the Young Turks, who had seized power, demanded the abdication of Abdülhamid in favour of his brother, Mehmed V, whose authority was a facade for the leaders of the Young Turks, Enver Pasha and Talat Pasha. After the revolution Austria-Hungary proclaimed the annexation of Bosnia-Herzegovina and Bulgaria proclaimed independence. The Austrian annexations were recognized by Constantinople in 1909 in return for the payment of a large sum. In 1911 war broke out with Italy which had invaded Tripolitania and Cyrenaica, then the Dodecanese in 1912. The sultanate renounced all territories conquered by Italy in the 1912 Peace of Lausanne. The 1912-1913 Balkan Wars put an end to the Ottoman presence in Europe, except for a band of territory around Constantinople. The Ottoman Empire entered the First World War alongside Germany and broke up definitively after the 1918 Mudros armistice. The peace treaty of Sèvres in 1920 reduced the once immense empire to Asia Minor and Istanbul, and the Dardanelles were placed under international administration.

The Republic of Turkey

The nationalist movement grew from the Young Turk movement and opposed the Greek occupation and the conditions agreed to by the Ottoman sultan at Sèvres. In 1920 a national assembly was convoked at Ankara and appointed Mustafa Kemal – who became Atatürk "Father of the Turks" in 1934 – as the head of a nationalist counter-government.

Mehmed VI abdicated in 1922 and the republic of Turkey was proclaimed on 23 July 1923; this followed the ratification of the Peace of Lausanne which provided for the withdrawal of all foreign troops from Turkey. Mustafa Kemal became president of the republic and the seat of government was transferred from Istanbul to Ankara (Angora until 1930).

Kemal undertook a vast campaign of modernisation of the country. Islam lost its rank as state religion by the constitutional reform of 1928, the wearing of the fez was banned and women obtained the right to vote as well as the right to appear unveiled in public. Islamic tribunals were abolished. Justice was reorganized along western lines and the Roman alphabet replaced Arabic script. When Kemal Atatürk died, in 1938, Ismet İnönü became head of state and enabled Turkey to stay out of the Second World War, apart from a symbolic declaration of war on Germany in 1945. After the war Turkey maintained privileged relations with the West, joining the Marshall Plan (1948) and then NATO (1952).

The Military in Power

President Adnan Menderes, who had been in power since 1950, was overthrown and executed by a military coup led by General Kemal Gürsel, in 1960. The military resumed power in 1971, overthrowing the government of Süleyman Demirel. An almost dictatorial regime was established, characterized by major political and social troubles. The 1980 coup (which was the second overthrow of Demirel) brought General Kenan Evren to power. He suspended all democratic institutions and persecuted the opposition. In 1982 a new presidential-style constitution was imposed, and general Evren became President of the republic. The conservative Turgut Ozal became premier. Martial law was partially lifted, only continuing to be applied in nine of the 67 provinces of the country. These regions, in the south-east, have been the scene of perpetual confrontations between the army and Kurdish separatists. After the western European countries had accused Turkey of human rights violations, a commission of inquiry was set up by Turkey's national assembly in September 1984. The commission returned its conclusions in November, reporting that torture continued to be practised frequently, though not systematically. At the end of the year the two main left-wing parties, the People's Party (HP) and the Social Democratic Party (SODEP) united. The SODEP had not been authorised to take part in the general elections of 1983, but the votes it obtained in the municipal elections of spring 1984 made it possible to estimate the new left-wing union's electoral support at 30 per cent.

The return to more normal parliamentary politics and some improvement in human rights led to closer relations with Europe. In November 1986 Turkey took over the chair of the Council of Europe for a six-month period and in April 1987 it applied formally to be considered for full membership of the European Community (EC). In general elections held on 29 November 1987, Prime Minister Turgut Ozal's government was re-elected.

Tuvalu

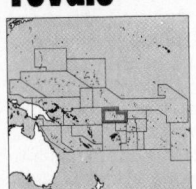

Oceania
9.5 sq. mi
Pop: 7,300
UN, CW

Capital: Funafuti (pop: 2850)
Official language: English, Tuvalu
Religion: Protestant (99 per cent)
System of govt: Constitutional monarchy; independent since 1 October 1978

Tuvalu, one of the smallest states in the world, is an archipelago of nine atolls in the middle of the Pacific Ocean, north of Fiji and east of the Solomon Islands. Tuvalu is peopled mainly by Polynesians, whose ancestors arrived there before 1000.

The Tuvalu islands were first visited by Europeans in 1586 when the Spanish navigator, Alvaro de Mendana de Neyra, landed. At the beginning of the 19th century the islands received the name Ellice Islands, by which they were known to Europeans before independence.

Britain annexed the Ellice Islands and installed a protectorate in 1892. The Ellice Islands were joined with the neighbouring Gilbert Islands to the north west in 1915, and integrated into the crown colony of the Gilbert and Ellice Islands.

Unlike the Gilbert Islands, the Ellice Islands escaped Japanese occupation during the Second World War. A movement for independence in the Ellice Islands developed, particularly after 1960, and the archipelago succeeded in obtaining its separation from the Gilbert Islands after a referendum in 1975. The Ellice Islands took on the name Tuvalu, while the Gilbert islands (which became independent in 1979) became known as Kiribati.

Independence was granted by Britain in 1978 and Tuvalu chose to remain within the Commonwealth, with Queen Elizabeth II as head of state. The islands' foreign policy and defence (Tuvalu has no armed forces) are still taken care of by London. A constitution came into force in the same year as independence.

Tomasi Puapua has been in charge of the Tuvalu government since 1981. Poor local resources, fishing, the cultivation of food stuffs and the export of copra – have led to emigration from the overpopulated islands, and Tuvalu has severe problems with maintaining a supply of fresh water. The country draws most of its income from money sent home by expatriate Tuvaluans who work abroad and from the issuing of special collectors' stamps.

Uganda

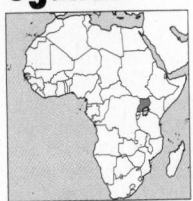

EAU
East Africa
91,343 sq. mi
Pop: 15.5 m
UN, CW, OAU

Capital: Kampala (pop: 458,000)
Official language: English,
Religions: Catholic (49 per cent), protestant (28 per cent), traditional beliefs (15 per cent) Moslem (6 per cent)
System of govt: Republic; independent since 9 October 1962

Several tribes of Hima stock-breeders penetrated into the territory of Uganda during the 16th and 17th centuries and subjugated the Bantu populations in a number of regions. By 1700 the empire of the Hima comprised the kingdoms of Buganda, Toro, Bunyoro and Ankole. The most important of these, Buganda, reached the height of its power between 1860 and 1884 under the reign of Mutesa I.

The explorers Speke and Grant got as far as Buganda in 1862. Christian missionaries were authorised to penetrate the country and Buganda started a permanent army. The death of Mutesa I marked the start of a conflict between moslems, protestants and catholics. An Anglo-German treaty (1890) gave the Hima kingdoms to Britain, which made Uganda a protectorate in 1896.

Indian workers arrived from 1900 to build railways. The Indians were later to play a key role in trade.

Independence

Although the preparations for independence were already at an advanced stage, King Mutesa II of Buganda demanded its acceleration in 1953. The British authorities decreed a state of emergency over the whole of the country and Mutesa II was banished. Under popular pressure the British allowed him to return to Uganda in 1955.

Buganda seceded from the protectorate of Uganda in 1960, but had to renounce independence under pressure from the other provinces of the protectorate which were disadvantaged economically. Independence was granted in 1962, and Dr Milton Obote became prime minister. A republic was proclaimed the following year and King Mutesa II became president. Dr Obote staged a coup in 1966 and the 1967 constitution then made Uganda a centralised republic.

A coup in 1971 brought an army officer, Idi Amin Dada, to power. The constitution was abrogated and political parties banned. Obote took refuge in Tanzania, and in 1972 an armed border conflict broke out between Uganda and Tanzania. The same year Idi Amin Dada expelled all British citizens of Asian origin from Uganda; 40,000 had left by 1973. British enterprises were nationalised. The collapse of the economy was aggravated by a number of conflicts with neighbouring countries, particularly Kenya.

The massacres organised under the Amin regime had already cost an estimated 300,000 lives when Britain broke off diplomatic relations with Uganda in 1976. Amin tried to annex part of Tanzania in 1978, prompting Tanzanian troops and Ugandan exiles to invade Uganda in early 1979.

In 1980 Amin fled, and the Ugandan exiles and the Tanzanians formed a provisional government led by Yusufu Lule. An army commission organised general elections for 1980 which were won, amid some controversy, by Obote. Massacres continued and almost a third of the country was under the control of various anti-government resistance groups.

Despite the foreign aid Obote was unable to redress the country's economic situation. He was overthrown by a coup on 29 July 1985 and replaced by Tito Okello, the head of the army. The new president attempted to negotiate a peace agreement with resistance movements and a ceasefire was signed on 17 December 1985. However, in January 1986 the resistance forces captured Kampala. Their leader, Yoweri Museveni, was elected president on 29 January 1986.

Pro-Amin rebel activity has continued in the north and Museveni has started reorganizing Uganda.

USSR

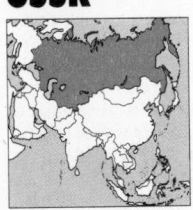

USSR
Europe, Asia
8,649,496 sq. mi
Pop: 286 m
UN, WP,
COMECON

Capital: Moscow (pop: 8.8 m)
Official language: Russian
Religions: Non-religious (51 per cent), Russian orthodox (31 per cent), Moslem (11 per cent)
System of govt: Federation of socialist republics since 30 December 1922

The first traces of human presence in the territory of the present-day USSR were found in Transcaucasia and the Caucasus and date back to the Palaeolithic era. There were later settlements in the Ukraine and Moldau (Vlatva) regions.

Large areas of the great plain of eastern Europe, the Urals and Siberia were inhabited 30,000 years ago by people using fire and fashioning tools from bone and horn in order to fish and hunt. While the tribes to the north remained hunter gatherers, the southern tribes – to the north of the Black Sea, in the Caucasus and the fertile regions of Central Asia – were engaged in the farming of crops and tending livestock from the fourth and third millennium BC.

During the course of the first millennium BC nomadic tribes settled with their herds in the deserts and steppes of Kazakhstan and Central Asia, and later in the regions to the north of the Black Sea and the Caspian Sea. Scythian mounted peoples seem to have dominated these regions from the seventh century BC, and their territory was invaded in the third century BC by the Sarmatians, originating from the Volga region.

From the sixth century Slavonic peoples migrated eastwards from their territories between the Dnieper and Vistula rivers.

The kingdom of Kiev

From the seventh century the small states in the north-west of modern Russia were embroiled in frequent quarrels and called upon mercenary Vikings (Varangians). The Vikings duly penetrated along the rivers Memel, Dvina and Volkhov, and set up small states around their commercial trading posts. The name "Russia" comes from the name the Byzantine Greeks gave to the Varangians – Rhos or Rus.

Russia's written history began in 852 when its name appeared for the first time in writing. In 862 the Varangian Rurik who had dominated the north of Russia from his base in Novgorod, founded the Rurik dynasty and a kingdom which survived until 1598. One of his descendants, Oleg the Wise, united north and south Russia and transferred his capital from Novgorod to Kiev.

The prince of Kiev, St Vladimir, was baptised into the orthodox church in 988 and obtained the title of grand prince from the Byzantine emperor. Although Kiev remained politically independent of the Byzantines, the Byzantine church made it the starting point for the evangelisation of Russia.

The decline of the kingdom of Kiev began after the death of Jaroslav the Wise (1019-54), a great builder and lawmaker. His skilful matrimonial policy had enabled him to ally the Rurik dynasty with the great royal families of Europe, and, under his reign, Kiev had become a highly influential spiritual and cultural centre. He ordered the compilation of the *Russkaya Pravda* (Russian Truth), a code of law which combined Byzantine written law and traditional Slavic law.

In 1037 Kiev had became the seat of an orthodox metropolitan (archbishop), and construction began, in the same year, of the church of St Sophia, which contains the oldest frescos and mosaics in Russian art. The oldest Russian cloister, a monastery cut into rock, was also established near Kiev, in this era (1051).

Grand Prince Vladimir II Monomachos succeeded in re-establishing Kiev's sovereignty over the whole of its territory between 1113 and 1125, but the dissolution of the kingdom into autonomous principalities recommenced after his death. The crown of Vladimir II, the "crown of Monomachos", later became the crown of the czars of Russia.

The Mongols to Ivan the Great

In May 1223 the Mongols destroyed an army of allied Russian princes near the river Kalka. The nomadic cavalry did not, however, exploit their victory and withdrew to the east until 1240, when the Mongol chief Batu Khan took Kiev and subjugated all the principalities to the south-west of Russia. Batu Khan had already seized the Bulgarian kingdoms of Kama and the Volga in 1236, Moscow and the old Russian principality of Ryazan in 1237 and the principality of Vladimir in 1238.

Novgorod was spared by the Mongol horde, but it had to pay tribute and recognise its sovereignty. Mongol domination isolated Russia from Europe in the following decades, while Novgorod and Pskov had to defend themselves against attacks from Swedes, Lithuanians and the Teutonic Knights. In 1242 the Russian Prince Alexander Nevski halted an army of Teutonic Knights on the frozen Lake Peipus.

In 1243 Batu Khan founded Sarai, the capital of the Golden Horde, on the lower Volga. The Mongol empire dominated eastern Europe and western Siberia until 1480. The Russian princes had to swear allegiance to the Golden Horde and their title of prince was granted by an edict of the khans, whose envoys were charged with the control of the principalities' policies.

The khan of the Golden Horde raised the Muscovite prince, Ivan Kalita, in 1328, to the title of grand prince. In 1327 Ivan had exploited a revolt by the Tver populations against Mongol tax levies in order to eliminate Moscow's only rival in its claim to the status of grand principality. Ivan's troops were party to the punitive Mongol expedition which marked the definitive end of the Tvers.

The growth of Moscow's domination was speeded by the transfer of the permanent seat of the "metropolitan of Kiev and all Russia" from Kiev to Moscow in 1325-26.

In 1380 the Grand Prince Dmitri Donskoy refused to pay Moscow's tribute to the horde, which he crushed in battle at Kulikovo on the Don. Despite the Mongol reconquest of Moscow in 1382 under Tokhtamish, Moscow became the symbol of Russian unity and the national struggle for independence. A century later the final break-up of the Golden Horde enabled Grand Prince Ivan III the Great to liberate the principalities from Mongol suzerainty. Ivan III made Moscow the principal power of eastern Europe and built the Kremlin, a fortress and symbol of the Muscovite principality's political and religious power. The building was completed in 1530 under the reign of Vassili III.

Ivan the Terrible

In 1547 the grand prince of Moscow, Ivan IV the Terrible, was crowned czar (emperor) "of all the Russias". He seized the Tartar and Moslem khanates of Kazan and Astrakhan and began the exploration and conquest of Siberia. However, the country was ruined by wars and the peasants, crippled by taxes, suffered under the czar's despotic rule. A futile war against Sweden and Poland for access to the Baltic Sea precipitated the decline of Russian power after the death of Ivan IV in 1584.

During the reign of his son, the insane Fyodor I Dimitri, the country was governed by Boris Godunov, who was eventually crowned czar in 1598 after the death in 1591 of Dimitri, the last of the Rurik dynasty.

In 1589 the czar had raised the metropolitan of Moscow, Iov, to the rank of patriarch. The independence of the Russian orthodox church had been recognised by the synod of Constantinople, and the patriarchy of Moscow was ranked fifth after Jerusalem. Not being of noble birth, Boris Godunov had to deal with the intrigues of the aristocracy, particularly the Romanovs. His son, Fyodor II Borisovich, who succeeded him in 1606, was assassinated a few weeks after his coronation, and the Muscovite army, led by Vasili Shuiski, had the "false Dimitri" crowned. This latter was, in fact, a Russian catholic who since 1604 had been passing himself off in Poland as the son of Czar Ivan IV, Fyodor I Dmitri (who died in 1591).

Supported by the Poles and by an army of discontented Cossacks, the imposter Dimitri succeeded in advancing as far as Moscow, and after his death in 1608 a second false Dimitri appeared. He, too, was supported by the Polish army and set up a government at Tushino, near Moscow. Fighting for the throne lasted until 1613 when the Zemski Sobor (assembly of nobles) elected the 16-year-old Mikhail Fedorovich Romanov as czar. This Romanov dynasty ruled Russia until 1917.

Peter and Catherine

In 1689 the 17-year-old Czar Peter I overthrew his sister Sophie, regent since 1682, and sent her to a convent. In 1697 Peter I made his first European voyage, which took him to Kurland, Prussia, Holland and England. On his return he imposed westernising reforms, such as the abolition of traditional Russian dress at court. He gave privileges to foreign experts – shipwrights, gunsmiths, clerks, teachers, soldiers – and set up technical schools and an academy of science. He tried to reform the bureaucracy on the basis of merit. He had many opponents, but pressed his reforms through with absolute power. The first Russian newspaper was published in 1703, but literacy remained something mainly for the ruling westernised elite.

In 1713 the new city of St Petersburg, Peter's "window on the west", became the capital of Russia, and the first commodities and currency market was opened there in the same year. The czar imposed a new system of writing, "bourgeois script", which combined the Latin and Cyrillic alphabets. In the same year (1710) the Treaty of Nystad put an end to the Northern War which had raged between Russia and Sweden since 1700. Russia obtained access to the Baltic and replaced Sweden as the dominant power there.

Peter died in 1725. After a palace revolution in 1741, Elizabeth Petrovna, Peter's illegitimate daughter, took power and ascended the throne under the name Catherine I. She chose as her successor her nephew Peter of Holstein Gottorp, and, in 1745, married him to the German Princess Sophie of Anhalt-Zerbst, the future Empress Catherine II (the Great). Elizabeth's reign was marked by the extravagance of the court, which was dominated by her favourites, and the country underwent a number of economic crises. It was during her reign that Russia entered into the system of European alliances. In 1775 she approved plans to found the first Russian university at Moscow.

Catherine II (1762-96) took part in the three partitions of Poland, which finally disappeared in 1795. The Peace of Kuchuk Kainarji (1774) enabled her to put an end to the war which had broken out against the Ottoman empire in 1768. Russia obtained the mouths of the rivers Don, Dnieper and Bug, and became the protector of orthodox Christians in the Balkans. In 1783 the Crimea was annexed and the Ottoman sultan again had to cede territory under the Peace of Iasi, namely the Black Sea coast between the southern Bug and Dniester rivers.

Catherine II's reign was also marked by a serious deterioration in the conditions of the peasants and serfs, and in 1773 a rebellion broke out, which was led by Emelyan Pugachev and supported by conservatives and poor Cossacks. Pugachev's manifesto, demanding the abolition of serfdom, enjoyed a great deal of support, but he was captured and executed in Moscow's Red Square in 1775.

Reforms and imperialism

In 1808, during the Napoleonic wars, Czar Alexander I annexed Finland. In 1812 Napoleon crossed the Klaipeda river, without declaring war, and penetrated deep into Russia. But the Russian campaign ended in disaster for Napoleon, whose forces succumbed in the face of the sheer size of the territories, and the scorched earth policy pursued by the Russian leader, Michael Kutuzov. Above all, Napoleon came up against Russia's staunchest ally: the winter.

One of the consequences of the "patriotic war" against the French, decreed by Alexander I, was the foundation of liberal secret societies, whose members came mainly from the young officers of the Imperial Guard, and who had been exposed to liberal principles during the campaigns that had taken them to Europe. Their main aims were the replacement of the czarist autocracy by a constitutional monarchy and the abolition of serfdom.

The "Decembrist" (Dekabristy) conspirators took advantage of Alexander I's death to stage an uprising, which was, however, brutally suppressed by Nicholas I in December 1825. He continued Russian encroachment on the Ottoman Empire and, after the Peace of Adrianople in 1829, the Ottomans abandoned most of the Danube delta, large areas of Armenia, and the principalities of Moldavia and Wallachia.

War broke out again between the two empires in 1853 as a response to Russia's activation of its rights of protectorate over orthodox Christians in the Ottoman empire, which Catherine the Great had secured in 1774 at Kutchuk Kainardji. The ensuing war was fought mainly in the Crimean, and saw France and Britain, who disliked the Ottoman empire but relished even less the prospect of a Russian one supplanting it, allied to the sultan. The war came to an end after the siege of Sebastopol (1855). The 1856 Peace of Paris, which formally settled the war, forced Russia to relinquish her rights of suzerainty over the Danubian principalities and to return the delta of the Danube and southern Bessarabia to Moldavia.

The end of the Crimean War and Alexander II's arrival on the throne marked the beginning of a new phase of reforms. The failure of the system of the balance of power caused relations between the European countries to be redefined, with Russia coming into conflict with Austria over the Balkans and drawing closer to France.

In 1861 the czar promulgated his manifesto on the liberation of the peasants. Almost 22 million Russian subjects attained their freedom from serfdom. Their economic ties, however, remained more or less unchanged, as they had little option but to carry on working for the same landlords.

In Poland, which had been joined by personal union to Russia since 1815 ("Congress Poland"), an uprising broke out in January 1863, which represented the Polish people's final attempt to attain independence in the 19th century. The revolt was crushed by Russian troops in 1864. An attempt to assassinate the czar in 1866 provoked the return of conservatism to Russian domestic policy, which had been growing more liberal.

Germany, Austria-Hungary and the Russian empire were joined, informally, through an agreement proposed by the German Chancellor Otto von Bismarck. This agreement was then replaced, in 1881, by the "League of the Three Emperors", which reaffirmed their solidarity against "revolution" and democratic ideas.

In 1877 the Russian secret police had begun to dismantle the socialist-inspired Narodnik movement. The first mass trial against the secret society members took place the same year, and 193 members of the "Liberty to the People" were sentenced. The day after the end of the trial the revolutionary, Vera Zasulich, mortally wounded the chief of police of St Petersburg.

The year 1878 saw the end of another war against the Ottoman empire, which had broken out a year earlier. The preliminary negotiations to the Peace of San Stefano, ending this war, extended Russia's Armenian territories and returned the Bessarabian regions which had been lost in 1856. The advantages gained by Russia in the Dardanelles by this treaty caused an international conference to be called at Berlin, largely at Britain's instigation, to revise the peace deal. The Congress of Berlin provided for Romania, Serbia and Montenegro to become independent; for Austria-Hungary to occupy the "protectorates" of Bosnia and Herzegovina; and for Britain to obtain a protectorate over Cyprus. Russia thererore had to abandon plans for a vast, Balkans-spanning "Great Bulgaria", over which the czar would have had a protectorship.

Bismarck played a major role in settling the affair and Russo-German tensions followed. In 1879, Germany and Austria-Hungary concluded a separate treaty of alliance.

In 1904 war broke out between Russia and Japan after Japan had attacked the Russian town of Port Arthur at the southernmost point of the peninsula of Liaodong in the Russian Far East. The conflict between the two powers had become increasingly inevitable with their clash of interests in Manchuria and Korea, and Russia, which had to send most of its warships from Europe, came off the worst.

The Russian defeat unleashed the "revolution" of 1905. The army opened fire on demonstrators in St Petersburg. Mutinies and riots spread across the whole of Russia, forcing Czar Nicholas II to guarantee the granting of a constitution, a parliament and individual freedom. The reforms proved to be superficial; the Duma (parliament) was generally in the pocket of the reactionary czarist faction and was frequently dismissed.

Revolution

The revolutionary movement, which had split into two factions, "Bolshevik" (Majority) and "Menshevik" (Minority), gained the upper hand in February 1917, with Nicholas II abdicating after a new wave of troubles and general strikes. A moderate provisional government was set up by Prince Lvov and then the social democrat (Menshevik) Alexander Kerensky became interim premier. Russia looked set to become a western-style democracy.

But it was not to be. On 7 November 1917 (25 October by the old Russian calender, hence "October Revolution"), the Marxists (Bolsheviks) revolutionary faction overturned the provisional government and seized power. Formerly in exile from the czarist regime in Switzerland, until allowed to return by the Germans, Vladimir Ilyich Ulyanov, known by his revolutionary name Lenin, became president of the Council of the People's Commissars (head of government). On 18 January 1918 the third Congress of Soviets (workers' councils) proclaimed the Russian Socialist Federated Soviet Republic (RSFSR).

A handful of Bolsheviks had pulled off a remarkable coup, but only controlled central Russia and some cities; the revolution was not recognised by the Ukraine or the Caucasus, and the domestic opposition was supported by the wartime Allies. The Treaty of Brest-Litovsk (3 March 1918) put an end to the new "Soviet" government's rigorous conditions on Russian participation in the First World War. "White" (anti-Bolshevik) army troops from the Baltic countries, the Ukraine, Crimea, the Caucasus, the Urals and Siberia, converged on Moscow at the end of 1918. However the Soviet Red Army managed to redress the situation in May

1919 and emerged as victors from the civil war, which ended in November 1920 as foreign powers gradually withdrew material support for the Whites.

The Union of Soviet Socialist Republics (USSR) was proclaimed on 30 December 1922. Lenin died in 1924 and was succeeded by a triumvirate consisting of Grigori Zinoviev, Leon Trotsky and Joseph Stalin. Stalin removed his two partners from power in 1927 and governed with dictatorial powers and frequent purges, mass trials and waves of executions, especially during the 1930s. Stalin's campaign against the kulaks, small private landowners, was particularly brutal, as was a partly engineered famine in the discontented Ukraine. Hundreds of thousands died in Stalin's ruthless drive to modernise and communise the USSR. After the Second World War his unlimited powers were joined by a personality cult which glorified the Soviet leader. Until his death Stalin dominated and totally planned every area in the life of Soviet society. He was planning a purge of middle-ranking party officials (including Leonid Brezhnev) even as he died in 1953.

Soviet superpower

The USSR was allied to Hitler at the beginning of the Second World War and profited from the invasion of Poland by occupying the east of the country in 1939. The Baltic countries, Finland and Romania gave in to the USSR. Despite the renewal of the German-Soviet agreement, Hitler invaded the USSR on 22 June 1941. After an initially rapid advance the German troops were subjected to a Soviet counter-offensive during the winter. The heroic resistance put up at Stalingrad, where the Germans capitulated in February 1943, was the turning point of the war.

The victory of the Allies and the USSR enabled Stalin to form a network of Soviet satellite states after the collapse of Hitler's Reich. Two blocs, East (Soviet) and West (US-aligned), had been defined and the "Cold War" set in. The path to military power and armament began. The Warsaw Pact was created in 1955. The launching of Sputnik I, the first object ever to be sent into space, in 1957 caused a shock in international public opinion.

Stalin had died in 1953 and the arrival of Nikita Khrushchev to power marked the beginning of a thaw in relations with the west. The abuse of power and the personality cult which had marked the Stalinist period were denounced. The figure of Lenin was restored and a policy of "destalinisation" inaugurated after the 20th Party Congress of 1956, at which Stalin was denounced. Control over the satellite states was relaxed until the Hungarian uprising of 1956, which was crushed by the Red Army. Khrushchev instigated the policy of "peaceful coexistence" between East and West, but an acute cri-

sis followed in 1962, when the USA demanded the dismantling of a Soviet missile base in Cuba. The conflict was resolved and the missiles went.

Brezhnev succeeded Khrushchev as party leader in 1964 and became head of state in 1977. Parallel to the establishment of a policy of detente with the west, major military installations were undertaken and internal opposition was silenced and suppressed. Attempts at liberalisation within the socialist states were harshly suppressed, either directly (the Warsaw Pact invasion of Czechoslovakia in 1968) or indirectly (the pressure put on Poland in the early 1980s).

The invasion of Afghanistan by Soviet troops (December 1979), and the installation of nuclear warheads (SS-20s) directed at Europe, during the Geneva disarmament talks, put an end to the period of political detente.

Yuri Andropov succeeded Brezhnev (died 1982) and halted the Geneva negotiations after NATO implemented its decision to compensate for the imbalance of forces in Europe.

Andropov died after barely a year in office. After the equally brief tenure of his successor, Konstantin Chernenko, 54-year-old Mikhail Gorbachev became general secretary of the party on 11 March 1985. He initiated a new policy of greater openness (glasnost) in regard to the whole state of the Soviet economy and society. The meeting between Mikhail Gorbachev and the US president, Ronald Reagan, at Geneva in November 1985 marked the changed attitude of the Soviet leaders. This was followed by further meetings between the two leaders in October 1986 in Iceland and again in Washington in December 1987, when a treaty was signed between the two superpowers eliminating their intermediate-range nuclear missile forces. This was subsequently ratified at a further summit meeting between them in Moscow in June 1988.

Along with this new attitude of the Soviet leaders towards foreign relations, there has also been some softening of their treatment of their Warsaw Pact allies, and at home a more liberal treatment of dissidents. Gorbachev authorised the USSR's first elections (1989), to a new Soviet legislature which would be in session for most of the year, in which many candidates were not from the ruling party and included some former dissidents. They included the veteran, scientist and noted dissident Dr Andrei Sakharov. In a speech to the European Parliament in early July 1989 Gorbachev explicitly ruled out the use of force to oppose reforms in Soviet bloc countries such as Poland and Hungary. However, increasing freedom in the USSR has been accompanied by a rising tide of labour unrest and of nationalist discontent in the republics, especially in Central Asia and in the Baltic states.

United Arab Emirates

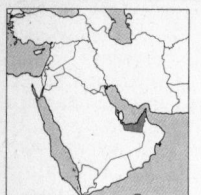

Near East
32,300 sq. mi
Pop: 1.8 m
UN, AL, OPEC

Capital: Abu Dhabi (pop: 450,000)
Official language: Arabic
Religion: Moslem (96 per cent)
System of govt: Federation of seven emirates; independent since 2 December 1971

The coast of the emirates off the Persian Gulf was known in the 19th century as the "Pirate Coast". Pirate activity and the slave trade represented the sole commercial outlets of a population inhabiting an arid environment.

The British East India Company put an end to piracy in 1820 and imposed an "eternal maritime peace" on the inhabitants of the coast in 1853. The protectorate of Britain, which at that point assumed control of its foreign affairs, was officially recognised by the emirates with the birth of the "Trucial States", in 1892.

This situation was changed by the discovery of oil in the emirates of Abu Dhabi, Dubai and Sharjah. Oil has been produced in Abu Dhabi since 1962. In 1968 six Emirates – Abu Dhabi, Dubai, Sharjah, Fujeira, Ajman and Umm-al Quwain – united in a federation which proclaimed its independence in 1971 and was joined by the emirate of Ras al-Khaima in 1972. At the same time as the announcement of the creation of the federation, Britain announced its intention of evacuating all its bases "East of Suez" in 1971. The military, judicial and monetary systems were unified (a unit of currency, the dirham, was created) and a federal government set up in Abu Dhabi. Its first president, Zayid ibn-Sultan al-Nahyan, was re-elected for five years in 1976. The emirates were recognised by Saudi Arabia (1974) and Iran (1975) after these two countries had secured beneficial territorial modifications.

Zayid's project for more extensive unification, with the abolition of internal frontiers for example, aroused a serious domestic crisis in 1979 which led to the nomination of Emir Rashid ibn Said al-Maktum, the ruler of Dubai and opposed to the project, to the post of prime minister.

The temporary resource of oil remains the emirates' principal source of wealth. In 1987 the oil rich emirate of Sharjah survived an internal crisis when it was agreed that its ruler, who had been overthrown, should be reinstated and his brother made his official successor. The emirate occupies a vital strategic position close to the Straits of Hormuz in the Gulf.

In November 1987 the UAE was one of more than 15 Arab states which restored full diplomatic relations with Egypt, with whom ties had been severed since the Egyptian-Israeli peace agreement. In 1988 the emirates were severely hit by the worldwide drop in oil prices, leading to budgetary restrictions to bring down its growing deficit.

United Kingdom

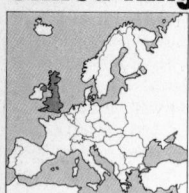

GB
Western Europe
94,226 sq. mi
Pop: 55.8 m
UN, CW, EC,
NATO, OECD

Capital: London (pop: 6.7 m)
Official language: English
Religions: Anglican, other Protestant, Catholic, Moslem
System of govt: Constitutional monarchy; Queen Elizabeth II reigned since 6 February 1952

In the third millenium BC a people from Iberia erected megaliths on the south and west coasts of the British Isles, which was already inhabited by different peoples. Celts began arriving around 600 BC and their influence became more marked after 500 BC.

Later waves of settlement occurred c.250 BC (settlers of La Tene origin) and C.100 BC (Belgic peoples). The links of the latter with the tribesmen of north-east Gaul helped to prompt the Roman invasion under Julius Caesar in 55 BC. Roman colonisation began with the invasion of Claudius in 43. The Roman presence remained until the last troops withdrew in 407, without ever having been able to conquer fully Ireland or Scotland.

Germanic peoples in their turn arrived from across the channel: Angles, Saxons and Jutes, from (roughly) northern Germany and southern Denmark. After fierce fighting they managed to create seven kingdoms in central and eastern England: Mercia, Sussex, Essex, Wessex, East Anglia, Kent and Northumbria. Celtic populations retreated west to Wales and Cornwall with some leaving Britain to colonise Armorica (Brittany) in Gaul.

The Welsh fought among themselves and against the "Saxons" for many centuries. King Edward I killed Llywelyn ap Gruffydd, the last Welsh prince of Wales, near Builth in December 1282. He then crowned his son, the Black Prince, as prince of Wales in 1301. This ended hopes of an independent Wales, which was united with England by acts of 1536 and 1543 – passed, ironically by an English king from a Welsh dynasty, the Tudors.

The conversion of the Anglo-Saxons to Christianity started at the end of the sixth century. The missionary St Augustine, sent by Rome in 601, established himself at Canterbury and the city became the religious centre of the island. A number of attempts were made at uniting the Anglo-Saxon kingdoms, and it was Alfred the Great, king of Wessex (871-99), who finally succeeded. He and his successors had to combat raids from the Danes who finally conquered England in 1016 under King Canute (Knut).

The attachment of England to the Scandinavian kingdom lasted only until the accession of Edward the Confessor in 1042. His death in 1065 was followed by a succession dispute, resolved in 1066 by the victory of William the Conqueror, the duke of Normandy, over King Harold at Hastings. His victory resulted in England developing links with France rather than Scandinavia; these links were reinforced by the accession of Henry of Anjou as Henry II in 1154 and his marriage to Eleanor of Aquitaine, making the king of England the most powerful vassal of the king of France.

Henry invaded Ireland in 1171 and claimed overlordship of Scotland and Wales. After his death his sons Richard I (the Lionheart, 1189-99) and John (known as Lackland, 1199-1216) found themselves in conflict with the feudal barons. John conceded their rights in the Magna Carta (1215). At the same time relations with France deteriorated, giving rise finally to what became known as the Hundred Years War.

The Hundred Years War

Edward III, crowned in 1327, asserted his rights to the French crown and war broke out between the two countries in 1339. The war was not resolved until 1453, and England lost all her continental lands apart from Calais. The war with France reinforced English nationalist feeling and French cultural influence suffered a sharp decline. The financial burden imposed by the war also encouraged the development of parliament, which had the acknowledged right to approve national taxation.

At the end of the Hundred Years War England was shaken by a serious internal political crisis. In 1455 the War of the Roses broke out with the houses of York and Lancaster, two branches of the Plantagenet dynasty, contesting the throne. The victory of the Welsh claimant, Henry Tudor, (1485-1509) in 1485 against Richard III of York put an end to the war. Henry became Henry VII and his marriage to Elizabeth of York united the two families.

The Tudor dynasty

In spite of rival claimants, Henry VII was successful in securing his dynasty. The reign of his son Henry VIII (1491-1547) saw the schism with Rome which arose after a quarrel with the pope, who had refused to annul the marriage of the king, who was still without heir, to Catherine of Aragon. In 1534 the king made himself head of an independent Anglican Church and proceeded to dissolve England's monasteries.

On the death of King Henry VIII in 1547 his son Edward VI was only nine years old. On the death of Edward VI his sister, Mary Tudor, became queen. She tried, without success, to reintroduce catholicism into the country, and even married Philip II of Spain. On her death in 1558 France made a vain attempt to place Mary Stuart, daughter of the king of Scotland, on the English throne, which was filled instead by Elizabeth I, the daughter of Henry VIII and Anne Boleyn.

The Anglican Church was restored in 1559 by the queen, whose reign lasted until 1603 and was an age of both cultural splendour and economic prosperity. Maritime trade boomed. Virginia, the first English colony in North America, was established in 1584. The British East India Company appeared in 1600.

Scotland to 1603

The Romans never conquered Scotland, and Hadrian's Wall (begun 121) and the earthen Antonine Wall (begun 142) are the most striking markers of the Roman frontier almost anywhere in the former empire. Christianity came earlier to Scotland than to England (c.400).

After 500 the Scots, a Celtic people in Ireland, arrived in Dalriada (central south-west Scotland) and formed a rival kingdom to that of the Picts. The first Anglo-Saxon interference in Scotland began between c.600-700 and the first Viking raids in the 780s. The Vikings occupied outer Scotland for many centuries until King James III annexed Orkney and Shetland in 1472.

Dalriada and the Pictish lands were united in 843 by Kenneth MacAlpin, regarded as the first king of what was then called Scotia – Scotland. Conflict with the Anglo-Saxons was now a permanent feature of Scottish affairs, and King Macbeth (1040-57) – a better king than he is reputed – was overthrown by Malcolm III with Anglo-Saxon aid. English-style feudalism was introduced in the early 1100s by King David I and Alexander I, although England's Richard I accepted Scottish independence in 1189.

In c.1200 Scottish parliaments are mentioned for the first time. English intervention continued; Edward I selected John Balliol, an Anglo-Norman lord, for the vacant Scottish throne. But Balliol signed a treaty with France in 1296 and was deposed by Edward the same year. An anti-English campaign began in 1297 under William Wallace, and then, after Wallace's execution, continued by Robert Bruce, crowned king of Scots in 1306. Bruce routed the English at Bannock Burn in 1314 and ruled until 1329.

In 1412 Scotland's first university, St Andrew's, was founded, followed by Glasgow (1451) and Aberdeen (1495). This was a time of a great cultural flowering, and the reigns of James IV (1488-1513) and James V (1513-42) mark the high point of scottish literature. In 1503 James IV married Margaret Tudor, Henry VIII's sister, and the thrones moved closer together. James died at Flodden Field against the English in 1513, and James V also died after a battle against the old foe (Solway Moss, 1542). The Reformation began to take hold in lowland Scotland around this time, and its leading figure was the fiery John Knox, who was exiled to France from 1547-59. He returned, and the Scottish Parliament declared protestantism to be the state religion. The unpalatably catholic Mary, queen of Scots, daughter of James V, arrived from France to assume her throne in 1561, but was deposed in 1567 and fled to England. Considered a threat to the English throne, she was executed in England in 1587. But her removal made her son, James VI, heir to both thrones and in 1603 he achieved by right what English monarchs had long sought by force: the union of crowns. James VI of Scotland and I of England was persuaded to call his new joint realm "Great Britain".

Stuarts and civil war

The status of Anglicanism as the state church was reaffirmed in 1604. The Gunpowder Plot, a Catholic conspiracy led by Guy Fawkes and Robert Catesby, was discovered a year later and the plotters executed.

From 1612 the king surrounded himself with favourites. Robert Carr, earl of Somerset from 1613, played an important role in the government. Parliaments summoned by the king in 1614 and 1621 because of his financial difficulties were immediately dissolved. George Villiers, the future duke of Buckingham, replaced Somerset as favourite in 1616. At peace with Spain since 1604, James I refused to split with Madrid on the outbreak of the Thirty Years War in 1618. However, English diplomacy was turned against Spain by Buckingham, whose influence increased from 1624. But the expedition of the English fleet to Cadiz under

Charles I (1625-49) ended in disaster in 1625. Despite the king's marriage with Henrietta Maria, daughter of Henry IV of France, relations with France became strained from 1626.

Charles I had already dissolved two parliaments, but a financial crisis forced him to call a third (1628-29), and to give his nominal consent to the Petition of Right which it presented. The prayer book of Archbishop Laud, unacceptable to Puritans (the term used for particularly austere protestants), was imposed in 1637 and marked the opening of a period of severe persecution of the Puritans, many of whom emigrated to North America.

Scotland, however, revolted against Laud's episcopalian measures and the king, unable to master the situation (the First Bishop's War), had to accept the Treaty of Berwick in 1639 and the Scottish Covenant, accompanied by the abolition of bishoprics in Scotland. Charles I raised a new army against the Scots who, however, were victorious at Newburn in August 1640 (Second Bishop's War).

The king's only means for a new campaign was to convoke parliament. The Long Parliament was composed in the Commons largely of Puritans; met in November and immediately sent Laud to the Tower of London. Anti-royal measures taken by parliament gathered a strong Anglican party around Charles I, who then alienated support by negotiating with the Irish catholics. In June 1642 parliament presented the king with the "Nineteen Propositions" – an absolute ultimatum removing all his powers. Charles I's refusal sparked the English Civil War.

The parliamentary army won several victories in 1643 and 1644, with Oliver Cromwell playing a decisive role in the victory of Marston Moor in July 1644. Parliament's alliance with Scotland brought it under the banner of presbyterianism. The Scots captured the king in May 1646 and returned him to England where he was executed on 30 January 1649. Cromwell brutally suppressed Ireland and Scotland, which had provided support for Charles' son, the future Charles II. The Long Parliament was dissolved in 1653 and on 16 December Cromwell published "The Instrument of Government", which established the Protectorate, uniting England, Scotland and Ireland. Cromwell died on 3 September 1658. His son Richard succeeded him but gave up office in May 1659.

Restoration

General George Monk recalled King Charles II from exile in France and he returned to London in May 1660. He ruled more or less absolutely – he rarely called parliament – but stabley.

He was succeeded by his brother, the catholic James II, in 1685. The catholic authoritarianism of his regime provoked a new revolt of parliament,

which called upon the king's nephew and son-in-law, the Dutch stadholder (which means leader) William of Orange, who was married to James' daughter Mary.

William and Mary landed in England in 1688 and James II took refuge in France. Once king, William III and Mary recognised the rights of parliament in the Bill of Rights. William ruled alone after the death of Queen Mary in 1694.

Britain: a world power

William was succeeded by Mary's sister Anne (1702-14). In her reign, in 1707, the Scottish parliament was abolished and the two kingdoms united with one parliament at Westminster (London). Catholics (in effect, the remaining Stuarts) were forbidden to inherit the throne in 1712. She died childless and the succession passed to the elector of Hanover, a descendant of one of James I's daughters.

King George I spoke no English and preferred Hanover to Britain. He entrusted state affairs to his cabinet, led by Robert Walpole from 1721-42, regarded as the first prime minister, who reformed the administrative structure of the country, pursued a favourable trade policy and restored the state's finances. Scotland was discontented with English rule; Jacobite (pro-Stuart) rebellions broke out in Scotland in 1715 and 1745, after the last of which the Highlands, the main centre of Jacobite feeling, were ruthlessly suppressed.

A new war with France broke out in 1755. The foreign secretary, William Pitt the Elder (Lord Chatham), succeeded in winning from France all her lands in North America, as well as her territories in southern India. These were augmented by Senegal in 1763 and the Lesser Antilles under the Treaty of Paris, which put an end to the Seven Years War. Britain was now unrivalled as a world power. In 1783, however, it had to recognise the loss of the North American colonies (except Canada) after the War of Independence.

The escalation of the Industrial Revolution brought about a new shock soon followed by that of the French Revolution. Numerous radical movements sprang up in Britain's industrial centres and, in the face of the supposed threat represented by revolutionary France, the government introduced measures to curb "Jacobinism". Britain took part in four coalitions against Napoleon and destroyed the Franco-Spanish fleet at Trafalgar in 1805. The failure of Napoleon's Continental System (a trade embargo against Britain) was closely followed by the French defeat at Waterloo.

Industrial nation

At the same time as the Industrial Revolution which developed between 1750 and 1850, Britain underwent an unprecedented growth in population. The expansion of trade and manufac-

turing, along with the discoveries in engineering and their industrial application, radically altered the traditional way of life. Britain was "the first industrial nation", as a later historian put it.

Developments in agriculture led to a massive exodus from the country to the towns. The textile industry was the first to adapt to new technology, putting an end to cottage-based industry and concentrating industrial activity in factories.

Towards the middle of the 19th century these had reached a scale which prompted the first social welfare measures. The ten hour working day was made law in 1850. The Reform Act of 1832 may have added few people to the franchise, but was an essential step to greater parliamentary reform and democracy. A Second Reform Act followed in 1867, which doubled the electorate by giving the vote to ratepayers, and the first Trades Union Congress met in 1868. The Liberal Party, headed by William Gladstone, was in power four times from 1868 to 1894. He introduced compulsory schooling for everyone, reformed the army and breathed new life into the economy with monetary and fiscal reforms. He also tried, and failed, to give Ireland home rule (autonomy).

The Conservative Benjamin Disraeli was prime minister from 1874 to 1880. It was under his direction that British imperialist policy was given a boost, with India being made an empire in 1876. Britain abandoned protectionism. Apart from one interruption due to the First World War, the age of free trade lasted from 1846 until 1932.

Imperial zenith and decline

The Boer War broke out in 1899 as a result of the imperialist policy pursued by the Conservative government in South Africa. The Boers were defeated in 1902, and Transvaal and Orange Free State were annexed. After a reign of 64 years, Queen Victoria died in 1901 and was succeeded by King Edward VII (1901-1910). The Liberals returned to power in 1905 and important social welfare laws were passed. When the House of Lords opposed the budget presented by the government in 1911, the Parliament Bill was pushed through to remove its right of veto (although it still has delaying powers).

George V was crowned in 1910 and political conflicts continued to worsen under his reign which lasted until 1936. It was under these conditions that the First World War broke out. Under the Treaty of Versailles in 1919, Britain gained some German colonies and several territories formerly belonging to the defeated Ottoman empire, under a League of Nations mandate. About a quarter of the Earth's surface at that time belonged to Britain.

The war had changed British society and its political parties. The Liberals lost the "social concern" vote to the rising Labour Party (formed 1900). The right to vote was granted to all taxpaying men over the age of 21 and to all women over 30 with husbands who paid tax; The full female franchise was not achieved until 1928. Ireland, which had openly rebelled in and after 1916, was finally given self-government in 1921 – or at least, part of Ireland.

The Labour Party formed a government for the first time in 1922. The General Strike of 1926 was followed by the world economic crisis of 1929. The government of national unity formed in 1931 took strict measures to restucture the economy. In the same year the Statute of Westminster turned the British Empire into the Commonwealth of Nations, a community of nations held together by the British crown and economic interdependence. The dominions of Canada, Australia, Newfoundland, New Zealand and South Africa,

became independent. Privileges granted to Poland by Britain and France led the country into the Second World War in September 1939. Britain, led from 1940 by Winston Churchill, succeeded in maintaining the war effort against German bombing and in gaining the material support of the USA before its actual entry into the war.

The Second World War marked the definitive end of British supremacy in Europe and overseas. Beginning with India in 1947, the British colonies were more or less willingly given their independence in the years following the 1945 victory and remained, for the most part, within the Commonwealth.

Since 1945

The Labour Party of Clement Attlee won the 1945 election and nationalised the most important sectors of

the British economy. Some of these nationalisations were annulled on the return to power of Winston Churchill and the conservatives in 1951. He retired in 1955 and Anthony Eden was briefly premier until the Suez crisis – the death throes of Anglo-French imperialism – forced him from office. His successor, the urbane and wily Harold Macmillan, began the decolonisation of Africa in earnest from 1957. He resigned in 1963 and was briefly succeeded by Sir Alec Douglas-Home until Labour returned to power under harold Wilson in 1964.

In 1969 crisis flared in Northern Ireland, and the government of Edward Heath (1970-74) faced the worst years of the troubles, scrapping the separate Northern Ireland executive. In 1973 Heath took Britain into the EEC (long opposed by France under De Gaulle). Wilson remained in office until his

retirement in 1976 when he was replaced by James Callaghan (1974-79). Callaghan faced an uphill battle against the effects of a deepening world recession, which sparked inflation and industrial unrest, despite increased revenues from North Sea oil. He lost in 1979 to Margaret Thatcher, the Conservative leader since 1975, who has been re-elected twice since. She introduced tough monetarist policies to control inflation and returned many longpublic utilities to the private sector.

Ireland continues to feature high on the national agenda. For the first time since 1922 Dublin was given a consultative role in Ulster's affairs by the Anglo-Irish Agreement in 1985. The future of one of the last colonial territories, Hong Kong, was agreed in 1984 with China, which will take over sovereignty in 1997.

United States of America

USA
North America
3,539,289 sq. mi
Pop: 243.7 m
UN, NATO,
OAS, OECD

Capital: Washington (pop: 626,000)
Official language: English
Religions: Protestants (40 per cent), Catholics (30 per cent), Jews
System of govt: Presidential Federal Republic since the Constitution of 17 September 1787

The origins of the first inhabitants of North America are still uncertain. They were probably Asian peoples who arrived on the continent in a number of waves from 30,000 BC onwards after crossing over the glaciated Bering Strait. The first evidence of these peoples dates back to between 12,000 and 8000 BC. The hunter-gatherers followed the hunters in between 7000 BC and 5000 BC. Whilst the cultures of South and Central America were flowering into splendid civilizations the peoples of the North remained largely nomadic with no agricultural base. The Iroquois seem to have developed a social structure which went beyond the tribal stage. Around the year 1000 AD the Norwegian navigator, Leif Eriksson, was cast onto the North American coast by a storm as he was bound for Greenland.

But the historical date for the discovery of America is that of the arrival of Christopher Columbus within sight of the island of Guanahani (El Salvador) on 12 October 1492. Giovanni (John) Caboto reached the coasts of the future New England in 1498 whilst in English service. In 1513 Ponce de Leon reconnoitred the coast of Florida.

The Mississippi was discovered by Hernando de Soto in 1539. The Spaniard, Vasquez de Coronados explored the territory of Arkansas between the years 1540 and 1542. The first fixed European colony on the territory of the present-day United States was finally established in 1565 when Pedro Menendez de Aviles and 600 settlers arrived in Saint Augustine in Florida. The north of the continent was divided between England, France, Spain and Russia until the middle of the 18th century.

The Thirteen English Colonies

After suffering a series of setbacks during the 16th century the English colonisers succeeded in establishing in 1607 the first permanent British American settlement in Jamestown, Virginia; Virginia became a British colony in 1624. In 1620 the Mayflower carrying 120 puritan emigrants from England, the Pilgrim Fathers, landed at Cape Cod near present-day Provincetown and then proceeded towards Plymouth. The new arrivals agreed in the Mayflower Compact that each of them had the right to expect just treatment from the government they would establish. The Mayflower Compact has remained the symbol in American history of the first agreement between free men leading to the founding of an autonomous government.

The Dutch settled in New York after 1623. Later the colonies od New York, New Hampshire, Massachussets, Maryland, Connecticut, Rhode island, New Haven, Delaware, North Carolina, New Jersey, South Carolina, Pennsylvania and Georgia had all appeared by the middle of the 18th century. The extension of these territories undertaken by the poorest settlers was characterized by an unremitting struggle against the Indian peoples. In 1700 the colonies of the North, in New England, numbered some 94,000 inhabi-

tants living from a variety of agriculture and stockbreeding and from the trade (and smuggling) in wood, molasses and rum. The South (Maryland, Virginia, North and South Carolina, Georgia) numbered 108,000 inhabitants in 1700 and its economy developed on a base of tobacco, rice and indigo plantations which exploited a black labour force. Between North and South, in Pennsylvania, Delaware, New York and New Jersey, the population stood at 53,000 in 1700. The majority were French, Dutch, and Swedes. This middleground occupied a pivotal position between the Puritan North and the Anglican South with its completely distinct social and cultural structures.

At the same time as the English colonies were developing, the French also settled on the North American continent; Detroit was founded by the French in 1701 and Louisiana became a colony in 1731. The English colonies were thus trapped between the French to the north and the west and the Spanish colonies in the south. The rivalry between France and England culminated in the Seven years War of 1756-1763.

The Fight for Independence

Tension between the British colonies and Great Britain worsened after the Seven years War. England, which considered its colonies solely as a source of raw materials, toughened the measures which, from the 17th century onwards had restricted their freedom to manufacture their own products or to engage in commerce. These measures were then augmented by the introduction of further legislation designed to limit the autonomy of the settlers. Crisis point was reached when the Stamp Act was promulgated in 1765, imposing a tax on documents and printed matter of all kinds on the northern colonies. The response of the settlers to this law was that they could not be subject to

a tax which had not previously been discussed with their elected representatives.

After a wave of protests and violent demonstrations the representatives of nine of the 13 colonies demanded the repeal of the Stamp Act. Succumbing to this pressure, the British parliament was forced to abrogate the law in 1766, yet reaffirmed its authority to impose laws on the colonies.

Thereafter, the transatlantic controversy was seldom quiet. The colonists regarded the army of 6,000 British soldiers in the colonies after 1763 with great suspicion. British authorities defended the army as necessary to preserve peace especially after Pontiac's Rebellion (1763-65), which had been lauched by the Indian leader Pontiac to expel the British from the continent and restore French rule. There was also controversy within the colonies concerning the privileges of the Church of England. Certain factions believed that there was an Anglican plot against religious liberty. They viewed their colonial tie to a morally corrupt and affluent Britain as detrimental to their movement towards liberty.

In the following years, Acts introduced higher customs duties on the most common products, promoting the colonies to boycott British products. Customs levies were abolished in 1770, with the exception of a symbolic tax on tea. After street fighting between settlers and British soldiers in Boston from the British garrison led to the death of five Bostonians, settlers set up anti-British committees and one of their leaders Samuel Adams organized the "Boston Tea Party" in 1773. Disguised as Indians, the Bostonians attacked the ships of the East India Company and threw 342 cases of tea overboard. London decided to close the port of Boston until the damage had been paid for, decreed the dissolution of the Massachussets Colonial Assembly and stationed additional troops. The British troops attempt to take control of the area around Boston led to the first confrontation with the American militia at Lexington in 1775. The British troops immediately seized the town of Concord 20 miles (30 kilometres) to the north-west of Boston with the intention of destroying the arms depot. The English soldiers had to retreat after suffering heavy losses.

The War of Independence had started. The second Continental Congress at Philadelphia in May 1775 united the delegates of 12 colonies, the exception being the colony of Georgia. The Congress proclaimed the formation of a continental army based on the militia and placed George Washington at its head. The British parliament announced the blockade of the American colonies and King George III declared the colonies to be in a state of "rebellion".

Independence

On 4 July 1776 the second Congress of Philadelphia proclaimed the independence of the North American colonies. Despite numerous successes, the British regular troops were unable to gain the upper hand against the American civilians mainly on account of their poor knowledge of the terrain and the extensiveness of the country. Washington possessed at most only 17,000 badly trained and underequipped volunteers and thus was forced to avoid pitched battles. But the American militia knew the country and could move about it freely. The American victory at Saratoga (1777) induced the French to enter the war on the American side in 1778. She was then joined in 1779 by Spain. The English General Charles Cornwallis surrendered to the Franco-American troops on 19 October 1781, and the Articles of Confederation were ratified, announcing the birth of the United States of America. The War of independence was officially ended by the Treaty of Paris in 1783 and Great Britain recognized the independence of the 13 American States.

Consolidation and expansion

In 1787 the Convention at Philadelphia established the Constitution of the United States, which became an association of autonomous states gathered within a federal framework. The constitution came into force in 1788.

In 1789 General George Washington became the first president of the United States. Washington DC, a new city founded in 1790 and named after him, was chosen to be the federal capital. In 1791 ten additional constitutional articles, or amendments, the Bill of Rights, extended the scope of public and individual freedom (such as freedom of the press, of expression and of religion). The dollar became the national currency in 1792.

In 1793 the engineer Eli Whitney invented the cotton gin, which made the US cotton industry the most productive in the world. In the same year Washington declared the neutrality of the United States in the conflict between a coalition of European states and revolutionary France, banning any act of hostility towards either of the warring parties. The trade restrictions imposed during the fourth war of the European Coalition during the Napoleonic Wars led to tension between England and the United States, which placed an embargo on the import of a number of English products in 1806. In 1812 the United States made a vain attempt to expel the English from North America by attacking Canada. Washington was burnt during the war, which was ended in 1814 by the Treaty of Ghent, which maintained the status quo.

In an attempt to prevent European powers intervening in South America, which had been thrown into unrest by independence movements, President James Monroe made it clear in the 1820s that the United States would not tolerate Old World interference in the affairs of the New World.

US territory trebled in area between 1780 and 1860. By 1865 23 new states had joined the 13 original colonies. In 1803 Louisiana – a huge strip of land from the Canadian border to the Gulf of Mexico – had been bought from France in the biggest sale of land ever recorded in history.

The conquest of the western territories was accompanied by unremitting war with the Indians. The construction of a transport network (including roads, canals and steamboats after 1807, railways after 1826) made the conquest of new territories easier.

After the British grip on the American economy had been broken, American producers demanded that the US Congress introduce protectionist measures as a response to the closure of the European market. The American economy thus became, on the one hand, private and liberal and, on the other, protectionist. The nature of the country's two main fields of activity, agriculture and maritime transport, made the opening up of export markets a necessity. The government had to guarantee both the Atlantic trade routes and those to the west.

The question of slavery soon led to rifts within the union. In order to avoid a preponderance of slave states or free states in the Senate, new states were accepted in alternation depending on their attitude to slavery.

The conflict grew worse following the war against Mexico; the United States had annexed Texas, part of Mexico declared independent by English-speaking settlers, in 1845 and Mexico itself was defeated in 1847. Mexico was forced, in return for indemnity, to cede all its territories to the north of the Rio Grande, or half of its total area.

The quarrel about the nature, pro or anti-slavery, of the new territories led to the passage of the Kansas-Nebraska Act of 1854 which left the question of slavery to the decision of the new states themselves; this idea came to be known as "popular sovereignty". The Republican Party, which was opposed to the extension of slavery, was founded in the same year, and in 1857 the Supreme Court ruled that Congress had the right to abolish slavery in any territory of the United States.

Abraham Lincoln won the election of 1860 for the Republicans. The southern states, feeling themselves to be endangered economically by a possible abolition of slavery, seceded from the Union, thereby setting off the American Civil War. In 1861 the southern states formed the Confederacy (the Confederate States of America) and elected Jefferson Davis as their rival president. After much bloodshed and destruction the war ended in 1865 with the victory of the northern states, and slavery was abolished throughout the United States. Lincoln did not live long after the Union's victory; he was assassinated the same year by a fanatic from the south.

Reconstruction and expansion

The American Civil War was the first war involving armies consisting of more that a million men. The cost was 617,000 dead and the virtual ruination of the south. Its role as the world's leading cotton producer disappeared as Europe, suddenly deprived of cotton, had turned to other sources of supply such as India.

The death of Lincoln (14 April 1865) and the election of the southern Democrat Andrew Johnson had prevented the realisation of the plan of reconstruction intended by the Republicans. Fearing an alliance of the south and west, a radical movement led by industrialists Thaddeus Stevens and Jay Cooke attempted to impose much more rigorous conditions of peace: absolute racial equality, protectionism and tighter customs regulations. The Reconstruction Act of 2 March 1867 entrusted the administration of the southern states to military governors.

The former Union general, Ulysses S Grant, was elected to the presidency (1869-77), a development which served to heighten radical pressure against the south. The "carpetbaggers" (northern adventurers) and scalawags (southern rebels favourable to the blacks) seized power in the southern states. Racist southerners founded a string of secret societies (such as the Ku Klux Klan, founded in 1866, or the Knights of the White Camelia) for the propagation of their views. Using oppressive measures to prevent the black population from voting, the southern rebels, who had been granted an amnesty in 1872, recovered power in their states in 1877.

Despite the serious monetary and financial difficulties which followed the war economic expansion took off again after 1875. The restoration of the plantations was made possible by the granting of a new status (share-cropping) to the blacks, whilst immigration fuelled the country's growth. The Homestead Act (1862) granted an area of 160 acres to any one who had cultivated it for at least five years.

The United States took in three million immigrants between 1870 and 1880 and eight million between 1870 and 1900, mainly from Europe, the largest single group coming from the British Isles with Italians and Germans also forming sizeable immigrant communities.

The first Americans – the so-called "Red Indians" – shared little of the new prosperity of the United States. The massacre of 200 Sioux, mostly women and children, at Wounded Knee in 1890 represented the tragic culmination of the fight against the indigenous peoples of North America, who had been all but deprived of land as the republic advanced westward.

A world power

The imperialist phase of American politics began in 1898 under President William McKinley when the United States, acting in the name of commercial interests, took part in the Cuban struggle for independence from Spain, annexing Hawaii and Wake Island during the course of the ensuing war with Spain. The former Spanish colonies of Puerto Rico, Guam and the Philippines became protectorates.

President McKinley was assassinated in 1901. The United States became a major naval power under the presidency of his vice-president and successor Theodore Roosevelt (1901-08), assuring itself of the territory of the Panama Canal and affirming its policing role in the affairs of South America. The two main methods of American imperialism at the time were "dollar diplomacy" (exerting economic pressure on a country followed by political pressure) and what Roosevelt called the "Big Stick" method. Wherever political troubles broke out, America intervened militarily, justifying itself with the necessity of protecting the security of its citizens.

The 20th century

In 1917 American intervention in the First World War under President Woodrow Wilson (1912-19) was decisive. In 1918 Wilson announced his "Fourteen Points" for post-war peace, founded on self-determination and international cooperation. Governments were enjoined to form a League of Nations which would allow the peaceful settlement of international conflicts. The United States, however, refused to sign the Treaty of Versailles (1919) or to join the League of Nations. This was the start of the United States' retreat into isolation during the course of the 1920s. After the Wall Street Crash of 1929 the United States slipped into the grim years of the "Depression".

The election of President Franklin D Roosevelt in 1933 brought a major change in policy. He opened diplomatic relations with the USSR in 1933 and introduced his "New Deal" to tackle the economy. This implied the introduction of liberal interventionist and welfare policies. Roosevelt was president an unprecedented four times between 1933 and his death in 1945.

The 1939-45 war saw the emergence of the United States and the USSR as indisputably the world's greatest powers. A founding member of the UN in 1945, the United States was to play a key role in the organisation. The Cold War saw the emergence of a number of localised conflicts (such as the Korean War, 1951-53) and a wave of anti-communist hysteria.

John Fitzgerald Kennedy became the first catholic president of the United States in 1961. On the domestic front he attempted to develop a more equitable policy towards the blacks and the poor. In foreign policy he tried to reach a military balance with the USSR and initiated nuclear test ban negotiations. He had, however, to come to terms with two serious crises in Cuba after the Bay of Pigs landing (April 1961) and after the installation of Soviet nuclear missile bases (October 1962). Between these two events was the Berlin crisis, which followed the construction of the wall (August 1961). After his assassination in Dallas (22 November 1963) his successors Lyndon B. Johnson (1963-69) and Richard M. Nixon (Republican, 1969-74) respectively escalated and ended US involvement in the Vietnam War.

The American space programme saw Neil Armstrong become the first man on the moon on 21 July 1969. Under Nixon relations relaxed with both the People's Republic of China (February 1972) and with the USSR. President Nixon was forced to resign in 1974 after the Watergate scandal. Gerald Ford held office until 1976, and then Jimmy Carter (1977-81) continued international detente and mediated in the Israeli-Egyptian Peace Treaty of 1979. The seizure of the American embassy in Iran by "students" and his failure to secure their release dogged his last year of office and almost certainly caused his downfall.

The Reagan years

The arrival of President Ronald Reagan in the White House in 1981 marked the United States' return to conservative policies. In 1983 Reagan made clear his intention of strengthening the military power of the United States. But his policies faced both opposition in Congress and a body of public opinion favourable to east-west detente. American intervention on the Caribbean island of Grenada (October 1983) and the overt support given to the anti-Sandinista rebels against Nicaragua signalled the United States' determination not to tolerate communism in its own back yard.

But the end of 1987 saw an agreement between the superpowers, when on 8 December in Washington Reagan and Gorbachev signed the INF Treaty banning intermediate-range nuclear missiles. This treaty was ratified at a further meeting in Moscow (May-June 1988) between the two leaders. President Reagan was succeeded by his vice-president, George Bush, on 20 January 1989.

Uruguay

ROU
South America
72,172 sq. mi
Pop: 2.97 m
UN, LAIA, OAS

Capital: Montevideo (pop: 1.24 m)
Official language: Spanish
Religions: Catholic (66 per cent), non-religious (30 per cent)
System of govt: Republic since the constitution of 24 August 1966

In 1515 the Spaniard Juan Diaz de Solis reached the Rio de la Plata (River Plate), but the Spanish were dissuaded from settling there by poor resources, and a hostile indigenous people, the Charruas. Colonisation eventually began at the start of the 17th century. The Charruas were exterminated or assimilated, and have now disappeared.

After the introduction of livestock (1603) the first European colonists were the gauchos, nomadic cattle farmers. In 1724 the Spaniards founded Montevideo on the Atlantic coast as an outpost in the struggle against the Portuguese. In 1776 the region was attached to the Spanish vice-royalty of the River Plate.

After the Spanish authorities in the vice-royalty had been overthrown in 1810, Jose Artigas took the leadership of the struggle against the supremacy of Buenos Aires, and seized Montevideo in 1814, where he set up the first national government in 1815. In 1817 the city was occupied by the Portuguese. The independence movement turned against Brazil, which annexed the country in 1821. There was an insurrection against Brazil in 1825. The eastern republic (Uruguay) was proclaimed in 1828, after Britain forced Brazil and Argentina to recognise the country's independence in the wake of the war of 1825-27. In 1830 Uruguay was given a constitution.

In the 19th century Uruguay's history was totally dominated by the continual rivalry between Brazil and Argentina for conquest of the country, as well as by the rivalry between the liberals (reds: *colorados*) and the conservatives (whites: *blancos*). Uruguay was not political stable until the presidency of Jose Batlle y Ordonez (1903-07 and 1911-17), who laid the foundations of modern Uruguay, and whose reforms brought back a measure of peace and stimulated the republic's growth.

President Gabriel Terra's regime encountered the economic crisis of the 1930s and, after the constitutional reform of 1933, became a dictatorship which was to last until 1938. During the Second World War the country's economy was dominated by Britain and the USA.

A national council ruled from 1952 until 1956. A state of emergency was imposed in 1965 in response to the guerrilla activity pursued by the Tupamaros, and direct presidential rule was established in 1966. A fall in the value of the peso in 1968 marked the beginning of a serious economic crisis, with 90 per cent of the Uruguayan population living below the poverty line in 1970.

In 1971 President Pacheco Areco put the struggle against the guerrilla movement in the army's hands. In 1976 President Bordaberry's civilian government was overthrown by the military, and replaced by an interim regime headed by Aparicio Mendez.

In 1980 a new constitution proposed by the ruling junta was turned down by the electorate and protests increased, culminating in the largest demonstration in Uruguay's history at Montevideo in November 1983, when 400,000 people demonstrated against the junta.

The Colorado Party headed by Julio Sanguinetti won the free presidential elections of 25 November 1984, marking the return to democracy after 11 years of military-backed direct rule. He introduced a wide-ranging plan to combat inflation.

Sanguinetti's five-year term of office ends in November 1989. The elections held then will be contested by a broad range of opposition parties including the Tupamaros, who were granted an amnesty in 1985.

Vanuatu

Oceania
5,700 sq. mi
Pop: 145,000
UN, CW

Capital: Port Vila (pop: 15,100)
Official languages: Bislama, English, French
Religion: Protestant (majority)

System of govt: Republic; independent since 30 July 1980

Vanuatu is a Melanesian archipelago, made up of around 60 islands and inhabited by Melanesians and Polynesians. It was first visited by Europeans (Portuguese) in 1606, and James Cook gave the group the name New Hebrides in 1774. In the 19th century numerous French colonists from New Caledonia settled there, causing unrest among Australian settlers. France and Britain guaranteed the archipelago's independence in 1878. Rivalry continued between the French and British communities and an Anglo-French condominium was established in 1906. During the 1920s a large Vietnamese workforce was brought into the coffee, copra and cocoa plantations. The joint authorities granted autonomy to the New Hebrides in anticipation of independence (July 1980).

Before independence opposition between French and English speakers led to the threat of the secession of the island of Espiritu Santo. The Rev Walter Lini of the left-wing Vanuaatu Pati party, representing the slight majority of English speakers, was elected in November 1979, and then again in 1983 and 1987.

In December 1988 President George Ati Sokomanu, attempted to dismiss Lini and replace him as prime minister with his nephew Barak Sope. This led to Sope and the president's arrest on a charge of inciting mutiny. In March 1989 both were convicted and jailed.

Vanuatu is one of the leaders of the anti-nuclear movement in the South Pacific. Its agricultural production cannot meet all the needs of its population; fishing is being developed.

Vatican

V
Southern Europe
108.7 acres
Pop: 1,000

Capital: Vatican City (pop: 1,000)
Official languages: Latin, Italian
Religion: Catholic
System of govt: Monarchy (papacy); sovereignty recognised 11 February 1929

In the sixth century the bishop of Rome was already the largest landowner of Italy, as a result of numerous gifts which illustrated the generosity of the Roman emperors and aristocracy. The temporal power of the popes was established properly by Pope Gregory the Great (590-604), who considerably extended the papal state and introduced its communal administration.

Theoretically, however, the owner of these lands was Christ's apostle, St Peter, whose representative was the head of the church. The official name of the territories owned by the bishops of Rome was therefore Patrimonium Petri (Patrimony of St Peter). Usually, though, the pope's expanded lands were later more usually known as the Papal States.

Foundation of the Papal State

In 754 Pepin the Short, the king of the Franks, promised Pope Stephen II he would guarantee his ownership of the Eastern Roman (Byzantine) duchy of Rome (between Gaeta, the Tiber and Todi). In 756 Pepin forced the king of the Lombards, Aistulf, to relinquish several regions of Romagna, the former Byzantine exarchate of Ravenna, and Pentapolis (Rimini, Pesaro, Fano, Senigaglia and Ancona), which he entrusted to the pope.

These "gifts" opened the era of the Papal State. The popes turned from Constantinople, and linked themselves instead, to the Frankish kingdom. In 774 Charlemagne ratified the 754 agreement, but after his coronation as Holy Roman emperor he regarded the Papal States as a privileged territory belonging to the empire, and the bishop of Rome as the first imperial bishop.

The document called "The Donation of Constantine" appeared between 750 and 800, in which the Emperor Constantine the Great was supposed to have delegated to Pope Sylvester I (314-335) imperial sovereignty over Rome and all the Italian and western provinces. This forgery enabled the popes to demand sovereignty over all the empire's independent territories, as well as the highest rank in the hierarchy of temporal sovereigns. The forgery was not exposed until the 15th century.

In practice, the popes were unable to escape the rival influences of the German kings, Roman emperors and the Italian and Roman nobility. The struggle between the pope and the Holy Roman emperor reached its first climax during the pontificate of Gregory VII, who imposed his will on the emperor over the question of investiture by forbidding the investiture of bishops by kings and emperors.

The Papal States underwent the period of their greatest expansion under Innocent III (1198-1216), who benefitted from the struggle for power within the empire following the death of Henry VI and was able to almost double the land under his control. In 1201 he acquired from Otto IV the inheritance of Matilda of Tuscany (bequeathed to the Holy See in 1077), comprising Tuscany and several important towns in Lombardy. When Frederick II was elected emperor, he recognised the pope's acquisitions in the Golden Bull of Eger (1213). The boundaries recognised by Frederick remained the limits of the Papal States until 1870.

In the 14th century the papacy fell under the influence of the kings of France, who brought the popes to Avignon (1309-77). The return of the popes to Rome provoked a schism which was not resolved until the Council of Constance in 1415. The Papal States were governed in an absolutist fashion during the 15th and 16th centuries. During the Renaissance papal patronage attracted a number of prestigious artists, scientists, architects and engineers to the papal court. In 1527 Rome was sacked by Emperor Charles V's imperial troops, following the papal alliance with France.

The popes of the 15th and 16th centuries sought to reconstitute the unity of their states, which had fallen under the sovereignty of local dynasties, during the schism and the wars of the late fifteenth century. After the Thirty Years War, Rome's political influence was progressively diminished, and Italy became once again the stage for rivalries between the European powers. The Habsburgs assured their domination over Italy after the War of the Spanish succession (1700-14).

Relations between the Holy See (as the pope's jurisdiction is also called) and the principal powers were determined by a number of concordats in the 18th century. After the French Revolution, uprisings broke out in the Papal States. The Roman Republic was founded (1798) under French occupation and the pope was taken into captivity in France. The Papal States were annexed by Napoleon in 1809, which caused European feeling to shift in the pope's favour, and the Papal States were restored by the Congress of Vienna in 1815.

The re-establishment of the pope's territorial sovereignty was unwelcomed within the Papal States themselves, and tensions were increased by the pope's lack of sympathy for the ideal of a united Italy. In 1849 a republic was proclaimed in Rome, but the pope, Pius IX, was restored by a French expeditionary force. Italian troops seized Rome during the Franco-Prussian War of 1870; Rome was proclaimed capital of the united kingdom of Italy. The pope retained sovereignty over the Vatican, the Lateran and Castel Gandolfo. The Vatican's sovereignty and the freedom to carry out its religious offices were guaranteed by law.

Treaties with Italy

As a protest against the occupation of Rome, the popes declared themselves "prisoners of the Vatican". The "Roman question" was not resolved until the 1929 Lateran accords, which were signed by Pope Pius XI and Benito Mussolini, and contained the pope's formal renunciation of the Papal States and his recognition of Rome as the Italian capital. The Fascist state, for its part, recognised the sovereignty of the state and city of the Vatican, and compensated the church for its loss of land.

In January 1984 diplomatic relations with the USA were restored after over a century. A month later a renewed concordat was signed with Italy.

The Vatican enjoys important customs advantages and its inhabitants are exempt from tax. Its main resources are gifts from the faithful and the financial returns on its investments.

Venezuela

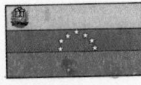

YV
South America
352,143 sq. mi
Pop: 15.1 m
UN, LAIA, OAS, OPEC, LAES

Capital: Caracas (pop: 1.8 m)
Official language: Spanish
Religion: Catholic (96 per cent)
System of govt: Republic; independent since 5 July 1811

Columbus sighted the coast of present-day Venezuela in 1498 on his third voyage to the Americas. The country's exploration began the following year with the expedition led by a Spaniard, Alonso de Ojeida, who succeeded in reaching Lake Maracaibo and gave the country its name (Venezuela is Spanish for "Little Venice") after seeing the raised huts constructed there by the local people.

Pearls were the only source of wealth to be exploited by the Spanish, and in 1528 Charles V granted a concession on the hinterland to the German Welser company, which explored the country in search of Eldorado. True colonisation of Venezuela did not begin until after the Germans had left in 1556.

Plantations (tobacco, cocoa, then tea and cotton) and trade assured the rapid growth of the colonies. The three Spanish colonies founded during the 16th century – Venezuela to the west, Nueva Andalucia to the east and Trinidad-Orinoco to the south – were all united in 1777 to form the captaincy-general of Venezuela. At the end of the 18th century a Creole aristocracy appeared, the Mantouans. One of their members, Francisco de Miranda, provoked the 1806 uprising after having pleaded in vain for Venezuela's independence in Europe.

Independence

After the failure of the first Venezuelan uprising, the fight for South American independence was taken up again in 1810 with the Caracas uprising led by Simon Bolivar and Miranda. The congress assembled by Bolivar at Caracas in 1811 proclaimed the independence of the republic of Venezuela. The first republic was immediately defeated by the Spanish but a second republic was proclaimed in 1813. After Bolivar had succeeded in freeing New Granada from the Spanish, by his victory at Boyaca (1819), the union of Venezuela and New Granada was proclaimed in December 1819 by the Congress of Angostura (the future Ciudad Bolivar). Bolivar became the first president of the republic of Gran Colombia.

Venezuela seceded in 1831 and proclaimed the third republic with General Jose Paez as its first president.

The military in power

Until the 20th century Venezuelan history was marked by political instability and military dictatorships were frequent. Under the dictator General Juan Gomez (1908-35) the country attained a degree of political stability and economic growth, due largely to the discovery of oil. While oil was being exploited agriculture was neglected, and Venezuela remained dependent on foreign foodstuffs. US and Anglo-Dutch firms controlled most of the country's economic activity.

The army kept power after Gomez' death in 1936. General Eleaze Contras brought in a socialist-inspired constitution. Venezuela entered the Second World War on the side of the Allies, but did not really engage in battle until February 1945.

The Democratic Action Party arrived in power in 1945, but was overthrown by a military coup in 1948. In 1952 a new coup brought Colonel Marcos Jimenez to power, and his regime became a dictatorship in 1953. Wishing to extend his mandate unconstitutionally in 1958, he was overthrown after a general strike and a people's uprising.

A temporary junta was in power until the election in December of Romulo Betancourt, leader of the Demo-

cratic Action Party. Although his election as president had been supported by the left-wing parties, Betancourt soon turned against them and in 1961 he introduced a new constitution which abolished a number of fundamental liberties.

The return to democracy

The first opposition candidate to gain power in a democratic way was Rafael Caldera, who, from 1969 onwards, tried to curb the clandestine activities of the communists and set up a policy of appeasement towards the parties of the left. In 1971 the Venezuelan parliament passed an act for the nationalisation of

all oil company properties, which was to be implemented by 1983.

The social democrat Carlos Perez was elected president in 1974. In the same year the government annulled the mining concessions of the US companies US Steel and Bethlehem Steel. The nationalisation of oil started in 1976. The christian socialist Luis Campins was elected president in 1979 and faced a fall in oil revenue and a huge exodus of capital; measures included a moratorium on national debt repayment.

The Democratic Action Party won an unexpectedly large majority in the elections at the end of the year. The first priority of Jaime Lusinchi's gov-

ernment was the economic crisis. The national debt problem needed to be resolved without resorting to the austerity measures proposed by the IMF. Venezuela's oil wealth made possible the conclusion of agreements with the country's creditors. But the debt problem still remained a persistant burden and on 31 December 1988 the outgoing President Lusinchi announced a moratorium on the repayment of almost all of Venezuela's foreign bank debt, which totalled around $30 billion. Earlier the same month former President Carlos Perez, the candidate of the ruling Democratic Action Party, was elected president for a five-year term.

Vietnam

VN
South East Asia
127,245 sq. mi
Pop: 62.3 m
UN, COMECON

Capital: Hanoi (pop: 2.9 m)
Official language: Vietnamese
Religions: Buddhist (majority), Catholic
System of govt: People's republic; reunited 2 July 1976

The first historically known dynasty of present-day Vietnam was that of the Sino-Vietnamese kingdom of Au Lac, founded in 257 BC in the delta of the Red River near Hanoi. In 207 BC the Thu'c dynasty became the Trieu dynasty, which was overthrown in 111 BC by the Chinese Emperor Wudi, of the Han dynasty. The region was annexed by China and divided into three commanderies: Hop Pho, Giao Chi and Cu'u Chan.

From the second century Buddhism spread deep into the country. A feudal aristocracy developed along Chinese lines and the country was shaken by repeated uprisings against the Chinese and by the invasions of the Indianised Chams from Champa in present-day south-central Vietnam (c.780) and the Nanzhao army from Yunnan, who took Hanoi in 863.

The first dynasties

In 939 the Vietnamese, led by a peasant, Ngo Vu'o'ng Quyen, expelled the Chinese. The Ngo dynasty (ruled 939-68) founded an Annamite kingdom. In 968, during the reign of Dinh Bo Linh, the kingdom took the name Dai Viet and Buddhism became the state religion. Ly Cong Uan, first king of the Ly dynasty (1009-1225) established his capital at Thang-Long (Hanoi).

The kingdom expanded under the

Tran dynasty (1225-1413), repelling a number of Mongol invasions. In 1406 the Chinese took advantage of a number of peasant revolts to invade the Dai Viet kingdom. In 1428 independence was regained by a peasant, Le Loi, who founded the second Le dynasty (1428-1527 and 1533-1789).

In 1471 the Le seized the Champa kingdom. Le Thanh Tong (1460-97) gave the country a definitive legal and administrative structure and imposed his suzerainty on the Lao kingdoms of the Mekong.

Thereafter, however, rivalry between two families of the court nobility, the Nguyen and the Trinh, led to the country's political division, the north being controlled by the Trinh and the south by the Nguyen.

French colonialisation

During the 16th century Dutch, Portuguese and French merchants and missionaries established themselves in Dai-Viet. Their deliveries of arms exacerbated the rivalry between the Nguyen and the Trinh. In 1773 a decisive people's revolt broke out in the south, led by the three Tay-son brothers. Supported by the majority of the population, the revolt ended, in 1778, with the fall of the Nguyen and Trinh families and then the fall of the Le dynasty itself.

The brothers divided Dai-Viet into Annam, Cochin-China and Tongking. In 1802, however, the Tay-son were overthrown by Nguyen Anh, supported by the French. It was under the reign of Gia Long, of the Nguyen dynasty, in 1803 that the Dai-Viet first received its modern name from China which had been asked to invest the new empire. Because they had been unable to obtain territorial concessions, and because of the repeated persecution of Christians, the French invaded Vietnam in 1858 and occupied Cochin-China after taking Saigon (1859). The Nguyen dynasty capitulated in 1862 and conceded Cochin-China, the richest province of Vietnam, by the Treaty of Saigon.

After signing a protectorate agreement with the Khmer kingdom (Cambodia) of King Norodom I in 1863, the French invasion of the north of the country began in 1873 with an expedition to Tongking. Tongking and Annam became protectorates in 1883. In 1887 the protectorates of Annam, Tongking and Cambodia, together with Cochin-China, were brought together to form French Indochina.

French defeat in the Second World War and the Japanese occupation of Vietnam provoked a nationalist uprising in the country. In 1945 Ho Chi Minh proclaimed the democratic republic of Vietnam, but the French reoccupied Saigon after the Japanese defeat. Despite an accord concluded with the democratic republic of Vietnam in 1946, according to which the democratic republic of Vietnam obtained the status of a free state within the French Union, France began recolonising the area and met with political and military resistance from Vietnamese rebels (Indochina War 1946-54).

The Vietnam Wars

The Viet Minh offensive, which became the Lien Viet (United National Front, open to non-Marxists) in 1951, ended with the French capitulation at Dien Bien Phu (7 May 1954). The ceasefire reached at Geneva (20 July) divided the country along the 17th parallel. On 9 October the French troops evacuated Hanoi, which Ho Chi Minh established as capital of the communist North Vietnam. Meanwhile a republic was proclaimed at Saigon by the catholic Ngo Dinh Diem, who installed a dictatorial right-wing regime, supported by the USA (1955).

In 1960 Vietnamese resistance movements against the South Vietnamese regime joined to form the National Liberation Front (NLF), including the Viet Cong (Vietnam Cong San, Vietnamese communists). Ngo Dinh Diem died in a military coup of 1963. There was a succession of military governments until 1965. General Nguyen Van Thieu

became head of state in 1965.

After the naval encounter in the Gulf of Tongking, in which two American destroyers were bombarded after having repeatedly provoked North Vietnamese naval units (1964), the USA intervened militarily on the side of South Vietnam. Systematic bombing of North Vietnam was carried out. The Tet joint offensive, reuniting the Viet Cong and the North Vietnamese troops, damaged US prestige in 1968.

During the subsequent Paris peace talks, US President Richard Nixon extended the fighting into neighbouring Cambodia (1970) and Laos (1971), and provoked the "Vietnamisation" of the war by giving massive support to the South's armed forces. The USA withdrew from the war by the Paris agreement of 1973. Saigon fell in April 1975 and the PRG (Provisional Revolutionary Government formed in 1969) took power.

The socialist republic of Vietnam

Vietnam was united in 1976 and Ton Duc Thang, former president of the democratic republic, was elected president of the socialist republic of Vietnam. In 1977 the restructuring of the economy and agriculture caused the relocation of several million people. Vietnam was admitted to the UN in 1978.

A conflict broke out in 1977 with Pol Pot's Kampuchea (Cambodia), supported by China. Vietnamese troops began an offensive on 25 December 1978, took Phnom Penh a month later, and overthrew the regime of the Khmer Rouge. The war which broke out against China in February 1979 led to the suspension of economic aid by the western countries, except Sweden and France, and Vietnam turned to the USSR for support.

A Vietnamese commitment to withdraw all its troops from Cambodia by 1990 was announced in 1985, but implementation has been slow. However, in January 1989 Vietnamese efforts to withdraw accelerated, bringing hope of an end to the Cambodian conflict.

Yemen Arab Republic (North Yemen)

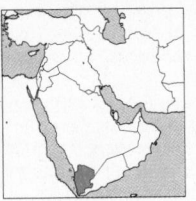

Near East
73,300 sq. mi
Pop: 8.38 m
UN, AL

Capital: San'a (pop: 427,000)
Official language: Arabic
Religion: Moslem (100 per cent)
System of govt: Islamic republic since October 1962

The first of the four Saba kingdoms which succeeded each other in Yemen was formed in the seventh century BC. The Saba kingdoms owed their wealth to their production of perfumes and to Yemen's geographical position between the Red Sea and the Indian Ocean.

Conquered in the fourth century by the kingdom of Aksum, Yemen then fell under Ethiopian domination in the sixth century and Persian in c. 570, becoming no more than a satrapy (Persian province).

From 630 onwards Yemen became part of the Islamic caliphate, until in the mid-ninth century it regained its independence under a series of local Moslem dynasties. From 1517 the local Arab dynasties had to accept Ottoman domination, but the prospering country soon regained its autonomy under the Zaydite imams (1635). From the beginning of the 19th century Egypt and Britain controlled the country, contributing to the restoration of Ottoman authority (1862).

After the fall of the Ottoman empire at the end of the First World War, the area was attached in 1926 to Saudi Arabia; the Zaydite imam was able to retain independence, but had to recognise the border of the British protectorate of Aden in 1934.

From 1956 Yemen drew closer to Egypt. The attempted integration with the United Arab Republic (1958) failed in 1961. A Yemeni republic was proclaimed during a civil war which broke out after the death of the Imam Ahmad in September 1962. Supported by Saudi Arabia, his heir Muhammad al-Badr continued the struggle against the republican regime until 1969. President-elect Colonel Ali Abdullah Salah has governed Yemen since 1978.

North Yemen's political life has been marked by poor relations with Aden (South Yemen), from the armed conflict of February 1979 to the failure of the plan for reunification in January 1980, which was followed by a number of further moves towards reconciliation. These, however, suffered a setback resulting from the January 1986 South Yemen civil war, when North Yemen sheltered the deposed South Yemeni President Ali Nasir Mohammed. Attempts to resolve these problems are still continuing.

Southern Yemen

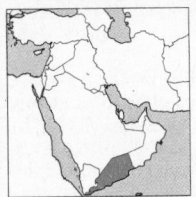

ADN
Near East
130,065 sq. mi
Pop: 2.5 m
UN, AL,
COMECON
(observer)

Capital: Aden (pop: 318,000)
Official language: Arabic
Religion: Moslem (99 per cent)
System of govt: People's republic since

30 November 1967

Aden, present-day South Yemen, was conquered in 1839 by the British who ran southern Arabia from India until 1937. The country became an autonomous British colony in 1947, and was shaken by violent nationalist troubles in 1963. The struggle of the National Liberation Front (NLF) led to the proclamation of independence and the break from the British in 1967.

The first president of South Yemen, Qahtan as-Shaabi, was overthrown in June 1969 by the left wing of the NLF.

The new regime signed co-operation agreements with socialist countries. After violent conflicts Saudi Arabia annexed the oil region of al-Wadiyya the same year. The NLF's policies became more radical after the overthrow of premier Mohammed Ali Haytham in 1971.

President Salim Ali Rubayyi, was judged to be too moderate and was executed in 1978. He was replaced as president by Ali Nasir Mohammed. Relations with the Saudis and North Yemen became more acrimonious and an inter-Yemen war erupted in February 1979.

Holding all principal offices of state from October 1980, Mohammed confirmed the country's ties with Ethiopia and Libya, but adopted a conciliatory tone towards its neighbours, which including meetings with President Salah of North Yemen to discuss reunification. He was deposed in January 1986 in a coup attempt which developed into a virtual civil war. Heidar al-Ahas, who succeeded him, was elected president in December 1986. Talks with North Yemen on reunification have been continuing, but the fact that the deposed Mohammed has been given refuge there has proved a stumbling block.

Yugoslavia

YU
South East
Europe
96,835 sq. mi
Pop: 23.4 m
UN, OECD
(special status)

Capital: Belgrade (pop: 1.45 m)
Official languages: Serbo-Croat, Slovene, Macedonian
Religions: Serbian orthodox (34 per cent), Catholic (26 per cent), Moslem (10 per cent)
System of govt: Federal republic since 29 November 1945

The territory of present-day Yugoslavia was once part of the ancient Greek Empire, before being absorbed into the Roman Empire; and in Constantine's division of the Roman Empire became part of Byzantium sphere. From the early 7th century she experienced the invasion of Slavic tribes (Serbs and Croats), who conquered Macedonia and several regions of Greece, and made themselves independent under the Nemanjid dynasty (1180).

By the reign of Stefan IX Dusan in 1331-1355 the Serbs dominated all of the Balkans. Their defeat at the hands of the Ottoman army at Kosovo (1389) marked the beginning of a domination which was to last until 1918 for a large part of present-day Yugoslavia.

Serbia was totally subjugated. It became a Turkish province in 1459, followed later in the century by Bosnia and Hercegovina. Serbian nationalism never really slept through the Ottoman centuries, but each time it asserted itself, it was savagely repressed, until the early nineteenth century when European public opinion made such repressions politically impossible.

A large scale Serbian national uprising was launched in 1804 by Karadjordje, who seized Belgrade and proclaimed himself Prince of Serbia (1808-1813), though Serbian and Croatian independence was not officially recognized until the 1878 Congress of Berlin.

The Ottoman Empire retained Macedonia, while Austria-Hungary imposed its sovereignty in Slovenia and over most of Croatia. Then in 1908 the Habsburg dual monarchy annexed Bosnia and Hercegovina.

At the beginning of the 20th century Serbia led the struggle for independence against the Ottomans, annexing Macedonia after Serbia's victories over Turkey and Bulgaria in 1912 and 1913.

The kingdom of Yugoslavia

Balkan nationalist struggles culminated in the assassination on 28 June 1914 of the Austrian archduke Franz Ferdinand, the heir of Emperor Franz Joseph, at Sarajevo, in Bosnia. The assassin, Gavrilo Princip, belonged to the Serbian nationalist secret society called "Black Hand".

Austria-Hungary, and then Bulgaria, declared war on Serbia on 28 July. Alliances brought other countries into the war, and by the time it was over eleven million were dead. After the German, Austrian and Turkist defeat, the king of Serbia, Peter I Karageorgevich proclaimed the Kingdom of Serbs, Croats and Slovenes (SHS) on 1 December 1918.

The SHS kingdom soon fell prey to internal nationalist rivalry. The existence of large minorities of Germans, Hungarians, Turks and Albanians only added to the already complicated cultural, religious and economic differences of the Slavs.

Alexander I, who succeeded Peter I in 1921, installed a dictatorship in 1929, and changed the name of the SHS kingdom to Yugoslavia and parliament was suppressed in 1931.

The King Alexander I was assassinated in October 1934 by the Oustacha, a nationalist Croatian and Macedonian secret society. The regency for the 11-year-old Peter II was exercised by Prince Paul.

The influence of the Axis powers continued to grow in Yugoslavia during the 1930s, with democratic government with new elections by secret ballot being re-established in 1939. On the outbreak of the Second World War Yugoslavia remained neutral. The government, under the regent Prince Paul, announced the adherence of Yugoslavia to the Axis pact.

The government was overthrown by a military coup in March 1941 and the young king Peter II was installed. German troops invaded Yugoslavia on 6 April in cooperation with Bulgarian, Hungarian, and Italian forces. Yugoslavia 's military surrendered on 17 April and the government evacuated Belgrade. Serbia and Croatia were organized as puppet states, and the remainder of the country was divided among Germany, Hungary, Bulgaria and Italy.

Resistance movements were formed. General Draza Mihajlovic assembled the royalist tchetniks, while Josip Broz or 'Tito', secretary of the Communist Party, and a veteran of both the Russian and Spanish civil wars, organised the "partisans". Despite terrible repression, Tito's liberation army continued to survive.

In November 1942 the Yugoslav National anti-fascist Liberation Council met openly in Bihac, Croatia, and on 20 October 1944 the partisans and Red Army liberated Belgrade. The National Committee for Liberation, formed by Tito in 1943, joined with the royalist government-in-exile in London to form the first government of free Yugoslavia in March 1945. The royalist ministers, however, soon left the government.

The November elections gave 90 per cent of votes to the communist-directed Popular Front, the only party to present any candidates. The new assembly proclaimed a republic on 29 November 1945.

The Republic of Yugoslavia

The newly adopted constitution of 31 January 1946 closely resembled that of the Soviet Union. Yugoslavia was declared a federal people's republic, and was recognized by the Western powers, although its leanings, from the start were decidedly pro-Soviet. The opposition was eliminated in 1946. General Draza Mihajlovic, the royalist resistance leader, was captured, tried for collaboration and – despite Western

protests – shot on 17 July. Archbishop Stepinac, the catholic leader of Croatia, was also tried for collaboration, and sentenced to 16 years hard labour.

Yugoslavia regained her 1919 borders and the territories taken by Mussolini's Italy in 1920. The regime set a huge agrarian reform in motion and nationalised the essential sectors of the economy.

Tito refused to align himself with a strict Stalinist policy, however, preferring to make Yugoslavia a neutral socialist state, independent of the USSR. The USSR duly severed relations with Belgrade, expelled her from membership within the Communist Information Bureau (Cominform) and organised an economic blockade in 1948. Tito denied the Cominform charges before a congress of the Yugoslav Communist Party, and as a counter move opened relations with the western countries and accepted aid from them. As a final gesture the Soviet Union denounced its treaty of friendship with Yugoslavia, with its satellites subsequently following their example. Relations with Italy improved after the abandonment of demands for Trieste, as did relations with Greece and Turkey (Treaty of Bled 1954).

Self-government by workers' councils in the country's larger towns was continued while Tito fought internal communist opposition, removing Milovan Djilas from the Central Committee in 1954. Relations with the USSR re-opened briefly, after Stalin's death, in the Khruschev era with their request that there be a resumption of normal diplomatic relations. These rela-

tions thawed under Brezhnev.

The federal parliament unanimously approved an extensive constitutional reform in April 1963. The new constitution renamed the country "The Socialist Federal Republic of Yugoslavia", comprising the six federal republics of Slovenia, Croatia, Bosnia, Herzegovina, Montenegro, Serbia and Macedonia, to which were added the two autonomous provinces in Serbia – Kosovo and Vojvodina. Further constitutional amendments provided for a Communist-controlled state, and created the post of premier.

Tito was re-elected for the fifth time, contrary to the provisions of the constitution, by a unanimous vote in May 1967. New measures of liberalisation were announced by Tito in 1969, permitting – for example – voters to reject the candidates on the official party list and to propose candidates of their own.

A collective presidency of 22 members, reduced to nine from 1974, would govern after Tito's death. This policy provoked a renewal of Croatian separatist attempts. The troubles which broke out at Zagreb in 1971 degenerated into a riot; as a result Croatian nationalists and liberal Serbs were eliminated from the upper echelons of the party.

Tito was elected life-president of the state and of the party in May 1974, shortly after the promulgation of a new constitution.

The rapprochement with Moscow, which finally accepted the Titoist doctrine of non-interference in the country's affairs, had led to an important economic agreement in 1972.

Relations with the Federal Republic of Germany and Bulgaria, which in the latter case had been tense because of demands on Macedonia, were also improved.

When Tito died, on 4 May 1980, his succession was organised on the collegiate principal. The presidency would rotate in succession among the members of the collective presidency, each president holding office for a year.

Yugoslavia's new leaders were confronted by an alarming economic situation, an astronomical national debt, a new militancy amongst the nationalities, and persistent communal troubles in Kosovo. These troubles have all continued and grown steadily worse throughout the 1980s.

Inflation, which had reached 80 per cent in the second half of 1985, had reached 175 per cent in November 1987 and by October 1988 almost 200 per cent. Together with inflation there have been strikes, regular devaluation and the need to seek IMF help concerning the country's inability to meet debt repayments.

There was trouble in the two autonomous provinces of Serbia, culminating in serious strikes and rioting in February and March 1989 in Kosovo, where ethnic Albanians demanded the rejection of planned changes to the constitution.

The changes, a response to nationalism led by the fiery Serbian party leader, Slobodan Milosevic, were approved in summer 1989, and increase Serbian control in Kosovo. Slobodan Milosevic, tipped as a future Yugoslav leader, subsequently adopted a moderate tone.

Zaïre

ZRE
Central Africa
905,365 sq. mi
34.6 m
UN, OAU

Capital: Kinshasa (pop: 2.7 m)
Official language: French
Religions: Catholic (50 per cent), Protestant (20 per cent), traditional beliefs (20 per cent)
System of govt: Republic; independent since 30 June 1960

Zaire takes its name from the Zaire river, otherwise called the Congo River, after the Kongo people who live near its mouth. Archaeology shows that neolithic farmers were living in large villages north of the Zaire river as early as the sixth century BC. This population was converted to Iron Age farming, which flourished on the plateaux

margins of savannah grasslands with the tropical forests of the Zaire basin.

The Kongo kingdom, with origins in the 14th century, flourished between 1500 and 1665 when it was effectively destroyed by Portuguese invasions.

Further south-east, the Kuba and Lele kingdoms of the 17th-19th centuries claimed origins from rulers who came up the Kasai river from the Zaire. The Luba and Lunda kingdoms on the southern margins of the Zaire basin originated in the 14th and 16th centuries respectively, but have cultural traditions that can be traced to at least the 11th century.

In 1879 the Welsh-American Henry Stanley, under mandate from the Belgian king, Leopold II, began the exploration of the Zaire basin, which was claimed as the personal property of Leopold II after the signing of treaties with different potentates. The independent state of the Congo was recognised by the African Conference of European powers at Berlin in 1884-85. In 1908 Leopold II was forced to surrender sovereignty over the Congo to

the Belgian state, after the brutal exploitation of the native population in his name had been made public.

Belgium granted its colony of the Congo independence in 1960. The republic of the Congo was proclaimed, with Joseph Kasavubu as president and Patrice Lumumba as prime minister. A wave of riots, strikes and confrontations swept across the country. The rich mining province of Katanga proclaimed its independence under Moise Tshombe. Lumumba was dismissed the same year and assassinated in January 1961 after a coup staged by Colonel Mobutu, but he remained in power for only a few months. The secession of Katanga and the civil war did not come to an end until the intervention by UN forces ended in 1963.

Tshombe became prime minister of the whole country in 1964, but was replaced by Kasavubu in 1965. Mobutu took power again a month later, proclaimed himself president and set up a policy of "authenticity" to place his nominees in key positions.

In 1971 Congo and Katanga were

renamed Zaire and Shaba resectively. Troops coming into the country from Angola – made up of members of the National Front for the Liberation of the Congo (former Katangans) – invaded Shaba in 1977. The attack was pushed back, thanks to Moroccan contingents and French support. A new attack led to direct intervention by France and Belgium at Kolwezi in 1978.

Relations between Zaïre and Angola became very strained because of Kinshasa's support for UNITA, which was also supported by South Africa. In 1983 the rapprochement between Zaire and Israel was formalised, and Zaire continued to provide air-bases for US zones in return for US political support.

The intervention by Zaire's troops in the conflict of the Chad government in 1983 provoked harsh criticism of Kinshasa from the OAU. Mobutu was re-elected in 1984 and has since been faced with considerable difficulties concerning repayment of the country's foreign debts. However, he has been able to obtain reschedulings of the debt repayments.

Zambia

Z
Southern Africa
290,586 sq. mi
Pop: 7.1 m
UN, CW, OAU

Capital: Lusaka (pop: 538,000)
Official language: English
Religions: Christian (72 per cent), traditional beliefs (27 per cent)
System of govt: Republic; independent since 24 October 1964

Zambia takes its name from the river Zambezi, which rises in the north-west of the country. Mining and metallurgy on the copper belt of the Zambia-Zaire border became intensive around 1000, to supply copper for export to the Indian Ocean and for regional trade of ornaments.

The first large state in the area of Zambia was the Lozi (Barotse) kingdom of the upper Zambezi flood-plain around the 17th century. This flourished until about 1840, when it was conquered by Koldo invaders who had come from what is now South Africa via Botswana. The Koldo, however, were overthrown in a Lozi revolution of 1864.

Meanwhile the eastern half of Zambia saw the extension of the Chewa kingdom from southern Malawi, and the rise of Bemba and Lunda states in the 18th century. But the Bemba and Luba were subjected to increasing violence from Swahili slave-traders in the 19th century, while the Chewa were conquered by Mpezeni's Ngoni invaders (ultimately from South Africa, via what is now Tanzania) in about 1870.

The Scottish explorer David Livingstone reconnoitred the Lozi country between 1851 and 1855, and the northeast of the country between 1866 and 1871. Agents of Cecil Rhodes' British South Africa Company (BSAC) concluded several agreements with eastern chiefs and the Lozi King Lewanika in the 1890s.

In 1901 the BSAC founded the two British protectorates of North-Western Rhodesia (including Barotseland) and North-Eastern Rhodesia, in 1899, joining them in 1911 to form Northern Rhodesia. It became a crown colony in 1924.

Copper mining on Zambia's copper belt developed rapidly in 1929-32, some 20 years later than copper mining in the Congo's Katanga province. As a result the country developed a white industrial population in addition to white farmers settled along the railways.

Northern Rhodesia was joined with Southern Rhodesia and Nyasaland in the Central African Federation of 1953, which, like similar colonial federations elsewhere, Britain intended to bring to independence as a single unit. This provoked nationalist protests in Northern Rhodesia as well as in Nyasaland, because of the predominance of white settlers and of Southern Rhodesia. Sir Roy Welensky, the prime minister of the new federation, rejected British proposals in 1961 that would have given Africans better and greater representation in the Northern Rhodesian legislature. Britain widened the franchise to most, but not all Africans, that June. But Northern Rhodesia decided, like Nyasaland (Malawi), to secede from the federation, which was dissolved in 1963. The copper mining companies recognised the realities of African nationalism, and Northern Rhodesia became the independent republic of Zambia in 1964 after the electoral victory of Kenneth Kaunda, head of the United National Independence Party (UNIP). A single-party system was installed by Kaunda in 1972 and he supported the nationalist movements of Zimbabwe, Namibia, Angola and South Africa among others.

Zambia had to enter closer relations with South Africa, however, during the 1982 economic crisis, due to the country's total dependence on its neighbours for energy and transport. The crisis has continued throughout the 1980s, with Zambia being compelled to adhere to strict conditions for debt repayment laid down by the International Monetary Fund (IMF). In May 1987 Kaunda broke with the austerity measures imposed by the IMF and introduced currency revolution, price controls and restricted payments to foreign creditors. In November 1988 he began his sixth term as president of one of Africa's most stable countries.

Zimbabwe

ZW
Southern Africa
150,699 sq. mi
Pop: 8.6 m
UN, CW, OAU

Capital: Harare (pop: 681,000)
Official language: English
Religions: Christian (44 per cent), traditional beliefs (40 per cent)
System of govt: Republic; independent since 18 April 1980

Zimbabwe takes its name from the civilisation based on the stone citadel of Great Zimbabwe, which flourished between c.1200 and 1450. In its wake two rival states arose among the Shona peoples of the Zimbabwe plateau, the Togwa state in Butwa to the southwest, and the Munhumutapa state to the north-east.

The Munhumutapa state was subjected by Portuguese traders on the Zambezi during the 17th century. The Togwa state was conquered by Rozvi rulers, former subjects of Munhumutapa, in about 1685. The 18th century saw many small wars of disruption following population growth and migrations among northern and eastern Shona. The early 19th century saw the invasion of powerful new military forces from south of the Limpopo – the Rozvi state being conquered by Ndebele (Matabele) invaders in 1838-40. The Ndebele were later followed by prospector-settlers organised in the British South Africa Company (BSAC) headed by Cecil Rhodes. Shona country (Mashonaland) was occupied in 1890, and Ndebele country (Matabeleland) was conquered in 1893-94, after which the country as a whole became known as Rhodesia. Ndebele and Shona risings were put down.

The colony became self-governing in 1923 under white rule. It joined Northern Rhodesia and Nyasaland in 1953 in the Central African Federation. This was dominated by Southern Rhodesia, where the white minority was entrenched by a system of racial discrimination. African nationalists won the federation's dissolution in 1963.

Southern Rhodesia declared unilateral independence under its white minority government in November 1965, after the African nationalists had divided themselves into conflicting political parties, the Zimbabwe African People's Party (ZAPU) and the Zimbabwe African National Union (ZANU). The regime of prime minister, Ian Smith, was maintained despite world pressure and opposition within Africa. The principle of racial segregation was made explicit in the 1969 republican constitution. But the liberation of Mozambique in 1974 strengthened the African liberation movements of Zimbabwe. South Africa, wishing to establish a "peace zone" along its borders, began to waver in its military and economic support, and Smith's regime found itself under increasing pressure. Joshua Nkomo (ZAPU) and Robert Mugabe (ZANU) unified the nationalist movements and intensified the guerrilla war within a Patriotic Front. Smith negotiated at Geneva in 1976, but opted for an "internal solution" after reaching an agreement with the African leaders Bishop Abel Muzorewa, and Ndabaningi Sithole (founder of ZANU).

The whites retained a veto on constitutional questions. Muzorewa became prime minister of Zimbabwe-Rhodesia in 1979, unrecognised internationally. War intensified until a conference in London in late 1979 brought about legal independence after an interim return to nominal British rule. Robert Mugabe's ZANU party won the pre-independence elections of 1980 with an overwhelming majority, and formed a government with some ZAPU and white minsters. In 1982 the capital, Salisbury, was renamed Harare. Then in September of 1987 a constitutional amendment abolished seats reserved for whites in parliament under the 1980 deal, and in November 1987 another amendment combined the posts of president and prime minister. Robert Mugabe, premier since independence, was sworn in for a 6 year term in December. That same month ZAPU and ZANU agreed to merge, ending often violent local rivalries and making the country a virtual one-party state.

Abbreviations

AL Arab League
ANZUS Australia, New-Zealand, US
ASEAN Association of South East Asian Nations
CARICOM Caribbean Community and Common Market
CFA African Financial Community currency
CMEA Council for Mutual Economic Assistance (or Comecon)
CW Commonwealth
ECOWAS Economic Community of West African States
EC European Community
EFTA European Free Trade Association
GCC Gulf Cooperation Council
LAES Latin American Economic System
LAIA Latin American Integration Association
NATO North Atlantic Treaty Organisation
NC Nordic Council
OAS Organisation of American States
OAU Organisation of African Unity
OECD Organisation for Economic Cooperation and Development
OPEC Organisation of Petroleum Exporting Countries
UN United Nations
WP Warsaw Pact

General Index

Page numbers in roman type indicate references in the text, those in italic type references in chronologies, and those in bold type references in essays.

Australopithecines – Bechuanaland

Take port in German New Guinea 1914 *1060a*
"Emden" sunk off Sumatra 1914 *1060a*
Allied forces establish themselves at Gallipoli 1915 *1062a*
Allies retreat from Dardanelles disaster 1915 1063a
Australian troops capture Jericho 1918 1067d
£10,000 prize for first flight from Britain in under 30 days 1075b
Scheme to encourage large-scale immigration 1925 *1086a*
Cobham flies 28,000 miles round trip to Australia *1088b*
Equal status with Britain in British Commonwealth 1926 1088c
Canberra Parliament building opened by Duke of York 1927 *1090a*
- Flying Doctor service inaugurated 1928 1091a
- 7,000 mile non-stop flight from California to Brisbane 1928 t1093c
- Two halves of the Sydney Harbour Bridge are joined 1930 *1096b*
- Amy Johnson flies solo England to Australia 1930 1096c
- Wonder racehorse Phar Lap dies in United States 1932 1098d
- Sydney Harbour Bridge opened 1931 *1100a*
- New South Wales Governor dismisses Prime minister Lang 1932 1100c
- Bodyline bowling threatens England relations beyond Cricket 1101c
- Menzies is new Prime minister 1939 1114d
- Two cities shelled by Japanese 1942 *1124a*
- Menzies becomes PM 1949 *1136c*
- British atomic bomb test off Monte Bello islands 1952 *1136d*
- Holt succeeds Menzies as PM 1966 *1140d*
- Gorton PM 1967 *1141a*
- Whitlam PM 1972 *1142b*
- Whitlam sacked 1975 *1142d*
- Fraser PM 1975 *1143a*
- Hawke PM 1983 *1144c*
- National History 1150

Australopithecines 15a
Australopithecus afarensis *14a*, 15d
Australopithecus africanus *14a*
Australopithecus boisei *14a*, 15a
Australopithecus robustus *14a*
Austria
- Frederick III crowned Holy Roman Emperor 1453 *426a*
- Protestant peasants revolt 1627 593a
- Hungary becomes province of Austria 1671 *648a*
- Siege of Vienna fails 1683 661c
- Receives large concessions from the Turks 1699 *672a*
- Forms alliance against fear of union of France and Spain 1701 *672b*
- Triumphs over Turks at Belgrade 1717 681a
- Agrees Treaty of Belgrade 1739 689d
- War of the Austrian Succession 1742 690c
- Reversal of the results of the War of the Austrian Succession *694b*, *696a*
- Machiavellian Prince von Kaunitz made chancellor 1753 701b
- Makes further alliance with Russia against Prussia 1757 *704a*
- Signs treaty of friendship with traditional enemy France 1756 705a
- Battles during 1760 *706b*
- Troops burn and pillage Berlin 1760 706c
- Battles with Prussia 1762 *708a*
- Signs truce with Prussia 1762 *708a*
- Emperor Josef II demands control over papal texts 1767 *716a*
- Signs alliance with Ottoman empire against Russia 1771 *720b*
- Obtains large part of Poland by negotiation 1772 720c
- Mesmer uses hypnotism for medical purposes 1774 *724b*
- Torture abolished by Josef II 1776 728c
- Agrees on boundary changes set out in Treaty of Teschen 1779 *734a*
- Empress Maria Theresa dies 1780 734c
- Talks with Russia to create front against Turks 1780 *736a*
- Salzburg court fails to appreciate talent of Mozart 1781 737a
- Josef II continues positive reforms 1783 *740b*
- Josef II to allow freedom of religious worship 1784 742c
- Treaty of Versailles ends conflict with Netherlands 1785 *744a*
- Guilds abolished by Josef II 1786 *744b*
- Catholic Church urged to use the vernacular by emperor 1786 *744b*
- Josephine code promulgated 1787 *748b*
- Styria and Carniola revolt against Josef II 1789 *754b*
- Austrian troops occupy Brussels 1789 *754b*
- Enlightened but failed ruler Josef II dies 1790 759a
- Starts to reconquer rebellious Belgian states 1790 *760b*
- Reverses against France 1792 *772a*
- Forms part of coalition of European states against France 1793 *774a*
- Agrees with Russia on handling of Venetian possessions 1794 *782a*
- Forms first alliance against France 1794 *786a*
- Army beaten by Napoleon in northern Italy 1796 790c
- With Russia and Prussia eliminates Poland as a country 1795 791c
- Surrenders to Napoleon in Italy 1797 795a
- Forms second military alliance against France 1798 *796b*
- Coalitions against Napoleon's France grow wider 1799 796c
- Ends war with France 1801 *804a*
- Vienna home of modern music 1803 807a
- Loses crucial Battle of Austerlitz to French 1805 811c
- Declares war on France 1808 *816a*
- Metternich aims for new balance of power 1809 819a
- Bankrupted by speculation and military costs 1811 *822a*
- Agrees alliance with France 1812 *822b*
- Signs armistice with Russia 1813 *824b*
- Declares war on France 1813 *826b*
- Riots oust Metternich 1848 899b
- Constitutional power conceded to electoral chamber 1848 901b
- Emperor abdicates in favour of son Franz Josef 1848 902b
- Turns on Hungary 1848 903d
- Kremsier constituion drawn up 1849 *906a*
- Avoids war with Prussia 1850 909c
- Stalemate after bloody battle in Italy 1859 929c
- Constitution established by Diet dissolved 1861 *934a*
- Archduke of Austria becomes King of Mexico 1864 944d
- Signs secret treaty with France against Prussia 1866 *948b*
- Crushed by formidable Prussian army 1866 949a
- Unites with Hungary under one monarch by Ausgleich 1867 951a
- Czech deputies withdraw from Parliament 1868 *954a*
- Emperor rejects Bohemian demands for "Hungarian" position 1871 *964a*
- Bismarck engineers their joining League of the Three Emperors 967a
- Coalition cabinet led by von Taaffe *980a*
- In Dual Alliance with Germany 1879 981c
- Fire during "Tales of Hoffmann" at Vienna Opera House kills 400 *984b*
- Bruckner's Seventh Symphony huge success 1884 *990b*
- Imperial heir dies in suspicious circumstances 1889 1001a
- Prime minister resigns over suffrage bill 1893 *1010a*
- Empress assassinated in Geneva *1022a*
- Renault wins first Paris-Vienna motor car race 1902 *1030a*
- Universal suffrage is granted 1905 *1036b*
- For war period see World War I 1059
- Berg shows new ideas with dissonant music 1085c
- New schilling unit for currency 1925 *1086a*
- Brutal political rioting in Vienna 1927 1089d
- Riots put down 1927 *1090a*
- Coup d'etat by national guard fails 1931 *1098b*
- Dolfuss bans all Nazi organisations 1933 *1102a*
- Chancellor Dollfuss murdered in own office 1934 1105c
- Unsuccessful Nazi coup 1934 1105c
- Gives Hitler tremendous welcome 1938 *1112a*
- Leading Jews are sent to Dachau concentration camp 1938 *1112a*
- Incorporated into Germany 1938 1113a
- Anti-Jewish moves follow Anschluss 1938 1113b
- Sovereignty restored 1955 *1138c*
- Waldheim president 1986 *1145b*
- National History 1151

Austro-Hungarian Empire (see Austria, Hungary)
Autographs of Yoshiwara Beauties, The (diptych) by Masanobu 662c
Automobile Association *1034b*
Autumn (painting) by Fragonard 719b
Autun, Bishop of (see Talleyrand)
Avaris 57c
Avars 305b
Avebury 42a
Avenant, Sir Willam d' *634a*
Averroists *382a*
Avicenna 338d
Avidius Cassius *232b*, *234a*, *234b*
Avignon
- New home for Clement V 1309 389c
- Meister Eckhan dies 1327 391d
- Simone Martini dies 1344 *392a*
- New papal palace nearly complete 1342 393a
- Petrarch's early life 1374 400d
- Papal consuls resign 1790 *758b*
- Seeks union with France 1790 *760a*
- Formally joined to France 1791 *766b*

Avila, Teresa de *522a*
Aviles, Pedro Menendez de *518a*, 519c, *528a*
Avitus *264b*
Avoggadro, Amadeo 819c
Avvakum 625a, 659a
Awakening of Spring, The (play) by Wedekind *1006b*
Awbek ben Ashfaga 655c
Awdaghost *332a*, 333c, *340a*
Awole *758a*
Axe, War of the *896b*
Axum
- Kingdom founded c550 BC *104a*
- Information in guide book 106 225b
- Powerful kingdom under Aphlas c250 *244b*
- Allies with Romans against Meroe 350 *252b*
- Commerical centre 330 253a
- Supports coptic patriarch 454 *264a*
- Ethiopians abandon Axum 319c
- Repulses invading queen of Damot c980 *330a*

Ayacati *430a*
Ayacucho, Battle of *850b*, 852c
Ayllon, Lucas Vasquez *478a*
Ayub Khan 982c
Azana, Manuel 1100d
Azeglio, Massimo d' *908b*
Azores, Battle of the *548a*
Azov, Siege of 1695 *668a*
Aztecs (see also Mexico)
- New city Tenochtitlan 393c
- Aztecs forge triple alliance 416d
- Drought and Faminine c1455 428d
- Aztec war 1473 *430a*
- Sacrifices to Huitzilopochtli 435a
- Montezuma II 1502 *446a*
- Conquered by Spaniards 1519 467c
- Moctezuma captured 467c
- Seige of Tenochtitlan 468c
- Montezuma deposed 1520 469c
- Surrender to Spaniards again 1521 469c
- Fall of Tenochtitlan 470b
- Execution of Cuauhtemoc *472a*

Azuchi Castle 535d

B

Baal 74c
Baal Ammon 157d
Babak *308a*
Babbage, Charles 869d, 886c
Babeuf, Francois *790b*, *792b*
Babington, Anthony *542a*
Babur *446a*, 454b, 479a, *480a*, *482a*, *482b*, 482c, 501d, 668c
Babylon
- Taken by Assyrians under Ashurbanipal 648 BC 19c
- Soothsayers power c1800 BC 55c
- First war with Assyria c1345 Bc *66a*
- Assyrian king takes power c1225 BC *68a*
- Loss of faith in gods c1200 BC 70b
- Captured by Elamites c1180 BC 71b
- Crushes Assyria c811 BC *74a*
- Assyrians crush rebellion c694 BC 82b
- City destroyed c689 BC *84a*
- Nabopolassar crowned king 626BC 92a
- Nebuchadrezzar II's cabinet of counsellors c605 BC *94a*
- Transformed by Nebuchadrezzar II c605 BC 95a
- Nabonidus leaves Babylon in Belshazzar's control c550 BC *102a*
- Conquered by Cyrus the Great 539 BC *104a*
- Cyrus the Great repatriates the Jews c538 BC 105a
- Xerxes puts down revolt against Persian rule 482 BC 114a
- Taken by Moslems 641 286c

Babylonians 95a, 95d, 101c
Bacchanalia 169a
Bacchiads 93c
Bacchus 169a
Bacchus and Ariadne (painting) by Titian 490d
Bacchylides *116a*
Bacciochi, Felix 826c
Bach, Carl Philipp Emanuel 698b, 751c
Bach, Johann Sebastian *682a*, *684a*, *686a*, 691c, 698b
Bach, John Sebastian *858a*
Bach, Wilhelm Friedemann 698b
Bach-i-Sachao *1092b*
Backgammon Players, The (painting) by Hals 595d
Baclk Hawk, Chief *866a*
Bacon, Francis *556a*, 567a, *580a*, *582b*, 583a, *584b*, *592a*, *592b*, *744a*
Bacon, Nathaniel *654a*
Bacon, Roger 385a, 387a
Bactria *146a*, *172b*, 181d, *210a*
Bad Axe, Battle of *866a*
Badajoz Conference *474a*
Baden-Powell, Robert 1027b
Badli-ki-Serai, Battle of 925c
Badoglio, Pietro 1127a
Badrinath 306d
Baedeker, Karl *882a*
Baeyer, Adolf von *978b*
Baffin, William *578a*
Bagaran 317d
Baghaya 292d
Baghdad
- Chosen as Abbasid capital 762 300c
- Chosen again as capital 892 *316a*
- Massacre follows capture by Mongols 1258 379b

Baghdad, Battle of 1534 534c
Bahadur Shah *676a*, 677a, 925c
Bahamas
- National History 1152

Bahia 591c
Bahman Shah *394a*
Bahrain
- National History 1152

Bahram II *246b*, 247d
Bai Ling 819a
Bailen, Battle of *814b*
Baillie, Joanna *874b*
Bailly, Jean-Sylvian 755d
Baines, Thomas 920c
Bairam Khan 510c, *514a*
Baird, James Logie 1089b
Baird, Sir David 811a
Baji Rao Peshwa 688c
Baker, Mathew 521c
Baker, Sir Samuel *968b*
Bakunin, Mikhail 945a, 967d
Balaclava, Battle of *918b*, 919a
Balakirev 999b
Balakot, Battle of *860a*
Balbinus 241b, *244a*
Balboa, Vasco Nunez de 457c, 465d, 473a
Balbuena *546b*
Balcombe, Betsy 835b
Balcombe, William 835b
Baldaya, Afonso 419c
Baldwin II of Byzantium 381c
Baldwin III of Jerusalem *354a*
Baldwin IV of Jerusalem *356a*, *358a*
Baldwin V of Flanders *340a*, *342a*
Baldwin VI of Flanders *342a*
Baldwin IX *368a*
Baldwin of Bouillon *346a*
Baldwin, Stanley 1081a, *1082a*, 1107a
Balearic Islands *58a*, *176b*
Balewa, Abubakar Tafawa *1140d*
Balfour Declaration 1067d, 1094d
Balfour, Arthur *1030b*, *1036b*, *1050b*, 1067d, *1096a*
Baliqiao, Battle of *932a*
Balitung 318c
Ballad of Reading Gaol, The (poem) by Wilde *1020b*
Ballads and Romances (book) by Goethe *802b*
Ballads and other Poems (poems) by Longfellow *886b*
Ballets Russes 1045d, 1048c
Ballynamuck, Battle of *796a*
Balmaceda, Manuel *1006a*
Balmart, Jacques 746d
Balta-Liman, Convention of *906a*
Baltimore, Battle of *830b*
Baltimore, Lord *592b*, *594a*, *600b*, 609d
Balzac, Honore de *870b*, 909b
Bamba, Battle of 548c
Ban Chao *218b*, *222a*, *222b*, 222c, *224a*, *226a*
Ban Gu *222b*, *226a*
Ban Yong *228a*
Bandaranaike, Sirimavo *1139c*
Bandung conference *1138c*
Bangladesh
- Wins independence from Pakistan 1971 *1142a*
- Cyclone and tidal wave kill over 10,000 1985 *1145a*
- National History 1152

Bani-Sadr, Abolhassan *1144a*, *1144b*
Bank of England 667a, *814b*
Banks, Joseph 721b
Banning-Cocq, Frans 627c
Bannockburn, Battle of *388a*
Banshee (ship) 938d
Banting, Frederick 1079d
Bantu
- Language 148a
- Expansion 149a

Bantu people *172b*
Bao Dai *1136c*
Bara, Joseph 783a
Baratieri 1019c
Barbados
- British settlers 1627 *592b*
- National History 1153

Barbalissus, Battle of 245b
Barbarossa, Khayr al-Din *460a*, *464a*, *482a*, *486a*, *488b*, 489a, *498b*, 499b
Barbastro, Luis Cancer de *504a*
Barber of Seville, The (opera) by Rossini 858d
Barber of Seville, The (play) by Beaumarchais *726a*, *798a*
Barbon, Praise-God *624a*
Barbotin, Abbot 774c
Barbuda
- National History 1149

Barca, Pedro Calderan de la (see Calderan)
Barcelona, Treaty of *440a*, *482a*
Barchester Towers (book) by Trollope *926a*
Bardas Phocas *330a*
Bardi 393b
Bardiya 105a
Bardo, Treaty of 985c, *988a*
Bare and ye Cubb, Ye (play) *640a*
Barention, Charles de *752b*
Barents, Willem *556a*, 556c
Bari, Siege of *342a*
Baring, Sir Evelyn 1008d
Barker, Robert 573d
Barlow, Arthur 547a
Barnard, Christiaan *1141a*
Barnardo, Thomas John *1036a*
Barnato, Barney 999c
Barnet, Battle of 431a
Baro 440b
Barrabas 211a
Barrack Room Ballads (book) by Kipling 1030d
Barrett, Elizabeth *1002a*
Barrie, James *1034b*
Barros, Joao de *522b*
Barry, Charles 884c
Barry, James 946b
Barry, Madame du *718b*, *780a*
Barrymore, John 1090d
Barsbay al-Zahiri 419d
Bart, Jean *666b*
Bartas, Guillaume du *536a*
Bartered Bride, the (opera) by Smetena *948b*
Bartholin, Erasmus Bertelsen *646b*
Bartholomew Fair (play) by Jonson 577a
Bartholomew's Day Massacre, St *526b*, 527a
Bartok, Bela *1134a*
Bartram, John *710b*
Barwalde, Treaty of *598a*
Bascio, Matteo de *478a*
Basil I *314a*, 317c, 317d
Basil II *330a*, 331c, *332a*, *334a*, *336a*, *336a*, 337a
Basil's Cathedral, St *514b*, 515c
Basileus (see Heraclius)
Basilian Academy *608b*
Basilicas 252c
Basle, Council of *416a*, *422a*
Basle, Treaty of *788a*
Basra 286d
Bass, George 830d
Bassano *548a*
Bassano, Battle of 790c
Bassein, Treaty of *806a*
Batan Grande *312a*
Bateman, Hester *784b*
Bathelemy, Jean Jacques *750b*
Bathers at Asnieres (painting) by Seurat 991a
Bathoen 1017c
Bathory, Stephen *524b*, *528a*, *528b*, 540c
Batista, Fulgencio *1136d*
Battle of the Boyne, The (painting) by Gow 666c
Battle of the Saints, The (painting) by Whitcombe 739a
Battleship Potemkin (film) by Eisenstein *1086b*
Battuta, Ibn 398d
Batu Khan 375a
Baudelaire, Charles *926a*, *950b*
Bauer, George (Agricola) *482b*
Bautzen, Battle of *826a*
Bautzen, Peace of 337d
Bavaria
- Agrees on boundary changes set out in Treaty of Teschen 1779 *734a*
- Elector maintained on throne by Napoleon 1805 *810a*
- Changes sides to oppose Napoleon 1813 *828a*
- King Ludwig II set to bankrupt state with castle building 1869 955a
- Ring cycle at Festival the musical event of the decade 1876 973c
- Liszt, greatest pianist of the day and musical pioneer dies 996c

Bavarian Succession, War of the *730b*, *734a*
Bawa Jan Gwarzo *786b*
Baxter, John 885a
Baxter, Richard *622a*
Bayajida 355d
Bayard, Chevalier de 472d
Baybars *382a*, 383a
Bayer, Johann 565d
Bayeux Tapestry 343c
Bayezid 402b, *406a*, 407c, 408d, *410a*, 410c, *512b*, 521b
Bayezid II *432a*, 432b, *456a*, 478d
Bayju 377c
Bayle, Pierre *656b*, *658b*, *660b*, 669a
Bayreuth Festival 973c
Bazaine, General *964b*
Bazzi, Giovanni *504a*
Beach at Egmond-aan-Zee, The (painting) by Van Ruysdael 595c
Beach, Sylvia *1080b*
Beachy Head, Battle of *664b*
Beaker folk 45c
Beale, Dorothea 909b
Beardsley, Aubrey 1021c
Beatlemania *1140b*
Beaton, Cardinal *500b*
Beatrice 389c
Beatus of Liebana 327c
Beaufort Scale *812b*
Beaufort, Francis *812b*
Beauharnais, Eugene de *810a*
Beauharnais, Hortense 826c
Beauharnais, Josephine de *790b*
Beaulieu, Edict of 533c
Beaumarchais, Pierre de *726a*, *742a*, *742b*
Beaumarchais, Pierre de *798a*
Beaumont, Francis 577b
Beaux Stratagem, The (play) by Farquhar 675a
Bebel, August 971d, *978b*, 1007d
Beccaria, Marquis of 711c
Becher, Johann *646a*
Bechuanaland
- Protectorate divided from Colony 1885 *994b*
- Three kings visit Britain in bid to save their lands 1895 1017c

France – France

- Louis X succeeds Philip the Fair, 1314 *388a*
- Pope moves to Avignon, 1309 389c
- War against England 1337 *390a*
- Truce with England 1340 *392a*
- England wins at Crecy, 1346 394b
- Essay on Hundred Years' War **398**
- King captured by English, 1356 399a
- Territory ceded to England, 1358 *400a*
- Jacquerie peasant revolt crushed 1358 401a
- Taxes provoke uprisings, 1382 405a
- Revolt against taxation 1382 405a
- Anti-Jewish decree 1394 *408a*
- England wins at Agincourt, 1415 415a
- Peace treaty with England, 1420 415c
- Beat English at Orleans 1429 416b
- Joan of Arc burnt at stake 1431 417a
- Rule by England ends 1453 427a
- French army defeated in Italy 1495 443b
- Pope Julius II creates Holy League to fight France 1511 454b
- Beaten at Pavia by forces of the Holy Roman Empire 1525 457a
- Agrees perpetual peace with Switzerland 1515 *460a*
- Utter defeat of Swiss avenges Novara 1515 461a
- Field of the Cloth of Gold 1520 469a
- French defeated at Pavia 1525 475a
- Glittering intellect at Court of Navarre 1527 478c
- Paris as capital 1528 *480a*
- Peace of Cambrai with Holy Roman Empire 1529 *482a*
- Charles V invades Provence 1536 *488b*
- French replaces Latin as official language 1539 *494a*
- Edict of Villiers ends painting strike 1539 *494b*
- Renaissance architecture 496c
- Peace with the Holy Roman Empire 1544 498c
- Peace of Ardres with England 1546 *500b*
- Unnecessary massacre of Waldensians 1545 500c
- Reign of King Francis 503c
- Henry II continues war against Emperor Charles V 1552 506c
- Treaty of Cambrai 1559 512c
- King Henry II fatally wounded at tournament 1559 512c
- Catherine de Medici becomes Regent 1560 515c
- Civil Religious War 1562 517a
- Cruelty of religious wars 1562 517a
- Peace of Amboise ends religious war 1563 517c
- Settlement in Florida destroyed by Spanish 1565 519c
- Second War of Religion ends 1568 *520b*
- Royalist forces defeat Huguenots 1569 *522a*
- Third war of religion ends 1570 *522b*
- Fourth war of religion ends 1573 *526b*
- St Bartholomew's Day Massacre 1572 527a
- Reign of Charles IX *528a*
- Fifth war of religion *528b*
- French Duke voted King of Poland 1573 529a
- Fifth war of religion ends 1576 *532a*
- Absolute authority of King debated 1576 532b
- Catholics turn against Huguenots 1576 533c
- Seventh war of religion ends 1580 *536b*
- Protestant rights withdrawn 1585 540c
- Eighth war of religion 1587 *542a*
- War of the Three Henries 1587 *542a*
- Henry III forced to flee 1588 543d
- Domination of politics by Catherine de Medici *544a*
- Revolt of the Croquants supressed 1592 *548b*
- Estates-General calls for a Catholic King 1593 *548b*
- End of the wars of religion 1593 549a
- King Henry IV rejects Protestantism 1593 549a
- Henry IV assassinated 1610 572c
- Freethinking monk and scholar burned to death 1619 581a
- Marie de Medici leads rebellion against her son Louis XIII 1619 581c
- Woman writer asserts right to sexual equality 1622 584c
- Signs Treaty of Paris against Spain 1623 *588b*
- Peasants "Croquants" rebellion 1624 *590b*
- Princess Henrietta Maria to marry King Charles I of England 591a
- Task force keeps route open through the Alps 1628 593c
- Huguenots barred from settling in French colonies 1628 *594a*
- Huguenot towns put down one by one 1629 *594b*
- Academy founded by Louis XIII 1635 *600b*
- Declares war on Habsburgs in Spain 1635 *600b*
- Joins Thirty Year War by declaring war on Spain 1635 600c
- Further Croquants uprisings 1637 *604a*
- Descartes publishes major work on his philosophy 1637 605a
- Invaded by three countries 1636 605c
- Normandy peasants revolt 1639 606c
- Cardinal Richelieu mourned by few 1642 610c
- First victory over Spain for 100 years 1643 612c
- Attack by Catholics on Jesuit beliefs 1643 612c
- Fronde uprising 1648 *616a*
- Fronde movement revolt 1649 621a
- Cardinal Mazarin and Louis XIV evade the Fronde 1649 621a
- Two women vie for power 1652 623a
- Combines with England to take Dunkirk 1658 629c
- Peace of the Pyrenees ends war with Spain 1659 *630a*
- Cardinal Mazarin dies 1661 635a
- Port Royal nuns defy Louis XIV 1664 639c
- New trade tariff to handicap Dutch and British 1667 645a
- Spanish Netherlands seized by magnificent army 1667 645c
- Lorraine occupied 1670 *648a*
- Moliere dies on stage 1673 649c
- Alsace reconquered 1675 *652b*
- Works of same name influence Racine to stop writing 1677 654c
- Partial victory over Dutch 1679 655a
- Ends war with Dutch 1679 655a
- Canal du Midi completed 1681 *656b*
- Government company sells slaves 1679 656c
- Huguenots excluded from trade and court 1682 *658b*
- Hugeunots forced to give up their religion 1681 658c
- Court moved by Louis XIV to Versailles 1682 659a
- St Cyr convent school for girls founded 1684 660c
- Protestant churches to be demolished 1685 661a
- Receives Luxembourg from Spain 1684 661a
- Edict of Nantes revoked 1685 661a
- Undeclared war on Holy Roman Empire 1688 *662b*
- Negro Code offers slaves better treatment 1685 663c
- Academie clash over modern arts 1687 663d
- Declares war on Netherlands 1688 *664a*
- Grand Alliance formed against France 1689 664b
- Defeat the Grand Alliance in Battle at Fleurus 1690 *664b*
- War declared by England 1689 665a
- Beaten by Grand Alliance *666a*
- Fleet breaks English blockade *666b*
- Ends nine year war with Grand Alliance 1697 669b
- Champagne developed 1698 669d
- War against English settlements in New England 1704 *672a*
- Camisard Protestant revolt 1702 *672b*
- Fear of Union with Spain unites enemies 1702 673c
- Crushing defeat at Battle of Blenheim 1704 674d
- Income tax – the "tenth" introduced 1710 *676b*
- Decisive defeat at Malplaquet 1709 677a
- British Invasion of French Canada fails 1711 678d
- Signs Triple Alliance against Spain 1717 *680a*
- Louis XIV dies 1715 680c
- Society satirized by Baron de Montesquieu 1721 682d
- Financial scandals and panic 1720 683a
- Fleury's dangerous foreign policies 1726 *684b*
- Regent Duke of Orleans dies of apoplexy 1723 685a
- Death of Cardinal Fleury 1743 *694a*
- Poised for war with Britain over India 1743 695d
- Troops occupy Brussels 1746 *696a*
- Diderot's "Philosophic Thoughts" burnt 1746 *696a*
- Occupy Austrian Flanders 1747 *696b*
- Marsal Saxe dies 1750 698c
- Lose key siege to British and Indians at Arcot 1751 698d
- First volume of Encyclopedie published 1751] 699a
- Death of de Montesquieu who challenged divine right of Kings 702d
- Winning war against Britain in North American colonies 1755 703a
- Extravagence of court of Louis XV 1755 703b
- Offers peace in India to British 1754 703c
- Signs treaty of friendship with traditional enemy Austria 1756 705a
- Agriculture seen by economists as key to nation's wealth 1758 705d
- Lose to Anglo-Hanoverian forces at Minden 1759 *706a*
- Loses decisive battle in India 1760 *706a*
- Loses Quebec to British 1759 707a
- Parliament condemns Jesuits 1761 *708a*
- Cedes Upper Louisiana to Spain 1762 *708a*
- Rousseau advocates equality before the law 1762 708c
- Treaty of Paris ends colonial ambitions in North America 1763 709c
- Death of Madame de Pompadour 1764 *710a*
- Porcelain factory at Sevres 1764 *710a*
- Military Academy founded *710a*
- Jesuit order disbanded by Louis XV 1764 *710b*
- Voltaire clears executed man's name 1765 710c
- Death of Rameau 1764 711b
- Takes Lorraine from Poland on death of King 1766 *712a*
- Seance de la Flagellation 1766 *712a*
- Artillery reformed 1766 *712b*
- Purchases Corsica from Genoa 1768 *716a*
- Corsican leader Paoli exiled 1769 717a
- Bougainville completes voyage round the world 1769 *718a*
- Dauphin marries Marie Antoinette of Austria 1770 *718b*
- Mass resignation of Members of Paris parliament 1770 *718b*
- Choiseul falls from power 1770 *718b*
- Flourishes and loses inhibitions under Louis XV 1770 719b
- Radical reform of legal system 1771 720c
- Establishment attacks on the Encyclopedie 1772 723a
- Louis XVI succeeds Louis XV 1774 *724a*
- Turgot urges free circulation of grain within France 1774 *724a*
- Flour war unrest compromises Turgot's reforms 1775 *726b*
- First French daily newspaper published 1776 *728b*
- Reforming Turgot dismissed 1776 728c
- Recognises independence of USA 1777 *730a*
- Enters war with USA against Britain 1778 *730a*
- Loan of 80 million livres necessary 1778 *730b*
- Swiss banker made comptroller-general 1777 730c
- Buffon suggests species are changed by their environment 1778 731d
- Provincial assembly created 1779 *734a*
- Last remaining serfs on royal land are freed 1779 *734a*
- Necker attempts to reform royal household finances 1780 *734b*
- Serfdom and torture abolished 1789 734c
- Sends troops to America 1780 *736a*
- Louis XVI attempts reorganisation of the prison system 1780 *736a*
- Financial crisis deepens 1780 *736b*
- France joins American colonists cause 1780 737d
- Necker's Compte-rendu is received with controversy 1781 *738a*
- Rousseau dies in exile 1781 *738a*
- "Les Liaisons Dangereuses" is instant publishing scandal 1782 *738b*
- Financial problems of the state deepen 1783 *740a*
- Intervenes to settle Crimea dispute 1784 *742a*
- Public ministerial arguments over state finance 1784 *742b*
- Introduces trade import barriers 1785 *744a*
- Queen Marie Antoinette's extravagance unpopular 1785 745a
- Mont Blanc conquered by climbers 746c
- Struggle against national bankruptcy 1786 747c
- National deficit total 112 million livres 1787 *748a*
- Louis XVI agrees Edict of Toleration 1787 *750a*
- Louis XVI challenges Paris Parliament 1788 *750a*
- Parliament stripped of all legislative powers 1788 *750b*
- Provincial parliaments revolt 1788 *750b*
- Food riots as economy disintegrates 1787 750c
- Lomenie declares state bankrupt 1788 *752a*
- Estates-General to meet for first time for 174 years 1788 753a
- Poverty of peasants appreciated in Britain 1788 753c
- Necker acts to avoid famine 1789 *754a*
- Third Estate becomes National Assembly 1789 *754b*
- Books of Grievances are full 1789 754c
- Third Estate bourgeoisie demand a hearing 1789 755a
- Third Estate swears oath in Tennis Court 1789 755c
- Necker dismissed and then recalled 1789 *756a*
- National Assembly faced by provincial arson campaign 1789 *756a*
- Deputies impose martial law 1789 *756b*
- Louis XVI moves troops against Third Estate 1789 756c
- Assembly approves Declaration of the Rights of Man 1789 756c
- Paris mob storms the Bastille 1789 757a
- Feudal privileges to go 1789 757d
- Sailors' Mutiny at Toulon creates crisis in Navy 1789 *758a*
- National Guard created 1789 *758a*
- Protestants given equal voting rights with Catholics 1789 *758a*
- Assembly jeers Robespierre plea for universal suffrage 1790 *758b*
- Divided into 83 Departments 1790 *758b*
- St Etienne made President of the Assembly 1790 *758b*
- Red Book reveals Louis XVI extravagance 1790 *758b*
- Newspapers and political clubs flourish 1789 758c
- Louis XVI approves nationalisation of clergy property 1790 759c
- Civil Constitution of the Clergy promulgated 1790 759c
- Assembly breaks 1775 alliance with Austria 1790 *760a*
- Revolt at Nancy put down, 300 killed 1790 *760b*
- Tricolour chosen for the flag 1790 *760b*
- Decimal system chosen 1790 *760b*
- National police – gendarmerie – created 1791 *764a*
- Pius VI threatens priests 1791 *764b*
- Louis XVI flees but is arrested 1791 765c
- Feuillants expelled from society 1791 *766a*
- Royalists take and barricade themselves inside Arles 1791 *766a*
- National Legislative Assembly holds first meeting 1791 *766b*
- Louis XVI signs Constitution abolishing absolute monarchy 1791 767b
- Social and economic impact of Revolution 1791 767d
- Split between Jacobins and Girondists 1792 *768b*
- Assembly agrees use of guillotine *768b*
- Ministry dominated by Girondins formed 1792 *768b*
- Girondins oust Jacobins from political power 1792 769a
- Declares war on Austria 1792 *770a*
- Revolutionary commune formed in Paris 1792 *770a*
- Assembly legalises divorce 1792 *770b*
- Guillotine to give less brutal execution 1792 770c
- Mob takes over, seizes Tuileries, insults Louis XVI 1792 771a
- Threat to the Revolution from abroad grows 1792 771c
- Successes against French and Prussians 1792 *772a*
- "Marseillaise" written 1792 *772a*
- First attacks by Prussians resisted 1792 773a
- Monarchy abolished 1792 773c
- Republic declared 1792 773c
- Use of "Citoyen" as greeting 1792 773c
- Annexes Nice 1793 *774a*
- Declares war on Britain and Netherlands 1793 *774a*
- Annexes Monaco 1793 *774a*
- Faces coaltiion of 8 European powers 1793 *774a*
- Declares war on Spain 1793 *774a*
- Anti-Republic revolt in the Vendee 1793 *774a*
- Jacobins oust Girondins 1793 *774b*
- Counter-revolution movement starts 1793 774c
- Louis XVI guillotined 1793 775a
- Women discharged from military service 1793 775d
- Essay on French Revolution **776**
- Republican forces capture Marseilles 1793 *778a*
- Moderate Girondin leaders guillotined 1793 778c
- Girondin leaders die singing Marseillaise 1793 778c
- Rise of Robespierre to power 1793 779b
- French army active all over Europe 1793 *780a*
- Vendee military rebellion defeated at Savenay 1793 *780a*
- Robespierre supports policy of Terror 1793 *780a*
- Revolutionary calendar introduced 1793 780b
- Women's contribution to the Revolution 1793 780b
- Male backlash ignores women's role in Revolution 1793 780b
- Europe united against her 1793 781a
- Terror takes over Paris 1793 781c
- Wages and prices fixed in economic crisis 1793 781c
- Leader of the Vendee revolt killed 1794 *782a*
- Leading Herbetists guillotined 1794 *782b*
- Counter-Revolutionaries systematically wiped out 1794 782c
- Committee of Public Safety acquires total authority 1794 782c
- Revolution celebrated artistically 1794 783a
- Desmoulins guillotined 1794 *784a*
- Assembly members guillotined 1794 *784a*
- Princess Elisabeth guillotined 1794 *784a*
- Great Terror recognised in law 1794 *784b*
- Robespierre arrested 1794 *784b*
- Doubtful celebration of the Supreme Being 1794 784c
- Indulgents tried and guillotined 1794 785a
- Danton guillotined on flimsy evidence 1794 785a
- Army invades Piedmont 1794 785a
- Beats Austrian army twice 1794 785c
- Robespierre himself guillotined 1794 786c
- The Terror ends 1794 787a
- Convention in control again 1794 787a
- Revolution influences all of Europe 1794 787b
- Royalists and republicans agree ceasefire in Brittany 1795 *788a*
- Food riots 1795 *788a*
- Public mood swings away from sans-culottes to reactonaries 1795 *788a*
- Agrees end to hostilities with Prussia 1795 *788a*
- Convention takes harsh measures against rioters 1795 *788a*
- Royalists agree not to take up arms against the republic again *788b*
- White Terror sweeps across the country 1795 *788b*
- Metric system introduced 1795 788c
- Recognises and controls Batavia Republic 1795 789b
- New constitution drops universal suffrage 1795 789d
- Signs peace treaty with Spain 1795 *790a*
- New coinage based on the Franc created 1795 *790a*
- Executive Directory replaces the Convention 1795 *790a*
- Napoleon wins battle after battle in Italy 1796 *790b*
- Communes fail to overthrow the Directory 1796 *790b*
- Savoy and Nice are ceded to the Republic 1796 *790b*
- Austrian army beaten by Napoleon in Northern Italy 1796 790c
- Napoleon continues devasting conquests in Italy 1797 *792b*
- Extends rule over Italian Cisalipine republic 1797 793c
- Royalist politicians ousted by Augereau 1797 793c
- Napoleon proposes and then abandons Invasion of England 1798 *794a*
- Napoleon placed in charge of invasion of Egypt 1798 *794a*
- Austria surrenders in Italy to Napoleon 1797 795a
- Alliances form against Napoleon 1799 796c
- Loses sea battle with US Navy 1799 797c
- Directory forced to resign 1799 *798a*
- Royalist leaders meet to consider resuming hostilities 1799 *798b*
- Napoleon seizes power 1799 799c
- Essay on Napoleon and his legacy **800**
- Napoleonic Wars mapped 801a
- New constitution making Napoleon First Consul is approved 1800 *802a*
- Army success leads to power for Napoleon in Italy 1800 *802a*
- Undeclared naval war with USA ends 1800 *802a*
- Concordat signed between Pius VII and Napoleon 1801 803b
- Eliminates all the second coalition states except Britain 1801 *804a*
- Treaty signed with Britain much to French advantage 1802 805a
- Napoleon made Consul for Life 1802 805b
- Bank of France granted privilege of issuing paper money 1803 *806a*
- Army encamped at Boulogne prior to invading England 1803 *806b*
- Enables USA to make the Louisiana Purchase 1803 807a

Great Britain – Great Britain

– Forms alliance against France and Austria 1787 *748b*
– Corruption charges laid against Warren Hastings 1787 749a
– Ex-slave calls for trade and not exploitation 1787 749c
– Cartwright's weaving machine patented 1787 751b
– Convicts deported to Australia 1788 753c
– Poverty of French peasants appreciated in Britain 1788 753c
– George III recovers sanity 1789 *754a*
– Canal system grows rapidly c1790 760c
– Burke denounces French Revolution 1790 761c
– Blake devises illuminated printing 1790 764c
– Paine claims French Revolution right and just 1791 765a
– Parliament votes against banning slavery 1791 765a
– Riot caused by Bastille Day celebrations 1791 *766a*
– Boswell's unvarnished "Life of Johnson" published 1791 768c
– "Bounty" mutineers tried 1792 769c
– Radical pamphlets inspired by the French Revolution 1792 *772c*
– Male fury at call for women's rights 1792 772c
– France declares war on Britain and Netherlands 1793 *774a*
– Forms part of coalition of European states against France 1793 *774a*
– Elaborate mission fails to persuade Chinese to trade 1793 779a
– Cornwallis consolidates power in India 1793 779c
– Attempt to colonise Cape Verde Islands fails 1793 *782a*
– Corsica proclaims George III its King 1794 *782a*
– Withdrawal from American Indian territories agreed 1794 782c
– Signs Treaty of The Hague against France 1794 *784a*
– Noted silversmith, Hester Bateman, dies 1794 *784b*
– Forms first alliance against France 1794 *786a*
– Disagreements with Prussia about fighting the French 1794 *786a*
– Habeas Corpus Act suspended 1794 *786b*
– Death of Boswell 1795 789a
– Builder of largest pottery in the world dies 1795 789b
– Radical societies incite riots 1795 789d
– French emigrees plan invasion of France from England 1795 *790a*
– Spanish fleet beaten at Cape St Vincent 1797 *792a*
– Mutinies sweep through Navy 1797 792c
– Wordsworth and Coleridge change poetic conventions 1798 *794b*
– Smuggling flourishes c1798 794c
– Forms second military alliance against France 1798 *796b*
– Greatest threat to mankind is population growth states Malthus 796c
– Coalitions against Napoleon's France grow wider 1799 796c
– Victory against Napoleon's fleet does not save Egypt 1798 797a
– Workers' Associations banned 1799 798c
– Tea becomes the Nation's drink and also a good tax earner c1800 802c
– Sole survivor of the second coalition against France 1801 *804a*
– First census shows population of 10.4 million in 1801 *804b*
– Pitt the Younger has to resign 1801 804c
– Speaker Addington becomes Prime minister 1801 804c
– Treaty signed with French much to French advantage 1802 805a
– Wedgwood and Davy develop elementary photography 1802 805d
– Formally abrogates Treaty of Amiens and declares war on France *806b*
– French Army encamped at Boulogne prior to invading England 1803 *806b*
– Parliament takes first step against child labour in factories 806c
– Emmet Irish rebellion fails 1803 807c
– Turner elected youngest Royal Academician 1803 *808a*
– William Blake publishes "Jerusalem" 1804 *808b*
– William Pitt the Younger dies 1806 *810b*
– French troops wait at Boulogne to invade 1805 810c
– Battle of Trafalgar decisive victory at sea against French 1805 811a
– Cape Colony seized from Dutch 1806 811a
– Cabinet decrees blockade of European coast 1806 *812a*
– Ministry of All the Talents collapses suddenly 1807 813a
– Slave trade legally abolished 1807 813c
– Loses Russian support after Treaty of Tilsit 1807 *814a*
– Sets aggressive attitude to all neutral countries over blockade *814a*
– Anti-slavery patrol at Sierra Leone 1808 814d
– Napoleon's blockade only works in theory 1807 815c
– Army lands in Portugal to start Peninsular War 1808 815c
– Still at odds with USA over merchant shipping 1809 *816b*
– Battle and Evacuation of Corunna saves British army 1809 817c
– Pioneer of schools for poor dies 1810 *818a*
– Economic crisis forces use of paper money 1811 *822a*
– Luddites smash machinery 1811 822c
– Regency established during George III illness 1811 822c
– USA declares war 1812 823b
– Prime Minister assassinated in House of Commons 1812 823c
– Prime Minister assassinated 1812 *824a*
– USA declares war 1812 *824a*
– Peace made with Sweden and Russia 1812 *824a*
– Jane Austen's work published anonymously 1813 825d
– Moves to reduce power of the East India Company 1813 827a
– Humiliating defeat by US Navy 1813 828c
– Stephenson builds his first colliery locomotive 1814 829c
– Funds alliance against Napoleon with £5 million 1814 *830a*
– British troops seize and burn Washington DC 1814 830c
– Treaty of Ghent to end war with USA 1814 *832a*
– Corn Law passed to protect agriculture of country 1815 834c
– Davy safety lamp to prevent methane gas explosions underground 835a
– Napoleon's final defeat at Waterloo 1815 835a
– Spa Fields riots over electoral reform 1816 *836a*
– Poor diplomacy ruins trade mission to China 1816 836c
– Year rich in romantic poetry 1816 837b
– Prince Regent stoned in London Park 1817 837b
– Government to crack down on dissenters 1817 837c
– Ricardo lays down Iron Law of Wages 1817 837d
– Coercion Acts passed 1817 *838a*
– Habeas Corpus Act suspended 1817 *838a*
– Manchester Blanketeers try to march on London 1817 *838a*
– Nash builds Regent Street and Brighton Pavilion 1818 838c
– Defeat of Marathas gives complete mastery of India 1818 839c
– So-called Six Laws passed 1819 *842a*
– Prince Regent succeeds as George IV *842a*
– Peterloo massacre 1819 842c
– Cato Street conspiracy against Cabinet foiled 1820 843a
– George III the "Farmer" dies at 81 in 1820 843a
– George IV bans Queen from Coronation and cortege from City 1821 845b
– King and Queen of Hawaii die on visit to Britain 1823 *850a*
– Society for Prevention of Cruelty to Animals founded 1824 *850b*
– Captures Rangoon 1824 850c
– Trade unions and strikes again to be allowed 1824 851a
– Pepys' Diary published 1825 *852b*
– First serious defeat of a major power by indigenous Africans 853a
– Gold Coast forces wiped out 1824 853a
– Stockton and Darlington Railway opened 1825 853b
– George Canning dies 1827 *854b*
– Lord Liverpool leaves after 15 years as premier 1827 855d
– Wellington and Peel form Tory government 1828 *856a*
– "The Spectator" published 1828 *856b*
– Carlyle draws attention to German literature 1828 *856b*
– Thomas Arnold appointed head of Rugby school 1828 *856b*
– Catholic Emancipation Act passed 1829 857a
– Determined to end Indian widows' suicide by suttee 1829 857c
– William IV succeeds George IV *858b*
– Wellington's resignation ends 50 years of Tory rule 1830 *860a*
– Farmworkers riot 1830 *860a*
– Bloody Assizes act harshly 1830 *860a*
– Pressure for electoral reform mounts 1830 861a
– Rioting caused by slow pace of electoral reform 1831 863a
– First, second and third Reform Bills divide Parliament 1831 863b
– Reform Act passed 1832 *866a*
– Great actor Edmund Kean dies 1833 *866b*
– Laws passed to reduce exploitation of children in factories 866c
– Electoral Reform forced through against House of Lords wishes 867a
– Factory Inspectors to be appointed by law 1833 *868a*
– Attempt to create trade union covering all trades 1833 *868a*
– Keble calls for radical changes in Church of England 1833 869c
– Babbage makes practical analytical engine 1833 869d
– Robert Peel takes over from Lord Grey as prime minister 1834 *870b*
– Tolpuddle Martyrs received exemplary deportation sentences 1834 *870b*
– Plans for Workhouses cause public outcry 1834 870c
– Lord Melbourne becomes Prime Minister 1835 *872a*
– Municipal Reform Act will creat new corporations for towns 1835 873d
– Locomotive (5 miles per hour) Act passed 1836 *874b*
– Royal Vauxhall balloon crosses the channel 1836 *876a*
– The Brimingham Political Union demands universal suffrage 1837 *876a*
– Queen Victoria shows independence in first days on throne 1837 877d
– John Constable dies, a painter highly acclaimed in his lifetime *878a*
– Trade treaty with Ottoman Empire 1838 *878a*
– Social conscience by novel writer Dickens 1837 879a
– People's Charter put forward 1838 879a
– Concern that deported convicts corrupt Asutralian settlers 1838 879b
– Infant Custody Act gives mothers access to their children 1839 *880b*
– Protests against Corn Laws grow 1839 880c
– Campaign for Free Trade 1839 880d
– Fox Talbot develops practical photographs 1839 881a
– Releuctantly claim New Zealand as colony 1840 883a
– Awards Canada independence under a Governor General 1840 883d
– Rowland Hill brings in Uniform penny postage and stamps 1840 883d
– Dickens popularity continues 1840 *884a*
– Chinese opium war row grows 1840 885b
– Cook runs first excursion 1841 885d
– Sir Robert Peel succeeds Lord Melbourne as Prime minister 1841 *886a*
– Miners' Assocation of G B and Ireland formed 1841 *886b*
– Parliament reject 3 million signature Chartists petition 1842 *886b*
– Treaty of Nanjing ends Opium War with China 1842 *886b*
– Opium war ends in complete success 1842 887a
– Agreement reached over border between Canada and USA 1842 887a
– Chartist riots more serious and widespread 1842 887b
– Income Tax 1842 *888a*
– Rule extends over three continents 1843 889a
– Law to stop scandal of children and women in mines 1842 889a
– Co-operative movement starts in Rochdale 1844 891c
– Young Men's Christian Association formed 1844 891c
– Sir Robert Peel Prime Minister again 1845 *892a*
– First black governor of a colonial territory in Sierra Leone *892b*
– Unpopular Corn Laws repealed 1846 *894a*
– Agrees with USA to end joint occupation of Oregon territory *894a*
– Free Traders win Commons vote to repeal hated Corn Laws 1846 894c
– Peel loses premiership after Free Traders win 1846 894c
– Vintage age of English novels 1847 897c
– Little support for Chartist rally to confront government 1848 899d
– Pre-Raphaelite Brotherhood of painters 1848 *902a*
– Agrees with USA on joint protective role in Central America *908a*
– Great painter Turner dies 1851 *908b*
– Pope restores regular Catholic hierarchy in Britain 1850 *908b*
– Public Library Act passed 1850 *908b*
– Blockades Greece on dubious grounds 1850 908c
– Act to discourage restoration of Catholic hierarchy 1851 *910a*
– "America" wins first America's Cup yachting race 1851 *910a*
– Palmnerston dismissed for not consulting colleagues 1851 *910b*
– Amalgamated Society of Engineers formed 1851 *910b*
– Essay on the Great Exhibition as peak of Britain's power **912**
– Great Exhibition as the peak of power – Essay **912**
– Conservative minority government 1852 *914a*
– Lord Aberdeen forms coalition government 1852 *914b*
– Soldier-statesman Duke of Wellington dies aged 83, 1852 914c
– Declares war on Russia over Crimea 1854 *918a*
– Agrees Reciprocity Treaty with USA 1854 *918a*
– Mismanagement of Crimean War brings down government 1855 *920a*
– Daily Telegraph and Courier published 1855 *920b*
– Limited Liability Companies are formed 1856 *922b*
– Declares war on China 1857 *922b*
– Prince Albert made Prince Consort 1857 *924a*
– Opium War with China re-opened 1857 927a
– De Rothschild admitted as MP after being elected 6 times 1858 *928a*
– Lord Palmerston forms his second ministry 1858 *928b*
– Strong reactions to Darwin's "The Origin of Species" 1859 928c
– Samuel Smiles urges Self-Help 1859 929c
– Popular craze for mediaeval times 1859 930c
– Declares its neutrality in the American Civil War 1861 *934a*
– Prince Albert dies 1861 *934b*
– Use of steel plates in shipbuilding 1862 938d
– Football Association separates Soccer from Rugby 1862 *940b*
– Army medical chief was a woman 1865 946b
– 80 year old Lord Palmerston dies suddenly 1865 948c
– Speed of Clippers change trade across the world 1866 948c
– First petition for women's suffrage presented to parliament *950a*
– Further Reform Act passed 1867 *952a*
– Disraeli takes over from Lord Derby as Premier 1868 *952b*
– Irish bomb campaign 953a
– Gladstone becomes Prime Minister 1868 *954a*
– First Trades Union Congress meeting divided on action 1868 955c
– Trade unions development 955c
– Married Women's Property Act passed 1869 956c
– William Morris leads revolution in home decoration 1869 956d
– ELementary education for all children 1870 *958b*
– Dickens dies from overwork 1870 958c
– Trade Unions granted legal status 1871 *962a*
– Secret ballot introduced 1871 *964b*
– Napoleon III dies at Chislehurst 1873 *966a*
– Divorced women given access to their children 1873 *966b*
– Factory Act cuts maximum working week to 56.5 hours 1874 *968a*
– Disraeli becomes PM 1874 969a
– Disraeli at 70 Prime Minister again 1874 969b
– Peaceful picketing authorised 1875 *970b*
– Webb swims Channel to France 1875 970c
– Disraeli forces through purchase of Suez Canal shares 1875 971a
– Political division over Bulgarian massacres 1876 972c
– Contraception campaign 1877 976b
– Damages of one farthing for Whistler in Ruskin libel suit 1878 *978a*
– William Booth founds Salvation Army 1878 979b
– Triumphant return of Disraeli from Berlin Congress 1878 979c
– Gladstone takes over as Prime Minister from Disraeli 1880 *982a*
– Iolanthe the first production to have electric illumination 1882 *986b*
– Second Married Women's Property Act passed 1882 *986b*
– Maxim invents rapid firing machine gun 1884 *990b*
– Further Reform Act passed 1884 *990b*
– Parliamentary seats to reflect population of constituencies *990b*
– White-slave trade in women exposed 1885 990c
– Politicians argue over Gordon's death at Khartoum 1885 995b
– Lord Salisbury succeeds Gladstone as Prime Minister 1886 *996a*
– Gladstone resigns 1886 996b
– Irish problems bring down another British government 1886 996c
– London's Bloody Sunday 1887 998b
– Queen Victoria's Golden Jubilee celebrations 1887 999a
– Football League formed 1888 1001c
– Football league 1888 1001c
– Great Dock strike 1889 1003c
– Prince of Wales appears as witness in Tranby Croft case 1891 *1006a*
– Liberal party adopts new policies 1891 *1006a*
– Great poverty amidst wealth in London and New York 1891 1007b
– Conditions of the poor 1007c
– Gladstone forms his fourth government 1892 *1008a*
– Keir Hardie elected MP for West Ham 1892 1009a
– Kier Hardie in Parliament 1009a
– Irish Home Rule Bill rejected by House of Lords 1893 *1010a*
– Gladstone replaced by Lord Rosebery 1894 *1010b*
– Blackpool resort 1014c
– Blackpool Tower opened 1894 1014d
– Wilbe jailed 1895 1015a
– Lord Salisbury forms his third ministry 1895 *1016a*
– Success of H G Wells' novel "The Time Machine" based on science *1016b*
– Kaiser's message to Kruger causes tremendous row 1896 *1016b*
– Gas for cooking and lighting in widespread use c1895 1017a
– Daily Mail launched 1896 *1018b*
– Queen Victoria's Diamond Jubilee marks 60 years' reign 1897 1018c
– Victoria's Jubilee 1897 1018c
– Aubrey Beardsley, dies aged 26: Art Nouveau story 1898 1021d
– Joseph Chamberlain seeks alliances with public, speech 1898 1022d
– Labour Party created 1900 *1024b*
– Successon of defeats in Boer War with few successes 1899-1900 *1024b*
– Makes large gains in scramble for West Africa 1024d
– Dictionary of National Biography completed 1900 *1026a*
– Optimism as new century starts 1026b
– House of Lords rule unions liable for losses caused by strikes *1028a*
– End of an era as Queen Victoria dies 1901 1029b
– Queen Victoria dies 1901 1029b
– Arthur Balfour becomes prime minister 1902 *1030b*
– Education Act puts schools in hands of boroughs and counties *1030b*
– Anglo-Japanese alliance agreed 1902 1031c
– Chamberlain seeks preferential tarriffs within British Empire *1032a*
– Signs Entente Cordiale with France 1904 *1032b*
– Women form political pressure groups 1903 1033c
– Russian fleet attacks Dogger Bank fishing trawlers 1904 *1034a*
– Russia will pay compensation for Dogger Bank incident 1905 *1034b*
– Automobile Association formed 1905 *1034b*
– Campbell-Bannerman will lead Liberal government 1905 *1036b*
– Liberals have landslide victory in General Election 1906 *1038a*
– Liberals sweep electoral board 1906 1039d
– Asquith becomes Liberal Prime Minister 1908 *1042a*
– Emergency measures to cope with unemployment 1908 *1042a*
– Kaiser endorses retraction of Daily Telegraph interview 1908 *1042b*
– Court of Appeal rules Unions may not put funds to political use *1042b*
– Kenneth Grahame writes masterpiece "The Wind in the Willows" *1042b*
– First old age pensions are paid 1908 *1042b*
– Acclaim for Elgar's work is universal 1908 1042d
– Kaiser gives gratuitous offence via Daily Telegraph interview 1043c
– Northcliffe, owner of The Times, prophesies war with Germany *1044a*
– Latest H G Wells' book banned by many libraries 1909 *1044b*
– Lloyd George produces People's Budget 1909 1044c
– Essay on British rule in India **1046**
– India the Jewel in the crown – Essay 1046a
– King George V suceeds King Edward VII 1910 *1048a*
– Asquith appeals to King for enough peers to pass Reform Bill *1048b*
– Labour party elect Ramsay MacDonald as their head *1048b*
– Force-feeding of imprisoned suffragettes 1910 1049c
– House of Lords deprived of its right of veto 1911 *1050a*
– Official Secrets Act passed 1911 *1050a*
– National Insurance Act passed *1050b*
– Churchill appointed First Lord of Admiralty 1911 *1050b*

R

Photo Credit Index

Jacket

1: Bridgeman Art Library – 2: Bridgeman Art Library – 3: Robert Harding Picture Library – 4: Giraudon – 5: Michael Holford Photographs – 6: Bridgeman Art Library – 7: Robillard – 8: Bridgeman Art Library – 9: Susan Griggs Agency – 10: Popperfoto – 11: Michael Holford Photographs – 12: Michael Holford Photographs – 13: Bridgeman Art Library – 14: Michael Holford Photographs – 15: Bridgeman Art Library – 16: Bridgeman Art Library – 17: Michael Holford Photographs – 18: Bridgeman Art Library – 19: Michael Holford Photographs – 20: Robert Harding Picture Library – 21: Bridgeman Art Library – 22: Robert Harding Picture Library – 23: Michael Holford Photographs – 24: Explorer – 25: Ancient Art and Architecture Collection – 26: Susan Griggs Agency – 27: Michael Holford Photographs – 28: Ann Ronan Picture Library – 29: Michael Holford Photographs – 30: Popperphoto – 31: Bridgeman Art Library – 32: Michael Holford Photographs

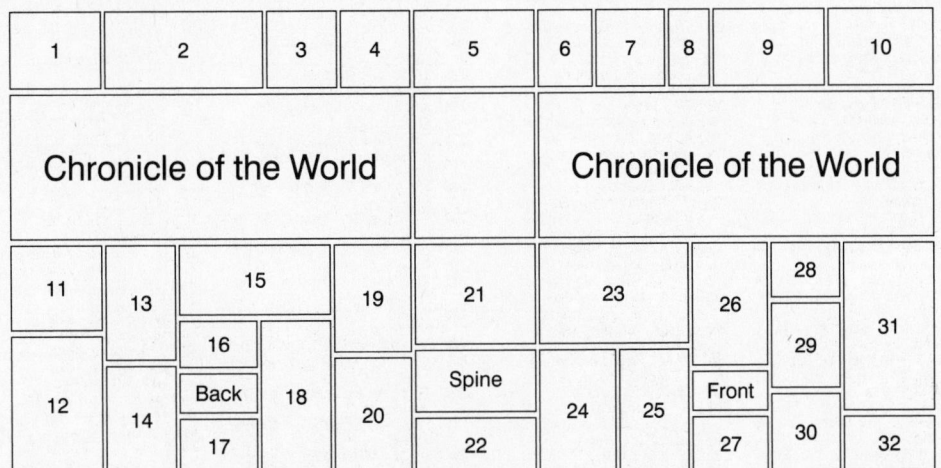

Agencies

Some agency names have been abbreviated in this index. The list below provides full names of pictures agencies:

Ann Ronan: Ann Ronan Picture Library
Art and Architecture: Ancient Art and Architecture Collection
Chronique: Editions Chronique, Paris
Forman: Werner Forman Archive
Granger: Granger Collection, New York
Harding: Robert Harding Picture Library
Holford: Michael Holford Photographs
Mary Evans: Mary Evans Picture Library
Newark: Peter Newark's Pictures
Topham: Topham Picture Library
Rex: Rex Features

Every effort has been made to trace the Copyright of the photographs, paintings and illustrations used in this publication. If an error has been made inadvertently in these picture credits, we apologise and ask the copyright older to contact Chronicle Communications Ltd so that it can be investigated and, where necessary, corrected. The large number of illustrations used in this book regrettably makes it impossible to acknowledge the many individual museums and art galleries who hold the various objects and paintings which appear in the photographs supplied by the agencies and libraries credited on these pages.

The position of the pictures are indicated by two letters: B: Bottom, T: Top, M: Middle, L: Left, R: Right, X: Middle Left, Y: Middle Right. When the pictures are not framed to the usual size, the positions of the pictures are completed by a number (i.e. BR1, BR2, BR3).

Photo Credit Index

Photo Credit Index

1296